G

LOS ANGELES CO.

LOS ANGELES COUNTY
1990 *Thomas Guide*®

TABLE OF CONTENTS

LOS ANGELES ORANGE COMBINATION	TBM 4054	**$22.95**
LOS ANGELES VENTURA COMBINATION	TBM 4053	**$22.95**
LOS ANGELES	TBM 3054	**$13.95**

HOW TO USE THE THOMAS GUIDE PAGE AND GRID SYSTEM

Finding Your Destination

- Use the Street Index to find the page number and grid location of a street name.

- Use the Cities and Communities or Points of Interest Index to find the page number and grid of a specific destination.

Planning Your Route

- Use the Key Maps or the Foldout Map to go from city to city, or to find what page your destination is on.

- Follow a street page to page by using the "See Map" page number in the border of each page.

COMO USAR EL SISTEMA DE PAGINA Y CUADRADO DEL THOMAS GUIDE

Encontrando Su Destinación

- Se puede usar el Indice de Calle para encontrar el número de página y locación del cuadrado del nombre de la calle.

- Se puede usar los Indices de las Ciudades y las Comunidades, o de Puntos de Interés para encontrar el número de página y el cuadrado de la destinación específica.

Planeando Su Ruta

- Se puede usar el Mapa Clave o el Mapa Doblado para viajar de ciudad a ciudad, o para encontrar la página de su destinación.

- Se puede usar el número de página con las palabras "See Map" se encuentran al borde de cada página para seguir una calle de página a página.

LIST OF ABBREVIATIONS

AL................ALLEY	CR................CRESCENT	KPN.....KEY PENINSULA NORTH	RDG................RIDGE
AR................ARROYO	CRES................CRESCENT	KPS.....KEY PENINSULA SOUTH	RES................RESERVOIR
ARR................ARROYO	CSWY................CAUSEWAY	L................LA	RIV................RIVER
AV................AVENUE	CT................COURT	LN................LANE	RV................RIVER
AVD................AVENIDA	CTE................CORTE	LP................LOOP	RO................RANCHO
AVD D LS......AVENIDA DE LOS	CTO................CUT OFF	LS................LAS, LOS	S................SOUTH
BCH................BEACH	CTR................CENTER	MDW................MEADOW	SN................SAN
BL................BOULEVARD	CV................COVE	MHP.........MOBILE HOME PARK	SPG................SPRING
BLVD................BOULEVARD	CY................CANYON	MNR................MANOR	SPGS................SPRINGS
CEM................CEMETERY	CYN................CANYON	MT................MOUNT	SQ................SQUARE
CIR................CIRCLE	D................DE	MTN................MOUNTAIN	SRA................SIERRA
CK................CREEK	DL................DEL	MTWY................MOTORWAY	ST................SAINT
CL................CALLE	DR................DRIVE	MTY................MOTORWAY	ST................STREET
CL DL................CALLE DEL	DS................DOS	N................NORTH	STA................SANTA
CL D LS................CALLE DE LAS	E................EAST	PAS................PASEO	STA................STATION
CALLE DE LOS	EST................ESTATE	PAS DE................PASEO DE	TER................TERRACE
CL EL................CALLE EL	EXPWY................EXPRESSWAY	PAS DL................PASEO DEL	THTR................THEATER
CLJ................CALLEJON	EXT................EXTENSION	PAS D LS......PASEO DE LAS	TK TR...........TRUCK TRAIL
CL LA................CALLE LA	FRWY................FREEWAY	PASEO DE LOS	TR................TRAIL
CL LS................CALLE LAS	FRW................FREEWAY	PGD................PLAYGROUND	VIA D................VIA DE
CALLE LOS	FY................FREEWAY	PK................PARK	VIA D LS...............VIA DE LAS
CM................CAMINO	GN................GLEN	PK................PEAK	VIA DE LOS
CM D................CAMINO DE	GRDS................GROUNDS	PKWY................PARKWAY	VIA DL...........VIA DEL
CM D LA..........CAMINO DE LA	GRN................GREEN	PL................PLACE	VIS................VISTA
CM D LS........CAMINO DE LOS	GRV................GROVE	PT................POINT	VLG................VILLAGE
CAMINO DE LOS	HTS................HEIGHTS	PY................PARKWAY	VLY................VALLEY
CMTO................CAMINITO	HWY................HIGHWAY	PZ................PLAZA	VW................VIEW
CN................CANAL	HY................HIGHWAY	RCH................RANCH	W................WEST
COM................COMMON	JCT................JUNCTION	RCHO................RANCHO	WK................WALK
		RD................ROAD	WY................WAY

LEGEND

LOS ANGELES CO.

LEGEND

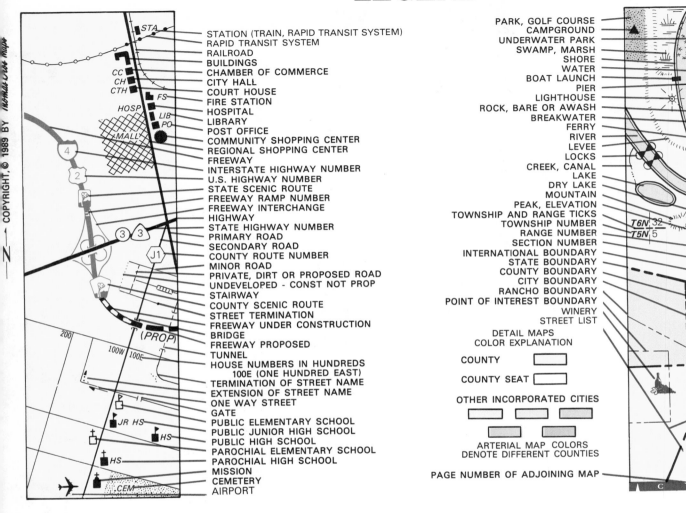

STATION (TRAIN, RAPID TRANSIT SYSTEM)
RAPID TRANSIT SYSTEM
RAILROAD
BUILDINGS
CHAMBER OF COMMERCE
CITY HALL
COURT HOUSE
FIRE STATION
HOSPITAL
LIBRARY
POST OFFICE
COMMUNITY SHOPPING CENTER
REGIONAL SHOPPING CENTER
FREEWAY
INTERSTATE HIGHWAY NUMBER
U.S. HIGHWAY NUMBER
STATE SCENIC ROUTE
FREEWAY RAMP NUMBER
FREEWAY INTERCHANGE
HIGHWAY
STATE HIGHWAY NUMBER
PRIMARY ROAD
SECONDARY ROAD
COUNTY ROUTE NUMBER
MINOR ROAD
PRIVATE, DIRT OR PROPOSED ROAD
UNDEVELOPED - CONST NOT PROP
STAIRWAY
COUNTY SCENIC ROUTE
STREET TERMINATION
FREEWAY UNDER CONSTRUCTION
BRIDGE
FREEWAY PROPOSED
TUNNEL
HOUSE NUMBERS IN HUNDREDS
100E (ONE HUNDRED EAST)
TERMINATION OF STREET NAME
EXTENSION OF STREET NAME
ONE WAY STREET
GATE
PUBLIC ELEMENTARY SCHOOL
PUBLIC JUNIOR HIGH SCHOOL
PUBLIC HIGH SCHOOL
PAROCHIAL ELEMENTARY SCHOOL
PAROCHIAL HIGH SCHOOL
MISSION
CEMETERY
AIRPORT

PARK, GOLF COURSE
CAMPGROUND
UNDERWATER PARK
SWAMP, MARSH
SHORE
WATER
BOAT LAUNCH
PIER
LIGHTHOUSE
ROCK, BARE OR AWASH
BREAKWATER
FERRY
RIVER
LEVEE
LOCKS
CREEK, CANAL
LAKE
DRY LAKE
MOUNTAIN
PEAK, ELEVATION
TOWNSHIP AND RANGE TICKS
TOWNSHIP NUMBER
RANGE NUMBER
SECTION NUMBER
INTERNATIONAL BOUNDARY
STATE BOUNDARY
COUNTY BOUNDARY
CITY BOUNDARY
RANCHO BOUNDARY
POINT OF INTEREST BOUNDARY
WINERY
STREET LIST

DETAIL MAPS
COLOR EXPLANATION

COUNTY

COUNTY SEAT

OTHER INCORPORATED CITIES

ARTERIAL MAP COLORS
DENOTE DIFFERENT COUNTIES

PAGE NUMBER OF ADJOINING MAP

T6N 32
T5N 5
1192'
(DRY)

R1W R1E
12 7

SEE 23 MAP

SEE Ⓐ C6

1 KEN DR
2 TAFT AV
3 BAY CT

C   D
SEE 17 MAP

SCALE OF MAP PAGES
(UNLESS OTHERWISE SHOWN)

0   ¼   ½   ¾   1   2 MILES
KILOMETERS
0 .1 .2   .5   1   2
0   1000 2000   5000   10000 FEET

MALL
P MW S

MAJOR DEPARTMENT STORES

B	BROADWAY
BF	BUFFUMS
BK	BULLOCKS
IM	I MAGNIN
M	MAY CO
MW	MONTGOMERY WARDS
N	NORDSTROM
O	OHRBACHS
P	J C PENNEY
R	ROBINSONS
S	SEARS

LOS ANGELES CO.

CITIES

1990 LOS ANGELES COUNTY CITIES AND COMMUNITIES INDEX

FOR CURRENT INFORMATION
CONTACT LOS ANGELES COUNTY
POPULATION RESEARCH SECTION
HALL OF RECORDS, ROOM 1101, 974-6476

ESTIMATED POPULATION INCORPORATED CITIES	7,671,785
ESTIMATED POPULATION UNINCORPORATED AREAS	978,515
ESTIMATED TOTAL POPULATION	8,650,300

COMMUNITY NAME	ABBR	POST OFFICE NAME	P.O. ABBR	EST. SQ. MI.	EST. POP.	MI. TO L.A.	MAP PAGE
ACTON		ACTON	ACT			46.8	189
AGOURA		AGOURA	AGO			32.2	100A
* AGOURA HILLS	AGH	AGOURA	AGO	7.97	19,400		102
AGUA DULCE		SAUGUS	SAU			43.8	181
* ALHAMBRA	ALH	ALHAMBRA	ALH	7.62	74,900	8.0	37
ALTADENA		ALTADENA	ALT			14.1	20
ANTELOPE ACRES		LANCASTER	LAN			64.3	146
* ARCADIA	ARC	ARCADIA	ARC	11.36	49,100	16.5	28
ARLETA		PACOIMA	PAC			18.2	8
* ARTESIA	ART	ARTESIA	ART	1.62	14,950	18.8	82
ATHENS		LOS ANGELES 44	LA44			11.5	57
ATWATER VILLAGE		LOS ANGELES 39	LA39			7.0	35
* AVALON	AVA	AVALON	AVA	1.25	2,490	44.2	77
* AZUSA	AZU	AZUSA	AZU	8.83	38,250	24.5	86
BALDWIN HILLS		LOS ANGELES 8	LA08			10.5	50
* BALDWIN PARK	BAP	BALDWIN PARK	BAP	6.77	63,300	17.7	39
BASSETT		LA PUENTE	LPUE			15.2	48
BEL AIR ESTATES		LOS ANGELES 77	LA77			14.0	32
* BELL	BELL	BELL	BELL	2.81	28,250	8.1	53
* BELLFLOWER	BLF	BELLFLOWER	BLF	6.14	60,900	17.7	66
* BELL GARDENS	BG	BELL	BELL	2.39	38,300	9.1	53
BELMONT SHORE		LONG BEACH 3	LB			26.7	76
BEVERLY GLEN		LOS ANGELES 24	LA			14.5	32
* BEVERLY HILLS	BH	BEVERLY HILLS	BH	5.69	34,300	10.9	33
BIG MOUNTAIN RIDGE		ACTON	ACT			50	182
BIG PINES		WRIGHTWOOD	WTWD			61.2	J
BIXBY KNOLLS		LONG BEACH 7	LB			15.7	70
BOUQUET CANYON		VAL VERDE	VAL			34.8	124
BOYLE HEIGHTS		LOS ANGELES 33	LA33			2.3	45
* BRADBURY	BRAD	DUARTE	DUA	1.99	930	21.1	29
BRENTS JUNCTION		CALABASAS	CAL			28.9	100A
BRENTWOOD		LOS ANGELES 49	LA49			15.1	41
* BURBANK	BUR	BURBANK	BUR	17.13	93,800	10.9	17
CALABASAS		CALABASAS	CAL			26.2	100
CALABASAS HIGHLANDS		CALABASAS	CAL			26.7	100
CALABASAS PARK		CALABASAS	CAL			26.2	100
CANOGA PARK		CANOGA PARK	CAN			25.7	12
CANYON COUNTRY	CYN	CANYON COUNTRY	CYN			40.6	125
* CARSON	CAR	CARSON	CAR	19.24	88,800	18.5	69
CASTAIC		CASTAIC	CAST			39.2	123
CASTELLAMMARE		PACIFIC PALISADES	PP			19.8	40
CENTURY CITY		LOS ANGELES 67	LA67			12.9	42
* CERRITOS	CER	ARTESIA	ART	8.78	58,400	18.8	82
CHARTER OAK		COVINA	COV			26.0	89
CHATSWORTH		CHATSWORTH	CHA			30.5	6
CHINATOWN		LOS ANGELES 12	LA12				44
CITY TERRACE		LOS ANGELES 63	LA63			4.0	45
* CLAREMONT	CLA	CLAREMONT	CLA	11.09	36,550	32.4	91
* COMMERCE	CMRC	LOS ANGELES 40	LA40	6.54	11,700	7.0	53
* COMPTON	COM	COMPTON	COM	10.11	93,000	11.6	64
CORNELL		AGOURA	AGO			35.9	106
COUNTRY CLUB PARK		LOS ANGELES 19	LA19				43
* COVINA	COV	COVINA	COV	6.99	43,250	22.9	88
CRENSHAW		LOS ANGELES 8	LA08				51
* CUDAHY	CDY	BELL	BELL	1.07	20,700	12.2	59
* CULVER CITY	CUL	CULVER CITY	CUL	4.97	40,950	10.9	50
DEL SUR		LANCASTER	LAN			60.2	158
DEL VALLE		SAUGUS	SAU			39.4	126
DENIS		PALMDALE	PALM			51.8	172
* DIAMOND BAR	DBAR	POMONA	POM	14.78	28,045	31.1	97
DOMINGUEZ		LONG BEACH	LB			15.7	70
* DOWNEY	DOW	DOWNEY	DOW	12.69	86,800	13.0	60
* DUARTE	DUA	DUARTE	DUA	6.57	21,350	19.8	29
EAGLE ROCK		LOS ANGELES 41	LA41			8.2	26
EAST LOS ANGELES		LOS ANGELES 22	LA22			5.1	45
EAST SAN PEDRO		SAN PEDRO	SP			25.1	79
ECHO PARK		LOS ANGELES 26	LA26				35
ELIZABETH LAKE		PALMDALE	PALM			55.6	157
* EL MONTE	ELM	EL MONTE	ELM	9.56	95,400	12.3	47
EL NIDO		REDONDO BEACH	RB			17.4	67
EL PORTO		MANHATTAN BEACH	MB			20.5	62
* EL SEGUNDO	ELS	EL SEGUNDO	ELS	5.50	15,750	19.5	56
EL SERENO		LOS ANGELES 32	LA32			5.2	36
ENCINO		ENCINO	ENC			16.9	21
FAIRMONT		LANCASTER	LAN			65.5	J
FERNWOOD		TOPANGA	TOP			24.2	109
FIVE POINTS		EL MONTE	ELM			24.1	47
FLORENCE		LOS ANGELES 1	LAO1			6.1	52
FORREST PARK		SAUGUS	SAU			40.6	125
FOX HILLS		CULVER CITY	CUL			11.6	50
* GARDENA	GAR	GARDENA	GAR	5.36	50,900	14.2	63
GLASSELL PARK		LOS ANGELES 65	LA65			5.9	35
* GLENDALE	GLEN	GLENDALE	GL	30.48	166,100	7.1	25
* GLENDORA	GLDR	GLENDORA	GLDR	19.04	47,400	25.9	87
GLENVIEW		TOPANGA	TOP			27.6	109
GORMAN		LANCASTER	LAN			65.1	H
GRANADA HILLS		SAN FERNANDO	SF			21.2	7
GREEN VALLEY		SAUGUS	SAU			50.8	157A
HACIENDA HEIGHTS		LA PUENTE	LPUE			21.6	85
HANCOCK PARK		LOS ANGELES 20	LA20			6.8	43
HARBOR CITY		HARBOR CITY	HAC			23.1	73
* HAWAIIAN GARDENS	HG	HAWAIIAN GARDENS	HG	1.00	12,350	21.8	81
* HAWTHORNE	HAW	HAWTHORNE	HAW	5.90	67,400	15.2	57
* HERMOSA BEACH	HB	HERMOSA BEACH	HB	1.36	19,750	21.0	62
* HIDDEN HILLS	HH	CALABASAS	CAL	1.67	1,950	27.1	100
HIGHLAND PARK		LOS ANGELES 42	LA42			6.1	36
HOLLYDALE		SOUTH GATE	SOG			12.8	59
HOLLYWOOD		LOS ANGELES 28	LA28			6.8	34
HOLLYWOOD RIVIERA		REDONDO BEACH	RB			23.4	67
* HUNTINGTON PARK	HPK	HUNTINGTON PARK	HPK	3.01	51,200	5.2	53
HYDE PARK		LOS ANGELES 43	LA43			12.8	51
* INDUSTRY	IND	LA PUENTE	LPUE	11.84	370	22.0	48
* INGLEWOOD	ING	INGLEWOOD	IN	9.11	102,300	13.0	57
* IRWINDALE	IRW	BALDWIN PARK	BAP	9.47	1,230	18.5	39
KAGEL CANYON		SAN FERNANDO	SF			18.5	3
KOREATOWN		LOS ANGELES	LAO6				43
* LA CANADA FLINTRIDGE	LCF	LA CANADA FLNTRDG	LCF	8.60	20,800	13.1	19
LA CRESCENTA		GLENDALE	GLEN			12.1	11
LADERA HEIGHTS		LOS ANGELES 56	LA56			13.2	50
* LA HABRA HEIGHTS	LHH	LA HABRA	LAH	6.39	5,450	23.6	84
LAKE HUGHES		LAKE HUGHES	LH			58.8	157
LAKE LOS ANGELES		LANCASTER	LAN			53.4	174
LAKEVIEW		PALMDALE	PALM			45.7	183
LAKE VIEW TERRACE		SAN FERNANDO	SF			24.0	9
* LAKEWOOD	LKD	LAKEWOOD	LKD	9.54	76,500	19.5	71
* LA MIRADA	LAM	LA MIRADA	LAM	7.77	42,600	19.6	83
* LANCASTER	LAN	LANCASTER	LAN	55.69	82,200	56.0	160
LANG		SAUGUS	SAU			37.1	125
* LA PUENTE	LPUE	LA PUENTE	LPUE	3.44	33,550	18.5	48
* LA VERNE	LAV	LA VERNE	LAV	7.92	30,500	31.2	90
* LAWNDALE	LAW	LAWNDALE	LAW	1.93	27,300	19.4	63
LENNOX		INGLEWOOD	ING			15.6	57
LITTLEROCK		LITTLEROCK	LR			49.3	184
LLANO		LLANO	LLAN			59.5	187
* LOMITA	LOM	LOMITA	LOM	1.89	20,300	21.5	73
* LONG BEACH	LB	LONG BEACH	LB	49.71	419,800	23.9	75
LONGVIEW		PEARBLOSSOM	PEAR			56.0	185
LOS ALTOS		LONG BEACH	LB15			24.2	76
* LOS ANGELES	LA	LOS ANGELES	LA	468.7	3,400,500		44
- -LOS ANGELES COUNTY	CO			4083			
LOS FELIZ		LOS ANGELES 27	LA27				34
LOS NIETOS		SANTA FE SPRINGS	SFS			15.2	61
* LYNWOOD	LYN	LYNWOOD	LYN	4.84	53,700	10.6	59
MALIBU BEACH		MALIBU	MAL			27.3	114
MALIBU BOWL		MALIBU	MAL			32.9	113
MALIBU HILLS		MALIBU	MAL			32.3	113
MALIBU JUNCTION		AGOURA	AGO			33.9	102
MALIBU LAKE		AGOURA	AGO			37.8	107

* INDICATES INCORPORATED CITY   MILES ARE ESTIMATED FROM DOWNTOWN CIVIC CENTER

1990 LOS ANGELES COUNTY
CITIES AND COMMUNITIES INDEX

FOR CURRENT INFORMATION
CONTACT LOS ANGELES COUNTY
POPULATION RESEARCH SECTION
HALL OF RECORDS, ROOM 1101, 974-6476

ESTIMATED POPULATION INCORPORATED CITIES 7,671,785
ESTIMATED POPULATION UNINCORPORATED AREAS 978,515
ESTIMATED TOTAL POPULATION 8,650,300

COMMUNITY NAME	ABBR	POST OFFICE NAME	P.O. ABBR	EST. SQ. MI.	EST. POP.	MI. TO L.A.	MAP PAGE
MALIBU RIVIERA		MALIBU	MAL			35.1	110
MALIBU VISTA		MALIBU	MAL			32.8	112
* MANHATTAN BEACH	MB	MANHATTAN BEACH	MB	3.87	35,300	22.0	62
MARINA DEL REY		MARINA DEL REY	MDR			11.4	49
MAR VISTA		LOS ANGELES 66	LA66			12.7	49
MAYFAIR		LAKEWOOD	LKD			18.6	71
* MAYWOOD	MAY	MAYWOOD	MAY	1.18	24,650	7.9	53
MID-CITY		LOS ANGELES 16	LA16				42
MINT CANYON		CANYON COUNTRY	CYN			40.0	125
MIRALESTE		PALOS VERDES PEN	PVP			25.0	78
MISSION HILLS		SAN FERNANDO	SF			19.7	8
MONETA		GARDENA	GAR			14.6	63
* MONROVIA	MON	MONROVIA	MON	13.80	34,000	19.1	29
* MONTEBELLO	MTB	MONTEBELLO	MTB	8.36	58,200	9.2	54
MONTECITO HEIGHTS		LOS ANGELES 31	LA31				36
MONTE NIDO		CALABASAS	CAL			30.3	108
MONTEREY HILLS		LOS ANGELES 32	LA32				36
* MONTEREY PARK	MPK	MONTEREY PARK	MPK	7.72	64,600	7.8	46
MONTROSE		MONTROSE	MONT			11.7	18
MORNINGSIDE PARK		INGLEWOOD	ING5			13.4	57
MOUNT OLYMPUS		LOS ANGELES 46	LA46			8.4	33
MOUNT WASHINGTON		LOS ANGELES 65	LA65			7.9	36
MOUNT WILSON		MOUNT WILSON	MV			20.7	20A
NAPLES		LONG BEACH 3	LB03			29.0	80
NEENACH		LANCASTER	LAN			72.7	H
NEWHALL		NEWHALL	NEW			29.8	127
NORTH HOLLYWOOD		NORTH HOLLYWOOD	NHO			13.3	16
NORTH LONG BEACH		LONG BEACH 5	LB05			16.6	70
NORTHRIDGE		NORTHRIDGE	NOR			24.0	7
* NORWALK	NWK	NORWALK	NWK	9.36	90,800	15.7	82
NORWOOD VILLAGE		EL MONTE	ELM			14.3	38
OBAN		LANCASTER	LAN			61.1	148
OCEAN PARK		SANTA MONICA	SM05			15.5	49
OLIVE VIEW		SAN FERNANDO	SF42			28.0	2
PACIFIC PALISADES		PACIFIC PALISADES	PP			18.5	40
PACOIMA		PACOIMA	PAC			19.0	8
PALISADES HIGHLANDS		PACIFIC PALISADES	PP			22.0	30
* PALMDALE	PALM	PALMDALE	PALM	61.65	45,850	47.8	172
PALMS		LOS ANGELES 34	LA34			10.7	42
* PALOS VERDES ESTATES	PVE	PALOS VERDES PEN	PVP	4.75	15,000	27.4	72
PANORAMA CITY		VAN NUYS	VAN			18.1	8
* PARAMOUNT	PAR	PARAMOUNT	PAR	4.80	44,450	16.5	65
PARK LA BREA		LOS ANGELES 36	LA36			8.3	43
* PASADENA	PAS	PASADENA	PAS	23.00	132,200	10.2	27
PEARBLOSSOM		PEARBLOSSOM	PEAR			56.4	185
PEARLAND		PALMDALE	PALM			46.9	184
PHILLIPS RANCH		POMONA	POM			32.1	94
PICO		NEWHALL	NEW			32.8	126
* PICO RIVERA	PR	PICO RIVERA	PR	8.22	57,300	13.5	54
PINETREE		SAUGUS	SAU			42.9	125
PLAYA DEL REY		PLAYA DEL REY	PDR			17.8	55A
* POMONA	POM	POMONA	POM	22.97	119,900	31.3	94
PORTER RANCH		NORTHRIDGE	NOR			20.2	1
PORTUGUESE BEND		PALOS VERDES PEN	PVP				77
QUARTZ HILL		LANCASTER	LAN			51.7	171
RANCHO DOMINGUEZ		RANCHO DOMINGUEZ	ROD			12.0	70
* RANCHO PALOS VERDES	RPV	PALOS VERDES PEN	PVP	13.50	46,000	27.0	72
RANCHO PARK		LOS ANGELES 64	LA64			11.9	42
RAVENNA		ACTON	ACT			52.2	189
* REDONDO BEACH	RB	REDONDO BEACH	RB	6.34	64,700	22.7	67
RESEDA		RESEDA	RES			21.7	14
* ROLLING HILLS	RH	PALOS VERDES PEN	PVP	2.98	2,090	24.8	73
* ROLLING HILLS ESTATES	RHE	PALOS VERDES PEN	PVP	3.44	7,875	23.2	73
ROOSEVELT		LANCASTER	LAN			65.6	161
* ROSEMEAD	RM	ROSEMEAD	RM	5.00	47,700	10.9	38
ROWLAND HEIGHTS		LA PUENTE	LPUE			20.3	98
SANDBERG		LAKE HUGHES	LH			59.9	H
* SAN DIMAS	SAD	SAN DIMAS	SAD	15.30	32,500	29.0	89
* SAN FERNANDO	SF	SAN FERNANDO	SF	2.40	20,700	20.8	2

COMMUNITY NAME	ABBR	POST OFFICE NAME	P.O. ABBR	EST. SQ. MI.	EST. POP.	MI. TO L.A.	MAP PAGE
* SAN GABRIEL	SGAB	SAN GABRIEL	SGAB	4.09	34,900	10.4	37
* SAN MARINO	SMAR	PASADENA	PAS	3.75	13,800	10.5	37
SAN PEDRO		SAN PEDRO	SP			25.2	78
* SANTA CLARITA	SCLR	SANTA CLARITA	SCLR	39.40	115,700	26.0	127
* SANTA FE SPRINGS	SFS	SANTA FE SPRINGS	SFS	8.70	16,400	13.6	61
* SANTA MONICA	SM	SANTA MONICA	SM	8.10	96,500	15.9	40
SAUGUS		SAUGUS	SAU			31.7	124
SAWTELLE		LOS ANGELES 25	LA25			13.0	41
SEMINOLE HOT SPRINGS		AGOURA	AGO			37.4	106
SEPULVEDA		SAN FERNANDO	SF			20.8	15
SHERMAN OAKS		VAN NUYS	VAN			12.8	22
* SIERRA MADRE	SMAD	SIERRA MADRE	SMAD	2.93	11,250	16.6	28
* SIGNAL HILL	SH	LONG BEACH 6	LB06	2.14	8,150	23.0	75
SILVER LAKE		LOS ANGELES 39	LA26				35
SLEEPY VALLEY		SAUGUS	SAU			40.8	H
SOLEDAD		SAUGUS	SAU			38.3	188
* SOUTH EL MONTE	SELM	EL MONTE	ELM	2.80	18,700	12.0	47
* SOUTH GATE	SOG	SOUTH GATE	SOG	7.32	79,200	9.7	59
* SOUTH PASADENA	SPAS	SOUTH PASADENA	SPAS	3.47	24,500	7.3	36
SOUTH SAN GABRIEL		ROSEMEAD	RM			11.0	46
STUDEBAKER		NORWALK	NWK			14.7	60
STUDIO CITY		NORTH HOLLYWOOD	NHO			11.2	23
SULPHUR SPRINGS		CANYON COUNTRY	CYN			37.9	125
SUNLAND		SUNLAND	SUN			18.7	10
SUN VALLEY		SUN VALLEY	SV			15.4	16
SYLMAR		SAN FERNANDO	SF			23.6	2
SYLMAR SQUARE		SAN FERNANDO	SF			23.9	2
SYLVIA PARK		TOPANGA	TOP			26.2	109
TARZANA		TARZANA	TAR			20.1	21
* TEMPLE CITY	TEC	TEMPLE CITY	TEC	3.85	31,900	13.4	38
TERMINAL ISLAND		SAN PEDRO	SP			24.8	79
TOLUCA LAKE		NORTH HOLLYWOOD	NHO			10.5	24
TOPANGA		TOPANGA	TOP			25.4	109
TOPANGA PARK		TOPANGA	TOP			27.1	109
* TORRANCE	TOR	TORRANCE	TOR	19.93	142,200	19.1	68
TROUSDALE ESTATES		BEVERLY HILLS	BH			11.2	33
TUJUNGA		TUJUNGA	TU			16.1	11
UNIVERSAL CITY		NORTH HOLLYWOOD	NHO			9.6	24
VALENCIA		VALENCIA	VAL			31.1	127
VALINDA		LA PUENTE	LPUE			18.0	92
VAL VERDE		SAUGUS	SAU			41.4	123
VALYERMO		VALYERMO	VAL			62.0	192
VAN NUYS		VAN NUYS	VAN			16.4	15
VASQUEZ ROCKS		SAUGUS	SAU			49.6	181
VENICE		VENICE	VEN			15.3	49
VERDUGO CITY		GLENDALE 8	GL08			12.6	18
* VERNON	VER	LOS ANGELES 58	LA58	5.01	80	4.8	52
VIEW PARK		LOS ANGELES 43	LA43			7.6	51
* WALNUT	WAL	WALNUT	WAL	8.61	26,400	27.7	97
WALNUT PARK		HUNTINGTON PARK	HPK			6.4	52
WALTERIA		TORRANCE	TOR			22.4	73
WARNER CENTER		WOODLAND HILLS	WOH			25.0	12
WATTS		LOS ANGELES 2	LA02			8.6	58
WESTCHESTER		LOS ANGELES 45	LA45			14.9	56
* WEST COVINA	WCOV	WEST COVINA	WCOV	16.14	94,200	20.0	92
WEST HILLS		CANOGA PARK	CAN			30.1	5
* WEST HOLLYWOOD	WHOL	LOS ANGELES 69	LA69	1.98	38,400	8.8	33
WESTLAKE		LOS ANGELES 57	LA57				44
* WESTLAKE VILLAGE	WLVL	THOUSAND OAKS	THO	5.44	8,025	35.0	102
WEST LOS ANGELES		LOS ANGELES 25	LA25			12.4	41
WESTWOOD		LOS ANGELES 24	LA24			13.1	41
* WHITTIER	WHI	WHITTIER	WHI	12.31	74,100	14.7	55
WILLOWBROOK		COMPTON	COM			10.2	58
WILMINGTON		WILMINGTON	WIL			22.3	74
WINDSOR HILLS		LOS ANGELES 43	LA43			9.0	51
WINNETKA		CANOGA PARK	CAN			24.3	12
WOODLAND HILLS		WOODLAND HILLS	WOH			23.5	13
WOODSIDE VILLAGE		WEST COVINA	WCOV			20.0	92

* INDICATES INCORPORATED CITY

MILES ARE ESTIMATED FROM DOWNTOWN CIVIC CENTER

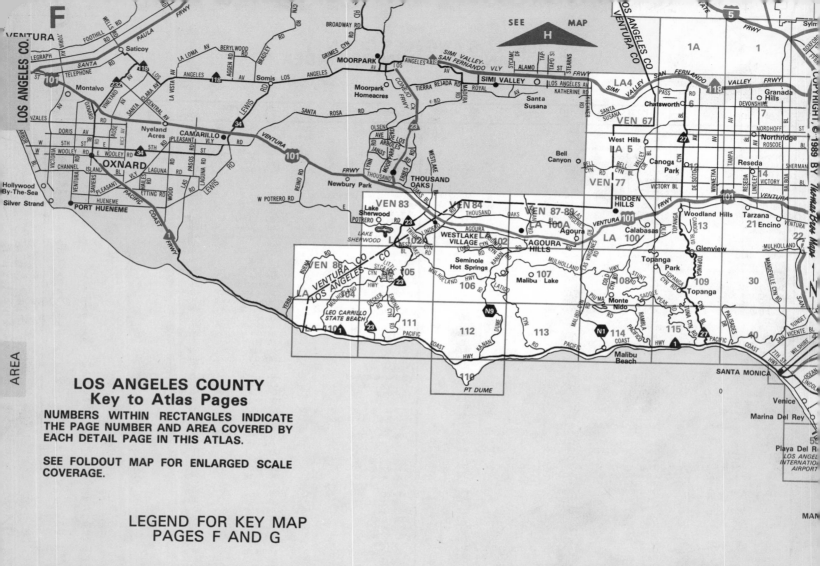

LOS ANGELES COUNTY
Key to Atlas Pages

NUMBERS WITHIN RECTANGLES INDICATE
THE PAGE NUMBER AND AREA COVERED BY
EACH DETAIL PAGE IN THIS ATLAS.

SEE FOLDOUT MAP FOR ENLARGED SCALE
COVERAGE.

LEGEND FOR KEY MAP
PAGES F AND G

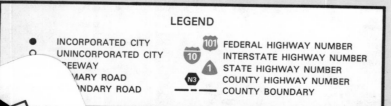

LEGEND

- INCORPORATED CITY
- UNINCORPORATED CITY
- FREEWAY
- PRIMARY ROAD
- SECONDARY ROAD

101 FEDERAL HIGHWAY NUMBER
10 INTERSTATE HIGHWAY NUMBER
1 STATE HIGHWAY NUMBER
N3 COUNTY HIGHWAY NUMBER
— — — COUNTY BOUNDARY

SCALE FOR KEY MAPS F AND G
ONE INCH EQUALS 5.7 MILES

MILES
KILOMETERS

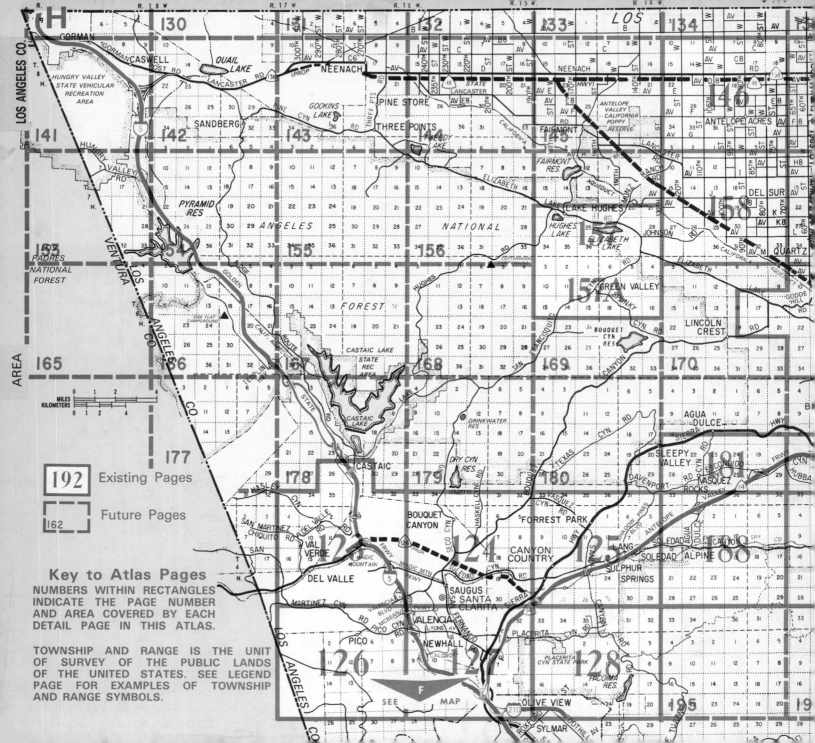

Key to Atlas Pages
NUMBERS WITHIN RECTANGLES
INDICATE THE PAGE NUMBER
AND AREA COVERED BY EACH
DETAIL PAGE IN THIS ATLAS.

TOWNSHIP AND RANGE IS THE UNIT
OF SURVEY OF THE PUBLIC LANDS
OF THE UNITED STATES. SEE LEGEND
PAGE FOR EXAMPLES OF TOWNSHIP
AND RANGE SYMBOLS.

192 Existing Pages

162 Future Pages

MILES
KILOMETERS

SEE   F   MAP

DOWNTOWN LOS ANGELES

LOS ANGELES CO.

DOWN-TOWN

MILES 0 1/8 1/4 1/2
FEET   0 660' 1320' 2640'

POINTS OF INTEREST

#	Name	Grid
1	AHMANSON THEATRE	D-2
27	A T & T BUILDING	C-3
2	ATLANTIC-RICHFIELD PLAZA	C-3
3	BANK OF AMERICA DATA CENTER	D-1
4	BANK OF AMERICA TOWER	C-3
6	BANK OF CALIFORNIA HEADQRTRS	C-3
5	BILTMORE HOTEL	C-3
85	BIXEL BUILDING	B-3
6	BOARD OF EDUCATION	D-2
	BROADWAY PLAZA	D-2
93	BRUNSWIG SQUARE	E-4
	BULLOCK'S CORP HEADQUARTERS	C-4
10	BUNKER HILL TOWERS	C-2
11	CALIFORNIA MART	C-5
90	CALIFORNIA PLAZA	
12	CALTRANS	D-3
13	CENTRAL LIBRARY	C-3
14	CHAMBER OF COMMERCE	C-2
15	CHINATOWN	E-1
89	CITICORP PLAZA	B-3
16	CITY HALL	E-3
17	CITY HALL EAST	E-3
18	CITY HALL SOUTH	E-3
19	CITY NATIONAL BANK	C-4
20	CIVIC CENTER LAW BUILDING	D-3
21	CONVENTION CENTER	A-4
22	COUNTY CRIMINAL COURTS	D-2
23	COUNTY HEALTH BUILDING	D-2
24	COUNTY HEALTH DEPARTMENT HQ	D-2
25	COUNTY OFFICES	D-2
26	COURTHOUSE	D-2
28	WELLS FARGO CENTER	C-3
	DEPARTMENT OF WATER & POWER	D-2
30	DOROTHY CHANDLER PAVILION	D-2
31	EL PUEBLO STATE HISTORIC PARK	E-2
32	EMPLOYMENT DEVELOPMENT DEPT	B-5
33	FEDERAL BUILDNG & POST OFFICE	E-2
34	FEDERAL COURTHOUSE	E-2
96	FEDERAL RESERVE	C-4
35	FIRE STATIONS	
92	GRAND CENTRAL MARKET	D-3
94	GRAND FINANCIAL PLAZA	C-4
37	GREYHOUND & TRAILWAYS DEPOT	D-4
38	HALL OF ADMINISTRATION	D-2
39	HALL OF JUSTICE	E-2
40	HALL OF RECORDS	D-2

#	Name	Grid
41	HERALD-EXAMINER	C-5
42	HILTON HOTEL	B-3
43	HOSPITALS	
99	HOTEL TOKYO	E-3
8	HYATT REGENCY HOTEL	C-3
44	INTERNATIONAL JEWELRY CENTER	C-3
86	INTERNATIONAL TOWER	B-4
	JUNIPERO SERRA BUILDING	D-3
49	LAW LIBRARY	D-2
50	LITTLE TOKYO	E-3
51	LOS ANGELES CHILDRENS MUSEUM	E-2
52	LOS ANGELES FLOWER MART	D-4
100	L.A. METRO BLUE LINE	B-4
84	L.A. THEATRE CENTER	D-4
47	L.A. TRADE-TECH COLLEGE	A-6
54	L.A. VISITORS & CONV. BUREAU	C-3
	(IN MANULIFE BUILDING)	
48	L.A. WORLD TRADE CENTER	C-2
53	MARK TAPER FORUM	D-2
54	MISSION CHURCH	E-2
90	MUSEUM OF CONTEMPORARY ART	D-3
	NEW OTANI HOTEL	E-3
55	OLVERA STREET	E-2
56	ONE WILSHIRE BUILDING	C-3
57	PACIFIC BELL	B-3
	PACIFIC STOCK EXCHANGE	C-2
59	PARKER CENTER	E-3
	PICO HOUSE	E-2
61	PLAZA	E-2
62	POST OFFICES	
97	PREMIERE TOWERS	D-4
	PROMENADE TOWERS	C-2
88	ST VINCENT'S SQUARE	C-4
63	SECURITY PACIFIC BUILDING	C-3
64	SECURITY PACIFIC NATL BANK HQ	C-3
65	SEVENTH MARKET PL	C-3
95	SHERATON GRANDE HOTEL	C-2
	SOUTHERN CALIFORNIA GAS CO	C-4
67	SO CALIF RAPID TRANSIT HQ	D-3
	TEMPORARY CONTEMPORARY	E-3
68	TERMINAL ANNEX POST OFFICE	E-2
69	TERMINAL MARKET	E-6
70	THE L.A. MART	B-6
71	THOMAS BROS. MAPS STORE	C-3
72	TIMES-MIRROR SQUARE	D-3
73	TRAFFIC COURT BUILDING	B-6
74	TRANSAMERICA CENTER	B-5
	U C L A EXTENSION	B-4
76	UNION BANK BUILDING	C-3
77	UNOCAL CENTER	B-2
78	UNION STATION	E-2
79	WELLER COURT SHOPPING CENTER	E-3
80	WELLS FARGO BUILDING	C-3
81	WESTERN PACIFIC BUILDING	C-5
7	WESTIN-BONAVENTURE HOTEL	C-3
82	WILCOX BUILDING	C-3
83	YMCA SITE	C-3

UNION STATION
THE COAST STARLIGHT
THE DESERT WIND
THE SUNSET LTD
THE SAN JOAQUINS
(BUS CONNECTION)
THE SAN DIEGANS
SOUTHWEST CHIEF

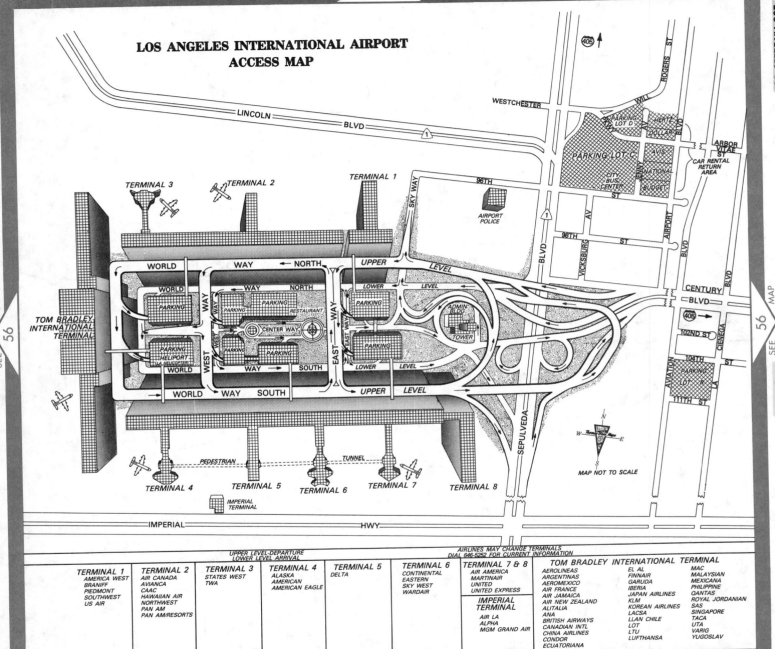

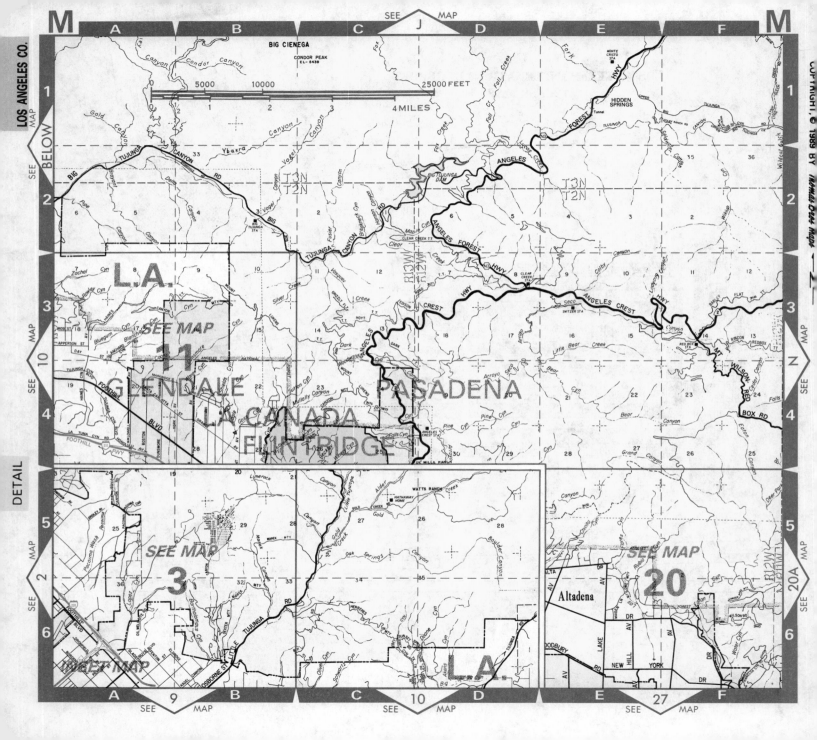

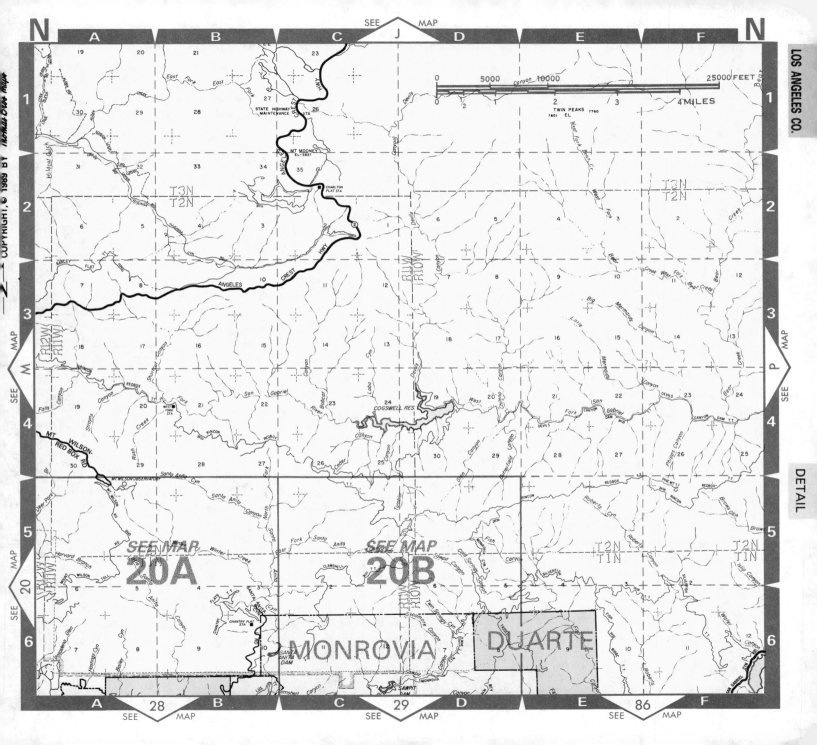

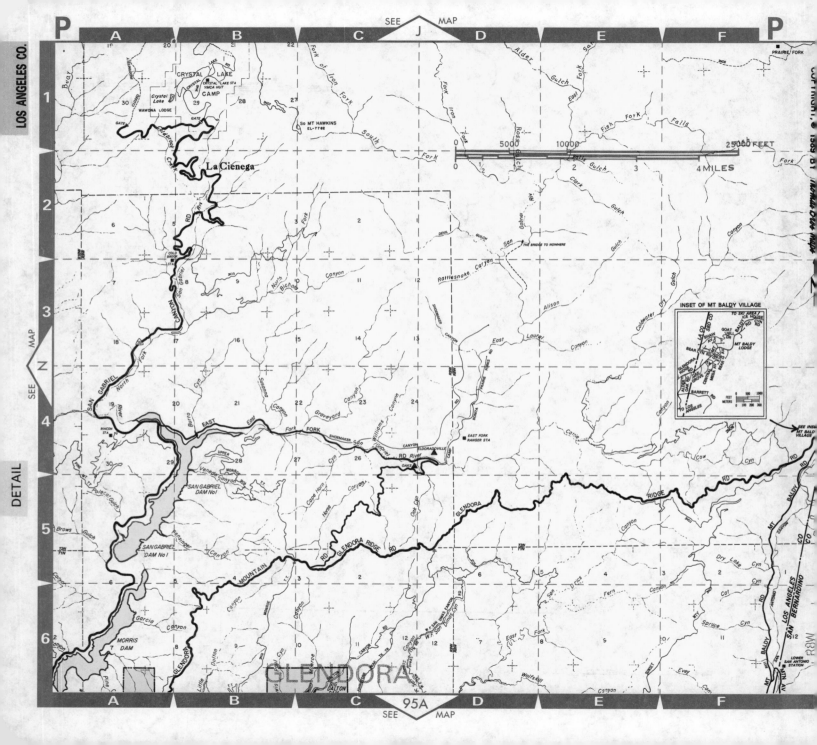

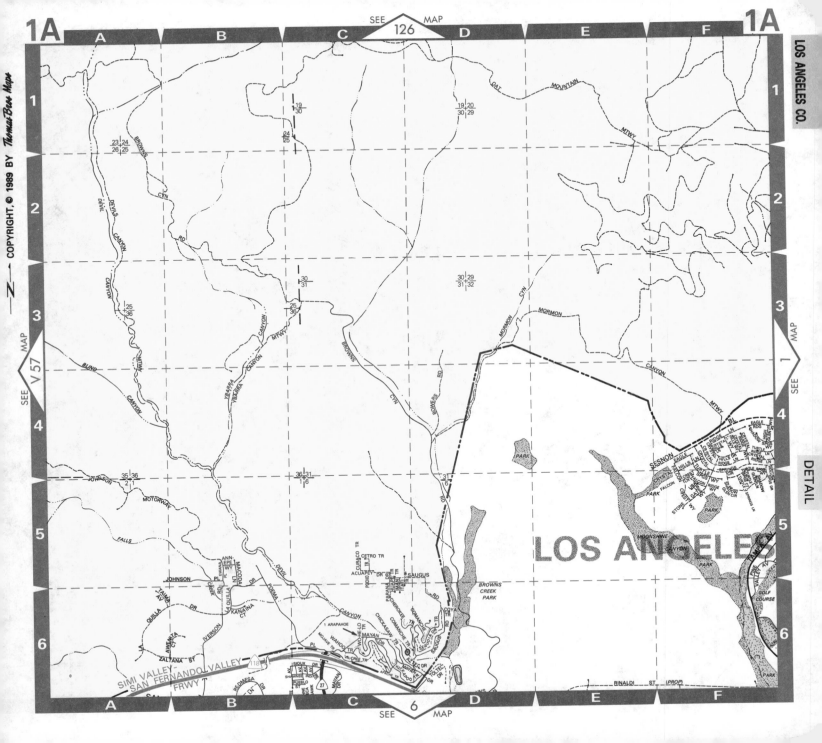

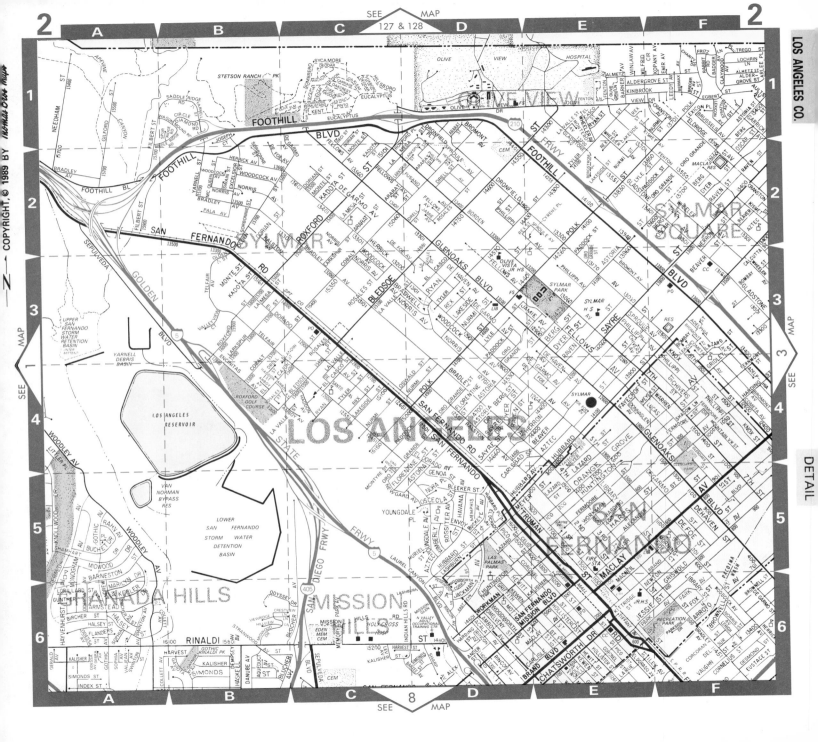

DETAIL

SEE MAP 2

LOS ANGELES

SAN FERNANDO

KAGEL CANYON

LAKEVIEW TERRACE

ANGELES NATIONAL FOREST

VETERANS MEMORIAL PARK

EL CARISO REGIONAL PARK

EL CARISO GOLF COURSE

LOS ANGELES MISSION COLLEGE (SITE)

GLENHAVEN MEMORIAL PARK

SHOLOM MEM PARK

DEXTER PARK

ANGELES NATIONAL FOREST BOUNDRY

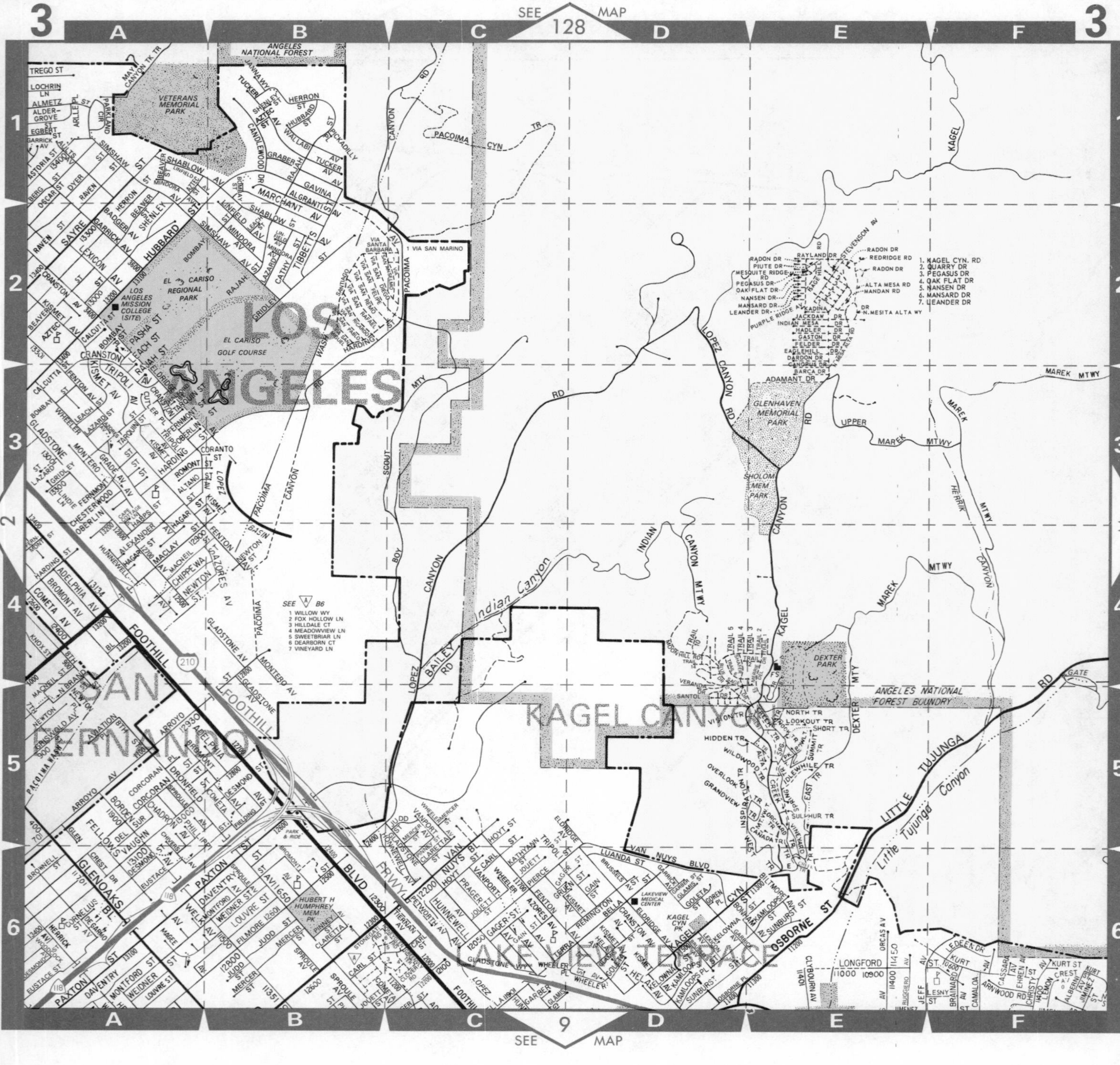

HUBERT H HUMPHREY MEM

LAKEVIEW MEDICAL CENTER

Little Tujunga Canyon

Indian Canyon

Pacoima Canyon

Lopez Canyon Rd

Kagel Canyon Rd

Marek Mtwy

Foothill Blvd

Osborne St

Van Nuys Blvd

SEE B6
1 WILLOW WY
2 FOX HOLLOW LN
3 HILLDALE CT
4 MEADOWVIEW LN
5 SWEETBRIAR LN
6 DEARBORN CT
7 VINEYARD LN

1. KAGEL CYN. RD.
2. QUARRY DR
3. PEGASUS DR
4. OAK FLAT DR
5. NANSEN DR
6. MANSARD DR
7. LEANDER DR

RADON DR
PIUTE DR
MESQUITE RIDGE RD
PEGASUS DR
OAK FLAT DR
NANSEN DR
MANSARD DR
LEANDER DR
RAYLAND DR
REDRIDGE RD
RADON DR
ALTA MESA RD
MANDAN RD
N. MESITA ALTA WY
KADINA
JACKDAW DR
INDIAN MESA
HADLER DR
GASTON DR
FELDER DR
EAGLEHILL DR
DARDON DR
SHOOFLY DR
BARCA DR
ADAMANT DR

LOS ANGELES CO.

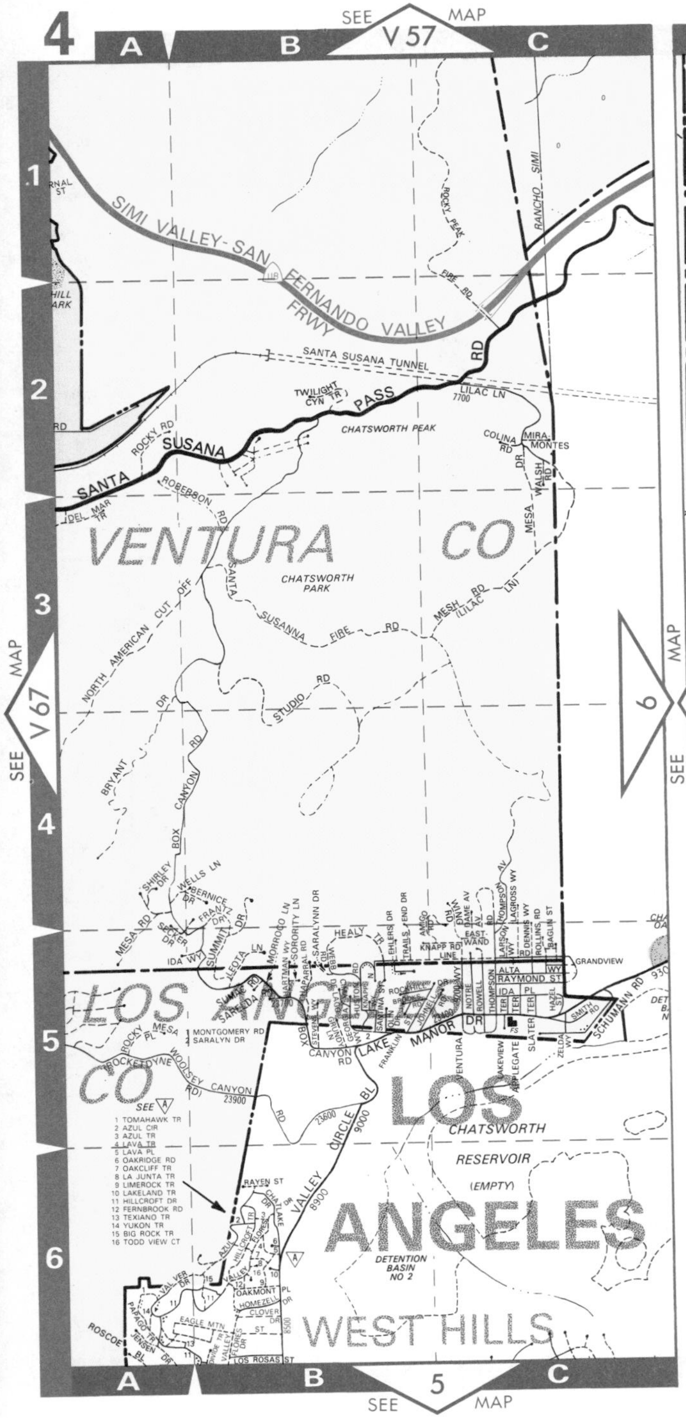

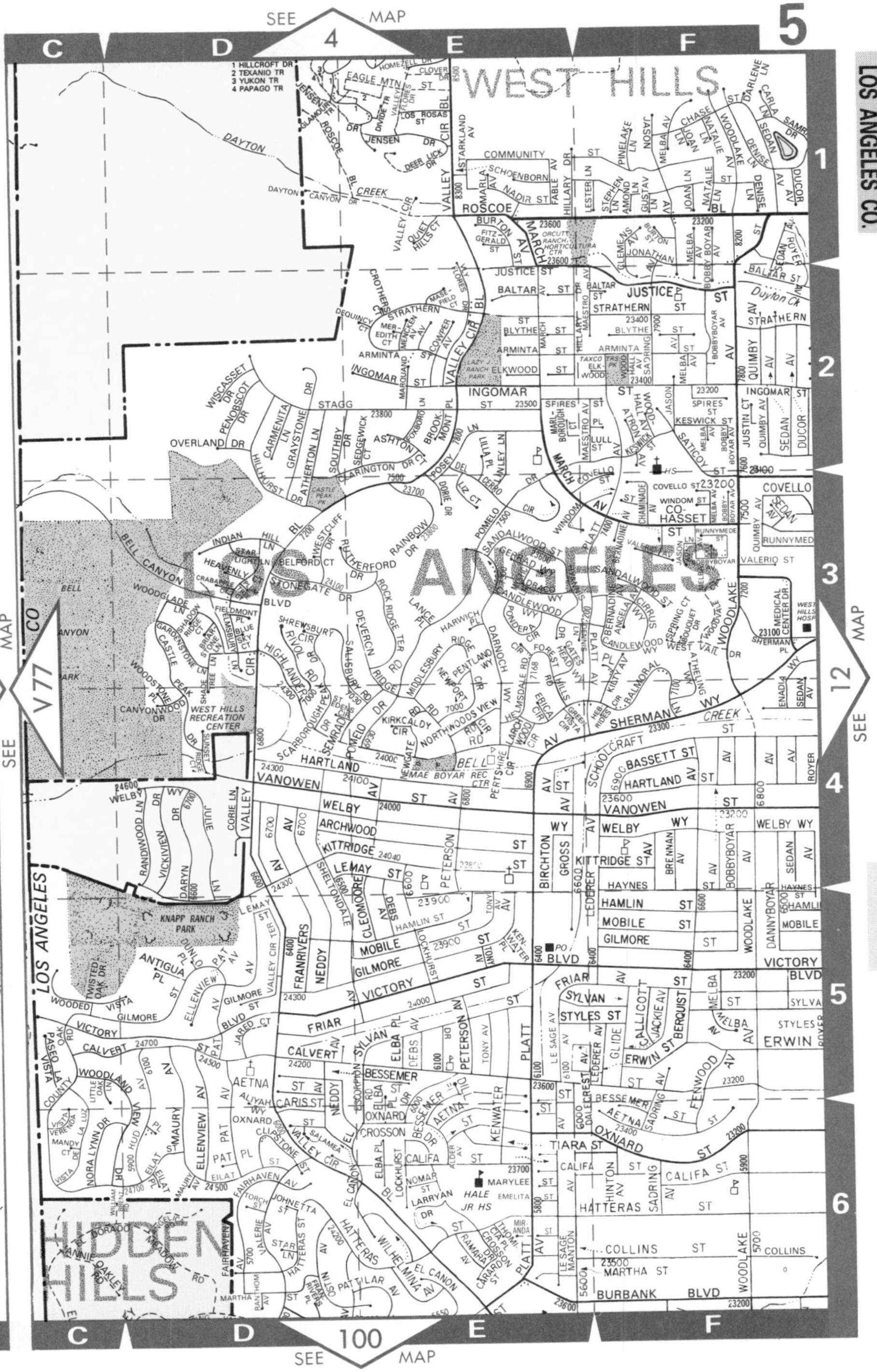

SEE MAP V 57

SEE MAP 4

WEST HILLS

4 A B C | C D E F 5

1 HILLCROFT DR
2 TEXANIO TR
3 YUKON TR
4 PAPAGO TR

SIMI VALLEY-SAN FERNANDO VALLEY FRWY

RANCHO SIMI

SANTA SUSANA TUNNEL

LILAC LN

TWILIGHT CYN

CHATSWORTH PEAK

COLINA RD

MIRA MONTES

SANTA SUSANA

ROBERTSON RD

WALSH

MESA

VENTURA CO

CHATSWORTH PARK

NORTH AMERICAN CUT-OFF

SUSANNA

FIBE RD

MESH RD

LILAC LN

STUDIO RD

BRYANT

CANYON

SEE MAP V 67

SEE MAP 6

LOS ANGELES CO

SEE MAP V 77

BELL CANYON

WEST HILLS RECREATION CENTER

CANYONWOOD DR

LOS ANGELES

ROSCOE

WEST HILLS

COMMUNITY

JUSTICE

STRATHERN

BLYTHE

ARMINTA

INGOMAR

STAGG

OVERLAND DR

HARTLAND

VANOWEN

WELBY

ARCHWOOD

KITTRIDGE

LEMAY

CLEEMORE

MOBILE

GILMORE

VICTORY

FRIAR

CALVERT

BESSEMER

OXNARD

CALIFA

HATTERAS

COVELLO

HASSET

SHERMAN WY

WOODLAKE

VANOWEN ST

WELBY WY

HAMLIN ST

GILMORE

VICTORY BLVD

SYLVAN ST

STYLES ST

ERWIN

BURBANK BLVD

MANOR

CANYON LAKE

RAYMOND ST

WEST HILLS

LOS ANGELES CO

LOS ANGELES

CHATSWORTH RESERVOIR (EMPTY)

DETENTION BASIN NO 2

WEST HILLS

KNAPP RANCH PARK

HIDDEN HILLS

ELLENVIEW

WOODLAND

OXNARD

FAIRHAVEN

HALE JR HS

MARYLEE

1 TOMAHAWK TR
2 AZUL DR
3 AZUL TR
4 LAVA TR
5 LAVA PL
6 OAKRIDGE RD
7 OAKCLIFF DR
8 LIMEROCK TR
9 LIMEROCK TR
10 LAKELAND TR
11 HILLCROFT DR
12 FERNBROOK RD
13 TEXIANO TR
14 YUKON TR
15 BIG ROCK CT
16 TODD VIEW CT

A B C | C D E F

SEE MAP 5

SEE MAP 100

LOS ANGELES CO.

DETAIL

SIMI VALLEY-SAN FERNANDO-VALLEY FRWY

SANTA SUSANA PASS RD

Santa Susana Pass Wash

CHATSWORTH PARK NORTH

CHATSWORTH PARK SOUTH

OAKWOOD CEMETERY

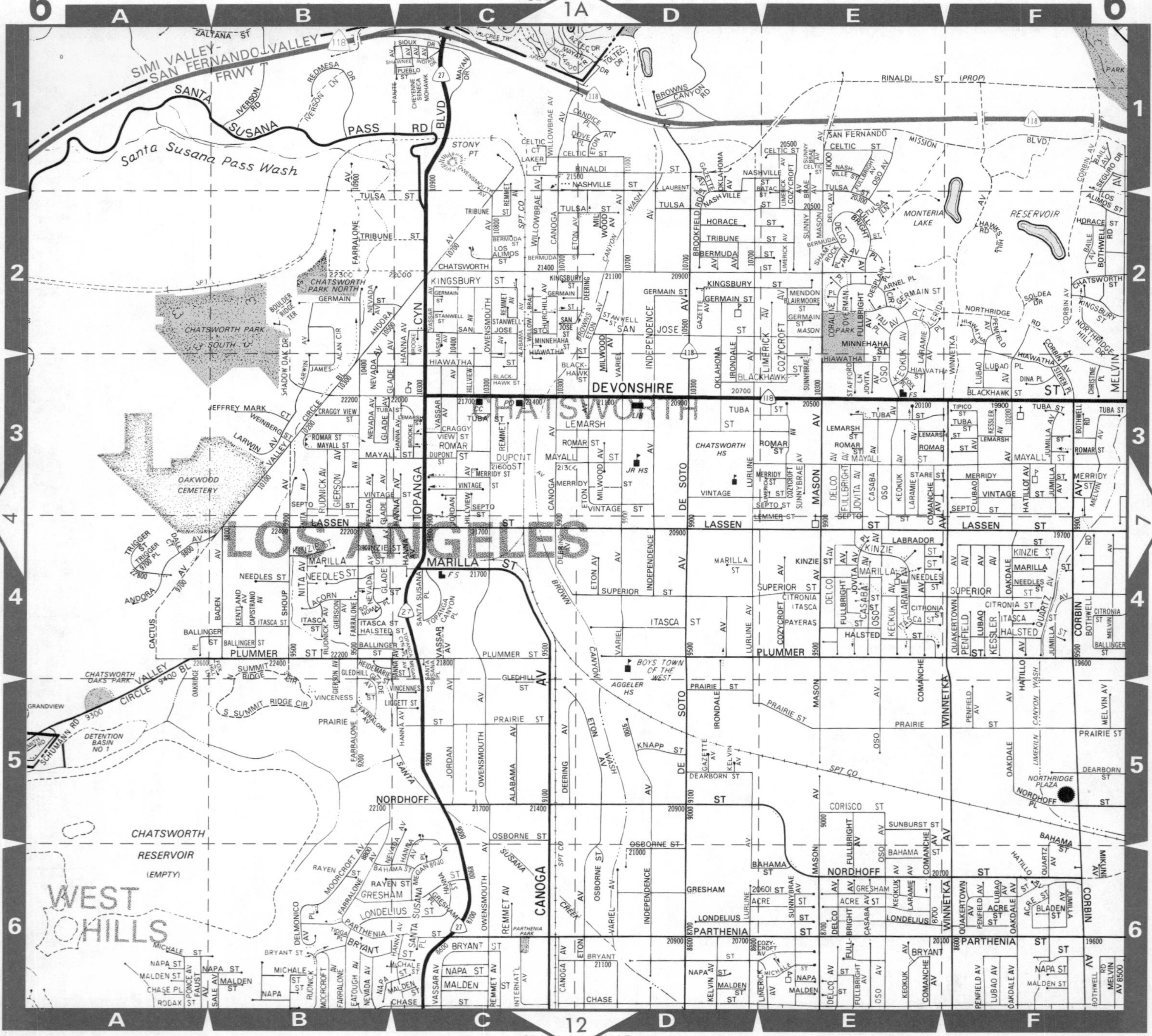

LOS ANGELES

CHATSWORTH

DEVONSHIRE

CHATSWORTH HS

JR HS

MONTERIA LAKE

RESERVOIR

BOYS TOWN OF THE WEST

AGGELER HS

NORTHRIDGE PLAZA

CHATSWORTH OAKS PARK

DETENTION BASIN NO 1

GRANDVIEW

CHATSWORTH RESERVOIR (EMPTY)

WEST HILLS

LASSEN

PLUMMER

NORDHOFF

PARTHENIA

SEE MAP 7

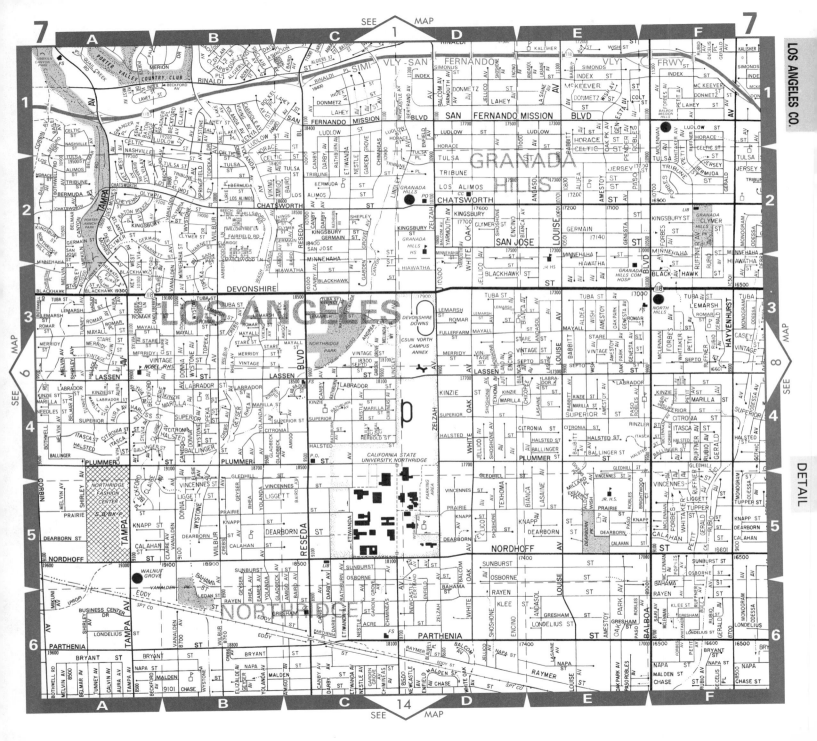

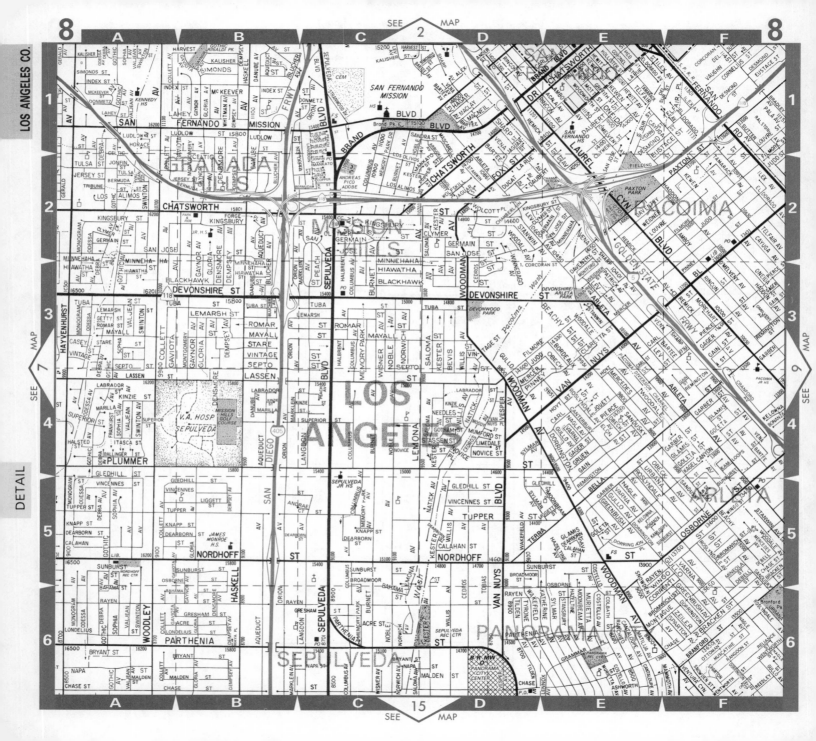

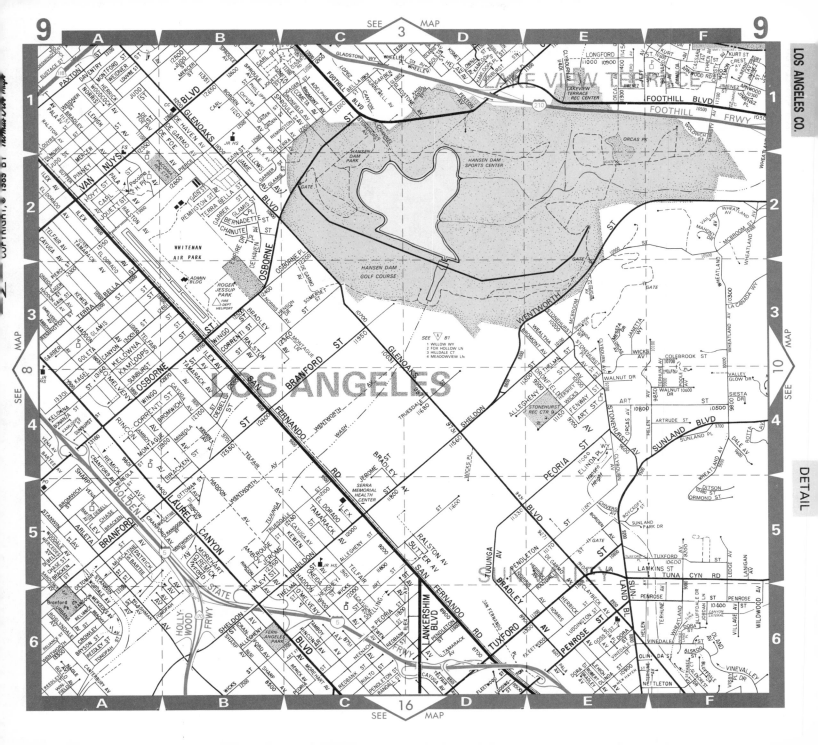

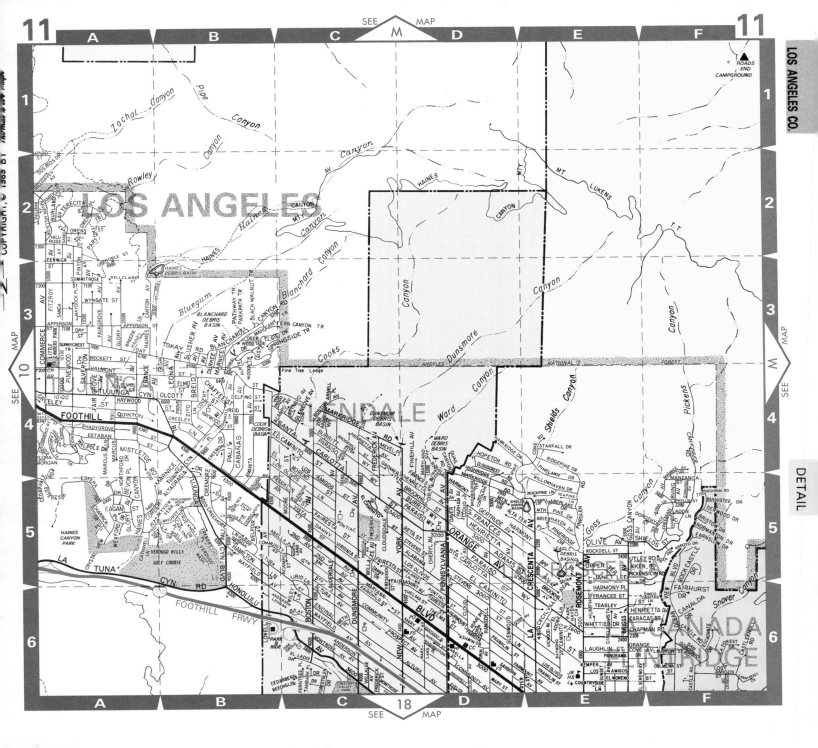

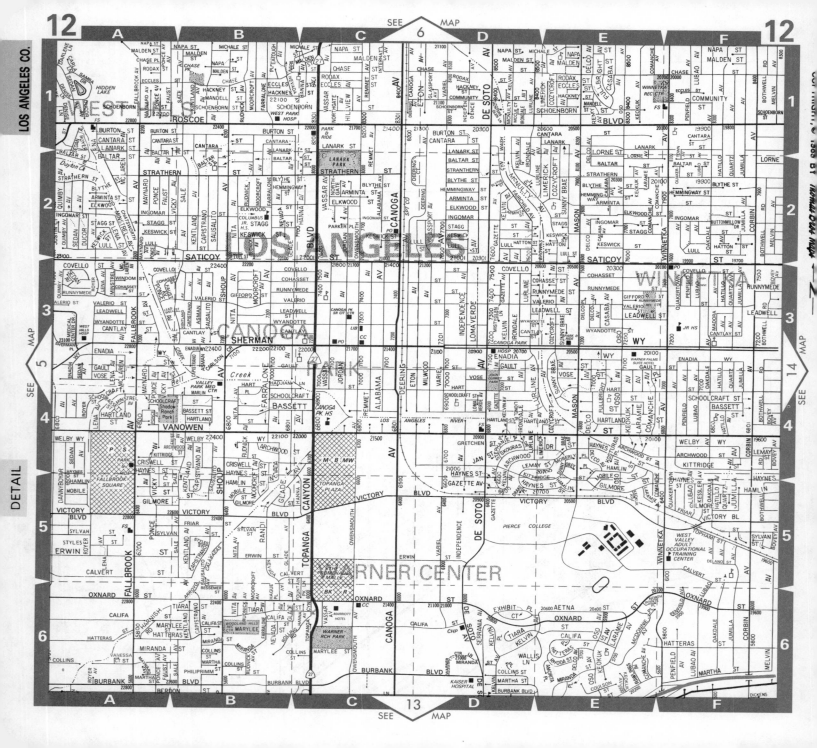

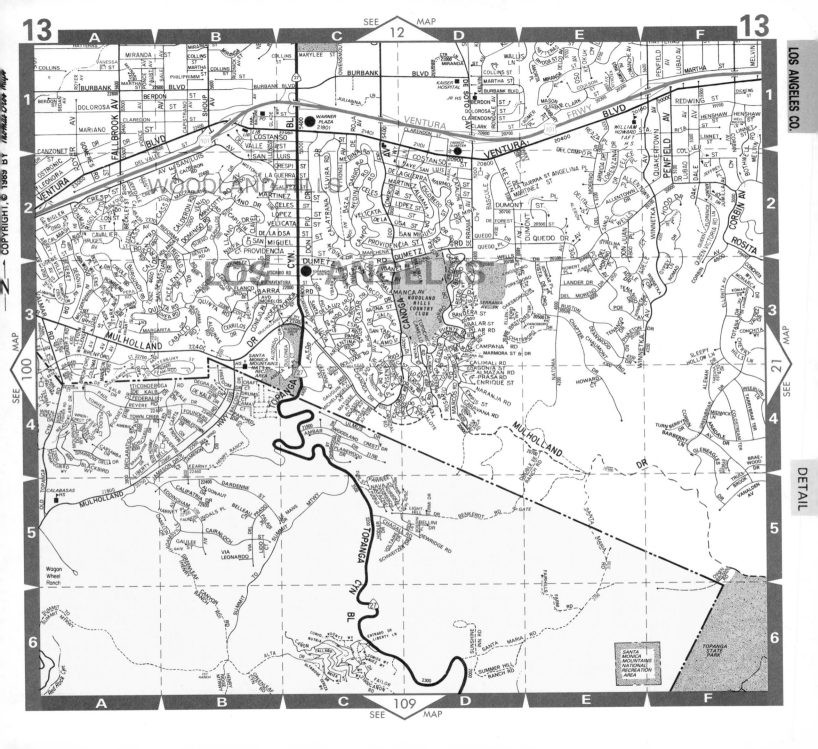

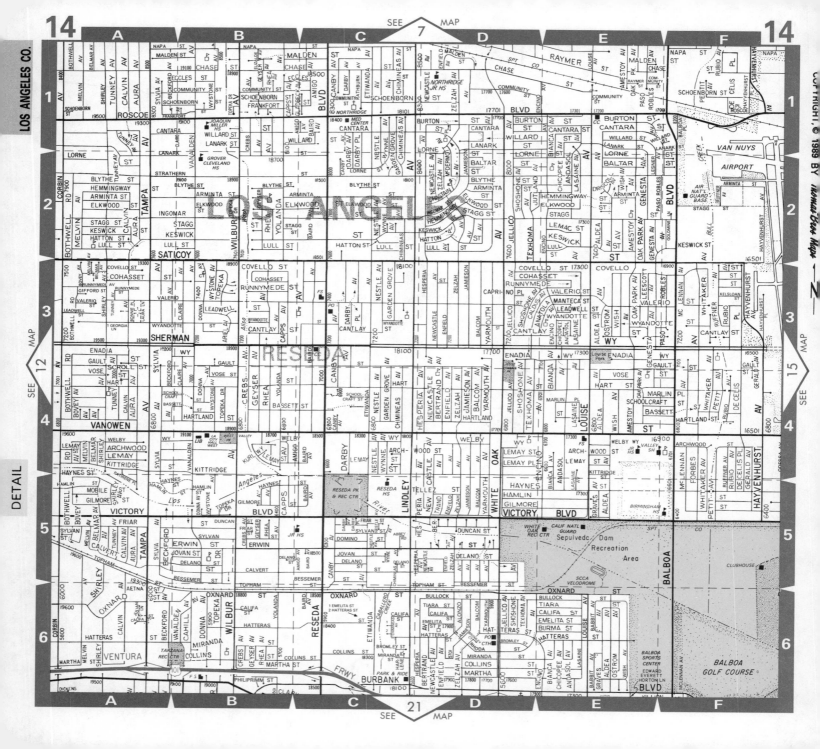

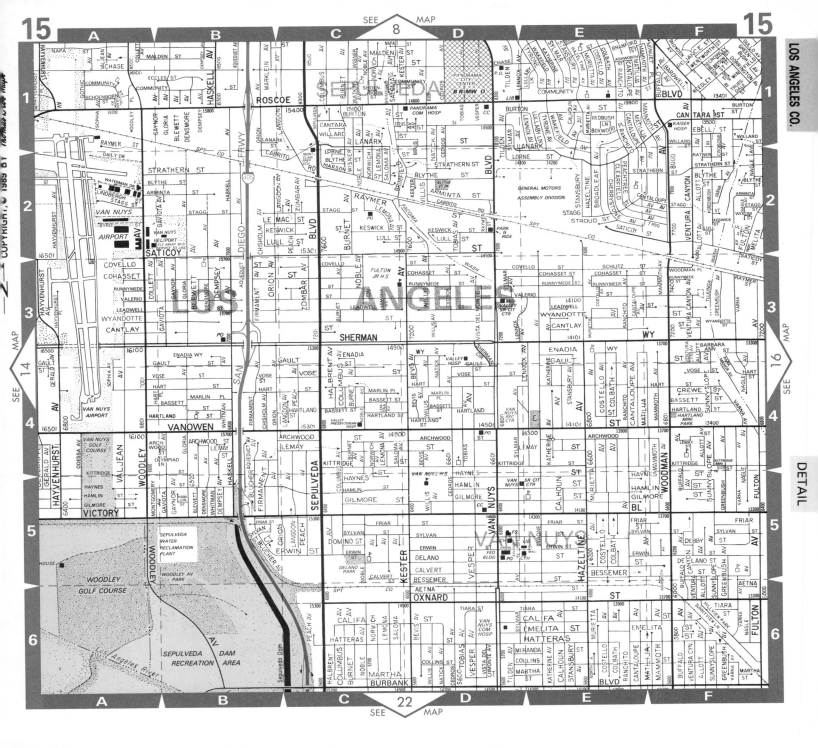

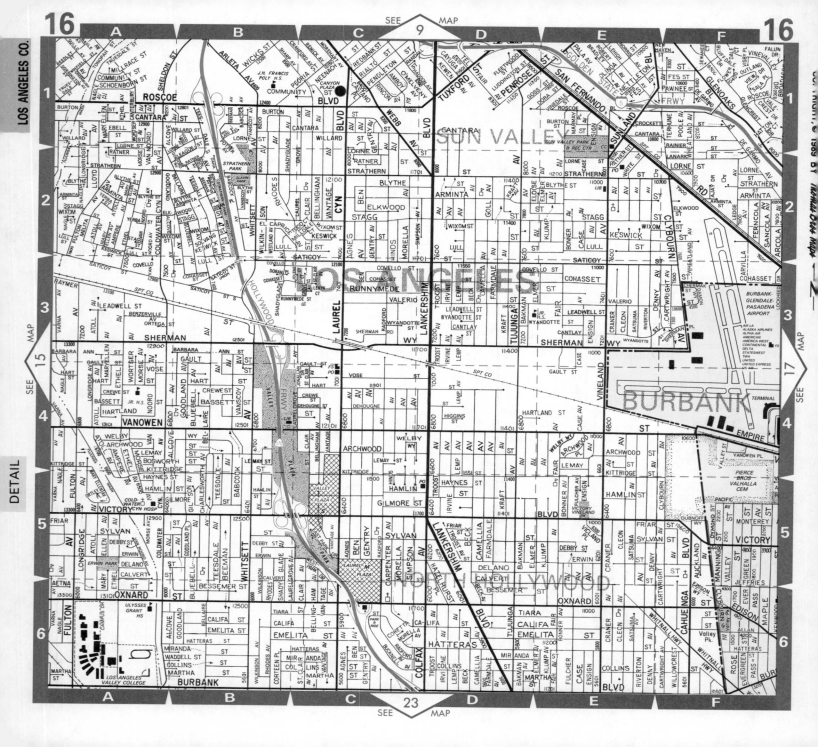

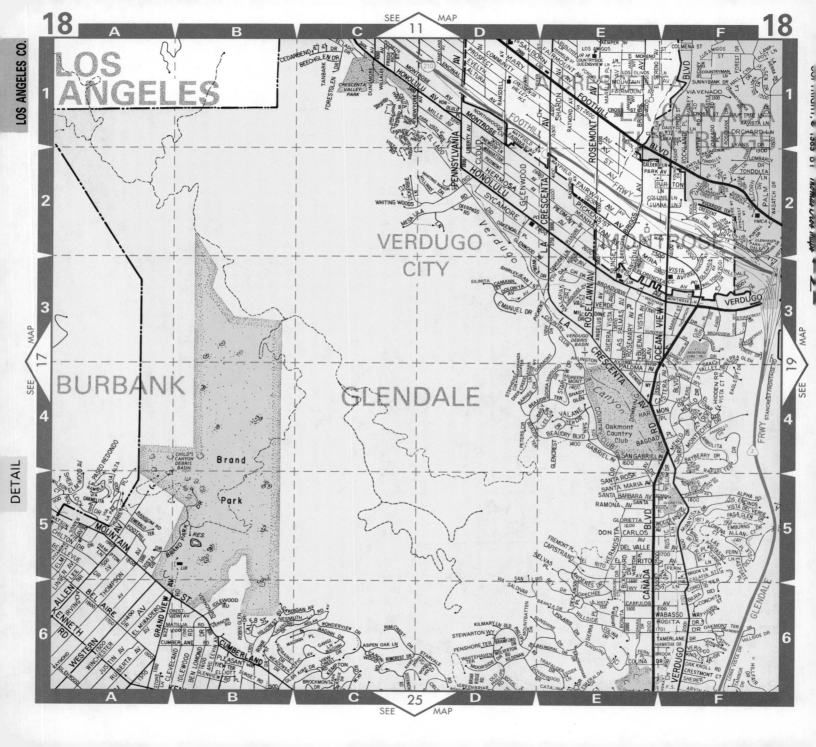

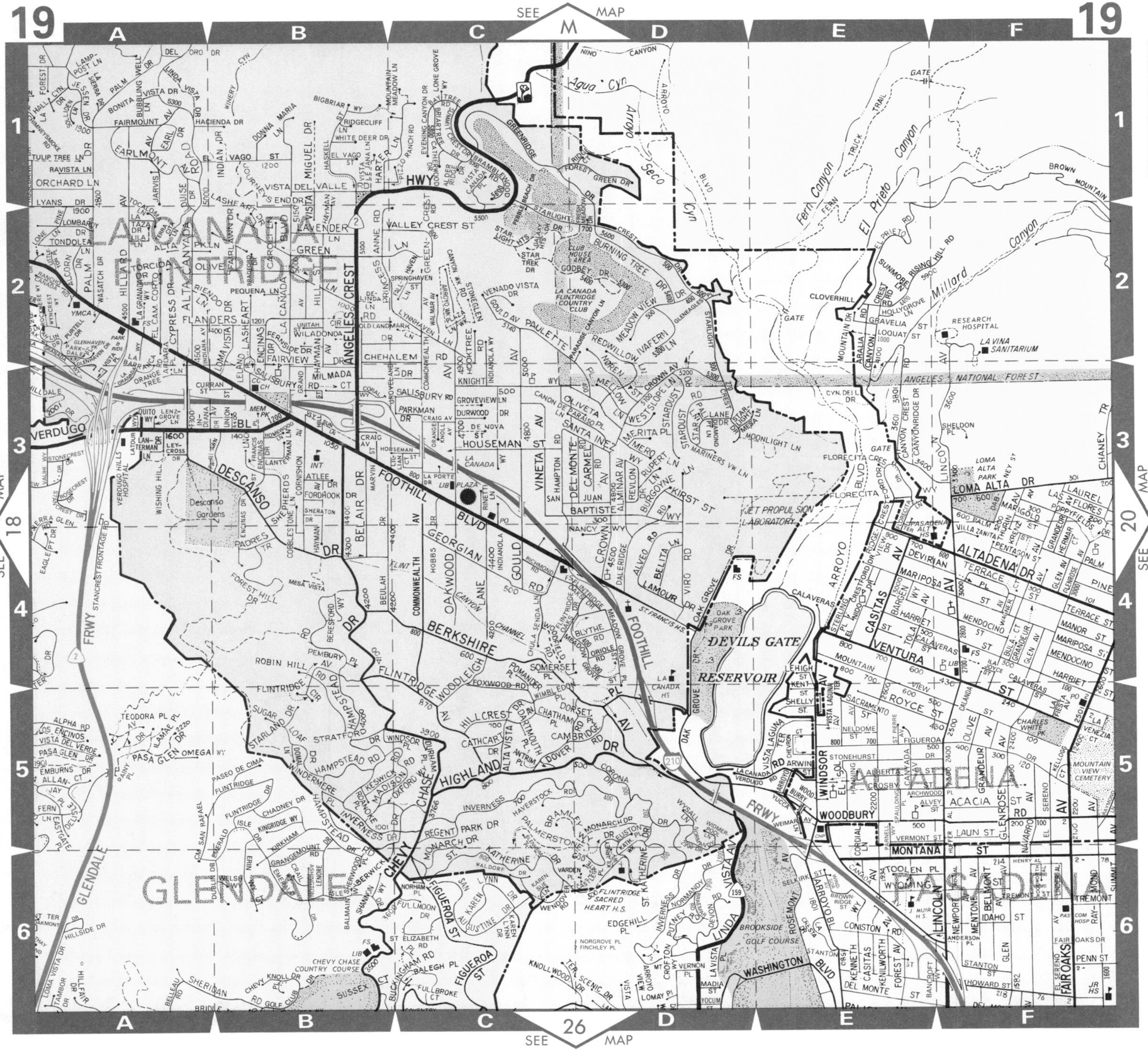

LOS ANGELES CO.

DETAIL

SEE MAP M

LA CANADA FLINTRIDGE

GLENDALE

PASADENA

ALTADENA

LA CANADA FLINTRIDGE COUNTRY CLUB

JET PROPULSION LABORATORY

DEVILS GATE RESERVOIR

FOOTHILL BLVD

ANGELES NATIONAL FOREST

Oak Grove Park

Descanso Gardens

Brookside Golf Course

Chevy Chase Country Course

SEE 18 MAP

SEE 20 MAP

SEE 26 MAP

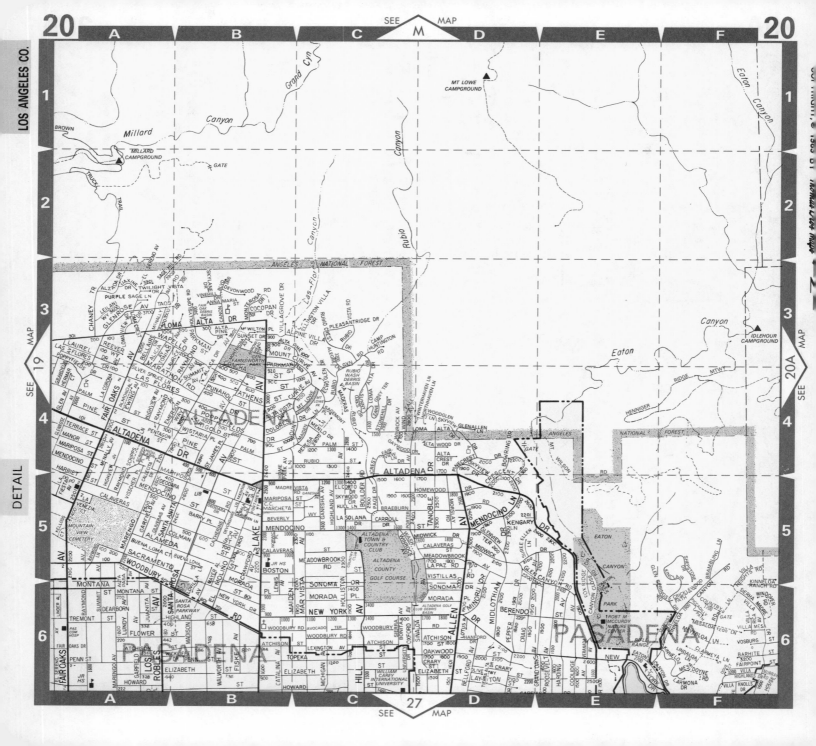

SEE MAP N

Eaton Canyon

Deer Park Brook

MT WILSON RED BOX
GATE

MT WILSON OBSERVATORY 5710

Santa

Anita

SANTA

ANITA

Canyon

SPRUCE GROVE CAMPGROUND
CASCADE CAMPGROUND

Winter

MT. WILSON

E

Creek

HOEGEE CAMPGROUND

Harvard Branch

RD

MT. WILSON RD

IDLEHOUR CAMPGROUND

TRUCK

FLATS

TRAIL

STA

GATE

Lillie

CHANTRY

Santa

Anita

Canyon

Glen

Pasadena

Canyon

Bailey

Hastings Canyon

ANITA

CANYON RD

SANTA ANITA DAM

SANTA

MONROVIA

ANGELES NATIONAL FOREST

WILDERNESS PARK

SIERRA MADRE

ARCADIA

Clamshell Canyon

PASADENA

VILLA HEIGHTS RD
KINNELOA RANCH RD
WINDOVER
SIERRA MADRE
SHAW RANCH RD
VILLA
VILLA MESA

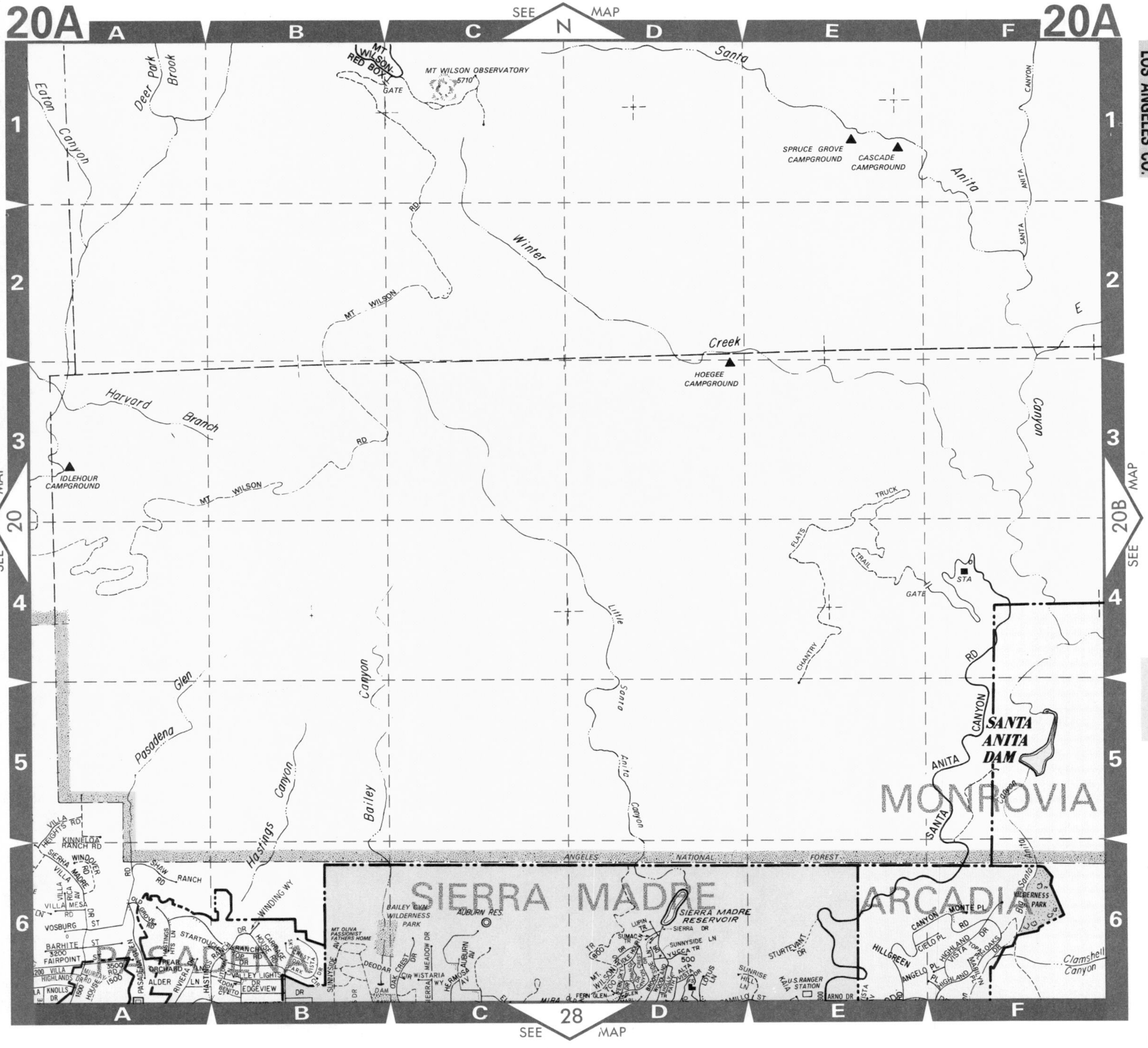

VOSBURG

BARHITE
FAIRPOINT
5200

WINDING WY

BAILEY CYN WILDERNESS PARK

MT OLIVA PASSIONIST FATHERS HOME

AUBURN RES.

SIERRA MADRE RESERVOIR
SIERRA DR

STURTEVANT DR

HILLGREEN

CIELO PL

HIGHLAND

MONTE PL

ANGELO PL

SUNRISE

U.S. RANGER STATION

DETAIL

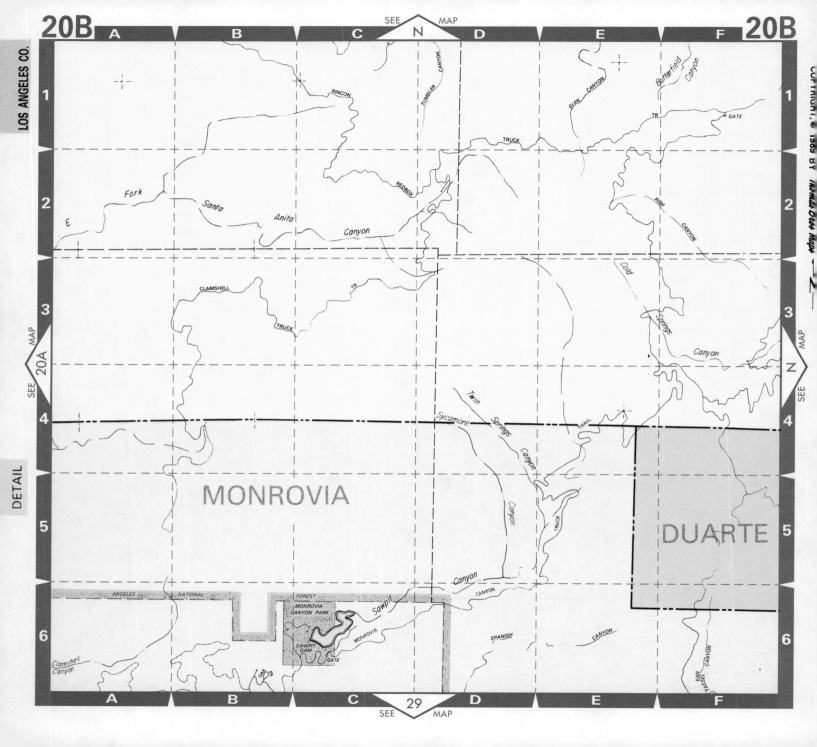

LOS ANGELES

SANTA MONICA MOUNTAINS

ENCINO RESERVOIR

STATE OWNED LANDS

SAN VICENTE MOUNTAIN PARK

TOPANGA STATE PARK

MULHOLLAND DR

BALBOA GOLF COURSE

CLUBHOUSE ENCINO GOLF CO

EL CABALLERO COUNTRY CLUB

BRAEMAR COUNTRY CLUB

TARZANA

ENCINO

BURBANK BLVD

VENTURA BLVD

VENTURA FRWY 101

MEDICAL CENTER OF TARZANA

TARZANA SQUARE

BALBOA SPORTS CENTER

VENTURA

ROSITA ST

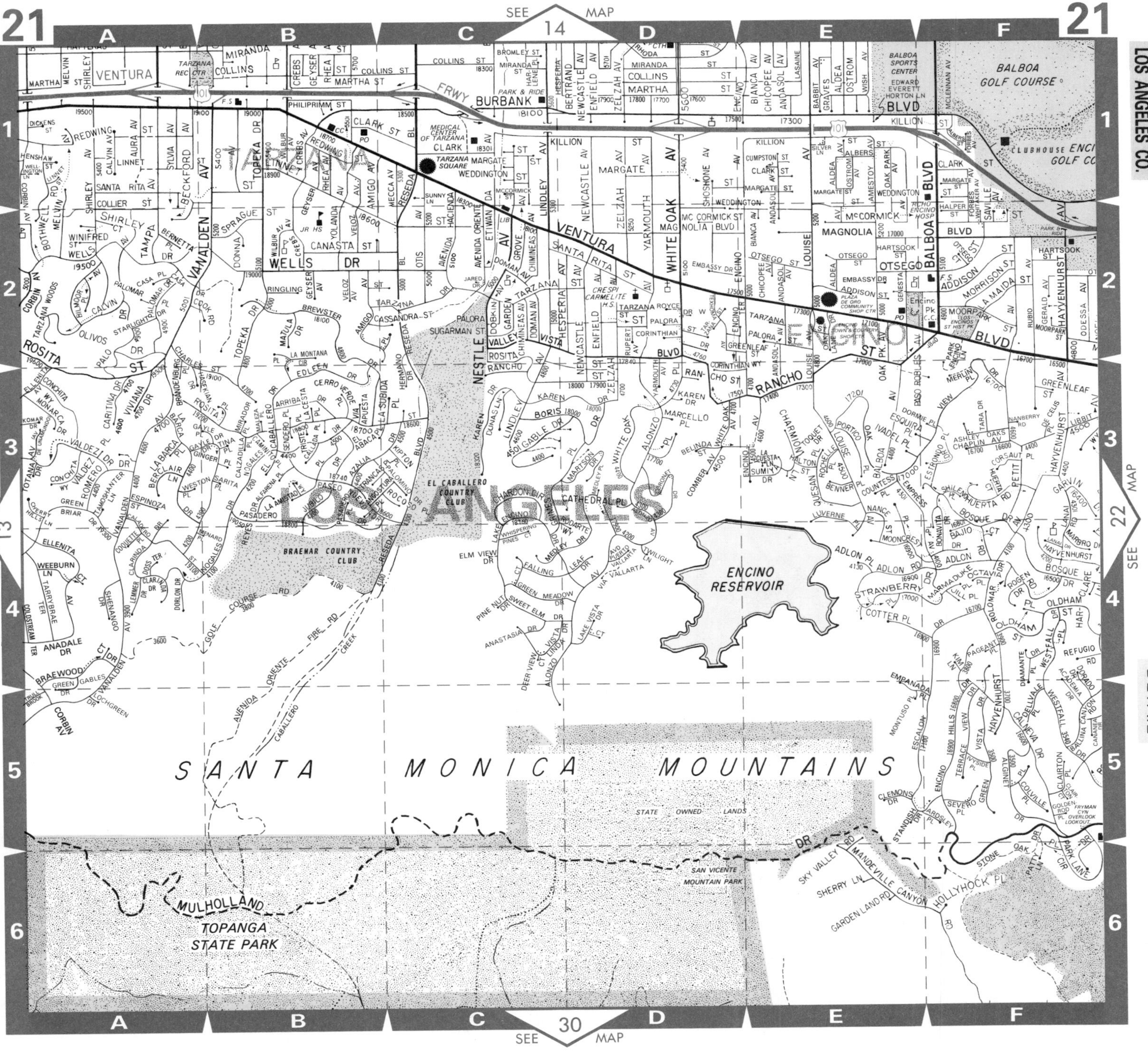

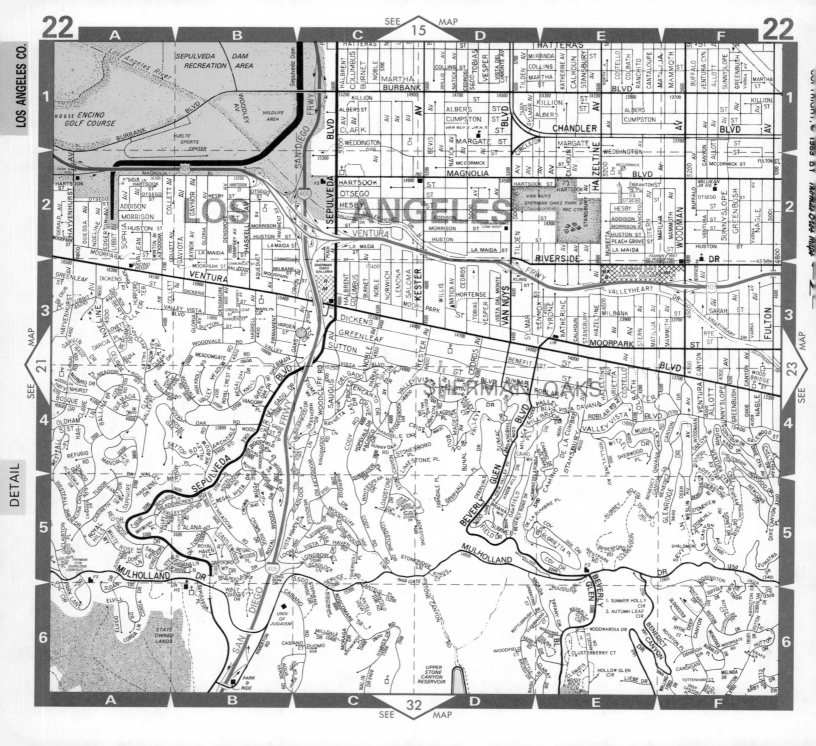

LOS ANGELES CO.

DETAIL

SEE MAP 17

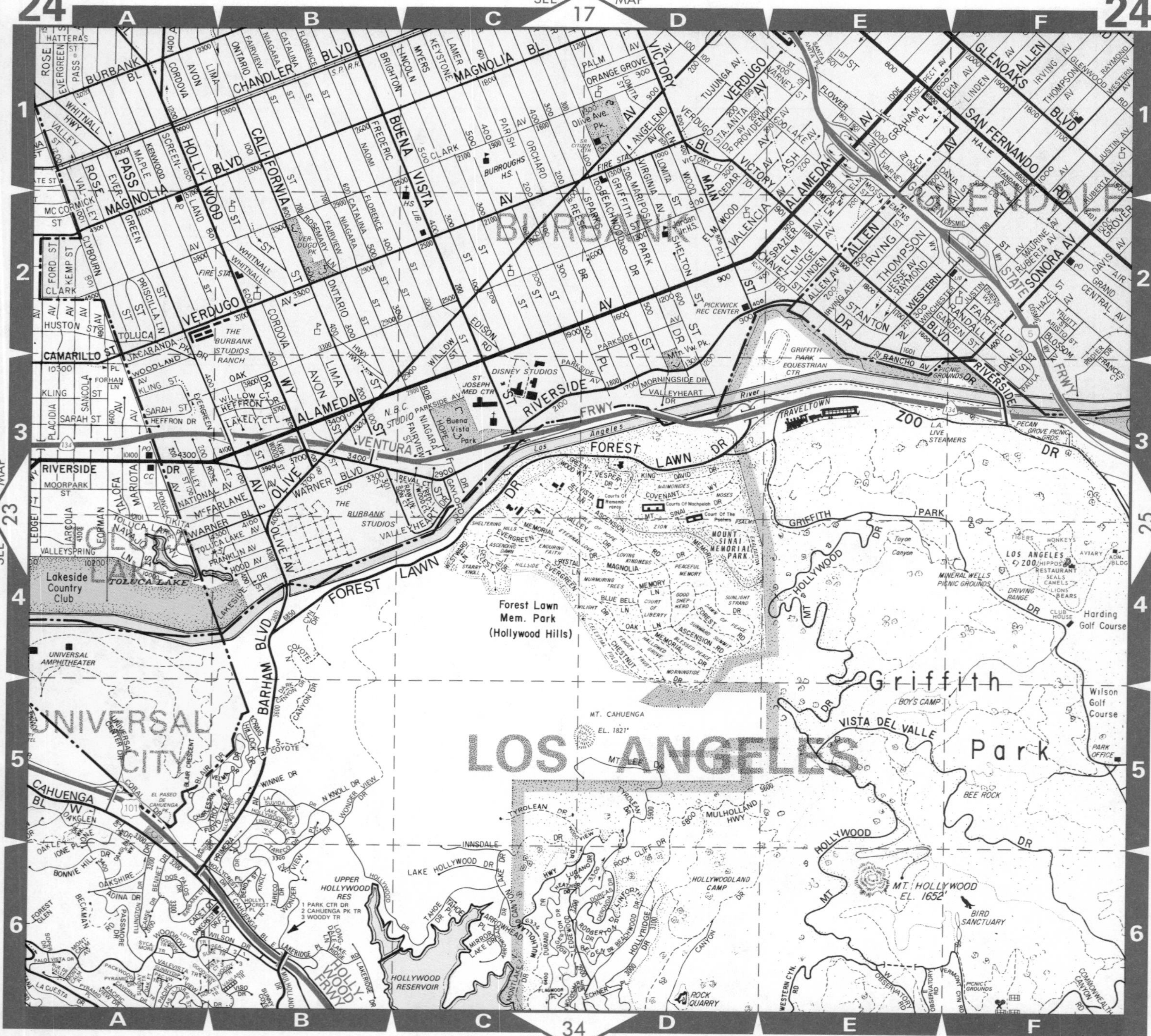

SEE MAP 23

SEE MAP 25

SEE MAP 34

BURBANK

GLENDALE

LOS ANGELES

Griffith Park

UNIVERSAL CITY

Forest Lawn Mem. Park (Hollywood Hills)

THE BURBANK STUDIOS

Lakeside Country Club

TOLUCA LAKE

Universal Amphitheater

LA ZOO

LOS ANGELES ZOO

Harding Golf Course

Wilson Golf Course

Park Office

MT. CAHUENGA EL. 1821'

MT. LEE

MT. HOLLYWOOD EL. 1652

Bird Sanctuary

Bee Rock

Rock Quarry

Hollywood Reservoir

Upper Hollywood Res.

Lake Hollywood Dr

Hollywoodland Camp

Boy's Camp

Vista Del Valle

Travel town

Griffith Park Equestrian Ctr

Pickwick Rec Center

Disney Studios

St Joseph Med Ctr

Burroughs H.S.

NBC Studio

Buena Vista Park

Olive Ave. Pk.

Mount Sinai Memorial Park

Forest Lawn Dr

Barham Blvd

Ventura Frwy

Riverside Frwy

Hollywood Frwy

Cahuenga Bl

Los Angeles River

Hollywood Dr

GLENDALE

Griffith Park

LOS ANGELES

ANGELES

SEE MAP 24

SEE MAP 26

DETAIL

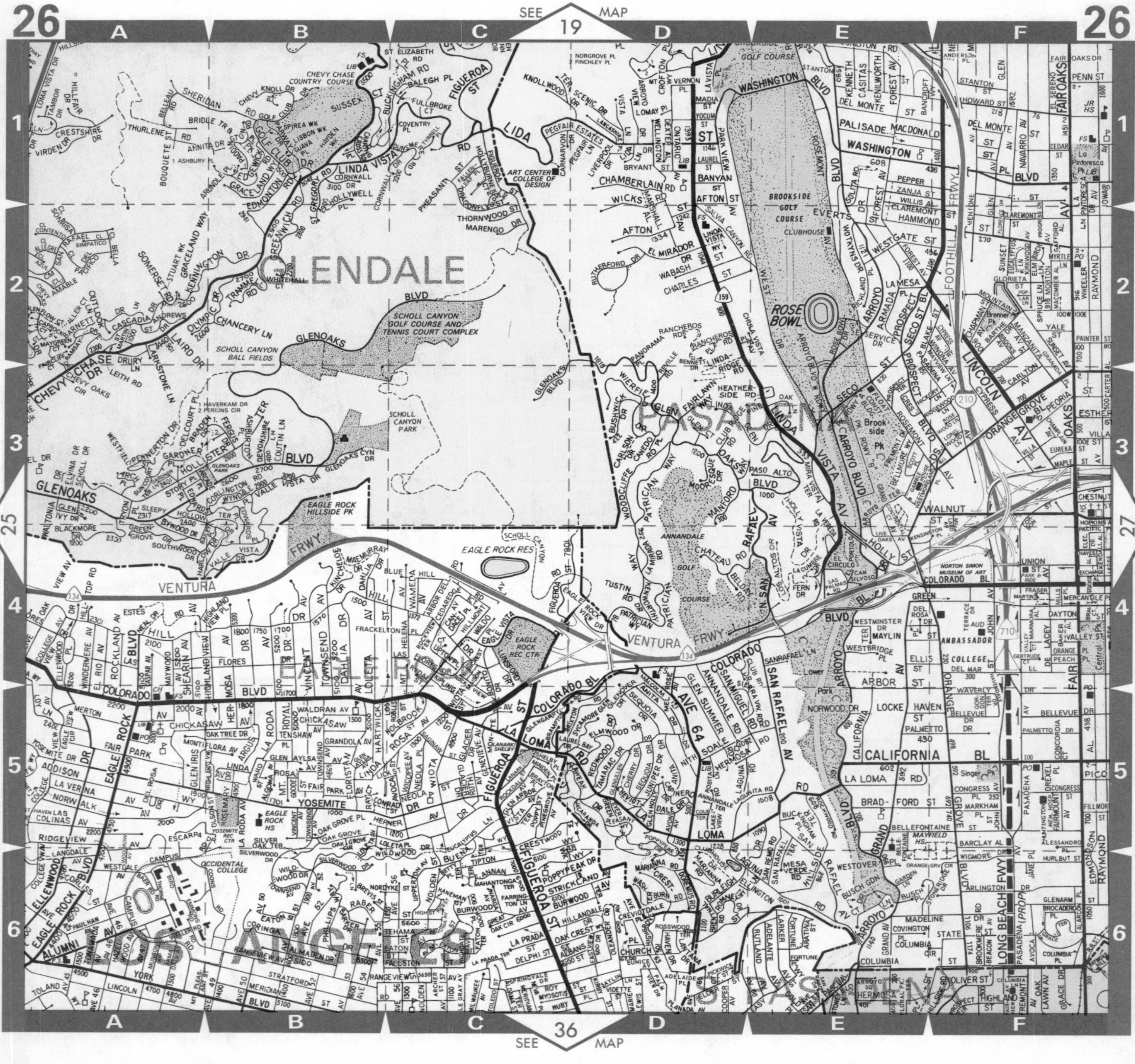

LOS ANGELES CO.

DETAIL

SEE MAP 25
SEE MAP 27

GLENDALE

PASADENA

LOS ANGELES

SO PASADENA

Chevy Chase Country Course

Scholl Canyon Golf Course and Tennis Court Complex

Scholl Canyon Ball Fields

Scholl Canyon Park

Eagle Rock Hillside Pk

Eagle Rock Res

Ventura Frwy

Brookside Golf Course

Brookside Golf Course Clubhouse

ROSE BOWL

Annandale Golf Course

Norton Simon Museum of Art

Eagle Rock Rec Ctr

Occidental College

Eagle Rock HS

Yosemite

Art Center College of Design

Washington Blvd

Glenoaks Blvd

Colorado Blvd

Figueroa St

York Blvd

Eagle Rock Blvd

California Bl

Lincoln Av

Orange Grove Av

Foothill Frwy

Long Beach Fwy

Ventura Frwy

Ambassador College

Mayfield HS

Pasadena (Prop) Fwy

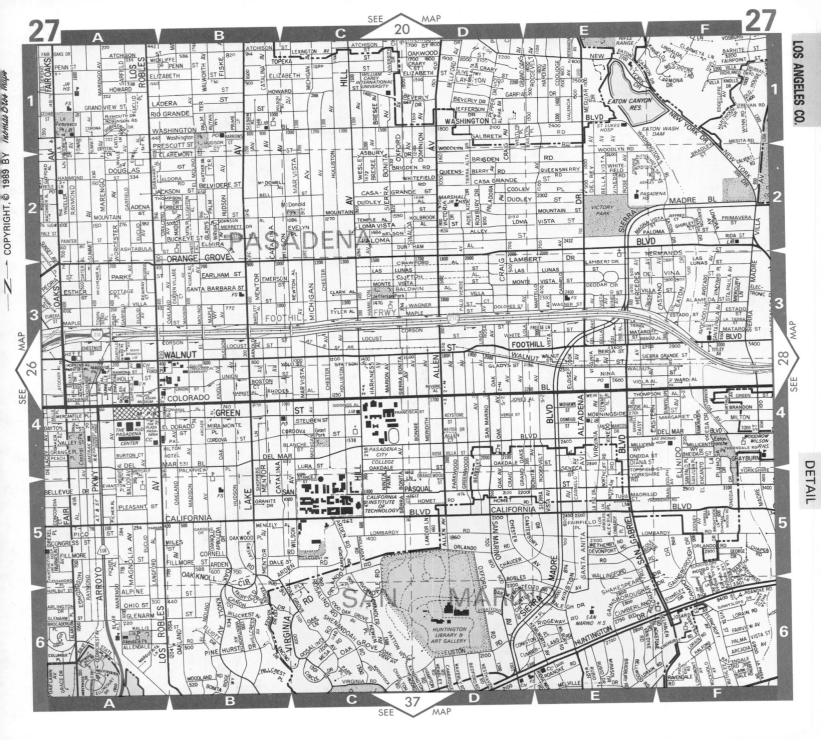

LOS ANGELES CO.

DETAIL

A   B   C   D   E   F

1 2 3 4 5 6

Major area labels:

- SIERRA MADRE
- PASADENA
- ARCADIA
- MON (Monrovia)

Major roads:

- FOOTHILL BLVD / FOOTHILL FRWY
- COLORADO BLVD
- HUNTINGTON DR
- BALDWIN AV
- MICHILLINDA AV
- ROSEMEAD BLVD
- DUARTE RD
- SANTA ANITA AV
- CALIFORNIA ST
- SAN PASQUAL ST
- CAMPUS DR
- SIERRA MADRE BLVD
- GRAND VIEW
- ORANGE GROVE AV
- MONTECITO AV
- RAMONA AV
- ARBOLADA DR
- HACIENDA DR
- HIGHLAND OAKS DR

Landmarks:

- Santa Anita Park
- Santa Anita Fashion Park
- Santa Anita Golf Course
- Arboretum / State & Los Angeles Co.
- Arcadia Park
- Methodist Hosp.
- City Hall / Civic Center
- Eaton Golf Course

SEE MAP 27 (left side)
SEE MAP 29 (right side)

MON (Monrovia)

Clamshell Canyon

U.S. Ranger Station

DETAIL

TOPANGA STATE PARK

E. TOPANGA FIRE T.T

EAGLE SPGS FIRE RD

LOS ANGELES

STATE OWNED LANDS

SEE MAP 109

MANDEVILLE CANYON

STATE OWNED LANDS

MERRIMAC

MOUNTAIN CREST LN

CANYONBACK

MANDEVILLE

Mandeville Canyon

CANYON 0092

RD 2500

SEE MAP 32

Kenter

Rustic

Sullivan

Canyon

TOPANGA STATE PARK

CANYON BD

CANYON

TEMESCAL

KENTER RD

MICHAEL

AVD DE HERENCIA

PALISADES

PALISADES DR

PALISADES CIR

PALISADES T.T

AVD DE YNEZ

AVD DE CORTEZ

CALLE DE SEVILLA

SANTA YNEZ CANYON PK

TOPANGA STATE PK

MONTE GRANDE

BOSQUE DR

CHASTAIN PKWY

CUESTA LINDA DR

CALLE ABOVADA

1 PASEO DE LA RISA
2 PASEO PUETO BELLO

AVD DE SANTA YNEZ

CALLE DE MADRID

MONTE VERDE

CUMBRE ALTA CT

MONTE HERMOSO DR

PIEDRA MORADA DR

SANTA YNEZ CANYON PARK

PALISADES HIGHLANDS

CORDELIA

WESTRIDGE RD

BANYAN

LA CONDESA

PESQUERA

WESTRIDGE RD

RAYWOOD

CHERYL PL

BAYLISS

OBELIA

PONDEROSA DR

JEFFERSONIA WY

CHALON

CHALON DR 3300

MANDEVILLE

CHALON RD

ARBUTUS WY

STRADELLA RD

KENTER AV

NADA

RUSTIC CYN PARK

SULLIVAN CYN PARK

QUEENSFERRY RD

RAYLISS

SULLIVAN

TANNERS RD

RIVERS RD

OLNEY

WYCHN

GLENMERE RD

HONEYWOOD RD

TEAKWOOD RD

BOCA DE CANON LN

ERIC

HEARD PL

WESTRIDGE RD

STIPA WY

OAKPORT RD

KIMBERLY LN

32   32

LOS ANGELES CO.

SEE MAP 22
SEE MAP 41
SEE MAP 30
SEE MAP 33

DETAIL

LOS ANGELES

BEVERLY GLEN

BEL AIR ESTATES

BEVERLY HILLS

UPPER STONE CANYON RESERVOIR

STONE CANYON RESERVOIR

STATE OWNED LANDS

MOUNTAINGATE GOLF COURSE NORTH

MOUNTAINGATE GOLF COURSE SOUTH

CHALON CAMPUS MT ST MARYS COLLEGE

CRESTWOOD HILLS PARK

BLUEGRASS LN

UCLA

BEL AIR COUNTRY CLUB

MARYMOUNT

SAWTELLE RES

Los Angeles Country Club

BRIAR WOOD

BEVERLY GLEN PARK

WESTLAKE SCHOOL FOR GIRLS

SEPULVEDA BLVD

SAN DIEGO FRWY

BEVERLY GLEN

BENEDICT CANYON

SUNSET BLVD

VETERAN AV

MONTANA AV

BEL AIR SUMMIT HOTEL

Holmby Pk

STUDENT REC AREA

DRAKE STADIUM

PAULEY PAVILION

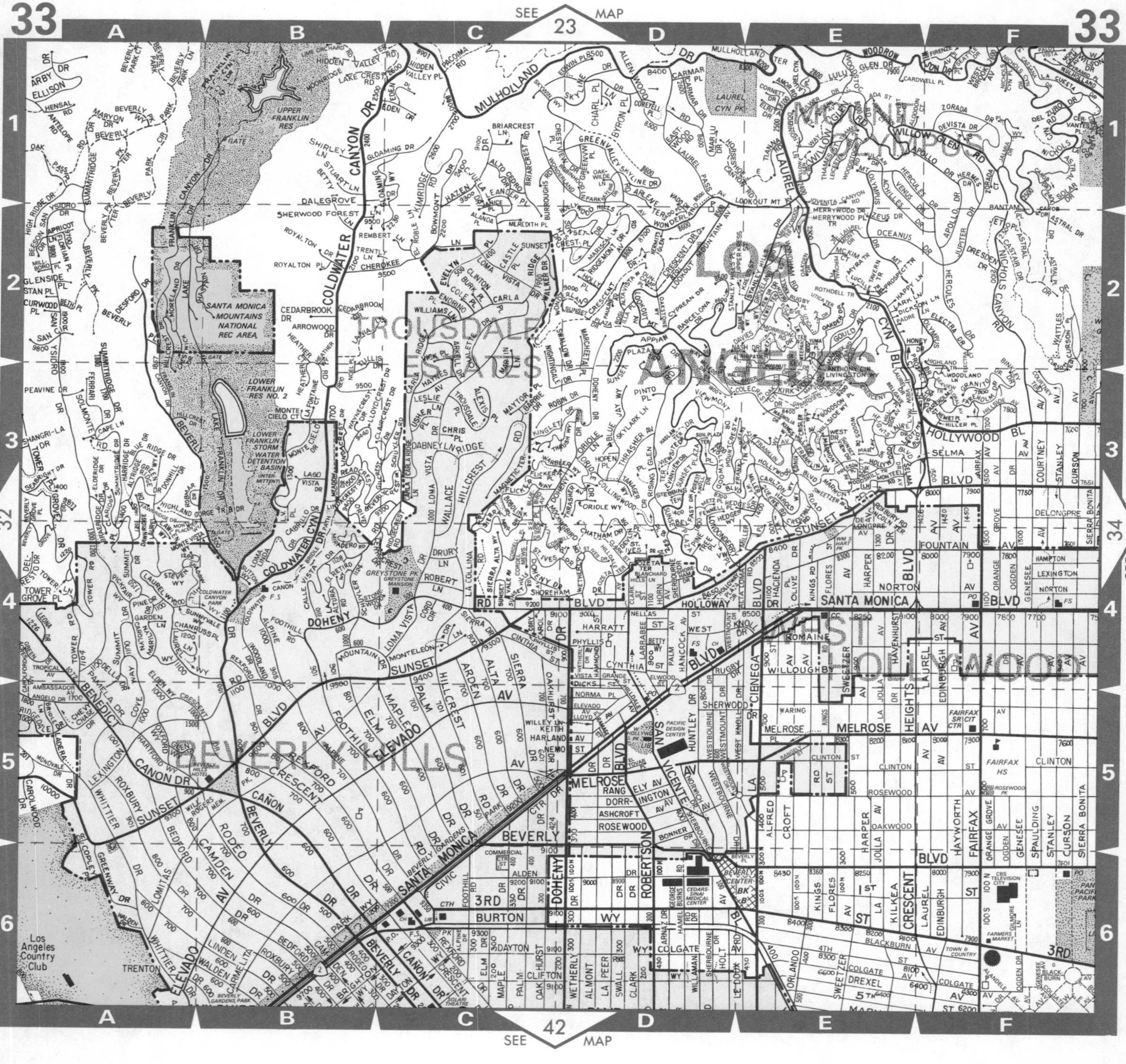
SEE MAP 23
A
B
C
D
E
F
1
2
3
4
5
6
SEE MAP 32
SEE MAP 34
SEE MAP 42
MULHOLLAND
DR
UPPER FRANKLIN RES
SANTA MONICA MOUNTAINS NATIONAL REC AREA
LOWER FRANKLIN RES NO. 2
LOWER FRANKLIN STORM WATER DETENTION BASIN
FRANKLIN CANYON DR
COLDWATER CANYON DR
TROUSDALE ESTATES
LOS ANGELES
MOUNT OLYMPUS
LAUREL CYN PK
LAUREL CANYON BLVD
NICHOLS CANYON RD
HOLLYWOOD BL
SUNSET BLVD
SANTA MONICA BLVD
WEST HOLLYWOOD
BEVERLY HILLS
MELROSE AV
BEVERLY BLVD
3RD ST
BURTON WY
WILSHIRE
DOHENY DR
ROBERTSON BLVD
LA CIENEGA BLVD
SAN VICENTE BLVD
CRESCENT HEIGHTS BLVD
FAIRFAX AV
LAUREL AV
LA BREA
GREYSTONE PK
GREYSTONE MANSION
BEVERLY HILLS HOTEL
PACIFIC DESIGN CENTER
CEDARS-SINAI MEDICAL CENTER
BEVERLY CENTER
FAIRFAX HS
CBS TELEVISION CITY
FARMERS MARKET
PAN PACIFIC PARK
Los Angeles Country Club
BEVERLY GARDENS PARK
FOUNTAIN AV
ROMAINE
WILLOUGHBY
CLINTON
ROSEWOOD
BLACKBURN
COLGATE
DREXEL
CANON DR
BEVERLY DR
REXFORD DR
CRESCENT DR
RODEO
CAMDEN
BEDFORD
ROXBURY
WHITTIER
LOMITAS
SIERRA BONITA
CURSON
STANLEY
SPAULDING
GENESEE
OGDEN
ORANGE GROVE
HAYWORTH
EDINBURGH
KILKEA
HARPER
KINGS
FLORES
SWEETZER
ORLANDO
HOLLOWAY
SHOREHAM
HILLCREST
LOMA VISTA
WALLACE
BENEDICT
SUMMITRIDGE
BEVERLY
TOWER RD
ELEVADO
CHRIS PL
DABNEY LN
HERCULES
JUPITER
APOLLO
OCEANUS
WONDERLAND AV
LOOKOUT MT AV
WOODROW WILSON DR
HIGHLAND
FOOTHILL
ALPINE
ELM
MAPLE
PALM
ALTA
ARDEN
SIERRA
TRENTON
CLARK
WETHERLY
ALMONT
LA PEER
SWALL
WESTBOURNE
WESTMOUNT
HUNTLEY DR
HANCOCK AV
LARRABEE
NORTON
HAMPTON
LEXINGTON
DELONGPRE
SELMA
WARING

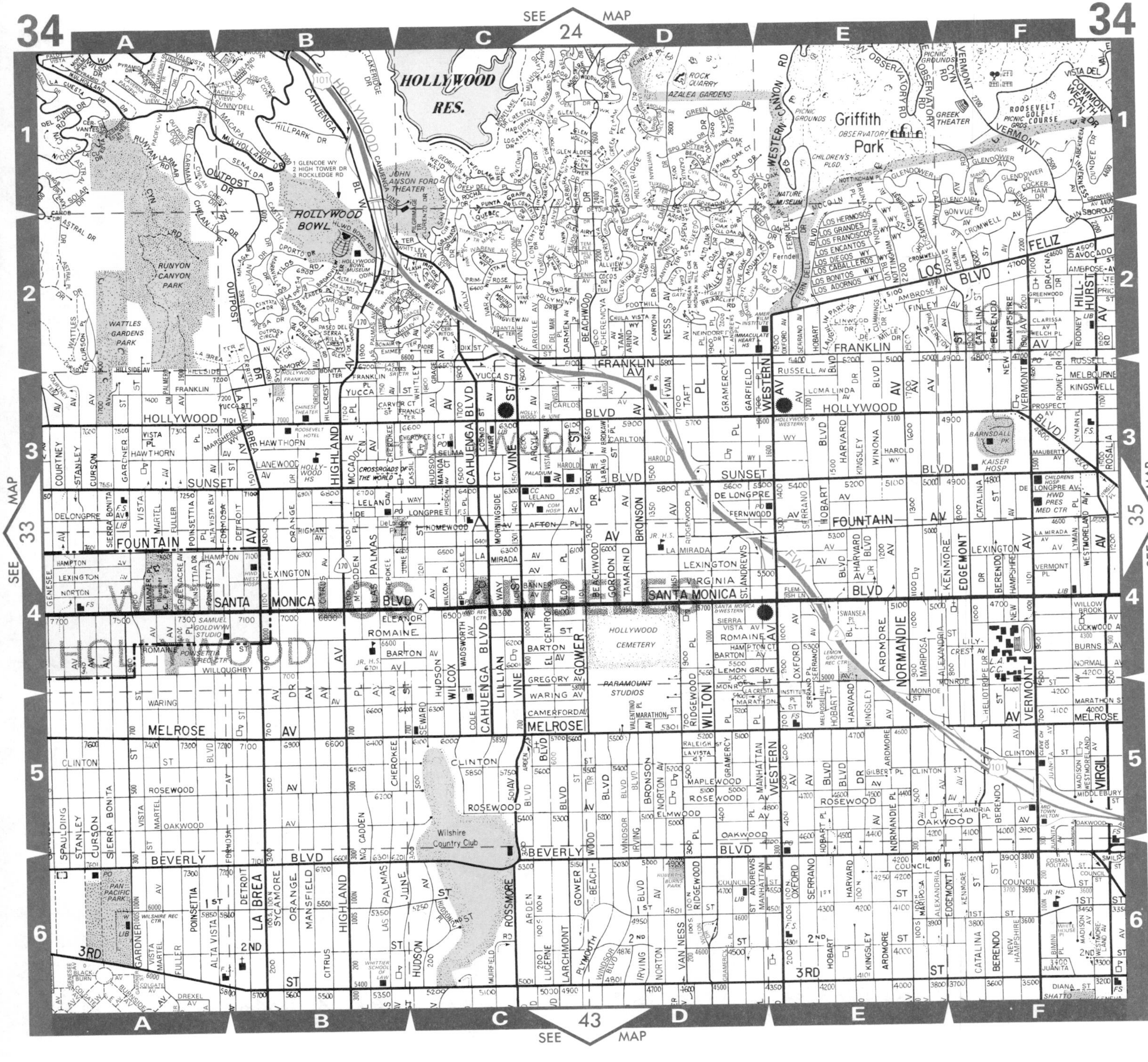

SEE MAP 24

SEE MAP 43

DETAIL

COPYRIGHT, © 1989 BY Thomas Bros. Maps

HOLLYWOOD RES.

Griffith Park

Griffith Observatory

Greek Theater

Hollywood Bowl

John Anson Ford Theater

Runyon Canyon Park

Wattles Gardens Park

Azalea Gardens

Rock Quarry

Nature Museum

Roosevelt Golf Course

HOLLYWOOD BLVD

SUNSET BLVD

SANTA MONICA BLVD

MELROSE AV

BEVERLY BLVD

FOUNTAIN AV

FRANKLIN AV

Paramount Studios

Hollywood Cemetery

Wilshire Country Club

Samuel Goldwyn Studio

Kaiser Hosp

Childrens Hosp

Barnsdall Pk

Pan Pacific Park

Crossroads of the World

Chinese Theater

Roosevelt Hotel

Hollywood High S

LOS FELIZ BLVD

VERMONT AV

WESTERN AV

NORMANDIE AV

CAHUENGA BLVD

VINE ST

HIGHLAND AV

LA BREA AV

LARCHMONT

ROSSMORE

3RD ST

2ND ST

1ST ST

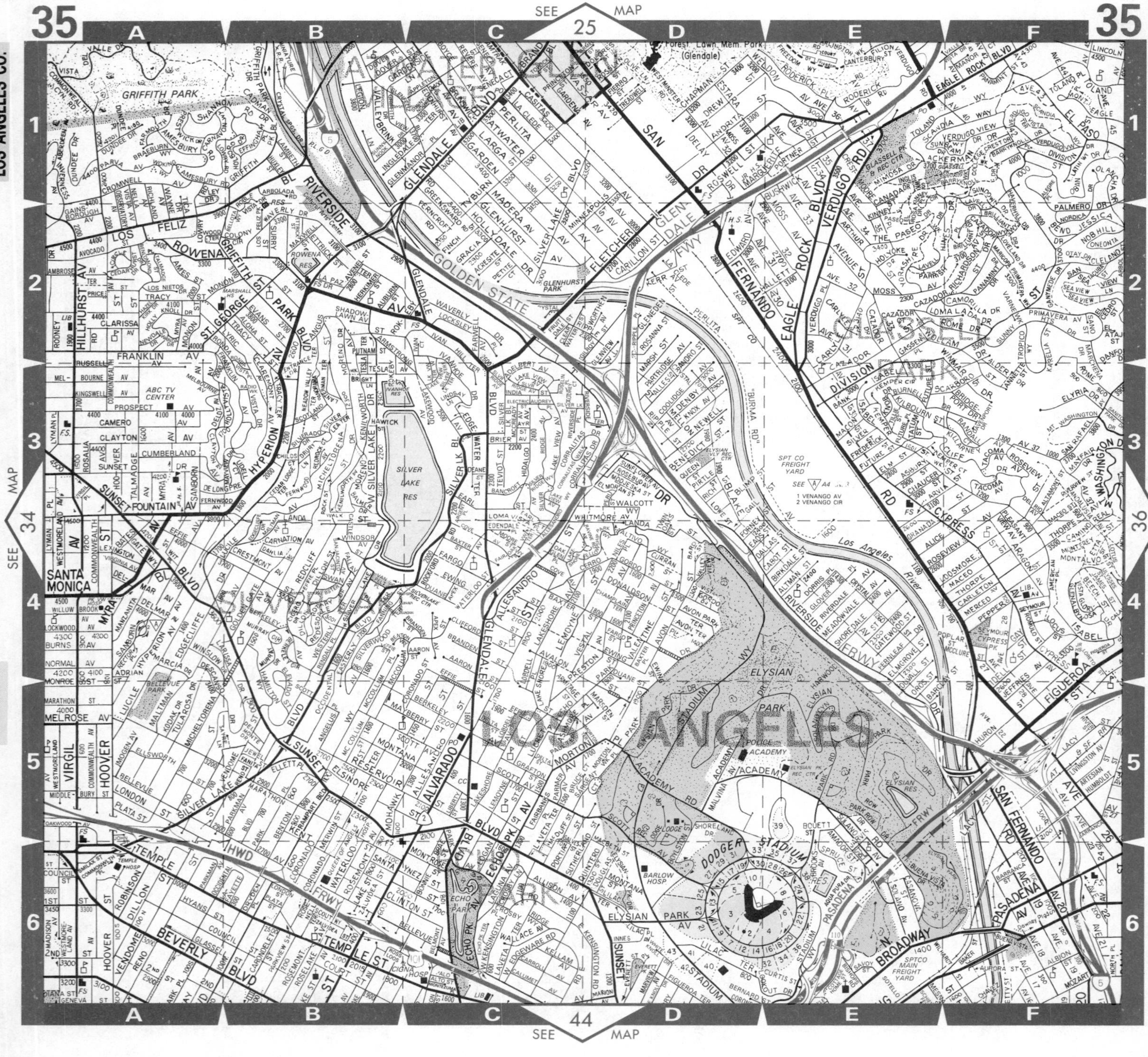

LOS ANGELES CO.

DETAIL

SEE MAP 25

SEE MAP 34

SEE MAP 36

SEE MAP 44

GRIFFITH PARK

ATWATER

GLENDALE

GOLDEN STATE FWY

Forest Lawn. Mem. Park (Glendale)

EAGLE ROCK BLVD

VERDUGO RD

SAN FERNANDO RD

LOS ANGELES RIVER

SILVER LAKE RES

SILVER LAKE

SANTA MONICA BLVD

SUNSET BLVD

ABC TV CENTER

HYPERION AV

ELYSIAN PARK

LOS ANGELES

POLICE ACADEMY

ELYSIAN RES

DODGER STADIUM

BEVERLY BLVD

TEMPLE ST

ECHO PARK

SUNSET BLVD

BROADWAY

RIVERSIDE DR

PASADENA FWY

SPT CO FREIGHT YARD

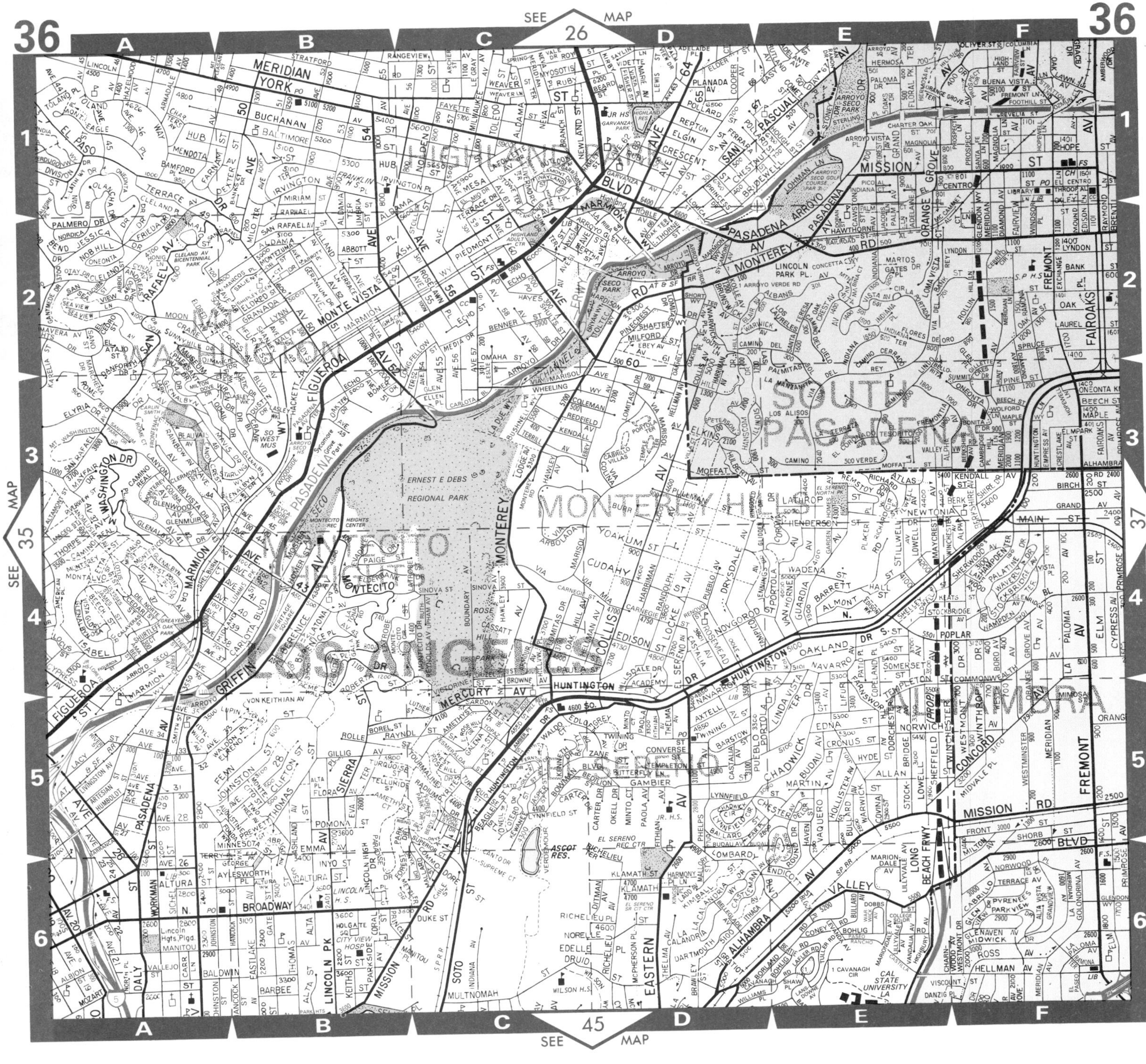
SEE MAP 26
SEE MAP 45
SEE MAP 35
SEE MAP 37
DETAIL
LOS ANGELES
SOUTH PASADENA
ALHAMBRA
MONTEREY HILLS
MONTECITO HEIGHTS
EL SERENO
HIGHLAND PARK
MT WASHINGTON
ERNEST E DEBS REGIONAL PARK
ARROYO SECO PARK
ASCOT RES.
CAL STATE UNIVERSITY LA
WILSON H.S.
LINCOLN H.S.
FIGUEROA ST
PASADENA FRWY
MONTEREY RD
HUNTINGTON DR
MISSION RD
VALLEY BLVD
EASTERN AV
FREMONT AV
LONG BEACH FRWY
YORK BLVD
MARMION WY
MONTE VISTA ST
BROADWAY

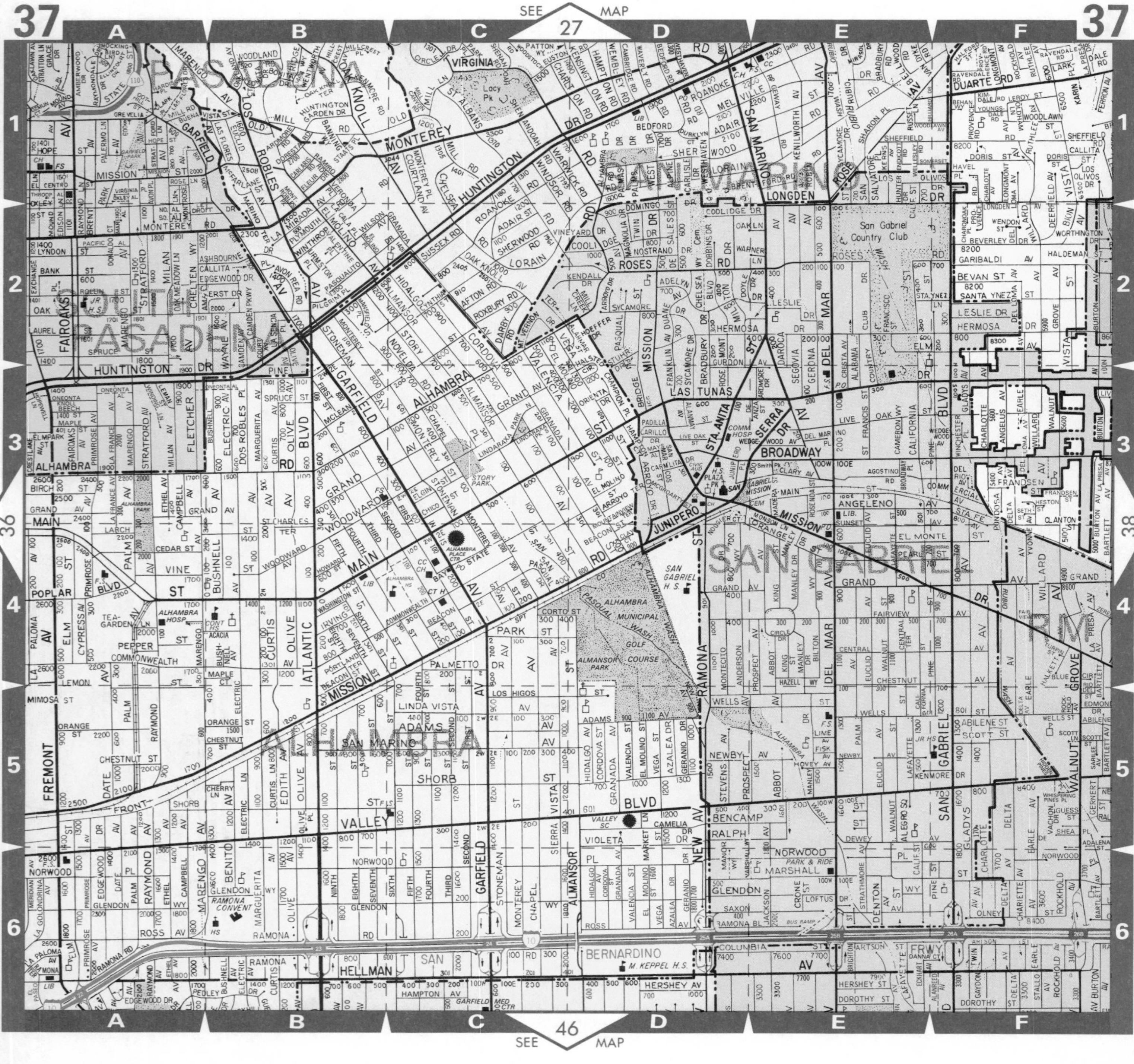

LOS ANGELES CO.

DETAIL

PASADENA

SOUTH PASADENA

SAN MARINO

San Gabriel Country Club

ALHAMBRA

SAN GABRIEL

Story Park

Alhambra Municipal Golf Course

Almansor Park

SEE MAP 36

SEE MAP 38

BROADWAY

MAIN ST

HUNTINGTON DR

GARFIELD BLVD

VALLEY BLVD

MISSION RD

LAS TUNAS

San Bernardino FRWY

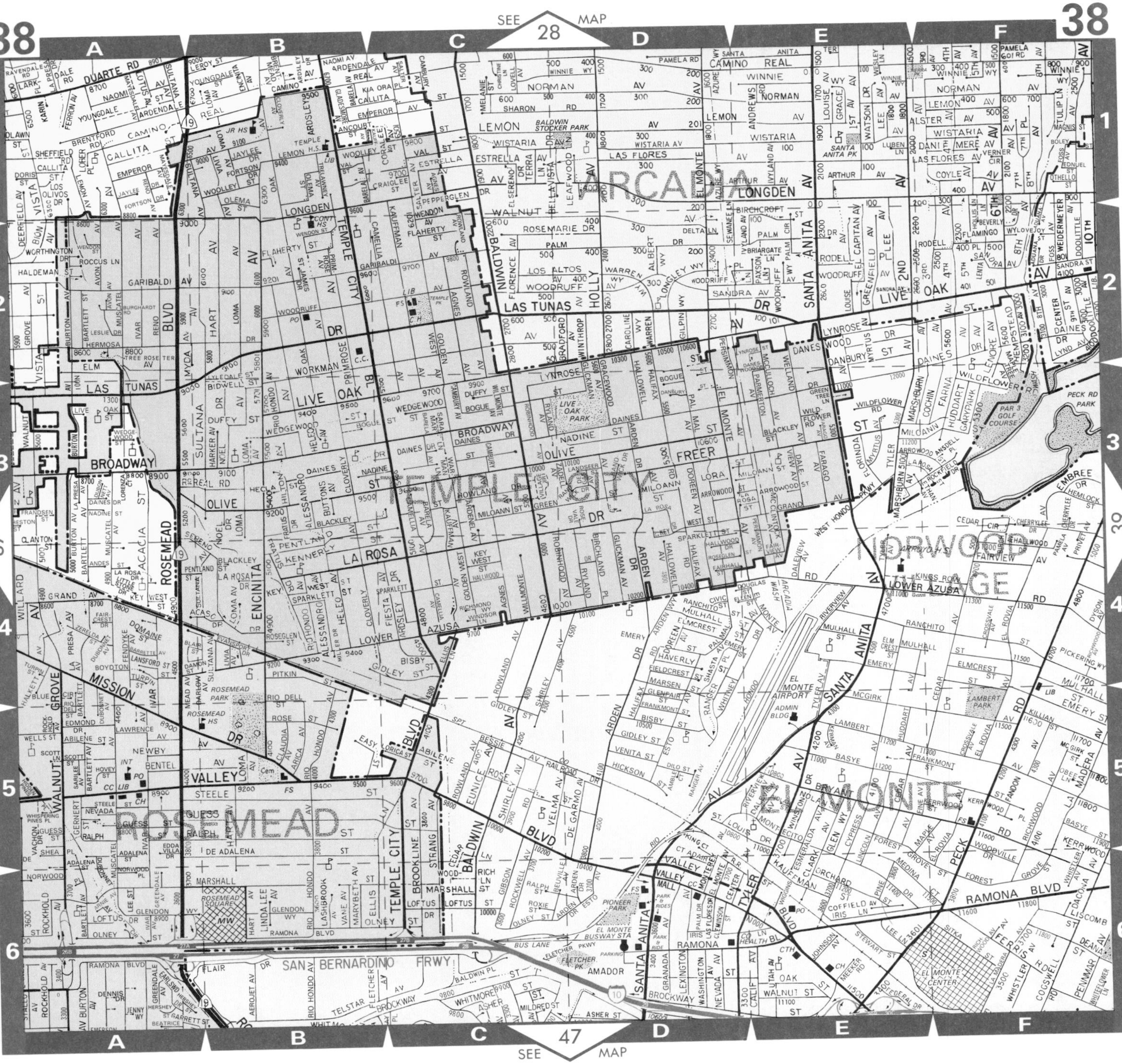

ARCADIA

TEMPLE CITY

ROSEMEAD

EL MONTE

NORWOOD FAIRVIEW VILLAGE

BROADWAY

LIVE OAK

LAS TUNAS

MISSION

VALLEY

DUARTE RD

SANTA ANITA AV

BALDWIN AV

ROSEMEAD BLVD

TEMPLE CITY BLVD

RAMONA BLVD

PECK RD

CAMINO REAL

LOWER AZUSA RD

LIVE OAK AV

FREER

PAR 3 GOLF COURSE

EL MONTE AIRPORT

LIVE OAK PARK

ROSEMEAD PARK

BALDWIN STOCKER PARK

SAN BERNARDINO FRWY

EL MONTE BUSWAY STA

VALLEY MALL

DETAIL

COPYRIGHT © 1983 BY THOMAS BROS. MAPS

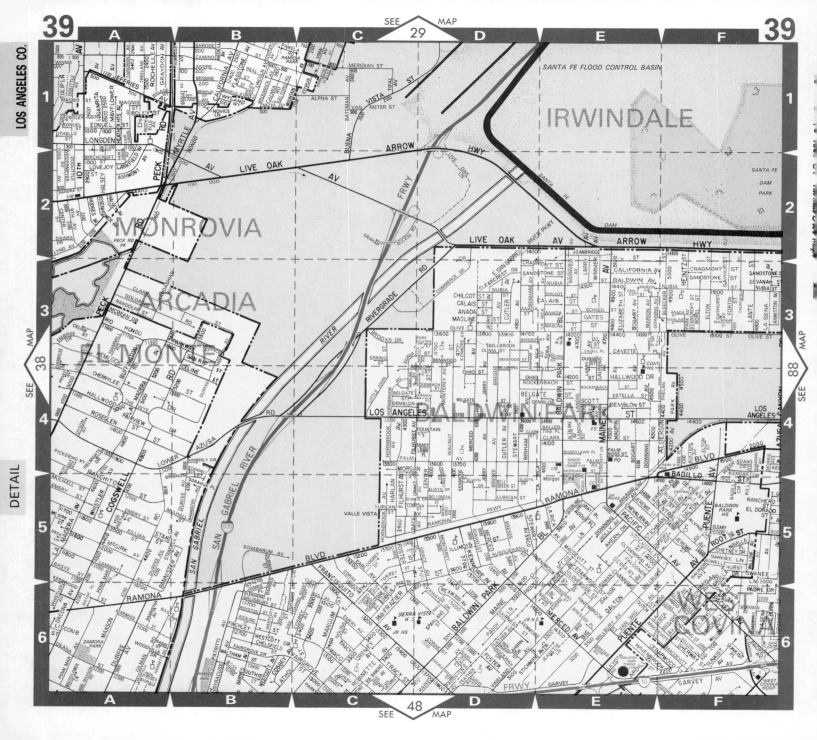

TOPANGA STATE PARK

TOPANGA STATE PK

TOPANGA STATE PARK

SANTA YNEZ CANYON PK

WILL ROGERS STATE HISTORIC PARK

RUSTIC CYN PARK

SULLIVAN CYN PARK

LOS ANGELES

SUNSET BLVD

PACIFIC COAST HWY

PALISADES BEACH RD

SANTA MONICA

Pacific Ocean

WILL ROGERS STATE BEACH

TAHITIAN TERRACE TRAILER PARK

WILL ROGERS

SANTA MONICA STATE BEACH

PALISADES HS

RIVIERA COUNTRY CLUB

RIVIERA RANCH

ALLENFORD AV

MONTANA AV
WASHINGTON AV
CALIFORNIA AV
BROADWAY
COLORA...

20TH ST
14TH ST
LINCOLN BLVD
7TH ST
OCEAN AV

SEE MAP 115
SEE MAP 41
SEE INSET MAP PAGE 49
SEE 49 MAP

1 TERRACE CIR
2 DRIFTWOOD DR
3 DRIFTWOOD PL
4 SHORE DR
5 TERRACE PL
6 WESTVIEW LN
7 PACIFIC AV
8 OCEAN VW
9 KONTIKI WY
10 KIKI PL
11 TAHITI WY
12 COCO PL

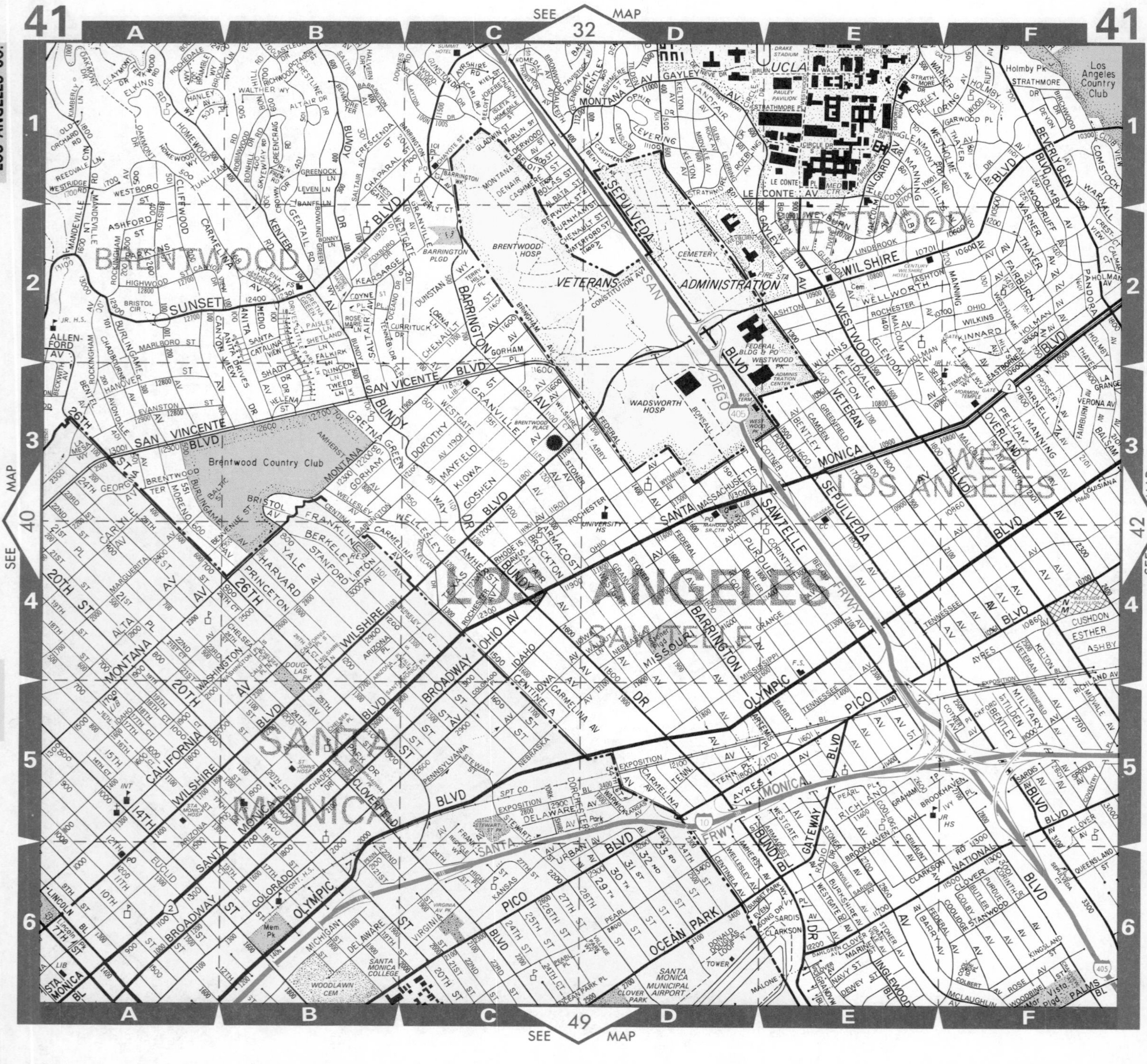

LOS ANGELES CO.

DETAIL

SEE MAP 40

SEE MAP 42

BRENTWOOD

SANTA MONICA

LOS ANGELES

SANTA MONICA

WEST LOS ANGELES

WESTWOOD

UCLA

Brentwood Country Club

Los Angeles Country Club

VETERANS ADMINISTRATION

Brentwood Hosp

Wadsworth Hosp

Santa Monica College

Woodlawn Cem

Santa Monica Municipal Airport

Ocean Park

SUNSET BLVD

SAN VICENTE BLVD

WILSHIRE BLVD

OLYMPIC BLVD

PICO BLVD

SANTA MONICA BLVD

NATIONAL BLVD

SEPULVEDA BLVD

BARRINGTON AV

BUNDY DR

SAWTELLE

OVERLAND AV

San Diego Frwy (405)

Los Angeles Frwy (10)

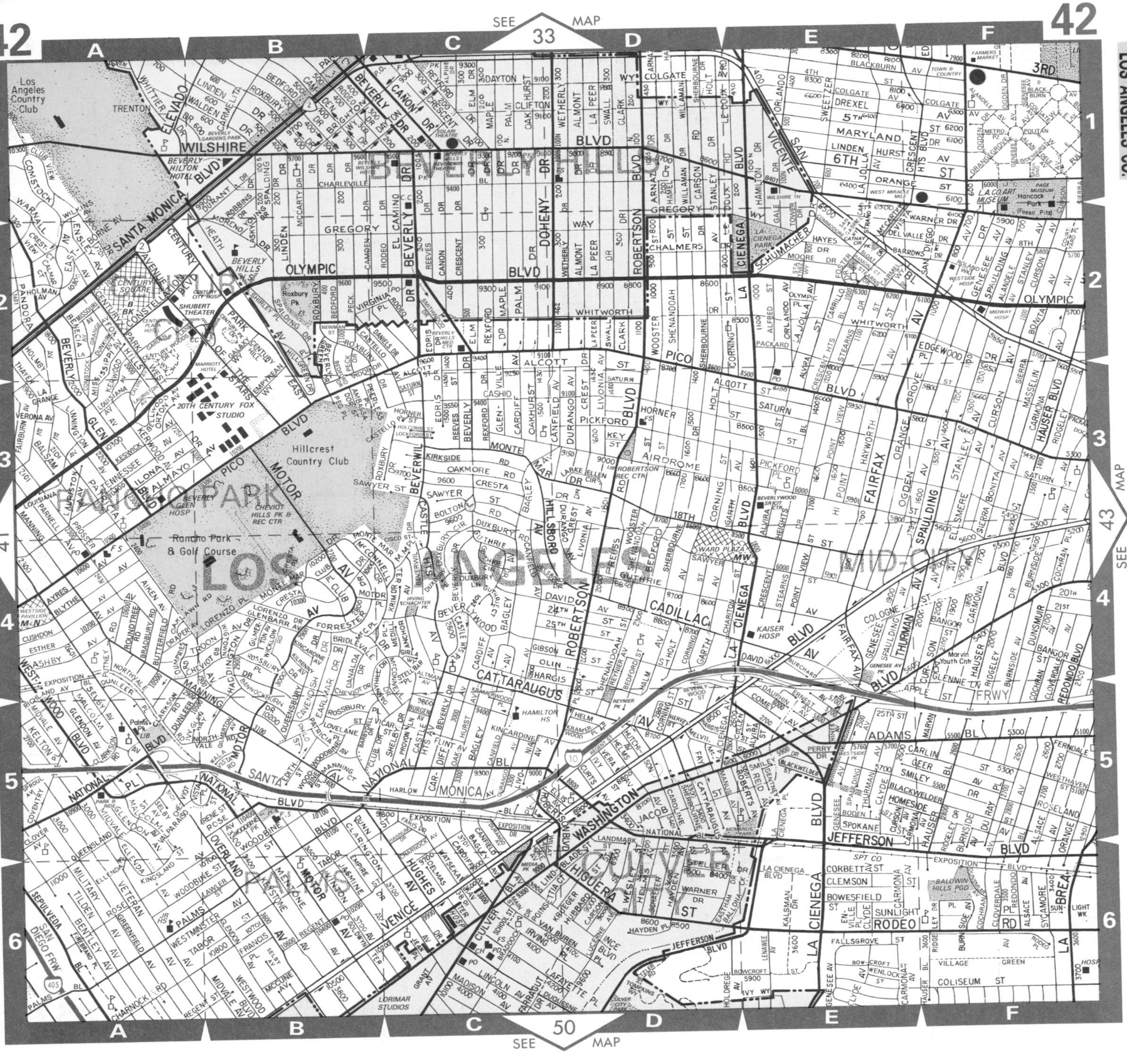

LOS ANGELES

RANCHO PARK

Los Angeles Country Club

Hillcrest Country Club

Rancho Park & Golf Course

20th Century Fox Studio

CULVER CITY

MID-C

CADILLAC

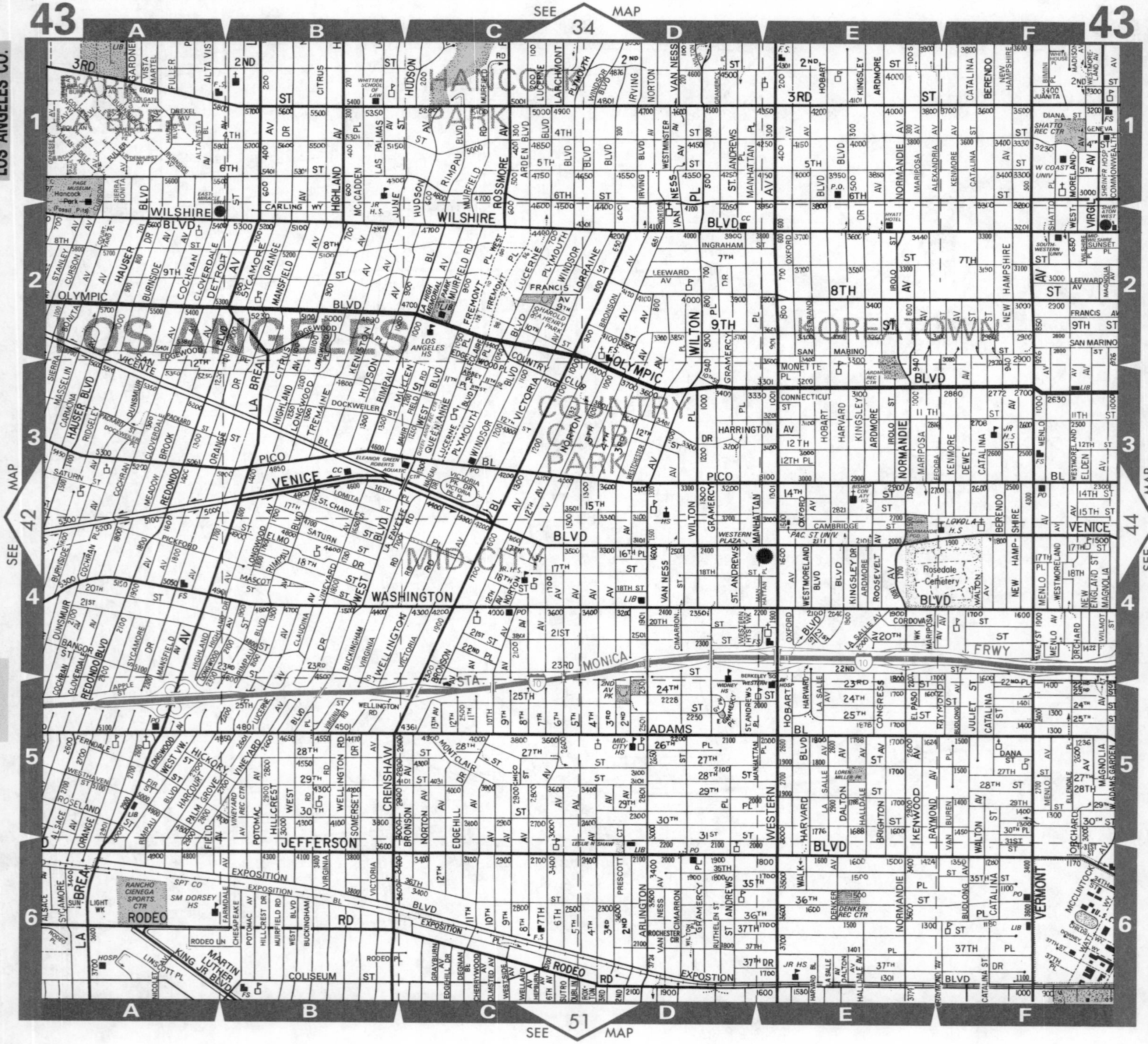

DETAIL

HANCOCK PARK

LOS ANGELES

KOREATOWN

COUNTRY CLUB PARK

MID CITY

WILSHIRE BLVD

OLYMPIC BLVD

PICO BLVD

VENICE BLVD

WASHINGTON BLVD

SANTA MONICA FRWY

ADAMS BLVD

JEFFERSON BLVD

EXPOSITION BLVD

RODEO RD

COLISEUM

VERMONT

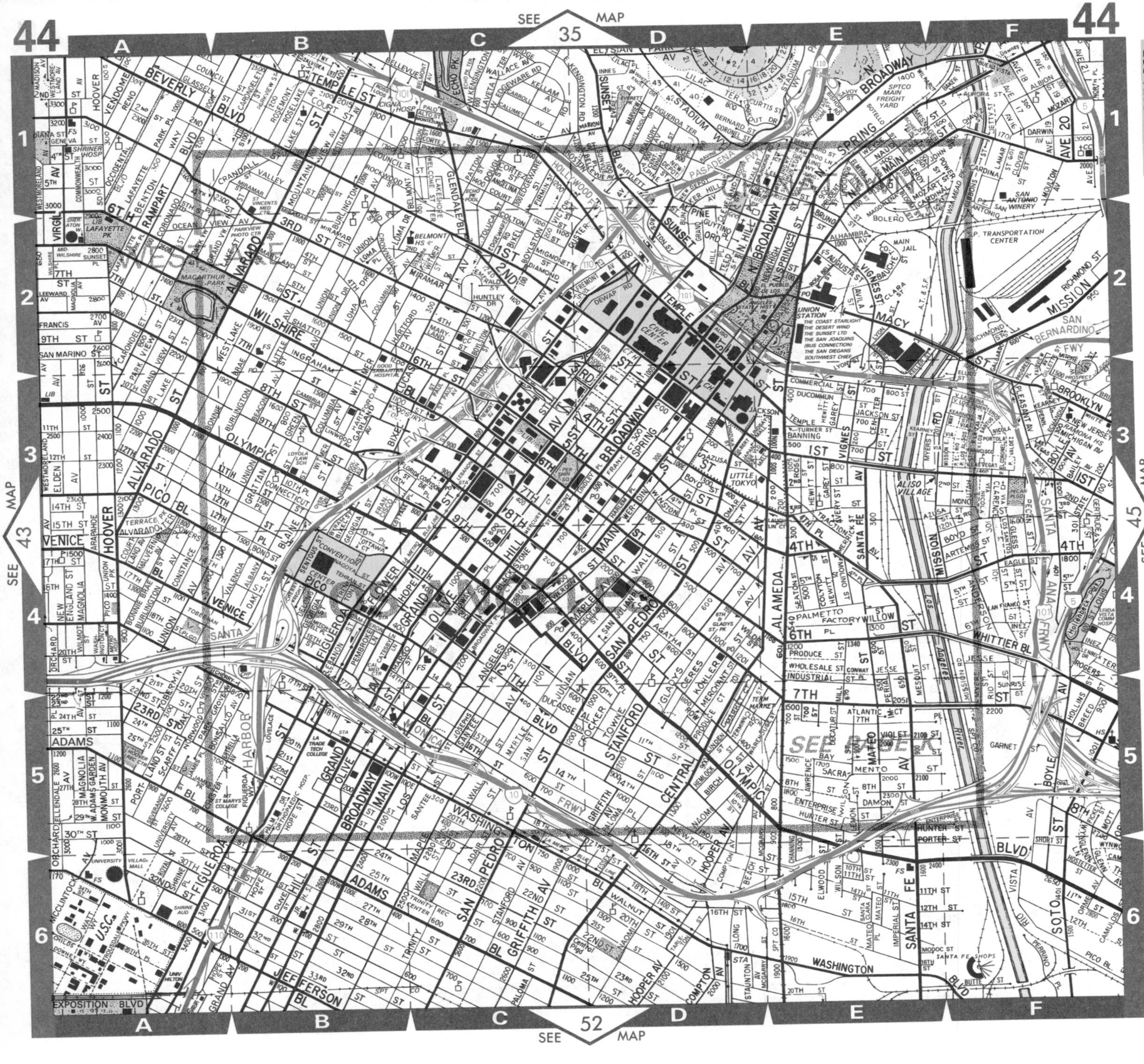

LOS ANGELES CO.

DETAIL

LOS ANGELES

COPYRIGHT, © 1969 BY Thomas Bros.

SEE MAP 43

SEE MAP 45

BEVERLY BLVD

WILSHIRE

OLYMPIC

PICO BL

VENICE

ADAMS

JEFFERSON

WASHINGTON

U.S.C.

UNION STATION
THE COAST STARLIGHT
THE DESERT WIND
THE SUNSET LTD
THE SAN JOAQUINS
(BUS CONNECTION
THE SAN DIEGANS
SOUTHWEST CHIEF)

MACY

MISSION

SAN BERNARDINO FWY

LITTLE TOKYO

CIVIC CENTER

Main Jail

L.A. TRANSPORTATION CENTER

BROADWAY

SPRING

MAIN

HILL

GRAND

HOPE

FLOWER

FIGUEROA

HARBOR

ALVARADO

HOOVER

VERMONT

TEMPLE ST

SUNSET

MacArthur Park

Lafayette Pk

Exposition Blvd

ALISO VILLAGE

SANTA FE

WHITTIER BL

LINCOLN PK

Lincoln Park

LA CO USC MEDICAL CENTER
U.S.C. SCHOOL OF MEDICINE

HAZARD PARK

MARENGO

San Bernardino FWY

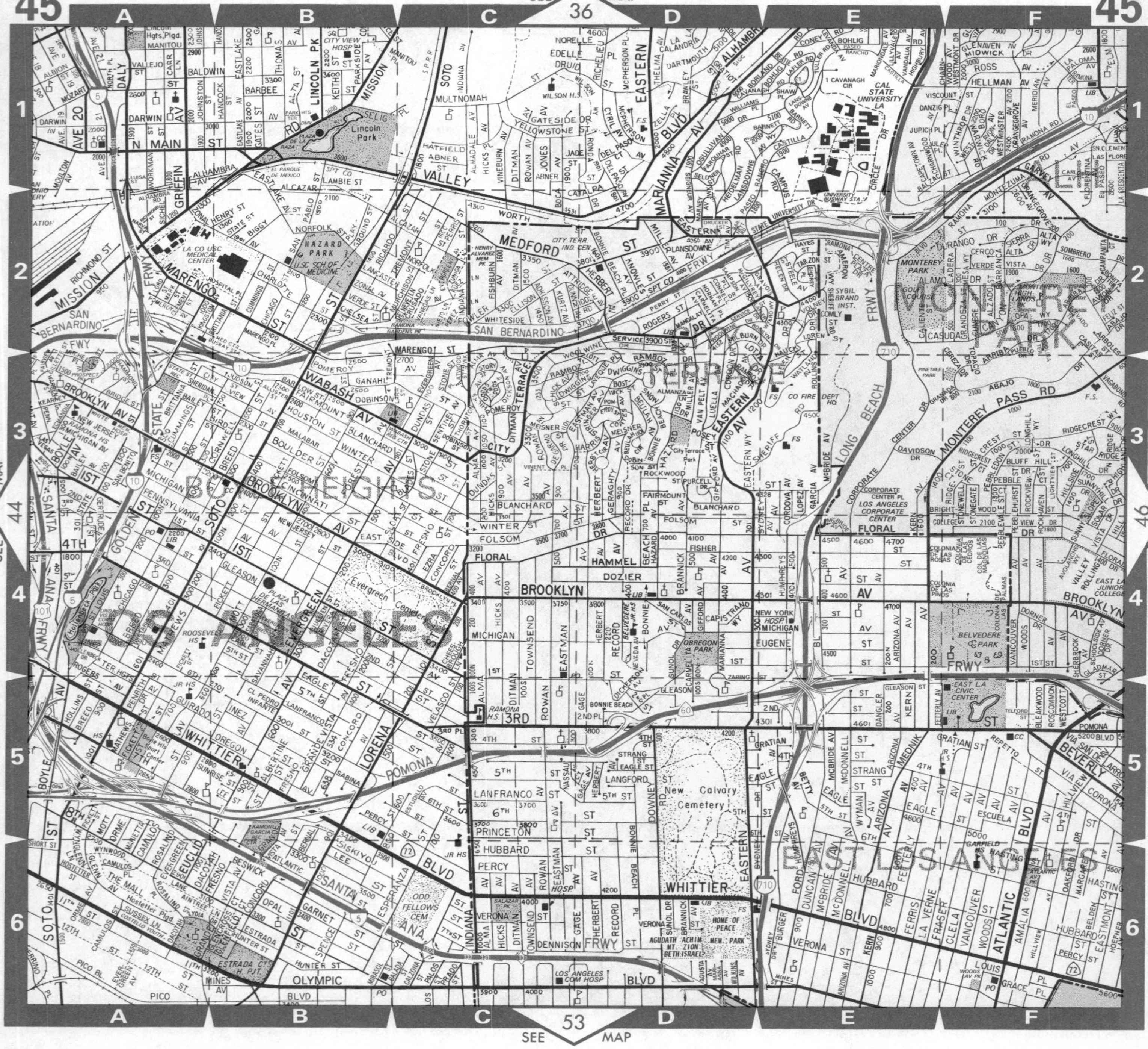

MISSION FWY

MEDFORD ST

CITY TERR. IND. CEN.

BOYLE HEIGHTS

WABASH AV

BROOKLYN

LOS ANGELES

4TH

WHITTIER

EVERGREEN CEMETERY

BROOKLYN AV

BROOKLYN

FLORAL

HAMMEL

DOZIER

MICHIGAN

EUGENE

OBREGON PARK

NEW YORK HOSP MICHIGAN

RAMONA HS

DITMAN

3RD

POMONA

LORENA

LANFRANCO AV

New Calvary Cemetery

WHITTIER

EAST LOS ANGELES

BELVEDERE PARK

EAST L.A. CIVIC CENTER

BEVERLY

BLVD

EAST LA JUNIOR COLLEGE

ATLANTIC

ODD FELLOWS CEM.

HOME OF PEACE

LOS ANGELES COM HOSP

OLYMPIC BLVD

BLVD

MONTEREY PARK

CAL STATE UNIVERSITY

CAVANAGH CIR

MONTEREY PARK

MONTEREY PASS RD

ALHAMBRA

MARIANNA AV

EASTERN

SANTA ANA FWY

TERRACE

EASTERN AV

FLORAL DR

CORPORATE CENTER
LOS ANGELES CORPORATE CENTER

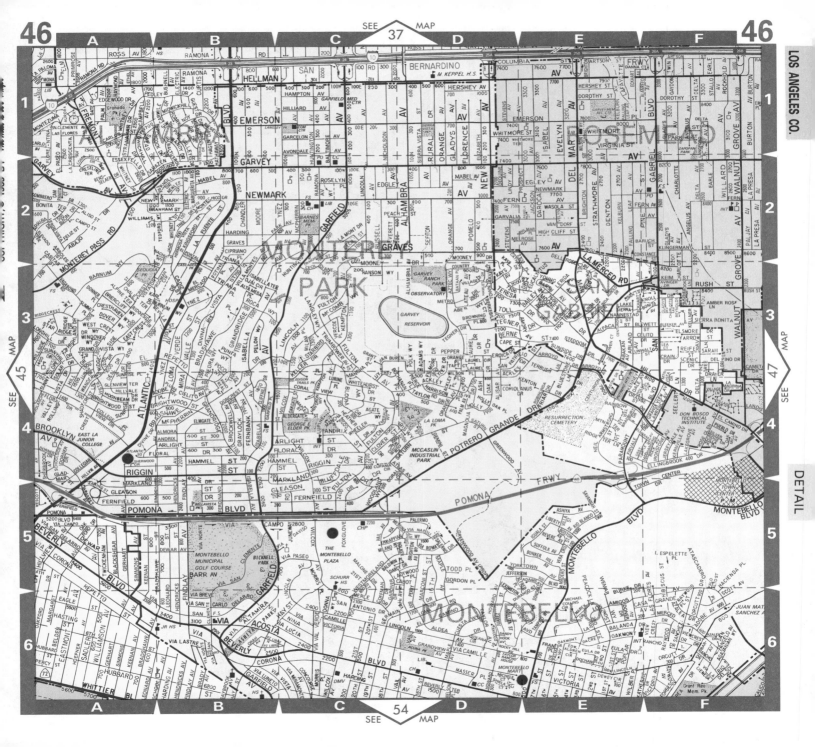

LOS ANGELES CO.

DETAIL

A B C D E F

SEE MAP 46

SEE MAP 48

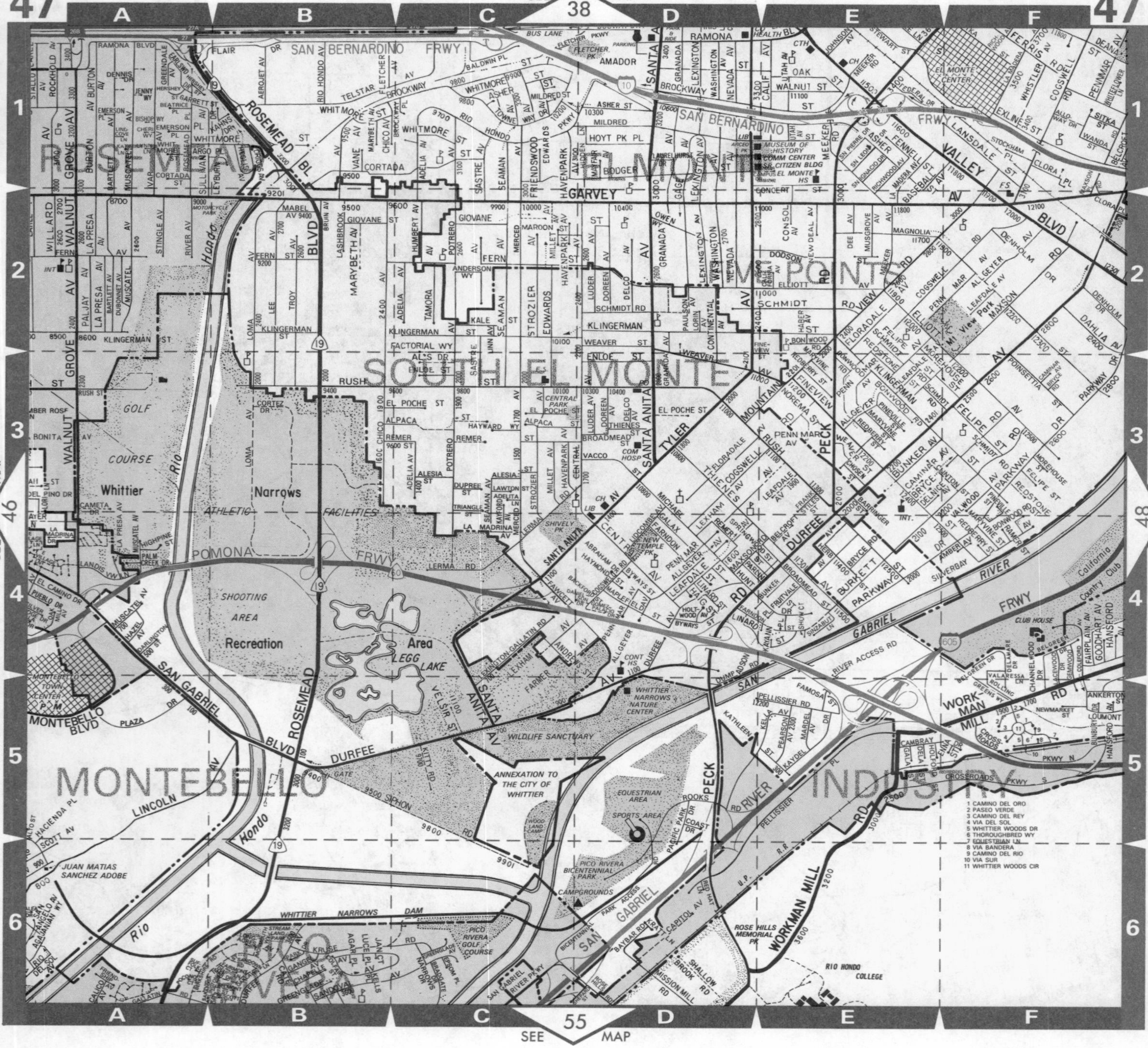

ROSEMEAD

EL MONTE

SOUTH EL MONTE

FIVE POINTS

WHITTIER Narrows

MONTEBELLO

PICO RIVERA

INDUSTRY

San Bernardino Frwy

Pomona Frwy

Rosemead Blvd

Garvey Ave

Durfee Ave

San Gabriel River Frwy

Whittier Narrows Dam

Legg Lake

Whittier Narrows Nature Center

Wildlife Sanctuary

Annexation to the City of Whittier

Pico Rivera Bicentennial Park

Equestrian Sports Area

Whittier Narrows Golf Course

Workman Mill Rd

Rose Hills Memorial Pk

Rio Hondo College

Juan Matias Sanchez Adobe

Montebello Plaza

Montebello Town Center

Golf Course

Athletic Facilities

Shooting Area

Recreation Area

Rio Hondo

San Gabriel River

1 Camino Del Oro
2 Paseo Verde
3 Camino Del Rey
4 Via Del Sol
5 Whittier Woods Dr
6 Thoroughbred Wy
7 Equestrian Ln
8 Via Bandera
9 Camino Del Rio
10 Via Sur
11 Whittier Woods Cir

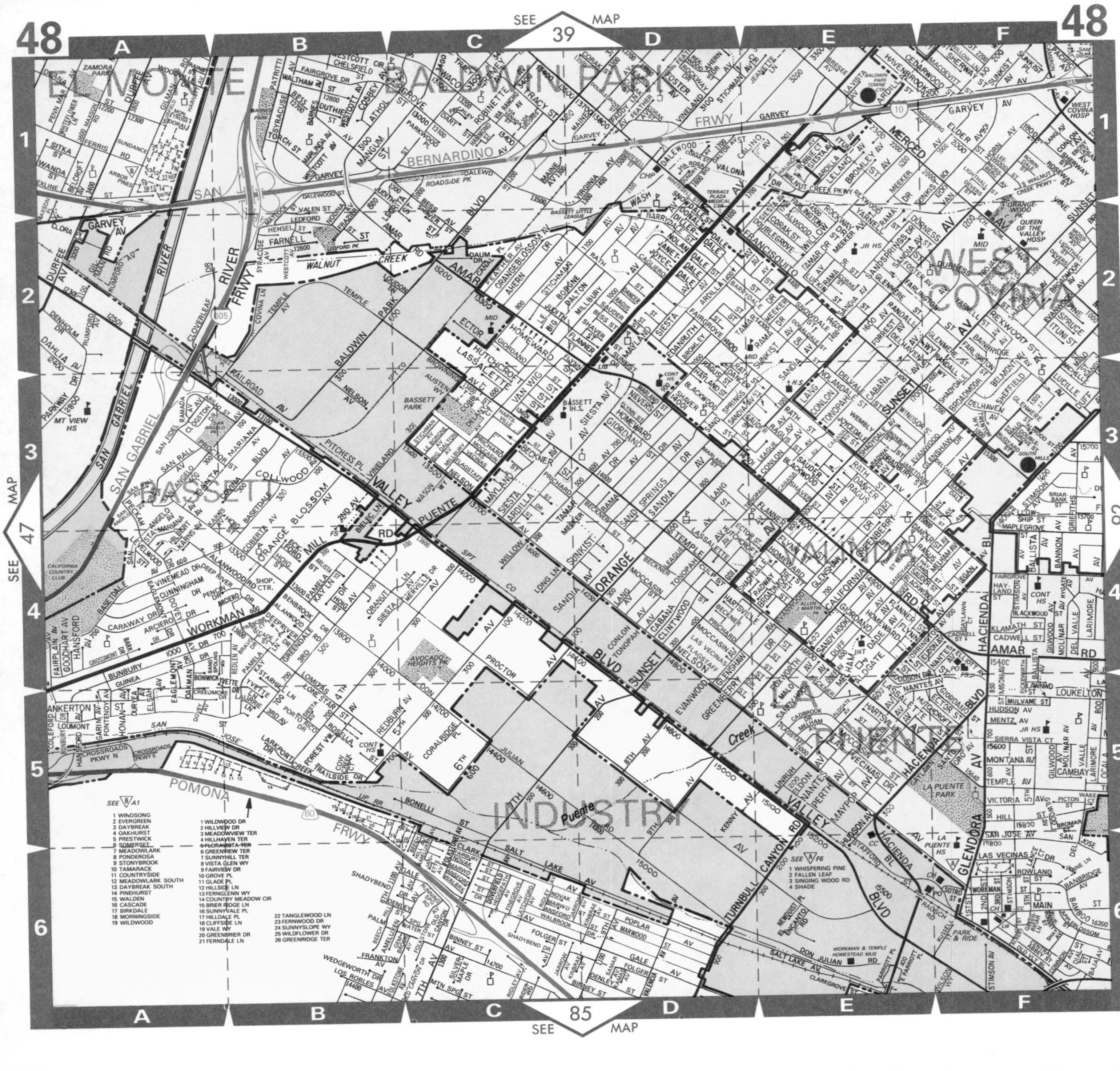

EL MONTE BALDWIN PARK WEST COVINA

BASSETT LA PUENTE VALINDA

INDUSTRY

SAN BERNARDINO FRWY GARVEY AV

SAN GABRIEL RIVER FRWY

POMONA FRWY

SEE MAP 47 · SEE MAP 92

SEE MAP 85

DETAIL

SEE 8 A1
SEE Y F6

#		#	
1	WINDSONG	1	WILDWOOD DR
2	EVERGREEN	2	HILLVIEW DR
3	DAYBREAK	3	MEADOWVIEW TER
4	OAKHURST	4	HILLHAVEN TER
5	PRESTWICK	5	FLORAVISTA TER
6	SOMERSET	6	GREENVIEW TER
7	MEADOWLARK	7	SUNNYHILL TER
8	PONDEROSA	8	VISTA GLEN WY
9	STONYBROOK	9	FAIRVIEW DR
10	TAMARACK	10	GROVE PL
11	COUNTRYSIDE	11	GLADE PL
12	MEADOWLARK SOUTH	12	HILLSIDE LN
13	DAYBREAK SOUTH	13	FERNGLENN WY
14	PINEHURST	14	COUNTRY MEADOW CIR
15	WALDEN	15	BRIER RIDGE LN
16	CASCADE	16	SUNNYSLOPE PL
17	BIRKDALE	17	HILLDALE PL
18	MORNINGSIDE	18	CLIFFSIDE LN
19	WILDWOOD	19	VALE WY
		20	GREENBRIER DR
		21	FERNDALE LN
		22	TANGLEWOOD DR
		23	FERNWOOD DR
		24	SUNNYSLOPE WY
		25	WILDFLOWER DR
		26	GREENRIDGE TER

#	
1	WHISPERING PINE
2	FALLEN LEAF
3	SINGING WOOD RD
4	SHADE

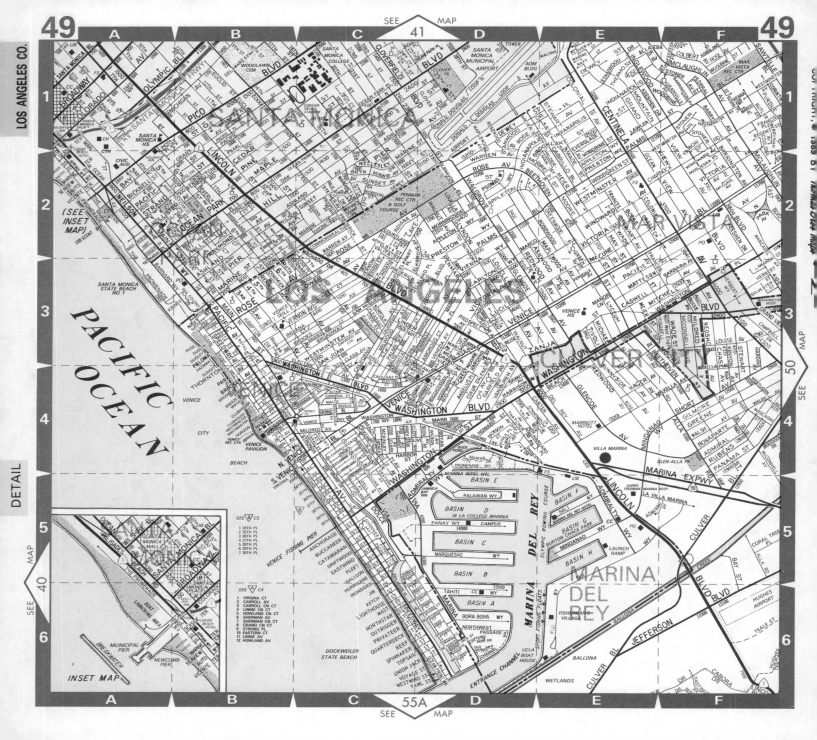

A B C D E F

LOS ANGELES

BALDWIN HILLS

CULVER CITY

WEST LOS ANGELES COLLEGE

LOS ANGELES

CULVER CITY

FOX HILLS

LADERA HEIGHTS

INGLEWOOD

BALDWIN HILLS

Kenneth Hahn State Recreation Area

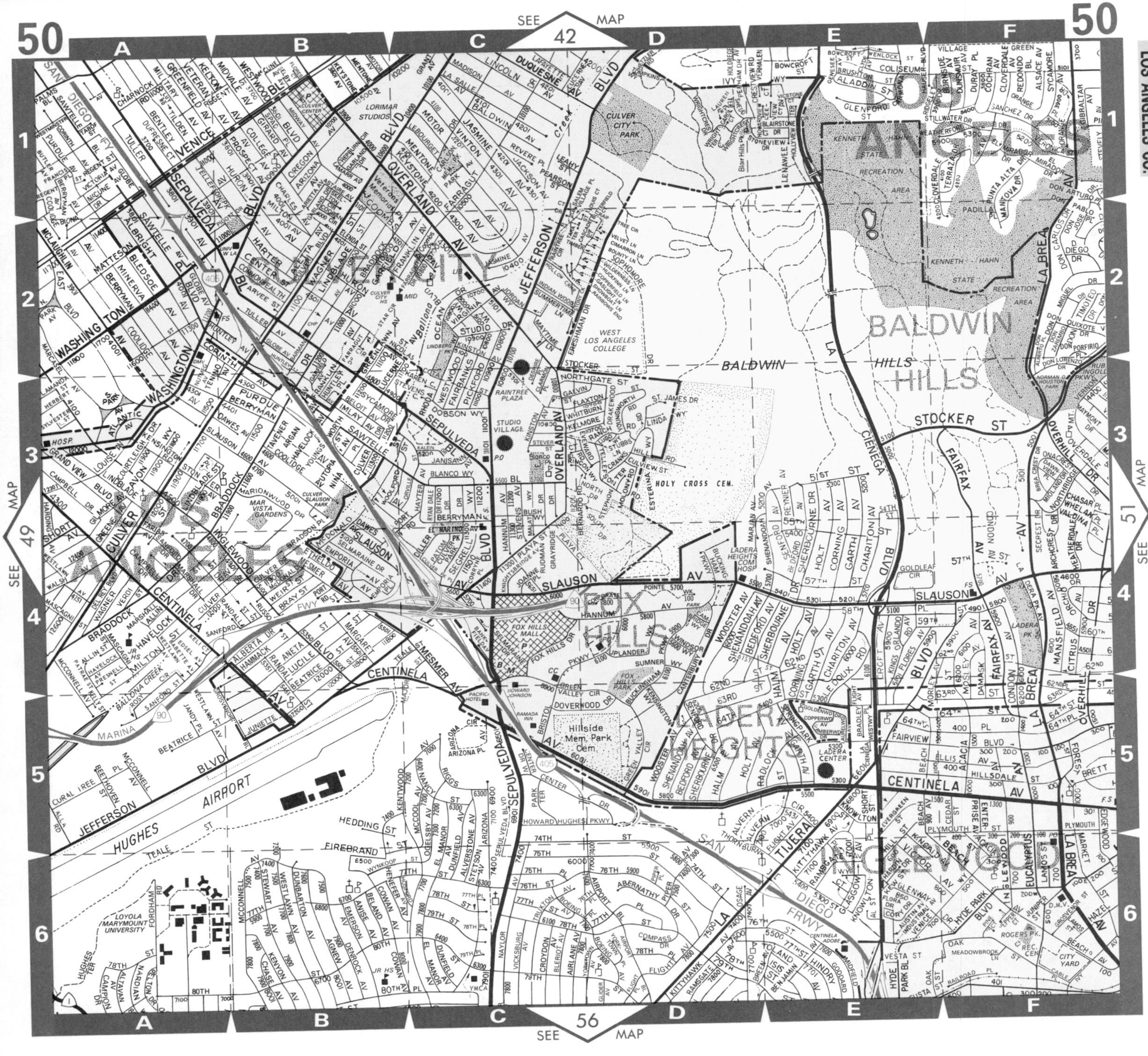

Culver City Park

Holy Cross Cem.

Fox Hills Mall

Hillside Mem. Park Cem.

Loyola Marymount University

HUGHES AIRPORT

MARINA

Studio Village

Raintree Plaza

VENICE BLVD
WASHINGTON BLVD
JEFFERSON BLVD
SEPULVEDA BLVD
OVERLAND AV
CENTINELA AV
SLAUSON AV
STOCKER ST
LA CIENEGA BLVD
FAIRFAX AV
LA BREA AV
OVERHILL DR
CENTINELA AV
SAN DIEGO FRWY

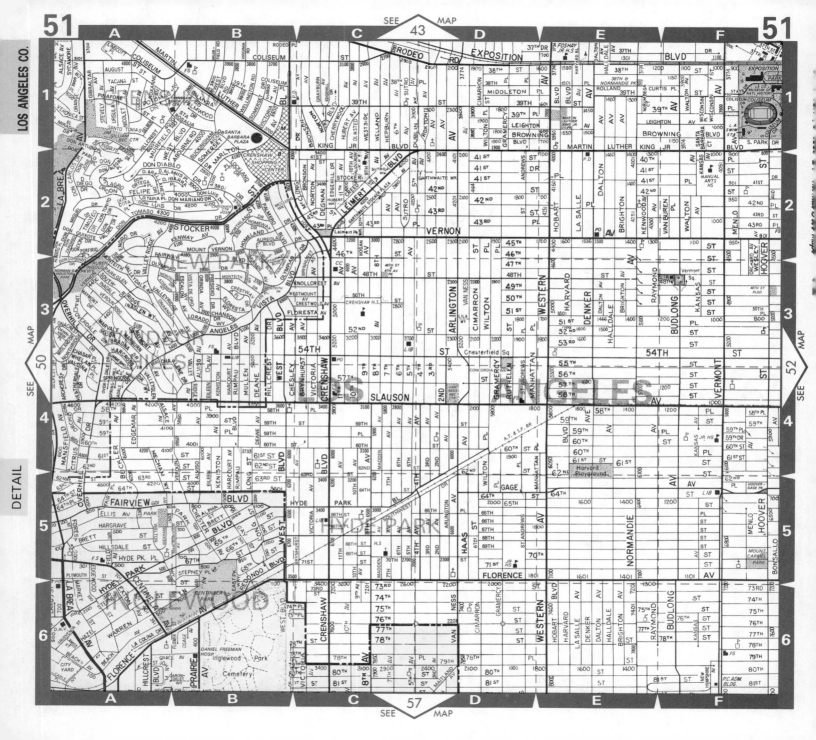

LOS ANGELES

VERNON

HUNTINGTON PARK

SEE MAP 45

LOS ANGELES CO.

DETAIL

SEE MAP 52

SEE MAP 54

LOS ANGELES

VERNON

MAYWOOD

HUNTINGTON PARK

COMMERCE

BELL

BELL GARDENS

CUDAHY

OLYMPIC

WASHINGTON

BANDINI

SLAUSON

FRUITLAND

LEONIS BLVD

FLORENCE

GAGE

ATLANTIC BL

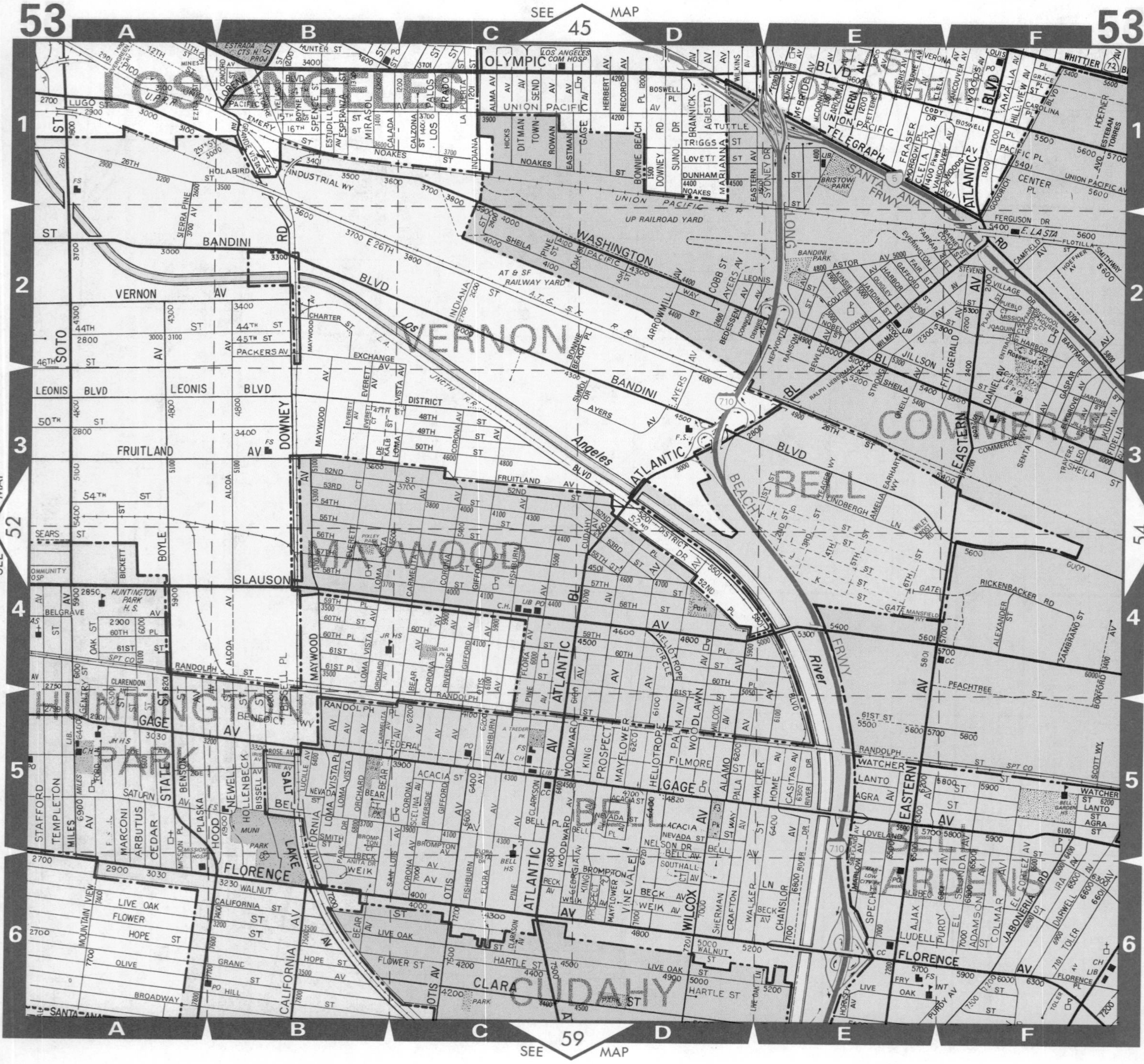

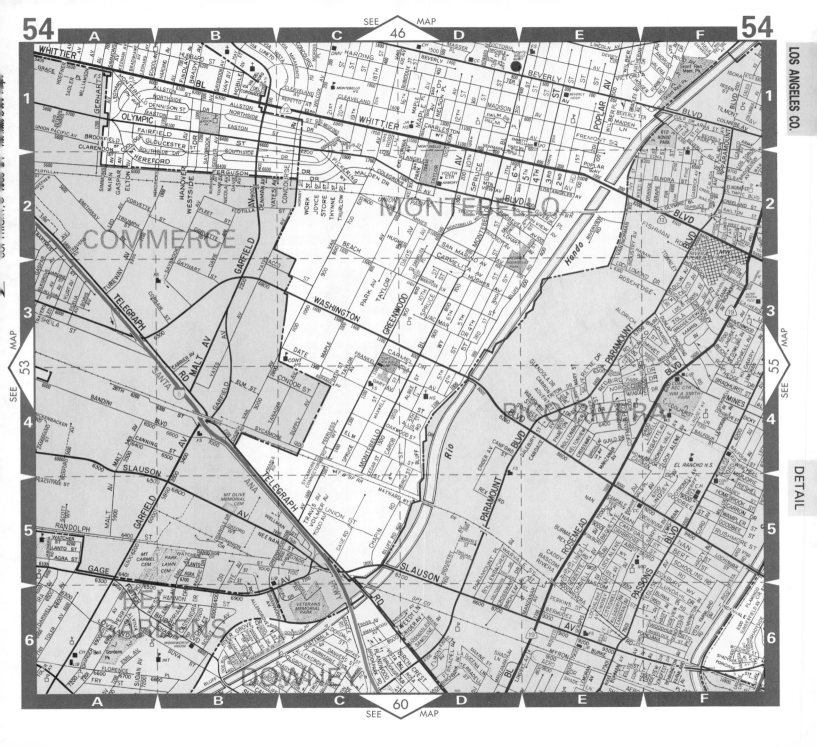

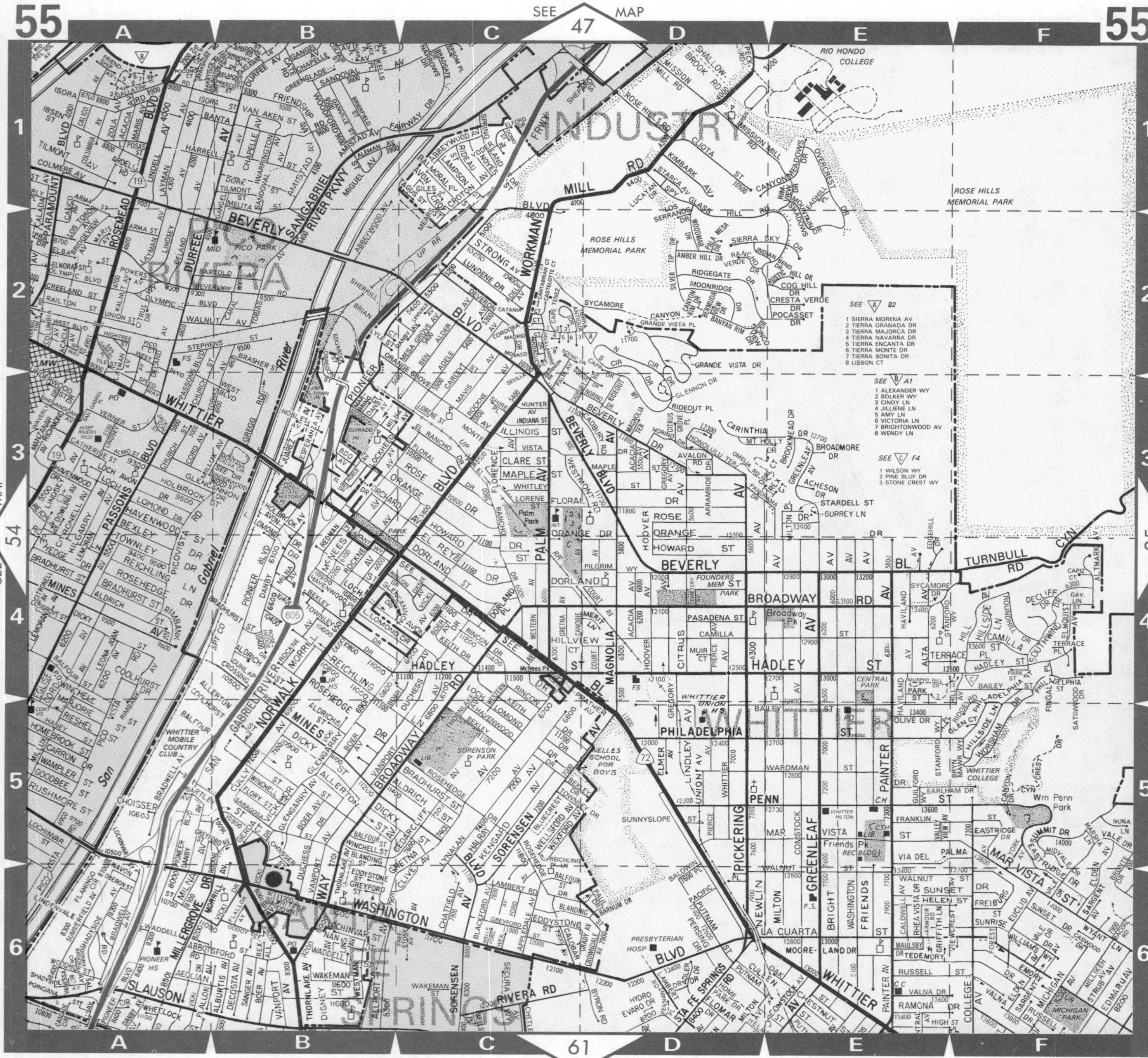

SEE MAP 47
SEE MAP 54
SEE MAP 85
SEE MAP 61
INDUSTRY
PICO RIVERA
WHITTIER
SANTA FE SPRINGS
RIO HONDO COLLEGE
ROSE HILLS MEMORIAL PARK
WHITTIER MOBILE COUNTRY CLUB
NELLES SCHOOL FOR BOYS
SUNNYSLOPE
WHITTIER COLLEGE
WHITTIER UNION HS
PRESBYTERIAN HOSP
Palm Park
Broadway Pk
CENTRAL PARK
Friends Pk
Wm Penn Park
SORENSEN PARK
MICHIGAN PARK
PICO PARK
BEVERLY BLVD
WHITTIER BLVD
WASHINGTON BLVD
SLAUSON
TURNBULL CYN RD
MILL RD
WORKMAN MILL RD
SAN GABRIEL RIVER PKWY
NORWALK BLVD
HADLEY ST
PHILADELPHIA ST
BROADWAY
MAR VISTA ST
SEE A D2
1 SIERRA MORENA AV
2 TIERRA GRANADA DR
3 TIERRA MAJORCA DR
4 TIERRA NAVARRA DR
5 TIERRA ENCANTA DR
6 TIERRA MONTE DR
7 TIERRA BONITA DR
8 LISBON CT
SEE B A1
1 ALEXANDER WY
2 BOLKER WY
3 CINDY LN
4 JILLIENE LN
5 AMY LN
6 VICTORIA LN
7 BRIGHTONWOOD AV
8 WENDY LN
SEE C F4
1 WILSON WY
2 PINE BLUF DR
3 STONE CREST WY

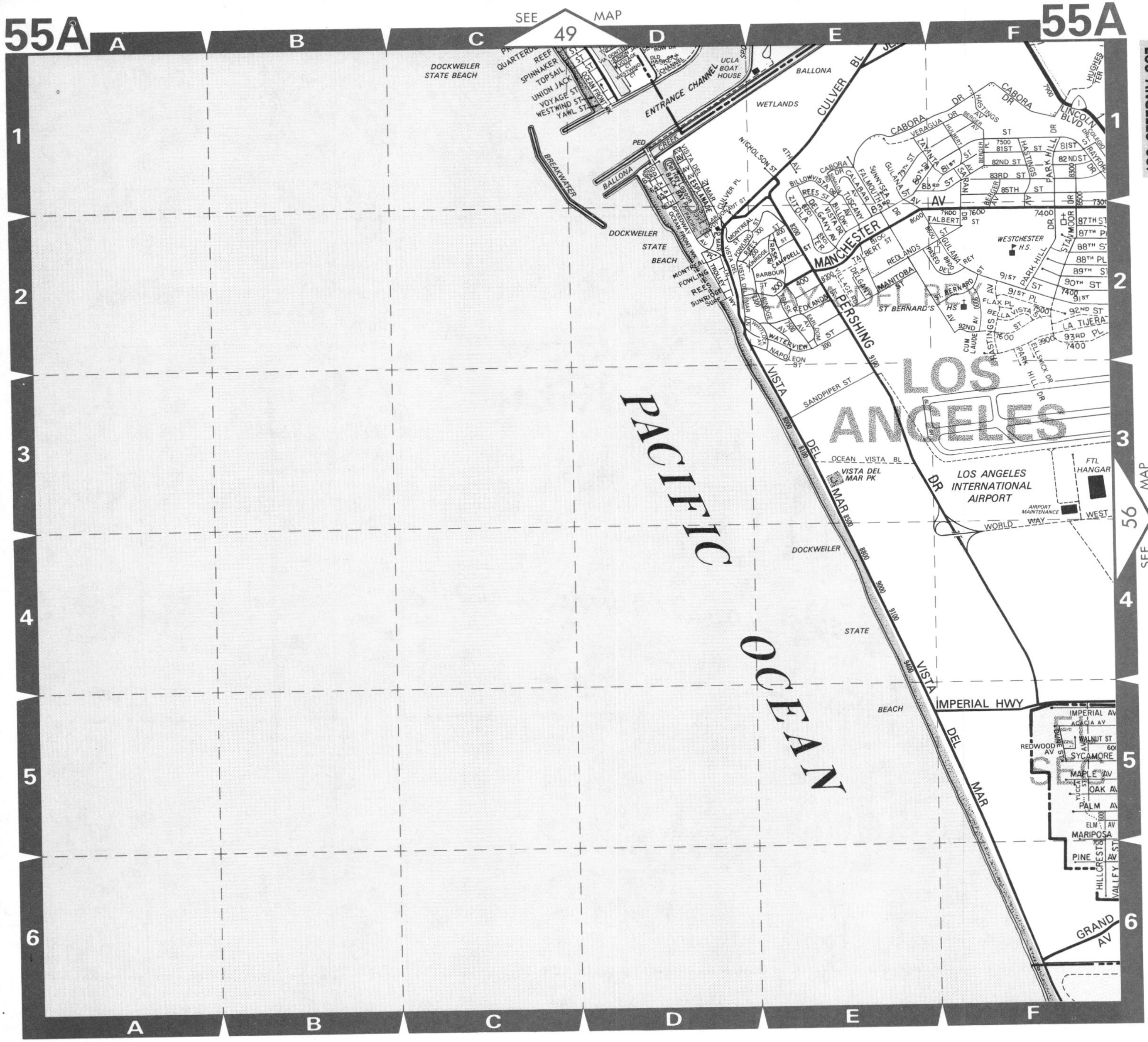

SEE MAP 49

A B C D E F

1

2

3

4

5

6

DOCKWEILER STATE BEACH

Dockweiler State Beach

PACIFIC OCEAN

LOS ANGELES

LOS ANGELES INTERNATIONAL AIRPORT

FTL HANGAR

AIRPORT MAINTENANCE

WORLD WAY WEST

DOCKWEILER STATE BEACH

IMPERIAL HWY

IMPERIAL AV
ACACIA AV
WALNUT ST
SYCAMORE
MAPLE AV
OAK AV
PALM AV
ELM AV
MARIPOSA
PINE AV
REDWOOD AV

GRAND AV

WESTCHESTER H.S.

MANCHESTER

PERSHING

DEL REY

ENTRANCE CHANNEL

BALLONA CREEK

WETLANDS

CULVER BL

LINCOLN BLVD

UCLA BOAT HOUSE

BREAKWATER

VISTA DEL MAR

VISTA DEL MAR PK

OCEAN VISTA BL

SANDPIPER ST

ST BERNARD'S

A B C D E F

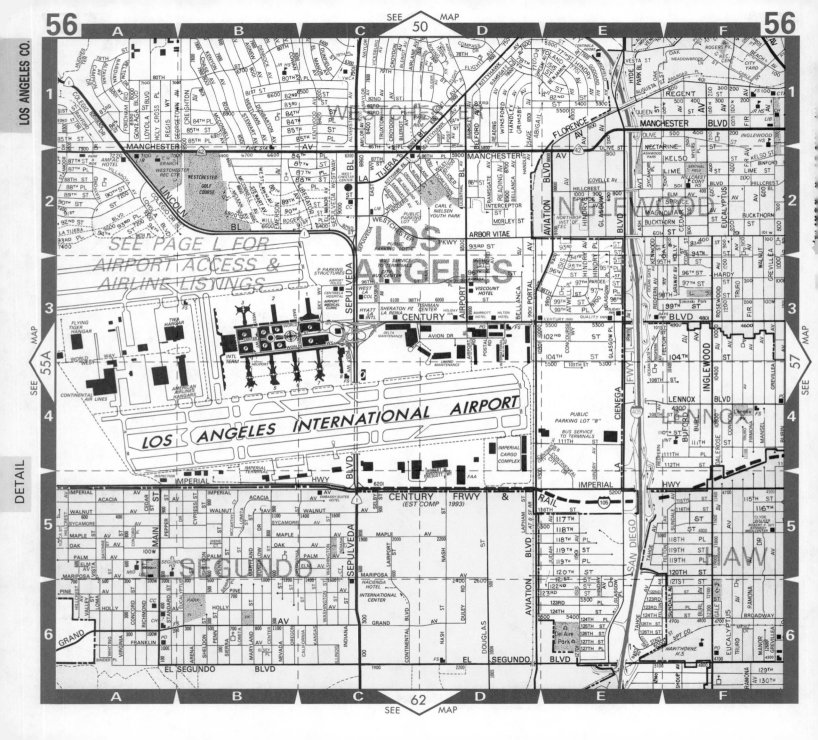

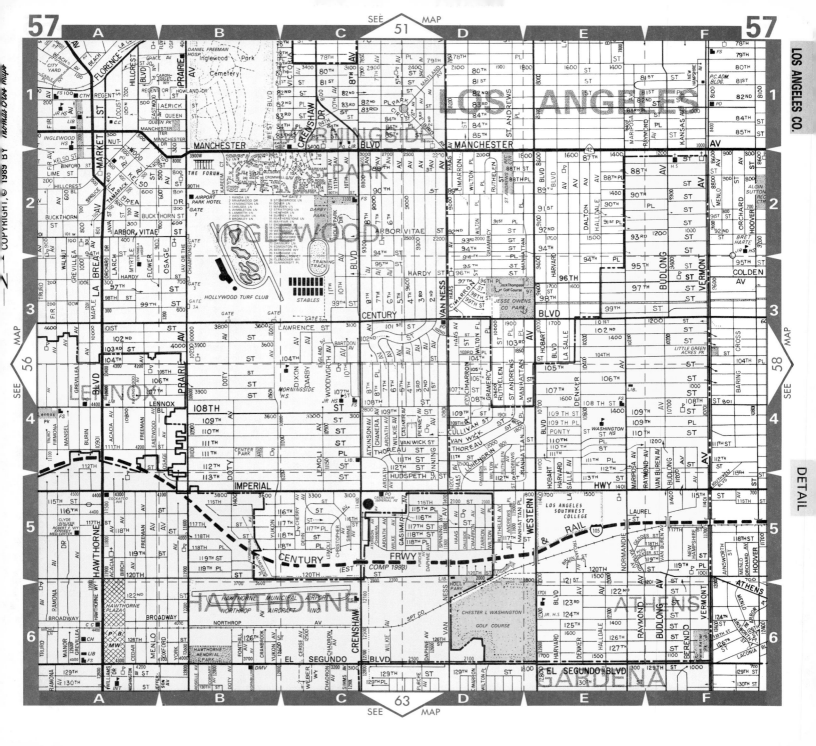

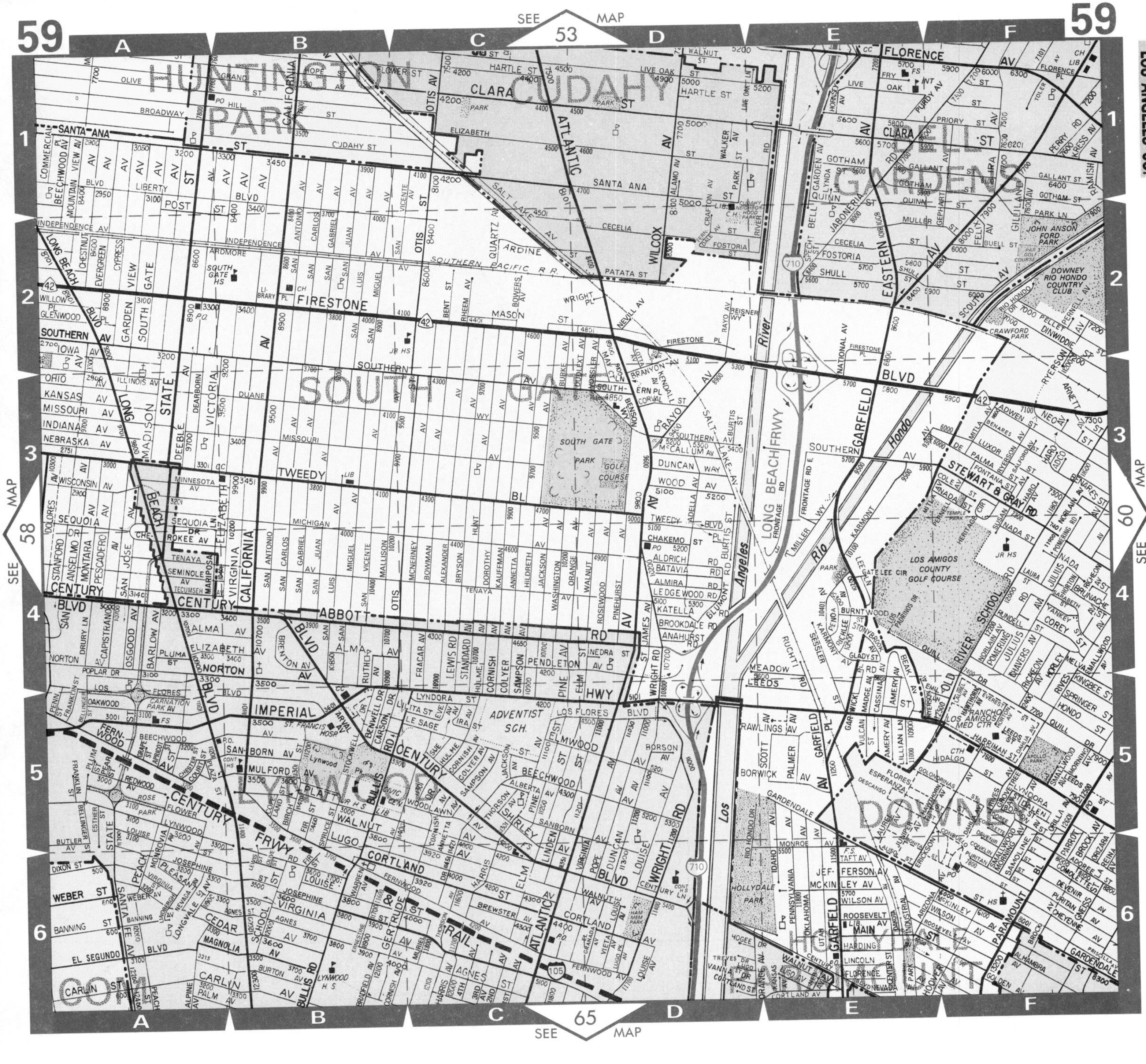

HUNTINGTON PARK

CUDAHY

CLARA

FLORENCE AV

BELL GARDENS

SOUTH GATE

DOWNEY RIO HONDO COUNTRY CLUB

JOHN ANSON FORD PARK

LYNWOOD

DOWNEY

Los Amigos County Golf Course

South Gate Park Golf Course

CENTURY BLVD

IMPERIAL

FIRESTONE BLVD

SOUTHERN AV

TWEEDY BL

ABBOTT RD

ATLANTIC AV

GARFIELD AV

PARAMOUNT BLVD

LONG BEACH FRWY

CENTURY FRWY

Los Angeles River

Rio Hondo

SANTA ANA

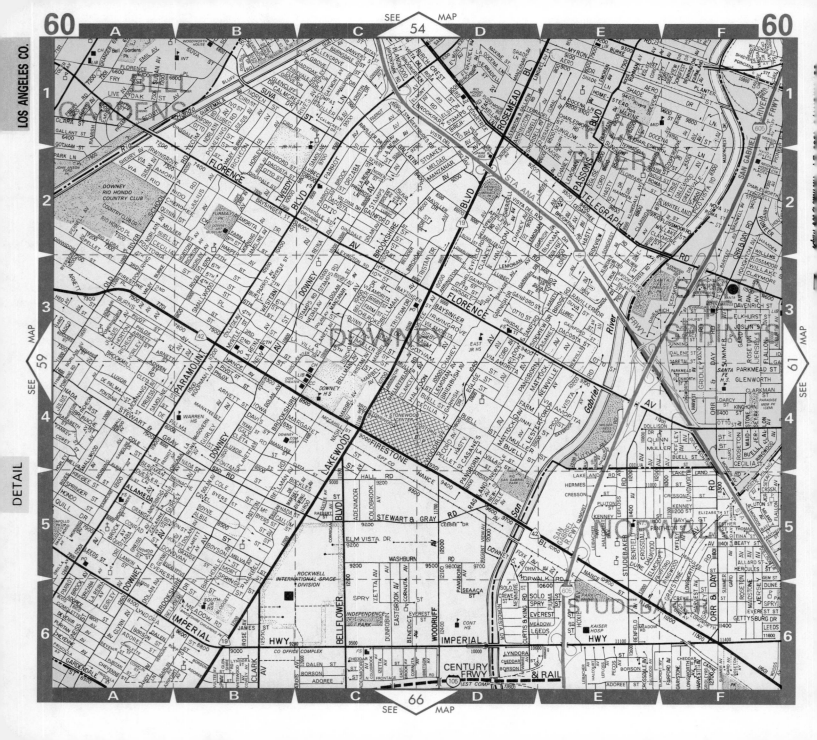

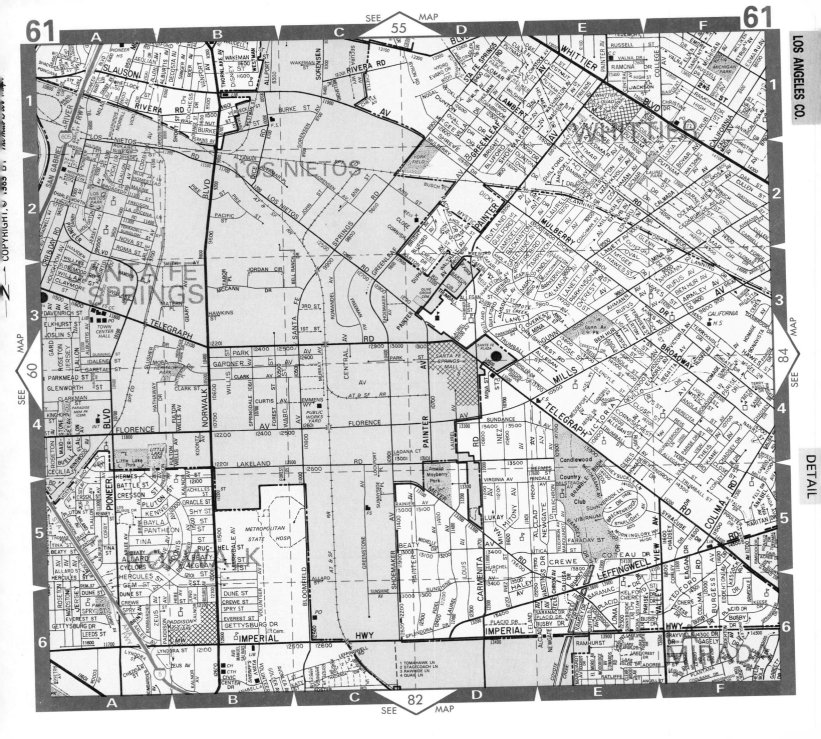

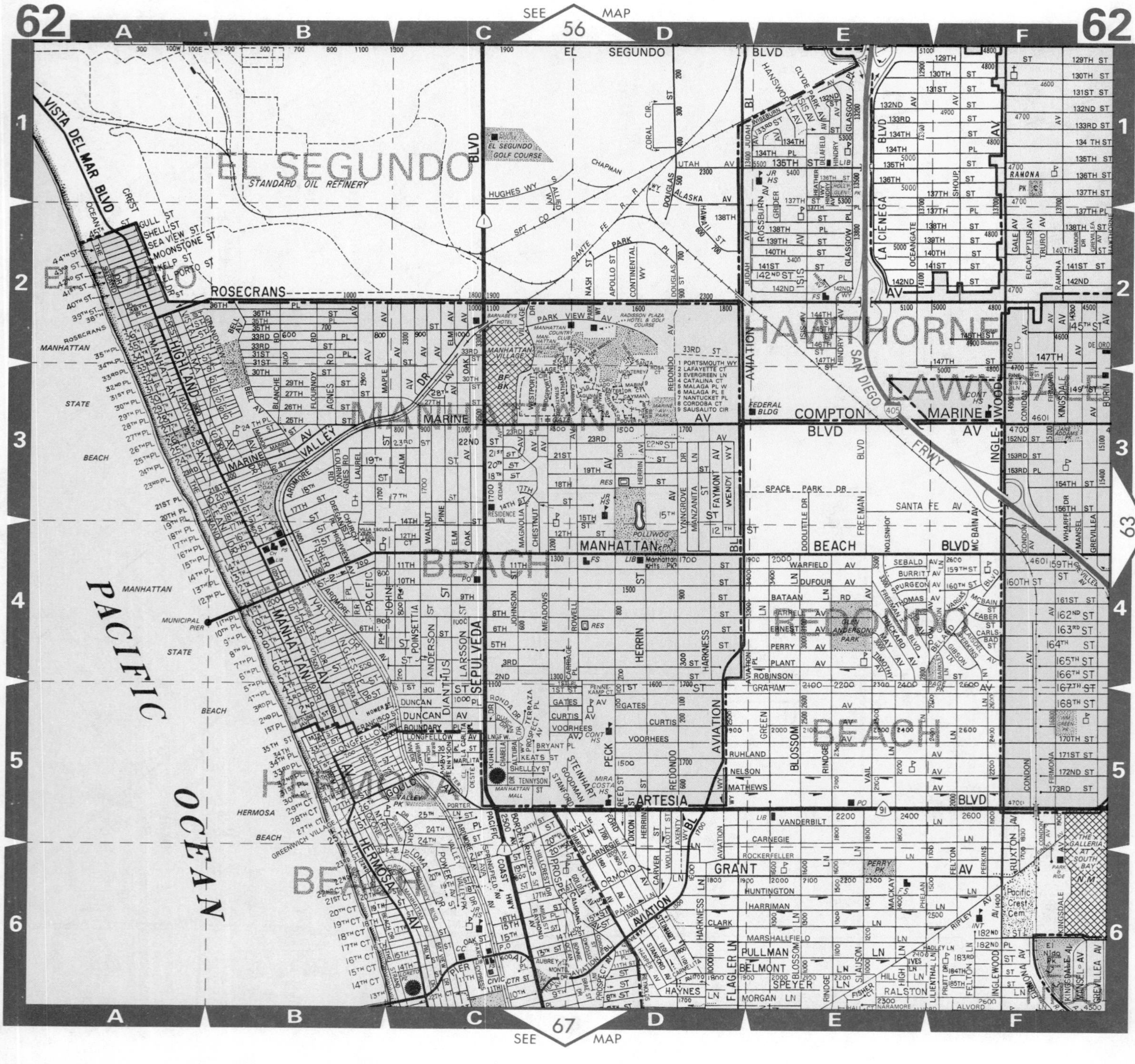

LOS ANGELES CO.

DETAIL

EL SEGUNDO BLVD

EL SEGUNDO
STANDARD OIL REFINERY

EL SEGUNDO GOLF COURSE

VISTA DEL MAR BLVD

ROSECRANS

MANHATTAN

PACIFIC OCEAN

MANHATTAN BEACH

MANHATTAN COUNTRY CLUB

PARK VIEW
RADISSON PLAZA HOTEL & GOLF COURSE

HAWTHORNE

LAWNDALE

MARINE AV
COMPTON BLVD

MANHATTAN BEACH

POLLIWOG

MANHATTAN

REDONDO BEACH

SAN DIEGO FRWY 405

INGLEWOOD

HERMOSA BEACH

HERMOSA BEACH

MIRA COSTA

ARTESIA BLVD

PACIFIC COAST HWY

AVIATION

GRANT

PULLMAN
BELMONT
SPEYER

PACIFIC CREST CEM.

THE GALLERIA AT SOUTH BAY

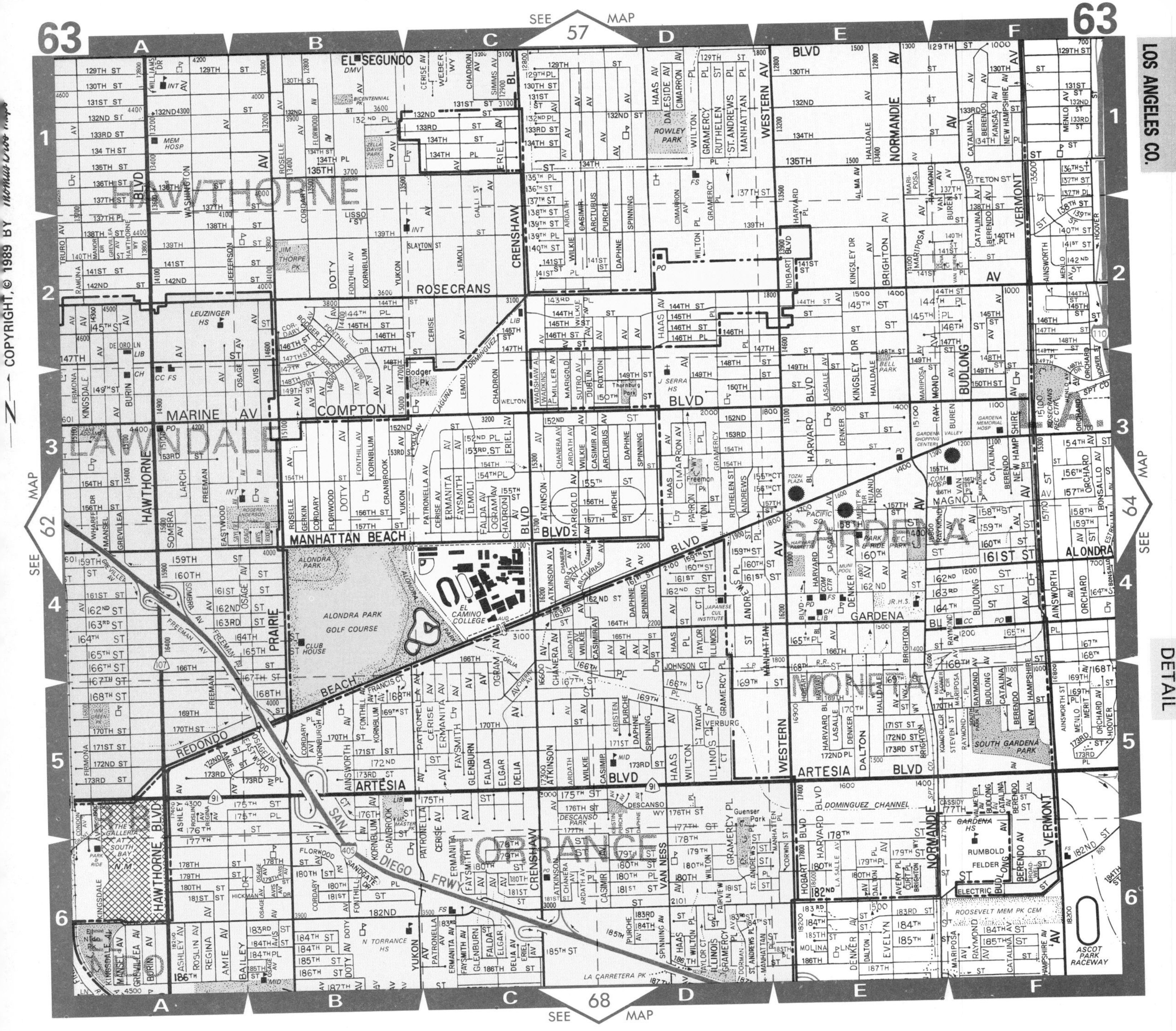

SEE MAP 57

SEE MAP 68

SEE MAP 62

SEE MAP 64

DETAIL

HAWTHORNE

LAWNDALE

EL SEGUNDO

GARDENA

TORRANCE

MANHATTAN BEACH

ALONDRA PARK

ALONDRA PARK GOLF COURSE

EL CAMINO COLLEGE

THE GALLERIA SOUTH BAY

ASCOT PARK RACEWAY

ROOSEVELT MEM PK CEM

ROSECRANS

MARINE AV

COMPTON

REDONDO

BEACH

ARTESIA BLVD

MANHATTAN BEACH BLVD

GARDENA

SOUTH GARDENA PARK

DOMINGUEZ CHANNEL

SAN DIEGO FRWY

LOS ANGELES CO.

DETAIL

SEE MAP 58

SEE MAP 63

SEE MAP 65

SEE MAP 69

EL SEGUNDO BLVD

ROSECRANS

COMPTON

COMPTON AIRPORT

ALONDRA BLVD

GARDENA BLVD

REDONDO BEACH BL

ARTESIA BLVD

REDONDO BEACH BLVD

CARSON

VICTORIA ST

CALIFORNIA STATE UNIVERSITY DOMINGUEZ HILLS

VELODROME

ASCOT PARK RACEWAY

HARBOR FRWY

FIGUEROA ST

BROADWAY

MAIN ST

SAN PEDRO ST

AVALON BLVD

CENTRAL AV

WILMINGTON AV

ALAMEDA ST

WILMINGTON ST

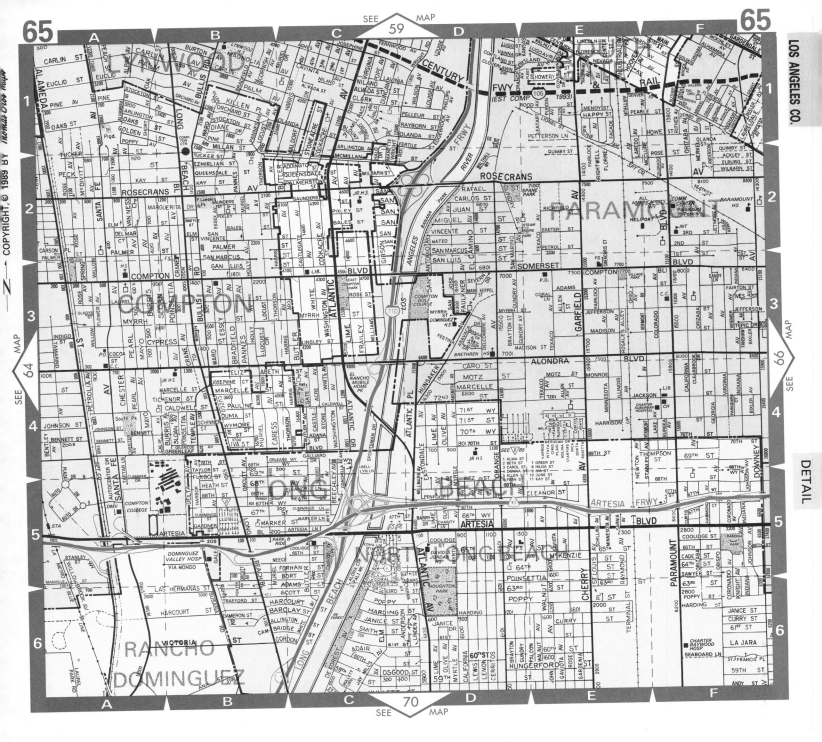

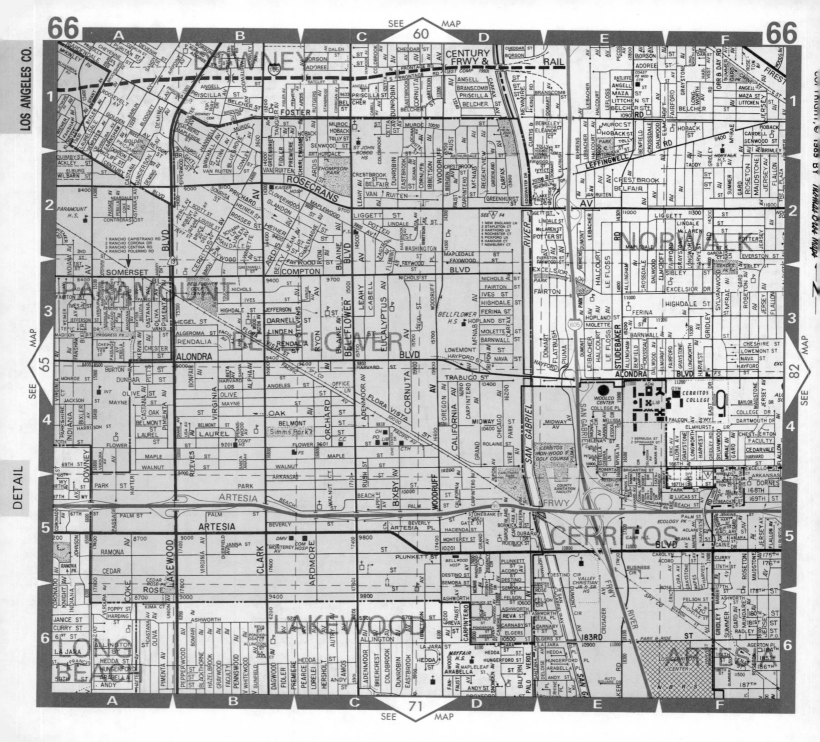

LOS ANGELES CO.

DETAIL

SEE MAP 63

SEE MAP 73

SEE MAP 67

SEE MAP 69

COPYRIGHT, © 1989 BY Thomas Bros. Maps

LOS ANGELES

TORRANCE

COLUMBIA REGIONAL PARK

OIL REFINERY

OIL TANKS

LA CARRETERA PK

ROOSEVELT MEM PK CEM

ASCOT PARK RACEWAY

OLD TOWNE MALL

SAN DIEGO FRWY

190TH ST

DEL AMO BLVD

TORRANCE BLVD

CARSON

SEPULVEDA

LOMITA BLVD

HAWTHORNE BLVD

PRAIRIE AV

CRENSHAW BLVD

WESTERN AV

NORMANDIE AV

VERMONT AV

HARBOR FRWY

MADRONA MARSH NATURE PRESERVE

CHARLES WILSON COM PARK

DEL AMO FASHION CENTER

PLAZA DEL AMO

CIVIC CENTER

TORRANCE HS

TORRANCE MEM HOSP

LA CO HARBOR-UCLA MED CTR

ALPINE VILLAGE

BARON ST

DELTHORNE PARK

PUEBLO PLAYGROUND & PARK

CHARTER PACIFIC MED CTR

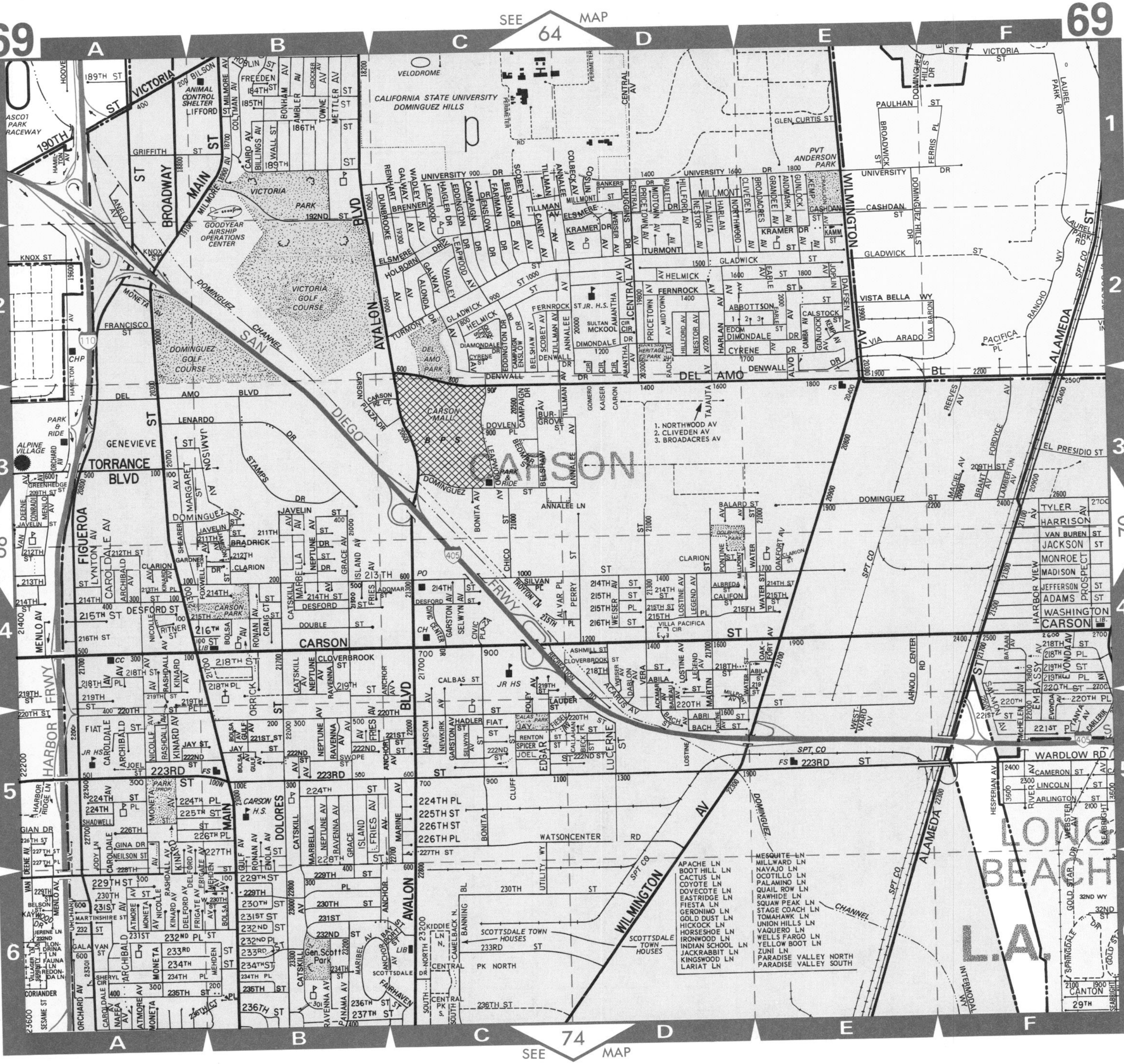

CALIFORNIA STATE UNIVERSITY
DOMINGUEZ HILLS

CARSON

LONG BEACH
L.A.

TORRANCE BLVD

HARBOR FRWY

SAN DIEGO FRWY

VICTORIA GOLF COURSE

DOMINGUEZ GOLF COURSE

ASCOT PARK RACEWAY

GOODYEAR AIRSHIP OPERATIONS CENTER

ANIMAL CONTROL SHELTER

Alpine Village

PARK & RIDE

CARSON MALL

DEL AMO PARK

PVT ANDERSON PARK

SCOTTSDALE TOWN HOUSES

Gen. Scott Park

WATSONCENTER RD

1. Northwood Av
2. Cliveden Av
3. Broadacres Av

MESQUITE LN
APACHE LN
BOOT HILL LN
CACTUS LN
COYOTE LN
DOVECOTE LN
EASTRIDGE LN
FIESTA LN
GERONIMO LN
GOLD DUST LN
HICKOCK LN
HORSESHOE LN
IRONWOOD LN
INDIAN SCHOOL LN
JACKRABBIT LN
KINGSWOOD LN
LARIAT LN
MILLWARD LN
NAVAJO LN
OCOTILLO LN
PALAMINO LN
QUAIL ROW LN
RAWHIDE LN
SQUAW PEAK LN
STAGE COACH LN
TOMAHAWK LN
UNION HILLS LN
VAQUERO LN
WELLS FARGO LN
YELLOW BOOT LN
ZUNI LN
PARADISE VALLEY NORTH
PARADISE VALLEY SOUTH

SEE MAP 68
SEE MAP 70
SEE MAP 74

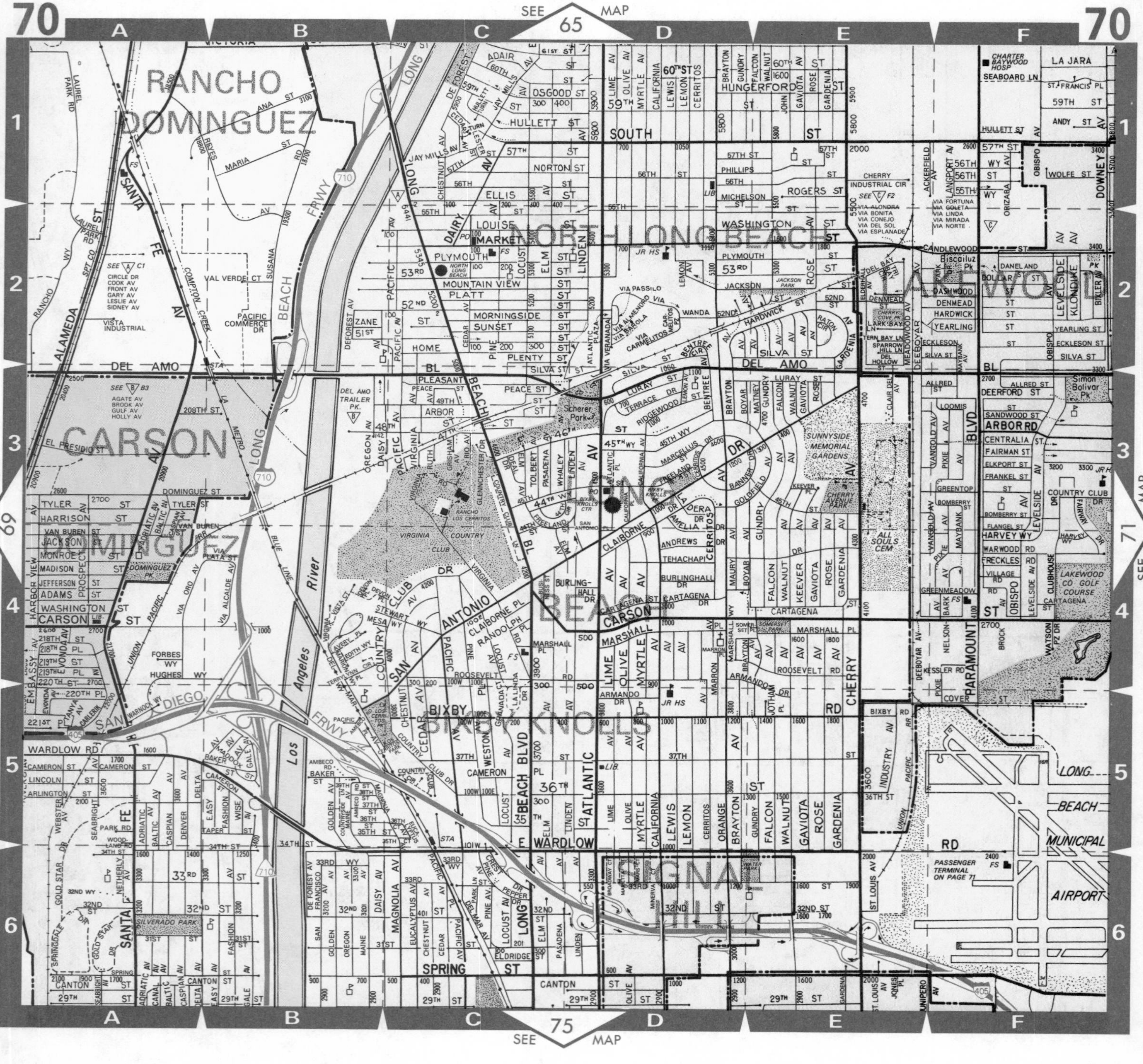

RANCHO DOMINGUEZ

CARSON

DOMINGUEZ

NORTH LONG BEACH

LAKEWOOD

LONG BEACH

SIGNAL HILL

BIXBY KNOLLS

LONG BEACH MUNICIPAL AIRPORT

La JARA

CHARTER BAYWOOD HOSP

SUNNYSIDE MEMORIAL GARDENS

ALL SOULS CEM

LAKEWOOD CO GOLF COURSE

Virginia Country Club

Silverado Park

Scherer Park

PASSENGER TERMINAL ON PAGE 71

Copyright © 1969 by Thomas Bros. Maps

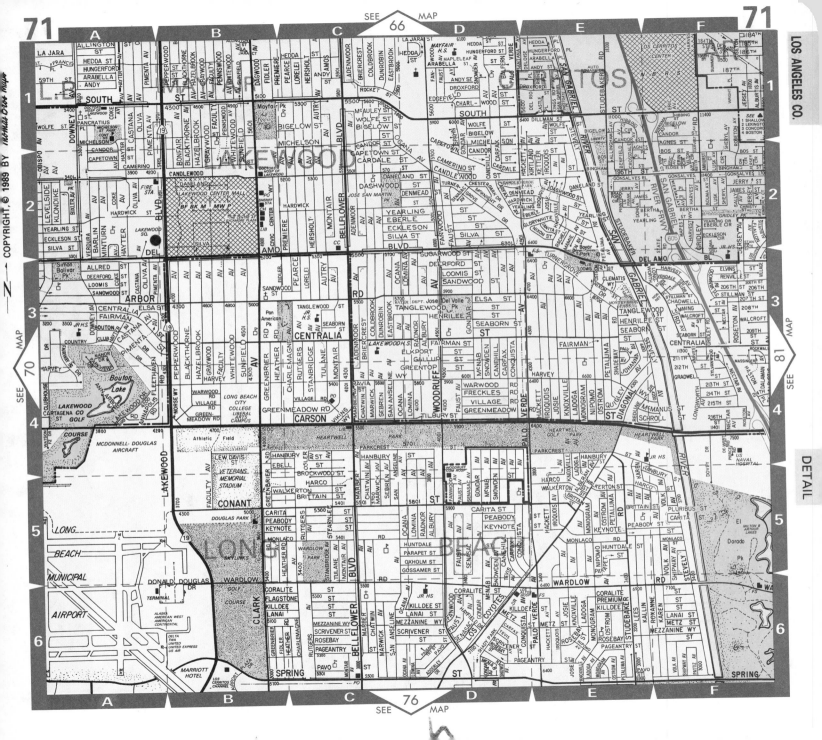

PACIFIC OCEAN

MALAGA COVE

Flat Rock Pt.

BLUFF COVE

PALOS VERDES ESTATES

PALOS VERDES DR

MALAGA COVE PT.

Rocky Pt.

LUNADA BAY

Resort Pt.

Palos Verdes H.S.

PALOS VERDES GOLF COURSE

PALOS VERDES TENNIS CLUB

CLUB HOUSE

TORRANCE

PACIFIC COAST HWY

SOUTH TORRANCE H.S.

PACIFIC COAST HWY

LA SELVA

PALOS VERDES

ROLLING HILLS ESTATES

Rolling Hills H.S.

CRENSHAW BLVD

HAWTHORNE BLVD

RANCHO PALOS VERDES

Hesse Park

Los Verdes Golf Course

Highridge Park

ROLLING HILLS

COPYRIGHT © 1969 BY Thomas Bros. Maps

DETAIL

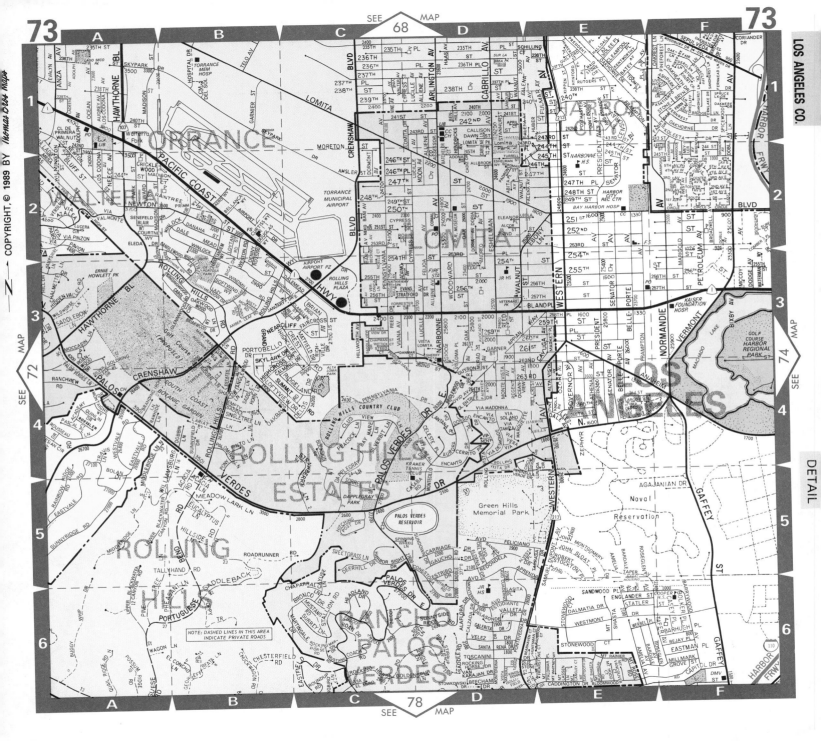

LOS ANGELES CO.

DETAIL

SEE MAP 69
SEE MAP 73
SEE MAP 75
SEE MAP 79

A   B   C   D   E   F

1   2   3   4   5   6

CARSON

SEPULVEDA BLVD

WILMINGTON

LOMITA

PACIFIC COAST HWY

LOS ANGELES

Banning Park

Banning Residence Museum

East Wilmington Greenbelt

Harbor Regional Park Golf Course

Los Angeles Harbor College

ANAHEIM ST

Wilmington Town Sq.

HARBOR FRWY

FIGUEROA ST

MAIN ST

WILMINGTON BLVD

AVALON BLVD

BROAD AV

ALAMEDA ST

DOMINGUEZ

TERMINAL

HENRY FORD AV

JOHN S GIBSON BLVD

MITSUI CONTAINER TERMINAL

LIGHTHOUSE

KS LINES CONTAINER TERMINAL

LOS ANGELES CONTAINER TERMINAL

AMERICAN PRESIDENT LINES CONTAINER TERMINAL

WEST BASIN

EAST BASIN

SLIP NO. 5

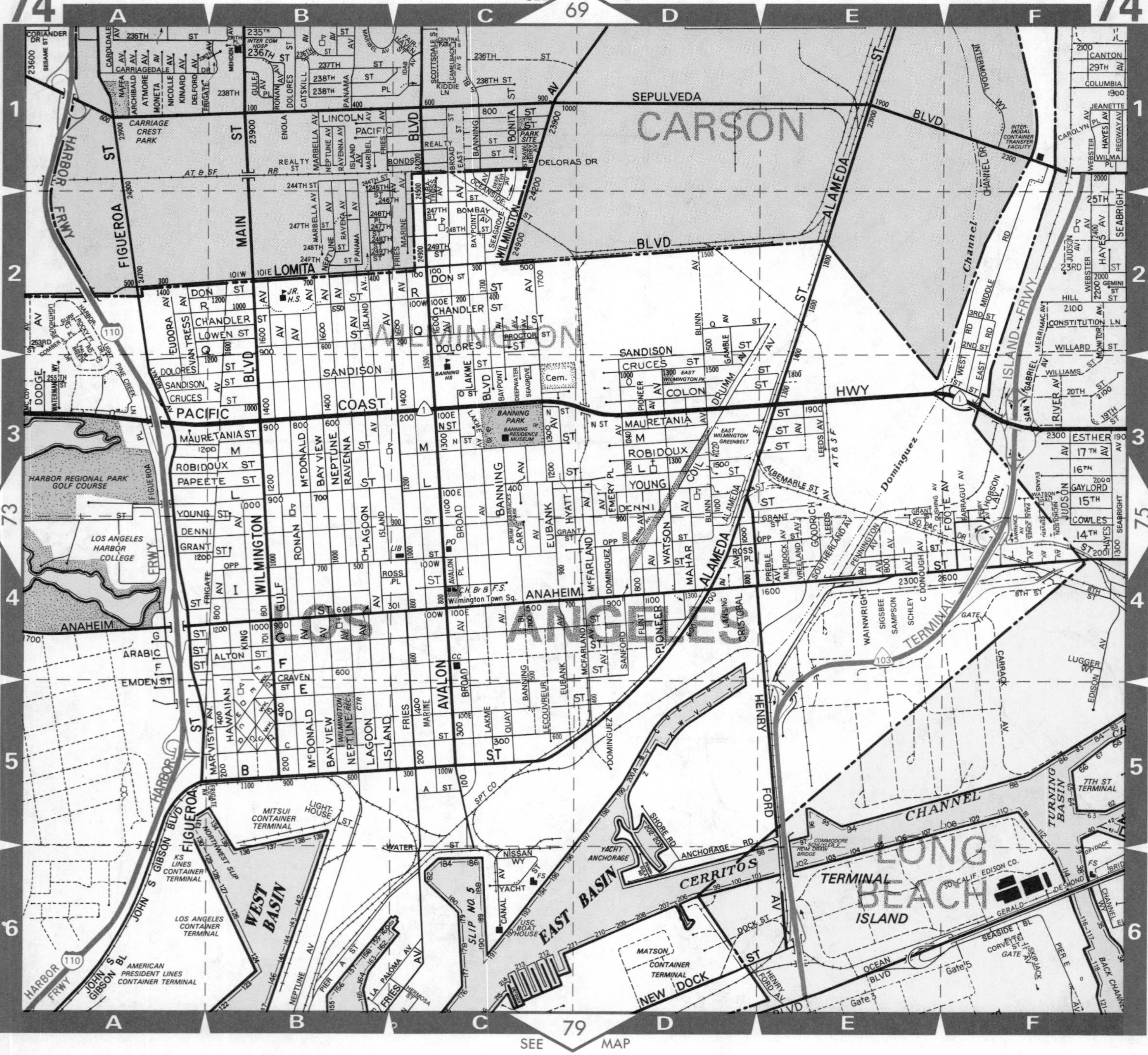

NISSAN WY

YACHT ANCHORAGE

ANCHORAGE RD

CERRITOS CHANNEL

MATSON CONTAINER TERMINAL

NEW DOCK

TERMINAL ISLAND

LONG BEACH

TURNING BASIN

7TH ST TERMINAL

CHANNEL

Calif Edison Co.

OCEAN BLVD

SEASIDE BL

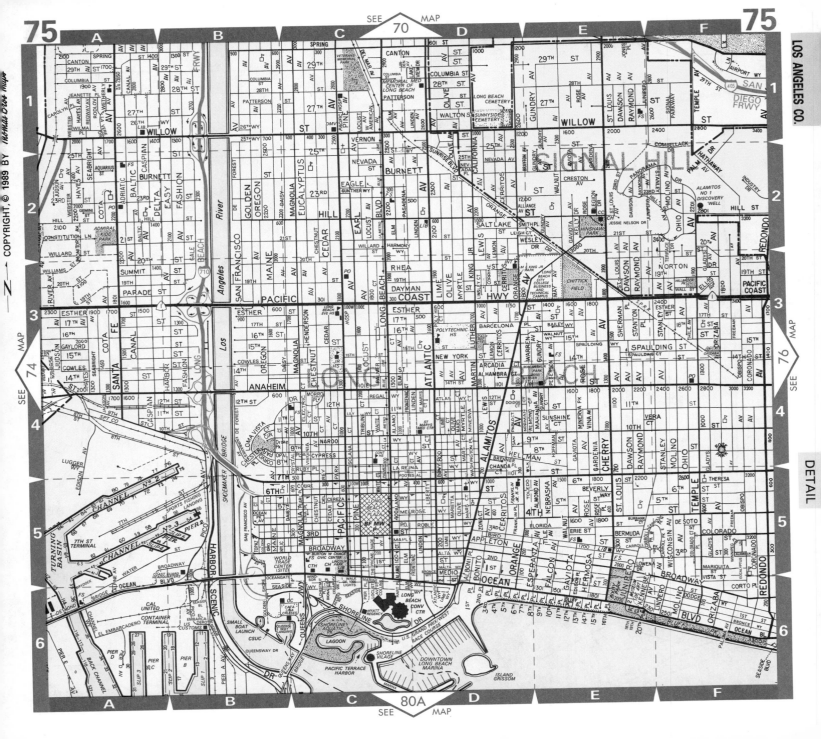

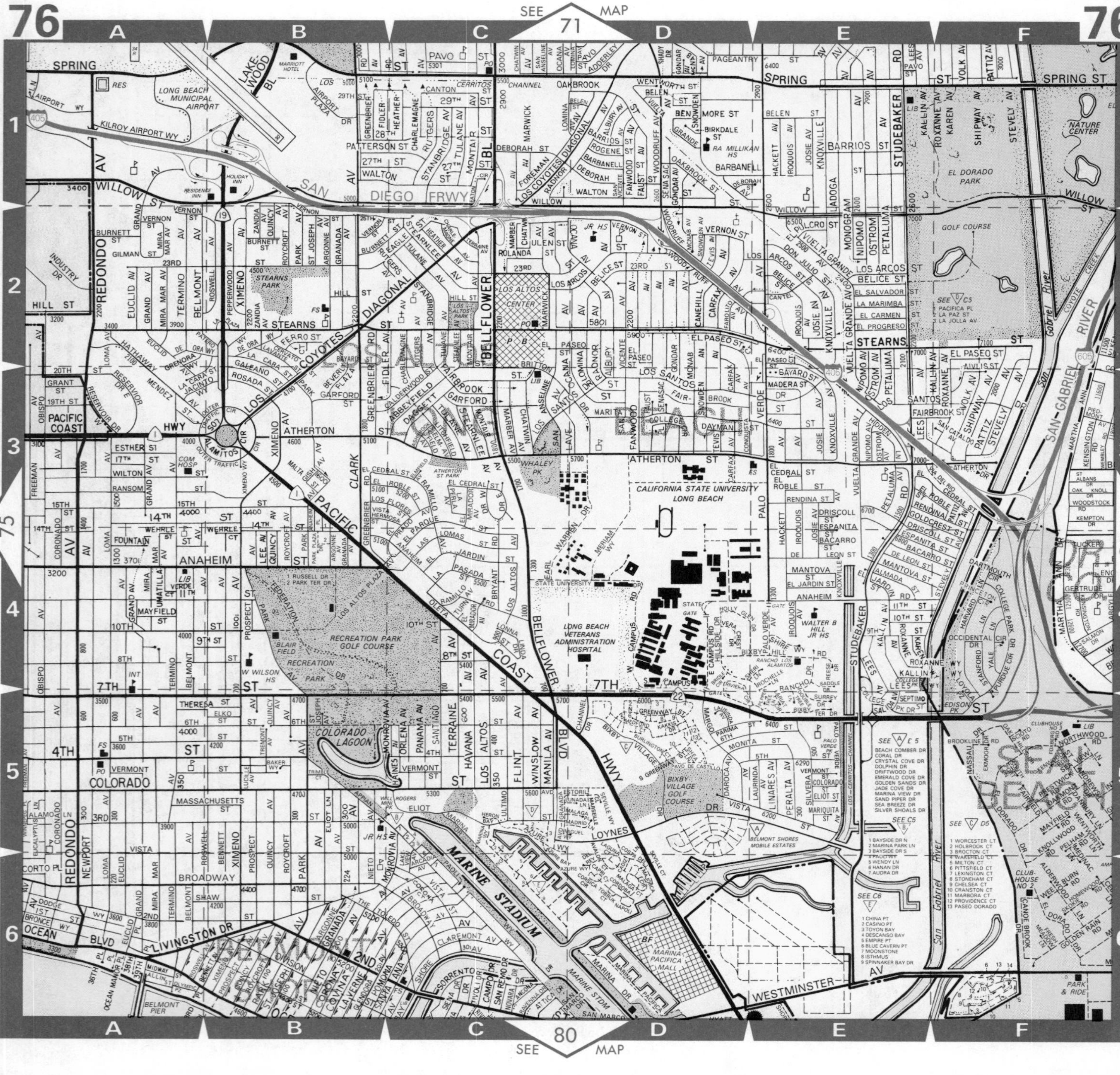

SEE MAP 71

LOS ANGELES CO.

DETAIL

1 2 3 4 5 6

Long Beach Municipal Airport

SAN DIEGO FRWY

EL DORADO PARK

GOLF COURSE

STEARNS

CALIFORNIA STATE UNIVERSITY LONG BEACH

Long Beach Veterans Administration Hospital

Recreation Park Golf Course

Colorado Lagoon

MARINE STADIUM

SEAL BEACH

SAN GABRIEL RIVER

PACIFIC COAST HWY

SPRING ST

WILLOW ST

STEARNS

ATHERTON ST

ANAHEIM

7TH ST

COLORADO

BROADWAY

OCEAN BLVD

LIVINGSTON DR

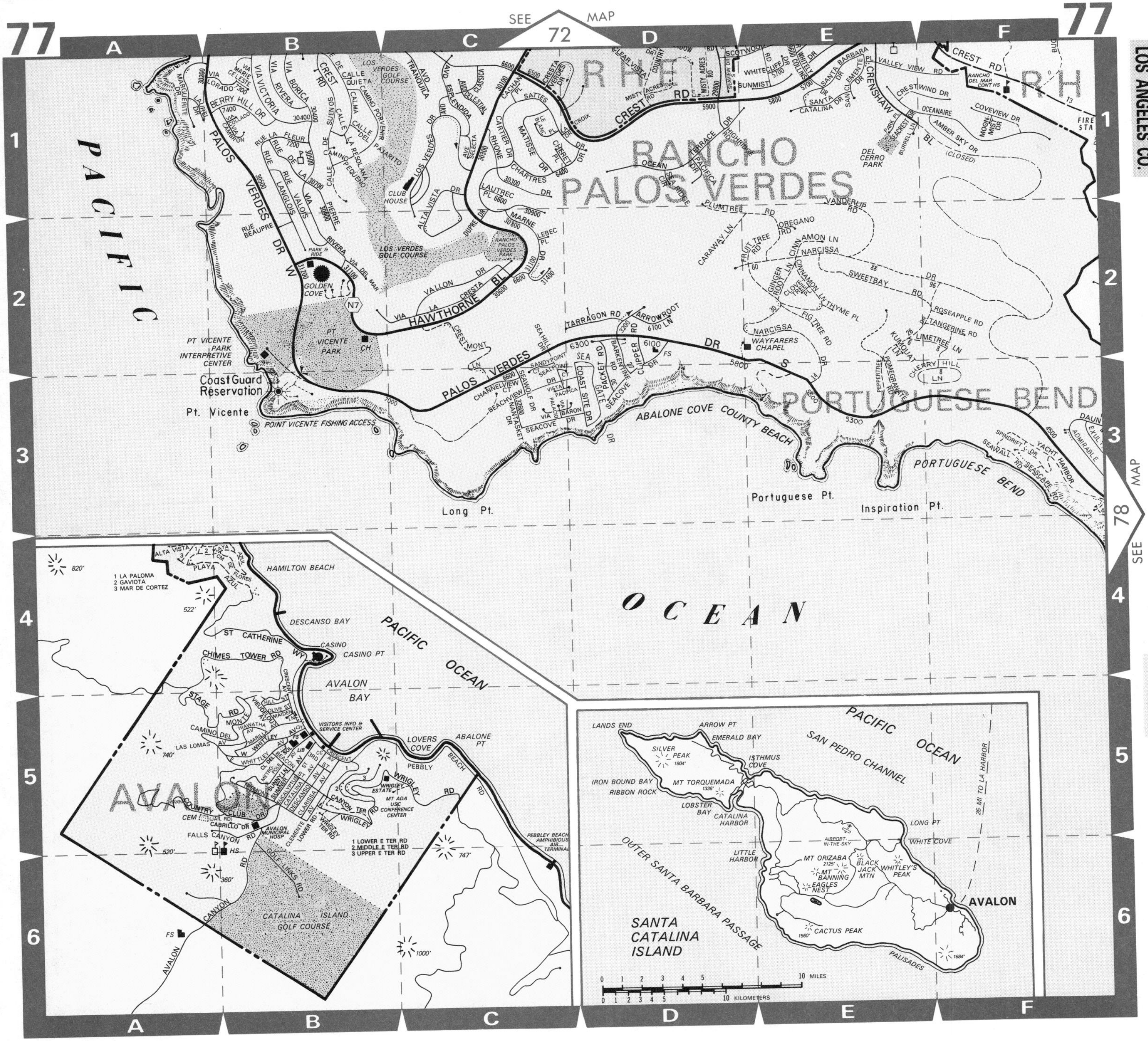

A B C D E F

R P V

RANCHO PALOS VERDES

PACIFIC

PALOS VERDES DR W

CLUB HOUSE

LOS VERDES GOLF COURSE

GOLDEN COVE

PT VICENTE PARK INTERPRETIVE CENTER

PT VICENTE PARK

Coast Guard Reservation

Pt. Vicente

POINT VICENTE FISHING ACCESS

HAWTHORNE BL

PALOS VERDES DR S

Del Cerro Park

WAYFARERS CHAPEL

PORTUGUESE BEND

ABALONE COVE COUNTY BEACH

Long Pt.

Portuguese Pt.

Inspiration Pt.

PORTUGUESE BEND

FIRE STA

R H

OCEAN

PACIFIC OCEAN

1 LA PALOMA
2 GAVIOTA
3 MAR DE CORTEZ

HAMILTON BEACH

DESCANSO BAY

ST CATHERINE WY

CASINO

CASINO PT

CHIMES TOWER RD

AVALON BAY

STAGE RD

VISITORS INFO & SERVICE CENTER

LOVERS COVE

ABALONE PT

PEBBLY BEACH

LAS LOMAS

AVALON

COUNTRY CLUB

CABRILLO DR

FALLS CANYON

HS

AVALON MUNICIPAL HOSP

1 LOWER E TER RD
2 MIDDLE E TER RD
3 UPPER E TER RD

PEBBLEY BEACH AMPHIBIOUS AIR TERMINAL

CATALINA ISLAND GOLF COURSE

AVALON CANYON RD

GOLF LINKS RD

PACIFIC OCEAN

LANDS END

ARROW PT

EMERALD BAY

SILVER PEAK 1804'

ISTHMUS COVE

SAN PEDRO CHANNEL

IRON BOUND BAY

RIBBON ROCK

MT TORQUEMADA 1336'

CATALINA HARBOR

LOBSTER BAY

LONG PT

WHITE COVE

AIRPORT IN THE SKY

LITTLE HARBOR

MT ORIZABA 2125'

MT BANNING

EAGLES NEST

BLACK JACK MTN

WHITLEY'S PEAK

26 MI TO LA HARBOR

AVALON

OUTER SANTA BARBARA PASSAGE

CACTUS PEAK 1560'

PALISADES

1684'

SANTA CATALINA ISLAND

0 1 2 3 4 5 10 MILES

0 1 2 3 4 5 10 KILOMETERS

LOS ANGELES CO.

DETAIL

COPYRIGHT © 1989 BY Thomas Bros. Maps

A B C D E F

ROLLING HILLS

PALOS VERDES

RANCHO PALOS VERDES

MIRALESTE

SAN PEDRO

LOS ANGELES

FIRE STA

HACKAMORE RD

CREST

HILLS

OPEN BRAND RD

FLYING MANE RD

EASTFIELD

PARK PLAZA

MAC ARTHUR PARK

PECK PARK & REC CTR

HARBOR HIGHLANDS PARK

CRESTWOOD ST

ELBERON AV

SUMMERLAND

WESTERN AV

HARBOR VIEW AV

FRIENDSHIP PARK

MARTIN BOGDANOVICH REC CTR

PALOS VERDES COLLEGE

VISTA DEL MAR

PALOS VERDES DR

PASEO DEL MAR

SAN PEDRO H.S.

DANA JR H.S

MARY STAR OF THE SEAS H.S.

SAN PEDRO & PENINSULA HOSP

25TH ST

PALOS VERDES SHORELINE PK (PROP)

PALOS VERDES SHORES GOLF COURSE

DICHA

ANCHOVY

WHITE POINT PARK

ROYAL PALMS STATE BEACH

WHITE POINT

FORT MACARTHUR UPPER RESERVATION

ANGELS GATE PARK

PT. FERMIN PARK

HISTORIC LIGHTHOUSE

GAFFEY

CABRILLO AV

PASEO DEL MAR

CATALINA CHANNEL

PACIFIC OCEAN

HARBOR FRWY

110

SEE MAP 77

SEE MAP 79

A B C D E

1 2 3 4 5 6

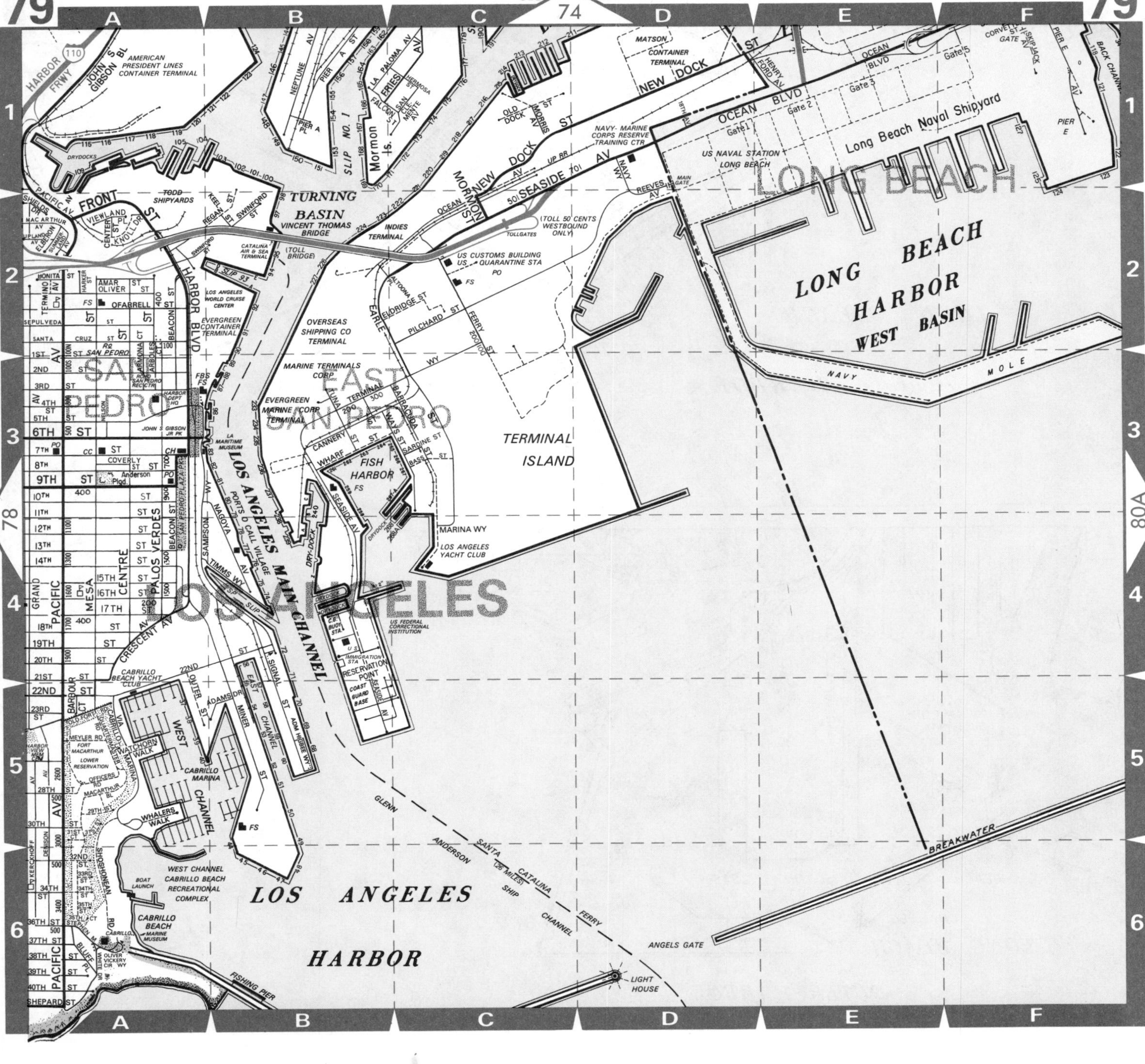

HARBOR FRWY
110
JOHN S. GIBSON BL
AMERICAN PRESIDENT LINES CONTAINER TERMINAL

PIER E
BACK CHANNEL

CORVET / SHIP JACK GATE
PIER E

NEPTUNE AV
PIER A ST
LA PALOMA AV
FRIES AV

MATSON CONTAINER TERMINAL
NEW DOCK ST

OCEAN BLVD
Gate 5

DRYDOCKS
PACIFIC AV
SHIELDS
FRONT
VIEWLAND CENTER
TODD SHIPYARDS

OLD DOCK AV
MORMON Is.

HENRY FORD AV
OCEAN BLVD
Gate 2
Long Beach Naval Shipyard

PIER E

TURNING BASIN
VINCENT THOMAS BRIDGE
(TOLL BRIDGE)
Catalina Air & Sea Terminal

INDIES TERMINAL

US NAVY
Gate 1
US Naval Station Long Beach

LONG BEACH

BONITA
TERMINO
AMAR
OLIVER
O'FABRELL ST
HARBOR BLVD
BEACON

Los Angeles World Cruise Center
Evergreen Container Terminal

NAVY- MARINE CORPS RESERVE TRAINING CTR
SEASIDE
(TOLL 50 CENTS WESTBOUND ONLY)
Tollgates

US Customs Building
US QUARANTINE STA
PO

MAIN GATE
REEVES AV

LONG BEACH HARBOR
WEST BASIN

SEPULVEDA
SANTA CRUZ
1ST AV
SAN PEDRO
2ND
3RD
AV 4TH ST
5TH
SAN PEDRO
6TH ST

Overseas Shipping Co Terminal

Marine Terminals Corp

EARLE
ELDRIDGE BRIDGE
PILCHARD WY

FERRY PO
PORTOLA

NAVY MOLE

7TH PO
8TH ST
COVERLY ST
9TH ST
Anderson Plgd
SAN PEDRO PLAZA PK
10TH
400
11TH
12TH
13TH
14TH
CENTRE
PALOS VERDES
MESA
15TH ST
16TH
17TH
18TH
19TH ST
20TH
GRAND
PACIFIC

LA MARITIME MUSEUM
LOS ANGELES MAIN CHANNEL
PORTS O CALL VILLAGE

Evergreen Marine Corp Terminal

CANNERY
WHARF
FISH HARBOR
SEASIDE AV
SARDINE ST
BASS ST
BARRACUDA

EAST SAN PEDRO

TERMINAL ISLAND

LOS ANGELES

MARINA WY
LOS ANGELES YACHT CLUB

21ST
22ND ST
23RD ST
BARROW
CRESCENT AV

CABRILLO BEACH YACHT CLUB
22ND
OUTER ST
ADAMS DR
MINER ST
EAST CHANNEL

US FEDERAL CORRECTIONAL INSTITUTION

US FEDERAL
IMMIGRATION STA
RESERVATION POINT
COAST GUARD BASE

MEYLER BD
FORT MacARTHUR
HARBOR VIEW AV
LOWER RESERVATION
OFFICERS
WEST CHANNEL
WATCHORN WALK
CABRILLO MARINA
TIMMS WY
SIGNAL ST
ADAM MARINE WY

28TH
30TH
WHALERS WALK
FS

32ND ST
WEST CHANNEL CABRILLO BEACH RECREATIONAL COMPLEX
BOAT LAUNCH

34TH ST
35TH
36TH ST
37TH ST
PACIFIC
38TH ST
39TH ST
40TH ST
SHEPARD ST

CABRILLO BEACH
CABRILLO MARINE MUSEUM
OLIVER VICKERY CIR WY

LOS ANGELES HARBOR

GLENN
ANDERSON
SANTA CATALINA 26 MILES
SHIP
FERRY
CHANNEL

BREAKWATER

ANGELS GATE
LIGHT HOUSE

FISHING PIER

SEE MAP 78

SEE MAP 80A

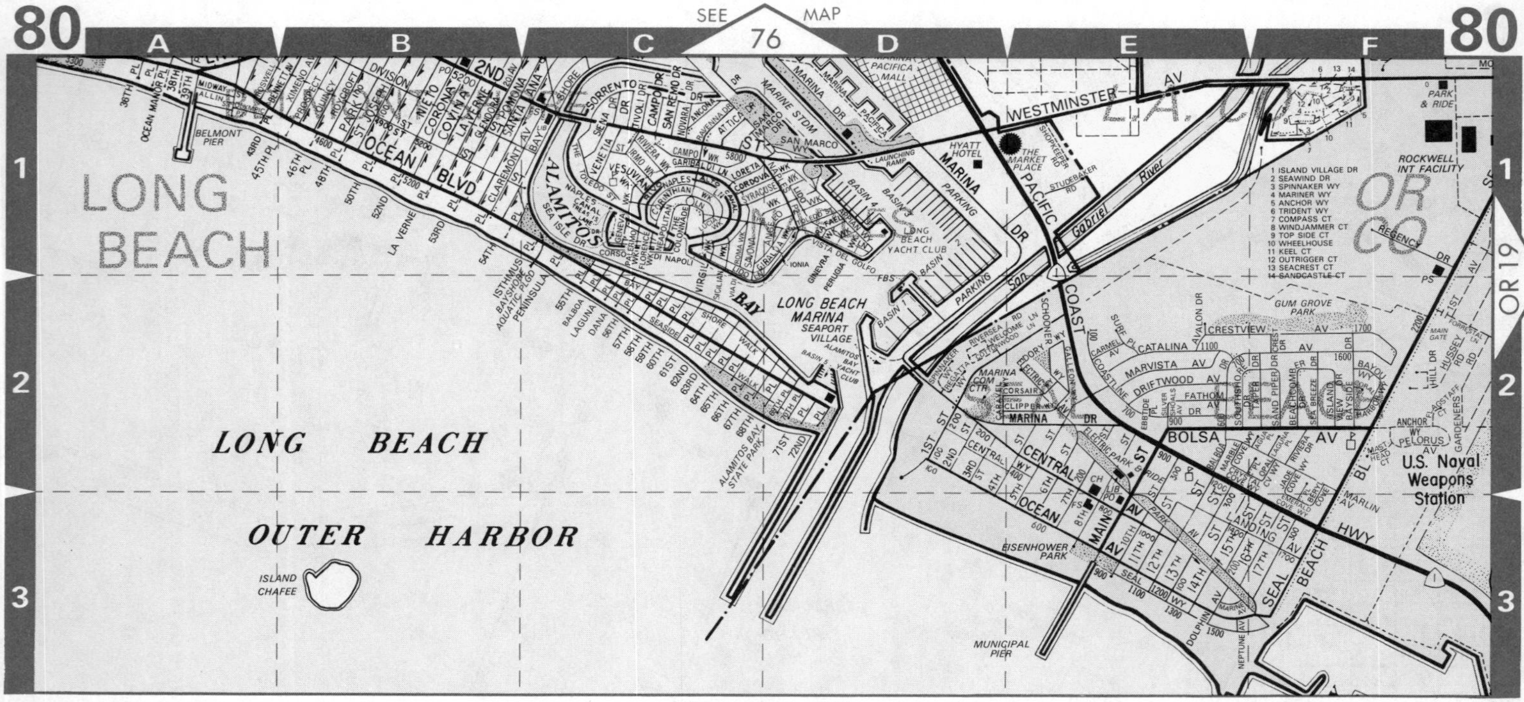

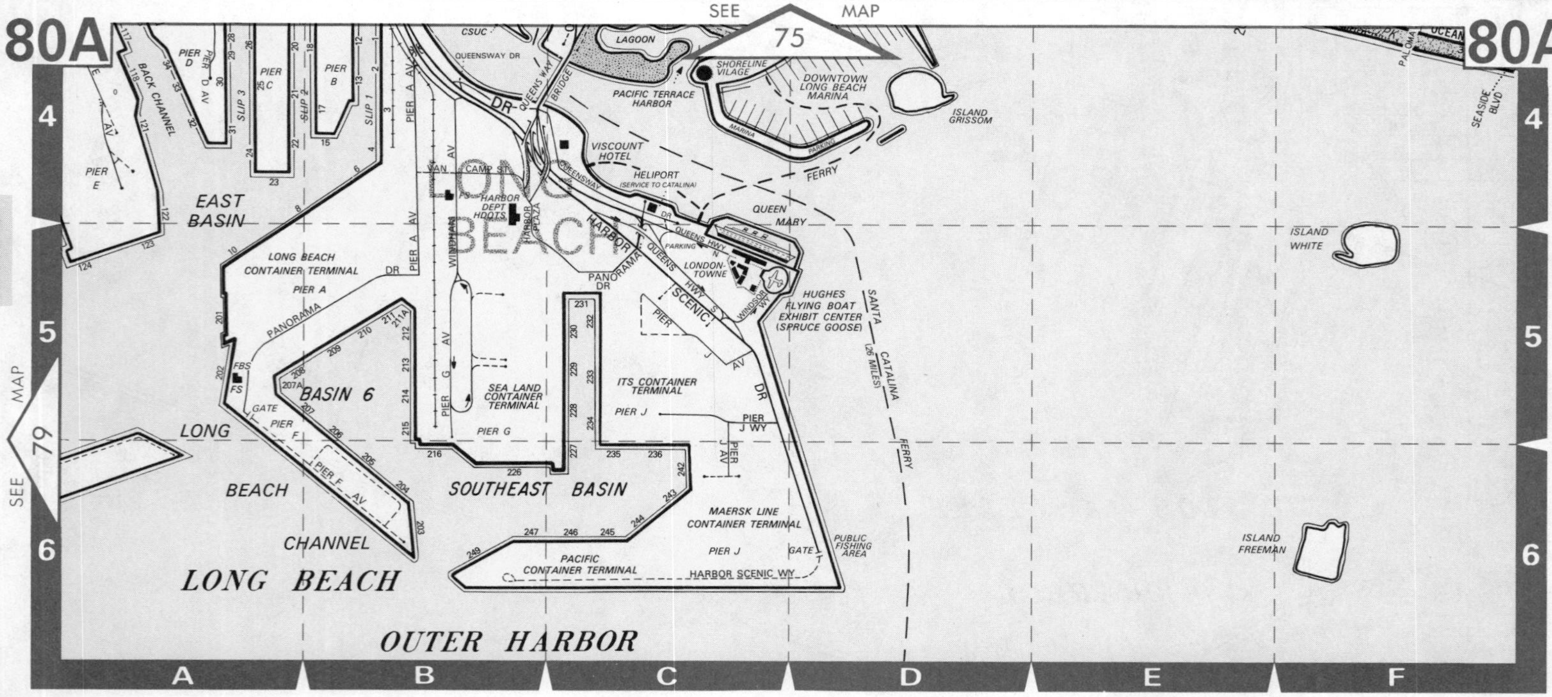

LOS ANGELES CO.

SEE MAP 76

LONG BEACH

LONG BEACH OUTER HARBOR

ISLAND CHAFEE

OCEAN BLVD

ALAMITOS BAY

LONG BEACH MARINA SEAPORT VILLAGE

Long Beach Yacht Club

Alamitos Bay Yacht Club

Alamitos Bay State Park

HYATT HOTEL

THE MARKET PLACE

WESTMINSTER AV

L.A. CO

OR CO

PACIFIC

COAST

San Gabriel River

MARINA

PARKING

ROCKWELL INT FACILITY

1 ISLAND VILLAGE DR
2 SEAWIND DR
3 SPINNAKER WY
4 MARINER WY
5 ANCHOR WY
6 TRIDENT WY
7 COMPASS CT
8 WINDJAMMER CT
9 TOP SIDE CT
10 WHEELHOUSE
11 KEEL CT
12 OUTRIGGER CT
13 SEACREST CT
14 SANDCASTLE CT

GUM GROVE PARK

CRESTVIEW

CATALINA AV

MARVISTA AV

DRIFTWOOD AV

FATHOM

MARINA DR

BOLSA AV

U.S. Naval Weapons Station

CENTRAL AV

OCEAN

MAIN AV

SEAL

BEACH

EISENHOWER PARK

MUNICIPAL PIER

SEE MAP 19

SEE MAP 75

DETAIL

SEE MAP 79

BACK CHANNEL

PIER D

PIER C

PIER B

SLIP 3

SLIP 1

PIER E

EAST BASIN

LONG BEACH CONTAINER TERMINAL

PIER A

PANORAMA

Basin 6

GATE

PIER F

SEA LAND CONTAINER TERMINAL

PIER G

LONG BEACH CHANNEL

PIER F AV

SOUTHEAST BASIN

PACIFIC CONTAINER TERMINAL

ITS CONTAINER TERMINAL

PIER J

PIER J WY

MAERSK LINE CONTAINER TERMINAL

PIER J

GATE

PUBLIC FISHING AREA

HARBOR SCENIC WY

CSUC

QUEENSWAY DR

LAGOON

SHORELINE VILLAGE

PACIFIC TERRACE HARBOR

DOWNTOWN LONG BEACH MARINA

ISLAND GRISSOM

VISCOUNT HOTEL

HELIPORT (SERVICE TO CATALINA)

CAMP ST

VAN

HARBOR DEPT HDQTRS

LONG BEACH

QUEEN MARY

LONDON TOWNE

FERRY

HUGHES FLYING BOAT EXHIBIT CENTER (SPRUCE GOOSE)

SANTA CATALINA (26 MILES)

FERRY

SCENIC DR

PANORAMA DR

ISLAND WHITE

ISLAND FREEMAN

SEASIDE BLVD

OCEAN

OUTER HARBOR

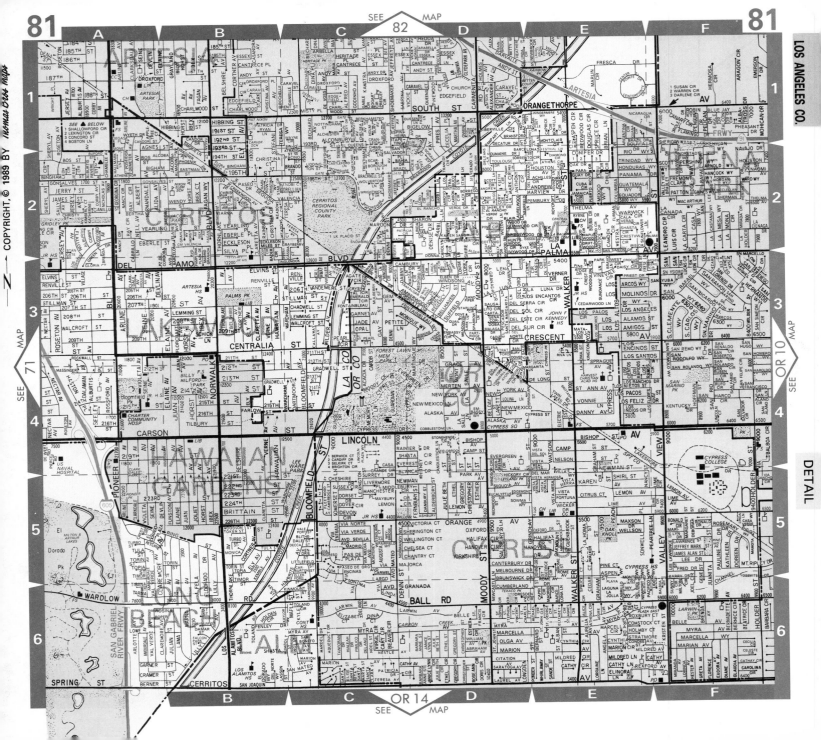

SEE MAP 61

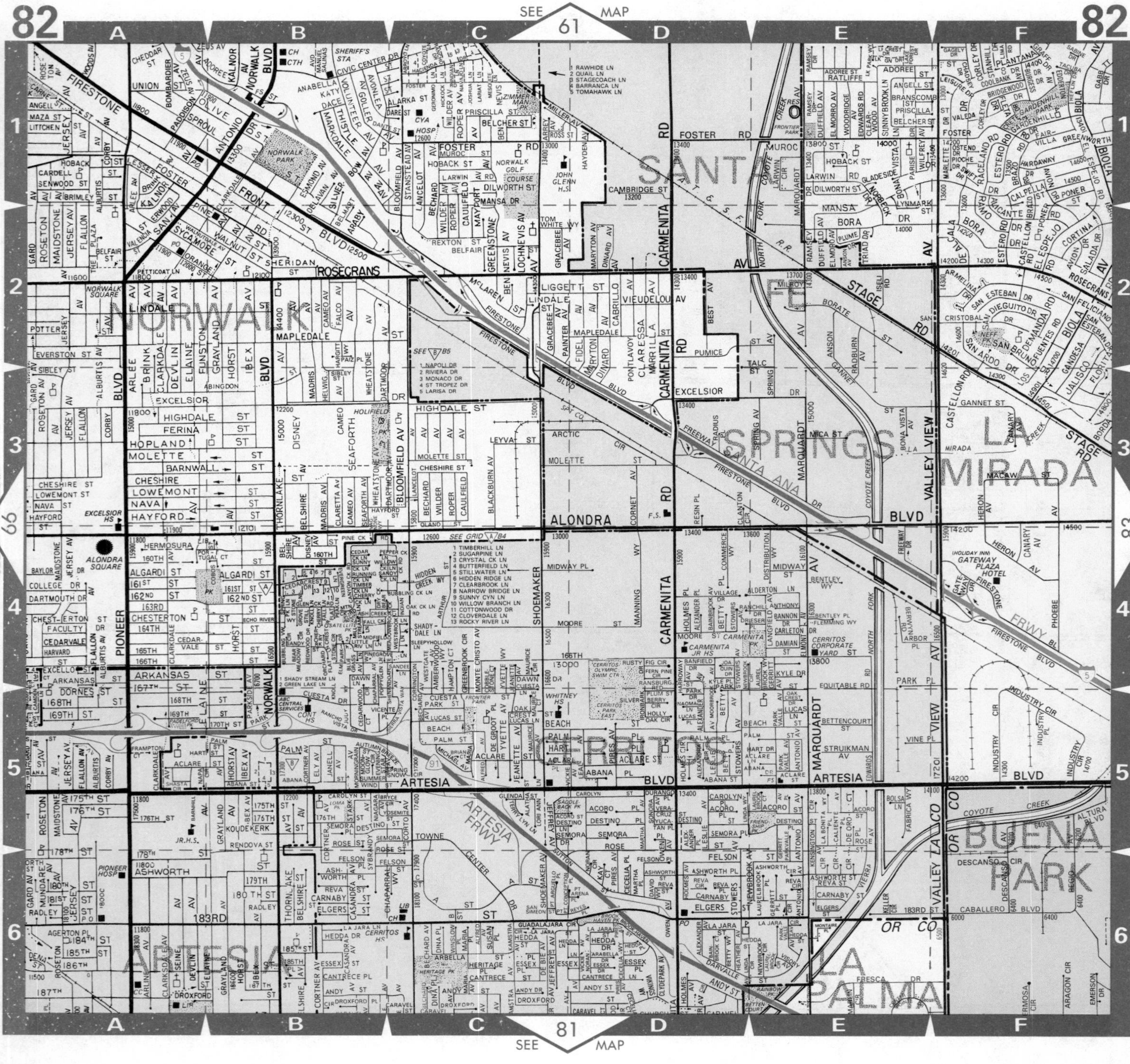

A   B   C   D   E   F

LOS ANGELES CO.

DETAIL

SEE MAP 66

SEE MAP 83

COPYRIGHT © 1969 BY THOMAS BROS. MAPS

NORWALK

SANTA FE SPRINGS

LA MIRADA

ARTESIA

CERRITOS

BUENA PARK

LA PALMA

FIRESTONE BLVD

ROSECRANS AV

ALONDRA BLVD

ARTESIA BLVD

ARTESIA FRWY

FIRESTONE FRWY

SANTA ANA FRWY

SEE MAP 81

ORANGE CO.

LA MIRADA

FULLERTON

BUENA PARK

VALENCIA

LOS ANGELES CO. / ORANGE CO.

ARTESIA BLVD

ROSECRANS AV

ALONDRA

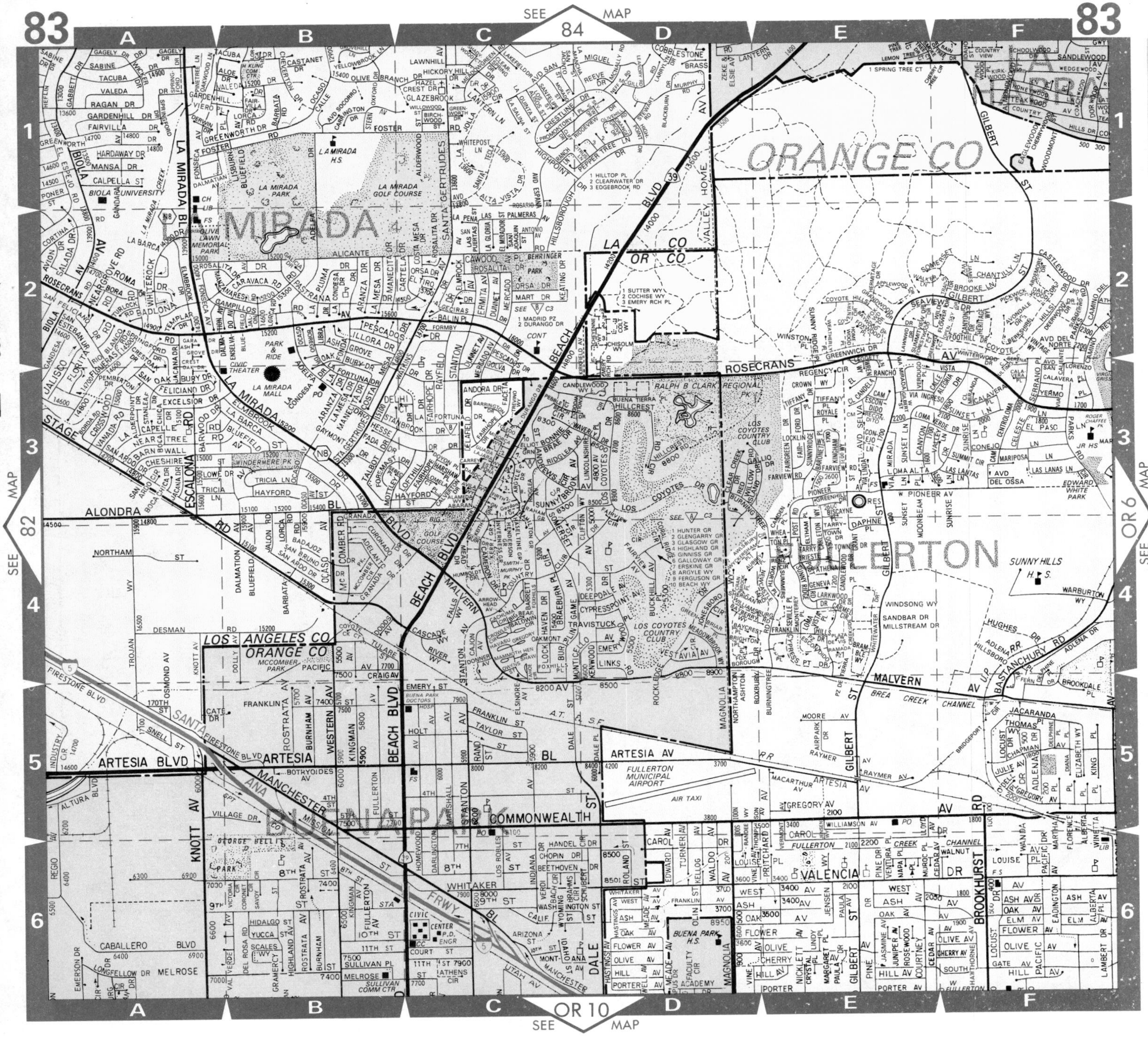

COMMONWEALTH

MALVERN AV

ARTESIA AV

FULLERTON MUNICIPAL AIRPORT

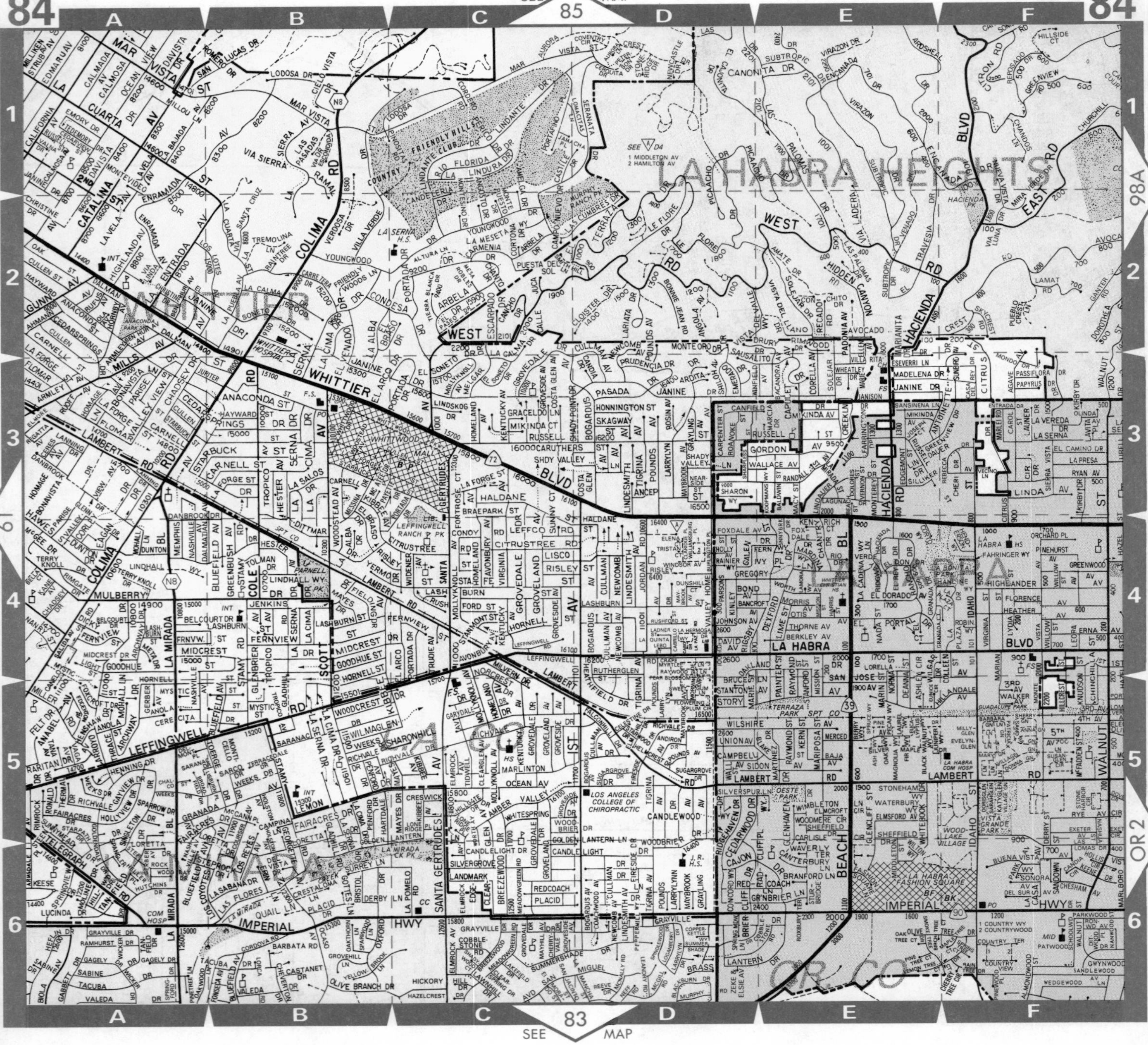

SEE 85 MAP
SEE 83 MAP
SEE 61 MAP
SEE 98A MAP
SEE OR 2 MAP
A B C D E F
1 2 3 4 5 6
WHITTIER
LA HABRA HEIGHTS
LA HABRA
LA MIRADA
LA CO.
OR. CO.
WHITTIER BLVD
COLIMA RD
LAMBERT RD
LEFFINGWELL
IMPERIAL HWY
HACIENDA BLVD
BEACH BLVD
LA HABRA BLVD
WEST RD
EAST RD
FRIENDLY HILLS COUNTRY CLUB
WHITTWOOD MALL
LOS ANGELES COLLEGE OF CHIROPRACTIC
LA HABRA FASHION SQUARE
LA MIRADA CK PK
WHITTIER HOSPITAL
LA HABRA COM HOSP

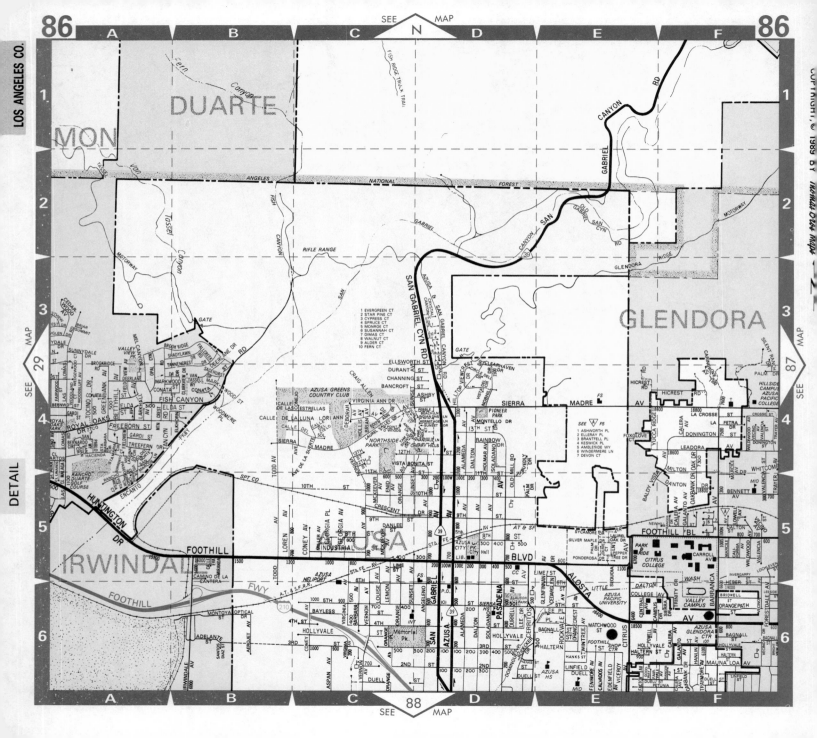

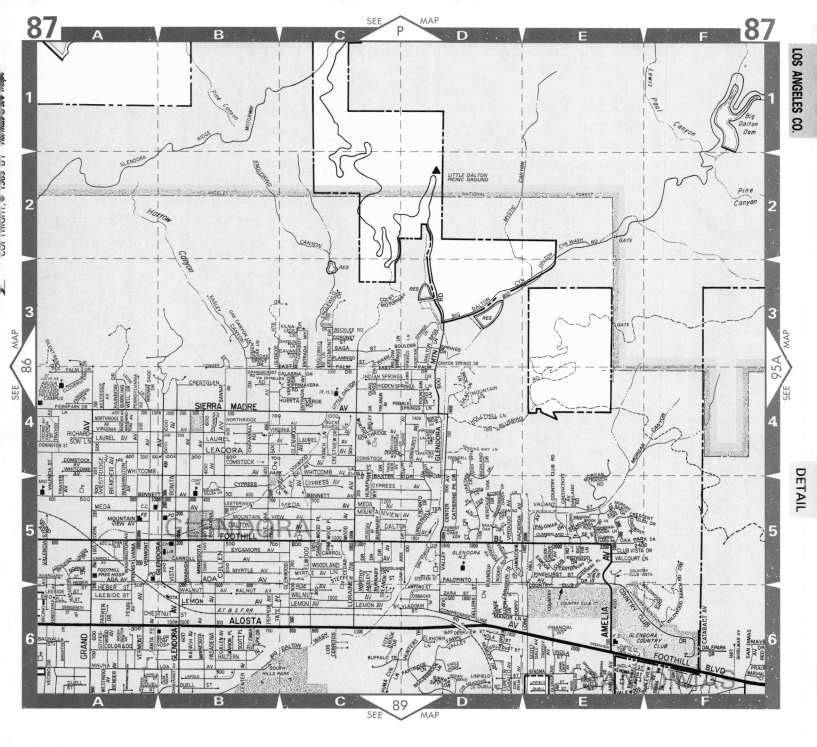

SEE MAP 86

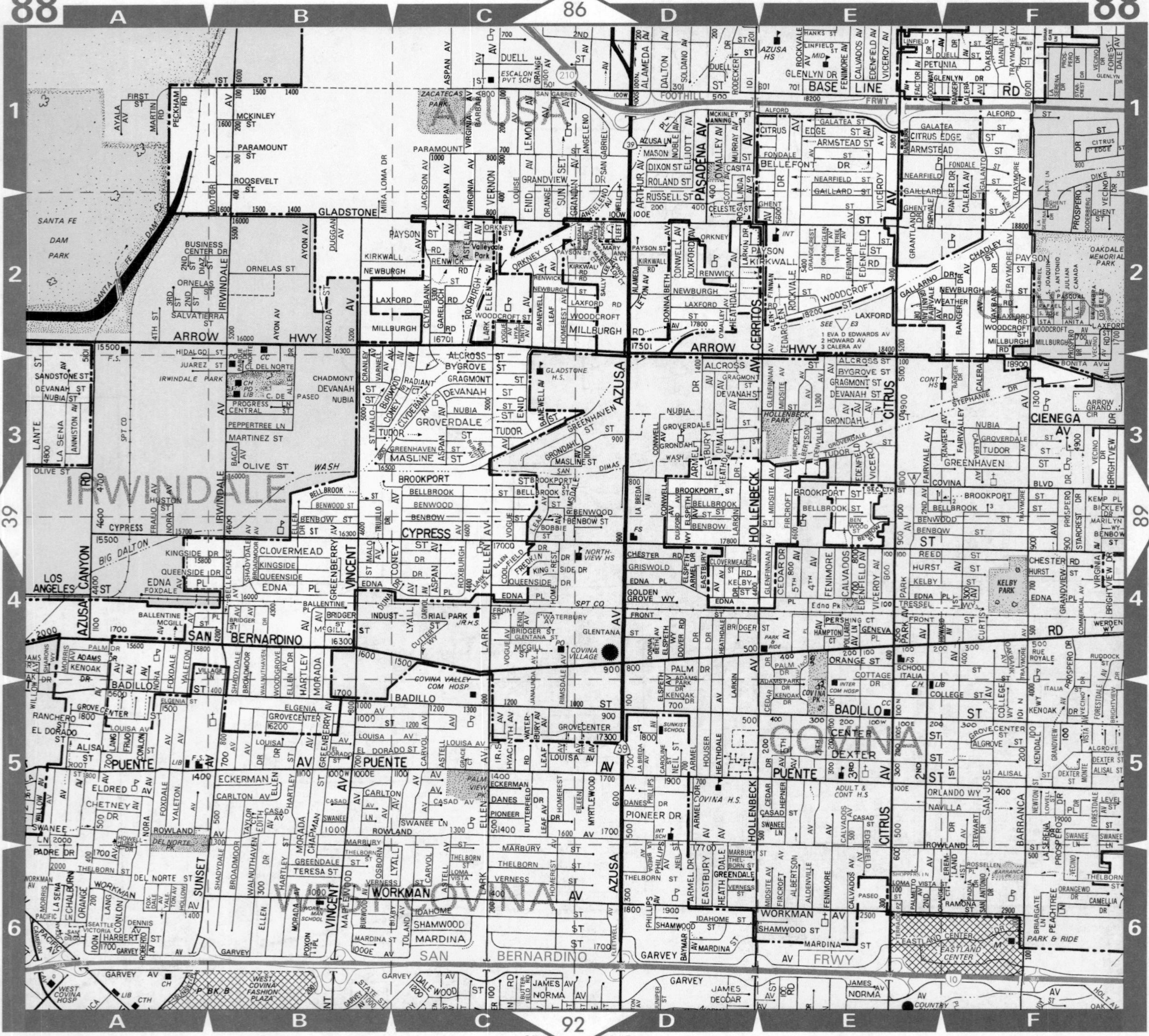

LOS ANGELES CO.

DETAIL

AZUSA

IRWINDALE

COVINA

PUENTE

WEST COVINA

WORKMAN

SAN BERNARDINO FRWY

SANTA FE DAM PARK

SEE MAP 39

SEE MAP 89

SEE MAP 92

COPYRIGHT © 1989 BY Thomas Bros. Maps

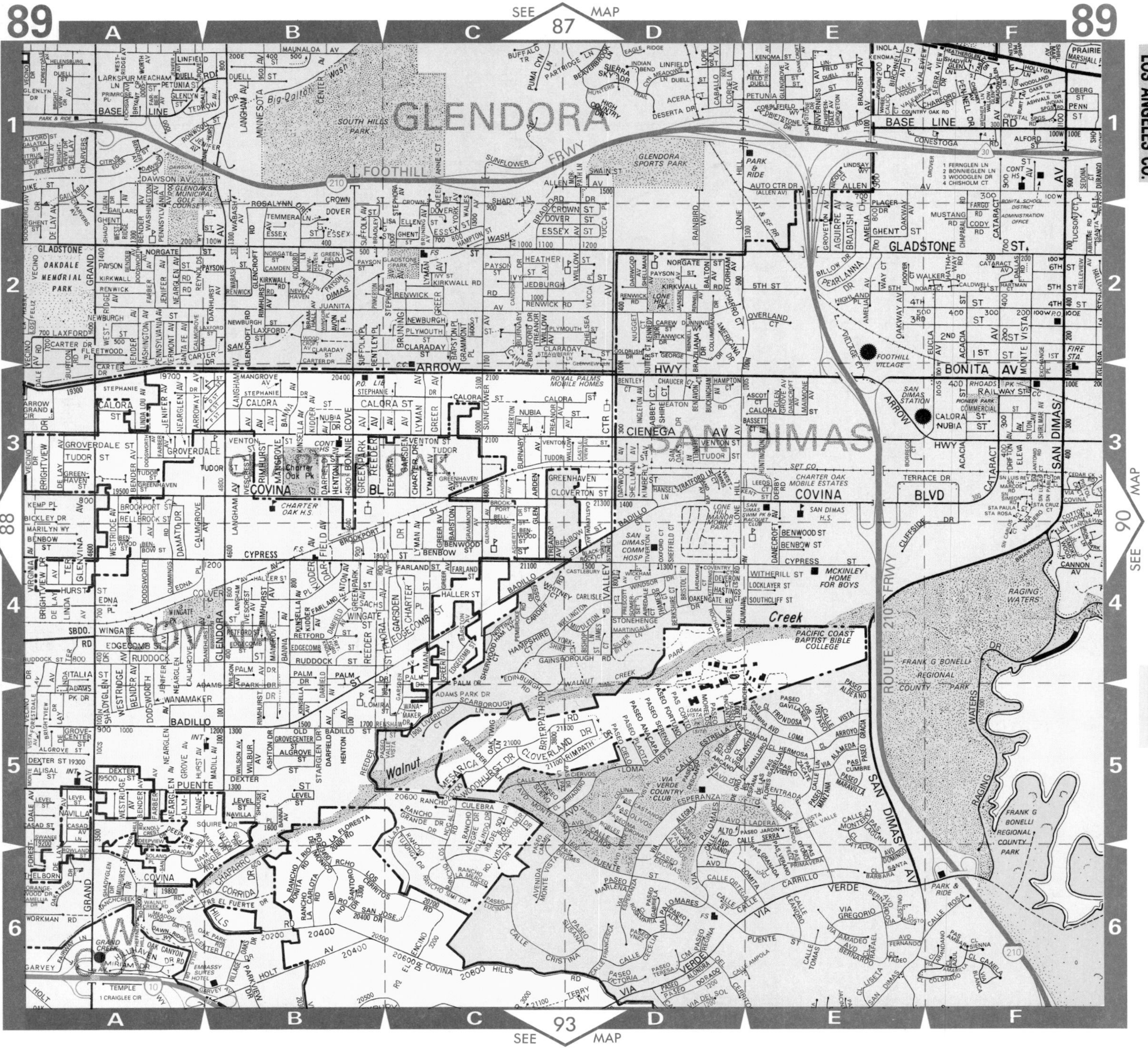

SEE MAP 87

LOS ANGELES CO.

DETAIL

GLENDORA

SAN DIMAS

CHARTER OAK

COVINA

Foothill Frwy

BASE LINE

GLADSTONE ST.

BONITA AV

ARROW HWY

CALORA

VENTON

CYPRESS

BADILLO

PUENTE

Walnut Creek

Route 210 Frwy

Frank G Bonelli Regional County Park

RAGING WATERS

Pacific Coast Baptist Bible College

McKINLEY HOME FOR BOYS

San Dimas H.S.

Charter Oak H.S.

Oakdale Memorial Park

Glendoaks Municipal Golf Course

South Hills Park

Glendora Sports Park

Foothill Village

San Dimas Station

VIA VERDE COUNTRY CLUB

SEE MAP 88

SEE MAP 90

COPYRIGHT, © 1989 BY Thomas Bros. Maps

SEE MAP 93

SEE MAP 95A

LOS ANGELES CO.

DETAIL

SEE MAP 89

SEE MAP 91

SEE MAP 94

FOOTHILL BLVD

BASE LINE RD

BASE LINE

GLADSTONE

BONITA AV

SAN DIMAS

ARROW

LA VERNE

FOOTHILL BLVD

WILLIAMS

CLAREMONT

LEROY BOYS HOME

WAGON HORSE AV

LIVE OAK CANYON DR

METROPOLITAN WATER DISTRICT PASEO

MAPLEWOOD

UNIV OF LA VERNE

3RD ST

BONITA

ARROW HWY

WALNUT

ORANGE

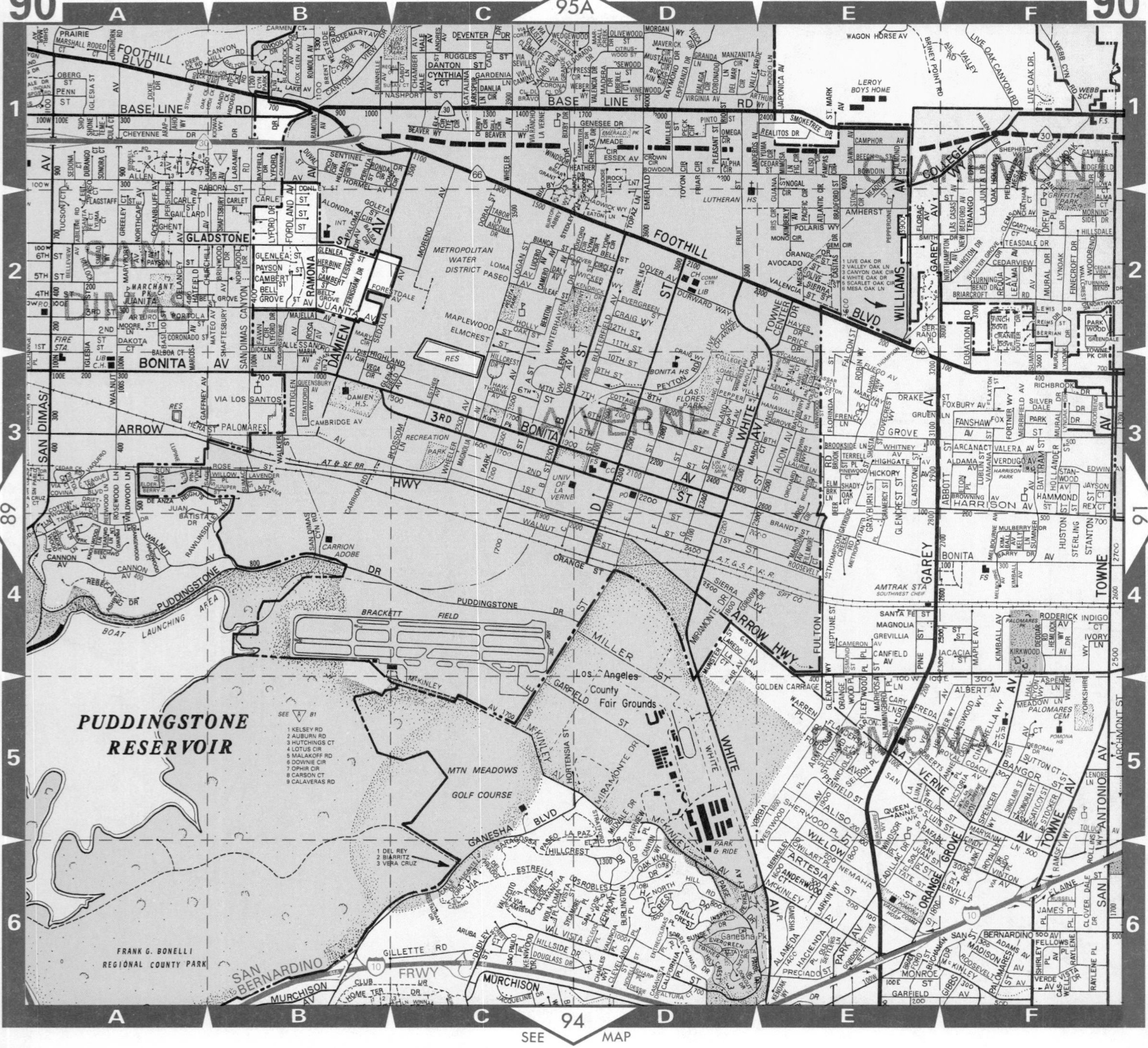

GAREY

TOWNE

AMTRAK STA
SOUTHWEST CHIEF

PUDDINGSTONE
RESERVOIR

PUDDINGSTONE DR

BRACKETT FIELD

BOAT LAUNCHING AREA

MTN MEADOWS
GOLF COURSE

Los Angeles
County Fair Grounds

GANESHA BLVD

McKINLEY

WHITE

POMONA

TOWNE AV

ORANGE GROVE AV

GARFIELD

FRANK G. BONELLI
REGIONAL COUNTY PARK

SAN BERNARDINO FRWY

MURCHISON

1 KELSEY RD
2 AUBURN RD
3 HUTCHINGS CT
4 LOTUS CIR
5 MALAKOFF DR
6 DOWNE CIR
7 OPHIR CIR
8 CARSON CT
9 CALAVERAS RD

1 DEL REY
2 BIARRITZ
3 VERA CRUZ

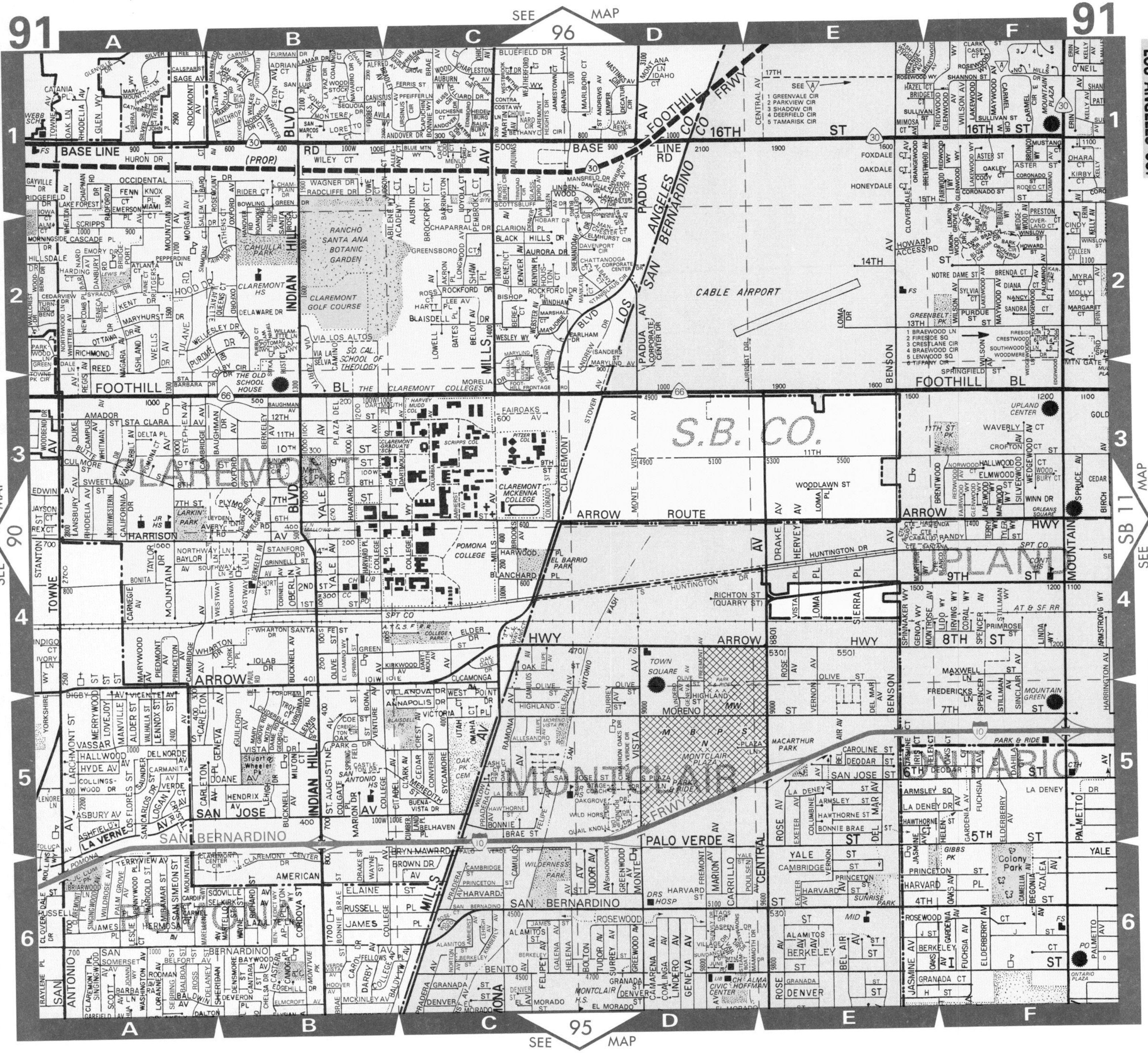

LOS ANGELES CO.

DETAIL

SEE MAP 90

SEE MAP 95

SB 11 SEE MAP

Rancho Santa Ana Botanic Garden

Claremont Golf Course

Claremont HS

The Old School House

So. Cal. School of Theology

The Claremont Colleges

Pomona College

Claremont McKenna College

CLAREMONT

UPLAND

MONTCLAIR

ONTARIO

S.B. CO.

CABLE AIRPORT

Upland Center

BASE LINE RD

FOOTHILL BL

FOOTHILL

ARROW ROUTE

ARROW HWY

SAN BERNARDINO

FOOTHILL FRWY

MONTCLAIR FRWY

SEE 88 MAP

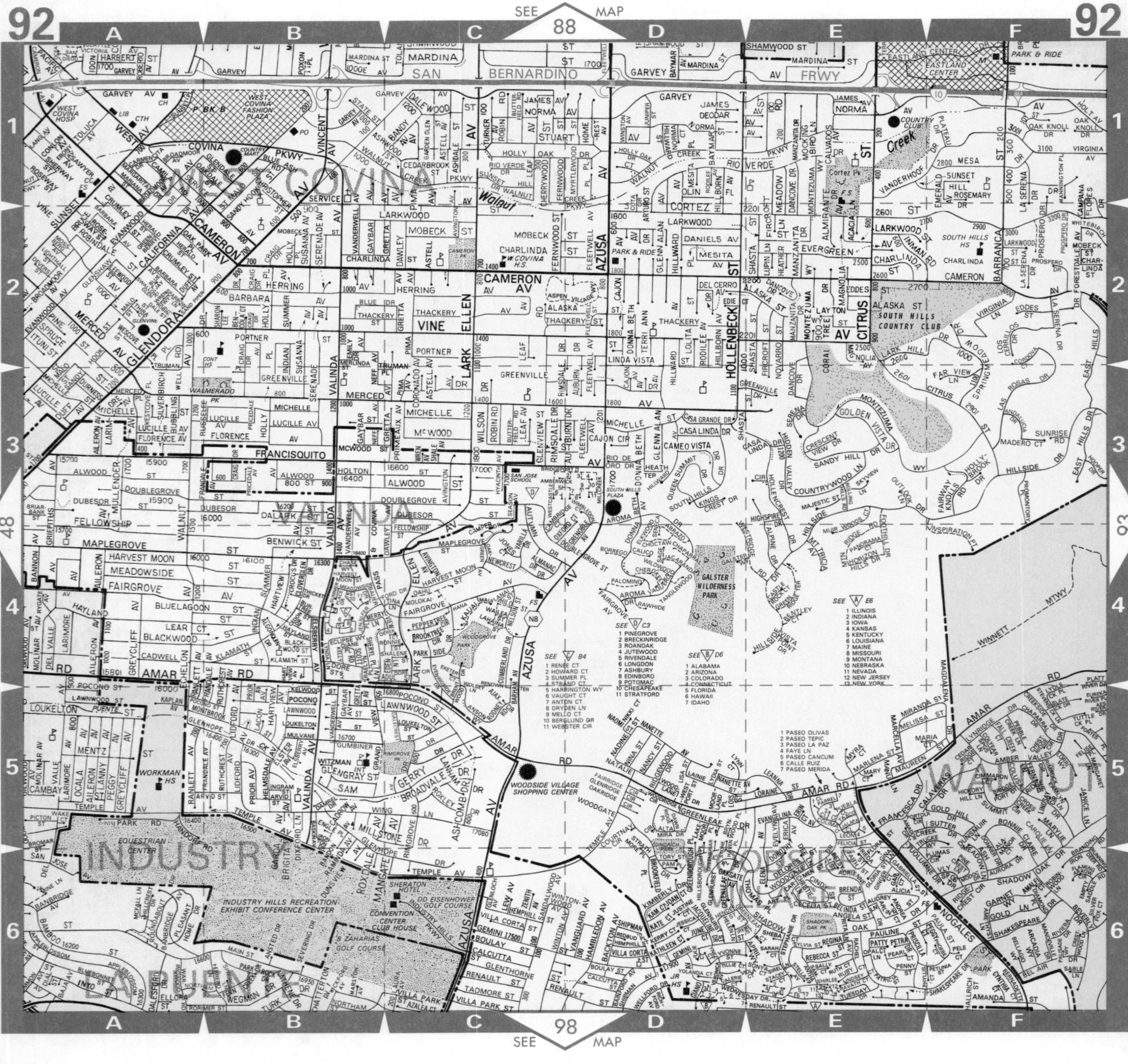

SEE 48 MAP

SEE 93 MAP

SEE 98 MAP

DETAIL

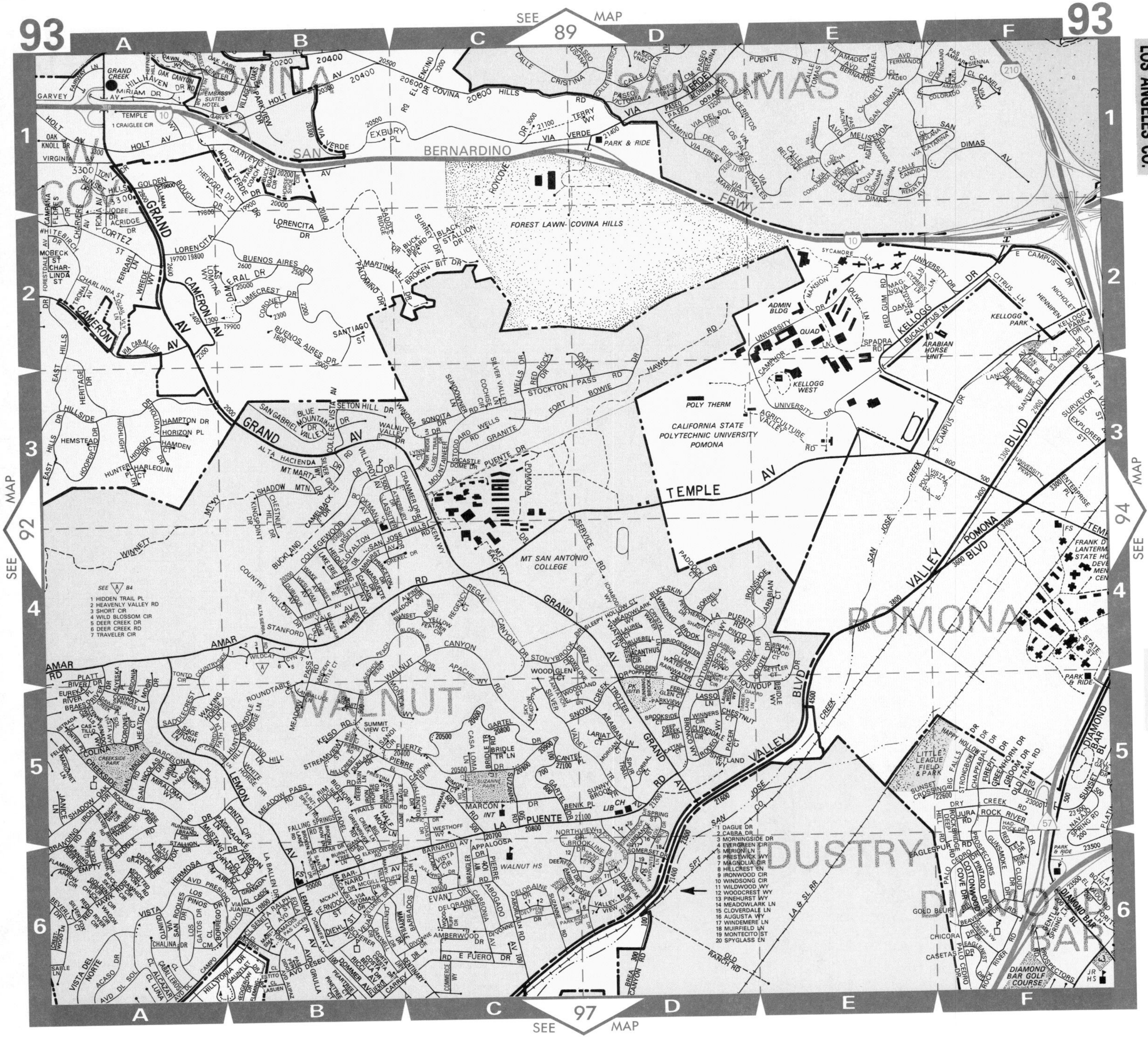

COVINA

SAN DIMAS

GRAND CREEK

FOREST LAWN- COVINA HILLS

SAN BERNARDINO FRWY

CALIFORNIA STATE POLYTECHNIC UNIVERSITY POMONA

KELLOGG PARK

ARABIAN HORSE UNIT

ADMIN BLDG

QUAD

KELLOGG WEST

AGRICULTURE VALLEY

POLY THERM

TEMPLE AV

MT SAN ANTONIO COLLEGE

POMONA

WALNUT

LA PUENTE

INDUSTRY

DIAMOND BAR

AMAR RD

GRAND AV

VALLEY BLVD

SAN JOSE CREEK

DIAMOND BAR GOLF COURSE

LITTLE LEAGUE FIELD & PARK

FRANK D LANTERMAN STATE HOSP DEVELOPMENTAL MEN CEN

SEE A 84
1 HIDDEN TRAIL PL
2 HEAVENLY VALLEY RD
3 SHORT CIR
4 WILD BLOSSOM CIR
5 DEER CREEK DR
6 DEER CREEK RD
7 TRAVELER CIR

1 DAGUE DR
2 CABRA DR
3 MORNINGSIDE DR
4 EVERGREEN CIR
5 MERION LN
6 PRESTWICK WY
7 MAGNOLIA CIR
8 HILLCREST DR
9 IRONWOOD CIR
10 WINDSONG CIR
11 WILDWOOD WY
12 WOODCREST WY
13 PINEHURST WY
14 MEADOWLARK LN
15 CLOVERDALE LN
16 AUGUSTA WY
17 WINDEMERE LN
18 MUIRFIELD LN
19 MONTECITO ST
20 SPYGLASS EN

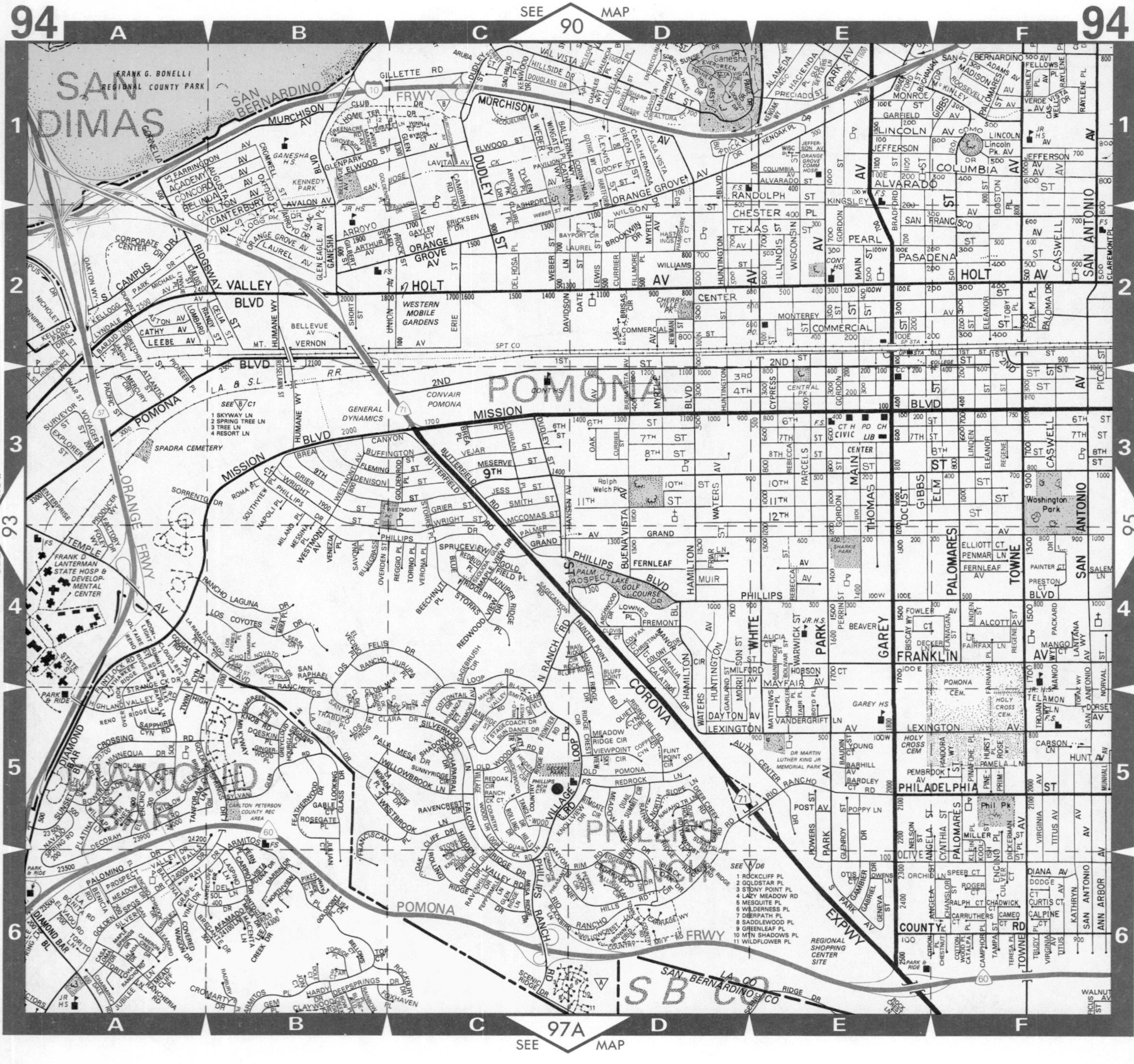

LOS ANGELES CO.

DETAIL

SAN DIMAS

POMONA

DIAMOND BAR

PHILLIPS RANCH

FRANK G. BONELLI REGIONAL COUNTY PARK

San Bernardino Frwy

SEE MAP 90

SEE MAP 97A

SEE MAP 93

SEE MAP 95

L.A. CO.
S B CO.

COPYRIGHT © 1969 BY THOMAS BROS. MAPS

LOS ANGELES CO.

DETAIL

POMONA

MONTCLAIR

ONTARIO

SAN BERNARDINO CO.

CHINO

MISSION BLVD

HOLT AV

HOLT BLVD

STATE ST

PHILLIPS ST

FRANCIS AV

FRANKLIN AV

PHILADELPHIA ST

OLIVE ST

WALNUT AV

COUNTY RD

RAMONA

CENTRAL AV

MAGNOLIA

MOUNTAIN AV

PALMETTO

BELLEVUE CEM

INDIAN HILL MALL

CHINO TOWN CENTER

PLYMOUTH

CHINO COMM HOSP

FWY

COPYRIGHT, © 1989 BY Thomas Bros. Maps

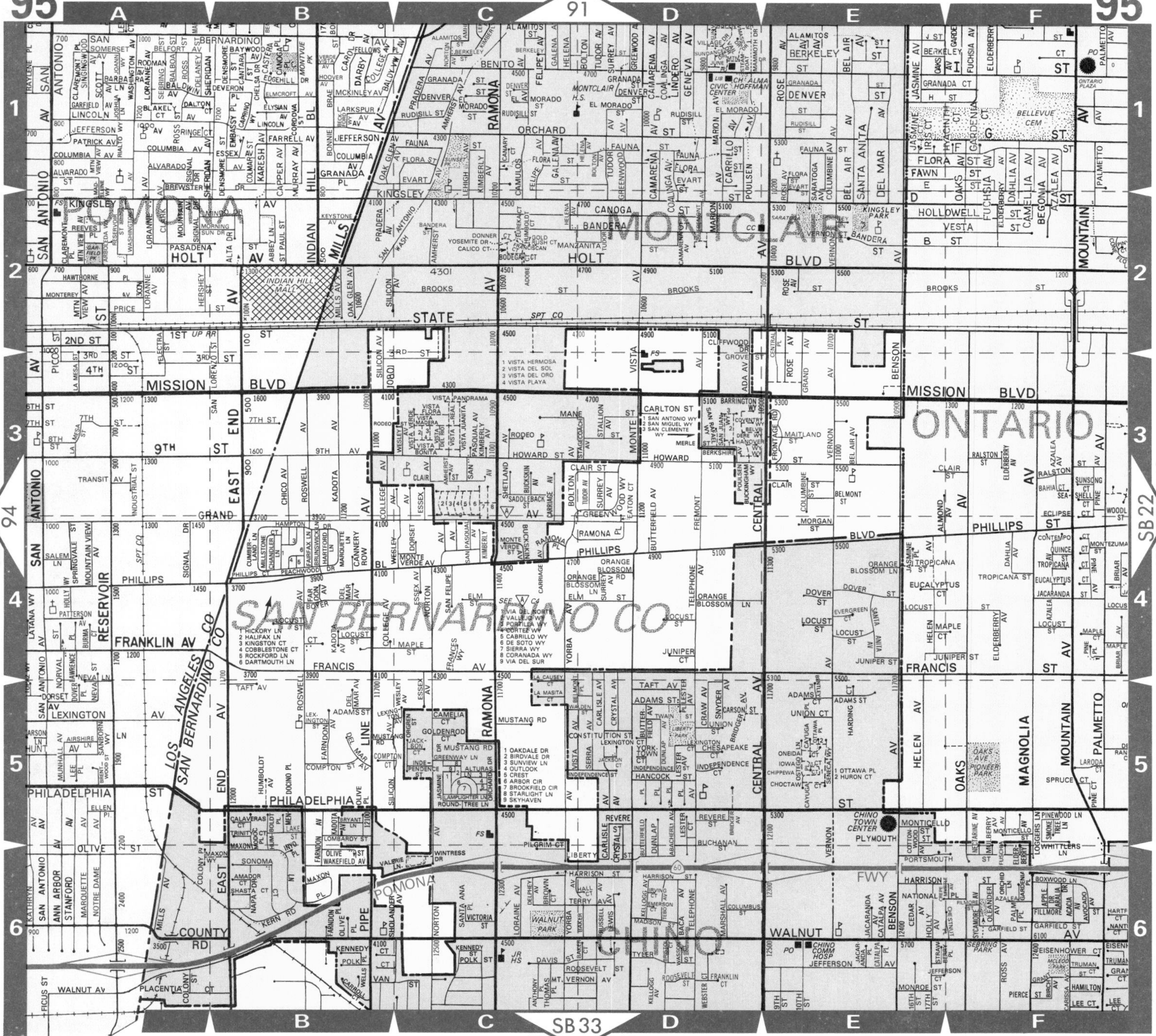

SEE MAP 94

SEE MAP SB 22

SEE MAP SB 33

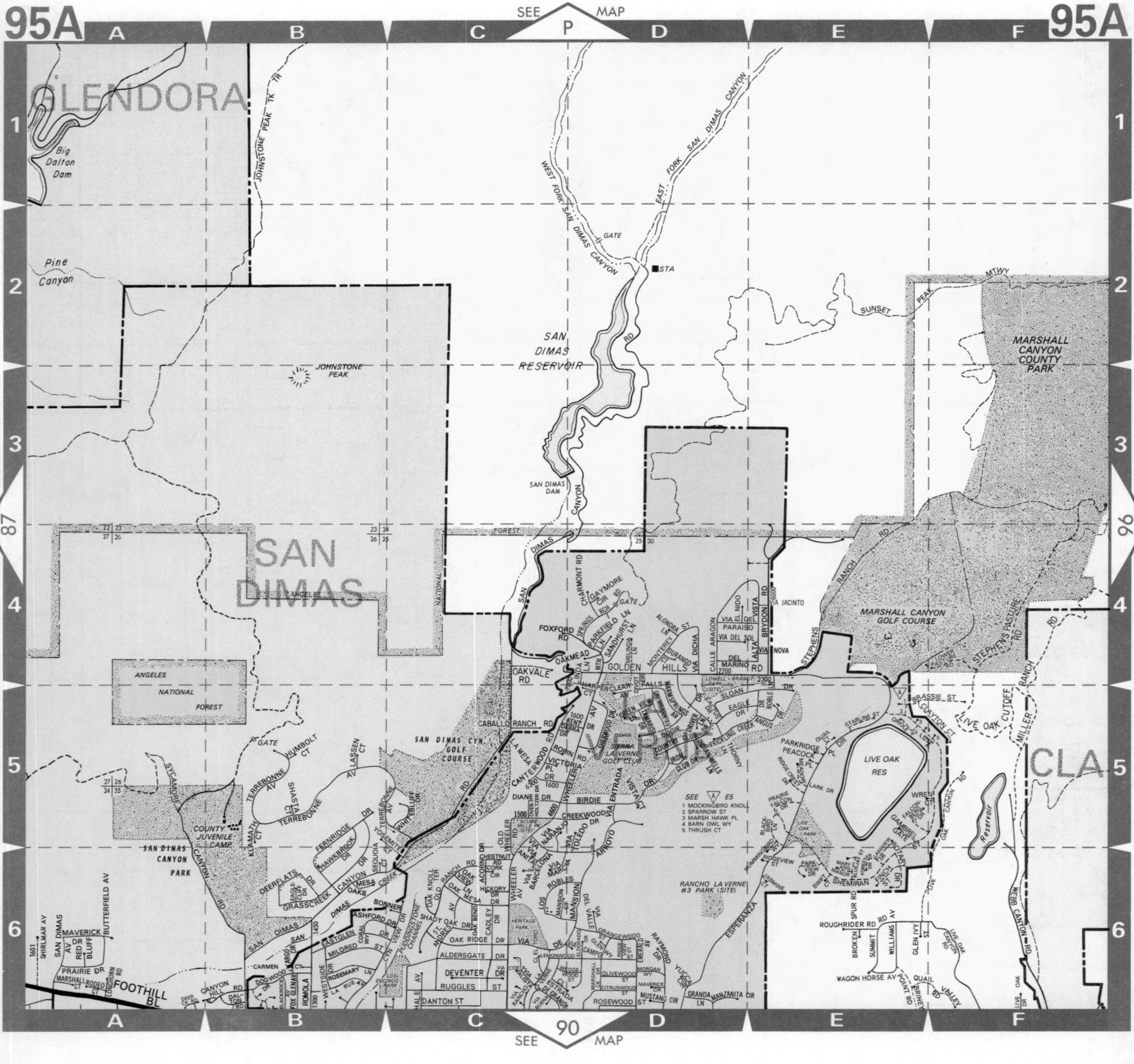

LOS ANGELES CO.

DETAIL

COPYRIGHT © 1989 BY Thomas Bros. Maps

SEE MAP P

SEE MAP 90

GLENDORA

Big Dalton Dam

Pine Canyon

JOHNSTONE PEAK TK TR

JOHNSTONE PEAK

WEST FORK SAN DIMAS CANYON

EAST FORK SAN DIMAS CANYON

GATE

STA

SAN DIMAS RESERVOIR

SUNSET PEAK

MTWY

MARSHALL CANYON COUNTY PARK

SAN DIMAS

ANGELES NATIONAL FOREST

SAN DIMAS DAM

SAN DIMAS CANYON

FOREST

NATIONAL

ANGEL

MARSHALL CANYON GOLF COURSE

STEPHENS PASTURE

RANCH RD

STEPHENS

SEE MAP 87

SEE MAP 96

SAN DIMAS CANYON PARK

COUNTY JUVENILE CAMP

SYCAMORE

TERREBONNE AV

SHASTA

TERREBONNE

KLAMATH

LASSEN CT

HUMBOLT CT

GATE

SAN DIMAS CYN. GOLF COURSE

DEEPFLATS

GRASSCREEK

HAWKBROOK DR

FERNRIDGE DR

SEQUOIA

MESA OAKS

CANYON

DIMAS

CREEK

WHITBLUR

TERREBONNE

YOSEMITE

CANYON

FOXFORD RD

OAKMEAD RD

OAKVALE RD

CABALLO RANCH RD

CHARMONT RD

CLAYMORE CIR

GATE

PARKFIELD LN

SANDHURST LN

GOLDEN HILLS

HARPER

CLEAR

FALLS

LA VERNE

SIERRA LAVERNE GOLF CLUB

VICTORIA

CANTERWOOD

ROBIN

LA MESA

DIANE

BIRDIE

CREEKWOOD DR

BARCELONA

NAPA

TOLEDO

MARCIA

CHESTNUT

ACORN

CORK

OAK MESA

HICKORY

SHADY OAK

OAK RIDGE

ROBLES

LOS ROBLES

MANSION

DEL VALLE

VIA

HERITAGE PARK

CADLEY

VIA

ALDERSGATE DR

DEVENTER DR

RUGGLES ST

DANTON ST

HALE AV

ROSEWOOD

OLIVEWOOD ST

MUSTANG CIR

GRANDA LN

MANZANITA CIR

RANCHO LAVERNE #3 PARK (SITE)

ESPERANZA

ALONDRA ST

MONTEREY

VIA DICHA

CALLE ARAGON

VIA DEL SOL

VIA DEL PARAISO

EL NIDO

BRYDON RD

DEL VISTA

VIA JACINTO

DEL MARINO

VIA NOVA

STEPHENS DR

SLOAN

EAGLE DR

ANGUS

TRICKLING CREEK

ROBLE

PARKRIDGE DR

PEACOCK

CLUB RD

QUAIL

STERLING ST

BRASSIE ST

CLAYTON ST

ORCHID

LIVE OAK RES

WREN

PRAIRIE

CLARK DR

LIVE OAK CUTOFF

MILLER

RANCH RD

CLA

SEE E5
1 MOCKINGBIRD KNOLL
2 SPARROW ST
3 MARSH HAWK PL
4 BARN OWL WY
5 THRUSH CT

ROUGHRIDER RD

BROKEN SPUR RD

WILLIAMS ST

SUMMIT

GLEN IVY

WAGON HORSE AV

QUAIL

LIVE OAK

VALLEY

WEBB CANYON RD

POINT

RESERVOIR

SHIRLMAR AV

SAN DIMAS AV

BUTTERFIELD AV

MAVERICK

REDBLUFF DR

PRAIRIE DR

MARSHALL

RODEO RD

FOOTHILL BL

CANYON HILLS

FOX GLENN

ROMOLA

ROSEMARY LN

WESTSIDE

MILDRED ST

CARMEN

ASHFORD DR

BONNER

CHANNING

HUDDINGSTONE DR

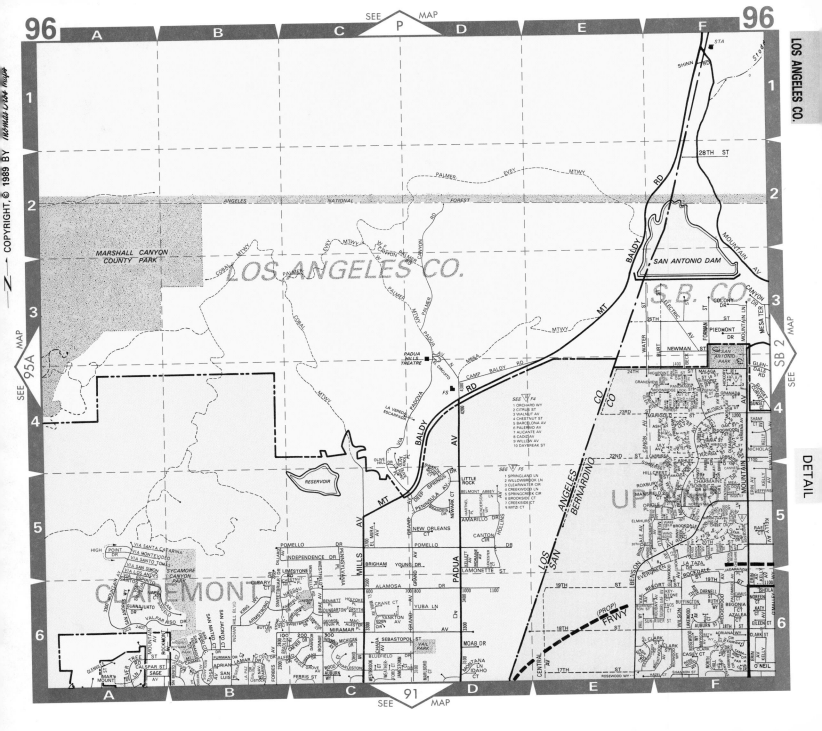

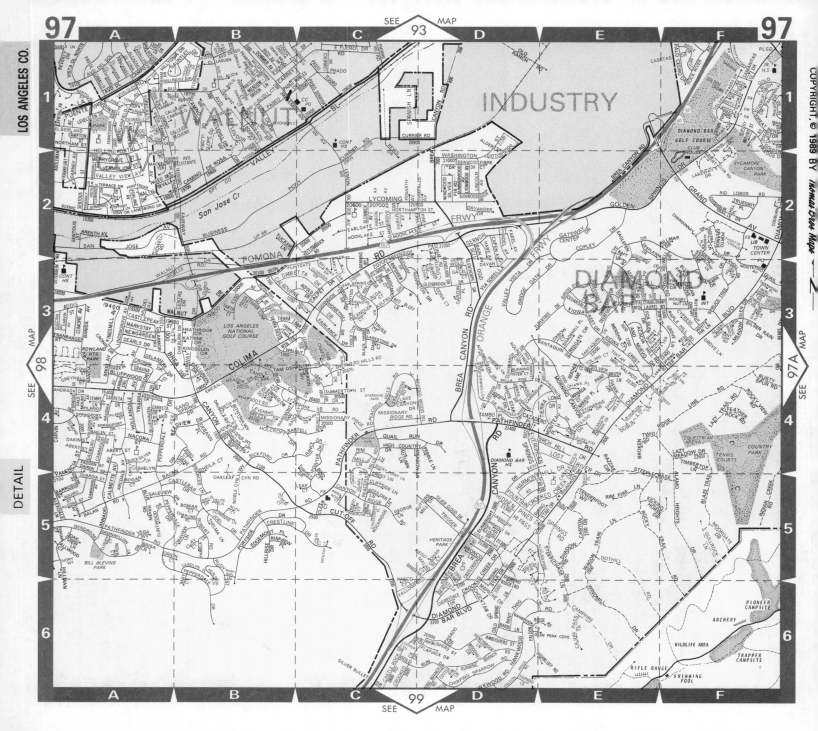

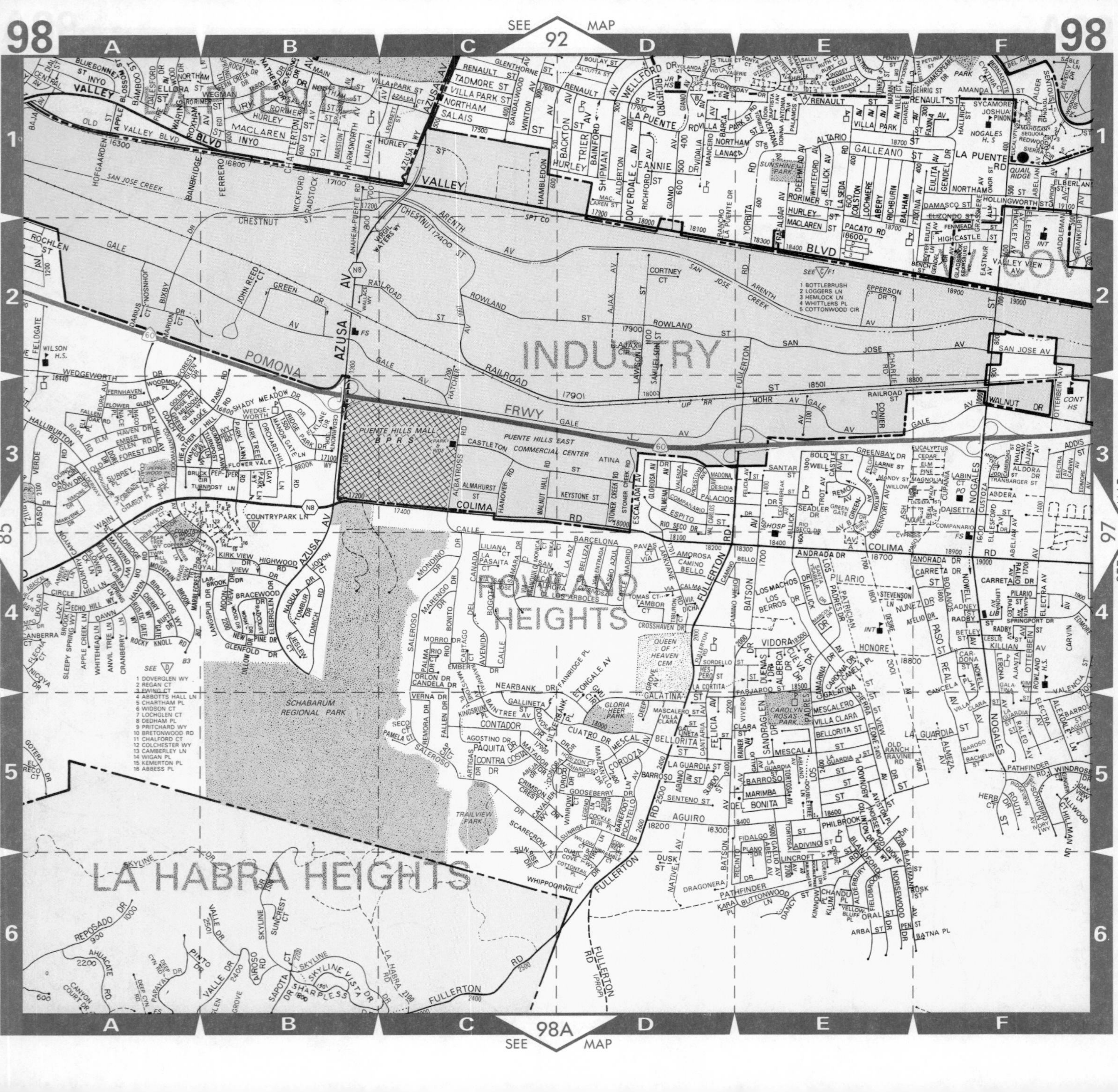

SEE MAP 92
SEE MAP 85
SEE MAP 97
SEE 98A MAP
LOS ANGELES CO.
DETAIL
INDUSTRY
ROWLAND HEIGHTS
LA HABRA HEIGHTS
LA PUENTE
WEST COVINA
PUENTE HILLS MALL
PUENTE HILLS EAST COMMERCIAL CENTER
SCHABARUM REGIONAL PARK
TRAILVIEW PARK
QUEEN OF HEAVEN CEM
GLORIA HEER PARK
CAROLYN ROSAS PARK
SUNSHINE PARK
POMONA FRWY
VALLEY BLVD
COLIMA RD
AZUSA AV
FULLERTON RD
NOGALES ST
SAN JOSE CREEK
SEE C F1
1 BOTTLEBRUSH
2 LOGGERS LN
3 HEMLOCK LN
4 WHITTLERS PL
5 COTTONWOOD CIR
SEE D
1 DOVERGLEN WY
2 REGAN CT
3 EWING CT
4 ABBOTTS HALL LN
5 CHARTHAM PL
6 WIDSON CT
7 LOCHGLEN CT
8 DEDHAM PL
9 PRITCHARD WY
10 BRETONWOOD RD
11 CHALFORD CT
12 COLCHESTER WY
13 CAMBERLEY LN
14 WIGAN PL
15 KEMERTON PL
16 ABBESS PL

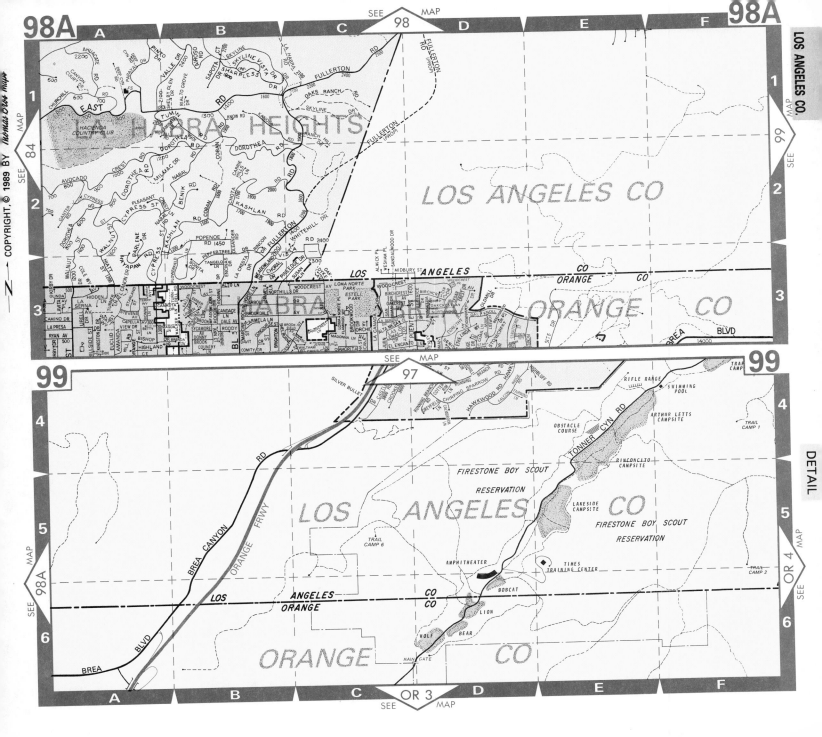

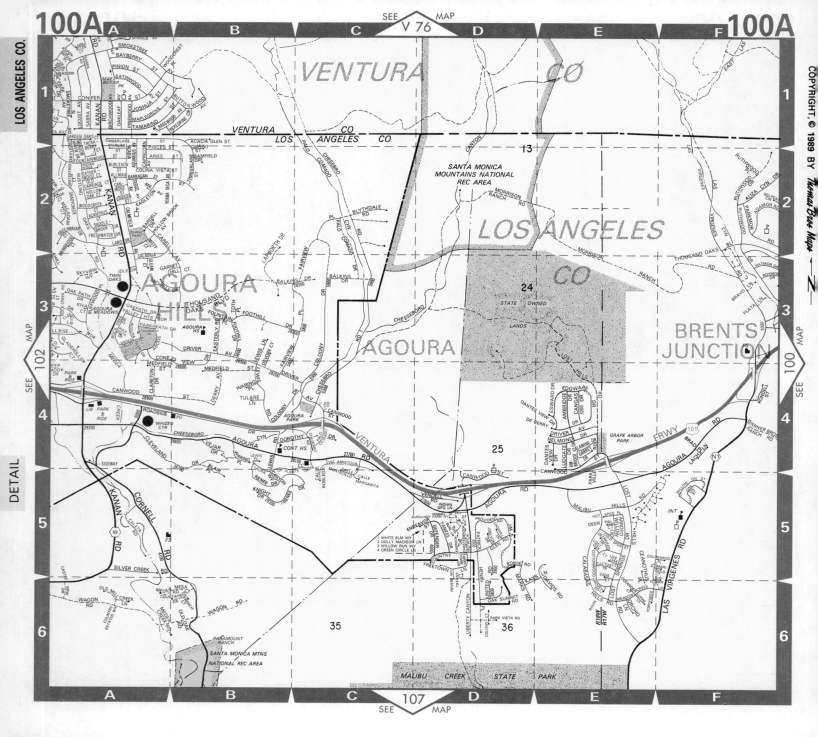

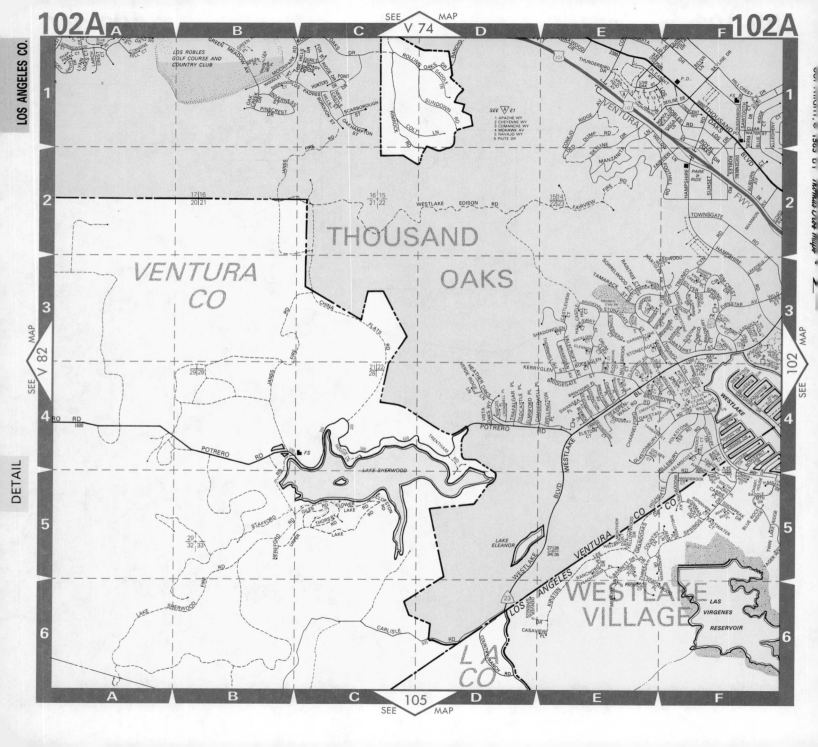

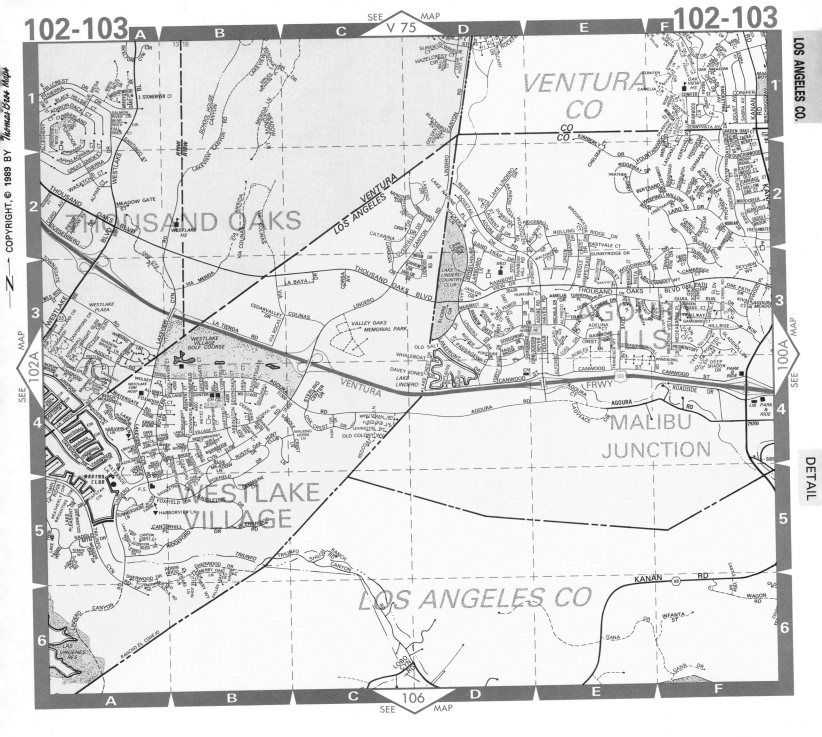

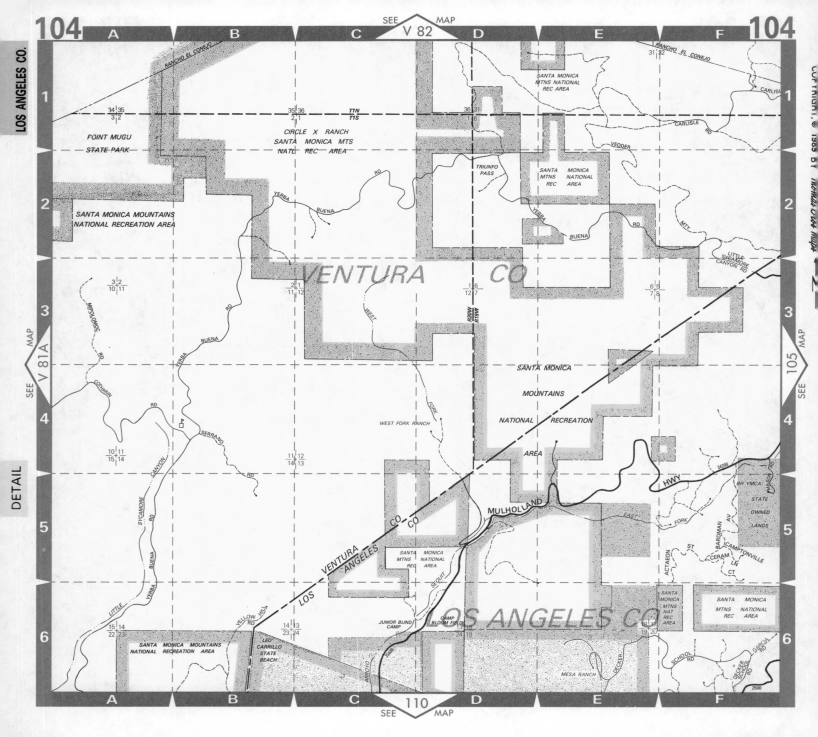

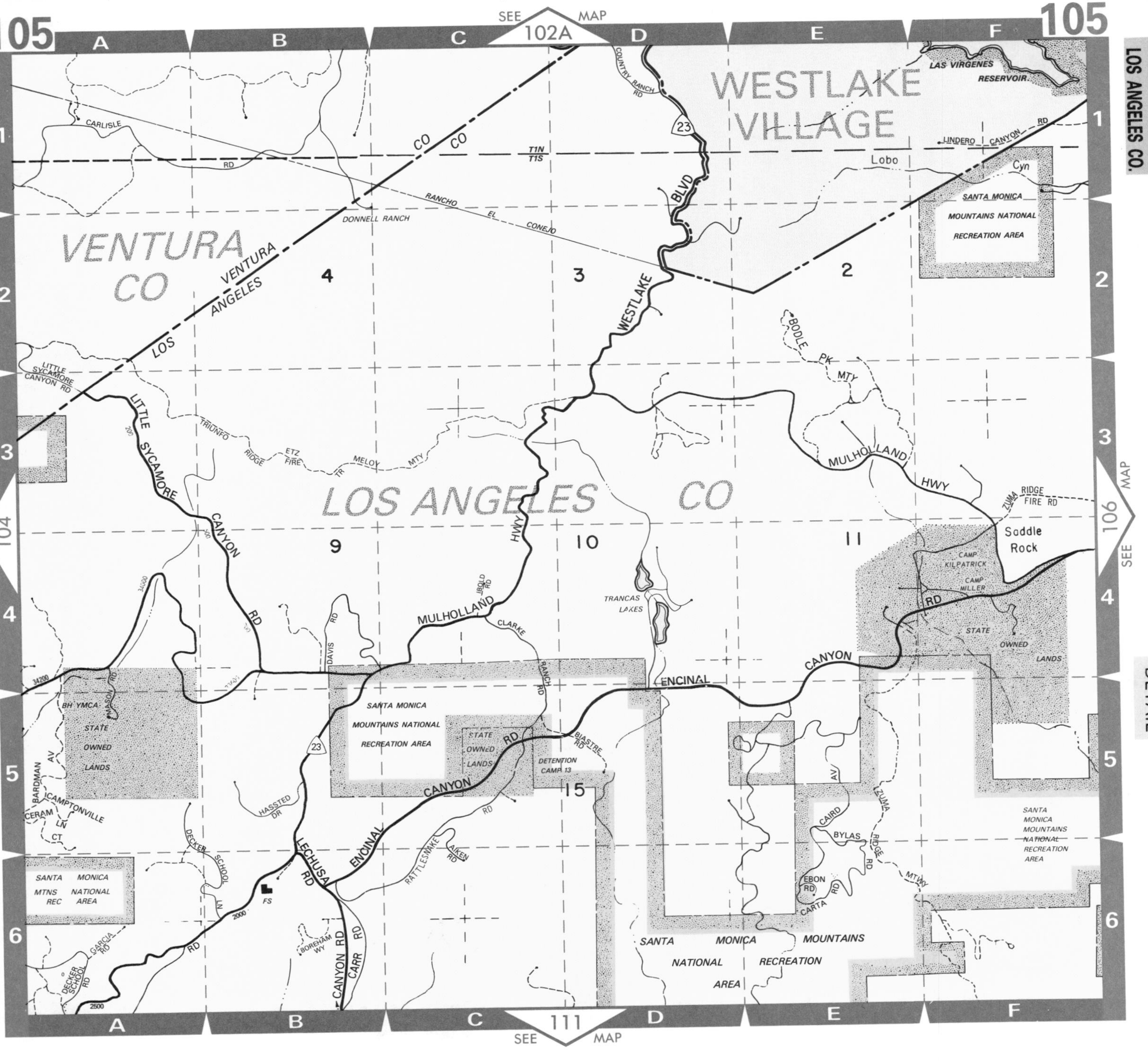

WESTLAKE VILLAGE

LAS VIRGENES RESERVOIR.

COUNTRY RANCH RD

23

Lobo Cyn

LINDERO CANYON RD

SANTA MONICA MOUNTAINS NATIONAL RECREATION AREA

CARLISLE RD

CO CO RD

T1N T1S

RANCHO EL CONEJO

VENTURA CO

DONNELL RANCH

LOS ANGELES VENTURA

WESTLAKE BLVD

4

3

2

LITTLE SYCAMORE CANYON RD

LITTLE SYCAMORE CANYON RD

TRIUNFO RIDGE

ETZ FIRE TR

MELOY MTY

LOS ANGELES CO

BODLE PK MTY

MULHOLLAND HWY

ZUMA RIDGE FIRE RD

Saddle Rock

9

10

11

HWY

OLD RD

CLARKE

MULHOLLAND

DAVIS RD

TRANCAS LAKES

CAMP KILPATRICK

CAMP MILLER

STATE OWNED LANDS

RD

ENCINAL CANYON

BH YMCA STATE OWNED LANDS

PASQUI RD

SANTA MONICA MOUNTAINS NATIONAL RECREATION AREA

23

ENCINAL

RANCH RD

STATE OWNED LANDS

RD

BIASTRE RD

DETENTION CAMP 13

15

CAIRD AV

ZUMA RIDGE RD

SANTA MONICA MOUNTAINS NATIONAL RECREATION AREA

5

BARDMAN AV

CAMPTONVILLE

CERAM LN

CT

HASSTED DR

DECKER SCHOOL LN

LECHUSA RD

CANYON

ENCINAL

RD

RATTLESNAKE RD

AIKEN RD

BYLAS

EBON RD

CARTA

ZUMA MTWY

FS

SANTA MONICA MTNS NATIONAL REC AREA

GARCIA RD

DECKER SCHOOL RD

2000

BOREHAM WY

CANYON RD

CARR RD

SANTA MONICA MOUNTAINS NATIONAL RECREATION AREA

6

2500

3200

3600

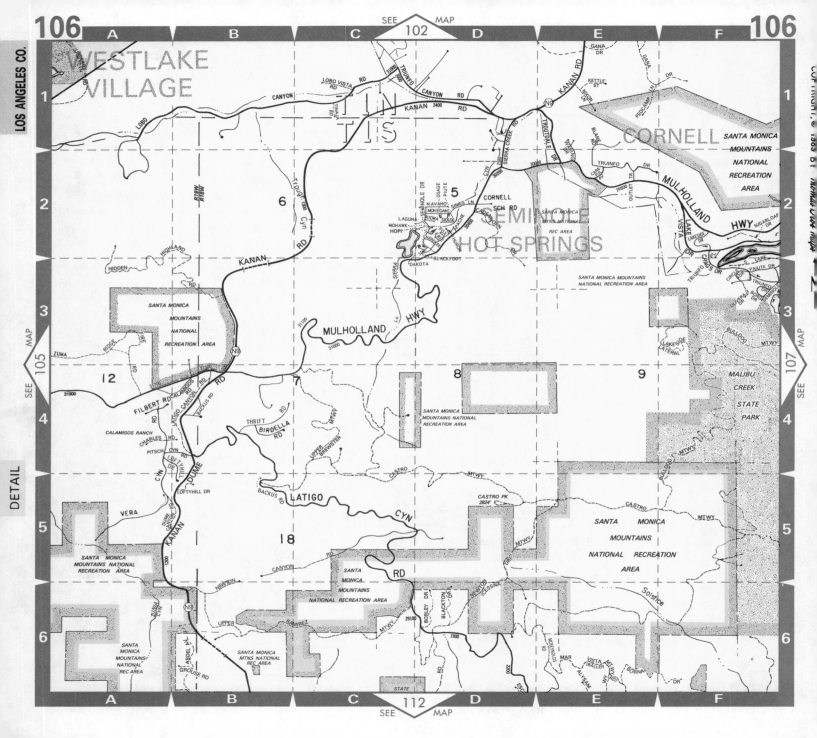

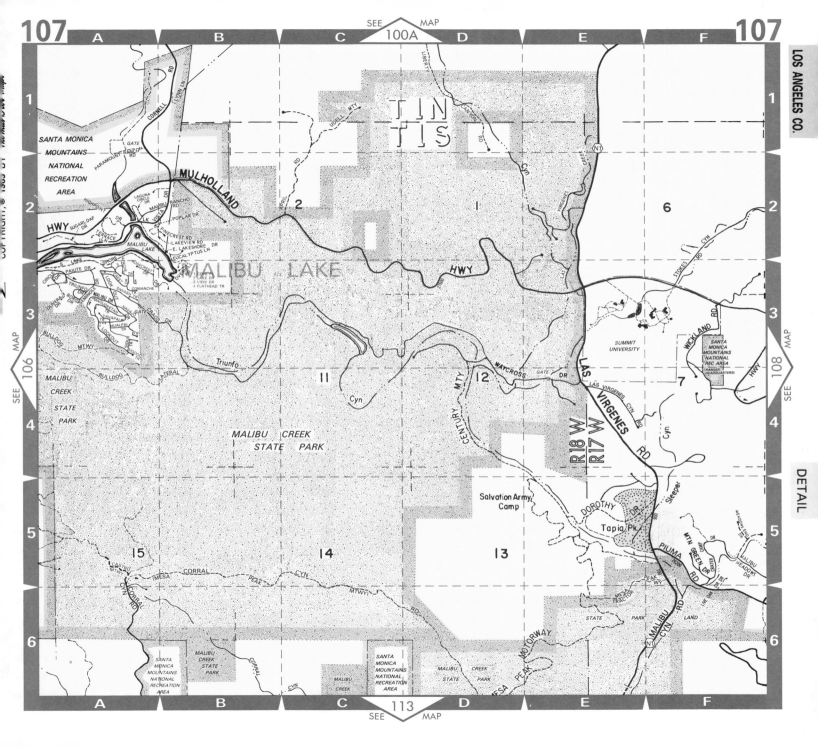

SEE MAP 100A

SEE MAP 113

SEE MAP 106

SEE MAP 108

TIN TIS

SANTA MONICA MOUNTAINS NATIONAL RECREATION AREA

MULHOLLAND HWY

MALIBU LAKE

MALIBU CREEK STATE PARK

MALIBU CREEK STATE PARK

MALIBU CREEK STATE PARK

SANTA MONICA MOUNTAINS NATIONAL RECREATION AREA

SANTA MONICA MOUNTAINS NATIONAL RECREATION AREA

SANTA MONICA MOUNTAINS NATIONAL REC AREA (RANGER HEADQUARTERS)

SUMMIT UNIVERSITY

Salvation Army Camp

Tapia Pk.

LAS VIRGENES RD

R18 W R17 W

Triunfo Cyn

WICKLAND RD

MAYCROSS

CENTURY MTY

DOROTHY DR

PIUMA RD

MTN GREEN DR

MALIBU CYN RD

MALIBU MEADOWS DR

MESA PEAK MOTORWAY

Sleeper

Cornell Rd

Lynn Ln

1 6

I 6

11 12 7

14 13

15

13

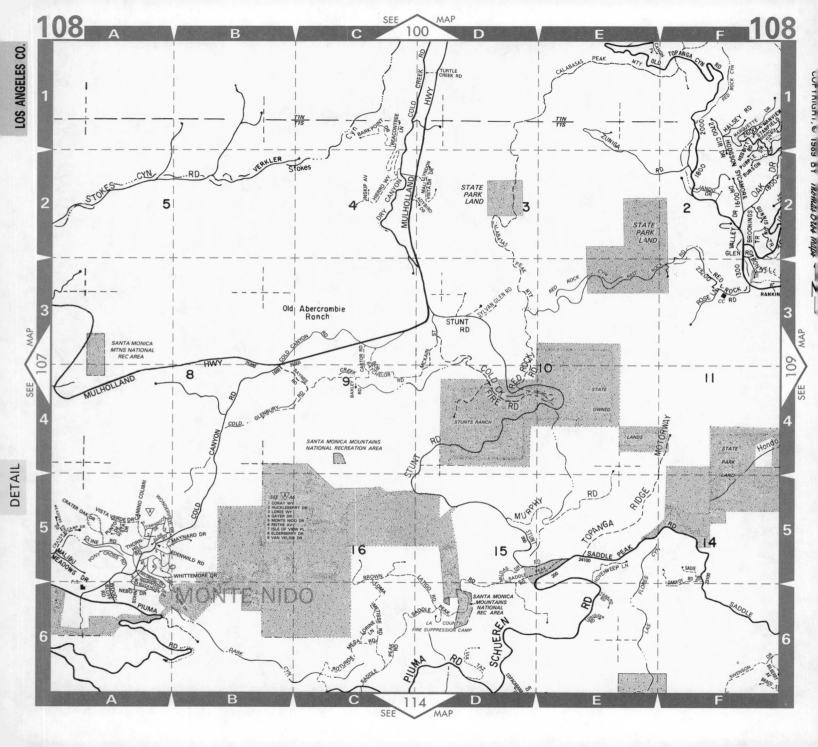

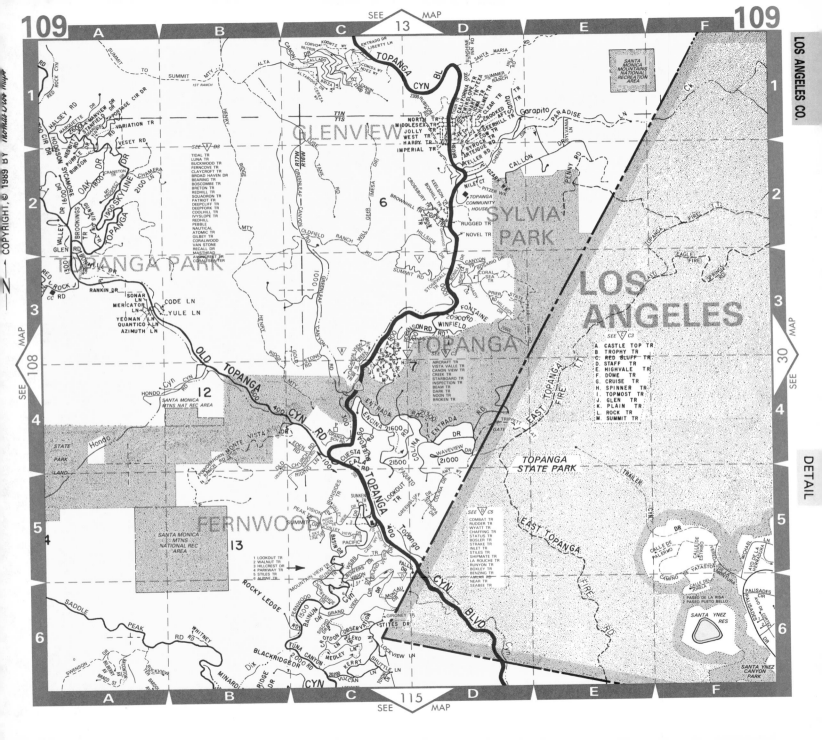

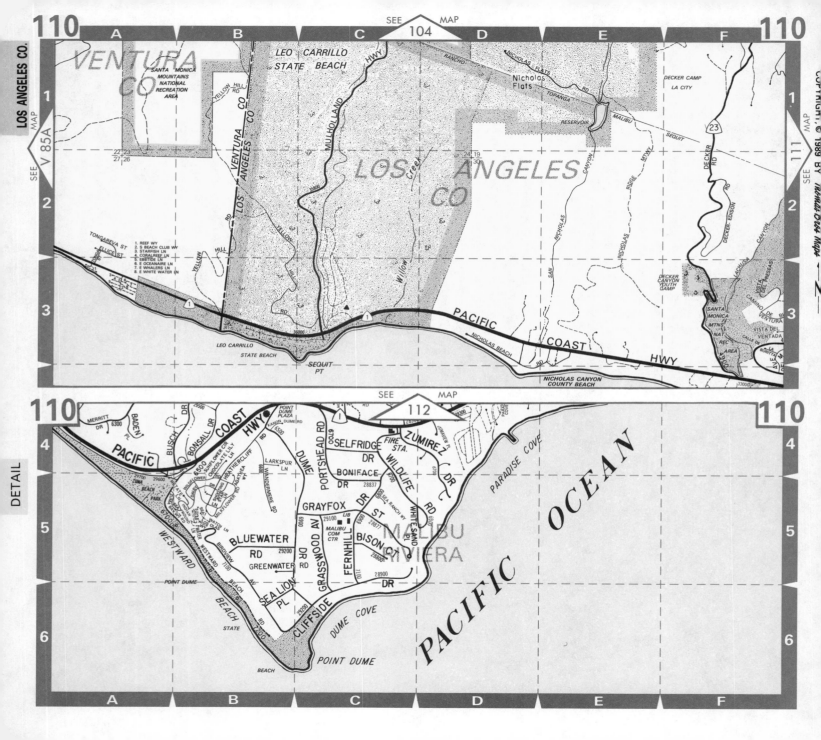

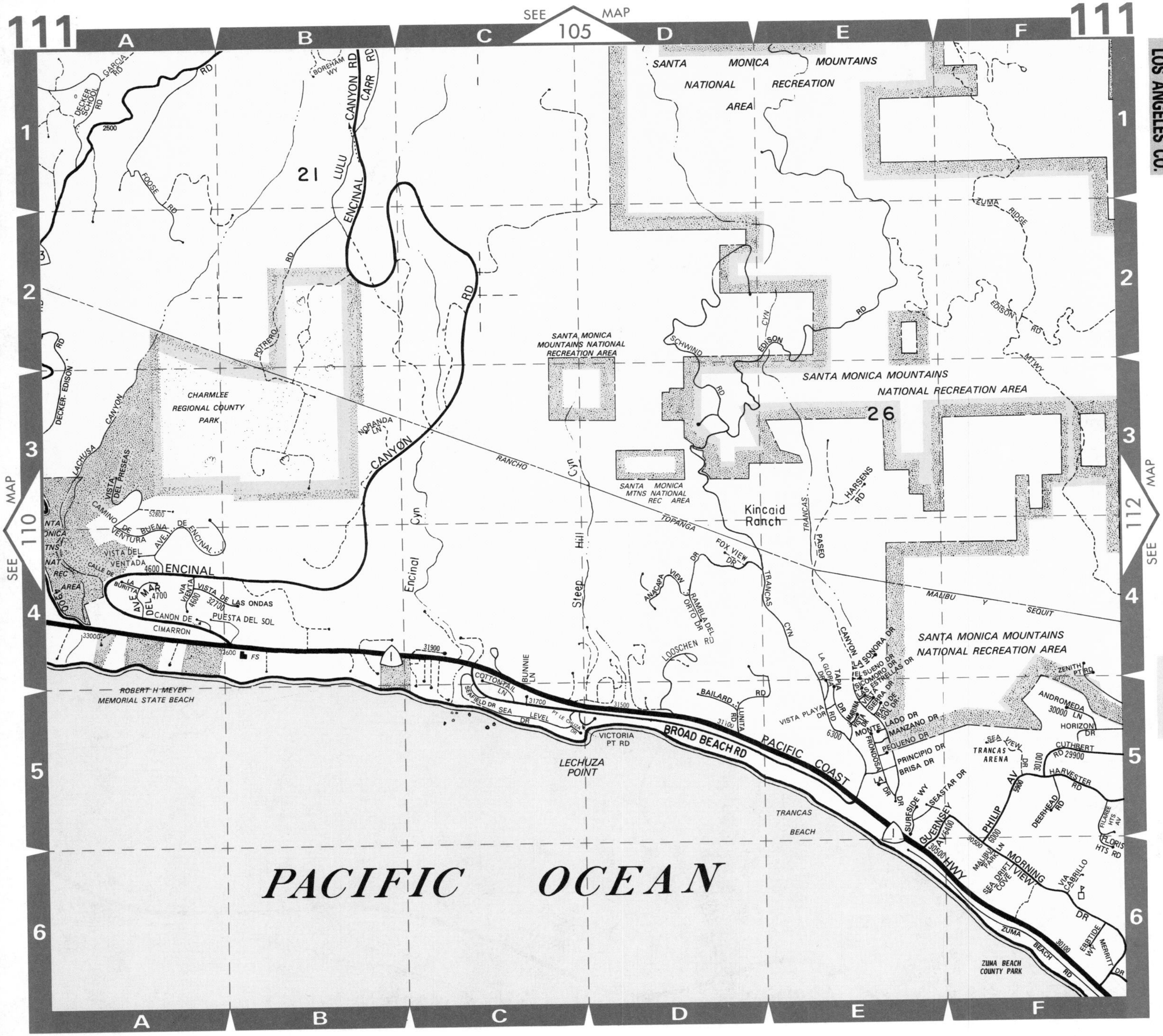

DECKER SCHOOL RD

GARCIA RD

2500

FOOSE RD

DECKER - EDISON RD

BOREHAM WY

LULU CANYON

ENCINAL CANYON RD

CARR RD

21

POTRERO RD

CANYON RD

SANTA MONICA MOUNTAINS NATIONAL RECREATION AREA

CHARMLEE REGIONAL COUNTY PARK

LECHUSA CANYON

VISTA DEL FRESNES

CAMINO DE BUENA VENTURA

VISTA DEL VENTADA

CALLE DE

52600

SANTA MONICA MTNS NAT REC AREA

NORANDA LN

CANYON

RANCHO

Encinal Cyn

Steep Hill

Cyn

TOPANGA

Santa Monica Mountains National Recreation Area

SCHWIND

EDISON CYN

EDISON RD

RD

MTWY

ZUMA RIDGE

EDISON RD

Santa Monica Mountains National Recreation Area

26

HARSENS RD

Kincaid Ranch

TRANCAS

PASEO

FOX VIEW DR

MALIBU

SEQUIT

Santa Monica Mountains National Recreation Area

ENCINAL

4600

AVE DEL MAR 4700

VIA VISTA 4600

VISTA DE LAS ONDAS 32700

PUESTA DEL SOL

CANON DE

BURITTO

CIMARRON

33000

31600

FS

31900

COTTONTAIL LN

BUNNIE LN

BEFIELD DR SEA LEVEL DR

31700

PT LE CRUSE

31500

ROBERT H MEYER MEMORIAL STATE BEACH

VICTORIA PT RD

LECHUZA POINT

BROAD BEACH RD

ZENITH PT RD

ANDROMEDA 30000 LN

HORIZON DR

CUTHBERT RD 29900

PACIFIC COAST

SEA VIEW

TRANCAS ARENA

HARVESTER RD

PHILIP AV

DEERHEAD RD

FILARE HTS AV

FLORIS HTS RD

LOODSCHEN RD

BAILARD RD

VISTA PLAYA DR

MONTE LADO DR

MANZANO DR

PEQUENO DR

PRINCIPIO DR

BRISA DR

6300

ANACAPA VIEW DR

RAMBLA DE ORTO DR

CANYON RD

LA GLORIA

TRANCAS CYN

TAPIA DR

EL SUENO DR

DESCONCO DR

SIERRA DE LAS ESTRELLAS DR

SURFSIDE WY

SEASTAR DR

GUERNSEY AV

BEACH HWY

MORNING VIEW DR

MALIBU

VIA CABRILLO

DR

EBTIDE

MERRITT DR

TRANCAS BEACH

ZUMA BEACH RD

ZUMA BEACH COUNTY PARK

PACIFIC OCEAN

SEE MAP 110

SEE MAP 112

DETAIL

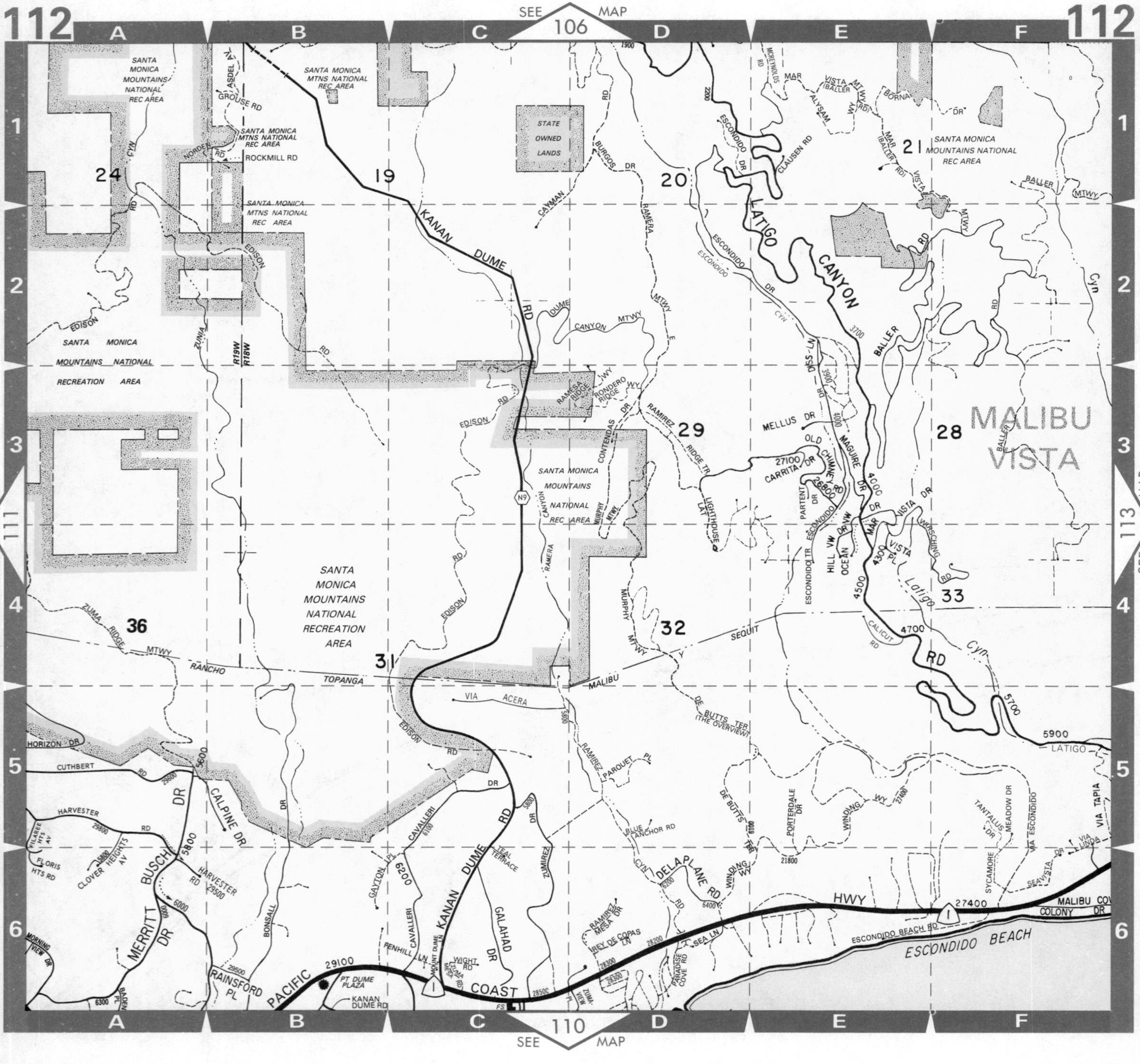

112   A   B   C   SEE MAP 106   D   E   F   112

DETAIL

Row 1

SANTA MONICA MOUNTAINS NATIONAL REC AREA

24

SANTA MONICA MTNS NATIONAL REC AREA

SANTA MONICA MTNS NATIONAL REC AREA

STATE OWNED LANDS

19

20

21

SANTA MONICA MOUNTAINS NATIONAL REC AREA

ASDEL AV

GROUSE RD

NORDEN RD

ROCKMILL RD

SANTA MONICA MTNS NATIONAL REC AREA

KANAN DUME RD

CAYMAN

BURGOS DR

RAMERA MTWY

CLAUSEN RD

ESCONDIDO DR

MORNINGSIDE RD

MAR VISTA (BALLER) WY

ALYSAM

MAR (BALLER) VISTA RD

BORNA

DR

BALLER MTWY

Row 2

EDISON

SANTA MONICA MOUNTAINS NATIONAL RECREATION AREA

ZUMA RD

R19W R18W

RD

KANAN DUME RD

CANYON MTWY

ESCONDIDO DR

CYN

ESCONDIDO DR

LATIGO CANYON

BALLER

Cyn

Row 3

SEE MAP 111

SANTA MONICA MOUNTAINS NATIONAL RECREATION AREA

RAMSA RIDGE HWY

RONDERO WY

EDISON RD

CONTENDAS DR

RAMIREZ

RIDGE TR

29

SANTA MONICA MOUNTAINS NATIONAL REC AREA

N9

MURPHY MTWY

RAMERA

LIGHTHOUSE LATIGO

MELLUS DR

OLD CHIMNEY RD

CARRITA DR

27100

MAGUIRE DR

ESCONDIDO

PARTENT DR

HILL VW DR VW

OCEAN

MAR VISTA DR

VISTA PL

4300 4500 4600

WOSCHING RD

28

33

MALIBU VISTA

BALLER MTWY

SEE MAP 113

Row 4

ZUMA RIDGE MTWY

RANCHO

36

EDISON RD

SANTA MONICA MOUNTAINS NATIONAL RECREATION AREA

TOPANGA

3

VIA ACERA

MURPHY MTWY

32

SEQUIT

MALIBU

DE BUTTS TER (THE OVERVIEW)

ESCONDIDO TR

4500

4700

CALICUT RD

LATIGO CYN RD

5700

5900 LATIGO

Row 5

HORIZON DR

CUTHBERT

CALPINE DR

BUSCH DR

5600

EDISON RD

CAVALLERI DR

RAMIREZ

PARQUET PL

BLUE HARBOR RD

DE BUTTS DR

PORTERDALE DR

WINDING WY

21800

TANTALUS LDR

MEADOW DR

VIA ESCONDIDO DR

VIA TAPIA

VIA LIBRA

SYCAMORE MEADOW DR

SEA VISTA

HARVESTER

FILARETE HTS AV

CLOVER HEIGHTS AV

29500

HARVESTER RD 29500

5800

BONSALL DR

GAYTON PL

CAVALLERI LN

KANAN DUME RD

GALAHAD DR

DELAPLANE RD

WINDING WY

6400

Row 6

MORNING VIEW DR

FLORIS HTS RD

6300

BADEN PL

MERRITT DR

RAINSFORD PL

PACIFIC

PT. DUME PLAZA

29100

KANAN DUME RD

PENHILL LN

MOUNT DUME RD

WIGHT RD

COAST HWY

FS 11

RAMIREZ MESA DR

TREE DE COPAS

28300

PARADISE VIEW

ZUMA VIEW

SEA LN

27400

ESCONDIDO BEACH RD

ESCONDIDO BEACH

MALIBU COVE COLONY DR

112   A   B   C   SEE MAP 110   D   E   F

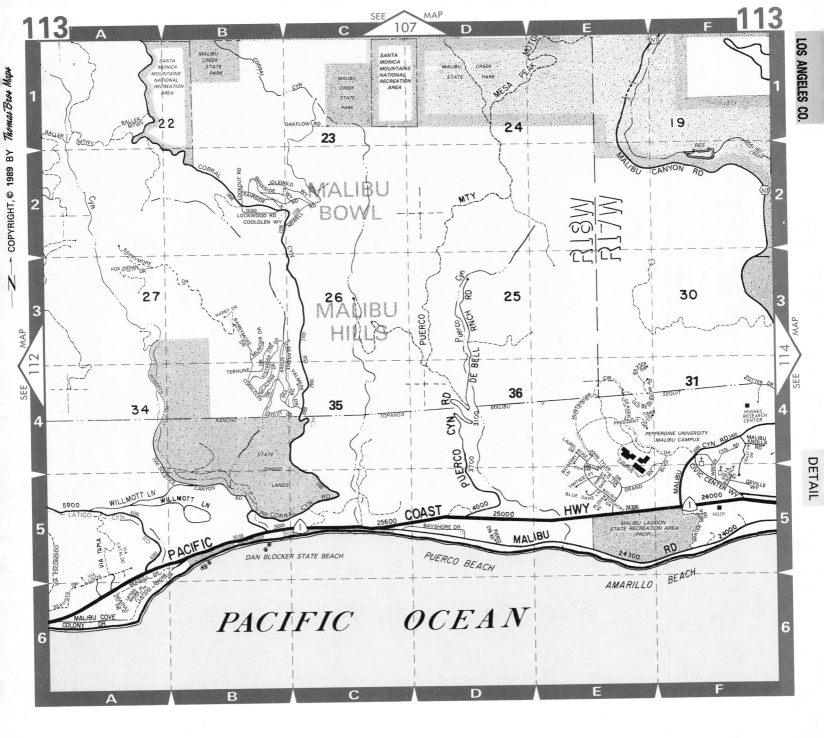

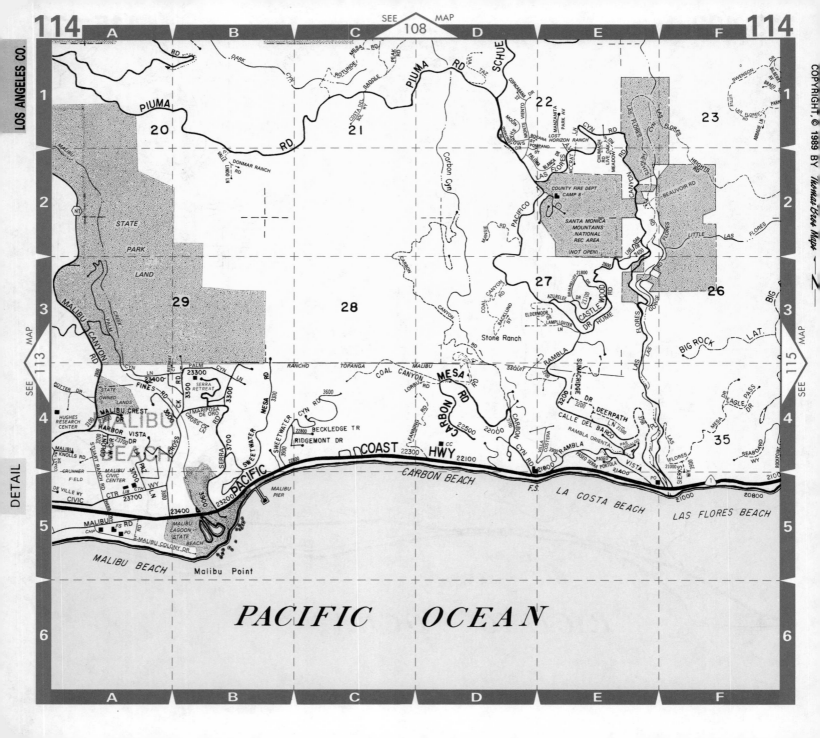

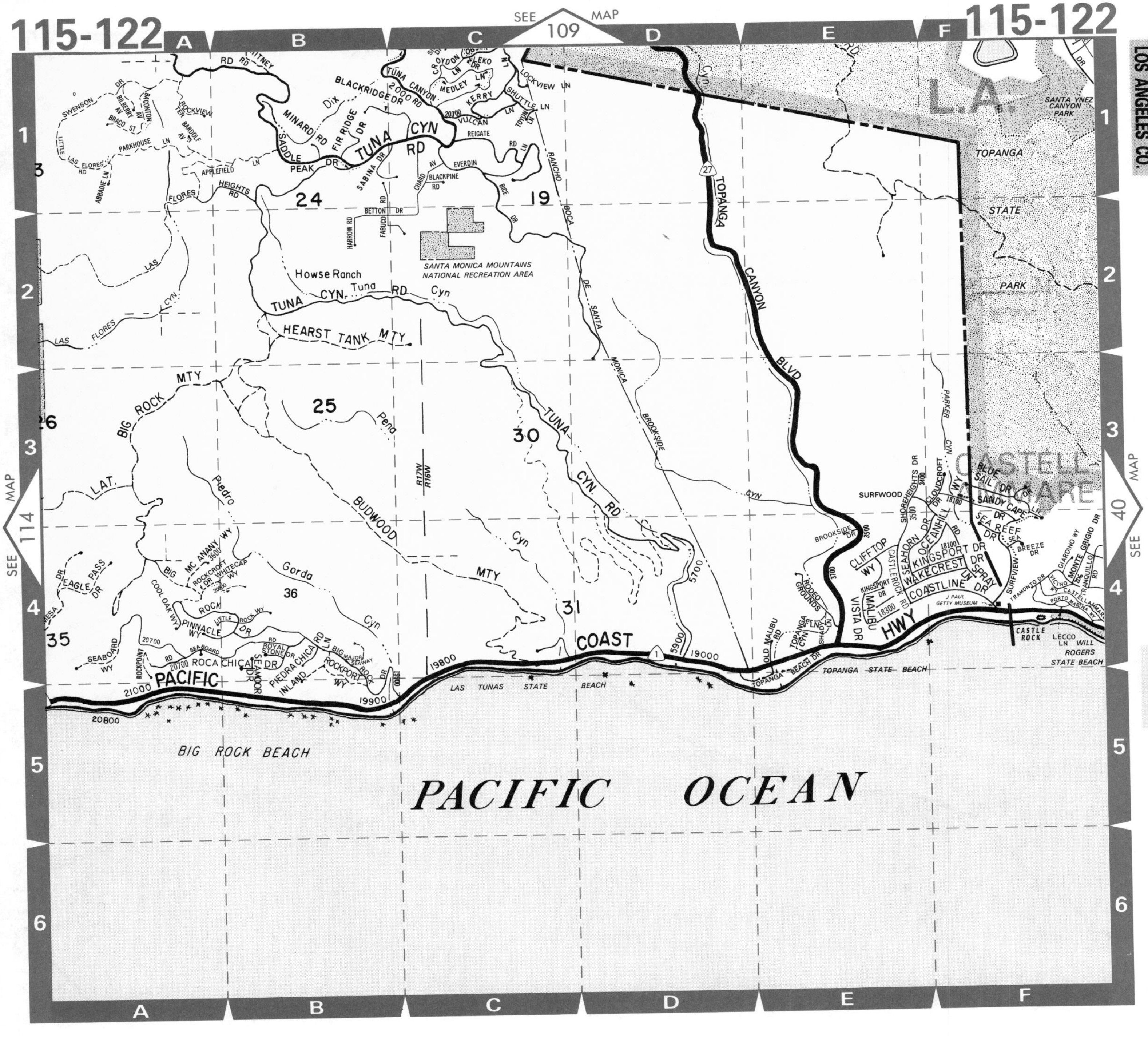

LOS ANGELES CO.

DETAIL

L.A.

Santa Ynez Canyon Park

TOPANGA

STATE

PARK

SWENSON DR
MOUNTAIN VIEW AV
BILBERRY AV
BRACO ST
BECKVIEW
WHITNEY RD RD
RD

LITTLE LAS FLORES RD
BARIQUE LN
PARKHOUSE LN
ABADIE LN
APPLEFIELD LN
HEIGHTS RD
FLORES

MINARD RD
SADDLE PEAK DR
FIR RIDGE DR
DIX
TUNA CANYON
COCO RD
BLACKRIDGE DR
SABINA DR
TUNA CYN RD

S DR
CYOON LN
COYOON LN
ALEKO LN
MEDLEY LN
KERRY
VULCAN AV
REIGATE
EVERDIN
BLACKPINE RD
CHINO
BETTON DR
FABIADO RD
HARROW RD

LOCKVIEW LN
SHUTTLE LN
RANCHO
TOPANGA
RICE DR
ROCA

24

19

Santa Monica Mountains National Recreation Area

Howse Ranch

TUNA CYN Tuna RD Cyn

HEARST TANK MTY

BIG ROCK MTY

26

25

Piedro

Pena

LAT.

BUDWOOD

R17W R16W

Cyn

DE SANTA MONICA

BROOKSIDE

TUNA CYN RD

Cyn

30

27

TOPANGA CANYON BLVD

PARKER CYN

CASTELLA MARE

BLUE SAIL DR
SANDY CAPE
SEA REEF DR
SURFWOOD
SHOREHEIGHTS DR
DROUGHCROFT WY
CLIFFTOP WY
KINGSPORT DR
SEAHORN DR
OCEANHILL
CASTLEROCK RD
WAKECREST DR
COASTLINE DR
MALIBU VISTA DR
RODEO GROUNDS
BROOKSIDE DR
GIARDINO WY
MONTE GRIGIO DR
SEA BREEZE DR
SURFVIEW DR
TRAMONTO DR
PORTO ASHOLY LN

J. PAUL GETTY MUSEUM

CASTLE ROCK

LECCO LN
WILL ROGERS STATE BEACH

40

EAGLE PASS DR
MESA WY
BIG ROCK DR
MC ANANY WY
ROCKCROFT
WHITECAP WY
PINNACLE WY
COOL OAK WY
ROCA CHICA DR
SEABOARD WY
ROCKMOUNT WY
PIEDRA CHICA DR
BIG ROCK
SEAWAY
LITTLE ROCK WY
ROYAL STONE
ROCKPORT WY
INLAND

36

31

Gorda Cyn

MTY

COAST

1

5900

19000

OLD MALIBU RD
TOPANGA CYN LN
TOPANGA BEACH DR

HWY

35

20700
20800
21000
19900
19800
LAS TUNAS STATE BEACH
TOPANGA STATE BEACH

PACIFIC

BIG ROCK BEACH

PACIFIC OCEAN

N

SEE MAP 114

SEE MAP 40

1 2 3 4 5 6

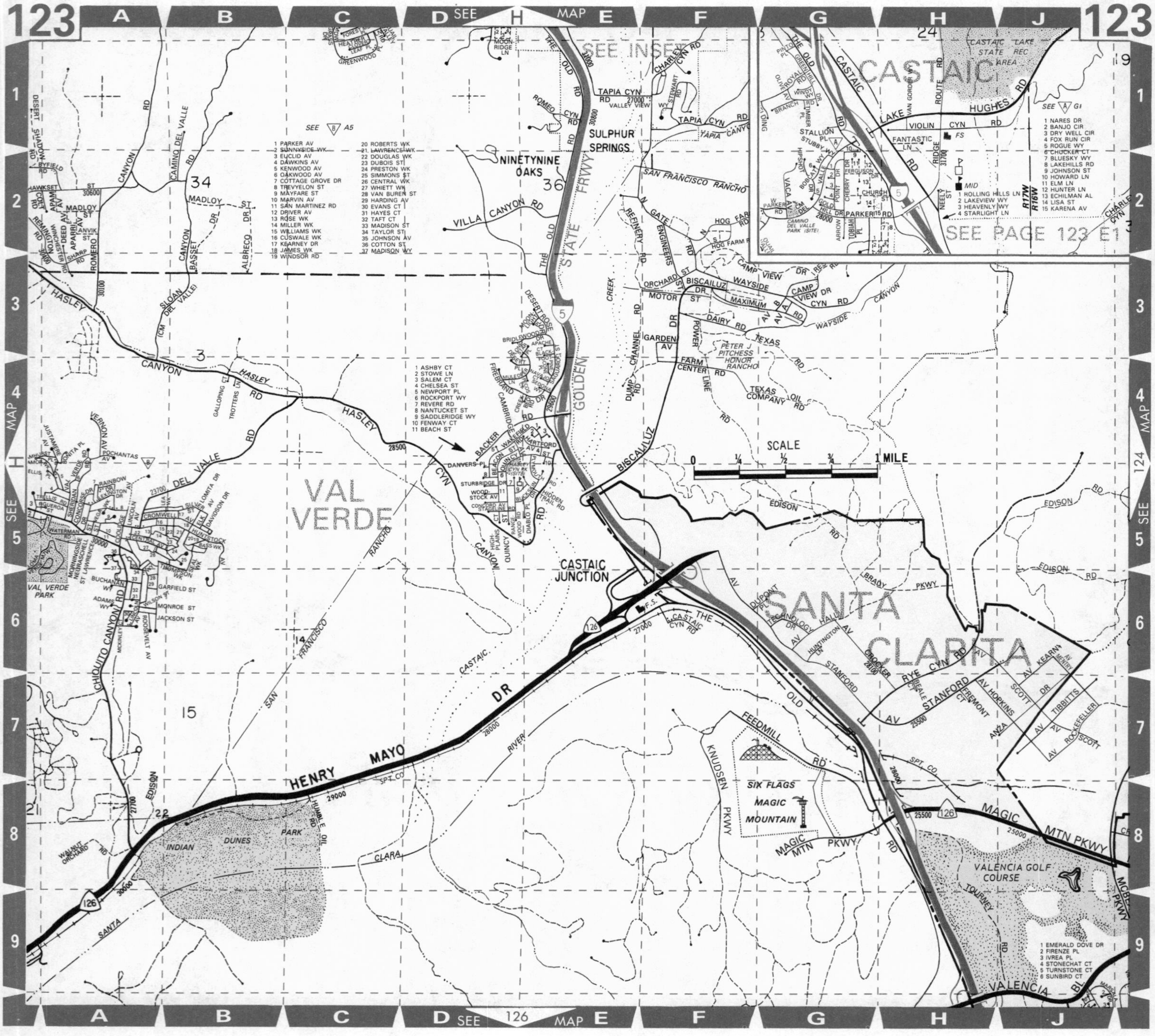

LOS ANGELES CO.

DETAIL

SEE INSET

SEE PAGE 123 E1

CASTAIC

CASTAIC LAKE STATE REC AREA

1 NARES DR
2 BANJO CIR
3 DRY WELL CIR
4 FOX RUN CIR
5 ROGUE WY
6 CHUCKER CT
7 BLUESKY WY
8 LAKEHILLS AV
9 JOHNSON ST
10 HOWARD LN
11 ELM LN
12 HUNTER LN
13 ECHILMAN AL
14 LISA ST
15 KARENA AV

MID
1 ROLLING HILLS LN
2 LAKEVIEW WY
3 HEAVENLY WY
4 STARLIGHT LN

1 PARKER AV
2 SUNNYSIDE WK
3 EUCLID AV
4 DAWKINS AV
5 KENWOOD AV
6 OAKWOOD AV
7 COTTAGE GROVE DR
8 TREVELON ST
9 MAYFARE ST
10 MARVIN AV
11 SAN MARTINEZ RD
12 DRIVER AV
13 ROSE AV
14 MILLER WK
15 WILLIAMS AV
16 CUSWALE WK
17 KEARNEY DR
18 JAMES WK
19 WINDSOR RD
20 ROBERTS WK
21 LAWRENCE WK
22 DOUGLAS WK
23 DUBOIS ST
24 PRESTON WK
25 SIMMONS ST
26 CENTRAL WK
27 WHIETT ST
28 VAN BUREN ST
29 HARDING AV
30 EVANS CT
31 HAYES CT
32 TAFT CT
33 MADISON ST
34 TAYLOR ST
35 JOHNSONS AV
36 COTTON ST
37 MADISON WY

1 ASHBY CT
2 STOWE LN
3 SALEM CT
4 CHELSEA ST
5 NEWPORT PL
6 ROCKPORT WY
7 REVERE RD
8 NANTUCKET ST
9 SADDLERIDGE WY
10 FENWAY CT
11 BEACH ST

VAL VERDE

VAL VERDE PARK

NINETYNINE OAKS

SULPHUR SPRINGS

CASTAIC JUNCTION

SANTA CLARITA

SIX FLAGS MAGIC MOUNTAIN

VALENCIA GOLF COURSE

INDIAN DUNES PARK

HENRY MAYO DR

SCALE
0 ¼ ½ ¾ 1 MILE

1 EMERALD DOVE DR
2 FIRENZE PL
3 IVREA PL
4 STONECHAT CT
5 TURNSTONE CT
6 SUNBIRD CT

VALENCIA

SEE 126 MAP

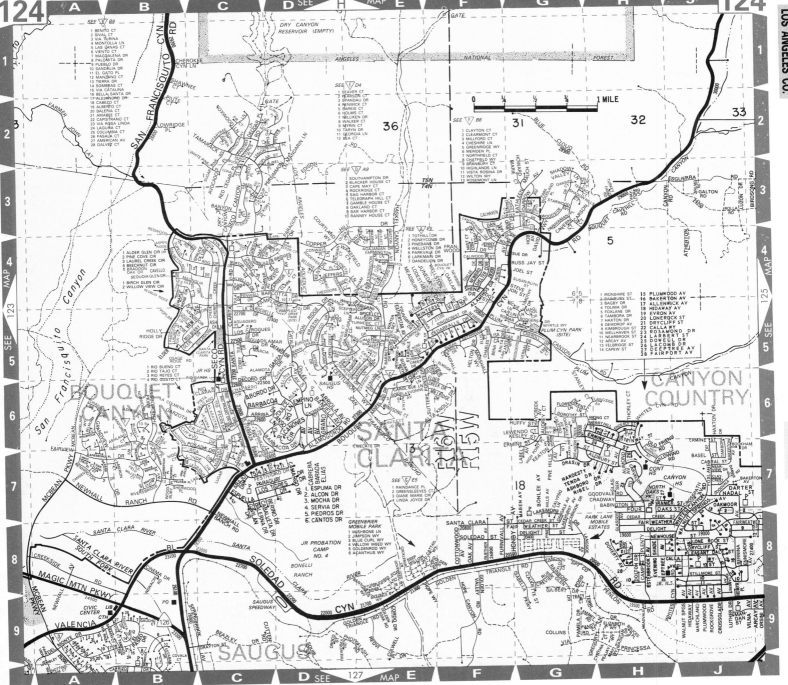

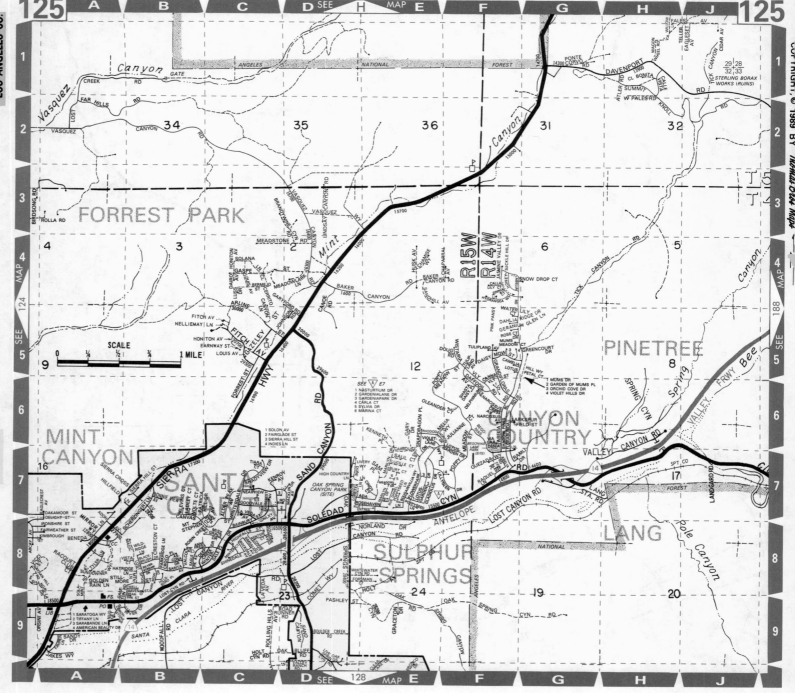

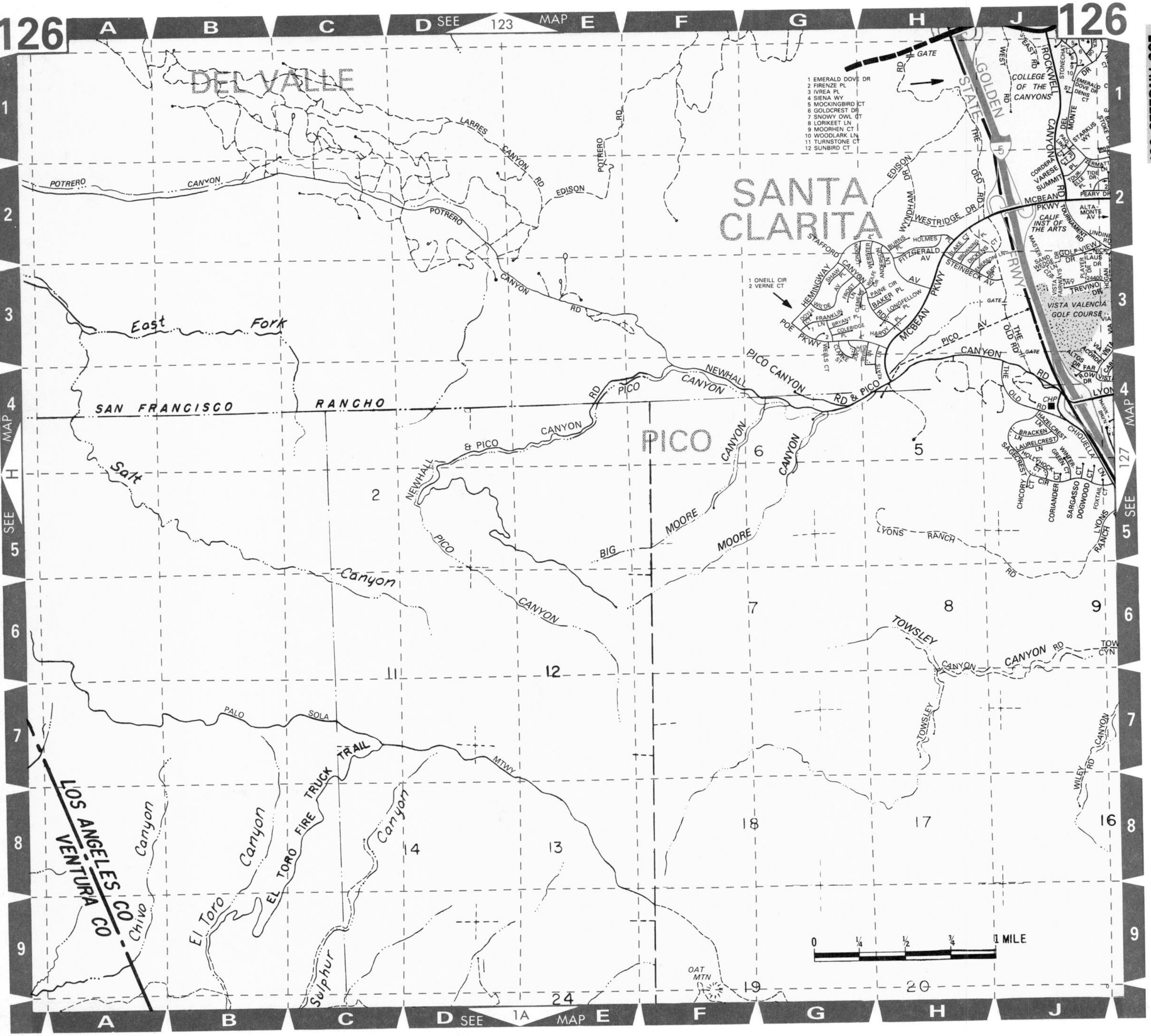

DEL VALLE

SANTA CLARITA

PICO

SAN FRANCISCO RANCHO

East Fork

Salt

POTRERO CANYON

POTRERO CANYON

LARRES CANYON RD

EDISON

COLLEGE OF THE CANYONS

CALIF INST OF THE ARTS

VISTA VALENCIA GOLF COURSE

GOLDEN STATE

MCBEAN PKWY

PICO CANYON

NEWHALL & PICO CANYON

BIG MOORE CANYON

MOORE CANYON

LYONS RANCH

TOWSLEY CANYON RD

TOW CYN

PALO SOLA

EL TORO FIRE TRUCK TRAIL

MTWY

El Toro Canyon

Chivo Canyon

Sulphur

OAT MTN

LOS ANGELES CO. VENTURA CO.

1. Emerald Dove Dr
2. Firenze Pl
3. Ivrea Pl
4. Siena Wy
5. Mockingbird Ct
6. Goldcrest Dr
7. Snowy Owl Ct
8. Lorikeet Ln
9. Moorhen Ct
10. Woodlark Ln
11. Turnstone Ct
12. Sunbird Ct

1 Oneill Cir
2 Verne Ct

DETAIL

1 MILE
0   ¼   ½   ¾

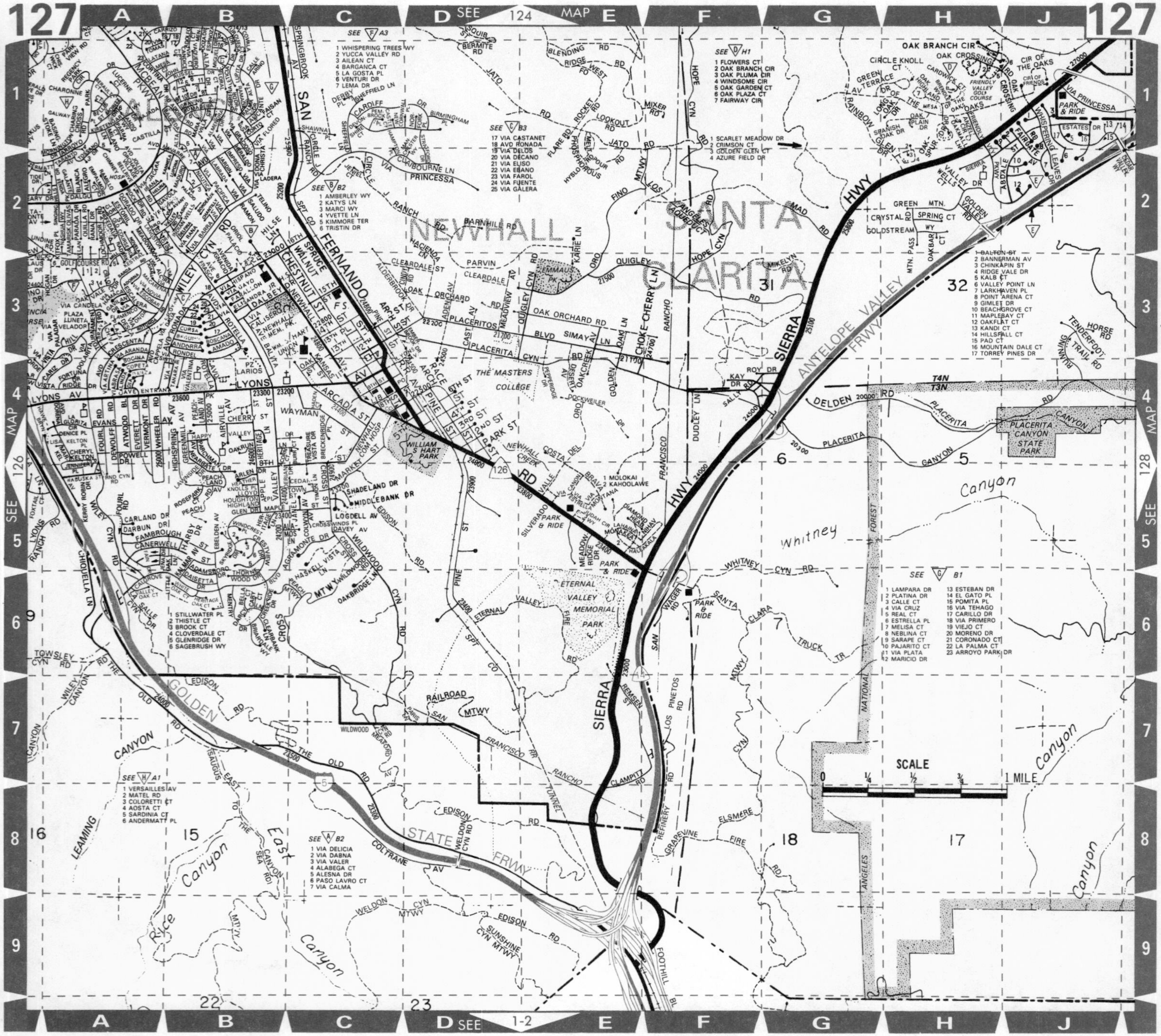

COPYRIGHT, © 1985 BY THOMAS BROS. MAPS

SEE F A3
1 WHISPERING TREES WY
2 YUCCA VALLEY RD
3 AILEAN CT
4 BARGANICA CT
5 LA GOSTA PL
6 VENTURI DR
7 LEMA DR

SEE B3
17 VIA CASTANET
18 AVD RONADA
19 VIA DELOS
20 VIA DECANO
21 VIA EUSO
22 VIA EBANO
23 VIA FAROL
24 VIA FUENTE
25 VIA GALERA

SEE B2
1 AMBERLEY WY
2 KATYS LN
3 MARCI WY
4 YVETTE LN
5 KIMMORE TER
6 TRISTIN DR

SEE D H1
1 FLOWERS CT
2 OAK BRANCH CIR
3 OAK PLUMA CIR
4 WINDSOME CIR
5 OAK GARDEN CT
6 OAK PLAZA CT
7 FAIRWAY CIR

1 SCARLET MEADOW DR
2 CRIMSON CT
3 GOLDEN GLEN CT
4 AZURE FIELD DR

OAK BRANCH CIR

PARK & RIDE

NEWHALL

SANTA CLARITA

32
1 BALFON ST
2 BANNERMAN AV
3 CHINKAPIN ST
4 RIDGE VALE DR
5 KALE CT
6 VALLEY POINT LN
7 LARKHAVEN PL
8 POINT ARENA CT
9 GIMLET DR
10 BEACHGROVE CT
11 MAPLEBAY CT
12 OAKFLAT CT
13 KANDI CT
14 HILLSFALL CT
15 PAD CT
16 MOUNTAIN DALE CT
17 TORREY PINES DR

31

SIERRA HWY

ANTELOPE VALLEY FRWY

6 **5**

PLACERITA CANYON STATE PARK

DELDEN RD

1 MOLOKAI CT
2 KAHOOLAWE

WILLIAM S HART PARK

ETERNAL VALLEY MEMORIAL PARK

PARK & RIDE

Whitney Canyon

SEE G B1
1 LAMPARA DR
2 PLATINA DR
3 CALLE C
4 VIA CRUZ
5 VIA REAL CT
6 ESTRELLA PL
7 MELISA CT
8 NEBLINA CT
9 SARAPE CT
10 PAJARITO CT
11 VIA PLATA
12 MARICIO DR
13 ESTEBAN DR
14 EL GATO PL
15 POMITA PL
16 VIA TEHAGO
17 CARILLO DR
18 VIA PRIMERO
19 VIEJO CT
20 MORENO DR
21 CORONADO CT
22 LA PALMA CT
23 ARROYO PARK DR

Stillwater
1 STILLWATER PL
2 THISTLE CT
3 BROOK CT
4 CLOVERDALE CT
5 GLENRIDGE DR
6 SAGEBRUSH WY

GOLDEN STATE FRWY

SEE H A1
1 VERSAILLES AV
2 MATEL RD
3 COLORETTI CT
4 AOSTA CT
5 SARDINIA CT
6 ANDERMATT PL

SEE B2
1 VIA DELICIA
2 VIA DABNA
3 VIA VALER
4 ALABEGA CT
5 ALESNA DR
6 VIA CALMA

SCALE
0 ¼ ½ ¾ 1 MILE

16 **15** **18** **17**

SEE 126 MAP

SEE 128 MAP

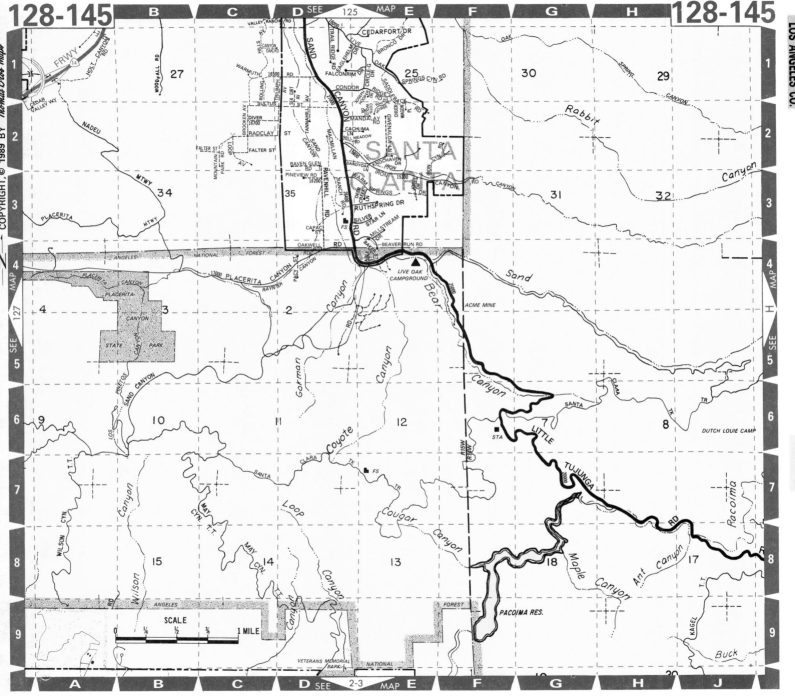

SANTA CLARITA

SCALE
0   1/4   1/2   3/4   1 MILE

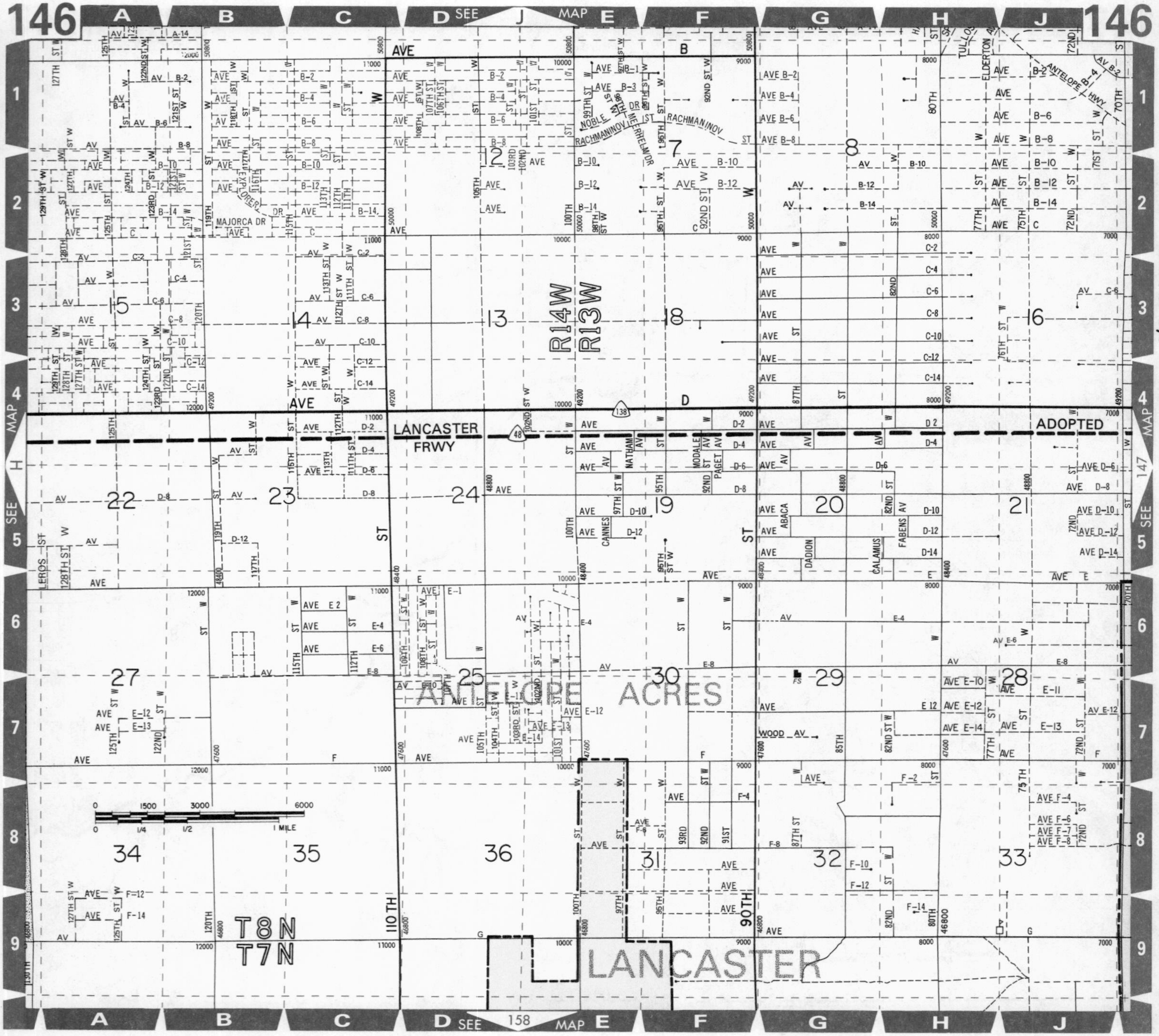

DETAIL

146 A B C D SEE J MAP E F G H J 146

COPYRIGHT, © 1989 BY Thomas Bros. Maps

AVE

LANCASTER FRWY

LANCASTER

ANTELOPE ACRES

R14W R13W

T8N
T7N

ADOPTED

SEE 147 MAP

SEE H MAP

SEE 158 MAP

A B C D SEE E MAP F G H J

0 1500 3000 6000
0 1/4 1/2 1 MILE

15 14 13 18 16

22 23 24 19 20 21

27 25 30 29 28

34 35 36 31 32 33

2 7 8

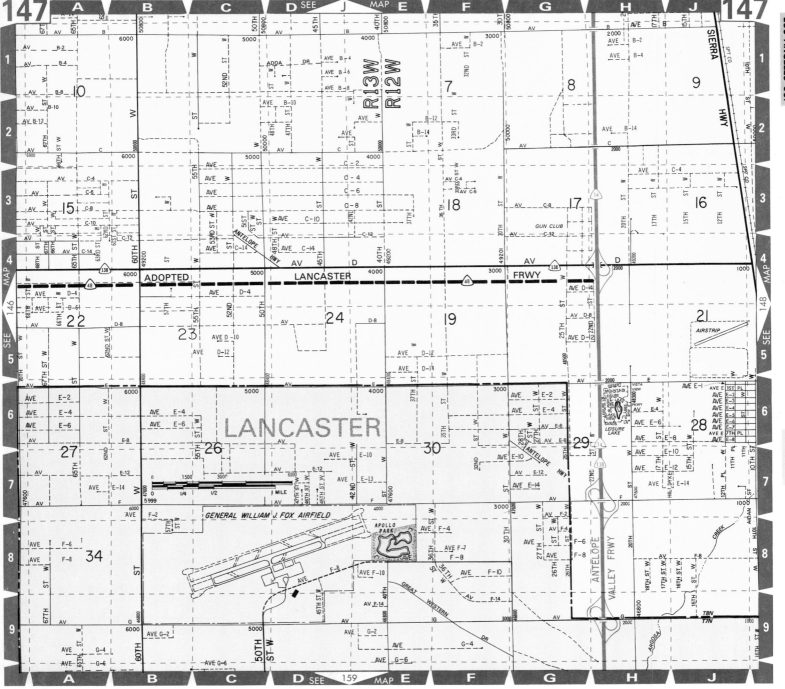

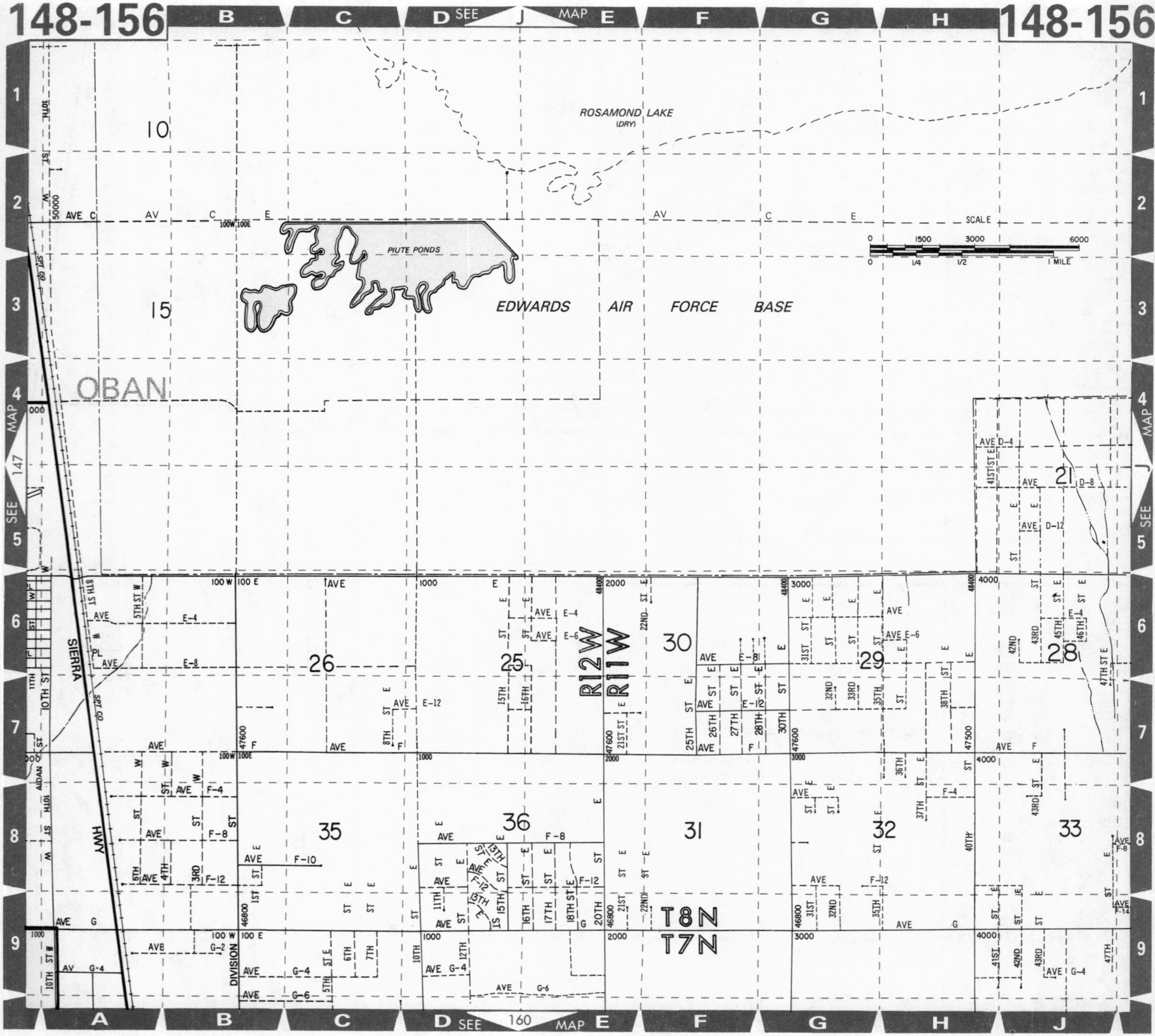

LOS ANGELES CO.

COPYRIGHT © 1989 BY Thomas Bros Maps

10TH ST W
1ST ST W
50000

AVE C AV C E 100W 100E

AVE C E

1

ROSAMOND LAKE (DRY)

SCALE
0 1500 3000 6000
0 1/4 1/2 1 MILE

2

PIUTE PONDS

15 EDWARDS AIR FORCE BASE

3

OBAN

SEE 147 MAP

006

AVE D-4
41ST ST E
AVE D-8
21
AVE D-12

4

SEE MAP

5

DETAIL

8TH ST W
5TH ST W
100 W 100 E AVE 1000 E 22ND ST E 2000 31ST ST 3000 4000
SIERRA
AVE AVE E-4 30
E-4 R12W R11W
AVE E-6
E-8 26 25 30 E-8 29 28
10TH ST
15TH ST 16TH ST 31ST ST 32ND 33RD 35TH 38TH 42ND 43RD 45TH 46TH ST E 47TH ST E
AVE E-12 AVE
8TH ST F 15TH ST 21ST ST 25TH ST 26TH 27TH 28TH 30TH 32ND 33RD 35TH 36TH

6

7

47600 F 47600 F 47500 F

AVE F AVE 1000 F 2000 3000 4000 AVE F
ST W AVE F-4 ST E 36TH ST F-4 43RD ST E AVE F-8

35 36 31 32 33 AVE F-8

AVE F-8
AVE F-10
6TH 4TH 3RD F-12 1ST ST 11TH 15TH 16TH 17TH 18TH ST E 20TH 22ND ST E 31ST 32ND 35TH ST E 41ST
SIERRA HWY F-12 46800 F-12 AVE F-14

8

AIDAN HIGH 10TH ST

46800 DIVISION

AVE G 100 W 100 E 1000 2000 3000 4000
AV G-2
AVE G-4 5TH ST 6TH 7TH 10TH 12TH AVE G-4 31ST 32ND 41ST 42ND 43RD AVE G-4 47TH
G-6 AVE G-6 T8N
AVE G-6 T7N

9

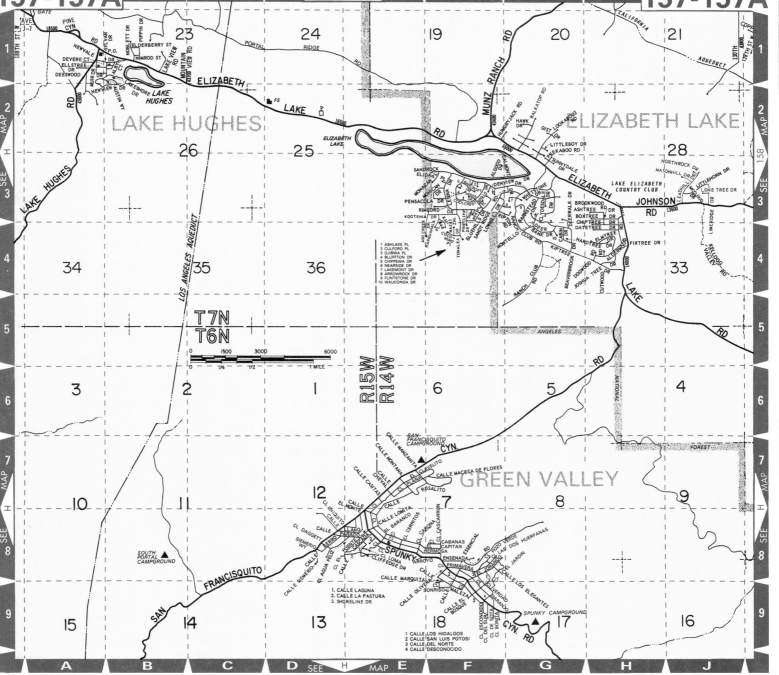

DETAIL

LAKE HUGHES

ELIZABETH LAKE

GREEN VALLEY

SPUNKY

SEE H MAP

1 ASHLAKE PL
2 CULFORD PL
3 OJIBWA PL
4 BLUFFTON DR
5 CHIPPEWA DR
6 NEARSIDE DR
7 LAKEMONT DR
8 ARROWROCK DR
9 FLINTSTONE DR
10 WAUCONDA DR

T7N
T6N

R15W
R14W

0   1500   3000   6000
1/4   1/2   1 MILE

1. CALLE LAGUNA
2. CALLE LA PASTURA
3. SHORELINE DR

1 CALLE LOS HIDALGOS
2 CL SAN LUIS POTOSI
3 CALLE DEL NORTE
4 CALLE DESCONOCIDO

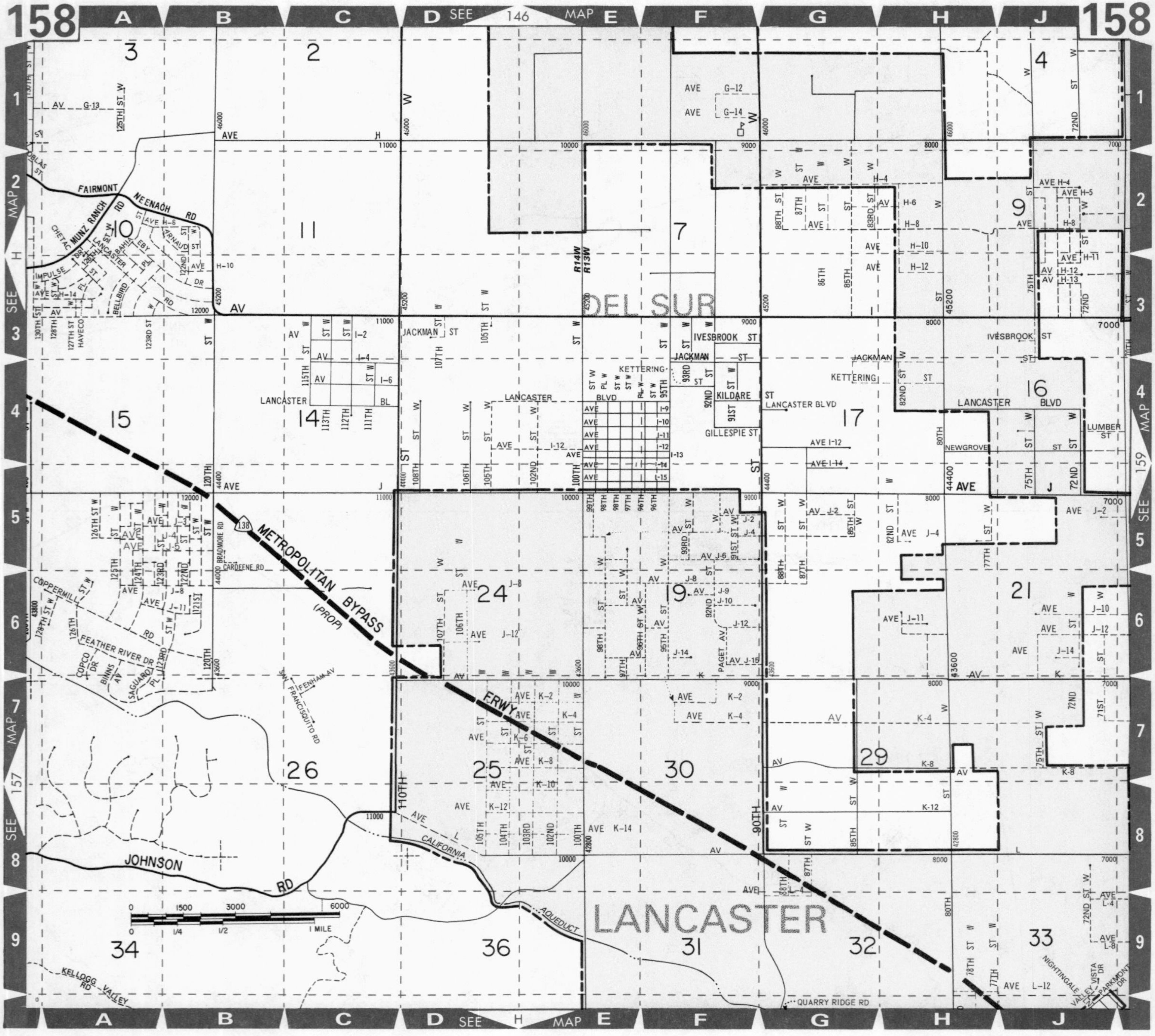

LOS ANGELES CO.

DETAIL

SEE H MAP

SEE 157 MAP

SEE 159 MAP

SEE H MAP

DEL SUR

LANCASTER

METROPOLITAN BYPASS (PROP)

FRWY

FAIRMONT

NEENACH RD

MUNZ RANCH RD

CHET AC

IMPULSE AVE

BELLBIRD

JOHNSON RD

KELLOGG VALLEY RD

FEATHER RIVER DR

COPPERMILL

COPCO DR

SAGUARO

BINNS

BRAEMORE RD

CARDEENE RD

SAN FRANCISQUITO RD

SAN FENTHAM AV

CALIFORNIA

AQUEDUCT

LANCASTER BLVD

JACKMAN ST

KETTERING

KILDARE ST

GILLESPIE ST

IVESBROOK ST

NEWGROVE

LUMBER ST

PAGET AV

QUARRY RIDGE RD

NIGHTINGALE

VALLEY VISTA DR

138

Map grid numbers: 3, 2, 4, 10, 11, 7, 9, 15, 14, 17, 16, 26, 24, 19, 21, 25, 30, 29, 34, 36, 31, 32, 33

Scale: 0 1500 3000 6000 / 1/4 1/2 1 MILE

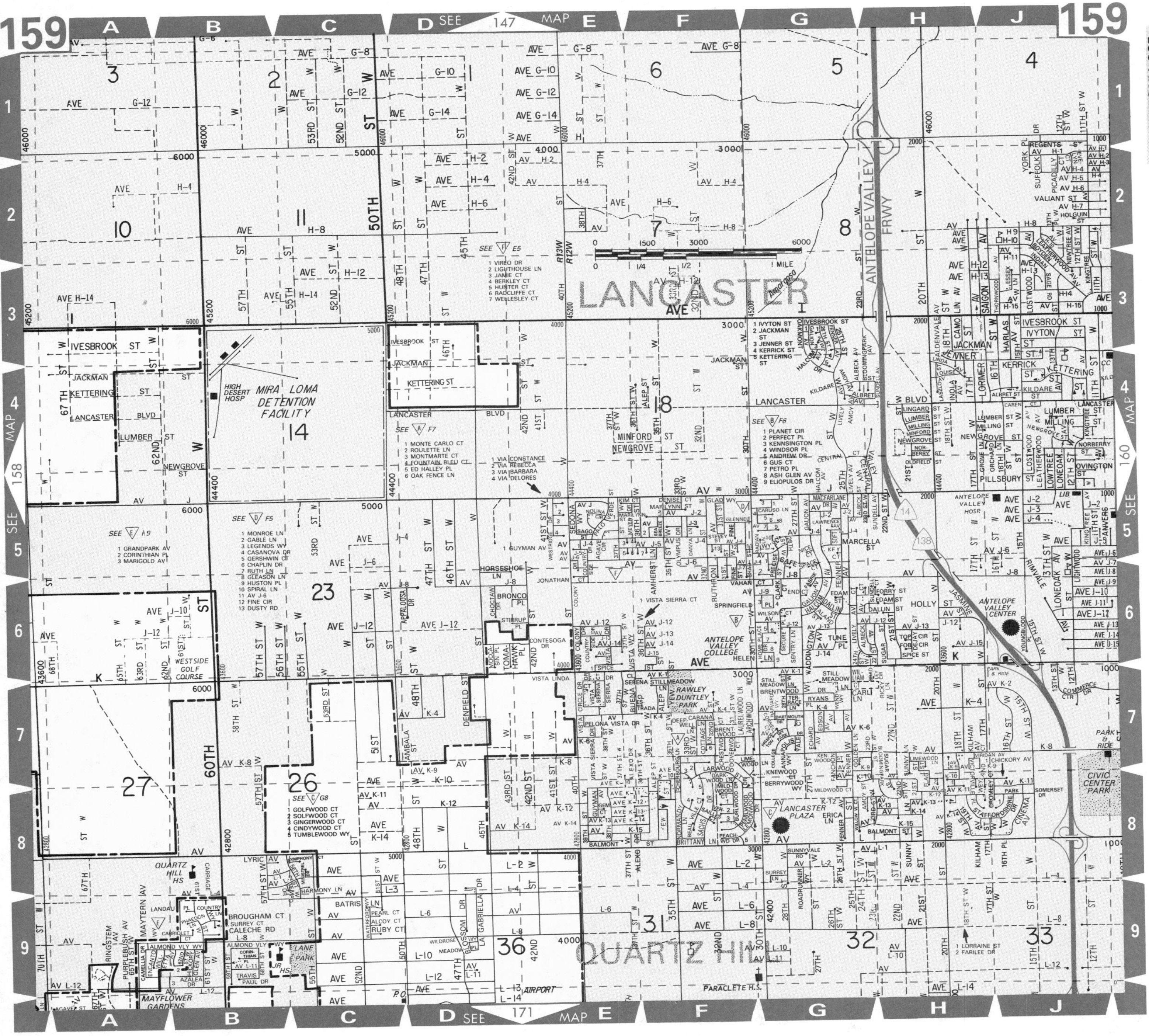

LANCASTER

QUARTZ HILL

LOS ANGELES CO.

DETAIL

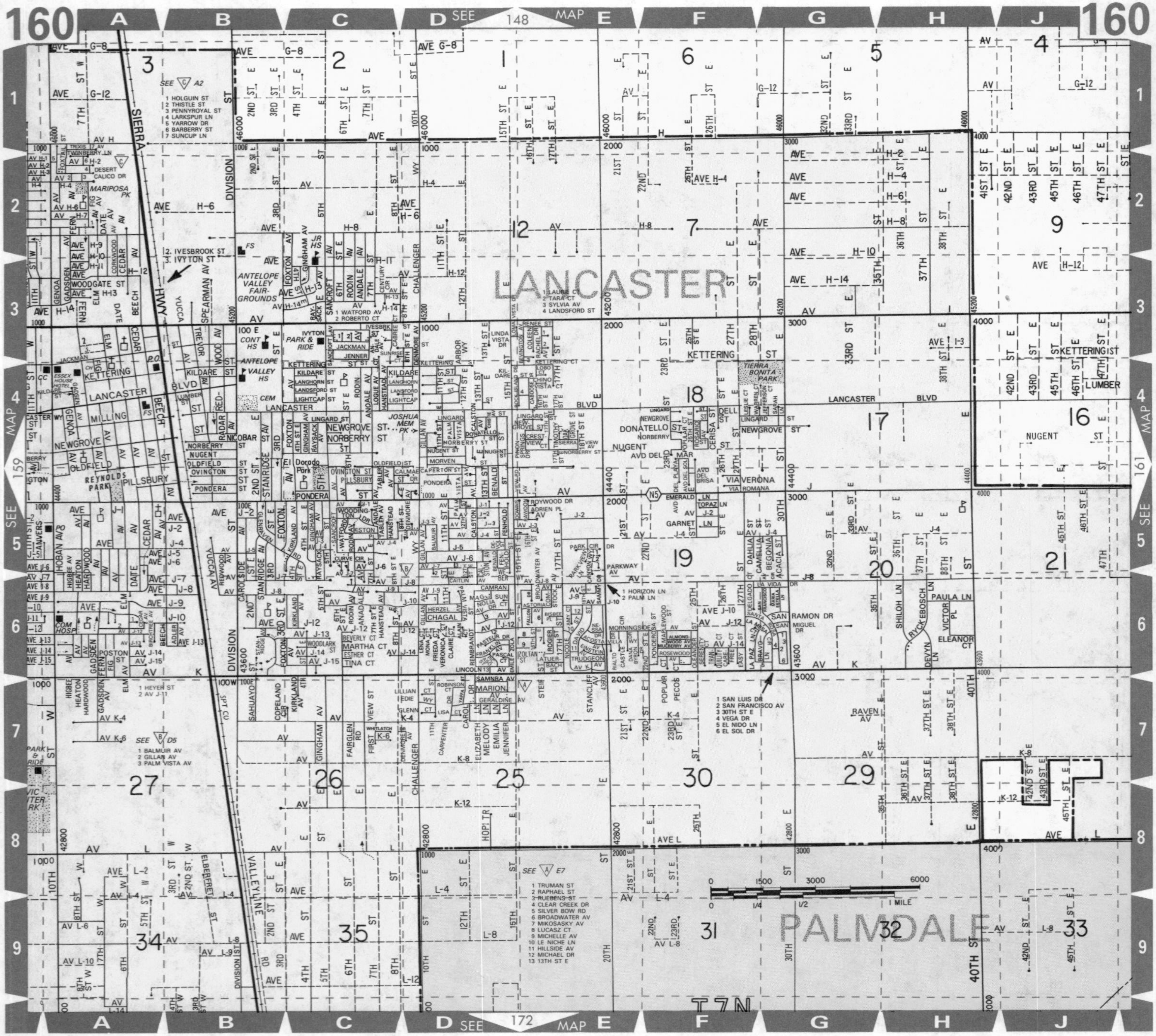

LOS ANGELES CO.

DETAIL

SEE 148 MAP

LANCASTER

PALMDALE

SEE 159 MAP

SEE 161 MAP

SEE 172 MAP

COPYRIGHT © 1989 BY THOMAS BROS. MAPS

T7N

3 2 1 6 5 4

12 7 9

18 17 16

19 20 21

27 26 25 30 29

34 35 31 32 33

SIERRA HWY

DIVISION ST

VALLEY LINE

ANTELOPE VALLEY FAIRGROUNDS

ANTELOPE VALLEY HS

LANCASTER BLVD

KETTERING ST

NEWGROVE ST

NUGENT ST

DONATELLO

TIERRA BONITA PARK

JOSHUA MEM PK

REYNOLDS PARK

MARIPOSA PK

PARK & RIDE

COM HOSP

VIC CENTER

0 1500 3000 6000

0 1/4 1/2 1 MILE

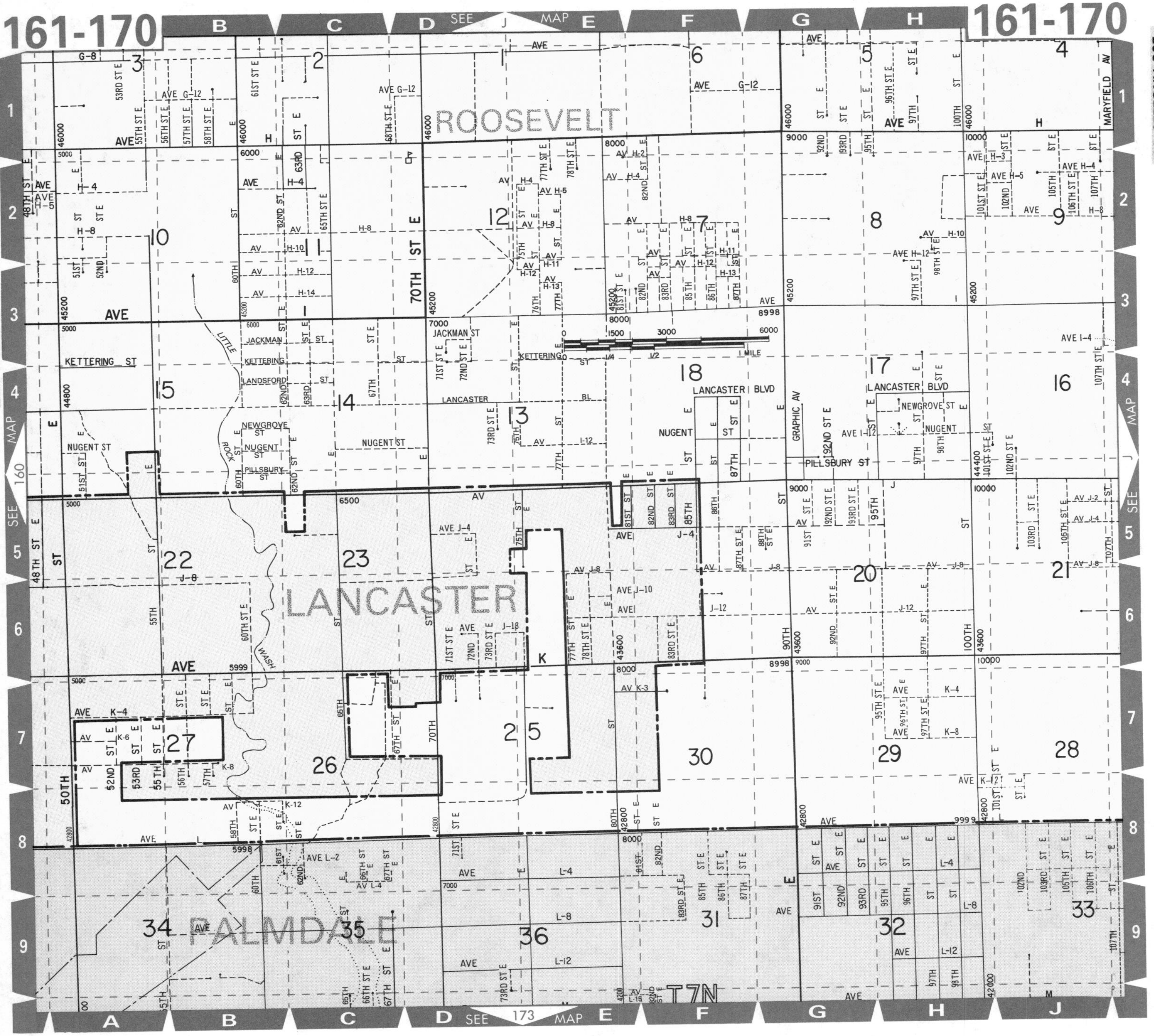

LOS ANGELES CO.

DETAIL

SEE MAP

ROOSEVELT

LANCASTER

PALMDALE

AVE

KETTERING ST

JACKMAN ST

KETTERING

LANDSFORD

NEWGROVE ST

NUGENT ST

PILLSBURY ST

LANCASTER BLVD

LANCASTER BLVD

GRAPHIC AV

NUGENT

NEWGROVE ST

PILLSBURY ST

MARYFIELD AV

WASH

LITTLE ROCK

T7N

SEE 173 MAP

SEE 160 MAP

SEE MAP

70TH ST E

50TH ST

48TH ST

3 2 1 6 5 4

10 12 7 8 9

15 14 13 18 17 16

22 23 20 21

27 26 25 30 29 28

34 35 36 31 32 33

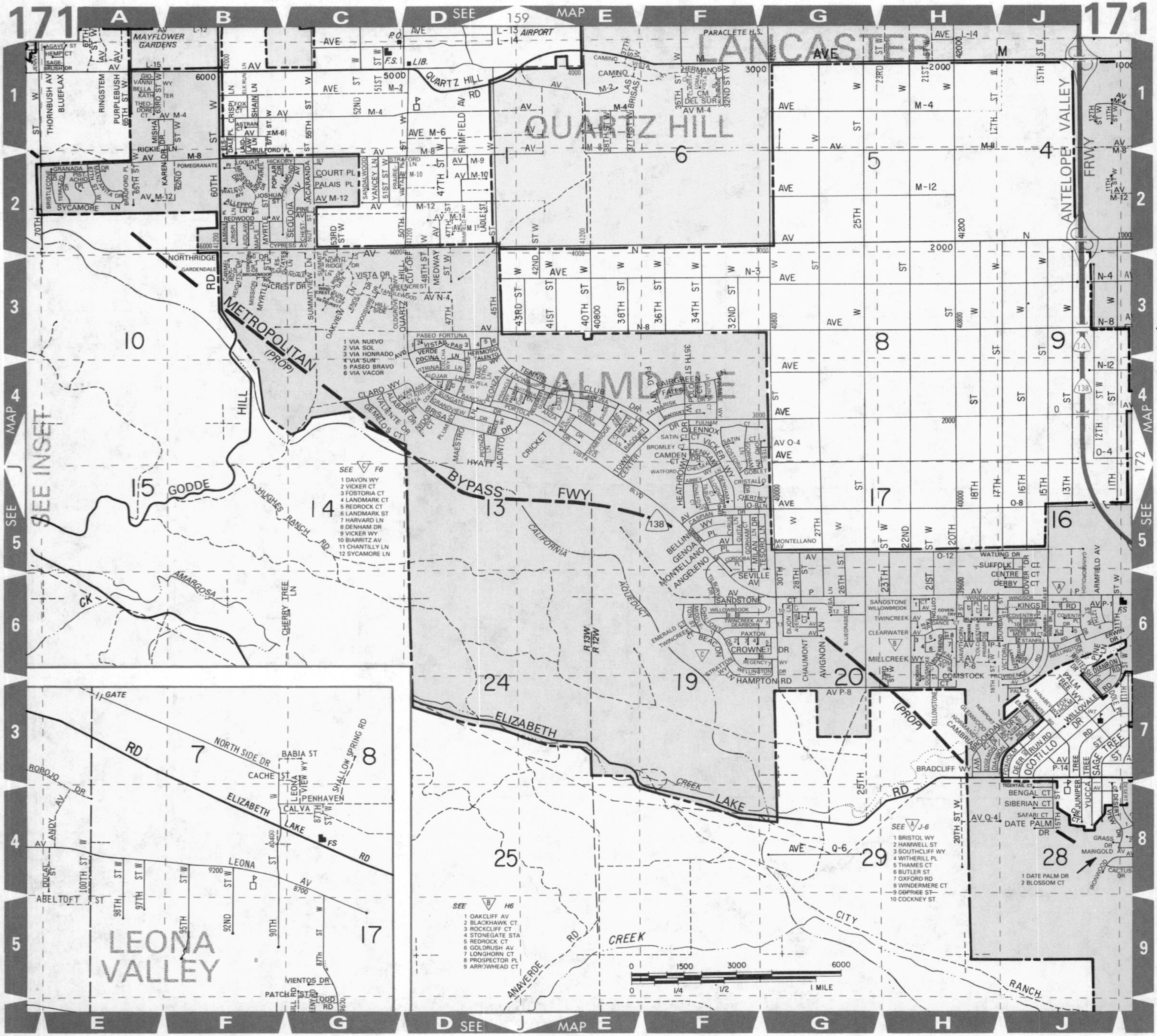

LOS ANGELES CO.

DETAIL

LANCASTER

QUARTZ HILL

PALMDALE

LEONA VALLEY

SEE INSET

METROPOLITAN (PROP)

BYPASS FWY

ELIZABETH LAKE

ANTELOPE VALLEY FRWY

COPYRIGHT, © 1989 BY Thomas Bros Maps

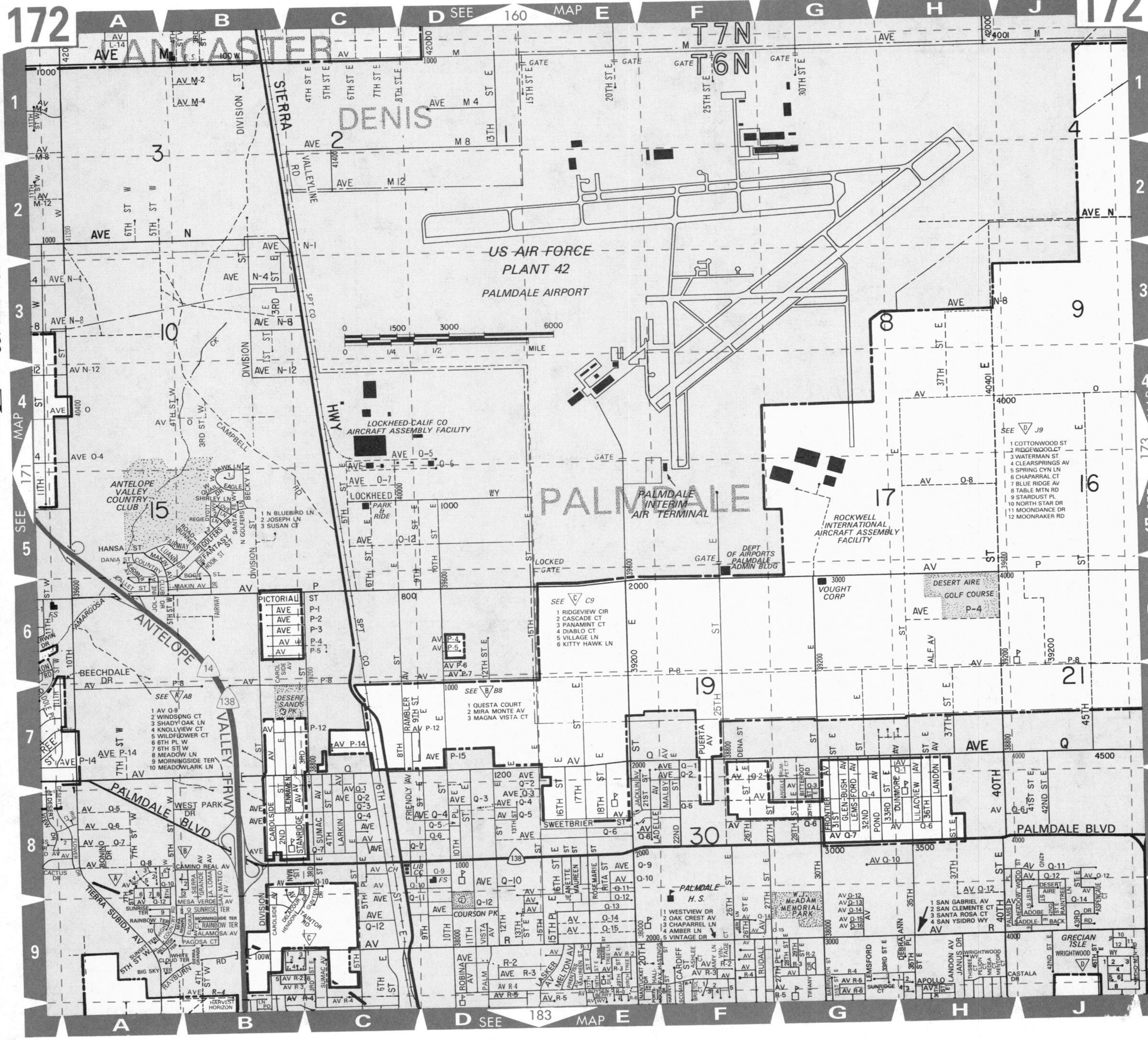

LANCASTER

DENIS

US AIR FORCE
PLANT 42
PALMDALE AIRPORT

PALMDALE

LOCKHEED-CALIF CO
AIRCRAFT ASSEMBLY FACILITY

ANTELOPE
VALLEY
COUNTRY
CLUB

PALMDALE
INTERIM
AIR TERMINAL

DEPT
OF AIRPORTS
PALMDALE
ADMIN BLDG

ROCKWELL
INTERNATIONAL
AIRCRAFT ASSEMBLY
FACILITY

VOUGHT
CORP

DESERT AIRE
GOLF COURSE

ANTELOPE

PALMDALE FRWY

PALMDALE BLVD

WEST PARK DR

PALMDALE
H.S.

MEMORIAL
PARK

COURSON PK

PALMDALE BLVD

GRECIAN ISLE

SEE MAP 160

SEE MAP 183

SEE 171 MAP

SEE 173 MAP

1 RIDGEVIEW CIR
2 CASCADE CT
3 PANAMINT CT
4 DIABLO CT
5 VILLAGE LN
6 KITTY HAWK LN

1 QUESTA COURT
2 MIRA MONTE AV
3 MAGNA VISTA CT

1 COTTONWOOD ST
2 RIDGEWOOD CT
3 WATERMAN ST
4 CLEARSPRINGS AV
5 SPRING CYN LN
6 CHAPARRAL CT
7 BLUE RIDGE AV
8 TABLE MTN RD
9 STARDUST PL
10 NORTH STAR DR
11 MOONDANCE DR
12 MOONRAKER RD

1 WESTVIEW DR
2 OAK CREST AV
3 CHAPARREL LN
4 AMBER LN
5 VINTAGE DR

1 SAN GABRIEL AV
2 SAN CLEMENTE CT
3 SANTA ROSA CT
4 SAN YSIDRO WY

1 N BLUEBIRD LN
2 JOSEPH CT
3 SUSAN CT

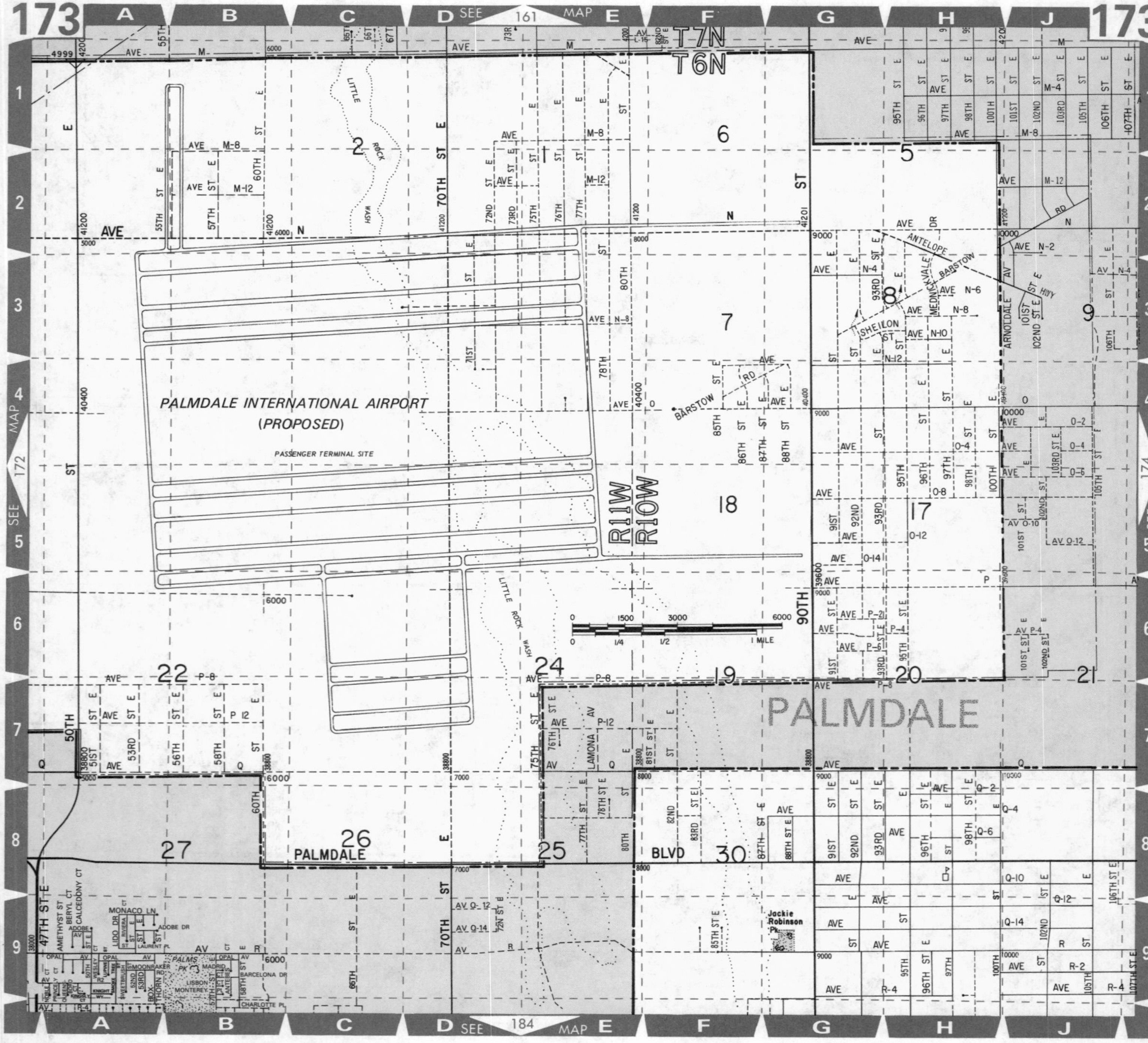

LOS ANGELES CO.

DETAIL

A B C D E F G H J

SEE 161 MAP

SEE 184 MAP

T7N
T6N

PALMDALE INTERNATIONAL AIRPORT
(PROPOSED)

PASSENGER TERMINAL SITE

R11W
R10W

PALMDALE

PALMDALE BLVD

LITTLE ROCK WASH

SEE 172 MAP

SEE 174 MAP

Jackie Robinson Pk.

0   1500   3000   6000
0   1/4   1/2   1 MILE

2 1 6 5
7 8 9
18 17
22 24 19 20 21
26 25 30 27

ANTELOPE BARSTOW MEDIAVALE SHEILON ARNOLDALE

50TH ST E
47TH ST E
70TH ST E
90TH
95TH 96TH 97TH 98TH 100TH 101ST 102ND 103RD 105TH 106TH 107TH

N

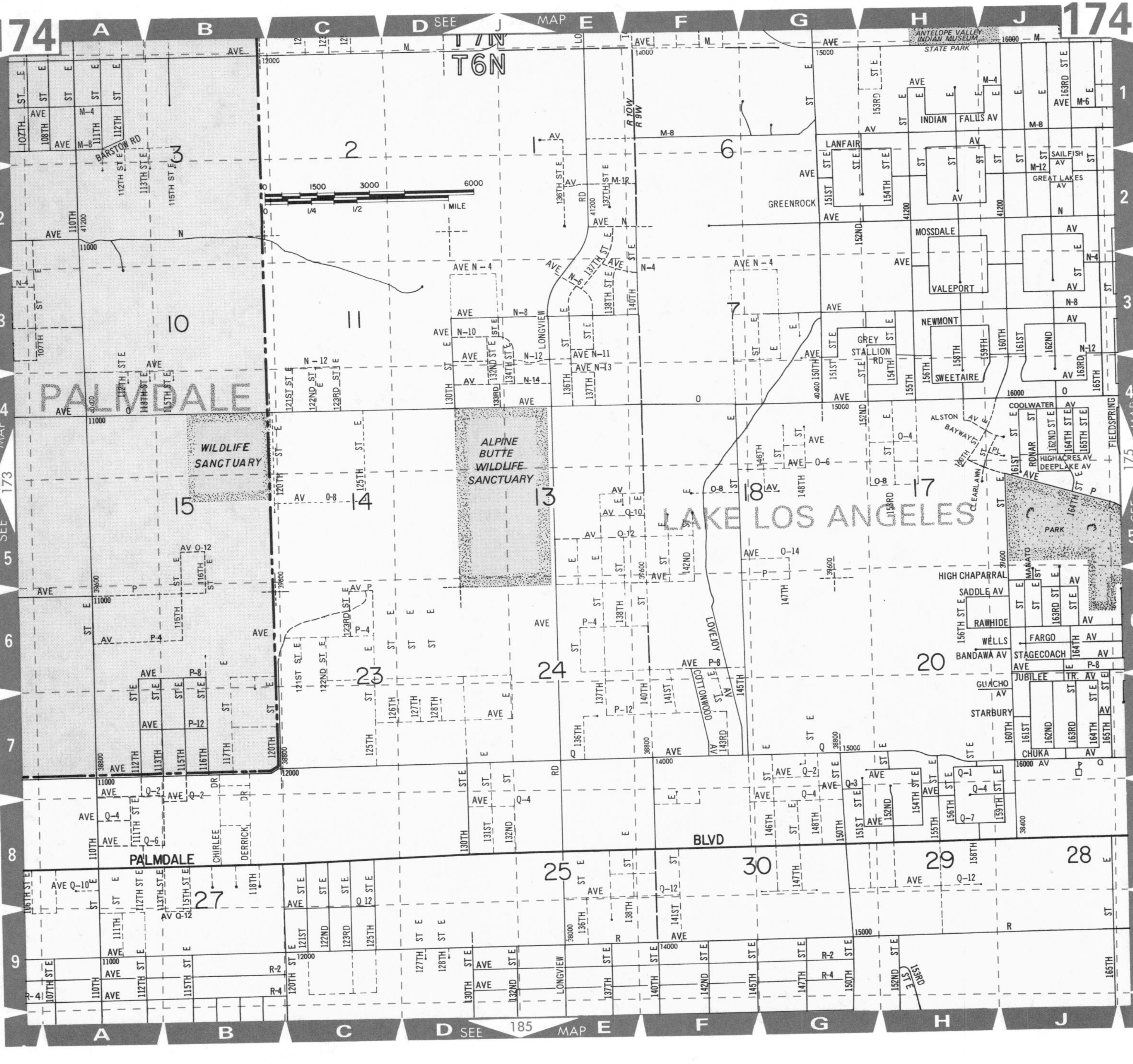

A B C D E F G H J

SEE MAP

T7N
T6N

COPYRIGHT, © 1989 BY Thomas Bros. Maps

N

SEE 173 MAP

SEE 175 MAP

ANTELOPE VALLEY INDIAN MUSEUM STATE PARK

PALMDALE

WILDLIFE SANCTUARY

ALPINE BUTTE WILDLIFE SANCTUARY

LAKE LOS ANGELES

PARK

Scale: 1/4 1/2 1 MILE (1500 3000 6000)

3 2 6

10 11 7

15 14 13 18 17

23 24 20

27 25 30 29 28

PALMDALE BLVD

Street / place labels:
107TH ST E, 108TH AVE, 110TH ST E, 111TH AVE, 112TH ST E, 113TH ST E, 115TH ST E, 116TH ST E, 117TH ST E, 120TH ST E, 121ST ST E, 122ND ST E, 123RD ST E, 125TH ST E, 126TH ST E, 127TH ST E, 128TH ST E, 130TH ST E, 131ST, 132ND ST E, 136TH ST E, 137TH ST E, 138TH ST E, 140TH, 141ST, 142ND, 143RD, 145TH, 146TH, 147TH, 148TH, 150TH, 151ST, 152ND, 153RD, 154TH, 155TH, 156TH, 158TH, 159TH, 160TH, 161ST, 162ND, 163RD ST E, 164TH, 165TH ST E, 166TH

BARSTOW RD

AVE M-4, M-8, N, N-4, N-8, N-10, N-11, N-12, N-13, N-14, O, O-4, O-6, O-8, O-12, O-14, P, P-4, P-8, P-12, Q, Q-2, Q-4, Q-6, Q-7, Q-10, Q-12, R, R-2, R-4

LONGVIEW

LANFAIR AV, INDIAN FALLS AV, SAILFISH, GREAT LAKES, GREENROCK, MOSSDALE, VALEPORT, NEWMONT, GREY STALLION RD, SWEETAIRE, COOLWATER, ALSTON AV, BAYWAY, CLEARLAWN, BONAR, HIGHACRES AV, DEEPLAKE AV, FIELDSPRING, MANATO, HIGH CHAPARRAL, SADDLE AV, RAWHIDE, FARGO, WELLS, BANDAWA AV, STAGECOACH, GUACHO AV, JUBILEE TR AV, STARBURY, CHUKA, CHIRLEE DR, DERRICK DR

LOVEJOY, COTTONWOOD

LOS ANGELES CO.

DETAIL

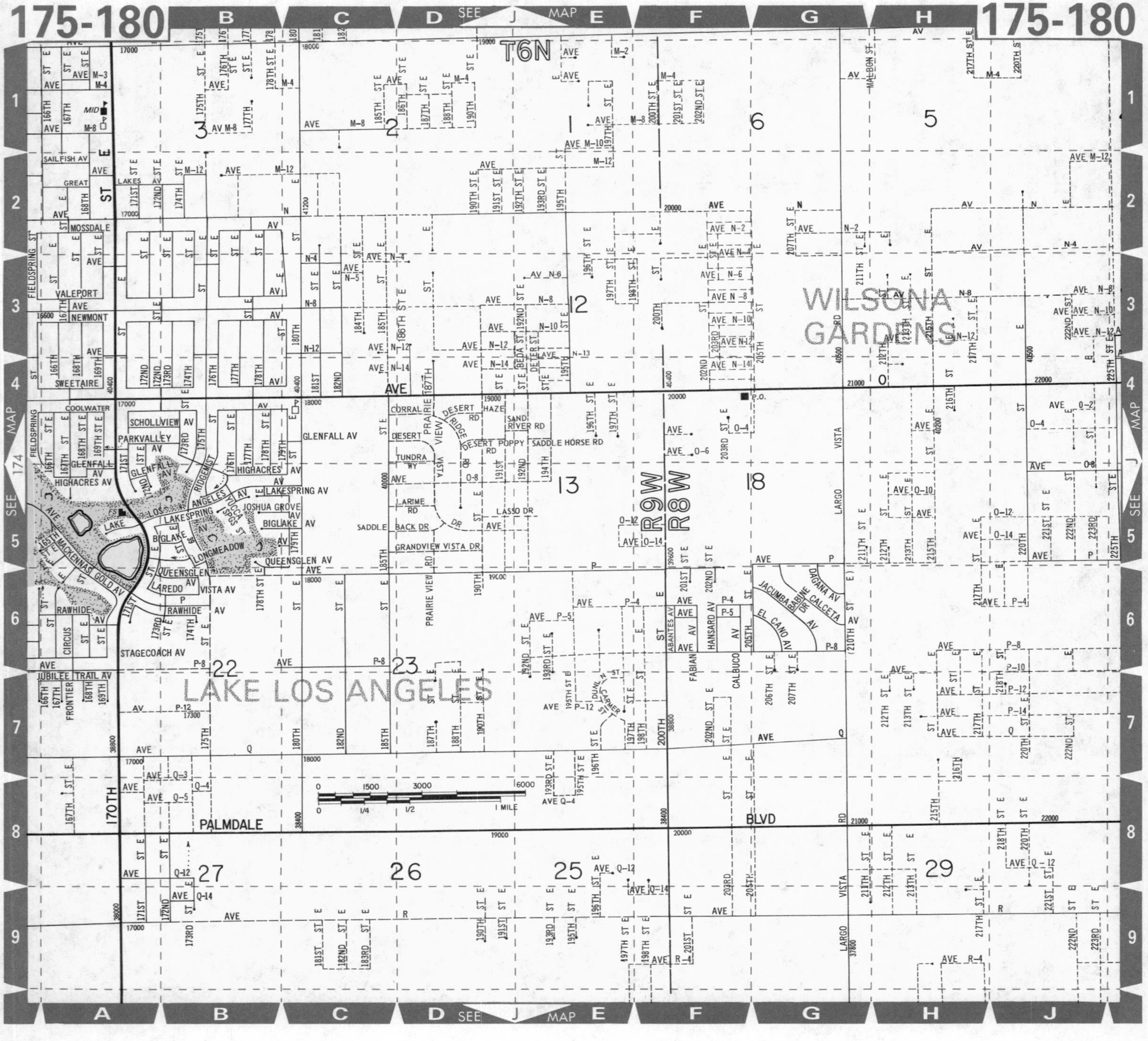

T6N

WILSONA GARDENS

LAKE LOS ANGELES

R9W   R8W

PALMDALE BLVD

SEE 174

SEE J

SEE MAP J

3   2   1   6   5

12   13   18

22   23

27   26   25   29

0   1500   3000   6000

0   1/4   1/2   1 MILE

170TH

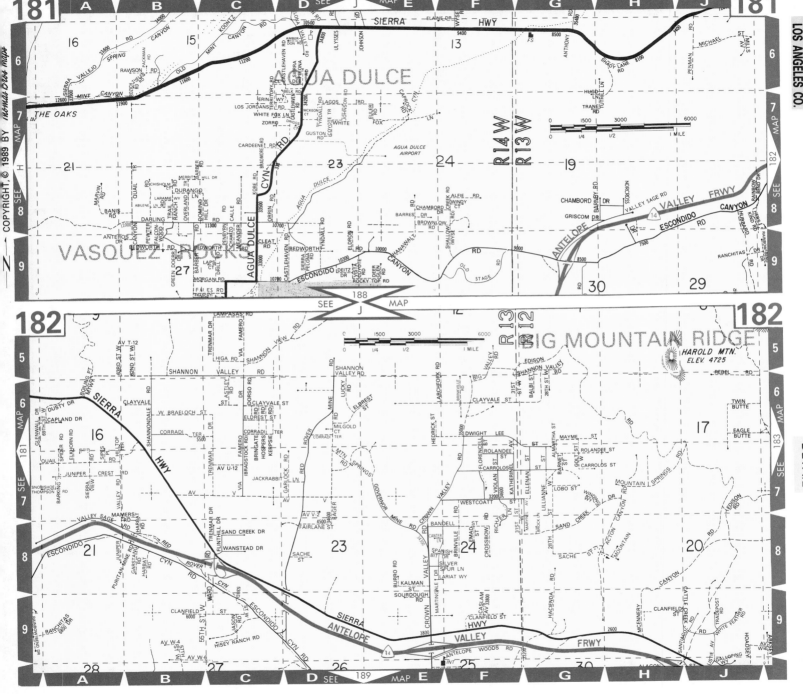

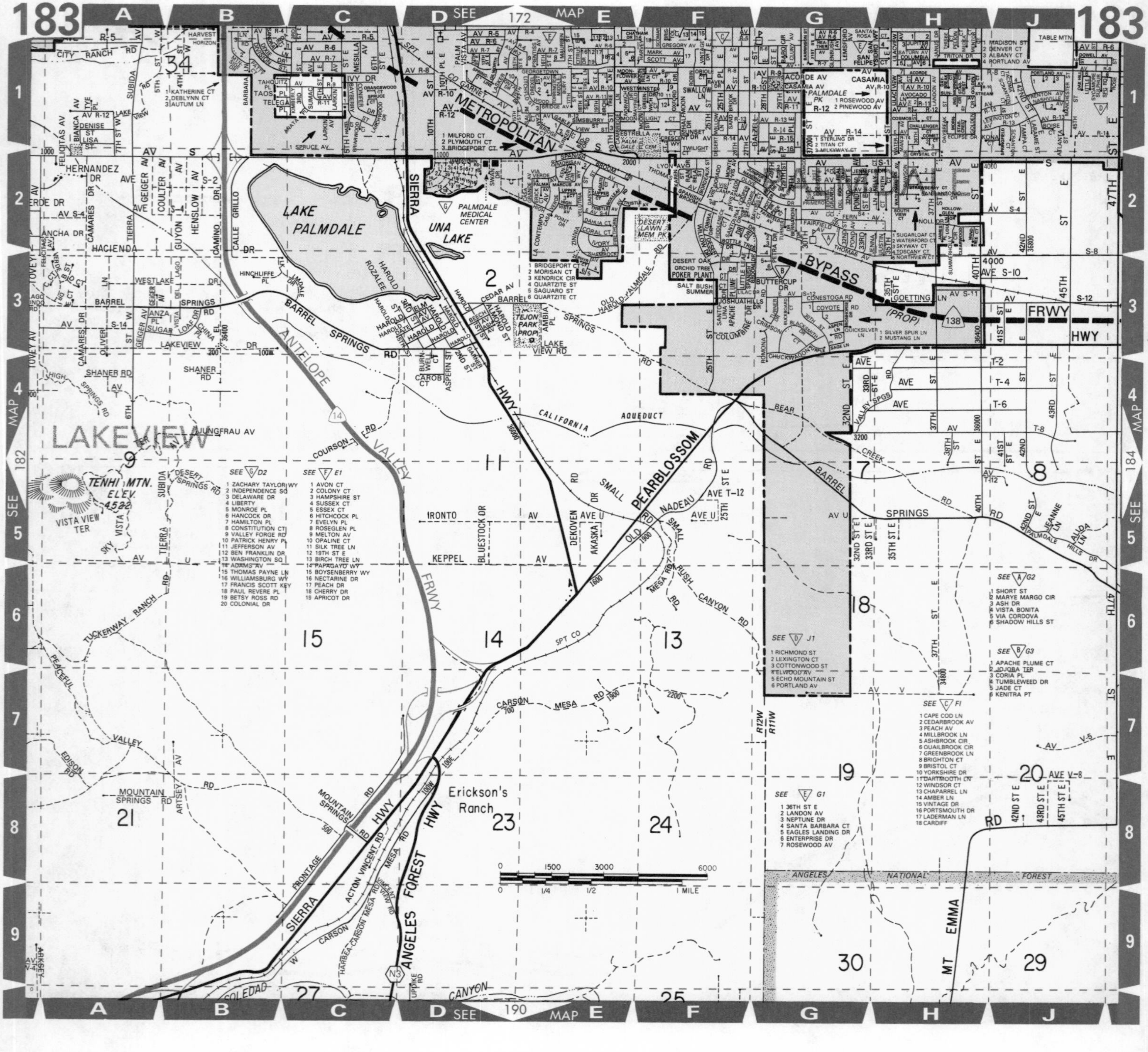

LOS ANGELES CO.

SEE 172 MAP

METROPOLITAN AV

PALMDALE

BYPASS (PROP) FRWY HWY

138

Lake
PALMDALE

UNA LAKE

SIERRA HWY

Palmdale Medical Center

DESERT LAWN MEM PK

SALT BUSH SUMMER

JOSHUAHILLS DR

CALIFORNIA AQUEDUCT

ANTELOPE VALLEY FRWY

BARREL SPRINGS RD

LAKEVIEW

TENHI MTN.
ELEV. 4522

VISTA VIEW TER

SEE 182 MAP

9

H

PEARBLOSSOM

SMALL CANYON RD

IRONTO AV

KEPPEL AV

DEKOVEN AV

AKASKA

OLD NADEAU RD

AVE T-12

AVE U

15

14

13

18

19

20 AVE V-8

21

23 Erickson's Ranch

24

SIERRA HWY

ANGELES FOREST HWY

MOUNTAIN SPRINGS RD

CARSON MESA RD

SOLEDAD CANYON

27

30

MT EMMA RD

MT EMMA

29

ANGELES NATIONAL FOREST

SEE 184 MAP

SEE 190 MAP

0 1500 3000 6000
0 1/4 1/2 1 MILE

SEE D2
1 ZACHARY TAYLOR WY
2 INDEPENDENCE SQ
3 DELAWARE DR
4 LIBERTY
5 MONROE PL
6 HANCOCK DR
7 HAMILTON PL
8 CONSTITUTION CT
9 VALLEY FORGE RD
10 PATRICK HENRY PL
11 JEFFERSON AV
12 BEN FRANKLIN DR
13 WASHINGTON SQ
14 ADAMS AV
15 THOMAS PAYNE LN
16 WILLIAMSBURG WY
17 FRANCIS SCOTT KEY
18 PAUL REVERE PL
19 BETSY ROSS RD
20 COLONIAL DR

SEE E1
1 AVON CT
2 COLONY CT
3 HAMPSHIRE ST
4 SUSSEX ST
5 ESSEX CT
6 HITCHCOCK PL
7 EVELYN PL
8 ROSEGLEN PL
9 MELTON AV
10 OPALINE CT
11 SILK TREE LN
12 19TH ST E
13 BIRCH TREE LN
14 PAPRGAYE WY
15 BOYSENBERRY WY
16 NECTARINE DR
17 PEACH DR
18 CHERRY DR
19 APRICOT DR

SEE J1
1 RICHMOND ST
2 LEXINGTON CT
3 COTTONWOOD ST
4 PELWROLL WY
5 ECHO MOUNTAIN ST
6 PORTLAND AV

SEE G2
1 SHORT ST
2 MARYE MARGO CIR
3 ASH AV
4 VISTA BONITA
5 VIA CORDOVA
6 SHADOW HILLS ST

SEE G3
1 APACHE PLUME CT
2 JOJOBA TER
3 CORIA PL
4 TUMBLEWEED DR
5 JADE CT
6 KENITRA PT

SEE FI
1 CAPE COD LN
2 CEDARBROOK AV
3 PEACH AV
4 MILLBROOK LN
5 ASHBROOK CIR
6 QUAILBROOK LN
7 GREENBROOK LN
8 BRIGHTON CT
9 BRISTOL CT
10 YORKSHIRE DR
11 DARTMOUTH LN
12 WINDSOR CT
13 CHAPARREL LN
14 AMBER LN
15 VINTAGE DR
16 PORTSMOUTH DR
17 LADERMAN LN
18 CARDIFF

SEE G1
1 36TH ST E
2 LANDON AV
3 NEPTUNE DR
4 SANTA BARBARA CT
5 EAGLES LANDING DR
6 ENTERPRISE DR
7 ROSEWOOD AV

PALMDALE
PK
1 ROSEWOOD AV
2 PINEWOOD AV

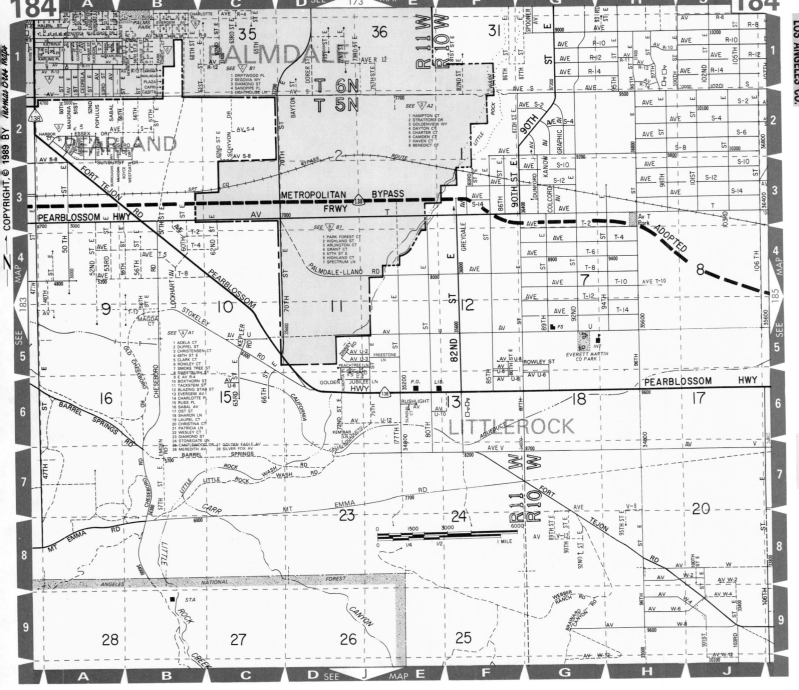

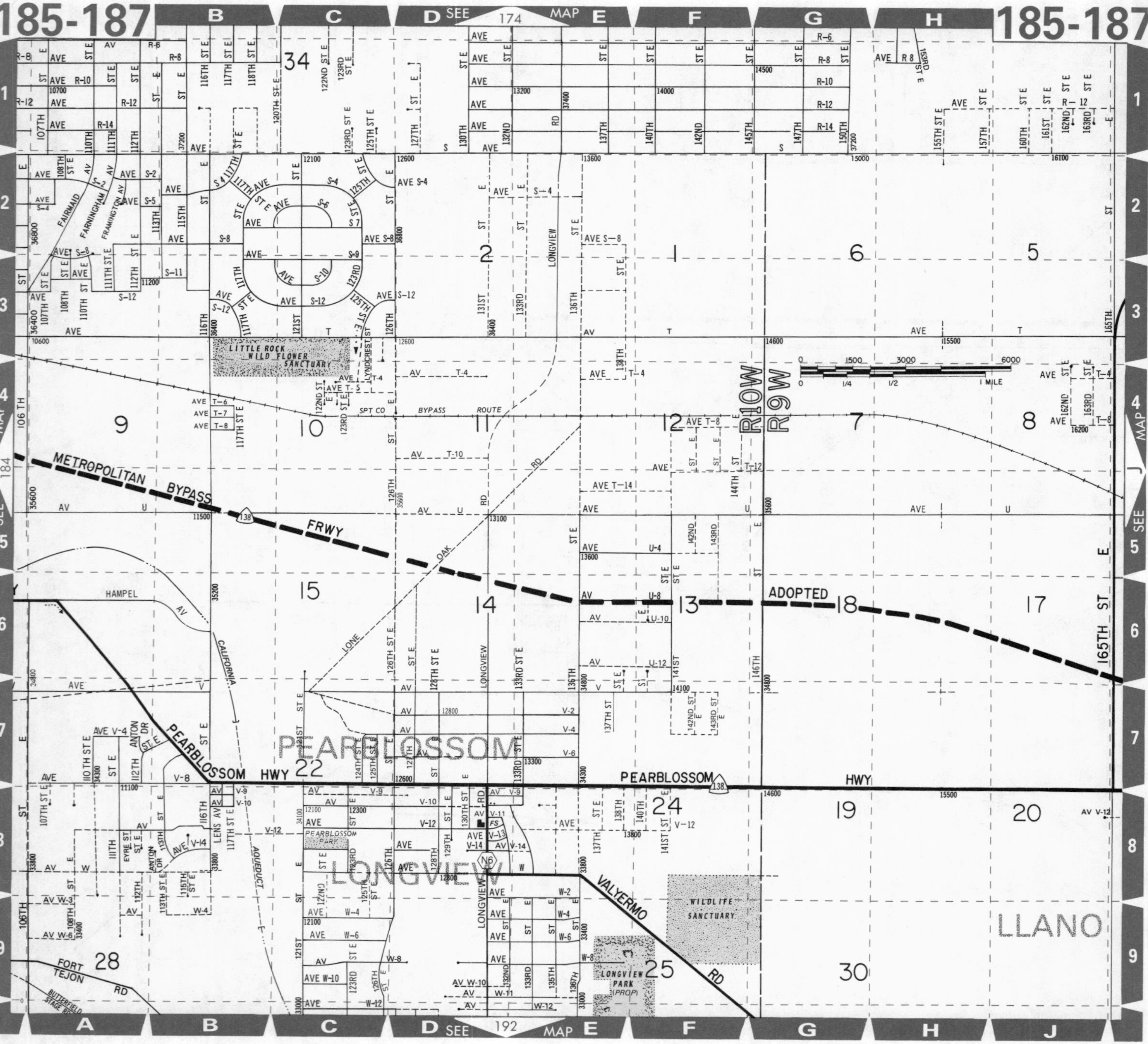

LOS ANGELES CO.

DETAIL

SEE 174 MAP

A B C D E F G H J

34

LITTLE ROCK WILD FLOWER SANCTUARY

METROPOLITAN BYPASS FRWY

R10W R9W

ADOPTED

PEARBLOSSOM HWY

PEARBLOSSOM

PEARBLOSSOM HWY

LONGVIEW

VALYERMO RD

WILDLIFE SANCTUARY

LLANO

PEARBLOSSOM PARK

LONGVIEW PARK (PROP)

FORT TEJON RD

BUTTERFIELD STAGE RD

0 1500 3000 6000
0 1/4 1/2 1 MILE

SEE 184 MAP

SEE MAP

165TH ST E

9 10 11 12 7 8

15 14 13 18 17

22 24 19 20

28 25 30

2 1 6 5

SEE 192 MAP

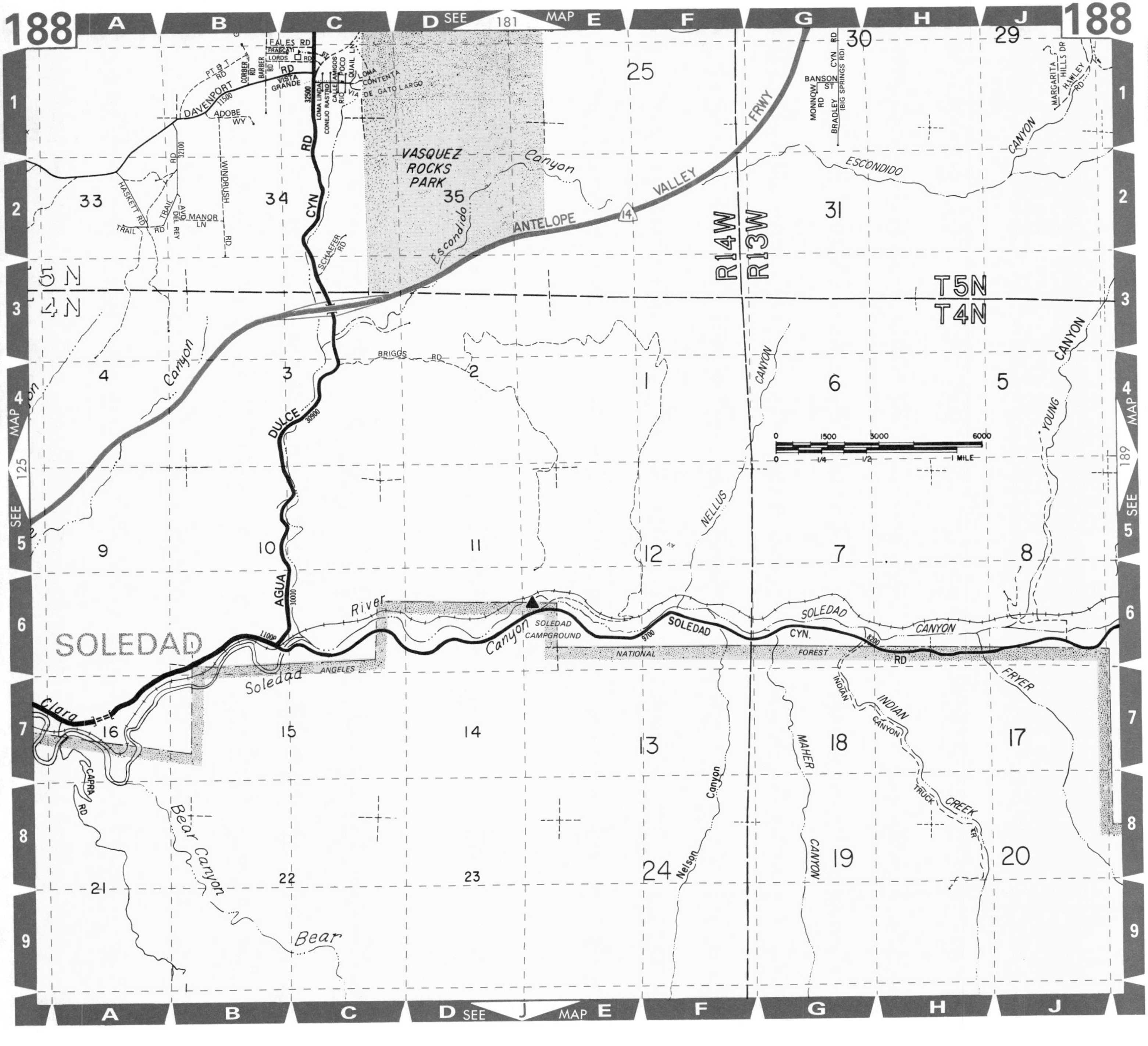

LOS ANGELES CO.

DETAIL

SEE MAP 125

SEE 189 MAP

FALES RD
THARP RD
LORDS RD
PT 9 T
RD
CORBER RD
BARBER RD
ADOBE WY
VISTA GRANDE
CONEJO RD
LOMA LINDA RD
CALLE LA MOS
RIO HONDO COCO
VIA DE QUAIL
LOMA CONTENTA
DE GATO LARGO

DAVENPORT

33 34

VASQUEZ ROCKS PARK

25

35

Canyon

Escondido

ANTELOPE

VALLEY

FRWY

14

ESCONDIDO

BANSON CYN RD
BANSON ST
MONNOW RD
BRADLEY (BIG SPRINGS RD)

30 29

MARGARITA
MARGARITA HILLS DR
HAWLEY RD

31

R14W R13W

T5N T4N

WINDRUSH RD

HASKETT RD
TRAIL RD
AVG MANOR LN
AVG DEL REY

SCHAEFER RD

CYN RD

BRIGGS RD

Canyon

4 3 2 1 6 5

YOUNG CANYON

0 1500 3000 6000
0 1/4 1/2 1 MILE

DULCE

AGUA

NELLUS CANYON

9 10 11 12 7 8

SOLEDAD

River

Soledad

Canyon

Angeles

SOLEDAD CAMPGROUND

NATIONAL

5700

SOLEDAD

CYN.

FOREST

SOLEDAD

3300

CANYON

RD

FRYER

Clara

16 15 14 13 18 17

CARRA RD

Bear Canyon

MAHER CANYON

Nelson Canyon

INDIAN CANYON

INDIAN

TRUCK CREEK

21 22 23 24 19 20

Bear

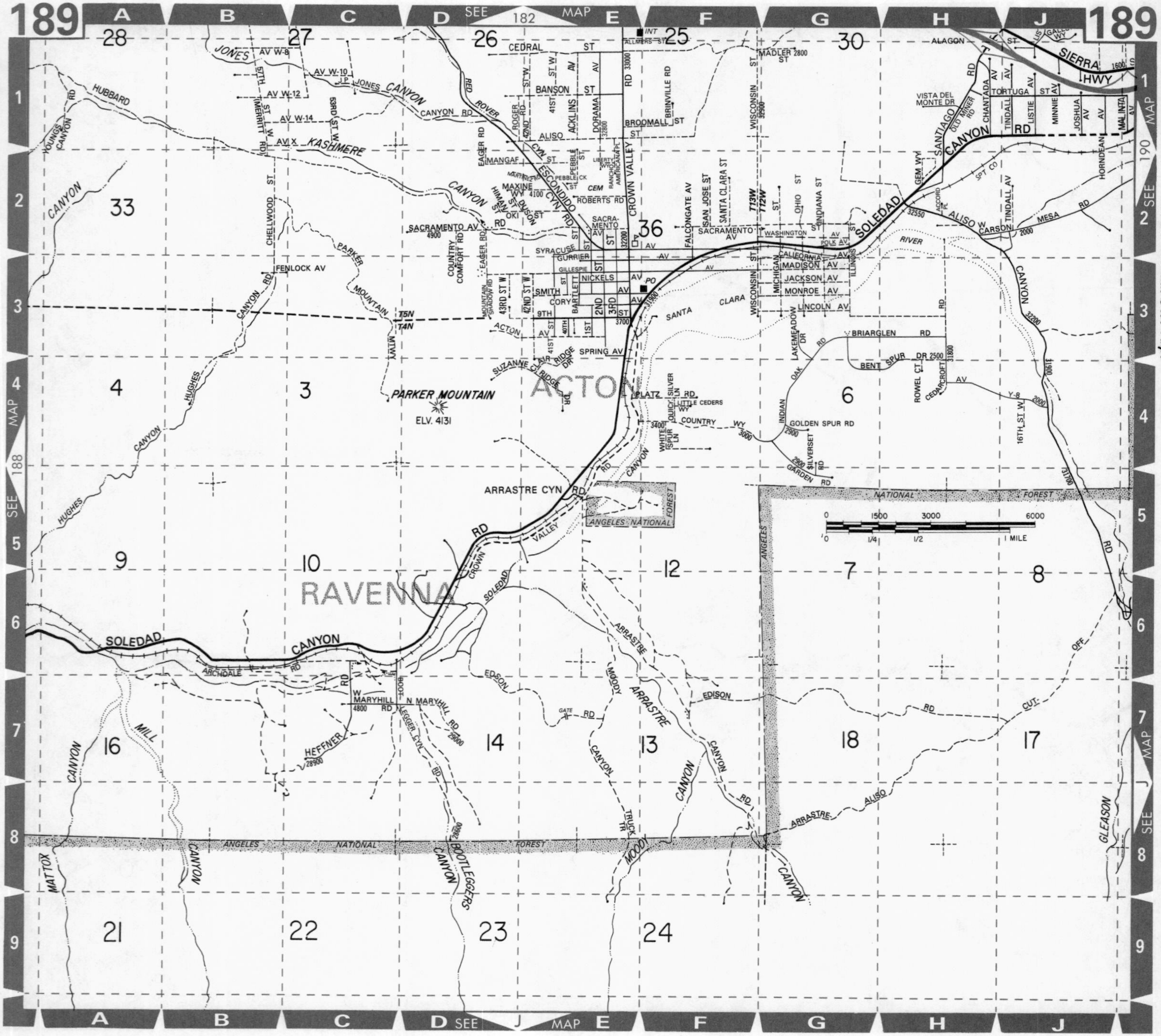

LOS ANGELES CO.

189

SEE 182 MAP

189

COPYRIGHT © 1989 BY Thomas Bros. Maps

SEE 190 MAP →

DETAIL

A B C D E F G H J

28 27 26 25 30

SIERRA HWY

1

JONES AV W-8
8TH ST W
JONES CANYON
AV W-10
J.F.
AV W-12
63RD ST W
TIMBERIT RD
CANYON RD
RED ROVER
AV W-14
AV X
KASHMERE
CEDRAL ST
BANSON ST
ST W
AV
41ST ST W
ACKLINS ST
DORAMA ST
RD 33000
BRINVILLE RD
BRODMALL ST
WISCONSIN 22900
MADLER 2800 ST
ALAGON
VISTA DEL MONTE DR
CHANTADA AV
TORTUGA AV
TINDALL RD
LISTIE AV
MINNIE AV
JOSHUA AV
MALINTA
GALL WY
SANTIAGO CANYON RD
GEM WY
OLD RIVER RD
SPT CO
HUBBARD RD
YOUNGS CANYON RD
MERRITT RD

2

33
CANYON RD
CHELLWOOD
ECONDIDO CYN RD
ESCONDIDO CANYON RD
EAGER RD
MANGAF
PEBBLE
MAXINE WY 4100
HIMA WY
DENISON
OKI
CEM
CROWN VALLEY
LIBERTY ST
RANCHO
MINT
SANTA CLARA ST
SAN JOSE ST
FALCONGATE AV
ROBERTS RD
SACRAMENTO AV
OHIO ST
INDIANA ST
SOLEDAD
RIVER
ALISO W
CARSONI RD
MESA 2000
GEM WY
ACCORD
SANTIAGO CANYON RD
AV 17550

3

PARKER
FENLOCK AV
COUNTRY COMFORT RD
EAGER RD
MOUNTAIN
T5N T4N
SACRAMENTO AV 4900
3RD ST W
SMITH
CORY
SYRACUSE
GURRIER
GILLESPIE
NICKELS
BARTLET
MOUNTAIN SHADOW RD
43RD ST W
2ND ST W
9TH
41ST ST
40TH
1ST
2ND
3RD ST
ST
PO
SACRAMENTO AV
WASHINGTON AV
CALIEORNIA AV
MADISON AV
MICHIGAN
WISCONSIN
JACKSON AV
MONROE AV
LINCOLN AV
SANTA CLARA
BRIARGLEN RD
LAKEMEADOW DR
OAK
INDIAN
CANYON RD 33200

4

4
3
PARKER MOUNTAIN
ELV. 4131
HUGHES CANYON RD
SUZANNE
RIDGE DR
PLATZ
ACTON
SILVER RD
LITTLE CEDERS LN
CHURCH LN
WHITE FISHER LN
COUNTRY WY 3600
SPRING AV
ARRASTRE CYN RD
CANYON RD
BENT SPUR DR
GOLDEN SPUR RD
ROWEL CT 2500
CEDARCROFT AV
SILVERSET
GARDEN RD
6
16TH ST W
Y-8 2000
11800

5

9
10
HUGHES CANYON RD
CROWN
SOLEDAD CANYON RD
VALLEY RD
ARRASTRE CYN RD
ANGELES NATIONAL FOREST
12
NATIONAL
FOREST
1500 3000 6000
0 1/4 1/2 MILE
7
8
ANGELES CANYON RD

6

RAVENNA
SOLEDAD
CANYON
ARCHDALE RD
ARRASTRE
CANYON
OFF

7

16
MILL CANYON
HEFFNER 28900
W MARYHILL RD 4800
N MARYHILL RD 29000
BOOGY
LEGGER CYN RD
EDSON RD
GATE RD
14
MOODY
ARRASTRE CANYON
13
EDISON RD
18
ARRASTRE RD
ALISO CANYON
17
GLEASON CANYON

8

MATTOX CANYON
CANYON
ANGELES
NATIONAL
BOOTLEGGERS CANYON
FOREST
MOODY CANYON
ARRASTRE CANYON

9

21
22
23
24

A B C D E F G H J
SEE J MAP

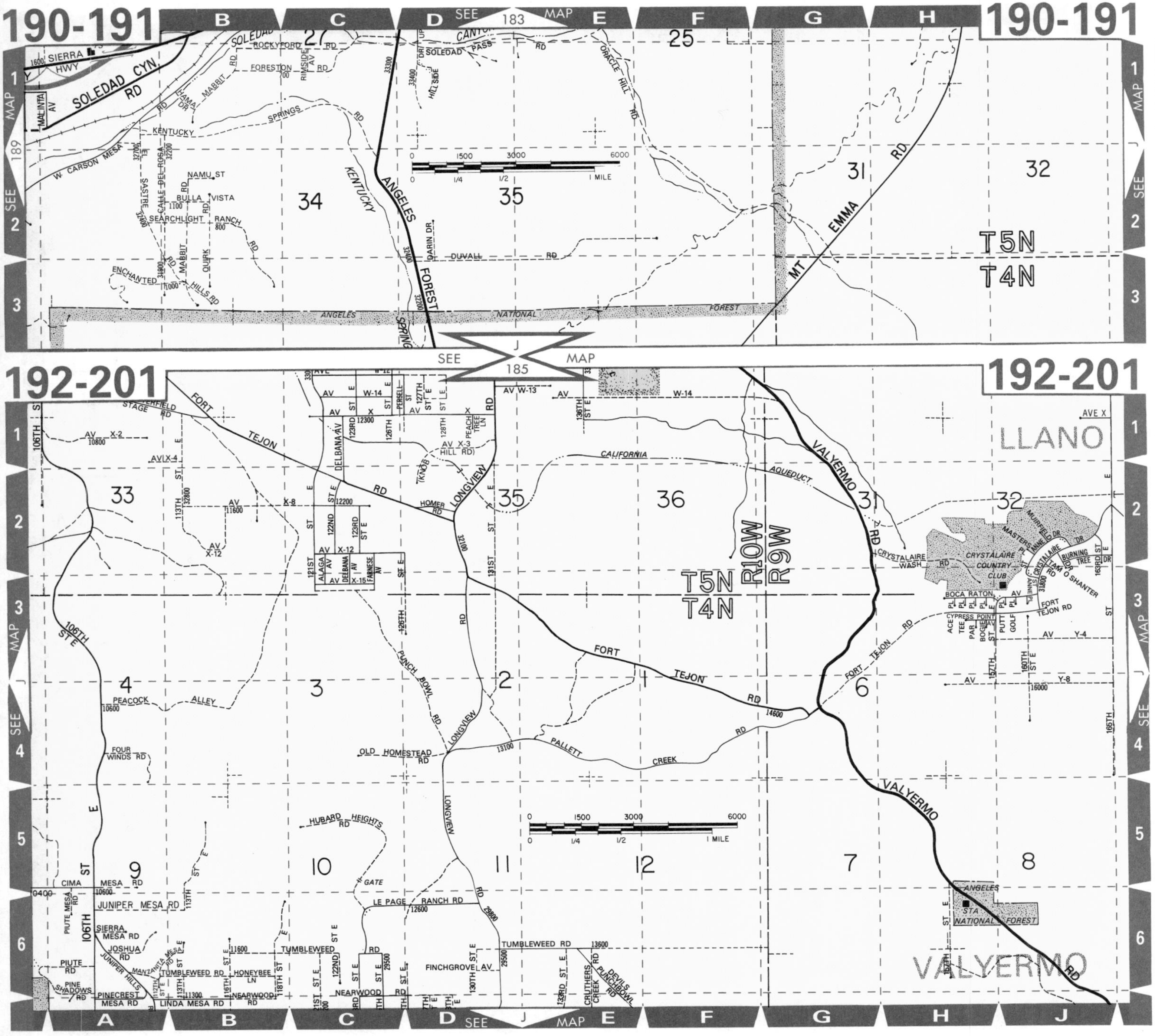

LOS ANGELES CO.

A B C D SEE 183 MAP E F G H

SEE MAP 189

Y

1600 SIERRA HWY

MALINTA AV

SOLEDAD CYN RD

SOLEDAD RD ROCKYFORD 27

CANYON SOLEDAD PASS RD 25

FORESTON 700

RIMSIDE RD

DRIFT

HILLSIDE

3300

3900

ORACLE HILL RD

MABBIT RD

PLAMA DR

EMMA DR

KENTUCKY

SPRINGS RD

W. CARSON MESA RD

CALLE DEL ROBO

SASTRE RD

BULLA VISTA

NAMU ST

1100

SEARCHLIGHT 1300

RANCH RD 800

QUIRK RD

34

KENTUCKY

ANGELES

35

31

32

T5N
T4N

ENCHANTED 11000

MABBIT RD

HILLS RD

DUVALL RD

DARIN DR

FOREST SPRINGS 3200 3200

MT EMMA RD

ANGELES NATIONAL FOREST

1 2 3

0 1500 3000 6000
0 1/4 1/2 1 MILE

SEE J MAP

SEE 185 MAP

A B C D SEE J MAP E F G H J

SEE MAP

DETAIL

106TH ST

ENFIELD RD

STAGE RD

FORT

AVE X-2 10800

AV X-4

TEJON

330 AVE

W-14

PERSELL ST E

127TH ST E

128TH ST E

PEACH TREE LN

AV W-13 AV

136TH ST E

W-14

AVE X

LLANO

VALYERMO RD

AQUEDUCT

CALIFORNIA

33

113TH ST E 12000

AV X-12 11600

AV X-12

AV K-8

DELBANA AV

123RD ST

12300

126TH ST E

123RD

AV X-3 HILL RD

TKIKI

HOMER RD

LONGVIEW

35

191ST ST

36

31

32

CRYSTALAIRE WASH

MASTERS

CRYSTALAIRE COUNTRY CLUB

TAM O SHANTER DR

BURNING TREE DR

T5N
T4N

R10W
R9W

BOCA RATON PL

121ST ST

ALAGA AV

DELBANA

FINESSE AV

122ND RD

126TH ST E

RD

4

PEACOCK 10600

3

PUNCH BOWL RD

2

FORT

1

TEJON

RD 14600

6

CYPRESS POINT PL

TEE AV

BOGEE ST

PUTT PL

GOLF PL

ACE PL

FORT TEJON RD

152ND ST E

160TH ST E

AV Y-4

AV Y-8

16000

ALLEY

FOUR WINDS RD

OLD HOMESTEAD RD

13100

PALLETT CREEK

LONGVIEW

VALYERMO

CIMA MESA RD 10600

9

JUNIPER MESA RD

113TH ST E

HUBABD HEIGHTS RD

GATE

10

LE PAGE RANCH RD 12600

11

TUMBLEWEED RD 13600

12

7

ANGELES STA NATIONAL FOREST

8

VALYERMO

0400

106TH ST E

SIERRA MESA RD

JOSHUA RD

JUNIPER HILLS RD

PIUTE MESA RD 10600

11600

MANZANITA

TUMBLEWEED RD

HONEYBEE LN

118TH ST E

NEARWOOD RD

122ND ST E

126TH ST E

130TH ST E

FINCHGROVE AV

133RD ST E

CRUTHERS CREEK RD

DEVILS PUNCH BOWL RD

PIUTE RD

PINE SHADOWS

PINECREST RD

MESA RD

LINDA MESA RD

21ST ST E 11300

0 1500 3000 6000
0 1/4 1/2 1 MILE

1990 LOS ANGELES COUNTY
ZIP CODE POSTAL ZONES

LOS ANGELES CO.

COMMUNITY	ZIP CODE	PAGE	GRID	COMMUNITY	ZIP CODE	PAGE	GRID
AGOURA	91301	202	C4	MANHATTAN BEACH	90266	204	A3
ALHAMBRA	91801-91803	203	F4	MARINA DEL REY	90292	204	A1
ALTADENA	91001	203	F2	MAYWOOD	90270	203	E6
ARCADIA	91006-91007	205	A1	MONROVIA	91016	205	B1
ARTESIA	90701	204	F3	MONTEBELLO	90640	203	F5
AZUSA	91702	205	C1	MONTEREY PARK	91754	203	F5
BALDWIN PARK	91706	205	B2	MONTROSE	91020	203	D2
BELL	90201	204	E2	NORTH HOLLYWOOD	91601-91609	203	B3
BELLFLOWER	90706	204	E3	NORTHRIDGE	91324-91330	202	F2
BEVERLY HILLS	90210-90213	203	B4	NORWALK	90650	204	F3
BURBANK	91501-91506	203	C2	PACIFIC PALISADES	90272	202	E5
CALABASAS	91302	202	C4	PACOIMA	91331	203	A1
CANOGA PARK	91303-91307	202	D2	PALOS VERDES PEN	90274	204	A5
CARSON	90745-90747	204	C4	PARAMOUNT	90723	204	E3
CHATSWORTH	91311	202	D1	PASADENA	91101-91126	203	F3
CLAREMONT	91711	205	F2	PICO RIVERA	90660	204	F1
COMPTON	90220-90224	204	D3	PLAYA DEL REY	90293	204	A2
COVINA	91722-91724	205	D2	POMONA	91765-91769	205	E3
CULVER CITY	90230-90232	203	B6	REDONDO BEACH	90277-90278	204	A4
DIAMOND BAR	91765	205	E4	RESEDA	91335	202	E3
DOWNEY	90240-90242	204	E2	ROSEMEAD	91770	203	F5
DUARTE	91010	205	B1	SAN DIMAS	91773	205	D2
EAGLE ROCK	90041	203	E3	SAN FERNANDO	91340-91345	202	F1
EL MONTE	91731-91734	205	A3	SAN GABRIEL	91775-91776	203	F4
EL SEGUNDO	90245	204	A2	SAN PEDRO	90731-90733	204	C6
ENCINO (VAN NUYS)	91316	202	F4	SANTA FE SPRINGS	90670	204	F2
GARDENA	90247-90249	204	C3	SANTA MONICA	90401-90406	202	F6
GLENDALE	91201-91214	203	D3	SIERRA MADRE	91024	205	A1
GLENDORA	91740	205	D1	SOUTH GATE	90280	204	D2
HARBOR CITY	90710	204	C5	SOUTH PASADENA	91030	203	E4
HAWAIIAN GARDEN	90716	204	F4	SUNLAND	91040	203	B2
HAWTHORNE	90250	204	B3	SUN VALLEY	91352	203	B2
HERMOSA BEACH	90254	204	A3	TARZANA	91356	202	E4
HUNTINGTON PARK	90255	204	D1	TEMPLE CITY	91780	205	A2
INGLEWOOD	90301-90310	204	B2	TOPANGA	90290	202	D4
LA CANADA-FLINTRIDGE	91011	203	E2	TORRANCE	90501-90510	204	B4
LA HABRA HEIGHTS	90631	205	C5	TUJUNGA	91042	203	D1
LAKEWOOD	90712-90716	204	E4	VAN NUYS	91401-91436	203	A3
LA MIRADA	90637-90639	205	B6	VENICE	90291	204	A6
LA PUENTE	91744-91748	205	B4	VERDUGO CITY	91046	203	D2
LA VERNE	91750	205	E1	WALNUT	91789	205	D3
LAWNDALE	90260-90261	204	B3	WEST COVINA	91790-91793	205	C3
LOMITA	90717	204	B5	WESTLAKE VILLAGE	91361	202	A4
LONG BEACH	90801-90840	204	D5	WHITTIER	90601-90608	205	A4
LOS ANGELES	90001-90089	203	C6	WILMINGTON	90744	204	C5
LYNWOOD	90262	204	D2	WOODLAND HILLS	91364-91367	202	D3
MALIBU	90265	202	B5				

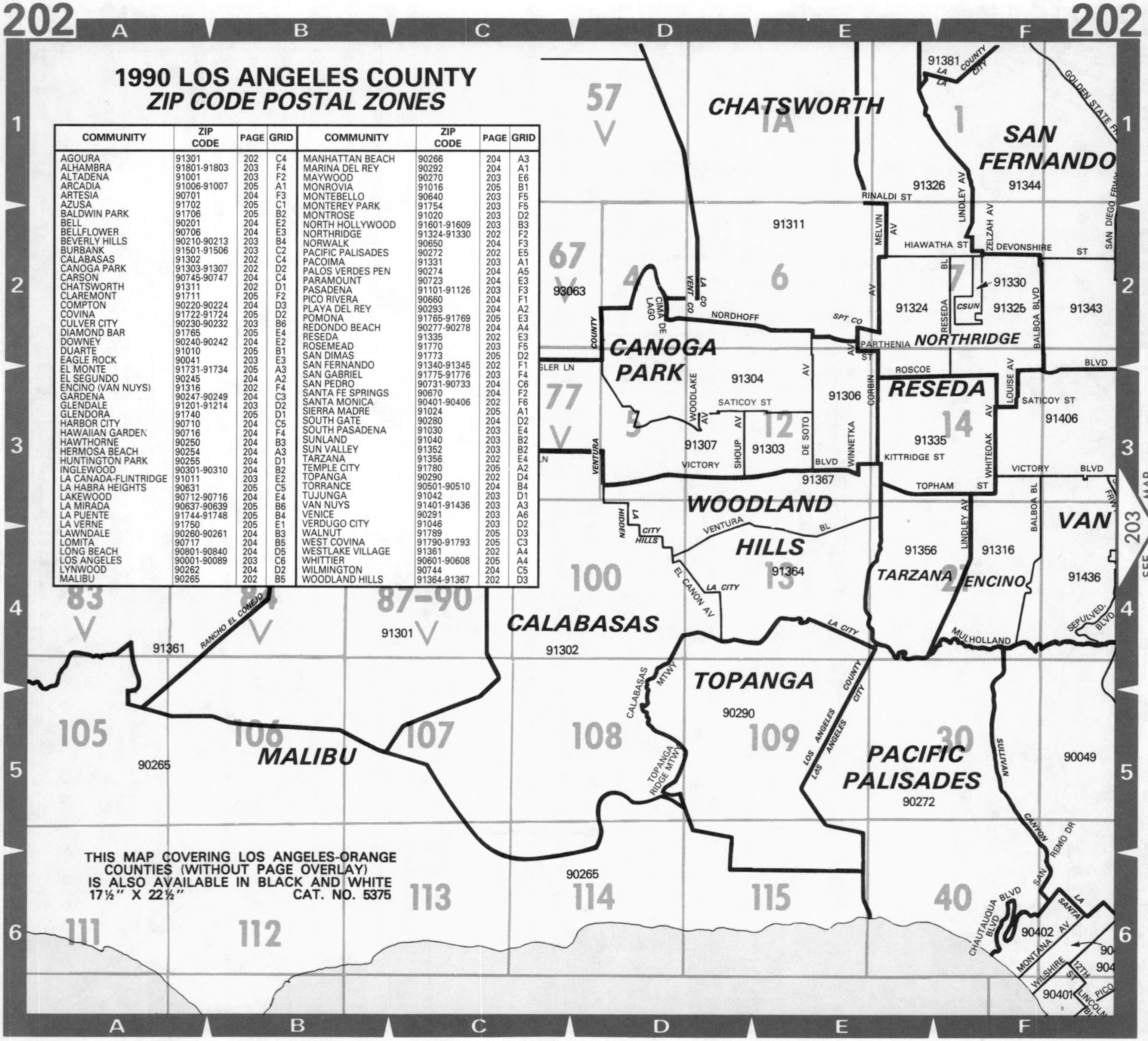

THIS MAP COVERING LOS ANGELES-ORANGE
COUNTIES (WITHOUT PAGE OVERLAY)
IS ALSO AVAILABLE IN BLACK AND WHITE
17½" X 22½"   CAT. NO. 5375

ZIP FRWY

CHATSWORTH

SAN FERNANDO

91381
91326
91344
91311
91324
91330
91325
91343

NORTHRIDGE

CANOGA PARK

RESEDA

91304
91306
91335
91307
91303
91367
91356
91316
91406
91436

WOODLAND HILLS

TARZANA

VAN

ENCINO

91364

CALABASAS

91302

TOPANGA

90290

PACIFIC PALISADES

90272

MALIBU

90265

90265

90049

90402
90401

57
67
77
83
84
87-90
91301
91361
100
105
106
107
108
109
30
113
114
115
40
111
112
1A
1
6
7
4
5
12
14
13
2

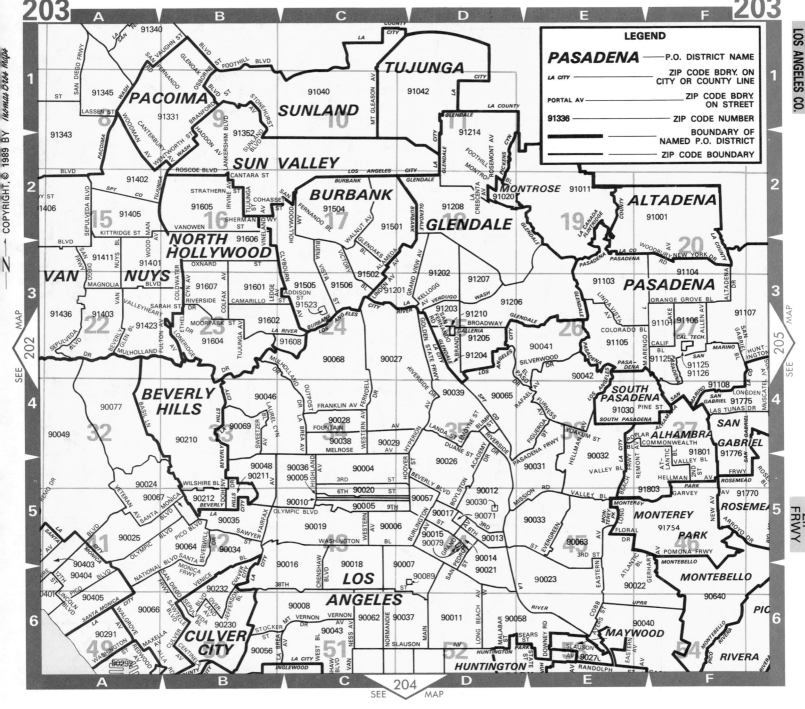

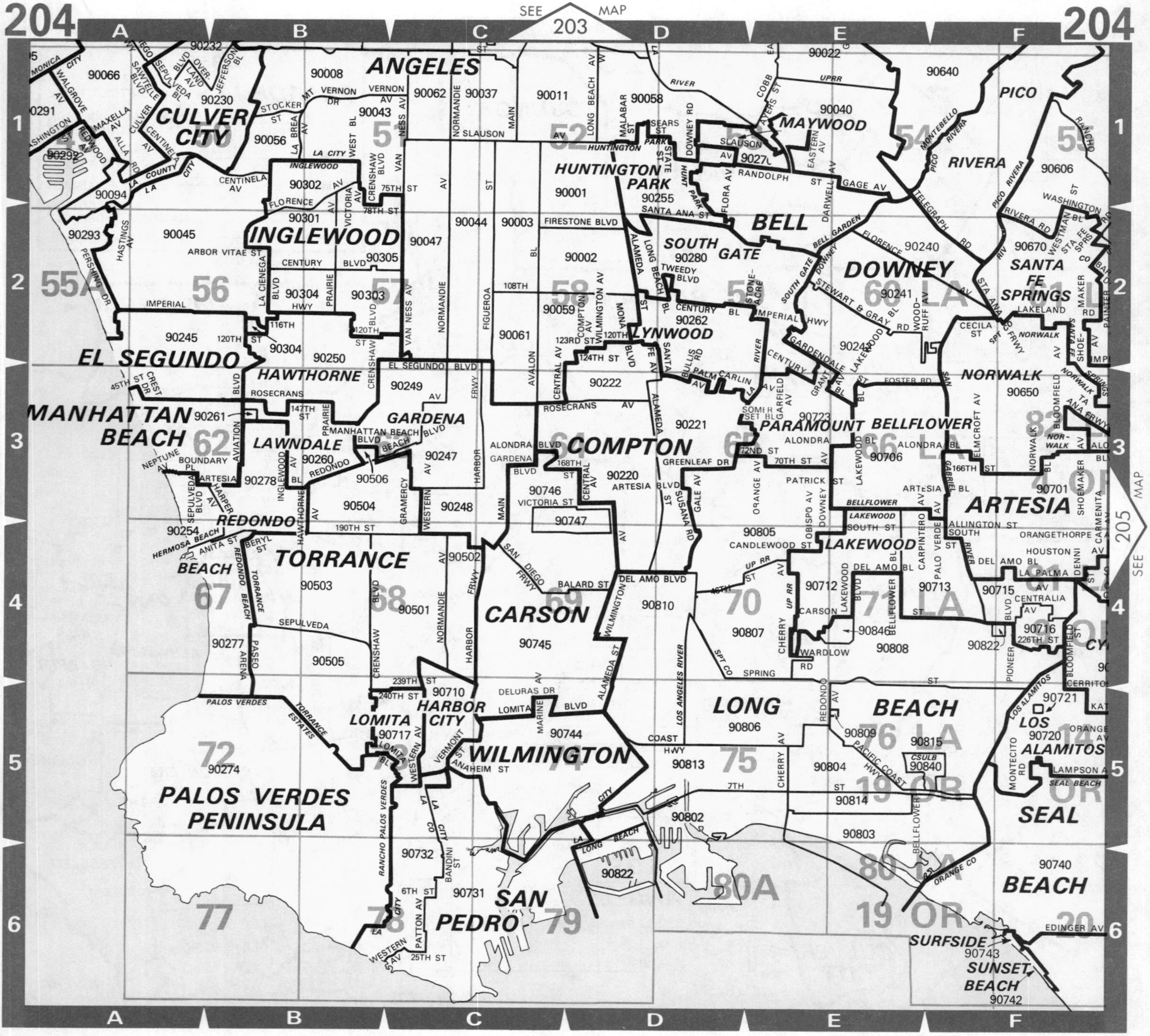

LOS ANGELES CO.

ZIP-FRWY

SEE MAP 203
SEE MAP 205

A B C D E F

1 2 3 4 5 6

CULVER CITY
ANGELES
VERNON
MAYWOOD
PICO RIVERA
HUNTINGTON PARK
BELL
SOUTH GATE
DOWNEY
SANTA FE SPRINGS
INGLEWOOD
LYNWOOD
EL SEGUNDO
HAWTHORNE
MANHATTAN BEACH
GARDENA
LAWNDALE
COMPTON
PARAMOUNT BELLFLOWER
NORWALK
ARTESIA
REDONDO BEACH
TORRANCE
CARSON
LAKEWOOD
PALOS VERDES PENINSULA
LOMITA
HARBOR CITY
WILMINGTON
LONG BEACH
LOS ALAMITOS
SAN PEDRO
SEAL BEACH
SURFSIDE
SUNSET BEACH

Map reference numbers: 51 52 53 54 55 55A 56 57 58 59 61 62 63 64 65 66 67 68 69 70 71 72 74 75 76 77 78 79 80A 81 19 20

ZIP codes: 90066, 90232, 90230, 90008, 90062, 90037, 90011, 90022, 90640, 90056, 90043, 90058, 90040, 90291, 90094, 90302, 90301, 90001, 90255, 90027, 90240, 90606, 90045, 90044, 90003, 90002, 90280, 90262, 90670, 90047, 90305, 90059, 90061, 90241, 90245, 90304, 90303, 90222, 90221, 90242, 90249, 90250, 90723, 90650, 90261, 90706, 90701, 90260, 90247, 90220, 90805, 90716, 90278, 90506, 90248, 90746, 90747, 90712, 90713, 90715, 90504, 90254, 90503, 90502, 90810, 90807, 90808, 90822, 90277, 90501, 90745, 90846, 90721, 90505, 90710, 90717, 90744, 90806, 90809, 90815, 90720, 90274, 90813, 90804, 90840, 90802, 90803, 90814, 90740, 90732, 90731, 90743, 90742

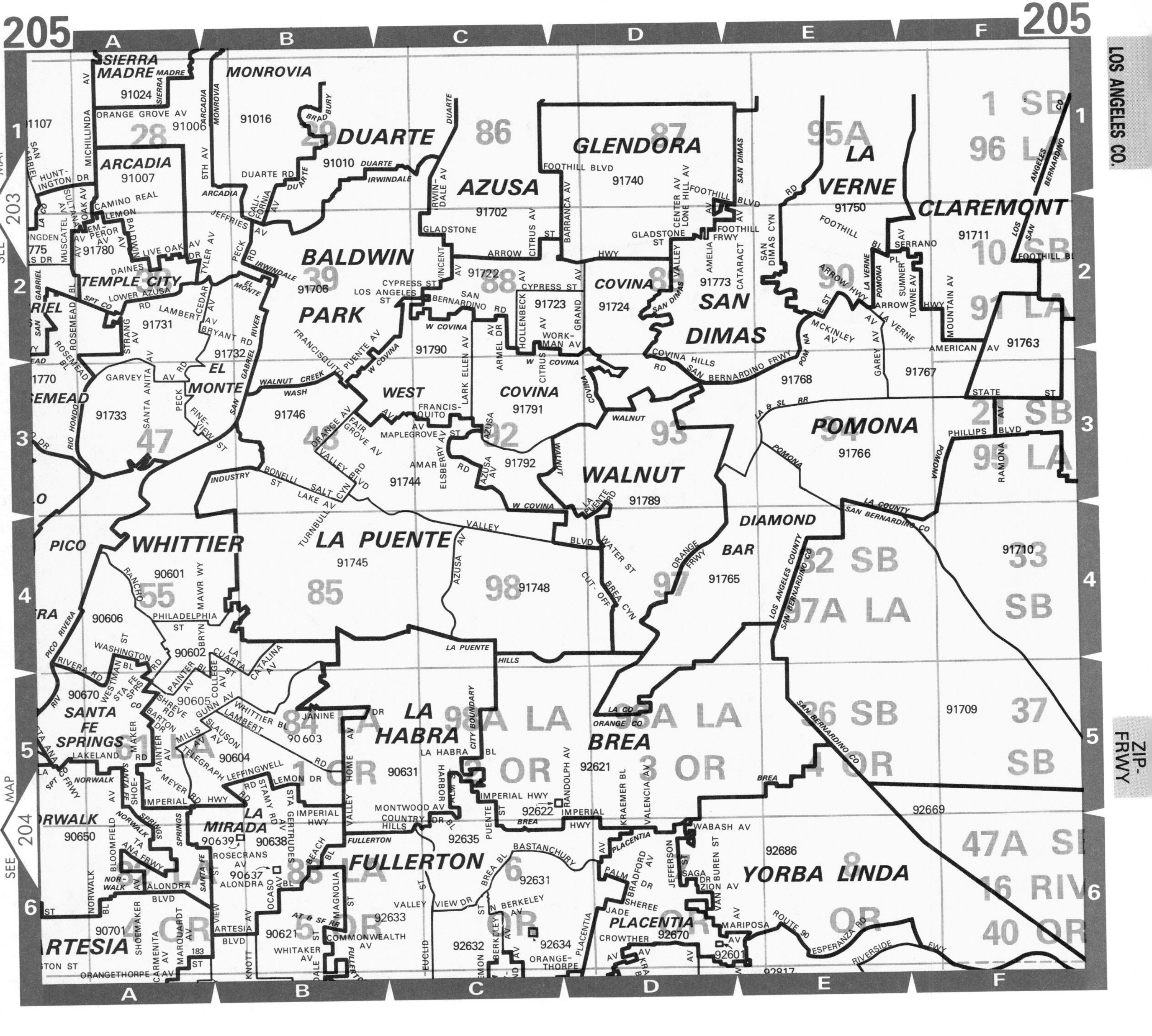

LOS ANGELES CO.

ZIP-FRWY

© COPYRIGHT, © 1989 BY Thomas Bros Maps

SEE MAP 203

SEE MAP 204

A B C D E F

1

SIERRA MADRE 91024
ORANGE GROVE AV
91107
ARCADIA 91007
HUNTINGTON DR
91780
91775

MONROVIA 91006 91016
DUARTE 91010
BRADBURY
IRWINDALE
DUARTE RD

86

GLENDORA 91740
FOOTHILL BLVD

87

95A

LA VERNE 91750

1 SB
96 LA

CLAREMONT 91711
FOOTHILL
10 SB

2

28
ARCADIA
TEMPLE CITY 91780
91731 91732
EL MONTE

29
BALDWIN PARK 91706
39
LOS ANGELES ST
SAN BERNARDINO

AZUSA 91702
GLADSTONE
ARROW HWY 91722
88
CYPRESS ST 91723
W COVINA 91790

COVINA 91724
SAN DIMAS 91773
GLADSTONE ST

85
SAN DIMAS
COVINA HILLS RD
SAN BERNARDINO FRWY

90
ARROW HWY
POMONA
LA VERNE
91763 91767

91 LA

3

47
91733
RIO HONDO

48
91746
WALNUT CREEK WASH
WEST COVINA 91790
FRANCISQUITO AV
MAPLEGROVE AV
AMAR
91744

92
AZUSA 91792

93
WALNUT 91789

94
POMONA 91766
94
PHILLIPS BLVD
RAMONA

2 SB
95 LA

4

WHITTIER
90601 90606
55
PICO

LA PUENTE 91745
85

98 91748
TURNBULL VALLEY

DIAMOND BAR 91765
97

ORANGE FRWY
LOS ANGELES COUNTY
SAN BERNARDINO CO

82 SB
07A LA

33 SB

91710

5

SANTA FE SPRINGS
90670 90605 90602 90604 90603
84 LA
1 LA

LA HABRA 90631
98A LA

BREA 92621 92635
36 SB
4 OR

92669

91709
37 SB

6

NORWALK 90650
LA MIRADA 90638 90639 90637
83 LA
4 OR
ARTESIA 90701 90621
5 OR

FULLERTON 92633 92632
6
92631
92634

PLACENTIA 92670 92601
8
YORBA LINDA 92686 92817
ROUTE 90

47A SB
16 RIV
40 OR

A B C D E F

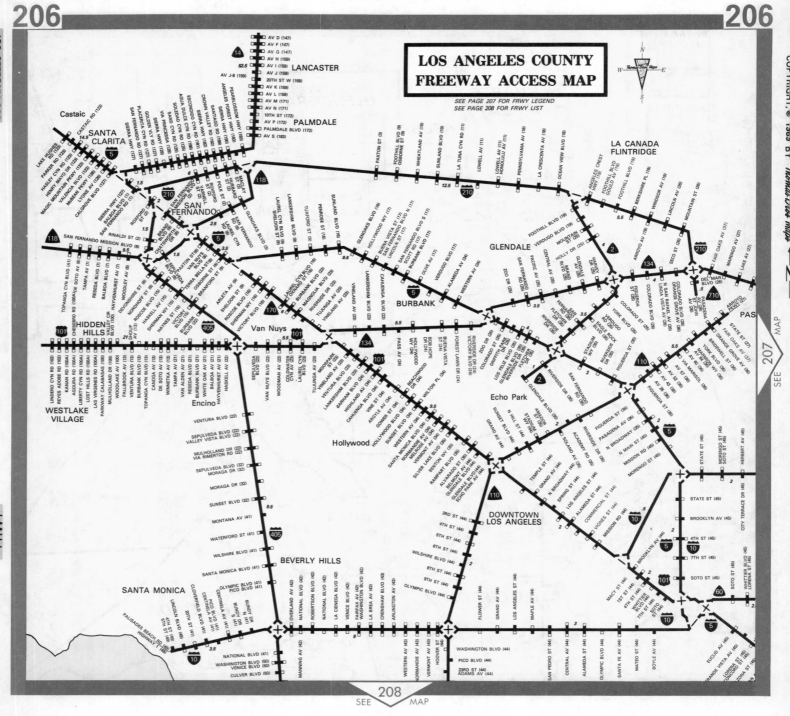

LOS ANGELES CO.

ZIP-FRWY

LOS ANGELES COUNTY FREEWAY ACCESS MAP

SEE PAGE 207 FOR FRWY LEGEND
SEE PAGE 208 FOR FRWY LIST

Copyright, © 1983 BY Thomas Bros. Maps

SEE 207 MAP

SEE 208 MAP

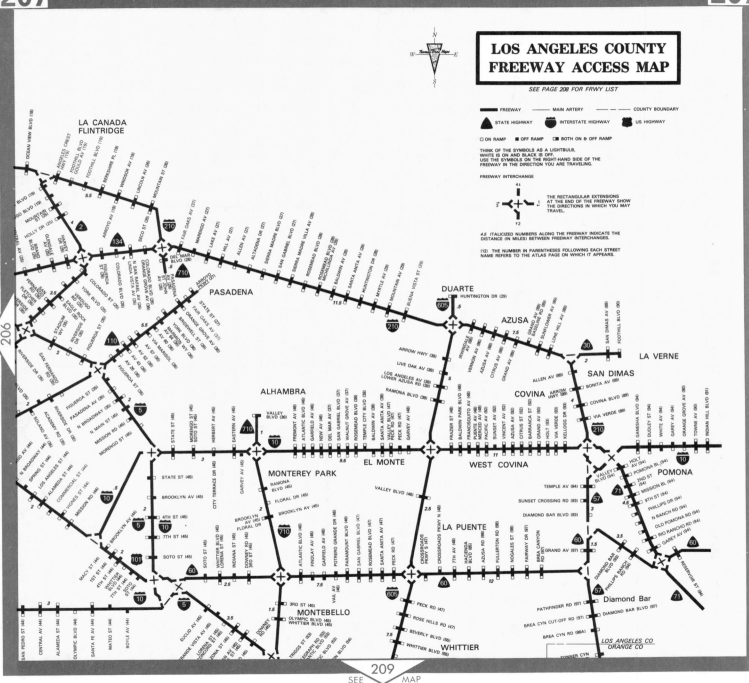

LOS ANGELES COUNTY FREEWAY ACCESS MAP

SEE PAGE 208 FOR FRWY LIST

SEE MAP 206

Hollywood

SEPULVEDA BLVD (22)
VALLEY VISTA BLVD (22)
MULHOLLAND DR (22)
VIA RIMERTON RD (22)
SEPULVEDA BLVD (32)
MORAGA DR (32)
MORAGA DR (32)
SUNSET BLVD (32)
MONTANA AV (41)
WATERFORD ST (41)
WILSHIRE BLVD (41)
SANTA MONICA BLVD (41)

9.5

405

SANTA MONICA

BEVERLY HILLS

SUNSET BLVD
HOLLYWOOD BLVD
WESTERN AV (36)
SANTA MONICA BLVD (36)
NORMANDIE AV (36)
MELROSE AV (36)
SILVER LAKE BLVD (36)
VERMONT AV (36)
BENTON WY (36)
RAMPART BLVD (36)
ALVARADO ST (36)
BELMONT AV (36)
GLENDALE BLVD (36)
ECHO PARK AV (36)

DOWNTOWN
LOS ANGELES

TEMPLE ST (44)
GRAND AV (44)
N BROADWAY (44)
SPRING ST (44)
N MAIN ST (44)
LOS ANGELES ST (44)
ALAMEDA ST (44)
COMMERCIAL ST (44)
VIGNES ST (44)
MISSION RD (44)

HOLLYWOOD FRWY
SUNSET BLVD
SOLANO AV (39)
ACADEMY RD (39)
RIVERSIDE DR (39)
PASADENA
N BROADWAY (45)
N MAIN ST (45)
MISSION RD (45)
MORENGO ST (45)

MORENGO ST
SOTO ST (45)
HERBERT AV (45)

STATE ST (45)
BROOKLYN AV (45)
CITY TERRACE DR (45)

STATE ST (45)
4TH ST (45)
7TH ST (45)
SOTO ST (45)

WHITTIER BLVD (45)
LORENA ST (45)

110

10

101

5

10

60

5

3

2.5

3.5

3RD ST (44)
4TH ST (44)
5TH ST (44)
6TH ST (44)
WILSHIRE BLVD (44)
8TH ST (44)
9TH ST (44)
OLYMPIC BLVD (44)

OVERLAND AV (42)
NATIONAL BLVD (42)
ROBERTSON BLVD (42)
NATIONAL BLVD (42)
LA CIENEGA BLVD (42)
VENICE BLVD (42)
FAIRFAX AV (42)
WASHINGTON BLVD (42)
LA BREA AV (43)
CRENSHAW BLVD (43)
ARLINGTON (43)

WESTERN AV (43)
NORMANDIE AV (43)
VERMONT AV (44)
HOOVER ST (44)

FLOWER ST (44)
GRAND AV (44)
LOS ANGELES ST (44)
MAPLE AV (44)

SAN PEDRO ST (44)
CENTRAL AV (44)
ALAMEDA ST (44)
OLYMPIC BLVD (44)
SANTA FE AV (44)
MATEO ST (44)
BOYLE AV (44)

EUCLID AV (46)
GRANDE VISTA AV (46)
LORENA ST (46)
CONCORD ST (46)
CALZONA ST (46)
DITMAN AV (46)
INDIANA ST (46)
OLYMPIC BLVD

ATLANTIC BLVD
BANDINI BLVD

WASHINGTON BLVD

FLORENCE AV

FIRESTONE BLVD

IMPERIAL HWY

PICO BLVD (41)
LINCOLN BLVD (41)
CENTINELA AV (41)
5TH ST (41)
4TH ST (41)
20TH ST (41)
CLOVERFIELD BLVD (41)
BUNDY DR S (41)
BUNDY DR (41)
PALISADES BEACH RD
HIGHWAY 1 (40)

10

3.5

NATIONAL BLVD (41)
WASHINGTON BLVD (50)
VENICE BLVD (50)
CULVER BLVD (50)
SAWTELLE BLVD (50)
BRADDOCK DR (50)
JEFFERSON BLVD (50)

CULVER CITY

MANNING AV (42)

3.5

SLAUSON AV (50)

90

.5

2.5

LINCOLN BLVD (49)
MINDANAO WY (49)
CENTINELA AV (50)

JEFFERSON BLVD (50)
SEPULVEDA BLVD (50)
HOWARD HUGHES PKWY (50)
LA TIJERA BLVD (50)

FLORENCE AV (56)
MANCHESTER BLVD (56)
LA CIENEGA BLVD (56)
MANCHESTER BLVD (56)
CENTURY BLVD (56)
IMPERIAL HWY (56)

INGLEWOOD

WASHINGTON BLVD (44)
PICO BLVD (44)
23RD ST (44)
ADAMS AV (44)

110

ADAMS AV (44)
EXPOSITION AV (52)
37TH ST (52)
MARTIN LUTHER KING JR BLVD (52)
VERNON AV (52)
51ST ST (52)
SLAUSON AV (52)
GAGE AV (52)
FLORENCE AV (52)
MANCHESTER AV (58)
CENTURY BLVD (58)
IMPERIAL HWY (58)
EL SEGUNDO BLVD (58)
ROSECRANS AV (64)
REDONDO BEACH BLVD (64)

VERNON

11.5

MAIN ST (64)
AVALON BLVD (64)
CENTRAL AV (64)
WILMINGTON AV (64)
ACACIA AV (65)
ALAMEDA ST (65)
SANTA FE (65)
LONG BEACH BLVD (65)

COMPTON

ALONDRA BLVD (65)
ATLANTIC AV (65)

CENTURY BLVD (58)
ROSECRANS AV (65)

91

13

405

GARDENA

EL SEGUNDO BLVD (60)
ROSECRANS AV (62)
INGLEWOOD AV (60)
HAWTHORNE BLVD (60)
REDONDO BEACH BLVD (60)
ARTESIA BLVD (60)
CRENSHAW BLVD (68)
WESTERN AV (68)
NORMANDIE AV (68)
VERMONT AV (68)

ARTESIA BLVD (64)

190TH ST (64)
VICTORIA ST (64)

CARSON

CARSON ST (69)
WILMINGTON AV (69)
ALAMEDA ST (69)
SANTA FE (70)

ARTESIA BLVD (65)
LONG BEACH BLVD (70)
DEL AMO BLVD (70)
PACIFIC AV (70)

40

3.5

1

TORRANCE

110

TORRANCE BLVD (69)
CARSON ST (69)
220TH ST (69)
223RD ST (69)

FIGUEROA ST (69)
MAIN ST (69)
AVALON BLVD (69)

PACIFIC AV (70)
WARDLOW RD (75)
WILLOW ST (75)
PACIFIC COAST HWY (75)
ANAHEIM ST (75)
PICO AV (75)
HARBOR SCENIC DR (75)
9TH ST (75)
7TH ST (75)
6TH ST (75)
3RD ST (75)
BROADWAY (75)
OCEAN BLVD (75)
SHORELINE DR (75)

5.5

SEPULVEDA BLVD (74)
PACIFIC COAST HWY (74)
ANAHEIM ST (74)
C ST (74)
JOHN GIBSON AV (79)
PACIFIC AV (78)

7.5

SEPULVEDA BLVD (74)
ANAHEIM ST (74)
HENRY FORD AV (74)
NEW DOCK ST (74)
OCEAN BLVD (74)

103

3.5

WILLOW ST (75)

LONG BEACH

710

PACIFIC

OCEAN

SEE MAP 209

San Pedro

GAFFEY ST (78)
FERRY ST (79)
FRONT ST (79)

SEASIDE AV (79)
SEASIDE AV (79)

LONG BEACH HARBOR

Freeway Legend

2	GLENDALE FRWY
5	GOLDEN STATE FRWY / SANTA ANA FRWY
10	SANTA MONICA FRWY / SAN BERNARDINO FRWY
14	ANTELOPE VALLEY FRWY
22	GARDEN GROVE FRWY
30	FOOTHILL FRWY
57	ORANGE FRWY
60	POMONA FRWY
71	CORONA EXPWY
90	MARINA FRWY
91	REDONDO BEACH FWY / ARTESIA FRWY
101	VENTURA FRWY / HOLLYWOOD FRWY
103	TERMINAL ISLAND FRWY
110	PASADENA FRWY / HARBOR FRWY
110	HARBOR FRWY
118	SIMI VALLEY-SAN FERNANDO VALLEY FRWY
134	VENTURA FRWY
170	HOLLYWOOD FRWY
210	FOOTHILL FRWY
405	SAN DIEGO FRWY
605	SAN GABRIEL RIVER FRWY
710	LONG BEACH FRWY
710	LONG BEACH FRWY

N
W E
S
Thomas Bros Maps

LOS ANGELES COUNTY FREEWAY ACCESS MAP

SEE PAGE 207 FOR FRWY LEGEND

COPYRIGHT © 1989 BY Thomas Bros Maps

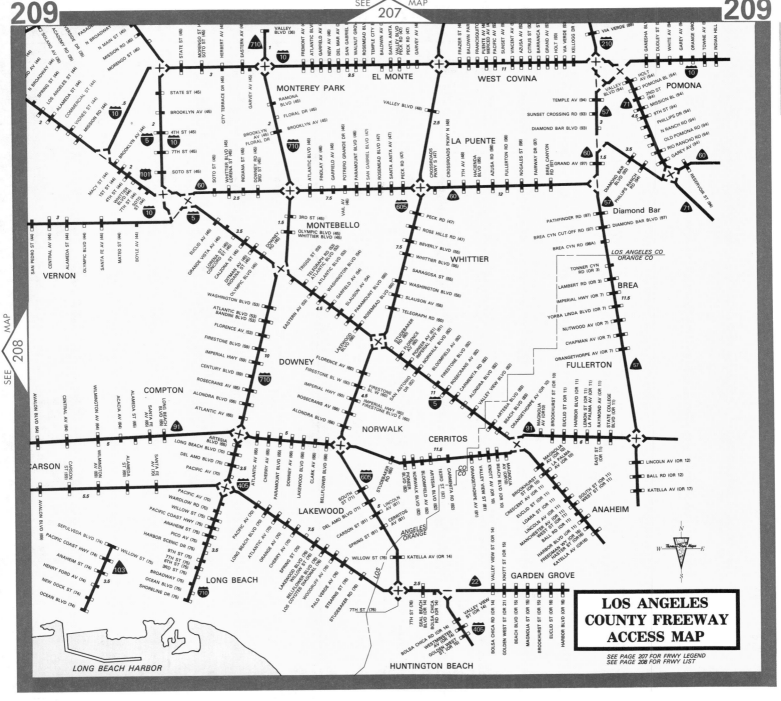

LOS ANGELES CO.

SEE MAP 207

SEE MAP 208

ZIP-FRWY

COPYRIGHT, © 1989 BY Thomas Bros. Maps

LOS ANGELES
COUNTY FREEWAY
ACCESS MAP

SEE PAGE 207 FOR FRWY LEGEND
SEE PAGE 208 FOR FRWY LIST

1990 LOS ANGELES COUNTY STREET INDEX

A

STREET	CITY	P.O. ZONE	BLOCK	PAGE	GRID
A ST	CER	ART		82	C6
A ST	HAW	HAW		57	D5
A ST	LA	WIL	100	74	C5
A ST	LAV	LAV	1700	90	C3
AARON ST	LA	LA26		35	C4
ABACA AV	CO	LAN	47600	146	G5
ABAJO DR	MPK	MPK	1600	45	F3
ABAJO DR	MPK	MPK	1400	46	A2
ABAJO DR	SCLR	SAU	26600	124	C7
ABAKAN AV	CO	RM		46	E3
ABALAR ST	LA	WOH	20900	13	D3
ABALONE AV	LA	SP	3400	78	D5
ABALONE AV	TOR	TOR	1700	68	D5
ABANA PL	CER	ART	13100	82	D5
ABANA ST	ART	ART	11500	66	F5
ABANA ST	CER	ART	11300	66	F5
ABANA ST	CER	ART	12000	82	A5
ABANO AV	CO	LPUE		98	D5
ABANTES AV	CO	LAN	38800	175	F6
ABARGO ST	LA	WOH	4000	13	D3
ABASCAL DR	CO	LPUE		85	F4
ABBADIE LN	CO	TOP		115	A1
ABBESS PL	CO	LPUE		98	A5
ABBEY CT	SAD	SAD	100	89	D3
ABBEY LN	PALM	PALM		171	F5
ABBEY LN	POM	POM	500	95	B2
ABBEY PL	LA	LA19	4500	43	C3
ABBEY RD	LA	RES		14	C5
ABBEY ST	LPUE	LPUE	15900	48	F6
ABBEY WY	LAV	LAV		90	C2
ABBEYFIELD ST	LB	LB15	5200	76	C3
ABBEYVILLE AV	LA	WOH	4700	13	A3
ABBEYVILLE AV	LA	WOH	4700	100	F2
ABBEYWOOD AV	CO	WHI	3700	55	C1
ABBEYWOOD AV	PR	PR	4200	55	B2
ABBINGTON CT	WLVL	THO	4200	102	B4
ABBOT AV	SGAB	SGAB	600	37	E4
ABBOTSFORD RD	CO	WHI	10900	55	A6
ABBOTSFORD RD	PR	PR	8700	54	E5
ABBOTSWOOD DR	RPV	PVP	6500	72	C5
ABBOTT PL	LA	LA42		36	B2
ABBOTT RD	LYN	LYN	3600	59	B4
ABBOTT RD	SOG	SOG	5100	59	B4
ABBOTT ST	POM	POM	2800	90	F3
ABBOTTSHALL LN	CO	LPUE		98	A5
ABBOTTSON ST	CAR	CAR	1500	69	E2
ABDALE ST	SCLR	SAU	19200	127	J2
ABDERA ST	CO	LPUE	19000	98	F3
ABE WY	MPK	MPK		46	D3
ABEJA DR	CO	LPUE	17800	98	C5
ABELIA RD	CO	CYN		125	F7
ABELIAN AV	CO	LPUE	400	98	F4
ABELLA ST	CO	GL14	3100	11	D6
ABELLA ST	GLEN	GL14	3900	11	B5
ABERDEEN AV	LA	LA27	4500	34	F1
ABERNATHY DR	LA	LA45	5700	50	D6
ABERT ST	CO	LPUE	19400	97	A4
ABERY AV	CO	LPUE	200	98	E1
ABETO AV	CO	LPUE	2600	98	E6
ABIGAIL PL	LA	LA45	7900	56	E1
ABILA ST	CAR	CAR	1400	69	D4
ABILENE LN	CO	SAU		181	B8
ABILENE RD	SAD	SAD	700	90	A2
ABILENE ST	RM	RM	8600	37	F5
ABILENE ST	RM	RM	8600	38	C5
ABILENE ST	SGAB	SGAB	900	37	F5
ABILENE WY	CLA	CLA	1900	91	C2
ABINGDON ST	NWK	NWK	11800	82	B3
ABINGTON DR	LA	BH		22	F6
ABISKO DR	CO	WHI	10600	61	E4
ABITA AV	LOM	LOM	24700	73	D2
ABLANO AV	CO	LPUE	2400	98	E6
ABLE ST	CO	CYN		128	E4
ABNER ST	LA	LA32	4100	45	C1
ABOGADO AV	WAL	WAL	200	93	C6
ABONADO PL	CO	LPUE	2500	98	E5
ABORDO DR	SCLR	SAU	22500	124	C6
ABORLA LN	WAL	WAL	200	93	C6
ABOURNE RD	LA	LA08	4000	51	B2
ABRAHAM DR	SELM	ELM	10900	47	D4
ABRAZO	WCOV	WCOV		92	D4
ABRAZO DR	RPV	PVP	30100	78	B2
ABRI ST	CAR	CAR	1600	69	D5
ABRIGO AV	LA	LA31	2700	36	B6
ABUELA PL	CO	LPUE		85	F4
ACACIA	LA	SF42		2	C1
ACACIA AV	BLF	BLF		66	D6
ACACIA AV	CO	IN04	10800	57	A5
ACACIA AV	HAW	HAW	12600	57	A5
ACACIA AV	MON	MON	100	29	A3
ACACIA AV	PR	PR	4900	54	F2
ACACIA AV	PR	PR	4000	55	A1
ACACIA AV	TOR	TOR	600	68	C4

STREET	CITY	P.O. ZONE	BLOCK	PAGE	GRID
ACACIA AV	WHI	WHI	5500	55	D4
ACACIA AV E	ELS	ELS	200	56	B5
ACACIA AV E	GLEN	GL05	100	25	D5
ACACIA AV N	COM	COM	100	64	F2
ACACIA AV S	COM	COM	100	64	F4
ACACIA AV W	ELS	ELS	100	56	A5
ACACIA AV W	GLEN	GL04	100	25	C5
ACACIA CT	COM	COM	1500	64	E5
ACACIA CT	CO	SAU		124	C2
ACACIA LN	RH	PVP	1	73	B5
ACACIA LN	WCOV	WCOV	600	92	E2
ACACIA RD	RH	PVP		73	B5
ACACIA ST	ALH	ALH	1500	37	A3
ACACIA ST	BELL	BELL	4000	53	C5
ACACIA ST	CO	ALT	200	19	F5
ACACIA ST	CO	LA56	6200	50	F5
ACACIA ST	CO	SGAB	4900	38	A4
ACACIA ST	ING	IN02	800	50	F6
ACACIA ST	LA	LA56	6300	50	F5
ACACIA ST	LAN	LAN		160	G5
ACACIA ST	MPK	MPK		46	D4
ACACIA ST	SMAD	SMAD	280	28	D1
ACACIA ST E	POM	POM	200	90	F4
ACACIA ST N	SAD	SAD	100	89	F3
ACACIA ST S	SAD	SAD	100	89	F3
ACACIA ST W	POM	POM	100	90	F4
ACACIA GLEN ST	AGH	AGO		100A	B2
ACACIA HILL RD	DBAR	POM	1600	97	E3
ACADEMIA DR	LA	ENC	16400	22	A4
ACADEMY AV	POM	POM	2200	94	A1
ACADEMY CT	CLA	CLA	1900	91	C2
ACADEMY DR	CO	PVP	26500	73	A4
ACADEMY DR	LA	LA12		35	D5
ACADEMY DR	RPV	PVP	26700	72	F4
ACADEMY PL	GLEN	GL06	1900	25	F3
ACADEMY RD	LA	LA12		35	D5
ACADEMY RD	LA	LA26		35	D5
ACADEMY ST	LA	LA32		36	D5
ACADIA AV	AGH	AGO		100A	A2
ACALA AV	LA	SF	11100	2	D6
ACALA AV	LA	SF	11100	8	E1
ACAMA ST	LA	NHO	10700	23	D4
ACAMPO AV	GLEN	GL14		11	C4
ACAMPO ST	GLEN	GL14		11	C5
ACANA RD	RPV	PVP	27900	72	C4
ACANTHUS CIR	WAL	WAL		93	D4
ACANTHUS CT	AGH	AGO		100A	A2
ACANTHUS WY	SCLR	SAU		124	E8
ACANTO PL	LA	LA49		32	B5
ACANTO ST	LA	LA49		32	C5
ACAPULCO DR	CO	WHI	13400	61	D3
ACARI DR	LA	LA49		41	C1
ACARUS AV	CAR	CAR	21700	69	D4
ACASO DR	TEC	TEC	9000	38	B4
ACASO DR	WAL	WAL		97	A1
ACCESS RD	LB	LB02		75	C6
ACCO ST	CMRC	LA40	6800	54	B3
ACCO ST	MTB	MTB	1700	54	B3
ACCORD PL	CO	ACT		189	H2
ACCRA ST	LA	NOR		7	B1
ACE PL	CO	LLAN		192	H3
ACERA CT	CO	GLDR		89	D1
ACFOLD DR	CO	WAL		97	B3
ACHESON DR	WHI	WHI		55	E3
ACHILLES DR	LA	LA46		33	E1
ACHILLES ST	NWK	NWK	12100	61	B5
ACKERFIELD AV	LB	LB05		70	E1
ACKERMAN DR	LA	LA65		35	F1
ACKLEY PL	MPK	MPK	1700	46	D4
ACKLEY ST	CO	SGAB		46	D4
ACKLEY ST	MPK	MPK	400	46	D4
ACKLEY ST	PAR	PAR	8200	65	F2
ACKLINS AV	CO	ACT		189	E1
ACKMAR AV	CAR	CAR	21900	69	D4
ACLARE CIR	CER	ART	11300	66	F5
ACLARE LN	CER	ART	13600	82	E5
ACLARE PL	CER	ART	13000	82	C5
ACLARE ST	ART	ART	11400	66	F5
ACLARE ST	CER	ART	11900	82	A5
ACME WK	LA	LA31		36	B4
ACOLITO PL	DBAR	POM		94	A5
ACOMA DR	CAR	CAR	700	64	C4
ACORDE AV	PALM	PALM		183	G1
ACORN CIR	MON	MON	100	29	C2
ACORN CT	SCLR	NEW		127	C4
ACORN DR	LAV	LAV		95A	C6
ACORN LN	GLDR	GLDR	1600	87	D5
ACORN ST	LA	CHA		6	B4
ACORO PL	CER	ART	13000	82	D5
ACORO ST	BLF	BLF	10400	66	D5
ACORO ST	CER	ART	11000	66	F5
ACORO ST	CER	ART	13000	82	E5
ACOSTA AV	LAN	LAN		160	E6
ACRE ST	LA	CAN	20100	6	E6
ACRE ST	LA	NOR	17900	6	F6
ACRE ST	LA	NOR	17900	7	C6

STREET	CITY	P.O. ZONE	BLOCK	PAGE	GRID
ACRE ST	LA	SF	14900	8	C6
ACRESITE ST	LA	LA39	2900	35	C2
ACRIDGE DR	WCOV	WCOV	3400	93	A2
ACTAEON ST	CO	MAL		104	F6
ACTINA AV	BLF	BLF	13700	66	B2
ACTON AV	CO	ACT		189	E3
ACTON CANYON RD	CO	ACT		182	H8
ACTON VINCNT RD	CO	PALM		183	C9
ACUAPEY DR	CO	CHA		1A	C5
ACUNA DR	CO	LPUE	3000	85	C4
ADA AV E	GLDR	GLDR	100	87	B5
ADA AV W	GLDR	GLDR	100	87	A5
ADA ST	SCLR	CYN		125	D7
ADA ST	LA	LA46	2600	33	E1
ADAGIO CT	LA	LA77		32	B1
ADAIR ST	LA	LA11	1900	44	C6
ADAIR ST	LA	LA11	4099	52	B2
ADAIR ST	LB	LB05	100	65	C6
ADAIR ST	SMAR	PAS	1100	37	C2
ADALE PL	CO	LA43	5600	51	A4
ADALIA AV	CO	LPUE	1500	85	C1
ADAMANT DR	CO	SF		3	E3
ADAMO AV	LOM	LOM	25300	73	C3
ADAMOR RD	CO	CAL		100	A2
ADAMS AV	MTB	MTB		46	E5
ADAMS AV	PALM	PALM		183	D2
ADAMS AV	POM	POM		94	F1
ADAMS AV E	ALH	ALH	1	37	C5
ADAMS AV E	POM	POM	300	90	F6
ADAMS AV W	ALH	ALH	200	37	C5
ADAMS BLVD	CUL	CUL	5800	42	E5
ADAMS BLVD E	LA	LA11	100	44	B6
ADAMS BLVD E	LA	LA11		52	C1
ADAMS BLVD W	LA	LA07	100	43	D5
ADAMS BLVD W	LA	LA07	100	44	A5
ADAMS BLVD W	LA	LA16	5100	42	E5
ADAMS BLVD W	LA	LA16	4400	43	D5
ADAMS BLVD W	LA	LA18	1700	43	D5
ADAMS DR	BAP	BAP		39	F4
ADAMS DR	LA	SP		79	B5
ADAMS DR	WCOV	WCOV	1800	88	A4
ADAMS ST	CAR	LB10	2500	69	F4
ADAMS ST	CAR	LB10	2600	70	A4
ADAMS ST	CO	GL14	2800	11	D5
ADAMS ST	PAR	PAR	7300	65	E3
ADAMS ST	SMAD	SMAD	100	28	C2
ADAMS ST E	LB	LB05	100	65	B6
ADAMS ST N	GLEN	GL06	100	25	D5
ADAMS ST S	GLEN	GL05	100	25	D5
ADAMS ST W	LB	LB05	1	65	B6
ADAMS WY	CO	CAST	29500	123	A6
ADAMS WY	MPK	MPK	1700	46	D3
ADAMSBORO DR	SCLR	NEW	23600	127	B5
ADAMS GARDEN W	LA	LA07		44	A5
ADAMSGROVE AV	DBAR	WAL	800	97	C2
ADAMSON AV	BG	BELL	6500	53	F6
ADAMS PARK DR	CO	COV	19200	89	A5
ADAMS PARK DR	COV	COV	400	88	E5
ADAMS PARK DR	COV	COV	800	89	A5
ADAMSVILLE AV	CO	WOH		13	B5
ADANA ST	COM	COM	2300	65	C4
ADCO AV	DOW	DOW	11500	59	F3
ADDA DR	CO	LAN	4000	147	D1
ADDERLEY DR	LB	LB08	5800	71	D6
ADDERLEY DR	LB	LB08	5800	76	D1
ADDINGTON ST	CO	COM	4200	65	C2
ADDINGTON WY	CO	LA43	4600	51	B3
ADDIS ST	CO	LPUE		97	A3
ADDIS ST	CO	LPUE	19000	98	F3
ADDISON RD	PVE	PVP	1500	72	A4
ADDISON ST	LA	ENC	15700	21	F2
ADDISON ST	LA	ENC	16600	22	A2
ADDISON ST	LA	NHO	10400	23	B2
ADDISON ST	LA	VAN	14900	22	D2
ADDISON ST	LA	VAN	12900	23	A2
ADDISON WY	LA	LA41	2000	26	A5
ADDLEMAN AV	CO	LPUE		97	A1
ADDLEMAN AV	CO	LPUE	300	98	F1
ADEL AV	DBAR	WAL		97	D2
ADEL WY	CO	WHI	10300	61	E4
ADELA CT	PALM	PALM		184	B5
ADELAIDE DR	PAS	PAS	800	27	D2
ADELAIDE DR	SM	SM	100	40	E5
ADELAIDE PL	LA	LA42	6300	26	D6
ADELAIDE PL	SM	SM	700	40	E5
ADELAINE AL	SPAS	SPAS		36	E1
ADELAINE AV	SPAS	SPAS	700	36	E2
ADELANTE AV	LA	LA42	900	26	E6
ADELANTE AV	LA	LA42		36	E1
ADELANTE ST	IRW	AZU		86	B6
ADELBERT AV	LA	LA39		35	C3
ADELE AV	CO	WHI	5200	55	C2
ADELE AV	WHI	WHI	5600	55	C3
ADELE CT	LA	WOH		13	F3
ADELE DR	LA	WOH		13	E3
ADELFA DR	LAM	LAM	13500	83	B1

STREET	CITY	P.O. ZONE	BLOCK	PAGE	GRID
ADELHART ST	CO	LPUE	15500	85	D3
ADELIA AV	ELM	ELM	2400	47	C1
ADELIA AV	SELM	ELM	1400	47	C1
ADELINA CT	AGH	AGO		102	E3
ADELITA DR	CO	LPUE	2600	85	D4
ADELITA LN	SELM	ELM	9900	47	C3
ADELITA ST	MTB	MTB		46	D6
ADELLA AV	SOG	SOG	9500	59	D3
ADELPHIA AV	LA	PAC	11900	3	A5
ADELPHIA AV	LA	PAC	11200	9	C1
ADELPHIA AV	LA	SF	13600	2	F3
ADELPHIA AV	LA	SF	11900	3	B5
ADELYN DR	SGAB	SGAB	400	37	D2
ADEN AV	SCLR	NEW	24700	127	D3
ADENA ST	PAS	PAS	300	27	A2
ADENMOOR AV	BLF	BLF	16500	66	C4
ADENMOOR AV	DOW	DOW	11600	60	C5
ADENMOOR AV	DOW	DOW	13200	66	C1
ADENMOOR AV	LKD	LKD	5901	66	C6
ADENMOOR AV	LKD	LKD	4300	71	C2
ADERNO WY	LA	PP		40	B4
ADGER DR	CO	WHI	14000	61	E4
ADINA DR	LA	LA68	3300	24	A6
ADIVINO ST	CO	LPUE	18500	98	E5
ADKINS AV	LA	LA32		36	E6
ADKISSON AV	CO	LA63	1400	45	C2
ADLER AV	LA	WOH		5	E6
ADLER AV	LAN	LAN	43600	160	B6
ADLER DR	WHI	WHI		55	D6
ADLER DR	WHI	WHI		61	D1
ADLON PL	LA	ENC	4100	21	E4
ADLON RD	LA	ENC	16500	21	F4
ADMIRABLE DR	RPV	PVP	3900	78	A3
ADMIRAL AV	LA	LA66		49	F4
ADMIRAL AV	LA	VEN		49	E5
ADM HIGBEE WY	LA	SP		79	B5
ADMIRALTY WY	CO	MDR		49	E5
ADNA AV	CO	LPUE	1600	85	C1
ADNEY ST	CO	LPUE	18900	98	F4
ADOBE AV	PALM	PALM		173	A9
ADOBE AV	MTB	MTB	800	46	F6
ADOBE DR	PALM	PALM		172	J9
ADOBE DR	PALM	PALM		173	A9
ADOBE PL	MPK	MPK	700	46	B4
ADOBE ST	LA	LA12	900	44	E1
ADOBE WY	CO	SAU		188	B1
ADOLFO CT	SCLR	VAL		127	B1
ADOLPH AV	TOR	TOR	22900	67	F6
ADOLPH AV	TOR	TOR	22900	68	A6
ADOLPH AV	TOR	TOR	24200	72	F1
ADOLPH AV	TOR	TOR	24200	73	A1
ADOMAR ST	CAR	CAR	500	69	C4
ADON AV	SCLR	CYN	27900	125	A7
ADONA DR	LOM	LOM	2100	73	D2
ADONIS AV	NWK	NWK	11300	61	B5
ADOREE ST	DOW	DOW	7700	59	F5
ADOREE ST	DOW	DOW	8000	60	A6
ADOREE ST	DOW	DOW	8300	66	C1
ADOREE ST	LAM	LAM	13800	61	E6
ADOREE ST	LAM	LAM	13800	82	E1
ADOREE ST	NWK	NWK	10600	60	E6
ADOREE ST	NWK	NWK	10600	66	E1
ADORNOS WY	BUR	BUR		17	C2
ADOUE PL	BAP	BAP	14100	39	E5
ADRIA MARU LN	CAR	CAR		64	B6
ADRIAN CT	CLA	CLA	400	91	B1
ADRIAN PL	LA	SF		1	E5
ADRIAN ST	LA	LA29		35	A4
ADRIATIC AV	CAR	LB10	21000	70	A3
ADRIATIC AV	LB	LB10	3400	70	A5
ADRIATIC AV	LB	LB10	2000	75	A2
ADRIEN PL	LAN	LAN	1600	160	E5
ADRIENNE DR	WCOV	WCOV		92	E6
ADSON PL	SELM	ELM	1500	47	D4
ADUANA AV	CO	ARC		38	F2
ADUANA DR	CO	ARC	2800	38	F2
ADUL ST	WCOV	WCOV	16800	92	B4
ADVENT ST	PR	PR	8300	54	E4
ADWEN ST	DOW	DOW	7100	59	F3
ADWEN ST	DOW	DOW	7300	60	A3
ADYE LN	RPV	PVP		72	D5
AEGEAN ST	NWK	NWK	12100	61	B5
AEOLIAN ST	CO	WHI	10900	55	A6
AEOLIAN ST	CO	WHI	11600	61	A1
AERICK ST	ING	IN01	600	57	B1
AERO DR	PR	PR	9000	54	E6
AERO DR	PR	PR	9000	60	E1
AERO WY	TOR	TOR		73	B2
AEROJET AV	AZU	AZU		86	B6
AEROJET AV	ELM	ELM	3200	47	B1
AETNA ST	LA	TAR	19300	14	A6
AETNA ST	LA	VAN	13300	15	D6
AETNA ST	LA	VAN	13300	16	E6
AETNA ST	LA	WOH	23200	5	F6
AETNA ST	LA	WOH	20200	12	E6
AFAMADO LN	DBAR	POM		94	B6

STREET	CITY	P.O. ZONE	BLOCK	PAGE	GRID
AFELIO DR	CO	LPUE	18700	98	F4
AFT TR	CO	TOP	1700	109	D1
AFTON PL	LA	LA28	6100	34	C4
AFTON RD	SMAR	PAS	900	37	C2
AFTON ST	PAS	PAS	1100	26	D2
AGAJANIAN DR	CO	SAU		124	E4
AGAJANIAN DR	LA	SP		73	E5
AGAJANIAN WY	MTB	MTB	700	46	F6
AGAR PL	PR	PR	9300	47	B6
AGAR PL	PR	PR	9300	55	B1
AGATE AV	CAR	LB10		70	A3
AGATE CT	PALM	PALM		183	E2
AGATE ST	RB	RB	400	67	D2
AGATE WY	MPK	MPK	300	46	C4
AGATHA ST	LA	LA21		44	D4
AGATHEA WY	CO	MAL		110	B4
AGAVE AV	LHH	LAH		84	F3
AGAVE CIR	LAN	LAN		159	E5
AGAVE ST	CO	LAN	42000	171	A1
AGAVE WY	PAR	PAR		65	E4
AGERTON PL	ART	ART		66	F6
AGNER AV	CO	MONT		18	E2
AGNER AV	GLEN	MONT	3700	18	E2
AGNES AV	LA	NHO	7800	16	C2
AGNES AV	LA	NHO	4200	23	C4
AGNES AV	LYN	LYN	3300	59	B6
AGNES AV	TEC	TEC	5700	38	C2
AGNES PL	CER	ART		71	E2
AGNES RD	MB	MB	1500	62	B3
AGNES ST	CER	ART		71	E2
AGNES ST	CER	ART		81	A1
AGNES ST	LYN	LYN	4100	59	C6
AGNEW AV	LA	LA45	7400	50	B6
AGNEW AV	LA	LA45	7900	56	B1
AGNOLO DR	CO	RM	2100	46	E3
AGOSTA DR	CO	LPUE	15600	85	D4
AGOSTINO DR	CO	LPUE	1700	98	C5
AGOSTINO RD	SGAB	SGAB		37	E3
AGOURA CT	AGH	AGO		102	E4
AGOURA RD	AGH	AGO		100A	B4
AGOURA RD	AGH	AGO		102	E4
AGOURA RD	CO	AGO		100A	F4
AGOURA RD	CO	CAL		100	A4
AGOURA RD	CO	CAL		100A	F4
AGOURA RD	WLVL	THO		102	B4
AGOURA GLEN DR	AGH	AGO		100A	A3
AGRA ST	BG	BELL	5500	53	E5
AGRA ST	CMRC	LA40	6700	54	B5
AGRAMONTE DR	SCLR	NEW		127	C5
AGRCULTR VLY RD	CO	POM		93	E3
AGUADERO PL	SCLR	SAU	22600	124	C5
AGUA DULC CY RD	CO	SAU		181	C9
AGUA DULC CY RD	CO	SAU		188	B6
AGUILAR ST	LA	LA65		25	E6
AGUILAR WY	LA	LA65		25	E6
AGUIRO ST	CO	LPUE		97	A5
AGUIRO ST	CO	LPUE	18200	98	D5
AGUIRRE AV	SAD	SAD	700	89	E2
AGUSTA AV	CO	LA23	1100	53	D1
AHERN DR	BAP	BAP	3400	39	E5
AHERN DR	BAP	BAP	3100	48	D1
AHERN DR	CO	LPUE	800	48	C2
AHLIN DR	LCF	LCF	2000	18	F2
AHMANN AV	WHI	WHI	8900	61	F2
AHMANN AV	WHI	WHI		84	A2
AHTENA DR	DBAR	WAL	1100	97	C3
AHUACATE DR	LHH	LAH	2000	98A	A1
AIDA PL	LA	WOH		13	A3
AIDAN ST	CO	LAN	47600	147	J7
AIGLON ST	LA	PP		40	C3
AIKEN AV	LA	LA64	2500	42	A4
AIKEN RD	CO	GL14		11	F5
AIKEN RD	CO	MAL		105	C6
AILEAN CT	SCLR	VAL		127	C1
AILERON AV	CO	LPUE	1200	92	A4
AILERON AV	LPUE	LPUE	600	92	A4
AINSWORTH AV	TOR	TOR	16700	63	B5
AINSWORTH ST	LA	GAR	13500	63	F2
AINSWORTH ST	LA	LA44	11800	57	F6
AINTREE LN	LA	LA23	3100	45	A6
AIR WY	GLEN	GL01	1400	24	F2
AIR WY	GLEN	GL01	900	25	A2
AIRCRAFT TR	CO	TOP		109	D4
AIRDROME ST	LA	LA19	5500	42	D3
AIRDROME ST	LA	LA35	5900	42	D3
AIREDALE CT	SAD	SAD		89	D4
AIRLANE AV	LA	LA45	7800	50	C6
AIRLANE AV	LA	LA45	7800	56	C1
AIRLIE DR	LA	TU		10	F1
AIRLINE WY	CO	GAR	500	64	B4
AIROLE WY	LA	LA77		32	D4
AIROSO RD	LHH	LAH	2400	98	B6
AIROSO RD	LHH	LAH	2400	98A	B1
AIRPOINT AV	DOW	DOW	12800	66	A1
AIRPORT AV	SM	SM	2400	49	D1

STREET	CITY	P.O. ZONE	BLOCK	PAGE	GRID
AIRPORT BLVD	LA	LA45	7400	50	D6
AIRPORT BLVD	LA	LA45	7800	56	D3
AIRPORT DR	TOR	TOR		73	B2
AIRPORT LN	LB	LB06		75	F1
AIRPORT RD	LA	LA45		56	D3
AIRPORT WY	LB	LB06		75	F1
AIRPORT WY	LB	LB06		76	A1
AIRPORT PZ DR	LB	LB15		71	B6
AIRPORT PZ DR	LB	LB15		76	B1
AIRSHIRE LN	POM	POM	800	95	A5
AIRVILLE AV	SCLR	NEW	24600	127	B4
AIVLIS ST	LB	LB15	7000	76	F2
AJANTA AV	CO	LPUE	1100	98	F3
AJAX AV	BG	BELL	6200	53	E6
AJAX AV	IND	LPUE	1000	98	D2
AJAX CIR	IND	LPUE		98	D2
AJAX CIR	WCOV	WCOV		92	C4
AJAY DR	LA	SV		16	F2
AKASKA DR	CO	PALM		183	E5
AKELEY DR N	GLDR	GLDR	600	87	C4
AKELEY DR S	GLDR	GLDR	100	87	C5
AKKER DR	CO	PALM		157	F8
AKRON PL	CLA	CLA	1300	91	C2
AKRON ST	LA	PP		40	B3
AL ST	LA	LA45		50	E6
ALABAMA AV	CO	LA59	11600	58	D5
ALABAMA AV	LA	CAN	6800	12	C4
ALABAMA AV	LA	CHA	10300	6	C2
ALABAMA ST	CO	GL14	2700	11	D5
ALABAMA ST	GLEN	GL14	3200	11	D5
ALABAMA ST	SGAB	SGAB	100	37	E2
ALABAMA ST	WCOV	WCOV		92	D4
ALABAR DR	PALM	LAN		171	C4
ALABASTRO DR	SCLR	VAL		124	C6
ALABEGA CT	SCLR	VAL		127	C8
ALACA DR	CO	ALT	3100	20	B4
ALADA DR	DBAR	POM		94	A6
ALADDIN ST	LA	LA08	5600	50	E1
ALAFLORA DR	RPV	SP	27900	73	D6
ALAGA AV	CO	PEAR	32400	192	C2
ALAGON ST	CO	PALM		189	H1
ALAHMAR ST	ALH	ALH	400	37	D2
ALAHMAR TER	SGAB	SGAB	340	37	D2
ALAIN CT	LAN	LAN		160	D6
ALAMANOR CT	WAL	WAL		92	F6
ALAMEDA AV	AZU	AZU	300	86	D6
ALAMEDA AV	AZU	AZU		88	D2
ALAMEDA AV	GLEN	GL01	1100	17	F6
ALAMEDA AV E	BUR	BUR	100	17	F6
ALAMEDA AV E	BUR	BUR	1	24	B3
ALAMEDA AV N	AZU	AZU	100	88	D1
ALAMEDA AV W	BUR	BUR	100	17	F6
ALAMEDA AV W	BUR	BUR	4000	24	B3
ALAMEDA PL	POM	POM		90	E6
ALAMEDA PL	POM	POM		94	E1
ALAMEDA ST	CAR	LB10	20400	69	E5
ALAMEDA ST	CAR	LB10	23800	74	E2
ALAMEDA ST	CO	ALT	200	20	A5
ALAMEDA ST	DOW	DOW	8000	60	A5
ALAMEDA ST	HPK	HPK	5800	52	E1
ALAMEDA ST	LYN	LYN		58	E1
ALAMEDA ST	PAS	PAS	3000	27	F3
ALAMEDA ST	POM	POM	1400	90	E6
ALAMEDA ST	SOG	SOG	9200	58	E1
ALAMEDA ST	VER	LA58	2600	52	E1
ALAMEDA ST N	COM	COM	3100	58	E6
ALAMEDA ST N	COM	COM	100	64	F1
ALAMEDA ST N	LA	LA12	100	44	E4
ALAMEDA ST S	CAR	LB10	20500	69	E5
ALAMEDA ST S	CO	COM	12400	58	E1
ALAMEDA ST S	CO	COM	12900	64	F1
ALAMEDA ST S	CO	COM	18000	65	A1
ALAMEDA ST S	CO	COM	18500	70	A2
ALAMEDA ST S	CO	LA01	7200	52	E1
ALAMEDA ST S	CO	LA01	7900	58	E1
ALAMEDA ST S	CO	LA02	8600	58	E1
ALAMEDA ST S	COM	COM	100	65	A1
ALAMEDA ST S	LA	LA12	100	44	E4
ALAMEDA ST S	LA	LA13	300	44	E4
ALAMEDA ST S	LA	LA21	600	44	E4
ALAMEDA ST S	LA	LA58	1900	52	E1
ALAMINOS DR	SCLR	SAU		124	E5
ALAMITAS AV	MON	MON	1100	29	A5
ALAMITOS AV	LB	LB02	1	75	D4
ALAMITOS AV	LB	LB06	1800	75	D4
ALAMITOS AV	LB	LB13	700	75	D4
ALAMO AV	BELL	BELL	6200	53	D5
ALAMO AV	CDY	BELL	8100	59	D1
ALAMO AV	MAY	MAY	5800	53	D5
ALAMO CT	LB	LB13		75	C5
ALAMO CT	LYN	LYN	11200	58	F4
ALAMO DR	GLEN	GL07	1500	25	E1
ALAMO DR	MPK	MPK	2000	45	E2
ALAMO LN	LB	LB04	3100	75	F5
ALAMO ST	LA	WOH		13	C3
ALAMOGORDO RD	SCLR	SAU	21800	124	D6

STREET	CITY	P.O. ZONE	BLOCK	PAGE	GRID
ALAMO HTS DR	DBAR	POM		97	F5
ALAMOS LN	SCLR	NEW		127	C5
ALAMOSA AV	PALM	PALM		172	B9
ALAMOSA DR	CLA	CLA	300	96	C6
ALAMOTA DR	SCLR	SAU		124	C5
ALANA DR	LA	VAN		22	B5
ALAND ST W	LAN	LAN	2600	159	G6
ALANDA PL	LA	BH		33	C2
ALANDELE AV	LA	LA36	800	42	F2
ALANDELE AV	LA	LA36	6400	42	F1
ALANMAY AV	SGAB	SGAB	100	37	D3
ALANREED AV	RM	RM	3200	46	F1
ALANWOOD RD	CO	LPUE	13100	48	B4
ALARCON PL	PAS	PAS	1000	26	F6
ALARKA ST	NWK	NWK	12500	82	C1
ALASKA AV	ELS	ELS	1900	62	D1
ALASKA AV	TOR	TOR		68	C3
ALASKA ST	WCOV	WCOV	1600	92	E2
ALATAR DR	LA	WOH		13	C3
ALATHA ST	CER	ART	17400	82	C5
ALAYA DR	SCLR	SAU		124	D6
ALBA ST	LA	LA58	5500	52	E4
ALBADA CT	CO	CAL		100	F3
ALBANY CT	CLA	CLA		91	D2
ALBANY CT	PALM	PALM		183	J1
ALBANY ST	HPK	HPK	5900	52	E5
ALBANY ST	LA	LA15		44	B4
ALBARIZA PL	DBAR	POM		97	F2
ALBATA ST	LA	LA49		41	C1
ALBATROSS AV	LA	WIL	24400	74	C1
ALBATROSS RD	IND	LPUE	1400	98	C3
ALBECK AV	LAN	LAN	43700	159	H6
ALBECK CT	LAN	LAN		159	G6
ALBEDO ST	CO	LPUE		85	C4
ALBEE ST	MTB	MTB	700	54	D4
ALBEMARLE ST	LA	WIL		74	E3
ALBERAN AV	LB	LB08	3800	71	E5
ALBERCA DR	CO	LPUE	2000	98	E4
ALBERNI AV	LA	SF		10	A1
ALBERS PL	LA	VAN		23	A1
ALBERS ST	LA	ENC	16800	21	E1
ALBERS ST	LA	NHO	11400	23	B1
ALBERS ST	LA	VAN	12900	22	D1
ALBERS ST	LA	VAN	12900	23	A1
ALBERS ST	LA	WOH		100	E1
ALBERT AV	CER	ART	19200	81	A2
ALBERT AV	POM	POM	100	90	F5
ALBERT AV	TOR	TOR	22000	67	E5
ALBERT ST	LPUE	LPUE	100	48	F6
ALBERT WY	ARC	ARC	2400	38	D2
ALBERTA AV	LA	VEN	1900	49	C4
ALBERTA AV	LYN	LYN	4000	59	C5
ALBERTA DR	LA	CUL	12000	50	B4
ALBERTA PL	CO	LR		184	D6
ALBERTA ST	CO	ALT		19	E5
ALBERTA ST	LA	SP		78	E4
ALBERTA ST	TOR	TOR	2800	68	E6
ALBERTINE ST	LA	LA23	800	45	B5
ALBERTO CT	SCLR	VAL		124	A2
ALBERTONI ST	CAR	CAR	100	64	B5
ALBERTSON AV	CO	COM	13900	64	D2
ALBERTSON AV	CO	COV	3200	88	E3
ALBERTSON AV	COM	COM	400	64	D2
ALBERTSON AV N	COV	COV	1200	88	E3
ALBERTSON AV S	COV	COV	300	88	E6
ALBIA ST	DOW	DOW	7900	60	A4
ALBION ST	LA	LA31	2000	35	F6
ALBION ST	LA	LA31	1700	44	F1
ALBONA PL	POM	POM	500	93	F3
ALBONI PL	LB	LB02	1	75	D6
ALBRECQ DR	CO	CAST		123	B3
ALBREDA ST	CAR	CAR	1600	69	D4
ALBRET AV	LAN	LAN		159	G4
ALBRET ST W	LAN	LAN	1500	159	H4
ALBRIGHT AV	CUL	LA66	4000	50	A2
ALBRIGHT ST	LA	PP		40	D3
ALBRO ST N	LA	SP		78	E2
ALBURTIS AV	ART	ART	18600	81	A1
ALBURTIS AV	ART	ART	16600	82	A5
ALBURTIS AV	CER	ART	19400	81	A2
ALBURTIS AV	CO	WHI	8300	55	B6
ALBURTIS AV	CO	WHI	8300	61	B1
ALBURTIS AV	LKD	LKD	19700	81	A2
ALBURTIS AV	LKD	LKD	20500	81	A4
ALBURTIS AV	NWK	NWK	11000	61	A5
ALBURTIS AV	NWK	NWK	11000	82	A1
ALBURTIS AV	SFS	SFS	9000	61	A2
ALBURY AV	LB	LB08	3600	71	D5
ALBURY AV	LB	LB15	2000	76	D3
ALBURY AV	LKD	LKD	4300	71	D3
ALBURY ST	SCLR	SAU	19500	124	H7
ALBYN CT	CO	LH		157	B6
ALCADE ST	CO	LPUE		48	B4
ALCALDE DR	GLEN	GL07	1000	25	E1
ALCALDE WY	GLEN	GL07	900	25	E1
ALCAMO DR	CO	CAL		100	E5

STREET	CITY	P.O. ZONE	BLOCK	PAGE	GRID
ALCAZAR ST	LA	LA33	2200	45	C2
ALCHESTER ST	CER	ART	12700	81	C1
ALCIMA AV	LA	PP		40	C3
ALCLAD AV	CO	WHI	10700	61	D5
ALCOA AV	VER	LA58	4300	53	B4
ALCOBA ST	CER	ART	12000	81	B2
ALCON DR	SCLR	SAU	26800	124	D7
ALCONA ST	CO	LPUE		97	A5
ALCONBURY ST	CER	ART	12700	81	C1
ALCOR ST	LOM	LOM		73	D2
ALCORN DR	LCF	LCF	4500	19	A2
ALCOTT AV	POM	POM	500	94	F4
ALCOTT ST	LA	LA35	6000	42	E3
ALCOVE AV	LA	NHO	3900	16	A2
ALCOVE AV	LA	NHO	3900	23	A2
ALCOY CT	CO	LAN		159	C9
ALCROSS ST	CO	COV	16700	88	C3
ALCROSS ST	COV	COV	17700	88	D3
ALCYONA DR	LA	LA68	2100	34	C2
ALDA CT	DBAR	WAL		97	C3
ALDAMA AV	POM	POM	100	90	F3
ALDAMA ST	LA	LA42		36	B2
ALDAMA TER	LA	LA42		36	B2
ALDBURY CT	LA	BH		32	F1
ALDBURY ST	SCLR	CYN	19500	124	H7
ALDEA AV	LA	ENC	5000	14	E6
ALDEA AV	LA	ENC	5000	21	E1
ALDEA AV	LA	NOR	9100	7	E3
ALDEA AV	LA	SF	10300	1	E6
ALDEA AV	LA	SF	10300	7	E2
ALDEA AV	LA	VAN	6400	14	E2
ALDEA DR	MTB	MTB		46	D6
ALDEN DR	BH	BH	9100	33	C6
ALDEN DR	LA	LA48		33	C6
ALDEN RD	CLA	CLA	600	91	B3
ALDENVALE AV	LAN	LAN		159	H3
ALDENVILLE AV	CO	COV	4900	88	E3
ALDENVILLE AV N	COV	COV	1300	88	E3
ALDENVILLE AV S	COV	COV	300	88	E6
ALDER	WCOV	WCOV		98	F1
ALDER CT	AZU	AZU	200	86	C3
ALDER DR	LA	LA65		35	F3
ALDER LN	IND	WAL	600	97	D1
ALDER LN	PAS	PAS	3600	20A	A3
ALDER LN	PAS	PAS	3600	28	A1
ALDER ST	POM	POM	2400	91	A5
ALDERBROOK DR	SCLR	NEW	24600	127	C3
ALDERBURY DR	CO	LPUE	18600	98	E6
ALDERDALE ST	DOW	DOW	7700	54	C6
ALDERGATE ST	MPK	MPK		46	C4
ALDER GLEN CIR	SCLR	VAL		124	B4
ALDERGROVE ST	LA	SF		2	F1
ALDER PEAK AV	SCLR	CYN		125	C7
ALDERPOINT DR	LAM	LAM		83	A3
ALDER RIDGE DR	LCF	LCF	4700	19	C1
ALDERSGATE DR	CO	LAV	1500	95A	C6
ALDERSGATE DR	LAV	LAV	1500	95A	C6
ALDERSON AV	BAP	BAP	4200	39	F4
ALDERTON AV	CO	LPUE	300	98	D1
ALDERTON LN	CER	ART	13600	82	E4
ALDERWOOD RD	CO	PALM		157	H9
ALDERWOOD ST	LAM	LAM		83	C1
ALDGATE AV	CO	LPUE	600	48	E4
ALDGATE AV	LPUE	LPUE	300	48	E5
ALDINE CT	LA	SP		78	E4
ALDIS ST	CO	LA01	1400	58	D1
ALDIS ST	POM	POM	500	94	A2
ALDON AV	LAV	LAV	2400	90	E3
ALDORA DR	CO	LPUE	19000	98	F3
ALDREN CT	AGH	AGO		102	D3
ALDRICH RD	SOG	SOG	5100	59	D4
ALDRICH ST	CO	WHI	10500	55	B4
ALDRICH ST	PR	PR	8700	54	E3
ALDRICH ST	PR	PR	9400	55	A4
ALEDO DR	LA	WOH	4400	13	C3
ALEGRE LN	CO	ALT	3200	20	C3
ALEGRE PL	LA	LA65		35	F2
ALEGRIA AV	PAS	PAS	3500	28	A1
ALEGRIA AV E	SMAD	SMAD	1	28	B1
ALEGRIA AV W	SMAD	SMAD	1	28	B1
ALEGRIA PL	SMAR	PAS	600	27	E5
ALEGRO DR	SCLR	VAL		127	A2
ALEGRO SQ	SGAB	SGAB	1600	37	E5
ALEJANDRO DR	SCLR	VAL		124	A1
ALEMAN AV	PR	PR	3800	55	B1
ALEMAN DR	LA	TAR	14000	13	F4
ALENE DR	LA	TU		10	F4
ALENE WK	LA	TU	9800	10	F4
ALEP ST	LAN	LAN	42800	159	F8
ALERION PL	LA	WOH		13	E2
ALESIA ST	SELM	ELM	9900	47	C3
ALESNA DR	SCLR	VAL		127	C8
ALESSANDRO AV	LAV	LAV	800	90	B2
ALESSANDRO AV	TEC	TEC	4800	38	B3
ALESSANDRO PL	PAS	PAS	99	26	F5
ALETHEA DR	LA	SUN	11000	10	E1

STREET	CITY	P.O. ZONE	BLOCK	PAGE	GRID
ALETHEA DR	LA	TU	11300	10	E1
ALETA WY	PALM	LAN		171	C4
ALETTA AV	CUL	CUL	10900	50	B2
ALEXANDER AV	CER	ART	18900	81	D1
ALEXANDER AV	CER	ART	16600	82	D5
ALEXANDER AV	LYN	LYN	10600	59	C4
ALEXANDER AV	SOG	SOG	8900	59	C4
ALEXANDER CIR	CER	ART	18700	81	D1
ALEXANDER PL	CER	ART	17700	82	D6
ALEXANDER ST	CMRC	LA40		53	F4
ALEXANDER ST	GLEN	GL03	500	25	B3
ALEXANDER ST	LA	SF	12800	3	A4
ALEXANDER ST	LA	SF	14800	8	D1
ALEXANDER ST	SF	SF	100	2	E5
ALEXANDER WY	PR	PR		55	E3
ALEXANDRA CIR	CER	ART	17200	82	D5
ALEXANDRA CT	CO	CAL		100	D5
ALEXANDRIA AV	CO	HAC	24200	73	F2
ALEXANDRIA AV	CO	TOR	22300	68	F6
ALEXANDRIA AV N	LA	LA04	100	34	E6
ALEXANDRIA AV N	LA	LA27	1300	34	E3
ALEXANDRIA AV N	LA	LA29	700	34	E5
ALEXANDRIA AV S	LA	LA04	100	34	E6
ALEXANDRIA AV S	LA	LA20	300	43	E1
ALEXANDRIA PL	LA	LA04		34	E5
ALEXDALE LN	CO	LPUE	2100	98	F5
ALEXIS PL	BH	BH	1500	33	C3
ALEXO DR	LAN	LAN	42800	159	E8
ALF AV	CO	PALM		172	H6
ALFARENA PL	LA	TAR		21	B3
ALFELD AV	CO	LA61		64	B2
ALFIE RD	CO	SAU		181	F8
ALFONSO DR	AGH	AGO		102	E4
ALFORD ST	AZU	AZU	18500	88	E1
ALFORD ST	CO	AZU	18000	88	F1
ALFORD ST	CO	GLDR	19000	88	F1
ALFORD ST	CO	GLDR	19100	89	A1
ALFORD ST	SAD	SAD	100	89	F1
ALFRED AV	CER	ART	18700	81	C1
ALFRED AV	CER	ART	17000	82	C5
ALFRED DR	CLA	CLA		91	C1
ALFRED DR	CLA	CLA		96	B6
ALFRED PL	MTB	MTB		46	E5
ALFRED ST	LA	LA35	1000	42	E2
ALFRED ST	LA	LA48	300	33	E5
ALFRED ST	LA	LA69	700	33	E5
ALFRED ST	WHOL	LA48	500	33	E5
ALFREDO CT	AGH	AGO		102	E3
ALGARDI ST	NWK	NWK	11800	82	A4
ALGECIRAS DR	LAM	LAM	14600	83	C2
ALGER ST	LA	LA39	4300	25	B5
ALGEROMA ST	BLF	BLF	9000	66	B3
ALGIERS ST	LA	NOR		7	B1
ALGINET DR	LA	ENC	3100	21	F5
ALGINET PL	LA	ENC	16700	21	F5
ALGODON CT	LA	LA46		33	E1
ALGOMA AV	LA	LA41	4900	26	B5
ALGONAUT DR	CO	WOH		13	B5
ALGONQUIN DR	CO	LPUE	1100	92	B4
ALGOOD DR	CO	PALM		157	F8
ALGRANTI AV	LA	SF		3	B1
ALGROVE ST	COV	COV	300	88	F5
ALGROVE ST	COV	COV	1400	89	B5
ALGUNAS RD	LA	WOH		13	B3
ALHAMA DR	LA	WOH	4100	13	D2
ALHAMBRA AV	COM	COM	1700	65	A1
ALHAMBRA AV	LA	LA12	1000	44	E2
ALHAMBRA AV	LA	LA31	1800	45	A1
ALHAMBRA AV	LA	LA32	5000	36	D6
ALHAMBRA AV	PAR	PAR	8000	59	F6
ALHAMBRA AV	PAR	PAR	8000	65	F1
ALHAMBRA AV	PAR	PAR	8000	66	A1
ALHAMBRA AV N	MPK	MPK	100	46	D2
ALHAMBRA AV S	MPK	MPK	100	46	D2
ALHAMBRA CT	LA	VEN	1100	49	C4
ALHAMBRA CT	LB	LB13	1100	75	D4
ALHAMBRA RD	LA	LA31		45	A2
ALHAMBRA RD	SMAR	PAS	1800	37	D1
ALHAMBRA RD	SPAS	SPAS	1300	36	F3
ALHAMBRA RD E	ALH	ALH	1	37	C3
ALHAMBRA RD N	SGAB	SGAB	300	37	C3
ALHAMBRA RD W	ALH	ALH	1	36	F3
ALHAMBRA RD W	SGAB	SGAB	1100	37	C3
ALICANTE	POM	POM		90	C6
ALICANTE DR	CO	CAL		100	C5
ALICANTE DR	SCLR	VAL		127	B1
ALICANTE RD	LAM	LAM	14300	82	F2
ALICANTE RD	LAM	LAM	15000	83	B2
ALICE AV	CO	COM	11800	65	D1
ALICE AV	LYN	LYN	11800	65	D1
ALICE ST	ARC	ARC	1	28	E5
ALICE ST	LA	LA65		35	E4
ALICIA AV	CO	ALT	3200	20	A3
ALICIA CT	POM	POM		94	E4
ALICIA ST	WCOV	WCOV		92	E6
ALIDA AV	CER	ART	19500	81	A2

STREET	CITY	P.O. ZONE	BLOCK	PAGE	GRID
ALIDA LN	CO	PALM		183	J5
ALINE WY	CO	CAL		108	B5
ALISAL CT	LA	SM		40	E4
ALISAL LN	LA	SM		40	E4
ALISAL ST	COV	COV	400	88	F5
ALISAL ST	WCOV	WCOV	1700	88	A5
ALISAR AV	MPK	MPK	1600	46	D4
ALISO CIR	LAV	LAV		90	E1
ALISO ST	CO	ACT		189	E1
ALISO ST	DOW	DOW	7400	59	E5
ALISO ST	LA	LA12		44	E2
ALISO ST	MPK	MPK	300	46	A2
ALISO ST E	POM	POM	100	90	E5
ALISO ST W	POM	POM	100	90	E5
ALISO CANYON RD	CO	PALM		189	H2
ALISO VILLAGE	LA	LA33		44	E3
ALISU CT	WAL	WAL		97	B1
ALIWIN ST	DOW	DOW	9700	60	E3
ALIX AV	CO	LA01	7900	58	E1
ALIYAH WY	LA	WOH		5	D6
ALIZIA CYN DR	CO	CAL		100	A2
ALIZONDO DR	LA	WOH		13	C3
ALLA RD	CUL	LA66	4000	49	E3
ALLA RD	LA	LA66	3900	49	E3
ALL AMER CTY WY	PAR	PAR		65	E2
ALLAN AV	BUR	BUR	3900	16	F6
ALLAN AV	BUR	BUR	3500	17	A6
ALLAN ST	LA	LA32		36	E5
ALLANJAY PL	GLEN	GL08	2100	18	F5
ALLARD ST	NWK	NWK	11600	60	F5
ALLARD ST	NWK	NWK	11600	61	A5
ALLARD ST	SFS	SFS	12600	61	C5
ALLASEBA DR	LA	LA66	11800	49	E1
ALLBROOK ST	LOM	LOM	2000	73	D2
ALLEGAN ST	CO	WHI	13300	61	D3
ALLEGANY CT	CLA	CLA		91	C1
ALLEGHENY ST	LA	SV	10000	9	E4
ALLEN AV	CO	ALT	1900	20	D6
ALLEN AV	CO	PAS	1500	20	D6
ALLEN AV	GLDR	GLDR	1100	89	C1
ALLEN AV	GLEN	GL01	1000	17	F6
ALLEN AV	GLEN	GL01	1300	18	A6
ALLEN AV	GLEN	GL01	100	24	E2
ALLEN AV	PAR	PAR		65	E4
ALLEN AV	SMAR	PAS	500	27	D5
ALLEN AV E	SAD	SAD	100	90	A1
ALLEN AV N	PAS	PAS	1	27	D4
ALLEN AV S	PAS	PAS	1	27	D4
ALLEN AV W	SAD	SAD	100	89	E1
ALLEN CT	PAS	PAS	1800	27	D4
ALLEN DR	IRW	BAP	5000	88	B3
ALLEN ST	PAR	PAR		65	E3
ALLENBY CT	WLVL	THO		102	A4
ALLENDALE RD	PAS	PAS	200	27	A6
ALLENFORD AV	LA	LA49	1400	40	F2
ALLENGROVE ST	DOW	DOW	7200	54	C6
ALLENGROVE ST	DOW	DOW	7200	60	C1
ALLENHURST ST	CO	LA61		64	B2
ALLENTON AV	CO	LPUE	2600	85	E5
ALLENTOWN DR	LA	WOH		13	E2
ALLENTOWN PL	LA	WOH		13	E2
ALLENWICK AV	SCLR	CYN	27400	124	H5
ALLENWOOD RD	LA	LA46	8400	33	D1
ALLEPPO LN	PALM	LAN		171	B2
ALLER CT	GLEN	GL06		25	F2
ALLERTON ST	CO	WHI	10600	55	B5
ALLERTON ST	CO	WHI	13600	61	E3
ALLESANDRO ST	LA	LA26	1300	35	C4
ALLESANDRO ST	LA	LA39	2000	35	C4
ALLESANDRO WY	LA	LA39	2200	35	C4
ALLGEYER AV	ELM	ELM	2200	47	E3
ALLGEYER AV	SELM	ELM	1200	47	D4
ALLIANCE AV	SH	LB06		75	E2
ALLIED WY	ELS	ELS		62	C1
ALLIENE AV	LOM	LOM	24100	73	D3
ALLIENE AV	TOR	TOR	23800	73	D1
ALLIN ST	LA	CUL	11700	50	A4
ALLIN ST	LA	LA66	12400	50	A4
ALLIN ST	LB	LB03	3900	80	A1
ALLINGHAM AV	CER	ART		71	E2
ALLINGHAM AV	NWK	NWK	14400	66	E3
ALLINGTON ST	BLF	BLF	10400	66	C6
ALLINGTON ST	LB	LB05	100	65	B6
ALLINGTON ST	LB	LB05	3800	66	A6
ALLINGTON ST	LKD	LKD	5500	66	C6
ALLIS DR	MTB	MTB	400	54	D4
ALLISON AV	LA	LA26		35	C6
ALLISON DR	SCLR	SAU		124	E5
ALLMAN PL	CO	COV		93	A1
ALLMAN ST	AGH	AGO		100A	A2
ALLMERS ST	CO	ACT		189	E1
ALLOTT AV	LA	VAN	5600	15	F2
ALLOTT AV	LA	VAN	4100	22	F4
ALLPORT AV	SFS	SFS	8100	55	B6
ALLPORT AV	SFS	SFS	8100	61	B1

212
1990 LOS ANGELES COUNTY STREET INDEX
ALLRED ST — ANADALE DR

LOS ANGELES CO.

STREET	CITY	P.O. ZONE	BLOCK	PAGE	GRID
ALLRED ST	LKD	LKD	2400	70	F3
ALLRED ST	LKD	LKD	2400	71	A3
ALLSTON ST	CO	LA22	5800	54	B1
ALLSTON ST	MTB	MTB	2200	54	B1
ALLVIEW TER	LA	LA68	2300	34	D2
ALLWOOD CT	CO	LPUE		97	A5
ALLWOOD CT	CO	LPUE		98	F5
ALMA AV	GAR	GAR	13500	63	E1
ALMA AV	LYN	LYN	3300	59	A4
ALMA AV	MB	MB	2200	62	A2
ALMA AV N	CO	LA63	100	45	C5
ALMA AV S	CO	LA23	800	45	C6
ALMA AV S	CO	LA63	100	45	C5
ALMA CT	CLA	CLA	1100	90	F2
ALMA ST	GLEN	GL02	700	25	B2
ALMA ST	LB	LB05		65	D4
ALMA ST S	LA	SP	700	78	E4
ALMADA ST	LB	LB15	6700	76	E4
ALMADALE AV	LA	LA32	2000	45	C1
ALMADEN CT	LA	LA77		32	E1
ALMADEN DR	LA	LA42	4900	26	B6
ALMADIN AV	CER	ART	19300	81	B2
ALMAHURST ST	IND	LPUE		98	C3
ALMANAC DR	WCOV	WCOV	17300	92	C4
ALMANSOR ST N	ALH	ALH	1	37	C3
ALMANSOR ST S	ALH	ALH	1	37	C3
ALMANZA LN	CO	LA63	4000	45	D3
ALMAR AV	LA	PP	400	40	C4
ALMAR PLAZA	LA	PP	16000	40	C4
ALMA REAL DR	LA	PP	200	40	D5
ALMAROSA AV	TOR	TOR	23000	68	C6
ALMARTHA ST	CO	PALM		182	G6
ALMAYO AV	LA	LA64	10200	42	A3
ALMAZAN RD	LA	WOH	20000	13	D4
ALMENA AV	CO	LPUE	1400	98	D3
ALMENDRA DR	SCLR	VAL		127	B1
ALMERIA ST	LA	SP	3100	78	E6
ALMERTENS PL	ING	IN03	11900	57	B5
ALMETZ ST	LA	SF		2	F1
ALMETZ ST	LA	SF		3	A1
ALMEZA AV	CO	LPUE	1700	98	F5
ALMIDOR AV	LA	WOH	4700	100	F2
ALMINAR AV	LCF	LCF	4700	19	D3
ALMIRA RD	SOG	SOG	5100	59	D4
ALMIRANTE DR	WCOV	WCOV	600	92	E2
ALMO ST	PR	PR	9200	55	A3
ALMOLOYA DR	LA	PP	500	40	D4
ALMOND AL	CO	ALT	3000	20	A4
ALMOND AV	LB	LB02	400	75	E5
ALMOND AV	MON	MON	400	29	B4
ALMOND AV	PALM	LAN		171	C2
ALMOND CT	LB	LB13	1000	75	D4
ALMOND DR	PALM	PALM		183	G7
ALMOND ST	LAV	LAV		90	E1
ALMOND ST E	COM	COM	100	64	F3
ALMOND ST W	COM	COM	100	64	F3
ALMOND VLY WY	CO	LAN		159	A9
ALMONDWOOD AV	LAN	LAN		160	F6
ALMONOR ST	CO	LPUE		98	F1
ALMONT DR N	BH	BH	100	42	D2
ALMONT DR N	LA	LA48	100	33	D6
ALMONT DR N	WHOL	LA69	600	33	D6
ALMONT DR S	BH	BH	100	42	D2
ALMONT DR S	LA	LA48	100	33	D6
ALMONT ST	LA	LA32	5100	36	E4
ALMORA ST	MPK	MPK	200	46	B4
ALOE DR	LAM	LAM	15000	83	B1
ALOHA CIR	LB	LB05		65	C5
ALOHA DR	LA	PP		40	C4
ALOHA ST	LA	LA27	3700	35	B2
ALOJAR LN	PALM	LAN		171	D4
ALOMAR DR	LA	VAN	3600	23	A4
ALONDA DR	CAR	CAR	19700	69	C2
ALONDRA BLVD	BLF	BLF	8700	66	B3
ALONDP 3LVD	BLF	BLF	9000	66	B3
ALONDRA BLVD	LAM	LAM	14200	82	C3
ALONDRA BLVD	LAM	LAM	14500	83	A4
ALONDRA BLVD	NWK	NWK	10600	66	E4
ALONDRA BLVD	NWK	NWK	10600	82	C3
ALONDRA BLVD	PAR	PAR	6400	65	E4
ALONDRA BLVD	PAR	PAR	8400	66	B3
ALONDRA BLVD	SFS	SFS	13000	82	C3
ALONDRA BLVD E	CO	COM	600	64	A4
ALONDRA BLVD E	CO	COM	4600	65	E4
ALONDRA BLVD E	CO	GAR	100	64	A4
ALONDRA BLVD E	COM	COM	100	64	D4
ALONDRA BLVD E	COM	COM	700	65	E4
ALONDRA BLVD W	CO	GAR	100	64	A4
ALONDRA BLVD W	COM	COM	100	64	D3
ALONDRA BLVD W	LA	GAR	500	63	F4
ALONDRA BLVD W	LA	GAR	500	64	A4
ALONDRA CIR	LAV	LAV		90	B2
ALONDRA DR	LA	PP	800	40	A3
ALONDRA LN	LAV	LAV		95A	D4
ALONZO AV	LA	ENC	4500	14	D6
ALONZO AV	LA	ENC	4200	21	D4
ALONZO AV	LA	RES	6100	14	D6
ALONZO PL	LA	ENC	17000	21	D3
ALORA AV	CER	ART	17400	66	F6
ALORA AV	NWK	NWK	16600	66	F5
ALORA AV	NWK	NWK	16300	66	F5
ALOSTA AV	AZU	AZU	600	86	E6
ALOSTA AV	CO	AZU	18100	86	E6
ALOSTA AV E	GLDR	GLDR	100	87	B6
ALOSTA AV W	GLDR	GLDR	100	87	B6
ALP TR	LA	TU		11	B4
ALPACA ST	CO	RM	7800	46	E3
ALPACA ST	SELM	ELM	9600	47	C3
ALPERN DR	CO	LPUE	14900	85	C1
ALPHA AV	BLF	BLF	15900	66	B4
ALPHA AV	CO	PAS	1400	27	D1
ALPHA AV	SPAS	SPAS	1800	36	F3
ALPHA CIR	LAV	LAV		90	D1
ALPHA RD	GLEN	GL08	1800	18	F5
ALPHA RD	GLEN	GL08	2000	19	A5
ALPHA ST	ING	IN02	900	51	B5
ALPHA ST	IRW	DUA		39	C1
ALPHA ST	LA	LA32		36	F4
ALPHINGTON AV	CER	ART	19000	81	C1
ALPINE AV	LB	LB02	100	75	A6
ALPINE AV	LYN	LYN	12100	59	A6
ALPINE DR	BH	BH	300	33	B5
ALPINE DR	SMAR	PAS	1800	37	D1
ALPINE DR	WCOV	WCOV	1300	92	E4
ALPINE ST	LA	LA12	1000	44	D1
ALPINE ST	PAS	PAS	200	27	A6
ALPINE TER	MPK	MPK	1000	46	A3
ALPINE TR	CO	TOP	1200	109	B6
ALPINE WY	LA	TU	7300	10	F1
ALPINE MDW CIR	WAL	WAL		93	C4
ALPINE VILLA DR	CO	ALT	900	20	C3
ALS DR	SELM	ELM	9700	47	C2
ALSACE AV	LA	LA08	3800	50	F1
ALSACE AV	LA	LA16	3600	42	F6
ALSACE AV	LA	LA16	2900	43	A5
ALSACE AV	LA	LA19	1800	43	A4
ALSACE AV	LA	LA43	5800	51	A4
ALSINA ST	CO	LA61		64	B2
ALSKOG ST	LA	SV		9	F6
ALSTER AV	ARC	ARC	200	38	F1
ALSTON AV	CO	LAN		174	H4
ALTA AV	SM	SM	100	40	E5
ALTA AV	SM	SM	1500	41	A4
ALTA AV	WHI	WHI	6500	55	E4
ALTA DR	BH	BH	500	33	C5
ALTA DR	CO	TOP	21900	13	C6
ALTA DR	SCLR	VAL		127	B1
ALTA DR	POM	POM	600	95	B2
ALTA PL	LA	LA31		36	B5
ALTA ST	ARC	ARC	1	28	E5
ALTA ST	LA	LA31	2300	36	B6
ALTA ST	LA	LA31	1900	45	B1
ALTA ST	MON	MON	500	29	A4
ALTA TER	CO	GL14	2800	11	D5
ALTA TR	CO	SF		3	E5
ALTA WY	CO	CHA		4	C5
ALTA WY	LB	LB03	100	75	D5
ALTA CANYADA RD	LCF	LCF	4300	19	A2
ALTA CREST DR	CO	ALT	1700	20	D4
ALTA CUESTA CR	DBAR	POM		97A	B1
ALTADENA DR E	CO	ALT	1	20	A4
ALTADENA DR N	CO	ALT	1700	20	C4
ALTADENA DR N	CO	PAS	1200	27	E4
ALTADENA DR N	PAS	PAS	1	27	C5
ALTADENA DR S	PAS	PAS	1	27	E4
ALTADENA DR W	CO	ALT	1	19	F4
ALTAGRACIA DR	LA	TU		11	B5
ALTA HACINDA DR	WAL	WAL	20200	93	B3
ALTAIR DR	LA	LA49		41	B1
ALTAIR PL	LA	VEN	400	49	C4
ALTA KNOLL DR	SCLR	SAU		124	F6
ALTALAKE AV	BAP	BAP	4300	39	E4
ALTA LOMA RD	WHOL	LA69	1000	33	E4
ALTA LOMA TER	LA	LA68	6700	34	B2
ALTA MADERA DR	SCLR	VAL		127	B1
ALTAMAR PL	SFS	SFS	12000	61	B2
ALTAMERE AV	SCLR	CYN	27300	124	J8
ALTA MESA DR	LA	NHO		23	B5
ALTA MESA PL	LA	NHO		23	B5
ALTA MESA PL	MPK	MPK	700	46	B3
ALTA MESA RD	CO	SF		3	E2
ALTAMIRA CIR	WCOV	WCOV		92	D5
ALTAMIRA DR	WCOV	WCOV		92	D5
ALTAMIRA LN	PVE	PVP	1600	72	D4
ALTA MIRA PL	POM	POM		94	B4
ALTAMONT ST	LA	LA65		35	F3
ALTAMONT ST	LA	LA65		36	A3
ALTAMONTE AV	SCLR	VAL		127	A2
ALTA MURA RD	LA	PP		40	F2
ALTANO ST	LA	SF		3	A3
ALTA OAKS DR	ARC	ARC	1600	28	E2
ALTA PARK LN	LCF	LCF	1400	19	A2
ALTAPASA AV	CO	ALT		20	A6
ALTAPASA AV	PAS	PAS		20	A6
ALTA PASEO	BUR	BUR	1200	17	F4
ALTA PINE DR	CO	ALT	200	20	B3
ALTARIDGE DR	CO	TOP	21600	109	C1
ALTARIO ST	CO	LPUE	18300	98	E1
ALTA SIERRA RD	WAL	WAL		93	B4
ALTATA DR	LA	PP		40	D5
ALTA TUPELO	CO	CAL		100	D4
ALTAVAN AV	LA	LA45	7800	56	A1
ALTA VIEW DR	LA	LA28		23	E5
ALTA VISTA	AVA	AVA		77	A4
ALTA VISTA	LAV	LAV		95A	E4
ALTA VISTA AV	ARC	ARC	900	29	A6
ALTA VISTA AV	LA	LA46		33	D2
ALTA VISTA AV	LOM	LOM	26200	73	E4
ALTA VISTA AV	SPAS	SPAS	300	36	E2
ALTA VISTA AV N	MON	MON	100	29	A4
ALTA VISTA AV S	MON	MON	100	29	A4
ALTA VISTA BL N	LA	LA36	100	34	A6
ALTA VISTA BL N	LA	LA46	700	34	A6
ALTA VISTA BL S	LA	LA36	100	43	A1
ALTA VISTA CIR	SPAS	SPAS	500	36	E2
ALTA VISTA DR	ALH	ALH	1700	36	F6
ALTA VISTA DR	CO	ALT	900	20	B4
ALTA VISTA DR	GLEN	GL05	600	25	D6
ALTA VISTA DR	LAM	LAM		83	C1
ALTA VISTA DR	LCF	LCF	3900	19	C5
ALTA VISTA DR	POM	POM		90	D6
ALTA VISTA DR	RPV	PVP		77	C2
ALTA VISTA DR	SMAD	SMAD		20A	D3
ALTA VISTA DR	SMAD	SMAD	500	28	D1
ALTA WOOD DR	CO	ALT	1600	20	D4
ALTENA DR	SCLR	SAU		124	E5
ALTERN ST	ARC	ARC	100	28	F6
ALTERN ST	ARC	ARC	1100	29	A6
ALTERN ST E	CO	MON	100	29	A6
ALTERN ST W	CO	MON	100	29	A6
ALTIVO WY	LA	LA26		35	D4
ALTMAN AV	LA	LA34	3800	42	C4
ALTMAN ST	LA	LA31		35	E4
ALTMARK AV	WHI	WHI	6000	55	F4
ALTO CIR	RPV	PVP	6000	72	D5
ALTO CEDRO DR	LA	BH		33	C1
ALTON ST	LA	WIL	1000	74	B4
ALTO OAK DR	LA	LA68	2300	34	D2
ALTOONA PL	LA	SP		79	B2
ALTOS DR	CO	VAL		126	J4
ALTRIDGE DR	LA	BH	1400	33	A3
ALTURA AV	CO	GL14	2300	18	D1
ALTURA AV	CO	GL14	2600	18	D1
ALTURA AV	GLEN	GL14	3200	11	C6
ALTURA AV	LA	TU	6200	11	B5
ALTURA CT	POM	POM	700	90	D6
ALTURA LN	WHI	WHI	15800	84	C2
ALTURA RD	ARC	ARC	1	28	B4
ALTURA ST	LA	LA31		36	A6
ALTURA TER	ARC	ARC	1100	28	B4
ALTURA WK	LA	LA31		36	B6
ALTURA WY	MB	MB	400	62	C5
ALUMNI AV	LA	LA41	2000	26	A6
ALVA DR	LA	PP		40	D4
ALVADA ST	LYN	LYN	4200	65	C1
ALVAR PL	CAR	CAR	21400	69	D4
ALVARADO AV	POM	POM	100	95	A1
ALVARADO ST E	POM	POM	100	94	E1
ALVARADO ST E	POM	POM	1000	95	A1
ALVARADO ST N	LA	LA26	400	35	C5
ALVARADO ST N	LA	LA26	100	44	B2
ALVARADO ST N	LA	LA39	1900	35	C5
ALVARADO ST S	LA	LA06	900	44	A3
ALVARADO ST S	LA	LA57	100	44	B2
ALVARADO ST W	POM	POM	100	94	E1
ALVARADO TER	LA	LA06		44	A3
ALVAREZ DR	RPV	PVP	27900	72	D4
ALVARO ST	CO	LA59	11600	58	D6
ALVARO ST	LA	LA59	11200	58	D5
ALVEO RD	LCF	LCF	4500	19	D4
ALVERN CIR	LA	LA45		50	D5
ALVERN ST	LA	LA45		50	D5
ALVERSTONE AV	LA	LA45	7000	50	C6
ALVERSTONE AV	LA	LA45	7900	56	C1
ALVESTA PL	RPV	SP	27600	73	D5
ALVEY ST	CO	ALT	400	19	E5
ALVINA ST	BG	BELL	6700	54	A6
ALVINE LN	BAP	BAP	14900	39	F5
ALVIRA ST	LA	LA34	2600	42	E3
ALVIRA ST	LA	LA35	1000	42	E3
ALVISO AV	CO	LA43	5400	51	B4
ALVISO AV	ING	IN02	1400	51	B5
ALVISO AV	LA	LA43	5800	51	B5
ALVO AV	CAR	CAR	19800	69	E2
ALVORD LN	RB	RB	2400	67	E1
ALWICK PL	CO	BREA		98A	C3
ALWOOD ST	CO	LPUE	15700	92	A3
ALWOOD ST	CO	WCOV	17000	92	C3
ALWOOD ST	WCOV	BAP	14500	48	E2
ALWOOD ST E	WCOV	WCOV	600	92	B3
ALWOOD ST W	WCOV	WCOV	1900	48	E2
ALYESKA PL	WAL	WAL		93	A5
ALYSAM WY	CO	MAL		112	E1
ALZADA DR	CO	ALT		20	A3
ALZADO ST	MPK	MPK	400	45	F2
AMABEL ST	LA	LA65		36	A2
AMABLE	LA	SP		78	C4
AMABLE CT	SCLR	VAL		124	B7
AMADO	LA	SP		78	C4
AMADOR CIR	WAL	WAL		92	E5
AMADOR PL	LA	LA12		35	E6
AMADOR ST	CLA	CLA	900	91	A3
AMADOR ST	CO	CLA		91	A3
AMADOR ST	ELM	ELM	10600	38	D6
AMADOR ST	LA	LA12		35	E6
AMALFI CT	LA	SM		40	E5
AMALFI CT	WAL	WAL		92	F6
AMALFI DR	LA	PP	700	40	E3
AMALFI DR	LA	SM	100	40	E5
AMALIA AV	CO	LA22	300	45	F6
AMALIA AV	CO	LA22	1000	53	F1
AMANDA DR	LA	NHO		23	D5
AMANDA ST	WCOV	WCOV		92	F6
AMANDA ST	WCOV	WCOV		98	F1
AMANITA AV	LA	TU		11	B4
AMANTHA AV	CAR	CAR	17600	64	D6
AMANTHA AV	CAR	CAR	19400	69	D2
AMANTHA AV	COM	COM	100	64	D3
AMAPOLA AV	TOR	TOR	600	68	C4
AMAPOLA CT	TOR	TOR		68	C3
AMAPOLA LN	LA	LA77		32	E5
AMAR RD	BAP	BAP	13100	48	C2
AMAR RD	CO	LPUE	13400	48	C2
AMAR RD	CO	LPUE	15800	92	A4
AMAR RD	IND	LPUE	13200	48	C2
AMAR RD	LPUE	LPUE	13700	48	C2
AMAR RD	LPUE	LPUE	15700	92	A4
AMAR RD	WAL	WAL		92	F5
AMAR RD	WCOV	WCOV		92	E5
AMAR ST	LA	SP	1300	78	E2
AMAR ST	LA	SP	200	79	A2
AMARGOSO DR	CO	LPUE	17400	98	D5
AMARILLO DR	CLA	CLA		96	D5
AMARILLO DR	GLEN	GL08	2000	18	F4
AMATE DR	LHH	LAH	1500	84	E2
AMBALA ST	LAN	LAN	42800	159	D7
AMBAR DR	CO	WOH		13	C4
AMBASSADOR AV	BH	BH		32	F4
AMBASSADOR AV	BH	BH	1700	33	A5
AMBASSADOR DR	LA	HAC		73	E1
AMBASSADOR ST	LA	LA35	1400	42	B3
AMBAZAC WY	LA	LA77		32	D5
AMBECO RD	LB	LB06	3900	70	B4
AMBER AV	ELM	ELM		47	F4
AMBER CIR	CO	CAL		100	B2
AMBER LN	BUR	BUR	1800	17	D3
AMBER LN	PALM	PALM		172	F9
AMBER LN	PALM	PALM		183	H8
AMBER PL	LA	LA32		36	C5
AMBER ST	BLF	BLF	10300	66	D6
AMBERDON RD	CO	SAU		181	D6
AMBER GATE DR	RPV	PVP	27900	72	C4
AMBER HILL DR	CO	WHI		55	D2
AMBER LEAF RD	TOR	TOR		73	B3
AMBERLEY WY	SCLR	VAL		127	C2
AMBERLY DR	ING	IN01		57	B2
AMBER RIDGE LN	WAL	WAL		93	C6
AMBER ROSE LN	RM	RM		46	F3
AMBER SKY DR	RPV	PVP	30400	77	F1
AMBER TREE LN	CO	LPUE		98	A4
AMBER VALLEY DR	WAL	WAL		92	F5
AMBER VALLEY DR	WHI	WHI	15800	84	C5
AMBERWICK	WCOV	WCOV		92	C3
AMBERWICK PL	DBAR	POM		97A	A3
AMBERWOOD DR	DUA	DUA		29	E5
AMBERWOOD DR	ING	LA56		50	E5
AMBERWOOD DR	SPAS	SPAS	1600	37	A1
AMBERWOOD DR	WAL	WAL		93	C6
AMBERWOOD LN	LA	NOR		7	B3
AMBERWOOD WY	CER	ART	16600	82	C4
AMBIA PL	CO	PALM		183	E3
AMBLE CT	ELM	ELM		38	D5
AMBLER AV	CAR	CAR	16900	64	B5
AMBLER AV	CO	COM	18600	69	B1
AMBLESIDE WY	GLDR	GLDR		86	E4
AMBOY AV	LA	PAC	10400	8	F2
AMBOY AV	LA	PAC	9800	9	A4
AMBOY AV	LA	SF	11600	2	D6
AMBOY AV	LA	SF	11100	8	E1
AMBOY AV	LA	SV	9700	9	B5
AMBOY AV	LA	SV	8300	16	C1
AMBRIDGE DR	CO	AGO		100A	E1
AMBROSE AV	LA	LA27	4500	34	F2
AMBROSE AV	LA	LA27	4200	35	A2
AMBROSE TER	LA	LA27	4400	35	A2
AMBUSHERS ST	DBAR	POM		97	D6
AMBY PL	HB	RB	2800	62	C5
AMEBCO RD	LB	LB06		70	B5
AMELGA DR	WHI	WHI	8200	84	C1
AMELGADO DR	CO	LPUE	2200	85	E4
AMELIA AV	LA	SP		73	E6
AMELIA AV	LA	SP		78	E1
AMELIA AV	SAD	SAD	100	89	E2
AMELIA AV N	GLDR	GLDR	1200	89	E2
AMELIA AV S	GLDR	GLDR	100	87	E6
AMELIA DR	AGH	AGO		102	E3
AMELIA DR	LB	LB07	1000	70	D3
AMELIA ERHRT WY	BELL	BELL		53	E3
AMELUXEN AV	CO	LPUE	900	48	C6
AMELUXEN AV	CO	LPUE	1400	85	B1
AMERICA WY	CO	WOH		13	A4
AMERICAN AV	CO	VAL		124	A2
AMERICAN AV E	POM	POM	100	91	B6
AMERICAN AV W	LB	LB06		75	C1
AMERICAN AV W	POM	POM	100	91	B6
AMERICAN PL	LA	LA65	600	35	F4
AMERICANA DR	SAD	SAD	100	89	D2
AMERON WY	MPK	LA63		45	E2
AMERY AV	SOG	SOG	10600	59	E5
AMES ST	LA	LA27	2000	35	A2
AMESBURY RD	LA	LA27	3400	35	A1
AMESTOY AV	LA	ENC	5000	21	E1
AMESTOY AV	LA	NOR	8500	7	E6
AMESTOY AV	LA	NOR	8300	14	E1
AMESTOY AV	LA	SF	11500	1	E6
AMESTOY AV	LA	SF	10300	7	E2
AMESTOY AV	LA	VAN	6800	14	E4
AMETHYST CT	LA	LA32	4000	36	B5
AMETHYST LN	WAL	WAL		92	F6
AMETHYST ST	LA	LA32	2900	36	C5
AMETHYST ST	PALM	PALM		173	A9
AMETHYST ST	RB	RB	1200	67	D2
AMEY ST	LA	LA07	2000	43	F4
AMHERST AV	LA	LA25	1200	41	C4
AMHERST AV	LA	LA49	800	41	C4
AMHERST AV	LA	LA64	2200	41	D5
AMHERST DR	BUR	BUR	100	17	D4
AMHERST DR	SPAS	SPAS	1900	37	A2
AMHERST LN	LAN	LAN		159	F6
AMHERST ST	CLA	CLA	100	90	E2
AMHERST ST	LAV	LAV	400	90	E2
AMHURST CT	CER	ART		71	F2
AMHURST DR	WAL	WAL		93	B4
AMHURST PL	CO	CAST		123	A4
AMIDON PL	LA	TU	10800	11	A2
AMIE AV	TOR	TOR	17100	63	A5
AMIE AV	TOR	TOR	18500	68	A1
AMIGO	LA	SP		78	C5
AMIGO AV	LA	NOR	11300	1	B6
AMIGO AV	LA	NOR	8700	7	C6
AMIGO AV	LA	RES	6400	14	B4
AMIGO AV	LA	TAR	4800	21	B2
AMIGO PL	LA	TAR	4700	21	C2
AMIGO RD	CO	CHA		4	C5
AMIGOS DR	BUR	BUR	3000	17	C2
AMIRANTE DR	LA	SP	2200	78	C4
AMISTAD AV	PR	PR	3900	55	B1
AMLAR RD	CO	TOP		109	D6
AMOND LN	LA	CAN	8300	5	F1
AMOR RD	LA	LA46	8100	33	E1
AMOR WK	CO	CAST		123	A5
AMORET DR	LA	TU	9500	10	F4
AMORITA PL	LA	WOH	5700	12	E6
AMOROSO CT	LA	VEN		49	D3
AMOROSO PL	LA	VEN	700	49	D3
AMORY AV	CO	RM	1600	46	E3
AMOS AV	LKD	LKD	5900	66	C6
AMOS AV	LKD	LKD	6199	71	C1
AMOY AV	LAN	LAN		159	G4
AMOY ST	LAN	LAN	42900	159	G8
AMPERE AV	LA	NHO	6600	16	A4
AMSDELL AV	CO	WHI	9200	61	D2
AMSDELL AV	WHI	WHI	8600	61	E2
AMSLER ST	TOR	TOR	2400	73	C2
AMY CT	LAN	LAN		160	E6
AMY DR	WAL	WAL		93	C5
AMY LN	PALM	PALM		172	F9
AMY LN	PR	PR		55	E3
AMY WY	CO	TOP		109	D5
ANA ST	CO	COM		65	B6
ANA ST	CO	COM	2800	70	B1
ANABAS AV	LA	SP	2300	78	D5
ANABEL AV	CO	WHI	11200	84	A5
ANABELLA ST	NWK	NWK	12500	82	B1
ANACAPA PL	WAL	WAL		93	A5
ANACAPA VIEW DR	CO	MAL	31300	111	D4
ANACONDA ST	WHI	WHI	14400	84	A2
ANADA ST	BAP	BAP	13600	39	D3
ANADALE DR	LA	TAR	19600	13	F4

INDEX

COPYRIGHT, © 1989 BY Thomas Bros Maps

213

1990 LOS ANGELES COUNTY STREET INDEX

ANADEL AV — ARDARA PL

LOS ANGELES CO.

INDEX

STREET	CITY	P.O. ZONE	BLOCK	PAGE	GRID
ANADEL AV	CO	LPUE		97	A3
ANAHEIM PL	LB	LB04	1400	76	B3
ANAHEIM RD E	LB	LB15	5100	76	C4
ANAHEIM ST E	LA	WIL	100	74	A4
ANAHEIM ST E	LB	LB04	2000	75	B4
ANAHEIM ST E	LB	LB04	5199	76	A4
ANAHEIM ST E	LB	LB13	100	75	B4
ANAHEIM ST W	LA	HAC	1100	73	F4
ANAHEIM ST W	LA	WIL	100	74	A4
ANAHEIM ST W	LB	LB13	100	75	B4
ANAHM-PUENTE RD	IND	LPUE	700	98	B2
ANAHURST RD	SOG	SOG	5200	59	D4
ANASTASIA DR	LA	ENC		21	C4
ANATA PL E	CO	PALM	300	183	C1
ANATOLA AV	LA	VAN	7200	14	E3
ANAVERDE RD	CO	PALM		171	E9
ANCEP ST	WHI	WHI	16200	84	D3
ANCHOR AV	CAR	CAR	22100	69	B6
ANCHOR AV	LA	LA64	2600	42	C4
ANCHOR WY	LB	LB03		80	F1
ANCHORAGE RD	LA	WIL		74	D6
ANCHORAGE ST	LA	VEN		49	C5
ANCHOVY AV	LA	SP	1900	78	C4
ANCIENT TITL CT	WAL	WAL		93	B4
ANCONA DR	LAV	LAV		90	C2
ANCONA DR	LB	LB03		76	C6
ANCONA DR	LB	LB03		80	C1
ANCOURT ST	CO	ARC	9600	38	B1
ANDALE AV	LAN	LAN	44300	160	C4
ANDALUCIA CT	WHI	WHI	5200	55	C2
ANDALUCIA DR	WCOV	WCOV		92	F2
ANDALUSIA AV	LA	LA65	600	35	F3
ANDALUSIA AV	LA	VEN	500	49	C4
ANDASOL AV	LA	ENC	4700	21	E1
ANDASOL AV	LA	NOR	8700	7	E6
ANDASOL AV	LA	NOR	7800	14	E2
ANDASOL AV	LA	SF	11500	1	E5
ANDASOL AV	LA	SF	10300	7	E2
ANDENES DR	GLEN	GL08	1300	18	E6
ANDENVALE AV	LAN	LAN	45100	159	H4
ANDERBERG AV	DOW	DOW	12100	60	A5
ANDERMATT PL	SCLR	VAL		127	A8
ANDERS AV	CO	LPUE	1200	85	E2
ANDERSON AV	COM	COM	1600	64	D5
ANDERSON AV	GLEN	GL14	3600	11	C6
ANDERSON AV	LB	LB05	6100	65	C6
ANDERSON LN	CO	VAL		126	H3
ANDERSON PL	PAR	PAR	8100	65	F2
ANDERSON PL	PAS	PAS	400	19	E6
ANDERSON ST	MB	MB	200	62	C4
ANDERSON ST	PAR	PAR	13900	65	F2
ANDERSON ST	VER	LA58		52	E4
ANDERSON ST N	LA	LA33	100	44	F4
ANDERSON ST S	LA	LA23	600	44	F4
ANDERSON ST S	LA	LA33	100	44	F4
ANDERSON WY	ELM	ELM	9800	47	C2
ANDERSON WY	SGAB	SGAB	500	37	D4
ANDERWOOD CT	POM	POM	300	90	E6
ANDES ST	CO	RM	8700	38	A4
ANDIRON DR	CO	WHI	16400	84	D5
ANDMARK AV	CAR	CAR	19000	69	E1
ANDORA AV	LA	CHA	9600	6	B2
ANDOVER AV	SAD	SAD		89	D3
ANDOVER DR	BUR	BUR	100	17	D4
ANDOVER DR	CLA	CLA		91	C1
ANDRADA DR	CO	LPUE	19300	97	A4
ANDRADA DR	CO	LPUE	18500	98	E4
ANDRAE CT	LA	SF	15500	8	B5
ANDRE ST	CO	DUA	500	39	B1
ANDREA CIR	LA	NOR		7	C3
ANDREA CT	WCOV	WCOV		92	E6
ANDREA LN	ARC	ARC	1	28	E2
ANDREO AV	LOM	LOM	25000	73	D2
ANDREO AV	TOR	TOR	1700	68	D5
ANDREW AV	LA	SF	11700	2	A6
ANDREW DR	CLA	CLA		91	D2
ANDREW DR	LAN	LAN		159	G4
ANDREWS DR	LB	LB07	1000	70	D4
ANDREWS RD	ARC	ARC	1600	38	E1
ANDREWS ST	SELM	ELM	11000	47	C4
ANDRITA ST	LA	LA65	3000	35	D1
ANDRIX ST E	MPK	MPK	100	46	C4
ANDRIX ST W	MPK	MPK	200	46	B4
ANDROMEDA LN	CO	MAL	30000	111	F5
ANDRUS AV	TOR	TOR	5600	67	E3
ANDRUSS PL	MTB	MTB	300	54	F1
ANDRY DR	PAR	PAR		66	A3
ANDY AV	CO	PALM		171I	E4
ANDY DR	CER	ART	12800	81	C1
ANDY ST	CER	ART	10600	71	E1
ANDY ST	CER	ART	12300	81	B1
ANDY ST	LB	LB05	3100	70	F1
ANDY ST	LB	LB05	3500	71	A1
ANDY ST	LKD	LKD	4300	71	A1
ANELO AV	CAR	GAR	18900	69	A1
ANETA ST	CO	LA66	12400	50	B4

STREET	CITY	P.O. ZONE	BLOCK	PAGE	GRID
ANETA ST	LA	CUL	11800	50	B4
ANGELA AV	LA	CAN		5	F3
ANGELA ST	POM	POM	2100	94	F5
ANGELA ST	WCOV	WCOV		92	E6
ANGELAINE WY	LA	SF		1	E4
ANGELAYVONNE AV	SCLR	SAU		124	E6
ANGELCREST DR	CO	LPUE	700	85	D2
ANGELENO AV E	BUR	BUR	100	17	E6
ANGELENO AV E	SGAB	SGAB	100	37	E3
ANGELENO AV N	AZU	AZU	100	86	D5
ANGELENO AV N	AZU	AZU	1199	88	D1
ANGELENO AV S	AZU	AZU	100	88	D1
ANGELENO AV W	BUR	BUR	1	24	D1
ANGELENO AV W	SGAB	SGAB	100	37	E3
ANGELENO PL	PALM	PALM		171	F5
ANGELES CST CIR	LCF	LCF		19	B2
ANGELES CRST HY	LCF	LCF	4500	19	B2
ANGELES CRST HY	CO			M	C3
ANGELES CRST HY	CO			N	C2
ANGELES FRST HY	CO	PALM		183	D9
ANGELES FRST HY	CO	PALM		190	C2
ANGELES FRST HY	CO			M	F3
ANGELES VSTA BL	CO	LA08	4100	51	B3
ANGELES VSTA BL	CO	LA43	4400	51	B3
ANGELE TRMPT CT	PALM	PALM		172	G8
ANGELICA RD	HH	CAL		5	D6
ANGELICA RD	HH	CAL		100	D1
ANGELINA PL	LA	WOH	20300	13	E2
ANGELINA ST	LA	LA12	1100	44	C1
ANGELINA ST	LA	LA26	1300	44	C1
ANGELL ST	DOW	DOW	9100	66	B1
ANGELL ST	LAM	LAM	14100	82	E1
ANGELL ST	NWK	NWK	10500	66	D1
ANGELL ST	NWK	NWK	11700	82	A1
ANGELO AV	BH	BH		32	F5
ANGELO AV	BH	BH		33	A5
ANGELO CIR	LA	BH	10100	32	F4
ANGELO DR	BH	BH	1700	32	F5
ANGELO DR	LA	LA77		22	E6
ANGELO DR	LA	LA77		32	E3
ANGELO PL	ARC	ARC	200	20A	E3
ANGELO PL	ARC	ARC	200	28	E1
ANGELO WK	LB	LB03	1	80	D1
ANGELO VIEW DR	LA	BH		32	F4
ANGELUS AV	CO	SGAB	5500	37	F3
ANGELUS AV	GLEN	GL08	3400	18	E3
ANGELUS AV	LA	LA26	1300	35	B5
ANGELUS AV	RM	RM	2200	46	F2
ANGELUS AV	SGAB	SGAB	5600	37	F3
ANGELUS PL	LA	VEN	600	49	D4
ANGOLA AV	LHH	LAH	1500	84	D2
ANGOSTO DR	WHI	WHI	8200	84	C1
ANGOSTURA PL	LA	TAR	4300	21	B3
ANGUS DR	LAV	LAV		95A	E5
ANGUS ST	LA	LA39	2700	35	B2
ANILLO ST	CER	ART		81	A2
ANISE AV	LA	LA45	7700	50	B6
ANITA AV	CO	PAS	3700	28	B5
ANITA AV	LA	LA49	100	41	B2
ANITA DR	BELL	BELL	3500	53	B6
ANITA DR	PAS	PAS	100	26	D5
ANITA ST	MON	MON	600	29	A5
ANITA ST	RB	RB	300	67	D2
ANITA CREST DR	ARC	ARC	1800	28	D2
ANITA DR 1	LA	LA49		41	B2
ANITA DR 2	LA	LA49		41	B2
ANITA DR 3	LA	LA49		41	B2
ANITA DR 4	LA	LA49		41	B2
ANITA DR 5	LA	LA49		41	B2
ANKARA CT	LA	NOR		1	C6
ANKERTON ST	CO	WHI	13100	47	F5
ANKERTON ST	CO	WHI	13100	48	A5
ANN ST	LA	LA12	100	44	E1
ANN ST	SFS	SFS	9000	61	C2
ANN ST E	LA	LA12	100	44	E1
ANN ST W	LA	LA12	100	44	E1
ANNABELLA ST	NWK	NWK		61	B6
ANNADEL AV	CO	LPUE	1200	97	A4
ANNALEE AV	CAR	CAR	19000	69	D1
ANNALEE LN	CAR	CAR		69	C3
ANNA MARIA ST	CO	ALT	300	20	B3
ANNAN TER	LA	LA42	6200	26	C6
ANNAN TR	LA	LA42		26	C6
ANNAN WK	LA	LA42		26	C6
ANNAN WY	LA	LA42	5900	26	C6
ANNANDALE LN	AZU	AZU	300	86	D4
ANNANDALE RD	PAS	PAS	100	26	D5
ANNANDALE TER	PAS	PAS		26	D5
ANNAPOLIS CT	LAV	LAV		90	E3
ANNAPOLIS DR	CLA	CLA	100	91	C5
ANNAPOLIS RD	LKD	LKD	4100	71	A4
ANNAPOLIS WY	LAN	LAN		159	G7
ANN ARBOR AV	POM	POM	2100	94	F6
ANN ARBOR AV	POM	POM	2100	95	A6
ANN ARBOR RD	LKD	LKD	3900	71	A4
ANNE PL	POM	POM		90	F5

STREET	CITY	P.O. ZONE	BLOCK	PAGE	GRID
ANNE FREDA ST	SCLR	CYN	17200	125	C8
ANNELLEN ST	CO	LPUE	15800	85	E3
ANNEPE WY	CO	CHA		1A	B5
ANNETTA AV	LYN	LYN	11300	59	C5
ANNETTA AV	SOG	SOG	8900	59	C4
ANNETTE ST	LA	LA65	3500	35	F3
ANNETTE JO CIR	SCLR	SAU		124	E6
ANNHURST AV	CLA	CLA		91	D1
ANNIE OAKLEY RD	HH	CAL		5	D6
ANNIE OAKLEY RD	HH	CAL		100	D1
ANNISTON AV	BAP	BAP	4800	88	A3
ANNITA DR	GLEN	GL06	1500	26	A1
ANNRITA AV	TOR	TOR	20500	67	E3
ANOAKIA LN	ARC	ARC	700	28	C3
ANOKA DR	LA	PP	1000	40	C3
ANOKA PL	LA	PP		40	C3
ANOKA PL	LA	WOH		13	C3
ANOLA ST	CO	WHI	12900	61	D2
ANOLA ST	CO	WHI	14900	84	A5
ANO NUEVO DR	DBAR	POM		97	E3
ANSDELL PL	CO	ARC	5200	38	F3
ANSEL WK	LA	LA45		50	A6
ANSFORD ST	CO	LPUE	14500	48	C6
ANSLEY AV	CO	MON	2500	39	B1
ANSMITH AV	PAR	PAR	15900	65	D4
ANSON AV	SFS	SFS	14200	82	E2
ANSON WY	WCOV	WCOV		92	C5
ANSTED DR	LPUE	LPUE	400	92	B6
ANTEBES CT	PALM	PALM		173	B9
ANTELO PL	LA	LA77	15200	22	C6
ANTELO RD	LA	LA77	3100	22	C6
ANTELOPE HWY	CO	LAN		146	J1
ANTELOPE HWY	CO	LAN	2000	147	G7
ANTELOPE HWY	CO	PALM		173	H2
ANTELOPE HWY	PALM	PALM		173	H2
ANTELOPE RD	LA	BH		32	F1
ANTELOPE RD	LA	BH		33	A1
ANTELOPE VLY FY	CO			125	F7
ANTELOPE VLY FY	CO			147	H8
ANTELOPE VLY FY	CO			181	G9
ANTELOPE VLY FY	CO			182	D9
ANTELOPE VLY FY	CO			183	C3
ANTELOPE VLY FY	CO			188	E2
ANTELOPE VLY FY	LAN	LAN		159	H3
ANTELOPE VLY FY	PALM	PALM		172	A6
ANTELOPE WDS RD	CO	ACT		182	F9
ANTELO VIEW DR	LA	LA77		22	C6
ANTENA DR	DBAR	WAL		97	C3
ANTEROS DR	CO	SAU		181	A9
ANTHONY CIR	LA	LA46	8300	33	E3
ANTHONY DR	CER	ART		82	E4
ANTHONY PL	LA	BH	9900	32	F3
ANTHONY RD	CO	SAU		181	G6
ANTIBES CT	LA	LA49		32	B5
ANTIGUA DR	BUR	BUR	2800	17	C2
ANTIGUA PL	LA	CAN		5	D5
ANTIOCH RD	CLA	CLA	2300	91	B2
ANTIOCH ST	LA	PP	15200	40	D3
ANTISANA PL	CO	LPUE	2800	85	E4
ANTLER DR	DBAR	POM		97	F1
ANTOINETTE DR	LHH	LAH	1200	84	F3
ANTON CT	WCOV	WCOV		92	C4
ANTON DR	CO	PEAR	34500	185	A7
ANTONIO AV	CER	ART	17200	82	E5
ANTONIO ST	TOR	TOR	3000	68	B4
ANTRIM PL	LCF	LCF	400	19	C5
ANTWERP AV	CO	LA01	7900	58	D1
ANTWERP AV	CO	LA59	11600	58	D5
ANTWERP ST	CO	LA59	11600	58	D5
ANTWERP ST	LA	LA02	9600	58	D3
ANTWERP ST	LA	LA59	11100	58	D4
ANVERS AV	LAN	LAN	43800	160	A5
ANVIK ST	CO	CAST		123	A2
ANVIL TREE LN	CO	LPUE		98	A4
ANZA AV	TOR	TOR	19100	67	F2
ANZA AV	TOR	TOR	23500	72	F2
ANZA DR	CO	VAL		123	H7
ANZA PL	CO	PALM		183	B3
ANZAC AV	CO	COM	12300	58	E6
ANZAC AV	COM	COM	1600	64	E1
ANZAC AV	LA	LA02	9200	58	E4
ANZAC AV	LA	LA59	10700	58	E4
ANZAC CIR	COM	COM		64	E3
ANZEL CIR	SCLR	NEW		127	H1
ANZIO RD	LA	LA77	11000	32	C4
ANZIO WY	SCLR	VAL		127	A1
AOSTA CT	SCLR	VAL		127	A8
APACHE	CO	AGO		106	D2
APACHE	CO	TOP		13	C5
APACHE CT	CO	CAST		123	E3
APACHE LN	CAR	CAR		69	D6
APACHE TR	CO	AGO		107	A3
APACHE TR	CO	CHA		6	C1
APACHE WY	WAL	WAL		93	C4
APACHE PLUME DR	PALM	PALM		183	J6
APAM AV	CO	CAST		123	A2

STREET	CITY	P.O. ZONE	BLOCK	PAGE	GRID
APARRI AV	CO	CAST		123	A2
APEX AV	LA	LA39	1900	35	C4
APHRODITE	WCOV	WCOV		48	F2
APOLLO	WCOV	WCOV		48	F2
APOLLO AV	PALM	PALM		172	H9
APOLLO DR	LA	LA46		33	F1
APOLLO PL	CO	PALM		157	F8
APOLLO ST	ELS	ELS	800	62	D2
APPALOOSA DR	LAN	LAN		159	D6
APPALOOSA DR	WAL	CLA		96	C6
APPALOOSA DR	WAL	WAL		93	C6
APPALOOSA LN	RH	PVP	1	73	A6
APPALOOSA WY	LA	SUN		10	B3
APPELBY ST	LA	VEN		49	C2
APPERSON ST	LA	SUN	7800	10	E3
APPERSON ST	LA	TU	6400	10	E3
APPERSON ST	LA	TU	6700	11	A3
APPIAN WY	LA	LA46	8500	33	D2
APPIAN WY	LB	LB03	4800	76	B5
APPIAN WY	LB	LB03		80	D1
APPIAN WY	LOM	LOM	25800	73	D3
APPIAN WY	MTB	MTB		46	D5
APPIAN WY	SM	SM	1600	49	A2
APPIAN WY	SM	SM	1600	49	B6
APPLE AV	TOR	TOR	2300	68	D5
APPLE ST	SCLR	NEW	24400	127	B5
APPLE ST	LA	LA16	5200	42	F5
APPLE ST	LA	LA16	5100	43	A5
APPLE BLSSOM ST	LPUE	LPUE	16100	92	A6
APPLEBY ST	DOW	DOW	9100	60	D2
APPLE CREEK LN	CO	LPUE		98	A4
APPLECROSS AV	CO	AZU	5500	88	D2
APPLEDALE AV	CO	WHI	7600	55	C6
APPLEGATE TER	CO	CHA		4	C5
APPLETON ST	LA	LA39	3300	35	C1
APPLETON ST	LB	LB02	900	75	D5
APPLETON ST	LB	LB03	2000	75	D5
APPLETON WY	LA	LA66	12400	49	D2
APPLETON WY	LA	VEN		49	D2
APPLETON WY	POM	POM	1700	91	B6
APPLETREE CT	CER	ART	19100	81	A1
APRA ST	COM	COM		64	E6
APRICOT DR	PALM	PALM		183	C6
APRICOT DR	PALM	PALM		183	E1
APRICOT LN	LA	BH	9700	33	A2
APRICOT PL	CO	SAU		124	C3
APRICOT ST	LYN	LYN	11200	59	A5
APRIL CT	LOM	LOM		73	D1
APRIL LN	LA	TU		10	F1
APRIL RD	CO	AGO		107	C2
APRIL WY	WCOV	WCOV		92	E6
APRILIA AV	CO	COM	14300	64	C2
APRILIA AV	COM	COM	100	64	C3
APSLEY RD	PVE	PVP	700	72	B3
APTOS AV	CO	LPUE	2900	85	C4
AQUA PURA DR	LA	LA12		35	E6
AQUARIUS AV	AGH	AGO		100A	A2
AQUARIUS ST	LB	LB10	1800	75	A2
AQUA VERDE CIR	LA	LA77	15600	22	B6
AQUA VERDE DR	LA	LA77	15600	22	B6
AQUA VISTA DR	RPV	PVP		78	B4
AQUA VISTA ST	LA	NHO	10700	23	D4
AQUEDUCT AV	LA	ENC	4700	22	B2
AQUEDUCT AV	LA	SF	8700	8	B6
AQUEDUCT AV	LA	SF	8300	15	B1
AQUEDUCT AV	LA	VAN	6500	15	B4
AQUINAS AV	CLA	CLA		91	C1
ARABELLA DR	CER	ART	13100	82	D6
ARABELLA LN	CER	ART	13000	82	D6
ARABELLA ST	CER	ART	12600	82	C6
ARABELLA ST	LB	LB05	3500	71	A1
ARABELLA ST	LKD	LKD	4300	66	D6
ARABELLA ST	LKD	LKD	4300	71	A1
ARABIAN CT	WAL	WAL		93	D4
ARABIAN LN	WAL	WAL		93	D5
ARABIC ST	LA	WIL	1300	74	A4
ARABY AV	NWK	NWK	13800	82	B2
ARAGON AV	LA	LA65		35	F4
ARAGON CT	LA	VEN	400	49	C4
ARALIA DR	POM	POM	1700	94	D4
ARALIA RD	CO	ALT	4100	19	E2
ARAMAC AV	CO	RM		46	E3
ARANBE AV	CO	COM	13000	64	E1
ARANBE AV	COM	COM	100	64	E1
ARANZA DR	LAM	LAM	14300	83	B3
ARAPAHO WY	SAD	SAD		90	A1
ARAPAHOE	CO	CHA		1A	C6
ARAPAHOE ST	LA	LA06	900	44	A4
ARAPAHOE ST	LA	LA07	1900	44	A4
ARARAT ST	LA	SF	14600	2	C2
ARATINA ST	LA	LA42	900	26	E6
ARAVACA DR	PAR	PAR	15500	65	D3
ARBA ST	CO	LPUE		98	E6
ARBELA DR	WHI	WHI	15700	84	C2
ARBELLA DR	CER	ART	13200	81	D1
ARBELLA LN	CER	ART	13000	81	D1

STREET	CITY	P.O. ZONE	BLOCK	PAGE	GRID
ARBELLA PL	CER	ART	10700	71	E1
ARBELLA PL	CER	ART	12900	81	C1
ARBOL LN	LA	LA68	6800	34	B2
ARBOL ST	LA	LA65		36	A2
ARBOLADA DR	ARC	ARC	200	28	D3
ARBOLADA RD	LA	LA27		35	B1
ARBOLADO CT	MB	MB		62	B4
ARBOLEDA DR	PAS	PAS		27	B5
ARBOLEDA ST	CO	PAS	3700	28	B3
ARBOLEDA WY	POM	POM	500	95	A2
ARBOLES CT N	LA	SP	100	79	A3
ARBOLES CT S	LA	SP	100	79	A3
ARBOLES DR	GLEN	GL07	1500	25	E1
ARBOLES ST	MPK	MPK	500	45	F2
ARBOLES ST	MPK	MPK	500	46	A2
ARBOR CT	WAL	WAL		93	D4
ARBOR DR	GLEN	GL02	1600	25	C1
ARBOR LN	PALM	PALM		184	A1
ARBOR PL	CER	ART	14100	82	E4
ARBOR PL	LA	LA44		57	F6
ARBOR RD	LB	LB08	4300	71	A3
ARBOR RD	LKD	LKD	2700	70	F3
ARBOR RD	LKD	LKD	3300	71	A3
ARBOR ST	PAS	PAS	400	26	E4
ARBOR ST E	LB	LB05	100	70	C3
ARBOR ST W	LB	LB05	1	70	C3
ARBOR WY	LAN	LAN		160	D4
ARBOR DELL RD	LA	LA41	1100	26	C4
ARBOR PINES	ELM	ELM		48	A1
ARBOR VITAE ST	ING	IN05	2200	57	C2
ARBOR VITAE ST	LA	LA45	5600	56	D2
ARBOR VTAE ST E	ING	IN01	100	57	A2
ARBOR VTAE ST W	ING	IN01	100	56	D2
ARBRAMAR AV	LA	PP		40	C4
ARBUCKLE AV	LA	SF		8	D1
ARBURY DR	DBAR	POM		97	E3
ARBUTUS DR	LA	LA49		30	E5
ARBUTUS ST	HPK	HPK	6000	53	A5
ARBUTUS ST E	COM	COM	200	64	D2
ARBUTUS ST W	COM	COM	300	64	D2
ARBUTUS WY	LA	LA49		30	E5
ARBY DR	LA	BH	9600	32	F1
ARBY DR	LA	BH	9600	33	A1
ARCADE AL	PAS	PAS	1	27	B4
ARCADE PL	GLEN	GL06	400	26	A3
ARCADIA AV	ARC	ARC	500	28	A6
ARCADIA AV	CO	SGAB	8400	27	F6
ARCADIA AV	CO	SGAB	8700	28	A6
ARCADIA AV	LB	LB03	300	76	C6
ARCADIA CT	LB	LB13	1100	75	D4
ARCADIA DR	LA	SP	300	78	E3
ARCADIA ST	SCLR	NEW	24300	127	C4
ARCADIA ST	SCLR	VAL	24700	127	C4
ARCADIA ST	LA	LA12		44	E2
ARCADIA TER	SM	SM	1	49	B6
ARCADIA TER	SM	SM	1	49	A2
ARCADIA WY	WAL	WAL		92	F6
ARCANA CT	POM	POM	100	90	F3
ARCANA RD	LA	WOH		13	D3
ARCAY AV	SCLR	CYN	27500	124	H5
ARCAY AV	SCLR	CYN	27100	124	J9
ARCAY AV	SCLR	CYN		125	A8
ARCDALE AV	CO	LPUE	2000	97	A4
ARCH DR	LA	NHO		23	E4
ARCH PL	GLEN	GL06	500	26	A3
ARCH ST	SCLR	NEW	24000	127	C3
ARCHCREST DR	CO	LA43	5500	50	F4
ARCHDALE RD	CO	SAU		189	B7
ARCHDALE RD	LA	ENC		22	B4
ARCHER ST	LA	LA42		36	C1
ARCHERY WY	WLVL	THO		102	B5
ARCHIBALD AV	CAR	CAR	21200	69	A4
ARCHIBALD AV	CAR	CAR	23600	74	A1
ARCHWAY DR	CO	WHI	10900	84	A4
ARCHWOOD DR	POM	POM	1300	94	D4
ARCHWOOD PL	CO	ALT	400	19	E5
ARCHWOOD PL	LA	NHO		16	E4
ARCHWOOD ST	LA	CAN	23700	5	E4
ARCHWOOD ST	LA	CAN	19700	12	B4
ARCHWOOD ST	LA	NHO	10900	16	C4
ARCHWOOD ST	LA	RES	17900	14	C4
ARCHWOOD ST	LA	VAN	16500	14	E4
ARCHWOOD ST	LA	VAN	13800	15	D4
ARCHWOOD ST	LA	VAN	13200	16	A4
ARCHWOOD WY	LAN	LAN		159	F7
ARCIERO DR	CO	LPUE		48	B4
ARCIERO DR	CO	WHI	600	48	A4
ARCO PL	PVE	PVP	1500	72	C4
ARCOLA AV	LA	NHO	4200	23	F4
ARCOLA AV	LA	SV	7800	17	A2
ARCOS DR	LA	WOH		13	C3
ARCTIC CIR	SFS	SFS	13000	82	C3
ARCTURUS AV	CO	GAR	15200	63	D3
ARCTURUS AV	GAR	GAR	12800	63	D1
ARDARA PL	LCF	LCF	4400	19	A2

STREET	CITY	P.O. ZONE	BLOCK	PAGE	GRID
ARDATH AV	CO	GAR	15200	63	C3
ARDATH AV	GAR	GAR	12900	63	C1
ARDATH AV	HAW	IN03	11600	57	C5
ARDATH AV	ING	IN03	11800	57	C5
ARDATH AV	TOR	GAR	16200	63	C5
ARDATH AV	TOR	TOR	16700	63	C5
ARD EEVIN AV	GLEN	GL02		25	B1
ARDELL RD	PR	PR	8900	55	A1
ARDEN AV	GLEN	GL02	600	25	B2
ARDEN AV	GLEN	GL03	100	25	C2
ARDEN BLVD N	LA	LA04		34	C6
ARDEN BLVD S	LA	LA04	100	43	C1
ARDEN BLVD S	LA	LA05	600	43	C1
ARDEN BLVD S	LA	LA20	300	43	C1
ARDEN DR	BH	BH	500	33	C5
ARDEN DR	CO	ELM	4300	38	D5
ARDEN DR	ELM	ELM	3600	38	C6
ARDEN DR	TEC	TEC	4800	38	D4
ARDEN PL	LA	LA04		34	C5
ARDEN RD	PAS	PAS	600	27	B5
ARDEN WY	ELM	ELM	4600	38	D4
ARDENDALE AV	CO	SGAB	8600	38	A1
ARDENEL AV	TEC	TEC	5200	38	C4
ARDILLA AV	BAP	BAP	3400	39	E6
ARDILLA AV	CO	LPUE	1100	48	D2
ARDILLA AV	LPUE	LPUE	300	48	C3
ARDILLA AV N	WCOV	WCOV	200	39	E6
ARDILLA AV S	WCOV	WCOV	1300	48	E1
ARDINE ST	CDY	BELL	4600	59	C2
ARDINE ST	DOW	DOW	9500	60	D5
ARDINE ST	SOG	SOG	4600	59	C2
ARDIS AV	BLF	BLF	13600	66	B2
ARDIS AV	DOW	DOW	12500	60	B6
ARDIS AV	DOW	DOW	12900	66	C1
ARDITA DR	WHI	WHI	16500	84	D3
ARDMORE AV	BLF	BLF	16100	66	C5
ARDMORE AV	GLEN	GL02	1400	25	B1
ARDMORE AV	HB	RB	1000	62	C5
ARDMORE AV	HB	RB	100	67	C1
ARDMORE AV	MB	MB	2100	62	B4
ARDMORE AV	SOG	SOG	2700	58	F2
ARDMORE AV	SOG	SOG	2900	59	A2
ARDMORE AV N	LA	LA04	100	34	E6
ARDMORE AV N	LA	LA29	700	34	E4
ARDMORE AV S	LA	LA04	100	34	E6
ARDMORE AV S	LA	LA05	600	43	E1
ARDMORE AV S	LA	LA06	900	43	E3
ARDMORE AV S	LA	LA20	300	43	E1
ARDMORE CT	SAD	SAD		89	D4
ARDMORE DR	SGAB	SGAB	100	37	E3
ARDMORE RD	SMAR	PAS	2700	37	B1
ARDSHEAL DR	LHH	LAH	2000	84	E1
ARDSHEAL DR	LHH	LAH	2300	85	E6
ARDSLEY DR	CO	ARC	6800	38	B1
ARDSLEY DR	TEC	TEC	4700	38	C4
ARDSLEY PL	LA	ENC		21	F5
ARDWICK ST	LA	WOH		13	A4
ARDWICK ST	LA	WOH		100	F4
ARENA ST	ELS	ELS	100	56	B6
ARENTH AV	IND	LPUE	19300	97	A2
ARENTH AV	IND	LPUE	17200	98	C2
ARGAN AV	LA	CUL	11200	50	B3
ARGENT PL	LA	LA39	2200	35	C3
ARGENTINE RD	LA	WOH		13	C3
ARGO CIR	LAV	LAV		95A	B6
ARGO PL	RM	RM	9000	47	A1
ARGONAUT ST	LA	VEN		55A	D2
ARGONIA PL	WAL	WAL		93	A5
ARGONNE AV	LB	LB03	200	76	B6
ARGONNE AV	LB	LB04	1300	76	B4
ARGONNE AV	LB	LB14	300	76	B6
ARGONNE AV	LB	LB15	2200	76	B2
ARGOS ST	AGH	AGO		100A	A3
ARGOSY WY	LA	LA68	2400	34	D2
ARGUS DR	LA	LA41	5000	26	B5
ARGYLE	PALM	PALM		171	E4
ARGYLE AV	LA	LA28	1600	34	C3
ARGYLE AV	LA	LA68	1900	34	C2
ARI LN	LA	LA49		32	A3
ARIAN	PALM	PALM		171	J7
ARICA AV	RM	RM	4000	38	B5
ARIEL AV	LA	RES	7200	14	B3
ARIELLA DR	CO	CAL		100	C5
ARIES ST	AGH	AGO		100A	A2
ARILLO ST	CO	LPUE	12900	48	A3
ARIMO LN	LA	LA77		32	E3
ARISTO PL	LA	SF		1	D4
ARISTO ST	GLEN	GL01	1300	24	F2
ARIZONA AV	CUL	CUL	10800	50	B1
ARIZONA AV	LA	LA45		50	C5
ARIZONA AV	SM	SM	100	40	F6
ARIZONA AV	SM	SM	700	41	A5
ARIZONA AV	SOG	SOG	11700	59	E6
ARIZONA AV N	CO	LA22	100	45	E5
ARIZONA AV S	CO	LA22	100	45	E5
ARIZONA AV S	CO	LA22	1100	53	E1

STREET	CITY	P.O. ZONE	BLOCK	PAGE	GRID
ARIZONA CIR	LA	LA45		50	C5
ARIZONA PL	LA	LA45		50	C5
ARIZONA PL	SM	SM	2900	41	B4
ARIZONA PL S	SM	SM		41	B4
ARIZONA ST	WCOV	WCOV		92	D4
ARKANSAS ST	ART	ART	11600	82	A4
ARKANSAS ST	BLF	BLF	9400	66	B5
ARKELL DR	BH	BH	500	33	C2
ARKLEY DR	DBAR	WAL	1000	97	C3
ARKSEY	CO	ACT		182	J9
ARKSEY	CO	ACT		183	A9
ARLAND AV	CO	RM	1500	46	E3
ARLEE AV	NWK	NWK	11000	61	A5
ARLEE AV	NWK	NWK	13500	82	A3
ARLEE AV	SFS	SFS	9100	61	A2
ARLEE PL	LA	SF		2	F1
ARLEN DR	SCLR	NEW	23400	127	B5
ARLENE TER	LA	LA46	8700	33	D1
ARLETA AV	LA	PAC	9400	8	E3
ARLETA AV	LA	PAC	9000	9	A5
ARLETA AV	LA	SF	10500	8	D2
ARLETA AV	LA	SV	8400	16	B1
ARLIGHT ST E	MPK	MPK	100	46	C4
ARLIGHT ST W	MPK	MPK	200	46	B4
ARLINE AV	ART	ART	18500	81	A1
ARLINE AV	ART	ART	17900	82	A6
ARLINE AV	CER	ART	18900	81	A1
ARLINE AV	HG	LKD	21700	81	A5
ARLINE AV	LKD	LKD	20300	81	A3
ARLINE ST	CO	CYN	30000	125	C5
ARLINE ST	WCOV	WCOV		92	E6
ARLINGTON AV	GLEN	GL08	1500	18	E3
ARLINGTON AV	LA	LA08	3800	51	D3
ARLINGTON AV	LA	LA18	1900	43	D6
ARLINGTON AV	LA	LA19	1000	43	D6
ARLINGTON AV	LA	LA43	4400	51	D3
ARLINGTON AV	LYN	LYN	4500	65	C1
ARLINGTON AV	TOR	TOR	22900	68	D6
ARLINGTON AV	TOR	TOR	23500	73	D1
ARLINGTON CT	PALM	PALM		184	D4
ARLINGTON DR	CLA	CLA		90	F2
ARLINGTON DR	PAS	PAS	100	26	F6
ARLINGTON DR	PR	PR		47	B6
ARLINGTON DR	PR	PR		55	B1
ARLINGTON ST	COM	COM	900	65	A1
ARLINGTON ST	LB	LB10	2100	69	F5
ARLINGTON ST	LB	LB10	1400	70	A5
ARLISTA ST	CO	LPUE	13700	48	B4
ARLOTTE AV	LB	LB08	2900	81	A6
ARMA ST	PR	PR	8500	54	F1
ARMA ST	PR	PR	8700	55	A2
ARMACOST AV	LA	LA25	1200	41	C4
ARMACOST AV	LA	LA64	2400	41	E5
ARMADA DR	PAS	PAS	900	26	E2
ARMADA RD	ARC	ARC	300	28	C5
ARMADALE AV	LA	LA42	1500	26	A6
ARMADALE AV	LA	LA42	1300	36	A1
ARMAGA SPG RD	RPV	PVP	5700	72	D5
ARMANDO DR	LB	LB07	600	70	D5
ARMEL DR	CO	COV	3200	88	D3
ARMEL DR N	COV	COV	100	88	D5
ARMEL DR S	COV	COV	100	88	D5
ARMELINA DR	LAM	LAM	14300	82	F2
ARMFIELD AV	CO	PALM	39400	171	J6
ARMIDA DR	LA	WOH		13	E2
ARMIJO ST W	CO	MON	100	29	A6
ARMINGTON AV	CO	LPUE	1300	85	F2
ARMINTA ST	LA	CAN	23200	5	F2
ARMINTA ST	LA	CAN	19700	12	A2
ARMINTA ST	LA	NHO	11400	16	D2
ARMINTA ST	LA	NOR	17400	14	D2
ARMINTA ST	LA	RES	17700	14	A2
ARMINTA ST	LA	SV	10200	16	D2
ARMINTA ST	LA	SV	10100	17	A2
ARMINTA ST	LA	VAN	17100	14	E2
ARMINTA ST	LA	VAN	14500	15	D2
ARMITAGE AV	ING	IN01		57	B2
ARMITAGE ST	LA	LA26		35	C5
ARMITOS PL	DBAR	POM		94	B5
ARMITOS PL	DBAR	POM		97A	B1
ARMLEY AV	CO	WHI	9600	61	F3
ARMLEY AV	WHI	WHI	9100	84	A2
ARMONA CT N	LA	SP	100	79	A3
ARMONA CT S	LA	SP	100	79	A3
ARMOUR AV	LA	LA32		36	C4
ARMOUR LN	RB	RB	1600	67	D1
ARMOUR PL	GLEN	GL08	2100	18	E6
ARMOUR RD	WHI	WHI	8200	55	E6
ARMOUR ST	POM	POM	2000	90	E5
ARMOURDALE AV	LB	LB08	2900	81	A6
ARMSDALE AV	CO	WHI	11900	61	F6
ARMSDALE AV	LAM	LAM	11700	61	F6
ARMSTEAD ST	AZU	AZU	900	88	E1
ARMSTEAD ST	CO	AZU	18000	88	E1
ARMSTEAD ST	CO	GLDR	19100	88	F1
ARMSTEAD ST	CO	GLDR	19300	89	A1

STREET	CITY	P.O. ZONE	BLOCK	PAGE	GRID
ARMSTEAD ST	LA	SF	17000	1	F6
ARMSTEAD ST	LA	SF	16200	2	A6
ARMSTRONG AV	LA	LA39		35	C3
ARMSTRONG DR	CLA	CLA		96	B6
ARNAUD ST	CO	LAN	45500	158	B2
ARNAZ DR	LA	LA48	300	33	D6
ARNAZ DR N	BH	BH	100	42	D1
ARNAZ DR S	BH	BH	100	42	D1
ARNEL PL	LA	CHA		6	E2
ARNELL PL	GLEN	GL14	3700	11	C4
ARNETT ST	DOW	DOW	7300	60	A3
ARNIE AV	RM	RM		38	A6
ARNIE LN	CO	PVP		73	B3
ARNO DR	SMAD	SMAD		28	E1
ARNO WY	LA	PP		40	B4
ARNOLD AL	PAS	PAS	200	27	B3
ARNOLDALE AV	PALM	PALM	40900	173	J3
ARNOLD CTR RD	CAR	LB10	21700	69	E4
ARNWOOD RD	LA	SF	10300	9	F1
ARNWOOD RD	LA	SF	9800	10	A1
AROMA DR	WCOV	WCOV		92	D3
AROMITIAS CIR	PVE	PVP		72	C2
ARRAMBIDE DR	WHI	WHI	5500	55	D3
ARRASTRE-ALISO	CO	SAU		189	G8
ARRASTRE CYN RD	CO	ACT	29900	189	E5
ARREY AV	NWK	NWK	13300	82	C1
ARRIBA DR	LA	TAR		21	B3
ARRIBA DR	MPK	MPK	1400	45	F2
ARRIBA DR	MPK	MPK	1400	46	A2
ARRIBA DR	SCLR	SAU	22500	124	C6
ARRINGTON AV	DOW	DOW	8800	60	D3
ARRINGTON AV	PR	PR	8100	60	D1
ARRIOLA AV	SCLR	SAU	27300	124	D6
ARROW HWY	AZU	AZU	400	88	D2
ARROW HWY	BAP	BAP	14300	39	E2
ARROW HWY	CO	AZU	16500	88	A2
ARROW HWY	CO	COV	16500	88	A2
ARROW HWY	CO	COV	19700	89	C3
ARROW HWY	IRW	BAP	14000	39	E2
ARROW HWY	IRW	BAP	15500	88	A2
ARROW HWY	LAV	LAV	700	90	C3
ARROW HWY E	CLA	CLA	100	91	A4
ARROW HWY E	COV	COV	200	88	D2
ARROW HWY E	COV	COV	700	89	C3
ARROW HWY E	POM	POM	100	90	D4
ARROW HWY E	POM	POM	800	91	A4
ARROW HWY E	SAD	SAD	100	90	A3
ARROW HWY W	CLA	CLA	100	91	A4
ARROW HWY W	COV	COV	300	88	D2
ARROW HWY W	POM	POM	100	90	D4
ARROW HWY W	POM	POM	800	91	A4
ARROW HWY W	SAD	SAD	100	89	F3
ARROWAY AV	CO	COV	5000	89	A3
ARROW GRAND CIR	COV	COV		88	F3
ARROW GRAND CIR	COV	COV		89	A3
ARROWHEAD CT	CO	ALT	3200	20	B3
ARROWHEAD CT	PALM	PALM		171	D5
ARROWHEAD DR	LA	LA68	3100	24	C6
ARROWHEAD LN	RHE	PVP		72	D6
ARROWHEAD PL	LA	LA68	6300	24	C6
ARROWMILL AV	CMRC	LA23	2400	53	D2
ARROWOOD DR	LA	BH	9600	33	B2
ARROWOOD ST	CO	ARC	11200	38	E3
ARROWOOD ST	TEC	TEC	10600	38	D3
ARROW POINT DR	CO	CAST	31400	123	G2
ARROWROCK DR	CO	PALM		157	E9
ARROWROOT LN	RPV	PVP	6100	77	D2
ARROYO AV	LA	SF	12800	3	A5
ARROYO AV	POM	POM	1300	94	B2
ARROYO AV	SF	SF	400	2	F6
ARROYO AV	SF	SF	700	3	A5
ARROYO BLVD	PAS	PAS		19	E5
ARROYO BLVD N	PAS	PAS	1500	19	E6
ARROYO BLVD N	PAS	PAS	100	26	E2
ARROYO BLVD S	PAS	PAS	100	26	E6
ARROYO CIR	PVE	PVP	1900	72	C2
ARROYO DR	CO	RM	7700	46	E4
ARROYO DR	CO	WHI	10800	84	A5
ARROYO DR	LA	LA42	5700	36	C2
ARROYO DR	LAM	LAM	11600	84	A5
ARROYO DR	MPK	MPK	1100	46	E3
ARROYO DR	MTB	MTB	100	46	E4
ARROYO DR	MTB	MTB	8500	47	A4
ARROYO DR	PAS	PAS	600	26	E4
ARROYO DR	POM	POM	2100	94	B2
ARROYO DR	RM	RM		47	A4
ARROYO DR	SPAS	SPAS	200	36	E2
ARROYO DR N	SGAB	SGAB	200	37	D3
ARROYO DR S	SGAB	SGAB	300	37	D3
ARROYO LN	NWK	NWK	12800	61	C6
ARROYO LN	NWK	NWK	12800	82	C1
ARROYO PKWY N	PAS	PAS	1	27	A5
ARROYO PKWY S	PAS	PAS	101	27	A5
ARROYO SQ	SPAS	SPAS	400	36	E1
ARROYO ST	LA	SF	12800	3	A5
ARROYO TER	ALH	ALH	900	37	D3

STREET	CITY	P.O. ZONE	BLOCK	PAGE	GRID
ARROYO TER	PAS	PAS	100	26	E3
ARROYO WK	LCF	LCF		19	C2
ARROYO BL W RDY	PAS	PAS		26	E2
ARROYO GLEN	LA	LA42		36	D2
ARROYO GLEN	LA	LA42		36	D2
ARROYO GLEN	LA	LA42		36	D2
ARROYO GLEN	LA	LA42		36	D2
ARROYO GLEN ST	LA	LA42		36	D2
ARROYO PARK DR	SCLR	VAL		127	H6
ARROYO PARK DR	POM	POM	1000	94	C1
ARROYO SECO AV	LA	LA65		36	A4
ARROYO VERDE RD	SPAS	SPAS	1000	36	D2
ARROYO VERDE ST	LA	LA42		36	D2
ARROYO VIEW DR	PAS	PAS	1300	26	D1
ARROYO VISTA DR	SM	SM	100	40	E5
ARROYO VISTA PL	SPAS	SPAS		36	E1
ARR WILLOW LN	CO	CAL		100A	E5
ART PL	WCOV	WCOV		92	E6
ART ST	LA	SUN	10500	9	E4
ART ST	LA	SV	10900	9	C6
ARTEIQUE RD	CO	TOP	1500	109	D2
ARTEMIS PL	LA	LA64		41	D5
ARTEMUS ST	LA	LA33		44	F4
ARTESIA BLVD	ART	ART	11400	66	B5
ARTESIA BLVD	ART	ART	11500	82	B5
ARTESIA BLVD	BLF	BLF	8500	66	B5
ARTESIA BLVD	CAR	CAR		64	C5
ARTESIA BLVD	CAR	GAR	100	64	A5
ARTESIA BLVD	CAR	GAR	100	64	A5
ARTESIA BLVD	CER	ART	10700	66	B5
ARTESIA BLVD	CER	ART	12300	82	B5
ARTESIA BLVD	COM	COM		64	E5
ARTESIA BLVD	COM	COM	100	65	A5
ARTESIA BLVD	GAR	GAR	1000	63	E5
ARTESIA BLVD	LA	GAR	700	63	E5
ARTESIA BLVD	LA	GAR	500	64	A5
ARTESIA BLVD	LAM	LAM	14200	82	B5
ARTESIA BLVD	LAM	LAM	14600	83	A5
ARTESIA BLVD	LAW	LAW	4500	62	D5
ARTESIA BLVD	MB	MB	1100	62	D5
ARTESIA BLVD	RB	RB	900	62	D5
ARTESIA BLVD	TOR	TOR	1800	63	B5
ARTESIA BLVD E	LB	LB05	100	65	A5
ARTESIA BLVD W	LB	LB05	100	65	A5
ARTESIA CT	BLF	BLF	17300	66	C5
ARTESIA LN	LB	LB05	300	65	C5
ARTESIA PL	BLF	BLF	9900	66	C5
ARTESIA ST	CAR	CAR	600	64	C5
ARTESIA ST E	POM	POM	100	90	E6
ARTESIA ST W	POM	POM	100	90	E6
ARTESIAN ST	LA	LA31		35	F5
ARTHUR AV	ARC	ARC	10000	38	E1
ARTHUR AV	AZU	AZU	300	88	D2
ARTHUR AV	PAR	PAR	13700	65	E2
ARTHUR AV	POM	POM	1900	94	B2
ARTHUR ST	CER	ART		82	C4
ARTHUR ST	LA	LA65		35	E2
ARTHUR WY	LAV	LAV		90	E1
ARTHURDALE AV	BLF	BLF	9500	66	C2
ARTHURS CT	CO	PVP		73	B4
ARTIGAS DR	CO	LPUE	2200	98	C5
ARTINE DR	SCLR	SAU		124	D5
ARTRUDE ST	LA	SUN		9	F4
ARTSEY AV	CO	PALM		182	B8
ARTSON ST	RM	RM	7800	46	F1
ARTURO ST	SAD	SAD		90	A2
ARTURO ST	WCOV	WCOV	400	92	D1
ARUBA CT	POM	POM	1400	90	C6
ARUNDEL DR	LA	WOH		13	F2
ARUNDEL PL	LA	WOH		13	F2
ARUNDLE PL	GLEN	GL06	1600	26	A1
ARVADA ST	TOR	TOR	3800	67	E1
ARVAL AV	LYN	LYN	11000	59	B5
ARVEE ST	CUL	CUL	4200	50	B2
ARVIA ST	LA	LA65		35	F3
ARVID ST	CO	LPUE	16400	92	A5
ARVIDA DR	LA	SF		1	D4
ARVILLA AV	LA	BUR	7500	16	F3
ARVILLA AV	LA	SV	7700	16	F3
ARVIN DR	GLEN	GL08	1800	25	F1
ARWIN ST	PAS	PAS	800	19	E5
ARWOLINDA WY	CO	CAL		100	D3
ARYE PL	LA	SF	17200	1	E4
ASBURY AV	POM	POM	800	91	A5
ASBURY DR	PAS	PAS	1400	27	C2
ASBURY ST	LA	LA65		35	E3
ASCONA DR	SCLR	CYN		125	B8
ASCOT AV	LA	LA11		52	D4
ASCOT CT	SAD	SAD		89	E3
ASCOT WK	LA	LA03		52	B5
ASDEL AV	CO	MAL		112	B1
ASDER LN	ARC	ARC	900	28	D3
ASH	CO	LP48		98	E3
ASH AV	BUR	BUR	50	24	E1
ASH AV N	ING	IN01	100	56	E2
ASH AV S	ING	IN01	100	56	E2

STREET	CITY	P.O. ZONE	BLOCK	PAGE	GRID
ASH CT	CO	SAU		124	C2
ASH DR	MPK	MPK	1600	46	D4
ASH DR	PALM	PALM		183	J6
ASH ST	CMRC	LA23	2400	53	D2
ASH ST	LA	LA42		36	C2
ASHBORO DR	SCLR	CYN	28000	124	G7
ASHBOURNE DR	SMAR	PAS	2100	37	B2
ASHBOURNE DR	SPAS	SPAS	2000	37	A2
ASHBRIDGE DR	CO	HAC		73	F1
ASHBRIDGE LN	CO	HAC		73	F1
ASHBROOK AV	LB	LB15	1800	76	C3
ASHBROOK CIR	PALM	PALM		183	H7
ASHBURTON PL	GLEN	GL06	400	26	B3
ASHBURY	WCOV	WCOV		92	D4
ASHBURY PL	GLEN	GL06	1600	26	A1
ASHBY AV	LA	LA64	10600	42	A4
ASHBY CT	CO	SAU		123	D4
ASHBY CT	SAD	SAD		90	A4
ASHBY ST	AZU	AZU	300	86	C4
ASHCOMB DR	CO	LPUE	600	92	C5
ASH CREEK DR	CO	PALM		157	E9
ASH CREEK LN	SCLR	VAL	22900	124	C5
ASH CREEK RD	CER	ART	12200	82	B4
ASHCROFT AV	WHOL	LA48	8700	33	D5
ASHDALE AV	LA	LA49		32	C6
ASHDALE LN	LA	NHO		23	C6
ASHDALE PL	LA	LA49		32	C6
ASHDALE ST	WCOV	WCOV	100	92	C1
ASHER ST	ELM	ELM	9800	47	C1
ASHERTON DR	CO	COV		89	C3
ASHERTON DR	CO	SAD	4600	89	C4
ASHFIELD AV	POM	POM	800	91	A5
ASHFIELD PL	CO	VAL		124	B6
ASHFORD DR	LAV	LAV		95A	B6
ASHFORD ST	LA	LA49		41	A2
ASHFORK PL	RPV	PVP	26400	72	D3
ASH GLEN AV	LAN	LAN		159	G5
ASHGLEN CIR	SCLR	VAL		124	B5
ASHGROVE DR	LAM	LAM	15000	83	B2
ASHINGTON DR	GLEN	GL06		19	B6
ASHIYA AV	MTB	MTB		46	E5
ASHLAKE PL	CO	PALM		157	E9
ASHLAND AV	CLA	CLA	1400	91	A2
ASHLAND AV	LA	LA31		36	B5
ASHLAND AV	SM	SM	100	49	B2
ASHLAND CT	CO	VAL		124	B6
ASHLEE CT	PALM	PALM		172	F9
ASHLEY AV	TOR	TOR	18200	63	A6
ASHLEY DR	PAS	PAS		27	F2
ASHLEY OAKS	LA	ENC	16600	21	F3
ASHLEY RIDGE RD	HH	CAL		100	C2
ASH MEADOW DR	WAL	WAL		92	F6
ASHMILL ST	CAR	CAR	1200	69	D4
ASHMONT AV	CO	ARC	2800	39	A2
ASHMORE PL	LA	LA26		35	C5
ASHPARK LN	CO	HAC		73	F1
ASHPORT ST	POM	POM	1000	94	C2
ASHTABULA ST	PAS	PAS	300	27	A2
ASHTON AV	LA	LA24		41	E2
ASHTON CT	LA	CAN		5	E2
ASHTON DR	COV	COV	100	89	B5
ASHTREE DR	CO	PALM		157	H8
ASHVALE DR	SAD	SAD	100	89	F1
ASHWIN DR	CO	GL14	3000	11	D6
ASHWOOD AV	LA	LA66		49	D2
ASHWOOD ST	WCOV	WCOV	1100	92	B1
ASHWORTH CIR	CER	ART	10700	66	E6
ASHWORTH CIR	CER	ART	13700	82	E6
ASHWORTH PL	CER	ART	12300	82	B6
ASHWORTH PL	GLDR	GLDR		86	E4
ASHWORTH ST	ART	ART	11800	82	A6
ASHWORTH ST	BLF	BLF	10400	66	D6
ASHWORTH ST	CER	ART	11300	66	F6
ASHWORTH ST	CER	ART	13300	82	D6
ASHWORTH ST	LA	VAN		15	E1
ASHWORTH ST	LB	LB05	3800	66	A6
ASHWORTH ST	LKD	LKD	3800	66	B6
ASILOMAR BLVD	LA	PP		40	C4
ASMAN AV	LA	CAN		12	B3
ASMUSSEN AV	NWK	NWK	11500	60	F5
ASPAN AV	CO	AZU	5500	88	C2
ASPAN AV	CO	COV	4300	88	C3
ASPAN AV N	AZU	AZU	200	86	C6
ASPAN AV N	AZU	AZU	100	88	C1
ASPAN AV S	AZU	AZU	300	88	C2
ASPEN AV	BLF	BLF		66	D6
ASPEN CIR	POM	POM		94	C6
ASPEN CIR	SFS	SFS		60	F3
ASPEN CT	CO	SAU		124	C2
ASPEN DR	LA	LA68	2400	34	D2
ASPEN DR	MON	MON		29	B3
ASPEN LN	PALM	PALM		183	G3
ASPEN LN	POM	POM		90	F5
ASPEN ST	LAV	LAV		90	A3
ASPEN WY	CO	CAL		100	D6

ASPEN WY

STREET	CITY	P.O. ZONE	BLOCK	PAGE	GRID
ASPEN WY	RHE	PVP		72	D5
ASPENCADE CT	PALM	PALM		172	F3
ASPEN GROVE LN	DBAR	POM		97	F3
ASPEN KNOLL DR	DBAR	POM		97	F2
ASPEN OAK LN	GLEN	GL02		18	C6
ASPEN RIDGE CT	SCLR	VAL		124	B4
ASPENVIEW CT	WLVL	THO		102A	F5
ASPEN VLG WY	WCOV	WCOV		92	D2
ASPENWOOD CT	DBAR	WAL		97	C5
ASPERN ST	CO	PALM		183	D4
ASTAIRE AV	CO	CUL	4000	50	B1
ASTELL AV	CO	AZU	5500	88	C2
ASTELL AV S	WCOV	WCOV	300	88	C1
ASTELL AV S	WCOV	WCOV	100	92	C1
ASTER TR	CO	CAL		100	C5
ASTERIA ST	TOR	TOR	4900	67	E3
ASTI ST	DUA	DUA	1300	29	D5
ASTLEY RD N	CO	ACT		182	C6
ASTON AV	POM	POM	2400	94	A2
ASTOR AV	CMRC	LA40	4700	53	E2
ASTORIA DR	LAN	LAN		160	E6
ASTORIA DR	LA	SF	14600	2	D4
ASTORIA ST	LA	SF	13400	2	D3
ASTORIA ST	LA	SF	13200	3	A1
ASTRA ST	CO	RM		46	E4
ASTRAL DR	LA	LA46		33	F1
ASTRAL PL	LA	LA46		33	F1
ASTRAN CT	CO	LAN		171	B1
ASTRO C ONIZUKA	LA	LA12		44	D3
ASTUTO DR	PALM	LAN		171	C4
ASUNCION ST	LA	NOR		1	B1
ATARA ST E	MON	MON	100	29	B6
ATARA ST W	CO	MON	200	29	A6
ATARA ST W	MON	MON	100	29	B6
ATASCADERO PL	MTB	MTB	900	46	F5
ATCHISON ST	CO	PAS	100	20	D6
ATCHISON ST	PAS	PAS	200	20	A6
ATFORD ST	RPV	SP	28700	78	D1
ATGLEN ST	CO	LPUE	15700	85	F2
ATHEL DR	LA	CAN		5	F3
ATHELING WY	LA	HAC	26200	73	E4
ATHENA AV	LA	LA39		48	F2
ATHENA ST	WCOV	WCOV		48	A2
ATHENE DR	CER	ART	11800	81	A1
ATHENIAN WY	CO	LA43	4000	51	A3
ATHENS BLVD	CO	LA61	400	58	A6
ATHENS BLVD	LA	LA61	700	57	C4
ATHENS BLVD	LA	LA44	500	58	A6
ATHENS CT	CLA	CLA		91	B2
ATHENS ST	CO	ALT	400	20	B4
ATHENS WY	CO	LA61	12000	58	A6
ATHENS WY	LA	LA61	11300	58	A6
ATHERTON AV	LB	LB15	7100	76	F3
ATHERTON LN	LA	CAN		5	D3
ATHERTON ST	LB	LB15	4600	76	B3
ATHERTON CYN RD	SCLR	SAU		124	J4
ATHOL ST	BAP	BAP	3200	39	B6
ATHOL ST	BAP	BAP	3100	48	A1
ATINA DR	CO	LPUE	18000	98	D3
ATITLAN DR	GLEN	GL06	600	25	E3
ATKINS DR	LA	LPUE	15800	85	E4
ATKINSON AV	HAW	IN03	11600	57	C4
ATKINSON AV	ING	IN02	10900	57	C4
ATKINSON AV	TOR	TOR	16200	63	C3
ATLANTA AV	LA	NOR		7	A2
ATLANTA CT	CLA	CLA	800	91	A2
ATLANTA DR	PALM	PALM		183	J1
ATLANTIC AV	BELL	BELL	6200	53	C6
ATLANTIC AV	CDY	BELL	7200	53	C4
ATLANTIC AV	CDY	BELL	7500	59	C1
ATLANTIC AV	CO	COM	12900	65	C3
ATLANTIC AV	COM	COM		65	C3
ATLANTIC AV	CUL	LA66	11800	50	D4
ATLANTIC AV	LB	LB02	100	75	D4
ATLANTIC AV	LB	LB02	300	75	D4
ATLANTIC AV	LB	LB05	1800	75	D4
ATLANTIC AV	LB	LB05	5100	70	D5
ATLANTIC AV	LB	LB06	1800	75	D4
ATLANTIC AV	LB	LB07	3000	70	D5
ATLANTIC AV	LB	LB13	700	75	D4
ATLANTIC AV	LYN	LYN	10600	59	C6
ATLANTIC AV	LYN	LYN	11700	65	C1
ATLANTIC AV	SOG	SOG	8600	59	C1
ATLANTIC BLVD	BELL	BELL	2700	53	D3
ATLANTIC BLVD	CMRC	LA40	2000	53	D3
ATLANTIC BLVD	CO	LA22	5100	53	D3
ATLANTIC BLVD	MAY	MAY	5200	53	C4
ATLANTIC BLVD N	ALH	ALH	100	37	B4
ATLANTIC BLVD N	CO	LA22	100	46	A4
ATLANTIC BLVD S	MPK	ALH	100	37	B4
ATLANTIC BLVD S	ALH	ALH	100	46	A4
ATLANTIC BLVD S	CO	LA22	200	46	A5
ATLANTIC BLVD S	CO	LA22	900	53	A1
ATLANTIC BLVD S	MPK	LA22	100	46	A4
ATLANTIC CIR	LAV	LAV		90	E2
ATLANTIC CT	LA	LA21	2000	44	E5
ATLANTIC DR	COM	COM	1200	65	C4
ATLANTIC DR	LB	LB05	6600	65	C5
ATLANTIC PL	PAR	PAR	4400	70	D3
ATLANTIC PL	PAR	PAR	15901	65	C5
ATLANTIC PZ	LB	LB05	600	70	D2
ATLANTIC ST	LA	LA23	3000	45	B5
ATLANTIC ST	POM	POM		94	A3
ATLANTIC WY	LB	LB02	1	75	D6
ATLANTIDA DR	CO	LPUE	16100	85	E3
ATLAS AV	MPK	MPK		46	C4
ATLAS ST	LA	LA32		36	E3
ATLAS WY	LB	LB13	1400	45	D4
ATLEE DR	LCF	LCF	1000	19	B3
ATLER RD	CO	SAU		125	H2
ATLIN ST	DUA	DUA	1900	29	E4
ATMORE ST	CAR	CAR	23200	69	A6
ATMORE AV	CAR	CAR	23500	74	A1
ATOLL AV	LA	NHO	6000	16	A4
ATOLL AV	LA	VAN	6000	16	A3
ATOLL AV	LA	VAN		23	A3
ATOMIC TR	CO	TOP		5	F2
ATRON AV	LA	CAN		1400	93	C5
ATTERBURY DR	WAL	WAL	1400	93	C5
ATTICA DR	LB	LB03	206	80	C1
ATTILLA RD	LA	SM	14100	40	E5
ATTRIDGE AV	CO	LA63	1400	45	D4
ATWATER AV	LA	LA39		77	A6
ATWATER CYN RD	GLEN	GL08	2900	18	F5
ATWELL PL	LA	LA45		56	E2
ATWOOD BLVD	SCLR	NEW	24600	127	A4
ATWOOD ST	LA	LA63		45	C3
ATWOOD ST	LA	LA63		45	C3
ATWOOD WK	LA	LA63		45	C3
ATWOOD WY	TOR	TOR		68	E5
AUBREY CT	LA	VN23		22	E5
AUBREY RD	LA	VN23		22	E5
AUBURN AV	SMAD	SMAD	1	28	C2
AUBURN DR	WCOV	WCOV	1000	92	D3
AUBURN LN	SMAD	SMAD	300	28	C1
AUBURN RD	SAD	SAD		80	B4
AUBURN RD	LA	LA39		35	B2
AUBURN WY	CLA	CLA		91	C1
AUBURN WY	CLA	CLA		96	C6
AUCKLAND AV	LA	NHO	5600	16	F5
AUCKLAND AV	LA	NHO	4400	23	F3
AUCKLAND AV	BAP	BAP	12700	39	B6
AUCKLAND AV	BAP	BAP	4200	39	F4
AUCTION AV	LB	LB03		39	C6
AUDRA DR	LA	LA63	400	18	B6
AUDRAINE DR	GLEN	GL02	400	18	A6
AUDREY AV	TOR	TOR	22900	63	A6
AUDREY AV	TOR	TOR	23800	73	A1
AUDREY CT	SCLR	CYN		124	G6
AUDREY LN	WCOV	WCOV		92	E6
AUDREY PL	LA	LA39		35	C3
AUDUBON AV	SMAD	SMAD	400	28	D1
AUGUST ST	LA	LA08	4500	51	A1
AUGUSTA ST	ING	IN02	600	56	E1
AUGUSTA ST	LA	LA12		44	E2
AUGUSTA WY	POM	POM	1100	94	B1
AUGUSTA WY	WAL	WAL		93	D6
AUGUSTINE CT	LA	LA31		36	A5
AUGUSTINE CT	LA	SF		3	A1
AULTS AV	LA	SF		3	A1
AUMOND AV	SCLR	CYN	28000	124	H7
AURA AV	LA	NOR	8500	14	A3
AURA AV	LA	NOR	8300	14	A1
AURA AV	LA	RES	6200	14	A5
AURA ST	LA	TAR	5300	21	A5
AUREOLA BLVD	CO	LA08	3600	51	B2
AURORA DR	CLA	CLA	60500	91	C2
AURORA DR	RHE	PVP		73	D4
AURORA DR	WAL	WAL		92	F6
AURORA ST	LA	LA12		44	F1
AURORA ST	ALH	ALH	2500	46	E1
AURORA TER	PAR	PAR		65	E4
AURORA WY	WHI	WHI		84	C1
AURORA CREST DR	ING	IN02	800	56	D5
AUSTIN CT	LA	CLA		91	C2
AUSTIN CT	LA	WOH		22	A2
AUSTIN ST	LA	LH		157	B7
AUSTIN WY	LA	LA39		35	A5
AUTO DR N	COM	COM		65	A5
AUTO DR S	COM	COM		65	A5
AUTO WY	SM	SM	1	49	A2
AUTOCENTER DR	COM	COM		65	A5
AUTO CENTER DR	GLDR	GLDR		93	D5
AUTO CENTER DR	POM	POM		94	D5
AUTO EMPORIUM	CER	ART	10000	71	E1
AUTO SQUARE DR	LB	LB03	4700	71	C3
AUTRY AV	LKD	LKD	5900	66	C5
AUTRY AV	LKD	LKD	4900	71	C1
AUTUM LN	PALM	PALM		183	B1
AUTUMN DR	WCOV	WCOV	17100	92	C4
AUTUMN LN	CO	POM		97	C4
AUTUMN LN	PAS	PAS		28	A1
AUTUMNBREEZE ST	CER	ART		82	B5
AUTUMNGLOW DR	DBAR	POM		97	A3
AUTUMN HILL RD	DBAR	POM		97A	A3
AUTUMN LEAF CIR	LA	LA77		22	E6
AUTUMN MOON DR	CO	LPUE	14400	85	C6
AVA AV	HB	RB	1900	62	C6
AVALO DR	CO	LPUE	3000	85	D4
AVALON AV	POM	POM	2100	94	B1
AVALON BLVD	CAR	CAR	14300	64	B6
AVALON BLVD	CAR	CAR	16100	64	C4
AVALON BLVD	CAR	CAR	16900	64	B6
AVALON BLVD	CO	CAR	21000	69	C2
AVALON BLVD	CO	CAR	23700	74	C5
AVALON BLVD	CO	LA61	12000	58	B6
AVALON BLVD	CO	LA61	12800	64	B6
AVALON BLVD	LA	LA03	5800	52	B4
AVALON BLVD	LA	LA03	7900	58	B2
AVALON BLVD	LA	LA11	3400	52	B4
AVALON BLVD	LA	LA61	10700	58	B1
AVALON BLVD	LA	WIL	24500	74	C5
AVALON BLVD	LA	WIL	100	74	C5
AVALON BLVD S	LA	WIL	100	74	C5
AVALON CT	LB	LB03		74	C3
AVALON PL	LA	WIL	800	74	C5
AVALON ST	LA	LA26		35	C4
AVALON CYN RD	CO	AVA		77	A6
AVENEL ST	LA	LA39		35	B2
AVENEL TER	LA	LA39		35	B2
AVENGER PL	RPV	PVP	32200	78	B6
AVENIDA ALIPAZ	WAL	WAL	100	93	B6
AVENIDA ALIPAZ	WAL	WAL		97	B6
AVENIDA ALTISMA	RPV	PVP	7000	78	B6
AVENIDA AMADIS	WAL	WAL	19800	93	B6
AVENIDA ANILLO	RPV	PVP	29000	72	C6
AVENIDA APRENDA	RPV	SP	1700	73	D5
AVD ASOLEADA	CO	CAL		100	D5
AVENIDA ATEZADA	TOR	TOR	200	72	E1
AVENIDA BALITA	SCLR	VAL		127	B3
AVD BARCELONA	CER	ART	20000	81	B3
AVD BERNARDO	SAD	SAD		89	E6
AVENIDA CALLADA	CO	CAL		100	C5
AVENIDA CAPPELA	RPV	PVP		72	C6
AVD CELESTIAL	RPV	PVP		72	C6
AVD CLASSICA	RPV	PVP	30000	78	C1
AVENIDA COLINA	SAD	SAD		89	D5
AVENIDA CONEJO	AZU	AZU	1400	86	C4
AVENIDA CORONA	RPV	SP	30400	78	C1
AVD CRESCENTA	SCLR	VAL		127	D1
AVD CUADERNO	CO	SP	27800	73	D6
AVENIDA CUMBRE	CO	CAL		100	D5
AVD DE AZALEA	RPV	PVP		78	C2
AVD DE CALMA	RPV	PVP	30000	78	C2
AVD DE CAMELIA	RPV	PVP		78	C2
AVD DE CASTILLO	LB	LB03		35	A6
AVD DE CORTEZ	LA	PP		30	A6
AVD DE CORTEZ	CO	PP		109	F6
AVD DE ENCINAL	CO	MAL	4500	111	A4
AVENIDA DE JOSE	TOR	RB		72	D7
AV D L HERADURA	CO	PP		30	A5
AV D L MERCED E	MTB	MTB	100	46	F6
AV D L MERCED W	MTB	MTB	100	46	F6
AVD D LA RAMBLA	WAL	WAL		97	A1
AVD D LA SUERTE	LAN	LAN		160	F5
AVD DEL BRISA	LA	LA03		97	A1
AVD DEL CAMPO	WAL	WAL	19400	97	A1
AVD DEL CANADA	CO	LPUE		98	C4
AVD DELEITANTE	WAL	WAL		97	B2
AVENIDA DEL MAR	CO	MAL	4700	111	A4
AVENIDA DEL MAR	LAN	LAN		160	F4
AVD DEL MESA	RPV	SP	27600	73	D5
AVD DEL NORTE	LAN	RB	200	160	F6
AVD DEL PLAYA	LAN	LAN		160	F6
AVENIDA DEL REY	CO	SAU		188	B2
AVENIDA DEL SOL	LAN	LAN		160	F4
AVENIDA DEL SOL	LA	NHO	3600	23	A1
AVENIDA DEL SOL	LA	NHO		1	B5
AVD DE MAGNOLIA	RPV	PVP		78	B2
AVD DE NOGAL	RPV	PVP		78	C2
AVD DE OLIVA	RPV	PVP		78	C2
AVENIDA DE OLMA	RPV	PVP		78	C2
AVENIDA DE ROSA	RPV	PVP		78	D5
AVD DE STA YNEZ	LA	PP		30	A6
AVENIDA DESEO	WAL	WAL	20000	93	D1
AVENIDA DESEO	WAL	WAL	20000	93	D1
AVD DE UNAMUNDO	LA	TAR	4500	13	D1
AVENIDA DOMINGO	SAD	SAD		89	D1
AVENIDA DORENA	SCLR	NEW	25200	127	A4
AVD ELEGANTE	RPV	PVP		78	C2
AVENIDA ENTRANA	SCLR	VAL		127	A4
AVD ENTRANA	SCLR	VAL		127	A4
AVD ESCALERA	WCOV	WCOV		85	C1
AVENIDA ESPANA	LAM	LAM		83	D1
AVD ESPLENDIDA	RPV	PVP		72	C2
AVD ESPLENDOR	WAL	WAL	300	97	B1
AVD ESTEBAN TOR	CMRC	LA22		53	F1
AVENIDA ESTORIL	LB	LB03		76	D5
AVENIDA ESTUDIANTE	RPV	SP	1800	73	D6
AVD FELICIANO	RPV	SP	1800	73	D5
AVD FERNANDO	SAD	SAD		89	E1
AVD FERNANDO	SCLR	VAL		127	B2
AVENIDA FRASCA	LB	LB03		76	C5
AVENIDA GRANADA	WAL	WAL		93	B6
AVENIDA GRULLA	WAL	WAL		97	B1
AVD HACIENDA	WAL	TAR	5000	21	C2
AVENIDA IGNACIO	SCLR	VAL		127	B3
AVENIDA JOLITA	SCLR	VAL		127	A2
AVENIDA LADERA	SAD	SAD		89	D5
AVD LOMA VISTA	SAD	SAD		89	D5
AVENIDA LOMITA	SAD	SAD		89	D6
AVD MAGNIFICA	RPV	PVP	29000	72	C6
AVD MANL SALINS	NWK	NWK	12600	61	B6
AVD MANL SALINS	NWK	NWK	12600	82	B1
AVD MELISENDA	PVE	SP		72	A5
AVENIDA MIROLA	PVE	SP	400	72	A5
AVD MONTE VISTA	SCLR	VAL		127	B2
AVD ORNT FR RD	LA	TAR		21	B5
AVD PAMPLONA	CER	ART	20100	81	B3
AVD PRESIDIO	WAL	WAL		93	A6
AVD PURTO VLRTA	LA	LANC	17800	21	D4
AVD RANCHEROS	POM	POM		94	B4
AVD REFINIDA	RPV	PVP	29000	72	C6
AVENIDA RONADA	SCLR	VAL		127	D2
AVENIDA RONDEL	SCLR	VAL		127	B3
AVENIDA ROTELLA	SAD	SAD		89	D5
AVENIDA SANDI	SAD	SAD		89	D5
AVD SAN MIGUEL	LAM	LAM		84	C6
AVD SAN MIGUEL	LAM	LAM		84	C6
AVD SANTA TECLA	LA	SF	15800	83	C1
AVENIDA SELECTA	RPV	PVP	30000	77	C1
AVENIDA SOCORRO	LAM	LAM	15400	83	C1
AVENIDA TERRAZA	SCLR	SAU		124	C6
AVD TRANQUILA	RPV	PVP	30000	72	C2
AVENIDA VELARTE	SCLR	VAL	23000	127	B2
AVD VERDE VISTA	SAD	SAD		89	D6
AVD VISTA VERDE	PALM	LAN		171	D3
AVENIR CT	PALM	PALM		171	D3
AVENTINE WY	CO	WAL	1800	97	B4
AVENUE A	CO	CAST		123	G3
AVENUE A	CO	LPUE		98	E4
AVENUE A	RB	RB	500	67	D5
AVENUE A	RB	RB	100	67	D5
AVENUE A	TOR	TOR	5600	67	D5
AVENUE A-14 W	CO	LAN	1500	146	B1
AVENUE B	CO	CAST		123	G3
AVENUE B	CO	LPUE		98	E4
AVENUE B	RB	RB	500	67	D5
AVENUE B	RB	RB	100	67	D5
AVENUE B	TOR	TOR		67	D5
AVENUE B W	CO	LAN	1200	146	J1
AVENUE B-1 W	CO	LAN		146	J1
AVENUE B-2 W	CO	LAN	1000	147	H1
AVENUE B-3 W	CO	LAN		146	F6
AVENUE B-4 W	CO	LAN		146	E6
AVENUE B-5 W	CO	LAN		146	D2
AVENUE B-6 W	CO	LAN		146	D2
AVENUE B-7 W	CO	LAN		146	D1
AVENUE B-8 W	CO	LAN		146	D1
AVENUE B-10 W	CO	LAN		146	D2
AVENUE B-11 W	CO	LAN		146	D2
AVENUE B-12 W	CO	LAN	1000	146	D2
AVENUE B-12 W	CO	LAN		146	D1
AVENUE B-13 W	CO	LAN		146	D1
AVENUE B-13 E	CO	LAN		147	H1
AVENUE B-14 W	CO	LAN		146	D1
AVENUE B-14 W	CO	LAN		147	D1
AVENUE C	RB	RB	500	67	E5
AVENUE C	CO	LAN	500	146	D5
AVENUE C	TOR	TOR		67	E5
AVENUE C	CO	VAL		67	E5
AVENUE C-2 W	CO	LAN	11000	146	H3
AVENUE C-2 W	CO	LAN		147	H3
AVENUE C-3 W	CO	LAN		146	E6
AVENUE C-4 W	CO	LAN	8000	147	J8
AVENUE C-5 W	CO	LAN		147	J8
AVENUE C-6 W	CO	LAN		146	H3
AVENUE C-6 W	CO	LAN		147	A3
AVENUE C-7 W	CO	LAN		147	H3
AVENUE C-8 W	CO	LAN		146	H3
AVENUE C-8 W	CO	LAN		146	H3
AVENUE C-9 W	CO	LAN		147	H3
AVENUE C-9 W	CO	LAN		147	H3
AVENUE C-10 W	CO	LAN		147	A3
AVENUE C-10 W	CO	LAN		146	C4
AVENUE C-12 W	CO	LAN	8000	146	H4
AVENUE C-12 W	CO	LAN		147	D3
AVENUE C-12 W	CO	LAN	1000	147	D3
AVENUE C-14 W	CO	LAN	8000	146	H4
AVENUE C-14 W	CO	LAN		147	D3
AVENUE CROCKER	CO	VAL		123	G6
AVENUE D	RB	RB	1000	67	E5
AVENUE D	CO	LAN	100	67	D5
AVENUE D W	CO	LAN	1000	146	F4
AVENUE D W	CO	LAN		147	H4
AVENUE D-2 W	CO	LAN		146	C4
AVENUE D-3 W	CO	LAN		146	C4
AVENUE D-4 E	CO	LAN	4000	148	H4
AVENUE D-4 W	CO	LAN		146	C4
AVENUE D-4 W	CO	LAN		147	A4
AVENUE D-6 W	CO	LAN		147	A4
AVENUE D-6 W	CO	LAN		146	J5
AVENUE D-7 W	CO	LAN		146	J5
AVENUE D-8 E	CO	LAN	4000	148	J5
AVENUE D-8 W	CO	LAN	1000	146	J5
AVENUE D-9 W	CO	LAN		146	J5
AVENUE D-10 W	CO	LAN		147	C5
AVENUE D-10 W	CO	LAN		146	C5
AVENUE D-11 W	CO	LAN		147	A5
AVENUE D-12 E	CO	LAN	4000	148	J5
AVENUE D-12 W	CO	LAN		146	C5
AVENUE D-12 W	CO	LAN		147	C5
AVENUE D-13 W	CO	LAN		146	C5
AVENUE D-14 W	CO	LAN		147	C5
AVENUE E	CO	LAN	1000	147	E5
AVENUE E	RB	RB	100	67	D5
AVENUE E E&W	CO	LAN	100	148	H6
AVENUE E-1 W	CO	LAN	100	147	J6
AVENUE E-1 W	CO	LAN		146	C6
AVENUE E-2 W	CO	LAN		147	J6
AVENUE E-3 W	CO	LAN		146	C6
AVENUE E-3 E	CO	LAN	100	148	E6
AVENUE E-4 E	CO	LAN		148	E6
AVENUE E-4 W	CO	LAN		147	J6
AVENUE E-5 W	CO	LAN		146	C6
AVENUE E-5 E	CO	LAN		147	J6
AVENUE E-6 E	CO	LAN		146	C6
AVENUE E-6 W	CO	LAN		147	J6
AVENUE E-6 W	CO	LAN	2000	147	G8
AVENUE E-7 W	CO	LAN		146	J6
AVENUE E-7 W	CO	LAN		147	J6
AVENUE E-8 E	CO	LAN		148	E6
AVENUE E-8 W	CO	LAN		146	J6
AVENUE E-10 E	CO	LAN		148	B7
AVENUE E-10 W	CO	LAN		146	D7
AVENUE E-11 W	CO	LAN		147	J7
AVENUE E-11 W	CO	LAN		146	J7
AVENUE E-12 E	CO	LAN	100	148	F7
AVENUE E-12 W	CO	LAN		146	J7
AVENUE E-12 W	CO	LAN		147	H7
AVENUE E-13 W	CO	LAN		146	J7
AVENUE E-13 W	CO	LAN		147	J7
AVENUE E-14 E	CO	LAN		148	G7
AVENUE E-14 W	CO	LAN		147	H7
AVENUE E-14 W	CO	LAN		146	D7
AVENUE F	RB	RB	100	67	D5
AVENUE F E&W	CO	LAN	9000	146	H7
AVENUE F	CO	LAN	700	148	H8
AVENUE F-2 W	CO	LAN	11000	146	H3
AVENUE F-2 W	CO	LAN		147	H3
AVENUE F-2 W	CO	LAN	100	148	G8
AVENUE F-4 E	CO	LAN		148	J8
AVENUE F-4 W	CO	LAN		147	J8
AVENUE F-5 W	CO	LAN		148	J8
AVENUE F-5 W	CO	LAN		146	

1990 LOS ANGELES COUNTY STREET INDEX

STREET	CITY	P.O. ZONE	BLOCK	PAGE	GRID
AVENUE F-5 W	CO	LAN		147	G8
AVENUE F-6 E	CO	LAN	100	148	B8
AVENUE F-6 W	CO	LAN		146	J8
AVENUE F-6 W	CO	LAN		147	G8
AVENUE F-7 W	CO	LAN		146	J8
AVENUE F-7 W	CO	LAN		147	G8
AVENUE F-8	CO	LAN		147	H8
AVENUE F-8 E	CO	LAN	100	148	E8
AVENUE F-8 W	CO	LAN		146	J8
AVENUE F-8 W	CO	LAN		147	G8
AVENUE F-8 W	CO	LAN	100	148	B8
AVENUE F-10 E	CO	LAN	100	148	C8
AVENUE F-10 W	CO	LAN		146	G8
AVENUE F-10 W	CO	LAN	100	147	F8
AVENUE F-11 W	CO	LAN		146	G8
AVENUE F-12 E	CO	LAN	100	148	E8
AVENUE F-12 W	CO	LAN		146	G8
AVENUE F-12 W	CO	LAN		146	A9
AVENUE F-12 W	CO	LAN	100	148	B8
AVENUE F-13 W	CO	LAN		146	A9
AVENUE F-14	CO	LAN		148	J9
AVENUE F-14 W	CO	LAN		146	A9
AVENUE F-14 W	CO	LAN	3000	147	F9
AVENUE F-15 W	CO	LAN	3500	147	F9
AVENUE G	LAN	LAN		147	A9
AVENUE G	RB	RB	100	67	D5
AVENUE G E	CO	LAN	100	148	A9
AVENUE G W	CO	LAN	100	148	A9
AVENUE G-2 W	CO	LAN	100	148	B9
AVENUE G-4 E	CO	LAN	100	148	C9
AVENUE G-4 W	CO	LAN		147	A9
AVENUE G-4 W	CO	LAN	100	148	A9
AVENUE G-5 W	CO	LAN		147	A9
AVENUE G-6 E	CO	LAN	100	148	C9
AVENUE G-6 W	CO	LAN		147	A9
AVENUE G-8 E	CO	LAN		160	A1
AVENUE G-8 W	CO	LAN		159	E1
AVENUE G-8 W	CO	LAN		160	A1
AVENUE G-9 W	CO	LAN		159	E1
AVENUE G-10 W	CO	LAN		159	E1
AVENUE G-10 W	CO	LAN	4000	159	E1
AVENUE G-11 W	CO	LAN		159	E1
AVENUE G-12 E	CO	LAN		160	A1
AVENUE G-12 W	LAN	LAN		158	F1
AVENUE G-12 W	CO	LAN		159	E1
AVENUE G-12 W	CO	LAN		160	A1
AVENUE G-13 W	LAN	LAN		158	F1
AVENUE G-13 W	CO	LAN		159	E1
AVENUE G-14 W	LAN	LAN		158	F1
AVENUE G-14 W	CO	LAN		159	E1
AVENUE H	RB	RB	100	67	D5
AVENUE H E	LAN	LAN	4000	160	F1
AVENUE H E&W	LAN	LAN	100	160	F1
AVENUE H W	CO	LAN	4000	159	E1
AVENUE H W	LAN	LAN	1000	159	E1
AVENUE H-1 W	LAN	LAN		159	J2
AVENUE H-1 W	LAN	LAN	1000	159	J2
AVENUE H-2	LAN	LAN		161	F2
AVENUE H-2 E	LAN	LAN		160	H2
AVENUE H-2 W	CO	LAN		159	C3
AVENUE H-2 W	LAN	LAN		159	J2
AVENUE H-2 W	LAN	LAN		160	H2
AVENUE H-3 E	CO	LAN		161	J2
AVENUE H-3 E	LAN	LAN		160	H2
AVENUE H-3 W	CO	LAN		159	C3
AVENUE H-3 W	LAN	LAN		159	J2
AVENUE H-3 W	LAN	LAN		160	H2
AVENUE H-4 E	CO	LAN	4000	160	G2
AVENUE H-4 E	CO	LAN		161	J2
AVENUE H-4 E	LAN	LAN		160	H2
AVENUE H-4 W	CO	LAN		159	C3
AVENUE H-4 W	LAN	LAN		158	H2
AVENUE H-4 W	LAN	LAN		159	J2
AVENUE H-4 W	LAN	LAN		160	H2
AVENUE H-5 E	CO	LAN		161	J2
AVENUE H-5 E	LAN	LAN		160	H2
AVENUE H-5 W	LAN	LAN		158	H2
AVENUE H-5 W	CO	LAN		159	C3
AVENUE H-5 W	LAN	LAN		159	J2
AVENUE H-5 W	LAN	LAN		160	H2
AVENUE H-6 E	LAN	LAN		160	H2
AVENUE H-6 W	CO	LAN		159	C3
AVENUE H-6 W	LAN	LAN		158	H2
AVENUE H-6 W	LAN	LAN		159	J2
AVENUE H-6 W	LAN	LAN		160	H2
AVENUE H-7 E	LAN	LAN		160	H2
AVENUE H-7 W	LAN	LAN		158	H2
AVENUE H-7 W	LAN	LAN		159	J2
AVENUE H-7 W	LAN	LAN		160	H2
AVENUE H-8 E	LAN	LAN		160	H2
AVENUE H-8 W	CO	LAN	4000	159	B2
AVENUE H-8 W	LAN	LAN		158	H2
AVENUE H-8 W	LAN	LAN		159	J2
AVENUE H-8 W	LAN	LAN		160	H2
AVENUE H-9 W	LAN	LAN		158	H2
AVENUE H-9 W	LAN	LAN		159	J2
AVENUE H-9 W	LAN	LAN	100	160	A2
AVENUE H-10 E	LAN	LAN	100	160	G3
AVENUE H-10 W	LAN	LAN		158	H2
AVENUE H-10 W	LAN	LAN		159	J2
AVENUE H-10 W	LAN	LAN	100	160	A2
AVENUE H-11	LAN	LAN		159	J3
AVENUE H-11 E	LAN	LAN		161	F2
AVENUE H-11 E	LAN	LAN		160	A3
AVENUE H-11 W	LAN	LAN		158	J3
AVENUE H-11 W	LAN	LAN		160	A3
AVENUE H-12 E	CO	LAN	4000	160	J3
AVENUE H-12 E	LAN	LAN		161	E3
AVENUE H-12 E	LAN	LAN		160	A3
AVENUE H-12 W	CO	LAN		159	C3
AVENUE H-12 W	LAN	LAN		158	J3
AVENUE H-12 W	LAN	LAN		159	J3
AVENUE H-12 W	LAN	LAN		160	A3
AVENUE H-13 E	LAN	LAN		161	E3
AVENUE H-13 E	LAN	LAN		160	A3
AVENUE H-13 W	CO	LAN		159	C3
AVENUE H-13 W	LAN	LAN		158	J3
AVENUE H-13 W	LAN	LAN		159	J3
AVENUE H-13 W	LAN	LAN		160	A3
AVENUE H-14	CO	LAN		161	B3
AVENUE H-14 E	LAN	LAN		160	A3
AVENUE H-14 W	LAN	LAN		159	J3
AVENUE H-14 W	LAN	LAN		160	A3
AVENUE H-15 W	LAN	LAN		159	J3
AVENUE HALL	CO	VAL		123	G6
AVENUE HOPKINS	CO	VAL		123	H7
AVENUE I	RB	RB		67	D6
AVENUE I E	CO	LAN	4000	160	G3
AVENUE I E&W	LAN	LAN	100	160	B3
AVENUE I W	CO	LAN	4000	159	A3
AVENUE I W	LAN	LAN	1000	159	F3
AVENUE I-2 W	CO	LAN		158	C3
AVENUE I-3 E	LAN	LAN	3000	160	H3
AVENUE I-3 W	CO	LAN		158	C3
AVENUE I-4 W	CO	LAN		158	C3
AVENUE I-9	CO	LAN		158	F4
AVENUE I-10	CO	LAN		158	F4
AVENUE I-11	CO	LAN		158	F4
AVENUE I-12	CO	LAN		158	F4
AVENUE I-12 E	CO	LAN	9000	161	G4
AVENUE I-13	CO	LAN		158	F4
AVENUE I-15 W	LAN	LAN	9500	158	F5
AVENUE J E	CO	LAN	4000	160	F5
AVENUE J E&W	LAN	LAN	100	160	B5
AVENUE J W	LAN	LAN	4000	159	B5
AVENUE J W	LAN	LAN	1000	159	F5
AVENUE J-1 E	LAN	LAN		160	D5
AVENUE J-2	CO	LAN		161	J5
AVENUE J-2 E	LAN	LAN		160	D5
AVENUE J-2 W	LAN	LAN		159	J5
AVENUE J-3 E	LAN	LAN		160	D5
AVENUE J-3 W	CO	LAN		158	B5
AVENUE J-3 W	LAN	LAN		159	J5
AVENUE J-4 E	LAN	LAN		160	D5
AVENUE J-4 E	LAN	LAN		161	F5
AVENUE J-4 W	CO	LAN		158	B5
AVENUE J-4 W	LAN	LAN	4000	159	C5
AVENUE J-4 W	LAN	LAN		159	J5
AVENUE J-4 W	LAN	LAN		160	D5
AVENUE J-5 E	LAN	LAN		160	D5
AVENUE J-5 W	CO	LAN		158	B5
AVENUE J-5 W	LAN	LAN		159	J5
AVENUE J-5 W	LAN	LAN		160	D5
AVENUE J-6	LAN	LAN		159	B6
AVENUE J-6 E	LAN	LAN	100	160	C5
AVENUE J-6 W	LAN	LAN	4000	159	C5
AVENUE J-6 W	LAN	LAN		159	J5
AVENUE J-6 W	LAN	LAN	100	160	B5
AVENUE J-7 E	LAN	LAN		160	A6
AVENUE J-7 W	LAN	LAN		159	J6
AVENUE J-7 W	LAN	LAN	100	160	B6
AVENUE J-8 E	CO	LAN	4000	160	G5
AVENUE J-8 E	LAN	LAN		161	F5
AVENUE J-8 E	LAN	LAN		160	A6
AVENUE J-8 W	LAN	LAN	4000	159	D6
AVENUE J-8 W	LAN	LAN		159	J6
AVENUE J-9	LAN	LAN		159	G6
AVENUE J-9 E	LAN	LAN		160	A6
AVENUE J-9 W	LAN	LAN		159	J6
AVENUE J-9 W	LAN	LAN		160	A6
AVENUE J-10	LAN	LAN		161	F6
AVENUE J-10 E	LAN	LAN		160	A6
AVENUE J-10 W	LAN	LAN		158	J6
AVENUE J-10 W	LAN	LAN	4000	159	B6
AVENUE J-10 W	LAN	LAN		159	J6
AVENUE J-10 W	LAN	LAN		160	A6
AVENUE J-11 E	LAN	LAN		160	A6
AVENUE J-11 W	LAN	LAN		158	J6
AVENUE J-11 W	LAN	LAN		159	J6
AVENUE J-11 W	LAN	LAN		160	A6
AVENUE J-12	LAN	LAN		161	F6
AVENUE J-12	LAN	LAN		160	D6
AVENUE J-12 E	LAN	LAN		160	A6
AVENUE J-12 W	CO	LAN	4000	159	A6
AVENUE J-12 W	LAN	LAN		158	J6
AVENUE J-12 W	LAN	LAN		159	J6
AVENUE J-12 W	LAN	LAN		160	A6
AVENUE J-13 E	LAN	LAN		161	D6
AVENUE J-13 E	LAN	LAN		160	A6
AVENUE J-13 W	LAN	LAN		158	J6
AVENUE J-13 W	LAN	LAN		159	J6
AVENUE J-13 W	LAN	LAN		160	A6
AVENUE J-14 E	LAN	LAN		160	A6
AVENUE J-14 W	LAN	LAN		158	J6
AVENUE J-14 W	LAN	LAN		159	J6
AVENUE J-14 W	LAN	LAN		160	A6
AVENUE J-15 E	LAN	LAN		160	A6
AVENUE J-15 W	LAN	LAN		159	J6
AVENUE J-15 W	LAN	LAN		160	A6
AVENUE K E	CO	LAN	4000	160	F6
AVENUE K E&W	LAN	LAN	100	160	F6
AVENUE K W	CO	LAN	4000	159	A6
AVENUE K-1 W	LAN	LAN	2700	159	G7
AVENUE K-2 W	LAN	LAN		158	E7
AVENUE K-2 W	LAN	LAN	2500	159	J7
AVENUE K-3 E	LAN	LAN	8000	161	F7
AVENUE K-3 W	LAN	LAN		158	E7
AVENUE K-4 E	LAN	LAN	100	160	C7
AVENUE K-4 E	LAN	LAN		161	A7
AVENUE K-4 W	LAN	LAN		158	E7
AVENUE K-4 W	LAN	LAN	4000	159	D7
AVENUE K-4 W	LAN	LAN	1000	159	H7
AVENUE K-5 W	LAN	LAN		158	E7
AVENUE K-6 E	CO	LAN		161	A7
AVENUE K-6 E	LAN	LAN	100	160	C7
AVENUE K-6 W	LAN	LAN		158	E7
AVENUE K-6 W	LAN	LAN	2300	159	G7
AVENUE K-7 W	LAN	LAN		158	E7
AVENUE K-8 E	LAN	LAN	100	160	C7
AVENUE K-8 E	LAN	LAN	4000	160	J7
AVENUE K-8 W	LAN	LAN		158	E7
AVENUE K-8 W	LAN	LAN	100	159	E7
AVENUE K-8 W	LAN	LAN	4000	159	B7
AVENUE K-9 W	LAN	LAN		158	E7
AVENUE K-9 W	LAN	LAN		159	D7
AVENUE K-10 W	LAN	LAN		158	E7
AVENUE K-10 W	LAN	LAN		159	D7
AVENUE K-10 W	LAN	LAN	2100	159	E8
AVENUE K-11 W	LAN	LAN		159	F8
AVENUE K-12 E	CO	LAN	4000	160	H8
AVENUE K-12 E	LAN	LAN	100	160	C8
AVENUE K-12 W	LAN	LAN		159	E8
AVENUE K-12 W	LAN	LAN		159	F8
AVENUE K-13 W	LAN	LAN		159	E8
AVENUE K-13 W	LAN	LAN		159	F8
AVENUE K-14 W	LAN	LAN		159	E8
AVENUE K-14 W	LAN	LAN		159	F8
AVENUE K-15 W	LAN	LAN		159	F8
AVENUE KEARNY	CO	VAL		123	J6
AVENUE L E	LAN	LAN	4000	160	J8
AVENUE L E	PALM	PALM	1500	160	D8
AVENUE L E&W	LAN	LAN	100	160	B8
AVENUE L W	LAN	LAN	4000	159	E8
AVENUE L-1	LAN	LAN		159	B8
AVENUE L-1 W	LAN	LAN	1100	159	G8
AVENUE L-2 E	PALM	PALM		161	C8
AVENUE L-2 W	CO	LAN		159	D8
AVENUE L-2 W	LAN	LAN	1000	159	F8
AVENUE L-2 W	LAN	LAN	100	160	A8
AVENUE L-3 W	CO	LAN		159	D8
AVENUE L-4	LAN	LAN		158	J8
AVENUE L-4 E	LAN	LAN	100	160	B9
AVENUE L-4 E	PALM	PALM	1500	160	E8
AVENUE L-4 E	PALM	PALM		161	C8
AVENUE L-4 W	CO	LAN		159	D8
AVENUE L-4 W	LAN	LAN	1000	159	F8
AVENUE L-6	LAN	LAN		160	A9
AVENUE L-6 W	CO	LAN		159	D9
AVENUE L-6 W	LAN	LAN	3000	159	F9
AVENUE L-7 W	LAN	LAN		159	D9
AVENUE L-8	LAN	LAN		158	J9
AVENUE L-8 E	LAN	LAN	100	160	B9
AVENUE L-8 E	PALM	PALM	1000	160	D9
AVENUE L-8 E	PALM	PALM		161	E9
AVENUE L-8 W	CO	LAN	4000	159	F9
AVENUE L-8 W	CO	LAN		159	D9
AVENUE L-8 W	LAN	LAN		160	B9
AVENUE L-9 W	LAN	LAN		159	D9
AVENUE L-9 W	LAN	LAN		160	B9
AVENUE L-10	LAN	LAN		159	G9
AVENUE L-10 W	CO	LAN		159	D9
AVENUE L-10 W	LAN	LAN	100	160	A9
AVENUE L-11	LAN	LAN		159	B9
AVENUE L-11 W	LAN	LAN		159	D9
AVENUE L-11 W	LAN	LAN		159	G9
AVENUE L-12 E	LAN	LAN	100	160	D9
AVENUE L-12 E	PALM	PALM		161	E9
AVENUE L-12 W	LAN	LAN	7000	158	J9
AVENUE L-12 W	LAN	LAN	4000	159	A9
AVENUE L-12 W	CO	LAN		159	D9
AVENUE L-12 W	LAN	LAN	1000	159	J9
AVENUE L-12 W	LAN	LAN	100	160	B9
AVENUE L-13 W	CO	LAN		159	D9
AVENUE L-14 W	CO	LAN		159	D9
AVENUE L-14 W	CO	LAN	4500	171	D1
AVENUE L-14 W	LAN	LAN	1000	171	H1
AVENUE L-15	PALM	LAN	6000	171	A1
AVENUE L-15	PALM	PALM		173	F1
AVENUE L-15 W	CO	LAN	6600	171	A1
AVENUE M	CO	LAN	12000	174	C1
AVENUE M E	PALM	PALM	1000	172	F1
AVENUE M E&W	LAN	LAN	100	172	B1
AVENUE M W	CO	LAN	4000	171	F1
AVENUE M W	LAN	LAN	1000	171	F1
AVENUE M-2	PALM	PALM		172	B1
AVENUE M-2 E	CO	LAN	19500	175	E1
AVENUE M-2 W	CO	LAN	6000	171	C1
AVENUE M-2 W	CO	LAN	3500	171	E1
AVENUE M-3 E	CO	LAN		175	A1
AVENUE M-4	CO	LAN		172	A1
AVENUE M-4	CO	LAN		175	H1
AVENUE M-4	PALM	LAN		171	B1
AVENUE M-4 E	CO	LAN	10700	174	J1
AVENUE M-4 E	CO	LAN		175	A1
AVENUE M-4 E	CO	PALM	9500	173	J1
AVENUE M-4 E	PALM	PALM	1000	172	D1
AVENUE M-4 E	PALM	PALM	11000	174	A1
AVENUE M-4 W	CO	LAN	1100	171	H1
AVENUE M-6 E	CO	LAN	16200	174	J1
AVENUE M-6 W	CO	LAN	1100	171	D1
AVENUE M-8	PALM	LAN	6000	171	B2
AVENUE M-8 E	CO	LAN	15000	174	J1
AVENUE M-8 E	CO	PALM	5500	173	B1
AVENUE M-8 E	PALM	PALM	100	172	D2
AVENUE M-8 E	PALM	PALM	10000	173	J1
AVENUE M-8 W	CO	LAN	1100	171	H2
AVENUE M-9 W	CO	LAN	4600	171	D2
AVENUE M-10 E	CO	LAN	19500	175	E1
AVENUE M-10 W	CO	LAN	4500	171	D2
AVENUE M-12 E	CO	LAN	15000	174	J2
AVENUE M-12 E	CO	PALM	5500	173	B2
AVENUE M-12 E	PALM	PALM	100	172	C2
AVENUE M-12 E	PALM	PALM	10000	173	J2
AVENUE M-12 W	CO	LAN	2000	171	H2
AVENUE M-14 W	CO	LAN	4700	171	D2
AVENUE M-15	CO	LAN	4700	171	D2
AVENUE MENTRY	CO	VAL		123	J6
AVENUE MORELOS	LA	WOH	22000	13	B3
AVENUE N	CO	LAN		175	H2
AVENUE N	PALM	LAN	5000	171	B2
AVENUE N E	CO	LAN	12000	174	E2
AVENUE N E	CO	PALM	4500	172	J2
AVENUE N E	PALM	PALM	10000	173	J2
AVENUE N E&W	PALM	PALM	100	172	B2
AVENUE N W	CO	PALM	1200	171	J2
AVENUE N-1 E	PALM	PALM	100	172	C2
AVENUE N-2 E	CO	LAN	20200	175	F2
AVENUE N-2 E	PALM	PALM	10000	173	J2
AVENUE N-3 W	CO	PALM	3000	171	F3
AVENUE N-4 E	CO	LAN	13000	174	D3
AVENUE N-4 E	CO	LAN		175	C3
AVENUE N-4 E	CO	LAN		175	F3
AVENUE N-4 E	CO	PALM	9000	173	G3
AVENUE N-4 E	PALM	PALM	100	172	B3
AVENUE N-4 W	CO	PALM	1200	171	J3
AVENUE N-4 W	PALM	PALM	1000	172	A3
AVENUE N-5	CO	LAN		175	F3
AVENUE N-6	CO	LAN		175	F3
AVENUE N-6 E	CO	LAN		174	E3
AVENUE N-6 E	CO	PALM		173	H3
AVENUE N-7	CO	LAN		175	F3
AVENUE N-7 E	CO	PALM		173	H3
AVENUE N-8	CO	LAN		175	F3
AVENUE N-8 E	CO	LAN	13000	174	E3
AVENUE N-8 E	CO	PALM	3700	172	H3
AVENUE N-8 E	CO	PALM		173	H3
AVENUE N-8 E	PALM	PALM	100	172	B3
AVENUE N-8 W	CO	PALM	1200	171	J3
AVENUE N-8 W	PALM	PALM	1000	172	A3
AVENUE N-9	CO	LAN		175	F3
AVENUE N-9 E	CO	PALM		173	H3
AVENUE N-10	CO	LAN		175	F3
AVENUE N-10 E	CO	LAN	13000	174	D3
AVENUE N-10 E	CO	PALM		173	H3
AVENUE N-10 E	PALM	PALM	100	172	B4
AVENUE N-11	CO	LAN		175	F3
AVENUE N-11 E	CO	LAN	13600	174	E3
AVENUE N-11 E	CO	PALM		173	H3
AVENUE N-12 E	CO	LAN	12000	174	E3
AVENUE N-12 E	CO	LAN		175	F3
AVENUE N-12 E	CO	PALM		173	H3
AVENUE N-12 W	CO	PALM	1000	172	A4
AVENUE N-13 E	CO	LAN	13000	174	E4
AVENUE N-14 E	CO	LAN	13000	174	E4
AVENUE O	PALM	PALM		172	A4
AVENUE O E	CO	LAN	13000	174	F4
AVENUE O E	CO	PALM	3400	172	J4
AVENUE O E	PALM	PALM	100	172	D4
AVENUE O E	PALM	PALM	10000	173	J4
AVENUE O W	CO	PALM	1000	172	A4
AVENUE O-2 E	CO	PALM	22000	175	J4
AVENUE O-2 E	PALM	PALM	10000	173	J4
AVENUE O-4	PALM	PALM		172	A4
AVENUE O-4 E	CO	PALM	9000	173	G4
AVENUE O-4 E	CO	PALM	15000	174	H4
AVENUE O-4 E	CO	PALM		175	F4
AVENUE O-4 E	PALM	PALM	10000	173	J4
AVENUE O-4 W	CO	PALM	1000	172	A4
AVENUE O-5 E	CO	PALM		175	F4
AVENUE O-5 E	PALM	PALM	100	172	D4
AVENUE O-6 E	CO	PALM	14500	174	G4
AVENUE O-6 E	CO	PALM		175	F4
AVENUE O-6 E	PALM	PALM	100	172	D5
AVENUE O-6 E	PALM	PALM	10000	173	J5
AVENUE O-7 E	PALM	PALM	100	172	C4
AVENUE O-8	PALM	LAN		171	F5
AVENUE O-8	CO	PALM	2700	172	H5
AVENUE O-8 E	CO	PALM	12000	174	C5
AVENUE O-8 E	PALM	PALM	10000	173	H5
AVENUE O-8 W	CO	PALM	1000	172	A5
AVENUE O-10	PALM	PALM	10000	173	J5
AVENUE O-10 E	CO	PALM	13500	174	E5
AVENUE O-10 E	CO	PALM		175	H5
AVENUE O-12 E	CO	PALM	9000	173	G5
AVENUE O-12 E	CO	PALM	13500	174	E5
AVENUE O-12 E	CO	PALM		175	J5
AVENUE O-12 W	CO	PALM	1500	171	H5
AVENUE O-12 E	PALM	PALM	500	172	C5
AVENUE O-12 W	PALM	PALM	700	171	H5
AVENUE O-13 E	CO	PALM		175	J5
AVENUE O-14 E	CO	PALM		175	J5
AV OF CHAMPIONS	ING	IN05	400	57	B3
AV OF THE OAKS	SCLR	NEW	19000	127	H1
AV OF THE STARS	LA	LA67	1800	42	A2
AVENUE P	PALM	PALM		171	F6
AVENUE P E	CO	PALM	100	172	D6
AVENUE P E	CO	PALM	16000	174	J5
AVENUE P E	PALM	PALM		172	C6
AVENUE P E	PALM	PALM	10000	173	H6
AVENUE P W	CO	PALM	1000	172	D6
AVENUE P W	PALM	PALM	100	172	D6
AVENUE P-1 E	CO	PALM		172	C6
AVENUE P-1 W	CO	PALM	1100	171	J6
AVENUE P-2 E	CO	PALM		172	C6
AVENUE P-3 E	CO	PALM		172	C6
AVENUE P-3 E	CO	PALM		173	G6
AVENUE P-4	PALM	PALM		171	H6
AVENUE P-4 E	CO	PALM		172	C6
AVENUE P-4 E	CO	PALM		173	G6
AVENUE P-4 E	CO	PALM	12000	174	C6
AVENUE P-4 E	CO	PALM		175	F6
AVENUE P-4 E	PALM	PALM	11000	174	A6
AVENUE P-5 E	CO	PALM		172	C6
AVENUE P-5 E	CO	PALM		173	G6
AVENUE P-5 E	CO	PALM		175	F6
AVENUE P-6	PALM	PALM		171	H6
AVENUE P-6 E	CO	PALM		172	D6
AVENUE P-6 E	CO	PALM		173	G6
AVENUE P-7 E	CO	PALM		172	D6
AVENUE P-8	PALM	PALM		172	C7
AVENUE P-8 E	CO	PALM		173	E7
AVENUE P-8 E	CO	PALM	16000	174	F6
AVENUE P-8 E	PALM	PALM	100	172	C7
AVENUE P-8 E	PALM	PALM	7500	173	E7
AVENUE P-8 E	PALM	PALM	11200	174	B6
AVENUE P-8 W	PALM	PALM	2000	171	G7
AVENUE P-8 W	PALM	PALM	100	172	B7
AVENUE P-10 E	CO	PALM	22000	175	J7
AVENUE P-12	CO	PALM	17000	175	A7
AVENUE P-12 E	CO	PALM	100	172	B7
AVENUE P-12 E	CO	PALM		173	E7
AVENUE P-12 E	CO	PALM	12000	174	E7
AVENUE P-12 E	PALM	PALM	7500	173	E7
AVENUE P-12 E	PALM	PALM	11200	174	B7
AVENUE P-14 E	CO	PALM	21000	175	J7
AVENUE P-14 E	PALM	PALM	400	172	C7
AVENUE P-14 W	CO	PALM	1000	172	A7
AVENUE P-14 W	PALM	PALM	100	172	A7
AVENUE P-15 E	CO	PALM	800	172	D7
AVENUE Q E	CO	LAN	12000	174	J7
AVENUE Q E	PALM	PALM	100	172	C7
AVENUE Q E	PALM	PALM	300	172	C7
AVENUE Q E	PALM	PALM	4700	173	A8
AVENUE Q W	CO	PALM	1000	172	A7
AVENUE Q W	PALM	PALM	100	172	A7
AVENUE Q-1 E	CO	PALM	3300	172	H7
AVENUE Q-1 W	CO	PALM	1100	171	J8
AVENUE Q-2 E	CO	PALM	2500	172	G8
AVENUE Q-2 E	CO	PALM		173	H8

1990 LOS ANGELES COUNTY STREET INDEX 217

AVENUE Q-2 E AYRES AV

LOS ANGELES CO.

STREET	CITY	P.O. ZONE	BLOCK	PAGE	GRID
AVENUE Q-2 E	PALM	PALM		172	D8
AVENUE Q-3 E	CO	PALM	100	172	C8
AVENUE Q-3 E	CO	PALM		173	H8
AVENUE Q-3 E	CO	PALM	15000	174	G8
AVENUE Q-3 E	CO	PALM	17100	175	B8
AVENUE Q-3 E	PALM	PALM		172	D8
AVENUE Q-4	PALM	PALM		171	J8
AVENUE Q-4 E	CO	PALM	100	172	C8
AVENUE Q-4 E	CO	PALM		173	H8
AVENUE Q-4 E	CO	PALM		174	A8
AVENUE Q-4 E	CO	PALM	17000	175	B8
AVENUE Q-4 E	PALM	PALM		172	D8
AVENUE Q-5 E	CO	PALM	1500	172	F8
AVENUE Q-5 E	CO	PALM		173	H8
AVENUE Q-5 E	CO	PALM		174	A8
AVENUE Q-5 E	CO	PALM	17100	175	B8
AVENUE Q-5 E	PALM	PALM		172	D8
AVENUE Q-6 E	CO	PALM	2500	172	G8
AVENUE Q-6 E	CO	PALM		173	H8
AVENUE Q-6 E	CO	PALM		174	A8
AVENUE Q-6 E	PALM	PALM		172	D8
AVENUE Q-6 W	CO	PALM	2500	171	G8
AVENUE Q-7 E	CO	PALM	100	172	C8
AVENUE Q-7 E	CO	PALM	3000	172	G8
AVENUE Q-7 E	PALM	PALM		172	D8
AVENUE Q-8 E	PALM	PALM		172	D8
AVENUE Q-8 W	PALM	PALM		172	A8
AVENUE Q-9 E	PALM	PALM		172	D8
AVENUE Q-9 W	PALM	PALM		172	A7
AVENUE Q-10 E	CO	PALM	100	172	C8
AVENUE Q-10 E	CO	PALM	9000	173	J8
AVENUE Q-10 E	PALM	PALM		172	D8
AVENUE Q-10 W	PALM	PALM		172	A8
AVENUE Q-11 E	PALM	PALM	800	172	C9
AVENUE Q-12	CO	LR		173	G9
AVENUE Q-12	PALM	PALM		173	D9
AVENUE Q-12 E	CO	LR		173	J9
AVENUE Q-12 E	PALM	PALM		172	G9
AVENUE Q-12 W	PALM	PALM		172	A9
AVENUE Q-13 E	CO	LR		173	J9
AVENUE Q-13 E	PALM	PALM		172	G9
AVENUE Q-14	CO	LR		173	G9
AVENUE Q-14	PALM	PALM		173	D9
AVENUE Q-14 E	CO	LR		173	J9
AVENUE Q-14 E	PALM	PALM		172	G9
AVENUE Q-15 E	PALM	PALM		172	G9
AVENUE Q-16 E	PALM	PALM		172	G9
AVENUE R	CO	LR		173	G9
AVENUE R	PALM	PALM		173	D9
AVENUE R E	CO	LLAN	18000	175	D9
AVENUE R E	CO	PALM	3700	172	H9
AVENUE R E	PALM	PALM	500	172	D9
AVENUE R E&W	CO	PALM	100	172	D9
AV ROCKEFELLER	CO	CAL		123	J7
AVENUE R-1 E	PALM	PALM	1500	172	E9
AVENUE R-2	PALM	PALM		173	A9
AVENUE R-2 E	CO	LR		173	J9
AVENUE R-2 E	CO	LR		174	B9
AVENUE R-2 E	CO	PALM		174	G9
AVENUE R-2 E	PALM	PALM	100	172	D9
AVENUE R-3 E	CO	LR		174	B9
AVENUE R-3 E	CO	PALM		174	G9
AVENUE R-3 E	PALM	PALM	100	172	D9
AVENUE R-4	PALM	PALM		183	E1
AVENUE R-4 E	CO	LR		173	J9
AVENUE R-4 E	CO	LR		174	B9
AVENUE R-4 E	CO	PALM	8700	173	H9
AVENUE R-4 E	CO	PALM		174	G9
AVENUE R-4 E	PALM	PALM	100	172	C9
AVENUE R-4 E	PALM	PALM		184	B5
AVENUE R-5 E	PALM	PALM	100	183	C1
AVENUE R-5 W	CO	PALM	700	183	A1
AVENUE R-5 W	PALM	PALM	1000	183	A1
AVENUE R-6	PALM	PALM		172	E9
AVENUE R-6	PALM	PALM		172	G9
AVENUE R-6 E	CO	PALM	10000	184	J1
AVENUE R-6 E	CO	PALM		185	G1
AVENUE R-6 E	PALM	PALM	100	183	C1
AVENUE R-7 E	CO	PALM		185	G1
AVENUE R-7 E	PALM	PALM	100	183	C1
AVENUE R-8	CO	LR		184	J1
AVENUE R-8 E	CO	PALM	3500	183	H1
AVENUE R-8 E	CO	PALM		185	G1
AVENUE R-8 E	PALM	PALM	100	183	C1
AVENUE R-8 E	PALM	PALM	4700	184	C1
AVENUE R-9	CO	LR		184	J1
AVENUE R-9 E	CO	PALM	300	183	C1
AVENUE R-9 E	CO	PALM		185	G1
AVENUE R-9 E	PALM	PALM	2800	183	G1
AVENUE R-10	CO	LR		184	J1
AVENUE R-10 E	CO	PALM		185	G1
AVENUE R-10 E	PALM	PALM	1000	183	D1
AVENUE R-11	CO	LR		184	J1
AVENUE R-11	PALM	PALM	2900	183	G1
AVENUE R-11	PALM	PALM	4700	184	A1
AVENUE R-11 E	CO	PALM	100	183	C1

STREET	CITY	P.O. ZONE	BLOCK	PAGE	GRID
AVENUE R-11 E	CO	PALM		185	G1
AVENUE R-12	CO	LR		184	J1
AVENUE R-12 E	CO	PALM	3000	183	G1
AVENUE R-12 E	PALM	PALM	4700	184	B1
AVENUE R-12 E	CO	PALM		185	G1
AVENUE R-12 E	PALM	PALM	100	183	C1
AVENUE R-12 E	PALM	PALM	6100	184	E1
AVENUE R-13	CO	LR		184	J1
AVENUE R-13	PALM	PALM	2800	183	G1
AVENUE R-13 E	CO	PALM		185	G1
AVENUE R-14	CO	LR		184	J1
AVENUE R-14	PALM	PALM	2800	183	G1
AVENUE R-14 E	CO	PALM	3000	183	J1
AVENUE R-14 E	CO	PALM		185	G1
AVENUE R-15	CO	PALM		183	G1
AVENUE R-16	CO	PALM		183	G1
AVENUE S E	CO	PALM	3000	183	G1
AVENUE S E	PALM	PALM	1000	183	F2
AVENUE S E	PALM	PALM	6000	184	D1
AVENUE S E&W	CO	PALM	100	183	F2
AVENUE S-1	PALM	PALM		183	G2
AVENUE S-2	PALM	PALM		183	G2
AVENUE S-2 E	CO	PALM	8700	184	G2
AVENUE S-2 W	CO	PALM	200	183	B2
AVENUE S-3	PALM	PALM		183	G2
AVENUE S-4	CO	PALM		184	A2
AVENUE S-4	PALM	PALM		183	A2
AVENUE S-4 E	CO	PALM	4000	183	J2
AVENUE S-4 E	PALM	PALM		183	E2
AVENUE S-4 W	CO	PALM	200	183	B2
AVENUE S-5 E	CO	PALM	11200	185	A2
AVENUE S-6 E	CO	PALM	9600	184	J2
AVENUE S-7 E	CO	PALM	11700	185	C2
AVENUE S-8 E	CO	PALM	3700	183	J2
AVENUE S-9 E	CO	PALM	11700	185	C2
AVENUE S-10 E	CO	PALM	4000	183	J3
AVENUE S-11 E	CO	PALM	10700	185	B3
AVENUE S-12 E	CO	PALM	4000	183	J3
AVENUE S-12 E	PALM	PALM		183	G3
AVENUE S-14 E	CO	PALM	8200	184	F3
AVENUE S-14 W	CO	PALM	600	183	A3
AVENUE SAN LUIS	LA	WOH	20900	13	D2
AVENUE SAN LUIS	LA	WOH	23000	100	F2
AVENUE SCOTT	CO	VAL		123	H6
AVENUE STANFORD	CO	VAL		123	G6
AVENUE T E	CO	PALM	5600	184	E3
AVENUE T E	PALM	PALM		184	B3
AVENUE T-2 E	CO	LR	8700	184	G3
AVENUE T-2 E	CO	PALM		183	J4
AVENUE T-3 E	CO	PALM		183	J4
AVENUE T-4 E	CO	LR	8700	184	G4
AVENUE T-4 E	CO	PALM		183	J4
AVENUE T-4 E	CO	PEAR		185	E4
AVENUE T-5 E	CO	PALM		183	J4
AVENUE T-5 E	CO	PALM	5700	184	B4
AVENUE T-6 E	CO	LR	8700	184	G4
AVENUE T-6 E	CO	PALM		183	J4
AVENUE T-7 E	CO	PALM		183	J4
AVENUE T-8 E	CO	LR	8700	184	G4
AVENUE T-8 E	CO	PALM		183	J4
AVENUE T-10	CO	PEAR		185	D4
AVENUE T-10 E	CO	LR	8700	184	H4
AVENUE T-12	CO	PALM		183	J5
AVENUE T-12	CO	SAU	6200	182	B5
AVENUE T-12 E	CO	LR	8700	184	G4
AVENUE T-14 E	CO	LR	8700	184	H5
AVENUE TIBBITTS	CO	VAL		123	J7
AVENUE U	CO	PALM		183	B5
AVENUE U	CO	PEAR		185	D5
AVENUE U E	CO	LR	7300	184	F5
AVENUE U E	CO	PALM	6200	184	C5
AVENUE U E	CO	PALM	13600	185	F5
AVENUE U-2 E	CO	LR	7300	184	E5
AVENUE U-3 E	CO	LR	7300	184	E5
AVENUE U-4 E	CO	LR	8500	184	F5
AVENUE U-4 E	CO	PALM	13600	185	F5
AVENUE U-5	CO	LR		184	F5
AVENUE U-6 E	CO	LR	8700	184	G6
AVENUE U-6 E	CO	PALM	6200	184	C6
AVENUE U-8 E	CO	PEAR	10700	185	E6
AVENUE U-10 E	CO	LR	8000	184	E6
AVENUE U-12	CO	ACT		182	C7
AVENUE U-12	CO	LR		184	D6
AVENUE U-12 E	CO	PEAR	11600	185	E6
AVENUE V	CO	PALM		183	H7
AVENUE V	CO	SAU		182	C7
AVENUE V E	CO	LR	7300	184	F7
AVENUE V E	CO	PEAR	10600	185	D7
AVENUE V-2	CO	ACT		182	D7
AVENUE V-2 E	CO	PEAR		185	E7
AVENUE V-3 E	CO	PEAR		185	E7
AVENUE V-4 E	CO	LR	11000	185	A7
AVENUE V-4 E	CO	PEAR		185	E7
AVENUE V-5	CO	PALM		183	J7
AVENUE V-5 E	CO	PEAR		185	E7
AVENUE V-6 E	CO	PEAR	13000	185	E7

STREET	CITY	P.O. ZONE	BLOCK	PAGE	GRID
AVENUE V-6 E	CO	PEAR		185	E7
AVENUE V-8 E	CO	LR	8900	184	G7
AVENUE V-8 E	CO	LR	10600	185	B7
AVENUE V-9 E	CO	PEAR	11600	185	B8
AVENUE V-10 E	CO	PEAR		185	D8
AVENUE V-11 E	CO	PEAR		185	D8
AVENUE V-12 E	CO	LR	8900	184	G8
AVENUE V-12 E	CO	PEAR		185	D8
AVENUE V-13 E	CO	PEAR		185	D8
AVENUE V-14 E	CO	PEAR		185	D8
AVENUE W E	CO	LR	9600	184	H8
AVENUE W E	CO	PEAR	10600	185	A8
AVENUE W-2 E	CO	LR	9600	184	H8
AVENUE W-2 E	CO	PEAR	13100	185	E8
AVENUE W-3 E	CO	PEAR	10600	185	A9
AVENUE W-4	CO	ACT		182	J9
AVENUE W-4	CO	LR		184	H9
AVENUE W-4 E	CO	PEAR	13100	185	E9
AVENUE W-5 E	CO	PEAR		185	E9
AVENUE W-6 E	CO	LR		184	H9
AVENUE W-6 E	CO	PEAR	10600	185	A9
AVENUE W-6 E	CO	PEAR		185	E9
AVENUE W-7 E	CO	LR		184	H9
AVENUE W-7 E	CO	PEAR		185	E9
AVENUE W-8	CO	LR		184	H9
AVENUE W-8 E	CO	ACT		189	C1
AVENUE W-8 E	CO	LR		184	H9
AVENUE W-8 E	CO	PEAR	12100	185	D9
AVENUE W-8 E	CO	PEAR		185	E9
AVENUE W-9 E	CO	ACT		189	C1
AVENUE W-9 E	CO	PEAR		185	E9
AVENUE W-10 E	CO	ACT		189	C1
AVENUE W-10 E	CO	PEAR	12100	185	C9
AVENUE W-10 E	CO	PEAR		185	E9
AVENUE W-11 E	CO	ACT		189	C1
AVENUE W-11 E	CO	PEAR	12100	185	C9
AVENUE W-11 E	CO	PEAR		185	E9
AVENUE W-12	CO	LR		184	J9
AVENUE W-12 E	CO	ACT		189	C1
AVENUE W-12 E	CO	PEAR	12100	185	C9
AVENUE W-12 E	CO	PEAR		185	E9
AVENUE W-13	CO	PEAR		192	D1
AVENUE W-13 E	CO	ACT		189	C1
AVENUE W-14 E	CO	ACT		189	C1
AVENUE W-14 E	CO	PEAR	12100	192	C1
AVENUE X E	CO	LLAN	16200	192	J1
AVENUE X E	CO	PEAR	12100	192	C1
AVENUE X-2	CO	LR		192	A1
AVENUE X-3 E	CO	PEAR	12900	192	D1
AVENUE X-4	CO	LR		192	A1
AVENUE X-8 E	CO	PEAR	12100	192	B2
AVENUE X-12	CO	LR		192	B2
AVENUE X-12 E	CO	PEAR	12100	192	C2
AVENUE X-15 E	CO	PEAR	12100	192	C2
AVENUE Y-4 E	CO	LLAN	16000	192	J3
AVENUE Y-8	CO	LLAN	16000	192	J3
AVENUE Y-8	CO	SAU		189	H4
AVENUE 16 S	LA	LA31	100	44	F1
AVENUE 17 S	LA	LA31	100	44	F1
AVENUE 18 N	LA	LA31	100	35	F6
AVENUE 18 S	LA	LA31	100	35	F6
AVENUE 18 S	LA	LA31	300	44	F1
AVENUE 19 N	LA	LA31	100	35	F6
AVENUE 19 S	LA	LA31	100	35	F6
AVENUE 19 S	LA	LA31	500	44	F1
AVENUE 20 S	LA	LA31	100	35	F6
AVENUE 20 S	LA	LA31	200	44	F1
AVENUE 20 S	LA	LA31	100	45	A1
AVENUE 21 N	LA	LA31	100	35	F6
AVENUE 21 S	LA	LA31	200	36	A6
AVENUE 21 S	LA	LA31	600	44	F1
AVENUE 21 S	LA	LA31	600	45	A1
AVENUE 22 N	LA	LA31	100	35	F6
AVENUE 22 N	LA	LA65	500	35	F5
AVENUE 22 S	LA	LA31	100	36	A6
AVENUE 23 N	LA	LA31	100	36	A5
AVENUE 23 S	LA	LA31	100	36	A5
AVENUE 24 S	LA	LA31	100	36	A6
AVENUE 25 N	LA	LA31	100	36	A5
AVENUE 26 E	LA	LA31		36	A6
AVENUE 26 W	LA	LA31	100	36	A5
AVENUE 26 W	LA	LA65	500	35	F5
AVENUE 27 W	LA	LA31	100	36	A5
AVENUE 27 W	LA	LA65	600	35	F4
AVENUE 28 E	LA	LA31	100	36	A5
AVENUE 28 W	LA	LA31	100	36	A5
AVENUE 28 W	LA	LA65	500	35	F4
AVENUE 29 W	LA	LA31	100	36	A5
AVENUE 30 W	LA	LA31	100	36	A5
AVENUE 30 W	LA	LA65	1900	35	E3
AVENUE 31 E	LA	LA31	100	36	A5
AVENUE 31 W	LA	LA31	100	36	A5
AVENUE 31 W	LA	LA65	2100	35	E2
AVENUE 32 E	LA	LA31	100	36	A5
AVENUE 32 W	LA	LA65	2400	35	E2
AVENUE 33 E	LA	LA31	100	36	A5

STREET	CITY	P.O. ZONE	BLOCK	PAGE	GRID
AVENUE 33 W	LA	LA31	100	36	A5
AVENUE 33 W	LA	LA65	2000	35	E2
AVENUE 34 W	LA	LA31	100	36	A5
AVENUE 34 W	LA	LA65	2500	35	E2
AVENUE 35 E	LA	LA31	100	36	A5
AVENUE 35 W	LA	LA65	2500	35	E2
AVENUE 36 E	LA	LA31	100	36	A4
AVENUE 36 W	LA	LA65	2900	35	E1
AVENUE 37 E	LA	LA31	100	36	A4
AVENUE 37 W	LA	LA65	800	35	F3
AVENUE 37 W	LA	LA65	100	36	A4
AVENUE 38 E	LA	LA31	100	36	A4
AVENUE 38 E	LA	LA65	2800	35	E1
AVENUE 38 W	LA	LA65	100	36	A4
AVENUE 39 E	LA	LA31	100	36	A4
AVENUE 40	LA	LA65		25	E5
AVENUE 40 E	LA	LA31	100	36	B4
AVENUE 40 W	LA	LA65	3700	35	E1
AVENUE 41 E	LA	LA31	100	36	B4
AVENUE 41 W	LA	LA65	4500	25	E5
AVENUE 41 W	LA	LA65	100	36	A4
AVENUE 42	LA	LA65		25	E5
AVENUE 42	LA	LA65	3500	35	F1
AVENUE 42 E	LA	LA31	100	36	B4
AVENUE 42 E	LA	LA65		36	A4
AVENUE 42 W	LA	LA65	100	36	B4
AVENUE 43 E	LA	LA31	100	36	B4
AVENUE 43 W	LA	LA41	3800	25	F6
AVENUE 43 W	LA	LA65	3800	25	F6
AVENUE 43 W	LA	LA65		35	F1
AVENUE 43 W	LA	LA65	100	36	B4
AVENUE 44 E	LA	LA31	100	36	B4
AVENUE 44 N	LA	LA41	1400	35	F1
AVENUE 44 W	LA	LA65	100	36	A3
AVENUE 45 E	LA	LA31	100	36	B4
AVENUE 45 N	LA	LA41	1400	25	F6
AVENUE 45 W	LA	LA65	100	36	B3
AVENUE 46	LA	LA41	1300	36	A1
AVENUE 46 N	LA	LA41	1400	26	A6
AVENUE 46 W	LA	LA65	400	36	A3
AVENUE 47 N	LA	LA42	1500	26	A6
AVENUE 47 N	LA	LA42	1400	36	A1
AVENUE 48 N	LA	LA42		36	B2
AVENUE 49	LA	LA41	800	36	A1
AVENUE 49 N	LA	LA42	1400	26	B6
AVENUE 49 N	LA	LA42	100	36	B2
AVENUE 49 S	LA	LA42	100	36	B2
AVENUE 50 N	LA	LA42	1400	26	B6
AVENUE 50 N	LA	LA42	100	36	B2
AVENUE 50 S	LA	LA42	100	36	B2
AVENUE 51 N	LA	LA42	1400	26	B6
AVENUE 51 N	LA	LA42	100	36	B2
AVENUE 51 S	LA	LA42		36	B3
AVENUE 52 N	LA	LA42	1400	26	B6
AVENUE 52 N	LA	LA42	100	36	B3
AVENUE 52 S	LA	LA42	100	36	B3
AVENUE 53 N	LA	LA42	1600	26	B6
AVENUE 53 N	LA	LA42	100	36	B2
AVENUE 53 S	LA	LA42	100	36	B2
AVENUE 54 N	LA	LA42	1500	26	B6
AVENUE 54 N	LA	LA42	100	36	B1
AVENUE 54 S	LA	LA42	100	36	C3
AVENUE 55 N	LA	LA42	1500	26	B6
AVENUE 55 N	LA	LA42	100	36	C2
AVENUE 55 S	LA	LA42	100	36	C3
AVENUE 56 N	LA	LA42	1300	26	C6
AVENUE 56 N	LA	LA42	100	36	C2
AVENUE 56 S	LA	LA42	100	36	C2
AVENUE 57	LA	LA42		36	C3
AVENUE 57 N	LA	LA42	1100	26	C6
AVENUE 57 N	LA	LA42	100	36	C2
AVENUE 57 S	LA	LA42	100	36	C2
AVENUE 58 N	LA	LA42	100	36	C2
AVENUE 58 S	LA	LA42	100	36	C2
AVENUE 59 N	LA	LA42	100	36	C2
AVENUE 59 S	LA	LA42	100	36	C2
AVENUE 60 N	LA	LA42	100	36	C2
AVENUE 60 S	LA	LA42	100	36	C2
AVENUE 61 N	LA	LA42	100	36	C2
AVENUE 61 S	LA	LA42	100	36	C2
AVENUE 62 N	LA	LA42	100	36	D1
AVENUE 63 N	LA	LA42	800	26	D6
AVENUE 63 N	LA	LA42	100	36	D1
AVENUE 63 S	LA	LA42	100	36	D1
AVENUE 64	PAS	PAS	100	26	D5
AVENUE 64 N	LA	LA42	800	26	D5
AVENUE 64 N	LA	LA42	100	36	D1
AVENUE 64 S	LA	LA42	100	36	D1
AVENUE 65 N	LA	LA42	800	26	D6
AVENUE 65 N	LA	LA42	100	36	D1
AVENUE 66 N	LA	LA42	800	26	D6
AVENUE 66 N	LA	LA42	100	36	D1
AVENUE 66 N	PAS	PAS		26	D6
AVENUE 66 S	LA	LA42	100	36	D2
AVENUE 67 N	LA	LA42	100	36	D1
AVERILL AV	LA	SP		78	E4

STREET	CITY	P.O. ZONE	BLOCK	PAGE	GRID
AVERILL PARK DR	LA	SP		78	D4
AVERY CIR	CER	ART		81	B3
AVERY PL	GAR	GAR	17900	63	E6
AVERY PL	LB	LB07	500	70	B4
AVERY RD	CLA	CLA		91	A3
AVERY ST	LA	LA13		44	E3
AVIATION BLVD	CO	HAW	12000	56	D6
AVIATION BLVD	CO	HAW	13500	62	D5
AVIATION BLVD	CO	IN04	11600	56	D6
AVIATION BLVD	HAW	HAW	13200	62	D5
AVIATION BLVD	ING	IN01		56	E2
AVIATION BLVD	LA	LA45	9200	56	D6
AVIATION BLVD	RB	RB	1200	62	D6
AVIATION BLVD N	ELS	ELS	100	56	D6
AVIATION BLVD N	MB	MB	100	62	D5
AVIATION BLVD S	ELS	ELS	100	62	D5
AVIATION BLVD S	MB	MB	100	62	D5
AVIATION PL	SF	SF40		3	A5
AVIATION WY	MB	MB	500	62	D5
AVIGNON LN	PALM	PALM		171	G6
AVILA ST	LA	LA12		44	E2
AVILA WY	CLA	CLA		91	B1
AVINGER DR	RM	RM		46	F3
AVINGTON AV	CO	LPUE	1300	92	C3
AVINGTON AV	WCOV	WCOV	500	92	C2
AVION DR	LA	LA45	5700	56	D3
AVION DR	LAM	LAM	13600	82	F2
AVION DR	MPK	MPK	1300	45	F2
AVIS AV	LAW	LAW	14300	63	B3
AVIS AV	TOR	TOR	18100	63	B6
AVIS AV	TOR	TOR	20400	68	B3
AVIS CT	TOR	TOR	22400	68	B5
AVISTON PL	CO	LPUE	2600	98	E5
AVIVA CT	LA	SF		1	E5
AVOCA AV	PAS	PAS	1000	26	F6
AVOCA ST	LA	LA41	4700	26	C5
AVOCADO AV	PAR	PAR	15300	66	A3
AVOCADO AV	PAS	PAS	400	27	F3
AVOCADO LN	PALM	PALM		183	H1
AVOCADO LN	PAS	PAS	300	27	F3
AVOCADO LN	RHE	PVP		72	D5
AVOCADO PL	CO	SAU		124	C3
AVOCADO PL	MON	MON	200	28	F3
AVOCADO ST	LA	LA27		35	A2
AVOCADO ST	LAV	LAV		90	E2
AVOCADO ST	LOM	LOM	25800	73	D3
AVOCADO TER	CO	LPUE	2000	85	C2
AVOCADO TER	CO	PAS	1200	20	C6
AVOCADO CREST E	LHH	LAH	100	84	E2
AVOCADO CREST E	LHH	LAH	800	98A	A2
AVOCADO CREST W	LHH	LAH	200	84	E2
AVOCADO HILL WY	CO	LPUE		85	C4
AVOLANCHE WY	MPK	MPK		45	F4
AVOLANCHE WY	MPK	MPK		46	A4
AVON AV	CO	SGAB	6300	38	A2
AVON AV	PAS	PAS	400	26	D5
AVON AV	TEC	SGAB	5900	38	A2
AVON CT	PALM	PALM		183	C5
AVON PL	GLDR	GLDR	5300	89	B2
AVON PL	LA	LA26	1400	35	D4
AVON PL	SPAS	SPAS	1000	37	A2
AVON RD	PVE	PVP	600	72	A3
AVON SQ	PVE	PVP	600	72	A3
AVON ST	LA	LA26	1900	35	D4
AVON ST N	BUR	BUR	1400	17	A6
AVON ST N	BUR	BUR	100	24	B3
AVON ST S	BUR	BUR	100	24	B3
AVON TER	LA	LA26	1400	35	D4
AVON WY	LA	LA66	11800	50	A3
AVONBURY AV	WHI	WHI	10500	84	C4
AVONCREST TR	CO	TOP		109	B2
AVONCROFT ST	CO	WHI	9900	55	C1
AVONDALE AV	LA	LA49	200	41	A3
AVONDALE AV	MPK	MPK	100	46	C1
AVONDALE DR	ALH	ALH	2200	45	F1
AVONDALE RD	SMAR	PAS	900	27	C6
AVONGLEN TER	GLEN	GL06	700	25	E3
AVONLEA AV	NWK	NWK	12900	61	B6
AVONLEA AV	NWK	NWK	12900	82	B1
AVONOAK TER	GLEN	GL06	700	25	E3
AVON PARK TER	LA	LA26	1400	35	D4
AVONREA RD	SMAR	PAS	1300	37	B2
AVORA ST	CO	MON	100	29	A6
AWENITA CT	CO	CHA		1A	B6
AXENTY WY	RB	RB	1700	62	D6
AXTELL ST	LA	LA32	4800	36	D5
AYALA AV	IRW	BAP		88	A1
AYARS CYN WY	GLEN	GL08		18	D4
AYERS AV	CMRC	LA40	2200	53	D2
AYERS AV	CO	LA22	2600	53	D3
AYERS WY	BUR	BUR		17	F4
AYLESWORTH PL	LA	LA31	3100	36	B6
AYON AV	IRW	BAP	5100	88	B2
AYR ST	LA	LA39	2200	35	C3
AYRES AV	LA	LA64	10700	41	D5

INDEX

218

1990 LOS ANGELES COUNTY STREET INDEX

AYRES AV — BARNETT DR

LOS ANGELES CO.

STREET	CITY	P.O. ZONE	BLOCK	PAGE	GRID
AYRES AV	LA	LA64	10500	42	A4
AYRSHIRE RD	LA	LA49		32	C6
AZALEA CT	LPUE	LPUE		92	C6
AZALEA CT	LPUE	LPUE		98	C1
AZALEA DR	ALH	ALH	1000	37	D6
AZALEA DR	LAN	LAN		159	A9
AZALEA DR	MTB	MTB	900	46	F6
AZALEA WY	CO	TOR		68	F5
AZALIA DR	LA	TAR	4400	21	B3
AZARIA AV	CO	LPUE	2800	85	D4
AZIMUTH LN	CO	TOP	800	109	A3
AZORES AV	LA	SF	11600	3	B4
AZORES PL	RPV	SP	2700	78	C3
AZTEC	CO	TOP		13	C5
AZTEC DR	CO	CHA		6	C1
AZTEC ST	LA	SF	14100	2	E4
AZTEC ST	LA	SF	13000	3	A2
AZTEC WY	MPK	MPK		46	D3
AZUCENA RD	LA	WOH	4700	13	B3
AZUL CIR	LA	CAN		4	B6
AZUL DR	LA	CAN		4	B6
AZUL TR	LA	CAN		4	B6
AZURE PL	LA	LA49		32	B6
AZURE WY	ARC	ARC	1400	38	D1
AZURE WY	LB	LB03		76	D5
AZURE BAY	LB	LB03		76	C5
AZURE FIELD DR	SCLR	NEW		127	F2
AZURELEE RD	CO	MAL	21600	114	D3
AZUSA AV	CO	AZU	5100	88	D3
AZUSA AV	CO	LPUE	400	92	D4
AZUSA AV	CO	LPUE	2400	98	B4
AZUSA AV	COV	COV	100	88	D3
AZUSA AV	IND	LPUE	100	92	C6
AZUSA AV	IND	LPUE	500	98	B2
AZUSA AV	WCOV	WCOV	800	92	C4
AZUSA AV N	AZU	AZU	200	86	D6
AZUSA AV N	AZU	AZU	100	88	D3
AZUSA AV N	COV	COV	100	88	D6
AZUSA AV N	WCOV	WCOV	100	88	D6
AZUSA AV S	AZU	AZU	100	88	D3
AZUSA AV S	WCOV	WCOV	100	92	D2
AZUSA LN	AZU	AZU	100	88	D1
AZUSA ST	LA	LA12	300	44	D3
AZUSA ST	LA	LA33	1200	44	F3
AZUSA WY	LPUE	LPUE	600	98	C1
AZUSA SN GAB RD	AZU	AZU	1400	86	D3
AZUSA SN GAB RD	CO	AZU	7600	86	D3
AZUSA CANYON RD	IRW	BAP	4400	88	A4
AZUSA CANYON RD	WCOV	WCOV	1100	88	A4
AZZURE CT	LA	LA77		32	B1

B

STREET	CITY	P.O. ZONE	BLOCK	PAGE	GRID
B ST	CER	ART		82	C6
B ST	CO	PALM		183	A3
B ST	LAV	LAV	1900	90	C3
B ST E	LA	WIL	100	74	B5
B ST W	LA	WIL	100	74	B5
BABBITT AV	LA	ENC	5600	14	E6
BABBITT AV	LA	ENC	5700	21	E1
BABBITT AV	LA	NOR	9500	7	E4
BABBITT AV	LA	SF	11400	1	E6
BABBITT AV	LA	SF	10300	7	E1
BABCOCK AV	LA	NHO	6200	16	B5
BABCOCK AV	LA	NHO	4200	23	B4
BABER AV	ART	ART	17000	66	F5
BABETTE AV	LA	LA66	5100	50	A4
BABIA ST	CO	PALM	8900	171I	G3
BABINE DR	CO	PALM	39300	175	G6
BABINGTON ST	SCLR	CYN	19500	124	H7
BACA AV	IRW	BAP	4700	88	B3
BACANORA AV	WHI	WHI	9900	84	E3
BACARRO ST	LB	LB15	6500	76	E4
BACH PL	LA	NOR		1	B6
BACH ST	CAR	CAR	1400	69	D5
BACHELIN ST	CO	LPUE	18900	98	F5
BACHRY PL	LA	SUN		10	C2
BACK BAY PL	LA	MDR		55A	D1
BACKER RD	CO	SAU		123	D4
BACKFORD ST	SELM	ELM	10900	47	C4
BACKLUND ST	CO	MAL		114	D3
BACKTON AV N	CO	LPUE	100	92	D6
BACKTON AV S	CO	LPUE	300	98	D1
BACKUS AV	CO	PAS	1	28	A4
BACON RD	WHI	WHI	7700	85	A6
BACONTON AV	CO	TOP		115	A1
BADAJOZ DR	LAM	LAM	15300	83	B4
BADEAU AV	CAR	CAR	21900	69	D4
BADEN AV	LA	CHA	9300	6	B4
BADEN PL	CO	MAL	29700	110	A4
BADER CIR	CER	ART		81	B3
BADGER AV	LA	SF		2	F1
BADGER AV	LA	SF		3	A2
BADILLO CIR	BAP	BAP		39	F5
BADILLO ST	BAP	BAP	14700	39	F5
BADILLO ST	CO	COV	15600	88	A5

STREET	CITY	P.O. ZONE	BLOCK	PAGE	GRID
BADILLO ST	SAD	SAD	1300	89	C4
BADILLO ST E	COV	COV	100	88	E5
BADILLO ST E	COV	COV		89	A5
BADILLO ST E	WCOV	WCOV	1000	88	C5
BADILLO ST W	COV	COV	100	88	E5
BADILLO ST W	WCOV	WCOV	1000	88	C5
BADLONA DR	LAM	LAM	14900	83	A2
BADMINTON AV	CO	WHI	9200	61	D2
BAELEN ST	CO	LPUE	19000	97	A4
BAER RD	LA	LA41		26	A6
BAFT LN	DBAR	POM		97	E2
BAGBY DR	SCLR	CYN		124	H5
BAGDAD PL	GLEN	GL08	1800	18	E4
BAGLEY AV	LA	CUL	3800	42	C5
BAGLEY AV	LA	LA34	2000	42	C4
BAGLEY AV	LA	LA35	1700	42	C3
BAGNALL ST	AZU	AZU	900	86	D6
BAGNALL ST	GLDR	GLDR	19000	86	E6
BAHAMA AV	CO	COM	14400	64	C2
BAHAMA AV N	COM	LA59	1800	64	C1
BAHAMA ST	LA	CAN	20100	6	E6
BAHAMA ST	LA	NOR	19700	6	F5
BAHAMA ST	LA	NOR	17800	7	D6
BAHAMA ST	LA	SF	16600	7	F6
BAHAMA ST	LA	SF	15000	8	C6
BAHIA DR	CER	ART	13000	81	C2
BAHIA ST	CO	LAN	45500	158	A2
BAILARD RD	CO	MAL	31100	111	D5
BAILE AV	LA	CHA		7	A2
BAILEY AV	CO	RM	1800	46	E3
BAILEY DR	TOR	TOR	17800	63	A6
BAILEY PL	GLEN	GL06	100	26	A4
BAILEY RD	CO	SF		3	C4
BAILEY ST	LA	LA33		45	A3
BAILEY ST	WHI	WHI	12100	55	D5
BAILEY WY	LB	LB13	1500	75	E3
BAIN AV	DBAR	WAL		97	D2
BAINBRIDGE	AGH	AGO		100A	A2
BAINBRIDGE AV	LA	LA77		32	E5
BAINBRIDGE AV	WCOV	WCOV	900	48	F2
BAINBRIDGE CT	AGH	AGO		102	F2
BAINBRIDGE ST	POM	POM	1700	94	E4
BAINBROOK AV	CER	ART		82	D4
BAINBROOK CT	CER	ART	18400	82	D6
BAINBROOK CT	WLVL	THO		102	B4
BAINBURY ST	SCLR	CYN		124	H5
BAINBURY ST	SCLR	CYN	16600	125	C8
BAINFORD AV	CO	LPUE	400	92	D6
BAINFORD AV	CO	LPUE	100	98	D1
BAINTREE AV	CO	LPUE	17900	98	C5
BAINUM DR	CO	TOP	1500	109	C6
BAIRD AV	CO	LA02	9200	58	D3
BAIRD AV	LA	NOR	11400	1	C6
BAIRD AV	LA	NOR	8700	7	C6
BAIRD AV	LA	RES	6400	14	C6
BAIRD AV	LA	TAR	6000	14	C6
BAIRD RD	LA	LA46		33	E2
BAIRNSDALE ST	DOW	DOW	7200	54	C6
BAIS PL	CO	LPUE		85	F4
BAJA AV	LPUE	LPUE	300	92	A6
BAJA AV	LPUE	LPUE	300	98	A1
BAJADA DR	SCLR	VAL		127	A1
BAJIO CT	LA	ENC	16700	21	F4
BAJIO RD	LA	ENC	16700	21	F4
BAKER AL	PAS	PAS	100	27	A4
BAKER PL	CO	NEW		126	H3
BAKER ST	CO	CYN		128	E4
BAKER ST	LB	LB06	600	70	B5
BAKER ST	LB	LB10	1300	70	B5
BAKER ST	LA	LA12		44	F1
BAKER CANYON RD	CO	SAU	16000	125	D4
BAKERTON AV	SCLR	CYN	27500	124	J7
BAKMAN AV	LA	NHO	5700	16	D6
BAKMAN AV	LA	NHO	4000	23	D4
BAKMAN AV	LA	SV	7200	16	D3
BALA CT	CO	ALT		20	B5
BALAN RD	CO	LPUE	2000	97	A5
BALANDA DR	MTB	MTB	100	46	E6
BALARD ST	CAR	CAR	1600	69	D3
BALASSI RD	CO	LPUE		85	F4
BALBI ST	CO	PALM		182	G6
BALBOA AV	GLEN	GL06	600	25	D3
BALBOA AV	LA	ENC	4400	21	E3
BALBOA BLVD	LA	ENC	5600	14	F5
BALBOA BLVD	LA	ENC	4900	21	F2
BALBOA BLVD	LA	NOR	9900	7	F6
BALBOA BLVD	LA	NOR	8300	14	F5
BALBOA BLVD	LA	SF	11400	1	F4
BALBOA BLVD	LA	SF	8300	7	F6
BALBOA BLVD	LA	SF	8300	14	F5
BALBOA BLVD	LA	VAN	6400	14	F5
BALBOA CT	SAD	SAD		90	A2
BALBOA DR	ARC	ARC	700	28	B5
BALBOA PL	LA	VAN		14	F1
BALBOA PL	LB	LB03	1	80	C2
BALBOA ST	POM	POM	1400	91	A6

STREET	CITY	P.O. ZONE	BLOCK	PAGE	GRID
BALBOA ST	POM	POM	1400	95	A1
BALCOM AV	LA	ENC	5800	14	D6
BALCOM AV	LA	NOR	8900	7	D6
BALCOM AV	LA	RES	6100	14	D5
BALCOM ST	LA	SF	11200	7	D1
BALCONY DR	CO	WOH		13	B4
BALDER DR	CO	CAL		100	E5
BALDWIN AL	PAS	PAS	400	27	C3
BALDWIN AV	BAP	BAP	14400	39	E3
BALDWIN AV	CO	ELM	4500	38	C5
BALDWIN AV	CUL	CUL	4100	50	C1
BALDWIN AV	ELM	ELM	3500	38	C5
BALDWIN AV	POM	POM	1000	95	A1
BALDWIN AV	TEC	TEC	4800	38	C4
BALDWIN AV N	ARC	ARC	100	28	C6
BALDWIN AV N	SMAD	SMAD	100	28	C3
BALDWIN AV S	ARC	ARC	100	28	C6
BALDWIN AV S	ARC	ARC	1500	38	C2
BALDWIN AV S	SMAD	SMAD	100	28	C3
BALDWIN PL	ELM	ELM		47	C1
BALDWIN PL	MTB	MTB		46	C5
BALDWIN PL	WHI	WHI	800	55	D6
BALDWIN ST	LA	LA31	2700	45	A1
BALDWIN PARK BL	BAP	BAP	3100	39	D6
BALDWIN PARK BL	BAP	BAP	1100	48	B2
BALDWIN PARK BL	CO	LPUE	800	48	B2
BALDWIN PARK BL	IND	LPUE	100	48	B2
BALDY VIEW AV	POM	POM	1600	91	B6
BALDY VIEW AV	POM	POM	900	95	B1
BALDY VISTA AV	CO	GLDR	7200	86	E5
BALEGH PL	GLEN	GL06	3100	26	C1
BALERIA CT	SCLR	VAL		124	B7
BALERIA DR	LA	SP		78	D4
BALERNA DR	SCLR	SAU	26300	124	C7
BALES ST E	CO	COM	4600	65	C2
BALES ST E	COM	COM	1800	65	B2
BALFERN AV	BLF	BLF	17100	66	D5
BALFERN AV	LKD	LKD	6000	66	D6
BALFOUR LN	LA	WOH		13	A2
BALFOUR ST	CO	WHI	10500	55	B5
BALFOUR ST	PR	PR	9000	54	F4
BALFOUR ST	PR	PR	9400	55	A4
BALHAM AV	CO	LPUE	300	98	E1
BALI DR	WCOV	WCOV	3200	97	A2
BALI LN	LA	PP		40	C4
BALI WY	CO	MDR	13500	49	E5
BALIN PL	LAM	LAM	15700	83	C2
BALKINS DR	AGH	AGO		100A	B3
BALL AV	CAR	GAR	16100	64	B4
BALL AV	CO	GAR	15100	64	B4
BALLARD ST	LA	LA32		36	D5
BALLENA DR	DBAR	POM	100	94	A6
BALLENTINE PL	BAP	BAP	14100	39	E4
BALLENTINE PL	CO	COV	15800	88	A4
BALLER MTWY	CO	MAL		112	F1
BALLER RD	CO	MAL		112	E1
BALLERINA PL	POM	POM	1300	94	C1
BALLINA DR	LA	ENC	3900	22	A4
BALLINA CYN RD	LA	ENC	3800	22	A5
BALLINGER ST	LA	CHA	19700	6	B4
BALLINGER ST	LA	NOR	17100	7	E4
BALLINGER ST	LA	SF	16500	7	F4
BALLINGER ST	LA	SF	16300	8	A4
BALLISTA AV	CO	LPUE	1200	48	F4
BALLISTA AV	LPUE	LPUE	900	48	F4
BALMAIN WY	GLEN	GL06	3500	19	B6
BALMER DR	LA	LA39		35	B3
BALMONT ST	LAN	LAN	2200	159	E8
BALMORAL DR	GLEN	GL07		25	E1
BALMORAL LN	LA	CAN		5	F4
BALMORAL ST	CO	WHI	9900	55	C1
BALMUIR AV	LAN	LAN		160	A7
BALMUIR AV	LAN	LAN	44100	160	D5
BALSA CIR	LAV	LAV		90	B2
BALSAM AV	LA	LA25	2100	42	A3
BALSAM AV	LA	LA64	2200	42	A3
BALTA DR	SCLR	SAU		124	F5
BALTAR ST	LA	CAN	23400	5	F2
BALTAR ST	LA	CAN	19900	12	F2
BALTAR ST	LA	NOR	17500	14	D2
BALTAR ST	LA	RES	17600	14	D2
BALTAR ST	LA	VAN	16900	14	E2
BALTIC AV	CAR	LB10	21000	70	A3
BALTIC AV	LB	LB10	2900	70	A6
BALTIC AV	LB	LB10	400	75	A2
BALTIC ST	LA	LA49		41	A3
BALTIMORE AV	MPK	MPK	100	46	C1
BALTIMORE ST	LA	LA42		36	B1
BALTON AV	SAD	SAD	500	89	D2
BALTUSROL DR	ALH	ALH	2400	46	B1
BALZAC ST	ALH	ALH	3200	45	E1
BAMBI PL	LA	SF		4	E5
BAMBOO LN	LA	LA12	400	44	E1
BAMBOO ST	LPUE	LPUE	16000	92	A6
BAMBOO ST	LPUE	LPUE	16000	98	A1
BAMFIELD DR	AGH	AGO		100A	B2

STREET	CITY	P.O. ZONE	BLOCK	PAGE	GRID
BAMFORD PL	LA	LA42		36	A1
BANBRIDGE AV N	LPUE	LPUE	100	92	A6
BANBRIDGE AV S	LPUE	LPUE	600	98	A1
BANBROOK LN	DBAR	POM		97	D6
BANBURY PL	LA	LA65		25	F6
BANCROFT AV	LA	LA39		35	C3
BANCROFT ST	AZU	AZU	300	86	C4
BANCROFT WY	PAS	PAS		19	E6
BANCROFT WY	PAS	PAS	1500	26	E1
BANDA DR	PAR	PAR	6600	65	D3
BANDANA DR	DBAR	POM	21200	97	D5
BANDAWA AV	CO	LAN		174	H6
BANDELL ST	CO	SAU		182	F8
BANDERA AV	CO	LA59	11600	58	E5
BANDERA AV	COM	COM	1700	64	E1
BANDERA ST	CO	LA02	8600	58	E3
BANDERA ST	LA	LA02	9200	58	E3
BANDERA ST	LA	LA58	5200	52	E4
BANDERA ST	LA	WOH	20900	13	D3
BANDINI BLVD	BELL	BELL	4800	53	D3
BANDINI BLVD	CMRC	LA40	5600	53	F4
BANDINI BLVD	CMRC	LA40	6000	54	A4
BANDINI BLVD	VER	LA23	2900	53	A2
BANDINI BLVD	VER	LA40	4500	53	B2
BANDINI ST N	LA	SP	100	78	F3
BANDINI ST S	CO	SP	100	78	F3
BANDON AV	CO	LPUE	400	92	B6
BANDRA PL	RPV	SP	27600	73	D5
BANDY AV	WCOV	WCOV	100	92	C1
BANEWELL AV	CO	AZU	5100	88	C2
BANEWELL AV	CO	COV	4900	88	C3
BANFF LN	LA	LA49		41	B1
BANFIELD DR	CER	ART	13400	82	D4
BANGLE RD	DOW	DOW	7800	54	C6
BANGOR ST	LA	LA16	5200	42	F4
BANGOR ST	LA	LA16	5100	43	A4
BANGOR ST	POM	POM	200	90	F5
BANI AV	LOM	LOM	25300	73	C3
BANIDA AV	CO	LPUE	1100	97	A4
BANIS RD	CO	SAU		181	A8
BANJO CIR	CO	CAST		123	J1
BANK ST	LA	LA65		35	E3
BANK ST	SPAS	SPAS	700	36	F2
BANK ST	SPAS	SPAS	1600	37	A2
BANKERS DR	CAR	CAR	1000	69	D1
BANKFIELD AV	CUL	CUL	5600	50	C4
BANKS CT DR	LA	LA42		36	B1
BANNA AV	CO	COV	5000	89	B3
BANNA AV	COV	COV	100	89	B4
BANNA AV	GLDR	GLDR	700	87	B4
BANNER AV	LA	LA38	6200	34	C4
BANNER DR	LB	LB07	4400	70	D3
BANNERMAN AV	SCLR	NEW	19200	127	H3
BANNER RIDGE RD	DBAR	POM		97A	A2
BANNING AV	LYN	LYN	3100	59	A6
BANNING BLVD	CAR	CAR	23000	69	C6
BANNING BLVD	CAR	CAR	23500	74	C1
BANNING BLVD	LA	WIL	200	74	C5
BANNING ST	COM	COM		58	F6
BANNING ST	LA	LA12	500	44	E3
BANNING WY	DBAR	WAL	1100	97	C3
BANNING WY	PAS	PAS	1600	37	B1
BANNING WY	SMAR	PAS	1600	37	B1
BANNISTER AV	ELM	ELM	4100	39	A5
BANNOCKBURN DR	LA	LA64	2900	42	B4
BANNON AV	CO	LPUE	1200	48	F4
BANNON AV	CO	LPUE	1200	92	A4
BANNON DR	CER	ART		82	E4
BANSON ST	CO	ACT		189	E1
BANSON ST	CO	SAU		188	G1
BANTA RD	PR	PR	9000	55	A1
BANTAM PL	LA	LA46		33	F2
BANUELA AV	SCLR	SAU	27200	124	D6
BANYAN DR	LA	LA49		30	E5
BANYAN PL	CO	SAU		124	C3
BANYAN ST	PAS	PAS	1100	26	D1
BANYAN RIM DR	CO	WHI		55	D2
BAPTISTE WY	LCF	LCF	200	19	D3
BARA RD	GLEN	GL08	1800	18	F6
BARADA AV	SCLR	SAU	26800	124	D7
BARATA ST	CO	LPUE	15300	85	D3
BARBACOA DR	SCLR	SAU	22100	124	C6
BARBACOA PL	SCLR	SAU		124	D6
BARBADOS DR	WAL	WAL		93	C6
BARBAKER LN	MON	MON	800	29	C5
BARBANELL ST	LB	LB15	5800	76	D1
BARBARA AV	AZU	AZU	200	86	C6
BARBARA AV	AZU	AZU	100	88	C1
BARBARA AV	LA	LA66		49	F3
BARBARA AV	WCOV	WCOV	800	92	A1
BARBARA CT	LA	LA68	3100	24	A6
BARBARA LN	PALM	PALM		183	B1
BARBARA LN	POM	POM	900	95	A1
BARBARA ST	LA	SP		78	E6
BARBARA ST	RB	RB	900	67	E4
BARBARA ST	TOR	TOR	21800	67	E4

STREET	CITY	P.O. ZONE	BLOCK	PAGE	GRID
BARBARA ANN ST	LA	NHO	13300	15	F3
BARBARA ANN ST	LA	NHO	12500	16	B3
BARBATA RD	LAM	LAM	13200	83	B1
BARBATA RD	LAM	LAM	12600	84	B6
BARBEE ST	LA	LA31		45	B1
BARBER AV	ART	ART		66	F6
BARBER RD	CO	SAU		181	B9
BARBER RD	CO	SAU		188	B1
BARBERRY DR	DBAR	POM		97	F2
BARBERRY LN	LA	TAR		13	F4
BARBERRY ST	LAN	LAN		160	B1
BARBI LN	DBAR	POM		97	D6
BARBOUR CT	LA	SP		79	A5
BARBOUR ST	LA	VEN		55A	E2
BARBYDELL DR	LA	LA64	3100	42	B5
BARCA AV	CO	LPUE	300	98	D1
BARCA DR	CO	SF		3	E3
BARCELONA CT	CO	AGO		100	C4
BARCELONA DR	LA	LA46		33	D2
BARCELONA DR	PALM	PALM		173	B9
BARCELONA PL	LB	LB13	1200	75	D3
BARCELONA PL	WAL	WAL		93	A5
BARCLAY AL	PAS	PAS	200	26	F5
BARCLAY AV	COM	COM	500	64	D3
BARCLAY ST	LA	LA31		35	E5
BARCLAY ST E	LB	LB05	100	65	B6
BARCLAY ST W	LB	LB05	100	65	B6
BARCOTTA DR	SCLR	SAU		124	D4
BARCROFT DR	CO	PALM		157	F8
BARD CT	CLA	CLA		91	A1
BARD ST	HB	RB		62	C6
BARD ST	HB	RB	800	67	C1
BARD ST	LA	LA26	2400	35	D4
BARDALE AV	LA	SP		73	E6
BARDELL DR	AGH	AGO		100A	A2
BARDLEY CT	POM	POM		94	E5
BARDMAN AV	CO	MAL		105	A6
BARDOLF AV	CO	TOP		115	A1
BARDWELL AV	LA	VAN		15	F1
BAREFOOT LN	CO	LPUE		98	D5
BARELA AV	CO	ARC	6700	38	B1
BARELA AV	TEC	TEC	5100	38	B1
BARFORD AV	CO	LPUE	1000	85	F2
BARGANCA CT	SCLR	VAL		127	C1
BARGEN WY	CO	ALT	2900	19	E4
BARHAM AV	WCOV	WCOV		92	C4
BARHAM BLVD	LA	LA68	3200	24	A6
BARHAM TER	LA	LA68	3200	24	A5
BAR HARBOR CT	SCLR	VAL		124	E3
BARHILL AV	POM	POM		94	E5
BARHITE ST	CO	PAS	3200	20	F6
BARHITE ST	CO	PAS	3200	20A	A3
BARHITE ST	CO	PAS	3200	27	F1
BARHITE ST	CO	PAS	3200	28	A1
BARHUGH PL	LA	SP		73	F6
BARI WY	LA	VEN		49	C5
BARING CROSS ST	LA	LA44	8600	57	F4
BARJUD AV	POM	POM	2400	94	A2
BARK DR	CO	WHI		48	A4
BARKENTINE RD	RPV	PVP	300	77	D3
BARKER DR	DBAR	POM		97A	B2
BARKER DR	LA	LA42	5200	26	B6
BARKER WAY	LB	LB14	4400	76	B5
BARKERVILLE AV	CO	WHI	9300	61	E3
BARKING SPDR RD	CO	SAU		182	A7
BARKLEY LN	RB	RB	2800	62	F4
BARKPOINT DR	CO	CAL		108	C1
BARKSTONE DR	RPV	PVP	26100	72	D3
BARLETTA DR	CO	LPUE	15700	85	D4
BARLY FLT TK TR	CO			M	F3
BARLY FLT TK TR	CO			N	A3
BARLIN AV	DOW	DOW	12600	60	A6
BARLIN AV	DOW	DOW	12900	66	A1
BARLIN AV	LKD	LKD	4900	71	A2
BARLING ST	LA	SUN		10	A4
BARLOCK AV	LA	LA49		32	C6
BARLOW AV	LYN	LYN	10700	59	A4
BARLOW ST	LA	LA33		45	B3
BARMAN AV	CUL	CUL	10700	50	B2
BARMAN AV	LA	CUL	11300	50	B2
BARMORE CT	GLEN	GL06		25	F2
BARNABY RD	LA	LA77	500	32	D5
BARNARD AV	CLA	CLA		91	A2
BARNARD AV	WAL	WAL	20200	93	B6
BARNARD WY	SM	SM	2400	49	A3
BARNBY RD	CO	SAU		181	H8
BARNER AV	LA	SF		2	E1
BARNES AV	BAP	BAP	3300	39	B6
BARNES CIR	GLEN	GL08		18	D4
BARNES LN	LA	LA46		33	E3
BARNESTON CT	LA	SF	17300	1	E5
BARNESTON ST	LA	SF	17000	1	E5
BARNESTON ST	LA	SF	16200	2	A5
BARNET ST	CO	PALM		182	G7
BARNETT DR	GLEN	GL06	2300	26	A2

INDEX

219

1990 LOS ANGELES COUNTY STREET INDEX

BARNETT RD — BELCOURT DR

LOS ANGELES CO. — INDEX

STREET	CITY	P.O. ZONE	BLOCK	PAGE	GRID
BARNETT RD	LA	LA32	1800	45	E1
BARNETT WY	LA	LA32	2000	45	D1
BARNEY CT	HB	RB	1	67	D1
BARNEY ST	CMRC	LA40	5200	53	E2
BARNHART AL	PAS	PAS	1000	27	A2
BARNHILL AV	CER	ART		82	A5
BARNHILL RD	SCLR	NEW		127	D2
BARN OWL WY	LAV	LAV		95A	D5
BARNSLEY AV	LA	LA45		56	D1
BARNSTEAD DR	CO	PALM		157	G8
BARNSTON ST	LA	SF	16400	1	E5
BARNUM DR	WHI	WHI		55	D6
BARNUM WY	MPK	MPK		46	A2
BARNWALL ST	BLF	BLF	10300	66	D3
BARNWALL ST	LAM	LAM	14800	83	A3
BARNWALL ST	NWK	NWK	10600	66	E3
BARNWALL ST	NWK	NWK	11600	82	A3
BARO CIR	PALM	PALM	37600	183	G1
BARODA DR	LA	LA77		32	F5
BARON ST	CO	TOR	900	68	F3
BARONSGATE RD	WLVL	THO	4300	102	B4
BARR AV	MTB	MTB	3200	46	B5
BARRACUDA ST	LA	SP	400	79	C3
BARRAGAN ST	AGH	AGO		100A	A2
BARRANCA AV	CO	AZU	6100	86	F6
BARRANCA AV	CO	AZU	5600	88	F5
BARRANCA AV	CO	COV	4800	88	F5
BARRANCA AV	CO	GLDR	6900	86	F6
BARRANCA AV	GLDR	GLDR	5200	88	F5
BARRANCA AV N	COV	COV	100	88	F5
BARRANCA AV S	COV	COV	100	88	F5
BARRANCA DR	MPK	MPK	100	45	F2
BARRANCA LN	NWK	NWK		61	C6
BARRANCA LN	NWK	NWK		82	C1
BARRANCA RD	BRAD	DUA	100	29	D3
BARRANCA ST	LA	LA31		35	F6
BARRANCA ST N	WCOV	WCOV	100	92	F2
BARRANCA ST S	WCOV	WCOV	100	92	F2
BARREL SPGS RD	CO	PALM	100	183	C3
BARREL SPGS RD	CO	PALM	4700	184	A6
BARRES DR	CO	SAU		181	E8
BARRETT DR	SCLR	SAU		124	E5
BARRETT DR	WLVL	THO		102A	E5
BARRETT RD	LA	LA32		36	E4
BARRETTE AV	RM	RM	8800	38	A4
BARRIE DR	BH	BH	400	33	C3
BARRINGER ST	SELM	ELM	11400	47	E4
BARRINGTON AV N	LA	LA49	100	41	B1
BARRINGTON AV S	LA	LA25	1200	41	C2
BARRINGTON AV S	LA	LA49	100	41	C2
BARRINGTON AV S	LA	LA64	2000	41	E5
BARRINGTON AV S	LA	LA66	3100	41	D4
BARRINGTON AV S	LA	LA66	3400	49	F2
BARRINGTON CT	CLA	CLA	1900	91	C2
BARRINGTON CT	LA	LA49		41	C1
BARRINGTON PL	LA	LA49	100	41	C1
BARRINGTON WK	LA	LA49		41	C1
BARRINGTON WY	GLEN	GL06	1300	25	E4
BARRINSON ST	PALM	PALM		172	G9
BARRINSON ST	PALM	PALM		183	G1
BARRIOS ST	LB	LB15	5800	76	D1
BARRON AV	COM	COM	100	64	E3
BARRON ST	COM	COM		64	E3
BARROSO ST	CO	LPUE	19200	97	A5
BARROSO ST	CO	LPUE	18200	98	E5
BARROWS CT	PAS	PAS	800	27	B1
BARROWS DR	LA	LA48	6100	42	F2
BARRY AV	LA	LA25	1200	41	D3
BARRY AV	LA	LA49	1100	41	D3
BARRY AV	LA	LA64	2200	41	E5
BARRY AV	LA	LA66	3100	41	E6
BARRY AV	LA	LA66	3600	49	F1
BARRY DR	LB	LB05	600	65	D5
BARRY DR	POM	POM	300	90	F4
BARRY PL	CO	ALT	600	20	B5
BARRYDALE ST	CO	LPUE	13900	48	D2
BARRYKNOLL DR	LA	LA65		35	F1
BARRYKNOLL WK	LA	LA65		35	F1
BARRYMORE DR	CO	MAL	2700	113	B3
BARRYWOOD AV	LA	SP		73	F6
BARSTON AV	COV	COV	900	89	C4
BARSTON PL	GLDR	GLDR	1600	89	C2
BARSTOW RD	PALM	PALM	11100	174	A1
BARSTOW RD E	CO	PALM	8500	173	F4
BARSTOW RD E	PALM	LAN	10000	173	H3
BARSTOW ST	LA	LA32		36	D5
BART AV	CO	HAW	12700	56	E6
BARTDON AV	ING	IN03	3200	57	C3
BARTEE AV	LA	PAC	9500	8	F3
BARTEE AV	LA	PAC	9000	9	A5
BARTEE AV	LA	SF		2	C6
BARTEE AV	LA	SF	10400	8	C1
BARTHE DR	PAS	PAS		26	F2
BARTLETT AL	PAS	PAS	300	27	B3
BARTLETT AV	CO	SGAB	5000	38	A4
BARTLETT AV	RM	RM	3600	38	A6

STREET	CITY	P.O. ZONE	BLOCK	PAGE	GRID
BARTLETT AV	RM	RM	2400	47	A2
BARTLETT DR	TOR	TOR	5600	67	E3
BARTLETT ST	CO	ACT		189	E3
BARTLETT ST	CO	SGAB	5900	38	A2
BARTLETT ST	LA	LA12	600	44	D1
BARTLEY AV	CO	WHI	7600	55	A5
BARTLEY AV	SFS	SFS	9400	60	F3
BARTMUS ST	CMRC	LA40	5700	54	A2
BARTO DR	LA	SF		1	E3
BARTOLO AV	MTB	MTB	600	46	F6
BARTOLO AV	PR	PR	9300	55	B2
BARTON AV	LA	LA38		34	C4
BARTON CIR	SFS	WHI	13200	61	D3
BARTON LN	CO	MONT	2200	18	F2
BARTON RD	CO	WHI	12900	61	C2
BARTON RD	SFS	SFS	13100	61	C2
BARTON RD	WHI	WHI	8300	61	E1
BARUCH ST	RM	RM	8100	46	F2
BARWOOD DR	LAM	LAM	15001	83	A3
BASCOM ST	PR	PR	9000	54	E6
BASCULE AV	LA	WOH	4900	13	D2
BASEBALL AV	ELM	ELM	3000	47	E1
BASEL ST	SCLR	CYN		124	J7
BASE LINE RD	AZU	AZU	600	88	E1
BASE LINE RD	CO	AZU	18500	88	E1
BASE LINE RD	CO	GLDR	19000	88	E1
BASE LINE RD	CO	LAV		90	C1
BASE LINE RD	LAV	LAV	900	90	C1
BASE LINE RD E	CLA	CLA	100	91	A1
BASE LINE RD E	GLDR	GLDR	2100	89	E1
BASE LINE RD E	SAD	SAD	100	90	A1
BASE LINE RD W	CLA	CLA	100	91	A1
BASE LINE RD W	GLDR	GLDR	100	89	A1
BASE LINE RD W	SAD	SAD	100	89	E1
BASE LINE TR	LA	LA68	2800	34	A1
BASETDALE AV	CO	LPUE	100	48	B3
BASETDALE AV	CO	WHI	600	48	A4
BASHFORD ST	LA	PP		40	D3
BASHOR ST	DUA	DUA	2300	29	F4
BASIL LN	LA	LA77		22	D6
BASIL LN	LA	LA77		32	D1
BASILIO ST	SAD	SAD	100	90	A2
BASIN DR	CO	TOP	700	109	C5
BASIN ST	LA	SP	700	78	F1
BASINGSTOKE LN	SCLR	VAL		127	A1
BASINVIEW AV	BAP	BAP	5000	39	E3
BASKIN AV	CO	LPUE		92	B6
BASS ST	LA	SP	300	79	C3
BASS WK	CO	CAST		123	B5
BASSET DR	CO	CAST		123	B3
BASSETT CT	SAD	SAD		89	E3
BASSETT ST	LA	CAN	23400	5	F4
BASSETT ST	LA	CAN	19700	12	F4
BASSETT ST	LA	NHO	12700	16	B4
BASSETT ST	LA	RES	18300	14	B4
BASSETT ST	LA	VAN	16600	14	E4
BASSETT ST	LA	VAN	13400	15	F4
BASSO TER	GLEN	GL02	1500	25	C1
BASSWOOD AV	RPV	PVP	26100	72	E4
BASYE ST	ELM	ELM	10000	38	E5
BASYE ST	ELM	ELM	11900	39	A5
BATAAN AV	CAR	LB10	21700	69	F4
BATAAN PL	MPK	MPK		46	D3
BATAAN RD	RB	RB	1900	62	E4
BATAC ST	LA	CHA	20600	6	E1
BATAVIA RD	SOG	SOG	5100	59	D4
BATCHELOR CT	LOM	LOM		73	D1
BATEMAN AV	IRW	BAP	2400	39	C1
BATES AV	LA	LA27	1300	35	A4
BATES AV	LA	LA29	1000	35	A4
BATES PL	CLA	CLA	1300	91	C2
BATEY AV	LA	HAC	23500	73	E1
BATEY PL	LA	HAC	1300	73	E1
BATHURST ST	LA	NOR		1	C6
BATNA PL	CO	LPUE		98	F6
BATON ROUGE AV	LA	NOR		7	A2
BATON ROUGE PL	LA	NOR		7	A2
BATRIS CT	CO	CAL		100	F4
BATRIS LN	CO	LAN		159	C9
BATSON AV	CO	LPUE	1400	98	D5
BATTERY ST	LA	SP	600	78	F1
BATTLE ST	NWK	NWK	11800	61	A5
BATTRAM ST	POM	POM	2800	90	F3
BAUCHARD CT	CAR	CAR	17400	64	C5
BAUCHET ST	LA	LA12		44	E2
BAUDIN DR	POM	POM	1900	94	E5
BAUER DR	WCOV	WCOV		92	B4
BAUGHMAN AV	CLA	CLA	400	91	B3
BAUGHMAN DR	CLA	CLA	1100	91	B3
BAXARD PL	CO	VAL		124	A7
BAXLEY RD	CO	CAL		108	C4
BAXTER DR	CO	MAL		113	E4
BAXTER DR	GLDR	GLDR	1100	87	C5
BAXTER PL	LA	LA26		35	D4
BAXTER ST	LA	LA26	1500	35	C4
BAXTER ST	LA	LA39	1900	35	C4

STREET	CITY	P.O. ZONE	BLOCK	PAGE	GRID
BAY ST	CO	MDR	5100	49	F5
BAY ST	LA	LA21	1500	44	E5
BAY ST	SM	SM	1	49	A2
BAYARD ST	LB	LB15	5700	76	E3
BAYBAR RD	CO	WHI		47	D6
BAYBERRY	CER	ART		81	B2
BAYBERRY CT	LAV	LAV		90	E3
BAYBERRY DR	GLEN	GL08	1900	18	F4
BAYBERRY LN	CO	MAL		113	E4
BAYBERRY PL	LA	VAN		22	A5
BAYBERRY ST	PALM	PALM		183	C1
BAY CLUB DR	LA	PP		40	B4
BAYCREST DR	RPV	PVP	29200	72	C6
BAYEND DR	RPV	SP	29000	78	D1
BAYER PL	LA	WOH		100	F1
BAYFIELD DR	SAD	LAV		90	B1
BAYLA ST	NWK	NWK	11200	60	F5
BAYLA ST	NWK	NWK	11700	61	A5
BAYLESS ST	AZU	AZU	500	86	C6
BAYLISS CT	PALM	PALM		183	G2
BAYLISS RD	LA	LA49		30	E6
BAYLOR AV	CLA	CLA	700	91	A4
BAYLOR DR	NWK	NWK	11400	66	F4
BAYLOR DR	NWK	NWK		82	A4
BAYLOR ST	DUA	DUA	1900	29	E4
BAYLOR ST	LA	PP		40	B3
BAYMAR AV N	WCOV	WCOV	100	88	D6
BAYMAR ST S	WCOV	WCOV	100	92	D1
BAY MARE LN	RHE	PVP		73	C4
BAYNES RD	CO	CAL		108	C4
BAYONNE ST	ELS	ELS	600	56	A5
BAYOU AV	BLF	BLF	14900	66	B3
BAYPOINT AV	LA	WIL	24400	74	C2
BAYPORT CIR	POM	POM		94	D2
BAYPORT DR	TOR	TOR		68	C5
BAYPORT DR S	TOR	TOR		68	C5
BAYPORT ST	CAR	CAR	500	69	B6
BAYRIDGE RD	RPV	PVP	5300	72	E3
BAY SHORE AV	LB	LB03	200	76	C6
BAY SHORE AV	LB	LB03	1	80	C1
BAYSHORE DR	CO	MAL		113	D5
BAY SHORE WK	LB	LB03	5500	80	C2
BAYSIDE DR	NWK	NWK		66	E2
BAYSIDE DR N	LB	LB03		76	E5
BAYSIDE DR S	LB	LB03		76	E5
BAYSINGER ST	DOW	DOW	7800	60	B2
BAY STATE ST E	ALH	ALH	1	37	C4
BAY STATE ST W	ALH	ALH	1	37	C4
BAYTON ST	CO	PALM	37200	184	D2
BAY TREE RD	LCF	LCF		19	C1
BAYVIEW AV	LA	WIL	1400	74	B5
BAYVIEW DR	HB	RB	1300	62	C6
BAYVIEW DR	HB	RB	100	67	C1
BAY VIEW DR	MB	MB	100	62	A3
BAYWATER AV	LA	SP	2800	78	F5
BAYWAY PL	CO	LAN	15900	174	H4
BAYWOOD AV	POM	POM		91	B6
BAYWOOD AV	POM	POM	1200	95	B1
BAYWOOD CT	LA	LA77		32	E1
BAYWOOD ST	LA	LA39	4000	25	B5
BAZA AV	LA	WOH	5000	13	C2
BEA CT	SCLR	SAU		124	D2
BEACH AV	LA	VEN	2200	49	C4
BEACH AV	LA	VEN	13300	49	E4
BEACH AV E	ING	IN02	100	50	F6
BEACH AV E	ING	IN02	100	51	A6
BEACH AV W	ING	IN02	100	50	F6
BEACH AV W	ING	IN02	100	51	A6
BEACH BLVD	LAM	LAM	13500	83	C2
BEACH CT	LA	VEN	2300	49	C4
BEACH DR	HB	RB	1300	62	B6
BEACH DR	HB	RB	100	67	C1
BEACH ST	BLF	BLF	9400	66	C5
BEACH ST	CER	ART	11200	66	F5
BEACH ST	CER	ART	12600	82	C5
BEACH ST	CO	LA01	7200	52	D6
BEACH ST	CO	LA01	7900	58	D1
BEACH ST	CO	LA02	8600	58	D3
BEACH ST	CO	SAU		123	D5
BEACH ST	ING	IN02	1000	50	E5
BEACH ST	LA	LA02	9200	58	D3
BEACH ST	MTB	MTB	1100	54	C2
BEACH ST	SM	SM	200	49	B2
BEACHCOMBER DR	LB	LB03	6100	76	E5
BEACHCOMBER RD	RPV	PVP	32500	77	E3
BEACHFRONT LN	WLVL	THO		102	A4
BEACHGROVE CT	SCLR	NEW	19200	127	H3
BEACHLAKE LN	WLVL	THO		102	A4
BEACHMEADOW LN	WLVL	THO		102	A4
BEACHSIDE DR	RPV	PVP	5500	72	E6
BEACHVIEW DR	RPV	PVP		77	C3
BEACHVIEW LN	WLVL	THO		102	A4
BEACHWOOD DR	LA	LA68	2900	24	D6
BEACHWOOD DR N	BUR	BUR	400	17	C5
BEACHWOOD DR N	BUR	BUR	100	24	D2
BEACHWOOD DR N	LA	LA04	100	34	C6

STREET	CITY	P.O. ZONE	BLOCK	PAGE	GRID
BEACHWOOD DR N	LA	LA28	1300	34	D3
BEACHWOOD DR N	LA	LA38	1100	34	D3
BEACHWOOD DR N	LA	LA68	1900	34	D2
BEACHWOOD DR S	BUR	BUR	100	24	D2
BEACHWOOD DR S	LA	LA04	100	34	C6
BEACHWOOD TER	LA	LA68	2100	34	D2
BEACHY AV	LA	PAC	9400	8	E3
BEACHY AV	LA	PAC	9000	9	A6
BEACON AV	LA	LA15	900	44	B3
BEACON AV	LA	LA17	700	44	B3
BEACON AV	SPAS	SPAS	200	26	F6
BEACON LN	PALM	PALM		171	F6
BEACON PL	CO	PAS	1	28	A4
BEACON ST	AVA	AVA	200	77	B5
BEACON ST	CO	SAU		123	D5
BEACON ST E	ALH	ALH	1	37	C4
BEACON ST N	LA	SP	100	79	A4
BEACON ST S	LA	SP	100	79	A4
BEACON ST W	ALH	ALH	1	37	C4
BEACONSFIELD CT	WLVL	THO		102	B4
BEACONTREE LN	CO	CAL		108	C1
BEAGLE ST	LA	LA32		36	C5
BEAK AV	SOG	SOG	10500	59	E4
BEALBY HEATN RD	HH	CAL		100	D2
BEALE CT	CO	VAL		123	H7
BEALE ST	LA	LA12	1500	44	E1
BEAM TR	CO	TOP		109	D4
BEAR AV	BELL	BELL	6200	53	B6
BEAR AV	CDY	BELL	7200	53	B6
BEAR AV	HPK	HPK	6000	53	C4
BEAR CT	BELL	BELL	3700	53	B5
BEARCREEK LN	CER	ART	16000	82	B4
BEAR CREEK RD	CO	PALM		183	G4
BEARD ST	LA	LA42	6200	36	D1
BEARDSLEE ST	DUA	DUA	1200	29	D4
BEARING TR	CO	TOP		109	B2
BEAR MEADOW CIR	CER	ART		82	B4
BEARS DEN RD	DBAR	POM		97A	A3
BEAR VALLEY	POM	POM		94	C5
BEATIE PL	LA	LA32		36	E6
BEATRICE PL	RM	RM	8900	47	A1
BEATRICE ST	CO	LA66	12300	50	B4
BEATRICE ST	LA	CUL	11800	50	B4
BEATRICE ST	LA	LA66	12400	50	A5
BEATY AV	CO	WHI	13000	61	C5
BEATY ST	NWK	NWK	11400	60	F5
BEATY ST	NWK	NWK	11500	61	A5
BEAU CT	CO	SAU		124	D4
BEAUCOURT AV	CO	LR		192	B6
BEAUCOURT AV	CO	VALY		192	E6
BEAUCROFT CT	WLVL	THO		102	B4
BEAUDINE AV	SOG	SOG	8800	58	F2
BEAUDRY AV N	LA	LA12	100	44	C2
BEAUDRY AV S	LA	LA12	100	44	C2
BEAUDRY AV S	LA	LA17	300	44	C2
BEAUDRY BLVD	GLEN	GL08	1200	18	E4
BEAUDRY TER	GLEN	GL08		18	D4
BEAUFAIT AV	LA	NOR		1	B4
BEAUVAIS AV	LA	LA65		36	A3
BEAUVAIS RD	RPV	SP	4600	78	D3
BEAU VILLE CT	LAN	LAN		159	F8
BEAUVOIR RD	CO	MAL		114	F2
BEAVER CT	POM	POM	100	94	E4
BEAVER ST	LA	SF	13400	2	E4
BEAVER ST	LA	SF	13000	3	A2
BEAVER WY	LAV	LAV		90	C1
BEAVERBROOK DR	CO	PALM		157	G9
BEAVERBROOK LN	GLDR	GLDR		87	D6
BEAVERBROOK LN	GLDR	GLDR		89	D1
BEAVERHEAD DR	DBAR	POM		93	F6
BEAVER RUN RD	CO	CYN	15700	128	E4
BEAZLEY DR	SCLR	SAU		124	C9
BECHARD AV	CER	ART		81	C1
BECHARD AV	CER	ART	19000	81	C2
BECHARD AV	CER	ART	16800	82	C5
BECHARD AV	NWK	NWK	13400	82	C2
BECK AV	BELL	BELL		53	D6
BECK AV	LA	NHO	5600	16	D3
BECK AV	LA	NHO	4000	23	D1
BECK ST	CAR	CAR		69	D5
BECKENHAM LN	ING	IN01		57	B2
BECKETT ST	LA	SUN	7800	10	E3
BECKETT ST	LA	TU	7600	10	E3
BECKETT ST	LA	TU	6800	11	A3
BECKFORD AV	LA	NOR	8500	7	A5
BECKFORD AV	LA	NOR	8400	14	A1
BECKFORD AV	LA	RES	6100	14	A4
BECKFORD AV	LA	TAR	5800	14	A6
BECKFORD AV	LA	TAR	5200	21	A1
BECKFORD PL	LA	NOR		7	A5
BECKFORD WY	POM	POM	1200	95	B2
BECKLEDGE TR	CO	MAL	22800	114	C4
BECKLEE RD	GLDR	GLDR	900	87	C3
BECKLEY ST	LA	WOH		13	A2
BECKMAN RD	LA	LA68		24	A6
BECKNEL AV	LOM	LOM	25300	73	C2

STREET	CITY	P.O. ZONE	BLOCK	PAGE	GRID
BECKNER ST	CO	LPUE	13500	48	C3
BECKNER ST	LPUE	LPUE	13700	48	E5
BECKVILLE ST	CO	DUA	700	29	B6
BECKVILLE ST	DUA	DUA	800	29	C6
BECKWITH AV	LA	LA49	1400	40	F3
BECKWORTH AV	TOR	TOR	19000	67	F2
BECKY LN	PALM	PALM		172	B5
BEDA ST	CO	LAN		175	E4
BEDEL ST	LA	WOH		13	D3
BEDESSEN AV	CMRC	LA40	2300	53	D2
BEDFORD AV	CO	LA56	5100	50	E4
BEDFORD CT	PALM	PALM		183	E1
BEDFORD DR	BH	BH	300	33	A6
BEDFORD DR	LA	LA35	1000	42	B2
BEDFORD DR N	BH	BH	300	42	B1
BEDFORD DR S	BH	BH	100	42	B2
BEDFORD RD	SMAR	PAS	1300	27	D6
BEDFORD RD	SMAR	PAS	1500	37	D1
BEDFORD ST	LA	LA34	1900	42	D4
BEDFORD ST	LA	LA35	800	42	D4
BEDFORD WY	CO	SAU		124	E4
BEDFORDHURST CT	WLVL	THO	31700	102	B4
BEDILION ST	LA	LA32		36	C5
BEDMAR ST	CAR	CAR	1000	69	C3
BEDWORTH RD	CO	SAU		181	C9
BEE AV	AGH	AGO		100A	A2
BEECH AV	LAN	LAN	43700	160	B6
BEECH AV	TOR	TOR	600	68	C4
BEECH ST	LA	LA65	400	36	A4
BEECH ST	LAV	LAV		90	E1
BEECH ST	SPAS	SPAS	1100	36	F3
BEECH ST	SPAS	SPAS	1400	37	A3
BEECHAM DR	RPV	SP	2000	78	D1
BEECH CREEK CIR	SCLR	VAL		124	C4
BEECHDALE DR	CO	PALM	1000	172	A7
BEECHFIELD DR	RPV	PVP	6900	72	B4
BEECHGATE DR	RHE	PVP	28000	72	F5
BEECHGATE DR	RPV	PVP	27900	72	F5
BEECHGLEN DR	GLEN	GL14	3700	18	C1
BEECH HILL AV	CO	LPUE	900	48	B6
BEECH HILL AV	CO	LPUE	1500	85	B1
BEECH HILL DR	CO	LPUE	1600	85	B1
BEECH KNOLL RD	LA	LA46		33	E2
BEECHLEY AV	LB	LB05	6700	65	C5
BEECHNUT CIR	SCLR	VAL		124	B4
BEECHNUT PL	POM	POM		94	C4
BEECHTREE LN	LA	NOR		7	B2
BEECHWOOD AV	LYN	LYN	2900	59	A5
BEECHWOOD AV	SOG	SOG	8100	58	F1
BEECHWOOD LN	SAD	SAD		90	A4
BEECHWORTH AV	MON	MON	300	29	B2
BEEHIVE AV	BRAD	DUA	200	29	D3
BEELER AV	LA	WOH		100	E1
BEEMAN AV	LA	NHO	5900	16	B5
BEEMAN AV	LA	NHO	4200	23	B3
BEEMAN ST	LA	NHO		16	B1
BEESON DR	LA	BH		32	F2
BEESON DR	LA	BH	9800	33	A2
BEETHOVEN ST	CUL	LA66	4000	49	E3
BEETHOVEN ST	LA	LA66	3400	49	E2
BEETHOVEN ST	LA	LA66	5400	50	A5
BEGONIA AV	LA	LA42	1500	26	C6
BEGONIA ST	LAN	LAN		160	G5
BEGONIA WY	CO	TOR		68	F5
BEGONIAS LN	CO	CYN	14800	125	F7
BEHAN WY	CO	SGAB	8200	37	F1
BEHRENS AV	NWK	NWK	12600	60	E6
BEHRENS AV	NWK	NWK	12800	66	E1
BEIRUT AV	LA	PP	300	40	C4
BEJAY PL	LA	SP		73	F6
BEKINS WY	GLEN	GL02		25	A3
BEKNEL AV	LOM	LOM	25300	73	C2
BEL TER	LA	LA49		32	B5
BELA ST	PALM	PALM		183	F2
BEL AIR CT	LA	LA77		32	E4
BEL AIR DR	LCF	LCF	4300	19	B3
BEL AIR DR	WAL	WAL		92	F6
BEL AIR DR	WAL	WAL		98	F1
BEL AIR PL	LA	LA77	1100	32	E4
BEL AIR RD	LA	LA77	700	32	E3
BEL AIR TER	LA	LA77		32	E3
BEL AIRE DR	GLEN	GL01	1500	18	A6
BEL AIRE DR N	BUR	BUR	100	17	D3
BEL AIRE DR S	BUR	BUR	100	17	D3
BL AIR CST RD N	LA	LA49		32	B2
BL AIR CST RD S	LA	LA49		32	B2
BELAND AV	LA	LA45	7700	50	B6
BELAND BLVD	RB	RB	2500	62	F4
BELBERT CIR	CO	CAL	5800	100	A2
BELBURY DR	DBAR	WAL	1000	97	C3
BELCHER ST	DOW	DOW	9100	66	B1
BELCHER ST	LAM	LAM	14000	82	E1
BELCHER ST	NWK	NWK	10900	66	E1
BELCHER ST	NWK	NWK	11600	82	C1
BELCOURT DR	CO	WHI	14800	84	A4

1990 LOS ANGELES COUNTY STREET INDEX

STREET	CITY	P.O. ZONE	BLOCK	PAGE	GRID
BELCROFT AV	ELM	ELM	3400	48	A1
BELCROFT AV	SELM	ELM	1800	47	E4
BELDAY RD	PAS	PAS	100	26	D4
BELDEN AV	CO	LA22	400	46	A6
BELDEN DR	LA	LA68	2900	24	D6
BELDEN DR	LA	LA68	2700	34	C1
BELDOVE CT	CO	SAU		124	D4
BELEN ST	LB	LB15	5800	76	C1
BELFAIR ST	BLF	BLF	9800	66	C2
BELFAIR ST	NWK	NWK	11000	66	E2
BELFAIR ST	NWK	NWK	11700	82	A2
BELFAST DR	LA	LA69		33	D3
BELFORD AV	LA	LA45	8100	56	D1
BELFORD CT	LA	CAN		5	D3
BELFOREST DR	CAR	GAR	16900	64	B5
BELFORT AV	POM	POM	1100	91	A6
BELFORT AV	POM	POM	1000	95	A1
BELGATE ST	BAP	BAP	13300	39	C4
BELGRAVE AV	HPK	HPK	1900	52	E4
BELGRAVE AV	HPK	HPK	2800	53	A4
BELGREEN DR	CO	WHI	1200	47	F4
BELHAM CT	WLVL	THO		102	B4
BELHAVEN AV	CO	LA59	12700	58	C6
BELHAVEN AV	CO	LA59	12800	64	C1
BELHAVEN AV	COM	LA59	1900	64	C1
BELHAVEN PL	CLA	CLA	100	91	C5
BELHAVEN RD	SMAR	PAS	1200	27	F6
BELHAVEN ST	CO	LA02	9200	58	C2
BELHAVEN ST	LA	LA59	11000	58	C5
BELHURST AV	LB	LB05		65	C5
BELICE ST	LB	LB05	6800	65	C5
BELICE ST	LB	LB15	5800	76	D2
BELINDA AV	POM	POM	2300	94	A1
BELINDA ST	LA	ENC	17600	21	D3
BELINDA ST	WCOV	WCOV		92	E6
BELITA LN	LCF	LCF	4500	19	D4
BELK RD	CO	SAU		181	D7
BELL AV	BELL	BELL		53	B5
BELL AV	CO	LA01	7200	52	E6
BELL AV	CO	LA01	7900	58	E1
BELL AV	MB	MB	2400	62	B2
BELL PL	BELL	BELL	4400	53	C5
BELL ST	LAV	LAV	1700	90	D2
BELL ST	PAS	PAS	800	27	B2
BELLA CT	SCLR	NEW		127	B6
BELLA CT	CO	WHI		61	F4
BELLA CT	CO	WHI		84	A4
BELLA DR	LA	BH	1400	32	F3
BELLAGIO DR	LA	LA24		32	D6
BELLAGIO PL	LA	LA77	11000	32	D5
BELLAGIO RD	LA	LA49	11000	32	E5
BELLAGIO RD	LA	LA77	10400	32	E5
BELLAGIO TER	LA	LA49		32	C5
BELLAGIO WY	LA	LA24		32	D6
BELLAGIO WY	WAL	WAL		92	F6
BELLA KATH TER	PALM	LAN		171	A1
BELLAIRE AV	LA	NHO	5600	16	B4
BELLAIRE AV	LA	NHO	4100	23	B2
BELLAIRE DR	CO	ALT	3200	20	A3
BELLANCA AV	LA	LA45	8600	56	D3
BELLANCA WY	TOR	TOR		73	B2
BELLA PINE DR	DBAR	POM		97	D4
BELLA SANTA DR	SCLR	VAL		124	A1
BELLA VISTA AV	PAS	PAS	200	27	E3
BELLA VISTA DR	ARC	ARC	1900	38	C1
BELLA VISTA DR	CO	CAL		100	C5
BELLA VISTA ST	LA	LA45	7500	55A	F2
BELLA VISTA ST	MON	MON	300	29	A5
BELLAVISTA TER	SMAD	SMAD	200	28	D2
BELLA VISTA WY	LA	LA68	6500	34	C2
BELLBIRD PL	CO	LAN	45200	158	A3
BELLBROOK ST	BAP	BAP	13600	39	D3
BELLBROOK ST	CO	COV	16200	88	B3
BELLBROOK ST	CO	COV	19600	89	A3
BELLBROOK ST	CO	SAD	1700	89	C3
BELLBROOK ST	COV	COV	1100	88	C3
BELL CANYON BL	LA	CAN		5	D3
BELLCLAIRE ST	LA	TU	6800	11	A3
BELLDER DR	DOW	DOW	9500	60	A6
BELLE DR	LA	BH		32	E2
BELLEAU CT	CO	WOH		13	B5
BELLEAU RD	GLEN	GL06	1400	26	A1
BELLECHASSE AV	CO	COV	4200	88	B4
BELLEFONT DR	CO	AZU	18000	88	E1
BELLEFNTAINE PL	PAS	PAS	800	26	E5
BELLEFNTAINE ST	PAS	PAS	100	26	E5
BELLEGLADE AV	LA	LA32		36	D6
BELLEMARE AV	TOR	TOR	19800	67	F2
BELLE PORTE AV	LA	HAC	25000	73	E3
BELLERIVE DR	SCLR	VAL		127	A2
BELLE RIVER DR	CO	LPUE		85	C4
BELLEVIEW AV	SAD	SAD	500	89	F2
BELLEVIEW AV	SAD	SAD	500	90	A2
BELLEVUE AV	LA	LA12	1100	44	D1
BELLEVUE AV	LA	LA26	1400	35	A5
BELLEVUE AV	LA	LA26	1200	44	C1

STREET	CITY	P.O. ZONE	BLOCK	PAGE	GRID
BELLEVUE AV	POM	POM	1300	94	B1
BELLEVUE DR	GLEN	GL01	2000	17	F5
BELLEVUE DR	GLEN	GL01	1900	18	A5
BELLEVUE DR E	PAS	PAS	100	27	A5
BELLEVUE DR W	PAS	PAS	100	26	F5
BELLEZE	LA	SP		78	C5
BELLFIELD WY	LA	LA68		23	E5
BELLFLOWER AV	LA	NHO	4400	23	E3
BELLFLOWER BLVD	BLF	BLF	13400	66	C3
BELLFLOWER BLVD	DOW	DOW	11400	60	C6
BELLFLOWER BLVD	DOW	DOW	12700	66	C3
BELLFLOWER BLVD	LB	LB08	3000	71	C6
BELLFLOWER BLVD	LB	LB14	300	76	C5
BELLFLOWER BLVD	LB	LB15	1700	76	C2
BELLFLOWER BLVD	LKD	LKD	4100	71	C2
BELLFORD AV	CO	PAS	1600	20	D6
BELLFORD AV	CO	PAS	1300	27	D1
BELL GARDEN AV	BG	BELL	7700	59	E1
BELLGAVE PL	LA	LA69		33	E3
BELLGREEN ST	BAP	BAP	13900	39	D5
BELL GROVE ST	CO	LAV	700	90	B2
BELL GROVE ST	SAD	SAD	600	90	A2
BELLINGER ST	LYN	LYN	10900	58	F5
BELLINGHAM AV	LA	NHO	5600	16	C4
BELLINGHAM AV	LA	NHO	4100	23	C2
BELLINI DR	CO	TOP		13	D5
BELLINI WY	PALM	PALM		171	F5
BELLINO DR	LA	PP		40	A3
BELLIS DR	SCLR	VAL		127	A1
BELL-LYN LN	LB	LB05		65	C4
BELLMAN AV	DOW	DOW	10200	60	C3
BELLMARIN DR	LA	SP	300	78	E3
BELLMORE WY	PAS	PAS	300	26	E3
BELLORITA ST	CO	LPUE	18200	98	D5
BELLOTA AV	PAR	PAR	15100	66	A3
BELLOTA WY	LA	LA27		35	B2
BELLOWS CT	DBAR	POM		94	B6
BELL RANCH DR	SFS	SFS		61	C3
BELLWOOD AV	LA	LA64	10200	42	A3
BELLWOOD RD	SMAR	PAS	1300	27	E6
BELMAR AV	LA	NOR	9700	7	A4
BELMAR AV	LA	RES	6200	14	A4
BELMART AV	NWK	NWK		82	B2
BELMONT AV	LA	LA26	100	44	C1
BELMONT AV	LB	LB03	100	76	A2
BELMONT AV	LB	LB04	700	76	A2
BELMONT AV	LB	LB15	2100	76	A2
BELMONT AV	PAS	PAS	1600	19	F6
BELMONT AV	WCOV	WCOV	1100	48	F3
BELMONT CT	AGH	AGO		102	E2
BELMONT LN	RB	RB	1700	62	E6
BELMONT PL	CER	ART		81	C2
BELMONT CT	CO	VAL		124	A6
BELMONT ST	BLF	BLF	8700	66	B4
BELMONT ST	PR	PR		47	B6
BELMONT ST	PR	PR		55	B1
BELMONT ST N	GLEN	GL06	100	25	D4
BELMONT ST S	GLEN	GL05	100	25	D4
BELMNT ABBEY LN	CLA	CLA		96	D5
BELOIT AV	CLA	CLA	1300	91	C2
BELOIT AV	LA	CUL	4700	50	B3
BELOIT AV	LA	LA25	1500	41	D3
BELOIT AV	LA	LA49	100	41	C1
BELRIDGE CT	WAL	WAL		93	B5
BELSHAW AV	CAR	CAR	19000	69	C1
BELSHIRE AV	ART	ART	18700	81	B1
BELSHIRE AV	ART	ART	17400	82	B6
BELSHIRE AV	CER	ART	18900	81	B1
BELSHIRE AV	CER	ART	17300	82	B6
BELSHIRE AV	HG	LKD	21400	81	B4
BELSHIRE AV	LKD	LKD	20300	81	B3
BELSHIRE AV	NWK	NWK	15500	82	B3
BELSIZE PL	AGH	AGO		102	D2
BELSON ST	CO	TOR	700	68	F6
BELTON DR	LA	LA45	7900	50	A6
BELTON DR	LA	LA45	7900	56	A1
BELVEDERE CT	CER	ART		66	F5
BELVIDERE ST	PAS	PAS	600	27	B2
BELVOIR AV	LA	TU		11	B5
BEMIS ST	LA	LA39	4000	25	B5
BEN AV	LA	NHO	5700	16	C5
BEN AV	LA	NHO	4200	23	C3
BEN CT	SCLR	SAU		124	F3
BENA CT	SCLR	SAU		124	F5
BENALD AV	LAN	LAN	44200	160	D5
BEN ALDER AV	CO	WHI	5700	55	B3
BEN ALDER AV	WHI	WHI	5300	55	C2
BENARES PL	LA	SV		17	A1
BENARES ST	DOW	DOW	7100	59	F3
BEN AVON CT	SAD	SAD		89	D3
BENAVON ST	CO	WHI	10400	55	A6
BENBOW ST	BAP	BAP	13400	39	D4
BENBOW ST	CO	COV	16200	88	B4
BENBOW ST	CO	COV	19600	89	C4
BENBOW ST	COV	COV	100	88	E4
BENBOW ST	COV	COV	700	89	A4

STREET	CITY	P.O. ZONE	BLOCK	PAGE	GRID
BENBOW ST	SAD	SAD	900	89	E4
BENBROOK DR	CO	LPUE	13600	48	B4
BENCAMP ST E	SGAB	SGAB	100	37	D5
BENCAMP ST W	SGAB	SGAB	100	37	D5
BENCH ST	CO	LPUE		98	F2
BENCHLEY CT	WLVL	THO	31900	102	A4
BENCOLA CT	WCOV	WCOV	900	92	B2
BEND DR	LA	LA65		35	F2
BENDA PL	LA	LA68	3200	24	B6
BENDA ST	LA	LA68	3200	24	B6
BENDER AV	CO	COV	3600	89	A5
BENDER AV	COV	COV	100	89	A5
BENDER AV N	GLDR	GLDR	300	87	A5
BENDER AV S	GLDR	GLDR	700	87	A6
BENDER AV S	GLDR	GLDR		89	A1
BENDIGO DR	RPV	PVP	3500	78	B3
BENECIA AV	LA	LA25	1800	42	A2
BENECIA AV	LA	LA64	2200	42	A2
BENEDA LN	SCLR	CYN	17800	125	A8
BENEDICT AV	CLA	CLA	2000	91	C2
BENEDICT AV	DOW	DOW	12300	60	C6
BENEDICT CT	CO	PALM		184	E2
BENEDICT ST	LA	LA39	2700	35	D3
BENEDICT WY	HPK	HPK		53	B5
BENEDICT WY	POM	POM	1700	91	B6
BENEDICT CYN DR	BH	BH	900	33	A5
BENEDICT CYN DR	LA	BH	2600	22	E6
BENEDICT CYN DR	LA	BH	1300	32	F1
BENEDICT CYN DR	LA	VAN	3800	22	E5
BENEDICT CYN LN	LA	VAN		22	F4
BENEFIT ST	LA	VAN	14400	22	D3
BENFIELD AV	CER	ART	19000	71	E2
BENFIELD AV	DOW	DOW	10800	60	E5
BENFIELD AV	NWK	NWK	11200	60	E5
BENFIELD AV	NWK	NWK	12800	66	E1
BENFIELD PL	DBAR	POM		97A	B1
BENGAL CT	PALM	PALM		171	J8
BENHAM AV	BAP	BAP	4000	39	D3
BENHILL AV	LOM	LOM	24000	73	D1
BEN HUR AV	CO	WHI	9600	61	F3
BEN HUR AV	WHI	WHI	6800	84	A2
BENICIA RD	DBAR	POM	100	94	A6
BENIK PL	WAL	WAL	21000	93	D5
BENIK RD	LHH	LAH	1600	98A	B2
BENITO AV	ALH	ALH	900	37	B6
BENITO CT	SCLR	VAL		124	A1
BENJAMIN AV	LA	LA45	5300	56	E1
BENKERDT RD	CO	TOP		13	D5
BEN LOMOND DR	GLEN	GL02	1600	18	B6
BEN LOMOND DR	GLEN	GL02	1500	25	B1
BEN LOMOND DR	LA	LA27	2200	35	A2
BEN LOMOND PL	LA	LA27		35	A2
BENMORE ST	LB	LB15	6000	76	D1
BENMORE TER	LA	LA49		41	B1
BENNER AV	TOR	TOR	22400	68	B5
BENNER CT	TOR	TOR	23000	68	B6
BENNER PL	LA	ENC	17200	21	E3
BENNER ST	LA	LA42	5600	36	C2
BENNETT AV	CO	GLDR	19000	86	F5
BENNETT AV	LB	LB03	100	76	A6
BENNETT AV	LB	LB04	700	76	B6
BENNETT AV E	GLDR	GLDR	100	87	A5
BENNETT AV W	GLDR	GLDR	100	87	A5
BENNETT DR	LA	LA68	3200	24	A6
BENNETT DR	PAS	PAS	1200	26	D2
BENNETT PL	CLA	CLA		96	C6
BENNETT ST	CO	COM	3700	65	A4
BENNETT ST E	COM	COM	100	64	F4
BENNETT ST E	COM	COM	200	65	A4
BENNETT ST W	COM	COM	100	64	E4
BEN NEVIS AV	NWK	NWK	13200	82	C1
BENNINGTON AV	PR	PR	7100	54	F6
BENNINGTON AV	PR	PR	7800	60	F1
BENNINGTON CT	CER	ART		66	F5
BENNINGTON DR	CO	VAL		124	A7
BENOWE SCOTI RD	GLEN	GL07	600	25	D1
BENRUD ST	CO	DUA		39	B1
BENRUD ST	CO	MON	200	39	B1
BENSON ST	HPK	HPK	6200	53	A5
BENSON WY	SOG	SOG	9200	59	D3
BENT ST	SOG	SOG	8600	59	C2
BENTEL AV	LA	LA49	300	41	A3
BENTEL AV	RM	RM	8900	38	A5
BENTGRASS WY	SCLR	SAU		124	E8
BENTLEY AV	COM	COM		64	F4
BENTLEY AV	CUL	CUL	3800	50	A1
BENTLEY AV N	LA	LA49	100	32	D6
BENTLEY AV S	LA	LA25	1400	41	E3
BENTLEY AV S	LA	LA34	3300	42	A6
BENTLEY AV S	LA	LA34	3600	50	A1
BENTLEY AV S	LA	LA49	100	32	D6
BENTLEY AV S	LA	LA49	300	41	D1
BENTLEY AV S	LA	LA64	2200	41	F5
BENTLEY CIR	LA	LA49		32	D6
BENTLEY CT	SAD	SAD	1400	89	D3
BENTLEY CT	SM	SM	3000	49	B2

STREET	CITY	P.O. ZONE	BLOCK	PAGE	GRID
BENTLEY CT	WCOV	WCOV		92	E4
BENTLEY PL	CER	ART		82	E4
BENTLEY PL	GLDR	GLDR	1600	89	B2
BENTLEY WY	CER	ART		82	E4
BENT OAK RD	DBAR	POM		97	F3
BENTON AV	LAV	LAV		90	C2
BENTON CT	CO	VAL		124	B7
BENTON WY N	LA	LA26	100	35	B6
BENTON WY S	LA	LA57	100	44	A1
BENTONGROVE DR	CO	WHI	13600	61	D3
BENTREE AV	LB	LB07	4500	70	D3
BENTREE CIR	LB	LB07	5000	70	D2
BENT SPUR DR	CO	ACT	2500	189	G4
BENT TWIG LN	DBAR	POM		97	D6
BENVENUE ST	LA	LA49	12900	41	A4
BENWELL DR	LYN	LYN	11000	59	B5
BENWICK ST	CO	LPUE	16200	92	B4
BENWOOD ST	BAP	BAP	14000	39	D3
BENWOOD ST	CO	COV	16200	88	B3
BENWOOD ST	CO	SAD	1800	89	C4
BENWOOD ST	SAD	SAD	900	89	E4
BENWOOD ST E	COV	COV	100	88	E4
BENWOOD ST E	COV	COV		89	C4
BENWOOD ST W	COV	COV	900	88	D3
BENZ RD	SCLR	SAU		124	F4
BENZING TR	CO	TOP	20200	109	D6
BEQUETTE AV	PR	PR	6300	54	F4
BEQUETTE ST	PR	PR	7800	54	E6
BERAN ST	TOR	TOR	4900	67	E5
BERAULT CT	SCLR	VAL		127	A1
BERCLAIR LN	LA	TAR		21	A3
BERDON ST	LA	WOH	20600	13	D1
BERDON ST	LA	WOH	23300	100	F1
BEREA CT	CLA	CLA	1400	91	C2
BEREA PL	LA	PP	1300	40	D3
BERENDO AV	CO	HAC	24300	73	F2
BERENDO AV	LA	LA44	11100	57	F6
BERENDO AV	CO	TOR	20400	68	F3
BERENDO AV	GAR	GAR	12900	63	F1
BERENDO ST	CO	ALT	2100	20	D6
BERENDO ST N	LA	LA04	100	34	F6
BERENDO ST N	LA	LA27	1300	34	F4
BERENDO ST N	LA	LA29	700	34	F5
BERENDO ST S	LA	LA04	100	43	F1
BERENDO ST S	LA	LA05	600	43	F2
BERENDO ST S	LA	LA06	900	43	F4
BERENDO ST S	LA	LA20	300	43	F1
BERENICE AV	LA	LA31	3800	36	B4
BERENICE PL	LA	LA31	3700	36	B4
BERESFORD RD	LA	VN23		22	E5
BERESFORD WY	LCF	LCF	4200	19	B4
BERG ST	LA	SF	13100	2	E3
BERG ST	LA	SF	13400	3	A1
BERGAMO DR	LA	ENC	4300	22	A3
BERGAMO PL	LA	ENC	16200	22	B3
BERGEN AV	BLF	BLF	13800	66	D2
BERGER PL	LA	PDR	8000	55A	F1
BERGLUND DR	WCOV	WCOV		92	D4
BERGMAN LN	DOW	DOW	8000	60	A4
BERGSTROM PL	LA	SF	14100	2	E2
BERIA ST	LA	NOR		7	C1
BERINO DR	SCLR	SAU	26300	124	D7
BERKEBILE CT	MPK	MPK		46	D3
BERKELEY AV	CO	PAS		27	D5
BERKELEY AV	LA	LA26	1800	35	C5
BERKELEY AV	POM	POM		90	E5
BERKELEY AV N	CLA	CLA	100	91	B3
BERKELEY AV N	PAS	PAS	100	27	D4
BERKELEY AV S	CLA	CLA	100	91	B4
BERKELEY AV S	PAS	PAS	100	27	D4
BERKELEY CIR	LA	LA26	3000	35	B4
BERKELEY CT	LAN	LAN		159	D3
BERKELEY CT	NWK	NWK		66	E1
BERKELEY CT	SM	SM		41	C4
BERKELEY DR	GLEN	GL05	1100	25	E6
BERKELEY DR	LA	VEN	1000	49	D4
BERKELEY SQ	LA	LA18	1	43	D4
BERKELEY ST	SM	SM	800	41	B4
BERKHAMSTED ST	CER	ART	12800	81	C1
BERKSHIRE AV	LA	LA32	4300	36	F3
BERKSHIRE AV	LCF	LCF	200	19	C4
BERKSHIRE AV	SPAS	SPAS	2000	36	F3
BERKSHIRE CT	SAD	SAD		89	D4
BERKSHIRE DR	LA	LA32	3500	36	F3
BERKSHIRE DR	PALM	PALM		171	J6
BERKSHIRE PL	LCF	LCF	200	19	C4
BERKSHIRE RD	PR	PR		47	A6
BERKSHIRE RD	PR	PR		55	A1
BERKSHIRE WY	ING	IN01		57	B2
BERKSHIRE WY	POM	POM	1900	90	E5
BERMAX AV	LA	SF	13900	2	F1
BERMEJO ST	CO	CYN		125	C4
BERMITE RD	SCLR	SAU		127	D1
BERMUDA CT	MB	MB		62	D3
BERMUDA ST	CER	ART	11000	66	E5
BERMUDA ST	LA	CHA	20300	6	E2

STREET	CITY	P.O. ZONE	BLOCK	PAGE	GRID
BERMUDA ST	LA	CHA	19600	7	A2
BERMUDA ST	LA	NOR	18000	7	C2
BERMUDA ST	LA	SF	16600	7	F2
BERMUDA ST	LA	SF	15800	8	B2
BERMUDA ST	LB	LB02	1900	75	E5
BERMUDA ST	LB	LB14	2000	75	E5
BERMUDA VIEW DR	CO	WHI		55	D2
BERMUDEZ ST	PR	PR	9000	54	E6
BERN PL	LA	PP		40	B4
BERNADETTE CT	WCOV	WCOV		92	F6
BERNADETTE CT	WCOV	WCOV		98	F1
BERNADETTE ST	LA	PAC	12400	9	B2
BERNADETTE ST	WCOV	WCOV		98	F1
BERNADINE AV	LA	CAN	7200	5	F3
BERNAL AV N	LA	LA63	400	45	C4
BERNAL AV S	LA	LA23	700	45	B5
BERNAL AV S	LA	LA63	400	45	B5
BERNARD AV	LA	VEN	200	49	B3
BERNARD ST	LA	LA12	400	44	E1
BERNARDIN DR	PALM	PALM		183	G2
BERNARDINO AV	CO	WHI	10200	55	B3
BERNARDO CIR	DUA	DUA		86	A4
BERNARDO RD	CUL	CUL	10800	50	D3
BERNAU AV	CLA	CLA	800	91	A6
BERNE ST	CO	RM	7300	46	D3
BERNER ST	LB	LB08	7800	81	A6
BERNETTA PL	LA	TAR	19200	21	A2
BERNICE DR	RPV	SP	29500	78	E2
BERNICE PL	TOR	TOR	21700	67	E4
BERNINA AV	SCLR	CYN	27500	124	J8
BERNIST AV	TOR	TOR	19800	67	F2
BERNWOOD ST	DUA	DUA	2600	29	F4
BERQUIST AV	LA	CAN	6400	5	F5
BERQUIST AV	LA	WOH	6100	5	F5
BERRIAN ST	CLA	CLA	400	90	F2
BERRIAN ST	POM	POM	300	90	F2
BERRY AV	MON	MON	900	29	C4
BERRY CT	LA	NHO	3800	23	D5
BERRY DR	LA	NHO	3200	23	D5
BERRY HILL DR	RPV	PVP	7100	72	B6
BERRY HILL DR	RPV	PVP	7100	77	B1
BERRYMAN AV	CUL	CUL	4000	50	C3
BERRYMAN AV	LA	CUL	4400	50	B3
BERRYMAN AV	LA	LA66	3700	49	F1
BERRYMAN AV	LA	LA66	3800	50	A2
BERRYWOOD WY	LAN	LAN		159	G8
BERSA ST	PAS	PAS	2500	27	E3
BERT ST E	PR	PR	9400	54	F5
BERTELLA DR	LA	ENC	16200	22	A3
BERTHA PL	CER	ART	11200	71	F2
BERTHA ST	CER	ART	11300	71	F2
BERTHA ST	CER	ART	11800	81	A2
BERTHA ST	LA	LA42	6200	36	C2
BERTRAND AV	LA	ENC	5700	14	D6
BERTRAND AV	LA	NOR	9000	7	D6
BERTRAND AV	LA	RES	6300	14	D4
BERTRAND AV	LA	SF	11200	7	D1
BERTRAND DR	AGH	AGO		102	F2
BERWICK DR	LCF	LCF	3600	19	B6
BERWICK PL	CO	VAL		124	B7
BERWICK ST	LA	LA49	11300	41	C1
BERWYN RD	CER	ART		82	E4
BERYL CT	PALM	PALM		173	A9
BERYL ST	LA	LA32	2800	36	C5
BERYL ST	RB	RB	1	67	D2
BERZERVILLE AV	LA	NHO		16	A3
BESS AV	BAP	BAP	12600	48	B1
BESS ST	CO	LPUE	13700	48	D2
BESSEMER ST	LA	ENC	17600	14	D5
BESSEMER ST	LA	NHO	11300	16	B6
BESSEMER ST	LA	RES	17700	14	D5
BESSEMER ST	LA	VAN	13400	15	E5
BESSEMER ST	LA	WOH	23200	5	F6
BESSEMER ST	LA	WOH	22400	12	B5
BESSIE AV	ELM	ELM	9900	38	C5
BEST AV	SFS	SFS	14300	82	D2
BESTOR BLVD	LA	PP	14600	40	D3
BESWICK ST	LA	LA23	3300	45	B6
BETA AV	BLF	BLF	15900	66	B4
BETH PL	GLEN	GL14	4200	11	C6
BETH PL	LA	BH	9700	33	A2
BETH ST	LB	LB05		65	D4
BETHANY CIR	CLA	CLA		91	C1
BETHANY RD	BUR	BUR	200	17	D4
BETHEL CT	CLA	CLA		91	C1
BETLEY ST	CO	LPUE	18900	98	F4
BETSY ST	WCOV	WCOV		92	E6
BETSY ROSS RD	PALM	PALM		183	D2
BETTENCOURT ST	CER	ART	13800	82	E5
BETTON DR	CO	TOP		115	B2
BETTY AV	CER	ART	16700	82	D5
BETTY AV	CO	LA22	400	45	E5
BETTY DR	LA	LA32	3200	36	C5
BETTY LN	LA	BH	2200	33	B1
BETTY PL	CER	ART	16300	82	D4

1990 LOS ANGELES COUNTY STREET INDEX

STREET	CITY	P.O. ZONE	BLOCK	PAGE	GRID
BETTY PL	LA	LA42	5700	26	C6
BETTY WY	CER	ART	18400	82	D6
BETTY WY	WHOL	LA69	8800	33	D4
BETTYHILL AV	DUA	DUA	200	86	A4
BETTY JEAN AV	BLF	BLF	14700	66	B2
BETTY LOU LN	LA	TU	10100	10	E2
BEULAH AV	CO	LA63	1000	45	D3
BEULAH CIR	CO	LA63	1000	45	D3
BEULAH DR	LCF	LCF	4200	19	B4
BEULAH ST	GLEN	GL02		25	B2
BEUVILLE AV	ELM	ELM	3600	38	C6
BEVAN ST	CO	SGAB	8200	37	F2
BEVERLY AV	SM	SM	2400	49	B2
BEVERLY BLVD	BH	BH	9100	33	C5
BEVERLY BLVD	CO	LA22	5000	45	F5
BEVERLY BLVD	CO	LA22	5300	46	A5
BEVERLY BLVD	CO	WHI	10100	55	B2
BEVERLY BLVD	LA	LA04	3400	34	A6
BEVERLY BLVD	LA	LA04	3300	35	A6
BEVERLY BLVD	LA	LA26	1400	44	A1
BEVERLY BLVD	LA	LA36	7600	33	C5
BEVERLY BLVD	LA	LA36	6700	34	A6
BEVERLY BLVD	LA	LA48	7900	33	C5
BEVERLY BLVD	LA	LA57	1800	44	A1
BEVERLY BLVD	PR	PR	8300	54	D1
BEVERLY BLVD	PR	PR	8800	55	B2
BEVERLY BLVD	WHI	WHI	10300	55	D3
BEVERLY BLVD	WHOL	LA69	8700	33	C5
BEVERLY BLVD E	MTB	MTB	100	54	D1
BEVERLY BLVD W	MTB	MTB	1500	46	B6
BEVERLY BLVD W	MTB	MTB	100	54	D1
BEVERLY CT	LA	LA49	100	41	C1
BEVERLY CT	LAN	LAN		160	C6
BEVERLY DR	ARC	ARC	600	38	F2
BEVERLY DR	CO	PAS	1600	27	D1
BEVERLY DR	CO	SGAB	8200	37	F2
BEVERLY DR	LA	BH		23	A6
BEVERLY DR	WAL	WAL		92	F6
BEVERLY DR	WAL	WAL		93	A6
BEVERLY DR	WAL	WAL		97	A1
BEVERLY DR	WAL	WAL		98	F1
BEVERLY DR	WHI	WHI	10800	55	D3
BEVERLY DR N	BH	BH	200	33	B5
BEVERLY DR N	BH	BH	200	42	C1
BEVERLY DR N	LA	BH	1300	33	A2
BEVERLY DR S	BH	BH	100	42	C1
BEVERLY DR S	LA	LA34	2000	42	C3
BEVERLY DR S	LA	LA35	1100	42	C3
BEVERLY PL	LA	BH	1900	33	B2
BEVERLY PL	LA	LA48	8500	33	D6
BEVERLY PL	WHOL	LA48	8500	35	D6
BEVERLY PZ	LB	LB15	1900	76	B3
BEVERLY RD	PR	PR	8500	54	F1
BEVERLY RD	PR	PR	8800	55	B2
BEVERLY ST	BLF	BLF	9400	66	B5
BEVERLY TER	MTB	MTB	200	54	D1
BEVERLY WY	CO	ALT	900	20	B5
BEVERLY WY	LB	LB02	1800	75	E5
BEVERLYCREST DR	LA	BH	9300	33	B3
BEVERLY ESTS DR	LA	BH	1200	32	F4
BEVRLY ESTS TER	LA	BH	1200	32	F4
BEVERLY GLEN BL	LA	LA77	2700	22	D5
BEVERLY GLEN BL	LA	VAN	3300	22	D5
BEVERLY GN BL N	LA	LA77	100	32	E4
BEVERLY GN BL S	LA	LA24	800	41	F1
BEVERLY GN BL S	LA	LA25	1800	42	A2
BEVERLY GN BL S	LA	LA64	2200	42	A2
BEVERLY GN BL S	LA	LA77	100	32	E4
BEVERLY GN CIR	LA	LA77		22	E6
BEVERLY GLEN PL	LA	LA77	2100	32	E2
BEVERLY GRN DR	LA	LA35	1200	42	B2
BEVERLY GRN DR	LA	LA35	1200	42	E2
BEVERLY GRV DR	LA	BH	9900	32	F4
BEVERLY GRV DR	LA	BH	9800	33	A4
BEVERLY GRV PL	LA	BH	1300	32	F3
BEVERLY GRV PL	LA	BH	1300	33	A3
BEVERLY PARK	LA	BH		23	A6
BEVERLY PARK	LA	BH		33	A2
BEVERLY PK CIR	LA	BH		33	A1
BEVERLY PARK CT	LA	BH		23	A6
BEVERLY PARK CT	LA	BH		33	A1
BEVERLY PARK DR	LA	LA49	500	32	C6
BEVERLY PARK LN	LA	BH		23	A6
BEVERLY PARK LN	LA	BH		33	A1
BEVERLY PARK PL	PR	PR	8500	54	F1
BEVERLY PK TER	LA	BH		33	A2
BEVERLY PARK WY	LA	BH		33	A1
BEVERLY RDG DR	LA	VAN	3500	22	D5
BEVERLY VIEW DR	LA	BH	1200	32	F4
BEVERLY VIEW PL	LA	BH		32	F4
BEVERLYWOOD ST	LA	LA34	8500	42	C4
BEVERLYWOOD ST	LA	LA64	9800	42	C4
BEVERWIL DR	BH	BH	400	42	C3
BEVERWIL DR	LA	LA34	2100	42	C3
BEVERWIL DR	LA	LA35	1100	42	C3
BEVINGTON AV	LAN	LAN		160	E4

STREET	CITY	P.O. ZONE	BLOCK	PAGE	GRID
BEVIS AV	LA	SF	9900	8	D3
BEVIS AV	LA	VAN	5600	15	D4
BEVIS AV	LA	VAN	5300	22	D1
BEVON PL	LA	TU	9500	11	A5
BEWLEY AV	CMRC	LA40	2400	53	E2
BEXLEY DR	PR	PR	8800	54	F3
BEXLEY DR	PR	PR	9300	55	A4
BEXLEY DR E	CO	WHI	10400	55	B4
BIAK CT	TOR	TOR	22500	67	F5
BIANCA AV	CO	PALM		183	A1
BIANCA AV	LA	ENC	5800	14	E6
BIANCA AV	LA	ENC	5100	21	E2
BIANCA AV	LA	NOR	9300	7	E3
BIANCA AV	LA	NOR	8100	14	E1
BIANCA AV	LA	SF	11500	1	E6
BIANCA AV	LA	SF	10500	7	E2
BIANCA AV	LA	VAN	6800	14	E4
BIANCA ST	LAV	LAV		90	C2
BIARRITZ	POM	POM		90	B6
BIARRITZ AV	PALM	PALM		171	C5
BIASTRE RD	CO	MAL	32200	105	D5
BICE DR	CO	TOP		115	C1
BICENTENNIAL PK	PR	PR		47	D6
BICKETT ST	HPK	HPK	3500	53	A4
BICKETT ST	VER	LA58	5400	53	A4
BICKFORD DR	CO	WAL		97	B4
BICKLEY DR	COV	COV	700	89	A3
BICKNELL ST	SM	SM	1	49	A2
BIDWELL ST	TEC	TEC	9100	38	B3
BIELEC LN	IND	LPUE	100	48	B3
BIENVENEDA AV	LA	PP	500	40	B3
BIENVENEDA PL	LA	PP		40	B2
BIG BEND AV	LA	SUN	10700	10	D2
BIGBRIAR WY	LCF	LCF	800	19	B1
BIGBY AV	DOW	DOW	8300	60	C3
BIGBY ST	DOW	DOW	8500	60	C3
BIG CANYON PL	LA	SP	1200	78	E3
BIG CREEK LN	WAL	WAL		93	B5
BIG DALTON AV	BAP	BAP	3300	39	E6
BIG DALTON AV	BAP	BAP	1600	48	D1
BIG DALTON AV	CO	LPUE	200	48	D2
BIG DALTN CY RD	CO	GLDR		87	D3
BIGELOW CIR	CER	ART	11000	71	E1
BIGELOW RD	TOR	TOR		73	B3
BIGELOW ST	CER	ART	13000	81	D1
BIGELOW ST	CER	ART	13000	81	D1
BIGELOW ST	LKD	LKD	5200	71	D1
BIG FALLS DR	DBAR	POM		93	F5
BIG FIR LN	GLDR	GLDR		87	E5
BIGGY ST	LA	LA33	1300	45	B2
BIG HORN LN	WAL	WAL		93	B5
BIGLAKE AV E	CO	LAN	17100	175	B5
BIGLER ST	LA	WOH	23000	13	A2
BIGLER ST	LA	WOH	23000	100	F2
BIG OAK DR	LA	NHO	3900	23	D5
BIG ROCK DR	CO	MAL	20000	115	A4
BIG ROCK MTWY	CO	MAL	2000	115	A3
BIG ROCK TR	LA	CAN	8500	4	A6
BIG ROCK LATERL	CO	MAL		114	F3
BIG SKY DR	CO	VALY		192	G9
BIG SKY TER	PALM	PALM		172	A9
BIG SPRINGS RD	CO	SAU		188	G1
BIGSTONE PL	WLVL	THO		102A	E5
BIG TJNGA CY RD	LA	TU	11700	10	E1
BIG TJNGA TK TR	CO			M	B2
BIG VALLEY RD	CO	ALT		182	F5
BILBERRY AV	CO	TOP		115	A1
BILL CODY RD	HH	CAL	5500	100	C2
BILLINGS AV	CAR	CAR	18400	69	B1
BILLINGS DR	CAR	CAR	16900	64	B5
BILLINGS ST	COM	COM	2600	64	C4
BILLOW DR	SAD	SAD	500	89	E2
BILLOWVISTA DR	LA	VEN	8100	55A	E1
BILMOOR AV	LA	TAR	4900	21	A2
BILMOOR PL	LA	TAR	19400	21	A2
BILOXI AV	LA	NHO	4500	23	F1
BILSON ST	CAR	CAR	100	64	B6
BILTMORE AV	LA	SF	11600	3	E6
BILTON WY	SGAB	SGAB	700	37	E4
BIMINI AV	CER	ART		66	E5
BIMINI PL	LA	LA04	100	34	F6
BINA CT	SPAS	SPAS		36	E2
BIND CT	CO	WAL		97	C4
BINDER PL	ELS	ELS	500	56	A6
BINDEWALD RD	TOR	TOR	9600	67	E6
BINFORD ST	ING	IN01	100	57	E4
BING CT	CO	LPUE		97	B4
BINGHAM ST	ART	ART	12200	81	B2
BINGHAM ST	CER	ART	11000	71	E2
BINGHAM ST	CER	ART	11500	81	A2
BINKLEY DR	LA	LA46	1800	33	F3
BINNEY ST	CO	LPUE	14600	48	C6
BINNEY ST	CO	LPUE	15000	85	D1
BINNS AV	CO	LAN	43600	158	A6
BINTON LN	RPV	PVP		72	D5
BIOLA AV	LAM	LAM	14300	82	F1

STREET	CITY	P.O. ZONE	BLOCK	PAGE	GRID
BIOLA AV	LAM	LAM	13000	83	A1
BIOLA AV	LAM	LAM	12600	84	A6
BION AV	CO	SGAB	6200	37	F2
BIONA CT	LB	LB02		75	C6
BIONA DR	LA	LA66	11300	50	A2
BIRCH AV	ELM	ELM	4900	38	F4
BIRCH AV	GLEN	GL01	1400	17	F5
BIRCH AV	HAW	HAW	11400	57	A5
BIRCH CT	LA	LA21		44	D5
BIRCH LN	PAS	PAS		26	F2
BIRCH ST	ALH	ALH	2400	36	F3
BIRCH ST	LA	LA21	800	44	D5
BIRCH ST	LYN	LYN	11100	59	B5
BIRCH ST	MTB	MTB	14100	54	D5
BIRCH WY	CO	LPUE		98	E3
BIRCHBARK AV	DOW	DOW	8800	60	C2
BIRCHBARK AV	PR	PR	8200	54	D6
BIRCHBARK AV	PR	PR	8300	60	D1
BIRCHCREST RD	DOW	DOW	7800	54	D6
BIRCHCREST RD	DOW	DOW	8000	60	D1
BIRCHCROFT ST	ARC	ARC	100	38	E2
BIRCHCROFT ST	CO	ARC	1000	39	A2
BIRCHDALE AV	DOW	DOW	9500	60	B5
BIRCHER ST	LA	SF	16400	1	F6
BIRCHER ST	LA	SF	16200	2	A6
BIRCHFIELD AV	RPV	PVP	26100	72	E3
BIRCH GLEN CIR	SCLR	VAL		124	B4
BIRCH HILL DR	DBAR	POM	21000	97	E4
BIRCHLAND PL	TEC	TEC	4800	38	D4
BIRCHLEAF AV	DOW	DOW	8600	60	D1
BIRCHLEAF AV	PR	PR	6600	54	E4
BIRCHLEAF AV	PR	PR	8200	60	D1
BIRCHLEAF ST	PR	PR	8800	54	D6
BIRCH LOG WY	CO	LPUE		98	A4
BIRCHMAN DR	RPV	PVP	6600	72	C4
BIRCHMONT DR	RPV	PVP	5800	72	D3
BIRCHNELL AV	SAD	SAD		87	E6
BIRCHNELL AV	SAD	SAD	1100	89	E1
BIRCHTON AV	LA	CAN	6500	5	E4
BIRCHTREE AV	LAN	LAN	43600	160	A6
BIRCH TREE LN	PALM	PALM		172	E9
BIRCH TREE LN	PALM	PALM		183	C5
BIRCH TREE LN	PALM	PALM		183	E1
BIRCHWOOD DR	LA	LA24	800	41	E2
BIRCHWOOD ST	LAM	LAM		83	C1
BIRD RD	LA	LA41	4500	26	A6
BIRD ST	LA	LA33	2100	45	A3
BIRD WY	LB	LB02	900	75	D5
BIRDELLA RD	CO	MAL		106	B4
BIRDIE DR	LAV	LAV		95A	D5
BIRDS EYE DR	DBAR	POM		97	E2
BIRDSONG RD	SCLR	SAU		124	J3
BIRDVALE DR	DOW	DOW	9100	66	B1
BIRDVIEW AV	CO	MAL	6800	110	B5
BIRKDALE	ELM	ELM		48	A6
BIRKDALE ST	LA	LA31	2300	35	E4
BIRKDALE ST	LB	LB15	6100	76	D1
BIRKHALL AV	BLF	BLF	13600	66	B2
BIRMINGHAM PL	SCLR	SAU		127	D1
BIRMINGHAM RD	BUR	BUR	200	17	D4
BISBEE PL	LAN	LAN		160	E6
BISBY ST	CO	ELM	10400	38	D6
BISBY ST	ELM	ELM		38	D5
BISBY ST	TEC	TEC	9500	38	C4
BISCAILUZ DR	CO	CAST		123	E4
BISCAY WY	POM	POM	1500	94	E4
BISHOP LN	SAD	SAD		89	D4
BISHOP PL	CLA	CLA		91	C2
BISHOP RD	TOR	TOR	4900	67	F2
BISHOP WY	RM	RM		47	A1
BISHOPS RD	LA	LA12		35	E6
BISHOPS RD	LA	LA12		44	E1
BISMARCK AV	LA	NOR	10700	7	A2
BISON CT	CO	MAL	28800	110	C5
BISSELL PL	HPK	HPK	6200	53	B5
BISSELL ST	BELL	BELL	6400	53	B5
BISSELL ST	HPK	HPK	6200	53	B5
BITHYNIA WY	CO	WAL	1800	97	B4
BITTER LAKE ST	CAR	CAR	900	64	C5
BITTERROOT RD	PALM	PALM		172	G8
BIXBY AV	BLF	BLF	16800	66	C5
BIXBY AV	LA	HAC	25600	73	F3
BIXBY AV	WCOV	WCOV	100	88	C6
BIXBY DR	IND	LPUE	900	98	A2
BIXBY DR	LAV	LAV		90	C1
BIXBY RD	LKD	LKD	2200	70	E5
BIXBY RD E	LB	LB07	100	70	C5
BIXBY RD W	LB	LB07	100	70	C5
BIXBY HILL RD	LB	LB15		76	D4
BIXBY TER DR	LB	LB15		76	E5
BIXBY VILLGE DR	LB	LB03		76	D5
BIXEL ST N	LA	LA26	100	44	C2
BIXEL ST S	LA	LA15	1000	44	C3
BIXEL ST S	LA	LA17	300	44	B3
BIXEL ST S	LA	LA26	100	44	C2
BIXLER AV	DOW	DOW	13400	66	A1

STREET	CITY	P.O. ZONE	BLOCK	PAGE	GRID
BIXLER AV	LKD	LKD	5100	70	F2
BIXLER AV	PAR	PAR	15300	65	F4
BIZET PL	LA	WOH	4700	13	A2
BLACKBERRY CT	PALM	PALM		171	H6
BLACKBIRD LN	LAV	LAV		95A	E5
BLACKBIRD LN	POM	POM		94	D6
BLACK BIRD WY	CO	CAL		13	A4
BLACKBRUSH DR	SCLR	CYN	17700	125	B8
BLACKBURN AV	LA	LA36	6100	43	A1
BLACKBURN AV	LA	LA48	7900	33	E6
BLACKBURN AV	NWK	NWK	15200	82	C3
BLACKBURN DR	LAM	LAM		83	D1
BLACKBURN ST	LAM	LAM		84	D6
BLACKR HOUSE CT	SCLR	VAL		124	E3
BLACK FOOT	CO	AGO		106	D3
BLACKFOOT CT	CO	CAST		123	E4
BLACKFORD AV	CO	WHI	7800	55	C6
BLACKFRIAR RD	LA	WOH	4500	13	A3
BLACKHAWK CT	PALM	PALM		171	D9
BLACK HAWK DR	DBAR	WAL		97	C3
BLACKHAWK ST	LA	CHA	20600	6	D3
BLACKHAWK ST	LA	NOR	18100	7	C3
BLACKHAWK ST	LA	SF	16500	7	F3
BLACKHAWK ST	LA	SF	14700	8	C3
BLACK HILLS DR	CLA	CLA	600	91	C2
BLACKHORSE DR	RPV	PVP	4800	72	E4
BLACKLEY ST	TEC	TEC	9100	38	E3
BLACKMORE DR	GLEN	GL06	2100	26	A4
BLACK OAK DR	LA	LA68	5400	34	E2
BLACK OAK DR	POM	POM		94	D6
BLACKPINE RD	CO	TOP		115	B1
BLACKRIDGE DR	CO	TOP		115	B1
BLACKROCK AV	LAV	LAV		90	B1
BLACKROCK CT	SAD	COV		89	D4
BLACKSHEAR AV	CO	LA22	200	46	A5
BLACKSMITH CIR	POM	POM		94	C5
BLACKSMITH DR	PALM	PALM		183	G3
BLK STALLION DR	CO	COV		93	C2
BLACKSTONE CT	LA	LA15	900	44	C4
BLACKSTONE RD	SMAR	PAS	1200	27	F6
BLACKTHORNE AV	LB	LB08	4200	71	B3
BLACKTHORNE AV	LKD	LKD	5900	66	B6
BLACKTHORNE AV	LKD	LKD	5400	71	B1
BLACKTON DR	CO	MAL		106	D6
BLACK WALNUT TR	LA	TU		11	B3
BLACKWELDER ST	CUL	CUL	5800	42	E5
BLACKWELDER ST	LA	LA16	5100	42	F5
BLACKWOOD ST	CO	LPUE	14100	48	D3
BLACKWOOD ST	CO	LPUE	15800	92	A4
BLACKWOOD ST	LPUE	LPUE	15500	48	F4
BLADEN ST	LA	NOR	19800	6	F6
BLADES ST	LA	LA63	700	45	C3
BLAINE AV	BLF	BLF	14500	66	C3
BLAINE ST	LA	LA15	900	44	B3
BLAIR AV	SPAS	SPAS	1200	36	D2
BLAIR CRES	LA	LA68	3300	24	A5
BLAIR DR	LA	LA68	3200	24	A5
BLAIR PL	AGH	AGO		100A	B5
BLAIR ST	RM	RM		38	A4
BLAIR WY	TOR	TOR		73	A2
BLAIRMOORE ST	LA	CHA		6	E2
BLAIRSTONE DR	CUL	CUL	5900	50	E1
BLAIRWOOD DR	LA	NHO	12900	23	A4
BLAISDELL AV	RB	RB	2800	62	F4
BLAISDELL DR	CLA	CLA	100	91	C2
BLAKE AV	LA	LA31	1000	35	D3
BLAKE AV	LA	LA39	1800	35	D3
BLAKE CT	CO	VAL		126	H2
BLAKE PL	GLEN	GL02		25	B2
BLAKE ST	PAS	PAS	400	26	F2
BLAKELY PL	CO	VAL		124	B6
BLAKEMAN AV	CO	LPUE	2600	98	E6
BLAKESLEE AV	LA	NHO	5200	23	E2
BLAKLEY AV	CO	COM	12500	58	D6
BLAKLEY AV	CO	LA59	12100	58	D6
BLAKLEY CT	POM	POM	1000	95	A1
BLANCA WY	SCLR	VAL		127	A2
BLANCHARD DR	GLEN	GL08	2300	18	C6
BLANCHARD PL	CLA	CLA	500	91	C4
BLANCHARD ST	CO	LA22	4300	45	C3
BLANCHARD ST	CO	LA63	3200	45	C3
BLANCHARD ST	LA	LA33	2700	45	B3
BLANCHARD ST	LA	LA63	3000	45	B3
BLANCHARD CY RD	LA	TU	6200	11	B3
BLANCHRD HLS LN	WHOL	LA69		33	D4
BLANCHE PL	LA	SF	16900	1	F4
BLANCHE RD	MB	MB	2100	62	B3
BLANCHE ST	CO	PAS	3700	28	B4
BLANCHE ST	PAS	PAS	100	27	C4
BLANCO AV	LA	WOH	5300	100	D1
BLANCO WY	CUL	CUL	5300	50	C3
BLAND PL	LOM	LOM	1900	73	D3
BLANDFORD DR	CO	LPUE	2600	98	E5
BLANDIN ST	LA	SF	15600	2	B3
BLANDING ST	CO	WHI	11400	55	B5
BLANDWOOD RD	DOW	DOW	7900	54	C6

STREET	CITY	P.O. ZONE	BLOCK	PAGE	GRID
BLANDWOOD RD	DOW	DOW	8000	60	C1
BLANE RD	CO	AGO		106	E1
BLANTYRE DR	LA	BH	9700	23	A6
BLAUVELT PL	LA	NOR		7	D6
BLAZE TR	DBAR	POM		97	F5
BLAZING STAR DR	CO	LPUE	1600	85	D2
BLAZING STAR ST	PALM	PALM		184	B6
BLEAKWOOD AV	CO	LA22		45	F5
BLEAKWOOD AV	MPK	MPK	100	45	F5
BLEDSOE AV	CUL	LA66	4000	50	A2
BLEDSOE AV	LA	LA66	3800	50	A2
BLEDSOE ST	LA	SF	14200	2	C3
BLEECKER ST	BAP	BAP	4800	39	F3
BLEEKER AV	CO	RM	8200	46	F3
BLEEKER ST	LA	SF	14700	2	D5
BLENARM DR	DBAR	WAL		97	C3
BLENBURY DR	DBAR	POM		97	E3
BLENDING RD	SCLR	SAU		127	E1
BLENEFIELD PL	DBAR	POM		94	B6
BLENEFIELD PL	DBAR	POM		97A	B1
BLENHEIM PL	LCF	LCF		19	C5
BLENHEIM ST	BAP	BAP	12600	39	B6
BLERIOT AV	LA	LA45	7800	50	C6
BLERIOT AV	LA	LA45	7900	56	C1
BLEWETT AV	LA	SF	8300	15	B1
BLEWETT AV	LA	VAN	6400	15	B3
BLEWETT ST	CO	RM	8000	46	F3
BLIMP ST	LA	LA39	2600	35	D3
BLINN AV	LA	WIL	1000	74	D4
BLISS CIR	CLA	CLA		91	C1
BLISS ST	CO	COM	1900	64	E1
BLISS CANYON RD	BRAD	DUA	100	29	D3
BLITHEDALE ST	LB	LB08	8300	81	C5
BLIX ST	LA	NHO	10600	23	E3
BLOCK PL	LA	LA32	2300	36	E6
BLODGETT AV	DOW	DOW	12200	60	B6
BLODGETT AV	DOW	DOW	13000	66	A1
BLOOM DR	MPK	MPK	200	46	C4
BLOOM ST	LA	LA12	100	44	E1
BLOOMDALE ST	DUA	DUA	900	29	F5
BLOOMFIELD AV	CER	ART	18500	81	C4
BLOOMFIELD AV	CER	ART	15900	82	C4
BLOOMFIELD AV	HG	LKD	21600	81	C4
BLOOMFIELD AV	LKD	LKD	20300	81	C4
BLOOMFIELD AV	NWK	NWK	12600	61	C6
BLOOMFIELD AV	NWK	NWK	12700	82	C4
BLOOMFIELD AV	SFS	SFS	9800	61	C6
BLOOMFIELD ST	LA	NHO	10400	23	E3
BLOOMFIELD ST	LA	VAN	13100	23	E3
BLOOMFIELD ST	LB	LB08		81	C5
BLOOMINGPARK ST	LAN	LAN	43000	159	H8
BLOOMINGTON AV	LA	BUR	7500	17	A3
BLOOMWOOD RD	LA	SP	800	78	E1
BLOOMWOOD RD	RPV	SP	1100	78	E1
BLOSSOM CT	PALM	PALM		171	J8
BLOSSOM CT	RB	RB	2100	67	E1
BLOSSOM DR	LAN	LAN		159	D9
BLOSSOM LN	LAV	LAV	2000	90	C3
BLOSSOM LN	RB	RB	1000	62	E6
BLOSSOM LN	RB	RB	500	67	E1
BLOSSOM ST	GLEN	GL01	1300	24	F2
BLOUNT PL	LYN	LYN	4500	65	C1
BLUCHER AV	LA	SF	11500	2	B6
BLUCHER AV	LA	SF	10300	8	B1
BLUCHER AV	LA	VAN	6200	15	B5
BLUCHER CT	LA	VAN	15400	15	B5
BLUE CIR	RM	RM	8600	37	F4
BLUE DR	WCOV	WCOV	900	92	B2
BLUE ANCHOR RD	CO	MAL		112	D5
BLUE ASH RD	WCOV	WCOV	800	92	B1
BLUEBELL AV	LA	NHO	6000	16	B3
BLUEBELL AV	LA	NHO	4200	23	B2
BLUEBELL CT	WAL	WAL		93	D4
BLUEBIRD AV	LA	LA69	1400	33	C3
BLUEBIRD DR	CO	CAL		100	F4
BLUEBIRD LN N	PALM	PALM		172	B5
BLUEBIRD RD	CO	GLDR		87	D4
BLUEBONNET ST	LPUE	LPUE		48	F6
BLUEBONNET ST	LPUE	LPUE		92	A6
BLUEBONNET ST	LPUE	LPUE	16100	98	A1
BLUE CANYON DR	LA	NHO		23	D5
BLUE CLOUD RD	CO	SAU		124	G2
BLUECREST LN	CO	WHI	11800	55	C5
BLUE CURL WY	SCLR	CYN		124	E8
BLUE DANE LN	CO	MAL		113	E5
BLUEFIELD AV	CO	WHI	10400	55	B4
BLUEFIELD AV	LAM	LAM	12800	83	B1
BLUEFIELD AV	LAM	LAM	11900	84	A6
BLUEFIELD DR	CLA	CLA		96	C6
BLUEFLAX AV	CO	LAN		171	A1
BLUEGRASS LN	CER	ART		82	B4
BLUEGRASS LN	LA	LA49	900	32	A6
BLUEGRASS PL	POM	POM	900	94	B4
BLUEGRASS WY	LA	LA49	900	32	A6
BLUEGRASS WY	PALM	PALM		171	G6

COPYRIGHT, © 1989 BY Thomas Bros Maps

222
LOS ANGELES CO.

1990 LOS ANGELES COUNTY STREET INDEX

BLUEGROVE AV
BRADSHAWE PL

STREET	CITY	P.O. ZONE	BLOCK	PAGE	GRID
BLUEGROVE AV	BLF	BLF	13700	66	B1
BLUEGROVE AV	DOW	DOW	13000	66	B1
BLUEHAVEN DR	CO	LPUE	1500	97	A4
BLUE HAVEN RD	CO	LPUE		97	A5
BLUE HEIGHTS DR	LA	LA69	1800	33	D2
BLUE HILL RD	LA	LA41	1200	26	C4
BLUEHILLS DR	CO	PALM		157	F9
BLUE IRIS LN	CO	MAL		110	B5
BLUE JAY CIR	WCOV	WCOV		92	A2
BLUEJAY LN	SFS	SFS	10900	61	A1
BLUEJAY ST	LAV	LAV		95A	E6
BLUEJAY WY	LA	LA69	1400	33	D3
BLUELAGOON ST	CO	LPUE	16100	92	A4
BLUE MEADOW LN	WLVL	THO		102	B4
BLUEMOUND RD	RHE	PVP	5100	72	E3
BLUE MTN DR	WAL	WAL	20400	93	B3
BLUE MTN WY	CLA	CLA		91	C1
BLUE PALM LN	DBAR	POM		97	F3
BLUE RIDGE AV	PALM	PALM		172	J9
BLUERIDGE DR	LA	BH	1400	33	A3
BLUE RIDGE DR	LA	PP		94	C4
BLUERIDGE LN	WAL	WAL		94	D5
BLUE ROCK RIDGE	WLVL	THO		102A	F5
BLUE SAGE DR	CO	SF	11200	3	D4
BLUE SAIL DR	LA	PP	18000	115	F3
BLUE SKY CT	LA	CAN		5	D3
BLUE SKY RD	CO	LPUE	14700	85	C3
BLUESKY WY	CO	CAST		123	J2
BLUESTOCK DR	CO	PALM		183	D5
BLUESTONE LN	MPK	MPK	1700	46	E4
BLUEWATER RD	CO	MAL	29200	110	B5
BLUFF CT	DBAR	POM		97A	B3
BLUFF PL	LA	SP		79	A6
BLUFF PL	LB	LB03	1700	75	E6
BLUFF RD	DOW	DOW	8800	54	B6
BLUFF RD	MTB	MTB	100	54	D4
BLUFF ST	TOR	TOR	3800	72	F2
BLUFF ST	TOR	TOR	4000	73	A2
BLUFFDALE DR	LA	SV	8500	9	F6
BLUFFDALE DR	LA	SV		16	F1
BLUFFDALE DR	MPK	MPK	300	46	C4
BLUFFHILL DR	MPK	MPK	1600	45	F3
BLUFF POINT CIR	POM	POM		94	D4
BLUFFSIDE DR	LA	NHO	10600	23	E4
BLUFFTON DR	CO	PALM		157	E9
BLUFFWOOD ST	CO	LPUE	19400	97	A4
BLUFORD AV	CO	WHI	9700	61	D2
BLUFORD AV	WHI	WHI	8600	61	D2
BLUMONT RD	SOG	SOG	10200	59	D4
BLYTHDALE RD	AGH	AGO		100A	C2
BLYTHE AV	LA	LA64	10500	42	A4
BLYTHE RD	LCF	LCF	200	19	D4
BLYTHE ST	LA	CAN	23200	5	F2
BLYTHE ST	LA	CAN	19800	12	F2
BLYTHE ST	LA	NHO	11400	16	E2
BLYTHE ST	LA	NOR	17400	14	D2
BLYTHE ST	LA	RES	17700	14	D2
BLYTHE ST	LA	SV	11200	16	E2
BLYTHE ST	LA	VAN	13400	15	A2
BLYTHE ST	LA	VAN		15	F2
BLYTHEWOOD DR	RPV	PVP	28300	72	C5
BOARDMAN LN	LA	BH	2400	32	E1
BOAZ ST	LA	LA11	3200	52	C1
BOB ST	MON	MON	100	29	B6
BOB BATCHELR RD	CO	CAL		108	C3
BOBBIE ST	COV	COV	1100	88	C4
BOBBYBOYAR AV	LA	CAN	6400	5	F5
BOBCAT WY	CO	CAST		123I	D9
BOB HOPE DR	BUR	BUR		24	C3
BOBOLINK PL	LA	LA69	1300	33	C3
BOBOLINK WY	POM	POM	1900	90	F6
BOBSTONE DR	LA	VAN	3700	22	F5
BOCA AV	LA	LA32	1700	45	C1
BOCA CHICA DR	LAM	LAM	15100	83	A3
BOCA D CANON LN	LA	LA49	13100	30	F6
BOCANA ST	CO	MAL		114	E1
BOCA RATON AV	CO	LLAN		192	H3
BOCCACCIO AV	LA	VEN	500	49	D4
BOCKDALE AV	SCLR	CYN		125	C8
BODA PL	LA	WOH	5000	100	E2
BODEN ST	LA	LA16	5500	42	E5
BODGER AV	HAW	HAW	14400	63	B2
BODGER ST	ELM	ELM	10000	47	D1
BODIE ST	LA	LA33	100	44	F3
BODLE PARK MTWY	CO	MAL		105	E2
BOEING AV	LA	LA45	7600	50	C6
BOEING AV	LA	LA45		56	D1
BOEING PL	LA	LA45	6000	50	C6
BOER AV	CO	WHI	6700	55	B5
BOER AV	CO	WHI	8300	61	B1
BOER AV	SFS	SFS	8000	55	B6
BOGARDUS AV	CO	WHI	11700	84	D5
BOGARDUS AV	LAM	LAM	12600	84	D6
BOGARDUS AV	WHI	WHI	9800	84	D3
BOGART AV	BAP	BAP	4100	39	E3
BOGART CIR	CER	ART	18900	81	C1

STREET	CITY	P.O. ZONE	BLOCK	PAGE	GRID
BOGIE DR	LAV	LAV		95A	D5
BOGIE PL	CO	LLAN		192	H3
BOGIE ST	PALM	PALM		172	B5
BOGUE DR	GLEN	GL08	2600	18	F5
BOGUE ST	TEC	TEC	9500	38	D3
BOHLIG RD	GLEN	GL07	500	25	D1
BOHLIG RD	LA	LA32	5000	36	E6
BOILING PT MTWY	CO	SAU		182	A6
BOISE AV	CUL	LA66	4000	49	F3
BOISE AV	LA	LA66	3600	49	E2
BOISE CT	PALM	PALM		183	J1
BOLAN LN	CO	PVP	26900	73	A4
BOLANOS AV	CO	LPUE	1700	98	F4
BOLAR AV	CO	LPUE		85	F4
BOLAS ST	LA	LA49	11300	41	C1
BOLD ST	CO	LPUE		98	E3
BOLERO LN	LA	LA12	1400	44	E2
BOLEY ST	CO	ARC	900	38	F1
BOLEY ST	CO	ARC	900	39	A1
BOLEY ST	MON	MON	1200	39	A1
BOLIVAR RD	LA	WOH	4500	13	C3
BOLIVAR ST	POM	POM	1700	94	E4
BOLKER PL	LA	SP	1800	73	F6
BOLKER WY	MTB	MTB		46	C5
BOLKER WY	PR	PR		55	E3
BOLLENBACHER AV	PR	PR	6400	54	D6
BOLLENBACHER DR	PR	PR	7600	54	E4
BOLLING AV	LAV	LAV		90	D3
BOLLINGER DR	LA	PP	16700	40	B3
BOLSA AV	CAR	CAR	22000	69	B5
BOLSA LN	CER	ART	14000	82	E5
BOLSA ST	CAR	CAR	21000	69	B4
BOLTON RD	LA	LA34	9300	42	C3
BOMAR CT	CO	LPUE		97	B5
BOMBARDIER AV	NWK	NWK		61	A6
BOMBARDIER AV	NWK	NWK	12600	82	A1
BOMBAY AV	LA	WIL	24700	74	C2
BOMBAY ST	LA	SF	13800	2	F3
BOMBAY ST	LA	SF	12800	3	A2
BOMBERRY ST	LKD	LKD	2500	70	F3
BOMER DR	LA	LA42	5100	36	B3
BONAIR PL	LA	LA68	6600	34	B2
BONANZA CT	POM	POM		94	C5
BONANZA ST	LA	PAC	13300	8	F4
BONANZA ST	LA	PAC	13200	9	A4
BONAPARTE AV	LA	LA66	12600	49	F4
BONAVISTA AV	SFS	SFS	15000	82	E3
BONAVISTA LN	CO	WHI	10200	61	F4
BONAVISTA LN	CO	WHI	9900	84	A3
BONAVISTA LN	LAM	LAM	13000	82	E1
BONAVISTA LN	WHI	WHI	9200	84	A3
BONAVITA DR	LA	ENC	4200	21	F4
BONAVITA PL	LA	ENC	4200	21	F3
BOND ST	LA	LA15	1300	44	B4
BONDS ST	CAR	CAR	500	74	B1
BONELLI ST	IND	LPUE		48	C5
BONFAIR AV	BLF	BLF	15900	66	B4
BONFAIR RD	LKD	LKD	5400	71	B1
BONFIELD AV	LA	NHO	7800	16	B2
BONHAM AV	CAR	CAR	17200	64	B5
BONHAM AV	CAR	CAR	18600	69	B1
BONHAM AV	LA	SF	11500	3	D6
BONHILL RD	LA	LA49	600	32	B6
BONHILL RD	LA	LA49	200	41	B1
BON HOMME RD	CO	WOH		13	A4
BONIFACE DR	CO	MAL	28800	110	C4
BONILLA DR	CO	TOP	1000	109	D3
BONINO DR	PALM	PALM		172	A8
BONITA AV	BUR	BUR	1700	17	C4
BONITA AV	CAR	CAR	21000	69	C3
BONITA AV	CO	PAS	200	27	E5
BONITA AV	GLDR	GLDR	700	88	F3
BONITA AV	LAV	LAV	900	90	C3
BONITA AV	POM	POM	800	91	A4
BONITA AV	SMAR	PAS	100	27	E5
BONITA AV E	POM	POM	100	90	E4
BONITA AV E	SAD	SAD	100	90	A3
BONITA AV E	SMAD	SMAD	1	28	C2
BONITA AV W	CLA	CLA	100	91	A4
BONITA AV W	POM	POM	100	90	E4
BONITA AV W	SAD	SAD	100	89	F3
BONITA AV W	SMAD	SMAD	1	28	C2
BONITA DR	GLEN	GL08	1900	18	E6
BONITA DR	LHH	LAH		98A	B3
BONITA DR	PAS	PAS	600	37	B1
BONITA DR	SPAS	SPAS	600	36	F3
BONITA PL	CO	CAST		123	A5
BONITA ST	ARC	ARC	1	28	E5
BONITA ST	CAR	CAR	21500	69	C5
BONITA ST	CAR	CAR	23900	74	C1
BONITA ST	DOW	DOW	7700	59	E6
BONITA ST	LA	SP	500	79	A2
BONITA ST	MON	MON	500	29	A5
BONITA TER	LA	LA68	6800	34	B3
BONITA TER	MPK	MPK	1400	45	F2
BONITA VISTA DR	LCF	LCF	1700	19	A1

STREET	CITY	P.O. ZONE	BLOCK	PAGE	GRID
BONITO AV	LB	LB02	100	75	D5
BONLEE AV	SCLR	CYN	27000	124	G7
BONNELL DR	CO	TOP	1400	109	A3
BONNER AV	LA	NHO	6000	16	E6
BONNER AV	LA	NHO	5500	23	E1
BONNER AV	LA	SV	7700	16	E2
BONNER CT	LAV	LAV		95A	B6
BONNER DR	WHOL	LA48	8700	33	D5
BONNEVILLE RD	HH	CAL	5400	100	D2
BONNIE AV N	PAS	PAS	1	27	D4
BONNIE AV S	PAS	PAS	1	27	D4
BONNIE PL	LA	RES		14	A3
BONNIE BCH PL N	CO	LA63	100	45	D4
BONNIE BCH PL S	CO	LA23	600	45	D6
BONNIE BCH PL S	CO	LA23	1200	53	D1
BONNIE BCH PL S	CO	LA63	100	45	D6
BONNIE BCH PL S	VER	LA23	2600	53	C2
BONNIE BRAE AV	CLA	CLA	2900	91	C1
BONNIE BRAE AV	CLA	CLA	3200	96	C6
BONNIE BRAE ST	HB	RB	1200	62	D6
BONNIE BRAE ST	POM	POM	1600	91	B6
BONNIE BRAE ST	POM	POM	1000	95	B1
BONNIE BRE ST N	LA	LA26	400	35	C6
BONNIE BRE ST N	LA	LA26	100	44	B1
BONNIE BRE ST S	LA	LA06	900	44	B3
BONNIE BRE ST S	LA	LA57	100	44	B3
BONNIE CLARE DR	WAL	WAL		92	F5
BONNIE COVE AV	CO	COV	4600	89	B3
BONNIE COVE AV	COV	COV	4500	89	B3
BONNIE COVE AV	GLDR	GLDR	5200	89	B3
BONNIEGLEN LN	SAD	GLDR		89	F1
BONNIE HILL DR	LA	LA68	3300	23	F6
BONNIE HILL DR	LA	LA68	3200	24	A6
BONNIE JEAN RD	LHH	LAH		84	D2
BONNIE VALE AV	PR	PR	6300	54	F4
BONNIE VALE PL	PR	PR	7000	54	E5
BONNIE VIEW AV	SCLR	CYN	28200	125	B7
BONNY LN	LA	LA49	12100	41	B2
BONNYBROOK TER	GLEN	GL07		25	D1
BONNYWOOD PL	BUR	BUR	100	17	D5
BONSALL	CO	LA25		41	D3
BONSALL DR	CO	MAL		110	B4
BONSALL DR	CO	MAL		112	B6
BONSALLO AV	LA	GAR	15400	64	A3
BONSALLO AV	LA	LA07	1900	44	B5
BONSALLO AV	LA	LA44	5800	52	A5
BONVUE AV	LA	LA27	4700	34	F2
BONWICK DR	CO	WHI	13500	48	A4
BONWOOD RD	ELM	ELM	11100	47	E3
BOOKHAM DR	SCLR	CYN		124	J7
BOOKMAN AV	WAL	WAL	1400	93	B3
BOONE AV	LA	VEN	2300	49	D4
BOOTHILL LN	CAR	CAR		69	D6
BOOTLEGGR CY RD	CO	SAU		189	D7
BORA DR	LAM	LAM	13800	82	E2
BORA DR	LAM	LAM	14600	83	A2
BORA DR	SFS	SFS	13600	82	E2
BORA BORA WY	CO	MDR		49	D6
BORAGE CT	SCLR	SAU		124	E5
BORATE ST	SFS	SFS	13800	82	E2
BORCO WY	LA	LA77		32	D5
BORDA RD	LAM	LAM	15200	83	A3
BORDEAUX AV	LA	PAC	9900	8	E3
BORDEAUX ST	PALM	PALM		183	F2
BORDEN AV	HB	RB	2100	62	C5
BORDEN AV	LA	PAC	11300	3	B6
BORDEN AV	LA	PAC	10900	9	B1
BORDEN AV	LA	SF	12600	2	D2
BORDEN AV	LA	SF	11800	3	A5
BORDEN AV	LA	SV	9200	9	E5
BORDER AV	TOR	TOR	600	68	D3
BOREGO DR	LAM	LAM	14700	83	B2
BOREHAM WY	CO	MAL		111	B1
BOREL ST	BAP	BAP	4800	39	F3
BOREL ST	LA	LA31	3700	36	B5
BORG DR	CO	AGO		107	A3
BORGOS PL	LA	PP	14800	40	D4
BORIS AV	CMRC	LA40	2500	54	A3
BORIS DR	LA	ENC	17900	21	C3
BORK AV	CO	LPUE	1500	98	A3
BORLAND RD	LA	LA32	5000	36	D6
BORLEY DR	CO	MAL		106	D6
BORNA DR	CO	MAL		112	E1
BORREGO	WCOV	WCOV		92	D4
BORREGO CT	SAD	SAD		89	E3
BORSON ST	DOW	DOW	7800	59	F5
BORSON ST	DOW	DOW	8200	60	A6
BORSON ST	NWK	NWK	10500	60	D6
BORT ST	LB	LB05	300	65	B5
BORT ST E	LB	LB05	100	65	C5
BORT ST W	LB	LB05	100	65	B5
BORWICK AV	SOG	SOG	5500	59	E5
BORWICK ST	BLF	BLF	10500	66	D5
BOS PL	CER	ART	11000	71	E2
BOS ST	CER	ART	11000	71	E2
BOSCOMBE TR	CO	TOP		109	B2

STREET	CITY	P.O. ZONE	BLOCK	PAGE	GRID
BOSLER TR	CO	TOP	19500	109	D5
BOSQUE DR	LA	ENC	16500	21	F4
BOSQUE DR	LA	ENC	16000	22	A4
BOSTON AV	GLEN	GL14	4000	11	C4
BOSTON AV	MTB	MTB		46	E5
BOSTON CT	PAS	PAS	800	27	B4
BOSTON LN	CER	ART		81	A1
BOSTON PL	POM	POM	800	94	F1
BOSTON ST	CO	ALT	900	20	B5
BOSTON ST	LA	LA12	800	44	D2
BOSTON ST	LA	LA26	1200	44	D1
BOSTWICK ST	CO	LA63	3700	45	D3
BOSWELL PL	CO	LA22	5100	53	F1
BOSWELL PL	CO	LA23	4300	53	D1
BOSWELL PL	LA	SF	17200	1	E3
BOSWORTH ST	LA	NHO	12700	16	A4
BOTANY ST E	DOW	DOW	7700	54	C6
BOTHWELL RD	LA	CHA	10000	6	F2
BOTHWELL RD	LA	CHA	10000	7	A2
BOTHWELL RD	LA	NOR	8400	7	A6
BOTHWELL RD	LA	NOR	8300	14	A1
BOTHWELL RD	LA	RES	6300	14	A4
BOTHWELL RD	LA	TAR	5100	13	F1
BOTTLEBRUSH	WCOV	WCOV		98	E2
BOTTLEBRUSH DR	LA	LA77		22	D6
BOTTLEBRUSH DR	LA	LA77		32	D1
BOTTLE TREE DR	PALM	PALM		183	F3
BOUETT ST	LA	LA12	1800	35	E5
BOUGAINVLLIA WY	CO	CYN	28900	125	E7
BOUGHTON PL	LA	NHO	12100	23	B5
BOULAY ST	CO	LPUE	17000	92	C6
BOULAY ST	CO	LPUE	17000	98	D1
BOULDER LN	DBAR	POM		97	C5
BOULDER RD	CO	ALT	2400	20	C5
BOULDER ST	LA	LA33	2400	45	B3
BOULDER ST	LA	LA63	3000	45	B3
BOULDER CK RD	CO	CYN		125	D9
BOULDER RDG TER	LA	CHA	10500	6	B2
BOULDER SPGS DR	GLDR	GLDR		87	D3
BOUMA AV	CER	ART	19500	71	F2
BOUMA CT	CER	ART	20100	71	F2
BOUNDARY AV	LA	LA32	3500	36	C4
BOUNDARY PL	MB	MB	800	62	C5
BOUNTY LN	CUL	CUL		50	D2
BOUQUET DR	LA	CAN		5	F3
BOUQUET CYN RD	CO	SAU	26000	124	D6
BOUQUET CYN RD	SCLR	SAU		124	D6
BOUQUETE ST	GLEN	GL06	1500	26	A1
BOURDET AV	WAL	WAL	400	97	B1
BOUTON DR	LKD	LKD	3600	71	A3
BOVEY AV	LA	RES	7500	12	F3
BOVEY AV	LA	RES	6200	14	A4
BOW AV	TOR	TOR	1100	68	D4
BOWCREEK DR	DBAR	POM		94	B6
BOWCREEK DR	DBAR	POM		97A	B1
BOWCROFT ST	LA	LA16	5600	42	E6
BOWDOIN ST	LA	PP	15400	40	C3
BOWDOIN ST	LAV	LAV		90	E1
BOWEN AV N	COM	COM	100	65	B3
BOWEN AV S	COM	COM	500	65	B3
BOWEN DR	WHI	WHI		85	A5
BOWER CASCAD PL	DBAR	POM		94	A5
BOWERS AV	SOG	SOG	8600	59	C2
BOWERS DR	CO	CHA		1A	D4
BOWERS DR	CO	TOP	19500	109	C5
BOWESFIELD ST	LA	LA16	5600	42	E6
BOWFIN AV	LA	SP	2500	78	D5
BOWIE RD	AGH	AGO		100A	D5
BOWIE RD	RH	PVP	1	78	B1
BOWLING GRN DR	CLA	CLA	400	91	B1
BOWLNG GRN WY N	LA	LA49	100	41	B2
BOWLNG GRN WY S	LA	LA49	100	41	B1
BOWMAN AV	SOG	SOG	8900	59	C4
BOWMAN BLVD	LA	LA32	4400	36	C5
BOWMAN KNOLL DR	WLVL	THO		102A	F5
BOWMONT DR	LA	BH	2200	33	C2
BOWMORE AV	LA	NOR		1	B5
BOWMORE PL	LA	NOR		1	B4
BOWRING DR	CO	ALT	2600	20	D4
BOWSPRIT CIR	WLVL	THO		102A	F5
BOX CANYON RD	CO	CHA		4	B5
BOXCOVE PL	DBAR	POM		97A	B1
BOXELDER LN	CO	COV		89	C5
BOXFORD AV	CMRC	LA40	3400	53	F4
BOXFORD AV	CMRC	LA40	3400	54	A4
BOXHILL TR	CO	TOP	1300	109	D2
BOXLEAF RD	PALM	PALM		183	E2
BOXLEY TR	CO	TOP		109	D5
BOXTHORN ST	PALM	PALM		173	A9
BOXTHORN ST	PALM	PALM		184	A5
BOXTREE DR	CO	PALM		157	H8
BOXWOOD LN	CO	SAU		124	C2
BOXWOOD PL	LA	VAN	13900	15	E1
BOYAR AV	LB	LB07	4100	70	D4
BOYAR AV	WHI	WHI		61	F2
BOYCE AV	LA	LA39		25	C6

STREET	CITY	P.O. ZONE	BLOCK	PAGE	GRID
BOYCE AV	LA	LA39	3600	35	C1
BOYD PL	POM	POM	1800	94	E5
BOYD ST	LA	LA13	200	44	D3
BOYD ST	LA	LA33	1400	44	F4
BOYDEN AV W	LAN	LAN	1200	159	J3
BOYDTON ST	RM	RM	8800	38	A4
BOYER LN	CO	LPUE		98	F2
BOYLE AV N	LA	LA33	100	45	A3
BOYLE AV S	LA	LA23	600	44	F5
BOYLE AV S	LA	LA33	100	45	A3
BOYLE AV S	VER	LA58	4500	53	A4
BOYLSTON ST	PAS	PAS	800	27	B2
BOYLSTON ST N	LA	LA12		35	D6
BOYLSTON ST N	LA	LA26	100	44	C2
BOYLSTON ST S	LA	LA12	100	44	C2
BOYLSTON ST S	LA	LA17	300	44	C2
BOYNE ST	DOW	DOW		60	B5
BOYNE ST	LA	LA23		53	B1
BOYNTON ST	GLEN	GL05	1000	25	D6
BOY SCOUT MTY	CO	SF		3	C4
BOYSENBERRY WY	PALM	PALM		183	C6
BOYSON ST	DOW	DOW	8200	60	B5
BRACE ST	LA	BUR	2900	17	C2
BRACE CANYON RD	BUR	BUR		17	C2
BRACEWOOD DR	CO	LPUE		98	B4
BRACKEN LN	CO	NEW		126	J4
BRACKEN ST	LA	PAC	13500	8	F6
BRACKEN ST	LA	PAC	12700	9	B4
BRACKNELL ST	CER	ART	12900	81	C2
BRACO ST	CO	TOP		115	A1
BRAD CT	CLA	CLA		91	B1
BRAD PL	CO	CAL		100A	F4
BRADBOURNE AV	DUA	DUA	800	29	E4
BRADBURY AV	DUA	DUA	1200	29	C5
BRADBURY AV	MON	MON	200	29	C4
BRADBURY DR	MTB	MTB		46	E4
BRADBURY DR	SGAB	SGAB	100	37	D3
BRADBURY LN	CO	MON	100	29	A6
BRADBURY RD	LA	LA64	10500	42	A4
BRADBURY RD	SMAR	PAS	1300	27	E6
BRADBURY ST	WCOV	WCOV	1200	48	E3
BRADBURY HLS LN	BRAD	DUA		29	E4
BRADBURY HLS RD	BRAD	DUA	1700	29	E4
BRADCLIFF WY	PALM	PALM		171	H7
BRADDOCK DR	CUL	CUL	9600	42	C6
BRADDOCK DR	CUL	CUL	9900	50	B2
BRADDOCK DR	LA	CUL	11300	50	B3
BRADDOCK DR	LA	LA66	12400	50	A4
BRADDON OAK DR	SCLR	VAL		124	B4
BRADEN DR	GLEN	GL06		26	A3
BRADENHALL DR	CAR	CAR	300	64	B5
BRADFIELD AV	CO	COM	15900	65	B3
BRADFIELD AV	LYN	LYN	12000	59	B6
BRADFIELD AV	LYN	LYN	12300	65	B1
BRADFIELD AV N	COM	COM	100	65	B3
BRADFIELD AV S	COM	COM	100	65	B3
BRADFORD AV	ARC	ARC	2700	38	D2
BRADFORD CIR	CER	ART		71	E2
BRADFORD DR	GLDR	GLDR	1000	89	C2
BRADFORD DR	LCF	LCF	1200	19	B2
BRADFORD PL	LA	SF	12000	1	E5
BRADFORD PL	PALM	LAN		171	A2
BRADFORD ST	LAV	LAV		90	E2
BRADFORD ST	PAS	PAS	400	26	E5
BRADFORD ST	POM	POM	700	94	E1
BRADGATE DR	PR	PR	9400	47	C6
BRADGATE DR	PR	PR	9400	55	C1
BRADHURST ST	CO	WHI	10400	55	C5
BRADHURST ST	PR	PR	8700	54	F3
BRADHURST ST	PR	PR	9400	55	A4
BRADISH AV	GLDR	GLDR	900	89	E1
BRADISH AV	SAD	SAD	700	89	E2
BRADLEY AV	CLA	CLA	2300	96	B6
BRADLEY AV	LA	PAC	11100	8	F1
BRADLEY AV	LA	PAC	9800	9	B3
BRADLEY AV	LA	SF	11400	1	F2
BRADLEY AV	LA	SF	11400	2	B2
BRADLEY AV	LA	SV	8500	9	D6
BRADLEY AV	LA	SV	8400	16	E1
BRADLEY AV	MTB	MTB	400	54	E1
BRADLEY CIR	LAN	LAN		159	H7
BRADLEY CT	GLDR	GLDR	1200	89	C2
BRADLEY PL	LA	LA56		50	E5
BRADLEY ST	PAS	PAS		27	F2
BRADLEY CYN RD	CO	SAU		188	G1
BRADMORE RD	CO	LAN	11800	158	B5
BRADMORE RD	CO	SAU		181	C7
BRADNA DR	CO	LA43	5400	51	A3
BRADNER PL	LA	NOR	11100	7	B1
BRADOAKS AV	MON	MON	500	29	C3
BRADRICK DR	CAR	CAR	200	69	B3
BRADSHAWE AV	CO	LA22	500	46	A6
BRADSHAWE AV	CO	LA22	700	54	A1
BRADSHAWE AV	MPK	MPK	600	46	B3
BRADSHAWE PL	MPK	MPK	900	46	B3

STREET	CITY	P.O. ZONE	BLOCK	PAGE	GRID
BRADSHAWE ST	MTB	MTB	400	46	B5
BRADSON PL	LA	CUL	11500	50	B4
BRADSTOCK RD	CO	ACT		182	C6
BRADWELL AV	CO	WHI	7700	55	B4
BRADWELL AV	WHI	WHI	8400	61	A1
BRADWELL AV	SF	SF	13000	2	D3
BRADWELL AV	SFS	SF	9400	80	F2
BRADY AV	LA	LA22	600	46	B6
BRADY AV	CO	LA22	600	46	B6
BRADY AV	MTB	MTB	400	46	B6
BRADY PKWY	CO	VAL		92	B4
BRAEBURN RD	CO	ALT	1400	20	C5
BRAEBURN WY	LA	LA27	4000	35	A1
BRAEHOLM PL	HB	RB	600	62	C5
BRAELOCK ST W	CO	ACT		182	B6
BRAEMAR CT	AGH	AGO		102	F2
BRAEMAR RD	PAS	SF	1800	19	A4
BRAEMORE PL	LA	NOR		1	A5
BRAEMORE RD	LA	NOR		1	A5
BRAEPARK ST	WHI	WHI		84	C3
BRAERIDGE DR	LA	BH	1300	33	A4
BRAES RIVER DR	WAL	WAL		92	F5
BRAES RIVER DR	WAL	WAL		93	A5
BRAEWOOD CT	LA	TAR		21	A4
BRAEWOOD DR	BRAD	DUA	700	29	D4
BRAEWOOD DR	LA	TAR		13	F4
BRAEWOOD DR	LA	TAR		21	A4
BRAIDED MANE DR	DBAR	POM		97A	A4
BRAIDWOOD DR	RPV	PVP	28000	72	C4
BRAINARD AV	SF	SF	11300	1	F1
BRAINARD CYN RD	CO	LR		184	D9
BRALEY CT	PAS	PAS	1	27	A4
BRAMANTE PZ	RPV	PVP		78	C2
BRAMBLE CT	CO	LPUE		98	B6
BRAMBLE WY	LA	LA49	800	32	A6
BRAMBLE WY	SCLR	SAU		124	E6
BRAMBLE BUSH AV	CO	WHI		61	C1
BRAMBLEWOOD RD	LCF	LCF	5600	19	C1
BRAMFORD CT	CO	PAS	2200	20	F5
BRAMFORD LN	DBAR	POM		97A	B2
BRAMFORD DR	GLEN	GL07		18	D6
BRAMHALL AV	GLDR	GLDR		89	B2
BRAMLEY AV	LCF	LCF	500	19	D5
BRAMPTON RD	LA	LA41	1300	26	C4
BRAMPTON RD	PAS	PAS	1300	26	C4
BRANBURY CT	CO	VAL		124	F3
BRANCH RD	CO	CAST		123	G2
BRANCH ST	LA	LA42	200	26	C1
BRANCH OAK CT	GLDR	GLDR		89	D5
BRANCH OAK DR	GLDR	GLDR	1700	87	D5
BRAND BLVD	LA	SF	14400	8	C1
BRAND BLVD N	GLEN	GL02	900	25	C4
BRAND BLVD N	GLEN	GL03	100	25	C4
BRAND BLVD N	SF	SF	100	25	C4
BRAND BLVD S	SF	SF	100	25	D5
BRANDEIS DR	CLA	CLA		96	D5
BRANDEN ST	CLA	LA26	1900	35	C4
BRANDENBURG PL	LA	TAR	4800	21	A3
BRANDING IRON LN	RHE	PVP	1	73	A4
BRANDING IRON RD	WAL	WAL		93	A5
BRANDO ST	CER	ART		81	C2
BRANDON ST	CO	PAS	3200	28	A4
BRANDON ST	PAS	PAS	3000	27	F4
BRAND PARK DR	GLEN	GL01		18	B5
BRANDT ST	LAV	LAV		90	E4
BRANDYWINE DR	CO	WOH		13	A4
BRANDY WINE WY	TOR	TOR		73	B2
BRANDYWINE CY RD	CO	CYN		125	D3
BRANFORD ST	LA	PAC	13500	8	F6
BRANFORD ST	LA	PAC	12400	9	A5
BRANFORD ST	LA	SV	11800	9	C3
BRANFORD ST	LA	VAN	13800	8	F6
BRANHAM ST	MPK	MPK	1700	47	A6
BRANNICK AV N	CO	LA63	400	45	D6
BRANNICK AV S	CO	LA23	900	45	D6
BRANNICK AV S	CO	LA23	1100	53	D1
BRANSCOMB ST	DOW	DOW	10100	66	D1
BRANSCOMB ST	LAM	LAM	14100	82	E1
BRANSCOMB ST	NWK	NWK	10500	66	E1
BRANT AV	LA	LB10	20900	69	F3
BRANTA DR	GLEN	GL08		18	E6
BRANTFELL PL	GLDR	GLDR		86	E4
BRANTLEY CT	LA	VAN	13900	22	E2
BRANTON PL	LA	VAN		13	F3
BRANYON AV	SOG	SOG	4900	59	F3
BRASHER ST	PR	PR	9500	55	B2
BRASILIA DR	CO	CYN		125	D2
BRASSIE ST	CO	LAV		95A	B3
BRASS LANTRN DR	LAM	LAM	16500	84	D6
BRAVO LN	LA	LPUE		98	B3
BRAVO LN	CO	CAL		100	A3
BRAVO LN	CO	CAL		100A	F1
BRAVO ST	LA	LA32		160	G6
BRAWLEY PL	LA	LA32	2100	45	D1
BRAXTON PL	LA	SF	12600	1	E4
BRAXTON ST	LA	SF	17100	1	E4
BRAY ST	LA	CUL	11800	50	B4
BRAYTON AV	LB	LB05	5900	65	D6
BRAYTON AV	LB	LB05	5200	70	D5
BRAYTON AV	LB	LB07	3300	70	D5
BRAYTON AV	SH	LB08	2600	75	D2
BRAYTON AV	SH	LB07	3300	70	D5
BRAYTON PL	LA	LA41	4800	26	D5
BRAZIL ST	PAR	PAR	15500	65	D3
BRAZIL ST	CER	ART	13000	81	D2
BRAZIL ST	CO	COM		64	D2
BRAZIL ST	LA	LA39	4500	25	B4
BRAZILIANA DR	SAD	SAD	100	89	D3
BRAZO RD	LAM	LAM	13400	82	F1
BRAZOS PL	DBAR	POM		97	D4
BREA PL	POM	POM	500	94	C3
BREA CYN CUTOFF	CO	LPUE	1200	97	B3
BREA CYN CUTOFF	CO	WAL	1600	97	B3
BREA CANYON RD	CO	WAL	100	93	D6
BREA CANYON RD	DBAR	POM		99	B5
BREA CANYON RD	IND	WAL		93	D6
BREA CANYON RD	IND	WAL	300	97	E2
BREA CANYON RD	POM	POM	1800	94	B3
BREA CREST DR	CO	LA43	5100	50	F3
BRECKENRIDGE DR	DBAR	POM		99	B4
BRECKENRIDGE DR	CO	WHI	11400	61	E5
BRECKENRIDGE LN	SFS	SFS		60	F3
BRECKENRIDGE PL	SCLR	NEW	24600	127	C4
BRECKINRIDGE	WCOV	WCOV		92	E4
BREED ST N	LA	LA33	100	45	A4
BREED ST S	LA	LA33	600	45	A4
BREED ST S	LA	LA33	100	45	A4
BREEN AV	LA	LA45	7700	56	E1
BREEZE AV	LA	VEN	1	49	B4
BREEZE CT	LA	VEN		49	B4
BREEZEWOOD DR	CO	WHI	11900	84	C6
BREEZEWOOD DR	LAM	LAM	12600	84	C6
BREGANTE DR	LA	TU	10300	11	A3
BREGANTE DR	DBAR	POM	23900	94	A6
BREGER DR	LA	SF	13900	2	F1
BREIDT AV	LA	TU	10000	11	B4
BREMERTON WY	CO	LA61	12100	58	A6
BRENDA AV	LA	TU		81	A2
BRENDA CT	WCOV	WCOV		92	E4
BRENDLE WY	SCLR	NEW		127	H1
BRENFORD ST	LA	WOH	22700	13	A4
BRENNAN AV	LA	CAN	6600	5	F4
BRENNER DR	CAR	CAR	800	69	D4
BRENNER PL	LA	LB02	1000	75	D4
BRENT AV	SPAS	SPAS	500	37	A6
BRENT CT	LA	LAV		90	B1
BRENT PL	GLEN	GL03	300	25	B3
BRENT ST	CER	ART		81	C1
BRENTA PL	LA	VEN	2200	49	D3
BRENTFORD RD	CO	SGAB	8600	38	A1
BRENTMEAD AV	CO	ARC	6700	38	B1
BRENTMEAD RD	PAS	PAS	900	26	D6
BRENTON AV	LYN	LYN	3500	59	B4
BRENTRIDGE DR	LA	LA49		32	B5
BRENTRIDGE LN	LA	LA49		32	B5
BRENTWOOD AV	LAN	LAN		159	F7
BRENTWOOD DR	WCOV	WCOV		92	G5
BRENTWOOD DR	LAN	LAN		159	G7
BRENTWOOD ST	POM	POM		94	A3
BRENTWOOD TER	LA	LA24	12900	41	A3
BRENTWOOD TER	SM	SM	1200	40	F4
BRENTWD GRVE DR	LA	LA49		32	B5
BREON ST	POM	POM	1000	94	D1
BRESCIA AV	CLA	CLA		91	C1
BRESEE AV	BAP	BAP	3700	39	D4
BRESEE PL	BAP	BAP	14300	39	E6
BRESSER AV	DOW	DOW		65	D4
BRETON TR	CO	TOP		109	H3
BRETONWOOD RD	CO	LPUE		98	A5
BRETT PL	LA	SP		78	E1
BRETT ST	LA	IN02	23000	51	E1
BRETTON PL	LA	TAR		21	A3
BREVE WY	LA	PP	17400	40	A4
BREVIS ST	LA	LA42	5400	26	A1
BREWSTER DR	LYN	LYN	4200	59	C6
BREWSTER DR	LA	TAR	4600	21	A3
BRIAN AV	TOR	TOR	900	73	B1
BRIAN AV	POM	POM	1300	86	D6
BRIAN CT	CER	ART		81	C4
BRIAN CT	SCLR	SAU		124	F4
BRIAN LN	LA	VN36		22	A2
BRIAR PL	LA	LAV		90	B1
BRIAR ST	CO	LA61	10600	66	G1
BRIARBANK ST	CO	LPUE	15500	98	F3
BRIARBLUFF DR	CO	MAL	21400	114	F3
BRIARCLIFF LN	LA	NHO		23	D6
BRIARCLIFF RD	LA	LA68	5600	34	D2
BRIARCLIFF PL	MON	MON	600	29	B2
BRIAR CREEK RD	DBAR	POM		94	A5
BRIARCREST LN	LA	BH	9100	33	C1
BRIARCREST RD	LA	BH	2400	33	C1
BRIARCROFT RD	CLA	CLA	400	90	F2
BRIARDALE WY	SCLR	NEW		127	B6
BRIARGATE AV	ARC	ARC	1	38	E2
BRIARGATE LN	AZU	AZU		88	F2
BRIARGATE LN	CO	GLDR	6000	88	F1
BRIARGATE LN	COV	COV	700	88	F6
BRIAR GLEN RD	CO	SAU		125	E5
BRIARHAVEN DR	RPV	PVP	28800	72	C5
BRIARHURST DR	LA	LA46		23	E6
BRIAR KNOLL DR	GLEN	GL07	1700	25	D3
BRIAR RIDGE RD	LA	LA46		5	D3
BRIAR SUMMIT LN	LA	CAN		5	C6
BRIAR SUMMIT DR	DUA	DUA		29	F3
BRIAR SUMMIT DR	LCF	LCF	7700	23	E6
BRIARTREE DR	LCF	LCF	5700	19	C1
BRIARVALE LN	LA	NHO	11900	23	C6
BRIARWOOD CT	PALM	PALM		183	C1
BRIARWOOD CT	WAL	WAL		93	E4
BRIARWOOD DR	LA	LA77		32	E1
BRIARWOOD LN	LA	VAN	15400	22	C4
BRIARWOOD LN	TOR	TOR		73	B3
BRIARWOOD LN	GLEN	GL06	900	25	E2
BRIARWOOD LN	POM	POM		99	A6
BRIARWOOD LN	SAD	SAD	600	89	F4
BRIARWOOD ST	CER	ART	13200	81	D2
BRIDEWELL ST	LA	LA42	100	36	D1
BRIDGE RD	CO	NOR		1	A5
BRIDGE ST	SGAB	SGAB	100	37	D3
BRIDGE ST	LA	LA33	1400	45	A3
BRIDGE GATE DR	DBAR	POM		97	D3
BRIDGEPORT	MB	MB		62	C3
BRIDGEPORT	WCOV	WCOV		92	C3
BRIDGEPORT AV	CLA	CLA	1700	91	C1
BRIDGEPORT CT	PALM	PALM		183	D1
BRIDGEPORT CT	PALM	PALM		183	E3
BRIDGEPORT CT	WAL	WAL		93	F3
BRIDGEPORT WY	CO	COV		88	B4
BRIDGES ST	TOR	TOR	16000	69	E3
BRIDGES CT	COV	COV	400	88	B4
BRIDGES CT	SCLR	SAU		124	D4
BRIDGEVIEW AV	PR	PR	4500	54	F2
BRIDGEVIEW AV	PR	PR	4500	55	A2
BRIDGEWATER CT	AGH	AGO		93	D4
BRIDGEWATER DR	WAL	WAL	14200	93	D4
BRIDGEWOOD DR	LAM	LAM		82	F1
BRIDGEWOOD DR	LA	SF		2	B1
BRIDLE CIR	LB	LB15		76	D4
BRIDLE DR	DBAR	POM		99	B1
BRIDLE LN	BH	BH	1000	33	A5
BRIDLE PATH	GLEN	GL06		26	A1
BRIDLE PATH	BH	BH		33	B4
BRIDLE TR	GLEN	GL06		26	A1
BRIDLE WY	WAL	WAL		93	E4
BRIDLE GLEN ST	AGH	AGO		102	F3
BRIDLE PARK	GLEN	GL06		26	A1
BRIDLE PATH LN	WAL	WAL		93	A5
BRIDLE RIDGE RD	LA	SF		2	B1
BRIDLE TRAIL LN	WAL	WAL	20700	13	A4
BRIDLE TRAIL RD	HH	CAL		100	D2
BRIDLE TRAIL RD	WAL	WAL	700	93	A5
BRIDLEVALE DR	CO	LA65	10100	42	B4
BRIDLEWOOD CIR	RHE	PVP		73	D4
BRIDLEWOOD DR	CO	CAST		123	E3
BRIDLEWOOD ST	CO	GLDR	19000	88	D4
BRIDWELL ST	CO	GLDR	19300	88	D4
BRIER AV	LA	LA39	2200	35	D3
BRIER AV	LA	LA46	8400	33	E3
BRIER WY	SCLR	SAU		124	E3
BRIERBUSH AV	DOW	DOW		65	D4
BRIERCLIFF WY	MPK	MPK	1000	46	A3
BRIERCREST AV	LKD	LKD	5900	66	D3
BRIERCREST AV	LKD	LKD	4300	71	C1
BRIERFIELD ST	PR	PR	9500	55	B1
BRIERHAVEN DR	CO	GL14		89	C5
BRIERPATH DR	CO	COV	3800	88	B5
BRIER RIDGE LN	CO	LPUE		48	B5
BRIERSTONE PL	LA	CAN		92	E4
BRIGANTINE CIR	WLVL	THO		102A	F3
BRIGANTINE CIR	CER	ART		81	C4
BRIGDEN RD	PAS	PAS	1500	27	D3
BRIGGS AV	CO	GL14	4500	89	C5
BRIGGS AV	CO	GL14	4500	89	C5
BRIGGS AV	LCF	LCF	4500	89	C5
BRIGGS RD	CO	SAU	30300	188	C4
BRIGHM YOUNG DR	CLA	CLA	600	96	C5
BRIGHT AV	CO	WHI	9700	61	D2
BRIGHT AV	WHI	WHI	5800	55	B6
BRIGHT AV	WHI	WHI	8100	61	D1
BRIGHT LN	LA	LA39	2800	35	B3
BRIGHTLY ST	BLF	BLF	9100	66	B2
BRIGHTON AV	GAR	GAR	13900	63	E2
BRIGHTON AV	LA	GAR	18700	68	E1
BRIGHTON AV	LA	LA18	2600	43	E5
BRIGHTON AV	LA	LA47	7200	51	E6
BRIGHTON AV	LA	LA62	3900	51	E2
BRIGHTON AV	LA	TOR	20800	68	E4
BRIGHTON CT	PALM	PALM		183	H7
BRIGHTON ST	RM	RM	2500	46	E2
BRIGHTON ST	SGAB	SGAB	1900	37	E6
BRIGHTON ST N	BUR	BUR	700	17	B3
BRIGHTON ST N	BUR	BUR	100	24	B1
BRIGHTON ST S	BUR	BUR	100	24	B1
BRIGHTON WY	BH	BH	9300	42	B1
BRIGHTON WY	GAR	GAR	16900	63	E5
BRIGHTON WY	MTB	MTB		46	D5
BRIGHTONWOOD AV	PR	PR		55	E3
BRIGHTSIDE AV	DUA	DUA	1500	29	D5
BRIGHTSIDE LN	PAS	PAS	600	27	F6
BRIGHTVIEW DR	CO	COV		88	A6
BRIGHTVIEW DR	CO	GLDR	5700	89	A1
BRIGHTVIEW DR	CO	COV	100	89	A5
BRIGHTWATER PL	LA	HAC	23100	68	E6
BRIGHTWELL AV	PAR	PAR	13900	65	E2
BRIGHTWOOD CT	LA	VAN	9300	7	E5
BRIGHTWOOD ST	MPK	MPK	1800	45	F3
BRIGHTWOOD ST	MPK	MPK	400	46	A4
BRIGITA AV	CO	LPUE	400	92	B6
BRILL DR	LA	NHO	11300	23	F5
BRILLIANT DR	LA	LA65	3700	35	F2
BRILLIANT PL	LA	LA65	3700	35	F2
BRILLIANT WY	LA	LA65	3900	35	F2
BRIMFIELD AV	LA	VAN	7800	15	C3
BRIMLEY ST	NWK	NWK	11500	66	A1
BRIMLEY ST	NWK	NWK	11600	82	A1
BRINDLE MARE RD	DBAR	POM		97A	A1
BINEY POINT RD	CO	LAV		95A	E6
BRINGATE RD	CO	ACT		182	C7
BRINGHAM AV	LA	LA49	800	41	E2
BRINK AV	NWK	NWK	11000	61	A5
BRINK AV	NWK	NWK	13400	82	A1
BRINKLEY AV	LA	LA13	1400	40	F3
BRINNON ST	CO	TOR	16000	69	B5
BRINSEY AV	DUA	DUA	800	29	D4
BRINVILLE RD	CO	SAU		182	F6
BRINVILLE RD	CO	SAU		189	F1
BRINWOOD DR	SAD	SAD	600	90	B2
BRISA DR	PALM	LAN		171	C4
BRISA LN	CO	LPUE		92	A5
BRISBANE CT	CO	CAL		100	B3
BRISBANE ST	CO	MON	100	29	B1
BRISBANE ST	CO	MON		171	A2
BRISTLECONE DR	PALM	LAN		171	A2
BRISTOL AV N	LA	LA49	100	41	A1
BRISTOL AV S	LA	LA49	100	41	A1
BRISTOL CIR N	LA	LA49	12700	41	A1
BRISTOL CIR S	LA	LA49	12700	41	A2
BRISTOL CT	PALM	PALM		172	F5
BRISTOL CT	PALM	PALM		183	H7
BRISTOL PKWY	CUL	CUL		50	C5
BRISTOL ST	SAD	SAD	300	89	D4
BRISTOL WY	CO	SAU		124	E4
BRISTOW DR	LCF	LCF	2100	11	F5
BRITTAIN ST	LA	LB08	5100	75	C5
BRITTANIA ST	LA	LA33		50	A2
BRITTANY LN	LAN	LAN		159	F8
BRITTON DR	LB	LB15	1800	76	D5
BRIXTON RD	PAS	PAS	1300	26	F5
BRIZA WY	DUA	DUA	1900	29	D4
BROACH AV	LA	WIL	1000	74	C5
BROAD AV	CAR	CAR	23900	74	C1
BROAD AV	LA	SV	8300	9	A4
BROADACRE DR	LA	LA65		36	A2
BROADACRE PL	LA	LA65		36	A2
BROADACRES AV	CO	CAR	19000	74	C1
BROADACRES AV N	COM	COM	100	69	E1
BROAD BEACH RD	SFS	SFS	31000	111	D3
BROADED ST	CO	LA65		36	A2
BROADFIELD DR	CO	LPUE		92	A5
BROADHAVEN DR	LA	TOP		109	H3
BROADLAWN DR	LA	DUA	3700	29	F3
BROADLEAF AV	SELM	SELM		55	D4
BROADMEAD ST	CO	COV	3900	88	B4
BROADMOOR AV	CO	COV		88	B4
BROADMOOR AV	CO	LPUE	600	92	B6
BROADMOOR AV N	WCOV	WCOV	100	92	B6
BROADMOOR AV S	WCOV	WCOV	100	92	B6
BROADMOOR AV S	WCOV	WCOV	600	92	A1
BROADMOOR RD	PALM	PALM		171	B3
BROADMOOR ST	LA	SF	15000	23	C5
BROADMOOR ST	LA	VAN	14400	8	D5
BROADMORE DR	WHI	WHI		55	E3
BROADVALE DR	CO	LPUE	17000	92	C5
BROADVIEW DR	GLEN	GL08	1400	25	E3
BROADVIEW TER	LA	LA68	2100	34	B2
BROADWATER AV	LAN	LAN		160	
BROADWAY	BUR	BUR	1100	17	C5
BROADWAY	CO	HPK	2400	58	F1
BROADWAY	CO	HPK	2900	59	A1
BROADWAY	CO	SGAB	8200	37	E3
BROADWAY	CO	SGAB	8500	38	A3
BROADWAY	CO	WHI	6300	55	B6
BROADWAY	CO	WHI	11400	61	F3
BROADWAY	HAW	HAW	4500	56	F6
BROADWAY	HAW	HAW	3100	57	A1
BROADWAY	HPK	HPK	3200	59	A1
BROADWAY	SFS	SFS	8000	55	B6
BROADWAY	SM	SM	700	41	A6
BROADWAY	SM	SM	100	49	A1
BROADWAY	SM	SM	100	49	B5
BROADWAY	TEC	TEC	8900	38	B3
BROADWAY	WHI	WHI	11400	55	D4
BROADWAY E	GLEN	GL05	100	25	D4
BROADWAY E	LB	LB02	100	75	C5
BROADWAY E	LB	LB03	2000	75	F6
BROADWAY E	LB	LB03	3300	76	B6
BROADWAY N	LA	LA31	1700	35	E6
BROADWAY N	LA	LA31		44	B6
BROADWAY N	RB	RB	100	67	D3
BROADWAY S	CAR	GAR	16100	64	A6
BROADWAY S	CO	GAR	18400	69	A1
BROADWAY S	CO	GAR	14300	64	A6
BROADWAY S	CO	LA61	12000	58	A6
BROADWAY S	CO	LA61	12900	64	A2
BROADWAY S	LA	LA03	5800	52	A3
BROADWAY S	LA	LA03	8000	58	A2
BROADWAY S	LA	LA07	1900	44	B5
BROADWAY S	LA	LA07	3400	52	B1
BROADWAY S	LA	LA12	100	44	B3
BROADWAY S	LA	LA13	300	44	D3
BROADWAY S	LA	LA14	600	44	D3
BROADWAY S	LA	LA15	900	44	D4
BROADWAY S	LA	LA31		44	B6
BROADWAY S	LA	LA37	3800	52	A3
BROADWAY S	LA	LA61	10700	58	A2
BROADWAY S	RB	RB	100	67	D4
BROADWAY W	GLEN	GL04	100	25	B4
BROADWAY W	LA	LA41	2700	25	F4
BROADWAY W	LB	LB02	100	75	C5
BROADWAY W	SGAB	SGAB	100	37	E3
BROADWAY AV	LA	SP	600	78	E3
BROADWAY AV	LB	LB02	1	75	D5
BROADWAY CT	SH	LB07	3300	70	D5
BROADWAY PL	LA	LA07	3600	52	B1
BROADWAY PL	LA	LA15	1000	44	C4
BROADWAY TER	LA	LA37	3800	52	B1
BROADWAY TER	SGAB	SGAB		37	E3
BROADWELL AV	CO	TOR	21000	68	F1
BROADWELL AV	GAR	GAR	17400	63	F5
BROADWELL AV	LA	HAC	25000	73	F1
BROADWICK ST	CO	COM		69	E1
BROCADERO PL	PAS	PAS	100	26	D5
BROCIUS ST	SCLR	SAU		124	D5
BROCK AV	DOW	DOW	12600	59	F6
BROCK AV	DOW	DOW	8900	65	C2
BROCK AV	LKD	LKD	4100	70	F1
BROCK LN	PAR	PAR	13100	65	F1
BROCK LN	CO	ACT		182	G8
BROCKMONT DR	GLEN	GL02	200	25	C2
BROCKPORT CT	CLA	CLA		91	C2
BROCKTON AV	LA	LA25	1200	41	C4
BROCKWAY PL	ELM	ELM	9600	47	D1
BROCKWAY ST	ELM	ELM	9600	47	D1
BROCKWELL AV	MPK	MPK		46	F4
BROCKWELL ST	LB	LB08	5100	76	C5
BROCTON CT	CO	COV		88	A6
BRODERICK AV	CO	DUA	2400	29	F3
BRODERICK AV	CO	DUA		30	A3
BRODIAEA AV	LA	LA24	20800	68	F2
BROKAW PL	LA	LA34		34	D3
BROKEN TR	CO	TOP	700	109	H3
BROKEN ARROW DR	DBAR	POM	21000	97	D4
BROKEN BIT DR	CO	CAL		100A	F1
BROKENBOW LN	RHE	PVP		73	F2
BROKEN BOW LN	WAL	WAL	500	93	A5
BROKEN FEATHR RD	DBAR	POM		97A	A4
BROKEN LANCE RD	WAL	WAL	500	93	A5
BROKEN SPUR RD	CO	CAL		95A	C2
BROKEN TWIG RD	DBAR	POM		97A	E4

STREET	CITY	P.O. ZONE	BLOCK	PAGE	GRID
BROMAR ST	LPUE	LPUE	15800	48	F5
BROMLEY AV	CO	LPUE	1000	48	D2
BROMLEY AV N	WCOV	WCOV	200	39	F6
BROMLEY AV S	WCOV	WCOV	1300	48	E1
BROMLEY CT	LA	ENC	17800	14	D6
BROMLEY CT	PALM	PALM		171	F4
BROMLEY LN	ING	IN01		57	B2
BROMLEY ST	LA	ENC	17500	14	D6
BROMLEY ST	LA	TAR	18100	14	C6
BROMONT AV	LA	PAC	11200	3	C6
BROMONT AV	LA	PAC	11200	9	C1
BROMONT AV	LA	SF	12600	2	D1
BROMONT AV	LA	SF	11900	3	A5
BROMONT AV	LA	SV	10100	9	E3
BROMPTON AV	BELL	BELL	3700	53	D6
BROMPTON CT	BELL	BELL	3700	53	B5
BROMWICH PL	LA	PAC	13400	8	F5
BROMWICH ST	LA	PAC	13500	8	F6
BROMWICH ST	LA	PAC	12400	9	B4
BRONCE WY E	LB	LB02	100	75	D5
BRONCE WY E	LB	LB03	2000	75	F6
BRONCE WY E	LB	LB03	3200	76	A6
BRONCO DR	CO	CYN		125	E9
BRONCO DR	CO	CYN		128	E1
BRONCO DR	RPV	PVP	2700	73	C6
BRONCO LN	DBAR	POM	21200	97	D5
BRONCO PL	LAN	LAN		159	D6
BRONCO WY	WAL	WAL		93	D5
BRONHOLLY DR	LA	LA68	2600	34	D1
BRONSON AV N	LA	LA04	300	34	D5
BRONSON AV N	LA	LA28	1300	34	D4
BRONSON AV N	LA	LA38	700	34	D5
BRONSON AV N	LA	LA68	1900	34	D4
BRONSON AV S	LA	LA05	600	43	D2
BRONSON AV S	LA	LA08	3800	51	C1
BRONSON AV S	LA	LA18	1900	43	D2
BRONSON AV S	LA	LA19	900	43	D2
BRONSON AV S	LA	LA20	500	43	D2
BRONSON HILL DR	LA	LA68	2200	34	D2
BRONTE DR	WHI	WHI		85	A6
BRONTE PL	LA	SF	17200	1	E3
BRONWOOD AV	LA	LA49	100	32	C6
BRONZE LN	LA	LA49	800	32	A6
BRONZE KNOLL RD	DBAR	POM		97A	A3
BROOK AV	CAR	LB10		70	A3
BROOK CT	SCLR	NEW		127	B6
BROOK LN	GLEN	GL08	1700	18	F5
BROOKBANK AV	CO	WHI	11100	61	E5
BROOKDALE LN	DUA	DUA		29	F3
BROOKDALE DR	PALM	PALM		171	H7
BROOKDALE LN	LA	NHO	11700	23	D6
BROOKDALE RD	LA	NHO	3000	23	C6
BROOKDALE RD	SOG	SOG	5200	59	D4
BROOKE AV	LA	CHA	10200	6	C3
BROOKEN AV	CO	CYN		128	C2
BROOKFIELD PL	WCOV	WCOV		92	D6
BROOKFIELD RD	LA	CHA	10800	6	D2
BROOKFIELD ST	CO	LA22	5800	54	A1
BROOKFORD AV	LA	WOH	4400	13	A3
BROOKFORD DR	RPV	PVP	6900	72	C4
BROOKGREEN RD	DOW	DOW	8000	60	C1
BROOKHAVEN AV	LA	LA64	10800	41	F5
BROOKHAVEN ST	CER	ART	13100	82	D6
BROOKHILL AV	CO	GL14	2700	11	E6
BROOKHILL ST	GLEN	GL14	3200	11	C4
BROOKHILL TER	GLEN	GL14	3600	11	C4
BROOKINGS TR	CO	TOP	1400	109	A2
BROOKLAKE ST	LA	LA66	12400	49	E1
BROOKLAWN DR	LA	LA77	1000	32	F4
BROOKLINE AV	RM	RM	3500	38	C6
BROOKLINE DR	WAL	WAL		93	C6
BROOKLYN AV	CO	LA22	4300	45	C4
BROOKLYN AV	CO	LA63	3600	45	C4
BROOKLYN AV	LA	LA33	1400	44	F3
BROOKLYN AV	LA	LA33	1600	45	A3
BROOKLYN AV	LA	LA63	3000	45	B3
BROOKLYN AV	MPK	MPK		45	F4
BROOKLYN AV	MPK	MPK		46	A4
BROOKLYN PL	LA	LA63	3300	45	C4
BROOKMEAD DR	WHI	WHI		55	E3
BROOKMERE RD	PAS	PAS	100	26	F6
BROOKMILL RD	DOW	DOW	7400	60	A3
BROOKMONT PL	LA	CAN		5	E2
BROOKPARK RD	DOW	DOW	7800	54	C6
BROOKPARK RD	DOW	DOW	7900	60	E2
BROOKPORT ST	BAP	BAP	14000	39	D3
BROOKPORT ST	CO	COV	16500	88	C3
BROOKPORT ST	CO	COV	19500	89	A3
BROOKPORT ST E	COV	COV	400	88	F3
BROOKPORT ST E	COV	COV	1000	89	A3
BROOKPORT ST W	COV	COV	1100	88	C3
BROOKRIDGE RD	DUA	DUA	200	86	B3
BROOKS AV	CLA	CLA		91	C4
BROOKS AV	LA	LA12	1700	35	E6
BROOKS AV	LA	VEN	1	49	B3
BROOKS AV	PAS	PAS	700	26	F2

STREET	CITY	P.O. ZONE	BLOCK	PAGE	GRID
BROOKS CT	LA	VEN		49	B4
BROOKS CT	LA	VEN		49	C3
BROOKS DR	BAP	BAP		39	C3
BROOKS RD	CO	CHA	23500	4	B5
BROOKSHIRE AV	DOW	DOW	9200	60	C2
BROOKSHIRE AV	DOW	DOW	12900	66	A1
BROOKSHIRE LN	LA	LA49		32	B2
BROOKSIDE CT	WAL	WAL		93	D5
BROOKSIDE DR	CO	MAL	3300	115	E3
BROOKSIDE LN	POM	POM	300	90	E3
BROOKSIDE LN	SMAD	SMAD	400	28	D1
BROOKTREE CIR	WCOV	WCOV		92	C4
BROOKTREE RD	LA	PP	700	40	E4
BROOKTREE RD	LA	SM	600	40	E4
BROOKVIEW DR	LA	NHO	10700	23	F4
BROOKWIN DR	POM	POM	1000	94	D2
BROOKWOOD DR	DBAR	POM		97A	B2
BROOKWOOD RD	CO	PALM		157	H8
BROOM WY	LA	LA49	800	32	A6
BROOMALL ST	CO	ACT		189	E1
BROUGHAM CT	CO	LAN		159	B9
BROUGHAM PL	CO	LP45		98	A3
BROWN DR	BUR	BUR	600	17	C3
BROWN DR	CLA	CLA	100	91	C6
BROWN RD	BUR	BUR	800	17	C3
BROWNDEER LN	RPV	PVP	7500	72	F4
BROWNE AV	LA	LA32	4500	36	C4
BROWNELL ST	LA	SF	13360	2	F6
BROWNELL ST	LA	SF	13400	2	F6
BROWNELL ST	LA	SF	13100	3	A6
BROWNFIELD LN	POM	POM		94	D6
BROWNHILL TR	CO	TOP		109	D2
BROWNING AV	POM	POM	100	90	F3
BROWNING BLVD	LA	LA37	1000	51	E1
BROWNING BLVD	LA	LA62	1400	51	D1
BROWNING PL	CO	VAL		126	H3
BROWNING PL	MPK	MPK	800	46	D3
BROWNING ST	CO	LPUE	13400	48	C3
BROWN LATIGO RD	CO	MAL		108	C5
BROWNLOW RD	CO	SAU		181	E8
BROWN MTN TK TR	CO	ALT		20	A1
BROWNRIDGE ST	PAS	PAS	700	19	E6
BROWNSAGE DR	GLDR	GLDR	700	87	A4
BROWNS CYN RD	CO	CHA		1A	C3
BROWNS CYN RD	LA	CHA		1A	C3
BROWNS CYN RD	LA	CHA		6	D1
BROWNSTONE ST	LA	SUN	7900	10	E2
BROWNWOOD PL	LA	LA77	15400	22	C6
BROXBOURNE TER	CO	GL14		11	D5
BROXTON AV	LA	LA24	900	41	E1
BRUCE AV	BLF	BLF	14400	66	B2
BRUCE AV	GLEN	GL02	1100	25	A1
BRUCE AV	WCOV	WCOV	800	92	A2
BRUCE CT	LA	LA26	1600	35	C5
BRUCE LN	BUR	BUR	1000	24	E1
BRUCES PL	CO	CYN		124	H9
BRUCK CIR	CO	LPUE	16700	98	A3
BRUGES AV	LA	WOH	4800	13	A2
BRUIN AV	SELM	ELM	2700	47	B2
BRUIN ST	CO	LA47		57	E5
BRUIN WALK	LA	LA24		32	D6
BRUNA PL	LA	LA27		34	E1
BRUNACHE ST	DOW	DOW	7500	60	A4
BRUNING AV	GLDR	GLDR	1200	89	C2
BRUNO ST	LA	LA12	100	44	E2
BRUNSWICK AV	LA	LA39	3900	25	B6
BRUNSWICK AV	LA	LA39	3600	35	C1
BRUNSWICK AV	SPAS	SPAS	1200	36	D2
BRUNTY LN	CO	LPUE		85	D1
BRUSH TR	CO	TOP		109	D2
BRUSHTON ST	LA	LA08	5600	50	E1
BRUSSELS AV	LA	SF	13600	2	F1
BRUSSELS AV	LA	SF	11400	3	D6
BRYAN AV	LA	VEN	2300	49	D4
BRYAN CIR	WAL	WAL		93	C6
BRYAN PL	LA	SF44		1	D5
BRYAN ST	LA	LA42		36	D2
BRYANT CIR	GLDR	GLDR	800	89	A1
BRYANT DR	LB	LB15	1400	76	C4
BRYANT PL	CO	NEW		126	G3
BRYANT PL	MB	MB	1200	62	C5
BRYANT RD	ELM	ELM	10800	38	E5
BRYANT RD	LB	LB15	900	76	C4
BRYANT ST	LA	CAN	19600	6	E6
BRYANT ST	LA	NOR	18400	7	A6
BRYANT ST	LA	SF	16600	7	F6
BRYANT ST	LA	SF	14900	8	B6
BRYANT ST	LA	VAN	14900	8	B6
BRYANT ST	PAS	PAS	1200	26	D1
BRYCE CIR	CER	ART	12400	82	B5
BRYCE RD	CO	ELM	1900	47	E4
BRYCE RD	ELM	ELM	2200	47	E3
BRYCE ST	LA	WOH	23000	13	A3
BRYCEDALE AV	DUA	DUA	1200	29	D5
BRYDON RD	LAV	LAV	6000	95A	E4
BRYMER CT	LA	NOR		1	B6

STREET	CITY	P.O. ZONE	BLOCK	PAGE	GRID
BRYMER LN	LA	NOR		1	C6
BRYMER ST	LA	NOR		1	B6
BRYN ATHYN WY	DBAR	POM		97A	B2
BRYNHURST AV	CO	LA43	4500	51	C3
BRYNHURST AV	LA	LA43	4500	51	C4
BRYN MAWR AV	SM	SM	1600	49	C2
BRYN MAWR CT	LA	LA68	2300	34	C2
BRYN MAWR DR	LA	LA68	6300	34	C2
BRYN MAWR RD	CLA	CLA	11000	91	C6
BRYN MAWR RD	LA	LA27	4700	34	F1
BRYN MAWR WY	WHI	WHI		55	F5
BRYNWOOD PL	WCOV	WCOV		92	D5
BRYON RD	LAV	LAV		95A	E4
BRYON RD	WHI	WHI		55	D6
BRYSON AV	SOG	SOG	8900	59	C4
BRYSON ST	LA	PAC	13200	9	A6
BRYSON ST	LA	VAN	13500	15	F1
BUBBLING CK LN	CER	ART	12400	82	B4
BUBBLING VW CIR	CER	ART		82	B4
BUBBLNG WELL DR	GLDR	GLDR	700	87	A4
BUBBLNG WELL LN	LCF	LCF	5200	19	A1
BUBBLNG WELL RD	WCOV	WCOV	1000	92	A3
BUCCANEER ST	LA	VEN		49	C5
BUCHANAN DR	POM	POM	1500	90	F6
BUCHANAN PL	MPK	MPK	1800	46	D4
BUCHANAN ST	LA	LA42	4800	36	B1
BUCHANAN WY	CO	CAST	29500	123	A6
BUCHET DR	LA	SF	16300	2	A5
BUCKBOARD CIR	WCOV	WCOV		93	B1
BUCKBOARD CT	PALM	PALM		183	G3
BUCKBOARD LN	GLDR	GLDR	500	87	C4
BUCKBOARD LN	RH	PVP	1	78	B1
BUCKBOARD PL	CO	COV		93	C2
BUCKEYE AV	LA	SF	12000	2	D5
BUCKEYE CT	CO	SAU		124	C2
BUCKEYE ST	PAS	PAS	300	27	B2
BUCKHORN DR	CO	CAL		108	A6
BUCKINGHAM AV	SAD	SAD		89	D3
BUCKINGHAM LN	LA	LA77		32	B2
BUCKINGHAM PKWY	CUL	CUL	5900	50	D5
BUCKINGHAM PL	GLEN	GL06	2000	26	B1
BUCKINGHAM PL	PAS	PAS	600	26	E5
BUCKINGHAM RD	GLEN	GL06	3000	26	B1
BUCKINGHAM RD	LA	LA08	3800	51	B1
BUCKINGHAM RD	LA	LA16	1900	43	B4
BUCKINGHAM RD	LA	LA19	1600	43	B4
BUCKLAND DR	WAL	WAL	20600	93	B4
BUCKLER AV	ING	IN02	1200	51	A5
BUCKLER AV	LA	LA43	5800	51	A5
BUCKLES ST	DOW	DOW	8600	60	C5
BUCKNELL AV	CLA	CLA	100	91	B5
BUCKNELL AV	LA	NHO	5600	16	C6
BUCKSKIN CIR	LAV	LAV		90	D1
BUCKSKIN CIR	WAL	WAL		93	A6
BUCKSKIN DR	CO	SAU		123	D5
BUCKSKIN DR	WAL	WAL		93	D4
BUCKSKIN LN	RHE	PVP	26800	73	C4
BUCKSKIN ST	PALM	PALM		171	H6
BUCKTHORN ST E	ING	IN01	100	57	A2
BUCKTHORN ST W	ING	IN01	100	56	F2
BUCKTHORN ST W	ING	IN01	100	57	A2
BUCKWOOD TR	CO	TOP		109	B2
BUD CT	SCLR	SAU		124	G3
BUDAU AV	LA	LA32	2700	36	E5
BUDAU PL	LA	LA32	5000	36	D5
BUDLEIGH DR	CO	LPUE	3000	85	E5
BUDLONG AV	CO	LA44	8600	57	F3
BUDLONG AV	CO	TOR	20400	68	F3
BUDLONG AV	GAR	GAR	12800	63	F3
BUDLONG AV	LA	LA07	1900	43	F6
BUDLONG AV	LA	LA37	3800	51	F3
BUDLONG AV	LA	LA44	5800	51	F6
BUDLONG AV	LA	LA44	7800	57	F3
BUDLONG PL	GAR	GAR	15500	63	F3
BUDWOOD MTWY	CO	MAL		115	B3
BUELL ST	BG	BELL	6000	59	F2
BUELL ST	DOW	DOW	7400	60	A2
BUELL ST	NWK	NWK		61	A4
BUELL ST	SFS	SFS	11400	60	F4
BUELL ST	SFS	SFS		61	A4
BUENA LOMA CT	CO	ALT	300	20	A5
BUENA LOMA ST	CO	ALT	500	20	B5
BUENA PARK DR	LA	NHO	3600	23	C5
BUENAVENTURA ST	LA	WOH	21900	13	B3
BUENA VISTA E	LA	LA31	1700	44	F1
BUENA VISTA W	LA	LA31	1700	44	F1
BUENA VISTA AV	GLEN	GL08	3400	18	E3
BUENA VISTA AV	POM	POM	100	94	D3
BUENA VISTA DR	CLA	CLA	100	91	C5
BUENA VISTA DR	LA	LA12		35	E6
BUENA VISTA LN	SPAS	SPAS	1400	36	F1
BUENA VISTA ST	DUA	DUA	800	29	D6
BUENA VISTA ST	IRW	BAP	2200	29	D6
BUENA VISTA ST	IRW	BAP	2300	39	C1
BUENA VISTA ST	MON	MON	700	29	D6
BUENA VISTA ST	SMAR	PAS	300	37	B1

STREET	CITY	P.O. ZONE	BLOCK	PAGE	GRID
BUENA VISTA ST	SPAS	SPAS	900	36	F1
BUENA VIS ST N	BUR	BUR	1000	17	B5
BUENA VIS ST N	BUR	BUR	100	24	B1
BUENA VIS ST S	BUR	BUR	100	24	B1
BUENA VISTA TER	LA	LA42	5700	26	C5
BUENA VISTA WY	LAN	LAN		159	E7
BUENOS AIRES DR	CO	COV	1800	93	B2
BUFF AV	CO	PAS	1	28	B4
BUFFALO AV	LA	VAN	5600	15	F6
BUFFALO AV	LA	VAN	4600	22	F1
BUFFALO TR	GLDR	GLDR		87	C6
BUFFINGTON RD	ELM	ELM	4900	39	A4
BUFFINGTON ST	POM	POM	1700	94	B3
BUFFWOOD PL	AGH	AGO		100A	A3
BUFORD AV	CO	IN04	10000	56	F4
BUFORD ST	CER	ART	11600	81	A2
BUGGY WHIP CIR	WAL	WAL		93	A5
BUGGY WHIP DR	RH	PVP	1	72	F6
BUHMAN AV	DOW	DOW	9000	60	E2
BUHMAN AV	PR	PR	7900	60	E1
BULA CT	CO	ALT	2700	19	F4
BULFORD PL	CO	LAN		171	B1
BULLARD AV	LA	LA32	2200	36	E6
BULLA VISTA	CO	PALM		190	B2
BULL CANYON RD	LA	SF	17600	1	D4
BULLDOG MTWY	CO	AGO		107	A3
BULLDOG MTWY	CO	MAL		106	F4
BULLDOG LATERAL	CO	MAL		107	A4
BULL FROG CIR	WAL	WAL		93	A5
BULLIS RD	LYN	LYN	11000	59	B5
BULLIS RD	LYN	LYN	12300	65	B1
BULLIS RD N	COM	COM	100	65	B3
BULLIS RD S	COM	COM	100	65	B3
BULLOCK ST	LA	ENC	16800	14	D6
BULOVA ST	TOR	TOR		67	F2
BULOVA ST	TOR	TOR	4500	68	A2
BULWER DR	LA	LA46	8000	33	E1
BULWER WY	LA	LA46	2600	33	E1
BUNAL DR	LA	VAN	3900	22	D4
BUNBURY DR	CO	WHI	700	48	A4
BUNDY DR N	LA	LA49	600	32	B6
BUNDY DR N	LA	LA49	100	41	B1
BUNDY DR S	LA	LA25	1200	41	C4
BUNDY DR S	LA	LA49	100	41	B2
BUNDY DR S	LA	LA64	2100	41	D5
BUNDY DR S	LA	LA66	3000	41	D5
BUNGALOW DR	ELS	ELS	100	56	B5
BUNGALOW PL	ARC	ARC	1000	29	A6
BUNKER AV	ELM	ELM	2100	47	E3
BUNKER AV	SELM	ELM	1500	47	E4
BUNKER CT	PALM	PALM		183	E1
BUNKER HILL AV	LA	LA17	300	44	D2
BUNKER HILL AV	MTB	MTB		46	E5
BUNNELLE AL	PAS	PAS		27	A4
BUNNELLE AV	LAV	LAV	1100	90	B1
BUNNIE LN	CO	MAL	4900	111	C4
BURBANK BLVD	LA	ENC	16800	21	C1
BURBANK BLVD	LA	NHO	10400	23	B1
BURBANK BLVD	LA	TAR	18100	21	C1
BURBANK BLVD	LA	VAN	12900	22	C1
BURBANK BLVD	LA	VAN	12900	23	B1
BURBANK BLVD	LA	WOH	20600	13	A1
BURBANK BLVD	LA	WOH	23000	100	F1
BURBANK BLVD E	BUR	BUR	100	17	B6
BURBANK BLVD W	BUR	BUR	100	17	B6
BURBANK BLVD W	BUR	BUR	3300	24	A1
BURCHARD AV	LA	LA34	5700	42	E4
BURCHETT ST	GLEN	GL02	600	25	B2
BURCHETT ST	GLEN	GL03	100	25	C3
BURCHETT ST	GLEN	GL06		25	C3
BURDICK DR	POM	POM	500	94	D1
BUR PUBLIC LAND	LA	SF		10	A1
BURGEN AV	LA	LA34	9800	42	C5
BURGER AV	CO	LA22	500	45	E6
BURGESS AV	CO	WHI	11800	61	F6
BURGESS AV	LAM	LAM	12600	61	F6
BURGESS AV	LAM	LAM	12800	82	F1
BURGHARDT RD	TEC	SGAB	8600	38	A2
BURGOS DR	CO	MAL		112	D1
BURGOYNE LN	LCF	LCF	4800	19	D3
BURGROVE ST	CAR	CAR	1100	69	C3
BURGUNDY RD	LA	WOH	4600	13	A3
BURGUNDY FRM WY	AGH	AGO		100A	D5
BURIN AV	CO	IN04	10400	57	A4
BURIN AV	ING	IN04	10000	57	A4
BURIN AV	LAW	LAW	14300	63	A3
BURIN AV	TOR	RB	18200	63	A6
BURIN AV	TOR	TOR	19900	67	F2
BURK PL	BH	BH	600	33	C2
BURKE AV	SOG	SOG	8900	59	C3
BURKE DR	MTB	MTB	200	46	E5
BURKE ST	CO	WHI	11400	61	B1
BURKE ST	PR	PR	9000	54	E6
BURKE ST	PR	PR	9200	60	E1
BURKE ST	SFS	SFS	11700	61	B1
BURKETT RD	ELM	ELM	2000	47	E4

STREET	CITY	P.O. ZONE	BLOCK	PAGE	GRID
BURKETT RD	SELM	ELM	1700	47	E4
BURKSHIRE AV	LA	LA64	2700	41	E6
BURL AV	CO	IN04	10000	56	F4
BURL AV	HAW	HAW	12100	56	F6
BURLAND AV	LA	TU	10800	11	A2
BURLEIGH DR	PAS	PAS	500	26	D6
BURLESON ST	AGH	AGO		100A	A2
BURLINGAME AV	LA	LA49	100	41	A3
BURLINGHALL DR	LB	LB07	500	70	D4
BURLINGTON AV N	LA	LA26	100	44	B2
BURLINGTON AV S	LA	LA06	900	44	A4
BURLINGTON AV S	LA	LA07	1900	44	A3
BURLINGTON AV S	LA	LA57	1900	44	B3
BURLINGTON CT	LB	LB03		76	D5
BURLINGTON PL	POM	POM	1600	90	D6
BURLINGTON PL	WHI	WHI		84	D4
BURLWOOD DR	LAN	LAN		159	F8
BURMA CT	POM	POM	1600	95	A4
BURMA RD	PR	PR	9000	54	E5
BURMA ST	LA	ENC	17300	14	E6
BURNABY DR	CO	GLDR	4800	89	C3
BURNABY DR	GLDR	GLDR	100	87	C6
BURNABY DR	GLDR	GLDR	1400	89	C2
BURNELL DR	LA	LA65	1600	35	E3
BURNELL OAKS LN	ARC	ARC	900	28	D3
BURNET AV	LA	SF	8500	8	C4
BURNET AV	LA	SF	8300	15	C1
BURNET AV	LA	VAN	5600	15	C4
BURNET AV	LA	VAN	4600	22	C3
BURNETT ST	LB	LB15		76	A2
BURNETT ST	SH	LB06	1000	75	C2
BURNETT ST E	LB	LB06	100	75	C2
BURNETT ST E	LB	LB15	4400	76	B2
BURNETT ST W	LB	LB06	100	75	A2
BURNETT ST W	LB	LB10	1200	75	A2
BURNHAM ST	LA	LA49	11300	41	C2
BURNING TREE DR	CO	LLAN		192	J2
BURNING TREE DR	LCF	LCF	5400	19	D2
BURNLEY PL	LA	BH		22	F6
BURNS AV	DOW	DOW	7400	60	A3
BURNS AV	LA	LA29	4200	34	F4
BURNS PL	CO	VAL		126	H2
BURNS,GEORGE RD	LA	LA48		33	D6
BURNSIDE AV	LA	LA08	3800	50	F1
BURNSIDE AV	LA	LA16	1900	42	F5
BURNSIDE AV	LA	LA19	1000	43	A4
BURNSIDE AV	LA	LA36	300	43	A1
BURNT TREE LN	WAL	WAL	20000	93	B6
BURNTWOOD ST	SOG	SOG	5700	59	E4
BURNWELL CT	CO	PALM		183	D4
BURR CT	SCLR	NEW		127	C4
BURR ST	LA	LA32	600	36	D4
BURRARD AV	CMRC	LA40	1500	54	B2
BURRELL LN	RPV	PVP		77	E1
BURRELL ST	LA	VEN	900	49	D4
BURRIS AV	COM	COM	100	65	A3
BURRITT AV	RB	RB	2400	62	E4
BURRITT WY	GLEN	GL14	3300	11	C4
BURRO RD	CO	SAU		182	E8
BURROUGHS RD	LA	LA46	9000	33	C1
BURROUGHS WY	CO	PALM		184	A3
BURSON RD	CO	TOP	2300	109	A2
BURT AV	SAD	SAD	1100	89	F1
BURT CT	CO	CYN		125	E7
BURTIS ST	SOG	SOG	9800	59	D4
BURTON AV	BUR	BUR	3100	17	A4
BURTON AV	CO	SGAB	6300	37	F3
BURTON AV	LYN	LYN	3200	65	B1
BURTON AV	RM	RM	3400	46	F1
BURTON AV	SGAB	SGAB	5600	38	A3
BURTON CT	PAS	PAS	200	27	A4
BURTON PL	LA	RES	8200	14	D1
BURTON PL	LAV	LAV		90	C2
BURTON RD	GLDR	GLDR	1700	89	A3
BURTON ST	BLF	BLF		66	A4
BURTON ST	LA	CAN	20900	12	A1
BURTON ST	LA	NHO	11900	16	B1
BURTON ST	LA	NOR	17300	14	E1
BURTON ST	LA	RES	17700	14	D1
BURTON ST	LA	SV	11000	16	E1
BURTON ST	LA	VAN	13400	14	E1
BURTON ST	LA	VAN	13400	15	C1
BURTON ST	LA	VAN	13300	16	A1
BURTON WY	BH	BH	11400	33	C6
BURTON WY	LA	LA48	8500	33	D6
BURTREE ST	CO	LPUE	16200	92	B4
BURWOOD AV	CO	COV	4900	88	B3
BURWOOD AV	LA	LA42	5800	26	C6
BURWOOD AV	WCOV	WCOV	300	88	B6
BURWOOD TER	LA	LA42	600	26	D6
BUSBY DR	CO	WHI	13600	61	E6
BUSCH DR	CO	MAL		110	A4
BUSCH DR	CO	MAL	5500	112	A5
BUSCH PL	PAS	PAS	500	26	E6
BUSCH PL	SFS	SFS	12900	61	D2

1990 LOS ANGELES COUNTY STREET INDEX

STREET	CITY	P.O. ZONE	BLOCK	PAGE	GRID
BUSCH GARDEN CT	PAS	PAS	1000	26	E6
BUSCH GARDEN DR	PAS	PAS	600	26	E6
BUSCH GARDEN LN	PAS	PAS	600	26	E6
BUSH WY	CUL	CUL	5600	50	C3
BUSHNELL AV	SPAS	SPAS	1600	37	A3
BUSHNELL AV N	ALH	ALH	100	37	B4
BUSHNELL AV S	ALH	ALH	2000	46	B1
BUSHNELL WY	LA	LA42	5400	36	C3
BUSHROD LN	LA	LA77	2300	32	D2
BUSHWICK DR	PAS	PAS	400	26	D3
BUSHWICK ST	LA	LA65	3200	35	E1
BUSINESS CIR	CER	ART		66	E5
BUSINESS PKWY	IND	WAL		97	B2
BUSINESS ST	LB	LB07	4100	70	C4
BUSINESS CTR DR	DUA	DUA		29	E5
BUSINESS CTR DR	IRW	BAP		88	A2
BUSINESS CTR DR	LA	NOR	19300	7	A6
BUSIRIS AV	NWK	NWK	12000	61	B6
BUTLER AV	CO	COM	12800	65	C2
BUTLER AV	COM	COM	1300	65	C4
BUTLER AV	LA	LA25	1400	41	D3
BUTLER AV	LA	LA64	2200	41	F6
BUTLER AV	LA	LA66	3100	41	F6
BUTLER AV	LA	LA66	3500	49	F1
BUTLER AV	LA	LA66	3500	50	A1
BUTLER AV	LB	LB05	6200	65	C6
BUTLER AV	LYN	LYN	2600	58	F5
BUTLER CT	CLA	CLA		96	B6
BUTLER ST	PALM	PALM		171	H8
BUTTE ST	CLA	CLA		91	A3
BUTTE ST	LA	LA58	2400	44	E6
BUTTE ST	LA	SP	600	78	E3
BUTTERCREEK DR	PAS	PAS		27	E2
BUTTERCUP DR	PALM	PALM		183	G3
BUTTERFIELD AV	LAV	LAV	800	90	D2
BUTTERFIELD AV	SAD	SAD		95A	A6
BUTTERFIELD CT	CUL	CUL		50	D2
BUTTERFIELD LN	CER	ART		82	C4
BUTTERFIELD RD	HH	CAL		100	C2
BUTTERFIELD RD	LA	LA64	10500	42	A4
BUTTERFIELD RD	POM	POM	500	94	C3
BUTTRFIELD RD N	WCOV	WCOV	500	88	C5
BUTTRFIELD RD S	WCOV	WCOV	100	92	C1
BUTTRFLD STG RD	CO	LR		185	A9
BUTTRFLD STG RD	CO	LR		192	A1
BUTTERFLY LN	LA	LA32	4600	36	D5
BUTTERNUT WY	DBAR	POM		97	F3
BUTTONS AV	TEC	TEC	5300	38	B3
BUTTONWILLOW DR	LA	CAN		12	F2
BUTTONWOOD LN	CO	LPUE		98	E6
BUTTRAM ST	CO	LPUE	15400	85	D4
BYCROFT ST	CO	LPUE	15000	85	C1
BYCROFT ST	CO	LPUE	16200	85	F2
BYERS ST	DOW	DOW	8300	60	B5
BYERTON CT	RPV	SP	1700	78	D1
BYFIELD RD	CO	SAU		123	A2
BYGROVE ST	COV	COV	16600	88	E3
BYLAS RD	CO	MAL		105	E5
BYNNER DR	LA	SP	400	78	D3
BYNUM ST	LB	LB08	8000	81	B6
BYRAM ST	LA	LA15	1000	44	B3
BYRD AV	ING	IN05	8300	57	D1
BYRD ST	LA	VAN		15	A2
BYRDON ST	LAV	LAV		95A	E4
BYROCK TR	CO	TOP	1700	109	D2
BYRON AV	LA	SF	12600	1	E4
BYRON CT	POM	POM		94	C1
BYRON DR	LAN	LAN		160	E6
BYRON PL	LA	LA46	2600	33	D1
BYRON RD	WHI	WHI	8100	55	D6
BYWAYS ST	SELM	ELM		47	D4
BYWOOD DR	GLEN	GL06	2400	26	A4
C					
C CT	CO	PALM		183	A3
C CT	LA	WIL		74	B5
C ST	CER	ART		82	C6
C ST	LAV	LAV	1800	90	C4
C ST	LA	WIL	100	74	B5
C ST E	LA	WIL	100	74	B5
C ST W	LA	WIL	100	74	B5
C WALK	LA	WIL		74	B5
CABALLERO RD	ARC	ARC	1400	28	D3
CABALLEROS LN	RH	PVP	1	78	B2
CABALLEROS RD	RH	PVP		78	B1
CABALLETA DR	SCLR	SAU	26300	124	C7
CABALLO AV	CO	GLDR	1400	87	D6
CABALLO AV	CO	GLDR	800	89	D1
CABALLO RD	LA	WOH	4500	13	B3
CABALLO RCH RD	SAD	LAV		95A	C5
CABANA AV	CO	LPUE	900	48	E3
CABANA AV	LPUE	LPUE	300	48	D4
CABANA AV	WCOV	WCOV	1500	48	E3
CABANA LN	LAN	LAN		159	F7
CABANAS AV	LA	TU	9600	11	B4
CABELL AV	BLF	BLF	14100	66	C3
CABELL AV	DOW	DOW	13200	66	C1
CABEZO CT	SCLR	VAL		124	B7
CABIN DR	CO	PALM		157	G9
CABIN ST	LA	SP	100	79	B2
CABINDA DR	CO	LPUE		85	B1
CABLE PL	ING	IN01		50	F6
CABLE PL	ING	IN01		56	F1
CABO DR	WHI	WHI		84	D4
CABO BLANCO DR	CO	LPUE		85	F5
CABOOSE DR	LAN	LAN		160	E4
CABORA DR	LA	LA45		55A	F1
CABORA DR	LA	VEN	7600	55A	E1
CABOT LN	LAV	LAV		90	C1
CABOT LN	MTB	MTB		46	D5
CABOT ST	LA	LA31	2300	35	E4
CABOT WY	LB	LB10	1300	70	A4
CABRA DR	WAL	WAL		93	D6
CABRAL ST	SCLR	CYN		124	J7
CABREE CT	LAN	LAN		160	C3
CABRERA AV	SCLR	SAU	26800	124	D7
CABRILLO AV	ALH	ALH	1500	36	F6
CABRILLO AV	LA	VEN		49	C4
CABRILLO AV	NWK	NWK	14300	82	D2
CABRILLO AV	TOR	TOR	1200	68	D6
CABRILLO AV	TOR	TOR	23900	73	D1
CABRILLO AV N	LA	SP	100	78	F4
CABRILLO AV S	LA	SP	100	78	F4
CABRILLO BLVD	LA	LA66	3200	49	E2
CABRILLO DR	AVA	AVA		77	B5
CABRILLO DR	BH	BH	1100	33	B4
CABRILLO DR	DUA	DUA	900	29	D4
CABRILLO DR	GLEN	GL07	900	25	D2
CABRILLO LN	CER	ART	17300	81	A3
CABRILLO RD	ARC	ARC	1	28	B5
CABRILLO ST	WHI	WHI		84	D4
CABRILLO VILLAS	LA	LA42		36	D3
CABRINI DR	LA	BUR		17	B2
CABRINI DR E	LA	BUR		17	B2
CABRINI DR W	LA	BUR		17	B2
CABRIOLE AV	LA	NOR	11300	1	B6
CABRIOLE AV	LA	NOR	11100	7	B1
CABRIOLET CT	CO	LAN		159	B9
CABRITO RD	LA	VAN	14500	15	C2
CACERAS ST	SCLR	SAU	22000	124	D6
CACHALOTE ST	LA	WOH	4100	13	D4
CACHAN PL	RPV	PVP	30200	77	C1
CACHE ST	CO	PALM	8900	171I	F3
CACHUMA LN	CO	CYN		128	E2
CACTUS AV	LA	CHA	9700	6	A4
CACTUS DR	LAV	LAV		95A	D5
CACTUS DR	PALM	PALM		171	J8
CACTUS LN	CAR	CAR		69	D6
CACTUS TR	CO	CAL		100A	E5
CADBROOK DR	LPUE	LPUE	300	48	E5
CADBURY RD	WHI	WHI		55	D3
CADDINGTON DR	RPV	SP	1400	78	D1
CADDY ST	PR	PR	9000	54	E5
CADE ST	LB	LB05	2800	65	F5
CADENHORN DR	CO	AGO		106	D2
CADET CT	LA	LA68	3100	24	A6
CADILLAC AV	LA	LA34	5700	42	D4
CADILLAC DR	POM	POM	1700	90	E6
CADISON ST	TOR	TOR		67	F1
CADISON ST	TOR	TOR	4500	68	A1
CADIZ CT	LA	VEN	400	49	C4
CADIZ DR	LOM	LOM	24500	73	D2
CADIZ LN	LB	LB03		76	D5
CADIZ ST	MPK	MPK	900	46	B3
CADLEY DR	CO	LAV	4000	95A	C6
CADLEY DR	LAV	LAV	1300	95A	C6
CADMAN DR	LA	LA27	3600	35	B1
CADMUS AV	CO	LA61		64	B2
CADROW AV	CO	LPUE	400	92	B5
CADWELL ST	CO	LPUE	15800	92	A4
CADWELL ST	LPUE	LPUE	15300	48	F4
CADWELL ST	LPUE	LPUE	15700	92	A4
CAERN AV	LA	TU	11400	10	F1
CAESAR AV	CO	PAS	1000	27	F6
CAFFEL WY	CO	WHI		61	D3
CAGLIERO ST	CO	LPUE	13400	48	D2
CAGNEY ST	LA	SF	17300	1	E4
CAHILL AV	LA	TAR	5600	14	B6
CAHILL PL	DBAR	POM		97A	F2
CAHILL ST	DBAR	POM		97	F2
CAHITA AV	CO	COM	14300	64	C2
CAHUENGA BLVD	LA	LA04	500	34	C5
CAHUENGA BLVD	LA	LA28	1300	34	C5
CAHUENGA BLVD	LA	LA38	700	34	C5
CAHUENGA BLVD	LA	LA68	4700	23	F3
CAHUENGA BLVD	LA	LA68	1900	34	C4
CAHUENGA BLVD	LA	NHO		16	F6
CAHUENGA BLVD	LA	NHO		23	F3
CAHUENGA BLVD E	LA	LA68		24	B6
CAHUENGA BLVD W	LA	LA68	3400	24	A5
CAHUENGA TER	LA	LA68	6500	34	B2
CAHUENGA PK TR	LA	LA68	6800	24	B6
CAINE DR	ART	ART	11400	66	F5
CAIRD AV	CO	MAL		105	E5
CAIRN AV	CO	COM	14300	64	C2
CAIRNGROVE AV	CO	GLDR	7700	86	F4
CAIRNLOCH ST	CO	WOH		13	B5
CAIRO AV	CAR	CAR	18000	64	B6
CAIRO AV	CAR	CAR	18700	69	B1
CAIRO WK	LA	VAN		22	D4
CAITHNESS ST	LA	NOR		1	B4
CAITLIN LN	SCLR	SAU		124	G5
CAJON AV	WCOV	WCOV	600	92	D2
CAJON CIR	WCOV	WCOV	1800	92	D3
CAJON PASS TR	DBAR	POM		97	E6
CALABAR AV	LA	VEN	8100	55A	E1
CALABASAS RD	CO	CAL		100	D3
CALABASAS HLS RD	CO	CAL		100A	E5
CALABASAS PEAK	CO	TOP		100	E6
CALABASH PL	LA	WOH	5000	13	A2
CALABASH ST	LA	WOH	22700	13	A2
CALABRIA DR	AGH	AGO		100A	A3
CALABRIA DR	GLDR	GLDR	700	87	C4
CALADA AV	PR	PR	4400	54	F2
CALADA ST	LA	LA23	1100	53	B1
CALADERO ST	LA	TAR	19100	21	A3
CALADRE AV	DOW	DOW	12200	60	A5
CALAFIA ST	GLEN	GL08	1800	18	F5
CALAHAN ST	LA	NOR	18700	7	B5
CALAHAN ST	LA	SF	16500	7	F5
CALAHAN ST	LA	SF	15900	8	A5
CALAHAN ST	LA	VAN	14100	8	D5
CALAIS ST	BAP	BAP	13600	39	D3
CALAMAR ST	TOR	TOR	1700	68	D5
CALAMIGOS RD	CO	MAL		106	B4
CALAMINE DR	CO	AGO		100A	E4
CALAMUS AV	CO	LAN	48500	146	G5
CALANDA AV	CO	ALT	2600	19	F4
CALATINA DR	POM	POM	1600	94	D4
CALATRANA DR	LA	WOH	5000	13	C2
CALAVERAS DR	WAL	WAL		92	F5
CALAVERAS RD	SAD	SAD		90	A1
CALAVERAS ST	LA	LA65	3700	36	A4
CALAVERAS ST E	CO	ALT	100	20	C5
CALAVERAS ST W	CO	ALT	100	19	F4
CALBAS ST	CAR	CAR	800	69	C4
CALBOURNE DR	DBAR	WAL	1000	97	B3
CALBUCO AV	CO	PALM	39200	175	F7
CALCEDONY CT	PALM	PALM		173	A9
CALCETA AV E	CO	LAN	20700	175	G6
CALCUTTA ST	CO	LPUE	17400	92	C6
CALCUTTA ST	LA	SF	13000	3	A2
CALDEN AV	SOG	SOG	8800	58	F2
CALDER DR	CO	GLDR	6800	87	A5
CALDERO LN	CO	MONT	2300	18	E2
CALDERON RD	LA	WOH	4700	13	B2
CALDERWOOD LN	PAS	PAS	700	28	A2
CALDERWOOD ST	LB	LB15	5100	76	C3
CALDORA AV	PAR	PAR	15600	65	D3
CALDUS AV	LA	VAN	7100	14	D3
CALDWELL AV	WHI	WHI		55	E6
CALDWELL CT	SAD	SAD		89	F2
CALDWELL ST E	COM	COM	100	65	B4
CALDWELL ST W	COM	COM	100	64	C4
CALEB ST	GLEN	GL02	500	18	B6
CALECHE RD	CO	LAN		159	B9
CALEDONIA WY	LA	LA65	4200	25	E6
CALENDA DR	LA	WOH	5100	100	F2
CALERA AV	CO	AZU	6000	88	F1
CALERA AV	CO	COV	4800	88	F3
CALERA AV	COV	COV	1000	88	F3
CALERA AV	GLDR	GLDR	100	86	F5
CALERA AV N	AZU	AZU	200	86	F6
CALERA AV S	AZU	AZU	300	88	F6
CALETA RD	CO	AGO		100A	E2
CALGARY LN	LA	LA77	1700	32	E2
CALGROVE BLVD	SCLR	NEW	23600	127	B6
CALHAVEN DR	SCLR	SAU		124	E5
CALHOUN AV	LA	VAN	5600	15	E6
CALHOUN AV	LA	VAN	4300	22	E1
CALIBURN DR	LA	LA02	600	58	C2
CALICO AV	PR	PR	4100	54	E2
CALICO AV	PR	PR	3900	55	A1
CALICO CT	SAD	SAD		89	E1
CALICO DR	WCOV	WCOV		92	D4
CALICUT RD	CO	MAL		112	E4
CALIENTE AV	CER	ART	17400	82	E5
CALIENTE CIR	CER	ART	17800	82	E5
CALIENTE PL	CER	ART	17600	82	E5
CALIENTE ST	MPK	MPK	400	45	E2
CALIFA PL	LA	WOH	5700	12	E6
CALIFA ST	LA	ENC	17300	14	E6
CALIFA ST	LA	NHO	10400	16	E6
CALIFA ST	LA	TAR	18100	14	C6
CALIFA ST	LA	VAN	13600	15	E6
CALIFA ST	LA	WOH	23000	5	E6
CALIFA ST	LA	WOH	20100	12	A6
CALIFON ST	CAR	CAR	1600	69	D4
CALIFORNIA AV	BAP	BAP	14400	39	E3
CALIFORNIA AV	BELL	BELL		53	B6
CALIFORNIA AV	BLF	BLF	16200	66	D4
CALIFORNIA AV	CO	ACT		189	G2
CALIFORNIA AV	CO	DUA	2100	29	B6
CALIFORNIA AV	CO	DUA	2300	39	B1
CALIFORNIA AV	CO	LPUE	600	48	E4
CALIFORNIA AV	CO	MON	2100	29	B6
CALIFORNIA AV	CO	MON	2300	39	B1
CALIFORNIA AV	COM	COM		65	A4
CALIFORNIA AV	ELM	ELM	3300	38	E6
CALIFORNIA AV	ELM	ELM	2600	47	E2
CALIFORNIA AV	GLDR	GLDR	100	86	F5
CALIFORNIA AV	HPK	HPK	7100	53	B6
CALIFORNIA AV	IND	LPUE	100	48	E4
CALIFORNIA AV	IRW	BAP		39	B1
CALIFORNIA AV	LA	VEN	500	49	C3
CALIFORNIA AV	LB	LB05	5900	65	D6
CALIFORNIA AV	LB	LB05	5400	70	D1
CALIFORNIA AV	LB	LB07	3400	70	D5
CALIFORNIA AV	LPUE	LPUE	300	48	E4
CALIFORNIA AV	LYN	LYN	10700	59	B4
CALIFORNIA AV	MON	MON	100	29	B5
CALIFORNIA AV	MON	MON	2500	39	B1
CALIFORNIA AV	MTB	MTB	100	54	D2
CALIFORNIA AV	PAR	PAR	15100	65	F4
CALIFORNIA AV	SH	LB06	2300	75	D2
CALIFORNIA AV	SH	LB07	3000	70	D6
CALIFORNIA AV	SM	SM	100	40	F6
CALIFORNIA AV	SM	SM	800	41	A5
CALIFORNIA AV	SOG	SOG	8100	59	B4
CALIFORNIA AV	WCOV	WCOV	1200	48	E4
CALIFORNIA AV	WCOV	WCOV	200	92	A2
CALIFORNIA AV	WHI	WHI	8300	61	F1
CALIFORNIA AV	WHI	WHI	7600	85	E4
CALIFORNIA AV E	GLEN	GL06	100	25	C3
CALIFORNIA AV W	GLEN	GL03	100	25	C3
CALIFORNIA BL	CO	PAS		28	A5
CALIFORNIA BL	SMAR	PAS	1700	27	D5
CALIFORNIA BL E	PAS	PAS	1	27	A5
CALIFORNIA BL W	PAS	PAS	1	26	E5
CALIFORNIA CT	LA	VEN		49	C3
CALIFORNIA DR	CLA	CLA	2800	91	A3
CALIFORNIA PL	LB	LB07	4400	70	D3
CALIFORNIA PL	POM	POM	1400	90	D6
CALIFORNIA PL	SM	SM		41	B4
CALIFORNIA PL	WHI	WHI		85	A6
CALIFORNIA PL S	SM	SM		41	B4
CALIFORNIA ST	ARC	ARC	1	28	E5
CALIFORNIA ST	CO	HPK	2400	52	F6
CALIFORNIA ST	CO	HPK	2700	53	B6
CALIFORNIA ST	ELS	ELS	100	56	B5
CALIFORNIA ST	HPK	HPK	3100	53	B6
CALIFORNIA ST	TOR	TOR		68	B3
CALIFORNIA ST N	BUR	BUR	1400	17	A5
CALIFORNIA ST N	BUR	BUR	100	24	B1
CALIFORNIA ST N	SGAB	SGAB	100	37	E3
CALIFORNIA ST S	BUR	BUR	100	24	B1
CALIFORNIA ST S	SGAB	SGAB	100	37	E3
CALIFORNIA TER	PAS	PAS	100	26	E5
CALIFORNIA TR	CO	TOP	1700	109	D1
CALIF INCLINE	SM	SM		40	E6
CALIMALI RD	LA	WOH	20900	13	D3
CALINO AV	BAP	BAP	1800	48	E1
CALIPATRIA DR	CO	WOH		13	B5
CALKIN ST	CO	LPUE	14600	85	C1
CALL ST	PR	PR	9200	54	E5
CALLA WY	SCLR	CYN	19000	124	H8
CALLADA PL	LA	TAR	4400	21	B3
CALLADO WY	CO	TOP		109	C1
CALLAHAN PL	CAR	CAR		69	D5
CALLA LILY CT	CO	CYN		125	F4
CALLAWAY AV	LKD	LKD	20300	81	C3
CALLE CT	SCLR	NEW		127	H6
CALLE ADRA	DUA	DUA		29	F4
CALLE ADRIANA	SAD	SAD		93	E1
CALLE AGATA	SAD	SAD		93	E1
CALLE AGOSTO	SAD	SAD		89	E6
CL AGUA FELIZ	CO	SAU		157A	D4
CALLE ALCAZAR	WAL	WAL		93	A6
CALLE ALICIA	WAL	WAL	20000	97	B1
CALLE ALLEGRE	GLEN	GL06		25	F2
CALLE ALTAMIRA	CO	CAL		100	D5
CALLE ALTO	SAD	SAD		89	D5
CALLE AMABLE	GLEN	GL06		25	F2
CALLE AMANDA	SAD	SAD		93	E1
CALLE AMIGO	PALM	PALM		183	G2
CALLE AMIGOS	CO	SAU		188	C1
CALLE AMPOLA	SAD	SAD		89	D6
CALLE AMPOLA	SAD	SAD		93	D1
CALLE AQUADUCTO	CO	LR		184	D7
CALLE ARAGON	LAV	LAV		95A	D4
CALLE ARANDANO	SAD	SAD		89	F6
CALLE ARANDANO	SAD	SAD		93	F1
CALLE ARBOLADA	LA	PP		30	B5
CALLE ARBOR	SCLR	VAL		127	A2
CALLE ARCANO	SAD	SAD		89	D5
CALLE ARDILLA	CO	CAL		100	D5
CALLE ARINO	SCLR	VAL		127	B1
CALLE ARROYO	CO	SAU		157A	E4
CALLE ARROYO	SAD	SAD		89	E5
CALLE AURORA	CO	LPUE		98	C4
CALLE AVENTURA	RPV	SP	2800	78	C3
CALLE AZUL	GLEN	GL06		25	F2
CALLE AZUL	SAD	SAD		89	F6
CALLE AZUL	SAD	SAD		93	F1
CALLE BAJA DR	WAL	WAL	19600	97	A1
CALLE BANDERA	SAD	SAD		89	E5
CALLE BARCELONA	CO	LPUE		98	C3
CALLE BECERRA	WAL	WAL	400	93	A6
CALLE BELICIA	SAD	SAD		93	E1
CALLE BELLA	GLEN	GL06		26	A2
CALLE BELLEZA	CO	LPUE		98	D4
CALLE BERRO	CO	SAU		157A	D4
CALLE BOGOTA	CO	LPUE		98	C4
CALLE BONITA	CO	SAU		125	H1
CALLE BONITA	CO	SAU		157A	F5
CALLE BONITA	PALM	PALM		183	G2
CALLE BORREGO	WAL	WAL		93	A6
CALLE CABALLERO	SAD	SAD		89	E5
CL CABALLEROS	WAL	WAL		93	A6
CALLE CABANAS	CO	SAU		157A	F4
CALLE CABRILLO	TOR	RB		67	E6
CALLE CADIZ	WAL	WAL		93	B6
CL CALIFORNIOS	LAN	LAN		171	F1
CALLE CAMPANA	WAL	WAL		97	A1
CALLE CANDIDA	SAD	SAD		93	E1
CALLE CANELA	SAD	SAD		89	F6
CALLE CANELA	SAD	SAD		93	F1
CALLE CANON	CO	CAL		100	D5
CALLE CARONA	CO	SAU		157A	E4
CALLE CARRILLO	SAD	SAD		89	D6
CALLE CASCADA	CO	SAU		157A	E4
CALLE CASCARRON	CO	SAU		157A	F4
CALLE CASITAS	CO	SAU		157A	E3
CALLE CATALINA	SAD	SAD		89	E6
CALLE CECELIA	SAD	SAD		89	D6
CALLE CECELIA	SAD	SAD		93	D1
CALLE CERRITO	CO	CYN		125	C4
CALLE CERRITOS	CO	SAU		157A	E4
CALLE CHEVAL	CO	SAU		157A	E3
CALLE CHIQUITO	CO	SAU		157A	D4
CALLE CIERVOS	SAD	SAD		89	C5
CALLE CINCO	MTB	MTB	400	54	D2
CALLECITA DR N	CO	ALT	2700	20	A4
CALLE CLARITA	LAN	LAN		171	F1
CALLE CLEMENTE	LAV	LAV		90	C1
CALLE COLIMA	WCOV	WCOV		92	E5
CALLE COLORADO	SAD	SAD		89	F6
CALLE COLORADO	SAD	SAD		93	F1
CALLE CONEJO	CO	CAL		100	D5
CALLE CONTENTO	GLEN	GL06		25	F2
CALLE CORONADO	DUA	DUA		29	D4
CALLE CORTA	CO	LPUE	15200	85	D2
CALLE CRESPI	SAD	SAD		89	E6
CALLE CRISTINA	SAD	SAD		89	C6
CALLE DAGGETT	CO	SAU		157A	D4
CL DE ANDALUCIA	TOR	RB	100	72	D1
CALLE DE ARAGON	TOR	RB	400	72	D1
CALLE D ARBOLES	TOR	RB	4900	72	D1
CL DE ARMONIA	SAD	SAD		89	E5
CALLE DE CABOS	POM	POM		94	C5
CL D CASTELLANA	TOR	RB		72	D1
CALLE DEE	CO	SAU		181	D7
CL DE ESTRIBO	LA	PP		109	F5
CALLE DE FELIPE	TOR	RB	400	72	E1
CALLE DE GRANDE	LAV	LAV		90	C1
CALLE DE GRANDE	LAV	LAV		95A	C6
CL D LA BURITTA	CO	MAL		111	A4
CL DE LA FUENTE	CO	LPUE	15200	85	D2
CL DE LA LUNA	AZU	AZU		86	B4
CL D LS ESTRLLS	AZU	AZU		86	B4
CL D LAS FLORES	SAD	SAD		89	E5
CALLE DEL BARCO	CO	MAL		114	E4
CALLE DEL BRAVO	LAV	LAV		90	C1
CALLE DEL CIELO	AZU	AZU		86	C4
CALLE DL JONELA	LA	PP		109	F6
CALLE DEL MAR	POM	POM		94	B4
CALLE DEL NORTE	CO	SAU		157A	E5
CALLE DEL NORTE	DUA	DUA		86	A4
CALLE DEL NORTE	IRW	BAP		88	B3
CL DEL OLIVIDA	SAD	SAD		89	D5
CL DEL PACIFICO	GLEN	GL06		25	F2
CL DL PAJARITO	RPV	PVP		77	B1
CL DEL REPOSO	WAL	WAL		97	B1
CALLE DEL ROJA	CO	PALM		190	B2
CALLE DEL SOL	AVA	AVA		77	B5
CALLE DEL SOL	AZU	AZU		86	C4
CALLE DEL SOL	PALM	PALM		183	G2
CALLE DEL SOL	POM	POM		94	B4
CALLE DEL SUR	CO	SAU		157A	F5

LOS ANGELES CO.

STREET	CITY	P.O. ZONE	BLOCK	PAGE	GRID
CALLE DE MADRID	LA	PP		30	A6
CALLE DE MADRID	TOR	RB	200	72	E1
CALLE DE MAYA	LAM	LAM	13400	83	B1
CALLE DE NORTE	IRW	BAP	16000	88	B3
CALLE DE ORO	POM	POM		90	C6
CALLE DE ORO	SAD	SAD		89	D5
CL DE PALERMO	LA	PP		109	F5
CALLE DE PASEO	IRW	BAP		88	B3
CL DE PRIMERA	TOR	TOR	4300	72	F1
CALLE DE REY	POM	POM		94	C5
CL DE RICARDO	TOR	RB	5100	72	E1
CALLE DE RODEO	POM	POM		94	C4
CALLE DESCANSO	WAL	WAL		97	A1
CL DESCONOCIDO	CO	SAU		157A	E5
CL DE SEVILLA	LA	PP		40	A1
CL DE SIRENAS	TOR	RB	100	72	D1
CALLE DE SOTA	CO	SAU		157A	F5
CL DESPENSERO	CO	LPUE	15200	85	D2
CALLE DE SUENOS	RPV	PVP		77	B1
CL EL BARANCO	CO	SAU		157A	E4
CALLE EL BOSQUE	CO	SAU		157A	F5
CALLE EL CAPITAN	CO	SAU		157A	F4
CL EL CLAVELITO	CO	SAU		157A	E3
CALLE EL FUENTE	CO	SAU		157A	E4
CALLE EL JARDIN	CO	SAU		157A	G4
CL EL JORANDO	CO	SAU		157A	F4
CALLE EL MONTE	CO	SAU		157A	E3
CALLE EL TORO	LAV	LAV		95A	C6
CALLE ESCONDIDO	CO	SAU		157A	F5
CALLE ESPANA	SAD	SAD		89	E5
CALLE ESSENCIAL	CO	SAU		157A	F4
CALLE ESTITO	WAL	WAL	19800	93	B6
CALLE ESTRADA	LAN	LAN		159	F7
CALLE ESTRADA	LAV	LAV		90	C1
CALLE ESTRADA	LAV	LAV		95A	C6
CALLE ESTRELLA	SAD	SAD		89	D5
CL EVA MIRANDA	IRW	BAP		86	B5
CALLE FORTUNA	WAL	WAL		93	A6
CALLE FRANCESCA	SAD	SAD		89	D6
CALLE FRONDOSA	SAD	SAD		89	E5
CALLE GALANTE	SAD	SAD		89	D5
CALLE GRANADA	DUA	DUA		29	D4
CALLE GRANADA	WAL	WAL		93	B6
CALLE GRANDE	PALM	PALM		183	G2
CALLE GRILLO	CO	PALM		183	B2
CALLE HERMOSA	CO	SAU		157A	F4
CALLE HERMOSA	SAD	SAD		89	E5
CALLE JALAPA	WCOV	WCOV		92	E5
CLJ CABRILLO	WAL	WAL		97	A1
CALLEJN PEQUENO	WAL	WAL		97	B1
CALLE JORANDO	CO	SAU		157A	F4
CALLE JUCA	LHH	LAH		84	C2
CALLE JUELA DR	LA	BH		33	C1
CALLE LAGO	WAL	WAL		93	B6
CALLE LAGUNA	CO	SAU		157A	E4
CL LA PASTURA	CO	SAU		157A	E5
CALLE LA PAZ	CO	LPUE		98	D4
CL LA RESOLANA	RPV	PVP		77	B1
CL LS DOS HUERF	CO	SAU		157A	G4
CALLE LASUEN	WAL	WAL	19800	93	B6
CALLE LEANDRO	SAD	SAD		89	E6
CALLE LEON	WCOV	WCOV		92	E5
CALLE LINARES	DUA	DUA		29	F4
CALLE LINARES	DUA	DUA		86	A4
CALLE LINDA	SAD	SAD		89	E5
CALLE LISETA	SAD	SAD		89	E6
CALLE LISETA	SAD	SAD		93	E1
CALLE LLANO	CO	SAU		157A	E4
CALLE LOMA	CO	SAU		157A	E4
CALLE LOMITA	CO	SAU		157A	E3
CALLE LORENA	SAD	SAD		93	E1
CL LOS ARBOLES	CO	LPUE		98	D4
CL LS ELEGANTES	CO	SAU		157A	G4
CL LOS HIDALGOS	CO	SAU		157A	E5
CALLE LUNA	WAL	WAL		97	A1
CL MACETA D FLR	CO	SAU		157A	F3
CALLE MADRID	CO	LPUE		98	D4
CALLE MALAGA	DUA	DUA		29	F5
CALLE MALAGA	DUA	DUA		86	A4
CALLE MALEZA	CO	SAU		157A	F5
CALLE MANZANITA	CO	SAU		157A	E3
CALLE MARGARITA	AGH	AGO		100A	C5
CALLE MARIPOSA	DUA	DUA		29	D4
CALLE MARISMA	WAL	WAL	19800	93	B6
CALLE MARQUITA	CO	SAU		157A	E4
CALLE MARSEILLE	LB	LB03		76	D5
CALLE MARTOS	DUA	DUA		29	F4
CALLE MAYOR	TOR	RB	100	72	E1
CALLE MAYOR	TOR	TOR		67	E6
CALLE MIRADERO	SAD	SAD		89	D5
CALLE MIRAMAR	RB	RB		67	D6
CALLE MIRAMAR	TOR	RB		67	D6
CALLE MIRAMAR	TOR	RB	100	72	D1
CALLE MONTANA	CO	SAU		157A	E3
CL MONTECILLO	AGH	AGO		100A	C5
CALLE MONTEREY	SAD	SAD		89	E5

STREET	CITY	P.O. ZONE	BLOCK	PAGE	GRID
CALLE NARANJO	CO	SAU		157A	F5
CALLE OLIVERA	CO	SAU		157A	E5
CALLE ORTEGA	SAD	SAD		89	D6
CALLE PAJAROS	SAD	SAD	1600	89	D5
CALLE PARADO	CO	SAU		157A	E4
CALLE PARREL	WCOV	WCOV		92	E5
CL PEDRO INFNTE	LA	LA63		45	B5
CALLE PETULA	SAD	SAD		93	E1
CALLE PLANA	CO	SAU		157A	E3
CL POZO VERDE	CO	SAU		157A	F4
CALLE PRIMAVERA	CO	SAU		157A	F4
CALLE PRIMAVERA	SAD	SAD		89	D6
CALLE PUEBLA	WCOV	WCOV		92	E5
CALLE QUIETA	RPV	PVP		77	B1
CALLE RAFAEL	SAD	SAD		89	E6
CALLE RAFAEL	SAD	SAD		93	E1
CALLE REAL	PALM	PALM		183	G2
CALLE REDONDA	CO	LPUE	15200	85	D2
CALLE REDONDA	WAL	WAL		97	A1
CALLE RENATA	SAD	SAD		93	E1
CALLE ROBLEDA	AGH	AGO		100A	C5
CALLE ROSA	SAD	SAD		89	F6
CALLE ROSALITO	CO	SAU		157A	F3
CALLE ROSAMARIA	SAD	SAD		89	D6
CALLE RUIZ	WCOV	WCOV		92	E5
CALLE SABINA	SAD	SAD		93	E1
CALLE SAN LUCAS	CO	LPUE		98	C4
C S LUIS POTOSI	CO	SAU		157A	E5
CL STA BARBARA	SAD	SAD		89	E6
CALLE SENITA	WAL	WAL		93	B6
CALLE SERENA	LAN	LAN		159	E7
CALLE SERRA	SAD	SAD		89	D6
CL SERRANONA	CO	CAL		100	D5
CALLE SIEMERIO	CO	SAU		157A	D4
CALLE SIENNA	SAD	SAD		89	F6
CALLE SIENNA	SAD	SAD		93	F1
CALLE SILVOSA	CO	LPUE		98	D4
CALLE SIMPATICO	GLEN	GL06		25	F2
CALLE SOLANA	SAD	SAD		93	D1
CALLE SOLIS	WAL	WAL	20000	97	B1
CALLE SONRISA	GLEN	GL06		25	F2
CALLE SONRISO	CO	SAU		157A	F5
CALLET ST	PALM	PALM	500	172	A6
CALLE TADEO	SAD	SAD		89	E6
CALLE TADEO	SAD	SAD		93	E1
CALLE TAXCO	WCOV	WCOV		92	E5
CALLE TOMAS	SAD	SAD		89	E6
CALLE TRELLA	SAD	SAD		93	E1
CALLE VAQUERO	GLEN	GL06	1200	25	E2
CALLE VERDAD	CO	SAU		157A	F5
CL VILLADA CIR	DUA	DUA		29	F4
CALLE VISTA	CO	SAU		125	H1
CALLE VISTA CIR	LA	NOR		1	C6
CALLE VISTA CT	LA	NOR		1	B5
CALLE VISTA DR	BH	BH		33	B4
CALLE VISTASO	SAD	SAD		89	E5
CALLICOTT AV	LA	CAN	6500	5	F5
CALLICOTT AV	LA	WOH	6100	5	F5
CALLISON ST	LOM	LOM	1900	73	D1
CALLITA PL	SMAR	PAS		37	B2
CALLITA ST	CO	ARC	9600	38	B1
CALLITA ST	CO	SGAB	8500	37	F1
CALLITA ST	CO	SGAB	8600	38	A1
CALLON DR	CO	TOP	20100	109	D2
CALMADA AV	CO	WHI	9300	61	E3
CALMADA AV	WHI	WHI	8800	61	F2
CALMADA AV	WHI	WHI	8100	84	A1
CALMADA AV	WHI	WHI	7600	85	A6
CALMAE DR	LAN	LAN	700	160	D5
CALMAR CT	LA	LA24	1500	42	A2
CALMBANK AV	LAV	LAV		95A	D5
CALMBROOK LN	DBAR	POM		99	D4
CALMCREST DR	DOW	DOW	7500	60	B1
CALMETTE AV	CO	LPUE	2000	97	A5
CALMFIELD AV	AGH	AGO		100A	A2
CALM GARDEN RD	CO	SAU		189	G4
CALMGROVE AV	CO	COV	3600	89	A5
CALMGROVE AV	COV	COV	400	89	A5
CALMGROVE AV	GLDR	GLDR	800	89	A2
CALMHILL DR	TOR	TOR	26000	73	B4
CALMIA RD	CO	DUA	2400	39	B1
CALMONT DR	CO	PALM		157	F8
CALMOSA AV	WHI	WHI	8700	61	F2
CALMOSA AV	WHI	WHI	8200	84	A1
CALMOSA AV	WHI	WHI	7600	85	A6
CALMVIEW AV	BAP	BAP	5000	39	F3
CALNEVA DR	LA	ENC	16400	21	F5
CALOBAR AV	CO	WHI	7800	55	C6
CALORA ST	CO	COV	19400	89	A3
CALORA ST	SAD	SAD	300	89	F3
CALPELLA ST	LAM	LAM	14400	82	F1
CALPELLA ST	LAM	LAM	14600	83	A1
CALPET DR	DBAR	WAL	20300	97	C3
CALPINE CT	POM	POM	800	94	F6
CALPINE DR	CO	MAL	5600	112	B5
CALSPAR ST	CO	CLA	700	96	A6

STREET	CITY	P.O. ZONE	BLOCK	PAGE	GRID
CALSTOCK ST	CAR	CAR	1800	69	E2
CALSTON AV	LAN	LAN	44100	160	D5
CALUMET AV	LA	LA26	1300	44	C1
CALUSA DR	CO	WHI	13700	61	E6
CALVA ST	CO	PALM	8500	171I	G4
CALVADOS AV	AZU	AZU	200	86	E6
CALVADOS AV	AZU	AZU	100	88	E1
CALVADOS AV	CO	COV	3200	88	E4
CALVADOS AV	WCOV	WCOV	100	92	E1
CALVADOS AV N	COV	COV	700	88	E4
CALVADOS AV S	COV	COV	500	88	E5
CALVELLO DR	SCLR	SAU	22600	124	C4
CALVELLO DR	SCLR	VL54		124	B4
CALVERT RD	PAS	PAS	3300	28	A2
CALVERT ST	LA	ENC	17600	14	B5
CALVERT ST	LA	NHO	10700	16	B5
CALVERT ST	LA	RES	17700	14	B5
CALVERT ST	LA	VAN	13700	15	D5
CALVERT ST	LA	VAN	12900	16	A5
CALVERT ST	LA	WOH	24400	5	D5
CALVERT ST	LA	WOH	19700	12	F5
CALVERTON DR	LAM	LAM	15400	83	C3
CALVERTON PL	LAM	LAM		83	C3
CALVIN AV	LA	LA25	10200	42	A2
CALVIN AV	LA	NOR	8500	7	A3
CALVIN AV	LA	NOR	8300	14	A1
CALVIN AV	LA	RES	6100	14	A5
CALVIN AV	LA	TAR	5800	14	A6
CALVIN AV	LA	TAR	4800	21	A2
CALWOOD ST	SCLR	SAU		124	F4
CALYPSO LN	SCLR	CYN	27200	124	G7
CALZADA DR	RPV	SP	28000	73	D6
CALZADILLA PL	LA	TAR	4500	21	B3
CALZONA ST	LA	LA23	1400	53	C1
CAMALOA AV	LA	SF	11300	9	F1
CAMANN ST	GLEN	GL08	1000	18	D3
CAMARES DR	CO	PALM	36300	183	A2
CAMARGO DR	SCLR	SAU	26800	124	D7
CAMARILLO PL	LA	NHO	10100	24	A3
CAMARILLO ST	LA	ENC	15400	22	B2
CAMARILLO ST	LA	NHO	10100	23	D3
CAMARILLO ST	LA	NHO	10100	24	A2
CAMARILLO ST	LA	VAN	14900	22	B2
CAMARINA DR	CO	LPUE	2100	98	E4
CAMARITAS DR	DBAR	POM	23000	97	F1
CAMAROSA DR	LA	PP	14900	40	D5
CAMAY CT	CO	WOH		13	B4
CAMBA AV	CAR	CAR	19700	69	E2
CAMBAY ST	LPUE	LPUE	15600	92	A5
CAMBERLEY LN	CO	LPUE		98	A5
CAMBERT ST	CO	LAV	700	90	B2
CAMBERT ST	SAD	SAD	600	90	B2
CAMBON AV	DBAR	WAL		97	C2
CAMBRAY DR	CO	WHI	12800	47	E5
CAMBRIA ST	LA	LA17	1500	44	B3
CAMBRIA WY	PALM	PALM		171	H7
CAMBRIDGE	MB	MB		62	C3
CAMBRIDGE AV	CLA	CLA	100	91	A3
CAMBRIDGE AV	CO	SAU		123	D4
CAMBRIDGE CT	AGH	AGO		102	F3
CAMBRIDGE CT	PALM	PALM		183	E1
CAMBRIDGE CT	WCOV	WCOV		92	C3
CAMBRIDGE DR	ARC	ARC	300	28	C4
CAMBRIDGE DR	BUR	BUR	400	17	C4
CAMBRIDGE DR	GLEN	GL05	1300	25	D6
CAMBRIDGE LN	PALM	PALM		183	E1
CAMBRIDGE PL	SPAS	SPAS	2000	36	F3
CAMBRIDGE RD	LCF	LCF		19	D5
CAMBRIDGE RD	SMAR	PAS	1300	27	D6
CAMBRIDGE RD	SMAR	PAS		37	D1
CAMBRIDGE ST	LA	LA06	2000	43	E4
CAMBRIDGE ST	LB	LB05	100	65	B6
CAMBRIDGE ST	SFS	SFS	13300	82	D1
CAMBRIDGE WY	CUL	CUL	5600	50	D4
CAMBRIDGE WY	TOR	TOR		68	C5
CAMBRIN RD	POM	POM	1300	94	C1
CAMBURY AV	ARC	ARC	1500	38	C1
CAMBURY AV	TEC	TEC	5400	38	C3
CAMDALE TER	PR	PR	9000	54	E5
CAMDEN AV	LA	LA25	1400	41	E3
CAMDEN AV	LA	LA64	2200	41	E3
CAMDEN AV	SPAS	SPAS	1700	37	B2
CAMDEN CT	CO	PALM		184	E2
CAMDEN CT	PALM	PALM		171	F4
CAMDEN DR	LA	LA35	1700	42	B2
CAMDEN DR N	BH	BH	400	33	B6
CAMDEN DR N	BH	BH	300	42	B1
CAMDEN DR S	BH	BH	100	42	B2
CAMDEN LN	CER	ART		66	F5
CAMDEN PKWY	SPAS	SPAS	1600	37	B2
CAMDEN PL	CO	VAL		124	A7
CAMDEN ST	CO	GLDR	20000	89	B2
CAMDEN ST	GLDR	GLDR	300	89	B2
CAMELBACK AV N	CAR	CAR	23200	69	C6
CAMELBACK AV S	CAR	CAR	23400	74	C1
CAMELBACK DR	WAL	WAL	20500	93	B3

STREET	CITY	P.O. ZONE	BLOCK	PAGE	GRID
CAMELIA DR	ALH	ALH	600	37	D5
CAMELIA HILL WY	CO	CYN		125	F5
CAMELLIA AV	LA	NHO	5600	16	D3
CAMELLIA AV	LA	NHO	4000	23	D4
CAMELLIA AV	TEC	TEC	5700	38	C4
CAMELLIA DR	COV	COV	600	88	F6
CAMELLIA DR	LAN	LAN		159	A9
CAMELLIA ST	LAN	LAN		160	G5
CAMELLIA WY	CO	TOR		68	F5
CAMELLO RD	LA	WOH	4300	13	D3
CAMELOT WY	LA	LA02	600	58	C2
CAMEO AV	NWK	NWK	14300	82	B3
CAMEO CT	POM	POM	100	94	F6
CAMEO PL	LA	SF	17200	1	E5
CAMEO VISTA DR	WCOV	WCOV	2000	92	D3
CAMERFORD AV	LA	LA38	5700	34	C5
CAMERINO ST	LKD	LKD	3600	71	A2
CAMERINO ST	LKD	LKD	5900	71	D2
CAMERO AV	LA	LA27	4000	35	A3
CAMERO AV	LAV	LAV		90	C2
CAMERON AV	CO	COV	1500	93	A2
CAMERON AV	CO	COV	19300	93	A2
CAMERON AV	POM	POM	100	90	E4
CAMERON AV	WCOV	WCOV		39	F5
CAMERON AV E	WCOV	WCOV	1000	92	B2
CAMERON AV W	WCOV	WCOV	1000	92	A2
CAMERON CT	CO	VAL		124	B7
CAMERON DR	PAS	PAS	800	27	C5
CAMERON DR	SMAR	PAS	800	27	C5
CAMERON LN	LA	LA15	400	44	B4
CAMERON PL	GLEN	GL07	300	25	D2
CAMERON PL	LB	LB07	100	70	C5
CAMERON ST	LB	LB10	2100	69	F5
CAMERON ST	LB	LB10	1200	70	B5
CAMERON WAY	SGAB	SGAB	200	37	E3
CAMERON CRST DR	DBAR	POM		94	A6
CAMERONS ST	CO	LPUE		98	F3
CAMETA DR	CO	RM	8600	46	F3
CAMETA DR	CO	RM	8600	47	A3
CAMFIELD AV	CMRC	LA40	2000	53	F2
CAMILA RD	WCOV	WCOV	1000	92	A1
CAMILLA ST	WHI	WHI	11800	55	D4
CAMILLO ST	SMAD	SMAD	200	28	D1
CAMINAR AV	ELM	ELM	2200	47	E3
CAMINAR AV	ELM	ELM		47	F3
CAMINATA LN	LHH	LAH	1300	98A	B1
CAMINITO LN	CO	GL14	4900	11	E6
CAMINITO PL	LA	TAR	4500	21	B3
CAMINO AV	CO	LPUE	3000	85	D4
CAMINO ARROYO	WAL	WAL		93	B6
CAMINO BELLO	CO	LPUE	18100	98	D4
CAMINO CERRADO	SPAS	SPAS	600	36	E2
CAMINO CODORNIZ	CO	CAL		100	D5
CAMINO COLIBRI	CO	CAL		108	A5
CM D BUENA VENT	CO	MAL	3500	111	A3
CM DE CARO	LA	HAC		73	F4
CM DE ENCANTO	TOR	RB	400	72	D1
CAMINO D FLORES	AVA	AVA		77	B4
CAMINO D GLORIA	WAL	WAL		97	B1
CM D LA CANTERA	IRW	BAP		86	B5
CM DE LA COSTA	RB	RB		67	D6
CM DE LA CUMBRE	LA	VAN		22	E4
CM DE LA CUMBRE	LA	VAN		22	D5
CM D LS COLINAS	TOR	RB		67	D6
CM DEL CAMPO	TOR	RB		67	D6
CM DEL CERRITOS	SAD	SAD		89	D6
CM DEL CERRITOS	SAD	SAD		93	D1
CM DEL CIELO	SPAS	SPAS		36	E2
CM DEL MONTE	AVA	AVA		77	A5
CAMINO DEL ORO	CO	WHI		47	F5
CAMINO DEL REY	CO	LPUE		47	F5
CAMINO DEL RIO	CO	WHI		47	F6
CAMINO DEL SOL	SPAS	SPAS		36	D2
CAMINO DEL SOL	TOR	TOR		73	B1
CAMINO DEL SUR	CO	LPUE		85	C4
CAMINO DEL SUR	LAN	LAN		171	F1
CAMINO DEL SUR	SAD	SAD		93	D1
CM DEL TOMASINI	CO	LPUE		85	C3
CAMINO DL VALLE	CO	CAST		123	G2
CAMINO DL VALLE	CO	SAU		123	B3
CAMINO DE MAYO	LA	HAC		73	E4
CAMINO DE ORO	LA	HAC		73	E4
CAMINO DE ROSA	WAL	WAL		97	B2
CM DE SOLANA	LA	VAN	3800	22	E4
CM DE TEODORO	WAL	WAL	500	97	A1
CM DE TEODORO	WCOV	WCOV	3500	97	A1
CM DE VILLAS	BUR	BUR	1600	17	F4
CM DE YATASTO	LA	PP		109	F5
CAMINO GROVE AV	ARC	ARC	600	28	F6
CAMINO HERMANOS	LAN	LAN		171	E1
CAMINO LARGO	CO	LPUE		85	E5
CAMINO LARGO	LA	HAC		73	E4
CAMINO LINDO	SPAS	SPAS	1500	36	E3
CAMINO PALMERO	LA	LA46	1700	34	A3
CAMINO PEQUENO	RPV	PVP		77	B1
CAMINO PLANO	CO	CAL		100	D5

STREET	CITY	P.O. ZONE	BLOCK	PAGE	GRID
CAMINO PORTAL	CO	CAL		100	D5
CAMINO PORVENIR	RPV	PVP		77	B1
CAMINO RASO	LA	HAC		73	F4
CAMINO REAL	ARC	ARC		28	C6
CAMINO REAL	CO	ARC	9600	38	B1
CAMINO REAL	CO	DUA	400	39	B1
CAMINO REAL	CO	MON	100	39	B1
CAMINO REAL	CO	SGAB	8600	38	B1
CAMINO REAL	LA	LA65		35	F4
CAMINO REAL	LA	LA65		36	A4
CAMINO REAL	RB	RB		67	D4
CAMINO REAL	TEC	TEC	9400	38	B1
CAMINO REAL E	ARC	ARC	100	38	E1
CAMINO REAL E	ARC	ARC	1000	39	B1
CAMINO REAL W	ARC	ARC	100	38	E1
CAMINO REAL AV	PALM	PALM		172	B8
CM SAN RAFAEL	GLEN	GL06		25	F2
CM SAN RAFAEL	GLEN	GL08		19	A6
CAMINO SILVOSO	PAS	PAS	500	26	E4
CAMINO VALENCIA	CER	ART	12000	81	B2
CAMINO VEGA	LA	HAC		73	E4
CAMINO VERDE	LA	HAC		73	F4
CAMINO VERDE	SPAS	SPAS	300	36	E3
CAMINO VIEJO	CO	LPUE	18300	98	D4
CAMINO VISTA	LA	HAC		73	E4
CAMINO VISTA	LAN	LAN		171	E1
CAMOLIN AV	LAN	LAN	44900	159	H3
CAMOMILE LN	SCLR	SAU		124	E5
CAMORILLA DR	LA	LA65	2100	35	F2
CAMORILLA ST	LA	VAN		22	B3
CAMPAIGN DR	CAR	CAR	19000	69	C1
CAMPANA RD	LA	WOH	20900	13	D3
CAMPANA ST	HB	RB	1400	62	D6
CAMPANA FLRS DR	WCOV	WCOV	500	92	F1
CAMPANITA CT	MPK	MPK	100	46	A2
CAMP BALDY RD	CO	CLA		96	D4
CAMPBELL AV N	ALH	ALH	400	37	A6
CAMPBELL AV S	ALH	ALH	1100	37	A6
CAMPBELL AV S	ALH	ALH	1100	46	A1
CAMPBELL AV S	ALH	ALH	2000	46	A1
CAMPBELL DR	CUL	LA66	4000	49	F3
CAMPBELL DR	LA	CUL	4600	50	A4
CAMPBELL DR	LA	LA66	4100	49	F3
CAMPBELL DR	LA	LA66	4300	50	A3
CAMPBELL RD E	PALM	PALM	100	172	B4
CAMPBELL RD W	PALM	PALM	100	172	B4
CAMPBELL ST	GLEN	GL07	1100	25	D2
CAMP BONITA P F	CO			P	D4
CAMPDELL ST	LA	VEN	400	55A	E2
CAMPER DR	WCOV	WCOV	1400	92	C4
CAMPESINA RD	ARC	ARC	400	28	B4
CAMPFIRE DR	DBAR	POM		97	E6
CAMPHOR AV	LAV	LAV		90	E1
CAMPHOR LN	CO	POM		93	E2
CAMPHOR PL	POM	POM	2300	94	F6
CAMP HUNTGTN RD	CO	ALT		20	C3
CAMPILLOS RD	LAM	LAM	15000	83	B2
CAMPINA LN	LAM	LAM	15200	84	B5
CAMPION DR	LA	LA45	7800	56	A1
CAMPION WK	LA	LA45		56	A1
CAMPO DR	LB	LB03	100	80	C1
CAMPO RD	LA	WOH	4900	13	C2
CAMPO ST	MPK	MPK	400	46	A2
CAMPO WK	LB	LB03	5500	80	C1
CAMPO NUEVO DR	WHI	WHI	16200	84	C2
CAMP PLENTY RD	SCLR	CYN	27400	124	H8
CAMPTON ST	CO	LPUE	19200	97	A1
CAMPTONVILLE LN	CO	MAL		105	A6
CAMPUS AV	CLA	CLA		91	A3
CAMPUS DR	ARC	ARC	1	28	D5
CAMPUS DR	AZU	AZU	6400	86	E6
CAMPUS DR E	CO	POM		93	F2
CAMPUS DR S	CO	POM		93	F3
CAMPUS DR S	POM	POM		93	F3
CAMPUS DR S	POM	POM	2400	94	A2
CAMPUS DR W	CO	POM		93	E3
CAMPUS RD	LA	LA32		45	E1
CAMPUS RD	LA	LA41	1600	26	A6
CAMPUS RD	LA	LA42	1400	26	A6
CAMPUS RD E	LB	LB15		76	D4
CAMPUS ST	GLEN	GL05	100	25	E4
CAMPUS WK	CO	MAL		113	E4
CAMPUS WY	GLEN	GL06		25	E2
CAMP VIEW DR	CO	CAST		123	F3
CAMRAN AV	LAN	LAN		160	D6
CAMROSE DR	LA	LA68	6800	34	B2
CAMULOS AV	GLEN	GL08	1500	18	E6
CAMULOS PL	LA	LA23	2700	45	A6
CAMULOS ST	LA	LA23	600	45	A6
CAMULOS ST	LA	LA33	400	45	A6
CAMWOOD AV	CO	LPUE	1700	97	A4
CANADA AV	PAS	PAS		19	E6
CANADA BLVD	GLEN	GL08	1900	18	E6
CANADA BLVD	GLEN	GL08	1500	25	E1
CANADA ST	LA	LA65	3500	35	E1

INDEX

COPYRIGHT, © 1989 BY Thomas Bros Maps

—Z— COPYRIGHT, © 1989 BY Thomas Bros Maps

STREET	CITY	P.O. ZONE	BLOCK	PAGE	GRID
CANADA TR	CO	SF	11900	3	E5
CANADA SOMBR RD	LHH	LAH	100	85	F6
CANAL AV	LA	WIL		74	C6
CANAL AV	LB	LB10	1800	75	A3
CANAL AV	LB	LB13	1300	75	A3
CANAL CT	LA	MDR		49	C5
CANAL PL	IND	LPUE	800	48	C2
CANAL ST	LA	VEN	1900	49	C4
CANAL WY	PR	PR	4500	55	B2
CANALDA DR	LCF	LCF	2200	11	F6
CANAL POINT RD	CO	LPUE	3000	85	C4
CANANEA DR	LA	ENC	3600	22	A5
CANARIAS DR	CO	LPUE	16400	85	F5
CANARY AV	LAM	LAM	15000	82	F3
CANASTA ST	LA	TAR	18600	21	B2
CANBERRA CT	CO	LPUE		85	F4
CANBY AV	LA	NOR	8500	7	C6
CANBY AV	LA	NOR	8300	14	C1
CANBY AV	LA	RES	6100	14	C3
CANCELA PL	CO	LPUE	18500	98	F5
CANCHO DR	LHH	LAH	900	84	C2
CANDACE AV	PR	PR	6500	54	E4
CANDACE PL	LA	LA41	5300	26	C4
CANDELA DR	CO	LPUE		98	C4
CANDELERIA DR	WHI	WHI		84	C2
CANDIA CT	LA	SF		1	D4
CANDIA DR	WHI	WHI	9900	84	D3
CANDIA ST	LA	SF	17400	1	E4
CANDICE PL	LA	CHA		6	D1
CANDISH AV	GLDR	GLDR	1400	89	C2
CANDLEBERRY LN	LA	NOR		7	A3
CANDLE FLAME CT	CO	WAL	20100	97	B4
CANDLELIGHT DR	CO	WHI	15800	84	C6
CANDLER CT	DBAR	WAL		97	C3
CANDLEWOOD DR	LA	SF	13800	3	B1
CANDLEWOOD RD	TOR	TOR		73	B2
CANDLEWOOD ST	LKD	LKD	2400	70	F2
CANDLEWOOD ST	LKD	LKD	3500	71	B2
CANDLEWOOD WY	LA	CAN	23400	5	F3
CANDOR DR	CER	ART	12100	81	B1
CANDOR ST	CER	ART	11000	71	E1
CANDOR ST	CER	ART	11900	81	A1
CANDOR ST	LKD	LKD	3600	71	A1
CANEDO AV	LA	NOR	9500	7	B4
CANEDO PL	PAS	PAS	400	26	D3
CANEHILL AV	BLF	BLF	17600	66	D6
CANEHILL AV	LB	LB08	3400	71	D5
CANEHILL AV	LB	LB15	2200	76	D2
CANEHILL AV	LKD	LKD	4300	66	D6
CANEHILL AV	LKD	LKD	5900	71	D2
CANELA PL	CO	LPUE	18900	98	E4
CANELO RD	CO	WHI	10800	84	A4
CANELONES DR	CO	LPUE	16200	85	F4
CANERWELL ST	SCLR	NEW	23600	127	A5
CANEY AV	CAR	CAR	19000	69	C2
CANFIELD AV	LA	CUL	3800	42	C5
CANFIELD AV	LA	LA34	2000	42	C5
CANFIELD AV	LA	LA35	1400	42	D3
CANFIELD AV	POM	POM	100	90	E4
CANFIELD RD	PAS	PAS	3700	28	B2
CANFORD ST	PR	PR	9000	54	E5
CANGAS DR	CO	AGO		100A	E4
CANISIUS CIR	CLA	CLA		91	B1
CANIZERO ST	LAN	LAN	1500	160	E4
CANMORE ST	AGH	AGO		100A	A2
CANNA RD	LA	LA49	12200	32	A5
CANNA VALLEY ST	CO	CYN		125	F5
CANNERY ST	LA	SP	100	79	B3
CANNES AV	CO	LAN	48600	146	E5
CANNING ST	CMRC	LA40	6400	54	A4
CANNON AV	SAD	SAD	100	90	A4
CANNON WY	POM	POM		90	D6
CANOBIE AV	WHI	WHI		55	C4
CANOE RD	CO	CYN		125	D4
CANOECOVE DR	DBAR	POM	23900	94	A6
CANOGA AV	LA	CAN	8500	6	C6
CANOGA AV	LA	CAN	6400	12	C2
CANOGA AV	LA	CHA	9100	6	C3
CANOGA AV	LA	WOH	5600	12	C6
CANOGA AV	LA	WOH	4000	13	D3
CANOGA DR	LA	WOH	4200	13	C4
CANOGA PL	POM	POM	1400	95	B1
CANON AV N	SMAD	SMAD	100	28	D2
CANON AV S	SMAD	SMAD	100	28	D2
CANON BLVD	CO	ALT	3400	20	B3
CANON DR	CO	CAL		100	F5
CANON DR	CO	TOP	21600	13	C6
CANON DR	LA	SP	1000	78	E3
CANON DR	PAS	PAS	700	27	B6
CANON DR	SMAD	SMAD	300	28	D1
CANON DR	SMAR	PAS	900	27	B6
CANON DR N	BH	BH	200	33	C6
CANON DR N	BH	BH	100	42	C1
CANON DR S	BH	BH	100	42	C2
CANON PL	CO	TOP		100	F6
CANON PL	SMAD	SMAD	1	28	D2
CANON CREST AV	LA	LA65	300	36	A3
CANON D CIMARON	CO	MAL		111	A4
CN D PARAISO LN	LCF	LCF	300	19	C3
CANONES CIR	SCLR	SAU	22100	124	D6
CANONES PL	SCLR	SAU		124	D6
CANONITA DR	LHH	LAH	2200	84	D1
CANON VIEW TR	CO	TOP		109	C4
CANONWOOD DR	GLEN	GL02		18	C6
CANOPUS DR	CO	SF		3	E3
CANSO LN	SCLR	SAU		124	D6
CANTABRIAN CT	WHI	WHI	5100	55	C2
CANTALOUPE AV	LA	VAN	8500	8	E6
CANTALOUPE AV	LA	VAN	5600	15	E6
CANTALOUPE AV	LA	VAN	5500	22	E1
CANTARA ST	LA	CAN	19900	12	F1
CANTARA ST	LA	NHO	11600	6	B1
CANTARA ST	LA	NHO	11800	16	A1
CANTARA ST	LA	NOR	17400	14	E1
CANTARA ST	LA	RES	17700	14	A1
CANTARA ST	LA	SV	10400	16	E1
CANTARA ST	LA	VAN	17000	14	E1
CANTARA ST	LA	VAN	14800	15	C1
CANTARA ST	POM	POM	1400	95	B1
CANTARIA AV	CO	LPUE	1700	98	D5
CANTATA DR	LA	LA68	2000	34	B2
CANTEL PL	WAL	WAL	21000	93	C5
CANTEL ST	LB	LB15	6300	76	E2
CANTER LN	CO	ACT		182	E8
CANTERBURY AV	LA	NHO	8200	16	A1
CANTERBURY AV	LA	PAC	8900	8	E4
CANTERBURY AV	LA	PAC	8700	9	A6
CANTERBURY AV	LA	SV	8300	9	A6
CANTERBURY AV	LA	SV	8300	16	A1
CANTERBURY AV	POM	POM	2200	94	B2
CANTERBURY DR	AGH	AGO		102	F2
CANTERBURY DR	CUL	CUL	5900	50	D5
CANTERBURY LN	GLDR	GLDR	2000	87	E5
CANTERBURY RD	SMAR	PAS	600	27	E5
CANTERHILL PL	WLVL	THO		102	A5
CANTERWOOD DR	SCLR	SAU		124	F3
CANTERWOOD RD	LAV	LAV		95A	C5
CANTLAY ST	LA	CAN	19700	12	A3
CANTLAY ST	LA	NHO	11500	16	D3
CANTLAY ST	LA	RES	18200	14	B3
CANTLAY ST	LA	SV	10700	16	E3
CANTLAY ST	LA	VAN	16600	14	D3
CANTLAY ST	LA	VAN	13500	15	E3
CANTLEWOOD DR	PALM	PALM		184	B7
CANTO DR	LA	LA32	4100	36	C6
CANTON CIR	CLA	CLA		96	D5
CANTON DR	LA	NHO	11200	23	D5
CANTON LN	LA	NHO	3300	23	D5
CANTON PL	LA	NHO	11600	23	D5
CANTON ST	SH	LB06	600	75	D1
CANTON ST E	LB	LB06	100	75	C1
CANTON ST E	LB	LB15	5200	76	C1
CANTON ST W	LB	LB10	1400	75	A1
CANTON WY	LA	NHO	3300	23	D5
CANTOS DR	SCLR	SAU	26300	124	D8
CANTRECE LN	CER	ART	13000	81	D1
CANTRECE PL	CER	ART	12300	81	B1
CANTRECE ST	CER	ART	12900	81	C1
CANTRELL AV	CO	WHI	10500	61	E4
CANTURA ST	LA	NHO	12100	23	B2
CANVAS ST	SCLR	CYN		125	C8
CANWOOD ST	AGH	AGO		102	D4
CANWOOD ST	CO	AGO		100A	E4
CANYADA AV	CO	ALT	2200	19	E5
CANYON BLVD N	MON	MON	100	29	B4
CANYON BLVD S	MON	MON	100	29	B4
CANYON DR	CO	CAL		100	E6
CANYON DR	GLEN	GL06	400	25	E3
CANYON DR	LA	LA28	1600	34	D2
CANYON DR	LA	LA68	1900	34	D2
CANYON DR	WHI	WHI		55	F5
CANYON LN	CO	CYN	16500	125	C5
CANYON MTY	CO			M	C4
CANYON RD	ARC	ARC		20A	E3
CANYON RD	ARC	ARC	2000	28	E1
CANYON TER	LA	LA68	2200	34	D2
CANYON TR	CO	TOP		109	D3
CANYON WK	LCF	LCF		19	C2
CANYON WY	AGH	AGO		100A	B5
CANYON WY	POM	POM	1700	90	D6
CANYONBACK RD	LA	LA49		32	A3
CANYON CLOSE RD	PAS	ALT	1900	20	E6
CANYON COURT RD	LHH	LAH		98A	A1
CANYON COVE	LA	LA68	5800	34	D2
CANYON CREEK RD	CER	ART	15900	82	B4
CANYON CREST CT	WLVL	THO		102	A5
CANYON CREST DR	CO	ALT	3300	19	E3
CANYON CREST DR	MON	MON		29	B2
CANYON CREST DR	SMAD	SMAD	600	28	D1
CANYON CREST RD	WHI	WHI		55	F5
CYN CUTOFF RD	DBAR	POM		97	B4
CANYON DELL DR	CO	ALT	4000	19	E3
CANYON HTS LN	LA	LA68	5900	34	D1
CANYON HILL RD	SAD	SAD		90	B1
CANYON HILL RD	SAD	SAD		95A	B6
CANYON LAKE DR	LA	LA68	3200	24	C6
CANYON MEADOWS	CO	WHI		55	E1
CANYON MDWS LN	GLDR	GLDR		87	D1
CANYON MDWS LN	GLDR	GLDR		89	D1
CANYON OAK CIR	POM	POM		90	E2
CANYON OAK DR	LA	LA68	2400	34	D1
CANYON OAK RD	CO	CYN		128	C1
CANYON PARK DR	DBAR	POM		97	E4
CANYON PARK LN	LAV	LAV		90	B1
CANYON QUAIL TR	CO	SAU		181	B9
CANYON RIDGE DR	CO	ALT	3400	19	E3
CANYON RIDGE DR	WLVL	THO		102	A5
CANYON RIDGE LN	LA	SF		1	E2
CANYON RIDGE RD	DBAR	POM		97	C5
CANYON RIM DR	CO	WHI		55	D2
CANYON RIM RD	POM	POM		94	C6
CANYONSIDE RD	CO	GL14	5500	11	F4
CYN SPRING LN	DBAR	POM		97A	A2
CANYON SPGS DR	GLDR	GLDR		87	D3
CANYON VIEW DR	LAV	LAV		90	B1
CANYON VIEW DR	LAV	LAV		95A	C6
CANYON VW DR N	LA	LA49	100	41	A2
CANYON VW DR S	LA	LA49	100	41	A2
CANYON VIEW LN	PAS	PAS		20	E5
CANYON VISTA DR	LA	LA65		36	A3
CANYON WASH DR	PAS	PAS	700	27	F2
CANYONWOOD DR	LA	CAN		5	D4
CANZONET ST	LA	WOH	23000	13	A1
CANZONET ST	LA	WOH	23200	100	F1
CAP CT	CO	LPUE		98	C5
CAPA DR	CO	LPUE	16200	85	F5
CAPAC ST	CO	CYN		128	D3
CAPE AV N	SAD	SAD		90	A2
CAPE LN	LA	BH		33	A3
CAPE ST	CO	RM	7300	46	D3
CAPE COD CT	CLA	CLA		91	C1
CAPE COD LN	PALM	PALM		183	H7
CAPE COTTAGE LN	LA	SF		3	A3
CAPEHART AV	DUA	DUA	1800	29	C6
CAPE HORN DR	AGH	AGO		102	D3
CAPELLO WY	LA	LA77	10600	32	D4
CAPE MAY CT	SCLR	VAL		124	E3
CAPEN AV	DBAR	WAL		97	D2
CAPERTON ST	LAN	LAN	1000	160	D5
CAPESWOOD DR	PVE	PVP	5700	72	D3
CAPE TENEZ DR	WHI	WHI		55	C2
CAPETOWN AV	ALH	ALH		45	E1
CAPETOWN ST	LKD	LKD	3600	71	A2
CAPEW ST	SCLR	CYN		124	H5
CAPINERO DR	PAS	PAS	1300	26	D5
CAPISTRANO AV	GLEN	GL08	1300	18	E5
CAPISTRANO AV	LA	CAN	6400	12	B2
CAPISTRANO AV	LA	CHA	9500	6	B4
CAPISTRANO AV	LA	WOH	5600	12	B6
CAPISTRANO AV	LA	WOH	5300	13	B1
CAPISTRANO AV	LYN	LYN	10700	59	A4
CAPISTRANO AV	SOG	SOG	10300	59	A4
CAPISTRANO CIR	GLEN	GL08	1700	18	E5
CAPISTRANO CT	SCLR	VAL		124	A2
CAPISTRANO LN	LA	NOR		1	A5
CAPISTRANO WY	CO	LA63	4200	45	D4
CAPISTRANO WY	LA	LA48	700	42	E1
CAPITAN	PALM	PALM		184	B1
CAPITOL AV	CO	WHI		47	D6
CAPITOL DR	LA	SP	700	78	F1
CAPIZ CT	WHI	WHI	13700	55	F4
CAPLAND DR	CO	SAU		182	A6
CAPPER AV	POM	POM	900	95	B1
CAPPS AV	LA	NOR	8300	14	B1
CAPPS AV	LA	RES	6400	14	B3
CAPRA RD	CO	SAU		188	A7
CAPRI	PALM	PALM		184	B1
CAPRI CT	LB	LB03		76	D5
CAPRI DR	LA	PP	1200	40	F2
CAPRI DR	WHI	WHI		55	C2
CAPRICORN AV	AGH	AGO		100A	A2
CAPRINO PL	LA	VAN	17600	14	D3
CAPRINO WY	POM	POM	1200	95	B1
CAPROCK CT	GLEN	GL06		25	F2
CAPROCK RD	CO	SAU		181	E7
CAPRON AV	CO	LPUE	300	98	F1
CAPSTAN CIR	WLVL	THO		102	A5
CAPTAINS PL	AGH	AGO		102	D4
CAPTAINS ROW	CO	MDR		49	D6
CAPUCHIN WY	CLA	CLA		91	C1
CAPULET AV	WHI	WHI	9800	84	E3
CAPULIN CT	LA	WOH	22200	13	B2
CARA PL	LA	SP		78	F2
CARACAS ST	CO	GL14	2300	11	F6
CARACOL DR	CO	LPUE	15700	85	D4
CARARD ST	LA	WOH	23700	5	E6
CARAVACA RD	LAM	LAM	15100	83	B2
CARAVANA RD	LA	WOH	4000	13	D4
CARAVEL CIR	CER	ART		81	B1
CARAVEL PL	CER	ART	12400	81	B1
CARAVEL ST	CER	ART		81	C1
CARAWAY DR	CO	WHI	500	48	A4
CARAWAY LN	RPV	PVP		77	D2
CARAWAY LN	SCLR	SAU		124	E6
CARBON CYN RD	CO	MAL	3700	114	D4
CARBONIA AV	WAL	WAL	200	93	C6
CARBON MESA RD	CO	MAL	21900	114	D4
CARBURTON ST	LB	LB08	8200	81	C5
CARCASSONNE RD	LA	LA77	600	32	D5
CARDALE ST	LKD	LKD	5700	71	C2
CARDAMINE DR	LA	TU	10900	10	E1
CARDAMINE PL	LA	TU	10900	10	F2
CARDAMINE ST	LA	TU		10	F2
CARDEENE RD	CO	LAN	11800	158	B5
CARDEENE RD	CO	SAU		181	C7
CARDELL ST	NWK	NWK	11700	82	A1
CARDENAS AV	LA	WOH	4700	13	C3
CARDIFF AV	LA	CUL	3800	42	C6
CARDIFF AV	LA	LA34	2600	42	C3
CARDIFF AV	LA	LA35	1100	42	C3
CARDIFF CT	POM	POM	1000	91	A6
CARDIFF DR	SCLR	SAU		127	C1
CARDIFF DR	SCLR	SAU		127	C4
CARDIFF RD	SAD	SAD		89	C4
CARDIFF ST	PALM	PALM		172	F9
CARDIGAN AV	GLEN	GL02	400	18	C6
CARDIGAN CT	LA	LA77		32	B1
CARDIGAN PL	LA	BH		22	F6
CARDILLO AV	CO	LPUE	2500	85	D3
CARDIN ST	WAL	WAL		93	C5
CARDINAL ST	LA	LA12	1300	44	F1
CARDINAL ST	LA	LA31	1700	44	F1
CARDONA DR	CO	LPUE	18600	98	E4
CARDOZA DR	WLVL	THO		102	C2
CARDWELL PL	LA	LA46	2700	23	E6
CARDWELL ST	LYN	LYN	4500	65	C1
CARDWICK CT	SCLR	NEW		127	H1
CAREFREE CT	LAN	LAN		160	F6
CAREFUL AV	CO	AGO		106	E2
CARELL AV	AGH	AGO		100A	A2
CAREN CT	LAN	LAN		159	J4
CARESS AV	CO	COM	15900	65	B4
CAREW ST	SAD	SAD	1100	89	D2
CAREY ST	LA	PP	14600	40	D3
CAREYBROOK DR	AGH	AGO		102	F2
CARFAX AV	BLF	BLF	13400	66	D2
CARFAX AV	DOW	DOW	12800	66	D1
CARFAX AV	LB	LB08	3000	71	D4
CARFAX AV	LB	LB15	1800	76	D2
CARFAX AV	LKD	LKD	4100	71	D1
CARGREEN AV	CO	LPUE		85	C5
CARGREEN LN	CO	ALT		20	B5
CARIBETH DR	LA	ENC	3400	22	A5
CARIBOU LN	LA	LA77	10300	32	E2
CARICIA DR	CO	LPUE	3000	85	D4
CARILLO DR	SCLR	VAL		127	H6
CARILLO DR	SGAB	SGAB	800	37	D3
CARILLON ST	LA	LA39	2700	35	D2
CARINTHIA DR	WHI	WHI		55	D3
CARIS ST	LA	WOH	24200	5	D6
CARITA ST	LB	LB08	5100	71	B5
CARITINA DR	LA	TAR	4500	21	A3
CARIZ DR	SCLR	VAL		127	A4
CARL PL	LA	PAC	12900	9	A2
CARL ST	LA	PAC	13600	8	E3
CARL ST	LA	PAC	12900	9	A2
CARL ST	LA	SF	12200	3	C6
CARLA CT	SCLR	CYN		125	D7
CARLA DR	GLEN	GL06	700	25	F2
CARLA LN	BH	BH	1100	33	C3
CARLA LN	LA	CAN	8400	5	F1
CARLA PL	CER	ART		66	E4
CARLAND DR	SCLR	NEW	24200	127	A5
CARLA RIDGE	BH	BH	1200	33	C2
CARLARIS RD	SMAR	PAS	2700	37	B1
CARLEEN CT	LA	TU		10	E1
CARLENE LN	LOM	LOM	24300	73	D1
CARLERIK ST	CAR	LB10	21800	70	A5
CARLET PL	SAD	SAD	500	90	B2
CARLET ST	CO	LAV	800	90	B2
CARLET ST	SAD	SAD	300	90	A2
CARLETON AV	CLA	CLA		91	A5
CARLETON AV	CLA	CLA	300	91	A5
CARLETON AV	LA	LA65	2600	35	F4
CARLETON DR	CER	ART		82	E4
CARLETON PL	CLA	CLA	500	91	A5
CARLEY AV	WHI	WHI	5300	55	C3
CARLI LN	LAN	LAN		159	G7
CARLIN AV	COM	COM	4100	65	B1
CARLIN AV	LYN	LYN	3100	65	A1
CARLIN ST	COM	COM	300	64	F1
CARLIN ST	LA	LA16	5300	42	F5
CARLING WY	LA	LA36	5000	43	B2
CARLISLE CT	SAD	SAD		89	C4
CARLISLE DR	SMAR	PAS	1800	37	D1
CARLISLE ST	SF	SF	400	2	E6
CARLOS AV	ALH	ALH	2700	45	F1
CARLOS AV	LA	LA28	5900	34	C3
CARLOS ST	ALH	ALH	1700	46	A1
CARLOTA BLVD	LA	LA31	3600	36	B4
CARLOTA BLVD	LA	LA42	5600	36	C3
CARLOW RD	TOR	TOR	23000	67	F6
CARLOW RD	TOR	TOR	23500	72	F1
CARLSBAD ST	LA	SF	14400	2	D5
CARLSBAD ST	RB	RB	2600	62	F4
CARLSON CIR	LA	CAN	22300	12	B4
CARLSON DR	PAS	PAS	400	26	D3
CARLSON LN	RB	RB	1600	67	D1
CARLTON AV	CO	LA61	12800	64	B1
CARLTON AV	PAS	PAS	100	26	F3
CARLTON AV	POM	POM	2300	94	A2
CARLTON AV E	WCOV	WCOV	1000	88	B5
CARLTON AV W	WCOV	WCOV	1200	88	B5
CARLTON DR	GLEN	GL05	1200	25	E4
CARLTON DR	ING	IN01		57	B2
CARLTON WY	LA	LA27	5400	34	D3
CARLTON WY	LA	LA28	5500	34	D3
CARLTON WY	LA	LA69	8400	33	E3
CARLTON WY	LA	VEN	2700	49	D3
CARLY CT	CO	LPUE		97	A4
CARLYLE AV	SM	SM	900	40	E5
CARLYLE AV	SM	SM	2000	41	A4
CARLYLE PL	LA	LA65	2200	35	E2
CARLYLE ST	LA	LA65	3000	35	E2
CARLYNN PL	LA	TU	9400	11	B5
CARMAN CREST DR	LA	LA68	2400	34	A1
CARMANITA AV	POM	POM	1000	91	A5
CARMAR DR	LA	LA46	2600	33	D1
CARMAR PL	LA	LA46	8300	33	D1
CARMEL CT	POM	POM	1000	91	A6
CARMEL DR	MTB	MTB	800	54	C4
CARMEL RD	LCF	LCF	4700	19	D3
CARMEL RD	PALM	PALM		171	B3
CARMEL ST	GLEN	GL04	1700	25	C6
CARMEL ST	LA	LA65	3000	35	D1
CARMEL WY	LA	LA36	900	42	E2
CARMELINA AV N	LA	LA49	100	41	A2
CARMELINA AV S	LA	LA25	1300	41	B4
CARMELINA AV S	LA	LA49	100	41	A2
CARMELINA AV S	LA	LA64	2200	41	D5
CARMELITA AV	BELL	BELL	6200	53	B5
CARMELITA AV	BH	BH	9100	33	B6
CARMELITA AV	CO	LA63	1500	45	D2
CARMELITA AV	HPK	HPK	5900	53	C4
CARMELITA AV	MAY	MAY	5100	53	C4
CARMELITA AV	MTB	MTB	800	54	D3
CARMELITA AV	RB	RB	1300	67	D1
CARMELITA AV N	CO	LA63	100	45	D4
CARMELITA AV S	CO	LA63	100	45	D4
CARMELITA CIR	MON	MON	900	29	C4
CARMELITA DR	SGAB	SGAB		37	D3
CARMELITA PL	ARC	ARC	1400	28	D3
CARMELITA PL	MTB	MTB	600	54	D3
CARMELITOS PZ	LB	LB06	900	70	D2
CARMELO AV N	PAS	PAS	200	27	E3
CARMELO AV S	CO	PAS	300	27	E5
CARMELYNN ST	TOR	TOR	4400	67	E2
CARMEN AV	LA	LA68	1900	34	C2
CARMEN CT	LAV	LAV		95A	B6
CARMEN DR	GLEN	GL07	1200	25	D2
CARMEN PL	LA	LA68	6100	34	C2
CARMEN ST	TOR	TOR	4100	67	E4
CARMEN ST	WCOV	WCOV		92	E6
CARMENCITA DR	WCOV	WCOV	700	92	A1
CARMEN CREST DR	LA	LA68	2400	34	A1
CARMENIA DR	WHI	WHI	15900	84	C2
CARMENITA LN	LA	CP04		5	D2
CARMENITA RD	CER	ART	18500	81	D1
CARMENITA RD	CER	ART	15900	82	D4
CARMENITA RD	NWK	NWK	14300	82	D3
CARMENITA RD	SFS	SFS	12600	61	D6
CARMENITA RD	SFS	SFS	12700	82	D2
CARMENITA RD	SFS	WHI	10500	61	D6
CARMER ST	CO	LAN		175	E7
CARMONA AV	LA	LA08	3800	50	E1
CARMONA AV	LA	LA16	1900	42	F4
CARNABY ST	BLF	BLF	10500	66	D6
CARNABY ST	CER	ART	10600	66	D6
CARNABY ST	CER	ART	12300	82	B6
CARNARVON DR	PAS	PAS	1300	26	C1
CARNATION AV	LA	LA26	3400	35	B4
CARNAVON WY	LA	LA27	3800	35	A1
CARNE ST	NWK	NWK	11300	60	F6
CARNEGIE AV	CLA	CLA		91	A4
CARNEGIE AV	SCLR	SAU		124	D4
CARNEGIE LN	RB	RB	900	62	E5
CARNEGIE ST	LA	LA32	4600	36	C4
CARNELIAN ST	RB	RB	100	67	D2
CARNELL ST	WHI	WHI	13400	61	E2

228

1990 LOS ANGELES COUNTY STREET INDEX

CARNELL ST — CEDAR AV

LOS ANGELES CO.

STREET	CITY	P.O. ZONE	BLOCK	PAGE	GRID
CARNELL ST	WHI	WHI	14300	84	B3
CARO ST	PAR	PAR	6600	65	D4
CAROB CT	CO	PALM		183	D4
CAROB DR	LA	LA46	2400	33	F1
CAROB ST	COM	COM	100	64	E5
CAROB WY	MTB	MTB	900	54	C4
CAROL CT	CUL	CUL	3900	50	D1
CAROL DR	LAN	LAN		160	D7
CAROL DR	POM	POM	1200	95	B1
CAROL DR	TOR	TOR	5100	67	E6
CAROL DR	WHOL	LA69	1000	33	C4
CAROL PL	LA	SF	12400	1	E4
CAROL ST	LB	LB05		65	D4
CAROLDALE AV	CAR	CAR	21200	69	A4
CAROLDALE AV	CAR	CAR	23600	74	A1
CAROLFORD WY	BH	BH		32	F4
CAROLFORD WY	BH	BH		33	A4
CAROLI LN	LCF	LCF	5100	19	B2
CAROLIE LN	WAL	WAL		92	F5
CAROLINA PL	CO	LA22	5100	53	F1
CAROLINA PL	LA	SP	3600	78	F6
CAROLINA ST	LA	SP	2400	78	F6
CAROLINE AV	CUL	CUL	3300	42	D5
CAROLINE ST	WCOV	WCOV	700	88	D5
CAROLINE WY	ARC	ARC	2700	38	D2
CAROL PARK PL	CO	GL14	2400	18	E1
CAROL PINE LN	CO	PAS		28	B4
CAROLSIDE AV	CO	PALM	38200	172	B9
CAROLSIDE AV	LAN	LAN	43600	160	B6
CAROL SUE LN	SCLR	SAU		124	E6
CAROLUS DR	LA	LA68	5800	34	D1
CAROLWOOD DR	ARC	ARC		28	E1
CAROLWOOD DR N	LA	LA77	100	32	F5
CAROLWOOD DR S	LA	LA77	100	32	F5
CAROLWOOD LN	TOR	TOR		73	B3
CAROLYN PL	CER	ART	12000	66	F5
CAROLYN PL	CER	ART	13500	82	D5
CAROLYN PL	CO	LPUE		97	B5
CAROLYN PL	LB	LB10	2000	75	A1
CAROLYN ST	CER	ART	12400	82	B5
CAROLYN WY	BH	BH	1000	33	A4
CAROLYN WY	GLEN	GL14	4900	11	C4
CARON CIR	CAR	CAR	20300	69	D3
CARONDELET ST N	LA	LA26	100	35	B6
CARONDELET ST S	LA	LA06	900	44	A2
CARONDELET ST S	LA	LA57	100	44	B1
CARONDELET WY	ING	IN01		57	B1
CARPENTER AV	LA	NHO	5600	16	C5
CARPENTER AV	LA	NHO	3800	23	C4
CARPENTER CT	LA	NHO	3900	23	C4
CARPINTERO AV	BLF	BLF	13600	66	D2
CARPINTERO AV	LKD	LKD	6100	66	D6
CARPIO DR	DBAR	POM		94	B6
CARR DR	GLEN	GL05	100	25	E4
CARR LN	LA	LA31	2200	45	A1
CARRACK AV	LB	LB13		74	F4
CARRALOS ST	CO	ACT		182	E7
CARRARA ST	CO	LPUE		85	E3
CARRETA DR	CO	LPUE	19400	97	A4
CARRETA DR	CO	LPUE	18700	98	F4
CARRETERA DR	WHI	WHI	15100	84	B2
CARREY RD	WAL	WAL	20500	93	B6
CARREY RD	WAL	WAL	20200	97	B1
CARRIAGE	LA	SF42		2	C1
CARRIAGE DR	RHE	PVP	2200	73	D5
CARRIAGE DR	RPV	SP	2100	73	D5
CARRIAGE LN	WAL	WAL		93	A5
CARRIAGE PL	CO	LPUE		98	A3
CARRIAGE PL	MB	MB	200	62	C4
CARRIAGE WY	CO	LAN		159	B8
CARRIAGE WY	POM	POM		94	D6
CARRIAGEDALE DR	CAR	CAR	100	74	A1
CARRIAGE HSE RD	PAS	PAS		28	B1
CARRIE LN	GLEN	GL08		18	F5
CARRIE PL	WLVL	THO		102A	F5
CARRIE HILLS LN	LHH	LAH		98A	B2
CARRIER AV	CMRC	LA40	2500	54	B3
CARRILLO DR	LA	LA48	900	42	E2
CARRINGTON CT	ING	IN01		57	B2
CARRINGTON DR	LAM	LAM		83	B1
CARRION RD	LCF	LCF	4500	90	B3
CARRISO DR	DBAR	POM		97	D4
CARRITA DR	CO	MAL		112	E3
CARRIZAL RD	LA	WOH	4100	13	C4
CARRIZO DR	SCLR	VAL		127	A1
CARRIZO DR	SCLR	VAL		124	B9
CARROLL AV	GLDR	GLDR	700	86	F5
CARROLL AV	LA	LA26	1300	44	C1
CARROLL AV	LA	VEN	400	49	B6
CARROLL AV E	GLDR	GLDR	100	87	B5
CARROLL AV W	GLDR	GLDR	100	87	A5
CARROLL DR	CO	ALT	1400	20	C5
CARROLL WY	PAS	PAS	600	27	F5
CARROLL CANAL	LA	VEN	200	49	C4
CARROLL CANL CT	LA	VEN	200	49	B6
CARROLL PARK E	LB	LB14		75	F5

STREET	CITY	P.O. ZONE	BLOCK	PAGE	GRID
CARROLL PARK N	LB	LB14		75	E5
CARROLL PARK S	LB	LB14		75	E5
CARROLL PARK W	LB	LB14		75	E5
CARROLOS ST	CO	PALM	2000	182	F7
CARRON DR	PR	PR	8500	54	E4
CARROUSEL DR	CO	CYN	15600	125	E6
CARRUTHERS CT	POM	POM	100	94	F6
CARSAMBA DR	CO	CAL		13	A4
CARSE DR	LA	LA68	3200	24	A6
CARSON CT	SAD	SAD		90	B5
CARSON CT	SCLR	SAU		124	G3
CARSON DR	LYN	LYN	11000	59	B5
CARSON LN	POM	POM	800	94	F5
CARSON LN	POM	POM	700	95	A5
CARSON PL	COM	COM		64	F2
CARSON RD N	BH	BH	100	42	D1
CARSON RD S	BH	BH	100	42	D1
CARSON ST	CUL	CUL	8800	42	D6
CARSON ST	HG	LKD	12000	81	A4
CARSON ST	LKD	LKD	2400	70	D4
CARSON ST	LKD	LKD	11300	71	C4
CARSON ST	LKD	LKD	3800	71	C4
CARSON ST	LKD	LKD	11600	81	A4
CARSON ST E	CAR	CAR	100	69	B4
CARSON ST E	LB	LB07	300	70	D4
CARSON ST E	LB	LB07	3500	71	C4
CARSON ST E	LB	LB08	4300	71	C4
CARSON ST W	CAR	CAR	100	69	B4
CARSON ST W	CAR	LB10	1900	69	B4
CARSON ST W	CO	TOR	700	68	B4
CARSON ST W	LA	TOR	1300	68	B4
CARSON ST W	LB	LB10	1000	70	A4
CARSON ST W	TOR	TOR	3900	67	F4
CARSON ST W	TOR	TOR	1700	68	B4
CARSON MSA RD E	CO	PALM	100	183	D7
CARSON MSA RD W	CO	PALM		183	C9
CARSON MSA RD W	CO	PALM		189	J2
CARSON MSA RD W	CO	PALM		190	A2
CARSON PLAZA CT	CAR	CAR		69	B3
CARSON PLAZA DR	CAR	CAR		69	B3
CARTA RD	CO	MAL		105	E6
CARTAGENA DR	LB	LB07	600	70	D4
CARTAGENA ST	LB	LB07	1200	70	D4
CARTAGENA ST	LKD	LKD	3200	70	F4
CARTAGO CT	CO	LPUE		98	C4
CARTELA DR	LAM	LAM	14300	83	C2
CARTER AL	PAS	PAS	600	27	A3
CARTER AV	LA	VEN	2900	49	D4
CARTER AV E	SMAD	SMAD	1	28	C1
CARTER AV W	SMAD	SMAD	1	28	C1
CARTER DR	GLDR	GLDR	100	89	A2
CARTER DR	LA	LA32	4500	36	D5
CARTESIAN CIR	CO	PVP		72	F4
CARTHAGE CT	CLA	CLA	1100	90	F2
CARTHAGE ST	LA	PP	15300	40	C4
CARTIER DR	RPV	PVP	30200	77	C1
CARTWRIGHT AV	LA	NHO	5600	16	F6
CARTWRIGHT AV	LA	NHO	4000	23	F3
CARTWRIGHT AV	LA	SV	7200	16	F3
CARTWRIGHT ST	PAS	PAS	3500	28	A2
CARUSO LN	LAN	LAN		159	G5
CARUTHERS ST	WHI	WHI	16000	84	C3
CARVEL DR	SCLR	CYN	27900	124	H7
CARVER CT	LA	LA28	6600	34	B3
CARVER DR	CLA	CLA		96	C6
CARVER ST	RB	RB	1500	62	D6
CARVIN AV	CO	LPUE	1100	97	A5
CARVOL AV	CO	COV	4300	88	C4
CARVOL AV	WCOV	WCOV	300	88	C5
CARWILE DR	ALH	ALH	2200	46	B1
CARY AV	LA	WIL	1000	74	C4
CARY CT	SCLR	NEW		127	B6
CARY LN	POM	POM	100	90	E5
CASA CT	PALM	PALM		171	E4
CASA DR	LA	TAR	4900	21	A2
CASA LN	LA	NOR		1	B5
CASA PL	LA	TAR	5000	21	A2
CASABA AV	LA	CAN	8500	6	E6
CASABA AV	LA	CAN	7300	12	E1
CASABA AV	LA	CHA	9500	6	E4
CASABA RD	RHE	PVP		73	D5
CASA BLANCA RD	LA	WOH	4000	13	D4
CASA CON VISTA	LA	SP		78	C5
CASAD AV	CO	COV		89	A5
CASAD AV E	WCOV	WCOV	1000	88	C5
CASAD AV W	WCOV	WCOV	1000	88	B5
CASAD ST E	COV	COV	600	88	D5
CASAD ST E	COV	COV		89	A5
CASAD ST W	COV	COV	200	88	D5
CASA DEL REY DR	LHH	LAH	1200	84	F3
CASA GRANDE AV	MTB	MTB	200	46	F6
CASA GRANDE AV	PALM	PALM		183	E2
CASA GRANDE DR	WCOV	WCOV	2000	92	D3
CASA GRANDE ST	PAS	PAS	1400	27	D2
CASA HERMOSA DR	POM	POM	900	94	D1
CASALE RD	LA	PP	1500	40	F2

STREET	CITY	P.O. ZONE	BLOCK	PAGE	GRID
CASALERO DR	LHH	LAH	2300	85	D6
CASA LINDA DR	WCOV	WCOV	1900	92	D3
CASA LOMA DR	DBAR	POM	23500	94	A6
CASA LOMA LN	WAL	WAL		93	C5
CASAMIA AV	PALM	PALM		183	G1
CASANDRA AV	CER	ART	18200	82	B6
CASANES AV	DOW	DOW	9100	60	E3
CASANOVA DR	LAN	LAN		159	B5
CASANOVA ST	LA	LA12	400	35	E6
CASA VERDE DR	PALM	PALM		183	E2
CASA VISTA DR	POM	POM	900	94	D1
CASCADA WY	LA	LA49	300	32	C5
CASCADE	ELM	ELM		48	A6
CASCADE AV	WAL	WAL		93	B4
CASCADE CIR	CO	WHI	10400	61	A1
CASCADE CT	CUL	CUL		50	D2
CASCADE CT	PALM	PALM		172	E6
CASCADE PL	CLA	CLA	1000	91	A2
CASCADE CYN DR	LA	SF		1	D4
CASCADIA DR	GLEN	GL06	2300	26	A2
CASCO CT	CO	LPUE		85	F5
CASE AV	LA	NHO	5600	16	E6
CASE AV	LA	SV	7200	16	E3
CASETAS DR	CO	POM		93	E6
CASETAS DR	DBAR	POM		93	F6
CASETAS DR	DBAR	POM		97	E1
CASEY PL	LA	SP	1800	73	F6
CASEY ST	LA	SF	16300	8	A3
CASHDAN ST	CAR	CAR	1800	69	E1
CASHDAN ST	CO	COM		69	E1
CASHIO ST	LA	LA35	8500	42	C3
CASHMERE ST	LA	LA49	11000	41	C1
CASHMERE TER	LA	LA24	500	41	D1
CASIANO CT	LA	LA77	15600	22	B6
CASIANO RD	LA	LA49	2500	22	B6
CASIANO RD	LA	LA49	950	32	B5
CASILINA DR	RPV	PVP	30700	78	B3
CASIMIR AV	CO	GAR	14400	63	D3
CASIMIR AV	GAR	GAR	12900	63	C1
CASIMIR AV	HAW	IN03	11400	57	C5
CASIMIR AV	ING	IN03	10900	57	C4
CASIMIR AV	TOR	GAR	16300	63	D5
CASIMIR AV	TOR	TOR	16800	63	D5
CASINO DR	CO	LPUE		85	C5
CASITA	PALM	PALM		184	B1
CASITA ST	AZU	AZU	500	88	D1
CASITAS AV	BELL	BELL	6200	53	E5
CASITAS AV	CO	ALT	2000	19	E4
CASITAS AV	LA	LA39	2900	35	C1
CASITAS AV	PAS	PAS	1500	19	E6
CASITAS DR	LAV	LAV		90	E2
CASITAS ST	MPK	MPK	400	45	F2
CASLAM AV	CO	ACT	33800	182	F9
CASPAR AV	LA	LA41	5000	26	A5
CASPIAN AV	CAR	LB10	21100	70	A4
CASPIAN AV	LB	LB10	3000	70	A6
CASPIAN AV	LB	LB10	1800	75	A2
CASPIAN AV	LB	LB13	1000	70	A6
CASPIAN AV	LB	LB13	1000	75	A4
CASPIAN DR	PALM	PALM		171	F5
CASS AV	LA	WOH	22200	13	A2
CASS PL	CO	HPK	2400	58	F1
CASSANDRA DR	BG	BELL	6500	54	B6
CASSANDRA ST	LA	TAR	18600	21	C2
CASSARA AV	LA	SF	11400	9	F1
CASSATT ST	LA	LA32	4500	36	C4
CASSIA CT	CER	ART		81	B3
CASSIDY ST	CAR	CAR	300	64	B5
CASSIDY ST	GAR	GAR	1000	63	F5
CASSIL PL	LA	LA28	1500	34	B3
CASSINA AV	SOG	SOG	10600	59	E5
CAST AV	SCLR	NEW		127	D3
CASTAC PL	LA	PP	800	40	B3
CASTAIC RD	CO	CAST	31900	123	G1
CASTAIC CYN RD	CO	VAL	28700	123	F6
CASTAIR DR	LA	LA46	2200	33	F2
CASTALA DR	PALM	PALM		172	H9
CASTALIA AV	LA	LA32	3200	36	D4
CASTANA AV	BLF	BLF	16200	66	A4
CASTANA AV	DOW	DOW	13300	66	A2
CASTANA AV	LKD	LKD	5900	66	A6
CASTANA AV	LKD	LKD	4600	71	A1
CASTANA AV	PAR	PAR	13400	66	A2
CASTANET DR	LAM	LAM		83	B1
CASTANO AV	PAS	PAS	300	27	F3
CASTANO PL	LA	SV	8300	16	C1
CASTELLAMMRE DR	LA	PP	17300	40	A4
CASTELLAMMRE DR	LA	PP	17800	115	F4
CASTELLO AV	LA	LA35	1100	42	B2
CASTELLO PL	LA	LA35	1500	42	B3
CASTELLON RD	LAM	LAM	14400	82	F2
CASTELOTTE CT	WHI	WHI	5100	55	C2
CASTERA AV	GLEN	GL08	3200	18	F4
CASTERA PL	POM	POM	1400	91	B6
CASTILE DR	WHI	WHI		84	C1
CASTILIAN DR	LA	LA68	2000	34	B2

STREET	CITY	P.O. ZONE	BLOCK	PAGE	GRID
CASTILLA CT	SCLR	VAL		127	B1
CASTILLO CT	WAL	WAL		92	F5
CASTILLO CT	WAL	WAL		93	A5
CASTILLO LN	LA	NOR		1	C6
CASTILLO ST	LA	WOH	21300	13	C3
CASTLE CIR	LAN	LAN		160	E6
CASTLE DR	POM	POM	2100	90	F5
CASTLE LN	LCF	LCF	4500	18	F2
CASTLE LN	PAS	PAS	1400	27	A1
CASTLE PL	BH	BH	400	33	C2
CASTLE PL	CER	ART		71	E1
CASTLE RD	LCF	LCF	5000	11	F6
CASTLE RD	LCF	LCF	4500	18	F1
CASTLE ST	LA	LA39	3000	35	B4
CASTLEBAR DR	CO	LPUE		85	E5
CASTLEBAR DR	CO	LPUE		97	B5
CASTLEBAY LN	LA	NOR		1	A4
CASTLEBAY PL	LA	NOR		1	A4
CASTLEBURY CT	SAD	SAD		89	D4
CASTLE CREST DR	LA	LA41		25	F5
CASTLE DOME DR	WAL	WAL		93	C3
CASTLEFORD LN	CER	ART	12700	81	C2
CASTLEGATE AV	CO	COM	14400	65	C2
CASTLEGATE AV N	COM	COM	1700	65	C2
CASTLEGATE AV S	COM	COM	900	65	C4
CASTLEGATE DR	LA	LA49		32	B6
CASTLEGATE PL	LCF	LCF		19	D6
CASTLEHAVEN RD	CO	SAU		181	D7
CASTLE HTS AV	LA	LA34	2000	42	C4
CASTLE HTS PL	LA	LA34	2600	42	C4
CASTLEHILL DR	AGH	AGO		102	F2
CASTLEHILL DR	WAL	WAL	400	97	B1
CASTLE KNOLL RD	LCF	LCF		11	F6
CASTLEMAN AV	LA	LA32	5000	36	D6
CASTLE PEAK DR	LA	CAN		5	D3
CASTLEPEAK ST	CO	LPUE	19500	97	A3
CASTLE ROCK CT	WCOV	WCOV		92	E4
CASTLEROCK RD	CO	MAL		115	E4
CASTLE ROCK RD	DBAR	POM	2200	97	D5
CASTLETON DR	CLA	CLA		91	B5
CASTLETON ST	IND	LPUE		98	C3
CASTLE TOP TR	CO	TOP	600	109	E3
CASTLEVIEW AV	CO	SAD		89	D3
CASTLE VIEW DR	CO	AGO		100A	A5
CASTLE VIEW DR	CO	AGO		102	F5
CASTLEWOOD DR	CO	MAL	21400	114	E3
CASTLEWOODS DR	LA	VAN	15610	22	B5
CASTLEWOODS PL	LA	VAN	3400	22	B5
CASTOR RD	CO	CAL		108	C4
CASTRO MTWY	CO	MAL		107	A5
CASUDA CYN DR	MPK	MPK	100	45	E2
CASWELL AV	CO	COM	14600	64	C2
CASWELL AV	COM	COM	400	64	C4
CASWELL AV	LA	LA66	12400	49	E3
CASWELL AV	POM	POM		94	F2
CASWELL AV N	POM	POM	500	94	F2
CASWELL ST S	POM	POM	100	94	F3
CASWOOD DR	WHI	WHI		55	F6
CATALA AV	SCLR	SAU		124	D5
CATALINA AV	AVA	AVA		77	B5
CATALINA AV	CO	WHI		85	B6
CATALINA AV	GAR	GAR	12800	63	F1
CATALINA AV	LA	GAR		68	F1
CATALINA AV	LAV	LAV	3900	90	C1
CATALINA AV	WHI	WHI		84	A2
CATALINA AV N	CO	PAS		20	B6
CATALINA AV N	PAS	PAS	1600	20	B6
CATALINA AV N	PAS	PAS	100	27	B2
CATALINA AV N	RB	RB	100	67	D2
CATALINA AV S	PAS	PAS	100	27	B5
CATALINA AV S	RB	RB	100	67	D5
CATALINA CT	MB	MB		62	D3
CATALINA DR	GLEN	GL07		25	E1
CATALINA ST	CO	TOR	20400	68	F3
CATALINA ST N	BUR	BUR	1100	17	B6
CATALINA ST N	LA	LA04	100	34	F6
CATALINA ST N	LA	LA27	1300	34	F3
CATALINA ST S	BUR	BUR	100	24	C3
CATALINA ST S	LA	LA04	100	34	F6
CATALINA ST S	LA	LA05	600	43	F1
CATALINA ST S	LA	LA06	900	43	F3
CATALINA ST S	LA	LA07	2200	43	F5
CATALINA ST S	LA	LA20	300	43	F1
CATALINA VISTA	LA	SP		78	C5
CATALON AV	LA	WOH	5000	13	D2
CATALONIA AV	LA	PP	500	40	A3
CATALPA AV	POM	POM	2500	94	F6
CATALPA RD	ARC	ARC	400	28	B4
CATALPA ST	LA	LA32	4400	45	C2
CATALUNA PL	PVE	PVP	1600	72	D4
CATALUNA SQ	PVE	PVP	1600	72	D4
CATAMARAN AV	CER	ART		66	E5
CATAMARAN ST	LA	VEN		49	C5
CATANIA CT	WHI	WHI	10600	55	C2
CATANIA PL	CO	CLA	800	91	A1
CATARACT AV	GLDR	GLDR	1300	87	F6

STREET	CITY	P.O. ZONE	BLOCK	PAGE	GRID
CATARACT AV N	SAD	SAD	100	89	F3
CATARACT AV S	SAD	SAD	100	89	F3
CATARINA DR	WLVL	THO		102	C2
CATARO DR	SCLR	SAU		124	D5
CATE RD	PR	PR	9300	47	B6
CATE RD	PR	PR	9500	55	B1
CATENIA DR	LA	SF	12200	1	F5
CATENIA PL	LA	SF	16800	1	F5
CATERINA CT	LA	SF		1	E4
CATESBY LN	LA	LA15	1300	44	B4
CATHANN PL	TOR	TOR	22300	67	F5
CATHANN ST	TOR	TOR	3900	67	E4
CATHAY ST	GLEN	GL08	1800	18	F6
CATHCART DR	LCF	LCF	700	19	C5
CATHEDRAL PL	LA	ENC	17800	21	D3
CATHEDRAL WY	POM	POM	900	94	C1
CATHERINE RD	CO	ALT	2300	20	B5
CATHERINE ST	PR	PR	9000	55	A3
CATHERINE PK DR	GLDR	GLDR	100	87	D5
CATHERWOOD CT	AGH	AGO		100A	A2
CATHERWOOD DR	LCF	LCF	5700	19	C1
CATHRYN DR N	CO	RM	2100	46	D3
CATHRYN PL	CO	RM	2200	46	D3
CATHWELL LN	LA	TU	9400	11	A5
CATHY AV	POM	POM	2600	94	A2
CATHY ST	LA	SF	12500	3	B2
CATO ST	LA	LA32	4400	36	C5
CATO WY	LA	LA32	4500	36	C5
CATSKILL AV	CAR	CAR	21000	69	B4
CATSKILL AV	CAR	CAR	23700	74	B1
CATSKILL RD	LA	SUN	9800	10	B4
CATTAIL CT	WAL	WAL		93	D5
CATTAIL WY	SCLR	CYN		124	E8
CATTARAUGUS AV	CUL	CUL	3200	42	D5
CATTARAUGUS AV	LA	LA34	3200	42	C4
CATTLE CREEK RD	CO	ACT		182	J9
CAULFIELD AV	NWK	NWK	13000	82	C2
CAVALIER ST	LA	WOH	22600	13	A2
CAVALIER WY	CO	LPUE		98	C5
CAVALLERI DR	CO	MAL		112	C5
CAVALLERI RD	CO	MAL		112	C6
CAVAN LN	GLDR	GLDR	700	87	B3
CAVANAGH CIR	LA	LA32	2200	45	E1
CAVANAGH RD	GLEN	GL07	500	25	D1
CAVANAGH RD	LA	LA32	5000	45	D1
CAVE WY	CO	TOP	19500	109	C5
CAVEHILL RD	SCLR	SAU		124	H3
CAVEL ST	DOW	DOW	8300	60	B5
CAVELL PL	BAP	BAP		39	E3
CAVENDISH DR	LA	LA64	2900	42	B4
CAVERN CT	SCLR	SAU		124	G3
CAVERNA DR	LA	LA68	7200	34	A1
CAVETTE PL	BAP	BAP	14400	39	E3
CAWOOD PL	LAM	LAM	15800	83	C2
CAWSTON ST	SPAS	SPAS	1000	36	E2
CAYENNE DR	SCLR	SAU		124	E5
CAYMAN CT	MB	MB		62	D3
CAYMAN RD	CO	MAL		112	C1
CAYUGA AV	LA	PAC	10500	8	F2
CAYUGA AV	LA	PAC	9800	9	B4
CAYUGA AV	LA	SV	8500	9	D6
CAYUGA AV	LA	SV	8500	16	D1
CAYUGA AV	LOM	LOM	25800	73	E3
CAYUSE LN	RPV	PVP	28200	73	C6
CAZADERO PL	DBAR	POM	21200	97	D4
CAZADOR CT	LA	LA65	3300	35	E2
CAZADOR DR	LA	LA65	2200	35	E2
CAZADOR ST	LA	LA65	2900	35	E3
CAZAUX DR	LA	LA68	5700	34	D1
CAZAUX PL	LA	LA68	2400	34	D1
CEANOTHUS PL	CO	CAL		100A	E6
CECELIA CT	CER	ART	18700	81	D1
CECELIA PL	CER	ART	19200	82	D6
CECELIA ST	BG	BELL	5600	59	E2
CECELIA ST	CDY	BELL	4500	59	D2
CECELIA ST	WCOV	WCOV		92	E6
CECELIA WY	CER	ART	18300	82	D6
CECIANA DR	CO	LPUE	2200	85	F3
CECIL ST	MPK	MPK	300	46	C2
CECILIA ST	DOW	DOW	7400	60	A2
CECILIA ST	LA	LA14	800	44	D4
CECILIA ST	SFS	SFS	11400	60	F4
CECILIA ST	SFS	SFS	11400	61	A4
CECILVILLE AV	CO	GL14	4800	11	E6
CECINA WY	LA	LA77	900	32	D4
CEDAR	CO	LP48		98	F3
CEDAR	LA	SF42		2	C1
CEDAR AV	CO	IN04		57	A4
CEDAR AV	ELM	ELM	3800	38	E5
CEDAR AV	HAW	HAW	12600	57	A6
CEDAR AV	LAN	LAN	43600	160	A6
CEDAR AV	LB	LB02	300	75	C5
CEDAR AV	LB	LB05	5100	70	C2
CEDAR AV	LB	LB06	2900	70	C6
CEDAR AV	LB	LB06	1800	75	C2

INDEX

229

1990 LOS ANGELES COUNTY STREET INDEX

CEDAR AV

CHARL PL

LOS ANGELES CO.

STREET	CITY	P.O. ZONE	BLOCK	PAGE	GRID
CEDAR AV	LB	LB07	3500	70	C5
CEDAR AV	LB	LB13	700	75	C3
CEDAR AV	LYN	LYN	3300	59	A6
CEDAR AV	MB	MB	1800	62	C3
CEDAR AV	MON	MON	100	29	B3
CEDAR AV E	BUR	BUR	100	17	E6
CEDAR AV N	ING	IN01	100	56	F2
CEDAR AV N	LB	LB02	100	75	C5
CEDAR AV S	ING	IN01	100	56	F2
CEDAR AV S	LB	LB02	100	75	C5
CEDAR AV W	BUR	BUR	200	24	D1
CEDAR CIR	BAP	BAP	3700	39	C6
CEDAR CIR	ELM	ELM	11300	38	F4
CEDAR CT	MTB	MTB	200	54	D2
CEDAR DR N	COV	COV	100	88	E4
CEDAR DR S	COV	COV	200	88	E5
CEDAR LN	ELM	ELM	9800	38	C5
CEDAR ST	ALH	ALH	1700	37	A4
CEDAR ST	BLF	BLF	8500	66	A5
CEDAR ST	ELS	ELS	900	56	A5
CEDAR ST	HPK	HPK	6200	53	A6
CEDAR ST	LA	LA65	400	36	A4
CEDAR ST	LAV	LAV		90	E1
CEDAR ST	MTB	MTB		54	C4
CEDAR ST	PAS	PAS	100	26	F1
CEDAR ST	SM	SM	700	49	B2
CEDAR ST E	COM	COM	100	64	E2
CEDAR ST N	GLEN	GL06	100	25	D4
CEDAR ST N	GLEN	GL07	900	25	D2
CEDAR ST N	ING	IN02	900	50	F5
CEDAR ST S	GLEN	GL05	100	25	D4
CEDAR ST S	ING	IN01		56	F2
CEDAR ST W	COM	COM	100	64	E2
CEDAR WK	LB	LB02	1	75	C6
CEDAR WY	LB	LB02		75	C5
CEDARBEND DR	GLEN	GL14	3700	18	B1
CEDARBLUFF DR	RPV	PVP	28300	72	C5
CEDARBREAK AV	CO	LPUE		98	E3
CEDARBROOK AV	PALM	PALM		183	H7
CEDARBROOK DR	LA	BH	9500	33	B2
CEDARBROOK ST	WCOV	WCOV	1100	92	C1
CEDARCLIFF AV	CO	WHI	7200	55	C5
CEDAR COURT RD	GLEN	GL07	1300	25	D2
CEDARCREEK LN	CER	ART	12400	82	B4
CEDAR CREEK RD	SAD	SAD		90	A3
CEDARCREEK ST	SCLR	CYN	19300	124	G8
CEDAR CREST AV	CLA	CLA	400	91	C5
CEDARCREST AV	SPAS	SPAS	1	27	A6
CEDARCREST DR	CER	ART	12400	82	B4
CEDARCROFT RD	CO	SAU		189	H4
CEDARDALE DR	DBAR	POM		97	E3
CEDARDALE DR	SFS	SFS	9800	60	F3
CEDAREDGE AV	LA	LA41	1200	26	C4
CEDAREDGE CT	LA	LA41	5400	26	C4
CEDARFALLS DR	SCLR	SAU	2100	124	F5
CEDARFORT DR	CO	CYN	15600	128	E1
CEDARGLEN DR	AZU	AZU	500	86	E6
CEDARGLEN DR	CO	AZU	5200	88	E2
CEDARGROVE AV	WHI	WHI		61	F2
CEDARHAVEN RD	AGH	AGO		102	E3
CEDARHILL RD	GLEN	GL02	1500	25	C1
CEDARHURST CIR	LA	LA27	4300	35	A2
CEDARHURST DR	LA	LA27	2100	35	A2
CEDARLANE DR	CO	LPUE	16200	85	F2
CEDAR LODGE TER	LA	LA39	1900	35	B3
CEDARMONT DR	CO	LPUE	17100	98	B3
CEDAR RIDGE CT	WAL	WAL		92	F5
CEDARSPRINGS DR	WHI	WHI	14400	84	A3
CEDARTOWN ST	SCLR	NEW	23200	127	C5
CEDARTREE RD	DOW	DOW	8400	60	D1
CEDAR TURN	LB	LB05	100	70	C1
CEDARVALE RD	LA	TU	9400	10	F4
CEDARVALE ST	NWK	NWK	11500	82	A4
CEDAR VALLEY DR	WLVL	THO		102	B3
CEDAR VALLEY WY	SCLR	NEW	26400	127	J2
CEDAR VALLEY WY	CO	NEW		128	A2
CEDARVIEW DR	CLA	CLA	200	90	F2
CEDARWOOD AV	CER	ART	16600	82	B5
CEDARWOOD AV	DUA	DUA		29	F3
CEDARWOOD AV	GLDR	GLDR	100	87	C5
CEDARWOOD CIR	CER	ART	16700	82	B5
CEDARWOOD CT	CER	ART	16900	82	B5
CEDARWOOD DR	POM	POM		94	D6
CEDARWOOD ST	BAP	BAP	14200	39	E5
CEDARWOOD ST	WCOV	WCOV	2200	39	E6
CEDON DR	CO	LPUE	1200	92	B4
CEDRAL ST	CO	ACT		189	E1
CEDRELA AV	PALM	PALM	37200	184	A2
CEDRIC PL	CO	LPUE	2600	98	E6
CEDROS AV	LA	SF	9600	8	D3
CEDROS AV	LA	VAN	8600	8	D6
CEDROS AV	LA	VAN	5700	15	D5
CEDROS AV	LA	VAN	4200	22	D3
CEEBEE DR	DOW	DOW	9500	60	D5
CEILHUNT AV	LA	LA64	2700	41	E5
CELES ST	LA	WOH	21200	13	C2

STREET	CITY	P.O. ZONE	BLOCK	PAGE	GRID
CELESTE PL	RHE	PVP	1	73	D4
CELESTE ST	AZU	AZU	400	88	D2
CELESTINE DR	CO	WHI	11500	84	D5
CELIA ST	POM	POM	100	94	B2
CELINDA PL	LA	ENC	16300	22	A3
CELINE ST	ELM	ELM	12000	39	B4
CELIS ST	SF	SF	600	2	D5
CELITA HWY	GLEN	GL14		18	C1
CELITO DR	CO	RM	8100	46	F3
CELLO DR	DBAR	POM		97	E3
CELTIC	LA	SF		8	C1
CELTIC CT	LA	CHA		6	C1
CELTIC ST	LA	CHA	19700	6	E1
CELTIC ST	LA	NOR	19300	7	A1
CELTIC ST	LA	SF	16700	7	F1
CELTIC ST	LA	SF	15300	8	A1
CELTIC WY	LA	NOR		1	C5
CEMETERY AV	WHI	WHI	6000	55	D4
CENDON DR	CO	LPUE		92	B4
CENSOR AV	LA	HAC	24100	73	E1
CENTENNIAL ST	LA	LA12	800	44	D1
CENTER AV	COM	COM	400	64	E4
CENTER AV	ELM	ELM	3600	38	D6
CENTER AV	GLDR	GLDR	700	89	B1
CENTER AV N	CO	HAC		73	F2
CENTER AV S	CO	HAC		73	F2
CENTER CT	LA	VEN	10	49	C4
CENTER DR	COM	COM	6700	65	A5
CENTER DR	LA	LA45		50	C5
CENTER DR W	LA	LA45		50	C5
CENTER PL	CO	LA22	5300	53	F1
CENTER PL	MB	MB	100	62	B4
CENTER ST	BAP	BAP	3900	39	D5
CENTER ST	CO	ARC	3000	38	F2
CENTER ST	CO	HPK	2100	58	E1
CENTER ST	CUL	CUL	4100	50	B2
CENTER ST	ELS	ELS	100	56	B6
CENTER ST	LA	LA12	100	44	E3
CENTER ST	SOG	SOG	11500	59	E6
CENTER ST	SOG	SOG	12500	65	E1
CENTER ST E	COV	COV	100	88	E5
CENTER ST E	POM	POM	100	94	D2
CENTER ST W	COV	COV	100	88	E5
CENTER ST W	POM	POM	100	94	D2
CENTER WY	LA	LA45	200	56	B3
CENTER WY	TOR	TOR		68	A5
CENTER CIR DR	CO	HAC		73	F2
CENTER COURT DR	COV	COV		89	B6
CENTER COURT DR	COV	COV		93	A1
CENTER PLAZA DR	MPK	MPK		45	E2
CENTERVIEW DR	CAR	CAR	300	64	B5
CENTINARY DR	WAL	WAL	300	93	B6
CENTINELA AV	ING	IN02	900	50	F5
CENTINELA AV	ING	IN02	300	51	A5
CENTINELA AV	LA	CUL	5800	50	B4
CENTINELA AV	LA	CUL	11800	50	B4
CENTINELA AV	LA	LA25	1200	41	C5
CENTINELA AV	LA	LA45	5400	50	E5
CENTINELA AV	LA	LA45	5200	50	E5
CENTINELA AV	LA	LA64	2000	41	C5
CENTINELA AV	LA	LA66	3300	49	E1
CENTINELA AV	LA	LA66	4300	50	A4
CENTINELA AV	SM	SM	800	41	B3
CENTRAL AL	SPAS	SPAS	1500	37	A1
CENTRAL AV	AZU	AZU	6400	86	E6
CENTRAL AV	BAP	BAP	14500	39	F5
CENTRAL AV	CAR	CAR	16800	64	D5
CENTRAL AV	CAR	CAR	19000	69	D2
CENTRAL AV	CAR	CAR	18600	69	D2
CENTRAL AV	CO	COM	14300	64	C2
CENTRAL AV	CO	CAST		123	A5
CENTRAL AV	DUA	DUA	900	29	C5
CENTRAL AV	ELM	ELM	2600	47	C3
CENTRAL AV	GLEN	GL02	900	25	C5
CENTRAL AV	LPUE	LPUE	15900	48	F6
CENTRAL AV	SFS	SFS		61	C4
CENTRAL AV	WHI	WHI	8300	61	E1
CENTRAL AV E	MON	MON	100	29	B5
CENTRAL AV E	SELM	ELM	10800	47	D4
CENTRAL AV E	SGAB	SGAB	100	37	E4
CENTRAL AV N	COM	COM	100	64	C2
CENTRAL AV N	GLEN	GL03	100	25	C4
CENTRAL AV N	LA	LA12	100	44	D5
CENTRAL AV N	SELM	ELM	1400	47	C3
CENTRAL AV S	CAR	CAR	16600	64	D6
CENTRAL AV S	CO	LA59	12000	58	C5
CENTRAL AV S	CO	LA59	12800	64	C2
CENTRAL AV S	COM	COM	100	64	C2
CENTRAL AV S	COM	LA59	13100	64	C2
CENTRAL AV S	GLEN	GL04	100	25	C5
CENTRAL AV S	LA	LA01	5800	52	C6
CENTRAL AV S	LA	LA01	7800	58	C2
CENTRAL AV S	LA	LA02	8600	58	C2
CENTRAL AV S	LA	LA11	1900	44	D5
CENTRAL AV S	LA	LA11	2500	52	C3
CENTRAL AV S	LA	LA12	100	44	D5

STREET	CITY	P.O. ZONE	BLOCK	PAGE	GRID
CENTRAL AV S	LA	LA13	300	44	D5
CENTRAL AV S	LA	LA21	600	44	D5
CENTRAL AV S	LA	LA59	10700	58	C5
CENTRAL AV W	MON	MON	100	29	A5
CENTRAL AV W	SGAB	SGAB	100	37	E4
CENTRAL CT	LAN	LAN		159	G4
CENTRAL CT	RB	RB	100	67	D3
CENTRAL ST	IRW	BAP	16000	88	B3
CENTRAL TER	SGAB	SGAB	400	37	E4
CENTRAL WK	CO	CAST		123	C2
CENTRALIA ST	LB	LB08	4300	71	C3
CENTRALIA ST	LKD	LKD	2700	70	F3
CENTRALIA ST	LKD	LKD	3300	71	A3
CENTRALIA ST	LKD	LKD	11300	71	F3
CENTRALIA ST	LKD	LKD	12700	81	B3
CENTRALIA ST	LKD	LKD	11500	81	B3
CENTRAL PARK N	CAR	CAR		69	C6
CENTRAL PARK S	CAR	CAR		69	C6
CENTRE CT	PALM	PALM		171	J6
CENTRE DR	IND	LPUE	900	97	B3
CENTRE ST N	LA	SP	100	79	A4
CENTRE ST S	LA	SP	100	79	A4
CENTRE PLAZA DR	MPK	MPK		45	E2
CENTURIA DR	RPV	PVP	27900	72	D4
CENTURION AV	CO	RM	7700	46	E4
CENTURION WY	SCLR	SAU		124	D5
CENTURY BLVD	DOW	DOW	8300	66	A2
CENTURY BLVD	ING	IN01	4601	56	C3
CENTURY BLVD	ING	IN01	4001	57	C3
CENTURY BLVD	ING	IN03	2200	57	C3
CENTURY BLVD	ING	IN04	4000	57	C3
CENTURY BLVD	ING	IN05	2201	57	C3
CENTURY BLVD	LYN	LYN	2600	58	F4
CENTURY BLVD	LYN	LYN	3000	59	A4
CENTURY BLVD	PAR	PAR		65	E1
CENTURY BLVD	PAR	PAR	8000	66	A2
CENTURY BLVD	SOG	SOG	2700	58	F4
CENTURY BLVD	SOG	SOG	3000	59	A4
CENTURY BLVD	SOG	SOG	7100	59	E6
CENTURY BLVD	SOG	SOG		65	E1
CENTURY BLVD E	CO	LA02	1200	58	D3
CENTURY BLVD E	LA	LA02	600	58	B3
CENTURY BLVD E	LA	LA03	100	58	B3
CENTURY BLVD W	CO	LA44	1000	57	C3
CENTURY BLVD W	CO	LA47	1400	57	C3
CENTURY BLVD W	LA	LA03	100	58	B3
CENTURY BLVD W	LA	LA44	600	57	C3
CENTURY BLVD W	LA	LA44	500	58	B3
CENTURY BLVD W	LA	LA45	5300	56	C3
CENTURY BLVD W	LA	LA47	1600	57	C3
CENTURY CIR	LAN	LAN		160	C3
CENTURY LN	LYN	LYN	5300	59	D6
CENTURY MTWY	CO	AGO		107	D4
CENTURY HILL	LA	LA67		42	B2
CENTURY PARK E	LA	LA25	1800	42	B2
CENTURY PARK E	LA	LA67	1800	42	B2
CENTURY PARK W	LA	LA25	1800	42	A2
CENTURY PARK LN	LA	LA67		42	B2
CENTURY WDS DR	LA	LA67		42	A2
CENTURY WDS WY	LA	LA67		42	A2
CERAM CT	CO	MAL		105	A6
CERCA DR	SCLR	VAL		124	C7
CERCO ALTA DR	MPK	MPK	1800	45	F2
CERECITA DR	CO	WHI	13900	61	E3
CERECITA DR	CO	WHI	15100	84	A5
CEREDO PL	LA	SF	17100	1	E5
CERES AV	CO	WHI		61	E4
CERES AV	LA	LA13	500	44	D4
CERES AV	LA	LA21	600	44	D4
CEREZA DR	MPK	MPK		45	F2
CEREZA WY	CO	TOP	22000	109	C1
CEREZA WY	LB	LB02	100	75	C5
CERISA ST	LAN	LAN		160	F4
CERISE AV	CO	GAR	15100	63	C3
CERISE AV	CO	HAW	13400	63	C2
CERISE AV	HAW	HAW	12500	57	C6
CERISE AV	HAW	HAW	13500	63	C2
CERISE AV	TOR	TOR	16600	63	C5
CERISE AV	TOR	TOR	18700	68	C1
CERISE AV	TOR	TOR	22500	68	C6
CERISE AV	TOR	TOR	800	68	C4
CERO DR	SCLR	SAU		124	F4
CERQUITA DR	WHI	WHI		84	D1
CERRILLOS DR	LA	WOH	4600	13	B2
CERRITO PL	RHE	PVP	1	73	D4
CERRITOS AV	AZU	AZU	5100	88	D2
CERRITOS AV	BLF	BLF	14000	66	B2
CERRITOS AV	LB	LB02	100	75	D5
CERRITOS AV	LB	LB05	5200	70	D1
CERRITOS AV	LB	LB06	1800	75	D3
CERRITOS AV	LB	LB07	3200	70	D5
CERRITOS AV	LB	LB13	700	75	D5
CERRITOS AV	SH	LB06	2200	75	D2
CERRITOS AV E	GLEN	GL05	100	25	C6
CERRITOS AV N	AZU	AZU	300	86	D6
CERRITOS AV N	AZU	AZU	100	88	D2

STREET	CITY	P.O. ZONE	BLOCK	PAGE	GRID
CERRITOS AV S	AZU	AZU	100	88	D2
CERRITOS AV W	GLEN	GL04	100	25	C6
CERRITOS CT	CLA	CLA		96	B6
CERRITOS DR	LB	LB07	4400	70	D3
CERRITOS PL	LA	LA68	6500	34	C2
CERRO WY	WAL	WAL	19600	97	A2
CERROCREST DR	LA	BH	1200	33	C4
CERRO GORDO ST	LA	LA26	1400	35	D4
CERRO GORDO ST	LA	LA39	1900	35	D4
CERRO VERDE PL	LA	TAR	4600	21	B3
CERRO VISTA DR	LA	TU	9400	11	B5
CERTA DR	RPV	PVP	6000	72	C4
CERVANTES PL	LA	LA46	7400	34	A1
CERVATO ST	LB	LB15	4400	76	B2
CERVERA AV	LA	WIL	800	74	F4
CESSNA DR	CO	MAL		106	D6
CETRO TR	CO	CHA		1A	C5
CEYLON AV	PR	PR	8500	60	E2
CEZANNE AV	LA	WOH	4300	13	C4
CEZANNE PL	LA	WOH	21600	13	C4
CHABELA DR	MB	MB	400	62	C5
CHADBOURNE AV	LA	LA49	200	41	A2
CHADLEY ST	CO	COV	18700	88	F2
CHADMONT ST	CO	COV	16500	88	B3
CHADNEY DR	GLEN	GL06		19	B5
CHADRON AV	CO	GAR	14700	63	C3
CHADRON AV	CO	HAW	14300	63	C3
CHADRON AV	HAW	HAW	12500	57	C6
CHADRON AV	HAW	HAW	13000	63	C1
CHADRON AV	LA	PAC	12000	3	A5
CHADSEY DR	CO	WHI	10700	61	F4
CHADSEY DR	LAM	LAM	12700	61	F6
CHADSEY DR	WHI	WHI	9800	84	A3
CHADSFORD DR	CO	VAL		124	A6
CHADWAY ST	SCLR	CYN	19500	124	H7
CHADWELL ST	LKD	LKD	11300	71	F3
CHADWELL ST	LKD	LKD	12500	81	C3
CHADWICK CIR	LA	LA32	2700	36	D5
CHADWICK CT	POM	POM	100	94	F6
CHADWICK DR	LA	LA32	2900	36	E5
CHADWICK WY	LAV	LAV		90	D2
CHAFFEE ST	LA	TU	6400	11	B4
CHAFFING TR	CO	TOP	20500	109	D5
CHAGAL AV	LAN	LAN		160	D6
CHAGALL RD	CO	TOP		13	C5
CHAKEMCO ST	SOG	SOG	5100	59	D4
CHALBURN AV N	WCOV	WCOV	200	88	A6
CHALCO ST	LAM	LAM	15000	84	A5
CHALET DR	BG	BELL	6400	54	B6
CHALET DR	CMRC	LA40	6200	54	B6
CHALET TER	LA	PP	16500	40	B3
CHALET TER	MPK	MPK	900	46	A3
CHALETTE DR	BH	BH	500	33	C2
CHALFONT CT	PALM	PALM		171	F5
CHALFONT DR	PALM	PALM		171	F6
CHALFORD CT	CO	LPUE		98	A5
CHALINA DR	WAL	WAL		93	A6
CHALLENGER ST	TOR	TOR		68	A2
CHALLENGER WY	LAN	LAN	42800	160	D7
CHALMERS DR	LA	LA35	8500	42	D2
CHALMERS PL	CO	CAL		100	A2
CHALMETTE LN	RHE	PVP	29500	72	F3
CHALON RD	LA	LA49	13100	30	F5
CHALON RD	LA	LA49	11100	32	C4
CHALON RD	LA	LA77	10600	32	D5
CHAMBER AV	LAV	LAV		90	C1
CHAMBERLAIN RD	PAS	PAS	1300	26	D1
CHAMBERLAIN ST	LA	SF	14000	8	D2
CHAMBERS ST	VER	LA58	2500	52	F3
CHAMBLEE AV	CER	ART	19300	81	A2
CHAMBORD DR	CO	SAU		181	E8
CHAMERA LN	CO	TOP		109	A2
CHAMINADE AV	LA	CAN	7500	5	F3
CHAMISE WY	CO	SAU		125	E4
CHAMIZO CALLE	CO	SAU		181	C9
CHAMPION PL	ALH	ALH	1	37	D3
CHAMPLAIN AV	PAS	PAS	400	26	F3
CHAMPLAIN DR	CLA	CLA		91	B1
CHAMPLAIN TER	LA	LA26	1600	35	D4
CHANCE ST	WCOV	WCOV		98	E1
CHANCERY LN	GLEN	GL06	2600	26	B2
CHANDA CT	LB	LB13	1000	75	D4
CHANDELEUR DR	LA	SP	1700	78	D3
CHANDELEUR DR	RPV	SP	2000	78	D3
CHANDELLE PL	DBAR	POM		97A	A1
CHANDELLE PL	LA	LA46	7700	23	F6
CHANDELLE RD	LA	LA46	3000	23	F6
CHANDLER AV N	MPK	MPK	100	46	B2
CHANDLER AV S	MPK	MPK	100	46	B2
CHANDLER BLVD	BUR	BUR	1100	17	B6
CHANDLER BLVD	BUR	BUR	2100	24	B1
CHANDLER BLVD	LA	NHO	10300	23	B1
CHANDLER BLVD	LA	VAN	13300	22	E1
CHANDLER BLVD	LA	VAN	12900	23	B1
CHANDLER PL	SMAR	PAS	1	27	C6
CHANDLER ST E	LA	WIL	100	74	C2

STREET	CITY	P.O. ZONE	BLOCK	PAGE	GRID
CHANDLER ST W	LA	WIL	100	74	B2
CHANDOS LN	LHH	LAH		84	F1
CHANDU PL	CO	LPUE		98	E6
CHANERA AV	CO	GAR	15200	63	C3
CHANERA AV	GAR	GAR	15800	63	C4
CHANERA AV	HAW	IN03	11500	57	C5
CHANERA AV	ING	IN03	10900	57	C4
CHANERA AV	TOR	GAR	16400	63	C5
CHANEY AV	DOW	DOW	9000	60	D2
CHANEY AV	PR	PR	8100	60	E1
CHANEY TR	CO	ALT	3400	20	A3
CHANNEL DR	CAR	LB10	24000	74	F1
CHANNEL DR	LB	LB14		76	D5
CHANNEL LN	LA	SM	14800	40	D5
CHANNEL RD	CO	CAST		123	E3
CHANNEL RD E	LA	SM		40	E4
CHANNEL RD W	LA	SM	100	40	D5
CHANNEL RD W	LA	SM	100	40	D5
CHANNEL ST	LA	SP	600	78	E1
CHANNEL WK	CO	MDR		49	D6
CHANNEL WY	LB	LB02		75	A6
CHANNELVIEW CT	RPV	PVP		77	C3
CHANNELWOOD DR	CO	WHI	1500	47	F4
CHANNING ST	AZU	AZU	300	86	C4
CHANNING ST	BAP	BAP	14300	39	E5
CHANNING ST	LA	LA21	700	44	E6
CHANNING ST	WCOV	WCOV	2200	39	F6
CHANRUSS PL	BH	BH	1200	33	A4
CHANSLOR AV	BELL	BELL	6400	53	E6
CHANSLOR ST	POM	POM	2300	94	F6
CHANSON DR	CO	LA43	3800	51	B3
CHANTADA AV	CO	PALM		189	H1
CHANTILLY LN	PALM	PALM		171	C5
CHANTILLY RD	LA	LA77	900	32	D4
CHANTO DR	WHI	WHI		84	C2
CHANTRY DR	ARC	ARC	1700	28	E1
CHANUTE ST	LA	PAC	12400	9	B2
CHAPALA DR	LA	PP	400	40	D4
CHAPARAL RD	SAD	SAD		89	F2
CHAPARAL ST	LA	LA49	11700	41	B1
CHAPARRAL AV	CER	ART	16600	82	B5
CHAPARRAL AV	CO	SAU		125	E4
CHAPARRAL CT	PALM	PALM		172	J5
CHAPARRAL DR	CLA	CLA	400	91	C2
CHAPARRAL DR	POM	POM		94	C5
CHAPARRAL DR	WAL	WAL		92	F5
CHAPARRAL DR	WCOV	WCOV		92	D4
CHAPARRAL LN	RPV	PVP		73	C6
CHAPARRAL RD	CO	CHA		4	B5
CHAPARRAL RD	GLDR	GLDR	500	87	B4
CHAPARRAL RD	SMAD	SMAD	600	28	C1
CHAPARRAL WY	CER	ART	17800	82	B6
CHAPARREL LN	PALM	PALM		172	F9
CHAPARREL LN	PALM	PALM		183	H8
CHAPARRO DR	SCLR	SAU	22500	124	C6
CHAPARRO RD	COV	COV	500	89	B6
CHAPEA RD	CO	PAS	800	28	A5
CHAPEL AV N	ALH	ALH	100	37	C3
CHAPEL AV S	ALH	ALH	100	37	C3
CHAPEL HILL DR	CO	WAL		97	C3
CHAPELLE AV	PR	PR	3500	47	B6
CHAPELLE AV	PR	PR	4100	55	B1
CHAPIN LN	LA	SUN	8200	10	D4
CHAPIN RD	MTB	MTB	1500	54	C5
CHAPIN TR	LA	SUN		10	D4
CHAPIN WY	LA	SUN	8200	10	D4
CHAPLIN AV	LA	ENC	16700	21	F3
CHAPLIN DR	LAN	LAN		159	B5
CHAPMAN AV	PAS	PAS	800	26	F2
CHAPMAN RD	CLA	CLA	1700	91	A1
CHAPMAN RD	CO	GL14	2300	11	E6
CHAPMAN ST	LA	LA65	3100	35	D1
CHAPMAN ST	LOM	LOM	2400	73	C3
CHAPMAN ST	WCOV	WCOV	300	88	B5
CHAPMAN WY	ELS	ELS		62	D1
CHAPMAN WDS RD	PAS	PAS		27	F5
CHAPPARAL DR	DBAR	POM		93	F5
CHAPTER DR	LA	WOH	20500	13	E3
CHARA AV	CLA	CLA		96	C6
CHARD AV	CO	TOP		115	C1
CHARDON CIR	LA	ENC	18100	21	C3
CHARDONNAY DR	DBAR	POM		97	F2
CHARFORD ST	SAD	SAD	2300	89	F1
CHARIETTE AV	RM	RM	3400	37	F6
CHARING CRSS PL	GLEN	GL06	3100	26	B1
CHARING CRSS RD	SCLR	VAL		127	A1
CHARING CRSS RD	GLEN	GL06	3100	26	B1
CHARING CRSS RD	LA	LA24	10200	32	F6
CHARIOT PL	CO	LP45		98	A3
CHARITON AV	CO	LA56	5500	50	E4
CHARITON ST	LA	LA34	1900	42	D4
CHARITY DR	LA	SF		2	F1
CHARITY LN	LB	LB05	700	65	D5
CHARL LN	LA	LA46	8500	33	D1
CHARL PL	LA	LA46	2600	33	D1

INDEX

230

1990 LOS ANGELES COUNTY STREET INDEX

CHARLEMAGNE AV — CIELITO AV

LOS ANGELES CO.

INDEX

STREET	CITY	P.O. ZONE	BLOCK	PAGE	GRID
CHARLEMAGNE AV	BLF	BLF	13400	66	C1
CHARLEMAGNE AV	LB	LB08	3000	71	C4
CHARLEMAGNE AV	LB	LB15	2000	76	C1
CHARLEMONT AV	CO	LPUE	1100	85	E2
CHARLEMONT AV	LA	WOH	4300	13	A4
CHARLENE DR	CO	LA43	4000	51	A4
CHARLES AV	CUL	CUL	4000	50	B1
CHARLES DR	SCLR	SAU		124	F5
CHARLES RD	CO	MAL		106	A4
CHARLES ST	LA	TAR	19100	21	A2
CHARLES ST	PAS	PAS	1000	26	D2
CHARLES WY	POM	POM	1400	90	D6
CHARLESTON DR	CLA	CLA		96	C6
CHARLESTON WY	LA	LA68	3300	24	A5
CHARLESTON WY	MTB	MTB	1300	54	D1
CHARLESTOWN DR	CO	WOH		13	B4
CHARLESWORTH AV	LA	NHO	6600	16	B5
CHARLESWORTH RD	PR	PR	9200	60	E1
CHARLESWORTH RD	SFS	SFS	11000	61	A2
CHARLEVILLE BL	BH	BH	8500	42	B1
CHARLIE RD	IND	LPUE	900	98	E2
CHARLIE CYN RD	CO	CAST		123	J2
CHARLIE CYN RD	CO	SAU		123	F1
CHARLINDA ST	WCOV	WCOV	1000	92	B2
CHARLINDA ST	WCOV	WCOV		93	A2
CHARLINE PL	CO	LPUE		97	B5
CHARLMONT PL	LA	WOH	22700	13	A4
CHARLOMA DR	DOW	DOW	8300	60	D2
CHARLOTTE AV	CO	RM		46	F3
CHARLOTTE AV	CO	SGAB	5200	37	F3
CHARLOTTE AV	RM	RM	3400	37	F6
CHARLOTTE AV	RM	RM	2200	46	F3
CHARLOTTE AV N	SGAB	SGAB	100	37	F3
CHARLOTTE AV S	SGAB	SGAB	100	37	F3
CHARLOTTE DR	TOR	TOR	22300	67	E5
CHARLOTTE PL	PALM	PALM		173	B6
CHARLOTTE PL	PALM	PALM		184	B6
CHARLOTTE ST	LA	LA33	2000	45	B2
CHARLTON LN	LA	NOR		1	C6
CHARLTON RD	SMAR	PAS	1400	37	C1
CHARLWOOD CIR	CER	ART		81	D1
CHARLWOOD ST	ART	ART	12100	81	B1
CHARLWOOD ST	CER	ART	12200	81	B1
CHARLWOOD ST	LKD	LKD	6000	71	D1
CHARM ACRES PL	LA	PP	1100	40	D3
CHARMEL CT	LA	PP		40	A2
CHARMEL LN	LA	PP	16600	40	B2
CHARMEL PL	LA	PP		40	A1
CHARMINGDALE RD	DBAR	POM	800	97A	A1
CHARMION LN	LA	ENC	4500	21	E3
CHARMONT RD	LAV	LAV	1200	95A	D4
CHARNER ST	BG	BELL	6600	54	B6
CHARNOCK AV	LA	LA34	11000	42	C5
CHARNOCK RD	LA	LA34	10700	42	A6
CHARNOCK RD	LA	LA34		50	A1
CHARNOCK RD	LA	LA66	11200	49	E2
CHARNWOOD AV	ALH	ALH	1900	45	E1
CHARONNE CT	SCLR	VAL		127	A1
CHARONOAK PL	CO	SGAB	6200	37	F2
CHARRICK DR	LA	TU	9300	11	A5
CHARRICK PL	LA	TU	7000	11	A5
CHARRO CT	SAD	SAD	400	89	D2
CHARRON PL	CO	COM	400	64	C2
CHART TR	CO	TOP	1700	109	D1
CHARTER CT	CO	PALM		184	E2
CHARTER DR	COV	COV	500	89	C4
CHARTER ST	VER	LA58		53	B2
CHARTER OAK LN	LA	BH	10000	32	E2
CHARTER OAK ST	SPAS	SPAS	600	36	E1
CHARTERS AV	LA	LA42	4700	36	A1
CHARTHAM PL	CO	LPUE		98	A5
CHARTHOUSE CIR	WLVL	THO		102A	F5
CHARTRES DR	RPV	PVP	6500	77	C1
CHARVERS AV	GLDR	GLDR	5600	89	A1
CHARVERS AV	WCOV	WCOV	2600	93	A2
CHARWOOD PL	DBAR	POM		97A	A3
CHASAR PL	CO	LA43	4500	51	A3
CHASE AV	LA	LA45	7900	56	B1
CHASE AV	LA	LA66	4100	49	F3
CHASE PL	LA	CAN		6	A6
CHASE PL	LA	CAN	22700	12	A1
CHASE ST	LA	CAN	23200	5	F1
CHASE ST	LA	CAN	19700	6	F6
CHASE ST	LA	CAN	19700	12	F1
CHASE ST	LA	NOR	17000	14	E1
CHASE ST	LA	PAC	13400	8	F5
CHASE ST	LA	PAC	13000	9	A5
CHASE ST	LA	SF	16500	7	F6
CHASE ST	LA	SF	15000	8	B6
CHASE ST	LA	VAN	13800	8	E6
CHASE WY	WCOV	WCOV		92	B4
CHASHAN RD	CO	SAU		181	J6
CHASTAIN AV	LA	RES	7999	14	D2
CHASTAIN PKWY W	LA	PP		30	B5
CHATEAU CT	MON	MON	400	29	A2
CHATEAU RD	PAS	PAS	1000	26	D4

STREET	CITY	P.O. ZONE	BLOCK	PAGE	GRID
CHATEAU CREST	MON	MON	400	29	A2
CHATFIELD AV	CO	WHI	7700	55	C6
CHATFIELD WY	CO	VAL		124	F2
CHATHAM	MB	MB		62	C3
CHATHAM CT	CLA	CLA	1800	90	F2
CHATHAM DR	LA	LA69	8900	33	D4
CHATHAM DR	PALM	PALM		172	F9
CHATHAM DR	PALM	PALM		183	E1
CHATHAM LN	LA	NOR		1	C6
CHATHAM PL	LCF	LCF	600	19	C5
CHATLAKE DR	LA	CAN	8600	4	B6
CHATSBORO DR	LA	WOH		13	D3
CHATSWORTH DR	LA	SF	15000	8	D2
CHATSWORTH DR	SF	SF	200	2	E6
CHATSWORTH ST	LA	CHA	19600	6	F2
CHATSWORTH ST	LA	NOR	18000	7	A2
CHATSWORTH ST	LA	SF	16600	7	D2
CHATSWORTH ST	LA	SF	15100	8	A2
CHATTANOOGA AV	LA	PP	800	40	B3
CHATTANOOGA CT	CLA	CLA		91	D2
CHATTANOOGA PL	LA	PP	16500	40	B3
CHATTERTON AV	LPUE	LPUE	400	98	B1
CHATWIN AV	LB	LB08	3000	71	C4
CHATWIN AV	LB	LB15	1800	76	C2
CHATWIN AV	LKD	LKD	4100	71	C4
CHAUCER CT	SAD	SAD		89	D3
CHAUCER RD	SMAR	PAS		27	D5
CHAUCER ST	LA	LA65	3000	35	E3
CHAUCER WK	LA	LA65	3500	35	F3
CHAUMONT CT	PALM	PALM		171	G6
CHAUMONT RD	LA	WOH	4200	13	E3
CHAUNCEY DR	CER	ART	19000	81	C1
CHAUTAUQUA BLVD	LA	PP	100	40	D4
CHAVERS AV	DOW	DOW	12200	59	F4
CHAVEZ ST	BUR	BUR	1000	24	E2
CHAVEZ ST	GLEN	GL01	1900	24	E2
CHAVEZ ST	LA	LA12		44	F1
CHAVZ RAVINE PL	LA	LA12	900	44	D1
CHAYOTE ST	LA	LA49	11600	41	C1
CHEDDAR ST	DOW	DOW	9600	60	C6
CHEDDAR ST	NWK	NWK	10500	60	D6
CHEDDAR ST	NWK	NWK	11900	61	A6
CHEESBROUGH LN	LA	LA63	100	45	C4
CHEHALEM RD	LCF	LCF	800	19	C2
CHELAN DR	LA	LA68	2200	34	A2
CHELAN PL	LA	LA68	2200	34	A2
CHELAN WY	LA	LA68	7100	34	A2
CHELLA DR	CO	LPUE	16100	85	E5
CHELLWOOD ST	CO	SAU		189	B2
CHELMSFORD WY	ING	IN01		57	B2
CHELSA DR	POM	POM	1300	95	B1
CHELSEA	PALM	PALM		171	F5
CHELSEA AV	CER	ART		81	C1
CHELSEA AV	SM	SM	1000	41	B4
CHELSEA CT	AGH	AGO		102	E2
CHELSEA CT	LB	LB03		76	F5
CHELSEA CT	SM	SM	1000	41	B4
CHELSEA DR	LAV	LAV		90	D2
CHELSEA LN	ING	IN01		57	B2
CHELSEA PL	GLDR	GLDR		89	D2
CHELSEA PL	SM	SM	2400	41	B5
CHELSEA RD	ARC	ARC		28	D3
CHELSEA RD	PVE	PVP	1400	72	A4
CHELSEA RD	SMAR	PAS	1400	37	C2
CHELSEA ST	CO	SAU		123	D4
CHELSEA ST	LA	LA33	2400	45	B2
CHELSEA WY	SGAB	SGAB	400	37	D2
CHELSFIELD ST	BAP	BAP	12700	39	B6
CHELSWORTH LN	CER	ART	12900	81	C2
CHELTEN WY	SPAS	SPAS	1200	37	A2
CHELTENHAM DR	LA	VAN	13300	23	A4
CHENAULT ST	LA	LA49	11300	41	C2
CHENEY DR	CO	TOP	20500	109	D2
CHENIL CT	SCLR	SAU		124	E5
CHERAW DR	SCLR	SAU		124	D5
CHERBOURG LN	LAN	LAN		159	F7
CHERE DR	CO	WHI	14100	61	E6
CHEREMOYA AV	LA	LA68	1900	34	D2
CHERET PL	RPV	PVP	30300	77	D1
CHERI WY	RM	RM		47	A1
CHERIE PL	CAR	CAR	16800	64	D5
CHERITON DR	CAR	CAR	500	64	B5
CHERMAK ST	BUR	BUR		16	F3
CHEROKEE	CO	AGO		106	D2
CHEROKEE	CO	TOP		13	C5
CHEROKEE AV	LA	LA04	500	34	B5
CHEROKEE AV	LA	LA28	1300	34	B5
CHEROKEE AV	LA	LA38	700	34	B5
CHEROKEE AV	LYN	LYN	3100	59	A4
CHEROKEE AV	SOG	SOG	3100	59	A4
CHEROKEE CT	LA	LA28		34	B3
CHEROKEE DR	DOW	DOW	7400	60	C3
CHEROKEE DR	WCOV	WCOV		92	D4
CHEROKEE LN	GLEN	GL05	900	25	E5
CHEROKEE LN	LA	BH	9300	33	B2
CHEROKEE TR	CO	CHA		1A	C6

STREET	CITY	P.O. ZONE	BLOCK	PAGE	GRID
CHEROKEE CYN LN	SCLR	SAU		124	B1
CHERRY AV	ING	IN03	11400	57	C5
CHERRY AV	LB	LB02	100	75	E4
CHERRY AV	LB	LB05	5900	65	E6
CHERRY AV	LB	LB05	5200	70	E4
CHERRY AV	LB	LB06	1800	75	E4
CHERRY AV	LB	LB07	3000	70	E4
CHERRY AV	LB	LB13	700	75	E4
CHERRY AV	SH	LB06	1800	75	E1
CHERRY AV	TOR	TOR	16700	63	C5
CHERRY AV E	MON	MON	100	29	B5
CHERRY AV W	MON	MON	100	29	A5
CHERRY DR	CO	CAST	31700	123	D9
CHERRY DR	PALM	PALM		183	C6
CHERRY DR	PALM	PALM		183	E1
CHERRY DR	PAS	PAS	200	26	D5
CHERRY LN	ALH	ALH	1600	37	B5
CHERRY ST	SCLR	NEW	23400	127	B4
CHERRY ST	COM	COM		64	E2
CHERRY ST	GLEN	GL02	1100	25	B2
CHERRY ST	LA	LA15	1300	44	B4
CHERRY CREEK DR	SCLR	VAL	27300	124	C5
CHERRYCREEK LN	CER	ART	12400	82	B4
CHERRY CRST CIR	CER	ART		82	B4
CHERRYDALE DR	DBAR	POM		97	D6
CHERRY FALL LN	CER	ART		82	B4
CHERRY GATE WY	CO	LPUE		98	A4
CHERRY HILL LN	RPV	PVP	1	77	F3
CHERRY HILLS LN	AZU	AZU	300	86	D4
CHERRY HILLS LN	LA	TAR	4300	13	F3
CHERRY INDL CIR	LB	LB05	2000	70	E1
CHERRYLEE DR	ELM	ELM	11300	38	F4
CHERRYLEE DR	ELM	ELM	11600	39	A4
CHERRYSTONE AV	LA	VAN	7700	15	E2
CHERRY TREE LN	CO	PALM		171	C6
CHERRYVALE DR	LAM	LAM	12600	84	C6
CHERRYWOOD AV	LA	LA08	3800	51	C1
CHERRYWOOD AV	LA	LA18	3700	51	C1
CHERRYWOOD ST	WCOV	WCOV	100	92	C1
CHERTSEY LN	PALM	PALM		171	F5
CHERTY DR	RPV	PVP	6900	72	C4
CHERYL AV	GLEN	GL14	4700	11	D5
CHERYL DR	TOR	TOR	20400	67	E3
CHERYL PL	LA	LA49	2300	30	E5
CHERYL WY	RB	RB	600	67	E4
CHERYL KELTN PL	SCLR	NEW		127	A4
CHESAPEAKE	WCOV	WCOV		92	D4
CHESAPEAKE AV	LA	LA16	2800	43	B6
CHESEBORO RD	CO	PALM	34000	184	B7
CHESEBRO RD	AGH	AGO		100A	C4
CHESHIRE LN	CO	VAL		124	F2
CHESHIRE ST	LAM	LAM	14800	83	A3
CHESHIRE ST	NWK	NWK	11500	66	F3
CHESHIRE ST	NWK	NWK	11600	82	A3
CHESLEY AV	LA	LA43	5100	51	B4
CHESNEY AV	SAD	SAD	1200	89	F1
CHESSINGTON DR	ING	IN01		57	B2
CHESSON ST	DUA	DUA	1800	29	E4
CHESTER AV	ING	IN02	900	51	B5
CHESTER AV	SMAR	PAS	600	27	D5
CHESTER AV N	COM	COM	100	65	A4
CHESTER AV N	PAS	PAS	100	27	C4
CHESTER AV S	COM	COM	100	65	A4
CHESTER AV S	PAS	PAS	100	27	C4
CHESTER PL	LA	LA07		44	A5
CHESTER PL	LB	LB13	800	75	B4
CHESTER PL	POM	POM	300	94	E2
CHESTER RD E	COV	COV	600	88	F4
CHESTER RD W	COV	COV	1000	88	D4
CHESTER ST	GLEN	GL03	200	25	B3
CHESTER ST	LA	LA32	5000	36	E5
CHESTER ST	LYN	LYN	11200	59	A5
CHESTER ST	PAR	PAR	8700	66	A3
CHESTERBROOK WY	AGH	AGO		100A	D5
CHESTERFIELD RD	RH	PVP	1	73	B6
CHESTEROARK DR	LKD	LKD	6000	71	D2
CHESTERTON ST	NWK	NWK	11500	82	A4
CHESTERWOOD ST	LA	SF	13100	3	A3
CHESTNUT AV	LA	LA42	200	36	D1
CHESTNUT AV	LB	LB02	100	75	C5
CHESTNUT AV	LB	LB05	5500	70	C1
CHESTNUT AV	LB	LB06	2900	70	C6
CHESTNUT AV	LB	LB06	1800	75	C2
CHESTNUT AV	LB	LB07	3700	70	C6
CHESTNUT AV	LB	LB13	700	75	C4
CHESTNUT AV	MB	MB	1100	62	C4
CHESTNUT AV	RM	RM	8300	37	E4
CHESTNUT AV	SOG	SOG	8100	59	A2
CHESTNUT AV E	MON	MON	100	29	A4
CHESTNUT AV E	SGAB	SGAB	100	37	E4
CHESTNUT AV W	MON	MON	100	29	A4
CHESTNUT AV W	SGAB	SGAB	100	37	E4
CHESTNUT CT	WAL	WAL		93	D5
CHESTNUT LN	RHE	PVP	1	72	F6
CHESTNUT PL	LB	LB02		75	C6
CHESTNUT PL	POM	POM	2500	94	F6

STREET	CITY	P.O. ZONE	BLOCK	PAGE	GRID
CHESTNUT RD	LAV	LAV		95A	C6
CHESTNUT ST	ALH	ALH	1500	37	A5
CHESTNUT ST	BLF	BLF		66	D6
CHESTNUT ST	BUR	BUR	2100	17	C6
CHESTNUT ST	SCLR	NEW	24300	127	C3
CHESTNUT ST	GLDR	GLDR	100	87	B6
CHESTNUT ST	IND	LPUE	16900	98	B2
CHESTNUT ST	PALM	LAN		171	C2
CHESTNUT ST	PAS	PAS	1	27	A3
CHESTNUT ST	WHI	WHI	13000	61	E1
CHESTNUT ST E	GLEN	GL05	100	25	C5
CHESTNUT ST W	GLEN	GL04	100	25	C5
CHESTNUT WY	CO	CAL		100	D6
CHESTNUT CK DR	DBAR	POM	1700	97	E4
CHESTNUT HLL DR	WAL	WAL	1500	93	B3
CHESTNUTHILL PL	CLA	CLA		96	B6
CHESTRIDGE CIR	WAL	WAL		92	F5
CHESTWICK DR	CO	BH		33	A2
CHESWIC LN	LA	LA27	2200	34	F2
CHESWOLD LN	CO	SAU		124	E4
CHETAC ST	CO	LAN	12500	158	A2
CHETLE AV	SFS	SFS		61	C1
CHETLE AV	WHI	WHI		61	C1
CHETNEY DR	BAP	BAP	15000	39	F5
CHETNEY DR	WCOV	WCOV	1600	88	A5
CHETWOOD DR	LA	TU	7200	10	F2
CHEVALIER AV	BAP	BAP	14500	39	E5
CHEVERTON DR	LAM	LAM	12600	83	B1
CHEVIOT DR	LA	LA64	10300	42	A4
CHEVIOTDALE DR	PAS	PAS	1300	26	D5
CHEVIOTDALE PL	LA	LA42	600	26	D6
CHEVIOT VIS PL	LA	LA34	3100	42	A5
CHEVRON CT	PAS	PAS	800	19	E5
CHEVY CHASE DR	BH	BH	1000	33	A5
CHEVY CHASE DR	LA	LA39	3900	25	B5
CHEVY CHASE DR	LCF	LCF	3600	19	C6
CHEVY CHAS DR E	GLEN	GL05	100	25	D5
CHEVY CHAS DR N	GLEN	GL06	3400	19	C6
CHEVY CHAS DR N	GLEN	GL06	100	25	E5
CHEVY CHAS DR N	GLEN	GL06	2300	26	A3
CHEVY CHAS DR S	GLEN	GL05	100	25	E5
CHEVY CHAS DR W	GLEN	GL04	100	25	C5
CHEVY KNOLL DR	GLEN	GL06	1600	26	B1
CHEVY KNOLL PL	GLEN	GL06	1800	26	B1
CHEVY OAKS CIR	GLEN	GL06	2200	25	F3
CHEVY OAKS DR	GLEN	GL06		25	F2
CHEYENNE AV	CO	CHA		6	C1
CHEYENNE AV	DOW	DOW	8000	59	F6
CHEYENNE AV	DOW	DOW	8300	60	A6
CHEYENNE DR	SAD	SAD		90	A1
CHEYENNE ST	DOW	DOW		60	A6
CHEYENNE ST	LA	NOR	19200	7	A2
CHEYNE WELS CIR	WAL	WAL		93	A5
CHICAGO AV	BLF	BLF	16200	66	D4
CHICAGO ST N	LA	LA33	100	45	A4
CHICAGO ST S	LA	LA23	600	45	A4
CHICAGO ST S	LA	LA33	100	45	A4
CHICKASAW AV	LA	LA41	1500	26	A5
CHICKASAW TR	CO	CHA		1A	C6
CHICKORY DR	LAN	LAN		159	J7
CHICKORY LN	LA	LA49	1200	32	A5
CHICO AV	ELM	ELM	3100	47	B1
CHICO AV	SELM	ELM	1400	47	B3
CHICO ST	ALH	ALH	1	37	C3
CHICO ST	CAR	CAR	21000	69	C4
CHICO ST	LA	LA18	2800	43	C5
CHICOPEE AV	LA	ENC	5700	14	E6
CHICOPEE AV	LA	ENC	5000	21	E2
CHICOPEE AV	LA	NOR	9700	7	E4
CHICOPEE AV	LA	NOR	8000	14	E2
CHICOPEE AV	LA	VAN	7200	14	E3
CHICORA DR	DBAR	POM		93	F6
CHICORY CT	CO	NEW		126	J5
CHILCOT ST	BAP	BAP	13600	39	D3
CHILDS CT	LA	LA39	3300	35	B3
CHILDS WY	LA	LA07		44	A6
CHILE ST	LA	LA32	4000	36	C6
CHILTON DR	GLEN	GL01	2000	17	F5
CHILTON DR	GLEN	GL01	1900	18	A5
CHIMES AV	DUA	DUA	800	29	E4
CHIMINEAS AV	LA	NOR	11500	1	C6
CHIMINEAS AV	LA	NOR	8500	7	C6
CHIMINEAS AV	LA	NOR	8300	14	C1
CHIMINEAS AV	LA	RES	6200	14	C5
CHIMINEAS AV	LA	TAR	5700	14	C6
CHIMINEAS AV	LA	TAR	4900	21	C2
CHIMNEY ROCK RD	SCLR	VAL		127	A1
CHIMNEYSMOKE RD	LCF	LCF	2000	18	F1
CHINA PL	CO	PALM		183	B3
CHINKAPIN ST	SCLR	NEW	18900	127	H3
CHINO VISTA CT	LAN	LAN		160	E4
CHINOOK PL	DBAR	POM	23800	94	A6
CHIP	PALM	PALM		171	E4
CHIPPENDALE AV	GLDR	GLDR		89	C1
CHIPPEWA DR	CO	PALM		157A	E9
CHIPPEWA ST	LA	SF	12800	3	A4

STREET	CITY	P.O. ZONE	BLOCK	PAGE	GRID
CHIPTREE DR	CO	PALM		157	H8
CHIQUELLA LN	CO	NEW		126	J4
CHIQUELLA LN	SCLR	NEW		127	A6
CHIQUITA PL	GLEN	GL08	1800	18	F3
CHIQUITA ST	LA	NHO	10600	23	D4
CHIQUITO CYN RD	CO	SAU	28300	123	A6
CHIRLEE DR	CO	PALM	38400	174	B8
CHIRPNG SPARROW	DBAR	POM		99	D4
CHISHOLM AV	LA	VAN	6800	15	B4
CHISHOLM CT	CO	SAU		181	B8
CHISHOLM CT	SAD	SAD		89	F1
CHISHOLM TR DR	DBAR	POM		97	F2
CHISLEHURST DR	LA	LA27	2200	34	E2
CHISLEHURST PL	LA	LA27	2500	34	E2
CHISWICK CT	CO	VAL		127	A1
CHISWICK RD	PVE	PVP	500	72	A4
CHIVERS AV	LA	PAC	11700	3	A5
CHIVERS AV	LA	PAC	11000	9	B1
CHIVERS AV	LA	SF	12800	2	D2
CHIVERS AV	LA	SV		9	E5
CHIVERS ST	SF	SF	1900	2	F4
CHOCKTAW DR	DBAR	POM	21300	97	D6
CHOCLAT LILY LN	CO	MAL		110	B4
CHOCTAW	WCOV	WCOV		92	D4
CHOCTAW DR	LAN	LAN		159	D6
CHOISSER ST	CO	WHI	10600	55	A5
CHOKE CHERRY LN	SCLR	NEW	24400	127	F3
CHOLAME DR	DBAR	POM		94	A5
CHORAL DR	LHH	LAH	2100	98A	B3
CHOSEN ST	ELM	ELM	12200	47	E3
CHOTA RD	LHH	LAH	1700	98A	B2
CHOUINARD CIR	CLA	CLA		91	C1
CHRIS PL	BH	BH	400	33	C3
CHRISTENSEN CT	PALM	PALM		184	B5
CHRISTIANSEN AL	PAS	PAS	100	26	F4
CHRISTIE AV	LAN	LAN	44700	160	D4
CHRISTIE LN	WCOV	WCOV		92	E6
CHRISTINA AV	CER	ART	18700	81	B1
CHRISTINA CIR	CER	ART		81	B2
CHRISTINA CT	CER	ART	12400	81	B2
CHRISTINA CT	CO	CAL		100	C4
CHRISTINA CT	CO	PALM		184	B6
CHRISTINA CT	POM	POM	1200	94	D4
CHRISTINA ST	ARC	ARC	1	28	E6
CHRISTINA WY	CER	ART	19500	81	B2
CHRISTINE AV	TOR	TOR	20600	67	E3
CHRISTINE DR	WHI	WHI	13800	61	F1
CHRISTINE LN	ARC	ARC		28	C6
CHRISTINE LN	ARC	ARC		38	C1
CHRISTINE PL	LA	CHA	10300	6	F3
CHRISTINE WY	LA	TU	10900	10	E2
CHRISTOPHER AV	ING	IN03	11400	57	C5
CHRISTOPHER LN	CER	ART	12200	81	B2
CHRISTOPHER ST	WCOV	WCOV	800	92	B1
CHRISTY AV	LA	SF	11400	3	F6
CHRISTY AV	LA	SF	11100	9	F1
CHRISTY AV	LA	SUN	11100	9	F1
CHRISTY ST	CER	ART	11500	71	F2
CHRYSANTHMUM LN	LA	LA77	10200	32	E2
CHUCKER CT	CO	CAST		123	J1
CHUCK WAGON CIR	WAL	WAL		93	A6
CHUCKWAGON PL	CO	CYN		128	E2
CHUCKWAGON RD	PALM	PALM		183	G3
CHUCKWAGON RD	PVE	PVP	1	78	B1
CHUDLEIGH LN	GLEN	GL07		25	D1
CHUKA AV E	CO	LAN	16100	174	J7
CHULA ST	CO	MON	100	29	A6
CHULA SENDA LN	CO	PAS	4200	19	C4
CHULA VISTA AV	PAS	PAS	800	26	E2
CHULA VISTA PL	PAS	PAS	1000	26	D2
CHULA VISTA WY	LA	LA68	5900	34	D2
CHUMASH RD	CO	MAL		114	E2
CHUNG KING CT	LA	LA12	500	44	E1
CHUNG KING RD	LA	LA12	900	44	E1
CHURCH LN N	LA	LA49	100	32	C6
CHURCH LN S	LA	LA49	100	41	C1
CHURCH PL	LA	LA42	6200	26	D6
CHURCH RD	CMRC	LA40	3100	54	B4
CHURCH ST	BUR	BUR	1700	17	C4
CHURCH ST	CER	ART		81	D1
CHURCH ST	CO	CAST	27800	123	G2
CHURCH ST	LA	LA42	6200	26	D6
CHURCH ST	MB	MB	1300	62	B3
CHURCH ST	PAS	PAS	1000	26	D6
CHURCH ST	PR	PR	4800	55	A3
CHURCHILL AV	LA	CHA	10500	6	C2
CHURCHILL AV	SAD	SAD	500	90	B2
CHURCHILL RD	LHH	LAH	500	98A	A1
CHURCHILL RD	SMAD	SMAD	200	28	D1
CHURCHILL GLEN	SMAD	SMAD	200	28	D1
CHURCHS CT	BUR	BUR		17	E4
CICERO DR	LA	LA26	1600	35	B4
CIDAR AV	CO	SAU		125	J1
CIE CT	CO	PALM		171	J8
CIELITO AV	MPK	MPK	1700	46	B4

231

1990 LOS ANGELES COUNTY STREET INDEX

CIELITO DR — CLOVERLEAF PL

LOS ANGELES CO.

STREET	CITY	P.O. ZONE	BLOCK	PAGE	GRID
CIELITO DR	GLEN	GL07	1600	25	D1
CIELO CT	SCLR	VAL		127	A3
CIELO DR	LA	BH	10000	32	F3
CIELO PL	ARC	ARC	2200	28	E1
CIELO VISTA DR	WHI	WHI	8000	84	B1
CIENEGA AV	CO	COV	19000	88	F3
CIENEGA AV	CO	COV	19400	89	D3
CIENEGA AV	COV	COV	500	88	F3
CIENEGA AV	SAD	SAD	500	89	D3
CIMA DE LAGO	CO	CHA		4	B5
CIMA MESA RD	CO	LR	10400	192	A5
CIMARRON AV	GAR	GAR	12800	63	D1
CIMARRON AV	HAW	LA47	11500	57	D5
CIMARRON LN	CUL	CUL		50	D2
CIMARRON ST	CO	LA47	10400	57	D4
CIMARRON ST	LA	LA18	1900	43	D6
CIMARRON ST	LA	LA19	1600	43	D6
CIMARRON ST	LA	LA47	5800	51	D6
CIMARRON ST	LA	LA47	7800	57	D2
CIMARRON ST	LA	LA62	3800	51	D1
CIMMARON CT	WAL	WAL		92	F5
CIMMARRON WY	GAR	GAR		63	D3
CIMMERON TR	GLDR	GLDR	200	87	D5
CINCHRING RD	RH	PVP	1	78	A1
CINCINNATI ST	LA	LA33	2400	45	B3
CINCO DR	LA	NHO	11500	23	D5
CINCO CASITS LN	CO	GL14	2400	11	F6
CINCO ROBLES DR	DUA	DUA	1500	29	D6
CINCO VIEW DR	CO	WHI		55	D2
CINDERELLA DR	CLA	CLA	400	91	B5
CINDERELLA WY	POM	POM	2100	90	F5
CINDY CT	CO	CYN		125	E7
CINDY CT	POM	POM	300	90	F6
CINDY LN	LA	LA65	2700	25	F5
CINDY LN	PR	PR		55	E3
CINDY RD	SCLR	NEW		127	D3
CINDY ST	WCOV	WCOV		92	E6
CINDY LOU CT	AZU	AZU		88	D2
CINEMA AV	LAN	LAN		159	J8
CINEMA DR	SCLR	VAL		124	B8
CINKEL ST	MTB	MTB	1100	54	D3
CINNAMON LN	DUA	DUA		29	C6
CINNAMON LN	RPV	PVP	1	77	E2
CINTHIA ST	BH	BH	700	33	C4
CIPRIANO PL	MPK	MPK	700	46	B2
CIRCLE CT	HB	RB	200	62	C6
CIRCLE CT	LAV	LAV		90	D2
CIRCLE DR	BRAD	DUA	300	29	D3
CIRCLE DR	CO	AGO		106	F3
CIRCLE DR	HB	RB	2000	62	C6
CIRCLE DR	LA	LA32		45	E1
CIRCLE DR	LA	VAN	5300	22	D1
CIRCLE DR	LB	LB05		70	A2
CIRCLE DR	RB	RB	1700	67	E6
CIRCLE DR	SMAR	PAS	1300	37	C1
CIRCLE DR E	LA	LA24		32	E6
CIRCLE DR N	LA	LA24		32	E6
CIRCLE DR N	SGAB	SGAB	200	37	E4
CIRCLE DR N	WHI	WHI		55	D2
CIRCLE DR S	LA	LA24		41	E1
CIRCLE DR S	SGAB	SGAB	200	37	E4
CIRCLE DR S	WHI	WHI		55	D2
CIRCLE DR W	LA	LA24		32	D6
CIRCLE TR	CO	TOP	21600	109	C4
CIRCLE DELL DR	AZU	AZU	100	86	D4
CIR DIAMOND RD	CO	NEW		2	B1
CIRCLE G DR	CO	CYN	27000	128	E1
CIRCLE HILL LN	CO	LPUE		98	A4
CIRCLE J RCH RD	SCLR	SAU		127	C1
CIRCLE KNOLL CT	SCLR	NEW		127	H1
CIRCLE OAK DR	MON	MON	200	29	C3
CIR OF FRIENDS	SCLR	SAU	18900	127	J1
CIR OF THE OAKS	SCLR	SAU	26800	127	J1
CIRCLE RIDGE LN	CO	LPUE		85	C4
CIRCLET DR	RPV	PVP	28200	72	D5
CIRCLE VERDE DR	RPV	LOM	26800	73	D4
CIRCLE VIEW BL	CO	LA43	4400	51	B3
CIRCLE VISTA AV	CO	GL14	5000	11	E6
CIRIO WY	PAR	PAR	16600	65	E4
CIRO ST	DOW	DOW	7400	60	B1
CIRRUS WY	LA	CAN		5	F3
CISCO ST	LA	LA34	9700	42	C4
CISERO DR	CO	PALM		184	A2
CITADEL AV	CLA	CLA	500	91	C5
CITADEL DR	WAL	WAL	500	93	B5
CITRON PL	POM	POM	2500	94	F6
CITRON RD	LHH	LAH	2100	84	F1
CITRONELL AV	PR	PR	7200	54	E6
CITRONELL AV	PR	PR	5000	55	A3
CITRONIA ST	LA	CHA	19700	6	E4
CITRONIA ST	LA	NOR	17100	7	E4
CITRONIA ST	LA	SF	16600	7	F4
CITRUS AV	CO	AZU	6400	86	E6
CITRUS AV	CO	AZU	5100	86	E3
CITRUS AV	CO	COV	4600	88	E3
CITRUS AV	WHI	WHI	5300	55	D4
CITRUS AV N	AZU	AZU	200	86	E6
CITRUS AV N	AZU	AZU	100	88	E3
CITRUS AV N	COV	COV	100	88	E5
CITRUS AV N	LA	LA28	1300	34	B4
CITRUS AV N	LA	LA36	100	34	B4
CITRUS AV N	LA	LA38	700	34	B4
CITRUS AV S	AZU	AZU	100	88	E3
CITRUS AV S	CO	LA43	5800	51	A4
CITRUS AV S	COV	COV	100	88	E5
CITRUS AV S	LA	LA19	1000	43	B1
CITRUS AV S	LA	LA36	100	43	B1
CITRUS DR	PR	PR	4700	55	A2
CITRUS LN	CO	POM		93	F2
CITRUS LN	LAM	LAM		83	D1
CITRUS PL	SCLR	SAU		124	C2
CITRUS ST	LHH	LAH	1200	84	F3
CITRUS ST N	WCOV	WCOV	100	92	E2
CITRUS ST S	WCOV	WCOV	100	92	E2
CITRUS EDGE ST	AZU	AZU	900	88	E1
CITRUS EDGE ST	CO	AZU	18000	88	E1
CITRUS EDGE ST	CO	GLDR	19100	88	F1
CITRUS EDGE ST	GLDR	GLDR		89	A1
CITRUS GROVE PL	WHI	WHI		55	D3
CITRUSTREE RD	WHI	WHI	15600	84	C4
CITRUS VIEW AV	CO	DUA	2400	39	C1
CITRUS VIEW AV	DUA	DUA	1800	29	C6
CITRUS VIEW AV	IRW	DUA	2400	39	C1
CITRUSWOOD ST	LAV	LAV		90	D1
CITY RANCH RD	CO	PALM		171	G9
CITY RANCH RD	CO	PALM		183	A1
CITY TERRACE DR	CO	LA63	3200	45	C3
CITY VIEW AV	LA	LA33	1900	45	A3
CIVIC PZ	CAR	CAR		69	C4
CIVIC ST	CO	ELM	10600	38	D4
CIVIC ST	ELM	ELM	10600	38	D4
CIVIC CENTER DR	BLF	BLF	16600	66	C4
CIVIC CENTER DR	BH	BH		33	C6
CIVIC CENTER DR	CAR	CAR	21400	69	C4
CIVIC CENTER DR	DOW	DOW		60	B4
CIVIC CENTER DR	NWK	NWK	12200	61	B6
CIVIC CENTER DR	NWK	NWK		82	B1
CIVIC CENTER DR	TOR	TOR		68	B3
CIVIC CENTER PL	ARC	ARC		28	D5
CIVIC CENTER WY	CO	MAL		113	F5
CIVIC CENTER WY	CO	MAL	23700	114	A5
CIVIC CENTER WY	LKD	LKD		71	B2
CLAIBORNE DR	LB	LB07	600	70	D4
CLAIBORNE PL	LB	LB07	200	70	C4
CLAIBOURNE LN	SCLR	SAU		127	D2
CLAIRCREST DR	LA	BH	9300	33	B3
CLAIR DEL AV	LB	LB07	4900	70	E3
CLAIR DEL AV	LKD	LKD	4900	70	E3
CLAIRE AV	LA	NOR	9100	7	A4
CLAIRE AV	LA	NOR	8300	14	B1
CLAIRE AV	LA	RES	6800	14	B3
CLAIRE CT	LAN	LAN		160	D6
CLAIRE PL	POM	POM	900	94	C2
CLAIR RIDGE DR	CO	ACT		189	E4
CLAIRTON CT	LA	VAN		21	F5
CLAIRTON PL	LA	ENC	16500	21	F5
CLAMPITT RD	SCLR	NEW		127	E7
CLANCEY AV	DOW	DOW	9100	60	D3
CLANFIELD ST	CO	ACT		182	F9
CLANFIELD ST	CO	SAU		182	B9
CLANTON CIR	SFS	SFS		82	D3
CLANTON ST	CO	SGAB	8300	37	F4
CLARA ST	BG	BELL	5600	59	E1
CLARA ST	BG	BELL	6400	60	A1
CLARA ST	CDY	BELL	4100	59	C1
CLARA ST	LA	LA12	500	44	E2
CLARADAY ST	GLDR	GLDR	600	89	C2
CLARAY DR	LA	LA77		22	E6
CLARAY DR	LA	LA77		32	E1
CLARE ST	WHI	WHI	10800	55	C3
CLARELLEN ST	TOR	TOR	2700	73	B3
CLAREMONT AV	LA	LA27	2300	35	B3
CLAREMONT AV	LB	LB03	300	76	C6
CLAREMONT AV	LB	LB03	300	80	C1
CLAREMONT BLVD	CLA	CLA	100	91	C3
CLAREMONT DR	SCLR	SAU		124	D4
CLAREMONT PL	LB	LB03	1	80	B1
CLAREMONT PL	POM	POM	1700	91	A6
CLAREMONT PL	POM	POM	500	95	A1
CLAREMONT ST E	PAS	PAS	100	27	B2
CLAREMONT ST W	PAS	PAS	100	26	F2
CLARMNT CTR CIR	CLA	CLA		91	A6
CLAREMNT CTR DR	CLA	CLA	400	91	B6
CLAREMNT HTS DR	CLA	CLA		91	C1
CLAREMORE AV	LB	LB08	3000	81	A6
CLARENCE ST N	LA	LA33	100	44	F3
CLARENCE ST S	LA	LA23	600	44	F3
CLARENCE ST S	LA	LA33	100	44	F3
CLARENDON AV	HPK	HPK	2000	52	F4
CLARENDON AV	HPK	HPK	2700	53	A4
CLARENDON ST	CO	LA22	5800	54	A2
CLARENDON ST	LA	WOH	20600	13	D1
CLARENDON ST	LA	WOH	23300	100	F1
CLARESSA AV	NWK	NWK	14300	82	D2
CLARETON DR	AGH	AGO		100A	A4
CLARETTA AV	CER	ART	19700	81	B2
CLARETTA AV	HG	LKD	20700	81	B4
CLARETTA AV	LKD	LKD	21000	81	B3
CLARETTA AV	NWK	NWK	15500	82	B3
CLARETTA ST	LA	PAC	12500	3	B6
CLARETTA ST	LA	PAC	14100	8	E3
CLARETTA ST	LA	SF	12200	3	C6
CLARIDGE DR	LA	BH	1300	33	A4
CLARIDGE PL	WHI	WHI		84	D4
CLARIDGE RD	LA	NOR		7	B2
CLARIDGE ST	ARC	ARC	1700	28	D2
CLARIN ST	LA	WOH	20900	13	D3
CLARINDA AV	PR	PR	7800	60	E2
CLARINDA DR	LA	TAR	4300	21	A3
CLARINGTON AV	LA	CUL	3800	42	B5
CLARINGTON AV	LA	LA34	3400	42	B5
CLARINGTON DR	LA	CAN		5	E2
CLARION DR E	CAR	CAR	100	69	B4
CLARION DR W	CAR	CAR	100	69	A4
CLARION DR W	CO	TOR	900	68	F4
CLARION PL	CLA	CLA	500	91	C2
CLARION ST	CAR	CAR	1600	69	D4
CLARISSA AV	AVA	AVA		77	B5
CLARISSA AV	LA	LA27	4600	34	F2
CLARISSA AV	LA	LA27	4300	35	A2
CLARK AL	PAS	PAS		27	C3
CLARK AV	BLF	BLF	13400	66	B5
CLARK AV	BUR	BUR	900	24	C1
CLARK AV	CLA	CLA	500	91	C5
CLARK AV	CO	LPUE	14300	48	C6
CLARK AV	DOW	DOW	12300	60	B6
CLARK AV	DOW	DOW	12800	66	B5
CLARK AV	ELM	ELM	3600	38	E6
CLARK AV	LA	VEN	2300	49	C4
CLARK AV	LB	LB08	3000	71	B6
CLARK AV	LB	LB15	1400	76	B3
CLARK AV	LKD	LKD	6000	66	B5
CLARK AV	LKD	LKD	4900	71	B6
CLARK AV	POM	POM	100	95	A2
CLARK AV	SFS	SFS	12200	61	B4
CLARK CT	SCLR	SAU		124	D4
CLARK CT	LAN	LAN		159	G6
CLARK CT	PALM	PALM		184	B5
CLARK DR N	BH	BH	100	42	D1
CLARK DR N	LA	LA48	100	33	D6
CLARK DR S	BH	BH	100	42	D1
CLARK DR S	LA	LA35	1100	42	D2
CLARK DR S	LA	LA48	100	33	D6
CLARK LN	RB	RB	1300	62	D6
CLARK PL	SPAS	SPAS	1800	37	A1
CLARK ST	ARC	ARC	11600	39	A3
CLARK ST	BAP	BAP	14000	39	E4
CLARK ST	LA	ENC	16800	21	E1
CLARK ST	LA	TAR	18100	21	B1
CLARK ST	LA	VAN	14500	22	C1
CLARK ST	LA	WOH	19700	13	E1
CLARK ST	LYN	LYN	5100	65	C1
CLARK ST	SFS	SFS	12000	61	B4
CLARK ST	WHOL	LA69	1100	33	D4
CLARKDALE AV	ART	ART	18300	81	A1
CLARKDALE AV	ART	ART	16600	82	A4
CLARKDALE AV	HG	LKD	21700	81	A5
CLARKDALE AV	LKD	LKD	20300	81	A3
CLARKDALE AV	NWK	NWK	13100	82	A3
CLARKE ST	CO	NEW		126	G4
CLARKE RANCH RD	CO	MAL		105	C4
CLARKGROVE ST	CO	LPUE	15600	85	E1
CLARKMAN ST	SFS	SFS	11200	60	F4
CLARKMAN ST	SFS	SFS	11600	61	A4
CLARKSON AV	BELL	BELL	6200	53	C5
CLARKSON AV	CDY	BELL		53	C6
CLARKSON AV	MAY	MAY	6000	53	C5
CLARKSON RD	LA	LA64	11300	41	E6
CLARKSON RD	LA	LA64	10500	42	A5
CLARKVIEW DR	DUA	DUA	300	86	B4
CLARMEYA LN	CO	PAS	2900	20	F6
CLARMON PL	CUL	CUL	10700	50	C3
CLARO DR	WAL	WAL		93	C6
CLARO WY	PALM	LAN		171	C4
CLARY AV	SGAB	SGAB	100	37	E3
CLAUDE ST	CAR	CAR	700	64	C4
CLAUDE ST	COM	COM	100	64	F4
CLAUDETTE ST	CO	CYN		124	G8
CLAUDIA AV	RM	RM	4100	38	B5
CLAUDINA AV	LA	LA16	1900	43	B4
CLAUSEN RD	CO	MAL		112	E1
CLAVEL CT	LA	WOH	5000	13	B2
CLAWSON PL	LA	NHO		23	A5
CLAY CT	ALH	ALH	900	37	D4
CLAY CT	CO	LPUE		97	B5
CLAYBECK AV	LA	BUR	7500	17	A2
CLAYBECK AV	LA	SV	8900	9	E6
CLAYBECK AV	LA	SV	7800	17	A2
CLAYCLIFFE CT	CO	LPUE		85	D5
CLAYCREST DR	SCLR	CYN	18900	124	J7
CLAYCROFT TR	CO	TOP		109	B2
CLAYGATE CT	LA	LA77		32	B1
CLAY HILL AV	CO	LPUE	1500	98	A3
CLAYHORN DR	DBAR	POM		97A	A1
CLAYMONT DR	LA	LA49	700	32	A6
CLAYMORE ST	PR	PR	9100	60	E1
CLAYMORE ST	SFS	SFS	11500	60	F3
CLAYMORE ST	SFS	SFS	11500	61	A3
CLAYPOLE DR	CO	PALM		183	E4
CLAYTON AV	LA	LA27	3700	35	A3
CLAYTON CT	CO	LAV		95A	F5
CLAYTON CT	CO	VAL		124	F2
CLAYVALE ST	CO	ACT	5000	182	F6
CLAYVALE ST	CO	SAU		182	F6
CLAYWOOD AV	LA	SF	13900	2	F1
CLAYWOOD DR	DBAR	POM		94	B6
CLAYWOOD DR	DBAR	POM		97A	B1
CLEAR CT	DBAR	WAL		97	B5
CLEAR TR	CO	TOP	1700	109	D1
CLEARBANK LN	SCLR	NEW		127	B6
CLEARBROOK DR	PAR	PAR	15900	65	F4
CLEARBROOK LN	CER	ART		82	C4
CLEARBROOK PL	LA	NOR		7	B1
CLEARBROOK ST	LA	NOR		7	B1
CLEAR CREEK DR	LAN	LAN		160	E6
CLEAR CREEK LN	DBAR	POM		97A	A4
CLEAR CK CYN DR	DBAR	POM		97A	A2
CLEARCREST DR	BAP	BAP	13600	39	D3
CLEARDALE ST	SCLR	NEW	27600	127	D3
CLEAR FALLS AV	LAV	LAV		95A	D5
CLEARFIELD AV	LA	VAN	7700	15	E2
CLEARFORD CT	WLVL	THO		102	B4
CLEARGLEN AV	CO	WHI	11700	84	C5
CLEARGROVE DR	DOW	DOW	7200	60	B1
CLEARHAVEN DR	AZU	AZU	100	86	D4
CLEARLAKE DR	CO	CYN	27400	125	E9
CLEARLAWN ST	CO	LAN		174	H5
CLEARMONT CT	CO	VAL		124	F2
CLEAR OAK DR	LA	ENC	16100	22	A3
CLEARPOOL PL	LA	HAC	23400	68	E6
CLEARPOOL PL	LA	HAC	23500	73	E1
CLEAR RIVER LN	CO	LPUE		98	A4
CLEARSITE ST	TOR	TOR	5200	67	E5
CLEAR SPRING CT	DBAR	WAL		97	C3
CLEARSPRING DR	LAM	LAM	15900	83	C1
CLEARSPRINGS AV	PALM	PALM		172	J5
CLEAR VALLEY DR	LA	ENC	4100	22	A3
CLEAR VALLEY PL	LA	ENC	16100	22	A4
CLEAR VALLEY RD	HH	CAL	5700	100	D1
CLEAR VIEW DR	LA	BH	1500	32	F3
CLEAR VW CST DR	DBAR	POM		93	F6
CLEAR VISTA DR	RHE	PVP		72	D6
CLEARWATER AV	PALM	PALM		171	H6
CLEARWATER CT	WAL	WAL		93	D4
CLEARWATER DR	LAM	LAM		83	D1
CLEARWATER ST	LA	LA39	2700	35	C3
CLEARWOOD AV	LAM	LAM	12900	61	E6
CLEARWOOD AV	LAM	LAM	12900	82	E1
CLEARWOOD CT	LA	LA77		22	D6
CLEARWOOD CT	PALM	PALM		183	H2
CLEARY CT	CLA	CLA		96	B6
CLEARY DR	BAP	BAP	15000	39	F5
CLEAT RD	CO	SAU		181	C9
CLEE CT	AGH	AGO		102	F3
CLEGHORN DR	DBAR	POM		97A	A2
CLELA AV	CO	LA22	300	45	F6
CLELA AV	CO	LA22	1000	53	E1
CLELAND AV	LA	LA42	4900	36	A2
CLELAND AV	LA	LA65	4400	36	A2
CLELAND PL	LA	LA65	800	36	A1
CLEMATIS CT	LA	LA77		22	E6
CLEMATIS ST	LKD	LKD	6900	71	E3
CLEMENS AV	LA	CAN	8000	5	F1
CLEMENS CT	CO	VAL		126	G3
CLEMENT DR	GLEN	GL02	500	25	B2
CLEMENT ST	LA	LA33	1000	45	A2
CLEMENT ST	LA	VEN	2300	49	C4
CLEMENTE AV	AVA	AVA	300	77	B5
CLEMENTINA DR	CO	LPUE	2200	85	F3
CLEMINSON ST	ELM	ELM	3500	38	D6
CLEMMER DR	COM	COM	700	65	A4
CLEMONS DR	LA	ENC	17100	21	E5
CLEMSON AV	CLA	CLA	1700	90	F2
CLEMSON ST	LA	LA16	5500	42	E6
CLEO ST	BAP	BAP	12900	39	C5
CLEOMOORE AV	LA	CAN	6500	5	E5
CLEON AV	LA	NHO	5600	16	E5
CLEON AV	LA	NHO	4800	23	E2
CLEON AV	LA	SV	7200	16	E3
CLERENDON RD	LA	VN23		22	E5
CLERMONT ST	LA	LA65	4400	36	A3
CLETA ST	DOW	DOW	7800	60	A4
CLEVELAND AV E	MTB	MTB	200	54	E2
CLEVELAND AV W	MTB	MTB	100	54	C1
CLEVELAND PL	POM	POM	1600	94	D1
CLEVELAND RD	GLEN	GL02	1500	18	B6
CLEVELAND RD	GLEN	GL02	900	25	A2
CLEVELAND ST	LA	LA12	700	44	D1
CLEVELAND ST	POM	POM	1100	94	D1
CLEVIS RD	RPV	PVP	29000	78	C1
CLIFF DR	LA	LA65	1200	35	F3
CLIFF DR	LAM	LAM		83	C1
CLIFF DR	PAS	PAS	300	28	A2
CLIFFBRANCH DR	DBAR	POM		97	D4
CLIFFEDGE DR	CO	SAU		157A	E4
CLIFFHILL DR	MPK	MPK	1800	46	B4
CLIFFORD ST	LA	LA26	2100	35	C4
CLIFFSIDE DR	CO	MAL	28800	110	B6
CLIFFSIDE DR	SAD	SAD		89	E4
CLIFFSIDE LN	CO	LPUE		48	B5
CLIFFSIDE LN	DBAR	POM		97	C5
CLIFFSITE DR	RPV	PVP	3600	78	B3
CLIFFTOP WY	CO	MAL	18300	115	E4
CLIFFVIEW ST	DUA	DUA	800	29	C6
CLIFFWOOD AV N	LA	LA49	100	41	A1
CLIFFWOOD AV S	LA	LA49	100	41	A2
CLIFTON AL	PAS	PAS	1400	27	D3
CLIFTON PL	GLEN	GL08	3600	18	F3
CLIFTON ST	LA	LA31	400	36	B5
CLIFTON WY	BH	BH	8400	42	C1
CLIMBER DR	DBAR	WAL		97	C3
CLINE RD	CO	CAL		108	A5
CLINT PL	RPV	PVP	5800	72	D4
CLINTON PL	BH	BH	600	33	C2
CLINTON ST	ELM	ELM		47	F3
CLINTON ST	LA	LA04	4000	34	E5
CLINTON ST	LA	LA04	3800	35	A5
CLINTON ST	LA	LA26	1700	35	C6
CLINTON ST	LA	LA36	7600	33	F5
CLINTON ST	LA	LA36	6800	34	A5
CLINTON ST	LA	LA48	7900	33	E5
CLINTON ST	PAS	PAS	100	26	F2
CLINTON ST	WHOL	LA48	8300	33	E5
CLINTWOOD AV	CO	LPUE	900	48	D4
CLINTWOOD AV	LPUE	LPUE	300	48	D4
CLIOTA ST	CO	WHI	10300	55	D1
CLIPPER RD	RPV	PVP	1	77	D2
CLIPSTONE ST	LA	WOH	24300	5	D6
CLIVE AV	CO	WHI	7700	55	C6
CLIVEDEN AV	CAR	CAR	19000	69	E1
CLIVEDEN AV N	COM	COM	600	64	D2
CLIVEDEN AV S	COM	COM	400	64	D3
CLOCK ST	LA	LA21	1300	44	D5
CLOGSTON DR	CO	LPUE	100	48	A3
CLOISTER DR	LHH	LAH	1400	84	D2
CLONLEE AV	LA	SF	11600	1	F5
CLORA PL	ELM	ELM	12000	47	F1
CLORA PL	IND	ELM	12300	48	A2
CLORINDA DR	DBAR	WAL	1000	97	C3
CLOSE ST	CO	WHI	12900	61	C2
CLOUD AV	CO	GL14	4600	11	D6
CLOUD AV	CO	GL14	4200	18	D2
CLOUD AV	GLEN	GL14	3700	18	D2
CLOUD LN	LA	LA49	12500	32	A5
CLOUDCREST RD	CO	GL14	2900	11	D4
CLOUDCROFT DR	CO	MAL	3400	115	F3
CLOUDSDALE AV	GLEN	GL14	4700	11	C5
CLOUDS REST DR	DBAR	POM		94	A4
CLOUDY CT	CO	LPUE		97	A5
CLOVER AV	LA	LA34	11000	41	F6
CLOVER AV	LA	LA66	11300	41	E6
CLOVER DR	LA	CAN		4	B6
CLOVER DR	LA	CAN		5	E1
CLOVER RD	LA	PAC		3	C6
CLOVER ST	LA	LA31	600	44	F1
CLOVER ST	LAV	LAV		90	C2
CLOVER ST	MPK	MPK	2000	46	C4
CLOVER ST	SM	SM		49	D1
CLOVER TR	CO	CAL		100	E6
CLOVERBROOK ST	CAR	CAR	400	69	B4
CLOVERCLIFF DR	RPV	PVP	6700	72	C5
CLOVERDALE AV	LA	LA08	3800	50	F1
CLOVERDALE AV	LA	LA16	2100	42	F5
CLOVERDALE AV	LA	LA19	1000	43	A3
CLOVERDALE AV	LA	LA36	300	43	A2
CLOVERDALE CT	SCLR	NEW		127	B6
CLOVERDALE DR	POM	POM	1800	90	F6
CLOVERDALE LN	CER	ART	16100	82	C4
CLOVERDALE LN	WAL	WAL		93	D6
CLOVERFIELD BL	SM	SM	1400	49	C1
CLOVERGLEN AV	CO	LPUE		92	B4
CLOVER HGTS AV	CO	MAL	5800	112	A6
CLOVERHILL RD	CO	ALT	1100	19	E2
CLOVERLAND DR	CO	COV	21000	89	C5
CLOVERLAWN DR	PAR	SOG	7100	65	D1
CLOVERLAWN DR	SOG	SOG	7300	65	E1
CLOVERLEAF DR	BAP	BAP		48	A2
CLOVERLEAF DR	MON	MON	400	29	A2
CLOVERLEAF PL	CO	CAST		123	C1

INDEX

STREET	CITY	P.O. ZONE	BLOCK	PAGE	GRID
CLOVERLEAF WY	MON	MON	400	29	A2
CLOVERLY AV	TEC	TEC	4500	38	B4
CLOVERLY AV	TEC	TEC	4800	38	B3
CLOVERMEAD ST	CO	COV	16100	88	D4
CLOVERSIDE ST	BAP	BAP	14200	39	E6
CLOVERTON ST	CO	SAD	21300	89	D3
CLOVER VIEW DR	GLDR	GLDR	7600	87	A4
CLOVERWOOD CT	PALM	PALM		184	A1
CLOVERWOOD ST	BLF	BLF	9500	66	B2
CLOVE TREE PL	RPV	PVP		77	E2
CLOVIS AV	CO	LA59	12300	58	C6
CLOVIS AV	CO	LA59	12800	64	C1
CLOVIS AV	LA	LA02	9200	58	C4
CLOVIS AV	LA	LA59	10700	58	C4
CLOVIS CT	POM	POM	1300	94	D4
CLOVIS WY	LA	LA59	11600	58	C5
CLOY AV	LA	VEN	2300	49	C4
CLOYDEN RD	PVE	PVP	500	72	A4
CLOYDEN SQ	PVE	PVP	700	72	A4
CLUB DR	LA	LA64	2700	42	B5
CLUB DR	PAS	PAS	100	26	D4
CLUB DR	POM	POM		94	B1
CLUB PL	LA	LA64	10200	42	B4
CLUB RD	PAS	PAS	100	26	D4
CLUBHOUSE AV	LA	VEN	4	49	B4
CLUBHOUSE CT	LA	VEN	15	49	B4
CLUBHOUSE DR	LKD	LKD	4100	70	F4
CLUBHOUSE DR	PAS	PAS	1200	26	D6
CLUBHOUSE DR	WCOV	WCOV		97	A2
CLUBRIDGE RD	PAS	PAS	400	26	D3
CLUB TERRACE DR	POM	POM		90	B6
CLUB VIEW DR	LA	LA24	500	32	F6
CLUB VIEW DR	LA	LA24	1200	42	A1
CLUB VIEW LN	RHE	PVP		73	C4
CLUB VISTA DR	GLDR	GLDR	2300	87	E5
CLUFF ST	CAR	CAR		69	C5
CLUNE AV	LA	VEN	2800	49	C5
CLUNY AV	PALM	PALM	37600	183	G1
CLUSTER LN	RB	RB	500	67	E1
CLUSTERBERRY CT	LA	LA77		22	E6
CLYBOURN AV	BUR	BUR	1400	16	F6
CLYBOURN AV	BUR	BUR	100	24	A2
CLYBOURN AV	LA	NHO	5600	16	F6
CLYBOURN AV	LA	NHO	5200	23	F2
CLYBOURN AV	LA	NHO	4200	24	A2
CLYBOURN AV	LA	SF	11300	9	E1
CLYBOURN AV	LA	SUN	9800	9	E3
CLYBOURN AV	LA	SV		9	E4
CLYBOURN AV	LA	SV	7200	16	F2
CLYDE AV	LA	LA16	2000	42	E5
CLYDE AV	LA	LA19	1800	42	E5
CLYDE BANK AV	CO	AZU	5100	88	C2
CLYDE BANK AV	CO	COV	4800	88	B3
CLYDE PARK AV	CER	ART	18300	81	D1
CLYDE PARK AV	HAW	HAW	13000	62	E1
CLYDESDALE CIR	WAL	WAL		93	D5
CLYDESDALE DR	CO	PALM		157	G8
CLYDE WALKER WY	HAW	HAW		56	F5
CLYDEWOOD AV	BAP	BAP	14800	39	F6
CLYDEWOOD AV	WCOV	WCOV	2200	39	F6
CLYDEWOOD ST	BAP	BAP	14700	39	E5
CLYMAR AV	CO	COM	14300	64	C2
CLYMER ST	LA	NOR	18600	7	B2
CLYMER ST	LA	SF	16600	7	F2
CLYMER ST	LA	SF	14500	8	D2
COACH PL	CO	LP45		98	A3
COACH RD	RPV	PVP	1	73	C6
COACHELLA AV	LB	LB05	6700	65	C5
COACHMAN AV	CO	WHI	9200	61	E3
COACHMAN AV	WHI	WHI	8800	61	E2
COACHWOOD AV	LAM	LAM	12600	84	D6
COACHWOOD CT	CO	LPUE		98	A3
COAL CANYON RD	CO	MAL		114	D3
COALINGA CT	CLA	CLA	3100	91	B1
COALINGA CT	CLA	CLA		96	B6
COAST DR	CO	WHI		47	D5
COASTLINE DR	CO	MAL	18000	115	E4
COAST SITE DR	RPV	PVP	32600	77	D3
COAST VIEW DR	CO	MAL	3400	113	F4
COATES AV	CO	LA63	1200	45	D3
COBAL MTY	CO	CLA		96	C3
COBALT ST	LA	SF	14600	2	B3
COBAN RD	LHH	LAH	1500	98A	B2
COBB CT	CO	LPUE		48	C3
COBB ST	CMRC	LA40	2400	53	D2
COBBLE CT	PALM	PALM		171	E4
COBBLEFIELD WY	GLDR	GLDR		89	E1
COBBLE STONE CT	CER	ART	16600	82	C4
COBBLESTONE DR	AGH	AGO		102	F2
COBBLESTONE LN	LCF	LCF	4300	19	B4
COBBLESTONE RD	LAM	LAM	15800	84	C6
COBERTA AV S	CO	LPUE	300	48	B4
COBHAM CT	LA	LA77		32	B1
COBLE AV	CO	LPUE	1300	85	C1
COBOS ST	NWK	NWK		82	B4
COBRE WY E	LB	LB02	100	75	C5

STREET	CITY	P.O. ZONE	BLOCK	PAGE	GRID
COBRE WY W	LB	LB02	100	75	C5
COBURN AV	SMAD	SMAD	1	28	D2
COCHIN AV	CO	ARC	5300	38	F3
COCHISE CIR	WAL	WAL		93	C3
COCHRAN AV	LA	LA08	3800	50	F1
COCHRAN AV	LA	LA16	2100	42	F5
COCHRAN AV	LA	LA19	1000	43	A3
COCHRAN AV	LA	LA36	300	43	A2
COCHRAN PL	LA	LA19	1600	42	F4
COCINA LN	PALM	LAN		171	D4
COCKERHAM DR	LA	LA24	4500	34	F1
COCKLEBUR LN	SCLR	CYN		124	E8
COCKLEBUR PL	CO	LPUE		98	C5
COCKNEY ST	PALM	PALM		171	H9
COCO AV	LA	LA08	3800	51	A1
COCO PL	LA	PP		40	C2
COCOA ST E	COM	COM	100	64	F3
COCOA ST E	COM	COM	200	65	A3
COCOA ST W	COM	COM	100	64	F3
COCONINO PL	CO	PALM		157	F9
COCOPAN DR	CO	ALT	500	20	B3
COCOS DR	LA	LA68	6000	34	D2
CODE LN	CO	TOP	800	109	B3
CODY DR	CO	LA22	5000	53	E1
CODY RD	LA	VAN	3400	22	C4
CODY RD	SAD	SAD		89	F2
COE ST	CLA	CLA	100	91	B5
COEUR DALENE	LA	VEN	600	49	D4
COFFIELD AV	ELM	ELM	11300	38	E6
COFFMAN DR	MTB	MTB	800	46	C5
COFFMAN PICO RD	PR	PR	5700	54	E4
COGBURN LN	DBAR	POM		97A	A2
COG HILL DR	CO	WHI		55	E2
COGSWELL RD	ELM	ELM	4000	39	A5
COGSWELL RD	ELM	ELM	2100	47	E2
COGSWELL RD	SELM	ELM	1100	47	D3
COHASSET ST	BUR	BUR	2700	17	A3
COHASSET ST	LA	CAN	23100	5	F3
COHASSET ST	LA	CAN	20600	12	A3
COHASSET ST	LA	NHO	11400	16	B3
COHASSET ST	LA	RES	17700	14	A3
COHASSET ST	LA	SV	10600	16	F3
COHASSET ST	LA	SV	10500	17	A3
COHASSET ST	LA	VAN	16600	14	D3
COHASSET ST	LA	VAN	13700	15	D3
COIL AV	LA	WIL	1200	74	D3
COINER CT	IND	LPUE		98	E3
COKE AV	BLF	BLF	17400	66	A6
COKE AV	LB	LB05	5900	66	A6
COKE AV	LKD	LKD	4700	71	A2
COKE AV	PAR	PAR	14300	66	A2
COLBATH AV	LA	VAN	8500	8	E6
COLBATH AV	LA	VAN	5600	15	E5
COLBATH AV	LA	VAN	4100	22	E4
COLBECK AV	CAR	CAR	19000	69	D1
COLBERT AV	LA	LA66	3300	49	F1
COLBY AV	LA	LA25	1400	41	D4
COLBY AV	LA	LA64	2200	41	F6
COLBY AV	LA	LA66	3100	41	F6
COLBY DR	GLEN	GL05	1400	25	D6
COLBY MTY	GLDR	GLDR		87	C3
COLBY CIR DR	CLA	CLA	600	91	B3
COLCHA WY	PALM	LAN		171	D4
COLCHESTER CT	PALM	PALM		171	H6
COLCHESTER WY	CO	LPUE		98	A5
COLCHESTER WY	LA	NOR		1	C6
COLCORD AV	CO	PALM	36400	184	G3
COLDBROOK AV	BLF	BLF	13200	66	C2
COLDBROOK AV	DOW	DOW	11600	60	C5
COLDBROOK AV	DOW	DOW	12700	66	C1
COLDBROOK AV	LKD	LKD	5900	66	C6
COLDBROOK AV	LKD	LKD	4500	71	C3
COLD CANYON RD	CO	CAL	1600	108	B4
COLD CK FIRE RD	CO	CAL		108	D4
COLDEN AV E	LA	LA02	600	58	B3
COLDEN AV E	LA	LA03	100	58	B3
COLDEN AV W	LA	LA03	100	58	B3
COLDEN AV W	LA	LA44	600	57	F3
COLDEN AV W	LA	LA44	500	58	A3
COLD PLAINS DR	CO	LPUE		85	D5
COLD SPRING LN	DBAR	POM	21200	97	D5
COLD SPRINGS ST	CO	CAL		100A	E5
COLDSTREAM CT	DBAR	POM		97A	B2
COLDSTREAM TER	LA	TAR	4100	13	F4
COLDWATR CYN AV	LA	NHO	6400	16	A2
COLDWATR CYN AV	LA	NHO	3200	23	A5
COLDWATR CYN AV	LA	VAN	4800	23	A5
COLDWATR CYN DR	BH	BH	1100	33	B2
COLDWATR CYN DR	LA	BH	2500	23	C6
COLDWATR CYN DR	LA	VAN	5400	16	A5
COLDWATR CYN LN	LA	NHO	3100	23	B5
CLDWTR CY B PTH	BH	BH		33	B4
COLE AV	CO	PAS	3700	28	B4
COLE AV	LA	LA28	1300	34	C5
COLE AV	LA	LA38	700	34	C5
COLE PL	BH	BH	600	33	C2

STREET	CITY	P.O. ZONE	BLOCK	PAGE	GRID
COLE PL	CO	HPK	2400	58	F1
COLE PL	LA	LA28	1300	34	C4
COLE PL	LA	LA38	1200	34	C4
COLE RD	CO	WHI	10400	84	B4
COLE RD	WHI	WHI	9800	84	B4
COLE ST	DOW	DOW	7100	59	F3
COLE ST	DOW	DOW	7800	60	A4
COLEBROOK PL	CO	VAL		124	B7
COLEBROOK ST	LA	SUN	10500	9	F3
COLECREST DR	LA	LA69	8400	33	D3
COLEFORD AV	CO	LPUE	1400	47	F5
COLEGIO DR	CO	LPUE	16300	85	F3
COLEGIO DR	LA	LA45	8100	56	A1
COLEGROVE AV	MTB	MTB	1100	54	C2
COLEMAN AV	LA	LA42	500	36	D3
COLERIDGE DR	CO	PAS	2900	27	E5
COLERIDGE PL	CO	NEW		126	G3
COLFAIR ST	PR	PR	9300	47	B6
COLFAIR ST	PR	PR	9300	55	B1
COLFAX AV	LA	NHO	5600	16	D6
COLFAX AV	LA	NHO	4000	23	D4
COLFAX CT	POM	POM	1200	94	D4
COLGATE AV	LA	LA36	6200	33	D6
COLGATE AV	LA	LA48	6300	33	E6
COLGATE PL	CLA	CLA	500	91	B5
COLGIN CT	BUR	BUR	400	17	E6
COLIMA RD	CO	LPUE	15300	85	F4
COLIMA RD	CO	LPUE	19200	97	B4
COLIMA RD	CO	LPUE	16400	98	A3
COLIMA RD	CO	WAL	19300	97	B4
COLIMA RD	CO	WHI	10900	61	F5
COLIMA RD	CO	WHI	10200	84	A4
COLIMA RD	IND	LPUE	17200	98	C3
COLIMA RD	LAM	LAM	12700	61	F6
COLIMA RD	WHI	WHI	8000	84	B2
COLINA AL	LA	LA65		36	A3
COLINA CT	PALM	LAN		171	D4
COLINA DR	CO	TOP	20800	109	D4
COLINA DR	GLEN	GL08	1400	25	E1
COLINA DR	WAL	WAL		93	A5
COLINA TER	MPK	MPK	500	45	F2
COLINA WY	LA	LA77		22	E6
COLINA VISTA ST	AGH	AGO		100A	A2
COLINTON DR	CO	LPUE	2600	98	E5
COLISEUM DR N	LA	LA37	900	51	F1
COLISEUM DR N	LA	LA37	500	52	A1
COLISEUM DR S	LA	LA37	500	52	A1
COLISEUM PL	LA	LA08	3600	51	B1
COLISEUM ST	LA	LA16	5100	50	E1
COLISEUM ST	LA	LA16	3700	51	A1
COLISEUM ST	LA	LA18	2700	51	B1
COLLAMER DR	CAR	CAR	300	64	B5
COLLEGE AV	AZU	AZU	18500	86	E6
COLLEEN DR	LAN	LAN		160	E3
COLLEGE AV	CUL	CUL	3800	50	B1
COLLEGE AV	DOW	DOW	10800	60	B3
COLLEGE AV	POM	POM	1200	91	B6
COLLEGE AV	WHI	WHI	7300	55	F6
COLLEGE AV	WHI	WHI	8200	61	F1
COLLEGE AV N	CLA	CLA	100	91	B4
COLLEGE AV S	CLA	CLA	100	91	B5
COLLEGE CIR	LB	LB15	1800	76	D3
COLLEGE DR	GLEN	GL06		25	E2
COLLEGE DR	NWK	NWK	11400	66	F4
COLLEGE LN	LAV	LAV		90	D3
COLLEGE PL	CER	NWK	10800	66	E4
COLLEGE PL	LB	LB15	1800	76	D3
COLLEGE ST E	COV	COV	100	88	E5
COLLEGE ST E	LA	LA12	100	44	D1
COLLEGE ST W	COV	COV	100	88	E5
COLLEGE ST W	LA	LA12	100	44	D1
COLLEGE WY	CLA	CLA		90	F1
COLLEGE WY	CLA	CLA	400	91	C4
COLLEGE WY	COV	COV	100	88	F5
COLLEGE CRST DR	LA	LA65	3600	35	F1
COLLEGE CRST WK	LA	LA65		35	F1
COLLEGE PARK DR	LAN	LAN		159	G7
COLLEGE PARK DR	LB	LB15	6700	76	E5
COLLEGE SQ DR	LA	LA32		36	E6
COLLEGE VIEW AV	LA	LA41	4400	25	F4
COLLEGE VIEW DR	MPK	MPK	1400	45	F4
COLLEGE VIEW DR	MPK	MPK	1000	46	A4
COLLEGE VIEW LN	MPK	MPK	900	46	A4
COLLEGE VIEW PL	LA	LA41	1700	25	F6
COLLEGE VSTA AV	WAL	WAL	1800	93	B3
COLLEGEWOOD DR	WAL	WAL	20200	93	B4
COLLEGIAN AV	MPK	MPK		46	A4
COLLETT AV	LA	ENC	4500	22	A3
COLLETT AV	LA	SF	11400	2	A6
COLLETT AV	LA	SF	8500	8	A6
COLLETT AV	LA	VAN	7400	15	A3
COLLIER PL	LA	WOH	5200	13	F2
COLLIER ST	LA	TAR	19300	21	A1
COLLIER ST	LA	WOH	19700	13	F2
COLLINA STRADA	LA	LA77		32	B1
COLLINGSWOOD DR	POM	POM	800	91	A5

STREET	CITY	P.O. ZONE	BLOCK	PAGE	GRID
COLLINGWOOD CIR	CO	CAL		100	B2
COLLINGWOOD DR	LA	LA69	8800	33	D3
COLLINGWOOD PL	LA	LA69	1300	33	D3
COLLINS LN	CO	MONT	2300	18	F2
COLLINS PL	LA	WOH	5600	13	D1
COLLINS RD	SCLR	CYN		124	G9
COLLINS ST	LA	ENC	17100	14	D6
COLLINS ST	LA	ENC	17100	21	D1
COLLINS ST	LA	NHO	10500	16	E6
COLLINS ST	LA	TAR	18300	14	B6
COLLINS ST	LA	VAN	13400	15	D6
COLLINS ST	LA	VAN	13400	22	E1
COLLINS ST	LA	WOH	23200	5	F6
COLLINS ST	LA	WOH	20700	12	A6
COLLINS ST	LA	WOH	20700	13	A1
COLLINS ST	LA	WOH	23000	100	F1
COLLINS WY	LB	LB02		75	C6
COLLIS AV	LA	LA32	3500	36	D4
COLLIS AV	SPAS	SPAS	4930	36	D3
COLLWOOD AV	CO	LPUE	100	48	B3
COLMAN ST	CO	ALT	400	20	B5
COLMAR AV	BG	BELL	6200	53	F6
COLMAR ST	POM	POM	900	95	B1
COLMENA ST	CO	GL14	2200	11	F6
COLMERE AV	PR	PR	8700	55	A1
COLODNY DR	AGH	AGO		100A	C3
COLOGNE ST	LA	LA16	5600	42	E4
COLOMA AV	LA	WOH	4200	13	A3
COLON ST	LA	WIL	900	74	D3
COLONADE THE	LB	LB03		80	C1
COL D LS MAGNLS	CO	LA22		45	F4
COL D LS PALMAS	CO	LA22		45	F4
COL D LS ROSAS	CO	LA22		45	E4
COL D LS CEDROS	CO	LA22		45	F4
COL D LS PINOS	CO	LA22		45	E4
COLONIAL AV	CUL	LA66	4000	49	E2
COLONIAL AV	LA	LA66	3200	49	E2
COLONIAL DR	PALM	PALM		183	D2
COLONY CIR	LA	LA27	3200	35	B2
COLONY CT	CO	AGO		100A	D6
COLONY CT	PALM	PALM		183	C5
COLONY DR	LAN	LAN		159	E6
COLONY DR	POM	POM	1100	94	D4
COLONY DR	SMAD	SMAD	100	28	D2
COLONY VIEW CIR	CO	MAL	3200	114	A4
COLORADO AV	PAR	PAR	14100	65	F2
COLORADO AV	SM	SM	800	41	B6
COLORADO AV	SM	SM	100	49	B6
COLORADO AV	SM	SM	100	49	A1
COLORADO AV E	GLDR	GLDR	100	87	A6
COLORADO AV W	GLDR	GLDR	100	87	A6
COLORADO BLVD	ARC	ARC	300	28	B4
COLORADO BLVD	CO	PAS	3300	28	B4
COLORADO BLVD	LA	LA39	4500	25	B4
COLORADO BLVD	LA	LA41	2400	25	F4
COLORADO BLVD	LA	LA41	700	26	A5
COLORADO BLVD E	ARC	ARC	1	28	D4
COLORADO BLVD E	MON	MON	100	29	A4
COLORADO BLVD E	PAS	PAS	100	27	B4
COLORADO BLVD W	ARC	ARC	1	28	D4
COLORADO BLVD W	MON	MON	100	29	A4
COLORADO BLVD W	PAS	PAS	100	26	D4
COLORADO CT	LB	LB14		75	F5
COLORADO PL	ARC	ARC	200	28	D4
COLORADO PL	LB	LB14	300	75	F5
COLORADO PL	SM	SM	3100	41	C5
COLORADO ST	CLA	CLA	600	91	C3
COLORADO ST	LB	LB03		76	E5
COLORADO ST	LB	LB14	2800	75	F5
COLORADO ST	LB	LB14	3100	76	A5
COLORADO ST	WCOV	WCOV		92	D4
COLORADO ST E	GLEN	GL05	100	25	C4
COLORADO ST W	GLEN	GL04	100	25	C4
COLORETTI CT	SCLR	VAL		127	A8
COLSTON AV	CO	LPUE	200	98	E1
COLT	LA	SF42		2	C1
COLT RD	CO	CAST		123	A2
COLT RD	RPV	SP	2200	78	C1
COLT ST	LA	SF	17000	7	E1
COLTMAN AV	CAR	CAR	18000	64	B6
COLTMAN AV	CAR	CAR	18600	69	B1
COLTON ST	LA	LA12	1000	44	C1
COLTON ST	LA	LA26	1200	44	C1
COLTRANE AV	SCLR	NEW		127	C8
COLUMBIA AV	CLA	CLA		91	C3
COLUMBIA AV	LA	LA17	300	44	B3
COLUMBIA AV	LA	LA26	200	44	B3
COLUMBIA AV	PALM	PALM		183	H1
COLUMBIA AV	PR	PR	4100	54	F2
COLUMBIA AV E	POM	POM	100	94	F1
COLUMBIA AV E	POM	POM	700	95	A1
COLUMBIA AV W	POM	POM	300	94	E1
COLUMBIA CIR	PAS	PAS	10600	26	E6
COLUMBIA CT	SCLR	VAL		124	A2
COLUMBIA CT	LAV	LAV		90	E3
COLUMBIA DR	GLEN	GL05	1300	25	D6

STREET	CITY	P.O. ZONE	BLOCK	PAGE	GRID
COLUMBIA LN	SPAS	SPAS	1100	26	F6
COLUMBIA PL	LA	LA26	200	44	C2
COLUMBIA PL	PAS	PAS	1100	26	F6
COLUMBIA PL	TOR	TOR	700	68	D3
COLUMBIA RD	ARC	ARC	200	28	B5
COLUMBIA RD	LAV	LAV		90	E3
COLUMBIA ST	PAS	PAS	100	26	E6
COLUMBIA ST	RM	RM	7400	46	D1
COLUMBIA ST	SH	LB06	600	75	D1
COLUMBIA ST	SPAS	SPAS	500	26	E6
COLUMBIA ST	TOR	TOR	2700	68	B3
COLUMBIA ST E	LB	LB06	300	75	D1
COLUMBIA ST W	LB	LB06	700	75	B1
COLUMBIA ST W	LB	LB10	1700	75	A1
COLUMBIANA DR	SAD	SAD	100	89	D2
COLUMBINE DR	PALM	PALM		183	F3
COLUMBUS AV	LA	SF	8500	8	C4
COLUMBUS AV	LA	SF	8300	15	C1
COLUMBUS AV	LA	VAN	5600	22	C1
COLUMBUS AV	LA	VAN	4600	22	C3
COLUMBUS AV N	GLEN	GL02	1000	25	C2
COLUMBUS AV N	GLEN	GL03	100	25	C2
COLUMBUS AV S	GLEN	GL04	100	25	C4
COLUSA DR	WAL	WAL		92	F5
COLVEN RD	LA	SF	16800	1	F4
COLVER PL	COV	COV	1300	89	B4
COLVILLE PL	LA	ENC	3200	21	F5
COLWELL DR	LA	SV	10000	17	A2
COLWELL PL	SCLR	SAU		124	E9
COLWYN AV	SCLR	NEW	24200	127	C5
COLYEAR SPGS LN	WAL	WAL		92	F5
COLYER AV	LYN	LYN	10600	59	C5
COLYTON ST	LA	LA13	400	44	E4
COMADO CYN RD	AGH	AGO		100A	C4
COMAL CT	LOM	LOM		73	D2
COMANCHE	CO	TOP		13	C5
COMANCHE AV	LA	CAN	8500	6	E6
COMANCHE AV	LA	CAN	6400	12	E1
COMANCHE AV	LA	CHA	9600	6	E3
COMANCHE AV	LA	WOH	5600	12	E1
COMANCHE AV	LA	WOH	5600	13	E1
COMANCHE CIR	WAL	WAL		94	C6
COMANCHE PL	LA	CAN	20100	12	E4
COMANCHE TR	CO	AGO		107	A3
COMANCHE TR	CO	CHA		1A	C6
COMBAT TR	CO	TOP	19700	109	D5
COMBELLACK DR	SH	LB06		75	F2
COMBER AV	LA	ENC	4500	21	D3
COMBER PL	CO	HAC		73	F2
COMBER PL	LA	HAC		74	A2
COMERCIO AV	LA	WOH	5100	13	C2
COMERCIO LN	LA	WOH	5300	13	C2
COMERCIO WY	LA	WOH	5300	13	C2
COMET ST	LA	LA42	6700	36	E1
COMET WY	SCLR	CYN		125	D8
COMETA AV	LA	PAC	11300	3	B6
COMETA AV	LA	PAC	11100	9	C1
COMETA AV	LA	SF	12400	2	F3
COMETA AV	LA	SF	12200	3	B5
COMEY AV	LA	LA34	5900	42	E5
COMIDA WY	CO	TOP	21700	109	C1
COMISO DR	CO	LPUE	16300	85	F3
COMLY ST	CO	LA63	4300	45	E2
COMMERCE AV	LA	TU	9700	10	F3
COMMERCE CIR	BAP	BAP		39	D3
COMMERCE DR	IRW	BAP		39	C3
COMMERCE WY	CER	ART	15900	82	D4
COMMERCE WY	CMRC	LA40	2300	53	F3
COMMERCE WY	WAL	WAL		93	C6
COMMERCE WY	WAL	WAL		97	C1
COMMERCE CTR DR	LAN	LAN		159	J7
COMMERCIAL AV	COV	COV	500	88	F4
COMMERCIAL AV	SGAB	SGAB	800	37	F3
COMMERCIAL PL	SOG	SOG	8100	58	F1
COMMERCIAL ST	GLEN	GL03	500	25	B3
COMMERCIAL ST	LA	LA12	200	44	E3
COMMERCIAL ST	SAD	SAD		89	F3
COMMERCIAL ST E	POM	POM	100	94	E2
COMMERCIAL ST W	POM	POM	100	94	E2
COMMERCL CTR ST	BH	BH	400	33	C6
COMMODORE ST	LA	LA32	2500	36	C6
COMMODORE SLOAT	LA	LA48	6200	42	E2
COMMON AV	LPUE	LPUE	100	48	F6
COMMONWEALTH AV	CUL	CUL	4100	50	B2
COMMONWEALTH AV	LA	LA20		44	A1
COMMONWEALTH AV	LA	VEN	800	49	C2
COMMONWEALTH AV	LCF	LCF	4100	19	C4
COMMONWLTH AV E	ALH	ALH	100	37	C4
COMMONWLTH AV N	LA	LA04	100	35	A5
COMMONWLTH AV N	LA	LA27	1300	35	A3
COMMONWLTH AV N	LA	LA29	1100	35	A3
COMMONWLTH AV S	LA	LA04	100	44	A1
COMMONWLTH AV S	LA	LA05	600	44	A1
COMMONWLTH AV S	LA	LA20	300	44	A1
COMMONWLTH AV W	ALH	ALH	2200	36	F5

233
1990 LOS ANGELES COUNTY STREET INDEX
COMMONWLTH AV W
CORONEL LN
LOS ANGELES CO.

STREET	CITY	P.O. ZONE	BLOCK	PAGE	GRID
COMMONWLTH AV W	ALH	ALH	100	37	C4
COMMNWEALTH CIR	CUL	CUL		50	B2
COMMONWEALTH PL	LA	LA04	200	35	A6
COMMNWLTH CY DR	LA	LA27		34	F1
COMMNWLTH CY RD	LA	LA27		24	F6
COMMUNITY AV	CO	GL14	2400	18	D1
COMMUNITY AV	CO	GL14	2700	18	D1
COMMUNITY AV	GLEN	GL14	3200	11	C6
COMMUNITY CT	LA	SF	16200	15	A1
COMMUNITY ST	LA	CAN	23200	5	F1
COMMUNITY ST	LA	CAN	19700	12	D1
COMMUNITY ST	LA	NOR	17000	14	B1
COMMUNITY ST	LA	SF	15000	15	A1
COMMUNITY ST	LA	SV	12200	16	C1
COMMUNITY ST	LA	VAN	13600	15	C1
COMO DR	POM	POM	400	94	F1
COMO ST	CMRC	LA40	5000	53	E2
COMOLETTE AV	DOW	DOW	8000	59	F6
COMOLETTE AV	DOW	DOW	8000	60	A6
COMOLETTE ST	DOW	DOW	7800	59	F5
COMOLETTE ST	DOW	DOW	8400	60	A6
COMPANARIO DR	CO	LPUE	18000	98	D3
COMPAS ST	DOW	DOW		60	C1
COMPASS CT	LB	LB03		80	F1
COMPASS DR	LA	LA45	5800	50	D6
COMPO REAL DR	CO	LPUE		85	F4
CMPRSR PLT F RD	CO	NOR		1	A2
COMPROMISE LINE	GLDR	GLDR	1500	87	D6
COMPTON AV	CO	COM	12300	58	D6
COMPTON AV	CO	LA01	5800	52	D5
COMPTON AV	CO	LA01	7800	58	D2
COMPTON AV	CO	LA02	8600	58	D2
COMPTON AV	CO	LA59	11500	58	D5
COMPTON AV	COM	COM	2000	64	D1
COMPTON AV	LA	LA02	9100	58	D2
COMPTON AV	LA	LA11	1900	52	D2
COMPTON AV	LA	LA21	1200	44	D6
COMPTON BLVD	BLF	BLF	9000	66	B3
COMPTON BLVD	GAR	GAR	1000	63	B3
COMPTON BLVD	HAW	HAW	2000	62	E3
COMPTON BLVD	HAW	LAW	3600	63	B3
COMPTON BLVD	PAR	PAR	6400	65	E3
COMPTON BLVD	RB	RB	4800	62	E3
COMPTON BLVD E	CO	COM	4000	65	A3
COMPTON BLVD E	CO	GAR	100	64	B3
COMPTON BLVD E	COM	COM	100	64	F3
COMPTON BLVD E	COM	COM	200	65	A3
COMPTON BLVD W	CO	GAR	2200	63	A3
COMPTON BLVD W	CO	GAR	100	64	A2
COMPTON BLVD W	COM	COM	100	64	F3
COMPTON CT	COM	COM	13900	64	E2
COMSTOCK AV	GLDR	GLDR	1400	87	D4
COMSTOCK AV	LA	LA24	200	32	E6
COMSTOCK AV	LA	LA24	800	41	F1
COMSTOCK AV	LA	LA24	800	42	A1
COMSTOCK AV	LA	LA25	1800	42	A2
COMSTOCK AV	LAN	LAN		160	E6
COMSTOCK AV	WHI	WHI	5800	55	E5
COMSTOCK AV E	GLDR	GLDR	500	87	B4
COMSTOCK AV W	GLDR	GLDR	500	87	A4
COMSTOCK CT	PALM	PALM		171	H6
CONANT ST	LB	LB08	5100	71	B5
CONATA ST	DUA	DUA	2500	29	F4
CONATA ST	DUA	DUA	2800	86	A4
CONCERT ST	ELM	ELM	11000	47	E1
CONCETTA WY	SPAS	SPAS	1200	36	E2
CONCHA ST	CO	ALT	900	20	B4
CONCHITA ST	GLEN	GL08	2100	18	F6
CONCHITA WY	LA	TAR	4400	21	A3
CONCHITO DR	LHH	LAH	1500	84	E2
CONCORD AV	ALH	ALH	2600	36	F5
CONCORD AV	CO	SAU		123	D5
CONCORD AV	LA	LA32	5500	36	F5
CONCORD AV	MON	MON	400	29	A3
CONCORD AV	MTB	MTB		46	E6
CONCORD AV	POM	POM	2200	94	A1
CONCORD CT	PALM	PALM		171	B3
CONCORD LN	GLDR	GLDR	1400	89	B2
CONCORD PL	ELS	ELS	800	56	A5
CONCORD ST	CER	ART		81	A1
CONCORD ST	ELS	ELS	100	56	A6
CONCORD ST	GLEN	GL02	700	25	B3
CONCORD ST	GLEN	GL03	100	25	B3
CONCORD ST N	LA	LA63	400	45	C4
CONCORD ST S	LA	LA23	600	45	B6
CONCORD ST S	LA	LA23	1300	53	B1
CONCORD ST S	LA	LA63	100	45	B6
CONCORDIA CT	PAS	PAS	400	26	F5
CONCORDIA WK	LA	LA62	1900	51	D4
CONCORSE DR	CO	CAST	29000	123	A5
CONCOURSE AV	CMRC	LA22	1500	54	C2
CONCOURSE AV	CO	LA22	900	54	C2
CONCOURSE AV	MTB	MTB	300	46	C6
CONCOURSE AV	MTB	MTB	100	54	C1
CONCOURSE WY	LA	LA45		56	E3
CONDE DR	SCLR	VAL		124	C7

STREET	CITY	P.O. ZONE	BLOCK	PAGE	GRID
CONDESA DR	WHI	WHI	15400	84	B2
CONDON AV	CO	IN04	10100	56	F4
CONDON AV	CO	LA56	5700	50	F4
CONDON AV	HAW	HAW	11400	56	F5
CONDON AV	ING	IN04		56	F4
CONDON AV	LA	LA56	6200	50	F5
CONDON AV	LAW	LAW	14300	62	F4
CONDON AV	RB	RB	1500	62	F6
CONDOR ST	CMRC	LA22	7100	54	C4
CONDOR RIDGE RD	CO	CYN	15800	128	E1
CONE ST	CO	LPUE		97	A4
CONEJO AV	LA	WOH	4700	13	B3
CONEJO RASTRO	CO	SAU		188	C1
CONEJO VIEW DR	AGH	AGO		100A	A3
CONESTOGA DR	LAN	LAN		159	D6
CONESTOGA DR	RHE	PVP	27600	73	D5
CONESTOGA RD	PALM	PALM		183	G3
CONESTOGA RD	SAD	SAD		89	F1
CONEY AV	AZU	AZU	200	86	C5
CONEY AV	CO	COV	4400	88	B3
CONEY RD	LA	LA32	5200	36	E6
CONFERENCE ST	ELM	ELM	12000	39	B3
CONGRESS AV	LA	LA18	2000	43	E5
CONGRESS PL	PAS	PAS	600	26	F5
CONGRESS ST	PAS	PAS	100	26	F5
CONIFER DR	PALM	PALM		183	C1
CONIFER RD	GLDR	GLDR		87	B3
CONISTON PL	SMAR	PAS	2300	27	D6
CONISTON RD	PAS	PAS	500	19	E6
CONKLIN ST	DOW	DOW	7800	59	F6
CONKLIN ST	DOW	DOW	8400	60	A6
CONLE WY	CO	GL14	2300	18	E1
CONLON AV	CO	COV	3900	88	A5
CONLON AV	CO	LPUE	900	48	E3
CONLON AV	LPUE	LPUE	300	48	D4
CONLON AV N	WCOV	WCOV	100	88	A6
CONLON AV S	WCOV	WCOV	800	48	E3
CONNECTICUT ST	LA	LA06	3200	43	E3
CONNECTICUT ST	LA	LA15	1300	44	B3
CONNECTICUT ST	WCOV	WCOV		92	D4
CONNELL PL	CO	LA63	1500	45	D2
CONNIE CT	SCLR	CYN		125	C8
CONNIE RAE DR	ARC	ARC		28	F6
CONNOR AV	CMRC	LA40	2300	53	D2
CONNORS CT	CLA	CLA		91	D2
CONOVER ST	LA	SF	9300	10	B1
CONOVER FIRE RD	LA	SUN		10	C1
CONOY RD	WHI	WHI	15800	84	C4
CONQUEROR DR	RPV	PVP	32300	78	A3
CONQUISTA AV	CO	LB08	3700	71	D5
CONQUISTA AV	LB	LB08	3000	71	D5
CONQUISTA AV	LB	LB15	1800	76	D3
CONQUISTA AV	LKD	LKD	4100	71	D3
CONRAD ST	DOW	DOW	8000	60	A5
CONRAD ST	LA	LA41	1400	26	B5
CONRADI AV	CO	TOR	20900	68	F3
CONSOL AV	ELM	ELM	2800	47	E2
CONSTABLE AV	LA	SF	13100	1	E2
CONSTANCE ST	LA	LA15	1300	44	A4
CONSTANCE ST	PAS	PAS	1000	27	C4
CONSTANCE ST	RM	RM	8000	46	F2
CONSTELLTION BL	LA	LA67	10050	42	A2
CONSTITUTION AV	CO	LA49		41	D2
CONSTITUTION CT	PALM	PALM		183	D2
CONSTITUTION LN	LB	LB10	100	75	A2
CONSUELO RD	LA	WOH	4400	13	D3
CONSUELO ST	DOW	DOW	7600	59	F5
CONTADOR DR	CO	LPUE	17200	98	C5
CONTENDAS DR	CO	MAL		112	D3
CONTENTED LN	MON	MON	1300	28	F5
CONTERA RD	LA	ENC	4100	22	A4
CONTESSA AV	SCLR	SAU		124	F4
CONTINENTAL AV	SELM	ELM	2200	47	D2
CONTINENTAL BL	ELS	ELS	100	56	C6
CONTINENTAL CT	PAS	PAS		26	E3
CONTINENTAL WY	ELS	ELS	700	62	D2
CONTNTL CTY DR	LA	LA45		56	E4
CNTNTL CTY DR W	LA	LA45		56	E4
CONTOUR DR	LA	VAN	13300	22	F4
CONTOUR RD	LA	VAN		22	F4
CONTRA COSTA DR	CO	LPUE	17200	98	C5
CONTRA COSTA WY	CLA	CLA		91	C1
CONTRERAS ST	PAR	PAR	8500	66	A2
CONVERSE AL	PAS	PAS	300	27	B4
CONVERSE AV	CLA	CLA	400	91	C5
CONVERSE AV	CO	LA01	5800	52	D5
CONVERSE ST	LA	LA32	4700	36	D5
CONVOY ST	LA	VEN	100	55A	D2
CONWAY AV	LA	LA77	200	32	F5
CONWAY PL	CO	SAU		124	D4
CONWAY PL	LA	LA21	1800	44	E4
CONWAY SPGS LN	WAL	WAL		93	A5
CONWELL AV	CO	AZU	5000	88	D2
CONWELL AV	CO	COV	4600	88	D4
CONWELL AV	COV	COV	1100	88	D3
COOGAN CIR	CUL	CUL	4000	50	B2

STREET	CITY	P.O. ZONE	BLOCK	PAGE	GRID
COOK AV	LB	LB05		70	A2
COOK AV	PAS	PAS	100	27	E3
COOK RD	LA	TAR	19200	21	A2
COOK ST	CO	LA61	12800	64	B1
COOKACRE AV	CO	COM	12900	65	C2
COOKACRE AV	COM	COM	12800	65	C1
COOKACRE AV	LYN	LYN	12400	65	C1
COOKACRE ST	CO	COM	14700	65	C2
COOLBANK DR	LAM	LAM	14300	82	F1
COOLCREST DR	CO	PALM		157	F8
COOLEY PL	PAS	PAS	100	27	E2
COOLFIELD DR	CO	COV	17000	88	C4
COOLFIELD DR	COV	COV	100	88	C4
COOL GLEN WY	CO	MAL	26200	113	B2
COOLGROVE DR	DOW	DOW	7200	54	C6
COOLGROVE DR	DOW	DOW	7600	60	C1
COOL HAVEN CT	WLVL	THO		102	B4
COOLHEIGHTS DR	RPV	PVP	3400	78	B3
COOLHILL TR	CO	TOP		109	B2
COOLHURST DR	PR	PR	8700	54	F4
COOLHURST DR	PR	PR	9500	55	A4
COOLHURST ST	CO	WHI	10600	55	A4
COOLIDGE AV	CO	ALT	1700	20	E6
COOLIDGE AV	CO	CAST		123	A4
COOLIDGE AV	CO	PAS	1300	27	E1
COOLIDGE AV	CUL	CUL	4000	50	A2
COOLIDGE AV	LA	CUL	4600	50	B3
COOLIDGE AV	LA	LA64	2400	41	E5
COOLIDGE AV	LA	LA66	3100	41	F6
COOLIDGE AV	LA	LA66	3600	49	F1
COOLIDGE AV	LA	LA66	3700	50	A1
COOLIDGE AV N	LA	LA39	2700	35	D3
COOLIDGE DR	SGAB	SGAB	300	37	D2
COOLIDGE PL	LA	LA66	11500	41	F6
COOLIDGE ST	LB	LB05	300	65	C5
COOLIDGE WY	CO	LA22	5800	54	A1
COOL OAK WY	CO	MAL	20700	115	A4
COOL SPRINGS DR	DBAR	POM	21200	97	D5
COOLWATER AV E	CO	LAN	16100	174	H4
COOLWATER AV E	CO	LAN	16600	175	A4
COOMBS AV	CUL	CUL	4100	50	B1
COONS RD	LA	LA41		26	B6
COOPER AV	LA	LA42	800	36	D1
COOPER CT	LAV	LAV		90	B1
COOPER TER	PALM	PALM		183	F2
COOPERGROVE AV	PR	PR	8100	60	F2
COPA WY	MPK	MPK	1300	45	F2
COPACABANA ST	CO	MAL		114	D1
COPA DE ORO RD	LA	LA77	100	32	E5
COPCO DR	CO	LAN	43600	158	A6
COPELAND CIR	LAN	LAN		160	C7
COPELAND CT	SM	SM	600	49	B2
COPELAND PL	LA	LA32	3500	36	E5
COPELAND ST	LYN	LYN	11400	59	B5
COPERTO DR	LA	PP	200	40	A4
COPLEY DR	DBAR	POM		97	E2
COPLEY DR	LA	BH	100	33	A6
COPLEY PL	BH	BH	100	33	A6
COPPER	LA	SF		8	C2
COPPER ST	LA	SF	14800	8	D2
COPPER CYN CIR	POM	POM		94	D5
COPPER CYN DR	DBAR	POM	21200	97	C6
COPPERFIELD LN	CUL	CUL		50	D2
COPPER HILL DR	SCLR	SAU		124	C4
COPPER HILL DR	SCLR	SAU		124	F3
COPPER HILL RD	CO	LPUE		98	A4
COPPER KETTL WY	LAM	LAM	16400	84	D6
COPPER LNTRN DR	CO	LPUE	1500	85	D2
COPPER MTN DR	DBAR	POM		97A	A3
COPPERWOOD AV	ING	LA56		50	E5
COPRA LN	LA	PP		40	C4
COPRICE ST	PALM	PALM		171	H8
COQUETTE PL	LA	TAR	4300	21	A4
CORA ST	LA	SUN	7800	10	D3
CORAK ST	BAP	BAP	13200	39	C5
CORAK ST	BAP	BAP	13600	48	D1
CORAK ST	WCOV	BAP	14400	48	E2
CORAK ST	WCOV	WCOV	1800	48	E2
CORAL AV	COM	COM	300	64	E3
CORAL CIR	ELS	ELS		62	D1
CORAL CIR	MPK	MPK		46	C4
CORAL CT	PALM	PALM		183	E2
CORAL DR	CO	NHO		24	A5
CORAL DR	LA	LA68		23	F5
CORAL DR	LB	LB03		76	E5
CORAL LN	LB	LB05		65	C5
CORAL LN	PAR	PAR	7200	65	E3
CORAL LN	PR	PR	8100	60	E1
CORAL WY	CO	SAU		124	C3
CORAL ST	LA	LA31	2300	36	B6
CORAL WY	LAV	LAV		95A	B6
CORAL WY	LCF	LCF	4500	19	B3
CORALEE AV	CO	ARC	6500	38	C1
CORALES PL	CO	CYN		125	F7
CORALGLEN DR	CO	MAL	2800	113	B4
CORALINE CIR	LA	CHA	20300	6	E2

STREET	CITY	P.O. ZONE	BLOCK	PAGE	GRID
CORALINE PL	LA	CHA	10600	6	E2
CORALITE ST	LB	LB08	5100	71	B6
CORALREEF CIR	CER	ART		66	E5
CORALRIDGE PL	CO	LPUE		48	C5
CORAL RIDGE RD	RPV	SP	2600	78	C1
CORAL SEA TER	CO	TOP		109	B3
CORAL TREE DR	WCOV	WCOV	700	92	E2
CORALTREE LN	RHE	PVP		72	C6
CORAL TREE PL	LA	LA66	12800	50	A5
CORAL VIEW ST	MPK	MPK	100	46	C4
CORALWOOD TR	CO	TOP		109	B2
CORANTO ST	LA	SF	12900	3	B3
CORAVIEW LN	CO	LPUE		97	B5
CORAY WY	CO	CAL		108	B5
CORBER RD	CO	SAU		188	B1
CORBETT ST	LA	LA16	5600	42	E6
CORBIN AV	LA	CAN	6400	12	F3
CORBIN AV	LA	NOR	8700	6	F6
CORBIN AV	LA	NOR		7	A5
CORBIN AV	LA	TAR	5700	12	F6
CORBIN AV	LA	TAR	4800	13	F2
CORBIN AV	LA	WOH	5700	12	F6
CORBIN AV	LA	WOH	4100	13	F3
CORBY AV	ART	ART	18500	81	A1
CORBY AV	ART	ART	17200	82	A5
CORBY AV	CER	ART	19500	81	A2
CORBY AV	LKD	LKD	19700	81	A2
CORBY AV	NWK	NWK	11000	61	A5
CORBY AV	NWK	NWK	13400	82	A3
CORBY AV	SFS	SFS	9100	61	A2
CORCORAN PL	LA	SF	12950	3	A5
CORCORAN ST	LA	SF	13400	2	F6
CORCORAN ST	LA	SF	12900	3	A5
CORCORAN ST	LA	SF	14300	8	D2
CORD AV	DOW	DOW	9000	60	E3
CORD AV	PR	PR	6200	54	F5
CORD AV	PR	PR	5100	55	A3
CORD AV	PR	PR	7900	60	E2
CORD CIR	BH	BH		33	C4
CORDA DR	LA	LA49	3000	22	A6
CORDA LN	LA	LA49	2900	22	A6
CORDARY AV	CO	LAW	14500	63	B3
CORDARY AV	HAW	HAW	12800	63	B2
CORDARY AV	TOR	TOR	16900	63	B6
CORDARY AV	TOR	TOR	18700	68	B1
CORDARY AV	TOR	TOR	1300	68	B4
CORDELIA AV	CO	GLDR		87	D6
CORDELIA AV	CO	GLDR		89	D1
CORDELIA RD	LA	LA49	2500	30	E5
CORDELL DR	LA	LA69	9100	33	C4
CORDELL PL	LA	LA69	1300	33	C4
CORDELL MEWS	LA	LA69		33	C4
CORDELL MUSE	LA	LA69		33	C4
CORDERA CT	CO	VAL		126	J2
CORDERO AV	LA	TU	9400	11	A5
CORDERO RD	WHI	WHI		84	C1
CORDIAL LN	PAS	PAS	1900	19	E5
CORDILLERA DR	CO	CAL		100	C4
CORDO DR	SCLR	SAU		124	E9
CORDOBA CT	LB	LB03		76	D6
CORDOBA CT	MB	MB		62	D3
CORDOBA CT	WHI	WHI	10600	55	C2
CORDOBA PL	PALM	PALM		171	F5
CORDON DR	CO	LA63	1300	45	D3
CORDONA ST	CO	LPUE	18900	98	F4
CORDOVA AV	CO	LA22	800	45	E3
CORDOVA AV	GLEN	GL06	600	25	D3
CORDOVA AV	GLEN	GL07	1000	25	D2
CORDOVA CIR	LAV	LAV		90	D4
CORDOVA CT	LA	VEN	400	49	C4
CORDOVA CT	WCOV	WCOV		92	F2
CORDOVA RD	LAM	LAM	13100	84	B6
CORDOVA ST	LA	LA07	1600	43	E4
CORDOVA ST	LA	LA18	1900	43	E4
CORDOVA ST	PAS	PAS	100	27	B4
CORDOVA ST	POM	POM	1700	91	B6
CORDOVA ST	POM	POM	1200	95	B1
CORDOVA ST N	ALH	ALH	100	37	C2
CORDOVA ST N	BUR	BUR	100	24	A1
CORDOVA ST S	ALH	ALH	100	37	C2
CORDOVA ST S	BUR	BUR	100	24	A1
CORDOVA WK	LB	LB03	100	80	C1
CORDOZA AV	CO	LPUE	2200	98	D5
CORELLA AV	WHI	WHI	9800	84	E3
CORELLIAN CT	CER	ART		81	C2
CORETTA AV	LA	NHO	5800	16	C6
COREY ST E	DOW	DOW	7400	59	F4
COREYELL PL	LA	LA46	8400	33	D1
CORFU LN	LA	LA77	10400	32	E3
CORIA PL	PALM	PALM		183	J7
CORIANDER CT	CO	NEW		126	J5
CORIANDER DR	CO	HAC	700	73	F1
CORIANDER DR	CO	LA02	700	68	F6
CORIANDER DR	CO	TOR	600	69	A6
CORIE LN	CO	CAN	6700	5	D4
CORINA CT	CO	LPUE	15900	85	E4

STREET	CITY	P.O. ZONE	BLOCK	PAGE	GRID
CORINGA DR	LA	LA42	4900	26	B6
CORINNA DR	RPV	PVP	3000	78	C3
CORINTH AV	LA	CUL	4300	50	A2
CORINTH AV	LA	LA25	1500	41	E4
CORINTH AV	LA	LA64	2200	41	E4
CORINTH AV	LA	LA66	3100	41	F6
CORINTH AV	LA	LA66	3500	50	A1
CORINTHIAN DR	LA	ENC	17600	21	D2
CORINTHIAN PL	LAN	LAN		159	A5
CORINTHIAN PL	LAN	LAN		159	B9
CORINTHIAN WK	LB	LB03	1	80	C1
CORINTHIAN WY	LA	ENC		21	D3
CORINTHIAN WY	POM	POM	900	94	D1
CORIOLANUS DR	MPK	MPK	900	46	D4
CORISCO ST	LA	CHA	20200	6	E5
CORK CIR	LAV	LAV		95A	C6
CORK PL	LA	SF	14700	2	D6
CORK PL	SF	SF		2	D6
CORK ST	CO	PALM		183	E4
CORK ST	LA	SF	600	2	D6
CORKWOOD AV	LAN	LAN	45400	160	A3
CORLETT AV	CO	COM	14300	64	C2
CORLETT AV	CO	LA59	12900	64	C1
CORLETT AV N	COM	LA59	1900	64	C1
CORLETT AV S	COM	COM	500	64	C3
CORLEY DR	CO	WHI	10300	61	F5
CORLEY DR	CO	WHI	10700	61	F6
CORLEY DR	CO	WHI	10300	84	A4
CORLEY DR	LAM	LAM	12700	61	F6
CORLEY DR	LAM	LAM	12900	82	F1
CORLINGTON RD	GLEN	GL06	2500	26	B3
CORLISS ST	LA	LA41	4400	26	A6
CORMORANT BAY	LB	LB03		76	E6
CORNELIA ST	POM	POM	500	94	A1
CORNELIUS ST	LA	PAC	13300	3	A6
CORNELIUS ST	LA	PAC	13400	8	F1
CORNELL AV	CLA	CLA	100	91	B4
CORNELL CT	LAN	LAN		159	G7
CORNELL DR	ARC	ARC	1	28	E4
CORNELL DR	BUR	BUR	200	17	D4
CORNELL DR	GLEN	GL05	1000	25	D6
CORNELL RD	CO	AGO		100A	A5
CORNELL RD	CO	AGO		107	A1
CORNELL RD	PAS	PAS	600	27	B5
CORNELL SCHL RD	CO	AGO		106	D2
CORNET AV	SFS	SFS	15000	82	D3
CORNETT DR	LA	LA46	8100	33	E1
CORNHILL RD	SCLR	NEW		127	E2
CORNING AV	CO	LA56	5100	50	E4
CORNING ST	LA	LA34	1900	42	D4
CORNING ST	LA	LA35	1000	42	D2
CORNISH AV	LYN	LYN	10700	59	C5
CORNISH AV	LYN	LYN	12100	65	B1
CORNISHCREST DR	CO	WHI	12900	61	C2
CORNISHCREST RD	CO	WHI	13600	61	D3
CORNISHON AV	LCF	LCF	4300	19	B3
CORNUTA AV	BLF	BLF	13400	66	D2
CORNUTA AV	DOW	DOW	12100	60	C6
CORNUTA AV	DOW	DOW	12700	66	C1
CORNWALL DR	GLEN	GL06	3000	26	B1
CORNWALL PL	SCLR	SAU		127	D1
CORNWELL ST	LA	LA33	300	45	A3
CORO TER	GLEN	GL08	1800	18	F6
CORONA AV	BELL	BELL	6200	53	C5
CORONA AV	HPK	HPK	5900	53	C4
CORONA AV	LB	LB03		76	B6
CORONA AV	LB	LB03		80	B1
CORONA AV	MAY	MAY	5100	53	C4
CORONA AV	VER	LA58	4600	53	C3
CORONA CT	LB	LB03		76	C6
CORONA DR	GLEN	GL05	1200	25	E6
CORONA DR	LA	LA32	4100	36	E4
CORONA DR	LCF	LCF	300	19	D5
CORONA DR	PAS	PAS	100	27	A1
CORONA EXPWY	POM	POM		94	D5
CORONA ST	HB	RB	1200	62	D6
CORONA DEL MAR	LA	PP	14800	40	D5
CORONADO AV	LB	LB03	100	75	F5
CORONADO AV	LB	LB04	700	75	F4
CORONADO AV	LB	LB05	6200	65	F6
CORONADO AV	LB	LB14	300	75	F5
CORONADO AV	SH	LB04	1800	75	F4
CORONADO AV	WCOV	WCOV	1100	92	C3
CORONADO CT	SCLR	VAL		127	H6
CORONADO CT	MB	MB		62	D3
CORONADO DR	ARC	ARC	800	28	B5
CORONADO DR	GLEN	GL06	800	25	D2
CORONADO LN	LAV	LAV		90	D1
CORONADO ST	SAD	SAD	300	90	A2
CORONADO ST N	LA	LA26	200	35	B6
CORONADO ST N	LA	LA26	100	44	B1
CORONADO ST S	LA	LA57	100	44	A1
CORONADO TER	LA	LA26	400	35	B6
CORONEL CT	WAL	WAL		93	A5
CORONEL LN	PVE	PVP	1500	72	C4

INDEX

STREET	CITY	P.O. ZONE	BLOCK	PAGE	GRID
CORONEL PZ	PVE	PVP	100	72	C4
CORONEL ST	LA	LA12	700	44	E1
CORONEL ST	SF	SF	600	2	E6
CORONET AV	PAS	PAS	1000	28	A2
CORONET CT	CO	COV	2300	93	B2
CORONET DR	LA	ENC	4300	21	D3
CORONET ST	GLDR	GLDR	900	87	C3
CORPORAT CTR DR	CLA	CLA		91	D2
CORPORAT CTR DR	MPK	MPK		45	E3
CORPORAT CTR DR	POM	POM		94	A2
CORPORAT CTR PL	MPK	MPK		45	E3
CORPORATE PT WK	CUL	CUL	100	50	D4
CORRADI TER	CO	ACT	5500	182	B6
CORRAL CT	WAL	WAL		93	D5
CORRAL RD	GLEN	GL06		25	F2
CORRAL CYN RD	CO	MAL		107	A6
CORRAL CYN RD	CO	MAL	1600	113	A1
CORRALITAS DR	LA	LA39	2400	35	D3
CORRALITAS WK	LA	LA39	2100	35	D3
CORRAL RDG RD E	CO	LAN	18500	175	D4
CORRL SUNSHINE	CO	NEW		1	B1
CORREA WY	LA	LA49	1700	40	F1
CORREGIDOR ST	COM	COM	600	64	E3
CORRENTI ST	LA	PAC	13600	8	E6
CORRENTI ST	LA	PAC	12500	9	B3
CORRIDA DR	COV	COV	600	89	B6
CORRIGAN AV	DOW	DOW	11700	60	C5
CORRIGAN AV	DOW	DOW	13000	66	C1
CORRINE AV	LB	LB06		75	D3
CORRINGTON AV	CER	ART	13000	82	C5
CORRINNE LN	CO	WAL		97	B5
CORRY PL	SCLR	SAU		124	C5
CORRYNE PL	CUL	CUL	5600	50	C4
CORSA AV	WLVL	THO		102	C3
CORSAIR ST	CMRC	LA40		54	B3
CORSAUT PL	LA	ENC	16600	21	F3
CORSICA CIR	LB	LB03		76	D6
CORSICA DR	LA	PP	900	40	E3
CORSINI PL	RPV	SP	6400	78	D2
CORSO DI NAPOLI	LB	LB03	5500	80	C1
CORSON ST E	PAS	PAS	100	27	B3
CORSON ST W	PAS	PAS	100	26	F3
CORTA CALLE	CO	PAS	3700	28	B4
CORTA CRESTA DR	WAL	WAL		97	B1
CORTADA ST	ELM	ELM	9400	47	B1
CORTADA ST	RM	RM	8900	47	A1
CORTEEN PL	LA	NHO	5200	23	B2
CORTEZ DR	CO	ELM	9200	47	B3
CORTEZ DR	GLEN	GL07	1000	25	D2
CORTEZ RD	ARC	ARC	400	28	B5
CORTEZ ST	LA	LA26	1300	44	C1
CORTEZ ST	WCOV	WCOV	1800	92	D2
CORTEZ ST	WCOV	WCOV	3300	93	A2
CORTINA DR	SCLR	VAL		127	B1
CORTINA RD	LAM	LAM	14500	82	F2
CORTINA RD	LAM	LAM	14600	83	A2
CORTLAND AV	LYN	LYN	5100	59	C6
CORTLAND AV	PAR	PAR	7100	65	E1
CORTLAND AV	PAR	SOG	7200	65	E1
CORTLAND ST	LYN	LYN	3700	59	B6
CORTLAND ST	PAR	PAR	7100	65	D1
CORTNER AV	CER	ART	18800	81	B1
CORTNER AV	CER	ART	17200	82	B5
CORTNER AV	HG	LKD	22600	81	B5
CORTNER AV	LB	LB08	3500	81	B5
CORTNER AV	LKD	LKD	20700	81	B3
CORTNEY CT	IND	LPUE		98	D2
CORTO AV	CER	ART	17700	82	C5
CORTO PL	LB	LB03	3000	75	F6
CORTO RD	ARC	ARC	1	28	B4
CORTO ST	ALH	ALH	300	37	C4
CORTOLANE DR	CO	GL14	5300	11	D5
CORTONA DR	WHI	WHI		84	C2
CORVAL ST	SOG	SOG	4900	59	D3
CORVETTE ST	CMRC	LA40	6000	54	A2
CORVETTE ST	LB	LB02		74	F6
CORVO CT	LB	LB13	900	75	B4
CORVO WY	CO	TOP	21600	13	C6
CORVO WY	CO	TOP		109	C1
CORWIN AV	GLEN	GL06	600	25	F3
CORWIN ST	TOR	TOR	1800	63	E6
CORY AV	CO	ACT		189	E3
CORY AV	LA	LA69	1100	33	C4
CORY AV	WHOL	LA69	1000	33	C4
CORY DR	ING	IN02	700	50	E6
CORYDON DR	LA	LA17	900	44	C3
CORYDON ST E	COM	COM	2100	64	C3
COSBEY AV	BAP	BAP	3100	39	C6
COSGROVE ST	PR	PR	9300	54	F4
COSLIN AV	CAR	CAR	19000	69	D1
COSMIC WY	GLEN	GL01	1300	24	F2
COSMO ST	LA	LA28	1600	34	C3
COSMOPOLITAN ST	LA	LA04	3600	34	F6
COSSACKS PL	GLDR	GLDR	1300	87	D6
COSTA DR	CO	HAW	12600	56	E6
COSTA BELLA DR	WAL	WAL		97	B1

STREET	CITY	P.O. ZONE	BLOCK	PAGE	GRID
COSTA BRAVA	SCLR	NEW		127	E5
COSTA DEL REY	LB	LB03		76	D6
COSTA DEL SOL	LB	LB03		76	D5
COSTA DL SOL WY	CO	MAL		114	C1
COSTA GLEN AV	WHI	WHI	10100	84	C3
COSTA MESA DR	LAM	LAM	14300	83	C2
COSTANSO ST	LA	WOH	20900	13	B1
COSTELLO AV	LA	VAN	8500	8	E6
COSTELLO AV	LA	VAN	5600	15	E4
COSTELLO AV	LA	VAN	4200	22	E4
COSTILLA DR	DBAR	POM	21200	97	D5
COTA AV	TOR	TOR		68	C4
COTA AV N	LB	LB10	1800	75	A3
COTA AV N	LB	LB13	1300	75	A3
COTA ST	CUL	CUL	5000	50	C3
COTEAU DR	CO	WHI	13900	61	E5
COTNER AV	LA	LA25	1500	41	E3
COTNER AV	LA	LA64	2200	41	E3
COTSWOLD DR	CO	CYN		128	E2
COTTAGE DR	COV	COV	100	88	E4
COTTAGE LN	LAN	LAN		159	F7
COTTAGE PL	LA	LA15	900	44	C3
COTTAGE PL	LAV	LAV	1900	90	D3
COTTAGE PL	PAS	PAS	200	27	A3
COTTAGE ST	CO	HPK	7200	52	E6
COTTAGE ST	HPK	HPK	6100	52	E5
COTTAGE GRV AV	GLEN	GL05	1200	25	D5
COTTAGE GRV DR	CO	CAST		123	B2
COTTAGE HOME ST	LA	LA12		35	E6
COTTAGE HOME ST	LA	LA12	400	44	E1
COTTER AV	DUA	DUA	800	29	D5
COTTER PL	LA	ENC	16900	21	E4
COTTER RIM LN	DBAR	POM		99	D4
COTTON ST	CO	CAST	29600	123	C2
COTTONTAIL DR	POM	POM		94	C5
COTTONTAIL LN	CO	MAL	31700	111	C4
COTTONTAIL PL	CO	LPUE		98	D6
COTTONTAIL ST	PALM	PALM		171	H6
COTTONWOOD AV	SCLR	CYN	26600	124	F8
COTTONWOOD AV	CO	PALM	38800	174	F7
COTTONWOOD AV	LA	SUN	10700	10	B2
COTTONWOOD CIR	RHE	PVP		72	D5
COTTONWOOD CIR	WCOV	WCOV		98	E2
COTTONWOOD DR	CER	ART	16100	82	B4
COTTONWOOD LN	IND	WAL	21000	97	D1
COTTONWOOD LN	SAD	SAD	600	90	A3
COTTONWOOD PL	POM	POM	2500	94	F6
COTTONWOOD ST	PALM	PALM		172	J4
COTTONWOOD ST	PALM	PALM		183	G6
COTTONWOOD WY	WAL	WAL		93	D4
COTTONWD CVE DR	DBAR	POM		93	F6
COTTONWD GRV RD	CO	CAL		100A	E5
COUGAS CREEK RD	DBAR	POM		94	A4
COULSON ST	LA	WOH	20200	13	E1
COULTER AV	CO	PALM	36900	183	B2
COUNCIL ST	LA	LA04	3600	34	D6
COUNCIL ST	LA	LA26	2400	35	A6
COUNCIL ST	LA	LA26	1500	44	B1
COUNTESS PL	LA	ENC	17000	21	E3
COUNTRY LN	CO	LAN		159	B9
COUNTRY LN	CO	PAS	1700	20	F6
COUNTRY LN	RHE	PVP		72	D6
COUNTRY LN	WLVL	THO		102A	E5
COUNTRY PL	MPK	MPK	1000	46	D3
COUNTRY RD	MPK	MPK	700	46	D3
COUNTRY RD	POM	POM		94	B4
COUNTRY WY	CO	SAU		189	F4
COUNTRY CYN RD	CO	LPUE		98	A4
COUNTRY CLB CIR	LB	LB07		70	C5
COUNTRY CLUB CT	GLDR	GLDR	100	87	E6
COUNTRY CLUB DR	BUR	BUR	1100	17	F4
COUNTRY CLUB DR	CO	ALT	2200	20	C5
COUNTRY CLUB DR	DOW	DOW	7200	60	A2
COUNTRY CLUB DR	GLDR	GLDR	1900	87	E6
COUNTRY CLUB DR	GLEN	GL08	1600	18	E4
COUNTRY CLUB DR	LA	LA19	3100	43	C2
COUNTRY CLUB DR	LAV	LAV		95A	D5
COUNTRY CLUB DR	LB	LB07	3600	70	B4
COUNTRY CLUB DR	LKD	LKD	3300	71	A3
COUNTRY CLUB DR	PALM	PALM	39600	172	A6
COUNTRY CLUB DR	SGAB	SGAB	100	37	E2
COUNTRY CLUB LN	LB	LB07	4200	70	C3
COUNTRY CLUB RD	AVA	AVA		77	B5
CNTRY CLUB RD N	GLDR	GLDR	100	87	E6
CNTRY CLUB RD S	GLDR	GLDR	100	87	E6
COUNTRY CLB VIS	GLDR	GLDR		87	F5
COUNTRY CMFT RD	CO	ACT		189	D3
COUNTRY ESTS WY	CO	AGO		100A	A6
COUNTRY GLEN RD	AGH	AGO		100A	D5
CNTRY HOLLOW DR	WAL	WAL		93	B4
CNTRY KNOLL PL	CO	LPUE		85	C2
COUNTRYMAN LN	LCF	LCF	2100	18	F1
COUNTRY MEADOW	RHE	PVP		72	D6
COUNTRY MDW CIR	CO	LPUE		48	B5
COUNTRY MILE RD	POM	POM		94	D6
COUNTRY OAK RD	SAD	SAD		89	E1

STREET	CITY	P.O. ZONE	BLOCK	PAGE	GRID
COUNTRYPARK LN	CO	LPUE	17000	98	B3
COUNTRY RCH RD	CO	MAL		102A	D6
COUNTRY RCH RD	CO	MAL		105	D1
COUNTRY RDG RD	POM	POM		94	C5
COUNTRYSIDE	ELM	ELM		48	A6
COUNTRYSIDE DR	CO	AGO		100A	A6
COUNTRYSIDE DR	LAN	LAN		159	E5
COUNTRYSIDE DR	LAN	LAN		159	E6
COUNTRYSIDE DR	WAL	WAL		93	D6
COUNTRYSIDE LN	CO	GL14	2500	18	E1
COUNTRYSIDE LN	LB	LB06		70	B5
COUNTRY VIEW DR	DBAR	POM		97A	A3
COUNTRYWOOD AV	CO	LPUE	1400	98	A3
COUNTRY WOOD DR	POM	POM		94	C5
COUNTRYWOOD LN	WCOV	WCOV		92	E3
COUNTY RD	POM	POM	100	94	E6
COUNTY RD	POM	POM	900	95	A6
COUNTY LINE RD	CO	CHA		4	C5
COUNTY OAK RD	LA	WOH		5	C5
COURBET LN	LA	SF	13100	1	E3
COURBET ST	LA	SF	17100	1	E3
COURSER AV	LAM	LAM	11800	84	B5
COURSON RD	CO	PALM		183	C4
COURT AV	SPAS	SPAS	1700	37	B2
COURT AV	WHI	WHI	5800	55	D4
COURT PL	PALM	PALM		171	C2
COURT ST	LA	LA12	900	44	D2
COURT ST	LA	LA26	1200	44	C1
COURT ST	LYN	LYN	11200	59	A5
COURT ST	MON	MON		29	A3
COURT TER	PAS	PAS	1300	26	D5
COURT ADAIR	ELM	ELM		38	D5
COURTLAND AV	SMAR	PAS	2000	37	C1
COURTLAND ST	LA	LA06	1400	44	A4
COURTLAND ST	LA	VEN	100	49	C2
COURTLAND WY	CO	SAU		124	D4
COURTLEIGH DR	LA	LA66	11700	50	A3
COURTNAY CIR	WCOV	WCOV		92	D5
COURTNEY AV	LA	LA46	1500	33	F3
COURTNEY ST	LA	LA02	10100	58	D3
COURTNEY TER	LA	LA46	1800	33	F3
COURTNEY WY	TOR	TOR		73	A2
COURTYARD PL	LA	LA36		43	A2
COUTIN LN	GLEN	GL06	400	26	B3
COUTS AV	CMRC	LA40	2200	53	E2
COVALA CT	SCLR	VAL		124	B9
COVALA CT	SCLR	VAL		127	B1
COVE	PALM	PALM		171	E4
COVE AV	LA	LA39	2000	35	C4
COVE PL	CO	AGO		107	B3
COVE PL	DBAR	POM		97A	B1
COVE WY	BH	BH	1000	33	A5
COVE WY	LA	LA39	2200	35	C4
COVECREST DR	RPV	PVP	28400	72	D5
COVECREST WY	POM	POM	3100	90	E3
COVELLE AV	ING	IN01	700	56	E2
COVELLO ST	LA	BUR	9900	17	A3
COVELLO ST	LA	CAN	23100	5	F3
COVELLO ST	LA	CAN	19700	12	F3
COVELLO ST	LA	NHO	11900	16	C3
COVELLO ST	LA	RES	18700	14	B3
COVELLO ST	LA	SV	11200	16	E3
COVELLO ST	LA	VAN	16600	14	E3
COVELLO ST	LA	VAN	14100	15	E3
COVENTRY CIR	WHI	WHI		84	D1
COVENTRY CIR	WHI	WHI		85	D6
COVENTRY CT	SAD	SAD		89	D4
COVENTRY PL	GLEN	GL06	100	26	C1
COVENTRY PL	LA	LA64	10600	41	F5
COVENTRY PL	PALM	PALM		171	H6
COVENTRY PL	PALM	PALM		171	J6
COVER ST	LKD	LKD	2000	70	F5
COVERED WAGN DR	DBAR	POM	500	94	A6
COVERED WAGN LN	RHE	PVP		72	D6
COVERIDGE DR	RPV	PVP		72	D5
COVERLY ST	LA	SP		79	A3
COVERT AV	LA	TU	9900	11	B4
COVEVIEW DR	RPV	PVP	5000	77	F1
COVINA AV	LB	LB03	200	76	B6
COVINA AV	LB	LB03	100	80	B1
COVINA BLVD	CO	COV	17600	88	E3
COVINA BLVD	CO	COV	19500	89	B3
COVINA BLVD	CO	LPUE	100	48	B3
COVINA BLVD E	COV	COV	100	88	E3
COVINA BLVD E	SAD	SAD	100	89	E3
COVINA BLVD E	SAD	SAD	100	90	A3
COVINA BLVD W	COV	COV	100	88	E3
COVINA BLVD W	COV	COV	700	89	A3
COVINA BLVD W	SAD	SAD	300	89	E3
COVINA LN	CO	LPUE	100	48	B2
COVINA ST	LA	LA32	2900	36	E5
COVINA HILLS RD	CO	COV	19500	89	A6
COVINA HILLS RD	CO	COV	20600	93	C1
COVINA HILLS RD	COV	COV	1200	89	A6
COVINGTON PL	PAS	PAS	500	26	E6
COW TR	CO	TOP		109	D1

STREET	CITY	P.O. ZONE	BLOCK	PAGE	GRID
COWAN AV	LA	LA45	7500	50	B6
COWARMAN LN	TEC	TEC		38	C3
COWBELL CT	CO	LPUE		98	D5
COW CREEK CT	CO	LPUE		48	B5
COWGILL AL	PAS	PAS	300	27	A1
COWLES ST	LB	LB13	2000	74	F4
COWLES ST	LB	LB13	400	75	C3
COWLEY AV	BLF	BLF	13400	66	B2
COWLEY AV	DOW	DOW	12600	60	B6
COWLEY AV	DOW	DOW	12800	66	B1
COWLIN AV	CMRC	LA40	2100	53	E2
COWPER AV	LA	CAN		5	E2
COY DR	LA	VAN	3200	22	E5
COYA TR	CO	CHA		1A	D6
COYLE AV	ARC	ARC	300	38	F1
COYLE PL	LA	WOH	4000	13	B3
COYNE ST	LA	LA49	12000	41	B2
COYOTE DR	WAL	WAL		93	E4
COYOTE LN	CAR	CAR		69	D6
COYOTE LN	NWK	NWK	12800	61	C6
COYOTE LN	NWK	NWK	12800	82	C1
COYOTE RD	PALM	PALM		183	G3
COYOTE TR	CO	SAU		181	D7
COYOTE CYN DR	LA	LA68		24	B5
COYOTE CYN DR N	LA	LA68		24	B4
COYOTE SPGS DR	DBAR	POM		97A	A3
COZYCROFT AV	LA	CAN	8600	6	E6
COZYCROFT AV	LA	CAN	6700	12	E4
COZYCROFT AV	LA	CHA	9500	6	E4
CRABAPPLE CT	LA	CAN		5	D3
CRAFT CT	CO	WOH		13	B4
CRAFTON AV	BELL	BELL	6400	53	D6
CRAFTON AV	CDY	BELL	8200	59	D1
CRAFTSMAN RD	CO	CAL		100	E3
CRAGGY VIEW ST	LA	CHA	21800	6	C3
CRAGMONT ST	BAP	BAP	14000	39	E3
CRAGS DR	CO	AGO		106	F3
CRAIG AV	CO	ALT	1700	20	D6
CRAIG AV	LCF	LCF	700	19	B3
CRAIG AV N	CO	PAS	1200	27	D2
CRAIG AV N	PAS	PAS	100	27	D3
CRAIG AV S	CO	PAS	300	27	D5
CRAIG AV S	PAS	PAS	100	27	D5
CRAIG CT	CAR	CAR	21500	69	B4
CRAIG DR	LA	LA68	3200	24	B5
CRAIG DR	WCOV	WCOV	700	92	B2
CRAIG PL	LA	SP		78	D3
CRAIG WY	LAV	LAV	1900	90	D2
CRAIG ALLEN DR	AZU	AZU	1300	86	C4
CRAIGHURST TER	MPK	MPK	600	46	C2
CRAIGJON AV	CAR	CAR	19300	69	E2
CRAIGLEE CIR	WCOV	WCOV		89	A6
CRAIGLEE CIR	WCOV	WCOV	3500	93	A1
CRAIGLEE ST	TEC	TEC	9600	38	C1
CRAIGMITCHEL LN	LA	SUN	9800	10	B3
CRAIGTON AV	CO	LPUE	1700	85	E3
CRAIGVIEW AV	LA	LA66	3400	41	F6
CRAIL WY	GLEN	GL06		19	B6
CRAIN DR	CO	RM	8200	46	F3
CRAMER ST	LB	LB08	7400	81	A6
CRANBERRY LN	CO	LPUE		98	A4
CRANBROOK AV	CO	LAW	15200	63	B3
CRANBROOK AV	HAW	HAW	12400	57	B6
CRANBROOK AV	HAW	HAW	14800	63	B3
CRANBROOK AV	TOR	TOR	16700	63	B6
CRANBROOK AV	TOR	TOR	800	68	B3
CRANBROOK AV	TOR	TOR	18700	68	B1
CRANDALL ST	LA	LA57	200	44	B1
CRANE	POM	POM		90	F2
CRANE AV N	COM	COM	100	65	B3
CRANE AV S	COM	COM	100	65	B3
CRANE BLVD	LA	LA65	300	36	A2
CRANE CT	CLA	CLA	600	96	C6
CRANER AV	LA	NHO	5600	16	E5
CRANER AV	LA	NHO	4800	23	E2
CRANER AV	LA	SV	7200	16	E3
CRANFORD AV	LA	PAC	9900	8	F4
CRANFORD AV	LA	PAC	9000	9	A4
CRANFORD AV	LA	SV	8400	9	B6
CRANKS RD	CUL	CUL	10600	50	D3
CRANLEIGH ST	CER	ART		81	C1
CRANLEY AV	CO	COV	5000	88	B3
CRANMER DR	WAL	WAL	1400	93	C3
CRANSTON AV	LA	SF	13400	2	F2
CRANSTON AV	LA	SF	11600	3	D6
CRANSTON CT	LB	LB03		76	F5
CRANSTON TR	CO	TOP	1800	109	A2
CRAPE MYRTLE LN	WHI	WHI		84	D4
CRARY ST	CO	PAS	1600	27	D1
CRATER LN	LA	LA77	1500	32	E3
CRATER CAMP DR	CO	CAL		107	F5
CRATER OAK DR	CO	CAL		108	A5
CRAVATH CT	WCOV	WCOV		92	E6
CRAVELL AV	PR	PR	7200	54	E6
CRAVELL AV	PR	PR	8100	60	D1
CRAVEN ST	LA	WIL	900	74	B5

STREET	CITY	P.O. ZONE	BLOCK	PAGE	GRID
CRAVENS AV	TOR	TOR	700	68	D4
CRAWFORD AL	PAS	PAS	1400	27	D3
CRAWFORD AV	CO	ALT	2100	20	B5
CRAWFORD ST	LA	LA11	3600	52	B1
CREBS AV	LA	NOR	9200	7	B3
CREBS AV	LA	RES	6300	14	B5
CREBS AV	LA	TAR	5700	14	B6
CREBS AV	LA	TAR	5100	21	B1
CREE TR	CO	CHA		6	C1
CREED AV	LA	LA08	4000	51	C2
CREEDMORE DR	CO	WHI	13500	48	A4
CREEK TR	CO	SF	11800	3	E6
CREEK TR	CO	TOP	500	109	D4
CREEK TR N	CO	TOP		109	C4
CREEKBED RD	CO	CAST		123	E4
CREEKSIDE DR	SCLR	NEW		127	B6
CREEKSIDE DR	WAL	WAL		92	F5
CREEKSIDE DR	WAL	WAL		93	A5
CREEKSIDE RD	SCLR	VAL		124	A8
CREEKWOOD AV	CER	ART	12200	81	B2
CREEK WOOD DR	LAV	LAV		95A	D5
CREELAND ST	PR	PR	8600	54	F2
CREELAND ST	PR	PR	8700	55	A2
CREEMORE DR	LA	TU	9200	11	B5
CREEMORE LN	LA	TU	6400	11	B5
CREEMORE PL	LA	TU	9500	11	B5
CREIGHTON AV	LA	LA45	8100	56	B1
CREIGHTON CIR	CLA	CLA	200	91	B5
CRENSHAW BLVD	CO	GAR	14400	63	C2
CRENSHAW BLVD	CO	HAW	13200	63	C2
CRENSHAW BLVD	CO	PVP	25900	73	A4
CRENSHAW BLVD	HAW	HAW	11800	57	C6
CRENSHAW BLVD	HAW	HAW	13500	63	C2
CRENSHAW BLVD	ING	IN03	10000	57	C6
CRENSHAW BLVD	ING	IN05	7900	57	C6
CRENSHAW BLVD	LA	LA05	600	43	B5
CRENSHAW BLVD	LA	LA08	5800	51	C4
CRENSHAW BLVD	LA	LA16	1900	43	B5
CRENSHAW BLVD	LA	LA19	900	43	B5
CRENSHAW BLVD	LA	LA43	4400	51	C4
CRENSHAW BLVD	LOM	LOM	24000	73	C1
CRENSHAW BLVD	RHE	PVP	26400	73	A4
CRENSHAW BLVD	RPV	PVP	26700	72	E6
CRENSHAW BLVD	RPV	PVP		77	E1
CRENSHAW BLVD	TOR	TOR	16200	63	C6
CRENSHAW BLVD	TOR	TOR	18400	63	C6
CRENSHAW BLVD	TOR	TOR	300	68	C5
CRENSHAW BLVD	TOR	TOR	23500	73	C1
CRENSHAW DR	ING	IN05	8200	57	C1
CRENSHAW PL	TOR	TOR	18700	68	C1
CREOLE RD	LA	WOH	22700	13	A3
CRESCENDA ST	LA	LA49	11700	41	B1
CRESCENT AV	AVA	AVA	100	77	C5
CRESCENT AV	CO	MONT	2000	18	F2
CRESCENT AV	LA	SP	1600	79	A4
CRESCENT CT	PALM	PALM		183	F1
CRESCENT DR	AZU	AZU	300	86	C5
CRESCENT DR	CO	ALT	2000	20	D5
CRESCENT DR	GLEN	GL05	1200	25	D5
CRESCENT DR	LA	LA46	8400	33	D2
CRESCENT DR	MON	MON	700	28	F3
CRESCENT DR N	BH	BH	100	33	B5
CRESCENT DR N	BH	BH	100	42	C1
CRESCENT DR S	BH	BH	100	42	C2
CRESCENT DR S	BH	LA35	100	42	C2
CRESCENT PL	LA	VEN	1600	49	C4
CRESCENT ST	LA	LA42	6200	36	D1
CRESCENT ST	NWK	NWK	11800	82	A2
CRESCENT WY	PALM	PALM		183	F1
CRESCENT GLN DR	GLDR	GLDR	100	87	E5
CRSCNT HTS BL N	LA	LA46	700	33	E6
CRSCNT HTS BL N	LA	LA48	100	33	E6
CRSCNT HTS BL N	LA	LA69	1600	33	E3
CRSCNT HTS BL N	WHOL	LA46	1000	33	E6
CRSCNT HTS BL S	LA	LA34	1900	42	E4
CRSCNT HTS BL S	LA	LA35	1000	42	E2
CRSCNT HTS BL S	LA	LA48	300	42	F1
CRESCENT VW DR	WCOV	WCOV	18300	92	E3
CRESPI ST	LA	WOH	22000	13	A2
CRESSEY ST	COM	COM	300	64	E2
CRESSON ST	NWK	NWK	10800	60	E5
CRESSON ST	NWK	NWK	11600	61	A5
CREST CIR	LB	LB08	7800	81	A5
CREST CT	LA	BH		23	C6
CREST DR	CO	AGO		107	A3
CREST DR	CO	ALT	1300	20	C4
CREST DR	LA	LA34	1900	42	D3
CREST DR	LA	LA35	1100	42	D3
CREST DR	LB	LB07	3300	70	C6
CREST DR	MB	MB	3800	62	A2
CREST DR	MB	MB	100	62	B4
CREST DR	PALM	PALM		171	B3
CREST LN	DBAR	POM		97	C5
CREST PL	LA	BH		23	C6
CREST RD	RPV	PVP	5200	72	D6

STREET	CITY	P.O. ZONE	BLOCK	PAGE	GRID
CREST RD	RPV	PVP	5700	77	D1
CREST RD	RPV	PVP	2900	78	C3
CREST RD	TOR	TOR	25600	73	C3
CREST RD E	RH	PVP	1	78	B2
CREST RD W	RH	PVP	13	72	F6
CREST RD W	RH	PVP	1	78	B2
CREST WY	LA	LA68	2200	34	C2
CREST WY	POM	POM	1400	90	C6
CRESTA AV	SGAB	SGAB	100	37	E3
CRESTA DR	LA	LA35	9000	42	C3
CRESTA DR	LA	LA64	10000	42	C3
CRESTA PL	LA	LA64	2700	42	B4
CRESTALOMA LN	LAM	LAM	15300	84	B6
CRESTA VERDE DR	CO	WHI		55	E2
CRESTA VRDES DR	RHE	PVP		77	C1
CRESTBROOK CT	DBAR	POM		97A	B2
CRESTBROOK ST	BLF	BLF	9800	66	C2
CRESTBROOK ST	NWK	NWK	11000	66	E2
CRESTFIELD DR	DUA	DUA	800	29	F5
CRESTFORD DR	CO	ALT	2900	19	E4
CRESTFORD DR	PAS	ALT	3200	19	E3
CRESTGLEN RD	GLDR	GLDR	200	87	B4
CRESTHAVEN CT	AGH	AGO		102	F2
CRESTHAVEN DR	LA	LA42	800	26	D6
CRESTHAVEN DR	PAS	PAS	1100	26	D6
CRESTHAVEN WY	MPK	MPK	1100	46	A3
CRESTHILL RD	LA	LA69	8400	33	E3
CRESTLAKE AV	SPAS	SPAS	2000	36	F3
CRESTLAWN ST	LA	WOH	24300	100	D1
CRESTLINE DR	CO	WAL		97	B5
CRESTLINE DR	LA	LA49	500	41	B1
CRESTLINE DR	LAM	LAM		83	C1
CRESTLINE TER	ALH	ALH	2500	46	A2
CRESTMONT AV	LA	LA26	3500	35	B4
CRESTMONT CT	GLEN	GL08	1800	25	F1
CRESTMONT DR	DBAR	POM		97A	B3
CRESTMONT LN	RPV	PVP		77	C2
CRESTMOORE PL	LA	LA65	2400	35	E1
CRESTMOORE PL	LA	VEN	600	49	D4
CRESTOAK DR	LAM	LAM	14800	83	A3
CRESTON AV	SH	LB06	1600	75	E2
CRESTON CT	SCLR	CYN		125	B8
CRESTON DR	LA	LA68	2300	34	C1
CRESTON WY	LA	LA68	2400	34	C1
CREST RIDGE DR	BUR	BUR	3000	17	C2
CRESTRIDGE RD	RPV	PVP	28600	72	E5
CRESTSHIRE DR	GLEN	GL08	1900	25	F1
CRESTVALE DR	SMAD	SMAD	400	28	B1
CRESTVIEW AV	GLEN	GL02	900	18	B6
CRESTVIEW CT	DUA	DUA		29	F3
CRESTVIEW CT	LA	LA24	1400	41	F2
CRESTVIEW CT	LAN	LAN		160	E4
CRESTVIEW DR	SCLR	NEW		127	B5
CRESTVIEW DR	GLDR	GLDR	500	87	C4
CRESTVIEW DR	LA	LA46	2400	33	C1
CRESTVIEW DR	PAS	PAS	900	28	A2
CRESTVIEW LN	LA	SF		2	B6
CRESTVIEW PL	LA	LA46		33	C1
CRESTVIEW PL	MON	MON	400	29	B2
CRESTVIEW RD	CUL	CUL	3800	50	E1
CREST VISTA DR	MPK	MPK	700	46	A3
CRESTWAY DR	CO	LA43	3700	51	B3
CRESTWAY PL	CO	LA43	3700	51	B3
CRESTWIND DR	RPV	PVP	5200	77	F1
CRESTWOLD AV	CO	LA43	3400	51	C3
CRESTWOOD CT	LAN	LAN		159	F7
CRESTWOOD LN	WAL	WAL		92	F6
CRESTWOOD LN	WAL	WAL		93	A6
CRESTWOOD ST	LA	SP	600	78	F2
CRESTWOOD ST	RPV	SP	1800	78	D2
CRESTWOOD TER	LA	LA42	800	26	C5
CRESTWOOD WY	LA	LA42	6000	26	C5
CRESWICK DR	LAM	LAM	15800	84	C5
CRETE DR	LAM	LAM	13200	82	F1
CREWE ST	CO	WHI	13700	61	E5
CREWE ST	LA	NHO	12100	16	B4
CREWE ST	LA	VAN	13100	15	F4
CREWE ST	NWK	NWK	10500	60	D6
CREWE ST	NWK	NWK	11800	61	A6
CRICKET LN	PALM	PALM		171	E4
CRICKETT LN	BAP	BAP	4100	39	E4
CRICKLEWOOD PTH	CO	PAS	1	20	F6
CRICKLEWOOD ST	TOR	TOR	3100	73	A2
CRIDER AV	DOW	DOW	8600	54	D6
CRIDER AV	PR	PR	7200	54	D4
CRIMSON CT	PALM	PALM		183	G3
CRIMSON CT	SCLR	NEW		127	F2
CRIMSON CRST DR	CO	LPUE		98	C5
CRISLER WY	LA	LA69	1700	33	E3
CRISP CANYON RD	LA	VAN	4000	22	D4
CRISPI LN	CO	LAN		171	B1
CRISPI LN	PALM	PALM		171	B2
CRISTALINO ST	CO	LPUE	15500	85	D4
CRISTALLO	PALM	PALM		171	F5
CRISTOBAL AV	LA	WIL	800	74	D4
CRISWELL ST	LA	CAN	22100	12	A4

STREET	CITY	P.O. ZONE	BLOCK	PAGE	GRID
CROCKER AV	CAR	CAR	17200	64	B5
CROCKER AV	CAR	CAR	18600	69	B1
CROCKER AV	CO	LA61	13200	64	B1
CROCKER AV	CO	VAL		123	G6
CROCKER ST	LA	LA03	5800	52	B4
CROCKER ST	LA	LA03	8600	58	B2
CROCKER ST	LA	LA11	4300	52	B3
CROCKER ST	LA	LA13	300	44	D5
CROCKER ST	LA	LA21	600	44	D5
CROCKET BLVD	CO	LA01	7200	52	E6
CROCKET BLVD	CO	LA01	7900	58	E1
CROCKETT PL	LA	SV	10300	16	F1
CROCKETT ST	LA	SV	10800	16	F1
CROCO PL	SCLR	CYN		125	B8
CROCUS DR	CO	LPUE	16200	92	B4
CROESUS AV	CO	LA01	7900	58	E1
CROESUS AV	CO	LA59	11600	58	E5
CROESUS AV	LA	LA02	9200	58	E3
CROESUS AV	LA	LA59	10700	58	E4
CROFT AV N	LA	LA69	700	33	E5
CROFT AV N	WHOL	LA48	100	33	E5
CROFT AV S	CO	LA56	5800	50	E4
CROFT AV S	LA	LA48	100	33	E5
CROFT AV S	LA	LA56	6200	50	E4
CROFTER DR	DBAR	WAL		97	D3
CROFTON WY	PAS	PAS	1600	19	D6
CROLL CT	DBAR	POM		97	E3
CROMARTY DR	DBAR	POM		97A	A1
CROMER PL	LA	WOH	5500	13	E1
CROMLEY CT	LAN	LAN		159	J8
CROMWELL AV	CO	CAST	28800	123	A5
CROMWELL AV	LA	LA27	4700	34	E2
CROMWELL AV	LA	LA27	4000	35	A1
CROMWELL LN	ING	IN01		57	C2
CROMWELL ST	POM	POM	1100	94	B1
CRONE ST	SGAB	SGAB		37	E6
CRONIN DR	CO	LPUE	19500	97	A3
CRONUS ST	LA	LA32	5200	36	E5
CROOKED TR	CO	TOP	1700	109	D1
CROOKED ARRW DR	DBAR	POM	900	97A	A1
CROOKED ARRW LN	DBAR	POM		94	A6
CROOKED CK DR	DBAR	POM	2500	97	E5
CROOKED CK DR	DBAR	POM	3600	99	C4
CROOK SHANK DR	SCLR	SAU		124	C4
CROSBY LN	LA	LA26	1000	35	C6
CROSBY PL	LA	LA26	1500	35	C6
CROSBY ST	CO	ALT	200	19	E5
CROSNOE AV	LA	VAN	7900	15	F2
CROSS AV	LA	LA65	500	36	B2
CROSS MTWY	SCLR	NEW		127	C6
CROSS ST	CO	GL14	2400	18	E1
CROSS ST	SCLR	NEW	24100	127	C5
CROSS ST	LCF	LCF	2200	18	F1
CROSSBOW RD	CO	ACT		182	F8
CROSSBURY TR	CO	TOP	1300	109	D2
CROSS CREEK CIR	WAL	WAL		92	F5
CROSS CREEK LN	CO	MAL	3500	114	B4
CROSS CREEK RD	CO	MAL	3300	114	B4
CROSSDALE AV	CER	ART	19100	71	E2
CROSSDALE AV	DOW	DOW	10800	60	E5
CROSSDALE AV	NWK	NWK	11200	60	E5
CROSSDALE AV	NWK	NWK	12900	66	E1
CROSSFIELD DR	RHE	PVP	27500	72	E5
CROSSGLADE AV	SCLR	CYN	27200	124	J9
CROSSHAVEN DR	CO	LPUE	18100	98	D4
CROSSHILL AV	TOR	TOR	22600	67	E5
CROSSON DR	LA	WOH	23700	5	E6
CROSSPATH AV	SCLR	CYN	27700	124	J7
CROSSROADS PY E	IND	LPUE		48	A5
CROSSROADS PY N	IND	LPUE		47	F5
CROSSROADS PY N	IND	LPUE		48	A5
CROSSROADS PY N	IND	WHI		47	F5
CROSSROADS PY S	IND	LPUE		47	F5
CROSSROADS PY S	IND	WHI		47	F5
CROSSRDS OF WLD	LA	LA28	1500	34	B3
CROSSVALE AV	ELM	ELM	4300	38	F4
CROSSWAY DR	PR	PR	6300	54	E4
CROSSWINDS PL	CO	NEW		127	C5
CROSSWOOD RD	LAM	LAM	14800	83	A3
CROTHERS CT	LA	CAN		5	E2
CROTON AV	CO	WHI	3700	55	C1
CROWFOOT LN	DBAR	POM		97A	A4
CROWLEY ST	LA	PAC	12800	9	A6
CROWLEY ST	LA	VAN	13500	15	F1
CROWN AV	LCF	LCF	4500	19	D3
CROWN CIR	LAV	LAV		90	D1
CROWN CT	SCLR	SAU		124	F3
CROWN DR	LA	LA49	300	41	B1
CROWN ST	GLDR	GLDR	500	89	C2
CROWNDALE AV	CO	WHI	7900	55	D6
CROWNE DR	PALM	PALM		171	F6
CROWNE DR	PAS	PAS		27	E2
CROWNFIELD CT	WLVL	THO		102	B4
CROWNHILL AV	LA	LA26	1500	44	C2
CROWN POINT DR	DBAR	POM		97	F1
CROWNRIDGE DR	LA	VAN	3100	22	B5

STREET	CITY	P.O. ZONE	BLOCK	PAGE	GRID
CROWNRIDGE PL	LA	VAN	15600	22	B5
CROWN VALLEY RD	CO	ACT		182	E9
CROWN VALLEY RD	CO	ACT		189	E2
CROWN VALLEY RD	CO	SAU		189	E2
CROWNVIEW DR	RPV	PVP	2800	78	C2
CROWN VISTA DR	CO	GAR		64	A3
CROYDON AV	LA	LA45	7800	50	C6
CROYDON AV	LA	LA45	7900	56	C1
CROYDON LN	CO	TOP	20200	109	C6
CROYDON WK	LA	LA45		56	C1
CRUCES ST E	LA	WIL	900	74	D3
CRUCES ST W	LA	WIL	1000	74	A3
CRUISE TR	CO	TOP		109	E4
CRUMLEY ST	WCOV	WCOV	800	92	A1
CRUMMER CYN RD	CO	CAL		100	B2
CRUSADER AV	CER	ART		66	E6
CRUSADO LN	LA	LA33	1300	45	C2
CRUTHERS CK RD	CO	VALY		192	E6
CRYSTAL CT	LB	LB02	100	75	C4
CRYSTAL CT	LB	LB13	700	75	C4
CRYSTAL CT	PALM	PALM		183	H2
CRYSTAL LN	PAS	PAS	200	27	A1
CRYSTAL PL	POM	POM	2100	91	A5
CRYSTAL ST	LA	LA31	1100	35	E4
CRYSTAL ST	LA	LA39	2100	35	E4
CRYSTALAIRE DR	CO	LLAN		192	J2
CRYSTALAIRE PL	LA	SF	16900	1	F4
CRYSTLAIRE WASH	CO	LLAN		192	H2
CRYSTAL CYN DR	AZU	AZU	1700	86	D3
CRYSTAL COVE DR	LB	LB03		76	E5
CRYSTAL CK LN	CER	ART	16100	82	C4
CRYSTAL GLEN WY	LA	NOR		1	A4
CRYSTAL HLLS DR	LA	NOR		1A	F4
CRYSTAL HLLS LN	LA	NOR		1A	F4
CRYSTAL HLLS WY	LA	NOR		1A	F4
CRYSTAL LAKE RD	CO			H	B1
CRYSTAL LANTERN	CO	LPUE	14400	85	B1
CRYSTAL RDG LN	LA	NOR		1	A4
CRYSTAL RDG LN	LA	NOR		1A	F4
CRYSTAL RDG WY	LA	NOR		1	A4
CRYSTAL RDG WY	LA	NOR		1A	F4
CRYSTL SPGS CIR	LA	NOR		1	A4
CRYSTL SPGS CIR	LA	NOR		1A	F4
CRYSTAL SPGS DR	LA	LA27		25	A4
CRYSTAL SPGS DR	LA	LA27		35	B1
CRYSTAL SPGS RD	SAD	SAD		89	F1
CRYSTAL VIEW DR	LA	TU	9300	11	A5
CRYSTL WATER LN	WAL	WAL		93	D4
CUATRO DR	CO	LPUE	1700	98	D5
CUATRO MILPS ST	SCLR	VAL		124	C7
CUCAMONGA AV	CLA	CLA	300	91	C4
CUDAHY AV	MAY	MAY	5100	53	D4
CUDAHY ST	CO	HPK	2400	58	F1
CUDAHY ST	HPK	HPK	3200	59	B1
CUDAHY ST	LA	LA32	700	36	D4
CUERNAVACA PL	CLA	CLA	1300	91	C2
CUERVO DR	SCLR	VAL		124	B6
CUESTA DR	CER	ART	12200	82	B5
CUESTA LN	CER	ART	12900	82	C4
CUESTA ST	CER	ART	12600	82	C5
CUESTA WY	LA	LA77	400	32	E5
CUESTA WY	MTB	MTB		46	D6
CUESTA CALA RD	CO	TOP	19400	109	C4
CUESTA LINDA DR	LA	PP		30	A5
CULFORD PL	CO	PALM		157	E9
CULLEN AV N	GLDR	GLDR	100	87	B5
CULLEN AV S	GLDR	GLDR	100	87	B5
CULLEN ST	LA	LA34	2600	42	E5
CULLEN ST	WHI	WHI	12600	55	D6
CULLEN ST	WHI	WHI	12700	61	E1
CULLEN ST	WHI	WHI	14400	84	A2
CULLIVAN ST	CO	LA47	2000	57	D4
CULLIVAN ST	ING	IN03	2200	57	D4
CULLMAN AV	CO	WHI	11500	84	D5
CULLMAN AV	LAM	LAM	12600	84	D6
CULLMAN AV	WHI	WHI	9800	84	D4
CULLY AV	CO	WHI	7000	55	B5
CULMORE ST	CLA	CLA	800	91	A3
CULP DR	PR	PR		54	F1
CULP ST	LPUE	LPUE	14500	48	D4
CULPER CT	HB	RB	200	67	C1
CULTURA ST	SFS	SFS		61	A1
CULVER AV	COM	COM	100	64	F2
CULVER BLVD	CO	MDR		49	E6
CULVER BLVD	CO	MDR		55A	E1
CULVER BLVD	CUL	CUL	9000	42	C6
CULVER BLVD	CUL	CUL	10100	50	A4
CULVER BLVD	LA	LA66	12600	49	E6
CULVER BLVD	LA	LA66	11400	50	A4
CULVER BLVD	LA	VEN	100	55A	E1
CULVER CT	POM	POM		94	F6
CULVER DR	LA	CUL	11200	50	B4
CULVER PL	LA	VEN	6600	55A	D1
CULVER CENTER	CUL	CUL	3800	50	B1
CULVER PARK DR	CUL	CUL	11200	50	C4
CULVER PARK PL	CUL	CUL		50	C4

STREET	CITY	P.O. ZONE	BLOCK	PAGE	GRID
CULVIEW ST	CUL	CUL	5900	50	D3
CUMBERLAND AV	LA	LA27	3900	35	A3
CUMBERLAND DR	WCOV	WCOV		92	C4
CUMBERLAND LN	CO	CAL		100	B2
CUMBERLAND PL	CLA	CLA	700	91	C5
CUMBERLAND RD	GLDR	GLDR	1900	87	E5
CUMBERLAND RD	GLEN	GL02	100	25	B1
CUMBERLAND RD	SMAR	PAS	2300	27	E6
CUMBERLAND TER	GLEN	GL02	1500	25	C1
CUMBRE DR	LA	SP	1600	78	D4
CUMBRE ST	MPK	MPK	400	45	F2
CUMBRE ALTA CT	LA	PP		30	B6
CUMBRE ALTA CT	LA	PP		40	B1
CUMBRE VERDE CT	LA	PP		30	B6
CUMIN CT	SCLR	SAU		124	D5
CUM LAUDE AV	LA	VEN	9000	55A	F2
CUMMINGS DR	LA	LA27	1900	34	E2
CUMMINGS LN	LA	LA27	2000	34	E2
CUMMINGS LN	LB	LB05	200	65	B5
CUMMINGS RD	COV	COV	4300	89	A4
CUMMINGS ST	LB	LB05	200	65	B5
CUMMINGS ST N	LA	LA33	100	45	A3
CUMMINGS ST S	LA	LA33	100	45	A3
CUMNOCK PL	LA	NOR		1	B4
CUMORAH CRST DR	LA	WOH	23000	13	A3
CUMPSTON ST	LA	ENC	17300	21	E1
CUMPSTON ST	LA	NHO	10400	23	B1
CUMPSTON ST	LA	VAN	13300	22	D1
CUMPSTON ST	LA	VAN	12900	23	B1
CUNARD ST	LA	LA65	2600	25	F6
CUNNINGHAM DR	CO	WHI	500	48	A4
CUPANIA	CO	LP48		98	F3
CUPANIA CIR	MPK	MPK		46	C4
CURACO TR	CO	CHA		1A	C5
CURLEW CT	LA	LA65	4500	25	E5
CURRAN PL	POM	POM	500	94	C3
CURRAN ST	LA	LA26	1500	35	D4
CURRAN ST	LCF	LCF	1400	19	A3
CURRIER RD	IND	WAL	20600	97	C1
CURRIER ST N	POM	POM	500	94	D2
CURRIER ST S	POM	POM	600	94	D3
CURRITUCK DR	LA	LA49	11900	41	B2
CURRY AV	LA	SF	11400	1	E6
CURRY LN	ART	ART		66	F5
CURRY ST	LB	LB05	1700	65	E6
CURRY ST	LB	LB10	3200	65	F6
CURSON AV N	LA	LA36	300	34	A6
CURSON AV N	LA	LA46	700	34	A6
CURSON AV N	WHOL	LA46	900	34	A6
CURSON AV S	LA	LA16	1900	42	F4
CURSON AV S	LA	LA19	1000	42	F3
CURSON AV S	LA	LA36	300	42	F1
CURSON PL	LA	LA46	1900	34	A2
CURSON TER	LA	LA46	7600	34	A2
CURT PL	GAR	GAR	17900	63	E6
CURTIS AV	COV	COV	1300	88	F4
CURTIS AV	LB	LB05		65	F5
CURTIS AV	MB	MB	1900	62	D5
CURTIS AV	RB	RB	1900	62	D5
CURTIS AV	SFS	SFS		61	B4
CURTIS AV N	ALH	ALH	6600	37	B3
CURTIS AV S	ALH	ALH	100	37	B4
CURTIS AV S	ALH	ALH	2800	46	B1
CURTIS CT	GLDR	GLDR		87	E6
CURTIS CT	POM	POM		94	F6
CURTIS LN	ALH	ALH	800	37	B5
CURTIS ST	LA	LA12	500	44	E1
CURTIS& KING RD	NWK	NWK	12100	60	D6
CURTIS& KING RD	NWK	NWK	12800	66	D1
CURTISS WY	TOR	TOR		73	B2
CURTS AV	LA	LA34	3000	42	D5
CURVE CIR	LAN	LAN		160	C5
CURWOOD PL	LA	BH	9800	33	A2
CUSHDON AV	LA	LA64	10500	42	A4
CUSHING AV	LA	WIL	800	74	E4
CUSTER AV	LA	LA12	500	44	D2
CUSTOZA AV	CO	LPUE	1100	98	F3
CUSWALE WK	CO	CAST		123	C2
CUTHBERT RD	CO	MAL	29600	112	A5
CUTLER AV	BAP	BAP	4000	39	D4
CUTLER PL	LA	SF	13100	3	A3
CUTOFF CT	CO	WAL		97	B5
CUTTEN RD	SCLR	SAU		124	C9
CUTTER ST	LA	LA39	4500	25	B3
CUTTER WY	COV	COV		88	C4
CUTWOOD RD	CO	PALM		157	H9
CUZCO AV	COM	COM	1600	65	B4
CUZCO AV	CO	COM	16300	65	B4
CYCLOPS ST	NWK	NWK	11600	61	A5
CYNTHIA AV	LA	LA65	800	36	A2
CYNTHIA AV	PAS	PAS	900	28	B2
CYNTHIA CT	SCLR	CYN		124	H9
CYNTHIA CT	LAV	LAV	1600	90	C1
CYNTHIA CT	WCOV	WCOV		92	F6
CYNTHIA ST	ALH	ALH	300	37	C2
CYNTHIA ST	POM	POM	2100	94	F5

STREET	CITY	P.O. ZONE	BLOCK	PAGE	GRID
CYNTHIA ST	WHOL	LA69	8800	33	D4
CYPREAN DR	LA	LA46	2000	33	D2
CYPRESS	CO	LP48		98	E4
CYPRESS AV	ALH	ALH	300	37	A4
CYPRESS AV	BUR	BUR	1	17	D6
CYPRESS AV	ELM	ELM	3600	38	E5
CYPRESS AV	GLDR	GLDR	400	87	B5
CYPRESS AV	HB	RB	500	67	C1
CYPRESS AV	LA	LA65	500	35	F4
CYPRESS AV	PALM	PALM		171	B2
CYPRESS AV	PAS	PAS	100	26	F2
CYPRESS AV	PAS	PAS	500	28	A4
CYPRESS AV	SOG	SOG	8100	59	A2
CYPRESS AV E	MON	MON	100	29	B5
CYPRESS AV W	MON	MON	100	29	B5
CYPRESS CIR	COM	COM		64	E3
CYPRESS CIR	LAV	LAV		90	C1
CYPRESS CT	AZU	AZU	200	86	C3
CYPRESS DR	LCF	LCF	4500	19	A2
CYPRESS LN	CO	POM		93	E2
CYPRESS PL	CO	SAU		124	D2
CYPRESS ST	CO	COV	16000	88	C4
CYPRESS ST	CO	COV	19500	89	B4
CYPRESS ST	COV	COV	700	89	B4
CYPRESS ST	ELS	ELS	900	56	B5
CYPRESS ST	IRW	BAP	15500	88	A4
CYPRESS ST	LCF	LCF	4700	18	F1
CYPRESS ST	LHH	LAH	1200	98A	A2
CYPRESS ST	LOM	LOM	24500	73	D3
CYPRESS ST	SAD	SAD	700	89	E4
CYPRESS ST	TOR	TOR	22600	68	D6
CYPRESS ST	TOR	TOR	23700	73	D1
CYPRESS ST E	COM	COM	100	65	A3
CYPRESS ST E	COV	COV	100	88	C4
CYPRESS ST E	COV	COV		89	B4
CYPRESS ST E	GLEN	GL05	100	25	D6
CYPRESS ST N	POM	POM	100	94	E3
CYPRESS ST S	POM	POM	100	94	E3
CYPRESS ST W	COM	COM	100	64	F3
CYPRESS ST W	COV	COV	100	88	C4
CYPRESS ST W	GLEN	GL04	100	25	C6
CYPRESS WY	LB	LB02	100	75	C4
CYPRESS WY	PAS	PAS		26	F2
CYPRESS WY	RHE	PVP		72	E5
CYPRESS CIR DR	LOM	LOM		73	C2
CYPRESS GRVE LN	DBAR	POM		97	F3
CYPRESS PT AV	CO	LLAN	15000	192	H3
CYPRESS PT DR	LA	NOR		1	A6
CYPRESS RDG RD	SCLR	VAL		124	B4
CYRENE DR	CAR	CAR	1500	69	E2
CYRENE PL	LA	SF	14300	2	E2
CYRENE ST	CAR	CAR	900	69	C2
CYRIL AV	LA	LA32	1900	45	D1
CYRUS LN	ARC	ARC		28	D3
CYRUS LN	PALM	PALM		171	F5

D

STREET	CITY	P.O. ZONE	BLOCK	PAGE	GRID
D CT	CO	PALM		183	A3
D CT	LA	WIL	1000	74	B5
D ST	LAV	LAV	1800	90	D3
D ST E	LA	WIL	100	74	B5
D ST W	LA	WIL	100	74	B5
D WALK	LA	WIL	1000	74	B5
DAB CT	DBAR	WAL		97	C3
DABLON AV	CAR	CAR	21800	69	D4
DABNEY LN	BH	BH	400	33	C3
DABNEY ST	CO	ALT	3200	19	F3
DACE ST	NWK	NWK	12300	82	B1
DACIAN DR	CO	WAL	1800	97	B4
DACONA AV	ELM	ELM	3900	38	F6
DACOSTA ST	DOW	DOW	7700	60	B2
DACOTAH ST	LA	LA23	900	45	A6
DACOTAH ST	LA	LA63	100	45	B4
DACRE PL	MTB	MTB	300	46	E6
DADE AV E	CO	LPUE	700	48	E4
DADION AV	CO	LAN	48500	146	G5
DAEMAS PL	LA	SF	17200	1	E4
DAFFODIL AV	CO	CYN		125	F5
DAGANA AV	CO	LAN	20900	175	G6
DAGGETT ST	LB	LB15	5200	76	C3
DAGMAR AV	CO	LA61		64	B2
DAGUE DR	WAL	WAL		93	D6
DAGUERRE AV	CO	WOH		13	B4
DAGWOOD AV	LKD	LKD	5800	71	B1
DAHA PL	LA	NHO		16	B2
DAHL DR	CO	LPUE	3200	85	E5
DAHLGREN AV	LA	LA66	3000	41	E6
DAHLIA AV	ELM	ELM	12300	47	F2
DAHLIA AV	LA	LA26	3400	35	B4
DAHLIA CT	PALM	PALM		183	E2
DAHLIA DR	LA	LA41	5100	26	B4
DAHLIA ST	DOW	DOW	12700	59	F5
DAHLIA ST	LAN	LAN		160	F5
DAHLIA WY	CO	TOR		68	F5

236

1990 LOS ANGELES COUNTY STREET INDEX

DAHLIA RIDGE DR — DEEPSPRINGS DR

LOS ANGELES CO.

STREET	CITY	P.O. ZONE	BLOCK	PAGE	GRID
DAHLIA RIDGE DR	CO	CYN		125	F5
DAILY CIR	GLEN	GL08		18	D4
DAILY DR	LA	VAN	16100	15	A2
DAINES DR	ARC	ARC		38	F2
DAINES DR	CO	ARC	11000	38	F2
DAINES DR	CO	SGAB	8700	38	A3
DAINES DR	CO	TEC	11000	38	D3
DAINES DR	TEC	TEC	9400	38	B3
DAIREN ST	CO	LPUE	19200	97	A4
DAIRY AV	LB	LB05	5400	70	C2
DAIRY RD	CO	CAST		123	F3
DAISETTA DR	SCLR	NEW	23600	127	B6
DAISETTA ST	CO	LPUE	19000	98	F3
DAISY AV N	LB	LB02	100	75	B5
DAISY AV N	LB	LB05	4700	70	B3
DAISY AV N	LB	LB06	3000	70	B6
DAISY AV N	LB	LB06	1800	75	B4
DAISY AV N	LB	LB13	700	75	B4
DAISY AV N	PAS	PAS	100	27	E4
DAISY AV S	LB	LB02	100	75	B4
DAISY AV S	PAS	PAS	100	27	E4
DAISY LN	CO	GL14	2200	18	F1
DAISY PL	LA	NOR		1	B6
DAISY ST	PALM	PALM		183	E2
DAISY TR	CO	CAL		100	E6
DAISY MEADOW ST	CO	CYN		125	F5
DAKIN ST	CO	LPUE	19200	97	A4
DAKOTA	CO	AGO		106	C3
DAKOTA AV	SOG	SOG	11500	59	E6
DAKOTA CT	SAD	SAD		90	A2
DALADIER DR	RPV	SP	2000	78	D3
DALAMAN AV	LKD	LKD	21000	81	A4
DALARK ST	CO	LPUE	16200	92	B3
DALBERG ST	BLF	BLF	9000	66	B1
DALBEY DR	SCLR	VAL		127	B3
DALBO ST	DUA	DUA	2500	29	F4
DALE AV	GLEN	GL02	700	25	B3
DALE AV	LA	SUN	9600	10	A4
DALE CT	LA	CHA	22700	6	A4
DALE DR	MON	MON	1500	29	A5
DALE RD	CO	CAL		100	F5
DALE RD	GLDR	GLDR	1700	89	A3
DALE ST	PAS	PAS	900	27	B5
DALEBURY ST	PR	PR	8400	54	E4
DALECREST AV	LA	WOH	6100	5	E5
DALEGROVE DR	LA	BH	9500	33	B1
DALEHURST AV	LA	LA24	300	32	E6
DALEMEAD ST	TOR	TOR	2400	73	C3
DALEN ST	DOW	DOW	7800	59	F5
DALEN ST	DOW	DOW	8400	60	A6
DALEPARK DR	SAD	SAD	2700	87	F6
DALERIDGE RD	LCF	LCF	4500	19	D4
DALEROSE AV	CO	IN04	10000	56	F4
DALEROSE AV	HAW	IN04	11200	56	F4
DALEROSE AV	ING	IN04		56	F4
DALESFORD DR	LPUE	LPUE		92	A6
DALESFORD DR	LPUE	LPUE	400	98	A1
DALESIDE AV	GAR	GAR	12800	63	D1
DALESIDE AV	HAW	LA47	11600	57	D5
DALEVIEW AV	ELM	ELM	3800	38	E5
DALEVIEW AV	TEC	TEC	5000	38	E3
DALEWOOD AV	DOW	DOW	9000	60	E3
DALEWOOD AV	PR	PR	8300	60	F2
DALEWOOD ST	BAP	BAP	12900	48	C1
DALEWOOD ST	WCOV	WCOV	1100	92	C1
DALFSEN AV	CAR	CAR	19700	69	E2
DALGO DR	SCLR	VAL		127	A2
DALHART AV	COM	COM	2700	58	E6
DALKEITH AV	LA	LA49	300	41	C1
DALLAS RD	SAD	SAD		89	F2
DALLAS ST	LA	LA31	2300	35	E4
DALLIN ST	LAN	LAN	2400	159	G6
DALMAN ST	WHI	WHI	14500	84	A2
DALMATIA DR	LA	SP		73	E6
DALMATIAN AV	LAM	LAM	13600	83	A1
DALMATION AV	LAM	LAM		83	B4
DALMATION AV	CO	WHI	10300	84	A4
DALTON AV	AZU	AZU	200	86	D6
DALTON AV	AZU	AZU	100	88	D1
DALTON AV	GAR	GAR	15800	63	E5
DALTON AV	GLDR	GLDR	400	87	B5
DALTON AV	LA	LA18	2600	43	E5
DALTON AV	LA	LA47	7200	51	E6
DALTON AV	LA	LA47	8700	57	E2
DALTON AV	LA	LA62	3900	51	E2
DALTON AV	LA	TOR	20800	68	E4
DALTON CT	POM	POM	1100	95	A1
DALTON PL	GAR	GAR	18000	63	E6
DALTON RD	PVE	PVP	1600	72	A4
DALTON RD	SAD	SAD		90	B1
DALTON RD	SAD	SAD		95A	B6
DALTON ST	SCLR	NEW	19100	127	H3
DALTON ST	GLDR	GLDR	700	86	F5
DALTON SPGS DR	GLDR	GLDR		87	D3
DALWOOD AV	DOW	DOW	10800	60	E5
DALWOOD AV	NWK	NWK	11200	60	E5
DALWOOD AV	NWK	NWK	12900	66	E1
DALY AV	LAV	LAV		90	C2
DALY ST	LA	LA31	2200	36	A6
DALY ST	LA	LA31	1600	45	A1
DALZELL ST	PALM	PALM	37600	183	G1
DAMAR CT	SCLR	CYN		124	J7
DAMAR ST	LB	LB08	8000	81	B6
DAMASCO ST	CO	LPUE	18700	98	F1
DAMASK AV	CO	LA56	5900	50	F5
DAMASK AV	LA	LA56	6200	50	F5
DAMATO DR	COV	COV	4600	89	A4
DAMERAL DR	CO	COV	20000	93	B2
DAMERON ST	LB	LB05	100	65	B6
DAMIAN ST	CER	ART		82	E4
DAMIEN AV	CO	LAV	400	90	B2
DAMIEN AV	LAV	LAV	2100	90	B2
DAMIETTA DR	CO	WAL		97	B3
DAMON ST	LA	LA21	2100	44	E5
DAMON ST	RM	RM		38	A4
DAMON WY	BUR	BUR		16	F3
DAMREL DR	CO	LPUE	16700	92	B5
DAN CT	SCLR	SAU		124	F3
DANA AV	TOR	TOR	23100	68	D6
DANA CT	CLA	CLA		91	B1
DANA CT	TOR	TOR	23000	68	D6
DANA DR	LAN	LAN		160	E6
DANA PL	LB	LB03	1	80	C2
DANA ST	GLEN	GL01	1800	24	F1
DANA ST	LA	LA07	1400	43	F5
DANAHA ST	TOR	TOR	2800	73	B2
DANALDA DR	LA	LA64	2900	42	B4
DANBRIDGE ST	PR	PR	9000	54	E5
DANBROOK DR	CO	WHI	14400	84	A3
DANBROOK DR	WHI	WHI	12600	61	D1
DANBURY LN	ING	IN01		57	B2
DANBURY PL	LA	WOH	5500	13	E1
DANBURY RD	CLA	CLA	1700	91	A2
DANBURY ST	CO	ARC	11100	38	E2
DANBURY ST	TEC	TEC	10600	38	D3
DANBY AV	CO	WHI	8500	61	A1
DANBY AV	SFS	SFS	9000	61	A2
DANBY AV	WHI	WHI	5400	55	C2
DANCER ST	CO	LPUE	13600	48	D2
DANCOVE DR	WCOV	WCOV	400	92	E1
DANCY ST	CO	LPUE		98	E6
DANDELION DR	SCLR	SAU	27800	124	E4
DANECROFT AV	CO	GLDR	600	87	E6
DANECROFT AV	SAD	SAD	100	89	E4
DANEHURST AV	CO	COV	3500	89	B5
DANEHURST AV	COV	COV	400	89	B4
DANEHURST AV	GLDR	GLDR	800	89	B2
DANELAND ST	LKD	LKD	2400	70	F2
DANELAND ST	LKD	LKD	4400	71	B2
DANES DR E	WCOV	WCOV	1400	88	C5
DANESWOOD DR	CO	ARC	11100	38	E2
DANESWOOD DR	TEC	TEC	10800	38	E2
DANFORTH DR	LA	LA65	700	36	A2
DANGLER AV N	CO	LA22	100	45	E5
DANGLER AV S	CO	LA22	100	45	E5
DANIA ST	PALM	PALM	500	172	A5
DANIEL AV	CMRC	LA40	2500	53	F3
DANIELLE AV	CER	ART		81	C1
DANIELS AV	WCOV	WCOV	2000	92	D2
DANIELS DR	BH	BH	400	42	C2
DANIELS DR	LA	LA35	1100	42	C2
DANIELSON CT	CMRC	LA40		54	B5
DANIELSON DR	SELM	ELM		47	C4
DANIMERE AV	ARC	ARC	200	38	F1
DANLEE DR	AZU	AZU	400	86	C5
DANLIA CIR	LAV	LAV		90	C1
DANMAR CT	LOM	LOM		73	C3
DANNA CT	RM	RM		37	E6
DANNY DR	GLEN	GL14	3500	11	C5
DANNY ST	GLEN	GL14	3700	11	C5
DANNY WY	CO	SAU		124	E4
DANNYBOYAR AV	LA	CAN	6400	5	F5
DANNYHILL DR	LA	LA64	3000	42	C4
DANTE ST	NWK	NWK	12500	82	B1
DANTES VIEW DR	CO	AGO		100A	E5
DANTON DR	CO	GLDR	18500	86	F5
DANTON ST	LAV	LAV		90	C1
DANUBE AV	LA	SF	11400	2	B6
DANUBE AV	LA	SF	9700	8	B4
DANVERS PL	CO	SAU		123	D5
DANVERS ST	DOW	DOW	7700	60	C1
DANVILLE DR	CLA	CLA		91	D1
DANVILLE ST	PR	PR	9500	55	B1
DANYA LN	LAN	LAN		159	F5
DANZA ST	LA	WOH	4600	13	D3
DANZIG PL	ALH	ALH	3200	45	E1
DAPHNE AV	CO	GAR	14400	63	D3
DAPHNE AV	GAR	GAR	12900	63	D1
DAPHNE AV	HAW	LA47	12600	57	D6
DAPHNE AV	HAW	IN03	11800	57	D5
DAPHNE AV	TOR	GAR	16100	63	D4
DAPHNE AV	TOR	TOR	16900	63	D5
DAPPLE GRAY CIR	WAL	WAL		93	A6
DAPPLEGRAY LN	RHE	PVP	26800	73	C4
DARBUN DR	SCLR	NEW	24200	127	A5
DARBY AV	ING	IN03	10100	57	C4
DARBY AV	LA	NOR	11300	1	C6
DARBY AV	LA	NOR	8700	7	C6
DARBY AV	LA	NOR	8400	14	C1
DARBY AV	LA	RES	6300	14	C3
DARBY AV	POM	POM	1200	95	B1
DARBY PL	LA	RES	6300	14	C2
DARBY RD	SMAR	PAS	900	37	C2
DARCIA PL	LA	ENC	16200	22	A3
DARCY DR	MTB	MTB	1700	46	D5
DARCY LN	SCLR	NEW		127	B6
DARCY ST	SFS	SFS	11200	60	F4
DARDENNE ST	CO	WOH	22400	13	B5
DARDON DR	CO	SF		3	E2
DARE CT	DBAR	POM		97A	A2
DARE ST	NWK	NWK	12500	82	C1
DARFIELD AV	CO	COV	4800	89	B3
DARFIELD AV	COV	COV	100	89	B5
DARGAN ST	AGH	AGO		100A	A2
DARIEN PL	TOR	TOR	19500	67	F2
DARIEN ST	LA	WOH		13	A3
DARIEN ST	TOR	TOR	4600	67	F2
DARIEN ST	TOR	TOR	4500	68	A2
DARIN DR	CO	PALM		190	D2
DARIO AV	CO	CYN		125	C4
DARIUS AV	DBAR	WAL	800	97	C2
DARIUS CT	IND	LPUE	1300	98	B2
DARK TR	CO	TOP	21500	109	D4
DARK CANYON DR	LA	LA68		24	B5
DARKWOOD LN	LAN	LAN		159	F7
DARLA AV	LA	SF	12600	1	E4
DARLAN ST	CO	GAR	300	64	B3
DARLENE DR	LHH	LAH	1400	98A	A2
DARLENE LN	LA	CAN	8400	5	F1
DARLEY AV	CO	LPUE	1500	85	C1
DARLING RD	CO	SAU	10600	181	B8
DARLINGTON AV	LA	LA49	11600	41	B3
DARLINGTON ST	CO	RR	500	47	A4
DARLOW AV	RM	RM	4500	38	B4
DARNELL ST	BLF	BLF	9400	66	B3
DARNEY AV	CO	LPUE		97	A2
DARNOCH WY	LA	CAN	6900	5	E3
DAROCA AV	LB	LB14	300	76	D5
DAROCA AV	RM	RM	2500	46	E2
DAROCA AV	SGAB	SGAB	200	37	E2
DARREL DR	GLEN	GL02	100	25	C1
DARRIN DR	DBAR	POM		94	B6
DARRO RD	LA	WOH	5200	13	C2
DARROW AV	SCLR	SAU		124	G3
DART CT	AGH	AGO		102	D3
DART ST	BAP	BAP	13200	39	C6
DARTER DR	SCLR	CYN	18800	124	J7
DARTFORD PL	ING	IN01		57	B2
DARTFORD WY	LA	VAN	15800	22	B5
DARTMOOR AV	LKD	LKD	21100	81	C4
DARTMOOR AV	NWK	NWK	14400	82	B2
DARTMOUTH AV	LA	LA32	4900	36	D6
DARTMOUTH AV N	CLA	CLA	200	91	C3
DARTMOUTH AV S	CLA	CLA	200	91	C4
DARTMOUTH CT	LAV	LAV		90	E3
DARTMOUTH DR	GLEN	GL05	1300	25	D6
DARTMOUTH DR	LAN	LAN		159	G7
DARTMOUTH DR	NWK	NWK	11400	66	F4
DARTMOUTH LN	PALM	PALM		183	H8
DARTMOUTH PL	CLA	CLA	100	91	B3
DARTMOUTH PL	LCF	LCF	500	19	C5
DARTMOUTH RD	BUR	BUR	400	17	C4
DARVALLE ST	CER	ART	13400	82	D6
DARWELL AV	BG	BELL	6200	53	F6
DARWIN AV	LA	LA31	1800	45	A1
DARWOOD AV	SAD	SAD	100	89	D3
DARYL AV	LA	SF	12400	1	E4
DARYN DR	CO	CAN	6600	5	D4
DASHLEY ST	CO	CYN		125	D9
DASHWOOD ST	LKD	LKD	2000	70	F2
DASHWOOD ST	LKD	LKD	5800	71	E2
DATE AV	ALH	ALH	300	37	A5
DATE AV	ALH	ALH	2200	46	A1
DATE AV	LAN	LAN	44000	160	A6
DATE AV	TOR	TOR	1200	68	C4
DATE AV	TOR	TOR	22700	68	C6
DATE CIR	TOR	TOR	2500	68	C6
DATE ST	DUA	DUA		29	E5
DATE ST	MTB	MTB	100	54	C3
DATE ST	POM	POM	500	94	D2
DATE PALM DR	PALM	PALM		171	J8
DATETREE DR	CO	PALM		157	H9
DAUBERT ST	LA	SF	14000	8	E1
DAUM DR	IND	LPUE	13200	48	C2
DAUNTLESS DR	RPV	PVP	3900	78	A3
DAUPHIN AV	LA	LA34	5500	42	E5
DAVAN ST	DBAR	WAL		97	D3
DAVANA RD	LA	VAN	3800	22	E4
DAVANA TER	LA	VAN	13700	22	E4
DAVE DR	LA	SP		78	D3
DAVENPORT CIR	CLA	CLA		91	D2
DAVENPORT DR	LA	LA65		35	F3
DAVENPORT RD	CO	SAU	13900	125	H1
DAVENPORT RD	CO	SAU		188	B1
DAVENRICH ST	SFS	SFS	11000	60	F3
DAVENTRY ST	LA	PAC	12900	3	B6
DAVENTRY ST	LA	PAC	13500	8	E2
DAVENTRY ST	LA	PAC	13100	9	A1
DAVENTRY ST	LA	SF	12700	3	B6
DAVER AV	CO	GL14		11	D5
DAVERIC DR	PAS	PAS	1000	28	A2
DAVEY AV	SCLR	NEW	23000	127	C5
DAVEY JONES DR	AGH	AGO		102	D3
DAVID AV	LA	LA34	5800	42	E4
DAVID AV	LA	LA34	8900	42	C4
DAVID ST	LAN	LAN		160	E6
DAVID WY	CER	ART	18000	82	D6
DAVID WY	CO	SAU		124	G4
DAVIDS RD	CO	AGO		100A	E6
DAVIDSON DR	CO	SAU	29000	123	B5
DAVIDSON DR	MPK	MPK		45	E3
DAVIDSON DR	WHI	WHI	5300	55	C2
DAVIDSON LN	POM	POM	500	94	C2
DAVIE AV	CMRC	LA40	1500	54	B2
DAVIES DR	LA	BH	1300	32	E3
DAVIES WY	LA	LA46	2000	33	E2
DA VINCI AV	LA	WOH	4400	13	C4
DAVIS AV	GLEN	GL01	300	24	F2
DAVIS AV	GLEN	GL01	1000	25	A2
DAVIS AV	MTB	MTB	600	54	D3
DAVIS RD	CO	MAL	500	105	B4
DAVIS ST	DOW	DOW	8300	60	B4
DAVISTA DR	WHI	WHI	8100	84	A1
DAVON WY	PALM	PALM		171	C5
DAWES AV	CUL	CUL	5100	50	B3
DAWES AV	LA	CUL	4400	50	B3
DAWKINS AV	CO	CAST		123	C2
DAWLEY AV	CO	LPUE	1400	92	C4
DAWLEY AV	WCOV	WCOV	500	92	C2
DAWN	PALM	PALM		171	E4
DAWN AV	LAV	LAV		90	E1
DAWN DR	CER	ART	12900	82	C4
DAWN LN	CER	ART	12400	82	B4
DAWN ST	LOM	LOM	2000	73	D1
DAWN HAVEN RD	CO	LPUE		98	A4
DAWNRIDGE DR	LA	BH	1300	33	A4
DAWN RIDGE PL	WCOV	WCOV		92	D5
DAWN RIDGE WY	COV	COV		89	A6
DAWN RIDGE WY	COV	COV		93	A1
DAWNVIEW AV	POM	POM	3000	90	E3
DAWNVIEW PL	CO	LA43	5100	50	F3
DAWSON AV	GLDR	GLDR	100	89	A1
DAWSON AV	LB	LB04	700	75	E4
DAWSON AV	LB	LB06	1800	75	E4
DAWSON AV	LB	LB14	400	75	E4
DAWSON AV	SH	LB06	1800	75	E3
DAWSON CT	GLDR	GLDR		89	A1
DAWSON DR	PALM	PALM		183	H2
DAWSON ST	LA	LA26	200	44	C1
DAWSON WY	CLA	CLA		96	C6
DAWSON CREEK PL	WAL	WAL		93	A5
DAY ST	LA	SUN	7900	10	E3
DAY ST	LA	TU	7600	10	E3
DAY ST	LA	TU	6200	11	A3
DAYBREAK	ELM	ELM		48	A5
DAYBREAK S	ELM	ELM		48	A6
DAYBREAK CT	PALM	PALM		183	H1
DAYBREAK DR	WAL	WAL		93	D6
DAYBREAK ST	PALM	PALM		183	H1
DAYKIN ST	CO	LPUE		85	D2
DAYLIGHT DR	AGH	AGO		100A	A2
DAYMAN ST	LB	LB06	300	75	C3
DAYMAN ST	LB	LB15	6200	76	D3
DAYTON AV	POM	POM	900	94	D5
DAYTON CT	CO	PALM		184	E2
DAYTON ST E	PAS	PAS	100	26	F4
DAYTON ST W	PAS	PAS	100	26	F4
DAYTON WY	BH	BH	8800	33	C6
DAYTONA AV	CO	LPUE	2600	85	C3
DAYTONA CYN RD	LA	CAN		5	D1
DE ADALENA ST	RM	RM	8600	38	B5
DEAL DR	LB	LB07	4500	70	C3
DE ALCALA DR	LAM	LAM	13200	82	F2
DEAN CIR	LA	LA49		32	A3
DEANA ST	ELM	ELM	11800	38	F6
DEANA ST	ELM	ELM	12100	39	A6
DEANE AV	CO	LA43	5100	51	B4
DEANE AV	LA	LA43	5800	51	B4
DEANE ST	LA	LA39	2300	35	C3
DEANNA CT	GAR	GAR		63	F2
DEANNE DR	CO	LPUE	2400	85	E3
DEANWOOD DR	LA	WOH	4300	13	E3
DE ANZA DR	PALM	PALM		171	E4
DEANZA PL	ARC	ARC	1100	28	B4
DE ANZA ST	SGAB	SGAB	100	37	D3
DE ANZA HTS DR	SAD	SAD	100	90	A3
DEARBORN AV	PALM	PALM		171	F6
DEARBORN AV	SOG	SOG	8100	59	A3
DEARBORN CT	LA	PAC		3	B4
DEARBORN DR	LA	LA68	2500	34	C1
DEARBORN ST	LA	CHA	20700	6	D5
DEARBORN ST	LA	NOR	17100	7	E5
DEARBORN ST	LA	SF	16600	7	F5
DEARBORN ST	LA	SF	15300	8	C5
DEARBORN ST	LA	VAN	14100	8	E5
DEARBORN ST	PAS	PAS	216	20	A6
DEAUVILLA CT	CO	CAL		100	D5
DEBANN PL	CO	WAL	1700	97	B4
DEBBY ST	LA	NHO	11100	16	E5
DEBBY ST	LA	VAN	13300	15	F5
DEBBY ST	LA	VAN	12900	16	A5
DEBELL ST	LA	PAC	13500	8	F6
DEBELL ST	LA	PAC	12600	9	B4
DE BELL RCH RD	CO	MAL		113	D4
DE BERRY DR	CO	AGO		100A	D4
DE BIE AV	CER	ART	18400	81	C1
DE BIE DR	PAR	PAR		65	D1
DEBLYNN AV	CO	GAR	15400	64	B3
DEBLYNN CT	PALM	PALM		183	B1
DEBORAH AV	AZU	AZU	1300	86	C4
DEBORAH DR	POM	POM		90	F5
DEBORAH ST	LB	LB15	5500	76	D1
DEBORAH KAY LN	CO	LPUE	2200	85	D2
DEBRA AV	LA	SF	11400	2	A6
DEBRA AV	LA	SF	8700	8	A3
DEBRA DR	LAV	LAV		95A	D5
DEBRA LN	CER	ART	16000	66	E4
DEBRA ANN PL	PALM	PALM		172	H9
DEBS AV	LA	CAN	6500	5	E5
DEBS AV	LA	WOH	6100	5	E5
DEBSTONE AV	LA	VAN	3700	22	F5
DE BUTTS TER	CO	MAL	5500	112	D5
DE CAMP DR	LA	BH	1700	32	E3
DECATUR CIR	CLA	CLA		91	D1
DECATUR ST	LA	LA21	700	44	E5
DECCA ST	LB	LB08	8300	81	C5
DECELIS PL	LA	ENC	4600	21	F3
DECELIS PL	LA	SF	11400	1	F6
DECELIS PL	LA	SF	11400	7	F1
DECELIS PL	LA	SF	8300	14	F1
DECELIS PL	LA	VAN	6500	14	F4
DECENTE CT	LA	NHO	11400	23	D5
DECENTE DR	LA	NHO	11400	23	D5
DECI	LA	SF	15200	2	C1
DECIMA DR	CO	LPUE	3000	85	D4
DECK ST	LA	SP	100	79	B2
DECKER LN	POM	POM	100	94	E4
DECKER RD	CO	MAL	1900	105	A6
DECKER RD	CO	MAL	2600	110	F2
DECKER-EDISN RD	CO	MAL	3700	110	F2
DECKER SCHL LN	CO	MAL		105	A5
DECKER SCHL RD	CO	MAL		104	E6
DECLARATION AV	CO	WOH		13	A4
DECLIFF DR	WHI	WHI	13600	55	F4
DECORAH RD	DBAR	POM		94	A5
DECORO DR	SCLR	SAU	22500	124	C6
DECOSTA AV	CO	WHI	8300	55	B6
DECOSTA AV	CO	WHI	8800	61	B1
DECOSTA AV	SFS	SFS	8800	61	B1
DEDHAM PL	CO	LPUE		98	A5
DEE AV	ELM	ELM	2800	47	E2
DEE LN	WCOV	WCOV		92	E6
DEE ST	CO	GAR	14700	64	B3
DEEBLE AV	SOG	SOG	8100	59	A3
DEEBOYAR AV	LKD	LKD	4100	70	E3
DEED AV	CO	CAST		123	A2
DEEGAN PL	MB	MB		62	B3
DEELANE PL	TOR	TOR		67	F2
DEELANE ST	TOR	TOR	4600	67	F2
DEELANE ST	TOR	TOR	4500	68	A2
DEEPBROOK DR	RPV	PVP	5500	72	F4
DEEP CANYON DR	LA	BH	2900	22	F6
DEEP CANYON DR	LA	BH	2600	32	F1
DEEP CANYON PL	LA	BH		32	F1
DEEP CANYON RD	LHH	LAH	2000	98A	A1
DEEPCLIFF TR	CO	TOP		109	B2
DEEP CREEK DR	SCLR	CYN	28400	125	C8
DEEP CREEK RD	WAL	WAL		93	D5
DEEP DELL PL	LA	LA68	6300	34	C1
DEEPFORK TR	CO	TOP		109	B2
DEEP GROVE AV	CO	LPUE	2200	98	D4
DEEP HILL RD	DBAR	POM		93	F5
DEEPLAKE AV E	CO	LAN	16100	174	J5
DEEPLAWN DR	DBAR	POM		97	E2
DEEPMEAD AV	CO	LPUE	100	98	E1
DEEPRIVER DR	CO	LPUE		48	B4
DEEP SHADOW DR	AGH	AGO		102	F3
DEEP SPRINGS DR	CLA	CLA		96	D5
DEEPSPRINGS DR	DBAR	POM		94	B6

INDEX

1990 LOS ANGELES COUNTY STREET INDEX

237

DEEPSPRINGS DR — DESERTA DR

LOS ANGELES CO.

INDEX

STREET	CITY	P.O. ZONE	BLOCK	PAGE	GRID
DEEPSPRINGS DR	DBAR	POM		97A	B1
DEEPTREE AV	SCLR	CYN	27500	124	H8
DEEP VALLEY DR	RHE	PVP	500	72	E5
DEEPVIEW DR	COV	COV		89	A5
DEEPVIEW LN	CO	COV	19800	89	A5
DEEPWATER AV	LA	WIL	1400	74	C3
DEEPWELL RD	HH	CAL	24300	100	D1
DEER AV	LA	VAN	3900	22	F5
DEERBANK DR	CO	PALM		157	G9
DEERBROOK LN	LA	LA49	12300	32	A6
DEER BROOK ST	POM	POM		90	E3
DEER CREEK DR	WAL	WAL		93	A4
DEER CREEK LN	CO	CYN	28400	128	E3
DEER CREEK LN	GLEN	GL08		18	D4
DEER CREEK RD	POM	POM		94	D5
DEER CREEK RD	SAD	SAD		90	A1
DEER CREEK RD	SAD	SAD		95A	A6
DEER CREEK RD	WAL	WAL		93	A4
DEER CROSSNG DR	DBAR	POM		97A	A3
DEERFIELD AV	BLF	BLF		66	B5
DEERFIELD AV	CO	SGAB	6200	37	F2
DEERFIELD DR	WAL	WAL		93	C6
DEERFIELD LN	LA	NOR		7	A3
DEERFIELD PL	DBAR	POM		97A	B3
DEERFLATS DR	SAD	LAV	800	95A	B6
DEERFOOT DR	DBAR	POM		97	E3
DEERFORD ST	LKD	LKD	2400	70	F3
DEERFORD ST	LKD	LKD	5900	71	D3
DEERGLEN RD	CO	SAU		181	E9
DEERHAVEN DR	CO	LPUE	1500	85	D2
DEERHEAD RD	CO	MAL	5800	111	F5
DEERHILL DR	RHE	PVP	2500	73	C5
DEERHILL TR	CO	TOP	1600	109	D1
DEERHORN DR	LA	VAN		22	C4
DEERHORN RD	LA	VAN	15400	22	C4
DEERING AV	LA	CAN	7000	12	C2
DEERING AV	LA	CHA	9100	6	C4
DEERING CT	LA	CAN	7900	12	C2
DEERLANE DR	DUA	DUA	2800	86	A4
DEERLICK DR	LA	CAN	23900	5	E1
DEERMONT RD	GLEN	GL07	1700	25	C1
DEERPARK CT	WLVL	THO		102	B4
DEERPASS RD	GLEN	GL08	3600	18	D2
DEERPATH LN	CO	MAL	21500	114	E4
DEERPATH PL	POM	POM		94	E6
DEERPATH PL	POM	POM		97A	C1
DEERPEAK DR	CO	LPUE		85	E3
DEER RUN RD	CO	PALM	38800	171	J7
DEER SKIN LN	WAL	WAL		93	B5
DEER SPRING LN	DBAR	POM		97A	A2
DEER TRAIL CT	CO	CAL		100A	E5
DEER TRAIL DR	CO	LPUE		98	A4
DEERVALE DR	LA	VAN	3700	22	D4
DEERVALE PL	LA	VAN	14500	22	D5
DEERVIEW CT	AGH	AGO		102	F2
DEER VIEW CT	LA	ENC		21	C4
DEERVIEW ST	GLDR	GLDR	1700	87	D6
DEERWALK DR	CO	PALM		157	G8
DEERWEED TR	CO	CAL		100A	E5
DEERWOOD TR	LA	TU	6200	11	B3
DEESWOOD DR	CO	LH		157	A6
DEFENDER DR	AGH	AGO		100A	D5
DEFIANCE AV	CO	LA59	12200	58	D6
DEFIANCE AV	LA	LA02	9500	58	D3
DE FOE AV	LA	PAC	11100	9	B1
DE FOE AV	LA	SF	12760	2	E4
DE FOE AV	SF	SF	900	2	F5
DE FOREST AV	LB	LB05	5900	65	C6
DE FOREST AV	LB	LB05	5100	70	B2
DE FOREST AV	LB	LB06	1900	75	B2
DE FOREST AV	LB	LB13	800	75	B4
DEFOREST ST	LA	WOH	20500	13	D2
DE GARMO AV	ELM	ELM	3800	38	D5
DE GARMO AV	LA	PAC	11600	3	A6
DE GARMO AV	LA	PAC	10300	9	C3
DE GARMO AV	LA	SF	12600	2	E4
DE GARMO AV	LA	SF		3	A6
DE GARMO AV	LA	SV	9000	9	E5
DE GARMO AV	LA	SV	7900	16	F1
DE GARMO DR	CO	LA63	1000	45	C3
DE GARMO ST	SF	SF	700	2	F5
DEGAS AV	TEC	TEC	5200	38	D3
DEGAS PL	CER	ART	11800	81	A1
DEGNAN BLVD	LA	LA08	3800	51	C2
DEGNAN BLVD	LA	LA18	3600	43	C6
DEGOVIA AV	LA	WOH	4600	13	A3
DEGRASSE DR	CO	WOH		13	B4
DE GROOT PL	CER	ART	17000	82	C5
DE HAVEN AV	LA	PAC	10700	9	B2
DE HAVEN ST	SF	SF	700	2	F5
DE HAVILAND AV	LA	LA45	8800	56	C2
DEHN AV	ING	IN03	11400	57	C5
DEHOUGNE ST	LA	NHO	11600	16	C4
DEITZ DR	CO	SAU		181	D9
DEJAY ST	LAN	LAN		159	H6
DE KALB DR	CO	CAL		13	A4

STREET	CITY	P.O. ZONE	BLOCK	PAGE	GRID
DE KALB DR	CO	WOH	22300	13	B4
DE KALB ST	VER	LA58	4800	53	B3
DEKOVEN RD	CO	PALM		183	E5
DELA ST	CO	WHI		47	E5
DE LACEY AV N	PAS	PAS	100	26	F4
DE LACEY AV S	PAS	PAS	100	26	F4
DELACOUR DR	CO	PALM	38100	172	B9
DELACROIX RD	RPV	PVP	4900	72	E5
DE LA CUMBRE PL	LA	VAN	3500	22	D5
DELAFIELD AV	HAW	HAW	13200	62	E1
DE LA FUENTE ST	MPK	MPK	300	46	B3
DE LA GUERRA ST	LA	WOH	20700	13	D2
DE LA LUZ AV	LA	WOH	21800	13	C3
DELAMARE DR	CO	LPUE	19500	47	F4
DELAMERE DR	CO	LPUE	1500	97	A3
DEL AMO BLVD	CER	ART	11000	71	E3
DEL AMO BLVD	CER	ART	11800	81	A3
DEL AMO BLVD	LKD	LKD	2400	70	F2
DEL AMO BLVD	LKD	LKD	3300	71	E3
DEL AMO BLVD	LKD	LKD	11600	81	B3
DEL AMO BLVD E	CAR	CAR	1400	69	E3
DEL AMO BLVD E	CAR	GAR	500	69	E3
DEL AMO BLVD E	CAR	LB10	2600	70	A2
DEL AMO BLVD E	CO	COM	1900	69	E3
DEL AMO BLVD E	LB	LB05	100	70	A2
DEL AMO BLVD E	LB	LB07	600	70	E2
DEL AMO BLVD W	CAR	CAR	100	69	A3
DEL AMO BLVD W	CO	TOR	600	68	F3
DEL AMO BLVD W	LB	LB05	100	70	A2
DEL AMO BLVD W	TOR	TOR	3900	67	E2
DEL AMO BLVD W	TOR	TOR	1700	68	C2
DEL AMO CIR E	TOR	TOR	21400	68	A5
DEL AMO CIR N	TOR	TOR	3300	68	A4
DEL AMO CIR W	TOR	TOR	21400	68	A4
DEL AMO ST	RB	RB	1000	67	D2
DEL AMO WDS DR	CO	HAC	23500	73	F1
DELANCEY AV	SAD	SAD	400	90	A2
DELAND AV	PR	PR	4100	55	A2
DELANO ST	LA	ENC	17600	14	D5
DELANO ST	LA	NHO	10600	16	D5
DELANO ST	LA	RES	17700	14	D5
DELANO ST	LA	VAN	13500	15	F5
DELANO ST	LA	VAN	13000	16	A5
DELANO ST	LA	WOH	19700	12	F5
DELANY CT	CO	LPUE		48	C3
DELANY ST	POM	POM	1400	95	A1
DE LA OSA ST	LA	WOH	21200	13	B2
DE LA PALIZADA	WAL	WAL		97	A2
DELAPLANE RD	CO	MAL		112	D6
DEL ARROYO DR	LA	SV	9100	10	A5
DELASONDE DR	RPV	SP	1800	73	D6
DE LA TORRE WY	LA	LA23	1300	53	B1
DELAVAN AV	NWK	NWK	13500	82	B1
DELAWARE AV	LA	LA41	5100	25	F5
DELAWARE AV	SM	SM	1400	41	C5
DELAWARE DR	CLA	CLA	600	91	B2
DELAWARE DR	PALM	PALM		183	D2
DELAWARE RD	BUR	BUR	200	17	D4
DE LAY AV	CO	COV	3400	89	A6
DE LAY AV	CO	GLDR	5700	89	A1
DE LAY AV	GLDR	GLDR		89	A2
DE LAY AV N	COV	COV	100	89	A5
DE LAY AV S	COV	COV	600	89	A6
DELAY DR	LA	LA65	2900	35	D1
DELBANA AV	CO	PEAR	32400	192	C2
DEL BAY ST	LKD	LKD	2000	70	E2
DEL BONITA ST	CO	LPUE	18400	98	E5
DEL CAMPO PL	LA	WOH	20300	13	E2
DEL CERRO AV	WCOV	WCOV	2000	92	D2
DEL CERRO CIR	LA	CAN	23600	5	E3
DEL CERRO DR	WCOV	WCOV	800	92	D2
DELCO AV	ELM	ELM	2600	47	D2
DELCO AV	LA	CAN	6600	12	E4
DELCO AV	LA	CHA	9500	6	E3
DELCO AV	LA	WOH	5800	12	E6
DELCO AV	LA	WOH	5800	13	E1
DELCO AV	SELM	ELM	1800	47	D3
DELCO PL	LA	CAN		12	E3
DELCOMBRE AV	PAR	PAR	15500	65	D3
DEL COURT PL	GLEN	GL06	400	26	A3
DELDEN RD	CO	NEW	20000	127	G4
DE LEON ST	LB	LB15	6400	76	E4
DELEVAN DR	LA	LA65	2600	25	F6
DELFERN DR	LA	LA77	100	32	F5
DELFINO ST	LA	TU	6200	11	B4
DELFORD AV	CAR	CAR	22600	69	A5
DELFORD AV	CAR	CAR	22600	69	A5
DELFORD AV	CAR	CAR	23800	74	A1
DELFORD AV	DUA	DUA	1500	29	C6
DELFS LN	CO	WAL		97	B5
DELGADO CT	LAN	LAN		160	F6
DEL GADO DR	LA	VAN	15000	22	B4
DEL GADO PL	LA	VAN	15500	22	B4
DELGANY AV	LA	VEN	8100	55A	E2
DELHAVEN AV	WCOV	WCOV	1000	48	F3
DELHAVEN ST	WCOV	WCOV	1700	48	E2

STREET	CITY	P.O. ZONE	BLOCK	PAGE	GRID
DELHI CT	LAM	LAM	15700	83	B3
DEL HOLLOW ST	LKD	LKD	2000	70	E2
DELIA AV	LA	SV	7500	17	A3
DELIA AV	TOR	TOR	16400	63	C5
DELIBAN AV	LA	TU	10700	10	F2
DELICIA	LA	SP		78	C4
DELIGHT ST	SCLR	CYN	18500	124	G8
DELIGHT ST	SCLR	CYN		125	A7
DELINDA LN	LCF	LCF	900	19	B2
DELISLE CT	GLEN	GL08	2200	18	F5
DELITA DR	LA	WOH	20100	13	E2
DELITA PL	LA	WOH	5000	13	E2
DELL AV	BLF	BLF	14400	66	B2
DELL AV	CO	MDR	2000	49	C5
DELL DR	MPK	MPK	1200	46	A3
DELL ST	LAN	LAN		160	F4
DELLA DR	BH	BH		33	A4
DELLMONT DR	LA	TU	11400	10	F1
DELL OAK DR	LA	LA28	5500	34	D1
DEL LOMA AV	CO	SGAB		37	F2
DEL LOMA AV	SGAB	SGAB		37	F3
DELLROSE AV	CO	RM	7800	46	E3
DELLVALE PL	LA	ENC	3600	21	F5
DELLWOOD LN	LA	LA77	1800	32	E2
DEL MAR AV	CO	RM	1600	46	E3
DEL MAR AV	LA	LA29	3900	35	A4
DEL MAR AV	LB	LB07	2800	70	B4
DEL MAR AV	RM	RM	2400	46	E2
DEL MAR AV	SMAR	PAS	1400	37	E2
DEL MAR AV N	SGAB	SGAB	100	37	E2
DEL MAR AV S	SGAB	SGAB	100	37	E4
DEL MAR BLVD	CO	PAS	3300	28	A4
DEL MAR BLVD E	PAS	PAS	100	27	A4
DEL MAR BLVD W	PAS	PAS	100	26	F4
DEL MAR CIR	LAV	LAV		90	D1
DEL MAR CT	COM	COM	800	65	A2
DEL MAR DR	PR	PR		47	B6
DEL MAR DR	PR	PR		55	B1
DEL MAR RD	CO	MONT	2200	18	F2
DEL MARINO	LAV	LAV		95A	D4
DEL MARINO PL	SGAB	SGAB	100	37	E3
DELMAS TER	CUL	CUL	3800	42	C6
DELMAS TER	LA	LA34	3700	42	C6
DELMESA AV	CO	LPUE		85	E3
DELMONICO AV	LA	CAN	8600	6	B6
DELMONT PL	LAM	LAM	15000	84	A5
DEL MONTE DR	SCLR	VAL		124	A9
DEL MONTE DR	CO	VAL		126	J1
DEL MONTE DR	GLEN	GL07	1400	25	E2
DEL MONTE DR	LA	LA26	3000	35	B5
DEL MONTE RD	LCF	LCF	4800	19	D3
DEL MONTE ST	PAS	PAS	200	26	E1
DEL MORENO DR	LA	WOH	4600	13	E2
DEL MORENO PL	LA	WOH	4700	13	E2
DELNICE AV	ELM	ELM	2200	47	E3
DEL NORDE AV	POM	POM	1000	91	A5
DEL NORTE ST	LA	LA65	400	36	A4
DEL NORTE ST	WCOV	WCOV	1500	88	A6
DE LONG ST	LA	LA15	1300	44	B4
DE LONGPRE AV	LA	LA27	7500	34	F3
DE LONGPRE AV	LA	LA27	3800	35	A3
DE LONGPRE AV	LA	LA28	5500	34	D3
DE LONGPRE AV	LA	LA46	7500	33	F3
DE LONGPRE AV	LA	LA46	7100	34	A3
DE LONGPRE AV	WHOL	LA69	8300	33	E4
DELOR DR	LA	LA32	2900	36	E5
DELOR RD	LA	LA65	2700	25	F5
DELORAINE DR	WAL	WAL	20500	93	C6
DELORAS DR	CAR	CAR	700	74	C1
DELORES ST	WCOV	WCOV		92	E6
DEL ORO DR	LCF	LCF	1600	19	A1
DELOS DR	TOR	TOR	26100	73	C4
DELOUISE AV	CER	ART	18300	66	E6
DELOZ AV	LA	LA27	1700	35	A3
DEL PASO AV	LA	LA32	1800	45	D1
DEL PASO CT	LA	LA32	4700	45	D1
DELPHI ST	LA	LA42	6000	26	C6
DELPHINE DR	WAL	WAL		93	C6
DELPHINIUM AV	CO	CYN		125	F6
DEL PINO DR	CO	RM	8400	46	F3
DEL PRADO	POM	POM		90	C6
DEL PRADO DR	CO	LPUE	15300	85	C3
DELRESTO DR	LA	BH	1200	32	F4
DEL REY	POM	POM		90	B6
DEL REY AV	LA	VEN	4000	49	E4
DEL REY AV	PAS	PAS	200	27	B3
DEL REY BLVD	LA	LA66		50	A4
DEL REY CT	LB	LB02	100	75	C5
DEL REY CT	LB	LB13	700	75	C5
DEL REY DR	GLEN	GL07	900	25	D2
DEL RIO AV	LA	LA65	1000	35	F3
DEL RIO AV	SGAB	SGAB	800	37	F3
DEL RIO PL	CER	ART	18700	71	E1
DEL RIO PL	LA	SF	11900	1	F5
DELROSA DR	LA	LA41	2000	26	A5
DEL ROSA DR	PAS	PAS	100	26	E4

STREET	CITY	P.O. ZONE	BLOCK	PAGE	GRID
DEL ROSA PL	PAS	PAS	400	26	E4
DEL ROSA PL	POM	POM	500	94	C2
DEL SOL LN	DBAR	POM	100	94	A5
DEL SUR ST	LA	PAC	13700	8	E1
DEL SUR ST	LA	SF	13400	2	F6
DEL SUR ST	LA	SF	12900	3	A5
DELTA AV	CO	RM	1200	46	F4
DELTA AV	CO	SGAB	5300	37	F3
DELTA AV	LB	LB05	6600	65	B5
DELTA AV	LB	LB10	3000	70	A6
DELTA AV	LB	LB10	2000	75	A2
DELTA AV	RM	RM	3400	37	F6
DELTA AV	RM	RM	1700	46	F2
DELTA AV	SGAB	SGAB	1400	37	F5
DELTA DR	DBAR	POM		97A	B3
DELTA LN	ARC	ARC	100	38	D2
DELTA PL	CLA	CLA	800	91	A3
DELTA PL	RM	RM	3200	46	F1
DELTA ST	CO	RM		46	F4
DELTA ST	LA	LA26	1600	35	C5
DELUNA DR	RPV	PVP	3000	78	C3
DELVALE ST	CO	LPUE	14900	48	F3
DELVALE ST	WCOV	WCOV	1500	48	E3
DEL VALLE AV	CO	LPUE	1200	92	A4
DEL VALLE AV	GLEN	GL08	1600	18	E5
DEL VALLE AV	LPUE	LPUE	400	92	A6
DEL VALLE DR	LA	LA48	6100	42	F2
DEL VALLE RD	CO	SAU	28900	123	A5
DEL VALLE ST	LA	WOH	22000	13	A2
DEL VINA ST	PAS	PAS	2700	27	F3
DEL VISTA DR	CO	LPUE	2600	85	D4
DEL VISTA DR	LAM	LAM	11900	84	B6
DEL ZURO DR	LA	LA46	7400	33	F1
DEMANDA RD	LAM	LAM	14600	82	F2
DEMARET PL	LA	SF	16600	1	F5
DEMBLON ST	BAP	BAP	13300	39	C4
DEMETER AV	CER	ART	19100	81	A2
DE MILLE DR	LA	LA27	1900	34	E2
DE MINA ST	LA	WOH	20900	13	D2
DEMING AV	DOW	DOW	11700	60	C5
DEMING AV	DOW	DOW	12800	66	A1
DEMPSEY AV	LA	ENC	4400	22	B3
DEMPSEY AV	LA	SF	11300	2	B6
DEMPSEY AV	LA	SF	8500	8	B5
DEMPSEY AV	LA	SF	8300	15	B1
DEMPSEY AV	LA	VAN	6400	15	B5
DEMPSTER AV	DOW	DOW	13300	66	A1
DENA ST	ART	ART	18300	66	F6
DENA ST	CO	PALM		172	F7
DENAIR ST	LA	LA49	11300	41	C1
DENAIR ST	PAS	PAS	3600	28	B1
DENBIGH DR	LA	BH		22	F6
DENBO ST	PAR	PAR	8000	65	F1
DENBY AV	LA	LA39	2700	35	D3
DE NEVE DR	LA	LA24		32	D6
DE NEVE LN	LA	LA33	1300	45	C2
DE NEVE SQ	LA	LA77		32	F5
DENFIELD ST	LAN	LAN	42400	159	D7
DENHAM DR	PALM	PALM		171	C5
DENHOLM DR	ELM	ELM	12000	47	F2
DENHAM DR	PALM	PALM		171	F4
DENICE PL	SCLR	NEW		127	A4
DENISE CT	LAN	LAN		159	F5
DENISE LN	LA	CAN	8300	5	F1
DENISE ST	CO	PALM		183	A1
DENISON AV	LA	SP	2400	78	F6
DENISON ST	CO	LA22	6000	54	A1
DENISON ST	CO	LA23	3900	45	C6
DENISON ST	POM	POM	1700	94	B3
DENIVELLE CT	LA	TU		10	E1
DENIVELLE PL	LA	TU	11200	10	E1
DENIVELLE RD	LA	SUN	8000	10	E1
DENIVELLE RD	LA	TU	7700	10	E1
DENKER AV	CO	LA47	10000	57	E4
DENKER AV	GAR	GAR	14300	63	E3
DENKER AV	LA	GAR	18200	63	E6
DENKER AV	LA	GAR	18300	68	E1
DENKER AV	LA	LA18	3400	43	E6
DENKER AV	LA	LA18	3700	51	E3
DENKER AV	LA	LA47	5800	51	E6
DENKER AV	LA	LA47	7900	57	E4
DENKER AV	LA	LA62	3800	51	E3
DENKER AV	LA	TOR	20300	68	E5
DENLEY ST	CO	LPUE	14400	48	B6
DENLEY ST	CO	LPUE	15000	85	D1
DENMAN AV	CMRC	LA40	1500	54	B2
DENMEAD ST	LKD	LKD	2000	70	E2
DENMEAD ST	LKD	LKD	5800	71	D2
DENMORE AV	LAN	LAN	44200	160	D5
DENNI ST E	LA	WIL	100	74	D3
DENNI ST W	LA	WIL	100	74	B4
DENNING AV	DUA	DUA	1500	29	D5
DENNIS AV	CMRC	LA40	2300	53	D2
DENNIS AV	WCOV	WCOV		88	A6
DENNIS DR	RM	RM	8700	47	A1
DENNIS LN	LA	CAN	7200	5	E3

STREET	CITY	P.O. ZONE	BLOCK	PAGE	GRID
DENNIS RD	TOR	TOR	23000	67	F5
DENNIS WY	CO	CAN		4	C5
DENNISON AV	LA	SP		79	A5
DENNY AV	LA	NHO	5600	16	F5
DENNY AV	LA	NHO	4000	23	F1
DENNY AV	LA	SV	7300	16	F3
DENNY RD	TOR	TOR	24700	73	B3
DE NOVA ST	LCF	LCF	500	19	C3
DENOYA DR	SCLR	SAU	27300	124	C5
DENROCK AV	LA	LA45	7400	50	B6
DENROCK AV	LA	LA45	8000	56	B1
DENSLOW AV	LA	LA49	100	32	D6
DENSLOW AV	LA	LA49	400	41	D1
DENSMORE AV	LA	ENC	4300	22	B3
DENSMORE AV	LA	SF	8800	8	B3
DENSMORE AV	LA	SF	8300	15	B1
DENSMORE AV	LA	VAN	6400	15	B3
DENSMORE ST	POM	POM	800	91	B6
DENSMORE ST	POM	POM	800	95	B1
DENTON AV	LA	SF	12800	2	E4
DENTON AV	RM	RM	3000	46	E2
DENTON AV	SGAB	SGAB	1900	37	E6
DENVER AV	CLA	CLA	1600	91	C2
DENVER AV	LA	GAR	14300	64	A2
DENVER AV	LA	LA44	5800	52	A5
DENVER AV	LA	LA44	8600	58	A5
DENVER AV	LB	LB10		70	A5
DENVER CT	PALM	PALM		183	J1
DENVER ST	PAR	PAR	7800	65	E1
DENVER SPGS DR	WLVL	THO		102A	D6
DENVIEW DR	CO	PALM		157	F8
DENWALL DR	CAR	CAR	700	69	C2
DEODAR	LA	SF42		2	C1
DEODAR AV	WCOV	WCOV	2100	92	D1
DEODAR CIR	PAS	PAS	2500	27	E3
DEODAR CIR	SMAD	SMAD		28	B1
DEODAR LN	BRAD	DUA	1000	29	C3
DEODAR LN	BRAD	DUA	100	29	D3
DEODAR LN	MON	MON	1000	29	C3
DEODAR PL	CO	SAU		124	C2
DEODAR RD	POM	POM	2300	90	F4
DEODARA DR	CO	ALT	600	20	B5
DEODAR WEST	BRAD	DUA		29	C3
DEODORA AV	CO	COM		64	C3
DEOLINDA DR	CO	LPUE	2900	85	E4
DEON PL	LA	SF	12700	1	E4
DE ORA WY	LB	LB15	4300	76	A2
DE ORO CIR	CER	ART	17800	82	E5
DE ORO CT	CER	ART	17400	82	E5
DE ORO LN	LAW	LAW		63	A2
DE ORO PL	CER	ART	17600	82	E5
DE PALMA ST	DOW	DOW	7000	59	F3
DE PALMA ST	DOW	DOW	7700	60	A4
DE PALMA ST	SOG	SOG	6000	59	F3
DE PALMA WY	MTB	MTB	700	46	E6
DE PAUL RD	CLA	CLA	300	91	B5
DE PAUW AV	CLA	CLA	2000	91	C2
DE PAUW ST	LA	PP	15200	40	D4
DEQUINCY CT	LA	CAN		5	E2
DEQUINE AV	RM	RM	2700	46	D2
DERBY CIR	LAV	LAV		90	C1
DERBY CT	PALM	PALM		171	J6
DERBY LN	LAM	LAM	15400	84	B6
DERBY PL	SCLR	SAU		127	C1
DERBY PL	LA	LA65	4400	25	E5
DERBY RD	SAD	SAD		89	E3
DERBYSHIRE LN	CER	ART	18300	81	C2
DEREK CT	WCOV	WCOV		92	B4
DEREK DR	ARC	ARC		28	F6
DEREK DR	ARC	ARC		29	A6
DERIAN DR	SCLR	SAU	24300	127	C5
DERN AV N	COM	LA59	1900	64	C1
DE ROJA AV	LA	WOH	5300	13	C1
DERONDA DR	LA	LA68	3100	24	D6
DERRICK DR	CO	PALM	38400	174	B8
DERRINGER LN	DBAR	POM		97A	B4
DERRY AV	AGH	AGO		100A	B4
DERWENT AV	LA	NOR		1	B4
DERWENT PL	LA	NOR		1	B4
DERWIN DR	LAM	LAM	15000	83	A1
DERWOOD DR	LCF	LCF	2000	11	F5
DE SALES ST	SGAB	SGAB	500	37	D2
DE SANTIS AV	LA	SF		2	C4
DESCANSO AV	AVA	AVA	200	77	B5
DESCANSO DR	LA	LA26	3200	35	B5
DESCANSO DR	LCF	LCF	900	19	B3
DESCANSO PL	GLEN	GL08	2200	18	E6
DESCANSO ST	DOW	DOW	7400	59	F5
DESCANSO WY	TOR	TOR		63	D5
DESCENDING DR	CO	LPUE	2900	85	B3
DESERET DR	LA	WOH	4400	13	A2
DESERET DR	LA	WOH	4500	100	F3
DESERT AV	SCLR	NEW		127	E4
DESERT PL	CO	CAST		123	D4
DESERTA DR	CO	GLDR		89	D1

238

1990 LOS ANGELES COUNTY STREET INDEX

DESERT AIRE AV — DONNER PL

LOS ANGELES CO.

STREET	CITY	P.O. ZONE	BLOCK	PAGE	GRID
DESERT AIRE AV	PALM	PALM		172	J9
DESRT CALICO DR	LAN	LAN		160	A2
DESERT FLWR DR	PALM	PALM		172	A8
DESERT HZE RD E	CO	PALM	18800	175	D4
DESERT OAK DR	PALM	PALM		183	G3
DSRT POPPY RD E	CO	LAN	18900	175	D4
DESERT ROSE DR	CO	CAST		123	E3
DESERT SHADW RD	CO	CAST		123	A1
DESERT SPGS RD	CO	PALM		183	B5
DESERT VIEW DR	CO	PALM	38600	171	J8
DESERT VIEW DR	PALM	PALM	38500	171	J8
DESERT VIEW DR	PALM	PALM		172	A8
DESERT VISTA	CO	LAN		147	H6
DESERT VIS DR E	CO	LAN	18500	175	D4
DESERT WILLW DR	PALM	PALM		183	F3
DESERT WILLW LN	DBAR	POM		97	F2
DESERT WILLW LN	PALM	PALM		183	F1
DESFORD DR	LA	BH	2000	33	A2
DESFORD ST	CO	TOR	1100	68	F4
DESFORD ST E	CAR	CAR	300	69	B4
DESFORD ST W	CAR	CAR	100	69	A4
DESHIRE PL	CUL	CUL	10700	50	C3
DESIDIA ST	CO	LPUE	18200	98	D3
DESIRE AV	CO	LPUE	1700	98	E4
DESMAN RD	LAM	LAM	14800	83	A4
DES MOINES AV	LA	NOR	10400	7	A2
DESMOND ST	LA	PAC	13500	2	F6
DESMOND ST	LA	PAC	13200	3	A6
DESMOND ST	LA	PAC	13600	8	F1
DESMOND ESTS RD	LA	LA46	2600	34	A1
DE SOTO AV	LA	CAN	8500	6	D6
DE SOTO AV	LA	CAN	6200	12	D5
DE SOTO AV	LA	CHA	9100	6	D5
DE SOTO AV	LA	WOH	5600	12	D5
DE SOTO AV	LA	WOH	5300	13	D1
DE SOTO ST	LB	LB14	2700	75	F5
DESPLAIN PL	LA	CHA	10600	6	E2
DESSIE PL	POM	POM		94	D1
D ESTE DR	LA	PP	13500	40	F2
DESTINO CIR	CER	ART		66	E5
DESTINO LN	CER	ART	13000	82	D5
DESTINO PL	CER	ART	13000	82	C5
DESTINO ST	BLF	BLF	10200	66	D5
DESTINO ST	CER	ART	12400	82	B5
DESTOYA AV	CO	LPUE	1400	98	D3
DETER ST	CO	LAN		175	E4
DETOUR DR	LA	LA68	2400	34	D2
DETROIT ST N	LA	LA36	100	34	B6
DETROIT ST N	LA	LA46	700	34	B6
DETROIT ST N	WHOL	LA46	1100	34	B4
DETROIT ST S	LA	LA36	100	34	B6
DETROIT ST S	LA	LA36	200	43	A2
DEVANAH ST	BAP	BAP	15400	88	A3
DEVANAH ST	CO	COV	16500	88	B3
DEVANAH ST	COV	COV	500	88	D3
DEVENIR AV	DOW	DOW	8000	59	F6
DEVENIR AV	DOW	DOW	8100	60	A6
DEVENIR ST	DOW	DOW	7800	59	F6
DEVENIR ST	DOW	DOW	8300	60	A6
DEVENTER DR	CO	LAV	1500	90	C1
DEVERE CT	CO	LH		157	A6
DEVERON CT	SAD	SAD		89	D4
DEVERON DR	WHI	WHI	10300	55	C2
DEVERON PL	POM	POM	1200	95	B1
DEVERON RDG RD	LA	CAN	6900	5	E3
DEVERS ST	WCOV	WCOV	1200	48	F1
DEVILLE ST	PALM	PALM		184	B1
DE VILLE WY	CO	MAL	23900	113	F5
DEVILLO DR	CO	WHI	10200	61	E4
DVLS CY DM T TR	CO			N	E4
DEVILS CYN MTWY	CO	CHA		1A	A2
DEVILS PUNCHBWL	CO	VALY		192	E6
DEVIRIAN PL	CO	ALT	400	19	F4
DEVISTA DR	LA	LA46	7500	33	F1
DEVISTA PL	LA	LA46	2600	33	F1
DEVLIN AV	ART	ART	18500	81	A1
DEVLIN AV	ART	ART	17900	82	A6
DEVLIN AV	HG	LKD	21700	81	A5
DEVLIN AV	LKD	LKD	20300	81	A3
DEVLIN AV	NWK	NWK	14300	82	A3
DEVLIN DR	LA	LA69	1300	33	D4
DEVLIN PL	LA	LA69	8900	33	D4
DEVOL ST	LAN	LAN	44100	160	D5
DEVON AV	LA	LA24	700	41	F1
DEVON CT	GLDR	GLDR		86	E4
DEVON LN	CO	SAU		124	E4
DEVON PL	DBAR	POM		97A	B2
DEVON PL	LB	LB07	500	70	B4
DEVON RD	PAS	PAS	1600	19	D6
DEVONPORT LN	LA	LA77		32	B1
DEVONPORT RD	SMAR	PAS	2500	27	E5
DEVONSHIRE CT	SCLR	SAU		127	C1
DEVONSHIRE LN	CO	ALT	2500	20	B5
DEVONSHIRE LN	GLEN	GL06	400	26	B3
DEVONSHIRE ST	LA	CHA	19700	6	E3
DEVONSHIRE ST	LA	CHA	18900	7	B3
DEVONSHIRE ST	LA	NOR	17000	7	B3
DEVONSHIRE ST	LA	PAC	14200	8	D3
DEVONSHIRE ST	LA	SF	16600	7	B3
DEVONSHIRE ST	LA	SF	14300	8	B3
DEVONWOOD RD	CO	ALT	200	20	B3
DEVORE CT	AGH	AGO		100A	B3
DE VOSS AV	CER	ART	18700	81	C1
DEVYN LN	LAN	LAN		160	H6
DEWAP RD	LA	LA12	100	44	D2
DEWAR AV	CO	LA22	5200	46	A5
DEWAR AV	MTB	MTB	3200	46	B5
DEWDROP AV	SCLR	CYN	27300	124	H5
DEWERT RD	LB	LB22		71	F4
DEWEY AV	LA	LA06	900	43	F3
DEWEY AV	SGAB	SGAB	100	37	E5
DEWEY AV	TOR	TOR	21800	67	E4
DEWEY CIR	MTB	MTB	100	46	E6
DEWEY ST	LA	LA66	12000	49	D1
DEWEY ST	SM	SM	400	49	C2
DE WITT DR	LA	LA68	3200	24	B5
DE WOLFE RD	SCLR	NEW	24600	127	A4
DEXTER AL	PAS	PAS	1200	26	D1
DEXTER AV	ARC	ARC	1100	28	B3
DEXTER DR	SCLR	SAU		124	D4
DEXTER MTY	CO	SF		3	E5
DEXTER ST	BAP	BAP		39	F5
DEXTER ST	CO	COV	19500	89	A5
DEXTER ST	LA	LA42	900	36	B1
DEXTER ST E	COV	COV	100	88	E5
DEXTER ST E	COV	COV		89	B5
DEXTER ST W	COV	COV	100	88	E5
DIABLO CT	PALM	PALM		172	E6
DIABLO DR	CLA	CLA	600	91	B1
DIABLO PL	CO	SAU		123	E5
DIAL ST	LPUE	LPUE	300	98	A1
DIAMANTE DR	LA	ENC	16600	21	F4
DIAMANTE PL	LA	ENC	3700	21	F5
DIAMOND AV	SPAS	SPAS	900	36	F3
DIAMOND PL	WAL	WAL		92	F6
DIAMOND ST	ARC	ARC	1	28	E5
DIAMOND ST	LA	LA12	900	44	C2
DIAMOND ST	MON	MON	500	29	A5
DIAMOND ST	PALM	PALM		184	C1
DIAMOND ST	RB	RB	100	67	D3
DIAMOND BAR BL	DBAR	POM		93	F5
DIAMOND BAR BL	DBAR	POM		94	A5
DIAMOND BAR BL	DBAR	POM		97	E4
DIAMOND BAR BL	DBAR	POM		97A	A2
DIAMOND HEAD	SCLR	NEW		127	E5
DIAMOND HEAD LN	RPV	PVP	26800	72	E4
DIAMOND PT LN	LCF	LCF		19	D3
DIAMOND RDG RD	DBAR	POM		97	D5
DIAMONTE LN	RPV	SP	30300	78	C3
DIANA AV	POM	POM	100	94	F6
DIANA ST	LA	LA20	3200	43	F1
DIANA ST	PAS	PAS	2700	27	E4
DIANE AV	BLF	BLF		66	B4
DIANE DR	COM	COM	1600	65	B1
DIANE DR	LAV	LAV		95A	C5
DIANE PL	WCOV	WCOV	16400	92	B4
DIANE WY	LA	LA46	2000	33	D2
DIANE WY	MPK	MPK	100	46	C3
DIANE MARIE CIR	SCLR	SAU		124	E7
DIANORA DR	RPV	PVP	3100	78	C3
DIANRON RD	CO	PALM		171	J7
DIANRON RD	PALM	PALM		171	J7
DIANTHUS ST N	MB	MB	100	62	C5
DIANTHUS ST S	MB	MB	100	62	C5
DIAZ DR	SCLR	SAU	26500	124	D7
DIAZ ST	IRW	BAP		88	A2
DICE RD	SFS	SFS	8500	61	B2
DICHA	LA	SP		78	C4
DICKENS CT	CO	VAL		126	J3
DICKENS LN	LAV	LAV		90	B2
DICKENS ST	LA	ENC	15500	22	A3
DICKENS ST	LA	NHO	12900	23	A4
DICKENS ST	LA	TAR	19600	13	F1
DICKENS ST	LA	VAN	14100	22	C3
DICKERMAN PL	POM	POM	2200	94	F5
DICKERSON AV	CO	LA63	100	45	D5
DICKS ST	WHOL	LA69	8900	33	D5
DICKSON AV	CO	LA63	1200	45	C3
DICKSON CT	LA	LA24		32	E6
DICKSON CT	WAL	WAL		97	B1
DICKSON LN	LA	LA46		33	E2
DICKSON ST	LA	VEN	800	49	D4
DICKY ST	CO	WHI	10900	55	B5
DICKY ST	CO	WHI	13400	61	D2
DICKY ST	CO	WHI	14800	84	A4
DICKY ST	PR	PR	9400	55	A4
DICTURN ST	LA	LA65	2700	25	F6
DIEHL ST	WAL	WAL	20100	93	B6
DIGBY AV	POM	POM	800	91	A5
DIJON LN	PALM	PALM		171	G6
DIKE ST	GLDR	GLDR	800	88	F1
DIKE ST	GLDR	GLDR	19200	89	A1
DILL PL	LA	WOH	6100	5	E5
DILLARD AV	CLA	CLA	3600	96	B5
DILLER AV	CUL	CUL	5400	50	C4
DILLERDALE ST	CO	LPUE	14000	48	D2
DILLING ST	LA	NHO	11200	23	D4
DILLMAN ST	LKD	LKD	6500	71	E1
DILLON CT	LA	VEN	700	49	C3
DILLON ST N	LA	LA26	100	35	B4
DILLON ST N	LA	LA57		35	A6
DILLON ST S	LA	LA57	100	35	A6
DILLOW DR	CO	LPUE		98	B4
DILO ST	ELM	ELM		38	D5
DILWORTH ST	LAM	LAM	13800	82	E1
DILWORTH ST	NWK	NWK	12600	82	C1
DIMAS CT	AZU	AZU	1600	86	C3
DIMMICK AV	LA	VEN	200	49	B3
DIMMICK DR	LA	LA65	500	36	A2
DIMONDALE DR	CAR	CAR	800	69	D2
DINA PL	CER	ART	18800	81	C1
DINA PL	CER	ART	18300	82	C6
DINA PL	LA	CHA	19700	6	F3
DINARD AV	NWK	NWK	14300	82	D2
DINARD AV	SFS	SFS		82	D2
DINO CT	CO	CAL		100	D4
DINSDALE ST	DOW	DOW	7300	60	C2
DINWIDDIE ST	DOW	DOW	7000	59	F2
DINWIDDIE ST	DOW	DOW	7200	60	A2
DIONE WY	CO	LPUE	2600	98	E6
DISNEY AV	CO	WHI	8200	55	B6
DISNEY AV	NWK	NWK	14300	82	B3
DISS LN	CO	MAL	3700	112	E2
DISTRIBUTION WY	CER	ART	15900	82	E4
DISTRICT BLVD	CO	LA22	5900	53	D4
DISTRICT BLVD	CO	LA22	5100	53	C3
DISTRICT BLVD	VER	LA58	4200	53	B3
DITMAN AV N	CO	LA63	100	45	C5
DITMAN AV N	LA	LA32	2400	36	D6
DITMAN AV N	LA	LA32	1800	45	C1
DITMAN AV S	CO	LA23	1200	53	C1
DITMAN AV S	CO	LA63	100	45	C6
DITSON ST	LA	SUN	10300	9	F5
DITTMAR DR	WHI	WHI	13200	61	E2
DITTMAR DR	WHI	WHI	15200	84	B4
DIVAN PL	LA	NHO	12500	16	B2
DIVER ST	CO	CYN		128	C2
DIVERSEY DR	RPV	PVP	5400	72	E3
DIVIDE TR	LA	CAN		5	E1
DIVINA ST	LA	WOH	4300	13	D3
DIVINA VISTA ST	MPK	MPK	700	46	B3
DIVINE DR	MPK	MPK	2000	46	A4
DIVINO DR	CO	WAL		97	B3
DIVISION PL	LA	LA65	4100	35	F1
DIVISION ST	CO	LAN	46500	148	B9
DIVISION ST	CO	LAN	46000	160	B2
DIVISION ST	CO	PALM	38000	172	B9
DIVISION ST	LA	LA65	2800	35	E3
DIVISION ST	LAN	LAN	42100	160	B9
DIVISION ST	LAN	LAN	42000	172	B1
DIVISION ST	LB	LB03	4300	76	B6
DIVISION ST	LB	LB03		80	B1
DIVISION ST	PALM	PALM	38300	172	B9
DIVISION ST	PALM	PALM	37600	183	B1
DIVONNE DR	WAL	WAL	20500	93	C6
DIVOT DR	LAV	LAV		95A	D5
DIX ST	LA	LA68	6200	34	C2
DIXFORD LN	CO	LPUE	400	92	B5
DIXIE DR	PALM	PALM		183	B1
DIXIE DR	SAD	SAD	1100	90	A1
DIXIE CANYON AV	LA	VAN	3300	22	F4
DIXIE CANYON PL	LA	VAN	3500	23	A5
DIXON AV	ING	IN03	10100	57	C4
DIXON ST	AZU	AZU	100	88	D1
DIXON ST	COM	COM	300	58	F6
DIXON ST	GLEN	GL05	1400	25	E4
DIXON ST	RB	RB	1600	62	D5
DIXON TRAIL RD	HH	CAL		100	C2
DOAN DR	BUR	BUR	700	17	C6
DOANE AV	CLA	CLA	500	91	B5
DOBBIN LN	RHE	PVP	1	73	B4
DOBBINS DR	SGAB	SGAB	500	37	D2
DOBBINS PL	LA	LA49	13200	40	F3
DOBBS ST	LA	LA32	5400	36	E6
DOBINSON ST	CO	LA63	3900	45	D3
DOBINSON ST	LA	LA33	2600	45	B3
DOBINSON ST	LA	LA63	3100	45	C3
DOBKIN AV	LA	TAR	4900	21	C2
DOBLAS ST	CO	LAN		157	J2
DOBLE AV	CO	TOR	20800	68	F4
DOBLE AV	LA	HAC	25000	73	F2
DOBSON WY	CUL	CUL	5200	50	C3
DOCHAN CIR	MTB	MTB	100	46	E6
DOCK ST	LB	LB02		74	D6
DOCKWEILER DR	SCLR	NEW		127	E4
DOCKWEILER PL	LA	LA19	5300	43	A3
DOCKWEILER ST	LA	LA19	4500	43	B3
DODDS AV	CO	LA63	1200	45	C3
DODDS CIR	CO	LA63	1200	45	C3
DODGE AV	LA	HAC	25000	73	F3
DODGE CT	POM	POM	800	94	F6
DODGE WY	LB	LB03	2100	75	F6
DODRILL DR	CO	LPUE	15600	85	D3
DODSON AV	LA	SP	600	78	D4
DODSON ST	ELM	ELM	11000	47	E2
DODSWORTH AV	CO	COV	4900	89	A3
DODSWORTH AV	COV	COV	100	89	A5
DODSWORTH AV	GLDR	GLDR	800	89	A2
DOE ST	CO	PALM		183	E4
DOESKIN PL	DBAR	POM		94	B5
DOGWOOD	WCOV	WCOV		98	F1
DOGWOOD CT	CO	NEW		126	J5
DOGWOOD DR	LAV	LAV		90	B1
DOGWOOD PL	LA	LA42	1500	26	C6
DOGWOOD RD	CO	PALM		157	H9
DOHENY DR N	BH	BH	200	33	D6
DOHENY DR N	BH	BH	100	42	D2
DOHENY DR N	LA	LA48	100	33	D6
DOHENY DR N	WHOL	LA48	300	33	D6
DOHENY DR N	WHOL	LA69	600	33	D6
DOHENY DR S	BH	BH	100	42	D2
DOHENY DR S	LA	LA35	1100	42	D2
DOHENY DR S	LA	LA48	100	33	D6
DOHENY LN	CO	PALM		184	A2
DOHENY RD	BH	BH	300	33	B4
DOHENY RD	WHOL	LA69	9200	33	B4
DOHERTY AV	SCLR	CYN	27300	124	H8
DOIDGE CT	LB	LB13	1200	75	D4
DOLAN AV	DOW	DOW	9700	60	C2
DOLAN ST	DOW	DOW	10300	60	B4
DOLCEDO WY	LA	LA77	10500	32	D4
DOLE CT	DBAR	POM		94	B6
DOLE CT	DBAR	POM		97A	B1
DOLE PL	CO	PALM	38800	171	J7
DOLLAR ST	LKD	LKD	2400	70	F2
DOLLISON DR	DOW	DOW	11200	60	F4
DOLLISON DR	NWK	NWK	11800	60	F5
DOLLISON DR	NWK	NWK		61	A5
DOLLY AV	LAM	LAM	16500	83	B4
DOLLY MADISN LN	AGH	AGO		100A	C5
DOLO WAY	LA	LA77	700	32	D5
DOLONITA AV	CO	LPUE	3100	85	C4
DOLORES AV	SOG	SOG	9900	58	F3
DOLORES DR	CO	ALT	900	20	B4
DOLORES PZ	PVE	PVP	1800	72	B4
DOLORES RD	LA	SP	1100	78	E3
DOLORES ST	CAR	CAR	21000	69	B5
DOLORES ST	CAR	CAR	23500	74	B1
DOLORES ST	GLEN	GL04	1700	25	D6
DOLORES ST	LA	LA65	3000	35	D1
DOLORES ST	PAS	PAS	2100	27	D3
DOLORES ST E	LA	WIL	100	74	C2
DOLORES ST W	LA	WIL	1000	74	A3
DOLORITA AV	GLEN	GL08	1000	18	D3
DOLOROSA ST	LA	WOH	20600	13	D1
DOLOROSA ST	LA	WOH	23000	100	F1
DOLPHIN AV	LA	SP	2600	78	E5
DOLPHIN DR	LB	LB03		76	E6
DOLPHIN ST	LA	SP	1100	78	E3
DOLTON DR	SCLR	CYN	27400	124	H8
DOMAINE ST	RM	RM	8800	38	A4
DOMAL LN	LCF	LCF	3800	19	B5
DOMAN AV	LA	TAR	4900	21	C2
DOMART AV	NWK	NWK	12600	60	E6
DOMART AV	NWK	NWK	12800	66	E1
DOME TR	CO	TOP	21400	109	E4
DOMINGO DR	SGAB	SGAB	700	37	D2
DOMINGO RD	LA	WOH	22400	13	B2
DOMINGUEZ AV	LA	WIL	300	74	D5
DOMINGUEZ PL	AZU	AZU	200	86	D6
DOMINGUEZ ST	CAR	CAR	100	69	B3
DOMINGUEZ ST	CAR	LB10	1900	69	E3
DOMINGUEZ ST	CAR	LB10	2600	70	A3
DOMINGUEZ ST	TOR	TOR	2100	68	C3
DOMINGUEZ WY	TOR	TOR		68	C3
DOMNGUZ HLLS DR	CO	COM		69	E1
DOMNGUZ HLLS DR	COM	COM		64	E6
DOMINICA AV	LA	SF	11300	10	A1
DOMINION AV	CO	PAS	1300	27	D1
DOMINION AV	PAS	PAS	1100	27	D1
DOMINION CIR	CMRC	LA40		54	B5
DOMINION LN	LA	LA46	2500	33	E1
DOMINION WY	LA	LA46	8000	33	E1
DOMINO ST	LA	RES	18200	14	C5
DOMINO ST	LA	VAN	15100	15	C5
DOMINO HILL DR	CO	SAU		181	B8
DOMMER AV	WAL	WAL	100	93	B6
DOMO ST	CO	WHI	9900	55	C1
DON ST E	LA	WIL	100	74	C2
DON ST W	LA	WIL	1000	74	A2
DONA ALICIA PL	LA	NHO	11600	23	D5
DONA CECILIA DR	LA	NHO	11400	23	D6
DONA CHRSTNA PL	LA	NHO	3100	23	D6
DONA CLARA PL	LA	NHO	3100	23	E6
DONA CONCHTA PL	LA	NHO	3100	23	D6
DONA DOLORES PL	LA	NHO	11400	23	D5
DONA DOROTEA DR	LA	NHO	11300	23	D6
DONA ELENA PL	LA	NHO	3100	23	D6
DONA EMILIA DR	LA	NHO	2900	23	E6
DONA EVITA DR	LA	NHO	11400	23	D6
DONAHUE PL	ELM	ELM	12200	39	B5
DONAIRE WY	LA	PP	1100	40	B2
DONA ISABEL DR	LA	NHO	11200	23	E6
DON ALANIS PL	LA	LA08	4200	51	A2
DON ALBERTO PL	LA	LA08	4700	50	F3
DONALDALE ST	CO	LPUE	14000	48	D2
DONLD DGLS LP N	SM	SM		41	D6
DONLD DGLS LP N	SM	SM		49	D1
DONLD DGLS LP S	SM	SM		49	D1
DONALDO CT	SPAS	SPAS	1100	37	A2
DONALDSON ST	LA	LA26	1500	35	D4
DON ALEGRE PL	LA	LA08	4200	51	A2
DONA LISA DR	LA	NHO	11200	23	E5
DONA LOLA DR	LA	NHO	11200	23	D5
DONA LOLA PL	LA	NHO	3300	23	D5
DON ALVARADO DR	ARC	ARC	900	28	C3
DONA MARIA DR	LA	NHO	3100	23	D6
DONA MARTA DR	LA	NHO	3000	23	E6
DONA MEMA PL	LA	NHO	3100	23	D6
DONA NENITA PL	LA	NHO	3000	23	D6
DONA PEGITA DR	LA	NHO	11100	23	D5
DONA PEPITA PL	LA	NHO	11500	23	D6
DONA RAQUEL PL	LA	NHO	3200	23	D6
DON ARELLANS DR	LA	LA08	4200	51	A2
DONA ROSA DR	LA	NHO	3300	23	E5
DON ARTURO PL	LA	LA08	4500	51	A1
DONA SARITA PL	LA	NHO	3100	23	E6
DONA SOFIA DR	LA	NHO	3100	23	E6
DONA SUSANA DR	LA	NHO	2900	23	E6
DONATELLO ST	LAN	LAN	1200	160	D4
DONA TERESA DR	LA	NHO	11300	23	D6
DON BAPTISTA AV	CO	LPUE	300	98	E1
DON BENITO CT	PAS	PAS	3700	28	B1
DON CARLOS AV	GLEN	GL08	1600	18	E5
DON CARLOS DR	LA	LA08	4200	51	A2
DON COTA PL	LA	LA08	4400	51	A2
DONCREST ST S	MPK	MPK	1800	46	B4
DONCREST ST W	MPK	MPK	200	46	B4
DON DIABLO DR	ARC	ARC	900	28	C3
DON DIABLO DR	LA	LA08	3900	51	A2
DON DIEGO DR	LA	LA08	4500	51	A2
DON DOUGLAS DR	LB	LB08		71	A6
DONELLA CIR	LA	LA77	2300	32	C1
DONER DR	MTB	MTB	900	46	E6
DON FELIPE DR	LA	LA08	3700	51	A2
DON GEE CT	CO	SAU		124	E4
DONHILL DR	LA	BH	1400	33	A3
DONI RD	LA	SM		40	E5
DON IBARRA PL	LA	LA08	4000	51	A2
DONINGTON PL	LA	BH		22	F5
DONINGTON ST	CO	GLDR	18700	86	F4
DONINGTON ST	GLDR	GLDR	700	86	F5
DON JAY PL	CO	SGAB	7100	28	B6
DON JOSE DR	GLEN	GL07	900	25	E2
DON JOSE DR	LA	LA08	4100	51	A2
DON JUAN PL	LA	WOH	4800	13	E2
DON JULIAN RD	CO	LPUE	13100	48	B4
DON JULIAN RD	IND	LPUE	14400	48	B4
DON JULIAN RD	IND	LPUE	15500	85	E1
DON JULIO ST	LB	LB15	6400	76	E2
DONLEY ST	CO	LAV	700	90	B1
DON LORENZO DR	LA	LA08	4600	50	F3
DON LUIS DR	LA	LA08	4000	51	B2
DON MARIANO DR	LA	LA08	4100	51	B2
DONMAR RANCH RD	CO	CAL		114	B2
DONMETZ ST	LA	NOR	18100	7	C1
DONMETZ ST	LA	SF	16600	7	F1
DONMETZ ST	LA	SF	15400	8	C1
DON MIGUEL DR	LA	LA08	4400	51	A2
DON MILAGRO DR	LA	LA08	4400	51	A2
DONNA AV	CER	ART	19500	71	E2
DONNA AV	LA	RES	9300	7	B3
DONNA AV	LA	RES	6400	14	B4
DONNA AV	LA	TAR	5600	14	B6
DONNA AV	LA	TAR	5200	21	B2
DONNA CT	LA	RES	19000	14	B3
DONNA ST	LB	LB05		65	D4
DONNA WY	MTB	MTB	700	46	C6
DONNA ANTNIA AV	CO	LPUE	300	98	E1
DONNA BETH AV	CO	AZU	5200	88	D2
DONNA BETH AV	COV	COV	500	88	D4
DONNA BETH AV	WCOV	WCOV	600	92	D2
DONNAGLEN AV	SF	SF	1900	2	E4
DONNA MARIA LN	LCF	LCF		19	B1
DONNA YNEZ LN	LA	PP	16900	40	B3
DONNELLY AV	CO	SGAB	7100	28	A6
DONNER DR	WAL	WAL		92	F6
DONNER PL	CO	PALM		157	F8
DONNER PL	MPK	MPK	1200	46	A3

INDEX

STREET	CITY	P.O. ZONE	BLOCK	PAGE	GRID
DONNYBROOK CIR	CO	WHI	8300	55	A6
DONORA AV	TOR	TOR	19200	67	F2
DON ORTEGA PL	LA	LA08	4200	51	A2
DONOSA DR	CO	LPUE	1700	98	C5
DONOVAN ST	DOW	DOW	8200	60	A5
DON PABLO DR	ARC	ARC	1000	28	C3
DON PABLO PL	LA	LA08	4500	51	A2
DON PIO DR	LA	WOH	4500	13	C3
DON PORFIRIO PL	LA	LA08	4700	50	F2
DON QUIXOTE DR	LA	LA08	4500	51	A2
DON RICARDO	ARC	ARC	1000	28	B3
DON RICARDO DR	LA	LA08	4400	51	A1
DON ROBLES DR	ARC	ARC	900	28	C3
DON RUDOLFO PL	LA	LA08	4500	51	A2
DON TAPIA PL	LA	LA08	4200	51	A2
DON TIMOTEO DR	LA	LA08	4300	51	A2
DON TOMASO DR	LA	LA08	3800	51	A2
DON TONITO DR	LA	LA08	4300	51	A2
DON VALDES DR	LA	LA08	4500	51	A2
DONWAY DR	CO	WAL	20100	97	B4
DON ZAREMBO DR	LA	LA08	4500	51	A2
DOOLITTLE AV	ARC	ARC	2500	39	A2
DOOLITTLE AV	CO	ARC	2600	39	A2
DOOLITTLE DR	RB	RB	1100	62	E3
DORA ST	LA	SV	10500	9	F6
DORA ST	LA	SV	11200	16	E1
DORADO DR	SCLR	VAL		127	A2
DORADO DR	LA	ENC	16400	22	A4
DORADO DR	RPV	SP	1900	78	D1
DORADO PL	RHE	PVP	1	73	D4
DORAL	ELM	ELM		39	A6
DORAL	ELM	ELM		48	A1
DORAL AV	LA	NOR	11700	1	A5
DORAL PL	LA	NOR		1	A5
DORAL ST	LAV	LAV		90	C2
DORAMA AV	CO	ACT	32800	189	E1
DORAN PL	LA	NHO		16	B3
DORAN ST	SPAS	SPAS	1000	36	E2
DORAN ST E	GLEN	GL06	100	25	D3
DORAN ST W	GLEN	GL03	100	25	B3
DORA VERDUGO DR	GLEN	GL08		18	E4
DORCAS PL	LA	LA68	6100	24	D6
DORCHESTER AV	LA	LA32	2900	36	E5
DORCHESTER AV	SM	SM	1800	41	C5
DORE CIR	WCOV	WCOV		92	C4
DORE DR	CO	LPUE	2100	98	A3
DORE ST	WCOV	WCOV	16700	92	B4
DOREEN AV	ELM	ELM	4600	38	D4
DOREEN AV	ELM	ELM	2600	47	D2
DOREEN AV	SELM	ELM	2400	47	D3
DOREEN AV	TEC	TEC	4800	38	D3
DOREEN PL	LA	VEN	1000	49	D3
DOREMUS RD	PAS	PAS	1200	26	D6
DORER ST	PALM	PALM	37200	184	D1
DORESTA RD	SMAR	PAS	2700	37	B1
DORIA AV	LOM	LOM	25000	73	D2
DORIA CT	LOM	LOM	25000	73	D2
DORIAN ST	LA	SF	15200	2	C2
DORIC ST	LA	SF		1	D3
DORIE DR	LA	CAN		5	E3
DORILEE LN	LA	ENC	16200	22	A5
DORINA PL	LA	SF	12600	1	E4
DORION ST	DOW	DOW	8600	66	A2
DORIS ST	CO	SGAB	8200	37	F1
DORIS WY S	TOR	TOR	23000	67	E6
DORIS WY W	TOR	TOR	5200	67	E6
DORK ST	PR	PR	9300	55	B1
DORLAND PL	CO	WHI	6300	55	C4
DORLAND PL	WHI	WHI	5900	55	C4
DORLAND ST	WHI	WHI	10400	55	C4
DORLON DR	LA	TAR		21	A4
DORMAN AV	TOR	TOR	18200	63	D6
DORMIE PL	LA	ENC	16900	21	E3
DORMONT AV	TOR	TOR	24600	73	C2
DORNER DR	MPK	MPK		45	F4
DORNER DR	MPK	MPK		46	A4
DORNES ST	ART	ART	11600	82	A5
DORNIE ST	CO	GLDR	19300	87	A5
DORO PL	CO	TOP		100	F6
DOROTHEA RD	LHH	LAH	500	98A	A2
DOROTHY AV	SOG	SOG	8900	59	C4
DOROTHY DR	AGH	AGO		100A	B4
DOROTHY DR	CO	AGO		107	E5
DOROTHY DR	GLEN	GL02	1200	25	C2
DOROTHY RD	CO	TOP		100	F6
DOROTHY ST	SCLR	CYN		124	G6
DOROTHY ST	CO	GL14	2300	11	F5
DOROTHY ST	LA	LA49	11700	41	C3
DOROTHY ST	RM	RM	7800	46	E1
DOROTHY ST	WCOV	WCOV		92	E6
DORRINGTON AV	LA	PAC	8600	8	E5
DORRINGTON AV	LA	PAC	8600	15	F1
DORRINGTON AV	LA	VAN	8400	15	F1
DORRINGTON AV	WHOL	LA48	8700	33	D5
DORRINGTON PL	LA	PAC	9100	8	E5
DORRIS PL	LA	LA31	2200	35	E4

STREET	CITY	P.O. ZONE	BLOCK	PAGE	GRID
DORSET AV	POM	POM	800	95	A5
DORSET DR	TOR	TOR		68	C5
DORSET PL	LA	HAC	23100	68	E6
DORSET PL	LCF	LCF	300	19	D5
DORSEY ST	LA	LA11	4100	52	D2
DORSO RD	CO	ACT		182	C6
DORY CIR	CER	ART		66	E5
DOSHIER AV	ARC	ARC	100	28	E2
DOS PALOS DR	LA	LA68	3200	24	A6
DOS RIOS DR	LA	TU	7100	10	F2
DOS RIOS RD	DOW	DOW	6500	54	B6
DOS ROBLES PL	ALH	ALH	600	37	B3
DOSS CT	LA	SF		1	F3
DOSS TER	LA	TAR		21	A4
DOT ST	SCLR	SAU		124	F4
DOTHILL RD	DBAR	POM		97	E5
DOTY AV	CO	LAW	15100	63	B3
DOTY AV	HAW	HAW	11400	57	B6
DOTY AV	HAW	HAW	12800	63	B2
DOTY AV	ING	IN03	10000	57	B4
DOTY AV	TOR	TOR	17800	63	B6
DOTY AV	TOR	TOR	18400	68	B1
DOUBLE ST	CAR	CAR	300	69	B4
DOUBLE ST	TOR	TOR	1800	68	D4
DBL EE RANCH RD	LA	WOH		13	E4
DOUBLEGROVE ST	BAP	BAP	13200	39	C6
DOUBLEGROVE ST	BAP	BAP		48	D1
DOUBLEGROVE ST	CO	LPUE	15700	92	A3
DOUBLEGROVE ST	WCOV	BAP	14200	48	E2
DOUBLEGROVE ST	WCOV	WCOV	1800	48	E2
DOUBLEGROVE ST	WCOV	WCOV		92	C4
DOUBLETREE LN	CO	LPUE	2200	98	E5
DOUBLE TREE LN	LB	LB15		76	E5
DOUG RD	CO	CYN		125	E5
DOUGLAS AV	COM	COM	100	64	F2
DOUGLAS PL	LA	VEN	800	49	B3
DOUGLAS ST	ELM	ELM		38	E4
DOUGLAS ST	LA	LA26	500	35	D6
DOUGLAS ST	LA	LA26	100	44	C1
DOUGLAS ST	PAS	PAS	200	27	A2
DOUGLAS ST N	ELS	ELS		56	D6
DOUGLAS ST S	ELS	ELS		62	D1
DOUGLAS WK	CO	CAST	28900	123	C2
DOUGLAS WY	TOR	TOR		73	B2
DGLS, DNLD LP N	SM	SM		41	D6
DGLS, DNLD LP N	SM	SM		49	D1
DGLS, DNLD LP S	SM	SM		49	D1
DOUGLAS FIR RD	CO	CAL		100	E2
DOUGLASS DR	POM	POM		90	C6
DOVE	POM	POM		90	F2
DOVE CT	CO	PAS		27	F1
DOVE DR	LA	LA65	500	36	A3
DOVE PL	LA	CHA		6	D1
DOVECOTE LN	CAR	CAR		69	D6
DOVER AV	LAV	LAV	2000	90	D2
DOVER DR	PALM	PALM		171	J6
DOVER LN	ING	IN01		57	B2
DOVER PL	LA	LA39	3700	25	B6
DOVER PL	MB	MB		62	D3
DOVER PL	POM	POM	1700	95	A5
DOVER RD	COV	COV	500	88	D4
DOVER RD	LCF	LCF	4000	19	C5
DOVER ST	GLDR	GLDR	900	89	C2
DOVER ST	LA	LA39	3400	25	B6
DOVER WY	MPK	MPK	1100	46	A3
DOVERDALE AV	CO	LPUE	400	98	D1
DOVERFIELD AV	CO	LPUE	1000	48	C6
DOVERFIELD AV	CO	LPUE	1500	85	C1
DOVERGLEN WY	CO	LPUE		98	A4
DOVERRIDGE DR	RPV	PVP	29000	72	D5
DOVERWOOD CT	LAN	LAN		159	F7
DOVERWOOD CT	WLVL	THO	32000	102	A4
DOVERWOOD DR	CUL	CUL		50	C5
DOVERWOOD DR	GLEN	GL07		25	D1
DOVETAIL DR	AGH	AGO		102	D2
DOVEWEED WY	SCLR	SAU		124	E8
DOVEY AV	CO	WHI	900	48	A4
DOVEY DR	LB	LB08		71	F5
DOVLEN PL	CAR	GAR	800	69	C3
DOW AV	RB	RB	2800	62	F4
DOWEL AV	PALM	PALM		183	J1
DOWELL DR	SCLR	CYN	28000	124	H5
DOWLING AV	PR	PR	5500	54	F3
DOWNES RD	LA	LA49	400	32	B6
DOWNEY AV	BLF	BLF	17400	66	A4
DOWNEY AV	DOW	DOW	9200	60	A6
DOWNEY AV	LB	LB05	5800	70	F1
DOWNEY AV	LKD	LKD	4800	71	A3
DOWNEY AV	PAR	PAR	13100	66	A1
DOWNEY RD	CO	LA23	600	45	D5
DOWNEY RD	CO	LA23	1200	53	D1
DOWNEY RD	CO	LA23	3700	53	B2
DOWNEY RD	CO	LA58	5100	53	B3
DOWNEY RD	CO	LA63	300	45	D5
DOWNEY RD	VER	LA23	2500	53	B3
DOWNEY RD	VER	LA58	4300	53	B3

STREET	CITY	P.O. ZONE	BLOCK	PAGE	GRID
DOWNEY WY	LA	LA07		44	A6
DOWNEY& NWLK RD	DOW	DOW	9800	60	D5
DOWNEY& NWLK RD	NWK	NWK	10400	60	D5
DOWNY&SNFRD BRG	DOW	DOW	9800	60	D3
DOWNIE CIR	SAD	SAD		90	B4
DOWNING AV	BAP	BAP	4100	39	E4
DOWNING AV	GLEN	GL08	3200	18	E4
DOWNSVIEW RD	LAN	LAN	44300	160	D5
DOYLE CT	CO	NEW		126	G3
DOYLE DR	SGAB	SGAB	400	37	D2
DOYLE PL	LA	LA12	1000	44	E1
DOYNE RD	CO	PAS	2700	27	F1
DOYON PL	LAM	LAM	15700	83	C3
DOZIER ST	CO	LA22	4300	45	D4
DOZIER ST	CO	LA63	3700	45	D4
DRACENA DR	LA	LA27	1900	34	F2
DRACO WY	LA	CAN	23600	5	E3
DRADO	LA	SP		78	C5
DRAGON RD	LA	LA12		44	E2
DRAGONERA DR	CO	LPUE	18200	98	D6
DRAGONFLY ST	GLEN	GL06		26	C1
DRAILLE DR	TOR	TOR	22600	67	E5
DRAKE LN	LA	BH	9700	22	F6
DRAKE PL	LA	CAN	6500	12	D5
DRAKE RD	ARC	ARC	200	28	B5
DRAKE ST	CLA	CLA		91	B6
DRAKE ST	POM	POM	100	90	E3
DRAKEWOOD AV	CUL	CUL	10600	50	D3
DRAPER AV	LA	LA64	10500	42	A4
DRAPER DR	CO	LPUE		85	D5
DRASIN DR	SCLR	CYN	20000	124	G7
DRAYER LN	CO	RM	8400	46	F4
DRAYER LN	RM	RM	8600	46	F4
DRAYTON ST	SCLR	SAU	23000	124	C9
DRELL ST	LA	SF	14700	2	D2
DRESDEN AV	DUA	DUA	1100	29	E4
DRESDEN DR	LA	LA46		33	F2
DRESDEN PL	LA	SF	12000	1	E5
DRESSER RD	CO	CAL		108	E6
DREW PL	CLA	CLA	4000	90	F2
DREW ST	LA	LA65	3100	35	D1
DREXEL AV	LA	LA36	6100	42	E1
DREXEL AV	LA	LA36	5900	43	A1
DREXEL AV	LA	LA48	6300	33	E6
DREXEL AV	LA	LA48	6200	42	E1
DREXEL DR	WAL	WAL		93	B4
DREXEL PL	PAS	PAS	500	26	F5
DREXEL ST	PALM	PALM		183	E1
DRIESER PL	CER	ART	13600	82	E4
DRIFT DR	WLVL	THO		102	C2
DRIFTON AV	SAD	SAD	100	89	F3
DRIFTSTONE DR	GLDR	GLDR		89	E1
DRIFTWOOD DR	LB	LB03		76	E5
DRIFTWOOD DR	LA	PP		40	C2
DRIFTWOOD LN	RPV	PVP	29200	72	C6
DRIFTWOOD LN	SAD	SAD	600	90	A3
DRIFTWOOD PL	LA	PP		40	C2
DRIFTWOOD PL	PALM	PALM		184	C1
DRIFTWOOD ST	LA	VEN		49	C5
DRIGGS AV	RM	RM	3000	47	B1
DRIGGS CT	CO	SAU		181	D7
DRILL RD	CO	SAU		181	C9
DRISCOLL AV	LA	VAN	7900	14	E2
DRISCOLL ST	LB	LB15	6500	76	E3
DRIVER AV	AGH	AGO	26900	100A	E4
DRIVER AV	CO	CAST	29500	123	C2
DRIVER LN	LAV	LAV		95A	D5
DRONFIELD AV	LA	PAC	11600	3	A5
DRONFIELD AV	LA	PAC	11000	9	C1
DRONFIELD AV	LA	SF	12900	2	D1
DRONFIELD AV	LA	SF	11900	3	A5
DRONFIELD AV	LA	SV	9700	9	E4
DRONFIELD PL	LA	SF	13800	2	D1
DROVER CT	SAD	SAD		89	F1
DROXFORD CIR	CER	ART	12300	81	B1
DROXFORD PL	CER	ART	12400	81	B1
DROXFORD ST	ART	ART	11900	82	A6
DROXFORD ST	CER	ART	10600	71	E1
DROXFORD ST	CER	ART	13000	81	D1
DROXFORD ST	LKD	LKD	6000	71	D1
DRUCKER ST	CO	LA32	4200	45	D2
DRUID ST	LA	LA32	4600	45	C1
DRUMHILL DR	CO	LPUE	1500	85	D2
DRUMM AV	LA	WIL	1100	74	D3
DRUMM AV	LA	WIL		74	D4
DRUMMOND ST	LA	PP	14600	40	D4
DRUMS CT	CO	WOH		13	B4
DRURY CT	CLA	CLA		91	C1
DRURY DR	WHI	WHI	16700	84	E2
DRURY LN	BH	BH	400	33	C4
DRURY LN	GLEN	GL06	2400	26	A2
DRURY LN	LA	LA39	3200	35	B3
DRURY LN	LYN	LYN	10700	58	F4
DRUSILLA WY	CO	WAL	1800	97	B4
DRYAD RD	LA	PP	500	40	E4
DRYANDER DR	DBAR	WAL		97	D2

STREET	CITY	P.O. ZONE	BLOCK	PAGE	GRID
DRYBANK DR	RHE	PVP	27500	72	E5
DRYBROOK DR	CO	LPUE	15300	85	D2
DRY CY CD CK RD	CO	CAL		100	D6
DRY CY CD CK RD	CO	CAL		100	E5
DRY CY CD CK RD	CO	CAL		108	C2
DRYCLIFF ST	SCLR	CYN	19000	124	J8
DRYCREEK LN	CER	ART	16000	82	B4
DRY CREEK RD	DBAR	POM		93	F5
DRYDEN LN	WCOV	WCOV		92	B4
DRYDEN LN	WCOV	WCOV		92	C4
DRYDEN PL	LA	LA26	300	35	B6
DRYDEN ST E	GLEN	GL07	100	25	C2
DRYDEN ST W	GLEN	GL02	100	25	B2
DRYSDALE AV	LA	LA32	3800	36	D4
DRY WELL CIR	CO	CAST		123	J1
DUANE AV N	SGAB	SGAB	200	37	D2
DUANE ST	LA	LA26	1400	35	D4
DUANE ST	LA	LA39	2100	35	C4
DUANE WY	SOG	SOG	3200	59	B3
DUARTE RD	CO	SGAB	9000	28	A6
DUARTE RD	CO	SGAB	8200	37	F1
DUARTE RD	CO	SGAB	8600	38	A1
DUARTE RD	DUA	DUA	700	29	B5
DUARTE RD	IRW	BAP		29	E5
DUARTE RD	SMAR	PAS	2800	37	F1
DUARTE RD E	ARC	ARC	100	28	D6
DUARTE RD E	MON	MON	100	29	B5
DUARTE RD W	ARC	ARC	100	28	D6
DUARTE RD W	ARC	ARC	9400	28	B6
DUARTE RD W	MON	MON	100	29	B5
DUARTE ST	LA	LA58	5200	52	D4
DUBARRY DR	BLF	BLF		66	D5
DUBESOR ST	CO	LPUE	15700	92	A3
DUBLIN AV	CO	GAR	14400	63	D3
DUBLIN AV	GAR	GAR	14700	63	D3
DUBLIN AV	LA	LA08	3800	51	C1
DUBLIN DR	GLEN	GL06		19	B6
DUBLIN LN	CO	POM		97	E4
DUBNOFF WY	LA	NHO		16	F5
DUBOIS AV	LA	WOH	5300	100	E1
DUBOIS ST	CO	CAST		123	C2
DUBONNET AV	CO	SGAB	4900	38	A3
DUBONNET AV	RM	RM	3700	38	A6
DUBONNET AV	RM	RM	2400	47	A2
DUBUQUE AV	WAL	WAL	1300	93	B4
DUCASSE AL	LA	LA21	700	44	C5
DUCAT ST	LA	SF	14300	8	D2
DUCHESNE CT	CLA	CLA		91	C1
DUCHESS DR	CO	WHI	6400	55	B6
DUCHESS DR	CO	WHI	8400	61	B1
DUCOMMUN ST	LA	LA12	400	44	E3
DUCOR AV	LA	CAN	8300	5	F2
DUCOR AV	LA	CAN	7600	12	A2
DUDLEXT AV	SOG	SOG	8900	59	D3
DUDLEY AL	PAS	PAS	1400	27	C2
DUDLEY AV	LA	VEN	5	49	B3
DUDLEY CT	LA	VEN	15	49	B3
DUDLEY CT	LA	VEN		49	B3
DUDLEY DR	LA	LA32	4400	36	C5
DUDLEY LN	SCLR	NEW		127	F4
DUDLEY ST	PAS	PAS	2000	27	E2
DUDLEY ST N	POM	POM	1600	90	C6
DUDLEY ST N	POM	POM	500	94	C1
DUDLEY ST S	POM	POM	500	94	C3
DUDLEY WY	LA	LA32	4500	36	C5
DUELL ST	CO	AZU	18500	88	E1
DUELL ST	CO	GLDR	8900	88	E1
DUELL ST	CO	GLDR	19400	89	A1
DUELL ST E	AZU	AZU	500	88	D1
DUELL ST E	GLDR	GLDR	200	89	B1
DUELL ST W	AZU	AZU	100	88	C1
DUELL ST W	GLDR	GLDR	200	89	A1
DUENAS DR	CO	LPUE	2000	98	E4
DUENDE LN	LA	PP		40	B2
DUESLER LN	DOW	DOW	8000	60	A5
DUESLER ST	DOW	DOW	8100	60	A5
DUFF AV	CO	LPUE	600	48	E4
DUFF AV	LPUE	LPUE	500	48	E4
DUFF AV	WCOV	WCOV	800	92	A2
DUFFEL ST	PALM	PALM		184	B5
DUFFIELD AV	CO	WHI	12300	61	E6
DUFFIELD AV	LAM	LAM	12800	61	E6
DUFFIELD AV	LAM	LAM	12600	82	E1
DUFFY ST	TEC	TEC	9100	38	C3
DUFOUR ST	RB	RB	9900	62	E4
DUFRESNE CT	LA	LA34	3700	50	A1
DUGGAN AV	AZU	AZU		88	B2
DUKAS ST	LA	NOR		1	B6
DUKE AV	CLA	CLA		91	A3
DUKE LN	WAL	WAL		93	B4
DUKE ST	LA	LA31	3800	36	C6
DULCE LN	SCLR	SAU		124	D6
DULCET AV	LA	NOR	11300	1	B6
DULCET AV	LA	NOR	11100	7	B1
DULCE YNEZ LN	LA	PP	16900	40	B3
DULCINEA CT	LA	WOH		13	C4

STREET	CITY	P.O. ZONE	BLOCK	PAGE	GRID
DULEY RD	ELS	ELS	100	56	D6
DULIN AV	PR	PR	5100	54	F3
DULUTH LN	LA	LA77	1500	32	E3
DULZURA DR	CO	LPUE		85	F5
DUMA ST	CO	COM	3600	65	B4
DUMAINE AV	SAD	SAD	600	89	E4
DUME DR	CO	MAL	6500	110	B4
DUME CYN MTWY	CO	MAL		112	C2
DUME CANYON RD	CO	MAL		106	A5
DUMETZ RD	LA	WOH	20700	13	C3
DUMFRIES RD	LA	LA64	2700	42	A4
DUMONT AV	CER	ART	17400	66	E5
DUMONT AV	DOW	DOW	11000	60	E5
DUMONT AV	NWK	NWK	11200	60	E5
DUMONT AV	NWK	NWK	13900	66	E2
DUMONT PL	LA	WOH	5000	13	E2
DUMONT ST	LA	WOH	20500	13	D2
DUMP RD	CO	CAST		123	E4
DUMP RD	SELM	ELM		47	D4
DUNA DR	CO	COV	4400	88	B4
DUNAS LN	LA	TAR		21	C3
DUNBAR PL	LA	VAN		22	D4
DUNBAR ST	BLF	BLF	14400	66	A4
DUNBAR ST	PALM	PALM		171	H6
DUNBARTON AV	LA	LA45	7300	50	B6
DUNBARTON AV	LA	LA45	8000	56	B1
DUNBARTON PL	CLA	CLA		96	C6
DUNBLANE AV	LA	NOR		1	B5
DUNBROOKE AV	CAR	CAR	19000	69	C1
DUNCAMP PL	LA	LA46	8700	33	D2
DUNCAN AV	CMRC	LA22	1400	53	E1
DUNCAN AV	CO	LA22	600	45	E6
DUNCAN AV	CO	LA22	1100	53	E1
DUNCAN AV	LYN	LYN	11000	59	D6
DUNCAN AV	LYN	LYN	11700	65	C1
DUNCAN AV	MB	MB	800	62	C5
DUNCAN DR	MB	MB	1100	62	C5
DUNCAN PL	MB	MB	800	62	C5
DUNCAN ST	LA	RES	17700	14	D5
DUNCAN WY	SOG	SOG	5100	59	D3
DUNCANNON AV	DUA	DUA	800	29	D5
DUNDAS DR	LA	NHO	11200	23	E2
DUNDAS ST	CO	LA63	900	45	C3
DUNDAS ST	LA	LA63	1000	45	C3
DUNDEE DR	LA	LA27	4100	35	A1
DUNDEE PL	LA	LA27	2600	35	A1
DUNDRY AV	BAP	BAP	3800	39	F5
DUNDRY AV	BAP	BAP	1600	48	D1
DUNE LN	CO	CYN		125	D7
DUNE LN	LAV	LAV	3000	90	D2
DUNE ST	ELS	ELS		55A	F5
DUNE ST	NWK	NWK	11000	60	E5
DUNE ST	NWK	NWK	11600	61	A6
DUNEGAL CT	AGH	AGO		102	D2
DUNES	PALM	PALM		171	E4
DUNESMORE PL	CO	VAL		124	B6
DUNFIELD AV	LA	LA45	7100	50	C6
DUNFORD AV	CO	PALM	36400	184	G3
DUNFORD LN	ING	IN01		57	B2
DUNHAM AL	PAS	PAS	1500	27	D2
DUNHAM ST	CMRC	LA22	4600	53	D1
DUNHAM ST	CMRC	LA23	4500	53	D1
DUNHAM ST	CO	LA23	4400	53	D1
DUNIA ST	BAP	BAP	13300	39	C3
DUNKIRK AV	LA	LA25	10300	42	A2
DUNLAP CRSSG RD	CO	WHI	10500	55	B4
DUNLAP CRSSG RD	PR	PR	8600	54	F3
DUNLAPS DR	WAL	WAL		93	B5
DUNLEER DR	LA	LA64	10200	42	A5
DUNLEER PL	LA	LA64	2700	42	A4
DUNLIN ST	CO	LAN		175	E7
DUNLO PL	LA	CAN	6400	5	D5
DUNMAN AV	LA	WOH	4600	13	A2
DUNMORE AV	CO	PALM	38500	172	H8
DUNN AV	CO	LA63	1400	45	C2
DUNN DR	LA	CUL	3800	42	B5
DUNN DR	LA	LA34	3500	42	B5
DUNN ST	LA	SP	100	78	E2
DUNNET AV	LAM	LAM	14400	83	C2
DUNNICLIFFE CT	LA	NOR		1	C5
DUNNING ST	SFS	SFS	11000	60	F3
DUNNING ST	SFS	SFS	11600	61	A3
DUNNING WY	SAD	SAD	1100	89	D2
DUNOON LN	LA	LA49	12200	41	B3
DUNRAVEN CT	WLVL	THO	31700	102	B4
DUNROBIN AV	BLF	BLF	13400	66	C2
DUNROBIN AV	DOW	DOW	12100	60	C6
DUNROBIN AV	DOW	DOW	12700	66	C1
DUNROBIN AV	LKD	LKD	5900	66	C6
DUNROBIN AV	LKD	LKD	4500	71	C1
DUNSHILL CT	WHI	WHI		84	D4
DUNSMERE RD	GLEN	GL06	3900	26	C1
DUNSMORE AV	GLEN	GL14	4000	11	C6
DUNSMORE AV	GLEN	GL14	3900	18	C1
DUNSMUIR AV	LA	LA08	3800	50	F1

STREET	CITY	P.O. ZONE	BLOCK	PAGE	GRID
DUNSMUIR AV	LA	LA16	1900	42	F4
DUNSMUIR AV	LA	LA19	1000	43	A3
DUNSMUIR AV	LA	LA36	600	43	A3
DUNSMUIR LN	WAL	WAL		92	F5
DUNSTAN WY	LA	LA49	11600	41	C2
DUNSVIEW AV	CO	LPUE	400	92	B6
DUNSWELL AV	CO	LPUE	1100	85	E1
DUNTON DR	CO	WHI	13800	61	E2
DUNTON DR	CO	WHI	14800	84	A4
DUNTON DR	WHI	WHI	12600	61	D1
DUNURE PL	LA	NOR		1	A4
DUNWICH AV	CO	TOR	1100	68	F5
DUNWOOD RD	RHE	PVP	26300	72	E3
DUOMO VIA	LA	LA77	15500	22	C6
DUPAGE AV	CO	WHI		61	D3
DUPONT PL	POM	POM	500	94	A2
DUPONT PL	SCLR	VAL		123	G6
DUPONT ST	LA	CHA	21600	6	C3
DUPONT ST	POM	POM	100	94	A2
DUPRE DR	RPV	PVP		77	C2
DUPREE ST	SELM	ELM	9800	47	C3
DUQUE DR	LA	NHO	11500	23	D6
DUQUESNE AV	CUL	CUL	3900	42	C6
DUQUESNE AV	CUL	CUL	4200	50	C1
DURAND DR	LA	LA68	2900	24	C6
DURAND DR	LA	LA68	2800	34	C1
DURANGO AV	LA	LA34	1900	42	C5
DURANGO AV	LA	LA35	1900	42	D3
DURANGO CT	LAV	LAV		95A	D4
DURANGO CT	SAD	SAD		90	A1
DURANGO DR	MPK	MPK	2000	45	F2
DURANGO LN	CO	SAU		181	B8
DURANGO PL	CER	ART	13300	82	D5
DURANGO ST	MTB	MTB		46	D6
DURANT DR	BH	BH	9800	42	B1
DURANT ST	AZU	AZU	300	86	C4
DU RAY PL	LA	LA08	3800	50	F1
DU RAY PL	LA	LA16	2700	42	F5
DURAZNO DR	CO	LPUE	2000	85	F3
DURBIN ST	IRW	BAP		39	B5
DURFEE AV	CO	ELM	100	47	B5
DURFEE AV	ELM	ELM	3800	39	A6
DURFEE AV	ELM	ELM	2100	47	E3
DURFEE AV	ELM	ELM	3200	48	A2
DURFEE AV	PR	PR	3000	47	B6
DURFEE AV	PR	PR	3900	55	A2
DURFEE AV	SELM	ELM	1100	47	D4
DURHAM PL	CO	SAU		124	E4
DURHAM PL	LCF	LCF	3900	19	C5
DURHAM RD	LA	VN23		22	E5
DURKEE AV	LA	TU	10100	11	B3
DURKLYN CT	SMAR	PAS	1700	37	D1
DURNESS ST	BAP	BAP	14000	39	D6
DURNESS ST	WCOV	WCOV	1000	48	F2
DURNESS ST	WCOV	WCOV	800	92	A3
DURRELL AV	AZU	AZU	400	86	D6
DURWARD WY	LAV	LAV		90	D2
DURWOOD DR	LCF	LCF	500	19	C3
DURYEA AV	CO	WHI	1300	48	A5
DUSK ST	CO	LPUE		98	D6
DUSON ST	CO	ACT		189	E2
DUSSEN LN	CER	ART	13100	81	D1
DUSTIN DR	LA	LA65	400	36	B3
DUSTY DR	CO	SAU		182	A6
DUSTY RD	LAN	LAN		159	B6
DUTCH ST	BAP	BAP	14700	39	E6
DUTHIE ST	BAP	BAP	12800	48	B1
DUVAL ST	LAV	LAV		90	B1
DUVALL RD	CO	PALM		190	D2
DUVALL ST	LA	LA31	2100	35	E5
DUXBURY CIR	LA	LA34	2100	42	C3
DUXBURY LN	LA	LA34	9500	42	C4
DUXBURY PL	LA	LA34	2400	42	C4
DUXBURY RD	LA	LA34	9300	42	C3
DUXFORD AV	CO	AZU	5500	88	D2
DUXFORD AV	CO	COV	4600	88	D4
DWIGGINS ST	CO	LA63	3600	45	C3
DWIGHT AV N	COM	COM	100	64	D3
DWIGHT AV S	COM	COM	300	64	D3
DWIGHT DR	GLEN	GL07	1400	25	C1
DWIGHT LEE ST	CO	SAU		182	F6
DYER AV	CO	GL14	4500	11	D6
DYER LN	GLDR	GLDR		87	A5
DYER ST	CO	GL14	4400	18	D1
DYER ST	LA	SF	13500	2	F2
DYER ST	LA	SF	13200	3	A1
DYLAN PL	LA	NOR		1	B6
DYLAN ST	LA	NOR		1	B6
DYMOND ST	BUR	BUR	2100	16	F5
DYOTT WY	PALM	PALM		172	B5
DYSON AV	ELM	ELM	4800	39	A4

E

STREET	CITY	P.O. ZONE	BLOCK	PAGE	GRID
E AV	PALM	PALM		183	H1
E CIR	CO	HAC		73	F2
E CT	CO	PALM		183	A3
E CT	LA	WIL		74	B5
E ST	LAV	LAV	1800	90	D4
E ST	POM	POM	1500	90	C5
E ST E	LA	WIL	100	74	B5
E ST W	LA	WIL	100	74	B5
EADALL AV	CO	LA61		64	B2
EADBROOK DR	CO	LPUE	14500	85	B1
EADBURY AV	CO	LPUE	1700	97	A4
EADHILL PL	CO	WHI		55	E1
EADMER AV	PALM	PALM	39600	172	A6
EADS ST	LA	LA31	2300	35	D4
EAGAN DR	CO	WHI	11800	61	F5
EAGAN DR	CO	WHI	10200	84	A4
EAGAN ST	LA	TU	6800	11	A5
EAGER RD	CO	ACT	32000	182	D7
EAGLE	PALM	PALM		172	B5
EAGLE DR	LAV	LAV		95A	D5
EAGLE ST	CO	LA22	4300	45	D5
EAGLE ST	CO	LA22	5500	46	A6
EAGLE ST	CO	LA63	3600	45	D5
EAGLE ST	LA	LA33	1500	44	F4
EAGLE ST	LA	LA33	2700	45	B4
EAGLE ST	LA	LA63	3000	45	B4
EAGLE ST	LB	LB15	5100	76	C2
EAGLE ST E	LB	LB06	100	75	C2
EAGLE ST W	LB	LB06	100	75	C2
EAGLEBROOK DR	AGH	AGO		102	D3
EAGLECLIFF DR	SAD	LAV		95A	B6
EAGLECREST AV	SCLR	CYN	28000	125	A7
EAGLECREST PL	DBAR	WAL		97	C5
EAGLEDALE AV	LA	LA41	5100	25	F4
EAGLEFEN DR	DBAR	POM		97	E2
EAGLE GROVE AV	CLA	CLA		96	C6
EAGLEHAVEN CIR	RPV	PVP	31300	78	B4
EAGLEHELM DR	CO	CYN		128	D1
EAGLEHILL DR	CO	SF		3	E2
EAGLEMONT AV	CO	WHI	1000	48	A4
EAGLEMONT DR	CO	WHI	900	48	A4
EAGLE MTN ST	CO	CAN	24000	4	A6
EAGLE MTN ST	LA	CAN	24000	5	E1
EAGLENEST DR	DBAR	POM		93	F6
EAGLE NEST DR	DBAR	POM		97	F1
EAGLEPARK RD	CO	LPUE	1400	98	B3
EAGLE PASS DR	CO	MAL	20600	114	F4
EAGLE PEAK AV	SCLR	CYN	27900	125	B8
EAGLE POINT DR	GLEN	GL08	3400	18	F4
EAGLE RIDGE	GLDR	GLDR		87	D6
EAGLE RIDGE	GLDR	GLDR		89	D1
EAGLE RIDGE LN	LA	NOR		1	A4
EAGLE RIDGE LN	LA	NOR		1A	F4
EAGLE RIDGE WY	LA	NOR		1A	F4
EAGLE ROCK BLVD	LA	LA41	4300	25	F6
EAGLE ROCK BLVD	LA	LA41	4400	26	A6
EAGLE ROCK BLVD	LA	LA65	2900	35	E2
EAGLE RCK VW DR	LA	LA41	800	26	D4
EAGLESET AV	CO	SAU		125	H1
EAGLES LANDG DR	PALM	PALM		183	G8
EAGLE SPGS F RD	LA	PP		109	F3
EAGLESPUR RD	CO	POM		93	E6
EAGLESPUR RD	DBAR	POM		93	F6
EAGLETON ST	AGH	AGO		100A	A2
EAGLE VIEW CIR	LA	LA41	5000	25	F5
EAGLE VISTA DR	LA	LA41	800	26	C4
EAMES AV	LA	NOR	8900	7	B6
EARHART AV	LA	LA45	8800	56	C2
EARL AV	BAP	BAP	13000	39	C5
EARL AV	LB	LB06	2100	75	C2
EARL CT	LA	LA39	2200	35	C4
EARL DR	LCF	LCF	5100	19	A1
EARL ST	LA	LA39	2200	35	C3
EARL ST	TOR	TOR	20200	67	F3
EARLDOM AV	LA	VEN	6800	55A	E2
EARLE AV	CO	SGAB	5600	37	F3
EARLE AV	RM	RM	3800	37	F6
EARLE AV	RM	RM	2400	46	F2
EARLE AV	SGAB	SGAB	100	37	F3
EARLE CT	RB	RB	2200	67	E1
EARLE ST	LA	SP	200	79	B2
EARLE ST	RB	RB	500	67	E1
EARLGATE ST	DBAR	WAL	20700	97	C2
EARLHAM DR	CLA	CLA		91	D2
EARLHAM DR	WHI	WHI		55	E5
EARLHAM ST	LA	PP	15200	40	C4
EARLHAM ST	PAS	PAS	600	27	B3
EARLIE AV	CAR	CAR	19600	69	E2
EARLINGTON AV	DUA	DUA	1800	29	D6
EARLMAR DR	LA	LA64	3000	42	B5
EARLMONT AV	LCF	LCF	1500	19	A1
EARLS CT	LA	LA77		32	C1
EARLSWOOD DR	RM	RM	3200	47	A1
EARL WARREN DR	LB	LB40		76	C4
EARLY AV	TOR	TOR		68	B6
EARNFORD DR	CO	CAL		100	E5
EARNSHAW AV	DOW	DOW	13400	66	A1
EARNSLOW DR	LCF	LCF	2100	11	F5

STREET	CITY	P.O. ZONE	BLOCK	PAGE	GRID
EARNWAY ST	CO	CYN		125	C5
EASLEY CYN RD	GLDR	GLDR	700	87	B4
EAST AV	BUR	BUR	1000	17	D4
EAST BLVD	LA	LA66	3800	50	A2
EAST DR	CO	HAC		73	F2
EAST DR	NWK	NWK	15900	66	F4
EAST PKWY	ING	IN02	700	51	B5
EAST RD	CO	VAL		126	J1
EAST RD	LA	LB10		74	F2
EAST RD	LHH	LAH	100	84	F2
EAST RD	LHH	LAH	500	98A	A1
EAST ST	CAR	CAR	23900	74	C1
EAST TR	CO	SF	11700	3	E6
EAST WALK	LA	WIL	1000	74	B5
EAST WY	LA	LA45		56	C3
EASTBORNE AV	LA	LA24	10200	41	F2
EASTBROOK AV	BLF	BLF	13400	66	C2
EASTBROOK AV	DOW	DOW	12100	60	C6
EASTBROOK AV	DOW	DOW	12700	66	C1
EASTBROOK AV	LKD	LKD	5900	66	C6
EASTBROOK AV	LKD	LKD	4500	71	C1
EASTBURY AV	CO	COV	3200	88	D3
EASTBURY AV	COV	COV	1100	88	D3
EAST CYN MTWY	SCLR	NEW		127	B9
EAST CHANNEL RD	LA	SM	400	40	E4
EAST CREST WY	MPK	MPK	900	46	A3
EASTEDGE DR	GLEN	GL06		25	F3
EAST END AV N	POM	POM	100	95	B3
EAST END AV S	POM	POM	100	95	B3
EASTERLY RD	AGH	AGO		100A	B3
EASTERLY TER	LA	LA26	1400	35	B4
EASTERN AV	BELL	LA40	2800	53	F3
EASTERN AV	BG	BELL	6200	53	E6
EASTERN AV	BG	BELL	7300	59	E2
EASTERN AV	CMRC	LA23	1300	53	D1
EASTERN AV	CMRC	LA40	2100	53	F3
EASTERN AV	LA	LA32	2300	36	D6
EASTERN AV	PAS	PAS	1	27	F4
EASTERN AV N	CO	LA22	100	45	D5
EASTERN AV N	CO	LA32	1700	45	D2
EASTERN AV N	CO	LA63	900	45	D3
EASTERN AV N	LA	LA32	2000	45	D1
EASTERN AV S	CO	LA22	100	45	D5
EASTERN CT	LA	VEN	2300	49	B6
EASTERN WY	CO	LA22	900	45	D3
EASTERN CANAL	LA	VEN	2200	49	C4
EASTFIELD DR	RH	PVP	1	78	B2
EASTFORD AV	DUA	DUA	800	29	D5
EAST FORK RD	CO			P	B4
EASTGATE DR	DBAR	POM		97A	B2
EASTGATE PL	GLEN	GL08	2200	18	F5
EASTGLEN DR	LAV	LAV		95A	B6
EASTHAM DR	CUL	CUL	3500	42	D6
EAST HILLS DR	WCOV	WCOV		92	F2
EAST HILLS DR	WCOV	WCOV		93	A2
EASTLAKE AV	LA	LA31	2200	36	B6
EASTLAKE AV	LA	LA31	1800	45	B1
EASTLAKE AV	LA	LA33	1400	45	B1
EASTLAND CTR DR	WCOV	WCOV	100	88	E6
EASTLEIGH AV	CO	LPUE	1300	85	F2
EASTLYN PL	CO	PAS	1200	27	E1
EASTMAN AV	CMRC	LA23	1400	53	C1
EASTMAN AV	CO	LA23	1200	53	C1
EASTMAN AV N	CO	LA63	100	45	C4
EASTMAN AV S	CO	LA23	600	45	C5
EASTMAN AV S	CO	LA63	100	45	C4
EASTMAN PL	LA	SP	800	73	F6
EASTMAN ST	CER	ART	12000	81	B2
EASTMONT AV	CO	LA22	400	46	A6
EASTNOR AV	WCOV	WCOV	400	98	F2
EASTON DR	LA	BH	9800	32	F2
EASTON LN	CO	SAU		124	E4
EASTON ST	CO	LA22	5900	54	B1
EASTON ST	MTB	MTB	2100	54	B1
EASTONDALE AV	LB	LB05	6800	65	D4
EAST PARK DR	LA	NHO	6200	16	C5
EAST PARK WY	ING	IN02	700	51	B6
EASTRIDE LN	CAR	CAR		69	D6
EASTRIDGE DR	WHI	WHI	13800	55	F5
EASTRIDGE DR	WHI	WHI		85	A6
EAST SIDE BLVD	LA	LA63	3000	45	B4
EASTVALE CT	AGH	AGO		102	E2
EASTVALE RD	CO	PVP	26400	73	A4
EAST VIEW DR	LA	LA42	400	26	D6
EASTWAND	CO	CHA		4	C5
EASTWAY LN	CLA	CLA	300	91	B4
EASTWIND ST	LA	VEN		49	C5
EASTWOOD AV	CO	IN04	10800	57	A5
EASTWOOD AV	HAW	IN04	11000	57	A5
EASTWOOD AV	ING	IN01	100	57	A1
EASTWOOD AV	LAW	LAW	14500	63	A4
EASTWOOD AV	TOR	TOR	17100	63	B5
EASTWOOD AV	TOR	TOR	20300	68	A3
EASTWOOD CT	TOR	TOR	22400	68	A5
EASTWOOD RD	LA	LA46	8500	33	D1
EASTWOOD ST	TOR	TOR		68	B5

STREET	CITY	P.O. ZONE	BLOCK	PAGE	GRID
EASY AV	LB	LB10	3000	70	B6
EASY AV	LB	LB10	2000	75	B2
EASY ST	ELM	ELM	4000	38	B5
EASY ST	LAN	LAN		160	F6
EASY ST	LA	LA42	5000	26	E6
EATON CIR	LB	LB15		76	C1
EATON DR	PAS	PAS	200	27	F2
EATON LN	LAV	LAV		90	D2
EATON RD	SAD	SAD		89	D3
EATON ST	LA	LA42	5000	26	C6
EATON TER	LA	LA42	1400	26	C6
EATON CYN DR	PAS	PAS	2700	27	E1
EATOUGH AV	LA	CAN	8400	12	B1
EATOUGH PL	LA	CAN	8500	12	B1
EAU CLAIRE DR	RPV	PVP	5400	72	D4
EBB CT	SCLR	SAU		124	G5
EBBTIDE WY	CO	MAL	6400	111	F6
EBELDEN AV	SCLR	NEW		127	B5
EBELL ST	LA	NHO	13000	16	A1
EBELL ST	LA	VAN	13300	15	F1
EBELL ST	LB	LB08	5100	71	C4
EBERLE CIR	CER	ART	11400	71	F2
EBERLE PL	CER	ART	12200	81	B2
EBERLE ST	CER	ART	11800	81	A2
EBERLE ST	LKD	LKD	5700	71	E2
EBEY AV	LA	LA42	5400	36	D3
EBEY CYN TK TR	CO	SF	300	46	C6
EBON RD	CO	MAL		105	E6
EBONY AV	WCOV	WCOV	700	92	A1
EBONY LN	LOM	LOM	25000	73	D2
EBY DR	CO	LAN	12000	158	A2
ECCLES ST	LA	CAN	20400	12	E1
ECCLES ST	LA	NOR	18100	14	C1
ECCLES ST	LA	SF	15900	15	B1
ECHANDIA ST	LA	LA33	100	45	A3
ECHARD AV	LAN	LAN	43300	159	G7
ECHELON AV	CO	LPUE	800	92	A4
ECHELON PL	LA	SV	8300	17	A1
ECHILMAN AL	CO	CAST		123	J2
ECHO ST	LA	LA42	4900	36	B3
ECHO GLEN DR	CO	ALT		20	C4
ECHO HILL WY	CO	LPUE		98	A4
ECHO MTN ST	PALM	PALM		183	G6
ECHO PARK AV	LA	LA26	600	35	C6
ECHO PARK TER	LA	LA26	700	35	C6
ECHO RIVER WY	CER	ART		82	B4
ECKERMAN AV E	WCOV	WCOV	1000	88	C5
ECKERMAN AV W	WCOV	WCOV	1000	88	B5
ECKFORD ST	CO	LPUE	13500	48	B4
ECKHART AV	CO	RM	1600	46	E3
ECKHART AV	RM	RM	3100	46	E1
ECKHART AV	SGAB	SGAB	1900	37	E6
ECKLESON CIR	CER	ART	11400	71	F2
ECKLESON PL	CER	ART	12200	81	B2
ECKLESON ST	CER	ART	12400	81	B2
ECKLESON ST	LKD	LKD	2400	70	F2
ECKLESON ST	LKD	LKD	5700	71	C2
ECLIPSE DR	PALM	PALM		183	H1
ECLIPSE WY	WCOV	WCOV		92	B4
ECTOR ST	CO	LPUE	13300	48	C2
ECTOR ST	IND	LPUE	13300	48	C2
ECTOR ST	LPUE	LPUE	15300	48	E4
EDAM ST	LAN	LAN	2500	159	G6
EDANRUTH AV	CO	LPUE	1000	48	D2
EDDA VILLA DR	RM	RM	8900	38	A5
EDDERTON AV	CO	WHI	11700	61	F6
EDDERTON AV	CO	WHI	11200	84	A5
EDDERTON AV	LAM	LAM	12600	61	F6
EDDERTON AV	LAM	LAM		82	F1
EDDES ST	WCOV	WCOV	2500	92	E2
EDDINGHAM AV	CO	WOH		13	B5
EDDINGHILL DR	RPV	PVP	6500	72	C4
EDDINGTON DR	CAR	CAR	19000	69	C1
EDDLESTON DR	LA	NOR		1	C5
EDDRIDGE DR	DBAR	POM		97	E2
EDDY ST	LA	NOR		7	A6
EDDYSTONE ST	CO	WHI	11500	55	C6
EDELLE PL	LA	LA32	4600	45	C1
EDEN AV	GLEN	GL06	1900	25	F3
EDEN CIR	CLA	CLA		96	C6
EDEN DR	LA	BH	9400	33	C1
EDEN PL	LA	BH	2600	33	C1
EDEN RD	CO	TOP		109	C4
EDENBERG AV	LA	NOR		1	B6
EDENDALE PL	LA	LA39	2200	35	C4
EDENFIELD AV	AZU	AZU	200	86	E6
EDENFIELD AV	AZU	AZU	100	88	E1
EDENFIELD AV	CO	AZU	5400	88	E2
EDENFIELD AV	CO	COV	4700	88	E4
EDENFIELD AV N	COV	COV	700	88	E4
EDENFIELD AV S	COV	COV	500	88	E5
EDENHURST AV	LA	LA39	4000	25	B6
EDENHURST AV	LA	LA39	3500	35	C1
EDENVIEW LN	WCOV	WCOV	1000	92	C4
EDENWILD RD	CO	CAL		108	B5
EDGAR ST	CAR	CAR	21700	69	C5

STREET	CITY	P.O. ZONE	BLOCK	PAGE	GRID
EDGAR ST	LA	PP	16700	40	B3
EDGEBROOK AV	LYN	LYN	12200	65	D1
EDGEBROOK DR	WAL	WAL		94	D6
EDGEBROOK RD	LAM	LAM		83	D1
EDGECLIFF LN	CO	PAS	1400	27	F1
EDGECLIFFE DR	LA	LA26	900	35	A4
EDGECOMB ST	COV	COV	900	89	A4
EDGEFIELD ST	CER	ART		81	B1
EDGEFIELD ST	LKD	LKD	5900	71	D1
EDGEHILL DR	LA	LA08	3800	51	C1
EDGEHILL DR	LA	LA18	2600	43	C5
EDGEHILL DR	POM	POM	1200	95	B1
EDGEHILL DR	WHI	WHI	5800	55	E4
EDGEHILL PL	PAS	PAS	1400	19	D6
EDGELEY PL	LA	LA24	10500	41	E1
EDGEMAR AV	CO	LA43	5600	51	A4
EDGEMAR AV	LA	LA43	5600	51	A4
EDGEMERE DR	TOR	TOR	5300	67	E3
EDGEMONT DR	PALM	PALM		171	H7
EDGEMONT PL	CO	WAL		97	B5
EDGEMONT PL	GLDR	GLDR		87	E5
EDGEMONT ST N	LA	LA04	100	34	F6
EDGEMONT ST N	LA	LA27	1300	34	F4
EDGEMONT ST N	LA	LA29	700	34	F4
EDGEMONT ST S	LA	LA04	100	34	F6
EDGERIDGE DR	CO	LPUE	14300	85	B3
EDGERTON AV	LA	ENC	4900	22	A2
EDGEVIEW DR	PAS	PAS	3700	28	B1
EDGEVIEW DR	SMAD	SMAD	600	28	B1
EDGEWARE RD E	LA	LA26	300	44	C1
EDGEWARE RD W	LA	LA26	1000	35	C6
EDGEWARE RD W	LA	LA26	1000	44	C1
EDGEWATER DR	NWK	NWK		66	D2
EDGEWATER TER	LA	LA39	2300	35	C3
EDGEWICK RD	GLEN	GL06	2800	26	B1
EDGEWOOD DR	ALH	ALH	1200	37	A6
EDGEWOOD DR	SPAS	SPAS	1900	37	B2
EDGEWOOD PL	LA	LA19	5800	42	F2
EDGEWOOD PL	LA	LA19	4500	43	C2
EDGEWOOD ST	ING	IN02	400	51	A6
EDGEWORTH AV	CO	WHI	11900	84	C5
EDGLEY AV	MPK	MPK	300	46	C2
EDGWARE DR	CO	AGO	5200	100A	E4
ED HALLEY PL	LAN	LAN		159	D5
EDIE CT	WCOV	WCOV		92	D2
EDIE DR	DUA	DUA	800	29	F4
EDIE WY	LAN	LAN		160	D7
EDINBORO	WCOV	WCOV		92	D4
EDINBORO AV	CLA	CLA		91	C1
EDINBURGH AV N	LA	LA48	100	33	F6
EDINBURGH AV N	WHOL	LA46	1000	33	F4
EDINBURGH AV S	LA	LA48	100	33	F6
EDINBURGH CT	AGH	AGO		102	F2
EDINBURGH LN	GLEN	GL06		25	E2
EDINBURGH RD	SAD	SAD		89	C4
EDISON AV	LB	LB13		75	A5
EDISON BLVD	BUR	BUR	1300	16	F6
EDISON LN	SPAS	SPAS	900	36	F2
EDISON PL	GLEN	GL04		25	C5
EDISON PL	LB	LB02	100	75	E6
EDISON RD	BUR	BUR	100	24	C2
EDISON RD	CO	ACT		182	G5
EDISON RD	CO	ACT		183	A7
EDISON RD	CO	ACT		189	F7
EDISON RD	CO	CAST		123	G5
EDISON RD	CO	MAL		111	D2
EDISON RD	CO	MAL		112	A2
EDISON RD	CO	NEW		127	B7
EDISON RD	CO	SAU		124	D3
EDISON RD	CO	VAL		123	G5
EDISON RD	CO	VAL		126	H2
EDISON ST	LA	LA32	4500	36	D4
EDISON WK	LA	LA32	3900	36	E4
EDISON WY	COM	COM		64	F6
EDISON WY	LA	NHO	10500	16	F6
EDISN PTRERO RD	CO	VAL		126	E2
EDITH AV	ALH	ALH		37	B5
EDITH AV	WCOV	WCOV	800	88	B5
EDITH ST	LA	LA64	500	42	B5
EDITH WY	LB	LB07	4000	70	B4
EDITH ANN DR	AZU	AZU	600	86	C4
EDLEEN DR	LA	TAR	18700	21	B3
EDLOFT AV	LA	LA32	3200	36	C5
EDMARU AV	WHI	WHI	8200	61	F1
EDMARU AV	WHI	WHI	8100	84	A1
EDMINSTER DR	LAV	LAV		90	D1
EDMOND DR	RM	RM	8600	38	A5
EDMONDSON AL	PAS	PAS	100	27	A6
EDMONTON PL	ING	IN01		57	B2
EDMONTON RD	GLEN	GL06	2900	26	B1
EDMORE AV	CO	LPUE	1100	97	A5
EDMORE PL	LA	SV	9800	17	A1
EDMUND AV	CO	GL14	5800	11	F5
EDNA PL	CO	COV	15600	88	B4
EDNA PL	COV	COV	900	89	A4

241

1990 LOS ANGELES COUNTY STREET INDEX

EDNA PL E — EL MIRADOR ST

LOS ANGELES CO.

STREET	CITY	P.O. ZONE	BLOCK	PAGE	GRID
EDNA PL E	COV	COV	100	88	F4
EDNA PL W	COV	COV	100	88	D4
EDNA ST	LA	LA32	5200	36	E5
EDNA ST	PR	PR	8200	54	F2
EDNUEL ST	CO	ARC	900	38	F1
EDNUEL ST	CO	RM	1000	39	A1
EDOM ST	CAR	CAR	1500	69	E2
EDRA AV	BAP	BAP	4600	39	E3
EDRIS DR	LA	LA35	1200	42	C3
EDSEL AV	LA	LA66	5100	50	A4
EDSON AV	LAN	LAN	43300	159	G7
EDSON RD	CO	ACT		189	D6
EDUARDO ST	CO	WHI	10000	55	B2
EDWARD AV	LA	LA65	2900	35	D2
EDWARD ST	CO	LAN		157	J2
EDW E HORTON LN	LA	ENC	5500	21	E1
EDWARDS AV	ELM	ELM	2600	47	C1
EDWARDS AV	SELM	ELM	2000	47	C2
EDWARDS PL	GLEN	GL06	100	26	B3
EDWARDS RD	CER	ART	17100	82	E5
EDWARDS RD	LAM	LAM	12600	61	E6
EDWARDS RD	LAM	LAM	12800	82	E1
EDWIN AV	POM	POM	500	90	F3
EDWIN DR	LA	LA46	8400	33	C1
EDWIN PL	LA	LA46	3200	33	C1
EDWN ALDREN CIR	MTB	MTB	400	46	E6
EFFIE PL	LA	LA26	3200	35	B4
EFFIE ST	LA	LA26	1300	35	D5
EFFIE ST	LA	LA29	3900	35	A4
EFFINGHAM PL	LA	LA27	3700	35	B1
EGAN AV	CO	LPUE	1100	48	F4
EGBERT ST	CO	NEW		3	A1
EGBERT ST	LA	SF	13400	2	F1
EGIL AV	BAP	BAP	13000	39	C6
EGLEY AV	RM	RM	7400	46	E2
EGLISE AV	DOW	DOW	9000	60	E2
EGLISE AV	PR	PR	5500	55	A4
EGLISE AV	PR	PR	7900	60	E2
EHLERS DR	CO	CHA		4	B5
EHREN AV	LA	SF	11400	9	F1
EILAT PL	LA	WOH	5800	5	D6
EILAT ST	LA	WOH	24400	5	D6
EILEEN AV	CO	LA43	5400	51	B4
EILEEN AV	COV	COV		88	D5
EILEEN AV	LA	LA43	6000	51	B5
EILEEN AV	WCOV	WCOV	500	88	D5
EILINITA AV	GLEN	GL08	900	18	D3
EISENHOWER AV	CO	ARC	3000	39	A2
EL ABACA PL	LA	TAR	4500	21	B3
EL ADOBE LN	CO	GL14	5000	11	E6
ELAINE AV	ART	ART	18500	81	B1
ELAINE AV	ART	ART	16600	82	B5
ELAINE AV	CER	ART	19900	81	B2
ELAINE AV	CER	ART	17100	82	A5
ELAINE AV	HG	LKD	22500	81	B5
ELAINE AV	LKD	LKD	20600	81	B3
ELAINE AV	NWK	NWK	13700	82	A3
ELAINE DR	CO	SAU		181	F6
ELAINE ST	POM	POM	600	90	F6
ELAINE ST	POM	POM	1600	91	B6
ELANITA DR	LA	SP	1900	78	E5
EL ARBOLITA DR	GLEN	GL08	1900	18	F4
EL ARCO DR	WHI	WHI	9700	84	C4
EL ATAJO ST	LA	LA65	700	36	A2
ELBA PL	LA	WOH	6100	5	E5
ELBA ST	PR	PR	8600	54	F2
ELBA ST	PR	PR	8700	55	A2
EL BAILE PL	CO	LPUE	2000	85	E3
ELBEN AV	LA	SUN	9200	10	B5
ELBEN PL	LA	SUN	9200	10	B5
ELBERFRET ST	LAN	LAN	42000	160	B8
ELBERGLEN DR	CO	LPUE		98	B4
ELBERLAND ST	CO	LPUE	19000	97	A1
ELBERON AV	LA	SP	400	78	E2
ELBERON ST	RPV	SP	2200	78	D2
EL BONITO AV	GLEN	GL04	300	25	C6
EL BOSQUE CT	LA	PP		30	A5
EL BRASO DR	WHI	WHI	9800	84	B2
ELBURG ST	PAR	PAR	8200	65	F2
EL CABALLERO DR	LA	TAR	4400	21	B3
EL CABALLO DR	ARC	ARC	1000	28	B3
EL CAJON ST	LA	SF	15400	2	B4
EL CAJONITA DR	LHH	LAH	2000	84	D1
EL CAMINITO LN	CO	GL14	4800	11	E6
EL CAMINITO PL	GLEN	GL14	4700	11	C4
EL CAMINITO ST	CO	GL14	2600	11	D6
EL CAMINITO ST	GLEN	GL14	3400	11	C5
EL CAMINO	MTB	MTB		46	D6
EL CAMINO	POM	POM		90	C6
EL CAMINO AV	PAR	PAR	14300	65	D2
EL CAMINO DR	BH	BH	100	42	C1
EL CAMINO DR	CO	PALM	36000	183	B3
EL CAMINO DR	RM	RM		46	F4
EL CAMINO WY	CLA	CLA	100	91	B5
EL CAMINO CORTO	LCF	LCF	4400	19	A2
EL CM ESPLANADE	WAL	WAL	19600	97	A1

STREET	CITY	P.O. ZONE	BLOCK	PAGE	GRID
EL CAMPO DR	CO	PAS	800	27	F6
EL CANO AV	CO	LAN	20500	175	G6
EL CANON AV	LA	WOH		5	D6
EL CANON DR	LA	WOH		100	E1
EL CANTO DR	LA	LA41		25	F5
EL CAPITAN AV	ARC	ARC	2200	38	E2
EL CAPRICE AV	LA	NHO	7600	16	B2
EL CARMEN ST	LB	LB15	6700	76	E2
EL CASCO ST	LA	SF	14100	2	D3
EL CEDRAL ST	LB	LB15	5100	76	C3
EL CEDRO ST	LA	LA65	600	36	A2
EL CENTRO AV	LA	LA28	1300	34	C4
EL CENTRO AV	LA	LA38	700	34	C4
EL CENTRO ST	SPAS	SPAS	300	36	F1
EL CERCO PL	LA	PP	600	40	D4
EL CERRITO CIR	SPAS	SPAS	1200	36	F2
EL CERRITO PL	LA	LA28	1700	34	B2
EL CERRITO PL	LA	LA68	1900	34	B2
EL CERRO LN	LA	NHO	11600	23	D5
EL CIELO LN	BRAD	DUA	100	29	E3
EL CINO PL	GLEN	GL08	1800	18	F3
EL CIRCUITO	CO	CLA		96	D3
EL CIRCULO DR	PAS	PAS	100	26	E4
EL CONCHO LN	RH	PVP	1	78	B1
EL CONTENTO DR	LA	LA68	2200	34	C2
EL CORONADO	SPAS	SPAS	400	36	E3
EL CORTEZ AV	BG	BELL	6500	53	F6
EL CORTO DR	CO	ALT	1300	20	C5
ELDA ST	BRAD	DUA	2300	29	F4
ELDA ST	DUA	DUA	2500	29	F4
ELDA ST	DUA	DUA	2900	86	A4
ELDEN AV	LA	LA06	900	43	F3
ELDEN AV	WHI	WHI	8100	55	F6
ELDEN WY	BH	BH	1000	33	A5
ELDENA DR	RPV	SP	27600	73	D5
ELDER CT	LA	LA42	900	26	D6
ELDER DR	CLA	CLA	300	91	C4
ELDER ST	LA	LA42	6400	36	D1
ELDER ST	WCOV	WCOV	1900	48	F1
ELDERBANK DR	LA	LA31	3800	36	B4
ELDERBERRY DR	CO	CAL		108	A5
ELDERBERRY ST	CO	LH		157A	B6
ELDERBERRY ST	LAV	LAV		90	A3
ELDER CREEK DR	SCLR	SAU		124	F6
ELDERGLEN LN	CO	HAC		73	F1
ELDERHALL AV	LKD	LKD	4800	70	E2
ELDERIDGE DR	LA	BH	9700	33	A3
ELDERMOOR DR	CO	MAL		114	D3
ELDERTON AV	CO	LAN	7600	146	H1
ELDERTREE DR	DBAR	POM		97	E3
ELDER VIEW DR	SCLR	VAL	27500	124	B5
ELDERWAY DR	CO	LPUE	2100	98	A3
ELDERWOOD ST	LA	LA49	11300	41	C1
ELDON AV	CO	LPUE	1000	85	D1
ELDON AV	LPUE	LPUE	300	48	E5
ELDORA AV	LA	SUN	10100	10	D2
ELDORA PL	LA	SUN	11000	10	D2
ELDORA RD	PAS	PAS	400	27	B2
EL DORADO AV	LA	PAC	10300	8	F1
EL DORADO AV	LA	PAC	9900	9	A2
EL DORADO AV	LA	SF	12400	2	D4
EL DORADO AV	LA	SF	11200	8	E1
EL DORADO AV	LA	SV	9000	9	C5
ELDORADO CT	PALM	PALM		172	B9
ELDORADO CT	POM	WAL		94	B4
ELDORADO DR	LAV	LAV		95A	D6
EL DORADO DR	LB	LB08	3400	81	B6
EL DORADO PZ	LB	LB08	7800	81	A5
EL DORADO ST	ARC	ARC	1	28	E5
EL DORADO ST	MON	MON	800	28	E5
EL DORADO ST	PAS	PAS	400	27	B4
EL DORADO ST	TOR	TOR	2100	68	B4
EL DORADO ST E	WCOV	WCOV	1000	88	B5
EL DORADO ST W	WCOV	WCOV	1000	88	A5
ELDORADO MDW RD	HH	CAL		5	D6
ELDORADO MDW RD	HH	CAL		100	D1
ELDORADO MDW RD	HH	CAL	5800	100	C1
ELDRED AV	WCOV	WCOV	1600	88	A5
ELDRED ST	LA	LA42	4800	36	B2
ELDRED WK	LA	LA65		36	A2
ELDREST ST	CO	ACT		182	D6
ELDRIDGE AV	LA	SF	13500	2	F1
ELDRIDGE AV	LA	SF	11500	3	D6
ELDRIDGE ST	LB	LB07	100	70	C6
ELDRON RD	CO	SAU		181	D9
ELEANOR AV	LA	LA38	6000	34	B4
ELEANOR CT	LAN	LAN		160	H6
ELEANOR CT	NWK	NWK	10600	66	E1
ELEANOR LN	LB	LB05	200	65	C5
ELEANOR PL	LOM	LOM		73	D2
ELEANOR ST	LB	LB05	1200	65	D5
ELEANOR ST N	POM	POM	100	94	F3
ELEANOR ST S	POM	POM	100	94	F3
ELEANORE DR	GLEN	GL06	2000	25	F3
ELECTRA AV	CO	LPUE	1100	98	F3
ELECTRA CT	LA	LA46		33	F2

STREET	CITY	P.O. ZONE	BLOCK	PAGE	GRID
ELECTRA DR	LA	LA46	7800	33	F2
ELECTRA ST	POM	POM	100	95	A2
ELECTRIC AV	ALH	ALH	100	37	B4
ELECTRIC AV	LA	VEN	900	49	B3
ELECTRIC AV	MPK	MPK		46	B2
ELECTRIC AV N	ALH	ALH	1	37	B4
ELECTRIC AV S	ALH	ALH	1	37	B4
ELECTRIC AV S	ALH	ALH	2000	46	B1
ELECTRIC CT	LA	VEN		49	D4
ELECTRIC CT	LB	LB13	1100	75	C4
ELECTRIC DR	PAS	PAS	100	27	A4
ELECTRIC LN	ALH	ALH	1300	37	B5
ELECTRIC ST	LA	GAR	800	63	F6
ELECTRIC ST	LA	LA39	2200	35	C3
ELECTRONIC DR	PAS	PAS	3400	28	A3
ELECTRONICS PL	LA	LA39	4500	25	B4
ELEDA DR	TOR	TOR		73	A2
EL EMBARCADERO	LB	LB02	1000	75	A6
EL EMPINO DR	LHH	LAH	2200	85	E6
ELENA AV	RB	RB		67	C2
ELENA AV	WCOV	WCOV		92	E6
ELENA AV N	RB	RB77		67	D6
ELENA AV S	RB	RB77		67	C2
ELENA CT	WHI	WHI3		84	D4
ELENA ST	CER	ART		66	E4
EL ENCANTO DR	PAS	PAS	300	27	F5
EL ENCANTO RD	IND	LPUE	300	48	E6
EL ENCINO DR	DBAR	POM	100	94	A6
ELENDA ST	CUL	CUL	4000	50	B2
EL ESCORPION RD	LA	WOH	5600	5	E6
EL ESPEJO RD	LAM	LAM	13400	82	F2
ELEVA AV	SAD	SAD	100	89	F3
ELEVADO AV	ARC	ARC	1600	28	E2
ELEVADO AV	BH	BH	9100	33	A6
ELEVADO AV	WHOL	LA69	8900	33	D5
ELEVADO ST	LA	LA26	1400	35	B5
ELEVADO ST	PVE	PVP	2700	72	D2
ELEVADO TER	MPK	MPK	400	45	F2
ELFORD DR	CO	WHI	3600	55	C1
ELFSTONE CT	THO	THO		102A	F3
ELFWOOD	MON	MON	400	29	C2
ELGAR AV S	TOR	TOR	16700	63	C5
EL GATO PL	SCLR	VAL		124	A1
EL GATO PL	SCLR	VAL		127	H6
EL GAVILAN DR	CO	LPUE	15200	85	C3
ELGENIA AV	CO	COV	16100	88	B5
ELGENIA AV E	WCOV	WCOV	1000	88	B5
ELGENIA AV W	WCOV	WCOV	1000	88	B5
ELGENIA ST	WCOV	WCOV	1500	88	A5
ELGERS ST	BLF	BLF	10500	66	D6
ELGERS ST	CER	ART	10600	66	D6
ELGERS ST	CER	ART	12300	82	B6
ELGIN ST	ALH	ALH	1	37	C3
ELGIN ST	LA	LA42	6300	36	D1
EL GRACE ST	SFS	SFS	11000	60	F3
EL GRANADA AV	LYN	LYN	11600	59	D6
EL GRECO CT	CO	LPUE		85	F5
EL HITO CIR	LA	PP		40	B2
EL HITO CT	LA	PP		40	B2
EL HITO PL	LA	PP		40	B2
ELI PL	CO	LPUE	1700	98	A3
ELIAS AV	SCLR	SAU	26800	124	D7
ELIDA PL	CO	PALM		157	F8
ELINDA PL	LA	SV	10900	9	E4
ELINDA WY	LA	SV	9600	9	E4
ELIOPULOS DR	LAN	LAN		159	G5
ELIOT CT	CO	VAL		126	J3
ELIOT LN	LB	LB14	300	76	B5
ELIOT ST	LB	LB03		76	E5
ELIOT ST	LB	LB14	5500	76	C5
ELISA PL	LA	ENC	16200	22	A3
ELIZABETH AV	LYN	LYN	3300	59	A4
ELIZABETH AV	MPK	MPK	100	46	D1
ELIZABETH AV	SOG	SOG	8100	59	A3
ELIZABETH LN	LAN	LAN		160	D7
ELIZABETH ST	BAP	BAP	4800	39	E3
ELIZABETH ST	CDY	BELL	4200	59	C1
ELIZABETH ST	CO	COM	3600	65	B4
ELIZABETH ST	COM	COM	1400	65	B4
ELIZABETH ST	HPK	HPK	4200	59	C1
ELIZABETH ST	NWK	NWK	11400	60	F5
ELIZABETH ST	PAS	PAS	20	27	A1
ELIZABETH WY	SCLR	CYN		124	H9
ELIZABETH LK RD	CO	LH		157	C6
ELIZABETH LK RD	CO	PALM		157	H8
ELIZABETH LK RD	CO	PALM	8000	171	F4
ELIZABETH LK RD	CO	PALM	1100	171	D7
ELIZALDE AV	LA	NOR	8500	7	B6
ELIZONDO ST	CO	LPUE	18700	98	F1
EL JARDIN ST	LB	LB15	5300	76	C4
EL JARDIN ST	LB	LB15	6400	76	E4
ELK AV	CO	CAST		123	B5
ELK AV E	GLEN	GL05	100	25	D4
ELK AV W	GLEN	GL04	100	25	C4
ELK CIR	LAV	LAV		90	C1
ELK GROVE AV	CMRC	LA40	2400	53	F3

STREET	CITY	P.O. ZONE	BLOCK	PAGE	GRID
ELK GROVE AV	LA	VEN	1000	49	C2
ELK GROVE CIR	LA	VEN	1400	49	C2
ELKHART PL	LA	VEN	900	49	C3
ELKHILL DR	CO	LPUE	15300	85	D2
ELKHORN DR	DUA	DUA	200	86	B4
ELKHORN LN	GLDR	GLDR		87	D6
ELKHORN RD	CO	SAU		182	A7
ELKHURST ST	SFS	SFS	11000	60	F3
ELKINS AV	SMAD	SMAD	900	28	E1
ELKINS AV	SPAS	SPAS		36	D3
ELKINS PL	ARC	ARC	1	28	E1
ELKINS RD	LA	LA49	500	41	A1
ELKLAND PL	LA	VEN	900	49	D3
ELKLANE DR	CO	LPUE	1500	98	B3
ELKMONT DR	RPV	PVP	5000	72	E4
ELKO ST E	LB	LB14	4400	76	B5
ELKPORT ST	LKD	LKD	2700	70	F3
ELKPORT ST	LKD	LKD	5900	71	D3
ELKRIDGE DR	RPV	PVP	4700	72	F5
ELK RUN LN	LAN	LAN		171	B1
ELKS RAPID LN	DBAR	POM		94	A5
ELKWOOD	WCOV	WCOV		92	D4
ELKWOOD RD	WAL	WAL		93	B6
ELKWOOD ST	LA	CAN	23500	5	E2
ELKWOOD ST	LA	CAN	20900	12	D2
ELKWOOD ST	LA	NHO	11400	16	C2
ELKWOOD ST	LA	NOR	17300	14	E2
ELKWOOD ST	LA	RES	17700	14	D2
ELKWOOD ST	LA	SV	10600	16	F2
ELKWOOD ST	LA	SV	10100	17	A2
ELKWOOD ST	LA	VAN	17200	14	E2
ELLA RD	RPV	PVP	27900	72	C4
EL LADO DR	GLEN	GL08	3500	18	D2
EL LADO DR	GLEN	GL14	3600	11	C6
ELLEN DR	CO	COV	4000	88	B3
ELLEN DR	WCOV	WCOV	100	88	B6
ELLEN PL	POM	POM	1100	95	A5
ELLEN ST	ELM	ELM		38	E4
ELLEN ST	LB	LB05		65	D5
ELLEN WY	ARC	ARC	200	28	F5
ELLEN WY	CER	ART	19400	71	F2
ELLENAN ST	CO	ACT	34800	182	G7
ELLENBOGEN ST	LA	SUN	7800	10	E1
ELLENBORO WY	LA	WOH		13	D3
ELLENDA AV	LA	LA34	3200	42	A6
ELLENDA PL	LA	LA34	10800	42	A6
ELLENDALE PL	LA	LA07	1900	43	F5
ELLENITA AV	LA	TAR	4100	13	F3
ELLENITA AV	LA	TAR	4000	21	A3
ELLENVALE AV	LA	WOH	5300	100	D2
ELLENVIEW AV	LA	WOH	5900	5	D3
ELLENWOOD DR	LA	LA41	4400	25	F6
ELLENWOOD PL	LA	LA41	5100	26	A4
ELLERAY PL	GLDR	GLDR		86	E4
ELLERFORD ST	LB	LB08	8200	81	C5
ELLERY DR N	LA	SP	200	78	D3
ELLERY DR S	LA	SP	100	78	D3
ELLERY PL	LA	SP	200	78	D2
ELLESFORD AV	CO	LPUE	1500	98	F3
ELLESFORD AV	WCOV	WCOV	500	98	F2
ELLETT PL	LA	LA26	900	35	B5
ELLICE DR	CO	LPUE		85	E5
ELLINCOURT DR	SPAS	SPAS	1700	37	A1
ELLINGBROOK DR	MTB	MTB	100	46	F4
ELLINGTON DR	LA	LA68	3000	24	A6
ELLINGTON LN	PAS	PAS	800	26	D6
ELLNTN VILLA DR	CO	ALT	3300	20	C3
ELLINWOOD DR	TOR	TOR	21300	67	E5
ELLIOTT AV	AZU	AZU	100	88	D1
ELLIOTT AV	ELM	ELM	10700	47	E2
ELLIOTT AV	LPUE	LPUE	15300	48	F4
ELLIOTT AV	SELM	ELM		47	E2
ELLIOTT CT	POM	POM		94	F4
ELLIOTT DR	BUR	BUR	1700	17	C4
ELLIOTT DR	PAS	PAS	500	27	B6
ELLIOTT PL	GLEN	GL02	700	25	B1
ELLIOTT ST	LA	LA33		44	F3
ELLIS AV	LA	LA34	8900	42	C5
ELLIS AV	SH	LB04	1800	75	F3
ELLIS AV E	ING	IN02	100	50	F5
ELLIS AV E	ING	IN02	100	51	A5
ELLIS AV W	ING	IN02	100	50	F5
ELLIS CT	SCLR	SAU		124	F5
ELLIS DR	LA	LA68	3300	24	B5
ELLIS LN	ELM	ELM	4400	38	C4
ELLIS LN	RM	RM	3500	38	B6
ELLIS LN	TEC	TEC	4400	38	C4
ELLIS PL	CO	CAST		123	A5
ELLIS ST	LB	LB05	1	70	C1
ELLIS ST	PAS	PAS	400	26	E4
ELLISON DR	LA	BH	2700	33	A1
ELLISON ST	CO	LA63	3300	45	C2
ELLITA PL	LA	LA42	100	36	B2
EL LOBO CIR	CER	ART	7600	81	D2
ELLORA ST	LPUE	LPUE	16400	98	A1
ELLSMERE AV	LA	LA19	1400	42	F3

STREET	CITY	P.O. ZONE	BLOCK	PAGE	GRID
ELLSTREE DR	CO	LH		157	A6
ELLSWICK DR	LA	LA45	9300	55A	F2
ELLSWORTH ST	AZU	AZU	300	86	C3
ELLSWORTH ST	LA	LA26	3200	35	A5
ELLWOOD AV	GLDR	GLDR		87	C6
ELM	CO	LP48		98	F3
ELM	LA	SF42		2	C1
ELM AV	BUR	BUR	200	24	E2
ELM AV	CO	SGAB	8300	37	E2
ELM AV	CO	SGAB	8500	38	A2
ELM AV	CO	TEC	8800	38	A2
ELM AV	ELS	ELS	1400	56	C5
ELM AV	GLEN	GL01	1000	17	F6
ELM AV	ING	IN01	300	56	F2
ELM AV	LAN	LAN	43800	160	A6
ELM AV	LB	LB02	100	75	C5
ELM AV	LB	LB05	6100	65	C6
ELM AV	LB	LB05	4900	70	C2
ELM AV	LB	LB06	2100	75	C2
ELM AV	LB	LB07	3000	70	C6
ELM AV	LB	LB13	700	75	C5
ELM AV	MB	MB	1100	62	C4
ELM AV	SGAB	SGAB	500	37	E2
ELM AV	SMAD	SMAD		28	C1
ELM AV	TEC	TEC	8900	38	A2
ELM AV	TOR	TOR	600	68	C4
ELM AV	TOR	TOR	22600	68	C5
ELM CT	BUR	BUR	100	24	E1
ELM CT	CO	SAU		124	D2
ELM DR	CO	CAL		100	E5
ELM DR	LA	LA35	1100	42	C2
ELM DR N	BH	BH	100	33	B5
ELM DR S	BH	BH	100	42	C2
ELM LN	CO	CAST		123	J2
ELM LN	PAS	PAS		26	F2
ELM ST	ALH	ALH	1	36	F4
ELM ST	CMRC	LA40	7000	54	B4
ELM ST	LA	LA01	8300	58	E2
ELM ST	LA	LA02	8600	58	E2
ELM ST	LA	LA05	2700	35	E3
ELM ST	LA	LA65	2700	35	E3
ELM ST	LA	VEN	1200	49	D4
ELM ST	LYN	LYN	10700	59	C6
ELM ST	MTB	MTB	100	54	C4
ELM ST	POM	POM	100	94	F3
ELM ST E	COM	COM	100	65	A2
ELM ST W	COM	COM	100	64	E2
ELM WY	LB	LB02	1	75	C6
ELMA RD	CO	PAS	3700	28	B4
EL MANOR AV	LA	LA45	7200	50	C6
EL MANOR AV	LA	LA45	8000	56	C1
ELMBANK RD	RPV	PVP	5400	72	E3
ELMBRAKE LN	MTB	MTB	100	46	E4
ELMBRIDGE DR	RPV	PVP	27400	72	F4
ELMBROOK DR	LAM	LAM	13900	83	A2
ELMBROOK LN	POM	POM		90	E3
ELMCREST ST	CO	ELM	10700	38	D4
ELMCREST ST	ELM	ELM	10600	38	F4
ELMCREST ST	LAV	LAV	1500	90	C2
ELMCROFT AV	DOW	DOW	10900	60	E5
ELMCROFT AV	NWK	NWK	11200	60	E5
ELMCROFT AV	NWK	NWK	12900	66	E5
ELMCROFT AV	POM	POM	1400	95	B1
ELMDALE DR	RHE	PVP	4800	72	F3
ELMDALE PL	LA	SF	17200	1	E4
EL MEDIO AV	LA	PP	400	40	C4
EL MEDIO PL	LA	PP		40	C3
ELMER AV	LA	NHO	6000	16	E5
ELMER AV	LA	NHO	4000	23	E4
ELMER AV	LA	SV	7400	16	E3
ELMER AV	WHI	WHI	7000	55	D5
EL MERCADO AV	MPK	MPK	400	46	B3
EL MERRIE DL DR	CO	SF	11200	3	E4
ELMFIELD AV	LB	LB15	1600	76	C3
ELMGATE ST E	MPK	MPK	100	46	B4
ELMGATE ST W	MPK	MPK	100	46	B4
ELM GLEN CIR	SCLR	VAL	23000	124	C5
ELMGROVE DR	GLDR	GLDR		87	D4
ELMGROVE ST	LA	LA31	2200	35	E4
ELM HAVEN DR	CO	LPUE	16500	98	A3
ELM HILL DR	CO	WHI	11500	84	D5
ELMHURST AV	DUA	DUA	1200	29	E5
ELMHURST CIR	CLA	CLA		91	D2
ELMHURST DR	LA	TU	6400	11	B5
ELMHURST DR	NWK	NWK	11200	66	F4
EL MIO DR	LA	LA42	9500	36	C1
EL MIRA AV	CLA	CLA		96	C5
EL MIRA AV	CLA	CLA		96	C6
ELMIRA CT	CER	ART	19400	71	F2
ELMIRA ST	PAS	PAS	600	27	B2
EL MIRADERO AV	GLEN	GL01	1400	18	A6
EL MIRADOR AV	LB	LB15	1000	76	C3
EL MIRADOR DR	LA	LA08	5200	50	F1
EL MIRADOR DR	PAS	PAS	1200	26	D2
EL MIRADOR ST	LAM	LAM		83	C2

INDEX

242
1990 LOS ANGELES COUNTY STREET INDEX
ELMO AV
ERNEST AV

LOS ANGELES CO.

STREET	CITY	P.O. ZONE	BLOCK	PAGE	GRID
ELMO AV	TOR	TOR	22000	67	F5
ELMO ST	LA	TU	7200	10	F4
ELMO ST	LA	TU	6500	11	B4
EL MOLINO AV	CO	ALT	1900	20	B6
EL MOLINO AV	SMAR	PAS	1700	37	B2
EL MOLINO AV N	PAS	PAS	1600	20	B6
EL MOLINO AV N	PAS	PAS	100	27	B3
EL MOLINO AV S	PAS	PAS	100	27	B6
EL MOLINO AV S	PAS	PAS	1400	37	B2
EL MOLINO PL	SMAR	PAS	2000	37	B2
EL MOLINO ST N	ALH	ALH	100	37	C3
EL MOLINO ST S	ALH	ALH	100	37	C3
ELMONT AV	CER	ART		82	E4
ELMONT AV	DOW	DOW	8500	60	C1
ELMONT AV	PR	PR	8200	54	D6
EL MONTE AV	ARC	ARC	1000	28	D6
EL MONTE AV	ARC	ARC	1600	38	D1
EL MONTE AV	ELM	ELM	3600	38	D6
EL MONTE AV	TEC	TEC	4800	38	D4
EL MONTE ST	SGAB	SGAB	100	37	E4
EL MORADO ST	LAM	LAM		83	C1
EL MORADO ST	LAM	LAM		84	C6
EL MORAN ST	LA	LA39		35	D3
ELMORE AV	CO	WHI	9600	61	F4
EL MORENO	CO	GL14		18	E1
EL MORENO ST	CO	GL14	2300	11	E6
EL MORENO ST	GLEN	GL14	3700	11	C5
EL MORO AV	LAM	LAM	12800	82	E1
ELM PARK	PALM	PALM		171	J7
ELM PARK DR	CER	ART		82	B4
ELM PARK ST	SPAS	SPAS	1100	36	F3
ELMQUIST AV	WHI	WHI	6200	55	F4
ELMROCK AV	CO	WHI	11700	84	C5
ELMROCK AV	LAM	LAM	14000	83	C2
ELMROCK AV	LAM	LAM	12600	84	C6
ELMSBURY LN	LA	CAN		5	D3
ELMSIDE DR	SCLR	SAU		124	F5
ELMTREE DR	CO	PALM		157	H9
ELMTREE RD	LA	NOR		7	B2
ELM VIEW DR	LA	ENC		21	C4
ELM VISTA DR	DOW	DOW		60	C5
ELMWOOD AV	LA	LA04	4700	34	D5
ELMWOOD AV	LYN	LYN	4200	59	C5
ELMWOOD AV E	BUR	BUR	100	17	E6
ELMWOOD AV W	BUR	BUR	200	24	D2
ELMWOOD DR	PAS	PAS	300	26	D5
ELMYRA ST E	LA	LA12	100	44	E1
ELMYRA ST W	LA	LA12	100	44	E1
EL NIDO	LAV	LAV		95A	D4
EL NIDO AV	MON	MON	100	29	A3
EL NIDO AV	PAS	PAS	1	27	F5
EL NIDO DR	CO	ALT	2800	19	E4
EL NIDO LN	LAN	LAN		160	F6
ELNORA PL	LA	SF	11900	1	E5
ELNORA ST	PR	PR	8200	54	F2
EL NORTE AV	ARC	ARC	800	28	F5
EL NORTE ST E	MON	MON	100	29	B5
EL NORTE ST W	MON	MON	100	29	B5
EL OESTE ST	HB	RB	2600	62	C5
ELOISE AV	LA	SV	7900	16	D2
ELOISE AV	PAS	PAS	1	27	E4
ELOISE ST	CER	ART	11200	71	F2
ELON AV	LA	PAC	9600	8	E4
EL ORO LN	LA	PP	800	40	B3
EL ORO WY	LA	SF	11900	1	E4
EL PARAISO DR	POM	POM	1200	90	D6
EL PARQUE ST	LB	LB15	5100	76	C4
EL PASEO	ALH	ALH	2100	46	A1
EL PASEO CT	LB	LB15	6300	76	D2
EL PASEO DR	SCLR	VAL		124	B9
EL PASEO DR	WHI	WHI	15700	84	C2
EL PASEO RD	CO	SP	300	78	E3
EL PASEO ST	LB	LB15	5500	76	C2
EL PASO CT	SAD	SAD	800	90	A2
EL PASO DR	LA	LA42	800	36	A1
EL PASO DR	LA	LA65	1100	36	A1
EL PASO WK	LA	LA07	2200	43	E5
EL POCHE ST	SELM	ELM	9600	47	C3
EL PORTAL PL	MPK	MPK	800	46	B2
EL PORTAL RD	PVE	PVP	100	72	C3
EL PORTO ST	MB	MB	100	62	A2
EL PORTOLO	PAS	PAS	99	26	E4
EL PRADO AV	LB	LB15	5200	76	C3
EL PRADO AV	TOR	TOR	1200	68	D4
EL PRESIDIO ST	CAR	LB10	2500	70	A3
EL PRIETO RD	CO	ALT	4200	19	E2
EL PROGRESO ST	LB	LB15	6500	76	E2
EL PULCRO ST	LB	LB15	6500	76	E2
EL RANCHO DR E	WHI	WHI	10400	55	C3
EL RANCHO DR S	WHI	WHI	6000	55	C3
EL RCHO VRDE DR	CER	ART	4600	81	D2
EL REDONDO	RB	RB	100	67	D3
EL RENO ST	LA	LA31	300	36	B5
EL REPETTO DR	MPK	MPK	100	46	A3
EL REPOSO DR	LA	LA41	4500	25	F5
EL RETIRO WY	BH	BH	1100	33	B4
EL REY DR	WHI	WHI		55	C4
EL REY RD	LA	SP	1700	78	D3
EL RICO PL	DBAR	POM		94	B6
EL RINCON WY	CUL	CUL	5700	50	D3
EL RIO AV	LA	LA41	5100	26	A4
EL RIO VRDE CIR	CER	ART	7600	81	D2
EL RITA DR	LA	LA46		33	E1
EL RITO AV	GLEN	GL08	1300	18	E5
EL ROBLE DR	LA	LA41	2700	25	F5
EL ROBLE LN	LA	BH	2100	33	C2
EL ROBLE ST	LB	LB15	5100	76	C3
EL RODEO RD	RPV	PVP	29200	72	C5
EL ROSA DR	LA	LA65	2500	35	E2
ELROVIA AV	ELM	ELM	4000	38	F5
ELSA ST	LKD	LKD	3900	71	D3
ELSAH AV	CO	WHI	1100	48	A5
EL SALVADOR ST	LB	LB15	6700	76	E2
EL SASTRE RD	CO	PALM		190	A2
ELSBERRY AV	CO	LPUE	700	92	B5
ELSDALE PL	CO	LAN		171	B1
ELSDALE PL	PALM	PALM		171	B2
EL SEBO AV	CO	LPUE	3000	85	C4
EL SEGUNDO BL E	CO	COM	1900	58	E6
EL SEGUNDO BL E	CO	LA59	600	58	C6
EL SEGUNDO BL E	CO	LA61	100	58	C6
EL SEGUNDO BL E	COM	COM	1200	58	C6
EL SEGUNDO BL E	COM	COM	300	58	F6
EL SEGUNDO BL E	ELS	ELS	100	56	B6
EL SEGUNDO BL E	LYN	LYN	3100	59	A6
EL SEGUNDO BL W	CO	HAW	4800	56	D6
EL SEGUNDO BL W	CO	LA61	100	58	C6
EL SEGUNDO BL W	ELS	ELS	100	56	B6
EL SEGUNDO BL W	GAR	GAR	1000	57	E6
EL SEGUNDO BL W	HAW	HAW	4700	56	D6
EL SEGUNDO BL W	HAW	HAW	3100	57	C6
EL SEGUNDO BL W	LA	GAR	700	57	E6
EL SEGUNDO BL W	LA	GAR	500	58	C6
EL SELINDA AV	BG	BELL	6200	53	F6
EL SELINDA DR	CO	LPUE		85	C3
EL SERENO AV	CO	ALT	2100	19	F6
EL SERENO AV	CO	ALT	3600	20	A3
EL SERENO AV	CO	GL14	4800	18	E1
EL SERENO AV	LA	LA32	3500	36	D4
EL SERENO AV	PAS	PAS	1500	19	F6
EL SERENO AV	PAS	PAS	1300	26	F1
EL SERENO DR	ARC	ARC	2000	38	C1
ELSEY PL	ELS	ELS	1000	56	B6
ELSIE AV	LA	NOR	9400	7	B4
ELSIE ST	CO	LA01	7200	52	D6
ELSINORE ST	LA	LA26	2100	35	B5
ELSMERE DR	CAR	CAR	600	69	C2
ELSMERE CYN RD	CO	NEW		127	F8
ELSMORE DR	CO	RM	8200	46	F3
EL SOL AV	CO	ALT	2100	19	E5
EL SOL DR	LAN	LAN		160	F7
EL SOL PL	POM	POM	1900	90	E6
EL SONETO DR	WHI	WHI	14900	84	C3
ELSPETH AV	CO	COV	4600	88	D4
ELSPETH AV	COV	COV	100	88	D5
ELSPETH WY	COV	COV	500	88	D4
ELSTEAD ST	BAP	BAP	14600	39	F5
ELSTER AV	CO	LPUE	700	92	B5
ELSTON AV	DOW	DOW	8800	60	D1
EL SUENO DR	CO	MAL		111	E4
EL SUR ST	ARC	ARC	1000	29	A6
EL SUR ST	CO	DUA	500	29	B6
EL SUR ST E	CO	MON	300	29	B6
EL SUR ST E	MON	MON	100	29	B6
EL SUR ST W	CO	MON	100	29	A6
EL TERRAZA DR	LHH	LAH	900	84	D2
EL TESORITO	SPAS	SPAS	700	36	E3
EL TESORO CT	CO	LPUE		85	C3
EL TESORO PL	RPV	PVP	6400	78	D2
EL TIRO DR	LAM	LAM	15700	83	C2
ELTON AV	CO	LA22	1500	54	A2
ELTON CIR	CER	ART	19400	71	F2
ELTON ST	BAP	BAP	4200	39	F3
EL TORO CIR	CER	ART	7600	81	D2
EL TORO RD	CO	DUA		39	B1
EL TORO F TK TR	CO	NEW		126	B8
EL TOVAR DR	GLEN	GL08	3100	18	F4
EL TOVAR PL	WHOL	LA69	8700	33	D5
EL TRAVESIA DR	LHH	LAH	1600	84	E2
ELUSIVE DR	LA	LA46	8300	33	E2
ELVA AV	CO	LA59	12000	58	D6
ELVA AV	COM	COM	1500	64	D1
ELVA ST	CO	LA59	1200	58	D5
EL VADO RD	DBAR	POM		93	F6
EL VADO RD	DBAR	POM	100	94	A6
EL VAGO ST	LCF	LCF	1200	19	B1
EL VALLNCITO DR	WAL	WAL		93	C5
EL VECINO PL	POM	POM		94	B4
EL VENADO DR	CO	LPUE	2500	85	B2
EL VENADO DR	WHI	WHI	9500	84	B2
EL VERANO AV	LA	LA41	5000	25	F5
ELVIDO DR	LA	LA49	2900	22	A6
ELVILL DR	LA	LA49	3000	22	A6
ELVINA DR	GLEN	GL06	400	26	A3
ELVINS ST	LKD	LKD	11400	71	F3
ELVINS ST	LKD	LKD	12400	81	B3
ELVIRA AV	RB	RB	600	67	D4
ELVIRA RD	LA	WOH	5100	13	C2
ELVISTA CIR	ARC	ARC	1700	28	E2
EL VISTA CT	GLEN	GL08	2000	18	F4
EL VOLCAN PL	CO	LPUE	2500	85	E4
ELWOOD AV	PALM	PALM		183	G6
ELWOOD AV	POM	POM	1300	94	B1
ELWOOD AV N	GLDR	GLDR	100	87	C5
ELWOOD AV S	GLDR	GLDR	100	87	C5
ELWOOD ST	LA	LA21	1300	44	E6
ELWOOD ST	POM	POM		94	C1
ELWOOD ST	WHOL	LA69	800	33	D4
ELWYN DR	BAP	BAP	13800	39	D5
ELY AV	ART	ART	19000	81	B2
ELY AV	CER	ART	17200	82	B5
ELY AV	LB	LB08		81	B5
ELY AV	LKD	LKD	20700	81	B3
ELY AV	LKD	LKD	21400	81	B4
ELYRIA DR	LA	LA65	800	36	A3
ELYSIAN AV	POM	POM	1200	95	B1
ELYSIAN PARK AV	LA	LA26	1000	35	D6
ELYSIAN PARK DR	LA	LA26	1200	35	D6
ELZA DR	CO	LPUE		85	F5
ELZEVIR RD	LA	WOH	4200	13	D3
EMAD ST	CO	SAU		182	F8
EMANUEL DR	GLEN	GL08	3500	18	D3
EMBASSY AV	CAR	LB10	21800	69	F4
EMBASSY DR	LA	ENC	17000	21	E2
EMBASSY PL	POM	POM	900	95	B1
EMBER CT	AGH	AGO		102	D3
EMBER DR	CO	LPUE		98	C4
EMBERBROOK DR	SCLR	NEW		127	D3
EMBER GLEN RD	CO	LPUE	16500	98	A3
EMBREE DR	ELM	ELM	11500	39	A3
EMBURNS DR	GLEN	GL08	1800	18	F5
EMBURY ST	LA	PP	900	40	D3
EMDEN RD	CO	PALM	34800	184	B7
EMDEN ST	LA	WIL	1300	74	A5
EMELITA ST	LA	ENC	17300	14	E6
EMELITA ST	LA	NHO	11000	16	B6
EMELITA ST	LA	VAN	13500	15	E6
EMELITA ST	LA	WOH	23600	5	E6
EMENS WY	GLEN	GL01	1500	24	F2
EMERADO DR	WHI	WHI	9800	84	D3
EMERALD AV	LAV	LAV	3600	90	D1
EMERALD AV	LAV	LAV	4200	95A	D6
EMERALD AV	WCOV	WCOV	300	92	F1
EMERALD CIR	LKD	LKD		81	C3
EMERALD CT	PALM	PALM		171	F6
EMERALD DR	LA	LA26	1300	44	C2
EMERALD LN	LAN	LAN		160	F5
EMERALD ST	LA	LA26	200	44	C2
EMERALD ST	RB	RB	300	67	D3
EMERALD ST	TOR	TOR	3200	67	E3
EMERALD ST	TOR	TOR	4200	68	A3
EMERALD TER	GLEN	GL01	1800	18	A5
EMERALD WY	MPK	MPK	2000	46	C4
EMERALD COVE DR	LB	LB03	6100	76	E5
EMERALD DOVE DR	CO	VAL		123	J9
EMERALD DOVE DR	CO	VAL		126	G1
EMERALD DOVE DR	CO	VAL		126	J1
EMERALD ISLE DR	GLEN	GL08	3500	19	B6
EMERALD MDW DR	CO	WAL	20000	97	B4
EMERSON	PALM	PALM		171	J7
EMERSON AV	ALH	ALH	2300	46	B1
EMERSON AV	LA	LA45	7700	50	B6
EMERSON AV	LA	LA45	8000	56	B2
EMERSON AV E	MPK	MPK	100	46	B1
EMERSON AV W	MPK	MPK	100	46	B1
EMERSON CT	AGH	AGO		102	E3
EMERSON LN	CO	VAL		126	J3
EMERSON PL	CLA	CLA	900	91	A2
EMERSON PL	RM	RM	7400	46	E1
EMERSON PL	RM	RM	8900	47	A1
EMERSON ST	PAS	PAS	900	27	B3
EMERSON WY	CO	ALT	2900	20	A4
EMERY AV	BAP	BAP	13100	39	C6
EMERY PL	LA	WIL	1100	74	D3
EMERY ST	ELM	ELM	10500	38	E4
EMERY ST	ELM	ELM	11700	39	A5
EMERY ST	LA	LA23	3300	53	B1
EMIL AV	BG	BELL	6400	54	A6
EMIL AV	BG	BELL	7100	60	A1
EMIL AV	CMRC	LA40	6200	54	B5
EMILE ZOLA ST	LAN	LAN		160	D6
EMILIA LN	LAN	LAN		160	D7
EMILIA PL	LA	SP	1900	78	D3
EMILY DR	WCOV	WCOV	1000	92	B3
EMILY LN	DOW	DOW	7300	59	F5
EMILY ST	LA	SP	2600	78	E6
EMIR AV	LA	SF	13900	2	F1
EMMA AV	LA	LA31	3400	36	B5
EMMENS WY	SFS	SFS	12600	61	C4
EMMET RD	SCLR	CYN		124	G9
EMMET TER	LA	LA68	6600	34	B2
EMMETT WLLMS WY	MTB	MTB	500	54	D1
EMMONS RD	LA	LA41	4500	26	A6
EMORY DR	CLA	CLA		91	A2
EMORY DR	WHI	WHI	13800	55	F6
EMORY DR	WHI	WHI	13800	61	F1
EMORY DR	WHI	WHI	14300	84	A1
EMPALMO CT	SCLR	VAL		127	A2
EMPANADA PL	LA	ENC	1500	21	E4
EMPEROR AV	CO	ARC	9700	38	C1
EMPEROR AV	CO	SGAB	8800	38	A1
EMPEROR AV	TEC	TEC	9000	38	A1
EMPINO LN	SCLR	SAU	22100	124	D6
EMPIRE AV	BUR	BUR	3900	16	F4
EMPIRE AV	BUR	BUR	1800	17	A4
EMPIRE DR	LA	LA34	3600	42	B6
EMPIRE DR	LA	PAC	10600	9	B2
EMPIRE PL	LA	PAC	12400	9	B2
EMPIS ST	LA	WOH	4100	13	D4
EMPORIA AV	CUL	CUL	5100	50	B4
EMPRESS AV	LA	ENC	4100	21	E3
EMPRESS AV	SPAS	SPAS	2000	36	F3
EMPRESS RD	POM	POM	500	93	F2
EMPTY SADDLE LN	RHE	PVP	1	73	B4
EMPTY SADDLE RD	RHE	PVP	1	73	B4
EMPTY SADDLE RD	WAL	WAL		93	A6
EMPYREAN WY	LA	LA67	10000	42	B2
ENADIA WY	LA	CAN	19700	12	F3
ENADIA WY	LA	RES	17700	14	A3
ENADIA WY	LA	VAN	16900	14	D3
ENADIA WY	LA	VAN	13700	15	E3
ENCANADA DR	LHH	LAH	100	84	E1
ENCANTADOR	LA	SP		78	C4
ENCANTO	PALM	PALM		171	E4
ENCANTO DR	ARC	ARC	900	28	B4
ENCANTO DR	GLDR	GLDR	100	87	D5
ENCANTO DR	LA	VAN		22	C4
ENCANTO DR	RHE	PVP	1	73	D4
ENCANTO PKWY	AZU	AZU		86	A5
ENCANTO PKWY	DUA	DUA		86	A5
ENCANTO WY	CO	LAN		159	A9
ENCHANTED PL	LA	PP	16900	40	B3
ENCHANTED WY	LA	PP	600	40	B3
ENCHANTD HLS RD	CO	PALM		190	A2
ENCINA RD	CO	TOP	21300	109	C4
ENCINAL AV	CO	GL14	2400	18	D1
ENCINAL AV	CO	GL14	3000	18	D1
ENCINAL AV	GLEN	GL14	3400	11	C6
ENCINAL AV	GLEN	GL14	3200	18	D1
ENCINAL CYN RD	CO	MAL		105	D5
ENCINAL CYN RD	CO	MAL		111	A4
ENCINAS DR	LCF	LCF	4100	19	B2
ENCINAS DR	LHH	LAH		98A	B3
ENCINITA AV	CO	SGAB	6900	28	B6
ENCINITA AV	CO	SGAB	6700	38	B1
ENCINITA AV	RM	RM	4100	38	B4
ENCINITA AV	TEC	TEC	4800	38	B4
ENCINITAS AV	LA	SF	12600	2	B4
ENCINITAS AV N	MON	MON	100	29	B3
ENCINITAS AV S	MON	MON	100	29	B3
ENCINO AV	ARC	ARC	900	28	F6
ENCINO AV	LA	ENC	5600	14	E6
ENCINO AV	LA	ENC	4500	21	E2
ENCINO AV	LA	NOR	8600	7	D3
ENCINO AV	LA	NOR	7600	14	E2
ENCINO AV	LA	SF	11500	1	D6
ENCINO AV	LA	SF	10500	7	D2
ENCINO AV	LA	VAN	6400	14	E4
ENCINO AV	MON	MON	1100	28	F5
ENCINO CT	ARC	ARC	600	28	F6
ENCINO DR	ARC	ARC	600	28	F6
ENCINO DR	PAS	PAS	1311	27	B6
ENCINO PL	MON	MON	800	28	F5
ENCINO PL	POM	POM	2200	94	F6
ENCINO TER	LA	ENC	4700	21	D2
ENCINO WY	MON	MON	800	28	F5
ENCINO HILLS DR	LA	ENC	16700	21	F5
ENCINO HILLS PL	LA	ENC	3800	21	F5
END CT	LAN	LAN	2600	159	G6
ENDEAVOR ST	AGH	AGO		100A	C5
ENDERBY CT	CO	CAL		100	B3
ENDERLY ST	SCLR	CYN	19500	124	H6
ENDICOTT DR	CLA	CLA		91	D1
ENDICOTT RD	SMAR	PAS	1800	37	E1
ENDICOTT ST	LA	LA32	2400	36	E6
ENDRINO PL	BH	BH	600	33	C2
ENDSLEIGH AV	ING	IN01		57	B2
ENFIELD AV	LA	ENC	4800	14	D6
ENFIELD AV	LA	ENC	4900	21	D2
ENFIELD AV	LA	NOR	8500	7	D6
ENFIELD AV	LA	RES	6100	14	D3
ENFIELD AV	LA	SF	11000	7	D1
ENGINEERS ST	CO	CAST		123	F2
ENGLAND AV	ING	IN03	10100	57	C3
ENGLANDER ST	CO	GAR	500	64	B3
ENGLANDER ST	LA	SP	1000	73	E6
ENGLE PL	CO	LPUE	16700	92	B5
ENGLEWILD DR	GLDR	GLDR	1000	87	C3
ENGLEWILD LN	GLDR	GLDR	900	87	C3
ENGLISH OAKS DR	ARC	ARC		28	C3
ENGRACIA AV	TOR	TOR	800	68	D4
ENID AV	CO	AZU	5200	88	C3
ENID AV	COV	COV	4300	88	C4
ENID AV N	AZU	AZU	900	86	C5
ENID AV S	AZU	AZU	300	88	C2
ENLOE ST	SELM	ELM	9700	47	C3
ENNA ST	CO	WHI	2300	47	F5
ENNIS ST	LA	SUN	8400	10	D3
ENNISMORE AV	SCLR	CYN	27500	124	J8
ENOLA AV	CAR	CAR	22600	69	B5
ENOLA AV	CAR	CAR	23600	74	B1
ENORO DR	CO	LA08	4200	51	A2
ENRAMADA AV	WHI	WHI	8100	84	A2
ENRIQUE ST	LA	WOH	20900	13	D4
ENRIQUES DR	DBAR	POM		94	A6
ENROSE AV	LA	SP	100	78	D2
ENROSE AV	RPV	SP	28900	78	D1
ENSELVADO AV	LAM	LAM	14600	83	B2
ENSENADA DR	LA	WOH	4200	13	C4
ENSENADA PL	LA	WOH		13	C3
ENSENADA RD	CO	SAU		157A	F4
ENSIGN AV	LA	NHO	5600	16	E5
ENSIGN AV	LA	NHO	4400	23	E3
ENSIGN AV	LA	SV	7200	16	E1
ENSLEY AV	LA	LA24	1500	42	A2
ENSLOW DR	CAR	CAR	19000	69	C1
ENTERPRISE AV	ING	IN02	900	50	F5
ENTERPRISE DR	PALM	PALM		183	G8
ENTERPRISE PL	LYN	LYN		58	F5
ENTERPRISE PL	POM	POM		93	F3
ENTERPRISE PL	POM	POM		94	A3
ENTERPRISE ST	LA	LA21	1800	44	E5
ENTERPRISE WY	MON	DUA		29	C5
ENTRADA AV	LA	NOR		1	C6
ENTRADA CT	LA	NOR		1	C6
ENTRADA DR	LA	SM	100	40	D5
ENTRADA RD	CO	TOP	20800	109	C4
ENTRADA ST	CMRC	LA40		53	F2
ENTRADA WY	GLDR	GLDR	700	87	C4
ENTRADERO AV	TOR	TOR	19100	67	E2
ENTRADO DR	CO	TOP	21700	13	C6
ENTRADO DR	CO	TOP		109	C1
ENTRANCE DR	LA	LA27	2400	35	B3
ENTRECOLINAS PL	POM	POM	1600	94	D1
ENVILLE PL	LA	LA16	3500	42	E6
ENVOY ST	LA	SF	14800	2	D5
EOLA DR	WAL	WAL	400	93	B6
EPPERSON DR	IND	LPUE		98	E2
EPPING RD	PVE	PVP	400	72	A4
EPSILON ST	LA	WOH	22800	13	A2
EPSOM PL	PR	PR	9400	47	C6
EPSOM PL	PR	PR	9400	55	C1
EQUATION RD	CO	CLA	3700	90	F2
EQUATION RD	POM	POM	3600	90	F3
EQUESTRIAN LN	CO	LPUE		47	F6
EQUITABLE RD	CER	ART	13800	82	E4
EREMLAND DR	COV	COV	500	88	F6
ERIC AV	CER	ART	16900	66	F5
ERIC AV	CER	ART	19000	71	F2
ERIC DR	LA	LA49	2100	30	F6
ERICA AV	WCOV	WCOV		92	E6
ERICA CIR	LA	CAN	7000	5	E4
ERICA LN	LAN	LAN		159	G8
ERICK CT	PALM	PALM		183	E2
ERICKSEN DR	POM	POM	900	94	C2
ERICKSON AV	DOW	DOW	11800	59	E6
ERIE	CO	AGO		106	D2
ERIE ST	LB	LB02	1600	75	E5
ERIE ST	POM	POM	200	94	C2
ERIEL AV	CO	GAR	15100	63	C3
ERIEL AV	CO	HAW	13200	63	C1
ERIEL AV	TOR	TOR	1100	68	C4
ERIEL AV	TOR	TOR	18400	68	C1
ERIEL AV	TOR	TOR	22400	68	C6
ERIKA CT	CO	LPUE		98	C4
ERIN CIR	CER	ART	19400	71	F2
ERIN CT	GLEN	GL06		19	B6
ERIN CT	WCOV	WCOV		92	E5
ERIN LN	LAM	LAM	12100	84	B6
ERIN WY	CO	SAU		181	C7
ERIN WY	GLEN	GL06		19	B6
ERMANITA AV	CO	GAR	15200	63	C3
ERMANITA AV	TOR	TOR	16400	63	C5
ERMANITA AV	TOR	TOR	18300	68	C1
ERMINE ST	SCLR	CYN	19300	124	H6
ERMITA AV	LAM	LAM	14400	83	C2
ERMONT PL	SM	SM	700	40	E4
ERNEST AV	LA	LA34	5800	42	E5
ERNEST AV	RB	RB	1900	62	E4

INDEX

COPYRIGHT, © 1989 BY Thomas Bros Maps

1990 LOS ANGELES COUNTY STREET INDEX

—Z— COPYRIGHT, © 1989 BY Thomas Bros Maps

STREET	CITY	P.O. ZONE	BLOCK	PAGE	GRID
ERNESTINE AV	LYN	LYN	11100	59	B6
EROICA DR	MPK	MPK	900	46	D3
ERSKINE DR	LA	PP	500	40	C4
ERVILLA PL	POM	POM	1900	90	F6
ERVILLA ST	POM	POM	300	90	F6
ERWIN DR	PALM	PALM		171	J6
ERWIN ST	LA	NHO	10500	16	B5
ERWIN ST	LA	RES	17700	14	B5
ERWIN ST	LA	VAN	13300	15	D5
ERWIN ST	LA	VAN	12900	16	A5
ERWIN ST	LA	WOH	23000	5	F5
ERWIN ST	LA	WOH	20900	12	A5
ERWOOD AV	NWK	NWK	13600	82	A2
ESCALADA AV	CO	LPUE	1400	98	D3
ESCALANTE DR	LCF	LCF	5200	11	F6
ESCALERA	SCLR	VAL		127	A3
ESCALON AV	CO	LA43	4800	51	B3
ESCALON DR	LA	ENC	16700	21	E5
ESCALONA RD	LAM	LAM	14700	83	A3
ESCARPA DR	LA	LA41	1900	26	A5
ESCARPARDO DR	LHH	LAH	800	84	C2
ESCOBEDO DR	LA	WOH	4700	13	D2
ESCONDIDO DR	CO	MAL	2900	112	E3
ESCONDIDO ST	LA	WOH	21100	13	C4
ESCNDIDO BCH RD	CO	MAL		112	E6
ESCNDIDO CYN RD	CO	ACT		181	H8
ESCNDIDO CYN RD	CO	ACT		189	D2
ESCNDIDO CYN RD	CO	SAU		181	D9
ESCNDIDO CYN RD	CO	SAU		182	C9
ESCUELA	CO	LA22		45	F5
ESCUELA WY	PALM	LAN		171	D4
ESEVERRI LN	LHH	LAH	100	84	E3
ESGUERRA RD	SCLR	SAU		124	J3
ESHELMAN AV	LOM	LOM	23900	73	D2
ESHELMAN WY	LOM	LOM		73	D2
ESKO AV	LA	SF	11200	10	A1
ESMERALDA AV	ELM	ELM	3600	38	E5
ESMERALDA DR	GLEN	GL07	1100	25	E1
ESMERALDA ST	LA	LA32	4300	36	C5
ESMOND AV	NWK	NWK	13400	82	B1
ESMOND ST	POM	POM	2300	90	E4
ESPADA PL	DBAR	POM		97	D4
ESPANITA ST	LB	LB15	6500	76	E3
ESPANOL AV	MTB	MTB	1400	54	C4
ESPARTA WY	LA	SM	14100	40	E4
ESPARTA WY	SM	SM	100	40	E4
ESPARTO RD	LA	WOH	4600	13	C3
ESPELETTE PL	MTB	MTB	700	46	F5
ESPERA AV	LA	PP	500	40	A3
ESPERANZA AV	CO	WHI	5700	55	B3
ESPERANZA AV	LB	LB02	1	75	D6
ESPERANZA AV	SMAD	SMAD	1	28	C2
ESPERANZA DR	LAV	LAV		90	D1
ESPERANZA DR	LAV	LAV		95A	D6
ESPERANZA ST	DOW	DOW	7400	59	E5
ESPERANZA ST	LA	LA23	600	45	B6
ESPERANZA ST	LA	LA23	1300	53	B1
ESPERANZA TER	GLEN	GL08		18	D4
ESPINHEIRA DR	CER	ART	13000	81	C1
ESPINOSA CIR	PVE	PVP	1500	72	B4
ESPINOSA ST	LA	TAR	19300	21	A3
ESPINOZA DR	SCLR	VAL		127	B1
ESPITO ST	CO	LPUE	18100	98	D3
ESPLANADE	LA	VEN	6200	55A	D1
ESPLANADE	RB	RB	400	67	D4
ESPLANADE W	LA	VEN		49	C5
ESPUELLA DR	SCLR	SAU	22300	124	C7
ESPUMA DR	SCLR	SAU	26800	124	D7
ESQUILINE AV	CO	WAL	19800	97	B4
ESQUIRA PL	LA	ENC	16900	21	E3
ESSEX AV	LAV	LAV		90	D1
ESSEX AV	POM	POM	1200	95	B1
ESSEX CT	GLDR	GLDR		89	B2
ESSEX CT	PALM	PALM		183	C5
ESSEX DR	CER	ART	13100	81	D1
ESSEX DR	CO	PALM		184	A2
ESSEX LN	CER	ART	13000	81	C1
ESSEX LN	GLEN	GL07		25	E1
ESSEX LN	LAN	LAN		159	J3
ESSEX PL	CER	ART	12900	81	C1
ESSEX RD	SAD	SAD		89	C4
ESSEX ST	CER	ART	12300	81	B1
ESSEX ST	GLDR	GLDR	200	89	B2
ESSEX ST	LA	LA21	1400	44	D6
ESSEXFELLS DR	ALH	ALH	2600	46	A2
ESSEY AV	CO	COM	15900	65	B3
ESSEY AV N	COM	COM	800	65	B2
ESSEY AV S	COM	COM	100	65	B3
ESTABAN DR	SCLR	VAL		124	B9
ESTABAN ST	LA	TU	6600	11	A4
ESTABAN WY	LA	TU	9700	10	F4
ESTADO ST	PAS	PAS	2700	27	F3
ESTARA AV	LA	LA65	2700	35	D1
ESTATE CT	WAL	WAL		93	D4
ESTATES LN	CO	PVP		73	B4
ESTATES LN	PALM	PALM		171	C3

STREET	CITY	P.O. ZONE	BLOCK	PAGE	GRID
ESTEBAN DR	SCLR	VAL		127	H6
ESTEBAN RD	LA	WOH		13	D4
ESTELL AV	WCOV	WCOV		92	C1
ESTELLA AV	CER	ART	16000	66	E4
ESTELLA LN	LAN	LAN		160	G6
ESTELLA ST	BAP	BAP	14400	39	E4
ESTELLE AV	GLEN	GL02	600	25	B2
ESTEPA DR	LA	TU		10	F5
ESTEPA DR	LA	TU	6700	11	A5
ESTERBROOK AV	SCLR	CYN	27500	124	H8
ESTERINA WY	CUL	CUL	10600	50	D3
ESTERO RD	LAM	LAM	13500	82	F1
ESTES RD	LA	LA41	1900	26	A4
ESTHER AV	LA	LA64	10500	42	A4
ESTHER AV	LAV	LAV	2300	90	C3
ESTHER CT	LAN	LAN		160	C6
ESTHER ST	LYN	LYN	11600	59	A5
ESTHER ST	NWK	NWK		60	F5
ESTHER ST	PAS	PAS	1	27	A3
ESTHER ST E	LB	LB04	2500	75	E3
ESTHER ST E	LB	LB04	3600	76	A3
ESTHER ST E	LB	LB13	300	75	C3
ESTHER ST W	LB	LB13	2000	74	F3
ESTHER ST W	LB	LB13	500	75	A3
ESTHER VIEW DR	LOM	LOM	2400	73	C3
ESTO AV	CO	ELM	4200	38	D5
ESTO AV	ELM	ELM	3700	38	D6
ESTON PL	LAN	LAN	600	160	C5
ESTORIL ST	SCLR	VAL		127	A2
ESTRADA CT	WAL	WAL		92	F5
ESTRADA CT	WAL	WAL		93	A5
ESTRADA LN	LA	NOR		1	B5
ESTRADA ST	LA	LA23	3200	45	B6
ESTRELLA AV	ARC	ARC	600	38	C1
ESTRELLA AV	LA	GAR	13200	64	A1
ESTRELLA AV	LA	LA07	1900	44	B5
ESTRELLA AV	LA	LA44	5800	52	A5
ESTRELLA AV	MON	MON	1800	29	A5
ESTRELLA AV	TEC	TEC	9800	38	C1
ESTRELLA CT	PALM	PALM		183	E1
ESTRELLA PL	SCLR	NEW		127	H6
ESTRELLITA WY	LA	LA49	600	32	C5
ESTRIBO DR	RHE	PVP	2200	73	D5
ESTRONDO DR	LA	ENC	4400	21	F3
ESTRONDO PL	LA	ENC	4300	21	F3
ESTUDILLO AV	LA	LA23	1500	53	B1
ESTUDILLO AV	LA	LA63	400	45	C5
ESWARD DR	CO	AGO		100A	E4
ETRNAL VLY F RD	SCLR	NEW		127	D6
ETHAN AV	CO	ARC	5000	38	F3
ETHEL AV	ALH	ALH		37	A3
ETHEL AV	LA	NHO	6400	16	A2
ETHEL AV	LA	NHO	3800	23	A4
ETHEL AV	LA	VAN	5600	16	A6
ETHEL AV	LA	VAN	4600	23	A1
ETHEL ST	GLEN	GL07	1000	25	E2
ETHELDO AV	CUL	CUL	5200	50	B4
ETHELDO AV	LA	CUL	5100	50	B4
ETIWANDA AV	LA	NOR	8500	7	C5
ETIWANDA AV	LA	NOR	8300	14	C1
ETIWANDA AV	LA	RES	6100	14	C4
ETIWANDA AV	LA	TAR	5600	14	C6
ETIWANDA AV	LA	TAR	5100	21	C1
ETON AV	LA	CAN	8500	6	D6
ETON AV	LA	CAN	6400	12	D1
ETON AV	LA	CHA	9100	6	D3
ETON DR	BUR	BUR	400	17	C4
ETON PL	POM	POM	2900	90	F3
ETONGALE AV	CO	LPUE	2100	98	D4
ETTA ST	LA	LA65	600	36	A4
ETTRICK ST	LA	LA27	3100	35	B2
ETTRICK ST	LA	LA39	2900	35	B2
ETZ MELOY MTWY	CO	MAL		105	B3
EUBANK AV	LA	WIL	200	74	C5
EUCALYPTUS	CO	LP48		98	F3
EUCALYPTUS	LA	SF42		2	C1
EUCALYPTUS	WCOV	WCOV		98	F1
EUCALYPTUS AV	BLF	BLF	15100	66	C3
EUCALYPTUS AV	HAW	HAW	12700	56	F6
EUCALYPTUS AV	HAW	HAW	13800	62	F2
EUCALYPTUS AV	LB	LB06	3000	70	C6
EUCALYPTUS AV	LB	LB06	2000	75	C2
EUCALYPTUS AV N	ING	IN01	100	56	F2
EUCALYPTUS AV N	ING	IN02	300	50	F6
EUCALYPTUS AV S	ING	IN01	100	56	F2
EUCALYPTUS DR	CO	RM	2000	46	E3
EUCALYPTUS DR	ELS	ELS	100	56	B6
EUCALYPTUS LN	CO	AGO		107	B2
EUCALYPTUS LN	CO	POM		93	E2
EUCALYPTUS LN	LB	LB04		75	F5
EUCALYPTUS LN	LA	LA42	5800	26	C5
EUCALYPTUS LN	PAS	PAS		26	F2
EUCALYPTUS LN	RH	PVP	1	73	B5
EUCALYPTUS ST	AVA	AVA	300	77	B6
EUCALYPTUS ST	DOW	DOW	8400	60	A5
EUCALYPTUS WY	CO	RM	7300	46	E3

STREET	CITY	P.O. ZONE	BLOCK	PAGE	GRID
EUCLA AV N	SAD	SAD	100	89	F3
EUCLA AV S	SAD	SAD	100	89	F3
EUCLID AV	CO	DUA	500	29	B6
EUCLID AV	CO	CAST	29000	123	C2
EUCLID AV	LA	LA23	600	45	A6
EUCLID AV	LA	LA63	400	45	A6
EUCLID AV	LB	LB03	100	76	A6
EUCLID AV	LB	LB04	700	76	A6
EUCLID AV	LB	LB14	300	76	A6
EUCLID AV	LB	LB15	2000	76	A2
EUCLID AV	LYN	LYN	3100	65	A1
EUCLID AV	SGAB	SGAB	400	37	E5
EUCLID AV	SMAR	PAS	1600	37	B1
EUCLID AV	WHI	WHI	7800	55	F6
EUCLID AV N	PAS	PAS	100	27	A2
EUCLID AV S	PAS	PAS	100	27	A5
EUCLID CT	SM	SM		41	A5
EUCLID PL	PAS	PAS	1400	27	A1
EUCLID ST	COM	COM	300	64	F1
EUCLID ST	SM	SM	200	40	F5
EUCLID ST	SM	SM	900	41	A6
EUCLID ST	SM	SM	1800	49	B1
EUDORA AV	LA	WIL	1300	74	A2
EUGENE ST	CO	LA22	4300	45	D4
EUGENE ST	CO	LA63	4200	45	D4
EUGENE ST	LA	WOH	23000	13	A2
EULA DR	MTB	MTB	100	46	E6
EULALIA ST E	GLEN	GL05	100	25	C6
EULALIA ST W	GLEN	GL04	100	25	C6
EULER RD	CO	SAU		181	E7
EULITA AV	CO	LPUE	300	98	F1
EUNICE AV	ELM	ELM	3900	38	C5
EUNICE AV	LA	LA42	6300	26	D6
EUREKA AV	LB	LB05	6900	65	F4
EUREKA AV	PAR	PAR	16600	65	F4
EUREKA DR	LA	NHO	3700	23	E5
EUREKA ST	PAS	PAS	100	26	F3
EUREKA RIVER PL	WAL	WAL		92	F5
EUREKA RIVER PL	WAL	WAL		93	A5
EUROPA DR	CO	TOP		109	D5
EUSTACE ST	LA	PAC	12700	3	A6
EUSTACE ST	LA	PAC	13400	8	F1
EUSTON PL	LCF	LCF	400	19	D5
EUSTON RD	SMAR	PAS	1500	27	D6
EVA TER	LA	LA31	2800	36	B5
EVADALE DR	LA	LA31	3900	36	B4
EVA D EDWRDS AV	COV	COV		88	E2
EVALYN AV	TOR	TOR	21300	67	F4
EVALYN AV	TOR	TOR	23500	72	F1
EVANGELINA ST	WCOV	WCOV		92	E5
EVANS AV	SCLR	NEW	23700	127	A4
EVANS CT	CO	CAST		123	C2
EVANS CT	LOM	LOM	2300	73	C3
EVANS RD	LA	PP	14200	40	E2
EVANS ST	LB	LB13		74	F3
EVANS ST	LA	LA27	3800	35	B2
EVANSPORT DR	RM	RM	9000	38	B4
EVANSTON PL	PAS	PAS	100	27	A5
EVANSTON ST	LA	LA49	12700	41	A3
EVANT DR	WAL	WAL	20500	93	C6
EVANVIEW DR	LA	LA69	8800	33	D3
EVANWOOD AV	CO	LPUE	600	48	E4
EVANWOOD AV	LPUE	LPUE	300	48	D5
EVANWOOD AV	WCOV	WCOV	1200	48	F2
EVANWOOD AV	WCOV	WCOV	600	92	A2
EVARG AV	COM	COM	1200	64	D4
EVARO DR	WHI	WHI	12400	61	D1
EVE AV	LYN	LYN	11000	59	C5
EVELYN AV	GAR	GAR	17800	63	E6
EVELYN AV	LA	GAR	18200	63	E6
EVELYN AV	LA	GAR	18500	68	E1
EVELYN AV	RM	RM	2700	46	E1
EVELYN AV	WCOV	WCOV		92	E5
EVELYN CT	LAN	LAN		159	J2
EVELYN PL	BH	BH	400	33	C2
EVELYN PL	PALM	PALM		183	C5
EVELYN PL	PAS	PAS	1000	27	C2
EVELYN ST	CO	GL14	2500	18	D1
EVELYN ST	CO	GL14	3000	18	D1
EVENING BRZE DR	CO	WAL	20100	97	B4
EVENING CYN DR	LCF	LCF	5700	19	C1
EVNING SHADE AV	SCLR	CYN	27500	124	H8
EVNING SHADE DR	LA	SP		78	F2
EVENINGSIDE DR	WCOV	WCOV		92	C4
EVENINGSTAR AV	CER	ART		82	B5
EVENSONG DR	LA	SM		41	E6
EVENTIDE PL	LA	BH	1100	32	F4
EVERDIN LN	CO	TOP		115	C1
EVERDING MTWY	CO	TOP		115	C2
EVEREST ST	DOW	DOW	7400	59	F5
EVEREST ST	DOW	DOW	8300	60	A5
EVEREST ST	NWK	NWK	10400	60	D6
EVEREST ST	NWK	NWK	11600	61	A6
EVERETT AV	HPK	HPK	5900	53	B4
EVERETT AV	MAY	MAY	5100	53	B4
EVERETT AV	MPK	MPK	100	46	C2

STREET	CITY	P.O. ZONE	BLOCK	PAGE	GRID
EVERETT AV	VER	LA58	4700	53	B3
EVERETT CT	VER	LA58	4800	53	B3
EVERETT DR	SCLR	NEW	24600	127	A4
EVERETT PL	LA	LA26	1000	44	D1
EVERETT ST	LA	LA26	900	44	D1
EVERETT ST N	GLEN	GL06	100	25	D3
EVERETT ST N	GLEN	GL07	900	25	D2
EVERETT ST S	GLEN	GL05	100	25	D4
EVERGEM AV	PALM	PALM		184	B1
EVERGLADE ST	LA	LA66	12200	49	E1
EVERGREEN	ELM	ELM		48	A5
EVERGREEN AV	SOG	SOG	8100	59	A2
EVERGREEN AV	WCOV	WCOV	2200	92	E2
EVERGREEN AV E	MON	MON	100	29	A5
EVERGREEN AV N	LA	LA33	100	45	B4
EVERGREEN AV S	LA	LA23	600	45	B4
EVERGREEN AV S	LA	LA33	100	45	B4
EVERGREEN AV W	MON	MON	100	29	A5
EVERGREEN CIR	WAL	WAL		93	D6
EVERGREEN CT	AZU	AZU	200	86	C3
EVERGREEN DR	PAS	PAS	400	26	D5
EVERGREEN DR	POM	POM		90	D6
EVERGREEN LN	CER	ART		82	B4
EVERGREEN LN	CO	SAU		124	C3
EVERGREEN LN	MB	MB		62	D3
EVERGREEN ST	BUR	BUR	1400	17	A6
EVERGREEN ST	BUR	BUR	100	24	A1
EVERGREEN ST	DUA	DUA	900	29	C5
EVERGREEN ST	ING	IN02	500	50	E5
EVERGREEN ST	LAV	LAV		90	D2
EVERGRN SPGS DR	DBAR	POM	1800	97	D4
EVERINGTON ST	CMRC	LA40	5100	53	E2
EVERS AV	CO	COM	13900	64	D2
EVERS AV	COM	COM	600	64	D2
EVERS AV	LA	LA02	9600	58	D3
EVERS AV	LA	LA59	11100	58	D5
EVERSTON ST	NWK	NWK	11500	66	F2
EVERSTON ST	NWK	NWK	11600	82	A2
EVERTS ST	PAS	PAS	600	26	E2
EVEWARD RD	CUL	CUL	5700	50	D3
EVITA CT	AGH	AGO		102	E3
EVONDA AV	CAR	LB10	21700	69	F4
EVRON AV	SCLR	CYN	27300	124	H5
EWANA PL	CO	CHA		1A	B5
EWELL LN	ARC	ARC	1100	28	D6
EWING AV	CO	ALT	3000	20	A4
EWING CT	CO	LPUE		98	A4
EWING ST	LA	LA26	1400	35	C4
EWING ST	LA	LA39	1900	35	C4
EXA CT	CAR	CAR	17500	64	C5
EXBURY PL	CO	COV	20500	93	B1
EXCELENTE DR	LA	WOH	4700	13	B3
EXCELLO ST	ART	ART	11600	82	A4
EXCELSIOR DR	LAM	LAM	14600	83	A3
EXCELSIOR DR	NWK	NWK	10600	66	F3
EXCELSIOR DR	NWK	NWK	11600	82	A3
EXCELSIOR DR	SFS	SFS	13500	82	D3
EXCELSIOR ST	LA	SF	15700	2	B2
EXCHANGE AL	PAS	PAS	1	27	A4
EXCHANGE AV	VER	LA58	3400	53	B2
EXCHANGE LN	SPAS	SPAS	900	36	F2
EXCHANGE PL	SAD	SAD	100	89	F3
EXCHANGE ST	LA	LA39	5200	25	B4
EXETER CT	WCOV	WCOV		92	C4
EXETER PL	LA	NOR	17200	7	E5
EXETER ST	PAR	PAR	7200	65	E2
EXHIBIT CT	LA	WOH	20700	12	D6
EXHIBIT PL	LA	WOH	20700	12	D6
EXLINE ST	ELM	ELM	11500	47	F1
EXLINE ST	ELM	ELM	12200	48	A1
EXMOOR AV	COM	COM	1000	64	E4
EXMOOR PL	GLDR	GLDR	2000	87	E5
EXPLORER DR	CO	LAN	50500	146	B2
EXPLORER ST	POM	POM		94	A3
EXPOSITION BLVD	CUL	CUL	8800	42	C5
EXPOSITION BLVD	LA	LA07	900	43	D6
EXPOSITION BLVD	LA	LA07	400	44	A6
EXPOSITION BLVD	LA	LA16	5100	42	F6
EXPOSITION BLVD	LA	LA16	3600	43	B6
EXPOSITION BLVD	LA	LA18	1300	43	D6
EXPOSITION BLVD	LA	LA34	8900	42	C5
EXPOSITION BLVD	LA	LA64	10800	41	D5
EXPOSITION BLVD	LA	LA64	10400	42	A4
EXPOSITION BLVD	SM	SM	2800	41	C5
EXPOSITION DR	LA	LA34	9000	42	C5
EXPOSITION PL	LA	LA18	2400	43	C6
EXTON AV	ING	IN02	400	51	A6
EXULTANT DR	RPV	PVP	3900	78	A3
EYRE ST	CO	PEAR		185	A8
EZMIRLIAN ST	COM	COM	1400	65	B2
EZRA ST N	LA	LA63	400	45	C4
EZRA ST S	LA	LA23	1500	53	A1
F					
F CT	LA	WIL	1000	74	B5

STREET	CITY	P.O. ZONE	BLOCK	PAGE	GRID
F ST	LAV	LAV	1900	90	D3
F ST E	LA	WIL	100	74	B4
F ST W	LA	WIL	100	74	B4
FABENS AV	CO	LAN	48600	146	H5
FABER ST	RB	RB	2600	62	F4
FABIAN AV	CO	LAN	39200	175	F6
FABLE AV	LA	CAN	7800	5	E1
FABRICA WY	CER	ART	17400	82	E5
FABRIK AV	LAN	LAN	43900	159	G6
FABRY DR	CO	HAC		73	F1
FABUCO RD	CO	TOP		115	B2
FABUENO DR	CO	LPUE	2700	85	E4
FACADE AV	PAR	PAR	13700	65	E1
FACETA DR	LAM	LAM	14800	83	C3
FACILIDAD ST	CO	LPUE	15400	85	D3
FACTOR AV	AZU	AZU	300	86	E6
FACTOR AV	CO	AZU	6000	88	E1
FACTORIAL WY	SELM	ELM	9600	47	C2
FACTORY DR	POM	POM		94	A3
FACTORY PL	LA	LA13	1200	44	E4
FACULTY AV	BLF	BLF	15700	66	B3
FACULTY AV	LB	LB08	3700	71	B3
FACULTY AV	LKD	LKD	5900	66	B6
FACULTY AV	LKD	LKD	4900	71	B1
FACULTY DR	NWK	NWK	11600	82	A4
FADA DR	LAM	LAM	15600	83	B3
FADDEN ST	CO	LPUE	19200	97	A4
FAGAN AV	ART	ART	18800	81	B1
FAGAN AV	CER	ART	19000	81	B2
FAGAN WY	CER	ART	19500	81	B2
FAHREN LN	SCLR	CYN		125	A9
FAILOR CYN RD	CO	TOP		109	C1
FAIN DR	SCLR	NEW		127	A5
FAINRIDGE PL	CO	LPUE	2200	98	D4
FAIR AV	LA	NHO	5600	16	E6
FAIR AV	LA	NHO	4000	23	E4
FAIR AV	LA	SV	7200	16	E3
FAIR AV	POM	POM	2000	90	D5
FAIR PL	ING	IN02	1200	51	A5
FAIR PL	LA	LA43	6300	51	A5
FAIR ST	CMRC	LA40	5000	53	E2
FAIR ACRES DR	LAM	LAM	14600	84	A5
FAIRBANKS AV	LB	LB13		75	B4
FAIRBANKS PL	LA	LA26	1400	35	C5
FAIRBANKS WY	CUL	CUL	5000	50	C3
FAIRBANKS WY	CUL	CUL	10800	50	C3
FAIRBREEZE CIR	WLVL	THO		102	A4
FAIRBROOK ST	LB	LB15	5400	76	C3
FAIRBURN AV	LA	LA24	1200	41	F2
FAIRBURN AV	LA	LA25	1800	41	F2
FAIRBURY ST	CO	LPUE	14400	48	C6
FAIRCHILD AV	LA	CAN	7800	12	D2
FAIRCHILD ST	GLEN	GL14	3500	11	C6
FAIRCLIFF CT	GLEN	GL06		25	F2
FAIRCLIFF RD	CO	VAL		124	B4
FAIRCOURT LN	GLEN	GL03	700	25	B3
FAIRCOVE DR	RPV	PVP	29200	72	C6
FAIRCREST DR	RM	RM	8700	38	A4
FAIRCROSS ST	TOR	TOR	2400	73	C3
FAIRDALE AV	DUA	DUA	1500	29	D5
FAIRESTA ST	CO	GL14	3000	11	D6
FAIRESTA ST	GLEN	GL14	3200	11	C5
FAIRFAX AV	ING	IN01		50	F4
FAIRFAX AV N	LA	LA36	100	33	F6
FAIRFAX AV N	LA	LA46	700	33	F6
FAIRFAX AV N	WHOL	LA46	900	33	F6
FAIRFAX AV S	CO	LA56	5000	50	F3
FAIRFAX AV S	LA	LA16	2300	42	E4
FAIRFAX AV S	LA	LA19	1000	42	E3
FAIRFAX AV S	LA	LA34	1900	42	E3
FAIRFAX AV S	LA	LA36	100	33	F6
FAIRFAX AV S	LA	LA36	300	42	E3
FAIRFAX AV S	LA	LA56	6200	50	F4
FAIRFAX CT	POM	POM		94	F4
FAIRFAX LN	POM	POM	100	94	F4
FAIRFIELD AV	LA	LA68	2100	34	B2
FAIRFIELD AV	PALM	PALM		183	G2
FAIRFIELD CIR	PAS	PAS	700	27	B6
FAIRFIELD DR	CLA	CLA		96	B6
FAIRFIELD PL	SMAR	PAS	2500	27	E5
FAIRFIELD RD	LA	NOR		7	B2
FAIRFIELD ST	CO	LA22	5900	54	A1
FAIRFIELD ST	GLEN	GL01	1300	24	F2
FAIRFIELD ST	MTB	MTB	2100	54	A1
FAIRFORD AV	DOW	DOW	10800	60	F5
FAIRFORD AV	NWK	NWK	11200	60	F5
FAIRFORD AV	NWK	NWK	12800	66	F1
FAIRGATE AV	SCLR	SAU	26500	127	J1
FAIRGLADE ST	SCLR	CYN	16500	125	C6
FAIRGLEN RD	LAN	LAN	43200	160	C7
FAIRGRANGE DR	AGH	AGO		102	E3
FAIRGREEN AV	CO	ARC	2500	39	A1
FAIRGREEN AV	CO	MON	1900	29	A6
FAIRGREEN AV	CO	MON	2400	39	A1
FAIRGREEN LN	PALM	PALM		171	F4

1990 LOS ANGELES COUNTY STREET INDEX

STREET	CITY	P.O. ZONE	BLOCK	PAGE	GRID
FAIRGROUNDS ST	CMRC	LA40		53	F2
FAIRGROVE AV	CO	LPUE	13500	48	D2
FAIRGROVE AV	CO	LPUE	15800	92	A4
FAIRGROVE AV	LA	TU	10300	11	A3
FAIRGROVE AV	LPUE	LPUE	15100	48	F4
FAIRGROVE AV	LPUE	LPUE	15700	92	A4
FAIRGROVE AV	WCOV	WCOV	1200	92	C4
FAIRGROVE ST	BAP	BAP	12800	48	C1
FAIRHALL ST	TEC	TEC	10600	38	D4
FAIRHAVEN AV	LA	WOH	5600	100	D1
FAIRHAVEN CT	AGH	AGO		102	F2
FAIRHAVEN ST	CAR	CAR	23500	69	C6
FAIRHILL DR	RPV	SP	2100	78	D2
FAIRHLS FARM RD	CO	TOP		13	E6
FAIRHOPE DR	LAM	LAM	14900	83	C3
FAIRHURST DR	LCF	LCF	2100	11	F6
FAIRLANCE DR	DBAR	WAL		97	C3
FAIRLAND BLVD	CO	LA43	3600	51	B3
FAIRLAND CT	LA	SF	17400	1	E5
FAIRLANE ST	CO	ACT	4300	182	D8
FAIRLAWN DR	LCF	LCF	4300	19	B3
FAIRLAWN WY	PAS	PAS	1300	26	D3
FAIRLEE AV	BRAD	DUA	500	29	E4
FAIRLEE AV	DUA	DUA	1200	29	E5
FAIRLEE DR	LAN	LAN		159	H9
FAIRLOCK AV	PAR	PAR	13500	65	E1
FAIRMAID AV	CO	PALM		185	A2
FAIRMAN ST E	LKD	LKD	2700	70	F3
FAIRMAN ST E	LKD	LKD	3300	71	A3
FAIRMEADE RD	PAS	PAS	3500	28	A3
FAIRMONT AV	GLEN	GL03	500	25	B3
FAIRMONT DR	CLA	CLA		91	B2
FAIRMONT LN	PR	PR		47	B6
FAIRMONT LN	PR	PR		55	B1
FAIRMNT NECH RD	CO	LAN	12000	158	A2
FAIRMOUNT AV	CO	GL14	2800	11	D6
FAIRMOUNT AV	CO	GL14	2400	18	E1
FAIRMOUNT AV	GLEN	GL14	3300	11	C5
FAIRMOUNT AV	LCF	LCF	1600	19	A1
FAIRMOUNT AV	PAS	PAS	600	26	F5
FAIRMOUNT RD	BUR	BUR	400	17	D5
FAIRMOUNT ST	CO	LA63	3900	45	D3
FAIRMOUNT ST	LA	LA33	2400	45	B3
FAIRMOUNT ST	LA	LA63	3000	45	B3
FAIROAKS AV	CLA	CLA	500	91	C3
FAIR OAKS AV	CO	ALT	2000	20	A4
FAIR OAKS AV	PAS	PAS	2100	20	A6
FAIR OAKS AV	SPAS	SPAS	200	36	F2
FAIR OAKS AV N	PAS	PAS	100	26	F4
FAIR OAKS AV S	PAS	PAS	100	26	F4
FAIR OAKS DR	PAS	PAS	1	19	F6
FAIR OAKS PL	SPAS	SPAS	1400	36	F2
FAIR OAK VW TER	LA	LA39	2200	35	C4
FAIR PARK AV	LA	LA41	1500	26	A5
FAIRPLAIN AV	CO	WHI	1300	48	A4
FAIRPOINT ST	CO	PAS	3200	20	F6
FAIRPOINT ST	PAS	PAS	3400	20A	A3
FAIRPORT AV	SCLR	CYN	27400	124	H5
FAIRRIDGE CIR	WCOV	WCOV		92	D5
FAIRSIDE RD	CO	MAL		113	B2
FAIRTON ST	BLF	BLF	10300	66	D3
FAIRTON ST	NWK	NWK	10700	66	E3
FAIRTON ST	PAR	PAR	8300	65	F3
FAIRVALE AV	AZU	AZU	300	88	E2
FAIRVALE AV	CO	AZU	6100	86	E6
FAIRVALE AV	CO	AZU	6000	88	E2
FAIRVALE AV	CO	COV	4800	88	E3
FAIRVALLEY AV	COV	COV	4800	88	F3
FAIRVIEW AV	ARC	ARC	300	28	B6
FAIRVIEW AV	CO	SGAB	8500	27	F6
FAIRVIEW AV	CO	SGAB	8700	28	A6
FAIRVIEW AV	ELM	ELM	11300	38	F4
FAIRVIEW AV	LA	LA33	500	44	F3
FAIRVIEW AV	LOM	LOM	26200	73	D4
FAIRVIEW AV	RM	RM	8400	37	E4
FAIRVIEW AV	SMAD	SMAD	400	28	B1
FAIRVIEW AV	SPAS	SPAS	900	36	F2
FAIRVIEW AV	TEC	TEC	10700	38	E4
FAIRVIEW AV E	GLEN	GL07	100	25	C2
FAIRVIEW AV E	SGAB	SGAB	100	37	E4
FAIRVIEW AV W	GLEN	GL02	200	25	C2
FAIRVIEW AV W	SGAB	SGAB	100	37	E4
FAIRVIEW BLVD	CO	LA56	5300	50	E5
FAIRVIEW BLVD	LA	LA56	5200	50	E5
FAIRVIEW BLVD E	ING	IN02	100	50	E5
FAIRVIEW BLVD E	ING	IN02	100	51	A5
FAIRVIEW BLVD W	ING	IN02	100	50	E5
FAIRVIEW DR	CO	LPUE		48	B5
FAIRVIEW DR	CO	VAL		124	A6
FAIRVIEW DR	LCF	LCF	1000	19	B2
FAIRVIEW LN	CO	ALT	2700	20	C4
FAIRVIEW LN	TOR	TOR	18200	63	D6
FAIRVIEW PL	AGH	AGO		100A	C3
FAIRVIEW PL	POM	POM	1800	90	D5
FAIRVIEW ST	ELM	ELM	11900	39	A4
FAIRVIEW ST N	BUR	BUR	1100	17	B6

STREET	CITY	P.O. ZONE	BLOCK	PAGE	GRID
FAIRVIEW ST N	BUR	BUR	200	24	B2
FAIRVIEW ST S	BUR	BUR	300	24	C3
FAIRVIEW TER	SMAD	SMAD	400	28	B1
FAIRVILLA DR	LAM	LAM	14500	82	F1
FAIRVILLA DR	LAM	LAM	14600	83	A1
FAIRWAY AV	CO	GL14	2900	18	D1
FAIRWAY AV	CO	MONT	2500	18	E2
FAIRWAY AV	LA	NHO	3800	23	B4
FAIRWAY BLVD	CO	LA43	3600	51	A2
FAIRWAY CIR	SCLR	NEW		127	G1
FAIRWAY DR	CO	WAL	800	97	B2
FAIRWAY DR	IND	WAL	700	97	B2
FAIRWAY DR	LKD	LKD	4100	70	F3
FAIRWAY DR	MB	MB		62	D2
FAIRWAY DR	PALM	PALM		172	B5
FAIRWAY DR	PR	PR		55	C1
FAIRWAY LN	WCOV	WCOV	100	89	A6
FAIRWAY LN	WCOV	WCOV		93	A1
FAIRWAY KNLS RD	WCOV	WCOV	1600	92	F3
FAIRWEATHER ST	SCLR	CYN	18500	124	G8
FAIRWEATHER ST	SCLR	CYN		125	A8
FAIRWIND LN	DBAR	POM		99	D4
FAIRWOOD ST	DUA	DUA	400	29	F4
FAISAN CT	SCLR	VAL		127	B1
FAITH ST	WCOV	WCOV		92	E6
FALCO AV	NWK	NWK	14300	82	B2
FALCON AV	LB	LB02	100	75	E6
FALCON AV	LB	LB05	5900	65	D6
FALCON AV	LB	LB05	5200	70	E3
FALCON AV	LB	LB07	3400	70	E5
FALCON AV	SH	LB07	3300	70	E5
FALCON CIR	CER	ART	19600	81	B2
FALCON CT	PALM	PALM		171	H6
FALCON PL	LA	SF		1	E4
FALCON ST	LA	WIL	200	79	B1
FALCON ST	POM	POM	3200	90	E3
FALCON WY	CER	NWK	10900	66	E4
FALCONBURG DR	LAV	LAV		95A	E5
FALCONBURN WY	DBAR	POM		97	E3
FALCON CREST LN	LA	NOR		1A	F5
FALCON CREST WY	LA	NOR		1A	F4
FALCONER ST	BAP	BAP		39	E5
FALCONET DR	CO	CAL		100	E5
FALCONGATE AV	CO	SAU		189	F2
FALCONHEAD DR	RPV	PVP	3100	78	B3
FALCONHILL DR	CO	WHI	11300	84	D5
FALCON PARK ST	LB	LB08		81	B6
FALCON RIDGE DR	POM	POM		94	C6
FALCON RIDGE RD	DBAR	POM		97	D6
FALCON RIDGE RD	DBAR	POM		99	B5
FALCON RIDGE WY	LA	NOR		1A	F5
FALCONRIM DR	CO	CYN	15000	128	D1
FALCON ROCK PL	RPV	PVP	4800	72	F4
FALCONS VIEW DR	DBAR	POM		97A	B4
FALCONWOOD	CO	SAU		181	B9
FALDA AV	CO	GAR	15600	63	C4
FALDA AV	TOR	TOR	16000	63	C5
FALDA AV	TOR	TOR	18300	68	C1
FALENA AV	LOM	LOM	24500	73	E2
FALENA AV	TOR	TOR	22900	68	E6
FALENA AV	TOR	TOR	23500	73	D1
FALENA AV	TOR	TOR	24200	73	E1
FALES RD	CO	SAU		125	H1
FALES RD	CO	SAU		188	C1
FALKIRK LN	LA	LA49	12200	41	B2
FALL AV	LA	LA26	3000	35	B4
FALLBROOK AV	LA	CAN	6400	12	A1
FALLBROOK AV	LA	WOH	5600	12	A6
FALLBROOK AV	LA	WOH	5000	13	A1
FALL CREEK CT	WAL	WAL		92	F5
FALLCREEK LN	CER	ART		82	B4
FALLCREEK RD	DUA	DUA	200	86	B3
FALLEN DR	CO	LPUE		98	C5
FALLEN LEAF	LPUE	LPUE		48	E6
FALLENLEAF DR	TOR	TOR		73	B3
FALLENLEAF PL	GLEN	GL06		26	C1
FALLEN LEAF RD	ARC	ARC	800	28	B3
FALLEN LEAF WY	WLVL	THO		102	B6
FALLEN OAK RD	CO	LPUE	16500	98	A3
FALLHAVEN LN	LCF	LCF	5000	19	C2
FALLING LEAF AV	CO	RM	2100	46	E2
FALLING LEAF AV	RM	RM	2300	46	E2
FALLNG LEAF CIR	POM	POM		94	D6
FALLING LEAF DR	LA	ENC		21	D4
FALLING SPGS RD	WAL	WAL	20000	93	B5
FALLING STAR LN	SCLR	SAU		124	E6
FALLON DR	LAN	LAN		160	E6
FALLOW FIELD DR	DBAR	POM	2700	97	D5
FALLS	PALM	PALM		171	F4
FALLS DR	CO	TOP	600	109	C5
FALLS CANYON RD	AVA	AVA		77	B5
FALLSGROVE ST	LA	LA16	5600	42	E6
FALLSTON ST	LA	LA42	5500	26	C6
FALMOUTH AV	LA	PDR	8500	55A	E1
FALSTONE AV	CO	LPUE	1300	85	E2
FALTER ST	CO	CYN		128	C2

STREET	CITY	P.O. ZONE	BLOCK	PAGE	GRID
FALUN DR	LA	SV	10200	17	A1
FAMBROUGH ST	SCLR	NEW	23600	127	A5
FAMOSA ST	CO	WHI		47	E5
FAN CT	SCLR	SAU		124	G4
FANCHON AV	LAN	LAN	43200	159	G7
FANCHON LN	CO	CYN		124	G8
FANDON AV	ELM	ELM	4100	38	F5
FANE ST	SMAD	SMAD	300	28	D2
FANITA ST	LA	LA26	3000	35	B5
FANNING RD	CO	MAL		114	C4
FANNING ST	LA	LA26	1700	35	B4
FANO ST	ARC	ARC	1	28	E5
FANO ST	MON	MON	500	29	A5
FANSHAW AV	PAR	PAR	13400	65	F1
FANSHAW AV	POM	POM	100	90	F3
FANTASTIC LN	CO	CAST	28000	123	H1
FANTASY ST	PALM	PALM	500	172	A6
FANWOOD AV	CO	LB08	3700	71	D5
FANWOOD AV	LB	LB08	3200	71	D6
FANWOOD AV	LB	LB15	1800	76	D1
FANWOOD AV	LKD	LKD	6100	66	D6
FANWOOD AV	LKD	LKD	4900	71	D2
FAR PL	LA	LA32		36	D5
FARADAY ST	CO	WHI	13700	61	E5
FARAGO AV	TEC	TEC	5000	38	E3
FARBEN DR	DBAR	POM		97A	A1
FARBER AV	COV	COV		89	A5
FARBER AV	GLDR	GLDR	800	89	A1
FAREHOLM CT	LA	LA46	1700	33	F3
FAREHOLM DR	LA	LA46	7800	33	F3
FAREL AV	DBAR	WAL		97	D2
FARGO RD	SAD	SAD		89	F2
FARGO ST	LA	LA26	1600	35	C4
FARGO ST	LA	LA39	2100	35	C4
FAR HILLS RD	CO	SAU		125	A2
FARIAS AV	LA	CUL	4500	50	A3
FARIMAN DR	CAR	CAR	19000	69	C1
FARING RD	LA	LA77	300	32	F5
FARIS DR	LA	LA34	3600	42	C5
FARJARDO ST	CO	LPUE	18300	98	E5
FARLAND ST	COV	COV	1500	89	B4
FARLEY CT	BUR	BUR	400	17	E6
FARLEY CT	LA	NHO	3900	23	E5
FARLIN ST	LA	LA49	11300	41	C1
FARLINGTON ST	WCOV	WCOV	1400	48	E2
FARLOW ST	HG	LKD	12400	81	B4
FARLOW ST	LKD	LKD	12300	81	B4
FARM ST	DOW	DOW	7800	60	B2
FARM CENTER RD	CO	CAST		123	F4
FARMDALE AV	LA	LA16	2900	43	B6
FARMDALE AV	LA	NHO	5600	16	D3
FARMDALE AV	LA	NHO	4000	23	D4
FARMER AV	SELM	ELM	800	47	C5
FARMER JOHN LAT	CO	SAU		124	A2
FARMFIELD RD	CO	CAL		100	A2
FARMINGTON AV	LA	SUN	8600	10	C3
FARMINGTON LN	CO	SAU		124	E4
FARMLAND AV	PR	PR	7200	54	F6
FARMLAND AV	PR	PR	7100	60	F1
FARMOUTH DR	LA	LA27	3900	35	A1
FARMSTEAD	CO	LPUE	1100	85	E1
FARNA AV	ARC	ARC		38	F3
FARNA AV	CO	ARC	5100	38	F3
FARNAM PL	POM	POM	1500	94	F4
FARNAM ST	LA	LA42	900	36	A1
FARNDON ST	SELM	ELM	10900	47	D4
FARNELL ST	BAP	BAP	13000	48	B2
FARNELL ST	CO	BAP	12700	48	B2
FARNESE AV	CO	PEAR	32400	192	C2
FARNHAM AV	LB	LB08	3400	81	C6
FARNHAM LN	ING	IN01		57	B2
FARNINGHAM AV	CO	PALM		185	A2
FARNSWORTH AV	LA	LA32	3100	36	E5
FAROLITO AV N	LB	LB15	2200	76	D2
FARQUHAR ST	LA	LA32	4800	45	D1
FARRAGUT AV	LA	WIL	800	74	F3
FARRAGUT DR	CUL	CUL	9500	50	C1
FARRALONE AV	LA	CAN	8500	6	B6
FARRALONE AV	LA	CAN	6400	12	B1
FARRALONE AV	LA	CHA	9200	6	B5
FARRALONE AV	LA	WOH	5800	12	B6
FARRALONE AV	LA	WOH	5400	13	B1
FARRALONE PL	LA	CHA		6	B5
FARRAR ST	CMRC	LA40	5100	53	E2
FARRELL AV	POM	POM	1200	95	B1
FARRELL AV	RB	RB	1900	62	E4
FARRINGDON AV	POM	POM	2300	94	A1
FARRINGTON LN	LA	LA42	6000	26	C6
FARROW DR	CO	VAL		126	J4
FAR VIEW LN	WCOV	WCOV		92	F3
FARWELL AV	LA	LA39	2600	35	C2
FARWELL PL	SFS	SFS	12600	61	C3
FASHION AV	LB	LB10	3000	70	B6
FASHION AV	LB	LB10	1800	75	B2
FASHION AV	LB	LB13	900	75	B4
FASHION WY	TOR	TOR	3200	68	A4

STREET	CITY	P.O. ZONE	BLOCK	PAGE	GRID
FASTWATER CT	WLVL	THO		102A	F5
FAUBION PL	CO	WOH		13	B5
FAULKNER AV	PAR	PAR	15100	65	D3
FAUNA LN	CO	TOR		68	F6
FAUNA LN	CO	TOR		69	A6
FAUST AV	BLF	BLF	13400	66	D1
FAUST AV	CO	LB08	3700	71	D5
FAUST AV	DOW	DOW	12800	66	D1
FAUST AV	LA	CAN	6700	12	A2
FAUST AV	LA	CAN		12	A4
FAUST AV	LA	WOH	5600	13	A1
FAUST AV	LB	LB08	3100	71	D6
FAUST AV	LB	LB15	1800	76	D3
FAUST AV	LKD	LKD	4100	71	D4
FAWCETT AV	SELM	ELM	11000	47	C4
FAWN CIR	LAV	LAV		90	B2
FAWNDALE PL	LA	VAN	3600	22	D5
FAWNRIDGE DR	LA	BH	9600	33	A3
FAWNSKIN DR	RPV	PVP	27400	72	E5
FAWN SPRINGS LN	GLDR	GLDR		87	D4
FAWN VALLEY	GLDR	GLDR		87	D6
FAXINA AV	CO	LPUE	300	98	F2
FAY AV	CUL	CUL	3200	42	D5
FAY AV	LA	LA34	3200	42	D5
FAY CIR	CER	ART	11200	66	F6
FAY DR	GLEN	GL06	700	25	F2
FAY PL	PAS	PAS	1200	27	A1
FAYE LN	RB	RB	400	67	E4
FAYE LN	WCOV	WCOV		92	E5
FAYECROFT ST	SF	SF	800	2	E4
FAYETTE ST	LA	LA42	5600	36	C1
FAYMONT AV	MB	MB	1200	62	D3
FAYSMITH AV	CO	GAR	15200	63	C3
FAYSMITH AV	TOR	TOR	16600	63	C5
FAYSMITH AV	TOR	TOR	800	68	C4
FAYWOOD ST	NWK	NWK	10700	66	E2
FAYWOOD ST E	BLF	BLF	9000	66	B3
FEATHER AV N	BAP	BAP	3400	39	D6
FEATHER AV N	CO	LPUE	800	48	C2
FEATHER RIV DR	CO	LAN	12200	158	A6
FEATHER ROCK RD	DBAR	POM		97	F4
FEATHERSTAR AV	SCLR	SAU		124	E5
FEATHERSTONE LN	ING	IN01		57	B2
FEATHERWOOD DR	DBAR	POM		94	B5
FEDALA RD	SCLR	VAL		127	A2
FEDCAMP LN	CO	AGO		106	E1
FEDERAL AV	BELL	BELL	4100	53	B5
FEDERAL AV	LA	LA25	1200	41	D3
FEDERAL AV	LA	LA64	2200	41	E5
FEDERAL AV	LA	LA66	3000	41	E6
FEDERAL DR	ELM	ELM		47	E1
FEDERALIST RD	CO	WOH		13	A4
FEDERATION DR	LB	LB04		76	B4
FEDORA ST	LA	LA05	800	43	E3
FEDORA ST	LA	LA06	900	43	E3
FEEDMILL RD	CO	VAL		123	F7
FEENY RD	CO	PALM	39600	171I	G5
FEIJOA AV	LOM	LOM	25000	73	D3
FELA AV	LB	LB08	3400	81	B6
FELBAR AV	TOR	TOR	800	68	B4
FELBAR AV	TOR	TOR	18600	68	B1
FELBERG AV	CO	DUA	2000	29	B6
FELBRIDGE ST	SCLR	CYN	18800	124	H5
FELCH AV	CO	LPUE		98	E3
FELDER DR	CO	SF		3	E2
FELDER ST	GAR	GAR	1000	63	F6
FELICE PL	LA	WOH	5300	13	E2
FELICIA AV	CO	LPUE	1700	98	D5
FELICIA AV	IND	LPUE		98	E3
FELICIA ST	WCOV	WCOV		92	E5
FELICIDAD	LA	SP		78	C5
FELICITAS AV	CO	PALM	37100	183	A2
FELIPE ST	ELM	ELM	12100	47	E3
FELISE PL	WAL	WAL		92	F5
FELISE PL	WAL	WAL		93	A5
FELIX AV	BG	BELL	8000	59	F2
FELIZ ST	MPK	MPK	1400	46	A2
FELKER DR	TOR	TOR	20600	67	E3
FELLOWS AV	LA	PAC	11500	3	A5
FELLOWS AV	LA	PAC	10900	9	B2
FELLOWS AV	LA	SF	12700	2	E3
FELLOWS AV	LA	SF	11700	3	A5
FELLOWS PL	POM	POM	1600	90	F6
FELLOWSHIP ST	CO	LPUE	15400	48	F3
FELLOWSHIP ST	CO	LPUE	15700	92	A3
FELLOWSHP PK WY	LA	LA26	2200	35	D4
FELLOWSHP PK WY	LA	LA39	2300	35	D4
FELSON CIR	CER	ART	10700	66	E6
FELSON PL	CER	ART	12300	82	B6
FELSON ST	BLF	BLF	10300	66	D6
FELSON ST	CER	ART	12500	82	C6
FELT DR	CO	WHI		84	A5
FELTON AV	CO	HAW	12100	56	E6
FELTON AV	CO	IN04	10000	56	F3
FELTON AV	HAW	HAW	11600	56	E6
FELTON AV	ING	IN01	1000	56	F3

STREET	CITY	P.O. ZONE	BLOCK	PAGE	GRID
FELTON AV	LA	LA45	11400	56	E6
FELTON LN	RB	RB	1300	62	F6
FENDA WY	SCLR	VAL		127	A2
FENDALE AV	CO	WHI	13300	61	D5
FENDYKE AV	RM	RM	4400	38	A4
FENHILL LN	CO	MAL		112	C6
FENHOLD ST	LAN	LAN	44200	160	D5
FENIMORE AV	AZU	AZU	200	86	E6
FENIMORE AV	AZU	AZU	100	88	E1
FENIMORE AV	CO	AZU	5400	88	E2
FENIMORE AV	COV	COV	3200	88	E6
FENIMORE AV N	COV	COV	700	88	E4
FENIMORE AV S	COV	COV	600	88	E5
FENLOCK AV	CO	SAU		189	C3
FENMEAD ST	WCOV	WCOV	18900	98	F2
FENN CT	CLA	CLA	800	91	A1
FENN ST	LA	LA31	400	36	A5
FENNEL DR	PALM	PALM		183	G2
FENNELL PL	LA	LA69	8600	33	D3
FENNELL ST	ELM	ELM	11500	47	E1
FENNER AV	LAN	LAN	43200	159	G7
FENTER AV	LB	LB05	6300	65	B6
FENTON AV	LA	SF	13500	2	F2
FENTON AV	LA	SF	12800	3	B4
FENTON AV	LA	SF	11200	9	D1
FENTON LN	LA	SF		2	E1
FENWALL DR	SCLR	SAU		124	C4
FENWAY CT	CO	SAU		123	E5
FENWAY ST	LA	SV	10900	9	E4
FENWICK ST	LA	SUN	7800	10	C2
FENWICK ST	LA	TU		10	F2
FENWICK ST	LA	TU	7100	11	A3
FENWOOD AV	LA	WOH	6000	5	F6
FENWOOD AV	LA	WOH	5400	100	F1
FENWORTH CT	AGH	AGO		102	F2
FERAL AV	AGH	AGO		100A	A2
FERDINAND AV	MPK	MPK	2200	46	B5
FERGUS DR	GLEN	GL06	500	26	B3
FERGUSON DR	CMRC	LA40	5400	53	F2
FERGUSON DR	CMRC	LA40	5600	54	B2
FERGUSON DR	CO	CAST	27800	123	G2
FERGUSON DR	MTB	MTB	1700	54	B2
FERINA ST	BLF	BLF	10300	66	D3
FERINA ST	NWK	NWK	11000	66	E3
FERINA ST	NWK	NWK	11600	82	A3
FERMI DR	CO	TOP		13	D5
FERMO DR	LA	PP	1400	40	E2
FERMOORE DR	SF	SF	1500	2	F4
FERMOORE ST	SF	SF	200	2	E5
FERN AV	LAN	LAN	43600	160	A6
FERN AV	PALM	PALM		183	G2
FERN AV	RM	RM	7400	46	F2
FERN AV	RM	RM	8500	47	A2
FERN AV	TOR	TOR	1200	68	C4
FERN AV	TOR	TOR	22600	68	C5
FERN CT	AZU	AZU	200	86	C3
FERN DR	PAS	PAS	100	26	E4
FERN DR	SMAD	SMAD	600	28	D1
FERN LN	GLEN	GL08	1700	18	F5
FERN LN	WAL	WAL		92	F5
FERN PL	DBAR	POM		94	B6
FERN PL	LA	LA32	4600	36	C5
FERN ST	ELM	ELM	9700	47	C2
FERN ST	LB	LB05		65	D5
FERN ST	SELM	ELM	9200	47	B2
FERNADEL AV	PR	PR	8100	54	D6
FERNANDO CT	GLEN	GL04	400	25	C6
FERNANDOS CT	CO	PVP		73	B4
FERNBANK AV	MPK	MPK	1800	46	B4
FERNBROOK PL	GLEN	GL08	1600	18	E6
FERNBROOK RD	LA	CAN	8600	4	A6
FERNBUSH LN	LA	LA77		32	E3
FERN CANYON TR	LA	TU	6200	11	C3
FERNCOLA AV	LA	SV	7700	17	A2
FERNCOVE TR	CO	TOP		109	B2
FERN CREEK DR	LPUE	LPUE		92	B6
FERNCREEK DR	RHE	PVP	4700	72	F3
FERNCREST DR	CO	SAU		124	F6
FERNCROFT AV	CO	SGAB	6900	27	F6
FERNCROFT RD	LA	LA39	3400	35	C2
FERNDALE AV	CDY	BELL	8200	59	D2
FERNDALE AV	LA	LA66	12900	49	E3
FERNDALE LN	CO	LPUE		48	B5
FERNDALE ST	LA	LA16	4700	43	A5
FERN DELL DR	LA	LA68	2100	34	E2
FERNDELL PL	GLDR	GLDR		87	D4
FERN DELL PL	LA	LA68	2100	34	E2
FERNDOC ST	WAL	WAL	20000	93	B6
FERNFIELD DR	CO	LA22	5300	46	A5
FERNFIELD DR E	MPK	MPK	100	46	C5
FERNFIELD DR W	MPK	MPK	200	46	A5
FERN GLEN	SMAD	SMAD	600	28	D1
FERNGLEN AV	LA	TU	10100	10	F3
FERN GLEN CT	WAL	WAL		93	D5
FERNGLEN LN	SAD	GLDR		89	F1

COPYRIGHT, © 1989 BY Thomas Bros Maps

245
FERNGLEN WY
FLORISTAN AV

1990 LOS ANGELES COUNTY STREET INDEX

STREET	CITY	P.O. ZONE	BLOCK	PAGE	GRID
FERNGLEN WY	CO	LPUE		48	B5
FERN HAVEN RD	CO	LPUE	16500	98	A3
FERNHILL DR	CO	MAL	6100	110	C5
FERN HOLLOW DR	DBAR	POM	1900	97	D4
FERNLAKE DR	CO	HAC		73	F1
FERNLEAF AV E	POM	POM	500	94	F4
FERNLEAF AV W	POM	POM	100	94	D4
FERNLEAF ST	LA	LA31	2200	35	E4
FERNLEY DR	DUA	DUA	1200	29	F5
FERNMEAD LN	CO	HAC		73	F1
FERNMONT ST	LA	SF	13500	2	F4
FERNMONT ST	LA	SF	13100	3	A3
FERNPARK DR	GLDR	GLDR		87	A4
FERN PINE CIR	CER	ART		82	D4
FERNREST DR	CO	HAC	900	73	F1
FERNRIDGE DR	SAD	LAV	1700	95A	B6
FERNROCK ST	CAR	CAR	1100	69	C2
FERNSHAW DR	CO	LAV	400	90	B2
FERNSIDE DR	LCF	LCF	1200	19	B2
FERNTOP DR	LA	LA32	4500	36	C5
FERNTOWER AV	WCOV	WCOV	3700	97	A1
FERNTREE PL	GLEN	GL14	3900	18	C1
FERN TRUCK TR	CO	ALT		19	E1
FERNVIEW ST	CO	WHI	14100	61	E3
FERNVIEW ST	CO	WHI	14800	84	A4
FERNVIEW ST	WHI	WHI	15400	84	C4
FERNWOOD AV	LA	LA27	5400	34	D3
FERNWOOD AV	LA	LA27	3800	35	A3
FERNWOOD AV	LA	LA28	5500	34	D3
FERNWOOD AV	LA	LA39	3000	35	B3
FERNWOOD AV	LYN	LYN	2600	58	F5
FERNWOOD AV	LYN	LYN	3000	59	A5
FERNWOOD DR	CO	LPUE		48	B5
FERNWOOD ST	WCOV	WCOV	100	92	C2
FERNWOOD PAC DR	CO	TOP	300	109	C6
FERRARA ST	LA	LA42	6600	36	D1
FERRARI DR	LA	BH	1600	33	A3
FERRARI LN	WCOV	WCOV		93	A2
FERRERO LN	LPUE	LPUE	100	92	B6
FERRERO LN	LPUE	LPUE	600	98	B1
FERRIS AV	CO	LA22	200	45	E6
FERRIS AV	CO	LA22	1000	53	E1
FERRIS PL	CO	COM		69	E1
FERRIS RD	ELM	ELM	11600	38	F6
FERRIS RD	ELM	ELM	12100	48	A1
FERRIS ST	CLA	CLA	200	91	C1
FERRO CT	LB	LB15	4900	76	B2
FERRO ST	LB	LB15	4900	76	B2
FERRON AV	CO	SGAB	6600	38	A1
FERRY ST	LA	SP	100	79	C2
FERTILE ST	LYN	LYN	5400	65	D1
FES ST	LA	SV	10600	16	F1
FESTINA DR	PAR	PAR	6600	65	D3
FESTIVIDAD DR	SCLR	SAU	22200	124	D7
FESTIVIDAD DR	SCLR	VL54		124	C7
FETTERLY AV N	CO	LA22	100	45	E5
FETTERLY AV S	CO	LA22	100	45	E5
FETTERLY AV S	CO	LA22	1000	53	E1
FIAT ST E	CAR	CAR	900	69	C5
FIAT ST W	CAR	CAR	200	69	A5
FIAT ST W	CO	TOR	1000	68	F5
FIBRE CT	DBAR	WAL		97	D2
FICKETT ST N	LA	LA33	100	45	B3
FICKETT ST S	LA	LA23	600	45	A4
FICKETT ST S	LA	LA33	100	45	A4
FICKEWIRTH AV	LPUE	LPUE	900	48	F5
FICUS ST	POM	POM		97A	F1
FIDALGO ST	CO	LPUE	18200	98	E5
FIDDLENECK CT	PALM	PALM		183	F3
FIDEL AV	CO	WHI	11300	61	D6
FIDEL AV	NWK	NWK	14300	82	D2
FIDELIA AV	CMRC	LA40	2400	54	A3
FIDELIDAD DR	CO	LPUE	2200	85	F4
FIDLER AV	BLF	BLF	13300	66	B1
FIDLER AV	DOW	DOW	13100	66	B1
FIDLER AV	LB	LB08	3000	71	B6
FIDLER AV	LB	LB15	2000	76	C3
FIDLER AV	LKD	LKD	5900	66	B6
FIDLER AV	LKD	LKD	4900	71	B3
FIELD AV	ING	IN02	1100	51	A5
FIELD AV	LA	LA16	3000	43	A6
FIELDBROOK ST	CO	LPUE	18600	98	E6
FIELDCREST LN	PALM	PALM		171	E4
FIELDCREST ST	CO	ELM	10500	38	D4
FIELDGATE AV	CO	LPUE	1100	85	F2
FIELDING DR	WHI	WHI	10800	84	B4
FIELDING ST	LA	PAC		3	B5
FIELDING ST	LA	PAC	13400	8	E2
FIELDMONT PL	LA	CAN		5	D4
FIELDSPRING ST	CO	LAN	40000	174	J4
FIELDVIEW AV	DUA	DUA	300	86	A4
FIERRO CIR	CO	GL14		11	E5
FIERRO ST	LA	LA65	3000	35	D1
FIESEL AV	CAR	CAR		69	C5
FIESTA AV	TEC	TEC	4500	38	C4
FIESTA LN	CAR	CAR		69	D6
FIFE AV	LPUE	LPUE	500	98	A1
FIG	WCOV	WCOV		98	F1
FIG AV	LAN	LAN	43600	160	A6
FIG AV	MON	MON	100	29	B5
FIG CIR	LAV	LAV		90	E1
FIG CT	CO	SAU		124	C3
FIG ST	COM	COM	300	64	E1
FIGTREE RD	RPV	PVP	1	77	E2
FIGUERAS RD	LAM	LAM	14100	83	A2
FIGUEROA DR E	CO	ALT	10	19	E5
FIGUEROA DR W	CO	ALT	100	19	E5
FIGUEROA PL	LA	WIL	500	74	A3
FIGUEROA ST	CO	CAST	30300	123	A5
FIGUEROA ST	GLEN	GL06		19	C6
FIGUEROA ST	GLEN	GL06	3200	26	C1
FIGUEROA ST	LA	GAR	12800	64	A2
FIGUEROA ST	LA	WIL	200	74	A5
FIGUEROA ST	LCF	LCF	3600	19	C6
FIGUEROA ST N	LA	LA12	100	44	D2
FIGUEROA ST N	LA	LA41	7200	26	C5
FIGUEROA ST N	LA	LA42	6700	26	C6
FIGUEROA ST N	LA	LA42	4700	36	B3
FIGUEROA ST N	LA	LA65	1900	35	F5
FIGUEROA ST N	LA	LA65	3300	36	B3
FIGUEROA ST S	CAR	CAR	19600	69	A4
FIGUEROA ST S	CAR	CAR	22900	69	A4
FIGUEROA ST S	CAR	CAR	23500	74	A2
FIGUEROA ST S	CAR	GAR	19100	69	A4
FIGUEROA ST S	LA	LA03	5800	52	A3
FIGUEROA ST S	LA	LA03	7900	58	A3
FIGUEROA ST S	LA	LA07	1900	44	A6
FIGUEROA ST S	LA	LA07	3500	52	A1
FIGUEROA ST S	LA	LA12	100	44	B4
FIGUEROA ST S	LA	LA15	900	44	B4
FIGUEROA ST S	LA	LA17	300	44	B4
FIGUEROA ST S	LA	LA37	3800	52	A3
FIGUEROA ST S	LA	LA61	10700	58	A3
FIGUEROA TER	LA	LA12	700	44	D1
FIGUEROA WY	LA	LA07	2300	44	B5
FIJI WY	CO	MDR	13500	49	E5
FIJI WY	LA	VEN	13200	49	E5
FIKSE LN	CER	ART		81	D1
FILAREE HTS AV	CO	MAL	5800	111	F5
FILBERT RD	CO	MAL		106	A4
FILBERT ST	LA	SF	15900	2	A2
FILHURST AV	BAP	BAP	3900	39	C4
FILION ST	LA	LA65	3800	25	E6
FILION WK	LA	LA65	3900	25	E6
FILLMORE CT	LAV	LAV		90	E4
FILLMORE DR	MPK	MPK	1700	46	D3
FILLMORE PL	POM	POM	500	94	D2
FILLMORE ST	PAS	PAS	100	27	A5
FILMORE ST	BELL	BELL		53	D5
FILMORE ST	LA	PAC	12600	3	B6
FILMORE ST	LA	PAC	13500	8	D3
FILMORE ST	LA	PAC	12800	9	A1
FILMORE ST	LA	SF	12300	3	B6
FINANCIAL WY	GLDR	GLDR		87	E6
FINCH	POM	POM		90	F2
FINCH PL	LAV	LAV		95A	E5
FINCH ST	LAV	LAV		95A	E6
FINCH ST	LA	LA39	2900	35	C2
FINCHGROVE RD	CO	VALY		192	D6
FINCHLEY	BAP	BAP		48	C1
FINCHLEY PL	PAS	PAS	1300	19	D6
FINCHLEY ST	BAP	BAP	12600	39	B6
FINDLAY AV	CO	LA22	600	46	B6
FINDLAY AV	CO	LA22	700	54	B1
FINDLAY AV	MPK	MPK	2100	46	B5
FINDLAY AV	MTB	MTB	400	46	B6
FINE CIR	LAN	LAN		159	B6
FINE CIR	LAN	LAN		159	F5
FINE ST	LAN	LAN		159	F6
FINECREST DR	RPV	PVP	5800	72	D4
FINECROFT DR	CLA	CLA	1600	90	F2
FINEGROVE AV	CO	LPUE	1000	48	C6
FINEGROVE AV	CO	LPUE	1400	85	C1
FINEHILL AV	GLEN	GL14	5200	11	D4
FINES RD	CO	MAL		114	A4
FINEVALE DR	DOW	DOW	7200	54	B6
FINEVALE DR	DOW	DOW	7600	60	B1
FINEVIEW ST	ELM	ELM	11000	47	E3
FINEVIEW ST	SELM	ELM	11000	47	D3
FINGAL PL	WHI	WHI		55	F5
FINISTERRA PL	CO	LPUE		85	C3
FINK PL	LA	LA68	6400	34	C2
FINK ST	LA	LA68	2200	34	C2
FINLEY AV	LA	LA27	4300	34	E2
FINNEY CT	CO	GAR		64	B2
FIR AV	CO	LA01	8300	58	E2
FIR AV	CO	LA02	8600	58	E2
FIR AV N	ING	IN01	100	56	F1
FIR AV S	ING	IN01	100	56	F2
FIR CT	CO	SAU		124	C2
FIR ST	LA	LA16	4900	43	A5
FIR ST	LYN	LYN	11400	59	B6
FIR ST	PR	PR	4600	54	F2
FIRCROFT AV	CO	COV	4600	88	E3
FIRCROFT AV N	COV	COV	1300	88	E3
FIRCROFT AV S	COV	COV	600	88	E6
FIRCROFT ST	WCOV	WCOV	100	92	E1
FIREBIRD AV	CO	WHI	9200	61	D3
FIREBIRD AV	WHI	WHI	8700	61	E2
FIREBRAND DR	CO	CAST		123	D4
FIREBRAND PL	LA	LA34	3300	42	A6
FIREBRAND ST	LA	LA45	6400	50	B6
FIRE HOLLOW DR	DBAR	POM		97A	A3
FIRENZE AV	LA	LA46	7700	23	F6
FIRENZE PL	CO	VAL		123	J9
FIRENZE PL	CO	VAL		126	G1
FIRENZE PL	LA	LA46	2800	23	F6
FIREPIT DR	DBAR	POM		93	F5
FIRESIDE DR	CO	WHI	11500	84	D5
FIRESTONE BLVD	CO	LA01	1100	58	C1
FIRESTONE BLVD	CO	LA02	2100	58	C1
FIRESTONE BLVD	DOW	DOW	7000	59	B2
FIRESTONE BLVD	DOW	DOW	7300	60	C4
FIRESTONE BLVD	LAM	LAM	14200	82	F4
FIRESTONE BLVD	LAM	LAM	14700	83	A5
FIRESTONE BLVD	NWK	NWK	10500	60	C4
FIRESTONE BLVD	NWK	NWK	11700	82	A1
FIRESTONE BLVD	SFS	SFS	12600	82	D3
FIRESTONE BLVD	SOG	SOG	2200	58	C1
FIRESTONE BLVD	SOG	SOG	2900	59	B2
FIRESTONE PL	DOW	DOW	7400	60	A3
FIRESTONE PL	SOG	SOG	5000	59	D2
FIRESTONE PZ	SOG	SOG	8800	58	F2
FIRETHORN AV	PALM	PALM		183	E2
FIRE THORN CIR	DBAR	POM		97	F3
FIREWORKS RD	SCLR	SAU		124	D9
FIRMA CT	LA	SF	17300	1	E5
FIRMAMENT AV	LA	ENC	4000	22	B3
FIRMAMENT AV	LA	VAN	6400	15	B3
FIRMIN ST	LA	LA26	300	44	C1
FIRMONA AV	CO	IN04	10000	56	F4
FIRMONA AV	HAW	IN04	11300	56	F5
FIRMONA AV	ING	IN04	10000	56	F4
FIRMONA AV	LAW	LAW	14300	62	F5
FIRMONA AV	RB	RB	1000	62	F6
FIRMONA AV	RB	RB	500	67	F1
FIRMONA AV	TOR	TOR	19000	67	F1
FIR RIDGE DR	CO	TOP		115	B1
FIRST VIEW ST	LAN	LAN		160	C7
FIRTH AV	LA	LA49	600	32	B6
FIRTH BLVD	LA	LA02		58	D3
FIRTH DR	LA	BH	13400	22	F6
FIRTH WK	LA	LA02	10300	58	D3
FIRTHRIDGE RD	RPV	PVP	27900	72	D5
FIRTREE DR	CO	PALM		157	H9
FIRVALE AV	MTB	MTB	1600	46	E4
FIRWOOD CT	NWK	NWK		66	D2
FISCHER ST	GLEN	GL05	300	25	E5
FISHBURN AV	BELL	BELL	6200	53	C6
FISHBURN AV	CO	LA63	1500	45	C2
FISHBURN AV	HPK	HPK	5900	53	C4
FISHBURN AV	MAY	MAY	5200	53	C4
FISH CANYON RD	DUA	DUA		86	A4
FISHER AV	MB	MB	1100	62	B4
FISHER CT	RB	RB	2200	67	E1
FISHER ST	CO	LA22	4300	45	D4
FISHER ST	CO	LA63	4000	45	D4
FISHER ST	LA	LA42	300	36	D1
FISHERMNS WHARF	RB	RB	100	67	C3
FISH HARBOR WHF	LA	SP		79	C3
FISHMAN RD	PR	PR	8500	54	F2
FISH RDG TK TR	CO			N	E6
FISK AV	SGAB	SGAB	100	37	E5
FISK CT	RB	RB	700	67	F1
FISK LN	RB	RB	500	67	F1
FISK LN	RB	RB	2400	67	E1
FISKE AV	PAS	PAS	1600	20	B6
FISKE ST	LA	PP	800	40	D3
FITCH AV	CO	CYN	29700	125	C5
FITCH DR	LA	LA68	1900	34	B2
FITHIAN AV	LA	LA32	2600	36	D6
FITZGERALD AV	CMRC	LA40	2100	53	F2
FITZGERALD AV	CO	VAL		126	H3
FITZGERALD ST	LA	CAN		5	E1
FITZPATRICK RD	HH	CAL	24600	100	C1
FITZROY AV	LA	TU	10600	11	A3
FIUME WK	LA	VAN		22	C4
FIVE OAKS DR	SPAS	SPAS	500	36	E1
FLAG ST	LAN	LAN		159	H7
FLAG ST	LA	LA68	5800	34	D2
FLAG WY	PALM	PALM		171	F4
FLAGLER LN	RB	RB	1000	62	D6
FLAGLER LN	RB	RB	700	67	D1
FLAGLER LN	TOR	TOR	19200	67	D1
FLAGMOOR PL	LA	LA68	6400	34	C1
FLAGON ST	SFS	SFS	12600	61	B3
FLAGSTAFF ST	CO	LPUE	13500	48	C3
FLAGSTAFF ST	LPUE	LPUE	13700	48	C3
FLAGSTAFF ST	SAD	SAD	300	90	A2
FLAGSTONE AV	CO	DUA	2000	29	B6
FLAGSTONE AV	CO	DUA	2300	39	B1
FLAGSTONE ST	LB	LB08	5100	71	B6
FLAHERTY ST	TEC	TEC	9200	38	B2
FLAIR DR	ELM	ELM		47	B1
FLALLON AV	ART	ART	17200	82	A5
FLALLON AV	CO	WHI	8000	55	B6
FLALLON AV	CO	WHI	8400	61	A1
FLALLON AV	LKD	LKD	19700	81	A2
FLALLON AV	NWK	NWK	11100	61	A5
FLALLON AV	NWK	NWK	13300	82	A2
FLALLON AV	SFS	SFS	9100	61	A2
FLAMBEAU RD	RPV	PVP	5800	72	D4
FLAMNG ARRW CIR	WAL	WAL		93	A6
FLAMNG ARROW DR	RPV	PVP	27400	72	E5
FLAMINGO CIR	CO	WHI	10500	55	A6
FLAMINGO ST	GLDR	GLDR	900	87	C3
FLAMINGO ST	LA	WOH	22500	13	B4
FLAMINGO WY	ARC	ARC	500	38	F2
FLAMSTEAD DR	CO	LPUE	1500	85	E3
FLANAGAN ST	POM	POM	1500	94	F4
FLANCO RD	LA	WOH	22200	13	B3
FLANDERS AV	POM	POM	300	90	E5
FLANDERS RD	LCF	LCF	900	19	A2
FLANDERS ST	LA	SF	16600	1	E6
FLANDERS ST	LA	SF	16300	2	A6
FLANGEL ST	LKD	LKD	2400	70	F3
FLANNER ST	CO	LPUE	13600	48	D2
FLANNER ST	LPUE	LPUE	14400	48	E3
FLAPJACK DR	DBAR	POM		97	D6
FLARE RD	SCLR	SAU		127	E1
FLASHMAN AV	LA	PAC	8900	9	A6
FLATBUSH AV	NWK	NWK	12800	66	E3
FLATHEAD TR	CO	AGO		107	B3
FLAT PEAK LN	CER	ART		82	B4
FLAVIAN AV	TOR	TOR	19200	67	F2
FLAX PL	LA	LA45	7600	55A	F2
FLAXTON ST	CUL	CUL	10600	50	D3
FLAXTON ST	POM	POM	300	90	F3
FLECHA CT	CO	LPUE		85	F4
FLEET DR	SOG	SOG	13500	65	E1
FLEET ST	CMRC	LA40	6400	54	B2
FLEET ST	LA	VEN		49	C5
FLEETHAVEN RD	LKD	LKD	4100	71	A4
FLEETWELL AV	CO	AZU	5500	88	D2
FLEETWELL AV N	WCOV	WCOV	100	88	D6
FLEETWELL AV S	WCOV	WCOV	700	92	D2
FLEETWELL ST	WCOV	WCOV		92	D2
FLEETWING AV	LA	LA45	8900	56	C2
FLEETWOOD PL	GLDR	GLDR	400	89	A2
FLEETWOOD PL	POM	POM	2100	90	E5
FLEETWOOD ST	LA	SV	11000	9	E6
FLEETWOOD ST	LA	SV	11500	16	D1
FLEMING AV	BLF	BLF	14700	66	C3
FLEMING ST	POM	POM	1700	94	B3
FLEMINGTON DR	WCOV	WCOV		93	A6
FLEMINGTON DR	WCOV	WCOV		97	A1
FLEMISH LN	LA	LA29	5400	34	E4
FLEMMING WY	CER	ART		82	E4
FLETA DR	LAM	LAM	13200	82	F1
FLETCHER AV	ELM	ELM		47	B1
FLETCHER AV	SPAS	SPAS	1600	37	A3
FLETCHER DR	LA	LA39	2300	35	D2
FLETCHER DR	LA	LA65	2900	35	D2
FLETCHER PK WY	ELM	ELM	3400	47	C1
FLEUR DR	SMAR	PAS	2700	37	B1
FLICKER PL	LA	LA69	9200	33	C3
FLICKER WY	LA	LA69	9200	33	C3
FLIGHT AV	CO	LA56	6100	50	E5
FLIGHT AV	LA	LA45	7000	50	D6
FLIGHT AV	LA	LA45	7800	56	D1
FLIGHT AV	LA	LA56	6100	50	E5
FLIGHT PL	LA	LA45	7800	56	D1
FLINT AV	LA	LA34	9500	42	C5
FLINT AV	LA	WIL	500	74	D4
FLINT AV	LB	LB14		76	C5
FLINTGATE DR	DBAR	WAL	20300	97	C3
FLINTHILL DR	CO	SAU		182	C8
FLINTLOCK LN	WLVL	THO		102	C4
FLINTLOCK RD	DBAR	POM		94	A4
FLINTPOINT CIR	POM	POM		94	D5
FLINTRIDGE AV	LCF	LCF	700	19	C5
FLINTRIDGE CIR	LCF	LCF	1200	19	B5
FLINTRIDGE DR	GLEN	GL08		19	B5
FLINTRDG OKS DR	LCF	LCF	300	19	C4
FLINT ROCK RD	DBAR	POM		97A	A3
FLINT SPEAR RD	WAL	WAL		93	B5
FLINTSTONE DR	CO	PALM		157	E9
FLINTWOOD DR	CO	LPUE		97	A5
FLO LN	CO	CYN		124	G8
FLOMAR DR	WHI	WHI	12600	61	D1
FLOMAR DR	WHI	WHI	14700	84	B3
FLORA AV	BELL	BELL		53	C6
FLORA AV	HPK	HPK	5900	53	C6
FLORA AV	LA	LA31	3500	36	B5
FLORA AV	MAY	MAY	5900	53	C6
FLORA DR	ING	IN02	800	50	E6
FLORA ST	WCOV	WCOV		92	E5
FLORABUNDA RD	CO	CYN		125	F6
FLORAC AV	LAV	LAV	3900	90	E2
FLORADALE AV	ELM	ELM		47	E2
FLORADALE AV	SELM	ELM	1800	47	D3
FLORAL AV	LA	LA46	8000	33	F3
FLORAL AV E	ARC	ARC	100	28	E3
FLORAL AV W	ARC	ARC	100	28	E3
FLORAL CT	SCLR	NEW		127	B1
FLORAL DR	CO	LA22	4300	45	C4
FLORAL DR	CO	LA63	3300	45	C4
FLORAL DR	CO	WHI	10200	55	C3
FLORAL DR	WHI	WHI	10400	55	C3
FLORAL DR E	MPK	MPK	100	46	C4
FLORAL DR W	MPK	MPK	1400	45	F4
FLORAL DR W	MPK	MPK	100	46	B4
FLORALITA AV	LA	SUN	10200	10	D3
FLORAL PARK TER	SPAS	SPAS	400	36	E1
FLORAMORGAN TR	LA	TU		10	F4
FLORAMORGAN TR	LA	TU	7000	11	A4
FLORA VISTA DR	BELL	BELL	4200	53	C5
FLORA VISTA ST	ART	ART	11800	81	A1
FLORA VISTA ST	BLF	BLF	9200	66	B3
FLORAVISTA TER	CO	LPUE		48	B5
FLORCRAFT AV	LKD	LKD	20800	81	B3
FLORECITA CRES	PAS	ALT	3300	19	E3
FLORECITA DR	PAS	ALT	3100	19	E3
FLORECITA LN	PAS	ALT	700	19	E4
FLORECITA TER	PAS	ALT	600	19	E4
FLORECITA WY	PAS	ALT	700	19	E3
FLORENA CT	GLEN	GL08	2100	18	F5
FLORENCE AV	ARC	ARC	2200	38	C2
FLORENCE AV	BELL	BELL	3600	53	B6
FLORENCE AV	BG	BELL	5600	53	E6
FLORENCE AV	BG	BELL	6400	60	B2
FLORENCE AV	CO	WHI	13300	61	D4
FLORENCE AV	DOW	DOW	7200	60	B2
FLORENCE AV	HPK	HPK	2900	53	B6
FLORENCE AV	LA	LA44	800	51	C5
FLORENCE AV	MPK	MPK		46	D1
FLORENCE AV	PAR	PAR		65	F1
FLORENCE AV	SFS	SFS	11300	60	D3
FLORENCE AV	SFS	SFS	11700	61	A4
FLORENCE AV	SOG	SOG	5700	65	E1
FLORENCE AV	WCOV	WCOV	400	92	B3
FLORENCE AV	WHI	WHI	5500	55	C3
FLORENCE AV E	CO	HPK	2100	52	B5
FLORENCE AV E	CO	LA01	1100	52	B5
FLORENCE AV E	ING	IN01	100	57	A1
FLORENCE AV E	ING	IN02	800	51	A6
FLORENCE AV E	LA	LA01	600	52	B5
FLORENCE AV E	LA	LA03	100	52	B5
FLORENCE AV W	ING	IN01	200	56	E1
FLORENCE AV W	ING	IN01	100	57	A1
FLORENCE AV W	LA	LA03	100	52	C5
FLORENCE AV W	LA	LA43	2200	51	C5
FLORENCE AV W	LA	LA44	500	52	C5
FLORENCE AV W	LA	LA47	1400	51	C5
FLORENCE DR	PAS	PAS	1100	26	F2
FLORENCE LN	SCLR	CYN		124	G6
FLORENCE PL	BG	BELL	6200	53	F6
FLORENCE PL	BG	BELL	6300	54	A6
FLORENCE PL	GLEN	GL04	1000	25	C5
FLORENCE ST	BUR	BUR		24	B1
FLORENCE ST	PAR	PAR	8000	65	F1
FLORENCE WK	LB	LB03	1	80	C1
FLORENCELL ST	CO	ACT	34600	182	F7
FLORENCITA AV	CO	MONT	2200	18	F3
FLORENTINA AV	ALH	ALH	2300	45	F1
FLORENTINE ST	LA	SF	14700	2	C5
FLORES AV	CO	LA56	5900	50	E4
FLORES AV	LA	LA56	6200	50	E4
FLORES ST	DOW	DOW	7400	59	E5
FLORES ST N	LA	LA48	100	33	E6
FLORES ST N	WHOL	LA48	500	33	E6
FLORES ST N	WHOL	LA69	1100	33	E4
FLORES ST S	LA	LA48	100	33	E6
FLORES DE ORO	SPAS	SPAS	700	36	E2
FLORESTA AV	CO	LA43	3400	51	B3
FLORESTA PL	LA	PP		40	B1
FLORESTA WY	CO	LA43	3700	51	B3
FLORHAM AV	SAD	SAD	500	89	D2
FLORIAN PL	LA	BH	2200	33	A2
FLORIDA ST	LA	LA17	1000	44	C3
FLORIDA ST	LB	LB02	1200	75	E5
FLORIDA ST	LB	LB14	2000	75	E5
FLORIDA ST	WCOV	WCOV		92	D5
FLORINDA AV	CO	ARC	5600	38	E3
FLORINDA AV	CO	TEC	5000	38	E3
FLORINDA ST	POM	POM	3100	90	E3
FLORINE AV	PAR	PAR	13700	65	E2
FLORIS HTS RD	CO	MAL	5900	112	A6
FLORISTAN AV	LA	LA41	4800	26	B5

LOS ANGELES CO.
INDEX

STREET	CITY	P.O. ZONE	BLOCK	PAGE	GRID
FLORITA RD	LAM	LAM	14500	83	A3
FLORIZEL ST	LA	LA32	4400	36	C4
FLORPARK ST	PR	PR	9500	60	E2
FLORWOOD AV	CO	LAW	15100	63	B3
FLORWOOD AV	HAW	HAW	13000	63	B3
FLORWOOD AV	TOR	TOR	17800	63	B6
FLORWOOD AV	TOR	TOR	1200	68	B4
FLORWOOD AV	TOR	TOR	18700	68	B1
FLORY ST	CO	WHI	10800	55	B5
FLOSSMOOR RD	PR	PR	9800	60	D1
FLOSSMOOR RD	SFS	SFS	11200	60	F3
FLOTILLA ST	CMRC	LA40	5500	53	F2
FLOTILLA ST	CMRC	LA40	6400	54	B2
FLOURNOY RD	MB	MB	1800	62	B3
FLOWER AV	COM	COM		65	A3
FLOWER AV	DUA	DUA	1500	29	E5
FLOWER AV	LA	VEN	600	49	C3
FLOWER AV	TOR	TOR	1600	68	B4
FLOWER AV S	COM	COM	200	65	A3
FLOWER DR	LA	LA37	3800	52	A1
FLOWER ST	ARC	ARC	300	28	E4
FLOWER ST	BLF	BLF	8700	66	B4
FLOWER ST	BUR	BUR	100	17	E6
FLOWER ST	BUR	BUR	400	24	E1
FLOWER ST	CDY	BELL	3800	53	B6
FLOWER ST	CO	HPK	2400	52	F6
FLOWER ST	CO	HPK	2900	53	A6
FLOWER ST	CO	LA61	12400	58	A6
FLOWER ST	GLEN	GL01		24	E1
FLOWER ST	GLEN	GL01	900	25	A3
FLOWER ST	HPK	HPK	3200	53	A6
FLOWER ST	LA	LA03	5800	52	A4
FLOWER ST	LA	LA03	7900	58	A1
FLOWER ST	LA	LA07	1900	44	B4
FLOWER ST	LA	LA07	3600	52	A1
FLOWER ST	LA	LA15	900	44	B4
FLOWER ST	LA	LA17	500	44	B4
FLOWER ST	LA	LA37	4000	52	A2
FLOWER ST	LYN	LYN	3000	59	A5
FLOWER ST	PAR	PAR	8500	66	A4
FLOWER ST	PAS	PAS	200	20	A6
FLOWER ST N	ING	IN01	400	51	B6
FLOWER ST S	ING	IN01	500	57	A3
FLOWER CREEK LN	CO	LPUE		98	A4
FLOWERDALE CT	LA	SV	10300	16	F1
FLOWERFIELD LN	LHH	LAH		98A	B3
FLOWER GLEN DR	CO	LPUE	16500	98	A3
FLOWER HILL CIR	LA	SF		1	E5
FLOWER HILL LN	CO	LPUE		85	C4
FLOWERIDGE DR	RPV	PVP	31200	78	B4
FLOWRNG PLM CIR	WHI	WHI		84	D5
FLOWERPARK DR	CO	CYN	28900	125	E7
FLOWERS CT	SCLR	SAU		127	G1
FLOWER VALE LN	CO	LPUE	16900	98	B3
FLOYD ST	BUR	BUR	2000	17	B3
FLOYD TER	LA	LA68	3300	24	B5
FLOYE DR	LA	LA68	3100	23	F6
FLYING HILL PL	DBAR	POM		94	B5
FLYING MANE LN	RH	PVP	1	78	B2
FLYING MANE RD	RH	PVP	1	78	B2
FLYNN ST	CO	LPUE	13500	48	D3
FLYNN ST	LPUE	LPUE	13800	48	D3
FLYNN RANCH RD	LA	LA46		23	F6
FOB CIR	LAN	LAN		159	H6
FOIX AV	NWK	NWK	10600	60	D5
FOIX PL	LA	CHA	20200	6	E3
FOLEY AV	CAR	CAR	21800	69	C4
FOLEY WY	POM	POM		94	A4
FOLGER ST	CO	LPUE	14800	48	C6
FOLGER ST	CO	LPUE	15200	85	D1
FOLKSTONE AV	CO	LPUE	900	48	C6
FOLKSTONE AV	CO	LPUE	1400	85	B1
FOLKSTONE LN	LA	LA77		32	C1
FOLSOM ST	CO	LA22	4300	45	C4
FOLSOM ST	CO	LA63	3200	45	C4
FOLSOM ST	LA	LA33	2300	45	B3
FOLSOM ST	LA	LA63	3000	45	B3
FOND DR	LA	ENC	3100	22	A5
FONDA WY	LA	LA31	2700	36	A5
FONDALE ST	AZU	AZU	1000	88	E1
FONDALE ST	CO	AZU	18000	88	E1
FOND DU LAC RD	RPV	PVP	26600	72	E4
FONSECA AV	LAM	LAM	12700	83	A1
FONTAINBLEAU AV	LKD	LKD	4200	81	C3
FONTAINBLEAU CT	LAN	LAN		159	D5
FONTAINE RD	CO	TOP	20800	109	D3
FONTANA ST	DOW	DOW	7000	59	F3
FONTANA ST	DOW	DOW	7600	60	B4
FONTANET WY	CO	ALT		20	B5
FONTENELLE WY	LA	LA77	10500	32	D3
FONTENOY AV	CO	WHI	1300	48	A5
FONTES PL	WAL	WAL		92	F5
FONTES PL	WAL	WAL		93	A5
FONTEZUELA DR	CO	LPUE	2200	85	F4
FONTHILL AV	CO	LAW	15100	63	B3
FONTHILL AV	HAW	HAW	12400	57	B6
FONTHILL AV	HAW	HAW	14200	63	B2
FONTHILL AV	TOR	TOR	16800	63	B5
FONTHILL AV	TOR	TOR	800	68	B3
FONTHILL AV	TOR	TOR	18800	68	B1
FOOSE RD	CO	MAL		111	A1
FOOTE AV	LA	WIL	800	74	F4
FOOTES AL	LB	LB13		75	C5
FOOTHILL AV	SMAD	SMAD	200	28	D1
FOOTHILL BLVD	CO	AZU	1800	86	E5
FOOTHILL BLVD	CO	GL14	3000	11	B4
FOOTHILL BLVD	CO	GL14	2300	18	E1
FOOTHILL BLVD	CO	GL14	2600	18	E1
FOOTHILL BLVD	CO	PAS	3700	28	A3
FOOTHILL BLVD	GLDR	GLDR	1850	86	E5
FOOTHILL BLVD	GLEN	GL14	3200	11	B4
FOOTHILL BLVD	IRW	BAP	100	86	B5
FOOTHILL BLVD	LA	SF	13400	2	D1
FOOTHILL BLVD	LA	SF	12200	3	A5
FOOTHILL BLVD	LA	SF	10400	9	E1
FOOTHILL BLVD	LA	SF	10000	10	B2
FOOTHILL BLVD	LA	SF		127	F9
FOOTHILL BLVD	LA	SUN	7800	10	D3
FOOTHILL BLVD	LA	TU	7000	10	D3
FOOTHILL BLVD	LA	TU	6200	11	B4
FOOTHILL BLVD	LAV	LAV	100	90	D2
FOOTHILL BLVD	LCF	LCF	300	19	B3
FOOTHILL BLVD	PAS	PAS	2000	27	D3
FOOTHILL BLVD	PAS	PAS	3400	28	A3
FOOTHILL BLVD E	ARC	ARC	100	28	A3
FOOTHILL BLVD E	AZU	AZU	100	86	B5
FOOTHILL BLVD E	CLA	CLA	100	91	A3
FOOTHILL BLVD E	GLDR	GLDR	800	87	B5
FOOTHILL BLVD E	MON	MON	1900	29	A3
FOOTHILL BLVD E	POM	POM	100	90	D2
FOOTHILL BLVD E	SAD	SAD	100	90	A1
FOOTHILL BLVD W	ARC	ARC	100	28	A3
FOOTHILL BLVD W	AZU	AZU	100	86	B5
FOOTHILL BLVD W	CLA	CLA	100	91	A3
FOOTHILL BLVD W	GLDR	GLDR	100	87	B5
FOOTHILL BLVD W	MON	MON	100	29	A3
FOOTHILL BLVD W	POM	POM	100	90	D2
FOOTHILL BLVD W	SAD	SAD	100	90	A1
FOOTHILL DR	AGH	AGO		100A	B3
FOOTHILL DR	GLEN	GL01	1600	18	A5
FOOTHILL DR	LA	LA68	5700	34	D2
FOOTHILL DR	LA	LA68	5700	34	D2
FOOTHILL DR	WCOV	WCOV		92	E3
FOOTHILL FRWY	AZU	COV		88	D1
FOOTHILL FRWY	CO			18	D1
FOOTHILL FRWY	GLDR	GLDR		89	B1
FOOTHILL FRWY	IRW	BAP		86	A6
FOOTHILL FRWY	LA	LA		10	D4
FOOTHILL FRWY	LA	LA		11	B6
FOOTHILL FRWY	LA	SF		2	C1
FOOTHILL FRWY	LCF	LCF		19	D4
FOOTHILL FRWY	LCF	LCF		19	D4
FOOTHILL FRWY	MON	MON		29	B5
FOOTHILL FRWY	PAS	PAS		26	F2
FOOTHILL FRWY	PAS	PAS		27	B3
FOOTHILL FRWY	PAS	PAS		28	A3
FOOTHILL FRWY	SAD	SAD		90	A1
FOOTHILL FRWY	SF	SF		3	B5
FOOTHILL PL	LA	SF	9100	10	B1
FOOTHILL RD	BH	BH	200	33	C6
FOOTHILL ST	SPAS	SPAS	900	36	F1
FOOTHILL ST	SPAS	SPAS	1700	37	A1
FOOTHL FRNTG RD	CLA	CLA		91	C3
FORBES AV	CLA	CLA	2900	91	B1
FORBES AV	CLA	CLA	3100	96	B6
FORBES AV	LA	ENC	5200	21	F1
FORBES AV	LA	SF	8600	7	F2
FORBES AV	LA	VAN	6400	14	F4
FORBES AV	MTB	MTB	600	46	F6
FORBES AV	MTB	MTB	500	54	F1
FORBES WY	LB	LB10	1500	70	A4
FORD AV	POM	POM	100	90	E5
FORD AV	RB	RB	1000	62	D5
FORD BLVD	CO	LA22	1100	53	E1
FORD BLVD N	CO	LA22	100	45	E6
FORD BLVD S	CO	LA22	100	45	E6
FORD DR	WCOV	WCOV		92	B4
FORD LN	HPK	HPK	6500	53	A5
FORD PL	PAS	PAS	400	27	B4
FORD ST	BUR	BUR	800	24	A2
FORDHAM PL	CLA	CLA	400	91	B5
FORDHAM RD	LA	LA45	7600	56	A1
FORDHOOK DR	LCF	LCF	1000	19	B3
FORDLAND AV	CO	LAV	700	90	B2
FORDYCE AV	CAR	LB10	20400	69	F3
FORDYCE RD	LA	LA49	300	32	C6
FORECASTLE AV	WAL	WAL		97	A2
FORECASTLE AV	WCOV	WCOV	3400	97	A2
FOREMAN AV	LB	LB15	2600	76	C1
FOREMAST DR	LAM	LAM	15300	83	B3
FOREST AV	GLEN	GL05		25	C6
FOREST AV	LA	LA33	400	45	B3
FOREST AV	PAS	PAS	1100	26	E1
FOREST AV	SPAS	SPAS	600	36	E1
FOREST AV	WHI	WHI		55	F6
FOREST AV E	ARC	ARC	1	28	E3
FOREST AV W	ARC	ARC	1	28	E3
FOREST PL	SFS	SFS	11000	61	B5
FOREST ST	ING	IN02	1100	51	A5
FOREST ST	SFS	SFS	10400	61	B4
FOREST TR	CO	SF	12200	3	E5
FOREST CYN DR	DBAR	POM		97	F3
FOREST COVE LN	AGH	AGO		102	E3
FORESTDALE AV	CO	GLDR	6100	86	F6
FORESTDALE AV	CO	GLDR	5800	88	F1
FORESTDALE AV	CO	GLDR		89	A1
FORESTDALE AV	CO	LAV	1100	90	B2
FORESTDALE AV	COV	COV	100	88	F5
FORESTDALE AV	WCOV	WCOV	2600	92	F2
FORESTER DR	LAV	LAV		95A	E6
FOREST GATE CIR	CO	MAL		113	E5
FOREST GLEN	LA	LA68		23	F6
FOREST GLEN	LA	LA68		24	A6
FOREST GLEN DR	CO	LPUE	1500	98	A2
FORESTGLEN DR	GLEN	GL14		18	C1
FORESTGLEN LN	SAD	SAD		89	F1
FOREST GREEN DR	LCF	LCF		19	D1
FOREST GROVE ST	ELM	ELM	11200	38	E5
FOREST HILL DR	LCF	LCF		19	B4
FOREST HILLS DR	COV	COV		89	A6
FOREST HILLS DR	COV	COV		93	A1
FOREST HILLS RD	LA	CAN		5	E3
FOREST KNOLL DR	LA	LA69	1400	33	D3
FOREST LAWN DR	LA	LA27	5200	24	D3
FOREST LAWN DR	LA	LA68	5900	24	D3
FOREST MDW PL	CO	CAST		123	C1
FOREST OAKS DR	GLDR	GLDR	1500	87	D5
FORESTON RD	CO	PALM		190	B1
FOREST PARK DR	LA	LA32	2500	36	B6
FORESTRIDGE DR	AGH	AGO		102	D4
FORESTVIEW AV	CO	LPUE	700	48	B5
FORGE PL	LA	SF	15700	8	B2
FORHAN LN	LA	NHO	10100	24	A3
FORHAN ST E	LB	LB05	100	65	C5
FORHAN ST W	LB	LB05	100	65	C5
FORMAN AV	LA	NHO	4100	24	A4
FORMBY DR	LAM	LAM	15700	83	C2
FORMOSA AV	WHOL	LA46	1000	34	A4
FORMOSA AV N	LA	LA36	100	34	A6
FORMOSA AV N	LA	LA46	700	34	A6
FORMOSA AV S	LA	LA36	100	34	A6
FORNEY ST	LA	LA31	2300	35	D4
FORREST AV	WCOV	WCOV	1600	48	E2
FORREST ST	SCLR	CYN	16400	125	C6
FORRESTAL DR	RPV	PVP	32200	78	B3
FORRESTER DR	LA	LA64	2700	42	B4
FORRESTER DR	LOM	LOM	2300	73	C3
FORRY ST	LAN	LAN		159	H6
FORSMAN CT	SCLR	CYN		125	D8
FORSYTH PL	CLA	CLA		96	C6
FORSYTHE ST	LA	SUN	800	10	E2
FORSYTHE ST	LA	TU	7600	10	E2
FORT BOWIE DR	WAL	WAL		93	C3
FORTIN ST	BAP	BAP	4800	39	F3
FORT LEWIS DR	CLA	CLA	1400	90	F2
FORT LEWIS DR	POM	POM	300	90	F2
FORTNER WY	POM	POM		90	F3
FORTROSE CT	WHI	WHI		84	C4
FORTSON DR	CO	SGAB	8900	38	A1
FORT TEJON RD	CO	LLAN		192	J3
FORT TEJON RD	CO	LR	8200	184	G7
FORT TEJON RD	CO	PEAR	10600	185	A9
FORT TEJON RD	CO	PEAR		192	B1
FORT TEJON RD	CO	VALY		192	E3
FORT TEJON RD	PALM	PALM	4700	184	A2
FORTUNA CT	CO	LR		184	D5
FORTUNA CT	LA	LA11	5300	52	D3
FORTUNA DR	SCLR	VAL		127	A4
FORTUNA ST	LA	LA11	5300	52	D4
FORTUNE PL	LA	LA42	6700	26	E6
FORTUNE WY	LA	LA42	900	26	E6
FOSS AV	CO	ARC	2600	38	F2
FOSS AV	CO	ARC		39	A1
FOSTER AV	WCOV	WCOV	1800	48	E2
FOSTER AV E	BAP	BAP	13400	39	D6
FOSTER AV N	BAP	BAP	3700	39	C5
FOSTER CIR	BAP	BAP	3700	39	C4
FOSTER DR	LA	LA48	800	42	E2
FOSTER RD	DOW	DOW	9200	66	B1
FOSTER RD	LAM	LAM	13800	82	F1
FOSTER RD	LAM	LAM	15001	83	B1
FOSTER RD	NWK	NWK		61	C6
FOSTER RD	NWK	NWK	10600	66	E1
FOSTER RD	NWK	NWK	11600	82	C1
FOSTER RD	SFS	SFS	13400	82	C1
FOSTR BRIDGE BL	BG	BELL	6400	54	A6
FOSTR BRIDGE BL	DOW	DOW	6900	54	A6
FOSTORIA CT	PALM	PALM		171	C5
FOSTORIA DR	PALM	PALM		171	F4
FOSTORIA ST	BG	BELL	5600	59	E2
FOSTORIA ST	CDY	BELL	5100	59	D2
FOSTORIA ST	DOW	DOW	7400	60	A2
FOTINI PL	MPK	MPK	600	46	B3
FOUNDERS DR	CO	WOH		13	B4
FOUNTAIN AV	LA	LA28	5500	34	A4
FOUNTAIN AV	LA	LA29	4500	34	E4
FOUNTAIN AV	LA	LA29	3800	35	A3
FOUNTAIN AV	WHOL	LA46	7600	33	F4
FOUNTAIN AV	WHOL	LA46	7100	34	A4
FOUNTAIN AV	WHOL	LA69	8300	33	F4
FOUNTAIN CT	BAP	BAP		39	D4
FOUNTAIN PL	AGH	AGO		100A	B3
FOUNTAIN ST	LB	LB04	3600	76	A4
FOUNTAIN PK LN	LA	WOH	6000	12	C6
FOUNTAIN SPG LN	GLDR	GLDR		87	D4
FOUNTN SPGS RD	DBAR	POM	21000	97	D5
FOUNTAINWOOD ST	AGH	AGO		100A	A2
FOUNTAINWOOD ST	AGH	AGO		102	E2
FOURL RD	SCLR	NEW	24200	127	A5
FOUR OAKS ST	SCLR	CYN	19200	124	H7
FOUR WINDS RD	CO	LR		192	A4
FOWLER AV	POM	POM	300	94	E4
FOWLER DR	MON	MON	100	29	A3
FOWLER ST	CO	LA63	3200	45	C2
FOWLING ST	LA	VEN	100	55A	D2
FOX	CO	AGO		106	D2
FOX CT	LAN	LAN		171	B1
FOX PL	GLEN	GL06	600	25	D3
FOX ST	LA	SF	13900	8	D2
FOX ST N	SF	SF	400	2	F6
FOX ST S	SF	SF	200	8	D2
FOXBORO	LA	SF42		2	C1
FOXBORO DR	LA	LA49	11900	41	B2
FOXBORO DR	WAL	WAL		93	D6
FOXBORO LN	LA	CAN		5	E2
FOXBROOK DR	GLDR	GLDR		87	C6
FOXBURY AV	POM	POM	100	90	F3
FOXBURY WY	PR	PR	9000	54	F6
FOXCROFT DR	CO	WHI	11000	84	A5
FOXCROFT LN	WAL	WAL		93	D6
FOXCROFT PL	LA	SF	12300	1	E4
FOXDALE	IRW	BAP	15600	88	A4
FOXDALE AV	CO	COV	4000	88	A4
FOXDALE AV	WCOV	WCOV	300	88	A6
FOXFIELD DR	WLVL	THO	31800	102	A5
FOXFORD RD	LAV	LAV	1200	95A	C4
FOX GLEN AV	LAV	LAV		90	B1
FOX GLEN DR	DBAR	POM		97	E3
FOXGLOVE CT	GLDR	GLDR		86	E4
FOXGLOVE CT	WAL	WAL		93	C4
FOXGLOVE DR	MPK	MPK	2300	46	C5
FOXGLOVE RD	GLEN	GL06		26	C1
FOXHAVEN DR	DBAR	POM		94	B6
FOXHAVEN PL	DBAR	POM		97A	B1
FOX HILL LN	LA	CHA		6	B4
FOX HILLS DR	CUL	CUL		50	C4
FOX HILLS DR	LA	LA25	1800	42	A2
FOX HILLS DR	LA	LA64	2200	42	A2
FOX HOLLOW LN	LA	PAC		3	B4
FOX HOLLOW LN	LA	PAC		9	D3
FOXHOLM DR	CO	PALM	38800	171	J7
FOXHOLM DR	PALM	PALM		171	J7
FOX INDIAN RD	CO	MAL		113	A3
FOXKIRK RD	GLEN	GL06	700	25	F2
FOXLAKE AV	WCOV	WCOV	4000	97	A2
FOXLANE DR	SCLR	CYN	27700	124	J7
FOXLEY DR	WHI	WHI	12600	61	D1
FOXMOOR CT	WLVL	THO		102	A4
FOXPARK DR	CO	CLA	600	90	F3
FOXPARK DR	POM	POM	400	90	F3
FOXPOINT LN	RHE	PVP	5000	72	F3
FOX RIDGE DR	PAS	ALT	1900	20	E6
FOX RUN CIR	CO	CAST		123	J1
FOXTAIL CT	CO	NEW		126	J5
FOXTAIL DR	SM	SM	100	40	E4
FOXTAIL ST	LAN	LAN		160	A2
FOXTON AV	LAN	LAN	43600	160	B7
FOX VIEW DR	CO	MAL		111	D4
FOXWELL AV	CAR	CAR	21300	69	B4
FOXWOOD RD	LCF	LCF	600	19	C5
FOXWORTH AV	CO	LPUE	600	48	E4
FOXWORTH AV	LPUE	LPUE	400	48	E4
FRACAR AV	LYN	LYN	10600	59	C4
FRACKELTON PL	LA	LA41	1300	26	C4
FRAGANCIA AV	CO	LPUE	2600	85	D4
FRAIJO AV	IRW	BAP	4600	88	A4
FRAILEY AV	CO	COM	12800	65	C3
FRAME AV	CO	LPUE		85	C4
FRAMINGTON AV	CO	PALM		185	A2
FRAMPTON AV	LA	HAC	24000	73	E4
FRAMPTON AV	LA	TOR	22800	68	E6
FRAMPTON CT	ART	ART		82	A5
FRAN PL	MTB	MTB		46	E6
FRANCE AV	LA	TU	9900	11	A4
FRANCES AV	CO	GL14	2700	11	D5
FRANCES AV	GLEN	GL14	3200	11	D5
FRANCES AV	LA	LA66	3500	49	C2
FRANCES CT	GLEN	GL01	1000	24	F3
FRANCES LN	CO	LPUE		97	B5
FRANCES PL	LA	LA34	10700	42	B6
FRANCES ST	CO	GL14	2400	11	E6
FRANCESCA DR	WAL	WAL		92	E5
FRANCESCA DR	WCOV	WCOV		92	E5
FRNCS SCOTT KEY	PALM	PALM		183	D2
FRANCINA DR	LA	ENC	16300	22	A5
FRANCINE CT	CO	LPUE		48	B4
FRANCIS AV	LA	LA05	4200	43	C2
FRANCIS AV	LA	LA05	2700	44	A2
FRANCIS CT	TOR	TOR	16600	63	B5
FRANCIS PL	LA	LA34	10700	42	B6
FRANCIS PL	LA	LA66	11400	49	F1
FRANCISCA AV N	RB	RB	100	67	D2
FRANCISCA AV S	RB	RB	100	67	D3
FRANCISCA ST	PAS	PAS	1600	27	D4
FRANCISCA WY	AGH	AGO		102	E4
FRANCISCAN PL	POM	POM		94	B5
FRANCISCO ST	CAR	CAR	100	69	A2
FRANCISCO ST	CO	TOR	600	68	F2
FRANCISCO ST	LA	LA15	900	44	B3
FRANCISCO ST	LA	LA17	700	44	B3
FRANCISCO ST	LA	TOR	700	68	F2
FRANCISCO ST	LA	TOR	600	69	A2
FRANCISCO ST	MB	MB	400	62	B5
FRANCISCO ST	SGAB	SGAB	200	37	E2
FRANCISQUITO AV	BAP	BAP	13000	39	C5
FRANCISQUITO AV	BAP	BAP	13700	48	E2
FRANCISQUITO AV	CO	LPUE	15700	92	A3
FRANCISQUITO AV	LPUE	LPUE	15400	48	E2
FRANCISQUITO AV	WCOV	BAP	14100	48	E2
FRANCISQUITO AV	WCOV	WCOV	1000	48	E2
FRANCISQUITO AV	WCOV	WCOV		92	B3
FRANCITA AV	DUA	DUA	800	29	F4
FRANDALE AV	CO	LPUE	500	92	A5
FRANDALE AV	WCOV	WCOV	1400	92	A3
FRANDSEN ST	CO	SGAB	8300	37	F3
FRANK AV	CER	ART		71	E2
FRANK CT	LA	LA13	400	44	D3
FRANK ST	SM	SM	1900	41	C6
FRANKE ST	CAR	CAR	900	64	C5
FRANKEL AV	MTB	MTB	100	54	C4
FRANKEL ST	LKD	LKD	2500	70	F3
FRANKFORT ST	LA	NOR	18500	14	B1
FRANKFURT AV	CO	LPUE	300	97	A2
FRANKFURT AV	WCOV	WCOV		98	F2
FRANKIRST AV	LA	SF	9600	8	A4
FRANKLIN AV	BUR	BUR	4100	24	B4
FRANKLIN AV	CUL	CUL	10700	50	B3
FRANKLIN AV	ELS	ELS	100	56	A6
FRANKLIN AV	GLEN	GL14	3800	11	C5
FRANKLIN AV	LA	LA27	4500	34	D2
FRANKLIN AV	LA	LA27	3700	35	B3
FRANKLIN AV	LA	LA46	7100	34	A3
FRANKLIN AV	LA	LA68	5500	34	D2
FRANKLIN AV	LA	LA69		33	E3
FRANKLIN AV	LAN	LAN		160	D6
FRANKLIN AV	SGAB	SGAB	100	37	D2
FRANKLIN AV E	POM	POM	100	94	E4
FRANKLIN AV W	POM	POM	100	94	E4
FRANKLIN CT	GLEN	GL05	100	25	D4
FRANKLIN LN	CO	NEW		126	G3
FRANKLIN PL	LA	LA28	6700	34	B3
FRANKLIN PL	LB	LB02	400	75	D5
FRANKLIN PL	MON	MON	500	29	A2
FRANKLIN ST	CO	CHA	9200	4	B5
FRANKLIN ST	CO	GL14	2700	11	E6
FRANKLIN ST	GLEN	GL14	3800	11	C5
FRANKLIN ST	LYN	LYN	11100	58	F5
FRANKLIN ST	SM	SM	800	41	B4
FRANKLIN ST	WHI	WHI	13400	55	E5
FRANKLIN WY	LA	LA69	1700	33	E3
FRANKLIN, BEN DR	PALM	PALM		183	D2
FRANKLIN CYN DR	CO	BH	1900	33	A2
FRANKLIN CYN DR	LA	BH	2800	23	B6
FRANKLIN CYN DR	LA	BH	1700	33	A3
FRANKMONT ST	ELM	ELM	11300	38	F5
FRANKMONT ST	ELM	ELM	11900	39	A5
FRANK STILES ST	SELM	ELM		47	E3
FRANKTON AV	CO	LPUE	14400	48	B6
FRANKTON AV	CO	LPUE		85	B1
FRANLIE DR	LA	SUN	10600	10	C3
FRANRIVERS AV	LA	CAN	6400	5	D5
FRANRIVERS PL	LA	WOH	5500	10	D1
FRANWOOD DR	SCLR	SAU		124	F4
FRASCATI ST	CO	SAU		188	B1
FRASER AL	PAS	PAS	100	26	F4
FRASER AV	CO	LA22	300	45	E6
FRASER AV	CO	LA22	1000	53	E1
FRASER AV	LA	SF	12500	1	E4
FRASER AV	SM	SM	100	49	A2

247

1990 LOS ANGELES COUNTY STREET INDEX

FRASER PL — GARFIELD AV E

LOS ANGELES CO.

INDEX

STREET	CITY	P.O. ZONE	BLOCK	PAGE	GRID
FRASER PL	LA	SF	17400	1	E4
FRATUS DR	TEC	TEC	4800	38	B4
FRAZIER ST E	BAP	BAP	13400	39	C6
FRAZIER ST N	BAP	BAP	700	48	B2
FRECKLES RD	LKD	LKD	6000	71	D4
FRECKLES ST	LKD	LKD	2700	70	F4
FREDA AV E	POM	POM	100	90	F5
FREDERIC ST N	BUR	BUR	900	17	B3
FREDERIC ST N	BUR	BUR	100	24	B1
FREDERIC ST S	BUR	BUR	100	24	B1
FREDERICK AV	GLEN	GL14	4900	11	C4
FREDERICK ST	GLEN	GL14	4100	11	C6
FREDERICK ST	GLEN	GL14	4000	18	C1
FREDERICK ST	LA	LA65	2700	35	E3
FREDERICK ST	LA	VEN	100	49	C3
FREDERICK ST	SM	SM	3100	49	C2
FREDKIN DR	CO	COV	4400	88	C4
FREDKIN DR	COV	COV	1000	88	C4
FREDONIA DR	LA	LA68	3600	23	F5
FREDSON ST	SFS	SFS	11300	61	B2
FREEBORN ST	BRAD	DUA	2300	29	F4
FREEBORN ST	DUA	DUA	2500	29	F4
FREEBORN ST	DUA	DUA	2800	86	A4
FREEDEN ST	CAR	CAR	200	64	B6
FREEDOM DR	CO	WOH		13	B4
FREELAND ST	LB	LB07	400	70	C3
FREEMAN AV	CO	GL14	5500	11	F5
FREEMAN AV	CO	IN04	10300	57	A5
FREEMAN AV	HAW	HAW	11100	57	A5
FREEMAN AV	ING	IN04	10000	57	A5
FREEMAN AV	LAW	LAW	14400	63	A5
FREEMAN AV	LB	LB04	700	75	F5
FREEMAN AV	LB	LB14	300	75	F5
FREEMAN AV	SFS	SFS	9900	61	C3
FREEMAN AV	SH	LB04	1800	75	F3
FREEMAN BLVD	RB	RB		62	E4
FREEMAN DR	CLA	CLA		91	C1
FREEMANTLE LN	CO	CAL		100	B2
FREEPORT RD	RPV	PVP	26800	72	D4
FREER ST	CO	ARC	11200	38	D3
FREER ST	CO	TEC	1000	38	D3
FREER ST	TEC	TEC	10300	38	D3
FREESE LN	PAS	PAS		27	E3
FREESTONE AV	SFS	SFS	8000	55	C6
FREESTONE LN	CO	LR		184	E5
FREETOWN LN	AGH	AGO		100A	D5
FREEWAY DR	SFS	SFS	13400	82	D3
FREIBURG ST	WHI	WHI		55	F6
FREMONT AV	MPK	MPK		46	B2
FREMONT AV	SPAS	SPAS	200	36	F2
FREMONT AV N	ALH	ALH	100	36	F5
FREMONT AV N	LA	LA12	100	44	C2
FREMONT AV S	ALH	ALH	100	36	F5
FREMONT AV S	ALH	ALH	1900	46	A1
FREMONT AV S	LA	LA71	500	44	C3
FREMONT CT	CO	VAL		123	H7
FREMONT DR	PAS	PAS	500	26	E3
FREMONT LN	SPAS	SPAS	200	36	F1
FREMONT PL	GLEN	GL08	2400	18	E5
FREMONT PL	LA	LA05	50	43	C2
FREMONT PL W	LA	LA05	100	43	C2
FREMONT SQ	MTB	MTB	100	54	E1
FREMONT ST	POM	POM	900	94	D4
FRENCH AV	LA	LA65	100	36	A4
FRENCH CT	CO	AGO		100A	A6
FRENCH LN	POM	POM	300	90	E3
FRESHMAN DR	CO	CUL		50	D2
FRESH MEADOW DR	LCF	LCF	5400	19	D2
FRESHWATER DR	AGH	AGO		100A	A2
FRESHWIND CIR	WLVL	THO		102	A4
FRESNO ST N	LA	LA63	400	45	C4
FRESNO ST S	LA	LA23	600	45	B4
FRESNO ST S	LA	LA63	100	45	B4
FREY AV	LA	VEN	2300	49	C4
FRIAR CIR	LAV	LAV		90	D1
FRIAR DR	MPK	MPK		46	E4
FRIAR LN	POM	POM	900	94	D4
FRIAR ST	LA	NHO	10600	16	F5
FRIAR ST	LA	RES	18300	14	C5
FRIAR ST	LA	VAN	13300	15	F5
FRIAR ST	LA	WOH	23300	5	F5
FRIAR ST	LA	WOH	19700	12	F5
FRIARS LN	WLVL	THO		102	B5
FRIARSTONE CT	RPV	SP	28600	78	E1
FRIEDA CT	LAN	LAN		160	D6
FRIEDA DR	LA	LA65	4700	36	A2
FRIEDA ST	WCOV	WCOV		92	E6
FRIENDLY AV	PALM	PALM	38600	172	C8
FRIENDLY LN	WCOV	WCOV		97	A2
FRIENDLY VLY PY	SCLR	SAU	26400	127	H1
FRIENDLY WDS LN	WHI	WHI		84	B2
FRIENDS AV	WHI	WHI	5800	55	E6
FRIENDS AV	WHI	WHI	8300	61	E1
FRIENDS ST	LA	PP	15200	40	C4
FRIENDSHIP AV	PR	PR	9300	55	B1
FRIENDSHP PK DR	LA	SP		78	D4

STREET	CITY	P.O. ZONE	BLOCK	PAGE	GRID
FRIENDSWOOD AV	ELM	ELM	3100	47	C1
FRIES AV	CAR	CAR	21300	69	B4
FRIES AV	CAR	CAR	23900	74	B2
FRIES AV N	LA	WIL	100	74	C5
FRIES AV S	LA	WIL	100	74	C5
FRIES AV S	LA	WIL	700	79	C1
FRIGATE AV	CAR	CAR	22700	69	A5
FRIGATE AV	CAR	CAR	23500	74	A1
FRIGATE AV	LA	WIL	400	74	A4
FRIJO AV	CO	COV	3900	88	A5
FRIJO AV	WCOV	WCOV	700	88	A5
FRISCA DR	SCLR	VAL		124	C6
FRITZ LN	LA	SF		2	F1
FRONDOSA DR	CO	MAL	6000	111	E5
FRONT AV	LB	LB05		70	A2
FRONT ST	ALH	ALH	2500	36	F5
FRONT ST	ALH	ALH	700	37	A5
FRONT ST	ARC	ARC	200	28	E4
FRONT ST	LA	SP	100	79	A2
FRONT ST	NWK	NWK	11800	82	B1
FRONT ST E	COV	COV	100	88	E4
FRONT ST N	BUR	BUR	100	17	D5
FRONT ST S	BUR	BUR	100	17	D5
FRONT ST W	COV	COV	800	88	D4
FRONTAGE RD	CO	PALM		183	C8
FRONTAGE RD	SOG	SOG	9500	59	E3
FRONTAGE RD N	DOW	DOW		60	C6
FRONTAGE RD N	DOW	DOW		66	C1
FRONTAGE RD S	DOW	DOW		66	C1
FRONTENAC AV	LA	LA65	400	36	A3
FRONTENAC CT	LB	LB02	1	75	D5
FRONTENAC CT	LB	LB13	700	75	D5
FRONTERA DR	LA	PP	500	40	D4
FRONTIER AV	CO	PALM	38400	172	G8
FRONTIER RD	POM	POM		94	C5
FRNTIR CIRCS ST	CO	LAN	39100	175	A7
FROST AL	PAS	PAS	1	27	A4
FROST LN	CO	VAL		126	G3
FROSTBURG CIR	CLA	CLA		91	C1
FRUIT ST	LAV	LAV		90	D2
FRUITDALE ST	LA	LA39	2700	35	C2
FRUITLAND AV	MAY	MAY	3400	53	C3
FRUITLAND AV	VER	LA58	2500	52	F3
FRUITLAND AV	VER	LA58	3100	53	A3
FRUITLAND DR	LA	NHO	10800	23	E4
FRUIT TREE RD	RPV	PVP	1	77	E2
FRUITVALE AV	SELM	ELM	1600	47	E4
FRY ST	BG	BELL	5400	59	E1
FRY ST	BG	BELL	6600	60	A1
FRYMAN PL	LA	NHO	3300	23	C5
FRYMAN RD	LA	NHO	3000	23	C6
FUCHSIA AV	GLDR	GLDR	800	89	A1
FUEGO AV	POM	POM	100	90	E3
FUEGO ST	LB	LB05	200	65	B4
FUERO DR	WAL	WAL	21000	93	B6
FUERO DR E	WAL	WAL		97	C1
FUERTE DR	WAL	WAL	20300	93	C5
FUJITA ST	TOR	TOR		68	B6
FULCHER AV	LA	NHO	5600	16	E6
FULCHER AV	LA	NHO	5500	23	E1
FULHAM CT	PALM	PALM		171	F4
FULLBRIGHT AV	LA	CAN	8500	6	E6
FULLBRIGHT AV	LA	CAN	7300	12	E1
FULLBRIGHT AV	LA	CHA	9500	6	E3
FULLBRIGHT PL	LA	CHA	20300	6	E2
FULLBROKE CT	GLEN	GL06		26	C1
FULLER AV N	LA	LA36	100	34	A6
FULLER AV N	LA	LA46	700	34	A6
FULLER AV N	WHOL	LA46	1000	34	A6
FULLER AV S	LA	LA36	100	34	A6
FULLERFARM ST	LA	NOR	17700	7	D3
FULLERTON RD	CO	LPUE	1300	98	D6
FULLERTON RD	IND	LPUE	1100	98	D4
FULLERTON RD	LHH	LAH	2400	98	C6
FULLERTON RD	LHH	LAH	1300	98A	B2
FULLMOON DR	GLEN	GL06	3600	19	C6
FULLMOON ST	PALM	PALM		183	F1
FULMAR AV	TOR	TOR	23800	73	E1
FULTON AV	CO	PAS	1	28	A4
FULTON AV	LA	NHO	5600	16	A6
FULTON AV	LA	NHO	4200	23	A3
FULTON AV	LA	VAN	5600	16	A6
FULTON AV	LA	VAN	4100	23	A3
FULTON AV	MPK	MPK	700	46	C3
FULTON CT	LA	VAN		23	A2
FULTON RD	LAV	LAV	1800	90	E4
FULTON RD N	POM	POM	2300	90	E4
FULTON WELLS AV	SFS	SFS	10600	61	B4
FUNCHAL RD	LA	LA77	600	32	D5
FUNSTON AV	HG	LKD	22100	81	B5
FUNSTON AV	NWK	NWK	13400	82	A2
FURLONG LN	BRAD	DUA	100	29	D3
FURLONG PL	VER	LA58	3800	52	E2
FURMAN DR	CLA	CLA	400	91	B1
FURMAN PL	GLEN	GL06	1100	25	E2
FURNESS AV	LA	LA42	100	36	B2

STREET	CITY	P.O. ZONE	BLOCK	PAGE	GRID
FURNIVALL AV	SCLR	CYN	26900	124	F8
FUSANO AV	LA	SF	13400	2	D2
FUTURE PL	LA	LA65	3000	35	E3
FUTURE ST	LA	LA65	2700	35	E3
FYLER PL	LA	LA65	2700	25	F5
G					
G ST	BELL	BELL		53	E3
G ST	LAV	LAV	1900	90	D4
G ST E	LA	WIL	100	74	B4
G ST W	LA	WIL	100	74	B4
GABBETT DR	LAM	LAM	12800	83	A1
GABBETT DR	LAM	LAM	12600	84	A6
GABLE CIR	CER	ART	18900	81	C1
GABLE CT	DBAR	POM		94	B5
GABLE DR	LA	ENC	4400	21	C3
GABLE LN	LAN	LAN		159	B5
GABLE VIEW ST	PALM	PALM		183	E1
GABRIEL DR	POM	POM	2300	94	E6
GABRIELLA ST	WCOV	WCOV		92	E6
GACEL CT	DBAR	WAL		97	D3
GADSDEN AV	LAN	LAN	43600	160	A6
GADSHILL LN	AGH	AGO		100A	D5
GAFF CT	SCLR	SAU		124	E5
GAFFEY PL	LA	SP	500	78	F2
GAFFEY ST N	LA	SP	1600	73	F5
GAFFEY ST N	LA	SP	100	78	F2
GAFFEY ST S	LA	SP	100	78	F3
GAFFNEY AV	SAD	SAD	100	90	A3
GAFFORD AL	PAS	PAS	1000	27	A2
GAFFORD ST	CMRC	LA40	5000	53	E2
GAGE AV	BELL	BELL	3400	53	D5
GAGE AV	BG	BELL	5500	53	D5
GAGE AV	BG	BELL	6300	54	A5
GAGE AV	CMRC	LA40	7100	54	B6
GAGE AV	ELM	ELM	3000	47	D1
GAGE AV	HPK	HPK	1900	52	E5
GAGE AV	HPK	HPK	2800	53	A5
GAGE AV E	CO	LA01	1100	52	C5
GAGE AV E	LA	LA01	600	52	C5
GAGE AV E	LA	LA03	100	52	A5
GAGE AV N	CO	LA63	100	45	D5
GAGE AV S	CO	LA23	700	45	C6
GAGE AV S	CO	LA23	1200	53	D1
GAGE AV S	CO	LA63	100	45	D5
GAGE AV W	LA	LA03	100	52	A5
GAGE AV W	LA	LA44	800	51	D5
GAGE AV W	LA	LA44	500	52	A5
GAGE AV W	LA	LA47	1400	51	D5
GAGE RD	MTB	MTB	1800	54	C5
GAGELY DR	LAM	LAM	14200	61	E6
GAGELY DR	LAM	LAM	14800	84	A6
GAGER ST	LA	PAC	13600	8	F3
GAGER ST	LA	PAC	12200	9	C1
GAGER ST	LA	SF	11700	3	C6
GAIL CT	WCOV	WCOV		92	E6
GAIL ST	LA	LA31	2300	35	D4
GAILLARD ST	AZU	AZU	900	88	E2
GAILLARD ST	CO	AZU	18000	88	E2
GAILLARD ST	CO	LAV	700	90	B2
GAILLARD ST	GLDR	GLDR	100	89	A2
GAILLARD ST	SAD	SAD	300	90	A2
GAILXY AV	SCLR	CYN	28700	125	C8
GAIN ST	LA	PAC	13600	8	F3
GAIN ST	LA	PAC	12300	9	B2
GAIN ST	LA	SF	11700	3	C6
GAINFORD ST	DOW	DOW	7700	60	B2
GAINFORD ST	LA	WOH	23000	13	A2
GAINFORD ST	LA	WOH	23000	100	F2
GAINSBOROUGH AV	LA	LA27	4500	34	F2
GAINSBOROUGH AV	LA	LA27	4400	35	A2
GAINSBOROUGH DR	CO	PAS	800	27	F6
GAINSBOROUGH DR	PALM	PALM		171	H8
GAINSBOROUGH DR	SMAR	PAS	1200	27	E6
GAINSBOROUGH RD	SAD	SAD		89	C4
GALA ST	CO	WHI	2300	47	E5
GALA WK	LA	LA31	4000	36	B4
GALAHAD DR	CO	MAL	5700	112	C6
GALANTE WY	SCLR	VAL		127	A2
GALANTO AV	AZU	AZU	200	88	F1
GALANTO AV	CO	AZU	6100	86	F6
GALANTO AV	CO	AZU	5600	88	F1
GALANTO AV	GLDR	GLDR	100	86	F5
GALATEA ST	AZU	AZU	900	88	E1
GALATEA ST	CO	AZU	18000	88	E1
GALATEA ST	CO	GLDR	19000	88	F1
GALATEA ST	CO	GLDR	19000	89	A1
GALATINA ST	CO	LPUE	18000	98	F5
GALAVAN ST	CAR	CAR	600	69	A6
GALAX ST	SELM	ELM	10900	47	D4
GALAXY WY	LA	LA67	10000	42	B2
GALAXY HTS DR	LCF	LCF		19	C2
GALBRETH RD	CO	PAS	2000	27	D1
GALBRETH RD	PAS	PAS	1800	27	D1
GALE AV	CO	LPUE	14400	48	B6

STREET	CITY	P.O. ZONE	BLOCK	PAGE	GRID
GALE AV	CO	LPUE	15000	85	E1
GALE AV	CO	LPUE		98	F3
GALE AV	HAW	HAW	11400	56	F6
GALE AV	HAW	HAW	13800	62	F2
GALE AV	IND	LPUE	15200	98	A2
GALE AV	IND	LPUE	18500	98	E3
GALE AV	LB	LB05	6400	65	B5
GALE AV	LB	LB10	3000	70	B6
GALE AV	LB	LB10	1900	75	B2
GALE DR	BH	BH	100	42	E1
GALE PL	SM	SM	1	40	F4
GALEANO ST	LB	LB15		76	B3
GALECREST AV	CO	LPUE	700	92	C5
GALEMONT AV	CO	LPUE	800	85	E1
GALEN ST	DUA	DUA	900	29	C6
GALENA ST	LA	LA32	3400	36	C5
GALENDO PL	LA	WOH	21900	13	C3
GALENDO ST	LA	WOH	4600	13	C3
GALER PL	GLEN	GL06	400	25	E3
GALERITA DR	RPV	SP	1800	73	D6
GALESBURG ST	LA	SF	17000	1	F5
GALETON DR	SCLR	CYN	27700	125	B8
GALE VIEW DR	CO	LPUE		97	A5
GALEWOOD ST	LA	NHO	12900	23	A4
GALEWOOD ST	LA	VAN	13400	22	F4
GALEWOOD ST	LA	VAN	13200	23	A4
GALICIA DR	LAM	LAM	14300	83	B2
GALILEE ST	CO	WOH		13	B5
GALION AV	LAN	LAN	43900	159	G5
GALLANT ST	BG	BELL	5900	59	F1
GALLARDO ST	LA	LA33	500	44	F2
GALLARNO DR	CO	COV	18500	88	E2
GALLATIN RD	DOW	DOW	7900	60	C2
GALLATIN RD	PR	PR		47	A6
GALLATIN RD	PR	PR	8700	55	A1
GALLAUDET PL	LA	PP	14500	40	E3
GALLEANO ST	CO	LPUE	18600	98	E1
GALLEON ST	LA	VEN		49	C5
GALLI ST	HAW	HAW	13600	63	C1
GALLIARD DR	LB	LB05	300	65	C4
GALLINETA ST	CO	LPUE	17900	98	D5
GALLIO AV	CO	LPUE	2400	98	E5
GALLION AV	LAN	LAN		159	G3
GALLOPING CT	CO	CAST		123	B4
GALLOPING WY	CO	ACT		182	J9
GALLOPING COLT	WAL	WAL		93	A6
GALLOWAY ST	LA	PP	800	40	D3
GALLUP ST	LKD	LKD	5900	71	D3
GALSTER WY	WCOV	WCOV		92	D4
GALT RD	DOW	DOW	8300	60	B4
GALTON RD	SCLR	SAU		124	J3
GALVA AV	TOR	TOR	22900	67	F6
GALVESTON ST	LA	LA26	1400	35	C6
GALVEZ CT	SCLR	VAL		124	A2
GALVEZ ST	LA	WOH	22000	13	C2
GALVIN CT	CO	POM		97	F4
GALVIN ST	CUL	CUL	10700	50	C3
GALWAY AV	CAR	CAR	19000	69	C1
GALWAY PL	SCLR	VAL		127	A1
GAMBIER DR	POM	POM	1500	94	E5
GAMBIER ST	LA	LA32	4700	36	D5
GAMBLE AV	LA	WIL	1400	74	D2
GAMBLE HOUSE CT	SCLR	VAL		124	E3
GAMBREL GATE	LAV	LAV		95A	E5
GAMEBIRD CT	AGH	AGO		102	F3
GANA DR	CO	AGO		102	E6
GANA DR	CO	AGO		106	E1
GANADO DR	RPV	PVP	30100	78	B3
GANAHL ST	LA	LA33	2500	45	B3
GANAHL ST	LA	LA63	3000	45	B3
GANDARA AV	LAM	LAM	13300	83	A1
GANDESA RD	LAM	LAM	14500	82	F2
GANDESA RD	LAM	LAM	14100	83	A2
GANELON DR	CO	WOH		13	B5
GANESHA AV	CO	ALT	2300	20	C5
GANESHA BLVD	POM	POM	1400	90	C6
GANESHA BLVD	POM	POM	500	94	B2
GANESHA PL	POM	POM	1500	90	E6
GANGEL AV	PR	PR	3600	47	B6
GANGEL AV	PR	PR	4100	55	B2
GANGI LN	GLEN	GL02		18	C6
GANNET ST	LAM	LAM	14200	82	F3
GANNET ST	SFS	SFS	13900	82	E3
GANTER RD	LHH	LAH	1900	98A	A2
GANYMEDE DR	LA	LA65	700	35	F2
GAONA ST	LA	WOH	21400	13	C3
GARA DR	LAM	LAM	15000	83	A2
GARAGE DR	CO	TOP		109	B5
GARBER ST	LA	PAC	13500	8	E5
GARBER ST	LA	PAC	12500	9	A3
GARBER ST	LA	SF	11800	3	C6
GARBER ST	LA	SF	11900	9	C1
GARCELON AV	MPK	MPK		46	C1
GARCIA AV	CO	LA22	800	45	E3
GARCIA CT	NWK	NWK		66	F2
GARCIA RD	CO	MAL		105	A6

STREET	CITY	P.O. ZONE	BLOCK	PAGE	GRID
GARD AV	ART	ART	17900	66	F6
GARD AV	NWK	NWK	11800	60	F6
GARD AV	NWK	NWK	13500	66	F1
GARD AV	SFS	SFS	9900	60	F3
GARDA AV	CO	LPUE	400	92	B6
GARDEN AV	CO	CAST		123	F3
GARDEN AV	LA	LA39	4000	25	B6
GARDEN AV	LA	LA39	3100	35	C1
GARDEN LN	BH	BH	1000	33	A4
GARDEN LN	LA	LA67		42	A2
GARDEN LN	PAS	PAS	500	26	E6
GARDEN ST	GLEN	GL01	1300	24	F2
GARDENA AV	GLEN	GL04	1400	25	C6
GARDENA AV	GLEN	GL04	3550	35	C1
GARDENA AV	SH	LB06	2400	75	E2
GARDENA BLVD E	CAR	CAR	600	64	A4
GARDENA BLVD E	CAR	GAR	100	64	A4
GARDENA BLVD W	CAR	GAR	100	64	A4
GARDENA BLVD W	GAR	GAR	1000	63	E4
GARDENA BLVD W	LA	GAR	700	63	E4
GARDENA BLVD W	LA	GAR	500	64	A4
GARDENDALE LN	PALM	PALM		171	B3
GARDENDALE ST	BLF	BLF	9000	66	A1
GARDENDALE ST	DOW	DOW	8000	59	E5
GARDENDALE ST	DOW	DOW	8400	66	A1
GARDENDALE ST	PAR	PAR	8000	59	F6
GARDENDALE ST	PAR	PAR	8300	66	A1
GARDENDALE ST	SOG	SOG	5400	59	E5
GARDEN GLEN ST	WCOV	WCOV	100	92	C1
GARDEN GROVE AV	LA	NOR	8500	7	C2
GARDEN GROVE AV	LA	NOR	8300	14	C1
GARDEN GROVE AV	LA	RES	6800	14	C4
GARDEN GROVE AV	LA	TAR	4900	21	C2
GARDENHILL DR	LAM	LAM	14300	82	F1
GARDENHILL DR	LAM	LAM	14600	83	A1
GARDEN HOMES AV	LA	LA32	4200	36	E4
GARDENIA AV	LB	LB05	5900	65	E6
GARDENIA AV	LB	LB05	5800	70	E1
GARDENIA AV	LB	LB06	1800	75	E4
GARDENIA AV	LB	LB07	3400	70	E5
GARDENIA AV	LB	LB13	700	75	E4
GARDENIA LN	LAV	LAV		90	C1
GARDENIALANE DR	CO	CYN	15500	125	E6
GARDENIA PK DR	CO	CYN	15500	125	E6
GARDENLAND AV	BLF	BLF	13500	66	D2
GARDEN LAND RD	LA	LA49	13100	21	E6
GARDEN OAKS CT	AGH	AGO		100A	A1
GARDENSIDE LN	LA	LA39	3400	35	B1
GARDENSTONE LN	LA	CAN		5	D3
GARDEN TER LN	CO	LPUE		85	D4
GARDEN VIEW AV	SOG	SOG	8100	59	A2
GARDEN VLG CT	PAS	PAS	400	27	B3
GARDI ST	BRAD	DUA	2200	29	F4
GARDI ST	BRAD	DUA	2100	29	E4
GARDI ST	DUA	DUA	2500	29	F4
GARDI ST	DUA	DUA	3000	86	A4
GARDNER AV	SFS	SFS	12200	61	B3
GARDNER DR	MTB	MTB	800	46	C5
GARDNER LN	GLEN	GL06	2400	26	A3
GARDNER PL	GLEN	GL06	400	26	A3
GARDNER PL	GLEN	GL06	2300	26	A3
GARDNER ST	CAR	CAR	100	69	A4
GARDNER ST	LB	LB05	200	65	B5
GARDNER ST N	LA	LA36	100	34	A6
GARDNER ST N	LA	LA46	700	34	A3
GARDNER ST N	WHOL	LA46	900	34	A6
GARDNER ST S	LA	LA36	100	34	A6
GARELOCH AV	CO	AZU	5200	88	C2
GARETAL ST	SFS	SFS	11100	60	F3
GARETAL ST	SFS	SFS	11600	61	A3
GAREY AV	LAV	LAV	3600	90	E2
GAREY AV N	POM	POM	1400	90	E4
GAREY AV N	POM	POM	100	94	E4
GAREY AV S	POM	POM	100	94	E4
GAREY ST N	LA	LA12	300	44	E3
GAREY ST S	LA	LA12	100	44	E3
GARFIAS DR	CO	PAS	1900	27	D1
GARFIELD AV	ALH	ALH	100	37	C4
GARFIELD AV	BG	BELL	6400	54	A5
GARFIELD AV	BG	BELL	7200	59	E3
GARFIELD AV	CMRC	LA40	1900	54	B3
GARFIELD AV	CMRC	LA40	6200	54	A5
GARFIELD AV	CO	ALT	2000	20	A5
GARFIELD AV	CO	LA22	900	54	B3
GARFIELD AV	CUL	CUL	10700	50	B2
GARFIELD AV	DOW	DOW	12700	59	E6
GARFIELD AV	LA	VEN	900	49	D4
GARFIELD AV	PAR	PAR	13600	65	E3
GARFIELD AV	POM	POM	100	94	E1
GARFIELD AV	POM	POM	800	95	A1
GARFIELD AV	SMAR	PAS	1000	37	A1
GARFIELD AV	SOG	SOG	8600	59	E3
GARFIELD AV	SOG	SOG	13500	65	E3
GARFIELD AV	SPAS	SPAS	200	37	A1
GARFIELD AV E	GLEN	GL05	100	25	D5

1990 LOS ANGELES COUNTY STREET INDEX

STREET	CITY	P.O. ZONE	BLOCK	PAGE	GRID
GARFIELD AV N	MPK	MPK	100	46	C2
GARFIELD AV N	MTB	MTB		46	B5
GARFIELD AV N	MTB	MTB		54	B3
GARFIELD AV N	PAS	PAS	1600	20	A6
GARFIELD AV N	PAS	PAS	1	27	A3
GARFIELD AV S	MPK	MPK	100	46	C2
GARFIELD AV S	MTB	MTB	100	54	B3
GARFIELD AV S	PAS	PAS	1	27	A4
GARFIELD AV W	GLEN	GL04	100	25	C5
GARFIELD PL	LA	LA28	1700	34	D3
GARFIELD PL	MON	MON	100	28	F3
GARFIELD PL	MPK	MPK		46	B4
GARFIELD PL	SOG	SOG	10600	59	E5
GARFIELD ST	CO	CAST	29500	123	A6
GARFIELD ST	POM	POM	1300	90	D5
GARFORD ST	LB	LB15	5400	76	C3
GARIBALDI AV	CO	SGAB	8200	37	F2
GARIBALDI AV	CO	TEC	8800	38	A2
GARIBALDI AV	SGAB	SGAB	8500	38	A2
GARIBALDI AV	TEC	TEC	8900	38	B2
GARIBALDI LN	LB	LB03		80	C1
GARIN AV	CO	WHI	1300	48	A5
GARLAND AV	LA	LA17	700	44	B3
GARLAND CT	CO	VAL		124	A7
GARLAND DR	CUL	CUL	10700	50	B1
GARLAND ST	POM	POM	1700	94	D4
GARLOCK RD	CO	SAU		182	C7
GARNER ST	LB	LB08	7800	81	A6
GARNER ST	LOM	LOM	2000	73	D3
GARNET AV	PALM	PALM		183	D1
GARNET LN	LAN	LAN		160	F5
GARNET ST	LA	LA23	2200	44	F5
GARNET ST	LA	LA23	2900	45	B6
GARNET ST	RB	RB	100	67	D3
GARNET ST	TOR	TOR	5000	67	E3
GARNET ST	TOR	TOR	3200	68	A3
GARNET WY	WAL	WAL		92	F6
GARNET HILL CT	AGH	AGO		100A	A3
GARNIER ST	TOR	TOR		73	B1
GARNISH DR	DOW	DOW	9100	60	D3
GARNSEY ST	RB	RB	800	67	D2
GARO ST	CO	LPUE	15400	85	D1
GARONA DR	CO	LPUE	16400	85	F5
GARRET DR	CO	AGO		100A	E4
GARRET PL	LA	TU	11400	10	F1
GARRETT ST	RM	RM	9000	47	A1
GARRICK AV	LA	SF	13500	3	A2
GARRICK AV	PR	PR	4600	54	F2
GARRIS AV	LA	SF		1	D3
GARRISON DR	LA	LA42	6100	36	C1
GARSDEN AV	CO	COV	5000	89	C3
GARSDEN AV	COV	COV	500	89	C4
GARSTANG RD	CO	ACT		182	B8
GARSTON AV	CAR	CAR	21300	69	C5
GARTEL DR E	WAL	WAL	20400	93	C5
GARTEL DR N	WAL	WAL	500	93	C5
GARTH AV	CO	LA56	5100	50	E4
GARTH AV	LA	LA34	1900	42	D4
GARTH AV	LA	LA35	1600	42	E3
GARTHWAITE AV	LA	LA08	4100	51	C2
GARTHWAITE WK	LA	LA08	2600	51	D2
GARVALIA AV	RM	RM	7400	46	D2
GARVANZA AV	LA	LA42	6200	36	D1
GARVEY AV	ALH	ALH		45	F2
GARVEY AV	BAP	BAP	12200	48	B1
GARVEY AV	CO	COV		93	B1
GARVEY AV	COV	COV		89	A6
GARVEY AV	ELM	ELM	9800	47	D2
GARVEY AV	ELM	ELM	12200	48	A2
GARVEY AV	RM	RM	7400	46	B2
GARVEY AV	RM	RM	8600	47	D2
GARVEY AV	SELM	ELM	9200	47	D2
GARVEY AV	WCOV	WCOV		89	A6
GARVEY AV E	MPK	MPK	100	46	B2
GARVEY AV E	WCOV	WCOV	1000	92	D1
GARVEY AV E	WCOV	WCOV		93	A1
GARVEY AV W	MPK	MPK	100	46	B2
GARVEY AV W	WCOV	WCOV		48	F1
GARVEY AV W	WCOV	WCOV	1000	92	B1
GARVIN DR	LA	ENC	16400	22	A3
GARWICK PL	SOG	SOG	10700	59	E5
GARWOOD PL	LA	LA24	10500	41	F1
GARY AV	LB	LB05		70	A2
GARY AV	MTB	MTB	800	54	C4
GARY DR	CO	CYN		125	E6
GARYDALE DR	CO	WHI	15800	84	C5
GARYFORD RD	CO	CYN		125	C4
GARY PARK AV	CO	ARC	5200	38	F3
GARZA DR	SCLR	SAU	27100	124	D5
GARZON PL	DBAR	WAL		97	D3
GARZOTA DR	SCLR	SAU		124	B6
GARZOTA DR	SCLR	VAL		124	B6
GASLIGHT LN	CUL	CUL		50	D2
GASPAR AV	CMRC	LA40	2400	53	F3
GASPAR AV	CO	LA22	1500	54	A2
GASPE ST	CO	CYN		125	C4
GASSEN PL	LA	LA65	3300	35	E2
GASTINE PL	CO	TOR	900	68	F6
GASTON DR	CO	SF		3	E2
GATE RD N	CO	CAST		123	F2
GATE LEE CIR	SOG	SOG	5800	59	E4
GATES AV	MB	MB	1300	62	D5
GATES AV	RB	RB	1900	62	D5
GATES PL	SPAS	SPAS	1200	36	E2
GATES ST	BAP	BAP	14300	39	E3
GATES ST	LA	LA31	2200	36	B6
GATES ST	LA	LA31	1900	45	B1
GATES CANYON RD	CO	CAL		100	B2
GATESHEAD WY	LA	CAN	7100	5	E3
GATESIDE DR	LA	LA32	4400	45	C1
GATEWAY AV	LA	LA29	4100	35	A4
GATEWAY BLVD	LA	LA64	11400	41	E5
GATEWAY DR	LAM	LAM		82	F4
GATEWAY DR	MB	MB		62	D3
GATEWAY CITY DR	DBAR	POM		97	E2
GATEWOOD LN	SMAD	SMAD	400	28	B1
GATEWOOD ST	LA	LA31	2200	35	E4
GATEWOOD TER	SMAD	SMAD	400	28	B1
GATLIN AV	CO	LPUE	1100	85	D1
GATOS PL	PVE	PVP	800	72	C3
GATUN ST	LA	SP	700	78	F1
GAUCHO CT	SCLR	VAL		124	B9
GAUCHO DR	RHE	PVP	2200	73	D5
GAUCHO DR	RPV	SP	2100	73	D5
GAUGUIN AV	LA	WOH	4300	13	C4
GAULT ST	LA	LA	19900	12	E3
GAULT ST	LA	NHO	11100	16	E4
GAULT ST	LA	RES	17700	14	B3
GAULT ST	LA	VAN	16500	14	B3
GAULT ST	LA	VAN	13500	15	E4
GAUNTLET DR	WCOV	WCOV	3300	97	B1
GAVEA CIR	SCLR	VAL		127	A2
GAVILAN DR	SCLR	SAU	26300	124	C7
GAVINA AV	LA	SF	13700	3	B1
GAVIOTA	AVA	AVA		77	A4
GAVIOTA AV	LA	ENC	4600	22	B2
GAVIOTA AV	LA	SF		2	B6
GAVIOTA AV	LA	SF	8800	8	A6
GAVIOTA AV	LA	VAN	6400	15	B5
GAVIOTA AV	LB	LB02	100	75	E6
GAVIOTA AV	LB	LB05	6000	65	E6
GAVIOTA AV	LB	LB05	5800	70	E1
GAVIOTA AV	LB	LB07	3400	70	E3
GAVIOTA AV	LB	LB13	700	75	E4
GAVIOTA AV	SH	LB06		75	E2
GAY ST	LA	LA65	2800	35	F4
GAY ST N	ING	IN02	700	51	B5
GAYBAR AV	CO	LPUE	1800	92	B3
GAYBAR AV	CO	LPUE	900	92	B5
GAYBAR AV	WCOV	WCOV	400	92	B2
GAYBROOK AV	DOW	DOW		60	E4
GAYCREST AV	TOR	TOR	22500	67	E5
GAYDON AV	RM	RM	3500	37	F6
GAYDON AV	SGAB	SGAB	1900	37	F6
GAYER DR	CO	CAL		108	B5
GAYHART ST	CMRC	LA40	6400	54	B3
GAYHURST AV	BAP	BAP	5000	39	F3
GAYLAND AV	CO	LPUE	1100	85	E2
GAYLAWN CT	LPUE	LPUE	600	48	F4
GAYLE DR	LA	TAR	4200	21	B3
GAYLE PL	LA	TAR	19100	21	B3
GAYLEY AV	LA	LA24	400	41	D1
GAYLEY CT	POM	POM	1700	94	C2
GAYLIN ST	WHI	WHI		55	F4
GAYLORD CT	CO	CAL		100	B2
GAYLORD DR	BUR	BUR	500	24	C3
GAYLORD ST	LB	LB13	1200	75	A3
GAYMONT AV	DOW	DOW	9000	60	C1
GAYMONT DR	LAM	LAM	15600	83	B3
GAYMORE CIR	LAV	LAV	5300	95A	D4
GAYNOR AV	LA	ENC	4900	22	B2
GAYNOR AV	LA	SF	11400	2	B6
GAYNOR AV	LA	SF	9900	8	B3
GAYNOR AV	LA	SF	8300	15	B1
GAYNOR AV	LA	VAN	7400	15	B3
GAY PARK LN	CO	LPUE	2100	98	B3
GAYRIDGE ST	POM	POM	2800	90	E3
GAYTON PL	CO	MAL	6200	112	B6
GAYVIEW DR	LAM	LAM	2000	84	A5
GAYVILLE DR	CLA	CLA		90	F1
GAYVILLE DR	CO	CLA		90	F1
GAYWOOD DR	CO	ALT	1600	20	C4
GAZEBO CT	DBAR	POM		94	B5
GAZELEY ST	CO	CYN	16400	125	C5
GAZELLE ST	CO	PALM	1500	182	J2
GAZETTE AV	LA	CAN	6500	12	D5
GAZETTE AV	LA	CHA	9200	6	D5
GEARY AV	SFS	SFS	9900	61	B3
GEDDES ST	CO	LA44	1200	57	E5
GEER AV	LA	LA16	5300	42	F5
GEHRIG ST	WCOV	WCOV		98	E1
GEIGER AV	CO	PALM	36900	183	A2
GELBER PL	LA	LA08	4000	51	A1
GELLER DR	CO	CAL		100	E5
GEM CIR	LAV	LAV		90	E2
GEM CT	LAN	LAN		159	E8
GEM PL	DBAR	POM		97A	B1
GEM ST	NWK	NWK	11600	61	A5
GEM WY	CO	ACT		189	H2
GEMBROOK AV	CO	LPUE	1300	48	C6
GEMELOS CT	PALM	LAN		171	C4
GEMINI ST	CO	LPUE	17000	92	C6
GEMINI ST	LB	LB10	1900	75	A2
GEMINI ST	MPK	MPK		46	D4
GEMWOOD DR	CO	WHI	1400	47	F5
GENDEL DR	CO	LPUE	300	98	F1
GENE CT	CO	LPUE		97	B4
GENERAL AV	LA	SP	700	78	F2
GENERAL ST	RPV	SP	1900	78	D2
GEN T KOSCIUSZK	LA	LA12		44	D2
GENESEE AV N	LA	LA36	300	33	F5
GENESEE AV N	LA	LA46	700	33	F4
GENESEE AV N	WHOL	LA46	900	33	F4
GENESEE AV S	LA	LA16	1900	42	E4
GENESEE AV S	LA	LA19	1000	42	F2
GENESEE AV S	LA	LA36	300	42	F1
GENESEE DR	LAV	LAV		90	D1
GENESTA AV	LA	ENC	4800	21	E2
GENESTA AV	LA	NOR	10000	7	E3
GENESTA AV	LA	SF	10500	7	E2
GENESTA AV	LA	VAN	7000	14	E2
GENEVA AV	CLA	CLA	300	91	B5
GENEVA PL	COV	COV	100	88	E4
GENEVA ST	GLEN	GL06	100	25	D4
GENEVA ST	GLEN	GL07	900	25	D2
GENEVA ST	LA	LA20	3100	44	A1
GENEVA ST	POM	POM	2300	94	E6
GENEVA WK	LB	LB03		80	C1
GENEVIEVE AV	LA	LA41	4800	26	C5
GENEVIEVE ST	CAR	CAR	100	69	A3
GENOA AV	LAN	LAN	44400	160	A4
GENOA PL	PALM	PALM		171	F5
GENOA ST	ARC	ARC	1	28	E5
GENOA ST	LA	SF	14800	2	D5
GENOA ST	MON	MON	300	29	A5
GENOLA DR	CO	LPUE	2600	85	E4
GENTLE SPG LN	DBAR	POM		93	F6
GENTRY AV	LA	NHO	5600	16	C6
GENTRY AV	LA	NHO	4200	23	C3
GENTRY ST	HB	RB	300	67	D1
GENTRY ST	HPK	HPK	6300	53	A5
GEORGE CIR	CO	PAS	3200	27	F5
GEORGE LN	DBAR	POM		97	C5
GEORGE ST	LA	LA31	3100	36	B6
GEORGE BURNS RD	LA	LA48		33	D6
GEORGEFF RD	RH	PVP	1	78	A1
GEORGETOWN AV	LA	LA45	8000	56	A1
GEORGETOWN AV	PALM	PALM		183	E1
GEORGETOWN DR	SCLR	SAU		124	F5
GEORGETOWN PL	CLA	CLA		96	C6
GEORGETTE AV	LAM	LAM	11900	84	B5
GEORGETTE PL	LA	SF	16400	1	E4
GEORGIA AV	AZU	AZU	700	86	C5
GEORGIA AV	BELL	BELL	6800	53	D6
GEORGIA AV	CER	ART		81	A2
GEORGIA AV	PAR	PAR	15100	65	F4
GEORGIA CT	CLA	CLA	400	91	B5
GEORGIA LN	LA	RES		14	A3
GEORGIA LN	SCLR	SAU		124	D2
GEORGIA PL	AZU	AZU	700	86	C5
GEORGIA ST	LA	LA15	900	44	B4
GEORGIA WY	CO	CHA	9100	4	B5
GEORGIAN RD	CO	PAS	300	19	C4
GEORGIAN RD	LCF	LCF	300	19	C4
GEORGINA AV	SM	SM	100	40	F4
GEORGINA AV	SM	SM	2100	41	A4
GEORGINA CIR	CER	ART	19500	81	A2
GEORGIUS WK	LA	LA68	2400	34	C1
GEORGIUS WY	LA	LA68	8400	34	C1
GEPHART AV	BG	BELL	7600	59	F1
GERAGHTY AV	CO	LA63	700	45	D3
GERALD AV	LA	ENC	5000	21	F2
GERALD AV	LA	SF	11400	2	A6
GERALD AV	LA	SF	8800	7	F6
GERALD AV	LA	VAN	6400	14	F4
GERALDINE ST	LA	LA11	2600	52	D1
GERANIO DR	ALH	ALH	1000	37	D6
GERANIUM DR	LA	LA42		36	B2
GERANIUM GLN LN	CO	CYN		125	F5
GERARD DR	DBAR	POM		97	E3
GERBER AV	CO	WHI	11000	84	A5
GERBER AV	LAM	LAM	12000	84	A6
GERDA CT	CO	WHI	7700	55	B5
GERHART AV	CMRC	LA22	900	54	A1
GERHART AV	CO	LA22	300	46	A5
GERHART AV	CO	LA22	700	54	A1
GERHART AV	MPK	MPK	2100	46	A5
GERKIN AV	CO	LAW	15100	63	B3
GERKIN AV	HAW	HAW	14900	63	B3
GERKIN AV S	TOR	TOR	1200	68	B4
GERMAIN DR	MTB	MTB	1400	46	C6
GERMAIN ST	LA	CHA	20100	6	E2
GERMAIN ST	LA	NOR	18100	7	C2
GERMAIN ST	LA	SF	16800	7	E2
GERMAIN ST	LA	SF	14500	8	D2
GERMAINE LN	WLVL	THO		102	B5
GERMANIA CT	AGH	AGO		102	F2
GERNDAL ST	DBAR	WAL		97	D2
GERNERT ST	RM	RM	3900	38	A5
GERNSIDE DR	DBAR	WAL		97	C3
GERONA AV	SGAB	SGAB	100	37	E2
GERONIMO DR	RPV	PVP	28400	72	C5
GERONIMO LN	CAR	CAR		69	D6
GERONIMO LN	NWK	NWK	12800	82	C1
GERRAD WY	LA	CAN		5	E3
GERRITT AV	CER	ART	16600	82	E5
GERSHWIN CT	LAN	LAN		159	B5
GERSHWIN DR	LA	WOH	22800	13	A3
GERSHWIN PL	LA	WOH	4600	13	A3
GERTRUDA AV N	RB	RB	300	67	C2
GERTRUDA AV S	RB	RB	400	67	D4
GERTRUDE AV	CO	GL14	2900	11	D5
GERTRUDE CT	PAS	PAS	100	26	F4
GERTRUDE DR	LYN	LYN	11300	59	B6
GERTRUDE ST	LA	LA33	300	45	A4
GESELL ST	GLEN	GL02	1000	25	B2
GETTY ST	LA	SF	16300	8	A3
GETTY CENTER DR	LA	LA49		32	B5
GETTYSBURG CIR	CLA	CLA		91	D1
GETTYSBURG DR	NWK	NWK	11400	60	F6
GETTYSBURG DR	NWK	NWK	11600	61	A6
GEYSER AV	LA	NOR	8900	7	B5
GEYSER AV	LA	NOR	8300	14	B2
GEYSER AV	LA	RES	6300	14	B3
GEYSER AV	LA	TAR	5700	14	B6
GEYSER AV	LA	TAR	5000	21	B1
GHENT ST	AZU	AZU	900	88	E2
GHENT ST	CO	AZU	18000	88	E2
GHENT ST	CO	LAV	700	90	B2
GHENT ST	GLDR	GLDR	19000	88	F2
GHENT ST E	GLDR	GLDR	600	89	C2
GHENT ST E	SAD	SAD	300	90	A2
GHENT ST W	GLDR	GLDR		89	A2
GHENT ST W	SAD	SAD	500	89	E2
GIAN DR	CO	TOR	700	69	A5
GIANO AV	CO	LPUE	300	98	D1
GIANO AV	IND	LPUE	600	98	D1
GIANT OAK RD	WAL	WAL	20000	93	B6
GIARDINO WY	LA	PP	200	40	A3
GIBBONS ST	LA	LA31	600	44	F1
GIBBS AL	PAS	PAS	1	27	B4
GIBBS ST N	POM	POM	100	94	E3
GIBBS ST S	POM	POM	100	94	E3
GIBRALTAR AV	LA	LA08	3800	51	A1
GIBRALTAR DR	LA	BH	3100	23	A6
GIBSON AV	CO	COM	12600	65	C2
GIBSON AV	LYN	LYN	12800	65	C2
GIBSON CT	BUR	BUR		17	F4
GIBSON LN	RB	RB	2800	62	F4
GIBSON PL	SCLR	SAU		124	C4
GIBSON RD	ELM	ELM	3500	38	C6
GIBSON ST	LA	LA34	8800	42	C4
GIDDINGS AL	PAS	PAS	1300	27	C4
GIDE CT	DBAR	POM		97	E3
GIDLEY ST	CO	ELM	10500	38	D5
GIDLEY ST	ELM	ELM	9900	38	C5
GIDLEY ST	TEC	TEC	9500	38	C4
GIERSON AV	LA	CHA	9500	6	B4
GIFFORD AV	BELL	BELL	6200	53	C5
GIFFORD AV	CO	LA63	300	45	D4
GIFFORD AV	HPK	HPK	5900	53	C4
GIFFORD AV	MAY	MAY	5100	53	C4
GIFFORD AV	VER	LA58	4900	53	C4
GIFFORD ST	LA	CAN	20200	12	E3
GIFFORD ST	LA	RES	19500	14	A3
GIFLA DR	CO	COV	3500	89	B5
GILBERT DR	SCLR	CYN		124	G9
GILBERT PL	LA	LA04	4500	34	E5
GILBERT ST	POM	POM	900	94	B2
GILBRT LNDSY ML	LA	LA12		44	D3
GILBEY TR	CO	TOP	21000	109	B2
GILCREST DR	LA	BH	1500	33	B3
GILDAY DR	LA	LA68	6300	34	C1
GILES PL	CO	WHI	3900	55	C1
GILFORD ST	LA	SF	16000	2	A1
GILL CIR	LAV	LAV		90	C1
GILLAN AV	LAN	LAN	42100	160	D6
GILLESPIE AV	CO	ACT		189	C3
GILLESPIE ST	CO	LAN		158	F4
GILLETTE CRESNT	SPAS	SPAS	1700	36	F3
GILLETTE RD	POM	POM	1500	90	C6
GILLETTE ST	LA	LA33	600	44	F3
GILLIG AV	LA	LA31	3500	36	B5
GILLIG PL	LA	LA31	3100	36	B5
GILLILAND AV	BG	BELL	7800	59	F1
GILMAN RD	ELM	ELM	3800	39	A6
GILMAN RD	ELM	ELM	3100	48	A1
GILMAN RD	IND	ELM	3200	48	A2
GILMAN ST	LB	LB15		76	A2
GILMERTON AV	LA	LA64	2900	42	B4
GILMORE AV	LA	LA66	12400	49	F4
GILMORE AV	LA	LA66	12100	50	A3
GILMORE LN	LA	LA36	100	33	F6
GILMORE ST	LA	CAN	23600	5	F5
GILMORE ST	LA	CAN	22000	12	A5
GILMORE ST	LA	NHO	11500	16	C5
GILMORE ST	LA	RES	18500	14	A5
GILMORE ST	LA	VAN	16500	14	D5
GILMORE ST	LA	VAN	13600	15	E5
GILPIN WAY	ARC	ARC	2700	38	D2
GILROY ST	LA	LA39	2700	35	D2
GILSON AV	LA	NHO	6400	16	B5
GILWOOD AV	LPUE	LPUE	400	48	F4
GILWORTH ST	PALM	PALM	37700	183	D1
GIMLET DR	SCLR	NEW	19200	127	H3
GINA DR	CAR	CAR	300	69	A5
GINA LN	WCOV	WCOV		92	E6
GINEVRA WK	LB	LB03	200	80	D1
GINGER CT	CO	LPUE		97	A5
GINGER CT	CO	LPUE		98	F5
GINGER CT	WCOV	WCOV		92	E6
GINGER DR	LB	LB05	700	65	C6
GINGER PL	LA	TAR	19000	21	B3
GINGER WY	SCLR	SAU		124	D5
GINGER ROOT LN	RPV	PVP	1	77	E2
GINGERWOOD LN	LAN	LAN		159	C8
GINGERWOOD PL	DBAR	POM		94	B5
GINGHAM AV	LAN	LAN	43600	160	C7
GIN LING WY	LA	LA12	400	44	E1
GIORDANO ST	CO	LPUE	13400	48	C2
GIORDANO ST	LPUE	LPUE	13900	48	D3
GIOVANE ST	ELM	ELM	9800	47	C2
GIOVANE ST	SELM	ELM	9500	47	B2
GIOVANNI WY	PALM	LAN		171	A1
GIRALDA WK	LB	LB03	1	80	D1
GIRARD AV	CUL	CUL	3800	50	B1
GIRLA WY	LA	LA64	9900	42	C4
GIRONEY TR	CO	TOP		109	C6
GISH AV	LA	TU	10100	11	B3
GISH AV	LB	LB15	1500	76	B3
GIST DR	CO	PALM		157	G7
GIVEN PL	MTB	MTB	100	54	E2
GIVENS PL	LA	NOR	9400	7	E4
GLACIER DR	LA	LA41	4800	26	C5
GLAD WY	LAN	LAN		159	F5
GLADBECK AV	LA	NOR	8900	7	B6
GLADBECK AV	LA	NOR	8300	14	B1
GLADBROOK AV	WCOV	WCOV	600	98	F2
GLADDEN PL	LA	LA41	4300	25	F6
GLADE AV	LA	CAN	6400	12	B5
GLADE AV	LA	CHA	9400	6	B5
GLADE AV	LA	WOH	5600	12	B6
GLADE AV	LA	WOH	5400	13	B1
GLADE PL	CO	LPUE		48	B5
GLADEHOLLOW CT	AGH	AGO		102	F3
GLADESIDE DR	LAM	LAM	14000	82	E1
GLADESMORE AV	CO	ARC	6500	38	B1
GLADHILL RD	CO	WHI	10800	84	B5
GLADHILL RD	LAM	LAM	11900	84	B6
GLADIOLA DR	CO	CAL		100	E5
GLADIOLUS DR	CO	CYN	28900	125	E7
GLADMAR ST	MPK	MPK		46	A4
GLADSTONE AV	LA	SF	13000	2	E2
GLADSTONE AV	LA	SF	11600	3	C6
GLADSTONE AV	LA	SF	11500	9	D1
GLADSTONE ST	CO	AZU	16700	88	B2
GLADSTONE ST	CO	BAP	16400	88	B2
GLADSTONE ST	CO	LAV	700	90	B2
GLADSTONE ST	IRW	BAP	15800	88	B2
GLADSTONE ST	LAV	LAV	1200	90	B2
GLADSTONE ST	POM	POM	2900	90	E3
GLADSTONE ST E	AZU	AZU	100	88	B2
GLADSTONE ST E	GLDR	GLDR	100	89	A2
GLADSTONE ST E	SAD	SAD	100	90	A2
GLADSTONE ST W	AZU	AZU	100	88	B2
GLADSTONE ST W	GLDR	GLDR		88	B2
GLADSTONE ST W	GLDR	GLDR	100	89	A2
GLADSTONE ST W	SAD	SAD	100	89	E2
GLADSTONE WY	LA	SF	11400	3	C6
GLADWICK ST	CAR	CAR	700	69	C2
GLADWICK ST	CO	COM		69	E2
GLADWIN ST	LA	LA49	11300	41	C1
GLADY ST	SOG	SOG	5700	59	E4
GLADYS AV	CO	SGAB	5600	37	F3
GLADYS AV	CO	SGAB	1700	46	F3
GLADYS AV	LA	LA13	400	44	D5
GLADYS AV	LA	LA21	600	44	D5
GLADYS AV	LB	LB04	700	75	F4
GLADYS AV	LB	LB14	300	75	F4

1990 LOS ANGELES COUNTY STREET INDEX

STREET	CITY	P.O. ZONE	BLOCK	PAGE	GRID
GLADYS AV	MPK	MPK	100	46	D1
GLADYS AV	RM	RM	1800	46	F2
GLADYS AV	SH	LB06	1800	75	F3
GLADYS AV N	SGAB	SGAB	100	37	F3
GLADYS AV S	SGAB	SGAB	100	37	F3
GLADYS CT	PAS	PAS	700	27	B2
GLADYS DR	GLEN	GL06	1600	25	E2
GLADYS ST	COM	COM	300	65	A3
GLADYS ST	MON	MON	600	29	B4
GLADYS ST	PAS	PAS	2000	27	D3
GLAMIS PL	LA	PAC	12500	9	B2
GLAMIS ST	LA	PAC	13600	8	E5
GLAMIS ST	LA	PAC	12500	9	B2
GLAMIS ST	LA	SF	11500	3	D6
GLAMIS ST	LA	SF	11800	9	C1
GLAMOUR TR	CO	CAN		4	A6
GLAMOUR TR	LA	CAN		5	D1
GLANDON ST	BLF	BLF	9500	66	B2
GLASGOW AV	CO	HAW	12000	56	E6
GLASGOW AV	ING	IN01	100	56	E2
GLASGOW AV	LA	LA45	6900	50	E6
GLASGOW CT	LA	LA45	5300	50	E6
GLASGOW PL	HAW	HAW	100	62	E1
GLASGOW PL	LA	LA45	9300	56	E3
GLASGOW WY	LA	LA45	5200	50	E6
GLASSBORO AV	CLA	CLA		91	C1
GLASSELL ST	LA	LA26	2700	35	A6
GLASSER AV	SCLR	CYN	27500	124	H8
GLASSPORT AV	LA	CAN	7600	12	D2
GLAZEBROOK DR	LAM	LAM	15800	83	C1
GLEAM CT	AGH	AGO		100A	A3
GLEASON AV	LA	LA33	2500	45	B4
GLEASON AV	LA	LA63	3000	45	B4
GLEASON LN	LAN	LAN		159	B5
GLEASON ST	CO	LA22	4500	45	E5
GLEASON ST	CO	LA63	3900	45	D5
GLEASON ST	MPK	MPK	5400	46	A5
GLEASON ST E	MPK	MPK	100	46	C5
GLEASON ST W	MPK	MPK	200	46	A5
GLEDHILL ST	LA	CHA	22100	6	B4
GLEDHILL ST	LA	NOR	17400	7	B4
GLEDHILL ST	LA	SF	16500	7	F4
GLEDHILL ST	LA	SF	15800	8	A4
GLEDHILL ST	LA	VAN	14400	8	D5
GLEN AV	CO	ALT	2600	19	F4
GLEN AV	GLEN	GL06	600	25	F3
GLEN AV	PAS	PAS	1500	19	F6
GLEN AV	PAS	PAS	900	26	F2
GLEN AV	POM	POM	900	94	C1
GLEN CT	PAS	PAS	400	26	D3
GLEN CT	WHI	WHI		55	F5
GLEN PL	SPAS	SPAS	800	36	F2
GLEN RD	CO	TOP	1400	109	A2
GLEN TR	CO	TOP	500	109	E4
GLEN WY	BH	BH	900	33	A5
GLEN WY	CLA	CLA		91	A1
GLEN WY	ELM	ELM		38	E5
GLEN WY	LAV	LAV		95A	D6
GLENADA AV	CO	MONT	2100	18	F3
GLEN AIRE DR	GLEN	GL02	300	25	C1
GLEN AIRY	LA	LA68	6200	34	C2
GLENALBYN DR	LA	LA65	3400	36	A3
GLENALBYN PL	LA	LA65	600	36	A3
GLENALBYN WY	LA	LA65		36	B3
GLEN ALDER	LA	LA68	6100	34	C1
GLEN ALLEN LN	CO	ALT	1800	20	D4
GLENANDALE TER	GLEN	GL06		25	E3
GLEN ARBOR AV	LA	LA41	900	26	C5
GLEN ARDEN AV	CO	SAD	4800	89	C3
GLENARM ST E	PAS	PAS	100	27	A6
GLENARM ST W	PAS	PAS	100	26	F6
GLENAVEN AV	ALH	ALH	2900	36	F6
GLENAVON AV	LA	VEN	1300	49	D2
GLEN AYLSA AV	LA	LA41	1500	26	B5
GLENBARR AV	LA	LA64	10300	42	B4
GLENBRIDGE RD	WLVL	THO		102	B5
GLENBRIER AV	CO	WHI	10800	84	B4
GLENBROOK DR	DBAR	WAL		97	D3
GLENBURN AV	TOR	TOR	16600	63	C5
GLENBURY RD	CO	CAL		108	B4
GLENBUSH AV	CO	PALM	38400	172	G8
GLENBUSH AV	PALM	PALM		183	G1
GLENCAIRN RD	LA	LA27	4800	34	F1
GLENCANNON DR	PR	PR	9400	55	A3
GLENCANNON DR	WHI	WHI		55	B4
GLEN CANYON RD	CO	ALT	2100	20	D5
GLENCLAIRE DR	DBAR	WAL		97	D3
GLENCLIFF DR	DOW	DOW	7200	60	B1
GLENCOE AV	COM	COM		65	A4
GLENCOE AV	CUL	VEN	3900	49	D3
GLENCOE AV	LA	MDR	4000	49	E4
GLENCOE AV	LA	VEN	1500	49	D2
GLENCOE DR	ARC	ARC	1300	28	C3
GLENCOE ST	COM	COM	100	64	F4
GLENCOE WY	GLEN	GL08	1600	18	F4
GLENCOE WY	LA	LA68	1900	34	B1

STREET	CITY	P.O. ZONE	BLOCK	PAGE	GRID
GLENCOE WY	POM	POM	2100	90	E5
GLENCOE WY	TOR	TOR	24800	73	B2
GLENCOE HTS DR	GLDR	GLDR	900	87	B3
GLENCOVE AV	GLEN	GL14	4500	11	C5
GLENCOVE DR	CO	LPUE		85	E5
GLEN CREEK RD	CER	ART		82	B4
GLENCREST CIR	LA	BUR	9900	17	A2
GLENCREST DR	GLEN	GL08	3100	18	E4
GLENCREST DR	LA	BUR	9800	17	A2
GLENCREST DR	LA	SF	11800	3	A6
GLENCREST DR	LA	SV	8100	16	F1
GLENCREST DR	LA	SV	7600	17	A1
GLENCREST ST	POM	POM	2800	90	E3
GLENCREST TER	GLEN	GL08	1400	18	E4
GLENCROFT RD	GLDR	GLDR	1200	89	B2
GLENCROSS CT	LA	LA23		45	B6
GLEN CURTIS ST	CAR	CAR		69	E1
GLENDA ST	CER	ART	12500	82	C5
GLENDALE AV N	GLEN	GL06	100	25	D4
GLENDALE AV S	GLEN	GL05	100	25	D4
GLENDALE BLVD	LA	LA26	700	35	C5
GLENDALE BLVD	LA	LA26	100	44	C1
GLENDALE BLVD	LA	LA39	1900	35	C5
GLENDALE FRWY	LA	LA		35	D2
GLENDALE ST	WCOV	WCOV	1000	92	B1
GLENDOLA DR	PR	PR	8400	54	E4
GLENDON AV	LA	LA24	1000	41	E2
GLENDON AV	LA	LA25	1800	41	E2
GLENDON AV	LA	LA34	3000	42	A5
GLENDON AV	LA	LA64	2200	41	E2
GLENDON CT	SPAS	SPAS	800	36	F2
GLENDON LN	SPAS	SPAS	800	36	F2
GLENDON WY	RM	RM	8800	38	A6
GLENDON WY	SPAS	SPAS	1000	36	F2
GLENDON WY E	ALH	ALH	100	37	C6
GLENDON WY E	SGAB	SGAB	100	37	D6
GLENDON WY W	ALH	ALH	100	37	C6
GLENDON WY W	SGAB	SGAB	100	37	D6
GLENDORA AV	CO	COV	4600	89	B4
GLENDORA AV	CO	GLDR	5600	89	B4
GLENDORA AV	CO	LPUE	1400	48	F6
GLENDORA AV	CO	LPUE	1700	92	A2
GLENDORA AV	GLDR	GLDR		89	B4
GLENDORA AV	LPUE	LPUE	100	48	F6
GLENDORA AV	WCOV	WCOV	100	92	A2
GLENDORA AV N	COV	COV		89	B4
GLENDORA AV N	GLDR	GLDR	100	87	A5
GLENDORA AV N	LB	LB03	200	76	B6
GLENDORA AV N	LB	LB03	1	80	B1
GLENDORA AV S	COV	COV	100	89	B4
GLENDORA AV S	GLDR	GLDR	300	87	B6
GLENDORA AV S	GLDR	GLDR		89	B4
GLENDORA MTN RD	CO			P	B6
GLENDORA MTN RD	CO	GLDR		87	D4
GLENDORA MTN RD	GLDR	GLDR	400	87	D4
GLENDRA RDG MTY	CO	AZU		86	E3
GLENDRA RDG MTY	CO	GLDR		87	A2
GLENDRA RDG MTY	GLDR	GLDR		87	A2
GLENDOVER WY	ING	IN01		57	B2
GLENDOWER AV	LA	LA27	2400	34	F1
GLENDOWER PL	LA	LA27	2400	34	F1
GLENDOWER RD	LA	LA27	2700	34	F1
GLEN EAGLE AV	POM	POM	600	94	B2
GLENEAGLES DR	LA	TAR		13	F4
GLENEAGLES PL	LCF	LCF	400	19	D2
GLENEDEN ST	LA	LA39	2800	35	D2
GLENELDER AV	CO	LPUE	1100	85	F2
GLEN ELLEN PL	LA	LA42	5200	36	C3
GLENFAIR ST	CO	ELM	10500	38	D4
GLENFALL AV E	CO	LAN	16800	175	A5
GLENFELIZ BLVD	LA	LA39	3600	35	B1
GLENFIELD AV	LAV	LAV	2400	90	B3
GLENFIELD CT	LA	LA23		45	B6
GLENFINNAN AV	AZU	AZU	500	86	E6
GLENFINNAN AV	CO	AZU	5200	88	E2
GLENFINNAN AV	CO	COV	4400	88	E4
GLENFINNAN AV	COV	COV		88	E3
GLENFLOW CT	GLEN	GL06		25	F2
GLENFOLD DR	CO	LPUE		98	B4
GLENFORD AV	DUA	DUA	1500	29	D5
GLENFORD ST	LA	LA08	5600	50	E1
GLENGARRY AV	CO	WHI	6400	55	B5
GLENGARRY AV	WHI	WHI	6200	55	B5
GLENGARRY RD	PAS	PAS	1400	26	C5
GLENGRAY ST	CO	LPUE	16700	92	B5
GLEN GREEN	LA	LA68	2500	34	D1
GLEN GREEN TER	LA	LA68	2500	34	D1
GLENGROVE AV	CO	GLDR	700	87	E6
GLENGROVE AV	CO	GLDR	600	89	E1
GLENGROVE AV	GLDR	GLDR	100	87	E5
GLENGROVE AV	SAD	SAD	100	89	E3
GLENGYLE ST	CO	WHI	14000	61	E4
GLENHAVEN AV	ALH	ALH	2900	36	F6
GLENHAVEN DR	LA	PP	900	40	B3
GLENHAVEN DR	LCF	LCF	1900	19	A2
GLENHILL DR	LA	BUR	9800	17	B2

STREET	CITY	P.O. ZONE	BLOCK	PAGE	GRID
GLEN HOLLY	LA	LA68	6100	34	C1
GLEN HOLLY DR	PAS	PAS	300	26	D5
GLENHOPE DR	CO	LPUE	16100	92	B5
GLENHURST AV	LA	LA39	2900	35	C2
GLENHURST PL	WCOV	WCOV		92	D6
GLENHURST ST	WCOV	WCOV		92	D6
GLEN IRIS AV	LA	LA41	4900	26	A5
GLEN IVY DR	GLEN	GL06	2100	25	F3
GLEN IVY ST	CO	LAV	4700	95A	E6
GLENLEA ST	CO	LAV	700	90	B2
GLENLOCH AV	CO	LPUE	100	92	C6
GLENLYN DR	AZU	AZU	600	88	E1
GLENLYN DR	CO	AZU	18500	88	E1
GLENLYN DR	CO	GLDR	19000	88	F1
GLENLYN DR	CO	GLDR	19400	89	A1
GLENLYN ST	GLDR	GLDR		89	A1
GLENMANOR PL	LA	LA39	2900	35	B1
GLENMARK DR	CO	LPUE		85	E5
GLENMERE ST	WCOV	WCOV	1200	48	F2
GLENMERE WY	LA	LA49	800	32	A6
GLENMONT AV	LA	LA24	700	41	E1
GLENMONT DR	GLEN	GL07	1500	25	C1
GLENMORE BLVD	GLEN	GL06	600	25	F3
GLENMUIR AV	LA	LA65	4200	36	A3
GLENN AV	LA	LA23	2700	45	A6
GLENN AV	SM	SM	2900	49	C2
GLENN CT	LAN	LAN		160	D7
GLENN CT	SM	SM	3300	49	C2
GLENN DR	CO	WHI	13900	61	E2
GLENN DR	CO	WHI	14700	84	A3
GLENN PL	TOR	TOR	5700	67	E4
GLENN ALAN AV	WCOV	WCOV	500	92	D2
GLENNCHESTER DR	LB	LB05		70	C3
GLENNEL AV	LAN	LAN	3000	159	F5
GLENN HILL DR	CO	LPUE		85	C3
GLENNIE LN	LA	LA16	5500	42	F4
GLENNON DR	WHI	WHI		55	D3
GLENNWOOD CIR	TOR	TOR		73	B3
GLEN OAK	LA	LA68	6000	34	C1
GLENOAK AV	COV	GLDR		89	C4
GLEN OAK WK	LA	LA68	6100	34	C1
GLENOAKS BLVD	LA	BUR	7500	17	A2
GLENOAKS BLVD	LA	PAC	11500	3	A6
GLENOAKS BLVD	LA	PAC	10200	9	B1
GLENOAKS BLVD	LA	SF	12600	2	C2
GLENOAKS BLVD	LA	SF	11700	3	A6
GLENOAKS BLVD	LA	SV	8600	9	C3
GLENOAKS BLVD	LA	SV	8000	16	F1
GLENOAKS BLVD	LA	SV	7800	17	A2
GLEN OAKS BLVD	PAS	PAS	800	26	D3
GLENOAKS BLVD	SF	SF	400	2	E4
GLENOAKS BLVD E	GLEN	GL06	1000	25	D2
GLENOAKS BLVD E	GLEN	GL06	2200	26	A3
GLENOAKS BLVD E	GLEN	GL07	100	25	D2
GLENOAKS BLVD N	BUR	BUR	100	17	B3
GLENOAKS BLVD S	BUR	BUR	100	17	B3
GLENOAKS BLVD W	GLEN	GL01	1500	24	F1
GLENOAKS BLVD W	GLEN	GL01	1200	25	B2
GLENOAKS BLVD W	GLEN	GL02	100	25	B2
GLENOAKS CYN RD	GLEN	GL06	3000	26	B3
GLEN O PEACE PY	LA	TU	9400	10	F5
GLENOVER DR	PAS	PAS	1400	26	D5
GLEN PARK ST	POM	POM	1700	94	B1
GLEN PEAK COVE	DBAR	POM		97	D6
GLENRAVEN AV	CO	PALM	38600	172	B8
GLENRAVEN RD	LAN	LAN	44300	160	B5
GLENRIDE CIR	WCOV	WCOV		92	D5
GLENRIDGE AV	ALH	ALH	2900	36	F4
GLENRIDGE DR	SCLR	NEW		127	B6
GLENRIDGE DR	LA	VAN	3600	22	F5
GLENROCK AV	LA	LA24	500	41	D1
GLENROSE AV	CO	ALT	2000	19	F5
GLENROSE AV	CO	ALT	3000	20	A4
GLENROY AV N	LA	LA49	100	32	D6
GLENROY AV S	LA	LA49	100	32	C6
GLENROY PL	LA	LA49	200	32	C6
GLENROY ST	POM	POM	1900	94	E5
GLENSHAW AV	LPUE	LPUE	300	48	D4
GLENSHAW DR	CO	LPUE	700	48	E4
GLENSHAW DR	WCOV	WCOV	700	92	A2
GLENSHIRE RD	DOW	DOW	12600	60	B6
GLENSIDE PL	LA	BH	9700	33	A2
GLEN SPRINGS RD	CO	PAS		20	F6
GLENSTONE AV	CO	LPUE	1900	85	D2
GLEN SUMMER RD	PAS	PAS	100	26	D5
GLENTANA ST	COV	COV	800	88	D4
GLENTHORNE ST	CO	LPUE	17400	92	C6
GLENTHORPE DR	DBAR	WAL		97	D3
GLENTIES LN	LA	SUN	7900	10	E4
GLENTIES WY	LA	SUN	7900	10	E4
GLENTOWER	LA	LA68	6100	34	C1
GLENTOWER WK	LA	LA68	6100	34	C1
GLENTREE DR	LOM	LOM	2000	73	D4
GLENULLEN DR	PAS	PAS	200	26	D5
GLENVIA ST	GLEN	GL06		25	D3
GLENVIEW AV	LA	LA39	2700	35	D2

STREET	CITY	P.O. ZONE	BLOCK	PAGE	GRID
GLEN VIEW DR	ALH	ALH	1700	36	F6
GLENVIEW LN	GLDR	GLDR		89	D2
GLENVIEW RD	GLEN	GL02	700	25	B1
GLENVIEW RD	WCOV	WCOV	800	92	C3
GLENVIEW TER	CO	ALT	1900	20	D5
GLENVIEW TER	MPK	MPK	900	46	A4
GLENVILLE DR	CLA	CLA		91	A1
GLENVILLE DR	CLA	CLA		96	A6
GLENVILLE DR	LA	LA35	1100	42	C3
GLENVINA AV	CO	COV	4500	89	A4
GLENVISTA DR	GLEN	GL06	700	25	E3
GLENWALL DR	CO	SAU		182	A6
GLENWAY DR	ING	IN02	700	50	E6
GLENWICK AV	DBAR	WAL	800	97	C2
GLENWOLD DR	DBAR	WAL		97	D3
GLENWOOD AV	CO	GL14	4500	11	D6
GLENWOOD AV	CO	GL14	4400	18	D2
GLENWOOD AV	GLEN	GL14	3700	18	D2
GLENWOOD AV	LA	LA65	4200	36	A3
GLENWOOD AV N	GLDR	GLDR	300	87	C4
GLENWOOD AV S	GLDR	GLDR	100	87	C6
GLENWOOD DR	PALM	PALM		171	H7
GLENWOOD PL	SOG	SOG	2400	58	F2
GLENWOOD PL	SOG	SOG	2700	59	A2
GLENWOOD PL N	BUR	BUR	300	17	D6
GLENWOOD PL S	BUR	BUR	200	24	D1
GLENWOOD RD	GLEN	GL01	1800	17	F6
GLENWOOD RD	GLEN	GL01	1300	25	B2
GLENWOOD RD	GLEN	GL02	500	25	B2
GLENWD SPGS RD	SFS	SFS		60	F3
GLENWORTH ST	SFS	SFS	11200	60	F4
GLENWORTH ST	SFS	SFS	11600	61	A4
GLESS ST	LA	LA33	100	44	F4
GLICK CT	RB	RB	2200	67	E1
GLICKMAN AV	TEC	TEC	4800	38	D4
GLIDDEN DR	LA	LA32	4300	36	E4
GLIDE AV	LA	WOH	6100	5	F5
GLIDER AV	LA	LA45	7900	56	D1
GLOAMING DR	LA	BH	9400	33	B1
GLOAMING WY	LA	BH	2200	33	B1
GLOBE AV	CUL	CUL	3800	50	B2
GLOBE AV	LA	LA66	3600	50	A1
GLORIA AV	LA	ENC	4300	22	B2
GLORIA AV	LA	SF	8500	8	B6
GLORIA AV	LA	SF	8300	15	B1
GLORIA AV	LA	VAN	6400	15	B4
GLORIA CT E	LKD	LKD		81	A3
GLORIA RD	ARC	ARC	500	28	C3
GLORIA ST	WCOV	WCOV		92	E6
GLORIETA ST	PAS	PAS	100	26	F2
GLORIETTA AV	GLEN	GL08	1600	18	E5
GLORIETTA DR	LA	VAN	14400	22	E5
GLORIETTA PL	LA	VAN	3400	22	E5
GLORIOSA AV	CO	LPUE	1400	98	D3
GLORY AV	LA	TU	9300	11	A3
GLORYWHITE ST	LKD	LKD	6400	71	E2
GLOUCESTER DR	LA	BH		22	F6
GLOUCESTER ST	CO	LA22	6000	54	A1
GLOVER PL	LA	LA31	2200	35	E4
GLYNDON AV	LA	VEN	1500	49	D2
GLYNDON CT	LA	VEN	2100	49	D2
GLYNN AV S	DOW	DOW	12200	60	A5
GLYNN DR	LA	PP		40	B1
GNEISS AV	DOW	DOW	12100	60	A5
GNEISS ST	DOW	DOW	12600	60	A6
GNU CIR	CO	LPUE	2200	98	D4
GOBLET	PALM	PALM		171	F5
GODBEY DR	LCF	LCF	5300	19	C2
GODDARD AV	LA	LA45	7600	56	E1
GODDE HILL RD	PALM	LAN	41100	171	B5
GODINHO AV	CER	ART	18900	81	C1
GODOY ST	CO	WHI	10000	55	B6
GOETHE PL	LA	SF	12700	1	E4
GOETTING LN	CO	PALM		183	H3
GOLD LN	WAL	WAL		92	F6
GOLD PL	LA	LA42	6700	36	E1
GOLD BLUFF DR	CO	POM		93	E6
GOLDBLUFF DR	DBAR	POM		93	F6
GOLD CANYON DR	DBAR	WAL		97	C3
GOLD CREEK RD	CO			M	C5
GOLDCREST DR	CO	VAL		126	G1
GOLDCREST ST	LB	LB15	6900	76	E3
GOLDDUST LN	CAR	CAR		69	D6
GOLD DUST ST	GLDR	GLDR	1700	87	D6
GOLDEN AV	DOW	DOW	8500	66	A1
GOLDEN AV	HB	RB	1500	62	D6
GOLDEN AV	LA	LA17	800	44	B3
GOLDEN AV	PAR	PAR	8000	65	F1
GOLDEN AV	PAR	SOG	8000	65	F1
GOLDEN AV N	LB	LB02	1	75	B5
GOLDEN AV N	LB	LB06	3000	70	B6
GOLDEN AV N	LB	LB06	1800	75	B2
GOLDEN AV S	LB	LB02	1	75	B5
GOLDEN CIR	LA	SF		1	E4
GOLDEN CIR	PALM	PALM		183	H1
GOLDEN CT	PALM	PALM		183	H1

STREET	CITY	P.O. ZONE	BLOCK	PAGE	GRID
GOLDEN LN	LA	SF		1	E4
GOLDEN LN	LAN	LAN		159	G7
GOLDEN ST	COM	COM	900	65	A1
GOLDEN ARROW DR	RPV	PVP	4900	72	E5
GOLDEN BOUGH DR	CO	COV	19600	93	A1
GOLDN CARRGE LN	POM	POM	100	90	E5
GOLDN CROWN CIR	DBAR	POM		97	F1
GOLDENDALE DR	LAM	LAM	11600	84	A5
GOLDEN EAGLE AV	PALM	PALM		184	A1
GOLDEN GATE AV	LA	LA26	1400	35	B4
GOLDEN GLEN CT	SCLR	NEW		127	F2
GOLDEN GROVE WY	COV	COV	800	88	D4
GOLDEN HILLS RD	LAV	LAV	1200	95A	D4
GOLDN JUBLEE LN	CO	LR		184	D6
GOLDN LANTRN LN	CO	WHI	15800	84	C6
GOLDN LANTRN LN	LAM	LAM		84	B6
GOLDEN LEAF DR	WLVL	THO		102	A5
GOLDEN MALL N	BUR	BUR	100	17	D5
GOLDEN MALL S	BUR	BUR	100	17	D5
GOLDEN MDW DR	DUA	DUA	2300	29	F3
GOLDEN MDW DR	RPV	PVP	27100	72	C5
GOLDEN OAK LN	SCLR	NEW	24600	127	E4
GOLDEN OAK RD	SCLR	SAU		124	E9
GOLDEN POPPY CT	WAL	WAL		93	D4
GOLDN PRADOS DR	DBAR	POM		97	F1
GOLDN PRADOS DR	DBAR	POM		97A	A1
GOLDEN RAIN LN	SCLR	CYN	18400	125	A8
GOLDEN RIDGE LN	CO	LPUE		85	D5
GOLDENROD DR	WAL	WAL		93	D6
GOLDENROD PL	CO	CAL		100A	E5
GOLDENROD PL	LA	ENC	16500	21	F5
GOLDENROD PL	LA	ENC	16500	22	A5
GOLDENROD PL	POM	POM		94	C3
GOLDENROD WY	SCLR	SAU		124	E8
GOLDEN ROSE AV	CO	LPUE	1500	98	A3
GOLDENROSE ST	LA	SP		78	E2
GOLDEN SANDS DR	LB	LB03	6100	76	E5
GOLDEN SHORE	LB	LB02		75	B6
GOLDEN SPAR PL	RHE	PVP	1	72	F4
GOLDEN SPGS DR	DBAR	POM		94	A6
GOLDEN SPGS DR	DBAR	POM		97	E2
GOLDEN SPGS DR	DBAR	POM		97A	A1
GOLDEN SPUR CIR	WAL	WAL		93	A6
GOLDENSPUR LN	RPV	PVP	2300	78	C1
GOLDEN SPUR RD	CO	SAU		189	G4
GOLDEN STATE FY	BUR	BUR		17	B3
GOLDEN STATE FY	CO			123	E4
GOLDEN STATE FY	CO			126	J1
GOLDEN STATE FY	CO			127	B7
GOLDEN STATE FY	GLEN	GL01		24	E1
GOLDEN STATE FY	LA	LA		1	F1
GOLDEN STATE FY	LA	LA		2	A3
GOLDEN STATE FY	LA	LA		8	E2
GOLDEN STATE FY	LA	LA		9	A5
GOLDEN STATE FY	LA	LA		16	E1
GOLDEN STATE FY	LA	LA		25	A4
GOLDEN STATE FY	LA	LA		35	C2
GOLDEN STATE FY	LA	LA		45	A4
GLDN TRIANGL RD	SCLR	CYN	20500	124	D9
GOLDEN VLY LN	LA	SF		1	E2
GOLDEN VLY RD	SCLR	CYN	26500	124	F9
GOLDEN VLY RD	SCLR	NEW		127	H2
GOLDEN VIEW DR	CO	LPUE	1500	85	C2
GOLDENVIEW WY	CO	PALM		184	E2
GOLDEN VISTA DR	WCOV	WCOV	1800	92	E3
GOLDEN WEST AV	TEC	TEC	4800	38	C2
GOLDEN W AV N	CO	ARC	6700	28	C6
GOLDEN W AV N	CO	ARC	6500	38	C2
GOLDEN W AV S	ARC	ARC	200	28	C5
GOLDENWOOD DR	ING	LA56		50	E5
GOLDFIELD AV	LB	LB07	4400	70	E3
GOLDFIELD PL	POM	POM		94	C4
GOLD HILL DR	CO	CAST		123	G2
GOLD HILL DR	WAL	WAL		92	F5
GOLDLEAF CIR	CO	LA56		50	E4
GOLDMINE LN	LA	VAN		14	F2
GOLD NUGGET AV	DBAR	POM		97A	A2
GOLDPOINT PL	DBAR	POM		94	B6
GOLDRING PL	RHE	PVP	26300	73	A3
GOLDRING RD	ARC	ARC		39	A3
GOLD RUN DR	DBAR	POM		97	C6
GOLDRUSH AV	PALM	PALM		171	D9
GOLD RUSH DR	DBAR	POM		97A	A1
GOLDRUSH DR	SAD	SAD		89	D2
GOLDSMITH ST	SM	SM	3000	49	B2
GOLD STAR DR	LB	LB10	3200	70	A6
GOLDSTAR PL	POM	POM		94	E6
GOLDSTAR PL	POM	POM		97A	C1
GOLD STONE RD	CO	TOP		109	C4
GOLDSTREAM WY	SCLR	NEW		127	G2
GOLDWYN TER	LA	CUL	3800	42	B6
GOLETA ST	CO	COM	14900	64	C3
GOLETA ST	LA	PAC	13300	8	F4
GOLETA ST	LA	PAC	12900	9	A3
GOLETA ST	LA	SF	11600	3	D6

1990 LOS ANGELES COUNTY STREET INDEX

STREET	CITY	P.O. ZONE	BLOCK	PAGE	GRID
GOLETA ST	LAV	LAV		90	B2
GOLF PL	CO	LLAN		192	J3
GOLF CLUB DR	GLEN	GL06	1500	26	B1
GOLF COURSE RD	LA	TAR	3800	21	B4
GOLF COURSE RD	SCLR	VAL		127	A3
GOLFERS DR	PALM	PALM		172	B5
GOLF LINKS RD	AVA	AVA		77	B6
GOLF VIEW DR	CO	VAL		126	J3
GOLL AV	LA	NHO	7800	16	D2
GOLLER AV	NWK	NWK	12900	82	B1
GOLONDRINA PL	LA	WOH	4200	13	C4
GOLONDRINA ST	LA	WOH	21200	13	C4
GOLONDRINAS ST	DOW	DOW	7400	59	F5
GOLT ST W	CO	PALM		182	G6
GOLVA DR	LAM	LAM	16000	83	C3
GOMERES RD	LA	WOH	5100	13	A2
GOMERO CIR	CAR	CAR	20300	69	D3
GOMEZ-PALCIO DR	SELM	ELM		47	D4
GONA CT	DBAR	WAL		97	D3
GONDAR AV	CO	LB08	3700	71	D5
GONDAR AV	LB	LB08	3000	71	D6
GONDAR AV	LB	LB15	2000	76	D2
GONDAR AV	LKD	LKD	4300	71	D3
GONSALES ST	CER	ART	11500	81	A2
GONSALVES PL	CER	ART	11000	71	E2
GONSALVES ST	CER	ART	11300	71	F2
GONZAGA BLVD	LA	LA45	8000	56	A1
GONZALES DR	LA	WOH	23100	100	F2
GOODALL AV	CO	DUA	2000	29	B6
GOODALL AV	CO	DUA		39	B1
GOODBEE ST	PR	PR	8300	54	F5
GOODE AV	GLEN	GL06		25	C3
GOODE ST	LA	LA41	4800	26	B5
GOODHART AV	CO	WHI	1300	48	A4
GOODHOPE AV	LA	SP	400	78	D2
GOODHOPE PL	LA	SP	900	78	D3
GOODHUE ST	CO	WHI	14800	84	B4
GOODHUE ST	WHI	WHI	15400	84	B4
GOODLAND AV	LA	NHO	6800	16	B4
GOODLAND AV	LA	NHO	3600	23	B4
GOODLAND DR	LA	NHO	3600	23	B5
GOODLAND PL	LA	NHO	6200	16	B5
GOODLAND PL	LA	NHO	3700	23	B4
GOODMAN AV	RB	RB	1100	62	D5
GOODMAN AV	RB	RB	300	67	D1
GOODRICH AV	LA	WIL	900	74	E4
GOODRICH BLVD	CMRC	LA22	900	53	F1
GOODSON DR	LPUE	LPUE	700	48	E4
GOODSON PL	LA	LA69	8400	33	E3
GOODSPRING DR	AGH	AGO		102	D3
GOODVALE RD	SCLR	CYN	18900	124	H7
GOODVALE RD	SCLR	CYN	16500	125	C7
GOOD VIEW TR	LA	LA68	2900	34	A1
GOODWAY DR	CO	AZU	6000	88	E1
GOODWICK DR	WCOV	WCOV	3200	97	A1
GOODWIN AV	LA	LA39	3900	25	B5
GOOSEBERRY DR	CO	LPUE		98	D5
GORDON AV	GLDR	GLDR	100	87	D5
GORDON CT	POM	POM	1600	90	E6
GORDON PL	MTB	MTB	1400	46	D5
GORDON ST	LA	LA28	1300	34	D4
GORDON ST	LA	LA38	1100	34	D4
GORDON ST	LB	LB05		65	B6
GORDON ST N	POM	POM	100	94	E3
GORDON ST S	POM	POM	100	94	E3
GORDON TER	PAS	PAS	300	26	F5
GOREN PL	LA	SF		3	D6
GORGE RD	CO	MAL	100	114	E3
GORGONIA ST	LA	WOH	20900	13	D4
GORHAM AV	LA	LA49	11600	41	B3
GORHAM LN	PALM	PALM		171	F4
GORHAM LN	PALM	PALM		171	F5
GORHAM PL	LA	LA49	11600	41	C2
GORMAN AV	CO	LA59	11600	58	E5
GORMAN AV	LA	LA02	10300	58	E4
GORMAN AV	LA	LA59	10700	58	E4
GOSFORD AV	LA	NHO	8000	16	B2
GOSHEN AV	LA	LA49	11600	41	C3
GOSS ST	LA	SV	10800	9	E6
GOSS ST	LA	SV	11200	16	E1
GOSSAMER ST	LB	LB08	5700	71	D5
GOSS CANYON AV	CO	GL14	5500	11	E5
GOTERA DR	CO	LPUE		85	F5
GOTHAM ST	BG	BELL	5500	59	E1
GOTHAM ST	DOW	DOW	8500	60	D3
GOTHAM ST	LA	SF	14800	8	D4
GOTHIC AV	LA	SF	11500	2	A6
GOTHIC AV	LA	SF	8500	8	A6
GOTHIC AV	LA	SF	8300	15	A1
GOTHIC AV	LA	VAN	6800	15	A4
GOTHIC PL	LA	SF	16400	2	A5
GOTHIC WY	POM	POM	900	94	D1
GOTTES LN	LAM	LAM	11900	84	B6
GOUCHER ST	LA	PP	1300	40	D2
GOULD AV	HB	RB	400	62	C5
GOULD AV	LA	LA46	8100	33	E2
GOULD AV	LCF	LCF	4400	19	C4
GOULD TER	HB	RB	600	62	C5
GOVERNOR AV	LA	HAC	24200	73	E1
GOVERNR MINE RD	CO	ACT		182	D7
GOWER ST	LA	LA04	100	34	C6
GOWER ST	LA	LA28	1300	34	C4
GOWER ST	LA	LA38	700	34	C4
GOWER ST	LA	LA68	1900	34	D1
GOYA DR	RPV	SP	28700	78	D1
GOYA ST	LA	SF	17100	1	E3
GRABER AV	LA	SF	13700	3	B1
GRACE AV	ARC	ARC	1600	38	E1
GRACE AV	BAP	BAP	3700	39	D5
GRACE AV	CAR	CAR	21000	69	B5
GRACE AV	ING	IN01	300	51	A6
GRACE AV	LA	LA28	1800	34	C3
GRACE AV	LA	LA68	1900	34	C3
GRACE CT	WCOV	WCOV	700	88	C5
GRACE DR	SPAS	SPAS	200	26	F6
GRACE DR	SPAS	SPAS	300	36	F1
GRACE LN	LA	LA49		32	B5
GRACE PL	CO	LA22	5300	53	F1
GRACE TER	PAS	PAS	99	26	F6
GRACEBEE AV	NWK	NWK	14300	82	C2
GRACELAND WY	GLEN	GL06	2800	26	B1
GRACELDO LN	WHI	WHI	15900	84	C3
GRACETON DR	CO	CYN		125	E9
GRACEWOOD AV	TEC	ARC	5500	38	D3
GRACIA ST	LA	LA39	2900	35	C2
GRACIOSA DR	LA	LA68	5800	34	D2
GRACITA PL	LA	LA42	5300	36	B2
GRADE AV	LA	SF	13000	3	A3
GRADWELL ST	LKD	LKD	11300	71	F4
GRADWELL ST	LKD	LKD	12400	81	B4
GRADWELL ST	LKD	LKD	12600	81	C4
GRADY AV	CO	WHI	7900	55	D6
GRAFF DR	LAM	LAM	12700	61	F6
GRAFTON ST	LA	LA26	1600	35	C5
GRAGMONT ST	CO	COV	16700	88	C3
GRAGMONT ST	COV	COV	500	88	D3
GRAHAM AV	CO	LA01	7200	52	D6
GRAHAM AV	CO	LA01	8400	58	D3
GRAHAM AV	CO	LA02	8600	58	D3
GRAHAM AV	COM	COM		64	D1
GRAHAM AV	LA	LA02	9200	58	D3
GRAHAM AV	LA	LA59	11100	58	D4
GRAHAM AV	RB	RB	1900	62	E5
GRAHAM PL	BUR	BUR	100	24	E1
GRAHAM PL	GLEN	GL01	900	24	E1
GRAHAM PL	LA	LA64	11200	41	E5
GRAHAM ACCSS RD	IRW	BAP		39	C2
GRAIGLEE CIR	WCOV	WCOV		93	A1
GRAJUELO DR	SCLR	VAL		124	B7
GRAMERCY AV	TOR	TOR	1400	68	D4
GRAMERCY DR	LA	LA05	700	43	D2
GRAMERCY DR	LA	LA19	900	43	D2
GRAMERCY PL	GAR	GAR	12900	63	D1
GRAMERCY PL	TOR	TOR	16900	63	D5
GRAMERCY PL	TOR	TOR	18500	68	D1
GRAMERCY PL N	LA	LA04	100	34	D6
GRAMERCY PL N	LA	LA28	1700	34	D3
GRAMERCY PL N	LA	LA38	700	34	D5
GRAMERCY PL N	LA	LA68	1900	34	D3
GRAMERCY PL S	CO	LA47	10800	57	D4
GRAMERCY PL S	LA	LA04	100	34	D6
GRAMERCY PL S	LA	LA04	200	43	D1
GRAMERCY PL S	LA	LA05	600	43	D1
GRAMERCY PL S	LA	LA18	1900	43	D3
GRAMERCY PL S	LA	LA19	900	43	D3
GRAMERCY PL S	LA	LA20	300	43	D1
GRAMERCY PL S	LA	LA47	5800	51	D6
GRAMERCY PL S	LA	LA47	8000	57	D2
GRAMERCY PL S	LA	LA62	3800	51	D1
GRAMERCY PK	LA	LA18	2400	43	D5
GRAMERCY PK E	LA	LA18	2400	43	D5
GRAMERCY ST	POM	POM	2800	90	E3
GRAMMAR PL	LA	VAN	14100	8	E6
GRAMMONT AV	COV	COV	4600	89	C3
GRAMMONT PL	GLDR	GLDR	1600	89	C2
GRANADA AV	ELM	ELM	3400	38	D6
GRANADA AV	ELM	ELM	2900	47	D1
GRANADA AV	LAM	LAM	15000	84	B5
GRANADA AV	LB	LB03	100	76	B6
GRANADA AV	LB	LB04	1300	76	B4
GRANADA AV	LB	LB14	300	76	B6
GRANADA AV	LB	LB15	2200	76	B2
GRANADA AV	SELM	ELM	2200	47	D3
GRANADA AV	SMAR	PAS	700	37	C2
GRANADA AV N	ALH	ALH	100	37	C3
GRANADA AV S	ALH	ALH	100	37	C3
GRANADA CIR	LA	NOR		1	B5
GRANADA CT	LA	VEN	200	49	C4
GRANADA CT	LB	LB07		70	C5
GRANADA DR	MPK	MPK		45	E3
GRANADA DR	PALM	LAN		171	A2
GRANADA PL	PAS	PAS	100	26	F2
GRANADA PL	POM	POM	1600	95	B1
GRANADA ST	GLEN	GL05	500	25	D5
GRANADA ST	LA	LA42	4800	36	B2
GRANADA ST	LA	LA65	2600	35	E4
GRAND AV	BLF	BLF	16200	66	D4
GRAND AV	CLA	CLA	3300	96	C6
GRAND AV	CO	COV	3200	89	A6
GRAND AV	CO	COV	2500	93	A2
GRAND AV	CO	HPK	2400	52	F6
GRAND AV	CO	HPK	2800	53	B6
GRAND AV	DBAR	POM		97	F2
GRAND AV	DBAR	POM		97A	A2
GRAND AV	HPK	HPK	3200	53	B6
GRAND AV	IND	WAL		97	F2
GRAND AV	LA	ELS		55A	F6
GRAND AV	LB	LB03	100	76	A6
GRAND AV	LB	LB04	800	76	A4
GRAND AV	LB	LB14	300	76	A6
GRAND AV	LB	LB15	2200	76	A2
GRAND AV	LCF	LCF	4500	19	B3
GRAND AV	MON	MON	100	29	B3
GRAND AV	RM	RM	8300	37	F4
GRAND AV	RM	RM	8700	38	A4
GRAND AV	SPAS	SPAS	200	36	E1
GRAND AV	TEC	TEC	10700	38	E3
GRAND AV	WAL	WAL	1400	93	B3
GRAND AV E	ALH	ALH	100	37	B3
GRAND AV E	ELS	ELS	100	56	A6
GRAND AV E	POM	POM	100	94	D4
GRAND AV E	POM	POM	1000	95	B4
GRAND AV E	SGAB	SGAB	100	37	E4
GRAND AV N	COV	COV	100	89	A6
GRAND AV N	GLDR	GLDR	100	87	A6
GRAND AV N	LA	LA12	1200	44	C4
GRAND AV N	LA	SP	100	78	F2
GRAND AV N	PAS	PAS	100	26	E3
GRAND AV N	WCOV	WCOV	100	93	A1
GRAND AV S	COV	COV	100	89	A6
GRAND AV S	GLDR	GLDR	100	87	A6
GRAND AV S	GLDR	GLDR	800	89	A2
GRAND AV S	LA	LA03	10000	58	A4
GRAND AV S	LA	LA07	1900	44	B5
GRAND AV S	LA	LA07	3500	52	A1
GRAND AV S	LA	LA12	100	44	C4
GRAND AV S	LA	LA15	900	44	C4
GRAND AV S	LA	LA17	300	44	C4
GRAND AV S	LA	LA37	3800	52	A1
GRAND AV S	LA	LA61	10700	58	A4
GRAND AV S	LA	SP	100	78	F4
GRAND AV S	PAS	PAS	100	26	E6
GRAND AV S	WCOV	WCOV	100	93	A1
GRAND AV W	ALH	ALH	2400	36	F3
GRAND AV W	ALH	ALH	100	37	B3
GRAND AV W	ELS	ELS	100	56	A6
GRAND AV W	POM	POM	100	94	D4
GRAND AV W	SGAB	SGAB	300	37	D4
GRAND BLVD	CO	MAL		113	E5
GRAND BLVD	LA	VEN	200	49	C4
GRANDA LN	LAV	LAV		90	D1
GRAND CANAL	LA	VEN	2200	49	C4
GRAND CANAL CT	LA	VEN		49	B6
GRAND CENTRL AV	GLEN	GL01	1400	24	F2
GRAND CENTRL AV	GLEN	GL01	900	25	A2
GRANDEE AV	CAR	CAR	19000	69	E1
GRANDEE AV	CO	COM	12300	58	D6
GRANDEE AV	CO	LA59	12100	58	D6
GRANDEE AV	LA	LA02	9500	58	D4
GRANDEE AV	LA	LA59	11400	58	D5
GRANDEE AV N	COM	COM	2600	58	D6
GRANDEE AV N	COM	COM	600	64	D2
GRANDEE AV S	COM	COM	900	64	D4
GRANDEUR AV	CO	ALT	2200	19	F4
GRANDEUR DR	LA	SP	2100	78	D4
GRANDE VISTA AV	LA	LA23	600	45	B5
GRANDE VISTA AV	LA	LA23	1600	53	B1
GRANDE VISTA AV	LA	LA63	400	45	B5
GRANDE VISTA DR	WHI	WHI		55	D2
GRANDE VISTA PL	WHI	WHI		55	D2
GRANDEZA ST	MPK	MPK	400	45	F2
GRANDIFLORAS RD	CO	CYN	14800	125	F5
GRANDIN AV	AZU	AZU	300	88	C2
GRAND OAKS AV	CO	ALT	1680	20	E6
GRAND OAKS AV N	CO	PAS	1300	27	E1
GRAND OAKS AV N	PAS	PAS	1	27	D5
GRAND OAKS AV S	CO	PAS	200	27	D5
GRAND OAKS AV S	PAS	PAS	1	27	D5
GRANDOAKS DR	WLVL	THO		102A	E5
GRANDOLA AV	LA	LA41	1500	26	B5
GRANDPARK AV	LAN	LAN		159	A5
GRANDPOINT LN	RPV	PVP	2800	78	C2
GRANDRIDGE AV	MPK	MPK	500	46	B4
GRANDRIDGE PL	MPK	MPK	400	46	B4
GRAND RIM CT	DBAR	POM		97A	A2
GRAND SUMMIT RD	TOR	TOR	2400	73	B3
GRANDVIEW	CO	CHA		4	C5
GRANDVIEW AV	CO	RM	1000	46	F4
GRANDVIEW AV	GLEN	GL01	1500	18	A6
GRANDVIEW AV	GLEN	GL01	700	25	A2
GRANDVIEW AV	LA	VEN	2300	49	D3
GRANDVIEW AV	MB	MB	2100	62	A2
GRANDVIEW AV	MTB	MTB	1500	46	D6
GRAND VIEW AV E	ARC	ARC		28	E1
GRANDVIEW AV E	SMAD	SMAD	100	28	B1
GRANDVIEW AV N	COV	COV	700	88	F4
GRANDVIEW AV S	COV	COV	100	88	F5
GRAND VIEW AV W	ARC	ARC	2	28	E1
GRANDVIEW AV W	SMAD	SMAD	100	28	B1
GRAND VIEW BLVD	CUL	LA66	3900	49	E1
GRAND VIEW BLVD	LA	LA66	3000	49	E1
GRAND VIEW BLVD	LA	LA66	4200	50	A3
GRAND VIEW DR	ALH	ALH	1500	36	F6
GRANDVIEW DR	AZU	AZU	200	88	C1
GRAND VIEW DR	CO	TOP	500	109	C6
GRANDVIEW DR	CO	VAL		124	A6
GRANDVIEW DR	LA	LA46	4200	33	E3
GRANDVIEW DR	PALM	PALM		171	D4
GRANDVIEW LN	WCOV	WCOV		92	B5
GRAND VIEW ST	LA	LA06	900	44	A2
GRAND VIEW ST	LA	LA57	200	44	A2
GRANDVIEW ST	PAS	PAS	100	27	A1
GRANDVIEW TR	CO	SF	11300	3	D5
GRAND VISTA PL	MPK	MPK	1200	46	A3
GRAND VISTA WY	MPK	MPK	1200	46	A3
GRANGE ST	GLEN	GL02	800	25	A3
GRANGEMOUNT RD	GLEN	GL06		19	B6
GRANGER AV	BG	BELL	6600	54	A6
GRANGER PL	LA	NOR	11000	7	A1
GRANITE AV	MON	MON	400	29	B2
GRANITE DR	PAS	PAS	800	27	B5
GRANITE WELS DR	WAL	WAL		93	C3
GRANITO DR	LA	LA46		33	F3
GRANO AV	SCLR	SAU	27200	124	D6
GRANT AV	CUL	CUL	10100	42	C6
GRANT AV	DOW	DOW	13100	65	F1
GRANT AV	GLEN	GL02	800	25	B3
GRANT AV	LA	VEN	1100	49	D4
GRANT AV	RB	RB	1700	62	D6
GRANT AV	TOR	TOR	21300	67	F4
GRANT CT	PALM	PALM		184	D4
GRANT PL	LAV	LAV		90	C1
GRANT PL	SM	SM	1100	49	B1
GRANT ST	LYN	LYN	11100	58	F4
GRANT ST	MPK	MPK	1700	46	C3
GRANT ST	SH	LB04	3200	75	F3
GRANT ST	SM	SM	600	49	B2
GRANT ST E	LA	WIL	600	74	C4
GRANT ST W	LA	WIL	1200	74	A4
GRANTLAND DR	AZU	AZU	400	88	E2
GRANTLAND DR	CO	COV	5300	88	E2
GRANVIA ALTAMRA	PVE	PVP	900	72	C4
GRANVIA ALTAMRA	RPV	PVP	27900	72	D4
GRANVILLE AV	LA	LA25	1200	41	D4
GRANVILLE AV	LA	LA49	100	41	C3
GRANVILLE AV	LA	LA64	2200	41	E5
GRANVILLE AV	LA	LA66	3000	41	E6
GRANVILLE AV	LA	LA66	3200	49	E1
GRAPE AV	COM	COM	1600	64	E1
GRAPE CIR	COM	COM		64	E3
GRAPE PL	LA	LA68	6300	34	C1
GRAPE ST	CO	LA01	8300	58	E2
GRAPE ST	CO	LA02	8600	58	E2
GRAPE ST	LA	LA02	9200	58	E4
GRAPE ST	LA	LA59	10700	58	E5
GRAPE ST	LYN	LYN		59	A5
GRAPE ST	PR	PR	4600	54	F2
GRAPEVINE DR	DBAR	POM	23900	94	A6
GRAPEVINE FR RD	CO	NEW		127	F8
GRAPHIC AV	CO	LAN	44400	161	G4
GRAPHIC AV	CO	PALM	36800	184	G2
GRASS DR	PALM	PALM	1100	171	J8
GRASS DR	PALM	PALM		172	A8
GRASSCREEK DR	SAD	SAD	1600	95A	B6
GRASSMERE AV	CO	LPUE		98	F2
GRASSWOOD AV	CO	MAL	6900	110	C5
GRASSY AV	LPUE	LPUE		98	B1
GRATIAN ST	CO	LA22	4300	45	E5
GRATIOT ST	LA	LA32	2200	36	D6
GRATTAN ST	LA	LA15	900	44	B3
GRAVELIA ST	CO	ALT	1100	19	E2
GRAVELY CT	HB	RB	500	67	D1
GRAVES AV	LA	ENC	5600	14	E6
GRAVES AV	LA	ENC	5600	21	E1
GRAVES AV	LA	VAN	6400	14	E5
GRAVES AV	RM	RM	7400	46	C2
GRAVES AV E	MPK	MPK	100	46	C2
GRAVES AV W	MPK	MPK	100	46	B2
GRAVINA ST	CO	LPUE	19400	97	A4
GRAVINO RD	SCLR	VAL		127	B1
GRAVOIS AV	CO	LA63	1500	45	D2
GRAVOIS AV	LA	LA32	5200	45	E1
GRAYBURN AV	LA	LA08	3800	51	C1
GRAYBURN AV	LA	LA18	3600	51	C1
GRAYBURN RD	CO	PAS	3300	28	A4
GRAYBURN ST	POM	POM	2800	90	E3
GRAYCASTLE AV	MTB	MTB		46	E4
GRAYDON AV	CO	MON	1900	29	A6
GRAYDON AV	CO	MON	2400	39	A1
GRAYFOX ST	CO	MAL	28700	110	C5
GRAYLAND AV	ART	ART	18600	81	B1
GRAYLAND AV	ART	ART	17400	82	B6
GRAYLAND AV	CER	ART	19900	81	B2
GRAYLAND AV	CER	ART	17100	82	B5
GRAYLAND AV	NWK	NWK	14300	82	B2
GRAYLING AV	CO	WHI	11500	84	D6
GRAYLING AV	LAM	LAM	12600	84	D6
GRAYLING AV	WHI	WHI	10100	84	D3
GRAYLOCK AV	MPK	MPK	1800	46	B4
GRAYLOG ST	RPV	PVP	5500	72	E3
GRAYMOUTH LN	CO	TOR		68	F5
GRAYNOLD AV	GLEN	GL02	800	25	A2
GRAYRIDGE DR	CUL	CUL	11200	50	C4
GRAYSBY AV	LA	SP	2500	78	D5
GRAYSLAKE RD	RPV	PVP	26100	72	D3
GRAYSON AV	LA	VEN	2800	49	C5
GRAYSTONE AV	CER	ART	17400	66	F5
GRAYSTONE AV	CO	ART	16600	66	F5
GRAYSTONE AV	NWK	NWK	11700	60	F6
GRAYSTONE AV	NWK	NWK	12800	66	F1
GRAYSTONE DR	LA	CP04		5	D2
GRAYSTONE ST	LA	SUN	8000	10	E2
GRAYVILLE DR	LAM	LAM	14200	61	F6
GRAYVILLE DR	LAM	LAM	14700	84	A6
GRAYWOOD AV	LB	LB08	4300	71	B4
GRAYWOOD AV	LKD	LKD	6000	66	B6
GRAYWOOD AV	LKD	LKD	4900	71	B2
GREAT BEND DR	DBAR	POM		97	F1
GREAT LAKES AV	CO	LAN	16200	174	J2
GREAT LAKES AV	CO	LAN	16600	175	A2
GREAT OAK CIR	LA	LA42	5900	26	C6
GREAT WESTRN DR	CO	LAN	3000	147	E8
GREELEY CT	SAD	SAD		90	A2
GREELEY ST	LA	TU	7100	10	F4
GREELEY ST	LA	TU	6600	11	A4
GREEN AV	LA	LA17	800	44	B3
GREEN CT	LA	LA66	3700	49	E2
GREEN DR	IND	LPUE	17000	98	B2
GREEN LN	LCF	LCF	800	19	B2
GREEN LN	RB	RB	800	67	E1
GREEN ST	GLEN	GL05	800	25	D5
GREEN ST	TEC	TEC	10000	38	C3
GREEN ST E	CLA	CLA	100	91	B4
GREEN ST E	CO	PAS	3000	27	F4
GREEN ST E	CO	PAS	3400	28	A4
GREEN ST E	PAS	PAS	100	27	B4
GREEN ST W	CLA	CLA	100	91	B4
GREEN ST W	PAS	PAS	100	26	E4
GREENACRE AV	WHOL	LA46	1100	34	A4
GREENACRE RD	POM	POM	1800	94	B1
GREEN ACRES DR	BH	BH		32	F5
GREEN ACRES DR	BH	BH		33	A4
GREENBANK AV	DUA	DUA	200	86	A4
GREENBAY DR	CO	LPUE	18500	98	E3
GREENBERRY AV	CO	COV	3900	88	B5
GREENBERRY AV N	WCOV	WCOV	700	88	B5
GREENBERRY DR	CO	LPUE	700	48	E4
GREENBERRY DR	LPUE	LPUE	300	48	D5
GREENBERRY DR S	WCOV	WCOV	700	92	A2
GREENBLUFF DR	CO	TOP		109	C5
GREENBOROUGH PL	WCOV	WCOV		92	D6
GREENBRIAR CT	AGH	AGO		100A	A2
GREENBRIAR CT	AGH	AGO		102	F2
GREENBRIAR DR	LA	TAR	19600	13	F4
GREENBRIAR DR	LA	TAR	19300	21	A3
GREENBRIAR LN	LPUE	LPUE		48	F6
GREENBRIAR PL	WCOV	WCOV		92	D6
GREENBRIAR RD	GLEN	GL07	1700	25	D1
GREENBRIER AV	BLF	BLF	13400	66	B2
GREENBRIER DR	CO	LPUE		48	B5
GREENBRIER RD	LB	LB08	3000	71	B6
GREENBRIER RD	LB	LB15	1300	76	B4
GREENBROOK CIR	CER	ART	16600	82	C4
GREENBROOK DR	WAL	WAL		93	D6
GREENBROOK LN	PALM	PALM		183	H7
GREENBURN AV	LA	SUN	10500	10	E3
GREENBUSH AV	CO	WHI		84	B4
GREENBUSH AV	LA	NHO	7300	15	F3
GREENBUSH AV	LA	PAC	8800	8	E5
GREENBUSH AV	LA	VAN	5600	15	F6
GREENBUSH AV	LA	VAN		16	A1
GREENBUSH AV	LA	VAN	4100	22	F4
GREENCASTLE AV	CO	LPUE	1500	98	E3
GREEN CIRCLE LN	AGH	AGO		100A	C5
GREEN COACH RD	CO	LPUE	16400	98	A3
GREENCOURT DR	CO	CYN		125	G5
GREENCRAIG RD	LA	LA49	400	41	B1
GREENCREST	PALM	PALM		171	C3
GREENCREST RD	LCF	LCF	5100	19	C2

1990 LOS ANGELES COUNTY STREET INDEX

STREET	CITY	P.O. ZONE	BLOCK	PAGE	GRID
GREENCROFT AV	GLDR	GLDR	100	87	E5
GREENDALE AV	RM	RM	3700	38	A6
GREENDALE AV	RM	RM	3200	47	A1
GREENDALE DR	CO	LPUE		48	B4
GREENDALE DR	LA	LA77	10300	32	E4
GREENDALE LN	POM	POM	600	90	F2
GREENDALE ST	COV	COV	17800	88	D6
GREENDALE ST E	WCOV	WCOV	1000	88	B6
GREENDALE ST W	WCOV	WCOV	1000	88	B6
GREEN DOERR DR	CO	SAU		181	C9
GREENE AV	LA	LA66	12400	49	F4
GREENE AV	LA	LA66	12200	50	A3
GREENFIELD AV	ARC	ARC	1000	28	E6
GREENFIELD AV	ARC	ARC	2000	38	E2
GREENFIELD AV	LA	LA25	1400	41	E3
GREENFIELD AV	LA	LA34	3000	42	A6
GREENFIELD AV	LA	LA34	3600	50	A1
GREENFIELD AV	LA	LA49	100	32	D6
GREENFIELD AV	LA	LA64	2200	41	F4
GREENFIELD AV S	ARC	ARC	1000	28	E6
GREENFIELD AV S	ARC	ARC	2200	38	E2
GREENFIELD CT	GLDR	GLDR		89	B2
GREENFIELD PL	ARC	ARC	100	28	E6
GREEN GABLES DR	LA	TAR		21	A4
GREENGATE CT	WLVL	THO	4500	102	B4
GREENGATE DR	CO	LPUE		98	E3
GREENGLADE AV	PR	PR	3300	47	C6
GREEN GRASS CT	AGH	AGO		102	F3
GREENGROVE DR	GLEN	GL06		26	A4
GREENHAVEN ST	CO	COV	16600	88	C3
GREENHAVEN ST	CO	COV	19400	89	A3
GREENHAVEN ST	SAD	SAD	1100	89	C3
GREENHAVEN ST E	COV	COV		89	C3
GREENHAVEN ST W	COV	COV	900	88	D3
GREENHEDGE ST	CO	TOR	600	68	E3
GREEN HILL DR	CO	CAST		123	G2
GREENHILL RD	PAS	PAS	3300	28	A3
GREENHORN DR	DBAR	POM		93	F5
GREENHURST ST	BLF	BLF	10200	66	D2
GREENING AV	CO	WHI	9400	61	D2
GREENLAKE LN	CER	ART		82	B4
GREENLAWN AV	LA	CUL	11000	50	B2
GREENLEAF AV	CO	WHI		61	C3
GREENLEAF AV	SFS	SFS	9800	61	C3
GREENLEAF AV	WHI	WHI	5500	55	E6
GREENLEAF AV	WHI	WHI	8200	61	D1
GREENLEAF BL E	COM	COM	100	64	D4
GREENLEAF BL W	COM	COM	100	65	B4
GREENLEAF CT	WCOV	WCOV		92	E6
GREENLEAF DR	COM	COM	100	64	E4
GREENLEAF DR	WCOV	WCOV		92	D5
GREENLEAF PL	POM	POM		94	E6
GREENLEAF PL	POM	POM		97A	C1
GREENLEAF ST	LA	ENC	16500	21	F3
GREENLEAF ST	LA	ENC	15700	22	C3
GREENLEAF ST	LA	NHO	12900	23	A4
GREENLEAF ST	LA	VAN	14100	22	C3
GREENLEAF ST	WCOV	WCOV		92	D6
GREENLEAF CY RD	CO	TOP		13	B5
GREENLEAF CY RD	CO	TOP		109	B1
GREEN MEADOW DR	AGH	AGO		102	E2
GREEN MEADOW DR	LA	ENC		21	C4
GREENMEADOW RD	LB	LB08	4400	71	B4
GREENMEADOW RD	LKD	LKD	2700	70	F4
GREENMEADOW RD	LKD	LKD	6000	71	D4
GREEN MDWS AV	TOR	TOR	4400	72	F1
GREEN MDWS ST	TOR	TOR		67	E6
GREEN MILL AV	SCLR	NEW	24400	127	B4
GREENMONT DR	GLEN	GL08	1300	18	E4
GREEN MTN DR	SCLR	NEW		127	H2
GREEN OAK DR	LA	LA68	5500	34	D1
GREEN OAK LN	GLDR	GLDR		87	B3
GREEN OAK PL	LA	LA68	2600	34	D1
GREENOAKS DR	ARC	ARC		28	B3
GREENOCK LN	LA	LA49	12100	41	B1
GREENPARK AV	CO	COV	5000	89	B3
GREENPARK AV	COV	COV	600	89	B4
GREENPORT AV	CO	LPUE	1500	98	E3
GREENRIDGE DR	LA	BH	1400	33	A3
GREENRIDGE DR	LCF	LCF		19	C1
GREENRIDGE TER	CO	LPUE		48	B5
GREEN RIDGE TER	WCOV	WCOV		92	E4
GREENRIDGE WY	CO	VAL		124	F2
GREENRIVER RD	WAL	WAL		93	B5
GREENROCK AV E	CO	LAN	15100	174	G2
GREENSBORO CT	CLA	CLA	400	91	C2
GREENSIDE DR	DBAR	WAL		97	C3
GREENSLEEVES CT	SCLR	SAU		124	E7
GREEN SPRING LN	CO	LPUE		98	A4
GREENSTONE AV	NWK	NWK	13200	82	C2
GREENSTONE AV	SFS	SFS		61	C5
GREENSWARD RD	LA	LA39	3400	35	C2
GREEN TER DR	SCLR	NEW		127	G1
GREENTOP ST E	LKD	LKD	2400	70	F3
GREENTOP ST E	LKD	LKD	5900	71	D4
GREENTREE CT	LA	LA77		22	D6
GREEN TREE LN	TEC	TEC	11000	38	E3
GREENTREE RD	LA	PP	700	40	D4
GREENVALE AV	PR	PR	8100	60	F2
GREEN VLY CIR	CUL	CUL		50	D5
GREEN VALLEY RD	LA	LA46	2400	33	D1
GREENVALLEY TER	LA	PAC		3	C6
GRN VERDUGO DR	LA	SUN	9500	10	B3
GRN VERDGO F RD	LA	SUN		10	D4
GREENVIEW DR	GLDR	GLDR		87	E6
GREEN VIEW LN	LAV	LAV		95A	D5
GREEN VIEW PL	LA	LA46	2400	33	D1
GREENVIEW RD	CO	CAL		100	A2
GREENVIEW RD	LHH	LAH	400	84	F1
GREENVIEW TER	CO	LPUE		48	B5
GREENVILLE DR	WCOV	WCOV	600	92	B3
GREEN VISTA CIR	LA	CAN	7000	5	E4
GREEN VISTA DR	LA	ENC	3700	21	F5
GREENWATER RD	CO	MAL	29200	110	B5
GREENWAY DR	BH	BH	800	33	A6
GREENWAY ST N	LB	LB03		76	D5
GREENWAY ST S	LB	LB03		76	D5
GREENWELL ST	BLF	BLF	9300	66	B3
GREENWICH CT	DBAR	POM		97A	B2
GREENWICH CT	PALM	PALM		183	F1
GREENWICH RD	GLEN	GL06	2800	26	B2
GREENWICH VLG	HB	RB	2600	62	B5
GREENWILLOW LN	CO	LPUE		97	A5
GREENWOOD AV	BG	BELL	6300	54	B6
GREENWOOD AV	CMRC	LA40	3500	54	B5
GREENWOOD AV	CO	SGAB	8700	28	A6
GREENWOOD AV	LA	LA66	3500	49	E2
GREENWOOD AV	MPK	MPK		46	D4
GREENWOOD AV	TOR	TOR	1200	68	C4
GREENWOOD AV	TOR	TOR	22500	68	B6
GREENWOOD AV N	MTB	MTB	100	54	C3
GREENWOOD AV N	PAS	PAS	100	27	D4
GREENWOOD AV S	MTB	MTB	100	54	C3
GREENWOOD AV S	PAS	PAS	100	27	D4
GREENWOOD AV S	SMAR	PAS	500	27	D5
GREENWOOD PL	CO	CAST		123	C1
GREENWOOD PL	LA	LA27	4600	34	F2
GREENWORTH DR	LAM	LAM	14500	82	F1
GREENWORTH DR	LAM	LAM	14600	83	A1
GREER AV	CO	COV	5000	89	C3
GREER AV	COV	COV	300	89	C4
GREER AV	GLDR	GLDR	1400	89	C2
GREER RD	LA	WOH	4200	13	A3
GREER ST	LB	LB05		65	E4
GREG AV	LA	SV	7500	17	A2
GREGG RD	PR	PR	4800	55	B3
GREGORIO DR	CO	LPUE	16300	85	F3
GREGORY AV	LA	LA38	6100	34	C4
GREGORY AV	PALM	PALM		183	F1
GREGORY AV	WHI	WHI	5500	55	D5
GREGORY LN	SCLR	CYN		124	G9
GREGORY LN	SCLR	SAU		124	G9
GREGORY WY	BH	BH	8300	42	D1
GRENADA CT	MB	MB		62	D3
GRENADIER DR	LA	SP	1900	78	D4
GRENOBLE AV	WCOV	WCOV		92	D4
GRENOBLE ST	LA	SUN	8200	10	D3
GRENOBLE ST	LA	TU	6800	11	A3
GRENOLA ST	LA	PP	300	40	B4
GRENORA WY	LB	LB15	4000	76	A3
GRENVILLE CT	WLVL	THO	32000	102	A4
GRESHAM PL	LA	CAN	8800	6	C6
GRESHAM ST	LA	CAN	20100	6	E6
GRESHAM ST	LA	NOR	17000	7	E6
GRESHAM ST	LA	SF	16600	7	F6
GRESHAM ST	SF	SF	15200	8	C6
GRETCHEN PL	POM	POM	100	94	A2
GRETCHEN ST	LA	CAN	20800	12	D4
GRETNA AV	CO	WHI	6600	55	C6
GRETNA AV	WHI	WHI	6200	55	C4
GRETNA GREEN WY	LA	LA49	100	41	B2
GRETTA AV	CO	LPUE	900	92	C3
GRETTA AV	WCOV	WCOV	500	92	C2
GREVE DR	RPV	PVP	3600	78	B2
GREVELIA ST	SPAS	SPAS	800	36	F1
GREVELIA ST	SPAS	SPAS	1400	37	A1
GREVILLEA AV	CO	IN04	10100	57	A4
GREVILLEA AV	HAW	HAW	11100	57	A6
GREVILLEA AV	HAW	HAW	13800	62	F2
GREVILLEA AV	LAW	LAW	14300	63	A3
GREVILLEA AV	TOR	TOR	18200	63	A6
GREVILLEA AV	TOR	TOR	20000	68	A2
GREVILLEA AV N	ING	IN01	100	57	A3
GREVILLEA AV S	ING	IN01	100	57	A3
GREVILLIA ST E	POM	POM	100	90	E4
GREVILLIA ST W	POM	POM	100	90	E4
GREY DR	LA	LA32	4600	36	D5
GREYCLIFF AV	CO	LPUE	1000	92	A4
GREYCLIFF AV	LPUE	LPUE	600	92	A5
GREYCLOUD LN	DBAR	POM		94	B5
GREYCREST PL	DBAR	POM		97A	B3
GREYDALE AV	CO	PALM	36400	184	F4
GREYDALE AV	GLEN	GL03	700	25	B3
GREYFIELD LN	DBAR	POM		99	D4
GREYFORD ST	CO	WHI	10800	55	C6
GREY FOX RD	WAL	WAL		93	A6
GREYHALL ST	CO	LPUE		97	A4
GREY ROCK RD	AGH	AGO		102	F3
GREY STLLN RD E	CO	LAN	15200	174	G3
GREYSTONE AV E	MON	MON	100	29	B3
GREYSTONE AV W	MON	MON	100	29	B3
GREYSTONE CT	SAD	COV		89	D4
GRIDER AV	HAW	HAW	13300	62	E2
GRIDLEY PL	CER	ART	16700	66	F5
GRIDLEY RD	ART	ART	16900	66	F6
GRIDLEY RD	CER	ART	16700	66	F6
GRIDLEY RD	CER	ART	18700	71	F2
GRIDLEY RD	CO	ART	16600	66	F6
GRIDLEY RD	LKD	LKD	20700	71	F3
GRIDLEY RD	NWK	NWK	11900	60	F6
GRIDLEY RD	NWK	NWK	12800	66	F2
GRIDLEY RD	SFS	SFS	10100	60	F4
GRIDLEY ST	LA	SF	13300	2	F4
GRIDLEY ST	LA	SF	12400	3	A3
GRIER ST W	POM	POM	1700	94	B3
GRIFFIN AV	LA	LA31	2300	36	B4
GRIFFIN AV	LA	LA31	1700	45	A2
GRIFFITH AV	LA	LA11	1900	44	C6
GRIFFITH AV	LA	LA11	2600	52	C1
GRIFFITH AV	LA	LA21	1400	44	C6
GRIFFITH LN	WHI	WHI		55	E6
GRIFFITH ST	CAR	GAR	100	69	A1
GRIFFITH ST	SF	SF	700	2	D6
GRIFFITH ST	SF	SF	600	8	E1
GRIFFITH PK BL	LA	LA26	1500	35	B2
GRIFFITH PK BL	LA	LA27	2700	35	B2
GRIFFITH PK BL	LA	LA39	1900	35	B2
GRIFFITH PK DR	LA	LA27		24	E3
GRIFFITH PK DR	LA	LA27		25	A5
GRIFFITH PK DR	LA	LA27		35	B1
GRIFFTH PK DR N	BUR	BUR	500	17	C5
GRIFFTH PK DR N	BUR	BUR	100	24	D1
GRIFFTH PK DR S	BUR	BUR	100	24	D2
GRIFFITHS AV	CO	LPUE	1400	48	F3
GRIFFITHS AV	CO	LPUE	1400	92	A4
GRIFFITH VW DR	LA	LA39	3700	35	B1
GRIMES PL	LA	ENC	4200	21	C3
GRIMKE WK	LA	LA42	6100	36	C1
GRIMSBY AV	LA	LA45	8100	56	D1
GRINNELL DR	BUR	BUR	200	17	D5
GRINNELL DR	CLA	CLA	400	91	B4
GRISCOM DR	CO	SAU		181	G8
GRISHAM AV	LB	LB05	4600	70	C3
GRISMER AV	BUR	BUR	1500	17	C4
GRISWOLD AV	SF	SF	300	2	F6
GRISWOLD AV	SF	SF	900	3	A5
GRISWOLD RD	CO	COV	17700	88	D4
GRISWOLD RD	COV	COV	1000	88	D4
GRISWOLD ST	GLEN	GL05	300	25	E4
GRZLY FLTS TKTR	CO			M	C3
GROFF ST	POM	POM	800	94	D1
GROMER TER	GLEN	GL14	3400	11	C4
GRONDAHL ST	COV	COV	18000	88	E3
GROOM DR	DBAR	POM		93	F5
GROSS AV	LA	CAN	6300	5	E4
GROSSMONT DR	CO	WHI	900	48	A4
GROSVENOR BLVD	CO	LA66	5400	50	A5
GROSVENOR ST	ING	IN02	100	50	F6
GROTON DR	BUR	BUR	400	17	C3
GROUSE RD	CO	MAL		112	A1
GROVE AL	SMAD	SMAD		28	B1
GROVE LN	LAN	LAN		159	H5
GROVE LN	SMAD	SMAD	1	28	B2
GROVE PL	CO	LPUE		48	B5
GROVE PL	GLEN	GL06	400	25	E3
GROVE ST	LA	SUN	7800	10	D1
GROVE ST	LA	TU	7600	10	E1
GROVE ST	LAV	LAV	2600	90	E3
GROVE ST	SMAD	SMAD	100	28	B2
GROVE ST E	POM	POM	100	90	E3
GROVE ST W	POM	POM	100	90	E3
GROVECENTER ST	CO	COV	15600	88	A5
GROVECENTER ST	CO	COV	19300	89	A5
GROVECENTER ST	COV	COV	300	88	F5
GROVECENTER ST	COV	COV	1400	89	B5
GROVECENTER ST	WCOV	WCOV	1000	88	B5
GROVEDALE DR	CO	WHI	11300	84	C5
GROVEDALE DR	LAM	LAM	12600	84	C6
GROVEDALE DR	WHI	WHI	9800	84	C4
GROVEHILL LN	LAM	LAM	15300	84	B6
GROVELAND AV	CO	WHI	11300	84	C5
GROVELAND AV	WHI	WHI	10100	84	C4
GROVELAND DR	LA	LA46	2100	33	E2
GROVELAND LN	LCF	LCF	4700	19	B3
GROVEOAK PL	RPV	PVP	5900	72	D3
GROVEPARK DR	SCLR	SAU		124	E5
GROVER AV	GLEN	GL01	1000	25	A2
GROVERDALE ST	CO	COV	16700	88	C3
GROVERDALE ST	CO	COV	19400	89	A3
GROVERDALE ST	COV	COV	1300	88	D3
GROVERTON PL	LA	LA77	100	32	D6
GROVESIDE AV	CO	WHI	11300	84	C5
GROVESIDE AV	LAM	LAM	12600	84	C6
GROVESIDE AV	WHI	WHI	10100	84	C4
GROVESIDE PL	POM	POM	1300	94	B1
GROVESPRING DR	RPV	PVP	6900	72	C5
GROVETON AV	GLDR	GLDR		87	E6
GROVETON AV	SAD	SAD	700	89	E2
GROVETREE AV	DOW	DOW	12600	59	F5
GROVEVIEW LN	LCF	LCF	500	19	C3
GRUBSTAKE DR	DBAR	POM		97A	A2
GRUEN LN	POM	POM	100	90	E3
GRUEN ST	LA	PAC	13900	8	E4
GRUEN ST	LA	PAC	12400	9	B1
GRUEN ST	LA	SF	11700	3	C6
GRUNDY LN	CO	CHA		4	B5
GUACHO AV	CO	LAN	15800	174	J7
GUADALAJARA CIR	CER	ART		82	C6
GUADALAJARA PL	CLA	CLA		91	C2
GUADALUPE AV N	RB	RB	100	67	C2
GUADALUPE AV S	RB	RB	100	67	D3
GUADILAMAR DR	SCLR	SAU	22500	124	C5
GUANAJUATO DR	CLA	CLA	1000	96	A6
GUARDIA AV	LA	LA32	3900	36	E4
GUATEMALA AV	DOW	DOW		54	C6
GUATEMALA AV	DOW	DOW		60	B1
GUAVA PL	GLEN	GL06		26	B1
GUAVA ST	LAV	LAV		90	E2
GUERIN ST	LA	NHO	12000	23	C4
GUERNSEY AV	CO	MAL	6400	111	E5
GUESS ST	RM	RM	8500	38	A5
GUEST DR	ALH	ALH	2200	46	B1
GUILD DR	PR	PR	6500	54	E4
GUILDFORD LN	LA	NOR		1	C6
GUILDHALL CT	WLVL	THO	4400	102	B4
GUILFORD AV	CLA	CLA		91	B5
GUILFORD AV	CO	WHI	9400	61	D2
GUILFORD AV	WHI	WHI	8600	61	E2
GUILFORD LN	CO	SAU		124	E4
GUILFORD PL	LA	HAC		73	E1
GUILFORD WY	WHI	WHI		55	E5
GUINEA DR	CO	WHI	800	48	A4
GUIRADO ST	LA	LA23	2600	45	A5
GUITA CT	PALM	PALM		171	F5
GULANA AV	LA	VEN	7900	55A	E1
GULF AV	CAR	CAR	22200	69	B5
GULF AV	CAR	CAR	23700	74	B1
GULF AV	CAR	LB10		70	A3
GULF AV	LA	WIL	100	74	B4
GULFCREST DR	RPV	PVP	3400	78	B4
GULL ST	MB	MB	100	62	A2
GULLO AV	LA	PAC	8500	8	E5
GULLO AV	LA	VAN	8800	9	A6
GULLO AV	LA	VAN	8300	16	A1
GULLROCK LN	DBAR	POM		97	F5
GUMBINER DR	CO	LPUE	16600	92	B5
GUMTREE PL	CO	SAU		124	D2
GUNDERSON AV	DOW	DOW	13400	66	A2
GUNDRY AV	LB	LB05	5900	65	D6
GUNDRY AV	LB	LB05	5200	70	E3
GUNDRY AV	LB	LB07	3400	70	E5
GUNDRY AV	LB	LB13	1300	75	E3
GUNDRY AV	PAR	PAR	14300	65	D3
GUNDRY AV	SH	LB06	2100	75	E1
GUNDRY AV	SH	LB07	3300	70	E5
GUNDRY CT	LB	LB13	1100	75	E4
GUNLOCK AV	CAR	CAR	19000	69	E1
GUNLOCK AV	COM	COM	1000	64	E4
GUNN AV	CO	WHI	9400	61	E3
GUNN AV	WHI	WHI		61	E3
GUNN AV	WHI	WHI	8900	84	A2
GUNNELL AV	LA	SP	2500	78	D4
GUNNISON TR	CO	TOP	1500	109	A2
GUNSMOKE AV	POM	POM		94	C5
GUNSMOKE DR	DBAR	POM		93	F6
GUNSTON DR N	LA	LA49	100	32	C6
GUNSTON DR S	LA	LA49	100	32	C6
GUNTER RD	RPV	SP	28600	78	D1
GUNTHER ST	LA	SF	16600	1	F6
GUNTHER ST	LA	SF	16300	2	A6
GUNTHER WY	LB	LB06	100	75	C2
GUNTON DR	CO	PALM	38200	172	C9
GUN TREE DR	CO	LPUE		85	E5
GURDON AV	SGAB	SGAB	200	37	D3
GURLEY AV	DOW	DOW	11900	60	A6
GURNARD AV	LA	SP	3400	78	D5
GURRIER AV	CO	ACT		189	E3
GUS CT	LAN	LAN		159	G5
GUSTAV LN	LA	CAN	8300	5	F1
GUSTON RD	CO	SAU		181	D7
GUTHRIE AV	LA	LA34	8500	42	D4
GUTHRIE CIR	LA	LA34	2400	42	C4
GUTHRIE CT	LA	LA34	2200	42	C4
GUTHRIE DR	LA	LA34	2000	42	C4
GUYMAN AV	LAN	LAN		159	E5
GUYMAN AV	LAN	LAN	43000	159	E8
GUYON AV	CO	PALM	36900	183	B2
GUYSON ST	LOM	LOM	2000	73	D4
GUYTINO PL	LA	LA12		44	D2
GWENALDA LN	CO	CYN	26700	128	E2
GWENCHRIS CT	PAR	PAR	15000	65	E3
GWYNE LN	LA	LA77		32	B1
GWYNNE AV	NWK	NWK	11300	61	A5
GYPSY DR	CO	LPUE		85	C4
GYPSY LN	LA	WOH		13	F3
GYRAL DR	LA	TU	6200	11	B3
H					
H ST	BELL	BELL		53	E3
HAAS AV	CO	GAR	14400	63	D2
HAAS AV	CO	LA47	10200	57	D3
HAAS AV	GAR	GAR	12900	63	D1
HAAS AV	HAW	LA47	11500	57	D5
HAAS AV	LA	LA47	5800	51	D5
HAAS AV	LA	LA47	8600	57	D2
HAAS AV	TOR	GAR	16200	63	D4
HAAS AV	TOR	TOR	16900	63	D5
HAAS AV	TOR	TOR	18500	68	D1
HAAS AV	TOR	TOR	23400	68	D6
HAAS AV	TOR	TOR	23500	73	D1
HABER AV	CO	ELM	2300	47	E2
HACIENDA AV N	GLDR	GLDR	100	87	D5
HACIENDA AV S	GLDR	GLDR	100	87	D5
HACIENDA BLVD	CO	LPUE	800	85	E3
HACIENDA BLVD	IND	LPUE	100	48	E6
HACIENDA BLVD	LHH	LAH	1200	84	F2
HACIENDA BLVD	LHH	LAH	2300	85	E5
HACIENDA BLVD	LPUE	LPUE	300	48	E5
HACIENDA DR	ARC	ARC	1	28	D3
HACIENDA DR	DUA	DUA		86	A5
HACIENDA DR	LA	NHO	12700	23	A5
HACIENDA DR	LCF	LCF	1300	19	B1
HACIENDA DR	MON	MON	500	29	D4
HACIENDA DR	NWK	NWK	12700	61	C6
HACIENDA DR	NWK	NWK	12700	82	C1
HACIENDA DR E	CO	PALM	100	183	A3
HACIENDA DR W	CO	PALM	200	183	A3
HACIENDA LN	SCLR	NEW	24700	127	D3
HACIENDA PL	MTB	MTB	1000	46	F5
HACIENDA PL	POM	POM	1400	90	E6
HACIENDA PL	WHOL	LA69	1100	33	E4
HACIENDA RD	CO	ACT		182	G9
HACIENDA ST	BLF	BLF	10200	66	D5
HACKAMORE RD	RPV	PVP	1	78	B1
HACKERS LN	AGH	AGO		102	D2
HACKETT AV	LB	LB08	300	71	E5
HACKETT AV	LB	LB15	1200	76	E1
HACKETT AV	LKD	LKD	4100	71	E4
HACKETT PL	LA	LA42	100	36	B3
HACKLEY AV	WCOV	WCOV	500	98	F2
HACKNEY ST	LA	CAN	20400	12	B1
HADDINGTON DR	LA	LA64	2800	42	B4
HADDOCK DR	DBAR	POM	23000	93	F6
HADDON AV	LA	PAC	10300	8	F3
HADDON AV	LA	PAC	9500	9	A3
HADDON AV	LA	SF	12600	2	C4
HADDON AV	LA	SV	8700	9	C5
HADDON AV	LA	SV	8400	16	D1
HADEN CT	SCLR	NEW		127	C4
HADJIAN LN	LA	CAN	22100	12	B4
HADLER DR	CO	SF		3	E2
HADLER ST	CAR	CAR	800	69	C5
HADLEY AV	LA	NOR	10100	7	A3
HADLEY LN	RB	RB	2400	62	F6
HADLEY ST	CO	LPUE		85	C5
HADLEY ST	CO	WHI	11100	55	C4
HADLEY ST	WHI	WHI	11600	55	D4
HAGAR ST	LA	SF	12800	3	A3
HAGAR ST	LA	SF	14700	8	D1
HAGAR ST	SF	SF	100	2	E5
HAGEN DR	ALH	ALH	2300	46	B1
HAGEN PL	LA	SF	12300	1	F4
HAGER AV	LA	LA66	13000	49	E4
HAGUE CT	GLEN	GL04	1200	25	C5
HAGUE PL	LA	WOH	5900	12	B6
HAHN AV	GLEN	GL03	500	25	B3
HAIG ST	SELM	ELM	11200	47	D4
HAIGLER DR	CAR	CAR	19000	69	C1
HAINES AV	LB	LB14	300	76	C5
HAINES CYN AV	LA	TU	9400	11	A5
HAINES CYN MTY	LA	TU		11	B2
HALAGA CIR	LAV	LAV		90	D1
HALBRENT AV	LA	SF	10000	8	C3
HALBRENT AV	LA	VAN	5600	15	C6
HALBRENT AV	LA	VAN	4600	22	C3
HALBRITE AV	LB	LB08	22600	81	B6
HALCOM AV	LAN	LAN	43800	159	G6
HALCOURT AV	DOW	DOW	10800	60	E5

COPYRIGHT, © 1989 BY Thomas Bros Maps

1990 LOS ANGELES COUNTY STREET INDEX

STREET	CITY	P.O. ZONE	BLOCK	PAGE	GRID
HALCOURT AV	NWK	NWK	11200	60	E5
HALCOURT AV	NWK	NWK	12800	66	E3
HALCYON WY	POM	POM	2200	90	F5
HALDANE ST	WHI	WHI	15900	84	C3
HALDEMAN RD	LA	SM	30	40	E4
HALDEMAN ST	TEC	SGAB	8600	38	A2
HALDERMAN ST	LA	LA66	3300	49	E2
HALE AV	LAV	LAV		90	C1
HALE AV	LAV	LAV		95A	C6
HALE ST	GLEN	GL01	1700	24	F1
HALEAKALA	SCLR	NEW		127	E5
HALEDON AV	DOW	DOW	9100	60	C4
HALEN ST	PALM	PALM		184	A1
HALES CORNER RD	RPV	PVP	27400	72	E5
HALEY AV E	CO	WHI	13500	61	D6
HALEY ST	LA	SV	12300	9	B6
HALFMOON DR	PALM	PALM		183	F1
HALF MOON LN	WAL	WAL		93	B5
HALFORD ST	CO	SGAB	8200	37	F1
HALFORD ST	LA	SF	12900	3	A3
HALIFAX RD	CO	ELM	4400	38	D5
HALIFAX RD	TEC	TEC	4800	38	D4
HALIFAX ST	PALM	PALM		172	F9
HALINOR AV	BAP	BAP	3800	39	F5
HALINOR AV	BAP	BAP	1700	48	E1
HALINOR AV	WCOV	WCOV	1300	48	E1
HALISON PL	TOR	TOR	19800	67	E2
HALISON ST	TOR	TOR	4600	67	E2
HALKETT AV	RM	RM	4500	37	F4
HALKETT AV	RM	RM	4700	38	A4
HALKIRK ST	LA	NHO	12700	23	B4
HALL CT	RB	RB	2200	67	E1
HALL RD	DOW	DOW	9000	60	C5
HALL ST	LA	LA32	3900	36	E4
HALLACK AV	LA	NOR	9900	7	A4
HALL CANYON DR	LCF	LCF	2000	19	A1
HALLDALE AV	CO	LA47	9500	57	E2
HALLDALE AV	GAR	GAR	12800	63	E1
HALLDALE AV	LA	HAC	23100	68	E6
HALLDALE AV	LA	HAC	23500	73	E1
HALLDALE AV	LA	LA18	2600	43	E5
HALLDALE AV	LA	LA47	5800	51	E6
HALLDALE AV	LA	LA47	7900	57	E2
HALLDALE AV	LA	LA62	3900	51	E3
HALLDALE AV	LA	TOR	20300	68	E5
HALLER ST	COV	COV	20100	89	B4
HALLETT AV	LA	LA65	2900	35	E2
HALLGREEN DR	CO	WAL	1500	97	B4
HALLIBURTON RD	CO	LPUE	15800	85	E3
HALLIBURTON RD	CO	LPUE	16500	98	A3
HALLIDAY AV	LA	LA49	700	32	B6
HALLMARK LN	CER	ART		81	A2
HALLOCK AV	SAD	SAD	500	90	A2
HALLOWELL AV	TEC	ARC	5500	38	D4
HALLOWELL AV	TEC	TEC	4800	38	D4
HALLRICH ST	CO	LPUE	300	98	F1
HALLWOOD AV	POM	POM	800	91	A5
HALLWOOD DR	BAP	BAP	14400	39	E4
HALLWOOD DR	ELM	ELM	11300	38	F4
HALLWOOD DR	ELM	ELM	11600	39	A4
HALLWOOD DR	TEC	TEC	9800	38	C4
HALM AV	CO	LA56	5800	50	E5
HALM AV	LA	LA34	2300	42	D4
HALO DR	COM	COM	12600	65	C2
HALO DR	LYN	LYN	12300	65	C1
HALPER ST	LA	ENC	16800	21	F2
HALRAY AV	CO	WHI	7100	55	C5
HALSEY AV	CO	ARC	2800	39	A2
HALSEY RD	CO	TOP	2700	108	F1
HALSEY ST	LA	SF	16800	1	E6
HALSEY ST	LA	SF	16200	2	A6
HALSTEAD ST N	PAS	PAS	1	28	A4
HALSTEAD ST S	CO	PAS	100	28	A4
HALSTED CIR	ALH	ALH	1	37	D3
HALSTED ST	LA	CHA	19800	6	E4
HALSTED ST	LA	NOR	17100	7	E4
HALSTED ST	LA	SF	16600	7	F4
HALSTED ST	LA	SF	16300	8	A4
HALTERN AV	GLDR	GLDR	100	87	B6
HALTERN ST	AZU	AZU	100	86	E6
HALTERN ST	CO	GLDR	19000	86	F6
HALTON ST	LA	ENC	17300	21	E3
HALVERN DR	LA	LA49	400	41	B1
HAMA DR	CO	PALM		190	B1
HAMBLEDON AV	IND	LPUE	500	98	C1
HAMBLEDON AV N	CO	LPUE	100	92	D6
HAMBLEDON AV S	CO	LPUE	100	92	D6
HAMBLEDON AV S	CO	LPUE	300	98	C1
HAMDEN CT	WCOV	WCOV		93	A3
HAMDEN PL	SFS	SFS		61	A3
HAMDEN ST	PR	PR	9500	60	E2
HAMDEN ST	SFS	SFS	11500	61	A2
HAMEL DR N	BH	BH	100	42	D1
HAMEL DR S	BH	BH	100	42	D1
HAMEL RD N	LA	LA48	100	33	D6
HAMEL RD S	LA	LA48	100	33	D6

STREET	CITY	P.O. ZONE	BLOCK	PAGE	GRID
HAMER CT	CO	GL14	5500	11	F5
HAMILTON AV	CO	SP	300	78	E3
HAMILTON AV	CO	TOR	19600	69	A2
HAMILTON AV	LA	GAR	18800	69	A1
HAMILTON AV	LA	SP	700	78	E5
HAMILTON AV	LA	TOR	19600	69	A2
HAMILTON AV	PAS	PAS	100	27	C3
HAMILTON AV	WHI	WHI		84	D1
HAMILTON BLVD N	POM	POM	100	94	D4
HAMILTON BLVD S	POM	POM	100	94	D4
HAMILTON CT	CO	CAL		100	B2
HAMILTON DR	LA	TU	6300	11	B5
HAMILTON DR N	BH	BH	100	42	E1
HAMILTON DR S	BH	BH	100	42	E1
HAMILTON LN	GLEN	GL14	4000	11	B5
HAMILTON LN	LA	TU	4000	11	B5
HAMILTON PL	LA	SP	600	78	F5
HAMILTON PL	PALM	PALM		183	D2
HAMILTON RD	DUA	DUA	900	29	C5
HAMILTON WY	LA	LA26	3100	35	B5
HAMLET DR	MPK	MPK	600	46	D3
HAMLET ST	LA	LA42	100	36	D1
HAMLIN ST	LA	CAN	23200	5	F5
HAMLIN ST	LA	CAN	19700	12	F5
HAMLIN ST	LA	NHO	10800	16	C5
HAMLIN ST	LA	RES	19500	14	A5
HAMLIN ST	LA	VAN	17300	14	E5
HAMLIN ST	LA	VAN	16500	15	D5
HAMLINE PL	BUR	BUR	900	17	D3
HAMMACK ST	CO	LA66	12400	50	B4
HAMMACK ST	CUL	CUL	11700	50	B4
HAMMACK ST	LA	CUL	11800	50	B4
HAMMEL ST	CO	LA22	4300	45	D4
HAMMEL ST	CO	LA63	3700	45	D4
HAMMEL ST E	MPK	MPK	100	46	B4
HAMMEL ST W	MPK	MPK	200	46	B4
HAMMILL RD	ELM	ELM	5200	39	A3
HAMMOND AV	LB	LB05	6500	65	F5
HAMMOND ST	BAP	BAP		48	C1
HAMMOND ST	LA	LA33	1600	45	A3
HAMMOND ST	POM	POM	400	90	F3
HAMMOND ST	WHOL	LA69	800	33	D4
HAMMOND ST E	PAS	PAS	100	27	A2
HAMMOND ST W	PAS	PAS	100	26	E2
HAMNER DR	LA	LA77	15400	22	C6
HAMPDEN PL	LA	PP	600	40	D4
HAMPDEN TER	ALH	ALH	1	36	F4
HAMPEL AV	CO	PEAR		185	A6
HAMPSHIRE CT	POM	POM	700	94	D2
HAMPSHIRE CT	SAD	SAD		89	C4
HAMPSHIRE LN	RHE	PVP	25800	72	F3
HAMPSHIRE ST	PALM	PALM		183	C5
HAMPSTEAD RD	CO	PAS	3600	19	B5
HAMPTON AV	MPK	MPK	100	46	C1
HAMPTON AV	WHOL	LA46	7200	34	A4
HAMPTON CT	ALH	ALH	1	37	D3
HAMPTON CT	CER	ART	16600	82	C4
HAMPTON CT	CO	PALM		184	E2
HAMPTON CT	COV	COV	100	88	E4
HAMPTON CT	LA	LA38		34	D4
HAMPTON CT	LA	NOR		1	C5
HAMPTON CT	SAD	SAD		89	D3
HAMPTON DR	LA	VEN		49	B3
HAMPTON DR	WCOV	WCOV		93	A3
HAMPTON LN	CER	ART		66	F5
HAMPTON LN	GLEN	GL01	1900	18	A5
HAMPTON PL	SCLR	SAU		127	C1
HAMPTON RD	ARC	ARC	600	28	B3
HAMPTON RD	BUR	BUR	500	17	C3
HAMPTON RD	LCF	LCF	4500	19	C3
HAMPTON RD	PALM	PALM		171	F6
HAMPTON RD	PAS	PAS	3500	28	A3
HAMPTON RD	SMAR	PAS	1400	37	D1
HAMPTON ST	GLDR	GLDR	800	89	C2
HAMPTON ST	VER	LA58	4600	52	F3
HAMWELL ST	PALM	PALM		171	H8
HANA	WCOV	WCOV		92	C4
HANAN DR	LB	LB03		76	E6
HANAN WY	PR	PR	8300	54	F2
HANAWALT RD	CO	SAU		181	E9
HANAWALT ST	LAV	LAV		90	E3
HANBURY ST	LB	LB08	5100	71	C4
HANCOCK AV	WHOL	LA69	900	33	D4
HANCOCK DR	PALM	PALM		183	D2
HANCOCK ST	LA	LA31	2200	36	B6
HANCOCK ST	LA	LA31	1800	45	B1
HANCOCK WALK	LA	LA31	2500	36	B6
HANDLEY AV	LA	LA45	8000	56	D1
HANDORF RD	IND	LPUE		92	A5
HANDY DR	CO	LA02	8600	58	D2
HANEMAN ST	LA	LA42	5700	26	C6
HANEY PL	LA	LA49	13200	40	F2
HANEY ST	PR	PR	8400	54	E4
HANEY ST	PR	PR	9600	55	A5
HANFORD AV N	LA	SP	100	78	E3
HANFORD AV S	LA	SP	100	78	E3

STREET	CITY	P.O. ZONE	BLOCK	PAGE	GRID
HANFORD DR	CO	PAS	1800	20	D6
HANGING ROCK AV	MTB	MTB	1600	46	F4
HANKS ST	AZU	AZU	500	86	D6
HANLEY AV	LA	LA49	500	32	A6
HANLEY PL	LA	LA49	500	41	A1
HANLEY WY	LA	LA49	600	32	A6
HANLIN AV	CO	AZU	5700	86	F6
HANLIN AV	CO	AZU	6100	86	F6
HANLIN AV	CO	AZU	5700	88	F2
HANNA AV	LA	CAN	8500	6	C6
HANNA AV	LA	CAN	6400	12	C5
HANNA AV	LA	CHA	9300	6	C5
HANNA AV	LA	WOH	5900	12	C6
HANNING AV	CO	ALT	2300	19	E5
HANNON ST	BG	BELL	6500	54	B6
HANNON ST	DOW	DOW	7200	54	B6
HANNUM AV	CUL	CUL	5600	50	C4
HANNUM AV	CUL	CUL	11200	50	C4
HANNUM DR	LA	LA34	9800	42	C5
HANOVER AV	CO	LA22	900	54	B2
HANOVER CT	CER	ART		66	D2
HANOVER DR	BH	BH	1000	32	F5
HANOVER DR	LA	BH	1000	32	F5
HANOVER RD	CLA	CLA	2100	91	B2
HANOVER RD	IND	LPUE		98	C3
HANOVER ST	LA	LA49	12700	41	A3
HANSA ST	PALM	PALM	500	172	A5
HANSARD AV	CO	LAN	39200	175	F6
HANSCOM DR	SPAS	SPAS	1700	36	D3
HANSEL LN	SAD	SAD		89	D3
HANSEN AV	POM	POM	500	94	D3
HANSFORD AV	CO	LPUE	1200	48	A4
HANSOM AV	CAR	CAR	21800	69	C5
HANSTEAD AV	LAN	LAN	44400	160	C5
HANSWORTH AV	HAW	HAW	13200	62	E1
HANWELL AV	BLF	BLF	13100	66	B1
HANWELL AV	DOW	DOW	12700	66	B1
HAPPY LN	LA	LA46	8000	33	E2
HAPPY ST	PAR	PAR	7500	65	E1
HAPPY TR	CO	TOP	1600	109	D1
HAPPY HOLLOW RD	DBAR	POM		93	F5
HAPPYVALLEY DR	SCLR	NEW	23400	127	B4
HARBAT RD	CO	ACT		182	B8
HARBEA-CA MS RD	CO	PALM		183	C9
HARBERT ST	WCOV	WCOV	1500	92	A1
HARBOR AV	LB	LB05	6600	65	B5
HARBOR AV	LB	LB10	1800	75	B4
HARBOR AV	LB	LB13	1300	75	B4
HARBOR BLVD N	LA	SP	100	79	A2
HARBOR BLVD S	LA	SP	100	79	A2
HARBOR CT	CO	PALM		184	A2
HARBOR DR N	RB	RB	200	67	C2
HARBOR DR S	RB	RB	300	67	D4
HARBOR FWY	CO			69	A5
HARBOR FWY	LA	LA		44	B5
HARBOR FWY	LA	LA		52	A5
HARBOR FWY	LA	LA		58	A5
HARBOR FWY	LA	LA		64	A3
HARBOR FWY	LA	LA		74	A6
HARBOR FWY	LA	LA		78	F1
HARBOR PZ	LB	LB02		80A	B4
HARBOR ST	CMRC	LA40	5000	53	E2
HARBOR ST	LA	VEN	500	49	C4
HARBOR HILLS	LOM	LOM		73	E4
HARBORLIGHT DR	LA	HAC		74	A2
HARBOR RIDGE LN	CO	TOR		69	A5
HARBOR SCNIC DR	LB	LB02		75	B5
HARBOR SCNIC DR	LB	LB02		80A	C5
HARBOR SCNIC WY	LB	LB02		80A	C6
HARBOR SIGHT DR	RHE	PVP	2500	73	C5
HARBOR VW AV	CAR	LB10	21600	69	F4
HARBOR VW AV N	LA	SP	100	78	E3
HARBOR VW AV S	LA	SP	100	78	E3
HARBORVIEW LN	WLVL	THO	32100	102	A5
HARBOR VISTA DR	CO	MAL	23600	114	A4
HARBY DR	SCLR	NEW		127	B5
HARCLARE LN	LA	ENC	4000	22	A4
HARCO ST	CO	LB08	5900	71	C5
HARCO ST	LB	LB08	5100	71	C5
HARCOURT AV	CO	LA43	5200	51	B4
HARCOURT AV	LA	LA16	1900	43	A5
HARCOURT AV	LA	LA43	6000	51	B5
HARCOURT ST	CO	COM	2800	65	A6
HARCOURT ST	LB	LB05	100	65	B6
HARCROSS DR	CO	LA43	5400	51	A3
HARDAWAY DR	LAM	LAM	14500	82	F1
HARDAWAY DR	LAM	LAM	14600	83	A1
HARDESTY AV	SCLR	CYN	28000	124	G7
HARDIN DR	ING	IN02	600	50	E6
HARDING AV	CO	ALT	1700	20	E6
HARDING AV	CO	LA22	500	46	B6
HARDING AV	CO	LA22	500	54	B1
HARDING AV	CO	PAS	1300	27	E1
HARDING AV	CO	CAST	28000	123	C2
HARDING AV	LA	LA66	4400	49	F3
HARDING AV	LA	VEN	900	49	D3

STREET	CITY	P.O. ZONE	BLOCK	PAGE	GRID
HARDING AV	MPK	MPK	300	46	B2
HARDING AV	MTB	MTB	300	54	C1
HARDING AV	MTB	MTB	300	54	C1
HARDING AV	SF	SF	100	2	E5
HARDING AV	SOG	SOG	5700	59	E6
HARDING CT	CLA	CLA		91	A2
HARDING ST	LA	SF	14600	2	D6
HARDING ST	LA	SF	13000	3	A3
HARDING ST	LA	SF42		3	B2
HARDING ST	LB	LB05	400	65	F6
HARDING ST	LB	LB05	3300	66	A6
HARDISON PL	SPAS	SPAS	1800	37	A1
HARDISON WY	LA	LA42	400	36	D2
HARDTREE DR	CO	PALM		157	H9
HARDWICK ST	LB	LB07	1300	70	E2
HARDWICK ST	LKD	LKD	2400	70	F2
HARDWICK ST	LKD	LKD	3300	71	A2
HARDWOOD AV	LAN	LAN	43700	160	A7
HARDY DR	DBAR	POM		94	B6
HARDY DR	DBAR	POM		97A	B1
HARDY PL	CO	NEW		126	H3
HARDY ST	ING	IN05	2200	57	D3
HARDY ST E	ING	IN01	100	57	A3
HARDY ST W	ING	IN01	200	56	F3
HARDY ST W	ING	IN01	100	57	A3
HARE AV	DBAR	WAL		97	D2
HARGILL ST	BLF	BLF	9000	66	B2
HARGIS ST	LA	LA34	8500	42	C4
HARGITT WY	NWK	NWK		82	B2
HARGRAVE DR	LA	LA68	2500	34	C1
HARGRAVE ST	ING	IN02	300	51	A5
HARKER AV	TEC	TEC	5500	38	B3
HARKER ST	LA	SP	500	79	A2
HARKNESS AV	PAS	PAS	1	27	C4
HARKNESS LN	RB	RB	1000	62	D6
HARKNESS LN	RB	RB	100	67	D2
HARKNESS ST	MB	MB	200	62	D4
HARLAN AV	BAP	BAP	3900	39	C4
HARLAN AV	CAR	CAR	19000	69	D1
HARLAN AV	COM	COM	900	64	D4
HARLAND AV	WHOL	LA69	9000	33	C5
HARLAS AV	LAN	LAN	44800	159	J4
HARLEM PL	LA	LA13	400	44	D3
HARLEM PL	LA	LA14	600	44	D3
HARLENE DR	LA	ENC		22	A5
HARLENE PL	LA	TAR	5700	14	C6
HARLENE PL	LA	TAR	5700	21	C1
HARLEQUIN CT	WCOV	WCOV		93	A3
HARLESDEN CT	LA	LA46	2600	33	E1
HARLINE CT	CO	TOR		68	F5
HARLISS ST	LA	NOR	19100	7	A4
HARLOW AV	LA	LA34	9200	42	C5
HARLOW DR	GLEN	GL06	100	26	A4
HARMAN AV	CO	LA59	11600	58	E5
HARMAN DR	LA	TU		11	B5
HARMON PL	GLEN	GL08	1800	18	F4
HARMONY AV	LA	NHO	5200	23	E2
HARMONY LN	LA	LA32		36	D6
HARMONY LN	LAN	LAN		159	C8
HARMONY PL	CO	GL14	2400	11	D5
HARMONY WY	LB	LB06	300	75	C2
HARMONY HILL DR	DBAR	POM	2300	97	D5
HARMSWORTH AV	LPUE	LPUE	600	98	B1
HARNETT AV	ELM	ELM	3900	39	A6
HARNETT ST	LA	NOR	18900	7	B2
HARNEY PL	CO	WOH		13	B5
HARNISH RD	LA	WOH	5800	12	A6
HARO AV	DOW	DOW	11500	59	F3
HAROLD CIR	BUR	BUR	2300	17	C2
HAROLD WY	LA	LA27	5100	34	E3
HAROLD WY	LA	LA28	5500	34	D3
HAROLD WY	LA	LA69	8400	33	E3
HAROLD ALMND ST	CO	PALM	36600	183	D3
HAROLD ASH AV	CO	PALM	800	183	D3
HAROLD BEECH AV	CO	PALM	800	183	D3
HAROLD CEDAR AV	CO	PALM	800	183	D3
HAROLD DATE AV	CO	PALM	800	183	C3
HAROLD ELM AV	CO	PALM	800	183	D3
HAROLD GARNR ST	CO	PALM	36600	183	D3
HAROLD 1ST ST	CO	PALM	36600	183	D3
HAROLD 2ND ST	CO	PALM	36600	183	D4
HAROLD 3RD ST	CO	PALM	36600	183	C3
HAROLD 5TH ST	CO	PALM	36600	183	C3
HARP DR	CO	LPUE		85	E3
HARPER AV	DOW	DOW	7800	60	B2
HARPER AV	RB	RB	1100	62	D6
HARPER AV N	LA	LA46	700	33	E5
HARPER AV N	LA	LA48	100	33	E5
HARPER AV N	WHOL	LA46	900	33	E4
HARPER AV S	LA	LA48	100	33	E5
HARPER CT	LAV	LAV		95A	D5
HARPERS WY	TOR	TOR		68	D3
HARPS ST	LA	SF	13000	3	A3
HARPS ST	SF	SF	100	2	E5
HARPTREE DR	CO	CAL		100	E5
HARQUAHALA PL	CO	PALM		157	F9

STREET	CITY	P.O. ZONE	BLOCK	PAGE	GRID
HARRATT ST	WHOL	LA69	8800	33	D4
HARRELL ST	PR	PR	9000	55	A1
HARRIDGE DR	LA	BH	1400	33	A3
HARRIET ST	LA	LA21	2100	52	F1
HARRIET ST	LA	LA58	2400	52	F1
HARRIET ST	VER	LA58	2500	52	F1
HARRIET ST E	CO	ALT	100	20	A4
HARRIET ST W	CO	ALT	100	19	F4
HARRIMAN AV	LA	LA32	3500	36	D4
HARRIMAN AV	SPAS	SPAS	4900	36	D4
HARRIMAN LN	RB	RB	1700	62	D6
HARRIMAN ST	DOW	DOW	7600	59	F5
HARRINGTON AV	LA	LA06	3000	43	E3
HARRINGTON RD	GLEN	GL07	800	25	D2
HARRINGTON WY	WCOV	WCOV		92	B4
HARRINGTON WY	WCOV	WCOV		92	C4
HARRIS AV	CO	COM	14000	65	B2
HARRIS AV	CO	LA63	1000	45	D3
HARRIS AV	COM	COM	100	65	C4
HARRIS AV	LYN	LYN	10000	59	C6
HARRIS AV	LYN	LYN	12100	65	C1
HARRISON AV	CLA	CLA	400	91	A4
HARRISON AV	LA	VEN	1000	49	D4
HARRISON AV E	POM	POM	100	90	F3
HARRISON AV E	POM	POM	700	91	A4
HARRISON AV W	POM	POM	100	90	F3
HARRISON RD	MPK	MPK	500	46	D4
HARRISON ST	CAR	LB10	2500	69	F3
HARRISON ST	CAR	LB10	2600	70	A3
HARRISON ST	PAR	PAR	7600	65	E4
HARRLEE LN	TOR	TOR	23900	72	F1
HARROW RD	CO	TOP		115	B2
HARROWAY AV	CER	ART		82	D4
HARSENS RD	CO	MAL		111	E3
HARSHAW PL	LAM	LAM	15700	83	C3
HART AV	RM	RM	3800	38	B5
HART AV	SM	SM	100	49	A2
HART AV	TEC	TEC		38	B2
HART DR	CER	ART	13600	82	E5
HART PL	CER	ART	13000	82	C5
HART PL	LB	LB02	1	75	C6
HART PL	LA	VN06		15	B4
HART PL	MTB	MTB	600	54	D1
HART ST	ART	ART	11400	66	F5
HART ST	CER	ART		82	A5
HART ST	LA	CAN	19700	12	B4
HART ST	LA	NHO	11400	16	C4
HART ST	LA	RES	17700	14	A4
HART ST	LA	VAN	16600	14	E4
HART ST	LA	VAN	13400	15	F4
HARTCREST DR	RPV	PVP	6800	72	C5
HARTDALE AV	LAM	LAM	11800	84	B5
HARTDALE DR	CO	WHI		84	B5
HARTER AV	CUL	CUL	4000	50	B2
HARTER LN	LCF	LCF	5200	19	B1
HARTFIELD CT	WLVL	THO		102	B4
HARTFORD AV	CO	SAU		123	E5
HARTFORD AV	LA	LA17	400	44	C2
HARTFORD LN	CER	ART		66	D2
HARTFORD PL	POM	POM		94	D1
HARTFORD WY	BH	BH	900	33	A5
HARTGLEN PL	AGH	AGO		102	E3
HARTLAND ST	LA	CAN	23000	5	F4
HARTLAND ST	LA	CAN	20100	12	E4
HARTLAND ST	LA	NHO	13100	16	A4
HARTLAND ST	LA	RES	17700	14	B4
HARTLAND ST	LA	VAN	16800	14	F4
HARTLAND ST	LA	VAN	13400	15	F4
HARTLE ST	CDY	BELL	4200	53	C6
HARTLEY AV	CO	COV	3900	88	B5
HARTLEY ST	WCOV	WCOV	100	88	B6
HARTMAN CT	SAD	SAD		89	F2
HARTMAN WY	CO	CHA	9200	4	B5
HARTNEL PL	CLA	CLA		96	D5
HARTSOOK ST	LA	ENC	16500	21	F2
HARTSOOK ST	LA	ENC	15700	22	A2
HARTSOOK ST	LA	NHO	10800	23	C2
HARTSOOK ST	LA	VAN	13700	22	C2
HARTSOOK ST	LA	VAN	12900	23	A2
HARTSVILLE ST	CO	LPUE	13500	48	C3
HARTSVILLE ST	LPUE	LPUE	13700	48	C3
HARTT PL	CLA	CLA	100	91	C2
HARTVIEW AV	CO	LPUE	800	92	B4
HARTWICK ST	LA	LA41	4800	26	B5
HARTWOOD PT DR	PAS	PAS	1200	27	F1
HARTZELL ST	LA	PP	700	40	D3
HARVARD AV N	CLA	CLA	100	91	B3
HARVARD BLVD N	LA	LA04	1003	34	E6
HARVARD BLVD N	LA	LA27	1300	34	E3
HARVARD BLVD N	LA	LA29	700	34	E5
HARVARD BLVD S	CO	LA47	11100	57	E5
HARVARD BLVD S	GAR	GAR	14700	63	E3
HARVARD BLVD S	LA	LA04	100	34	E6
HARVARD BLVD S	LA	LA05	600	43	E3
HARVARD BLVD S	LA	LA06	900	43	E3

1990 LOS ANGELES COUNTY STREET INDEX

STREET	CITY	P.O. ZONE	BLOCK	PAGE	GRID
HARVARD BLVD S	LA	LA18	1900	43	E5
HARVARD BLVD S	LA	LA20	300	43	E3
HARVARD BLVD S	LA	LA47	5800	51	E6
HARVARD BLVD S	LA	LA47	7900	57	E3
HARVARD BLVD S	LA	LA62	3800	51	E3
HARVARD BLVD S	LA	TOR	20300	68	E6
HARVARD CT	LAV	LAV		90	E3
HARVARD DR	ARC	ARC	300	28	D4
HARVARD DR	NWK	NWK	11200	66	F4
HARVARD LN	PALM	PALM		171	C5
HARVARD PL	CLA	CLA		91	B4
HARVARD PL	GAR	GAR		63	E2
HARVARD PL	LA	VEN		49	D4
HARVARD RD	BUR	BUR	200	17	E5
HARVARD ST	BLF	BLF	9100	66	B4
HARVARD ST	SM	SM	800	41	B4
HARVARD ST E	GLEN	GL05	100	25	E4
HARVARD ST W	GLEN	GL04	100	25	B4
HARVARD WK	LA	LA18	3400	43	E5
HARVARD WY	LAN	LAN		159	G7
HARVEST AV	CER	ART	17300	66	F5
HARVEST AV	CER	ART	19500	71	F2
HARVEST AV	LKD	LKD	20300	71	F3
HARVEST AV	NWK	NWK	12000	60	F6
HARVEST AV	NWK	NWK	16600	66	F4
HARVEST AV	NWK	NWK	12800	66	F1
HARVEST AV	SFS	SFS	9900	60	F4
HARVEST CT	CO	LR		184	D5
HARVEST LN	PALM	PALM		183	B1
HARVEST ST	LA	SF	15500	8	B1
HARVEST WY	CER	ART	19900	71	F2
HARVESTER RD	CO	MAL	29600	112	A5
HARVEST MOON ST	CO	LPUE	15700	92	A4
HARVEST MOON ST	WCOV	WCOV		92	C4
HARVEY DR	GLEN	GL06	100	25	F3
HARVEY WY	LB	LB08	4300	71	B4
HARVEY WY	LKD	LKD	2700	70	F4
HARVEY WY	LKD	LKD	4200	71	B4
HARWICH PL	LA	CAN	23800	5	E3
HARWICK CT	CAR	CAR	17500	64	D6
HARWICK CT	CO	COM		64	D6
HARWILL AV	CAR	CAR	16200	64	C4
HARWOOD CT	SAD	SAD		90	A4
HARWOOD DR	SCLR	SAU		124	C4
HARWOOD PL	CLA	CLA	500	91	C4
HARWOOD ST	LA	LA31	2200	35	E4
HASEKIAN DR	LA	TAR	4800	21	B3
HASKELL AV	LA	ENC	4300	22	B3
HASKELL AV	LA	SF	11400	2	B6
HASKELL AV	LA	SF	8500	8	B6
HASKELL AV	LA	SF	8300	15	B1
HASKELL AV	LA	VAN	6400	15	B5
HASKELL ST	LCF	LCF	5200	19	B1
HASKELL CYN RD	SCLR	SAU		124	E4
HASKELL CYN RD	CO	SAU		124	E4
HASKELL VSTA LN	SCLR	NEW		127	C6
HASKETT RD	CO	SAU		188	A2
HASKINS AV	CO	COM	15400	64	C3
HASKINS AV	COM	COM	1400	64	C4
HASKINS LN	CAR	CAR	16100	64	C4
HASLAM TER	LA	LA69	1500	33	D3
HASLEY CYN RD	CO	SAU		123	A3
HASSTED DR	CO	MAL		105	B5
HASTAIN DR	CO	BH		33	A2
HASTING ST	CO	LA22	5200	45	F6
HASTINGS AV	LA	LA45	8100	55A	F1
HASTINGS CIR	CLA	CLA		91	D1
HASTINGS CT	POM	POM		94	D2
HASTINGS CT	SAD	SAD		89	D4
HASTINGS DR	CO	WHI	11900	61	E6
HASTINGS ST	PALM	PALM		172	F9
HASTINGS WY	LA	NOR		1	C6
HASTINGS HTS LN	PAS	PAS		20A	A6
HASTINGS RCH DR	PAS	PAS	300	28	A3
HASTON PL	LKD	LKD	21100	71	F4
HASTY AV	DOW	DOW	9100	60	E3
HASTY AV	PR	PR	7000	54	F5
HASTY AV	PR	PR	8200	60	E2
HATCHER AV	IND	LPUE	1200	98	C3
HATCHWAY ST	CO	COM	2000	64	E1
HATFIELD AV	SAD	SAD	400	90	A2
HATFIELD PL	LA	LA32	4100	45	C1
HATHAWAY AV	ALH	ALH	2100	46	B2
HATHAWAY AV	LB	LB15	1800	76	A2
HATHAWAY AV	MPK	MPK	500	46	B1
HATHAWAY AV	SH	LB06	2200	75	F2
HATHAWAY RD	SAD	SAD		89	F2
HATILLO AV	LA	CAN	6400	12	F2
HATILLO AV	LA	NOR	8800	6	F6
HATMOR DR	CO	CAL		100	A2
HATRIDGE LN	SCLR	CYN	17900	125	A8
HATTERAS ST	BUR	BUR	3900	16	F6
HATTERAS ST	LA	ENC	17100	14	D6
HATTERAS ST	LA	NHO	10600	16	D6
HATTERAS ST	LA	TAR	18300	14	A6
HATTERAS ST	LA	VAN	13300	15	C6
HATTERAS ST	LA	WOH	23000	5	F6
HATTERAS ST	LA	WOH	19700	12	F6
HATTERAS ST	LA	WOH	23000	100	D1
HATTON CT	LA	SV	10200	17	A1
HATTON PL	LA	RES	7700	14	D2
HATTON ST	LA	CAN	19900	12	E2
HATTON ST	LA	RES	19300	14	A2
HAUCK ST	CO	LA63	4300	45	E2
HAUSER BLVD	LA	LA16	1900	42	F4
HAUSER BLVD	LA	LA19	1100	42	F3
HAUSER BLVD	LA	LA19	1000	43	A3
HAUSER BLVD	LA	LA36	300	43	A2
HAVANA AV	LA	SF	12000	2	D5
HAVANA AV	LB	LB04	700	76	C5
HAVANA AV	LB	LB14	300	76	C5
HAVECO PL	CO	LAN	45200	158	A3
HAVEL PL	CO	SGAB	8200	37	F1
HAVELOCK AV	LA	CUL	11200	50	B3
HAVELOCK AV	LA	LA66	12400	50	A4
HAVEMEYER LN	RB	RB	1600	67	D1
HAVEN AV	ARC	ARC	100	28	E4
HAVEN CT	CO	PALM		184	E2
HAVEN ST	GLEN	GL08	1900	18	F6
HAVEN ST	LA	LA32	2600	36	E6
HAVEN WY	BUR	BUR	2700	17	C2
HAVENBROOK ST	BAP	BAP	14000	39	E6
HAVENBROOK ST	WCOV	WCOV	2200	48	E1
HAVENDALE DR	PAS	PAS	300	26	F4
HAVENHURST DR	LA	LA46	1400	33	E4
HAVENHURST DR	WHOL	LA46	900	33	E4
HAVENPARK AV	ELM	ELM	2600	47	C1
HAVENPARK AV	SELM	ELM	1500	47	C3
HAVENWOOD DR	CO	WHI	11400	55	C5
HAVENWOOD DR	PR	PR	9000	55	A3
HAVENWOOD PL	CO	WHI	10500	55	B4
HAVENWOOD ST	PR	PR	9400	55	A3
HAVERFORD AV	LA	PP	600	40	C4
HAVERHILL DR	LA	LA65	2300	35	F2
HAVERHILL WY	LA	LA65	2300	35	F2
HAVERKAMP DR	GLEN	GL06	500	26	B3
HAVERLY ST	CO	ELM	10500	38	D4
HAVERSTOCK RD	LCF	LCF		19	C5
HAVILAND AV	WHI	WHI	5800	55	E4
HAWAII AV	TOR	TOR		68	B3
HAWAII ST	ELS	ELS	100	62	D2
HAWAII ST	WCOV	WCOV		92	D5
HAWAIIAN AV	HG	LKD	21600	81	B4
HAWAIIAN AV	LA	WIL	200	74	B5
HAWAIIAN AV	LKD	LKD	20300	81	B3
HAWES ST	CO	WHI	13800	61	E3
HAWICK ST	LA	LA39	3000	35	B3
HAWK DR	CO	PALM		157	G7
HAWK LN	GLDR	GLDR	300	87	C5
HAWK LN W	PALM	PALM		172	B5
HAWK RD	WAL	WAL		93	D2
HAWKBROOK DR	SAD	SAD	1800	95A	B6
HAWKBRYN AV	SCLR	NEW		127	A4
HAWKDEN CT	GLEN	GL06		25	F2
HAWKHURST DR	RPV	PVP	26000	72	E4
HAWKINS AV	RB	RB	2400	62	E4
HAWKINS CIR	HPK	LA01		52	E5
HAWKINS ST	SFS	SFS		61	B3
HAWKRIDGE DR	CO	GL14		11	D4
HAWKSET ST	CO	CAST		123	A3
HAWKS HILL RD	LA	CHA		6	F2
HAWKSMOOR DR	RPV	PVP	31000	78	B3
HAWKSTONE AV	CO	WHI		61	D3
HAWKWOOD RD	DBAR	POM		99	D4
HAWLEY AV	LA	LA32	3800	36	C4
HAWLEY AV	LA	LA42	5300	36	C4
HAWLEY RD	CO	SAU		188	J1
HAWTHORN AV	DOW	DOW	12400	59	F5
HAWTHORN AV	LA	LA28	6700	34	B3
HAWTHORN AV	LA	LA46	7100	34	A3
HAWTHORN ST	PALM	PALM		171	H6
HAWTHORNE AV	LAV	LAV	1600	90	C3
HAWTHORNE AV	VER	LA58	4400	52	E3
HAWTHORNE BLVD	CO	IN04	10000	57	A5
HAWTHORNE BLVD	HAW	HAW	11000	57	A5
HAWTHORNE BLVD	HAW	HAW	12800	63	A3
HAWTHORNE BLVD	LAW	LAW	14300	63	A3
HAWTHORNE BLVD	RB	RB	17200	63	A6
HAWTHORNE BLVD	RHE	PVP		72	E4
HAWTHORNE BLVD	RHE	PVP		73	A3
HAWTHORNE BLVD	RPV	PVP	27400	72	C5
HAWTHORNE BLVD	RPV	PVP	30100	77	C2
HAWTHORNE BLVD	TOR	RB	17400	63	A6
HAWTHORNE BLVD	TOR	RB	18200	68	A3
HAWTHORNE BLVD	TOR	TOR	19000	68	A3
HAWTHORNE BLVD	TOR	TOR	23500	73	A1
HAWTHORNE LN	SPAS	SPAS	1000	36	E2
HAWTHORNE PL	POM	POM	700	95	A2
HAWTHORNE ST	GLEN	GL04	200	25	B4
HAWTHORNE ST	SPAS	SPAS	1000	36	E2
HAWTHORNE WY	HAW	HAW	12000	57	A6
HAWTHORNE WY	HAW	HAW	13800	63	A2
HAXBY CT	CAR	CAR	800	64	C5
HAXTON DR	SCLR	CYN	27700	124	H5
HAY AV	CO	LA22	600	54	B1
HAY ST	MTB	MTB	300	46	B6
HAYCREEK AV	SCLR	CYN		124	G6
HAYDEN AV	CUL	CUL	3500	42	D6
HAYDEN AV	NWK	NWK	13300	82	D1
HAYDEN PL	CUL	CUL		42	D6
HAYDEN WK	GLEN	GL06		26	B1
HAYES AL	PAS	PAS	1	27	A4
HAYES AV	LA	LA42	5900	36	C2
HAYES AV	LB	LB10	2300	75	A2
HAYES AV	LB	LB13	1300	75	A4
HAYES DR	LA	LA48	6400	42	E2
HAYES DR	LAV	LAV		90	E2
HAYES ST	CO	CAST	29600	123	C2
HAYES ST	CO	LA63	4400	45	E2
HAYFIELD DR	LB	LB08	3200	71	D6
HAYFORD ST	BLF	BLF	10200	66	D3
HAYFORD ST	LAM	LAM	15100	83	B3
HAYFORD ST	NWK	NWK	10600	66	E3
HAYFORD ST	NWK	NWK	11800	82	A3
HAYFORK RD	SCLR	SAU		124	H3
HAYLAND ST	CO	LPUE	14100	48	D3
HAYLAND ST	CO	LPUE	15800	92	A4
HAYLAND ST	LPUE	LPUE	15200	48	F4
HAYLAND ST	LPUE	LPUE	15700	92	A4
HAYLOFT PL	CO	LPUE		98	A4
HAYMAN AV	LCF	LCF	4300	19	B4
HAYMOND ST	SELM	ELM	10900	47	D4
HAYNES AV	BH	BH	500	33	C3
HAYNES LN	RB	RB	1600	67	D1
HAYNES ST	LA	CAN	23000	5	F4
HAYNES ST	LA	CAN	19800	12	F5
HAYNES ST	LA	NHO	11500	16	D5
HAYNES ST	LA	RES	18600	14	A5
HAYNES ST	LA	VAN	16500	14	D5
HAYNES ST	LA	VAN	13500	15	C5
HAYRIDE CT	CO	LPUE		98	D5
HAYTER AV	BLF	BLF	15900	66	A5
HAYTER AV	CUL	CUL	11200	50	C3
HAYTER AV	LKD	LKD	4300	71	A2
HAYTER AV	PAR	PAR	15000	66	A3
HAYVENHURST AV	LA	ENC	3600	21	F2
HAYVENHURST AV	LA	SF	11400	1	F6
HAYVENHURST AV	LA	SF	8500	7	F3
HAYVENHURST AV	LA	SF	8300	14	F1
HAYVENHURST AV	LA	VAN	6400	15	A5
HAYVENHURST DR	LA	ENC	4200	21	F4
HAYVENHURST DR	LA	ENC	4000	22	A4
HAYVENHURST PL	LA	SF	8300	14	F1
HAYVENHURST PL	LA	VAN		15	A3
HAYWARD ST	WHI	WHI	14200	61	F2
HAYWARD ST	WHI	WHI	14400	84	B3
HAYWARD WY	SELM	ELM		47	C3
HAYWOOD ST	LA	TU	6300	11	A4
HAYWORTH AV N	LA	LA48	100	33	F5
HAYWORTH AV N	WHOL	LA46	900	33	F5
HAYWORTH AV S	LA	LA35	1000	42	E3
HAYWORTH AV S	LA	LA48	100	33	F5
HAZARD AV	CO	LA63	400	45	D3
HAZBETH LN	GLEN	GL07	1500	25	C1
HAZEL AV	CO	RM	900	47	A4
HAZEL CT	PALM	PALM		183	C1
HAZEL ST	CO	CHA		4	C5
HAZEL ST	CO	SAU		124	C3
HAZEL ST	GLEN	GL01	500	24	F2
HAZEL ST	ING	IN02	100	51	A6
HAZEL WY	SGAB	SGAB		37	E4
HAZELBROOK AV	LB	LB08	4300	71	B3
HAZELBROOK AV	LKD	LKD	5900	66	B6
HAZELBROOK AV	LKD	LKD	4900	71	B1
HAZELBROOK RD	LA	NHO	3400	23	D5
HAZELCREST DR	LAM	LAM	15800	83	C1
HAZELCREST LN	CO	NEW		126	J4
HAZELHURST PL	LA	NHO	6000	16	D6
HAZELKIRK DR	LA	LA27	4200	35	A2
HAZELL WY	SGAB	SGAB	200	37	E4
HAZELRIDGE DR	RPV	PVP	27900	72	C4
HAZELTINE AV	LA	VAN	8500	8	E6
HAZELTINE AV	LA	VAN	5600	15	E5
HAZELTINE AV	LA	VAN	4100	22	E2
HAZELWOOD AV	LA	LA41	1400	26	A6
HAZELWOOD AV	LA	LA41	1400	36	A1
HAZEN DR	LA	BH	9100	33	C1
HEADLAND DR	RPV	PVP	1	73	C6
HEALY TR	CO	CHA		4	B5
HEARD PL	LA	LA49		40	F1
HEARST TANK MTY	CO	MAL	19700	115	B2
HEATH AV	BH	BH	200	42	B2
HEATH LN	LB	LB05	200	65	C5
HEATH ST	LB	LB05	200	65	B5
HEATH TER	WCOV	WCOV	1900	92	D3
HEATHDALE AV	CO	AZU	5100	88	D2
HEATHDALE AV	CO	COV	3200	88	D3
HEATHDALE AV N	COV	COV	100	88	D5
HEATHDALE AV S	COV	COV	100	88	D5
HEATHER AV	CER	ART	18300	82	D6
HEATHER AV	LB	LB15	2300	76	C2
HEATHER AV	PALM	PALM		183	G1
HEATHER CT	AGH	AGO		102	E2
HEATHER CT	LA	BH	1800	33	B2
HEATHER DR	LA	LA68	6300	24	C6
HEATHER DR	LAV	LAV	1500	90	C1
HEATHER DR	MPK	MPK	1900	46	C4
HEATHER LN	CO	CAST		123	C1
HEATHER LN	ING	IN01		57	B2
HEATHER LN	WCOV	WCOV	700	92	E2
HEATHER RD	LA	BH	9500	33	B3
HEATHER RD	LB	LB08	3000	71	B6
HEATHER RD	LB	LB15	2700	76	C1
HEATHER SQ	PAS	PAS	1100	27	B2
HEATHER ST	GLDR	GLDR	900	89	C2
HEATHER WY	HAW	HAW		62	E1
HEATHER WY	LA	BH	1800	33	B2
HEATHER WY	POM	POM	2100	90	F5
HEATHERCLIFF RD	CO	MAL	29100	110	B4
HEATHERDALE DR	CO	LA43	5600	51	A4
HEATHERFIELD DR	CO	LPUE		85	C4
HEATHERGLEN LN	SAD	GLDR		89	F1
HEATHER HTS AV	CO	ARC	2700	39	A1
HEATHER HTS AV	CO	MON	2500	39	A1
HEATHER HTS CT	MON	MON	200	29	A3
HEATHER HILL RD	CO	LPUE	1400	98	A3
HEATHER KNLS PL	SCLR	NEW	23400	127	B5
HEATHERLANE CT	DBAR	POM		97	E4
HEATHER RDG DR	GLEN	GL07	1500	25	D1
HEATHERSIDE RD	PAS	PAS	600	26	D3
HEATHERTON AV	CO	LPUE		98	E3
HEATHFIELD DR	WHI	WHI	16200	84	D4
HEATHRIDGE CIR	CO	WAL	19700	97	B3
HEATHROW DR	PALM	PALM		171	F5
HEATON AV	LAN	LAN	43700	160	A7
HEATON MOOR DR	WAL	WAL		93	A5
HEAVEN AV	LA	WOH	4700	100	F2
HEAVENLY CT	LA	CAN		5	D3
HEAVENLY WY	CO	CAST		123	H2
HEAVENLY VLY RD	WAL	WAL		93	A4
HEBE AV	NWK	NWK	12000	61	B6
HEBER ST	CO	GLDR	19000	86	F5
HEBER ST	CO	GLDR	19100	87	A5
HEBER ST	GLDR	GLDR	300	87	A6
HEBRIDES CIR	LA	CAN	7000	5	F4
HEBRON LN	LA	LA77	10400	32	E3
HECLA ST	TEC	TEC	9200	38	B3
HEDDA CIR	CER	ART	13700	82	E6
HEDDA DR	CER	ART	12300	82	B6
HEDDA LN	CER	ART	13000	82	D6
HEDDA PL	CER	ART	10700	71	E1
HEDDA PL	CER	ART	13200	82	D6
HEDDA ST	CER	ART	12900	82	C6
HEDDA ST	LB	LB05	3500	66	A6
HEDDA ST	LKD	LKD	3900	66	C6
HEDDING ST	LA	LA45	6400	50	B5
HEDGEPATH AV	CO	LPUE	1000	48	C6
HEDGEPATH AV	CO	LPUE	1300	85	C1
HEDGEROW DR	WCOV	WCOV	3400	97	B1
HEDGES PL	LA	LA69	8500	33	D3
HEDGES WY	LA	LA69	8500	33	D3
HEDGEWALL DR	WLVL	THO		102	D2
HEDGEWOOD DR	RPV	PVP	6800	72	C5
HEDGEWOOD PL	DBAR	POM		97A	B2
HEDRICK ST	CO	PALM		182	E6
HEFFNER RD	CO	SAU		189	C7
HEFFNER HILL RD	COV	COV		89	A6
HEFFRON DR	BUR	BUR	3700	24	B3
HEFLIN DR	LAM	LAM	12600	61	F6
HEFLIN DR	LAM	LAM	12800	83	A1
HEFLIN DR	LAM	LAM	12600	84	A6
HEGEL ST	BLF	BLF	9000	66	B3
HEGLIS AV	RM	RM	3000	47	B1
HEIDELBERG AV	WAL	WAL	1300	93	B4
HEIDELBURG LN	CLA	CLA		91	C1
HEIDEMARIE ST	LA	CHA		6	B4
HEIDI LN	CO	TOP		13	D5
HEIDI JO LN	SCLR	SAU		124	E6
HEIDLEMAN RD	LA	LA32	1800	45	D1
HEIGHTS DR	PALM	PALM		171	B3
HEINER ST	BLF	BLF	9200	66	B2
HEINTZ ST	BAP	BAP	5000	39	F3
HEISS ST	LA	WOH	23100	13	A3
HELA AV	LA	SF	11300	3	D6
HELA AV	LA	SF	11000	9	D1
HELBERTA AV	RB	RB	100	67	D3
HELBERTA AV N	RB	RB	100	67	D3
HELEN AV	LA	SUN	9600	9	F4
HELEN AV	LA	SV	8800	9	E6
HELEN DR	CO	LA63	5300	45	E2
HELEN LN	LAN	LAN		159	F6
HELEN LN	WCOV	WCOV		92	D6
HELEN PL	LA	SUN		9	F4
HELEN ST	WHI	WHI		55	E6
HELENA CIR	LAV	LAV		90	B1
HELENA ST	LA	LA49	12400	41	B3
HELENA DR 1	LA	LA49	12300	41	B2
HELENA DR 2	LA	LA49	12300	41	B2
HELENA DR 3	LA	LA49	12300	41	B2
HELENA DR 4	LA	LA49	12300	41	B2
HELENA DR 5	LA	LA49	12300	41	B2
HELENA DR 6	LA	LA49	12300	41	B2
HELENA DR 7	LA	LA49	12300	41	B2
HELENA DR 8	LA	LA49	12300	41	B2
HELENA DR 9	LA	LA49	12300	41	B2
HELENA DR 10	LA	LA49	12300	41	B2
HELENA DR 11	LA	LA49	12300	41	B2
HELENA DR 12	LA	LA49	12300	41	B2
HELENA DR 13	LA	LA49	12300	41	B2
HELENA DR 14	LA	LA49	12300	41	B2
HELENA DR 15	LA	LA49	12300	41	B2
HELENA DR 16	LA	LA49	12300	41	B2
HELENA DR 17	LA	LA49	12300	41	B2
HELENA DR 18	LA	LA49	12300	41	B2
HELENA DR 19	LA	LA49	12300	41	B2
HELENA DR 20	LA	LA49	12300	41	B2
HELENA DR 21	LA	LA49	12300	41	B2
HELENA DR 22	LA	LA49	12300	41	B2
HELENA DR 23	LA	LA49	12300	41	B2
HELENA DR 24	LA	LA49	12300	41	B2
HELENA DR 25	LA	LA49	12300	41	B2
HELENDALE AV	LA	TU	10100	10	F3
HELENSBURG ST	CO	GLDR	19200	89	A1
HELEO AV	TEC	TEC	4800	38	B3
HELIOS DR	LA	LA68	2200	34	C2
HELIOTROPE AV	BELL	BELL	6200	53	D5
HELIOTROPE AV	CO	LA22		53	D5
HELIOTROPE AV	MAY	MAY	5600	53	D5
HELIOTROPE AV N	MON	MON	100	29	B4
HELIOTROPE AV S	MON	MON	100	29	B4
HELIOTROPE CIR	MAY	MAY	4600	53	D4
HELIOTROPE DR	LA	LA04	300	34	F5
HELIOTROPE DR	LA	LA29	700	34	F5
HELLER PL	LAM	LAM	14900	84	A6
HELLMAN AV	LA	LA32	3600	36	C4
HELLMAN AV	LA	LA42	4900	36	D4
HELLMAN AV	RM	RM	7400	46	B1
HELLMAN AV E	ALH	ALH	100	46	B1
HELLMAN AV E	MPK	MPK	100	46	B1
HELLMAN AV W	ALH	ALH	2200	45	F1
HELLMAN AV W	ALH	ALH	100	46	B1
HELLMAN AV W	MPK	MPK	100	46	B1
HELLMAN ST	LB	LB13	1000	75	D4
HELM PL	RPV	PVP	32200	78	A3
HELMCREST DR	CO	WHI	16400	84	D5
HELMER DR	WHI	WHI	13000	61	E1
HELMET TR	CO	TOP		109	D1
HELMGATE DR	ELM	ELM		39	A4
HELMICK ST	CAR	CAR	700	69	D2
HELMOND DR	CO	AGO		100A	D4
HELMS AV	CUL	CUL	3200	42	D6
HELMS AV	LA	LA34	3000	42	D5
HELMS PL	LA	LA34	8900	42	D5
HELMSDALE AV	CO	LPUE	500	92	B5
HELMSDALE CIR	LA	CAN	7100	5	E3
HELMSDALE RD	LA	CAN	7000	5	E4
HELTON DR	SCLR	SAU		124	F5
HELWIG AV S	NWK	NWK	14400	82	B3
HEMET PL	LA	LA46	8000	33	F3
HEMINGER ST	GLEN	GL05	300	25	D6
HEMINGWAY AV	CO	VAL		126	G3
HEMLOCK LN	WCOV	WCOV		98	E2
HEMLOCK ST	ELM	ELM	11500	38	F3
HEMLOCK ST	ELM	ELM	11600	39	A3
HEMLOCK ST	LA	LA21	800	44	D5
HEMLOCK WY	POM	POM	2300	90	F4
HEMMINGWAY ST	LA	CAN	19800	12	F2
HEMMINGWAY ST	LA	NOR	17200	14	E2
HEMMINGWAY ST	LA	RES	17400	14	E2
HEMMINGWAY ST	LA	VAN	17200	14	E2
HEMP CT	CO	LAN	42000	171	A1
HEMPHILL ST	CO	LPUE	17400	92	D6
HEMPSTEAD AV	ARC	ARC	2800	38	F2
HEMPSTEAD AV	CO	ARC	3000	38	F2
HEMPSTEAD DR	AGH	AGO		102	E3
HEMSTEAD CT	WCOV	WCOV		93	A3
HENDEE ST	WCOV	WCOV		92	D6
HENDERSON AV	LB	LB06	1800	75	C3
HENDERSON AV	LB	LB13	1400	75	C3
HENDERSON ST	LA	LA32	5000	36	E4
HENDERSON WY	CLA	CLA		96	D5
HENDLEY DR	LA	NHO	11300	23	E5
HENDON DR	CO	PALM	38100	172	C9
HENDRICKS AV	CO	LA22	500	46	B6
HENDRICKS AV	CO	LA22	700	54	A2
HENDRICKS AV	LOM	LOM	24300	73	D1
HENDRICKS AV	MPK	MPK	1900	46	B4
HENDRICKS ST	MTB	MTB	500	46	B6
HENDRIE ST	LB	LB08	8300	81	C5

254

1990 LOS ANGELES COUNTY STREET INDEX

HENDRIX AV — HILLGATE DR

LOS ANGELES CO.

STREET	CITY	P.O. ZONE	BLOCK	PAGE	GRID
HENDRIX AV	CLA	CLA	500	91	B5
HENDRON WY	MPK	MPK	1800	46	C4
HENEFER AV	LA	LA45	7400	50	B6
HENLEY CT	WLVL	THO	4500	102	B4
HENLEY LN	LA	LA77		32	B1
HENNING DR	LAM	LAM	14700	84	A5
HENNIPEN ST	POM	POM	500	93	F2
HENNY AV	LA	SF	13600	2	D2
HENRIETTA AV	CO	GL14	2700	11	D5
HENRIETTA AV	GLEN	GL14	3200	11	C4
HENRIETTA ST	TOR	TOR	20200	67	E3
HENRILEE ST	LKD	LKD	5900	71	D3
HENRY AL	PAS	PAS	1	19	F6
HENRY CT	TOR	TOR	23200	68	C6
HENRY ST	LA	LA33	1300	45	B2
HENRY FORD AV	LB	LB02		79	E1
HENRY FORD AV	LA	WIL	100	74	E5
HENRY MAYO DR	CO	SAU	27000	123	C7
HENRY RANCH RD	CO	TOP		13	B5
HENRY RANCH RD	CO	TOP		109	B1
HENRY RANCH RD	CO	WOH		13	B4
HENRY RDG MTWY	CO	TOP	1000	109	B3
HENSAL RD	LA	BH	9700	32	F1
HENSAL RD	LA	BH	9700	33	A1
HENSEL ST	BAP	BAP	12700	48	B2
HENSHAW AV	CO	WHI	11300	84	A5
HENSHAW ST	LA	TAR	19700	13	F1
HENSLOW AV	CO	PALM	36900	183	B2
HENSON DR	LA	PAC		9	C3
HENTON AV	CO	COV	4800	89	B3
HENTON AV	COV	COV	100	89	B4
HENZIE PL	LA	SF	12400	1	E4
HEPBURN AV	LA	LA08	3800	51	C1
HEPBURN AV	LA	LA18	3700	51	C1
HEPBURN CIR	CUL	CUL	10700	50	B1
HEPNER AV	COV	COV	500	88	E5
HEPNER AV	LA	LA41	1300	26	B5
HEPWORTH AV	CMRC	LA40	2200	53	E2
HERA ST	SAD	SAD	300	90	A3
HERALD ST	WCOV	WCOV	800	92	A2
HERB CT	CO	LPUE		98	F5
HERB ST	CO	ELM	11300	47	E4
HERBERT AV	GLEN	GL06	1600	25	F3
HERBERT AV N	CO	LA63	100	45	D4
HERBERT AV N	LA	SP	800	78	F2
HERBERT AV S	CMRC	LA23	1400	53	D1
HERBERT AV S	CO	LA23	700	45	D6
HERBERT AV S	CO	LA23	1200	53	D1
HERBERT AV S	CO	LA63	100	45	D5
HERBERT AV S	LA	SP	800	78	F2
HERBERT CIR	CO	LA63	1000	45	D3
HERBERT ST	CUL	LA66	12200	49	F3
HERBERT ST	CUL	LA66	11300	50	A3
HERBERT ST	LA	LA66	12000	49	F3
HERBERT ST	PAS	PAS	500	27	B2
HERBERT WY	CUL	LA66	4100	49	F3
HERBINE ST	CO	LAV		90	B2
HERBOLD ST	LA	NOR		7	C4
HERCULES DR	LA	LA46	2000	33	F2
HERCULES ST	NWK	NWK	11100	60	F5
HERCULES ST	NWK	NWK	11500	61	A5
HEREFORD DR	CO	LA22	5800	54	A1
HEREFORD DR	MTB	MTB	1900	54	A1
HERITAGE CIR	DOW	DOW	11900	59	F4
HERITAGE DR	AGH	AGO		102	F2
HERITAGE DR	PAS	PAS		27	F2
HERITAGE DR	WCOV	WCOV		93	A3
HERITAGE LN	SCLR	NEW	24200	127	B4
HERITAGE PL	CER	ART		81	C1
HERITAGE OAK CT	SCLR	NEW		127	B6
HERITAGE OAK DR	GLDR	GLDR		87	D5
HERITAGE OKS DR	ARC	ARC	900	28	B3
HERITAGE PK DR	SFS	SFS		61	A4
HERKIMER ST	LA	LA39	2800	35	B2
HERLINDA LN	CO	LPUE		97	B5
HERMANO DR	LA	TAR		21	C3
HERMANOS ST	PAS	PAS	2700	27	F2
HERMAR CT	CO	ALT	3000	19	F4
HERMES DR	LA	LA46	7500	33	F1
HERMES ST	CO	WHI	13600	61	E4
HERMES ST	NWK	NWK	10800	60	E5
HERMES ST	NWK	NWK	11600	61	A4
HERMITAGE AV	LA	NHO	5200	23	C2
HERMITAGE DR	CO	LPUE		85	C5
HERMITAGE LN	AZU	AZU	300	86	D4
HERMITS GLEN	LA	LA46	2300	33	D2
HERMOSA AV	CO	MONT	2500	18	D2
HERMOSA AV	GLEN	GL14	2800	18	D2
HERMOSA AV	GLEN	MONT	2600	18	D2
HERMOSA AV	HB	RB	1300	62	B6
HERMOSA AV	HB	RB	100	67	C1
HERMOSA AV	LA	LA41	5000	26	B5
HERMOSA AV	LB	LB02	100	75	E6
HERMOSA AV	LB	LB02	300	75	E6
HERMOSA AV	POM	POM	1000	91	A6
HERMOSA AV N	SMAD	SMAD	1	28	C2
HERMOSA AV S	SMAD	SMAD	1	28	C2
HERMOSA DR	CO	SGAB	8500	38	A2
HERMOSA DR	SGAB	SGAB	8400	37	F2
HERMOSA DR	TEC	TEC	8800	38	A2
HERMOSA DR E	SGAB	SGAB	100	37	D2
HERMOSA DR W	SGAB	SGAB	100	37	D2
HERMOSA PL	SPAS	SPAS	400	36	E1
HERMOSA RD	PAS	PAS	1000	26	D5
HERMOSA ST	LA	WIL		79	C1
HERMOSA ST	SPAS	SPAS	200	36	E1
HERMOSA VIEW DR	HB	RB		62	C5
HERMOSA VSTA ST	MPK	MPK	300	46	B2
HERMOSILLA CT	CO	AGO		100	C4
HERMOSITA DR	GLEN	GL08	2300	18	E5
HERMOSURA ST	NWK	NWK	11800	82	B4
HERN DR	DBAR	WAL		97	C3
HERNANDEZ DR W	CO	PALM	800	183	A2
HEROIC DR	RPV	PVP	3600	78	B3
HERON AV	LAM	LAM		82	F3
HERON BAY	LB	LB03		76	C5
HERONDO ST	HB	RB	1	67	C2
HERONDO ST	RB	RB	100	67	C2
HERRICK AV	LA	PAC	11400	3	A6
HERRICK AV	LA	PAC	10900	9	A1
HERRICK AV	LA	SF	11500	2	F6
HERRICK AV	LA	SV	8800	9	E5
HERRIN AV	MB	MB	1800	62	D3
HERRIN ST	RB	RB	1500	62	D6
HERRIN ST N	MB	MB	100	62	D4
HERRIN ST S	MB	MB	100	62	D4
HERRING AV	WCOV	WCOV	600	92	B2
HERRON ST	LA	SF	13400	2	F2
HERRON ST	LA	SF	13000	3	A2
HERSHEY AV	MPK	MPK	700	46	D1
HERSHEY ST	LA	SV	11000	9	E4
HERSHEY ST	POM	POM	100	95	A2
HERSHEY ST	RM	RM	7800	46	E1
HERSHOLT AV	LB	LB08	4700	71	C2
HERSHOLT AV	LKD	LKD	5900	66	C6
HERSHOLT AV	LKD	LKD	4900	71	C2
HERSKIND RD	CO	SAU		181	J9
HERVEY ST	LA	LA34	8600	42	D5
HERZEL AV	LAN	LAN		160	D6
HESBY ST	LA	ENC	15500	22	B2
HESBY ST	LA	NHO	10800	23	C2
HESBY ST	LA	VAN	13600	22	E2
HESBY ST	LA	VAN	12900	23	A2
HESPERIA AV	LA	ENC	5600	14	D6
HESPERIA AV	LA	ENC	4900	21	D2
HESPERIA AV	LA	RES	6200	14	D5
HESPERIAN AV	LB	LB10	3600	69	F5
HESPERO ST	CO	LPUE	18200	98	D4
HESSE DR	LAM	LAM	15600	83	B3
HESTER AV	CO	WHI	10600	84	B4
HESTER AV	WHI	WHI	10200	84	B3
HESTON ST	CO	SGAB	8300	37	F3
HETZLER RD	CO	CUL	6200	42	D6
HETZLER RD	LA	CUL	6100	42	D6
HETZLER RD	LA	LA16	3600	42	D6
HEWITT AV	LA	SF	11200	8	E1
HEWITT ST	SF	SF	600	2	D6
HEWITT ST N	LA	LA12	500	44	E3
HEWITT ST S	LA	LA12	100	44	E3
HEWITT ST S	LA	LA13	300	44	E4
HEYER ST W	LAN	LAN	500	160	A7
HEYWOOD DR	SCLR	SAU		124	E5
HIATT ST	LHH	LAH		98A	A3
HIAWATHA AV	AVA	AVA	100	77	B5
HIAWATHA DR	GLEN	GL08	1700	18	F6
HIAWATHA ST	LA	CHA	19800	6	F3
HIAWATHA ST	LA	NOR	17900	7	C3
HIAWATHA ST	LA	SF	16800	7	E3
HIAWATHA ST	LA	SF	14700	8	C3
HIBBING ST	ART	ART	12000	81	B1
HIBBING ST	CER	ART		71	E1
HIBISCUS ST	MTB	MTB	900	46	F5
HICKMAN DR	TOR	TOR	4000	63	B6
HICKOCK LN	CAR	CAR		69	D6
HICKOCK LN	NWK	NWK	12800	82	C1
HICKORY AV	COM	COM	800	64	F2
HICKORY AV	POM	POM	200	90	E3
HICKORY AV	TOR	TOR	600	68	C4
HICKORY AV	TOR	TOR	22500	68	B5
HICKORY DR	LAV	LAV		95A	C6
HICKORY LN	PAS	PAS	500	26	F3
HICKORY PL	CO	SAU		124	C3
HICKORY ST	CO	LA01	8300	58	E2
HICKORY ST	CO	LA02	8600	58	E2
HICKORY ST	LA	LA02	9200	58	E3
HICKORY ST	LA	LA16	4700	43	A5
HICKORY ST	LA	LA59	10700	58	E4
HICKORY ST	PALM	LAN		171	B2
HICKORY GLEN AV	LAN	LAN		159	B9
HICKORY HILL DR	LAM	LAM	15800	84	C6
HICKORY HILL LN	WAL	WAL		92	F5
HICKORY NUT LN	DBAR	POM		97	F3
HICKS AV	LA	LA32	2000	45	C1
HICKS AV N	CO	LA63	100	45	C4
HICKS AV S	CMRC	LA23		53	C1
HICKS AV S	CO	LA23	800	45	C6
HICKS AV S	CO	LA23	1200	53	C1
HICKS AV S	CO	LA63	100	45	C4
HICKSON ST	CO	ELM	10400	38	D5
HICKSON ST	ELM	ELM	10400	38	D5
HICREST RD	CO	GLDR	18500	86	F4
HICREST RD	GLDR	GLDR	1100	86	F4
HIDALGO AV	LA	LA39	2200	35	C3
HIDALGO AV N	ALH	ALH	100	37	C2
HIDALGO AV S	ALH	ALH	100	37	C2
HIDALGO PL	CO	MAL		114	E4
HIDALGO ST	DOW	DOW	7500	59	F5
HIDALGO ST	IRW	BAP	15600	88	A3
HIDAWAY AV	SCLR	CYN	27200	124	H5
HIDAWAY AV	SCLR	CYN	27200	124	J9
HIDDEN LN	CO	PVP		73	B4
HIDDEN LN	ELM	ELM	3200	47	D1
HIDDEN LN	LB	LB15	1900	76	E3
HIDDEN TR	CO	SF	12200	3	D5
HIDDEN TR	LA	TU	10100	11	B4
HIDDEN CYN RD	LHH	LAH	1400	84	E2
HIDDEN CREEK RD	SAD	SAD		90	B1
HIDDENCREEK WY	CER	ART	12400	82	C4
HIDDN HGHLND RD	CO	AGO		106	A3
HIDDEN HLS CIR	POM	POM		94	C5
HIDDEN OAK DR	LA	SUN	10200	10	C3
HIDDEN PINE DR	CO	SGAB	7100	28	A6
HIDDEN PINES DR	DBAR	POM	21200	97	D5
HIDDEN PINES PL	RM	RM	1600	37	F5
HIDDEN PINES PL	RM	RM	1600	38	A5
HIDDEN RIDGE LN	CER	ART		82	C4
HIDDEN SPGS LN	GLDR	GLDR	1100	87	D4
HIDDEN TRAIL PL	WAL	WAL		93	A4
HIDDEN TRAIL RD	CO	SAU		123	E5
HIDDEN VLY DR	WCOV	WCOV	1200	92	E3
HIDDEN VLY PL	LA	BH	9400	33	C1
HIDDEN VLY RD	LA	BH	9500	33	B1
HIDDEN VLY RD	MON	MON	300	29	A2
HIDDEN VLY RD	POM	POM		94	C6
HIDDEN VLY RD	RHE	PVP	25900	72	F3
HIDEAWAY LN	WCOV	WCOV		97	A2
HIDEOUT DR	DBAR	POM	21200	97	D5
HIDEOUT DR	WCOV	WCOV		93	A3
HIERRO WY	CO	CAL		108	C2
HIGA RD	CO	ACT		182	C5
HIGBEE AV	LAN	LAN	43700	160	A6
HIGGINS CT	TOR	TOR		68	E3
HIGGINS ST	LA	NHO	11600	16	D4
HIGH LN	RB	RB	600	67	E1
HIGH PL	SM	SM	1900	41	C6
HIGH ST	ING	IN02	900	51	B6
HIGH ST	LA	LA42	5600	26	C6
HIGH ST	TOR	TOR		73	A2
HIGH ST E	WHI	WHI	13400	61	E1
HIGHACRES AV E	CO	LAN	16100	174	J4
HIGHACRES AV E	CO	LAN	16600	175	A5
HIGHBLUFF DR	DBAR	POM		97A	A3
HIGHBLUFF RD	DBAR	POM		97	D6
HIGHBLUFF RD	DBAR	POM		99	E4
HIGHBURY AV	LA	LA32	2200	36	E6
HIGHCASTLE ST	WCOV	WCOV	18900	98	F2
HIGH CHPRL AV E	CO	LAN	16000	174	H6
HIGHCLIFF DR	TOR	TOR	2500	73	B3
HIGHCLIFF ST	RM	RM	7600	46	E2
HIGHCLIFF TR	LA	TU	7000	11	A4
HIGH COUNTRY DR	DBAR	POM		97	C4
HIGH COUNTRY DR	GLDR	GLDR		89	D1
HIGH COUNTRY LN	CO	CYN		125	D7
HIGH COUNTRY RD	PALM	PALM		172	A9
HIGHCREST AV	LA	LA41	5100	26	C4
HIGHCREST DR	DBAR	POM		97A	B1
HIGHCROSS DR	TOR	TOR	26000	73	B4
HIGHDALE ST	BLF	BLF	9200	66	D3
HIGHDALE ST	NWK	NWK	11300	66	F3
HIGHDALE ST	NWK	NWK	11800	82	A3
HIGHFALLS ST	SCLR	CYN		125	C8
HIGHGATE AV	LA	LA42	1300	26	C6
HIGHGATE AV	POM	POM	100	90	E3
HIGH GLEN WY	LA	NOR		1	A4
HIGH GLEN WY	LA	NOR		1A	F4
HIGHGROVE AV	TOR	TOR	4300	72	F1
HIGHGROVE ST	TOR	TOR		67	E6
HIGHGROVE TER	LA	LA42	1000	26	D6
HIGH HILL DR	LA	TU	9700	10	F4
HIGH KNOB RD	DBAR	POM		94	B5
HIGH KNOLL DR	LA	ENC		22	B4
HIGH KNOLL RD	LA	ENC	15500	22	B4
HIGHLAND AV	CO	ALT	2300	20	C5
HIGHLAND AV	DUA	DUA	600	29	E5
HIGHLAND AV	GLEN	GL02	700	25	B2
HIGHLAND AV	MB	MB	200	62	A3
HIGHLAND AV	SM	SM	2600	49	B2
HIGHLAND AV	WHI	WHI	8600	84	A2
HIGHLAND AV E	SMAD	SMAD	100	28	B2
HIGHLAND AV N	LA	LA28	1300	34	B3
HIGHLAND AV N	LA	LA36	100	34	B6
HIGHLAND AV N	LA	LA38	700	34	B6
HIGHLAND AV N	LA	LA68	1900	34	B3
HIGHLAND AV S	LA	LA16	1900	43	A4
HIGHLAND AV S	LA	LA19	1000	43	B3
HIGHLAND AV S	LA	LA36	100	34	B6
HIGHLAND AV S	LA	LA36	200	43	B1
HIGHLAND AV W	SMAD	SMAD	100	28	B2
HIGHLAND CT	PALM	PALM		184	D4
HIGHLAND DR	GLDR	GLDR	400	87	D5
HIGHLAND DR	LA	LA16	1900	43	A4
HIGHLAND DR	LAV	LAV		90	B3
HIGHLAND DR	LCF	LCF	100	19	C5
HIGHLAND DR	MPK	MPK	1100	46	A3
HIGHLAND PL	MON	MON	100	29	A3
HIGHLAND PL	SAD	SAD		89	E2
HIGHLAND ST	PALM	PALM		184	D4
HIGHLAND ST	PAS	PAS	300	20	B6
HIGHLAND ST	SPAS	SPAS	1000	36	F1
HIGHLAND TR	LA	LA46	7900	33	F2
HIGHLANDER RD	LA	CAN	23700	5	D3
HIGHLAND GLN DR	SCLR	NEW		127	B5
HIGHLAND GOR DR	LA	BH	9600	33	A3
HIGHLAND GOR TR	LA	BH	9600	33	A3
HIGHLAND OAK DR	ARC	ARC	2300	20A	F3
HIGHLAND OKS DR	ARC	ARC	100	28	E2
HIGHLANDS DR	CO	PAS		20	F6
HIGHLANDS LN	CO	VAL		124	F3
HIGHLAND VLY RD	DBAR	POM		94	A5
HIGHLAND VW AV	LA	LA41	4900	26	A4
HIGHLAND VW DR	BUR	BUR	3100	17	C2
HIGHLAND VW PL	LA	LA41	5300	26	A4
HIGHLAND VIS DR	ARC	ARC	2100	20A	F3
HIGHLAWN PL	CO	ALT	100	20	A4
HIGHLIGHT DR	WCOV	WCOV		93	A3
HIGHLIGHT PL	LA	LA16	5300	42	F6
HIGHLINE RD	GLEN	GL05	800	25	E5
HIGH MESA DR	DUA	DUA	2300	29	F3
HIGHMORE AV	RPV	SP	29000	78	E1
HIGH OAK DR	LA	LA68	2300	34	D2
HIGH PEAK PL	AGH	AGO		102	E3
HIGHPINE ST	CO	RM	8600	47	A4
HIGHPLAINS CT	CO	SAU		123	D5
HIGH POINT DR	CLA	CLA		96	A5
HIGHPOINT DR	CO	AGO		107	A2
HIGHPOINT DR	LAM	LAM		83	C1
HIGH POINT DR	PALM	PALM		183	E2
HIGH POINT PL	SCLR	CYN		124	G7
HIGHPOINT RD	RPV	PVP	29600	78	C2
HIGHRIDGE DR	LA	BH		33	A2
HIGHRIDGE PL	LA	BH		33	A2
HIGHRIDGE RD	CO	GL14	2800	11	D4
HIGHRIDGE RD	HH	CAL		100	D1
HIGHRIDGE RD	RHE	PVP	27800	72	D5
HIGHRIDGE RD	RPV	PVP		72	D4
HIGHRIDGE RD	RPV	PVP		77	D1
HIGHRIM RD	CO	GL14	2100	11	F5
HIGHSPIRE DR	WCOV	WCOV	2200	92	E3
HIGHSPRING AV	SCLR	NEW	25100	127	B4
HIGH SPRINGS RD	CO	PALM		183	A4
HIGHTIDE DR	RPV	PVP	3400	78	B3
HIGHTOP DR	LA	TU		10	F4
HIGH TOR DR	CO	LPUE		85	E5
HIGH TOWER DR	LA	LA68	2000	34	B1
HIGHTREE RD	LA	SM	600	40	E4
HIGHTREE ST	PR	PR	9000	55	A2
HIGHVALE TR	CO	TOP	21400	109	E4
HIGH VALLEY PL	LA	ENC	16100	22	A4
HIGH VALLEY RD	LA	ENC	4100	22	A4
HIGHVIEW AV	CO	ALT	2600	20	A5
HIGHVIEW AV	MB	MB	800	62	B4
HIGH VIEW RIDGE	LA	NOR		1	A4
HIGH VISTA AV	PALM	PALM		183	E2
HIGHWATER RD	LA	SF	11800	1	D5
HWY ESPLANADE	MON	MON	800	29	A4
HIGHWOOD RD	CO	LPUE		98	B4
HIGHWOOD ST	LA	LA49	12700	41	A2
HIGMAN AV	LA	LA28	6800	34	B4
HIGUERA ST	CUL	CUL	8400	42	D6
HILARY LN	LA	BH	1100	32	F4
HILBERT AV	CO	LPUE	200	48	A4
HILDA AV	GLEN	GL05	1300	25	E5
HILDA ST	LB	LB05		65	E4
HILDRETH AV	SOG	SOG	8900	59	C4
HILE AV N	LB	LB04	1500	75	F3
HILGARD AV	LA	LA24	100	32	E6
HILGARD AV	LA	LA24	500	41	E1
HILL AV	CO	ALT	1900	20	C6
HILL AV	CO	PAS	1700	20	C6
HILL AV	WHI	WHI	6200	55	F4
HILL AV N	PAS	PAS	100	27	C1
HILL AV S	PAS	PAS	100	27	C4
HILL CT	SM	SM	400	49	B2
HILL DR	CO	RM	7800	46	E3
HILL DR	GLEN	GL06	500	25	F3
HILL DR	LA	LA41	2300	25	F4
HILL DR	LA	LA41	1100	26	A4
HILL DR	SPAS	SPAS	1600	36	D3
HILL LN	RB	RB	2300	62	E6
HILL LN	SPAS	SPAS	1300	36	F2
HILL PL	LA	LA12	600	44	D2
HILL RD	CO	CAL		100	F5
HILL RD	CUL	CUL	5900	50	D3
HILL ST	AVA	AVA	100	77	B5
HILL ST	CO	HPK	2400	52	F6
HILL ST	CO	HPK	2900	59	B1
HILL ST	HB	RB	100	67	C2
HILL ST	HPK	HPK	3200	59	B1
HILL ST	ING	IN02	500	50	E6
HILL ST	LCF	LCF	4500	19	B2
HILL ST	LPUE	LPUE	15400	48	F5
HILL ST	LPUE	LPUE		92	A5
HILL ST	MON	MON	300	29	B3
HILL ST	SH	LB06	1200	75	C2
HILL ST	SM	SM	600	49	B2
HILL ST E	LB	LB06	100	75	C2
HILL ST E	LB	LB15	5000	76	B2
HILL ST N	LA	LA12	100	44	D2
HILL ST S	LA	LA07	1900	44	B6
HILL ST S	LA	LA07	3400	52	A1
HILL ST S	LA	LA12	100	44	C4
HILL ST S	LA	LA13	300	44	C4
HILL ST S	LA	LA14	600	44	C4
HILL ST S	LA	LA15	900	44	C4
HILL ST S	LA	LA37	3800	52	A1
HILL ST W	LB	LB06	100	75	C2
HILL ST W	LB	LB10	2100	74	F2
HILL ST W	LB	LB10	1200	75	A2
HILLANDALE DR	LA	LA42	6000	26	C6
HILLARD AV	LCF	LCF	4400	19	A2
HILLARY DR	LA	CAN	7800	5	E2
HILLBORN	WCOV	WCOV	400	92	D1
HILLCASTLE LN	CO	TOR		68	F5
HILLCREST AV	ELS	ELS	300	56	A6
HILLCREST AV	GLEN	GL02	1700	18	B6
HILLCREST AV	GLEN	GL02	1400	25	B2
HILLCREST AV	LCF	LCF	600	19	C5
HILLCREST AV	LOM	LOM	26300	73	E4
HILLCREST AV	PAS	PAS	1100	27	B6
HILLCREST BLVD	ARC	ARC	300	28	F3
HILLCREST BLVD	MON	MON	700	28	F3
HILLCREST BLVD	MON	MON	100	29	A3
HILLCREST BL E	ING	IN01	100	57	A2
HILLCREST BL N	ING	IN01	300	51	A6
HILLCREST BL N	ING	IN01	100	57	A1
HILLCREST BL S	ING	IN01	100	57	A1
HILLCREST BL W	ING	IN01	100	56	E2
HILLCREST DR	CO	BH		33	A2
HILLCREST DR	CO	PALM		184	A2
HILLCREST DR	CO	TOP	700	109	B5
HILLCREST DR	HB	RB	1800	62	C6
HILLCREST DR	LA	BH		33	A2
HILLCREST DR	LA	BH		33	A3
HILLCREST DR	LA	LA08	3900	51	A2
HILLCREST DR	LA	LA16	1900	43	B6
HILLCREST DR	LA	LA43	4900	51	B4
HILLCREST DR	LAV	LAV	2700	90	C2
HILLCREST DR	LPUE	LPUE		92	A6
HILLCREST DR	POM	POM	900	90	C6
HILLCREST DR	WLVL	THO		102A	F1
HILLCREST LN	WAL	WAL		93	D6
HILLCREST PL	PAS	PAS	800	27	B6
HILLCREST PL	POM	POM	800	90	D6
HILLCREST RD	BH	BH	500	33	C3
HILLCREST RD	LA	LA28	1700	34	B3
HILLCREST RD	LA	LA68	1900	34	B3
HILLCREST ST	WAL	WAL		93	B5
HILLCREST WY	LA	LA68	6900	34	B2
HILLCROFT DR	LA	CAN		4	A6
HILLCROFT DR	LA	CAN	8300	5	D1
HILLCROFT RD	GLEN	GL07	900	25	D2
HILLCROFT TR	LA	CAN	8600	4	B6
HILLDALE AV	LA	LA69	1100	33	D4
HILLDALE AV	WHOL	LA69	800	33	D5
HILLDALE CT	LA	PAC		3	B4
HILLDALE CT	LA	PAC		9	D3
HILLDALE DR	CO	MONT	1900	18	F3
HILLDALE DR	LCF	LCF	1900	18	F3
HILLDALE PL	CO	LPUE		48	B5
HILLDYKE	CO	LAN	47600	147	J7
HILLEN DR	CLA	CLA		90	F1
HILLER PL	LA	LA46	1700	33	F3
HILLFAIR DR	GLEN	GL08	2000	25	F1
HILLFIELD LN	SCLR	CYN	28100	125	A7
HILLFORD AV	CAR	CAR	19000	69	D1
HILLFORD AV	CO	COM	13900	64	D2
HILLFORD AV N	COM	COM	400	64	D2
HILLFORD AV S	COM	COM	900	64	D4
HILLGATE DR	CO	WHI	15800	84	C5

INDEX

1990 LOS ANGELES COUNTY STREET INDEX

STREET	CITY	P.O. ZONE	BLOCK	PAGE	GRID
HILLGATE DR	LAM	LAM	15700	84	C5
HILLGREEN DR	BH	BH	400	42	B2
HILLGREEN DR	LA	LA35	1200	42	B2
HILLGREEN PL	ARC	ARC	200	28	E1
HILLGREEN PL	BH	BH	9800	42	B2
HILLGROVE DR	LA	BH	10000	32	F4
HILLGROVE PL	LA	BH	1200	32	F4
HILLHAVEN AV	LA	TU	9400	10	F4
HILLHAVEN DR	WCOV	WCOV		89	A6
HILLHAVEN DR	WCOV	WCOV	3400	93	A1
HILLHAVEN PL	LA	TU	9500	10	F5
HILLHAVEN TER	CO	LPUE		48	B5
HILLHURST AV	LA	LA27	1900	34	F2
HILLHURST AV	LA	LA27	1500	35	A2
HILLHURST DR	LA	CAN		5	D3
HILLIARD AV	MPK	MPK	100	46	C1
HILLIARD DR	SMAR	PAS	1600	37	E1
HILLMAN LN	CO	LPUE		97	A5
HILLMAN LN	CO	LPUE		98	F5
HILLMAR DR	DBAR	POM		97	E2
HILLMONT AV	LA	LA41	5300	26	C4
HILL OAK DR	LA	LA68	5600	34	D2
HILLOCK DR	LA	LA68	3200	24	B5
HILLPARK DR	LA	LA68	6700	34	B1
HILLRISE DR	AGH	AGO		102	F3
HILLRISE DR	CO	WAL		97	B5
HILLROSE CIR	LA	SUN	10600	10	C2
HILLROSE ST	LA	SUN	7800	10	D2
HILLROSE ST	LA	TU	7200	10	F2
HILLROSE ST	LA	TU	7000	11	A2
HILLSBORO	LA	SF42		2	C1
HILLSBORO AV	LA	LA34	2000	42	C3
HILLSBORO AV	LA	LA35	1800	42	C3
HILLSBORO DR	LA	LA34	9100	42	C4
HILLSBORO PL	SCLR	CYN		125	B8
HILLSBORO RD	LA	NOR		7	B2
HILLSBOROUGH DR	LAM	LAM		83	C2
HILLSBOROUGH PY	CO	VAL		124	B6
HILLSBOROUGH PL	WCOV	WCOV		92	D6
HILLSDALE DR	CLA	CLA	1100	90	F2
HILLSDALE DR	LA	LA32	4700	36	D4
HILLSDALE ST E	ING	IN02	300	51	A5
HILLSDALE ST W	ING	IN02	100	50	F5
HILLSFALL CT	SCLR	NEW		127	H3
HILLSIDE AV	LAN	LAN		160	E9
HILLSIDE AV	LA	LA28	7000	34	A3
HILLSIDE AV	LA	LA46	7800	33	F3
HILLSIDE AV	LA	LA46	7100	34	A3
HILLSIDE AV	LA	LA69	8100	33	E3
HILLSIDE CT	LHH	LAH	2200	84	F1
HILLSIDE DR	CO	TOP	20200	109	D2
HILLSIDE DR	GLEN	GL08	1300	18	E6
HILLSIDE DR	LB	LB15		76	D4
HILLSIDE DR	POM	POM	1000	94	C1
HILLSIDE DR	TOR	TOR		73	C3
HILLSIDE DR	WCOV	WCOV		92	F3
HILLSIDE DR	WCOV	WCOV		93	A3
HILLSIDE LN	CO	LPUE		48	B5
HILLSIDE LN	LA	SM	400	40	D5
HILLSIDE LN	RH	PVP	1	73	B5
HILLSIDE LN	WHI	WHI	6200	55	F5
HILLSIDE PL	POM	POM	1100	94	C1
HILLSIDE RD	PAS	PAS	1100	26	F6
HILLSIDE RD	SPAS	SPAS	200	26	F6
HILLSIDE ST	MPK	MPK	1000	45	F3
HILLSIDE TER	PAS	PAS	600	26	E6
HILLSIDE WY	LA	LA69	1700	33	E3
HILLSLOPE ST	LA	NHO	12100	23	C4
HILLTONIA DR	WCOV	WCOV		93	A6
HILLTONIA DR	WCOV	WCOV		97	A1
HILLTOP CIR	RPV	PVP		72	D4
HILLTOP CT	CO	SAU		124	G3
HILLTOP DR	AZU	AZU	1400	86	D4
HILLTOP PL	LAM	LAM		83	D1
HILL TOP RD	HH	CAL	5600	100	D1
HILLTOP RD	LA	LA41	5300	26	A4
HILLTOP TER	CO	SAU		182	A7
HILLTOP TER	PALM	PALM		172	A9
HILLTOP CLMB DR	CO	CAL		108	B6
HILLTREE RD	LA	SM	14600	40	D4
HILLVALE DR	MPK	MPK	900	46	A4
HILLVIEW AV	LA	CAN	8400	12	C1
HILLVIEW AV	LA	CHA	10000	6	C3
HILLVIEW AV	MPK	MPK		46	A4
HILLVIEW AV N	CO	LA22	100	46	A5
HILLVIEW AV S	CO	LA22	300	45	F5
HILLVIEW AV S	CO	LA22	100	46	A5
HILLVIEW AV S	CO	LA22	900	53	F1
HILLVIEW CT	WHI	WHI	11700	55	C4
HILLVIEW DR	CO	LPUE		48	B5
HILL VIEW DR	CO	MAL		112	E4
HILLVIEW LN	LA	SF		2	B6
HILL VIEW PL	LA	LA32	3500	36	C4
HILLVIEW PK AV	LA	VAN	5700	15	F6
HILLWARD AV	WCOV	WCOV	400	92	D2
HILLWARD ST	WCOV	WCOV	200	92	D1

STREET	CITY	P.O. ZONE	BLOCK	PAGE	GRID
HILLWAY DR	GLEN	GL08	3700	18	D2
HILLWOOD DR	CO	WHI	12200	84	A6
HILLWORTH AV	LOM	LOM	25800	73	C3
HILO CT	SCLR	VAL		127	A2
HILO ST	WCOV	WCOV		92	C4
HILSE LN	SCLR	NEW	23000	127	B2
HILTON AV	TEC	TEC	5400	38	B3
HILTON DR	BUR	BUR	1800	17	D3
HILTON HEAD DR	DBAR	POM		97	F1
HILTS AV	LA	LA24	900	41	E1
HIMAN ST	CO	SAU		189	D2
HIMBER PL	LA	HAC	23500	73	E1
HINCHLIFFE PL	CO	PALM		183	B3
HINDRY AV	CO	HAW	12000	56	E6
HINDRY AV	CO	LAW	14300	62	E2
HINDRY AV	HAW	HAW	13000	62	E2
HINDRY AV	ING	IN01	200	56	E2
HINDRY AV	LA	LA45	7700	56	E1
HINDRY PL	LA	LA45	9200	56	E3
HINDS AV	LA	NHO	6500	16	C5
HINES AL	PAS	PAS	700	27	B2
HINES AV	CUL	CUL	2600	42	E5
HINES DR	LA	LA65	2400	35	F2
HINNEN AV	CO	LPUE	1100	85	F2
HINSDALE AV	TOR	TOR	19200	67	E2
HINTON AV	LA	WOH	5900	5	F6
HINTON AV	LA	WOH	5300	100	F2
HI PASS DR	DBAR	POM	21200	97	D5
HI POINT ST	LA	LA34	1900	42	E3
HI POINT ST	LA	LA35	1000	42	E3
HIPSHOT DR	CO	CAST		123	G2
HIRONDELLE LN	LA	TU	9900	10	F4
HISEY RANCH RD	CO	ACT		182	C9
HITCHCOCK DR	ALH	ALH	22000	46	B1
HITCHCOCK PL	PALM	PALM		183	C5
HITCHING PST DR	RHE	PVP	1	73	C5
HITE ST	BLF	BLF	13700	66	C1
HOADSEY	CO	ACT		182	J9
HOB AV	SCLR	SAU		124	G4
HOBACK ST	BLF	BLF	9400	66	C1
HOBACK ST	LAM	LAM	13800	82	E1
HOBACK ST	NWK	NWK	11700	82	A1
HOBACK GLEN RD	HH	CAL	24500	100	D2
HOBAN AV	LAN	LAN	44000	160	A5
HOBART BLVD N	LA	LA04	100	34	E6
HOBART BLVD N	LA	LA27	1300	34	E3
HOBART BLVD N	LA	LA29	700	34	E6
HOBART BLVD S	CO	GAR	14000	63	E2
HOBART BLVD S	CO	LA47	10800	57	E5
HOBART BLVD S	GAR	GAR	16000	63	E5
HOBART BLVD S	LA	LA04	100	34	E6
HOBART BLVD S	LA	LA05	600	43	E3
HOBART BLVD S	LA	LA06	900	43	E3
HOBART BLVD S	LA	LA18	1900	43	E5
HOBART BLVD S	LA	LA20	300	43	E3
HOBART BLVD S	LA	LA47	6000	51	E6
HOBART BLVD S	LA	LA47	8600	57	E3
HOBART BLVD S	LA	LA62	3800	51	E2
HOBART BLVD S	LA	TOR	21100	68	E4
HOBART DR	CLA	CLA		91	C2
HOBART PL N	LA	LA04	300	34	E6
HOBBS DR	LCF	LCF	4400	19	C4
HOBSON AV	LB	LB13	1600	74	F4
HOBSON AV	LA	WIL	800	74	F4
HOBSON CT	CO	CAL		100	B2
HOBSON CT	POM	POM	500	94	E4
HOCKEY TR	LA	LA68	7100	34	A1
HODGES AV	CO	ARC	3000	39	A2
HODGSON CIR DR	CO	TOP	2600	108	F1
HODLER DR	CO	TOP		13	C5
HOEFFER DR	ALH	ALH	1200	37	D2
HOEFNER AV	CMRC	LA40	2000	53	F2
HOEFNER AV	CO	LA22	400	46	A6
HOFFMAN AV	CER	ART		66	E5
HOFFMAN AV	LB	LB13	800	75	E4
HOFFMAN ST	LA	NHO	12000	23	C4
HOFGAARDEN ST	LPUE	LPUE		98	A1
HOGAN DR	SCLR	VAL		127	A3
HOGAN WK	LA	LA08	4300	51	C2
HOGEE DR	PAR	SOG	7100	59	D6
HOG FARM RD N	CO	CAST		123	F2
HOG FARM RD S	CO	CAST		123	F2
HOIG ST	CO	LPUE	13500	48	B4
HOKE AV	CUL	CUL	3800	42	C6
HOLABIRD AV	LA	LA23	3300	53	B1
HOLANDA RD	LA	WOH	22600	13	B2
HOLBORN DR	CAR	CAR	700	69	C2
HOLBORO DR	LA	LA27	3500	35	B1
HOLBROOK AL	PAS	PAS	1600	27	D2
HOLBROOK CT	LB	LB03		76	F5
HOLBROOK ST	CO	WHI	10200	55	B3
HOLBROOK ST	LA	LA41	1400	26	C5
HOLBROOK ST	PR	PR	8600	54	F3
HOLBROOK ST	PR	PR	9400	55	A3
HOLCOMB ST	LA	LA35	9600	42	C3
HOLCROFT DR	CO	WAL		97	B4

STREET	CITY	P.O. ZONE	BLOCK	PAGE	GRID
HOLDMAN AV	SMAD	SMAD	1	28	D2
HOLDREGE AV	LA	LA16	3600	42	D6
HOLFORD ST	CO	WHI	2300	47	E5
HOLGATE SQ	LA	LA31	2300	36	B6
HOLGER DR	MTB	MTB	300	54	F1
HOLGUIN ST	LAN	LAN	1100	159	J2
HOLGUIN ST W	LAN	LAN	700	160	A2
HOLIDAY DR	WCOV	WCOV		93	A3
HOLLADAY RD	PAS	PAS	600	27	C5
HOLLADAY RD	SMAR	PAS		27	C5
HOLLAND AV	LA	LA42	400	36	B2
HOLLAND DR	LA	TU		10	F4
HOLLANDALE AV	CO	LPUE	1500	97	A4
HOLLANDER ST	POM	POM	2800	90	F3
HOLLENBECK AV	CO	COV	3200	88	D5
HOLLENBECK AV N	COV	COV	100	88	D5
HOLLENBECK AV S	COV	COV	100	88	D5
HOLLENBECK DR	LA	LA23	2000	44	F4
HOLLENBECK ST	HPK	HPK	6200	53	B5
HOLLENBECK ST	WCOV	WCOV	200	92	D2
HOLLENCREST CIR	WCOV	WCOV	2200	92	E3
HOLLENCREST DR	WCOV	WCOV	1200	92	E3
HOLLIFIELD CT	RPV	SP		78	D1
HOLLINGWORTH ST	CO	LPUE	19000	97	A1
HOLLINGWORTH ST	WCOV	WCOV	2900	97	A1
HOLLINGWORTH ST	WCOV	WCOV		98	F1
HOLLINS AV	CLA	CLA		96	D5
HOLLINS ST	LA	LA23	900	45	A5
HOLLIS AV	AZU	AZU	1300	86	C4
HOLLIS LN	ARC	ARC		38	F2
HOLLIS ST	CO	LPUE	15400	85	D2
HOLLISTER AV	LA	LA32	2800	36	E5
HOLLISTER AV	SM	SM	100	49	A2
HOLLISTER ST	SF	SF	600	2	E6
HOLLISTER TER	GLEN	GL06	2100	26	B3
HOLLISTON AV	CO	ALT	1900	20	C6
HOLLISTON AV N	PAS	PAS	1	27	C2
HOLLISTON AV S	PAS	PAS	1	27	C4
HOLLOW AV N	WCOV	WCOV	300	88	A6
HOLLOWAY DR	WHOL	LA69	8400	33	D4
HOLLOWAY PZ DR	WHOL	LA69	8600	33	D4
HOLLOW BROOK AV	AGH	AGO		100A	A2
HOLLOW CORNR LN	CUL	CUL		50	C2
HOLLOWELL AV	HB	RB	200	67	D1
HOLLOWELL AV	TEC	ARC	5500	38	D4
HOLLOW GLEN CIR	LA	LA77		22	E6
HOLLOWGLEN DR	PALM	PALM		183	H2
HOLLOW OAK CT	AGH	AGO		100A	A2
HOLLOW PINE DR	DBAR	WAL		97	C3
HOLLOW SPGS DR	LA	NOR		1	A5
HOLLOW SPGS DR	LA	NOR		1A	F5
HOLLY AV	ARC	ARC	900	28	D6
HOLLY AV	ARC	ARC	1500	38	D2
HOLLY AV	BAP	BAP	3600	39	E5
HOLLY AV	COM	COM	100	65	B3
HOLLY AV	LB	LB10		70	A3
HOLLY AV	MON	MON	200	29	C4
HOLLY AV E	ELS	ELS	100	56	B6
HOLLY AV W	ELS	ELS	100	56	A6
HOLLY CT	CO	SAU		124	D2
HOLLY DR	GLEN	GL06	1700	25	F3
HOLLY DR	LA	LA68	1900	34	C2
HOLLY PL	LA	LA46	8900	33	D2
HOLLY PL	WCOV	WCOV	700	92	B2
HOLLY ST	ING	IN01	900	56	F2
HOLLY ST	LAN	LAN		159	H6
HOLLY ST E	PAS	PAS	100	27	A4
HOLLY ST W	PAS	PAS	700	26	F4
HOLLY WY	POM	POM	1500	95	A4
HOLLYBROOK DR	WCOV	WCOV	18900	92	F3
HOLLYBURNE CT	GLEN	GL06		26	C1
HOLLYBUSH LN	LA	LA77		32	E4
HOLLY CREST DR	LA	LA68	3000	24	B6
HOLLY CREST PL	LA	LA68	3000	24	B6
HOLLYDALE DR	LA	LA39	3100	35	C2
HOLLY GLEN DR	LB	LB15		76	D4
HOLLYGLEN LN	SAD	SAD		89	F1
HOLLYGLEN PL	LA	NHO	12100	23	C4
HOLLYGROVE LN	CO	ALT	1000	19	E2
HOLLYHILL LN	GLDR	GLDR	1600	87	D4
HOLLY HILL TER	LA	LA68	2000	34	C2
HOLLYHOCK CT	CO	NEW		126	J4
HOLLYHOCK PL	LA	LA49	3700	21	F6
HOLLYHOCK ST	SFS	SFS	11200	60	F3
HOLLY KNOLL DR	LA	LA27	4000	35	A2
HOLLY LEAF WY	DBAR	POM		97	F3
HOLLYLINE AV	LA	VAN	3800	22	E4
HOLLYMONT DR	LA	LA68	6200	34	C2
HOLLY OAK CIR	CER	ART		82	D5
HOLLY OAK DR	LA	LA68	5600	34	D2
HOLLY OAK DR	MPK	MPK	1600	46	D4
HOLLY OAK DR	WCOV	WCOV	1400	92	C1
HOLLY OAK PL	MPK	MPK	800	46	D4
HOLLY OAK PL	WCOV	WCOV	300	92	C1
HOLLY OAK ST	LAV	LAV	1600	90	C2
HOLLYPARK DR	ING	IN05	3100	57	C2

STREET	CITY	P.O. ZONE	BLOCK	PAGE	GRID
HOLLYPARK PL	LA	LA39	3800	25	B6
HOLLY RIDGE DR	SCLR	VAL		124	B5
HOLLYRIDGE DR	LA	LA68	2900	24	D6
HOLLYRIDGE DR	LA	LA68	2100	34	D1
HOLLYRIDGE LOOP	LA	LA68	2100	34	D2
HOLLYSLOPE RD	CO	ALT	3400	20	B3
HOLLY TRAIL	SMAD	SMAD		28	D1
HOLLY TR PATH	SMAD	SMAD	600	28	D1
HOLLY TREE RD	CO	LPUE	14700	85	C3
HOLLYVALE ST	GLDR	GLDR	19000	86	F6
HOLLYVALE ST E	AZU	AZU	500	86	D6
HOLLYVALE ST W	AZU	AZU	600	86	C6
HOLLYVIEW DR	LAM	LAM	11600	84	A5
HOLLYVIEW TER	CUL	CUL	3800	50	E1
HOLLYVISTA AV	LA	LA27	1700	35	B3
HOLLY VISTA DR	PAS	PAS	800	26	E3
HOLLYWELL PL	GLEN	GL06	3100	26	B1
HOLLYWOOD BLVD	LA	LA27	4400	34	E3
HOLLYWOOD BLVD	LA	LA28	5500	34	E3
HOLLYWOOD BLVD	LA	LA46	7600	33	F3
HOLLYWOOD BLVD	LA	LA46	7500	34	A3
HOLLYWOOD BLVD	LA	LA69	8100	33	E3
HOLLYWOOD FRWY	LA	LA		16	B3
HOLLYWOOD FRWY	LA	LA		23	D2
HOLLYWOOD FRWY	LA	LA		24	B5
HOLLYWOOD FRWY	LA	LA		34	B1
HOLLYWOOD FRWY	LA	LA		35	B6
HOLLYWOOD FRWY	LA	LA		44	C1
HOLLYWOOD WY	BUR	BUR	1400	17	A6
HOLLYWOOD WY	BUR	BUR	100	24	A1
HOLLYWOOD WY	LA	BUR	7500	17	A2
HOLLYWOOD WY	LA	SV	7900	17	A2
HOLLYWOOD WY N	BUR	BUR	1400	17	A6
HOLLYWOOD WY N	BUR	BUR	100	24	A1
HOLLYWOOD WY S	BUR	BUR	100	24	A1
HOLLYWD BOWL RD	LA	LA28		34	B2
HOLLYWD HILL RD	LA	LA46	8700	33	D2
HOLMAN AV	LA	LA24	10300	41	E2
HOLMAR AV	AZU	AZU	1100	86	D4
HOLMBURY AV	CER	ART		81	C1
HOLMBY AV	LA	LA24	600	41	F1
HOLMBY PARK LN	LA	LA77		32	F5
HOLMES AV	CER	ART	18700	81	D1
HOLMES AV	CER	ART	17800	82	D6
HOLMES AV	CO	LA01	5826	52	D5
HOLMES AV	CO	LA01	7900	58	E2
HOLMES AV	CO	LA02	8600	58	E2
HOLMES AV	CO	LA59	11600	58	E5
HOLMES AV	COM	COM		64	E1
HOLMES AV	LA	LA02	9200	58	E3
HOLMES AV	LA	LA58	5000	52	D4
HOLMES CIR	CER	ART	17000	82	D5
HOLMES CIR	CO	LPUE		85	C5
HOLMES PL	CER	ART		82	D4
HOLMES PL	CO	VAL		126	H2
HOLMS CT	SCLR	SAU		124	D2
HOLSTON AV	LAM	LAM	11500	84	B5
HOLT AV	CO	COV	20300	89	B6
HOLT AV	CO	COV	20000	93	B1
HOLT AV	CO	CYN		125	E8
HOLT AV	CO	LA56	5100	50	E4
HOLT AV	COV	COV	1200	89	B6
HOLT AV	LA	LA34	1900	42	D4
HOLT AV	LA	LA35	800	42	D3
HOLT AV	LA	LA48	300	33	D6
HOLT AV	WCOV	WCOV	3200	92	F1
HOLT AV	WCOV	WCOV	3300	93	A1
HOLT AV E	POM	POM	100	94	F2
HOLT AV E	POM	POM	700	95	A2
HOLT AV W	POM	POM	100	94	C2
HOLT CANYON RD	SCLR	CYN		125	C9
HOLT CANYON RD	CO	CYN		128	A1
HOLTON ST	CO	LPUE	16400	92	B3
HOLTON ST	CO	WCOV	17000	92	B3
HOLTWOOD AV	SELM	ELM	1300	47	D4
HOLY CROSS PL	LA	LA45	8000	56	A1
HOLYOKE DR	LA	LA65	3300	35	E2
HOLYOKE PL	CLA	CLA		96	C6
HOMAGE AV	CO	WHI	9500	61	F4
HOMAGE AV	WHI	WHI	9300	84	A3
HOME AV	BELL	BELL	6200	53	E5
HOME ST E	LB	LB05	100	70	C2
HOME ST W	LB	LB05	1	70	C2
HOMEBROOK ST	PR	PR	9000	54	F4
HOMEDALE ST	LA	LA49	11200	32	C6
HOMELAND AV	CO	WHI	11300	84	C5
HOMELAND AV	WHI	WHI	10100	84	C3
HOMELAND DR	CO	LA08	3500	51	B2
HOME PARK AV	CO	ALT	2600	20	B5
HOME PARK DR	WHI	WHI	12600	61	D1
HOME PLACE DR	LAN	LAN		159	G6
HOMER RD	CO	PEAR		192	D2
HOMER ST	LA	LA31	3800	36	B4
HOMER ST	MB	MB	200	62	B5
HOMEREST AV	CO	AZU	5200	88	C2
HOMEREST AV	COV	COV	700	88	C4

STREET	CITY	P.O. ZONE	BLOCK	PAGE	GRID
HOMEREST AV N	WCOV	WCOV	100	88	C6
HOMEREST AV S	WCOV	WCOV	100	92	D1
HOMERIDGE DR	PALM	PALM		171	E4
HOMESIDE AV	LA	LA16	5300	42	F5
HOMESTEAD ST	PR	PR	9200	60	E1
HOMESTEAD ST	SFS	SFS	11300	61	A2
HOMET RD	PAS	PAS	1600	27	D5
HOMET RD	SMAR	PAS	1700	27	D5
HOME TERRACE DR	POM	POM		90	B6
HOME TERRACE DR	POM	POM		94	B1
HOMEWARD ST	CO	LPUE	13400	48	C2
HOMEWARD ST	LPUE	LPUE	14000	48	D3
HOMEWAY DR	CO	LA08	3600	51	B2
HOMEWOOD AV	LA	LA28	6300	34	C4
HOMEWOOD DR	CO	ALT	1500	20	D5
HOMEWOOD LN	LCF	LCF		19	B3
HOMEWOOD RD	LA	LA49	100	41	A1
HOMEWOOD WY	LA	LA49	12600	41	A1
HOMEWORTH DR	RPV	SP	1800	78	D1
HOMEZELL DR	LA	CAN	23900	4	B6
HOMEZELL PL	LA	CAN		4	B6
HOMEZELL PL	LA	CAN		5	E1
HOMYR PL	SCLR	CYN		124	J9
HONAN AV	CO	WHI	1300	48	A5
HONBY AV	SCLR	SAU	26900	124	G8
HONDO ST	DOW	DOW	7400	59	F5
HONDO ST	DOW	DOW	7800	60	A5
HONDO CANYON RD	CO	TOP		109	A4
HONDURAS ST	LA	LA11	4300	52	D3
HONEY DR	LA	LA46	7900	33	E2
HONEYBEE LN	CO	LR	14000	192	B6
HONEYBROOK LN	DBAR	POM		97	D6
HONEYCOMB DR	SCLR	SAU	27900	124	E4
HONEY CREEK RD	RPV	PVP	26500	72	F4
HONEYGLEN RD	LA	PAC		3	C6
HONEYHILL DR	DBAR	WAL		97	C3
HONEYSUCKLE LN	CO	WHI	14000	61	E5
HONEYSUCKLE HLL	CO	CYN		125	F4
HONEYWOOD RD	LA	LA49	900	32	A6
HONIG LN	LA	LA65		36	A2
HONITON AV	CO	CYN		125	C5
HONNEWELL AV	LA	SF42		3	C6
HONNINGTON ST	WHI	WHI	16200	84	D3
HONNOLD DR	SCLR	SAU		124	C4
HONOLULU AV	GLEN	GL14	2800	11	B6
HONOLULU AV	GLEN	GL14	2800	18	D2
HONOLULU AV	GLEN	MONT	2200	18	D2
HONOLULU AV	LA	TU	6300	11	B6
HONOLULU PL	GLEN	GL14	3200	18	D1
HONOLULU TER	WHI	WHI		55	D3
HONORE ST	CO	LPUE	18600	98	E4
HOOD AV	BUR	BUR	4100	24	B4
HOOD AV	HPK	HPK	6200	53	B5
HOOD DR	CLA	CLA	600	91	A2
HOOD DR	LA	WOH	4900	13	F2
HOOK LN	LA	BH	2100	32	E2
HOOK ST	PALM	PALM		172	B5
HOOKTREE RD	LCF	LCF	5000	19	C2
HOOPER AV	CO	LA01	5800	52	D6
HOOPER AV	CO	LA01	7800	58	C2
HOOPER AV	CO	LA02	8600	58	C2
HOOPER AV	LA	LA11	1900	44	D6
HOOPER AV	LA	LA11	2100	52	D1
HOOPER AV	LA	LA21	800	44	D6
HOOPER AV	LA	LA59	10900	58	D5
HOOPER DR	WCOV	WCOV		92	F3
HOOPER DR	WCOV	WCOV		93	A3
HOOPER PL	LA	LA11	2300	52	D1
HOOPER,JOSPH DR	SCLR	CYN		128	E1
HOOVER AV	POM	POM		91	B6
HOOVER AV	SOG	SOG	11700	59	E6
HOOVER AV	SOG	SOG	12400	65	E1
HOOVER AV	WHI	WHI	5500	55	D4
HOOVER CT	SAD	SAD		89	E2
HOOVER ST N	LA	LA04	100	35	A6
HOOVER ST N	LA	LA27	1300	35	A3
HOOVER ST N	LA	LA29	700	35	A5
HOOVER ST S	LA	GAR	12800	64	A2
HOOVER ST S	LA	LA04	100	44	A1
HOOVER ST S	LA	LA05	600	44	A1
HOOVER ST S	LA	LA06	900	44	A3
HOOVER ST S	LA	LA07	1900	44	A4
HOOVER ST S	LA	LA20	300	44	A1
HOOVER ST S	LA	LA37	3900	52	A2
HOOVER ST S	LA	LA44	5800	52	A5
HOOVER ST S	LA	LA44	7900	58	A5
HOOVER WY	SAD	SAD		89	E2
HOPE CT	SPAS	SPAS	700	36	F1
HOPE ST	CO	HPK	2400	52	F6
HOPE ST	CO	HPK	2700	53	A6
HOPE ST	HPK	HPK	3000	53	A6
HOPE ST	SPAS	SPAS	1000	36	F1
HOPE ST	SPAS	SPAS	1400	37	A1
HOPE ST N	LA	LA12	100	44	B4
HOPE ST S	LA	LA07	2300	44	B5

STREET	CITY	P.O. ZONE	BLOCK	PAGE	GRID
HOPE ST S	LA	LA07	3800	52	A1
HOPE ST S	LA	LA12	100	44	B4
HOPE ST S	LA	LA15	900	44	B4
HOPE ST S	LA	LA17	300	44	C3
HOPE WY	SCLR	CYN		124	E9
HOPE CANYON RD	SCLR	NEW		127	F2
HOPE CANYON RD	SCLR	SAU		124	F9
HOPELAND AV	DOW	DOW	10200	60	B2
HOPEN PL	LA	LA69	9000	33	D3
HOPETON RD	CO	GL14	5500	11	D4
HOPEVALE DR	LA	VAN	3800	22	C4
HOPEWELL LN	SPAS	SPAS	700	36	F1
HOPEWELL LN	SPAS	SPAS		37	A3
HOPI	CO	AGO		106	C2
HOPI ST	DBAR	POM		97	F1
HOPI TR	LAN	LAN		160	D8
HOPKINS AL	PAS	PAS	1	27	A3
HOPKINS AV	CO	VAL		123	J6
HOPKINS AV	HB	RB	300	67	D1
HOPKINS WY	RB	RB	500	67	C2
HOPLAND ST	BLF	BLF	10300	66	D3
HOPLAND ST	NWK	NWK	10800	66	E3
HOPLAND ST	NWK	NWK	11800	82	A3
HOPPER CT	CO	CAL		100	F3
HORACE	LA	SF		8	C1
HORACE ST	LA	CHA	19600	6	F2
HORACE ST	LA	NOR	18500	7	B1
HORACE ST	LA	SF	16500	7	F1
HORACE ST	LA	SF	700	8	A1
HORCADA PL	PVE	PVP	700	72	B2
HORIZON AV	LA	VEN	4	49	B4
HORIZON CT	CO	LP48		98	D5
HORIZON CT	LA	VEN	14	49	B4
HORIZON DR	CO	MAL	5200	112	A5
HORIZON LN	LAN	LAN		160	E5
HORIZON PL	WCOV	WCOV		93	A3
HORIZON RD	PALM	PALM		183	B1
HORIZON HLS DR	WCOV	WCOV		92	E4
HORLEY AV	DOW	DOW	8900	54	C6
HORLEY AV	DOW	DOW	12000	59	F4
HORLEY AV	DOW	DOW	900	60	A4
HORMEL AV	LAV	LAV		90	B1
HORN AV	WHOL	LA69	1100	33	D4
HORNBROOK AV	BAP	BAP	3900	39	C4
HORNBY AV	WHI	WHI	8900	84	A2
HORNBY ST	MTB	MTB	500	54	C2
HORNDEAN AV	CO	PALM		189	J2
HORNELL ST	CO	WHI		84	A4
HORNELL ST	WHI	WHI	15400	84	C4
HORNER ST	LA	LA35	6000	42	D3
HORNET PL	LKD	LKD		71	F3
HORNSEY AV	BG	BELL	7500	59	E1
HORSESHOE CIR	WCOV	WCOV		93	B1
HORSESHOE DR	CO	TOP	19700	109	B6
HORSESHOE LN	CAR	CAR		69	D6
HORSESHOE LN	LAN	LAN		159	D5
HORSESHOE LN	RHE	PVP		72	D6
HORSESHOE BEND	WAL	WAL		93	B4
HORSESHOE CY RD	LA	LA46	2400	33	D1
HORST AV	ART	ART	18600	81	B1
HORST AV	CER	ART	19500	81	B2
HORST AV	CER	ART	16600	82	B5
HORST AV	HG	LKD	21900	81	B5
HORST AV	LKD	LKD	20800	81	B3
HORST AV	NWK	NWK	13900	82	B2
HORTENSE ST	LA	NHO	10600	23	E3
HORTENSE ST	LA	VAN	14100	22	D3
HORTENSIA ST	POM	POM	1400	90	C5
HORTICULTURL DR	CO	LPUE	14600	85	C2
HORTON AV	DOW	DOW		59	F5
HORTON AV	DOW	DOW	10600	60	B2
HOSFORD AV	LA	LA45	7700	50	B6
HOSMER WK	LA	LA42	200	36	C1
HOSPERS RD	CO	ACT		182	C7
HOSPITAL DR	TOR	TOR		73	B1
HOSPITAL PL	LA	LA33	1900	45	A2
HOSS ST	DBAR	POM		97	F1
HOSTETTER ST	LA	LA23	2700	45	A6
HOT SPRINGS AV	SCLR	CYN	28100	124	H6
HOT SPRINGS PL	CO	CAL		100A	E5
HOUGH ST	LA	LA42	6600	36	E1
HOUGHTON AV	SFS	SFS	9200	60	F3
HOUGHTON AV	SFS	SFS	9200	61	A2
HOURGLASS PL	DBAR	POM		94	B5
HOUSEMAN ST	LCF	LCF	400	19	C3
HOUSER DR N	COV	COV	100	88	D5
HOUSER DR S	COV	COV	100	88	D5
HOUSTON CT	CLA	CLA	1600	91	C2
HOUSTON ST	LA	LA33	2400	45	B3
HOVENWEEP LN	CO	TOP		108	E5
HOVEY AV W	SGAB	SGAB	100	37	E5
HOVEY ST	RM	RM	8700	38	A5
HOWARD AV	COV	COV	500	88	F4
HOWARD AV	MTB	MTB	500	46	D6
HOWARD AV	TOR	TOR	21300	67	E4
HOWARD CT	BUR	BUR		17	D2

STREET	CITY	P.O. ZONE	BLOCK	PAGE	GRID
HOWARD CT	LA	WOH		13	E4
HOWARD CT	WCOV	WCOV		92	C4
HOWARD LN	CO	CAST		123	J2
HOWARD ST	ALH	ALH	500	37	B4
HOWARD ST	GLEN	GL06	100	25	D3
HOWARD ST	GLEN	GL07	900	25	D3
HOWARD ST	LA	VEN	700	49	D4
HOWARD ST	WHI	WHI	10800	55	C4
HOWARD ST E	PAS	PAS	100	27	B1
HOWARD ST W	PAS	PAS	100	26	F1
HOWRD HUGHES PY	LA	LA45		50	C5
HOWARD MARIE CT	CO	SAU		124	G3
HOWARDVIEW CT	CUL	CUL		50	E1
HOWE ST	PAR	PAR	7800	65	F1
HOWELL RD	IND	LPUE	1000	97	A2
HOWELLHURST DR	BAP	BAP	15000	39	F5
HOWELLHURST DR	WCOV	WCOV	1600	88	A6
HOWERY ST	SOG	SOG	7300	65	E1
HOWLAND AV	LA	VEN	400	49	B6
HOWLAND DR	ING	IN01	200	57	B1
HOWLAND DR	TEC	TEC	9800	38	C3
HOWLAND CANAL	LA	VEN		49	C4
HOWLAND CANL CT	LA	VEN	200	49	B6
HOWSLER PL	POM	POM	1800	94	E5
HOXIE AV	NWK	NWK	11500	60	E6
HOYA WY	PAR	PAR		65	E4
HOYT ST	LA	PAC	13700	8	E4
HOYT ST	LA	PAC	13000	9	A2
HOYT ST	LA	SF	12200	3	C6
HOYT PARK PL	ELM	ELM	10300	47	D1
HOYT TRUCK TR	CO			M	C3
HUALPAI TR	CO	AGO		107	A3
HUAPI TR	CO	CHA		1A	C6
HUB ST	LA	LA42	4700	36	A1
HUBARD HTS RD	CO	PEAR		192	C5
HUBBARD AV N	SF	SF	1	2	D5
HUBBARD AV S	SF	SF	1	2	D5
HUBBARD PL	LA	SF	12100	2	D5
HUBBARD RD	CO	ACT		189	A1
HUBBARD RD	CO	SAU		181	J9
HUBBARD RD	CO	SAU		189	A1
HUBBARD ST	CO	LA22	4400	45	E6
HUBBARD ST	CO	LA22	5300	46	A6
HUBBARD ST	CO	LA22	5700	54	B1
HUBBARD ST	CO	LA23	3700	45	C6
HUBBARD ST	CUL	CUL	8800	42	D6
HUBBARD ST	LA	SF	13400	2	E4
HUBBARD ST	LA	SF	12900	3	A2
HUBER AV	TOR	TOR	1100	68	E4
HUBER AV	TOR	TOR	22900	68	D6
HUBER AV	TOR	TOR	23800	73	E1
HUBERT AV	LA	LA08	3900	51	C1
HUBERT WK	LA	LA08		51	C2
HUCKFINN LN	CUL	CUL		50	D2
HUCKLEBERRY CIR	WAL	WAL		93	D4
HUCKLEBERRY DR	CO	CAL		108	B5
HUDDART AV	CO	ARC	5300	38	F3
HUDDART AV	ELM	ELM	5300	38	E5
HUDSON AV	IND	LPUE	100	48	E5
HUDSON AV	LPUE	LPUE	15600	48	F5
HUDSON AV N	LA	LA04	100	34	C6
HUDSON AV N	LA	LA28	1400	34	C3
HUDSON AV N	LA	LA38	700	34	C5
HUDSON AV N	PAS	PAS	1	27	B5
HUDSON AV S	LA	LA04	100	34	C6
HUDSON AV S	LA	LA05	600	43	C2
HUDSON AV S	LA	LA19	900	43	B3
HUDSON AV S	LA	LA20	300	43	C2
HUDSON AV S	PAS	PAS	1	27	B5
HUDSON CT	PAS	PAS	1	27	B1
HUDSON PL	LA	LA04	100	34	C6
HUDSON ST	PALM	PALM		184	A1
HUDSPETH ST	ING	IN03	2300	57	C5
HUERTA CT	LA	ENC	4400	21	F3
HUERTA DR	SCLR	VAL		124	B9
HUERTA RD	LA	ENC	16600	21	F3
HUERTA VERDE RD	GLDR	GLDR	700	87	C4
HUFFER AL	PAS	PAS		19	F6
HUFFY ST	SCLR	CYN		124	G6
HUGGINS DR	CAR	CAR	19000	69	D1
HUGHES AV	LA	CUL	3800	42	C6
HUGHES AV	LA	LA34	3500	42	C6
HUGHES AV	MTB	MTB	100	54	D3
HUGHES ST	MTB	MTB	1200	54	D2
HUGHES TER	LA	LA45		49	F6
HUGHES TER	LA	LA45		50	A6
HUGHES TER	LA	LA45		56	A1
HUGHES WY	LB	LB10		70	A4
HUGHES WY S	ELS	ELS		62	C1
HUGHES CYN RD	CO	ACT		189	B4
HUGHES HOWRD PY	LA	LA45		50	C5
HUGHES RANCH RD	CO	PALM		171	B5
HUGO AV	CO	LA59		58	E5
HUGO LN	CO	SAU		181	G7
HUGO REID DR	ARC	ARC	700	28	B4
HULA DR	LB	LB05	300	65	C5

STREET	CITY	P.O. ZONE	BLOCK	PAGE	GRID
HULA LN	LB	LB05	300	65	C5
HULA-HULA	LB	LB05	300	65	C5
HULBERT AV	LA	VEN	7900	55A	F1
HULBERT AV	SPAS	SPAS	2000	36	D3
HULL LN	CO	ALT	1300	20	C5
HULLETT ST	LB	LB05	100	70	C1
HULLETT TURN	LB	LB05	5800	70	C1
HULME AV	LYN	LYN	10600	59	C5
HUMANE WY N	POM	POM	100	94	B3
HUMANE WY S	POM	POM	100	94	B3
HUMBERT AV	ELM	ELM	2600	47	C2
HUMBERT AV	SELM	ELM	2700	47	C2
HUMBLE OIL RD	CO	SAU		123	C8
HUMBOLDT ST	LA	LA31	1800	35	F5
HUMBOLDT ST	LA	LA31	2300	36	A5
HUMBOLT CT	SAD	SAD		95A	B5
HUMBOLT WY	POM	POM		93	F2
HUME AV	CO	GL14	4600	11	D6
HUME RD	CO	MAL	2500	114	E3
HUMFORD AV	CO	LPUE	1900	85	D3
HUMMINGBIRD DR	LAV	LAV		95A	D6
HUMMINGBIRD LN	RH	PVP	1	78	C1
HUMMINGBIRD PL	POM	POM	2100	90	E5
HUMMING BIRD WY	CO	CAL		13	A4
HUMPHREY WY	CO	GL14	5000	11	E6
HUMPHREYS AV N	CO	LA22	100	45	E4
HUMPHREYS AV S	CO	LA22	100	45	E4
HUMPHREYS WY	GLDR	GLDR	300	87	C5
HUNGATE LN	ARC	ARC	800	28	C6
HUNGERFORD PL	CER	ART	10700	71	E1
HUNGERFORD ST	LB	LB05	1200	65	D6
HUNGERFORD ST	LB	LB05	3400	66	A6
HUNGERFORD ST	LB	LB05	1200	70	D1
HUNGERFORD ST	LB	LB05	3400	71	A1
HUNGERFORD ST	LKD	LKD	4300	66	D6
HUNGERFORD ST	LKD	LKD	4300	71	A1
HUNGRY JACK RD	CO	PALM		157	G7
HUNNEWELL AV	LA	SF	11600	3	A4
HUNNEWELL AV	LA	SF	11300	9	C1
HUNSAKER AV	PAR	PAR	15300	65	D4
HUNSTOCK AV	CO	CAST	29400	123	B5
HUNT AV	POM	POM	800	94	F5
HUNT AV	POM	POM	1000	95	A5
HUNT AV	SOG	SOG	8900	59	C4
HUNT LN	SPAS	SPAS	1800	36	F3
HUNT,MICHAEL DR	SELM	ELM		47	D3
HUNTCLIFF LN	DBAR	WAL		97	C4
HUNT CLUB LN	WLVL	THO	31600	102	B4
HUNTDALE ST	LB	LB08	5700	71	E5
HUNTER AV	WHI	WHI		55	C3
HUNTER CT	LAN	LAN		159	D3
HUNTER DR	SGAB	SGAB	700	37	E2
HUNTER LN	CO	CAST		123	J2
HUNTER PL	WCOV	WCOV		93	A3
HUNTER ST	LA	LA21	2000	44	E5
HUNTER ST	LA	LA23	3200	45	B6
HUNTER POINT RD	POM	POM		94	D4
HUNTERS TR	GLDR	GLDR		87	D6
HUNTERS GLEN LN	LA	CAN	8300	12	D1
HUNTERS HILL DR	WAL	WAL		93	B5
HUNTINGTON AV	SAD	SAD		89	E3
HUNTINGTON AV N	MPK	MPK	100	46	C2
HUNTINGTON AV S	MPK	MPK	500	46	C2
HUNTINGTON BLVD	POM	POM	500	94	D2
HUNTINGTON DR	CO	SGAB	8200	27	E6
HUNTINGTON DR	CO	SGAB	8500	28	B5
HUNTINGTON DR	DUA	DUA	900	29	A4
HUNTINGTON DR	DUA	DUA	2700	86	A5
HUNTINGTON DR	IRW	DUA	15400	86	A5
HUNTINGTON DR	SMAR	PAS	2200	27	E6
HUNTINGTON DR	SMAR	PAS	100	37	C1
HUNTINGTON DR	SPAS	SPAS	1100	36	C5
HUNTINGTON DR	SPAS	SPAS	1400	37	A3
HUNTINGTON DR E	ALH	ALH	100	37	A3
HUNTINGTON DR E	ARC	ARC	1	28	E4
HUNTINGTON DR E	MON	MON	100	29	A4
HUNTINGTON DR N	ALH	ALH	100	36	D4
HUNTINGTON DR N	LA	LA32	4200	36	A5
HUNTINGTON DR S	LA	LA32	4200	36	C5
HUNTINGTON DR W	ALH	ALH	1500	37	A3
HUNTINGTON DR W	ARC	ARC	1	28	B5
HUNTINGTON DR W	MON	MON	600	28	E4
HUNTINGTON DR W	MON	MON	100	29	A4
HUNTINGTON LN	CO	VAL		123	G6
HUNTINGTON LN	RB	RB	1700	62	D6
HUNTINGTON LN	SPAS	SPAS	1100	36	F3
HUNTINGTON ST N	POM	POM	100	94	D3
HUNTINGTON ST N	SF	SF	100	2	E5
HUNTINGTON ST S	POM	POM	100	94	D3
HUNTINGTON ST S	SF	SF	100	2	D6
HUNTNGTN GDN DR	PAS	PAS	700	37	B1
HUNTLEY AV	CUL	CUL	4100	50	B2
HUNTLEY CIR	SMAR	PAS	2100	27	D6
HUNTLEY DR	LA	LA26	1100	44	C2
HUNTLEY DR	WHOL	LA48	300	33	D5
HUNTLEY DR	WHOL	LA69	600	33	D5

STREET	CITY	P.O. ZONE	BLOCK	PAGE	GRID
HUNTLEY PL	CUL	CUL	11200	50	B3
HUNTSINGER CIR	CO	MAL		113	E4
HUNTSMAN CT	RPV	SP	1700	78	E1
HURCHEL CT	CO	WHI	13400	61	D5
HURFORD CT	AGH	AGO		102	D3
HURFORD TER	LA	ENC	4600	22	A3
HURLBUT ST	PAS	PAS	100	26	F6
HURLEY ST	CO	LPUE	17700	98	D1
HURLEY ST	LPUE	LPUE	16800	98	B1
HURLOCK AV	DUA	DUA	2000	29	C6
HURON	CO	AGO		106	D2
HURON AV	CUL	CUL	3800	50	B2
HURON DR	CLA	CLA	800	91	A1
HURON ST	LA	LA65	2000	35	F5
HURRICANE ST	LA	VEN		49	C6
HURST ST	CO	COV	19200	89	A4
HURST ST	COV	COV	100	88	E4
HURST ST	COV	COV	100	89	A4
HURST VIEW AV	MON	MON	400	29	B5
HURST VIEW ST	DUA	DUA	900	29	C6
HUSK AV	CO	CYN		125	E4
HUSK AV	CO	SAU		125	E4
HUSTON PL	LAN	LAN		159	B6
HUSTON RD	CO	CHA	9200	4	B5
HUSTON RD N	CO	CHA	9300	4	B5
HUSTON ST	IRW	BAP	15600	88	A3
HUSTON ST	LA	ENC	15400	22	A2
HUSTON ST	LA	NHO	10200	23	F2
HUSTON ST	LA	NHO	10100	24	A2
HUSTON ST	LA	VAN	13300	22	D2
HUSTON ST	LA	VAN	12900	23	A2
HUSTON ST	POM	POM	2800	90	F4
HUTCHCROFT ST	CO	LPUE	13400	48	C2
HUTCHCROFT ST	LPUE	LPUE	14500	48	D4
HUTCHINGS CT	SAD	SAD		90	B4
HUTCHINS DR	LAM	LAM	14900	84	A6
HUTCHISON AV	CUL	CUL	3200	42	D5
HUTCHISON AV	LA	LA34	3100	42	D5
HUTTON DR	LA	BH	2700	22	F6
HUTTON DR	LA	BH	2500	32	F1
HUTTON PL	LA	BH	3000	22	F6
HUXLEY ST	LA	LA27	3400	35	B1
HYACINTH AV	LA	AZU	5100	88	C2
HYACINTH AV	CO	WCOV	1700	92	C3
HYACINTH AV	COV	COV		88	C5
HYACINTH AV	WCOV	WCOV	700	88	C5
HYANNIS DR	LA	CAN	7200	5	E3
HYANS ST	LA	LA26	2700	35	A6
HYATT	PALM	PALM		171	D4
HYATT AV	LA	WIL	1000	74	C4
HYDE AV	POM	POM	800	91	A5
HYDE ST	LA	LA32	5300	36	E5
HYDE PARK BLVD	ING	IN02		56	E1
HYDE PARK BLVD	LA	LA43	2200	51	C5
HYDE PARK BLVD	LA	LA47	2000	51	C5
HYDE PARK BL E	ING	IN02	100	51	A6
HYDE PARK BL W	ING	IN02	100	50	F6
HYDE PARK CT	CER	ART		66	F5
HYDE PARK PL	ING	IN02	500	51	A5
HYDRANGEA WY	CO	CYN		125	F4
HYDRO DR	WHI	WHI		61	D1
HYLAND AV	ARC	ARC	1500	28	E2
HYLER AV	LA	LA41	2500	25	F6
HYNFORD PL	LA	HAC	23700	73	E1
HYPERION AV	LA	LA27	1800	35	B3
HYPERION AV	LA	LA29	700	35	A4
HYSCO RD	SCLR	SAU		127	E2
HYSSOP LN	SCLR	SAU		124	E5
HYTE RD	RPV	PVP	26600	72	D3
HYTHE CT	LA	BH		22	F6
I					
I ST	BELL	BELL		53	E4
I ST	LAV	LAV	2200	90	D4
I ST E	LA	WIL	100	74	E4
I ST W	LA	WIL	100	74	B4
IA LN	LA	WOH		13	A3
IANITA ST E	LKD	LKD	6500	71	E2
IBANEZ AV	LA	WOH	21300	13	C3
IBBETSON AV	BLF	BLF	13400	66	D2
IBBETSON AV	DOW	DOW	12600	60	D6
IBBETSON AV	DOW	DOW	12900	66	D1
IBBETSON AV	LKD	LKD	5900	66	D6
IBEX AV	ART	ART	17400	82	B5
IBEX AV	CER	ART	19000	81	B2
IBEX AV	CER	ART	17300	82	B5
IBEX AV S	ART	ART	18400	81	B1
IBEX AV S	HG	LKD	21700	81	B5
IBEX AV S	LKD	LKD	20700	81	B3
IBEX AV S	NWK	NWK	14300	82	B2
IBEX CT	CER	ART	19500	81	B2
IBOLD RD	CO	MAL		105	C4
IBSEN ST E	PR	PR	8700	55	A1
ICHABOD WY	WAL	WAL		93	D4
IDA AV	LA	LA66	12800	49	E3

STREET	CITY	P.O. ZONE	BLOCK	PAGE	GRID
IDA PL	CO	CHA		4	C5
IDA ST	LA	PP	500	40	B3
IDABEL AV	CAR	CAR	23500	74	C1
IDAHO AV	LA	LA25	11300	41	C4
IDAHO AV	SM	SM	100	40	F6
IDAHO AV	SM	SM	2599	41	A5
IDAHO AV	SOG	SOG	11300	59	E6
IDAHO CT	CLA	CLA		95	D1
IDAHO CT	CLA	CLA		96	D6
IDAHO ST	PAS	PAS	200	19	F6
IDAHO ST	WCOV	WCOV		92	D5
IDAHO ST N	BAP	BAP	3700	39	D5
IDAHOME ST	COV	COV	18000	88	D6
IDAHOME ST E	WCOV	WCOV	1000	88	C6
IDALENE ST	SFS	SFS	11100	60	F3
IDALENE ST	SFS	SFS	11700	61	A3
IDELL ST	LA	LA65	2300	35	F5
IDLE DR	AGH	AGO		100A	A3
IDLEHOUR LN	SMAD	SMAD	700	28	D1
IDLEWHILE TR	CO	SF	12000	3	E5
IDLEWILD WY	CO	MAL	26100	113	B2
IDLEWOOD RD	GLEN	GL02	800	25	A2
IDYLWILD AV	LA	LA31		36	A5
IGLESIA DR	LA	WOH	21400	13	C3
IGLESIA ST	SAD	SAD	100	90	A2
IGUALA ST	MTB	MTB		46	E5
ILA JOYCE ST	CO	ALT	300	19	F4
ILAMAE PL	GLEN	GL08	2800	19	A5
ILENE DR	ARC	ARC	100	28	E6
ILEX AV	LA	PAC	10300	8	F2
ILEX AV	LA	PAC	9900	9	B3
ILEX AV	LA	SF	11400	8	E1
ILEX AV	LA	SV	8800	9	C5
ILIFF ST	LA	PP	700	40	D3
ILLINOIS	WCOV	WCOV		92	E4
ILLINOIS AV	PAR	PAR	15100	65	E4
ILLINOIS AV	SOG	SOG	2400	58	F2
ILLINOIS AV	SOG	SOG	2700	59	A3
ILLINOIS CT	ELS	ELS	600	56	C5
ILLINOIS CT S	TOR	GAR	15900	63	D4
ILLINOIS CT S	TOR	TOR	17000	63	D5
ILLINOIS CT S	TOR	TOR	18200	68	D1
ILLINOIS DR	SPAS	SPAS	1800	36	D3
ILLINOIS ST	CO	ACT		189	G3
ILLINOIS ST	ELS	ELS	100	56	C6
ILLINOIS ST	POM	POM		94	E2
ILLINOIS ST E	BAP	BAP	13700	39	D5
ILLINOIS ST E	WHI	WHI	10800	55	C3
ILLORA DR	LAM	LAM	15400	83	B2
ILONA AV	LA	LA64	10300	42	A3
ILOPANGO DR	CO	LPUE	2800	85	E4
ILUSO AV	CO	WAL		97	B3
IMAN TR	CO	CHA		1A	C6
IMBLER CT	AGH	AGO		102	F2
IMLAY AV	LA	CUL	4700	50	B3
IMOGEN AV	LA	LA26	600	35	A5
IMPERIAL AV E	ELS	ELS	100	56	B5
IMPERIAL AV W	ELS	ELS	600	55A	F5
IMPERIAL AV W	ELS	ELS	100	56	A5
IMPERIAL DR	GLEN	GL07	1200	25	E1
IMPERIAL HWY E	CO	LA59	2400	58	B5
IMPERIAL HWY E	CO	WHI	13000	61	D6
IMPERIAL HWY E	CO	WHI	15900	84	C6
IMPERIAL HWY E	DOW	DOW	7400	59	E5
IMPERIAL HWY E	DOW	DOW	7900	60	B6
IMPERIAL HWY E	LA	LA59	600	58	B5
IMPERIAL HWY E	LA	LA61	100	58	B5
IMPERIAL HWY E	LAM	LAM	13800	61	D6
IMPERIAL HWY E	LAM	LAM	14700	84	C6
IMPERIAL HWY E	LYN	LYN	2600	58	B5
IMPERIAL HWY E	LYN	LYN	2800	59	B5
IMPERIAL HWY E	NWK	NWK	10400	60	D6
IMPERIAL HWY E	NWK	NWK	11600	61	B6
IMPERIAL HWY E	SFS	SFS	12600	61	B6
IMPERIAL HWY E	SOG	SOG	5100	59	E5
IMPERIAL HWY W	CO	IN04	4800	56	E5
IMPERIAL HWY W	CO	LA44	1000	57	F5
IMPERIAL HWY W	CO	LA47	1400	57	B5
IMPERIAL HWY W	HAW	HAW	3600	57	B5
IMPERIAL HWY W	HAW	IN04		56	E5
IMPERIAL HWY W	ING	IN03	2300	57	B5
IMPERIAL HWY W	LA	LA44	700	57	F5
IMPERIAL HWY W	LA	LA44	500	58	B5
IMPERIAL HWY W	LA	LA45	5200	56	B5
IMPERIAL HWY W	LA	LA61	100	58	B5
IMPERIAL HWY W	LA	VEN		55A	F5
IMPERIAL HWY W	LA	VEN	7300	56	B5
IMPERIAL ST	LA	LA21	600	44	E5
IMPERIAL TR	CO	TOP	1600	109	D2
IMPULSE DR	CO	LAN	12900	158	A3
INA DR	GLEN	GL06	1600	25	E2
INADALE AV	CO	LA43	4800	51	A3
INAGLEN WY	CO	LA43	5000	51	A3
INAVALE PL	LA	LA49	900	32	B5
INCA WY	PAR	PAR		65	E4

STREET	CITY	P.O. ZONE	BLOCK	PAGE	GRID
INCE BLVD	CUL	CUL	3900	42	D6
INDALS PL	CO	WOH		13	B5
INDEPENDENCE AV	CO	HPK	2600	58	F2
INDEPENDENCE AV	LA	CAN	8500	6	D6
INDEPENDENCE AV	LA	CAN	6400	12	D3
INDEPENDENCE AV	LA	CHA	9100	6	D4
INDEPENDENCE AV	LA	WOH	6200	12	D5
INDEPENDENCE AV	SOG	SOG	2600	58	F1
INDEPENDENCE AV	SOG	SOG	2900	59	A2
INDEPENDENCE DR	CLA	CLA	100	96	C5
INDEPENDENCE SQ	PALM	PALM		183	D2
INDEPENDENCA ST	LA	WOH	22000	13	B3
INDEX ST	LA	SF	18300	7	C1
INDEX ST	LA	SF	15600	8	A1
INDIA ST	LA	LA39	2100	35	C3
INDIAN DR	CO	CHA	5100	6	C1
INDIAN DR	LCF	LCF		19	B1
INDIAN LN	NWK	NWK	12900	82	C1
INDIANA	WCOV	WCOV		92	F4
INDIANA AV	CLA	CLA		96	C6
INDIANA AV	LA	LA32	1800	45	C1
INDIANA AV	LA	VEN	300	49	B3
INDIANA AV	LB	LB05	6200	65	F5
INDIANA AV	LCF	LCF	4400	19	A3
INDIANA AV	PAR	PAR	14700	65	F4
INDIANA AV	SOG	SOG	2400	58	F3
INDIANA AV	SOG	SOG	2700	59	A3
INDIANA AV	SPAS	SPAS	900	36	E2
INDIANA CT	ELS	ELS	700	56	C5
INDIANA CT	LA	VEN	1000	49	C3
INDIANA CT	SPAS	SPAS	500	36	E1
INDIANA PL	SPAS	SPAS	500	36	E2
INDIANA ST	ARC	ARC	100	28	E4
INDIANA ST	CO	ACT		189	G2
INDIANA ST	ELS	ELS	100	56	C6
INDIANA ST	WHI	WHI		55	C3
INDIANA ST N	CO	LA63	100	45	C6
INDIANA ST S	CMRC	LA23	1400	53	C1
INDIANA ST S	CO	LA23	600	45	C6
INDIANA ST S	CO	LA23	1200	53	C1
INDIANA ST S	CO	LA63	100	45	C6
INDIANA ST S	LA	LA23	1500	53	C1
INDIANA ST S	VER	LA23	2600	53	C2
INDIANA TER	SPAS	SPAS	500	36	E2
INDIANAPOLIS ST	LA	LA66	12400	49	E1
INDIAN BEND DR	CO	WHI		55	D2
INDIAN BEND	GLDR	GLDR		87	D1
INDIAN BEND	GLDR	GLDR		89	D1
INDIAN CYN MTY	CO	SF		3	D4
INDIAN CY TK TR	CO	SAU		188	G7
INDIAN CREEK RD	CER	ART	15900	82	B4
INDIAN CREEK RD	DBAR	POM		97A	A5
INDIAN DUNES LN	AZU	AZU	300	86	D4
INDIAN FALLS AV	CO	LAN	15600	174	H1
INDIAN HILL BL	POM	POM	1200	91	B5
INDIAN HILL BL	POM	POM	500	95	B2
INDIAN HIL BL N	CLA	CLA	100	91	B2
INDIAN HIL BL N	CLA	CLA	3200	96	B6
INDIAN HIL BL S	CLA	CLA	100	91	B5
INDIAN HILL LN	LA	CAN		5	D3
INDIAN HILLS RD	LA	SF	11500	2	C6
INDIAN MESA DR	CO	SF		3	E2
INDIAN MOUND RD	CO	MAL		110	B5
INDIAN OAK RD	CO	SAU		189	G4
INDIANOLA WY	LCF	LCF	4500	19	C3
INDIAN PEAK RD	RHE	PVP		72	E5
INDIAN PEAK RD	RPV	PVP	26600	72	E4
INDIAN RIDGE CT	AGH	AGO		100A	A2
INDIAN ROCK DR	RPV	PVP	27800	72	C4
INDIAN SGE RD W	LAN	LAN	1300	159	J3
INDIAN SCHL LN	CAR	CAR		69	D6
INDIAN SPG LN	AGH	AGO		100A	D5
INDIAN SPGS DR	GLDR	GLDR	1100	87	D4
INDIAN SPGS RD	SAD	SAD		89	F1
INDIAN SUMMR AV	CO	LPUE	1000	92	B4
INDIAN SUMMR AV	WCOV	WCOV	800	92	B2
INDIAN VLY RD	RPV	PVP	28200	72	D5
INDIAN WELL DR	DBAR	POM		97	F3
INDIAN WLLS CIR	SCLR	VAL		127	B2
INDIAN WELLS LN	LAV	LAV		95A	D5
INDIAN WOOD RD	CUL	CUL		50	C2
INDIES LN	SCLR	CYN	28800	125	C6
INDIGO	COM	COM		64	E3
INDIGO CT	POM	POM	700	90	F4
INDIGO ST E	COM	COM	100	64	F3
INDIGO ST W	COM	COM	100	64	F3
INDUSTRIAL AV	ING	IN02	400	50	E6
INDUSTRIAL AV	SOG	SOG	11700	59	E6
INDUSTRIAL AV	SOG	SOG	12300	65	E1
INDUSTRIAL ST	AZU	AZU	700	86	C5
INDUSTRIAL ST	LA	LA21	1200	44	E4
INDUSTRIAL ST	POM	POM	900	95	A3
INDUSTRIAL WY	LA	LA23	1700	53	B1
INDUSTRIL PK ST	COV	COV	16500	88	B4
INDUSTRY AV	LKD	LKD	3600	70	E5
INDUSTRY AV	PR	PR	7600	54	D5
INDUSTRY AV	PR	PR	5000	54	E3
INDUSTRY CIR	LAM	LAM		82	F5
INDUSTRY DR	SH	LB06		76	A2
INDUSTRY PL	LAM	LAM		82	F5
INDUSTRY WY	LYN	LYN	2400	58	F5
INDUSTRY HLS PY	CO	LPUE		92	C6
INEZ ST	CO	WHI	10600	61	D4
INEZ ST	LA	LA23	1900	44	F4
INEZ ST	LA	LA23	2000	45	B5
INEZ ST	LB	LB05	900	65	D5
INFANTA ST	CO	AGO		102	F6
INGLEDALE TER	LA	LA39	2900	35	B1
INGLENOOK	CER	ART		81	B3
INGLESIDE DR N	MB	MB	100	62	B4
INGLESIDE DR S	MB	MB	100	62	B4
INGLESIDE WY	CO	MAL	26100	113	B2
INGLETON AV	SAD	SAD	100	89	D3
INGLEWOOD AV	CO	HAW	12800	62	F3
INGLEWOOD AV	HAW	HAW	11600	56	F4
INGLEWOOD AV	HAW	HAW	13000	62	F3
INGLEWOOD AV	LA	HAW	11400	56	F4
INGLEWOOD AV	LAW	LAW	14300	62	F3
INGLEWOOD AV	RB	RB	1000	62	F6
INGLEWOOD AV	RB	RB	500	67	F1
INGLEWOOD AV	TOR	TOR	19000	67	F1
INGLEWOOD AV N	ING	IN01	100	56	F4
INGLEWOOD AV N	ING	IN02	600	50	F6
INGLEWOOD AV S	CO	IN04	10000	56	F4
INGLEWOOD AV S	ING	IN01	100	56	F4
INGLEWOOD BLVD	CUL	LA66	4100	50	A3
INGLEWOOD BLVD	LA	CUL	4500	50	A3
INGLEWOOD BLVD	LA	LA66	3000	41	E6
INGLEWOOD BLVD	LA	LA66	3200	49	E1
INGLEWOOD BLVD	LA	LA66	4000	50	A3
INGLIS DR	LA	LA65	3500	35	E1
INGLIS WK	LA	LA65		35	E1
INGOMAR ST	LA	CAN	23100	5	F2
INGOMAR ST	LA	CAN	19800	12	F2
INGOMAR ST	LA	RES	17600	14	A2
INGRAHAM ST	LA	LA05	3800	43	D2
INGRAHAM ST	LA	LA17	1000	44	B2
INGRAM ST	CO	LPUE	16400	92	B5
INGRES AV	LA	SF	13100	1	F3
INGRUM WY	TOR	TOR	19800	67	F2
INLAND LN	CO	MAL	20000	115	B4
INLET TR	CO	TOP		109	D5
INMAN RD	WCOV	WCOV	600	92	E2
INNES AV	LA	LA26	1100	35	D6
INNES PL	LA	VEN	1300	49	B4
INNSDALE DR	LA	LA68	6300	24	C5
INOLA AV	LAN	LAN	44800	159	H4
INOLA ST	GLDR	GLDR	1700	87	E6
INOLA ST	SAD	SAD	2300	87	E6
INSKEEP AV	LA	LA03	5800	52	B4
INSKIP AV	CO	CAL		108	C2
INSPECTION TR	CO	TOP	500	109	D4
INSPIRATION DR	POM	POM		90	D6
INSPIRATION PT	WCOV	WCOV		92	F4
INSPIRATION TR	CO	SF	11900	3	D5
INSPIRATION TR	CO	TOP	19500	109	B5
INSPIRATION WY	LA	TU	9500	10	F4
INSTAR PL	ELM	ELM	4100	39	A6
INSTITUTE PL	LA	LA29	5000	34	E5
INTERCEPTOR ST	LA	LA45		56	D2
INTERMODAL WY	CAR	LB10		69	F6
INTERMODAL WY	CAR	LB10		74	F1
INTERNATIONL AV	LA	CAN	8500	6	C6
INTERNATIONL AV	LA	CAN	8500	12	C1
INTERNATIONL RD	LA	LA45	10000	56	D3
INTREPID DR	RPV	PVP		78	A3
INVALE DR	GLEN	GL08		18	E3
INVERGARRY ST	CO	GLDR	19200	86	F5
INVERGARRY ST	CO	GLDR	19300	87	A5
INVERNESS AV	GLDR	GLDR	900	89	E1
INVERNESS AV	LA	LA27	2300	35	A1
INVERNESS DR	LCF	LCF	100	19	C5
INVERNESS DR	PAS	PAS	1300	19	D6
INVERNESS PL	GLDR	GLDR	200	87	E5
INWOOD DR	LA	VAN	13300	22	F5
INYO ST	LA	LA31	3600	36	B6
INYO ST	LPUE	LPUE		92	A6
INYO ST	LPUE	LPUE	16100	98	A1
IOLAB DR	CLA	CLA		91	B4
IONE DR	LA	LA68	3400	24	A6
IONE PL	LA	LA68	3200	24	A6
IONE WK	LA	LA68		24	A6
IONIA WK	LB	LB03		80	D1
IOWA	WCOV	WCOV		92	E4
IOWA AV	LA	LA25	11200	41	D4
IOWA AV	PAS	PAS	1300	27	A1
IOWA AV	SOG	SOG	2400	58	F2
IOWA AV	SOG	SOG	2700	59	A2
IOWA CT	CLA	CLA	1100	90	F2
IOWA ST	DOW	DOW	8300	60	B4
IOWA TR	CO	TOP	1700	109	D1
IPSWICH CT	LA	LA77		32	B1
IRA AV	BG	BELL	6400	53	F6
IRA AV	BG	BELL	7200	59	F1
IRA ST	LYN	LYN	3900	59	C5
IREDELL LN	LA	NHO		23	C6
IREDELL ST	LA	NHO	11900	23	C5
IRENA AV N	RB	RB	100	67	D3
IRENA AV S	RB	RB	100	67	D3
IRENE CT	ELS	ELS	500	56	B5
IRENE ST	LA	LA34	10400	42	B5
IRENE ST	WCOV	WCOV		92	D6
IRIS AV	BELL	BELL		53	B5
IRIS AV	COV	COV	100	88	C5
IRIS AV	TOR	TOR	22600	68	B5
IRIS AV	TOR	TOR	1400	68	B4
IRIS CIR	LA	LA68	6800	34	C2
IRIS CIR	LAV	LAV		90	E2
IRIS CT	PALM	PALM		172	A8
IRIS DR	LA	LA68	6500	34	C2
IRIS LN	ELM	ELM	10900	38	D6
IRIS PL	LA	LA68	6800	34	C2
IRIS WY	MPK	MPK	2100	46	D4
IRMA AV	LA	TU	10400	10	E3
IROLA DR	RHE	PVP	4700	72	F3
IROLO ST	LA	LA05	600	43	E3
IROLO ST	LA	LA06	900	43	E3
IRONBARK DR	CER	ART		82	D5
IRONBARK DR	DBAR	POM		97	F3
IRONBARK LN	SAD	SAD	700	90	A4
IRON CANYON RD	CO	CYN	15100	128	E3
IRON CLUB DR	LAV	LAV		95A	D5
IRONDALE AV	LA	CAN	6700	12	D2
IRONDALE AV	LA	CHA	9400	6	D4
IRONDALE AV	LA	WOH	5400	13	D1
IRONHORSE DR	PALM	PALM		183	G3
IRON HORSE RD	WAL	WAL		93	B5
IRONHORSE CY RD	DBAR	POM		97	F3
IRONSHIRE ST	SCLR	CYN	18500	124	H5
IRONSHIRE ST	SCLR	CYN		125	A8
IRONSHOE CT	WAL	WAL		93	D4
IRONSIDES ST	LA	VEN		49	C6
IRONSIDES TR	CO	TOP	19800	109	C5
IRONSTONE AV	MTB	MTB	1600	46	F4
IRONSTONE DR	SCLR	CYN		125	B9
IRONTO AV	CO	PALM		183	D5
IRONTON DR	CO	LPUE	16600	92	B5
IRONWOOD AV	PALM	PALM		171	J8
IRONWOOD CIR	WAL	WAL		93	D6
IRONWOOD DR	AGH	AGO		102	E2
IRONWOOD LN	CAR	CAR		69	D6
IRONWOOD ST	RPV	PVP	5300	72	D3
IROQUOIS AV	LB	LB08	3000	71	E5
IROQUOIS AV	LB	LB15	1200	76	E4
IROQUOIS AV	LKD	LKD	4100	71	E2
IRVINE AV	LA	NHO	5600	16	D6
IRVINE AV	LA	NHO	4200	23	D4
IRVING AV	CO	GL14	5800	11	F5
IRVING AV	GLEN	GL01	1100	17	F6
IRVING AV	GLEN	GL01	1300	18	A6
IRVING AV	GLEN	GL01	200	24	E2
IRVING BLVD N	LA	LA04	100	34	D6
IRVING BLVD N	LA	LA38	700	34	D6
IRVING BLVD S	LA	LA04	100	43	D1
IRVING BLVD S	LA	LA05	600	43	D1
IRVING BLVD S	LA	LA20	300	43	D1
IRVING DR	BUR	BUR	500	17	C3
IRVING LN	CO	NEW		126	H4
IRVING PL	CUL	CUL	4000	42	C6
IRVING ST	ALH	ALH	600	37	B4
IRVING ST	VER	LA58	3700	52	E2
IRVINGTON PL	LA	LA42	5000	36	B1
IRVINGTON TER	LA	LA42	5100	36	B1
IRWIN AV	CO	IN04	10000	56	E3
IRWINDALE AV	AZU	AZU	100	88	B2
IRWINDALE AV	CO	COV	3900	88	B3
IRWINDALE AV	IRW	AZU	6100	86	B6
IRWINDALE AV	IRW	AZU	6000	88	B2
IRWINDALE AV	IRW	BAP	4600	88	B3
IRWINGROVE DR	DOW	DOW	7200	60	A2
IRWINGROVE ST	DOW	DOW	9000	60	D3
ISABEL AV	RM	RM	3000	46	E1
ISABEL DR	LA	LA65	3000	35	E3
ISABEL ST	BUR	BUR	900	17	C5
ISABEL ST	LA	LA65		35	E3
ISABEL ST	LA	LA65		36	A4
ISABEL ST N	GLEN	GL06	100	25	D3
ISABEL ST N	GLEN	GL07	900	25	D3
ISABEL ST S	GLEN	GL05	100	25	D3
ISABELLA AV	MPK	MPK	800	46	B5
ISABELLA PKWY	CO	CYN		124	G8
ISABELLA TER	MPK	MPK	300	46	B3
ISELI RD	SFS	SFS	14300	82	E2
ISHIDA AV	CAR	CAR		64	C4
ISIS AV	CO	HAW	12000	56	E6
ISIS AV	CO	IN04	11600	56	E6
ISIS AV	CO	LAW	14300	62	E2
ISIS AV	HAW	HAW	13200	62	E2
ISIS AV	ING	IN01	300	56	E3
ISIS AV	LA	LA45	7700	56	E1
ISLAND AV	CAR	CAR	21300	69	B4
ISLAND AV	CAR	CAR	24200	74	B2
ISLAND AV	LA	WIL	100	74	B5
ISLANDIA AV	CER	ART	16000	66	E4
ISLAND VIEW DR	RPV	PVP	28800	72	C6
ISLAND VLG DR	LB	LB03		80	F1
ISLE OF VIEW PL	CO	CAL		108	B5
ISLETA ST	LA	LA49	11300	41	C1
ISORA RD	PR	PR	8700	55	A1
ISORA ST	PR	PR	9100	55	A1
ISTHMUS PL	LB	LB03	1	80	B2
ITALIA ST	COV	COV	100	88	E4
ITALIA ST	COV	COV	800	89	A4
ITAPETINGA LN	CER	ART	13000	81	C1
ITASCA ST	LA	CHA	19800	6	E4
ITASCA ST	LA	NOR	19200	7	A4
ITASCA ST	LA	SF	16600	7	F4
ITASCA ST	LA	SF	16200	8	A4
ITATI TR	CO	CHA		1A	C6
ITHACA AV	LA	LA32	4900	36	D6
ITUNI ST	BAP	BAP	14400	48	E1
ITUNI ST	WCOV	WCOV	1100	48	E1
IVA ST	CO	COM	3700	65	B4
IVA ST	LB	LB05		65	E4
IVADEL PL	LA	ENC	16900	21	E3
IVAFERN LN	LCF	LCF	5300	19	D2
IVAN CT	LA	LA39	2700	35	C2
IVANELL ST	LPUE	LPUE	500	48	E5
IVAN HILL TER	LA	LA39	2500	35	C2
IVANHOE DR	LA	LA39	2400	35	C3
IVAR AV	LA	LA28	1300	34	C3
IVAR AV	LA	LA68	1900	34	C2
IVAR AV	RM	RM	3500	38	A6
IVAR AV	RM	RM	3000	47	A1
IVAR AV	TEC	TEC	5900	38	A2
IVARENE AV	LA	LA68	6200	34	C2
IVERSON LN	CO	CHA		6	B1
IVERSON RD	CO	CHA		1A	B6
IVERSON RD	CO	CHA		6	B1
IVES LN	RB	RB	2300	67	E1
IVES ST E	BLF	BLF	9200	66	B3
IVES ST E	PAR	PAR	8300	65	F3
IVESBROOK ST	LAN	LAN		160	C3
IVESBROOK ST W	CO	LAN	4000	159	D3
IVESBROOK ST W	LAN	LAN	7000	158	F3
IVESBROOK ST W	LAN	LAN	1100	159	J3
IVESBROOK ST W	LAN	LAN	500	160	B2
IVESCREST AV	CO	COV	5000	89	B3
IVESCREST AV	COV	COV	400	89	B4
IVO ST	DOW	DOW	7400	60	B1
IVORY AV	PALM	PALM		183	E2
IVORY DR	DUA	DUA	2000	29	C6
IVORY LN	POM	POM	500	90	F4
IVORY WY	CO	LPUE		98	F5
IVREA PL	CO	VAL		123	J9
IVREA PL	CO	VAL		126	G1
IVY AV E	ING	IN02	100	51	A6
IVY AV N	MON	MON	100	29	B4
IVY AV S	MON	MON	100	29	B4
IVY AV W	ING	IN02	100	51	A6
IVY AV W	ING	IN02	100	56	F1
IVY CT	NWK	NWK	10600	66	D2
IVY CT	POM	POM	300	90	E3
IVY DR	PALM	PALM		183	C1
IVY PL	LA	LA64	11200	41	F5
IVY ST	CO	LA02	8600	58	E2
IVY ST	GLDR	GLDR	700	89	C2
IVY ST	GLEN	GL04	300	25	B4
IVY ST	LA	LA34	3000	42	D5
IVY ST	PR	PR	4600	54	E2
IVY WY	CUL	CUL	5900	50	D1
IVY BRIDGE RD	GLEN	GL07	1600	25	D1
IVYDALE CT	CO	PAS	3600	28	A5
IVY GLEN WY	LA	LA64	3100	42	A5
IVYHILL RD	CO	LPUE	16500	98	B3
IVYLAND AV	ARC	ARC	2100	38	E1
IVYSIDE PL	LA	ENC	16800	21	F5
IVYSLOPE TR	CO	TOP		109	B2
IVYTON ST	LAN	LAN		160	C3
IVYTON ST W	LAN	LAN	1100	159	J3
IVYTON ST W	LAN	LAN	700	160	B3
IZETTA AV	BLF	BLF	13400	66	C1
IZETTA AV	DOW	DOW	12100	60	C6
IZETTA AV	DOW	DOW	12700	66	C1
J					
J ST	BELL	BELL		53	E4
JABONERIA RD	BG	BELL	6200	53	F6
JABONERIA RD	BG	BELL	7200	59	E2
JACANA DR	LAM	LAM	14700	83	A3
JACARANDA	WCOV	WCOV		92	D4
JACARANDA AV	BUR	BUR	3000	24	A2
JACARANDA DR	PAS	PAS	500	26	D5
JACARANDA ST	PALM	LAN		171	C2
JACINTO	PALM	PALM		171	D4
JACINTO AV	LA	SF	11300	10	A1
JACINTO WY	LB	LB15	4100	76	A3
JACK PL	LA	SP	2200	73	E6
JACKDAW DR	CO	SF		3	E2
JACKIE AV	LA	CAN	6500	5	F5
JACKIE AV	LA	WOH	6100	5	F5
JACKLIN AV	PALM	PALM	38600	172	E7
JACKMAN AV	LA	SF	11600	2	D6
JACKMAN ST E	LAN	LAN	600	160	C3
JACKMAN ST E	LAN	LAN	7100	161	D3
JACKMAN ST W	LAN	LAN	7000	158	H3
JACKMAN ST W	LAN	LAN	1100	159	H3
JACKMAN ST W	LAN	LAN	4000	159	D4
JACKMAN ST W	LAN	LAN	100	160	A3
JACKRABBIT LN	CAR	CAR		69	D6
JACKRABBIT LN	CO	ACT		182	D7
JACKSON AV	AZU	AZU	300	88	C2
JACKSON AV	CO	ACT		189	G3
JACKSON AV	CUL	CUL	4000	50	C1
JACKSON AV	LB	LB10	1100	75	A4
JACKSON AV	LYN	LYN	10600	59	C5
JACKSON AV	RM	RM	2400	46	E2
JACKSON AV	SGAB	SGAB	1700	37	E6
JACKSON AV	SOG	SOG	900	59	C4
JACKSON PL	CO	SGAB	7200	28	B6
JACKSON PL	GLEN	GL06		25	D3
JACKSON PL	WHI	WHI		61	E1
JACKSON ST	BUR	BUR	1700	17	C4
JACKSON ST	CAR	LB10	2600	69	F4
JACKSON ST	CAR	LB10	2500	70	A4
JACKSON ST	CO	CAST		123	A6
JACKSON ST	LA	LA12	300	44	E3
JACKSON ST	LB	LB05	1100	70	D2
JACKSON ST	PAR	PAR	7200	65	E4
JACKSON ST	PAS	PAS	300	27	B2
JACKSON ST	PR	PR	9300	55	A3
JACKSON ST	WHI	WHI		61	E1
JACKSON ST N	GLEN	GL06	100	25	D3
JACKSON ST N	GLEN	GL07	900	25	D3
JACKSON ST S	GLEN	GL05	100	25	D4
JACKSTADT ST	LA	SP	3700	78	E6
JACMAR AV	WHI	WHI		61	E2
JACMAR DR	MTB	MTB	400	54	D3
JACOB AV	CER	ART	19100	81	B2
JACOB ST	CUL	CUL	6000	42	D5
JACOB HAMBLN RD	HH	CAL	24800	100	C2
JACOBS LN	SPAS	SPAS	1000	36	E2
JACON WY	LA	PP	600	40	B3
JACQUELINE DR	POM	POM		94	C1
JACQUELINE DR	WCOV	WCOV		92	D6
JACQUELINE PL	LA	SF		1	D4
JACQUES ST	TOR	TOR	4600	67	E4
JACUMBA AV E	CO	LAN	20500	175	G6
JADE AV	LKD	LKD		81	C3
JADE CT	PALM	PALM		183	J7
JADE ST	LA	LA32	4500	45	C1
JADE COVE DR	LB	LB03		76	E5
JADESTONE DR	LA	VAN	14800	22	D5
JADESTONE PL	LA	VAN	14900	22	C5
JADE TREE DR	MPK	MPK		46	B2
JAFFREY AV	CO	TOR	21400	68	F4
JAGUAR ST	LA	SF	14500	8	D2
JAIL RD	AVA	AVA		77	B5
JAKES WY	SCLR	CYN		125	A9
JALAPA DR	COV	COV		89	C5
JALEE CT	CO	WAL		97	C5
JALISCO RD	LAM	LAM	14200	83	A3
JALMIA DR	LA	LA46	2500	33	F1
JALMIA PL	LA	LA46	2500	33	F1
JALMIA WY	LA	LA46	7500	33	F1
JALON RD	LAM	LAM	14500	83	B2
JAMACHA PL	WHI	WHI		84	C1
JAMES AV	WCOV	WCOV	1500	92	C1
JAMES PL	CER	ART	11100	71	E2
JAMES PL	PALM	PALM		183	H2
JAMES PL	POM	POM	600	90	F6
JAMES PL	POM	POM	800	91	B6
JAMES ST	CER	ART	11600	81	A2
JAMES ST	DOW	DOW	9000	60	B6
JAMES ST	LA	LA65	400	36	A4
JAMES WK	CO	CAST	28900	123	C2
JAMES ALAN CIR	LA	CHA	22300	6	B3
JAMESON CT	SMAD	SMAD		28	B2
JAMESON DR	CO	WOH		13	B4
JAMESON PL	CO	WOH		13	B4
JAMESTOWN	MON	MON		29	B2
JAMESTOWN CT	CLA	CLA		91	C1
JAMESTOWN RD	BUR	BUR	500	17	C3
JAMESTOWN RD	PALM	PALM		183	D2
JAMIE AV	LA	PAC	10100	9	B2
JAMIE AV	LA	SF	12900	2	E3
JAMIE CT	LAN	LAN		159	D3
JAMIESON AV	LA	ENC	5700	14	D6

1990 LOS ANGELES COUNTY STREET INDEX

STREET	CITY	P.O. ZONE	BLOCK	PAGE	GRID
JAMIESON AV	LA	NOR	8300	14	D1
JAMIESON AV	LA	RES	6100	14	D3
JAMISON AV	CAR	CAR	20600	69	B3
JAMON LN	WAL	WAL		93	B6
JAN CT	PR	PR	9300	47	B6
JAN CT	PR	PR	9300	55	B1
JAN ST	LA	CAN	20800	12	D4
JANALINDA AV	COV	COV	300	88	C5
JANDO DR	CO	TOP	1600	108	F2
JANDY PL	LA	LA66	5300	50	A5
JANE PL	PAS	PAS	900	26	F6
JANEL AV	SCLR	NEW	24300	127	C5
JANELL AV	CER	ART		82	B5
JANET LN	TOR	TOR	23900	72	F1
JANET PL	LA	LA41		25	F5
JANETDALE ST	CO	LPUE	13500	48	D2
JANETDALE ST	WCOV	WCOV		48	E3
JANET LEE DR	CO	GL14	2300	11	E5
JANETTA WY	LA	SUN		9	E4
JANETTE AV	CO	LPUE	1000	48	C6
JANICE DR	LB	LB05	700	65	D6
JANICE LN	WAL	WAL		92	F5
JANICE LN	WAL	WAL		93	A5
JANICE PL	LA	BH	9100	33	C2
JANICE ST	LB	LB05	200	65	F6
JANINE DR	LHH	LAH	100	84	E3
JANINE DR	WHI	WHI	14100	61	F1
JANINE DR	WHI	WHI	14800	84	A2
JANIS ST	CAR	CAR	1100	64	D5
JANISANN AV	CUL	CUL	5200	50	C3
JANISON DR	LHH	LAH	17000	84	E3
JANLOR DR	AGH	AGO		102	D3
JANLU AV	CO	LPUE	1300	85	D2
JANNA ST	BLF	BLF		66	B5
JANNA WY	LA	SF		3	B1
JANNETTA AV	BUR	BUR	2100	17	B4
JANSEN AV	SAD	SAD	100	89	D2
JANSU PL	POM	POM	100	94	A2
JANUARY DR	TOR	TOR	25400	73	B3
JANUS DR	PALM	PALM		172	H9
JANUS DR	PALM	PALM		183	H1
JANVIER WY	CO	GL14	4800	18	E1
JAPNS VLG PZ ML	LA	LA12		44	D3
JAPONICA AV	CO	LAV	4100	90	E1
JARANA CT	SCLR	VAL		124	C6
JARDINE AV	LA	SUN	10100	10	E3
JARDINE ST	CMRC	LA40	4900	53	E2
JARED CT	LA	WOH	6100	5	D5
JARED DR	LA	LA49		21	C2
JARMAN PL	BAP	BAP	13400	39	D4
JARROW AV	CO	LPUE	1000	48	C6
JARVIS AV	CO	LA61	12800	64	B1
JARVIS AV	LCF	LCF	5000	19	A1
JARVIS ST	LA	LA12	1800	35	E6
JASMINE AV	CUL	CUL	3800	50	C1
JASMINE AV	LA	LA34	3400	42	B6
JASMINE AV	MON	MON	100	29	B4
JASMINE CT	LAV	LAV		95A	E6
JASMINE LN	LPUE	LPUE		48	F6
JASMINE ST	LAN	LAN		159	H6
JASMINE VLY DR	CO	CYN		125	F4
JASON AV	LA	CAN	7800	5	F1
JASON AV	LA	CAN		5	F3
JASON CIR	TOR	TOR	3600	68	A5
JASON LN	LA	CAN		5	F3
JASON PL	DBAR	POM		97A	B2
JASON RD	CO	ACT		182	C9
JASPER ST	LA	LA32	4400	36	C5
JATO RD	SCLR	SAU		127	D1
JAVA DR	LA	BH	13000	22	F5
JAVA DR	LA	BH		23	A5
JAVA ST	ING	IN01	800	57	A2
JAVALAMBRE DR	WHI	WHI	5100	55	C2
JAVELIN ST	CAR	CAR	100	69	B3
JAVELIN ST	CO	TOR	600	68	F3
JAXINE DR	CO	ALT	100	20	A3
JAY CT	MTB	MTB		54	D1
JAY CT N	MTB	MTB		46	D6
JAY PL	CO	TOR	22100	68	F5
JAY ST	CO	TOR	900	68	F5
JAY ST E	CAR	CAR	100	69	B5
JAY ST W	CAR	CAR	100	69	A5
JAYBROOK DR	RPV	SP	1800	78	D1
JAY CARROLL DR	SCLR	SAU		124	G5
JAYDEE CIR	LA	TU		10	E2
JAYHAWKER LN	DBAR	POM		94	A5
JAYLEE DR	CO	SGAB	8900	38	A1
JAYLEE DR	TEC	TEC	9100	38	B1
JAYMA LN	CO	GL14	2300	11	F5
JAYMILLS AV	LB	LB05	5900	65	C6
JAYMILLS AV	LB	LB05	5700	70	C1
JAYSEEL ST	LA	SUN	7800	10	E2
JAYSEEL ST	LA	TU	7600	10	E2
JAYSON CT	POM	POM	700	91	A3
JEAN LN	WLVL	THO		102A	F5
JEAN PL	CUL	CUL	3800	42	C6

STREET	CITY	P.O. ZONE	BLOCK	PAGE	GRID
JEAN PL	LA	CUL	3800	42	C6
JEANETTE AV	CER	ART	16600	82	C4
JEANETTE LN	BAP	BAP	3600	39	E6
JEANETTE PL	LA	SF	12000	1	E5
JEANETTE PL	LB	LB10	1800	75	A1
JEANETTE ST	PALM	PALM	38100	172	E9
JEANINE PL	LA	SF	16900	1	E4
JEANNE LN	CO	PALM		183	J5
JEANNE LN	LA	ENC	16000	22	B5
JEANNE TER	LA	TU		10	E1
JEANNIE DR	CO	LPUE	17900	98	D1
JEDBURGH ST	GLDR	GLDR	1000	89	C2
JED SMITH RD	HH	CAL	24500	100	C2
JEFF AV	LA	SF	11400	3	E6
JEFF AV	LA	SF	11300	9	F1
JEFF ST E	BLF	BLF	9000	66	B2
JEFFDALE AV	LA	WOH	5100	13	A2
JEFFERS LN	CO	SAU		124	D4
JEFFERSON AV	HAW	HAW	100	63	A2
JEFFERSON AV	PALM	PALM		183	D2
JEFFERSON AV	SOG	SOG	5700	59	E6
JEFFERSON AV E	POM	POM	100	94	E1
JEFFERSON AV E	POM	POM	700	95	A1
JEFFERSON AV W	POM	POM	100	94	E1
JEFFERSON BLVD	CO	CUL	11900	50	A5
JEFFERSON BLVD	CO	LA66	12300	50	A5
JEFFERSON BLVD	CO	MDR	13100	49	E6
JEFFERSON BLVD	CUL	CUL	9000	42	D6
JEFFERSON BLVD	CUL	CUL	10000	50	C2
JEFFERSON BLVD	CUL	CUL	11400	50	A5
JEFFERSON BLVD	LA	CUL	11700	50	A5
JEFFERSON BLVD	MTB	MTB	800	46	D5
JEFFERSON BL E	LA	LA11	100	52	B1
JEFFERSON BL W	LA	LA07	1000	43	B6
JEFFERSON BL W	LA	LA07	100	44	B6
JEFFERSON BL W	LA	LA16	5200	42	E5
JEFFERSON BL W	LA	LA16	3600	43	B6
JEFFERSON BL W	LA	LA18	1500	43	B6
JEFFERSON CT	LAN	LAN		160	G4
JEFFERSON DR	CO	PAS	1900	27	D1
JEFFERSON ST	BLF	BLF	9400	66	B3
JEFFERSON ST	CAR	LB10	2500	69	F4
JEFFERSON ST	CAR	LB10	2600	70	A4
JEFFERSON ST	PAR	PAR	7500	65	E3
JEFFERSON ST	PAR	PAR	8400	66	A3
JEFFERSON ST	TOR	TOR	2500	68	C5
JEFFERSONIA WY	LA	LA49	2200	30	E5
JEFFREY AV	CER	ART	17400	82	C5
JEFFREY CIR	CER	ART	19500	81	C2
JEFFREY CT	PAS	PAS	2900	27	F2
JEFFREY DR	TOR	TOR	5400	67	E3
JEFFREY PL	LA	WOH		13	F2
JEFFREY MARK CT	LA	CHA	22400	6	B3
JEFFRIES AV	ARC	ARC	1100	39	A1
JEFFRIES AV	BUR	BUR	3900	16	F5
JEFFRIES AV	BUR	BUR	2300	17	A5
JEFFRIES AV	CO	ARC	525	39	A1
JEFFRIES AV	CO	MON	100	39	A1
JEFFRIES AV	LA	LA65	2600	35	F5
JELLICK AV	CO	LPUE	400	98	E1
JELLICK AV	IND	LPUE	1100	98	E3
JELLICO AV	LA	ENC	5900	14	D6
JELLICO AV	LA	NOR	8600	7	D6
JELLICO AV	LA	NOR	7600	14	D2
JELLICO AV	LA	SF	11400	1	D5
JELLICO AV	LA	SF	1300	7	D1
JELLICO AV	LA	VAN	6700	14	D4
JENA DR	SCLR	NEW		127	B5
JENIEL CT	SCLR	SAU		127	C2
JENIFER AV	CO	COV	4900	89	A3
JENIFER AV	COV	COV	400	89	A5
JENIFER AV	GLDR	GLDR	800	89	A1
JENKINS DR	CO	WHI	15200	84	B4
JENKINS DR	WHI	WHI	15400	84	B4
JENKINS ST	ART	ART		66	F5
JENNA LN	PALM	PALM		183	H2
JENNER ST	LAN	LAN		160	C3
JENNER ST W	LAN	LAN	1400	159	H4
JENNIFER DR	PALM	PALM		183	G2
JENNIFER LN	LAN	LAN		160	D7
JENNIFER PL	SCLR	NEW		127	A5
JENNIFER PL	WCOV	WCOV		92	B4
JENNINGS DR	LA	LA32	4000	36	D4
JENNY AV	LA	LA45		56	D3
JENNY CT	SCLR	SAU		124	F4
JENNY LN	LAN	LAN		171	A1
JENNY WY	RM	RM		47	A1
JENSEN DR	LA	CAN	23900	5	E1
JEREMIE ST	BAP	BAP	14800	39	F5
JEREMY PL	LA	SF		1	D4
JERENE LN	CO	TOR		68	F6
JERENE LN	CO	TOR		69	A6
JERI LN	PALM	PALM		172	F9
JEROME ST	LA	SV	11900	9	B5
JERRY AV	BAP	BAP	3900	39	D4
JERRY PL	CER	ART	11000	71	E2

STREET	CITY	P.O. ZONE	BLOCK	PAGE	GRID
JERRY ST	CER	ART	11500	81	A2
JERSEY	LA	SF		8	C2
JERSEY AV	ART	ART	18600	81	A1
JERSEY AV	ART	ART	16600	82	A5
JERSEY AV	CER	ART	19500	81	A2
JERSEY AV	LKD	LKD	19700	81	A2
JERSEY AV	NWK	NWK	11100	61	A5
JERSEY AV	NWK	NWK	13500	82	A1
JERSEY AV	SFS	SFS	9400	61	A2
JERSEY CIR	CER	ART	19400	81	A2
JERSEY ST	LA	SF	16600	7	F2
JERSEY ST	LA	SF	16000	8	A2
JERSEYDALE AV	MTB	MTB	1600	46	F4
JESLEW CT	CO	LPUE		98	B4
JESS ST	POM	POM	1500	94	C3
JESS ST	SOG	SOG	4900	59	D2
JESSE AV	GLEN	GL01	100	24	E2
JESSE ST	LA	LA21	1500	44	E4
JESSE ST	LA	LA23	2200	44	F4
JESSEN DR	LCF	LCF	5000	19	A1
JESSICA CIR	CER	ART		66	E4
JESSICA CT	WCOV	WCOV		92	D6
JESSICA DR	LA	LA65	4500	36	A2
JESSICA PL	LA	SF		1	D4
JESSIE ST	SF	SF	1	2	E6
JESSIE NELSN DR	SH	LB06		75	E2
JET PL	LA	LA46		33	F2
JETMORE AV	PAR	PAR	13400	65	F1
JETTY ST	LA	LA31		44	F1
JEWEL ST	LA	LA26	3000	35	B5
JEWELL AV	VER	LA58	2800	52	F2
JEWETT DR	LA	LA46	1800	33	E2
JIB ST	LA	VEN		49	C6
JILL PL	LA	ENC	4000	21	F4
JILLIENE LN	PR	PR		55	E3
JILLSON ST	CMRC	LA40	4800	53	E2
JILLSON ST	CMRC	LA40	6000	54	A3
JIM BOWIE RD	AGH	AGO		100A	D5
JIM BRIDGER RD	HH	CAL	24700	100	C2
JIMENEZ PL	LA	SF		9	F1
JIMENEZ ST	LA	SF	10200	9	F1
JIMENEZ ST	LA	SF	9700	10	A1
JIMENO AV	LA	SF	12600	1	F4
JIMPSON WY	SCLR	CYN		124	E8
J LEE CIR	GLEN	GL08		18	E4
JOAN CT	WCOV	WCOV		92	D6
JOAN DR	CO	LPUE	1400	85	D2
JOAN LN	LA	CAN	8300	5	F1
JOANBRIDGE ST	BAP	BAP	14100	39	E2
JOANN WY	POM	POM		95	A1
JOANNA AV	CER	ART		66	E4
JOANNE PL	CUL	CUL		50	C4
JOAQUIN CT	CMRC	LA40		53	F2
JOAQUIN DR	BUR	BUR	2600	17	C2
JOAQUIN DR	CER	ART	13500	82	D4
JOAQUIN LN	CER	ART	13700	82	E4
JOAQUIN RD	ARC	ARC	300	28	C5
JODEE DR	WCOV	WCOV	3300	93	A1
JODI PL	SCLR	SAU		124	D5
JODI ST	CO	LPUE		98	F3
JODON CT	CO	LPUE		98	B4
JODY AV	CO	WHI	9700	61	D2
JODY LN	CAR	CAR		69	A5
JOEL DR	CO	LPUE		97	B5
JOEL ST	SCLR	SAU		124	G4
JOEL ST E	CAR	CAR	800	69	C5
JOEL ST W	CAR	CAR	300	69	A5
JOELLA ST	CO	DUA	700	29	B6
JOELLA ST	CO	MON	300	29	B6
JOELLA ST	DUA	DUA	800	29	C6
JOELTON DR	AGH	AGO		100A	D5
JOFFRE ST	LA	LA49	11300	41	C1
JOHANNA AV	LA	SUN	10100	10	A3
JOHANNA AV	LKD	LKD	4300	71	E4
JOHANNA PL	LA	SUN	9700	10	A3
JOHN AV	CO	LA02	8600	58	D2
JOHN AV	LB	LB05	5800	70	E1
JOHN AV	PAS	PAS	300	26	F5
JOHN PL	CLA	CLA		91	A1
JOHN ST	LA	LA26	3400	35	A6
JOHN ST	MB	MB	200	62	B4
JOHN ST	SFS	SFS	9000	61	C2
JOHN WY	LA	SP		73	D3
JOHN COLTER RD	HH	CAL	24500	100	D3
JOHN DODSON DR	AGH	AGO		102	E3
JOHNELL RD	CO	CHA		4	B5
JOHNETTA ST	LA	WOH	24300	5	D6
JOHN FREMONT RD	HH	CAL	24900	100	C2
JOHN MNTGMRY DR	LA	SP	27500	73	E5
JOHN REED CT	IND	LPUE		98	B2
JOHN RUSSELL DR	SCLR	VAL		127	B1
JOHNS CANYON RD	RH	PVP	1	72	F6
JOHN S GIBSN BL	LA	SP		74	A6
JOHN SLOAT PL	LA	SP	27600	73	E5
JOHNSON AL	PAS	PAS	700	27	B2
JOHNSON AV	CO	CAST		123	C2

STREET	CITY	P.O. ZONE	BLOCK	PAGE	GRID
JOHNSON AV	ELM	ELM		38	E6
JOHNSON AV	LB	LB05	6200	65	F5
JOHNSON CT	TOR	TOR	2000	63	D5
JOHNSON DR	IND	LPUE	16300	98	A2
JOHNSON MTWY	CO	CHA		1A	A5
JOHNSON PL	CO	CHA		1A	B5
JOHNSON RD	CO	CYN		125	D5
JOHNSON RD	CO	LAN		157	H8
JOHNSON RD	CO	SAU	35000	181	E6
JOHNSON RD W	CO	LAN	11000	158	A8
JOHNSON ST	CO	CAST	27800	123	J2
JOHNSON ST	MB	MB	200	62	C4
JOHNSON ST E	COM	COM	100	64	F4
JOHNSON ST E	COM	COM	200	65	A4
JOHNSON ST W	COM	COM	100	64	F4
JOHNSTON AV	RB	RB	2800	62	E4
JOHNSTON ST	LA	LA31	2200	36	A6
JOHNSTON ST	LA	LA31	1700	45	A1
JHNSTN PEAK TT	CO	GLDR		95A	B1
JOHN TYLER DR	CO	MAL		113	E4
JOJOBA TER	PALM	PALM		183	J6
JOLEE LN	RPV	PVP		72	D5
JOLENE CT	LA	NHO		16	C3
JOLETTE AV	LA	SF	12200	1	E4
JOLIET AV	HG	LKD	22100	81	B5
JOLINE AV	PALM	PALM	39600	172	A6
JOLLEY DR	BUR	BUR	2000	17	C3
JOLLY TR	CO	TOP		109	D1
JON CT	DBAR	POM		94	B6
JON CT	DBAR	POM		97A	B1
JON ST	CO	TOR	1200	68	F2
JONALLAN DR	LA	NHO		16	C4
JONATHAN CT	LAN	LAN		159	E6
JONATHAN ST	LA	CAN	23100	5	F1
JONES AL	PAS	PAS	2100	27	D4
JONES AV	LA	LA32	1800	45	C1
JONES CT	WCOV	WCOV		92	C4
JONES PL	SH	LB06		70	E6
JONES PL	SH	LB06		75	E1
JONESBORO DR	LA	LA49	1300	40	F3
JONESBORO PL	LA	LA49	13200	40	F3
JONES CANYON RD	CO	ACT		189	C1
JONFIN	LA	SF		8	C2
JONFIN ST	LA	SF	16200	8	A2
JONQUIL FLD RD	WLVL	THO		102	A5
JOPLIN AV	CAR	CAR	19600	69	E2
JORDAN AV	LA	CAN	6800	12	C4
JORDAN AV	LA	CHA	9100	6	C5
JORDAN CIR	SFS	SFS	12400	61	B3
JORDAN LN	LA	SV		9	F6
JORDAN RD	WHI	WHI	10600	84	D4
JORDAN WY	CUL	CUL	5000	50	C2
JORDERR AV	LA	LA46	8000	33	E1
JOSARD AV	CO	SGAB	8300	27	F6
JOSEL DR	CO	CYN		128	E3
JOSEPH CT	LA	SF		2	B1
JOSEPH LN	PALM	PALM		172	B5
JOSEPHINE CT	CO	COM	3600	65	B4
JOSEPHINE ST	LYN	LYN	5100	59	B6
JOSHUA	WCOV	WCOV		98	F1
JOSHUA AV	CO	PALM		189	J1
JOSHUA LN	NWK	NWK	12900	82	C1
JOSEPH HOOPR DR	SCLR	CYN		128	E1
JOSHUA LN	POM	POM		95	A1
JOSHUA RD	CO	LR		192	A6
JOSHUA ST	PALM	LAN		171	B2
JOSHUA GROVE AV	CO	LAN	17700	175	B5
JOSHUA HILLS DR	PALM	PALM		183	F3
JOSHUA TREE DR	CO	PALM		157	H9
JOSIE AV	LB	LB08	3000	71	E6
JOSIE AV	LB	LB15	1300	76	E4
JOSIE AV	LKD	LKD	4100	71	E4
JOSLIN ST	SFS	SFS	11000	60	F3
JOTHAM PL	LB	LB07	3800	70	E5
JOUETT ST	LA	PAC	13900	8	E4
JOUETT ST	LA	PAC	12300	9	B1
JOUETT ST	LA	SF	11800	3	C6
JOURNEYS END DR	LCF	LCF	1200	19	B1
JOVAN ST	LA	RES	18300	14	C5
JOVENITA CYN RD	LA	LA46	8000	33	E1
JOVITA AV	LA	CHA	9700	6	E3
JOVITA PL	LA	CHA	9800	6	E4
JOY ST	HB	RB	1000	62	D6
JOY ST	LA	LA42	200	36	B2
JOY ST	WCOV	WCOV		92	F1
JOYCE AV	ARC	ARC	200	28	F4
JOYCE PL	CO	NEW		126	G3
JOYCE ST	MTB	MTB	500	54	C2
JOYCEDALE ST	CO	LPUE	13500	48	D2
JOYCEDALE ST	WCOV	WCOV	1400	48	E3
JOYGLEN DR	CO	WHI	13600	61	D3
JUAN AV	HG	LKD	21000	81	B4
JUAN AV	HG	LKD	21400	81	B5
JUAN AV	TOR	TOR	4600	67	F6
JUAN BATISTA DR	SAD	SAD		90	A3
JUANITA AV	CO	SAD		89	B2

STREET	CITY	P.O. ZONE	BLOCK	PAGE	GRID
JUANITA AV	GLDR	GLDR	100	89	B2
JUANITA AV	PAS	PAS	1900	20	A6
JUANITA AV	RB	RB	1000	67	D5
JUANITA AV E	CO	LAV	700	90	B2
JUANITA AV E	SAD	SAD	300	90	A2
JUANITA AV N	LA	LA04	100	34	F6
JUANITA AV N	RB	RB	100	67	D3
JUANITA AV S	LA	LA04	200	34	F6
JUANITA AV S	RB	RB	100	67	D4
JUANITA AV W	GLDR	GLDR	19500	89	B2
JUANITA AV W	SAD	SAD	1100	89	B2
JUAREZ AV	CO	WHI	5700	55	B3
JUAREZ ST	IRW	BAP	15600	88	A3
JUAREZ ST	MTB	MTB		46	D6
JUBILEE LN	DBAR	POM		97A	A1
JUBILEE RUN RD	CO	VALY		192	G9
JUBILEE TR AV	CO	LAN	16600	175	A7
JUBILO DR	LA	TAR	4200	21	B3
JUBUEDLY DR	AZU	AZU	500	86	D4
JUDAH AV	CO	HAW	12000	56	E5
JUDAH AV	CO	IN04	11600	56	E5
JUDAH AV	HAW	HAW	13400	62	D2
JUDAH AV	LA	LA45	11400	56	E5
JUDAH CIR	SCLR	NEW		127	E5
JUDAH WY	SCLR	NEW		127	E5
JUDD ST	LA	PAC	12600	3	B6
JUDD ST	LA	PAC	13400	8	D3
JUDD ST	LA	PAC	12900	9	A1
JUDD ST	LA	SF	12300	3	C5
JUDILEE DR	LA	ENC	3300	22	A5
JUDITH ST	BAP	BAP	13000	48	B1
JUDITH ST	CO	LPUE	13400	48	C2
JUDSON AV	LB	LB10	2300	74	F2
JUDSON AV	LB	LB13	1500	74	F3
JUDSON CT	CLA	CLA	2400	91	C1
JUDSON ST	LA	LA33	600	45	A3
JUDY DR	RB	RB	500	67	D4
JUDY WY	CER	ART	16600	82	B5
JULEP PL	ALH	ALH	3200	45	E1
JULIA AV	RB	RB	700	67	E4
JULIAN AV	LB	LB08	3000	81	B6
JULIAN CT	DBAR	POM		94	B5
JULIAN LN	LA	TAR		14	A6
JULIANNA LN	LA	WOH		13	C1
JULIANNE CT	CO	CYN		125	F6
JULIE CT	WCOV	WCOV		92	D6
JULIE DR	CO	LPUE		97	A4
JULIE LN	CO	CAN	6600	5	D4
JULIET ST	LA	LA07	2200	43	F5
JULIUS AV	DOW	DOW	11700	59	F4
JULIUS AV	DOW	DOW	9600	60	B1
JULLIARD DR	CLA	CLA		91	C1
JULLIARD DR	WAL	WAL	20000	93	C6
JULLIEN ST	LA	LA63	100	45	B4
JUMILLA AV	LA	CAN	6400	12	F5
JUMILLA AV	LA	CHA	10000	6	F3
JUMILLA AV	LA	NOR	8700	6	F6
JUMILLA AV	LA	WOH	5700	12	F5
JUMILLA AV	LA	WOH	5100	13	F1
JUNALUSKA WY	LA	PP	15900	40	C3
JUNCTION ST	CO	LA01	5900	52	D4
JUNE CT	WCOV	WCOV		92	D6
JUNE LN	GLEN	GL08	1700	18	F5
JUNE ST	LB	LB05		65	D5
JUNE ST N	LA	LA04	100	34	B6
JUNE ST N	LA	LA28	1300	34	C4
JUNE ST N	LA	LA38	700	34	B6
JUNE ST S	LA	LA04	100	34	B6
JUNE ST S	LA	LA05	600	43	B2
JUNE ST S	LA	LA20	300	43	B2
JUNEAU PL	LA	WOH	20400	13	E3
JUNEDA DR	SCLR	SAU		124	E4
JUNEWAY RD	MPK	MPK	2300	46	C5
JUNEWOOD PL	DBAR	POM		97A	A1
JUNGFRAU AV	CO	PALM		183	B4
JUNGLE ST	LA	SUN		10	C2
JUNIETTE ST	CO	LA66	12400	50	B5
JUNIETTE ST	LA	CUL	11800	50	B5
JUNIPER AV	TOR	TOR	1600	68	B4
JUNIPER AV	TOR	TOR	22600	68	B5
JUNIPER DR	PALM	PALM		183	F2
JUNIPER DR	PAS	PAS	400	26	D5
JUNIPER ST	CO	LA02	8600	58	E3
JUNIPER ST	DOW	DOW	11800	59	E6
JUNIPER ST	ING	IN02	100	50	F6
JUNIPER ST	LA	LA02	10100	58	E4
JUNIPER ST	LA	LA59	10700	58	E4
JUNIPER ST	LAV	LAV		90	B3
JUNIPER ST	WCOV	WCOV	100	92	D1
JUNIPER CRST RD	CO	ACT		182	A7
JUNIPER HLLS RD	CO	LR	10600	192	A6
JUNIPER MESA RD	CO	LR	10600	192	A5
JUNIPERO AV	LB	LB03	100	75	E6
JUNIPERO AV	LB	LB04	700	75	E6
JUNIPERO AV	LB	LB14	300	75	E6

COPYRIGHT, © 1989 BY Thomas Bros Maps

1990 LOS ANGELES COUNTY STREET INDEX

STREET	CITY	P.O. ZONE	BLOCK	PAGE	GRID
JUNIPERO AV	SH	LB06	2900	75	E1
JUNIPERO DR	DUA	DUA	800	29	D4
JUNIPERO PL	SGAB	SGAB	300	37	D3
JUNIPERO SER DR	SGAB	SGAB		37	D4
JUNIPER RIDGE	POM	POM		94	C4
JUNIPER TREE RD	CO	PALM	38800	171	J8
JUNIPER VLY RD	CO	ACT		182	A8
JUNO AV	NWK	NWK	12000	61	B6
JUPITER AV	PALM	PALM		183	H1
JUPITER DR	LA	LA46	2300	33	F2
JUPITER ST	WHI	WHI	14800	84	B3
JURA RD	DBAR	POM		93	F5
JURADO AV	CO	LPUE	2300	85	D3
JURICH PL	ALH	ALH		45	E1
JUSTAMERE AV	CO	CAST	29200	123	A4
JUSTICE ST	LA	CAN	23400	5	F2
JUSTIN AV	GLEN	GL01	200	24	F2
JUSTIN CT	LA	CAN	7700	5	F2
JUSTIN CT	PALM	PALM		183	H2
JUSTINE CT	WCOV	WCOV		92	D6
JUTEWOOD	WCOV	WCOV		92	D4
JUTLAND AV	LA	NOR	9700	7	D4
JUTLAND AV	LA	NOR	7800	14	D2
K					
K ST	BELL	BELL		53	E4
KADIN DR	CO	SF		3	E2
KADLETZ RD	GLEN	GL14		18	C1
KADOTA ST	LA	SF	15700	2	C2
KAGAWA ST	LA	PP	800	40	D3
KAGEL CANYON RD	CO	SF		3	E4
KAGEL CANYON ST	LA	PAC	13300	8	F4
KAGEL CANYON ST	LA	PAC	12800	9	A3
KAGEL CANYON ST	LA	SF	11300	3	D6
KAGEL CANYON ST	LA	SF	11600	9	C1
KAGEL TRUCK TR	CO	SAU		128	J9
KAHLENBERG LN	LA	NHO	12700	23	B2
KAHNS DR	RM	RM	9000	47	B1
KAHOOLAWE	SCLR	NEW		127	E5
KAIA LN	SMAD	SMAD		28	E1
KAIBAB CT	CO	PALM		157	F9
KAILUA LN	LA	TU	10400	10	E3
KAISER CIR	CAR	CAR	20300	69	D3
KAKKIS DR	LB	LB03		76	D5
KALB CT	SCLR	SAU	18800	127	H3
KALE ST E	SELM	ELM	9800	47	C2
KALEIN DR	CUL	CUL	5200	50	C3
KALISHER ST	LA	SF	14700	2	D6
KALISHER ST	LA	SF	16600	7	E1
KALISHER ST	LA	SF	15600	8	B1
KALISHER ST	SF	SF	200	2	D6
KALLIN AV	LB	LB08	3000	71	E6
KALLIN AV	LB	LB15	800	76	E4
KALLIN WY	LB	LB15	6700	76	E4
KALMAN ST	CO	SAU		182	E8
KALMAR AV	SCLR	NEW		127	B6
KALMIA ST	CO	LA02	9200	58	E3
KALMIA ST	LA	LA02	10300	58	E4
KALMIA ST	LA	LA59	10700	58	E4
KALNOR AV	NWK	NWK	11000	61	B6
KALNOR AV	NWK	NWK	13300	82	B1
KALSMAN AV	CO	COM	13900	64	D2
KALSMAN AV	COM	COM	600	64	D2
KALSMAN DR	LA	LA16	3600	42	E6
KALUA DR	LA	SUN	10200	10	A4
KAM CT	WCOV	WCOV		92	D6
KAMAN CT	LA	SF		1	D5
KAMAS AV	CO	LPUE	1100	48	D6
KAMAS AV	CO	LPUE		85	D1
KAMLOOPS PL	LA	SF	11400	9	D1
KAMLOOPS ST	LA	PAC	13500	8	F4
KAMLOOPS ST	LA	PAC	12700	9	A4
KAMLOOPS ST	LA	SF	11400	3	D6
KAMLOOPS ST	LA	SF	11400	9	D1
KAMLYN LN	WAL	WAL		92	F5
KAMM ST	CAR	CAR	1900	69	E2
KAMSTRA AV	CER	ART	18400	81	C1
KAMSTRA AV	CER	ART	18300	82	C6
KANAN RD	AGH	AGO		100A	A4
KANAN RD	AGH	AGO		102	F4
KANAN RD	CO	AGO	2400	106	D1
KANAN RD	CO	MAL	1200	106	B3
KANAN DUME RD	CO	MAL		106	A5
KANAN DUME RD	CO	MAL		112	C6
KANDI CT	SCLR	NEW		127	H3
KANE AV	CO	WHI	10700	61	F4
KANAINA CT	CO	CHA		1A	B6
KANOLA RD	LHH	LAH	1700	98A	B1
KANON DUME RD	CO	MAL		110	B5
KANOW AV	CO	PALM	36800	184	G3
KANSAS	WCOV	WCOV		92	E4
KANSAS AV	GAR	GAR	13300	63	F1
KANSAS AV	LA	LA37	4000	51	F2
KANSAS AV	LA	LA44	5800	51	F6
KANSAS AV	LA	LA44	8300	57	F1
KANSAS AV	PAR	PAR	13600	65	E1
KANSAS AV	SM	SM	2300	41	C6
KANSAS AV	SOG	SOG	2400	58	F3
KANSAS AV	SOG	SOG	2700	59	A3
KANSAS ST	SCLR	NEW	24700	127	C4
KANSAS ST	ELS	ELS	100	56	C6
KAPLAN AV	IND	LPUE	16000	92	A5
KARA PL	CO	LPUE		98	E6
KARDASHIAN AV	ARC	ARC		39	A3
KAREEM CT	ING	ING		57	B2
KARELIA ST	LA	LA65	4000	35	F2
KAREN AV	LB	LB08	3000	71	F6
KAREN AV	LB	LB08	3000	76	F1
KAREN CIR	CUL	CUL	5100	50	C3
KAREN DR	LA	ENC	17600	21	D3
KAREN DR	LA	TAR	4500	21	C3
KAREN DR	LA	TAR	18300	21	C3
KAREN DR	PALM	LAN		171	B2
KAREN ST	BUR	BUR	1800	17	C3
KAREN ST	PALM	PALM		183	F2
KAREN WY	LB	LB15	800	76	E4
KARENA AV	CO	CAST		123	J2
KAREN LYNN DR	GLEN	GL06		19	C6
KAREN SUE LN	LCF	LCF	3600	19	C6
KARESH AV	POM	POM	500	95	B1
KARI WY	ARC	ARC		28	E6
KARIE LN	SCLR	NEW		127	E2
KARIN PL	CO	SGAB		27	A6
KARIN PL	CO	SGAB	6600	37	F1
KARL BURNUM WY	MPK	MPK	800	46	B3
KARLING PL	PALM	PALM		184	A1
KARMONT AV	SOG	SOG	9300	59	E4
KARNS AV	CO	LPUE	200	48	A4
KARROO WY	PAR	PAR		65	E4
KASHIWA CT	TOR	TOR		68	B6
KASHIWA ST	TOR	TOR		68	B6
KASHLAN RD	LHH	LAH	1300	98A	B2
KATE CT	WCOV	WCOV		92	D6
KATELLA RD	SOG	SOG	5100	59	D4
KATHERINE AV	LA	VAN	8500	8	E6
KATHERINE AV	LA	VAN	5600	15	E6
KATHERINE AV	LA	VAN	4400	22	E3
KATHERINE CT	CER	ART		81	A2
KATHERINE CT	PALM	PALM		183	B1
KATHERINE DR	MTB	MTB	400	54	E1
KATHERINE LN	ARC	ARC	700	28	C3
KATHERINEL ST	CO	ACT	34600	182	F8
KATHLEEN AV	SCLR	SAU		124	G3
KATHLEEN AV	CO	WHI	12300	47	E5
KATHLEEN CT	WCOV	WCOV		92	D6
KATHRYN AV	POM	POM	1900	94	F6
KATHRYN AV	TOR	TOR	23500	72	F1
KATHRYN ST	TOR	TOR	22400	67	F6
KATHY WY	TOR	TOR	2000	68	D6
KATHYANN ST	LA	SF	11800	3	C6
KATIE LN	RM	RM	3100	47	A1
KATRINA PL	PALM	PALM		184	A1
KATRINE CIR	CO	WAL	19700	97	B3
KATY ST	NWK	NWK	12500	82	B1
KATYS LN	SCLR	VAL		127	C2
KAUAI	WCOV	WCOV		92	C4
KAUFFMAN AV	CO	TEC	6500	38	B1
KAUFFMAN AV	SOG	SOG	8900	59	C4
KAUFFMAN AV	TEC	TEC	4900	38	C2
KAUFFMAN ST	ELM	ELM	11000	38	E6
KAWEAH DR	PAS	PAS	1500	26	D5
KAY AV	CER	ART	19000	81	D1
KAY CT	CER	ART	17800	82	D6
KAY DR	SCLR	NEW	20800	127	F4
KAY ST	COM	COM	800	65	A2
KAY ST	LB	LB05		65	D5
KAYANN PL	SELM	ELM	1500	47	E4
KAYDEL DR	CO	WHI	2200	47	E5
KAY FIORNTNO DR	LA	SP		78	D5
KAYFORD AV	SELM	ELM	1300	47	C4
KAYREID DR	CO	WHI	12100	61	E6
KAYS AV	CO	RM	2100	46	D3
KAYS AV	MPK	MPK	800	46	D3
KAYS LN	AGH	AGO		100A	D5
KAYS PL N	CO	RM	2200	46	D2
KAYWOOD DR	CO	TOR	700	68	F6
KEANSBURG AV	WCOV	WCOV	600	98	F2
KEARNEY DR	CO	CAST		123	C2
KEARNEY ST	LA	LA33	1100	44	F3
KEARNY ST	CO	WOH		13	B4
KEARSARGE ST	LA	LA49	11700	41	B2
KEATING DR	LAM	LAM	14300	83	C2
KEATON ST	SCLR	CYN	19800	124	G7
KEATS LN	CO	NEW		126	H4
KEATS ST	ALH	ALH	3200	36	F4
KEATS ST	LA	LA32	5400	36	F4
KEATS ST	MB	MB	1100	62	C5
KEEGAN AV	CAR	CAR	16900	64	D5
KEEL CT	LB	LB03		80	F1
KEEL ST	LA	SP	100	79	B2
KEELER DR	LA	SF	16200	2	A6
KEELER ST	BUR	BUR	1600	17	C4
KEELSON TR	CO	TOP	1300	109	D2
KEENAN AV	CO	LA22	500	46	A6
KEENAN ST	MTB	MTB	600	46	A5
KEENE AV	CO	COM	14300	64	C2
KEENE AV	CO	LA59	12800	64	C1
KEENE AV N	COM	LA59	1900	64	C1
KEENE AV S	CAR	CAR	17500	64	D5
KEENE AV S	COM	COM	300	64	D3
KEESE DR	CO	WHI	14200	61	F6
KEESE DR	CO	WHI	14700	84	A6
KEESHEN DR	LA	LA66	3200	49	E1
KEEVER AV	LB	LB07	4100	70	E4
KEEVER PL	LB	LB07	1500	70	E3
KEIM ST	RM	RM	8200	46	F3
KEITH AV	WHOL	LA69	8900	33	C5
KEITH CT	PALM	PALM		183	H2
KEITH DR	CO	WHI	11100	55	C4
KEITH ST	LA	LA31	2000	45	B1
KELBURN AV	CO	RM	2200	46	E2
KELBURN AV	RM	RM	2300	46	E2
KELBY ST	CO	COV	17800	88	D4
KELBY ST	COV	COV	200	88	E4
KELFIELD DR	DBAR	WAL		97	C3
KELFORD ST	CO	WHI	14000	61	E6
KELI CT	LA	LA66	5100	50	A4
KELLA AV	CO	WHI	2200	47	E5
KELLAM AV	LA	LA26	1300	44	C1
KELLAM LN	PR	PR	8400	60	D1
KELLER CIR	CER	ART		82	E6
KELLER RD	CO	TOP	20900	109	D2
KELLER ST	LA	LA12	700	44	E2
KELLER ST	MPK	MPK		46	C3
KELLERTON DR	CO	LPUE	1600	85	E3
KELLETT AV	CLA	CLA	1300	96	D5
KELLEY AV	LOM	LOM		73	C3
KELLNER AV	CO	RM	1700	46	F3
KELLOGG AV	GLEN	GL02	600	25	A3
KELLOGG CT	CO	ALT	2300	19	F5
KELLOGG DR	CO	POM		93	E2
KELLOGG PARK DR	POM	POM	2100	94	B2
KELLOGG VLY RD	CO	PALM		157	J9
KELLOGG VLY RD	CO	PALM		158	A9
KELLS PL	PR	PR	9300	47	B6
KELLWIL WY	DUA	DUA	1000	29	D6
KELLY CT	PALM	PALM		183	H2
KELLY DR	SH	LB06	2100	75	E2
KELLY LN	POM	POM	2700	90	F4
KELLY ST	LA	LA66		50	A5
KELLY WY	WCOV	WCOV		92	B4
KELMORE ST	CUL	CUL	10700	50	D3
KELOWNA ST	LA	PAC	13300	8	F4
KELOWNA ST	LA	PAC	12800	9	A3
KELOWNA ST	LA	SF	11400	3	D6
KELP ST	MB	MB	100	62	A2
KELSEY RD	SAD	SAD		90	B4
KELSEY ST	LA	NHO	11500	23	D4
KELSLOAN ST	LA	VAN	16600	14	F3
KELSO RD	WAL	WAL		93	B5
KELSO ST E	ING	IN01	100	57	A2
KELSO ST W	ING	IN01	100	56	F2
KELTON AV	LA	LA24	400	41	D1
KELTON AV	LA	LA25	1800	41	E3
KELTON AV	LA	LA34	3000	42	A5
KELTON AV	LA	LA34	3600	50	A1
KELTON AV	LA	LA64	2200	41	F4
KELTON AV	LA	LA64	2800	42	A5
KELTONVIEW DR	PR	PR	6400	54	D6
KELVIN AV	LA	CAN	8500	6	D6
KELVIN AV	LA	CAN	6500	12	D5
KELVIN AV	LA	CHA	9200	6	D5
KELVIN AV	LA	WOH	5600	12	D6
KELVIN AV	LA	WOH	4800	13	D2
KELVIN PL	LA	WOH	5700	12	D6
KELWOOD ST	CO	LPUE	16501	92	B4
KEM WY	WAL	WAL		93	C4
KEM BAR LN	CO	LR		184	D6
KEMBLE AV	LB	LB08	3400	81	B5
KEMERTON PL	CO	LPUE		98	A5
KEMP AV	CAR	CAR	19000	69	E1
KEMP AV N	COM	COM	100	64	E3
KEMP AV S	COM	COM	100	64	E3
KEMP PL	COV	COV	700	89	A3
KEMP ST	BUR	BUR	800	24	A2
KEMPER AV	CLA	CLA		91	D1
KEMPER AV	CO	GL14	2400	11	E6
KEMPER CIR	LA	LA65	1900	35	E3
KEMPER CT	LA	LA65	3000	35	F3
KEMPER ST	LA	LA65	1400	35	E3
KEMPTON AV	MPK	MPK	1800	46	C3
KEMPTON PL	MPK	MPK	200	46	C4
KEMPTON RD	GLEN	GL02	200	25	C1
KEN AV N	LKD	LKD	4900	71	E2
KENBRIDGE DR	CAR	CAR	500	64	B5
KENDALL AL	PAS	PAS	1	27	A4
KENDALL AV	LA	LA32	1000	36	C3
KENDALL AV	LA	LA32	5500	36	F3
KENDALL AV	LA	LA42	300	36	C3
KENDALL AV	SOG	SOG	8900	59	D3
KENDALL DR	SGAB	SGAB	1000	37	D2
KENDALL ST	LAV	LAV		90	E3
KENDALL WY	COV	COV	100	88	F5
KENDRICK CIR	PALM	PALM		183	E2
KENDRICK DR	LAV	LAV		90	C2
KENESAW AV	COM	COM	2700	58	D6
KENFEL DR	SCLR	SAU		124	E6
KENFIELD AV	LA	LA49	900	32	B6
KENGARD AV	CO	WHI	7100	55	C5
KENGARY LN	CO	ALT	2200	20	D5
KENILWORTH AV	LA	LA39	2000	35	B3
KENILWORTH AV	PAS	PAS	1500	19	E6
KENILWORTH AV	SMAR	PAS	1200	27	E6
KENILWORTH AV	SMAR	PAS	1700	37	E1
KENILWORTH AV N	GLEN	GL02	900	25	B2
KENILWORTH AV N	GLEN	GL03	100	25	B4
KENILWORTH AV S	GLEN	GL04	200	25	B4
KENILWORTH PL	SMAR	PAS		27	D6
KENILWORTH WK	LA	LA39	3200	35	B3
KENISTON AV	CO	LA43	4800	51	B4
KENISTON AV	LA	LA05	700	43	B2
KENISTON AV	LA	LA19	900	43	B2
KENISTON AV	LA	LA43	5800	51	B5
KENITRA PT	PALM	PALM		183	J7
KENMERE AV	BUR	BUR	1900	17	B4
KENMORE AV E	BAP	BAP	13600	39	D5
KENMORE AV N	LA	LA04	100	34	F4
KENMORE AV N	LA	LA04	100	34	F6
KENMORE AV N	LA	LA27	1300	34	F4
KENMORE AV N	LA	LA29	700	34	F4
KENMORE AV S	LA	LA04	100	34	F6
KENMORE AV S	LA	LA04	100	43	F1
KENMORE AV S	LA	LA05	600	43	F3
KENMORE AV S	LA	LA06	900	43	F3
KENMORE AV S	LA	LA20	300	43	F1
KENMORE CIR	BAP	BAP	14300	39	E6
KENMORE DR	SGAB	SGAB	600	37	F5
KENMORE RD	PAS	PAS	1400	37	B1
KENMORE ST N	BAP	BAP	3700	39	D5
KENNARD ST	CO	LPUE	15600	85	D2
KENNEBEC AV	LB	LB03	1	75	E6
KENNEDY DR	SAD	SAD	200	89	D2
KENNERLY ST	TEC	TEC	9200	38	B4
KENNETH DR	LA	LA32	3100	36	C5
KENNETH PL	CO	CYN		125	E6
KENNETH RD E	GLEN	GL07	100	25	B1
KENNETH RD N	BUR	BUR	100	17	E4
KENNETH RD S	BUR	BUR	100	17	E4
KENNETH RD W	GLEN	GL01	1700	17	F6
KENNETH RD W	GLEN	GL01	1400	18	A6
KENNETH RD W	GLEN	GL02	200	25	B1
KENNETH WY	PAS	PAS	1500	19	E6
KENNEY LN	NWK	NWK		61	A5
KENNEY ST	NWK	NWK	10800	60	E5
KENNEY ST	NWK	NWK	11700	61	A5
KENNEYDALE AV	CO	RM	1200	46	E4
KENNINGTON DR	GLEN	GL06	2600	26	A2
KENNSINGTON PL	LAN	LAN		159	G4
KENNY AV	CO	LPUE	100	48	D5
KENNY DR	LA	SF	12200	1	F5
KENOAK DR	BAP	BAP		39	F4
KENOAK DR	POM	POM	400	94	E1
KENOAK DR	WCOV	WCOV	1800	88	A4
KENOAK DR E	COV	COV	600	88	F5
KENOAK DR W	COV	COV	400	88	D5
KENOAK PL	POM	POM	300	94	E1
KENOAK WY	POM	POM		90	E6
KENOBI CT	CER	ART		81	C2
KENOMA ST	CO	GLDR	1800	87	E6
KENOMA ST	GLDR	GLDR	2000	87	E6
KENOMA ST	SAD	SAD	2300	87	E6
KENROSE CIR	CO	CAL		100	A3
KENROY AV	SCLR	CYN	28700	125	C7
KENSINGTON AV	CER	ART	17600	82	E6
KENSINGTON CIR	CER	ART	17400	82	E5
KENSINGTON LN	ING	IN01		57	B2
KENSINGTON PL	PAS	PAS	200	26	F4
KENSINGTON RD	LA	LA66	4300	50	A3
KENSINGTON RD	SM	SM	600	49	B2
KENSINGTON RD	SMAR	PAS	1400	37	D1
KENSINGTON RD E	LA	LA26	500	35	D6
KENSINGTON RD W	LA	LA26	500	35	C6
KENSINGTON RD W	LA	LA26	900	35	C6
KENSINGTON WY	CUL	CUL	5600	50	D5
KENSINGTON WY	MTB	MTB	200	54	C1
KENSLEY DR	ING	IN01		57	B2
KENT	LA	SF42		2	C1
KENT AV	TOR	TOR	21200	67	F4
KENT DR	BUR	BUR	500	17	C3
KENT DR	CLA	CLA	800	91	A2
KENT DR	LAV	LAV		95A	D5
KENT LN	SCLR	CYN		124	G6
KENT PL	GLEN	GL05	1300	25	E5
KENT ST	CO	ALT	900	19	E5
KENT ST	LA	LA26	1700	35	B5
KENT ST	SAD	SAD		89	E3
KENTER AV N	LA	LA49	1300	30	F5
KENTER AV N	LA	LA49	700	32	A6
KENTER AV N	LA	LA49	100	41	A1
KENTER AV S	LA	LA49	100	41	A1
KENTER WY	LA	LA49	900	32	A6
KENTFIELD CT	WLVL	THO	31700	102	B4
KENTLAND AV	LA	CAN	6100	12	B2
KENTLAND AV	LA	CHA	9500	6	B4
KENTLAND AV	LA	WOH	5800	12	B6
KENTON DR	MPK	MPK	1100	46	E4
KENTON LN	CO	SAU		124	D4
KENTUCKY	WCOV	WCOV		92	E4
KENTUCKY AV	CO	WHI	11300	84	C5
KENTUCKY AV	WHI	WHI	10100	84	C3
KENTUCKY DR	LA	LA68	3900	23	F5
KENTUCKY PL	GLEN	GL14	3200	11	D6
KENTUCKY SPG RD	CO	PALM		190	B1
KENTWOOD AV	LA	LA45	7000	50	B5
KENTWOOD AV	LA	LA45	8000	56	C1
KENTWORTHY AV	LA	HAC	23500	73	E1
KENWATER AV	LA	CAN	6500	5	E6
KENWATER AV	LA	WOH	5900	5	E6
KENWATER PL	LA	CAN		5	E5
KENWAY AV	CO	LA08	3900	51	B2
KENWOOD AV	CO	CAST		123	C1
KENWOOD AV	CO	TOR	20400	68	F3
KENWOOD AV	LA	LA07	2600	43	E5
KENWOOD AV	LA	LA37	4200	51	E2
KENWOOD DR	POM	POM	1400	90	C6
KENWOOD ST	BUR	BUR	1500	17	A6
KENWOOD ST	BUR	BUR	100	24	A1
KENWOOD ST	ING	IN01	900	56	E2
KENWOOD ST	SCLR	SAU		124	G7
KENWOOD ST N	GLEN	GL06	100	25	D4
KENWOOD ST S	GLEN	GL05	100	25	D4
KENWORTHY DR	PAS	PAS	100	26	D4
KENYA PL	LA	NOR	11000	7	A1
KENYA ST	LA	NOR	18600	7	B1
KENYON AV	LA	LA45	7800	50	B6
KENYON AV	LA	LA45	7900	56	B1
KENYON AV	LA	LA66	4100	49	F3
KENYON PL	CLA	CLA	1600	91	C2
KEOKUK AV	LA	CAN	8500	6	E6
KEOKUK AV	LA	CAN	8300	12	E1
KEOKUK AV	LA	CHA	9600	6	E4
KEOKUK AV	LA	WOH	5700	12	E6
KEOKUK AV	LA	WOH	5600	13	E1
KEPLER RD	CO	PALM	35500	184	C5
KEPPEL AV	CO	PALM		183	D5
KERCKHOFF AV	LA	SP	2600	78	F6
KERMAN AV	ELM	ELM	4200	38	E5
KERN AV N	CO	LA22	100	45	E5
KERN AV S	CO	LA22	100	45	E5
KERN AV S	CO	LA22	1000	53	E1
KERNS AV	SGAB	SGAB	700	37	E1
KERNS AV	SMAR	PAS	1900	37	E1
KERNVILLE AV	MTB	MTB	1600	46	F4
KERPSIE RD	CO	ACT		182	C7
KERR DR	GAR	GAR	1700	63	E3
KERR ST	LA	LA39	2700	35	D2
KERRICK ST W	LAN	LAN	1400	159	J4
KERRMOOR DR	WLVL	THO		102	D2
KERRWOOD PL	ELM	ELM	11600	38	F5
KERRWOOD ST	CO	ELM	11800	39	A5
KERRWOOD ST	ELM	ELM	11400	38	F5
KERRWOOD ST	ELM	ELM	11600	39	A6
KERRY CT	WCOV	WCOV		92	D6
KERRY LN	CO	TOP	1700	109	C6
KERRYHILL CT	AGH	AGO		102	F2
KERRY ROBIN DR	SCLR	NEW		127	A5
KERSTING CT	SMAD	SMAD	1	28	C2
KERVIN AV	PAR	PAR	15400	66	A3
KERWIN PL	LA	LA41	2500	25	F5
KERWOOD AV	LA	LA25	2000	42	A3
KERWOOD AV	LA	LA64	2200	42	A3
KESLEY ST	SCLR	CYN		124	G6
KESSLER AV	LA	CAN	6400	12	F5
KESSLER AV	LA	CHA	9500	6	F4
KESSLER RD	LKD	LKD	2400	70	F4
KESSOCK AV	CO	WHI	11800	61	F6
KESTER AV	LA	SF	9500	8	C2
KESTER AV	LA	VAN	8700	8	D5
KESTER AV	LA	VAN	5600	15	C5
KESTER AV	LA	VAN	4200	22	D3
KESTRAL DR	SCLR	VAL		127	A3
KESWICK AV	LA	LA64	10300	42	A3
KESWICK PL	GLDR	GLDR		86	E4
KESWICK RD	LCF	LCF	3800	19	B5
KESWICK ST	LA	CAN	23300	5	F2
KESWICK ST	LA	CAN	20500	12	A2
KESWICK ST	LA	NHO	11400	16	C2
KESWICK ST	LA	NOR	17300	14	E2

STREET	CITY	P.O. ZONE	BLOCK	PAGE	GRID
KESWICK ST	LA	RES	17700	14	B2
KESWICK ST	LA	SV	10400	16	E2
KESWICK ST	LA	SV	10000	17	A2
KESWICK ST	LA	VAN	16900	14	F2
KESWICK ST	LA	VAN	14500	15	D2
KETCH CT	LA	VEN		49	C5
KETCH ST	LA	VEN		49	C6
KETTERING ST E	CO	LAN	4000	160	J3
KETTERING ST E	CO	LAN	5000	161	A3
KETTERING ST E	LAN	LAN	300	160	C4
KETTERING ST W	LAN	LAN	7000	158	G4
KETTERING ST W	LAN	LAN	4000	159	D4
KETTERING ST W	LAN	LAN	1100	159	J4
KETTERING ST W	LAN	LAN	100	160	A4
KETTLE ST	CO	AGO		106	E1
KETTLER AV	LKD	LKD	5300	71	E2
KEVIN CT	LA	NOR		7	C3
KEVIN PL	SCLR	SAU		124	D5
KEVIN ST	LB	LB08	8200	81	B5
KEW DR	LA	LA46	2000	33	E2
KEW ST	ING	IN02	600	50	E6
KEWANEE ST	LA	LA32	4300	36	C5
KEWEN AV	LA	PAC	10600	8	F2
KEWEN AV	LA	PAC	9600	9	C5
KEWEN AV	LA	SF	11100	8	E1
KEWEN AV	LA	SV	8500	9	C6
KEWEN AV	LA	SV	8500	16	D1
KEWEN DR	PAS	PAS	100	27	B6
KEWEN PL	SMAR	PAS	1	27	C6
KEWEN ST	SF	SF	600	2	E6
KEWEN ST	SF	SF	600	8	E1
KEY CT	SCLR	SAU		124	G3
KEY CT	LAN	LAN	2500	159	G5
KEY ST	LA	LA35	8800	42	D3
KEY,FRNCS SCOTT	PALM	PALM		183	D2
KEYNOTE ST	LB	LB08	5100	71	B5
KEYSTONE AV	CUL	CUL	4100	50	C1
KEYSTONE AV	LA	LA34	3300	42	B6
KEYSTONE AV	POM	POM	1600	95	B2
KEYSTONE ST	IND	LPUE		98	D3
KEYSTONE ST	PAS	PAS	100	27	D4
KEYSTONE ST N	BUR	BUR	700	17	B2
KEYSTONE ST N	BUR	BUR	100	24	C1
KEYSTONE ST S	BUR	BUR	100	24	C1
KEY VISTA DR	SMAD	SMAD	400	28	B1
KEY WEST AV	LA	NOR	10300	7	A3
KEY WEST ST	CO	SGAB	8900	38	A4
KEY WEST ST	TEC	TEC	9200	38	B4
KIA ORA PL	CO	ARC	9800	38	C1
KIBBEE AV	CO	WHI	10800	84	C5
KIBBEE AV	LAM	LAM	11800	84	C5
KIBBEE AV	WHI	WHI	10400	84	B3
KICKAPOO TR	CO	CHA		6	C1
KICKING HRSE DR	DBAR	POM		97	E5
KIDD DR	DBAR	POM		97A	A1
KIDDER AV	CO	COV	5000	89	B3
KIDDER AV	COV	COV	600	89	B4
KIDDIE LN N	CAR	CAR	700	69	C6
KIDDIE LN S	CAR	CAR	700	74	C1
KIEL ST	LA	LA49	11300	41	C1
KIKI PL	LA	PP		40	C2
KILARNEY WY	LCF	LCF		19	D6
KILBOURN ST	LA	LA65	1600	35	E3
KILDARE ST	LAN	LAN		160	D4
KILDARE ST E	LAN	LAN	300	160	C4
KILDARE ST W	CO	LAN	9000	158	F4
KILDARE ST W	LAN	LAN	1200	159	J4
KILDARE ST W	LAN	LAN	100	160	B4
KILDONAN DR	GLEN	GL07		25	D1
KILFINAN PL	LA	NOR		1	B4
KILFINAN ST	LA	NOR		1	B4
KILGARRY AV	PR	PR	5500	54	F5
KILGARRY AV	PR	PR	5300	55	A4
KILHAM AV	LAN	LAN	42800	159	H8
KILHAM AV	LAN	LAN		159	J7
KILKEA DR N	LA	LA46	700	33	E6
KILKEA DR N	LA	LA48	100	33	E6
KILKEA DR S	LA	LA48	100	33	E6
KILLARNEY AV	LA	LA65	1300	35	F3
KILLDEE ST	LB	LB08	5100	71	B6
KILLEN CT	COM	COM	2300	65	B1
KILLEN PL	COM	COM	1600	65	B1
KILLIAN AV	CO	LPUE	18900	98	F4
KILLIAN ST	ELM	ELM	11300	38	F5
KILLIAN ST	ELM	ELM	11700	39	A5
KILLIMORE AV	LA	NOR		1	B6
KILLIMORE CT	LA	NOR		1	B5
KILLION ST	LA	ENC	16800	21	E1
KILLION ST	LA	NHO	11300	23	D1
KILLION ST	LA	TAR	18100	21	D1
KILLION ST	LA	VAN	13300	22	F1
KILLION ST	LA	VAN	12900	23	A1
KILLION ST	LA	WOH	23700	100	E1
KILLOCH PL	LA	NOR		1	B4
KILLOCH WY	LA	NOR		1	B5
KILMARY LN	GLEN	GL07		18	D6

STREET	CITY	P.O. ZONE	BLOCK	PAGE	GRID
KILNALECK LN	GLDR	GLDR	700	87	C3
KILPACK DR	CO	CAL		100	E5
KILRENNY AV	LA	LA64	10200	42	B4
KILROY AIRPT WY	LB	LB15		76	A1
KILTY AV	LA	CAN	7100	5	F3
KILTY PL	LA	CAN	23400	5	F3
KIM CT	CO	LP48		98	F4
KIM CT	LAN	LAN		159	E5
KIM LN	LA	ENC	3800	21	F4
KIMA CT	LKD	LKD		66	A6
KIMBALL AV	POM	POM	2300	90	F4
KIMBALL ST	LA	LA32	4900	36	D6
KIMBARK AV	CO	WHI	10300	55	D1
KIMBERLEY CY RD	CO	AGO		106	C1
KIMBERLEY CY RD	CO	MAL		106	B3
KIMBERLY AV	LA	LA02	10300	58	E4
KIMBERLY AV	LAV	LAV		90	E2
KIMBERLY AV	SAD	SAD	400	89	D3
KIMBERLY CIR	ELM	ELM		39	B4
KIMBERLY CT	CER	ART		81	A2
KIMBERLY DR	AGH	AGO		102	E1
KIMBERLY DR	WCOV	WCOV		92	D6
KIMBERLY LN	LA	LA49	1850	30	F6
KIMBERLY LN	PALM	PALM		183	C1
KIMBROUGH ST	SCLR	CYN	18500	124	H5
KIMBROUGH ST	SCLR	CYN		125	A8
KIMDALE LN	LA	LA46	7500	23	F6
KIMDALE RD	CO	SGAB	6500	37	F1
KIMLIN DR	GLEN	GL06	600	25	F3
KIMMORE TER	SCLR	VAL		127	C2
KIMRIDGE RD	LA	BH	2300	33	C1
KINARD AV	CAR	CAR	21200	69	A5
KINARD AV	CAR	CAR	23500	74	A1
KINBRACE ST	LA	NOR		1	B4
KINBRAE AV	CO	LPUE	800	48	C6
KINBRAE AV	CO	LPUE	1000	85	C1
KINBROOK ST	LA	SF	13700	2	E1
KINCAID ST	ING	IN02	800	50	E6
KINCARDINE AV	LA	LA34	9000	42	C5
KINCARDINE AV	LA	LA64	10200	42	B4
KINCHELOE DR	LA	LA41	5300	26	B4
KINCLAIR DR	CO	PAS	1900	20	F5
KING AV	BELL	BELL	6200	53	D6
KING AV	LA	WIL	200	74	B4
KING AV	MAY	MAY	5200	53	D5
KING CT	ELM	ELM	10700	38	D5
KING ST	LAV	LAV		90	E3
KING ST	MON	MON	800	28	F4
KING ST	MON	MON	500	29	A4
KING ST	SGAB	SGAB		37	E4
KING WY	CLA	CLA		96	B6
KING ARTHUR CT	RPV	PVP	28300	72	D5
KINGBEE ST	DOW	DOW	7900	59	F5
KINGBEE ST	DOW	DOW	7900	60	A5
KINGFISHER RD	CO	CAL		13	A4
KINGHAM CT	AGH	AGO		102	F2
KINGHORN ST	SFS	SFS	11400	60	F4
KINGHURST RD	CO	SGAB	8200	27	F6
KINGHURST RD	SMAR	PAS	2800	27	F6
KINGLAKE DR	DBAR	WAL		97	C3
KINGLET DR	LA	LA69	9200	33	C3
KINGMAN AV	LA	SM	600	40	E4
KINGMAN RD	SM	SM		40	E4
KING M L JR AV	LB	LB02	600	75	D3
KING M L JR AV	LB	LB06	1800	75	D4
KING M L JR AV	LB	LB13	700	75	D4
KING M L JR BL	LA	LA08	3700	51	A1
KING M L JR BL	LA	LA11	100	52	B1
KING M L JR BL	LA	LA16	4500	43	A6
KING M L JR BL	LA	LA37	800	51	E1
KING M L JR BL	LA	LA37	100	52	B1
KING M L JR BL	LA	LA62	1400	51	E1
KINGRIDGE WY	GLEN	GL06		19	B5
KINGS CT	LA	LA77		22	D5
KINGS PL	LA	LA32		36	D6
KINGS PL	WLVL	THO		102	B5
KINGS RD	CO	LA56	5800	50	E4
KINGS RD	PALM	PALM		171	J6
KINGS RD N	LA	LA48	100	33	E6
KINGS RD N	LA	LA69	700	33	E5
KINGS RD N	WHOL	LA48	500	33	E5
KINGS RD N	WHOL	LA69	800	33	E5
KINGS RD S	LA	LA48	100	33	E6
KINGS ROW	ELM	ELM		38	F4
KINGS WY	LA	LA69	1700	33	E3
KINGSBORO WY	LA	WOH		13	D3
KINGSBURY ST	LA	CHA	20600	6	D2
KINGSBURY ST	LA	CHA	18100	7	A2
KINGSBURY ST	LA	NOR	19400	7	A2
KINGSBURY ST	LA	SF	16400	7	F2
KINGSBURY ST	LA	SF	14500	8	C2
KINGSCREST DR	SCLR	SAU	20800	124	F5
KINGS CREST DR	WCOV	WCOV		92	D3
KINGSDALE AV	LAW	LAW	14300	62	F3
KINGSDALE AV	RB	RB	1800	62	F6
KINGSDALE AV	TOR	RB	18200	63	A6

STREET	CITY	P.O. ZONE	BLOCK	PAGE	GRID
KINGSDALE AV	TOR	RB	18200	67	F1
KINGSDALE AV	TOR	RB	18200	68	A1
KINGSDOWN CT	RPV	SP	1700	78	D1
KINGSFORD ST	MPK	MPK	300	46	B2
KINGSGLEN CIR	CO	WAL	19700	97	B3
KINGS HARBOR DR	RPV	PVP	6500	72	C5
KINGSHILL PL	CAR	CAR		64	C5
KINGSIDE DR	CO	COV	15700	88	A4
KINGSIDE DR	COV	COV	1000	88	C4
KINGSLAND ST	LA	LA34	10700	42	A6
KINGSLAND ST	LA	LA66	11300	41	F6
KINGSLEY AV E	POM	POM	100	94	E1
KINGSLEY AV E	POM	POM	700	95	A2
KINGSLEY AV W	POM	POM	100	94	E1
KINGSLEY DR	ARC	ARC	800	28	C5
KINGSLEY DR	GAR	GAR	14100	63	E2
KINGSLEY DR N	LA	LA04	100	34	E6
KINGSLEY DR N	LA	LA27	1300	34	E3
KINGSLEY DR N	LA	LA29	700	34	E5
KINGSLEY DR S	LA	LA04	100	34	E6
KINGSLEY DR S	LA	LA05	600	43	E3
KINGSLEY DR S	LA	LA06	900	43	E4
KINGSLEY DR S	LA	LA20	300	43	E3
KINGSLY CT	PALM	PALM		173	A9
KINGSMILL AV	CO	LPUE	1200	97	A3
KINGSPARK CT	WLVL	THO	32000	102	A4
KINGSPINE RD	RHE	PVP	4800	72	F3
KINGSPOINT DR	WAL	WAL	1600	93	B3
KINGSPORT DR	CO	MAL	18000	115	E4
KINGSRIDGE DR	RPV	SP		78	D3
KINGS ROW AV	CER	ART	18700	71	E1
KINGSRUN PL	CO	LPUE	17700	98	C5
KINGSTON AV	LA	LA33	1000	45	A2
KINGSTON CT	CO	CAL		100	B2
KINGSVIEW AV	CAR	CAR	16900	64	C5
KINGS VIEW DR	CO	LPUE		98	A4
KINGSWAY DR	BUR	BUR	800	17	C3
KINGSWELL AV	LA	LA27	4500	34	F3
KINGSWELL AV	LA	LA27	4400	35	A3
KINGSWOOD LN	CAR	CAR		69	D6
KINGSWOOD LN	LA	VAN	15300	22	C4
KINGSWOOD RD	LA	VAN	3800	22	C4
KINGTREE AV	LAN	LAN	44100	159	J5
KINMOUNT ST	LB	LB08	8200	81	C6
KINNARD AV	LA	LA24	10400	41	F2
KINNELOA AV	PAS	PAS		27	F4
KINNELOA CYN RD	CO	PAS	1700	20	F6
KINNELOA MSA RD	CO	PAS	1600	20	F6
KINNELOA RCH RD	CO	PAS		20	F5
KINNEY CIR	LA	LA65	3600	35	E2
KINNEY PL	LA	LA65	3600	35	E2
KINNEY ST	LA	LA65	3500	35	E2
KINNEY ST	SM	SM	100	49	B3
KINNEY PLAZA	LA	VEN		49	C4
KINNOW PL	CO	LPUE		98	E6
KINROSS AV	LA	LA24	10800	41	E2
KINSELLA AV	CO	COV	5000	89	B3
KINSELLA AV	COV	COV	100	89	B4
KINSIE ST	CMRC	LA40	4900	53	E2
KINSTON AV	CUL	CUL	5100	50	C2
KINZIE ST	LA	CHA	19700	6	F4
KINZIE ST	LA	NOR	17100	7	E4
KINZIE ST	LA	SF	16800	7	F4
KINZIE ST	LA	SF	14800	8	D4
KIOWA	CO	AGO		106	D2
KIOWA AV	LA	LA49	11600	41	C3
KIOWA WY	SAD	SAD		90	B1
KIOWA CREST DR	DBAR	POM		97	E3
KIP DR	LA	BH	9900	32	F3
KIPLING AV	LA	LA41	1000	26	C4
KIPPEN ST	LA	HAC	23700	73	E1
KIPTON PL	LA	TAR	18600	21	C3
KIPTREE DR	CO	PALM		157	G9
KIPWAY DR	DOW	DOW	12700	66	B1
KIRBY ST	LA	LA42	300	36	D1
KIRKBY RD	GLEN	GL08	1700	25	F1
KIRKCALDY CIR	LA	CAN	24000	5	E4
KIRKCOLM CT	LA	NOR		1	B5
KIRKCOLM LN	LA	NOR		1	B4
KIRKFIELD AV	LAM	LAM	13400	83	D3
KIRKHAM DR	GLEN	GL06		19	B5
KIRKLAND AV	LAN	LAN	44300	160	C5
KIRKLAND DR	LA	BH	2800	23	A6
KIRKSIDE RD	LA	LA35	9300	42	C3
KIRKTON PL	GLEN	GL07		25	D1
KIRK VIEW DR	CO	LPUE		98	B4
KIRKWALL RD	AZU	AZU	300	88	D2
KIRKWALL RD	CO	AZU	16500	88	B2
KIRKWALL RD	SAD	SAD	1100	89	D2
KIRKWALL RD E	GLDR	GLDR		89	B2
KIRKWALL RD W	GLDR	GLDR	19500	89	A2
KIRKWOOD AV	CLA	CLA	100	91	B4
KIRKWOOD AV	PAS	PAS	900	26	F2
KIRKWOOD AV	POM	POM	600	90	F4
KIRKWOOD DR	LA	LA46	8100	33	E3
KIRKWOOD LN	MON	MON	400	29	B2

STREET	CITY	P.O. ZONE	BLOCK	PAGE	GRID
KIRST ST	LCF	LCF	100	19	D3
KIRSTENGARY WY	SCLR	VAL		127	A1
KIRSTEN LEE DR	WLVL	THO		102A	E5
KIRTLAND AV	LKD	LKD	5300	71	E2
KIRUNA PL	LA	WOH	23600	100	E1
KISKA AV	CO	LPUE	2300	85	E4
KISMET AV	LA	SF	13300	2	F2
KISMET AV	LA	SF	12700	3	B3
KISMET AV	LA	SF	11300	9	D1
KIT CARSON RD	HH	CAL	24900	100	C1
KITFOX PL	SCLR	VAL		127	A2
KITTERING RD	SAD	SAD		89	D4
KITTRIDGE ST	BUR	BUR	2300	17	B5
KITTRIDGE ST	CO	CAN	24500	5	D4
KITTRIDGE ST	LA	CAN	23500	5	F4
KITTRIDGE ST	LA	CAN	19700	12	F4
KITTRIDGE ST	LA	NHO	10700	16	E4
KITTRIDGE ST	LA	RES	17700	14	B4
KITTRIDGE ST	LA	VAN	17200	14	E4
KITTRIDGE ST	LA	VAN	13300	15	E4
KITTRIDGE ST	LA	VAN	13200	16	A4
KITTRIDGE ST	SF	SF	1	2	E6
KITTY RD	CO	ELM	9700	47	C5
KITTYHAWK AV	LA	LA45	6900	50	E6
KITTYHAWK AV	LA	LA45	7600	56	D1
KITTY HAWK LN	PALM	PALM		172	E6
KITTYHAWK WK	LA	LA45	8500	56	D1
KITTYS LN	LA	TU		11	B5
KIVA CT	AGH	AGO		102	F3
KIVIK ST	LA	WOH	23500	100	E2
KLAMATH CT	SAD	SAD		95A	B5
KLAMATH PL	LA	LA32	4700	36	D6
KLAMATH ST	CO	LPUE	16000	92	B4
KLAMATH ST	LA	LA32	4600	36	D6
KLAMATH ST	LPUE	LPUE	15400	48	F4
KLEE ST	LA	NOR	17400	7	E6
KLEE ST	LA	SF	16800	7	F6
KLEIN PL	POM	POM	2200	94	F6
KLEINART LN	LA	BH	2400	32	E1
KLEVINS CT	SCLR	CYN		125	B7
KLINEDALE AV	DOW	DOW	9200	60	E3
KLINEDALE AV	PR	PR	8600	60	E2
KLING ST	BUR	BUR	4200	24	A3
KLING ST	LA	NHO	10300	23	C5
KLING ST	LA	NHO	10200	24	A3
KLING ST	LA	VAN	14400	22	D3
KLING ST	LA	VAN	12900	23	A3
KLINGERMAN ST	ELM	ELM	10900	47	E3
KLINGERMAN ST	RM	RM	8200	46	F2
KLINGERMAN ST	RM	RM	8600	47	A2
KLINGERMAN ST	SELM	ELM	9800	47	D2
KLINGERMAN ST	SELM	ELM	9200	47	D2
KLONDIKE AV	LKD	LKD	5100	70	F2
KLONDYKE AV	DOW	DOW	13400	66	A1
KLUM PL	CO	LPUE		98	E6
KLUMP AV	LA	NHO	5700	16	E5
KLUMP AV	LA	NHO	4100	23	E4
KLUMP AV	LA	SV	7700	16	E2
KNAPP ST	LA	CHA	20900	6	D5
KNAPP ST	LA	NOR	17200	7	E5
KNAPP ST	LA	SF	16500	7	F5
KNAPP ST	LA	SF	15900	8	A5
KNAPP WY	CO	CHA	9200	4	B5
KNEWOOD CT	LAN	LAN		159	G7
KNIGHT AV	LB	LB05	6200	65	F6
KNIGHT DR	AGH	AGO		100A	B5
KNIGHT WY	LCF	LCF	300	19	C3
KNIGHT WY	PALM	PALM		173	A9
KNIGHTSBRDGE AV	CUL	CUL		50	C4
KNIGHTSGATE RD	WLVL	THO	4500	102	B4
KNOB DR	LA	LA65	3000	35	E3
KNOB HILL AV	RB	RB	100	67	D4
KNOB HILL DR	LA	VAN	3500	22	D5
KNOB HILL RD	CO	PEAR		192	D1
KNOCHAVEN DR	CO	CYN	15700	128	E2
KNODE ST	TOR	TOR	22800	68	D6
KNOLL CT	DBAR	POM		97A	B3
KNOLL DR	DBAR	POM		97	F3
KNOLL DR	LA	LA68	3200	24	B5
KNOLL DR	LA	SP	200	79	A2
KNOLL DR	MPK	MPK	1100	46	B2
KNOLL DR	PALM	PALM		171	C3
KNOLLCREST AV	CO	LA43	3400	51	C3
KNOLLCREST DR	COV	COV		89	A5
KNOLL RIDGE DR	POM	POM		94	C6
KNOLL STONE CIR	CER	ART		82	B4
KNOLLVIEW CT	PALM	PALM		172	B9
KNOLLVIEW DR	POM	POM		94	C5
KNOLL VIEW DR	RPV	PVP	29600	78	C2
KNOLLWOOD AV	LAV	LAV	3100	90	D3
KNOLLWOOD DR	LA	SF	11900	1	F5
KNOLLWOOD DR	LA	SF	11900	2	A5
KNOLLWOOD DR	PAS	PAS	1500	26	C1
KNOLLWOOD LN	SAD	SAD	700	90	A4
KNOLLWOOD TER	PAS	PAS	1500	26	C1
KNOPF ST	CO	COM	2000	64	E1

STREET	CITY	P.O. ZONE	BLOCK	PAGE	GRID
KNOTT AV	LAM	LAM	15900	83	A4
KNOW RD	LHH	LAH		98A	B1
KNOWLES AV	CO	LA63	1500	45	D2
KNOWLTON PL	LA	LA45	6900	50	E6
KNOWLTON ST	LA	LA45	5200	50	E5
KNOX AV	LA	LA39	2600	35	D3
KNOX PL	CLA	CLA	800	91	A1
KNOX ST	CAR	GAR	100	69	A2
KNOX ST	CO	GAR	700	68	F2
KNOX ST	CO	GAR	600	69	A2
KNOX ST	SF	SF	1100	2	F4
KNOX ST	SF	SF	1100	3	A4
KNOXVILLE AV	LB	LB08	3000	71	E6
KNOXVILLE AV	LB	LB15	1200	76	E4
KNOXVILLE AV	LKD	LKD	4100	71	E4
KNUDSEN PKWY	CO	VAL	28000	123	F7
KOBE RD	CO	SAU		181	C8
KOBE FIRE RD	CO	NOR		1	B2
KODAK DR	LA	LA26	800	35	A5
KOHLER ST	LA	LA21	700	44	D4
KOLEETA DR	CO	HAC		73	F1
KOLLE AV	SPAS	SPAS	1200	36	D2
KOMAR DR	LA	TAR	19700	13	F3
KOMORI CIR	GAR	GAR	17000	63	F5
KONA CT	PALM	PALM		183	J1
KONA DR	COM	COM		64	D5
KONA LN	LB	LB05	100	65	C5
KONTIKI WY	LA	PP		40	C2
KONYA DR	TOR	TOR	5000	67	F2
KOOLISH ST	POM	POM	2200	94	F6
KOONTZ AV	SFS	SFS	10800	61	B4
KOONTZ RD	CO	SAU	35300	181	C6
KOONTZ WY	CO	TOP	21700	13	C6
KOONTZ WY	CO	TOP		109	C1
KOOPMAN AV	DOW	DOW	11400	60	B4
KOOTENIA DR	CO	PALM		157	E8
KOPANY AV	LA	SF	13900	2	F1
KORNBLUM AV	CO	LAW	15100	63	B3
KORNBLUM AV	HAW	HAW	11500	57	B5
KORNBLUM AV	HAW	HAW	12800	63	B2
KORNBLUM AV	TOR	TOR	16700	63	B5
KORNBLUM AV	TOR	TOR	800	68	B3
KORNBLUM AV	TOR	TOR	18600	68	B1
KOSTER AV	LA	VAN	3600	22	F4
KOSTURAS PL	LA	CAN	6600	12	E4
KOUDEKERK ST	ART	ART	12000	82	B5
KOURY DR	CO	LPUE		85	C4
KRAFT AV	LA	NHO	6200	16	D5
KRAFT AV	LA	NHO	4000	23	D4
KRAKE AL	PAS	PAS	500	27	B3
KRAMER DR	CAR	CAR	1100	69	D2
KRAMERWOOD PL	LA	LA34	8900	42	D5
KRATT LN E	CO	WHI	9800	47	D6
KREGMONT DR	GLDR	GLDR	900	87	C3
KRENZ AV	CO	ALT	3000	19	F4
KRESS AV	BG	BELL	6500	54	A6
KRESS AV	BG	BELL	7500	60	A1
KRESS ST	LA	LA46	2100	33	E2
KRIM DR	LA	LA64	2800	42	C4
KRISTIN AV	TOR	TOR	16500	63	D5
KRISTIN DR	DOW	DOW		54	C1
KRISTIN LN	SCLR	SAU		124	D5
KRISTOPHER PL	LA	NOR		1	B4
KRUEGER ST	CUL	CUL	8800	42	D6
KRUSE AV	MON	MON	200	29	B6
KRUSE RD	PR	PR	9300	47	B6
KUEN PL	LA	VAN		23	A1
KUHL DR	CMRC	LA40	7100	54	C6
KUHN DR	MB	MB	100	62	C5
KUMQUAT LN	RPV	PVP	1	77	E2
KURL WY	LA	RES	18600	14	B4
KURT AV	CMRC	LA40	2500	54	A3
KURT ST	LA	SF	10400	3	F6
KURT ST	LA	SF	10400	9	F1
KURT ST	LA	SF	10400	10	A1
KURTZ AV	CO	LA63	1400	45	C2
KWIS AV	CO	LPUE	1100	85	D2
KYLE CT	LA	CAN		5	F3
KYLE DR	CER	ART	13700	82	E4
KYLE PL	CER	ART	13500	82	D4
KYLE ST	LA	SUN	7800	10	E2
KYLE ST	LA	TU	7300	10	F2
L					
L ST E	LA	WIL	100	74	D3
L ST W	LA	WIL	100	73	F4
LA ALAMEDA AL	LA	SP		78	E2
LA ALAMEDA AV	LA	SP	100	78	E3
LA ALAMEDA AV	LA	SP	100	78	E3
LA ALAMEDA AV	LA	SP	900	78	E3
LA ALBA DR	WHI	WHI	10400	84	B2
LA ALTURA RD	BH	BH	1100	33	B4
LA AMISTAD PL	LA	TAR	18800	21	B3
LA AMISTAD WY	LA	TAR	4300	21	B3

1990 LOS ANGELES COUNTY STREET INDEX

1990 LOS ANGELES COUNTY STREET INDEX

STREET	CITY	P.O. ZONE	BLOCK	PAGE	GRID
LANAI ST	WCOV	WCOV		92	C4
LANARK ST	LA	CAN	19700	12	E1
LANARK ST	LA	LA41	1000	26	C5
LANARK ST	LA	NOR	17500	14	D1
LANARK ST	LA	RES	17700	14	D1
LANARK ST	LA	SV	10300	16	F2
LANARK ST	LA	SV	10000	17	A1
LANARK ST	LA	VAN	17000	14	E1
LANARK ST	LA	VAN	13600	15	E1
LANCASHIRE PL	PAS	PAS	1400	26	D1
LANCASTER AV	LA	LA33	2400	45	B2
LANCASTER BL E	CO	LAN	4000	160	G4
LANCASTER BL E	CO	LAN	4900	161	A4
LANCASTER BL E	LAN	LAN	100	160	B4
LANCASTER BL W	LAN	LAN	7200	158	H4
LANCASTER BL W	LAN	LAN	1100	159	H4
LANCASTER BL W	LAN	LAN	4000	159	D4
LANCASTER BL W	LAN	LAN	100	160	A4
LANCASTER CT	CLA	CLA		91	D1
LANCASTER DR	CLA	CLA		91	D1
LANCASTER RD	CO	LAN	12000	158	A3
LANCASTER WY	LAN	LAN	1000	159	J4
LANCE CT	LPUE	LPUE	300	48	F6
LANCE PL	LA	CAN		5	E3
LANCEBROOK DR	SCLR	CYN	27200	124	G8
LANCELOT AV	NWK	NWK	13300	82	C1
LANCELOT LN	LA	LA77		32	C1
LANCER AV	POM	POM	2800	93	F3
LANCER CT	LA	BH		32	E2
LANCEWOOD AV	CO	LPUE	1200	85	E2
LANDA LN	LA	LA39	2500	35	D4
LANDA ST	LA	LA31	1400	35	D4
LANDA ST	LA	LA39	3700	35	B4
LANDALE ST	LA	NHO	10600	23	E3
LANDALE ST	LA	VAN	13100	23	B3
LANDALUCE LN	WAL	WAL		93	B4
LANDAU LN	CO	LPUE		98	A3
LANDAU PL	CO	LAN		159	A9
LANDER DR	LA	WOH	20400	13	E3
LANDEROS AV	LAV	LAV		90	D1
LANDFAIR AV	LA	LA24	400	41	D1
LANDFAIR RD	PAS	PAS	3300	28	A2
LANDGARD RD	CO	CYN		125	J7
LANDINO DR	WLVL	THO		102	D2
LANDIS AV	BAP	BAP	4200	39	E4
LANDIS ST	BUR	BUR	1600	17	C4
LANDIS VIEW LN	CO	RM	8600	47	A4
LANDMARK CT	PALM	PALM		171	C5
LANDMARK DR	CO	WHI	15800	84	C6
LANDMARK ST	CUL	CUL	3900	42	D5
LANDMARK ST	PALM	PALM		171	C5
LANDON AV	CO	PALM	38400	172	H8
LANDON AV	PALM	PALM		183	H1
LANDOR LN	PAS	PAS	500	27	D5
LANDSEER ST	TEC	TEC		38	D3
LANDSFORD ST	CO	LAN		161	B4
LANDSFORD ST	LAN	LAN		160	E3
LANDSFORD ST E	LAN	LAN	300	160	C4
LANE CT	CLA	CLA	1800	90	F1
LANE CT	CO	VAL		124	B7
LANESBORO DR	WCOV	WCOV	3000	97	A2
LANESBORO PL	CO	VAL		124	A7
LANETT AV	CO	WHI	9400	61	E3
LANETT AV	SFS	SFS	10100	61	D3
LANEWOOD AV	ALH	ALH	1	36	F4
LANEWOOD AV	LA	LA28	7000	34	B3
LANFAIR AV E	CO	LAN	15100	174	G1
LANFRANCO ST	CO	LA63	3600	45	C5
LANFRANCO ST	LA	LA33	1700	44	F4
LANFRANCO ST	LA	LA33	2500	45	B5
LANFRANCO ST	LA	LA63	3000	45	B5
LANG AV	CO	COV	3900	88	A5
LANG AV	CO	LPUE	900	48	D3
LANG AV	LPUE	LPUE	300	48	D4
LANG AV N	WCOV	WCOV	100	88	A6
LANG AV S	WCOV	WCOV	700	48	F1
LANG AV S	WCOV	WCOV	700	92	A1
LANGDALE AV	LA	LA41	2400	25	F5
LANGDALE AV	LA	LA41	2300	26	A6
LANGDON AV	LA	SF	10500	8	C6
LANGDON AV	LA	SF	8300	15	C1
LANGDON AV	LA	VAN	6300	15	C5
LANGDON AV	LA	VAN	4600	22	C3
LANGFIELD CT	AGH	AGO		102	E3
LANGFORD AL	PAS	PAS	600	27	A5
LANGFORD PL	RM	RM	3000	46	F2
LANGFORD ST	CO	LA63	3900	45	D5
LANGHALL CT	AGH	AGO		102	F2
LANGHAM AV	CO	COV	5000	89	B3
LANGHAM AV	COV	COV	700	89	B4
LANGHAM AV	GLDR	GLDR	800	89	B1
LANGHILL DR	CO	LPUE	14400	85	B1
LANGHORN ST E	LAN	LAN	300	160	C4
LANGLEY	PALM	PALM		171	J7
LANGLEY ST	GLEN	GL05	300	25	E4
LANGLEY WAY	MPK	MPK	1000	46	C3

STREET	CITY	P.O. ZONE	BLOCK	PAGE	GRID
LANGMUIR AV	LA	SUN	10200	10	E3
LANGPORT AV	LB	LB05	5500	70	F1
LANGSIDE AV	SCLR	SAU	27000	124	G8
LANGSPUR CT	WLVL	THO	31800	102	B4
LANGSPUR DR	CO	LPUE		98	B4
LANG STATION RD	CO	CYN		125	G7
LANGSTON ST	SCLR	VAL		127	A2
LANHAM DR	CO	LPUE	600	92	C5
LANIA LN	LA	BH	9500	33	B2
LANIGAN AV	LA	SV		9	F5
LANIGAN AV	LA	SV		10	A5
LANKERSHIM BLVD	LA	LA28	3600	23	E5
LANKERSHIM BLVD	LA	NHO	5600	16	D5
LANKERSHIM BLVD	LA	NHO	3800	23	E2
LANKERSHIM BLVD	LA	SV	8500	9	D6
LANKERSHIM BLVD	LA	SV	8400	16	D3
LANKIN ST	DOW	DOW	8200	60	A5
LANNING DR	CO	WHI	13400	61	E2
LANNING DR	CO	WHI	14600	84	A3
LANNY AV	LPUE	LPUE	600	92	A5
LANSBURY AV	CLA	CLA	3000	91	A3
LANSDALE ST	ELM	ELM	11700	47	F1
LANSDOWNE AV	CO	LA32	1800	45	D2
LANSDOWNE AV	LA	LA32	1900	45	E1
LANSFORD ST	RM	RM	8800	38	A4
LANSING AV	LA	WIL	800	74	D4
LANTANA DR	LA	LA42	1000	26	D6
LANTANA PL	RHE	PVP		73	D4
LANTANA ST	COM	COM	2600	64	C4
LANTANA ST	LAV	LAV		90	B3
LANTANA WY	POM	POM	1600	94	F4
LANTE ST	BAP	BAP	4800	39	F3
LANTERMAN LN	LCF	LCF	1200	19	B3
LANTERMAN TER	LA	LA39	2400	35	B3
LANTERN LN	LAM	LAM	12600	83	C1
LANTO ST	BG	BELL	5500	53	E5
LANTO ST	BG	BELL	6200	54	A5
LANTO ST	CMRC	LA40	6700	54	B5
LANZIT AV	LA	LA59	600	58	C4
LANZIT AV	LA	LA61	100	58	C4
LA PALMA AV	PALM	PALM		183	E2
LA PALMA CT	SCLR	VAL		127	H6
LA PALMA LN	CO	SGAB	7000	28	A6
LA PALOMA	AVA	AVA		77	A4
LA PALOMA AV	ALH	ALH	1	36	F4
LA PALOMA AV	ALH	ALH	1900	45	F1
LA PALOMA AV	LA	WIL	600	74	B6
LA PASADA ST	LB	LB15	5300	76	C4
LA PASAITA CT	CO	LPUE		98	C4
LA PAZ DR	CLA	CLA		91	B1
LA PAZ DR	CLA	CLA		96	B6
LA PAZ DR	CO	PAS	500	27	E5
LA PAZ DR	LA	LA39	3000	35	B2
LA PAZ LN	CO	MAL		114	A5
LA PAZ LN	CO	POM		97	E6
LA PAZ LN	LAN	LAN		160	F6
LA PAZ RD	CO	ALT	1700	20	D5
LA PAZ RD	WHI	WHI		84	D4
LA PAZ ST	LB	LB03		76	F2
LA PEER DR N	BH	BH	100	42	D2
LA PEER DR N	LA	LA48	100	33	D6
LA PEER DR N	WHOL	LA69	600	33	D6
LA PEER DR S	BH	BH	100	42	D2
LA PEER DR S	LA	LA35	1100	42	D2
LA PENA AV	LAM	LAM		83	C2
LA PERLA AV	LB	LB15	1400	76	C3
LAPHAM ST	ELS	ELS	700	56	D5
LAPINE AV	SCLR	SAU		124	G3
L PINTORESCA DR	PAS	PAS	1200	26	F1
LAPLANTE WY	SCLR	SAU		124	F5
LA PLATA AV	CO	LPUE	1100	85	D2
LA PLAZA	LB	LB15	4100	76	B2
LA PLUMA DR	LAM	LAM	14300	83	B2
LA POMELO RD	LAM	LAM	12300	84	C6
LA PORTADA	SPAS	SPAS	700	36	E2
LA PORTE DR	LCF	LCF	700	19	C3
LA PORTE ST	ARC	ARC	1	28	E4
LA PRADA ST	LA	LA42	5900	26	C6
LA PRADA TER	LA	LA42		26	C6
LA PRESA AV	CO	SGAB	5400	38	A3
LA PRESA AV	RM	RM	4400	37	F4
LA PRESA AV	RM	RM	2400	46	F2
LA PRESA AV	RM	RM	2400	47	A2
LA PRESA DR	CO	PAS	700	27	F5
LA PRESA DR	CO	SGAB	6800	27	F6
LA PRESA DR	LA	LA68	6900	34	B2
LA PRESA DR	PAS	PAS	200	27	F4
LAPS CT	CO	SAU		181	C9
LA PUEBLA AV	WHI	WHI	8700	84	B2
LA PUENTE RD	CO	LPUE	17900	98	D1
LA PUENTE RD	CO	WCOV	19300	97	A1
LA PUENTE RD	CO	WCOV	19000	98	F1
LA PUENTE RD	WAL	WAL	19700	93	D5
LA PUENTE RD	WAL	WAL	19500	97	A1
LA PUENTE RD	WCOV	WCOV	19400	97	A1
LA PUERTA ST	LA	LA23	1100	53	C1

STREET	CITY	P.O. ZONE	BLOCK	PAGE	GRID
LA PUNTA DR	LA	LA68	6300	34	C1
LAPWORTH DR	AGH	AGO		100A	B3
LA QUILLA DR	CO	CHA		1A	A6
LA QUINTA CT	PALM	PALM		171	F4
LA QUINTA DR	GLDR	GLDR	200	87	E6
LA QUINTA ST	LAM	LAM		83	C1
LA QUINTA WY	WHI	WHI		84	D4
LARA ST	LA	LA33	1000	45	B3
LARAINE CIR	LA	SP		78	D3
LA RAMADA AV	ARC	ARC	1600	28	E2
LA RAMADA PL	POM	POM		94	A4
LA RAMBLA	BUR	BUR	900	18	A5
LARAMIE AV	LA	CAN	6400	12	E5
LARAMIE AV	LA	CHA	9600	6	E4
LARAMIE AV	LA	WOH	5700	12	E6
LARAMIE DR	SAD	SAD		90	B1
LARAMIE PL	LA	CHA	10500	6	E2
LARAMIE ST	PALM	PALM		183	J1
LARAMIE WY	CO	SAU		181	B8
LARAWAY AV	ING	IN01	1100	56	F3
LARBERT ST	SCLR	CYN	19800	124	H5
LARBOARD LN	AGH	AGO	5800	102	D3
LARBROOK DR	CO	LPUE		98	B4
LARCH AV	CO	IN04	10300	57	A4
LARCH AV	LAW	LAW	14300	63	A3
LARCH PL	LAV	LAV		90	C1
LARCH ST	ALH	ALH	1600	37	A4
LARCH ST	ING	IN01	700	57	A3
LARCHBLUFF DR	RPV	PVP	27400	72	E5
LARCHFORK RD	CO	PALM		182	E6
LARCHMONT BL N	LA	LA04	100	34	C6
LARCHMONT BL S	LA	LA04	100	34	C6
LARCHMONT ST	POM	POM	1500	91	A5
LARCHWOOD AV	CO	LPUE	800	85	E1
LARCHWOOD CIR	LA	CAN	6900	5	E4
LARCHWOOD DR	PALM	PALM		183	C1
LARCO WAY	GLEN	GL02	1500	25	C1
LAREDA VIS AV E	CO	LAN	17100	175	B6
LAREDO AV	PAR	PAR	14000	65	E2
LAREDO AV	POM	POM	600	90	D4
LAREDO DR	SAD	SAD		90	A1
LA REINA AV	DOW	DOW	9200	60	C2
LA REINA DR	LA	TU	6300	11	B5
LA REINA PL	LA	TU	9400	11	B5
LA REINA WY E	LB	LB13	100	75	C5
LA REINA WY W	LB	LB13	100	75	C5
LARGA AV	LA	LA39	3000	35	C1
LARGO AV N	COM	COM	1600	64	F1
LARGO AV S	CO	COM	13000	64	F1
LARGO VISTA RD	CO	LLAN		175	G9
LARIAT CIR	LB	LB15		76	E5
LARIAT CT	WAL	WAL		93	D5
LARIAT LN	CAR	CAR		69	D6
LARIAT LN	NWK	NWK	12900	82	C1
LARIAT LN	RHE	PVP	3400	73	B4
LARIAT WY	CO	ACT		182	F8
LA RIATA DR	LHH	LAH		84	D2
LA RIBA WY	LA	LA42	6200	36	D2
LA RICA AV E	BAP	BAP	14100	39	E5
LA RICA AV N	BAP	BAP	3900	39	D3
LARIME RD E	CO	LAN	18500	175	D5
LARIMORE AV	CO	LPUE	1200	92	A4
LARIMORE AV	LPUE	LPUE	600	92	A4
LARIMORE AV	WCOV	WCOV	1200	92	A3
LARISSA DR	LA	LA26	3200	35	B5
LARK CT	LA	LA65	700	36	A3
LARK LN	LA	LA46	8000	33	E2
LARK BAY LN	LKD	LKD	2000	70	E2
LARKDALE RD	CO	SGAB	8300	37	F1
LARKE ELLEN CIR	LA	LA35	9000	42	D3
LARK ELLEN AV	AZU	AZU		88	C2
LARK ELLEN AV	CO	AZU	5100	88	C2
LARK ELLEN AV	CO	COV	3900	88	C4
LARK ELLEN AV	CO	LPUE	1400	92	C4
LARK ELLEN AV	COV	COV		88	C4
LARK ELLEN AV N	WCOV	WCOV	100	88	C6
LARK ELLEN AV S	WCOV	WCOV	100	92	C2
LARK ELLEN LN	CO	COV		88	C4
LARKER AV	LA	LA42	900	26	E6
LARKFIELD AV	CO	ARC	2800	39	A2
LARKHALL AV	DUA	DUA	300	86	A4
LARKHAVEN PL	SCLR	NEW	19100	127	H3
LARK HILL DR	WCOV	WCOV		92	E2
LARKIN AV	CO	PALM	37300	183	C1
LARKIN AV	PALM	PALM	38400	172	C8
LARKIN AV	PALM	PALM	37600	183	C1
LARKIN DR	CO	AZU	5500	88	D2
LARKIN DR	CO	COV	4000	88	D4
LARKIN DR	COV	COV	100	88	D5
LARKIN PL	SM	SM	100	40	E4
LARKIN WY	POM	POM	1600	90	E6
LARKMAIN DR	SCLR	SAU	27800	124	E4
LARKPORT DR	CO	LPUE		48	B5
LARK SPRING TER	DBAR	POM		97	F3
LARKSPUR AV	POM	POM	1600	95	B1
LARKSPUR DR	PALM	PALM		171	J6

STREET	CITY	P.O. ZONE	BLOCK	PAGE	GRID
LARKSPUR LN	CO	MAL	21900	110	B4
LARKSPUR LN	GLDR	GLDR	19500	89	A1
LARKSPUR LN	LAN	LAN		160	B1
LARKSPUR LN	LAV	LAV		90	C1
LARKSPUR ST	LA	SF	14800	2	B3
LARKSPUR FLD ST	CO	CYN		125	G6
LARKSTONE DR	DBAR	WAL		97	C3
LARKSTONE LN	GLEN	GL06	900	26	A2
LARK TREE WY	CO	LPUE	1500	98	B3
LARKVALE DR	RPV	PVP	6900	72	C4
LARKVANE RD	CO	LPUE	1700	98	D4
LARKWOOD AV	LA	WOH	4500	13	A3
LARKWOOD ST	WCOV	WCOV	1000	92	B2
LARMAR RD	LA	LA68		34	A1
LARMONA DR	CO	PAS		27	F1
LARMOR AV	CO	LPUE	1200	97	A3
LARNE ST	CO	LPUE		98	E3
LARO DR	AGH	AGO		100A	A2
LARO DR	AGH	AGO		102	F2
LA ROCHA DR	LA	LA68	6300	34	C1
LA ROCHELLE DR	SCLR	SAU	22400	124	C5
LA RODA AV	LA	LA41	4700	26	B5
LA RONDA CIR	CO	LPUE		85	E3
LA ROSA DR	CO	SGAB	8900	38	A4
LA ROSA DR	TEC	TEC	9200	38	B4
LA ROSA DR	TEC	TEC		38	D3
LA ROSA RD	ARC	ARC	1100	28	B4
LA ROSA ST	CO	ARC	11200	38	F3
LA ROSA ST	TEC	TEC		38	D3
LA ROTONDA DR	RPV	SP	3000	78	B4
LA ROUCHE TR	CO	TOP	19800	109	D5
LARRABEE ST	LA	LA69	1300	33	D4
LARRABEE ST	WHOL	LA69	800	33	D4
LARRES CYN RD	CO	VAL		126	D2
LARRY AV N	BAP	BAP	4600	39	E3
LARRYAN DR	LA	WOH	5700	5	E6
LARRYLYN DR	CO	WHI	11800	84	D6
LARRYLYN DR	LAM	LAM	12600	84	D6
LARRYLYN DR	WHI	WHI	9800	84	D3
LARSON WY	CO	CHA		4	B4
LARSSON ST	MB	MB	200	62	C4
LA RUE AV	LAV	LAV		90	B1
LA RUE AV	LAV	LAV		95A	B6
LA RUE ST	LA	SF	12800	8	E1
LARWIN AV	LA	CHA	10300	6	B3
LARWIN CIR	SFS	SFS		82	E1
LARWIN RD	LAM	LAM	13800	82	E1
LARWIN RD	NWK	NWK	12600	82	C1
LARWOOD ST	LAN	LAN		159	F7
LA SABANA DR	LAM	LAM	15100	84	B6
LASAINE AV	LA	ENC	5600	14	E6
LASAINE AV	LA	NOR	8600	7	E6
LASAINE AV	LA	NOR	7700	14	E2
LASAINE AV	LA	SF		1	E6
LASAINE AV	LA	SF	11100	7	E1
LASAINE AV	LA	VAN	6500	14	E5
LA SALINA ST	LAM	LAM		83	C1
LA SALLE AV	CO	LA47	11000	57	E5
LA SALLE AV	CUL	CUL	4000	50	C1
LA SALLE AV	GAR	GAR		63	E3
LA SALLE AV	LA	LA18	1900	43	E5
LA SALLE AV	LA	LA47	7200	51	E6
LA SALLE AV	LA	LA47	8700	57	E3
LA SALLE AV	LA	LA62	3800	51	E2
LA SALLE AV	LA	TOR	20900	68	E3
LA SALLE CYN DR	SCLR	NEW		127	A6
LA SALOS DR	WHI	WHI	15200	84	B3
LAS ALTURAS ST	LA	LA68	2800	34	A1
LAS BRISAS	LAN	LAN		171	E1
LAS BRISAS CIR	POM	POM		94	D2
LAS BRISAS WY	CO	PAS	1000	27	F6
LAS CANOAS RD	LA	PP	1300	40	C2
LAS CASAS AV	CLA	CLA		90	F2
LAS CASAS AV	LA	PP	300	40	B4
LAS CASAS PL	LA	PP	16500	40	B3
LAS COLINAS AV	LA	LA41	2400	25	F5
LAS COLINAS AV	LA	LA41	2000	26	A5
LAS CRUCES DR	LA	VAN	4200	22	C4
LAS CUMBRES DR	WHI	WHI	16200	84	C2
LA SEDA RD	CO	LPUE	100	98	E1
LA SELVA PL	PVE	PVP	3400	72	E1
LA SENA AV	BAP	BAP	4800	39	F3
LA SENA AV	WCOV	WCOV	100	88	A6
LA SENA CT	POM	POM	600	90	D4
LA SENDA PL	SPAS	SPAS	1700	37	B2
LA SERENA DR	CO	GLDR	6000	88	F1
LA SERENA DR	COV	COV	500	88	F5
LA SERENA DR	WCOV	WCOV	400	92	F1
LA SERNA DR	CO	WHI	10300	84	B4
LA SERNA DR	LAM	LAM	11900	84	B5
LA SERNA DR	WHI	WHI	9400	84	B3
LS ESTRELLAS DR	CO	MAL	30600	111	E4
LAS FLORES AV	LAM	LAM	15200	84	B6
LAS FLORES AV	MTB	MTB	900	46	F6
LAS FLORES AV	SMAR	PAS	1600	37	B1
LAS FLORES AV E	ARC	ARC	100	38	D1

STREET	CITY	P.O. ZONE	BLOCK	PAGE	GRID
LAS FLORES AV W	ARC	ARC	100	38	D1
LAS FLORES CT	LA	LA34	3700	50	B1
LAS FLORES DR	ELM	ELM	3500	38	D6
LAS FLORES DR	GLEN	GL07	1500	25	E1
LAS FLORES DR	LA	LA41	2400	25	F4
LAS FLORES DR	LA	LA41	1200	26	C4
LAS FLORES DR	SPAS	SPAS	500	37	A1
LAS FLORES DR E	CO	ALT	100	20	A4
LAS FLORES DR W	CO	ALT	100	20	A4
LAS FLORES ST	ALH	ALH	2500	46	A1
LAS FLRS CYN RD	CO	MAL		114	E1
LS FLORS HTS RD	CO	MAL		114	F1
LS FLORS MSA DR	CO	MAL	20700	114	F4
LASH LN	LA	LA68	6600	34	C2
LASHBROOK AV	ELM	ELM	3000	47	B2
LASHBROOK AV	RM	RM	3500	38	B6
LASHBROOK AV	SELM	ELM	2700	47	B2
LASHBURN ST	LA	SF	600	2	D5
LASHBURN ST	WHI	WHI	15400	84	C4
LASHEART DR	LCF	LCF	4500	19	B1
LA SHELL DR	LA	TU	9400	11	B5
LASHER RD	HH	CAL	24000	100	D2
LAS HERMANAS ST	LB	LB05	2800	65	A6
LA SIERRA AV	WHI	WHI	8200	84	B1
LA SIERRA DR	LCF	LCF	5200	19	A1
LA SIERRA DR	POM	POM		94	B5
LA SIERRA DR E	ARC	ARC	100	28	F6
LA SIERRA DR W	ARC	ARC	100	28	E6
LA SIERRA WY	CLA	CLA		91	A1
LASITA PL	RPV	SP	1900	73	D6
LASKER AV	PALM	PALM	37800	172	E9
LASKER AV	PALM	PALM	37700	183	D1
LASKY DR	BH	BH	100	42	B2
LAS LANAS CT	SCLR	VAL		124	A1
LASLEY WK	LA	LA65	400	36	B3
LAS LOMAS AV	AVA	AVA	300	77	B5
LAS LOMAS AV	LA	PP	600	40	C3
LAS LOMAS PL	LA	PP	1200	40	C2
LAS LOMAS RD	DUA	DUA	700	29	F4
LAS LOMAS ST	LB	LB15	5200	76	C4
LAS LOMITAS DR	CO	LPUE	1900	85	D3
LAS LOMITAS WY	CO	COV		93	B2
LAS LUNAS ST	PAS	PAS	100	27	F3
LAS LUNITAS AV	LA	TU	10300	10	F2
LS MANANITAS DR	SCLR	VAL		124	B7
LAS MARIAS AV	CO	LPUE	2600	85	D4
LA SOLANA DR	CO	ALT	1300	20	C5
LA SOMBRA DR	LA	LA68	3400	24	B5
LA SONORA DR	CO	MAL		111	E4
LAS PALMAS AV	GLEN	GL08	3300	18	E3
LAS PALMAS AV	LA	LA28	1300	34	B2
LAS PALMAS AV	LA	LA68	1800	34	B2
LAS PALMAS AV N	LA	LA04	100	34	B6
LAS PALMAS AV N	LA	LA38	700	34	B6
LAS PALMAS AV S	LA	LA04	100	34	B6
LAS PALMAS RD	PAS	PAS	800	26	E4
LAS PALMERAS AV	LAM	LAM		83	C2
LAS PALMITAS	SPAS	SPAS	1700	36	E2
LAS PALOMAS DR	LHH	LAH	2200	84	E1
LAS PALOMAS DR	LHH	LAH	1700	85	D6
LAS PASADAS DR	WHI	WHI	8200	84	B1
LAS PILAS RD	LA	WOH	21300	13	D4
LASPINO LN	DBAR	POM		94	B6
LAS PLUMAS LN	LA	TU	7200	10	F4
LAS POSAS ST	PR	PR	8800	55	A1
LAS POSITAS RD	GLEN	GL08	2300	18	F5
LAS PUERTAS ST	LAM	LAM		83	C2
LAS PULGAS PL	LA	PP	1100	40	C3
LAS PULGAS RD	LA	PP	900	40	C3
LAS RIENDAS WY	CO	PAS	1000	27	F6
LAS ROCAS DR	SMAD	SMAD	400	28	D1
LAS ROSAS DR	WCOV	WCOV		92	F2
LASSALETTE ST	CO	LPUE	13400	48	C2
LASSALETTE ST	LPUE	LPUE	14300	48	D4
LASSEN AV	CLA	CLA		91	C2
LASSEN CT	SAD	SAD		95A	B5
LASSEN ST	LA	CHA	17600	6	B4
LASSEN ST	LA	NOR	17000	7	B4
LASSEN ST	LA	SF	14700	8	B4
LASSITER DR	WAL	WAL	1400	93	B3
LASSO DR	CO	LAN	19000	175	D5
LASSO DR	DBAR	POM	21200	97	D5
LASSO LN	WAL	WAL		93	D5
LAS TUNAS DR	ARC	ARC	100	38	C2
LAS TUNAS DR	CO	LPUE	14700	85	C2
LAS TUNAS DR	TEC	TEC	8800	38	A3
LAS TUNAS DR E	SGAB	SGAB	100	37	D3
LAS TUNAS DR E	SGAB	SGAB	1300	38	A3
LAS TUNAS DR W	SGAB	SGAB	100	37	D3
LA SUBIDA DR	CO	LPUE	15200	85	D3
LA SUBIDA PL	LA	TAR	4600	21	C3
LA SUVIDA DR	LA	LA68	3100	24	B5
LAS VECINAS DR	CO	LPUE	13400	48	C3
LAS VECINAS DR	LPUE	LPUE	13700	48	C3
LAS VEGAS AV	POM	POM	2000	90	E5

1990 LOS ANGELES COUNTY STREET INDEX

STREET	CITY	P.O. ZONE	BLOCK	PAGE	GRID
LAS VIRGENES RD	CO	AGO		100A	E6
LAS VIRGENES RD	CO	CAL		100	A3
LAS VIRGENES RD	CO	CAL		100A	F2
LAS VIRGENES RD	CO	CAL	900	107	E4
LAS VIRGENES RD	CO	MAL	700	107	E4
LASZLO ST	LAN	LAN		159	H4
LATANA CT	SCLR	VAL		127	B1
LA TAZA DR	LCF	LCF	1700	19	A2
LATCHFORD AV	CO	LPUE	900	48	C6
LATCHFORD AV	CO	LPUE	1400	85	C1
LA TERRAZA	SPAS	SPAS	400	36	E3
LATHAM ST	LA	LA11	5100	52	D3
LATHROP ST	LA	LA32	5000	36	E3
LA TIENDA RD	WLVL	THO	31600	102	B3
LA TIERRA CT	LA	NOR		1	B5
LA TIERRA ST	PAS	PAS	2600	27	F3
LATIGO LN	RHE	PVP	25900	72	F3
LATIGO CYN RD	CO	MAL		106	C5
LATIGO CYN RD	CO	MAL		112	E2
LATIGO CYN RD	CO	MAL	5900	113	A5
LATIGO SHORE DR	CO	MAL	26500	113	A6
LATIGO SHORE PL	CO	MAL		113	A6
LA TIJERA BLVD	CO	LA56	5800	50	E6
LA TIJERA BLVD	ING	IN02	1300	50	E6
LA TIJERA BLVD	LA	LA45	9800	55A	F2
LA TIJERA BLVD	LA	LA45	7800	56	C2
LA TIJERA BLVD	LA	LA56	6200	50	E6
LATIMER LN	LA	LA77		32	E2
LATIMER RD	LA	PP	1	40	E3
LATIN WY	LA	LA65	1000	35	F1
LATIUM WY	CO	WAL	19800	97	B4
LATONA AV	LA	LA31	4200	36	B4
LATONA RD	LA	LA31	4200	36	B4
LA TORRE DR	POM	POM		94	B5
LA TORTOLA DR	WAL	WAL	400	93	B6
LA TOUR WY	LCF	LCF		19	A3
LA TREMOLINA LN	WHI	WHI	8500	84	B2
LATROBE ST	LA	LA31	3600	36	B4
LA TUNA CYN RD	LA	SV	10400	9	F5
LA TUNA CYN RD	LA	SV	7100	10	E5
LA TUNA CYN RD	LA	SV	6300	11	A5
LAUDER ST	CAR	CAR	1100	69	D4
LAUDERDALE AV	GLEN	GL14	4000	11	C5
LAUGHLIN CT	LA	LA12		44	E3
LAUGHLIN ST	CO	GL14	2200	11	E6
LAUGHLIN PK DR	LA	LA27	1900	34	E2
LAUGHTON WY	LA	NOR		1	C5
LAUN ST	CO	ALT	200	19	F5
LAUNDY RD	GLDR	GLDR		87	F5
LAURA AV	HPK	HPK	1900	52	E4
LAURA AV	LPUE	LPUE	200	92	C6
LAURA AV	LPUE	LPUE	600	98	B1
LAURA LN	LA	RES		14	A3
LAURA ST	DOW	DOW	7400	59	F4
LAURA L PLNT DR	AGH	AGO		100A	B4
LAUREL AV	ARC	ARC	100	28	F3
LAUREL AV	CO	WHI	9200	61	E2
LAUREL AV	DOW	DOW	12300	59	E5
LAUREL AV	MB	MB	1100	62	B3
LAUREL AV	POM	POM	1500	94	B2
LAUREL AV	SFS	SFS	10600	61	D4
LAUREL AV E	GLDR	GLDR		87	B4
LAUREL AV E	GLDR	GLDR	400	87	C4
LAUREL AV E	SMAD	SMAD	1	28	C2
LAUREL AV N	LA	LA48	100	33	F6
LAUREL AV N	WHOL	LA46	1000	33	F4
LAUREL AV S	LA	LA48	100	33	F6
LAUREL AV S	WHI	WHI	8300	61	E2
LAUREL AV W	GLDR	GLDR	400	87	A4
LAUREL AV W	POM	POM	500	94	D2
LAUREL AV W	SMAD	SMAD	1	28	C2
LAUREL CIR	MPK	MPK	600	46	D3
LAUREL CT	CO	PALM		184	B6
LAUREL CT	WAL	WAL		93	D4
LAUREL DR	CO	ALT	1	20	A3
LAUREL DR	MPK	MPK	1500	46	D3
LAUREL DR	RPV	PVP		77	A1
LAUREL LN	BH	BH	1000	33	A4
LAUREL LN	LA	LA46		33	E3
LAUREL LN	LA	NHO	12000	23	C5
LAUREL LN	MON	MON		29	B2
LAUREL PL	CO	CAL		100	D6
LAUREL PL	CO	SAU		124	D2
LAUREL PL	LA	LA02	9700	58	E3
LAUREL PL	MPK	MPK	600	46	D3
LAUREL PL	SOG	SOG	2700	58	F2
LAUREL ST	BLF	BLF	8700	66	B4
LAUREL ST	CO	LA02	9200	58	E3
LAUREL ST	CO	LA44	9200	57	E5
LAUREL ST	CO	LAV		90	F1
LAUREL ST	PAS	PAS	1100	26	D1
LAUREL ST	SPAS	SPAS	1400	36	F2
LAUREL ST	SPAS	SPAS	1600	37	A2
LAUREL ST E	COM	COM	100	65	A3
LAUREL ST E	GLEN	GL05	100	25	C6
LAUREL ST W	COM	COM	100	64	E3

STREET	CITY	P.O. ZONE	BLOCK	PAGE	GRID
LAUREL ST W	GLEN	GL04	100	25	C6
LAUREL WY	BH	BH	1000	33	A4
LAUREL WY	LA	BH	1300	33	A4
LAUREL BAY DR	PAS	PAS	1800	26	D5
LAUREL BLUFF PL	AGH	AGO		102	E3
LAURELBROOK CIR	CER	ART		82	E6
LAURELBROOK WY	CER	ART	16600	82	E4
LAUREL CYN BLVD	LA	LA46	1500	33	E1
LAUREL CYN BLVD	LA	NHO	5600	16	C3
LAUREL CYN BLVD	LA	NHO	3000	23	D5
LAUREL CYN BLVD	LA	PAC	10000	8	E2
LAUREL CYN BLVD	LA	PAC	9400	9	B5
LAUREL CYN BLVD	LA	SF	11400	2	D6
LAUREL CYN BLVD	LA	SF	10800	8	E2
LAUREL CYN BLVD	LA	SV	8500	9	B5
LAUREL CYN PL	LA	LA46	2700	33	E1
LAUREL CK CIR	SCLR	VAL		124	B4
LAURELCREST DR	LA	NHO	11400	23	D5
LAURELCREST LN	CO	NEW		126	J4
LAURELCREST RD	LA	NHO	11400	23	D5
LAURELDALE AV	DOW	DOW	13000	66	A1
LAUREL GLEN CIR	SCLR	VAL		124	B5
LAUREL GROVE AV	LA	NHO	6000	16	B6
LAUREL GROVE AV	LA	NHO	3900	23	B3
LAUREL GROVE CT	LA	NHO		16	C3
LAUREL HILLS RD	LA	NHO	11800	23	C5
LAURELHURST DR	ELM	ELM	10600	47	D1
LAURELMONT DR	LA	LA46	8100	33	E2
LAURELMONT PL	LA	LA46	2300	33	E2
LAUREL OAK DR	AZU	AZU	900	86	E5
LAUREL PARK RD	CO	COM		70	A1
LAUREL PASS AV	LA	LA46	2400	33	D1
LAUREL RIDGE DR	CO	MAL		113	E4
LAURELRIM DR	DBAR	POM		97	E4
LAUREL TER DR	LA	NHO	12000	23	B4
LAURELVALE DR	LA	NHO	3400	23	D5
LAUREL VLY DR	AZU	AZU	1300	86	C4
LAUREL VIEW DR	LA	LA69	8000	33	E3
LAURELWOOD AV	ING	LA56		50	E5
LAURELWOOD DR	LA	NHO	11600	23	D4
LAURELWOOD LN	LAN	LAN		159	F7
LAURELWOOD WY	WAL	WAL		93	D5
LAUREN WY	CUL	CUL		50	D1
LAURENS AV	BAP	BAP	4100	39	E4
LAURENT ST	LA	CHA	20800	6	D2
LAURETTE ST	TOR	TOR	4700	67	E4
LAURICE AV	CO	ALT	3200	20	B3
LAURIE CT	LAN	LAN		160	E3
LAURIE DR	LA	NHO	11200	23	E5
LAURIE LN	LAV	LAV	2600	90	E3
LAURIE PL	LA	NHO	3400	23	E5
LAURINDA AV	LB	LB14	300	76	E5
LAURISTON AV	LA	LA25	10300	42	A3
LAURISTON AV	LA	LA64	10400	42	A3
LAURITA AV	CO	PAS	3700	28	A5
LAURRIE LN	CO	WHI	13700	48	B5
LAUSANNE RD	LA	LA77	700	32	D5
LAUSINDA AV	LB	LB03		76	D5
LAUTERBACH ST	LAN	LAN		160	E6
LAUTREC PL	RPV	PVP	6500	77	C1
LAVA PL	LA	CAN	8400	4	B6
LAVA TR	LA	CAN	8700	4	A6
LAVAGNA WY	LA	LA77	10600	32	D3
LA VALLE ST	LA	SF	14200	2	C4
LAVANTE ST	LB	LB15	4400	76	B2
LAVE AV	LB	LB15	1800	76	D3
LA VEDA AV	SCLR	CYN	28200	125	C7
LA VELA AV	WHI	WHI	8400	84	A2
LAVELL DR	LA	LA65	3500	35	F2
LAVENDER LN	LCF	LCF	1000	19	B2
LAVENDER PL	LAV	LAV		90	B3
LA VENEZIA CT	CO	ALT	1	20	A5
LA VENTA RD	WLVL	THO		102	A4
LA VEQUE ST	CO	LA63		45	D3
LA VERE DR	LB	LB10	2600	75	A1
LA VEREDA RD	PAS	PAS	100	26	E3
LA VEREDA ESCRP	CO	CLA		96	C4
LAVERNA AV	LA	LA41	2100	26	A5
LA VERNE AV	CO	LA22	300	45	E6
LA VERNE AV	CO	LA22	1000	53	E1
LA VERNE AV	LB	LB03	100	76	B6
LA VERNE AV	LB	LB03	1	80	B1
LA VERNE AV E	POM	POM	100	90	E5
LA VERNE AV E	POM	POM	800	91	A5
LA VERNE AV W	POM	POM	100	90	E5
LA VERNE PL	LB	LB03	1	80	B1
LAVETA TER	LA	LA26	600	35	C6
LAVETA TER	LA	LA26	300	44	C1
LA VIDA DR	LAN	LAN		160	G6
LA VILLA ST	DOW	DOW	8300	60	B3
LA VILLA MARINA	LA	VEN		49	E5
LA VINA WY	CO	PAS	1000	27	F6
LAVINIA AV	LYN	LYN	5100	65	C1
LA VISTA AV	BAP	BAP	1900	39	E6
LA VISTA CT	LA	LA04	5100	34	D5
LA VISTA PL	PAS	PAS	1600	19	D6

STREET	CITY	P.O. ZONE	BLOCK	PAGE	GRID
LA VISTA TER	GLEN	GL08	1400	18	E6
LA VISTA VERDE	RPV	SP	30300	78	C3
LAVITA AV	POM	POM	1500	94	C1
LA VITA CT	SCLR	VAL		124	B9
LAVON DR	LA	CAN	23500	5	E2
LAWFORD ST	GLDR	GLDR	1300	87	D6
LAWLEN WY	LA	BH	9600	33	A4
LAWLER ST	LA	LA34	10700	42	A6
LAWLER ST	LA	LA66	11900	49	E1
LAWNDALE DR	LA	LA65	2800	25	F5
LAWNHILL DR	LAM	LAM	15800	83	C1
LAWNSIDE DR	SCLR	NEW	23700	127	A5
LAWNWOOD ST	CO	LPUE	16300	92	B5
LAWNWOOD ST	LPUE	LPUE	15500	48	F5
LAWNWOOD ST	LPUE	LPUE	15700	92	A5
LAWRENCE AV	CO	RM	1000	46	F4
LAWRENCE AV	LAN	LAN		159	G5
LAWRENCE AV	LA	WIL	800	74	F4
LAWRENCE AV	RM	RM	8800	38	A5
LAWRENCE CIR	CLA	CLA		91	D1
LAWRENCE LN	LA	BH	10000	32	F4
LAWRENCE PL	POM	POM	1600	95	A4
LAWRENCE ST	ING	IN03	3300	57	C3
LAWRENCE ST	LA	LA21	700	44	E5
LAWRENCE WK	CO	CAST		123	C2
LAWSON PL	GLEN	GL02	300	25	C1
LAWSON ST	IND	LPUE	700	98	D3
LAWTON ST	SELM	ELM	9900	47	C3
LAXFORD RD	CO	AZU	16500	88	B2
LAXFORD RD	CO	COV	18500	88	D2
LAXFORD ST E	CO	GLDR		89	B2
LAXFORD ST W	GLDR	GLDR	100	89	A2
LAYMAN AV	PR	PR	3900	55	A1
LAYTON DR N	LA	LA49	100	41	C1
LAYTON DR S	LA	LA49	100	41	C1
LAYTON ST	CO	PAS	1800	27	D1
LAYTON WY	LA	LA49	300	32	C6
LAYTON WY	WCOV	WCOV	2400	92	E2
LA ZANJA DR	GLEN	GL07	1100	25	E2
LAZARD ST	LA	SF	13200	2	F3
LAZARD ST	LA	SF	12600	3	A3
LAZARD ST N	SF	SF	200	2	E5
LAZARD ST S	SF	SF	1	2	D5
LAZULITE LN	POM	POM	1200	91	B6
LAZY BROOK LN	CO	LPUE		98	A4
LAZY CREEK LN	RHE	PVP		72	F3
LAZY MEADOW DR	DBAR	POM		97	F4
LAZY MEADOW DR	TOR	TOR		73	B3
LAZY MEADOW RD	POM	POM		94	E6
LAZY MEADOW RD	POM	POM		97A	C1
LAZY OAK PL	AGH	AGO		102	F3
LAZY TRAIL LN	POM	POM		94	C5
LAZY TRAIL RD	DBAR	POM		97	F4
LEA CT	CO	RM		46	F3
LEA WK	CO	CAST		123	A5
LEACH ST	LA	SF	13400	2	F3
LEACH ST	LA	SF	12800	3	B2
LEACREST DR	RPV	PVP	28700	72	C5
LEADHILL DR	CO	PALM		157	J8
LEADORA AV	CO	GLDR	18500	86	F4
LEADORA AV	GLDR	GLDR	100	86	F4
LEADORA AV E	GLDR	GLDR	100	87	B4
LEADORA AV W	GLDR	GLDR	100	87	B4
LEADWELL ST	LA	CAN	23100	5	F3
LEADWELL ST	LA	CAN	19700	12	A3
LEADWELL ST	LA	NHO	11500	16	D3
LEADWELL ST	LA	RES	18700	14	B3
LEADWELL ST	LA	SV	11000	16	E3
LEADWELL ST	LA	VAN	17300	15	C3
LEADWELL ST	LA	VAN	13500	16	A3
LEAF AV	CO	AZU	5200	88	C2
LEAF AV N	COV	COV	900	88	C4
LEAF AV N	WCOV	WCOV	500	88	C6
LEAF AV S	COV	COV	100	88	C5
LEAF AV S	WCOV	WCOV	100	92	C1
LEAF ST	LAV	LAV		90	C2
LEAFDALE AV	ELM	ELM	2400	47	E3
LEAFDALE AV	SELM	ELM	1400	47	D4
LEAFWOOD DR	MON	MON	1600	28	F5
LEAFWOOD LN	ARC	ARC	1900	38	D1
LEAGUE AV	CO	LPUE	900	48	E3
LEAGUE AV	LPUE	LPUE	300	48	D4
LEAGUE ST	LA	NHO	12700	16	B2
LEAH CIR	RPV	PVP	28800	72	C5
LEAHY AV	BLF	BLF	14100	66	C3
LEAHY AV	DOW	DOW	13100	66	C1
LEAHY ST	CUL	CUL	4300	50	C1
LEAL AV	CER	ART	17000	82	D5
LEAL CIR	CER	ART	19400	81	D2
LEALMA AV	CLA	CLA	3800	90	F2
LEANDER DR	CO	LPUE	15900	85	E4
LEANDER DR	CO	SF		3	E2
LEANDER PL	LA	BH	9100	33	C1
LEANDRA LN	ARC	ARC	900	28	D3
LEANDRY RD	LAM	LAM		83	D1
LEANDRY RD	LAM	LAM		84	D6

STREET	CITY	P.O. ZONE	BLOCK	PAGE	GRID
LEANING OAK CT	GLDR	GLDR	1700	87	D5
LEANING PINE DR	DBAR	POM		97	D4
LEANNA DR	WCOV	WCOV		92	E5
LEANNE AV	MON	MON	1600	29	A5
LEANNE TER	CO	WAL		97	C3
LEAP CT	DBAR	WAL		97	C5
LEAPWOOD AV	CAR	CAR	19000	69	C1
LEAR CT	CO	LPUE	16100	92	A4
LEATA LN	LCF	LCF		18	F2
LEATART AV	PAR	PAR	13800	65	E1
LEATHERWOOD AV	LAN	LAN	43600	159	J7
LEAYN CT	LA	NHO		16	C3
LEBANON ST	LA	LA15	1300	44	B4
LEBANON ST	LA	LA17	600	44	C3
LEBEC PL	RPV	PVP	6000	77	C2
LE BERTHON ST	LA	SUN	7900	10	E2
LE BERTHON ST	LA	TU	7600	10	E2
LE BLANC PL	RPV	PVP	6500	77	C1
LEBO ST	WHI	WHI	16400	84	D4
LE BORGNE AV	CO	LPUE	200	48	C2
LE BOURGET AV	CUL	CUL	4100	50	C1
LECCO LN	LA	PP	17800	40	A4
LECCO LN	LA	TOP		115	F4
LECHNER PL	LA	LA68	6000	34	D1
LECHUSA RD	CO	MAL		105	B6
LE CLAIRE PL	LA	LA19	1000	43	C2
LE CONTE AV	LA	LA24	10400	41	D1
LE CONTE PL	LA	LA24		41	E1
LECOUVREUR AV	LA	WIL	200	74	C5
LEDA LN	ARC	ARC	300	28	F6
LEDAN ST	LA	NOR	18900	7	B6
LEDEEN DR	LA	SF	10600	3	F6
LEDERER AV	LA	CAN	6400	5	F5
LEDERER AV	LA	WOH	6100	5	F5
LEDFORD ST	BAP	BAP	12900	48	B2
LEDGE AV	BUR	BUR	5000	23	F4
LEDGE AV	LA	NHO	4200	23	F4
LEDGE AV	LA	SV	9000	9	F5
LEDGE AV	LA	SV	7800	16	F2
LEDGEWOOD DR	LA	LA68	2900	24	C6
LEDGEWOOD RD	SOG	SOG	5100	59	D4
LEDO WY	LA	LA49	600	32	D5
LE DOUX RD	CO	LA56	5800	50	E5
LE DOUX RD	LA	LA35	800	42	E1
LE DOUX RD	LA	LA48	400	33	D6
LE DOUX RD N	BH	BH	100	42	E1
LE DOUX RD S	BH	BH	100	42	E1
LE DROIT DR	SPAS	SPAS	2000	37	A2
LEE AV	ARC	ARC	1600	38	E1
LEE AV	CLA	CLA		91	C2
LEE AV	LB	LB04	1300	76	B4
LEE AV	SELM	ELM	2000	47	B2
LEE DR	AZU	AZU	400	86	D6
LEE DR	GLEN	GL01	1400	18	A5
LEE LN	ELM	ELM	11400	38	E6
LEE LN	SOG	SOG	10200	59	E4
LEE PL	AZU	AZU	600	86	E6
LEE PL	POM	POM	2000	95	A5
LEE ST	LA	LA23	2900	45	B5
LEE ST	RM	RM	3600	38	A6
LEE ST	TOR	TOR	4600	67	E4
LEEBE AV	POM	POM	2500	94	A2
LEE CREEK DR	DBAR	POM		94	B6
LEEDS AV	LA	WIL	1000	74	E4
LEEDS CT	SAD	SAD		89	E3
LEEDS ST	DOW	DOW	7900	59	F5
LEEDS ST	DOW	DOW	7900	60	A5
LEEDS ST	NWK	NWK	10400	60	E6
LEEDS ST	NWK	NWK	11600	61	A6
LEEDS ST	SOG	SOG	5600	59	D5
LEEDY AV	LA	SF	13900	2	F1
LEERIDGE TER	GLEN	GL06	500	25	E3
LEES AV	LB	LB08	3000	71	E6
LEES AV	LB	LB15	800	76	E4
LEES WY	LB	LB15	6800	76	E4
LEESCOTT AV	LA	VAN	7200	14	E3
LEESDALE AV	LA	HAC	26400	73	E4
LEESIDE ST	CO	GLDR	19200	86	F6
LEESIDE ST	CO	GLDR	19200	87	A6
LEESIDE ST	GLDR	GLDR	300	87	A6
LEEVIEW CT	CUL	CUL	3800	50	E1
LEEWARD AV	CER	ART		66	E5
LEEWARD AV	LA	LA05	3000	43	F2
LEEWOOD ST	WCOV	WCOV	1600	48	F1
LEEWOOD ST	WCOV	WCOV	1000	92	A2
LEFFCO RD	WHI	WHI	15600	84	C4
LEFFINGWELL RD	CO	WHI	13000	61	E5
LEFFINGWELL RD	CO	WHI	15300	84	A5
LEFFINGWELL RD	LAM	LAM	14500	61	E5
LEFFINGWELL RD	LAM	LAM	14500	84	A5
LEFFINGWELL RD	NWK	NWK	12600	61	C6
LEFFINGWELL RD	NWK	NWK	10700	66	E2
LEFFINGWELL RD	WHI	WHI	16000	84	C4
LEFLORE DR	LHH	LAH	1200	84	D2
LEFLOSS AV	DOW	DOW	10800	60	E5
LEFLOSS AV	NWK	NWK	11200	60	E5

STREET	CITY	P.O. ZONE	BLOCK	PAGE	GRID
LEFLOSS AV	NWK	NWK	13200	66	E1
LEGACY CT	LA	WOH		13	A2
LEGARY PL	LA	SP	700	78	D3
LEGEND AV	CAR	CAR	21300	69	D4
LEGEND LN	CO	LPUE		98	D5
LEGENDS WY	LAN	LAN		159	B5
LEGHORN AV	LA	VAN	5200	23	A2
LEGION DR	SH	LB06	2200	75	E2
LEGION LN	LA	LA39	3700	35	B1
LE GRANDE TER	LA	SP	1400	78	E4
LE GRAY AV	LA	LA42	900	36	C1
LEHIGH AV	LA	PAC	10900	9	A1
LEHIGH AV	LA	SF	11400	2	F6
LEHIGH AV	LA	SV	8400	9	E6
LEHIGH AV	LA	SV	8300	16	E1
LEHIGH DR	CLA	CLA	600	91	B5
LEHIGH ST	CO	ALT	900	19	E4
LEHMAN RD	GLEN	GL14	4000	11	C6
LEI DR	LB	LB05	100	65	C5
LEIBACHER AV	DOW	DOW	10900	60	E5
LEIBACHER AV	NWK	NWK	11500	60	E5
LEIBACHER AV	NWK	NWK	12800	66	E1
LEICESTER CT	CLA	CLA		96	D5
LEICESTER DR	LA	LA45	2500	33	E1
LEIGH CT E	LB	LB06	1200	75	D2
LEIGHTON AL	PAS	PAS	900	27	B2
LEIGHTON AV	LA	LA37	900	51	F1
LEIGHTON AV	LA	LA62	1500	51	D1
LEILANI WY	CO	ALT	3200	20	A3
LEIMERT BLVD	LA	LA08	4000	51	C2
LEI MIN WY	LA	LA12	400	44	E1
LEIR DR	CO	GL14	4500	18	E1
LEISURE DR	LAM	LAM	14200	82	F1
LEISURE LN	CO	LAN		147	H6
LEISURE LK PKWY	CO	LAN		147	H6
LEITH RD	GLEN	GL06	2300	26	A2
LEKNES DR	CO	CAL		108	A5
LEKO DR	CO	TOP		109	C6
LELA DR	DBAR	POM	24000	93	F6
LELAND AV	CO	WHI	10700	61	D6
LELAND AV N	WCOV	WCOV	200	39	F6
LELAND AV S	WCOV	WCOV	1300	48	E1
LELAND PL	LCF	LCF	4500	19	B3
LELAND ST N	LA	SP	400	78	E2
LELAND ST S	LA	SP	700	78	E5
LELAND WY	ARC	ARC	200	28	F6
LELAND WY	BUR	BUR	1000	17	C5
LELAND WY	LA	LA28	6200	34	C3
LELIA LN	LA	LA77		32	E3
LEMA DR	SCLR	VAL		127	C1
LEMAC ST	LA	NOR	17300	14	E2
LEMAC ST	LA	VAN	15300	15	B2
LEMAN ST	SPAS	SPAS	1900	37	A3
LE MANS DR	CO	TOP		13	C5
LEMAR PARK DR	GLDR	GLDR	600	87	B6
LEMARSH ST	LA	CHA	19700	6	F3
LEMARSH ST	LA	NOR	17400	7	D3
LEMARSH ST	LA	SF	16600	7	F3
LEMARSH ST	LA	SF	15200	8	B3
LEMAY PL	LA	VAN	17500	14	D4
LEMAY ST	LA	CAN	24200	5	D4
LEMAY ST	LA	CAN	20600	12	E4
LEMAY ST	LA	NHO	10800	16	E4
LEMAY ST	LA	RES	19600	12	F4
LEMAY ST	LA	RES	18100	14	C4
LEMAY ST	LA	VAN	17200	14	E4
LEMAY ST	LA	VAN	14100	15	E4
LEMMER DR	LA	TAR		21	A4
LEMMER ST	LA	CHA		6	E4
LEMMING ST	LKD	LKD	11300	71	F3
LEMMING ST	LKD	LKD	12000	81	B3
LEMOLI AV	CO	GAR	14600	63	C3
LEMOLI AV	CO	HAW	13100	63	C3
LEMOLI AV	HAW	HAW	13500	63	C3
LEMOLI AV	ING	IN03	10800	57	C4
LEMON AV	BRAD	DUA	1400	29	D4
LEMON AV	CO	SGAB	6300	38	A1
LEMON AV	GLDR	GLDR	100	87	B6
LEMON AV	IND	WAL	500	97	C3
LEMON AV	IND	WAL	600	97	C2
LEMON AV	LB	LB05	5900	65	D6
LEMON AV	LB	LB05	5200	70	D5
LEMON AV	LB	LB06	1800	75	D3
LEMON AV	LB	LB07	3400	70	D5
LEMON AV	LB	LB13	1300	75	D3
LEMON AV	SH	LB06	2200	75	D3
LEMON AV	TEC	TEC	9200	38	B1
LEMON AV	WAL	WAL	100	93	B5
LEMON AV	WAL	WAL	100	97	B1
LEMON AV E	ARC	ARC	100	38	D1
LEMON AV E	MON	MON	100	29	A4
LEMON AV N	AZU	AZU	500	86	C6
LEMON AV S	AZU	AZU	100	88	C1
LEMON AV W	ARC	ARC	100	38	D1
LEMON AV W	MON	MON	100	29	A4

264

1990 LOS ANGELES COUNTY STREET INDEX

LEMON DR LINDLEY AV

LOS ANGELES CO.

STREET	CITY	P.O. ZONE	BLOCK	PAGE	GRID
LEMON DR	LAM	LAM	15300	84	B5
LEMON ST	ALH	ALH	1700	37	A5
LEMON ST	CO	SAU		124	C2
LEMON ST	LA	LA21	1200	44	E5
LEMONA AV	LA	SF	8700	8	C5
LEMONA AV	LA	VAN	5600	15	C6
LEMONA AV	LA	VAN	4500	22	C3
LEMON CREEK DR	WAL	WAL		97	B1
LEMONCREST AV	LA	SF	11100	9	F1
LEMON GROVE AV	LA	LA29	4800	34	D4
LEMON GROVE AV	LA	LA38	5300	34	D4
LEMONWOOD DR	LAN	LAN		159	F8
LEMONWOOD ST	LAV	LAV		95A	C6
LEMORAN AV	DOW	DOW	9000	60	D2
LEMORAN AV	PR	PR	5500	54	F4
LEMORAN AV	PR	PR	5300	55	A4
LEMORAN AV	PR	PR	8000	60	E1
LEMOYNE ST	LA	LA26	1100	35	C4
LEMP AV	LA	NHO	5600	16	D6
LEMP AV	LA	NHO	4200	23	D4
LEMSFORD AV	CO	PALM	38400	172	G8
LEMSFORD AV	PALM	PALM	38000	172	G9
LEMSFORD AV	PALM	PALM		183	G1
LENA AV	LA	CAN		12	A3
LENA AV	LA	CAN	6800	12	A4
LENA AV	LA	WOH	6200	12	A5
LENA CT	LAN	LAN		160	D6
LENARDO DR	CAR	CAR		69	B3
LENAWEE AV	CUL	CUL	3800	50	E1
LENAWEE AV	LA	LA16	3600	42	E6
LENCHO PL	WAL	WAL	19600	97	A2
LE NICHE LN	LAN	LAN		160	E9
LENNON ST	CO	COM	800	64	C2
LENNON ST	CO	GAR	100	64	B2
LENNOX AV	LA	VAN	6800	15	E4
LENNOX AV	LA	VAN	4400	22	E3
LENNOX BLVD	CO	IN04	4500	56	F4
LENNOX BLVD	CO	IN04	4000	57	A4
LENNOX CT	PALM	PALM		171	F4
LENNOX ST	POM	POM	2400	91	A5
LENORE AV	CO	ARC	5400	38	F3
LENORE DR	GLEN	GL06	3500	19	B6
LENORE LN	POM	POM	700	90	F5
LENORE LN	POM	POM		91	A5
LENORE ST	TOR	TOR	4100	67	E4
LENS AV	CO	PEAR	34100	185	B8
LENTA LN	ARC	ARC	2200	38	F2
LENVALE AV	WHI	WHI		55	C2
LENZGROVE LN	LCF	LCF	4200	19	A3
LEO AV	CMRC	LA40	2100	54	A2
LEOLA ST	LOM	LOM	1800	73	D2
LEOLANG AV	LA	SUN	10300	10	E3
LEON CIR	CER	ART	19400	81	A2
LEONA AV	CO	PALM	8600	171I	F4
LEONA AV	LA	TU	10000	11	B4
LEONA DR	BH	BH	1200	33	A4
LEONA JOAN AV	PR	PR	6100	55	A4
LEONARD AV	CO	LA22	600	46	A6
LEONARD AV	CO	LA22	700	54	A1
LEONARD AV	PAS	PAS	1000	28	A2
LEONARD PL	CO	LA22	900	54	A1
LEONARD RD	LA	LA49	800	32	A6
LEONARD ST	MTB	MTB	600	46	B6
LEONA VIEW WY	CO	PALM	40500	171I	G4
LEONIS BLVD	VER	LA58	2600	52	F3
LEONIS BLVD	VER	LA58	2800	53	A3
LEONIS ST	CMRC	LA40	4500	53	D2
LEONORA DR	LA	WOH	22700	13	A2
LEONORA DR	LA	WOH	23000	100	F2
LEOPOLD AV	CO	LPUE	2600	85	E4
LEORITA ST	BAP	BAP	900	48	B2
LEOSE LN	GLDR	GLDR	200	87	A4
LEOTA ST	CO	HPK	2100	52	E6
LEOTI TER	LA	LA69	8100	33	E3
LE PAGE RCH RD	CO	VAL	12600	192	C5
LERDO AV	LA	SF	11500	1	D6
LERIDA PL	CO	RM	2000	46	E3
LERIDA PL	LA	CHA	10500	6	E2
LERMA RD	CO	ELM	1200	47	C4
LERMA RD	SELM	ELM	1300	47	C4
LERONA AV	CO	LPUE	1700	98	F4
LEROS ST	CO	LAN	48400	146	A6
LEROY AV	ARC	ARC	1	28	C6
LEROY ST	CO	ARC	9600	28	B6
LEROY ST	CO	SGAB	9000	28	B6
LEROY ST	CO	SGAB	8300	37	F1
LEROY ST	LA	LA12	100	44	E1
LESAGE AV	LA	WOH	5600	5	E6
LE SAGE AV	LA	WOH	5600	100	E1
LE SAGE ST	LYN	LYN	3600	59	C5
LESINA DR	CO	PALM		157	F8
LESLIE AV	CER	ART	16800	82	D5
LESLIE AV	LB	LB05		70	A2
LESLIE CT	LAN	LAN		160	F4
LESLIE CT	POM	POM	1700	91	A6
LESLIE DR	TEC	TEC	8700	38	A2

STREET	CITY	P.O. ZONE	BLOCK	PAGE	GRID
LESLIE DR E	SGAB	SGAB	800	37	E2
LESLIE DR W	SGAB	SGAB	200	37	E2
LESLIE LN	BH	BH	500	33	C3
LESLIE ST	CO	LPUE		98	F4
LESLIE WY	LA	LA42	200	36	C3
LESMAR DR	CO	LAV		90	B2
LESNER AV	LA	VAN	8000	14	E2
LESNY ST	LA	SF	10700	9	F1
LESSER ST	NWK	NWK	11800	82	A1
LESSERMAN ST	TOR	TOR	2500	68	C3
LESTER LN	LA	CAN	8300	5	F1
LESTER ST	LB	LB05	5700	70	C1
LESTERFORD AV	DOW	DOW	10000	60	D4
LESTERWEST WY	GLDR	GLDR	500	87	B5
LETA ST	LA	LA11	2600	52	D1
LETICIA DR	CO	LPUE	2600	85	D4
LETICIA DR	SCLR	VAL		127	B1
LETON AV	AZU	AZU		88	D2
LEUCADIA RD	LHH	LAH		85	F6
LEV AV	LA	PAC	9500	8	E3
LEV AV	LA	PAC	9000	9	A5
LEV AV	LA	SF		2	C6
LEV AV	LA	SF	10400	8	D2
LEVANDA AV	LA	LA32	2200	36	E6
LEVEL ST	CO	COV	19400	89	A5
LEVEL ST	COV	COV	700	89	A5
LEVELGLEN DR	WCOV	WCOV	2900	97	A1
LEVELSIDE AV	LKD	LKD	4100	70	F2
LEVELWOOD ST	CO	LPUE	13100	48	A4
LEVEN LN	LA	LA49	12100	41	B1
LEVERETT AV	LPUE	LPUE	200	98	C1
LEVERETT ST	LPUE	LPUE		98	C1
LEVERING AV	LA	LA24	400	41	D1
LEVICO WAY	LA	LA77	10600	32	D3
LEVINSON ST	CO	TOR	1100	68	F4
LEVITT LN	LA	VAN	4200	22	D4
LEW AV	CO	LPUE	100	92	C6
LEW DAVIS ST	LB	LB08	5000	71	B4
LEWENDO CT	SCLR	SAU		124	F6
LEWIS AV	CO	ALT	2000	20	B6
LEWIS AV	LAV	LAV		90	C2
LEWIS AV	LB	LB05	5900	65	D6
LEWIS AV	LB	LB05	5300	70	D1
LEWIS AV	LB	LB06	1800	75	D2
LEWIS AV	LB	LB07	3400	70	D5
LEWIS AV	LB	LB13	1000	75	D4
LEWIS AV	SH	LB06	3200	70	D5
LEWIS AV	SH	LB06	2300	75	D2
LEWIS CT	CLA	CLA	300	91	B5
LEWIS LN	AGH	AGO		100A	B3
LEWIS PL	AGH	AGO		100A	B4
LEWIS RD	AGH	AGO		100A	B3
LEWIS RD	LYN	LYN	10600	59	C4
LEWIS ST	LA	LA42	400	36	D1
LEWIS ST	LYN	LYN	10700	59	B5
LEWIS ST	POM	POM	500	94	D2
LEWIS TER	LA	LA46	2000	33	E2
LEWIS& CLARK RD	HH	CAL	24900	100	C2
LEWISTON ST	DUA	DUA	800	29	C6
LEXHAM AV	SELM	ELM	900	47	C4
LEXICON AV	LA	SF	13800	2	F1
LEXICON AV	LA	SF	11400	3	D6
LEXICON PL	LA	SF	13500	2	F1
LEXINGTON AV	CO	PAS	1100	20	C6
LEXINGTON AV	ELM	ELM	3400	38	D6
LEXINGTON AV	ELM	ELM	2600	47	D1
LEXINGTON AV	LA	LA29	4500	34	F4
LEXINGTON AV	LA	LA29	4200	35	A4
LEXINGTON AV	LA	LA38	5500	34	D4
LEXINGTON AV	MTB	MTB		46	D5
LEXINGTON AV	WHOL	LA46	7500	33	F4
LEXINGTON AV	WHOL	LA46	7100	34	A4
LEXINGTON AV E	POM	POM	100	94	E5
LEXINGTON AV E	POM	POM	900	95	A5
LEXINGTON AV W	POM	POM	100	94	E5
LEXINGTON CIR	CER	ART		81	A1
LEXINGTON CT	LB	LB03		76	F5
LEXINGTON CT	PALM	PALM		183	G6
LEXINGTON CT	PALM	PALM		183	J1
LEXINGTON DR	CO	CAST	30000	123	A5
LEXINGTON DR E	GLEN	GL06	100	25	C3
LEXINGTON DR W	GLEN	GL03	100	25	C3
LEXINGTON RD	BH	BH	1000	33	A5
LEXINGTON RD	DOW	DOW	8300	60	C2
LEXINGTON RD	PR	PR	4000	54	F2
LEXINGTON WY	WLVL	THO		102	C4
LEXGTN GALTN RD	CO	ELM	700	47	C4
LEXGTN GALTN RD	PR	PR	8300	60	D1
LEY DR	LA	LA27	3300	35	A1
LEYBURN DR	RM	RM	3000	47	B1
LEYCROSS DR	LCF	LCF	1600	19	A3
LEYDON AV	LA	WOH	4400	13	A3
LEYLAND DR	DBAR	POM		97A	B2
LEYTE DR	TOR	TOR	22200	67	F5
LEYTE DR	TOR	TOR	23500	72	F1
LEYVA ST	NWK	NWK	12900	82	C3

STREET	CITY	P.O. ZONE	BLOCK	PAGE	GRID
LIAHONA PL	LA	WOH	23200	13	A3
LIAHONA PL	LA	WOH	23200	100	F3
LIBBIT AV	LA	ENC	4400	21	F3
LIBBIT AV	LA	ENC	4500	22	A2
LIBBY WY	LA	LA68	5800	34	D2
LIBERATOR AV	LA	LA45	8600	56	C2
LIBERTY	PALM	PALM		183	D2
LIBERTY AV	GLEN	GL14	3900	18	D2
LIBERTY AV	MTB	MTB		46	E5
LIBERTY BLVD	SOG	SOG	2600	58	F1
LIBERTY BLVD	SOG	SOG	2800	59	A1
LIBERTY CT	LB	LB02	100	75	D5
LIBERTY CT	LB	LB02	300	75	D5
LIBERTY CT	LB	LB13	700	75	D5
LIBERTY LN	CO	TOP	2400	109	C1
LIBERTY ST	LA	LA26	1300	35	C5
LIBERTY WY	CO	ACT		189	E2
LIBERTY BELL RD	CO	WOH		13	A4
LIBERTY CYN RD	CO	AGO		100A	D6
LIBLEN AV	BLF	BLF	14500	66	B2
LIBRA DR	LAM	LAM	14300	83	B2
LIBRARY LN	SPAS	SPAS	1100	36	F1
LIBRARY PL	SOG	SOG	3500	59	B2
LIBRARY ST	SF	SF	500	2	E5
LIBRE PZ	MTB	MTB		46	B6
LICK ST	LA	LA41	1400	26	B5
LIDA LN	PAS	PAS	1100	26	D1
LIDA ST	PAS	PAS	1100	26	C1
LIDCOMBE AV	SELM	ELM	1400	47	D4
LIDDINGTON ST	CER	ART		81	B2
LIDFORD AV	CO	LPUE	500	92	B5
LIDO CT	CO	TOP		13	B5
LIDO DR	PALM	PALM		173	A9
LIDO LN	LB	LB03		80	C1
LIEBE DR	LA	BH	9900	32	E1
LIFFORD ST	CAR	CAR	100	64	B6
LIFUR AV	LA	LA32	3400	36	E5
LIGGETT ST	LA	CHA	22000	6	B5
LIGGETT ST	LA	NOR	18600	7	B5
LIGGETT ST	LA	SF	16600	7	F5
LIGGETT ST	LA	SF	15900	8	B5
LIGGETT ST	LA	VAN	14350	8	E5
LIGGETT ST	NWK	NWK	12900	82	C2
LIGHT ST	CO	WHI	13800	61	E3
LIGHT ST	CO	WHI	14500	84	A4
LIGHTCAP ST E	LAN	LAN	300	160	C4
LIGHTFOOT PL	RPV	PVP	26600	72	D3
LIGHTHALL ST	WCOV	WCOV	1300	48	F1
LIGHTHILL DR	CO	TOP		13	C5
LIGHTHOUSE CT	LA	VEN		49	D6
LIGHTHOUSE DR	CO	HAC		73	F2
LIGHTHOUSE DR	LA	HAC		74	A2
LIGHTHOUSE LN	LAN	LAN		159	D3
LIGHTHOUSE LN	PALM	PALM		184	C1
LIGHTHOUSE ST	LA	VEN		49	C6
LIGHTHOUSE ST	LA	WIL		74	B5
LIGHTHOUSE LAT	CO	MAL		112	D4
LIGHTVIEW ST	MPK	MPK		45	F3
LIGHTWOODS AV	LAN	LAN	44100	159	J5
LILA LN	LCF	LCF	1700	19	A2
LILA WY	LA	LA62		51	D3
LILAC CT	CO	SAU		124	C3
LILAC LN	CO	GLDR		87	D4
LILAC LN	GLEN	GL06	2000	25	F3
LILAC PL	LA	LA26	1200	35	D6
LILAC PL	POM	POM	900	94	B2
LILAC TER	CO	TOP		100	E6
LILAC TER	LA	LA12	800	35	D6
LILAC TER	LA	LA26	1200	35	D6
LILAC TR	CO	CAL		100	E6
LILACVIEW AV	CO	PALM	38500	172	H8
LILAC VIEW AV	PALM	PALM		183	H1
LILIANA CT	CO	LPUE		98	C4
LILIANO DR	SMAD	SMAD	1900	28	E1
LILIANO PL	SMAD	SMAD	1900	28	E1
LILIENTHAL AV	LA	LA45	8300	56	D2
LILIENTHAL LN	RB	RB	600	67	F1
LILITA ST	LYN	LYN	3600	59	C5
LILLA PL	LA	CAN		5	E2
LILLIAN CT	LCF	LCF	4500	19	C3
LILLIAN CT	LAN	LAN		160	C7
LILLIAN LN	SOG	SOG	10900	59	E5
LILLIAN PL	CO	LPUE		85	C4
LILLIAN ST	CO	LA01	5900	52	E4
LILLIAN ST	TOR	TOR	4900	67	E4
LILLIAN WY	LA	LA04	500	34	C5
LILLIAN WY	LA	LA38	700	34	C5
LILLIANNE ST	CO	ACT	34800	182	G7
LILLY AV	LB	LB08		81	B6
LILLY CT	LA	NOR		7	C4
LILLYGLEN DR	CO	CYN	15500	125	F7
LILLYVALE AV	LA	LA32	2200	36	E6
LILY WY E	LB	LB13	100	75	C4
LILY WY W	LB	LB13	100	75	C4
LILY CREST AV	LA	LA29	4600	34	F4
LIMA ST	LA	LA11	4300	52	D2

STREET	CITY	P.O. ZONE	BLOCK	PAGE	GRID
LIMA ST N	BUR	BUR	1900	17	A6
LIMA ST N	BUR	BUR	100	24	B3
LIMA ST N	SMAD	SMAD	100	28	C2
LIMA ST S	BUR	BUR	100	24	B3
LIMA ST S	SMAD	SMAD	100	28	C2
LIME AV	CO	COM	12800	65	C3
LIME AV	LB	LB02	100	75	D5
LIME AV	LB	LB05	5900	65	D4
LIME AV	LB	LB05	5300	70	D1
LIME AV	LB	LB06	1800	75	D3
LIME AV	LB	LB07	3400	70	D5
LIME AV	LB	LB13	700	75	D5
LIME AV	SGAB	SGAB		37	E5
LIME AV	SH	LB06		75	D1
LIME AV E	MON	MON	100	29	C4
LIME AV W	MON	MON	100	29	A4
LIME ST	AZU	AZU	500	86	C5
LIME ST	ING	IN01	400	56	F2
LIME WY	LB	LB02	1	75	D6
LIMECREST DR	CO	COV	19900	93	B2
LIMEDALE ST	LA	PAC	14600	8	D4
LIMEKILN CYN RD	CO	NOR		1	A2
LIMEKILN CYN RD	LA	NOR	10300	7	A2
LIME ORCHARD RD	LA	BH	9500	33	B1
LIMERICK AV	LA	CAN	8500	6	E6
LIMERICK AV	LA	CAN	6700	12	E4
LIMERICK AV	LA	CHA	10300	6	E3
LIMERIDGE DR	CO	PALM		157	J9
LIMEROCK TR	LA	CAN	8600	4	A6
LIMESTONE PL N	LA	VAN	14900	22	C4
LIMESTONE RD	CLA	CLA		96	C5
LIMETREE LN	RPV	PVP	1	77	F2
LIMEWOOD LN	LAN	LAN		159	F7
LIMEWOOD LN	LAN	LAN		159	H7
LINARD ST	SELM	ELM	11200	47	D4
LINARES AV	LB	LB14	300	76	E5
LINCOLN AV	CO	ACT		189	G3
LINCOLN AV	CO	ALT	2080	19	F3
LINCOLN AV	CO	DUA	2400	39	B1
LINCOLN AV	CO	CAST		123	A5
LINCOLN AV	CUL	CUL	4000	42	C6
LINCOLN AV	CUL	CUL		50	C1
LINCOLN AV	DBAR	WAL		97	D2
LINCOLN AV	ELM	ELM	3800	38	E5
LINCOLN AV	GLEN	GL05	300	25	E5
LINCOLN AV	LA	LA41	4400	36	A1
LINCOLN AV	LA	LA42	4700	36	A1
LINCOLN AV	LAN	LAN		160	D6
LINCOLN AV	PAS	PAS	1500	19	F6
LINCOLN AV	PAS	PAS	100	26	F2
LINCOLN AV	POM	POM	100	94	E1
LINCOLN AV	POM	POM	600	95	A1
LINCOLN AV	SOG	SOG	5700	59	E6
LINCOLN AV	TOR	TOR		68	D5
LINCOLN AV E	MTB	MTB	100	46	C6
LINCOLN AV E	MTB	MTB	800	47	A5
LINCOLN AV N	MPK	MPK	100	46	C2
LINCOLN AV S	MPK	MPK	100	46	C2
LINCOLN AV W	MTB	MTB	100	46	D6
LINCOLN BLVD	CO	MDR	4300	49	E5
LINCOLN BLVD	LA	LA45	8100	56	A2
LINCOLN BLVD	LA	MDR	4000	49	E5
LINCOLN BLVD	LA	VEN	100	49	B2
LINCOLN BLVD	SM	SM	200	40	E5
LINCOLN BLVD	SM	SM	1400	49	B2
LINCOLN CT	SM	SM	1100	40	F5
LINCOLN PL N	MON	MON	100	28	F3
LINCOLN PL S	MON	MON	100	28	F4
LINCOLN ST	CAR	CAR	300	74	B1
LINCOLN ST	LB	LB10	2100	69	F5
LINCOLN ST	LB	LB10	1500	70	A5
LINCOLN ST N	BUR	BUR	700	17	B3
LINCOLN ST N	BUR	BUR	100	24	C1
LINCOLN ST S	BUR	BUR	100	24	C1
LINCOLN TER	LA	LA69	8200	33	E3
LINCOLN WY	CO	CAST		123	A6
LINCOLN HIGH CT	LA	LA31	3800	36	B6
LINCOLN HIGH DR	LA	LA31	2400	36	B6
LINCOLN HIGH PL	LA	LA31	3800	36	B6
LINCOLN PK AV	LA	LA31	2300	36	B6
LINCOLN PK AV	LA	LA31	2000	45	B1
LINCOLN PK PL	SPAS	SPAS	1	36	E2
LINCROFT ST	CO	LPUE	18500	98	E6
LINDA AV	CER	ART		82	E6
LINDA AV	LAN	LAN		159	H4
LINDA CIR	CER	ART		82	D6
LINDA CT	PALM	PALM		183	B1
LINDA CT	WAL	WAL		93	A5
LINDA DR	TOR	TOR	19400	67	E2
LINDA DR	TOR	TOR		67	E4
LINDA LN	LAV	LAV		95A	C4
LINDA LN	SM	SM	2900	49	C2
LINDA TER	CO	COV	4500	89	A4
LINDA TER	COV	COV	200	89	A4
LINDA TER	LA	PP	16600	40	B3
LINDA WY	ARC	ARC	1200	28	F6

STREET	CITY	P.O. ZONE	BLOCK	PAGE	GRID
LINDA WY	CER	ART	17400	82	D5
LINDA WY	CUL	CUL	6000	50	D3
LINDACREST DR	BH	BH	1400	33	B3
LINDACREST DR	LA	BH	1500	33	B3
LINDA FLORA DR	LA	LA49	700	32	C2
LINDA FLORA DR	LA	LA77	1800	32	C2
LINDA GLEN DR	PAS	PAS	1100	26	D3
LINDA JOYCE DR	SCLR	SAU		124	E7
LINDALE ST	BLF	BLF	9900	66	C2
LINDALE ST	NWK	NWK	10600	66	E2
LINDALE ST	NWK	NWK	11600	82	A2
LINDA LEE AV	RM	RM	3600	38	B6
LINDALOA LN	CO	PAS	2900	20	F6
LINDA LOU AV	CO	COV	5000	89	A3
LINDAMERE DR	LA	LA77	10600	32	D3
LINDAMERE PL	LA	LA77	1600	32	D3
LINDA MESA RD	CO	LR	10900	192	B6
LINDANTE DR	WHI	WHI	8100	84	C1
LINDA RAE WY	ARC	ARC		28	E6
LINDARAXA PK N	ALH	ALH	700	37	C3
LINDARAXA PK S	ALH	ALH	700	37	C3
LINDA RIDGE RD	PAS	PAS	1100	26	D2
LINDA ROSA AV	LA	LA41	1600	26	B5
LINDA ROSA AV	PAS	PAS	200	27	D3
LINDA ROSA CT	PAS	PAS	1900	27	D3
LINDA VISTA AV	PAS	PAS		19	D6
LINDA VISTA AV	PAS	PAS	100	26	E3
LINDA VSTA AV E	ALH	ALH	100	37	C5
LINDA VSTA AV W	ALH	ALH	100	37	C5
LINDA VISTA DR	LCF	LCF	5200	19	A1
LINDA VISTA DR	LAN	LAN		160	D3
LINDA VISTA DR	WHI	WHI		85	A6
LINDA VISTA RD	GLEN	GL06	3100	26	B1
LINDA VISTA ST	WCOV	WCOV	1800	92	D2
LINDA VISTA TER	LA	LA32	3300	36	E5
LINDA VISTA WY	PAS	PAS	1000	26	D2
LINDBERGH AV	LYN	LYN	11600	59	A6
LINDBERGH LN	BELL	BELL		53	E3
LINDBERGH ST	LA	VAN	16100	15	A2
LINDBLADE DR	LA	CUL	4700	50	A3
LINDBLADE DR	LA	LA66	4200	50	A3
LINDBLADE PL	CUL	CUL	4500	50	A3
LINDBLADE ST	CUL	CUL	8900	42	C6
LINDBLADE ST	CUL	CUL	10800	50	B2
LINDBLADE ST	LA	CUL	11800	50	A3
LINDBROOK DR	LA	LA24	10300	41	E2
LINDCOVE LN	RM	RM	8700	47	A1
LINDELL AV	DOW	DOW	8800	60	D2
LINDELL AV	PR	PR	6400	54	F4
LINDELL AV	PR	PR	4100	55	A1
LINDELL AV	PR	PR	8100	60	E1
LINDEN AV	GLEN	GL01	1000	17	F6
LINDEN AV	GLEN	GL01	1000	24	F1
LINDEN AV	LA	VEN	1400	49	C3
LINDEN AV	LB	LB02	100	75	D4
LINDEN AV	LB	LB02	300	75	D5
LINDEN AV	LB	LB05	5100	70	D2
LINDEN AV	LB	LB06	2000	75	D2
LINDEN AV	LB	LB07	3100	70	D6
LINDEN AV	LB	LB13	700	75	D5
LINDEN AV E	BUR	BUR	100	24	E2
LINDEN AV W	BUR	BUR	100	24	E2
LINDEN CT	BUR	BUR	100	24	E1
LINDEN DR N	BH	BH	500	33	B6
LINDEN DR N	BH	BH	400	42	B2
LINDEN DR S	BH	BH	100	42	B1
LINDEN ST	BLF	BLF	9400	66	B3
LINDEN ST	LA	LA21	800	44	D5
LINDEN ST	LYN	LYN	11000	59	C6
LINDEN ST N	POM	POM	100	94	F4
LINDEN ST S	POM	POM	100	94	F3
LINDENCLIFF ST	CO	TOR	900	68	F6
LINDENGROVE AV	CO	LPUE	1200	97	A3
LINDENHURST AV	LA	LA36	5800	42	F1
LINDENHURST AV	LA	LA36	5700	43	A1
LINDENHURST AV	LA	LA48	6100	42	E1
LINDENVALE RD	CO	WHI	10400	55	A6
LINDENWOOD DR	CLA	CLA		91	C1
LINDENWOOD LN	LA	LA49	1000	32	A5
LINDER AL	PAS	PAS	1800	19	F6
LINDERO AV	LB	LB03	1	75	F6
LINDERO CYN RD	WLVL	THO		102	C3
LINDERO CYN RD	WLVL	THO		105	F1
LINDESMITH AV	LAM	LAM	12600	84	D6
LINDESMITH AV	WHI	WHI	10100	84	D4
LINDHALL WY	CO	WHI	14800	84	A4
LINDIE LN	LA	SF	12900	3	A3
LINDLEY AV	LA	ENC	5600	14	C5
LINDLEY AV	LA	ENC	4500	21	C3
LINDLEY AV	LA	NOR	8500	7	C6
LINDLEY AV	LA	NOR	8300	14	C5
LINDLEY AV	LA	RES	6100	14	C5
LINDLEY AV	LA	SF	10400	7	D2
LINDLEY AV	LA	TAR	5600	14	C5
LINDLEY AV	LA	TAR	4600	21	C3

INDEX

STREET	CITY	P.O. ZONE	BLOCK	PAGE	GRID
LINDLEY AV	WHI	WHI	6700	55	D5
LINDLEY PL	LA	LA13	500	44	D3
LINDO ST	LA	LA68	3100	24	B5
LINDSAY CIR	WAL	WAL		92	F5
LINDSAY LN	LA	LA39	2400	35	C3
LINDSAY WY	GLDR	GLDR		89	E1
LINDSAY CYN RD	CO	CYN		125	D3
LINDSEY AV	DOW	DOW	9000	60	E2
LINDSEY AV	PR	PR	5400	54	F3
LINDSEY AV	PR	PR	4000	55	A2
LINDSEY CT	WCOV	WCOV		92	E6
LINDSKOG DR	WHI	WHI	15700	84	C3
LINDY AV	RM	RM	2700	46	D2
LINFIELD AV	LA	SF	13500	3	B2
LINFIELD ST	AZU	AZU	18200	88	E1
LINFIELD ST	CO	AZU	18500	88	E1
LINFIELD ST	CO	GLDR	18900	88	F1
LINFIELD ST E	CO	GLDR	1700	89	D1
LINFIELD ST E	GLDR	GLDR	200	89	A1
LINFIELD ST W	GLDR	GLDR	100	89	A1
LINFORTH DR	LA	LA68	6000	24	D6
LINGARD ST E	LAN	LAN	300	160	C4
LINGARD ST W	LAN	LAN	2000	159	H4
LINK ST	LA	LA61	11400	58	B5
LINLEY LN	LA	CAN		5	E2
LINLEY ST	CO	TOR	900	68	F3
LINN AV N	SELM	ELM	2400	47	C2
LINNET ST	LA	TAR	18300	21	A1
LINNET ST	LA	WOH	19800	13	F1
LINNIE AV	LA	VEN	400	49	B6
LINNIE CANAL CT	LA	VEN	200	49	B6
LINNINGTON AV	LA	LA25	2000	42	A3
LINNINGTON AV	LA	LA64	2200	42	A3
LINS AV	CO	WHI	8200	55	B6
LINSCOTT PL	LA	LA16	4800	43	A6
LINSLEY CT	LB	LB06	1800	75	D3
LINSLEY ST	CO	COM	4000	65	C3
LINSLEY ST	COM	COM		65	C3
LINTON DR	CO	COV	3500	89	B5
LINVILLE AL	PAS	PAS	1100	27	A2
LINWALT ST	CO	RM		46	E3
LINWOOD AV	LA	LA17	1300	44	B3
LINWOOD AV	MON	MON	100	29	A3
LINWOOD DR	LA	LA27	5100	34	E2
LIONEL PL	LA	CAN	6700	12	D4
LIONEL ST	PAR	PAR	7200	65	E1
LIPTON AV	SM	SM	3000	41	B4
LIRIO LN	GLEN	GL14	3800	11	C5
LISA AV	BLF	BLF		66	B4
LISA CT	DBAR	POM		94	B6
LISA CT	LAN	LAN		160	D7
LISA LN	LA	NOR		1A	F5
LISA PL	LA	VAN	3400	22	C5
LISA ST	CO	CAST		123	J2
LISA ST	CO	PALM		183	E4
LISA ST	WCOV	WCOV		92	D5
LISA ELLEN ST	GLDR	GLDR	600	89	C2
LISA GAIL DR	SCLR	SAU		124	F5
LISA KELTON PL	SCLR	NEW		127	A4
LISBON CT	PALM	PALM		173	B9
LISBON CT	WHI	WHI	10600	55	E2
LISBON LN	LA	LA77		32	E3
LISBON WK	GLEN	GL06	2900	26	B1
LISBURN PL	LA	NOR		1	B4
LISBURN PL	LAM	LAM	13200	83	B1
LISBURN PL	LAM	LAM	11600	84	A5
LISCO PL	LA	LA46	2600	34	A1
LISCO ST	WHI	WHI	16000	84	C4
LISCOMB ST	ELM	ELM	11800	38	F6
LISETTE ST	LA	SF	17000	1	E4
LISMAN AV	CO	PALM	37800	172	C9
LISSO ST	HAW	HAW	3700	63	B2
LISTIE AV	CO	ACT		182	J9
LISTIE AV	CO	PALM		189	J1
LITA PL	LA	WOH	23000	100	F3
LITCHFIELD AV	LB	LB15	1800	76	C3
LITCHFIELD ST	PALM	PALM		183	E1
LITHUANIA DR	LA	SF	12300	1	E4
LITHUANIA PL	LA	SF	17200	1	E4
LITTCHEN ST	NWK	NWK	10900	66	F1
LITTLE ST	LA	LA17	600	44	B2
LITTLEBOW RD	RPV	PVP	5300	72	E4
LITTLEBOY DR	CO	PALM		157	G7
LTL CEDERS WY	CO	ACT		189	F4
LITTLEFIELD DR	CO	VAL		124	B7
LITTLEFIELD ST	LB	LB08	8300	81	C5
LTL HOLLOW RD	HH	CAL	24200	100	D2
LITTLEHORN DR	CO	PALM		157	J8
LITTLE JOHN LN	WLVL	THO		102	B5
LITTLE JOHN ST	BAP	BAP		39	C4
LITTLE LAKE RD	DOW	DOW	10700	60	E4
LTL LS FLRES RD	CO	TOP		114	F1
LITTLE LEAF DR	PALM	PALM		183	F3
LITTLE OAK LN	SCLR	NEW		127	B6
LITTLE OAK LN	LA	WOH		5	C6
LITTLE PARK LN	LA	LA49	200	41	B2

STREET	CITY	P.O. ZONE	BLOCK	PAGE	GRID
LITTLE QUAIL AV	DBAR	POM		97A	A2
LITTLER PL	LA	SF	12300	1	F4
LITTLE RIVER LN	CER	ART		82	B4
LITTLE ROCK	CLA	CLA		96	D5
LITTLE ROCK WY	CO	MAL	20300	115	B4
LTL ROCK WSH RD	CO	PALM	6000	184	B7
LITTLESTONE DR	CO	SGAB		38	A4
LTL SYCAMORE ST	PALM	PALM		183	J1
LTL SYCMR CY RD	CO	MAL	100	105	A3
LITTLETON PL	LCF	LCF	4500	19	A2
LTL TUJUNGA RD	CO	SAU		128	G6
LTL TUJUNGA RD	CO	SF		3	E5
LITTLE VAL RD	HH	CAL	24100	100	D1
LITTLE WOOD DR	RPV	PVP	27400	72	E5
LIVELY AV	LAN	LAN	43600	159	G6
LIVELY CT	LAN	LAN		159	G6
LIVE OAK AV	CO	ARC	4000	38	E2
LIVE OAK AV	CO	ARC	4100	39	B2
LIVE OAK AV	GLDR	GLDR	700	87	B3
LIVE OAK AV	GLDR	GLDR	100	87	B5
LIVE OAK AV	IRW	BAP	100	39	B2
LIVE OAK AV	SGAB	SGAB	500	37	D3
LIVE OAK AV	TEC	ARC	10000	38	B3
LIVE OAK AV	TEC	TEC	9000	38	B3
LIVE OAK AV E	ARC	ARC	100	38	E2
LIVE OAK AV E	SGAB	SGAB	100	37	E3
LIVE OAK AV E	SGAB	SGAB	8500	38	A3
LIVE OAK AV W	ARC	ARC	100	38	E2
LIVE OAK AV W	SGAB	SGAB	100	37	E3
LIVE OAK CT	CO	CAL		100A	E5
LIVE OAK CTO	CO	CLA		95A	F5
LIVE OAK DR	CO	CLA	3900	90	F1
LIVE OAK DR	CO	MAL		114	E2
LIVE OAK DR	POM	POM		90	E2
LIVE OAK DR E	LA	LA68	2300	34	D2
LIVE OAK DR W	LA	LA68	2100	34	D2
LIVE OAK LN	CDY	BELL		53	E6
LIVE OAK LN	IRW	DUA		39	D2
LIVE OAK ST	BG	BELL	5600	53	E6
LIVE OAK ST	BG	BELL	5600	59	E1
LIVE OAK ST	BG	BELL	6600	60	A1
LIVE OAK ST	CDY	BELL	3600	53	B6
LIVE OAK ST	CO	HPK	2400	52	F6
LIVE OAK ST	CO	HPK	2700	53	A6
LIVE OAK ST	CO	SGAB	8200	37	E3
LIVE OAK ST	CO	SGAB	8600	38	A3
LIVE OAK ST	HPK	HPK	3200	53	A6
LIVE OAK CYN RD	CO	LAV		90	F1
LIVE OAK CYN RD	LAV	LAV		95A	F6
LIVE OAK CIR DR	CO	MAL		107	F6
LIVE OAK MDW RD	CO	MAL		114	E2
LIVE OAKS AV	PAS	PAS	500	26	E4
LIVE OAK S C RD	CO	CYN	27700	125	D9
LIVE OAK S C RD	CO	CYN		128	E1
LIVE OAK VW AV	LA	LA41	5200	25	F4
LIVERMONT LN	DUA	DUA	800	29	F4
LIVERMORE TER	LA	LA42	200	36	C1
LIVERPOOL CT	SAD	SAD		89	C5
LIVERPOOL DR	PAS	PAS	1300	26	D1
LIVERY WY	CO	CYN		125	D7
LIVEWOOD LN	CO	HAC		73	F1
LIVIA AV	TEC	TEC	6300	38	B1
LIVINGSTON AV	LA	LA31		35	F5
LIVINGSTON DR	LB	LB03	3700	76	A6
LIVINGSTON WY	LA	LA46		33	E3
LIVIUS WY	CO	WAL	1800	97	B4
LIVONIA AV	LA	LA34	1900	42	D4
LIVONIA AV	LA	LA35	1400	42	D3
LIVORNO DR	LA	PP	16700	40	B4
LIZ CT	LA	CAN		5	E3
LLANO DR	LA	WOH	4800	13	B2
LLEWELLYN ST	LA	LA12	100	44	E1
LLOYD AV	LA	NHO	7800	16	A2
LLOYD LN	LA	LA68		34	B2
LLOYD PL	WHOL	LA69	8900	33	D5
LLOYDCREST DR	LA	BH	9300	33	B3
LLOYD HGHTON PL	SCLR	NEW	23400	127	B5
LLOYDS CT	PALM	PALM		171	F5
LOADSTONE DR	LA	VAN	3300	22	C5
LOBDELL PL	LA	LA26	1500	35	C5
LOBELIA WY	LA	LA49		30	E5
LOBER PL	CO	SGAB	6500	38	A1
LOBIVIA WY	PAR	PAR		65	E4
LOBO CT	LAN	LAN		160	E4
LOBO ST	CO	PALM		182	G7
LOBO CANYON RD	CO	AGO	31000	106	A1
LOBOS RD	LA	WOH	4100	13	C4
LOBO VISTA RD	CO	AGO		106	C1
LOBROOK DR	RPV	PVP	27900	72	C4
LOCH ALENE AV	PR	PR	6300	54	E5
LOCH AVON DR	CO	WHI	10100	55	B3
LOCH AVON DR	PR	PR	9200	55	A3
LOCH AVON DR	WHI	WHI	10800	55	B4
LOCHGLEN CT	CO	LPUE		98	A5
LOCHGREEN DR	LA	TAR		21	A5
LOCHINVAR DR	PR	PR	9200	54	F5

STREET	CITY	P.O. ZONE	BLOCK	PAGE	GRID
LOCHINVAR ST	CO	WHI	10500	55	A6
LOCHINVAR ST	PR	PR	9200	54	F5
LOCHLEVEN ST	CO	GLDR	19200	86	F5
LOCHLEVEN ST	CO	GLDR	19200	87	A5
LOCH LOMOND DR	CO	WHI	10200	55	B3
LOCH LOMOND DR	PR	PR	8300	54	E3
LOCH LOMOND DR	PR	PR	9200	55	A3
LOCH LOMOND DR	WHI	WHI	10800	55	B4
LOCHMERE AV	CO	LPUE	500	98	E1
LOCHMOOR RD	SCLR	VAL		127	A2
LOCHNEVIS AV	NWK	NWK	14100	82	C2
LOCHRIN LN	LA	SF	13400	2	F1
LOCHVALE DR	RPV	PVP	6000	72	D5
LOCINA LN	PALM	PALM		171	E4
LOCKE AV	LA	LA32	3500	36	D4
LOCKEARN ST	LA	LA49	700	32	B6
LOCKE HAVEN ST	PAS	PAS	400	26	E5
LOCKERBIE CT	GLEN	GL08	3800	18	C2
LOCKERBIE LN	GLEN	GL08	3700	18	C2
LOCKFORD ST	LA	LA35	9600	42	C3
LOCKHART AV	CO	PALM	36000	184	B5
LOCKHAVEN AV	LA	LA41	4800	25	F4
LOCK HAVEN WY	CLA	CLA		90	F1
LOCKHEED AV	CO	WHI	5700	55	B3
LOCKHEED AV	WHI	WHI		55	B3
LOCKHEED DR	LA	BUR	7500	17	A3
LOCKHEED WY	PALM	PALM	500	172	C5
LOCKHEED VW DR	BUR	BUR		17	E3
LOCKHURST DR	LA	CAN	6400	5	E5
LOCKHURST DR	LA	WOH	5900	5	E6
LOCKHURST DR	LA	WOH	5200	100	F1
LOCKLAND DR	LA	LA08	3700	51	B2
LOCKLAND PL	LA	LA08		51	B2
LOCKLAYER ST	SAD	SAD	700	89	E4
LOCKLENNA LN	RPV	PVP		72	C6
LOCKNESS AV	LA	GAR		68	E6
LOCKNESS AV	LA	HAC	23100	68	E6
LOCKNESS PL	LA	GAR		68	E6
LOCKPORT PL	SFS	SFS	11000	61	C4
LOCKRIDGE RD	LA	NHO	11900	23	C6
LOCKSLEY DR	CO	PAS	3500	28	A5
LOCKSLEY PL	LA	LA39	2600	35	C2
LOCKSLEY PL	LA	LA68	5800	34	D1
LOCKVIEW LN	CO	TOP		109	C6
LOCKWOOD AV	LA	LA29	4200	34	F4
LOCKWOOD RD	CO	MAL	26200	113	B2
LOCKWOOD RD	GLEN	GL08	1800	18	F5
LOCUST AV N	COM	COM	100	65	B3
LOCUST AV N	LB	LB02	1	75	C5
LOCUST AV N	LB	LB05	4900	70	C2
LOCUST AV N	LB	LB06	1800	75	C2
LOCUST AV N	LB	LB07	3100	70	C6
LOCUST AV N	LB	LB13	700	75	C3
LOCUST AV S	COM	COM	100	65	B3
LOCUST AV S	LB	LB02	1	75	C5
LOCUST CIR	COM	COM	500	65	B3
LOCUST DR	CO	CAL		100	E5
LOCUST ST	LA	LA65	500	35	F4
LOCUST ST	PAS	PAS	600	27	B3
LOCUST ST N	ING	IN01	100	57	A1
LOCUST ST N	POM	POM	100	94	E3
LOCUST ST S	ING	IN01	100	57	A1
LOCUST ST S	POM	POM	100	94	E3
LOCUST RDG CIR	SCLR	VAL		124	B5
LODESTAR DR	SCLR	SAU		124	E4
LODESTONE LN	CO	LPUE	15700	85	D4
LODGE AV	LA	LA42	5300	36	C3
LODGE POLE RD	DBAR	POM		97A	B3
LODI PL	LA	LA38	1100	34	C4
LODI CREEK RD	SAD	SAD		90	A1
LODOSA DR	WHI	WHI	15500	84	B1
LOFIELD CT	CO	PAS	3500	28	A4
LOFTHILL DR	LAM	LAM	14900	83	C3
LOFTUS DR	RM	RM	8600	38	C6
LOFTUS DR	SGAB	SGAB	7800	37	E6
LOFTUS ST	ELM	ELM	9800	38	C6
LOFTY GROVE DR	RPV	PVP	6900	72	C4
LOFTY HILL DR	CO	MAL		106	A4
LOFTYVIEW DR	TOR	TOR	2400	73	B4
LOGAN ST	LA	LA26	1100	35	C6
LOGAN ST	LAV	LAV		90	C2
LOGAN ST	POM	POM	2200	91	A5
LOGANBERRY DR	LAM	LAM	12600	84	D6
LOGANDALE DR	LA	LA68	6300	34	C1
LOGANRITA AV	ARC	ARC	900	29	A6
LOGANRITA AV	ARC	ARC	1500	39	A1
LOGANRITA AV	CO	ARC	2500	39	A1
LOGANSIDE DR	CO	LA47	1800	57	D5
LOGDELL AV	SCLR	NEW	24200	127	C5
LOGGERS LN	WCOV	WCOV		98	E2
LOGUE AV	LAN	LAN		160	C4
LOGUE CT	LAN	LAN		160	C3
LOGWOOD RD	WLVL	THO		102	D3
LOHART AV	MTB	MTB	300	54	D2
LOHENGRIN ST	CO	LA47	1800	57	D4
LOHMAN LN	SPAS	SPAS		36	E1

STREET	CITY	P.O. ZONE	BLOCK	PAGE	GRID
LOIS AV	LA	SP	900	78	F2
LOIS CIR	LAV	LAV		90	B2
LOIS LN	LA	SP		78	D3
LOIS ST	WCOV	WCOV		92	D5
LOLA AV	PAS	PAS	200	27	D3
LOLETA AV	LA	LA41	4600	26	B4
LOLETA PL	LA	LA41	4600	26	B5
LOLINA LN	LA	LA46	7500	23	F6
LOLITA ST	WCOV	WCOV	800	92	D2
LOMA AV	CO	SGAB	6700	38	B1
LOMA AV	LAV	LAV		90	C2
LOMA AV	LB	LB03	100	76	A6
LOMA AV	LB	LB04	700	76	A6
LOMA AV	LB	LB14	300	76	A5
LOMA AV	MON	MON	1100	29	A5
LOMA AV	RM	RM	4000	38	B5
LOMA AV	SELM	ELM	2000	47	B2
LOMA AV	TEC	TEC	4900	38	B2
LOMA DR	CO	WHI		61	E6
LOMA DR	HB	RB	1200	62	C6
LOMA DR	HB	RB	500	67	C1
LOMA DR	LA	LA17	300	44	B2
LOMA DR	LA	LA26	100	44	B2
LOMA LN	BAP	BAP	3700	39	C6
LOMA PL	LA	LA26	200	44	B2
LOMA RD	MTB	MTB		46	D6
LOMA ST	RB	RB	1200	67	E3
LOMA ALTA DR E	CO	ALT	100	20	A3
LOMA ALTA DR W	CO	ALT	100	19	F3
LOMACITAS LN	WHI	WHI		84	D1
LOMA CONTENTA	CO	SAU		188	C1
LOMA CREST	GLEN	GL05	1600	25	E6
LOMA CREST DR	CO	ALT	1	20	A3
LOMA LADA DR	LA	LA65	3400	35	F2
LOMA LINDA	CO	SAU		188	C1
LOMA LINDA AV	LA	LA27		34	E3
LOMA LINDA DR	BH	BH	1100	33	B4
LOMA LISA LN	ARC	ARC	900	28	C3
LOMA METISSE RD	CO	MAL		108	C6
LOMAS VERDES	LA	SP		78	C5
LOMA VERDE AV	LA	CAN	7200	12	D3
LOMA VERDE DR	ARC	ARC	1000	28	B3
LOMA VERDE MTWY	CO	CAST		123	A5
LOMA VERDE ST	MPK	MPK	700	46	B3
LOMA VIEW DR	CO	ALT	3400	20	A3
LOMA VISTA	LAN	LAN		171	F1
LOMA VISTA AV	BELL	BELL	6200	53	B5
LOMA VISTA AV	HPK	HPK	5900	53	B4
LOMA VISTA AV	MAY	MAY	5100	53	B4
LOMA VISTA AV	VER	LA58	4500	53	B3
LOMA VISTA CT	SPAS	SPAS	1100	36	E2
LOMA VISTA DR	ALH	ALH	2500	46	A1
LOMA VISTA DR	BH	BH	2000	33	C2
LOMA VISTA DR	GLEN	GL08		18	F6
LOMA VISTA DR	GLEN	GL08		25	F1
LOMA VISTA DR	LAN	LAN		160	D3
LOMA VISTA DR	LB	LB13	700	75	B4
LOMA VISTA DR	LCF	LCF	4500	19	B2
LOMA VISTA PL	BELL	BELL	6400	53	B5
LOMA VISTA PL	LA	LA39	2100	35	C4
LOMA VISTA ST	COV	COV	100	88	E6
LOMA VISTA ST	ELS	ELS	100	56	A6
LOMA VISTA ST	PAS	PAS	100	27	C2
LOMA VISTA ST	POM	POM		90	C6
LOMA VISTA ST	WCOV	WCOV	1300	88	C6
LOMAX LN	RB	RB	1600	67	D1
LOMAY PL	PAS	PAS	1300	26	D1
LOMBARD AV	LA	PP	300	40	D4
LOMBARD ST	POM	POM	100	94	E2
LOMBARDY BLVD	LA	LA32	2400	36	D6
LOMBARDY DR	LCF	LCF	1900	19	A2
LOMBARDY PL	SMAR	PAS	600	27	E5
LOMBARDY RD	CO	PAS	2700	27	F5
LOMBARDY RD	CO	PAS	3300	28	A5
LOMBARDY RD	PAS	PAS	1300	27	C5
LOMBARDY RD	SMAR	PAS	1700	27	C5
LOMELA CT	LAM	LAM	15700	83	C3
LOMELI LN	LAV	LAV	2300	90	D3
LOMINA AV	LB	LB08	3000	71	D5
LOMINA AV	LB	LB15	2000	76	D2
LOMINA AV	LKD	LKD	4100	71	D3
LOMIRA ST	CO	COV	20500	89	B5
LOMITA AV E	GLEN	GL05	100	25	D4
LOMITA AV W	GLEN	GL04	100	25	C4
LOMITA BLVD	CO	HAC	800	73	C1
LOMITA BLVD	LA	HAC	1300	73	C1
LOMITA BLVD	LOM	LOM	1700	73	C1
LOMITA BLVD	TOR	TOR		67	F5
LOMITA BLVD	TOR	TOR		68	A6
LOMITA BLVD	TOR	TOR	2500	73	C1
LOMITA BLVD E	CAR	CAR	100	74	B2
LOMITA BLVD E	LA	WIL	100	74	C2
LOMITA BLVD W	CAR	CAR	100	74	B2
LOMITA BLVD W	LA	WIL	100	74	B2
LOMITA CT	PAS	PAS	1400	37	B1
LOMITA DR	CO	CAST	29000	123	B5

STREET	CITY	P.O. ZONE	BLOCK	PAGE	GRID
LOMITA DR	LOM	LOM	24100	73	D1
LOMITA DR	PAS	PAS		37	B1
LOMITA ST	ELS	ELS	100	56	B6
LOMITA ST	LA	LA19	4500	43	B3
LOMITA ST N	BUR	BUR	300	17	D6
LOMITA ST N	BUR	BUR	100	24	D1
LOMITA ST S	BUR	BUR	200	24	D1
LOMITA PARK PL	LOM	LOM	2000	73	D1
LOMITAS AV	BH	BH	9400	33	A6
LOMITAS AV	CO	LPUE	13600	48	B4
LOMITAS DR	LA	LA32	3700	36	C4
LOMO DR	RPV	PVP	27900	72	C4
LOMOND AV	LA	LA24	400	32	F6
LOMORA AV	PAS	PAS	600	27	F2
LOMPOC ST	LA	LA65	2700	25	F5
LONDELIUS ST	LA	CAN	20100	6	E6
LONDELIUS ST	LA	NOR	19700	6	F6
LONDELIUS ST	LA	NOR	17400	7	E6
LONDELIUS ST	LA	SF	15800	8	A6
LONDON PL	CO	VAL		126	H3
LONDON ST	LA	LA26	2500	35	B6
LONDONDERRY PL	LA	LA46	1300	33	D4
LONDONDERRY VW	LA	LA69	1300	33	D4
LONDRINA LN	CO	TOR		69	A6
LONECREST DR	CO	LPUE	15800	85	E4
LONE EAGLE RD	WAL	WAL		93	B5
LONE GROVE WY	LCF	LCF		19	C1
LONE HILL AV	CO	GLDR	1300	87	E6
LONE HILL AV	CO	GLDR		89	D2
LONE HILL AV N	GLDR	GLDR	100	87	E6
LONE HILL AV N	SAD	SAD	100	89	D3
LONE HILL AV S	GLDR	GLDR	100	87	E6
LONE HILL AV S	GLDR	GLDR	1000	89	D2
LONE HILL AV S	SAD	SAD	100	89	D3
LONEOAK AV	LAN	LAN	43800	159	J6
LONE OAK DR	LA	SF		1	C4
LONE OAK RD	CO	PEAR		185	C6
LONE PINE LN	LCF	LCF	4500	18	F2
LONE RIDGE PL	CO	WHI	15800	84	C5
LONE RIDGE PL	LAM	LAM	15700	84	C5
LONE RIDGE RD	POM	POM		94	D6
LONEROCK ST	SCLR	CYN	27400	124	J8
LONESS AV S	CO	COM	14400	64	C2
LONESTAR PL	CO	CAST		123	E3
LONE STAR ST	CO	LPUE	14000	48	B5
LONE TREE DR	CO	PALM		157	J8
LONE VALLEY DR	RPV	PVP	4700	72	F4
LONG LN	IND	LPUE	100	48	C4
LONG PT	LB	LB03		76	C6
LONG ST	LA	LA43	6000	51	B5
LONG ST N	ING	IN02	700	51	B5
LONGACRE AV	LA	SF	12000	1	C4
LONGACRES AV	PR	PR		47	B6
LONG BEACH AV	LA	LA21	900	44	D6
LONG BEACH AV	LA	LA58	1900	44	D6
LONG BEACH AV	LA	LA58	2000	52	D4
LONG BEACH BLVD	LB	LB02	100	75	C5
LONG BEACH BLVD	LB	LB02	300	75	C5
LONG BEACH BLVD	LB	LB05	5900	65	B5
LONG BEACH BLVD	LB	LB05	4600	70	C3
LONG BEACH BLVD	LB	LB06	1800	75	C3
LONG BEACH BLVD	LB	LB07	3000	70	C6
LONG BEACH BLVD	LB	LB13	700	75	C5
LONG BEACH BLVD	LYN	LYN	9900	59	A3
LONG BEACH BLVD	LYN	LYN	12300	65	B1
LONG BEACH BLVD	SOG	SOG	8100	58	F2
LONG BEACH BLVD	SOG	SOG	8600	59	A2
LONG BEACH BL N	COM	COM	100	65	B2
LONG BEACH BL S	COM	COM	100	65	B2
LONG BEACH FRWY	CMRC	LA40		53	E2
LONG BEACH FRWY	LB	LB15		65	C6
LONG BEACH FRWY	LB	LB15		70	B4
LONG BEACH FRWY	LB	LB15		75	B4
LONG BEACH FRWY	MPK	MPK		45	E3
LONG BEACH FRWY	SOG	SOG		59	E4
LONGBOW CT	LA	VAN	3400	22	C5
LONGBOW DR	LA	LA77		22	B5
LONGBOW DR	LA	VAN	15300	22	C5
LONG CANYON RD	BRAD	DUA	100	29	D3
LONGDALE LN	LA	LA68	3000	24	B6
LONGDEN AV	CO	ARC	800	38	E1
LONGDEN AV	CO	ARC	900	39	A1
LONGDEN AV	CO	MON	100	39	A1
LONGDEN AV	CO	SGAB	8200	37	F1
LONGDEN AV	IRW	BAP	100	39	A1
LONGDEN AV	IRW	DUA	100	39	A1
LONGDEN AV	TEC	SGAB	8600	38	B1
LONGDEN AV	TEC	TEC	8800	38	B1
LONGDEN AV E	ARC	ARC	100	38	E1
LONGDEN AV W	ARC	ARC	100	38	E1
LONGDEN DR E	SGAB	SGAB	100	37	E2
LONGDEN DR W	SGAB	SGAB	100	37	E2
LONGDON	WCOV	WCOV		92	D4
LONGFELLOW AV	HB	RB	100	62	B5
LONGFELLOW AV	MB	MB	500	62	C5

STREET	CITY	P.O. ZONE	BLOCK	PAGE	GRID
LONGFELLOW DR	MB	MB	1100	62	C5
LONGFELLOW PL	CO	NEW		126	H3
LONGFELLOW PL	HB	RB	1	62	B5
LONGFELLOW ST	LA	LA42	5100	36	C3
LONGFELLOW ST	SM	SM	3100	49	B2
LONGFORD ST	LA	SF	10800	9	E1
LONGHILL DR	MPK	MPK	1400	45	F3
LONGHILL DR	RPV	PVP	27400	72	E5
LONGHILL WY	MPK	MPK	1000	45	F3
LONGHORN RD	SAD	SAD		90	A1
LONGHORN RD	SAD	SAD		95A	A6
LONGHORN CT	PALM	PALM		171	D9
LONGLEAF DR	LAM	LAM	12600	61	F6
LONGLEY WY	ARC	ARC	200	38	D2
LONGLEY WY	ARC	ARC	2600	38	D2
LONGMEADOW AV E	CO	PALM	17000	175	B5
LONGMONT AV	CO	SGAB	6300	37	F1
LONG OAK DR	SCLR	NEW		127	G1
LONGRIDGE AV	LA	NHO	6000	16	A5
LONGRIDGE AV	LA	NHO	3200	23	A4
LONGRIDGE AV	LA	VAN	6000	16	A5
LONGRIDGE AV	LA	VAN	4200	23	A4
LONGRIDGE PL	LA	VAN	3300	23	A5
LONGRIDGE TER	LA	VAN	3200	23	A6
LONGRDG ESTS DR	LA	NHO		23	A5
LONGVALE AV	LYN	LYN	11800	59	A6
LONG VALLEY RD	HH	CAL	23600	100	D2
LONG VALLEY RD	LA	WOH	23400	100	D2
LONGVIEW AV	LA	LA68	6300	34	C2
LONGVIEW DR	DBAR	POM		97A	B2
LONGVIEW RD	CO	LAN	38000	174	E3
LONGVIEW RD	CO	PALM	37000	174	E9
LONGVIEW RD	CO	PALM		185	D9
LONGVIEW RD	CO	PEAR	33400	185	D9
LONGVIEW RD	CO	PEAR	32800	192	D2
LONGVIEW RD	CO	VALY		192	D2
LONGVIEW VLY RD	LA	VAN	3600	22	D5
LONGWOOD AV	CLA	CLA	1300	91	C2
LONGWOOD AV	LA	LA05	700	43	B3
LONGWOOD AV	LA	LA16	1900	43	A5
LONGWOOD AV	LA	LA19	900	43	B3
LONGWOOD LN	PAS	PAS	500	26	F3
LONGWOOD PL	LA	LA19	1100	43	B2
LONGWORTH AV	DOW	DOW	10800	60	F5
LONGWORTH AV	LKD	LKD	20300	71	E2
LONGWORTH AV	NWK	NWK	11800	60	F5
LONGWORTH AV	NWK	NWK	12800	66	F1
LONGWORTH AV	SFS	SFS	9400	60	F4
LONGWORTH DR	LA	LA49	1300	40	F3
LONNA LINDA DR	LB	LB15	5500	76	C4
LONZO ST	LA	TU	7200	10	F1
LONZO ST	LA	TU		11	A2
LOOKABOUT RD	CO	PALM		157	G7
LOOKNG GLASS DR	DBAR	POM		94	B5
LOOKOUT DR	CO	AGO		107	A3
LOOKOUT DR	LA	LA12	600	44	E1
LOOKOUT DR	POM	POM		90	D6
LOOKOUT RD	CO	MAL	1800	113	B2
LOOKOUT RD	SCLR	SAU		127	E1
LOOKOUT TR	CO	SF	10800	3	E5
LOOKOUT TR	CO	TOP	19500	109	B5
LOOKOUT MTN AV	LA	LA46	8100	33	D2
LOOM PL	LA	VAN	15400	22	B5
LOOMIS CT	PALM	PALM		183	F2
LOOMIS ST	LKD	LKD	2400	70	F3
LOOMIS ST	LKD	LKD	3400	71	A3
LOOP AV	CO	CYN		128	C2
LOOSCHEN RD	CO	MAL		111	D4
LOOSMORE ST	LA	LA65	2600	35	F4
LOPE LN	CO	GLDR	1200	89	D1
LOPE LN	GLDR	GLDR	1400	87	D6
LOPEZ AV	CO	LA22	500	45	E3
LOPEZ ST	LA	WOH	21100	13	C2
LOPEZ CANYON RD	CO	SF	100	3	C4
LOQUAT LN	PALM	LAN		171	B2
LOQUAT ST	CO	ALT	1100	19	E2
LORA ST	TEC	TEC	10600	38	D3
LORADO WY	CO	LA43	3700	51	B3
LORAE PL	LA	LA68	5800	34	D1
LORAIN RD	CO	SGAB	8200	27	F6
LORAIN RD	SMAR	PAS	1000	37	C2
LORAINE AV	CO	GLDR	500	87	C6
LORAINE AV N	GLDR	GLDR	100	87	C6
LORAINE AV S	GLDR	GLDR	100	87	C6
LORAINE ST	WCOV	WCOV		92	E5
LORAINE ST E	GLEN	GL07	400	25	D2
LORAINE ST W	GLEN	GL02	200	25	C2
LORALYN DR	ARC	ARC	1	28	E2
LORANNE AV	POM	POM	100	95	A1
LORAY PL E	BAP	BAP	14300	39	E5
LORBU RD	CO	MAL	22300	114	D4
LORCA RD	LAM	LAM	13000	83	B1
LORD ST	LA	LA33	900	45	A2
LORDS RD	CO	SAU		188	C1
LOREE WY	CO	CAL		108	B5
LORELEI AV	LB	LB08	4700	71	C3

STREET	CITY	P.O. ZONE	BLOCK	PAGE	GRID
LORELEI AV	LKD	LKD	5900	66	C6
LORELEI AV	LKD	LKD	4900	71	C2
LORELLA AV	CO	GAR	15700	64	B3
LOREN AV N	AZU	AZU	700	86	B5
LOREN LN	CO	RM		46	E3
LOREN ST	CO	LA63	4300	45	E2
LORENA CT	CO	CAL		100	C5
LORENA ST	ARC	ARC	500	28	E4
LORENA ST N	LA	LA63	100	45	B5
LORENA ST S	LA	LA23	600	45	B5
LORENA ST S	LA	LA23	1200	53	B1
LORENA ST S	LA	LA63	100	45	B5
LORENCITA DR	CO	COV	19700	93	A2
LORENE ST	WHI	WHI	10500	55	C3
LORENZA CT	CO	SGAB	5400	38	A3
LORENZANA DR	LA	WOH	20200	13	E2
LORENZO CT	CO	CAL		100	D6
LORENZO DR	LA	LA64	10300	42	B4
LORENZO DR	LA	LA68	2300	34	C2
LORENZO PL	LA	LA64	10400	42	B4
LORENZO ST	POM	POM		95	B3
LORETA WK	LB	LB03	100	80	C1
LORETO DR	GLEN	GL07	1300	25	E2
LORETO ST	LA	LA65	400	36	A4
LORETTA DR	LAM	LAM	14900	84	B6
LORETTA LN	SCLR	CYN		125	D7
LORETTO CT	CLA	CLA		91	B1
LORI LN	CO	RM	1300	46	F4
LORI ANN AV	AZU	AZU	600	86	C4
LORI ANN LN	CER	ART	17400	82	C5
LORICA ST	RM	RM	9600	38	C5
LORIKEET LN	CO	VAL		126	G1
LORILLARD ST	LA	SF	16600	1	E6
LORIMER AV	LAN	LAN	44800	159	H4
LORIN AV	SELM	ELM	2400	47	D2
LORINDA DR	GLEN	GL06	900	25	E2
LORINE LN	CO	MAL		108	C6
LORING AV	LA	LA24	500	41	E1
LORING AV	LA	LA77	100	32	E5
LORNA LN	LA	LA49	500	41	C2
LORNA ST	TOR	TOR	5000	67	E3
LORNE ST	LA	CAN	19900	12	E2
LORNE ST	LA	NHO	11600	16	C2
LORNE ST	LA	NOR	17400	14	D2
LORNE ST	LA	RES	17800	14	D2
LORNE ST	LA	SV	10300	16	E2
LORNE ST	LA	SV	10300	17	A2
LORNE ST	LA	VAN	16400	14	E2
LORNE ST	LA	VAN	14200	15	D2
LORRAINE BLVD	LA	LA04	200	43	D2
LORRAINE BLVD	LA	LA05	600	43	D2
LORRAINE BLVD	LA	LA20	300	43	D2
LORRAINE RD	RPV	SP	4000	78	D2
LORRAINE ST	LAN	LAN		159	H7
LORRAINE ST	LYN	LYN	10700	58	F4
LORRAINE WK	LA	LA03	6200	52	B5
LORRI WY	WAL	WAL		92	F5
LOS ADORNOS WY	LA	LA27	5100	34	E2
LS ALAMITOS CIR	LB	LB04		76	B3
LOS ALIMOS ST	LA	CHA	19600	6	F2
LOS ALIMOS ST	LA	NOR	18000	7	A2
LOS ALIMOS ST	LA	SF	16500	7	D2
LOS ALIMOS ST	LA	SF	14900	8	C2
LOS ALISOS	SPAS	SPAS	300	36	E3
LOS ALISOS CIR	NWK	NWK		61	A5
LOS ALISOS ST	LAM	LAM		83	C1
LOS ALTOS AV	ARC	ARC	400	38	D2
LOS ALTOS AV	LB	LB04	700	76	C4
LOS ALTOS AV	LB	LB14	300	76	C5
LOS ALTOS AV	LB	LB15	1000	76	C4
LOS ALTOS DR	CO	LPUE	15100	85	D3
LOS ALTOS DR	PAS	PAS	100	26	E4
LOS ALTOS PL	LA	LA68	6800	34	B2
LOS ALTOS PZ	LB	LB15	5200	76	B4
LOS AMIGOS AV E	MTB	MTB	100	46	E6
LOS AMIGOS AV W	MTB	MTB	100	46	E6
LOS AMIGOS ST	CO	GL14	2300	11	E6
LOS AMIGOS ST	CO	GL14	2300	18	E1
LOS AMIGOS ST	GLEN	GL14	3200	11	C5
LOS AMIGOS ST	LCF	LCF		11	F6
LOS AMIGOS ST	LCF	LCF	2000	18	F1
LOS ANGELES AV	MON	MON	100	29	B5
LOS ANGELES AV	MON	MON		29	C5
LOS ANGELES AV	MTB	MTB	100	54	D2
LOS ANGELES ST	BAP	BAP	13200	39	C4
LOS ANGELES ST	BLF	BLF	9000	66	B4
LOS ANGELES ST	GLEN	GL04	700	25	C5
LOS ANGELES ST	IRW	BAP	15300	88	A4
LS ANGELES ST N	LA	LA12	100	44	D3
LS ANGELES ST S	CO	LA61	12200	58	B6
LS ANGELES ST S	LA	LA03	5800	52	B4
LS ANGELES ST S	LA	LA11	1900	44	C5
LS ANGELES ST S	LA	LA12	100	44	D3
LS ANGELES ST S	LA	LA13	300	44	D3
LS ANGELES ST S	LA	LA14	600	44	C4
LS ANGELES ST S	LA	LA15	900	44	C4

STREET	CITY	P.O. ZONE	BLOCK	PAGE	GRID
LOS ARBOLES LN	SMAR	PAS	500	27	E5
LOS ARCOS ST	LB	LB15	5600	76	D2
LOS BENTOS DR	CO	LPUE	2000	85	E3
LOS BERROS DR	CO	LPUE	18500	98	E4
LOS BONITOS WY	LA	LA27	5100	34	E2
LS CABALLROS WY	LA	LA	5100	34	E2
LS CERRILLOS DR	WCOV	WCOV	2900	92	F2
LOS CERRITOS RD	GLDR	GLDR	600	87	C6
LS CERITS PK PL	LB	LB07		70	C5
LOS CERROS DR	DBAR	POM	1800	97	D4
LOS CODONA AV	TOR	TOR	23100	68	A6
LOS CODONA AV	TOR	TOR	23800	73	A2
LOS COYOTES AV	LAM	LAM	11800	84	B6
LOS COYOTES BL	LKD	LKD	19700	81	A2
LOS COYOTES DR	POM	POM		94	B4
LS COYOTES DIAG	LB	LB08	3000	71	D6
LS COYOTES DIAG	LB	LB15	4500	76	B2
LS COYOTES DIAG	LKD	LKD	4100	71	D6
LOS DIEGOS WY	LA	LA	5100	34	E2
LOS ENCANTOS WY	LA	LA	5100	34	E2
LOS ENCINOS RD	GLEN	GL08	1800	18	F5
LOS ENCINOS WY	LA	WOH	23300	100	F2
LOS FELIS DR	POM	POM		94	C4
LOS FELIZ	GLDR	GLDR		88	F2
LOS FELIZ BLVD	LA	LA27	4400	34	E2
LOS FELIZ BLVD	LA	LA27	3600	35	A2
LOS FELIZ BLVD	LA	LA39	2800	25	B6
LOS FELIZ BLVD	LA	LA39	3200	35	A2
LOS FELIZ PL	LA	LA39	4100	25	C6
LOS FELIZ RD E	GLEN	GL05	100	25	C6
LOS FELIZ RD W	GLEN	GL04	100	25	C6
LOS FELIZ PARK	LA	LA27	3300	35	B2
LOS FLORES AV	LAM	LAM	15200	84	B6
LOS FLORES BLVD	LYN	LYN	2700	59	A5
LOS FLORES ST	LB	LB15	5100	76	B3
LOS FLORES ST	POM	POM	2100	91	A5
LS FRANCSCOS WY	LA	LA	5100	34	E2
LOS FUENTES RD	LAM	LAM	14300	82	F3
LOS GATOS DR	WAL	WAL		93	A6
LOS GRANDES WY	LA	LA	5100	34	E2
LOS HERMOSOS WY	LA	LA27	5100	34	E2
LOS HIGOS ST	ALH	ALH	1	37	C5
LOS JORDANS RD	CO	SAU		181	C7
LOS LAURELES	SPAS	SPAS	200	36	E2
LOS LIONES DR	LA	PP	300	40	A4
LOS LOTES AV	WHI	WHI	14900	84	A2
LOS MACHOS DR	CO	LPUE	18500	98	E4
LOS MOLINOS ST	CO	LPUE	15300	85	C4
LOS NIETOS DR	LA	LA27	4100	35	A2
LOS NIETOS RD	CO	WHI	13200	61	C2
LOS NIETOS RD	SFS	SFS	10900	61	A1
LOS OLAS WY	CO	MAL		110	B5
LOS OLIVOS	LA	SF		8	C1
LOS OLIVOS DR	CO	SGAB	8500	37	F1
LOS OLIVOS DR	SGAB	SGAB	500	37	E1
LOS OLIVOS LN	CO	GL14	2600	11	E6
LOS OLIVOS LN	CO	GL14	2400	18	E1
LOS OLIVOS LN	GLEN	GL14	3000	11	D5
LOS OLIVOS ST	LA	SF	15000	8	C2
LOS PADRES DR	CO	LPUE	1700	98	E4
LOS PADRES PL	POM	POM		94	B4
LOS PADRINOS DR	DOW	DOW	12200	59	E4
LOS PALACIOS DR	CO	LPUE	18000	98	D3
LOS PALOS ST	LA	LA23	1000	53	C1
LOS PINETOS RD	CO	NEW		127	F7
LOS PINOS DR	WAL	WAL		93	A6
LOS PINOS PL	POM	POM		94	B5
LOS REYES AV	LAM	LAM	11900	84	B6
LOS ROBLES	LAV	LAV		95A	C6
LOS ROBLES AV	CO	LPUE	14400	85	C1
LOS ROBLES AV	MON	MON		28	F5
LOS ROBLES AV	SMAR	PAS	1600	37	B1
LOS ROBLES AV N	PAS	PAS		20	A6
LOS ROBLES AV N	PAS	PAS	1	27	A1
LOS ROBLES AV S	PAS	PAS	1	27	A6
LOS ROBLES PL	POM	POM	1200	90	D6
LOS ROBLES ST	LA	LA41	4900	26	C5
LOS ROGUES DR	SCLR	SAU		124	C5
LOS ROSAS ST	LA	CAN	23900	5	E1
LOS SANTOS DR	LB	LB15	5600	76	C3
LOS SERRANOS DR	CO	WHI	10400	55	D2
LOST CANYON RD	CO	CYN	14600	125	F7
LOST CREEK RD	CO	SAU		125	A2
LOST HILLS RD	CO	AGO		100A	E4
LOST HILLS RD	CO	CAL		100A	E5
LOS TIGRES DR	SCLR	SAU	22300	124	C7
LOS TILOS RD	LA	LA68	6900	34	B2
LOSTINE AV	CAR	CAR	21300	69	D4
LOST OAK CT	CO	CAL		100A	E5
LOS TOROS AV	PR	PR	4600	54	F3
LOS TOROS AV	PR	PR	4400	55	A2
LOST RIDGE RD	DBAR	POM		97A	B1
LOST RIVER DR	DBAR	POM	21000	97	E4
LOST SPRINGS DR	CO	CAL		100A	E5
LOST SPRINGS RD	SCLR	CYN	27700	125	B8
LOST TRAIL DR	WAL	WAL		93	C3

STREET	CITY	P.O. ZONE	BLOCK	PAGE	GRID
LOS VERDES DR	RPV	PVP		77	C1
LOTONE ST	MON	MON	400	29	A2
LOTT AV	CO	LA63	1300	45	D3
LOTTA AV	SOG	SOG	8900	59	D2
LOTTA DR	CO	LA63	1300	45	D2
LOTUS AL	CO	PAS	1800	20	D6
LOTUS AV N	CO	PAS	1	28	A5
LOTUS AV N	CO	SGAB	6800	28	A6
LOTUS AV N	CO	SGAB	6700	38	A1
LOTUS AV S	CO	PAS	1	28	A5
LOTUS CIR	SAD	SAD		90	B4
LOTUS LN	SMAD	SMAD		28	D1
LOTUS ST	LA	LA65		36	A4
LOTUS GARDEN DR	CO	CYN	28900	125	E7
LOTUS PETAL CT	CO	CYN		125	F5
LOU LN	PALM	PALM		183	H2
LOU DILLON AV	CO	LA01	7600	52	E6
LOU DILLON AV	CO	LA01	7800	58	E1
LOU DILLON AV	CO	LA59	11600	58	E5
LOU DILLON AV	LA	LA02	10300	58	E4
LOU DILLON AV	LA	LA59	10700	58	E4
LOUDON LN	IND	LPUE	13100	48	B2
LOUELLA AV	LA	VEN	1500	49	D3
LOUIS AV	CO	CYN	29500	125	C5
LOUIS AV	CO	WHI	11500	61	D5
LOUIS PL	CO	LA22	5100	53	F1
LOUISA AV E	WCOV	WCOV	1000	88	C5
LOUISA AV W	WCOV	WCOV	1000	88	B5
LOUISE AV	ARC	ARC	1100	28	E6
LOUISE AV	ARC	ARC	1700	38	E2
LOUISE AV	CUL	LA66	12700	49	F3
LOUISE AV	CUL	LA66	11900	50	A3
LOUISE AV	LA	ENC	5600	14	E4
LOUISE AV	LA	ENC	4400	21	E3
LOUISE AV	LA	LA66	12300	49	F3
LOUISE AV	LA	LA66	11900	50	A3
LOUISE AV	LA	NOR	8500	7	E5
LOUISE AV	LA	NOR	7600	14	E4
LOUISE AV	LA	SF	11400	1	E6
LOUISE AV	LA	SF	10300	7	E2
LOUISE AV	LA	VAN	6400	14	E4
LOUISE AV	LAN	LAN		159	H4
LOUISE AV	LYN	LYN	11000	59	D6
LOUISE AV	LYN	LYN	11800	65	D1
LOUISE AV	TOR	TOR	4900	67	F6
LOUISE AV N	AZU	AZU	500	86	C6
LOUISE AV S	AZU	AZU	100	88	C2
LOUISE AV S	LYN	LYN	1500	59	D6
LOUISE DR	LCF	LCF	5000	19	A1
LOUISE ST	BLF	BLF	9000	66	B2
LOUISE ST	LYN	LYN	11000	59	B6
LOUISE ST E	LB	LB05	1	70	C2
LOUISE ST N	GLEN	GL06	100	25	C5
LOUISE ST N	GLEN	GL07	900	25	C5
LOUISE ST S	GLEN	GL05	100	25	C4
LOUISE ST W	LB	LB05	1	70	C2
LOUISE TER	GLEN	GL07	200	25	C1
LOUISIANA	WCOV	WCOV		92	E4
LOUISIANA AV	LA	LA25	10300	42	A3
LOUKELTON ST	CO	LPUE	16500	92	B5
LOUKELTON ST	LPUE	LPUE	15400	48	F5
LOUKELTON ST	LPUE	LPUE	15700	92	A5
LOUMONT ST	CO	WHI	700	48	A5
LOUVRE ST	LA	PAC	12600	3	B6
LOUVRE ST	LA	PAC	13200	8	F1
LOUVRE ST	LA	PAC	12900	9	A1
LOVAGE CT	SCLR	SAU		124	D5
LOVE LN	PALM	PALM		172	B5
LOVEJOY AV	CO	PALM	38800	174	F6
LOVEJOY ST	CO	ARC	800	38	F2
LOVEJOY ST	CO	ARC	1000	39	A2
LOVEJOY ST	POM	POM	2300	91	A5
LOVELACE AV	LA	LA07	1900	44	B5
LOVELAND DR	LA	LA65	2200	35	F2
LOVELAND ST	BG	BELL	5500	53	E5
LOVELAND ST	BG	BELL	6300	54	A6
LOVELANE PL	LA	LA64	10100	42	B5
LOVELL AV	ARC	ARC	1200	28	C6
LOVETT PL	LA	ENC	16200	22	A3
LOVETT ST	CMRC	LA23	4400	53	D1
LOVETT ST	CO	LA23	4300	53	D1
LOVILA LN	CO	ALT	2000	20	B6
LOWDER ST	LA	LA77		32	E3
LOWE DR	LAM	LAM	15000	83	A3
LOWE ST	LA	LA39	1800	35	D3
LOWE ST	LB	LB08	7400	81	A6
LOWELL AV	CLA	CLA	1300	91	C2
LOWELL AV	GLEN	GL14	3800	11	B6
LOWELL AV	GLDR	GLDR	100	86	F5
LOWELL AV	LA	LA32	2800	36	E4
LOWELL AV	SMAD	SMAD	1	28	C2
LOWELL ST	CO	COV	400	88	F5
LOWEMONT ST	BLF	BLF	10300	66	D3
LOWEMONT ST	NWK	NWK	11500	66	F3
LOWEMONT ST	NWK	NWK	11600	82	A3
LOWEN ST	LA	WIL	1000	74	A2

STREET	CITY	P.O. ZONE	BLOCK	PAGE	GRID
LOWENA DR	LB	LB03	200	75	E5
LOWER RD	AVA	AVA		77	B5
LOWER TER	AVA	AVA		77	B5
LOWER AZUSA RD	ARC	ARC	12300	39	A4
LOWER AZUSA RD	ELM	ELM	9600	38	F4
LOWER AZUSA RD	ELM	ELM	11600	39	A4
LOWER AZUSA RD	IRW	BAP	12400	39	A4
LOWER AZUSA RD	RM	RM	9000	38	B4
LOWER AZUSA RD	TEC	TEC	9300	38	B4
LWR BLACKWTR CY	RH	PVP		73	A5
LWR PAS L CRSTA	PVE	PVP		72	C3
LWR PASTURE RD	CO	LAV		95A	F4
LOWHILL DR	CO	PALM		157	F9
LOWMAN AV	DOW	DOW	8500	60	C1
LOWMAN AV	PR	PR	8200	54	D6
LOWNES PL	POM	POM	1200	94	D4
LOWRIDGE PL	CO	SAU		124	B2
LOWRY RD	LA	LA27	3200	35	A1
LOWTREE AV	LAN	LAN	44400	159	J5
LOXLEY PL	DBAR	WAL		97	D3
LOY LN	LA	LA41	2300	25	F5
LOYAL TR	LA	LA68	6900	24	A6
LOYALTON DR	WAL	WAL	20400	93	B4
LOYNES DR	LB	LB14		76	D5
LOYOLA BLVD	LA	LA45	8900	56	A2
LOYOLA CT	CLA	CLA		91	C1
LOYTAN ST	TOR	TOR	25200	73	B2
LUANA LN	CO	MONT	2200	18	F2
LUANDA ST	LA	SF	11700	3	D6
LUANN DR	PALM	PALM		172	B5
LUBAO AV	LA	CAN	8500	6	F6
LUBAO AV	LA	CAN	6400	12	F5
LUBAO AV	LA	CHA	9500	6	F4
LUBAO AV	LA	NOR	8800	6	F6
LUBAO AV	LA	WOH	5700	12	F6
LUBAO AV	LA	WOH	5100	13	F2
LUBAO PL	LA	CHA	11900	6	F3
LUBEC ST	BG	BELL	5500	53	E6
LUBEC ST	DOW	DOW	7300	60	B1
LUBEN LN	ARC	ARC		38	E1
LUBICAN ST	BAP	BAP	13400	39	C5
LUBLIN ST	POM	POM		90	F3
LUCANIA DR	RPV	PVP	30600	78	C3
LUCAS AV	LA	LA17	300	44	C3
LUCAS AV	LA	LA26	100	44	C3
LUCAS LN	CER	ART	12900	82	C5
LUCAS PL	CER	ART	13400	82	D5
LUCAS ST	CER	ART	11300	66	F5
LUCAS ST	CER	ART	12600	82	C5
LUCAS ST	SF	SF	700	2	F4
LUCASZ CT	LAN	LAN		160	E8
LUCAYAN DR	CO	WHI	4400	55	D1
LUCCA DR	LA	PP	13500	40	F2
LUCE PL	PR	PR	9300	47	B6
LUCE PL	PR	PR	9300	55	B1
LUCERA CIR	PVE	PVP	4300	73	A2
LUCERNE AV	CUL	CUL	9000	42	D6
LUCERNE AV	LA	CUL	11100	50	B3
LUCERNE AV	LA	LA16	2300	43	B5
LUCERNE BLVD N	LA	LA04	100	34	C6
LUCERNE BLVD S	LA	LA04	100	43	C1
LUCERNE BLVD S	LA	LA05	600	43	C1
LUCERNE BLVD S	LA	LA19	900	43	C2
LUCERNE BLVD S	LA	LA20	300	43	C1
LUCERNE CT	SCLR	VAL		127	A1
LUCERNE ST	CAR	CAR	22000	69	D5
LUCERO AV	LA	PP	500	40	A3
LUCERO AV	LAV	LAV		90	C2
LUCERO PL	LA	PP	500	40	A3
LUCIA AV	WHI	WHI		61	F2
LUCIA AV N	RB	RB	100	67	D2
LUCIA AV S	RB	RB	100	67	E3
LUCIA PL	LA	SV	8700	9	E6
LUCIA WALK	LB	LB03	5700	80	C1
LUCIEN ST E	CO	COM	2000	64	E1
LUCILE AV	LA	LA26	600	35	A5
LUCILE AV	LA	LA39	1800	35	B4
LUCILE ST	LA	CUL	11800	50	B4
LUCILLE AV	BELL	BELL		53	B5
LUCILLE AV	LA	LA66	12900	49	D3
LUCILLE AV	LA	VEN	900	49	D3
LUCILLE AV	LB	LB14	300	76	B5
LUCILLE AV	LOM	LOM	24300	73	D1
LUCILLE AV	TOR	TOR	23800	73	D1
LUCILLE AV	WCOV	WCOV	900	92	A3
LUCILLE CT	CO	CYN		125	E7
LUCILLE ST	ARC	ARC	1	28	E5
LUCILLE TR	LA	LA46	8000	33	E2
LUCINDA DR	CO	WHI	14700	84	A6
LUCKY RD	CO	ACT		182	D6
LUCRETIA AV	LA	LA26	1500	35	C5
LUCY CT	SCLR	SAU		124	D5
LUDDINGTON ST	LA	SV	10900	9	E6
LUDDINGTON ST	LA	SV	11200	16	D1
LUDELL ST	BG	BELL	5500	53	E6

1990 LOS ANGELES COUNTY STREET INDEX

STREET	CITY	P.O. ZONE	BLOCK	PAGE	GRID
LUDER AV	ELM	ELM	2600	47	D2
LUDER AV	SELM	ELM	1800	47	D3
LUDGATE DR	CO	AGO		100A	E5
LUDLOW	LA	SF		8	C1
LUDLOW ST	LA	NOR	18100	7	C1
LUDLOW ST	LA	SF	16600	7	D1
LUDLOW ST	LA	SF	15500	8	B1
LUELLA DR	CO	LA63	1300	45	D3
LUFKIN ST	WCOV	WCOV	1800	48	E2
LUGANO PL	LA	LA68	3300	24	C6
LUGAR DE ORO DR	SCLR	VAL		124	C7
LUGGER WY	LB	LB13		75	A4
LUGO AV	LYN	LYN	3600	59	B5
LUGO AV	PAR	SOG	7200	65	E1
LUGO ST	LA	LA23	2800	53	A1
LUGO ST	PAR	SOG	7100	65	D1
LUGO WY	CUL	CUL	10600	50	D3
LUGO PARK AV	LYN	LYN	11600	59	D6
LUIS DR	AGH	AGO		102	E3
LUISA ST	LA	LA31	2100	45	A1
LUJON ST	CO	LPUE	14600	85	C1
LUJON ST	CO	LPUE		85	E2
LUKAY ST	CO	WHI	13400	61	D5
LUKENS PL	GLEN	GL06	100	25	E4
LUKENS TRUCK TR	CO			M	B3
LULL ST	LA	BUR	9900	17	A2
LULL ST	LA	CAN	19900	12	A2
LULL ST	LA	NHO	11500	16	B2
LULL ST	LA	NOR	17400	14	E2
LULL ST	LA	RES	17900	14	C2
LULL ST	LA	SV	10700	16	E2
LULL ST	LA	VAN	13400	15	B2
LULLABY LN	LA	VAN	8000	15	E1
LULU CARR RD	CO	MAL		111	B1
LULU GLEN DR	LA	LA46	7800	33	E1
LUMBER ST E	CO	LAN	4600	160	J4
LUMBER ST W	LAN	LAN	7000	158	J4
LUMBER ST W	LAN	LAN	1100	159	J4
LUMBER ST W	LAN	LAN	4000	159	A4
LUMBER ST W	LAN	LAN	400	160	B4
LUNA PL	LA	SF	12300	1	E4
LUNA PL	LB	LB02	400	75	C5
LUNA TR	CO	TOP		109	B2
LUNADA CIR	RPV	LOM	26800	73	E4
LUNADA LN	LB	LB03		76	D5
LUNADA BAY PZ	PVE	PVP	700	72	A5
LUNADA RIDGE DR	RPV	PVP	28200	72	D5
LUNAR DR	MPK	MPK	1500	46	A4
LUNA VISTA DR	LA	PP		40	B2
LUND ST	LA	WOH	23600	100	E2
LUNDAHL DR	PR	PR	9500	54	F6
LUNDENE DR	CO	WHI	10200	55	C2
LUNDY AV	PAS	PAS	1700	20	A6
LUNITA RD	CO	MAL		111	D5
LUNSFORD DR	LA	LA41	5100	26	C4
LUPIN LN	GLDR	GLDR	300	87	D6
LUPIN LN	WCOV	WCOV	700	92	E2
LUPIN TER	LA	LA31	300	36	A5
LUPIN TR	SMAD	SMAD		20A	D3
LUPINE AV	MPK	MPK	1400	46	C4
LUPINE DR	TOR	TOR	22600	67	F5
LUPINE LN	CO	CAL		100A	E6
LUPINE PL	LAV	LAV		90	A3
LUPINE PL	MPK	MPK	300	46	C4
LUPINE ST	PALM	PALM		173	A9
LUPINE ST	PALM	PALM		184	A1
LUPIN HILL RD	HH	CAL	24100	100	D1
LUPIN HILL RD	LHH	LAH		85	D6
LUPITA DR	SCLR	VAL		127	B1
LURA ST	PAS	PAS	1000	27	C4
LURAY ST	LB	LB07	600	70	D3
LURIE PL	LA	NOR	10800	7	B2
LURING DR	GLEN	GL06	700	25	E2
LURLINE AV	LA	CAN	8500	6	D6
LURLINE AV	LA	CAN	6700	12	D2
LURLINE AV	LA	CHA	9100	6	D3
LUSE TANK RD	CO	TOP		109	C1
LUSK AV	CER	ART	19400	71	F2
LUSS DR	CO	CYN		125	C4
LUTGE AV	BUR	BUR	300	24	E2
LUTHER DR	SCLR	CYN	27200	124	J9
LUTHER ST	LA	LA31	3500	36	C5
LUTON DR	GLEN	GL06	500	25	E3
LUVERNE PL	LA	ENC	17200	21	E3
LUXOR ST	DOW	DOW	7000	59	F3
LUXOR ST	DOW	DOW	7300	60	A4
LUXOR ST	SOG	SOG	6000	59	F3
LUY RD	LA	LA34	3600	50	A1
LUY ST	MPK	MPK	1800	46	C4
LUZON DR	SCLR	SAU		124	J3
LUZZETTE ST	WAL	WAL		97	B1
LYALL AV	CO	COV	4300	88	C4
LYALL AV	WCOV	WCOV	300	88	C6
LYANS DR	LCF	LCF	1900	18	F1
LYCEUM AV	CUL	LA66	4000	49	E3
LYCEUM AV	LA	LA66	3800	49	E3

STREET	CITY	P.O. ZONE	BLOCK	PAGE	GRID
LYCOMING ST	DBAR	WAL	20600	97	C2
LYDIA DR	LA	LA23	3100	45	A6
LYDIA ST	WCOV	WCOV		92	D5
LYDLE CREEK PL	WAL	WAL		92	F5
LYFORD DR	CO	LAV		90	B2
LYFORD DR	LAV	LAV	2500	90	B2
LYFORD DR	SAD	LAV	900	90	B1
LYLE ST	LA	SF	13800	2	D3
LYLE ST	WHI	WHI	10200	55	B2
LYLEDALE ST	TEC	TEC	9100	38	B3
LYMAN AV	CO	COV	4800	89	C3
LYMAN AV	COV	COV	900	89	C4
LYMAN AV	GLDR	GLDR	1200	89	C2
LYMAN PL	LA	LA27	1300	34	F4
LYMAN PL	LA	LA29	1100	34	F4
LYMAN ST	CO	COV	4000	89	C4
LYMAN ST	COV	COV	400	89	C4
LYNALAN AV	CO	WHI	6800	55	C5
LYNBROOK AV	CO	LPUE	1900	85	E3
LYND AV	CO	ARC		38	F2
LYND AV	CO	ARC	4000	39	A2
LYNDA LN	BG	BELL	7900	59	E1
LYNDA LN	WCOV	WCOV		92	B4
LYNDALE AV	POM	POM	2400	94	A2
LYNDBROOK CT	WLVL	THO	31900	102	A4
LYNDCREST ST	CO	PEAR		185	C4
LYNDHURST AV	CO	LPUE	1300	85	F2
LYNDON DR	CO	CAL		108	D2
LYNDON ST	HB	RB	1	67	C2
LYNDON ST	SPAS	SPAS	800	36	F2
LYNDON WY	ARC	ARC	1100	28	D6
LYNDORA ST	DOW	DOW	7800	59	F5
LYNDORA ST	DOW	DOW	8300	60	A6
LYNDORA ST	LYN	LYN	3800	59	C5
LYNDORA ST	NWK	NWK	10500	60	D6
LYNDORA ST	NWK	NWK	11800	61	A6
LYNETTE LN	CO	SAU		124	D4
LYNGLEN DR	GLEN	GL06	1500	25	E3
LYNMARK ST	LAM	LAM	14000	82	E1
LYNN CIR	LAV	LAV		90	D2
LYNN CT	WAL	WAL		93	C3
LYNN CT	WCOV	WCOV		92	D5
LYNN LN	CO	AGO		107	B1
LYNN LN	RM	RM		47	A1
LYNN ST	LA	LA42	4800	36	B2
LYNNFIELD CIR	LA	LA32	2700	36	D5
LYNNFIELD ST	LA	LA32	4400	36	C5
LYNNGROVE DR	MB	MB	1100	62	D4
LYNNHAVEN LN	LCF	LCF	700	19	C2
LYNOAK DR	CLA	CLA		90	F3
LYNOAK DR	CO	CLA		90	F3
LYNOAK DR	POM	POM	3600	90	F3
LYNRIDGE DR	WAL	WAL		92	F5
LYNROSE ST	CO	ARC	11100	38	E2
LYNROSE ST	TEC	TEC	10000	38	C3
LYNTON AV	CAR	CAR	21200	69	A4
LYNTON AV	LA	WIL	1400	74	A2
LYNVUE PL	POM	POM	500	94	A2
LYNWOOD RD	LYN	LYN	3000	58	F5
LYNWOOD RD	LYN	LYN	2600	59	A5
LYON AV	PALM	PALM		183	F2
LYON ST	LA	LA12	700	44	E2
LYONS AV	CO	NEW		126	J4
LYONS AV	SCLR	NEW	22500	127	B4
LYONS RANCH RD	CO	NEW		127	A5
LYONWOOD AV	DBAR	WAL		97	D2
LYRIC AV	LAN	LAN		159	B8
LYRIC AV	LA	LA27	2100	35	B2
LYRIC AV	LA	LA39	2000	35	B2
LYSANDER DR	CAR	CAR	17500	64	C5
LYSTER AV	LA	NOR		1	B6
LYTELLE PL	LA	LA65	2700	25	F6

M

STREET	CITY	P.O. ZONE	BLOCK	PAGE	GRID
M ST E	LA	WIL	100	74	D3
M ST W	LA	WIL	100	74	D3
MABBIT RD	CO	PALM		190	B2
MABEL AV	SELM	ELM	9200	47	B2
MABEL AV E	MPK	MPK	700	46	D2
MABEL AV W	MPK	MPK	800	46	B2
MABEN AV	SCLR	CYN	27200	124	G7
MABERY RD	LA	SM	100	40	D5
MACADAM CT	AGH	AGO		100A	A2
MACADAM CT	AGH	AGO		102	F2
MACAFEE RD	TOR	TOR	4600	67	E6
MACAL PL	LA	LA68	6300	34	C2
MACALESTER DR	WAL	WAL	100	93	B6
MACALESTER PL	CLA	CLA		96	C6
MACAPA DR	LA	LA68	7000	34	B1
MACARTHUR AV	LA	SP	500	78	E2
MACARTHUR BLVD	LA	SP		79	A5
MACARTHUR ST	RPV	SP	1800	78	D2
MACAW ST	LAM	LAM		82	F3
MACBETH ST	LA	LA26	1400	35	D6
MACCULLOCH DR	LA	LA49	600	32	B6

STREET	CITY	P.O. ZONE	BLOCK	PAGE	GRID
MACDEVITT ST	BAP	BAP	14100	39	E6
MACDEVITT ST	WCOV	WCOV	2200	39	F6
MACDONALD AV	LA	LA49	700	32	B6
MACDONALD ST	PAS	PAS	200	26	E1
MACE PL	CO	LA01	7200	52	D6
MACENTA LN	DBAR	POM		94	B6
MACEO ST	LA	LA65	2600	35	F4
MACFARLANE DR	LAN	LAN		159	G5
MACFARLANE DR	LA	WOH	22200	13	B2
MACHADO AV	CO	LA63	1300	45	D3
MACHADO DR	LA	VEN	700	49	C2
MACHREA ST	LA	TU	7600	10	E3
MACIEL AV	CAR	LB10	20900	69	F3
MACKAY LN	RB	RB	1100	62	E6
MACKEL TER	WAL	WAL	19600	97	A2
MACKENNS GLD AV	CO	LAN	16500	175	A5
MACKESON CT	CAR	CAR	17900	64	C6
MACKLIN AV	SCLR	CYN	27800	125	D7
MACLAREN ST	CO	LPUE	18400	98	E2
MACLAREN ST	LPUE	LPUE	16800	98	B1
MACLAY AV N	SF	SF	100	2	E6
MACLAY AV S	SF	SF	100	2	D6
MACLAY ST	LA	SF	12500	3	A4
MACLAY ST	LA	SF	14400	8	D1
MACMILLN RCH RD	CO	CYN		128	D2
MACNEIL ST	LA	SF	12900	3	A4
MACNEIL ST	LA	SF	14600	8	D1
MACNEIL ST	SF	SF	100	2	E6
MACNEIL ST	SF	SF	1200	3	A5
MACODA LN	CO	CHA		1A	B5
MACOMBER AL	PAS	PAS	900	27	A2
MACON ST	LA	LA65	2700	35	E3
MACY ST E	LA	LA12	100	44	E2
MACY ST E	LA	LA33	1000	44	E2
MACY ST W	LA	LA12	100	44	E2
MAD RD	SCLR	NEW		127	G2
MADDEN AV	LA	LA43	7000	51	C5
MADDOX ST	LB	LB10	1200	70	B5
MADEIRA CT	CER	ART		81	D2
MADELEINE WY	POM	POM	800	95	A2
MADELENA DR	LHH	LAH	100	84	E3
MADELIA AV	LA	VAN	3900	22	D4
MADELINE DR	MON	MON	100	29	C3
MADELINE DR	PAS	PAS	200	26	E6
MADELINE CV DR	RPV	PVP		72	C5
MADERA AV	LA	LA39	3100	35	C2
MADERA DR	CO	LAV		90	C1
MADERA ST	LB	LB15	6400	76	E3
MADERA ST	SGAB	SGAB	300	37	E3
MADERO CT	WCOV	WCOV		92	F2
MADERO ST	MTB	MTB		46	E5
MADGE AV	SOG	SOG	10600	59	E5
MADIA ST	PAS	PAS	1100	26	D1
MADIGAN DR	SCLR	CYN		124	H9
MADILL AV	CO	COV	3600	89	B5
MADISON AV	CO	ACT		189	G3
MADISON AV	CO	ALT	2000	20	B5
MADISON AV	CUL	CUL	3900	42	C6
MADISON AV	CUL	CUL	4000	50	C1
MADISON AV	LAV	LAV		90	E4
MADISON AV	POM	POM	300	94	F1
MADISON AV	SOG	SOG	8100	59	A3
MADISON AV	WHI	WHI	8300	61	E1
MADISON AV E	MTB	MTB	100	54	D1
MADISON AV N	LA	LA04	200	34	F6
MADISON AV N	LA	LA29	700	34	F6
MADISON AV N	MON	MON	100	28	F3
MADISON AV N	PAS	PAS		20	B6
MADISON AV N	PAS	PAS	100	27	B5
MADISON AV S	LA	LA04	100	34	F6
MADISON AV S	MON	MON	100	28	F4
MADISON AV S	PAS	PAS	100	27	B5
MADISON AV W	MTB	MTB	100	54	D1
MADISON CT	TOR	TOR	3500	73	A2
MADISON RD	LCF	LCF	3700	19	B5
MADISON ST	CAR	LB10	2600	69	F4
MADISON ST	CAR	LB10	2700	70	A4
MADISON ST	CO	CAST	28700	123	C2
MADISON ST	PALM	PALM		183	J1
MADISON ST	PAR	PAR	7300	65	E3
MADISON ST	TOR	TOR	20200	68	A3
MADISON ST	TOR	TOR	20500	68	A3
MADISON ST	TOR	TOR	23200	68	A6
MADISON ST	TOR	TOR	23500	73	A2
MADISON WY	CO	CAST	30000	123	C3
MADISON WY	GLEN	GL05	300	25	D6
MADLER ST	CO	ACT	2800	189	G1
MADLOY ST	CO	CAST		123	B2
MADONA ST	CO	LPUE	18200	98	E3
MADORA AV	LA	CAN	7200	12	F3
MADRE LN	SMAD	SMAD	400	28	D1
MADRE ST	CO	PAS	1	28	A5
MADRE VISTA RD	CO	ALT	1000	20	B5
MADRID AV	TOR	TOR	100	68	C4
MADRID CT	PALM	PALM		173	B9
MADRID CT	WHI	WHI	10600	55	C2

STREET	CITY	P.O. ZONE	BLOCK	PAGE	GRID
MADRID LN	LB	LB03		76	D5
MADRILLO CT	PAS	PAS	2700	27	E5
MADRIS AV	NWK	NWK	14100	82	B3
MADRONA AV	TOR	TOR		68	B5
MADRONO LN	LA	LA77	300	32	E5
MAEMURRAY DR	LA	LA41	5400	26	B4
MAESTRO AV	LA	CAN	7600	5	F2
MAESTRO LN	PALM	LAN		171	D4
MAESTRO PL	LA	CAN	23400	5	F2
MAGDA CT	CO	PALM		184	B5
MAGDALENA DR	SCLR	VAL		124	A1
MAGDALENA DR	WCOV	WCOV		92	F5
MAGDALENA ST	LA	LA12	1300	44	E1
MAGEE AV	LA	PAC	11500	3	A6
MAGELLAN DR	LA	TOR	19500	68	F2
MAGELLAN RD	ARC	ARC	200	28	B5
MAGIC MTN LN	SCLR	CYN	27800	125	B8
MAGIC MTN PKWY	CO	VAL	25000	123	J8
MAGIC MTN PKWY	SCLR	VAL	23300	124	A8
MAGINN DR	GLEN	GL02	1700	18	C6
MAGINN PL	GLEN	GL02		18	C6
MAGNA CARTA RD	CO	CAL		13	B4
MAGNA VSTA AV E	ARC	ARC	100	28	E6
MAGNA VSTA AV W	ARC	ARC	100	28	E6
MAGNA VISTA CT	PALM	PALM		172	D7
MAGNA VISTA ST	PAS	PAS	2700	27	F2
MAGNETIC TER	LA	LA69	1600	33	C3
MAGNIS ST	ARC	ARC	800	38	F1
MAGNIS ST	CO	ARC	1200	39	A1
MAGNOLIA	CO	LP48		98	F3
MAGNOLIA AV	GAR	GAR		63	F3
MAGNOLIA AV	GLEN	GL04	100	25	C5
MAGNOLIA AV	ING	IN01		56	E2
MAGNOLIA AV	LA	LA05	700	44	A2
MAGNOLIA AV	LA	LA06	400	44	A4
MAGNOLIA AV	LA	LA07	1900	44	A5
MAGNOLIA AV	LAV	LAV	2300	90	C3
MAGNOLIA AV	LB	LB13	700	75	C2
MAGNOLIA AV	LYN	LYN	3300	59	A6
MAGNOLIA AV	MB	MB	1100	62	C4
MAGNOLIA AV	PAS	PAS	500	27	A5
MAGNOLIA AV	WCOV	WCOV	600	92	E2
MAGNOLIA AV	WHI	WHI	5400	55	D4
MAGNOLIA AV N	LB	LB02	100	75	C5
MAGNOLIA AV N	LB	LB02	300	75	C5
MAGNOLIA AV N	LB	LB06	3000	70	C6
MAGNOLIA AV N	LB	LB06	1800	75	C2
MAGNOLIA AV N	MON	MON	100	29	A5
MAGNOLIA AV S	LB	LB02	10	75	C5
MAGNOLIA AV S	MON	MON	100	29	A5
MAGNOLIA BLVD	LA	ENC	15400	21	D2
MAGNOLIA BLVD	LA	NHO	10300	23	A2
MAGNOLIA BLVD	LA	VAN	13300	22	D2
MAGNOLIA BLVD	LA	VAN	12900	23	A2
MAGNOLIA BLVD E	BUR	BUR	100	17	E5
MAGNOLIA BLVD W	BUR	BUR	100	17	E5
MAGNOLIA BLVD W	BUR	BUR	1200	24	A2
MAGNOLIA CIR	WAL	WAL		93	D6
MAGNOLIA CT	COM	COM	100	64	E3
MAGNOLIA CT	LA	LA07	2100	44	A4
MAGNOLIA DR	LA	LA46	8400	33	E3
MAGNOLIA DR	LAN	LAN		160	D6
MAGNOLIA DR	MPK	MPK	1700	46	D4
MAGNOLIA DR N	SGAB	SGAB	600	37	D2
MAGNOLIA LN	CO	POM		93	E2
MAGNOLIA LN	SPAS	SPAS	600	36	F1
MAGNOLIA LN E	ARC	ARC	800	29	A6
MAGNOLIA ST	ELM	ELM	11600	47	E2
MAGNOLIA ST	SPAS	SPAS	400	36	E1
MAGNOLIA ST E	COM	COM	100	64	E3
MAGNOLIA ST E	POM	POM	100	90	E4
MAGNOLIA ST W	COM	COM	300	64	E3
MAGNOLIA ST W	POM	POM	100	90	E4
MAGNOLIA TER	WHI	WHI		55	D3
MAGNOLIA WY	CO	SAU		124	C2
MAGNOLIA GN DR	SCLR	VAL		124	B4
MAGUIRE DR	CO	MAL	4000	112	E3
MAHALO PL	COM	COM		64	D5
MAHANNA AV	LB	LB13	1000	75	E4
MAHANTONGA TER	LA	LA42	700	26	C6
MAHAR AV	LA	WIL	800	74	D4
MAHOGANY	WCOV	WCOV		98	F1
MAHOGANY CT	DBAR	WAL		97	C3
MAHOGANY TR	LA	TU	10100	11	B3
MAHONIA AV	PALM	PALM	37200	184	A2
MAHONY DR	LA	SUN	10500	9	F2
MAHONY PL	LA	SF		1	D4
MAIDEN LN	AVA	AVA	100	77	B5
MAIDEN LN	CO	ALT	1900	20	C4
MAIDEN LN	LA	SF	16800	1	F5
MAIDEN LN	MTB	MTB	200	54	E1
MAIDSTONE AV	ART	ART	17500	66	F5
MAIDSTONE AV	NWK	NWK	11100	60	F6
MAIDSTONE AV	NWK	NWK	13500	66	F2
MAIDSTONE AV	SFS	SFS	10800	60	F4
MAIDSTONE CIR	LA	HAC		73	E1

STREET	CITY	P.O. ZONE	BLOCK	PAGE	GRID
MAIDSTONE PL	LA	HAC	23700	73	E1
MAIE AV	CO	LA01	7200	52	D6
MAIE AV	CO	LA01	7900	58	D2
MAIE AV	CO	LA02	8600	58	D2
MAIE AV	LA	LA02	9200	58	D3
MAIE AV	LA	LA59	11200	58	D5
MAIE AV N	COM	COM	100	64	D3
MAIE AV S	COM	COM	100	64	D3
MAIMONE AV	SAD	SAD	100	89	E3
MAIN ST	BUR	BUR	400	24	D1
MAIN ST	CO	TOR	20300	69	B1
MAIN ST	CUL	CUL	3800	42	C6
MAIN ST	ELS	ELS	100	56	A5
MAIN ST	LA	LA31	2000	45	A1
MAIN ST	LA	VEN	200	49	B3
MAIN ST	LPUE	LPUE	15700	48	F6
MAIN ST	LPUE	LPUE	16200	92	B6
MAIN ST	LPUE	LPUE	16900	98	B1
MAIN ST	SM	SM	1600	49	A2
MAIN ST	SOG	SOG	5400	59	E6
MAIN ST E	ALH	ALH	1	37	B4
MAIN ST E	SGAB	SGAB	100	37	E3
MAIN ST N	LA	LA12	100	44	E1
MAIN ST N	LA	LA31	1700	44	E1
MAIN ST N	POM	POM	100	94	E3
MAIN ST S	CAR	CAR	20000	69	B1
MAIN ST S	CAR	CAR	23500	74	B2
MAIN ST S	CAR	GAR	16100	64	B6
MAIN ST S	CAR	GAR	18400	69	B1
MAIN ST S	CO	GAR	14300	64	B6
MAIN ST S	CO	LA61	12000	58	B5
MAIN ST S	CO	LA61	12800	64	B2
MAIN ST S	LA	LA03	5800	52	B4
MAIN ST S	LA	LA03	7900	58	B2
MAIN ST S	LA	LA07	1900	44	B5
MAIN ST S	LA	LA07	3300	52	B4
MAIN ST S	LA	LA12	100	44	D3
MAIN ST S	LA	LA13	300	44	D3
MAIN ST S	LA	LA14	600	44	D3
MAIN ST S	LA	LA15	900	44	B5
MAIN ST S	LA	LA37	3800	52	B4
MAIN ST S	LA	LA61	10700	58	B5
MAIN ST S	POM	POM	100	94	E3
MAIN ST W	ALH	ALH	1	37	B4
MAIN ST W	SGAB	SGAB	100	37	E3
MAINE	WCOV	WCOV		92	E4
MAINE AV	BAP	BAP	3200	39	D6
MAINE AV	BAP	BAP	2900	48	C1
MAINE AV	LB	LB02	300	75	B5
MAINE AV	LB	LB02	100	75	B5
MAINE AV	LB	LB06	3000	70	B6
MAINE AV	LB	LB06	1800	75	B3
MAINE AV	LB	LB13	700	75	B5
MAINE RD	RPV	SP	4500	78	D2
MAINMAST DR	AGH	AGO		102	D3
MAINMAST PL	AGH	AGO		102	D3
MAINSAIL CIR	WLVL	THO		102A	F4
MAIREMONT DR	CO	WAL		97	B4
MAISON AV	LA	LA41	5100	26	C4
MAITLAND AV	ING	IN05	7900	57	D1
MAJELLA AV	LAV	LAV	200	90	B2
MAJESTIC ST	WCOV	WCOV		92	E3
MAJESTIC WY	GLEN	GL07	1500	25	E1
MAJOR ST	CO	CUL	11800	50	C5
MAJORCA CIR	LB	LB03		76	D6
MAJORCA DR	CO	LAN	11900	146	B2
MAJORCA PL	LA	LA49		32	B6
MAJOR SEAWAY	CO	MAL		115	B4
MAKEE AV	CO	LA01	5800	52	D5
MAKIN AV	PALM	PALM	39700	172	A5
MALABAR ST	CO	LA58	5200	52	F5
MALABAR ST	HPK	HPK	5900	52	F5
MALABAR ST	LA	LA33	2400	45	B3
MALABAR ST	LA	LA63	3000	45	B3
MALABAR ST	VER	LA58	5100	52	F5
MALAD CT	DBAR	POM		97	D5
MALAFIA DR	GLEN	GL08	3600	18	E3
MALAGA	PALM	PALM		184	B1
MALAGA CIR	CO	POM		97	D5
MALAGA CT	CO	CAL		100	C5
MALAGA CT	LB	LB03		76	D6
MALAGA LN	PVE	PVP	400	72	C2
MALAGA PL	LB	LB03		76	D5
MALAGA PL E	MB	MB		62	D3
MALAGA PL W	MB	MB		62	D3
MALAGA RD	LA	LA68	2200	34	B2
MALAGA WY	MB	MB		62	D3
MALAGA COVE PZ	PVE	PVP	1	72	D2
MALAKOFF RD	SAD	SAD		90	B4
MALAT WY	CUL	CUL	11200	50	C4
MALBON ST	CO	LAN		175	G1
MALBY AV	PALM	PALM	38500	172	F8
MALCOLM AV	LA	LA24	700	41	E2
MALCOLM AV	LA	LA25	1800	41	F3
MALCOLM AV	LA	LA34	3000	42	A5

268

1990 LOS ANGELES COUNTY STREET INDEX

MALCOLM AV — MARIGOLD AV

LOS ANGELES CO.

STREET	CITY	P.O. ZONE	BLOCK	PAGE	GRID
MALCOLM AV	LA	LA64	2200	41	F3
MALCOLM AV	LA	LA64	2700	42	A5
MALCOLM DR	PAS	PAS	100	26	D4
MALDEN DR	MTB	MTB	1700	54	C2
MALDEN LN	ING	IN01		57	B2
MALDEN ST	LA	CAN	19600	12	F1
MALDEN ST	LA	NOR	16900	14	E1
MALDEN ST	LA	NOR	17800	14	D1
MALDEN ST	LA	SF	15800	15	B1
MALDEN ST	LA	VAN	14900	15	C1
MALEZA PL	LA	TAR	4600	21	B3
MALGREN AV N	LA	SP	200	78	D2
MALGREN AV S	LA	SP	700	78	D3
MALIBU DR	CO	AGO		107	A3
MALIBU RD	CO	MAL	18000	113	D5
MALIBU RD	CO	MAL		114	A5
MALIBU CYN RD	CO	CAL		107	F6
MALIBU CYN RD	CO	CAL		113	E1
MALIBU CYN RD	CO	MAL		114	A4
MALIBU COLNY DR	CO	MAL		114	A5
MALIBU COLNY RD	CO	MAL		114	A5
MALIBU CNTRY DR	CO	MAL		113	E5
MALIBU CV COLNY	CO	MAL		113	A6
MALIBU CREST DR	CO	MAL	23800	114	A4
MALIBU HILLS RD	CO	AGO		100A	E5
MALIBU HILLS RD	CO	CAL		100A	E5
MALIBU KNOLS RD	CO	MAL		113	F4
MALIBU MDWS DR	CO	CAL		108	A5
MALIBU PARK LN	CO	MAL		111	F6
MALIBU RCHO RD	CO	AGO		107	A2
MALIBU VISTA DR	CO	MAL		115	E4
MALINTA AV	CO	PALM		190	A1
MALI VISTA DR	CO	CAL		108	D2
MALLARD ST	LA	LA32	2500	36	C6
MALLISON AV	LYN	LYN	10600	59	B4
MALLISON AV	SOG	SOG	9200	59	B4
MALLORY ST	LA	LA32	2500	36	D6
MALLOT PL	LA	SF	11900	1	F5
MALLOY AV	CAR	CAR	16200	64	C4
MALL THE	LA	LA23		45	A6
MALMO RD	SCLR	SAU		124	J3
MALO ST	WCOV	WCOV		92	A2
MALONE DR	MTB	MTB	700	46	C5
MALONE ST	LA	LA66	12200	41	E6
MALT AV	CMRC	LA40	2400	54	B4
MALTA ST	LA	LA42	4800	36	B2
MALTA ST	LB	LB15	4700	76	B3
MALTA WY	LB	LB04		75	D5
MALTBY PL	LA	HAC	23100	68	E6
MALTMAN AV	LA	LA26	600	35	B4
MALTON PL	CO	LPUE	15500	85	E3
MALVERN AV	LA	LA06	1400	44	A4
MALVINA AV	LA	LA12	1800	35	D5
MAMERS RD	CO	ACT		182	A7
MAMIE AV N	LKD	LKD	4900	71	E2
MAMMOTH AV	CER	ART	7900	81	C2
MAMMOTH AV	LA	VAN	5600	15	F6
MAMMOTH AV	LA	VAN	4100	22	F3
MANADA CT	DBAR	POM		97	E4
MANAGUA PL	CO	LPUE	2800	85	E4
MANATEE ST	DOW	DOW	8200	60	B4
MANATO ST	CO	PALM		174	J6
MANCERO AV	CO	LPUE	300	98	D1
MANCHA PL	MPK	MPK	300	46	C4
MANCHA WY	MPK	MPK	1700	46	C4
MANCHESTER AV E	CO	LA01	2200	58	E1
MANCHESTER AV E	LA	LA01	600	58	C1
MANCHESTER AV E	LA	LA03	100	58	C1
MANCHESTER AV W	LA	LA03	100	58	C1
MANCHESTER AV W	LA	LA44	700	57	D1
MANCHESTER AV W	LA	LA44	500	58	C1
MANCHESTER AV W	LA	LA45	5500	56	A1
MANCHESTER AV W	LA	LA47	1400	57	D1
MANCHESTER AV W	LA	VEN	7500	55A	E2
MANCHESTER BL E	ING	IN01	100	57	B1
MANCHESTER BL W	ING	IN01	200	56	E1
MANCHESTER BL W	ING	IN01	100	57	B1
MANCHESTER BL W	ING	IN05	2200	57	B1
MANCHESTER CT	CLA	CLA		91	D2
MANCHESTER CT	LA	LA44	8600	58	A2
MANCHESTER DR	ING	IN01	600	57	A1
MANCHESTER ST	PALM	PALM		183	J1
MANCHESTER TER	ING	IN01	500	57	A1
MANCHESTER WY	SCLR	SAU		127	D2
MANCO DR	CO	LPUE		85	E3
MANDALAY DR	CO	LA63	4100	45	D2
MANDALAY DR	LA	ENC	16200	22	A4
MANDALAY RD	CO	CYN		128	E2
MANDALE ST	BLF	BLF	9200	66	B2
MANDAN RD	CO	SF		3	E2
MANDAN ST	SCLR	CYN	18600	124	J9
MANDARIN CT	LA	SF	17100	1	E5
MANDARIN LN	CO	SAU		124	D2
MANDELL ST	LA	CAN	20400	12	B1
MANDERLY AV	WCOV	WCOV	4000	97	A2
MANDEVILLE DR	WAL	WAL		92	F6

STREET	CITY	P.O. ZONE	BLOCK	PAGE	GRID
MANDEVILLE LN	LA	LA49		40	F1
MANDEVLLE CY RD	LA	LA49	1600	21	E6
MANDEVLLE CY RD	LA	LA49	1900	30	F3
MANDEVLLE CY RD	LA	LA49	1600	40	F2
MANDY CT	LA	WOH		5	C6
MANDY ST	CO	LPUE		98	E3
MANE DR	DBAR	POM		97A	A1
MANECITA DR	LAM	LAM	14300	83	B2
MANETTE PL	CO	COM	12800	65	C2
MANETTE PL	COM	COM	12600	65	C2
MANETTE PL	LYN	LYN	12500	65	C2
MANFORD WY	PAS	PAS	300	26	D3
MANGAF ST	CO	SAU		189	D2
MANGATE AV	CO	LPUE	400	92	B6
MANGO CT	POM	POM	800	94	F4
MANGO WY	LA	LA49	1800	40	F1
MANGO WY	POM	POM	1600	94	F4
MANGROVE AV	CO	COV	4800	89	B3
MANGROVE AV	COV	COV	300	89	B4
MANGUM ST	BAP	BAP	3200	39	C6
MANGUM ST	BAP	BAP	3100	48	B1
MANHATTAN AV	CO	MONT	2500	18	E2
MANHATTAN AV	GLEN	GL14	2800	18	D2
MANHATTAN AV	GLEN	MONT	2600	18	E2
MANHATTAN AV	HB	RB	300	62	C6
MANHATTAN AV	HB	RB	100	67	C1
MANHATTAN AV	MB	MB	100	62	A3
MANHATTAN PL	TOR	TOR	17800	63	D6
MANHATTAN PL	TOR	TOR	18400	68	D1
MANHATTAN PL N	LA	LA04	100	34	D5
MANHATTAN PL N	LA	LA38	700	34	D5
MANHATTAN PL S	CO	LA47	10800	57	D4
MANHATTAN PL S	GAR	GAR	13000	63	D1
MANHATTAN PL S	LA	LA04	100	43	D1
MANHATTAN PL S	LA	LA05	600	43	D1
MANHATTAN PL S	LA	LA18	2600	43	D5
MANHATTAN PL S	LA	LA19	900	43	D4
MANHATTAN PL S	LA	LA20	300	43	D1
MANHATTAN PL S	LA	LA47	6000	51	D5
MANHATTAN PL S	LA	LA47	8900	57	D3
MANHATTAN PL S	LA	LA62	5100	51	D4
MANHATTN BCH BL	CO	GAR	2200	63	B4
MANHATTN BCH BL	CO	LAW	3600	63	B4
MANHATTN BCH BL	LAW	LAW	4500	62	D4
MANHATTN BCH BL	LAW	LAW	4000	63	B4
MANHATTN BCH BL	MB	MB	100	62	D4
MANHATTN BCH BL	RB	RB	1900	62	D4
MANILA AV	LB	LB14	200	76	C5
MANINGTON PL	WCOV	WCOV	400	92	F1
MANISTEE DR	LCF	LCF	2100	11	F5
MANITOBA ST	LA	VEN	8100	55A	E2
MANITOU AV	LA	LA31	2100	36	A6
MANITOU PL	LA	LA31	3800	36	B6
MANITOWAC DR	RPV	PVP	5300	72	E3
MANKATO	LA	SF		8	C2
MANKATO CT	CLA	CLA		91	D2
MANKATO ST	LA	SF	14900	8	D2
MANLEY CT	CO	CAL		100	A2
MANLEY DR	SGAB	SGAB	600	37	E5
MANNING AV	LA	LA24	700	41	E1
MANNING AV	LA	LA25	1800	41	F3
MANNING AV	LA	LA64	2200	42	A3
MANNING CT	LA	LA64	3300	42	B5
MANNING DR	LA	LA24		41	E1
MANNING ST	AZU	AZU	500	88	D1
MANNING ST	BUR	BUR	1800	16	F5
MANNING WY	CER	ART	15900	82	D4
MANNINGTON PL	WCOV	WCOV	500	92	F1
MANNIX DR	LA	LA46	8100	33	E2
MANOA CT	LA	LA28		34	C3
MANOLA WY	LA	LA68	5800	34	D2
MANOR CIR	POM	POM	1100	94	D4
MANOR CT	LA	LA65	4100	35	F1
MANOR DR	HAW	HAW	11800	56	F6
MANOR DR	HAW	HAW	13800	62	F2
MANOR DR	LKD	LKD	3900	71	A3
MANOR DR	MB	MB	2100	62	B3
MANOR LN	CO	SAU		188	B2
MANOR LN	GLDR	GLDR	1700	87	D6
MANOR LN	LA	LA66	12900	49	E3
MANOR ST E	CO	ALT	1	20	A4
MANOR ST W	CO	ALT	1	20	A4
MANOR WY	SGAB	SGAB	1700	37	D6
MANORGATE RD	CO	LPUE	1500	98	B3
MANSA DR	LAM	LAM	13800	82	E2
MANSA DR	LAM	LAM	14600	83	A1
MANSA DR	NWK	NWK	12800	82	C1
MANSARD DR	CO	SF		3	F2
MANSEL AV	CO	IN04	10000	57	A4
MANSEL AV	LAW	LAW	14300	62	F4
MANSEL AV	LAW	LAW	14300	63	A4
MANSEL AV	TOR	RB	18200	62	F6
MANSEL AV	TOR	TOR	20000	67	F2
MANSFIELD AV N	LA	LA28	1300	34	B6
MANSFIELD AV N	LA	LA36	100	34	B6
MANSFIELD AV N	LA	LA38	700	34	B6

STREET	CITY	P.O. ZONE	BLOCK	PAGE	GRID
MANSFIELD AV S	CO	LA43	5800	50	F4
MANSFIELD AV S	LA	LA16	2100	43	A4
MANSFIELD AV S	LA	LA19	1000	43	B2
MANSFIELD AV S	LA	LA36	100	34	B6
MANSFIELD AV S	LA	LA36	100	43	B2
MANSFIELD DR	BUR	BUR	2700	17	C3
MANSFIELD DR	CLA	CLA		91	D1
MANSFIELD PL	ALH	ALH	1000	37	B2
MANSFIELD WY	BELL	BELL		53	E4
MANSIE RD	CO	MAL		114	D2
MANSION CT	LAV	LAV		95A	C6
MANSION LN	CO	POM		93	E2
MANSON AV	LA	WOH	4200	13	A3
MANTECA ST	LA	VAN	17400	14	E3
MANTIS AV	LA	SP	1700	78	D4
MANTON AV	LA	WOH	5600	5	E6
MANTON AV	LA	WOH	5400	100	E1
MANTOVA DR	LA	LA08	4000	50	F2
MANTOVA ST	LB	LB15	6500	76	E4
MANTUA RD	LA	PP	200	40	B4
MANTUA WK	LA	PP	300	40	B4
MANU LN	WCOV	WCOV		92	E5
MANUEL AV	TOR	TOR	1300	68	D4
MANVIEW DR	CO	TOP		109	A1
MANVILLE ST	COM	COM	100	65	A5
MANVILLE ST	POM	POM	2400	91	A5
MANZANA AV	PAR	PAR	15300	66	A3
MANZANAR AV	DOW	DOW	8800	60	D2
MANZANAR AV	PR	PR	5200	54	F3
MANZANAR AV	PR	PR	8200	60	D1
MANZANARES RD	LAM	LAM	15000	83	B2
MANZANILLO DR	CO	LPUE	2200	98	D5
MANZANITA AV	PAS	PAS	700	26	F2
MANZANITA AV	SMAD	SMAD	100	28	B2
MANZANITA CIR	LAV	LAV		90	D1
MANZANITA DR	CO	LPUE	15300	85	D2
MANZANITA DR	PALM	LAN		171	A2
MANZANITA DR	WCOV	WCOV	100	92	E2
MANZANITA LN	MB	MB	1100	62	D4
MANZANITA ST	CO	GL14	2200	11	F5
MANZANITA ST	LA	LA27	1300	35	A4
MANZANITA ST	LA	LA29	800	35	A4
MANZANITA MS RD	CO	LR	10800	192	A6
MANZANITA PK AV	CO	MAL	1700	114	E1
MANZANO CT	SCLR	VAL		124	A1
MANZANO DR	CO	MAL	30700	111	E5
MAPACHE DR	DBAR	POM	21300	97	D6
MAPES AV	CER	ART	17200	66	F5
MAPES AV	CER	ART	19500	71	F2
MAPES AV	NWK	NWK	16600	66	F5
MAPLE	CO	LP48		98	F3
MAPLE AV	CAR	GAR	16100	64	B4
MAPLE AV	CMRC	LA22	2900	54	C3
MAPLE AV	CO	GAR	14300	64	B2
MAPLE AV	CO	LA61	14000	64	B2
MAPLE AV	ELM	ELM	3900	38	E5
MAPLE AV	ING	IN01	900	57	A3
MAPLE AV	LA	LA11	1900	44	C5
MAPLE AV	LA	LA11	3100	52	B1
MAPLE AV	LA	LA13	500	44	C5
MAPLE AV	LA	LA14	600	44	C5
MAPLE AV	LA	LA15	900	44	C5
MAPLE AV	MB	MB	2500	62	B3
MAPLE AV	POM	POM	2200	90	F4
MAPLE AV	TOR	TOR	1700	68	B4
MAPLE AV E	ELS	ELS	100	56	C5
MAPLE AV E	MON	MON	100	29	A4
MAPLE AV N	MTB	MTB	500	46	D5
MAPLE AV N	MTB	MTB	100	54	D1
MAPLE AV S	MTB	MTB	100	54	D1
MAPLE AV W	ELS	ELS	800	55A	F5
MAPLE AV W	ELS	ELS	100	56	A5
MAPLE AV W	MON	MON	100	29	A4
MAPLE CT	ALH	ALH	1500	37	B4
MAPLE DR	LA	LA46	8300	33	E3
MAPLE DR N	BH	BH	500	33	C5
MAPLE DR N	BH	BH	100	42	C1
MAPLE DR S	BH	BH	100	42	C1
MAPLE PL	MTB	MTB	200	54	D1
MAPLE ST	BLF	BLF	8700	66	A4
MAPLE ST	BUR	BUR	1400	17	A6
MAPLE ST	BUR	BUR	100	24	A1
MAPLE ST	CO	LA61	12200	58	B6
MAPLE ST	PALM	PALM		171	B2
MAPLE ST	SCLR	NEW	23200	127	B5
MAPLE ST	SM	SM	800	49	B2
MAPLE ST	SPAS	SPAS	1100	36	F3
MAPLE ST	WHI	WHI	11000	55	D3
MAPLE ST E	COM	COM	100	64	E2
MAPLE ST E	GLEN	GL05	100	25	D5
MAPLE ST E	PAS	PAS	100	27	A3
MAPLE ST W	COM	COM	300	64	E2
MAPLE ST W	GLEN	GL04	100	25	C5
MAPLE ST W	PAS	PAS	100	26	F3
MAPLE WY	LB	LB02		75	C5
MAPLE WY	PAS	PAS	300	27	B3

STREET	CITY	P.O. ZONE	BLOCK	PAGE	GRID
MAPLE WY	SPAS	SPAS	1200	36	F3
MAPLEBAY CT	SCLR	NEW	19300	127	H3
MAPLEDALE ST	BLF	BLF	10200	66	D2
MAPLEDALE ST	NWK	NWK	10700	66	E2
MAPLEDALE ST	NWK	NWK	11400	82	B2
MAPLEFIELD ST	SELM	ELM	10800	47	D4
MAPLEGATE ST	MPK	MPK		46	C4
MAPLEGROVE ST	CO	LPUE	15400	48	F4
MAPLEGROVE ST	CO	LPUE	15600	92	A4
MAPLEGROVE ST	LPUE	LPUE	15400	48	F4
MAPLEGROVE ST	WCOV	WCOV		92	C4
MAPLEHILL RD	DBAR	POM		97	F3
MAPLELEAF ST	LKD	LKD		71	D1
MAPLEPARK DR	RPV	PVP	28900	72	C5
MAPLE RIDGE CIR	SCLR	VAL		124	B4
MAPLESIDE ST	BLF	BLF	9000	66	B1
MAPLE SPRING DR	DBAR	POM	23500	94	A6
MAPLETON DR N	LA	LA77	100	32	F5
MAPLETON DR S	LA	LA77	100	32	F5
MAPLETREE AV	CO	ARC		38	F3
MAPLE VIEW DR	POM	POM		94	C4
MAPLEWOOD AV	BLF	BLF	9300	66	B2
MAPLEWOOD AV	LA	LA04	4400	34	D5
MAPLEWOOD AV	LA	LA66	3400	49	D2
MAPLEWOOD AV	WCOV	WCOV	100	88	B6
MAPLEWOOD LN	LA	NOR		7	B2
MAPLEWOOD ST	LAN	LAN		160	F6
MAPLEWOOD ST	LAV	LAV	1500	90	C2
MAQUOKETAH TR	CO	AGO		107	A3
MARACAIBO PL	CO	LPUE	15900	85	E4
MARAND ST	DUA	DUA	1300	29	D5
MARANVILLE CT	WCOV	WCOV		98	E1
MARATHON RD	CO	ALT	1	20	A4
MARATHON ST	LA	LA26	2100	35	A5
MARATHON ST	LA	LA29	4000	34	F5
MARATHON ST	LA	LA29	3900	35	A5
MARATHON ST	LA	LA38	5100	34	D5
MARAVILLA CT	SCLR	VAL		127	B1
MARAVILLA DR	LA	LA68	2200	34	B2
MARBEL AV	DOW	DOW	10600	60	C3
MARBELLA AV	CAR	CAR	21000	69	B4
MARBELLA AV	CAR	CAR	23900	74	B1
MARBELLA CT	CO	CAL		100	C5
MARBER AV	LB	LB08	3100	71	C6
MARBER AV	LB	LB15	1800	76	C3
MARBER AV	LKD	LKD	4100	71	C4
MARBLE DR	LA	VAN	15000	22	C4
MARBLECREST DR	CO	LPUE		98	A4
MARBORA CT	LB	LB03		76	F5
MARBRING CT	CO	WHI	5400	55	B3
MARBRISA AV	CO	HPK	7200	52	E6
MARBRISA AV	CO	HPK	7900	58	E1
MARBRISA AV	HPK	HPK	6100	52	E6
MARBRO DR	LA	ENC	16400	22	A4
MARBURN AV	CO	LA43	5000	51	A3
MARBURY ST	COV	COV	17800	88	D6
MARBURY ST E	WCOV	WCOV	1000	88	C6
MARBURY ST W	WCOV	WCOV	1000	88	B5
MARBY DR	CO	AGO		113	B3
MARC CT	DBAR	POM		97A	B2
MARCASEL AV	LA	LA66	3800	49	F2
MARCASEL AV	LA	LA66	3800	50	A2
MARCELINA AV	TOR	TOR	1300	68	D4
MARCELLA AV	WCOV	WCOV		92	E5
MARCELLA ST	LAN	LAN	2500	159	G5
MARCELLE ST	CO	COM	3600	65	B4
MARCELLE ST	COM	COM	1100	65	B4
MARCELLE ST	PAR	PAR	6600	65	D4
MARCELLO PL	LA	ENC	17700	21	D3
MARCELLUS ST	LB	LB07	1000	70	D3
MARCH AV	LA	CAN	7500	5	E2
MARCHANT AV	LA	SF	13600	3	B2
MARCHEETA PL	LA	LA69	1800	33	D2
MARCHENA DR	LA	LA65	4000	35	F2
MARCHENA ST	LA	WOH	21500	13	C2
MARCHETA ST	CO	ALT	800	20	B5
MARCHLAND AV	SCLR	CYN	27200	124	J9
MARCHMONT AV	CO	LPUE	1100	85	E1
MARCI WY	SCLR	VAL		127	C2
MARCIA DR	LA	LA26	3600	35	A4
MARCIA RD	GLEN	GL08	2900	18	F5
MARCILE AV	GLDR	GLDR	100	86	F5
MARCO CT	LA	VEN	700	49	D3
MARCO CT	LAV	LAV	2800	90	D3
MARCO PL	LA	LA66	12600	49	D2
MARCO PL	LA	VEN	700	49	D3
MARCOLA DR	CO	LPUE	18500	98	E4
MARCON DR	WAL	WAL	20600	93	C5
MARCONI ST	HPK	HPK	6300	53	A5
MARCONI ST	MTB	MTB	700	46	D6
MARCOS AV	SAD	SAD	100	90	A2
MARCOS RD	LA	WOH	4100	13	D4
MARCUS AV	LA	TU	9700	11	A4
MARCUS AV	PALM	PALM		183	E2
MARCUS LN	LA	TU	9700	11	A4
MAR DE CORTEZ	AVA	AVA		77	A4

STREET	CITY	P.O. ZONE	BLOCK	PAGE	GRID
MARDEL AV	CO	WHI	2200	47	E5
MARDINA ST	WCOV	WCOV	1000	88	C6
MAREK DR	MTB	MTB	200	46	E6
MAREK MTY	CO	SF		3	F3
MARELLEN PL	CO	GL14	4600	18	E1
MARELLEN WY	POM	POM	1700	91	A6
MARENDALE LN	ARC	ARC	1500	28	E2
MARENGO AL	SPAS	SPAS	1100	37	A2
MARENGO AV	CO	ALT	2080	20	A5
MARENGO AV	SPAS	SPAS	1000	37	A3
MARENGO AV N	ALH	ALH	100	37	A4
MARENGO AV N	PAS	PAS	1500	20	A6
MARENGO AV N	PAS	PAS	100	27	A2
MARENGO AV S	ALH	ALH	100	37	A4
MARENGO AV S	PAS	PAS	100	27	A6
MARENGO AV S	PAS	PAS	1200	37	A1
MARENGO DR	CO	LPUE		98	C4
MARENGO DR	GLEN	GL06		26	C2
MARENGO PL	LA	LA33	2100	45	B2
MARENGO ST	CO	LA63	3300	45	C2
MARENGO ST	LA	LA33	1500	45	A2
MARGARET AV	CO	LA22	300	45	F6
MARGARET AV	CO	LA22	200	46	A6
MARGARET AV	LA	CUL	5300	50	B4
MARGARET AV	MPK	MPK		46	A5
MARGARET CT	RB	RB		67	E1
MARGARET DR	PAS	PAS	2900	27	F4
MARGARET LN	SM	SM	2900	49	C2
MARGARET LN	WAL	WAL		92	F5
MARGARET LN	WAL	WAL		93	A5
MARGARET ST	CAR	CAR	20800	69	A3
MARGARET ST	DOW	DOW	8500	60	C4
MARGARITA DR	LA	WOH	22500	13	A3
MARGARITA DR	WCOV	WCOV	1100	92	A1
MARGARITA HL DR	CO	SAU		188	J1
MARGATE RD	PVE	PVP	1600	72	A4
MARGATE SQ	PVE	PVP	1	72	A4
MARGATE ST	LA	ENC	16800	21	D1
MARGATE ST	LA	NHO	10300	23	F1
MARGATE ST	LA	TAR	18200	21	C1
MARGATE ST	LA	VAN	13300	22	E1
MARGATE ST	LA	VAN	13100	23	A1
MARGAY AV	CAR	CAR	16900	64	C5
MARGO AV	LB	LB14	300	76	D5
MARGO ST	LA	LA15	1300	44	C4
MARGUERITA AV	MPK	MPK	100	46	B2
MARGUERITA AV	SM	SM	100	40	E5
MARGUERITA AV	SM	SM	1700	41	A4
MARGUERITA AV N	ALH	ALH	100	37	B3
MARGUERITA AV S	ALH	ALH	100	37	B6
MARGUERITA DR	COM	COM	1400	65	B2
MARGUERITA LN	PAS	PAS	200	27	A6
MARGUERITE DR	RPV	PVP		77	A1
MARGUERITE ST	LA	LA65	3200	35	E1
MARIA AV	CER	ART	17000	82	C5
MARIA AV	LA	CAN	7800	5	E2
MARIA AV	LAV	LAV	800	90	B3
MARIA AV	RB	RB	400	67	D2
MARIA AV N	RB	RB	300	67	E4
MARIA CIR	LAN	LAN		160	G6
MARIA CT	WCOV	WCOV		92	E5
MARIA PL	CER	ART	18300	82	C6
MARIA ST	BUR	BUR	1600	17	C4
MARIA ST	CO	COM	2900	70	B1
MARIALINDA ST	TOR	TOR	5500	67	E3
MARIAM PL	SCLR	SAU		124	D5
MARIAN PL	LA	VEN	2100	49	D3
MARIANA ST	WCOV	WCOV	1200	92	A1
MARIANITA DR	LHH	LAH	1300	84	E2
MARIANNA AV N	CO	LA63	100	45	D4
MARIANNA AV N	LA	LA32	1900	45	D1
MARIANNA AV S	CMRC	LA23	1200	53	D1
MARIANNA AV S	CO	LA23	1100	45	D6
MARIANNA AV S	CO	LA63	100	45	D4
MARIANNA RD	PAS	PAS	1300	26	D6
MARIANO ST	LA	WOH	22600	13	A1
MARIANO ST	LA	WOH	23000	100	E1
MARIBEL AV	CAR	CAR	23200	69	B6
MARIBEL AV	CAR	CAR	24200	74	B1
MARICIO DR	SCLR	NEW		127	H6
MARICOPA DR	LA	LA65	2200	35	F2
MARICOPA PL	TOR	TOR	2300	68	C3
MARICOPA ST	TOR	TOR	2200	68	C3
MARICOPA ST W	TOR	TOR	4200	67	E3
MARIE AV	LA	LA42	300	26	D6
MARIE AV	LA	LA42		36	D1
MARIE ELLEN AV	LHH	LAH	1200	84	E3
MARIETTA AV	CLA	CLA		91	B1
MARIETTA AV	CUL	CUL	10800	50	B1
MARIETTA CT	LB	LB02	20	75	D5
MARIETTA CT	SH	LB07	3300	70	D5
MARIETTA ST	LA	LA23	900	45	A5
MARIGOLD AV	CO	GAR	15400	63	C4
MARIGOLD AV	CO	TOR	21200	68	F4
MARIGOLD AV	GAR	GAR	14700	63	C3

INDEX

1990 LOS ANGELES COUNTY STREET INDEX

STREET	CITY	P.O. ZONE	BLOCK	PAGE	GRID
MARIGOLD AV	LAN	LAN		159	A9
MARIGOLD AV	LA	HAC	25000	73	F3
MARIGOLD AV	PALM	PALM		171	J8
MARIGOLD CT	CO	CAL		100A	F5
MARIGOLD ST	POM	POM	1700	91	A6
MARIGOLD ST E	CO	ALT	300	20	B4
MARIGOLD ST W	CO	ALT	300	19	F3
MARILLA AV	AVA	AVA	100	77	B5
MARILLA ST	LA	CHA		6	C4
MARILLA ST	LA	NOR	17100	7	E4
MARILLA ST	LA	SF	16600	7	F4
MARILLA ST	LA	SF	15500	8	B4
MARILYN DR	BH	BH	1000	33	A4
MARILYN DR	CO	CYN		125	E7
MARILYN DR	LA	SF	16200	2	A6
MARILYN LN	LA	ENC		22	B3
MARILYN PL	ARC	ARC	300	28	F1
MARILYN WY	COV	COV	800	88	F4
MARILYN WY	COV	COV	800	89	A4
MARILYNN ST	LAN	LAN		159	F5
MARIMBA ST	CO	LPUE	18400	98	E5
MARIN CT	MB	MB		62	D3
MARINA CT	CO	CYN		125	E6
MARINA DR	LA	SP	1800	78	D4
MARINA DR	LB	LB03		76	D6
MARINA DR	RHE	PVP	26000	72	F3
MARINA FRWY	LA	LA		50	A5
MARINA PL	LA	SP	2000	78	D4
MARINA WY	LB	LB03		76	C5
MARINA WY	LA	SP		79	C4
MARINA WY	RB	RB	1	67	C2
MARINA PACIFICA	LB	LB03		80	D1
MARINA PARK LN	LB	LB03		76	E5
MARINA VIEW DR	LB	LB03	6100	76	E5
MARINA VISTA DR	CO	MAL	31000	111	E5
MARINE AV	CAR	CAR	22300	69	C6
MARINE AV	CAR	CAR	24400	74	C2
MARINE AV	LA	WIL	100	74	C5
MARINE AV	MB	MB	100	62	C3
MARINE AV	LAW	LAW	4500	62	F3
MARINE AV	LAW	LAW	4000	63	A3
MARINE PL	MB	MB	100	62	B3
MARINE PL N	SM	SM		49	B2
MARINE ST	LA	LA66	12000	41	E6
MARINE ST	LA	LA66	12200	49	E1
MARINE ST	SM	SM	100	49	B3
MARINE TER	SM	SM	1	49	A2
MARINE WY	LB	LB02	100	75	C6
MARINER AV	TOR	TOR		68	A2
MARINER CIR	WLVL	THO		102	A4
MARINER DR	LA	SP		78	E5
MARINER WY	LB	LB03		80	F1
MARINERS VW LN	LCF	LCF		19	D3
MARINETTE RD	LA	PP	1200	40	D2
MARINETTE ST	TOR	TOR	1700	68	D5
MARINO TER	SMAR	PAS	1900	37	B2
MARION AV	BAP	BAP	4800	39	E3
MARION AV	LA	LA26	1100	44	D1
MARION AV	LAN	LAN		160	D7
MARION AV	PAS	PAS	1	27	C4
MARION AV	TOR	TOR	4900	67	F6
MARION CIR	BAP	BAP		39	E3
MARION CT	IND	IND		98	A2
MARION CT	IND	LPUE	1300	98	B2
MARION DR	CLA	CLA	500	91	B5
MARION DR	GLEN	GL05	1000	25	E6
MARION DR	RPV	PVP		73	C6
MARION PL	GLDR	GLDR	600	87	B6
MARION WY	LB	LB07	500	70	B4
MARIONDALE AV	LA	LA32	2200	36	E6
MARIONWOOD DR	LA	CUL	4700	50	B3
MARIOTA AV	LA	NHO	4300	24	A3
MARIPOSA AV	CO	HAC	24200	73	F2
MARIPOSA AV	CO	LA44	11100	57	E5
MARIPOSA AV	CO	TOR	20600	68	F3
MARIPOSA AV	GAR	GAR	13700	63	E2
MARIPOSA AV	LA	GAR	18400	63	F6
MARIPOSA AV	LA	GAR	18400	68	F1
MARIPOSA AV	SMAD	SMAD	100	28	B2
MARIPOSA AV E	ELS	ELS	100	56	C5
MARIPOSA AV N	LA	LA04	100	34	E6
MARIPOSA AV N	LA	LA27	1300	34	E4
MARIPOSA AV N	LA	LA29	700	34	E4
MARIPOSA AV S	LA	LA04	100	34	E6
MARIPOSA AV S	LA	LA05	600	43	E2
MARIPOSA AV S	LA	LA06	900	43	E3
MARIPOSA AV S	LA	LA07	1900	43	E4
MARIPOSA AV S	LA	LA20	300	43	E2
MARIPOSA AV S	LA	LA44	8000	57	E1
MARIPOSA AV W	ELS	ELS	100	56	A5
MARIPOSA LN	LYN	LYN	10400	59	A4
MARIPOSA LN	MTB	MTB	900	54	D3
MARIPOSA LN	SOG	SOG	10200	59	A4
MARIPOSA ST	GLEN	GL05	800	25	D5
MARIPOSA ST	POM	POM	2100	90	E5
MARIPOSA ST E	CO	ALT	100	20	B5
MARIPOSA ST N	BUR	BUR	100	17	C6
MARIPOSA ST N	BUR	BUR	100	24	D1
MARIPOSA ST S	BUR	BUR	100	24	D2
MARIPOSA ST W	CO	ALT	100	19	E4
MARIPOSA DE ORO	CO	MAL	23300	114	B4
MARIQUITA ST	LB	LB03	2700	75	F5
MARIQUITA ST	LB	LB14	6500	76	E5
MARIS AV	PR	PR	5500	54	F3
MARIS AV	PR	PR	4000	55	A1
MARISCAL LN	LA	LA46	2300	33	D2
MARITA ST	LB	LB15	5800	76	D3
MARITIME DR	RPV	PVP		78	A3
MARJAN AV	CO	LA56	5300	50	E4
MARJORAM CT	SCLR	SAU		124	D5
MARJORIE AV	CLA	CLA		91	C2
MARJORIE AV	TOR	TOR	21300	67	F4
MARJORIE ST	PR	PR	9400	55	A5
MARK AV	PALM	PALM		183	F1
MARK PL	LA	BH		32	E1
MARK ST	LA	LA33	1000	45	A2
MARKDALE AV	NWK	NWK	11800	61	B5
MARKDALE AV	NWK	NWK	13200	82	B1
MARKEL DR	SCLR	NEW		127	A4
MARKER LN	LB	LB05	300	65	C5
MARKER ST	LB	LB05	100	65	B5
MARKET AL	PAS	PAS		27	B4
MARKET CT	LA	LA21	700	44	D5
MARKET LN	ALH	ALH	1400	37	D6
MARKET PL	COM	COM	900	64	F4
MARKET PL	LOM	LOM	25900	73	E3
MARKET ST	SCLR	NEW	22800	127	C5
MARKET ST	GLEN	GL08	3500	18	F3
MARKET ST	LA	VEN	1	49	B4
MARKET ST E	LB	LB05	100	70	C2
MARKET ST N	ING	IN01	100	57	A2
MARKET ST N	ING	IN02	300	51	A6
MARKET ST S	ING	IN01	100	57	A2
MARKET ST W	LB	LB05	100	70	C2
MARKHAM LN	ING	IN01		57	C2
MARKHAM PL	PAS	PAS	200	26	F5
MARK KEPPEL ST	PAR	PAR	6500	65	D3
MARKLAND DR E	MPK	MPK	100	46	C4
MARKLAND DR W	MPK	MPK	100	46	A4
MARKLEIN AV	LA	SF	18500	8	B6
MARKLEIN AV	LA	SF	8500	15	B1
MARKRIDGE RD	CO	GL14	2800	11	D5
MARKRIDGE RD	GLEN	GL14	3400	11	C4
MARKS RD	CO	AGO		100A	D6
MARKSTAY ST	CO	LPUE	19500	97	A3
MARKTON ST	CO	LA61	300	64	B2
MARKWAY LN	POM	POM	200	90	E3
MARKWOOD ST	DUA	DUA	2100	29	F4
MARKWOOD ST	DUA	DUA	2100	86	A4
MARLA AV	LA	CAN	8300	5	E1
MARLAND ST	LPUE	LPUE	13900	48	D3
MARLAY DR	LA	LA69	1500	33	E3
MARLBORO CT	CLA	CLA		91	D1
MARLBORO ST	LA	LA49	12700	41	A2
MARLBOROUGH AV	ING	IN02	500	51	A5
MARLBOROUGH CT	LA	CAN	7600	5	E2
MARLBOROUGH TER	SMAD	SMAD		28	D1
MARLENA ST	WCOV	WCOV		92	E5
MARLETTE DR	LAM	LAM	12900	82	F1
MARLIES ST	AGH	AGO		100A	A2
MARLIN PL	LA	CAN	22200	12	B4
MARLIN PL	LA	VAN	16900	14	E4
MARLIN PL	LA	VAN	14700	15	C4
MARLINDA AV	BAP	BAP	3100	48	B1
MARLINTON DR	CO	WHI	15600	84	C5
MARLITA PL	HB	RB	700	62	C5
MARLOMA DR	RHE	PVP	4300	72	E3
MARLOW AV	BG	BELL	6500	53	E6
MARLTON AV	LA	LA08	3900	51	B2
MAR LU DR	LA	LA46	2600	33	D1
MARMADUKE PL	LA	ENC	16800	21	F4
MARMAY PL	LA	SV	8200	16	E1
MARMION WY	LA	LA42	4800	36	B2
MARMION WY	LA	LA65	3400	36	B2
MARMION WY	SPAS	SPAS	100	36	D2
MARMOL DR	LA	WOH	4900	13	D2
MARMONT AV	LA	LA69	1500	33	E3
MARMONT LN	LA	LA69	8200	33	E3
MARMORA AL	PAS	PAS	1	26	F4
MARMORA DR	LA	WOH	20900	13	D3
MARMORA ST	LA	WOH	20900	13	D3
MARNA AV	LB	LB08	3000	81	B6
MARNE DR	RPV	PVP	30700	77	C1
MARNEY AV	CO	LA32	1800	45	D2
MARNEY AV	LA	LA32	1800	45	D2
MARNEY WK	LA	LA32	1800	45	D2
MARNICE AV	LA	TU	9800	11	B4
MAROGE CIR	SCLR	SAU		124	G5
MARONDE WY	MPK	MPK	100	46	C3
MARONEY LN	LA	PP	1000	40	C3
MAROON ST	ELM	ELM	10100	47	C2
MARQUAND AV	LA	CAN		5	E2
MARQUARDT AV	CER	ART	15900	82	E5
MARQUARDT AV	CO	WHI	11400	61	E5
MARQUARDT AV	LAM	LAM	12700	61	E6
MARQUARDT AV	LAM	LAM	12800	82	E2
MARQUARDT AV	SFS	SFS	12600	61	E6
MARQUARDT AV	SFS	SFS	12700	82	E2
MARQUESAS WY	CO	MDR	13900	49	D5
MARQUETTE AV	POM	POM	2100	95	A6
MARQUETTE DR	CO	TOP	2500	109	A1
MARQUETTE DR	WAL	WAL		93	B4
MARQUETTE ST	LA	PP	500	40	B3
MARQUEZ AV	LA	PP	16600	40	B3
MARQUEZ PL	LA	PP	100	40	B4
MARQUEZ TER	LA	PP	16600	40	B3
MARR ST	LA	VEN	500	49	D4
MARRILLA AV	NWK	NWK	14300	82	D2
MARRON AV	LB	LB07	3800	70	D5
MARRON PL	LB	LB07	1100	70	D4
MARS CT	LB	LB02	400	75	D5
MARS CT	SH	LB07	3300	70	D6
MARS LN	LA	LA77		32	E3
MARSALA DR	SCLR	VAL	26000	123	J9
MARSDEN CT	CO	CAL		100	A2
MARSDEN ST	LA	LA26	1500	35	D5
MARSEN ST	CO	ELM	10400	38	D4
MARSEN ST	ELM	ELM	10600	38	D4
MARSH AV	CO	RM	7600	46	E3
MARSH ST	LA	LA39	2400	35	D3
MARSHA LN	WHI	WHI		55	F5
MARSHALL AL	PAS	PAS		26	D1
MARSHALL CT	CLA	CLA		91	C2
MARSHALL CT	LA	SP	100	78	F2
MARSHALL CT	SAD	SAD		90	A1
MARSHALL CT	SAD	SAD		95A	A6
MARSHALL DR	LA	CUL	4600	50	A4
MARSHALL PL	LB	LB07	200	70	D4
MARSHALL RD	TOR	TOR	21200	68	A4
MARSHALL ST	ELM	ELM	9800	38	C6
MARSHALL ST	LA	CUL	11900	50	A4
MARSHALL ST	LA	LA66	12400	50	A4
MARSHALL ST	RM	RM	8300	38	B6
MARSHALL ST E	SGAB	SGAB	100	37	E6
MARSHALL ST W	SGAB	SGAB	100	37	E6
MARSHALL WY	SCLR	SAU		124	F5
MARSHALL WY	LB	LB07	3900	70	D4
MARSHALL WY	SGAB	SGAB	1700	37	E6
MARSHALL CK DR	LAV	LAV		90	D1
MARSHALL CK DR	LAV	LAV		95A	D6
MARSHALLFLD LN	RB	RB	1300	62	E6
MARSHBURN AV	CO	ARC	5000	38	E3
MARSHFIELD WY	LA	LA46	7100	34	A3
MARSH HAWK PL	LAV	LAV		95A	D5
MARSON ST	LA	VAN	14900	15	C2
MARSTON AV	LPUE	LPUE	400	98	B1
MARSTON CT	SCLR	SAU		124	D4
MART DR	LAM	LAM	15900	83	C2
MARTEL AV N	LA	LA36	100	34	A6
MARTEL AV N	LA	LA46	700	34	A6
MARTEL AV N	WHOL	LA46	1000	34	A6
MARTEL AV S	LA	LA36	100	34	A6
MARTELLO ST	POM	POM	1700	91	B6
MARTELO AV	PAS	PAS	100	27	E3
MARTHA AV	CER	ART	19000	81	D1
MARTHA AV	CER	ART	17400	82	D5
MARTHA AV	TOR	TOR	2600	68	E6
MARTHA CIR	CO	PAS	3300	27	F5
MARTHA CT	LAN	LAN		160	C6
MARTHA PL	CER	ART	18200	82	D6
MARTHA ST	LA	ENC	17100	21	D1
MARTHA ST	LA	NHO	11300	23	E1
MARTHA ST	LA	TAR	18700	21	B1
MARTHA ST	LA	VAN	13300	22	F1
MARTHA ST	LA	WOH	23600	5	F6
MARTHA ST	LA	WOH	19700	13	A1
MARTHA ST	LA	WOH	23600	100	F1
MARTIN AL	PAS	PAS		26	F4
MARTIN LN	BH	BH	400	33	C2
MARTIN RD	IRW	BAP		88	A1
MARTIN ST	CAR	CAR	21000	69	D4
MARTIN ST	LA	LA32	5100	36	E5
MARTIN WY	CLA	CLA		91	C1
MARTINA AV	TOR	TOR	1700	68	D5
MARTINDALE AV	LA	SV	9000	10	A6
MARTINEZ RD	CO	ACT		189	D2
MARTINEZ ST	IRW	BAP		88	B3
MARTINEZ ST	LA	WOH	20800	13	E2
MARTINGAIL DR	CO	COV		93	B2
MARTINGALE DR	CO	ACT		182	E9
MARTINGALE DR	RPV	PVP		73	B6
MARTINGALE LN	SAD	SAD		89	D4
MARTN L KING AV	LB	LB02	600	75	D3
MARTN L KING AV	LB	LB06	1800	75	D4
MARTN L KING AV	LB	LB13	700	75	D4
MARTN L KING BL	LA	LA08	3700	51	A1
MARTN L KING BL	LA	LA11	100	52	B1
MARTN L KING BL	LA	LA16	4500	43	A6
MARTN L KING BL	LA	LA37	800	51	E1
MARTN L KING BL	LA	LA37	100	52	B1
MARTN L KING BL	LA	LA62	1400	51	E1
MARTINSHIRE ST	CAR	CAR	400	69	A6
MARTOS DR	SPAS	SPAS		36	E2
MARTSON DR	LA	ENC	4500	21	D3
MARVA AV	LA	SF		1	D4
MARVALE DR	CO	LA43		51	A3
MARVENE DR	CO	LPUE	16400	98	A4
MARVIEW AV	LA	LA12		44	D1
MARVIN AV	CO	CAST		123	C2
MARVIN AV	LA	LA16	1900	42	F4
MARVIN AV	LA	LA19	1700	42	F4
MARVIN RD	CO	SAU		181	A8
MARVIN ST	LCF	LCF	4500	19	B3
MAR VISTA AV	CO	ALT	1900	20	C6
MAR VISTA AV	CO	PAS	1700	20	C6
MAR VISTA AV	LA	WIL	200	74	A5
MAR VISTA AV	PAS	PAS	1500	20	C6
MAR VISTA AV	PAS	PAS	100	27	C2
MAR VISTA DR	CO	MAL		112	E3
MAR VISTA MTWY	CO	MAL		106	E6
MAR VISTA MTWY	CO	MAL		112	E1
MAR VISTA ST	WHI	WHI	12300	55	E5
MAR VISTA ST	WHI	WHI	14600	84	A1
MAR VISTA ST	WHI	WHI	14200	85	A6
MARWICK AV	LB	LB08	3000	71	C6
MARWICK AV	LB	LB15	2300	76	C2
MARWICK AV	LKD	LKD	4100	71	C4
MARWOOD DR	LA	LA65	4600	25	F5
MARWOOD ST	CO	LPUE	14400	48	C6
MARWOOD ST	CO	LPUE	15700	85	E1
MARY AV	CO	LA02	8600	58	D2
MARY AV	LA	LA02	10300	58	D4
MARY CIR	LAV	LAV		90	B2
MARY CT	WCOV	WCOV		92	E5
MARY ST	CO	GL14	2600	11	D6
MARY ST	CO	GL14	2400	18	D1
MARY ST	CO	GL14	2600	18	D1
MARY ST	GLEN	GL14	3300	11	D6
MARY ST	PR	PR	8400	54	E4
MARY ANN CT	AZU	AZU		88	D2
MARY ANN DR	RB	RB	500	67	E1
MARY ANN LN	CO	WAL		97	B5
MARYANN LN	POM	POM	300	90	F6
MARY ANN ST	GLEN	GL14	3200	11	C5
MARYANNA LN	MON	MON	600	29	A5
MARY ANN MANOR	LAV	LAV		95A	E6
MARY BELL AV	LA	SUN	10300	10	A3
MARYBETH AV	ELM	ELM	3100	47	B1
MARYBETH AV	RM	RM	3500	38	B6
MARYBETH AV	SELM	ELM	2600	47	B2
MARY ELLEN AV	LA	NHO	7000	16	A4
MARY ELLEN AV	LA	NHO	3900	23	A4
MARY ELLEN AV	LA	SV	8200	16	A1
MARY ELLEN AV	LA	VAN	6000	16	A5
MARY ELLEN AV	LA	VAN	4400	23	A3
MARYE MARGO CIR	PALM	PALM		183	J6
MARYGROVE RD	CLA	CLA	300	91	B5
MARYHILL RD N	CO	ACT	29000	189	D7
MARYHILL RD W	CO	ACT	4800	189	C7
MARYHURST DR	CLA	CLA	800	91	A2
MARY JEAN LN	CO	PVP		73	B3
MARYKNOLL AV	CO	WHI	9200	61	E3
MARYKNOLL AV	WHI	WHI	8700	61	E2
MARY KNOLL CIR	MON	MON	700	29	C3
MARYLAND AV	GLEN	GL14	4200	11	D6
MARYLAND AV	GLEN	GL14	4200	18	D1
MARYLAND AV N	GLEN	GL06	100	25	C3
MARYLAND AV N	GLEN	GL07	1100	25	C3
MARYLAND AV S	GLEN	GL05	100	25	C3
MARYLAND DR	LA	LA36	6000	42	E1
MARYLAND PL	GLEN	GL06	200	25	C3
MARYLAND ST	ELS	ELS	100	56	B6
MARYLAND ST	LA	LA17	1200	44	C2
MARYLAND ST	LA	LA57	1800	44	B2
MARYLEE ST	LA	WOH	23700	5	E6
MARYLEE ST	LA	WOH	21700	12	C6
MARYLIE LN	WAL	WAL		92	F5
MARYLIND AV	CLA	CLA	600	91	C2
MARYMOUNT LN	CLA	CLA		91	A1
MARYMOUNT PL	LA	LA24	100	32	E6
MARYNEL AV	CO	PALM		182	G8
MARYON DR	LA	BH	9500	33	A1
MARYPORT AV	SAD	SAD	600	90	A2
MARYTON AV	NWK	NWK	14300	82	D2
MARYTON AV	SFS	SFS		82	D2
MARYVILLE DR	WAL	WAL		93	B6
MARYVINE ST	ELM	ELM	11200	47	E3
MARYWOOD AV	CLA	CLA		91	A4
MARZELLA AV	LA	LA49	700	32	B6
MASCAGNI ST	LA	LA66	4400	49	F4
MASCAGNI ST	LA	LA66	4800	50	A4
MASCARELL AV	LA	SF	10800	8	D1
MASCOT ST	LA	LA19	4600	43	B4
MASEFIELD CT	LA	CAN		5	E2
MASLINE ST	BAP	BAP	13600	39	D3
MASLINE ST	CO	COV	16500	88	C3
MASLINE ST	COV	COV	900	88	C3
MASON AV	LA	CAN	8500	6	E6
MASON AV	LA	CAN	6400	12	E4
MASON AV	LA	CHA	9000	6	E3
MASON AV	LA	WOH	5400	13	E1
MASON CT	SCLR	SAU		124	C4
MASON CT	TOR	TOR	20200	67	E2
MASON RD	CO	MAL		105	A5
MASON ST	AZU	AZU	100	88	D1
MASON ST	SOG	SOG	4300	59	C2
MASON WY	IND	LPUE	200	48	C3
MASONCREST DR	PR	PR	8000	60	F2
MASONGATE DR	RHE	PVP	25900	72	F3
MASONHILL DR	CO	PALM		157	J8
MASSACHUSTTS AV	LA	LA24	10700	41	D3
MASSACHUSTTS AV	LA	LA25	11000	41	D3
MASSACHUSTTS ST	LB	LB14	3900	76	A5
MASSELIN AV	LA	LA19	1000	42	F3
MASSELIN AV	LA	LA36	700	42	F3
MASSENA AV	RB	RB	1600	67	E6
MASSER PL	MTB	MTB	800	46	D6
MASSEY AV	HB	RB	300	67	D2
MASSINGER ST	LKD	LKD	11700	81	A4
MAST CT	LA	VEN		49	D6
MAST ST	LA	VEN		49	C6
MASTER CUP WY	CO	VAL		126	J2
MASTERS PL	CO	LLAN		192	J2
MASTERSON CT	SCLR	SAU		124	E5
MASTHEAD TR	CO	TOP		109	B3
MATADOR DR	CO	LPUE	2400	98	C5
MATANA DR	SCLR	SAU		124	C4
MATARO ST	PAS	PAS	2600	27	E3
MATCHLEAF AV	CO	LPUE	1300	85	E2
MATCHWOOD PL	AZU	AZU	700	86	E6
MATCHWOOD ST	AZU	AZU	1000	86	E6
MATEL RD	SCLR	VAL		127	A2
MATEL RD	SCLR	VAL		127	A8
MATEO AV	SAD	SAD	100	90	B2
MATEO PL	LA	LA21	2000	44	E6
MATEO ST	LA	LA13	400	44	E5
MATEO ST	LA	LA21	600	44	E5
MATER DEI CIR	CLA	CLA		91	C1
MATERN PL	SFS	SFS		61	A3
MATFIELD DR	TOR	TOR	25800	73	C3
MATHER AV	LA	SUN	10200	10	E3
MATHEWS AV	MB	MB	1500	62	E5
MATHEWS AV	RB	RB	1900	62	E5
MATHEWS PL	LA	LA23	2500	45	A5
MATHEWS ST N	LA	LA33	100	45	A4
MATHEWS ST S	LA	LA23	600	45	A4
MATHEWS ST S	LA	LA33	100	45	A4
MATILIJA AV	LA	VAN	8500	8	E6
MATILIJA AV	LA	VAN	5600	15	E6
MATILIJA AV	LA	VAN	4200	22	E3
MATILIJA RD	GLEN	GL02	800	18	B6
MATISSE AV	LA	WOH	4100	13	C4
MATISSE DR	RPV	PVP		77	C1
MATLEY RD	LCF	LCF	4800	18	F1
MATLOCK AV	BAP	BAP	600	48	B2
MATNEY AV N	LB	LB07	4700	70	E3
MATRANGA PL	LA	SV	9100	10	A5
MATTESON AV	CUL	CUL	10900	50	A2
MATTESON AV	CUL	LA66	11300	50	A2
MATTESON AV	LA	LA66	12600	49	E3
MATTESON AV	LA	LA66	11400	50	A2
MATTHEWS PL	POM	POM	1800	94	E5
MATTHISEN AV	COM	COM	100	64	E3
MATTHISEN CIR	COM	COM		64	E3
MATTOCK AV	DOW	DOW	9800	60	D4
MATULA DR	LA	TAR	4900	21	B2
MAUBERT AV	LA	LA27	4600	34	F3
MAUCH ST	CO	SAU		124	G3
MAUDE AV	LA	SUN	9900	10	A4
MAUI	WCOV	WCOV		92	C4
MAULSBY DR	WHI	WHI	13400	55	E6
MAUNA LOA AV	AZU	AZU	900	86	F6
MAUNA LOA AV	CO	AZU	18500	86	F6
MAUNA LOA AV	CO	GLDR	19000	86	F6
MAUNA LOA AV	CO	GLDR	19200	87	A6
MAUNA LOA AV E	GLDR	GLDR	100	87	A6
MAUNA LOA AV W	GLDR	GLDR	100	87	A6
MAUNA LOA DR	MON	MON	100	29	A3
MAUPIN AV	BAP	BAP	4300	39	E4
MAUREEN ST	PALM	PALM	38200	172	E9
MAUREEN ST	PALM	PALM		183	E1
MAUREEN ST	WCOV	WCOV		92	E5
MAURETANIA ST E	LA	WIL	900	74	D3
MAURETANIA ST W	LA	WIL	1000	74	B3
MAURICE AV	CER	ART	17000	82	C5
MAURICE AV	CO	GL14	2200	11	F4
MAURICE CIR	CER	ART	16600	82	C4
MAURICE CT	CER	ART	16700	82	C5
MAURICE ST	MON	MON	900	29	C4

1990 LOS ANGELES COUNTY STREET INDEX

STREET	CITY	P.O. ZONE	BLOCK	PAGE	GRID
MAURINE AV	GLEN	GL01		24	F2
MAURITA PL	GLEN	GL06		25	D3
MAURY AV	LA	WOH	5800	5	D6
MAURY AV	LB	LB07	4200	70	D4
MAVERICK CIR	LAV	LAV		90	D1
MAVERICK CIR	LAV	LAV		95A	D6
MAVERICK CIR	POM	POM		94	C5
MAVERICK DR	SAD	SAD		95A	A6
MAVERICK LN	RH	PVP	1	78	B1
MAVIS AV	WHI	WHI	5400	55	C3
MAVIS DR	LA	LA65	300	36	A3
MAXELLA AV	LA	LA66	12500	49	E4
MAXFIELD ST	CO	TOR	1100	68	F5
MAXIMUM RD	CO	CAST		123	F3
MAXINE LN	CO	SAU		124	E4
MAXINE ST	PR	PR	8400	54	D6
MAXINE ST	PR	PR	8700	60	D1
MAXINE ST	SFS	SFS	11200	61	A2
MAXINE WY	CO	ACT	4100	189	D2
MAXSON PL	ELM	ELM	3300	47	F1
MAXSON PL	ELM	ELM		48	A1
MAXSON RD	ELM	ELM	3900	39	A6
MAXSON RD	ELM	ELM	3300	47	F1
MAXSON RD	ELM	ELM	3300	48	A1
MAXWELL ST	LA	LA27	2900	35	B2
MAXWELL ST	MTB	MTB	1000	54	C4
MAXWELLTON RD	LA	NHO	12000	23	C4
MAY AV	LB	LB06		75	E3
MAY AV	MON	MON	100	29	B3
MAY AV	RB	RB	2800	62	E4
MAY CT	CO	LPUE		97	A5
MAY CT	SOG	SOG	8900	59	D3
MAY ST	LA	LA66	3500	49	E2
MAY WY	SCLR	SAU		124	H9
MAYA PL	LA	SF43		8	B6
MAYALL ST	LA	CHA	19700	6	E3
MAYALL ST	LA	NOR	17000	7	E3
MAYALL ST	LA	SF	16500	7	E3
MAYALL ST	LA	SF	14800	8	C3
MAYAN DR	CO	CHA		1A	C6
MAYAN DR	LA	CHA		6	C1
MAYAPAN RD	LHH	LAH	1200	98A	A3
MAYBANK AV	LKD	LKD	4100	70	F3
MAYBERRY ST	LA	LA26	2300	35	C5
MAYBROOK AV	CO	WHI	11500	84	D6
MAYBROOK AV	WHI	WHI	10300	84	D3
MAYBROOK DR	LA	BH	1000	32	F4
MAY CYN TK TR	CO	NEW		128	C7
MAY CYN TK TR	CO	SF		3	A1
MAYCOTTE RD	LA	WOH	22400	13	B2
MAYCREST	SPAS	SPAS	2100	36	E4
MAYCREST AV	LA	LA32	4200	36	E4
MAYCROFT DR	RPV	PVP	6900	72	C4
MAYDEE ST	CO	DUA	500	29	B6
MAYDEE ST	CO	MON	300	29	B6
MAYDOCK PL	LA	TU	7000	11	A3
MAYER AL	CO	ALT	2000	20	B6
MAYERLING ST	LA	SF	17200	1	D5
MAYES DR	CO	WHI	11600	84	C5
MAYES DR	LAM	LAM	11800	84	C5
MAYES DR	WHI	WHI	10800	84	B4
MAYESDALE AV	CO	SGAB	6700	28	A6
MAYESDALE AV	CO	SGAB	6700	38	A1
MAYFAIR AV	ELM	ELM	3000	47	D1
MAYFAIR AV	POM	POM	500	94	E4
MAYFAIR DR	LA	LA65	3700	35	F3
MAYFAIR DR	PAS	PAS	3600	28	B3
MAYFAIR LN	ING	IN01		57	B2
MAYFARE ST	CO	CAST		123	C2
MAYFIELD AV	CO	GL14	2600	18	E2
MAYFIELD AV	CO	MONT	2400	18	E2
MAYFIELD AV	GLEN	GL14	3400	11	C6
MAYFIELD AV	LA	LA49	11600	41	C3
MAYFIELD AV	LA	TU	6200	11	B5
MAYFIELD CT	PALM	PALM		183	F1
MAYFIELD ST	LB	LB04	3700	76	A4
MAYFLOWER AV	ARC	ARC	900	29	A5
MAYFLOWER AV	ARC	ARC	1500	39	A1
MAYFLOWER AV	BELL	BELL	6200	53	D6
MAYFLOWER AV	CO	ARC	2600	39	A1
MAYFLOWER AV	MAY	MAY	5200	53	D5
MAYFLOWER AV	MON	MON	1700	29	A5
MAYFLOWER AV	MON	MON	100	29	A5
MAYFLOWER AV N	MON	MON	100	29	A5
MAYFLOWER AV S	MON	MON	100	29	A5
MAYFLOWER CIR	GAR	GAR		63	E5
MAYFLOWER CT	MON	MON	500	29	A3
MAYFLOWER DR	LA	SF	17400	1	E6
MAYFLOWER PL	BELL	BELL	6800	53	D6
MAYFLOWER RD	CLA	CLA	500	91	B3
MAYGREEN CT	GLEN	GL06		25	F2
MAYHILL AV	LAM	LAM	12600	84	C6
MAYLAND AV	BAP	BAP	3400	39	F6
MAYLAND AV	CO	LPUE	1000	48	D2
MAYLAND AV	LPUE	LPUE	300	48	C3
MAYLAND AV	WCOV	BAP	1600	48	D2
MAYLIN ST	PAS	PAS	400	26	E4
MAYME ST	CO	PALM		182	G6
MAYMONT DR	CO	LA43	4900	51	A3
MAYNARD AV	LA	CAN	6900	12	A4
MAYNARD AV	LA	WOH	5600	13	A1
MAYNARD DR	CO	CAL		108	B5
MAYNARD DR	DUA	DUA	900	29	E5
MAYNARD ST	GLEN	GL05	100	25	E4
MAYNARD WY	MTB	MTB	100	54	C5
MAYNE ST	BLF	BLF	8700	66	B4
MAYO AV N	COM	COM	100	65	A3
MAYO AV S	COM	COM	100	65	A3
MAYO ST	LA	LA42	900	36	A2
MAYOR DR	TOR	TOR	4600	67	F6
MAYPOP AV	LPUE	LPUE	300	48	E5
MAYPORT AV	NWK	NWK	13500	82	C2
MAYS AL	SGAB	SGAB		37	D3
MAYSTONE PL	CO	LPUE	2000	98	C4
MAYTERN AV	LAN	LAN		159	A9
MAYTIME LN	CUL	CUL		50	C2
MAYTOR PL	BH	BH	1100	33	C3
MAYVIEW DR	LA	LA27	1900	35	A3
MAYVIEW LN	PAS	PAS	100	26	F2
MAYWIND WY	CO	LPUE		98	A4
MAYWOOD AV	BELL	BELL	6200	53	B4
MAYWOOD AV	HPK	HPK	5900	53	B4
MAYWOOD AV	MAY	MAY	5100	53	B4
MAYWOOD AV	VER	LA58	4300	53	B2
MAYWOOD AV N	LA	LA41	4800	26	A4
MAZA ST	NWK	NWK	10900	66	F1
MAZATLAN AV	CO	ELM	4100	38	D5
MAZATZAL CT	CO	PALM		157	F9
MAZUR DR	RPV	PVP	26500	72	D4
MCALLISTER ST	LA	LA33	2100	45	B3
MCALPINE DR	CO	MAL	2800	113	B4
MCANANY WY	CO	MAL	3600	115	A4
MCATEE DR	WHI	WHI	10400	84	B3
MCAULEY ST	LKD	LKD	5700	71	C1
MCBAIN AV	RB	RB		62	F4
MCBAIN ST	RB	RB	2700	62	F4
MCBEAN DR	ELM	ELM	11600	39	A3
MCBEAN PKWY	CO	VAL		123	J8
MCBEAN PKWY	CO	VAL		124	A8
MCBEAN PKWY	CO	VAL		126	H3
MCBEAN PKWY	CO	VAL		126	H3
MCBEAN PKWY	SCLR	VAL		127	A2
MCBEAN PKWY	SCLR	VL55		124	A8
MCBRIDE AV	MPK	MPK	1000	45	E3
MCBRIDE AV N	CO	LA22	800	45	E3
MCBRIDE AV S	CMRC	LA22	1400	53	E1
MCBRIDE AV S	CO	LA22	300	45	E5
MCBRIDE AV S	CO	LA22	1000	53	E1
MCBROOM ST	LA	SUN	10300	9	F2
MCBROOM ST	LA	SUN	9800	10	A2
MCCADDEN PL N	LA	LA04	100	34	B5
MCCADDEN PL N	LA	LA28	1300	34	B4
MCCADDEN PL N	LA	LA38	700	34	B5
MCCADDEN PL S	LA	LA04	100	34	B5
MCCADDEN PL S	LA	LA05	600	43	B1
MCCADDEN PL S	LA	LA20	300	43	B2
MCCAHILL ST	DOW	DOW	8700	60	C4
MCCALLUM AV	SOG	SOG	5100	59	D3
MCCALLUM ST	DOW	DOW	8700	60	B5
MCCAMMET AL	SPAS	SPAS	800	36	E2
MCCANN DR	SFS	SFS	12200	61	B3
MCCANN PL	LAM	LAM	15200	84	B5
MCCARTHY CT	ELS	ELS	800	56	B5
MCCARTHY DR	LA	LA65	3200	25	E5
MCCARTHY VISTA	LA	LA48	700	42	E2
MCCARTY DR	BH	BH	100	42	B2
MCCLEAN DR	CO	ARC	6800	28	B6
MCCLELLAN DR	LA	LA25	1200	41	C4
MCCLELLAN DR	LA	LA49	1100	41	C4
MCCLEMONT AV	LA	TU	10100	10	F3
MCCLEMONT LN	LA	TU	10000	10	F4
MCCLINTOCK AV	LA	LA07	3200	43	F6
MCCLINTOCK AV	TEC	TEC	4900	38	E3
MCCLOUD DR	CO	PALM		157	J8
MCCLUNG DR	LA	LA08	3900	51	B2
MCCLUNG WK	LA	LA08	3500	51	B2
MCCLURE AV	PAR	PAR	13800	65	F1
MCCLURE ST	LA	LA65	2600	35	F4
MCCOLLUM PL	LA	LA26	1400	35	B5
MCCOLLUM ST	LA	LA26	1300	35	B5
MCCOMAS ST	POM	POM	1500	94	C3
MCCOMB WY	MPK	MPK	1000	46	C3
MCCONNELL AV	LA	LA45	7400	50	B6
MCCONNELL AV	LA	LA45	7900	56	B1
MCCONNELL AV	LA	LA66	4400	49	F5
MCCONNELL BLVD	CUL	LA66	4000	49	F3
MCCONNELL DR	LA	LA64	2700	42	B4
MCCONNELL PL	LA	LA64	10100	42	C4
MCCOOL AV	LA	LA45	7200	50	C5
MCCORMICK AL	PAS	PAS	100	26	F4
MCCORMICK ST	LA	ENC	16600	21	E2
MCCORMICK ST	LA	NHO	10300	23	F2
MCCORMICK ST	LA	TAR	18200	21	C1
MCCORMICK ST	LA	VAN	13300	22	F2
MCCORMICK ST	LA	VAN	13200	23	A2
MCCOY AV	LA	HAC	25000	73	F3
MCCRAY LN	CO	MAL		114	E2
MCCREADY AV	LA	LA39	2400	35	C3
MCCUE CT	LA	CAN	8300	12	D1
MCCULLOCH AV	ARC	ARC		38	E3
MCCULLOCH AV	TEC	TEC	5400	38	E3
MCCUNE AV	LA	LA34	10700	50	B1
MCCUNE AV	LA	LA66	11800	49	F2
MCCUNE AV	LA	LA66	11300	50	A1
MCDERMOTT AV	LA	RES	8000	14	D2
MCDIVITT AV	COM	COM	1100	65	A2
MCDONALD AV	LA	WIL	200	74	B5
MCDONALD ST	CUL	CUL	11200	50	B4
MCDONALD ST	LA	CUL	11700	50	B4
MCDONIE AV	LA	WOH	5600	12	E6
MCDONIE PL	LA	WOH	5900	12	E6
MCDONNELL AV	CMRC	LA22	1400	53	E1
MCDONNELL AV N	CO	LA22	100	45	E5
MCDONNELL AV S	CO	LA22	100	45	E5
MCDONNELL AV S	CO	LA22	1000	53	E1
MCDONOUGH AV	LA	WIL	800	74	E4
MCDOWELL AL	PAS	PAS	900	27	B2
MCDUFF ST	LA	LA26	1300	35	C6
MCENNERY CYN RD	CO	ACT		182	H9
MCFALL LN	LPUE	LPUE		92	A6
MCFARLAND AV	LA	WIL	200	74	D4
MCFARLANE AV	BUR	BUR	4100	24	A3
MCFARLANE ST	SMAR	PAS	1800	37	B1
MCGARRY ST	LA	LA21	800	44	E6
MCGARRY ST	LA	LA58	1900	52	D1
MCGEE DR	CO	WHI	13500	61	E2
MCGEE DR	WHI	WHI	12500	61	D1
MCGILL DR	WAL	WAL	20200	93	B6
MCGILL RD	LAM	LAM		83	D1
MCGILL RD	LAM	LAM		84	D6
MCGILL ST	CO	COV	15600	88	A4
MCGILVREY AV	CO	LA63	1400	45	D2
MCGIRK AV	ELM	ELM	10900	38	E5
MCGIRK ST	ELM	ELM	11600	38	F5
MCGIRK ST	ELM	ELM	11800	39	A5
MCGOVERN AV	DOW	DOW	11500	60	B4
MCGREW AL	PAS	PAS	600	27	A6
MCGROARTY DR	LA	SUN	7800	10	D3
MCGROARTY PL	LA	SUN	8200	10	D3
MCGROARTY ST	LA	SUN	7800	10	E3
MCGROARTY ST	LA	TU	7500	10	E3
MCGROARTY ST	SGAB	SGAB	500	37	D3
MCGROARTY TER	LA	TU	7500	10	F4
MCHELEN AV	CAR	LB10	21800	69	F5
MCHENRY RD	GLEN	GL06	300	25	E3
MCINTYRE ST	LA	SF		2	C5
MCKAIN ST	CO	CAL		108	D4
MCKAY DR	WAL	WAL	20200	93	B6
MCKEEVER AV	AZU	AZU	700	86	C5
MCKEEVER ST	LA	SF	17000	7	E1
MCKEEVER ST	LA	SF	15400	8	B1
MCKENDREE AV	LA	PP	14600	40	D3
MCKENZIE AV	LA	LA32	3500	36	C5
MCKENZIE ST	LB	LB05	1600	65	E5
MCKEON CT	CO	SAU		181	D7
MCKIM CT	LA	LA46	8100	33	E2
MCKINLEY AV	CAR	CAR	16100	64	C3
MCKINLEY AV	CO	COM	15200	64	C3
MCKINLEY AV	CO	LA59	12100	58	C6
MCKINLEY AV	CO	LA59	12900	64	C2
MCKINLEY AV	LA	LA01	6400	52	C6
MCKINLEY AV	LA	LA01	7800	58	C4
MCKINLEY AV	LA	LA02	8600	58	C4
MCKINLEY AV	LA	LA11	3400	52	C4
MCKINLEY AV	LA	LA59	10700	58	C4
MCKINLEY AV	LA	VEN	2300	49	C4
MCKINLEY AV	LAV	LAV	1700	90	C5
MCKINLEY AV	PAR	PAR	8000	59	F6
MCKINLEY AV	SOG	SOG	5500	59	E6
MCKINLEY AV E	POM	POM	100	90	E6
MCKINLEY AV E	POM	POM	1500	91	B6
MCKINLEY AV N	COM	LA59	1100	64	C2
MCKINLEY AV S	COM	COM	1100	64	C4
MCKINLEY AV W	POM	POM	100	90	E6
MCKINLEY CT	CO	CAST	28500	123	A6
MCKINLEY PL	LA	LA02	8600	58	C2
MCKINLEY PL	MON	MON	100	28	F3
MCKINLEY ST	AZU	AZU	1400	88	A1
MCKNIGHT DR	LKD	LKD	6000	71	D2
MCKOOL CIR	CAR	GAR	1300	69	D2
MCLAREN AV	LA	CAN	6900	12	A2
MCLAREN ST	NWK	NWK	10600	66	F2
MCLAREN ST	NWK	NWK	12800	82	C2
MCLAUGHLIN AV	LA	LA66	3300	49	F1
MCLAUGHLIN AV	LA	LA66	3800	50	A2
MCLEAN AV	LA	LA45	8800	56	B2
MCLEAN PL	LA	LA45	6800	56	B2
MCLEAN ST E	ALH	ALH	100	37	B3
MCLEAN ST W	ALH	ALH	100	37	B3
MCLENNAN AV	LA	ENC	5500	21	F1
MCLENNAN AV	LA	SF	8800	7	F6
MCLENNAN AV	LA	VAN	6400	14	F3
MCLENNAN AV	SF	SF	11400	1	F6
MCLEOD DR	LA	LA46	1800	33	D2
MCLEOD PL	POM	POM	1500	90	D6
MCMANUS AV	CUL	CUL	3200	42	D5
MCMANUS AV	LA	LA34	3200	42	D5
MCMANUS ST	LKD	LKD	7000	71	E4
MCMILLAN ST	COM	COM	1500	65	B1
MCMILLAN ST	LYN	LYN	4500	65	C2
MCNAB AV	BLF	BLF	13400	66	D3
MCNAB AV	BLF	BLF	13600	66	D5
MCNAB AV	CO	LB08	3700	71	D5
MCNAB AV	LB	LB15	1800	76	D3
MCNAB AV	LKD	LKD	4300	71	D2
MCNALLY AV	CO	ALT	2600	20	A4
MCNALLY RD	LAM	LAM		83	D1
MCNALLY RD	LAM	LAM		84	D6
MCNEES AV S	CO	WHI	6000	55	B4
MCNEES AV S	WHI	WHI	5800	55	B4
MCNERNEY AV	LYN	LYN	10600	59	C4
MCNERNEY AV	SOG	SOG	8900	59	C4
MCNULTY AV	LA	CAN	7700	12	D2
MCNULTY PL	LA	CAN	20700	12	D2
MCPHERRIN AV N	MPK	MPK	100	46	C2
MCPHERRIN AV S	MPK	MPK	100	46	C2
MCPHERSON AV	LA	LA32	2000	45	D1
MCPHERSON PL	LA	LA32	2000	45	D1
MCQUEEN ST	LA	SF	15800	2	B2
MCRAE AV	NWK	NWK	12800	66	F1
MCRAE DR	LA	SP	2100	78	C4
MCREYNOLDS RD	CO	MAL		106	E6
MCVINE AV	LA	SUN	10100	10	D3
MCVINE TR	LA	SUN	10000	10	D4
MCWILTON PL	CO	ALT	500	20	B3
MCWOOD ST	CO	LPUE	16400	92	B3
MCWOOD ST	WCOV	WCOV	1200	92	B3
MEACHAM ST	GLDR	GLDR	300	89	A1
MEAD AL	PAS	PAS	900	28	B2
MEAD AV	RM	RM	4500	38	A4
MEADBROOK ST	CAR	CAR	900	64	C6
MEADBURY DR	SCLR	SAU		124	E4
MEADCLIFF PL	DBAR	POM		94	A6
MEADCLIFF PL	DBAR	POM		97A	A1
MEADE CIR	LAV	LAV		90	D1
MEADE PL	LA	VEN	2200	49	D3
MEADOW DR	BH	BH	1400	33	B3
MEADOW DR	CO	CYN		125	E7
MEADOW LN	DBAR	POM		97	C4
MEADOW LN	MON	MON	300	29	C2
MEADOW LN	PALM	PALM		172	A9
MEADOW LN	POM	POM	400	90	F5
MEADOW PL	LAN	LAN		159	D9
MEADOW RD	DOW	DOW	8500	60	B6
MEADOW RD	NWK	NWK	10400	60	D6
MEADOW RD	SOG	SOG	5600	59	D4
MEADOW RD N	WCOV	WCOV	100	92	E1
MEADOW RD S	WCOV	WCOV	100	92	E1
MEADOW ST	LAV	LAV		90	E2
MEADOWBROOK AV	CO	ALT	1700	20	B5
MEADOWBROOK AV	LA	LA19	1000	43	A3
MEADOWBROOK LN	CER	ART		82	B4
MEADOWBROOK LN	GLDR	GLDR		87	E5
MEADOWBROOK LN	ING	IN02		50	F6
MEADOWBROOK LN	WAL	WAL		97	B1
MEADOWBROOK RD	CO	ALT	1100	20	C5
MEADOW CREEK LN	CO	CAL		100A	F6
MEADOWCREEK RD	SCLR	CYN	27800	124	G7
MEADOWCREST RD	LA	VAN	16100	22	A5
MEADOWDALE LN	RPV	PVP	5400	72	E6
MEADOW FALLS DR	DBAR	POM	23700	94	A6
MEADOWGATE RD	LA	ENC	15500	22	B3
MEADOWGATE RD	LA	VAN	15400	22	B3
MEADOW GLEN DR	DBAR	POM		97	F3
MEADOWGLEN LN	SAD	SAD		89	F1
MEADOW GLEN WY	CO	LPUE	1500	98	A3
MEADOW GRASS DR	CO	CAST		123	C1
MEADOWGREEN RD	CO	WHI	12300	84	C6
MEADOWGREEN RD	LAM	LAM	12900	83	C1
MEADOWGREEN RD	LAM	LAM	12600	84	C6
MEADOW GROVE PL	CO	PAS	300	19	D4
MEADOW GROVE ST	CO	PAS		19	D4
MEADOW HAVEN DR	AGH	AGO		100A	A1
MEADOWLAND DR	LHH	LAH		98A	B3
MEADOWLARK	ELM	ELM		48	A6
MEADOWLARK S	ELM	ELM		48	A6
MEADOWLARK AV	LA	SF		1	E3
MEADOWLARK DR	CO	CAL		13	A4
MEADOW LARK DR	LAV	LAV		95A	E5
MEADOWLARK LN	CO	CYN		125	D4
MEADOWLARK LN	PALM	PALM		172	A7
MEADOW LARK LN	RH	PVP	1	73	B5
MEADOWLARK LN	WAL	WAL		93	D6
MEADOWLARK WY	WAL	WAL		93	D4
MEADOWMIST DR	RPV	PVP	28200	72	D5
MEADOWMIST WY	AGH	AGO		102	F3
MEADOWMONT ST	SCLR	VAL		127	A3
MEADOW OAK DR	WLVL	THO		102	A5
MEADOW PASS RD	WAL	WAL		93	B5
MEADOW RDG CIR	POM	POM		94	D5
MEADOWRIDGE DR	CO	NEW		127	E5
MEADOW RIDGE PL	LA	ENC	4100	22	A4
MEADOW RIDGE RD	LA	ENC	16200	22	A4
MEADOWRIDGE WY	LA	ENC	16100	22	A4
MEADOWS AV N	MB	MB	100	62	C4
MEADOWS AV S	MB	MB	100	62	C4
MEADOWS CIR	CER	ART	19600	81	B2
MEADOWS CT	CER	ART		81	B2
MEADOWS DR	GLEN	GL02	400	25	B1
MEADOWS END DR	CO	CAL		107	F5
MEADOWSIDE ST	CO	LPUE	15800	92	A4
MEADOWSIDE ST	WCOV	WCOV		92	B4
MEADOWVALE AV	LA	LA31	2200	35	E4
MEADOW VLY TER	LA	LA39		35	B3
MEADOWVIEW CT	CO	PALM		184	A3
MEADOW VIEW DR	LA	ENC	16100	22	A3
MEADOW VIEW DR	LCF	LCF	400	19	D2
MEADOW VIEW DR	WAL	WAL		94	D5
MEADOWVIEW LN	LA	PAC		3	B4
MEADOWVIEW LN	LA	PAC		9	D3
MEADOW VIEW PL	LA	ENC	4300	22	A3
MEADOWVIEW TER	CO	LPUE		48	B5
MEADOW VISTA WY	AGH	AGO		102	F3
MEADOW WOOD AV	LKD	LKD	4900	70	E2
MEADOW WOOD DR	COV	COV		89	A6
MEADOW WOOD LN	LA	SF		1	F2
MEADOW WOOD ST	PALM	PALM		172	J9
MEADSTONE RD	CO	CYN		125	C4
MEADVALE AV	SCLR	CYN		124	H9
MEADVIEW AV	SCLR	NEW	24700	127	D3
MEADVILLE DR	LA	VAN	3300	22	C5
MEAFORD AV	CO	NEW		127	C7
MEALY AV	CER	ART		71	F2
MEALY ST	COM	COM	100	64	F2
MEANDER RD	CO	SAU		181	C9
MEANDERNG CK DR	DBAR	POM		97A	A2
MEARS PL	CO	WHI	3900	55	C2
MECATE DR	SCLR	SAU	20000	124	E7
MECCA AV	LA	TAR	5200	21	C1
MECHAM WY	LA	LA43	600	51	A4
MEDA AV E	GLDR	GLDR	100	87	A5
MEDA AV W	GLDR	GLDR	100	87	A5
MEDEA CT	PALM	PALM		172	H9
MEDEA CT	PALM	PALM		183	H1
MEDEABROOK PL	AGH	AGO		102	F3
MEDEA CREEK RD	CO	AGO		100A	A6
MEDEA MESA RD	CO	AGO		100A	B6
MEDEA VALLEY DR	AGH	AGO		100A	A3
MEDFIELD ST	AGH	AGO		100A	A4
MEDFORD CT	LB	LB03		76	D5
MEDFORD RD	PAS	PAS	900	28	B2
MEDFORD ST	CO	LA63	3200	45	C2
MEDFORD ST	LA	LA33	2400	45	C2
MEDFORD ST	MTB	MTB	1800	54	C1
MEDIA DR	LA	LA42	5500	36	C2
MEDWAY AV	PALM	PALM		171	D3
MEDICAL CTR DR	LA	CAN	7200	5	F3
MEDILL PL	LA	LA64	2600	42	C4
MEDINA CT	ELM	ELM	11200	38	E6
MEDINA DR	LA	WOH	4900	13	C2
MEDINA RD	LA	WOH	4900	13	C2
MEDINA ST	POM	POM	500	93	F2
MEDIO DR	LA	LA49	100	41	B2
MEDIO ST	LB	LB02	700	75	D6
MEDLEY DR	LA	ENC	17900	21	C4
MEDLEY LN	CO	TOP	20300	109	C6
MEDLEY PL	LA	ENC	4400	21	D3
MEDLOW AV	LA	LA41	2400	25	F6
MEDLOW AV	LA	LA65	2600	25	F6
MEDNICKVALE DR	CO	PALM	40800	173	H3
MEDNIK AV N	CO	LA22	100	45	E4
MEDNIK AV S	CO	LA22	100	45	E4
MEDWAY AV	CO	LAN	41200	171	D2
MEEKER AV	CO	BAP	1800	48	E2
MEEKER AV	CO	LPUE	1000	48	E2
MEEKER AV	ELM	ELM	11300	47	E2
MEEKER AV	LPUE	LPUE	500	48	C4
MEEKER AV	WCOV	WCOV	900	48	E1
MEEKER RD	ELM	ELM	2600	47	E1
MEERHELM DR	CO	LAN		146	E1
MEGAN AV	LA	CAN	8800	6	C6
MEGAN AV	LA	CHA	9400	6	C4
MEGAN PL	LA	CAN	8900	6	C6
MEGUIAR DR	CO	PAS	2600	27	E1
MEHDEN AV	CAR	CAR	22900	69	B6
MEIER ST	CUL	LA66	3900	49	E3
MEIER ST	LA	LA66	3300	49	E2
MEI LING WY	LA	LA12	900	44	E1
MEISNER ST	LA	LA63	3500	45	C3
MELA LN	RPV	PVP		72	E6

1990 LOS ANGELES COUNTY STREET INDEX

STREET	CITY	P.O. ZONE	BLOCK	PAGE	GRID
MELANIE LN	ARC	ARC	1400	28	C6
MELANIE LN	GLEN	GL14		11	D5
MELANIE ST	ARC	ARC		28	C6
MELANIE ST	ARC	ARC	1700	38	C1
MELBA AV	LA	CAN	6600	5	F5
MELBA AV	LA	WOH	6100	5	F5
MELBOURNE AV	LA	LA27	4600	34	F3
MELBOURNE AV	LA	LA27	3900	35	A3
MELBOURNE AV	POM	POM	2700	90	F4
MELBOURNE CT	CO	CAL		100	B2
MEL CANYON RD	DUA	DUA	200	86	A3
MELDAR AV	DOW	DOW	8800	60	D2
MELGAR DR	WHI	WHI	9800	84	C3
MELGRE AV	LA	WOH	5300	100	F1
MELHAM AV	CO	LPUE	700	48	E4
MELHAM AV	LPUE	LPUE	200	48	E4
MELHILL WY	LA	LA49	1800	40	F1
MELHORN DR	ALH	ALH	2300	46	B1
MELIA WY	CO	CYN		125	E6
MELINDA DR	LA	BH	9800	22	F6
MELINDA LN	LAV	LAV		95A	D4
MELINDA WY	LA	NOR		7	C3
MELISA CT	SCLR	NEW		127	H6
MELISSA ST	CO	TOR	900	68	F3
MELISSA ST	WCOV	WCOV		92	E5
MELITA AV	LA	NHO	7500	16	A2
MELITA ST	PR	PR	9300	55	B2
MELLISSA ST	CER	ART		66	E4
MELLO CT	WCOV	WCOV		92	C4
MELLON AV	LA	LA39	1900	35	D3
MELLOW LN	LCF	LCF	300	19	D3
MELLUS DR	CO	MAL	26800	112	E3
MELODI LN	SCLR	SAU		124	D6
MELODY LN	LAN	LAN		160	D7
MELROSE AV	GLEN	GL02	1000	25	C2
MELROSE AV	LA	LA29	4000	34	C5
MELROSE AV	LA	LA38	5000	34	C5
MELROSE AV	LA	LA46	7600	33	E5
MELROSE AV	LA	LA46	7100	34	A5
MELROSE AV	MON	MON	100	29	A3
MELROSE AV	PAS	PAS	100	26	D5
MELROSE AV	RM	RM	7500	46	E2
MELROSE AV	WHOL	LA69	8300	33	D5
MELROSE PL	LA	LA69	8400	33	E5
MELROSE WY E	LB	LB02	100	75	C5
MELROSE WY W	LB	LB02	100	75	C5
MELROSE HILL CT	LA	LA29	800	34	E5
MELTON AV	PALM	PALM	37800	172	E9
MELTON AV	PALM	PALM		183	E1
MELVA ST	DOW	DOW	7800	60	A4
MELVIL ST	LA	CUL	6100	42	D5
MELVIL ST	LA	LA34	6100	42	D5
MELVILLE AV	LA	SF	12400	1	D4
MELVILLE DR	SMAR	PAS	2100	37	D1
MELVILLE PL	LA	SF	17500	1	D4
MELVIN AV	LA	NOR	9300	7	A5
MELVIN AV	LA	NOR	8500	12	F1
MELVIN AV	LA	NOR	8300	14	A1
MELVIN AV	LA	RES	6200	14	A2
MELVIN AV	LA	TAR	5600	14	A6
MELVIN AV	LA	TAR	5100	21	A1
MELWOOD DR	GLEN	GL07	1400	25	D1
MEMO CT	LA	NOR		1	B5
MEMORY DR	LA	TU	7600	10	F1
MEMORY LN	WLVL	THO		102A	E6
MEMORY PARK AV	LA	SF	11500	2	C6
MEMORY PARK AV	LA	SF	8700	8	C6
MEMORY PARK DR	LA	SF	10700	8	C2
MEMPHIS AV	CO	WHI	10400	84	A4
MEMPHIS AV	LA	SF	12100	2	D5
MEMPHIS AV	WHI	WHI	9700	84	A4
MENARD PL	LA	TAR	19100	21	B4
MENCKEN AV	LA	CAN		5	E2
MENDEL DR	LA	SF	12500	1	E4
MENDEZ ST	LB	LB04	4000	76	A3
MENDIPS RDG RD	LA	NHO		23	D6
MENDOCINO CT	LA	LA65	4500	25	E5
MENDOCINO LN	CO	ALT	1900	20	D5
MENDOCINO ST E	CO	ALT	100	20	A5
MENDOCINO ST W	CO	ALT	1	19	F4
MENDON DR	RPV	SP	2000	78	D1
MENDON PL	LA	CHA	20400	6	E2
MENDOTA AV	LA	LA42	4700	36	A1
MENDOZA DR	SCLR	VAL		127	B1
MENDY ST	PAR	PAR	7400	65	E1
MENEELY AL	PAS	PAS	900	27	B5
MENLO AV	CO	TOR	20900	68	F3
MENLO AV	HAW	HAW	100	57	A6
MENLO AV	LA	GAR	12800	63	F1
MENLO AV	LA	LA06	900	43	F3
MENLO AV	LA	LA07	2000	43	F4
MENLO AV	LA	LA37	3800	51	F2
MENLO AV	LA	LA44	5800	51	F5
MENLO AV	LA	LA44	8600	57	F2
MENLO AV	LA	LA44	12000	58	A5
MENLO DR	CLA	CLA		91	C1

STREET	CITY	P.O. ZONE	BLOCK	PAGE	GRID
MENLO DR	CO	ALT	1100	20	C4
MENLO DR	GLEN	GL08	3000	18	F4
MENOMINEE PL	RPV	PVP	26600	72	D3
MENSHA CT	DBAR	POM		97	E3
MENTONE AV	CUL	CUL	4100	50	C1
MENTONE AV	LA	LA34	3300	42	B6
MENTONE AV	PAS	PAS	1000	26	F2
MENTOR AV N	PAS	PAS	100	27	B3
MENTOR AV S	PAS	PAS	10	27	B5
MENTOR CT	PALM	PALM		172	H9
MENTOR CT	PALM	PALM		183	H1
MENTRY DR	SCLR	NEW		127	B6
MENTZ ST	LPUE	LPUE	15400	48	F5
MENTZ ST	LPUE	LPUE	15600	92	A5
MERAMEC AV	LA	SP	1000	78	E2
MERCADO AV	LAM	LAM	14400	83	C2
MERCANTILE PL	ING	IN01	200	57	A1
MERCANTILE PL	PAS	PAS	1	27	A4
MERCATOR LN	CO	TOP	800	109	A3
MERCED AV	ELM	ELM	2600	47	C4
MERCED AV	SELM	ELM	1200	47	C4
MERCED AV E	BAP	BAP	13900	39	D5
MERCED AV E	WCOV	WCOV	400	92	B3
MERCED AV N	BAP	BAP	3700	39	D4
MERCED AV W	WCOV	WCOV	1200	48	E1
MERCED AV W	WCOV	WCOV	800	92	A2
MERCED PL	WCOV	WCOV		92	A3
MERCED ST	LA	LA65	2600	35	F4
MERCEDES AV	LA	PAC	9100	8	E4
MERCEDES AV	LA	PAC	8900	9	A6
MERCEDES AV	PAS	PAS	300	27	E3
MERCER CT	CLA	CLA		91	B1
MERCER ST	LA	PAC	12600	3	B6
MERCER ST	LA	PAC	13400	8	E3
MERCER ST	LA	PAC	12900	9	A2
MERCER ST	LA	SF	12300	3	C5
MERCHANT ST	LA	LA21	700	44	D5
MERCURY AV	LA	LA31	3700	36	C5
MERCURY AV	LA	LA32	4200	36	C5
MERCURY CIR	POM	POM		94	A3
MERCURY CT	LA	LA14	600	44	C3
MERCURY LN	PAS	PAS	400	27	F3
MEREDITH CT	LA	CAN		5	E2
MEREDITH PL	LA	BH	9000	33	C2
MEREDITH ST	CLA	CLA	100	91	C5
MERENDINO LN	PAS	PAS	1100	26	D2
MERIAM WY	LB	LB15		76	D4
MERIDEN PL	CO	VAL		124	F2
MERIDIAN AV	ALH	ALH	1	36	F5
MERIDIAN AV	ALH	ALH	1800	45	F1
MERIDIAN AV	SPAS	SPAS	300	36	F2
MERIDIAN DR	PAR	PAR		65	E4
MERIDIAN LN	SPAS	SPAS		36	F2
MERIDIAN ST	IRW	DUA	700	39	C1
MERIDIAN ST	LA	LA42	4900	36	B1
MERIDIAN TER	LA	LA42	500	36	C1
MERIDITH AV N	PAS	PAS	100	27	D4
MERIDITH AV S	PAS	PAS	100	27	D4
MERIMAC CT	CAR	CAR	17500	64	C5
MERION DR	LA	NOR		1	B6
MERION LN	WAL	WAL		93	D6
MERION WY	DBAR	WAL		97	C4
MERIT AV	LA	GAR	16800	63	F5
MERIT LN	WHI	WHI		55	D4
MERIT PL	TOR	TOR	3800	68	A5
MERITA PL	LCF	LCF	5000	19	D3
MERIT PARK DR	GAR	GAR		63	E4
MERIVALE LN	LA	PP	16600	40	B2
MERKEL AV	PAR	PAR	13100	65	F1
MERLE DR	MTB	MTB	1800	46	C6
MERLIN PL	LA	ENC		21	F3
MERLINDA ST	WCOV	WCOV	1000	92	B2
MERLON AV	CO	PAS	1	28	B4
MERMAID DR	LA	SP	1700	78	C4
MERO LN	LCF	LCF	200	19	D3
MERRETT DR	PAS	PAS		27	B2
MERRICK ST	LA	LA13	300	44	E4
MERRIDY ST	LA	CHA	19700	6	F3
MERRIDY ST	LA	NOR	17700	7	A3
MERRIFIELD AV	POM	CLA	3200	90	F3
MERRILL AV	GLEN	GL06	300	25	F3
MERRILL AV	SMAD	SMAD	100	28	C2
MERRILL DR	TOR	TOR	3000	68	B4
MERRILL ST	TOR	TOR	3900	67	F4
MERRIMAC AV	LB	LB10	2000	74	F2
MERRIMAC RD	LA	LA49	3400	30	F2
MERRIMAN DR	GLEN	GL02	1400	25	C1
MERRIT HILL DR	CO	SAU		181	B8
MERRITT DR	CO	MAL	6000	112	A6
MERRITT RD	CO	ACT		189	B1
MERRYGROVE ST	WCOV	WCOV	2900	97	A2
MERRYHILL ST	SCLR	CYN	19700	124	G6
MERRYL LN	WCOV	WCOV		92	B4
MERRY OAK LN	ARC	ARC	800	28	D3
MERRY OAK LN	WLVL	THO		102	B5
MERRYWOOD DR	LA	LA46	2200	33	E2

STREET	CITY	P.O. ZONE	BLOCK	PAGE	GRID
MERRYWOOD ST	POM	POM	2400	91	A5
MERRYWOOD TER	LA	LA46	2300	33	E2
MERRYWOOD TR	LA	LA46	8100	33	E2
MERSIN PL	SFS	SFS		61	A1
MERTON AV	LA	LA41	2000	26	A5
MERVILLE DR	CO	LPUE	200	48	C4
MERWIN ST	LA	LA26	800	35	B6
MESA AV	LA	LA42	5900	36	C1
MESA CIR	MON	MON	200	29	A2
MESA CT	SCLR	VAL		127	B1
MESA DR	CO	TOP		109	C2
MESA DR	WCOV	WCOV	2700	92	F1
MESA LN	PALM	PALM		171	G6
MESA MTY	CO	CLA		96	D3
MESA RD	CO	PALM		183	F6
MESA RD	LA	SM	200	40	E5
MESA RD	SMAR	PAS	1200	27	C6
MESA ST	TOR	TOR	4000	72	F2
MESA ST	TOR	TOR	3800	73	A2
MESA ST N	LA	SP	100	79	A4
MESA ST S	LA	SP	100	79	A4
MESA WY	LB	LB07	500	70	B4
MESA WY	MPK	MPK	100	45	F2
MESA ALTA RD	CO	SF		3	E2
MESABA DR	RPV	PVP	27000	72	D4
MESAGROVE AV	WHI	WHI	5400	55	C2
MESA LILA LN	GLEN	GL08	3600	18	D2
MESA LILA RD	GLEN	GL08	100	18	D2
MESALOA LN	CO	PAS	3000	20	F6
MESA OAK LN	POM	POM		90	E2
MESA OAKS DR	SAD	LAV		95A	B5
MSA OF THE OAKS	SCLR	NEW		127	H1
MESA PEAK MTWY	CO	MAL		107	B5
MSA PEAK TRK WY	CO	CAL		107	E6
MESARICA RD	CO	COV	21000	89	C5
MESARICA RD	SAD	COV	20700	89	C5
MESA RIDGE DR	POM	POM		94	C6
MESA ROBLES DR	CO	LPUE	16100	85	E3
MESA ROBLES DR	WHI	WHI	9400	84	C2
MESA VERDE AV	PALM	PALM		172	B9
MESA VERDE DR	BUR	BUR		17	C2
MESA VERDE RD	PAS	PAS	900	26	E6
MESA VISTA DR	LCF	LCF	4200	19	B4
MESCAL ST	CO	LPUE	17400	98	D5
MESCALERO ST	CO	LPUE	18200	98	E5
MESERVE ST	POM	POM	1500	94	C3
MESETA DR	LA	SUN		9	E4
MESILLA AV	PALM	PALM	37600	183	C1
MESITA AV	WCOV	WCOV	2000	92	D2
MESITA PL	WCOV	WCOV	400	92	D1
MESITA RD	PAS	PAS	1000	28	A1
MESITA WY	LA	SM		40	E4
MESITA ALTA WY	CO	SF		3	E2
MESMER AV	CO	CUL	5600	50	C4
MESMER AV	LA	CUL	5100	50	B4
MESNAGER ST	LA	LA12	200	44	F1
MESQUIT ST	LA	LA21	600	44	E5
MESQUITE LN	CAR	CAR		69	E5
MESQUITE LN	NWK	NWK	12800	61	C6
MESQUITE LN	NWK	NWK	12800	82	C1
MESQUITE PL	POM	POM		94	E6
MESQUITE PL	POM	POM		97A	C1
MESQUITE RD	CO	PALM	38800	171	J7
MESQUITE RDG RD	CO	SF		3	E2
MESSINA	MTB	MTB		46	D5
MESSINA DR	WHI	WHI	10300	84	B3
MESSINA PL	POM	POM	1200	94	B4
META DR	CO	WHI	14900	84	A4
METATE LN	CO	MAL		110	B4
METCALF AL	PAS	PAS		27	A4
METRO DR	MPK	MPK	700	46	D3
METRO ST	DOW	DOW	9500	60	E2
METROPOL DR	CO	LPUE		85	C5
METROPOLE AV	AVA	AVA	100	77	B5
METROPOLITAN PL	POM	POM	2700	90	E4
METROPOLITAN PZ	LA	LA36	5900	43	A1
METTLER AV	CAR	CAR	18000	64	B6
METTLER AV	CAR	CAR	18400	69	B1
METTLER AV	CO	LA61	13200	64	B1
METTLER DR	CAR	CAR	17100	64	B5
METTLER ST	LA	LA03	5800	52	B4
METTLER ST	LA	LA03	8600	58	B2
METTLER ST	LA	LA11	3600	52	B3
METZ PL	LA	LA69	8600	33	D3
METZ ST	LB	LB08	6200	71	F6
METZLER DR	LA	LA31	2400	36	B6
MEVEL PL	GLEN	GL14	3400	11	C4
MEXICO PL	PVE	PVP	700	72	B2
MEYER CT	HB	RB	1	67	D1
MEYER DR	LAN	LAN		159	E5
MEYER LN	RB	RB	500	67	E1
MEYER RD	CO	WHI	13100	61	D5
MEYER RD	SFS	WHI	13000	61	D5
MEYER ST N	SF	SF	200	2	D5
MEYER ST S	LA	SF	100	2	D5
MEYERLOA LN	CO	PAS	3100	20	F6

STREET	CITY	P.O. ZONE	BLOCK	PAGE	GRID
MEYLER AV	CO	HAC	24400	73	F2
MEYLER AV	CO	TOR	21300	68	F4
MEYLER RD	LA	SP		79	A5
MEYLER ST	CO	TOR	21500	68	F4
MEYLER ST N	LA	SP	100	78	F2
MEYLER ST S	LA	SP	100	78	F4
MEZZANINE WY	LB	LB08	5100	71	C6
MIAMI CT	CLA	CLA	800	91	A1
MIAMI WY	LA	PP	15800	40	C3
MICA ST	SFS	SFS		82	E3
MICAELA DR	AGH	AGO		102	E3
MICHAEL AV	CER	ART		82	C5
MICHAEL AV	CUL	LA66	3900	49	E3
MICHAEL AV	LA	LA66	3900	49	E3
MICHAEL DR	LAN	LAN		160	E6
MICHAEL DR	LAN	LAN		160	E9
MICHAEL LN	LA	PP		30	A5
MICHAEL PL	POM	POM	2400	94	A2
MICHAEL ST	CO	SAU		181	J6
MICHAEL CLN CIR	MTB	MTB		46	E6
MICHAEL HUNT DR	SELM	ELM		47	D3
MICHALE ST	LA	CAN	20500	6	E6
MICHELANGELO AV	LA	WOH	4200	13	C4
MICHELE CT	MTB	MTB		54	D1
MICHELE CT W	MTB	MTB		46	D6
MICHELLE AV	LAN	LAN		160	E8
MICHELLE CIR	CO	WHI	13100	61	D5
MICHELLE DR	AGH	AGO		100A	A3
MICHELLE DR	TOR	TOR	5000	67	F2
MICHELLE DR	TOR	TOR	3400	68	A3
MICHELLE ST	CER	ART		66	F6
MICHELLE ST E	WCOV	WCOV	1200	92	C3
MICHELLE ST W	WCOV	WCOV	800	92	A3
MICHELSON ST	LB	LB05	1200	70	D1
MICHELSON ST	LKD	LKD	3600	71	D1
MICHELTORENA ST	LA	LA26	400	35	A5
MICHELTORENA ST	LA	LA39	1900	35	B3
MICHENER AL	PAS	PAS	600	27	A3
MICHIGAN AV	CO	LA22	4300	45	E4
MICHIGAN AV	CO	LA63	3600	45	C4
MICHIGAN AV	LA	LA33	1500	45	A3
MICHIGAN AV	LYN	LYN	3200	59	B3
MICHIGAN AV	SM	SM	1400	41	B6
MICHIGAN AV	SM	SM	700	49	B1
MICHIGAN AV	SOG	SOG	3200	59	B3
MICHIGAN AV	WHI	WHI	8000	55	F6
MICHIGAN AV N	CO	PAS	1700	20	C6
MICHIGAN AV N	PAS	PAS	1600	20	C6
MICHIGAN AV N	PAS	PAS	1	27	C3
MICHIGAN AV S	PAS	PAS	1	27	C4
MICHIGAN AV S	WHI	WHI	8200	61	F1
MICHIGAN BLVD	CO	PAS	400	28	B5
MICHIGAN DR	CLA	CLA		96	C6
MICHIGAN ST	CO	ACT		189	G3
MICHILLNDA AV N	ARC	ARC	1	28	B5
MICHILLNDA AV N	CO	PAS	1	28	B5
MICHILLNDA AV N	PAS	PAS	200	28	B3
MICHILLNDA AV N	SMAD	SMAD	1	28	B3
MICHILLNDA AV S	ARC	ARC	1	28	B5
MICHILLNDA AV S	CO	PAS	1	28	B5
MICHILLNDA AV S	SMAD	SMAD	1	28	B3
MICHILLINDA DR	CO	PAS	3800	28	B5
MICHILLINDA WY	SMAD	SMAD	600	28	B1
MICHU LN	HAW	HAW		56	F6
MICHU LN	HAW	HAW		57	A6
MICON CIR	CO	GAR	15700	64	B3
MIDBURY ST	CO	BREA		98A	C3
MIDCREST DR	CO	WHI	14800	84	A4
MIDCREST DR	WHI	WHI	15400	84	B4
MIDDLE RD	CO	LA63	3700	45	C2
MIDDLE RD	LA	LB10		74	F2
MIDDLE TER	AVA	AVA	100	77	C5
MIDDLE BANK DR	SCLR	NEW	23000	127	C5
MIDDLEBROOK RD	TOR	TOR	1800	68	D6
MIDDLEBURY ST	LA	LA04	3700	34	F5
MIDDLEBURY ST	PALM	PALM		183	E1
MIDDLECOFF PL	LA	SF	12500	1	F4
MIDDLE CREST DR	AGH	AGO		102	E3
MIDDLECREST RD	RPV	PVP	5200	72	E6
MIDDLEGATE RD	WLVL	THO	3900	102	B4
MIDDLERIDGE LN	RH	PVP	1	73	A5
MIDDLERIDGE RD	RHE	PVP		73	A5
MIDLSBY RDG CIR	LA	CAN	7000	5	E3
MIDDLESEX LN	ING	IN01		57	C2
MIDDLESEX TR	CO	TOP		109	D1
MIDDLETON AV	WHI	WHI		84	D1
MIDDLETON PL	LA	LA62	1600	51	D1
MIDDLETON RD	SAD	SAD		89	D4
MIDDLETON ST	HPK	HPK	5900	52	F5
MIDDLETON ST	PALM	PALM		171	F6
MIDDLEWAY LN	CLA	CLA	300	91	B4
MIDFIELD AV	LA	LA45	7400	50	E6
MIDFIELD AV	LA	LA45	7600	56	E1
MIDFIELD LN	CER	ART		82	B4
MIDHURST DR	COV	COV	3300	89	A6
MIDLAND ST	LA	LA31	3800	36	A4

STREET	CITY	P.O. ZONE	BLOCK	PAGE	GRID
MIDLOTHIAN DR	CO	ALT	1800	20	D6
MIDLOTHIAN DR	CO	PAS	1600	20	D6
MIDSITE AV	CO	COV	3200	88	E3
MIDSITE AV	COV	COV	1300	88	E3
MIDTOWN AV	CAR	CAR	19200	69	D1
MIDVALE AV	LA	LA24	400	41	D1
MIDVALE AV	LA	LA25	1800	41	E3
MIDVALE AV	LA	LA34	3000	42	A5
MIDVALE AV	LA	LA34	3700	50	B1
MIDVALE AV	LA	LA64	2200	41	F5
MIDVALE AV	LA	LA64	2700	42	A5
MIDVALE DR	POM	POM	1800	90	D5
MIDVALE DR	WHI	WHI		55	F5
MIDVALE PL	ALH	ALH	3100	36	F5
MIDWAY AV	CER	ART	10700	66	E4
MIDWAY AV	CUL	CUL	3800	50	B1
MIDWAY PL	CER	ART	12600	82	C4
MIDWAY PL	LA	LA15	900	44	C4
MIDWAY ST	BLF	BLF	10200	66	D4
MIDWAY ST	CER	ART	13700	82	E4
MIDWAY ST	LB	LB03	3900	80	A1
MIDWAY THE	GLEN	GL08	1500	25	F1
MIDWICK DR	ALH	ALH	2800	36	F6
MIDWICK DR	CO	ALT	1400	20	D5
MIDWICK LN	LA	TAR	4100	13	F4
MIDWICKHILL DR	ALH	ALH	1200	46	A1
MIDWOOD CT	LAN	LAN		159	F8
MIDWOOD DR	CO	SF		2	B6
MIDWOOD DR	LA	SF	17000	1	E5
MIGNONETTE ST	LA	LA12	1000	44	D2
MIGUEL AV	CER	ART	19600	81	B2
MIGUEL AV	PR	PR	3900	55	B1
MIGUEL CT	SCLR	VAL		127	B1
MIGUEL WY	LB	LB03		76	D5
MIKELYN RD	SCLR	NEW		127	G3
MIKINDA CT	WHI	WHI	15900	84	C3
MIKOSASKY AV	LAN	LAN		160	E8
MIKUNI AV	LA	NOR	8900	7	A6
MILA DR	PAR	PAR		65	E4
MILACA PL	LA	VAN	4000	22	D4
MILAM PL	MPK	MPK	1200	46	C3
MILAN AV	SPAS	SPAS	500	37	A2
MILAN DR	PALM	PALM		171	G5
MILAN PL	LA	SP	1900	78	D3
MILANO	MTB	MTB		46	C5
MILANO AV	NWK	NWK	10900	60	F5
MILANO AV	NWK	NWK	10900	61	A5
MILANO LN	SCLR	VAL		127	A1
MILANO PL	POM	POM	1200	94	B4
MILANO WY	LA	SV	9900	17	A2
MILBANK ST	LA	ENC	15500	22	B3
MILBANK ST	LA	NHO	12300	23	B3
MILBANK ST	LA	VAN	13700	22	E3
MILBORO PL	LA	BH		33	A2
MILBURN DR	CO	LA63	4200	45	D2
MILBURN DR	LA	SV	9800	17	A1
MILDAS DR	CO	CAL		108	D5
MILDINE DR	GLEN	GL08	1400	18	E3
MILDRED AV	CUL	LA66	4100	49	F3
MILDRED AV	LA	VEN	100	49	C4
MILDRED AV	TOR	TOR	19300	67	E2
MILDRED DR	GLEN	GL06	1700	25	F2
MILDRED ST	ELM	ELM	10100	47	D1
MILDRED ST	LAV	LAV		95A	B6
MILDWOOD CT	LAN	LAN		159	F8
MILDWOOD CT	LAN	LAN		159	G8
MILES AV	HPK	HPK	5900	53	A5
MILES ST	CER	ART		81	B2
MILES ST	PAS	PAS	400	27	A5
MILFORD AV	POM	POM	900	94	D4
MILFORD CT	PALM	PALM		183	D1
MILFORD ST	GLEN	GL03	100	25	B3
MILFORD ST	LA	LA42	600	36	D2
MILGOLD CT	CO	ACT		182	D6
MILITARY AV	LA	LA34	3000	42	A6
MILITARY AV	LA	LA34	3700	50	A1
MILITARY AV	LA	LA64	2400	41	F5
MILKFLOWER RD	CO	MAL		110	B5
MILKYWAY PL	DBAR	POM		94	B5
MILL LN	DBAR	WAL		97	C4
MILL LN	SMAR	PAS	1100	37	C1
MILL RD	SPAS	SPAS	1900	37	A1
MILL ST	LA	LA21	600	44	E5
MILLAR DR	GLEN	GL06	1400	25	E3
MILLARD AV	PAS	PAS	100	26	F3
MILLARD PL	LA	NOR	17200	7	E5
MILLBORO PL	LA	BH		33	A2
MILLBRAE AV	DUA	DUA	1000	29	D5
MILLBRAE ST	DUA	DUA	1000	29	F5
MILLBROOK DR	LA	VAN	14200	22	E4
MILLBROOK LN	PALM	PALM		183	H7
MILLBURGH AV	GLDR	GLDR	800	88	F2
MILLBURGH RD	CO	AZU	16700	88	B2
MILLBURGH RD	CO	COV	18900	88	F2
MILLBURY AV	BAP	BAP	3300	39	E6

STREET	CITY	P.O. ZONE	BLOCK	PAGE	GRID
MILLBURY AV	CO	LPUE	200	48	D2
MILL CANYON RD	SMAR	PAS	1	37	C1
MILLCREEK	WCOV	WCOV		92	D3
MILL CREEK LN	SGAB	SGAB	400	37	D2
MILLCREEK WY	PALM	PALM		171	H6
MILLDALE CT	LA	NHO	12200	16	C2
MILLDALE DR	LA	LA77	15400	22	C6
MILLENNIUM WY	LA	LA42	5000	26	B6
MILLER AV	AZU	AZU	700	86	C5
MILLER AV	CO	LA63	900	45	D3
MILLER AV	GAR	GAR	14700	63	C3
MILLER AV	NWK	NWK	13300	82	C1
MILLER DR	LA	LA69	1300	33	E4
MILLER DR	TEC	TEC	9300	38	B4
MILLER PL	LA	LA69	1300	33	E4
MILLER RD	CO	WHI	11200	61	F5
MILLER ST	LAV	LAV		90	D1
MILLER ST	POM	POM	1300	90	D4
MILLER ST	POM	POM	400	94	F5
MILLER WK	CO	CAST		123	C2
MILLER WY	LA	LA69	1400	33	E3
MILLER WY	SOG	SOG	9800	59	E4
MILLERGROVE DR	CO	WHI	8000	55	A6
MILLERGROVE DR	CO	WHI	8500	61	A2
MILLERGROVE DR	SFS	SFS	8700	61	A2
MILLER RANCH RD	CLA	CLA		95A	F5
MILLER RANCH RD	CO	CLA		95A	F5
MILLET AV	ELM	ELM	2600	47	C2
MILLET AV	SELM	ELM	1400	47	C3
MILLETTE AV	WAL	WAL		97	B1
MILLFORD CT	CO	VAL		124	F2
MILLICENT WY	PAS	PAS	2700	27	F4
MILLIKEN AV	WHI	WHI	7900	55	F6
MILLIKEN AV	WHI	WHI		61	F1
MILLIKEN AV	WHI	WHI	8100	85	A6
MILLIKEN DR	SCLR	SAU		124	D2
MILLING ST W	LAN	LAN	1100	159	J4
MILLING ST W	LAN	LAN	100	160	A4
MILLIS ST	MTB	MTB	1900	54	C1
MILLMARK AV	LB	LB05	6600	65	D5
MILLMARK GRV ST	LA	SP	800	78	F1
MILL MEADOW RD	CO	CYN		128	E2
MILLMONT ST	CAR	CAR	1100	69	D1
MILLOU LN	WHI	WHI	14500	84	A1
MILLPOINT AV	CAR	CAR	21000	69	D4
MILLRACE AV	LYN	LYN	12300	65	C1
MILLRACE ST	LA	SV	13100	16	A1
MILLRIDGE DR	SCLR	SAU		124	F6
MILLRIDGE DR	WCOV	WCOV	3300	97	A1
MILL RUN	MON	MON		29	B2
MILLS AV	CO	SAU		181	J6
MILLS AV	CO	WHI	9600	61	E4
MILLS AV	GLEN	GL14	3100	18	D1
MILLS AV	WHI	WHI	8800	84	A3
MILLS AV N	CLA	CLA	100	91	C4
MILLS AV N	CLA	CLA	3100	96	C5
MILLS AV S	CLA	CLA	100	91	C4
MILLS PL	PAS	PAS	1	26	F4
MILLS PL	PAS	PAS		27	A4
MILLS ST	SM	SM	200	49	A2
MILLSTON CT	CO	VAL		124	B7
MILLSTONE DR	CO	LPUE	16900	92	B5
MILLSTREAM DR	CO	CYN	26100	128	E3
MILLSTREAM LN	CER	ART		82	B4
MILLUX AV	PR	PR	6200	54	F5
MILLUX AV	PR	PR	5000	55	A3
MILL VALLEY RD	SCLR	VAL		127	A3
MILL VALLEY RD	POM	POM		94	C5
MILLWARD LN	CAR	CAR		69	E6
MILMAC DR	LHH	LAH	1000	98A	A2
MILMADA DR	LCF	LCF	800	19	B3
MILMORE AV	CAR	CAR	18200	64	B6
MILMORE AV	CAR	CAR	18600	69	B1
MILNA AV	CO	WHI	5700	55	B3
MILNA AV	CO	WHI	8600	61	A1
MILNE DR	TOR	TOR	4600	67	E5
MILNER RD	LA	LA68	6700	34	B2
MILO CT	LAN	LAN		160	D5
MILO TER	LA	LA42	600	36	B2
MILOANN ST	CO	ARC	11200	38	E3
MILOANN ST	TEC	TEC	9800	38	D3
MILROY PL	SFS	SFS	13700	82	E2
MILSTEAD AV	CO	WHI	11200	61	E5
MILTON AV	ALH	ALH	1300	36	F6
MILTON AV	CUL	CUL	4100	50	B1
MILTON AV	WHI	WHI	5500	55	E6
MILTON AV	WHI	WHI	8200	61	D1
MILTON CT	CLA	CLA	400	91	B5
MILTON CT	LB	LB03		76	F5
MILTON CT	LA	LA65	500	36	A3
MILTON DR	CO	GLDR	18500	86	F4
MILTON DR	GLDR	GLDR	100	86	F4
MILTON DR	SGAB	SGAB	200	37	D2
MILTON PL	WHI	WHI	5700	55	E3
MILTON ST	CO	PAS	3200	27	F4
MILTON ST	CO	PAS	3200	28	A4
MILTON ST	CO	TOR	900	68	F3
MILTON ST	LA	LA66	12400	50	A4
MILTON ST	PAS	PAS	3100	27	F4
MILTON ST	PAS	PAS	3100	28	A4
MILTONWOOD AV	DUA	DUA	800	29	E4
MILVERN DR	CO	WHI	15900	84	C4
MILWAUKEE AV	LA	LA42	500	36	C1
MILWOOD AV	LA	CAN	6500	12	D4
MILWOOD AV	LA	CHA	9900	6	D3
MILWOOD AV	LA	VEN	500	49	C3
MIMOSA DR	LA	LA65	3500	35	E1
MIMOSA LN	LAV	LAV		90	E1
MIMOSA ST	ALH	ALH	2700	36	F5
MINA AV S	CO	WHI	9500	61	E3
MINARD RD	CO	TOP	2400	115	B1
MINA RICA DR	LA	TU	9500	11	B5
MINDANAO WY	CO	MDR		49	E5
MINDANAO WY	LA	VEN	13200	49	E4
MINDEN PL	LA	LA41	4800	26	C5
MINDO DR	POM	POM	1100	95	B2
MINDORA AV	LA	SF	13500	3	B2
MINDORA CT	LA	SF	17100	1	E5
MINDORA DR	TOR	TOR	4500	67	E5
MINEOLA ST	LA	PAC	13400	8	F5
MINEOLA ST	LA	PAC	12600	9	B4
MINER ST	LA	LA02	8800	58	E2
MINER ST	LA	SP	2200	79	B5
MINERVA AV	CUL	LA66	4000	50	A2
MINERVA AV	LA	LA66	3800	50	A2
MINERVA CT	LB	LB13	1000	75	D4
MINERVA CT	SH	LB07	3300	70	D6
MINERVA ST	LA	LA58	2200	52	F1
MINERVA ST	VER	LA58	2500	52	F1
MINERVA PARK	LB	LB13	1000	75	E4
MINES AV	LA	LA23	3200	53	A1
MINES AV	MTB	MTB	100	54	D2
MINES AV	PR	PR	8700	54	F3
MINES AV	PR	PR	9300	55	A4
MINES BLVD	CO	WHI	10800	55	B5
MINES ST	CO	LA22	4500	53	E1
MINFORD ST W	LAN	LAN	2000	159	H4
MINGUS DR	WLVL	THO		102	C2
MINK DR	DBAR	POM	24000	93	F6
MINNEAPOLIS ST	LA	LA39	3200	35	D2
MINNEHAHA ST	LA	CHA	20200	6	E2
MINNEHAHA ST	LA	NOR	18100	7	C2
MINNEHAHA ST	LA	SF	16500	7	F2
MINNEHAHA ST	LA	SF	14300	8	C2
MINNEQUA DR	DBAR	POM		94	A5
MINNESOTA AV	LB	LB05	6600	65	E5
MINNESOTA AV	LYN	LYN	3100	59	A3
MINNESOTA AV	PAR	PAR	15100	65	E4
MINNESOTA AV	SOG	SOG	3300	59	A3
MINNESOTA AV N	GLDR	GLDR	100	87	B5
MINNESOTA AV S	GLDR	GLDR	100	87	B5
MINNESOTA AV S	GLDR	GLDR	800	89	B1
MINNESOTA ST	LA	LA31	3000	36	A6
MINNIE AV	CO	PALM		189	J1
MINOA AV	CO	PAS	400	28	B5
MINOMINEE PL	RPV	PVP	26600	72	D3
MINORCA DR	LA	PP	1200	40	E3
MINORU DR	CO	ALT	1800	20	D6
MINSTREL AV	LA	CAN	6800	12	A2
MINSTREL DR	LAN	LAN		159	C8
MINT CANYON RD	CO	SAU	11500	181	C6
MINTER CT	SCLR	CYN		125	C8
MINTO CT	LA	LA32	2800	36	D5
MINTURN AV	LKD	LKD	4900	71	A2
MINUET PL	LA	VAN	8300	15	F1
MINUTEMAN WY	WLVL	THO		102	C4
MIOLAND DR	CO	LA43		50	F3
MIRA ST	HB	RB	1500	62	C6
MIRABEAU AV	LA	SP	100	78	D3
MIRACOSTA ST	LA	SP	1600	78	D3
MIRADERO RD	BH	BH	1100	33	B4
MIRADOR AV	LB	LB15		76	C3
MIRADOR PL	LA	TAR	4600	21	B3
MIRAFLORES AV	LA	SP	600	78	F1
MIRAGE	PALM	PALM		171	E4
MIRAGE LN	DBAR	POM		97A	A4
MIRALESTE DR	LA	SP	300	78	D3
MIRALESTE DR	RPV	SP	4000	78	C2
MIRALESTE PZ	RPV	SP		78	C2
MIRALINDA DR	CO	RM	1800	46	E3
MIRA LOMA AV	GLEN	GL04	300	25	C6
MIRA LOMA DR	AZU	AZU	300	88	C1
MIRALOMA WY	WAL	WAL		93	A5
MIRAMAR AV	CLA	CLA	100	96	B6
MIRA MAR AV	LB	LB03	100	76	A6
MIRA MAR AV	LB	LB04	700	76	A6
MIRA MAR AV	LB	LB14	300	76	A6
MIRA MAR AV	LB	LB15	2100	76	A2
MIRAMAR DR	CO	LPUE		85	C5
MIRAMAR DR	RB	RB	400	67	D4
MIRAMAR ST	LA	LA26	1200	44	C2
MIRAMAR ST	LA	LA57	1800	44	B1
MIRAMAR ST	POM	POM	1700	91	A6
MIRAMONTE AV	PALM	PALM		172	B9
MIRAMONTE AV	PALM	PALM		172	D7
MIRAMONTE AV E	SMAD	SMAD	100	28	C1
MIRAMONTE AV W	SMAD	SMAD	100	28	C1
MIRAMONTE BLVD	CO	LA01	5800	52	D6
MIRAMONTE BLVD	CO	LA01	7800	58	D1
MIRAMONTE DR	LAV	LAV		90	D4
MIRAMONTE DR	POM	POM	1900	90	D5
MIRA MONTE PL	PAS	PAS	600	27	B4
MIRANDA PL	LA	WOH	20500	13	E1
MIRANDA ST	LA	ENC	17400	14	D6
MIRANDA ST	LA	NHO	11200	16	D6
MIRANDA ST	LA	TAR	18100	14	B6
MIRANDA ST	LA	VAN	14300	15	E6
MIRANDA ST	LA	WOH	23600	5	F6
MIRANDA ST	LA	WOH	20300	12	E6
MIRANDA ST	LA	WOH	20300	13	D1
MIRANDA ST	WCOV	WCOV		92	E5
MIRASOL DR	SMAR	PAS	1400	27	E6
MIRASOL ST	LA	LA23	1100	53	B1
MIRA VALLE ST	MPK	MPK	800	46	B3
MIRA VERDE DR	LHH	LAH		84	F2
MIRA VISTA AV	CO	MONT	2200	18	F3
MIRA VISTA DR	GLEN	GL08	2700	18	F5
MIRA VISTA TER	PAS	PAS	300	26	E3
MIRIAM DR	WCOV	WCOV	3400	89	A6
MIRIAM DR	WCOV	WCOV		93	A1
MIRIAM ST	LA	LA42	5100	36	B1
MIRROR WY	SCLR	CYN	27800	125	A7
MIRROR LAKE DR	LA	LA68	6000	24	C6
MISHA DR	PALM	LAN		171	A1
MISS GRACE DR	SCLR	CYN		125	C8
MISSION AL	SPAS	SPAS		37	A1
MISSION BLVD E	POM	POM	100	94	C3
MISSION BLVD E	POM	POM	1000	95	A3
MISSION BLVD W	POM	POM	100	94	C3
MISSION DR	PALM	LAN		171	B2
MISSION DR	PALM	PALM		171	B3
MISSION DR	RM	RM	8400	37	E4
MISSION DR	RM	RM	8500	38	A4
MISSION DR E	SGAB	SGAB	100	37	E4
MISSION DR N	SGAB	SGAB	100	37	D3
MISSION DR S	SGAB	SGAB	100	37	D3
MISSION DR W	SGAB	SGAB	100	37	E4
MISSION PL	HPK	HPK	7000	53	A6
MISSION RD	ALH	ALH		36	F5
MISSION RD	GLEN	GL05	100	25	D6
MISSION RD	LA	CHA	21000	6	C1
MISSION RD E	ALH	ALH	100	37	B5
MISSION RD N	LA	LA31	1800	36	B6
MISSION RD N	LA	LA31	1800	45	A2
MISSION RD N	LA	LA33	100	44	F4
MISSION RD N	LA	LA33	900	45	A2
MISSION RD S	LA	LA23	600	44	F5
MISSION RD S	LA	LA33	100	44	F4
MISSION RD W	ALH	ALH	100	37	B5
MISSION ST	SMAR	PAS	1500	37	A1
MISSION ST	SPAS	SPAS	400	36	E1
MISSION ST	SPAS	SPAS	1400	37	A1
MISSION WY	CMRC	LA40		53	F2
MISSION EASTWAY	LA	LA33	100	44	F3
MISSION GLEN LN	LA	SF		2	D6
MISSION HLLS RD	LA	SF		2	C6
MISSION MILL RD	CO	WHI		47	D6
MISSION MILL RD	CO	WHI	9800	55	D1
MISSION RDG WY	LA	SF		1	D5
MISSIONRY RG RD	DBAR	POM		97	C3
MISSIONRY RG RD	DBAR	WAL		97	C4
MISSION TIERRA	LA	SF		1	F2
MISSISSIPPI AV	LA	LA25	10500	41	E4
MISSISSIPPI AV	LA	LA25	10200	42	A2
MISSOURI	WCOV	WCOV		92	E4
MISSOURI AV	LA	LA25	10300	41	D4
MISSOURI AV	LA	LA25	10300	42	A2
MISSOURI AV	SOG	SOG		58	F3
MISSOURI AV	SOG	SOG	2700	59	A3
MIST CT	SCLR	SAU		124	F4
MISTLETOE RD	LA	TU	9600	11	A4
MISTON DR	LA	WOH	22200	13	B2
MISTRIDGE DR	RPV	PVP	5500	72	E5
MISTY CT	AGH	AGO		100A	A2
MISTY CT	DBAR	POM		97A	B3
MISTY PL	CER	ART		81	C1
MISTY ACRES RD	RHE	PVP		72	D6
MISTYGLEN LN	LA	CAN	7300	12	D3
MISTY ISLE DR	GLEN	GL07	800	25	D1
MISTY MORNIN RD	TOR	TOR		73	B3
MITCHELL AV	LA	LA66	12000	49	E3
MITCHELL PL	LA	LA15	700	44	B4
MITCHELL PL	LA	LA33	1400	44	F3
MITLA AV	DOW	DOW	11600	59	F3
MITONY AV	CO	WHI	11200	61	D5
MIXER RD	SCLR	SAU		127	F1
MOAB DR	CLA	CLA	1000	96	D6
MOANA WALK	LA	VAN		22	D5
MOBECK ST	WCOV	WCOV	1200	92	C2
MOBERLY PL	LA	CAN	20400	12	E4
MOBILE AV	CO	LA22	700	54	B1
MOBILE ST	LA	CAN	23200	5	F5
MOBILE ST	LA	CAN	20100	12	E5
MOBILE ST	LA	RES	19500	14	A5
MOCCASIN LN	RHE	PVP		72	F3
MOCCASIN PL	LAN	LAN		159	D6
MOCCASIN ST	CO	LPUE	13400	48	C3
MOCCASIN ST	LPUE	LPUE	13800	48	D4
MOCHA DR	SCLR	SAU	26600	124	D7
MOCKINGBIRD CT	CO	VAL		126	G1
MOCKINGBIRD DR	SPAS	SPAS		37	A1
MOCKINGBIRD LN	SPAS	SPAS	100	27	A6
MOCKINGBRD LN N	WCOV	WCOV	100	92	E1
MOCKINGBRD LN S	WCOV	WCOV	100	92	E1
MOCKINGBIRD PL	LA	LA69	1400	33	C3
MOCKNGBRD HL DR	CO	LPUE	15300	85	C3
MOCKINGBIRD KNL	LAV	LAV		95A	D5
MOCO LN	LA	LA28	5300	34	E2
MODALE AV	CO	LAN	49000	146	F4
MODENA PL	AGH	AGO		102	D3
MODESTA AV	TOR	TOR	2700	68	D6
MODJESKA PL	LA	LA66	11900	49	F2
MODJESKA ST	LA	LA39	1900	35	D3
MODOC DR	WAL	WAL		92	F6
MODOC ST	LA	LA21	2400	44	F6
MODOC TR	CO	AGO		107	A3
MOFFATT ST	SPAS	SPAS	20	36	E3
MOHALL LN	CO	WHI	10500	84	A4
MOHAVE ROSE DR	CO	LAN	7000	171	A1
MOHAWK	CO	AGO		106	C2
MOHAWK	CO	TOP		13	C5
MOHAWK AV	CO	CHA		6	C1
MOHAWK ST	CO	PAS	3700	28	B4
MOHAWK ST	LA	LA26	1000	35	B5
MOHAWK ST	PAS	PAS	2400	27	E4
MOHEGAN	CO	AGO		106	D2
MOHICAN DR	CO	PALM		157	F8
MOHR AV	IND	LPUE	18400	98	E3
MOJAVE TR	CO	CHA		6	C1
MOJAVE SAGE ST	PALM	PALM		184	A1
MOLETTE ST	BLF	BLF	10300	66	D3
MOLETTE ST	NWK	NWK	10800	66	E3
MOLETTE ST	NWK	NWK	11800	82	A3
MOLETTE ST	SFS	SFS	13000	82	C3
MOLINA LN	LA	GAR	1600	68	E1
MOLINAR AV	LPUE	LPUE	600	92	A4
MOLINE DR	CO	WHI	12200	84	A6
MOLINO AV	LB	LB03	100	75	F6
MOLINO AV	LB	LB04	700	75	F4
MOLINO AV	LB	LB14	300	75	F6
MOLINO AV	SH	LB04	1800	75	F4
MOLINO AV	SH	LB06	2200	75	F2
MOLINO ST	LA	LA13	400	44	E4
MOLLYKNOLL AV	CO	WHI	11300	84	C5
MOLLYKNOLL AV	WHI	WHI	9800	84	C3
MOLOKAI	SCLR	NEW		127	E5
MOLOKAI	WCOV	WCOV		92	C4
MOLONY RD	CUL	CUL	10700	50	D3
MONA BLVD	LA	LA59	10700	58	E5
MONA BLVD N	COM	COM	1100	64	F1
MONA BLVD S	CO	COM	12400	58	F6
MONA BLVD S	CO	COM	12800	64	F1
MONA CT	LAN	LAN		160	D6
MONACAN PL	CO	PALM		157	E8
MONACO CT	WHI	WHI	10600	55	C2
MONACO DR	LA	PP	1200	40	F2
MONAKEA	SCLR	NEW		127	E5
MONARCA DR	LA	TAR	4600	13	F3
MONARCH DR	LCF	LCF	200	19	C6
MONARCH ST	PALM	PALM		184	A1
MONCADO DR	GLEN	GL07	1100	25	E2
MONDINO DR	CO	LPUE		98	C4
MONDO DR	LHH	LAH		84	F3
MONDON AV	NWK	NWK		61	A5
MONDON AV	SFS	SFS	11000	60	F4
MONERO DR	RPV	PVP	6100	72	C4
MONET AV	LA	WOH	4100	13	C4
MONET PL	CER	ART	11800	81	A2
MONETA AV	CAR	CAR	19900	69	A2
MONETA AV	CAR	CAR	23500	74	A1
MONETTE PL	LA	LA06	3200	43	E2
MONICA AV	LB	LB08	3500	81	B5
MONICA CIR	CER	ART		66	E4
MONICA CT	CO	LPUE		98	C4
MONICA WY	WAL	WAL		93	B5
MONITA ST	LB	LB14	6200	76	D5
MONITEAU PL	DBAR	POM		97	E4
MONITOR AV	LA	LA59	11100	58	E5
MONITOR AV	LB	LB10	2000	75	A2
MONLACO RD	LB	LB08	5100	71	B5
MONLACO ST	LB	LB08		71	F5
MONMOUTH AV	LA	LA07	2600	44	A5
MONMOUTH WY	PR	PR		47	B6
MONNOW RD	CO	SAU		188	G1
MONO CIR	LAV	LAV		90	E2
MONO ST	LA	LA33	1300	44	F3
MONOGRAM AV	LKD	LKD	4100	71	E4
MONOGRAM AV	LB	LB08	3000	71	E6
MONOGRAM AV	LA	SF	11400	1	F6
MONOGRAM AV	LA	SF	11400	2	A6
MONOGRAM AV	LA	SF	8700	8	A6
MONON ST	LA	LA27		35	B2
MONOVALE DR	LA	LA24	100	33	A5
MONROE AV	CO	ACT		189	G3
MONROE AV	SOG	SOG	5400	59	E6
MONROE CT	AZU	AZU	300	86	C3
MONROE LN	LAN	LAN		159	B5
MONROE PL	MON	MON	200	29	A3
MONROE PL	PALM	PALM		183	D2
MONROE ST	CAR	LB10	2500	69	F4
MONROE ST	CAR	LB10	2700	70	A4
MONROE ST	CO	CAST	29500	123	A6
MONROE ST	CO	ELM	5300	39	B3
MONROE ST	LA	LA29	4100	34	F5
MONROE ST	LA	LA38	5300	34	D5
MONROE ST	PAR	PAR	7500	65	E4
MONROE ST	POM	POM	100	94	E1
MONROVIA AV	LB	LB03	200	76	C6
MONROVIA AV	LB	LB14	400	76	C5
MONROVIA AV	LYN	LYN	11600	59	A6
MONROVISTA AV	MON	MON	400	29	B5
MONSON LN	SGAB	SGAB	500	37	E4
MONTAGUE LN	LA	PAC		9	C3
MONTAGUE ST	LA	PAC	13400	8	E6
MONTAGUE ST	LA	PAC	12000	9	A4
MONTAIGNE WY	CO	PVP		73	A4
MONTAIR AV	LB	LB08	3000	71	C6
MONTAIR AV	LB	LB15	1800	76	C3
MONTAIR AV N	LKD	LKD	4900	71	C2
MONTALVO ST	LA	LA65	3600	36	A4
MONTANA	WCOV	WCOV		92	E4
MONTANA AV	LA	LA49	11100	41	D1
MONTANA AV	LPUE	LPUE	15400	48	F5
MONTANA AV	SM	SM	100	40	E6
MONTANA AV	SM	SM	1500	41	A4
MONTANA LN	CLA	CLA		95	D1
MONTANA LN	CLA	CLA		96	D6
MONTANA ST	LA	LA26	1300	35	B5
MONTANA ST	MON	MON	100	29	A5
MONTANA ST E	PAS	PAS	100	19	F6
MONTANA ST E	PAS	PAS	100	20	A6
MONTANA ST W	PAS	PAS	100	19	F6
MONTNA CLVA CIR	PR	PR		55	B3
MONTANERO AV	CAR	CAR		64	C5
MONTARA AV	SOG	SOG	9900	58	F4
MONTAU DR	CO	TOP	19800	109	C6
MONTBROOK ST	CO	LPUE	16100	92	A5
MONTCALM AV	LA	LA46	2800	23	F6
MONTCALM AV	LA	LA46	2900	24	A6
MONTCLAIR ST	LA	LA18	3100	43	C5
MONTE PL	ARC	ARC		20A	F3
MONTE ST	LA	SF	15500	2	B3
MONT EAGLE PL	LA	LA41	4300	36	A1
MONTE ALTO PL	LA	PP		30	B6
MONTEBELLO BLVD	MTB	MTB		47	A5
MONTEBELLO BL N	MTB	MTB	500	46	E6
MONTEBELLO BL N	MTB	MTB	100	54	D2
MONTEBELLO BL S	MTB	MTB	100	54	D2
MONTEBELLO PKWY	CO	LA22	5800	54	A1
MONTEBELLO WY	MTB	MTB		54	D2
MONTE BONITO DR	LA	LA41	5000	26	C5
MONTE CARLO CT	LAN	LAN		159	D4
MONTECHICO DR	MPK	MPK	300	46	B2
MONTE CIELO CT	LA	BH		33	B3
MONTE CIELO DR	BH	BH	1100	33	B3
MONTE CIELO DR	LA	BH	1600	33	B3
MONTECILLO DR	RHE	PVP	1	73	D5
MONTECITO AV E	SMAD	SMAD	100	28	B2
MONTECITO AV W	SMAD	SMAD	100	28	B2
MONTECITO CIR	LA	LA31	1300	36	B4
MONTECITO CT	SMAD	SMAD		28	C2
MONTECITO DR	ELM	ELM	10800	38	E5
MONTECITO DR	GLEN	GL08	1900	18	F4
MONTECITO DR	LA	LA31	400	36	B4
MONTECITO DR	SGAB	SGAB	500	37	D5
MONTECITO DR	SMAR	PAS	2200	27	D6
MONTECITO ST	LA	LA31	2700	36	B5
MONTECITO ST	WAL	WAL		93	D6
MONTE CRISTO AV	CER	ART	16600	82	C4
MONTECRISTO DR	CO	LPUE	16300	85	F4
MONTE DIABLO LN	POM	WAL		94	B4
MONTEEL RD	LA	LA49	8200	33	E3
MONTEFINO AV	DBAR	POM		97	F3
MONTEGO DR	LA	LA49	1000	32	B5
MONTE GRANDE PL	LA	PP		30	A6
MONTE GRIGIO DR	LA	PP		40	A4
MONTE GRIGIO DR	LA	PP		115	F4
MONTE HRMOSO DR	LA	PP		30	B6
MONTE HRMOSO DR	LA	PP		40	B1

1990 LOS ANGELES COUNTY STREET INDEX

STREET	CITY	P.O. ZONE	BLOCK	PAGE	GRID
MONTEITH DR	CO	LA43	3700	51	A3
MONTE LADO DR	CO	MAL	30700	111	E5
MONTE LEON DR	BH	BH	800	33	C4
MONTE LEON LN	BH	BH	9300	33	C4
MONTE LEON WY	LA	NOR		1	B5
MONTELL CT	CO	LPUE		98	F3
MONTELLANO AV	CO	LPUE	2600	85	C4
MONTELLANO AV	PALM	PALM		171	F5
MONTELLO DR	AZU	AZU	300	86	D4
MONTELLO DR	CO	PALM		157	G9
MONTE MALAGA DR	RPV	PVP	5300	72	D3
MONTE MALAGA PZ	PVE	PVP		72	D3
MONTE MAR DR	LA	LA35	9000	42	C3
MONTE MAR DR	LA	LA64	10200	42	B4
MONTE MAR PL	LA	LA64	2600	42	C4
MONTE MAR TER	LA	LA64	2700	42	C4
MONTE NIDO AV	CO	CAL		108	B5
MONTE ORO DR	WHI	WHI	16600	84	D2
MONTE PLACENTIA	LA	BH	1300	33	A4
MONTE PUESTO DR	WHI	WHI	8200	84	C1
MONTERA DR	CO	LPUE	2000	85	E3
MONTEREINA DR	RPV	SP	27800	73	D6
MONTEREY AV	BLF	BLF		66	B5
MONTEREY AV	BUR	BUR	1500	17	A5
MONTEREY AV	ELM	ELM	3600	38	D6
MONTEREY AV	MON	MON	600	28	F4
MONTEREY AV	MON	MON	600	29	A4
MONTEREY AV E	BAP	BAP	13600	39	D5
MONTEREY AV E	POM	POM	100	94	E2
MONTEREY AV E	POM	POM	700	95	A2
MONTEREY AV N	BAP	BAP	3700	39	D5
MONTEREY AV W	POM	POM	100	94	E2
MONTEREY BLVD	HB	RB		62	C6
MONTEREY CT	MB	MB		62	D3
MONTEREY DR	CLA	CLA		91	B1
MONTEREY LN	SMAD	SMAD	1	28	D2
MONTEREY PL	ARC	ARC		28	E2
MONTEREY PL	BUR	BUR	2300	17	B5
MONTEREY PL	PALM	PALM		173	B9
MONTEREY PL	SMAR	PAS	1300	37	C1
MONTEREY RD	GLEN	GL06	300	25	D3
MONTEREY RD	LA	LA32	3400	36	C4
MONTEREY RD	LA	LA42	5300	36	C4
MONTEREY RD	SMAR	PAS	2300	37	C1
MONTEREY RD	SPAS	SPAS	100	36	E2
MONTEREY RD	SPAS	SPAS	1400	37	A2
MONTEREY ST	BLF	BLF	10200	66	D5
MONTEREY ST	LA	LA65	3500	36	A3
MONTEREY ST	LAV	LAV		95A	D4
MONTEREY ST	TOR	TOR	2500	68	B4
MONTEREY ST N	ALH	ALH	200	37	C3
MONTEREY ST S	ALH	ALH	1	37	C4
MONTEREY PSS RD	MPK	MPK	700	45	F3
MONTEREY PSS RD	MPK	MPK	300	46	A2
MONTERICO ST	LA	LA65	3800	36	A4
MONTERO AV	LA	SF	12300	3	A3
MONTEROSA AV	CO	ALT		20	B3
MONTEROSA DR	CO	ALT		20	B3
MONTESANO AV	CO	LPUE	15100	85	C4
MONTESINO DR	WHI	WHI	8200	84	C1
MONTE VERDE DR	ARC	ARC	800	28	B4
MONTE VERDE DR	CO	COV	2800	93	B1
MONTEVIDEO DR	WHI	WHI	14600	84	A1
MONTE VIENTO DR	CO	MAL		114	D1
MONTE VISTA AV	COV	COV	100	88	F5
MONTE VISTA AV	GLEN	GL02	500	25	B1
MONTE VISTA AV	LOM	LOM	26200	73	D4
MONTE VISTA AV	PALM	PALM		183	F2
MONTE VIS AV N	SAD	SAD	100	89	F3
MONTE VIS AV S	SAD	SAD	100	89	F3
MONTE VISTA BL	LA	TU	11200	10	F1
MONTE VISTA DR	CO	TOP	300	109	B4
MONTE VIS DR E	WHI	WHI		55	C3
MONTE VISTA LN	SMAD	SMAD		28	D2
MONTE VISTA RD	ARC	ARC	300	28	B4
MONTE VISTA ST	LA	LA42	4800	36	B2
MONTE VISTA ST	PAS	PAS	100	27	C3
MONTE VISTA WY	LA	BH	9600	33	A4
MONTEZUMA AV	ALH	ALH	2500	45	F1
MONTEZUMA AV	ALH	ALH	2100	46	A1
MONTEZUMA PL	LA	LA26		44	C1
MONTEZUMA ST	LA	LA42	5000	36	B2
MONTEZUMA WY	WCOV	WCOV	300	92	E1
MONTEZUMA WY	WCOV	WCOV	1900	92	E3
MONTFORD ST	LA	PAC	12600	3	B6
MONTFORD ST	LA	PAC	14100	8	E3
MONTFORD ST	LA	PAC	13100	9	A1
MONTFORD ST	LA	SF	12500	3	B6
MONTGOMERY AV	GLEN	GL02	1400	25	B1
MONTGOMERY AV	LA	SF	9900	8	B3
MONTGOMERY AV	LA	VAN	6400	15	A5
MONTGOMERY CIR	CLA	CLA		91	C2
MONTGOMERY DR	HB	RB	800	62	C6
MONTGOMERY RD	CO	CHA		4	B5
MONTGOMERY ST	DOW	DOW	12200	60	A5
MONTICELLO DR	LAM	LAM	11700	84	B5
MONTICELLO RD	CLA	CLA		96	C6
MONTIFLORA AV	LA	LA41	1800	26	B5
MONTLAKE DR	LA	LA68		24	C6
MONTLAKE DR	LA	LA68		34	C1
MONTLINE LN	LA	LA77	700	32	E4
MONTMARTE CT	LAN	LAN		159	D4
MONTOLLA LN	SCLR	VAL		124	A1
MONTOYA ST	IRW	AZU		86	B6
MONTREAL ST	LA	VEN	200	55A	D2
MONT ROBLES PL	SMAR	PAS	1800	37	B2
MONTROSE	ELM	ELM		39	A6
MONTROSE	ELM	ELM		48	A1
MONTROSE AV	CO	GL14	2000	18	D1
MONTROSE AV	GLEN	GL14	3400	11	C6
MONTROSE AV	GLEN	GL14	2800	18	D1
MONTROSE AV	GLEN	MONT	2600	18	D1
MONTROSE AV	SPAS	SPAS	700	37	A2
MONTROSE LN	GLEN	MONT	1800	18	F3
MONTROSE LN	SPAS	SPAS	1000	37	A2
MONTROSE ST	LA	LA26	1800	35	C6
MONTURA DR	DBAR	POM	600	97	F1
MONTUSO PL	LA	ENC	3700	21	E5
MONTVIEW CT	WLVL	THO		102A	E5
MONUMENT ST	LA	PP	900	40	D3
MONUMENT CYN DR	DBAR	POM	23000	97A	A2
MOODY ST	LA	VAN	14600	8	D4
MOODY CYN TK TR	CO	ACT		189	E7
MOON AV	LA	LA65	700	36	A2
MOON AV	LOM	LOM	24500	73	D2
MOONBEAM AV	LA	VAN	8800	8	E5
MOONBEAM DR	MPK	MPK	900	46	A4
MOONCREST DR	LA	ENC	16800	21	E4
MOONCREST PL	LA	ENC	4200	21	E4
MOONDANCE DR	PALM	PALM		172	J5
MOONEY DR	MPK	MPK	200	46	C2
MOONEY DR W	CO	RM	7100	46	E3
MOONFLOWER CT	PALM	PALM		183	E1
MOONGATE DR	RPV	PVP	6000	72	D5
MOONGLOW CIR	CER	ART		82	B5
MOONHILL RD	CO	SF		3	D4
MOONLAKE ST	DBAR	WAL	20700	97	C2
MOONLIGHT CT	PALM	PALM		183	E1
MOONLIGHT LN	LCF	LCF	100	19	D3
MOONLIGHT PL	CO	CAST		123	E3
MOONLIGHT SMT DR	DBAR	POM		94	A4
MOONMIST DR	RPV	PVP	30400	77	F1
MOONRAKER RD	PALM	PALM		172	J5
MOONRAKER RD	PALM	PALM		173	A9
MOONRIDGE DR	CO	WHI		55	D2
MOON RIDGE DR	LA	VAN		22	C4
MOONRIDGE LN	CO	CAST		123	D1
MOONRIDGE LN	PALM	PALM		183	E1
MOONRIDGE TER	LA	BH		23	B6
MOON SHADOWS DR	CO	MAL		114	D1
MOONSTONE CT	LA	LA32	2800	36	C5
MOONSTONE DR	LA	LA32	4200	36	C5
MOONSTONE ST	MB	MB	100	62	A2
MOON VIEW DR	CO	LPUE	2200	98	B4
MOORBROOK AV	CER	ART	16600	82	D5
MOORCRAFT AV	LA	CAN	6500	12	B1
MOORCROFT AV	LA	CAN	8500	6	B6
MOORCROFT AV	LA	WOH	5900	12	B6
MOORCROFT PL	LA	CAN	8700	6	B6
MOORE AV N	MPK	MPK	100	46	B2
MOORE AV S	MPK	MPK	100	46	B2
MOORE DR	LA	LA48	6400	42	E2
MOORE LN	SAD	SAD		90	A2
MOORE ST	CER	ART	12600	82	D4
MOORE ST	CUL	LA66	3900	49	F3
MOORE ST	GLEN	GL14	4500	11	C5
MOORE ST	LA	LA39	2200	35	C4
MOORE ST	LA	LA66	3300	49	E2
MOOREHAVEN DR	CAR	CAR	400	64	B5
MOORHEN CT	CO	VAL		126	G1
MOORELAND DR	WHI	WHI		55	E6
MOORESQUE DR	PAS	PAS	300	26	D3
MOORGATE DR	DBAR	POM		97	F5
MOORGATE RD	LA	BH		22	F6
MOORLAND PL	WCOV	WCOV		92	D5
MOORPARK ST	LA	ENC	16700	21	F2
MOORPARK ST	LA	ENC	15400	22	A2
MOORPARK ST	LA	NHO	10300	23	D3
MOORPARK ST	LA	NHO	10000	24	A3
MOORPARK ST	LA	VAN	13100	22	F3
MOORPARK WY	LA	NHO	4400	23	F3
MOORSHIRE DR	CER	ART	12700	81	C2
MOORSHIRE PL	CER	ART		81	C1
MOORSIDE DR	GLEN	GL07		25	D1
MORA DR	SFS	SFS		61	A4
MORADA AV	CO	COV	4000	88	B4
MORADA AV	WCOV	WCOV	100	88	B5
MORADA PL	CO	ALT	700	20	B6
MORADA ST	AZU	BAP		88	B2
MORADA ST	IRW	BAP	5200	88	B2
MORAGA DR	LA	LA49	2800	22	C6
MORAGA DR	LA	LA49	800	32	C5
MORAGA LN	LA	LA49		32	C4
MORAGA WK	LA	LA49		32	C5
MORAINE AV	CLA	CLA	3600	96	D5
MORAY AV	LA	SP	1800	78	D5
MOREHART AV	LA	PAC	10200	8	F3
MOREHART AV	LA	PAC	9000	9	B5
MOREHART AV	LA	SV	8500	16	C1
MOREHOUSE ST	ELM	ELM	12100	47	E3
MORELAND DR	CO	BH		33	A2
MORELIA DR	CLA	CLA	500	91	C2
MORELLA AV	LA	NHO	6200	16	C5
MORELLA AV	LA	NHO	4400	23	C3
MORELOS AV	LA	WOH		13	B3
MORENO AV	LA	LA49	500	41	A3
MORENO AV	LAV	LAV	600	90	C2
MORENO DR	BH	BH	100	42	B1
MORENO DR	SCLR	VAL		127	H6
MORENO DR	GLEN	GL07	1500	25	E1
MORENO DR	LA	LA39	1800	35	B3
MORESBY DR	TOR	TOR	4600	67	F5
MORETON ST	TOR	TOR	2400	73	C2
MORGAN AV	BUR	BUR	1800	17	C4
MORGAN AV	CLA	CLA	1800	91	A2
MORGAN AV	LA	LA11	3200	52	D4
MORGAN CT	WAL	WAL		93	D5
MORGAN LN	RB	RB	1600	67	E1
MORGAN LN	RH	PVP		72	F6
MORGAN RD	CO	SAU	11300	181	C9
MORGAN ST	BAP	BAP	14100	39	E5
MORGAN WY	LAV	LAV		90	D1
MORGANFIELD AV	WCOV	WCOV	3900	97	A1
MORGAN HILL CIR	LA	LA68	2000	34	D2
MORGAN HILL DR	LA	LA68	2000	34	D2
MORGAN RANCH DR	GLDR	GLDR		87	E5
MORGAN RANCH RD	GLDR	GLDR		87	E5
MORISAN AV	PALM	PALM		183	E3
MORISAN CT	PALM	PALM		183	E3
MORLAN PL	ARC	ARC	1	28	E4
MORLEY AV	CO	LA56	6200	50	F5
MORLEY AV	LA	LA56	6200	50	F5
MORLEY ST	LA	LA45	5700	56	D2
MORMON ST	LA	SP	100	79	C1
MORMON CYN MTWY	CO	CHA		1A	E3
MORMON CYN MTWY	LA	CHA		1A	E3
MORNING AV	DOW	DOW	12700	59	F6
MORNING AV	DOW	DOW	10300	60	A4
MORNING CIR	PALM	PALM		183	H1
MORNING CT	PALM	PALM		183	H1
MORNING CYN RD	DBAR	POM		97	E4
MORNINGLORY WY	CO	WHI	14000	61	E5
MORNING GLOW WY	LA	SV		10	A6
MORNINGRAIN AV	CER	ART		82	B5
MORNINGSIDE	ELM	ELM		48	A6
MORNINGSIDE AV	LAN	LAN		160	E6
MORNINGSIDE CT	LA	LA28	1300	34	C3
MORNINGSIDE CT	SF	SF	900	2	F5
MORNINGSIDE DR	BUR	BUR	1300	24	D3
MORNINGSIDE DR	CLA	CLA	1100	90	F2
MORNINGSIDE DR	CO	CAST	28900	123	A5
MORNINGSIDE DR	HB	RB	2500	62	B5
MORNINGSIDE DR	WAL	WAL		93	D6
MORNINGSIDE DR	WHI	WHI		84	D5
MORNINGSDE DR N	MB	MB	100	62	B4
MORNINGSDE DR S	MB	MB	100	62	B4
MORNINGSIDE ST	LB	LB05	1	70	C2
MORNINGSIDE ST	PAS	PAS	2500	27	E4
MORNINGSIDE TER	PALM	PALM		172	A7
MORNINGSIDE TER	PALM	PALM		172	B9
MORNINGSIDE WY	LA	LA66	13000	49	D2
MORNINGSIDE WY	LA	VEN	1200	49	D2
MORNING SUN AV	DBAR	WAL		97	C3
MORNING SUN DR	POM	POM	1100	95	B2
MORNINGTON DR	SCLR	VAL		127	A1
MORNING VIEW DR	CO	MAL	30000	111	F6
MORO BAY DR	RPV	PVP	28500	72	E6
MORPATH LN	GLDR	GLDR		89	D1
MORRILL AV	CO	WHI	6000	55	B4
MORRILL AV	CO	WHI	8400	61	A1
MORRILL AV	SFS	SFS	9100	61	A1
MORRIS AV	LA	SP		79	C1
MORRIS AV	WCOV	WCOV	100	88	A4
MORRIS PL	MTB	MTB	300	46	C5
MORRISON RD	LA	LA46		33	E2
MORRISON ST	LA	ENC	16700	21	F2
MORRISON ST	LA	ENC	15500	22	A2
MORRISON ST	LA	NHO	10800	23	B2
MORRISON ST	LA	VAN	13500	22	E2
MORRISON ST	LA	VAN	13100	23	A2
MORRISON ST	POM	POM	1700	94	D4
MORRISON RCH RD	CO	CAL		100A	E2
MORRO DR	CO	LPUE		98	C4
MORRO DR	LA	WOH	4100	13	D3
MORRO PL	LB	LB02		75	C4
MORROCO LN	CO	CHA		4	B5
MORROW PL	CO	LA22	1300	53	E1
MORSE AV	LA	NHO	6500	16	A4
MORSE AV	LA	NHO	4400	23	A3
MORSE AV	LA	VAN	6400	16	A5
MORSE AV	LA	VAN	4600	23	A3
MORSE DR	LA	SP	1600	78	D4
MORSLAY RD	CO	ALT	2300	20	D5
MORTIMER AV	HPK	HPK	2100	52	E5
MORTON AV	CO	LA01	7900	58	E1
MORTON AV	LA	LA26	1500	35	C5
MORTON AV	PAS	PAS	900	26	F2
MORTON CIR	CLA	CLA		91	C2
MORTON PL	LA	LA26	1400	35	D5
MORTON TER	LA	LA26	1500	35	C5
MORTON WALK	LA	LA26	1700	35	D5
MORVEN ST	LAN	LAN	1000	160	D4
MORY ST	DOW	DOW	8400	60	A5
MOSBY ST	LA	WOH	23000	13	A3
MOSCADA AV	CO	WAL		97	B3
MOSHER AV	LA	LA31	4300	36	B4
MOSLEY AV	CO	LA56	6200	50	F5
MOSLEY AV	LA	LA56	6200	50	F5
MOSS AV	LA	LA65	2100	35	D1
MOSS AV	SM	SM	100	49	B6
MOSS CIR	LAV	LAV		90	E3
MOSS ST N	BUR	BUR	400	17	D6
MOSS ST S	BUR	BUR	800	24	E1
MOSSBANK DR	RPV	PVP	5600	72	D4
MOSSBERG AV	WCOV	WCOV	1300	48	F2
MOSSBERG ST	BAP	BAP	14200	39	D5
MOSSDALE AV E	CO	LAN	15600	174	H2
MOSSDALE AV E	CO	LAN	16500	175	A2
MOSSY ROCK CIR	LA	LA77		22	E6
MOTOR AV	AZU	AZU	100	88	A2
MOTOR AV	CUL	CUL	4100	50	C1
MOTOR AV	IRW	BAP		88	B2
MOTOR AV	LA	CUL	3800	42	B6
MOTOR AV	LA	LA34	3200	42	B6
MOTOR AV	LA	LA64	2600	42	B3
MOTOR AV	LA	LA64	10100	42	B4
MOTOR ST	CO	CAST		123	F3
MOTT ST	SF	SF	700	2	D6
MOTT ST	SF	SF	600	8	E1
MOTT ST N	LA	LA33	100	45	B4
MOTT ST S	LA	LA23	600	45	A5
MOTT ST S	LA	LA33	100	45	B4
MOTTLEY DR	LAM	LAM	15000	83	C3
MOTZ ST	PAR	PAR	6500	65	D4
MOULTON AV	LA	LA31	600	44	F1
MOUND AV	SPAS	SPAS	400	36	F2
MOUND ST	LA	LA68	2000	34	C2
MOUND VIEW AV	LA	NHO	3700	23	C4
MOUND VIEW PL	LA	NHO	12000	23	C5
MOUNT ST	DBAR	POM		97	F1
MT ADA RD	AVA	AVA		77	C5
MOUNTAIN AV	CO	CLA	2900	91	A2
MOUNTAIN AV	CO	DUA	1200	29	C5
MOUNTAIN AV	CO	DUA	2300	39	B1
MOUNTAIN AV	CO	GL14	2300	18	E1
MOUNTAIN AV	CO	MON	2300	39	B1
MOUNTAIN AV	POM	POM	1700	91	A6
MOUNTAIN AV	POM	POM	600	95	A2
MOUNTAIN AV N	CLA	CLA	100	91	A4
MOUNTAIN AV N	CLA	CLA	2400	96	A6
MOUNTAIN AV N	CO	CLA	2900	91	A2
MOUNTAIN AV N	CO	CLA	3100	96	A6
MOUNTAIN AV N	MON	MON	100	29	C5
MOUNTAIN AV S	CLA	CLA	300	91	A6
MOUNTAIN AV S	MON	MON	100	29	C5
MOUNTAIN DR	BH	BH	500	33	B4
MOUNTAIN DR	CO	ALT	4200	19	E2
MOUNTAIN LN	CO	GLDR		87	D4
MOUNTAIN PL	CO	ACT		182	H8
MOUNTAIN PL	PAS	PAS	800	27	B2
MOUNTAIN ST E	GLEN	GL07	100	25	C2
MOUNTAIN ST E	GLEN	GL06	1500	25	C2
MOUNTAIN ST E	PAS	PAS	100	27	C2
MOUNTAIN ST W	GLEN	GL01	1600	18	A5
MOUNTAIN ST W	GLEN	GL02	700	18	A5
MOUNTAIN ST W	GLEN	GL02	100	25	C2
MOUNTAIN ST W	PAS	PAS	100	26	F2
MTN BROOK DR	CO	LPUE		98	A4
MTN CREEK RD	CER	ART	12400	82	B4
MTN CREST LN	LA	LA49		32	A3
MTN CREST RD	DUA	DUA	200	86	A4
MTN DALE CT	SCLR	NEW	18700	127	H3
MOUNTAINEER RD	WAL	WAL		93	C3
MOUNTNEERING LN	CO	TOR		68	F5
MTN GATE DR	CO	CAL		100	B2
MOUNTAINGATE DR	LA	LA49		32	A2
MOUNTAIN GRN DR	CO	CAL		107	F5
MTN LAUREL WY	DBAR	POM		97	E3
MTN MEADOW LN	LCF	LCF		19	C1
MOUNTAIN OAK DR	LA	LA68	2200	34	D2
MOUNTAIN PK DR	CO	CAL		100	D6
MOUNTAIN PK RD	CO	CYN		128	C3
MTN PASS RD	SCLR	NEW		127	H3
MTN PINE DR	CO	GL14		11	E5
MTN RIDGE RD	WCOV	WCOV		92	E4
MTN SHADOW RD	CO	ACT		189	D3
MTN SHADOWS DR	CO	WHI		55	E2
MTN SHADOWS PL	POM	POM		94	E6
MTN SHADOWS PL	POM	POM		97A	C1
MOUNTAINSIDE DR	PALM	PALM		183	B1
MTN SPRING ST	CO	LPUE		48	C6
MTN SPRING ST	CO	LPUE		85	D1
MTN SPRINGS RD	CO	ACT		182	G8
MTN SPRINGS RD	CO	PALM		183	C8
MTN SPGS RCH RD	LAV	LAV		95A	D4
MOUNTAIN TER LN	MTB	MTB		46	E4
MTN TRAIL AV N	SMAD	SMAD	100	28	D2
MTN TRAIL AV S	SMAD	SMAD	100	28	D2
MOUNTAIN VIEW	CO	LAN		147	H6
MTN VIEW AV	CO	HPK	7200	53	A6
MTN VIEW AV	CO	PAS	3500	28	B4
MTN VIEW AV	HPK	HPK	6900	53	A6
MTN VIEW AV	LA	LA66	3000	49	E1
MTN VIEW AV	MON	MON	700	29	C3
MTN VIEW AV	MTB	MTB	100	54	D2
MTN VIEW AV	SOG	SOG	8000	58	F1
MTN VIEW AV	SPAS	SPAS	1300	36	E2
MTN VIEW AV E	GLDR	GLDR	500	87	B5
MTN VIEW AV N	LA	LA26	100	44	B1
MTN VIEW AV N	POM	POM	100	95	A2
MTN VIEW AV S	LA	LA57	100	44	B1
MTN VIEW AV S	POM	POM	1300	95	A4
MTN VIEW AV W	GLDR	GLDR	200	87	A5
MTN VIEW DR	LAV	LAV		90	C3
MTN VIEW RD	CO	ELM	2100	47	D3
MTN VIEW RD	CO	LH		157	C6
MTN VIEW RD	ELM	ELM	2000	47	D3
MTN VIEW RD	SELM	ELM	1600	47	D3
MTN VIEW ST	CO	ALT	100	19	E5
MTN VIEW ST	SF	SF	1100	2	F4
MTN VIEW ST E	LB	LB05	100	70	C2
MTN VIEW ST W	LB	LB05	100	70	C2
MTN VIEW TER	ALH	ALH	900	37	D4
MTN VIEW TR	CO	SF		3	E5
MTN VIEW TR	CO	TOP		109	B6
MTN VISTA DR	CO	RM	1400	46	F4
MOUNTAIR AV	LA	TU	10000	10	F3
MT ANGELUS DR	LA	LA42	6100	36	C2
MT ANGELUS PL	LA	LA42	6100	36	C2
MT ANGELUS WK	LA	LA42		36	C2
MT BALDY RD	CLA	CLA		96	C5
MT BALDY RD	CO	CLA		96	C4
MOUNTBATTEN DR	GLEN	GL07		18	D6
MT BEACON TER	LA	LA68	2500	34	D1
MT CARMEL DR	CLA	CLA	100	96	B6
MT CARMEL DR	GLEN	GL06	400	25	F3
MOUNTCASTLE DR	LA	NHO	11100	23	E5
MOUNTCREST AV	LA	LA69	1600	33	D3
MOUNT CURVE AV	CO	ALT	500	20	C4
MT DUME LN	CO	MAL		112	C6
MT EMMA RD	CO	PALM		183	H9
MT EMMA RD	CO	PALM		184	A8
MT EMMA RD	CO	PALM		190	G3
MT GLEASON AV	LA	SUN	10100	10	E3
MT GLEASON AV	LA	TU	11400	10	E3
MT HELENA AV	LA	LA41	5000	26	C4
MT HOLLY DR	WHI	WHI		55	E3
MT HOLLYWOOD DR	LA	LA27		24	E4
MT HOLYOKE AV	LA	PP	300	40	C4
MT HOOD CT	RPV	SP	28500	78	E1
MT LANGLEY CT	RPV	SP	28500	78	E1
MT LASSEN LN	RPV	SP	28500	78	E1
MT LEE DR	LA	LA68	3700	24	D5
MT LOWE DR	CO	ALT	1000	20	C4
MT LUKENS TK TR	CO			M	C4
MT MARTY DR	WAL	WAL		93	B3
MT OLIVE DR	BRAD	DUA	100	29	F4
MT OLIVE DR	DUA	DUA	800	29	F3
MT OLIVE DR	DUA	DUA		29	F5
MT OLIVE LN	BRAD	DUA	2400	29	F4
MT OLYMPUS DR	LA	LA46	1700	33	E2
MT PALOMAR PL	RPV	SP	28500	78	E1
MT PLEASANT ST	LA	LA42	1400	26	A6
MT PLEASANT ST	LA	LA42	1400	36	A1
MT PROSPECT DR	CO	TOP	1900	109	A2
MT RAINIER RD	RPV	SP	1200	78	E1
MT ROSE RD	RPV	SP	28500	78	E1
MT ROYAL DR	LA	LA41	5100	26	B5
MT RUSHMORE RD	RPV	SP	28500	78	E1
MT SAC WY	WAL	WAL		93	C4
MT SAWTOOTH DR	RPV	SP	28500	78	E1
MT SHASTA DR	LA	SP		73	E6
MT SHASTA DR	RPV	SP	28500	78	E1
MT STEPHEN AV	SCLR	CYN		125	B8
MT TRICIA AV	WCOV	WCOV		92	E4
MT VANCOUVER CT	RPV	SP	28500	78	E1
MT VERNON AV	POM	POM	1800	94	B2
MT VERNON DR	CO	LA08	3400	51	B2
MT VERNON DR	CO	LA43	4300	51	A3

274

1990 LOS ANGELES COUNTY STREET INDEX

MT VERNON DR N — NELSON AV

LOS ANGELES CO.

STREET	CITY	P.O. ZONE	BLOCK	PAGE	GRID
MT VERNON DR N	SGAB	SGAB	300	37	C2
MT VERNON DR W	SGAB	SGAB	1300	37	C2
MT VERNON PL	PAS	PAS	1200	26	D1
MT WASHINGTN DR	LA	LA65	200	36	A3
MT WHITNEY WY	RPV	SP	28500	78	E1
MT WILSON RD	CO			20	E4
MT WILSON RD	CO			20A	A1
MT WILSON RD	CO			20A	E4
MT WILSON RD	PAS	PAS	2600	20	E4
MT WILSON TR	SMAD	SMAD		28	D1
MT WLSN-RDBX RD	CO			M	F4
MT WLSN-RDBX RD	CO			N	A4
MT WLSN-RDBX RD	CO			20A	B1
MOURNING DOV WY	CO	CAL		13	A4
MOY LN	LA	SUN	10000	10	E4
MOZART ST	LA	LA31	1700	45	A1
MUERDAGO RD	CO	TOP	100	109	C4
MUIR AV	POM	POM	1000	94	D4
MUIR CT	WHI	WHI		55	D4
MUIR DR	CO	LH		157	A6
MUIRFIELD	ELM	ELM		39	A6
MUIRFIELD	ELM	ELM		48	A1
MUIRFIELD DR	CO	LLAN		192	J2
MUIRFIELD LN	WAL	WAL		93	D6
MUIRFIELD RD	LA	LA04	100	43	C1
MUIRFIELD RD	LA	LA05	600	43	C1
MUIRFIELD RD	LA	LA08	3800	51	B1
MUIRFIELD RD	LA	LA16	3500	43	B6
MUIRFIELD RD	LA	LA19	900	43	C2
MUIRFIELD RD	LA	LA20	300	43	C1
MUIRKIRK DR	LA	NOR		1	B4
MUIR WOODS CT	WCOV	WCOV		92	E4
MULBERRY AV	LAN	LAN		160	F6
MULBERRY DR	CO	WHI	13000	61	E2
MULBERRY DR	CO	WHI	14700	84	A4
MULBERRY DR	LA	SUN	8700	10	C2
MULBERRY DR	POM	POM	300	90	F3
MULBERRY DR	WHI	WHI	12600	61	E2
MULBERRY GN DR	SCLR	VAL	23000	124	B5
MULBERRY LN	ING	IN01		57	B2
MULBERRY ST	COM	COM		64	F2
MULEDEER LN	CO	CAST		123	D4
MULFORD AV	LYN	LYN	3300	59	B5
MULHALL ST	ELM	ELM	10400	38	E4
MULHALL ST	ELM	ELM	11700	39	A5
MULHOLLAND	LA	VAN		22	D5
MULHOLLAND DR	LA	BH	13400	23	A5
MULHOLLAND DR	LA	BH	8900	23	B6
MULHOLLAND DR	LA	BH	8700	33	C1
MULHOLLAND DR	LA	ENC	16500	21	A6
MULHOLLAND DR	LA	ENC	15900	22	A5
MULHOLLAND DR	LA	LA46	7500	23	E6
MULHOLLAND DR	LA	LA46	8200	33	C1
MULHOLLAND DR	LA	LA46	7300	34	A1
MULHOLLAND DR	LA	LA49	16500	21	A6
MULHOLLAND DR	LA	LA49	15500	22	A5
MULHOLLAND DR	LA	LA68	6700	34	B1
MULHOLLAND DR	LA	LA77	14200	22	A5
MULHOLLAND DR	LA	TAR	19000	21	A6
MULHOLLAND DR	LA	VAN	13400	22	A5
MULHOLLAND DR	LA	WOH	20000	13	E4
MULHOLLAND DR	LA	WOH	23100	100	F2
MULHOLLAND HWY	CO	AGO		106	F2
MULHOLLAND HWY	CO	AGO		107	B2
MULHOLLAND HWY	CO	CAL	22800	13	A5
MULHOLLAND HWY	CO	CAL	23000	100	E5
MULHOLLAND HWY	CO	CAL		107	B2
MULHOLLAND HWY	CO	CAL		108	A4
MULHOLLAND HWY	CO	MAL		104	D5
MULHOLLAND HWY	CO	MAL		105	C4
MULHOLLAND HWY	CO	MAL		106	C3
MULHOLLAND HWY	CO	MAL		110	C1
MULHOLLAND HWY	CO	WOH	22200	13	A5
MULHOLLAND HWY	LA	LA27	5600	24	D5
MULHOLLAND HWY	LA	LA68	6100	24	D5
MULHOLLAND PL	LA	LA49	15700	22	B6
MULHOLLAND TER	LA	LA46	8100	23	D6
MULHOLLAND WY	LA	WOH	22000	13	B4
MULLAGHBOY DR	GLDR	GLDR	900	87	C3
MULLDAE AV	LA	SP	3400	78	D5
MULLEN AV	CO	LA43	4400	51	B3
MULLEN AV	LA	LA05	700	43	B3
MULLEN AV	LA	LA19	900	43	B3
MULLEN PL	LA	LA43	3700	51	B3
MULLENDER AV	CO	LPUE	1500	92	A3
MULLENDER AV	WCOV	WCOV	1300	92	A3
MULLER ST	BG	BELL	5600	59	E2
MULLER ST	DOW	DOW	7400	60	A2
MULLER ST	SFS	SFS	11400	60	E4
MULLIN AV	TOR	TOR		68	D4
MULTIVIEW DR	LA	LA68	3500	23	F5
MULTNOMAH ST	LA	LA32	4100	45	C1
MULVANE ST	CO	LPUE	16500	92	B5
MULVANE ST	LPUE	LPUE	15500	48	F5
MUMFORD ST	LA	PAC	14600	8	D4
MUMS DR	CO	CYN		125	G6
MUMS MEADOW CT	CO	CYN		125	F5

STREET	CITY	P.O. ZONE	BLOCK	PAGE	GRID
MUNDARE AV	ART	ART	18000	66	F6
MUNGER DR	CO	MAL	2700	113	B3
MUNHALL AV	POM	POM	1900	95	A6
MUNSON AV	LA	LA42	1500	26	A6
MUNSTER ST	POM	POM	2100	90	D4
MUNZ RANCH RD	CO	LAN		157	F7
MUNZ RANCH RD	CO	LAN	45300	158	A3
MUNZ RANCH RD	CO	PALM		157	F7
MURAD AV	LOM	LOM		73	D4
MURAL DR	CLA	CLA	1400	90	F3
MURAL DR	POM	POM	3200	90	F3
MURCHISON AV	POM	POM	800	94	C1
MURCHISON ST	LA	LA33	1300	45	B2
MURDOCK AV	LA	WIL	800	74	E4
MUREAU RD	CO	CAL		100	A3
MUREAU RD	CO	CAL		100	C3
MURIEL AV	CO	COM	14300	65	B2
MURIEL AV	COM	COM	500	65	B2
MURIEL AV	LB	LB05	6300	65	B5
MURIEL DR	LYN	LYN	11300	59	C6
MURIEL ST	LA	SF	14900	2	D2
MURIETTA AV	LA	VAN	8600	8	E6
MURIETTA AV	LA	VAN	5600	15	E6
MURIETTA AV	LA	VAN	3900	22	E2
MURIETTA DR	ARC	ARC	800	28	C4
MUROC ST	BLF	BLF	9200	66	B1
MUROC ST	LAM	LAM	13800	82	E1
MUROC ST	NWK	NWK	10900	66	E1
MUROC ST	NWK	NWK	12700	82	C1
MUROS PL	PVE	PVP	2000	72	B4
MURPHY MTWY	CO	MAL		112	D3
MURPHY RD	CO	MAL		108	D5
MURPHY RD	LAM	LAM		83	D1
MURPHY HILL DR	WHI	WHI1		55	E4
MURPHY RD	LAM	LAM		84	D6
MURPHYS LN	CO	LR		192	B7
MURPHYS LN	CO	VALY		192	D7
MURRAY AV	AZU	AZU	200	88	D1
MURRAY AV	POM	POM	900	95	B1
MURRAY AV	SFS	SFS	10000	61	C3
MURRAY CIR	LA	LA26	1500	35	B4
MURRAY DR	LA	LA26	1400	35	B4
MURRAY RD	PAS	PAS		28	A1
MUSCATEL AV	CO	RM	600	47	A4
MUSCATEL AV	CO	SGAB	6800	28	A6
MUSCATEL AV	CO	SGAB	4900	38	A4
MUSCATEL AV	RM	RM	3600	38	A6
MUSCATEL AV	RM	RM	2400	47	A1
MUSCATEL AV	TEC	TEC	5600	38	A2
MUSCATEL CIR	RM	RM		38	A6
MUSCATINE ST	LA	PAC	13600	8	F6
MUSCATINE ST	LA	PAC	12700	9	A5
MUSCATINE ST	LA	SV	12300	9	B5
MUSE DR	CO	COV	3500	89	B6
MUSEUM DR	LA	LA65	200	36	A3
MUSGROVE AV	ELM	ELM	2600	47	E2
MUSKINGUM AV	LA	PP	500	40	C3
MUSKINGUM PL	LA	PP	500	40	C4
MUSTANG	LA	SF42		2	C1
MUSTANG CIR	LAV	LAV		90	D1
MUSTANG CIR	WAL	WAL		93	B4
MUSTANG LN	PALM	PALM		183	G3
MUSTANG RD	RPV	PVP	1	73	C6
MUSTANG RD	SAD	SAD		89	F2
MUSTANG WY	LA	SUN		10	B3
MYDA AV	TEC	TEC	5800	38	A2
MYERS PL	ING	IN01	300	56	F2
MYERS ST N	BUR	BUR	700	17	B3
MYERS ST N	BUR	BUR	100	24	C1
MYERS ST N	LA	LA33	100	44	E3
MYERS ST S	BUR	BUR	100	24	C1
MYERS ST S	LA	LA23	600	44	F5
MYERS ST S	LA	LA33	100	44	E3
MYOSOTIS ST	LA	LA42	6000	36	C1
MYRA AV	LA	LA27	1500	35	A4
MYRA AV	LA	LA29	1000	35	A4
MYRA CT	WCOV	WCOV		92	E5
MYRA LN	CER	ART	16000	66	E4
MYRA TR	LA	LA46		33	E2
MYRIN CT	SCLR	SAU		124	D2
MYRNA ST	LA	NHO	10300	23	F1
MYRON ST	PR	PR	9100	54	E6
MYRON ST	PR	PR	9100	60	E1
MYRRH ST	CO	COM	4100	65	C3
MYRRH ST	PAR	PAR	6500	65	D3
MYRRH ST E	COM	COM	100	64	F3
MYRRH ST E	COM	COM	200	65	A3
MYRRH ST W	COM	COM	100	64	F3
MYRTLE AV	CO	MON	2200	29	B6
MYRTLE AV	GLDR	GLDR	400	87	C5
MYRTLE AV	HB	RB	2400	62	B5
MYRTLE AV	ING	IN01	600	57	A3
MYRTLE AV	IRW	BAP	2600	39	B1
MYRTLE AV	LB	LB05	5900	65	D6
MYRTLE AV	LB	LB05	5400	70	D1
MYRTLE AV	LB	LB06	1800	75	D3

STREET	CITY	P.O. ZONE	BLOCK	PAGE	GRID
MYRTLE AV	LB	LB07	3400	70	D5
MYRTLE AV	LB	LB13	1000	75	D4
MYRTLE AV	SH	LB06	2600	75	D1
MYRTLE AV	SH	LB07	3300	70	D5
MYRTLE AV N	MON	MON	100	29	B5
MYRTLE AV N	POM	POM	100	94	D2
MYRTLE AV S	MON	MON	100	29	B5
MYRTLE AV S	POM	POM	100	94	D2
MYRTLE LN	PAS	PAS	100	26	F2
MYRTLE ST	DOW	DOW	10400	60	B3
MYRTLE ST	GLEN	GL03	300	25	C3
MYRTLE ST	LA	LA15	1300	44	C5
MYRTLE ST	PALM	LAN		171	B2
MYRTLE ST	PALM	PALM		171	B3
MYRTLE ST	PR	PR	4600	54	F2
MYRTLE WY	SCLR	SAU		124	G5
MYRTLEWOOD AV N	WCOV	WCOV	700	88	D5
MYRTLEWOOD ST S	WCOV	WCOV	100	92	D1
MYRTUS AV	ARC	ARC		38	E2
MYRTUS AV	CO	ARC		38	E2
MYRTUS AV	CO	TEC	5100	38	E3
MYSTIC LN	LA	CAN		5	E3
MYSTIC ST	CO	WHI	13300	61	D2
MYSTIC ST	CO	WHI	14800	84	A4
N					
N ST	LA	WIL	100	74	C3
NABAL RD	LHH	LAH	1500	98A	B2
NACE PL	CO	LPUE	1500	98	A3
NACHI WY	MPK	MPK		46	B2
NACO PL	CO	LPUE	1500	98	A3
NACORA ST	CO	LPUE	19500	97	A4
NADA ST	DOW	DOW	7100	59	F3
NADA ST	DOW	DOW	7500	60	A4
NADAL ST	SCLR	CYN	18700	124	J7
NADEAU DR	LA	LA19	1400	43	C3
NADEAU ST	CO	HPK	2200	52	D6
NADEAU ST	CO	LA01	1100	52	D6
NADEU MTWY	CO	NEW		128	A2
NADINA ST	LA	SF	10300	10	A1
NADINE CIR	TOR	TOR	22600	68	B6
NADINE ST	CO	SGAB	8700	38	A3
NADINE ST	TEC	TEC	9500	38	D3
NADINE ST	WCOV	WCOV		92	D5
NADIR ST	CO	CAN	23600	5	E1
NADULA DR	CO	LPUE		98	B4
NAFFA AV	CAR	CAR	23500	74	A1
NAGLE AV	LA	NHO	6800	15	F4
NAGLE AV	LA	PAC	9700	8	E4
NAGLE AV	LA	SV	8300	16	A1
NAGLE AV	LA	VAN		8	F6
NAGLE AV	LA	VAN	5800	15	F6
NAGLE AV	LA	VAN	4100	22	F4
NAGOYA AV	LA	SP		79	B3
NAGOYA ST	LA	LA15		44	B4
NAIRN AV	CO	LA22	1500	54	A2
NALIN DR	LA	LA77	2400	22	C6
NALIN DR	LA	LA77	2300	32	C1
NALIN PL	LA	LA77	15500	32	C1
NAMU ST	CO	PALM		190	B2
NAN CT	DBAR	POM		97A	B2
NAN ST	CO	WHI	11400	55	B6
NAN ST	PR	PR	9000	54	E5
NAN ST	PR	PR	9100	54	F5
NANBERRY RD	LA	ENC	16600	21	F3
NANCE AV	DOW	DOW	8100	60	B3
NANCE ST	LA	ENC	17100	21	E3
NANCE ST	NWK	NWK	10800	60	E5
NANCY CIR	CER	ART	19500	81	A2
NANCY PL	SCLR	SAU		124	D4
NANCY RD	RPV	SP	6500	78	D2
NANCY ST	LA	LA45	6300	50	C5
NANCY ST	WCOV	WCOV		92	D5
NANCY WY	LCF	LCF	300	19	D4
NANCY LEE LN	TOR	TOR	23900	72	F1
NANDINA DR	PALM	PALM		183	F2
NANETTE AV	WCOV	WCOV		92	D5
NANETTE ST	LA	SF	16800	1	E4
NANNESTAD ST	CO	RM	7700	46	E3
NANRY ST	CO	WHI	14700	61	F4
NANSEN DR	CO	SF		3	E2
NANTASKET DR	RPV	PVP		77	C3
NANTES AV	CO	LPUE	1000	85	D1
NANTES AV	LPUE	LPUE	200	48	E5
NANTUCKET DR	PALM	PALM		172	E9
NANTUCKET DR	PALM	PALM		183	E1
NANTUCKET PL	MB	MB		62	D3
NANTUCKET ST	CO	SAU		123	D4
NAOMA LN	CER	ART	13400	82	D5
NAOMI AV	ARC	ARC	1	28	C6
NAOMI AV	CO	ARC	9400	28	B6
NAOMI AV	CO	LA01	6100	52	C5
NAOMI AV	CO	LA01	7900	58	C1
NAOMI AV	CO	SGAB	8700	38	A1
NAOMI AV	LA	LA11	1900	44	D6

STREET	CITY	P.O. ZONE	BLOCK	PAGE	GRID
NAOMI AV	LA	LA11	2300	52	C1
NAOMI AV	LA	LA21	800	44	D5
NAOMI ST	BUR	BUR	2200	17	B4
NAOMI ST	WCOV	WCOV		92	D5
NAOMI ST N	BUR	BUR	100	24	B1
NAOMI ST S	BUR	BUR	100	24	B1
NAPA CIR	CER	ART		82	A5
NAPA CT	CLA	CLA	2400	96	A6
NAPA ST	LA	CAN	19600	12	F1
NAPA ST	LA	NOR	17300	7	E6
NAPA ST	LA	NOR	18900	14	B1
NAPA ST	LA	SF	16500	7	F6
NAPA ST	LA	SF	15000	8	C6
NAPA ST	LA	VAN	14900	8	C6
NAPLES AV	LA	VEN	2500	49	D4
NAPLES LN	LB	LB03		80	C1
NAPLES PZ	LB	LB03	5800	80	D1
NAPLES ST	MON	MON	700	28	F5
NAPLES CANAL	LB	LB03	5400	80	C1
NAPOLEON ST	LA	VEN	100	55A	E2
NAPOLI CT	LB	LB03		76	D6
NAPOLI DR	LA	PP	700	40	E4
NAPOLI PL	POM	POM	1200	94	B3
NARAMORE WY	RB	RB		67	E1
NARANJA AV	PAR	PAR	15300	66	A3
NARANJA DR	GLEN	GL06	400	25	E3
NARANJA RD	LA	WOH	20900	13	D4
NARATO PL	DBAR	POM		97	E4
NARBONNE AV	LOM	LOM	24000	73	D3
NARBONNE AV	RPV	SP	27800	73	C6
NARBONNE AV	RPV	SP	28400	78	C1
NARCISSA DR	RPV	PVP		77	E2
NARCISSUS AV	CO	CYN	14800	125	F6
NARCSSUS CST AV	CO	CYN	14800	125	F6
NARCISUS CT	LA	VEN	2100	49	C4
NARDIAN WY	LA	LA45	7800	50	A6
NARDIAN WY	LA	LA45	7800	56	A1
NARDO WY E	LB	LB13	100	75	C4
NARDO WY W	LB	LB13	100	75	C4
NARES DR	CO	CAST		123	J1
NARINO DR	CO	PVP	3300	78	C3
NARROT ST	TOR	TOR	4600	67	F2
NARROT ST	TOR	TOR	4400	68	A2
NARROW BRDGE LN	CER	ART		82	C4
NARROWS DR	PR	PR	9200	47	C6
NARROWS DR	PR	PR	9200	55	C1
NARVA ST	LA	LA31	1700	45	A2
NASH AV	DOW	DOW	11200	60	C4
NASH DR	LA	LA46	8500	33	E2
NASH ST N	ELS	ELS	100	56	D6
NASH ST S	ELS	ELS	800	62	D2
NASHPORT AV	LAV	LAV		90	C1
NASHUA WY	SCLR	VAL		127	A2
NASHVILLE AV	CO	WHI	10500	84	A4
NASHVILLE AV	LAM	LAM	12200	84	A6
NASHVILLE AV	PALM	PALM		183	J1
NASHVILLE ST	LA	CHA	19700	6	D2
NASHVILLE ST	LA	NOR	19000	7	A1
NASSAU AV	CO	LA63	400	45	C5
NASSAU AV	LA	SUN	10200	10	D2
NASSAU AV	CO	LA63	400	45	C5
NASSAU PL	CLA	CLA		96	B6
NASTURTIUM DR	CO	CYN	15500	125	E6
NATALIE AV	WCOV	WCOV		92	D5
NATALIE DR	CO	WHI	14600	61	F5
NATALIE LN	LA	CAN	8300	5	F1
NATALIE WY	SCLR	SAU		124	E6
NATCHEZ ST	LA	SP	900	78	F1
NATHAM AV	CO	LAN	49000	146	E4
NATHAN HILL RD	SCLR	CYN		125	A8
NATHENE DR	LPUE	LPUE	300	92	B6
NATHENE DR	LPUE	LPUE	300	98	B1
NATICK AV	LA	SF	9500	8	D4
NATICK AV	LA	VAN	5600	15	D6
NATICK AV	LA	VAN	4600	22	D3
NATIONAL AV	BUR	BUR	4100	24	A3
NATIONAL AV	SOG	SOG	8800	59	E3
NATIONAL BLVD	CUL	CUL	8300	42	D5
NATIONAL BLVD	LA	LA34	8900	42	C5
NATIONAL BLVD	LA	LA64	10900	41	E6
NATIONAL BLVD	LA	LA64	10700	42	A5
NATIONAL PL	LA	LA34	10700	42	A5
NATIVE AV	CO	LPUE	2600	98	D6
NATOMA AV	LA	WOH	4100	13	E4
NAU AV	LA	NOR		1	B6
NAUD ST	LA	LA12	1400	44	E1
NAUSET CT	CAR	CAR	17500	64	C5
NAUSIKA AV	CO	LPUE		97	A4
NAUTICAL TR	CO	TOP		109	B2
NAUTILUS DR	RPV	PVP		78	A3
NAVA ST	BLF	BLF	10400	66	D3
NAVA ST	NWK	NWK	11500	66	F3
NAVAHO	CO	AGO		106	D2
NAVAHO TR LN	POM	POM		94	D5
NAVAJO	CO	TOP		13	C5
NAVAJO CT	CO	CAST		123	E4

STREET	CITY	P.O. ZONE	BLOCK	PAGE	GRID
NAVAJO LN	CAR	CAR		69	E6
NAVAJO LN	NWK	NWK		82	C1
NAVAJO PL	PVE	PVP	3600	72	E2
NAVAJO ST	LA	NHO	4200	24	A4
NAVAJO TR	CO	AGO		107	A3
NAVAJO SPG RD	DBAR	POM		93	F5
NAVAJO SPG RD	DBAR	POM		94	A5
NAVARRE CT	LA	VEN		49	C4
NAVARRO AV	CO	ALT	2080	19	F5
NAVARRO AV	PAS	PAS	1500	19	F5
NAVARRO AV	PAS	PAS	1200	26	F1
NAVARRO DR	CLA	CLA	3100	91	B1
NAVARRO ST	LA	LA32	4800	36	D5
NAVILLA PL	BAP	BAP	15100	39	F5
NAVILLA PL	CO	COV	19300	89	A5
NAVILLA PL	COV	COV	100	88	E5
NAVILLA PL	COV	COV	900	89	A5
NAVOJOA PL	SFS	SFS		61	A2
NAVY CT	LA	VEN	10	49	B3
NAVY ST	LA	LA66	11800	41	E6
NAVY ST	LA	VEN	1	49	B3
NAVY ST	SM	SM	600	49	B2
NAVY WY	LA	SP		79	D1
NAWA LN	NWK	NWK		66	F2
NAYLOR AV	LA	LA45	7400	50	C6
NAYLOR AV	LA	LA45	7800	56	C1
NEAL DR	LA	LA41	5300	26	A4
NEAPOLITAN LN E	LB	LB03		80	C1
NEAPOLITAN LN W	LB	LB03		80	C1
NEAR TR	CO	TOP		109	D6
NEARBANK DR	CO	LPUE	17900	98	C4
NEARBROOK ST	SCLR	CYN	18900	124	H5
NEARBROOK ST	SCLR	CYN	17900	125	B8
NEARCLIFF ST	TOR	TOR	2300	73	B3
NEARDALE ST	PAR	PAR	8500	66	A2
NEARFIELD ST	AZU	AZU	900	88	E1
NEARFIELD ST	CO	AZU	18000	88	E1
NEARGATE DR	SCLR	NEW	23400	127	B5
NEARGLEN AV	CO	COV	3600	89	A5
NEARGLEN AV	COV	COV	100	89	A5
NEARGLEN AV	GLDR	GLDR	1400	89	A2
NEARGROVE RD	LAM	LAM	14200	83	A2
NEARPOINT DR	WCOV	WCOV	3800	97	A1
NEARSIDE DR	CO	PALM		157	E9
NEARSIDE ST	WHI	WHI	16500	84	D3
NEARTREE RD	LAM	LAM	14800	83	A3
NEARVIEW DR	SCLR	CYN	18900	124	J7
NEARVIEW DR	SCLR	CYN	16500	125	C7
NEARWOOD RD	CO	LR		192	B6
NEARWOOD RD	CO	PEAR	12300	192	C6
NEBLINA CT	SCLR	VAL		127	H6
NEBO DR	CO	CAL		108	A6
NEBRASKA	WCOV	WCOV		92	E4
NEBRASKA AV	LA	LA25	11100	41	D4
NEBRASKA AV	LB	LB02	400	75	E5
NEBRASKA AV	PAR	PAR	13600	65	E1
NEBRASKA AV	SM	SM	2900	41	C5
NEBRASKA AV	SOG	SOG	2400	58	F3
NEBRASKA AV	SOG	SOG	2700	59	A3
NECTAR AV	LKD	LKD	20700	71	F3
NECTARINE DR	PALM	PALM		183	C6
NECTARINE ST	ING	IN01	300	56	E1
NEDDY AV	LA	CAN	6100	5	D5
NEDRA AV	DOW	DOW	10500	60	C3
NEDRA DR	LA	SF	12400	1	F4
NEDRA ST	LYN	LYN	4300	59	D4
NEECE AV	TOR	TOR	24000	73	A2
NEECE ST E	LB	LB05	100	65	B5
NEECE ST W	LB	LB05	100	65	B5
NEEDHAM ST	LA	SF	15400	1	F1
NEEDHAM ST	LA	SF	15400	2	A1
NEEDLES ST	LA	CHA	19700	6	F4
NEEDLES ST	LA	NOR	19600	7	A4
NEEDLES ST	LA	SF	14700	8	D4
NEELY ST	CO	CAST		123	H2
NEENACH ST	LA	SV	11700	9	C6
NEENAH ST	CMRC	LA40	7500	54	B5
NEFF AV	CO	LPUE	1800	92	B3
NEFF RD	LAM	LAM		83	D1
NEFF RD	LAM	LAM		84	D6
NEIL ST	WCOV	WCOV	400	88	D5
NEIL ARMSTNG ST	MTB	MTB		46	E4
NEILSON ST	CAR	CAR	300	69	A5
NEILSON WY	SM	SM	1900	49	A2
NEINDORFF DR	LA	LA68		34	D2
NEKO DR	LOM	LOM		73	C2
NEKOMA ST	LA	LA65	2600	25	F5
NELDOME ST	CO	ALT	600	19	E5
NELL AV	CER	ART		81	A2
NELLAS ST	WHOL	LA69	8800	33	D4
NELLA VISTA AV	LA	LA27	2200	35	A1
NELLIEMAY LN	CO	CYN		125	B5
NELROSE AV	LA	VEN	1100	49	D3
NELSON AL	PAS	PAS	1400	27	D2
NELSON AV	CO	LPUE	13400	48	C3

INDEX

1990 LOS ANGELES COUNTY STREET INDEX

STREET	CITY	P.O. ZONE	BLOCK	PAGE	GRID
NELSON AV	IND	LPUE	13200	48	B3
NELSON AV	LPUE	LPUE	13700	48	C3
NELSON AV	MB	MB	1500	62	D5
NELSON AV	RB	RB	1900	62	D5
NELSON DR	BELL	BELL	4700	53	D5
NELSON PL	MTB	MTB	200	54	D1
NELSON ST	LA	SP		79	A3
NELSON ST	POM	POM	2100	94	E6
NELSON ST	WCOV	WCOV		92	C4
NELSONBARK AV	LKD	LKD	4200	70	F4
NEMAHA ST	POM	POM	100	90	E6
NEMO ST	WHOL	LA69	9000	33	C5
NEO ST	DOW	DOW	7200	59	F3
NEO ST	DOW	DOW	7300	60	A3
NEOLA PL	LA	LA41	4800	26	C5
NEOLA ST	LA	LA41	900	26	C5
NEON WY	LA	SF	12600	1	D4
NEOSHO AV	CUL	LA66	4100	49	F3
NEOSHO AV	LA	LA66	4100	49	F3
NEPTUNE AV	CAR	CAR	21000	69	B4
NEPTUNE AV	CAR	CAR	24000	74	B1
NEPTUNE AV	MB	MB		62	B5
NEPTUNE AV N	LA	WIL	200	74	B5
NEPTUNE AV S	LA	WIL	100	74	B5
NEPTUNE AV S	LA	WIL	700	79	B1
NEPTUNE DR	PALM	PALM		183	G8
NEPTUNE ST	POM	POM	2300	90	E4
NESBITT RD	CO	TOP		109	A2
NESMUTH RD	GLEN	GL02	300	18	C6
NESSA DR	LAN	LAN		160	E6
NESTLE AV	LA	NOR	8500	7	C6
NESTLE AV	LA	NOR	8300	14	C1
NESTLE AV	LA	RES	6600	14	C4
NESTLE AV	LA	TAR	4900	21	C3
NESTOR AV	CAR	CAR	19000	69	D1
NESTOR AV	CO	COM	13900	64	D2
NESTOR AV N	COM	COM	100	64	D3
NESTOR AV S	COM	COM	100	64	D3
NETHERLY AV	LB	LB10	3200	70	A6
NETTLETON ST	LA	SV	10500	16	E1
NEURASCHEL ST	CO	CAST	28900	123	A5
NEVA LN	POM	POM	1100	95	A5
NEVA PL	LA	LA42	300	36	C1
NEVA ST	POM	POM	1800	95	A5
NEVADA	WCOV	WCOV		92	E4
NEVADA AV	CO	LA63	100	45	D4
NEVADA AV	ELM	ELM	3300	38	D6
NEVADA AV	ELM	ELM	2600	47	D1
NEVADA AV	LA	CAN	8500	6	B6
NEVADA AV	LA	CAN	6500	12	B4
NEVADA AV	LA	CHA	9600	6	B4
NEVADA AV	LA	WOH	5800	12	B6
NEVADA AV	LYN	LYN	11800	59	A6
NEVADA AV	RM	RM	8900	38	A5
NEVADA AV	SOG	SOG	5700	65	E1
NEVADA ST	BELL	BELL	3500	53	D5
NEVADA ST	ELS	ELS	100	56	B6
NEVADA ST	LB	LB06	200	75	C2
NEVADA ST	SH	LB06	900	75	D2
NEVERS ST	LPUE	LPUE	13900	48	D3
NEVETTE CT	SCLR	CYN		125	C7
NEVILL AV	SOG	SOG	8600	59	D2
NEVIN AV	LA	LA11	2400	52	D1
NEW AV	ALH	ALH	1000	37	D6
NEW AV	SGAB	SGAB	1400	37	D6
NEW AV N	MPK	MPK	100	46	D2
NEW AV S	MPK	MPK	100	46	D2
NEW ST	DOW	DOW	10700	60	B3
NEWACRE RD	SCLR	VAL		124	B8
NEWARK AV	LA	LA32		36	D6
NEWARK CT	CLA	CLA		96	D5
NEW BEDFORD AV	CLA	CLA		90	F2
NEWBIRD DR	SCLR	SAU	28200	124	F4
NEWBRIDGE CIR	CO	WAL	19800	97	B4
NEWBROOK AV	CER	ART	17800	82	D6
NEWBROOK CIR	CER	ART	16600	82	D5
NEWBURGH ST	AZU	AZU	100	88	D2
NEWBURGH ST	CO	AZU	16500	88	B2
NEWBURGH ST	CO	COV	18600	88	F2
NEWBURGH ST E	GLDR	GLDR	400	89	B2
NEWBURGH ST W	GLDR	GLDR	200	89	A2
NEWBURRY CT	CER	ART		66	D2
NEWBURY PL	PALM	PALM		184	B1
NEWBURY WY	DBAR	POM		97A	B1
NEWBY AV	RM	RM	8900	38	A5
NEWBY AV E	SGAB	SGAB	100	37	E5
NEWBY AV W	SGAB	SGAB	200	37	E5
NEWBY ST	GLEN	GL01	1000	25	A2
NEWCASTLE AV	LA	ENC	5700	14	D6
NEWCASTLE AV	LA	ENC	4800	21	D2
NEWCASTLE AV	LA	NOR	8500	7	D6
NEWCASTLE AV	LA	NOR	8500	14	D1
NEWCASTLE AV	LA	RES	6200	14	D5
NEWCASTLE AV	LA	SF	11500	1	D6
NEWCASTLE AV	LA	SF	11100	7	D1
NEWCASTLE CT	SCLR	SAU		127	D1

STREET	CITY	P.O. ZONE	BLOCK	PAGE	GRID
NEWCASTLE DR	WHI	WHI		84	D1
NEWCASTLE DR	WHI	WHI		85	D6
NEWCASTLE LN	CO	CAL		100	B2
NEW CENTURY DR	CO	GAR	15600	64	A3
NEWCOMB AV	LAM	LAM	12600	84	D6
NEWCOMB AV	WHI	WHI	9800	84	D4
NEWCOMB DR	LA	VAN	13300	22	F5
NEWCOMB PL	CLA	CLA	1500	91	A2
NEWCREST DR	WCOV	WCOV		92	C4
NEWCREST DR	WCOV	WCOV		92	C4
NEWDALE DR	LA	LA27	4200	35	A2
NEW DEAL AV	ELM	ELM	2700	47	E2
NEW DEPOT ST	LA	LA12	600	44	D1
NEWDOCK ST	LA	SP	400	79	C1
NEW DOCK ST	LB	LB02		79	C1
NEWELL RD	CO	MAL	1800	113	B2
NEWELL ST	HPK	HPK	6200	53	B5
NEWELL ST	LA	LA39	2600	35	D3
NEW ENGLAND LN	CER	ART		66	D2
NEW ENGLAND ST	LA	LA06	1700	44	A4
NEW ENGLAND ST	LA	LA07	1900	44	A4
NEWFIELD CT	CO	SAU		124	E4
NEWFIELD ST	CO	GAR	300	64	B3
NEWGARD AV	LA	SF	12100	2	D5
NEWGARDEN ST	CO	LPUE	19500	97	A3
NEWGATE AV	CO	WHI	10700	61	E5
NEWGATE RD	LA	CAN	6900	5	E4
NEWGROVE ST E	CO	LAN	9500	161	H4
NEWGROVE ST E	LAN	LAN	500	160	C4
NEWGROVE ST W	LAN	LAN	7200	158	H4
NEWGROVE ST W	LAN	LAN	4000	159	A4
NEWGROVE ST W	LAN	LAN	1100	159	H4
NEWGROVE ST W	LAN	LAN	100	160	A4
NEWHALL AV	SCLR	NEW	24300	127	C3
NEWHALL AV	SCLR	VAL		124	A9
NEWHLL&PC CY RD	CO	NEW		126	G4
NEWHALL RCH RD	SCLR	SAU		124	C7
NEWHALL RCH RD	CO	VAL		124	A7
NEW HAMPSHRE AV	CO	LA44	11100	57	F5
NEW HAMPSHRE AV	CO	TOR	20300	68	F3
NEW HAMPSHRE AV	GAR	GAR	13200	63	F1
NEW HAMPSR AV N	LA	LA04	100	34	F6
NEW HAMPSR AV N	LA	LA27	1300	34	F2
NEW HAMPSR AV N	LA	LA29	700	34	F4
NEW HAMPSR AV S	LA	LA04	100	43	F1
NEW HAMPSR AV S	LA	LA05	600	43	F2
NEW HAMPSR AV S	LA	LA06	900	43	F4
NEW HAMPSR AV S	LA	LA20	300	43	F2
NEW HAMPSR AV S	LA	LA44	7900	57	F1
NEWHAMPTON ST	CO	LPUE	15600	85	D3
NEWHAVEN CT	GLDR	GLDR		89	B2
NEWHAVEN LN	GLDR	GLDR	300	89	B2
NEWHAVEN RD	PAS	PAS	3500	28	A3
NEW HAVEN ST	LA	SV	10700	16	F1
NEW HIGH CT	RB	RB	200	67	D3
NEW HIGH ST	LA	LA12	300	44	E2
NEWHILL ST	GLDR	GLDR	1000	86	F5
NEWHOME AV	LA	SUN	10200	10	D3
NEWHOME PL	LA	SUN		10	D3
NEWHOUSE ST	SCLR	CYN	19500	124	H8
NEWINGTON ST	CO	DUA	600	29	B6
NEWINGTON ST	DUA	DUA	800	29	C6
NEW JERSEY	WCOV	WCOV		92	E4
NEW JERSEY ST	LA	LA33	1600	45	A3
NEWKIRK AV	CAR	CAR	21300	69	C5
NEWLAND ST	LA	LA42	200	36	D1
NEWLEE ST	MPK	MPK	1100	46	B2
NEWLIN AV	WHI	WHI	5500	55	D6
NEWLIN AV	WHI	WHI	8300	61	D1
NEWMAN AV E	ARC	ARC	1	28	E4
NEWMAN AV W	ARC	ARC	1	28	E4
NEWMAN ST	LA	LA35	9700	42	B2
NEWMAN ST	POM	POM	100	94	D2
NEWMANOR AV	POM	POM	1300	94	B1
NEWMARK AV	RM	RM	7400	46	E2
NEWMARK AV E	MPK	MPK	100	46	B2
NEWMARK AV W	MPK	MPK	100	46	B2
NEWMARKET ST	CO	WHI		47	F5
NEWMARK MALL	MTB	MTB	700	54	D1
NEWMIRE AV	NWK	NWK	11800	60	D6
NEWMIRE AV	NWK	NWK	12800	66	D1
NEWMONT AV E	CO	LAN	15100	174	H3
NEWMONT AV E	CO	LAN	16500	175	A3
NEW ORLEANS CT	CLA	CLA		96	D5
NEW PINE DR	CO	LPUE		98	B4
NEWPORT AV	LB	LB03	200	76	A6
NEWPORT AV	LB	LB04	700	76	A6
NEWPORT AV	LB	LB14	300	76	A6
NEWPORT AV	PAS	PAS	1600	19	F6
NEWPORT CIR	LA	CAN	7000	5	E4
NEWPORT PL	CO	SAU		123	D4
NEWPORT RD	PALM	PALM		171	H7
NEWQUIST PL	IND	LPUE	300	48	E6
NEWRIDGE DR	RPV	PVP	3300	78	C3
NEW ROCHELLE ST	WAL	WAL	20300	93	B4
NEWSTAR DR	RPV	PVP	28600	72	E6

STREET	CITY	P.O. ZONE	BLOCK	PAGE	GRID
NEWTON AL	PAS	PAS	400	27	C3
NEWTON AV	LB	LB05	6900	65	E5
NEWTON CT	CO	SAU		124	E4
NEWTON MTWY	CO	MAL		106	D5
NEWTON PL	SF	SF	700	3	A5
NEWTON ST	CO	LPUE	15400	85	D3
NEWTON ST	COV	COV	400	88	F5
NEWTON ST	LA	LA21	1300	44	D5
NEWTON ST	LA	SF	12800	3	A4
NEWTON ST	SF	SF	300	2	E6
NEWTON ST	SF	SF	900	3	A5
NEWTON ST	TOR	TOR	4800	67	E6
NEWTON ST	TOR	TOR	4000	72	F1
NEWTON ST	TOR	TOR	3000	73	A2
NEWTONIA DR	LA	LA32	5200	36	E4
NEWTREE AV	LAN	LAN	45400	159	J3
NEWVALE DR	CO	LH		157	A6
NEWVIEW DR	CO	LH		157	A7
NEWVILLE AV	DOW	DOW	9700	60	E3
NEW VISTA PL	CO	LPUE	14800	85	C1
NEW YORK	WCOV	WCOV		92	E4
NEW YORK AV	GLEN	GL14	4200	11	D5
NEW YORK AV	GLEN	GL14	3800	18	C1
NEW YORK DR	CO	ALT	700	20	B6
NEW YORK DR	CO	PAS	2600	20	E6
NEW YORK DR	CO	PAS	2700	27	E1
NEW YORK DR	PAS	PAS	2700	20	E6
NEW YORK DR	PAS	PAS	2700	27	E1
NEW YORK ST	CO	LA22	4300	45	E4
NEW YORK ST	LB	LB13	500	75	D4
NIAGARA AV	CER	ART	17400	82	B5
NIAGARA AV	CLA	CLA	1400	91	A2
NIAGARA ST N	BUR	BUR	600	17	B6
NIAGARA ST N	BUR	BUR	200	24	B2
NIAGARA ST S	BUR	BUR	100	24	C3
NIAGARA WY	LA	LA41	2400	25	F4
NICADA DR	LA	LA77	2800	22	E6
NICE CT	LAN	LAN		159	G5
NICHOLAS AV	CER	ART		81	A2
NICHOLAS LN	ARC	ARC		28	F6
NICHOLAS BCH RD	CO	MAL	32800	110	D3
NICHOLET ST	POM	POM	500	93	F2
NICHOLS ST	BLF	BLF	9200	66	D3
NICHOLS ST	POM	POM	2000	90	E5
NICHOLS CYN PL	LA	LA46	2800	23	F6
NICHOLS CYN PL	LA	LA46	2800	33	F1
NICHOLS CYN RD	LA	LA46	1700	23	F6
NICHOLS CYN RD	LA	LA46	1700	33	F2
NICHOLS FLAT RD	CO	MAL		110	E1
NICHOLSON AV	LA	WIL	800	74	F4
NICHOLSON AV	LB	LB13		74	F4
NICHOLSON AV N	MPK	MPK	100	46	C1
NICHOLSON AV S	MPK	MPK	100	46	C1
NICHOLSON ST	CO	MDR	100	55A	E1
NICKELS AV	CO	ACT		189	E3
NICKIE LN	SCLR	SAU		124	G5
NICKLAUS DR	SCLR	VAL		127	A3
NICOBAR ST W	LAN	LAN	100	160	B4
NICOLA AV	CMRC	LA40	1500	54	B2
NICOLE CT	GLDR	GLDR		89	E1
NICOLE ST	LAN	LAN		160	E6
NICOLET AV	LA	LA08	3800	51	A1
NICOLET AV	LA	LA16	3700	43	A6
NICOLET AV	LA	LA16	3700	51	A1
NICOLLE AV	CAR	CAR	23100	69	A4
NICOLLE AV	CAR	CAR	23500	74	A1
NICOYA DR	CO	LPUE		85	F4
NIDO CT	SCLR	VAL		124	B7
NIDO CT	PALM	LAN		171	D4
NIETO AV	LB	LB03	100	76	B6
NIETO AV	LB	LB03	100	80	B1
NIETO AV	LB	LB14	300	76	B6
NIETO LN	LA	LA33	1400	45	C2
NIGHTINGALE DR	LA	LA69	9200	33	C3
NIGHTINGALE LN	LAN	LAN		158	J9
NIHAV	SCLR	NEW		127	F5
NIKKI CT	WCOV	WCOV		92	D5
NILAND ST	LYN	LYN	5100	65	C1
NILE CT	CO	TOP	20900	109	D2
NILES PL	LA	LA26	2300	35	D4
NIMES PL	LA	LA77	800	32	E4
NIMES RD	LA	LA77	600	32	E4
NIMROD PL	LA	LA49	13100	40	F3
NIMROD ST	CO	LH		157	B6
NINA LN	ING	IN01		57	B2
NINA PL	LA	CUL	11300	50	B3
NINA ST	PAS	PAS	2500	27	E4
NINA ST	WCOV	WCOV		92	D5
NINDE PL	PAS	PAS	200	27	A3
NINFA CT	LA	WOH	22200	13	B2
NINITA PKWY	PAS	PAS	300	27	C5
NIODRARA DR	GLEN	GL08	1800	18	E6
NIPOMO AV	LB	LB08	3000	71	E6
NIPOMO AV	LB	LB15	1800	76	E3
NIPOMO AV	LKD	LKD	4100	71	E4
NISSAN WY	LA	WIL		74	C6

STREET	CITY	P.O. ZONE	BLOCK	PAGE	GRID
NITA AV	LA	CAN	6500	12	B5
NITA AV	LA	CHA	9700	6	B4
NITA AV	LA	WOH	5800	12	B6
NITA AV	LA	WOH	5800	13	B1
NITHSDALE RD	PAS	PAS	900	26	D5
NIXON LN	CO	AGO		106	E1
NIXON ST	LKD	LKD	6400	71	E2
NOAH CT	SAD	SAD		89	E2
NOAKES ST	CMRC	LA22	4600	53	D1
NOAKES ST	CMRC	LA23	3900	53	C1
NOAKES ST	LA	LA23	3600	53	B1
NOBEL ST	CMRC	LA40	4700	53	E2
NOB HILL DR	AZU	AZU	1300	86	D4
NOB HILL DR	LA	LA65	4600	36	A2
NOBLE AV	AZU	AZU	100	88	D1
NOBLE AV	LA	SF	8500	8	C6
NOBLE AV	LA	SF	8300	15	C1
NOBLE AV	LA	VAN	5600	15	C6
NOBLE AV	LA	VAN	4200	22	C3
NOBLE CT	PALM	PALM		173	A9
NOBLE DR	CO	LAN	9500	146	E1
NOBLE CYN WY	CO	LPUE		97	B5
NOBLES AV	CO	WHI	10000	55	B3
NOBLETT DR	CO	LH		157	B6
NOBLE VIEW DR	RPV	SP	2000	78	D2
NOEL DR	TEC	TEC	5300	38	B3
NOEL PL	LA	BH	1800	33	B3
NOELINE AV	LA	ENC	4200	22	A3
NOELINE WY	LA	ENC	4500	22	A3
NOELL CIR	CER	ART	19500	81	B2
NOELLE CT	LOM	LOM		73	C3
NOFRAL RD	LA	WOH	4900	13	D2
NOGAL AV	WHI	WHI	8600	61	D1
NOGAL CIR	LAV	LAV		90	E1
NOGALES DR	LA	TAR	4100	21	B3
NOGALES ST	CO	LPUE	400	98	F3
NOGALES ST	IND	LPUE	700	98	F3
NOGALES ST	WCOV	WCOV		92	E5
NOGALES ST	WCOV	WCOV	600	98	F3
NOHLES DR	LA	SUN		10	C2
NOKOMIS RD	RPV	PVP	4900	72	E4
NOLA PL	LA	SF		1	D4
NOLAN AV	GLEN	GL02	300	18	C6
NOLAN ST	ELM	ELM	11200	38	E5
NOLANDALE ST	CO	LPUE	13800	48	D2
NOLANDALE ST	WCOV	WCOV	1700	48	E3
NOLDEN ST	LA	LA41	500	26	C6
NOLDEN ST	LA	LA42	500	36	C1
NOLINA AV	BAP	LPUE	700	48	B2
NOLINA CIR	LAN	LAN		159	E5
NOLINA ST	BAP	BAP	3300	39	C6
NOLINA WY	PAR	PAR		65	E4
NOLL DR	PALM	PALM		183	H2
NOLTE CT	SCLR	CYN		125	B7
NOMAD DR	LA	WOH	4600	13	F2
NOMAR ST	LA	WOH	23900	5	E6
NONA LN	WHI	WHI		55	F5
NONPAREIL DR	PALM	LAN		171	B2
NOOK TR	CO	SF		3	E5
NOOK TR	CO	TOP	21500	109	D4
NORA AV	CO	COV	4000	88	A5
NORA AV	IRW	BAP	4600	88	A4
NORA AV	WCOV	WCOV	300	88	A5
NORA PL	LA	SF	15100	2	D5
NORAH AV	CER	ART	19400	81	D2
NORA LYNN DR	LA	CAN	5900	5	C6
NORAN AV	CER	ART	18300	82	D6
NORAN CIR	CER	ART	17800	82	D6
NORANDA LN	CO	MAL		111	B3
NORBECK DR	LAM	LAM	13700	82	E1
NORBERRY ST E	LAN	LAN	500	160	C4
NORBERRY ST W	LAN	LAN	1100	159	J4
NORBERRY ST W	LAN	LAN	100	160	B4
NORCO AV	BAP	BAP	4600	39	D3
NORCREST DR	CO	WHI	15900	84	C5
NORCROFT AV	LA	LA24	300	32	E6
NORCROSS DR	CO	SAU		181	H8
NORD ST	CO	COM	2000	64	E1
NORD ST	COM	COM	600	64	E1
NORDBY ST	CAR	CAR	800	64	C4
NORDEN RD	CO	MAL		112	A1
NORDESTA DR	NWK	NWK	12200	60	D6
NORDHOFF PL	LA	NOR	19700	6	F5
NORDHOFF ST	LA	CAN	20100	6	E6
NORDHOFF ST	LA	CHA	20500	6	C5
NORDHOFF ST	LA	NOR	19700	6	E6
NORDHOFF ST	LA	NOR	17000	7	D5
NORDHOFF ST	LA	PAC	13900	8	D5
NORDHOFF ST	LA	SF	16500	7	D5
NORDHOFF ST	LA	SF	14900	8	B5
NORDHOFF ST	LA	VAN	14100	8	D5
NORDICA DR	LA	LA65	900	36	A2
NORDLAND AV	LAV	LAV	2700	90	D3
NORDMAN ST	LOM	LOM	1900	73	D2
NORDYKE ST	LA	LA42	5400	26	B6
NORELLE ST	LA	LA32	4600	36	C6

STREET	CITY	P.O. ZONE	BLOCK	PAGE	GRID
NOREMA ST	ELM	ELM	2100	47	E3
NOREN ST	DOW	DOW	7400	60	B1
NOREN ST	LCF	LCF	300	19	D3
NORFIELD CT	LA	LA49		32	B2
NORFOLK AV	LA	VEN	900	49	C3
NORFOLK ST	LA	LA33	1400	45	B2
NORFORK PL	SCLR	SAU		127	D1
NORGATE ST	SAD	SAD	1100	89	D2
NORGATE ST E	GLDR	GLDR	100	89	A2
NORGATE ST W	GLDR	GLDR	100	89	A2
NORGROVE PL	PAS	PAS	1300	19	D6
NORHAM PL	GLEN	GL06	900	19	B6
NORINO DR	WHI	WHI		55	C3
NORLAIN AV	DOW	DOW	11700	59	F4
NORLAIN AV	DOW	DOW	9700	60	B1
NORLAND DR	CO	CYN		125	E8
NORLINA PL	LA	SF		1	D4
NORMA AV	WCOV	WCOV	1400	92	C1
NORMA CT	WCOV	WCOV		92	D1
NORMA PL	WHOL	LA69	8900	33	D5
NORMAL AV	LA	LA29	4200	34	F4
NORMAL AV	LA	LA29	4100	35	A4
NORMALLIN ST	TOR	TOR	2700	73	B3
NORMAN AV	WAL	WAL		93	C5
NORMAN AV E	ARC	ARC	100	38	C1
NORMAN AV W	ARC	ARC	1	38	C1
NORMAN CT	LB	LB13	1000	75	D4
NORMAN PL	CO	LA63	1500	45	D2
NORMAN PL	LA	LA49	800	32	B6
NORMAN PL	SM	SM	200	49	A2
NORMANDALE AV	CER	ART	19500	81	A2
NORMANDIE AV N	LA	LA04	100	34	E4
NORMANDIE AV N	LA	LA27	1300	34	E4
NORMANDIE AV N	LA	LA29	700	34	E4
NORMANDIE AV S	CO	HAC	23400	68	E5
NORMANDIE AV S	CO	HAC	23500	73	F3
NORMANDIE AV S	CO	LA44	8600	57	E5
NORMANDIE AV S	CO	TOR	22500	68	E5
NORMANDIE AV S	GAR	GAR	12800	63	E1
NORMANDIE AV S	LA	GAR	17700	63	E6
NORMANDIE AV S	LA	GAR	18300	68	E2
NORMANDIE AV S	LA	HAC	25000	73	F3
NORMANDIE AV S	LA	LA04	100	34	E4
NORMANDIE AV S	LA	LA05	600	43	E2
NORMANDIE AV S	LA	LA06	900	43	E3
NORMANDIE AV S	LA	LA07	1900	43	E6
NORMANDIE AV S	LA	LA20	300	43	E2
NORMANDIE AV S	LA	LA37	3800	51	E5
NORMANDIE AV S	LA	LA44	5800	51	E5
NORMANDIE AV S	LA	LA44	7800	57	E5
NORMANDIE AV S	LA	TOR	19000	68	E2
NORMANDIE PL	LA	LA04	300	34	E6
NORMANDY CT	PALM	PALM		171	H7
NORMANDY DR	LCF	LCF	2800	19	D6
NORMANDY DR	PAS	PAS	1400	19	D6
NORMANDY LN	LAN	LAN		159	F8
NORMANTON DR	LCF	LCF	2100	11	F5
NOROCO DR	PR	PR	6000	54	E4
NORRIS AV	LA	PAC	10200	9	B3
NORRIS AV	LA	SF	11400	2	F6
NORRIS AV	LA	SV	8700	9	E6
NORRIS AV	LA	SV	8400	16	E1
NORSALL CT	GLEN	GL06		25	F2
NORSE WY	LB	LB08	4100	71	B4
NORSEWOOD DR	CO	LPUE	2600	98	E6
NORTH AL	SPAS	SPAS	1900	37	A2
NORTH DR	CO	HAC		73	F2
NORTH DR	CUL	CUL		50	D3
NORTH PL	LA	LA31	2100	45	A1
NORTH ST	MON	MON	100	29	B2
NORTH TR	CO	SF		3	E5
NORTH TR	CO	TOP		109	D1
NORTHAM ST	CO	LPUE	19100	97	A1
NORTHAM ST	CO	LPUE	17400	98	C1
NORTHAM ST	CO	WCOV		98	F1
NORTHAM ST	LAM	LAM	14700	83	A4
NORTHAM ST	LPUE	LPUE	17100	98	B1
NORTHAMPTON AV	CLA	CLA		90	F2
NORTHAMPTON ST	DBAR	WAL		97	C2
NORTHBAY RD	RPV	PVP	28700	72	E6
NORTH BRAND BL	LA	SF	13200	3	A4
NORTH BRAND BL	SF	SF	900	3	A5
NORTHBROOK AV	SCLR	CYN	27000	124	G7
NORTHCAPE AV	SAD	SAD	500	90	A2
NORTH CIRCLE DR	WHI	WHI		55	D2
NORTHCLIFF RD	CO	PAS	300	27	E5
NORTHFIELD CT	CO	VAL		124	F2
NORTHFIELD ST	LA	PP	15900	40	C3
NORTHFORD DR	LA	TU	6800	11	A5
NORTHGATE AV	LA	CAN	7800	12	C2
NORTHGATE AV	SAD	SAD	600	90	A2
NORTHGATE ST	CUL	CUL	10700	50	D3
NORTHHAVEN LN	CO	ALT	2800	20	D4
NORTH HILL RD	POM	POM		90	D6
NORTH KNOLL DR	LA	LA68	3200	24	B6

STREET	CITY	P.O. ZONE	BLOCK	PAGE	GRID
NORTHLAND AV	GLEN	GL14	4300	11	C5
NORTHLAND DR	CO	LA08	3600	51	B2
NORTH PARK AV	LA	LA66	11800	50	A2
NORTH POINTE PL	LA	WOH		12	E6
NORTH RANCH RD	POM	POM		94	C4
NORTHRIDGE AV E	GLDR	GLDR	700	87	C4
NORTHRIDGE AV W	GLDR	GLDR	400	87	A4
NORTHRIDGE DR	CO	LA43	4200	51	A3
NORTHRIDGE DR	PALM	PALM		171	B3
NORTH RIDGE PL	MPK	MPK	1100	45	F3
NORTHRIDGE RD	LA	CHA	19700	6	F2
NORTHRDGE HL DR	LA	CHA	10600	6	F2
NORTHROCK DR	CO	PALM		157	J8
NORTHROP AV	HAW	HAW		57	B6
NORTHRUP AV	PAS	PAS		27	F4
NORTHSIDE DR	CO	LA22	5900	54	B1
NORTH SIDE DR	CO	PALM	9000	171I	F3
NORTHSIDE DR	MTB	MTB	1900	54	B1
NORTH SLOPE LN	POM	POM		94	D5
NORTHSTAR CT	LA	VEN		49	D6
NORTH STAR DR	PALM	PALM		172	J5
NORTHSTAR ST	LA	VEN		49	C6
NORTHUP AV	CO	PAS	1	27	F4
NORTHVALE RD	LA	LA64	10300	42	A5
NORTHVIEW AV	ARC	ARC	800	28	F3
NORTHVIEW CT	PALM	PALM		183	H2
NORTHVIEW DR	WAL	WAL		93	C5
NORTHVIEW PL	DBAR	POM		94	B6
NORTHVIEW TER	CO	LPUE		85	C3
NORTHWAY LN	CLA	CLA	600	91	A4
NORTHWESTERN DR	CLA	CLA	500	91	A3
NORTHWEST PASSG	CO	MDR		49	D6
NORTHWOOD AV	CAR	CAR	19000	69	E1
NORTHWOOD AV N	COM	COM	600	64	D2
NORTHWOOD AV S	CO	COM	13900	64	D2
NORTHWOOD AV S	COM	COM	400	64	D3
NORTHWOOD LN	POM	POM	700	90	F2
NORTHWOODS LN	GLEN	GL08		18	D1
NORTHWOOD VW RD	LA	CAN	23800	5	E4
NORTON AV	GLEN	GL02	800	25	A2
NORTON AV	LYN	LYN	2600	58	F4
NORTON AV	LYN	LYN	2900	59	A4
NORTON AV	WHOL	LA46	7600	33	E4
NORTON AV	WHOL	LA46	7500	34	A4
NORTON AV N	LA	LA04	100	34	D5
NORTON AV S	LA	LA04	100	34	D6
NORTON AV S	LA	LA05	600	43	D2
NORTON AV S	LA	LA08	3800	51	C1
NORTON AV S	LA	LA18	2800	43	C5
NORTON AV S	LA	LA19	900	43	C3
NORTON AV S	LA	LA20	300	43	D2
NORTON DR	SCLR	SAU		124	C4
NORTON DR	SH	LB06	2800	75	F3
NORTON ST	LB	LB05	100	70	C1
NORTON ST	TOR	TOR	5000	67	E2
NORUMBEGA CT	LA	LA37	3900	51	E1
NORUMBEGA DR	MON	MON	100	29	C3
NORUMBEGA RD	MON	MON	400	29	B2
NORVAL ST	POM	POM	1700	95	A4
NORWALK AV	LA	LA41	1900	25	F5
NORWALK AV	LA	LA41	2400	26	A5
NORWALK BLVD	ART	ART	18500	81	B4
NORWALK BLVD	ART	ART	17500	82	B5
NORWALK BLVD	CER	ART	19100	81	B4
NORWALK BLVD	CER	ART	16600	82	B5
NORWALK BLVD	CO	WHI	6000	55	B5
NORWALK BLVD	CO	WHI	8300	61	B4
NORWALK BLVD	HG	LKD	21400	81	B4
NORWALK BLVD	LKD	LKD	20300	81	B4
NORWALK BLVD	LB	LB08	3400	81	B4
NORWALK BLVD	NWK	NWK	11000	61	B4
NORWALK BLVD	NWK	NWK	13900	82	B5
NORWALK BLVD	SFS	SFS	9200	61	B4
NORWALK BLVD	WHI	WHI	5400	55	B5
NORWALK SQUARE	NWK	NWK		82	A2
NORWAY LN	LA	LA49	700	32	B6
NORWIC PL	CO	ALT	2200	20	B5
NORWICH AV	ALH	ALH	3100	36	E5
NORWICH AV	LA	LA32	5400	36	E5
NORWICH AV	LA	SF	8500	8	C6
NORWICH AV	LA	SF	8500	15	C1
NORWICH AV	LA	VAN	5700	15	C6
NORWICH AV	LA	VAN	4600	22	C3
NORWICH DR	CLA	CLA		91	B1
NORWICH DR	PALM	PALM		183	E1
NORWICH DR	WHOL	LA48	500	33	D5
NORWOOD CT	SAD	SAD	600	90	B2
NORWOOD DR	PAS	PAS	600	26	E5
NORWOOD DR	SAD	SAD	600	90	B2
NORWOOD PL	CO	VAL		124	B6
NORWOOD PL	RM	RM	8400	37	F6
NORWOOD PL	RM	RM	8800	38	A6
NORWOOD PL E	ALH	ALH	1	37	B6
NORWOOD PL E	SGAB	SGAB	100	37	E6
NORWOOD PL W	ALH	ALH	2300	36	F6
NORWOOD PL W	ALH	ALH	1	37	B6

STREET	CITY	P.O. ZONE	BLOCK	PAGE	GRID
NORWOOD PL W	SGAB	SGAB	100	37	E6
NORWOOD ST	LA	LA07	1900	44	A5
NOSTRAND DR	SGAB	SGAB	700	37	D2
NOTRE DAME AV	CO	CHA		4	C5
NOTRE DAME AV	POM	POM	2100	95	A6
NOTRE DAME RD	CLA	CLA		91	B5
NOTTEARGENTA RD	LA	PP	200	40	A4
NOTTINGHAM AV	LA	LA27	2200	34	E2
NOTTINGHAM CT	SCLR	VAL		124	A9
NOTTINGHAM CT	CO	VAL		127	A1
NOTTINGHAM LN	ING	IN01		57	B2
NOTTINGHAM LN	SAD	SAD		89	C4
NOTTINGHAM PL	LA	LA27		34	E1
NOTTINGHAM RD	WLVL	THO		102	A6
NOTTINGHAM ST	CER	ART	12700	81	C1
NOUGUIER CT	SGAB	SGAB	400	37	D4
NOVA CT	CO	LPUE		97	A5
NOVA ST	PR	PR	9700	60	E2
NOVA ST	SFS	SFS	11200	60	F2
NOVA ST	SFS	SFS	11600	61	A2
NOVAK ST	CO	LPUE	14400	48	C6
NOVAK ST	CO	LPUE	15700	85	E1
NOVARA DR	LB	LB03	200	80	C1
NOVARRO ST	WCOV	WCOV	900	92	E2
NOVATO PL	PVE	PVP	2500	72	D3
NOVEL CT	CO	LPUE		85	C5
NOVEL TR	CO	TOP		109	D2
NOVELA WY	SCLR	VAL		127	A2
NOVELDA RD	ALH	ALH	600	37	C2
NOVELL ST	POM	POM		94	D1
NOVGOROD ST	LA	LA32	5000	36	D4
NOVICE LN	MON	MON		39	B1
NOVICE PL	LA	SF	14800	8	D4
NOVICE ST	LA	PAC	14600	8	D4
NOVICE ST	LA	SF	14800	8	C4
NOWELL AV	CO	LPUE	1700	98	F4
NOWITA CT	LA	VEN		49	D3
NOWITA PL	LA	VEN	700	49	C3
NOYA PL	PVE	PVP	2000	72	B4
NOYES ST	CO	WHI	9900	55	C1
NOYON ST	DUA	DUA	1300	29	D6
NUANU DR	GAR	GAR	15500	63	E4
NUBIA DR	CO	COV		89	B3
NUBIA ST	BAP	BAP	13800	39	D3
NUBIA ST	BAP	BAP	15300	88	A3
NUBIA ST	CO	COV	16500	88	C3
NUBIA ST	CO	SAD	1600	89	D3
NUBIA ST	COV	COV	700	88	D3
NUBIA ST	SAD	SAD	300	89	F3
NUEVA VISTA DR	LHH	LAH		84	F1
NUEZ WY	CO	TOP	2400	13	C6
NUGENT DR	LA	SF	12400	1	E4
NUGENT PL	LA	SF	17100	1	E4
NUGENT ST E	CO	LAN	4000	160	J4
NUGENT ST E	LAN	LAN	100	160	B4
NUGENT ST E	LAN	LAN	8500	161	F4
NUGENT ST W	LAN	LAN	100	160	B4
NUGGET CT	SAD	SAD		89	D2
NUGGET DR	SCLR	CYN		125	A9
NUNEZ DR	CO	LPUE	18700	98	E4
NURMI ST	LA	SF	13700	2	C4
NUTMEG AV	LA	LA66	11300	50	A2
NUTMEG LN	SCLR	SAU		124	E5
NUTRIA WY	CO	TOP	21600	109	C1
NUTRIR WY	CO	TOP		109	C1
NUTWOOD ST	ING	IN01	100	57	A1
NYE AV	CMRC	LA40	6200	54	B5
NYLIC CT	LB	LB02	1	75	B5
NYLIC CT.	LB	LB13	700	75	B5
O					
O ST	LA	WIL	200	74	D3
OAHU	WCOV	WCOV		92	C4
OAK AV	CO	ARC	6700	28	B6
OAK AV	CO	ARC	6700	38	B2
OAK AV	SCLR	CYN	26600	124	F8
OAK AV	CO	SGAB	6600	28	B6
OAK AV	CO	SGAB	6600	38	B2
OAK AV	DUA	DUA	800	29	E4
OAK AV	MB	MB	1100	62	C4
OAK AV	POM	POM	100	94	D3
OAK AV	TEC	TEC	5700	38	B2
OAK AV E	ELS	ELS	100	56	B5
OAK AV N	PAS	PAS	1	27	D4
OAK AV S	CO	PAS	300	27	D5
OAK AV S	PAS	PAS	1	27	D5
OAK AV W	ELS	ELS	600	55A	F5
OAK AV W	ELS	ELS	100	56	A5
OAK CT	LA	LA46	8500	33	E3
OAK DR	CO	GLDR	7300	86	F4
OAK DR	CO	TOP	1600	109	A2
OAK DR	LCF	LCF	4200	18	F3
OAK LN	BRAD	DUA		29	C3
OAK LN	CO	CLA		91	A1
OAK LN	CO	POM		93	E2

STREET	CITY	P.O. ZONE	BLOCK	PAGE	GRID
OAK LN	SGAB	SGAB	400	37	E2
OAK LN	SMAR	PAS		27	C6
OAK PL	CO	MONT	4200	18	F3
OAK ST	BLF	BLF	8700	66	A4
OAK ST	BUR	BUR	2500	24	B3
OAK ST	CMRC	LA23	2400	53	C2
OAK ST	SCLR	NEW	22900	127	C4
OAK ST	ELM	ELM	11000	47	E1
OAK ST	GLEN	GL04	300	25	B4
OAK ST	HPK	HPK	6000	53	A4
OAK ST	ING	IN02	400	50	F6
OAK ST	ING	IN01		56	E1
OAK ST	LA	LA07	1900	44	A5
OAK ST	LA	LA15	1300	44	B4
OAK ST	LA	LA46		33	E3
OAK ST	LOM	LOM	24600	73	D3
OAK ST	LYN	LYN	12300	65	A1
OAK ST	PR	PR	4600	54	F2
OAK ST	SM	SM	1100	49	B2
OAK ST	SPAS	SPAS	1100	36	F2
OAK ST	SPAS	SPAS	1400	37	A2
OAK ST	TOR	TOR	1700	68	C5
OAK ST	WHI	WHI	12800	55	E6
OAK ST	WHI	WHI	12900	61	F1
OAK ST	WHI	WHI	14200	84	A2
OAK ST N	ING	IN01	100	56	F2
OAK ST S	ING	IN01	100	56	F2
OAK TER	LA	LA42	100	36	D2
OAK WY	CO	SAU		123	C3
OAKADO PL	LCF	LCF	4700	18	F1
OAKBANK AV	COV	COV	400	88	F4
OAKBANK DR	CO	AZU	6000	86	F6
OAKBANK DR	CO	AZU	6000	88	F1
OAKBANK DR	CO	COV	5200	88	F2
OAKBANK DR	CO	GLDR	6900	86	F5
OAKBANK DR	GLDR	GLDR	100	86	F5
OAKBAR CT	SCLR	NEW		127	H3
OAKBAY RD	TOR	TOR	26000	73	B4
OAK BEND DR	LA	TU	7200	10	F4
OAKBEND DR	LAV	LAV	1500	95A	C6
OAK BLUFF RD	CO	CYN		125	D9
OAK BRANCH CIR	SCLR	SAU		127	H1
OAKBRIDGE LN	SCLR	NEW		127	C6
OAKBROOK ST	LB	LB15	5800	76	D1
OAK BURL LN	AGH	AGO		100A	D5
OAKBURN DR	CO	WAL	1200	97	B3
OAKBURY DR	LAM	LAM	14900	83	A3
OAK CANYON AV	LA	VAN	13600	22	F4
OAK CANYON DR	CO	LPUE	14300	85	B2
OAK CANYON LN	GLDR	GLDR		87	B3
OAK CANYON RD	COV	COV		89	A6
OAK CANYON RD	COV	COV		93	A1
OAK CIRCLE DR	GLEN	GL08	1200	18	E3
OAKCLIFF AV	PALM	PALM		171	D9
OAKCLIFF DR	MON	MON	300	29	C2
OAK CLIFF DR	WAL	WAL		94	C6
OAKCLIFF TR	LA	CAN	23900	4	A6
OAKCREEK AV	SCLR	NEW	24600	127	E4
OAKCREEK LN	CER	ART	12400	82	C4
OAK CREEK RD	SAD	SAD		90	A1
OAKCREST	LA	SF42		2	C1
OAK CREST AV	PALM	PALM		172	F9
OAK CREST AV	SPAS	SPAS	1400	36	E2
OAK CREST DR	CER	ART	13700	82	E5
OAK CREST DR	LA	LA68	3100	24	A6
OAK CREST DR	SMAD	SMAD	500	20A	C3
OAK CREST DR	SMAD	SMAD	500	28	C1
OAK CREST DR	WLVL	THO		102	C4
OAK CREST ST	CER	ART	12900	82	C5
OAK CREST WY	LA	LA42	6100	26	D6
OAK CROSSING RD	SCLR	SAU	26500	127	H1
OAKDALE AV	CO	PAS	3700	28	B4
OAKDALE AV	LA	BUR	5700	12	F6
OAKDALE AV	LA	CAN	8500	6	F6
OAKDALE AV	LA	CAN	6400	12	F5
OAKDALE AV	LA	CHA	9500	6	F4
OAKDALE AV	LA	NOR	8700	6	F6
OAKDALE AV	LA	WOH	5000	13	F2
OAKDALE AV	MON	MON	700	29	C3
OAKDALE DR	CLA	CLA		91	C4
OAKDALE DR	SMAD	SMAD	500	28	D1
OAKDALE LN	ARC	ARC		28	D3
OAKDALE ST	CLA	CLA		91	C4
OAKDALE ST	CO	PAS	2000	27	D4
OAKDALE ST	PAS	PAS	1400	27	C4
OAKDALE ST	WCOV	WCOV	1000	92	A1
OAKDELL LN	LA	NHO	3100	23	D6
OAKDELL RD	LA	NHO	3200	23	D6
OAKDEN DR	LA	LA46	1800	33	E2
OAKDYKE AV	LHH	LAH		98A	C3
OAKENDALE PL	GLEN	GL14	2900	18	D2
OAKENGATE DR	GLEN	GL07		25	D1
OAKENGATE RD	SAD	SAD		89	D4
OAKFAIR LN	CO	HAC		73	F1
OAKFEN CT	AGH	AGO		102	D3
OAK FENCE LN	LAN	LAN		159	D5

STREET	CITY	P.O. ZONE	BLOCK	PAGE	GRID
OAKFERN LN	CO	HAC		73	F1
OAKFIELD DR	HH	CAL		100	E3
OAKFIELD DR	LA	VAN	3500	22	D5
OAKFIELD RD	HH	CAL		100	E3
OAKFLAT CT	SCLR	NEW		127	H3
OAK FLAT DR	CO	SF		3	E2
OAKFLOW RD	CO	MAL		113	C1
OAKFORD DR	CO	LA22	200	45	F6
OAK FOREST CIR	GLDR	GLDR		87	D5
OAKFOREST LN	CO	PAS	900	27	F5
OAKFORT AV	CAR	CAR	21200	69	E4
OAKGALE AV	SCLR	CYN	27200	124	G7
OAK GARDEN CT	SCLR	SAU		127	G1
OAKGATE ST	BLF	BLF		66	D5
OAKGATE ST	MPK	MPK		46	C4
OAKGLADE DR	MON	MON	700	29	B1
OAKGLEN AV	ARC	ARC	1100	28	E3
OAK GLEN AV	POM	POM	10500	95	B2
OAK GLEN DR	LA	LA68	3300	24	A5
OAK GLEN PL	LA	LA39	2000	35	C4
OAK GLEN RD	GLEN	GL08	2900	18	F5
OAK GLEN ST	CO	CAL		100A	F5
OAK GLEN WK	LA	LA68	3300	24	A6
OAKGREEN AV	WCOV	WCOV		92	C4
OAK GROVE	MON	MON		29	B2
OAK GROVE AV	SMAR	PAS	900	27	C6
OAK GROVE CIR	LA	LA41	4600	26	B5
OAK GROVE CT	GLEN	GL14		11	C6
OAK GROVE DR	CO	PAS	4000	19	D4
OAK GROVE DR	GLDR	GLDR		87	B3
OAK GROVE DR	LA	LA41	1000	26	B5
OAK GROVE PL	LA	LA41	1500	26	B5
OAK GROVE PL	SMAR	PAS		27	C6
OAK GROVE ST	LAN	LAN		160	E4
OAKHART DR	GLDR	GLDR	100	87	E5
OAKHAVEN DR	ARC	ARC	1600	28	E2
OAKHAVEN DR	DUA	DUA	2100	29	E4
OAKHAVEN LN	ARC	ARC	1100	28	E3
OAKHAVEN RD	ARC	ARC		28	E3
OAKHEATH DR	CO	HAC	1100	73	F1
OAKHEATH DR	LA	HAC	1300	73	F1
OAKHEATH PL	LA	HAC	23600	73	E1
OAK HIGHLAND DR	SCLR	NEW		127	H1
OAK HILL AV	LA	LA32	3600	36	C4
OAK HILL AV	LA	LA42	4900	36	D3
OAK HILL AV	SPAS	SPAS	1200	36	D2
OAK HILL LN	SPAS	SPAS	1	36	D2
OAK HILL PL	LA	LA42	6000	36	D3
OAK HILL PL	SPAS	SPAS	1300	36	D2
OAK HILL ST	PALM	PALM		183	J1
OAK HILL TER	SPAS	SPAS	1	36	D2
OAK HOLLOW RD	CLA	CLA		90	F1
OAK HOLLOW RD	CO	CAL		13	A4
OAKHORNE DR	CO	HAC	900	73	F1
OAKHORNE DR	LA	HAC	1400	68	E6
OAKHORNE DR	LA	HAC	1400	73	E1
OAKHURST	ELM	ELM		48	A5
OAKHURST AV	LA	LA34	2700	42	C5
OAKHURST DR	LA	LA35	1100	42	C3
OAKHURST DR N	BH	BH	200	33	C6
OAKHURST DR N	BH	BH	100	42	C1
OAKHURST DR S	BH	BH	100	42	C1
OAKHURST LN	ARC	ARC	200	28	D4
OAK KNOLL	BRAD	DUA	100	29	D3
OAK KNOLL AV	SMAR	PAS	1600	37	B1
OAK KNOLL AV N	PAS	PAS	100	27	B4
OAK KNOLL AV S	PAS	PAS	100	27	B4
OAK KNOLL AV S	PAS	PAS	1300	37	B1
OAK KNOLL CIR	PAS	PAS	600	27	B5
OAK KNOLL DR	GLDR	GLDR	400	87	D4
OAK KNOLL DR	POM	POM	1000	90	D6
OAK KNOLL DR	WCOV	WCOV	3200	92	F1
OAK KNOLL DR	WCOV	WCOV	1400	93	A1
OAK KNOLL RD	GLEN	GL08	1800	25	F1
OAK KNOLL TER	LAV	LAV		95A	C6
OAK KNOLL TER	PAS	PAS	1	37	B1
OAK KNOLL GDNS	PAS	PAS	1	27	B5
OAKLAND AV S	PAS	PAS	100	27	B5
OAKLAND AV S	PAS	PAS	1300	37	B1
OAKLAND CT	SCLR	VAL		124	E3
OAKLAND RD	GLDR	GLDR		87	E5
OAKLAND ST	LA	LA32	5100	36	E4
OAK LANE DR	LA	ENC	4900	21	E2
OAKLAR DR	SCLR	SAU		124	F4
OAKLAWN AV	SPAS	SPAS	200	36	F1
OAKLAWN LN	PR	PR		47	B6
OAKLAWN LN	PR	PR		55	B1
OAKLAWN PL	ARC	ARC	1400	28	C3
OAKLAWN PL	SPAS	SPAS	200	36	F1
OAKLAWN RD	ARC	ARC	1200	28	C3
OAKLAWN RD	LA	LA64	10500	42	A4
OAKLEAF	LA	SF42		2	C1
OAKLEAF AV	MON	MON	900	29	C3
OAKLEAF CYN RD	CO	LPUE		97	B4
OAKLEY DR	LA	LA68	3200	24	A6
OAKLEY RD	PVE	PVP	400	72	A5

STREET	CITY	P.O. ZONE	BLOCK	PAGE	GRID
OAKLEY WK	LA	LA68	3300	24	A6
OAKLON DR	RPV	PVP	4900	72	E5
OAKMALL LN	SCLR	NEW		127	H1
OAKMAN DR	CO	WHI	700	48	A4
OAKMEAD LN	LAV	LAV	1100	95A	D4
OAK MEADOW LN	SPAS	SPAS	1400	37	A2
OAK MEADOW RD	ARC	ARC	1300	28	D3
OAK MEADOW RD	SMAD	SMAD	1	28	D2
OAK MEADOW RD	SMAD	SMAD	100	28	D3
OAKMERE DR	CO	HAC		73	F1
OAK MESA DR	LAV	LAV	1500	95A	C6
OAKMILL AV	RM	RM		46	F4
OAKMONT DR	GLEN	GL08	1800	18	F6
OAKMONT DR	LA	LA49	1000	30	F6
OAKMONT DR	LA	LA49	1000	32	A6
OAKMONT DR	LA	LA49	600	41	A1
OAKMONT DR	LAN	LAN		159	G3
OAKMONT DR E	MTB	MTB	100	46	E6
OAKMONT DR W	MTB	MTB	100	46	E6
OAKMONT PL	LA	CAN	23900	4	B6
OAKMONT TER	GLEN	GL08		18	F6
OAKMONT VIEW DR	GLEN	GL08		18	D4
OAKMOOR ST	SCLR	CYN	18500	124	J7
OAKMOOR ST	SCLR	CYN		125	A7
OAKMORE RD	LA	LA35	9300	42	C3
OAK MTN MTWY	CO	NOR		1	A1
OAK ORCHARD RD	SCLR	NEW	21100	127	E3
OAK PARK AV	LA	ENC	4800	21	E2
OAK PARK AV	LA	NOR	10200	7	E3
OAK PARK AV	LA	NOR	8500	14	E1
OAK PARK AV	LA	SF	11000	7	E1
OAK PARK AV	LA	VAN	6800	14	E4
OAK PARK DR	GLDR	GLDR	2400	87	F5
OAK PARK DR W	CLA	CLA	100	91	B5
OAK PARK LN	LA	VAN		23	A2
OAK PARK PL	WCOV	WCOV	800	92	A2
OAK PARK RD	COV	COV		89	B6
OAK PARK RD	COV	COV		93	B1
OAK PASS RD	LA	BH	9700	32	F1
OAK PASS RD	LA	BH		33	A1
OAKPATH DR	AGH	AGO		100A	A3
OAK PATH DR	AGH	AGO		102	F3
OAK PLAIN DR	SCLR	NEW		127	H1
OAK PLAZA CT	SCLR	SAU		127	G1
OAK PLUMA CT	SCLR	SAU		127	G1
OAK POINT TR	LA	LA68	2900	34	A1
OAK RANCH CT	WLVL	THO		102	B5
OAKREST LN	CO	HAC	23500	73	F1
OAKRIDGE	LA	SF42		2	C1
OAKRIDGE CIR	WCOV	WCOV		92	D5
OAKRIDGE CT	WAL	WAL		97	B1
OAKRIDGE DR	GLEN	GL05	1200	25	D6
OAK RIDGE DR	LAV	LAV		95A	C6
OAKRIDGE PL	LA	CHA	9500	6	A4
OAKRIDGE RD	LA	CAN	23900	4	A6
OAKRIDGE TER	CO	CAL		100	D6
OAKRIM DR	WLVL	THO		102	D3
OAKROCK CT	LA	SF		1	D4
OAKROW DR	CO	LPUE	16400	98	A3
OAKROY RD	CO	TOP		108	F5
OAKRUN LN	SCLR	NEW		127	C4
OAKS AV	MON	MON	100	29	A3
OAKS PL	ARC	ARC	2000	28	F1
OAKS ST	COM	COM	300	65	A1
OAKSBORO CIR	LA	WOH		13	D3
OAKSHADE RD	BRAD	DUA	2200	29	E4
OAKSHIRE DR	LA	LA68	3100	24	A6
OAKSHORE DR	WLVL	THO		102	A4
OAKSIDE CT	CO	SAU		124	G3
OAKSIDE LN	GLEN	GL08	1200	18	E3
OAK SPG CYN RD	CO	CYN	28100	125	F9
OAK SPRINGS LN	LA	NOR		1	A4
OAKSPUR DR	SCLR	NEW		127	H1
OAKS RANCH RD	LHH	LAH	2300	98A	C1
OAKSTONE WY	LA	LA46	2000	33	D2
OAK SUMMIT RD	AGH	AGO		100A	D6
OAK TERRACE DR	LA	LA42	4900	36	B3
OAKTHORN LN	LAM	LAM	15300	84	B6
OAKTON WY	POM	POM		94	A2
OAKTREE CIR	GLDR	GLDR	100	87	D5
OAKTREE CT	GLDR	GLDR	1600	87	D5
OAK TREE DR	COV	COV		89	A6
OAKTREE DR	GLDR	GLDR	100	87	D5
OAK TREE DR	LA	LA41	1800	26	B5
OAKTREE LN	GLDR	GLDR	1600	87	D5
OAKTREE LN	RHE	PVP		72	E5
OAKTREE PL	GLDR	GLDR	1600	87	D5
OAKTREE TER	GLDR	GLDR	1600	87	D5
OAK TWIG LN	CO	COV		89	C5
OAK VALE DR	SCLR	VAL		127	A3
OAKVALE RD	SAD	LAV		95A	C4
OAK VALLEY RD	GLEN	GL08	1900	18	F4
OAK VIEW AV	SMAR	PAS		27	C6
OAK VIEW DR	LA	ENC	16600	21	F3
OAKVIEW LN	ARC	ARC	1800	28	D2

COPYRIGHT, © 1989 BY Thomas Bros Maps

277

1990 LOS ANGELES COUNTY STREET INDEX

OAKVIEW LN

ONEONTA AL

STREET	CITY	P.O. ZONE	BLOCK	PAGE	GRID
OAKVIEW LN	CO	LPUE		97	A5
OAKVIEW LN	CO	LPUE		98	F5
OAK VIEW LN	LAV	LAV	1400	95A	C6
OAKVIEW LN	PALM	PALM		171	C3
OAKVISTA CT	AGH	AGO		102	E3
OAK VISTA DR	GLEN	GL06	300	25	F3
OAKWATER ST	CO	TOR		68	F6
OAKWAY AV	SAD	SAD		89	E2
OAKWELL DR	WAL	WAL	100	93	B6
OAKWELL RD	CO	CYN		128	D4
OAKWILDE LN	LA	LA46	8800	33	D1
OAKWOOD	LA	SF42		2	C1
OAKWOOD AV	ARC	ARC	1600	28	E2
OAKWOOD AV	CO	CAST		123	C2
OAKWOOD AV	GLDR	GLDR	800	87	C4
OAKWOOD AV	GLEN	GL08	1800	18	F5
OAKWOOD AV	LCF	LCF	4200	19	C4
OAKWOOD AV	LA	LA04	3600	34	E5
OAKWOOD AV	LA	LA36	7600	33	E5
OAKWOOD AV	LA	LA36	6600	34	A5
OAKWOOD AV	LA	LA48	7900	33	E5
OAKWOOD AV	LA	VEN	1000	49	C3
OAKWOOD AV	LYN	LYN	2900	59	A5
OAKWOOD AV	SMAD	SMAD	1900	28	E2
OAKWOOD CT	LA	VEN		49	D4
OAKWOOD DR	ARC	ARC	1100	28	E3
OAKWOOD DR	SMAR	PAS	1000	27	D6
OAKWOOD LN	DUA	DUA		29	E5
OAKWOOD LN	LAM	LAM		83	A1
OAKWOOD LN	TOR	TOR		73	B3
OAKWOOD PL	PAS	PAS	800	27	B5
OAKWOOD PL	SMAD	SMAD	900	28	E1
OAKWOOD ST	CO	PAS	1600	20	D6
OAKWOOD ST	MTB	MTB	100	54	C4
OAKWOOD TR	CO	TOP		109	D2
OAKWOOD WY	WAL	WAL		93	D4
OAKWOOD RIDGE	LOM	LOM	2100	73	D3
OASIS DR	CO	TOR	1100	68	F6
OATES DR	DBAR	POM		97A	A2
OAT MTN MTWY	CO	CHA		1A	D1
OBAN DR	LA	LA65	900	36	A1
OBAR DR	CO	LPUE	500	48	A3
OBECK AV	LA	PAC	9300	8	E4
OBEE LN	ELM	ELM		38	F5
OBER AV	LOM	LOM	26200	73	D4
OBERG ST	SAD	SAD	100	90	A1
OBERLE CT	CO	LAV		90	C1
OBERLIN AV	CLA	CLA	100	91	B4
OBERLIN DR	GLEN	GL05	1000	25	E5
OBERLIN ST	LA	SF	12900	3	A4
OBERON ST	CO	WHI	10400	55	A6
OBERT AV	CO	WHI	11500	61	F5
OBISPO AV	LB	LB03	200	75	F5
OBISPO AV	LB	LB04	700	75	F5
OBISPO AV	LB	LB05	5900	65	F6
OBISPO AV	LB	LB05	5800	70	F1
OBISPO AV	LB	LB06	2500	75	F5
OBISPO AV	LB	LB14	300	75	F5
OBISPO AV	LKD	LKD	4100	70	F4
OBISPO AV	PAR	PAR	13300	65	F1
OBISPO AV	SH	LB04	1800	75	F4
OBISPO AV	SH	LB06	2200	75	F4
OBOE CIR	CO	LPUE		85	C3
OBREGON ST	CO	WHI	10000	55	B2
OBSERVATION DR	CO	TOP	19700	109	C6
OBSERVATORY AV	LA	LA27	2200	35	A1
OBSERVATRY RD E	LA	LA27		34	E1
OBSERVATRY RD W	LA	LA27		34	E1
OCALA AV	LPUE	LPUE	600	92	A5
OCAMPO DR	LA	PP	400	40	D4
OCANA AV	BLF	BLF	13400	66	C2
OCANA AV	LB	LB08	3000	71	C6
OCANA AV	LB	LB15	2000	76	D3
OCANA AV	LKD	LKD	4100	71	C4
OCASO AV	LAM	LAM		83	B4
OCASO AV	LAM	LAM	13000	83	B1
OCASO AV	LAM	LAM	12300	84	B6
OCCIDENTAL BL N	LA	LA26	100	35	B5
OCCIDENTAL BL S	LA	LA57	100	44	A1
OCCIDENTAL DR	CLA	CLA	1000	91	A1
OCEAN	WCOV	WCOV		88	A6
OCEAN AV	CO	WHI	15800	84	C5
OCEAN AV	LA	SM	100	40	E5
OCEAN AV	LA	SP	101	79	C2
OCEAN AV	LA	VEN	2200	49	C4
OCEAN AV	SM	SM	200	40	E6
OCEAN AV	SM	SM	1200	49	A2
OCEAN AV	SM	SM	1200	49	A5
OCEAN AV	TOR	TOR	21300	68	A5
OCEAN AV	TOR	TOR	23600	73	A1
OCEAN BLVD E	LB	LB02	100	75	D6
OCEAN BLVD E	LB	LB03	2000	75	D6
OCEAN BLVD E	LB	LB03	3300	76	A6
OCEAN BLVD E	LB	LB03	3900	80	B1
OCEAN BLVD W	LB	LB02		74	E6
OCEAN BLVD W	LB	LB02	100	75	A6

STREET	CITY	P.O. ZONE	BLOCK	PAGE	GRID
OCEAN BLVD W	LB	LB02		79	E1
OCEAN DR	CUL	CUL	10700	50	C2
OCEAN DR	HB	RB	900	62	D6
OCEAN DR	HB	RB	800	67	D1
OCEAN DR	MB	MB	100	62	A3
OCEAN WY	LA	SM	1	40	D5
OCEANAIRE DR	RPV	PVP	30000	77	F1
OCEANBLUFF AV	SAD	SAD	600	90	A2
OCEAN CREST CT	RPV	PVP		72	C6
OCEAN CREST DR	RPV	PVP	6500	72	C6
OCEAN FRONT WK	LA	VEN	100	49	B3
OCEAN FRONT WK	LA	VEN	6300	55A	D2
OCEANGATE	LB	LB02		75	B5
OCEAN GATE AV	CO	HAW	12800	62	E2
OCEAN GATE AV	CO	IN04	10000	56	E4
OCEAN GATE AV	HAW	LAW	14300	62	E2
OCEAN GATE AV	ING	IN01	1000	56	E3
OCEANGROVE DR	RPV	PVP		78	B3
OCEANHILL WY	CO	MAL	3400	115	E4
OCEAN MANOR PL	LB	LB03	1	80	A1
OCEANO DR	LA	LA49	200	41	B2
OCEANO PL	LA	LA49	11900	41	B2
OCEAN PARK AV	LB	LB02	800	75	B5
OCEAN PARK BLVD	LA	LA64	11800	41	D6
OCEAN PARK BLVD	SM	SM	2400	41	D6
OCEAN PARK BLVD	SM	SM	100	49	B2
OCEAN PARK PL N	SM	SM	1700	49	C1
OCEAN PARK PL S	SM	SM	1300	49	B2
OCEANPORT RD	RPV	PVP	28900	72	E6
OCEANRIDGE DR	RPV	PVP	28900	72	E6
OCEANSIDE ST	LA	WIL	800	74	C2
OCEAN TER DR	RPV	PVP		77	D1
OCEANUS DR	LA	LA46	7800	33	E2
OCEAN VIEW	LA	PP		40	C2
OCEAN VIEW AV	HB	RB	300	67	D1
OCEAN VIEW AV	LA	LA57	2100	44	A2
OCEAN VIEW AV	LA	LA66	3500	49	E2
OCEAN VIEW AV	LOM	LOM	26200	73	D4
OCEAN VIEW AV	MON	MON	700	29	C3
OCEAN VIEW AV	WHI	WHI	8700	61	F2
OCEAN VIEW AV	WHI	WHI	8200	84	A1
OCEAN VIEW AV	WHI	WHI	7700	85	A6
OCEAN VIEW BLVD	CO	MONT	3850	18	F3
OCEAN VIEW BLVD	GLEN	GL08	3400	18	F3
OCEAN VIEW BLVD	GLEN	MONT	3800	18	F3
OCEAN VIEW BLVD	LCF	LCF	4800	11	F6
OCEAN VIEW BLVD	LCF	LCF	4500	18	F3
OCEAN VIEW DR	CO	MAL	26500	112	E4
OCEAN VISTA BL	LA	PDR		55A	E3
OCONTO AV	RPV	PVP	5100	72	E4
OCOTILLO DR	CO	PALM	38800	171	J7
OCOTILLO LN	CAR	CAR		69	E6
OCTAGON ST	LA	LA49	12200	32	B6
OCTAVIA PL	LA	ENC	16700	21	F4
ODD RD	CO	PALM	8600	171I	G5
ODELL AV	LA	SUN	10200	10	D2
ODESSA AV	LA	ENC	4800	22	A2
ODESSA AV	LA	SF	11400	2	A6
ODESSA AV	LA	SF	8700	8	A6
ODESSA AV	LA	VAN	6400	15	A4
ODIN ST	LA	LA68	6400	34	B2
ODONNELL LN	LA	TU	9900	11	B4
ODYSSEY DR	LA	SF	15700	2	B6
OESTE AV	LA	NHO	3900	23	B5
OFARRELL ST E	LA	SP	100	78	E2
OFARRELL ST W	LA	SP	200	78	E2
OFFICE LN	BLF	BLF		66	C4
OFFLEY AV	DOW	DOW	10800	60	F4
OFFLEY AV	NWK	NWK	11700	60	F5
OGDEN DR N	LA	LA36	300	33	F6
OGDEN DR N	WHOL	LA46	900	33	F4
OGDEN DR S	LA	LA19	1000	42	F3
OGDEN DR S	LA	LA36	300	42	F1
OGELSBY AV	LA	LA45	7100	50	C6
OGRAM AV	CO	GAR	15500	63	C4
OGRAM AV	TOR	TOR	16600	63	C5
OHAN CT	DBAR	POM		97	D5
OHIO AV	CLA	CLA		96	C6
OHIO AV	LB	LB04	700	75	F5
OHIO AV	LB	LB14	400	75	F5
OHIO AV	LA	LA24	10500	41	F2
OHIO AV	LA	LA25	10900	41	D4
OHIO AV	PAR	PAR	15100	65	E3
OHIO AV	SH	LB04	2000	75	F2
OHIO AV	SOG	SOG	2400	58	F2
OHIO AV	SOG	SOG	2700	59	A2
OHIO ST	BAP	BAP	14000	39	D4
OHIO ST	CO	ACT		189	G2
OHIO ST	PAS	PAS	200	27	A6
OHM AV	NWK	NWK	10500	60	D5
OJAI CIR	MPK	MPK	700	46	B3
OJIBWA PL	CO	PALM		157	E9
OKEAN PL	LA	LA46	2900	23	E6
OKEAN TER	LA	LA46	8000	23	E6
OKELL DR	LA	LA32	2900	36	D5
OKI ST	CO	ACT		189	D2

STREET	CITY	P.O. ZONE	BLOCK	PAGE	GRID
OKLAHOMA AV	LA	CHA	10200	6	D3
OKLAHOMA AV	SOG	SOG	11300	59	E6
OKOBOJI DR	ARC	ARC	1100	28	B6
OLA AV	WHI	WHI	8900	84	A2
OLAF PL	LA	SF		1	D4
OLAF HILL DR	CO	LPUE		85	C5
OLANCHA DR	LA	LA65	900	36	A1
OLAND AV	LA	SV	8700	9	F6
OLAND ST	NWK	NWK	12600	82	C3
OLANDA ST	COM	COM	4200	65	C1
OLANDA ST	LYN	LYN	4300	65	C1
OLANDA ST	PAR	PAR	8200	65	F1
OLAS DR	LA	SP	1900	78	C4
OLCOTT ST	LA	TU	6300	11	B4
OLD BADILLO ST	COV	COV		89	B5
OLD BUCKBRD LN	LA	SV		10	A6
OLD CANYON DR	CO	LPUE	1100	48	C6
OLD CANYON DR	CO	LPUE		85	B1
OLD CARRIAGE CT	AGH	AGO		100A	A2
OLD CASTLE RD	WLVL	THO		102	B6
OLD CHESBORO RD	CO	PALM		184	B5
OLD CHIMNEY RD	CO	MAL	26800	112	E3
OLD CHURCH RD	CO	TOP		109	B4
OLD COLONY WY	WLVL	THO		102	C4
OLD COPPER LN	CO	LPUE		98	A4
OLD COURSE RD	SCLR	VAL		127	A2
OLD DOCK ST	LA	SP	400	79	C1
OLDEN ST	LA	SF	15500	2	B2
OLD FARM RD	HH	CAL		100	E2
OLDFIELD ST E	LAN	LAN	600	160	C5
OLDFIELD ST W	LAN	LAN	1100	159	H5
OLDFIELD ST W	LAN	LAN	100	160	B5
OLDFIELD RCH RD	CO	TOP		109	C2
OLD FOREST RD	CO	LPUE	16500	98	A3
OLD FORT RD	LA	SP		79	A5
OLD FRIEND RD	SCLR	SAU		124	H7
OLD GROVE RD	PAS	PAS	1600	20A	A3
OLDGROVE WY	PALM	PALM		171	C3
OLDHAM AV	CO	SGAB		37	F1
OLDHAM PL	LA	ENC	16600	21	F4
OLDHAM ST	LA	ENC	16300	21	F4
OLDHAM ST	LA	ENC	16300	22	A4
OLD HARBOR LN	CO	MDR		49	D6
OLD HARLD PLMDL	PALM	PALM		183	E3
OLD HOMESTD RD	CO	PEAR		192	C4
OLD HOUSE RD	PAS	PAS	1400	28	A1
OLD LANDMARK LN	LCF	LCF	800	19	B2
OLD MAIN ST	CO	GAR		64	B3
OLD MALIBU RD	CO	MAL	3700	115	E4
OLD MILL RD	AZU	AZU	1000	86	D4
OLD MILL RD	PAS	PAS	1000	37	B1
OLD MILL RD	SMAR	PAS	500	37	C1
OLD MILL CK LN	CO	AGO		100A	A6
OLD MINER RD	CO	ACT		189	H1
OLD MINT CYN RD	CO	SAU	11500	181	B6
OLD NADEAU RD	CO	PALM		183	E5
OLD OAK LN	ARC	ARC	1600	28	D2
OLD OAK LN	LA	LA49	13200	40	F2
OLD OAK LN	SMAD	SMAD	100	28	C3
OLD OAK RD	CO	AGO		100A	A6
OLD OAK RD	LA	LA49	1500	40	F2
OLD ORCHARD RD	LA	LA49	1800	40	F1
OLD ORCHARD RD	LA	LA49	1800	41	A1
OLD PHILLIPS RD	GLEN	GL07		18	D6
OLD PHILLIPS RD	GLEN	GL07	1800	25	D1
OLD POMONA RD	POM	POM		94	D5
OLD POST RD	WAL	WAL		93	B6
OLD RANCH RD	BRAD	DUA	1200	29	D3
OLD RANCH RD	IND	WAL		93	D6
OLD RANCH RD	IND	WAL		97	D1
OLD RANCH RD	LA	PP		40	F1
OLD RANCH RD	LAV	LAV		95A	C6
OLD RANCH RD	SMAD	SMAD		28	D1
OLD RANCH RD N	ARC	ARC	1	28	C4
OLD RANCH RD S	ARC	ARC	1	28	C5
OLD RCH RAV RD	CO	LPUE	18800	98	E5
OLD RESERVR RD	CO	MAL		113	E4
OLDRIDGE DR	CO	LPUE		98	A4
OLD RIV SCHL RD	DOW	DOW	11500	59	F4
OLD RIV SCHL RD	DOW	DOW	10200	60	A2
OLD SALT LN	AGH	AGO		102	D3
OLD SN GABRL CY	AZU	AZU	1200	86	E2
OLD SCANDIA LN	CO	CAL		100	E3
OLD SETTLERS LN	POM	POM	1400	94	E1
OLD STAGE RD	CO	SAU		181	F9
OLDSTONE CT	RPV	SP	1700	78	E1
OLD TPNGA CY RD	CO	CAL		100	F6
OLD TPNGA CY RD	CO	TOP		100	F6
OLD TPNGA CY RD	CO	TOP	1300	108	F1
OLD TPNGA CY RD	CO	TOP	100	109	B3
OLD TRAIL RD	DBAR	POM		93	F5
OLD VALLEY BLVD	LPUE	LPUE	15800	48	F6
OLD VALLEY BLVD	LPUE	LPUE		98	A1
OLD WOOD RD	POM	POM		94	C5
OLD 1ST ST	POM	POM	100	94	F2
OLEANDER AV N	COM	COM	100	64	F3

STREET	CITY	P.O. ZONE	BLOCK	PAGE	GRID
OLEANDER AV S	CO	COM	13000	64	E1
OLEANDER AV S	COM	COM	100	64	F4
OLEANDER CT	CO	CAL		100A	E6
OLEANDER CT	CO	CYN		125	F6
OLEANDER DR	LA	LA42	500	26	D6
OLEANDER LN	LA	VAN		22	F4
OLEANDER RD	LHH	LAH		98A	B2
OLEANDER ST	LAN	LAN		160	F6
OLEMA ST	TEC	TEC	9000	38	B1
OLETA ST	LB	LB15	5300	76	C4
OLETHA LN	LA	LA77	10200	32	D2
OLIN DR	CO	CHA	9100	4	B5
OLIN PL	WCOV	WCOV	2000	92	D1
OLIN ST	LA	LA34	8600	42	C4
OLINDA ST	LA	SV	10800	9	F6
OLINDA ST	LA	SV	10800	16	E1
OLIVA AV	LKD	LKD	4700	71	A3
OLIVA AV	LKD	LKD	5900	66	A6
OLIVA AV	PAR	PAR	15100	66	A3
OLIVA CT	CO	SAU		124	D4
OLIVAS PARK RD	SCLR	VAL		127	A2
OLIVE	LA	SF42		2	C1
OLIVE AV	CO	ALT	2300	19	F5
OLIVE AV	CO	CAST		123	G2
OLIVE AV	CO	GL14	2400	11	E5
OLIVE AV	LA	VEN	500	49	C4
OLIVE AV	LB	LB02	300	75	D5
OLIVE AV	LB	LB05	5900	65	D6
OLIVE AV	LB	LB05	5300	70	D1
OLIVE AV	LB	LB06	1800	75	D3
OLIVE AV	LB	LB07	3400	70	D4
OLIVE AV	LB	LB13	700	75	D5
OLIVE AV	SH	LB06	2700	75	D1
OLIVE AV	SH	LB07	3300	70	D5
OLIVE AV	SMAD	SMAD	1	28	C1
OLIVE AV	SPAS	SPAS	1800	37	B2
OLIVE AV E	BUR	BUR	100	17	E5
OLIVE AV E	MON	MON	100	29	A4
OLIVE AV N	ALH	ALH	100	37	B3
OLIVE AV N	LB	LB02	200	75	D5
OLIVE AV S	ALH	ALH	100	37	B4
OLIVE AV W	BUR	BUR	100	17	E5
OLIVE AV W	BUR	BUR	3300	24	B3
OLIVE AV W	MON	MON	100	28	F4
OLIVE AV W	MON	MON	100	29	A4
OLIVE CT	AZU	AZU	700	86	E5
OLIVE DR	PALM	PALM		183	F2
OLIVE DR	WHI	WHI		55	E5
OLIVE DR	WHOL	LA69	1100	33	E4
OLIVE LN	CO	POM		93	E2
OLIVE LN	LCF	LCF	1000	19	B2
OLIVE PL	ALH	ALH	1200	37	B5
OLIVE PL	MPK	MPK	700	46	D4
OLIVE ST	AVA	AVA	100	77	B5
OLIVE ST	BAP	BAP	13300	39	D3
OLIVE ST	BLF	BLF	8700	66	A4
OLIVE ST	CDY	BELL	4000	59	A1
OLIVE ST	CLA	CLA	100	91	B4
OLIVE ST	CO	HPK	2400	52	F6
OLIVE ST	CO	HPK	2700	53	A6
OLIVE ST	GLEN	GL06	100	25	E4
OLIVE ST	HPK	HPK	3200	53	A6
OLIVE ST	ING	IN01	100	56	E1
OLIVE ST	IRW	BAP	14800	39	D3
OLIVE ST	IRW	BAP		39	F3
OLIVE ST	IRW	BAP	15300	88	B3
OLIVE ST	LA	VEN	600	49	D4
OLIVE ST	LAV	LAV	2500	90	E2
OLIVE ST	LYN	LYN	11600	59	B6
OLIVE ST	NWK	NWK	11900	82	B1
OLIVE ST	TEC	TEC	9000	38	B3
OLIVE ST	TOR	TOR	2800	68	D6
OLIVE ST E	POM	POM	100	94	E5
OLIVE ST E	POM	POM	1000	95	A6
OLIVE ST S	LA	LA03	5800	52	A4
OLIVE ST S	LA	LA03	8400	58	A1
OLIVE ST S	LA	LA07	1900	44	B5
OLIVE ST S	LA	LA12	100	44	C4
OLIVE ST S	LA	LA13	300	44	C4
OLIVE ST S	LA	LA14	600	44	C4
OLIVE ST S	LA	LA15	900	44	C4
OLIVE ST S	LA	LA37	4200	52	A2
OLIVE ST W	POM	POM	100	94	E5
OLIVE WY	CO	PAS	1900	27	D1
OLIVE BRANCH DR	LAM	LAM	15400	83	B1
OLIVE GROVE AV	LA	SUN	10600	10	C2
OLIVE GROVE LN	LA	SF		2	E1
OLIVEGROVE PL	LA	SUN		10	C2
OLIVE HILL DR	CO	CLA		96	C4
OLIVEHILL RD	LAM	LAM		83	D1
OLIVE KNOLL PL	CO	CLA		96	C4
OLIVE POINT PL	CO	CLA		96	C4
OLIVER LN	CO	PALM	36300	183	A4
OLIVER ST	SPAS	SPAS	900	36	F1
OLIVER ST W	LA	SP	200	78	E2
OLIVERA DR	CO	AGO		107	A3

STREET	CITY	P.O. ZONE	BLOCK	PAGE	GRID
OLIVERA LN	SMAD	SMAD	100	28	D2
OLIVERAS AV	CO	ALT	2300	20	A5
OLIVETA PL	LCF	LCF	300	19	D3
OLIVE TREE LN	SMAD	SMAD		28	C1
OLIVE VIEW DR	LA	SF		2	E1
OLIVEWOOD ST	LAV	LAV		90	D1
OLIVIA TER	LA	SV	10000	17	A1
OLIVOS DR	LA	TAR	19300	21	A2
OLMSTEAD DR	GLEN	GL02	500	25	B1
OLMSTED AV	LA	LA08	3800	51	C1
OLMSTED AV	LA	LA18	3700	51	C1
OLNEY PL	BUR	BUR		17	C2
OLNEY ST	ELM	ELM	10100	38	C6
OLNEY ST	RM	RM	8300	37	F6
OLNEY ST	SGAB	SGAB	800	37	F6
OLNEY WY	LA	LA49	13100	30	F6
OLSON ST	LA	LA41	4700	26	B5
OLVERA ST	LA	LA12	1	44	E2
OLYMPIA PL	LA	NOR	10600	7	B2
OLYMPIA ST	LA	NOR	18900	7	A2
OLYMPIAD DR	CO	LA43	3400	51	B3
OLYMPIAD LN	LA	VAN		15	A4
OLYMPIC BLVD	BH	BH	8800	42	B2
OLYMPIC BLVD	MTB	MTB	400	54	A1
OLYMPIC BLVD	PR	PR	8300	54	E2
OLYMPIC BLVD	PR	PR	8700	55	A2
OLYMPIC BLVD	SM	SM	1100	41	B6
OLYMPIC BLVD	SM	SM	100	49	A1
OLYMPIC BLVD E	CMRC	LA22	5500	53	C1
OLYMPIC BLVD E	CMRC	LA22	5600	54	A1
OLYMPIC BLVD E	CO	LA22	4300	45	B6
OLYMPIC BLVD E	CO	LA22	4500	53	C1
OLYMPIC BLVD E	CO	LA22	5800	54	A1
OLYMPIC BLVD E	CO	LA23	3900	45	B6
OLYMPIC BLVD E	CO	LA23	3900	53	C1
OLYMPIC BLVD E	LA	LA15	100	44	B3
OLYMPIC BLVD E	LA	LA21	1000	44	D5
OLYMPIC BLVD E	LA	LA23	2500	44	D5
OLYMPIC BLVD E	LA	LA23	2600	45	B6
OLYMPIC BLVD E	LA	LA23	3100	53	C1
OLYMPIC BLVD W	LA	LA06	2600	43	D3
OLYMPIC BLVD W	LA	LA06	1800	44	B3
OLYMPIC BLVD W	LA	LA15	100	44	B3
OLYMPIC BLVD W	LA	LA19	3300	43	D3
OLYMPIC BLVD W	LA	LA35	8500	42	F2
OLYMPIC BLVD W	LA	LA36	5700	42	F2
OLYMPIC BLVD W	LA	LA36	5100	43	A2
OLYMPIC BLVD W	LA	LA48	6100	42	F2
OLYMPIC BLVD W	LA	LA64	10500	41	D5
OLYMPIC BLVD W	LA	LA64	10300	42	B4
OLYMPIC BLVD W	LA	LA67	10000	42	B2
OLYMPIC DR	GLEN	GL06	2600	26	A2
OLYMPIC PL	LA	LA35	6500	42	E2
OLYMPIC PL	SM	SM		49	A1
OLYMPIC PZ	LB	LB03		76	A6
OLYMPIC PZ	LB	LB03		80	A1
OLYMPIC WY	PR	PR	9100	55	A2
OLYMPUS	WCOV	WCOV		48	F2
OLYMPUS AV	CO	LPUE	800	85	E3
OLYMPUS DR	LAN	LAN		159	F5
OMAHA CT	CLA	CLA	300	91	C5
OMAHA ST	LA	LA42	5700	36	C2
OMALLEY AV	AZU	AZU	100	88	D1
OMALLEY AV	CO	AZU	5400	88	D1
OMALLEY AV	COV	COV	1100	88	D3
OMAR AV	LA	LA13	300	44	D3
OMAR ST	GLEN	GL02	700	25	B2
OMAR ST	POM	POM	500	94	A3
OMEGA CIR	LAV	LAV		90	D1
OMEGA WY	GLEN	GL08		19	A5
OMELIA RD	WHI	WHI		55	D3
OMELVENY AV	LA	PAC	9500	9	A3
OMELVENY AV	LA	PAC	10000	8	F3
OMELVENY AV	LA	SF	10900	8	E1
OMELVENY AV	LA	SV	8800	9	C6
OMELVENY AV	LA	SV	8500	16	C1
OMELVENY AV	SF	SF	700	2	D6
OMELVENY AV	SF	SF	600	8	E1
OMER LN	BUR	BUR	1000	24	E1
ONACREST DR	CO	LA43	5100	50	F3
ONAKNOLL AV	CO	LA43	4900	51	A3
ONARGA AV	LA	LA42	700	26	C6
ONAWA PL	DBAR	POM		97	E4
ONEAL CT	LA	NOR		7	C4
ONEIDA AV	LA	PAC	10200	8	F3
ONEIDA AV	LA	PAC	10300	9	A3
ONEIDA AV	LA	SF	11100	8	E1
ONEIDA AV	LA	SV	8800	9	C5
ONEIDA DR	PAS	PAS	300	27	F5
ONEIDA ST	CO	PAS	2400	27	E4
ONEIDA ST	PAS	PAS	2600	27	E4
ONEIL ST	LA	LA32	4300	36	C5
ONEILL AV	CMRC	LA40		53	E3
ONEILL CIR	CO	NEW		126	G3
ONEONTA AL	SPAS	SPAS		37	A3

LOS ANGELES CO.

INDEX

STREET	CITY	P.O. ZONE	BLOCK	PAGE	GRID
ONEONTA DR	LA	LA65	800	36	A2
ONEONTA DR	SPAS	SPAS	700	36	F3
ONEONTA KNOLL	SPAS	SPAS	1400	37	A3
ONIZUKA ST	LA	LA12		44	D3
ONLEE AV	SCLR	SAU		124	D5
ONRADO ST	TOR	TOR	2700	68	B4
ONTARE RD	ARC	ARC	1	28	E2
ONTARIO AV	LA	BUR	7500	17	B4
ONTARIO AV	PAS	PAS	1200	26	D1
ONTARIO ST	BUR	BUR	1300	17	B6
ONTARIO ST	BUR	BUR	200	24	B1
ONTEORA WY	LA	LA41	4900	25	F5
ONTIVEROS	SFS	SFS		61	B4
ONYX DR	LA	LA32	2500	36	C6
ONYX DR	PALM	PALM		183	D1
ONYX DR	WAL	WAL		93	C3
ONYX PL	LA	LA32	2700	36	B6
ONYX ST	TOR	TOR	5000	67	E3
ONYX ST	TOR	TOR	3200	68	B3
OPAL AV	LKD	LKD		81	C3
OPAL AV	PALM	PALM		173	A9
OPAL AV	PALM	PALM		173	B9
OPAL CT	WHI	WHI		55	E3
OPAL LN	WCOV	WCOV		92	E6
OPAL PL	LB	LB13	400	75	B4
OPAL ST	LA	LA23	2200	45	B6
OPAL ST	RB	RB	700	67	D4
OPAL ST	TOR	TOR	2900	68	B4
OPAL CANYON RD	DUA	DUA	200	86	A3
OPALINE CT	PALM	PALM		183	C5
OPECHEE WY	GLEN	GL08	1300	18	E6
OPENBRAND RD	RH	PVP	1	78	B2
OPEN CREST DR	SCLR	SAU		124	D5
OPHIR CIR	SAD	SAD		90	B4
OPHIR DR	LA	LA24	10900	41	D1
OPORTO DR	LA	LA68	6900	34	B2
OPP ST E	LA	WIL	100	74	D4
OPP ST W	LA	WIL	100	74	B4
OPTICAL DR	AZU	AZU		86	B6
ORACLE PL	LA	PP	14700	40	D2
ORACLE ST	NWK	NWK	12000	61	B5
ORACLE HILL RD	CO	PALM		190	E1
ORAH AV	MTB	MTB	500	46	B6
ORAL ST	CO	LPUE	18700	98	E6
ORANGE AV	CO	COV	3900	88	A6
ORANGE AV	CO	GL14	2400	11	D5
ORANGE AV	CO	LPUE	900	48	D4
ORANGE AV	GLEN	GL14	3200	11	D5
ORANGE AV	IND	LPUE	100	48	D4
ORANGE AV	LB	LB02	100	75	D5
ORANGE AV	LB	LB02	300	75	D5
ORANGE AV	LB	LB05	5900	65	D4
ORANGE AV	LB	LB05	5200	70	D1
ORANGE AV	LB	LB06	1800	75	D3
ORANGE AV	LB	LB07	3400	70	D5
ORANGE AV	LB	LB13	700	75	D5
ORANGE AV	LPUE	LPUE	300	48	D4
ORANGE AV	LYN	LYN	10600	59	C4
ORANGE AV	MON	MON	1200	29	D4
ORANGE AV	PAR	PAR	14300	65	D4
ORANGE AV	PAR	SOG	11400	59	D6
ORANGE AV	PAR	SOG		65	D1
ORANGE AV	PR	PR	8100	60	E2
ORANGE AV	SH	LB06	3100	70	D5
ORANGE AV	SH	LB06	2200	75	D2
ORANGE AV	SOG	SOG	9900	59	C4
ORANGE AV	TOR	TOR	2700	68	D5
ORANGE AV N	AZU	AZU	200	86	C5
ORANGE AV N	AZU	AZU	100	88	C1
ORANGE AV N	MPK	MPK	100	46	D1
ORANGE AV N	WCOV	WCOV	100	88	A6
ORANGE AV S	AZU	AZU	100	88	C2
ORANGE AV S	MPK	MPK	100	46	D3
ORANGE AV S	WCOV	WCOV	700	48	D4
ORANGE CT	COV	COV		88	E6
ORANGE DR	CO	WHI	10000	55	B3
ORANGE DR	LB	LB06		75	D2
ORANGE DR	SMAD	SMAD		28	D1
ORANGE DR	WHI	WHI	10300	55	C3
ORANGE DR N	LA	LA28	1300	34	B4
ORANGE DR N	LA	LA36	100	34	B6
ORANGE DR N	LA	LA38	700	34	B6
ORANGE DR S	LA	LA08	3800	51	A1
ORANGE DR S	LA	LA16	1900	43	A5
ORANGE DR S	LA	LA19	1000	43	A3
ORANGE DR S	LA	LA36	100	34	B6
ORANGE DR S	LA	LA36	200	43	B2
ORANGE FRWY	DBAR			99	B5
ORANGE FRWY	POM	POM		94	A3
ORANGE PL	AZU	AZU	300	86	C6
ORANGE PL	LA	LA08	5100	50	F1
ORANGE PL	MPK	MPK	600	46	D3
ORANGE PL	PAS	PAS	100	26	F4
ORANGE ST	ALH	ALH	1500	37	A5
ORANGE ST	CO	RM	8000	46	E4
ORANGE ST	CO	WHI	8600	61	B1

STREET	CITY	P.O. ZONE	BLOCK	PAGE	GRID
ORANGE ST	COV	COV	100	88	E4
ORANGE ST	DOW	DOW	8000	60	A5
ORANGE ST	LA	LA48	6100	42	F1
ORANGE ST	LAV	LAV	1900	90	E2
ORANGE ST	NWK	NWK	11800	82	A2
ORANGE ST	PR	PR	4600	54	F2
ORANGE ST	RM	RM	8300	46	E4
ORANGE ST	SGAB	SGAB	100	37	E4
ORANGE ST N	GLEN	GL03	100	25	C4
ORANGE ST S	GLEN	GL04	100	25	C6
ORANGE BLSSM AV	CO	LPUE	100	48	B4
ORANGE COVE AV	CO	GL14	2300	11	F6
ORANGECREST AV	AZU	AZU	300	86	E6
ORANGECREST AV	CO	AZU	5300	88	E2
ORANGECREST RD	GLDR	GLDR		87	B4
ORANGEDALE AV	CO	MONT	3800	18	E3
ORANGEDALE AV	GLEN	MONT	3800	18	E3
ORANGEGLEN AV	CO	AZU	5500	88	E2
ORANGE GROVE AV	ALH	ALH	400	36	F5
ORANGE GROVE AV	ALH	ALH	2100	45	F1
ORANGE GROVE AV	CO	LPUE	14300	85	B1
ORANGE GROVE AV	GLEN	GL05	600	25	D4
ORANGE GROVE AV	SF	SF	1	2	E5
ORANGE GROVE AV	SPAS	SPAS	100	36	E2
ORANGE GROVE AV	WHI	WHI	10200	55	B2
ORANGE GRV AV E	ARC	ARC	1	28	B3
ORANGE GRV AV E	BUR	BUR	1	17	E5
ORANGE GRV AV E	SMAD	SMAD	100	28	B3
ORANGE GRV AV N	LA	LA36	300	33	F6
ORANGE GRV AV N	LA	LA46	700	33	F6
ORANGE GRV AV N	POM	POM	1500	90	E6
ORANGE GRV AV N	WHOL	LA46	900	33	F4
ORANGE GRV AV S	LA	LA19	1000	42	E3
ORANGE GRV AV S	LA	LA36	300	42	F1
ORANGE GRV AV W	ARC	ARC	1	28	B2
ORANGE GRV AV W	BUR	BUR	200	24	D1
ORANGE GRV AV W	POM	POM	100	94	D1
ORANGE GRV AV W	SMAD	SMAD	100	28	B3
ORANGE GRV BL E	PAS	PAS	1	27	B2
ORANGE GRV BL N	PAS	PAS	1	26	F3
ORANGE GRV BL S	PAS	PAS	1	26	F4
ORANGE GRV CIR	PAS	PAS	300	26	F6
ORANGE GROVE DR	LAM	LAM		83	D1
ORANGE GROVE PL	SPAS	SPAS	800	36	F2
ORANGE GRV TER	BUR	BUR	1	17	F4
ORANGE GRV TER	SPAS	SPAS	700	36	E1
ORANGE KNOLL AV	LCF	LCF	4600	19	C3
ORANGEPATH ST	CO	GLDR	19000	86	F6
ORANGEPATH ST	CO	GLDR	19200	87	A6
ORANGE TREE LN	LCF	LCF	1600	19	A3
ORANGEWOOD CT	PALM	PALM		183	C1
ORANGEWOOD DR	COV	COV	600	88	F6
ORANGEWOOD LN	ARC	ARC		28	E2
ORANGEWOOD LN	SAD	SAD	700	90	A4
ORANGEWOOD PL	POM	POM	2100	90	E5
ORANGEWOOD ST	LAV	LAV		95A	D6
ORANGEWOOD ST	PAS	PAS	1700	27	D5
ORANUT LN	CO	LPUE	300	48	B4
ORBIT CT	CO	LPUE		98	F5
ORCAS AV	LA	SF	11400	3	E6
ORCAS AV	LA	SF	11100	9	E1
ORCAS AV	LA	SUN	9700	9	E4
ORCHARD AV	BELL	BELL	6200	53	B5
ORCHARD AV	BLF	BLF	15900	66	C4
ORCHARD AV	CAR	CAR	22800	69	A6
ORCHARD AV	CO	TOR	20800	69	A3
ORCHARD AV	CO	WHI	10100	55	B3
ORCHARD AV	GLEN	GL06	1700	25	F3
ORCHARD AV	HPK	HPK	6100	53	B5
ORCHARD AV	LA	GAR	14300	63	F3
ORCHARD AV	LA	LA06	1300	43	F4
ORCHARD AV	LA	LA07	1900	43	F4
ORCHARD AV	LA	LA37	4400	51	F3
ORCHARD AV	LA	LA44	8600	57	F2
ORCHARD AV	LA	LA44	12000	58	A5
ORCHARD AV	LYN	LYN	3300	65	B1
ORCHARD AV	WHI	WHI	10500	55	B3
ORCHARD CT	LAV	LAV	2600	90	E3
ORCHARD DR	ING	IN01	900	57	A3
ORCHARD DR N	BUR	BUR	600	17	C6
ORCHARD DR N	BUR	BUR	200	24	C1
ORCHARD DR S	BUR	BUR	100	24	C1
ORCHARD LN	LAN	LAN		159	J5
ORCHARD LN	LCF	LCF	1900	19	A1
ORCHARD PL	SOG	SOG	2700	58	F2
ORCHARD ST	CO	CAST		123	F3
ORCHARD ST	COM	COM	1300	65	B1
ORCHARD ST	ELM	ELM	11100	38	E6
ORCHARD TR	CO	SF	11900	3	E5
ORCHARD FLAT LN	CER	ART		82	B4
ORCHARD HILL LN	CO	LPUE	1500	98	B3
ORCHARDVIEW CT	WLVL	THO	4300	102	B4
ORCHARD VLG RD	SCLR	VAL		127	A2
ORCHID AV	LA	LA28	1700	34	B3
ORCHID AV	LA	LA68	1900	34	B3
ORCHID DR	CO	LA43	4500	51	A4

STREET	CITY	P.O. ZONE	BLOCK	PAGE	GRID
ORCHID LN	BUR	BUR	1800	17	B3
ORCHID LN	CO	CAL		100A	E6
ORCHID LN	LB	LB05	200	65	C5
ORCHID LN	POM	POM	100	94	E6
ORCHID COVE DR	CO	CYN		125	G6
ORCHID TREE DR	PALM	PALM		183	F3
ORCUT LSE TR RD	CO	NEW		1	B2
ORCUT LSE TR RD	CO	SF		1	C3
ORCUTT AV	LB	LB05	6400	65	B5
ORCUTT DR	MTB	MTB	400	46	F6
ORD CT N	LB	LB02	10	75	B6
ORD CT N	LB	LB02	300	75	B5
ORD CT S	LB	LB02	10	75	B6
ORD ST	LA	LA12	100	44	D2
ORDCO ST	SCLR	SAU		124	D9
OREGANO CIR	SCLR	SAU		124	E5
OREGANO RD	RPV	PVP	1	77	E2
OREGON AV	BLF	BLF	16200	66	D4
OREGON AV	CUL	CUL	10700	50	B1
OREGON AV	LA	LA23	2700	45	B5
OREGON AV	LB	LB05	4800	70	B3
OREGON AV	LB	LB06	3000	70	B6
OREGON AV	LB	LB06	1800	75	B2
OREGON AV	LB	LB13	1300	75	B4
OREGON CT	TOR	TOR		68	B3
OREGON ST	ELS	ELS	100	56	B6
OREO PL	LA	PP	800	40	C3
OREY PL	LA	CAN	20400	12	E4
ORGAN LN	CO	MONT		18	F2
ORIENTA DR	ALH	ALH	1200	37	D3
ORILLA AV	DOW	DOW	12700	59	F5
ORILLA AV	LA	LA65	3200	25	E5
ORIN AV	CO	GL14	4600	11	D6
ORINDA AV	CO	LA43	4800	51	B3
ORINOCO PL	CO	LPUE	2900	85	E4
ORIOLE AV	LAV	LAV		95A	E5
ORIOLE CT	PALM	PALM		183	F1
ORIOLE DR	LA	LA69	1400	33	D3
ORIOLE LN	LA	LA69	1500	33	D3
ORIOLE RD	LCF	LCF	300	19	D4
ORIOLE WY	LA	LA69	9000	33	D3
ORION AV	LA	SF	8500	8	B6
ORION AV	LA	SF	8300	15	B1
ORION AV	LA	VAN	6200	15	B5
ORION AV	LA	VAN	4600	22	B3
ORION CT	CO	LPUE		97	A5
ORIS ST E	CO	COM	100	64	E2
ORIZABA AV	DOW	DOW	9100	60	A6
ORIZABA AV	LB	LB03	100	75	F6
ORIZABA AV	PAR	PAR	13300	65	F3
ORIZABA AV	SH	LB06	1800	75	F3
ORIZABA AV N	LB	LB03	100	75	F6
ORIZABA AV N	LB	LB04	700	75	F3
ORIZABA AV N	LB	LB05	5500	70	F1
ORIZABA AV N	LB	LB14	300	75	F6
ORIZABA AV S	LB	LB05	6200	65	F5
ORKNEY ST	AZU	AZU		88	D2
ORKNEY ST	CO	AZU	16800	88	C2
ORLANDO AV N	LA	LA48	100	33	E6
ORLANDO AV N	LA	LA69	700	33	E6
ORLANDO AV N	WHOL	LA48	500	33	E6
ORLANDO AV N	WHOL	LA69	1000	33	E6
ORLANDO AV S	CO	LA56	5800	50	E4
ORLANDO AV S	LA	LA35	1000	42	E2
ORLANDO AV S	LA	LA48	100	33	E6
ORLANDO AV S	LA	LA48	400	42	E1
ORLANDO DR	ARC	ARC	1400	28	C3
ORLANDO PL	SMAR	PAS	900	27	C6
ORLANDO RD	CO	PAS	3000	27	F5
ORLANDO RD	PAS	PAS	2900	27	F5
ORLANDO RD	SMAR	PAS	900	27	C6
ORLANDO WY	COV	COV	200	88	F5
ORLEANS WY	LB	LB05		65	B4
ORLENA AV	LB	LB14	300	76	C5
ORLON AV	LA	PP	1100	40	C2
ORLON DR	CO	LPUE		98	C4
ORME AV	LA	LA23	600	45	A5
ORMOND LN	RB	RB	900	62	D6
ORMOND ST	LA	SUN	10300	9	F5
ORMSKIRK AV	LA	NOR		1	B4
ORNA DR	LA	SF	17400	1	E4
ORNELAS ST	IRW	BAP	1580	88	B2
ORO TER	LA	SP	700	78	E3
ORO FINO MTWY	SCLR	NEW		127	E2
ORO GRANDE ST	LA	SF	14300	2	C4
OROS ST	LA	LA31	2100	35	E5
OROSCO DR	GLEN	GL07	1500	25	E1
OROVISTA AV	LA	SUN	10100	10	D3
OROZCO ST	LA	SF	17000	1	E3
ORR & DAY RD	NWK	NWK	11200	60	F5
ORR & DAY RD	NWK	NWK	12800	66	F1
ORR & DAY RD	SFS	SFS	9500	60	F2
ORRICK AV	CAR	CAR	21300	69	B4
ORRIN RD	CO	SAU		181	C8
ORRINGTON AV	LPUE	LPUE	800	48	E4
ORRVILLE AV	LA	WOH	5400	100	E1

STREET	CITY	P.O. ZONE	BLOCK	PAGE	GRID
ORSA DR	LAM	LAM	15700	83	C2
ORSINI AV	SCLR	CYN	27400	124	J9
ORTEGA PL	LA	SP	1700	78	D4
ORTEGA ST	LA	NHO		16	A3
ORTLEY PL	LA	VAN	13100	16	A5
ORTON AV	LA	LA64	10200	42	A3
ORUM RD	LA	LA49	11400	32	C4
ORVILLE ST	CUL	CUL	11100	50	C3
OSAGE	CO	AGO		106	D2
OSAGE AV	CO	IN04	10600	57	A5
OSAGE AV	HAW	IN04	11300	57	A5
OSAGE AV	ING	IN01		51	B6
OSAGE AV	LA	LA45	7300	50	D6
OSAGE AV	LA	LA45	7600	56	D1
OSAGE AV	LAW	LAW	14500	63	A3
OSAGE AV	TOR	TOR	16900	63	B5
OSAGE AV	TOR	TOR	20500	68	B3
OSAGE AV N	ING	IN01	400	57	B3
OSAGE AV S	ING	IN01	300	57	B3
OSAGE RIDGE RD	SCLR	VAL	23000	124	B5
OSBORN AV	WCOV	WCOV	300	88	B6
OSBORNE PL	LA	PAC	12000	9	C3
OSBORNE ST	LA	CAN	20900	6	D5
OSBORNE ST	LA	NOR	17000	7	C5
OSBORNE ST	LA	PAC	13400	8	F5
OSBORNE ST	LA	PAC	12100	9	B3
OSBORNE ST	LA	SF	11100	3	E6
OSBORNE ST	LA	SF	16600	7	F5
OSBORNE ST	LA	SF	14100	8	E5
OSBORNE ST	LA	SF	11300	9	D1
OSBORNE ST	LA	VAN	14000	8	E5
OSCAR ST	LA	SF	13300	2	F2
OSCEOLA ST	GLEN	GL05	900	25	E5
OSCEOLA ST	LA	SF	14800	2	D5
OSGOOD AV	LYN	LYN	10700	59	A4
OSGOOD ST	LB	LB05	100	70	C1
OSLER AV	LB	LB08	3900	71	C4
OSMOND AV	LAM	LAM	16600	83	A5
OSO AV	LA	CAN	8500	6	E6
OSO AV	LA	CAN	6400	12	E3
OSO AV	LA	CHA	9200	6	E4
OSO AV	LA	WOH	5600	12	E6
OSO AV	LA	WOH	5500	13	E1
OST ST	PALM	PALM		184	B6
OSTEND DR	LAM	LAM	14200	82	F1
OSTIA WY	CO	WAL	19800	97	B4
OSTIN AV	LA	WOH	5500	100	D1
OSTROM AV	LA	ENC	5600	14	E6
OSTROM AV	LA	ENC	5300	21	E1
OSTROM AV	LA	SF	11400	1	E6
OSTROM AV	LA	VAN	7200	14	E3
OSTROM AV	LB	LB08	3000	71	E5
OSTROM AV	LB	LB15	1800	76	E2
OSTROM AV	LKD	LKD	4100	71	E3
OSTRONIC DR	LA	WOH	22800	13	A2
OSTRONIC DR	LA	WOH	23000	100	F2
OSTRONIC PL	LA	WOH		100	F2
OSULLIVAN DR	LA	LA32	4800	45	D1
OSWALD ST	LA	SF	14700	2	C4
OSWEGO ST	LA	SUN	7800	10	D2
OSWEGO ST	PAS	PAS	2300	27	E4
OTAY DR	LA	LA65	4500	36	A2
OTERO DR	LA	LA32	4300	36	C5
OTHELLO ST	CO	ARC	800	38	F1
OTHELLO ST	CO	ARC	900	39	A1
OTIS AV	BELL	BELL	6200	53	C5
OTIS AV	CDY	BELL	7200	53	C5
OTIS AV	CDY	BELL	7500	59	C1
OTIS AV	HPK	HPK	5900	53	C5
OTIS AV	LA	TAR	5000	21	C2
OTIS CT	POM	POM	300	94	E6
OTIS ST	HPK	HPK	7800	59	C1
OTIS ST	LYN	LYN	10600	59	B4
OTIS ST	SOG	SOG	8100	59	B4
OTSEGO CT	LA	ENC	5100	21	F2
OTSEGO ST	LA	ENC	16700	21	F2
OTSEGO ST	LA	ENC	15500	22	A2
OTSEGO ST	LA	NHO	10400	23	C2
OTSEGO ST	LA	VAN	13300	22	F2
OTSEGO ST	LA	VAN	12900	23	A2
OTT PL	BAP	BAP	4400	39	E4
OTTERBEIN AV	CO	LPUE	1000	98	F3
OTTO ST	BG	BELL	6700	60	A1
OTTO ST	DOW	DOW	7700	60	B2
OTTO ST	SFS	SFS	11400	60	F4
OTTOMAN ST	LA	PAC	13600	8	F6
OTTOMAN ST	LA	PAC	13000	9	A5
OTTOMAN ST	LA	SV	12900	9	B5
OTTONE WY	LA	LA77	10500	32	D3
OTTOWA CT	LA	LA15	1000	44	B4
OTTOWA DR	CLA	CLA		91	A2
OUTER DR	POM	POM		90	F2
OUTER ST	LA	SP	2300	79	A5
OUTR TRAFFC CIR	LB	LB04		76	B3
OUTLAND VIEW DR	LA	SV	8300	16	F1
OUTLET TR	CO	AGO	2200	106	E2

STREET	CITY	P.O. ZONE	BLOCK	PAGE	GRID
OUTLOOK AV	LA	LA42	6100	36	C1
OUTLOOK LN	GLEN	GL06	1000	26	A2
OUTLOOK LN	WCOV	WCOV		92	E3
OUTPOST CIR	LA	LA68	1900	34	B2
OUTPOST DR	LA	LA28	1800	34	A2
OUTPOST LN	CO	PAS		20	F6
OUTPOST LN	PAS	PAS		20	F6
OUTPOST COVE DR	LA	LA68	7200	34	A1
OUTRIDER RD	RH	PVP	29200	78	C1
OUTRIGGER CIR	CER	ART		66	E5
OUTRIGGER CT	LA	VEN		49	D6
OUTRIGGER CT	LB	LB03		80	F1
OUTRIGGER ST	LA	VEN		49	C6
OVADA PL	LA	LA49	11300	32	C6
OVAL DR	CO	WHI	13900	61	E2
OVAL DR	WHI	WHI	12600	61	D1
OVERCREST DR	CO	WHI		55	E1
OVERCREST RD	CO	MAL		114	D1
OVERDALE DR	CO	LA43	5000	51	A3
OVERDEN ST	POM	POM		94	B4
OVEREST AV	CO	WHI	9900	61	E3
OVERFALL DR	WLVL	THO		102	C2
OVERHILL DR	CO	LA43	5000	51	A3
OVERHILL DR	ING	IN02	1300	51	A5
OVERHILL DR	LA	LA43	6200	50	F5
OVERHILL RD	CO	AGO		107	B3
OVERHOLTZER DR	LAV	LAV		95A	C5
OVERING DR	LA	WOH	5400	100	E1
OVERLAND AV	CUL	CUL	3900	50	C1
OVERLAND AV	CUL	CUL	10800	50	C3
OVERLAND AV	LA	LA25	1800	41	F3
OVERLAND AV	LA	LA34	3000	42	B5
OVERLAND AV	LA	LA64	2200	41	F3
OVERLAND AV	LA	LA64	2300	42	B5
OVERLAND CT	SAD	SAD		89	E2
OVERLAND TR	CO	SAU		181	B8
OVERLAND DR	LA	CAN		5	D2
OVERLOOK TR	CO	SF	11900	3	D5
OVERLOOK RDG RD	DBAR	POM		94	A5
OVERMAN AV	LA	CHA	10500	6	E2
OVERTON ST	LA	LA15	1000	44	B3
OVID AV	LOM	LOM	26400	73	D4
OVINGTON ST E	LAN	LAN	600	160	C5
OVINGTON ST W	LAN	LAN	1100	159	H5
OVINGTON ST W	LAN	LAN	100	160	B5
OWEN AV	CER	ART		82	D5
OWEN CT	CO	RM		46	E3
OWEN WY	ELM	ELM	10500	47	D2
OWEN BROWN RD	LA	WOH		13	F5
OWENS LN	POM	POM	100	94	E6
OWENS PL	LA	TU	10700	11	A2
OWENS ST	LA	SUN		10	C2
OWENS ST	LA	SUN	7800	10	D2
OWENS ST	LA	TU	7500	10	D2
OWENS ST	LA	TU	6900	11	A2
OWENSMOUTH AV	LA	CAN	8500	6	C5
OWENSMOUTH AV	LA	CAN	6400	12	C4
OWENSMOUTH AV	LA	CHA	9100	6	C3
OWENSMOUTH AV	LA	WOH	5800	12	C6
OWOSSO AV	HB	RB	900	62	D6
OXBOW CT	DBAR	POM		97	E3
OXFORD AV	CLA	CLA	800	91	B3
OXFORD AV	CLA	CLA		96	B6
OXFORD AV	CLA	CLA	3100	96	B6
OXFORD AV	CO	ALT	1900	20	C6
OXFORD AV	CO	CLA	2800	91	B2
OXFORD AV	CO	PAS	1500	20	C6
OXFORD AV	CO	PAS	1300	27	C1
OXFORD AV	HAW	HAW	11400	57	A6
OXFORD AV	LA	VEN	600	49	D4
OXFORD AV	PAS	PAS	1100	27	D1
OXFORD AV N	LA	LA04	100	34	E6
OXFORD AV N	LA	LA27	1900	34	E2
OXFORD AV N	LA	LA29	700	34	E4
OXFORD AV S	LA	LA04	100	34	E6
OXFORD AV S	LA	LA05	600	43	E2
OXFORD AV S	LA	LA06	900	43	E3
OXFORD AV S	LA	LA18	1900	43	E4
OXFORD AV S	LA	LA20	300	43	E2
OXFORD CIR	LAV	LAV		90	D2
OXFORD CT	SAD	SAD		89	D4
OXFORD CT	WCOV	WCOV		92	C4
OXFORD DR	ARC	ARC	300	28	C4
OXFORD DR	LAM	LAM	11900	84	B6
OXFORD DR	PALM	PALM		183	F1
OXFORD PL	POM	POM	1100	94	B1
OXFORD RD	PALM	PALM		171	H8
OXFORD RD	SMAR	PAS	800	27	D6
OXFORD WY	BH	BH	900	33	A5
OXFORD WY	CMRC	LA40		54	B5
OXFORD WY	LCF	LCF	1000	19	C5
OXHOLM ST	LB	LB08	5700	71	D5
OXLEY AL	SPAS	SPAS	1700	37	A2
OXLEY ST	SPAS	SPAS	1100	36	F2
OXLEY ST	SPAS	SPAS	1500	37	A2

STREET	CITY	P.O. ZONE	BLOCK	PAGE	GRID
OXNARD ST	LA	ENC	16800	14	E6
OXNARD ST	LA	NHO	10400	16	A6
OXNARD ST	LA	TAR		16	F2
OXNARD ST	LA	TAR	18100	14	A6
OXNARD ST	LA	VAN	13300	15	D6
OXNARD ST	LA	VAN	12900	16	A6
OXNARD ST	LA	WOH	23100	5	F6
OXNARD ST	LA	WOH	19700	12	F6
OXSEE AV	WHI	WHI		55	C4
OZARK WK	CO	TOP	20900	109	A3
OZETA TER	LA	LA69	1200	33	D4
OZMUN CT	SPAS	SPAS	1400	36	F1
OZONE AV	LA	HAC	26200	73	E4
OZONE AV	LA	VEN	1	49	B3
OZONE AV	SM	SM	900	49	C2
OZONE CT	HB	RB	2300	62	B4
OZONE ST	LA	SM		49	C2
OZONE ST	SM	SM	400	49	B3

P

STREET	CITY	P.O. ZONE	BLOCK	PAGE	GRID
PABLO PL	PVE	PVP	1700	72	C2
PACATO RD	CO	LPUE	18600	98	D2
PACE AV	CO	LA02	9200	58	D3
PACE AV	LA	LA02	10400	58	D4
PACE AV	LA	LA59	10800	58	D4
PACER CT	WAL	WAL		93	D5
PACHECO DR	LA	VAN	3900	22	C4
PACIFIC AL	SPAS	SPAS	900	37	E5
PACIFIC AV	BAP	BAP	14300	39	E5
PACIFIC AV	BLF	BLF	9400	66	E4
PACIFIC AV	BUR	BUR	3900	16	F5
PACIFIC AV	BUR	BUR	1400	17	A5
PACIFIC AV	LA	LA66	11800	49	E3
PACIFIC AV	LA	VEN	100	49	B3
PACIFIC AV	LA	VEN	6200	55A	D2
PACIFIC AV	LA	LB02	100	75	C5
PACIFIC AV	LB	LB05	4700	70	C6
PACIFIC AV	LB	LB06	3000	70	C6
PACIFIC AV	LB	LB06	1800	75	C5
PACIFIC AV	LB	LB13	3200	70	C6
PACIFIC AV	LB	LB13	700	75	C5
PACIFIC AV	MB	MB	500	62	B4
PACIFIC AV	RB	RB	300	67	A1
PACIFIC AV	WCOV	WCOV	1900	39	F6
PACIFIC AV	WCOV	WCOV		92	A1
PACIFIC AV N	GLEN	GL02	1600	18	C6
PACIFIC AV N	GLEN	GL02	300	25	B4
PACIFIC AV N	GLEN	GL03	100	25	B4
PACIFIC AV N	LA	SP		79	A6
PACIFIC AV S	GLEN	GL04	100	25	B4
PACIFIC AV S	LA	SP	100	79	A6
PACIFIC BLVD	CO	HPK	7200	52	F6
PACIFIC BLVD	COM	COM	600	64	E2
PACIFIC BLVD	HPK	HPK	5200	52	F2
PACIFIC BLVD	VER	LA58	2400	52	F2
PACIFIC CIR	LAV	LAV		90	E2
PACIFIC CT	LA	VEN	3500	49	C5
PACIFIC DR	CMRC	LA40		54	B5
PACIFIC DR	CO	TOP		109	C5
PACIFIC DR	WAL	WAL		93	C5
PACIFIC LN	TOR	TOR	700	68	C3
PACIFIC LN	WCOV	WCOV	1800	88	A6
PACIFIC PL	CO	LA22	5300	53	F1
PACIFIC PL	LB	LB06	3200	70	C6
PACIFIC PL	LA	PP		40	C2
PACIFIC PL	PAS	PAS	1	27	A3
PACIFIC PL	WHI	WHI		55	D6
PACIFIC PL N	SM	SM		49	B1
PACIFIC ST	CAR	CAR	400	74	B1
PACIFIC ST	POM	POM		94	A3
PACIFIC ST	SFS	SFS		61	B2
PACIFIC ST	SM	SM	1	49	A1
PACIFIC TER	SM	SM		49	A2
PACIFIC TER	SM	SM		49	B6
PACIFIC WY	CMRC	LA40	4100	53	D2
PACIFIC WY	CMRC	LA40	4500	53	D2
PACIFICA AV	WLVL	THO		184	A1
PACIFICA AV	PALM	PALM		102A	A6
PACIFICA DR	RPV	PVP		77	D1
PACIFICA DR	CO	COM		69	F2
PACIFICA PL	LB	LB14		76	F2
PACIFIC CST HWY	CO	MAL		111	D6
PACIFIC CST HWY	CO	MAL		112	A6
PACIFIC CST HWY	CO	MAL		112	B6
PACIFIC CST HWY	CO	MAL		113	B5
PACIFIC CST HWY	CO	MAL		114	B5
PACIFIC CST HWY	HB	RB	900	62	C5
PACIFIC CST HWY	LA	HAC	700	73	B2
PACIFIC CST HWY	LA	HAC	500	74	A3
PACIFIC CST HWY	LA	PP	14800	40	C4
PACIFIC CST HWY	LA	WIL	100	74	A3
PACIFIC CST HWY	LB	LB03	5600	76	D2
PACIFIC CST HWY	LB	LB03		80	E1
PACIFIC CST HWY	LB	LB04	2000	75	B3
PACIFIC CST HWY	LB	LB04	3100	76	A3
PACIFIC CST HWY	LB	LB06	100	75	B3
PACIFIC CST HWY	LB	LB10	2200	74	A3
PACIFIC CST HWY	LB	LB10	1200	75	B3
PACIFIC CST HWY	LOM	LOM	1700	73	B2
PACIFIC CST HWY	TOR	TOR	5000	67	D2
PACIFIC CST HWY	TOR	TOR	4300	72	F1
PACIFIC CST HWY	TOR	TOR	2500	73	B2
PACIFIC CMRCE DR	CO			70	B2
PACIFIC GTWY DR	LA	TOR	19000	68	F2
PACIFIC PARK DR	CO	WHI	3200	47	D5
PACIFIC VIEW DR	LA	LA68	6800	34	A1
PACIFIC VIEW TR	LA	LA68	2800	34	C2
PACINO ST	CER	ART		23	A6
PACKARD DR	POM	POM	1300	94	F4
PACKARD ST	LA	LA19	5400	42	E2
PACKARD ST	LA	LA19	5000	43	A3
PACKARD ST	LA	LA35	5900	42	D2
PACKERS AV	VER	LA58	3400	53	B2
PACKET RD	RPV	PVP	1	77	B6
PACKMAN RD	CO	SAU		181	B6
PACKSADDLE LN	WAL	WAL		88	A5
PACKSADDLE RD	RH	PVP	1	78	A2
PACKWOOD TR	LA	LA68	7200	34	A1
PACOIMA CT	LA	NHO	12000	23	C4
PACOIMA RD	LA	SF	17700	3	C2
PACOIMA CYN RD	CO	SF	12400	3	B4
PACOIMA CYN RD	LA	SF		3	C1
PACOIMA CYN TR	CO	SF		128	D4
PACY ST	SCLR	NEW		127	H3
PAD CT	GLEN	GL06		26	B1
PADDINGTON PL	GLEN	GL06		26	B1
PADDISON AV	NWK	NWK	11000	61	A4
PADDISON AV	NWK	NWK	13200	82	A1
PADDOCK CT	WAL	WAL		93	D4
PADDOCK ST	LA	SF	13700	2	D4
PADDY LN	BAP	BAP	3200	39	D4
PADILLA PL	LA	LA19	4400	50	F2
PADILLA ST	SGAB	SGAB	300	53	D3
PADONIA AV	LHH	LAH	1200	84	E2
PADOVA DR	CO	LPUE	15800	85	C1
PADRE DR	WCOV	WCOV	1700	88	A6
PADRE LN	LA	LA46	8000	33	F2
PADRE TER	LA	LA46	6600	34	C2
PADRES TR	LCF	LCF		19	B4
PADRINO AV	CO	WAL		97	B3
PADRON PL	LOM	LOM	24600	73	D2
PADUA AV	CLA	CLA	1300	91	D1
PADUA AV	CLA	CLA	3500	96	D5
PADUA DR	CO	COV	4300	96	D3
PADUA DR	COV	COV	600	88	F6
PAGE DR	CO	ALT	2300	20	C5
PAGEANT PL	LA	ENC	16700	21	F4
PAGEANT ST	DOW	DOW	8100	60	C1
PAGEANTRY ST	LB	LB08	5100	71	C6
PAGET AV	CO	LAN	48900	146	F5
PAGET AV	LA	LA31		158	F6
PAGODA CT	LA	LA31	1000	36	B4
PAGODA PL	PALM	PALM		172	B9
PAGOSA CT	LA	LA31		36	B4
PAIGE DR	POM	POM	800	90	D6
PAIGE ST	LA	LA31		36	B4
PAINE CIR	CO	VAL		126	H3
PAINE CT	CLA	CLA	1600	91	A2
PAINT BRUSH LN	CO	WHI	9100	61	D2
PAINTER AV	NWK	NWK	13400	82	C2
PAINTER AV	SFS	SFS	10000	61	D4
PAINTER AV	WHI	WHI	5800	55	E5
PAINTER AV	WHI	WHI	8200	61	E1
PAINTER CT	POM	POM	800	94	F4
PAISLEY AV	LA	NOR		1	
PAISLEY LN	LA	LA49	12200	41	B5
PAISLEY PL	CO	CHA		1	B1
PAIUTE DR	CO	AGO		107	A3
PAIZ PL	NWK	NWK		82	B2
PAJARITO CT	SCLR	VAL		127	E1
PALA AV	BELL	BELL	6200	53	A5
PALA AV	CO	PAL	10900	94	
PALA AV	LA	SF		2	B2
PALA AV	MAY	MAY	6100	53	D5
PALACE	LA	PALM		171	J7
PALACEITE DR	SCLR	VAL		124	A3
PALACIOS ST	LA	SP	1700	78	D4
PALADORA AV	PAS	PAS		27	D2
PALAIS PL	CO	PALM		171	C2
PALAIS PL	CO	TOP		13	B5
PALA MAL AV	CO	WHI		55	D2
PALA MESA DR	LA	POM		94	B6
PALA MESA DR	LA	NOR		1	B6
PALA MESA DR	CAR	CAR		69	E6
PALAMINO LN	LA	HAC		74	

STREET	CITY	P.O. ZONE	BLOCK	PAGE	GRID
PALAMOS AV	CO	LPUE	300	98	E1
PALATINE DR	ALH	ALH	1	36	F4
PALAWAN WY	LA	MDR	13900	49	D5
PALENCIA AV	LA	WOH	4800	13	D3
PALERMO DR	CO	AGO		100	C4
PALERMO LN	SPAS	SPAS	600	37	A1
PALERMO WK	LB	LB03	1	80	C1
PALES RD W	CO	SAU		125	H2
PALI AV	LYN	LYN	9200	11	B5
PALI DR	LB	TU	500	65	C6
PALIMINO DR	DBAR	POM		94	A6
PALI PT LN	LCF	LCF		19	D3
PALISADE ST	PAS	PAS	200	26	E1
PALISADE WY	WAL	WAL		92	F6
PALISADES AV	SM	SM		40	E6
PALISADES CIR	LA	PP		30	A5
PALISADES CT	LA	PP		30	A5
PALISADES DR	LA	PP		30	A5
PALISADES DR	LA	PP		40	A2
PALISADES BH RD	SM	SM	100	40	E6
PALISADES BH RD	SM	SM	1000	49	E6
PALISAIR PL	LA	PP	1000	40	C3
PALJAY AV	RM	RM	2400	47	A2
PALLETT CK RD	CO	VAL	13100	192	E4
PALLETT MESA RD	CO	VAL		98	F3
PALM AV	BAP	BAP	13000	39	C4
PALM AV	BELL	BELL	6200	53	D5
PALM AV	CO	LPUE	14400	48	B4
PALM AV	CO	LPUE	14800	85	C1
PALM AV	LYN	LYN	3200	65	A1
PALM AV	MAY	MAY	6100	53	D5
PALM AV E	BUR	BUR	100	17	E5
PALM AV E	ELS	ELS	500	56	C5
PALM AV S	ALH	ALH	100	37	A5
PALM AV S	ALH	ALH	2100	46	A1
PALM AV W	BUR	BUR	100	17	D6
PALM AV W	ELS	ELS	100	56	C5
PALM AV W	MON	MON	100	29	C3
PALM CIR	ARC	ARC	2200	38	E2
PALM CT	CER	ART	13600	82	E5
PALM CT	CO	SAU		124	B5
PALM DR	SM	SM	1600	49	A1
PALM DR	SPAS	SPAS	600	37	B6
PALM DR	LA	PALM	37700	183	D1
PALM DR	ALT	ALT	2000	20	C5
PALM DR	ELM	ELM	3500	38	D2
PALM DR	GLEN	GL02	3000	25	B2
PALM DR	HB	RB	1200	62	C5
PALM DR	RB	RB	100	67	C1
PALM DR E	COV	COV	1300	89	B2
PALM DR N	BH	BH	300	33	C5
PALM DR N	BH	BH	100	42	C1
PALM DR S	BH	BH	100	42	C1
PALM DR W	ARC	ARC	100	38	E2
PALM DR W	COV	COV	300	89	A2
PALM LN	GLDR	GLDR	500	87	A4
PALM LN	LAN	LAN		160	E5
PALM LN	RB	RB	900	62	D6
PALM PL	CER	ART	13000	82	D5
PALM PL	CO	HPK	2400	58	F1
PALM PL	MTB	MTB	1000	54	F1
PALM PL	SOG	SOG	2500	58	F1
PALM ST	BLF	BLF	8700	66	B5
PALM ST	CER	ART	12100	82	D6
PALM ST	CO	ALT	100	20	A4
PALM ST E	COM	COM	100	64	D2
PALM ST W	CO	ALT	100	19	C4
PALM ST W	CO	ALT	100	20	A4
PALM TER	PAS	PAS	100	64	F3
PALM WY	DAM	DAM		68	A3
PALMA DR	CO	LPUE		85	C4
PALMA ALTA DR	CO	SCLR		127	B1
PALMARIS AV	LA	POM		94	F3
PALMAS	PALM	PALM	1800	37	D1
PALMAS DR	SMAR	SGAB	8500	23	C3
PALM VSTA E	SGAB	SGAB	8500	23	C3
PALM BREEZE LN	LA	HAC		74	

STREET	CITY	P.O. ZONE	BLOCK	PAGE	GRID
PALM CANYON LN	CO	MAL	23200	114	A3
PALMCREEK DR	CO	RM	8600	47	A4
PALMDALE BLVD E	CO	LAN	17200	175	B8
PALMDALE BLVD E	CO	PALM	100	172	A8
PALMDALE BLVD E	CO	PALM	5000	173	C8
PALMDALE BLVD E	CO	PALM	10700	174	A8
PALMDALE BLVD E	CO	PALM	16600	175	B8
PALMDALE BLVD E	PALM	PALM	300	172	A8
PALMDALE BLVD E	PALM	PALM	100	172	A8
PALMDALE BLVD W	CO	PALM		183	J5
PALMDLE LLAN RD	CO	LR	7000	184	D2
PALMDLE LLAN RD	CO	LR		184	D4
PALMER AV	COM	COM	300	64	E2
PALMER AV E	GLEN	GL05	100	25	C5
PALMER AV W	GLEN	GL04	100	25	C5
PALMER CT	LB	LB02	300	75	C4
PALMER CT	LB	LB13	700	75	C4
PALMER DR	CO	LA65	2600	25	E5
PALMER DR	CO	COM	4000	65	B2
PALMER ST	COM	COM	100	64	F2
PALMER ST	COM	COM	300	65	B2
PALMER ST	POM	POM	1500	94	C3
PALMERA AV	LA	PP		40	C3
PALMER CYN RD	CO	CLA		96	D3
PALMR-EVEY	CO	LA08		51	B2
PALMERO BLVD	CO	LA08	4200	51	B2
PALMERO DR	LA	LA65	4100	36	A2
PALMERSTON PL	LA	LA27	1900	34	E2
PALMERSTONE DR	CO	COM	400	19	C5
PALMERSTONE ST	CO	COM	4200	65	C2
PALMETTO DR	ALH	ALH	1	37	A5
PALMETTO DR	PAS	PAS	100	26	E5
PALMETTO ST	LA	LA13	1100	44	B5
PALMETTO RDG DR	SCLR	VAL		124	B4
PALM GROVE AV	LA	LA16	1900	43	A5
PALM GROVE AV	POM	POM	1700	91	A6
PALM HILL LN	BRAD	DUA	150	29	D3
PALMILLA DR	CO	CAL		100	C4
PALMROSE ST	BAP	BAP	14400	39	E4
PALMS BLVD	LA	LA34	10000	48	B6
PALMS BLVD	LA	LA66	11600	49	C3
PALMS BLVD	LA	VEN	600	49	C3
PALMS PL	PALM	PALM		172	A9
PALM TREE WY	CO	PALM	38900	171	J7
PALM VIEW DR	LA	LA42	800	16	C6
PALM VIEW PL	PAS	PAS	600	27	B4
PALM VISTA AV	CO	SAU		124	B5
PALM VISTA AV	LA	PALM	44300	160	D5
PALM VISTA AV	PALM	PALM	37800	172	D9
PALM VISTA AV	PALM	PALM	37700	173	D1
PALMWOOD DR	CO	LA08	4000	51	B1
PALMYRA RD	LA	LA08	4000	51	B1
PALO DR	ARC	ARC	800	28	B5
PALO ALTO DR	ARC	ARC	800	28	B5
PALO ALTO ST	LA	LA26	1600	44	C1
PALO CEDRO DR	MTB	MTB	100	46	F5
PALO CEDRO DR	DBAR	POM		97	F1
PALO CEDRO DR	SH	LB06	2600	75	F2
PALO CMDO CY RD	AGH	AGO		100A	C4
PALOMA AV	GLEN	GL08	100	18	C3
PALOMA AV	LA	LA02	9800	58	C3
PALOMA AV	LA	VEN	1	49	B2
PALOMA CT	LAV	LAV		90	B2
PALOMA CT	LA	VEN	10	49	B3
PALOMA DR	ARC	ARC		28	B5
PALOMA DR	POM	POM	400	36	F2
PALOMA DR	SPAS	SPAS	400	36	C1
PALOMA ST	LA	LA11	1200	44	C5
PALOMA ST	PAS	PAS	1	27	C2
PALOMAR DR	GLDR	GLDR	1900	87	E3
PALOMAR DR	LA	TAR	4900	21	D4
PALOMAR PL	LA	TAR	19300	21	D4
PALOMAR RD	SMAR	PAS	700	27	D3
PALOMARES ST N	POM	POM	100	94	B2
PALOMARES ST S	POM	POM	100	94	B3
PALOMINO	WCOV	WCOV		92	C1
PALOMINO DR	CO	SF		9	F1
PALOMINO CT	CO	DBAR	23500	21	D3
PALOMINO LN	RHE	PVP		73	B4
PALOMINTO AV	GLDR	GLDR		87	D5
PALORA ST	LA	ENC	17300	21	D5
PALO SOL F TKTR	CO	NEW		126	
PALOS VERDES BL	TOR	RB	100	67	D6
PALOS VERDES BL	TOR	TOR		67	D6

STREET	CITY	P.O. ZONE	BLOCK	PAGE	GRID
PALOS VERDES BL	TOR	TOR	5300	67	E5
PALOS VRDS DR E	RPV	PVP	26200	73	C4
PALOS VRDS DR E	RPV	PVP	27700	73	C6
PALOS VRDS DR E	RPV	PVP	28900	78	C1
PALOS VRDS DR N	LA	SP	1500	73	A4
PALOS VRDS DR N	LOM	LOM	1800	73	A4
PALOS VRDS DR N	PVE	PVP	2700	72	E2
PALOS VRDS DR N	PVE	PVP	2700	72	D2
PALOS VRDS DR N	RHE	PVP	4300	72	D2
PALOS VRDS DR N	RHE	PVP	2500	73	A4
PALOS VRDS DR S	RPV	PVP	4500	77	C2
PALOS VRDS DR S	RPV	PVP	3200	78	A3
PALOS VRDS DR W	PVE	PVP	200	72	B3
PALOS VRDS DR W	RPV	PVP	30200	77	B2
PALOS VERDES LN	RHE	PVP	2	73	A3
PALO VERDE AV	BLF	BLF	100	79	A4
PALO VERDE AV	BLF	BLF	17900	66	D6
PALO VERDE AV	CER	ART		66	D6
PALO VERDE AV	CO	LB08	3000	71	E6
PALO VERDE AV	LB	LB15	1200	76	E4
PALO VERDE AV	LKD	LKD	5900	66	D6
PALO VERDE AV	LKD	LKD	4100	71	D4
PALO VERDE DR	LA	LAN		159	E5
PALO VERDE DR	PAS	PAS	300	27	D3
PALO VISTA DR	LA	LA46	7400	23	F6
PALO VISTA DR	RPV	PVP		78	B4
PAM CT	SCLR	SAU		124	G4
PAM PL	WCOV	WCOV		92	D6
PAMELA AV	ELM	ELM	5000	38	F4
PAMELA CIR	ARC	ARC		28	B5
PAMELA C	CO	LPUE		98	C5
PAMELA DR	BH	BH		33	A5
PAMELA DR	SCLR	CYN		124	G9
PAMELA DR	SCLR	SAU		124	G9
PAMELA LN	CO	LPUE		97	B5
PAMELA LN	POM	POM	500	94	F5
PAMELA RD	CO	DUA	400	29	B6
PAMELA RD E	ARC	ARC	1	28	E6
PAMELA RD W	ARC	ARC	1	28	E6
PAMELA ST	RM	RM		46	E2
PAMELA KAY LN	CO	LPUE	300	48	B4
PAMELA KAY LN	CO	WHI	700	48	B4
PAMPAS CIR	LA	LAV		90	E1
PAMPAS RD	LA	WOH	4300	13	C3
PAMPAS RICAS BL	LA	PP	14800	40	C3
PAMPLICO DR	SCLR	SAU	22600	124	C4
PAMPLICO DR	SCLR	VAL		124	B5
PANAMA AV	CAR	CAR	23100	69	B6
PANAMA AV	LB	LB14	300	76	C5
PANAMA CT	PALM	PALM		172	E6
PANAMINT CT	LA	LA65		36	A2
PANAMINT DR	LA	LA65	4200	35	F1
PANAY WY	LA	MDR	13900	49	D5
PANCHO PL	LHH	LAH	2400	85	F3
PANDO DR	CO	LPUE	2000	85	F3
PANDORA AV	LA	LA24	1400	41	F2
PANDORA AV	LA	LA25	1800	41	F2
PANDORA ST	POM	POM	1900	94	F5
PANDY CT	SCLR	CYN		124	G9
PANGBORN AV	DOW	DOW	9500	60	D4
PANNES AV	CO	COM	15900	65	B3
PANNES AV	CO	COM	800	65	B3
PANNES AV N	COM	COM	100	65	B3
PANORAMA CT	ARC	ARC		92	E4
PANORAMA DR	CO	GL14	2300	11	F6
PANORAMA DR	LB	LB02		80A	A5
PANORAMA DR	SH	LB06	2000	75	E2
PANORAMA PL	WHI	WHI		55	E2
PANORAMA PL	PAS	PAS	700	26	D2
PANORAMA TER	CO	LA39	2100	35	B3
PANSY DR	CO	CAL		100	D5
PANSY PL	DBAR	POM		97A	F1
PANTERA DR	DBAR	POM		97A	F1
PANTHEON ST	NWK	NWK	11200	61	F5
PANTHEON ST	NWK	NWK	11600	61	A5
PAOLA AV	LA	LA32	2900	36	D5
PAOLI WY	LB	LB03	5200	76	D2
PAOLINO DR	CO	VAL		126	J1
PAPAGAYO WY	PALM	PALM		183	C6
PAPAGO TR	LA	CAN		4	A6
PAPAGO TR	LA	CAN		98	A6
PAPAYA DR	LHH	LAH	2000	98	A6
PAPAYA DR	LA	WIL	1000	98A	A4
PAPEETE PL	LA	TAR	18200	21	C4
PAPYRUS DR	CO	TOP		109	A6
PAQUITA DR	CO	LPUE	17800	98	C5
PAQUITO	CO	TOP		109	
PAR PL	CO	LLAN	30800	192	H3

280

LOS ANGELES CO.

1990 LOS ANGELES COUNTY STREET INDEX

PARADA DR

PASEO LUCINDA

STREET	CITY	P.O. ZONE	BLOCK	PAGE	GRID
PARADA DR	SCLR	VAL		127	A2
PARADE ST	LB	LB10	1100	75	A3
PARADISE DR	LA	LA32	2600	36	B5
PARADISE LN	CO	TOP	20200	109	E1
PARADISE LN	LB	LB05	900	65	C6
PARADISE CYN LN	LCF	LCF	5100	19	D2
PARADISE VLY N	CAR	CAR		69	E6
PARADISE VLY S	CAR	CAR		69	E6
PARADISE VLY RD	HH	CAL		100	E2
PARAGON DR	SCLR	SAU		124	D4
PARAGUAY DR	SCLR	SAU	22200	124	C7
PARAISO ST	LA	SP	1100	78	F1
PARAISO WY	CO	GL14	2700	11	D5
PARAISO WY	GLEN	GL14	3300	11	C4
PARALTA AV	LA	WOH	5200	13	D2
PARAMOUNT BLVD	DOW	DOW	12500	59	F6
PARAMOUNT BLVD	DOW	DOW	8500	60	B4
PARAMOUNT BLVD	LB	LB05	5900	65	F6
PARAMOUNT BLVD	LB	LB05	5400	70	F4
PARAMOUNT BLVD	LKD	LKD	4200	70	F4
PARAMOUNT BLVD	MTB	MTB		46	E4
PARAMOUNT BLVD	PAR	PAR	13800	65	F6
PARAMOUNT BLVD	PR	PR	5000	54	E3
PARAMOUNT BLVD	SOG	SOG	13000	59	F6
PARAMOUNT BLVD	SOG	SOG	13200	65	F6
PARAMOUNT DR	LA	LA68	2000	34	B2
PARAMOUNT PL	PR	PR	7500	54	D6
PARAMOUNT ST	AZU	AZU		88	C1
PARAMNT RCH RD	CO	AGO		107	A2
PARANA DR	CO	CHA		1A	C6
PARAPET ST	LB	LB08	5700	71	D5
PARCELS ST N	POM	POM	100	94	E3
PARCELS ST S	POM	POM	100	94	E3
PARCHED DR	CO	WOH		13	B4
PARCHER PL	GLEN	GL06	1900	25	F2
PARCHER TR	LA	TU	9600	10	F4
PARCHER TR	LA	TU	9600	11	A4
PARCHMAN AV	SCLR	NEW	24800	127	B4
PARDEE ST	LA	LA45	5200	56	D3
PARHAM AV	CO	GL14	5000	11	D5
PARIMA ST	LB	LB14		76	D5
PARION CT	LA	WOH	5200	100	E1
PARIS LN	SCLR	NEW		127	D7
PARISE DR	CO	WHI	10200	61	F4
PARISE DR	CO	WHI	10200	84	A3
PARISE DR	LAM	LAM	12900	82	E1
PARISE DR	WHI	WHI	9100	84	A3
PARISH PL N	BUR	BUR	600	17	C5
PARISH PL N	BUR	BUR	100	24	C1
PARISH PL S	BUR	BUR	100	24	C1
PARK AV	ARC	ARC	900	28	D6
PARK AV	BAP	BAP	4800	39	F3
PARK AV	CO	MONT	2300	18	E2
PARK AV	COV	COV	500	88	E4
PARK AV	CUL	CUL	10400	50	C1
PARK AV	GLEN	GL05	1100	25	E5
PARK AV	HB	RB	2200	62	C5
PARK AV	ING	IN02	600	51	B5
PARK AV	IRW	BAP	4200	39	F4
PARK AV	LA	LA26	1600	35	C6
PARK AV	LA	LA66	11800	49	F2
PARK AV	LA	PP		40	C4
PARK AV	LA	VEN	1	49	B4
PARK AV	LAV	LAV	1400	90	C3
PARK AV	LB	LB03	100	76	B6
PARK AV	LB	LB03	100	80	B1
PARK AV	LB	LB04	1300	76	B4
PARK AV	LB	LB14	300	76	B6
PARK AV	LB	LB15	1500	76	B2
PARK AV	MPK	MPK	400	46	C2
PARK AV	RB	RB	200	67	D3
PARK AV	SF	SF	1	2	E6
PARK AV	SFS	SFS	12200	61	C3
PARK AV	SMAD	SMAD	1	28	B2
PARK AV	SPAS	SPAS	600	37	A2
PARK AV N	LA	LA66	11800	50	A2
PARK AV N	MTB	MTB	100	54	D2
PARK AV N	POM	POM	100	94	E6
PARK AV S	LA	LA66	11800	50	A3
PARK AV S	MTB	MTB	100	54	D2
PARK AV S	POM	POM	100	94	E6
PARK CIR	ING	IN05	8200	57	C1
PARK CIR	LB	LB13	900	75	B4
PARK CT	LA	VEN	16	49	B4
PARK CT	LB	LB13	200	75	C5
PARK DR	BELL	BELL	6800	53	B6
PARK DR	CER	ART	13400	82	D5
PARK DR	LA	LA26	1700	35	D5
PARK DR	LKD	LKD	5200	70	F2
PARK DR	PR	PR		47	B6
PARK DR	SM	SM	1400	41	B5
PARK LN	BG	BELL	6100	59	F2
PARK LN	CO	LA01	8300	58	D1
PARK LN	LB	LB07	3100	70	C6
PARK PL	BAP	BAP	4200	39	F4
PARK PL	CER	ART		82	E4
PARK PL	CO	MONT	3800	18	F3
PARK PL	ELS	ELS		62	D2
PARK PL	GLEN	GL08	3700	18	F3
PARK PL	HPK	HPK	2600	52	F4
PARK PL	LA	VEN	100	49	B4
PARK PL	MB	MB		62	C2
PARK PL	MONT	MONT		18	F3
PARK PL	RPV	PVP		77	E1
PARK PL	SMAR	PAS	1400	37	C1
PARK RD	IND	LPUE		92	A5
PARK RD	LA	LA12		35	E5
PARK RD	LB	LB10	1700	70	A5
PARK ROW	LA	LA12	600	35	E5
PARK ROW	LA	VEN	1500	49	B4
PARK ROW	LA	VEN	1500	49	C4
PARK ST	ALH	ALH	1	37	C4
PARK ST	BLF	BLF	8500	66	B5
PARK ST	CDY	BELL	7900	59	D1
PARK ST	CER	ART	11200	66	E5
PARK ST	CER	ART	12100	82	B5
PARK ST	SCLR	NEW	22300	127	D4
PARK ST	RM	RM	8200	46	F1
PARK ST	SFS	SFS	13000	61	C3
PARK ST	TOR	TOR	23400	73	A2
PARK ST	WHI	WHI	13400	55	E4
PARK TER	LA	LA45		50	C5
PARK WY	BH	BH	1200	33	B6
PARK WY	MB	MB		62	D2
PARK WY E	ING	IN01	700	51	B6
PARK ADELFA	CO	CAL	23400	100	F3
PARK ALISAL	CO	CAL		100	F4
PARK ALLEGRA	CO	CAL		100	F3
PARK ANDORRA	CO	CAL		100	E4
PARK ANTIGUA	CO	CAL		100	E4
PARK ANTONIO	CO	CAL		100	E4
PARK ARROYO	LA	WOH		100	F3
PARK ATHENA	CO	CAL		100	D4
PARK AURORA	CO	CAL		100	E4
PARK BASILICO	CO	CAL		100	F4
PARK BELMONTE	CO	CAL		100	E4
PARK BLANCO	CO	CAL		100	F3
PARK BLU	CO	CAL		100	F3
PARK BOWL TR	CO	SF		3	E5
PARKBROOK LN	GLDR	GLDR		87	A4
PARKBYRN PL	CO	SGAB		28	B6
PARK CAPRI	CO	CAL		100	E3
PARK CASINO	CO	CAL		100	E4
PARK CENTER DR	LA	LA68	2900	24	B6
PARK CENTER DR	LA	LA68	2900	34	B1
PARK CENTER TR	LA	LA68		24	B6
PARK CENTER ST	BAP	BAP		39	D3
PARK CIRCLE DR	LAN	LAN		160	E5
PARK CLIFF ST	DOW	DOW		66	A2
PARK COLUMBO	CO	CAL		100	E4
PARK CONTESSA	CO	CAL		100	F4
PARK CORDERO	CO	CAL		100	F3
PARK CORNICHE	CO	CAL		100	F4
PARK CORONA	CO	CAL		100	F4
PARKCREST ST	LB	LB08	5100	71	C4
PARKDALE PL	LCF	LCF	1900	19	A2
PARK DULCE	LA	WOH		100	F3
PARKE ST	PAS	PAS	200	27	A3
PARK ENCINO LN	LA	ENC	4700	21	F2
PARK ENSENADA	CO	CAL		100	F4
PARK ENTRADA	CO	CAL		100	D4
PARKER AL	PAS	PAS	300	27	A5
PARKER AV	CO	SAU	28800	123	C3
PARKER AV	MON	MON	500	29	A4
PARKER DR	GLDR	GLDR	500	87	A6
PARKER PL	CO	LPUE		48	B3
PARKER PL	LA	CAN		12	C2
PARKER RD	CO	CAST	27800	123	G2
PARKER ST N	LA	SP	100	78	F4
PARKER ST S	LA	SP	1300	78	E6
PARKER MTN MTWY	CO	ACT		189	C2
PARKERTON DR	CO	PALM	34800	182	J3
PARK ESPERANZA	CO	CAL		100	F4
PARK ESTE	LA	WOH		100	F3
PARKFIELD LN	LAV	LAV	5100	95A	D4
PARK FOREST CT	PALM	PALM		184	B1
PARK FORTUNA	CO	CAL		100	F4
PARK FRONT WK	LA	LA11	400	52	B3
PARKGLEN AV	CO	LA43	4800	51	A3
PARK GRANADA	CO	CAL		100	D4
PARK GRANADA BL	CO	CAL	4500	100	E3
PARK GROVE AV	LA	LA07	1900	44	A5
PARK HACIENDA	CO	CAL		100	F4
PARK HAVEN CIR	CO	GL14	5000	11	E6
PARKHEATH DR	AGH	AGO		100A	A3
PARK HTS TER	LA	LA31	3400	45	B1
PARK HELENA	CO	CAL		100	F4
PARK HERMOSA	CO	CAL		100	F4
PARK HILL DR	LA	LA45	8000	55A	F1
PARKHOUSE LN	CO	TOP		115	A1
PARKHURST DR	RPV	PVP	3300	78	B3
PARKINSON AV	CO	WHI	9900	61	E3
PARK JACARANDA	CO	CAL	23400	100	F3
PARK JAZMIN	CO	CAL	23400	100	F4
PARKLAND CIR	LA	SF		3	A1
PARKLAND DR	CO	LPUE	15800	85	E5
PARK LANE CIR	LA	LA49	16500	21	F5
PARK LANE DR	LA	LA49	16500	21	F5
PARK LANE PL	LA	LA49	16600	21	F5
PARKLANE WY	CO	VAL		124	A6
PARK LAWN RD	CO	LPUE	1500	98	B3
PARK LIDO	CO	CAL		100	F4
PARK LIVORNO	CO	CAL		100	F3
PARKLYNN DR	RPV	PVP	6300	72	C5
PARK MADRID	CO	CAL		100	E4
PARK MALLORCA	CO	CAL		100	E4
PARKMAN AV	LA	LA26	300	35	A6
PARKMAN DR	LCF	LCF	800	19	C3
PARKMAN ST	CO	ALT	200	20	B3
PARK MANOR AV	LA	NHO	7000	15	F4
PARK MARBELLA	CO	CAL		100	D4
PARK MARCO POI.O	CO	CAL		100	F3
PARK MARIPOSA	CO	CAL		100	F2
PARKMEAD ST	SFS	SFS	11200	60	F4
PARKMEAD ST	SFS	SFS	11600	61	A4
PARK MEADOW DR	SCLR	CYN		125	B8
PARK MELINDA	CO	CAL		100	F4
PARK MILANO	CO	CAL		100	E4
PARK MIRAMAR	CO	CAL		100	D4
PARK MIRASOL	CO	CAL		100	F3
PARK MONACO	CO	CAL		100	E3
PARK MONTE NORD	CO	CAL		100	F3
PARKMOR RD	CO	CAL		100	A2
PARKMOUNT DR	GLEN	GL06	1900	25	F2
PARK OAK CT	LA	LA68	2500	34	D1
PARK OAK DR	LA	LA68	2400	34	D1
PARK OAK PL	LA	LA68	5600	34	D1
PARK OESTE	CO	CAL		100	F5
PARK OLIVO	CO	CAL	23400	100	F3
PARK ORA	CO	CAL		100	F4
PARK PALOMA	CO	CAL		100	F4
PARKPATH TR	LA	TU	6300	11	B3
PARK PINTA	CO	CAL		100	F4
PARK PLAZA DR	LB	LB04		76	B4
PARK PRIVADO	LA	WOH		100	F3
PARKRIDGE DR	GLEN	GL02	1600	25	C1
PARKRIDGE DR	WAL	WAL		93	C6
PARKRIDGE LN	SCLR	CYN		125	B8
PARKRIDGE PL	LAV	LAV		95A	E5
PARK RIVIERA	CO	CAL		100	D4
PARK ROADWAY A	PAS	PAS		26	E3
PARK ROADWAY B	PAS	PAS		26	E3
PARK ROCK DR	LPUE	LPUE		92	B6
PARK ROSE AV	DUA	DUA	1300	29	C6
PARK ROSE AV	DUA	DUA	2300	39	C1
PARK ROSE AV	MON	MON	200	29	C3
PARK ROSE AV S	MON	MON		29	C4
PARK ROSSO	CO	CAL		100	D4
PARK ROW DR	LA	LA12		35	E5
PARK SERENA	CO	CAL		100	F3
PARK SEVILLA	CO	CAL		100	F3
PARKSHIRE CT	PAR	PAR	16400	65	F4
PARKSIDE AV	BUR	BUR	1300	24	D2
PARKSIDE AV	CER	ART	16600	82	B5
PARKSIDE AV	LA	LA31	2100	36	B6
PARKSIDE CIR	WCOV	WCOV		92	C4
PARKSIDE DR	SF	SF	300	2	F6
PARKSIDE DR	WCOV	WCOV		92	C4
PARK SIENNA	CO	CAL		100	E4
PARK SOLDI	CO	CAL		100	F4
PK SOMERSET DR	LAN	LAN	1700	159	J8
PARK SORRENTO	CO	CAL		100	E3
PARKSOUTH ST	CO	CAL		100	E5
PARK SPRING LN	DBAR	POM		97A	A2
PARK TERRA	CO	CAL		100	F3
PARK TERRACE DR	LB	LB04		76	B4
PARK TERRACE DR	WLVL	THO		102	C4
PARKVALE DR	SCLR	SAU		124	E4
PARKVALLE AV	CER	ART	16700	82	E5
PARKVALLE CIR	CER	ART	18200	82	E6
PARKVALLE PL	CER	ART	17300	82	E6
PARKVALLEY AV E	CO	LAN	16900	175	A4
PARK VERDI	CO	CAL		100	F4
PARK VERONA	CO	CAL		100	F3
PARK VICENTE	CO	CAL		100	F4
PARK VIEW AV	MB	MB		62	C2
PARK VIEW AV	PAS	PAS	1000	26	D1
PARKVIEW CT	WAL	WAL		93	D4
PARKVIEW DR	ALH	ALH	1800	36	F6
PARKVIEW DR	COV	COV		93	B1
PARKVIEW DR	LKD	LKD	4300	71	A3
PARKVIEW DR	LAV	LAV		95A	E6
PARK VIEW RD	CO	VAL		127	A1
PARK VIEW RD	SCLR	VAL		124	A9
PARK VIEW ST N	LA	LA26	100	35	B6
PARK VIEW ST S	LA	LA06	900	44	A2
PARK VIEW ST S	LA	LA57	100	44	A2
PARKVILLE RD	CO	AGO		100A	E5
PARK VISTA CIR	PAS	PAS		20A	B3
PARK VISTA DR	GLEN	GL14	3200	18	D1
PARK VISTA DR	PAS	PAS		20A	B3
PARK VISTA PL	GLEN	GL14		18	D1
PARK VISTA RD	CO	AGO		100A	D6
PARKWAY DR	ELM	ELM	2100	47	E4
PARKWAY DR	SELM	ELM	1800	47	E4
PARKWAY TR	CO	TOP	1100	109	B5
PARK WESTERN DR	LA	SP	1100	78	E1
PARK WESTERN PL	LA	SP	1200	78	E1
PARKWOOD AV N	PAS	PAS	1	27	D4
PARKWOOD AV S	PAS	PAS	1	27	D5
PARKWOOD DR	GLEN	GL02	200	25	C2
PARKWOOD DR	LA	LA77	300	32	F5
PARKWOOD LN	GLEN	GL08	1300	25	C2
PARKWOOD LN	POM	POM	600	90	F2
PARKWOOD PL	BAP	BAP	13100	48	C1
PK WOODLAND PL	CO	SAU		124	G3
PARKYNS ST	LA	LA49	12700	41	A2
PARLIN ST	SELM	ELM	11200	47	D4
PARMA CT	SCLR	VAL		127	A1
PARMA PL	LA	PP	700	40	E4
PARMELEE AV	CO	COM	13900	64	D2
PARMELEE AV	CO	LA01	6300	52	D6
PARMELEE AV	CO	LA02	9200	58	D3
PARMELEE AV	CO	LA59	11600	58	D5
PARMELEE AV	COM	COM	1500	64	D2
PARMELEE AV	LA	LA02	10400	58	D4
PARMELEE AV	LA	LA59	11200	58	D5
PARMER AV	LA	LA26	1500	35	C5
PARMERTON AV	TEC	TEC	5300	38	E3
PARNA WY	PAR	PAR		65	E4
PARNELL AV	LA	LA25	1800	41	F3
PARNELL AV	LA	LA64	2200	41	F3
PARNELL WY	CO	ALT	2000	19	E6
PARNES AV	CO	PEAR		192	C2
PARQUE DL NORTE	IRW	BAP	5000	88	B3
PARQUET PL	CO	MAL		112	D5
PARR AV	LA	SUN	10100	10	D2
PARRAL PL	LA	VAN	4200	22	C4
PARRIOTT PL	IND	LPUE	400	85	E1
PARRIOTT PL E	IND	LPUE	400	85	E1
PARRISH AV	LA	LA65	3500	35	F2
PARRON AV	GAR	GAR	14700	63	D3
PARROT AV	DOW	DOW	12600	59	F6
PARROT AV	DOW	DOW	8900	60	C2
PARSONS TR	LA	TU	6800	11	A2
PARTENT DR	CO	MAL	4000	112	E3
PARTHENIA PL	LA	NOR	18400	7	C6
PARTHENIA PL	LA	SF	8600	8	C6
PARTHENIA ST	LA	CAN	20100	6	D6
PARTHENIA ST	LA	NOR	19600	6	D6
PARTHENIA ST	LA	NOR	17000	7	D6
PARTHENIA ST	LA	SF	16500	7	F6
PARTHENIA ST	LA	SF	15000	8	B6
PARTHENIA ST	LA	VAN	13900	8	D6
PARTRIDGE AV	LA	LA39	2700	35	D3
PARTRIDGE LN	GLDR	GLDR		87	D6
PARVA AV	LA	LA27	4000	35	A1
PARVIN DR	SCLR	NEW		127	D3
PARWAY DR	GLEN	GL06	1500	26	B1
PASADA DR	WHI	WHI	16200	84	D3
PASADENA AV	LA	LA31	1700	35	F6
PASADENA AV	LA	LA31	2100	36	A5
PASADENA AV	LB	LB06	1800	75	C2
PASADENA AV	LB	LB07	3000	70	C3
PASADENA AV	SPAS	SPAS	100	36	D2
PASADENA AV N	AZU	AZU	200	86	D6
PASADENA AV N	AZU	AZU	100	88	D1
PASADENA AV N	GLDR	GLDR	100	87	B5
PASADENA AV N	PAS	PAS	100	26	F3
PASADENA AV S	AZU	AZU	100	88	D1
PASADENA AV S	GLDR	GLDR	100	87	B5
PASADENA AV S	PAS	PAS	100	26	F5
PASADENA FRWY	LA	LA		35	E6
PASADENA FRWY	LA	LA		36	B3
PASADENA FRWY	LA	LA		44	D1
PASADENA FRWY	SPAS	SPAS		37	A1
PASADENA ST	WHI	WHI	12300	55	D4
PASADENA ST E	POM	POM	100	94	E2
PASADENA ST E	POM	POM	1000	95	A2
PASADENA ST W	POM	POM	100	94	E2
PASADENA AV TER	LA	LA42	4800	36	B3
PASADENA GLN RD	CO	PAS	1500	20A	A3
PASADENA GLN RD	CO	PAS	1500	28	A1
PASADERO DR	LA	TAR	18600	21	B3
PASADERO PL	LA	TAR	4200	21	B3
PASADO DR	DBAR	POM		97	D6
PASA GLEN DR	GLEN	GL08	1800	18	F5
PASA GLEN DR	GLEN	GL08	2200	19	A5
PASALA CT	SCLR	VAL		124	A2
PASATIEMPO LN	CO	HAC		73	F1
PASCAL CT	LAN	LAN		160	D6
PASCAL PL	CO	PVP		73	A4
PASCO CT	DBAR	POM		97	C6
PASEO AV	LAV	LAV		90	C2
PASEO DR	CER	ART	12300	81	B2
PASEO DR	LA	LA65	3500	35	E2
PASEO ST	COV	COV	100	88	E6
PASEO ST	PAR	PAR	8500	66	A3
PASEO WK	LA	LA65		35	E2
PASEO ALAMOS	SAD	SAD		89	D6
PASEO ALDEANO	SAD	SAD		89	E5
PASEO ALICIA	SAD	SAD		89	D6
PASEO ALONDRA	SAD	SAD		89	D6
PASEO ALONDRA	SAD	SAD		93	D1
PASEO AMBAR	SAD	SAD		89	F6
PASEO AMBAR	SAD	SAD		93	F1
PASEO ANACAPA	SAD	SAD		89	D5
PASEO AZUL	CO	LPUE		98	D4
PASEO BRAVO	PALM	LAN		171	D4
PASEO CANCUM	WCOV	WCOV		92	E5
PASEO CANYON DR	CO	MAL	6000	111	E4
PASEO CARMEL	SAD	SAD		89	C6
PASEO CASTANOS	SAD	SAD		89	D5
PASEO CIELO	SAD	SAD		89	D5
PASEO COMERCIO	WAL	WAL		93	C6
PASEO COMERCIO	WAL	WAL		97	C1
PASEO CORRIDO	SAD	SAD		89	D5
PASEO CORTO	SAD	SAD		89	D5
PASEO CUMBRE	SAD	SAD		89	E5
PASEO DE ARENA	TOR	RB	500	72	E1
PAS DE CASTANA	RPV	PVP		78	C2
PASEO DE CIMA	GLEN	GL08		19	B5
PASEO DE GRACIA	TOR	RB	100	67	D6
PAS DE GRANADA	TOR	TOR	100	72	E1
PAS D L CONCHA	TOR	RB	100	67	D6
PAS D L PALIZDA	WAL	WAL	500	97	A2
PASEO DE LA PAZ	SAD	SAD		89	D5
PAS DE LA PLAYA	RB	RB		67	D6
PAS DE LA PLAYA	TOR	RB		67	D6
PAS DE LA PLAYA	TOR	RB	300	72	D1
PAS DE LA PLAZA	LA	LA12	100	44	E2
PAS DE LA RISA	LA	PP		30	A6
PAS DE LA RISA	LA	PP		109	F6
PAS D LS DLCIAS	RB	RB		67	D6
PAS D LS DLCIAS	TOR	RB		67	D6
PAS D LS ESTRLS	TOR	RB	300	72	D1
PAS D LS TRTUGS	TOR	RB	4000	72	E1
PAS D LS TRTUGS	TOR	TOR	4900	72	F1
PAS DEL CABALLO	WAL	WAL		97	A1
PASEO DEL CAMPO	PVE	PVP	2100	72	D2
PASEO DEL MAR	LA	SP	500	78	E6
PASEO DEL MAR	PVE	PVP	200	72	A4
PASEO DEL MAR	RPV	PVP		78	B4
PASEO DELORES	SAD	SAD		89	C6
PAS D LS REYES	TOR	RB	500	72	D1
PASEO DEL PRADO	WAL	WAL		97	B1
PASEO DEL REY	LA	VEN	8700	55A	F2
PASEO DEL SERRA	LA	LA68	6900	34	B2
PASEO DEL SOL	CO	CAL		100	C6
PASEO DEL SOL	PVE	PVP	1800	72	C3
PASEO DE PABLO	TOR	RB	5000	72	E1
PASEO DE PAVON	TOR	TOR	4900	72	E1
PASEO DE PINO	RPV	PVP		78	C2
PASEO DE ROCHA	CO	LPUE	16300	85	F3
PASEO DESCANSO	SAD	SAD		89	D5
PAS DE SEVILLA	WAL	WAL		97	A2
PASEO DE SUENOS	TOR	RB	100	72	D1
PASEO D TERRADO	DBAR	POM		97	F2
PASEO DORADO	LB	LB03		76	F5
PASEO DORADO	SAD	SAD		89	D6
PASEO DORADO	SAD	SAD	1200	93	D1
PAS EL CORONEL	LA	LA33	100	44	F3
PASEO EL RIO	LA	LA33	100	44	F3
PASEO ENCANTO	SAD	SAD	1300	89	D5
PASEO ENCINAS	SAD	SAD		89	D6
PASEO FELIZ	SAD	SAD		89	E6
PASEO FORTUNA	PALM	LAN		171	D3
PASEO FORTUNO	SAD	SAD		89	D5
PASEO GABRIELA	SAD	SAD		89	D6
PASEO GRACIA	SAD	SAD		89	E5
PASEO GRANADA	CER	ART	20100	81	B3
PASEO GRANADA	SAD	SAD		89	E6
PAS GRANDE CIR	DUA	DUA		86	A5
PASEO HERMOSO	PALM	LAN		171	D3
PASEO HIDALGO	CO	MAL	3800	114	E4
PASEO ISABELLA	SAD	SAD		89	E5
PASEO JACINTA	SAD	SAD		93	E1
PASEO JARDIN	SAD	SAD		89	E5
PASEO LA CRESTA	PVE	PVP	1000	72	C3
PASEO LAGUNA	SAD	SAD		89	E5
PASEO LA PAZ	POM	POM		90	C5
PASEO LA PAZ	WCOV	WCOV		92	E5
PASEO LA VISTA	LA	WOH		5	C5
PASEO LAVRO CT	SCLR	VAL		127	C8
PASEO LA ZANJA	LA	LA33	300	44	F3
PAS LOS ALISOS	LA	LA33	100	44	F3
PAS LS GAVILANS	SAD	SAD		89	E5
PASEO LUCER	WAL	WAL	19800	93	B6
PASEO LUCINDA	SAD	SAD		89	C6

INDEX

281

1990 LOS ANGELES COUNTY STREET INDEX

PASEO LUNADO

PEPPER BROOK WY

LOS ANGELES CO.

INDEX

STREET	CITY	P.O. ZONE	BLOCK	PAGE	GRID
PASEO LUNADO	PVE	PVP	500	72	A5
PASEO MADRONAS	SAD	SAD		89	D5
PASEO MANZANA	SAD	SAD		89	E5
PASEO MARAVILLA	SAD	SAD		89	E5
PASEO MARLENA	SAD	SAD		89	D6
PASEO MERIDA	WCOV	WCOV		92	E5
PASEO MIRAMAR	LA	PP	300	40	A3
PASEO MORALES	SAD	SAD		89	D5
PASEO MUNDO	SAD	SAD		89	E5
PASEO NOGALES	SAD	SAD		89	D5
PASEO NUEVO DR	LA	TAR	18600	21	B3
PASEO OLIVAS	WCOV	WCOV		92	E5
PASEO OLIVOS	SAD	SAD		89	D5
PASEO OTONO	SAD	SAD		89	E6
PASEO PERDIDO	WAL	WAL		93	B6
PASEO PERDIDO	WAL	WAL		97	B1
PASEO PLACITA	SAD	SAD		89	D5
PASEO PORTOLA	CO	MAL	21400	114	E4
PASEO PRIMARIO	CO	CAL		100	C5
PAS PUETO BELLO	LA	PP		30	A6
PAS PUETO BELLO	LA	PP		109	F6
PAS RO CASTILLA	LA	LA32		36	E6
PAS RO CASTILLA	LA	LA32		45	D2
PASEO REDONDO	BUR	BUR	1200	18	A5
PASEO REGINA	SAD	SAD		89	D6
PASEO REGINA	SAD	SAD		93	D1
PASEO ROBLES	SAD	SAD		89	D5
PASEO ROBLES	WAL	WAL		97	B1
PASEO SERENO	SAD	SAD		89	D5
PASEO SERRA	CO	MAL	21500	114	E4
PASEO SOMBRA	SAD	SAD		89	E5
PASEO SONRISA	WAL	WAL		97	C1
PASEO SUENO	SAD	SAD		89	C5
PASEO SUSANA	SAD	SAD		89	D6
PASEO TEPIC	WCOV	WCOV		92	E5
PASEO TERESA	SAD	SAD		89	D6
PASEO TERESA	SAD	SAD		93	D1
PASEO TERRAZA	SCLR	SAU		124	C7
PASEO TESORO	WAL	WAL		97	C1
PASEO THE	LA	LA65	3300	35	E2
PASEO VALDES	LA	LA33	120	44	F3
PAS VALLE VISTA	SAD	SAD		89	C5
PASEO VERANO	SAD	SAD		89	E6
PASEO VERDE	CO	WHI		47	F5
PASEO VICTORIA	SAD	SAD		89	D6
PASEO VIENTO	SAD	SAD		89	E5
PASEO YNEZ	SAD	SAD		89	D6
PASEO ZACATE	SAD	SAD		89	E5
PASHA PL	LA	SF	13300	3	A2
PASHA ST	LA	SF	13300	3	A2
PASKENTA RD	LA	PP	1200	40	D2
PASO ALTO RD	PAS	PAS	1000	26	E3
PASO REAL AV	CO	LPUE	1700	98	F4
PASO ROBLES AV	LA	ENC	4800	21	F3
PASO ROBLES AV	LA	NOR	8500	7	E6
PASO ROBLES AV	LA	NOR	8300	14	E1
PASO ROBLES AV	LA	SF	11400	1	E6
PASO ROBLES AV	LA	SF	10300	7	E2
PASO ROBLES AV	LA	VAN	7300	14	E2
PASO VERDE	CO	LPUE	1900	85	F3
PASQUAL AV	SGAB	SGAB	200	37	D2
PASQUAL PL	SGAB	SGAB	100	37	D2
PASQUALITO DR	SMAR	PAS	1300	37	B2
PASS AV	BUR	BUR	1200	17	A6
PASS AV	BUR	BUR	1200	24	A1
PASS& COVINA RD	CO	LPUE	1400	92	B4
PASS& COVINA RD	WCOV	WCOV		92	B4
PASSAGE AV	BLF	BLF	16800	66	A5
PASSAGE AV	PAR	PAR	14300	66	A2
PASSAGEWAY PL	AGH	AGO		102	D3
PASSAIC ST	HPK	HPK	6200	53	A5
PASSIFLORA DR	LHH	LAH		84	F3
PASSMORE DR	LA	LA68	2900	24	A6
PASSONS BLVD	DOW	DOW	8700	60	E2
PASSONS BLVD	PR	PR	6200	54	F5
PASSONS BLVD	PR	PR	4800	55	A3
PASSONS BLVD	PR	PR	7900	60	E2
PASTEL PL	LA	NHO	3700	23	D5
PASTEUR DR	LAN	LAN		160	D6
PASTRANA DR	LAM	LAM	15200	83	B2
PAT AV	LA	WOH	5900	5	D6
PAT PL	LA	WOH	24500	5	D6
PATAGONIA DR	LCF	LCF	2100	18	F2
PATATA ST	CDY	BELL	4700	59	D2
PATATA ST	SOG	SOG	4800	59	D2
PATCH ST	CO	PALM	8700	171I	G5
PATERO WY	LB	LB15	4000	76	A2
PATHFINDER RD	CO	LPUE		97	A5
PATHFINDER RD	CO	LPUE	18600	98	E6
PATHFINDER RD	CO	WAL		97	B5
PATHFINDER RD	DBAR	POM		97	C4
PATHFINDER RD	DBAR	POM	21000	97	D4
PATHWAY TR	LA	TU		11	B3
PATIO PL	LA	LA32	3600	36	E4
PATIRENE PL	LA	RES	19300	14	A5
PATOM DR	CUL	CUL	11200	50	C4

STREET	CITY	P.O. ZONE	BLOCK	PAGE	GRID
PATRAE ST	LA	LA66	4800	50	A4
PATRICE PL	LA	GAR		64	A6
PATRICIA AV	LA	LA25	2100	42	A3
PATRICIA AV	LA	LA64	3200	42	B5
PATRICIA DR	CER	ART	12400	81	B1
PATRICIA LN	CO	PALM		184	B6
PATRICIA ST	WCOV	WCOV		92	E6
PATRCIA HILL DR	SCLR	CYN		125	B7
PATRICIAN WY	LA	LA41	5300	26	D4
PATRICIAN WY	MON	MON	400	29	A2
PATRICIAN WY	PAS	PAS	100	26	D3
PATRICIAN VW DR	CO	LPUE	2000	98	E4
PATRICK AV	LA	PAC	10300	8	E3
PATRICK AV	LA	PAC	9000	9	A5
PATRICK AV	POM	POM	800	95	A1
PATRICK ST	TOR	TOR	5000	67	F2
PATRICK HNRY PL	AGH	AGO		100A	D6
PATRICK HNRY PL	PALM	PALM		183	D2
PATRIOT TR	CO	TOP		109	B2
PATRITTI AV N	BAP	BAP	3000	39	B6
PATRITTI AV N	BAP	BAP	3300	48	B1
PATRONELLA AV	CO	GAR	15200	63	C3
PATRONELLA AV	TOR	TOR	16600	63	B5
PATRONELLA AV	TOR	TOR	18000	68	C1
PATTERSON AV	GLEN	GL02	726	25	B3
PATTERSON AV	GLEN	GL03	300	25	B3
PATTERSON AV	POM	POM	500	95	A4
PATTERSON DR	MON	MON	300	29	A2
PATTERSON PL	LA	PP		40	D4
PATTERSON ST	SH	LB06	600	75	D1
PATTERSON ST E	LB	LB06	300	75	B1
PATTERSON ST E	LB	LB15	5100	76	B1
PATTERSON ST W	LB	LB06	700	75	C1
PATTIE ST	COM	COM	1400	65	B2
PATTIGLEN AV	LAV	LAV	2400	90	B3
PATTILAR AV	LA	WOH	5500	100	D1
PATTIZ AV	LB	LB08	3000	71	F6
PATTIZ AV	LB	LB15	1600	76	F3
PATTON AV N	LA	SP	100	78	E3
PATTON AV S	LA	SP	100	78	E3
PATTON CT	SMAR	PAS		27	C6
PATTON RD	DOW	DOW	11400	60	B5
PATTON ST	LA	LA26	200	44	C1
PATTON WY	SMAR	PAS		27	C6
PATTY CT	PALM	PALM		183	B1
PATTY CT	WCOV	WCOV		92	E6
PATTY LN	LA	LA49		21	F6
PAUL AV	TOR	TOR	21500	67	E4
PAUL DR	WHI	WHI		55	D6
PAUL TER	LA	LA26		35	C5
PAULA AV	GLEN	GL01	300	24	F3
PAULA DR	SM	SM	2900	49	C2
PAULA LN	LAN	LAN		160	H6
PAULA ST	LA	LA32	4600	36	C5
PAULA ST	LKD	LKD	4400	71	E3
PAULA ST	WCOV	WCOV		92	F6
PAULCREST DR	LA	LA46	3000	23	E6
PAULETTE PL	LCF	LCF	400	19	C2
PAULETTE PL	LA	SF	16900	1	E4
PAULHAN AV	LA	LA41	4500	26	A6
PAULHAN ST	CO	COM		69	F1
PAULINA AV	RB	RB	400	67	D2
PAULINE AV	LA	LA46	2000	33	D2
PAULINE ST	CO	COM	3600	65	B4
PAULINE ST	WCOV	WCOV		92	E6
PAUL JONES AV	LA	WIL		74	F4
PAUL REVERE DR	CO	CAL	22700	13	A4
PAUL REVERE DR	CO	WOH	22400	13	A4
PAUL REVERE PL	PALM	PALM		183	D2
PAULSEN AV	COM	COM	100	64	E2
PAULSEN CIR	COM	COM		64	E3
PAULSON AV	SELM	ELM	2400	47	D2
PAUMA VALLEY DR	LA	NOR		1	A6
PAVAS CT	CO	LPUE		98	D4
PAVIA PL	LA	PP	1300	40	E2
PAVILION DR	POM	POM	1000	94	C1
PAVO ST	LB	LB08	5300	71	D6
PAVO ST	LB	LB08	5300	76	D1
PAVO ST	LB	LB08		76	E1
PAVO REAL AV	MPK	MPK	1600	46	B4
PAWNEE	CO	TOP		13	C5
PAWNEE ST	LA	SV	10600	16	F1
PAXSON LN	ARC	ARC	2500	38	E2
PAXTON AV	PALM	PALM		171	F6
PAXTON ST	LA	PAC	12600	3	A6
PAXTON ST	LA	PAC	12900	8	E2
PAXTON ST	LA	PAC	13000	9	A1
PAXTON ST	LA	SF	12800	3	A6
PAYERAS ST	LA	CHA	20200	6	E4
PAYETTE DR	WHI	WHI	10300	84	C3
PAYNE AV	CO	TOR	21300	68	F4
PAYNE, THOMS LN	PALM	PALM		183	D2
PAYSON ST	CO	AZU	16600	88	D2
PAYSON ST	CO	COV	18800	88	F2
PAYSON ST	CO	LAV	700	90	B2
PAYSON ST E	AZU	AZU	100	88	D2

STREET	CITY	P.O. ZONE	BLOCK	PAGE	GRID
PAYSON ST E	GLDR	GLDR	100	89	B2
PAYSON ST E	SAD	SAD	200	90	A2
PAYSON ST W	AZU	AZU	300	88	D2
PAYSON ST W	GLDR	GLDR	100	89	B2
PAYSON ST W	SAD	SAD	1200	89	D2
PEABODY ST	LB	LB08	5100	71	B5
PEACE ST E	LB	LB05	300	70	C3
PEACE ST W	LB	LB05	1	70	C3
PEACEFUL HLS RD	DBAR	WAL		97	C4
PEACEFUL VLY RD	CO	PALM		183	A7
PEACH	LA	SF		8	C1
PEACH AV	LA	SF	9800	8	C4
PEACH AV	LA	VAN	5800	15	C4
PEACH AV	LA	VAN	4800	22	C3
PEACH AV	PALM	PALM		183	H7
PEACH CT	CO	SAU		124	C2
PEACH DR	PALM	PALM		183	C6
PEACH MTWY	SCLR	NEW		127	C6
PEACH PL	PAS	PAS	100	26	F4
PEACH RD	SCLR	NEW		127	B5
PEACH ST	COM	COM	500	64	E2
PEACH ST	LYN	LYN	11000	59	A6
PEACH ST	MPK	MPK	300	46	C2
PEACH BLOSSM RD	WAL	WAL		93	B4
PEACH GROVE ST	LA	NHO	10800	23	E2
PEACH GROVE ST	LA	VAN	13900	22	E2
PEACHLAND AV	SCLR	NEW	24600	127	B4
PEACHTREE AV	LA	VAN	7700	15	E2
PEACHTREE LN	ARC	ARC	400	28	F6
PEACHTREE LN	COV	COV	700	88	F6
PEACHTREE LN	CO	LR		184	D5
PEACH TREE LN	CO	PEAR		192	D1
PEACHTREE ST	CMRC	LA40	5700	53	F4
PEACHWOOD PL	WLVL	THO		102A	E5
PEACOCK AL	CO	LR		192	A4
PEACOCK CT	CO	CAL		13	A4
PEACOCK LN	MTB	MTB	200	46	E6
PEACOCK LN	RHE	PVP		73	C4
PEACOCK PL	LAV	LAV		95A	E5
PEACOCK RDG DR	PVE	PVP	27900	72	D5
PEACOCK RDG RD	PVE	PVP		72	D5
PEAJAY WY	SCLR	CYN		124	H9
PEAK CT	DBAR	POM		97A	B2
PEAK TR	CO	TOP		109	B5
PEALE DR	CO	WOH		13	B4
PEAR CT	CO	SAU		124	C3
PEAR ST	COM	COM	300	64	E2
PEAR ST	LYN	LYN	11400	59	A5
PEAR BLOSSOM CT	WHI	WHI		84	D5
PEARBLOSSOM HWY	CO	LLAN	14500	185	E7
PEARBLOSSOM HWY	CO	LR	7000	184	C4
PEARBLOSSOM HWY	CO	PALM		183	F5
PEARBLOSSOM HWY	CO	PALM	4700	184	A3
PEARBLOSSOM HWY	CO	PEAR	10600	185	B7
PEARBLOSSOM HWY	PALM	PALM		183	F5
PEARCE AV	LB	LB08	4700	71	C3
PEARCE AV	LKD	LKD	4900	71	C3
PEARL AV	MON	MON	400	29	B3
PEARL AV N	COM	COM	100	65	A3
PEARL AV S	COM	COM	100	65	A3
PEARL CIR	LKD	LKD		81	C3
PEARL CT	CO	LAN		159	C9
PEARL CT	WCOV	WCOV		92	E6
PEARL PL	LA	LA64	11600	41	E5
PEARL PL	LB	LB02		75	C5
PEARL PL	PAS	PAS	300	27	A3
PEARL PL	SM	SM	2400	41	C6
PEARL ST	LA	LA64	11200	41	D6
PEARL ST	RB	RB	100	67	D4
PEARL ST	SGAB	SGAB	100	37	E4
PEARL ST	SM	SM	2000	41	D6
PEARL ST	SM	SM	800	49	B1
PEARL ST	TOR	TOR	5600	67	E4
PEARL ST E	POM	POM	100	94	E2
PEARL ST W	POM	POM	100	94	E2
PEARLANNA DR	SAD	SAD	500	89	E2
PEARLE ST	PAR	PAR	7800	65	E1
PEARLWOOD DR	LAN	LAN		159	F8
PEAR ORCHARD LN	PAS	PAS		28	A1
PEARSON AV	CO	WHI	2200	47	E5
PEARSON CT	SCLR	SAU		124	D2
PEARSON PL	LA	SUN	10500	10	B3
PEARSON ST	CUL	CUL	4300	50	C1
PEARTREE CT	WAL	WAL		93	B6
PEARTREE CT	WAL	WAL		97	B1
PEARTREE LN	RHE	PVP		72	D6
PEAR TREE WY	CO	LPUE		98	A4
PEARWOOD AV	LA	SF	11600	2	D6
PEARY DR	SCLR	VAL		127	A2
PEAVINE DR	LA	BH	9700	33	A3
PEBBLE CT	MPK	MPK	2000	45	F3
PEBBLE LN	DBAR	POM		97	D4
PEBBLE ST	CO	ACT		189	E2
PEBBLE TR	LA	TOP		109	B2
PEBBLE WY	PALM	PALM		171	F4
PEBBLE BEACH DR	LCF	LCF		19	C2

STREET	CITY	P.O. ZONE	BLOCK	PAGE	GRID
PEBBLE BEACH LN	AZU	AZU	300	86	D4
PEBBLE BEACH PL	LA	NOR	19100	1	A5
PEBBLE CREEK LN	WAL	WAL		92	F5
PEBBLE CREEK ST	CO	ACT		189	E2
PEBBLEDON ST	MPK	MPK	1100	45	F3
PEBBLE HURST ST	MPK	MPK	1300	45	F3
PEBBLESHIRE RD	GLEN	GL07		25	D1
PEBBLE SPGS LN	GLDR	GLDR		87	D4
PEBBLE VALE ST	MPK	MPK	1300	45	F3
PEBBLEWOOD DR	DBAR	POM		97A	B2
PEBBLY BEACH RD	AVA	AVA	600	77	C5
PECAN PL	CO	SAU		124	C3
PECAN ST	LA	LA23	600	44	F3
PECAN ST	LA	LA33	100	44	F3
PECAN GROVE DR	DBAR	POM		97	F3
PECK AV	LA	SP	2500	78	F6
PECK AV N	MB	MB	100	62	D5
PECK AV S	MB	MB	100	62	D5
PECK CIR	LAV	LAV		90	D1
PECK CT	PALM	PALM		183	G2
PECK DR	BH	BH	100	42	B2
PECK DR	LA	LA35	1000	42	B2
PECK RD	ARC	ARC	5300	39	A3
PECK RD	CO	ELM	1100	47	D5
PECK RD	CO	WHI	700	47	D5
PECK RD	ELM	ELM	3400	38	F6
PECK RD	ELM	ELM	4800	39	A3
PECK RD	ELM	ELM	2100	47	E3
PECK RD	IND	WHI		47	D5
PECK RD	IRW	BAP		39	A2
PECK RD	MON	MON	1800	29	A5
PECK RD	MON	MON	2400	39	A2
PECK RD	SELM	ELM	2000	47	E3
PECK ST	COM	COM	300	65	A2
PECKAM DR	CO	LPUE	13000	48	A3
PECKHAM RD	AZU	AZU	100	88	A1
PECOS AV	NWK	NWK	12600	60	E6
PECOS AV	NWK	NWK	12800	66	E1
PECOS CT	CO	CAST		123	E4
PECOS CT	LAN	LAN		160	F6
PEDLEY DR	ALH	ALH	1400	46	A1
PEDRO PL	PVE	PVP	1800	72	C2
PEEKABOO RD	CO	PALM		157	G7
PEERLESS PL	LA	LA35	1400	42	B3
PEERLESS WY	MTB	MTB		54	C4
PEG PL	LA	LA35	1400	42	B3
PEGASUS DR	CO	SF		3	F2
PEGFAIR LN	PAS	PAS	1300	26	C1
PEGFAIR EST DR	PAS	PAS	1400	26	C1
PEGGY AV	LPUE	LPUE	600	92	A5
PEGGY CT	WCOV	WCOV		92	F6
PEGGY JOYCE LN	SCLR	SAU		124	E6
PELANCONI AV	GLEN	GL02	800	25	A2
PELE CT	WCOV	WCOV		92	F6
PELHAM AV	LA	LA25	1800	41	F3
PELHAM AV	LA	LA64	2200	41	F3
PELHAM PL	CO	VAL		124	B7
PELHAM PL	LA	LA68	2700	34	D1
PELICAN AV	LA	SP	1700	78	D4
PELICAN BAY	LB	LB03		76	E6
PELION CT	PALM	PALM		172	H9
PELION CT	PALM	PALM		183	H1
PELLET ST	DOW	DOW	7000	59	F2
PELLET ST	DOW	DOW	7100	60	A2
PELLEUR ST	LYN	LYN	4600	65	D1
PELLISSIER PL	IND	WHI		47	E5
PELLISSIER RD	CO	WHI	12200	47	E5
PELON WY	MPK	MPK	1000	46	B3
PELONA VLY RD	CO	SAU		181	D6
PELONA VISTA DR	LAN	LAN		159	E7
PELTON AV S	PAR	PAR	13800	65	E1
PELUSO AV	LA	SUN	10700	10	B2
PEMBERTON DR	LAM	LAM	14900	83	A3
PEMBINA RD	RPV	PVP	27000	72	E4
PEMBRIDGE CT	LA	LA49		32	B2
PEMBROKE CT	CLA	CLA		91	C2
PEMBROKE LN	LA	LA15	1400	44	B4
PEMBROKE RD	SAD	SAD		89	C4
PEMBROOK AV	POM	POM	300	94	E5
PEMBROOK DR	PAS	PAS	400	28	B3
PEMBROOK PL	SCLR	SAU		127	C1
PEMBURY PL	LCF	LCF	4100	19	B4
PEN ST	CO	LPUE	18800	98	E6
PENARTH AV	DBAR	WAL	800	97	C2
PENBYRN RD	CO	SAU		181	C9
PENCIN DR	CO	LPUE		48	A4
PENDER AV	LA	SF	11000	7	E1
PENDLETON AV	LYN	LYN	4500	59	C4
PENDLETON AV	SOG	SOG	5100	59	C4
PENDLETON ST	LA	SV	10900	9	D5
PENDLETON ST	LA	SV	11800	16	C1
PENFIELD AV	LA	CAN	8500	6	F6
PENFIELD AV	LA	CAN	6400	12	F4
PENFIELD AV	LA	CHA	9500	6	F4
PENFIELD AV	LA	NOR	8700	6	F6
PENFIELD AV	LA	WOH	5600	12	F6

STREET	CITY	P.O. ZONE	BLOCK	PAGE	GRID
PENFIELD AV	LA	WOH	5100	13	F2
PENFIELD ST	POM	POM	100	90	E5
PENFOLD ST	LB	LB05	600	65	C5
PENFORD DR	CO	WHI		84	B5
PENFORD DR	LAM	LAM	11800	84	B5
PENGRA ST	DUA	DUA	1300	29	D6
PENHAVEN LN	CO	PALM	8500	171I	G4
PENHILL CT	GLEN	GL06		25	F2
PENHOLM DR	CO	ELM		48	A2
PENINSULA AV	CLA	CLA		96	D5
PENINSULA PL	LB	LB03	1	80	C2
PENINSULA RD	LA	WIL		74	D6
PENINSLA VDE DR	RPV	LOM	1800	73	D4
PENLAND PL	HH	CAL	24100	100	D2
PENLAND RD	HH	CAL	5600	100	D2
PENLON RD	SCLR	CYN		124	H9
PENMAN RD	CO	SAU		181	J6
PENMAR AV	LA	VEN	1300	49	D3
PENMAR CT	LA	VEN	2200	49	D3
PENMAR LN	POM	POM	100	94	F4
PENN ST	ELS	ELS	100	56	B6
PENN ST	LYN	LYN	11100	58	F5
PENN ST	PAS	PAS		27	A1
PENN ST	SAD	SAD	100	90	A1
PENN ST	WHI	WHI	12300	55	D5
PENNANT PL	WHI	WHI	12500	61	D1
PENNEKAMP CT	MB	MB		62	D5
PENNELL DR	SAD	SAD	1100	89	F1
PENNERTON DR	GLEN	GL06	2300	26	A3
PENNEY AV	ING	IN03	10900	57	D4
PENNINGTON AV	LA	WIL	500	74	E4
PENN MAR AV	ELM	ELM	3700	39	A6
PENN MAR AV	ELM	ELM	2200	47	E3
PENN MAR AV	SELM	ELM	1200	47	D4
PENNSWOOD AV	BLF	BLF	16600	66	B4
PENNSWOOD AV	LKD	LKD	5900	66	B6
PENNSWOOD AV	LKD	LKD	5600	71	B1
PENNSYLVANIA AV	GLEN	GL14	4000	11	D5
PENNSYLVANIA AV	GLEN	GL14	3800	18	D2
PENNSYLVANIA AV	LA	LA33	1300	45	A3
PENNSYLVANIA AV	LOM	LOM	24000	73	C3
PENNSYLVANIA AV	SM	SM	2000	41	B6
PENNSYLVANIA AV	SOG	SOG	11300	59	E6
PENNSYLVANIA AV	TOR	TOR	22700	68	C6
PENNSYLVANIA AV	TOR	TOR	23500	73	C3
PENNSLVNIA AV N	GLDR	GLDR	100	87	A5
PENNSLVNIA AV S	GLDR	GLDR	100	87	A5
PENNSLVNIA AV S	GLDR	GLDR		89	A2
PENNSYLVANIA DR	LOM	LOM	26000	73	C3
PENNSYLVANIA DR	RHE	PVP	26100	73	C4
PENNSYLVANIA LN	GLDR	GLDR		87	A4
PENNSYLVANIA PL	CLA	CLA	3500	96	C5
PENNY LN	CER	ART		71	E2
PENNY RD	CO	TOP	1200	109	E2
PENNY ST	WCOV	WCOV		92	E6
PENNYROYAL ST	LAN	LAN		160	B1
PENNYWOOD PL	POM	POM	1700	91	A6
PENOBSCOT DR	LA	CAN		5	D2
PENRIDGE PL	ING	IN01		57	B2
PENRITH DR	LA	LA23	600	45	A5
PENROD DR	AGH	AGO		102	D3
PENROD DR	CAR	CAR		64	C6
PENROSE AV	CO	COM	13000	64	F1
PENROSE CT	DBAR	POM		97A	B3
PENROSE ST	LA	SV	10300	9	F6
PENROSE ST	LA	SV	10200	10	A6
PENROSE ST	LA	SV	11200	16	D1
PENSACOLA DR	CO	PALM		157	E8
PENSHORE TER	GLEN	GL07		18	D6
PENTAGON ST E	CO	ALT	200	20	A4
PENTAGON ST W	CO	ALT	400	19	F4
PENTLAND ST	TEC	TEC	9000	38	B4
PENTLAND WY	LA	CAN	23900	5	E3
PEONIA RD	LA	WOH	4800	13	B3
PEONZA LN	PALM	LAN		171	D4
PEORIA ST	LA	SV	10900	9	E4
PEORIA ST	LA	SV	12000	16	B1
PEORIA ST E	PAS	PAS	100	27	A3
PEORIA ST W	PAS	PAS	100	26	F3
PEORIA ST W	PAS	PAS	100	27	A3
PEPPER AV	GLDR	GLDR	300	87	B6
PEPPER AV	LA	LA65	2600	35	F4
PEPPER CT	ING	IN02		50	F6
PEPPER DR	CO	ALT	1700	20	D6
PEPPER DR	CO	PAS	1300	27	D1
PEPPER DR	LB	LB07	100	70	C6
PEPPER PL	CO	SAU		124	D2
PEPPER ST	ALH	ALH	1700	37	A4
PEPPER ST	BUR	BUR	1400	17	A6
PEPPER ST	ELS	ELS	800	56	A5
PEPPER ST	LAV	LAV	2300	90	D3
PEPPER ST	MPK	MPK	700	46	D3
PEPPER ST	PAS	PAS	100	26	E1
PEPPER WY	GLEN	GL05	800	25	D5
PEPPER BROOK WY	CO	LPUE	16500	98	B3

STREET	CITY	P.O. ZONE	BLOCK	PAGE	GRID
PEPPERCORN DR	SCLR	SAU		124	D5
PEPPER CREEK LN	CER	ART		82	B4
PEPPERDALE DR	CO	LPUE	1900	97	A4
PEPPERDINE CT	LAV	LAV		90	E2
PEPPERDINE LN	CLA	CLA		91	A2
PEPPERGLEN DR	ARC	ARC	700	38	C1
PEPPERHILL RD	PAS	PAS		28	A2
PEPPERIDGE DR	SCLR	NEW		127	E4
PEPPERMILL LN	POM	POM		94	C6
PEPPER MILL WY	LAM	LAM	12600	84	D6
PEPPERTREE CIR	WCOV	WCOV		92	C4
PEPPERTREE CT	WAL	WAL		97	B1
PEPPER TREE DR	AZU	AZU	900	86	E5
PEPPERTREE DR	LHH	LAH		98A	B3
PEPPERTREE DR	RPV	PVP		77	E3
PEPPERTREE LN	IRW	BAP	16000	88	B3
PEPPER TREE LN	LAM	LAM		83	D1
PEPPERTREE LN	LB	LB15		76	E5
PEPPER TREE PL	TOR	TOR	22800	68	D6
PEPPERWOOD AV	BLF	BLF	13300	66	B2
PEPPERWOOD AV	LB	LB08	4200	71	B3
PEPPERWOOD AV	LB	LB15	2200	76	B2
PEPPERWOOD AV	LKD	LKD	5900	66	B6
PEPPERWOOD AV	LKD	LKD	4900	71	B2
PEPPERWOOD CIR	POM	POM		94	D6
PEPPERWOOD LN	DUA	DUA		29	E5
PEQUENA LN	LCF	LCF	1200	19	B2
PEQUENO DR	CO	MAL		111	E5
PEQUENO PL	LA	PP	16600	40	B2
PERA RD	LA	WOH	22700	13	A3
PERALTA AV	LB	LB14	300	76	E5
PERCH ST	LA	SP	1700	78	D4
PERCHERON DR	WAL	WAL		93	D4
PERCIVAL PL	LA	LA46	2200	33	E2
PERCY ST	CO	LA22	5400	45	F6
PERCY ST	CO	LA23	3900	45	C6
PERCY ST	LA	LA23	3300	45	B5
PERDIDO LN	LA	LA77	2500	32	E1
PEREZ LN	LA	LA33	1400	45	C2
PEREZ PL	BAP	LPUE		48	A2
PEREZ PL	IND	LPUE		48	A2
PERFECT PL	LAN	LAN		159	G4
PERHAM DR	CUL	CUL	3800	50	E1
PERICO DR	WHI	WHI		84	C1
PERILLA AV	PAR	PAR	14300	66	A2
PERIMETER RD	CAR	CAR		64	D6
PERKINS	TOR	TOR		68	A3
PERKINS AV	CO	WHI	11500	61	B1
PERKINS CIR	GLEN	GL06	2500	26	B3
PERKINS DR	ARC	ARC	1	28	E2
PERKINS LN	RB	RB	1500	62	F6
PERKINS ST	PR	PR	9100	54	E6
PERLITA AV	LA	LA39	4000	25	B5
PERLITA AV	LA	LA39	1900	35	C1
PERLITA ST	LAV	LAV		90	B1
PERNELL AV	DOW	DOW	10900	59	F2
PERRIN ST	POM	POM		94	E4
PERRINO PL	LA	LA23	1600	52	F1
PERRIS ST	LA	LA33	1600	45	C2
PERRY AV	LA	WIL		74	F3
PERRY AV	MTB	MTB	800	46	D6
PERRY AV	RB	RB	1900	62	E4
PERRY CT	CLA	CLA		91	B1
PERRY DR	CUL	CUL	5800	42	E5
PERRY RD	BG	BELL	6400	54	A6
PERRY RD	BG	BELL	7000	60	A1
PERRY ST	CAR	CAR	21000	69	D4
PERRY ST	CO	LA63	3900	45	D2
PERSELL ST	CO	PEAR		192	D1
PERSHING CT	COV	COV	200	88	E4
PERSHING DR	LA	VEN	7000	55A	E2
PERSHORE AV	SAD	SAD	600	90	A2
PERSIMMON AV	ARC	ARC		38	D3
PERSIMMON AV	ELM	ELM	4500	38	E4
PERSIMMON AV	TEC	TEC	4800	38	E4
PERSIMMON LN	CO	SAU		124	D2
PERSING DR	WHI	WHI	12500	55	D6
PERTH AV	LPUE	LPUE	200	48	E5
PERTSHIRE CIR	LA	CAN	6900	5	E4
PERU ST	LA	LA39	2300	35	D3
PERUGIA WK	LB	LB03		80	D2
PERUGIA WY	LA	LA77	500	32	D5
PESCADERO AV	SOG	SOG	9900	59	A4
PESCADORES AV	LA	SP	1700	78	D4
PESCADOS DR	LAM	LAM	15500	83	B2
PESQUERA DR	LA	LA49	2400	30	E5
PETALUMA AV	LB	LB08	3000	71	E6
PETALUMA AV	LB	LB15	1600	76	E2
PETALUMA AV	LKD	LKD	4200	71	E4
PETALUMA DR	LA	SV	8300	17	A1
PETALUMA PL	LA	SV	10200	17	A1
PET CEMETERY RD	CO	CAL		100	D3
PETERS CIR	GLEN	GL08		18	D4
PETERSEN RD	CO	SAU		181	D6
PETERSON AV	LA	CAN	6500	5	E4
PETERSON AV	LA	WOH	6100	5	E5

STREET	CITY	P.O. ZONE	BLOCK	PAGE	GRID
PETERSON AV	LB	LB13	1300	75	E4
PETERSON AV	SPAS	SPAS	100	36	D3
PETERSON DR	WHI	WHI		84	D1
PETERSON DR	WHI	WHI		85	D6
PETIT AV	LA	ENC	4300	21	F3
PETIT AV	LA	SF	8600	7	F6
PETIT AV	LA	SF	8400	14	F1
PETIT AV	LA	VAN	6400	14	F4
PETITE CT	LA	LA39	3000	35	C2
PETRA CT	WCOV	WCOV		92	E6
PETRA DR	PALM	PALM		183	G2
PETRO PL	LAN	LAN		159	G5
PETROL ST	PAR	PAR	7200	65	E2
PETROLEUM AV	CO	TOR	22800	68	F6
PETROLEUM AV	LA	HAC	25000	73	F3
PETROLIA AV	COM	COM	900	65	A4
PETTERSON LN	PAR	PAR	7200	65	E1
PETTICOAT LN	NWK	NWK	11600	82	A2
PETULA PL	CER	ART		66	E4
PETUNIA ST	CO	AZU	18600	88	E1
PETUNIA ST	CO	GLDR	1900	89	E1
PETUNIA ST	GLDR	GLDR	200	89	A1
PETUNIA ST	WCOV	WCOV		92	F6
PETWORTH AV	LA	SF		3	C6
PEWTER CT	CO	LPUE		98	A4
PEWTER RD	CO	SAU		181	B9
PEYTON AV	BUR	BUR	1600	17	C4
PEYTON RD	LAV	LAV	2000	90	D3
PFEIFFER LN	CLA	CLA		91	C1
PFLUEGER AV	GLDR	GLDR	100	87	C5
PHAEDON LN	CO	LAN		159	B9
PHAETON AV	PR	PR	6200	54	E4
PHAETON AV	LA	WOH	20100	13	E3
PHANTOM DR	RPV	PVP	32200	78	B3
PHEASANT DR	LA	LA65	600	36	A3
PHEASANT LN	RH	PVP	1	73	A6
PHEASANT RD	POM	POM		94	C6
PHEASANT ST	GLEN	GL06		26	C1
PHELAN AV	BAP	BAP	4400	39	F4
PHELAN LN	RB	RB	1200	62	E6
PHELAN LN	RB	RB	500	67	F1
PHELPS AV	LA	LA32	2700	36	D5
PHILADELPHIA ST	WHI	WHI	12000	55	D5
PHILADLPHA ST E	POM	POM	100	94	F5
PHILADLPHA ST E	POM	POM	900	95	A5
PHILADLPHA ST W	POM	POM	100	94	F5
PHILBERT DR	LA	LA77	1600	32	E3
PHILBROOK AV	CO	VAL		124	A6
PHILBROOK ST	CO	LPUE	18600	98	E5
PHILIP AV	CO	MAL	5800	111	F5
PHILIPRIMM ST	LA	TAR	18600	21	B1
PHILIPRIMM ST	LA	WOH	22100	13	B1
PHILIPRIMM ST	LA	WOH	22200	100	D1
PHILLIPPI AV	LA	PAC	11600	3	B6
PHILLIPPI AV	LA	PAC	11100	9	B1
PHILLIPPI AV	LA	SF	12800	2	E3
PHILLIPPI AV	LA	SF	11700	3	B6
PHILLIPPI ST	SF	SF	1200	2	F4
PHILLIPS AV	LYN	LYN	11800	65	D1
PHILLIPS AV	WCOV	WCOV	200	88	D5
PHILLIPS BLVD E	POM	POM	100	94	D4
PHILLIPS BLVD E	POM	POM	1000	95	A4
PHILLIPS BLVD W	POM	POM	100	94	D4
PHILLIPS DR	POM	POM	1900	94	B3
PHILLIPS ST	LB	LB05	1200	70	E1
PHILLIPS WY	LA	LA42	1700	26	B6
PHILLIPS RCH RD	POM	POM		94	C6
PHILO ST	LA	LA64	3200	42	B5
PHILRICH CIR	CO	CAL	26000	100	A2
PHLOX ST	DOW	DOW	7400	60	B4
PHOEBE AV	LAM	LAM		82	F4
PHOEBE CT	WCOV	WCOV		92	F6
PHOENIX DR	CER	ART	12000	81	B2
PHOENIX DR	IND	LPUE	16000	85	F1
PHOSPHOROUS RD	SCLR	SAU		127	E2
PHOTOFLASH RD	SCLR	SAU		124	D9
PHYLLIS AV	WHOL	LA69	9000	33	D4
PHYLLIS AV	WCOV	WCOV		92	E6
PHYLLIS CT	BH	BH		33	C4
PHYLLIS ST	CO	GL14	2200	11	F5
PICAACHO DR	LHH	LAH	500	84	D1
PICADILLY CT	LAN	LAN		159	J2
PICARDIE RD	RPV	PVP	6200	78	C1
PICASO ST	LAN	LAN		160	D6
PICASSO AV	LA	WOH	4100	13	C4
PICASSO PL	LA	WOH	21400	13	C4
PICCADILLY PATH	CO	PAS		20	F6
PICCOLO ST	CO	PAS	3100	27	F5
PICHER AL	PAS	PAS	100	27	A5
PICKADILLY PL	LA	SF		3	B1
PICKENS ST	GLEN	MONT	2600	18	E2
PICKENS CYN RD	CO	GL14	2300	11	E5
PICKERING AV	WHI	WHI	5400	55	D5
PICKERING WY	ELM	ELM	11600	39	A4
PICKERING WY	MTB	MTB	300	54	C2
PICKFAIR WY	BH	BH	1100	33	A4

STREET	CITY	P.O. ZONE	BLOCK	PAGE	GRID
PICKFORD LN	CER	ART		66	D2
PICKFORD PL	LA	LA35	6000	42	E3
PICKFORD ST	LA	LA19	5300	42	D3
PICKFORD ST	LA	LA19	4500	43	A4
PICKFORD ST	LA	LA35	5900	42	D3
PICKFORD ST	LA	LA64	11200	41	E5
PICKFORD WY	CUL	CUL	5000	50	C3
PICKNEY DR	CO	CAL		13	A4
PICKWICK ST	LA	LA42		26	D6
PICO AL	SPAS	SPAS	500	36	F1
PICO AV	CO	NEW		126	H3
PICO AV	LB	LB02	300	75	B6
PICO AV	LB	LB13	700	75	B6
PICO BLVD	SM	SM	1600	41	C6
PICO BLVD	SM	SM	1	49	B1
PICO BLVD E	LA	LA15	100	44	B4
PICO BLVD E	LA	LA23	2800	45	A6
PICO BLVD E	LA	LA23	2900	53	A1
PICO BLVD W	LA	LA06	2300	43	D3
PICO BLVD W	LA	LA06	1800	44	A3
PICO BLVD W	LA	LA15	100	44	B4
PICO BLVD W	LA	LA19	5400	42	F3
PICO BLVD W	LA	LA19	3100	43	D3
PICO BLVD W	LA	LA21	700	44	B4
PICO BLVD W	LA	LA35	5900	42	E3
PICO BLVD W	LA	LA64	10600	41	E5
PICO BLVD W	LA	LA64	10300	42	B3
PICO BLVD W	LA	LA67	10000	42	B3
PICO CIR	LAV	LAV		90	B1
PICO CT	PR	PR	9200	55	A2
PICO PL	SM	SM	600	49	A1
PICO ST	PAS	PAS	1	27	A5
PICO ST	POM	POM	100	95	A3
PICO ST	SF	SF	600	2	E6
PICO ST	SF	SF	600	8	E1
PICO CYN RD	CO	NEW	24600	126	G4
PICO VISTA RD	DOW	DOW	9000	60	E4
PICO VISTA RD	PR	PR	7200	54	F6
PICO VISTA RD	PR	PR	5100	55	A4
PICO VISTA RD	PR	PR	8300	60	F2
PICTON ST	LPUE	LPUE	15800	48	F5
PICTORIAL ST E	PALM	PALM	100	172	B6
PICTURESQUE DR	LA	NHO	11600	23	D4
PIEDMNT MESA DR	CLA	CLA		90	F2
PIEDMONT AV	CLA	CLA	100	91	A4
PIEDMONT AV	CO	MONT	2700	18	E2
PIEDMONT AV	GLEN	GL06	400	25	D3
PIEDMONT AV	GLEN	GL14	2800	18	D2
PIEDMONT AV	GLEN	MONT	2600	18	E2
PIEDMONT AV	LA	LA42	5800	36	C2
PIEDRA WY	MPK	MPK	1400	46	B3
PIEDRA CHICA RD	CO	MAL	20000	115	B4
PIEDRA MRDA DR	LA	PP		30	B6
PIEDROS DR	SCLR	SAU	26600	124	D7
PIER AV	HB	RB	100	62	C6
PIER AV	HB	RB	100	67	C1
PIER AV	SM	SM	400	49	B3
PIER PL	LB	LB02	1	75	C6
PIER A AV	LB	LB02		75	B6
PIER A ST	LA	WIL	300	74	B6
PIER A ST	LA	WIL		79	B1
PIER A WY	LB	LB02		80A	B5
PIER B AV	LA	LA02		75	B6
PIER C AV	LA	LA02		75	A6
PIERCE AV	WHI	WHI	6200	55	D5
PIERCE PL	MPK	MPK	1800	46	D4
PIERCE RD	LB	LB22		71	F4
PIERCE ST	LA	PAC	12200	3	C6
PIERCE ST	LA	PAC	13300	8	E4
PIERCE ST	LA	PAC	12200	9	B2
PIERCE ST	LA	SF	11600	3	C6
PIER D AV	LB	LB02		75	A6
PIER E AV	LB	LB02		75	A6
PIER E AV	LB	LB02		80A	C3
PIER F AV	LB	LB02		80A	B6
PIER G AV	LB	LB02		80A	B5
PIER J AV	LB	LB02		80A	C5
PIER J WY	LB	LB02		80A	C5
PIERMONT DR	CO	LPUE	1700	85	F3
PIERRE RD	WAL	WAL	100	93	C6
PIERRE RD	WAL	WAL		97	C1
PIETRO DR	CO	LPUE	2800	85	D4
PIGOTT DR	CUL	CUL	11100	50	B2
PIKE ST	SFS	SFS		61	B2
PIKES CT	DBAR	POM		94	B6
PILAR RD	LA	WOH	20900	13	D3
PILARIO ST	CO	LPUE	19300	97	A4
PILARIO ST	CO	LPUE	18600	98	E4
PILCHARD ST	LA	SP	200	79	B3
PILGRIM PL	SMAR	PAS		37	B2
PILGRIM WY	MON	MON	300	28	F4
PILGRIM WY	WHI	WHI		55	C4
PILGRIMAGE TR	LA	LA68	2400	34	C2
PILLSBURY ST E	CO	LAN	9000	161	G5
PILLSBURY ST E	LAN	LAN	600	160	C5
PILLSBURY ST W	LAN	LAN	1100	159	J5

STREET	CITY	P.O. ZONE	BLOCK	PAGE	GRID
PILLSBURY ST W	LAN	LAN	100	160	A5
PIMA AV	WCOV	WCOV	200	92	C1
PIMENTA AV	BLF	BLF	16400	66	A4
PIMENTA AV	LKD	LKD	5900	66	A6
PIMENTA AV	LKD	LKD	4600	71	A3
PIMENTA AV	PAR	PAR	15100	66	A3
PIN CT	SCLR	SAU		124	G3
PINAFORE PL	POM	POM	1900	94	F5
PINAFORE ST	LA	LA08	4000	51	A1
PINALE LN	PVE	PVP	2600	72	D2
PINCKARD AV	RB	RB	2800	62	E4
PINE	CO	LP48		98	F3
PINE AV	BELL	BELL	6200	53	C5
PINE AV	COM	COM	300	64	F1
PINE AV	COM	COM	300	65	A1
PINE AV	ELM	ELM	3700	38	E6
PINE AV	LYN	LYN	10700	59	C4
PINE AV	LYN	LYN	3200	65	A1
PINE AV	MAY	MAY	5200	53	C5
PINE AV	MB	MB	1100	62	C4
PINE AV	PALM	LAN		171	C2
PINE AV E	ELS	ELS	100	56	B6
PINE AV N	LB	LB02	1	75	C5
PINE AV N	LB	LB05	5100	70	C2
PINE AV N	LB	LB06	1800	75	C5
PINE AV N	LB	LB07	3100	70	C6
PINE AV N	LB	LB13	700	75	C5
PINE AV S	LB	LB02	1	75	C5
PINE AV W	ELS	ELS	100	56	A6
PINE CT	ING	IN02		50	F6
PINE DR	BH	BH	1100	33	A4
PINE DR	TOR	TOR	600	68	C3
PINE LN	CO	PALM		171	J6
PINE PL	SOG	SOG	2600	58	F1
PINE ST	CMRC	LA23	2400	53	C2
PINE ST	COM	COM		65	B1
PINE ST	SCLR	NEW	23900	127	D4
PINE ST	CO	RM	2100	46	F2
PINE ST	HB	RB	500	67	D1
PINE ST	LYN	LYN	11000	59	C5
PINE ST	NWK	NWK	1200	82	B2
PINE ST	POM	POM	2300	90	E4
PINE ST	PR	PR	4000	54	F2
PINE ST	RM	RM	2700	46	F2
PINE ST	SGAB	SGAB	100	37	F4
PINE ST	SM	SM	700	49	B2
PINE ST	SPAS	SPAS	1100	36	F3
PINE ST	WCOV	WCOV	800	92	A2
PINE ST E	ALH	ALH	100	37	B3
PINE ST E	CO	ALT	100	20	A4
PINE ST N	SGAB	SGAB	100	37	E3
PINE ST S	SGAB	SGAB	100	37	E3
PINE ST W	ALH	ALH	100	37	B3
PINE ST W	CO	ALT	100	20	A4
PINEBANK DR	SCLR	SAU		124	E4
PINE BLUFF DR	PAS	PAS	900	28	A2
PINE BLUFF DR	WHI	WHI1		55	E3
PINEBLUFF PL	WLVL	THO		102A	F5
PINE CANYON RD	CO	LH		157	A6
PINECASTLE DR	RPV	PVP	28500	72	E6
PINECLIFF DR	CO	PALM		157	F9
PINECONE PL	CO	CAST		123	E4
PINECONE RD	CO	GL14	5400	11	E5
PINE COVE CIR	SCLR	VAL		124	B4
PINE CREEK LN	LA	HAC		74	A3
PINE CREEK RD	CER	ART	12400	82	B4
PINECREST DR	CO	ALT	1900	20	D4
PINE CREST DR	LA	LA42	6000	36	D2
PINECREST DR	SPAS	SPAS	1	36	D2
PINE CREST LN	WAL	WAL		92	F6
PINECREST RD	CO	AGO		107	B2
PINECRST MSA RD	CO	LR	10600	192	A6
PINECROFT DR	CO	CLA	3800	90	F2
PINEEDGE DR	LHH	LAH	1100	98A	C3
PINEFALLS AV	DBAR	WAL		97	D2
PINEFALLS DR	WCOV	WCOV	2900	97	A1
PINEFOREST LN	CO	HAC		73	F1
PINEGLEN RD	CO	GL14		11	E5
PINEGROVE	WCOV	WCOV		92	D4
PINE GROVE AV	LA	LA42	900	26	C5
PINEGROVE LN	CER	ART		82	B4
PINEGROVE E	CER	ART		82	B4
PINEGROVE W	CER	ART		82	B4
PINEHILL LN	DBAR	POM		97	D4
PINE HILLS AV	SCLR	CYN	27100	124	G7
PINE HOLLOW RD	CO	CAL	4100	13	A4
PINEHURST	ELM	ELM		48	A6
PINEHURST AV	LYN	LYN	10600	59	D4
PINEHURST AV	SOG	SOG	9900	59	D4
PINEHURST DR	PAS	PAS	600	27	B6
PINEHURST PL	POM	POM	1900	94	F5
PINEHURST RD	LA	LA68	1900	34	B2
PINEHURST ST	GLDR	GLDR	1900	87	E6
PINEHURST WY	WAL	WAL		93	D6
PINEKNOLL AV	LA	HAC	26400	73	E4
PINELAKE LN	LA	CAN	8400	5	F1

STREET	CITY	P.O. ZONE	BLOCK	PAGE	GRID
PINELAND AV	LAV	LAV	2700	90	D3
PINELAWN DR	CO	GL14		11	E4
PINE MT TK TR	CO			N	F5
PINE NEEDLES	AZU	AZU	1200	86	D4
PINE NUT DR	LA	ENC		21	C4
PINE OAK LN	PAS	PAS		26	E3
PINEPARK CIR	CO	HAC	23600	73	F1
PINERIDGE DR	CO	GL14		11	E5
PINERIDGE DR	LA	SF	16500	1	F5
PINERIDGE PL	CO	GL14	2700	11	E5
PINE SHADOWS RD	CO	LR	10500	192	A6
PINETREE CT	WAL	WAL		93	B6
PINETREE CT	WAL	WAL		97	B1
PINE TREE LN	CO	RM	1300	46	F3
PINETREE LN	LAM	LAM		83	A1
PINE TREE LN	MON	MON		29	B2
PINE TREE LN	RH	PVP	1	73	A6
PINE TREE PL	LA	LA69	8600	33	D4
PINE VALLEY AV	LA	NOR	18900	1	A5
PINE VALLEY DR	ALH	ALH	2400	46	B1
PINE VALLEY PL	LA	NOR		1	A6
PINEVIEW RD	CO	CYN		128	D3
PINEVILLE ST	ELM	ELM	12100	47	E3
PINE VISTA LN	LAW	LAW	4700	62	F3
PINEWOOD AV	LA	TU	9700	11	A4
PINEWOOD AV	PALM	PALM		183	G1
PINEWOOD CIR	CER	ART	18700	81	D1
PINEWOOD CT	POM	POM		90	E3
PINEWOOD LN	GLEN	GL14	3000	18	D1
PINEWOOD LN	SAD	SAD	700	90	A4
PINEWOOD PL	GLDR	GLDR	100	87	C5
PINKERTON RD	GLDR	GLDR	1500	89	C2
PINK PANSY	CO	CYN		125	F5
PINNACLE PL	LA	NHO		23	C6
PINNACLE WY	CO	MAL	20600	115	A4
PINNACLE WY	PALM	PALM		171	D4
PINNEY ST	LA	PAC	12500	3	B6
PINNEY ST	LA	PAC	13200	8	F2
PINNEY ST	LA	PAC	12900	9	A2
PINNEY ST	LA	SF	12200	3	C5
PINON	WCOV	WCOV		98	F1
PINON SPGS DR	LAN	LAN		160	E4
PINOSITAS RD	WHI	WHI	8200	84	C1
PINTADO DR	DBAR	POM		93	F6
PINTO	LA	SF42		2	C1
PINTO CIR	WAL	WAL		93	A5
PINTO DR	LHH	LAH	1100	98	A6
PINTO LN	RHE	PVP	1	73	B4
PINTO PL	CO	CAST		123	G1
PINTO PL	LA	LA69	8800	33	D3
PINTO RD	RH	PVP	1	78	A2
PINTO ST	LAV	LAV		90	D1
PINTO WY	WAL	WAL		93	D4
PINTO MESA DR	DBAR	POM		94	B6
PINTORESCA DR	LA	PP	200	40	B4
PINTURA DR	CO	LPUE	15000	85	D3
PINYON AV	LA	TU	10300	11	A3
PINYON PL	LAV	LAV		90	A3
PIOCHE DR	LAM	LAM	14200	82	F1
PIONEER AV	LA	WIL	400	74	D4
PIONEER AV	TOR	TOR		68	A2
PIONEER BLVD	ART	ART	16600	82	A5
PIONEER BLVD	CER	ART	19400	81	A2
PIONEER BLVD	CO	WHI	4800	55	B3
PIONEER BLVD	CO	WHI	8500	61	A1
PIONEER BLVD	LB	LB08		81	A5
PIONEER BLVD	LKD	LKD	20200	81	A5
PIONEER BLVD	NWK	NWK	11000	61	A5
PIONEER BLVD	NWK	NWK	13100	82	A5
PIONEER BLVD	SFS	SFS	9000	61	A2
PIONEER BLVD	WHI	WHI	5700	55	B3
PIONEER DR	GLEN	GL03	300	25	C3
PIONEER DR	WCOV	WCOV	1400	88	C5
PIONEER PL	POM	POM		94	A3
PIPER AV	LA	LA45	7300	50	D6
PIPER PL	LA	LA45	7500	50	D6
PIPPIN DR	CO	LH		157	B6
PIRATE DR	RPV	PVP	3700	78	B3
PIRES AV	CER	ART	19400	81	D1
PIRES AV	CER	ART	17100	82	D5
PIRTLE ST	LA	LA39	2600	35	D3
PIRU ST	CO	COM	2000	64	E1
PIRU ST	CO	LA61	300	64	B1
PIRU ST	COM	COM	1700	64	D1
PISA PL	LA	SP	1900	78	D3
PISANI PL	LA	VEN	2000	49	D4
PISCES ST	AGH	AGO		100A	F2
PISTACHIO PL	PALM	LAN		171	A2
PISTOL CREEK CT	SAD	SAD		90	A3
PITAYA WY	PAR	PAR		65	E4
PITCAIRN WY	TOR	TOR	24800	73	B2
PITCHER RD	LA	LA68	2500	34	C1
PITCHESS PL	IND	LPUE	13300	48	B3
PITKIN ST	RM	RM	9200	38	B4
PITMAN AV	GLEN	GL02	1000	25	B2

283

1990 LOS ANGELES COUNTY STREET INDEX

PITSCH CYN RD
PRESTON AV
LOS ANGELES CO.

STREET	CITY	P.O. ZONE	BLOCK	PAGE	GRID
PITSCH CYN RD	CO	MAL		106	A4
PITTS AV	BLF	BLF	15900	66	A4
PITTS AV	PAR	PAR	15500	66	A4
PITTSFIELD CT	LB	LB03		76	F5
PITZER WK	CO	TOP	1500	109	D2
PIUMA AV	CER	ART	16200	66	E4
PIUMA AV	NWK	NWK	12000	60	E6
PIUMA AV	NWK	NWK	14300	66	E3
PIUMA RD	CO	CAL		107	F6
PIUMA RD	CO	CAL		114	A1
PIUMA RD	CO	MAL		107	F6
PIUMA RD	CO	MAL		114	A1
PIUTE	CO	AGO		106	D2
PIUTE CT	CO	SAU		124	B2
PIUTE DR	CO	SF		3	E2
PIUTE RD	CO	LR	10500	192	A6
PIUTE MESA RD	CO	LR		192	A6
PIVOT ST	DOW	DOW	7400	60	A3
PIXIE AV	LKD	LKD	3900	70	F3
PIXLEY ST	CO	COM	4500	65	C2
PIXLEY ST	COM	COM	1600	65	B2
PIZARRO ST	LA	LA26	1500	44	C1
PIZZO RANCH RD	LCF	LCF	5200	19	C1
PLACENTIA DR	CO	LPUE	1900	85	F3
PLACER DR	SAD	SAD		89	E1
PLACER PL	LA	LA32	4400	36	E4
PLACERITA MTWY	CO	NEW		128	A3
PLACERITA CY RD	CO	NEW	20300	127	G4
PLACERITA CY RD	CO	NEW		128	C4
PLACERITOS BLVD	SCLR	NEW	21100	127	D3
PLACID DR	CO	WHI	13400	61	D6
PLACID DR	CO	WHI	16000	84	C6
PLACIDIA AV	LA	NHO	4400	23	F3
PLACITA PL	SFS	SFS		61	A2
PLAID WY	PAR	PAR		65	E4
PLAIN TR	CO	TOP	500	109	E4
PLAINFIELD DR	RPV	PVP	28200	72	C5
PLAINVIEW AV	LA	TU	10000	10	E1
PLANADA AV	LA	LA42	6300	36	D1
PLANET CIR	LAN	LAN	44000	159	G4
PLANETT AV	DOW	DOW	10600	60	C3
PLANEWOOD DR	CO	WOH		13	C4
PLANO DR	CO	LPUE	2700	98	E6
PLANT AV	RB	RB	1900	62	E4
PLANTANA DR	LAM	LAM	14200	61	F6
PLANTANA DR	LAM	LAM	14200	82	F1
PLANTATION LN	WAL	WAL		93	C5
PLANTER ST	PR	PR	9400	60	F1
PLASKA AV	HPK	HPK	6200	53	A5
PLATA LN	CO	CAL		100	A3
PLATA ST	LA	LA26	3400	35	A5
PLATEAU AV	MPK	MPK	600	46	D3
PLATEAU DR	LA	SUN	10700	10	C2
PLATEAU DR	WCOV	WCOV	200	92	F1
PLATINA DR	DBAR	POM	100	94	A5
PLATINA DR	SCLR	VAL		127	H6
PLATT AV	LA	CAN	6400	5	E5
PLATT AV	LA	WOH	5600	5	E6
PLATT AV	LA	WOH	5600	100	E1
PLATT AV	LYN	LYN	3300	59	B5
PLATT ST	LB	LB05	1	70	C2
PLATT RIVER DR	WAL	WAL		92	F4
PLATT RIVER DR	WAL	WAL		93	A4
PLATZ RD	CO	ACT		189	F4
PLAYA CT	CUL	CUL		50	C4
PLAYA ST	CUL	CUL	11200	50	C4
PLAYA AZUL	AVA	AVA		77	A4
PLAYER DR	CO	VAL		126	J3
PLAYGROUND ST	LA	LA33	1400	45	B2
PLAZA	PALM	PALM		184	B1
PLAZA DR	COM	COM		65	A4
PLAZA DR	MTB	MTB		47	A5
PLAZA LN	LCF	LCF	700	19	C2
PLAZA ST	CMRC	LA40		53	F2
PLAZA ST	LYN	LYN	11200	59	A5
PLAZA WK	LCF	LCF		19	C2
PLAZA ANDRES	PVE	PVP		72	B5
PLAZA CHIVA	SCLR	VAL		127	A3
PLAZA D CORDOBA	CER	ART	20000	81	A3
PLAZA DEL AMO	LA	TOR	1300	68	E5
PLAZA DEL AMO	TOR	TOR		68	B5
PLAZA DEL AMO	TOR	TOR	1700	68	D4
PLAZA DL CAMINO	CLA	CLA		91	B3
PLAZA DE MADRID	CER	ART	20100	81	B3
PLAZA ESCOVAR	SCLR	VAL		127	B3
PLAZA FRANCISCO	PVE	PVP		72	B5
PLAZA GAVILAN	SCLR	VAL		127	A3
PLAZA LARIOS	SCLR	NEW		127	B4
PLAZA LIBRE	MTB	MTB	2500	46	B6
PLAZA LUNETA	SCLR	VAL		127	A3
PZ SAN ANTONIO	LA	LA31	1700	44	F1
PLEASANT AV	LA	LA33	1200	44	F3
PLEASANT ST	LAV	LAV		90	D1
PLEASANT ST	LYN	LYN	3200	59	A6
PLEASANT ST	PAS	PAS	200	27	A5
PLEASANT ST E	LB	LB05	100	70	C3
PLEASANT ST W	LB	LB05	1	70	C3
PLEASANT WY	CO	WHI	10500	55	B3
PLEASANT WY	PAS	PAS	1500	26	D5
PLEASANT CST LN	LHH	LAH	1500	98A	A2
PLEASNT DALE ST	SCLR	CYN	19000	124	J8
PLEASNT HILL DR	RHE	PVP		72	F3
PLEASNT HILL LN	SMAD	SMAD	400	28	D1
PLEASNT HOME DR	LPUE	LPUE	100	92	A6
PLEASANT MDW RD	DBAR	POM		97A	A4
PLEASANT RDG DR	CO	ALT	900	20	C3
PLEASANT VW AV	LA	LA65	1100	35	F4
PLEASANT VW AV	LA	VEN	900	49	C3
PLEASANT VW TER	GLEN	GL02	700	25	B1
PLEASURE WY	GLEN	MONT	3700	18	E2
PLENTY ST	LB	LB05	200	70	C2
PLEVKA AV	CO	LA02	8600	58	D2
PLOVER WY	CO	MAL		113	E5
PLUM AV	TOR	TOR	2000	68	C5
PLUM ST	COM	COM	300	64	E2
PLUM ST	LYN	LYN	11400	59	A5
PLUM WY	PALM	PALM		171	D4
PLUMA ST	LYN	LYN	3100	59	A4
PLUMA WY	MPK	MPK	600	46	B4
PLUMAS CIR	WAL	WAL		92	F6
PLUMAS ST	GLEN	GL05	1400	25	E5
PLUMAS ST	LA	LA65	3100	25	E5
PLUM CYN RD	CO	SAU		124	F5
PLUME DR	LAM	LAM	13900	82	E2
PLUMMER PL	WHOL	LA46	1100	34	A4
PLUMMER ST	LA	CHA	19700	6	B4
PLUMMER ST	LA	NOR	17000	7	E4
PLUMMER ST	LA	SF	16400	7	E4
PLUMMER ST	LA	SF	14800	8	A4
PLUMMER ST	LA	VAN	14300	8	A4
PLUMOSA DR	PAS	PAS	300	27	F5
PLUMTREE CT	LA	CAN		5	D3
PLUMTREE LN	LA	NOR		7	B2
PLUMTREE RD	RPV	PVP	1	77	D2
PLUMWOOD AV	SCLR	CYN	27200	124	J9
PLUNKETT ST	BLF	BLF	10100	66	C5
PLURIBUS ST	LB	LB08	7100	71	F5
PLUTON ST E	NWK	NWK	10800	60	E5
PLUTON ST E	NWK	NWK	11500	61	A5
PLYMOUTH BLVD N	LA	LA04	100	34	C6
PLYMOUTH BLVD S	LA	LA04	100	34	C6
PLYMOUTH BLVD S	LA	LA04	100	43	C1
PLYMOUTH BLVD S	LA	LA05	600	43	C2
PLYMOUTH BLVD S	LA	LA19	900	43	C3
PLYMOUTH BLVD S	LA	LA20	300	43	C2
PLYMOUTH CT	PALM	PALM		183	D1
PLYMOUTH DR	PAS	PAS	200	27	A1
PLYMOUTH RD	CLA	CLA	600	91	B3
PLYMOUTH RD	CO	SAU		123	E4
PLYMOUTH RD	SMAR	PAS	400	37	B2
PLYMOUTH ST	GLDR	GLDR	400	89	C2
PLYMOUTH ST E	ING	IN02	100	50	F5
PLYMOUTH ST E	ING	IN02	100	51	A5
PLYMOUTH ST E	LB	LB05	100	70	C2
PLYMOUTH ST W	ING	IN02	100	50	F5
PLYMOUTH ST W	LB	LB05	100	70	C2
POCAHANTAS AV	CO	CAST	30000	123	A4
POCASSET DR	CO	WHI		55	E2
POCATELLO AV	CO	LPUE	2200	98	D5
POCHO TR	CO	CHA		1A	C5
POCO WY	MPK	MPK	300	46	B3
POCONO CT	PR	PR		47	A6
POCONO CT	PR	PR		55	A1
POCONO ST	CO	LPUE	16000	92	C5
POCONO ST	LPUE	LPUE	15700	92	A4
PODD CT	SCLR	CYN		124	G9
POE AV	LA	WOH	4400	13	E3
POE PKWY	CO	NEW		126	G3
POEMA PL	CO	CHA		1A	B6
POINCIANA ST	CO	WHI	10600	55	A6
POINCIANA ST	CO	WHI	10600	61	A1
POINCIANA ST	PR	PR	9600	54	F6
POINDEXTER ST	CO	LA44	1200	57	E5
POINSETTIA AV	MON	MON	100	29	B3
POINSETTIA AV N	COM	COM	100	65	B3
POINSETTIA AV N	MB	MB	100	62	C4
POINSETTIA AV S	COM	COM	100	65	B3
POINSETTIA AV S	MB	MB	100	62	C4
POINSETTIA CT	CUL	CUL	9000	42	D6
POINSETTIA DR	WHOL	LA46	1100	34	A4
POINSETTIA PL N	LA	LA36	100	34	A6
POINSETTIA PL N	LA	LA46	700	34	A3
POINSETTIA PL N	WHOL	LA46	1000	34	A4
POINSETTIA PL S	LA	LA36	100	34	A6
POINSETTIA ST	ELM	ELM		47	F3
POINSETTIA ST	LB	LB05	1200	65	D6
POINT ARENA CT	SCLR	NEW	19100	127	H3
POINT ARENA PL	CER	ART		82	D6
PT ARGUELLO PL	CER	ART		82	C6
POINTCEDAR DR	WCOV	WCOV		97	A2
PT CONCPTION PL	CER	ART		82	C6
POINTED OAK PL	AGH	AGO		102	F3
POINTER DR	CO	WAL		97	C4
POINTER LN	LA	LA77		32	E2
PT O WOODS DR	AZU	AZU	500	86	C4
POINT REYES PL	CER	ART		82	C6
POINT VIEW ST	LA	LA34	1900	42	E4
POINT VIEW ST	LA	LA35	1000	42	E3
POKER PLANT CT	PALM	PALM		183	F3
POLA WK	LA	LA65		36	A3
POLARIS DR	GLEN	GL08		18	E6
POLARIS WY	LAV	LAV		90	E2
POLK AV	CO	ACT		189	G2
POLK ST	LA	SF	13600	2	D4
POLK WY	MPK	MPK	1700	46	D3
POLLARD LN	COV	COV	500	88	E4
POLLARD ST	LA	LA42	6400	36	D1
POLLOCK ST	CO	RM	1200	46	E4
POLLY AV	CO	LAW		63	C3
POLO CT	PALM	PALM		171	F4
POLY HI CT	LB	LB13		75	D3
POLYNESIAN DR	LB	LB05	800	65	C6
POLY VISTA	POM	POM		93	E3
POMANDER PL	LCF	LCF	600	19	C4
POMEGRANATE PL	PALM	LAN		171	B2
POMEGRANATE RD	RPV	PVP	1	77	E3
POMELLO DR	CLA	CLA	600	96	C5
POMELO AV	MPK	MPK	300	46	D2
POMELO DR	LA	CAN	6900	5	E3
POMERING RD	DOW	DOW	11800	59	F4
POMERING RD	DOW	DOW	9600	60	A3
POMEROY AV	LA	LA33	1600	45	B3
POMEROY ST	CO	LA63	3300	45	C3
POMITA PL	SCLR	VAL		127	H6
POMONA AV	LB	LB03	200	76	B6
POMONA AV	LB	LB03	1	80	B1
POMONA AV E	MON	MON	100	29	B5
POMONA AV W	MON	MON	100	29	B5
POMONA BLVD	CO	LA22	5100	45	F5
POMONA BLVD	CO	LA22	5200	46	A5
POMONA BLVD	MTB	MTB	2200	46	A5
POMONA BLVD	POM	POM	3300	93	F4
POMONA BLVD	POM	POM	1600	94	A3
POMONA BLVD E	MPK	MPK	100	46	A5
POMONA BLVD W	MPK	MPK	100	46	A5
POMONA CT	CLA	CLA	800	91	A3
POMONA DR	WAL	WAL		93	C3
POMONA FRWY	CO			47	B4
POMONA FRWY	CO			48	A5
POMONA FRWY	CO			85	D1
POMONA FRWY	IND	LPUE		98	B2
POMONA FRWY	LA	LA		45	C5
POMONA FRWY	MPK	MPK		46	A5
POMONA ST	LA	LA31	3400	36	B5
POMONA MALL E	POM	POM	100	94	E2
POMONA MALL W	POM	POM	100	94	E2
POMPANO ST	CO	MAL		114	E1
POMPEII WY	LA	BUR		17	B1
PONCA AV	LA	NHO	4300	24	A3
PONCE AV	LA	CAN	6400	12	A2
PONCE AV	LA	WOH	5600	12	A5
PONCE AV	LA	WOH	5200	13	A1
POND AV	CO	PALM	38400	172	G8
POND AV	PALM	PALM		183	G2
POND CIR	LAV	LAV		90	B1
PONDERA CIR	LA	CAN	7200	5	E3
PONDERA ST E	LAN	LAN	300	160	C5
PONDERA ST W	LAN	LAN	100	160	B5
PONDEROSA	ELM	ELM		48	A6
PONDEROSA CT	LKD	LKD		66	B6
PONDEROSA DR	AZU	AZU	900	86	E5
PONDEROSA DR	LA	LA49	13200	30	E5
PONDEROSA LN	RHE	PVP	5000	72	F3
PONDEROSA ST	BLF	BLF	10300	66	D6
PONDEROSA ST	LAN	LAN		160	F6
PONDOSA AV	CO	SGAB	5300	37	F4
PONER ST	LAM	LAM	14300	82	F1
PONER ST	LAM	LAM	14300	83	A1
PONET DR	LA	LA28	2100	34	E2
PONTE CORVO RD	CO	SAU		125	G1
PONTENOVA AV	CO	LPUE	800	85	E3
PONTEVEDRA DR	RPV	SP	27800	73	D6
PONTIAC ST	CO	GL14	3100	11	D6
PONTIAC ST	CO	GL14	2600	18	E1
PONTIAC ST	GLEN	GL14	3200	11	C5
PONTINE AV	CAR	CAR	21000	69	D4
PONTIUS AV	LA	LA25	1500	41	E3
PONTIUS AV	LA	LA64	2200	41	E3
PONTLAVOY AV	NWK	NWK	14300	82	D2
PONTOON PL	LA	LA49	13100	40	F3
PONTY ST	CO	LA47	1600	57	E4
PONY LN	RHE	PVP	1	73	B4
PONY RANCH RD	DUA	DUA	1600	29	D5
POOLE AV	LA	SUN	9900	9	F4
POOLE AV	LA	SV	8300	16	F1
POPE AV	LYN	LYN	10900	59	D6
POPE AV	LYN	LYN	11700	65	C1
POPENOE RD	LHH	LAH	1200	98A	B2
POPLAR AV	CO	LPUE	15000	48	D6
POPLAR AV	MTB	MTB	700	46	E6
POPLAR AV	MTB	MTB	100	54	E1
POPLAR BLVD	ALH	ALH	2200	36	F4
POPLAR BLVD	LA	LA32	5300	36	F4
POPLAR CIR	PALM	LAN		171	B2
POPLAR CT	LAN	LAN		160	F4
POPLAR CT	LAN	LAN		160	F6
POPLAR DR	CO	AGO		107	B2
POPLAR DR	LYN	LYN	2900	59	A4
POPLAR LN	PAS	PAS	100	26	F2
POPLAR PL	CO	HPK	2400	58	F1
POPLAR PL	SOG	SOG	2500	58	F1
POPLAR ST	CO	SAU		124	D2
POPLAR ST	LA	LA65	2600	35	F4
POPLAR ST E	COM	COM	200	64	E2
POPLAR ST W	COM	COM	100	64	E2
POPLAR WY	MTB	MTB	100	54	E2
POPLAR GLEN CIR	SCLR	VAL		124	B5
POPPY AV	COM	COM	900	65	A1
POPPY AV	MON	MON	100	29	C3
POPPY DR	CO	TOP		100	E5
POPPY LN	GLDR	GLDR	300	87	D6
POPPY LN	POM	POM	300	94	E5
POPPY ST	LA	LA42	900	26	C5
POPPY ST	LB	LB05	200	65	C6
POPPY ST	LB	LB05	2900	65	F6
POPPY ST	LB	LB05	3700	66	A6
POPPY TR	RH	PVP	1	73	B6
POPPY FLDS DR E	CO	ALT	300	20	B4
POPPY FLDS DR W	CO	ALT	200	19	F3
POPPY FLDS DR W	CO	ALT	100	20	A3
POPPYGLEN LN	CER	ART		82	B4
POPPY MEADOW ST	CO	CYN		125	E5
POPPY PEAK DR	LA	LA42	6100	26	C6
POPPY PEAK DR	PAS	PAS	1400	26	D5
POPPY PEAK WK	LA	LA42	6200	26	C6
POPPYSEED LN	CO	CYN	28900	125	E7
POPPYSEED PL	CO	CAL		100A	F6
POPS RD	DUA	DUA	1200	29	D5
POPULUS AV	PALM	PALM	37200	184	A2
PORT RD	CO	LA66	12400	50	B4
PORT RD	CUL	CUL	11400	50	C3
PORT RD	LA	CUL	11800	50	B4
PORTAC RIDGE RD	CO	LH		157	C6
PORTADA DR	CO	WHI	11000	84	C4
PORTADA DR	WHI	WHI	9300	84	C3
PORTAFINO PL	WHI	WHI		84	C1
PORTAGE CIR DR	CO	TOP	22800	109	A1
PORTAL AV	LA	LA45	8600	56	D3
PORTER AV	CO	ALT	2300	20	C5
PORTER LN	HB	RB	400	62	C5
PORTER ST	GLEN	GL05	300	25	E5
PORTER ST	LA	LA21	2300	44	E6
PORTERDALE DR	CO	MAL		112	E5
PORTER VLY DR	LA	NOR	11300	1	A6
PORTER VLY DR	LA	NOR		7	A1
PORTIA ST	LA	LA26	1300	35	C6
PORTICO PL	LA	ENC	4400	21	E3
PORTLAND AV	PALM	PALM		183	J1
PORTLAND ST	LA	LA07	2100	44	A5
PORTLAND TER	ALH	ALH	800	37	B4
PORTNER ST	LA	LA65	3300	35	E1
PORTNER ST E	WCOV	WCOV	1000	92	C2
PORTNER ST W	WCOV	WCOV	900	92	B2
PORTOBELLO DR	TOR	TOR	2500	73	B3
PORTOFINO PL	LA	LA77	10800	32	D3
PORTOFINO WY	RB	RB	1	67	C3
PORTO GRANDE DR	DBAR	POM		97	F2
PORTOLA AV	GLEN	GL06	600	25	D3
PORTOLA AV	LA	LA32	3200	36	E4
PORTOLA AV	TOR	TOR	600	68	D4
PORTOLA CIR	WAL	WAL		92	F5
PORTOLA CT	POM	WAL		94	B4
PORTOLA DR	ARC	ARC	900	28	B5
PORTOLA DR	DUA	DUA	1000	29	D4
PORTOLA DR	LA	BH	9800	32	F2
PORTOLA DR	PALM	PALM		171	E4
PORTOLA ST	SAD	SAD	300	90	A2
PORTOLA TER	LA	LA42		36	D3
PORTOLA TR	LA	BH	9800	32	F2
PORTO MARINA WY	LA	PP	17500	115	F4
PORTO RICO DR	CO	LPUE	13900	48	B5
PORTSHEAD RD	CO	MAL	5800	110	C4
PORTSIDE DR	CO	WAL		97	B5
PORTSIDE PL	AGH	AGO		102	D3
PORTSMOUTH DR	PALM	PALM		172	F9
PORTSMOUTH DR	PALM	PALM		183	F1
PORTSMOUTH RD	LA	SP	2300	78	E5
PORTSMOUTH WY	MB	MB		62	D3
PORTUGAL CT	NWK	NWK		82	B4
PORTUGUSE BD RD	RH	PVP	1	73	A6
PORTUGUSE BD RD	RH	PVP		78	A2
POSADA DR	SCLR	VAL		124	C6
POSEIDON	WCOV	WCOV		48	F2
POSEIDON AV	CER	ART	19100	81	A2
POSETANO RD	LA	PP	17400	40	A4
POSEY LN	LA	CAN		5	E2
POSEY ST	CO	LA63		45	D3
POSEY WY	RPV	PVP	6900	72	C5
POSSUM RIDGE RD	RHE	PVP	1	78	A1
POST AV	POM	POM	500	94	E5
POST AV	TOR	TOR	1300	68	D4
POST ST	SOG	SOG	3100	59	A1
POST WY	LA	LA45		56	C4
POSTAL RD	LA	LA45		56	D3
POSTMASTER AV	LA	HAC	24200	73	E1
POSTON ST	LAN	LAN	700	160	A6
POTOMAC	WCOV	WCOV		92	D4
POTOMAC AV	LA	LA08	3900	51	A1
POTOMAC AV	LA	LA16	2800	43	B6
POTOMAC DR	LA	LA08	4000	51	A1
POTOMAC WY	CLA	CLA		91	B2
POTOSI AV	LA	NHO	3600	23	A5
POTRERO AV	ELM	ELM	2500	47	C3
POTRERO AV	SELM	ELM	1200	47	C3
POTRERO RD	CO	MAL		111	B2
POTRERO CYN RD	CO	VAL		126	D1
POTRERO GRDE DR	CO	RM	900	46	D4
POTRERO GRDE DR	MPK	MPK	300	46	D4
POTRILLO RD	RH	PVP	2200	73	D5
POTTER AV	LA	NHO	8200	16	B2
POTTER DR	CO	MAL		114	A4
POTTER DR	PALM	PALM		183	G2
POTTER ST	BLF	BLF	9800	66	C2
POTTER ST	NWK	NWK	10600	66	E2
POTTER ST	NWK	NWK	11500	82	A2
POTTER FIRE RD	CO	NOR		1	A3
POULTER DR	CO	WHI	14600	61	F5
POUNDS AV	CO	WHI	11500	84	D6
POUNDS AV	WHI	WHI	9800	84	D3
POWDERHN RCH RD	CO	TOP		109	B4
POWELL AV	AZU	AZU		86	E6
POWELL DR	SCLR	NEW	23700	127	A4
POWER ST	HB	RB	1700	62	C6
POWER ST	LA	LA12		44	F1
POWER LINE RD	CO	CAST		123	F3
POWERS AV	PR	PR	9100	55	A2
POWERS PL	LA	LA06		44	A3
POWERS ST	POM	POM	2100	94	E5
POXON PL	WCOV	WCOV		88	B6
POYNETTE ST	GLEN	GL14	3500	18	C1
POZO DR	CO	LPUE		85	F5
PRA DR	PR	PR	8600	54	F2
PRADO ST	LA	LA23	1000	53	C1
PRAGER AV	LA	SF	11400	3	C6
PRAIRIE AV	CO	LAW	15200	63	B4
PRAIRIE AV	HAW	HAW	11200	57	B4
PRAIRIE AV	HAW	HAW	12800	63	B4
PRAIRIE AV	LAW	LAW	15800	63	B4
PRAIRIE AV	TOR	TOR	16900	63	B4
PRAIRIE AV	TOR	TOR	18300	68	B1
PRAIRIE AV N	ING	IN01	200	51	B6
PRAIRIE AV N	ING	IN01	100	57	B1
PRAIRIE AV S	ING	IN01	100	57	B1
PRAIRIE AV S	ING	IN03	10000	57	B4
PRAIRIE AV S	ING	IN04	10001	57	B4
PRAIRIE DR	SAD	SAD		95A	A6
PRAIRIE PL	GLDR	GLDR	100	87	D5
PRAIRIE ST	LA	CHA	20300	6	E5
PRAIRIE ST	LA	NOR	17000	7	D5
PRAIRIE FLCN DR	LAV	LAV		95A	E5
PRAIRIE VIEW RD	CO	PALM	39600	175	D6
PRAIRIEVISTA PL	CO	LAN		171	C2
PRASA RD	LA	WOH	4200	13	D4
PRATHER AV	WHI	WHI	11500	55	D5
PREBLE AV	LA	WIL	800	74	E4
PRECIADO ST	POM	POM	300	94	E1
PRECISE ST	LAN	LAN		159	G6
PREMIERE AV	BLF	BLF	13400	66	B2
PREMIERE AV	DOW	DOW	13100	66	B1
PREMIERE AV	LKD	LKD	4900	71	C2
PREMIERE AV	LB	LB08	4700	71	C2
PREMIUM ST	LB	LB08	6700	71	E6
PRENTISS AV	PALM	PALM	37800	172	E9
PRESADO DR	DBAR	POM		97	E4
PRESCOTT AV	SAD	SAD		89	D4
PRESCOTT CT	LA	LA18	3000	43	D6
PRESCOTT ST	PAS	PAS	400	27	B1
PRESCOTT ST	PR	PR		47	B6
PRESCOTT ST	PR	PR		55	B1
PRESIDENT AV	LA	HAC	23500	73	E1
PRESIDENT DR	CO	MAL		113	E4
PRESIDIO DR	CO	LA08	4400	51	B3
PRESIDIO DR	CO	LA43	4700	51	B3
PRESLEY CIR	CER	ART	18900	81	C1
PRESNELL ST	LA	LA66	12600	50	A4
PRESSON PL	LA	LA69	8200	33	E3
PRESTINA WY	WAL	WAL		93	B5
PRENTISS AV	PALM	PALM		183	E1
PRESTON AV	LA	LA26	1800	35	D4

INDEX

284

1990 LOS ANGELES COUNTY STREET INDEX

PRESTON CT

RAILROAD AV

LOS ANGELES CO.

STREET	CITY	P.O. ZONE	BLOCK	PAGE	GRID
PRESTON CT	POM	POM	800	94	F4
PRESTON WK	CO	CAST		123	C2
PRESTON WY	LA	LA66	12400	49	E2
PRESTON WY	LA	VEN	1200	49	D2
PRESTON TRLS AV	LA	NOR	11700	1	A5
PRESTWICK	ELM	ELM		48	A5
PRESTWICK DR	LA	LA27	3700	35	A1
PRESTWICK WY	WAL	WAL		93	D6
PREUSS RD	LA	LA34	1900	42	D4
PREUSS RD	LA	LA35	1600	42	D4
PREWETT ST	LA	LA31	2700	36	B5
PRIAM DR	BG	BELL	6500	54	B6
PRIAM DR	BG	BELL	7400	60	A1
PRICE AV	POM	POM	900	95	A2
PRICE DR	BUR	BUR	600	17	C3
PRICE DR	LAV	LAV		90	E2
PRICE ST	LA	LA27	4300	35	A2
PRICEDALE AV	WCOV	WCOV	1000	92	B3
PRICETOWN AV	CAR	CAR	19000	69	D1
PRICHARD ST	BLF	BLF	9200	66	B2
PRICHARD ST	CO	LPUE	13500	48	C3
PRICHARD ST	DOW	DOW	8400	66	A1
PRICHARD ST	LPUE	LPUE	13600	48	E5
PRIER RD	CO	TOP		109	D3
PRIMAVERA AV	LA	LA65	3600	35	F2
PRIMAVERA RD	GLDR	GLDR	700	87	C4
PRIMAVERA ST	PAS	PAS	3100	27	F2
PRIMAVERA WK	LA	LA65		35	F2
PRIME CT	PAS	PAS	1300	27	B1
PRIMEAUX AV	WCOV	WCOV	1200	92	C3
PRIMERA AV	LA	LA68	3200	24	B6
PRIMERA PL	LA	LA68	3200	24	B6
PRIMM WY	TOR	TOR	3300	73	B2
PRIMROSE AV	CO	MON	2200	29	B6
PRIMROSE AV	LA	LA68	6100	34	C2
PRIMROSE AV	SPAS	SPAS	1900	37	A4
PRIMROSE AV	TEC	TEC	5700	38	B3
PRIMROSE AV N	ALH	ALH	1	37	A4
PRIMROSE AV N	MON	MON	100	29	B4
PRIMROSE AV S	ALH	ALH	1	37	A4
PRIMROSE AV S	MON	MON	100	29	B4
PRIMROSE AV S	MON	MON	2300	39	A1
PRIMROSE CT	PALM	PALM		171	H6
PRIMROSE LN	DOW	DOW	8100	60	C2
PRIMROSE PL	GLDR	GLDR	19500	89	A1
PRIMROSE WY	POM	POM	1900	94	F5
PRINCE AV	CO	LA02	8600	58	D2
PRINCE ST	LA	LA31	2300	36	B6
PRINCELY CT	PALM	PALM		173	A9
PRINCES DR	GLEN	GL07	1500	25	E1
PRINCESS DR	LA	LA42	6700	36	D1
PRINCSS ANNE RD	LCF	LCF	5000	19	B2
PRINCETON AV	CLA	CLA	100	91	A4
PRINCETON AV	LA	LA26	2100	35	D4
PRINCETON CT	LAV	LAV		90	E3
PRINCETON DR	GLEN	GL05	1100	25	E6
PRINCETON DR	LA	VEN	900	49	D4
PRINCETON DR	WAL	WAL		93	B4
PRINCETON RD	ARC	ARC	500	28	D4
PRINCETON ST	CO	LA23	3700	45	C5
PRINCETON ST	GLEN	GL04	1800	35	C1
PRINCETON ST	SM	SM	800	41	B4
PRINCETON WY	LAN	LAN		159	G7
PRINCIPIA DR	GLEN	GL06	1000	25	E2
PRINCIPIO DR	CO	MAL		111	E5
PRIOR AV	CO	LPUE	500	92	B4
PRIORY ST	BG	BELL	5500	59	F1
PRISCILLA AV	DOW	DOW	8000	59	F6
PRISCILLA DR	WCOV	WCOV		92	E6
PRISCILLA LN	BUR	BUR	600	24	A2
PRISCILLA ST	DOW	DOW	8400	60	A6
PRISCILLA ST	DOW	DOW	8400	66	B1
PRISCILLA ST	LAM	LAM	14100	82	E1
PRISCILLA ST	NWK	NWK	10500	66	D1
PRISCILLA ST	NWK	NWK	12800	82	C1
PRISCILLA WY	CLA	CLA	600	91	A3
PRISMO DR	LA	LA65	2600	25	F6
PRITCHARD WY	CO	LPUE		98	A5
PRIVATEER CT	LA	VEN		49	D6
PRIVATEER ST	LA	VEN		49	C6
PRIVET AV	ELM	ELM	5000	39	A4
PROCK ST	POM	POM	900	94	C2
PROCTOR AV	CO	LPUE	13800	48	C4
PROCTOR AV	IND	LPUE	14100	48	C4
PROCTOR ST	CO	LPUE	13000	48	A3
PROCTOR ST	LA	WIL	400	74	C2
PRODUCE CT	LA	LA21	800	44	D5
PRODUCE ROW	LA	LA21	1200	44	D5
PRODUCE ST	LA	LA21		44	E4
PRODUCER WY	POM	POM		94	A3
PROGRESS LN	IRW	BAP		88	B3
PROGRESS LN	PAS	PAS	1200	26	F2
PROGRESS PL	LA	LA33	400	44	F2
PROMENADE	LA	LA44		51	F6
PROMENADE WY	CO	MDR		49	D4
PROMENADE THE	SM	SM	1100	49	A2

STREET	CITY	P.O. ZONE	BLOCK	PAGE	GRID
PROMONTORY PL	AGH	AGO		102	F3
PROMONTORY PL	LAM	LAM		83	C1
PROMONTORY PL	WCOV	WCOV		92	F3
PROMONTORY RD	LA	LA49		32	A3
PRONDALL CT	CAR	CAR	17500	64	C5
PROSA CT	CO	WAL		97	B3
PROSPECT	PALM	PALM		171	J7
PROSPECT AV	BELL	BELL	6200	53	D5
PROSPECT AV	BUR	BUR	1	24	E1
PROSPECT AV	CAR	LB10	21000	70	A4
PROSPECT AV	CO	GL14	2400	18	D1
PROSPECT AV	CO	GL14	2600	18	D1
PROSPECT AV	CUL	CUL	3800	50	B1
PROSPECT AV	GLEN	GL14	3200	11	D6
PROSPECT AV	HB	RB	800	62	D6
PROSPECT AV	HB	RB	100	67	D1
PROSPECT AV	LA	LA27	4600	34	F3
PROSPECT AV	LA	LA27	3900	35	A3
PROSPECT AV	LA	VEN	2200	49	D3
PROSPECT AV	LB	LB03	100	76	B6
PROSPECT AV	LB	LB04	1000	76	B4
PROSPECT AV	LB	LB14	300	76	B6
PROSPECT AV	MAY	MAY	6000	53	D5
PROSPECT AV	MB	MB	400	62	C5
PROSPECT AV	MON	MON	200	29	B2
PROSPECT AV	RB	RB	1000	67	E6
PROSPECT AV	RM	RM	2700	46	E2
PROSPECT AV	SGAB	SGAB	1000	37	E5
PROSPECT AV	SM	SM	2900	49	C2
PROSPECT AV	SPAS	SPAS	500	36	F1
PROSPECT AV N	RB	RB	100	67	D2
PROSPECT AV S	RB	RB	100	67	E3
PROSPECT BLVD	PAS	PAS	400	26	E2
PROSPECT CIR	SPAS	SPAS	400	36	F1
PROSPECT CR	PAS	PAS	600	26	E3
PROSPECT DR	GLEN	GL05	700	25	D6
PROSPECT DR	LA	LA46	1700	33	F3
PROSPECT DR	POM	POM	1100	94	D4
PROSPECT DR	SPAS	SPAS	800	36	F1
PROSPECT LN	SPAS	SPAS	600	36	F1
PROSPECT SQ	PAS	PAS	400	26	E3
PROSPECT TER	PAS	PAS	400	26	E3
PROSPECT TR	LA	LA46	2000	33	E2
PROSPECTOR PL	PALM	PALM		171	D9
PROSPECTORS RD	DBAR	POM		93	F6
PROSPECT VLY DR	DBAR	POM	23500	94	A6
PROSPERO DR	CO	GLDR	5800	88	F1
PROSPERO DR	GLDR	GLDR	5100	88	F2
PROSPERO DR	WCOV	WCOV		92	F2
PROSPERO DR N	COV	COV	100	88	F3
PROSPERO DR S	COV	COV	400	88	F6
PROSSER AV	LA	LA25	1800	41	F3
PROSSER AV	LA	LA25	1800	42	A3
PROSSER AV	LA	LA64	2200	42	A3
PROVENCE RD	CO	SGAB	6300	37	F1
PROVIDENCE CT	LB	LB03		76	F5
PROVIDENCE PL	CLA	CLA		91	A1
PROVIDENCE RD	PALM	PALM		171	J6
PROVIDNCIA AV E	BUR	BUR	100	17	F5
PROVIDNCIA AV W	BUR	BUR	100	24	D1
PROVIDENCIA ST	LA	WOH	21200	13	B2
PROVIDENT RD	AGH	AGO	27000	100A	D5
PROVO AV	LA	TU	9900	11	B4
PROVON LN	LA	LA34	3200	42	C5
PRUDENCIA DR	WHI	WHI	16300	84	D3
PRUDENT ST	LA	LA12		44	E1
PRUESS AV	DOW	DOW	11400	60	A4
PRUITT DR	RB	RB	500	67	F1
PRUITT DR	TOR	TOR	19000	67	F2
PRYOR PL	LA	HAC	23100	68	E6
PSOMAS WY	LA	LA66	13000	49	D2
PUDDINGSTONE DR	LAV	LAV	800	90	A4
PUDDINGSTONE DR	SAD	SAD	100	90	A4
PUEBLA DR	GLEN	GL07	1500	25	E1
PUEBLO AV	LA	LA32	3100	36	D5
PUEBLO CT	CLA	CLA		91	B2
PUEBLO CT	CMRC	LA40		53	F2
PUEBLO DR	SCLR	VAL		124	A1
PUEBLO DR	MPK	MPK		45	F2
PUEBLO DR	RM	RM		46	F4
PUEBLO ST	CO	CHA		6	C1
PUEBLO CREST LN	LHH	LAH		84	F2
PUENTE AV	BAP	BAP	3500	39	E6
PUENTE AV	BAP	BAP	1500	48	C3
PUENTE AV	CO	LPUE	300	48	C3
PUENTE AV	IND	LPUE	100	48	C3
PUENTE AV E	WCOV	WCOV	1000	88	B5
PUENTE AV W	WCOV	WCOV	1000	88	A5
PUENTE RD	LA	WOH	20900	13	D3
PUENTE ST	CO	COV		89	A5
PUENTE ST	LHH	LAH		98A	C3
PUENTE ST	SAD	COV		89	D6
PUENTE ST E	COV	COV	100	88	E5
PUENTE ST E	COV	COV	1100	89	B5
PUENTE ST W	COV	COV	100	88	E5
PUERCO MTY	CO	MAL	1100	113	D3

STREET	CITY	P.O. ZONE	BLOCK	PAGE	GRID
PUERCO CYN RD	CO	MAL	3100	113	D4
PUERTA AV	CO	PALM	38600	172	F8
PUERTA DL NORTE	PVE	PVP	100	72	D2
PUERTO DEL MAR	LA	PP	400	40	C4
PUESTA DEL SOL	CO	MAL	4900	111	A4
PUESTA DEL SOL	POM	POM		90	C6
PUESTA DEL SOL	WHI	WHI	15900	84	C2
PULIDO CT	CO	CAL	4100	13	A4
PULLMAN LN	RB	RB	1700	67	E1
PULLMAN ST	LA	LA32	900	36	D3
PULLMAN ST	LA	LA42	200	36	D3
PUMA CANYON LN	GLDR	GLDR		87	C6
PUMA CANYON LN	GLDR	GLDR		89	C1
PUMICE ST	NWK	NWK	13400	82	D2
PUMICE ST	SFS	SFS	13600	82	D2
PUNAHOU ST	CO	ALT	300	20	B4
PUNCH BOWL RD	CO	PEAR		192	D3
PUNTA PL	PVE	PVP	1700	72	C3
PUNTA WY	MPK	MPK	1100	46	B3
PUNTA ALTA DR	LA	LA08	4000	50	F2
PUNTA DEL ESTE	CO	LPUE	2000	85	F3
PUNTO DE VIS DR	CO	CAL		108	A5
PURCELL DR	CO	LA63	4100	45	D3
PURCHE AV	CO	GAR	14400	63	D5
PURCHE AV	GAR	GAR	12800	63	D1
PURCHE AV	HAW	IN03	11800	57	D5
PURCHE AV	TOR	TOR	16900	63	D5
PURDIN AV	PAR	PAR	13800	65	E1
PURDUE AV	CUL	CUL	5100	50	B3
PURDUE AV	LA	CUL	4300	50	B3
PURDUE AV	LA	LA25	1500	41	D4
PURDUE AV	LA	LA64	2200	41	E4
PURDUE AV	LA	LA66	3000	41	F6
PURDUE AV	LA	LA66	3400	49	F1
PURDUE AV	LA	LA66	3500	50	A1
PURDUE DR	CLA	CLA	600	91	A2
PURDY AV	BG	BELL	6400	53	F6
PURDY AV	BG	BELL	7300	59	E1
PURITAN AV	DOW	DOW	8000	59	F6
PURITAN ST	DOW	DOW	7800	59	F6
PURITAN ST	DOW	DOW	8300	60	A6
PURITAN MINE RD	CO	ACT		182	A8
PURPLE DR	CO	TOP		109	A2
PURPLEBUSH AV	LAN	LAN	42200	159	A9
PURPLEBUSH AV	CO	LAN	42000	171	A1
PURPLE RIDGE AV	CO	SF		3	E2
PURPLE RIDGE DR	RPV	PVP	6900	72	C5
PURPLE SAGE LN	CO	ALT	1	20	A3
PURPLE SAGE LN	PALM	PALM		183	G3
PURTELL DR	LCF	LCF	4300	19	A2
PURVIS DR	BUR	BUR	2500	17	C3
PUTNAM ST	LA	LA39	2800	35	B3
PUTNAM ST	WHI	WHI	12300	55	D6
PUTNAM ST	WHI	WHI	12600	61	D1
PUTNEY LN	ING	IN01		57	C2
PUTNEY RD	LA	LA64	10500	42	A4
PUTNEY RD	PAS	PAS	1600	19	D6
PUTT PL	CO	LLAN	30800	192	J3
PYRAMID DR	LA	LA46	7300	34	A1
PYRAMID PL	LA	LA46	7300	33	F1
PYRENEES DR	ALH	ALH	1600	36	F6
PYRITES ST	LA	LA32	2800	36	C5

Q

STREET	CITY	P.O. ZONE	BLOCK	PAGE	GRID
Q ST E	LA	WIL	100	74	C2
Q ST W	LA	WIL	100	74	C2
QUADRO VECCHIO	LA	PP	200	40	A4
QUAIL CT	LAV	LAV		95A	E5
QUAIL DR	LA	LA65	400	36	A3
QUAIL DR W	PALM	PALM		172	B5
QUAIL LN	CO	SAU		188	C1
QUAIL LN	LAM	LAM		84	B6
QUAIL LN	NWK	NWK	12800	61	56
QUAIL LN	NWK	NWK	12800	82	C1
QUAIL RD	CO	SAU		182	A7
QUAILBROOK CIR	PALM	PALM		183	H7
QUAIL CANYON RD	GLEN	GL14		11	D4
QUAIL COVE WY	CO	LPUE		98	D6
QUAIL CREEK LN	POM	POM		94	C5
QUAIL CREEK PL	LA	NOR		1	A6
QUAIL CREEK RD	LA	NOR	11300	1	A6
QUAILHILL DR	RPV	PVP	28200	72	D5
QUAIL HOLLOW CT	AZU	AZU	1300	86	C4
QUAIL RIDGE RD	RH	PVP	1	78	A1
QUAIL ROW LN	CAR	CAR		69	E6
QUAIL RUN DR	AGH	AGO		102	E3
QUAIL RUN DR	DBAR	POM		97	A2
QUAIL SPGS PATH	GLDR	GLDR	800	87	D4
QUAIL SUMIT CIR	POM	POM		94	D5
QUAIL SUMMIT DR	DBAR	POM		97A	A3
QUAIL VALLEY LN	WCOV	WCOV		93	A2
QUAIL VALLEY RD	CO	CAST		123	C1
QUAIL VALLEY RD	CO	LAV		90	F1
QUAILWOOD DR	RPV	PVP	29300	72	E6
QUAINT ST	AGH	AGO		100A	B2

STREET	CITY	P.O. ZONE	BLOCK	PAGE	GRID
QUAKERTOWN AV	LA	CAN	6400	12	F5
QUAKERTOWN AV	LA	CHA	9500	6	F4
QUAKERTOWN AV	LA	NOR	8700	6	F6
QUAKERTOWN AV	LA	WOH	5100	13	F1
QUANTICO LN	CO	TOP	800	109	A3
QUAN YIN CT	LA	LA12		44	E2
QUAN YIN RD	LA	LA12		44	E2
QUARRY DR	CO	SF		3	F2
QUARRY RIDGE RD	LAN	LAN	8900	158	G9
QUARTERDECK CT	LA	VEN		49	D6
QUARTERDECK ST	LA	VEN		49	C6
QUARTERHORSE LN	RHE	PVP		72	D6
QUARTERMASTR CT	LA	SP		79	A5
QUARTERMASTR RD	LA	SP		79	A5
QUARTZ AV	LA	CAN	8600	6	F6
QUARTZ AV	LA	CAN	6400	12	F5
QUARTZ AV	LA	CHA	9500	6	F4
QUARTZ AV	LA	NOR	8700	6	F6
QUARTZ AV	SOG	SOG	8400	59	C2
QUARTZ HILL CTO	PALM	PALM	40800	171	D3
QUARTZ HILL CTO	PALM	LAN		171	D3
QUARTZ HILL RD	CO	LAN	4300	171	D1
QUARTZITE CT	PALM	PALM		183	E3
QUARTZITE ST	PALM	PALM		183	E3
QUARY LN	CO	POM		97	C5
QUAY AV	LA	WIL	100	74	C5
QUEBEC DR	LA	LA68	6200	34	C2
QUEDO DR	LA	WOH	20400	13	E2
QUEDO PL	LA	WOH	4800	13	D2
QUEEN ST	LA	LA39	2600	35	D3
QUEEN ST E	ING	IN01	100	57	B1
QUEEN ST W	ING	IN01	100	56	E1
QUEEN ANNE CT	GLDR	GLDR	1200	89	C1
QUEEN ANNE PL	LA	LA19	1000	43	C3
QUEEN ANNES WK	POM	POM	1900	90	E5
QUEEN FLORNC LN	LA	WOH	4800	13	F2
QUEEN OAK DR	LA	ENC		22	B4
QUEENRIDGE DR	RPV	PVP	6000	72	D5
QUEENS CT	CER	ART	18700	81	D1
QUEENS CT	CLA	CLA	1400	91	B2
QUEENS CT	LA	LA69	1700	33	E3
QUEENS HWY N	LB	LB02		80A	C5
QUEENS HWY S	LB	LB02		80A	C5
QUEENS RD	LA	LA69	1400	33	F3
QUEENS WY	AGH	AGO		102	F3
QUEENS WY	LA	LA69	1400	33	F3
QUEENS WY	LB	LB02		75	C6
QUEENS WY	LB	LB02		80A	C4
QUEENSBERRY RD	PAS	PAS	1800	27	D2
QUEENSBORO CT	PALM	PALM		173	A9
QUEENSBOROGH LN	LA	LA49		32	B2
QUEENSBOROUG ST	CER	ART	12700	81	C2
QUEENSBURY AV	LAV	LAV		90	B3
QUEENSBURY DR	LA	LA64	2900	42	B4
QUEENSCLIFF CT	CO	CAL		100	B3
QUEENSDALE ST	CO	COM	4200	65	C2
QUEENSDALE ST	COM	COM	1500	65	B2
QUEENSFERRY RD	LA	LA49	2100	30	E6
QUEENSGLEN AV E	CO	PALM	17100	175	B6
QUEENSIDE DR	CO	COV	15700	88	A4
QUEENSIDE DR	COV	COV	1000	88	C4
QUEENSLAND ST	LA	LA34	10700	42	A5
QUEEN SUMMIT DR	WCOV	WCOV		92	D3
QUEENSVIEW LN	CO	GL14	2500	18	E1
QUEENSWAY DR	LB	LB02		75A	B6
QUEENSWAY DR	LB	LB02		80A	C4
QN VICTORIA RD	LA	WOH	4700	13	F2
QUEMADA RD	LA	ENC	16200	22	A4
QUESAN PL	LA	ENC	17200	21	E3
QUESTA CT	PALM	PALM		172	D7
QUEZADA WY	CO	CYN		125	F7
QUICK SILVER LN	CO	ACT		189	F4
QUICKSILVER LN	CO	LPUE		97	A4
QUICKSILVER LN	PALM	PALM		183	G3
QUIET CYN CIR	POM	POM		94	D5
QUIET CREEK LN	DBAR	POM		97A	A1
QUIET HILLS CIR	POM	POM		94	C6
QUIET HILLS CT	LA	CAN		5	E1
QUIET HILLS RD	POM	POM		94	C6
QUIET HOLLOW RD	POM	POM		94	D5
QUIGLEY AV	LKD	LKD	4100	71	E4
QUIGLEY AV N	CO	PAS	1	28	B4
QUIGLEY AV S	CO	PAS	1	28	B4
QUIGLEY RD	SCLR	NEW		127	E3
QUIGLEY ST	CMRC	LA40	4900	53	E2
QUIGLEY CYN RD	SCLR	NEW	24700	127	D3
QUILL AV	LA	SUN	10200	10	D3
QUILL DR	DOW	DOW	7200	59	F5
QUILL DR	DOW	DOW	7800	60	A5
QUILLA RD	SCLR	VAL		127	A2
QUIMBY AV	LA	CAN	7400	5	F3
QUIMBY ST	PAR	PAR	7300	65	E2
QUINCE CIR	CO	LPUE	16400	98	A3
QUINCY AV	LB	LB03	100	76	B6
QUINCY AV	LB	LB04	1300	76	B4
QUINCY AV	LB	LB14	300	76	B5

STREET	CITY	P.O. ZONE	BLOCK	PAGE	GRID
QUINCY AV	LB	LB15	2400	76	B2
QUINCY ST	CO	SAU		123	D5
QUINLIN DR	CO	PVP		73	A4
QUINN PL	SCLR	SAU		124	E5
QUINN ST	BG	BELL	5500	59	E1
QUINN ST	DOW	DOW	7400	60	A2
QUINN ST	SFS	SFS	11400	60	E4
QUINNELL DR	WCOV	WCOV	2900	97	A1
QUINTA RD	LA	WOH	22300	13	A3
QUINTERO ST	LA	LA26	1300	35	D6
QUINTON LN	LA	TU	6500	11	A4
QUIRK RD	CO	PALM		190	B2
QUIROZ CT	IND	WAL		97	B3
QUITO LN	LA	LA77	10400	32	E2
QUITO WY	LCF	LCF	1800	19	A3
QUIXLEY ST	CAR	CAR	19800	69	C2
QUOIT ST	DOW	DOW	8000	60	A5

R

STREET	CITY	P.O. ZONE	BLOCK	PAGE	GRID
R ST E	LA	WIL	100	74	C2
R ST W	LA	WIL	100	74	C2
RABBIT RD	LA	SF		2	F1
RABER ST	LA	LA42	5200	26	B6
RABORN ST	SAD	SAD	500	90	A2
RACE ST	SCLR	NEW	23900	127	D4
RACELAND RD	LAM	LAM	13400	82	F1
RACHEL AV	LKD	LKD	4900	71	E2
RACHEL AV	LAN	LAN		160	E3
RACHEL AV	WCOV	WCOV		92	E6
RACHMANINOV ST	CO	LAN	9000	146	F1
RACIMO DR	CO	WHI	12900	61	D2
RACINE AV	PAR	PAR	13600	65	E1
RACINE AV E	PAR	PAR	7500	65	E1
RACQUET CT	PALM	PALM		171	F4
RACQUET LN	PALM	PALM		171	E4
RACQUET CLUB CT	SCLR	CYN		125	A8
RADA RD	CO	LPUE	1500	98	A3
RADAR AV	LAN	LAN	44700	160	B4
RADBARD ST	CAR	CAR	900	64	C5
RADBROOK CT	RPV	SP		73	E6
RADBROOK PL	SCLR	VAL		127	A2
RADBURN AV	SFS	SFS	14500	82	E2
RADBURY PL	DBAR	POM		94	B6
RADBURY PL	DBAR	POM		97A	B1
RADBY ST	CO	LPUE	18900	98	F4
RADCLAY DR	CO	WAL		97	B4
RADCLAY ST	CO	CYN		128	C2
RADCLIFF DR	WAL	WAL		93	C6
RADCLIFFE AV	LA	PP	500	40	C4
RADCLIFFE CT	LAN	LAN		159	D3
RADCLIFFE DR	CLA	CLA	100	91	B1
RADCOCK AV	CO	LA56		50	E5
RADCOURT DR	CO	LPUE		98	B4
RADFALL CT	SCLR	SAU		124	F5
RADFORD AV	CLA	CLA	1800	91	A2
RADFORD AV	LA	NHO	5600	16	C5
RADFORD AV	LA	NHO	4000	23	C3
RADFORD PL	MON	MON	1600	29	A5
RADIAN LN	LAN	LAN		159	G5
RADIAN WY	LAN	LAN		159	G5
RADIANT CT	CO	COV	16600	88	C3
RADIO DR	LA	LA64	11700	41	E6
RADIO WK	LA	LA27		35	B3
RADIUM DR	LA	LA32	4300	36	C5
RADIUS PL	SFS	SFS		82	D3
RADLETT AV	CAR	CAR	19000	69	D1
RADLEY ST	ART	ART	11500	66	F6
RADLEY ST	ART	ART	11500	82	A6
RADLOCK AV	CO	LA56	5300	50	D5
RADNOR AV	LB	LB08	3600	71	D5
RADNOR AV	LB	LB15	2000	76	D2
RADNOR AV	LKD	LKD	4300	71	D3
RADON DR	CO	SF		3	E2
RADSTOCK AV	LPUE	LPUE	600	98	B1
RADWAY AV	CO	LPUE	600	48	E4
RADWAY AV	LPUE	LPUE	500	48	E4
RADWAY AV	WCOV	WCOV	1900	48	E3
RADWIN AV	LA	SUN	10600	10	B2
RAEBERT ST	DOW	DOW	9000	60	C5
RAELYN PL	WCOV	WCOV		92	B4
RAFAEL DR	ARC	ARC		28	B3
RAFAEL TER	GLEN	GL08		18	F4
RAFAEL WK	LB	LB03	200	80	D1
RAGAN DR	LAM	LAM	14500	83	A1
RAGLAND AV	DOW	DOW	1100	60	D5
RAGLEY ST	CO	LPUE	15700	85	E2
RAGUS ST	CO	LPUE	13600	48	D2
RAHN AV	LA	SF	12100	2	A5
RAHN AV	LB	LB05	6200	65	B6
RAILROAD AL	SPAS	SPAS	300	36	E2
RAILROAD AV	BAP	BAP	3800	39	E5
RAILROAD AV	SCLR	NEW		127	D4
RAILROAD AV	IND	LPUE	13000	48	B3
RAILROAD AV	MON	MON	100	29	B5

INDEX

285

1990 LOS ANGELES COUNTY STREET INDEX

RAILROAD DR

REDBUD PL

LOS ANGELES CO.

INDEX

STREET	CITY	P.O. ZONE	BLOCK	PAGE	GRID
RAILROAD DR	ELM	ELM	10100	38	C5
RAILROAD MTY	SCLR	NEW		127	D7
RAILROAD PL	ING	IN01	300	56	F1
RAILROAD PL	MB	MB	800	62	B4
RAILROAD ST	ELM	ELM	10900	38	D6
RAILROAD ST	GLEN	GL04	1400	25	C6
RAILROAD ST	IND	LPUE	17200	98	B2
RAILROAD ST	IND	LPUE	18900	98	E3
RAILROAD ST	PAS	PAS		27	A6
RAILTON ST	PR	PR	8600	54	F2
RAILTON ST	PR	PR	8700	55	A2
RAILWAY ST	SAD	SAD		89	F3
RAINBIRD WY	GLDR	GLDR		89	D2
RAINBOW AV	LA	LA65	400	36	A3
RAINBOW CT	CER	ART	19500	81	B2
RAINBOW DR	AZU	AZU	300	86	D4
RAINBOW DR	CO	CAST	30000	123	A5
RAINBOW DR	GLDR	GLDR	700	87	A4
RAINBOW DR	LA	CAN	23700	5	E3
RAINBOW PL	DBAR	POM		94	B6
RAINBOW PL	DBAR	POM		97A	B1
RAINBOW TER	PALM	PALM		172	A9
RAINBOW WY	CER	ART		81	B2
RAINBOW BEND DR	CO	ACT	33400	181	J8
RAINBOW BEND DR	CO	ACT	33400	182	A9
RAINBOW CRST DR	AGH	AGO		102	D3
RAINBOW GLEN DR	SCLR	CYN		124	G8
RAINBOW GLEN DR	SCLR	NEW		127	G1
RAINBOW HILL DR	AGH	AGO		102	D2
RAINBOW RDG CIR	LA	SF		1	E5
RAINBOW RDG RD	CO	PVP	27200	73	A5
RAINBOW RDG RD	POM	POM		94	D5
RAINBOWS END	CUL	CUL		50	D2
RAINBOW TER LN	MTB	MTB		46	E4
RAINBOW VIEW DR	AGH	AGO		102	D3
RAINDANCE PL	SCLR	SAU		124	E7
RAINER AV	CO	LPUE		98	E5
RAINEY PL	GLEN	GL08	2800	19	A5
RAINIER AV	CO	WHI	13000	61	C5
RAINIER ST	LA	SV	10300	16	F1
RAINS ST	ELM	ELM	12400	39	A6
RAINSBURY AV	CAR	CAR	17400	64	C6
RAINSFORD PL	CO	MAL	29500	112	B6
RAINTREE AV	TOR	TOR	3200	73	A2
RAINTREE CIR	CUL	CUL		50	C2
RAINTREE DR	WHI	WHI		84	B2
RAINTREE LN	CO	SAU		124	C2
RAINTREE LN	LA	NOR		7	B2
RAINTREE LN	PALM	PALM		172	J9
RAINWATER LN	WAL	WAL		93	D4
RAINWOOD DR	DBAR	WAL		97	D2
RAJAH ST	LA	SF	12800	3	B2
RAJRUTANA AV	LA	SUN		10	C2
RALEIGH DR	SMAR	PAS	2400	27	E6
RALEIGH ST	GLEN	GL05	400	25	D5
RALEIGH ST	LA	LA04	5100	34	D5
RALEO AV	CO	LPUE	1100	98	F4
RALL AV	BAP	BAP	3200	39	D6
RALL AV	CO	LPUE	300	48	A3
RALPH CT	POM	POM	100	94	F6
RALPH ST	ELM	ELM	10200	38	C6
RALPH ST	RM	RM	8700	38	A5
RALPH ST	WAL	WAL	19900	93	B6
RALPH ST W	SGAB	SGAB	200	37	D5
RALSTON AV	LA	PAC	9600	9	B3
RALSTON AV	LA	SF	12200	2	D4
RALSTON AV	LA	SV	9100	9	D5
RALSTON LN	RB	RB	2300	67	E1
RAMA DR	CO	LPUE	1300	48	E2
RAMA DR	LPUE	LPUE	500	48	D3
RAMA DR	WCOV	WCOV	1400	48	E2
RAMADA AV	CO	LPUE	100	48	A3
RAMADA DR	SCLR	VAL		127	B1
RAMAGE ST	WHOL	LA69	700	33	D5
RAMARA AV	LA	WOH	5600	5	E6
RAMBLA DL OR DR	CO	MAL		111	D4
RAMBLA ORIENTA	CO	MAL	3800	114	E4
RAMBLA PACIFICO	CO	MAL	1100	114	E3
RAMBLA VISTA	CO	MAL	21300	114	E4
RAMBLER AV	PALM	PALM	38800	172	C7
RAMBLING RD	CO	COV	19800	89	B6
RAMBOZ DR	CO	LA63	3500	45	D3
RAMBOZ PL	CO	LA63	1300	45	D3
RAMER ST	ELM	ELM	12500	47	F4
RAMERA MTWY E	CO	MAL		112	D2
RAMESA RIDGE	CO	MAL		112	D3
RAMHURST DR	LAM	LAM	13700	61	E6
RAMHURST DR	LAM	LAM	14700	84	A6
RAMILLO AV	LB	LB15	1200	76	C3
RAMILLO WY	SCLR	VAL		127	A2
RAMINDA AV	CO	LPUE	400	92	B6
RAMIREZ ST	LA	LA12	400	44	E2
RAMIREZ CYN RD	CO	MAL	5800	112	D5
RAMIREZ MESA DR	CO	MAL	28200	112	D6
RAMIREZ RDG TR	CO	MAL		112	D3
RAMIRO RD	SMAR	PAS	1600	37	B1
RAMISH AV	BG	BELL	7500	60	A1
RAMLI DR	CO	CYN		125	F7
RAMO DR	LAM	LAM	14300	82	F2
RAMON CT	CMRC	LA40	5800	54	B5
RAMONA AV	CO	LAV		90	B2
RAMONA AV	GLEN	GL08	1600	18	E5
RAMONA AV	HAW	HAW	12900	56	F6
RAMONA AV	HAW	HAW	13000	62	F2
RAMONA AV	LAV	LAV	1900	90	B3
RAMONA AV	MPK	MPK	100	46	C2
RAMONA AV	SMAD	SMAD	100	28	B2
RAMONA AV	SPAS	SPAS	1500	36	F2
RAMONA BLVD	BAP	BAP	12600	39	B5
RAMONA BLVD	ELM	ELM	10600	38	D6
RAMONA BLVD	ELM	ELM	12000	39	A6
RAMONA BLVD	MPK	MPK	4500	45	E2
RAMONA BLVD	RM	RM	8600	38	B6
RAMONA BLVD	RM	RM		47	A1
RAMONA BLVD	SGAB	SGAB	100	37	D6
RAMONA CT	CLA	CLA		91	C4
RAMONA CT	LA	LA48	6300	42	E2
RAMONA DR	WHI	WHI	13400	61	E1
RAMONA PKWY	BAP	BAP		39	D5
RAMONA PL	PAS	PAS	100	27	F4
RAMONA RD	ARC	ARC	1200	28	E3
RAMONA RD E	ALH	ALH	100	37	B6
RAMONA RD E	ALH	ALH	100	46	B1
RAMONA RD W	ALH	ALH	100	37	B6
RAMONA RD W	ALH	ALH	2600	45	F1
RAMONA RD W	ALH	ALH	100	46	B1
RAMONA ST	BLF	BLF	8500	66	A5
RAMONA ST	COV	COV	300	88	F6
RAMONA ST	PAS	PAS	200	27	A3
RAMONA ST	SGAB	SGAB	400	37	D5
RAMONA TER	ALH	ALH	1900	36	F6
RAMOS PL	LA	PP	14900	40	D5
RAMPART BLVD N	LA	LA26	100	35	B5
RAMPART BLVD S	LA	LA57	100	44	A1
RAMSAY DR	GLEN	GL06	2300	26	A2
RAMSDELL AV	CO	GL14	4600	11	D6
RAMSDELL AV	CO	GL14	4100	18	D1
RAMSDELL AV	GLEN	GL14	3700	18	D1
RAMSEY DR	CO	WHI	11400	61	E5
RAMSEY DR	LAM	LAM	12600	61	E6
RAMSEY DR	LAM	LAM	12600	82	E1
RAMSEY WY	POM	POM	2000	90	F6
RAMSGATE AV	LA	LA45	7000	50	E6
RAMSGATE AV	LA	LA45	7800	56	D2
RAMSGATE PL	LA	LA45	7000	50	E6
RAMS HORN CT	GLEN	GL07		25	D1
RAN DR	PALM	PALM		183	F2
RANA DR	SCLR	VAL		127	A2
RANBURN AV	AZU	AZU	200	88	E1
RANCE DR	CO	WAL		97	C4
RANCH LN	GLDR	GLDR	500	87	C4
RANCH LN	LAM	LAM		83	C1
RANCH LN	LA	PP	700	40	E4
RANCH RD	CO	TOP		13	B4
RANCH RD	CUL	CUL	10600	50	D3
RANCH CLUB RD	CO	PALM		157	G8
RANCH CREEK CT	POM	POM		94	C5
RANCHCREEK RD	COV	COV	19500	89	A6
RANCHERIA RD	DBAR	POM	800	94	A6
RANCHERIA RD	DBAR	POM		97A	A1
RANCHERO RD	RPV	PVP	1	78	A2
RANCHERO ST	WCOV	WCOV	1800	88	A5
RANCHEROS PL	PAS	PAS	800	26	D2
RANCHEROS RD	PAS	PAS	1100	26	D2
RANCHGROVE DR	WLVL	THO		102A	E5
RANCH HILL DR	LHH	LAH		98A	C1
RANCHILL DR	CER	ART	13600	82	E4
RANCHITAS DR	CO	ACT		181	J9
RANCHITAS DR	CO	ACT	6800	182	A9
RANCHITO AV	LA	VAN	8500	8	E6
RANCHITO AV	LA	VAN	5600	15	E6
RANCHITO AV	LA	VAN	4800	22	E2
RANCHITO RD	MON	MON	500	29	D4
RANCHITO ST	ELM	ELM	10400	38	D4
RANCHITO ST	ELM	ELM	11700	39	A5
RANCHO AV	GLEN	GL01	1500	24	E2
RANCHO DR	LB	LB15		76	E5
RANCHO DR	MTB	MTB	200	46	F6
RANCHO DR	NWK	NWK		61	C6
RANCHO DR	NWK	NWK		82	C1
RANCHO RD	ARC	ARC	900	28	D3
RANCHO RD	DUA	DUA		86	A4
RANCHO RD	SMAD	SMAD	1	28	D2
RANCHO ST	LA	ENC	17000	21	E3
RANCHO ST	LA	TAR	18100	21	C2
RANCHO WY	CO	COM		69	F2
RANCHO ADOBE RD	SCLR	VAL		127	B1
RCHO ALEGRE DR	COV	COV		89	C5
RO AMERICANA PL	CO	ACT		189	E2
RANCHO ARROYO	PAR	PAR		65	F1
RCHO BONITA RD	CO	COV		89	B6
RCHO CABALLO DR	LA	LA		10	A3
RCHO CANADA RD	LCF	LCF	2100	18	F2
RCHO CANADA RD	LCF	LCF		19	A2
RO CAPISTRNO RD	PAR	PAR		66	A2
RCHO CENTINA RD	PAR	PAR		66	A2
RO CLEMENTE DR	PAR	PAR		66	A3
RCHO CORONA DR	PAR	PAR		66	A2
RANCHO CORTO DR	COV	COV		89	C5
RCHO CULEBRA DR	COV	COV		89	C5
RO D L VISTA BL	PALM	LAN		171	D4
RO DL MONICO RD	CO	COV	3200	89	B6
RANCHO DEL ORO	PAR	PAR		65	F1
RCHO DEL SOL DR	COV	COV		89	C5
RO EL ENCINO DR	CO	COV	3200	89	C6
RO EL FUERTE DR	COV	COV		89	B6
RCHO GRANDE DR	COV	COV		89	C5
RCHO JURUPA PL	POM	POM		94	B4
RCHO L CARLA RD	CO	COV	3200	89	B6
RCHO LA FLOR RD	CO	COV		89	B5
RCHO LAGUNA DR	POM	POM		94	B4
RO LA MERCED DR	COV	COV		89	C6
RCHO LA PUENTE	CO	LPUE	700	98	D2
RANCHO LINDO DR	COV	COV		89	C5
RO LS CERITS RD	CO	COV		89	B6
RO LS NOGALS RD	COV	COV		89	C6
RCHO NOVATO DR	POM	POM		94	B4
RCHO OBISPO RD	PAR	PAR		66	A3
RANCHO PODEROSA	PAR	PAR		65	F1
RCHO POLERMO RD	PAR	PAR		66	A2
RANCHO REAL RD	TEC	TEC	9000	38	A3
RO RIO BNITA RD	CO	COV		89	B6
RCHO SN JOSE DR	CO	COV	20400	89	B6
RCHO SANTORO DR	CO	COV	3300	89	B6
RANCHO SERENA	PAR	PAR		66	A3
RANCHO SIMI DR	COV	COV		89	C6
RCHO SINALOA DR	COV	COV		89	A6
RCHO TUJUNGA DR	COV	COV		89	C5
RANCHO VALERO	PAR	PAR		65	F1
RANCHO VERDE	PAR	PAR		66	A3
RANCHO VERDE DR	CO	WHI		55	D2
RANCHO VISTA BL	PAS	PAS	100	27	B5
RANCHO VISTA BL	PALM	PALM		171	D4
RANCHO VISTA DR	CER	ART	12400	82	B5
RANCHO VISTA DR	COV	COV		89	C6
RANCHO VISTA ST	PAR	PAR		66	A3
RANCH TOP RD	PAS	PAS	3700	20A	A3
RANCHVIEW RD	RHE	PVP	1	72	F4
RANCHWOOD PL	DBAR	POM		97A	B2
RAND CT	LA	VAN	4000	22	F4
RAND DR	LA	VAN	13400	22	F4
RANDA LN	ING	IN01		57	B2
RANDALL CT	LA	LA65		35	F3
RANDALL ST	GLEN	GL01	1300	24	F2
RANDALL ST	LA	CUL	5300	50	B4
RANDALL ST	LA	SV	10900	9	E6
RANDALL ST	LA	SV	11800	16	C1
RANDALL WY	WCOV	WCOV	1300	48	E2
RANDI AV	LA	CAN	6400	12	B5
RANDIWOOD LN	CO	CAN	6600	5	D4
RANDOLPH AV	LA	LA32	3600	36	D4
RANDOLPH AV	PAS	PAS	500	27	F5
RANDOLPH PL	BELL	BELL	3500	53	B5
RANDOLPH PL	LB	LB07	200	70	C4
RANDOLPH ST	ARC	ARC		39	A3
RANDOLPH ST	BELL	BELL	3900	53	C5
RANDOLPH ST	CMRC	LA40	5500	53	E5
RANDOLPH ST	CMRC	LA40	6000	54	A5
RANDOLPH ST	CO	LA01	1700	52	D4
RANDOLPH ST	CO	LA22	5200	53	C5
RANDOLPH ST	HPK	HPK	1900	52	F4
RANDOLPH ST	HPK	HPK	2700	53	A4
RANDOLPH ST	MAY	MAY	4300	53	C5
RANDOLPH ST	POM	POM	300	94	E1
RANDOLPH ST	VER	LA58	3100	53	A4
RANDOLPH ST E	GLEN	GL07	100	25	D2
RANDOLPH ST W	GLEN	GL02	100	25	D2
RANDOM LN	DUA	DUA	800	29	E4
RANDSBURG ST	CER	ART	13400	82	D5
RANDWICK DR	TEC	TEC	10200	38	D3
RANDY ST	POM	POM	100	94	B2
RANETTO PL	LA	SF	11200	10	A1
RANGE CT	DBAR	POM		97A	B3
RANGE RD	LA	LA65	2600	25	F6
RANGE HORSE LN	RHE	PVP	5000	72	E3
RANGELY AV	WHOL	LA48	8700	33	D5
RANGELY ST	WHOL	LA48	8400	33	E5
RANGER AV	COV	COV		88	F3
RANGER AV	ELM	ELM	4300	38	D5
RANGER DR	AZU	AZU	300	88	F2
RANGER DR	CO	AZU	6000	86	F6
RANGER DR	CO	AZU	6000	88	F1
RANGER DR	GLDR	GLDR	100	86	F5
RANGETON DR	DBAR	WAL		97	C3
RANGEVIEW AV	LA	LA42	4800	26	B6
RANGEVIEW DR	GLEN	GL01	1900	18	A5
RANGEWOOD RD	CO	SAU		123	D5
RANGOON ST	LA	PAC	13300	8	F6
RANGOON ST	LA	PAC	12900	9	B5
RANIER ST	SCLR	CYN	19100	124	H7
RANKIN DR	CO	TOP		109	A3
RANLETT AV	CO	LPUE	500	92	A5
RANMORE DR	CO	LPUE	16400	98	A3
RANNEY HOUSE CT	SCLR	VAL		124	E3
RANONS AV	LA	LA65	4000	25	E6
RANSOM RD	GLEN	GL01	1700	18	A5
RANSOM ST	CMRC	LA40	2200	53	E2
RANSOM ST	LB	LB04	3200	76	A3
RANSON WY	MPK	MPK	300	46	C3
RANTHOM AV	LA	WOH	5500	100	D1
RAPALLO AV	LA	SP	600	78	D3
RAPHAEL ST	LA	LA42	5000	36	B2
RAPHAEL ST	LAN	LAN		160	E8
RAPID BROOK RD	DBAR	POM		97A	A2
RAPIDVIEW DR	DBAR	WAL		97	C3
RAQUEL LN	CO	CYN		125	F7
RAQUET CLUB RD	DBAR	POM		97	F2
RARITAN DR	CO	WHI	14700	84	A5
RASHDALL AV	CAR	CAR	21800	69	A4
RASIC RIDGE RD	GLEN	GL07	900	25	D1
RASKIN DR	CO	LPUE		97	A4
RATH ST	CO	LPUE	13300	48	D2
RATHBURN AV	LA	NOR	8900	7	C5
RATHBURN AV	LA	NOR	8300	14	C1
RATLIFFE ST	DOW	DOW	9100	66	B1
RATLIFFE ST	LAM	LAM		61	E6
RATLIFFE ST	LAM	LAM	13800	82	E1
RATLIFFE ST	NWK	NWK	10500	66	E1
RATNER ST	LA	NHO	11900	16	C2
RATNER ST	LA	SV	10900	16	E2
RATNER ST	LA	VAN	13400	15	F2
RATON CIR	LB	LB07	5000	70	E2
RATTLESNAKE RD	CO	MAL		105	C6
RAUSCH RD	IND	LPUE		48	E6
RAVEN AV	LAN	LAN		160	G7
RAVEN DR	PALM	PALM		183	F1
RAVEN ST	LA	SF	13200	2	F2
RAVEN ST	LA	SF	13100	3	A2
RAVENCREST CIR	POM	POM		94	C5
RAVENDALE RD	CO	SGAB	8200	37	F1
RAVENFALL AV	CO	LPUE	2400	98	C4
RAVEN GLEN RD	CO	CYN	16200	128	D2
RAVENHILL DR	POM	POM		94	C6
RAVEN HILL RD	CO	CYN	26100	128	D3
RAVENNA AV	CAR	CAR	21300	69	B4
RAVENNA AV	CAR	CAR	23600	74	B1
RAVENNA AV	LA	WIL	1000	74	B3
RAVENNA DR	LB	LB03	100	80	C1
RAVENSPUR DR	RPV	PVP	5600	72	D4
RAVENSWOOD AV	CO	IN04	10400	57	A4
RAVENSWOOD LN	LA	LA49		32	B2
RAVENSWOOD WY	POM	POM	2100	90	F5
RAVENWOOD CT	DBAR	WAL		97	C5
RAVENWOOD CT	LA	LA77		32	E1
RAVIA ST	LKD	LKD	5500	71	C4
RAVILLER DR	DOW	DOW	7700	60	C1
RAVIN CT	CO	CAL		100A	E6
RAVINE RD	LA	LA26	2300	35	D4
RAVINNA	MTB	MTB		46	C5
RAVISTA LN	LCF	LCF	1900	19	A1
RAVOLI DR	LA	PP	1000	40	E3
RAWDON AV	LAN	LAN	44300	160	E5
RAWHIDE	WCOV	WCOV		92	D4
RAWHIDE AV E	CO	LAN	16000	174	H6
RAWHIDE AV E	CO	PALM	16600	175	A6
RAWHIDE CIR	WAL	WAL		93	A6
RAWHIDE LN	CAR	CAR		69	E6
RAWHIDE LN	NWK	NWK	12700	61	C6
RAWHIDE LN	NWK	NWK	12700	82	C1
RAWHIDE LN	RHE	PVP		73	A4
RAWHIDE ST	POM	POM		94	C5
RAWLINGS AV	LA	WOH	5600	12	E6
RAWLINGS AV	LA	WOH	5600	13	E1
RAWLINGS AV	SOG	SOG	5600	59	E5
RAWLINSDALE LN	SAD	SAD	500	90	A4
RAWLINSON CT	BUR	BUR	300	24	C3
RAWSON CT	CO	WHI		61	E4
RAWSON RD	CO	SAU		181	B6
RAY CIR	CER	ART	19500	81	A2
RAY CT	SCLR	SAU		124	F3
RAY CT	LA	LA41	4800	26	B5
RAYBET RD	LA	LA77	10400	22	D6
RAYBORN ST	LYN	LYN	4600	65	D1
RAYBURN RD	CO	PALM		172	B9
RAYBURN RD	PALM	PALM		172	B9
RAYEN ST	LA	CAN	23900	4	B6
RAYEN ST	LA	CAN	22000	6	B6
RAYEN ST	LA	NOR	17000	7	F6
RAYEN ST	LA	PAC	13500	8	E5
RAYEN ST	LA	SF	16500	7	F6
RAYEN ST	LA	SF	15000	8	B6
RAYEN ST	LA	VAN	14200	8	D6
RAYFIELD DR	LAM	LAM	14500	83	C3
RAYFORD DR	LA	LA45	8000	56	A1
RAYLAND DR	CO	SF	11200	3	E2
RAYLAND DR	CO	TOR	900	68	F6
RAYLENE PL	POM	POM		94	F1
RAYLENE PL	POM	POM	1300	95	A1
RAYMER ST	LA	NHO	13300	15	F3
RAYMER ST	LA	NHO	12500	16	A3
RAYMER ST	LA	NOR	17200	7	E6
RAYMER ST	LA	NOR	17100	14	E1
RAYMER ST	LA	VAN	14500	15	C2
RAYMOND AV	CO	ALT	2100	20	A4
RAYMOND AV	CO	GL14	4800	11	E6
RAYMOND AV	CO	GL14	4200	18	E2
RAYMOND AV	CO	LA44	11100	57	E5
RAYMOND AV	CO	TOR	20400	68	F3
RAYMOND AV	GAR	GAR	13500	63	F1
RAYMOND AV	GLEN	GL01	1200	18	A6
RAYMOND AV	GLEN	GL01	200	24	E2
RAYMOND AV	GLEN	MONT	4000	18	E2
RAYMOND AV	HB	RB	1600	62	C6
RAYMOND AV	LA	GAR	18400	63	F6
RAYMOND AV	LA	GAR	18400	68	F1
RAYMOND AV	LA	LA07	1900	43	E5
RAYMOND AV	LA	LA37	4000	51	E3
RAYMOND AV	LA	LA44	5800	51	E6
RAYMOND AV	LA	LA44	8300	57	E1
RAYMOND AV	LB	LB04	700	75	E4
RAYMOND AV	LB	LB05	6200	65	E5
RAYMOND AV	MON	MON	1500	29	B5
RAYMOND AV	PAS	PAS	1500	20	A6
RAYMOND AV	PAS	PAS	100	27	A2
RAYMOND AV	PAS	PAS	100	27	A6
RAYMOND AV	SH	LB06	1800	75	E1
RAYMOND AV	SM	SM	600	49	B2
RAYMOND AV N	ALH	ALH	100	37	A5
RAYMOND AV S	ALH	ALH	100	37	A5
RAYMOND CT	SM	SM	400	49	B2
RAYMOND DR	CO	PAS	400	28	B5
RAYMOND DR	LAV	LAV		90	D1
RAYMOND DR	LAV	LAV		95A	D6
RAYMOND LN	CO	ALT	2200	20	A5
RAYMOND LN	SPAS	SPAS	800	37	A2
RAYMOND PL	GAR	GAR	16800	63	F5
RAYMOND ST	CO	CHA		4	C5
RAYMOND ST	COM	COM	100	64	E4
RAYMONDALE DR	SPAS	SPAS	300	37	A1
RAYMOND HILL RD	SPAS	SPAS	1600	27	A6
RAYNETA DR	LA	VAN	15000	22	C4
RAYNOL ST	LA	LA32	3700	36	B5
RAYO AV	SOG	SOG	8800	59	D3
RAYO DE SOL DR	CO	MAL	30600	111	E4
RAYSACK AV	LAN	LAN	44100	160	C5
RAYWOOD AV	MTB	MTB	400	46	F6
RAYWOOD DR	LA	LA49	13750	30	E5
RAYWOOD LN	WHI	WHI		84	D4
RAYWOOD PL	MTB	MTB	900	46	F6
RAZZAK CIR	DBAR	POM		97	E4
REA DR	MTB	MTB	600	46	F6
REA DR	MTB	MTB	500	54	F1
READCREST DR	LA	BH	9300	33	B3
READING AV	LA	LA45	7900	56	D2
REAL AV	HB	RB	800	67	C1
REAL CT	SCLR	NEW		127	H6
REALITOS DR	CO	LAV	500	90	E1
REALTY ST	CAR	CAR	300	74	B1
REATA LN	RH	PVP	1	78	B1
REATA PL	DBAR	POM		97	E5
REAZA PL	LA	WOH	20300	13	E1
REBECCA AV	GLEN	GL14	4500	11	C5
REBECCA DR	SAD	SAD		90	A4
REBECCA ST	WCOV	WCOV		92	E6
REBECCA ST N	POM	POM	100	94	E4
REBECCA ST S	POM	POM	100	94	E4
REBUD PL	CO	LPUE	17800	92	D6
RECADO RD	LHH	LAH	1400	84	E3
RECALL DR	CO	TOP		109	B2
RECINTO AV	CO	LPUE	2400	98	D6
REC LODGE DR	LA	LA26	1200	35	D5
RECORD AV N	CO	LA63	100	45	D4
RECORD AV S	CO	LA23	600	45	D6
RECORD AV S	CO	LA23	1200	53	D1
RECORD AV S	CO	LA63	300	45	D4
RECORD DR	CO	LA63	700	45	D3
RECREATION RD	CAR	CAR		69	D4
RECTOR PL	LA	LA29	900	35	A4
RECYCLE WY	SM	SM		41	C6
REDBANK ST	LA	SV	11800	9	C6
REDBEAM AV	TOR	TOR	19300	67	E2
REDBERRY ST	ELM	ELM	11200	47	E3
REDBIRD DR	PR	PR	6000	54	E4
RED BLUFF CT	SAD	SAD		95A	A6
REDBLUFF DR	CO	CAL		100	A3
RED BLUFF LN	DBAR	WAL		97	C3
RED BLUFF TR	CO	TOP		109	E4
REDBOX TRUCK TR	CO			N	E5
REDBUD PL	POM	POM		94	C4

1990 LOS ANGELES COUNTY STREET INDEX

STREET	CITY	P.O. ZONE	BLOCK	PAGE	GRID
REDBUD RDG CIR	SCLR	VAL	27500	124	B4
REDBURN AV	CO	LPUE	500	48	C5
REDBUSH LN	LA	VAN	8100	15	E1
RED CEDAR DR	WAL	WAL	20000	93	B6
RED CEDAR PL	CO	SAU		124	C3
REDCLIFF ST	LA	LA26	1600	35	B4
REDCLIFF ST	LA	LA39	1900	35	B4
RED CLOUD DR	DBAR	POM		93	F5
REDCOACH LN	CO	WHI	16000	84	C6
REDCOAT LN	WLVL	THO		102	C4
REDDING AV	CO	RM	1700	46	E3
REDELL AV	CO	MON	2100	29	B6
REDESDALE AV	LA	LA26	1600	35	B4
REDESDALE AV	LA	LA39	1900	35	B4
REDFERN AV	CO	IN04	10000	56	F4
REDFERN AV	ING	IN01	1000	56	E3
REDFIELD AV	LA	LA42	400	36	C3
RED FIR LN	DBAR	POM		97	F3
REDGATE CIR	DBAR	POM		97	E3
RED GUM LN	CO	POM		93	E2
RED HAT LN	IND	WHI		47	D6
RED HAWK RD	WAL	WAL		93	A6
REDHILL TR	CO	TOP		109	C3
REDLANDS AV	CLA	CLA		91	B1
REDLANDS ST	LA	VEN	7800	55A	E2
REDLEN AV	CO	WHI	700	48	B4
RED LINE DR	LKD	LKD	4100	71	E4
REDMAN AV	CO	WHI	6000	55	B4
REDMAN AV	WHI	WHI	5500	55	B4
REDMESA DR	CO	CHA		1A	B6
REDMESA DR	CO	CHA		6	B2
REDMONT AV	LA	TU	10000	10	F4
RED OAK CIR	POM	POM		94	C5
RED OAK DR	LA	LA68	5300	34	E2
REDONDA LN	CO	TOR		68	F6
REDONDELA DR	RPV	SP	1800	73	D5
REDONDO AV	LB	LB03	100	76	A6
REDONDO AV	LB	LB04	700	76	A2
REDONDO AV	LB	LB06	2300	76	A2
REDONDO AV	LB	LB14	300	76	A6
REDONDO AV	LB	LB15	2200	76	A2
REDONDO AV	SH	LB04	1800	76	A2
REDONDO AV N	MB	MB	100	62	D5
REDONDO AV S	MB	MB	100	62	D5
REDONDO BLVD	ING	IN02	800	51	B6
REDONDO BLVD	LA	LA08	3800	50	F1
REDONDO BLVD	LA	LA16	2300	42	F6
REDONDO BLVD	LA	LA16	1900	43	A5
REDONDO BLVD	LA	LA19	10000	43	A3
REDONDO BCH BL	GAR	GAR	1000	63	B5
REDONDO BCH BL	LA	GAR	700	63	B5
REDONDO BCH BL	LA	GAR	500	64	B3
REDONDO BCH BL	LAW	LAW	4000	63	B5
REDNDO BCH BL E	CO	COM	600	64	B3
REDNDO BCH BL E	CO	GAR	100	64	B3
REDNDO BCH BL W	CO	GAR	100	64	B3
REDONDO BCH FWY	CAR	CAR		64	B5
RED PLUM CIR	MPK	MPK		46	C4
RED PLUM ST	CER	ART		82	D4
REDPOST CT	DBAR	POM		97	E3
REDRIDGE RD	CO	SF		3	E2
RED RIVER CIR	WAL	WAL		93	A6
REDROCK CT	LA	LA39	2100	35	B3
REDROCK CT	PALM	PALM		171	C5
REDROCK CT	PALM	PALM		171	D9
RED ROCK DR	WAL	WAL		93	C3
REDROCK LN	POM	POM		94	D5
REDROCK RD	CO	TOP	23100	108	D4
RED ROSE DR	LA	ENC	3300	22	A5
RED ROV MINE RD	CO	ACT		182	D8
REDSTONE ST	ELM	ELM	12000	47	E2
REDVIEW DR	SCLR	SAU		124	E9
REDWILLOW LN	LCF	LCF	5000	19	D3
REDWING ST	LA	TAR	19500	13	F1
REDWING ST	LA	TAR	18700	21	B1
REDWING ST	LA	WOH	19700	13	F1
REDWOOD AV	BLF	BLF		66	D6
REDWOOD AV	CUL	LA66	3900	49	E4
REDWOOD AV	ELS	ELS		55A	F5
REDWOOD AV	LA	LA66	3400	49	D2
REDWOOD AV	LAN	LAN	44100	160	B6
REDWOOD AV	LYN	LYN	3000	59	A5
REDWOOD AV	PALM	PALM		171	B2
REDWOOD CT	BUR	BUR	400	24	C3
REDWOOD DR	CER	ART		82	B4
REDWOOD DR	GLDR	GLDR	2100	87	E5
REDWOOD DR	PAS	PAS	200	26	D5
REDWOOD LN	SAD	SAD	600	90	A4
REDWOOD LN	WCOV	WCOV		98	F1
REDWOOD GLEN RD	SCLR	VAL		124	B3
REDWOOD VIEW DR	POM	POM		94	C4
REED DR	CLA	CLA	800	91	A2
REED DR	LOM	LOM	25500	73	C3
REED ST	COV	COV	100	88	E4
REED ST	LOM	LOM	25800	73	D3
REED ST	RB	RB	1700	62	D5

STREET	CITY	P.O. ZONE	BLOCK	PAGE	GRID
REEDER AV	CO	COV	5000	89	C3
REEDER AV N	COV	COV	100	89	B5
REEDER AV S	COV	COV	100	89	B5
REEDLEY ST	LA	PAC	13200	9	A6
REEDLEY ST	LA	VAN	13300	9	A6
REEDLEY ST	LA	VAN	13300	15	F1
REEDVALE LN	LA	LA49	1700	40	F1
REEDVIEW DR	CO	WAL	19500	97	B4
REEF CT	LA	VEN		49	D6
REEF ST	LA	VEN		49	C6
REEFTON CT	CO	CAL		100	B2
REES ST	LA	VEN	100	55A	D2
REESE DR	LB	LB14		76	E4
REESE PL N	BUR	BUR	200	17	C5
REESE PL N	BUR	BUR	100	24	C2
REESE PL S	BUR	BUR	100	24	C2
REESE RD	TOR	TOR	4600	67	E6
REEVE DR	LAM	LAM		83	D1
REEVE RD	PR	PR	7700	54	E6
REEVE ST E	COM	COM	100	64	F4
REEVE ST W	COM	COM	100	64	F4
REEVER WY	CO	ALT	1	20	A3
REEVES AV	BLF	BLF	16600	66	B4
REEVES AV	CAR	LB10		69	F3
REEVES AV	LA	SP		79	D1
REEVES DR	BH	BH	100	42	C2
REEVES PL	GLEN	GL05	800	25	D5
REEVES PL	POM	POM	800	95	A2
REEVES ST	LA	LA35	1400	42	C3
REEVESBURY DR	LA	BH	9900	32	E2
REFINERY RD	CO	CAST		123	E2
REFINERY RD	CO	NEW		127	F8
REFORMA RD	LA	WOH	4600	13	B2
REFUGIO RD	LA	ENC	16400	21	F4
REFUGIO RD	LA	ENC	16400	22	A4
REGAL CT	LAV	LAV		90	C1
REGAL PL	LA	LA68	3600	23	F5
REGAL WY E	LB	LB13	100	75	C4
REGAL WY W	LB	LB13	100	75	C4
REGALADO ST	CO	LPUE	15300	85	D3
REGAL CANYON DR	WAL	WAL		93	C4
REGALO RD	LA	WOH	4700	13	B2
REGAL OAK DR	LA	ENC	4100	22	B4
REGAL VISTA DR	LA	VAN	3700	22	B5
REGAL WOODS PL	LA	VAN	15700	22	B5
REGAN CT	CO	LPUE		98	A4
REGAN ST	LA	SP	700	79	B1
REGATTA AV	CO	WHI	9600	61	F4
REGENCY CIR	BLF	BLF	17600	66	D5
REGENCY CT	WAL	WAL		93	C4
REGENCY PL	CO	PALM		184	A2
REGENCY WY	LA	SF44		1	D5
REGENCY WY	PALM	PALM		171	F6
REGENCY PK CIR	SCLR	VAL		127	A1
REGENE ST	POM	POM	300	94	F3
REGENT AV	LOM	LOM	26000	73	D4
REGENT CIR	ING	IN01	200	57	A1
REGENT ST	HPK	HPK	5900	52	E5
REGENT ST	LA	LA34	9300	42	A6
REGENT ST	LA	LA34	10900	50	B1
REGENT ST	LA	LA66	11400	49	F1
REGENT ST	LA	LA66	11200	50	A1
REGENT ST E	ING	IN01	100	57	A1
REGENT ST W	ING	IN01	200	56	F1
REGENT ST W	ING	IN01	100	57	A1
REGENT PK DR	CO	PAS	300	19	C5
REGENTS CT	WLVL	THO	4500	102	B4
REGENTS ST	LAN	LAN		159	J1
REGENTVIEW AV	BLF	BLF	13400	66	D2
REGENTVIEW AV	DOW	DOW	11900	60	D5
REGENT VIEW DR	BLF	BLF	17800	66	D6
REGGIO PL	POM	POM		94	C4
REGIE LN	PALM	PALM		172	B5
REGINA AV	TOR	TOR	17900	63	A6
REGINA CT	LA	LA44	8700	58	A2
REGINA ST	WCOV	WCOV		92	E6
REGIS AV	CLA	CLA	1300	91	A3
REGIS WY	LA	LA45	8000	56	A1
REGWAY AV	LB	LB10	2600	75	A1
REICHLING LN	CO	WHI	10400	55	B4
REICHLING LN	PR	PR	8600	54	F3
REICHLING LN	PR	PR	9100	55	A4
REICHLING ST	CO	LPUE	15500	85	D5
REID AV	CUL	CUL	3000	42	E5
REID ST	LA	TU	6200	11	B4
REIFER ST	CO	RM	8300	46	F3
REIGATE RD	CO	TOP		115	C1
REIMS ST	CLA	CLA	1300	90	F2
REIMS ST	POM	POM	300	90	F2
REINA CT	CO	CAL		100	D5
REINHART AV	CAR	CAR	19000	69	C1
REINWAY CT	PAS	PAS	300	27	A3
REIS ST	CO	WHI	12900	61	D2
REISNER WY	SOG	SOG		59	D2
REITER DR	PAS	PAS	1800	27	D4
REITHE AV	CO	CAL		108	B5

STREET	CITY	P.O. ZONE	BLOCK	PAGE	GRID
REKLAW DR	LA	NHO	3700	23	C4
RELIANCE ST	LA	PAC	13300	8	F6
RELIANCE ST	LA	PAC	13000	9	A6
REMAH VISTA DR	GLEN	GL07	1500	25	D1
REMBERT LN	LA	BH		33	B2
REMBRANDT ST	LAN	LAN	43600	160	D6
REMER ST	SELM	ELM	10000	47	C3
REMEY AV	BAP	BAP	3400	39	C6
REMICK AV	LA	PAC	9800	8	E2
REMICK AV	LA	PAC	9000	9	A4
REMICK AV	LA	SF	10900	8	D1
REMICK AV	LA	SV	8500	9	C6
REMICK AV	LA	SV	8500	16	C1
REMINGTON RD	CO	CAST		123	A2
REMINGTON ST	LA	PAC	13300	8	E4
REMINGTON ST	LA	PAC	12200	9	C1
REMINGTON ST	LA	SF	11700	3	D6
REMMET AV	LA	CAN	8400	6	C6
REMMET AV	LA	CAN	6800	12	C4
REMMET AV	LA	CHA	10100	6	C3
REMO AV	CO	LPUE		98	E3
REMORA DR	CO	LPUE		98	C4
REMSEN ST	SCLR	NEW		127	E7
REMSTOY DR	LA	LA32	5100	36	E3
REMUDA DR	GLDR	GLDR	1200	87	D6
REMY AV	LA	CAN	8300	12	E1
REMY PL	BUR	BUR		17	D2
RENAULT ST	CO	LPUE	17400	98	C1
RENDALIA ST	BLF	BLF	9000	66	B3
RENDALL PL	LA	LA26	1500	35	B4
RENDINA ST	LB	LB15	6400	76	E3
RENDOVA ST	ART	ART	12000	82	B5
RENEE CT	WCOV	WCOV		92	C4
RENEE DR	AGH	AGO		100A	B5
RENEE ST	LAN	LAN		160	E3
RENFREW RD	LA	LA49	12200	41	B1
RENNELL AV N	SAD	SAD	100	89	D2
RENNELL AV S	SAD	SAD	100	89	D2
RENNIE AV	LA	VEN	200	49	B3
RENO AV	CO	SGAB	6300	38	A2
RENO AV	TEC	TEC	5700	38	A2
RENO ST N	LA	LA26	100	35	A6
RENO ST S	LA	LA57	100	44	A1
RENOA AV	SOG	SOG	10200	59	E4
RENOAK WY	ARC	ARC	200	28	D4
RENO RIDGE DR	DBAR	POM		94	A4
RENO RIDGE LN	DBAR	POM		94	A5
RENOVO ST	LA	LA32	4900	36	D4
RENOWN TER	WCOV	WCOV		92	C4
RENSHAW ST	CO	COV		89	C5
RENSHAW ST	COV	COV	1800	89	C5
RENSSELAER DR	ALH	ALH	2000	46	A2
RENTON ST E	CAR	CAR	900	69	C5
RENVILLE ST	LKD	LKD	11400	71	F3
RENVILLE ST	LKD	LKD	12200	81	B3
RENWICK CT	SCLR	SAU		124	C2
RENWICK RD	CO	AZU	16500	88	C2
RENWICK RD	SAD	SAD	1400	89	D2
RENWICK RD E	AZU	AZU	500	88	D2
RENWICK RD E	GLDR	GLDR	100	89	B2
RENWICK RD W	AZU	AZU	200	88	C2
RENWICK RD W	GLDR	GLDR	200	89	A2
REPASADO DR	LHH	LAH		85	F6
REPETTO AV	MTB	MTB	2200	54	C1
REPETTO ST	CO	LA22	5000	45	F5
REPETTO ST	CO	LA22	5400	46	A5
REPOSA LN	CO	ALT	2800	20	C4
REPOSADO DR	LHH	LAH	100	84	F1
REPOSADO DR	LHH	LAH	900	98	A6
REPPERT CT	LA	LA46	2600	33	E1
REPTON ST	LA	LA42	6300	36	D1
REPUBLIC ST	LA	LA12	100	44	E2
REQUA AV	CLA	CLA	3800	90	F2
RESEDA BLVD	LA	NOR	12000	1	B4
RESEDA BLVD	LA	NOR	8500	7	C5
RESEDA BLVD	LA	NOR	8300	14	C6
RESEDA BLVD	LA	RES	6100	14	C6
RESEDA BLVD	LA	TAR	5600	14	C6
RESEDA BLVD	LA	TAR	4100	21	C1
RESERVOIR DR E	LB	LB04	1800	76	A3
RESERVOIR DR W	LB	LB04	1800	76	A3
RESERVOIR ST	LA	LA26	1900	35	B5
RESERVOIR ST N	POM	POM	100	95	A4
RESERVOIR ST S	POM	POM	100	95	A4
RESIN PL	SFS	SFS	15700	82	D3
RESOLANO DR	LA	PP	600	40	A3
RESORT LN	POM	POM		94	B3
RESTAURANT DR	POM	POM		90	C6
RESTHAVEN DR	LA	LA41	2400	25	F5
RETA ST	GLEN	GL14	3300	11	D5
RETFORD ST	COV	COV	1300	89	B4
RETFORD KNOLL	COV	COV		89	B4
RETREAT CT	CO	MAL		114	A4
REVA CIR	CER	ART	13400	82	D6
REVA CT	LKD	LKD		66	B6
REVA PL	CER	ART	10700	66	E6

STREET	CITY	P.O. ZONE	BLOCK	PAGE	GRID
REVA PL	CER	ART	13500	82	D6
REVA ST	BLF	BLF	10500	66	D6
REVA ST	CER	ART	12300	82	B6
REVA ST	LKD	LKD	5900	66	D6
REVAL CT	BUR	BUR	3000	24	C3
REVELLO DR	LA	PP	17400	40	A4
REVERE AL	PAS	PAS	1700	27	D4
REVERE AV	LA	LA39	3600	25	C6
REVERE AV	MTB	MTB		46	E5
REVERE PL	CUL	CUL	4200	50	C1
REVERE RD	CO	SAU		123	D4
REVERE ST	CER	ART		81	A2
REVERE WY	CO	AGO		100A	D5
REVERE, PAUL PL	PALM	PALM		183	D2
REVERIE RD	LA	TU	9300	10	F5
REVILLE RD	PAS	PAS	1400	26	D2
REVLON DR	LCF	LCF	4800	19	D3
REVUELTA WY	LA	LA77	10400	32	E5
REX CT	POM	POM	700	90	F3
REX CT	WHI	WHI		55	E3
REX RD	PR	PR	8200	54	D5
REX ST	LA	SF	13900	2	D3
REXALL AV	CO	WHI	8100	55	B6
REXBON RD	LA	SF	18000	1	D5
REXFORD AV	PAS	PAS	1100	28	B2
REXFORD CT	DBAR	POM		97A	B1
REXFORD DR	LA	LA35	1100	42	C3
REXFORD DR N	BH	BH	200	33	B5
REXFORD DR N	BH	BH	100	42	C1
REXFORD DR S	BH	BH	100	42	C2
REXFORD PL	CO	VAL		124	B6
REXTON ST	NWK	NWK	12500	82	C2
REXWOOD AV.	BAP	BAP	13500	39	D6
REXWOOD ST	BAP	BAP	13800	39	D6
REXWOOD ST	WCOV	WCOV	1200	48	E1
REY ALBERTO CT	CO	CAL		100	C5
REY DE COPAS LN	CO	MAL	26000	112	D6
REYDON AV	DOW	DOW	8900	66	A1
REYES AV	CO	COM	18600	70	A1
REYES DR	IND	WAL		97	C1
REYES DR	LA	TAR	4200	21	B3
REYES ADOBE RD	AGH	AGO		102	D2
REYNARD AV	GLEN	GL14	4900	11	C4
REYNIER AV	CO	LA56	5000	50	E3
REYNIER AV	LA	LA34	2500	42	D5
REYNOLDS AV	CO	RM	1700	46	F3
REYNOLDS AV	LA	LA32	3600	36	C4
REYNOLDS DR	BUR	BUR		17	C2
REYNOLDS DR	GLEN	GL05	1200	25	D5
REYNOLDS DR	TOR	TOR	20800	67	F5
REYNOLDS LN	RB	RB	300	67	D1
REYNOLDS WY	GLDR	GLDR	1200	89	B2
REYNOSA DR	TOR	TOR	1800	68	D6
RHAPSODY RD	CO	WAL	20100	97	B4
RHEA AV	LA	NOR	9300	7	B5
RHEA AV	LA	NOR	8400	14	B1
RHEA AV	LA	RES	6300	14	B5
RHEA AV	LA	TAR	5700	14	B6
RHEA AV	LA	TAR	5300	21	B1
RHEA ST	LB	LB06	300	75	C3
RHEA VISTA DR	WHI	WHI		55	E6
RHEEM AV	SOG	SOG	8600	59	C2
RHINE PL	CER	ART	18700	71	E1
RHINESTONE DR	LA	VAN	14900	22	C5
RHODA CIR	CER	ART		81	B3
RHODA ST	LA	ENC	17500	14	D6
RHODA ST	LA	WOH	20500	12	E6
RHODA WY	CUL	CUL	10900	50	C3
RHODE ISLAND AV	LA	LA25	12000	41	C4
RHODELIA AV	CLA	CLA	2800	91	A4
RHODES AL	PAS	PAS	900	27	C4
RHODES AV	LA	NHO	5600	16	B6
RHODES AV	LA	NHO	3800	23	B4
RHODES AV	LA	NHO		23	B2
RHODES LN	BAP	BAP	3600	39	B6
RHODES ST	HB	RB	1800	62	C6
RHODESIA AV	LA	SUN	10500	10	E3
RHODODENDRON DR	CO	CYN	15500	125	E6
RHONE DR	RPV	PVP	30300	77	C1
RIAL LN	LA	LA77	1700	32	D2
RIALTO AV	LA	VEN	400	49	C4
RIALTO CT	LA	VEN	600	49	C3
RIALTO DR	LAN	LAN		160	E6
RIALTO ST	LA	SV	11800	9	C6
RIALTO ST	LA	SV		16	C1
RIALTO WY	POM	POM	1000	95	A1
RIALTO GROVE DR	LHH	LAH	2100	98A	B1
RICARDO CT	LAV	LAV	2600	90	E3
RICARDO ST	LA	LA33	1200	45	B2
RICCI AV	WAL	WAL		97	B1
RICE ST	LA	LA42	1800	26	C6
RICH LN	RPV	PVP		78	D3
RICH ST	LA	LA39	2600	35	D3
RICHARD CIR E	LA	LA32	4400	36	E4
RICHARD CIR W	LA	LA32	4400	36	E4
RICHARD DR	LA	LA32	4400	36	E3

STREET	CITY	P.O. ZONE	BLOCK	PAGE	GRID
RICHARD PL	GLEN	GL06	1200	25	E3
RICHARD ST	BUR	BUR	1800	17	D3
RICHARD ST	POM	POM	1700	91	B6
RICHARDSON DR	LA	LA65	3600	35	F2
RICHARDSON LN	GLDR	GLDR		87	A4
RICHARDSON WK	LA	LA65	3700	35	F2
RICHBROOK DR	CO	CLA	500	90	F3
RICHBROOK DR	POM	POM	500	90	F3
RICHBURN AV	CO	LPUE	300	98	E1
RICHDALE AV	CO	LPUE	1900	85	E2
RICHELIEU AV	LA	LA32	2200	36	D6
RICHELIEU PL	LA	LA32	4600	36	C6
RICHELIEU TER	LA	LA32	4600	36	C6
RICHEON AV	DOW	DOW	12000	59	F5
RICHEON AV	DOW	DOW	9600	60	B2
RICHEY DR	LCF	LCF	2200	18	F1
RICHFIELD ST	PAR	PAR	7200	65	E2
RICHFORD AV	CO	LPUE	100	98	D1
RICHGROVE CT	WLVL	THO	32000	102	A4
RICHLAND AV	GLEN	GL06	200	25	E3
RICHLAND AV	LA	LA27	2200	35	A1
RICHLAND AV	LA	LA64	10700	41	E5
RICHLAND AV	LA	LA64	10700	42	A4
RICHLAND PL	PAS	PAS	99	26	E2
RICHLEE AV	SOG	SOG	10200	59	E4
RICHMOND CT	CO	CAL		100	A2
RICHMOND CT	HPK	HPK		52	E5
RICHMOND DR	CLA	CLA	800	91	A2
RICHMOND DR	PR	PR	5000	54	F3
RICHMOND RD	LCF	LCF	400	19	C4
RICHMOND ST	ELS	ELS	100	56	A6
RICHMOND ST	LA	LA33	500	44	F2
RICHMOND ST	PALM	PALM		183	G6
RICHMOND WY	TEC	TEC		38	C4
RICHTER LN	CO	ALT		182	F8
RICHVALE DR	CO	WHI	16300	84	D5
RICHVALE DR	LAM	LAM	14600	84	A5
RICHVIEW DR	CO	LPUE	3100	85	E5
RICHVILLE DR	TOR	TOR	25800	73	C3
RICHWOOD AV	ELM	ELM	3700	38	F6
RICHWOOD AV	ELM	ELM	4700	39	A4
RICHWOOD AV	ELM	ELM	3000	47	E2
RICHWOOD DR	LA	LA49	12200	32	B6
RICKENBACKER RD	BELL	BELL		53	E4
RICKENBACKER RD	CMRC	LA40		54	A4
RICKIE LN	PALM	LAN		171	A1
RICKNEY DR	CO	WOH	4100	13	A4
RICKY LN	LAN	LAN		159	H7
RICO PL	PVE	PVP	1700	72	B4
RIDA ST	PAS	PAS	3100	27	F2
RIDDLE AV	COM	LA59	1900	64	C1
RIDEAU ST	CO	WHI	9900	55	C1
RIDEOUT PL	WHI	WHI		55	D3
RIDEOUT WY	WHI	WHI		55	D3
RIDER CT	CLA	CLA	400	91	B1
RIDERWOOD AV	CO	LPUE	1000	48	C6
RIDERWOOD AV	CO	LPUE	1300	85	C1
RIDERWOOD DR	LA	SUN	8800	10	C2
RIDERWOOD VW E	LA	SUN		10	C2
RIDERWOOD VW W	LA	SUN		10	C2
RIDGE CIR	LA	LA49	12300	32	A2
RIDGE CT	LCF	LCF		19	D1
RIDGE DR	BRAD	DUA	400	29	D3
RIDGE DR	GLEN	GL06	600	25	F2
RIDGE DR	LA	LA49	2000	32	A2
RIDGE RD	SCLR	SAU		127	E1
RIDGE RD	LA	LA49	12400	32	A2
RIDGE RD	WHI	WHI	13600	55	F5
RIDGE WY	LA	LA26	1400	35	C6
RIDGE WY	PAS	PAS	1300	37	B1
RIDGEBLUFF CT	RPV	PVP	27900	72	D4
RIDGEBROOK CT	RPV	PVP	27900	72	D4
RIDGEBROOK DR	AGH	AGO		102	E2
RIDGEBYRNE CT	RPV	PVP	6400	72	C4
RIDGECLIFF LN	LCF	LCF		19	B1
RIDGECOVE CT	RPV	PVP	27900	72	D4
RIDGE CREST CIR	POM	POM		94	D5
RIDGECREST CIR	WAL	WAL		92	F6
RIDGECREST CT	MPK	MPK	1200	45	F3
RIDGE CREST DR	LAV	LAV		95A	E5
RIDGECREST DR	POM	POM		94	D5
RIDGE CREST LN	CER	ART	13300	81	D1
RIDGECREST RD	LA	BH	1300	33	C4
RIDGECREST ST	MPK	MPK	900	45	F3
RIDGECREST ST	MPK	MPK	900	46	A3
RIDGECREST WY	MPK	MPK	1500	46	A3
RIDGECROFT CT	RPV	PVP	28400	72	C5
RIDGEDALE DR	BH	BH		32	F5
RIDGEDALE DR	BH	BH	1000	33	A5
RIDGEFALLS CT	RPV	PVP	28300	72	C4
RIDGEFERN CT	RPV	PVP	28100	72	C4
RIDGEFIELD CT	CO	SAU		124	E4
RIDGEFIELD DR	CLA	CLA		90	F1
RIDGEFIELD DR	CLA	CLA		91	A1
RIDGEFORD DR	WLVL	THO		102	B5

287

1990 LOS ANGELES COUNTY STREET INDEX

RIDGEFOREST CT — ROCK RIVER DR

LOS ANGELES CO.

STREET	CITY	P.O. ZONE	BLOCK	PAGE	GRID
RIDGEFOREST CT	RPV	PVP	28000	72	D4
RIDGEGATE DR	CO	WHI		55	D2
RIDGEGATE DR	RPV	PVP	6000	72	D4
RIDGEGATE LN	PALM	PALM		171	C3
RIDGEGLADE CT	RPV	PVP	6300	72	D4
RIDGEGROVE DR	SCLR	SAU		124	E5
RIDGEHAVEN CT	RPV	PVP	28300	72	C5
RIDGELAND RD	TOR	TOR	2400	73	B4
RIDGELEY DR	LA	LA08	3800	50	F1
RIDGELEY DR	LA	LA16	1900	42	F5
RIDGELEY DR	LA	LA19	1100	42	F3
RIDGELEY DR	LA	LA19	1000	43	A3
RIDGELEY DR	LA	LA36	600	43	A3
RIDGE LINE RD	DBAR	POM		97	F4
RIDGE LINE RD	DBAR	POM		97A	A3
RIDGEMAR CT	RPV	PVP	6300	72	D4
RIDGEMIST ST	CO	LAN	39900	175	B5
RIDGEMONT DR	CO	MAL	3800	114	C4
RIDGEMONT DR	LA	LA46	2100	33	D2
RIDGEMONT LN	WAL	WAL		93	D6
RIDGEMOOR DR	LA	NHO	3800	23	D5
RIDGE OAK DR	LA	LA68	5500	34	D1
RIDGE PARK DR	CO	LPUE	1500	98	B3
RIDGEPATH CT	RPV	PVP	6300	72	D4
RIDGEPINE DR	CO	GL14		11	E4
RIDGEPOINT CT	RPV	PVP	28100	72	D4
RIDGE ROUTE RD	CO	CAST		123	H1
RIDGESIDE CIR	MPK	MPK	800	46	A3
RIDGESIDE DR	MON	MON	600	29	B1
RIDGESIDE DR	MPK	MPK	800	46	A3
RIDGE TER LN	MTB	MTB		46	E4
RIDGETHORN CT	RPV	PVP	28100	72	C4
RIDGETREE AV	WAL	WAL		97	B1
RIDGE VALE	SCLR	NEW		127	H3
RIDGEVIEW AV	CO	LPUE		98	F5
RIDGEVIEW AV	LA	LA41	2500	25	F5
RIDGEVIEW AV	LA	LA41	2000	26	A5
RIDGEVIEW CIR	PALM	PALM		172	E6
RIDGEVIEW DR	CO	ALT	2700	19	E4
RIDGEVIEW DR	GLEN	GL07	1500	25	D1
RIDGEVIEW DR	LAM	LAM		83	D1
RIDGEVIEW ST	LAV	LAV		95A	D6
RIDGEVIEW ST	LAV	LAV		95A	E6
RIDGEWAY DR	GLEN	GL02	1500	25	B1
RIDGEWAY RD	LA	SF	17500	1	D5
RIDGEWAY RD	SMAR	PAS	1500	37	E1
RIDGEWAY ST	POM	POM	100	94	A2
RIDGEWOOD CT	PALM	PALM		172	J4
RIDGEWOOD CT	POM	POM		94	C5
RIDGEWOOD DR	WCOV	WCOV		92	D5
RIDGEWOOD LN	PAS	PAS	500	26	F3
RIDGEWOOD PL	LA	LA28	1300	34	D4
RIDGEWOOD PL	LA	LA38	700	34	D5
RIDGEWOOD PL N	LA	LA04	100	34	D5
RIDGEWOOD PL S	LA	LA04	100	34	D6
RIDGEWOOD ST	LB	LB07	1000	70	D3
RIDING LN	CO	TOP		109	C5
RIDLEY AV	CO	LPUE	1000	48	C6
RIDLEY AV	CO	LPUE	1000	85	C1
RIDPATH DR	LA	LA46	8300	33	D2
RIEGEL DR	ALH	ALH	2300	46	B1
RIEGO DR	DBAR	POM		97	D5
RIENDO LN	LCF	LCF	1500	19	A2
RIESHEL ST	PR	PR	9600	55	A5
RIGALI AV	LA	LA39	4000	25	B6
RIGEL DR	SCLR	CYN	28000	124	G7
RIGGER RD	AGH	AGO		102	D3
RIGGIN ST E	MPK	MPK	100	46	C4
RIGGIN ST W	MPK	MPK	100	46	A4
RIGGS PL	LA	LA45		50	C5
RIGOLETTO ST	LA	WOH	4900	13	A2
RIM LN	DBAR	POM		97	C4
RIM LN	DBAR	WAL		97	C4
RIM RD	DUA	DUA	2300	29	F3
RIM RD	PAS	PAS	500	28	A2
RIMBANK AV	PR	PR	5500	55	A5
RIM CANYON RD	LA	SUN	7800	10	E1
RIMCREST DR	CO	LPUE		85	D5
RIMCREST RD	GLEN	GL02		18	C6
RIMERTON RD	LA	LA77		22	B6
RIMFIELD AV	CO	LAN	41500	171	D2
RIM FIRE LN	DBAR	POM		97	E5
RIMFORD DR	CO	PALM		157	F8
RIMFORD PL	DBAR	POM		97A	B3
RIMGATE CIR	POM	POM		94	D5
RIMGATE DR	CO	WHI	14400	61	F4
RIMGATE DR	CO	WHI		84	A4
RIMGROVE DR	CO	LPUE	400	92	C5
RIMHILL RD	GLEN	GL14	3200	11	D4
RIMHURST AV	CO	COV	4800	89	B3
RIMHURST AV	COV	COV	300	89	B4
RIMHURST AV	GLDR	GLDR	1300	89	B2
RIMMELE DR	LA	BH	9800	32	E3
RIMMER AV	LA	PP	1200	40	D3
RIMPATH DR	CO	COV	21100	89	D5
RIMPAU BLVD	CO	LA43	5100	51	B4
RIMPAU BLVD	LA	LA04	200	43	C1
RIMPAU BLVD	LA	LA05	600	43	C1
RIMPAU BLVD	LA	LA16	1900	43	A5
RIMPAU BLVD	LA	LA19	900	43	B3
RIMPAU BLVD	LA	LA20	300	43	C1
RIMPAU BLVD	LA	LA43	5800	51	B5
RIM RIDGE RD	WAL	WAL		93	B5
RIMROCK CIR	WAL	WAL		92	F5
RIM ROCK DR	CO	LAN		157A	J8
RIMROCK DR	LAM	LAM	11700	84	A5
RIMSDALE AV	CO	AZU	5500	88	C2
RIMSDALE AV	COV	COV	1100	88	C3
RIMSDALE DR	WCOV	WCOV	1000	92	C3
RIMSIDE AV	CO	PALM		190	C1
RIMVALE AV	LAN	LAN	43700	159	J6
RIMVIEW DR	CO	WHI		55	E1
RIMVIEW PL	CO	WAL		97	B5
RIMWOOD DR	WHI	WHI	16800	84	E3
RINALDI PL	LA	NOR	18200	7	C1
RINALDI PL	LA	NOR	18400	7	C1
RINALDI ST	LA	CHA	19600	6	E1
RINALDI ST	LA	NOR	18100	7	A1
RINALDI ST	LA	SF	16500	1	D6
RINALDI ST	LA	SF	14600	2	B6
RINARD AV	CO	COV	4400	88	D4
RINCON AV	CO	MONT	4100	18	F2
RINCON AV	LA	PAC	10000	8	F3
RINCON AV	LA	PAC	9500	9	A4
RINCON AV	LA	SF	11300	2	D6
RINCON AV	LA	SF	11100	8	D1
RINCON AV	LA	SV	8800	9	B5
RINCON AV	LA	SV	8400	16	C1
RINCON DR	CO	WHI	11100	55	C4
RINCON DR	LHH	LAH		98A	B2
RINCON DR	WHI	WHI	10800	55	C4
RINCON LN	PVE	PVP	800	72	C2
RINCONIA DR	LA	LA68	2400	34	C1
RNCN RDBX TK TR	CO			M	F3
RNCN RDBX TK TR	CO			N	A4
RINDGE AV	LA	VEN	7000	55A	E2
RINDGE LN	RB	RB	1000	62	E6
RINDGE LN	RB	RB	500	67	E1
RINETTI LN	LCF	LCF	4500	19	C3
RING ST	LB	LB08	7800	81	B5
RINGBIT RD	RH	PVP	1	78	B2
RINGE CT	POM	POM	1000	95	A1
RINGER PL	CO	LPUE	15300	85	D1
RINGGOLD DR	LA	LA32	4300	36	D3
RINGLING ST	LA	TAR	18600	21	B2
RINGSTEM AV	CO	LAN	42000	171	A1
RINGSTEM AV	LAN	LAN	42200	159	A9
RINGWOOD AV	NWK	NWK	11500	60	F5
RINGWOOD AV	SFS	SFS	10800	61	A4
RINZLER ST	LA	SF	16900	7	E4
RIO AV	LB	LB05	4600	70	C3
RIO CT	CO	LPUE		98	C4
RIO ST	LA	LA23	600	44	F5
RIO ST	LAV	LAV		90	D1
RIO BLANCO AV	MTB	MTB		46	E5
RIO BLANCO RD	LAM	LAM	14500	83	A2
RIO BONITO DR	CO	LPUE		98	C4
RIO BOSQUE DR	SCLR	VAL		124	C6
RIO BRANCA DR	CO	LPUE	2300	85	E3
RIO BUENO CT	SCLR	VAL		124	B5
RIO CHICO DR	SCLR	VAL		124	C6
RIO CLARA DR	SCLR	VAL		124	B6
RIO CLARO DR	CO	LPUE	2800	85	D4
RIO DELL ST	RM	RM	8600	38	B5
RIO DEL SOL AV	MTB	MTB	500	46	F6
RIO DE ORO DR	WCOV	WCOV	1900	92	D3
RIO FLORA PL	DOW	DOW	7000	60	A2
RIO FLORIDA DR	WHI	WHI		84	C1
RIO GARZA DR	SCLR	VAL		124	B6
RIO GRANDE ST	PAS	PAS	400	27	B1
RIO GUSTO CT	SCLR	VAL		124	B6
RIO HONDO AV	ELM	ELM		47	B1
RIO HONDO AV	RM	RM	3400	38	B6
RIO HONDO AV	TEC	TEC	4800	38	B4
RIO HONDO DR	DOW	DOW	7100	59	F2
RIO HONDO DR	SOG	SOG	11300	59	D6
RIO HONDO PKWY	ELM	ELM	1600	39	A3
RIO HONDO PKWY	ELM	ELM	9700	47	C1
RIO HONDO PL	DOW	DOW	7100	60	A2
RIO LEMPA DR	CO	LPUE		85	F5
RIO LINDA DR	RPV	PVP	6200	72	D4
RIO LOBOS RD	DBAR	POM		97	F2
RION TR	CO	TOP	1300	109	D2
RIO PECOS DR	SCLR	VAL		124	C6
RIO POCO	CO	SAU		188	C1
RIO PRADO DR	SCLR	VAL		124	C6
RIO RANCHO RD	POM	POM		94	C6
RIO REYES CT	SCLR	VAL		124	B5
RIOS ST	LA	WOH	20900	13	D3
RIO SECO DR	CO	LPUE	18100	98	D3
RIO TAJO CT	SCLR	VAL		124	B5
RIO VERDE DR	WCOV	WCOV	1400	92	E1
RIO VISTA AV	LA	LA23	1200	44	F6
RIPLEY AV	RB	RB	2300	62	F6
RIPLEY AV	RB	RB	1700	67	E1
RIPON AV	BLF	BLF	15900	66	D3
RIPPLE PL	LA	LA39	2800	35	D2
RIPPLE ST	LA	LA39	1800	35	D2
RIPTON RD	CO	PALM		157	G8
RISA DR	GLEN	GL08	2200	18	F5
RISA PL	GLEN	GL08	1800	18	F5
RISING DR	LA	LA32	4000	36	B5
RISING GLEN PL	LA	LA69	8800	33	D3
RISING GLEN RD	LA	LA69	1400	33	D3
RISING HILL RD	CO	ALT	4300	19	E2
RISING HILL RD	POM	POM		94	D5
RISING STAR DR	DBAR	POM	2600	97	D5
RISLEY ST	WHI	WHI	15600	84	C4
RISTA DR	AGH	AGO		102	E3
RITA AV	HPK	HPK	5900	52	F5
RITA LN	WCOV	WCOV		92	E6
RITA ST	PALM	PALM	38200	172	E9
RITA ST	RB	RB	700	67	E4
RITCHIE ST	LB	LB08	7800	81	A5
RITNER ST	CAR	CAR	100	69	A4
RITNER ST	CO	TOR	1100	68	F4
RITTER ST	DBAR	POM		97	F1
RIVAS CANYON RD	LA	PP	900	40	E3
RIVENDALE	WCOV	WCOV		92	D4
RIVER AV	CO	RM		47	A2
RIVER AV	LB	LB10	3600	69	F5
RIVER AV	LB	LB10	2000	74	F3
RIVER AV	RM	RM	2500	47	A2
RIVER CIR	SCLR	CYN		125	B9
RIVER DR	BELL	BELL	6200	53	E5
RIVER ST	LA	LA31	400	35	F5
RIVER ST	LA	LA65	500	35	F5
RIVERA PL	PVE	PVP		72	B6
RIVERA RD	CO	WHI	10800	61	A1
RIVERA RD	PR	PR	9000	54	E6
RIVERA RD	SFS	SFS	11900	55	C6
RIVERA RD	SFS	SFS	12000	55	C6
RIVERA RD	SFS	SFS	11600	61	A1
RIVERA RD	WHI	WHI	12100	61	C1
RIVERA ST	LA	LA63	100	45	B4
RIVER ACCESS RD	CO	WHI		47	E4
RIVERBEND ST	PALM	PALM		171	H6
RIVERDALE AV	LA	LA31	2200	35	E4
RIVERDALE DR	GLEN	GL04	300	25	B5
RIVER FARM DR	WLVL	THO		102	A5
RIVERGRADE RD	BAP	BAP		39	C3
RIVERGRADE RD	CO	BAP		39	C3
RIVERGRADE RD	CO	BAP	900	48	B2
RIVERGRADE RD	CO	LPUE	200	48	B2
RIVERGRADE RD	IRW	BAP		39	C3
RIVER GROVE DR	DOW	DOW		54	B6
RIVERS RD	LA	LA49	13100	30	F6
RIVERSBRIDGE WY	CO	VAL		124	B7
RIVERSIDE AV	BELL	BELL	6200	53	C5
RIVERSIDE AV	HPK	HPK	5900	53	C4
RIVERSIDE DR	BUR	BUR	400	24	C3
RIVERSIDE DR	GLEN	GL01	1500	24	F3
RIVERSIDE DR	LA	LA27		24	F3
RIVERSIDE DR	LA	LA27	3100	35	B2
RIVERSIDE DR	LA	LA31	900	35	E4
RIVERSIDE DR	LA	LA39	1800	35	B2
RIVERSIDE DR	LA	NHO	10000	23	D2
RIVERSIDE DR	LA	NHO	10100	24	A3
RIVERSIDE DR	LA	VAN	13300	22	E2
RIVERSIDE DR	LA	VAN	12900	23	A2
RIVERSIDE PL	LA	LA39	2400	35	C3
RIVERSIDE TER	LA	LA39	2500	35	D3
RIVERTON AV	LA	NHO	5600	16	E6
RIVERTON AV	LA	NHO	3800	23	E3
RIVERTON AV	LA	SV	7200	16	E3
RIVERVIEW AV	ELM	ELM	600	38	D5
RIVER VIEW RD	MTB	MTB	100	54	E2
RIVERVIEW ST	LA	LA31		35	F3
RIVERWOOD DR	LA	SUN		10	D1
RIVERWOOD TER	LA	SUN		10	D1
RIVES AV	DOW	DOW	8500	54	C6
RIVES AV	DOW	DOW	12000	59	F5
RIVES AV	DOW	DOW	9000	60	C1
RIVIERA AV	LA	VEN	1100	49	C4
RIVIERA CIR	LB	LB15		76	D4
RIVIERA CIR	PAS	PAS	1200	28	A1
RIVIERA CT	PALM	PALM		173	A9
RIVIERA DR	PAS	PAS	1500	20A	A3
RIVIERA DR	PAS	PAS	900	28	A2
RIVIERA DR	WAL	WAL		92	F6
RIVIERA WK	LB	LB03	5500	80	C1
RIVIERA WY	TOR	TOR	5400	67	E6
RIVIERA RCH RD	LA	LA49	13100	40	F2
RIVKIND LN	LA	SUN	10100	10	A2
RIVO ALTO CANAL	LB	LB03	1	80	C1
RIVOL RD	LA	CAN	7000	5	D3
RIXFORD AV	LAW	LAW	15700	63	B4
ROA DR	CAR	CAR	16900	64	B5
ROADRUNNER LN	CO	LR	16000	192	B7
ROAD RUNNER RD	SCLR	CYN		125	C9
ROADRUNNER RD	RH	PVP	1	73	B5
ROAD RUNNER ST	PALM	PALM		172	B5
ROADRUNNER WY	LAN	LAN		159	G9
ROADS END	GLEN	GL05	300	25	D6
ROADSIDE DR	AGH	AGO		100A	B4
ROADSIDE DR	AGH	AGO		102	D4
ROAN DR	RPV	PVP	28600	73	C6
ROANOAK	WCOV	WCOV		92	D4
ROANOKE PL	CO	PAS	1100	19	B5
ROANOKE RD	CLA	CLA	2100	91	B2
ROANOKE RD	CO	SGAB	8500	27	F6
ROANOKE RD	SMAR	PAS	800	37	C2
ROANOKE ST	LHH	LAH		84	D3
ROANWOOD DR	RHE	PVP	26300	73	A3
ROARK DR	ALH	ALH	2200	46	B1
ROB CIR	WAL	WAL		93	C4
ROBALO AV	LA	SP	2400	78	D5
ROBBIE CT	BAP	BAP	14300	48	E1
ROBBINS DR	ARC	ARC	400	28	F6
ROBBINS DR	BH	BH	9900	42	B1
ROBERT AV	BLF	BLF	14400	66	B2
ROBERT AV	LA	SV	8400	9	E6
ROBERT AV	LA	SV	8400	16	E1
ROBERT LN	BH	BH	400	33	C4
ROBERT PL	LA	WOH	20400	13	E3
ROBERT RD	CO	LPUE		97	B5
ROBERT RD	TOR	TOR	23000	67	E6
ROBERTA ST	CER	ART		66	E4
ROBERTA ST	LA	LA31	3600	36	B4
ROBERT GUY RD	HH	CAL	24700	100	C2
ROBERTO AV	WCOV	WCOV	100	88	A6
ROBERTO CT	LAN	LAN		160	C3
ROBERTO LN	LA	LA77	1100	32	D4
ROBERTS AV	CUL	CUL	3100	42	E5
ROBERTS RD	CO	ACT		189	E2
ROBERTS RD	CO	MAL		113	A4
ROBERTS ST E	POM	POM	200	90	F5
ROBERTS WK	CO	CAST	28900	123	C1
ROBERTSON BLVD	CUL	CUL	3700	42	C5
ROBERTSON BL N	BH	BH	100	42	D2
ROBERTSON BL N	LA	LA48	100	33	D6
ROBERTSON BL N	WHOL	LA48	300	33	D6
ROBERTSON BL N	WHOL	LA69	600	33	D6
ROBERTSON BL S	BH	BH	100	42	D2
ROBERTSON BL S	LA	LA34	1900	42	D4
ROBERTSON BL S	LA	LA35	400	42	D2
ROBERTSON BL S	LA	LA35	1100	42	D4
ROBERTSON BL S	LA	LA48	100	33	D6
ROBERTSON PL	LA	LA34	2900	42	C5
ROBT STOCKTN PL	LA	SP	27700	73	E5
ROBERTS VIEW PL	LA	NHO	3600	23	D5
RBT W PRESCT WY	LA	LA45		56	D5
ROBIDOUX ST E	LA	WIL	900	74	D3
ROBIDOUX ST W	LA	WIL	1000	74	A3
ROBIN AV	BAP	BAP	4100	39	E5
ROBIN AV	SCLR	SAU		124	F4
ROBIN DR	LA	LA69	9200	33	D3
ROBIN LN	LOM	LOM		73	C2
ROBIN LN	PALM	PALM		183	F1
ROBIN RD	LAV	LAV		95A	C5
ROBIN RD	SMAR	PAS	1800	37	E1
ROBIN RD	WCOV	WCOV	100	92	C1
ROBIN ST	CO	LA59	11600	58	D5
ROBIN WY	IND	LPUE	16000	85	F1
ROBIN WY	POM	POM	3100	90	E3
ROBINA AV	PALM	PALM	37800	172	D9
ROBINBROOK PL	DBAR	POM		97A	A3
ROBIN CREST CT	SCLR	CYN		125	B8
ROBINCROFT DR	PAS	PAS	200	27	A1
ROBINDALE ST	WCOV	WCOV	1700	48	F1
ROBINDALE ST	WCOV	WCOV	1000	92	A2
ROBINETTE AV	BAP	BAP	3400	39	C6
ROBINETTE AV	BAP	BAP	3200	48	C1
ROBIN GLEN DR	GLEN	GL02		18	B6
ROBIN HILL RD	LCF	LCF	3900	19	B4
ROBINHOOD AV	TEC	TEC	4800	38	C3
ROBINHOOD LN	LA	LA46		33	D1
ROBIN HOOD PL	WLVL	THO		102	B5
ROBINLINDA LN	CO	RM	1700	46	E4
ROBINLINDA LN	MPK	MPK		46	E4
ROBIN OAKS TER	DBAR	POM		97	E3
ROBINSON CT	LAN	LAN		160	D7
ROBINSON RD	CO	TOP	700	109	D3
ROBINSON RD	PAS	PAS	200	27	A1
ROBINSON ST	LA	LA26	100	35	A6
ROBINSON ST	RB	RB	1900	62	E4
ROBINVIEW LN	RPV	PVP	28500	72	F6
ROBINWOOD DR	LA	LA49	400	41	B1
ROBINWOOD LN	WAL	WAL		92	F6
ROBLAR PL	LA	VAN	14200	22	E4
ROBLAR RD	LA	VAN	14000	22	E4
ROBLE AV	LA	LA42	6900	36	D2
ROBLE LN	LAV	LAV		95A	E5
ROBLE WY	LB	LB02		75	C5
ROBLES AV	SMAR	PAS	2200	27	D5
ROBLES LN	AGH	AGO		102	E3
ROBLE VISTA DR	LA	LA27	3800	35	B2
ROBLIN ST	CAR	CAR	100	64	B6
ROBMAR DR	LA	BH	1400	33	A3
ROBOJO DR	CO	PALM		171I	E4
ROBRUCE DR	CO	LPUE		85	D3
ROBRUCE LN	CO	LPUE	2100	85	D3
ROBSON ST	SM	SM	1700	49	C2
ROCA DR	GLEN	GL07	1500	25	E1
ROCA WY	MPK	MPK	100	46	B3
ROCA CHICA DR	CO	MAL	20100	115	A4
ROCCA CT	LA	LA77		32	E4
ROCCA PL	LA	LA77	10500	32	D4
ROCCA WY	LA	LA77	10500	32	E4
ROCCUS LN	TEC	SGAB	8600	38	A2
ROCHDALE CT	SAD	SAD		89	D4
ROCHEDALE LN	LA	LA49	12300	32	A6
ROCHEDALE WY	LA	LA49	700	32	A6
ROCHELLE AV	CER	ART		81	C1
ROCHELLE AV	CO	MON	2200	29	A6
ROCHELLE AV	CO	MON	2400	39	A1
ROCHELLE AV	MON	MON	2600	39	A1
ROCHELLE LN	LB	LB15		76	E4
ROCHELLE PL	LA	ENC	4400	21	E3
ROCHESTER AV	LA	LA24	10200	41	E2
ROCHESTER AV	LA	LA25	11400	41	C4
ROCHESTER CIR	LA	LA18	1900	43	D6
ROCHESTER CT	CER	ART		66	D2
ROCHLEN ST	CO	LPUE	15200	85	D1
ROCK LN	LAV	LAV		90	D1
ROCK ST	LA	LA26	2100	35	B3
ROCK TR	CO	TOP	500	109	E4
ROCKBLUFF DR	RHE	PVP	4600	72	F3
ROCK BLUFF RD	POM	POM		94	C4
ROCK BRIDGE RD	DBAR	POM		93	F6
ROCKBURY DR	DBAR	POM		94	B6
ROCKBURY DR	DBAR	POM		97A	B1
ROCK CASTLE DR	CO	GL14	5100	11	F5
ROCKCLIFF CT	PALM	PALM		171	D9
ROCKCLIFF DR	LA	LA68	6100	24	D6
ROCKCLIFF PL	POM	POM		94	E6
ROCKCLIFF PL	POM	POM		97A	C1
ROCK CREEK RD	AGH	AGO		102	F3
ROCK CREST LN	POM	POM		94	E6
ROCK CREST LN	POM	POM		97A	E1
ROCKCROFT DR	CO	MAL		115	A4
ROCKDALE AV	LA	LA41	900	26	C5
ROCKDELL ST	CO	GL14	2300	11	E5
ROCKENBACH ST	BAP	BAP	13300	39	E4
ROCKERFELLER LN	RB	RB	1700	62	E6
ROCKET RD	SCLR	SAU		127	E1
ROCKET ST	LKD	LKD	5500	71	C1
ROCKETDYNE RD	CO	CAN		4	A5
ROCKFIELD DR	CO	ARC	11200	38	F3
ROCKFOLD DR	CO	LPUE		85	C2
ROCKFORD DR	CLA	CLA	600	91	C2
ROCKFORD RD	LA	LA39	1900	35	C4
ROCK GLEN AV	GLEN	GL05	1400	25	E4
ROCK GLEN AV	LA	LA41	2700	25	E4
ROCKGROVE AV	SCLR	CYN	27200	124	J9
ROCK HAVEN ST	MPK	MPK	1300	45	F3
ROCKHILL DR	CO	CHA	23500	4	B5
ROCKHILL DR	CO	LPUE	14700	85	C2
ROCKHOLD AV	CO	SGAB	6700	27	F6
ROCKHOLD AV	CO	SGAB	6700	37	F1
ROCKHOLD AV	RM	RM	3300	37	F6
ROCKHOLD AV	RM	RM	3300	46	F1
ROCKHURST LN	RPV	PVP	5500	72	F4
ROCKINGHAM AV N	LA	LA49	100	41	A2
ROCKINGHAM AV S	LA	LA49	100	41	A2
ROCKINGHORSE DR	RPV	SP	2100	73	D6
ROCKINGHORSE RD	RPV	PVP	1	73	C6
ROCKING HRSE RD	WAL	WAL		93	A5
ROCK ISLAND DR	LAN	LAN		160	E4
ROCKLAND AV	LA	LA41	5100	26	A4
ROCKLAND PL	CO	MONT	4100	18	F2
ROCKLAND PL	LCF	LCF	4500	18	F1
ROCKLEDGE RD	LA	LA68	2100	34	B1
ROCKMEAD CT	CO	LPUE		85	C4
ROCKMERE WY	LCF	LCF	4400	18	F2
ROCKMILL RD	CO	MAL		112	B1
ROCKMONT AV	CO	CLA	2900	91	A1
ROCKNE AV	CO	WHI	6100	55	B4
ROCKNE AV	WHI	WHI	5400	55	C3
ROCK PARK DR	RPV	PVP	7000	72	C5
ROCKPINE LN	CO	GL14		11	E5
ROCKPOINT RD	CO	MAL	20600	115	A4
ROCKPORT WY	CO	MAL	20100	115	B4
ROCKPORT WY	CO	SAU		123	D4
ROCKRIDGE CT	SCLR	VAL		124	E3
ROCKRIDGE LN	DBAR	POM		97	C5
ROCK RIDGE TER	LA	CAN	7100	5	E3
ROCKRIDGE TER	LCF	LCF	2100	18	F2
ROCK RIVER DR	DBAR	POM		93	F5

INDEX

COPYRIGHT, © 1989 BY Thomas Bros maps

1990 LOS ANGELES COUNTY STREET INDEX

STREET	CITY	P.O. ZONE	BLOCK	PAGE	GRID
ROCK RIVER RD	DBAR	POM		93	F6
ROCK RIVER RD	DBAR	POM		97	F1
ROCK ROSE ST	CO	MON	100	29	A5
ROCK TREE DR	AGH	AGO		100A	A3
ROCKVALE AV	AZU	AZU	200	86	E6
ROCKVALE AV	AZU	AZU	5500	88	E1
ROCKVALE AV	CO	AZU	5300	88	E2
ROCKVALLEY RD	RPV	PVP	4000	72	E4
ROCK VIEW CT	MPK	MPK	1800	45	F3
ROCKVIEW DR	TOR	TOR	5100	67	E5
ROCKVIEW ST	LA	LA41	1100	26	C4
ROCK VIEW ST	MPK	MPK	1200	45	F3
ROCKVIEW TER	CO	TOP		109	A6
ROCKVIEW TER	CO	TOP		115	A1
ROCKVIEW TER	LA	LA41	5300	26	C4
ROCK VISTA DR	AGH	AGO		100A	A3
ROCKWALL ST	LKD	LKD	11700	81	A3
ROCKWAY DR	BAP	BAP	13400	39	D6
ROCKWAY DR	BAP	BAP	13800	48	D1
ROCKWAY DR E	WCOV	BAP	14500	48	E2
ROCKWELL AV	ELM	ELM	3600	38	C6
ROCKWELL CYN RD	CO	VAL		126	J1
ROCKWOOD RD	PAS	PAS	600	26	E5
ROCKWOOD ST	CO	LA63	3900	45	D3
ROCKWOOD ST	LA	LA26	1500	44	C1
ROCKYFORD RD	CO	PALM		190	B1
ROCKY HILL AV	MTB	MTB		46	D6
ROCKY KNOLL RD	CO	LPUE		98	A4
ROCKY LEDGE RD	CO	TOP		109	B6
ROCKY MESA PL	CO	CAN		4	A5
ROCKY MTN WY	SFS	SFS		60	F3
ROCKY POINT LN	DBAR	POM		97	C4
ROCKY POINT PL	PVE	PVP	2200	72	A5
ROCKY POINT RD	LA	HAC		74	A2
ROCKY POINT RD	PVE	PVP	100	72	A5
ROCKYRIVER LN	CER	ART	16100	82	C4
ROCKY TOP RD	CO	SAU		181	D9
ROCKY TRAIL RD	DBAR	POM		97	E5
ROCKY VIEW RD	DBAR	POM		97	F4
ROCOSO PL	LA	TAR	18600	21	C3
ROCTON DR	PAS	PAS		27	E2
ROD AV	LA	WOH	5900	5	D6
ROD PL	LA	WOH	24600	5	D6
RODARTE WY	LA	ENC	18000	21	D3
RODAX ST	LA	CAN	20400	12	E1
RODECKER DR	AZU	AZU	200	86	D6
RODECKER DR	AZU	AZU	100	88	D1
RODEFFER PL	CO	SAU		124	D4
RODELL PL E	ARC	ARC	1	38	E2
RODELL PL W	ARC	ARC	1	38	E2
RODEO CT	SAD	SAD		90	A1
RODEO DR	LA	LA35	1100	42	C2
RODEO DR N	BH	BH	300	33	B6
RODEO DR N	BH	BH	200	42	B1
RODEO DR S	BH	BH	100	42	C2
RODEO LN	LA	LA16	4500	43	A6
RODEO LN	LAV	LAV	4000	90	E1
RODEO PL	LA	LA16	5100	42	F6
RODEO PL	LA	LA16	5100	43	A6
RODEO RD	ARC	ARC	800	28	E3
RODEO RD	GLDR	GLDR	100	87	D5
RODEO RD	LA	LA16	5100	42	E6
RODEO RD	LA	LA16	3600	43	A6
RODEO RD	LA	LA18	1800	43	C6
RODEO WY	WAL	WAL		93	D5
RODEO GROUNDS	CO	MAL	3700	115	E4
RODERICK AV	POM	POM	400	90	F4
RODERICK PL	LA	LA65	3000	35	E1
RODERICK RD	LA	LA65	3600	35	E1
RODGERS DR	SCLR	SAU		124	G5
RODGERTON DR	LA	LA68	6000	24	D6
RODIER DR	GLEN	GL01	400	24	F3
RODILEE AV	WCOV	WCOV	300	92	D2
RODIN AV	LAN	LAN	44300	160	C5
RODIN PL	LA	LA41	2900	25	F5
RODLOY AV	LB	LB10	2700	75	A1
RODMAN AV	POM	POM	1000	95	A1
RODMAN CIR	MPK	MPK	700	46	B3
RODNEY DR	LA	LA27	1500	34	F3
RODNEY RD	WCOV	WCOV		92	C4
ROEBLING AV	LA	LA24	10900	41	D1
ROEBUCK ST	BLF	BLF	10600	66	D5
ROELLE RD	IND	LPUE	19300	97	A3
ROELLE RD	IND	WAL	19600	97	A3
ROESSLER CT	CO	PVP		73	A4
ROGAN CT	CO	LPUE		97	A5
ROGEN DR	LA	ENC	4000	21	F4
ROGENE ST	LB	LB15	5800	76	D1
ROGER CT	POM	POM	100	94	F6
ROGER CT	PR	PR	8600	54	E3
ROGER RD	CO	ACT		189	D1
ROGERS AV	LA	LA23	2200	45	A4
ROGERS PL	BUR	BUR	1700	17	C4
ROGERS ST	CO	LA63	3900	45	D2
ROGERS ST	LB	LB05	1600	70	E1
ROGIER ST	LAN	LAN		160	E6
ROGOWAY LN	CO	PVP		73	B3
ROGUE WY	CO	CAST		123	J1
ROHR ST	GLEN	GL02	1700	18	B6
ROJAS ST	CO	LPUE	15300	85	D3
ROKEBY ST	LA	LA39	2600	35	B2
ROLAINE ST	BLF	BLF		66	D4
ROLAND ST	AZU	AZU	100	88	D1
ROLAND WK	LA	LA36	6000	42	F2
ROLANDA ST	LB	LB15	5500	76	C2
ROLANDEE ST	CO	SAU		182	F7
ROLKEL PL	LA	NOR	11100	7	B1
ROLLA RD	SCLR	SAU		124	J3
ROLLA RD	CO	SAU		125	A3
ROLLND CRTIS PL	LA	LA37		51	E1
ROLLND CRTIS PL	LA	LA62		51	E1
ROLLANDO DR	RHE	PVP	4300	72	F3
ROLLE ST	LA	LA31	3600	36	B5
ROLLIN ST	SPAS	SPAS	800	36	F2
ROLLIN ST	SPAS	SPAS	1400	37	A2
ROLLING RD	LA	WOH	5700	12	B6
ROLLING GRNS WY	CO	LPUE	1500	47	F5
ROLLING HILL DR	MPK	MPK	1400	46	A4
ROLLING HLLS AV	CO	CYN		128	C1
ROLLING HLLS AV	SCLR	CYN		125	C9
ROLLING HLLS DR	POM	POM		94	C5
ROLLING HLLS LN	CO	CAST		123	H2
ROLLING HLLS RD	RHE	PVP	26100	73	B4
ROLLING HLLS RD	TOR	TOR	25400	73	B3
ROLLING HLLS RD	WCOV	WCOV		92	E3
ROLLING KNLL DR	DBAR	POM		97A	A3
ROLLING MDWS LN	RHE	PVP	4900	72	F3
ROLLING MDWS RD	RHE	PVP	4900	72	F3
ROLLING RDG DR	AGH	AGO		102	E2
ROLLING RDG DR	BUR	BUR	2900	17	C2
ROLLING RDG DR	POM	POM		94	C6
ROLLINGRIDGE RD	RPV	PVP	5200	72	E3
ROLLING VIEW RD	HH	CAL		100	D2
ROLLING VIS DR	RPV	LOM		73	D4
ROLLINGWOOD DR	RHE	PVP	1	72	E3
ROLLINS DR	CO	LA63	1300	45	E3
ROLLINS RD	CO	CHA		4	C5
ROLLINS WY	POM	POM	2100	90	F6
ROLOMAR DR	LA	ENC	4100	21	F4
ROLYN PL	ARC	ARC	1	28	E4
ROMA CT	LA	VEN		49	C5
ROMA DR	LAM	LAM	14700	83	A2
ROMA PL	POM	POM		94	B3
ROMA ST	PR	PR	9700	60	E2
ROMA ST	SFS	SFS	11200	60	F2
ROMA ST	SFS	SFS	11600	61	A2
ROMAINE ST	LA	LA29	4900	34	D4
ROMAINE ST	LA	LA38	5400	34	B4
ROMAINE ST	LA	LA69	8300	33	E4
ROMAINE ST	WHOL	LA46	7500	33	E4
ROMAINE ST	WHOL	LA46	7100	34	B4
ROMAINE ST	WHOL	LA48	7000	34	B4
ROMAINE ST	WHOL	LA69	8300	33	E4
ROMANDEL AV	SFS	SFS	9900	61	C3
ROMANO PL	TOR	TOR	23100	67	F6
ROMANY DR	LA	PP	13500	40	F2
ROMAR LN	SCLR	SAU		124	G5
ROMAR PL	LA	SF	19300	7	A3
ROMAR ST	LA	CHA	19700	6	F3
ROMAR ST	LA	NOR	17000	7	E3
ROMAR ST	LA	SF	16500	7	F3
ROMAR ST	LA	SF	15000	8	C3
ROMBERG PL	LA	WOH	4600	13	A3
ROME CT	LA	LA65	3900	36	A3
ROME DR	LA	LA65	2000	35	F2
ROME DR	LA	LA65	700	36	A3
ROMEO CYN RD	CO	CAST		123	E1
ROMERO CT	WAL	WAL		93	A5
ROMERO DR	LA	TAR	4300	21	A3
ROMERO DR	WHI	WHI	14700	84	B1
ROMERO CYN RD	CO	CAST		123	A2
ROMNEY DR	DBAR	WAL		97	D3
ROMNEY DR	PAS	PAS	1100	26	D6
ROMNEY WY	PAS	PAS	1200	26	D6
ROMOLA AV	LAV	LAV	1100	90	B1
ROMOLA AV	LAV	LAV	1500	95A	B6
ROMOLA AV	SAD	LAV	1700	95A	B6
ROMONA RD	PALM	PALM		183	G3
ROMONT ST	LA	SF	12900	3	A6
ROMULO ST	LA	LA65	600	35	F4
ROMULUS DR	GLEN	GL05	1200	25	E5
ROMULUS DR	LA	LA65	3200	25	E5
RON RIDGE DR	SCLR	SAU		124	D4
RONALD AV	TOR	TOR	19000	67	E2
RONALD DR	CO	WHI	11700	61	F5
RONALD DR	LAM	LAM	11700	84	A5
RONALD DR	SFS	WHI	11700	61	F5
RONAN AV	CAR	CAR	21300	69	B4
RONAN AV	CAR	CAR	23600	74	B1
RONAN AV	LA	WIL	1000	74	B4
RONAR ST	CO	LAN	40000	174	J4
RONDA CIR	LAV	LAV		90	B1
RONDA DR	LA	LA32	1800	45	C1
RONDA DR	MB	MB	1100	62	C5
RONDA VISTA DR	LA	LA27	2200	35	B3
RONDA VISTA PL	LA	LA27	3800	35	B3
RONDELL ST	CO	CAL		100	A4
RONDELL ST	CO	CAL		100A	F4
RONDERO RDG WY	CO	MAL		112	D3
RONDOUT ST E	LA	LA12	100	44	E1
RONDOUT ST W	LA	LA12	100	44	E1
RONMAR PL	LA	WOH	4700	13	E3
RONNIE ST	CO	LPUE	16800	92	B4
RONSARD RD	RPV	SP	2100	78	D1
RONWOOD ST	GLDR	GLDR		89	B1
ROOD ST	PAR	PAR	7200	65	E1
ROOKS RD	IND	WHI		47	D5
ROOSEVELT AV	CO	ALT	1680	20	E6
ROOSEVELT AV	CO	CAST	28400	123	A6
ROOSEVELT AV	DOW	DOW	8400	66	A1
ROOSEVELT AV	LA	LA06	1600	43	E4
ROOSEVELT AV	MTB	MTB	100	54	D2
ROOSEVELT AV	POM	POM	200	90	F6
ROOSEVELT AV	SOG	SOG	5700	59	E6
ROOSEVELT AV E	POM	POM		94	F1
ROOSEVELT AV N	CO	PAS	1200	27	E1
ROOSEVELT AV N	PAS	PAS	100	27	E5
ROOSEVELT AV S	CO	PAS	300	27	E5
ROOSEVELT AV S	PAS	PAS	100	27	E5
ROOSEVELT RD	LB	LB07	100	70	C4
ROOSEVELT ST	AZU	AZU	1500	88	B1
ROOSEVELT ST	LAV	LAV		90	E4
ROOT ST	BAP	BAP	15000	39	F5
ROOT ST	WCOV	WCOV	1800	88	A5
ROPER AV	NWK	NWK	13500	82	C2
ROPER ST	LB	LB08	7800	81	A6
RORIMER ST	CO	LPUE	18400	98	E1
RORIMER ST	LPUE	LPUE	16600	98	A1
ROSA AV	LAV	LAV	2500	90	B2
ROSA RD	LA	WOH	4800	13	A2
ROSABELL ST	CUL	LA66	4000	49	E3
ROSABELL ST	LA	LA12	800	44	E2
ROSADA ST	LB	LB15	4300	76	B3
ROSALES AL	PAR	PAR	15500	65	E3
ROSALES ST	LA	SF	14600	2	D2
ROSALIA RD	LA	LA27	1500	35	A3
ROSALIND AV	LA	LA23	1100	45	A6
ROSALIND PL	LA	LA23	2900	45	A6
ROSALIND RD	SMAR	PAS	800	27	C6
ROSALINDA AV	AZU	AZU	300	88	D2
ROSALITA DR	LAM	LAM	15000	83	A2
ROSALYNN DR	GLDR	GLDR	200	89	B1
ROSAMOND DR	SCLR	CYN	27800	124	H5
ROSANNA CT	CO	TOR		68	F6
ROSANNA ST	LA	LA39	2800	35	D2
ROSARIO AV	LAM	LAM		83	C1
ROSARIO AV	LAN	LAN		160	F4
ROSARIO DR	CO	TOP	1000	109	D3
ROSARIO RD	LA	WOH	4100	13	D4
ROSCOE BLVD	LA	CAN	23000	5	E1
ROSCOE BLVD	LA	CAN	19700	12	B1
ROSCOE BLVD	LA	NHO	11800	16	A1
ROSCOE BLVD	LA	NOR	17000	14	A1
ROSCOE BLVD	LA	SF	16400	14	A1
ROSCOE BLVD	LA	SF	15000	15	B1
ROSCOE BLVD	LA	SV	10200	16	A1
ROSCOE BLVD	LA	SV	9900	17	A1
ROSCOE BLVD	LA	VAN	16600	14	A1
ROSCOE BLVD	LA	VAN	13400	15	B1
ROSCOE PL	LA	SF	16500	14	F1
ROSCOMARE	LA	LA77		22	C6
ROSCOMARE RD	LA	LA49	2900	22	C6
ROSCOMARE RD	LA	LA77	2200	22	C6
ROSCOMARE RD	LA	LA77	900	32	C4
ROSCOMMON AV	CO	LA22	100	45	F5
ROSCOMMON AV	MPK	MPK		45	F5
ROSE AL	PAS	PAS	2700	27	E4
ROSE AV	BELL	BELL	3300	53	B5
ROSE AV	DOW	DOW	12400	60	B6
ROSE AV	LA	LA34	10500	42	B5
ROSE AV	LA	LA66	11300	49	D2
ROSE AV	LA	VEN	100	49	B3
ROSE AV	LB	LB02	400	75	E4
ROSE AV	LB	LB05	5200	70	E2
ROSE AV	LB	LB07	3400	70	E5
ROSE AV	LB	LB13	700	75	E4
ROSE AV	PAS	PAS	900	27	E2
ROSE AV	SGAB	SGAB	700	37	E1
ROSE AV	SH	LB06	2100	75	E2
ROSE AV	SH	LB06	2200	75	E2
ROSE AV	SMAR	PAS	2000	37	E1
ROSE AV N	COM	COM	100	65	A3
ROSE AV S	COM	COM	100	65	A3
ROSE CIR	CER	ART		66	E6
ROSE CT	LA	VEN		49	C3
ROSE CT	LA	VEN		49	B3
ROSE DR	GLDR	GLDR	1000	87	C3
ROSE DR	WHI	WHI		55	D3
ROSE LN	CO	TOP		108	F3
ROSE LN	MTB	MTB	100	54	C1
ROSE LN	SPAS	SPAS	1900	37	A1
ROSE PL	LB	LB02	400	75	E5
ROSE ST	BLF	BLF	8500	66	A6
ROSE ST	CER	ART	12000	66	F5
ROSE ST	CER	ART	12200	82	B5
ROSE ST	COM	COM	4700	65	C3
ROSE ST	CO	COM	4300	65	C3
ROSE ST	ELM	ELM	9900	38	C5
ROSE ST	LA	LA12	100	44	E3
ROSE ST	PALM	PALM		183	J1
ROSE ST	PALM	PALM		184	A1
ROSE ST	PAR	PAR	7800	65	F2
ROSE ST	RM	RM	9200	38	B5
ROSE ST N	BUR	BUR	1300	16	F6
ROSE ST N	BUR	BUR	1000	23	F1
ROSE ST N	BUR	BUR	100	24	A1
ROSE ST S	BUR	BUR	100	24	A1
ROSE WK	CO	CAST		123	C2
ROSE WY	WCOV	WCOV		92	A1
ROSEAPPLE RD	RPV	PVP	1	77	F2
ROSEBANK DR	LCF	LCF	4700	18	F1
ROSEBAY ST	LB	LB08	5300	71	C6
ROSEBERRY AV	CO	HPK	7200	52	E6
ROSE BOWL DR	PAS	PAS	800	26	E2
ROSEBROOK LN	RM	RM		46	F3
ROSEBUD AV	LA	LA39	1900	35	D3
ROSECOURT DR	CO	CYN		125	F5
ROSECRANS AV	ELS	ELS	500	62	B2
ROSECRANS AV	MB	MB	100	62	B2
ROSECRANS AV E	BLF	BLF	9000	66	B2
ROSECRANS AV E	CO	COM	1200	64	C2
ROSECRANS AV E	CO	COM	4300	65	A2
ROSECRANS AV E	CO	GAR	100	64	C2
ROSECRANS AV E	CO	LA59	600	64	C2
ROSECRANS AV E	COM	COM	100	64	C2
ROSECRANS AV E	COM	COM	300	65	A2
ROSECRANS AV E	COM	LA59	700	64	C2
ROSECRANS AV E	DOW	DOW	8700	66	B2
ROSECRANS AV E	LAM	LAM	14200	82	B2
ROSECRANS AV E	LAM	LAM	14500	83	A2
ROSECRANS AV E	NWK	NWK	10600	66	B2
ROSECRANS AV E	NWK	NWK	11400	82	B2
ROSECRANS AV E	PAR	PAR	6600	65	A2
ROSECRANS AV E	PAR	PAR	8300	66	B2
ROSECRANS AV E	SFS	SFS	13100	82	B2
ROSECRANS AV W	CO	GAR	1700	63	C2
ROSECRANS AV W	CO	GAR	100	64	C2
ROSECRANS AV W	CO	HAW	5200	62	B2
ROSECRANS AV W	COM	COM	100	64	C2
ROSECRANS AV W	GAR	GAR	1000	63	C2
ROSECRANS AV W	HAW	HAW	4500	62	B2
ROSECRANS AV W	HAW	HAW	3100	63	C2
ROSECRANS AV W	LA	GAR	600	63	C2
ROSECRANS AV W	LA	GAR	500	64	C2
ROSECRANS AV W	LAW	LAW	4500	62	B2
ROSECRANS AV W	LAW	LAW	4000	63	C2
ROSECRANS PL	MB	MB	100	62	A2
ROSECREST DR	CO	AGO		107	A3
ROSECREST DR	GLEN	GL08	2000	18	F3
ROSEDALE AV	GLEN	GL01	1100	25	A2
ROSEDELL DR	SCLR	SAU		124	E5
ROSEGATE PL	DBAR	POM		94	B5
ROSEGLEN AV	LA	SP	1600	73	E6
ROSE GLEN AV	RM	RM		46	F4
ROSEGLEN PL	PALM	PALM		183	C5
ROSEGLEN ST	ELM	ELM	11600	39	A4
ROSEGLEN ST	TEC	TEC	9200	38	D4
ROSEHAVEN LN	CO	CYN	15600	125	E7
ROSEHEDGE DR	CO	WHI	10400	55	B4
ROSEHEDGE DR	PR	PR	8600	54	E3
ROSEHEDGE DR	PR	PR	9100	55	A4
ROSEHEDGE DR	WHI	WHI		55	C5
ROSEHEDGE LN	ING	IN01		57	C2
ROSEHILL DR E	LA	LA32		36	C5
ROSEHILL DR W	LA	LA32		36	C5
ROSEHILLS RD	CO	WHI	9900	55	C1
ROSEHILLS RD	IND	WHI	10000	55	C1
ROSELAKE AV	LA	LA26	100	44	B1
ROSELAND ST	LA	LA16	4900	42	F5
ROSELAWN AV	GLEN	GL08	3400	18	E3
ROSELAWN AV	POM	POM	100	94	B3
ROSELAWN PL	LA	LA42	100	36	C2
ROSE LEE CT	SCLR	SAU		124	E6
ROSELIN PL	LA	LA39		35	C3
ROSELLA ST	CO	LPUE	14000	48	B5
ROSELLE AV	CO	LAW	15100	63	B3
ROSELLE AV	HAW	HAW	100	63	B1
ROSELLE AV	HAW	HAW	12800	63	B1
ROSELLE AV	TOR	TOR	18800	68	B1
ROSELLI ST	BUR	BUR	600	17	F6
ROSELYN PL	MPK	MPK	100	46	C2
ROSELYN WY	MPK	MPK	100	46	C2
ROSE MARIE DR	ARC	ARC	400	38	C2
ROSE MARIE LN	LA	LA49	12000	41	B2
ROSEMARIE ST	PALM	PALM	38300	172	E9
ROSEMARY AV	GLEN	GL08	3400	18	E3
ROSEMARY DR	LA	LA41	4800	26	B5
ROSEMARY DR	WCOV	WCOV	2800	92	F1
ROSEMARY LN	BUR	BUR	500	24	B2
ROSEMARY LN	LAV	LAV		95A	B6
ROSEMEAD AV	LA	LA32	3700	36	D4
ROSEMEAD BLVD N	CO	ELM	100	47	B5
ROSEMEAD BLVD N	CO	PAS	100	28	A6
ROSEMEAD BLVD N	CO	SGAB	6700	28	A6
ROSEMEAD BLVD N	CO	SGAB	6600	38	A4
ROSEMEAD BLVD N	ELM	ELM	3000	47	B1
ROSEMEAD BLVD N	PAS	PAS	200	28	A3
ROSEMEAD BLVD N	RM	RM	3300	38	A4
ROSEMEAD BLVD N	RM	RM	3100	47	B1
ROSEMEAD BLVD N	SELM	ELM	2000	47	B5
ROSEMEAD BLVD N	TEC	SGAB	4900	38	A4
ROSEMEAD BLVD N	TEC	TEC	5500	38	A4
ROSEMEAD BLVD S	CO	PAS	100	28	A4
ROSEMEAD BLVD S	CO	PR	3000	47	B5
ROSEMEAD BLVD S	CO	PR	3900	55	A2
ROSEMEAD BLVD S	PR	PR	4900	54	E5
ROSEMEAD BLVD S	PR	PR	4000	55	A2
ROSEMEAD BLVD S	PR	PR	7900	60	D1
ROSEMEAD PL	RM	RM	3000	47	A1
ROSEMONT AV	CO	GL14	4600	11	E6
ROSEMONT AV	CO	GL14	4200	18	E2
ROSEMONT AV	CO	MONT	4100	18	E2
ROSEMONT AV	GLEN	MONT	3800	18	E2
ROSEMONT AV	LA	LA26	100	35	B6
ROSEMONT AV	PAS	PAS	1400	19	E6
ROSEMONT AV	PAS	PAS	200	26	E3
ROSEMONT BLVD	SGAB	SGAB	100	37	D3
ROSEMONT LN	CO	VAL		124	F3
ROSEMOUNT AV	CLA	CLA		91	B1
ROSEMOUNT RD	GLEN	GL07	900	25	D1
ROSENDA ST	SGAB	SGAB	400	37	E3
ROSENELL TER	LA	LA26	400	35	B6
ROSEPARK CT	SCLR	NEW		127	B5
ROSES RD E	SGAB	SGAB	100	37	D2
ROSES RD W	SGAB	SGAB	100	37	D2
ROSETA DR	CO	TOP	1000	109	D3
ROSETON AV	ART	ART	17000	66	F5
ROSETON AV	CER	ART	19200	81	A1
ROSETON AV	LKD	LKD	20300	71	F3
ROSETON AV	NWK	NWK	11800	60	F6
ROSETON AV	NWK	NWK	12800	66	F2
ROSETON AV	SFS	SFS	10100	60	F3
ROSETTA WY	PAR	PAR		65	E4
ROSEVALE DR	TEC	TEC	5100	38	D3
ROSEVIEW AV	LA	LA65	2600	35	F3
ROSE VILLA ST	CO	PAS	2000	27	D4
ROSE VILLA ST	PAS	PAS	1400	27	D4
ROSEWAY ST	WCOV	WCOV	1200	48	F1
ROSEWOOD AV	ING	IN01	900	56	F3
ROSEWOOD AV	LA	LA04	3900	34	E5
ROSEWOOD AV	LA	LA36	7500	33	E5
ROSEWOOD AV	LA	LA36	6600	34	A5
ROSEWOOD AV	LA	LA48	7900	33	D5
ROSEWOOD AV	LA	LA66	3200	49	D1
ROSEWOOD AV	LAN	LAN		160	E6
ROSEWOOD AV	LYN	LYN	1060	59	D4
ROSEWOOD AV	PALM	PALM		183	G1
ROSEWOOD AV	SOG	SOG	9900	59	D4
ROSEWOOD AV	WHOL	LA48	8500	33	D5
ROSEWOOD CIR	WHOL	LA46		33	E5
ROSEWOOD DR	MON	MON	1600	28	F5
ROSEWOOD LN	PAS	PAS	500	26	F3
ROSEWOOD LN	SAD	SAD	600	90	A4
ROSEWOOD ST	CO	LAV		90	C1
ROSEWOOD ST	LAV	LAV		95A	D6
ROSILLA PL	LA	LA46	2000	33	D2
ROSILYN DR	CO	LA63	4200	45	E2
ROSIN AV	WHI	WHI	10100	84	D3
ROSINA ST	LB	LB08	7800	81	A6
ROSITA AV	BUR	BUR	1700	17	C4
ROSITA DR	GLEN	GL08	1800	18	F6
ROSITA LN	PAS	PAS	300	26	D5
ROSITA PL	LA	TAR	4700	21	B3
ROSITA PL	PVE	PVP	2100	72	C2
ROSITA ST	LA	ENC	17900	21	C2
ROSITA ST	LA	TAR	18600	21	A2
ROSLIN AV	TOR	TOR	17200	63	A5
ROSLYNDALE AV	LA	PAC	8800	8	E4
ROSLYNDALE AV	LA	PAC	8500	9	A6
ROSLYNDALE CT	LA	PAC	14100	8	E4
ROSNICK PL	LA	SF	17000	1	E4
ROSS AV E	ALH	ALH	600	37	D6
ROSS AV W	ALH	ALH	2300	36	F6
ROSS AV W	ALH	ALH	1800	37	A6
ROSS AV W	ALH	ALH	2400	45	F1
ROSS CT	CLA	CLA	100	91	C2
ROSS PL	LA	WIL	1500	74	B4
ROSS PL	SMAD	SMAD	1	28	B2
ROSS ST	GLEN	GL07	400	25	D2
ROSS ST	NWK	NWK	13000	82	C1

1990 LOS ANGELES COUNTY STREET INDEX

STREET	CITY	P.O. ZONE	BLOCK	PAGE	GRID
ROSS ST	POM	POM	1200	95	A1
ROSS ST	VER	LA58	2000	52	E2
ROSS, BETSY RD	PALM	PALM		183	D2
ROSSBURN AV	HAW	HAW	13700	62	E2
ROSSBURY PL	LA	LA64	10000	42	B4
ROSSELLEN PL	COV	COV	300	88	F6
ROSSER ST	BLF	BLF	9200	66	B2
ROSSFORD AV	LKD	LKD	19700	81	A2
ROSSFORD AV	LKD	LKD	20500	81	A4
ROSSINI PL	CO	TOP		13	D5
ROSSITER AV	LA	SF	12000	2	D5
ROSS LOOS PL	LA	LA26		44	B1
ROSSLYN ST	GLEN	GL04		35	D1
ROSSLYN ST	LA	LA65	3000	35	D1
ROSSMORE AV N	LA	LA04	100	34	C6
ROSSMORE AV S	LA	LA04	100	43	C1
ROSSMORE AV S	LA	LA05	600	43	C1
ROSSMORE AV S	LA	LA20	300	43	C1
ROSSMOYNE AV	GLEN	GL07	1000	25	D2
ROSSWOOD TER	LA	LA42	6300	26	D6
ROSWELL AV	LB	LB03	100	76	A6
ROSWELL AV	LB	LB04	700	76	A6
ROSWELL AV	LB	LB14	300	76	A6
ROSWELL AV	LB	LB15	2200	76	A2
ROSWELL CT	CO	VAL		124	B7
ROSWELL ST	LA	LA65	3000	35	D1
ROSY CIR	LA	LA66		50	A5
ROTARY DR	LAV	LAV		95A	E6
ROTARY DR	LA	LA26	1600	35	B4
ROTHDELL TR	LA	LA46	8000	33	E2
ROTHROCK DR	RPV	PVP	28200	72	C5
ROTTA AV	LA	SUN	9700	9	F4
ROTTA AV	LA	SUN		10	A4
ROTUNDA RD	SCLR	VAL		127	A3
ROTUNDE MESA RD	CO	MAL		108	C6
ROTUNDE MESA RD	CO	MAL		114	C1
ROUGE ST	LA	SV	12600	9	B5
ROUGHRIDER RD	CO	LAV		95A	E6
ROULETTE LN	LAN	LAN		159	D4
ROUND DR	LA	LA32	2600	36	E6
ROUNDABOUT DR	LPUE	LPUE		92	A6
ROUND CYN RD	SCLR	NEW		127	A5
ROUNDHILL DR	WHI	WHI		55	F4
ROUND HILL LN	WAL	WAL		93	B5
ROUND MEADOW RD	CO	CAL		100	C3
ROUND MEADOW RD	HH	CAL	5100	100	C3
ROUND ROCK DR	DBAR	POM	2500	97	E5
ROUNDTABLE CT	WAL	WAL		93	B5
ROUND TOP DR	LA	LA65	4500	25	F5
ROUNDTREE AV	WAL	WAL		97	B1
ROUNDTREE CIR	DBAR	POM		97	D3
ROUNDUP DR	WAL	WAL		93	E5
ROUNDUP RD	GLDR	GLDR	100	87	D5
ROUNDUP RD	RH	PVP	1	78	C1
ROUND VALLEY DR	LA	VAN	14500	22	D4
ROUNTREE RD	LA	LA64	10500	42	A4
ROUSSEAU LN	CO	PVP		73	A4
ROUTE 103 FRWY	LA	LA		74	E4
ROUTH DR	CO	LPUE		98	F5
ROW ALLEY	PAS	PAS	1900	19	F6
ROW CT	SCLR	SAU		124	G3
ROWAN AV N	CO	LA63	100	45	C5
ROWAN AV N	LA	LA32	1800	45	C1
ROWAN AV S	CMRC	LA23	1400	53	C1
ROWAN AV S	CO	LA23	600	45	C6
ROWAN AV S	CO	LA23	1100	53	C1
ROWAN AV S	CO	LA63	100	45	C5
ROWAN CT	PALM	PALM		171	H6
ROWEL CT	CO	ACT		189	H4
ROWELL AV	CO	CHA		4	C5
ROWELL AV N	MB	MB	100	62	D4
ROWELL AV S	MB	MB	100	62	D4
ROWENA AV	LA	LA27	3100	35	A2
ROWENA AV	LA	LA39	2700	35	A2
ROWLAND AV	ARC	ARC	1800	38	C2
ROWLAND AV	CO	ELM	4500	38	C4
ROWLAND AV	ELM	ELM	3900	38	C4
ROWLAND AV	TEC	TEC	5700	38	C2
ROWLAND AV E	WCOV	WCOV	1000	88	B5
ROWLAND AV W	WCOV	WCOV	1000	88	A5
ROWLAND ST	CO	COV	19200	88	E6
ROWLAND ST	CO	COV	19200	89	A6
ROWLAND ST	IND	LPUE	17500	98	C2
ROWLAND ST	LPUE	LPUE	15800	48	F6
ROWLAND ST E	COV	COV	100	88	E6
ROWLAND ST W	COV	COV	100	88	E6
ROWLEY CT	PALM	PALM		184	B5
ROWLEY PL	LA	TU	7200	10	F2
ROWLEY ST	CO	LR	8700	184	G5
ROXABEL ST	SFS	SFS	11100	61	A1
ROXANNE AV	LA	LA08	3900	51	A1
ROXANNE AV	LB	LB08	3000	71	F6
ROXANNE AV	LB	LB15	800	76	F3
ROXANNE WY	LB	LB15	6800	76	E4
ROXANNE BCH RD	CO	MAL		111	C4
ROXBURGH AV	CO	AZU	5100	88	C4

STREET	CITY	P.O. ZONE	BLOCK	PAGE	GRID
ROXBURGH AV	CO	COV	4600	88	C4
ROXBURGH PL	LA	NOR		1	B4
ROXBURY DR	LA	LA35	1000	42	B2
ROXBURY DR	PAS	PAS	800	27	D2
ROXBURY DR N	BH	BH	500	33	A5
ROXBURY DR N	BH	BH	400	42	B1
ROXBURY DR S	BH	BH	100	42	B2
ROXBURY RD	LA	LA69	8200	33	E3
ROXBURY RD	SMAR	PAS	900	37	C2
ROXBURY ST	LA	SP	3600	78	F6
ROXBURY ST	WCOV	WCOV	1200	48	E3
ROXCOVE DR	RHE	PVP	27500	72	E5
ROXDALE AV	CO	LPUE	400	92	B6
ROXFORD PL	LA	SF		2	C2
ROXFORD ST	LA	SF	14900	2	B3
ROXHAM AV	LPUE	LPUE	600	98	A1
ROXIE ST	ELM	ELM	10200	38	C6
ROXLEY DR	CO	LPUE		92	C5
ROXTON AV	CO	GAR	14400	63	D3
ROXTON AV	GAR	GAR	14700	63	D3
ROXTON AV	LA	LA08	3800	51	D1
ROXTON AV	LA	LA18	3700	51	D1
ROY DR	SCLR	NEW	20800	127	F4
ROY ST	LA	LA42	6000	36	C1
ROYAL BLVD	CO	TOR	20900	68	F4
ROYAL BLVD	GLEN	GL07	1400	25	E1
ROYAL CT	LA	VEN	700	49	B3
ROYAL CT	PALM	PALM		184	A1
ROYAL RD	CO	CAST		123	G2
ROYAL ST	LA	LA07	3000	44	A6
ROYAL COACH AV	POM	POM	200	90	F5
ROYAL CREST PL	LA	ENC	4100	22	B4
ROYAL GLEN RD	WLVL	THO	4400	102	A4
ROYAL HAVEN PL	LA	VAN	15800	22	B5
ROYAL HILLS DR	LA	ENC	16300	22	A5
ROYALL RD	LHH	LAH		98A	B1
ROYAL MEADOW PL	LA	VAN	15800	22	B5
ROYAL MEADOW RD	LA	VAN	3600	22	B5
ROYAL MOUNT DR	LA	ENC	16000	22	A4
ROYAL OAK PL	LA	ENC	3900	22	A4
ROYAL OAK RD	LA	ENC	15600	22	A4
ROYAL OAKS DR	BRAD	DUA	1400	29	D4
ROYAL OAKS DR	CO	DUA	1700	29	D4
ROYAL OAKS DR	DUA	DUA	1200	29	D4
ROYAL OAKS DR	DUA	DUA	2600	86	A4
ROYAL OAKS DR	MON	MON	400	29	C4
ROYAL PALMS DR	LA	SP		78	D5
ROYAL RIDGE RD	LA	VAN	15500	22	B4
ROYAL STONE DR	CO	MAL		115	B4
ROYALTON DR	LA	BH		33	B2
ROYALTON PL	LA	BH		33	B2
ROYALTY DR	POM	POM	1900	90	F6
ROYAL VIEW RD	CO	LPUE		98	A4
ROYALVIEW ST	DUA	DUA	400	29	F4
ROYAL WOODS DR	LA	VAN	3100	22	B4
ROYAL WOODS PL	LA	VAN	15500	22	B4
ROYCE CT	CO	PALM		184	B3
ROYCE CT	LA	BH		22	F6
ROYCE DR W	LA	ENC		21	D2
ROYCE ST	CO	ALT	400	19	E5
ROYCETON CT	WLVL	THO	32000	102	A4
ROYCOVE DR	CO	COV	3000	93	C1
ROYCROFT AV	LB	LB03	100	76	B6
ROYCROFT AV	LB	LB03	300	80	B1
ROYCROFT AV	LB	LB04	1300	76	B4
ROYCROFT AV	LB	LB14	300	76	B5
ROYCROFT AV	LB	LB15	2300	76	B2
ROYCROFT ST	LA	SUN	10800	9	E5
ROYER AV	LA	CAN	6400	12	A5
ROYER AV	LA	WOH	6200	12	A5
ROYER AV	LA	WOH	5300	13	A2
ROYMOR DR	CO	CAL		100	A3
ROYSTON PL	LA	BH		22	F6
ROYSTON ST	BAP	BAP	12700	39	B6
ROYWOOD DR	LAN	LAN	1600	160	E5
ROZALEE ST	CO	PALM		183	C3
ROZICH RD	CO	SAU		181	B6
ROZIE AV	LA	WOH	5400	100	E1
RUBENS AV	LA	LA66	12400	49	F4
RUBERTA AV	GLEN	GL01	300	24	F2
RUBERTA AV	GLEN	GL01	1000	25	A1
RUBICON RD	CO	TOP		109	D1
RUBIDOUX ST	MTB	MTB	300	54	D1
RUBIO AV	LA	ENC	4600	21	F2
RUBIO AV	LA	SF	11400	1	F6
RUBIO AV	LA	SF	8500	7	F6
RUBIO AV	LA	SF	8500	14	F1
RUBIO AV	LA	VAN	6500	14	F4
RUBIO DR	SMAR	PAS	1400	37	E1
RUBIO ST	CO	ALT	1000	20	C4
RUBIO CANYON RD	CO	ALT	3000	20	C4
RUBIO CREST DR	CO	ALT		20	C3
RUBIO VISTA RD	CO	ALT		20	C3
RUBY CT	CO	LAN		159	C9
RUBY CT	WCOV	WCOV		92	E6
RUBY PL	LA	LA42	6000	36	C1

STREET	CITY	P.O. ZONE	BLOCK	PAGE	GRID
RUBY PL	LB	LB13		75	C4
RUBY PL	TOR	TOR	5600	67	E4
RUBY ST	LA	LA42	6200	36	D1
RUBY ST	RB	RB	100	67	D4
RUBY ST	RB	RB	800	67	E4
RUBY ST	TOR	TOR	4900	67	E4
RUCHEL ST	NWK	NWK	12100	61	B5
RUCHTI RD	SOG	SOG	10600	59	E4
RUDALL AV	PALM	PALM	37800	172	F9
RUDDER TR	CO	TOP		109	D5
RUDDOCK ST	CO	COV		89	C4
RUDDOCK ST	COV	COV	19000	88	F4
RUDDOCK ST	COV	COV	700	89	A4
RUDELL RD	BUR	BUR		17	F4
RUDMAN DR	CUL	CUL	11200	50	C4
RUDNICK AV	LA	CAN	8500	6	B6
RUDNICK AV	LA	CAN	6700	12	B4
RUDNICK AV	LA	CHA	9500	6	B3
RUDNICK AV	LA	WOH	5700	12	B6
RUDNICK AV	LA	WOH	5700	13	B1
RUDY ST	CO	LPUE		97	B5
RUDYARD ST	WCOV	WCOV	900	48	F3
RUE BEAUPRE	RPV	PVP		77	B2
RUEBENS ST	LAN	LAN		160	E8
RUE CREVIER	CO	CYN		124	G8
RUE DANIEL	CO	CYN		125	E7
RUE D LA PIERRE	RPV	PVP	30500	77	B1
RUE DE VALLE	AZU	AZU		88	D2
RUE DE VALLEE	LA	LA68		24	A6
RUE ENTREE	CO	CYN		125	E7
RUE GODBOUT	RPV	PVP	7100	72	B6
RUE LA FLEUR	RPV	PVP		77	B1
RUE LANGLOIS	RPV	PVP	30500	77	B2
RUELAS ST	IRW	DUA	2400	29	C6
RUELAS ST	IRW	DUA	2400	39	C1
RUE LE CHARLENE	RPV	SP		78	D3
RUE L CHARLNE E	LA	SP		78	D3
RUE L CHARLNE E	RPV	SP		78	D3
RUE ROYALE	COV	COV	500	88	F4
RUETHER AV	SCLR	CYN	26800	124	F8
RUE VALOIS	RPV	PVP	30600	77	B2
RUEZ LN	LA	LA33	1500	45	C2
RUFF DR	CO	LPUE		98	A4
RUFFNER AV	LA	SF	11400	1	F6
RUFFNER AV	LA	SF	8700	7	F6
RUFFNER AV	LA	VAN	6500	14	F4
RUFUS AV	CO	WHI	9400	61	E3
RUFUS AV	WHI	WHI	8900	84	A2
RUGBY AV	HPK	HPK	5900	52	F5
RUGBY DR	WHOL	LA69	8500	33	D4
RUGBY PL	LA	LA46	8300	33	E2
RUGGED TR	CO	TOP		109	D2
RUGGIERO AV	LA	SF	11400	3	E6
RUGGIERO AV	LA	SF	11300	9	E1
RUGGLES ST	LAV	LAV		90	C1
RUGGLES ST	LAV	LAV		95A	C6
RUHLAND AV	MB	MB	1500	62	D5
RUHLAND AV	RB	RB	1900	62	D5
RUIZ PL	CO	LPUE	2200	85	F3
RUMBOLD ST	GAR	GAR	1000	63	F6
RUMFORD AV	ELM	ELM		48	A2
RUMFORD AV	IND	ELM	3000	48	A2
RUMSON ST	CO	LPUE	15700	85	E2
RUNDELL ST E	DOW	DOW	7400	59	F4
RUNNING BRCH RD	DBAR	POM		99	D4
RUNNING BRAND	WAL	WAL		93	A5
RUNNING BRND RD	RH	PVP	1	78	A2
RUNNING BRND RD	RH	PVP	1	78	A2
RNNING BROOK LN	WAL	WAL		93	D5
RUNNINGCREEK LN	CER	ART	12400	82	B4
RUNNING DEER RD	WAL	WAL		93	A6
RUNNING HRSE RD	CO	NEW		127	J4
RUNNING RIV CT	DBAR	POM		97	D4
RUNNING SPGS RD	CO	LPUE	14400	48	C6
RUNNYMEDE ST	LA	CAN	23100	5	F3
RUNNYMEDE ST	LA	CAN	20100	12	E3
RUNNYMEDE ST	LA	NHO	11700	16	C3
RUNNYMEDE ST	LA	RES	18600	14	B3
RUNNYMEDE ST	LA	SV	11100	16	C3
RUNNYMEDE ST	LA	VAN	16600	14	D3
RUNNYMEDE ST	LA	VAN	13500	15	E3
RUNYAN CYN RD	LA	LA68	1900	34	A1
RUNYON TR	CO	TOP	19900	109	D5
RUOFF AV	CO	WHI	10000	61	F4
RUOFF AV	WHI	WHI	9400	84	A3
RUPERT AV	LA	ENC	4900	21	D2
RUPERT LN	LCF	LCF	4900	19	D3
RUPP RD	DOW	DOW	8700	60	A6
RURAL DR N	MPK	MPK	100	46	D1
RURAL DR S	MPK	MPK	100	46	D1
RUSH ST	BLF	BLF	17000	66	C5
RUSH ST	CO	RM	8100	46	F3
RUSH ST	CO	RM	8500	47	B3
RUSH ST	RM	RM	8200	46	F3
RUSH ST	SELM	ELM	9100	47	B3
RUSH CANYON RD	CO	PALM		183	F6

STREET	CITY	P.O. ZONE	BLOCK	PAGE	GRID
RUSHFORD ST	WHI	WHI	15700	84	C4
RUSHING DR	LA	SF		1	D4
RUSHLIGHT AV	CO	LR		184	E6
RUSHMORE ST	PR	PR	9600	54	F5
RUSK ST	CO	LPUE	18800	98	F6
RUSKIN ST	SM	SM	3000	49	B2
RUSS PL	PALM	PALM		184	B6
RUSSELEE DR	WCOV	WCOV	900	92	A2
RUSSELL AV	LA	LA27	4600	34	E3
RUSSELL AV	LA	LA27	4000	35	A3
RUSSELL AV	MPK	MPK	100	46	C2
RUSSELL DR	LB	LB04	1400	76	B4
RUSSELL PL	POM	POM	500	90	F6
RUSSELL PL	POM	POM	800	91	A6
RUSSELL ST	AZU	AZU	100	88	D2
RUSSELL ST	IND	LPUE		48	F6
RUSSELL ST	WHI	WHI	13400	61	F1
RUSSELL ST	WHI	WHI	15800	84	C3
RUSSET LN	SMAR	PAS	1700	37	E1
RUSSETT AV	LA	SUN	10200	10	D3
RUSS JAY ST	SCLR	SAU		124	G4
RUSSO ST	LA	CUL		50	B4
RUST CT	CLA	CLA		91	B3
RUSTIC CT	DBAR	POM		97A	B3
RUSTIC DR	LA	LA65	400	36	B3
RUSTIC LN	GLEN	GL08	2700	18	F5
RUSTIC RD E	LA	SM		40	D5
RUSTIC RD W	LA	SM		40	D5
RUSTIC GATE WY	CO	LPUE		98	A4
RUSTIC GLEN DR	POM	POM		94	C6
RUSTIC HILL DR	CO	WHI		55	E2
RUSTIC OAK DR	WLVL	THO		102	B4
RUSTLER LN	RHE	PVP	4800	72	F3
RUSTLNG OAKS RD	AGH	AGO		100A	A2
RUSTON RD	LA	WOH	19900	13	E3
RUSTY FIG CIR	CER	ART		82	D4
RUSTY PUMP RD	DBAR	POM		97A	A4
RUSTY SPUR RD	DBAR	POM		97A	A4
RUTAN WY	PAS	PAS	1300	27	B1
RUTGERS AV	DOW	DOW	13000	66	C1
RUTGERS AV	LB	LB08	3000	71	C6
RUTGERS AV	LB	LB15	2000	76	C2
RUTGERS CT	CLA	CLA	1600	91	A2
RUTGERS CT	WAL	WAL		93	B4
RUTGERS PL	LA	HAC		73	E1
RUTH AV	LA	LA41	4800	26	C5
RUTH AV	LA	VEN	200	49	B3
RUTH AV	LB	LB05	4600	70	C3
RUTH AV	LYN	LYN	10600	59	B4
RUTH CT	CO	WAL		97	B5
RUTH CT	WCOV	WCOV		92	E3
RUTH LN	LAN	LAN		159	B5
RUTHBAR DR	HAW	HAW	3700	63	B3
RUTHCREST AV	CO	LPUE	500	92	B5
RUTHELEN AV	CO	LA47	10800	57	D5
RUTHELEN ST	GAR	GAR	13000	63	D1
RUTHELEN ST	LA	LA18	3600	43	D6
RUTHELEN ST	LA	LA47	8600	57	D2
RUTHELEN ST	LA	LA62	5100	51	D4
RUTHER AV	PAR	PAR	13900	65	F1
RUTHER AV	SOG	SOG	13400	65	F1
RUTHERFORD CT	ING	IN01		57	B2
RUTHERFORD DR	LA	CAN		5	D3
RUTHERFORD DR	LA	LA68	2600	34	D1
RUTHERFORD DR	PAS	PAS		26	D2
RUTHERGLEN ST	WHI	WHI	16200	84	D4
RUTHLEE AV	CO	SGAB	6400	37	F1
RUTHRON AV	LAN	LAN		159	F5
RUTHSPRING DR	CO	CYN	15700	128	E3
RUTHUPHAM AV	LA	LA31	3600	36	C4
RUTHVEN LN	LA	LA77	10200	32	E2
RUTHWOOD DR	CO	CAL		100	A2
RUTHWOOD PL	CO	CAL		100	A1
RUTLAND AV	CO	WHI	9400	61	D2
RUTLAND AV	LA	LA42	900	26	E6
RUTLEDGE PL	LA	SV	10000	17	A2
RUXTON AV	RB	RB	1600	62	F6
RYAN LN	CER	ART	12400	81	B1
RYAN ST	LA	SF	14000	2	D3
RYANDALE DR	CUL	CUL	11200	50	C4
RYANS PL	LAN	LAN		159	G7
RYCKEBOSCH LN	LAN	LAN		160	H6
RYDAL ST	LA	LA41	1200	26	C4
RYE ST	LA	NHO	11200	23	E3
RYE ST	LA	VAN	13600	22	F3
RYE CANYON RD	CO	VAL		123	H6
RYERSON AV	DOW	DOW	10900	59	F3
RYERSON AV	DOW	DOW	10900	60	A3
RYGATE AV	LPUE	LPUE	1100	92	A4
RYLAND AV	TEC	TEC	4800	38	D4
RYNGLER RD	LA	NHO		23	C4
RYON AV	BLF	BLF	14700	66	C2

S

STREET	CITY	P.O. ZONE	BLOCK	PAGE	GRID
S CIR	CO	HAC		73	F2
SABADO CT	SCLR	VAL		124	A9
SABAL AV	PALM	PALM	37200	184	A2
SABAL AV	PALM	PALM		184	B6
SABAL ST	PALM	PALM		184	A1
SABANA DR	DBAR	POM	600	97	F1
SABANA LN	LA	ENC	16000	22	A5
SABBIADORO WY	LA	PP	17700	40	A3
SABINA DR	CO	TOP	2300	115	B1
SABINA ST	LA	LA23	3400	45	C5
SABINE DR	LAM	LAM	14400	61	F6
SABINE DR	LAM	LAM	14400	84	A6
SABLE AV	LA	SUN	10600	10	C2
SABLE LN	WAL	WAL		92	F6
SABLE LN	WAL	WAL		93	A6
SABLE LN	WAL	WAL		97	A1
SABLE LN	WAL	WAL		98	F1
SABRINA AV	CER	ART	18700	81	C1
SABRINA CT	CER	ART	19500	81	C2
SACHE ST	CO	ACT		182	G8
SACHS DR	LAN	LAN	42800	159	F8
SACHS PL	COV	COV	20600	89	B4
SACO ST	VER	LA58	2900	52	E2
SACRAMENTO AV	CO	SAU		189	F2
SACRAMENTO ST	CO	ACT		189	F2
SACRAMENTO ST	LA	LA21	1600	44	E5
SACRAMENTO ST E	CO	ALT	100	20	A5
SACRAMENTO ST W	CO	ALT	700	19	E5
SADDLE AV	CO	LAN		174	H6
SADDLE DR	LB	LB15		76	E4
SADDLE RD	RHE	PVP	27600	73	D6
SADDLE RD	RPV	PVP		73	D6
SADDLE BCK DR E	CO	LAN	18500	175	C5
SADDLEBACK RD	CO	CYN		128	E2
SADDLEBACK RD	PALM	PALM		172	J9
SADDLEBACK RD	RH	PVP	1	73	B6
SADDLEBOW LN	RHE	PVP	25900	72	F3
SADDLEBROOK DR	AGH	AGO		100A	A2
SADDLE CREEK RD	HH	CAL		100	E2
SADDLECREST DR	WAL	WAL		93	A5
SADDLECREST LN	WLVL	THO		102	B4
SADDLE HORN LN	RHE	PVP	1	73	B4
SADDLE HRS RD E	CO	LAN	19200	175	E4
SADDLE MTN DR	WLVL	THO		102	A5
SADDLE PEAK RD	CO	CAL	21400	108	D5
SADDLE PEAK RD	CO	MAL	1100	108	C6
SADDLE PEAK RD	CO	MAL		114	C1
SADDLE PEAK RD	CO	TOP	23100	108	F6
SADDLE PEAK RD	CO	TOP		115	B1
SADDLE RIDGE DR	CO	COV		93	C2
SADDLE RIDGE LN	WAL	WAL		93	B5
SADDLE RIDGE RD	CO	NEW		2	B1
SADDLERIDGE WY	CO	SAU		123	D5
SADDLERIM RD	DBAR	POM		97A	A2
SADDLE TREE DR	WLVL	THO		102	B5
SADDLE VIEW DR	LOM	LOM	25900	73	C3
SADDLEWOOD PL	POM	POM		94	E6
SADDLEWOOD PL	POM	POM		97A	C1
SADIE RD	CO	TOP		108	F5
SADLER AV N	CO	LA22	100	46	A6
SADLER AV S	CO	LA22	100	46	A6
SADLER AV S	CO	LA22	700	54	A1
SADRING AV	LA	CAN	7800	5	F2
SADRING AV	LA	WOH	5800	5	F6
SADRING AV	LA	WOH	5300	100	F2
SAED ST	POM	POM	900	94	B2
SAFARI CT	PALM	PALM		171	J8
SAFARI DR	CO	WHI		61	D3
SAFE CIR	LAN	LAN	2800	159	G6
SAFFRON LN	SCLR	SAU		124	E5
SAGA ST	GLDR	GLDR	900	87	C3
SAGAMORE WY	LA	LA65	3800	25	E5
SAGE	WCOV	WCOV		92	D4
SAGE AV	CLA	CLA	800	91	A1
SAGE AV	CO	CLA	700	91	A1
SAGE CT	CO	CAL		100A	E5
SAGE LN	LA	SM	200	40	E5
SAGE PL	GLDR	GLDR	300	87	D6
SAGE ST	LAV	LAV		90	B3
SAGEBANK ST	CAR	CAR	900	64	C6
SAGEBRUSH CIR	POM	POM		94	C4
SAGEBRUSH DR	CO	LAN	42000	171	A1
SAGE BRUSH LN	WAL	WAL		93	A5
SAGEBRUSH WY	SCLR	NEW		127	B6
SAGE CANYON RD	WAL	WAL		94	C4
SAGECREST CIR	CO	NEW		126	J4
SAGE HILL RD	CO	ALT		20	A3
SAGE HILL RD	CO	SF		3	E2
SAGEHURST DR	DUA	DUA	400	86	B3
SAGEMONT PL	CO	ALT	1200	20	C4
SAGE TREE ST	CO	PALM	38600	171	J7
SAG HARBOR CT	SCLR	VAL		124	E3
SAGINAW ST	LA	LA41	1200	26	C5
SAGO ST	LAN	LAN		159	E5
SAGUARO PL	CO	LAN	43600	158	A7
SAGUARO ST	CO	CAST		123	E4

STREET	CITY	P.O. ZONE	BLOCK	PAGE	GRID
SAGUARO ST	PALM	PALM		183	E3
SAHUAYO ST	LAN	LAN		160	B7
SAIGON AV	LAN	LAN	45200	159	J3
SAILBOAT CIR	AGH	AGO		102	D3
SAILFISH AV	CO	LAN	16200	174	J2
SAILFISH AV	CO	LAN	16600	175	A2
SAILVIEW LN	WLVL	THO		102	A4
ST ALBANS AV	SPAS	SPAS	100	36	E2
ST ALBANS RD	SGAB	SGAB	500	37	C1
ST ALBANS RD	SMAR	PAS	1000	37	C1
ST ALBANS ST	LA	LA42	6100	26	C6
ST ANDRES AV	LAV	LAV	1300	90	C1
ST ANDRES AV	LAV	LAV	1400	95A	C6
ST ANDREWS AV	CLA	CLA		91	D1
ST ANDREWS DR	GLEN	GL06	2500	26	A2
ST ANDREWS LN	AZU	AZU	300	86	D5
ST ANDREWS PL N	LA	LA04	100	34	D6
ST ANDREWS PL N	LA	LA28	1300	34	D4
ST ANDREWS PL N	LA	LA38	700	34	D6
ST ANDREWS PL S	CO	LA47	10800	57	D4
ST ANDREWS PL S	GAR	GAR	12900	63	D1
ST ANDREWS PL S	LA	LA04	100	34	D6
ST ANDREWS PL S	LA	LA05	600	43	D1
ST ANDREWS PL S	LA	LA18	2400	43	D5
ST ANDREWS PL S	LA	LA19	900	43	D4
ST ANDREWS PL S	LA	LA20	300	43	D1
ST ANDREWS PL S	LA	LA47	5900	51	D5
ST ANDREWS PL S	LA	LA47	7800	57	D1
ST ANDREWS PL S	LA	LA62	3800	51	D4
ST ANDREWS PL S	TOR	TOR	17800	63	D6
ST ANDREWS PL S	TOR	TOR	18300	68	D1
ST ANNE DR	CO	LLAN	30800	192	J2
ST AUGUSTINE AV	CLA	CLA	300	91	B5
ST BERNARD ST	LA	VEN	8000	55A	F2
ST BONAVNTRE AV	CLA	CLA	300	91	B5
ST CATHERINE WY	AVA	AVA	100	77	B5
ST CATHERINE WY	CLA	CLA		91	A1
ST CHARLES PL	LA	LA19	4200	43	B3
ST CHARLES ST	VER	LA58	4400	52	E3
ST CHARLES TER	ALH	ALH	1100	37	B4
ST CLAIR AV	LA	NHO	5600	16	C6
ST CLAIR AV	LA	NHO	4100	23	C4
ST CLOUD RD	LA	LA77	300	32	E4
ST DENIS CT	CO	VAL		126	J1
ST EDENS CIR	LA	CAN	24200	5	D4
ST ELIZABETH RD	GLEN	GL06	3500	19	C6
ST ELMO DR	LA	LA19	4500	43	B4
ST ESTABAN ST	LA	TU	6600	11	A4
ST FRANCIS PL	LB	LB05	3200	70	F1
ST FRANCIS PL	LCF	LCF	4400	19	B3
ST FRANCIS ST	SGAB	SGAB	100	37	E3
ST FRANCIS TER	LA	LA68	6600	34	B3
ST GEORGE DR	SAD	SAD	1100	89	D2
ST GEORGE ST	LA	LA27	2300	35	A2
ST GREGORY RD	GLEN	GL06	2900	26	B1
ST IRMO WK	LB	LB03	5500	80	C1
ST IVES CT	DBAR	POM		97A	B2
ST IVES DR	LA	LA69	9100	33	C4
ST IVES DR	LA	LA69	9100	33	C4
ST IVES DR	LA	LA69	8700	33	D4
ST IVES PL	LA	LA69	1200	33	C4
ST JAMES AV	SOG	SOG	10400	59	D4
ST JAMES CIR	BAP	BAP	13400	39	C5
ST JAMES CT	SAD	SAD		89	D4
ST JAMES DR	CUL	CUL		50	D3
ST JAMES DR	TEC	TEC	6100	38	B2
ST JAMES PL	BAP	BAP	12700	39	B6
ST JAMES PL	CO	ALT	2600	20	B4
ST JAMES PL	LA	LA07	2500	44	A5
ST JAMES PK	LA	LA07	1	44	A5
ST JOHN AV	PAS	PAS	500	26	F5
ST JOHN PL	CLA	CLA		91	A1
ST JOHN PL	ING	IN01	500	57	A1
ST JOHN ST	LA	LA12		44	F1
ST JOHNSWOOD DR	CO	WOH		13	C4
ST JOSEPH AV	LB	LB03	100	76	B6
ST JOSEPH AV	LB	LB03	100	80	B1
ST JOSEPH AV	LB	LB14	300	76	B6
ST JOSEPH AV	LB	LB15	2300	76	B2
ST JOSEPH ST E	ARC	ARC	1	28	E4
ST JOSEPH ST W	ARC	ARC	1	28	E4
ST JOSEPHS PL	LA	LA15	1300	44	C5
ST KATHERINE DR	LCF	LCF	200	19	C6
ST KATHERINE WK	LCF	LCF	400	19	D6
ST LAURENT DR	AGH	AGO		102	D2
ST LAURENT PL	PALM	PALM		173	A9
ST LAWRENCE ST	CO	SAU		123	C3
ST LOUIS AV	LB	LB04	700	75	E5
ST LOUIS AV	LB	LB05	6300	65	E5
ST LOUIS AV	LB	LB08	3000	70	E6
ST LOUIS AV	LB	LB14	400	75	E5
ST LOUIS AV	SH	LB06	1800	75	E3
ST LOUIS CT	CUL	CUL		50	D1
ST LOUIS DR	ELM	ELM	10700	38	D5
ST LOUIS PL	LB	LB05	6200	65	E6
ST LOUIS ST N	LA	LA33	100	45	A4

STREET	CITY	P.O. ZONE	BLOCK	PAGE	GRID
ST LOUIS ST S	LA	LA23	600	45	A4
ST LOUIS ST S	LA	LA33	100	45	A4
ST MALO AV	CO	COV	4500	88	B4
ST MALO AV	CO	LPUE	1100	48	F3
ST MALO AV	LPUE	LPUE	500	48	E5
ST MALO ST	WCOV	WCOV	1500	48	F3
ST MALO ST	WCOV	WCOV	600	92	A2
ST MARK AV	CO	LAV	4300	90	E1
ST MARTIN LN	GLEN	GL06	1000	26	A2
ST MARYS CT	LB	LB13	1000	75	D4
ST MORITZ DR	SCLR	VAL		127	A1
ST NICOLAS AV	LA	CUL	4600	50	C2
ST PANCRTIUS PL	LKD	LKD	3500	71	A1
ST PAUL AV	LA	LA17	600	44	C3
ST PAUL PL	LA	LA17	600	44	C3
ST PAUL ST	POM	POM	500	95	B2
ST PIERRE AV	CO	ALT	2400	19	E5
ST PIERRE RD	LA	LA77	200	32	E5
ST SUSAN PL	LA	LA66	3500	49	F1
ST THIRA CT	WCOV	WCOV		92	A2
ST TROPEZ DR	LA	LA49		32	B6
ST VINCENT CT	LA	LA14	600	44	C3
ST VLADIMIR ST	GLDR	GLDR	1300	87	D6
SAL AV	CO	WHI		61	A1
SALA PL	LA	SV	10300	17	A1
SALADA DR	LAM	LAM	13800	82	F2
SALADA DR	LAM	LAM	13800	83	A2
SALAIS ST	CO	LPUE	17400	98	C1
SALAIS ST	LPUE	LPUE	16900	98	B1
SALAMANCA AV	LA	WOH	21400	13	C3
SALAMEA AV	LA	WOH	5900	5	D6
SALAZAR DR	CO	LPUE	16000	85	E3
SALCEDA RD	SCLR	VAL		127	B1
SALDEE DR	CAR	CAR	17100	64	B5
SALE AV	LA	CAN	6400	12	B2
SALE AV	LA	WOH	5600	12	B6
SALE AV	LA	WOH	5100	13	B2
SALE PL	CO	HPK	2400	58	F1
SALEM CT	CLA	CLA	1800	91	A2
SALEM CT	CO	SAU		123	D4
SALEM CT	PALM	PALM		183	E1
SALEM DR	LA	SF	17100	1	E5
SALEM LN	CLA	CLA		95	A4
SALEM LN	POM	POM		94	F4
SALEM ST	GLEN	GL03	300	25	B3
SALEM VLG CT	CUL	CUL		50	D1
SALEM VLG DR	CUL	CUL		50	D1
SALEM VLG PL	CUL	CUL		50	D1
SALERNO	MTB	MTB		46	D5
SALERNO DR	LA	PP	400	40	B4
SALEROSO DR	CO	LPUE		98	C4
SALFORD AV	DOW	DOW	11600	59	F3
SALIDA AV	CO	WHI	700	84	A3
SALIDA AV	LB	LB15	5000	76	E5
SALIENT DR	LA	LA42		36	B2
SALINAS AV	COM	LA59	1900	64	C1
SALISBURY CT	LCF	LCF	1000	19	B3
SALISBURY LN	CLA	CLA		91	C1
SALISBURY RD	LA	CAN	7000	5	D3
SALISBURY RD	LCF	LCF	800	19	B3
SALISBURY ST	BAP	BAP	12700	39	B6
SALLY AV	CER	ART	19500	71	F2
SALLY CT	WCOV	WCOV		92	E6
SALLY RD	SCLR	NEW	24500	127	F4
SALLY LEE AV	AZU	AZU		88	D2
SALMON AV	CAR	LB10	21800	69	F4
SALOMA AV	LA	SF	9500	8	D4
SALOMA AV	LA	VAN	8500	8	C6
SALOMA AV	LA	VAN	5600	15	C6
SALOMA AV	LA	VAN	4500	22	C3
SALONICA ST	LA	LA42	6700	36	D2
SALTAIR AV N	LA	LA49	100	41	B1
SALTAIR AV S	LA	LA25	1200	41	C4
SALTAIR AV S	LA	LA49	100	41	B2
SALTAIR PL	LA	LA49	12000	41	B2
SALTAIR TER	LA	LA49	11900	41	B2
SALT BUSH CT	PALM	PALM		183	F3
SALTEE AV	TOR	TOR	20100	67	F2
SALTER AV	CO	ARC	6700	38	C1
SALTER AV	TEC	TEC	6300	38	C1
SALTILLO ST	LA	WOH	4100	13	C3
SALT LAKE AV	BELL	BELL	6400	53	B5
SALT LAKE AV	CDY	BELL	7900	59	C1
SALT LAKE AV	HPK	HPK	6400	53	B5
SALT LAKE AV	HPK	HPK	7600	59	C1
SALT LAKE AV	IND	LPUE	14600	48	C6
SALT LAKE AV	IND	LPUE	15500	85	E1
SALT LAKE AV	LA	NOR	11000	7	B1
SALT LAKE AV	SOG	SOG	9500	59	D3
SALT LAKE PL	LA	NOR	18800	7	B1
SALT LAKE ST	LB	LB06	1000	75	D2
SALTO DR	CO	LPUE	1900	85	F3
SALUDA AV	LA	TU	9600	11	B5
SALVATIERRA ST	IRW	BAP	15800	88	A2
SALVIA CYN RD	PAS	PAS	1000	26	D2
SALVIN AV	SCLR	CYN		125	C9

STREET	CITY	P.O. ZONE	BLOCK	PAGE	GRID
SAM PL	CO	CYN		125	E7
SAMANTHA AV	WCOV	WCOV		92	E6
SAMAR AV	CO	LPUE	1100	48	D6
SAMARA DR	CO	LPUE		98	C4
SAMARKAND PL	GLEN	GL08	1800	18	F6
SAM GERRY DR	CO	LPUE	16600	92	B5
SAMMY DR	LAN	LAN		160	E6
SAMOA AV	LA	TU		10	F2
SAMOA AV	LA	TU	9700	11	A3
SAMOA PL	LA	TU		10	F3
SAMOA PL	LA	TU	7100	11	A2
SAMOA WY	LA	PP		40	C4
SAMOLINE AV	DOW	DOW	12400	59	F6
SAMOLINE AV	DOW	DOW	8700	60	C2
SAMOLINE AV	PR	PR	8200	54	D6
SAMOLINE LN	DOW	DOW	12000	60	A4
SAMPAN CIR	CER	ART		66	E5
SAMPSON AV	LA	WIL	800	74	E4
SAMPSON AV	LYN	LYN	10600	59	C5
SAMPSON PL	CO	LA63	1500	45	D2
SAMPSON WY	LA	SP		79	A4
SAMRA AV	LAN	LAN		160	D7
SAMRA DR	LA	CAN	8300	5	F1
SAMUAL DR	SCLR	SAU		124	G5
SAMUEL ST	TOR	TOR	22700	68	A6
SAMUEL DUPNT AV	LA	SP	27400	73	E5
SAMUELSON ST	CO	LPUE	1100	98	D2
SAN CIR	LA	BH	9700	33	A2
SAN ANDREAS AV	LA	LA65	4400	36	A2
SAN ANDRES WY	CLA	CLA	3300	96	A6
SAN ANGELO AV	CO	LPUE	100	48	A3
SAN ANGELO AV	MTB	MTB	600	46	F6
SAN ANGELO DR	CLA	CLA		96	A6
SAN ANSELINE AV	LB	LB08	3000	71	C5
SAN ANSELINE AV	LB	LB15	1700	76	C3
SAN ANSELINE AV	LKD	LKD	4100	71	C4
SAN ANSELMO AV	SOG	SOG	9900	58	F4
SAN ANTONIO	GLDR	GLDR		88	F2
SAN ANTONIO AV	LAM	LAM		83	C2
SAN ANTONIO AV	PAR	PAR	14700	65	D2
SAN ANTONIO AV	SOG	SOG	8100	59	B4
SAN ANTNIO AV N	POM	POM	700	91	A6
SAN ANTNIO AV N	POM	POM	100	95	A2
SAN ANTNIO AV S	POM	POM	100	95	A2
SAN ANTONIO DR	COV	COV	600	88	F6
SAN ANTONIO DR	MTB	MTB	2000	46	C6
SAN ANTONIO DR	NWK	NWK	12800	82	A2
SAN ANTONIO DR	PALM	PALM		183	H2
SAN ANTNIO DR E	LB	LB07	100	70	C4
SAN ANTNIO DR W	LB	LB07	100	70	C4
SAN ANTONIO PL	LB	LB07	600	70	D3
SAN ANTONIO RD	ARC	ARC	200	28	E4
SAN ANTONIO RD	SAD	SAD		89	F3
SAN ARDO CIR	LAM	LAM	15500	83	A3
SAN ARDO DR	LAM	LAM	14300	82	F2
SAN ARDO DR	LAM	LAM	14500	83	A3
SAN ARDO ST	TOR	TOR	1700	68	D5
SN AUGUSTINE DR	GLEN	GL06		19	C6
SAN BENITO CT	CLA	CLA		91	B1
SAN BENITO ST	LA	LA33	200	45	A3
SN BERNARDINO E	COV	COV	100	88	A4
SN BERNARDINO E	COV	COV	600	89	A4
SN BERNARDINO W	COV	COV	100	88	A4
SN BERNARDNO AV	POM	POM	300	90	F6
SN BERNARDNO AV	POM	POM	700	91	A6
SN BERNARDNO FY	ALH	ALH		37	D6
SN BERNARDNO FY	ALH	ALH		46	D1
SN BERNARDNO FY	BAP	BAP		48	C1
SN BERNARDNO FY	CO			45	C2
SN BERNARDNO FY	CO			93	B1
SN BERNARDNO FY	ELM	ELM		38	B6
SN BERNARDNO FY	ELM	ELM		47	D1
SN BERNARDNO FY	LA	LA12		44	F2
SN BERNARDNO FY	POM	POM		91	A5
SN BERNARDNO FY	SAD	SAD		90	B6
SN BERNARDNO FY	SAD	SAD		94	B1
SN BERNARDNO FY	WCOV	WCOV		88	C6
SN BERNARDNO FY	WCOV	WCOV		92	C1
SN BERNARDNO RD	CO	COV	15600	88	A4
SN BERNARDNO RD	WCOV	WCOV	1100	88	A4
SAN BLAS AV	LA	WOH	4300	13	C3
SANBORN AV	CO	GL14	2700	18	D1
SANBORN AV	LA	LA27	1300	35	A3
SANBORN AV	LA	LA29	800	35	A3
SANBORN AV	LA	VEN	2800	49	C5
SANBORN AV	LYN	LYN	3100	59	B5
SANBORN AV	LYN	LYN	3100	59	C5
SANBORN WY	POM	POM	1900	95	A5
SAN BRUNO DR	LAM	LAM	14300	82	F2
SAN BRUNO DR	LAM	LAM	14600	83	B4
SAN CARLOS AV	SOG	SOG	8100	59	B4
SAN CARLOS CT	SAD	SAD		89	F4
SAN CARLOS DR	POM	POM	2200	91	A5
SAN CARLOS RD	ARC	ARC	900	28	D3
SAN CARLOS ST	CO	COM	4900	65	C2
SAN CARLOS ST	CO	LA63	3900	45	D4

STREET	CITY	P.O. ZONE	BLOCK	PAGE	GRID
SAN CARLOS ST	COM	COM	4900	65	C2
SAN CARLOS ST	PAR	PAR	6500	65	C2
SAN CATALDO AV	LB	LB15	1800	76	F3
SANCHEZ DR	GLEN	GL03		25	C3
SANCHEZ DR	LA	LA08	5100	50	F1
SANCHEZ ST	LA	LA12	400	44	E2
SANCHEZ ST	MTB	MTB	700	46	F6
SAN CLEMENTE AV	ALH	ALH	2000	46	A1
SAN CLEMENTE AV	LA	WIL	700	79	C1
SAN CLEMENTE CT	PALM	PALM		172	H9
SAN CLEMENTE DR	RPV	PVP		72	E6
SAN CLEMENTE DR	RPV	PVP		77	E1
SAN CLEMENTE PL	RPV	PVP		72	E6
SAN CLEMENTE PL	RPV	PVP		77	E1
SANCOLA AV	LA	NHO	4400	24	A3
SANCOLA AV	LA	SV	7700	17	A2
SN CRISTOBAL DR	LAM	LAM	14200	82	F2
SANCROFT AV	LAN	LAN	44200	160	C6
SANDAL LN	LA	LA77	10400	32	E3
SANDALIA DR	SCLR	VAL		124	A1
SANDALWOOD AV N	CO	LPUE	100	92	C6
SANDALWOOD AV S	CO	LPUE	100	92	C6
SANDALWOOD AV S	CO	LPUE	300	98	C1
SANDALWOOD DR	LHH	LAH		98A	C3
SANDALWOOD PL	CO	LAN		171	C2
SANDALWOOD PL	GLDR	GLDR	100	87	C5
SANDALWOOD ST	LA	CAN	23300	5	F3
SAND BROOK DR	PALM	PALM		183	F1
SAND BROOK DR	RPV	PVP	5800	72	D3
SAND CANYON RD	SCLR	CYN	27500	125	D7
SAND CANYON RD	CO	CYN		128	D1
SAND CANYON RD	CO	NEW		128	B9
SANDCASTLE CT	LB	LB03		80	F1
SANDCREEK DR	CO	SAU		182	C8
SAND CREEK RD	CO	ACT		182	G8
SANDEE LN	CER	ART	12400	82	C4
SANDEFUR ST	DUA	DUA	1200	29	D5
SANDEL AV	CO	GAR	15400	64	B3
SANDERS ST	CLA	CLA		91	D2
SANDGATE DR	TOR	TOR	3600	63	B6
SANDHILL AV	CAR	CAR	700	64	C5
SANDHILL AV	CO	CYN		125	E4
SANDHURST LN	CO	HAC		73	F1
SANDHURST LN	LAV	LAV	1100	95A	D4
SANDI CIR	WAL	WAL		93	B5
SANDIA AV	CO	LPUE	900	48	D3
SANDIA AV	LPUE	LPUE	300	48	C4
SANDIA AV S	WCOV	WCOV	1400	48	E2
SANDI CREEK RD	SAD	SAD		90	B1
SAN DIEGO	WCOV	WCOV		88	A6
SAN DIEGO CT	CLA	CLA	2400	96	B6
SAN DIEGO FRWY	CAR	CAR		69	B2
SAN DIEGO FRWY	CO			41	D2
SAN DIEGO FRWY	CO			56	E5
SAN DIEGO FRWY	HAW	HAW		62	E3
SAN DIEGO FRWY	LA	LA		22	C1
SAN DIEGO FRWY	LA	LA		32	B5
SAN DIEGO FRWY	LA	LA		42	A6
SAN DIEGO FRWY	LA	LA		50	A1
SAN DIEGO FRWY	LB	LB15		70	A5
SAN DIEGO FRWY	TOR	TOR		63	B5
SAN DIEGO FRWY	TOR	TOR		68	D1
SAN DIEGO WY	LA	LA48	700	42	F2
SAN DIEGUITO DR	LAM	LAM	14400	82	F2
SAN DIMAS AV	SAD	SAD		93	F1
SAN DIMAS AV N	SAD	SAD	100	89	F3
SAN DIMAS AV N	SAD	SAD	1600	95A	A6
SAN DIMAS AV S	SAD	SAD	100	89	F3
SAN DIMAS CY RD	CO	LAV		95A	C4
SAN DIMAS CY RD	LAV	LAV		90	B4
SAN DIMAS CY RD	LAV	LAV		95A	B6
SN DIMS CY RD N	SAD	SAD	100	90	B3
SN DIMS CY RD N	SAD	SAD		95A	B6
SN DIMS CY RD S	SAD	SAD	100	90	B3
SANDISON ST E	LA	WIL	200	74	B3
SANDISON ST W	LA	WIL	100	74	B3
SANDLAKE AV	CAR	CAR	17400	64	C6
SANDLOCK ST	PR	PR	8800	54	E4
SANDOVAL AV	PR	PR	3200	47	C6
SANDOVAL AV	PR	PR	3800	55	B1
SANDOWN RD	PR	PR		47	B6
SANDOWN RD	PR	PR		55	B1
SANDPIPE PL	PALM	PALM		184	C1
SAND PIPER	WCOV	WCOV		92	A2
SANDPIPER CT	WLVL	THO		102A	F5
SANDPIPER DR	LB	LB03		76	D6
SANDPIPER ST	LA	VEN	200	55A	E3
SANDPIPER ST	WAL	WAL		93	D6
SANDPIPER BAY	LB	LB03		76	E6
SANDPOINT CT	CAR	CAR	800	64	C5
SANDRA AV E	ARC	ARC	100	38	E2
SANDRA AV W	ARC	ARC	100	38	D2
SANDRA LN	PALM	PALM		183	B1
SANDRA ST	CO	ARC	4100	38	F2
SANDRA ST	CO	ARC	4100	39	A2
SANDRA ST	LA	SF	14900	8	D1

STREET	CITY	P.O. ZONE	BLOCK	PAGE	GRID
SANDRA GLEN DR	CO	LPUE	2200	98	E5
SAND RIDGE RD	DBAR	POM		97A	A3
SANDRINGHAM CT	LA	NOR		1	C6
SANDRINGHAM DR	GLEN	GL07		25	E1
SAND RIVER RD E	CO	LAN	19100	175	E4
SANDROCK DR	CO	PALM		157	F8
SANDS LN	CO	LAN		147	H6
SAND SPOLING AV	CO	WHI		48	A4
SAND SPRING DR	CO	LPUE		97	B4
SANDSPRINGS DR	CO	LPUE	1000	48	D3
SANDSPRINGS DR	LPUE	LPUE	500	48	D3
SANDSPRINGS DR	WCOV	WCOV	1400	48	E2
SANDSTONE CT	PALM	PALM		171	F6
SANDSTONE CT	PALM	PALM		171	H6
SANDSTONE DR	GLDR	GLDR		89	E1
SANDSTONE ST	BAP	BAP	13900	39	D3
SANDSTONE ST	BAP	BAP	15300	88	A3
SAND TRAP DR	AGH	AGO		102	D2
SANDUSKY AV	LA	PAC	9000	8	F5
SANDUSKY AV	LA	PAC	9000	9	A5
SAND WEDGE LN	CO	VAL		126	J3
SANDWOOD PL	LA	SP	800	73	E6
SANDWOOD ST	LB	LB08	5200	71	B3
SANDWOOD ST	LKD	LKD	2700	70	F3
SANDWOOD ST	LKD	LKD	3200	71	A3
SANDY DR	SCLR	CYN		125	A9
SANDY LN	DOW	DOW	12900	66	A1
SANDY LN	LA	ENC	16100	22	A5
SANDY LN	PAR	PAR		65	F3
SANDY CAPE DR	CO	MAL	18100	115	F3
SANDY CAPE DR	LA	PP	18000	115	F3
SANDYCREEK DR	WLVL	THO		102A	E5
SANDYCREEK LN	CER	ART	12400	82	B4
SANDY HILL DR	WCOV	WCOV	18200	92	E3
SANDY HOOK AV	CO	LPUE	600	48	E4
SANDY HOOK AV	LPUE	LPUE	500	48	E5
SANDY HOOK AV	MTB	MTB		46	D6
SANDY HOOK ST	WCOV	WCOV	400	92	A2
SANDYOAK LN	CO	CYN		128	E2
SANDY POINT CT	RPV	PVP		77	C3
SANDY RIDGE RD	CO	PALM		157	F9
SANDY ROCK ST	CER	ART		82	B4
SAN ESTEBAN DR	LAM	LAM	14300	82	F2
SAN ESTEBAN DR	LAM	LAM	14700	83	A2
SN FELICIANO DR	LA	WOH	4500	13	B3
SN FELICIANO DR	LAM	LAM	14300	82	F2
SN FELICIANO DR	LAM	LAM	14600	83	A2
SN FELICIANO PL	LA	WOH		13	B2
SAN FELIPE CT	PALM	PALM		183	H1
SAN FELIPE ST	LAM	LAM		83	C1
SAN FELIPE ST	POM	POM	200	90	E5
SAN FERNANDO BL	LA	BUR	7500	17	A3
SN FERNNDO	BUR	BUR	500	17	D5
SN FERNNDO BL S	BUR	BUR	300	17	D5
SAN FERNANDO CT	CLA	CLA		96	B6
SAN FERNANDO PL	LA	SV		9	D6
SAN FERNANDO RD	SCLR	NEW	23400	127	B1
SAN FERNANDO RD	SCLR	SAU	25300	127	B1
SAN FERNANDO RD	GLEN	GL01	6400	24	F1
SAN FERNANDO RD	GLEN	GL01	6100	25	B3
SAN FERNANDO RD	GLEN	GL02	5600	25	B3
SAN FERNANDO RD	GLEN	GL03	5200	25	B3
SAN FERNANDO RD	GLEN	GL04	3700	25	B3
SAN FERNANDO RD	GLEN	GL04	3500	35	D1
SAN FERNANDO RD	LA	LA31	100	35	F5
SAN FERNANDO RD	LA	LA65	500	35	F5
SAN FERNANDO RD	LA	PAC	10800	8	F1
SAN FERNANDO RD	LA	PAC	9800	9	B3
SAN FERNANDO RD	LA	SF	13800	1	F1
SAN FERNANDO RD	LA	SF	11100	2	D4
SAN FERNANDO RD	LA	SV	8500	9	D6
SAN FERNANDO RD	LA	SV	7400	16	E1
SAN FERNANDO RD	SF	SF	600	2	D4
SN FERNNDO RD W	LA	LA39	4700	25	B3
SN FERNNDO MALL	SF	SF	700	2	E6
SN FRNDO MSN BL	LA	CHA	19600	6	E1
SN FRNDO MSN BL	LA	NOR	18100	7	C1
SN FRNDO MSN BL	LA	SF	14500	2	E6
SN FRNDO MSN BL	LA	SF	16500	7	D1
SN FRNDO MSN BL	LA	SF	14500	8	B1
SN FRNDO MSN BL	SF	SF	200	2	E6
SAN FIDEL AV	CO	LPUE		48	A3
SANFORD AV	LA	WIL	400	74	D5
SANFORD DR	LA	CUL	4600	50	A4
SANFORD ST	LA	CUL	12000	50	B4
SANFORD ST	LA	LA66	12400	50	A4
SANFORD WY	CO	VAL		124	B6
SN FRANCISCO AV	LAN	LAN		160	F7
SN FRANCISCO AV	LAN	LAN		160	G6
SN FRANCISCO AV	LB	LB02	400	75	B5
SN FRANCISCO AV	LB	LB06	2900	70	B6
SN FRANCISCO AV	LB	LB06	1800	75	B3
SN FRANCISCO AV	LB	LB13	1300	75	B3
SN FRANCISCO AV	POM	POM	200	94	F2
SN FRANCQ CY RD	CO	SAU	28000	124	B2

1990 LOS ANGELES COUNTY STREET INDEX

STREET	CITY	P.O. ZONE	BLOCK	PAGE	GRID
SN FRANCQ CY RD	CO	SAU		157A	B5
SN FRANCQ CY RD	SCLR	SAU	28600	124	B2
SAN GABRIEL	GLDR	GLDR		88	F2
SAN GABRIEL AV	CER	ART	17400	66	E5
SAN GABRIEL AV	CER	ART	18300	71	E1
SAN GABRIEL AV	GLEN	GL08	1600	18	E4
SAN GABRIEL AV	LB	LB10	1900	74	F3
SAN GABRIEL AV	LB	LB13	1500	74	F3
SAN GABRIEL AV	PALM	PALM		172	H9
SAN GABRIEL AV	SOG	SOG	8100	59	B4
SN GABRIEL AV N	AZU	AZU	200	86	D6
SN GABRIEL AV N	AZU	AZU	100	88	D1
SN GABRIEL AV S	AZU	AZU	100	88	D1
SAN GABRIEL BL	CO	ELM	9300	47	A5
SAN GABRIEL BL	CO	RM	2000	46	F3
SAN GABRIEL BL	CO	RM	100	47	A5
SAN GABRIEL BL	CO	SGAB	1400	37	F5
SAN GABRIEL BL	PAS	PAS	100	27	E5
SAN GABRIEL BL	RM	RM	2000	46	F2
SAN GABRIEL BL	SGAB	SGAB	100	37	F5
SAN GABRIEL BL	SMAR	PAS	1200	27	E5
SAN GABRIEL CT	SMAD	SMAD	100	28	D2
SAN GABRIEL PL	AZU	AZU	100	88	C1
SAN GABRIEL PL	PR	PR		54	F3
SAN GABRIEL PL	PR	PR	4800	55	A3
SAN GABRIEL WY	LA	LA48	800	42	E2
SN GBRIEL CY RD	AZU	AZU	7600	86	D3
SN GBRIEL CY RD	CO	AZU	7600	86	D3
SN GABRL RIV FY	CER	ART		66	E4
SN GABRL RIV FY	CER	ART		71	F2
SN GABRL RIV FY	CO			55	B5
SN GABRL RIV FY	DOW	DOW		60	E5
SN GABRL RIV FY	IRW	BAP		39	B5
SN GABRL RIV FY	LB	LB15		81	A6
SN GABRL RIV FY	LKD	LKD		71	F2
SN GABRL RIV FY	NWK	NWK		60	E5
SN GABRL RIV FY	NWK	NWK		66	E4
SN GABRL RIV FY	SFS	SFS		60	F2
SN GABRL RIV PY	IND	PR		55	B1
SN GABRL RIV PY	PR	PR		55	B1
SN GABRL R PY E	BAP	BAP	3400	39	B6
SN GABRL VLY DR	WAL	WAL	20100	93	B3
SANGAMON AV	LA	SV	7900	17	A2
SANGER AV	CO	WHI	8300	55	B6
SANGER AV	CO	WHI	8400	61	B1
SAN GORGONIO RD	LCF	LCF	2200	11	F6
SAN IGNACIO DR	ELM	ELM	3000	47	E1
SANITRIUM PK DR	LA	LA65		36	F3
SAN JACINTO CT	CLA	CLA	2400	96	B6
SAN JACINTO ST	LA	LA26	1800	35	B4
SAN JACINTO ST	LAM	LAM		83	C1
SAN JACINTO ST	LAM	LAM		84	C6
SAN JOAQUIN	GLDR	GLDR		88	F2
SAN JOAQUIN CT	CLA	CLA		91	B1
SAN JOAQUIN CT	CLA	CLA		96	B6
SAN JOAQUIN RD	CO	COV	3300	89	A6
SAN JOAQUIN ST	LAM	LAM		83	C2
SAN JOSE	GLDR	GLDR		88	F2
SAN JOSE AV	BUR	BUR	1	17	D5
SAN JOSE AV	CO	LPUE	19000	98	F2
SAN JOSE AV	IND	LPUE	19200	97	A2
SAN JOSE AV	IND	LPUE	18500	98	E2
SAN JOSE AV	LPUE	LPUE	15800	48	F6
SAN JOSE AV	LPUE	LPUE	16000	92	A6
SAN JOSE AV	LYN	LYN	10700	59	A4
SAN JOSE AV	PAR	PAR	14500	65	D3
SAN JOSE AV	SOG	SOG	10400	59	A4
SAN JOSE AV E	CLA	CLA	100	91	B5
SAN JOSE AV N	COV	COV	100	88	F5
SAN JOSE AV S	COV	COV	100	88	F5
SAN JOSE AV W	CLA	CLA	100	91	B5
SAN JOSE DR N	GLDR	GLDR	100	87	D5
SAN JOSE DR S	GLDR	GLDR	100	87	D5
SAN JOSE PL	POM	POM	1600	90	D6
SAN JOSE ST	CO	SAU		189	F2
SAN JOSE ST	LA	CHA	20600	6	D2
SAN JOSE ST	LA	NOR	18100	7	C2
SAN JOSE ST	LA	SF	16500	7	D2
SAN JOSE ST	LA	SF	14300	8	D2
SAN JOSE HLS RD	WAL	WAL	2100	93	B4
SAN JUAN AV	LA	VEN	200	49	C3
SAN JUAN AV	SOG	SOG	8100	59	B4
SAN JUAN CIR	DUA	DUA		86	A4
SAN JUAN DR	ARC	ARC		28	D4
SAN JUAN PL	PAS	PAS	300	27	F5
SAN JUAN ST	CO	COM	4700	65	D2
SAN JUAN ST	COM	COM	4700	65	D2
SAN JUAN ST	PAR	PAR	6500	65	D2
SAN JUAN ST	POM	POM	200	90	E6
SAN JUAN WY	LCF	LCF	300	19	C3
SAN JULIAN	GLDR	GLDR		88	F2
SAN JULIAN PL	LA	LA14	500	44	D4
SAN JULIAN ST	LA	LA13	500	44	C5
SAN JULIAN ST	LA	LA14	600	44	C5
SAN JULIAN ST	LA	LA15	900	44	C5
SAN LEANDRO DR	DBAR	POM	600	94	A6

STREET	CITY	P.O. ZONE	BLOCK	PAGE	GRID
SAN LEON DR	ELM	ELM	3000	47	E1
SANLO PL	LA	WOH	5000	13	E2
SAN LORENZO ST	LA	SM	600	40	E4
SAN LORENZO ST	POM	POM	100	95	B3
SAN LUCAS CT	SAD	SAD		89	F3
SAN LUCAS DR	WHI	WHI	8000	84	B1
SAN LUIS AV	BELL	BELL	6800	53	B6
SAN LUIS AV	LA	WOH	20900	13	D2
SAN LUIS AV	LA	WOH	23000	100	F2
SAN LUIS AV	LYN	LYN	10600	59	B4
SAN LUIS AV	SOG	SOG	8100	59	B4
SAN LUIS DR	LAN	LAN		160	F7
SAN LUIS PL	CLA	CLA		91	B1
SAN LUIS ST	CO	COM	4000	65	B3
SAN LUIS ST	COM	COM	1600	65	B3
SAN LUIS ST	PAR	PAR	6400	65	D3
SAN LUIS ST	POM	POM	200	90	E5
SAN LUIS REY DR	GLEN	GL08	1100	18	E6
SAN LUIS REY DR	SAD	SAD		89	F3
SAN LUIS REY RD	ARC	ARC	200	28	E4
SAN MARCO CIR	LA	LA68	6400	34	C2
SAN MARCO DR	LA	LA68	2200	34	C2
SAN MARCO DR	LB	LB03	200	80	D1
SAN MARCO WY	LB	LB03	5800	80	D1
SAN MARCOS DR	PAS	PAS	2500	27	E4
SAN MARCOS LN	DUA	DUA		86	A4
SAN MARCOS PL	CLA	CLA		91	B1
SAN MARCOS PL	LA	LA42	4800	36	A2
SAN MARCOS RD	SAD	SAD		89	F3
SAN MARCOS ST	SGAB	SGAB	200	37	D3
SAN MARCUS ST	CO	COM	1600	65	D2
SAN MARCUS ST	PAR	PAR	6400	65	D2
SAN MARINO AV	CO	PAS	200	27	D5
SAN MARINO AV	MTB	MTB	800	54	D3
SAN MARINO AV	PAR	PAR	14800	65	D2
SAN MARINO AV	SMAR	PAS	500	27	D5
SAN MARINO AV	SMAR	PAS	1600	37	E1
SAN MARINO AV E	ALH	ALH	100	37	C5
SAN MARINO AV N	PAS	PAS	1	27	D4
SAN MARINO AV N	SGAB	SGAB	100	37	E1
SAN MARINO AV S	PAS	PAS	1	27	D4
SAN MARINO AV S	SGAB	SGAB	100	37	E1
SAN MARINO AV W	ALH	ALH	100	37	C5
SAN MARINO ST	LA	LA06	2700	43	E2
SAN MARINO ST	LA	LA06	2500	44	A2
SAN MARINO ST	LA	LA19	3500	43	E2
SAN MARTINEZ RD	CO	CAST	30000	123	C2
SAN MATEO AV	PALM	PALM		172	B9
SAN MATEO CT	CLA	CLA	2400	96	B6
SAN MATEO ST	CO	COM	4000	65	D2
SAN MATEO ST	PAR	PAR	6400	65	D2
SAN MIGUEL AV	LA	VEN	700	49	C3
SAN MIGUEL AV	LYN	LYN	10600	59	B4
SAN MIGUEL AV	SOG	SOG	8100	59	B4
SAN MIGUEL CT	MB	MB		62	D2
SAN MIGUEL DR	ARC	ARC	100	28	E4
SAN MIGUEL DR	LAN	LAN		160	G6
SAN MIGUEL RD	PAS	PAS	100	26	D4
SAN MIGUEL RD	WAL	WAL		93	A5
SAN MIGUEL ST	CO	COM	4900	65	C2
SAN MIGUEL ST	LA	WOH	21000	13	D2
SAN MIGUEL ST	PAR	PAR	6500	65	D2
SAN NICOLAS DR	RPV	PVP	27900	72	C4
SAN NICOLAS DR	WAL	WAL		93	A5
SANO CT	ARC	ARC	1100	28	B5
SANO ST	LA	LA65	3700	35	F2
SAN OAKS DR	SAD	SAD	100	89	D3
SAN ONOFRE DR	LA	PP	1600	40	F2
SAN PABLO CT	LB	LB13	800	75	D4
SAN PABLO CT	SAD	SAD		89	F3
SAN PABLO DR	GLEN	GL07	1400	25	E1
SAN PABLO ST	LA	LA33	1300	45	B2
SAN PABLO ST	POM	WAL		94	B4
SAN PABLO WY	DUA	DUA		86	A4
SAN PALO PL	PAS	PAS	300	27	F5
SAN PASCUAL AV	LA	LA42	100	36	D1
SAN PASCUAL AV	SPAS	SPAS	300	26	E6
SAN PASQUAL	GLDR	GLDR		88	F2
SAN PASQUAL DR	ALH	ALH	400	37	C4
SAN PASQUAL ST	CO	PAS	1900	27	C5
SAN PASQUAL ST	CO	PAS	3300	28	A5
SAN PASQUAL ST	PAS	PAS	800	27	C5
SAN PATRICIO DR	MPK	MPK	900	46	D3
SAN PEDRO PL	LA	LA11	4100	52	B2
SAN PEDRO ST	CAR	CAR	16500	64	B4
SAN PEDRO ST	CO	GAR	14300	64	B2
SAN PEDRO ST N	LA	LA12	100	44	D4
SAN PEDRO ST S	CO	LA61	12000	58	B5
SAN PEDRO ST S	CO	LA61	12800	64	B2
SAN PEDRO ST S	LA	LA03	5800	52	B5
SAN PEDRO ST S	LA	LA03	7800	58	B5
SAN PEDRO ST S	LA	LA11	1900	44	C6
SAN PEDRO ST S	LA	LA11	2800	52	B1
SAN PEDRO ST S	LA	LA12	100	44	D4
SAN PEDRO ST S	LA	LA13	300	44	D4
SAN PEDRO ST S	LA	LA14	600	44	D4

STREET	CITY	P.O. ZONE	BLOCK	PAGE	GRID
SAN PEDRO ST S	LA	LA15	900	44	C6
SAN PEDRO ST S	LA	LA61	10700	58	B5
SAN PIERRE DR	ELM	ELM	3100	47	E1
SAN RAFAEL	GLDR	GLDR		88	F2
SAN RAFAEL	PAS	PAS	100	26	E4
SAN RAFAEL AV	GLEN	GL02	1000	25	C2
SAN RAFAEL AV	LA	LA42	4200	36	A2
SAN RAFAEL AV	LA	LA65	3700	36	A2
SAN RAFAEL AV	PAS	PAS	100	26	E5
SAN RAFAEL LN	PAS	PAS	900	26	E4
SAN RAFAEL RD	ARC	ARC	1	28	E5
SAN RAFAEL ST	CO	COM	4900	65	C2
SAN RAFAEL ST	CO	COM	4900	65	D2
SAN RAFAEL ST	PAR	PAR	6600	65	D2
SAN RAFAEL ST	POM	POM	200	90	E5
SAN RAFAEL TER	PAS	PAS	700	26	E6
SAN RAMON DR	LAN	LAN		160	G6
SAN RAMON DR	LA	LA42	6700	26	E6
SAN RAMON DR	LA	LA42	6700	36	E1
SAN RAMON DR	RPV	PVP	2700	78	C3
SAN RAPHAEL PL	POM	POM		94	B4
SAN REMO DR	LA	PP	1300	40	F2
SAN REMO DR	LB	LB03	200	80	C1
SAN REMO RD	PAS	PAS	700	26	E6
SAN RIO ST	ELM	ELM	12000	39	B4
SAN ROQUES DR	WAL	WAL		93	A6
SAN SALVADOR PL	CER	ART	13000	81	C2
SN SALVATORE PL	SGAB	SGAB	700	37	E1
SN SALVATORE PL	SMAR	PAS	1900	37	E1
SAN SEBASTIAN	TOR	RB		72	D1
SN SEBASTIAN DR	LA	WOH	4700	13	A3
SN SEBASTIAN DR	LA	WOH	4700	13	A3
SAN SIMEON RD	ARC	ARC	500	28	C4
SAN SIMEON RD	SAD	SAD		89	F3
SAN SIMEON ST	CER	ART		82	C6
SAN SIMEON ST	POM	POM		91	A6
SANTA ANA AV	BLF	BLF	15300	66	B4
SANTA ANA AV	LB	LB03		76	C6
SANTA ANA AV	LB	LB03		80	C1
SANTA ANA BLVD	CO	LA59	2400	58	E4
SANTA ANA BLVD	LA	LA02	1700	58	E4
SANTA ANA BLVD	LA	LA59	1900	58	E4
SANTA ANA FRWY	CMRC	LA40		53	E1
SANTA ANA FRWY	CMRC	LA40		54	B4
SANTA ANA FRWY	DOW	DOW		60	D2
SANTA ANA FRWY	LA	LA		44	F4
SANTA ANA FRWY	LA	LA		45	B6
SANTA ANA FRWY	LAM	LAM		83	A5
SANTA ANA FRWY	NWK	NWK		61	A6
SANTA ANA FRWY	SFS	SFS		82	D3
SANTA ANA ST	CDY	BELL	4200	59	D1
SANTA ANA ST	CO	HPK	2400	58	F1
SANTA ANA ST	HPK	HPK	3200	59	A1
SANTA ANA ST	SOG	SOG	2600	58	F1
SANTA ANA ST	SOG	SOG	2900	59	A1
SANTA ANITA	GLDR	GLDR		88	F2
SANTA ANITA AV	CO	ALT	2100	20	A5
SANTA ANITA AV	CO	ELM		47	C5
SANTA ANITA AV	CO	PAS	200	27	E5
SANTA ANITA AV	ELM	ELM	3600	38	D6
SANTA ANITA AV	ELM	ELM	2600	47	D3
SANTA ANITA AV	SELM	ELM	1100	47	C4
SANTA ANITA AV	SMAD	SMAD	1900	28	E5
SANTA ANITA AV	SMAR	PAS	500	27	E5
SANTA ANITA AV	TEC	TEC	5000	38	E4
STA ANITA AV E	BUR	BUR	100	17	E5
STA ANITA AV N	ARC	ARC	100	28	E5
STA ANITA AV S	ARC	ARC	100	28	E5
STA ANITA AV S	ARC	ARC	1600	38	E2
STA ANITA AV W	BUR	BUR	200	24	D1
SANTA ANITA CT	SMAD	SMAD	100	28	D2
SANTA ANITA PL	BUR	BUR		17	E6
STA ANITA ST N	SGAB	SGAB	100	37	D3
STA ANITA ST S	SGAB	SGAB	100	37	D3
STA ANITA ST W	SGAB	SGAB	600	37	D3
STA ANITA TER E	ARC	ARC	1	28	E6
STA ANITA TER W	ARC	ARC	1	28	E6
STA ANITA CY RD	CO	ARC		20A	F2
STA BARBARA AV	GLEN	GL08	1600	18	E5
STA BARBARA CIR	DUA	DUA		86	A4
STA BARBARA CT	LA	LA37		51	F1
STA BARBARA CT	PALM	PALM		183	C8
STA BARBARA DR	CLA	CLA	600	91	A3
STA BARBARA DR	RPV	PVP		72	E6
STA BARBARA DR	RPV	PVP		77	E1
STA BARBARA PZ	LA	LA08	1	51	B1
STA BARBARA ST	PAS	PAS	600	27	B3
SANTA BELLA RD	RHE	PVP	1	72	F4
SANTA BIANCA DR	CO	LPUE	16300	85	F3
STA CARLOTTA ST	CO	GL14	2900	11	D5
STA CARLOTTA ST	GLEN	GL14	3200	11	C4
STA CATALINA DR	RPV	PVP		72	E6
STA CATALINA DR	RPV	PVP		77	E1
STA CATALINA VW	LA	LA49	12400	41	B2
SANTA CLARA AV	CLA	CLA	700	91	A3
SANTA CLARA AV	LA	VEN	400	49	C3

STREET	CITY	P.O. ZONE	BLOCK	PAGE	GRID
SANTA CLARA DR	POM	POM		94	B5
SANTA CLARA ST	ARC	ARC	1	28	E4
SANTA CLARA ST	SCLR	CYN		124	F8
SANTA CLARA ST	CO	SAU		189	F2
SANTA CLARA ST	LA	LA21	1900	44	E6
STA CLARA TK TR	CO	NEW		127	F6
STA CLARA TK TR	CO	NEW		128	C7
STA CLARITA RD	SCLR	SAU	26900	124	C5
SANTA CRUZ CT	LA	SP		78	E2
SANTA CRUZ CT	MB	MB		62	C2
SANTA CRUZ CT	SAD	SAD		89	F3
SANTA CRUZ CT	TOR	TOR	2100	68	C5
SANTA CRUZ RD	ARC	ARC	100	28	D4
SANTA CRUZ ST E	LA	SP	100	79	A2
SANTA CRUZ ST W	LA	SP	500	78	E2
SANTA CRUZ ST W	LA	SP	100	79	A2
SAN TAELA CT	LA	WOH	4500	13	C3
SANTA FE AV	CAR	LB10	21000	70	A1
SANTA FE AV	CO	COM		70	A1
SANTA FE AV	CO	HPK	7200	52	E6
SANTA FE AV	CO	HPK	7900	58	F1
SANTA FE AV	CO	LA58	5700	52	E3
SANTA FE AV	GLDR	GLDR	600	87	A6
SANTA FE AV	GLDR	GLDR	1600	89	A2
SANTA FE AV	HPK	HPK	5900	52	E6
SANTA FE AV	LB	LB10	2900	70	A6
SANTA FE AV	LB	LB10	1800	75	A4
SANTA FE AV	LB	LB13	900	75	A4
SANTA FE AV	LYN	LYN	11800	59	A5
SANTA FE AV	RB	RB	2300	62	E3
SANTA FE AV	SGAB	SGAB	800	37	F4
SANTA FE AV	SOG	SOG	8600	58	F1
SANTA FE AV	TOR	TOR	1900	68	C5
SANTA FE AV	TOR	TOR	2100	68	D5
SANTA FE AV	VER	LA58	5700	52	E4
SANTA FE AV E	AZU	AZU	100	86	D5
SANTA FE AV N	COM	COM	100	65	A2
SANTA FE AV N	LA	LA12	100	44	E4
SANTA FE AV S	COM	COM	100	65	A5
SANTA FE AV S	LA	LA12	100	44	E4
SANTA FE AV S	LA	LA13	300	44	E4
SANTA FE AV S	LA	LA21	600	44	E6
SANTA FE AV S	LA	LA58	2100	52	E3
SANTA FE AV W	AZU	AZU	700	86	C5
SANTA FE CT	SAD	SAD	700	90	A2
SANTA FE LN	SPAS	SPAS	700	36	F1
SANTA FE PL	MON	MON	1800	29	B5
SANTA FE ST	CLA	CLA	400	91	B4
SANTA FE ST	POM	POM	100	90	E4
SANTA FE ST	WHI	WHI	15300	84	C4
SANTA FE WY	PALM	PALM		172	B5
STA FE SPGS RD	SFS	SFS	9400	61	C2
STA FE SPGS RD	WHI	WHI	8100	55	D6
STA FE SPGS RD	WHI	WHI	8200	61	D1
STA GERTRUDE AV	CO	WHI	11200	84	C4
STA GERTRUDE AV	LAM	LAM	12900	83	C2
STA GERTRUDE AV	LAM	LAM	11800	84	C6
STA GERTRUDE AV	WHI	WHI	9800	84	C4
STA GERTRUDE RD	DOW	DOW	8000	60	C1
SANTA INEZ WY	LCF	LCF	300	19	D3
SANTA LUCIA DR	LA	WOH	4500	13	C3
SANTA LUNA DR	RPV	SP	30500	78	C3
SANTA LUNA DR	RPV	SP	30500	78	C3
STA MARGARTA DR	ARC	ARC	1300	28	C3
SANTA MARIA AV	GLEN	GL08	1600	18	E5
SANTA MARIA CIR	DUA	DUA		86	A4
SANTA MARIA RD	ARC	ARC	500	28	D4
SANTA MARIA RD	CO	TOP	200	13	D6
SANTA MARIA RD	LA	WOH		13	E5
STA MARIANA AV	CO	LPUE	100	48	B3
SANTA MONICA BL	BH	BH	9100	33	C6
SANTA MONICA BL	BH	BH	9500	42	A2
SANTA MONICA BL	LA	LA25	10400	41	D3
SANTA MONICA BL	LA	LA25	10000	42	A2
SANTA MONICA BL	LA	LA29	4500	34	D4
SANTA MONICA BL	LA	LA29	4000	35	A4
SANTA MONICA BL	LA	LA38	5500	34	D4
SANTA MONICA BL	SM	SM	600	41	A6
SANTA MONICA BL	SM	SM	100	49	A5
SANTA MONICA BL	WHOL	LA46	7500	33	E4
SANTA MONICA BL	WHOL	LA46	7100	34	A4
SANTA MONICA BL	WHOL	LA48	7000	34	A4
SANTA MONICA BL	WHOL	LA69	8300	33	E4
SANTA MONICA FY	LA	LA		42	B5
SANTA MONICA FY	LA	LA		43	C5
SANTA MONICA FY	LA	LA		44	A4
SANTA MONICA FY	SM	SM		41	C6
SANTA MONICA FY	SM	SM		49	A1
STA MONICA PL N	SM	SM		41	C4
SANTANA AV	CER	ART	18300	66	E6
SANTA PAULA AV	PAS	PAS	200	27	F3
SANTA PAULA CT	SAD	SAD		89	F3
SANTA PAULA PL	GLEN	GL08	1700	18	F5
SANTAQUIN DR	DBAR	POM		97	E3
SANTAR ST	CO	LPUE	18400	98	E3
SANTA RENA DR	RPV	SP	1800	73	D6

STREET	CITY	P.O. ZONE	BLOCK	PAGE	GRID
SANTA RITA ST	CO	COM	600	64	C2
SANTA RITA ST	LA	ENC	17700	21	D2
SANTA RITA ST	LA	TAR	19000	21	A1
SANTA RITA ST	LA	WOH	19800	13	F1
SANTA ROSA AV	CO	ALT	2000	20	A6
SANTA ROSA AV	GLEN	GL08	1500	18	E5
SANTA ROSA AV	PAS	PAS	1800	20	A6
SANTA ROSA CIR	LAN	LAN		160	G6
SANTA ROSA CT	CLA	CLA	1800	91	B2
SANTA ROSA CT	MB	MB		62	D2
SANTA ROSA CT	PALM	PALM		172	H9
SANTA ROSA CT	PALM	PALM		183	H1
SANTA ROSA CT	SAD	SAD		89	F3
SANTA ROSA RD	ARC	ARC	200	28	D4
STA ROSALIA DR	LA	LA08	3700	51	B1
SANTA SUSANA PL	LA	CAN	8600	6	C6
SANTA SUSANA PL	LA	CHA		6	C4
STA SUSANA P RD	CO	CHA		4	A2
STA SUSANA P RD	CO	CHA		6	B1
SANTA TERESA	SPAS	SPAS	1400	36	E2
SANTA YNEZ DR	ARC	ARC	100	28	E4
SANTA YNEZ LN	SGAB	SGAB	600	37	F2
SANTA YNEZ ST	CO	SGAB	8200	37	F2
SANTA YNEZ ST	LA	LA26	1800	35	C6
SANTA YNEZ WY	LA	LA36	900	42	E2
STA YSABELA DR	CO	LPUE	1700	98	E4
SANTEE ST	LA	LA11	1900	44	C5
SANTEE ST	LA	LA14	700	44	C5
SANTEE ST	LA	LA15	900	44	C5
SANTEZ DR	POM	POM	2800	93	F3
SANTIAGO AV	LB	LB04	700	76	C5
SANTIAGO AV	LB	LB14	300	76	C5
SANTIAGO DR	CER	ART	4600	81	D2
SANTIAGO RD	CO	ACT		182	H9
SANTIAGO RD	CO	ACT		189	H1
SANTIAGO ST	CO	COV	2000	93	B2
SANTINA ST	CO	CHA	9100	4	B5
STO DOMINGO AV	DUA	DUA	1200	29	E5
SANTOL DR	CO	SF	11300	3	D4
SANTOLINA DR	PALM	PALM		183	F2
SANTOLINA DR	PALM	PALM		183	F3
SANTONA DR	RPV	PVP	28000	72	C4
SANTO ORO AV	LPUE	LPUE	600	48	F5
SANTOS DIAZ ST	IRW	BAP		86	B6
SANTO TOMAS DR	LA	LA08	3900	51	A1
SAN VICENTE AV	LB	LB15	1800	76	D3
SAN VICENTE BL	SM	SM	100	40	E5
SN VICENTE BL N	BH	BH	100	42	E1
SN VICENTE BL N	LA	LA48	100	33	D5
SN VICENTE BL N	WHOL	LA48	300	33	D5
SN VICENTE BL N	WHOL	LA69	600	33	D5
SN VICENTE BL S	LA	LA48	100	33	D5
SN VICENTE BL S	LA	LA48	400	42	F2
SN VICENTE BL W	LA	LA19	5500	42	E1
SN VICENTE BL W	LA	LA19	4700	43	A3
SN VICENTE BL W	LA	LA36	6000	42	E1
SN VICENTE BL W	LA	LA48	6100	42	E1
SN VICENTE BL W	LA	LA49	11400	41	A3
SAN VICENTE CIR	WAL	WAL		93	B6
SAN VICENTE DR	WAL	WAL		93	B6
SAN VICENTE RD	ARC	ARC	500	28	C4
SAN VINCENTE AV	LYN	LYN	10500	59	B4
SAN VINCENTE AV	SOG	SOG	8100	59	B4
SAN VINCENTE ST	CO	COM	4000	65	B2
SAN VINCENTE ST	COM	COM	1600	65	B2
SAN VINCENTE ST	COM	COM	1600	65	B2
SAN VINCENTE ST	PAR	PAR	6500	65	D2
SAN YSIDRO DR	BH	BH	1100	33	A4
SAN YSIDRO DR	LA	BH	1300	33	A2
SAN YSIDRO WY	PALM	PALM		172	H9
SAN YSIDRO WY	PALM	PALM		183	H1
SAO PAULO PL	POM	POM	1400	90	C6
SAPOTA DR	LHH	LAH	2100	98	B6
SAPOTA DR	LHH	LAH	2100	98A	B1
SAPPHIRE DR	LA	ENC	3400	22	A5
SAPPHIRE ST	RB	RB	100	67	D4
SAPPHIRE CYN RD	DBAR	POM		94	A5
SARA DR	TOR	TOR	3400	67	E3
SARA DR	TOR	TOR	3400	68	A3
SARABANDE LN	SCLR	CYN		125	A9
SARABETH ST	DOW	DOW	7500	59	F4
SARAGOSA ST	CO	WHI	10400	55	B5
SARAGOSSA	POM	POM		90	C6
SARAH CT	WCOV	WCOV		92	E6
SARAH LN	LAN	LAN		160	G4
SARAH ST	CO	RM	8300	46	F3
SARAH ST	LA	BUR	4200	24	A3
SARAH ST	LA	NHO	10300	23	F3
SARAH ST	LA	NHO	10000	24	A3
SARAH ST	LA	VAN	13300	22	F3
SARAH ST	LA	VAN	12900	23	A3
SARALYNN DR	CO	CHA		4	B5
SARA MAR LN	TEC	TEC	5400	38	C3
SARAN DR	LA	VEN	8100	55A	F1
SARANAC DR	CO	WHI	13600	61	E6

STREET	CITY	P.O. ZONE	BLOCK	PAGE	GRID
SARANAC DR	CO	WHI	15300	84	B5
SARANAC DR	LAM	LAM	15000	84	B5
SARANDI GRND DR	CO	LPUE	2300	85	E3
SARANNE ST	CO	GL14	22	18	F1
SARAPE CT	SCLR	VAL	127	81	B1
SARATOGA ST	PR	PR		47	A6
SARATOGA ST	PR	PR		55	A1
SARATOGA ST N	LA	LA33	100	45	B4
SARATOGA ST S	LA	LA33	200	45	B4
SARATOGA WY	SCLR	CYN		125	A9
SARAZEN DR	ALH	ALH	1200	46	B2
SARAZEN PL	LA	SF	12200	1	F5
SARBONNE RD	LA	LA77	600	32	D5
SARCO DR	LAM	LAM	15200	84	B5
SARDA RD	SCLR	VAL		127	A3
SARDINE ST	LA	SP	300	79	C3
SARDINIA CT	LA		127	81	A8
SARDIS AV	LA	LA64	11000	41	C4
SARDONYX ST	LA	LA32	4300	36	C5
SARELDA RD	CO	CAN	4	4	B5
SARGASSO CT	CO	NEW		126	J5
SARGENT AV	WHI	WHI	7900	55	F1
SARGENT AV	WHI	WHI	8200	61	F1
SARGENT CT	LA	LA26	1600	35	D5
SARGENT PL	LA	LA26	1500	35	D5
SARGENT ST	LAV	LAV		90	D2
SARI AV	LA	SF	8700	7	F6
SARI PL	LA	SF	9700	7	F4
SARILEE AV	RM	RM	4000	38	A5
SARITA AV	SCLR	CYN	17400	125	B9
SARITA PL	LA	TAR	19100	21	B3
SARKIS CT	SCLR	SAU		124	D2
SARNIA AV	LB	LB05	6600	65	E5
SARTELL DR	CO	WAL		97	B4
SARTORI AV	TOR	TOR	600	68	D3
SASTRE AV	ELM	ELM	2500	47	C1
SASTRE AV	SELM	ELM	2000	47	C3
SATICOY ST	LA	BUR	9900	17	A3
SATICOY ST	LA	CAN	23000	5	F2
SATICOY ST	LA	CAN	19700	12	A4
SATICOY ST	LA	NHO	13300	15	F3
SATICOY ST	LA	NHO	11400	16	C3
SATICOY ST	LA	RES	17700	14	A2
SATICOY ST	LA	SV	10700	16	C3
SATICOY ST	LA	VAN	16500	14	A2
SATICOY ST	LA	VAN	13400	15	E2
SATICOY ST	LA	VAN	13500	15	E2
SATICOY ST	LA	VAN	15300	15	A2
SATICOY ST	POM	POM	2100	90	F6
SATIN CT	PALM	PALM		171	F4
SATINWOOD DR	SCLR	SAU		124	F5
SATINWOOD DR	WHI	WHI		55	F5
SATSUMA AV	LA	NHO	5600	16	E6
SATSUMA AV	LA	NHO	4200	23	E4
SATSUMA AV	LA	SV	7200	16	E3
SATTES DR	RPV	PVP	5900	77	C1
SATURN AV	HPK	HPK	2000	52	E5
SATURN AV	HPK	HPK	2700	53	A5
SATURN AV	PALM	PALM		183	H1
SATURN ST	LA	LA19	5300	42	B4
SATURN ST	LA	LA19	4500	43	B4
SATURN ST	LA	LA35	5900	42	B3
SATURN ST	MPK	MPK		46	D4
SAUDER ST	CO	LPUE	13500	48	D2
SAUGUS AV	LA	VAN	4000	22	B2
SAUGUS RD	CO	CHA		1A	D6
SAUGUS T SEA RD	CO	NEW		127	B7
SAUGUS T SEA RD	CO	SF		1	B1
SAUL CT	CO	CYN		125	E7
SAUNDERS ST	LA	COM	4100	65	C4
SAUNDERS ST	LA	COM	1600	65	B5
SAUNDERS ST	POM	POM	2300	91	A5
SAUSALITO AV	LA	CAN	6500	12	B5
SAUSALITO AV	LA	WOH	6000	12	B6
SAUSALITO CIR	MB	MB		62	D3
SAVAGE AV	WHI	WHI	16700	84	D3
SAVANNAH ST	DOW	DOW	9700	60	D1
SAVANNAH ST	MTB	MTB		46	E5
SAVANNAH ST N	LA	LA33	100	45	B4
SAVANNAH ST S	LA	LA33	100	45	B4
SAVARONA WY	CAR	CAR		64	B6
SAVILLE AV	LA	ENC	5200	21	F1
SAVONA PL	POM	POM		94	B4
SAVONA ST	LA	LA77	10800	32	D2
SAVONA WK	LB	LB03		80	C1
SAVOY ST	LA	LA12	400	44	F4
SAWPIT LN	BRAD	DUA		29	C3
SAWTELLE BLVD	CUL	CUL	3800	50	B3
SAWTELLE BLVD	CUL	CUL	4500	50	B4
SAWTELLE BLVD	LA	LA25	1500	41	B3
SAWTELLE BLVD	LA	LA64	2200	41	B4
SAWTELLE BLVD	LA	LA66	3000	41	B3
SAWTELLE BLVD	LA	LA66	3500	50	A1
SAWYER AV	CUL	WCOV	1400	92	A1
SAWYER ST	LA	LA19	5800	42	D4
SAWYER ST	LA	LA35	6000	42	D4
SAWYER ST	LB	LB05	2800	65	F6
SAXON AV E	SGAB	SGAB	100	37	D6
SAXON AV W	SGAB	SGAB	100	37	D6
SAXON DR	LA	LA65	2600	25	B4
SAYBROOK AV	CMRC	LA40	2000	54	B3
SAYBROOK AV	CO	LA22	600	54	B2
SAYLER AV	LAW	LAW	15700	63	A4
SAYLIN LN	LA	LA42	6200	36	D1
SAYRE DR	LA	SF		2	E3
SAYRE LN	LA	LA26	800	35	B5
SAYRE ST	LA	SF	13400	2	E3
SAYRE ST	LA	SF	13000	3	A1
SAYUAYO ST	LAN	LAN	43600	160	B1
SCADLOCK LN	LA	VAN	3400	22	C4
SCALLION DR	SCLR	SAU		124	D5
SCAMOCKER RD	SCLR	NEW	25100	127	G3
SCANDIA WY	LA	LA65	3800	35	B1
SCANNEL AV	LA	TOR	21500	67	E4
SCARBORO ST	LA	LA65	3300	35	B3
SCARBOROUGH LN	CER	ART	12900	81	C2
SCARBOROUGH LN	SAD	SAD		89	C5
SCARBRG PEAK DR	LA	CAN	6900	5	D4
SCARECROW PL	CO	LPUE		98	C5
SCARFF ST	LA	LA07	2300	44	A5
SCARLET MDW DR	SCLR	NEW		127	F2
SCARLET OAK CIR	POM	POM		90	E2
SCELINA AV	BELL	BELL	6500	53	C5
SCENARIO LN	LA	LA77	10200	32	D2
SCENIC AV	LA	LA68	6000	34	C4
SCENIC AV	CO	RM	8300	46	F4
SCENIC DR	GLEN	GL05	1200	25	E6
SCENIC DR	PAS	PAS	1400	26	D1
SCENIC DR	WCOV	WCOV		97	A2
SCENIC DR	WHI	WHI		55	C2
SCENIC DR E	MON	MON	100	29	B2
SCENIC DR W	MON	MON	100	29	B2
SCENIC PL	LA	PP	16900	40	B3
SCENIC RIDGE DR	POM	POM		94	B4
SCENIC RIDGE DR	POM	POM		94	E6
SCENIC RIDGE DR	POM	POM		97A	C1
SCEPTER LN	SCLR	SAU		124	D5
SCHABARUM AV	IRW	BAP		39	B5
SCHABARUM DR	IRW	BAP		88	A1
SCHADER DR	SM	SM	2200	41	B5
SCHAEFER RD	CO	SAU		188	C2
SCHAEFER ST	CUL	CUL	3500	42	D6
SCHARN LN	BLF	BLF	9200	66	B2
SCHERER LN	WAL	WAL	100	93	B6
SCHERZINGER LN	SCLR	CYN	17600	125	A8
SCHICK AV	CO	LA63		45	C3
SCHICK LN	LKD	LKD	12100	81	B3
SCHIEFFELIN ST	LA	LA12		44	F1
SCHILLING LN	LB	LB05	6600	65	E5
SCHILLING ST	TOR	TOR		68	D6
SCHINNER ST	COM	COM	1300	65	B4
SCHLEY AV	LA	WIL	800	74	E4
SCHLITZ ST	LA	VAN		15	E2
SCHMIDT AV	CO	ELM	10300	47	D2
SCHMIDT RD	ELM	ELM	10900	47	D2
SCHOENBORN ST	LA	CAN	23100	5	F1
SCHOENBORN ST	LA	CAN	20200	12	E1
SCHOENBORN ST	LA	NOR	17900	14	C1
SCHOENBORN ST	LA	SF	16500	14	F1
SCHOENBORN ST	LA	SF	15000	15	C1
SCHOENBORN ST	LA	SV	13100	16	A1
SCHOLL DR	GLEN	GL06	300	26	A3
SCHOLL CYN RD	LA	LA41	7800	26	C3
SCHOLLVIEW AV E	CO	LAN	17100	175	D4
SCHOOL AV	CO	LA22	500	48	A6
SCHOOL AV	CO	LA22	700	54	A1
SCHOOL ST	BAP	BAP	14300	39	E3
SCHOOL ST	CO	COV	100	64	D3
SCHOOL ST	CO	COV	100	88	E4
SCHOOL ST	GLEN	GL02	1300	25	B2
SCHOOL ST	LYN	LYN	11600	59	B6
SCHOOLCRAFT ST	LA	CAN	23000	5	F1
SCHOOLCRAFT ST	LA	CAN	19700	12	A4
SCHOOLCRAFT ST	LA	RES	18300	14	A4
SCHOOLCRAFT ST	LA	VAN	16900	14	A1
SCHOOLING RD	LA	PR	9500	54	F5
SCHOOLSIDE AV	MPK	MPK		46	E6
SCHOONER DR	RPV	VEN		49	C5
SCHROLL ST	LKD	LKD	7000	71	F1
SCHUELEN ST	CO	MAL	500	108	D6
SCHUMACHER DR	LA	LA48	700	42	F2
SCHUMANN RD	LA	CAL		100	D3
SCHUYKILL DR	CO	CHA		4	D5
SCHUYLER RD	CO	WOH		13	A4
SCHUYLER RD	BH	BH	1000	33	C3
SCHWEITZER DR	BH	BH	1300	33	C3
SCHWIND RD	CO	TOP		13	D5
SCHYVON DR	CO	MAL		111	D2
SCOBEY AV	CO	PALM		184	D3
	CAR	CAR	19000	69	C1
SCOFIELD DR	GLEN	GL05	1100	25	E5
SCOTGROVE DR	RPV	PVP	6500	72	D6
SCOTLAND ST	LA	LA39	3000	35	B3
SCOTMIST DR	RPV	PVP	6000	72	D5
SCOTMONT DR	LA	TU	9400	11	A5
SCOTSVIEW DR	RPV	PVP	28300	72	C5
SCOTT AV	AZU	AZU	300	88	D2
SCOTT AV	CO	VAL		123	J6
SCOTT AV	CO	WHI	10800	84	B4
SCOTT AV	LA	LA26	1000	35	C5
SCOTT AV	MTB	MTB	500	46	F5
SCOTT AV	PALM	PALM		183	F1
SCOTT AV	POM	POM	1200	95	A1
SCOTT AV	SOG	SOG	11200	59	E5
SCOTT AV	WHI	WHI	10000	84	B4
SCOTT LN	RM	RM	8500	38	A5
SCOTT PL	ARC	ARC		28	F6
SCOTT PL	BAP	BAP	14300	39	E4
SCOTT PL	GLDR	GLDR	600	87	B6
SCOTT PL	LA	LA26	2800	35	B5
SCOTT PL	PAS	PAS	200	26	E3
SCOTT RD	BUR	BUR	900	17	C3
SCOTT RD	LA	BUR		17	B2
SCOTT RD	WCOV	WCOV		92	B4
SCOTT ST	LA	LA26		35	B6
SCOTT ST	RM	RM	8600	37	F5
SCOTT ST E	LB	LB05	100	65	B6
SCOTT ST W	LB	LB05	100	65	B6
SCOTT TR	LA	LA69	1500	33	F3
SCOTT WY	CMRC	LA40		54	A5
SCOTT WY	LA	BUR		17	B2
SCOTTDALE AV	CO	GLDR	1300	87	E6
SCOTT ROBTSN RD	HH	CAL		100	D2
SCOTTSBLUFF DR	CA	CA		91	C1
SCOTTSDALE DR	CAR	CAR	700	69	B6
SCOTTSDALE DR N	CAR	CAR	23200	69	C6
SCOTTSDALE DR S	CAR	CAR	23400	74	C1
SCOTWOOD DR	RHE	PVP	5500	72	F6
SCOTWOOD DR	RPV	PVP	5500	72	E6
SCOUT AV	BG	BELL	6500	54	B6
SCOUT AV	BG	BELL	6200	59	F2
SCOUT WY	BG	BELL	7200	60	A1
SCOUT WY	LA	LA26	2200	35	B6
SCOVILLE AV	LA	SUN	10100	10	D2
SCOVILLE AV	POM	POM	1200	91	A6
SCRANTON CT	PALM	PALM		183	J1
SCREENLAND DR	BUR	BUR	1400	17	A6
SCREENLAND DR	BUR	BUR	100	24	A1
SCRIBNER AV	CO	WHI	9900	61	D3
SCRIPPS DR	CLA	CLA	400	91	A2
SCRIPPS LN	CO	ALT	2700	20	A4
SCRIPPS PL	CO	ALT	2700	20	A4
SCRIVENER ST	LB	LB08	5300	71	C6
SCROLL ST	CO	LB08	7000	71	E4
SCUDDER CT	CAR	CAR	17500	64	D6
SEA LN	CO	MAL		112	D6
SEAACA ST	DOW	DOW		60	D6
SEABEC CIR	LA	PP	15800	40	C4
SEABEE TR	CO	TOP		109	D6
SEA BISCUIT CT	WAL	WAL		93	B5
SEABOARD RD	LB	LB05		65	F6
SEABOARD RD	CO	MAL	20400	115	A4
SEABORN AV	LKD	LKD	6100	71	D3
SEABORN ST	LKD	LKD	6100	71	D3
SEA BREEZE DR	CO	MAL	2700	113	A4
SEA BREEZE DR	LA	PP	17900	115	F4
SEA BREEZE LN	LAN	LAN		159	F5
SEABREEZE WY	LB	LB03	6100	76	A1
SEABRIGHT AV	LB	LB10	2900	70	A6
SEABRIGHT AV	LB	LB10	2200	75	A2
SEABRIGHT AV	LB	LB13	1300	75	A4
SEABRIGHT DR	LA	BH	1400	33	A4
SEABRIGHT DR	LA	BH	1400	33	A4
SEABRIGHT PL	LA	BH	1400	33	A4
SEABROOK LN	AGH	AGO		100A	A3
SEABRYN DR	RPV	PVP		77	F4
SEABURY LN	LA	LA77	10200	32	D2
SEACLIFF DR	RPV	PVP	3200	78	A3
SEACLIFFE AV	LA	TU		11	B5
SEA COLONY DR	SM	SM		49	B3
SEACOVE DR	RPV	PVP	1700	78	A3
SEACREST CT	LB	LB03		80	C1
SEACREST DR	RPV	PVP	5400	72	D6
SEA DAISY DR	CO	MAL		110	B4
SEADLER DR	CO	LPUE		98	E3
SEA DRIFT COVE	CO	MAL		111	F6
SEAFARER CIR	LA	SP		79	D5
SEAFIELD DR	CO	MAL	33000	111	C4
SEAFORTH AV	NWK	NWK	11100	81	B1
SEA GATE DR	RPV	PVP	32600	77	D3
SEA GIRT AV	CO	CYN		128	D1
SEAGLEN DR	RPV	PVP	3400	78	B3
SEAGREEN DR	DBAR	POM		94	B5
SEAGROVE AV	CAR	CAR	24200	74	C2
SEAGULL DR	LA	WIL	1400	74	C3
SEAHALL DR	CO	MAL		113	A6
SEAHORSE WY	RPV	PVP	32500	77	C3
SEAHORN DR	LA	MAL	3600	115	A6
SEAHORSE LN	RPV	PVP	4100	78	A4
SEAHURST RD	RHE	PVP		72	F4
SEA ISLE DR	LB	LB03		80	C1
SEA LEVEL DR	CO	MAL	31500	111	C4
SEA LION PL	CO	MAL	29200	110	B6
SEALPOINT CT	RPV	PVP		77	C3
SEAMAN AV	ELM	ELM	2600	47	C1
SEAMAN AV	SELM	ELM	2000	47	C3
SEAMOOR DR	CO	MAL		115	B4
SEAMOUNT DR	RPV	PVP	28400	72	C5
SEAPINE LN	CO	GL14		11	E5
SEA RANCH WY	CO	MAL		110	C5
SEA RAVEN DR	RPV	PVP	32200	78	B3
SEARCHLIGHT RD	CO	PALM		190	B2
SEA REEF DR	LA	PP	18000	115	F3
SEA RIDGE DR	RPV	PVP		77	D1
SEARIDGE DR	CO	MAL	2700	113	B6
SEARLS DR	CO	LPUE	19500	97	A3
SEAROCK LN	CO	TOP		109	A1
SEARS ST	VER	LA58		52	F4
SEARS WY	PAS	PAS		28	B3
SEASCAPE RD	RPV	PVP		77	F3
SEASHELL WY	RPV	PVP	28000	72	F5
SEASIDE AV N	LA	SP	700	79	B3
SEASIDE AV S	LA	SP		79	B3
SEASIDE BLVD	LB	LB22		75	B6
SEASIDE TER	SM	SM	1	49	B6
SEASIDE WY	LB	LB03	5500	80	C2
SEASIDE WY E	LB	LB03	5500	75	B6
SEASIDE WY W	LB	LB02	300	75	B6
SEASIDE HTS DR	RPV	PVP	5500	72	E6
SEASPRAY DR	RPV	PVP	29200	72	C6
SEA SPRING DR	CO	LPUE		85	F3
SEASTAR DR	CO	MAL	6400	111	E5
SEATON CT	LA	LA13	400	44	E4
SEATTLE AV	WCOV	WCOV		88	A6
SEATTLE DR	LA	LA46	2800	75	A6
SEATTLE PL	LA	LA46	7600	23	F6
SEAVER AV	CLA	CLA	1300	91	C1
SEAVER DR	CO	MAL		113	A6
SEAVIEW AV	LA	PP		40	C4
SEA VIEW AV	LA	LA65	4100	36	A2
SEA VIEW DR	CO	MAL		111	F5
SEA VIEW DR	LA	LA65	4100	36	A2
SEAVIEW DR N	RHE	PVP	100	77	D1
SEAVIEW DR S	RHE	PVP	100	77	D1
SEA VIEW LN	LA	LA65	4100	36	A2
SEAVIEW ST	MB	MB	100	62	A2
SEAVIEW TER	SM	SM	1	49	A2
SEAVIEW TR	LA	LA46	1700	33	F3
SEAVIEW WY	CO	MAL	26800	112	F6
SEAWALL RD	RPV	PVP		77	F3
SEAWATCH LN	CO	MAL		110	B4
SEAWIND DR	LB	LB03		80	B4
SEA WIND PL	CO	WOH		13	B4
SEAWOLF DR	RPV	PVP		77	F3
SEBALD AV	RB	RB	2400	62	E4
SEBASTOPOL ST	CO	CLA		96	C6
SEBEC DR	CO	LAM	15600	83	C2
SEBREN AV	LKD	LKD	3700	71	C4
SEBREN AV	LKD	LKD	6100	76	A1
SEBRING CT	LA	LA77		32	D2
SECLUSION LN	LA	GL07	600	25	E5
SECO CT	CO	LPUE		98	E3
SECO ST	PAS	PAS	400	26	E3
SECO CANYON RD	CO	MAL		123	C3
SECO CANYON RD	SCLR	SAU	26800	124	C3
SECO CANYON RD	SCLR	VL54		124	C3
SECREST DR	CO	MAL		115	B4
SECTION CTR ST	CO	LPUE	18300	88	C2
SECURA WY	SFS	SFS	8200	61	C1
SECURE PL	LAN	LAN	43600	159	A6
SECURITY AV	LA	BUR	7500	17	C3
SEDALIA AV	CO	WHI	9500	55	B4
SEDALIA AV	LAV	LAV	2400	90	C5
SEDAN AV	LA	CAN		12	A6
SEDAN AV	LA	RES	8400	5	A5
SEDAN AV	LA	WOH	6600	13	A4
SEDGE CT	CO	MAL	5500	13	A4
SEDGEWICK CT	SAD	SAD		89	E5
SEDONA CT	CO	LPUE		98	E3
SEDONA DR	CO	LPUE		98	E3
SEE DR	CO	WHI	11100	55	D4
SEE DR	PR	PR	9500	55	D3
SEE DR	WHI	WHI	10800	55	D4
SEELERT LN	CO	RM	1300	46	F4
SEELEY PL	LKD	LKD	21000	81	A4
SEEP WILLOW WY	SCLR	CYN		124	E8
SEFTON AV	MPK	MPK	100	28	B1
SEGAL ST	CER	ART		81	C2
SEGOVIA AV	SGAB	SGAB	100	37	D5
SEGOVIA WY	PALM	PALM		184	C1
SEGRELL WY	CUL	CUL	11200	50	C4
SEGURO DR	CO	CHA	10800	6	F1
SEIGNEUR AV	LA	LA32	1800	45	D1
SEINE AV	ART	ART	18400	81	A1
SEINE AV	ART	ART	17900	82	A6
SEINE AV	HG	LKD	21000	81	A5
SEINE AV	LKD	LKD	20300	81	A3
SEKIO AV	CO	LPUE		97	A4
SELANDIA LN	CAR	CAR		64	B6
SELBY AV	LA	LA24	1000	41	D3
SELBY AV	LA	LA25	1800	41	C3
SELBY AV	LA	LA34	3000	42	A4
SELBY AV	LA	LA34	3700	50	B1
SELBY AV	LA	LA64	2200	41	C3
SELBY AV	LA	LA64	2400	41	C4
SELBY ST	ELS	ELS	900	56	C6
SELDNER ST	LA	LA32	1800	45	D1
SELDON PL	POM	POM	2000	90	F1
SELFLAND AV	BG	BELL		53	E6
SELFRIDGE DR	CO	MAL	28800	110	C4
SELIG PL	LA	LA31		45	B1
SELKIRK LN	POM	POM	1100	91	A4
SELKIRK LN	CO	LPUE	10200	32	D2
SELLERS ST	PAS	PAS	700	19	E6
SELMA AV	LA	LA28	6000	34	C3
SELMA AV	LA	LA34	3700	50	B1
SELMA AV	LA	LA46	7600	23	F6
SELVAS PL	GLEN	GL08	1200	18	F5
SELWYN AV	CAR	CAR	21300	69	F1
SELWYN AV	LYN	LYN	3300	59	A4
SEMINOLE AV	SOG	SOG	2500	58	F4
SEMINOLE AV	SOG	SOG	2700	59	A4
SEMINOLE CIR	LA	NOR		1	A6
SEMINOLE PL	LA	NOR		1	A6
SEMORA CIR	CER	ART		82	B5
SEMORA PL	CER	ART	13000	82	B5
SEMORA ST	BLF	BLF	12300	82	B5
SEMORA ST	BLF	BLF	10200	66	D6
SEMORA ST	CER	ART	10600	66	D6
SEMORA ST	CER	ART	12500	82	B5
SEMRAD RD	LA	CAN	6900	5	D4
SENA CT	SCLR	VAL		124	B6
SENADALE ST	CO	LPUE	15600	97	B2
SENALDA RD	LA	LA68	7000	34	B1
SENASAC AV	LB	LB08	3700	71	D4
SENASAC AV	LB	LB15	3100	76	D1
SENASAC AV	LKD	LKD	5100	71	D2
SENATOR AV	LA	HAC	24200	73	E3
SENDA PAJARO	CO	CAL		100	D5
SENDA SALVIO	CO	CAL		100	D5
SENDE RANCHO PL	LA	TAR		21	B3
SENDERO PL	LA	TAR	4500	21	B3
SENECA	WCOV	WCOV		92	D4
SENECA AV	CO	CHA		6	D3
SENECA AV	LA	LA39	3600	25	C6
SENECA CT	CLA	CLA	3400	25	C1
SENECA CT	CLA	CLA	1500	91	A1
SENECA PL	DBAR	POM		97A	B2
SENECA ST	CO	PAS	2300	27	E4
SENEFELD DR	TOR	TOR	3500	73	A4
SENFORD AV	CO	LA56	5100	50	C4
SENITA WY	PAR	PAR		65	E4
SENTA AV	CMRC	LA40	2200	53	B3
SENTAR RD	LA	WOH	22400	13	B2
SENTENO ST	CO	LPUE	18200	98	C5
SENTINEL AV	CO	LA63		45	C3
SENTINEL AV	LAV	LAV		90	B3
SENTNEY AV	CUL	CUL	2800	42	E5
SENTOUS AV	CO	LA39	3600	25	C6
SENTOUS AV	IND	LPUE		97	B3
SENTOUS AV	LA	BUR		17	A5
SENTOUS PL	WCOV	WCOV	600	97	B3
SENTOUS ST	LA	CHA		6	D3
SENTRY DR	DBAR	POM		97A	B1
SENTRY LN	LAN	LAN	43600	159	G6
SENWOOD DR	BLF	BLF	9600	66	C2
SENWOOD ST	NWK	NWK	11500	66	F1
SENWOOD ST	NWK	NWK	11600	82	A1
SEPTIMO ST	LB	LB15	6700	76	E1
SEPTO ST	LA	CHA	19900	6	F3
SEPTO ST	LA	NOR	17000	7	F3
SEPTO ST	LA	SF	16900	7	F3
SEPULVEDA BLVD	CO	CUL	14700	50	C4

1990 LOS ANGELES COUNTY STREET INDEX

STREET	CITY	P.O. ZONE	BLOCK	PAGE	GRID
SEPULVEDA BLVD	CO	HAC	900	68	B5
SEPULVEDA BLVD	CO	HAC	900	68	B5
SEPULVEDA BLVD	CO	HAC	800	73	F1
SEPULVEDA BLVD	CO	LA49		41	D1
SEPULVEDA BLVD	CUL	CUL	3800	50	A1
SEPULVEDA BLVD	LA	CUL	4800	50	B2
SEPULVEDA BLVD	LA	ENC	3700	22	B4
SEPULVEDA BLVD	LA	HAC	1300	68	F6
SEPULVEDA BLVD	LA	LA25	1500	41	E3
SEPULVEDA BLVD	LA	LA34	3400	50	A1
SEPULVEDA BLVD	LA	SF	12900	2	A3
SEPULVEDA BLVD	LA	SF	8500	8	C6
SEPULVEDA BLVD	LA	SF	8300	15	C5
SEPULVEDA BLVD	LA	VAN	5600	15	C5
SEPULVEDA BLVD	LA	VAN	3100	22	B5
SEPULVEDA BLVD	LB	LB10	1600	74	F1
SEPULVEDA BLVD	TOR	TOR	1700	68	B5
SEPULVEDA BL E	CAR	CAR	100	74	D1
SEPULVEDA BL E	CAR	LB10	1000	74	D1
SEPULVEDA BL N	ELS	ELS	100	56	C5
SEPULVEDA BL N	LA	LA49		22	B5
SEPULVEDA BL N	LA	LA49	100	32	B4
SEPULVEDA BL N	MB	MB	100	62	C4
SEPULVEDA BL S	CO	LA25	1200	41	D1
SEPULVEDA BL S	ELS	ELS	100	56	C5
SEPULVEDA BL S	ELS	ELS	100	62	C4
SEPULVEDA BL S	LA	LA34	3000	41	F6
SEPULVEDA BL S	LA	LA34	3100	42	A6
SEPULVEDA BL S	LA	LA45	6500	50	C5
SEPULVEDA BL S	LA	LA45	7900	56	C5
SEPULVEDA BL S	LA	LA49	100	41	D1
SEPULVEDA BL S	LA	LA64	2200	41	E3
SEPULVEDA BL S	MB	MB	100	62	C4
SEPULVEDA BL W	CAR	CAR	100	74	D1
SEPULVEDA BL W	CO	TOR	900	68	B5
SEPULVEDA BL W	CO	TOR	800	73	F1
SEPULVEDA BL W	CO	TOR	700	74	D1
SEPULVEDA BL W	LA	TOR	1300	68	B5
SEPULVEDA BL W	TOR	TOR	3700	67	E5
SEPULVEDA CT	LA	LA34	3200	41	F6
SEPULVEDA LN	LA	VAN		22	A5
SEPULVEDA PL	LA	LA49		22	B6
SEPULVEDA PL	LA	VAN	8100	15	C1
SEPULVEDA ST	LA	SP	200	78	E2
SEPULVEDA WY	LA	LA49		32	C6
SEPULVEDA WY	TOR	TOR	2200	68	D5
SEPULVEDA E WY	LA	LA45	8700	56	C2
SEPULVEDA W WY	LA	LA45	8600	56	C2
SEQUIT DR	CO	MAL	2800	113	B4
SEQUOIA AV	CER	ART	19500	81	B2
SEQUOIA AV	PALM	LAN		171	C2
SEQUOIA CIR	WCOV	WCOV		98	F1
SEQUOIA CT	CLA	CLA		91	B1
SEQUOIA CT	SAD	SAD		95A	B6
SEQUOIA DR	CLA	CLA		91	B1
SEQUOIA DR	CO	CHA		1A	D6
SEQUOIA DR	COM	COM		64	E6
SEQUOIA DR	LYN	LYN	2700	59	A3
SEQUOIA DR	PAS	PAS	100	26	D5
SEQUOIA DR	SOG	SOG	2500	58	F3
SEQUOIA DR	SOG	SOG	2900	59	A3
SEQUOIA LN	AZU	AZU	700	86	E5
SEQUOIA ST	LA	LA39	3900	25	B5
SEQUOIA GLEN	POM	POM		94	C4
SEQUOIA GLEN DR	SCLR	VAL	27500	124	B4
SERANATA DR	WHI	WHI		84	D1
SERAPIS AV	PR	PR	7400	54	E6
SERAPIS AV	PR	PR	7900	60	E1
SERENA DR	SCLR	VAL		127	B1
SERENA DR	WCOV	WCOV		92	E3
SERENADE AV	WCOV	WCOV	600	92	B2
SERENITY CT	LAN	LAN		160	F6
SERENITY LN	CO	TOR		68	F6
SERENO DR	TEC	TEC	4900	38	A4
SERPENTINE ST	RB	RB	700	67	D4
SERRA DR	POM	POM		94	B4
SERRA RD	CO	MAL	3200	114	B4
SERRANIA AV	LA	WOH	5700	12	D6
SERRANIA AV	LA	WOH	4800	13	D2
SERRANO AV N	LA	LA04	100	34	E6
SERRANO AV N	LA	LA27	1300	34	E3
SERRANO AV N	LA	LA29	900	34	E4
SERRANO AV S	LA	LA04	100	34	E6
SERRANO AV S	LA	LA05	600	43	E2
SERRANO AV S	LA	LA06	900	43	E2
SERRANO AV S	LA	LA20	300	43	E2
SERRANO PL	LA	LA29		34	E5
SERRANO PL	POM	POM	100	90	F2
SERVER AV	CO	LA22	900	54	B2
SERVIA DR	SCLR	SAU	26600	124	D7
SERVICE AV E	WCOV	WCOV	900	92	B1
SERVICE AV W	WCOV	WCOV	800	92	A1
SERVICE DR	PAS	PAS	700	26	E2
SERVICE RD	WAL	WAL		93	D4
SERVICE ST	CO	LA63	3700	45	D2
SESAME ST	CO	LA02		68	F6

STREET	CITY	P.O. ZONE	BLOCK	PAGE	GRID
SESAME ST	CO	TOR	23200	69	A6
SESAME ST	CO	TOR	23200	74	A1
SESMAS ST	DUA	DUA	1200	29	F4
SESNON AV	CO	LPUE	1600	92	C3
SESNON BLVD	LA	NOR		1	B4
SESNON BLVD	LA	NOR		1A	F4
SESNON BLVD	LA	SF	17100	1	C4
SESPE AV	LA	VAN	4200	22	D4
SESSLER ST	SOG	SOG	10200	59	E4
SETH ST	CO	SGAB	8300	37	F3
SETON CT	CLA	CLA		91	B1
SETON HILL DR	WAL	WAL	20400	93	B3
SETTLER CT	WAL	WAL		93	E4
SEVEN HILLS DR	LA	TU	10700	10	F2
SEVEN HILLS PL	LA	TU	7200	10	F2
SEVENOAKS CT	WLVL	THO	4400	102	B4
SEVERANCE ST	LA	LA07	2600	44	A5
SEVERING DR	LPUE	LPUE	400	92	B6
SEVERN DR	PAR	PAR	6800	65	D3
SEVERO PL	LA	ENC	16800	21	F5
SEVERRI LN	LHH	LAH		84	E2
SEVERY ST	DOW	DOW	8100	60	C2
SEVILLA	RHE	PVP		72	D5
SEVILLA CT	WHI	WHI	5300	55	C3
SEVILLA ST	MPK	MPK	1100	46	A3
SEVILLE AV	CO	HPK	7200	52	F6
SEVILLE AV	HPK	HPK	5600	52	F5
SEVILLE AV	PALM	PALM		171	F5
SEVILLE AV	SOG	SOG	8000	58	F1
SEVILLE AV	VER	LA58	4300	52	F3
SEVILLE CT	LA	VEN	400	49	C4
SEVILLE CT	LB	LB03		76	D6
SEVILLE WY	LB	LB03		76	D5
SEVY LN	LA	VAN	3200	22	F5
SEWANEE CT	LA	SV	8500	16	F1
SEWANEE LN	ARC	ARC	2200	38	D2
SEWARD ST	LA	LA04	600	34	C5
SEWARD ST	LA	LA28	1300	34	C5
SEWARD ST	LA	LA38	700	34	C5
SEWELL AL	PAS	PAS		27	E4
SEYMOUR PL	MON	MON	100	29	B2
SEYMOUR ST	LA	LA65	3300	35	F4
SHABLOW AV	LA	SF	13500	3	B2
SHAD PL	LA	SP	3700	78	C5
SHAD ST	LAN	LAN		159	F5
SHADE	LPUE	LPUE		48	E6
SHADE LN	PR	PR	8900	60	E1
SHADE LN	SFS	SFS	11000	61	A2
SHADED WOOD RD	DBAR	WAL		97	C4
SHADEHILL PL	DBAR	POM		97	E3
SHADELAND DR	SCLR	NEW		127	C5
SHADE TREE LN	LA	CAN		5	D4
SHADEWAY RD	LKD	LKD	4200	71	E4
SHADOW LN	MON	MON		29	B2
SHADOW LN	RHE	PVP	1	73	B4
SHADOW LN	SF	SF	1000	2	F4
SHADOW WAY	LA	SUN	9800	10	B4
SHADOW CYN DR	DBAR	POM		97	E5
SHADOWCREST PL	DBAR	POM		97A	A3
SHADOW GLEN CIR	LA	NOR		1	A5
SHADOW GLEN CIR	LA	NOR		1A	F5
SHADOW GLEN LN	LA	NOR		1	A5
SHADOW GLEN LN	LA	NOR		1A	F5
SHADOWGROVE RD	PAS	PAS	3500	28	A2
SHADOW HILL DR	LA	SUN	9900	10	A3
SHADOW HILL WY	BH	BH	1000	33	A4
SHADOW HILLS CT	CO	SAU		124	G3
SHADOW HILLS ST	PALM	PALM		183	J6
SHADOW ISLND DR	LA	SUN	9700	10	B4
SHADOWLAWN AV	LA	LA39	2800	35	B2
SHADOW MTN DR	LA	PP		40	B2
SHADOW MTN RD	WAL	WAL	20100	93	B3
SHADOW OAK DR	LA	CHA	10300	6	B3
SHADOW OAK DR	WAL	WAL		92	F6
SHADOW OAK DR	WAL	WAL		93	A5
SHADOW OAK DR	WCOV	WCOV		92	D6
SHADOW PINE BL	CO	CYN	29000	125	F6
SHADOW RIDGE CT	LA	CAN		5	D3
SHADOW RIDGE LN	CO	LPUE		85	C4
SHADOW SPGS WY	LA	NOR		1	A4
SHADOW SPGS WY	LA	NOR		1A	F4
SHADOW VLY LN	CO	SAU		124	G3
SHADOWVIEW DR	POM	POM		94	C5
SHADOW WOOD DR	RPV	PVP	26600	72	E4
SHADWELL ST	CAR	CAR	400	69	A5
SHADY DR	LA	LA49	12400	41	B2
SHADY LN	CO	MAL		115	E4
SHADY LN	CO	TOP	20700	109	D3
SHADY LN	GLDR	GLDR	900	89	C1
SHADY PL	DBAR	POM		97A	B1
SHADYBEND DR	CO	LPUE	14400	48	B6
SHADYBEND DR	CO	LPUE	15200	85	D1
SHADYBROOK DR	LA	BH	1200	32	F4
SHADYCOVE AV	LA	BUR	7700	17	B2
SHADYCREEK DR	AGH	AGO		100A	A2
SHADY CREST LN	MPK	MPK	1600	46	A4

STREET	CITY	P.O. ZONE	BLOCK	PAGE	GRID
SHADYCROFT AV	TOR	TOR	22200	67	E5
SHADYDALE AV	CO	COV	3900	88	B4
SHADYDALE AV	CO	LPUE	600	48	D4
SHADYDALE AV	LPUE	LPUE	400	48	D4
SHADYDALE AV N	WCOV	WCOV	100	88	A6
SHADYDALE AV S	WCOV	WCOV	1000	48	F2
SHADYDALE LN	CER	ART		82	C4
SHADY ELM TER	DBAR	POM		97	E3
SHADYGLADE AV	LA	NHO	6000	16	B6
SHADYGLADE AV	LA	NHO	4000	23	B4
SHADYGLEN DR	COV	COV	100	89	A5
SHADY GLEN DR	GLDR	GLDR		89	A2
SHADYGLEN LN	SAD	SAD		89	F1
SHADYGLEN RD	GLEN	GL08		18	E4
SHADY GROVE PL	CO	CAL		100	B1
SHADYGROVE ST	LA	TU	6600	11	A4
SHADY HILLS DR	DBAR	POM		97	E4
SHADY HOLLOW CT	LA	NOR		1	A4
SHADY HOLLOW LN	LA	NOR		1	A4
SHADY LANE RD	CO	SAU		181	H6
SHADYLAWN DR	DUA	DUA	3200	86	A3
SHADYLAWN PL	BAP	BAP	13500	39	E4
SHADY MEADOW DR	CO	LPUE	16900	98	B3
SHADY MOSS CT	WAL	WAL		93	D4
SHADYOAK CT	POM	POM		90	E3
SHADYOAK DR	DOW	DOW	7200	54	B6
SHADYOAK DR	DOW	DOW	7600	60	B1
SHADY OAK DR	LAV	LAV	1400	95A	C6
SHADY OAK LN	PALM	PALM		172	A7
SHADY OAK RD	LA	NHO	3600	23	C5
SHADY OAKS DR	MON	MON		29	B2
SHADYPARK DR	LB	LB08	3000	71	D6
SHADY POINT DR	WHI	WHI	10000	84	D3
SHADY RIDGE LN	DBAR	POM		97A	A5
SHADYSIDE AV	CO	WHI	8100	61	A1
SHADYSPRING DR	LA	BUR	7700	17	A2
SHADY SPRING PL	LA	BUR		17	A2
SHADY SPGS CT	LA	NOR		1	A4
SHADY STREAM LN	CER	ART		82	B4
SHADY VALLEY LN	WHI	WHI	16100	84	C3
SHADYVIEW DR	SCLR	CYN		125	C7
SHADY VISTA RD	RHE	PVP	1	72	F4
SHADYWOOD CT	LAM	LAM	15800	83	C1
SHAFER PL	CO	SF	12400	3	D4
SHAFTER WY	LA	LA42	600	36	D2
SHAFTESBURY AV	SAD	SAD	400	90	B2
SHAIN LN	CO	LAN		171	B1
SHAKESPEARE DR	CO	PAS	3000	27	E6
SHAKESPEARE DR	SMAR	PAS	2700	27	E6
SHAKESPEARE DR	WAL	WAL		92	F6
SHAKESPEARE DR	WCOV	WCOV		92	E6
SHALE AV	CO	LPUE	1800	92	C3
SHALE HOLLOW LN	DBAR	POM		97A	A3
SHALENE ST	CO	LPUE	16800	92	B4
SHALLOT CT	SCLR	SAU		124	E5
SHALLOWBROOK RD	CO	WHI	10100	55	D1
SHALLOW CK RD	CO	SAU		181	F9
SHALLOWFORD CIR	CER	ART	19300	81	A1
SHALLOW SPG RD	CO	PALM	40500	171I	G3
SHALOMERE AV	LA	VAN	13600	22	F5
SHAMHART DR	LA	SF	16300	2	A5
SHAMROCK AV	CO	MON	1800	29	B5
SHAMROCK AV	PALM	PALM		183	E3
SHAMROCK AV N	MON	MON	100	29	C4
SHAMROCK AV S	MON	MON	100	29	C4
SHAMROCK PL	LA	CHA	20400	6	E2
SHAMWOOD ST	COV	COV	18000	88	E6
SHAMWOOD ST	WCOV	WCOV	1000	88	C6
SHANER RD W	CO	PALM	600	183	A4
SHANGRI-LA DR	SCLR	CYN		125	A8
SHANGRI LA DR	LA	BH	9900	32	F3
SHANLEY AV	LA	LA42	200	36	B2
SHANNON LN	CO	POM		97	F4
SHANNON RD	LA	LA27	3600	35	A1
SHANNON WY	GLEN	GL08	3600	19	B6
SHANNONDALE RD	CO	SAU		182	B6
SHANNON VLY RD	CO	ACT		182	B5
SHANNON VIEW RD	CO	ACT		182	C5
SHARON AV	CO	GL14	4400	18	E1
SHARON AV	LA	SUN	10700	10	B2
SHARON DR	POM	POM	100	90	E5
SHARON LN	CO	PALM		184	B6
SHARON PL	SMAR	PAS	1700	37	E1
SHARON RD	ARC	ARC	200	38	C1
SHARON ST	CER	ART		66	F6
SHARONHILL DR	CO	WHI	15600	84	C5
SHARON LEE DR	WCOV	WCOV	800	92	B2
SHARONS WY	BAP	BAP		39	F4
SHARP AV	LA	PAC	9700	8	F3
SHARP AV	LA	PAC	9100	9	A4
SHARP AV	LA	SF		2	D6
SHARP AV	LA	SF	10700	8	D1
SHARP AV	LA	SV	8500	9	B6
SHARP AV	LA	SV	8300	16	B1
SHARP PL	POM	POM		94	D1
SHARP RD	CO	CAST		123	A3

STREET	CITY	P.O. ZONE	BLOCK	PAGE	GRID
SHARPE CT	SCLR	NEW		127	H6
SHARPLESS CT	LHH	LAH	2200	98	B6
SHARPLESS DR	LHH	LAH	1800	98	B6
SHARYNNE LN	TOR	TOR	4600	67	E5
SHASTA CIR	CER	ART		82	A5
SHASTA CIR N	LA	LA65	3000	25	E6
SHASTA CIR S	LA	LA65	3000	25	E6
SHASTA CT	SAD	SAD		95A	B5
SHASTA PL	ELM	ELM	4400	38	D4
SHASTA ST	POM	POM	3000	90	E3
SHASTA ST	WCOV	WCOV	600	92	E2
SHASTA DAISY PL	CO	CYN		125	F6
SHATTO PL	LA	LA05	600	43	F2
SHATTO PL	LA	LA20	400	43	F2
SHATTO ST	LA	LA17	1200	44	B2
SHAUER ST	CO	COM	2000	64	E1
SHAVER ST	BAP	BAP	13000	48	C1
SHAVER ST	CO	LPUE	13600	48	D2
SHAW PL	CLA	CLA	1300	91	C2
SHAW PL	CO	VAL		126	G3
SHAW PL	LA	LA32	2200	45	E1
SHAW ST	LB	LB03	4100	76	B6
SHAWNA PL	SCLR	SAU		127	C1
SHAWNEE CT	CO	SAU		124	B1
SHWNEE INDN DR	CO	CHA		6	B1
SHAW RANCH RD	CO	PAS	3500	20A	A3
SHAY AV	LPUE	LPUE	100	48	F6
SHEA LN	LB	LB03		76	D5
SHEA PL	RM	RM	8500	37	F5
SHEARER AV	CAR	CAR	20600	69	A4
SHEARIN AV	LA	LA41	5000	26	A4
SHEARWATER LN	CO	MAL		110	B4
SHEBA CT	WCOV	WCOV		92	E6
SHEDD TER	CUL	CUL	3800	50	D1
SHEELIN LN	GLDR	GLDR	700	87	C3
SHEFFIELD AV	LA	LA32	3100	36	E5
SHEFFIELD AV	WCOV	WCOV	1400	48	F3
SHEFFIELD CT	SAD	SAD		89	D4
SHEFFIELD LN	SCLR	SAU		127	C1
SHEFFIELD LN	LA	NOR		1	C6
SHEFFIELD RD	CO	SGAB	8200	37	F1
SHEFFIELD RD	SMAR	PAS	2700	37	E1
SHEFFIELD WY	LA	NOR		1	C6
SHEFFORD ST	CO	LPUE	15300	85	D2
SHEILA CT	CO	LPUE		97	B4
SHEILA CT	WAL	WAL		93	C5
SHEILA ST	CMRC	LA23	4000	53	C2
SHEILA ST	CMRC	LA40	4500	53	E3
SHEILA ST	CMRC	LA40	6000	54	A3
SHEILON ST E	CO	PALM	9200	173	G3
SHELBOURNE WY	TOR	TOR		68	C5
SHELBURN CT	LA	LA65	4000	36	A4
SHELBY DR	LA	LA34	3000	42	C5
SHELBY PL	LA	LA41	4800	26	C5
SHELBY GLEN DR	LHH	LAH	2100	98A	B1
SHELDON PL	CO	ALT		19	F3
SHELDON ST	ELS	ELS	100	56	B6
SHELDON ST	LA	SV	11100	9	D4
SHELDON ST	LA	SV	8300	16	A1
SHELFORD DR	CER	ART		81	C2
SHELL AV	LA	VEN	1400	49	C3
SHELL ST	MB	MB	100	62	A2
SHELLCREEK PL	WLVL	THO		102A	F5
SHELLEY ST	LA	LA32	5300	36	E4
SHELLEY ST	MB	MB	1100	62	C5
SHELLMAN AV	SAD	SAD	100	89	D3
SHELLY ST	CO	ALT	900	19	E5
SHELLYFIELD RD	DOW	DOW	9300	60	D2
SHELLY VISTA DR	LA	TU	11500	10	F1
SHELTER COVE DR	SCLR	SAU		124	F4
SHELTER GRV DR	CLA	CLA	3800	90	F2
SHELTON ST N	BUR	BUR	300	17	C6
SHELTON ST S	BUR	BUR	500	24	D2
SHELTONDALE AV	LA	CAN	6400	5	D4
SHELTONDALE AV	LA	WOH	6300	5	D4
SHELYN DR	CO	LPUE	19600	97	A4
SHEMIRAN ST	LAV	LAV		95A	E6
SHENANDOAH AV	CER	ART	16600	82	B5
SHENANDOAH AV	CO	LA56	5100	50	E4
SHENANDOAH AV	PR	PR	8800	54	F3
SHENANDOAH DR	CLA	CLA		91	D2
SHENANDOAH LN	GLDR	GLDR	2200	87	E5
SHENANDOAH RD	SMAR	PAS	1100	27	C6
SHENANDOAH RD	SMAR	PAS	1600	37	C1
SHENANDOAH ST	LA	LA34	1900	42	D4
SHENANDOAH ST	LA	LA35	800	42	D2
SHENANGO DR	LA	TAR	19400	21	A4
SHENLEY ST	LA	SF	13000	3	A2
SHEPARD ST	IND	WHI1		47	D6
SHEPARD ST	IND	WHI1		55	C1
SHEPARD ST	LA	SP	500	78	F6
SHEPHERD DR	DUA	DUA	1500	29	D5
SHEPHERD WY	CLA	CLA		90	F1
SHEPHERD HLS RD	CO	WAL		97	C4
SHEPHERDS LN	LCF	LCF	4200	19	B3
SHEPLEY PL	LA	NOR	18200	7	C2

STREET	CITY	P.O. ZONE	BLOCK	PAGE	GRID
SHEPSTONE DR	CO	PAS		20	F5
SHERATON DR	LCF	LCF	1100	19	B3
SHERBOURNE DR	CO	LA56	5100	50	E4
SHERBOURNE DR	CUL	CUL	3200	42	D5
SHERBOURNE DR	LA	LA34	1900	42	D4
SHERBOURNE DR	LA	LA35	800	42	D4
SHERBOURNE DR	LA	LA48	100	33	D6
SHERBOURNE DR	LA	LA48	100	42	D1
SHERBOURNE DR	WHOL	LA48	300	33	D5
SHERBROOK AV	MPK	MPK		45	F4
SHERER LN	GLEN	GL08	1800	25	F1
SHERER PL	COM	COM	100	64	E3
SHERI LN	LB	LB15		76	E4
SHERIDAN AV	POM	POM	800	95	B1
SHERIDAN PL	LA	LA33	2000	45	A3
SHERIDAN RD	CO	CAST	29000	123	A5
SHERIDAN RD	GLEN	GL06	1500	26	A1
SHERIDAN ST	LA	LA33	1900	45	A3
SHERIDAN ST	NWK	NWK	12200	82	B2
SHERIDELL AV	DOW	DOW	9100	60	D2
SHERIDELL AV	PR	PR	8400	60	D1
SHERIDGE DR	LA	VAN	3600	22	C5
SHERIFF RD	CO	LA63	4200	45	D3
SHERIFF RD	MPK	LA63		45	E2
SHERINGHAM LN	LA	LA49		32	B2
SHERLOCK DR	BUR	BUR	900	18	A5
SHERMAN AV	CO	GAR	100	64	A5
SHERMAN AV	LA	VEN	200	49	B6
SHERMAN AV	MON	MON	1100	29	B5
SHERMAN CIR	LA	VAN	14500	15	D3
SHERMAN DR	CAR	CAR	300	64	B5
SHERMAN LN	GLEN	GL07	900	25	D2
SHERMAN PL	LA	CAN	23100	5	F3
SHERMAN PL	LA	SV	10600	16	F3
SHERMAN PL	LB	LB04	1500	75	E3
SHERMAN RD	LA	NHO	11900	16	C3
SHERMAN WY	BELL	BELL	6400	53	D6
SHERMAN WY	LA	CAN	23200	5	F4
SHERMAN WY	LA	CAN	19700	12	B3
SHERMAN WY	LA	NHO	11400	16	A3
SHERMAN WY	LA	RES	17700	14	B3
SHERMAN WY	LA	SV	10600	16	A3
SHERMAN WY	LA	VAN	13400	15	C3
SHERMAN CANL CT	LA	VEN	400	49	B6
SHERMAN GRV AV	LA	SUN	10100	10	D3
SHERMAN OAKS AV	LA	VAN	4200	22	B3
SHERMAN OAKS CR	LA	ENC	4400	22	C3
SHERNOLL PL	LA	VAN	3400	22	C5
SHERRILL ST	WHI	WHI		55	B2
SHERRY AV	DOW	DOW	10300	60	A2
SHERRY LN	LA	LA49	13100	21	E6
SHERVIEW DR	LA	VAN	3800	22	C4
SHERVIEW PL	LA	VAN	15000	22	C4
SHERWAY ST	WCOV	WCOV	1600	48	F1
SHERWIN WY	LAV	LAV	2400	90	E3
SHERWOOD AV	ALH	ALH	3000	36	F4
SHERWOOD CIR	MPK	MPK	600	46	A4
SHERWOOD CT	SAD	SAD		89	C4
SHERWOOD DR	LAV	LAV		95A	D5
SHERWOOD DR	WHOL	LA69	8500	33	D5
SHERWOOD DR	WLVL	THO		102	B6
SHERWOOD PL	CO	VAL		124	B7
SHERWOOD PL	GLEN	GL06		19	B6
SHERWOOD PL	LA	VAN	3800	22	E4
SHERWOOD PL	POM	POM	200	90	E5
SHERWOOD RD	SMAR	PAS	900	37	C2
SHERWOOD FST LN	LA	BH	9500	33	B2
SHERYL AV	CER	ART	19500	71	F2
SHERYL AV	CER	ART	19200	81	A2
SHERYL CIR	CAR	CAR	600	69	A6
SHERYL CIR	CER	ART	19400	81	A2
SHERYL PL	WCOV	WCOV		92	B4
SHETLAND LN	LA	LA49	12100	41	B2
SHETLAND WY	WAL	WAL		93	D5
SHIELA CT	MTB	MTB		54	D1
SHIELA CT W	MTB	MTB		46	D6
SHIELDS DR	LA	SP		78	F2
SHIELDS DR	LA	SP		79	A2
SHIELDS ST	CO	GL14	2200	11	F5
SHILENO PL	LA	ENC	16800	21	F3
SHILOH AV	WHI	WHI	9900	84	D3
SHILOH LN	LAN	LAN		160	H6
SHILOH RANCH RD	CO	AGO		102	C5
SHINE DR	SCLR	SAU		124	F4
SHINEDALE DR	SCLR	CYN		125	C8
SHINING AV	CO	SGAB	6900	28	B6
SHINN RD	CO	CLA		96	F1
SHIPLEY GLEN CT	LA	LA42	5000	36	B2
SHIPLEY GLEN DR	LA	LA42	5000	36	B2
SHIPMAN AV N	CO	LPUE	100	92	D6
SHIPMAN AV S	CO	LPUE	100	92	D6
SHIPMAN AV S	CO	LPUE	300	98	D1
SHIPMATE TR	CO	TOP	1500	109	D5
SHIPWAY AV	LB	LB08	3000	71	F6
SHIPWAY AV	LB	LB15	1800	76	F3

STREET	CITY	P.O. ZONE	BLOCK	PAGE	GRID
SHIRE CT	SAD	SAD	100	89	D3
SHIRE PL	WHI	WHI		55	C3
SHIRE WY	LB	LB15		76	E4
SHIRE OAKS DR	RPV	PVP	6000	72	D5
SHIRLEE ST	WCOV	WCOV		92	E6
SHIRLEY AV	CO	ELM	4300	38	C5
SHIRLEY AV	ELM	ELM	3900	38	C5
SHIRLEY AV	LA	NOR	8500	7	A6
SHIRLEY AV	LA	NOR	8300	14	A1
SHIRLEY AV	LA	TAR	5700	14	A6
SHIRLEY AV	LA	TAR	5000	21	A1
SHIRLEY AV	LYN	LYN	3800	59	C5
SHIRLEY CT	LA	TAR	19400	21	A2
SHIRLEY CT	PAS	PAS	2900	27	F2
SHIRLEY LN	LA	BH	9500	33	B1
SHIRLEY LN	PALM	PALM		172	B5
SHIRLEY PL	BH	BH	400	42	B2
SHIRLEY PL	POM	POM	1500	90	F6
SHIRLEYJEAN ST	GLEN	GL08	1000	18	D3
SHIRLMAR AV N	SAD	SAD	1600	87	F6
SHIRLMAR AV S	SAD	SAD	300	89	F3
SHOEMAKER AV	CER	ART	18400	81	C2
SHOEMAKER AV	CER	ART	15900	82	C4
SHOEMAKER AV	NWK	NWK	14300	82	C4
SHOEMAKER AV	SFS	SFS	10400	61	C5
SHOEMAKER AV	SFS	SFS	12600	82	C4
SHOEMAKER AV	WHI	WHI	8600	61	D2
SHOEMAKER CY RD	CO			P	C4
SHOOTNG STAR LN	CO	MAL		110	B5
SHOPKEEPER RD	LB	LB03		80	E1
SHOPPERS LN	COV	COV	100	88	E6
SHOPPERS LN	PAS	PAS	200	27	B5
SHORB ST	ALH	ALH	2600	36	F6
SHORB ST E	ALH	ALH	100	37	C5
SHORB ST W	ALH	ALH	100	37	C5
SHORE DR	LA	PP		40	C2
SHORE RD	LA	WIL		74	D5
SHOREDALE AV	LA	LA31	2200	35	E4
SHOREHAM DR	LA	LA69	8900	33	C4
SHOREHAM DR	WHOL	LA69	8700	33	D4
SHOREHEIGHTS DR	CO	MAL	3400	115	E3
SHORELAND DR	LA	LA12	1600	35	D5
SHORELINE DR	CO	SAU		157A	E5
SHORELINE DR	LB	LB02		75	C6
SHORELINE DR	NWK	NWK		66	D2
SHOREVIEW DR	RPV	PVP	5500	72	D4
SHOREWOOD RD	RPV	PVP	26600	72	D4
SHOREY PL	CO	LA63	1500	45	E2
SHORT AV	COM	COM	1700	65	A1
SHORT AV	LA	LA66	12400	49	F4
SHORT AV S	COM	COM	12700	65	A1
SHORT CIR	WAL	WAL		93	A4
SHORT ST	ARC	ARC	1200	29	A6
SHORT ST	CLA	CLA		91	B4
SHORT ST	CO	HPK	2300	58	E1
SHORT ST	CO	PALM		183	J6
SHORT ST	CO	WHI	8700	61	B1
SHORT ST	ING	IN02	500	50	E5
SHORT ST	LA	LA23	2600	44	F6
SHORT ST	LA	SM	14800	40	D5
SHORT ST	POM	POM		94	B2
SHORT TR	CO	SF		3	E5
SHORT TR	CO	TOP	400	109	D5
SHORT WY	LA	LA42	6500	36	D2
SHORT WY	SPAS	SPAS	1	36	D2
SHOSHONE AV	LA	ENC	5800	14	D6
SHOSHONE AV	LA	ENC	5200	21	D1
SHOSHONE AV	LA	NOR	8500	7	D3
SHOSHONE AV	LA	NOR	7800	14	D2
SHOSHONE AV	LA	SF	11500	1	D6
SHOSHONE AV	LA	SF	10500	7	D3
SHOSHONE AV	LA	VAN	6800	14	D4
SHOSHONE CT	SAD	SAD		90	A1
SHOSHONEAN RD	LA	SP		79	A5
SHOTGUN LN	DBAR	POM		97A	B3
SHOUP AV	CO	HAW	12800	62	F1
SHOUP AV	HAW	HAW	14200	62	F1
SHOUP AV	LA	CAN	6400	12	B5
SHOUP AV	LA	CHA	9200	6	B4
SHOUP AV	LA	WOH	5600	12	B5
SHOUP AV	LA	WOH	5300	13	B1
SHOUSE AV	COV	COV	300	89	B5
SHOW CT	SELM	ELM	1500	47	E4
SHOWBOAT LN	CUL	CUL		50	D2
SHREVE RD	WHI	WHI	12600	61	D1
SHREWSBURY CIR	LA	CAN	24300	5	D3
SHRINE PL	LA	LA07	3000	44	A6
SHRODE ST	ARC	ARC	400	29	A6
SHRODE ST	CO	DUA	400	29	B6
SHRODE ST	CO	DUA	400	39	B1
SHRODE ST	CO	MON	100	29	B6
SHROPSHIRE CT	WLVL	THO	4300	102	B4
SHULL ST	BELL	BELL	5600	59	E2
SHULL ST	BG	BELL	5600	59	E2
SHULMAN AV	WHI	WHI	8400	61	D1
SHULTS ST	LA	LA42	300	36	C2

STREET	CITY	P.O. ZONE	BLOCK	PAGE	GRID
SHURTLEFF CT	LA	LA65	3500	36	A4
SHUTTLE LN	CO	TOP	20100	115	C1
SHY ST	NWK	NWK	12100	61	B5
SIBERIAN CT	PALM	PALM		171	J8
SIBERT ST	SFS	SFS	11100	61	A1
SIBLEY ST	NWK	NWK	11200	66	F3
SIBLEY ST	NWK	NWK	11700	82	B3
SICHEL ST	LA	LA31	2300	36	A6
SICHEL ST	LA	LA31	1700	45	A1
SICILIAN WK	LB	LB03	1	80	C2
SICO MORO DR	CO	MAL	30600	111	E5
SIDEVIEW DR	DOW	DOW	9000	60	E2
SIDEVIEW DR	PR	PR	7400	54	F6
SIDEVIEW DR	PR	PR	7900	60	E1
SIDEWAY RD	AGH	AGO		100A	A4
SIDLEE PL	LA	HAC	23400	68	E6
SIDLEE PL	LA	HAC	23500	73	E1
SIDNEY AV	LB	LB05		70	A2
SIDNEY AV	PAS	PAS	600	27	F5
SIDNEY DR	LA	VAN	13300	22	F5
SIDWELL ST	LA	SF	17700	1	D4
SIEMERIO WY	CO	SAU		157A	D4
SIENA CT	CLA	CLA	3200	91	B1
SIENA DR	LB	LB03	100	80	C1
SIENA WY	CO	VAL		126	G1
SIENA WY	LA	LA77	600	32	E5
SIERKS WY	CO	MAL	3900	114	F5
SIERRA CIR	WCOV	WCOV		98	F1
SIERRA DR	AZU	AZU	6400	86	E6
SIERRA DR	BH	BH	500	33	C5
SIERRA DR	CAR	COM		64	D6
SIERRA DR	SMAD	SMAD		20A	D3
SIERRA HWY	SCLR	CYN	14700	125	C6
SIERRA HWY	CO	LAN	49400	147	J1
SIERRA HWY	CO	LAN	46500	148	A4
SIERRA HWY	CO	LAN	42100	160	A1
SIERRA HWY	CO	LAN	42000	172	B1
SIERRA HWY	SCLR	NEW		127	E7
SIERRA HWY	CO	PALM	38800	172	B1
SIERRA HWY	CO	PALM		183	C9
SIERRA HWY	CO	PALM		190	A1
SIERRA HWY	CO	SAU		181	E6
SIERRA HWY	CO	SAU		182	D9
SIERRA HWY	LAN	LAN	46000	160	A1
SIERRA HWY	PALM	PALM	37800	172	B1
SIERRA HWY	PALM	PALM		183	D2
SIERRA LN	LA	NOR		1	A5
SIERRA PL	ELS	ELS	500	56	B6
SIERRA PL	GLEN	GL08	2000	18	E6
SIERRA PL	SMAD	SMAD	1	28	C2
SIERRA PL	TOR	TOR	1000	68	C3
SIERRA ST	ELS	ELS	100	56	B6
SIERRA ST	LA	LA31	2600	36	B5
SIERRA ST	LAV	LAV		90	E2
SIERRA ST	TOR	TOR	2500	68	C3
SIERRA TER	MON	MON	800	29	C4
SIERRA WY	BAP	BAP	14800	39	F6
SIERRA WY	LAV	LAV	2500	90	D4
SIERRA ALTA WY	LA	LA69	1100	33	C4
SIERRA ALTA WY	MPK	MPK	1800	45	F2
SIERRA ALTA WY	WHOL	LA69	1100	33	C4
SIERRA ANCHA DR	CO	PALM	1000	183	A2
SRA BLANCA DR	MON	MON	900	28	F5
SRA BONITA AV	CO	PAS	1800	20	C6
SRA BONITA AV	CO	RM	8200	46	F3
SRA BONITA AV	LA	LA19	1000	42	F2
SRA BONITA AV	LA	LA36	300	34	A6
SRA BONITA AV	LA	LA36	500	43	A2
SRA BONITA AV	LA	LA46	700	34	A6
SRA BONITA AV	WHOL	LA46	900	33	F5
SRA BONITA AV	WHOL	LA46	900	34	A6
SRA BONITA AV N	PAS	PAS	100	27	C2
SRA BONITA AV S	PAS	PAS	100	27	C5
SRA BONITA LN	PAS	PAS	1600	27	C5
SIERRA CYN WY	CO	LPUE		85	F4
SIERRA CREEK RD	CO	AGO		106	D1
SIERRA CREST WY	CO	LPUE		85	E4
SIERRA CROSS AV	SCLR	CYN	28200	125	A7
SIERRA ESTS DR	SCLR	NEW	18700	127	H2
SIERRA GLEN RD	GLEN	GL08	3400	18	F3
SIERRA GRNDE AV	PALM	PALM		172	B8
SIERRA GRNDE ST	CO	PAS	3700	28	B3
SIERRA GRNDE ST	PAS	PAS	2700	27	E3
SIERRA HILL ST	SCLR	CYN	16500	125	C6
SIERRA KEYS DR	SMAD	SMAD	300	28	B1
SIERRA LEONE AV	CO	LPUE	1800	98	E5
SIERRA MADRE AV	AZU	AZU	100	86	D4
SIERRA MADRE AV	CO	AZU	18000	86	D4
SIERRA MADRE AV	CO	GLDR	18600	86	D4
SRA MADRE AV E	GLDR	GLDR	100	87	B4
SRA MADRE AV W	GLDR	GLDR	100	87	B4
SIERRA MADRE BL	CO	PAS	300	27	D6
SIERRA MADRE BL	PAS	PAS	100	27	D6
SIERRA MADRE BL	PAS	PAS	2700	27	E2
SIERRA MADRE BL	SMAR	PAS	500	27	D6
SRA MADRE BL E	ARC	ARC	100	28	E2

STREET	CITY	P.O. ZONE	BLOCK	PAGE	GRID
SRA MADRE BL E	PAS	PAS	3300	28	B2
SRA MADRE BL E	SMAD	SMAD	100	28	B2
SRA MADRE BL W	ARC	ARC	100	28	E2
SRA MADRE BL W	SMAD	SMAD	100	28	B2
SRA MDR VLLA AV	PAS	PAS	1	28	A2
SRA MDR VLLA DR	CO	PAS	1600	20A	A3
SIERRA MAR DR	LA	LA69	9200	33	C3
SIERRA MAR PL	LA	LA69	9400	33	C3
SIERRA MDW DR	SMAD	SMAD	500	28	C1
SIERRA MESA RD	CO	LR	10600	192	A6
SRA MORENA AV	WHI	WHI		55	E2
SRA MORENA CT	LA	NOR		1	B6
SIERRA OAKS DR	ARC	ARC	300	28	D3
SIERRA PASS WY	CO	LPUE		85	F4
SIERRA PEAK WY	CO	LPUE		85	E4
SRA PELONA RD	CO	SAU		181	D6
SRA PELONA RD	CO	SAU		181	D9
SIERRA PINE AV	VER	LA23	2600	53	A2
SIERRA RIDGE WY	CO	LPUE		85	F4
SIERRA SKY DR	CO	WHI		55	D2
SIERRA SKY DR	GLDR	GLDR		87	D6
SIERRA SKY DR	GLDR	GLDR		89	D1
SIERRA TRAIL CT	CO	LPUE		85	F4
SRA VALLEJO RD	CO	SAU	33600	181	A7
SIERRA VIEW AV	LAN	LAN		160	E4
SIERRA VIEW DR	SAD	SAD	1100	89	F1
SIERRA VIEW RD	CO	SAU		182	A7
SIERRA VIEW RD	PAS	PAS	100	26	E5
SIERRA VILLA DR	LA	LA41	4900	25	F4
SIERRA VISTA AV	ALH	ALH	600	37	C6
SIERRA VISTA AV	CO	PAS	500	27	E5
SIERRA VISTA AV	GLEN	GL08	3400	18	E3
SIERRA VISTA AV	LA	LA29	5300	34	D4
SIERRA VISTA AV	LA	LA38	5400	34	D4
SIERRA VISTA AV	MON	MON	400	29	B3
SIERRA VISTA AV	SMAR	PAS	100	27	E5
SIERRA VISTA CT	LPUE	LPUE	15400	48	F5
SIERRA VISTA DR	LAN	LAN	43600	159	E7
SIERRA VISTA DR	LHH	LAH	1300	84	F3
SIERRA VISTA DR	RB	RB	400	67	D4
SIERRA VIS ST N	MPK	MPK	100	46	D1
SIERRA VIS ST S	MPK	MPK	100	46	D1
SIERRA VISTA WY	CER	ART	16700	82	C5
SIERRA WOODS DR	SMAD	SMAD	200	28	B2
SIESTA AV	BAP	BAP		39	F6
SIESTA AV	BAP	BAP		48	E1
SIESTA AV	LPUE	LPUE	300	48	C3
SIESTA AV	WCOV	BAP	1600	48	E2
SIESTA AV	WCOV	WCOV	1300	48	E1
SIESTA AV N	CO	LPUE	1000	48	D2
SIESTA AV S	CO	LPUE	200	48	B4
SIESTA DR	LA	SUN	10400	9	F4
SIESTA DR	LA	SUN		10	A4
SIGMAN ST	CO	LPUE	15500	85	E2
SIGNAL DR N	POM	POM	600	95	A2
SIGNAL DR S	POM	POM	1300	95	A4
SIGNAL PKWY	SH	LB06	2600	75	F1
SIGNAL PL	LA	SP	2100	79	B4
SIGNAL ST	LA	SP	1400	79	B4
SIGNATURE DR	LA	SF	17000	1	E5
SIGSBEE AV	LA	WIL	800	74	E4
SILENT RANCH DR	GLDR	GLDR		86	F3
SILENT RANCH DR	GLDR	GLDR		87	A4
SILICA DR	CO	PALM	38900	171	J7
SILK TREE LN	PALM	PALM		172	E9
SILK TREE LN	PALM	PALM		183	C5
SILK TREE LN	PALM	PALM		183	E1
SILL RD	CO	PALM	39600	171I	G5
SILMAN ST	CO	LPUE	15500	85	E2
SILTON AV	SAD	SAD	100	89	F3
SILVA PL	CER	ART		81	B2
SILVA ST	LB	LB05	300	70	C2
SILVA ST	LB	LB07	600	70	D2
SILVA ST	LKD	LKD	2400	70	F2
SILVA ST	LKD	LKD	3200	71	A2
SILVAN PL	CAR	CAR		69	C4
SILVER LN	LA	ENC		21	E1
SILVER ST	CO	CAST	29500	123	B5
SILVER ST	HB	RB	1500	62	D6
SILVER ST	LA	LA65	2800	35	E3
SILVERA AV	LB	LB14	300	76	E5
SILVERADO	SCLR	NEW		127	E5
SILVERADO DR	LA	LA39	3100	35	B3
SILVER ARROW DR	RPV	PVP	4800	72	E5
SILVER BANK PL	CO	LPUE	2200	98	C5
SILVERBAY AV	ELM	ELM	1800	47	F4
SILVR BERRY CIR	CER	ART		82	D5
SILVERBIRCH PL	WCOV	WCOV	1000	92	A3
SILVER BIT CIR	SAD	SAD		89	D4
SILVERBIT LN	RHE	PVP		73	C4
SILVER BOW AV	NWK	NWK	13600	82	B1
SILVER BOW RD	LAN	LAN		160	E8
SILVR BRIDLE RD	WAL	WAL		93	A5
SILVER BULLT DR	DBAR	POM	21200	97	C6
SILVER BULLT DR	DBAR	POM		99	C4
SILVER CLOUD DR	DBAR	POM	21200	97	D5

STREET	CITY	P.O. ZONE	BLOCK	PAGE	GRID
SILVER CREEK RD	CO	AGO		100A	A5
SILVER CREST WY	WAL	WAL		93	B3
SILVERDALE DR	CO	CLA	600	90	F3
SILVERDALE DR	POM	POM	400	90	F3
SILVER EAGLE RD	RHE	PVP	26100	72	F3
SILVERETTE DR	PR	PR	6300	54	E4
SILVER FIR RD	DBAR	WAL	800	97	D2
SILVERFSH TK TR	CO			N	E5
SILVER FOX AV	PALM	PALM		184	A1
SILVER FOX CT	WAL	WAL		92	F6
SILVER FOX CT	WAL	WAL		93	A6
SILVERGROVE DR	CO	WHI	15800	84	C6
SILVER HAWK DR	DBAR	POM		97	E3
SILVERLAKE AV	LA	LA39	2100	35	C3
SILVER LAKE BL	LA	LA04	200	35	A5
SILVER LAKE BL	LA	LA26	300	35	A5
SILVER LAKE BL	LA	LA39	1900	35	C4
SILVERLAKE CT	LA	LA39	2500	35	C3
SILVERLAKE DR W	LA	LA26	1700	35	B3
SILVERLAKE DR W	LA	LA39	1900	35	B3
SILVERLAKE TER	LA	LA39	2500	35	C3
SILVER LNTRN DR	CO	LPUE	1500	85	D2
SILVER LEA TER	LA	LA39	3000	35	B3
SILVERLEAF DR	RHE	PVP	4100	73	A4
SILVER MAPLE DR	AZU	AZU	900	86	E5
SILVERMAPLE DR	CO	LPUE	1100	48	C6
SILVER MOON LN	RPV	PVP	27000	72	E4
SILVER OAK TER	LA	LA41	1600	26	B5
SILVER RAIN DR	DBAR	POM		97	F3
SILVER RIDGE AV	LA	LA39	2200	35	C3
SILVER RIDGE DR	RM	RM		46	F4
SILVER RIDGE WY	LA	LA39	2300	35	C3
SILVR SADDLE LN	RHE	PVP	1	72	F4
SILVERSET RD	CO	SAU		189	G4
SILVER SHOAL DR	LB	LB03		76	D6
SILVER SPRAY DR	DBAR	POM	23700	94	A6
SILVER SPG DR	RHE	PVP	1	72	E4
SILVER SPG LN	DBAR	POM		97A	A2
SILVR SPRUCE LN	CO	ALT	1	20	A4
SILVER SPUR LN	CO	ACT		182	E8
SILVER SPUR LN	PALM	PALM		183	G3
SILVERSPUR RD	RHE	PVP	600	72	E4
SILVERSPUR RD	RPV	PVP	26200	72	E4
SILVER STAR LN	CO	CYN		128	E3
SILVER STRAND	HB	RB	2400	62	B5
SILVERSTREAM DR	SCLR	CYN	17700	125	B8
SILVER TIP DR	CO	WHI		55	D2
SILVERTIP DR	DBAR	POM		97A	B2
SILVERTON AV	LA	TU	10000	11	A4
SILVER TREE LN	CLA	CLA		91	A1
SILVER TREE RD	CLA	CLA		91	A1
SILVER TREE RD	GLDR	GLDR		87	E5
SILVER TREE ST	CO	CLA	700	96	A6
SILVER VLY AV	AGH	AGO		102	F3
SILVER VLY LN	WAL	WAL		93	C3
SILVER VLY TR	WAL	WAL		93	D5
SILVERWOOD DR	LA	LA41	1400	26	B6
SILVERWOOD LN	LA	LA42	1900	26	B6
SILVERWOOD LN	POM	POM		94	C5
SILVERWOOD TER	LA	LA26	1500	35	B4
SILVIA AV	LAN	LAN		160	E3
SILVIUS AV	LA	SP	1200	78	E5
SIMAY LN	SCLR	NEW	21200	127	E3
SIMES LN	CO	AGO		106	D2
SIMI VALLEY FWY	CO	CHA		4	A1
SIMI VALLEY FWY	CO	CHA		6	A1
SIMMONS AV	CMRC	LA22	1500	54	A1
SIMMONS AV	CO	LA22	500	46	A6
SIMMONS AV	CO	LA22	700	54	A1
SIMMONS AV	MTB	MTB	200	46	A5
SIMMONS CT	CLA	CLA	1700	91	A2
SIMMONS ST	CO	CAST		123	C2
SIMMS AV	HAW	HAW	12800	63	C1
SIMMS AV	ING	IN03	11400	57	C5
SIMON CT	WAL	WAL		93	C5
SIMONDS ST	LA	SF		1	D6
SIMONDS ST	LA	SF		2	A6
SIMONDS ST	LA	SF	16600	7	E1
SIMONDS ST	LA	SF	15600	8	B1
SIMPSON AV	LA	NHO	5700	16	C5
SIMPSON AV	LA	NHO	4400	23	D3
SIMPSON PL	CO	CAL		100	B2
SIMS CT	CO	SAU		124	D4
SIMS PL	DBAR	POM		97A	A3
SIMSALIDO AV	SCLR	CYN		125	C8
SIMSBURRY ST	PALM	PALM		183	F1
SIMSHAW AV	LA	SF	13900	3	A1
SINALOA AV	CO	ALT	1900	20	D6
SINALOA AV	CO	PAS	1300	20	D6
SINALOA AV	PAS	PAS	400	27	D2
SINALOA DR	GLEN	GL07	1300	25	E2
SINALOA RD	LA	VEN	8100	55A	E1
SINATRA ST	CER	ART	12500	81	C2
SINCLAIR AV	GLEN	GL06	100	25	E3
SINCLAIR AV	LA	NOR		1	B6
SINCLAIR PL	LA	NOR		1	B6

STREET	CITY	P.O. ZONE	BLOCK	PAGE	GRID
SINCLAIR ST	POM	POM	2100	90	F5
SINGING HLLS DR	SCLR	VAL		127	A2
SINGING HLLS DR	LA	NOR	19300	1	A6
SINGING WIND RD	DBAR	POM		97	F3
SINGINGWOOD AV	POM	POM	1700	91	A6
SINGINGWOOD AV	POM	POM	1200	95	A1
SINGINGWOOD DR	ARC	ARC	700	28	B3
SINGINGWOOD DR	TOR	TOR		73	B3
SINGING WOOD RD	LPUE	LPUE		48	E6
SINGLETON DR	LAM	LAM	11600	84	A5
SINGLETREE LN	RHE	PVP	1	73	B4
SINO AV	DUA	DUA	800	29	F4
SINOVA ST	LA	LA31	4000	36	B4
SINOVA ST	LA	LA32	4400	36	C4
SINZABUT LN	SELM	ELM	1600	47	E4
SIOUX	CO	AGO		106	D2
SIOUX DR	CO	CHA		6	C1
SIOUX TR	CO	AGO		107	A3
SIPES PL	CO	SAU		182	A7
SIPHON RD	CO	PR	9400	47	B5
SIREL LN	WCOV	WCOV		92	E6
SIR HENRY	LA	SF42		2	C1
SIRIUS DR	CO	LPUE		97	B5
SISAL PL	CO	LPUE	2900	85	E4
SISCHO DR	CO	TOP	19900	109	C6
SISKIYOU ST	LA	LA23	3400	45	B6
SISSON AL	PAS	PAS	1300	27	B1
SISTER ELSIE DR	LA	TU	6000	11	B3
SITKA CT	CLA	CLA		91	B3
SITKA ST	ELM	ELM	11600	38	F6
SITKA ST	ELM	ELM	12000	47	F1
SIVAL CT	SCLR	VAL		124	A1
SIWANOY DR	ALH	ALH	1400	46	B1
SIWASH TR	CO	AGO		107	A3
SKABO AV	CO	WHI	8600	61	B1
SKAGWAY ST	WHI	WHI	16200	84	D3
SKELTON CIR	CUL	CUL	4000	50	B1
SKILLEN AL	PAS	PAS	1	27	A4
SKIPJACK AV	LB	LB02		74	F6
SKOURAS DR	LA	CAN	20500	12	D4
SKY CT	DBAR	POM		97A	B1
SKY LN	LA	LA49	12200	32	A5
SKY WY	LA	LA45		56	C3
SKYBURST	PALM	PALM		171	C3
SKYCREST DR	PAS	PAS		20A	B3
SKYCREST RD	LHH	LAH	300	84	F2
SKYEWIAY RD	LA	LA49	300	41	B1
SKYHILL DR	LA	LA68	7700	23	F5
SKYLAND DR	SMAD	SMAD	600	28	D1
SKYLAND RD	LA	SUN		10	D1
SKYLANE DR	CO	ALT	3600	20	B3
SKYLARK DR	TOR	TOR	25700	73	B3
SKYLARK LN	LA	LA69	1400	33	D3
SKYLINE DR	BUR	BUR	1	17	F4
SKYLINE DR	CO	LPUE	14100	85	B2
SKYLINE DR	LA	LA46	8500	33	D1
SKYLINE DR	LHH	LAH		85	E5
SKYLINE DR	LHH	LAH	1500	98	B6
SKYLINE DR	LHH	LAH		98A	C1
SKYLINE LN	POM	POM		94	D5
SKYLINE TER	CO	TOP		109	C5
SKYLINE TR	CO	TOP		109	C5
SKYLINE VIEW DR	CO	MAL		113	E4
SKYLINE VSTA DR	LHH	LAH	1800	98A	B1
SKY MEADOW PL	WAL	WAL		93	C5
SKYPARK DR	TOR	TOR		73	B1
SKYRIDGE DR	SCLR	NEW		127	B5
SKY RIDGE LN	CO	LPUE		85	C4
SKYTOP RD	LA	ENC	15900	22	A4
SKY VALLEY RD	LA	LA49		21	E6
SKYVIEW CIR	POM	POM		94	D5
SKYVIEW DR	CO	ALT	1600	20	D4
SKYVIEW DR	LAM	LAM		83	D1
SKYVIEW LN	WCOV	WCOV		92	E3
SKYVIEW TER	LA	TU	9500	11	B5
SKYVIEW WY N	AGH	AGO		100A	A3
SKYVIEW WY N	AGH	AGO		102	F3
SKY VISTA TER	CO	PALM		183	A5
SKYWAY CT	PALM	PALM		183	H2
SKYWAY LN	POM	POM		90	C6
SKYWAY LN	POM	POM		94	B3
SKYWIN WY	LA	LA46		33	C1
SKYWOOD CIR	CO	ALT	1300	20	C5
SLATE CREEK DR	WAL	WAL		92	F5
SLATER AV	CO	COM	12400	58	D6
SLATER AV	CO	LA59	12200	58	D6
SLATER AV	COM	COM		58	D6
SLATER AV	COM	COM	1800	64	D1
SLATER AV	LA	LA59	11000	58	D4
SLATER ST	CO	LA59	11600	58	D5
SLATER TER	CO	CHA		4	C5
SLAUSON AV	MTB	MTB	1800	54	A4
SLAUSON AV E	BELL	LA40	5300	53	B4
SLAUSON AV E	CMRC	LA40	5400	53	B4
SLAUSON AV E	CMRC	LA40	5900	54	A4

295

1990 LOS ANGELES COUNTY STREET INDEX

SLAUSON AV E

SPRUCEVIEW

LOS ANGELES CO.

STREET	CITY	P.O. ZONE	BLOCK	PAGE	GRID
SLAUSON AV E	CO	LA01	1100	52	C4
SLAUSON AV E	CO	WHI	10400	61	A1
SLAUSON AV E	HPK	HPK	1900	52	C4
SLAUSON AV E	HPK	HPK	2700	53	B4
SLAUSON AV E	LA	LA11	100	52	C4
SLAUSON AV E	MAY	MAY	3500	53	B4
SLAUSON AV E	PR	PR	8200	54	D5
SLAUSON AV E	SFS	SFS	11600	61	A1
SLAUSON AV E	VER	LA58	3300	53	B4
SLAUSON AV E	WHI	WHI	12400	61	A1
SLAUSON AV S	CUL	CUL	5100	50	B4
SLAUSON AV S	LA	CUL	4400	50	A3
SLAUSON AV S	LA	LA66	4300	50	A3
SLAUSON AV W	CO	LA43	4500	50	D4
SLAUSON AV W	CO	LA43	3700	51	C4
SLAUSON AV W	CO	LA56	4700	50	D4
SLAUSON AV W	CUL	CUL	5700	50	D4
SLAUSON AV W	LA	LA03	100	52	C4
SLAUSON AV W	LA	LA43	2200	51	C4
SLAUSON AV W	LA	LA44	700	51	C4
SLAUSON AV W	LA	LA44	500	52	C4
SLAUSON AV W	LA	LA47	1400	51	C4
SLAUSON LN	RB	RB	1000	62	E6
SLAYTON ST	HAW	HAW	3400	63	B2
SLEEPY HOLLW CT	WAL	WAL		93	D4
SLEEPY HOLLW DR	GLEN	GL06	2400	26	A3
SLEEPYHOLLOW LN	CER	ART		82	C4
SLEEPY HOLLW LN	LA	TAR	19700	13	F3
SLEEPY HOLLW PL	GLEN	GL06	2900	26	A3
SLEEPY HOLW TER	GLEN	GL06	100	26	A3
SLEEPY SPG WY	CO	LPUE		98	A4
SLICERS CIR	AGH	AGO		102	D3
SLOAN AV N	COM	COM	100	65	B4
SLOAN AV S	COM	COM	100	65	B4
SLOAN DR	LA	LA49	16300	22	A5
SLOAN DR	LAV	LAV		95A	D5
SLOAN PL	CO	CAL		100	B2
SLOAN CANYON RD	CO	CAST		123	B2
SLOAN CANYON RD	CO	SAU		123	A3
SLOAT ST	LA	LA63	400	45	B4
SLOPE DR	WAL	WAL	500	97	B1
SLUSHER AV	LA	TU	10100	11	B3
SLUSHER DR	SFS	SFS		61	A3
SMALL RD	CO	PALM		183	E5
SMALLWOOD AV	DOW	DOW	8600	54	C6
SMALLWOOD AV	DOW	DOW	12000	59	F6
SMALLWOOD AV	DOW	DOW	8900	60	C1
SMEAD WY	SAD	SAD	500	90	A2
SMILAX ST	LA	LA04	3500	35	A6
SMILEY CT	SCLR	SAU		124	D4
SMILEY DR	CUL	CUL	5700	42	E5
SMILEY DR	LA	CUL	5300	42	E5
SMILEY DR	LA	LA16	5300	42	F5
SMITH AV	CO	ACT		189	E3
SMITH AV	SFS	SFS	11500	61	B3
SMITH DR	CLA	CLA		90	E2
SMITH PL	LB	LB06	1200	75	D2
SMITH RD	CO	CHA		4	C5
SMITH ST	BELL	BELL	3500	53	B5
SMITH ST	LA	LA31	3300	36	A5
SMITH ST	LB	LB05	300	65	C6
SMITH ST	POM	POM	1500	94	C3
SMITH HILL LN	LHH	LAH		84	C2
SMITHWAY ST	CMRC	LA40	5600	54	A2
SMITHWOOD DR	BH	BH	400	42	C2
SMITHWOOD DR	LA	LA35	1200	42	C2
SMOKETREE DR	CO	LAV	500	90	D1
SMOKE TREE ST	PALM	PALM		173	A9
SMOKE TREE ST	PALM	PALM		184	B5
SMOKEWOOD LN	SAD	SAD	500	90	A4
SMOKIE LN	CER	ART	12000	81	B1
SNAPDRAGON PL	CO	CYN	29100	125	E6
SNEAD DR	ALH	ALH	1700	46	A1
SNELL ST	LAM	LAM	14800	83	A5
SNELLING ST	LA	SV	11700	9	C6
SNOW DR	CO	LA63	3900	45	D3
SNOWBIRD CIR	CER	ART	4400	81	C2
SNOW CREEK DR	WAL	WAL		93	C5
SNOWDALE ST	CO	LPUE	13600	48	D1
SNOWDEN AV	CO	LB08	3700	71	D5
SNOWDEN AV	LA	PAC	8500	8	E6
SNOWDEN AV	LA	PAC	8500	15	F1
SNOWDEN AV	LB	LB08	3000	71	D6
SNOWDEN AV	LB	LB15	2900	76	D1
SNOWDEN AV	LB	LB15	1800	76	D3
SNOWDEN AV	LB	LB15	2200	76	D2
SNOWDEN AV	LKD	LKD	4300	71	D4
SNOW DROP CT	CO	CYN		125	G4
SNOWPEAK DR	WLVL	THO		102A	F5
SNOWY OWL CT	CO	VAL		126	G1
SNWSH THMPSN RD	CO	SAU		182	A7
SOBRECOLINAS PL	POM	POM	800	94	D1
SODERBERG AV	GLDR	GLDR	5600	88	F2
SODERBERG AV	GLDR	GLDR		89	A2
SOFT AV	LAN	LAN	44100	159	G5
SOFTWIND DR	DBAR	POM		97A	B3

STREET	CITY	P.O. ZONE	BLOCK	PAGE	GRID
SOFTWIND WY	AGH	AGO		102	F3
SOFTWIND WY	TOR	TOR		73	B3
SOHN DR	CO	CAL		108	A6
SOLAMINT RD	SCLR	CYN	27800	125	A8
SOLANA CIR	MTB	MTB		46	D6
SOLANA CT	LB	LB13	1	75	C4
SOLANA LN	CO	SAU		125	C4
SOLANO AV	LA	LA12	400	35	E5
SOLANO PL	CO	COV	19600	89	A6
SOLANO CYN DR	LA	LA12	1900	35	E5
SOLAR DR	LA	LA46	2300	33	F2
SOLAR DR	MPK	MPK	1400	45	F3
SOLDANO AV	AZU	AZU	300	86	D6
SOLDANO AV	AZU	AZU	100	88	D1
SOLDANO DR	AZU	AZU	300	86	D4
SOLDON CT	SCLR	CYN		124	H6
SOLEDAD ST	SCLR	CYN	20500	124	F8
SOLEDAD CYN RD	CO	ACT		189	A6
SOLEDAD CYN RD	SCLR	CYN	14600	125	D7
SOLEDAD CYN RD	CO	PALM		189	G2
SOLEDAD CYN RD	CO	PALM		190	A1
SOLEDAD CYN RD	SCLR	SAU	19000	124	C8
SOLEDAD CYN RD	CO	SAU		188	F6
SOLEDAD CYN RD	CO	SAU		189	A6
SOLEDAD PASS RD	CO	PALM		190	D1
SOLEJAR DR	WHI	WHI		84	E3
SOLERA LN	DBAR	POM		97	F2
SOLITA RD	PAS	PAS	1100	26	E1
SOLLIDEN LN	LCF	LCF	5100	19	A1
SOLMONTE RD	LA	BH	1500	33	A3
SOLO ST	NWK	NWK	10400	60	D6
SOLON AV	SCLR	CYN		125	C6
SOLSTICE CYN RD	CO	MAL	3300	113	A4
SOLTAIRE ST	DBAR	POM		94	A4
SOLVANG ST	LA	NHO	12500	16	B2
SOL VISTA LN	RPV	PVP	27900	73	D6
SOL VISTA WY	WAL	WAL		93	A5
SOLWAY ST	GLEN	GL06	500	25	F2
SOMBRA AV	LAW	LAW	15600	63	A4
SOMBRA DR	GLEN	GL08	1700	18	F5
SOMBRA TER	LA	SUN	9700	10	B3
SOMBRAS CT	SCLR	VAL		124	B6
SOMBRA VLY DR	LA	SUN	9600	10	B3
SOMBRERO	LA	SF42		2	C1
SOMBRERO DR	MPK	MPK	1600	45	F2
SOMBRERO DR	MPK	MPK	1300	46	A2
SOMBRERO RD	MON	MON	500	29	D4
SOMERA RD	LA	LA77	900	32	D4
SOMERS AV	LA	LA65	4000	25	E6
SOMERSET	ELM	ELM		48	A5
SOMERSET AV	POM	POM	800	95	A1
SOMERSET BL	PAR	PAR		65	E3
SOMERSET BL	PAR	PAR		66	A3
SOMERSET DR	LA	LA08	3800	51	B1
SOMERSET DR	LA	LA16	2600	43	B6
SOMERSET DR	SAD	SAD		89	D4
SOMERSET DR	WAL	WAL		93	D6
SOMERSET DR	WCOV	WCOV		97	A2
SOMERSET PL	LB	LB07	1300	70	E4
SOMERSET PL	LCF	LCF	400	19	C4
SOMERSET PL	SMAR	PAS	2700	37	E1
SOMERSET RD	GLEN	GL06	2600	26	A2
SOMERSET ST	LA	LA32		36	E4
SOMERSET ST	LA	PAC	5300	9	C3
SOMMA WY	LA	LA77	10600	32	D4
SONAR LN	CO	TOP	800	109	A3
SONATA LN	LA	LA42	4800	36	B2
SONGBIRD LN	CO	LPUE		98	F5
SONGFEST DR	DOW	DOW	9100	60	E2
SONGFEST DR	PR	PR	7400	54	F6
SONGFEST DR	PR	PR	8600	60	E2
SONNET PL	CO	LPUE		85	D3
SONOITA DR	WAL	WAL		93	C3
SONOMA DR	CO	ALT	1100	20	C6
SONOMA PL	LA	CHA	22100	6	B4
SONOMA ST	TOR	TOR		68	B4
SONOMA WY	LA	NOR		1	A5
SONORA AV	CER	ART	17400	82	D5
SONORA AV	GLEN	GL01	300	24	F2
SONORA AV	GLEN	GL01	1000	25	A1
SONORA CT	SAD	SAD		90	A1
SONORA PL	CLA	CLA		91	B1
SONORA ST	MTB	MTB		46	E5
SONORA ST	POM	POM	2100	90	F5
SONRISA ST	BLF	BLF	9100	66	B2
SONYA CT	WCOV	WCOV		92	E6
SOPER DR	LA	LA46	2800	23	F6
SOPHIA AV	LA	ENC	4700	22	A3
SOPHIA AV	LA	SF	11500	2	A6
SOPHIA AV	LA	SF	8700	8	A6
SOPHIA AV	LA	SF	8300	15	A1
SOPHIA AV	LA	VAN	7000	15	A4
SOPHOMORE DR	CO	CUL		50	D2
SORBONNE ST	LA	SF	15700	2	B2
SORDELLO ST	CO	LPUE	18200	98	D4
SORENSEN AV	CO	WHI	6900	55	C5

STREET	CITY	P.O. ZONE	BLOCK	PAGE	GRID
SORENSEN AV	SFS	SFS	8000	55	C6
SORENSEN AV	SFS	SFS	8300	61	C1
SORENSEN AV	WHI	WHI	6700	55	C5
SORIANO DR	CO	LPUE	16200	85	E4
SOROCK ST	CO	TOR	900	68	F6
SORORITY LN	CO	CHA		4	B5
SORREL CT	WAL	WAL		93	D4
SORREL LN	RHE	PVP	2500	73	C5
SORRENTO CT	DUA	DUA		86	A4
SORRENTO DR	LA	PP	1500	40	F2
SORRENTO DR	LB	LB03	200	80	C1
SOTELLO ST	LA	LA12	100	44	E1
SOTO ST	HPK	HPK	5600	52	F2
SOTO ST N	LA	LA32	2000	36	C6
SOTO ST N	LA	LA32	1800	45	C1
SOTO ST N	LA	LA33	100	45	A4
SOTO ST S	LA	LA23	600	45	A6
SOTO ST S	LA	LA23	1700	52	F2
SOTO ST S	LA	LA33	100	45	A4
SOTO ST S	VER	LA23	2600	52	F2
SOTO ST S	VER	LA58	3600	52	F2
SOTRO ST	IND	LPUE		48	E6
SOURDOUGH RD	CO	ACT	3800	182	E8
SOUTH AL	SPAS	SPAS	1900	37	A2
SOUTH AV	CO	LA01	5800	52	D5
SOUTH DR	CO	HAC		73	F2
SOUTH DR	CUL	CUL		50	D3
SOUTH LN	SPAS	SPAS	1	36	D2
SOUTH ST	ART	ART	11600	81	C1
SOUTH ST	CER	ART	10900	71	D1
SOUTH ST	CER	ART	11500	81	D1
SOUTH ST	GLEN	GL02	500	25	B2
SOUTH ST	LB	LB05	100	70	D1
SOUTH ST	LKD	LKD	4100	71	A1
SOUTHALL CT	BELL	BELL	4900	53	D6
SOUTHALL LN	BELL	BELL	4900	53	D6
SOUTHAMPTON CT	LA	LA49		32	B2
SOUTHAMPTON DR	SCLR	VAL		124	E3
SOUTHBY DR	LA	CAN		5	D2
SOUTH CIRCLE DR	WHI	WHI		55	D2
SOUTHCLIFF ST	SAD	SAD	700	89	E4
SOUTHCLIFF WY	PALM	PALM		171	H8
SOUTHCOAST DR	WAL	WAL		93	C5
SOUTHERLAND AV	LA	WIL	800	74	E4
SOUTHERN AV	SOG	SOG	2400	58	F2
SOUTHERN AV	SOG	SOG	2700	59	B2
SOUTHERN LN	SOG	SOG	4800	59	D3
SOUTHERN PL	SOG	SOG	4800	59	D3
SOUTHERN PAC DR	LA	WIL	2200	74	E4
SOUTHFIELD DR	RH	PVP	1	78	B2
SOUTH GATE AV	SOG	SOG	8100	59	A2
SOUTH HILLS DR	WCOV	WCOV	1200	92	D3
SOUTH PARK AV	LA	LA66	11800	50	A3
SOUTH PARK DR	LA	LA37		51	F1
SOUTH PARK DR	LA	LA37		52	A1
SOUTH PARK LN	GAR	GAR		63	F5
SOUTHRIDGE AV	CO	LA43	4800	51	A3
SOUTHSHORE PL	WLVL	THO		102A	F5
SOUTHSIDE DR	CO	LA22	5900	54	A2
SOUTHSIDE DR	MTB	MTB	2000	54	B2
SOUTHVIEW CT	PALM	PALM		183	H2
SOUTHVIEW PL	POM	POM	800	94	B3
SOUTHVIEW RD	ARC	ARC	700	28	C5
SOUTHVIEW RD	CO	SGAB	8900	28	B6
SOUTHWAY LN	CLA	CLA	600	91	B4
SOUTHWEST BLVD	LA	LA44		57	F5
SOUTHWEST DR	LA	LA43	2200	51	C5
SOUTHWIND DR	WHI	WHI		55	F4
SOUTHWINDS DR	LA	SP	1700	78	E4
SOUTHWOOD DR	GLEN	GL06		26	A4
SOVEREIGN LN	ING	IN01		57	C2
SPACE CT	LAN	LAN		159	G6
SPACE PARK DR	RB	RB	1900	62	E3
SPAD PL	CUL	CUL	3800	50	B1
SPADRA RD	CO	POM		93	E2
SPAHN AV	LKD	LKD	5300	71	D1
SPALDING DR	BH	BH	100	42	B1
SPANDAU DR	SCLR	SAU		124	D2
SPANGLER PL	LAM	LAM	14800	84	A5
SPANISH LN	CO	WAL	300	97	C1
SPANISH LN	IND	WAL	300	97	C1
SPANISH BIT DR	CO	ACT		182	E8
SPANISH BRM DR	PALM	PALM		183	E2
SPANISH BRM DR	PALM	PALM		183	F2
SPANISH BRM DR	PALM	PALM		183	G3
SPANISH OAK DR	SCLR	NEW		127	H1
SPANNER ST	MON	MON	100	29	B6
SPARKLETT ST	TEC	TEC	9200	38	B4
SPARKS ST N	BUR	BUR	300	17	C6
SPARKS ST N	BUR	BUR	100	24	D2
SPARKS ST S	BUR	BUR	100	24	D2
SPARLAND ST	BAP	BAP	3400	39	D6
SPARR BLVD	GLEN	GL08	3000	18	F4
SPARROW DR	LAM	LAM	14900	84	A5
SPARROW LN	WCOV	WCOV		92	A2
SPARROW ST	LAV	LAV		95A	D5

STREET	CITY	P.O. ZONE	BLOCK	PAGE	GRID
SPARROW DELL DR	CO	CAL		13	A4
SPARROW HILL LN	LKD	LKD	2000	70	E2
SPARTA DR	RPV	SP	2100	78	D1
SPARTA DR	RPV	SP	2200	78	D1
SPARTON AV	LA	PAC	8500	8	F6
SPARTON AV	LA	PAC	8500	15	F1
SPARTON AV	LA	VAN	8400	8	F6
SPARTON AV	LA	VAN	8300	15	F1
SPARWOOD LN	LAM	LAM	15300	84	B6
SPAULDING AV N	LA	LA36	300	33	F5
SPAULDING AV N	LA	LA46	700	33	F5
SPAULDING AV N	WHOL	LA46	900	33	F5
SPAULDING AV S	LA	LA16	1900	42	E4
SPAULDING AV S	LA	LA19	1000	42	F3
SPAULDING AV S	LA	LA36	500	42	F1
SPAULDING CT	LB	LB04	2100	75	E4
SPAULDING PL	CO	ALT	2100	19	E5
SPAULDING ST	LB	LB04	2100	75	E3
SPAULDING WY	LB	LB04	2100	75	E3
SPAZIER AV	GLEN	GL01	1000	17	F6
SPAZIER AV W	BUR	BUR	100	24	E2
SPEARING AV	LA	SP	3500	78	C5
SPEARMAN AV	LAN	LAN	44700	160	B3
SPECHT AV	BG	BELL	6200	53	E6
SPECHT ST	BG	BELL	8200	59	E2
SPECTRUM LN	PALM	PALM		184	D4
SPEEDWAY	LA	VEN	100	49	B3
SPEEDWAY	LA	VEN	6200	55A	D2
SPEEDWAY	PR	PR	8700	54	F2
SPEEDWAY	PR	PR	9200	55	A3
SPEEDWAY	SM	SM	2400	49	B3
SPEER CT	POM	POM	100	94	F6
SPENCE ST	LA	LA23	600	45	B6
SPENCE ST	LA	LA23	1200	53	B1
SPENCER AV	POM	POM	2100	90	F5
SPENCER CT	CO	CAL		100	A2
SPENCER DR	COV	COV		89	B6
SPENCER PL	DBAR	POM		97A	C1
SPENCER ST	GLEN	GL02	200	25	C1
SPENCER ST	RB	RB	800	67	D3
SPENCER ST	TOR	TOR	3900	67	E3
SPENCER ST	TOR	TOR	3200	68	A3
SPERRY ST	LA	LA39	4500	25	B3
SPEYER LN	RB	RB	1700	62	E6
SPEYER LN	RB	RB	1700	67	E1
SPEZIA PL	LA	PP	1200	40	E3
SPICE CT	SCLR	SAU		124	E5
SPICE ST	LAN	LAN		159	F6
SPICE ST	LAN	LAN		159	H6
SPICER ST	CAR	CAR	1000	69	C5
SPICEWOOD LN	CO	HAC		73	F1
SPINDLEWOOD DR	LAM	LAM	12600	84	D6
SPINDRIFT DR	RPV	PVP		77	F3
SPINKS CYN RD	DUA	DUA	100	29	E3
SPINKS RANCH RD	CO	DUA	700	29	E4
SPINNAKER CT	LA	VEN		49	D6
SPINNAKER ST	CER	ART		66	E4
SPINNAKER ST	LA	VEN		49	C6
SPINNAKER WY	LB	LB03		80	F1
SPINNER TR	CO	TOP		109	E4
SPINNING AV	GAR	GAR	12900	63	D2
SPINNING AV	HAW	IN03	11500	57	D5
SPINNING AV	LA	LA47	11500	57	D5
SPINNING AV	TOR	TOR	16100	63	D4
SPINNING AV	TOR	TOR	18500	68	D1
SPINNING WHL LN	RHE	PVP	2200	73	C5
SPINNING WHL RD	WAL	WAL		93	A5
SPIRAL LN	LAN	LAN		159	B6
SPIRAL LN	LAN	LAN		159	G5
SPIRAL WY	LAN	LAN		159	G5
SPIREA WK	GLEN	GL06		26	B1
SPIRES ST	LA	CAN	23200	5	F2
SPIROS DR	LA	LA49		32	C5
SPIROS PL	LA	LA49		32	C5
SPLENDORA DR	CO	WHI	13000	61	D6
SPOKANE ST	LA	LA16	5500	42	E5
SPOLETO DR	LA	SM	400	40	E5
SPOONER AV	CO	PALM	37200	184	G1
SPORTSMAN DR	COM	COM	1300	65	C4
SPOTTED PONY RD	WAL	WAL		93	A6
SPRAGUE ST	COM	COM	1300	64	D1
SPRAGUE ST	LA	TAR	19000	21	B2
SPRAY LN	CO	MAL	3600	115	F4
SPREADNG OAK DR	LA	LA68	5600	34	D2
SPRECKELS CT	RB	RB	2900	67	F1
SPRECKELS LN	RB	RB	1600	67	D1
SPRING AV	CO	ACT		189	E3
SPRING AV	CO	GAR	14600	64	B3
SPRING AV	COM	COM	100	65	A3
SPRING AV	SFS	SFS		82	E2
SPRING CT	LA	CAN		5	F3
SPRING ST	BAP	BAP		39	C3
SPRING ST	CLA	CLA	100	91	B4
SPRING ST	WAL	WAL		93	D5
SPRING ST E	LB	LB06	100	70	C6
SPRING ST E	LB	LB08	5100	71	B6

STREET	CITY	P.O. ZONE	BLOCK	PAGE	GRID
SPRING ST E	LB	LB15	6000	71	B6
SPRING ST E	LB	LB15	7500	81	A6
SPRING ST E	SH	LB06	600	70	C6
SPRING ST N	LA	LA12	100	44	D3
SPRING ST N	LA	LA31	1700	44	E1
SPRING ST S	CO	LA61	12100	58	B6
SPRING ST S	CO	LA61	12900	64	B1
SPRING ST S	LA	LA03	9400	58	B4
SPRING ST S	LA	LA12	100	44	D3
SPRING ST S	LA	LA13	300	44	D3
SPRING ST S	LA	LA14	600	44	D3
SPRING ST S	LA	LA61	10700	58	B4
SPRING ST W	LB	LB06	100	70	C6
SPRING ST W	LB	LB10	1900	69	F6
SPRING ST W	LB	LB10	1200	70	A6
SPRING TR	CO	SF		3	E5
SPRINGBROOK AV	SCLR	SAU	25600	124	C9
SPRINGBROOK AV	SCLR	SAU		127	C1
SPRING CYN LN	PALM	PALM		172	J5
SPRING CYN RD	CO	CYN		125	H6
SPRINGCREEK RD	RPV	PVP	26700	72	D4
SPRINGDALE AV	SFS	SFS	10400	61	B3
SPRINGDALE DR	CO	LA43	4400	51	A4
SPRINGDALE DR	LB	LB10		70	A6
SPRINGDALE ST	SFS	SFS	10400	61	B4
SPRINGER ST	DOW	DOW	5800	59	F5
SPRINGER ST	DOW	DOW	5800	60	A5
SPRINGFIELD AV	HB	RB	1900	62	C6
SPRINGFIELD AV	LA	NOR	10700	7	B2
SPRINGFIELD PL	LAN	LAN		159	F6
SPRINGFIELD ST	CLA	CLA	300	91	B5
SPRINGFIELD ST	PALM	PALM		183	J1
SPRINGFORD DR	LA	SV	8300	17	A1
SPRINGFORD DR	LAM	LAM	13100	83	A1
SPRINGFORD DR	LAM	LAM	12600	84	A6
SPRING HAVEN ST	LCF	LCF	800	19	C2
SPRINGHILL PL	CO	LA43	5600	51	A4
SPRINGLAND DR	CO	WHI	9900	55	C1
SPRINGLAND DR	PR	PR	9900	55	C1
SPRINGLET TR	LA	LA68	3000	24	A6
SPRINGLINE DR	PALM	PALM		183	D1
SPRINGMEADOW DR	WCOV	WCOV	900	92	F2
SPRING OAK DR	LA	LA68	5700	34	D1
SPRING OAK TER	LA	LA68	5700	34	D1
SPRINGPARK AV	CO	LA56	6400	50	E5
SPRING PARK LN	CER	ART		82	B4
SPRING POINT DR	BRAD	DUA	500	29	F4
SPRINGPORT DR	CO	LPUE	19300	97	A4
SPRINGPORT DR	CO	LPUE	19200	98	F4
SPRINGSIDE TR	LA	TU	6200	11	C3
SPRINGSNOW CIR	CER	ART		82	C5
SPRING TREE LN	POM	POM		90	C6
SPRING TREE LN	POM	POM		94	B3
SPRINGVALE DR	LA	LA42	5800	26	C6
SPRINGVALE ST	POM	POM		95	A4
SPRING VLY RD	HH	CAL		100	C1
SPRING VLY RD	HH	CAL		100	D1
SPRINGVIEW DR	CO	WHI	12000	84	A6
SPRINGVIEW DR	LAM	LAM	11700	84	A6
SPRINGWATER ST	CO	LPUE	14400	48	B6
SPRINGWOOD DR	DBAR	POM		97A	B3
SPRINGWOOD ST	SELM	ELM	11200	47	D4
SPRONG LN	LPUE	LPUE		92	B6
SPROUL AV	LA	LA64	10800	41	F5
SPROUL ST	NWK	NWK	11800	82	A1
SPROULE AV	LA	PAC	11300	3	B6
SPROULE AV	LA	PAC	11100	9	C1
SPROULE AV	LA	SF	12900	2	E3
SPROULE AV	LA	SF	11900	3	B6
SPRUCE AV	PALM	PALM		183	C1
SPRUCE AV E	ING	IN01	100	57	A2
SPRUCE AV N	MTB	MTB	100	54	D2
SPRUCE AV S	MTB	MTB	100	54	D2
SPRUCE AV W	ING	IN01	200	56	F2
SPRUCE CT	AZU	AZU	1600	86	C3
SPRUCE CT	PALM	PALM		183	C1
SPRUCE LN	PAS	PAS	900	26	F2
SPRUCE ST	ALH	ALH	1100	37	B3
SPRUCE ST	BLF	BLF		66	D6
SPRUCE ST	SCLR	NEW	24500	127	C3
SPRUCE ST	LA	LA12	600	35	E6
SPRUCE ST	LYN	LYN	11300	59	B5
SPRUCE ST	MTB	MTB	700	54	D3
SPRUCE ST	PR	PR	8500	54	F2
SPRUCE ST	SPAS	SPAS		36	F2
SPRUCE ST	SPAS	SPAS	1200	37	A2
SPRUCE ST	WCOV	WCOV	800	92	A2
SPRUCE ST E	COM	COM	100	64	D2
SPRUCE ST W	COM	COM	300	64	D2
SPRUCE WY	RHE	PVP		72	D5
SPRUCE CK CIR	SCLR	VAL		124	C4
SPRUCEGROVE DR	RPV	PVP	28500	72	C5
SPRUCELAKE DR	CO	HAC		73	F1
SPRUCE TREE DR	DBAR	POM		97	F3
SPRUCEVIEW	POM	POM		94	C4

INDEX

1990 LOS ANGELES COUNTY STREET INDEX

STREET	CITY	P.O. ZONE	BLOCK	PAGE	GRID
SPRUCEWOOD LN	LA	LA77		32	E2
SPRY ST E	DOW	DOW	9600	60	C6
SPRY ST E	NWK	NWK	10400	60	D6
SPRY ST E	NWK	NWK	11600	61	A6
SPUNKY CYN RD	CO	SAU	13000	157A	E4
SPUR LN	RH	PVP	1	78	A1
SPURGEON AV	RB	RB	2400	62	F4
SPUR RIDGE RD	CO	NEW		2	B1
SPUR TRAIL AV	WAL	WAL		93	D5
SPY GLASS DR	LA	NOR		1	A6
SPYGLASS LN	WAL	WAL		93	D6
SPY GLASS HL RD	CO	WHI	10300	55	D2
SQUADRON TR	CO	TOP		109	B2
SQUAW PEAK LN	CAR	CAR		69	E6
SQUAW VALLEY WY	CER	ART	7800	81	C2
SQUIB ST	SCLR	SAU		124	D9
SQUIB ST	SCLR	SAU		127	D1
SQUIRE DR	CO	COV	19800	89	B6
STAATS PL	PAS	PAS	1600	37	B1
STACEY CT	WCOV	WCOV		92	E6
STACY ST	CO	HAW	4900	56	E6
STADIA HILL LN	RPV	PVP	29000	72	D6
STADIUM WY	LA	LA12		35	D6
STADIUM WY	LA	LA12		44	D1
STADIUM WY	LA	LA26		35	D5
STAFF CT	CO	GAR	15000	64	B3
STAFF TR	CO	TOP		109	E4
STAFFORD AV	HPK	HPK	5900	52	F5
STAFFORD LN	LA	CHA	10300	6	E3
STAFFORD ST	IND	LPUE		48	E6
STAFFORD CYN RD	CO	VAL		126	G3
STAFFORDSHRE DR	LAN	LAN	42900	159	J8
STAGE RD	AVA	AVA		77	B5
STAGE RD	CO	LAM	15300	83	A3
STAGE RD	LAM	LAM	14200	82	E2
STAGE RD	LAM	LAM	14500	83	A3
STAGE RD	SFS	SFS	13800	82	E2
STAGECOACH AV E	CO	LAN	16100	174	J6
STAGECOACH AV E	CO	LAN	16600	175	A6
STAGECOACH DR	POM	POM		94	C5
STAGECOACH DR	WCOV	WCOV		93	B1
STAGE COACH LN	CAR	CAR		69	E6
STAGECOACH LN	NWK	NWK	12700	61	C6
STAGECOACH LN	NWK	NWK	12700	82	C1
STAGECOACH RD	RHE	PVP	1	72	F3
STAGELINE RD	CO	SAU		123	D5
STAGG ST	LA	CAN	23500	5	E2
STAGG ST	LA	CAN	19700	12	E2
STAGG ST	LA	NHO	11400	16	C2
STAGG ST	LA	NOR	17300	14	E2
STAGG ST	LA	RES	17700	14	D2
STAGG ST	LA	SV	10600	16	E2
STAGG ST	LA	SV	10100	17	A2
STAGG ST	LA	VAN	16900	14	E2
STAGG ST	LA	VAN	13300	15	E2
STAGIO DR	CO	MON	1900	29	A6
STALLION CIR	WAL	WAL		93	A5
STALLION PL	CO	CAST		123	G2
STALLION RD	RPV	PVP	1	73	C6
STALLO AV	RM	RM	3300	46	F1
STALWART DR	RPV	PVP	3900	78	A3
STAMPER PL	BUR	BUR		17	C2
STAMPS AV	DOW	DOW	9300	60	C2
STAMPS DR	CAR	CAR		69	B3
STAMPS RD	DOW	DOW	8700	60	C3
STAMY RD	CO	WHI	10300	84	B4
STAMY RD	LAM	LAM	11400	84	B5
STAN PL	LA	BH	9800	33	A2
STANBRIDGE AV	BLF	BLF	13400	66	C1
STANBRIDGE AV	DOW	DOW	12900	66	C1
STANBRIDGE AV	LB	LB08	3400	71	C5
STANBRIDGE AV	LB	LB15	2100	76	C2
STANBROOK DR	LAM	LAM	15600	83	C3
STANCLIFF AV	LAN	LAN		160	E7
STANCREST DR	GLEN	GL08	3500	18	F3
STANCREST FR RD	GLEN	GL08	3300	18	F4
STANCROFT AV	BAP	BAP	4800	39	F3
STANDARD AV	GLEN	GL01	1700	24	F1
STANDARD AV	LYN	LYN	10600	59	C4
STANDARD ST	ELS	ELS	100	56	A6
STNDRD OIL F RD	CO	NOR		1	A2
STANDELL AV	ELM	ELM	4400	39	A5
STANDISH DR	LA	ENC	3400	21	E5
STANDISH ST	ARC	ARC	1300	29	A6
STANDISH ST	CO	MON	100	29	A6
STANFIELD DR	CO	TOP		109	A1
STANFILL RD	PALM	PALM		171	J6
STANFORD AV	CO	COM	14300	64	C2
STANFORD AV	CO	LA59	12400	58	C6
STANFORD AV	CO	VAL		123	G6
STANFORD AV	COM	COM	1500	64	C1
STANFORD AV	LA	LA01	6400	52	C6
STANFORD AV	LA	LA01	7800	58	C1
STANFORD AV	LA	LA02	8900	58	C4
STANFORD AV	LA	LA11	1900	44	C6
STANFORD AV	LA	LA11	2700	52	C1

STREET	CITY	P.O. ZONE	BLOCK	PAGE	GRID
STANFORD AV	LA	LA13	400	44	D5
STANFORD AV	LA	LA21	600	44	D5
STANFORD AV	LA	LA59	10700	58	C4
STANFORD AV	LA	VEN	2900	49	D4
STANFORD AV	LYN	LYN	10700	58	F4
STANFORD AV	LYN	LYN	10700	59	A4
STANFORD AV	POM	POM	2100	94	F6
STANFORD AV	POM	POM	2100	95	A6
STANFORD AV	RB	RB	1100	62	D6
STANFORD AV	SOG	SOG	9200	58	F4
STANFORD CT	WAL	WAL		93	B4
STANFORD DR	ARC	ARC	400	28	C4
STANFORD DR	CLA	CLA	400	91	B4
STANFORD DR	GLEN	GL05	1400	25	E6
STANFORD PL	WHI	WHI		55	E5
STANFORD RD	BUR	BUR	400	17	C4
STANFORD ST	SM	SM	800	41	B4
STANFORD WY	WHI	WHI	6200	55	E5
STANGATE ST	LKD	LKD	11600	81	A2
STANHILL DR	LAM	LAM	12700	61	F6
STANHILL DR	LAM	LAM	12800	82	F1
STANHURST AV	LOM	LOM	24000	73	D1
STANHURST AV	TOR	TOR	23800	73	D1
STANISLAUS CIR	CLA	CLA		91	D2
STANLEAF DR	LAM	LAM	15000	83	A3
STANLEY AV	GLEN	GL06	1100	25	E3
STANLEY AV	LB	LB04	700	75	F5
STANLEY AV	LB	LB05	6900	65	E5
STANLEY AV	LB	LB14	600	75	F5
STANLEY AV	SH	LB06	1800	75	F2
STANLEY AV N	LA	LA36	300	33	F6
STANLEY AV N	LA	LA46	700	33	F6
STANLEY AV N	WHOL	LA46	900	33	F6
STANLEY AV S	LA	LA19	1000	42	F3
STANLEY AV S	LA	LA36	700	42	F2
STANLEY CT	SCLR	CYN		124	G6
STANLEY DR N	BH	BH	100	42	D1
STANLEY DR S	BH	BH	100	42	D1
STANLEY ST	COM	COM	200	65	A5
STANLEY WY	COM	COM		65	A5
STANLEY HLLS DR	LA	LA46	2000	33	E2
STANLEY HLLS PL	LA	LA46	2000	33	D2
STANMONT ST	WHI	WHI	15800	84	C4
STANMOOR DR	LA	LA45	8200	55A	F2
STANRIDGE AV	CO	PALM	38400	172	C8
STANRIDGE AV	LAN	LAN	43600	160	B6
STANSBURY AV	LA	VAN	8500	8	E6
STANSBURY AV	LA	VAN	5600	15	E4
STANSBURY AV	LA	VAN	4000	22	E4
STANSBURY WY	LA	LA11	3200	52	D1
STANSTEAD AV	NWK	NWK	13400	82	C1
STANTON AV	GLEN	GL01	1700	24	E2
STANTON AV	LAM	LAM	14400	83	C3
STANTON DR	LA	LA41	4500	25	F5
STANTON PL	LB	LB04	1500	75	E3
STANTON ST	PAS	PAS	200	26	F1
STANTON ST	POM	POM	2800	90	F4
STANWELL ST	LA	CHA	21100	6	D2
STANWICK DR	SAD	SAD	1100	89	D2
STANWIN AV	LA	PAC	9200	8	E3
STANWIN AV	LA	PAC	8800	9	A5
STANWIN AV	LA	SF	10600	8	D2
STANWOOD AV	POM	POM	400	90	F3
STANWOOD DR	LA	LA66	11300	41	F6
STANWOOD DR	LA	LA66	11900	49	D1
STANWOOD PL	LA	LA66	12400	49	E1
STAPLETON CT	CER	ART		66	D2
STAR CIR	CER	ART		81	C2
STAR CIR	CUL	CUL		50	B2
STAR CT	DBAR	POM		94	B6
STAR CT	DBAR	POM		97A	B1
STAR LN	LA	WOH	5700	100	D1
STAR ST	ELM	ELM	12200	39	A5
STAR WY	CER	ART		81	C2
STARBIRD DR	MPK	MPK	100	46	C3
STARBOARD TR	CO	TOP		109	D4
STARBUCK ST	WHI	WHI	13400	61	E1
STARBUCK ST	WHI	WHI	14800	84	A3
STARBURY AV	CO	LAN	16000	174	H7
STARCA AV	CO	WHI	10300	55	D1
STARCREST CT	PALM	PALM		183	H1
STARCREST DR	CO	GLDR	6000	88	F1
STARCREST DR	COV	COV	900	88	F4
STARCREST DR	DUA	DUA		29	F3
STARCREST ST	PALM	PALM		183	H1
STARDALE DR	SCLR	SAU		124	E5
STARDELL ST	WHI	WHI	12800	55	E3
STARDUST DR	DBAR	POM		97A	B3
STARDUST PL	LA	SF	16900	1	F4
STARDUST PL	PALM	PALM		172	J5
STARDUST RD	LCF	LCF	5200	19	D3
STARE ST	LA	CHA	20201	6	E3
STARE ST	LA	NOR		7	A3
STARE ST	LA	NOR	17000	7	E3
STARE ST	LA	SF	14700	8	B3
STARFALL DR	CO	GL14		11	E4

STREET	CITY	P.O. ZONE	BLOCK	PAGE	GRID
STAR FIRE WY	PAR	PAR		65	E4
STARGAZER AV	LA	SP	3600	78	C5
STARGLEN DR	COV	COV	3800	89	B5
STARHAVEN AV	DUA	DUA	1300	29	C6
STARHAVEN ST	DUA	DUA	1300	29	D6
STARHILL LN	CO	LPUE	13700	48	B4
STARK AV	CER	ART	18700	81	B1
STARK AV	CER	ART	7200	82	B5
STARK AV	LA	WOH	4500	13	A3
STARKLAND AV	CO	CAN	7800	5	E2
STARKLAND ST	LA	CAN		5	E1
STARKUS WY	CO	VAL		126	J1
STARLAND DR	LCF	LCF	3900	19	B5
STARLANE DR	LCF	LCF		19	D3
STARLIGHT AV	CO	WHI	11400	61	E5
STARLIGHT CIR	BUR	BUR	1900	17	D3
STARLIGHT DR	LA	TAR	19300	21	A2
STARLIGHT LN	CO	CAST		123	H2
STARLIGHT LN	LA	CAN		5	D3
STARLGHT CST DR	LCF	LCF		19	D2
STARLGHT MSA DR	LCF	LCF		19	D3
STARLINE DR	RPV	PVP	3200	78	C3
STARLING ST	LAV	LAV		95A	E5
STARLING WY	LA	LA65	4500	36	A3
STARLIT LN	MON	MON	1000	29	C2
STARLITE DR	BRAD	DUA	10	29	D3
STAR O INDIA LN	CAR	CAR		64	B6
STARPATH DR	LAM	LAM	14600	84	A5
STAR PINE CT	AZU	AZU	200	86	C3
STAR RIDGE DR	MPK	MPK		46	A3
STARS AV OF THE	LA	LA67	1800	42	A2
STARSHINE RD	DBAR	WAL	1700	97	C4
STARSTONE DR	RPV	PVP	6900	72	C5
STARTOUCH DR	PAS	PAS	3600	28	A1
STARTREE LN	CO	SAU		124	C2
STARTREK DR	LCF	LCF		19	C2
STARVALE RD	GLEN	GL07	1800	25	D1
STARVIEW DR	GLEN	GL08	3200	18	E4
STARWOOD DR	CO	WHI	16200	84	D5
STARWOOD WY	CO	SAU		124	G3
STASSEN ST	LA	SF	14800	8	D4
STASSI LN	LA	SM	500	40	E5
STATE DR	LA	LA37	800	51	F1
STATE DR	LA	LA37	500	52	A1
STATE RD	CER	ART	20200	71	F2
STATE ST	GLEN	GL03	500	25	B3
STATE ST	HPK	HPK	6200	53	A5
STATE ST	HPK	HPK	7600	59	A3
STATE ST	LYN	LYN	10700	59	A4
STATE ST	POM	POM		93	F4
STATE ST	POM	POM		94	A4
STATE ST	SOG	SOG	8100	59	A3
STATE ST	SPAS	SPAS	1600	37	A1
STATE ST	WCOV	WCOV	100	92	B1
STATE ST E	PAS	PAS	1	27	A6
STATE ST N	LA	LA33	100	45	A3
STATE ST S	LA	LA33	100	45	A3
STATE ST W	PAS	PAS	1	26	F6
STATE UNIV DR	CO	LA32	4300	45	D2
STATE UNIV DR	LA	LA32	5100	45	D2
STATE UNIV DR	LB	LB15	5600	76	D4
STATLER ST	LA	SP	800	73	E6
STATUS TR	CO	TOP		109	D5
STAUNTON AV	LA	LA21	1600	44	D6
STAUNTON AV	LA	LA58	1900	44	D6
STAUNTON AV	LA	LA58	1900	52	D1
STEARNLEE AV	LB	LB08	3600	71	C5
STEARNLEE AV	LB	LB15	1800	76	C2
STEARNS DR	LA	LA34	1900	42	E4
STEARNS DR	LA	LA35	1000	42	E3
STEARNS DR	LA	LA48	900	42	E2
STEARNS PZ	LB	LB15		76	C2
STEARNS ST	LB	LB15	3500	76	E2
STEBBINS TER	LA	LA69	1400	33	D3
STEDDOM DR	CO	RM	7600	46	E3
STEDLEY PL	LAV	LAV		90	D1
STEDMAN PL	MON	MON	100	29	B3
STEED CT	LOM	LOM	2400	73	C3
STEELE AV	CO	LA63	1500	45	E2
STEELE ST	RM	RM	8700	38	A5
STEELE ST	TOR	TOR		67	F2
STEEN PL	LAM	LAM	11800	84	A5
STEEP CYN RD	DBAR	POM		97A	A2
STEEPLECHASE LN	DBAR	POM		97	E5
STEFANI AV	CER	ART	8400	81	B1
STEFFEN ST	GLDR	GLDR	1100	87	D5
STEFFEN ST	GLDR	GLDR	1100	87	C5
STEIF ST	LAN	LAN		160	E7
STEINBECK AV	CO	VAL		126	H3
STEINER AV	SM	SM	3000	49	C2
STEINHART AV	RB	RB	1100	62	D5
STEINWAY ST	SCLR	CYN	19500	124	G6
STELLA AV	WCOV	WCOV		92	E6
STELLBAR PL	LA	LA64	9900	42	C4
STELLER DR	CUL	CUL	8400	42	D6
STEPHANIE DR	CO	COV	19700	89	C3

STREET	CITY	P.O. ZONE	BLOCK	PAGE	GRID
STEPHANIE DR	COV	COV	18600	88	F3
STEPHANIE DR	LA	CAN	20700	12	D4
STEPHANIE DR	WCOV	WCOV		92	E6
STEPHANIE PL	LA	CAN		12	D4
STEPHEN AV	CLA	CLA	1100	91	A3
STEPHEN LN	LA	CAN	8300	5	F1
STEPHEN RD	BUR	BUR	600	17	C3
STEPHN WHITE DR	LA	SP	3600	79	A6
STEPHENS CIR	GLEN	GL08		18	D4
STEPHENS ST	IND	LPUE	16100	85	F1
STEPHENS ST	PR	PR	9300	55	A2
STEPHNS PSTR RD	CO	CLA		95A	F4
STEPHENS RCH RD	CO	LAV	5700	95A	E4
STEPHN S WSE DR	LA	LA77		22	C6
STEPHON TER	CUL	CUL	10700	50	D3
STEPHORA AV	CO	COV	5000	89	C3
STEPHORA AV	COV	COV	400	89	C4
STEPHORA AV	GLDR	GLDR	1200	89	C2
STEPHORA DR	COV	COV	100	89	C4
STEPNEY PL	ING	IN02	700	51	B5
STEPNEY ST	ING	IN02	200	51	B6
STEPROCK DR	LAM	LAM	14800	84	A6
STERLING DR	BAP	BAP	4000	39	E5
STERLING DR	PALM	PALM		183	G1
STERLING PL	CO	ALT	2800	19	E4
STERLING PL	SPAS	SPAS	500	36	E1
STERLING ST	POM	POM	2800	90	F4
STERLING CTR DR	WLVL	THO	31400	102	C4
STERN AV	LA	VAN	4200	22	E3
STERN AV	LAM	LAM	13400	83	B1
STETSON	LA	SF42		2	C1
STETSON AL	PAS	PAS	1400	27	C3
STETSON AV	LA	LA45	7600	50	C6
STEUBEN ST	PAS	PAS	1000	27	C4
STEVEANN ST	TOR	TOR	4900	67	E4
STEVE JON ST	SCLR	SAU		124	G4
STEVELY AV	LA	LA08	3800	51	A1
STEVELY AV	LKD	LKD	4100	71	E3
STEVELY AV N	LB	LB08	3000	71	F5
STEVELY AV N	LB	LB15	800	76	F3
STEVEN DR	LA	ENC	3100	22	A5
STEVEN PL	LA	CHA	10300	6	F3-
STEVEN ST	GAR	GAR	17000	63	F5
STEVEN WY	BH	BH	1200	33	A4
STEVENS AV	BLF	BLF	15100	66	C3
STEVENS AV	CUL	CUL	11200	50	C3
STEVENS AV	RM	RM	2400	46	D2
STEVENS AV	SGAB	SGAB	1300	37	D5
STEVENS CIR	CUL	CUL	5100	50	C3
STEVENS PL	CMRC	LA40	5300	53	F2
STEVENS ST	CO	GL14	2700	11	D5
STEVENS ST	GLEN	GL14	3300	11	D5
STEVENS WY	CO	CHA		4	B5
STEVENS CK LN	WAL	WAL		92	F5
STEVENSON LN	CO	LPUE		98	E4
STEVER CT	CUL	CUL	5700	50	C3
STEVER ST	CUL	CUL	10800	50	C3
STEVEY ST	LAN	LAN		159	F5
STEWART AL	PAS	PAS	1	27	E4
STEWART AV	BAP	BAP	3800	39	D4
STEWART AV	LA	LA45	7400	50	B6
STEWART AV	LA	LA45	7900	56	B1
STEWART AV	LA	LA66	3200	49	E2
STEWART AV	LA	LA66	4100	49	F3
STEWART DR	COV	COV	500	88	F5
STEWART RD	CO	CAST		123	F1
STEWART RD	LAM	LAM		83	D1
STEWART ST	ELM	ELM	11300	38	E6
STEWART ST	ELM	ELM	11700	47	E1
STEWART ST	SM	SM	1600	41	C5
STEWART WY	LB	LB07	200	70	B4
STEWART-GRAY RD	DOW	DOW	7000	59	F3
STEWART-GRAY RD	DOW	DOW	7400	60	A4
STEWARTON DR	LA	NOR	12000	1	B5
STEWARTON WY	GLEN	GL07		18	D6
STICHMAN AV	BAP	BAP	3200	39	E5
STICHMAN AV	CO	LPUE	2000	48	C2
STILES TR	CO	TOP		109	D5
STILL KNOLL LN	CER	ART		82	B4
STILLMAN ST	LKD	LKD	11400	71	F3
STILLMAN ST	LKD	LKD	12200	81	B3
STILL MDW LN W	LAN	LAN	2500	159	G7
STILLMORE ST	SCLR	CYN		124	J8
STILLMORE ST	SCLR	CYN	17700	125	B8
STILLWATER DR	LA	LA08	5300	50	F1
STILLWATER PL	SCLR	NEW		127	B6
STILLWELL AV	LA	LA32	4100	36	E4
STIMSON AV N	CO	LPUE	1400	48	F4
STIMSON AV N	LPUE	LPUE	100	48	F6
STIMSON AV S	CO	LPUE	1100	85	E2
STIMSON AV S	IND	LPUE	100	48	F6
STIMSON AV S	IND	LPUE	300	85	E2
STINGLE AV	RM	RM	2600	47	A2
STIPA WY	LA	LA49	1800	40	F1
STIRRUP DR	DBAR	POM		97	F1
STIRRUP LN	RPV	PVP	28400	73	D6

STREET	CITY	P.O. ZONE	BLOCK	PAGE	GRID
STIRRUP PL	LAN	LAN		159	D6
STIRRUP RD	RPV	PVP	28400	73	D6
STITES DR	CO	TOP	20000	109	C6
STITESWOOD AV	GLDR	GLDR	600	87	A6
STOAKES AV	DOW	DOW	8800	60	D2
STOCKBRIDGE AV	ALH	ALH	1	36	F4
STOCKBRIDGE AV	LA	LA32	2900	36	E5
STOCKDALE ST	BAP	BAP	14700	39	E5
STOCKER AL	PAS	PAS		27	A4
STOCKER PL	LA	LA08	3000	51	C2
STOCKER PZ	LA	LA08	2800	51	C2
STOCKER ST	CO	CUL		50	D2
STOCKER ST	CO	LA08		51	B2
STOCKER ST	CO	LA56		50	F3
STOCKER ST	LA	LA08	3000	51	B2
STOCKER ST	POM	POM	2100	90	F5
STOCKER ST E	GLEN	GL07	100	25	C2
STOCKER ST W	GLEN	GL02	100	25	C2
STOCKHAM PL	ELM	ELM	11900	47	F1
STOCKTON AV	LYN	LYN	3200	65	B1
STOCKTON ST	COM	COM	1600	65	B1
STOCKTON ST	COM	COM	3200	65	A1
STOCKTN PASS RD	WAL	WAL		93	C3
STOCKWELL DR	LYN	LYN	11000	59	B5
STOCKWELL ST	CO	COM	1900	64	E1
STOCKWELL ST	COM	COM	600	64	E1
STODDARD PL	POM	POM	2000	90	E5
STODDRD WELS RD	WAL	WAL		93	C3
STOKELEY RD	CO	PALM	5700	184	B5
STOKES CYN RD	CO	CAL		100	C5
STOKES CYN RD	CO	CAL		107	F2
STOKOWSKI DR	RPV	SP	28600	78	D1
STOLL DR	LA	LA42	5600	36	C2
STONE CIR	LAV	LAV		90	E2
STONE CT	MPK	MPK	2200	45	F3
STONE LN	GLEN	GL02		25	A1
STONE ST	LA	LA63	900	45	C3
STONEACRE AV	COM	COM	1600	65	C4
STONEACRE ST	CO	COM	12900	65	C1
STONEACRE ST	LYN	LYN	12400	65	C1
STONEBANK ST	BLF	BLF		66	D5
STONEBRIDGE LN	ING	IN01		57	B2
STONEBRYN DR	CO	HAC		73	F1
STONE CANYON AV	LA	VAN	3700	22	C4
STONE CANYON RD	LA	LA77	100	32	D2
STONECHAT CT	CO	VAL		123	J9
STONECLIFF CIR	CO	HAC	23700	73	F1
STONECLIFF LN	CO	HAC	23800	73	F1
STONECOURT CIR	CO	HAC	23700	73	F1
STONE CREEK RD	SAD	SAD		90	A1
STONECREST DR	AGH	AGO		102	D3
STONECREST PL	DBAR	POM		97A	B3
STONECREST RD	RHE	PVP	29300	72	E6
STONECREST RD	RPV	PVP	29342	72	E6
STONE CREST WY	WHI	WHI1		55	E3
STONEGATE	THO	THO		102A	E3
STONEGATE CIR	POM	POM		94	C5
STONEGATE DR	LA	CAN		5	D3
STONEGATE LN	PALM	PALM		184	A1
STONEGATE RD	LA	PAC		3	B6
STONEGATE ST	MPK	MPK	1300	45	F3
STONEGATE ST	PALM	PALM		171	D9
STONE GATE WY	LA	NOR		1A	F5
STONEGLEN RD	LCF	LCF	5100	19	C2
STONE GROVE LN	CER	ART		82	B4
STONEHAM CT	LB	LB03		76	F5
STONEHAVEN CT	LA	NOR		1	B5
STONEHAVEN PL	WCOV	WCOV		92	D5
STONEHAVEN WY	LA	LA49	100	41	B2
STONEHENGE DR	SAD	SAD		89	D4
STONEHENGE LN	LA	LA49		32	B2
STONEHILL CT	CLA	CLA		96	B6
STONEHILL DR	CO	ALT	2800	20	C4
STONEHILL LN	LA	LA49	900	32	A6
STONEHILL PL	LA	VAN	3500	22	F5
STONE HOUSE RD	ARC	ARC	1800	28	E2
STONE HOUSE RD	SMAD	SMAD	1900	28	E1
STONEHURST AV	LA	SUN	9500	9	E4
STONEHURST AV	LA	SV	9500	9	E3
STONEHURST DR	CO	ALT	400	19	E5
STONEHURST PL	LA	SV	9900	9	E3
STONELEY DR	CO	PAS	3000	27	F6
STONEMAN AV N	ALH	ALH	100	37	C3
STONEMAN AV S	ALH	ALH	100	37	C3
STONE OAK DR	LA	LA49		21	F6
STONEPINE DR	DBAR	POM		97	E4
STONER AV	LA	CUL	4500	50	A3
STONER AV	LA	LA25	1200	41	C3
STONER AV	LA	LA64	2200	41	C3
STONER AV	LA	LA66	3200	49	F1
STONER CREEK RD	IND	LPUE		98	D3
STONERIDGE DR	PAS	PAS	900	26	F6
STONERIDGE DR	WHI	WHI		84	D1
STONERIDGE DR	WHI	WHI		85	D6
STONERIDGE LN	LA	VAN		22	C5

1990 LOS ANGELES COUNTY STREET INDEX

— Z — COPYRIGHT, © 1989 BY Thomas Bros Maps

STREET	CITY	P.O. ZONE	BLOCK	PAGE	GRID
STONERIDGE PL	LA	VAN	13200	23	A4
STONESBORO PL	LA	VAN	14900	22	C4
STONEVIEW DR	CUL	CUL	3900	50	E1
STONEVIEW DR	LA	VAN	13500	22	F5
STONEWALL TR	CO	TOP	21000	109	D3
STONEWELL ST	MPK	MPK	1300	45	F3
STONEWOOD CT	LA	SP		73	E6
STONEWOOD DR	BH	BH	3500	33	B4
STONEWOOD DR	DUA	DUA		29	E5
STONEWOOD DR	LA	VAN	3500	22	C5
STONEWOOD ST	DOW	DOW	15300	60	C4
STONEWOOD TER	LA	VAN		22	C5
STONEY DR	SPAS	SPAS	4000	36	E1
STONEY LN	LA	LA49		32	A3
STONEYBROOK DR	LA	VAN		22	C4
STONEY HILL RD	LA	LA49		32	A3
STONINGTON LN	CO	SAU		124	E4
STONYBROOK	ELM	ELM		48	A6
STONYBROOK AV	SOG	SOG	10400	59	E4
STONYBROOK DR	WAL	WAL		93	C4
STONY CREEK RD	CUL	CUL		50	D2
STONY POINT PL	POM	POM		94	E6
STONY POINT PL	POM	POM		97A	C1
STONYVALE RD	CO			M	B2
STORE ST	MTB	MTB	500	54	C2
STORK PL	LKD	LKD		71	C9
STORM PKWY	TOR	TOR		68	E6
STORRS PL	POM	POM	900	94	C3
STORY PL	ALH	ALH	300	37	C2
STORY PL	GLEN	GL06	2500	26	A3
STORY ST	CO	LA63	3200	45	C3
STOVALL AV	CO	LPUE	1100	85	D1
STOVER AV	CO	CLA	1300	91	D3
STOWE CT	CLA	CLA	2400	91	B1
STOWE LN	CO	SAU		123	D4
STOWE TER	LA	LA42	300	36	C1
STOWELL LN	LA	BH	10000	32	E2
STOWERS AV	CER	ART	16300	82	D4
STOWKOWSKI DR	RPV	SP		78	D1
STRADA CORTA RD	LA	LA77	200	32	E5
STRADA VECCHIA	LA	LA77	800	32	E4
STRADELLA CT	LA	LA77	10600	32	D4
STRADELLA RD	LA	LA77	700	32	C2
STRAFORD LN	CO	LAN		171	C2
STRAKE TR	CO	TOP		109	D5
STRANAHAN DR	ALH	ALH	2200	46	A1
STRAND CT	WCOV	WCOV		92	C4
STRAND ST	SM	SM	1	49	A2
STRAND THE	HB	RB	1300	62	C6
STRAND THE	HB	RB	100	67	C1
STRAND THE	MB	MB		62	A2
STRAND THE	MB	MB		62	A4
STRANG AV	RM	RM	3500	38	C6
STRANG ST	CO	LA22	4600	45	E5
STRANG ST	CO	LA63	3900	45	D5
STRANGE CK RD	DBAR	POM		94	A4
STRANWOOD AV	LA	SF	11400	2	B6
STRANWOOD AV	LA	SF	11000	8	C1
STRATFORD	MB	MB		62	C3
STRATFORD	WCOV	WCOV		92	D5
STRATFORD AV	SPAS	SPAS	600	37	A2
STRATFORD CIR	LA	LA49		32	B2
STRATFORD DR	CO	PALM		184	E2
STRATFORD DR	SCLR	SAU		127	D2
STRATFORD DR	LCF	LCF	100	19	B5
STRATFORD DR	LOM	LOM		73	C3
STRATFORD LN	ING	IN01		57	B2
STRATFORD LN	SAD	SAD		89	D3
STRATFORD LN	SPAS	SPAS		37	A1
STRATFORD PL	POM	POM	1800	90	D5
STRATFORD RD	LA	LA42	4800	36	B1
STRATFORD RD	SMAR	PAS	2000	37	D6
STRATFORD WY	LAV	LAV		90	B3
STRATHERN ST	LA	CAN	23100	5	F2
STRATHERN ST	LA	CAN	19700	12	E2
STRATHERN ST	LA	NHO	13100	15	F2
STRATHERN ST	LA	NHO	11400	16	C2
STRATHERN ST	LA	NOR	17300	14	A2
STRATHERN ST	LA	RES	17700	14	A2
STRATHERN ST	LA	SV	10200	16	F2
STRATHERN ST	LA	VAN	16900	14	A2
STRATHERN ST	LA	VAN	13200	15	F2
STRATHMORE AV	CO	SGAB	2200	46	E2
STRATHMORE AV	RM	RM	1900	46	E2
STRATHMORE AV	SGAB	SGAB	1800	37	F6
STRATHMORE DR	LA	LA24	10300	32	D5
STRATHMORE DR	LA	LA24	10700	41	D1
STRATHMORE PL	LA	LA24		41	E1
STRATHMORE PL	WCOV	WCOV		92	D5
STRATTON AL	PAS	PAS	1	27	A4
STRATTON AV	LA	SF	13800	2	F1
STRATTON LN	SPAS	SPAS		36	F1
STRATTON LN	SPAS	SPAS		37	A1
STRATTON WY	PALM	PALM		171	F6
STRAWBERRY AV	CAR	CAR		74	C1
STRAWBERRY CT	PALM	PALM		183	H2
STRAWBERRY DR	LA	ENC	16900	21	E4
STRAWBERRY LN	GLDR	GLDR		89	C2
STRAWBERRY LN	RHE	PVP	27000	73	C4
STRAWBERRY PL	LA	ENC	4000	21	E4
STRAWBRRY HL DR	AGH	AGO		102	E3
STRAW FLOWER LN	DBAR	POM		97	F3
STREAMVIEW ST	WAL	WAL		93	B5
STRELNA PL	LA	WOH	20300	13	E2
STRETTO WY	LA	PP	17500	40	A4
STRICKLAND AV	LA	LA42	6100	26	C6
STRINGER AV	CO	LA63	1000	45	D3
STROHM AV	LA	NHO	4200	23	F1
STRONG AV	CMRC	LA40	2200	53	E3
STRONG AV	CO	WHI	10200	55	C2
STRONGBOW DR	DBAR	POM		93	F5
STRONGS DR	LA	VEN	1800	49	C4
STRONGS PL	LA	VEN	3000	49	B6
STROUD ST	LA	VAN	13900	15	E2
STROZIER AV	ELM	ELM	1300	47	C2
STROZIER AV	SELM	ELM	2300	47	C2
STRUB AV	WHI	WHI	8200	55	F6
STRUB AV	WHI	WHI	8200	61	F1
STRUB AV	WHI	WHI	8300	61	F1
STRUB AV	WHI	WHI	8100	85	A6
STRUIKMAN RD	CER	ART	13800	82	E5
STUART AV	WCOV	WCOV	1200	92	C1
STUART LN	LA	BH	9500	33	B1
STUART WK	GLEN	GL06		25	A2
STUART RANCH RD	CO	MAL	23400	114	A4
STUBBS LN	CUL	CUL		50	D3
STUBBY WY	CO	CAST		123	G1
STUDEBAKER RD	CER	ART	16700	66	E3
STUDEBAKER RD	CER	ART	18300	71	E1
STUDEBAKER RD	CER	NWK	15900	66	E3
STUDEBAKER RD	DOW	DOW	10500	60	E5
STUDEBAKER RD	LB	LB08	3000	71	E6
STUDEBAKER RD	LB	LB14	300	76	E4
STUDEBAKER RD	LB	LB15	700	76	E4
STUDEBAKER RD	LKD	LKD	20300	71	E2
STUDEBAKER RD	NWK	NWK	11200	60	E5
STUDEBAKER RD	NWK	NWK	12800	66	E3
STUDIO DR	CUL	CUL	10600	50	C2
STUHR DR W	SGAB	SGAB		37	D2
STULMAN ST	CO	GAR	14900	64	B2
STUNT RD	CO	CAL		108	D3
STURBRIDGE DR	CO	SAU		123	D5
STURGESS DR	TOR	TOR	19200	67	E2
STURTEVANT DR	SMAD	SMAD		28	D1
STYLES ST	LA	WOH	2200	5	E5
STYLES ST	LA	WOH	22400	12	B5
SUANA DR	RPV	SP	2000	78	D3
SUBIDO ST	CO	LPUE	18200	98	D5
SUBTROPIC DR	LHH	LAH	1600	84	E1
SUCCESS AV	CO	LA59	11500	58	D5
SUCCESS AV	LA	LA02	9200	58	D3
SUCCESS AV	LA	LA59	11400	58	D5
SUDAN AV	BG	BELL	7200	60	A1
SUDBURY CT	CO	COM	17400	64	C5
SUE AV	LYN	LYN	11000	59	C5
SUE DR	SCLR	SAU		124	G4
SUENO RD	LA	WOH	22400	13	B2
SUFFOLK AV	GLDR	GLDR	1200	89	C2
SUFFOLK AV	MTB	MTB		46	E5
SUFFOLK AV	SMAD	SMAD	1	28	C2
SUFFOLK CT	PALM	PALM		171	H5
SUFFOLK CT	PR	PR		47	A6
SUFFOLK CT	PR	PR		55	A1
SUFFOLK DR	LA	BH		22	F6
SUFFOLK DR	LAN	LAN		159	J2
SUFFOLK LN	ING	IN01		57	C2
SUFFOLK PL	GLDR	GLDR	1600	89	B2
SUGAR ST	LAN	LAN	43000	159	H8
SUGARGROVE DR	CO	WHI	16200	84	D5
SUGAR GUM RD	CO	LPUE	14700	85	C3
SUGARHILL DR	RHE	PVP	4500	72	F3
SUGARLOAF CT	PALM	PALM		183	H2
SUGARLOAF DR	CO	AGO		107	A2
SUGAR LOAF DR	CO	PALM		183	B3
SUGAR LOAF DR	LCF	LCF	1300	19	B5
SUGARMAN ST	LA	TAR	18200	21	D2
SUGARPINE LN	CER	ART		82	C4
SUGARPINE PL	DBAR	POM		97	E5
SUGAR PINE WY	CO	SAU		124	C2
SUGARWOOD ST	LKD	LKD	6000	71	D3
SULLIVAN AV	RM	RM	3000	47	A1
SULLY DR	LA	SV	10000	17	A1
SULPHUR TR	CO	SF	11000	3	E5
SULPHUR SPG RD	PALM	PALM		183	J1
SULPHR SPG F RD	CO	SF		1	C3
SULTAN CIR	CAR	GAR	1300	69	D2
SULTANA AV	CO	SGAB	6700	28	A6
SULTANA AV	CO	SGAB	6600	38	A1
SULTANA AV	RM	RM	4500	38	B4
SULTANA AV	TEC	TEC	4900	38	A3
SULTUS ST	CO	CYN		128	C2
SUMAC AV	CO	PALM	37300	183	C1
SUMAC AV	PALM	PALM	38400	172	C8
SUMAC AV	PALM	PALM	37700	183	C1
SUMAC DR	LA	VAN	3900	22	D4
SUMAC LN	LA	SM	300	40	E5
SUMAC RD	CO	CAN		4	B5
SUMAC ST	LAV	LAV		90	B3
SUMAC TR	SMAD	SMAD		28	D1
SUMAC RIDGE DR	CO	MAL	3100	114	E3
SUMATRA DR	LA	VAN	13300	22	F5
SUMIYA DR	LA	ENC	17400	21	E3
SUMMER AV	ART	ART	18000	66	F6
SUMMER AV	NWK	NWK	11800	60	F6
SUMMER AV	NWK	NWK	12800	66	F1
SUMMER AV	SFS	SFS	10000	60	F3
SUMMER PL	WCOV	WCOV		92	B4
SUMMER PL	WCOV	WCOV		92	C4
SUMMERFIELD AV	CO	WHI	8000	55	A6
SUMMERFIELD DR	LA	VAN	3500	22	D5
SUMMER HILL DR	CO	LA43	5500	51	A4
SUMMR HL RCH RD	CO	TOP		13	D6
SUMMERHOLLY CIR	LA	LA77		22	E6
SUMMERHOLLY CIR	PALM	PALM		183	H2
SUMMERLAND AV	LA	SP	700	78	E2
SUMMERLAND PL	LA	SP	700	78	F2
SUMMERLAND ST	RPV	SP	1900	78	D2
SUMMER LAWN WY	CO	LPUE	1500	98	B3
SUMMER LILAC DR	PALM	PALM		183	F3
SUMMERPLACE DR	WCOV	WCOV		92	B4
SUMMERSET PL	ING	IN01		57	B2
SUMMERSHADE DR	LAM	LAM	15900	84	C6
SUMMER SHORE LN	WLVL	THO		102	A5
SUMMERTIME LN	CUL	CUL		50	C2
SUMMERTOWN ST	DBAR	WAL		97	C4
SUMMERWIND DR	PALM	PALM		171	J6
SUMMERWIND ST	CER	ART		82	B5
SUMMERWOOD AV	DBAR	WAL		97	D2
SUMMIT AV	CO	ALT	2080	20	A6
SUMMIT AV	PAS	PAS	1500	20	A6
SUMMIT AV	PAS	PAS	200	27	A2
SUMMIT CIR	LA	BH		23	C6
SUMMIT CT	LA	BH		23	C6
SUMMIT DR	BH	BH	1000	33	A6
SUMMIT DR	CO	CAL		100	E6
SUMMIT DR	CO	TOP	19900	109	C5
SUMMIT DR	SPAS	SPAS	600	36	F3
SUMMIT DR	WHI	WHI		55	F5
SUMMIT DR	CO	VAL		126	J2
SUMMIT PL	LA	BH		23	C6
SUMMIT PL	MPK	MPK	900	46	A3
SUMMIT PL	PALM	PALM		171	C3
SUMMIT RD	CO	LAV		95A	E6
SUMMIT RD	CO	TOP	21000	109	D5
SUMMIT ST	LB	LB10	1300	75	A3
SUMMIT TR	CO	SF	12200	3	E5
SUMMIT TR	CO	TOP	21400	109	E4
SUMMIT CREST DR	LCF	LCF	5700	19	C1
SUMMIT KNOLL RD	CO	SAU		125	H1
SUMMT RDG CIR N	LA	CHA		6	B4
SUMMT RDG CIR S	LA	CHA		6	B5
SUMMITRIDGE DR	DBAR	POM		97A	B2
SUMMITRIDGE DR	LA	BH	1300	33	A2
SUMMIT RIDGE DR	WAL	WAL		92	F5
SUMMITRIDGE PL	LA	BH	1200	33	A4
SUMMITROSE ST	LA	TU	7200	10	F3
SUMMITROSE ST	LA	TU	7000	11	A3
SUMT TO SUMT MY	CO	TOP		13	A6
SUMT TO SUMT MY	CO	TOP		100	F6
SUMMIT VIEW CT	WAL	WAL		93	B5
SUMMITVIEW LN	PALM	PALM		171	C3
SUMNER AV	AVA	AVA	100	77	B5
SUMNER AV	CLA	CLA	1600	90	F3
SUMNER AV	SCLR	SAU		124	C4
SUMNER AV	LA	LA41	5200	25	F4
SUMNER AV	POM	POM	3600	90	F4
SUMNER AV	CUL	CUL	5600	50	D4
SUMNER WY	LA	LA42	200	36	C2
SUMPTER DR	LAN	LAN		160	D6
SUN CT	LA	LA65	3800	35	F1
SUNBEAM DR	LHH	LAH	1200	84	F3
SUNBIRD AV	CO	VAL		123	J9
SUNBIRD CT	CO	VAL		126	G1
SUNBIRD CT	PALM	PALM		171	C3
SUNBLUFF	DBAR	POM		97	E3
SUNBLUFF DR	DBAR	POM	2300	97	D5
SUNBRIGHT DR	LA	BH	10100	32	F4
SUNBROOK DR	CO	PALM		184	A2
SUNBURST DR	LA	CAN	20100	6	E5
SUNBURST ST	LA	NOR	19700	6	E6
SUNBURST ST	LA	NOR	17000	7	E5
SUNBURST ST	LA	PAC	13600	8	F4
SUNBURST ST	LA	PAC	12700	9	A4
SUNBURST ST	LA	SF	11200	3	E6
SUNBURST ST	LA	SF	16600	7	F5
SUNBURST ST	LA	SF	15000	8	C5
SUNBURST ST	LA	SF	11400	9	D1
SUNBURST ST	LA	VAN	14100	8	D5
SUNBURY ST	LA	LA15	900	44	B3
SUN COURT TER	GLEN	GL06	500	26	A3
SUNCREST CT	LHH	LAH	1600	98	B6
SUNCUP LN	LAN	LAN		160	B1
SUNDALE AV	HAW	HAW	300	56	F6
SUNDALE AV	LA	HAW	11400	56	F5
SUNDALE DR	LA	TU	7200	10	F4
SUNDANCE	ELM	ELM		48	A1
SUNDANCE AV	CO	WHI	13300	61	D4
SUNDANCE CT	PALM	PALM		171	H6
SUNDANCE DR	POM	POM		94	C5
SUNDANCE ST	WAL	WAL		93	D6
SUNDAY TR	LA	LA68	2800	24	A6
SUNDELL AV	LAN	LAN	44300	159	H5
SUNDERLAND DR	LA	SF	17100	1	E5
SUNDIAL CT	CO	LR		184	E6
SUNDIAL LN	LA	BH	10000	32	F4
SUNDOWN DR	LA	LA65	2400	35	F1
SUNDOWN DR	RHE	PVP	27600	73	D5
SUNDOWNER LN	WAL	WAL		93	C3
SUNDOWNER WY	SCLR	CYN		125	A8
SUNFIELD AV	LB	LB08	4300	71	B3
SUNFIELD AV	LKD	LKD	5400	71	B1
SUNFLOWER AV	CO	COV	4300	89	C3
SUNFLOWER AV	COV	COV	900	89	C3
SUNFLOWER AV	GLDR	GLDR	1200	89	C3
SUNFLOWER AV	LA	LA39	1900	35	D3
SUNFLOWER CIR	CO	MAL		110	B4
SUNFLOWER CT	CO	CAL		100A	F5
SUNFLOWER PL	CLA	CLA		96	C6
SUNGATE DR	PALM	PALM		171	D4
SUNGLOW ST	PR	PR	9200	60	E1
SUNGLOW ST	SFS	SFS	11600	61	B2
SUNGLOW WY	LA	SV		10	B6
SUNKEN TR	CO	TOP	19500	109	C5
SUNKIST AV	CO	LPUE	900	48	E2
SUNKIST AV	LPUE	LPUE	300	48	D4
SUNKIST AV N	WCOV	WCOV	100	39	F6
SUNKIST AV S	WCOV	WCOV	800	48	F1
SUNKIST DR	LPUE	LPUE		48	D2
SUNKIST PL W	WCOV	WCOV	2000	39	F6
SUNLAND BLVD	LA	SUN	9500	9	F4
SUNLAND BLVD	LA	SUN	9700	10	A4
SUNLAND BLVD	LA	SV	8600	9	E5
SUNLAND BLVD	LA	SV	8100	16	E1
SUNLAND PL	LA	SV	9500	9	F4
SUNLAND WY	LA	SUN	10000	10	B3
SUNLAND PARK DR	LA	SUN	10700	9	E5
SUNLIGHT PL	LA	LA16	5100	42	E6
SUNLIGHT WK	LA	LA16	5100	42	F6
SUNMIST DR	RPV	PVP	5500	72	E6
SUNMORE LN	CO	ALT	1000	19	E2
SUN MUN WY	LA	LA12	900	44	E1
SUNNY CT	WHI	WHI	16100	84	C4
SUNNY LN	AVA	AVA		77	B5
SUNNY LN	LA	TAR		21	C1
SUNNY LN	LAN	LAN		159	H7
SUNNY LN	LAN	LAN		159	H8
SUNNYBANK DR	LCF	LCF	2000	18	F1
SUNNYBRAE AV	LA	CAN	8400	6	E6
SUNNYBRAE AV	LA	CAN	6500	12	E2
SUNNYBROOK LN	CO	WHI	10200	61	F4
SUNNYBROOK LN	LAM	LAM	13000	61	E6
SUNNYBROOK LN	LAM	LAM	13000	82	E1
SUNNY BROOK TR	WAL	WAL		93	D5
SUNNY CANYON LN	CER	ART		82	C4
SUNNY COVE	LA	LA68	6800	34	B1
SUNNYCREEK LN	CER	ART	12400	82	B4
SUNNYCREST CT	DBAR	POM		97A	B2
SUNNYCREST DR	LA	LA65	4400	25	E5
SUNNYCREST TR	LA	TU	7000	11	A3
SUNNYDALE DR	CO	PALM		157	G8
SUNNYDALE DR	DUA	DUA	2600	86	A3
SUNNYDELL TR	LA	LA68	6900	34	A1
SUNNYDIP TR	LA	LA68	7200	34	A1
SUNNYFIELD DR	RHE	PVP	1	73	B4
SUNNY GLEN RD	TOR	TOR		73	B3
SUNNY GLENN WY	CO	SGAB	8500	27	F6
SUNNY HTS DR	LA	LA65	1600	35	F2
SUNNYHILL DR	LA	LA65	600	36	A2
SUNNYHILL DR	MPK	MPK	1300	45	F3
SUNNYHILL PL	DBAR	POM		97A	B2
SUNNYHILL TER	CO	LPUE		48	B5
SUNNY LEAF LN	LOM	LOM		73	D3
SUNNYMEAD DR	LAM	LAM	14600	84	A5
SUNNYNOOK DR	LA	LA39	2900	35	B3
SUNNY OAK RD	LA	VAN	3900	22	C4
SUNNY OAKS CIR	CO	ALT	1200	20	C4
SUNNY POINT PL	RPV	PVP	5200	72	E5
SUNNYRIDGE CIR	POM	POM		94	C5
SUNNYRIDGE DR	AGH	AGO		102	E3
SUNNYRIDGE RD	CO	PVP	27100	73	A5
SUNNYRIDGE RD	RPV	PVP	27300	72	F5
SUNNYSEA DR	LA	VEN	8200	55A	F2
SUNNYSIDE AV	LA	LA66	4100	49	E4
SUNNYSIDE AV N	SMAD	SMAD	100	28	B2
SUNNYSIDE AV S	SMAD	SMAD	100	28	B2
SUNNYSIDE LN	SMAD	SMAD	600	28	D1
SUNNYSIDE PL	SFS	WHI		61	C5
SUNNYSIDE TER	LA	SP	1400	78	E4
SUNNYSIDE WK	CO	CAST	28900	123	C2
SUNNYSDE RDG RD	PVE	PVP	2200	73	D6
SUNNYSLOPE AV	LA	VAN	5600	15	F6
SUNNYSLOPE AV	LA	VAN	4000	22	F2
SUNNYSLOPE AV N	PAS	PAS	1	27	F4
SUNNYSLOPE AV S	PAS	PAS	1	27	F4
SUNNYSLOPE BLVD	CO	PAS	3100	27	F5
SUNNYSLOPE BLVD	PAS	PAS	3100	27	F5
SUNNYSLOPE DR	CO	SGAB	8400	27	F6
SUNNYSLOPE DR	MPK	MPK	1300	45	F4
SUNNYSLOPE PL	MPK	MPK	1300	45	F3
SUNNYSLOPE RD	POM	POM		94	D5
SUNNYSLOPE ST	WHI	WHI		55	D5
SUNNYSLOPE WY	CO	LPUE		48	B5
SUNNYVALE PL	CO	LPUE		48	B5
SUNNYVALE RD	LAN	LAN		159	G8
SUNNYVALE WY	BH	BH		33	A4
SUNNYVIEW LN	LA	VAN	13400	15	F6
SUNNYVIEW ST	TOR	TOR	9500	67	E5
SUNNYVIEW TER	CO	LPUE		85	F3
SUNNYWOOD LN	LA	LA46	7500	23	F6
SUNOL DR N	CO	LA63	100	45	D4
SUNOL DR S	CO	LA23	900	45	D6
SUNOL DR S	CO	LA23	1200	53	D1
SUNOL DR S	CO	LA63	100	45	D4
SUNOL DR S	VER	LA23	2700	53	C3
SUNRIDGE CT	PALM	PALM		172	G9
SUNRIDGE ST	LA	VEN	100	55A	D2
SUNRISE BLVD	LB	LB06	600	75	D2
SUNRISE CT	LAN	LAN		160	C3
SUNRISE DR	CO	LPUE		98	D5
SUNRISE DR	MPK	MPK	1300	46	A4
SUNRISE DR	WHI	WHI		55	F6
SUNRISE PL	MPK	MPK	1400	46	A3
SUNRISE RD	WCOV	WCOV		92	F3
SUNRISE ST	LA	LA23	2300	44	F5
SUNRISE ST	LA	LA23	2900	45	A5
SUNRISE TER	PALM	PALM		172	A9
SUNRISE HILL LN	SMAD	SMAD		28	D1
SUNRISE RDG LN	CO	LPUE		85	C4
SUNRIVER DR	DBAR	POM		97A	B1
SUN ROSE ST	LAV	LAV		90	A3
SUNSET AV	CO	GL14	4600	18	E3
SUNSET AV	CO	LPUE	600	48	D4
SUNSET AV	CO	MONT	3800	18	E3
SUNSET AV	GLEN	MONT	3700	18	E3
SUNSET AV	IND	LPUE	100	48	D4
SUNSET AV	LA	VEN	300	49	B3
SUNSET AV	LPUE	LPUE	300	48	D4
SUNSET AV	PAS	PAS	700	26	F2
SUNSET AV	SGAB	SGAB	100	37	E4
SUNSET AV	SM	SM	1200	49	C2
SUNSET AV N	AZU	AZU	500	86	C5
SUNSET AV N	WCOV	WCOV	100	88	A6
SUNSET AV S	AZU	AZU	100	88	C1
SUNSET AV S	WCOV	WCOV	900	48	E3
SUNSET AV S	WCOV	WCOV	100	92	A1
SUNSET BLVD	ARC	ARC	500	28	B5
SUNSET BLVD N	CO	ARC	6700	28	B6
SUNSET BLVD W	BH	BH	9200	33	C4
SUNSET BLVD W	LA	LA12	200	44	D2
SUNSET BLVD W	LA	LA24	10000	32	D6
SUNSET BLVD W	LA	LA24	10000	33	A5
SUNSET BLVD W	LA	LA26	1200	35	B5
SUNSET BLVD W	LA	LA26	1200	44	D1
SUNSET BLVD W	LA	LA27	4400	34	D3
SUNSET BLVD W	LA	LA27	4300	35	A3
SUNSET BLVD W	LA	LA28	5500	34	D3
SUNSET BLVD W	LA	LA29	3900	35	A3
SUNSET BLVD W	LA	LA46	7500	33	E4
SUNSET BLVD W	LA	LA46	7100	34	A3
SUNSET BLVD W	LA	LA49	11000	32	D6
SUNSET BLVD W	LA	LA49	13000	40	E3
SUNSET BLVD W	LA	LA49	11300	41	A2
SUNSET BLVD W	LA	PP	13200	40	E3
SUNSET BLVD W	WHOL	LA46	8200	33	E4
SUNSET BLVD W	WHOL	LA69	8300	33	E4
SUNSET CT	LA	VEN		49	B4
SUNSET CT	LA	VEN	10	49	C3
SUNSET DR	AZU	AZU	1300	86	D4
SUNSET DR	CO	ALT	500	20	B3
SUNSET DR	HB	RB	600	67	C1
SUNSET DR	LA	LA27	3800	35	A3
SUNSET DR	PALM	PALM		183	F1
SUNSET DR	POM	POM	700	90	D6
SUNSET DR	WHI	WHI		55	E6
SUNSET PL	LA	LA05	2800	44	A2
SUNSET PL	WCOV	WCOV		92	A1
SUNSET PL N	MON	MON	100	28	F3
SUNSET PL S	MON	MON	100	28	F4
SUNSET RD	GLEN	GL02	500	25	B1

STREET	CITY	P.O. ZONE	BLOCK	PAGE	GRID
SUNSET ST	LB	LB05	1	70	C2
SUNSET TER	PALM	PALM		172	A9
SUNSET TR	CO	TOP	19700	109	C6
SUNSET BLUFF RD	WAL	WAL		93	B4
SUNSET CYN DR N	BUR	BUR	100	17	E4
SUNSET CYN DR S	BUR	BUR	100	17	E4
SUNSET CREST DR	LA	LA46	2100	33	C2
SUNSET CREST PL	LA	LA46	8800	33	C2
SUNSET CRSSG RD	DBAR	POM		93	E5
SUNSET CRSSG RD	DBAR	POM		94	A5
SUNSET HTS DR	LA	LA46	2200	33	D2
SUNSET HILL DR	WCOV	WCOV	1400	92	C1
SUNSET HILL DR	WCOV	WCOV	3300	93	A1
SUNSET HILLS RD	LA	LA69	1100	33	C4
SUNSETPARK WY	LA	SM		41	E6
SUNSET PEAK MTY	CO	LAV		95A	E2
SUNSET PLAZA DR	LA	LA69	1200	33	D3
SUNSET PLAZA PL	LA	LA69	8700	33	D3
SUNSET PZ TER	LA	LA69	8700	33	D3
SUNSET RDG CIR	LA	SF		1	E5
SUNSET RIDGE CT	LA	CAN		5	D4
SUNSET RIDGE DR	POM	POM		94	D4
SUNSET RIDGE LN	CO	LPUE		85	C4
SUNSET VALE AV	LA	LA69	1100	33	C4
SUNSET VIEW DR	LA	LA69	8300	33	E3
SUNSHINE AV	CO	WHI	13000	61	D6
SUNSHINE AV	SFS	SFS	12900	61	C6
SUNSHINE CT	GLEN	GL08		18	E6
SUNSHINE CT	LA	NHO	3800	23	D5
SUNSHINE CT	LB	LB13	1400	75	E4
SUNSHINE DR	GLEN	GL08		18	E6
SUNSHINE MTY	CO	SF		1	B1
SUNSHINE TER	LA	NHO	11100	23	C5
SUNSHINE CY MTY	CO	NEW		127	D9
SUNSHINE INN RD	CO	TOP		13	D6
SUNSHINE INN RD	CO	TOP		109	D1
SUNSIDE DR	CO	RM	7600	46	E3
SUNSIDE ST	LA	SP	1200	78	E3
SUNSTONE PL	LA	VAN	15500	22	C5
SUNSTREAM AV	PALM	PALM		183	H1
SUNSWEPT DR	LA	NHO	3600	23	B4
SUN VALLEY CT	AGH	AGO		102	F3
SUNVIEW DR	GLEN	GL08	1500	18	F3
SUNVUE PL	LA	LA12	1100	44	D1
SUNWOOD DR	DBAR	WAL		97	D2
SUPERBA AV	LA	VEN	600	49	C3
SUPERIOR AV	LA	VEN	2200	49	D3
SUPERIOR CT	LA	LA32	4100	36	C6
SUPERIOR ST	LA	CHA	19700	6	F4
SUPERIOR ST	LA	NOR	17000	7	E4
SUPERIOR ST	LA	SF	16400	7	F4
SUPERIOR ST	LA	SF	15300	8	B4
SUPI	CO	TOP		13	C5
SUPPLY AV	CMRC	LA22	2700	54	C4
SUPREME CT	LA	LA32	4100	36	C6
SUREE ELLEN LN	CO	ALT	2200	20	D5
SURF CT	CO	HAC		73	F2
SURF CT	LA	HAC		74	A2
SURF ST	LA	VEN	50	55A	D2
SURFSIDE WY	CO	MAL	6400	111	E5
SURFVIEW DR	LA	PP	100	115	F4
SURFWOOD RD	CO	MAL	3400	115	E3
SURREY CT	CO	LAN		159	B9
SURREY DR	CO	COV		93	C2
SURREY DR	LB	LB15		76	E5
SURREY LN	ING	IN01		57	B2
SURREY LN	LAM	LAM	15400	84	B6
SURREY LN	LAN	LAN		159	G8
SURREY LN	RPV	PVP	1	73	C6
SURREY LN	WHI	WHI		55	E3
SURREY PL	CO	LP45		98	A3
SURRY ST	LA	LA27	3000	35	B2
SURVEYOR ST	POM	POM		94	A3
SUSAN AV	BLF	BLF	14400	66	B2
SUSAN AV	DOW	DOW	11600	59	F4
SUSAN AV	DOW	DOW	10300	60	A2
SUSAN CT	LAV	LAV		90	C1
SUSAN CT	PALM	PALM		172	B5
SUSAN DR	LA	SF	11800	1	F5
SUSAN PL	CER	ART	18300	82	C6
SUSANA AV	RB	RB	400	67	E4
SUSANA AV	TOR	TOR	22000	67	E5
SUSANA RD	CO	COM	18600	70	B2
SUSANA RD	COM	COM	17400	65	B6
SUSANA RD	LB	LB05	17900	65	B6
SUSANA RD	LB	LB05		70	B2
SUSAN BETH WY	SCLR	SAU		124	E5
SUSAN CAROLE DR	SCLR	SAU		124	F5
SUSANNA AV	WCOV	WCOV	600	92	B2
SUSANNAH CT	AZU	AZU	200	86	C3
SUSANNE MARIE	AZU	AZU		88	D2
SUSAN RUTH ST	SCLR	SAU		124	G4
SUSQUEHANNA AV	BAP	BAP	13900	39	D5
SUSSEX CT	GLEN	GL06		26	B1
SUSSEX CT	PALM	PALM		183	C5
SUSSEX LN	ING	IN01		57	C2

STREET	CITY	P.O. ZONE	BLOCK	PAGE	GRID
SUSSEX LN	LA	LA23	2900	45	A6
SUSSEX RD	SMAR	PAS	800	37	C2
SUTHERLAND ST	LA	LA26	1300	35	D6
SUTRO AV	GAR	GAR	14700	63	C3
SUTRO AV	LA	LA08	3800	51	C2
SUTRO AV	LA	LA18	3700	43	C6
SUTRO AV	LA	LA18	3700	51	C2
SUTRO WK	LA	LA08		51	C2
SUTTER AV	LA	PAC	11100	8	F1
SUTTER AV	LA	PAC	10600	9	A2
SUTTER AV	LA	SV	9200	9	D5
SUTTER CT	SAD	SAD		89	D2
SUTTER CREEK	MON	MON		29	B2
SUTTER CREEK DR	WAL	WAL		92	F5
SUTTERS MILL DR	DBAR	POM		97	D5
SUTTERS PNTE DR	SCLR	SAU		124	E6
SUTTON CT	POM	POM	300	90	F5
SUTTON PL	LA	VAN	4300	22	C4
SUTTON ST	CER	ART		82	D6
SUTTON ST	LA	ENC	15300	22	B3
SUTTON ST	LA	VAN	14600	22	C3
SUTTON WY	BH	BH	1100	33	B4
SUVA ST	BG	BELL	6500	54	B6
SUVA ST	DOW	DOW	7300	60	B1
SUZANNE RD	WAL	WAL	100	93	C5
SUZANNE RDG DR	CO	ACT		189	D4
SWAIN ST	GLDR	GLDR	1200	89	D1
SWAIN ST	LA	SF	15800	2	B2
SWALL DR N	BH	BH	100	33	D6
SWALL DR N	BH	BH	100	42	D1
SWALL DR N	LA	LA48	100	33	D6
SWALL DR N	WHOL	LA48	200	33	D6
SWALL DR S	BH	BH	100	42	D1
SWALL DR S	LA	LA35	1100	42	D1
SWALL DR S	LA	LA48	100	33	D6
SWALLOW DR	LA	LA69	9200	33	D2
SWALLOW LN	PALM	PALM		183	F1
SWALLOW GLEN	WCOV	WCOV		92	A2
SWAN DR	PALM	PALM		183	D2
SWAN PL	LA	LA26	2900	35	B4
SWANEE LN	BAP	BAP	15100	39	F5
SWANEE LN	CO	COV	19300	89	A5
SWANEE LN E	COV	COV	600	88	F5
SWANEE LN E	WCOV	WCOV	1000	88	B5
SWANEE LN W	COV	COV	400	88	D5
SWANEE LN W	WCOV	WCOV	1000	88	B5
SWANSEA PL	LA	LA29		34	E4
SWARTHMORE AV	LA	PP	300	40	D4
SWARTHMORE CT	CLA	CLA		96	D5
SWARTHMORE DR	GLEN	GL06	1100	25	E2
SWEET PL	CO	LPUE	15600	85	E2
SWEET ST	CO	LPUE	15800	85	E3
SWEETAIRE AV E	CO	LAN	15200	174	H4
SWEETAIRE AV E	CO	LAN	16500	175	A4
SWEETBAY RD	RPV	PVP	1	77	E2
SWEETBRIAR DR	CLA	CLA		96	B6
SWEETBRIAR DR	GLEN	GL06	1100	25	E2
SWEETBRIAR LN	LA	PAC		3	B4
SWEETBRIER ST E	PALM	PALM	1500	172	E8
SWEETBRUSH ST	PALM	PALM		173	A9
SWEETBUSH ST	PALM	PALM		184	B5
SWEET ELM DR	LA	ENC		21	C4
SWEETGRASS LN	RHE	PVP	2600	73	C5
SWEET GUM LN	WHI	WHI		84	D5
SWEETLAND ST	CLA	CLA	900	91	A3
SWEETWATR CY RD	CO	MAL	3300	114	B4
SWEETWTR MSA RD	CO	MAL	3300	114	B4
SWEETZER AV N	LA	LA48	100	33	E6
SWEETZER AV N	LA	LA69	700	33	E5
SWEETZER AV N	LA	LA69	1400	33	E3
SWEETZER AV N	WHOL	LA69	800	33	E5
SWEETZER AV S	LA	LA48	100	33	E6
SWEETZER AV S	LA	LA48	300	42	E1
SWENSON DR	CO	TOP		115	A1
SWIFT CT	LAV	LAV		95A	E6
SWIFT DR	LAM	LAM	14200	82	F1
SWINFORD ST	LA	SP	200	79	B2
SWINTON AV	LA	ENC	4800	22	A2
SWINTON AV	LA	SF	11500	2	A6
SWINTON AV	LA	SF	8700	8	A6
SWISS TR	DUA	DUA		29	F4
SWOPE ST	CAR	CAR	300	69	B5
SYBLE AV	BLF	BLF	14300	66	B2
SYBRANDY AV	CER	ART	17400	82	B6
SYCAMORE	CO	LP48		98	F3
SYCAMORE	LA	SF42		2	C1
SYCAMORE	WCOV	WCOV		98	F1
SYCAMORE AV	CLA	CLA	200	91	C5
SYCAMORE AV	CO	PAS		28	A4
SYCAMORE AV	GLDR	GLDR	400	87	B5
SYCAMORE AV	GLEN	GL01	1400	17	F5
SYCAMORE AV	GLEN	GL14	2800	18	D2
SYCAMORE AV	GLEN	MONT	2600	18	D2
SYCAMORE AV	SPAS	SPAS	1000	36	D2
SYCAMORE AV E	ARC	ARC	100	28	E3
SYCAMORE AV E	ELS	ELS	200	56	B5

STREET	CITY	P.O. ZONE	BLOCK	PAGE	GRID
SYCAMORE AV N	LA	LA28	1300	34	B6
SYCAMORE AV N	LA	LA36	100	34	B6
SYCAMORE AV N	LA	LA38	700	34	B6
SYCAMORE AV N	LA	LA68	1900	34	B6
SYCAMORE AV S	LA	LA08	3800	50	F1
SYCAMORE AV S	LA	LA08	3800	51	A1
SYCAMORE AV S	LA	LA16	1900	43	A5
SYCAMORE AV S	LA	LA19	1000	43	B2
SYCAMORE AV S	LA	LA36	100	34	B6
SYCAMORE AV S	LA	LA36	200	43	B2
SYCAMORE AV W	ARC	ARC	100	28	E3
SYCAMORE AV W	ELS	ELS	700	55A	F5
SYCAMORE AV W	ELS	ELS	100	56	A5
SYCAMORE DR	AZU	AZU	900	86	E5
SYCAMORE DR	CO	TOP	1600	108	F2
SYCAMORE DR	LA	CUL	4900	50	B3
SYCAMORE DR	LAV	LAV	2500	90	E3
SYCAMORE DR	SMAR	PAS	1800	37	E1
SYCAMORE DR	WHI	WHI	13500	55	E4
SYCAMORE DR N	SGAB	SGAB	100	37	D3
SYCAMORE DR W	SGAB	SGAB	600	37	D2
SYCAMORE LN	BRAD	DUA		29	D3
SYCAMORE LN	CO	POM		93	E2
SYCAMORE LN	PALM	LAN		171	A2
SYCAMORE LN	PALM	PALM		171	C5
SYCAMORE LN	RHE	PVP		72	D5
SYCAMORE PL	ING	IN01	500	56	E2
SYCAMORE PL	POM	POM	1600	90	C6
SYCAMORE PL	SMAD	SMAD	200	28	D1
SYCAMORE RD	LA	SM		40	D5
SYCAMORE ST	CMRC	LA40	6900	54	B4
SYCAMORE ST	CO	PAS	3700	28	B4
SYCAMORE ST	MTB	MTB	100	54	B4
SYCAMORE ST	NWK	NWK	11900	82	A2
SYCAMORE TR	LA	LA68	7100	24	A6
SYCAMORE CANYON	CO	WHI		55	D2
SYCAMORE CYN RD	SAD	SAD	1500	95A	A5
SYCAMORE CYN RD	SAD	SAD	1500	95A	A5
SYCAMORE CON RD	MTB	MTB		54	C5
SYCAMORE CK DR	SCLR	VAL	27300	124	C5
SYCAMORE GLEN	PAS	PAS	200	26	D5
SYCAMORE GLEN	PAS	PAS	200	26	D5
SYCAMORE MDW DR	CO	MAL		112	F6
SYCAMORE MDW DR	CO	MAL		112	F6
SYCAMORE PK DR	LA	LA31		36	B4
SYDNEY AV	CO	LA22		45	E4
SYDNEY DR N	CO	LA22	700	45	D6
SYDNEY DR S	CMRC	LA22	1400	53	E1
SYDNEY DR S	CO	LA22	900	45	D6
SYLMAR AV	LA	VAN	9300	8	D5
SYLMAR AV	LA	VAN	5800	15	D6
SYLMAR AV	LA	VAN	4400	22	D3
SYLVAN DR	CO	LH		157	B6
SYLVAN LN	GLEN	GL08	2300	18	F6
SYLVAN ST	LA	NHO	10700	16	C5
SYLVAN ST	LA	RES		12	F5
SYLVAN ST	LA	RES	18200	14	C5
SYLVAN ST	LA	VAN	13300	15	F5
SYLVAN ST	LA	VAN	13100	16	A5
SYLVAN ST	LA	WOH	23000	5	E5
SYLVAN ST	LA	WOH	22200	12	B5
SYLVAN GLEN RD	CO	CAL		108	D3
SYLVAN GLEN RD	DBAR	POM		94	B5
SYLVANIA LN	CO	TOP	1700	109	E1
SYLVANOAK DR	GLEN	GL06	700	25	E3
SYLVANWOOD AV	LKD	LKD	20300	71	F3
SYLVANWOOD AV	NWK	NWK	13900	66	F4
SYLVESTER ST S	LA	LA66	4100	49	F3
SYLVESTER ST W	LA	LA66	12000	49	F3
SYLVIA AV	LA	NOR	9600	7	A4
SYLVIA AV	LA	NOR	8300	14	A1
SYLVIA AV	LA	RES	6100	14	A5
SYLVIA AV	LA	TAR	5400	21	A1
SYLVIA DR	CO	CYN		125	E6
SYLVIA ST	WCOV	WCOV		92	E6
SYLVIAN LN	LAV	LAV		90	B3
SYMPHONY CT	LAN	LAN		159	C8
SYRACUSE AV	BAP	BAP	3400	39	B6
SYRACUSE AV	BAP	BAP	3000	48	B1
SYRACUSE AV	CO	ACT		189	E2
SYRACUSE DR	CLA	CLA	800	91	A2
SYRACUSE DR	CO	WHI	14100	61	F5
SYRACUSE WK	LB	LB03	100	80	C1
SYRINGA ST	SFS	SFS	11200	60	F3

T

STREET	CITY	P.O. ZONE	BLOCK	PAGE	GRID
TABARD RD	CO	CAL		108	E6
TABLE MTN RD	PALM	PALM		172	J5
TABLE MTN RD	PALM	PALM		183	J1
TABLER AV	LAN	LAN	44500	160	C5
TABOR LN	LAV	LAV		90	C2
TABOR PL	SFS	SFS		61	B3
TABOR ST	LA	LA34	9800	42	B6
TABOR ST	LA	LA66	11000	49	F1
TABOR ST	LA	LA66	11200	50	A1

STREET	CITY	P.O. ZONE	BLOCK	PAGE	GRID
TACANA ST	LA	LA08	4700	51	A1
TACKABERRY CT	AGH	AGO		100A	A1
TACKSTEM ST	PALM	PALM		184	B6
TACOMA AV	LA	LA65	3500	35	F3
TACOMA CT	PALM	PALM		183	J1
TACUBA DR	LAM	LAM	14500	82	F1
TACUBA DR	LAM	LAM	15000	83	A1
TACUBA ST	LA	LA65	800	36	A2
TADDY ST	NWK	NWK	11200	66	F2
TADMORE ST	CO	LPUE	17400	98	C1
TAFT AV	LA	LA28	1600	34	D3
TAFT AV	LA	LA68	1900	34	D3
TAFT AV	SOG	SOG	5700	59	E6
TAFT CT	CO	CAST	28600	123	C2
TAFT CT	MPK	MPK	600	46	D3
TAFT WY	SM	SM	700	49	A1
TAGUS ST	CO	WHI	9900	55	C1
TAHITI AV	LA	PP		40	C2
TAHITI WY	CO	MDR	13800	49	D6
TAHITIAN TER	LA	PP		40	C4
TAHOE AV	CO	HAW	11700	56	E6
TAHOE DR	LA	LA68	6300	24	C6
TAHOE PL	LA	LA68	3200	24	C6
TAHQUITZ PL	CO	PALM		183	B1
TAHQUITZ PL	LA	PP	500	40	C4
TAIMA AV	CO	CHA		1A	A6
TAINTOR RD E	CO	PALM	100	172	B9
TAJAUTA AV	CAR	CAR	19000	69	D1
TAJAUTA AV	CO	COM	13800	64	D3
TAJAUTA AV N	COM	COM	100	64	D3
TAJAUTA AV S	COM	COM	100	64	D3
TALBERT ST	LA	VEN	7800	55A	E2
TALBOT DR	LAM	LAM	15100	83	B3
TALC ST	SFS	SFS	13600	82	D2
TALENTO WY	PALM	LAN		171	D4
TALISMAN ST	TOR	TOR	4400	68	A2
TALLAC DR	ARC	ARC	800	28	C4
TALL PINE DR	DUA	DUA	2300	29	F3
TALLYHAND RD	RH	PVP		73	A5
TALLYRAND DR	DBAR	POM		97A	B2
TALMADGE ST	LA	LA27	1300	35	A2
TALOFA AV	LA	NHO	4300	24	A3
TALOGA ST	CO	LPUE	15500	85	D4
TALUS PL	LA	BH		23	C6
TAMAR DR	CO	LPUE	1400	48	E2
TAMAR DR	LPUE	LPUE	500	48	C3
TAMAR DR	WCOV	WCOV	1600	48	E2
TAMARAC DR	PAS	PAS	300	26	D5
TAMARACK	ELM	ELM		48	A6
TAMARACK AV	LA	PAC	10400	8	F2
TAMARACK AV	LA	PAC	9800	9	A2
TAMARACK AV	LA	SF	11200	8	E1
TAMARACK AV	LA	SV	8800	9	C5
TAMARACK AV E	ING	IN01	100	57	A2
TAMARACK AV W	ING	IN01	100	57	A2
TAMARACK LN	CO	SAU		124	C2
TAMARACK LN	CO	SAU		124	C3
TAMARIND AV	LA	LA28	1300	34	D4
TAMARIND AV	LA	LA38	1100	34	D4
TAMARIND AV	LA	LA68	1900	34	D2
TAMARIND AV N	COM	COM	100	64	F4
TAMARIND AV S	COM	COM	100	64	F4
TAMARISK DR	LAV	LAV		95A	D5
TAMARISK DR	PALM	PALM		171	F4
TAMARISK PL	SCLR	VAL		127	A2
TAMARIX DR	CO	LPUE	14700	85	C2
TAMBO PL	DBAR	POM	21000	97	D4
TAMBOR CT	CO	LPUE		98	D4
TAMBOR DR	GLEN	GL08	2100	25	F1
TAMBORA DR	SCLR	CYN	27700	124	H5
TAMCLIFF AV	CAR	CAR	17800	64	C6
TAMERLANE DR	GLEN	GL08	1800	18	F6
TAMORA AV	CO	ELM	1100	47	C2
TAMORA AV	SELM	ELM	2400	47	C2
TAM OSHANTER DR	AZU	AZU	1200	86	C4
TAM OSHANTER DR	CO	WAL		97	B4
TAMOSHANTER LN	LA	TAR	4300	21	A3
TAM OSHANTER RD	CO	LLAN		192	J2
TAMPA AV	LA	NOR	11300	1	A5
TAMPA AV	LA	NOR	8500	7	A5
TAMPA AV	LA	NOR	8300	14	A2
TAMPA AV	LA	RES	6100	14	A2
TAMPA AV	LA	TAR	6000	14	A5
TAMPA AV	LA	TAR	5100	21	A2
TAMPA CT	PALM	PALM		183	J1
TAMPA ST	POM	POM	2300	94	F6
TAMPICO AV	LA	LA32	3800	36	D4
TAMPICO DR	SCLR	VAL		124	B9
TAMPICO WY	MTB	MTB		46	E6
TAMWORTH AV	CO	SGAB	7200	28	A6
TANA AV	CO	WHI	11500	61	F5
TANAGER AV	CMRC	LA40	2800	54	B4
TANAGER WY	LA	LA69	1400	33	D3
TANBARK PL	GLEN	GL14	3900	18	C1
TAN CANYON RD	DUA	DUA	500	86	A4
TANDEM WY	TOR	TOR	25200	73	B3

STREET	CITY	P.O. ZONE	BLOCK	PAGE	GRID
TANFIELD DR	LAM	LAM	12600	84	A6
TANFORAN LN	DBAR	POM		94	A5
TANGELO LN	LHH	LAH		98A	B3
TANGENT LN	LKD	LKD		71	F3
TANGERINE RD	RPV	PVP	1	77	F2
TANGIER AV	BLF	BLF	13400	66	B1
TANGIER PL	POM	POM	500	93	F2
TANGLEWOOD	PALM	PALM		171	C3
TANGLEWOOD	WCOV	WCOV		92	D4
TANGLEWOOD DR	POM	POM		94	C5
TANGLEWOOD DR	SAD	SAD	100	89	F4
TANGLEWOOD DR	SAD	SAD	100	90	A4
TANGLEWOOD LN	CO	LPUE		48	B5
TANGLEWOOD LN	RHE	PVP	3400	73	B4
TANGLEWOOD ST	LB	LB08	5300	71	C3
TANGLEWOOD ST	LKD	LKD	5700	71	D3
TANNA HILL AV	CO	CYN		128	D2
TANNENCREST DR	DUA	DUA	2900	86	A3
TANNERBERG CT	CAR	CAR	900	64	C5
TANNER BRIDG RD	LA	LA77		32	D3
TANNERS RD	LA	LA49	13100	30	F6
TANOBLE DR	CO	ALT	2300	20	D5
TAN PAN DR	CO	TOP		100	F6
TANTALUS DR	CO	MAL	6100	112	F5
TANYA AV	CAR	LB10		70	A5
TAOS CIR	CER	ART	4400	81	C2
TAOS PL	CO	PALM		183	B1
TAOS RD	CO	ALT	1	20	A3
TAPER AV	COM	COM	400	64	C3
TAPER AV	LA	SP	1600	73	E6
TAPER ST	LB	LB10	1200	70	A5
TAPIA DR	CO	MAL	6200	111	E4
TAPIA CYN RD	CO	SAU	27000	123	E1
TARA CT	LAN	LAN		160	E3
TARA DR	LA	ENC	4500	21	F3
TARA TER	CUL	CUL		50	D2
TARANTO AV	SCLR	VAL		127	A2
TARANTO WY	LA	LA77	10600	32	D3
TARAPACA RD	RPV	SP	30600	78	C3
TARCUTO WY	LA	LA77	800	32	D5
TARECO DR	LA	LA68	3200	24	B6
TARLETON ST	LA	LA11	1900	44	D6
TARLETON ST	LA	LA21	1600	44	D6
TARMA ST	LB	LB08	7400	81	A6
TARO WY	LA	LA77	800	32	D5
TARQUIN ST	LA	SF	12900	3	A3
TARR PL	POM	POM	1800	94	E5
TARRAGON RD	RPV	PVP	6300	77	D2
TARRANT AV	CAR	CAR	16300	64	C4
TARRANT AV	CO	COM	15200	64	C3
TARRASA DR	RPV	SP	27600	73	E5
TARRON AV	HAW	LA47	11500	57	D5
TARRYBRAE TER	LA	TAR	4100	13	F4
TARRYGLEN LN	SAD	SAD		89	F1
TARRYTON AV	CO	WHI	9200	61	E3
TARRYTOWN LN	AGH	AGO		100A	D6
TARTA CT	CO	WAL		97	B3
TARTAR LN	COM	COM	1600	65	A5
TARYN DR	SCLR	SAU		124	D2
TARZANA DR	LA	TAR	18300	21	C2
TARZANA ST	LA	ENC	17400	21	D2
TARZANA ST	LA	TAR	18100	21	C2
TARZANA ESTS DR	LA	TAR		13	F4
TARZANA WOODS	LA	TAR	4900	21	A2
TARZON ST	CO	LA63	4400	45	E2
TASMAN AV	POM	POM	300	90	F5
TASSEL MTY	MON	MON		29	F1
TATE AV	GLDR	GLDR	300	87	B6
TATE ST	POM	POM	100	90	E6
TATUM ST	LA	LA65	3000	35	E3
TAU PL	LA	CHA	20300	6	E2
TAVENER AV	LA	CUL	11200	50	B3
TAVERN TR	LA	LA46	2100	33	E2
TAVISTOCK AV	LA	LA49	200	32	C6
TAWNY CT	DBAR	POM		97	E3
TAYLOR AV N	MTB	MTB	500	46	D6
TAYLOR AV N	MTB	MTB	100	54	D2
TAYLOR AV S	MTB	MTB	100	54	D2
TAYLOR CT	TOR	GAR	16200	63	D4
TAYLOR CT	TOR	TOR	16900	63	D4
TAYLOR CT	WCOV	WCOV	500	88	B5
TAYLOR DR	CLA	CLA	300	91	A4
TAYLOR DR	MPK	MPK	500	46	D4
TAYLOR PL	TOR	TOR		63	D5
TAYLOR ST	CO	CAST	29500	123	C2
TAYLOR ST	LB	LB05		65	B4
TAYLOR ST	MON	MON	100	29	B6
TAYLR,ZACHRY WY	PALM	PALM		183	D2
TEAGARDEN LN	ALH	ALH	2000	37	A4
TEAGUE DR	SAD	SAD	200	90	A3
TEAK ST	LA	LA16	5700	42	E5
TEAKWOOD LN	SAD	SAD	700	90	A4
TEAKWOOD RD	LA	LA49	700	32	A6
TEAL TER	CO	MAL		112	C5
TEALE ST	CO	CUL		50	B4

—Z— COPYRIGHT, © 1989 BY Thomas Bros Maps

STREET	CITY	P.O. ZONE	BLOCK	PAGE	GRID
TEALE ST	CO	MDR	11800	49	F6
TEASDALE DR	CLA	CLA	300	90	F2
TEASLEY ST	CO	GL14	2300	11	E6
TEAZLE CYN RD	LA	SUN		10	B3
TECHNOLOGY DR	SCLR	VAL		123	G6
TECUM RD	DOW	DOW	9700	60	B1
TECUMSEH AV	LYN	LYN	3200	59	A4
TECUMSEH AV	SOG	SOG	3100	59	A4
TEDEMORY DR	WHI	WHI	13400	55	E6
TEDFORD DR	CO	WHI	14000	61	F6
TEDFORD WY	MPK	MPK	400	46	B2
TEDREGAL CT	CO	CAL		100	D4
TEDROW DR	GLDR	GLDR	100	89	B1
TEE PL	CO	LLAN		192	H3
TEED ST	LA	LA12	600	44	D2
TEESDALE AV	LA	NHO	6000	16	B1
TEESDALE AV	LA	NHO	4200	23	B2
TEGNER DR	CO	RM	7200	46	D3
TEGNER DR	MPK	MPK	700	46	D3
TEHACHAPI DR	LB	LB07	800	70	D4
TEHAMA ST	LA	LA42	5500	26	C6
TEHRAN ST	LA	LA15	700	44	B4
TEJON PL	PVE	PVP	300	72	C2
TELAMON LN	POM	POM	800	94	F5
TELECHRON AV	CO	WHI	10800	61	E5
TELEGA PL	CO	PALM		183	B1
TELEGRAPH RD	CMRC	LA22	4600	53	E1
TELEGRAPH RD	CMRC	LA23	4500	53	E1
TELEGRAPH RD	CMRC	LA40	5700	54	A3
TELEGRAPH RD	CO	LA23	4300	53	E1
TELEGRAPH RD	CO	WHI	13200	61	E4
TELEGRAPH RD	DOW	DOW	8000	54	B5
TELEGRAPH RD	DOW	DOW	8100	60	E2
TELEGRAPH RD	LAM	LAM	14500	61	F4
TELEGRAPH RD	LAM	LAM	14600	84	A5
TELEGRAPH RD	MTB	MTB	7100	54	B5
TELEGRAPH RD	PR	PR	7900	54	B5
TELEGRAPH RD	PR	PR	8000	60	E2
TELEGRAPH RD	SFS	SFS	11200	60	E2
TELEGRAPH RD	SFS	SFS	11500	61	A3
TELEGRAPH HL CT	SCLR	VAL		124	E3
TELFAIR AV	LA	PAC	10200	8	F2
TELFAIR AV	LA	PAC	9700	9	A3
TELFAIR AV	LA	SF	12300	2	B3
TELFAIR AV	LA	SF	11000	8	E1
TELFAIR AV	LA	SV	8500	9	C5
TELFAIR AV	LA	SV	8300	16	D1
TELFAIR PL	LA	PAC	13500	8	F1
TELFAIR PL	LA	SF		8	F1
TELFORD ST	CO	LA22	5000	45	F5
TELLEFSON RD	CUL	CUL	5700	50	D3
TELLEM DR	LA	PP	1000	40	B2
TELLER AV	CO	SAU		125	H1
TELLEZ ST	LA	RES	17900	14	D5
TELLGATE DR	DBAR	POM		93	F5
TELLGATE DR	DBAR	POM		94	A5
TELLURIDE ST	LA	LA31	4100	36	B5
TELLURIDE ST	LA	LA32	4299	36	B5
TELO AV	TOR	TOR		68	B6
TELSTAR AV	ELM	ELM	9500	47	B1
TEMECULA CT	SAD	SAD		90	A1
TEMECULA ST	LA	PP		40	C3
TEMESCAL CYN RD	LA	PP		30	B6
TEMESCAL CYN RD	LA	PP		40	C3
TEMMA CT	CO	CAL		100	F4
TEMMERA LN	GLDR	GLDR	200	89	B2
TEMPE WY	WLVL	THO		102	A5
TEMPLAR DR	LAM	LAM	14900	83	A2
TEMPLE AL	PAS	PAS	1400	27	C2
TEMPLE AV	CO	LPUE	13300	48	C2
TEMPLE AV	CO	LPUE	16100	92	A5
TEMPLE AV	CO	POM		93	D3
TEMPLE AV	COM	COM	1600	65	B4
TEMPLE AV	IND	LPUE	13100	48	C2
TEMPLE AV	LB	LB03	100	75	F5
TEMPLE AV	LB	LB04	700	75	F5
TEMPLE AV	LB	LB06	2400	75	F5
TEMPLE AV	LB	LB14	300	75	F5
TEMPLE AV	LPUE	LPUE	13700	48	C2
TEMPLE AV	LPUE	LPUE	15600	92	A5
TEMPLE AV	POM	POM		93	D3
TEMPLE AV	POM	POM		94	A4
TEMPLE AV	SH	LB06	1800	75	F3
TEMPLE AV	WAL	WAL		93	B4
TEMPLE AV	WCOV	WCOV		92	D5
TEMPLE ST	LA	LA04	3500	35	A6
TEMPLE ST	LA	LA12	200	44	D2
TEMPLE ST	LA	LA26	1800	35	B6
TEMPLE ST	LA	LA26	1200	44	C1
TEMPLE TER	LA	LA42		36	D3
TEMPLE WY	WCOV	WCOV		89	A6
TEMPLE WY	WCOV	WCOV		93	A1
TEMPLE WY E	LA	LA24		41	F2
TEMPLE WY N	LA	LA24		41	F2
TEMPLE CITY BL	CO	ARC	6500	38	B2
TEMPLE CITY BL	CO	SGAB		28	B6
TEMPLE CITY BL	ELM	ELM	4200	38	C6
TEMPLE CITY BL	RM	RM	3500	38	C6
TEMPLE CITY BL	TEC	TEC	4300	38	B2
TEMPLE HILL DR	LA	LA68	6000	34	C2
TEMPLETON ST	HPK	HPK	5900	52	F5
TEMPLETON ST	LA	LA32	4700	36	D5
TEMPO DR	LAN	LAN		159	B8
TEMRE LN	CO	LPUE		97	A4
TENANGO DR	CLA	CLA		90	F2
TENANGO DR	LA	WOH	4500	13	E3
TENAYA AV	LYN	LYN	3200	59	A4
TENAYA AV	SOG	SOG	3100	59	A4
TENDA DR	SCLR	CYN	28000	124	G7
TENDERFOOT WY	DBAR	POM		97	E5
TENDRFOOT TR RD	CO	NEW		127	J3
TENDILLA AV	LA	WOH	4900	13	C2
TENINO AV	LA	LA66		50	B2
TENNEB DR	LA	LA49	300	41	B2
TENNESSEE AV	LA	LA64	10700	41	E4
TENNESSEE AV	LA	LA64	10300	42	A3
TENNESSEE PL	LA	LA64	11500	41	D5
TENNEYSON DR	AGH	AGO		102	F2
TENNIS CLUB DR	PALM	PALM		171	D4
TENNYSON PL	HB	RB	2700	62	C5
TENNYSON PL	LA	SF	17200	1	E3
TENNYSON ST	MB	MB	1100	62	C5
TENSHAW PL	LA	LA41	1700	26	B5
TEODORA PL	GLEN	GL08	2000	19	A5
TEPIC DR	PAR	PAR	8400	65	F3
TEPIC RD	LA	WOH	4100	13	D4
TEPOCA RD	LA	WOH	4400	13	D3
TERBUSH DR	MPK	MPK	1300	46	E3
TERECITA PL	LA	TU		11	A2
TERECITA RD	LA	TU	10700	11	A2
TERESA AV	CO	SGAB	7200	46	D3
TERESA CT	CER	ART	19600	81	C2
TERESA PL	POM	POM	2500	94	F6
TERESA ST	WCOV	WCOV	1000	88	B6
TERESA WY	CER	ART	19000	81	B1
TERESAS LN	CO	PVP		73	B4
TERESINA DR	CO	LPUE	2500	85	E3
TERESITA CIR	MON	MON	900	29	C4
TERHUNE AV	LA	SUN	9900	9	F4
TERHUNE AV	LA	SV	8300	16	F1
TERHUNE DR	CO	MAL	2700	113	B3
TERI AV	TOR	TOR	800	68	B3
TERMINAL RD	AVA	AVA		77	B5
TERMINAL ST	LA	LA21	700	44	D5
TERMINAL ST	LB	LB06	6100	65	E6
TERMINAL WY	LA	SP	100	79	B3
TERMINO AV	LA	SP	400	78	F2
TERMINO AV N	LB	LB03	100	76	A6
TERMINO AV N	LB	LB04	700	76	A6
TERMINO AV N	LB	LB14	300	76	A6
TERMINO AV N	LB	LB15	2100	76	A6
TERMINO AV S	LB	LB03	100	76	A6
TERN BAY LN	LKD	LKD	2000	70	E2
TERRA LN	ARC	ARC	1800	38	C1
TERRA BELLA ST	LA	PAC	13300	8	D5
TERRA BELLA ST	LA	PAC	12200	9	B2
TERRA BELLA ST	LA	SF	11600	3	C6
TERRA BELLA ST	LA	SF	11800	9	B2
TERRA BELLA ST	LA	VAN	14200	8	D5
TERRACE AV	ALH	ALH	2800	36	F6
TERRACE CIR	LA	PP		40	C2
TERRACE CT	CO	SAU		124	G3
TERRACE DR	CO	GL14	5500	11	F5
TERRACE DR	LA	LA42	5900	36	C2
TERRACE DR	LA	PP		40	C4
TERRACE DR	LB	LB07	700	70	D3
TERRACE DR	PAS	PAS	100	26	F4
TERRACE DR	RHE	PVP		72	D5
TERRACE DR	SAD	SAD		89	E3
TERRACE DR	SH	LB06	2000	75	F3
TERRACE DR	WCOV	WCOV		97	A2
TERRACE LN	CO	AGO		107	A2
TERRACE LN	LA	LA42	300	36	B2
TERRACE LN	LAN	LAN		159	G7
TERRACE PL	LA	PP		40	C2
TERRACE PL	WHI	WHI	13500	55	E4
TERRACE ST E	CO	ALT	100	20	A4
TERRACE ST W	CO	ALT	100	19	F4
TERRACEDALE DR	LAM	LAM	15200	84	B5
TERRACE HTS AV	LA	LA23	2200	45	A4
TERRACE VIEW DR	LA	ENC	3500	21	F5
TERRACE VIEW DR	MON	MON		28	F3
TERRACE 49	LA	LA42	700	36	A1
TERRACE 52	LA	LA42	200	36	C3
TERRACITA LN	LCF	LCF	4900	19	A2
TERRA COTTA WY	PAR	PAR		65	E4
TERRADELL ST	PR	PR	8300	60	D1
TERRADELL ST	SFS	SFS	10900	60	F2
TERRADELL ST	SFS	SFS	11000	61	A2
TERRADO DR	MON	MON	500	29	D4
TERRADO PZ	COV	COV		88	E6
TERRAINE AV	LB	LB04	700	76	C5
TERRAINE AV	LB	LB14	400	76	C5
TERRAINE AV	LB	LB15	2400	76	C2
TERRAZA DR	LA	LA08	4100	50	F1
TERRAZA PL	MB	MB	100	62	C5
TERRAZA TER	WAL	WAL	19600	97	A1
TERRAZZO DR	PALM	LAN		171	A2
TERREBONNE AV	SAD	LAV		95A	B5
TERRELL PL	POM	POM		90	E3
TERRI DR	SCLR	CYN		124	G9
TERRI ANN DR	WCOV	WCOV	600	92	D2
TERRILL AV	LA	LA42		36	C3
TERRITORY RD	CO	SAU		181	C7
TERRY PL	LA	LA31	3000	36	A6
TERRY WY	CO	COV	21100	93	D1
TERRY WY	COV	COV		89	D6
TERRY HILL PL	LA	LA49	11600	41	C2
TERRYKNOLL DR	CO	WHI	14200	61	F3
TERRYKNOLL DR	CO	WHI	14600	84	A4
TERRY LYN LN	CER	ART	17400	82	C5
TERRY LYNN AV	CO	LPUE		85	C3
TERRYLYNN CIR	LB	LB07		70	B4
TERRY LYNN PL	LB	LB07	600	70	B4
TERRYVIEW AV	POM	POM	800	91	A6
TERRYVIEW DR	LA	NHO	10900	23	E5
TERZILLA PL	LA	LA65	3200	25	E5
TESLA AV	LA	LA39	2700	35	B3
TESLA TER	LA	LA39	2400	35	B3
TESLA WK	LA	LA39	2800	35	B3
TESORO LN	PALM	PALM		171	F4
TESORO LN	PALM	PALM		171	G5
TETLEY ST	CO	LPUE	15400	85	D3
TETON DR	CO	LPUE	14500	85	C3
TETON ST	GAR	GAR	1100	63	F1
TEVIOT ST	LA	LA39	2300	35	C3
TEVIS AV	LB	LB08	3000	71	D6
TEVIS AV	LB	LB15	1800	76	D2
TEXACO AV	PAR	PAR	14300	65	E2
TEXANIO TR	LA	CAN	24100	5	D1
TEXAS AV	LA	LA25	11600	41	C4
TEXAS RD	CO	CAST		123	G3
TEXAS ST	DOW	DOW	8300	60	B4
TEXAS ST	POM	POM	400	94	E2
TEXAS TR	CO	TOP	1700	109	D1
TEXAS OIL CO RD	CO	CAST		123	F4
TEXCOCO ST	MTB	MTB		46	D6
TEXHOMA AV	LA	ENC	5900	14	D6
TEXHOMA AV	LA	ENC	4800	21	D2
TEXHOMA AV	LA	NOR	9300	7	D4
TEXHOMA AV	LA	NOR	7600	14	D2
TEXHOMA AV	LA	VAN	6800	14	D4
THACKERY AV	WCOV	WCOV	1300	92	C2
THACKERY ST	WCOV	WCOV	1000	92	B2
THAMES CT	PALM	PALM		171	H8
THAMES CT	SAD	SAD		89	D4
THAMES PL	LA	LA46	2500	33	E1
THAMES ST	LA	LA46	2500	33	E1
THATCHER AV	LA	VEN	2900	49	D4
THAXTON AV	CO	LPUE	3200	85	E4
THAYER AV	LA	LA24	600	41	F2
THAYER AV	LA	LA25	1800	41	F2
THE COLONADE	LB	LB03	1	80	C1
THEIS AV	CO	WHI	10700	61	F4
THELBORN ST	CO	COV	17800	88	F6
THELBORN ST	COV	COV	600	88	D6
THELBORN ST E	WCOV	WCOV	1000	88	C6
THELBORN ST W	WCOV	WCOV	1000	88	A6
THELEN RD	CO	SAU		181	B6
THELMA AV	LA	LA32	2100	36	D6
THELMA LN	CO	LPUE		97	B5
THELMA ST	CO	GL14	3100	11	D6
THELMA ST	GLEN	GL14	3200	11	D6
THELMA ST	LA	SV	10100	9	E3
THE MALL	LA	LA23	2800	45	A6
THE MIDWAY	GLEN	GL08	1500	25	F1
THEO AV	TOR	TOR	4800	67	F6
THEODORA DR	CO	COV	2800	93	B1
THEODORE CT	CO	SAU		124	D4
THEODORE CT	PALM	LAN		171	A1
THE OLD RD	CO	CAST		123	G2
THE OLD RD	CO	NEW		127	C7
THE OLD RD	CO	SAU		123	F6
THE OLD RD	CO	VAL		126	H1
THE OVERVIEW	CO	MAL		112	D5
THE PASEO	LA	LA65	3300	35	E2
THE PIKE	LB	LB02		75	C6
THE PLAZA	NWK	NWK	14100	82	A2
THE PROMENADE	SM	SM	1100	49	A2
THERESA LN	SMAD	SMAD		28	D1
THERESA ST	LA	LA65	200	36	A4
THERESA ST	LB	LB14	2800	75	F5
THERMAL DR	LAM	LAM	11600	84	A5
THERMO ST	LA	LA66	12000	49	E1
THE STRAND	HB	RB	1300	62	C6
THE STRAND	HB	RB	100	67	C1
THE STRAND	MB	MB	3900	62	A2
THE STRAND	MB	MB	100	62	A4
THE TOLEDO	LB	LB03	5000	76	B6
THE TOLEDO ST	LB	LB03	5400	80	C1
THE VISTA	LA	LA49		32	A3
THE WYE	ELM	ELM	11800	39	A4
THICKET DR	CO	LPUE	16200	92	B4
THIENES AV	CO	ELM	11300	47	D3
THIENES AV	SELM	ELM	10400	47	D3
THISBE CT	PALM	PALM		172	H9
THISBE CT	PALM	PALM		183	H1
THISTLE AV	NWK	NWK	13100	82	B1
THISTLE AV	PALM	PALM		183	E2
THISTLE CT	SCLR	NEW		127	B6
THISTLE ST	LAN	LAN		160	B1
THISTLEWOOD WY	RPV	SP	28600	78	E1
THOMAS AV	PALM	PALM		183	F2
THOMAS AV	RB	RB	2400	62	F4
THOMAS PL	NWK	NWK		60	F5
THOMAS PL	WCOV	WCOV		92	E6
THOMAS RD	CO	SAU		181	J6
THOMAS ST	LA	LA31		36	B6
THOMAS ST	LA	LA31	2200	45	B1
THOMAS ST N	POM	POM	200	94	E3
THOMAS ST S	POM	POM	100	94	E3
THOMAS PAYNE LN	PALM	PALM		183	D2
THOMICIA PL	LA	WOH	5700	5	E6
THOMPSON AL	PAS	PAS	2700	27	F4
THOMPSON AV	GLEN	GL01	1300	18	A6
THOMPSON AV	GLEN	GL01	200	24	E2
THOMPSON CT	CO	MONT	2000	18	F3
THOMPSON CT	GLEN	MONT	2000	18	F3
THOMPSON DR	PAS	PAS	500	27	B2
THOMPSON RD	CO	CHA		4	C5
THOMPSON ST	LB	LB05	2400	65	F4
THOMPSON WK	CO	CAST		123	B6
THOMPSON CREEK	POM	POM		90	E2
THOMPSON CK RD	POM	POM		90	E4
THOREAU ST	CO	LA47	1800	57	D4
THOREAU ST	ING	IN03	2300	57	C4
THORLEY CT	SCLR	CYN		124	H6
THORLEY PL	PVE	PVP	2100	72	A5
THORLEY RD	PVE	PVP	2100	72	A4
THORNBURGH AV	TOR	TOR	16800	63	B5
THORNBURGH PL	TOR	TOR	3900	63	B5
THORNBURN ST	LA	LA45	5200	50	D5
THORNBUSH AV	CO	LAN	42000	171	A1
THORNCREST DR	GLEN	GL07	1700	25	D1
THORNCROFT WY	ING	IN01		57	B2
THORNDALE RD	CO	PAS	3300	28	A4
THORNDIKE RD	PAS	PAS	2700	27	F5
THORNE RD	LA	LA41		26	A6
THORNE ST	LA	LA42	200	36	D2
THORNEWOOD DR	SCLR	NEW		127	B6
THORNHILL RD	CO	CAL		108	A5
THORNHURST AV	GLDR	GLDR	300	87	D4
THORNLAKE AV	ART	ART	17400	82	B6
THORNLAKE AV	CER	ART		81	B2
THORNLAKE AV	CO	WHI	6800	55	C5
THORNLAKE AV	CO	WHI	8100	61	B1
THORNLAKE AV	LB	LB08		81	B6
THORNLAKE AV	LKD	LKD	20300	81	B3
THORNLAKE AV	NWK	NWK	14600	82	B3
THORNTON AV	BUR	BUR	2300	17	B4
THORNTON AV	LA	VEN	1	49	B4
THORNTON CT	LA	VEN	15	49	B4
THORNTON PL	LA	VEN	100	49	B4
THORNTON ST	LA	LA63	1000	45	C3
THORNWOOD AV	LAN	LAN	45400	159	J3
THORNWOOD ST	GLEN	GL06		26	C2
THORNY LN	LAV	LAV		95A	D5
THOROUGHBRED WY	CO	LPUE		47	F5
THORPE AV	LA	LA65	2600	35	F4
THORSON AV	CO	COM	11800	65	B3
THORSON AV	LYN	LYN	11800	59	C5
THORSON AV	LYN	LYN	11200	65	B2
THORSON AV N	COM	COM	700	65	B3
THORSON AV S	COM	COM	100	65	B3
THOUSAND OKS BL	AGH	AGO		100A	B3
THOUSAND OKS BL	AGH	AGO		102	E3
THOUSAND OKS BL	CO	CAL	26000	100	A2
THOUSAND OKS BL	CO	CAL		100A	F2
THOUSAND OKS BL	WLVL	THO	30400	102	C3
THOUSAND OKS DR	LA	TU	7500	10	E3
THRACE DR	CO	WHI	11200	84	A5
THRASHER AV	LA	LA69	8800	33	D3
THREE PALMS ST	CO	LPUE	15400	85	E2
THREE RANCH RD	DUA	DUA	1000	29	D5
THREE SPGS DR	WLVL	THO		102A	E5
THRIFT RD	CO	MAL		106	B4
THROOP AL	SPAS	SPAS	700	36	F1
THRUSH CT	LAV	LAV		95A	D5
THRUSH WY	LA	LA69	9200	33	D3
THRUST DR	CO	WAL		97	C4
THUNDER TR	DBAR	POM		97A	B2
THUNDERBIRD AV	LA	NOR	11700	1	A5
THURBER PL	BUR	BUR	1000	18	A5
THURBER PL	GLEN	GL01	1600	18	A5
THURIN AV	CO	ALT	3000	19	F4
THURLENE RD	GLEN	GL06	1400	26	A1
THURLOW ST	MTB	MTB	500	54	C2
THURMAN AV	LA	LA16	1900	42	E4
THURMAN AV	LA	LA19	1800	42	E4
THURSTON AV N	LA	LA49	100	32	C6
THURSTON AV S	LA	LA49	100	32	C6
THURSTON CIR	LA	LA49	11300	32	C6
THURSTON PL	LA	LA49	11300	32	C6
THYME PL	RPV	PVP	1	77	E2
THYNNE ST	MTB	MTB	500	54	C2
TIANNA RD	LA	LA46		33	E1
TIARA CT	SCLR	CYN		125	C7
TIARA ST	LA	ENC	16800	14	E6
TIARA ST	LA	NHO	10400	16	D6
TIARA ST	LA	VAN	13400	15	F6
TIARA ST	LA	WOH	23500	5	E6
TIARA ST	LA	WOH	20300	12	D6
TIBANA ST	LB	LB08	7400	81	A5
TIBBETTS ST	LA	SF	12400	3	B2
TIBURON CT	CO	LPUE		98	D4
TIBURON CT	MB	MB		62	D2
TICA DR	LA	LA27	3300	35	A1
TICATICA DR	CO	LPUE	2600	85	E4
TICHENOR E	COM	COM	1100	65	B4
TICHENOR ST E	COM	COM	100	64	F4
TICHENOR ST W	COM	COM	100	64	F4
TICK CANYON RD	CO	SAU		125	G4
TICONDEROGA RD	CO	WOH		13	A4
TIDAL TR	CO	TOP	1300	109	B2
TIDE DR	SCLR	VAL		127	A2
TIDWELL AV	CO	WHI	11500	84	C5
TIERNAN AV	LA	SF		3	C6
TIERRA DR	SCLR	VAL		124	B6
TIERRA ALTA DR	CO	PAS	1300	27	D1
TIERRA ALTA DR	PAS	PAS	1000	27	D2
TIERRA ANTIGUA	WHI	WHI		55	C2
TIERRA BLNCA DR	WHI	WHI	9400	84	C2
TIERRA BONIT DR	WHI	WHI		55	E2
TIERRA CIMA	CO	WAL		97	B3
TIERRA ENCANTA	WHI	WHI		55	E2
TIERRA GRNAD DR	WHI	WHI		55	E2
TIERRA LOMA DR	DBAR	POM	1800	97	E4
TIERRA LUNA	CO	WAL		97	B3
TIERRA MAJOR DR	WHI	WHI		55	E2
TIERRA MONTE DR	WHI	WHI		55	E2
TIERRA NAVAR DR	WHI	WHI		55	E2
TIERRA SIESTA	CO	WAL		97	B3
TIERRA SUBIDA	PALM	PALM		172	A9
TIERRA SUBDA AV	CO	PALM	37800	172	A9
TIERRA SUBDA AV	CO	PALM		183	A2
TIFAL AV	IRW	BAP	2400	39	C1
TIFFANY AV	SF	SF	600	2	E6
TIFFANY CIR	LA	LA77		22	E6
TIFFANY CIR	PALM	PALM		172	G9
TIFFANY CT	CO	AGO		100A	D6
TIFFANY CT	TOR	TOR		68	A5
TIFFANY LN	SCLR	CYN		125	A9
TIFFANY LN	TOR	TOR	3600	68	A5
TIFFANY LN	WCOV	WCOV		97	A2
TIFFANY TER	ARC	ARC	700	28	F6
TIFFIN WY	CLA	CLA		91	B3
TIGER TR	CO	TOP	1700	109	D1
TIGERTAIL CT	PALM	PALM		171	J8
TIGERTAIL RD	LA	LA49	500	32	A5
TIGERTAIL RD	LA	LA49	100	41	B2
TIGRINA AV	CO	WHI	11500	84	D6
TIGRINA AV	LAM	LAM	12600	84	D6
TIGRINA AV	WHI	WHI	10100	84	D3
TIKI WK	LB	LB05	100	65	C5
TIKITA PL	LA	NHO	10000	24	A4
TILBURY DR	PALM	PALM		171	F5
TILBURY DR	PALM	PALM		171	F6
TILBURY ST	HG	LKD	12000	81	B4
TILBURY ST	LKD	LKD	5500	71	D4
TILBURY ST	LKD	LKD	12300	81	B4
TILDEN AV	CUL	CUL	3800	50	A1
TILDEN AV	LA	LA34	3200	42	A6
TILDEN AV	LA	LA34	3500	50	A1
TILDEN AV	LA	LA49	200	32	D6
TILDEN AV	LA	LA64	2500	41	F5
TILDEN AV	LA	VAN	8500	8	D6
TILDEN AV	LA	VAN	5600	15	D6
TILDEN AV	LA	VAN	4600	22	D2
TILE AV	LB	LB02	300	75	E5
TILE ST	PR	PR	9100	55	A2
TILFORD CT	LA	SF	17400	1	E5
TILLIE CT	WCOV	WCOV		92	D6
TILLIE ST	LA	LA65	3000	35	E3
TILLMAN AV	CAR	CAR	19000	69	C1
TILMONT AV	PR	PR	8700	54	F1
TILMONT AV	PR	PR	8700	55	A1
TILMONT ST	PR	PR	9300	55	A1
TIM AV	CO	LA32	1700	45	D2
TIMBER LN	WCOV	WCOV		98	F1

1990 LOS ANGELES COUNTY STREET INDEX

STREET	CITY	P.O. ZONE	BLOCK	PAGE	GRID
TIMBER PL	CO	CAST		123	G2
TIMBERCREEK LN	CER	ART	12400	82	B4
TIMBERHILL LN	CER	ART		82	C4
TIMBERLAKE DR	CO	GL14		11	E5
TIMBERLAKE TER	CUL	CUL		50	D2
TIMBERLAND LN	WAL	WAL		93	D5
TIMBERLANE ST	AGH	AGO		100A	A1
TIMBERLINE LN	DBAR	WAL		97	C5
TIMBERRIDGE CT	WLVL	THO		102A	F5
TIMBER RIDGE DR	LA	SF		1	F2
TIMBER RIDGE LN	WAL	WAL		93	C3
TIMBERTOP LN	DBAR	POM		97	F4
TIMMONS TR	LA	LA68	6400	34	C2
TIMMS WY	LA	SP		79	B4
TIMON LN	SCLR	NEW		127	C5
TIMOR ST	LB	LB08	7400	81	A5
TIMOTHY AV	RB	RB	2800	62	E4
TIMOTHY CT	LAN	LAN		160	E4
TIMOTHY DR	SCLR	SAU		124	G5
TIMPANGOS DR	CO	CAL		108	A5
TIN DR	DBAR	POM		97A	A1
TINA CT	LAN	LAN		160	C6
TINA LN	WCOV	WCOV		92	C4
TINA PL	LA	TAR	19000	21	B3
TINA ST	NWK	NWK	11400	60	F5
TINA ST	NWK	NWK	11700	61	A5
TINAJA RD	CO	AGO		106	B1
TINDALL AV	CO	ACT		189	J1
TINDALO RD	ARC	ARC	800	28	E3
TINER CT	CO	MAL		113	E4
TINKER AV	LA	TU	10200	10	E3
TINKER ST	WCOV	WCOV		98	E1
TINTAH DR	DBAR	POM		97	E3
TIOGA DR	DBAR	POM		97	F1
TIOGA PL	LA	CAN	22000	6	B6
TIONE RD	LA	LA77	900	32	D4
TIPICO ST	LA	CHA	20000	6	F3
TIPTON TER	LA	LA42	700	26	C6
TIPTON WY	LA	LA42	5800	26	C6
TITAN CT	PALM	PALM		183	G1
TITIAN AV	LA	SF	12800	1	E3
TITLEY AV	PAS	PAS	100	27	F3
TITUS AV	POM	POM	1900	94	F5
TITUS ST	LA	VAN	14400	15	D1
TIVERTON AV	LA	LA24	900	41	E2
TIVERTON CT	SAD	SAD		89	D4
TIVOLI AV	CUL	LA66	3900	49	E3
TIVOLI AV	LA	LA66	3900	49	E3
TIVOLI DR	LB	LB03	100	80	C1
TOBERMAN ST	LA	LA07	1900	44	A4
TOBERMAN ST	LA	LA15	1300	44	A4
TOBIAH PL	CO	CAST		123	G2
TOBIAS AV	LA	VAN	8500	8	D6
TOBIAS AV	LA	VAN	5600	15	D1
TOBIAS AV	LA	VAN	4400	22	D3
TOBIAS AV	PR	PR	4100	55	B2
TOBIN WY	LA	VAN	15800	22	B5
TOBIRA DR	PALM	PALM		183	F2
TOBRUK CT	LB	LB03		76	D6
TOBY PL	POM	POM		94	F2
TOCALOMA LN	LCF	LCF	4800	19	A2
TOCINO DR	DUA	DUA	300	86	A4
TODD AV	AZU	AZU	700	86	B5
TODD AV	CMRC	LA22	3600	54	C5
TODD CT	LA	NHO	12200	16	C2
TODD PL	LAV	LAV		90	D1
TODD PL	MTB	MTB	1400	46	D5
TODD VIEW CT	LA	CAN		4	A6
TOERGE DR	LAM	LAM	11500	84	B5
TOKAY RD	LA	TU	6400	11	B3
TOKEN ST	LB	LB08	8100	81	B5
TOLA AV	CO	ALT	2700	19	E4
TOLA ST	MTB	MTB	800	54	C4
TOLAND AV	LA	LA45	7700	56	E1
TOLAND AV	WCOV	WCOV	100	88	C6
TOLAND PL	LA	LA41	4300	35	F1
TOLAND WY	LA	LA41	4300	35	F1
TOLAND WY	LA	LA41	4400	36	A1
TOLAND WY	LA	LA42	4700	36	A1
TOLAND WY	LA	LA65	3700	35	F1
TOLANI CT	DBAR	POM		97	E3
TOLBERT AV	LB	LB07	4500	70	C3
TOLEDO CT	LA	VEN	200	49	C4
TOLEDO DR	GLEN	GL07	1400	25	E1
TOLEDO ST	LA	LA42	400	36	C1
TOLEDO WK	LB	LB13	700	75	D5
TOLENAS DR	LA	NHO	12500	23	B5
TOLER AV	BG	BELL	6500	53	F6
TOLIMA DR	SCLR	CYN	27700	124	H5
TOLL DR	CO	RM	7200	46	D3
TOLLHOUSE CT	RPV	SP		78	E1
TOLLY ST	BLF	BLF	9500	66	C1
TOLLY ST	NWK	NWK	10600	66	E2
TOLMAN DR	CO	WHI	15000	84	B4
TOLMIE AV	CMRC	LA40	1500	54	B2
TOLTEC DR	LA	CHA		6	D1

STREET	CITY	P.O. ZONE	BLOCK	PAGE	GRID
TOLTEC WY	LA	LA42	6000	36	D2
TOLUCA AV	POM	POM	500	90	F5
TOLUCA AV	TOR	TOR	20300	67	E3
TOLUCA AV	WCOV	WCOV		92	A1
TOLUCA RD	LA	NHO	4200	23	F4
TOLUCA ST N	LA	LA26	100	44	C2
TOLUCA ST S	LA	LA26	100	44	C2
TOLUCA ESTS DR	LA	NHO	4100	23	F4
TOLUCA LAKE AV	BUR	BUR	4100	24	B4
TOLUCA LAKE AV	LA	NHO	9900	24	A4
TOLUCA LAKE LN	BUR	BUR	4200	24	A4
TOLUCA PARK DR	BUR	BUR	500	24	A2
TOMAHAWK LN	CAR	CAR		69	E6
TOMAHAWK LN	NWK	NWK	12700	61	C6
TOMAHAWK LN	NWK	NWK	12700	82	C1
TOMAHAWK PL	LAN	LAN		159	D6
TOMAHAWK TR	LA	CAN	8400	4	A5
TOMAS CT	CO	LPUE		98	D4
TOMBUR DR	CO	LPUE		98	B4
TOMICH RD	CO	LPUE		98	B4
TOM LEE AV	TOR	TOR	19200	67	E2
TOMLINSON RD	CO	TOR	22800	68	E6
TOMPKINS WY	CO	CUL	1	42	D6
TOM WHITE WY	NWK	NWK	13000	82	C2
TONALEA DR	CO	PALM		157	F9
TONAWANDA AV	LA	LA41	1500	26	A6
TONDOLEA LN	LCF	LCF	1900	18	F2
TONI DR	WCOV	WCOV	3000	93	A1
TONIA AV	CO	ALT	3200	20	A3
TONIBAR ST	NWK	NWK	10700	66	E2
TONNER DR	POM	POM	700	90	D6
TONNER CYN RD	CO	BREA		99	E4
TONONI AV	GLEN	GL02		25	B2
TONOPAH AV	CO	LPUE	900	48	E3
TONOPAH AV	LPUE	LPUE	300	48	D4
TONOPAH AV	WCOV	WCOV	1500	48	E3
TONOPAH ST	LA	PAC	12900	9	A6
TONOPAH ST	LA	VAN	13300	16	A1
TONTO CIR	WAL	WAL		93	A4
TONY AV	LA	CAN	6400	5	E5
TONY AV	LA	WOH	6100	5	E5
TOOLEN PL	PAS	PAS		19	E6
TOOMEY PL	LA	HAC	1300	73	E1
TOP CIR	LAN	LAN		159	H6
TOP CT	DBAR	POM		94	B6
TOPACIO DR	MPK	MPK		45	F2
TOPANGA BCH DR	CO	MAL	18600	115	E4
TOPANGA CYN BL	CO	CHA	11000	6	C3
TOPANGA CYN BL	CO	TOP		13	C5
TOPANGA CYN BL	CO	TOP	100	109	C5
TOPANGA CYN BL	LA	CAN	8500	6	C3
TOPANGA CYN BL	LA	CAN	6400	12	C5
TOPANGA CYN BL	LA	CHA	9100	6	C3
TOPANGA CYN BL	LA	PP		115	D1
TOPANGA CYN BL	LA	WOH	5600	12	C5
TOPANGA CYN BL	LA	WOH	4400	13	C4
TOPANGA CYN LN	CO	MAL	3400	115	E4
TOPANGA CYN PL	LA	CHA	9500	6	C4
TOPANGA CYN PL	LA	WOH	5800	12	C6
TPNGA FIRE RD E	LA	PP		109	E5
TPNGA FIRE TT E	LA	PP		109	E4
TOPANGA RDG MTY	CO	TOP		108	E5
TOPANGA SCHL RD	CO	TOP	22000	109	D4
TOPANGA SKLN DR	CO	TOP	1500	109	A2
TOPAZ CT	LB	LB02		75	B5
TOPAZ LN	LAN	LAN		160	F5
TOPAZ LN	LAV	LAV		90	D2
TOPAZ PL	ARC	ARC	300	28	F1
TOPAZ ST	LA	LA32	4400	36	C5
TOPAZ ST	RB	RB	100	67	D4
TOPAZ WY	POM	POM	1800	94	F4
TOPAZ WY	POM	POM	1800	95	A4
TOPE AV	SOG	SOG	8900	58	F2
TOPEKA DR	LA	NOR	9700	7	B4
TOPEKA DR	LA	NOR	8300	14	B1
TOPEKA DR	LA	RES	6100	14	B6
TOPEKA DR	LA	TAR	5700	14	B6
TOPEKA DR	LA	TAR	4800	21	B2
TOPEKA ST	PAS	PAS	900	20	C6
TOPEKA ST	PAS	PAS	900	27	C1
TOPHAM ST	LA	CAN	20000	12	E5
TOPHAM ST	LA	ENC	17700	14	B6
TOPHAM ST	LA	RES	17900	14	B6
TOPHAM ST	LA	TAR	18100	14	B6
TOPHAM ST	LA	WOH	19700	12	F5
TOPIA ST	LB	LB08	7400	81	A5
TOPLEY LN	LA	SUN	7900	10	E3
TOPLEY LN	LA	TU	7500	10	F3
TOPMOST TR	CO	TOP	500	109	E4
TOPOCHICO DR	LA	WOH	21000	13	D3
TOPOCK ST	GLEN	GL04	1800	35	C1
TOPOCK ST	LA	LA39	3400	35	C1
TOPPINGTON DR	LA	BH		22	F6
TOPRAIL LN	RPV	PVP	29000	78	C1
TOPSAIL CT	LA	VEN		49	D6
TOPSAIL ST	LA	VEN		49	C6

STREET	CITY	P.O. ZONE	BLOCK	PAGE	GRID
TOPSFIELD ST	CO	PAS	2600	27	E4
TOPSFIELD ST	PAS	PAS	2600	27	E4
TOP SIDE CT	LB	LB03		80	F1
TOPSIDE PL	DBAR	POM		94	B6
TOQUET DR	LA	ENC	17300	21	E3
TORCH ST	BAP	BAP	12700	48	B1
TORCH ST	LA	WOH	24200	5	D6
TORCHWOOD PL	WLVL	THO		102A	E6
TORCIDA DR	LCF	LCF	1600	19	A2
TORIN ST	LB	LB08	7400	81	B5
TORINO PL	POM	POM		94	C4
TORINO ST	MTB	MTB		46	D5
TORITO LN	DBAR	POM	900	94	A6
TORO DR	CO	LPUE	2400	98	C5
TORRANCE BLVD	CO	TOR	600	68	F3
TORRANCE BLVD	LA	TOR	1400	68	D3
TORRANCE BLVD	RB	RB	100	67	F4
TORRANCE BLVD	TOR	TOR	4200	67	F4
TORRANCE BLVD	TOR	TOR	1700	68	B4
TORRANCE BLVD E	CAR	CAR	100	69	A3
TORRANCE BLVD W	CAR	CAR	100	69	A3
TORRANCE PL	LA	TOR	1300	68	E3
TORREON DR	LA	WOH	4200	13	C4
TORREON PL	LA	WOH	4100	13	C4
TORREPINES PL	AGH	AGO		102	E3
TORRES DR	GLEN	GL07	1300	25	E1
TORREY CIR	BAP	BAP	3700	39	C6
TORREY ST	BAP	BAP	3800	39	C5
TORREY PINES DR	SCLR	NEW	26400	127	H4
TORREYSON DR	LA	LA46	7700	23	E6
TORREYSON PL	LA	LA46		23	E6
TORRINGTON ST	PALM	PALM		183	E1
TORTOSA AV	CO	LPUE	2400	98	E6
TORTUGA ST	CO	ACT		189	J1
TORTUOSO WY	LA	LA77	700	32	E4
TORY ST	WCOV	WCOV		92	D6
TOSCA RD	LA	WOH	4200	13	D4
TOSCANINI DR	RPV	SP	1400	78	D1
TOSCANY CT	PALM	PALM		183	H2
TOSSANO DR	SCLR	VAL		127	A1
TOTANA DR	LA	TAR		21	A3
TOTH PL	AGH	AGO		100A	B3
TOTHILL DR	SCLR	SAU		124	E4
TOTTENHAM CT	LA	BH		32	F1
TOUCAN ST	TOR	TOR	4400	68	A2
TOUCHWOOD AV	BLF	BLF	14900	66	B3
TOULON DR	LA	PP	800	40	E3
TOURELLE PL	CO	VAL		126	J2
TOURMALINE ST	LA	LA32	4300	36	C5
TOURNAMENT RD	SCLR	VAL		127	A3
TOURNEY RD	CO	SAU		123	H8
TOVEY AV	CO	PALM	34800	183	A3
TOWER DR	BH	BH	100	42	E1
TOWER LN	LA	BH		33	A4
TOWER RD	BH	BH	1100	33	A4
TOWER GROVE DR	LA	BH		32	F3
TOWER GROVE DR	LA	BH	1100	33	A3
TOWER GROVE PL	LA	BH	9800	33	A4
TOWERS ST	TOR	TOR	4600	67	E2
TOWHEE DR	CO	CAL		13	A4
TOWN AV	MPK	MPK		46	D3
TOWN & CNTRY RD	POM	POM		94	D6
TOWN CENTER DR	MTB	MTB		46	F5
TOWN CENTER DR	PALM	PALM		171	E5
TOWN CRIER RD	CO	WOH	22600	13	A4
TOWNE AV	CAR	CAR	18200	64	B6
TOWNE AV	CAR	CAR	18600	69	B1
TOWNE AV	CLA	CLA	1300	91	A4
TOWNE AV	CO	CLA	2900	91	A4
TOWNE AV	CO	LA61	12800	64	B1
TOWNE AV	LA	LA03	5800	52	B4
TOWNE AV	LA	LA03	7800	58	B1
TOWNE AV	LA	LA11	4400	52	B4
TOWNE AV	LA	LA13	300	44	D5
TOWNE AV	LA	LA21	600	44	D5
TOWNE AV	LA	LA61	10700	58	B4
TOWNE AV N	POM	POM	1400	90	F5
TOWNE AV N	POM	POM	2500	91	A4
TOWNE AV N	POM	POM	100	94	F4
TOWNE AV S	POM	POM	100	94	F4
TOWNE AV S	POM	POM	2800	97A	F1
TOWNE CT	CAR	CAR	17300	64	B5
TOWNE ST	GLEN	GL08	1700	25	F1
TOWNE CENTER DR	CER	ART		82	C6
TOWNE CENTER DR	LAV	LAV		90	E2
TOWNE PARK CIR	POM	POM		90	F3
TOWNE WAY DR	ELM	ELM	9800	47	C1
TOWNLEY DR	CO	WHI	10400	55	B4
TOWNLEY DR	PR	PR	8600	54	F3
TOWNLEY DR	PR	PR	9300	55	A4
TOWNSEND AV	LA	LA41	4700	26	B4
TOWNSEND AV N	CO	LA63	100	45	C4
TOWNSEND AV S	CO	LA23	800	45	C6
TOWNSEND AV S	CO	LA23	1200	53	C1
TOWNSEND AV S	CO	LA63	100	45	C4
TOWNSEND PL	PAS	PAS	200	27	A3

STREET	CITY	P.O. ZONE	BLOCK	PAGE	GRID
TOWNSITE DR	WCOV	WCOV	3200	97	A1
TOWSLEY CYN RD	CO	NEW		126	H7
TOYON	WCOV	WCOV		98	F1
TOYON CIR	LAV	LAV		90	D1
TOYON LN	CO	POM		93	E2
TOYON LN	CO	TOP	20000	109	C6
TOYON LN	CO	TOP	20000	115	C1
TOYON RD	SMAD	SMAD	200	28	C1
TOYOPA DR	LA	PP	200	40	D4
TRABUCO PL	POM	POM		94	B5
TRABUCO ST	BLF	BLF	10200	66	D3
TRACTION AV	LA	LA13	500	44	E3
TRACY CT	SCLR	CYN		124	G9
TRACY ST	BAP	BAP	13100	39	C6
TRACY ST	BAP	BAP	13200	48	C1
TRACY ST	LA	LA27	3700	35	A2
TRACY ST	LA	LA39	3600	35	B2
TRACY TER	LA	LA27	2200	35	B3
TRADEPOST RD	CO	ACT		182	J9
TRAFALGAR AV	CO	LPUE	300	98	E2
TRAFALGER DR	GLEN	GL07		25	E1
TRAFFORD ST	LB	LB05	1	65	B6
TRAGNIEW LN	LA	CAN	23650	5	E2
TRAIL RD	CO	SAU		188	B2
TRAIL CREEK DR	AGH	AGO		102	E3
TRAILER CYN DR	LA	PP		109	E5
TRAILER CY F RD	LA	PP		30	A5
TRAIL RANCH RD	CO	SAU		181	B8
TRAILRIDER DR	RPV	PVP	28200	72	C5
TRAIL RIDGE CIR	POM	POM		94	D4
TRAIL RIDGE RD	CO	CYN		128	D1
TRAILS END DR	CO	CHA		4	C5
TRAILS END RD	WAL	WAL		93	B5
TRAILSIDE DR	CO	LPUE		48	B5
TRAILWAY LN	AGH	AGO		102	F3
TRAIL 1	CO	SF		3	D4
TRAIL 2	CO	SF		3	D4
TRAIL 3	CO	SF		3	D4
TRAIL 4	CO	SF		3	D4
TRAIL 5	CO	SF		3	D4
TRAIL 6	CO	SF		3	D4
TRAIL 7	CO	SF		3	D4
TRAIL 8	CO	SF		3	D4
TRAIL 9	CO	SF		3	D4
TRAIL 10	CO	SF		3	D4
TRAIL 11	CO	SF		3	D4
TRAIL 12	CO	SF		3	D4
TRAIL 13	CO	SF		3	D4
TRAIL 14	CO	SF		3	D4
TRAIL 15	CO	SF		3	D4
TRAIL 16	CO	SF		3	D4
TRAIL 17	CO	SF		3	D4
TRAIL 18	CO	SF		3	D4
TRAIL 19	CO	SF		3	D4
TRAIL 20	CO	SF		3	D4
TRAIL 21	CO	SF		3	D4
TRAMMELL RD	GLEN	GL06	2600	26	B2
TRAMONTO DR	LA	PP	17300	40	A4
TRAMONTO DR	LA	PP	17900	115	F4
TRANA CIR	CO	CAL		100	A2
TRANBARGER ST	CO	LPUE	19000	98	F3
TRANCAS PL	LA	TAR	4400	21	B3
TRANCAS CYN RD	CO	MAL	6300	111	E4
TRANE RD	CO	SAU		181	G7
TRANQUIL DR	LA	TU	7200	10	F5
TRANQUIL PL	LA	TU	7200	10	F5
TRANQUILITY CT	LAN	LAN		160	F6
TRANQUILLO RD	LA	PP	200	115	F4
TRANSIT AV	POM	POM	1200	95	A3
TRASK AV	LA	VEN	7000	55A	E2
TRAUB AV	CO	LA59	13200	64	C1
TRAVELER CIR	WAL	WAL		93	A4
TRAVERS AV	CMRC	LA40	2400	54	A3
TRAVIS AV	CMRC	LA22	3500	54	C5
TRAVIS LN	CO	PVP	27100	73	A4
TRAVIS ST	LA	LA49	900	32	B6
TRAVIS PAUL DR	LAN	LAN		159	B9
TRAYER AV	GLDR	GLDR	300	87	A5
TRAYMORE AV	CO	AZU	6100	86	F6
TRAYMORE AV	CO	AZU	5600	88	F1
TRAYMORE AV	CO	COV	4800	88	F2
TRAYMORE AV	COV	COV	400	88	F4
TREADWELL ST	LA	LA65	3000	35	D1
TREANOR AV	CO	COV	5000	89	C3
TREANOR AV	SAD	SAD	700	89	D4
TREANOR AV N	GLDR	GLDR	300	87	C4
TREANOR AV S	GLDR	GLDR	100	87	C6
TREANOR AV S	GLDR	GLDR	1400	89	C2
TREASURE TR	LA	LA68	6800	24	A6
TREASURE IS DR	LB	LB03	5500	80	C1
TREASURE IS LN	LB	LB03	5500	80	C1
TREASURE VISTA	SCLR	NEW		127	C5
TREBERT PL	LA	TU	9400	11	B5
TREE LN	POM	POM		90	C6
TREE LN	POM	POM		94	B3
TREEFERN DR	DUA	DUA	2900	86	A4

STREET	CITY	P.O. ZONE	BLOCK	PAGE	GRID
TREE HOLLW GLEN	AGH	AGO		102	F4
TREELANE AV	CO	ARC	2600	39	A1
TREELANE AV	CO	MON	2200	29	A6
TREELANE AV	CO	MON	2400	39	A1
TREE ROSE TER	TEC	SGAB	5800	38	A2
TREETOP CIR	DBAR	POM		97	D4
TREGO PL	LA	SF	13400	2	F1
TREGO ST	LA	SF	13300	2	F1
TRELAWNEY AV	TEC	TEC	6300	38	B1
TRELLIS RD	CO	CAST	30200	123	A5
TREMAINE AV	LA	LA05	700	43	B3
TREMAINE AV	LA	LA19	900	43	B3
TREMONT AV	LB	LB14	300	76	B5
TREMONT ST	AVA	AVA	100	77	B5
TREMONT ST	LA	LA33	1000	45	B2
TREMONT ST E	PAS	PAS	1	20	A6
TREMONT ST W	PAS	PAS	1	19	F6
TREND CT	DBAR	WAL		97	C3
TREND TER	GLEN	GL14	4900	11	C5
TRENMAR DR	CO	SAU		182	C8
TRENT CT	LA	LA65	2700	25	F6
TRENT WY	LA	LA65	4100	25	F6
TRENTHAM AV	CER	ART	19200	81	C2
TRENTLY LN	LA	BH		33	B2
TRENTON AV	GLEN	GL06	1500	25	F3
TRENTON AV	PALM	PALM		183	J1
TRENTON CT	GLDR	GLDR	300	89	B2
TRENTON DR	BH	BH	600	42	A1
TRENTON ST	LA	LA15	1100	44	B4
TRENTON WY	WCOV	WCOV	1000	48	F3
TRESSEL WY	COV	COV		88	F4
TRESSY AV	CO	GLDR		87	E6
TRESSY AV	CO	GLDR		89	E1
TREVAN RD	PAS	PAS	3300	28	A1
TREVES DR	PAR	SOG	7100	59	D6
TREVINO DR	CO	VAL		126	J3
TREVOR AV	LAN	LAN	44400	160	B3
TREVYELON ST	CO	CAST	30000	123	C2
TRIAD DR	CO	LAM	13900	82	E2
TRIANA PL	MPK	MPK	700	46	B3
TRIANA ST	MPK	MPK	600	46	B2
TRIANGLE DR	CMRC	LA40		54	B5
TRIANGLE PL	GLEN	GL08	3300	18	F3
TRIANGLE ST	SELM	ELM	9800	47	C3
TRI BAY CIR	LKD	LKD	5200	70	E2
TRIBUNE CT	LB	LB02	10	75	C4
TRIBUNE CT	LB	LB13	1700	75	C4
TRIBUNE PL	LA	SF	17900	7	C2
TRIBUNE ST	LA	CHA	20600	6	E2
TRIBUNE ST	LA	NOR	18000	7	C2
TRIBUNE ST	LA	SF	16500	7	F2
TRIBUNE ST	LA	SF	16200	8	A2
TRICIA LN	LAM	LAM	15000	83	A3
TRICKLING CK DR	LAV	LAV		95A	D5
TRIDENT WY	LB	LB03		80	F1
TRIER AV	CO	LPUE	700	98	D1
TRIGGER LN	DBAR	POM	21200	97	D5
TRIGGER PL	LA	CHA	9700	6	A4
TRIGGER ST	LA	CHA	22700	6	A4
TRIGGS ST	CO	LA23	4100	53	D1
TRIMBLE CT	LB	LB14	300	76	B5
TRIMBLE CT	LB	LB14	4800	76	B5
TRIMINGHAM ST	CER	ART	19200	81	C2
TRINIDAD CIR	CLA	CLA		91	C1
TRINIDAD RD	LA	WOH	4000	13	D4
TRINITY DR	CO	AZU	6400	86	E6
TRINITY LN	CLA	CLA		91	D2
TRINITY ST	CO	LA61	12100	58	B6
TRINITY ST	LA	LA11	1900	44	C6
TRINITY ST	LA	LA11	3200	52	B2
TRINITY ST	LA	LA15	1600	44	C6
TRINO WY	LA	PP	200	40	B4
TRIPOLI AV	LA	SF	11600	3	D6
TRIPPETT LATRAL	CO	TOP		109	D4
TRISTAN AV	DOW	DOW	10800	60	C4
TRISTAN CT	WHI	WHI3		84	D4
TRISTAN DR	DOW	DOW	9800	60	C3
TRISTE PL	LA	TAR	4500	21	B3
TRISTIN DR	SCLR	VAL	19200	127	C2
TRITON DR	PALM	PALM		183	H1
TRITON DR	PR	PR	6400	54	E4
TRIUMPH AV	CO	CYN		128	D2
TRIUMPH ST	CMRC	LA40	5900	54	A2
TRIUNFO DR	CO	AGO		106	E2
TRIUNFO DR	CO	AGO		107	A3
TRIUNFO PL	CO	AGO		106	F3
TRIUNFO CYN RD	CO	AGO		102	C5
TRIUNFO CYN RD	CO	AGO	3000	106	C1
TRIUNFO CYN RD	WLVL	THO		102	A5
TRIUNFO CYN RD	WLVL	THO		102A	F4
TRIXIS AV	LAN	LAN		160	A2
TROJAN AV	CO	LA47		57	E5
TROJAN ST	PR	PR	8400	54	D5
TROJAN WY	LAM	LAM	15900	83	A5
TROJAN WY	POM	POM	1700	94	F5

STREET	CITY	P.O. ZONE	BLOCK	PAGE	GRID
TROJAN WY	WCOV	WCOV	1200	48	F2
TROLLEY PL	LA	VEN	6900	55A	D2
TROLLEY WY	LA	VEN	6900	55A	D2
TRONA AV	WCOV	WCOV	300	93	A1
TROON AV	LA	LA64	10400	42	A4
TROOST AV	LA	NHO	5600	16	D3
TROOST AV	LA	NHO	4000	23	D2
TROPHY TR	CO	TOP	600	109	E4
TROPICAL DR	BH	BH		32	F4
TROPICAL AV	BH	BH		33	A4
TROPICAL AV	CO	SAU	10300	84	B4
TROPICAL AV	PAS	PAS	1100	28	B2
TROPICAL DR	LA	NHO	3900	23	D5
TROPICO AV	WHI	WHI	10200	84	F2
TROPICO WY	LA	LA65	4000	35	F2
TROSA ST	LA	SF	17200		7
TROT AV	CO	LPUE		98	E3
TROTTER CT	WAL	WAL		93	D5
TROTTERS LN	CO	CAST		123	B4
TROTWOOD AV	RPV	SP	29500	78	D2
TROTWOOD AV N	LA	SP	100	78	D2
TROTWOOD AV S	LA	SP	1000	78	D2
TROUSDALE PKWY	LA	LA89		44	A6
TROUSDALE PL	BH	BH	300	33	C3
TROUTDALE DR	CO	AGO		106	E1
TROWBRIDGE CT	WLVL	THO	3900	102	B4
TROY AV N	SELM	ELM	2000	47	B3
TROY CT	CLA	CLA		91	B5
TROY DR	LA	LA68	3200	24	A5
TROYTON LN	CAR	CAR		69	C4
TRUBA AV	SOG	SOG	9200	58	F3
TRUCK WY	MTB	MTB	800	54	D2
TRUCKEY WY	WAL	WAL		92	F6
TRUDGEON AV	LAN	LAN		160	E6
TRUDI LN	BUR	BUR	3000	17	B2
TRUDIE AV	WHI	WHI	10900	84	C4
TRUDIE DR	RPV	SP	1800	78	D1
TRUDY DR	LA	BH	2900	22	F6
TRUDY PL	POM	POM	2500	94	F6
TRUE AV	DOW	DOW	9200	60	E3
TRUE AV	PR	PR	7800	60	F2
TRUE PL	DBAR	POM		97	F2
TRUEGRIT PL	DBAR	POM		97A	F2
TRUE KNOLL DR	LA	TU	9400	11	F1
TRUESDALE ST	LA	SV	11500	9	C4
TRUESDALE ST	LA	VAN	13200	16	B4
TRUITT ST	GLEN	GL01	1300	18	F2
TRUJILLO DR	CO	COV	4500	88	B4
TRULLBROOK DR	CO	SAU		13	F5
TRUMAN CT	CO	SAU		124	D4
TRUMAN DR	WCOV	WCOV	300	92	A1
TRUMAN ST	LAN	LAN		160	E8
TRUMAN ST	SF	SF	700	2	E5
TRUMBALL ST	CO	WHI	13200	61	D3
TRUMBOWER AV	MPK	MPK	1400	46	F3
TRURO AV	CO	IN04	10400	56	F4
TRURO AV	HAW	HAW	11400	56	F6
TRURO AV	HAW	HAW	13800	62	F2
TRURO AV	ING	IN01	900	56	F3
TRUSS ST	DBAR	WAL		97	C3
TRUXTON AV	LA	LA45	7600	50	C6
TRUXTON AV	LA	LA45	7900	56	C1
TRYON PL	GLEN	GL06	3500	34	D2
TRYON RD	LA	LA68	5600	34	D2
TUALLITAN RD	LA	LA49	5000	41	E3
TUBA ST	LA	CHA	20100	6	E3
TUBA ST	LA	NOR	17100	7	E3
TUBA ST	LA	SF	16500	7	F3
TUBA ST	LA	SF	14800	8	D3
TUBEWAY AV	CMRC	LA40	2000	54	A3
TUCKAWAY LN	LA	DUA	11000	29	D6
TUCKER AV	LA	SF	13800	3	B1
TUCKER LN	IND	WAL	13800	97	B2
TUCKER ST	COM	COM	300	65	A3
TUCKERWY RCH RD	CO	PALM		183	A7
TUCSON DR	SAD	SAD	800	90	A7
TUDOR DR	LA	ENC	16300	22	C4
TUDOR ST	CO	COV	16500	88	B3
TUDOR ST	CO	COV	19300	89	A3
TUDOR ST	COV	COV	1200	89	C3
TUDOR ST	SAD	SAD	1100	90	C3
TUESDAY DR	WCOV	WCOV		92	E1
TUFTS AV	BUR	BUR	400	17	B6
TUFTS CIR	WAL	WAL		93	B6
TUJUNGA AV	LA	BUR	300	17	D6
TUJUNGA AV	LA	NHO	5600	16	D3
TUJUNGA AV	LA	NHO	4000	23	D2
TUJUNGA AV	LA	SV	7800	9	D6
TUJUNGA AV	LA	SV	7800	16	D1
TUJUNGA AV	BUR	BUR	300	17	D6
TUJUNGA AV	LA	SUN	5600	10	E6
TUJUNGA CYN BL	LA	TU	10100	10	F2
TUJUNGA CYN BL	LA	TU	9100	11	B4
TUJUNGA CYN PL	LA	TU	9700	11	B4
TUJUNGA VLY ST	LA	SUN		10	D2
TULA ST	SCLR	SAU		124	C4
TULANE AV	LB	LB08	7400	81	A5
TULANE AV	LB	LB08	3400	71	C5
TULANE AV	LB	LB15	1800	76	C3
TULANE RD	CLA	CLA	1300	91	A2
TULARE AV	BUR	BUR	1500	17	B3
TULARE LN	AGH	AGO		100A	B4
TULARE PL	LB	LB02	1	75	A4
TULAROSA DR	LA	LA26	600	124	C3
TULIP CT	CO	SAU		124	C4
TULIP LN	ARC	ARC	1800	38	F1
TULIPLAND AV	CO	CYN		125	F5
TULIP TREE LN	CO	LPUE		98	D6
TULIP TREE WY	LCF	LCF	1900	18	F1
TULLER AV	LA	LA34	3800	50	B2
TULLER AV	LA	LA34	3500	50	A1
TULLER RD	LA	LA32	2200	45	E1
TULLIS DR	LA	BH	9500	33	B3
TULLOS AV W	LA	LAN	7700	146	H1
TULSA AV	CLA	CLA		8	C2
TULSA AV	LA	CHA		96	B6
TULSA LN	LA	CHA		7	D2
TULSA PL	LA	SF	17900	7	D2
TULSA ST	LA	CHA	19700	6	D2
TULSA ST	LA	NOR	18500	7	F2
TULSA ST	LA	SF	16500	7	F2
TULSA ST	LA	SF	15500	8	F2
TUMBLEWEED DR	PALM	PALM		183	J7
TUMBLEWEED RD	CO	VAL	12300	192	E6
TUMBLEWEED RD	CO	VAL	13100	192	E6
TUMBLEWEED WY	SCLR	SAU		124	E3
TUMIN RD	LHH	LAH	1900	98A	B1
TUNA ST	LA	SP	400	79	B3
TUNA CANYON RD	CO	MAL		115	C3
TUNA CANYON RD	CO	TOP		109	C6
TUNA CANYON RD	CO	TOP		115	B1
TUNBRIDGE CT	LA	LA49		32	B2
TUNDRA WY E	LAN	LAN	18500	175	D4
TUNE PL W	LAN	LAN	2400	159	C6
TUNNEY AV	LA	NOR	8500	14	A1
TUNNEY AV	LA	NOR	8300	14	A1
TUNNEY AV	LA	RES	6200	14	A5
TUOLUMNE DR	WAL	WAL		92	E6
TUPELO LN	LA	LA77	10200	32	E2
TUPELO RDG DR	SCLR	VAL		124	E3
TUPPER ST	LA	SF	16500	7	F3
TUPPER ST	LA	SF	14900	8	E3
TUPPER ST	LA	SF	14300	8	D3
TURBO ST	LB	LB08	7400	81	A5
TURK DR	LA	LPUE	16800	98	E1
TURKEY FARM RD	SCLR	SAU		124	H3
TURLOCK RD	LAM	LAM	14800	83	A4
TURMERIC ST	SCLR	SAU		124	C5
TURMONT ST	CAR	CAR	600	69	C2
TURNBERRY DR	LA	SUN	10600	10	F4
TURNBOW DR	LA	SUN		48	D6
TURNBULL CYN RD	CO	LPUE		98	E4
TURNBULL CYN RD	CO	LPUE	1000	85	C3
TURNBULL CYN RD	IND	LPUE	100	98	D6
TURNER CT	WCOV	WCOV	100	92	C1
TURNER DR	GLEN	GL08	1700	18	F3
TURNER ST	PALM	PALM		183	G2
TURNER ST	LA	LA12	400	44	E3
TURNERGROVE DR	LKD	LKD	5900	71	D2
TURNING BEND DR	CLA	CLA	1000	92	F2
TURNPOST LN	CO	LPUE	1600	98	D3
TURN POST LN	POM	POM		94	D5
TURNSTONE CT	LA	VAL		123	J9
TURNSTONE CT	CO	VAL		126	G1
TURPIN ST	RM	RM	8500	2	F6
TURQUESA DR	SCLR	VAL		124	B9
TURQUOISE DR	SCLR	VAL		124	B9
TURQUOISE LN	LAV	LAV	1200	40	B2
TURQUOISE ST	LA	LA31	4100	36	B5
TURQUOISE ST	LA	LA32	4400	36	B5
TURRELL ST	LOM	LOM	1900	73	C1
TURTLE CREEK DR	CO	CAL		108	C1
TURTLE RIDGE DR	LA	NOR		1A	F4
TURTLE RIDGE LN	LA	NOR		1A	F4
TURTLE RIDGE PL	LA	NOR		1A	F4
TURTLE SPGS CT	LA	NOR		1A	A5
TURTLE SPGS LN	LA	NOR		1A	A5
TURTLE SPGS WY	LA	NOR		1A	A5
TUSCAN CT	LA	SF	17400	7	D2
TUSCAN DR	LA	VEN	8100	55A	C2
TUSCANY AV	PAS	PAS		28	A1
TUSTIN RD	LA	VAN	14600	22	A1
TUTHILL LN	CO	SAU		181	H1
TUTTLE ST	CMRC	LA23	5000	53	D1
TUTTLE ST	CO	LA23	4400	53	D1
TUTTLE CREEK PL	WAL	WAL		92	F6
TUXEDO TER	LA	LA68	5500	34	D1
TUXFORD PL	LA	SV	10800	9	F5
TUXFORD ST	LA	SV	10400	9	D1
TUXFORD ST	LA	SV	11500	16	D1
TWEED LN	LA	LA49		41	E3
TWEEDY BLVD	LYN	LYN	3100	59	B3
TWEEDY BLVD	SOG	SOG	2500	58	F3
TWEEDY BLVD	SOG	SOG	2751	59	B3
TWEEDY LN	DOW	DOW	8500	54	D6
TWEEDY LN	DOW	DOW	9000	60	D1
TWEEDY PL	SOG	SOG	5300	59	D4
TWICKENHAM AV	CO	LA22	200	46	A5
TWILIGHT CT	PALM	PALM		183	F1
TWILIGHT LN	LA	ENC	17800	21	D3
TWILIGHT VIS DR	CO	ALT	100	20	A3
TWIN AV	RM	RM	3400	37	F6
TWIN AV	SGAB	SGAB	1100	37	F6
TWINBERRY LN	LAN	LAN		160	A5
TWIN CANYON LN	DBAR	POM		94	A5
TWIN CREEK AV	PALM	PALM		171	F6
TWINCREEK AV	PALM	PALM		171	H6
TWIN CREEK CT	PALM	PALM		171	F6
TWIN HILL DR	CO	LPUE		94	A5
TWIN HILLS AV	LA	NOR	11400	1	A6
TWIN HILLS PL	LA	NOR		1	A6
TWINING ST	LA	LA32	4500	36	D5
TWIN LAKE RIDGE	WLVL	THO		102A	F5
TWIN OAK ST	LA	LA26	2500	35	D4
TWIN OAKS RD	HH	CAL	5100	100	E1
TWIN PALMS DR	SGAB	SGAB	500	37	D1
TWIN PALMS DR	SMAR	PAS		37	D1
TWIN PINES LN	DBAR	POM		94	A5
TWINSLOPE TR	CO	TOP	1700	109	D1
TWIN SPRING LN	DBAR	POM		97A	A2
TWINTREE AV	AZU	AZU	200	86	E6
TWINTREE AV	AZU	AZU	5500	88	E2
TWISTED OAK DR	LA	LA31		5	C5
TWO TREE AV	PVE	PVP	700	72	B5
TYBURN RD	GLEN	GL04	3300	36	B5
TYBURN ST	LA	LA39	2900	35	C1
TYBURN ST	LA	LA39	2900	35	C1
TYE CIR	LAV	LAV		90	C1
TYE PL	CO	PALM		183	A1
TYLEEN PL	POM	POM	1000	94	C1
TYLER AL	PAS	PAS	1200	27	C3
TYLER AV	CO	ARC		38	C5
TYLER AV	ELM	ELM	1100	47	C5
TYLER AV	CO	TEC	5301	38	E1
TYLER AV	ELM	ELM	3400	38	D6
TYLER AV	ELM	ELM		47	D1
TYLER AV	ELM	ELM	2400	47	D3
TYLER AV	SELM	ELM	1600	47	D3
TYLER AV	MPK	MPK	1700	46	D3
TYLER LN	CO	SAU		125	A4
TYLER ST	CAR	LB10	24600	69	F3
TYLER ST	GLEN	GL05	10300	70	A3
TYLER ST	LA	LA37	13800	2	D3
TYNDALL RD	CO	SAU	33100	181	D7
TYNEBOURNE CT	WLVL	THO	31800	102	B4
TYRELL PL	GLEN	GL06	3100	18	E3
TYRONE AV	LA	VAN	8500	8	D6
TYRONE AV	LA	VAN	8500	15	D1
TYRONE AV	LA	VAN	5600	15	D5
TYRONE AV	LA	VAN	4300	22	D1
TYROLEAN DR	LA	SF		1	D4
TYSON PL	LA	SF		1	D4
U					
UCLAN DR	BUR	BUR	600	17	D4
UDELL CT	LA	LA27	3800	35	D2
UDELL MTY	CO	AGO		105	B2
UDINE WY	LA	LA77	100	32	E5
UHEA RD	LA	WOH	22500	13	A3
ULEN ST	LB	LB15	5000	76	C1
ULMUS DR	CO	WOH		13	C4
ULTIMO AV	LB	LB04	700	76	C5
ULTIMO AV	LB	LB14	300	76	C5
ULYSSES RD	CO	SAU		181	D1
ULYSSES ST	LA	LA65	300	36	A4
UMATILLA AV	LA	LB04	1100	76	A4
UMBRIA ST	LA	LA42	1400	42	E2
UMEO RD	LA	PP	1500	40	E2
UNDERHILL DR	GLDR	GLDR	1100	87	B5
UNDERHILL TER	GLDR	GLDR	1400	87	B5
UNDERWOOD ST	PR	PR	8800	54	F3
UNDERWOOD ST	PR	PR	8800	55	A3
UNDINE AV	SCLR	VAL		127	A4
UNION AV	POM	POM	900	94	C1
UNION AV	WHI	WHI		55	D5
UNION AV	LA	LA26	3100	35	D5
UNION AV	LA	LA07		44	C1
UNION AV S	LA	LA15	300	44	C3
UNION AV S	LA	LA17	300	44	B2
UNION AV S	LA	LA26	100	44	C4
UNION DR	LA	LA17	400	44	B2
UNION PL	LA	LA17	300	44	B2
UNION PL	LA	LA26	100	44	B2
UNION PL	LCF	LCF	4400	19	B3
UNION ST	MTB	MTB	700	54	C5
UNION ST	NWK	NWK	11800	82	A1
UNION ST	PR	PR	9000	55	A2
UNION ST E	PAS	PAS	100	27	B4
UNION ST W	PAS	PAS	100	26	F4
UNION ST W	PAS	PAS	100	27	B4
UNION HILLS LN	CAR	CAR		69	E6
UNION JACK ST	LA	VEN		49	C6
UNION PACFIC AV	CMRC	LA22	5400	53	F1
UNION PACFIC AV	CMRC	LA22	5600	54	A1
UNION PACFIC AV	CO	LA22	4600	53	E1
UNION PACFIC AV	CO	LA23	3900	53	C1
UNION PACFIC AV	CO	LA23	3200	53	A1
UNION PACFIC PL	LA	LA23		53	F5
UNIT ST	LA	LA59	11200	58	C5
UNITAH ST	LCF	LCF	1100	19	B2
UNITED RD	AGO	AGO		100A	D6
UNIVERSAL PL	LA	NHO		23	F5
UNIVERSL CTR DR	CO	NHO		24	A5
UNIVERSL CTR DR	LA	LA68		24	A5
UNIVERSL TER PY	LA	NHO		23	F5
UNIVERSITY AV	BUR	BUR	100	17	D4
UNIVERSITY AV	LA	LA07	3400	44	A4
UNIVERSITY CIR	CLA	CLA	400	91	B3
UNIVERSITY DR	CAR	CAR	900	69	C1
UNIVERSITY DR	CO	COM		69	C1
UNIVERSITY DR	CO	POM		93	E2
UNIVERSITY DR	PAS	PAS	1600	20	C6
UNIVERSITY DR	PAS	PAS	1600	27	C1
UNIVERSITY PKWY	POM	POM		93	F3
UNRUH AV	IND	LPUE		48	E5
UNSER ST	PR	PR	8600	54	E4
UPDIKE RD	CO	PALM		183	D9
UPLAND AV	LA	LA31	3300	36	B5
UPLAND AV	RPV	SP	500	78	D2
UPLANDER WY	CUL	CUL	6000	50	D4
UPPER CT	PALM	PALM		183	E2
UPPER PL	CO	GL14		11	E5
UPPER TER	CO	GL14	2400	11	E5
UPPER TER	AVA	AVA	100	77	B5
UPR BLCKWTR CYN	RH	PVP	1	73	A6
UPR BLKWR CY RD	RH	PVP		73	A6
UPPER BREW MTWY	CO	MAL		106	C4
UPPER MESA RD	LA	SM	300	40	B6
UPR RAMIREZ MTY	CO	MAL		106	B6
UPPERTON AV	CO	LA42	1700	26	C6
UPPERTON PL	CO	LA42	1900	26	C6
UPTON CT	LA	LA41	5200	26	C4
UPTON PL	LA	LA41	1200	26	C4
URBAN AV	SM	SM	2800	41	C6
URBANA AV	CO	PAC	9300	8	E4
URBANA AV	CO	PAC	8800	9	A4
URBANDALE AV	SCLR	SAU		124	E5
URMISTON PL	SMAR	PAS	2000	28	E3
URQUIDEZ AV	GLEN	GL08	3600	18	E3
URSINUS CIR	CLA	CLA		91	B5
URSULA AV	LA	LA08	3900	51	A1
USHER PL	BH	BH	400	33	C3
UTAH AV	ELM	ELM	3200	47	C1
UTAH AV	ELS	ELS	1900	62	D1
UTAH AV	SOG	SOG	11300	59	C6
UTAH CT	CLA	CLA	300	91	C5
UTAH ST N	LA	LA33	100	44	F3
UTAH ST S	LA	LA33	100	44	F3
UTICA DR	LA	LA46	2000	33	E2
UTICA PL	CO	WHI	13500	61	E5
UTICA ST	CO	WHI		63	E1
UTICA TER	LA	LA46		33	E1
UTILITY WY	CO	TOR		69	C6
UTLEY RD	CO	GL14	3200	11	E4
UTOPIA RD	CO	CUL	11200	50	B3
V					
VACA AV	CO	CAST		123	G2
VACCARO AV	TOR	TOR	20500	71	F5
VACCO ST	SELM	ELM		47	D6
VACHON DR	RM	RM	3800	37	F6
VADO DR	LA	LA46	2400	33	D2
VADO PL	LA	LA46	8600	33	D2
VAGA AV	WHI	WHI		84	F6
VAGABOND RD	MPK	MPK	1000	46	A3
VAGNONE WY	CER	ART	15900	81	C3
VAHAN CT	LAN	LAN		159	G6
VAIL AV	CMRC	LA40	6400	53	F1
VAIL AV	WHI	WHI	900	55	D5
VAIL AV	CO	LA26	3100	55	D5
VAIL AV N	LA	LA07		44	A3
VAIL AV N	LA	LA15	300	44	A3
VAIL AV N	LA	LA17	300	44	B2
VAIL AV N	MTB	MTB	400	54	C3
VAIL AV S	LA	LA26	100	44	A4
VAIL DR	LA	SUN	10500		9
VAIL DR	SFS	SFS		60	F3
VAIL ST	CER	ART	4400	81	C2
VAIL ST	ARC	ART	700	38	C1
VAIL ST	TEC	TEC	9600	38	B1
VALAHO DR	LA	TU	7200	10	F3
VALAHO LN	LA	TU	7200	10	F4
VALANE DR	GLEN	GL08	1400	18	E4
VALARESSA LN	CO	LPUE	1700	47	F4
VAL CARLOS AV	CO	LPUE	1400	98	D3
VALCOURT DR	SCLR	CYN		125	B8
VALCOURT LN	GLDR	GLDR	2300	87	E5
VALDARES DR	CO	LPUE		85	C3
VALDERAS DR	GLEN	GL08	2000	18	F3
VALDEMAR DR	LA	TAR	19500	21	A3
VALDEZ PL	LA	TAR	4500	21	A3
VALDEZ PL	CO	TOP		100	F5
VALDINA DR	DOW	DOW	8100	60	C2
VALDINA PL	CO	LA43	4500	51	A4
VALE AV	WHI	WHI	1900	55	F5
VALE DR	WHI	WHI	7600	85	A5
VALE WY	CO	LPUE		48	B5
VALEBROOK PL	SAD	SAD	1100	89	F1
VALECREST DR	LA	SV	8300	16	F1
VALEDA DR	LAM	LAM	14200	82	F1
VALEDA DR	LAM	LAM	14600	83	A1
VALEMONT AV	CO	LPUE		97	A4
VALEMOUNT AV	CO	LPUE	1700	97	A4
VALEN ST	BAP	BAP		48	B1
VALENCIA AV	CO	LPUE	800	48	D6
VALENCIA AV	CO	LPUE	1000	85	D1
VALENCIA AV	CO	LPUE	1300	97	E1
VALENCIA AV	BUR	BUR	200	17	E6
VALENCIA AV E	BUR	BUR		24	D2
VALENCIA AV W	BUR	BUR		24	D2
VALENCIA BL	SCLR	VAL		124	A9
VALENCIA BLVD	SCLR	VAL	1300	124	A9
VALENCIA CT	LAV	LAV		90	D1
VALENCIA DR	COV	COV	100	88	E5
VALENCIA PL	POM	POM	1300	90	D6
VALENCIA PL	CER	ART		81	C2
VALENCIA ST	CO	LPUE	1900	98	F5
VALENCIA ST	GLDR	GLDR	100	87	A5
VALENCIA ST	LA	LA15	900	44	B4
VALENCIA ST	LA	LA17	600	44	B4
VALENCIA ST	LAV	LAV		90	E2
VALENCIA ST E	NWK	NWK	11800	82	A2
VALENCIA ST S	ALH	ALH	100	37	D5
VALENCIA WY	ARC	ARC	1100	28	F5
VALENTINE PL	GLEN	GL02	400	18	B2
VALENTINE PL	SMAR	PAS	2000	35	D4
VALENTINE ST	LA	LA26	2000	35	D4
VALENTINO PL	LA	LA38	700	34	D5
VALENZA AV	CO	LAN	16500	175	H3
VALEPORT AV	CO	LAN	15600	174	H3
VALEPORT AV E	LB	LB08	8300	81	C1
VALERA AV	MTB	MTB	400	54	F1
VALERIA DR	CO	TOR	300	90	F1
VALERIE AV	WCOV	WCOV		92	D6
VALERIE CT	LA	CAN	23300	5	E3
VALERIO AV	LA	CAN	19700	5	E3
VALERIO ST	LA	NHO	11400	16	C2
VALERIO ST	LA	RES	17700	14	A3
VALERIO ST	LA	SV	10600	16	E3
VALERIO ST	LA	VAN	16600	14	A3
VALERIO ST	LA	VAN	13700	15	D3
VALEVIEW AV	SAD	SAD	1200	87	F6
VALEVIEW AV	SAD	SAD	1200	89	F1
VALEVIEW DR	DBAR	POM		97A	B3
VALEVISTA TR	LA	LA68	2900	24	A6
VALEVISTA TR	LA	LA68	2900	34	A1
VALEWOOD ST	BUR	BUR	2300	89	F1
VALHALLA DR	POM	POM	2400	91	A5
VALIANT ST	GLDR	GLDR	2000	87	E5
VALIANT ST	LAN	LAN	1000	159	J2
VALIANT ST W	LAN	LAN	1000	159	J2
VALIDO RD	ARC	ARC	400	28	B4
VALIENTE DR	PALM	PALM		171	C4
VALIHI WY	GLEN	GL08	3600	18	F3
VALINDA AV	CO	LPUE	900	48	F5
VALINDA AV	CO	WCOV	400	92	B2
VALITA ST	LA	ENC	4600	22	A9
VALJEAN AV	LA	SF	11400	2	A6
VALJEAN AV	LA	SF	8500	2	A6
VALJEAN AV	LA	SV	8300	15	A1
VALJEAN AV	LA	VAN	6400	15	A5
VALLE DR	LHH	LAH	2100	98A	B1
VALLE DR	POM	POM		90	C6
VALLECITO DR	CO	LPUE	1600	98	D3

302

LOS ANGELES CO.

1990 LOS ANGELES COUNTY STREET INDEX

VALLECITO DR — VERDE CT

STREET	CITY	P.O. ZONE	BLOCK	PAGE	GRID
VALLECITO DR	LA	SP	1800	78	D4
VALLE CNTNTO DR	CO	LPUE	15800	85	E4
VALLE DEL ORO	SCLR	NEW		127	E5
VALLEJO DR	GLEN	GL06	200	25	E4
VALLEJO ST	LA	LA31	2100	45	A1
VALLE LINDO LN	CO	CAL		114	B2
VALLETA DR	RPV	SP	1800	73	D6
VALLE VERDE CT	LAV	LAV		90	E1
VALLE VISTA AV	BAP	BAP	13400	39	C5
VALLE VISTA AV	MON	MON	200	29	B3
VALLE VISTA DR	GLEN	GL06	2700	26	B3
VALLE VISTA DR	LA	LA65	2900	25	E6
VALLE VISTA DR	SMAD	SMAD		28	D1
VALLEY BLVD	CO	ELM	12100	47	F1
VALLEY BLVD	CO	LPUE	12900	48	B3
VALLEY BLVD	CO	WAL	21100	93	E5
VALLEY BLVD	CO	WAL	9600	97	B1
VALLEY BLVD	CO	WAL	19300	97	B1
VALLEY BLVD	ELM	ELM	9800	38	A5
VALLEY BLVD	ELM	ELM	11400	47	F1
VALLEY BLVD	IND	ELM	12500	48	B3
VALLEY BLVD	IND	LPUE	13400	48	B3
VALLEY BLVD	IND	LPUE		85	F1
VALLEY BLVD	IND	LPUE	17400	98	C1
VALLEY BLVD	LA	LA31	3500	45	C1
VALLEY BLVD	LA	LA32	5000	36	E6
VALLEY BLVD	LA	LA32	4000	45	C1
VALLEY BLVD	LPUE	LPUE		98	A1
VALLEY BLVD	POM	POM	3300	93	E4
VALLEY BLVD	POM	POM	2200	94	B2
VALLEY BLVD	POM	WAL	3600	93	D6
VALLEY BLVD	RM	RM	8300	38	B5
VALLEY BLVD	WCOV	WCOV	19300	97	B1
VALLEY BLVD E	ALH	ALH	100	37	B5
VALLEY BLVD E	SGAB	SGAB	100	37	B5
VALLEY BLVD W	ALH	ALH	2500	36	E6
VALLEY BLVD W	ALH	ALH	100	37	B5
VALLEY BLVD W	SGAB	SGAB	100	37	B5
VALLEY CT	PAS	PAS	100	26	F4
VALLEY DR	CO	TOP	1500	108	F2
VALLEY DR	HB	RB	1000	62	C6
VALLEY DR	HB	RB	100	67	C1
VALLEY DR N	MB	MB	100	62	B3
VALLEY DR S	MB	MB	100	62	B4
VALLEY ST	BUR	BUR	1500	16	F5
VALLEY ST	SCLR	NEW	24200	127	B5
VALLEY ST	ELS	ELS	300	56	A6
VALLEY ST	LA	LA57	2000	44	B1
VALLEY ST	PAS	PAS	100	26	F4
VALLEY ST N	BUR	BUR	100	24	A3
VALLEY ST S	BUR	BUR	100	24	A3
VALLEYBRINK RD	LA	LA39		35	B1
VALLEY CYN RD	CO	CYN		125	H6
VALLEY CTR AV	CO	COV	4600	89	D4
VALLEY CTR AV N	GLDR	GLDR	100	87	D5
VALLEY CTR AV N	SAD	GLDR	700	89	D4
VALLEY CTR AV S	GLDR	GLDR	100	87	D5
VALLEY CTR AV S	GLDR	GLDR	1400	89	D1
VALLEY CTR AV S	SAD	SAD	800	89	D4
VALLEY CNTRL WY	LAN	LAN		159	H4
VALLEY CIR BLVD	LA	CAN	8500	4	B6
VALLEY CIR BLVD	LA	CAN	6300	5	D5
VALLEY CIR BLVD	LA	CHA	9200	4	B6
VALLEY CIR BLVD	LA	CHA	9300	6	A5
VALLEY CIR BLVD	LA	WOH	5600	5	D6
VALLEY CIR BLVD	LA	WOH	5900	5	D5
VALLEY CIR BLVD	LA	WOH	4900	100	F2
VALLEY CIR TER	LA	CAN	6400	5	D5
VALLEYCREST RD	LA	NHO	11650	23	D6
VALLEY CREST ST	LCF	LCF	800	19	C2
VALLEYDALE AV	CO	LA43	4900	51	A3
VALLEY FALLS RD	LA	VAN	3500	22	A5
VLY FLORES DR	LA	CAN	8500	4	B6
VLY FLORES DR	LA	CAN	8400	5	E1
VALLEY FORGE RD	PALM	PALM		183	D2
VALLEY GLEN WY	CO	LA43	5600	51	A4
VALLEY GLOW DR	LA	SUN	10300	9	F4
VALLEY GLOW DR	LA	SUN		10	A4
VALLEY HEART DR	BUR	BUR	1300	24	D3
VALLEYHEART DR	LA	NHO	10600	23	C4
VALLEYHEART DR	LA	VAN	13300	22	E3
VALLEYHEART DR	LA	VAN	13100	23	A4
VALLEYHRT DR N	LA	VAN		22	C2
VALLEY HTS DR	AGH	AGO		100A	A3
VALLEY HOME AV	CO	WHI	11500	84	D4
VALLEY HOME AV	LAM	LAM	13400	83	D2
VALLEY HOME AV	WHI	WHI	1000	84	D4
VALLEY HOME RD	LA	VAN	3500	22	B5
VLY LIGHTS DR	PAS	PAS	3700	28	B1
VALLEYLINE RD	LAN	LAN	42100	160	B8
VALLEYLINE RD	PALM	PALM	41400	172	C2
VALLEY MALL	ELM	ELM		38	D6
VALLEY MDW PL	LA	ENC	15700	22	B4
VALLEY MDW RD	LA	ENC	3700	22	B4
VALLEY MDW RD	LA	VAN	3100	22	B5
VALLEY OAK CT	SCLR	NEW		127	A6

STREET	CITY	P.O. ZONE	BLOCK	PAGE	GRID
VALLEY OAK DR	LA	LA68	5600	34	D2
VALLEY OAK LN	POM	POM		90	E2
VALLEY PARK AV	HB	RB	1700	62	C6
VALLEY POINT LN	SCLR	NEW	26400	127	H3
VALLEY RANCH RD	SCLR	CYN	16200	125	C9
VALLEY RANCH RD	CO	CYN		128	C1
VALLEY RIDGE AV	CO	LA43	4400	51	A3
VALLEY SAGE RD	CO	SAU		181	H8
VALLEY SAGE RD	CO	SAU		182	A7
VALLEY SPG LN	LA	NHO	10300	23	B4
VALLEY SPG LN	LA	NHO	11100	23	E4
VALLEY SPG LN	LA	NHO	10000	24	A4
VALLEY SPG PL	LA	NHO		23	E4
VALLEY SPGS DR	WAL	WAL		92	F6
VALLEY SPGS RD	CO	PALM	36000	183	G4
VALLEY SUN LN	LCF	LCF		19	B3
VALLEY VIEW AV	CER	ART	17300	82	F6
VALLEY VIEW AV	CO	LPUE	19200	97	A2
VALLEY VIEW AV	CO	WHI	10700	61	F4
VALLEY VIEW AV	CO	WHI	10200	84	A3
VALLEY VIEW AV	LAM	LAM	12600	61	F6
VALLEY VIEW AV	LAM	LAM	12900	82	E3
VALLEY VIEW AV	MON	MON	700	29	C3
VALLEY VIEW AV	PAS	PAS	900	28	B2
VALLEY VIEW AV	SFS	SFS	14300	82	E3
VALLEY VIEW AV	WCOV	WCOV		97	A2
VALLEY VIEW AV	WCOV	WCOV	19000	98	F2
VALLEY VIEW AV	WHI	WHI	7400	55	E5
VALLEY VIEW AV	WHI	WHI	8900	84	A3
VALLEYVIEW CT	LA	SF		2	B3
VALLEY VIEW DR	CO	TOP	19500	109	C5
VALLEY VIEW DR	LA	LA26	2300	35	D4
VALLEYVIEW DR	WAL	WAL		93	D6
VALLEY VIEW RD	CO	CAL		100	E5
VALLEY VIEW RD	GLEN	GL02	1200	25	C1
VALLEY VIEW RD	RPV	PVP		72	E6
VALLEY VIEW RD	SPAS	SPAS	700	36	E3
VALLEY VIEW WY	CO	CAST		123	E1
VALLEY VW CREST	BUR	BUR	1800	17	D3
VALLEY VISTA BL	LA	ENC	17700	21	C2
VALLEY VISTA BL	LA	ENC	15500	22	B3
VALLEY VISTA BL	LA	NHO	13100	23	A4
VALLEY VISTA BL	LA	TAR	18100	21	C2
VALLEY VISTA BL	LA	VAN	13300	22	E4
VALLEY VISTA BL	LA	VAN	13200	23	A4
VALLEY VISTA CT	LA	VAN	4100	22	D4
VALLEY VISTA DR	DBAR	POM		97	D3
VALLEY VISTA DR	LAN	LAN		158	J9
VALLEY VISTA DR	MPK	MPK	1400	46	A4
VAL VISTA ST	POM	POM	600	90	C6
VALLEY WELLS CT	SCLR	NEW		127	H2
VALLEYWOOD RD	LA	VAN	15000	22	A5
VALLOMBROSA DR	CO	PAS	500	28	A5
VALLON DR	RPV	PVP	6700	77	C2
VALMAR RD	LA	WOH	4200	100	F3
VALMERE DR	CO	MAL	2900	113	B3
VALMEYER AV	CO	GAR	17400	63	F5
VALMONT DR	MON	MON	500	29	B2
VALMONT PL	MON	MON	500	29	B2
VALMONT ST	LA	SUN	7800	10	E3
VALMONT ST	LA	TU	7100	10	E3
VALMONT ST	LA	TU	6400	11	A3
VALMONTE AV	PVE	PVP	3700	72	E2
VALMONTE PZ	PVE	PVP	3900	72	F2
VALNA DR	WHI	WHI	13400	61	E1
VALONA DR	BAP	BAP	1700	48	D1
VALOR PL	RPV	PVP	32200	78	A3
VALPARAISO DR	CLA	CLA	600	96	A6
VALPARAISO ST	LA	LA34	10500	42	A5
VALPICO PL	DBAR	POM		97	E4
VALPREDA ST	BUR	BUR	1800	17	C4
VAL VERDE AV	LB	LB08	3000	81	A6
VAL VERDE CT	CO	COM	3000	70	B2
VAL VERDE CT	GLEN	GL08	3600	18	E3
VALVERDE DR	LA	CAN	8400	4	A6
VAL VERDE PL	GLEN	GL08	1400	18	E3
VAL VERDE RD	CO	CAST	29000	123	A5
VALWOOD AV	ELM	ELM	2200	47	F3
VALYERMO RD	CO	PEAR		185	E8
VALYERMO RD	CO	PEAR		192	H5
VALYERMO RD	CO	VAL		192	G1
VAMANA ST	POM	POM	2800	90	F3
VANADA RD	LAM	LAM		83	A3
VAN AKEN ST	PR	PR	9300	55	B1
VANALDEN AV	LA	NOR	8500	7	B6
VANALDEN AV	LA	NOR	8300	14	B2
VANALDEN AV	LA	RES	6100	14	B5
VANALDEN AV	LA	TAR	3800	13	F5
VANALDEN AV	LA	TAR	5700	14	B6
VANALDEN AV	LA	TAR	3900	21	A3
VANANBEV WY	CO	PALM		171	J7
VAN BUREN AV	CO	LA44	11100	57	F5
VAN BUREN AV	GAR	GAR	13600	63	F2
VAN BUREN AV	LA	VEN	1000	49	D4
VAN BUREN CT	GAR	GAR		63	F2
VAN BUREN DR	MPK	MPK	400	46	C3

STREET	CITY	P.O. ZONE	BLOCK	PAGE	GRID
VAN BUREN PL	CUL	CUL	3900	42	C6
VAN BUREN PL	LA	LA07	2600	43	F5
VAN BUREN PL	LA	LA37	4200	51	F2
VAN BUREN ST	CAR	LB10	2500	69	F4
VAN BUREN ST	CAR	LB10	2600	70	A3
VAN BUREN ST	CO	CAST		123	C2
VAN CAMP ST	LB	LB02		80A	B4
VANCE ST	LA	PP	200	40	D5
VANCEBORO CT	LA	WOH		13	E3
VANCOUVER AV	CO	LA22	100	45	F6
VANCOUVER AV	CO	LA22	900	53	F1
VANCOUVER AV	MPK	MPK		45	F5
VANDA WY	LA	SUN		9	E3
VANDALIA AV	LA	LA32	2200	36	E6
VAN DEENE AV	CO	TOR	20800	68	F3
VANDEMERE ST	LKD	LKD	12200	81	C3
VANDERBILT AV	CLA	CLA	900	91	A3
VANDERBILT LN	RB	RB	1800	62	E5
VANDERBILT PL	GLEN	GL05	1500	25	E6
VANDERGRIFT LN	POM	POM	500	94	E5
VANDERHILL RD	TOR	TOR	4600	67	E6
VANDERHOOF DR	WCOV	WCOV	2600	92	E1
VANDERLIP DR	RPV	PVP	1	77	E2
VANDERWELL AV	CO	LPUE	700	92	B5
VANDERWELL AV	WCOV	WCOV	600	92	B2
VANDORF PL	LA	ENC	15600	22	B4
VANDORF ST	RM	RM	7700	46	E2
VAN DYKE RD	SMAR	PAS	1300	27	E6
VANE AV	ELM	ELM	3100	47	B1
VANE AV	RM	RM	3500	38	B6
VANEGAS LN	LA	LA33	1300	45	C2
VANESSA CIR	CO	WHI	8500	55	A6
VANESSA CT	LA	WOH		12	A6
VANETTA DR	LA	NHO	4100	23	B4
VANETTA PL	LA	NHO	4100	23	B4
VAN GOGH ST	LA	SF	17100	1	E3
VANGOLD AV	LKD	LKD	4300	70	E3
VAN GORDER WY	CO	CAST		123	H1
VANGUARD AV	CO	LPUE	100	92	D6
VAN HORN AV	WCOV	WCOV	800	48	F1
VAN HORNE AV	LA	LA32	3800	36	E4
VAN HORNE LN	RB	RB	1600	67	D1
VAN KARAJAN DR	RPV	SP	1800	78	D1
VANLAND TR	LA	LA68	6900	34	B1
VAN METER ST	CO	MON	500	39	B1
VAN METER ST	IRW	BAP	900	39	C1
VANNA DR	PAR	PAR	7100	65	D1
VAN NESS AV	COM	COM	700	65	A2
VAN NESS AV N	LA	LA04	100	34	D6
VAN NESS AV N	LA	LA38	700	34	D6
VAN NESS AV N	LA	LA68	1300	34	D2
VAN NESS AV N	LA	LA68	1900	34	D3
VAN NESS AV S	CO	GAR	14300	63	D2
VAN NESS AV S	CO	LA47	10000	57	D3
VAN NESS AV S	GAR	GAR	12800	63	D2
VAN NESS AV S	HAW	LA47	11400	57	D6
VAN NESS AV S	ING	IN03	10001	57	D3
VAN NESS AV S	ING	IN05	7600	51	D6
VAN NESS AV S	ING	IN05	7901	57	D3
VAN NESS AV S	LA	LA04	100	34	D6
VAN NESS AV S	LA	LA05	600	43	D2
VAN NESS AV S	LA	LA18	3500	43	D6
VAN NESS AV S	LA	LA19	1200	43	D4
VAN NESS AV S	LA	LA20	300	43	D2
VAN NESS AV S	LA	LA47	5800	51	D6
VAN NESS AV S	LA	LA62	3800	51	D3
VAN NESS AV S	TOR	TOR	16000	63	D6
VAN NESS AV S	TOR	TOR	18500	68	D2
VAN NESS WY	TOR	TOR	300	68	D3
VAN NOORD AV	LA	NHO	6500	16	A4
VAN NOORD AV	LA	NHO	3900	23	A3
VAN NOORD AV	LA	VAN	6100	16	A5
VAN NOORD AV	LA	VAN	4600	23	A3
VAN NORMAN RD	PR	PR	5200	54	E2
VAN NUYS BLVD	LA	PAC	12300	3	C6
VAN NUYS BLVD	LA	PAC	13400	8	E4
VAN NUYS BLVD	LA	PAC	12500	9	A2
VAN NUYS BLVD	LA	SF	12000	3	C6
VAN NUYS BLVD	LA	VAN	9600	8	D6
VAN NUYS BLVD	LA	VAN	5600	15	D5
VAN NUYS BLVD	LA	VAN	4200	22	D3
VAN NUYS PL	LA	VAN	14600	8	D4
VANORA DR	LA	SUN	10600	10	C3
VANOWEN PL	BUR	BUR	4100	16	F4
VANOWEN ST	BUR	BUR	3900	16	A4
VANOWEN ST	BUR	BUR	2500	17	A4
VANOWEN ST	LA	BUR	10600	16	A4
VANOWEN ST	LA	CAN	23000	5	E4
VANOWEN ST	LA	CAN	19700	12	A4
VANOWEN ST	LA	NHO	10600	16	A4
VANOWEN ST	LA	RES	17700	14	A4
VANOWEN ST	LA	VAN	16500	14	A4
VANOWEN ST	LA	VAN	13300	15	B4
VAN PELT AV	CO	LA63	900	45	D3
VAN PELT PL	LA	LA26	2900	35	B4
VANPORT AV	CO	WHI	6700	55	B5

STREET	CITY	P.O. ZONE	BLOCK	PAGE	GRID
VANPORT AV	CO	WHI	8300	61	B1
VANPORT AV	LA	SF	11400	3	C6
VAN RUITEN ST	BLF	BLF	9200	66	B2
VAN RUITEN ST	NWK	NWK	10700	66	E2
VANS ST	PAR	PAR	8700	66	A3
VANSCOY AV	LA	NHO	6800	16	B4
VANSTONE TR	CO	TOP	21000	109	D2
VANTAGE AV	LA	NHO	5600	16	C4
VANTAGE AV	LA	NHO		16	C5
VANTAGE AV	LA	NHO	3700	23	C4
VANTAGE PT TER	CO	MAL		113	E5
VAN TASSEL WY	DUA	DUA	3300	86	B4
VAN TRESS AV	LA	WIL	1500	74	A2
VAN VELSIR DR	CO	CAL		108	B5
VAN WICK ST	CO	LA47	1900	57	D4
VAN WICK ST	ING	IN03	2300	57	C4
VAN WICKLIN AV	LA	SF		2	C4
VAN WIG AV	BAP	BAP	1500	39	E6
VANWIG AV	CO	LPUE	500	48	C3
VAQUERO	WCOV	WCOV		92	D4
VAQUERO AV	LA	LA32	2800	36	E6
VAQUERO CT	SCLR	VAL		127	B1
VAQUERO LN	CAR	CAR		69	E6
VAQUERO LN	GLEN	GL06		25	F2
VAQUERO RD	ARC	ARC	200	28	C4
VAQUERO RD	MON	MON	500	29	D4
VARA PL	LA	SF		1	D5
VARDEN PL	LCF	LCF		19	C6
VARDEN ST	LA	ENC	15300	22	B3
VARDEN ST	LA	VAN	15300	22	B3
VARESE CT	CO	VAL		126	J2
VARGAS WY	RB	RB	2500	62	F4
VARIATION TR	CO	TOP		109	A1
VARIEL AV	LA	CAN	6400	12	D4
VARIEL AV	LA	CHA	9500	6	D3
VARIEL AV	LA	WOH	5600	12	D6
VARIEL AV	LA	WOH	5500	13	D1
VARILLA DR	WCOV	WCOV		92	C4
VARNA AV	LA	NHO	7000	15	F3
VARNA AV	LA	PAC	8700	8	F5
VARNA AV	LA	VAN	5600	15	F5
VARNA AV	LA	VAN	4500	22	F3
VARNE WK	LA	LA65		35	F2
VARNELL AV	CO	COV	5100	88	B3
VARNEY ST N	BUR	BUR	400	17	D6
VARNEY ST S	BUR	BUR	400	17	D6
VARNEY ST S	BUR	BUR	400	24	E1
VARSITY DR	WAL	WAL	20400	93	B4
VASANTA WY	LA	LA68	2200	34	C2
VASCONES DR	CO	LPUE	1900	85	F3
VASQUEZ WY	CO	CYN		125	D3
VASQUEZ CYN RD	CO	SAU	16300	125	A2
VASSAR AV	GLEN	GL04	1800	35	D1
VASSAR AV	LA	CAN	8500	6	C6
VASSAR AV	LA	CAN	7000	12	C4
VASSAR AV	LA	CHA	10200	6	C3
VASSAR AV	LA	WOH	5900	12	C6
VASSAR CT	LAV	LAV		90	E3
VASSAR LN	WAL	WAL		93	B4
VASSAR ST	CLA	CLA	800	91	A5
VASSAR ST	POM	POM	800	91	A5
VAUGHN ST	LA	PAC	14000	8	E1
VAUGHN ST	LA	SF	13400	2	F6
VAUGHN ST	LA	SF	12700	3	A6
VAUGHN ST	LA	SF	13500	8	F1
VAUGHT CT	WCOV	WCOV		92	C4
VECINO AV	CO	GLDR	6500	86	F6
VECINO AV	GLDR	GLDR	600	87	A4
VECINO AV	GLDR	GLDR	1700	88	F2
VECINO AV N	GLDR	GLDR	100	86	F5
VECINO DR	CO	COV	4000	88	F3
VECINO DR	CO	GLDR	5600	88	F2
VECINO DR N	COV	COV	100	88	F5
VECINO DR S	COV	COV	400	88	F6
VEDADO AV	LA	NHO	3900	23	B5
VEDANTA PL	LA	LA68	1900	34	C2
VEDANTA TER	LA	LA68	6300	34	C2
VEGA CIR	LAV	LAV		90	B3
VEGA DR	LAN	LAN		160	F7
VEGA ST N	ALH	ALH	100	37	D6
VEGA ST S	ALH	ALH	100	37	D6
VEGA WK	CO	CAST		123	A5
VEGA WY	CO	LPUE		97	A5
VEJAR DR	AGH	AGO		100A	B4
VEJAR RD	WAL	WAL	20100	93	B6
VEJAR ST	POM	POM	1300	94	C3
VELA PL	PR	PR	6500	54	E4
VELAN DR	SCLR	VAL		127	A2
VELASCO ST	LA	LA23	1200	53	B1
VELASCO ST	LA	LA63	100	45	C5
VELEZ DR	RPV	SP	1800	73	D6
VELICATA ST	LA	WOH	21200	13	B2
VELMA AV	ELM	ELM	4000	38	C5
VELMA DR	LA	LA68	3200	24	A5
VELMA LN	LA	BH	10000	32	E2
VELOZ AV	LA	TAR	5000	21	B2

STREET	CITY	P.O. ZONE	BLOCK	PAGE	GRID
VELSIR ST	CO	ELM	11000	47	C5
VELUTINA WY	PALM	PALM		183	E2
VELVET LN	CUL	CUL		50	D2
VENA AV	LA	PAC	9500	8	F4
VENA AV	LA	PAC	9000	9	A5
VENA AV	LA	SF	10900	8	D1
VENADO DR	LHH	LAH	1600	84	E2
VENADO WY	WAL	WAL		93	F5
VENADO VISTA DR	LCF	LCF	500	19	C2
VENANGO AV	LA	LA29	900	35	E3
VENANGO CIR	LA	LA29	900	35	E3
VENDALE DR	LKD	LKD		71	F3
VENDELL RD	AGH	AGO		100A	D5
VENDOME ST N	LA	LA26	100	35	A5
VENDOME ST S	LA	LA57	100	35	A6
VENDOME ST S	LA	LA57	100	44	A1
VENETIA DR	LB	LB03	100	80	C1
VENEZIA AV	LA	VEN	500	49	D3
VENEZIA CT	LA	VEN		49	D4
VENEZIA PL	POM	POM		94	B4
VENICE AV	MON	MON	1500	28	F5
VENICE BLVD	CUL	CUL	10700	50	A1
VENICE BLVD	CUL	LA66	11300	50	A1
VENICE BLVD	LA	CUL	8900	42	C6
VENICE BLVD	LA	LA06	1500	43	F4
VENICE BLVD	LA	LA06	1200	44	A4
VENICE BLVD	LA	LA15	100	44	B4
VENICE BLVD	LA	LA19	5200	42	C6
VENICE BLVD	LA	LA19	2300	43	B3
VENICE BLVD	LA	LA34	5900	42	C6
VENICE BLVD	LA	LA34	10700	50	A1
VENICE BLVD	LA	LA66	11600	49	D3
VENICE BLVD	LA	LA66	11400	50	A1
VENICE BLVD	LA	VEN	600	49	C4
VENICE BLVD N	LA	VEN	100	49	B4
VENICE BLVD S	LA	VEN	100	49	B4
VENICE WY	ING	IN02	300	50	F6
VENICE WY	LA	VEN	100	49	B4
VENIDO RD	LA	WOH	22400	13	B2
VENITA ST	CO	ELM	10400	38	D5
VENTANA AV	CO	LPUE	300	98	E1
VENTON ST	CO	COV	20000	89	B3
VENTON ST	COV	COV	20600	89	C3
VENTON ST	SAD	SAD	700	89	D3
VENTURA BLVD	CO	CAL		100	D3
VENTURA BLVD	LA	ENC	17500	21	D2
VENTURA BLVD	LA	ENC	15500	22	B3
VENTURA BLVD	LA	NHO	12100	23	C4
VENTURA BLVD	LA	TAR	18100	21	D2
VENTURA BLVD	LA	VAN	15900	22	B3
VENTURA BLVD	LA	WOH	23000	13	A2
VENTURA BLVD	LA	WOH	24000	100	F2
VENTURA CT	LA	NHO	12300	23	B4
VENTURA FRWY	AGH	AGO		100A	C4
VENTURA FRWY	BUR	BUR		24	B3
VENTURA FRWY	CO			100	C3
VENTURA FRWY	CO			102	C4
VENTURA FRWY	GLEN	GL01		25	C3
VENTURA FRWY	LA	LA		13	C1
VENTURA FRWY	LA	LA		21	A1
VENTURA FRWY	LA	LA		22	C2
VENTURA FRWY	LA	LA		23	B3
VENTURA FRWY	LA	LA		24	B3
VENTURA FRWY	LA	LA		26	A4
VENTURA FRWY	WLVL	THO		102	C4
VENTURA PL	LA	NHO	12000	23	C4
VENTURA ST	CO	ALT	1	19	E4
VENTURA WY	CO	CHA	9200	4	C5
VENTURA CYN AV	LA	PAC	8400	15	F2
VENTURA CYN AV	LA	VAN	5600	15	F6
VENTURA CYN AV	LA	VAN	3300	22	F5
VENTURI DR	SCLR	VAL		127	C1
VENUS DR	LA	LA46	2300	33	E1
VERA AV	LA	LA34	3100	42	D5
VERA CT	LB	LB04	2300	75	E4
VERA ST	CAR	CAR	21000	69	D4
VERA CANYON RD	CO	MAL		106	A5
VERA CREST DR	LB	LB15		76	D4
VERA CRUZ	POM	POM		90	B6
VERACRUZ ST	CER	ART	13300	82	D5
VERA CRUZ ST	MTB	MTB		46	E5
VERADA AV	LA	SF	11600	1	E6
VERAGUA DR	LA	VEN	7700	55A	F1
VERANADA AV	CO	ALT	1600	20	E6
VERANDA DR	CO	SF	12500	3	D4
VERANO DR	GLDR	GLDR	700	87	C4
VERANO RD	LA	LA77	10900	32	C4
VERBECK ST	CO	WHI	11600	61	B1
VERBECK ST	SFS	WHI	11600	61	B1
VERBENA DR	LA	LA68	2500	34	D1
VERBURG CT	TOR	TOR	2000	63	D5
VERCOE PL	MPK	MPK	1200	46	C3
VERDANT ST	LA	LA39	3900	25	B5
VERDE CT	LB	LB04	3900	76	A4
VERDE CT	POM	POM	1000	91	A5

INDEX

COPYRIGHT, © 1989 BY Thomas Bros Maps

1990 LOS ANGELES COUNTY STREET INDEX

STREET	CITY	P.O. ZONE	BLOCK	PAGE	GRID
VERDE DR	CO	PALM		183	A3
VERDE DR	GLEN	GL07	1500	25	E1
VERDE ST	LA	LA33	2400	45	B2
VERDE ST	PAS	PAS	2000	27	D4
VERDEMOUR AV	LA	LA32	4400	36	C5
VERDE OAK DR	LA	LA68	2100	34	D2
VERDE RIDGE RD	RPV	PVP	6300	72	C5
VERDE VISTA AV	POM	POM	500	91	B6
VERDE VISTA DR	MPK	MPK	1700	45	F2
VERDE VISTA DR	MPK	MPK	1200	46	A2
VERDE VISTA DR	POM	POM	600	90	F6
VERDI ST	LA	LA66	12400	50	A4
VERD OAKS DR	GLEN	GL05	1400	25	E5
VERDOSA DR	WHI	WHI	8300	84	B2
VERDUGO AV	GLDR	GLDR	100	87	D5
VERDUGO AV	POM	POM	300	90	F3
VERDUGO AV E	BUR	BUR	1	17	E5
VERDUGO AV W	BUR	BUR	1	24	D1
VERDUGO BLVD	GLEN	GL08	1800	19	A3
VERDUGO BLVD	GLEN	MONT	2000	18	F3
VERDUGO BLVD	LCF	LCF	1200	19	A3
VERDUGO CT	GLEN	GL08	2200	18	E6
VERDUGO DR	BUR	BUR	400	24	D1
VERDUGO PL	LA	LA65	3100	35	E2
VERDUGO RD	GLEN	GL08	1500	25	F1
VERDUGO RD	LA	LA65	2900	35	E2
VERDUGO RD N	GLEN	GL06	100	25	E5
VERDUGO RD N	GLEN	GL08	1700	18	F6
VERDUGO RD S	GLEN	GL05	100	25	E5
VERDUGO CIR DR	GLEN	GL06	1000	25	E2
VERDUGO CST CIR	LA	TU	7200	10	F4
VERDUGO CSTL DR	LA	SUN	7200	10	E4
VERDUGO KNLS PL	GLEN	GL08	1800	18	F6
VERDUGO LOMA DR	GLEN	GL08	1800	25	F1
VERDUGO SPG LN	BUR	BUR	1100	17	F4
VERDUGO VIEW DR	LA	LA65	3900	35	F1
VERDUGO VIEW WY	LA	LA65		35	F1
VERDUGO VIS DR	GLEN	GL08	1800	25	F1
VERDUGO VIS TER	LA	LA65	3400	35	F1
VERDUGO WDS HWY	GLEN	GL14		18	C1
VERDUN AV	CO	LA43	4800	51	A3
VERDUN AV	LA	LA43	5700	51	A5
VERDURA AV	DOW	DOW	12600	60	A6
VERDURA AV	DOW	DOW	13000	66	A1
VERDURA AV	LB	LB05	6200	66	A6
VERDURA AV	LKD	LKD	4900	71	A2
VERDURA AV	PAR	PAR	14900	66	A3
VEREDA D L MONT	LA	PP		109	F5
VERHALEN CT	CUL	CUL		50	E1
VERKLER	CO	CAL		108	B2
VERMILION CK RD	SAD	SAD		90	A1
VERMILLION ST	WCOV	WCOV	2900	97	A2
VERMONT AV	PAR	PAR	15100	65	F4
VERMONT AV N	GLDR	GLDR	100	87	A5
VERMONT AV N	LA	LA04	100	34	F5
VERMONT AV N	LA	LA27	1300	34	F5
VERMONT AV N	LA	LA29	700	34	F5
VERMONT AV S	CO	HAC	23600	73	F3
VERMONT AV S	CO	LA44	8600	57	F3
VERMONT AV S	CO	TOR	22200	68	F5
VERMONT AV S	GAR	GAR	12800	63	F2
VERMONT AV S	GLDR	GLDR	100	87	A5
VERMONT AV S	GLDR	GLDR	1600	89	A2
VERMONT AV S	LA	GAR	12800	63	F2
VERMONT AV S	LA	HAC	25000	73	F3
VERMONT AV S	LA	LA04	100	34	F5
VERMONT AV S	LA	LA05	600	43	F6
VERMONT AV S	LA	LA06	900	43	F2
VERMONT AV S	LA	LA07	1900	43	F6
VERMONT AV S	LA	LA20	300	43	F6
VERMONT AV S	LA	LA37	3800	51	F4
VERMONT AV S	LA	LA37	3800	51	F4
VERMONT AV S	LA	LA44	5800	51	F4
VERMONT AV S	LA	LA44	9600	57	F3
VERMONT AV S	LA	TOR	19500	68	F2
VERMONT DR	SCLR	NEW	25000	127	A4
VERMONT PL	LA	LA29	4600	34	F4
VERMONT PL	POM	POM	1600	90	D6
VERMONT ST	CO	ALT	400	19	E5
VERMONT ST	LB	LB14	6300	76	E5
VERMONT CYN RD	LA	LA27		24	E6
VERMONT CYN RD	LA	LA27	2700	34	F1
VERNA DR	CO	LPUE		98	C5
VERNAL WY	SCLR	SAU		124	G5
VERNE AV	HG	LKD	21600	81	B4
VERNE AV	LKD	LKD	20700	81	B3
VERNE AV	LKD	LKD	21000	81	B3
VERNE CT	CO	NEW		126	G3
VERNER CIR	ARC	ARC	500	38	F1
VERNER ST	PR	PR	9100	55	A3
VERNESS ST	COV	COV	17800	88	D6
VERNESS ST	WCOV	WCOV	1100	88	B6
VERNETTE AV	LA	SF		1	E4
VERNON AV	CO	CAST	29000	123	A4
VERNON AV	LA	VEN	300	49	B3
VERNON AV E	LA	LA11	100	52	B2
VERNON AV E	LA	LA58	1600	52	D2
VERNON AV E	VER	LA58	2000	52	F2
VERNON AV E	VER	LA58	3000	53	A2
VERNON AV N	AZU	AZU	100	86	C6
VERNON AV N	AZU	AZU	100	88	C1
VERNON AV S	AZU	AZU	100	88	C1
VERNON AV W	LA	LA08	2100	51	D2
VERNON AV W	LA	LA37	800	51	D2
VERNON AV W	LA	LA37	100	52	B2
VERNON AV W	LA	LA62	1400	51	D2
VERNON CT	LA	VEN	900	49	C3
VERNON RD	GLEN	GL02	1800	18	B6
VERNON ST	LB	LB06	200	75	C1
VERNON ST	LB	LB15	3900	76	A2
VERNON ST	SH	LB06	900	75	C1
VERONA AV	LA	LA25	10500	42	A3
VERONA LN	PALM	PALM		171	F5
VERONA PL	POM	POM		94	C4
VERONA ST	CO	LA22	4400	45	E6
VERONA ST	CO	LA22	4700	53	E1
VERONA ST	CO	LA23	3800	45	C6
VERONDA PL	SMAR	PAS		37	B1
VERONICA AV	WCOV	WCOV		92	D6
VERONICA CT	LAN	LAN		160	D6
VERONICA LN	LOM	LOM		73	C3
VERONICA ST	LA	LA08	5100	50	F1
VERSAILLES AV	SCLR	VAL		127	A8
VERSAILLES CT	LAN	LAN		159	F8
VERWOOD AV	GLEN	GL14	5000	11	C4
VESELICH AV	LA	LA39	3900	25	B6
VESEY RD	CO	TOP	2100	109	A1
VESPER AV	LA	PAC	9700	8	D4
VESPER AV	LA	VAN	5600	15	D5
VESPER AV	LA	VAN	4400	22	D3
VESTA AV	CO	COM	13000	64	E1
VESTA ST	ING	IN02	700	56	E1
VESTAL AV	LA	LA26	1900	35	D4
VESTONE WY	LA	LA77	10500	32	D3
VESUVIAN WK	LB	LB03	5500	80	C1
VETERAN AV	LA	LA24	100	32	D6
VETERAN AV	LA	LA24	300	41	D1
VETERAN AV	LA	LA25	1800	41	E3
VETERAN AV	LA	LA34	3000	42	A6
VETERAN AV	LA	LA34	3600	50	A1
VETERAN AV	LA	LA64	2200	41	F4
VETS CT	AGH	AGO		102	D2
VEVA WY	CO	CAL		100	A2
VIA ACALONES	PVE	PVP	2200	72	C3
VIA ACERA	CO	MAL	28200	112	B5
VIA ACORDE	CO	VAL		126	J4
VIA ACOSTA	MTB	MTB	2400	46	B6
VIA ADARME	PVE	PVP	300	72	F2
VIA ADORNA	SCLR	VAL		127	A3
VIA ALAMEDA	PVE	PVP	100	72	D2
VIA ALAMEDA	SAD	SAD		89	E5
VIA ALAMEDA	TOR	RB	100	72	D2
VIA ALAMITOS	PVE	PVP	2100	72	C3
VIA ALCALDE AV	LB	LB10		70	B4
VIA ALCANCE	PVE	PVP	200	72	F2
VIA ALCIRA	SCLR	VAL		127	B3
VIA ALEGRE	SAD	SAD		89	D5
VIA ALISTA	LAV	LAV		90	C1
VIA ALISTA	LAV	LAV		95A	C6
VIA ALMAR	PVE	PVP	300	72	C2
VIA ALMENDRO	LB	LB05	600	70	D2
VIA ALONDRA	LB	LB05		70	E1
VIA ALONDRA	PVE	PVP	4200	72	F2
VIA ALTA	BUR	BUR	1000	18	A5
VIA ALTAMIRA	MTB	MTB	500	46	B6
VIA ALVARADO	PVE	PVP	2700	72	A6
VIA AMADEO	SAD	SAD		89	E6
VIA AMADEO	SAD	SAD		93	E1
VIA AMADO	SCLR	VAL		127	B3
VIA AMADOR	PVE	PVP	2300	72	B5
VIA AMARILLA	SAD	SAD		89	F6
VIA AMARILLA	SAD	SAD		93	F1
VIA AMISTAD	POM	POM		90	C6
VIA AMISTOSA	AGH	AGO		100A	C4
VIA AMORITA	DOW	DOW	7200	60	A2
VIA AMOROSA	CO	LPUE	18100	98	D4
VIA ANACAPA	PVE	PVP	2200	72	A5
VIA ANDORRA	SCLR	VAL		127	B3
VIA ANDRES	PVE	PVP		72	B5
VIA ANITA	LA	PP		40	C2
VIA ANITA	LAV	LAV		95A	C6
VIA ANITA	PVE	PVP	2400	72	D2
VIA ANITA	TOR	TOR	100	72	D1
VIA ANSELMO	LA	SF		3	B2
VIA APUESTA	LA	TAR	4600	21	B3
VIA ARABELLA	SAD	SAD		93	E1
VIA ARADO	CO	COM	1900	69	E2
VIA ARANDA	SCLR	VAL		127	A3
VIA ARBOLADA	LA	LA32		36	C4
VIA ARBOLADA	LA	LA42		36	C3
VIA ARCO	PVE	PVP	1500	72	C4
VIA ARDILLA	PVE	PVP	100	72	F1
VIA AROMITAS	PVE	PVP	1700	72	C2
VIA ARRIBA	PVE	PVP	1600	72	C2
VIA ARROYO	LAV	LAV	1600	95A	C5
VIA ARROYO	PVE	PVP	1900	72	C2
VIA ARTINA	SCLR	VAL		127	A4
VIA ASTURIAS	PVE	PVP		72	B5
VIA AVANT	SCLR	VAL		127	B2
VIA AZALEA	PVE	PVP	4300	72	F2
VIA BALBOA	PVE	PVP		72	C3
VIA BANDERA	CO	LPUE		47	F6
VIA BANDINI	PVE	PVP	400	72	A5
VIA BARBARA	LAN	LAN		159	D4
VIA BARCELONA	LAV	LAV		95A	C6
VIA BARCELONA	PVE	PVP		72	B5
VIA BAROLA	LB	LB05	600	70	D2
VIA BARON	CO	COM	19900	69	E2
VIA BARON	RPV	PVP		77	C3
VIA BARRA	SCLR	VAL		127	B3
VIA BARRI	PVE	PVP	2800	72	A6
VIA BEGUINE	SCLR	VAL		127	B3
VIA BERNARD	LA	BUR	9560	17	C1
VIA BLANCA	SAD	SAD		89	F6
VIA BLANCA	SAD	SAD		93	F1
VIA BOCINA	SCLR	VAL		127	A4
VIA BODEGA	PVE	PVP	500	72	E2
VIA BONITA	LB	LB05		70	E1
VIA BONITA	TOR	RB	200	67	D6
VIA BORDEAUX	SCLR	VAL		127	B2
VIA BORICA	PVE	PVP	3000	72	B6
VIA BORICA	RPV	PVP	5000	72	B6
VIA BORONADA	PVE	PVP	1500	72	B4
VIA BOSCANA	SCLR	VAL		127	B3
VIA BRAMANTE	RPV	SP	4000	78	C2
VIA BRASA	SCLR	VAL		127	A4
VIA BRAVA	SCLR	VAL		127	A3
VIA BREVE	MTB	MTB	3000	46	B6
VIA BUENA	LAV	LAV		90	C1
VIA BUENA	LAV	LAV		95A	C6
VIA BUENA	PVE	PVP	3000	72	B6
V BUENA VENTURA	TOR	RB	100	67	D6
VIA CABALLOS	CO	COV		93	A2
VIA CABRILLO	CO	MAL		111	F6
V CABRILLO MRNA	LA	SP		79	A5
VIA CALETA	PVE	PVP	700	72	A6
VIA CALINDA	SCLR	VAL		127	A4
VIA CALISERO	SCLR	VAL		127	B3
VIA CALMA	CO	LPUE	18100	98	D4
VIA CALMA	SCLR	VAL		127	C8
VIA CAMBRON	RPV	PVP	30200	77	B1
VIA CAMILLE	MTB	MTB	2200	46	C6
VIA CAMILLE	SAD	SAD		93	E1
VIA CAMINO	LAV	LAV		90	C1
VIA CAMPESINA	PVE	PVP	2300	72	D2
VIA CAMPO	CO	LA22	5200	46	A5
VIA CAMPO	LAV	LAV		95A	D6
VIA CAMPO	MTB	MTB	5600	46	B5
VIA CANADA	RPV	PVP	6200	78	C2
VIA CANADA	SAD	SAD		89	E5
VIA CANDELA	SCLR	VAL		127	A3
VIA CANDICE CT	SCLR	VAL		127	B1
VIA CANON	SCLR	NEW		127	E5
VIA CANTARE	LA	LA77		32	B1
VIA CAPAY	PVE	PVP	100	72	D2
VIA CAPRI	LA	BUR	7700	17	C2
VIA CARDELINA	PVE	PVP	3700	72	F2
VIA CARMELITA	BUR	BUR	1000	18	A5
VIA CARMELITOS	LB	LB05		70	D2
VIA CARRILLO	PVE	PVP	2200	72	B5
VIA CASSANO	LA	BUR	7780	17	B2
VIA CASTANET	SCLR	VAL		127	D2
VIA CASTILLA	PVE	PVP		72	B5
VIA CATALDO	CO	MAL		113	A5
VIA CATALINA	SCLR	VAL		124	A1
VIA CATALINA	LA	BUR	7750	17	B2
VIA CATALUNA	PVE	PVP	1100	72	C3
VIA CATARINA	SAD	SAD		93	E1
VIA CERRITOS	PVE	PVP	2000	72	C4
VIA CERRO	MTB	MTB	3000	46	B6
VIA CHANTILLY	SCLR	VAL		127	B2
VIA CHAPPARO	CO	CAL		100	D5
VIA CHICO	PVE	PVP	400	72	D2
VIA CHINO	PVE	PVP	1600	72	B2
VIA CIEGA	RPV	SP	6300	78	C3
VIA CIELO	CO	LPUE		85	C2
VIA CLASICO	SCLR	VAL		127	B2
VIA CLEMENTE	CO	LA22	700	54	B1
VIA CLEMENTE	MTB	MTB	700	46	B5
VIA COLINA	LA	LA42		36	D3
VIA COLINAS	WLVL	THO	31500	102	C3
VIA COLINITA	LA	SP	2100	78	D2
VIA COLINITA	RPV	SP	6300	78	D2
VIA COLLADO	RPV	PVP	7300	77	B1
VIA COLORIN	PVE	PVP	200	72	F2
VIA COLUSA	PVE	PVP	100	72	E2
VIA COLUSA	TOR	TOR	100	72	E1
VIA CONCORDIA	SAD	SAD		93	E1
VIA CONEJO	LB	LB05		70	E1
VIA CONEJO	PVE	PVP	800	72	C2
VIA CONSTANCE	LAN	LAN		159	D4
VIA COPETA	SCLR	VAL		127	A4
VIA CORDOVA	LA	SP		78	E1
VIA CORDOVA	PALM	PALM		183	J6
VIA CORONA	CO	LA22	5100	45	F5
VIA CORONA	CO	LA22	5400	46	A5
VIA CORONA	LAV	LAV		90	C1
VIA CORONA	MTB	MTB	2200	46	B6
VIA CORONA	TOR	TOR	4700	72	F1
VIA CORONEL	PVE	PVP	800	72	B4
VIA CORSA	SCLR	VAL		127	B3
VIA CORTA	LAV	LAV		95A	C6
VIA CORTA	LAV	POM		90	C1
VIA CORTA	PVE	PVP	300	72	D2
VIA CORTO	SCLR	VAL		127	B1
VIA COSTA VERDE	RPV	PVP		72	D5
VIA CREMA	LA	BUR	9340	17	B1
VIA CRESTA	LA	PP		40	C2
VIA CRUZ	SCLR	NEW		127	H6
VIA CURVA	PVE	PVP	1100	72	B4
VIA DABNA	SCLR	VAL		127	C8
VIA DALIA	SCLR	VAL		127	B3
VIA DANZA	SCLR	VAL		127	A4
VIA DAVALOS	PVE	PVP	1400	72	B5
VIA DAVISO	MTB	MTB		46	C5
VIA DE ANZAR	RPV	SP		78	D1
VIA DECANO	SCLR	VAL		127	D1
V D GATO LARGO	CO	SAU		188	C1
VIA DE L GUERRA	PVE	PVP	2800	72	B6
VIA DE LA PAZ	LA	PP	300	40	C4
VIA DE LAS OLAS	LA	PP	15200	40	C5
VIA DE LA VISTA	RHE	PVP	1	72	E4
VIA DEL COLLADO	TOR	RB	5600	72	E1
VIA DL CORONADO	CO	LA22	6500	54	B1
VIA DELFINA	SCLR	VAL		127	B2
VIA DELICIA	SCLR	VAL		127	C8
VIA DEL LLANO	CO	CAL		100	D5
VIA DEL MAR	RPV	PVP		77	B2
VIA DEL MONTE	PVE	PVP	500	72	C2
VIA DELORES	BAP	BAP	3300	39	C6
VIA DELORES	BAP	BAP	3300	48	C1
VIA DELORES	LAN	LAN		159	D4
VIA DEL ORO	CO	LA22	700	54	B1
VIA DELOS	SCLR	VAL		127	D1
VIA DEL PALMA	WHI	WHI		55	E5
VIA DEL PARAISO	LAV	LAV		95A	D4
VIA DEL PLAZA	RPV	SP	6300	78	C2
VIA DEL PRADO	CO	TOP		13	B5
VIA DEL PUENTE	PVE	PVP	200	72	C2
VIA DEL REY	SPAS	SPAS	1200	36	E3
VIA DEL RIO	LB	LB15		76	F3
VIA DEL RIO	PALM	PALM		183	G2
VIA DEL SOL	CO	LPUE		47	F5
VIA DEL SOL	LAV	LAV		95A	D4
VIA DEL SOL	LB	LB05		70	E1
VIA DEL SOL	SAD	SAD		89	D6
VIA DEL SOL	SAD	SAD	1200	93	D1
VIA DEL VALLE	LAV	LAV		95A	D6
VIA DEL VALLE	TOR	RB	5300	72	E1
VIA DE MANSION	LAV	LAV		95A	C6
VIA DE PAJARO	DBAR	POM		97A	B2
VIA DESCA	SCLR	VAL		127	A3
VIA DESCANSO	PVE	PVP	1200	72	B4
VIA DESMONDE	LOM	LOM		73	D4
VIA DIA	SCLR	VAL		127	A4
VIA DICHA	CO	LPUE	18100	98	D4
VIA DICHA	LAV	LAV		95A	D4
VIA DI ROMA WK	LB	LB03	1	80	C2
VIA DOLARITA	SCLR	VAL		127	A4
VIA DOLCE	LA	VEN		49	C5
V DONA CHRISTA	SCLR	VAL	25200	127	B2
VIA DONTE	LA	VEN		49	D6
VIA EBANO	SCLR	VAL		127	D1
VIA EL CAMINO	BAP	BAP	4700	39	E3
VIA EL CHICO	TOR	RB	100	67	E6
VIA EL CHICO	TOR	TOR	100	72	E1
VIA ELEVADA	PVE	PVP	2700	72	D2
VIA ELISANDRA	SCLR	VAL		127	B3
VIA ELISO	SCLR	VAL		127	D1
VIA EL MIRO	RPV	PVP	2800	78	C1
VIA EL PRADO	RB	RB	1700	67	D6
VIA EL SERENO	TOR	RB	4800	72	E1
VIA EL TORO	TOR	RB	100	72	D1
VIA ENCANTO	LOM	LOM		73	D4
VIA ENTRADA	CO	LPUE		98	D4
VIA ENTRADA	LAV	LAV	4600	95A	D5
VIA ESCONDIDA	WHI	WHI	15000	84	B1
VIA ESCONDIDO	CO	MAL	5900	112	F6
VIA ESCOVAR	SCLR	VAL		127	A3
VIA ESPERANZA	SAD	SAD		89	D5
VIA ESPLANADE	LB	LB05		70	E1
VIA ESQUINA	CO	CAL		100	D5
VIA ESTRADA	PVE	PVP	600	72	A5
VIA ESTRELLA	SCLR	NEW		127	E5
VIA ESTRELLA	POM	POM		90	C6
VIA ESTRELLITA	GLDR	GLDR	800	87	B4
VIA ESTRELLITA	TOR	RB	100	67	D6
VIA ESTUDILLO	PVE	PVP	1700	72	B4
VIA FAMERO DR	CO	SAU		182	C7
VIA FARALLON	SCLR	VAL		127	B3
VIA FAROL	SCLR	VAL		127	D1
VIA FERNANDEZ	PVE	PVP	2000	72	C3
VIA FERRARA	LA	BUR	9310	17	B1
VIA FLAMENCO	SCLR	VAL		127	A3
VIA FLORED	SCLR	VAL	22900	127	B1
VIA FLORENCE	LA	PP	300	40	A3
VIA FLORESTA	LA	PP		40	B2
VIA FOGGIA	LA	BUR	7800	17	C1
VIA FORTUNA	LB	LB05		70	E1
VIA FORTUNA	PVE	PVP	900	72	B5
VIA FRANCISCA	LA	SP		78	E1
VIA FRANCISCO	LA	LA33	1200	44	F3
VIA FRASCATI	RPV	SP	4200	78	C2
VIA FRESA	SAD	SAD	2300	93	D1
VIA FUENTE	SCLR	VAL		127	D2
VIA GABRIEL	PVE	PVP	1200	72	D3
VIA GALERO	SCLR	VAL		127	D2
VIA GALICIA	PVE	PVP		72	B5
VIA GARDENIA	CO	CYN	14800	125	F6
VIA GARFIAS	PVE	PVP	1600	72	B4
VIA GAVILAN	PVE	PVP	4000	72	F2
VIA GAVOLA	SCLR	VAL		127	B2
VIA GAYO	SCLR	VAL		127	B3
VIA GENOVA	LA	BUR	7780	17	B2
VIA GOLETA	LB	LB05		70	E1
VIA GOLETA	PVE	PVP	1000	72	B5
VIA GORRION	PVE	PVP	500	72	F2
VIA GRACIOSO	SCLR	VAL	25500	127	B1
VIA GRANADA	RHE	PVP	28300	72	D5
VIA GRANATE	SMAD	SMAD		28	E1
VIA GREGORIO	SAD	SAD		89	E6
VIA GUADALANA	PVE	PVP	2200	72	C3
VIA HALCON	CO	CAL		100	D5
VIA HAMACA	SCLR	VAL		127	A3
VIA HELINA	SCLR	VAL		127	A2
VIA HERALDO	SCLR	VAL	25500	127	B2
VIA HISPANO	SCLR	VAL		127	B3
VIA HONRADO	PALM	LAN		171	D3
VIA HORCADA	PVE	PVP	700	72	B2
VIA HORQUILLA	PVE	PVP	600	72	D2
VIA IMPRESO	SCLR	VAL	25500	127	B2
VIA IRANA	SCLR	VAL		127	A2
VIA JACARA	SCLR	VAL		127	A2
VIA JACINTO	LAV	LAV		95A	E4
VIA JARDIN	SCLR	VAL	25500	127	B2
VIA JOSE	PVE	PVP	100	72	D2
VIA JUANA	SCLR	VAL		127	A3
VIA JUANITA	WAL	WAL		93	B6
VIA JUSTINO	SAD	SAD		89	E6
VIA KANNELA	SCLR	VAL		127	B2
VIA LABRADA	SCLR	VAL	25500	127	B2
VIA LA BREA	PVE	PVP	2200	72	C3
VIA LA CIENEGA	MTB	MTB	800	46	F6
VIA LA CIMA	RPV	PVP		72	D5
VIA LA CIRCULA	TOR	RB	100	67	D6
VIA LA CRESTA	RPV	PVP	30500	77	C2
VIA LA CUESTA	PVE	PVP		72	D3
VIA LADERA	SCLR	VAL	22900	127	B2
VIA LADERA	LHH	LAH	1700	84	E2
VIA LADO	TOR	TOR	4100	72	F1
VIA LANDETA	PVE	PVP	1200	72	B4
VIA LA PALOMA	RPV	SP	6600	78	D2
VIA LA PAZ	BUR	BUR		18	A5
VIA LA PAZ	LA	SP		78	E1
VIA LA REINA	LA	LA33	1200	44	F3
VIA LARGAVISTA	PVE	PVP	4000	72	F2
VIA LA ROCCA	RPV	PVP		72	D5
VIA LA SELVA	CLA	CLA		91	B2
VIA LA SELVA	PVE	PVP	2400	72	E2
VIA LA SELVA	TOR	RB	400	72	D1
VIA LA SOLEDAD	TOR	RB	100	72	D1
VIA LASTRE	MTB	MTB	3000	46	B6
VIA LAS VEGAS	LA	LA33	1200	44	F3
VIA LAS VEGAS	PVE	PVP	100	72	E2
VIA LATINA	LA	BUR	7930	17	B1
VIA LAZO	PVE	PVP	1500	72	B3
VIA LEON	PVE	PVP	1500	72	B4
VIA LEONARDO	CO	TOP		13	B5
VIA LIDO PL	POM	POM	1900	90	F6
VIA LINDA	CO	MAL		113	A5
VIA LINDA	LB	LB05		70	E1
VIA LINDA	WHI	WHI	8700	84	A2
VIA LINDA VISTA	TOR	RB	200	67	D6
VIA LOPEZ	PVE	PVP	1500	72	B3
VIA LORADO	RPV	PVP	7300	72	B6
VIA LORENZO	RPV	SP	6500	78	D2
VIA LOS ALTOS	CLA	CLA	300	91	B2
VIA LOS ALTOS	TOR	TOR	300	72	E1
VIA LOS ANDES	CLA	CLA	2400	96	A5

STREET	CITY	P.O. ZONE	BLOCK	PAGE	GRID
V LOS MIRADORES	TOR	RB		67	E6
V LOS MIRADORES	TOR	RB	500	72	E1
VIA LOS PALOS	SAD	SAD	2300	93	D1
V LS PIMENTEROS	LA	LA33	1200	44	F3
VIA LOS SANTOS	SAD	SAD	700	90	B3
VIA LS SANTOS E	LA	LA33	1400	44	F3
VIA LS SANTOS S	LA	LA33	300	44	F4
VIA LUCIA	LA	PP	400	40	A3
VIA LUCIA	MTB	MTB	2400	46	C6
VIA LUNA DR	LHH	LAH		84	F2
VIA LUNETO	MTB	MTB	400	46	B6
VIA LUPONA	SCLR	VAL		127	B2
VIA MACARENA	SCLR	VAL		127	A3
VIA MACHADO	PVE	PVP	1600	72	B4
VIA MADERAS	CO	ALT	2900	20	C4
VIA MADONNA	LOM	LOM		73	D4
VIA MADRID	LAV	LAV		90	C1
VIA MADURO	SCLR	VAL		127	B2
VIA MAGDALENA	LA	BUR	7900	17	B2
VIA MAJORCA	RHE	PVP	28200	72	D5
VIA MALAGA	TOR	RB	300	72	D1
VIA MALONA	RPV	PVP		72	D5
VIA MARCIA	SCLR	SAU		124	C5
VIA MARCIA	LAV	LAV		95A	C6
VIA MARGARITA	PVE	PVP	1300	72	C4
VIA MARGARITA	SAD	SAD		93	E1
VIA MARGATE	PVE	PVP	800	72	B4
VIA MARIA	LA	PP	300	40	A3
V MARIE CELESTE	RPV	PVP	7200	72	B6
VIA MARINA	CO	MDR	4000	49	D5
VIA MARIPOSA	SAD	SAD	2400	93	D1
VIA MARISOL	LA	LA32		36	C4
VIA MARISOL	LA	LA42		36	C3
VIA MARQUETTE	LOM	LOM		73	D4
VIA MARTINEZ	PVE	PVP	1500	72	B4
VIA MATEO	PVE	PVP		72	D4
VIA MEDIA	PVE	PVP	400	72	C2
VIA MESA GRANDE	TOR	RB	100	72	D1
VIA MIA	LA	LA32		36	D4
VIA MIGUEL	PVE	PVP		72	B6
VIA MILAND	LA	BUR	9550	17	L1
VIA MIRABEL	PVE	PVP	1000	72	C3
VIA MIRADA	LB	LB05		70	E1
VIA MIRADA	PVE	PVP	900	72	D3
VIA MIRAMONTE	MTB	MTB	400	46	C6
VIA MIRAMONTE	MTB	MTB	300	54	C1
VIA MIROLA	PVE	PVP		72	B5
VIA MONDO	CO	COM		65	B5
VIA MONIQUE	LA	BUR	9350	17	B2
VIA MONTANA	BUR	BUR	100	17	F4
VIA MONTANA	SCLR	NEW		127	E5
VIA MONTE D ORO	TOR	RB	100	72	D1
VIA MONTE D ORO	TOR	TOR		67	D6
VIA MONTE MAR	PVE	PVP	1400	72	C2
VIA MONTES AV	MPK	MPK		46	B3
VIA MONTEVIDEO	CLA	CLA	2400	96	A5
VIANA AV	LOM	LOM	25800	73	C3
VIA NAPOLI	LA	BUR	7700	17	B2
VIA NAPOLI	MTB	MTB		46	D5
VIA NARANJO	LAV	LAV		95A	C5
VIA NAUTICA	SCLR	VAL	25500	127	B2
VIA NAVAJO	PVE	PVP	100	72	E2
VIA NAVARRA	LA	SP		78	E1
VIA NEVE	PVE	PVP	2800	72	A6
VIA NICOLA E	LA	LA33	1200	44	F3
VIA NICOLA S	LA	LA33	100	44	F3
VIA NICOLAS	LA	PP	300	40	A3
VIA NINA	MTB	MTB	2400	46	C6
VIA NIVEL	PVE	PVP	3900	72	F2
VIA NOGALES	PVE	PVP	900	72	C3
VIA NOLA	LA	BUR	9760	17	B2
VIA NORTE	LB	LB05		70	E1
VIA NORTE	MTB	MTB	300	46	B6
VIA NORTE AV	MPK	MPK	2300	46	B5
VIA NOVA	LAV	LAV		95A	E4
VIA NOVA	LOM	LOM		73	D4
VIA NOVIA	SCLR	VAL		127	A3
VIA NUEVO	PALM	LAN		171	D3
VIA OLEADAS	PVE	PVP	1	72	A5
VIA OLIVERA	PVE	PVP	1800	72	B5
VIA ONDA	SCLR	VAL		127	A3
VIA OPATA	PVE	PVP	3900	72	F2
VIA ORIOL	SCLR	VAL		127	B2
VIA ORO AV	LB	LB10		70	A4
VIA PACHECO	PVE	PVP	1800	72	A4
VIA PACIFICA	SCLR	VAL	25100	127	B2
VIA PADOVA	CO	CLA	3900	96	C4
VIA PALACIO	SCLR	VAL		127	B2
VIA PALACIO	RPV	PVP		77	C3
VIA PALADAR	SCLR	VAL		127	A3
VIA PALERMO	MTB	MTB		46	D5
VIA PALESTRA	PVE	PVP		72	B5
VIA PALOMARES	SAD	SAD		89	D5
VIA PALOMINO	PVE	PVP	3300	72	E2
VIA PANORAMA	PVE	PVP	900	72	D3
VIA PARO	PVE	PVP	600	72	F2

STREET	CITY	P.O. ZONE	BLOCK	PAGE	GRID
VIA PASCUAL	TOR	RB	100	72	D1
VIA PASEO	MTB	MTB	2400	46	C5
VIA PASQUAL	PVE	PVP	100	72	D1
VIA PASSILO	LB	LB05	5100	70	D2
VIA PATRICIA	LA	BUR	9340	17	B2
VIA PAVIA	LA	BUR	9760	17	B2
VIA PAVION	PVE	PVP	3900	72	F2
VIA PENA	PVE	PVP	400	72	A5
VIA PERGOLA	RPV	PVP		72	D5
VIA PICAPOSTE	PVE	PVP	3900	72	F2
VIA PIMA	PVE	PVP	4000	72	F2
VIA PINALE	PVE	PVP	2300	72	D2
VIA PINZON	PVE	PVP	4200	73	A2
VIA PLATA	SCLR	NEW		127	H6
VIA PLATA ST	LB	LB10		70	A4
VIA PZ LIBRE N	MTB	MTB		46	B6
VIA PZ LIBRE S	MTB	MTB		46	B6
VIA PLAZA SIENA	RPV	PVP		78	D2
VIA POMPEII	LA	BUR	8000	17	B1
VIA PORTO GRNDE	RPV	PVP		72	D5
VIA PORTOLA	LA	LA33	1200	44	F3
VIA PRADERA	CO	CAL		100	D5
VIA PRIMERO	SCLR	VAL		127	H6
VIA PRIMERO	PALM	PALM		183	G2
VIA PRINCESSA	SCLR	SAU		124	G9
VIA PRINCESSA	SCLR	SAU		127	J1
VIA PROVIDENCIA	BUR	BUR		17	F5
VIA QUINTO	WAL	WAL		93	A6
VIA RAFAEL	PVE	PVP	2400	72	D3
VIA RAMON	SCLR	VAL	25200	127	B2
VIA RAMON	PVE	PVP	2400	72	D2
VIA RANA	SCLR	VAL		127	B2
VIA RANCHO AV	BAP	BAP		48	C1
VIA RANCHO RD	DBAR	POM		94	A6
V RO LA VERNE	LAV	LAV	3900	90	C1
V RO LA VERNE	LAV	LAV		95A	C6
VIA RAZA	SCLR	VAL		124	A9
VIA REBECCA	LAN	LAN		159	D4
VIA REGATA	CO	MDR		49	D4
VIA RICARDO	LA	BUR	9520	17	C1
VIA RIMINI	LA	BUR	9630	17	B3
VIA RINCON	PVE	PVP	900	72	D2
VIA RIO NIDO	DOW	DOW	7200	60	A2
VIA RIVERA	PVE	PVP	2100	72	B5
VIA RIVERA	RPV	PVP	30000	72	B6
VIA RIVERA PZ	PVE	PVP	2100	72	B5
VIA RIVIERA	TOR	RB	100	72	D1
VIARNA ST	CER	ART	12200	81	B2
VIA ROCAS	WLVL	THO		102	B3
VIA ROMA	LA	BUR		17	B2
VIA ROMA	MTB	MTB	7900	46	D5
VIA ROMALES	SAD	SAD	1000	93	E1
VIA ROMANA	LAN	LAN		160	F5
VIA ROMERO	PVE	PVP	1000	72	B5
VIA RONALDO	LA	BUR	7760	17	C1
VIA ROSA	BAP	BAP		48	D1
VIA ROSA	LA	BUR	7750	17	C1
VIA ROSA	PVE	PVP	2200	72	C2
VIA ROSA LINDA	SCLR	VAL		124	A1
VIA SALDIVAR	GLEN	GL08	2000	18	D6
VIA SALERNO	LA	BUR	9420	17	C1
VIA SALUDO	SCLR	VAL	25200	127	B2
VIA SAN CARLO	MTB	MTB	2800	46	B6
VIA SANCHEZ	PVE	PVP	2500	72	B5
VIA SN CLEMENTE	MTB	MTB	300	46	B6
VIA SAN DELARRO	CO	LA22	5200	46	A5
VIA SAN DELARRO	MTB	MTB		46	B6
VIA SAN DIEGO	LA	SF		3	B2
VIA SAN FELIPE	LA	SF		3	B2
VIA SAN JOSE	CO	LPUE		98	C4
VIA SAN MARINO	LA	SF		3	B2
VIA SAN MIGUEL	LA	SF		3	B2
VIA SAN PABLO	LA	SF		3	B2
VIA SAN RAFAEL	LA	SF		3	B2
VIA SAN REMO	LA	SF		3	B2
VIA SAN RICARDO	LA	SF		3	B2
V SAN SEBASTIAN	TOR	RB	300	72	D1
VIA SAN SIMON	CLA	CLA	2400	96	A5
VIA STA BARBARA	LA	SF		3	B2
V STA CATARINA	CLA	CLA	2400	96	A5
VIA SANTA CRUZ	WHI	WHI	8600	84	B2
VIA SANTA YNEZ	LA	PP	500	40	B3
VIA SANTIAGO	LA	SF		3	B2
VIA SANTO TOMAS	CLA	CLA	2400	96	A5
VIA SEBASTIAN	LA	SP		78	E1
VIA SEGO	TOR	RB	100	67	E6
VIA SEGO	TOR	TOR	100	72	E1
VIA SEGOVIA	PVE	PVP	2800	72	A6
VIA SEGUNDA	PVE	PVP	2600	72	D2
VIA SERRA RAMAL	WHI	WHI	8400	84	B1
VIA SEVILLA	LAV	LAV		90	C1
VIA SEVILLA	RHE	PVP	100	72	D5
VIA SEVILLA	TOR	RB	100	72	E1
VIA SIENA	LA	BUR	9720	17	B2
VIA SIENA	RPV	SP	6500	78	D2
VIA SINALOA	CLA	CLA	3400	96	A6

STREET	CITY	P.O. ZONE	BLOCK	PAGE	GRID
VIA SISTINE	SCLR	VAL		127	B4
VIA SOBRANTE	PVE	PVP	2400	72	D3
VIA SOL	PALM	LAN		171	D3
VIA SOLA	PVE	PVP	2800	72	A6
VIA SOLANO	LOM	LOM		73	D4
VIA SOLANO	PVE	PVP	3900	72	F2
VIA SOMONTE	PVE	PVP	700	72	C2
VIA SONOMA	PVE	PVP	2400	72	D3
VIA SONOMA	RPV	PVP	2400	72	D3
VIA SORELLA	DBAR	WAL		97	D3
VIA SORRENTO	LA	BUR	7700	17	B2
VIA STEFANO	LA	BUR	7900	17	C2
VIA SUBIDA	RPV	SP		78	C2
VIA SUN	PALM	LAN		171	D4
VIA SUR	CO	LPUE		47	F6
VIA TAMPA	LOM	LOM		73	D4
VIA TANARA	SCLR	VAL		127	B4
VIA TAPIA	CO	MAL	6000	113	A5
VIA TAZ	CO	MAL		108	D6
VIA TAZ	CO	MAL		114	D1
VIA TECOLOTE	CO	CAL		100	D5
VIA TEHAGO	SCLR	VAL		127	H6
VIA TEJON	PVE	PVP	2500	72	D2
VIA TELINO	SCLR	VAL	25200	127	B2
VIA TERRAZA	SCLR	SAU		124	C6
VIA TIVOLI	LA	BUR	9520	17	C1
VIA TOLEDO	LAV	LAV		95A	D5
VIA TOMAS	SCLR	VAL		127	A1
VIA TOMAS DR	WAL	WAL	21000	93	B6
VIA TORINO	LA	BUR	9630	17	B2
VIA TORTONA	LA	BUR	7800	17	C2
VIA TRANQUILO	CO	LPUE		98	C4
VIA TURINA	SCLR	VAL		124	A1
VIA UDINE	LA	BUR	7800	17	B2
VIA VALDES	PVE	PVP	2600	72	B5
VIA VALENCIA	TOR	TOR		67	D6
VIA VALENTINA	SCLR	VAL		127	B4
VIA VALER	SCLR	VAL		127	C8
VIA VALLARTA	LA	ENC	17800	21	D4
VIA VALMONTE	PVE	PVP	3700	72	E2
VIA VALMONTE	TOR	TOR		73	A2
VIA VALOR	PALM	LAN		171	D4
VIA VAL VERDE	MTB	MTB		46	C6
VIA VAQUERO	SAD	SAD		89	F3
VIA VAQUERO	SAD	SAD		90	A3
VIA VELADOR	SCLR	VAL		127	A3
VIA VELARDO	RPV	SP	2200	78	D1
VIA VENADO	LCF	LCF	2100	18	F1
VIA VENADO ST	BAP	BAP		48	C1
VIA VENEZIA	LA	BUR	9420	17	B2
VIA VENTANA	PVE	PVP	900	72	B5
VIA VERA	LOM	LOM		73	D4
VIA VERANADA	LB	LB05	5100	70	D2
VIA VERDAD	PALM	LAN		171	D4
VIA VERDE	CO	COV	20300	93	C1
VIA VERDE	SAD	SAD		93	D1
VIA VERDE AV	PALM	PALM		183	E2
VIA VERDEROL	PVE	PVP		72	F2
VIA VERITA AV	CO	LPUE	2100	85	D3
VIA VERITA DR	CO	LPUE	15300	85	D3
VIA VERONA	LAN	LAN		160	F5
VIA VERONA	LA	BUR	8000	17	C1
VIA VERONA	LA	LA77	10800	32	D3
VIA VICO	RPV	SP	4000	78	D2
VIA VICTORIA	PVE	PVP	2900	72	B6
VIA VICTORIA	RPV	PVP	30100	77	B1
VIA VIENTA	CO	MAL	4500	111	A4
VIA VIGO	RB	RB		67	D6
VIA VISALIA	PVE	PVP	1300	72	C3
VIA VISTA	MTB	MTB	500	46	C6
VIA VISTA	MTB	MTB	100	54	B1
VIA WANDA	LB	LB05	600	70	D2
VIA YOLANDA	LA	BUR	9400	17	B1
VIA ZIBELLO	LA	BUR	9700	17	B2
VIA ZUMAYA	PVE	PVP	1500	72	B5
VIA ZURITA	CLA	CLA	1300	91	B2
VIA ZURITA	PVE	PVP	1500	72	B4
VIBURNUM DR	CO	WHI	14100	61	E5
VICAR ST	LA	LA34	9800	42	C5
VICASA DR	CO	CAL		100	F4
VICCI ST	SCLR	CYN	18700	124	J9
VICCI ST	SCLR	CYN		125	A8
VICENTE AV	POM	POM	900	91	A5
VICENTE PL	CER	ART		82	B5
VICENTE TER	SM	SM	1	49	A2
VICENZA WY	LA	LA77	10800	32	D3
VICEROY AV	AZU	AZU	100	86	E6
VICEROY AV	AZU	AZU	100	88	E1
VICEROY AV	CO	AZU	5400	88	E2
VICEROY AV	CO	COV	4600	88	E4
VICEROY AV	COV	COV	700	88	E4
VICINO WY	LA	PP	17800	115	F4
VICK PL	BH	BH	500	33	C2
VICKER CT	PALM	PALM		171	C5
VICKER WY	PALM	PALM		171	C5
VICKER WY	PALM	PALM		171	F4

STREET	CITY	P.O. ZONE	BLOCK	PAGE	GRID
VICKERS DR	GLEN	GL08	1800	18	F4
VICKI DR	CO	WHI	7000	55	B5
VICKI DR	CO	WHI	8400	61	A1
VICKI DR	SFS	SFS	7900	55	B6
VICKI DR	SFS	SFS	9100	61	A2
VICKI DR	WHI	WHI	6200	55	C4
VICKIE AV	CER	ART	18400	81	D1
VICKIE AV	CER	ART	17000	82	C5
VICKIE PL	CER	ART	19300	81	D2
VICKIVIEW DR	CO	CAN		5	D4
VICKSBURG AV	LA	LA45	7800	50	C6
VICKSBURG AV	LA	LA45	7900	56	C1
VICKY AV	LA	CAN	6400	12	A4
VICKY AV	TOR	TOR	21500	67	F4
VICLAND PL	LA	NHO	6300	16	E5
VICSTONE CT	CUL	CUL	5800	50	E1
VICTOR AV	ING	IN02	800	50	E6
VICTOR PL	LAN	LAN		160	H6
VICTOR ST	LA	LA12	400	44	D1
VICTOR ST	TOR	TOR	20200	67	E3
VICTORIA	WCOV	WCOV		88	A6
VICTORIA AV	CO	LA08	4100	51	C4
VICTORIA AV	CO	LA43	4700	51	C4
VICTORIA AV	CO	WHI	10000	61	E4
VICTORIA AV	ING	IN05	7400	51	C6
VICTORIA AV	ING	IN05	7800	57	C1
VICTORIA AV	LA	LA05	800	43	C3
VICTORIA AV	LA	LA08	3800	51	B1
VICTORIA AV	LA	LA16	1900	43	B4
VICTORIA AV	LA	LA19	900	43	C3
VICTORIA AV	LA	LA43	5100	51	C5
VICTORIA AV	LA	LA66	11300	49	E2
VICTORIA AV	LA	LA66	11300	50	A1
VICTORIA AV	LA	VEN	500	49	D3
VICTORIA AV	LPUE	LPUE	15400	48	F5
VICTORIA AV	SOG	SOG	8100	59	A3
VICTORIA AV E	MTB	MTB	100	54	E1
VICTORIA AV W	MTB	MTB	100	46	C6
VICTORIA AV W	MTB	MTB	100	54	E1
VICTORIA DR	ARC	ARC	800	28	C5
VICTORIA DR	PAS	PAS	800	27	D2
VICTORIA LN	PR	PR		55	E3
VICTORIA LN	SMAD	SMAD	1	28	C2
VICTORIA PL	BUR	BUR	800	17	D3
VICTORIA PL	CLA	CLA	300	91	C5
VICTORIA PL	LAV	LAV		95A	C5
VICTORIA PL	PVE	PVP	1000	72	B6
VICTORIA ST	CO	COM	1900	64	E6
VICTORIA ST	CO	COM		65	B6
VICTORIA ST	COM	COM		64	F6
VICTORIA ST	LB	LB05	100	65	B6
VICTORIA ST	PALM	PALM		171	J7
VICTORIA ST E	CAR	CAR	1300	64	D6
VICTORIA ST E	CAR	GAR	100	64	D6
VICTORIA ST W	CAR	GAR	100	64	A6
VICTORIA WY	POM	POM		90	F5
VICTORIA PK DR	LA	LA19	4300	43	C3
VICTORIA PK PL	LA	LA19	4300	43	C3
VICTORIA PT RD	CO	MAL		111	D4
VICTORINE ST	LA	LA31		36	B5
VICTORVILLE PL	LAN	LAN		159	J7
VICTORVILLE PL	LAN	LAN	42900	159	J8
VICTORY BLVD	BUR	BUR	3900	16	F5
VICTORY BLVD	BUR	BUR	900	17	A5
VICTORY BLVD	GLEN	GL01	1500	24	D1
VICTORY BLVD	LA	NHO	10500	16	A5
VICTORY BLVD	LA	RES	17700	14	A5
VICTORY BLVD	LA	VAN	16400	14	D5
VICTORY BLVD	LA	VAN	13300	15	A5
VICTORY BLVD	LA	VAN	13100	16	A5
VICTORY BLVD	LA	WOH	23000	5	E5
VICTORY BLVD	LA	WOH	19700	12	A5
VICTORY BLVD N	BUR	BUR	100	17	D5
VICTORY BLVD S	BUR	BUR	100	24	D1
VICTORY CT	BUR	BUR	300	24	D1
VICTORY PL	BUR	BUR	1000	17	C5
VICTORY TRCK BL	GLEN	GL01		24	F3
VICTORY TRCK BL	GLEN	GL10		25	A3
VICWOOD AV	CO	GL14	4800	11	E6
VIDALIA AV	CO	LPUE	300	98	D1
VIDETTE ST	LA	LA42	6200	36	D1
VIDOR DR	LA	LA35	9800	42	B2
VIDORA DR	CO	LPUE	18400	98	E4
VIEJO CT	SCLR	VAL		127	H6
VIELLA AV	GLDR	GLDR	1400	88	F2
VIENNA WY	LA	LA66		49	F1
VIENNA WY	LA	VEN	1200	49	D3
VIENTO CT	SCLR	VAL		124	A1
VIENTOS DR	CO	PALM	8700	171I	G5
VIENTO VERNO DR	DBAR	POM	21200	97	D4
VIERO PL	LAM	LAM	15100	83	A1
VIERRA AV	CER	ART	17600	82	E6
VIETA AV	LYN	LYN	11600	59	D6
VIEUDELOU AV	AVA	AVA		77	B4
VIEUDELOU AV	NWK	NWK	13200	82	D2
VIEW DR	BUR	BUR	600	17	F5

STREET	CITY	P.O. ZONE	BLOCK	PAGE	GRID
VIEW DR	CO	AGO		107	B3
VIEW DR	WCOV	WCOV		97	A2
VIEW LN	DBAR	POM		97A	B1
VIEW PL	HB	RB		62	D6
VIEW CREST DR	AZU	AZU	100	86	D4
VIEWCREST DR	BUR	BUR		17	D2
VIEWCREST DR	MTB	MTB	300	46	F6
VIEWCREST DR	WHI	WHI		55	F6
VIEW CREST RD	GLEN	GL02	300	25	C1
VIEWCREST RD	LA	NHO	12000	23	C5
VIEWFIELD AV	CO	LPUE	3300	85	D5
VIEWLAKE LN	WLVL	THO		102	A4
VIEWLAND PL	LA	SP	200	79	A2
VIEWMONT DR	LA	LA69	1600	33	D3
VIEW PARK AV	BLF	BLF		66	D4
VIEWPOINT CIR	POM	POM		94	D5
VIEWPOINT DR	LA	TU	9700	10	F4
VIEW POINTE DR	WLVL	THO		102	A5
VIEWPOINTE LN	WAL	WAL		93	D6
VIEWRIDGE LN	LA	SF		2	B6
VIEWRIDGE RD	CO	TOP		13	C5
VIEWSITE DR	LA	LA69	1500	33	D3
VIEWSITE TER	LA	LA69	1500	33	D3
VIGILANCE DR	RPV	PVP	3500	78	B3
VIGNES ST N	LA	LA12	100	44	E3
VIGNES ST S	LA	LA12	100	44	E3
VIKING AV	LA	NOR		1	B6
VIKING AV	LA	NOR	10100	7	B3
VIKING WY	LB	LB08	4100	71	C4
VIKINGS WY	CER	ART	18600	81	D1
VILLA CT	SPAS	SPAS		36	D3
VILLA DR	WHI	WHI	8700	61	D1
VILLA ST	MTB	MTB		46	E5
VILLA ST E	PAS	PAS	100	27	F3
VILLA ST W	PAS	PAS	100	26	F3
VILLA WY	LAN	LAN		160	E6
VILLA WY	LAV	LAV	2400	90	D3
VILLA ALTA PL	CO	LPUE	2600	85	E4
VILLA CANYON RD	CO	CAST	30400	123	D2
VILLA CLARA ST	CO	LPUE	18200	98	F5
VILLA CORTA ST	CO	LPUE	17000	92	C6
VILLA COSTERA	CO	MAL	3900	114	E4
VILLA ESCUELA	MB	MB		62	B4
VILLA FLORES DR	CO	LPUE	16000	85	E4
VILLAGE AV	LA	SV	8800	9	F6
VILLAGE CIR	MB	MB		62	C3
VILLAGE CIR	TEC	TEC	5200	38	C3
VILLAGE CT	SAD	SAD		89	E2
VILLAGE CT	TOR	TOR	21400	68	A4
VILLAGE DR	CER	ART	13400	82	D4
VILLAGE DR	CMRC	LA40		53	F2
VILLAGE DR	MB	MB		62	C2
VILLAGE DR	MPK	MPK	700	46	D3
VILLAGE LN	PALM	PALM		172	E6
VILLAGE LN	TOR	TOR	3800	68	A4
VILLAGE LN	WCOV	WCOV		88	B4
VILLAGE LN E	RM	RM		46	F4
VILLAGE PL	MPK	MPK	700	46	D3
VILLAGE RD	LA	VEN	8600	55A	E2
VILLAGE RD	LB	LB08	4400	71	B4
VILLAGE RD	LKD	LKD	2700	70	F4
VILLAGE RD	LKD	LKD	5500	71	D4
VILLAGE WY	LA	SP		78	D3
VILLGE BROOK RD	WLVL	THO	31800	102	B4
VILLAGE CTR DR	MB	MB		62	D3
VILLAGE CTR RD	WLVL	THO		102	B4
VILLAGE CIRCLE	MB	MB		62	C3
VILLAGE GREEN	LA	LA16	5100	42	F6
VILLAGE GRN DR	LKD	LKD		81	A3
VILLAGE LOOP RD	POM	POM		94	C5
VILLAGE OAKS DR	COV	COV		89	B6
VILLAGE OAKS DR	COV	COV		93	B1
VILLAGE PARK DR	SM	SM		41	D6
VILLAGER LN	CO	TOR		68	F6
VILLAGE SCHL RD	WLVL	THO	31600	102	B4
VILLA GRANDE RD	CO	LPUE	15800	85	E4
VILLA GROVE DR	CO	ALT		20	B3
VILLA GROVE DR	LA	PP		40	E3
VILLA HTS RD	CO	PAS		20	F5
VILLA HTS RD	CO	PAS		20A	A2
VLA HIGHLNDS DR	CO	PAS		27	F1
VILLA KNOLLS DR	CO	PAS		20	F6
VILLA MARIA RD	CLA	CLA		91	B1
VILLA MESA RD	CO	PAS		20	F6
VILLA MESA RD	CO	PAS		20A	A3
VILLA MONTE AV	MPK	MPK		46	B3
VILLANOVA AV	LA	LA45	8700	56	A2
VILLANOVA DR	CLA	CLA	100	91	C5
VLA PACIFCA CIR	CAR	CAR		69	D4
VILLA PARK DR	RM	RM		46	F4
VILLA PARK ST	CO	LPUE		92	C6
VILLA PARK ST	CO	LPUE	17400	98	C1
VILLA PARK ST	LPUE	LPUE		92	C6
VILLA PARK ST	LPUE	LPUE	17100	98	C1
VILLA RICA AV	CO	PAS		20	F6

1990 LOS ANGELES COUNTY STREET INDEX

STREET	CITY	P.O. ZONE	BLOCK	PAGE	GRID
VILLA RICA AV	CO	PAS		20A	A3
VILLA RITA DR	LHH	LAH		84	E2
VILLA RITA DR	WHI	WHI		84	E3
VILLA ROSA DR	RPV	PVP	6300	72	D4
VILLA VERDE DR	WHI	WHI	8200	84	B2
VILLA VIEW	LA	PP		40	E3
VILLAWOOD CIR	CO	CAL		100	B2
VILLA WOODS DR	LA	PP		40	E3
VILLA WOODS PL	LA	PP		40	E3
VILLA ZANITA	CO	ALT		19	F4
VILLEBOSO AV	LA	WOH	5200	13	B1
VILLENA AV	LA	WOH	21400	13	C3
VILLEROY AV	WAL	WAL		93	B3
VILNA AV	SCLR	CYN	27500	124	J9
VIMY RD	LA	SF	11500	1	D6
VINA AV	LB	LB13	1000	75	E4
VINCENNES ST	LA	CHA	22100	6	B5
VINCENNES ST	LA	NOR	19100	7	B5
VINCENNES ST	LA	SF	16800	7	F5
VINCENNES ST	LA	SF	15500	8	B5
VINCENNES ST	LA	VAN	14600	8	D5
VINCENT AV	CO	COV	4400	88	B4
VINCENT AV	COV	COV	100	88	B4
VINCENT AV	LA	LA41	4700	26	B5
VINCENT AV N	WCOV	WCOV	100	88	B6
VINCENT AV S	WCOV	WCOV	100	92	B1
VINCENT PL	CO	LA63	3500	45	C3
VINCENT PK	RB	RB	600	67	D3
VINCENT ST	RB	RB	400	67	D3
VINCENT WY	GLEN	GL05	1100	25	E6
VINCENT VIEW RD	CO	PALM		183	C9
VINE AL	PAS	PAS	200	27	E3
VINE AV	BELL	BELL		53	B5
VINE AV	TOR	TOR	2700	68	C5
VINE AV	TOR	TOR	23700	73	C1
VINE AV E	WCOV	WCOV	500	92	C2
VINE AV W	WCOV	WCOV	1000	92	A2
VINE PL	CER	ART		82	E5
VINE ST	ALH	ALH	1400	37	A4
VINE ST	GLEN	GL04	300	25	C4
VINE ST	LA	LA28	1300	34	C5
VINE ST	LA	LA38	700	34	C5
VINE ST	LA	LA68		34	B1
VINE ST	LA	LA68	1900	34	C5
VINE WY	LA	LA68	6200	34	C2
VINEBURN AV	LA	LA32	1700	45	C1
VINEDALE ST	LA	SV	10500	9	F6
VINEDALE ST	LA	SV	11200	16	E1
VINEDO AV N	PAS	PAS	100	27	E4
VINEDO AV S	PAS	PAS	100	27	E4
VINEHILL DR	CO	ALT	200	20	B3
VINELAND AV	BAP	BAP	3100	39	D6
VINELAND AV	BAP	BAP	1400	48	D1
VINELAND AV	CO	LPUE	600	48	B3
VINELAND AV	IND	LPUE	100	48	B3
VINELAND AV	LA	BUR	7100	16	E4
VINELAND AV	LA	NHO	5600	16	E4
VINELAND AV	LA	NHO	3700	23	E4
VINELAND AV	LA	SV	7200	16	E4
VINELAND PL	LA	NHO		23	E3
VINEMEAD DR	CO	LPUE	500	48	A4
VINETA AV	LCF	LCF	4500	19	C3
VINEVALE AV	BELL	BELL	6200	53	D6
VINEVALE AV	MAY	MAY	6000	53	D6
VINEVALLEY DR	LA	SV	8600	9	F6
VINEVALLEY DR	LA	SV	8300	16	F1
VINEWOOD ST	CO	LAV		90	C1
VINEYARD AV	DUA	DUA	200	29	F4
VINEYARD AV	LA	LA16	1900	43	B5
VINEYARD AV	LA	LA19	1600	43	B4
VINEYARD DR	SGAB	SGAB	1000	37	D2
VINEYARD LN	LA	PAC		3	B4
VINEYARD PL	PAS	PAS	400	27	F3
VINEYARD TR	CO	SF	11800	3	E6
VINTAGE CT	PALM	PALM		172	F9
VINTAGE DR	PALM	PALM		172	F9
VINTAGE DR	PALM	PALM		183	F1
VINTAGE ST	LA	CHA		6	D3
VINTAGE ST	LA	NOR	17000	7	E3
VINTAGE ST	LA	SF	16500	7	F3
VINTAGE ST	LA	SF	14700	8	D3
VINTON AV	CUL	CUL	4100	50	C1
VINTON AV	LA	LA34	3500	42	B6
VINTON AV	POM	POM	300	90	F6
VIOLA AL	PAS	PAS	2700	27	F4
VIOLA AV	GLEN	GL02	1100	25	C2
VIOLA CT	WCOV	WCOV		92	D6
VIOLA PL	LA	VEN		49	D4
VIOLA PL	POM	POM		90	C6
VIOLA WY	GLEN	GL02		25	C2
VIOLAN ST	CO	ACT	34600	182	F7
VIOLET AL	LA	LA58		52	E2
VIOLET AV	MON	MON	100	29	A4
VIOLET ST	LA	LA21	1900	44	E5
VIOLETA AV	HG	LKD	20700	81	A5
VIOLETA AV	LKD	LKD	20300	81	A3
VIOLETA DR	ALH	ALH	600	37	D6
VIOLET HILLS DR	CO	CYN		125	G6
VIOLET LANE WY	CO	CYN	15500	125	E6
VIOLIN CYN RD	CO	CAST	27600	123	H1
VIRAZON DR	LHH	LAH	1600	84	E1
VIRDEN DR	GLEN	GL08	2000	25	F1
VIREO DR	LAN	LAN		159	D3
VIREO DR	LA	LA69	1300	33	C3
VIRETTA LN	LA	LA77	10300	32	E3
VIRGIL AV	BLF	BLF		66	C3
VIRGIL AV N	LA	LA04	100	34	F5
VIRGIL AV N	LA	LA27	1300	34	F5
VIRGIL AV N	LA	LA29	700	34	F5
VIRGIL AV S	LA	LA04	100	34	F5
VIRGIL AV S	LA	LA05	600	44	A2
VIRGIL AV S	LA	LA20	300	44	A2
VIRGIL PL	LA	LA27	1300	35	A3
VIRGIL WK	LB	LB03	1	80	C2
VIRGIL WATRS WY	IND	LPUE	800	98	C2
VIRGINIA AV	BAP	BAP	3900	39	F5
VIRGINIA AV	BAP	BAP	1300	48	D1
VIRGINIA AV	BLF	BLF	15100	66	B4
VIRGINIA AV	BUR	BUR	100	24	D1
VIRGINIA AV	CO	COM	11700	65	C1
VIRGINIA AV	CO	WHI	13600	61	E5
VIRGINIA AV	COV	COV	900	88	F4
VIRGINIA AV	CUL	CUL	10600	50	C2
VIRGINIA AV	GLEN	GL02	1100	25	B2
VIRGINIA AV	LA	LA29	5200	34	D4
VIRGINIA AV	LA	LA29	4200	35	A4
VIRGINIA AV	LA	LA38	5500	34	D4
VIRGINIA AV	LAV	LAV		90	D1
VIRGINIA AV	LB	LB05	4600	70	C3
VIRGINIA AV	LYN	LYN	3600	59	B6
VIRGINIA AV	LYN	LYN	11350	59	D6
VIRGINIA AV	LYN	LYN	11700	65	C1
VIRGINIA AV	PAR	PAR	15100	65	F4
VIRGINIA AV	POM	POM	1900	94	F5
VIRGINIA AV	SM	SM	2000	41	C6
VIRGINIA AV	SOG	SOG	8100	59	B4
VIRGINIA AV	WCOV	WCOV	3000	92	F1
VIRGINIA AV	WCOV	WCOV	3200	93	A1
VIRGINIA AV	WHI	WHI	10300	84	C4
VIRGINIA AV E	GLDR	GLDR	100	87	A4
VIRGINIA AV N	AZU	AZU	200	86	C6
VIRGINIA AV N	PAS	PAS	100	27	E4
VIRGINIA AV S	AZU	AZU	100	88	C1
VIRGINIA AV S	CO	PAS	200	27	E4
VIRGINIA AV S	PAS	PAS	1	27	E4
VIRGINIA AV W	GLDR	GLDR	100	87	A4
VIRGINIA CT	LA	VEN	10	49	B6
VIRGINIA CT	LB	LB02	100	75	C4
VIRGINIA CT	LB	LB02	300	75	C4
VIRGINIA CT	LB	LB13	700	75	C4
VIRGINIA DR	ARC	ARC	1	28	E2
VIRGINIA LN	WCOV	WCOV		92	F2
VIRGINIA PL	BH	BH	9500	42	B2
VIRGINIA PL	GLEN	GL04	1000	25	C5
VIRGINIA PL	SPAS	SPAS	1700	37	A1
VIRGINIA RD	CLA	CLA	300	91	B5
VIRGINIA RD	LA	LA08	3800	51	B1
VIRGINIA RD	LA	LA16	1900	43	B5
VIRGINIA RD	LA	LA19	1600	43	B5
VIRGINIA RD	LB	LB07	3900	70	C4
VIRGINIA RD	SMAR	PAS	1000	27	C6
VIRGINIA RD	SMAR	PAS	1400	37	C1
VIRGINIA ST	ELS	ELS	100	56	A6
VIRGINIA ST	GLEN	GL14	3600	11	C5
VIRGINIA ST	LYN	LYN	3100	59	A6
VIRGINIA ST	PR	PR	8800	54	F2
VIRGINIA ST	RM	RM		46	E1
VIRGINIA ANN DR	AZU	AZU	500	86	C4
VIRGINIA VIS CT	LB	LB07	4000	70	B4
VIRIDAN AV	LAN	LAN		159	J7
VIRO RD	LCF	LCF	4500	19	D4
VISALIA AV	CAR	CAR	16100	64	C4
VISALIA AV	CO	COM	14700	64	C3
VISALIA AV	COM	COM	1300	64	C4
VISBY PL	LA	SV	8500	17	A1
VISCANIO RD	LA	WOH	21900	13	B3
VISCANO DR	GLEN	GL07	1100	25	E2
VISCO CT	SCLR	SAU		124	G3
VISCOUNT ST	ALH	ALH	3200	45	E1
VISION DR	CO	TOP	19600	109	C6
VISION TR	CO	SF		3	D5
VISION TR	CO	TOP	19700	109	C5
VISLOMA PL	LOM	LOM		73	D3
VISO DR	LA	LA68	6900	34	B1
VISROY AV	CER	ART		82	E6
VISSCHER PL	CO	ALT	2600	20	A5
VISTA AV	ARC	ARC	2000	28	E1
VISTA AV	PAS	PAS	100	27	E3
VISTA AV	SMAD	SMAD	1900	28	E1
VISTA CIR	WAL	WAL		93	B6
VISTA CT	GLEN	GL05	1200	25	D5
VISTA CT	GLEN	GL14	3800	11	C5
VISTA CT	LAV	LAV		95A	D5
VISTA CT	SCLR	CYN		125	B8
VISTA DR	CLA	CLA	400	91	B5
VISTA DR	GLEN	GL01	1600	18	A5
VISTA DR	MB	MB	100	62	A2
VISTA DR	PALM	PALM		171	C3
VISTA DR	TOR	TOR		68	A3
VISTA LN	PAS	PAS	1300	26	D1
VISTA LN	WCOV	WCOV		97	A2
VISTA PL	ALH	ALH		36	F4
VISTA PL	CO	MAL	4200	112	E3
VISTA PL	LA	LA42	300	36	D1
VISTA PL	LA	LA46	7400	34	A3
VISTA PL	LA	VEN	100	49	B3
VISTA PL	LCF	LCF	4300	19	A3
VISTA RD	GLEN	GL14		18	C2
VISTA RD	LHH	LAH	2100	98A	C3
VISTA ST	LB	LB03	2800	75	F6
VISTA ST	LB	LB03	3200	76	A5
VISTA ST	LB	LB14	6200	76	D5
VISTA ST	SGAB	SGAB	5700	37	F2
VISTA ST N	CO	SGAB	6700	27	F6
VISTA ST N	CO	SGAB	5700	37	F1
VISTA ST N	LA	LA36	100	34	A6
VISTA ST N	LA	LA46	700	34	A5
VISTA ST N	WHOL	LA46	1000	34	A5
VISTA ST S	LA	LA36	100	34	A6
VISTA TER	LA	PP		40	C4
VISTA TR	LA	LA68		24	A6
VISTA BELLA WY	CO	COM	1900	69	E2
VISTA BONITA	PALM	PALM		183	J6
VIS BONITA AV N	GLDR	GLDR	100	87	B5
VIS BONITA AV S	GLDR	GLDR	100	87	B5
VISTA BONITA ST	AZU	AZU	300	86	C4
VISTA BUENA DR	DBAR	POM		94	B6
VISTA CAMPANA	PALM	PALM		183	F2
VISTA CANADA PL	LCF	LCF	5100	19	C1
VISTA CERRITOS	CO	CAL		100	D5
VISTA CIRCLE CT	LAN	LAN		159	E7
VISTA CIRCLE DR	SMAD	SMAD	1	28	D1
VISTA COYOTE RD	CO	SAU		181	D9
VISTA CREST DR	LA	LA68	3000	24	B6
VISTA DEL CIR	AZU	AZU	1400	86	D4
VISTA DE LA LUZ	LA	WOH		5	C5
VISTA DL ARR DR	CO	GL14	5400	11	F5
VIS D LAS ONDAS	CO	MAL		111	A4
VIS DELGADO DR	SCLR	VAL		124	B6
VISTA DEL GOLFO	LB	LB03	1	80	D1
VISTA DEL LAGO	CO	PALM		183	B3
VISTA DEL LLANO	LHH	LAH		84	E2
VISTA DEL MAR	LA	PDR		55A	E3
VISTA DEL MAR	LA	VEN	6000	55A	E2
VISTA DEL MAR	RB	RB	100	67	D6
VISTA DEL MAR	RPV	PVP		78	C4
VISTA DL MAR AV	LA	LA28	1700	34	C2
VISTA DL MAR AV	LA	LA68	1900	34	C2
VISTA DL MAR BL	ELS	ELS		62	A1
VISTA DL MAR DR	GLEN	GL08	3100	18	F4
VISTA DL MAR LN	LA	VEN	6800	55A	D2
VISTA DL MAR PL	LA	LA68	2200	34	C2
VIS DL MONTE AV	LA	VAN	5600	15	D6
VIS DL MONTE AV	LA	VAN	4500	22	D3
VIS DL MONTE DR	CO	ACT		189	H1
VISTA DEL NORTE	WAL	WAL		97	A1
VISTA DL PARQUE	TOR	RB	100	67	D6
VIS DEL PRESEAS	CO	MAL		111	A3
VISTA DL RIO AV	DOW	DOW	8300	60	D1
VISTA DL RIO DR	DOW	DOW	9200	60	D2
VIS DEL ROSA AV	DOW	DOW		60	D1
VIS DEL ROSA ST	DOW	DOW	7800	54	C6
VIS DEL ROSA ST	DOW	DOW	7900	60	C1
VISTA DEL SOL	TOR	RB	1200	72	D1
VISTA DEL VALLE	ARC	ARC	1700	28	E2
VISTA DEL VALLE	LHH	LAH	1400	84	D2
VIS DL VALLE DR	LA	LA27		24	E5
VIS DL VALLE DR	LA	LA27		25	A6
VIS DL VALLE DR	LA	LA27		35	A1
VIS DL VALLE RD	LCF	LCF	1000	19	B1
VISTA DEL VEGAS	TOR	TOR	5000	72	F1
VIS DEL VENTADA	CO	MAL		111	A4
VIS DL VERDE DR	GLEN	GL08	1800	18	F5
VISTA DE ORO AV	CO	LA43		51	B3
VISTA DE ORO AV	LA	WOH		13	E3
VISTA DE ORO PL	LA	WOH	20500	13	D3
VISTA DORADO	PALM	PALM		183	F2
VISTA EL RINCON	PALM	PALM		183	F2
VIS ENCANTDA DR	SCLR	VAL		124	B6
VIS FAIRWAYS DR	CO	VAL		126	J3
VISTA GLEN WY	CO	LPUE		48	B5
VIS GLORIOSA DR	LA	LA65	400	36	A4
VIS GLORIOSA DR	SAD	SAD		89	E5
VISTA GORDO DR	LA	LA26	2300	35	D4
VISTA GRANDE	BUR	BUR		17	E3
VISTA GRANDE	CO	SAU		188	C1
VISTAGRANDE DR	LA	PP		40	B2
VISTA GRANDE ST	WHOL	LA69	8900	33	D4
VISTA GRANDE WY	LA	NOR		1	A5
VISTA HAVEN PL	LA	VAN	15400	22	B5
VISTA HAVEN RD	LA	VAN	3300	22	C5
VISTA HERMOSA	LB	LB15	5200	76	B3
VIS HERMOSA DR	WAL	WAL		93	A6
VISTA HILLS DR	SCLR	VAL		127	A3
VISTA INDUSTRIA	CO	COM	2500	70	A2
VIS LAGUNA CIR	DUA	DUA		86	A4
VIS LAGUNA TER	PAS	PAS	2300	19	E5
VISTA LARGO	TOR	TOR	4200	72	F1
VIS LE JANA LN	LCF	LCF	5200	19	B1
VISTA LEON	PALM	PALM		183	F2
VISTA LINDA DR	LA	ENC		21	C4
VISTA LINDA DR	LAN	LAN	4000	159	E7
VISTA LOMITA LN	LOM	LOM	2200	73	D3
VISTA MADERA	RPV	SP		78	D1
VISTA MESA CT	DUA	DUA		86	A5
VISTA MESA DR	RPV	SP	2700	78	C3
VISTA MIGUEL DR	LCF	LCF	5100	19	B1
VISTA MONTANA	TOR	TOR	4100	72	F1
VISTA MORAGA	LA	LA49		32	C4
VISTA PACIFICA	LA	PP		40	A3
VISTA PACIFICA	RPV	PVP		77	C3
VIS PACIFICA ST	CO	MAL		113	F5
VISTA PLAYA DR	CO	MAL		111	E5
VISTA POINT DR	WCOV	WCOV		92	E4
VISTA RAMBLA	WAL	WAL	100	97	A1
VISTA REAL DR	RHE	PVP	1	73	D4
VISTA RIDGE	BUR	BUR	1100	17	D3
VISTA RIDGE DR	SCLR	VAL		127	A4
VISTA ROSINA DR	SCLR	VAL		124	F3
VISTA SERENA CT	LAN	LAN	43600	159	E7
VISTA SERENA CT	LAN	LAN	43600	159	E7
VISTA SERENA DR	LAN	LAN	43600	159	E7
VISTA SIERRA DR	CO	MAL	30600	111	E4
VISTA SIERRA DR	LAN	LAN		159	E7
VIS SUPERBA DR	LA	LA65	4400	25	E5
VISTA TIERRA	RPV	SP		78	D1
VISTA VALLE TR	CO	TOP		109	D4
VISTA VERDE DR	CO	CAL		108	A5
VISTA VERENDA	LA	WOH		5	C6
VISTA VIEW TER	CO	PALM		183	A5
VISTILLAS RD	CO	ALT	1700	20	D5
VITRINA LN	PALM	LAN		171	D4
VITRINA LN	PALM	PALM		171	E4
VIVA DR	LA	TU	7200	10	F4
VIVERO DR	CO	LPUE	2000	98	E5
VIVIAN AV	CO	SAU		123	F1
VIVIANA DR	LA	TAR	4700	21	A3
VOGUE AV	CO	AZU	5100	88	C2
VOGUE AV	COV	COV	4200	88	C4
VOLADOR PL	LA	SP	100	78	D3
VOLANTE DR	ARC	ARC	800	28	B4
VOLETTA PL	LA	NHO	5500	23	B1
VOLK AV	CO	LB08	3000	71	F6
VOLK AV	LB	LB08	3000	71	F5
VOLK AV	LB	LB15	1800	76	F3
VOLMER AV	CMRC	LA22	3500	54	C5
VOLNEY DR	CO	LA63	1300	45	E2
VOLTAIRE DR	CO	TOP		13	C5
VOLTARA CT	CO	AGO		100	C4
VOLUNTEER AV	NWK	NWK	11600	61	B6
VOLUNTEER AV	NWK	NWK	12100	82	B1
VON KEITHIAN AV	LA	LA31	300	36	B5
VOORHEES AV	MB	MB	1300	62	D5
VOORHEES AV	RB	RB	1900	62	D5
VOSBURG ST	CO	PAS	3200	20A	A3
VOSE ST	LA	CAN	20300	12	A4
VOSE ST	LA	NHO	11700	16	C4
VOSE ST	LA	RES	17700	14	A4
VOSE ST	LA	VAN	16900	14	E4
VOSE ST	LA	VAN	13400	15	C4
VOSSLER AV	SOG	SOG	8900	59	D3
VOYAGE CT	LA	VEN		49	D6
VOYAGE ST	LA	VEN		49	C6
VOYAGER CIR	LA	SP		78	E5
VOYAGER ST	POM	POM		94	A3
VOYAGER ST	TOR	TOR		68	A2
VREELAND AV	LA	WIL	800	74	E4
VUELTA PL	PVE	PVP	1300	72	C3
VUELTA GRNDE AV	LB	LB15	1400	76	D1
VULCAN DR	LA	LA46	7900	33	E1
VULCAN LN	CO	TOP	20000	115	C1
VULCAN ST	SOG	SOG	10900	59	E5
VULTEE AV	BLF	BLF	13100	66	B1
VULTEE AV	DOW	DOW	10000	60	C5
VULTEE AV	DOW	DOW	12600	66	B1
W					
W CIR	CO	HAC		73	F2
WABASH AV	GLDR	GLDR		89	B2
WABASH AV	LA	LA33	2200	45	B3
WABASH AV	LA	LA63	3000	45	B3
WABASH AV N	GLDR	GLDR	100	87	B5
WABASH AV S	GLDR	GLDR	100	87	B5
WABASH ST	GLDR	GLDR	1400	89	B2
WABASH ST	PAS	PAS	1000	26	D2
WABASSO WY	GLEN	GL08	1400	18	F6
WABUSKA ST	SCLR	NEW		127	A5
WACO AV	BAP	BAP	12800	39	C6
WACO AV	BAP	BAP	13100	48	C1
WADDELL ST	CO	WHI	10900	55	A6
WADDELL ST	LA	NHO	12800	16	A6
WADDINGTON AV	LAN	LAN	43600	159	G6
WADE AV	TOR	TOR	23200	68	C6
WADE ST	CUL	LA66	4000	49	F3
WADE ST	LA	LA66	3300	49	E2
WADENA ST	LA	LA32	5000	36	E4
WADKINS AV	CO	GAR	14300	63	C3
WADKINS AV	GAR	GAR	14700	63	C3
WADLEY AV	CAR	CAR	19000	69	C1
WADSHAW AL	GAR	GAR	14700	63	C3
WADSWORTH AV	CO	COM	14900	64	C2
WADSWORTH AV	CO	LA59	12300	58	C6
WADSWORTH AV	COM	COM	900	64	C4
WADSWORTH AV	LA	LA01	7200	52	C6
WADSWORTH AV	LA	LA01	7800	58	C2
WADSWORTH AV	LA	LA02	8700	58	C2
WADSWORTH AV	LA	LA11	3200	52	C3
WADSWORTH AV	LA	LA59	10900	58	C5
WADSWORTH AV	SM	SM	100	49	A2
WADSWORTH PL	LA	LA38		34	C4
WAGER RD	CO	NEW		127	F6
WAGNER CT	CO	ALT	2800	19	F4
WAGNER DR	CLA	CLA	100	91	B1
WAGNER PL	CER	ART	12000	81	B2
WAGNER ST	CUL	CUL	10800	50	B2
WAGNER ST	LA	CUL	11800	50	A4
WAGNER ST	LA	LA66	12400	50	A4
WAGNER ST	PAS	PAS	1600	27	E3
WAGON LN	RH	PVP	1	73	A6
WAGON RD	CO	AGO		100A	A5
WAGON HORSE AV	CO	LAV		95A	E6
WAGON MOUND RD	CO	NEW		2	B1
WAGON TRAIL RD	DBAR	POM	23500	97A	A1
WAGON TRAIN LN	DBAR	POM		97	E5
WAGON WHEEL CT	SAD	SAD		89	E1
WAGON WHEEL RD	CO	SAU		125	H1
WAGONWHEEL RD	GLDR	GLDR	100	87	D5
WAHOO TR	CO	CHA		1A	C6
WAILEA ST	WCOV	WCOV		92	C4
WAIN PL	CO	LPUE		98	A3
WAINWRIGHT AV	LA	WIL	800	74	E4
WAITE CT	LB	LB02	400	75	C5
WAITE CT	LB	LB13	700	75	C4
WAKE CT	LPUE	LPUE	16000	92	A5
WAKECREST DR	CO	MAL	18000	115	E4
WAKEFIELD AV	LA	VAN	8500	8	D6
WAKEFIELD AV	LA	VAN	8000	15	E1
WAKEFIELD CT	CO	SAU		124	D4
WAKEFIELD CT	LB	LB03		76	F5
WAKEFIELD RD	CO	SAU		123	D4
WAKE FOREST AV	WAL	WAL	1300	93	B4
WAKEMAN ST	CO	WHI	11500	61	B1
WAKEMAN ST	SFS	SFS	11800	61	C1
WALA VISTA RD	LA	LA64	10300	42	B5
WALBROOK DR	CO	LPUE	14500	48	C6
WALBROOK DR	CO	LPUE	15000	85	D1
WALBURG ST	CO	WHI		61	D3
WALCOTT WY	LA	LA39	1900	35	D3
WALCROFT ST	LKD	LKD	11300	71	F3
WALCROFT ST	LKD	LKD	11600	81	A3
WALDEN	ELM	ELM		48	A6
WALDEN DR	BH	BH	500	33	A6
WALDEN DR	BH	BH	500	42	B1
WALDO AV	PAS	PAS	300	27	A5
WALDO CT	LA	LA32	4500	36	C5
WALDO PL	LA	LA41	5300	26	C4
WALDON PL	LA	LA31	300	36	A5
WALDORF DR	COM	COM	1500	65	C1
WALDORF DR	LCF	LCF	700	19	C6
WALDORF DR	LYN	LYN	12100	65	C1
WALDRAN AV	LA	LA41	1500	26	B5
WALES AV	GLDR	GLDR	1200	89	C2
WALES ST	PALM	PALM		171	J7
WALFORD CT	AGH	AGO		102	E3
WALGROVE AV	LA	LA66	700	49	D2
WALKATOP RD	CO	PALM		157	G7
WALKER AV	BELL	BELL	6200	53	E5
WALKER AV	CDY	BELL	7700	59	D1
WALKER AV	MAY	MAY	5900	53	E5
WALKER AV	MON	MON	1800	29	B6
WALKER AV S	LA	SP	300	78	E3
WALKER AV S	LA	SP	100	78	E5
WALKER CT	SCLR	SAU		124	D2
WALKER CT	SCLR	SAU		124	D4
WALKER DR	BH	BH	400	33	C2
WALKER RD	SAD	SAD		89	F2
WALKER ST	BELL	BELL	6400	53	D6
WALKER ST	LAV	LAV	400	90	B3

306

1990 LOS ANGELES COUNTY STREET INDEX

WALKERTON ST — WELBY WY

LOS ANGELES CO.

STREET	CITY	P.O. ZONE	BLOCK	PAGE	GRID
WALKERTON ST	LB	LB08	5100	71	B5
WALKNG HORSE LN	WAL	WAL		93	A5
WALKNG HORSE LN	WLVL	THO		102	C4
WK OF 1000 LGTS	LB	LB02		75	C6
WALL ST	CAR	CAR	17200	64	B5
WALL ST	CAR	CAR	18600	69	B1
WALL ST	CO	LA61	12200	58	B6
WALL ST	LA	LA03	5800	52	B5
WALL ST	LA	LA03	8100	58	B4
WALL ST	LA	LA11	2100	44	C6
WALL ST	LA	LA11	3600	52	B3
WALL ST	LA	LA13	300	44	D4
WALL ST	LA	LA14	600	44	D4
WALL ST	LA	LA15	900	44	C5
WALL ST	LA	LA61	10700	58	B4
WALL ST	SH	LB04	2600	75	F3
WALLABI AV	LA	SF	13800	3	B1
WALLACE AV	LA	LA26	1400	35	C6
WALLACE WY	IND	LPUE	1000	98	B2
WALLACE RIDGE	BH	BH	1000	33	C3
WALLCREST DR	CLA	CLA	1500	90	F2
WALLINGFORD DR	LA	BH		22	F6
WALLINGFORD DR	LA	BH		32	F1
WALLINGFORD RD	CO	PAS	3000	27	E5
WALLINGFORD RD	SMAR	PAS	2500	27	E5
WALLINGTON CT	WLVL	THO	32000	102	A4
WALLIS LN	LA	WOH	5700	12	D6
WALLIS ST	PAS	PAS	100	27	A6
WALMAR AV	LCF	LCF	5000	19	C2
WALNUT	LA	SF42		2	C1
WALNUT AV	ARC	ARC	100	38	C2
WALNUT AV	BUR	BUR	200	17	D4
WALNUT AV	CO	LPUE	1400	92	A3
WALNUT AV	GLDR	GLDR	500	87	B6
WALNUT AV	ING	IN01	600	57	A3
WALNUT AV	LA	VEN	1500	49	D3
WALNUT AV	LB	LB02	300	75	E5
WALNUT AV	LB	LB05	5900	65	E6
WALNUT AV	LB	LB05	5200	70	E1
WALNUT AV	LB	LB06	1800	75	E5
WALNUT AV	LB	LB07	3000	70	E5
WALNUT AV	LB	LB13	700	75	E5
WALNUT AV	LYN	LYN	4400	59	C6
WALNUT AV	LYN	LYN	3600	59	B5
WALNUT AV	MB	MB	1200	62	C3
WALNUT AV	MTB	MTB	400	54	D2
WALNUT AV	PAR	PAR	7200	65	E1
WALNUT AV	POM	POM	900	95	A6
WALNUT AV	PR	PR	4600	55	A2
WALNUT AV	PR	PR	9300	55	A2
WALNUT AV	SH	LB06	2000	75	E5
WALNUT AV	SOG	SOG	9800	59	D4
WALNUT AV	WCOV	WCOV	1300	92	A4
WALNUT AV E	ELS	ELS	100	56	B5
WALNUT AV E	MON	MON	100	29	A4
WALNUT AV N	SAD	SAD	100	90	A2
WALNUT AV S	SAD	SAD	100	90	A3
WALNUT AV W	ELS	ELS	100	56	A5
WALNUT AV W	MON	MON	700	28	F4
WALNUT AV W	MON	MON	100	29	A4
WALNUT CT	AZU	AZU	200	86	C3
WALNUT CT	BLF	BLF	17000	66	C5
WALNUT CT	CO	PAS	200	28	B4
WALNUT CT	LA	VEN	2100	49	D3
WALNUT DR	CO	LA01	7200	52	E6
WALNUT DR	CO	LA01	7200	58	E1
WALNUT DR	CO	LPUE	19200	97	A3
WALNUT DR	CO	LPUE	19000	98	F3
WALNUT DR	CO	PAS	300	28	B4
WALNUT DR	CO	WAL	19600	97	A3
WALNUT DR	IND	LPUE		97	A3
WALNUT DR	IND	WAL		97	A3
WALNUT DR	LA	LA46	8400	33	E3
WALNUT DR	LA	SUN	10700	9	F4
WALNUT LN	LA	LA25	11900	41	D4
WALNUT ST	BAP	BAP	3900	39	D5
WALNUT ST	BELL	BELL	4200	53	B6
WALNUT ST	BLF	BLF	8700	66	B4
WALNUT ST	CAR	CAR	200	64	C5
WALNUT ST	CDY	BELL	3600	53	B6
WALNUT ST	CO	HPK	2400	52	F6
WALNUT ST	CO	HPK	2700	53	B6
WALNUT ST	SCLR	NEW	24300	127	C3
WALNUT ST	CO	PAS	3500	28	B4
WALNUT ST	CO	WHI	11400	61	B1
WALNUT ST	COM	COM	100	64	E5
WALNUT ST	ELM	ELM	11000	47	E1
WALNUT ST	GLDR	GLDR	200	87	B6
WALNUT ST	HPK	HPK	2900	53	B6
WALNUT ST	LA	LA11	1300	44	D6
WALNUT ST	LAV	LAV	1800	90	C4
WALNUT ST	LHH	LAH	1200	84	F3
WALNUT ST	LHH	LAH	1200	98A	A2
WALNUT ST	LOM	LOM	23800	73	D3
WALNUT ST	NWK	NWK	12000	82	B2
WALNUT ST	SGAB	SGAB	900	37	E5

STREET	CITY	P.O. ZONE	BLOCK	PAGE	GRID
WALNUT ST	TOR	TOR	22900	68	D6
WALNUT ST	TOR	TOR	4300	72	F1
WALNUT ST	TOR	TOR	23600	73	D1
WALNUT ST	WHI	WHI	12500	55	E6
WALNUT ST E	CAR	CAR	100	64	B5
WALNUT ST E	PAS	PAS	100	27	B3
WALNUT ST W	CAR	GAR	100	64	A5
WALNUT ST W	PAS	PAS	100	26	E3
WALNUT TER	CO	HPK	2200	52	E6
WALNUT TR	CO	TOP	19500	109	B5
WALNUT WY	LB	LB13	1400	75	E3
WALNUT WY	PALM	LAN		171	B2
WALNUT CYN RD	WAL	WAL		93	B4
WALNUT CREEK CT	WCOV	WCOV	1800	92	D1
WALNUT CK PKWY	BAP	BAP	14100	48	E1
WALNUT CK PKY W	WCOV	WCOV	1400	48	F1
WALNUT CREEK PL	WCOV	WCOV	300	92	D1
WALNUT CREEK RD	COV	COV		89	A6
WALNUTDALE AV	NWK	NWK	11900	82	A2
WALNUT GROVE AV	CO	RM	3300	37	F5
WALNUT GROVE AV	CO	RM	1000	46	F3
WALNUT GROVE AV	CO	RM	1000	47	A3
WALNUT GROVE AV	CO	SGAB	5100	37	F3
WALNUT GROVE AV	RM	RM	3400	37	F5
WALNUT GROVE AV	RM	RM	1000	46	F3
WALNUT GROVE AV	SGAB	SGAB		37	F3
WALNUT HALL RD	IND	LPUE		98	C3
WALNUTHAVEN DR	CO	COV	3900	88	B5
WALNUTHAVEN DR	WCOV	WCOV	100	88	B6
WALNUT LEAF DR	CO	WAL		97	B3
WALNT ORCHRD RD	CO	SAU		123	A8
WALNUT PARK DR	COM	COM		64	D5
WALNUT PARK WY	COM	COM		64	D5
WALNUT RIDGE DR	AGH	AGO		102	E3
WALNUT SPG AV	SCLR	CYN	27200	124	J9
WALNUT VLY DR	WAL	WAL	20700	93	B3
WALPOLE DR	LA	TU	7000	11	A4
WALSH AV	LA	LA66	12500	49	F4
WALSH AV	LA	LA66	12400	50	A4
WALT DISNEY DR	LA	LA49		22	B6
WALTER AV	TOR	TOR	23700	73	C1
WALTER ST	CO	HPK	2100	52	E6
WALTHALL AV	CO	WHI	9600	61	D3
WALTHALL WY	PAR	PAR		65	D2
WALTHAM ST	BAP	BAP	12700	48	B1
WALTHER WY	LA	LA49	600	41	B1
WALTON AV	LA	LA06	1700	43	F4
WALTON AV	LA	LA07	2800	43	F5
WALTON AV	LA	LA37	3800	51	F1
WALTON ST	LB	LB15	5100	76	B1
WALTON ST	SH	LB06	700	75	D1
WALTONIA DR	CO	MONT	1900	18	F2
WALTONIA DR	GLEN	GL06	300	25	F3
WALTON OAKS	CO	MONT		18	F2
WALWORTH AV	PAS	PAS	1600	20	B6
WAMEDA AV	LA	LA41	5400	26	C4
WAMPLER ST	PR	PR	8300	54	F5
WANAMAKER DR	COV	COV	900	89	A5
WANDA DR	LA	LA27	4100	35	A2
WANDA ST	ELM	ELM	12000	47	F1
WANDA PARK DR	LA	BH	9800	32	F1
WANDERER DR	LA	SP	2200	78	C4
WANDERING DR	MPK	MPK	900	46	A4
WANDERMERE RD	CO	MAL	6500	110	B4
WANETTE AV	BLF	BLF	14900	66	B3
WANSTEAD DR	CO	ACT		182	C8
WAPELLO ST	CO	ALT	1	20	A3
WARBLER PL	LA	LA69	9100	33	C3
WARBLER WY	LA	LA69	9100	33	C3
WARD AL	PAS	PAS	2900	27	F4
WARD AV N	COM	COM	1900	65	B1
WARD AV S	COM	COM	100	65	B3
WARD RD	CO	SAU		182	C9
WARD ST	LA	LA41	4900	26	B5
WARD ST	SFS	SFS	10600	61	B4
WARD ST	TOR	TOR	22300	68	A5
WARD ST	TOR	TOR	23500	73	A2
WARD WY	IND	LPUE		85	F1
WARDELL AV	DUA	DUA	1800	29	C5
WARDHAM AV	HG	LKD	21900	81	B5
WARDHAM AV	LKD	LKD	20300	81	C3
WARDHAM AV	LKD	LKD	21000	81	C4
WARDLOW RD	LB	LB08	5100	71	B5
WARDLOW RD	LB	LB08	7800	81	A6
WARDLOW RD E	LB	LB07	100	70	C5
WARDLOW RD W	CAR	LB10	1500	70	A5
WARDLOW RD W	LB	LB06	400	70	C5
WARDLOW RD W	LB	LB10	2100	69	F5
WARDLOW RD W	LB	LB10	1500	70	A5
WARDMAN ST	WHI	WHI	12300	55	E5
WAREHOUSE ST	LA	LA21	700	44	E5
WARFIELD AV	RB	RB	1900	62	E4
WARING AV	LA	LA38	5700	34	C5
WARING AV	LA	LA46	7500	33	E5
WARING AV	LA	LA46	7100	34	A5
WARING AV	LA	LA69	8300	33	E5

STREET	CITY	P.O. ZONE	BLOCK	PAGE	GRID
WARING DR	CO	AGO		106	E2
WARING PL	AGH	AGO		100A	B4
WARINGWOOD RD	LPUE	LPUE		92	A6
WARINGWOOD RD	LPUE	LPUE	600	98	A1
WARMAN LN	TEC	TEC	5400	38	C3
WARMOUTH ST	LA	SP	2500	78	C5
WARMSIDE AV	TOR	TOR	22200	67	E5
WARMSPRINGS AV	LAV	LAV		95A	D5
WARM SPRINGS DR	CO	CYN	15700	128	E3
WARMUTH RD	CO	CYN		128	C1
WARN AV	LA	SV	9100	10	A5
WARNALL AV	LA	LA24	1300	41	F1
WARNER AV	LA	LA24	400	41	F1
WARNER BLVD	BUR	BUR	2900	24	A4
WARNER DR	CUL	CUL	8400	42	D6
WARNER DR	LA	LA48	6100	42	F2
WARNER LN	SGAB	SGAB	400	37	D2
WARNR BR RCH RD	CO	CAL		100	A4
WARNER CTR LN	LA	WOH		12	D6
WARNICK RD	RPV	PVP	29100	72	C5
WARNOCK WY	LB	LB10	1600	70	A5
WARREN AV	LA	LA66	13000	49	D2
WARREN AV	LA	VEN	800	49	C2
WARREN AV	LB	LB13	1300	75	E3
WARREN AV	LYN	LYN	11600	59	B6
WARREN CT	LAN	LAN		160	F4
WARREN LN	ING	IN02	300	51	A6
WARREN PL	POM	POM	400	90	E5
WARREN ST	LA	LA33	1300	44	F3
WARREN ST	SF	SF	1100	2	F4
WARREN WY	ARC	ARC	300	38	D2
WARRINGTON AV	DUA	DUA	1800	29	C6
WARRINGTON AV	PR	PR	4000	55	B1
WARRINGTON DR	LA	SF	17200	1	E5
WARRIOR DR	RPV	PVP	27300	72	E5
WARVALE ST	PR	PR	8400	54	D5
WARWICK AV	LA	LA32	2200	36	E5
WARWICK AV	SM	SM	1800	41	D5
WARWICK AV	SPAS	SPAS	1	36	D2
WARWICK PL	SPAS	SPAS	1	36	D2
WARWICK RD	ALH	ALH	2300	45	F1
WARWICK RD	SMAR	PAS	1700	37	C1
WARWICK ST	POM	POM	1500	94	E4
WARWOOD RD	LB	LB08	4500	71	B4
WARWOOD RD	LKD	LKD	2600	70	F4
WARWOOD RD	LKD	LKD	6000	71	D4
WASATCH AV	CUL	LA66	4000	49	E2
WASATCH AV	LA	LA66	3500	49	E2
WASATCH DR	LCF	LCF	4400	19	A2
WASECA ST	CO	LPUE	15500	85	D4
WASHBURN RD	DOW	DOW	9000	60	C5
WASHBURN RD	PAS	PAS	1400	26	D6
WASHINGTON AV	CO	ACT		189	G2
WASHINGTON AV	CO	COM	15100	65	C3
WASHINGTON AV	COM	COM	900	65	C4
WASHINGTON AV	ELM	ELM	2600	47	D1
WASHINGTON AV	GLDR	GLDR	5600	89	A2
WASHINGTON AV	HAW	HAW	12800	63	A1
WASHINGTON AV	LYN	LYN	10600	59	C4
WASHINGTON AV	POM	POM	500	95	A1
WASHINGTON AV	SM	SM	100	40	F6
WASHINGTON AV	SM	SM	1100	41	A4
WASHINGTON AV	SOG	SOG	9900	59	C4
WASHINGTON AV	TOR	TOR	2000	68	C5
WASHINGTON AV	WHI	WHI	5800	55	E6
WASHINGTON AV	WHI	WHI	8100	61	E1
WASHINGTON AV N	GLDR	GLDR	300	87	A5
WASHINGTON AV S	GLDR	GLDR	100	87	A5
WASHINGTON BLVD	CMRC	LA22	5900	54	C3
WASHINGTON BLVD	CO	PAS	1900	27	D1
WASHINGTON BLVD	CO	WHI	10500	55	B6
WASHINGTON BLVD	CUL	CUL	5800	42	D5
WASHINGTON BLVD	CUL	CUL	10500	50	A3
WASHINGTON BLVD	CUL	LA66	12000	49	E3
WASHINGTON BLVD	CUL	LA66	11300	50	A3
WASHINGTON BLVD	CUL	VEN	13200	49	E3
WASHINGTON BLVD	LA	VEN	900	49	C4
WASHINGTON BLVD	MTB	MTB	100	54	C3
WASHINGTON BLVD	PR	PR	8000	54	C3
WASHINGTON BLVD	SFS	WHI	11100	55	B6
WASHINGTON BLVD	WHI	WHI	12100	55	B6
WASHINGTON BL E	CMRC	LA22	4500	53	C2
WASHINGTON BL E	CMRC	LA23	3900	53	C2
WASHINGTON BL E	LA	LA15	100	44	B5
WASHINGTON BL E	LA	LA21	700	44	B5
WASHINGTON BL E	LA	LA21	1900	52	E1
WASHINGTON BL E	LA	LA23	2600	52	E1
WASHINGTON BL E	LA	LA23	2700	53	C2
WASHINGTON BL E	PAS	PAS	100	27	D1
WASHINGTON BL E	VER	LA23	3200	53	C2
WASHINGTON BL W	LA	LA07	1400	43	B4
WASHINGTON BL W	LA	LA07	1200	44	B5
WASHINGTON BL W	LA	LA15	100	44	B5
WASHINGTON BL W	LA	LA16	5300	42	D5
WASHINGTON BL W	LA	LA16	4200	43	B4
WASHINGTON BL W	LA	LA18	1900	43	B4

STREET	CITY	P.O. ZONE	BLOCK	PAGE	GRID
WASHINGTON BL W	PAS	PAS	100	26	E1
WASHINGTON CIR	BUR	BUR	2300	17	B4
WASHINGTON CT	LA	LA07	1900	44	A4
WASHINGTON PL	CUL	CUL	11000	50	A2
WASHINGTON PL	GLEN	GL14	3200	11	D6
WASHINGTON PL	LA	LA66	11800	49	F3
WASHINGTON PL	LA	LA66	11300	50	A2
WASHINGTON PL	LB	LB13	700	75	D5
WASHINGTON PL	PAS	PAS	100	26	E1
WASHINGTON PL	SM	SM	2400	41	A4
WASHINGTON SQ	PALM	PALM		183	D2
WASHINGTON ST	ALH	ALH	600	37	B4
WASHINGTON ST	BLF	BLF	1000	66	C2
WASHINGTON ST	CAR	LB10	2500	69	F4
WASHINGTON ST	CAR	LB10	2600	70	A4
WASHINGTON ST	DBAR	WAL		97	D2
WASHINGTON ST	ELS	ELS	100	56	C5
WASHINGTON ST	LA	VEN	100	49	C5
WASHINGTON ST	LB	LB05	1200	70	D2
WASHINGTON WY	LA	VEN	1700	49	C4
WASOLA ST	RM	RM	7700	46	E2
WATCHER ST	BG	BELL	5500	53	E5
WATCHER ST	BG	BELL	6200	54	A5
WATCHER ST	CMRC	LA40	6700	54	B5
WATCHORN WK	LA	SP		79	A5
WATER AV	COM	LA59	2000	64	D1
WATER ST	CAR	CAR	21000	69	E4
WATER ST	LA	WIL		74	B6
WATER ST	LB	LB02	1100	75	A6
WATERBURY AV	COV	COV	100	88	C5
WATERBURY ST	LA	WOH	22500	13	B3
WATERCRESS LN	WAL	WAL		93	D4
WATERFORD CT	PALM	PALM		183	H2
WATERFORD DR	CO	VAL		124	B7
WATERFORD ST	LA	LA49	11300	41	C2
WATERFORD WY	CO	LAN		159	C9
WATERGATE CT	WLVL	THO	31900	102	A4
WATERGATE RD	WLVL	THO	32000	102	A4
WATER LILY CT	CO	CYN		125	F4
WATERLOO ST	LA	LA26	600	35	B6
WATERLOO ST	LA	LA39	1900	35	C4
WATERMAN AV	PALM	PALM		183	H2
WATERMAN DR	LA	VAN	16100	15	A2
WATERMAN RD	CO	SAU	30100	123	C3
WATERMAN ST	PALM	PALM		172	J5
WATERMAN WY	LA	HAC		73	F3
WATERMAN WY	LA	HAC		74	A3
WATERS AV	POM	POM	900	94	D3
WATERSIDE LN	WLVL	THO		102	A4
WATERTREE CT	AGH	AGO		100A	A2
WATERVIEW ST	LA	VEN	100	55A	E2
WATFORD AV	LAN	LAN	44300	160	C5
WATFORD WY	PALM	PALM		171	F5
WATKINS AV	LA	SF		15	C1
WATKINS DR	LAM	LAM	14400	83	C3
WATLAND AV	CO	LA63	1200	45	E3
WATLING DR	PALM	PALM		171	H5
WATSEKA AV	CUL	CUL	3800	42	C6
WATSEKA AV	LA	LA34	3600	42	C6
WATSON AL	LB	LB13		74	F3
WATSON AV	CER	ART		81	D1
WATSON AV	LA	WIL	600	74	D4
WATSON AV	TOR	TOR	1700	68	D4
WATSON AV	WHI	WHI		61	F2
WATSON DR	ARC	ARC	1600	38	E1
WATSON ST	GLEN	GL01	2000	17	F5
WATSON WY	WHI	WHI		61	F2
WATSONCENTER RD	CAR	CAR	700	69	C5
WATSONIA CT	LA	LA68	6700	34	B2
WATSONIA TER	LA	LA68	2000	34	B2
WATSONIA TR	CO	CAL		100	E5
WATSON PLAZA DR	LKD	LKD		70	F4
WATSON PLAZA DR	LKD	LKD		71	A4
WATT WY	LA	LA89		43	F6
WATT WY	LA	LA89		44	A6
WATTLERS DR	LA	LA28		34	A2
WATTLES DR	LA	LA46	1900	33	F2
WATTS AV	CO	LA59	10700	58	F5
WAUCONDA DR	CO	PALM		157	E9
WAUKESHA PL	RPV	PVP	5900	72	D4
WAUPACA RD	RPV	PVP	5300	72	E4
WAVECREST AV	LA	VEN	1	49	B4
WAVECREST CT	LA	VEN	10	49	B4
WAVERLY DR	ALH	ALH	1	36	F4
WAVERLY DR	LA	LA27	3100	35	B2
WAVERLY DR	LA	LA39	2600	35	B2
WAVERLY DR	PAS	PAS	100	26	F4
WAVERLY DR	PR	PR	5000	54	F3
WAVERLY RD	SMAR	PAS	1300	27	D6
WAVERLY RD	SMAR	PAS	1500	37	D1
WAVERLY GLEN WY	CO	LPUE	16700	98	A3
WAVEVIEW DR	CO	TOP	20800	109	D4
WAWONA PL	LA	LA41	2700	25	F5
WAWONA ST	LA	LA41	4500	25	F5
WAWONA ST	LA	LA65	3800	25	E6
WAXWING DR	LA	LA46		33	C4

STREET	CITY	P.O. ZONE	BLOCK	PAGE	GRID
WAYCROSS DR	CO	CAL		107	D3
WAYLAND CT	CLA	CLA		91	C4
WAYLAND ST	LA	LA42	200	36	C1
WAYMAN ST	SCLR	NEW	24400	127	C4
WAYNE AV	LA	LA27	2200	35	A1
WAYNE AV	SPAS	SPAS	1400	37	B3
WAYNE AV	TOR	TOR	20000	67	E2
WAYNE CIR	CER	ART		81	C1
WAYNE ST	CLA	CLA		91	B6
WAYNE ST	POM	POM	1700	91	B6
WAYNECREST DR	LA	BH	1600	33	B3
WAYS ST	LA	SP	300	79	B3
WAYSIDE DR	LA	SUN	9100	10	B2
WAYSIDE PL	DBAR	POM		94	B6
WAYSIDE ST	CO	COM	2000	64	E1
WAYSIDE CYN RD	CO	CAST		123	F3
WEALTHA AV	LA	SV	9800	9	E3
WEATHER RD	CO	COV	18800	88	F2
WEATHERFORD CT	CLA	CLA		91	C1
WEATHERFORD DR	LA	LA08	5200	50	F1
WEATHERLY CIR	WLVL	THO		102	A4
WEAVER AV	SELM	ELM	10500	47	D2
WEAVER LN	LA	LA42	5900	36	C1
WEAVER ST	ELM	ELM	12100	47	E3
WEAVER ST	LA	LA42	5800	36	C1
WEAVER ST	SELM	ELM	10300	47	D2
WEBB AV	LA	NHO	8000	16	C1
WEBB AV	LA	SV	8300	16	C1
WEBB RD	CO	CHA		4	B5
WEBB TR	CO	TOP	19500	109	C5
WEBB WY	CO	MAL		114	A5
WEBB CANYON RD	CLA	CLA		95A	F6
WEBB CANYON RD	CO	CLA		90	F1
WEBB CANYON RD	CO	CLA		95A	F6
WEBBER RANCH RD	CO	LR		184	G9
WEBER AV	LA	NOR		1	C6
WEBER AV	LYN	LYN	3100	59	A6
WEBER PL	LA	NOR		1	C6
WEBER ST	COM	COM	300	58	F6
WEBER ST	POM	POM	500	94	C2
WEBER WY	HAW	HAW		63	C1
WEBER WY	LAN	LAN		160	D5
WEBER WY	LAV	LAV		90	C1
WEBSTER AV	CLA	CLA		91	C2
WEBSTER AV	LA	LA26	1700	35	B4
WEBSTER AV	LB	LB10	3500	70	A5
WEBSTER AV	LB	LB10	2200	74	F2
WEBSTER CIR	WCOV	WCOV		92	D4
WEBSTER PL	CO	VAL		126	H3
WEBSTER WY	SMAD	SMAD	100	28	C2
WEDDINGTON ST	LA	ENC	16800	21	E1
WEDDINGTON ST	LA	NHO	10300	23	C1
WEDDINGTON ST	LA	TAR	18200	21	C1
WEDDINGTON ST	LA	VAN	13300	22	E1
WEDDINGTON ST	LA	VAN	13000	23	C1
WEDGEPORT AV	CO	WHI	10500	61	E4
WEDGEWOOD AV E	SGAB	SGAB	800	37	F3
WEDGEWOOD AV W	SGAB	SGAB	200	37	E3
WEDGEWOOD CT	DUA	DUA	400	86	A3
WEDGEWOOD PL	LA	LA68	6700	34	B2
WEDGEWOOD ST	CO	SGAB	8700	38	A3
WEDGEWOOD ST	LAV	LAV		95A	D6
WEDGEWOOD ST	TEC	TEC	9100	38	B3
WEDGEWORTH DR	CO	LPUE	14600	85	C1
WEDGEWORTH DR	CO	LPUE	16400	98	A3
WEEBURN CT	LA	TAR	19500	13	F4
WEEBURN LN	LA	TAR	19600	13	F4
WEEKS DR	CO	WHI	15500	84	B5
WEEKS DR	LAM	LAM	14700	84	A5
WEEPAH TER	LA	LA46	8400	33	E2
WEEPAH WY	LA	LA46	1800	33	E2
WEEPING WLLW DR	AGH	AGO		102	F2
WEEPING WLLW LN	CO	LPUE	2400	85	D2
WEGMAN DR	LPUE	LPUE	16800	98	B1
WEHNER LN	SAD	SAD	1100	89	F1
WEHRLE ST	LB	LB04	3800	76	A4
WEID PL	LA	LA68	2400	34	C1
WEID WY	LA	LA68		34	C1
WEIDERMEYER AV	CO	ARC	2800	38	F2
WEIDLAKE DR	LA	LA68	6300	34	C1
WEIDNER ST	LA	PAC	12600	3	A6
WEIDNER ST	LA	PAC	13500	8	E2
WEIDNER ST	LA	PAC	12800	9	A1
WEIGAND AV	LA	LA02	10300	58	E4
WEIGAND AV	LA	LA59	10700	58	E4
WEIGHT AL	PAS	PAS		27	A5
WEIK AV	BELL	BELL	3500	53	D6
WEIMAR AV	CO	ALT		19	E5
WEIR AL	PAS	PAS	2500	27	E4
WEIR ST	LA	CUL	11800	50	B4
WEISER AV	CAR	CAR	19300	69	D2
WELBY WY	CO	CAN	24500	5	D4
WELBY WY	LA	CAN	2300	5	F4
WELBY WY	LA	CAN	19700	12	A4
WELBY WY	LA	NHO	11000	16	A4

INDEX

1990 LOS ANGELES COUNTY STREET INDEX

STREET	CITY	P.O. ZONE	BLOCK	PAGE	GRID
WELBY WY	LA	RES	17700	14	D4
WELBY WY	LA	VAN	17200	14	E4
WELCH PL	LA	LA27	4600	34	F2
WELCOME ST	LA	LA26	200	44	C1
WELDON AV	LA	LA65	3000	35	E1
WELDON CYN MTWY	CO	NEW		1	B1
WELDON CYN MTWY	CO	NEW		127	C9
WELDON CYN RD	CO	NEW		127	D8
WELFLEET LN	CO	SAU		124	E4
WELK AV	LA	PAC	11500	3	A6
WELK AV	LA	PAC	11000	9	B1
WELL ST	CO	LPUE		98	E3
WELLAND AV	ARC	ARC		38	E3
WELLAND AV	LA	LA08	3800	51	C1
WELLAND AV	LA	LA18	3700	51	C1
WELLAND AV	TEC	TEC	5300	38	E3
WELLBROOK DR	WLVL	THO		102A	E5
WELLER DR	LA	WOH	5200	100	F2
WELLER PL	LA	WOH		100	F2
WELLER RD	LA	LA41	4800	26	A6
WELLER ST	LA	LA12	100	44	D3
WELLESLEY AV	LA	LA25	1200	41	C4
WELLESLEY AV	LA	LA49	800	41	B3
WELLESLEY AV	LA	LA64	2200	41	D6
WELLESLEY CT	LAN	LAN		159	D3
WELLESLEY DR	CLA	CLA	600	91	A2
WELLESLEY DR	CO	CAL		100	B2
WELLESLEY DR	GLEN	GL05	1400	25	D6
WELLESLEY DR	SM	SM	1600	49	C2
WELLESLEY RD	SMAR	PAS	1900	37	E1
WELLFLEET AV	CAR	CAR	17400	64	D6
WELLFORD DR	CO	LPUE	17900	98	D1
WELLHAVEN ST	SCLR	CYN	18700	124	H5
WELLHAVEN ST	SCLR	CYN	17900	125	B8
WELLINGTON AV	PAS	PAS	1000	26	D1
WELLINGTON CT	CO	CAL		100	A2
WELLINGTON DR	PALM	PALM		171	F6
WELLINGTON DR	PALM	PALM		171	J6
WELLINGTON LN	LA	TAR		13	F1
WELLINGTON LN	LA	TAR		21	A1
WELLINGTON RD	LA	LA08	3800	51	B1
WELLINGTON RD	LA	LA16	1906	43	B4
WELLINGTON RD	LA	LA19	1600	43	B4
WELLINGTON RD	SAD	SAD		89	C4
WELLMAN ST	CMRC	LA40	7500	54	B5
WELLS AV	CLA	CLA	1400	91	A2
WELLS CT	CO	NEW		126	G4
WELLS DR	LA	TAR	18400	21	B2
WELLS DR	LA	WOH	19700	13	E2
WELLS ST E	SGAB	SGAB	100	37	E5
WELLS ST W	SGAB	SGAB	100	37	D5
WELLS FRGO AV E	CO	LAN	16000	174	H6
WELLS FARGO LN	CAR	CAR		69	E6
WELLSFORD AV	CO	WHI	7200	55	C6
WELLSFORD PL	SFS	SFS		61	C1
WELLSPRING DR	DBAR	POM		97	D4
WELLSTON DR	SCLR	SAU	27900	124	E4
WELLWORTH AV	LA	LA24	10400	41	E2
WELSH WY	GLEN	GL08		19	B6
WELTON AL	GAR	GAR	2700	63	C3
WELTON WY	ING	IN02	600	51	A5
WEMAR WY	MTB	MTB	900	46	E6
WEMBLEY CT	SCLR	VAL		124	A9
WEMBLEY RD	SMAR	PAS	1300	27	D6
WEMBLEY RD	SMAR	PAS	1500	37	D1
WEMBLY ST	WCOV	WCOV	1200	48	E3
WENDON ST	CO	SGAB	8300	37	F2
WENDON ST	TEC	SGAB	8700	38	A2
WENDOVER DR	LA	BH		22	F6
WENDOVER RD	LCF	LCF	600	19	C6
WENDOVER RD	PAS	PAS	600	19	C6
WENDY DR	CER	ART	12200	81	B2
WENDY DR	TOR	TOR	20600	67	E3
WENDY LN	LB	LB03		76	E6
WENDY LN	PR	PR		55	E3
WENDY ST	CER	ART	12000	81	B2
WENDY WY	LAN	LAN		159	G7
WENDY WY	MB	MB	1200	62	D3
WENGER AL	PAS	PAS	2500	27	F3
WENHAM RD	CO	PAS	300	27	E5
WENLOCK ST	LA	LA16	5600	50	E1
WENTIFF CT	CO	WAL		97	C5
WENTWORTH AV	LA	PAC	12900	9	B5
WENTWORTH AV	PAS	PAS	1100	27	B6
WENTWORTH ST	LA	PAC	13300	8	F6
WENTWORTH ST	LA	PAC	12700	9	A6
WENTWORTH ST	LA	SUN	10300	9	F2
WENTWORTH ST	LA	SUN	7800	10	D2
WENTWORTH ST	LA	TU	7500	10	D2
WENTWORTH ST	LA	VAN	13500	15	F1
WENTWORTH ST	LB	LB15	5800	76	D1
WENTZEL WY	LA	SF		1	E3
WENWOOD ST	LAV	LAV		90	E3
WERBEL PL	LA	SP	1000	73	E6
WERDIN PL	LA	LA12	200	44	D3
WERDIN PL	LA	LA13	300	44	D3
WERDIN PL	LA	LA14	800	44	C4
WERDIN PL	LA	LA15	900	44	C4
WERNER ST	LB	LB13	1200	75	D4
WESCOTT AV	LA	SUN	8500	10	D2
WESHAM PL	CO	BREA		98A	C3
WESLEY AV	LA	LA37	4100	51	F3
WESLEY AV	PAS	PAS	1000	27	C2
WESLEY CT	PALM	PALM		173	A9
WESLEY DR	LB	LB06	1200	75	D2
WESLEY LN	ARC	ARC		28	E6
WESLEY LN	ARC	ARC		38	E1
WESLEY LN	PALM	PALM		184	A1
WESLEY ST	CUL	CUL	3400	42	D6
WESLEY WY	CLA	CLA	500	91	C2
WESLEYAN AV	WAL	WAL	1300	93	B4
WESLEY GROVE AV	CO	DUA	2000	29	B6
WESLEY GROVE AV	CO	DUA		39	B1
WESLIN AV	LA	VAN	3500	22	F5
WEST AV	CO	HAC		73	F2
WEST BLVD	CO.	LA43	4900	51	B4
WEST BLVD	ING	IN02	6401	51	B5
WEST BLVD	ING	IN05	7400	51	B5
WEST BLVD	ING	IN05	7800	57	B1
WEST BLVD	LA	LA08	3800	51	B1
WEST BLVD	LA	LA16	1900	43	B5
WEST BLVD	LA	LA19	1000	43	B4
WEST BLVD	LA	LA43	5100	51	B4
WEST BLVD	PR	PR	8700	54	F2
WEST BLVD	PR	PR	8900	55	A2
WEST DR	CO	HAC		73	F2
WEST DR	LA	LA69	8300	33	E3
WEST DR	PAS	PAS	600	26	E2
WEST DR	SMAR	PAS	1600	37	D1
WEST RD	CO	VAL		126	J1
WEST RD	LA	LB10		74	F2
WEST RD	LHH	LAH	100	84	C2
WEST RD	WHI	WHI	2000	84	C2
WEST TR	CO	SF	11800	3	E6
WEST TR	CO	TOP	1600	109	D1
WEST WY	LA	LA45		56	B3
WESTBORO AV	ALH	ALH	300	36	F5
WESTBORO AV	ALH	ALH	2100	45	F1
WESTBORO ST	LA	LA49	12700	41	A1
WESTBOURNE DR	WHOL	LA48	300	33	D5
WESTBOURNE DR	WHOL	LA69	600	33	D5
WESTBRIDGE PL	PAS	PAS	600	26	E4
WESTBROOK AV	LA	LA46	2800	33	F1
WESTBROOK CT	CLA	CLA		91	C1
WESTBROOK LN	CER	ART		82	B4
WESTBROOK LN	POM	POM		94	B5
WESTBURY DR	LA	SF	17000	1	E4
WESTBURY LN	ING	IN01		57	B2
WESTCASTLE	WCOV	WCOV		92	C3
WESTCHESTER DR	LA	WOH	10800	13	D3
WESTCHESTER PL	LA	LA05	800	43	D3
WESTCHESTER PL	LA	LA19	900	43	D3
WESTCHESTER PKWY	LA	LA45		56	C2
WESTCLIFF DR	LA	CAN		5	D3
WESTCOATT ST	CO	SAU		182	F7
WESTCOTT AV	BAP	BAP	3400	39	B6
WESTCOTT AV	BAP	BAP	3000	48	B1
WESTCOTT AV	CO	LA22	100	45	F5
WESTCOTT AV	MPK	MPK		45	F5
WESTCOTT CIR	BAP	BAP	12800	39	B6
WESTCOVE DR	LA	LA49	13300	40	F2
WESTCOVE PL	WCOV	WCOV		92	A2
WEST COVINA PKY	WCOV	WCOV		88	A6
WEST COVINA PKY	WCOV	WCOV		92	A1
WEST CREST WY	MPK	MPK	1200	46	A3
WESTDALE AV	LA	LA41	4400	26	A6
WESTERLY TER	LA	LA26	1100	35	B4
WESTERN AV	DOW	DOW	10200	60	B3
WESTERN AV	GLEN	GL01	1300	18	A6
WESTERN AV	GLEN	GL01	100	24	E2
WESTERN AV	LA	SP		73	E5
WESTERN AV	WHI	WHI	5900	55	C4
WESTERN AV N	LA	LA04	100	34	D5
WESTERN AV N	LA	LA27	1300	34	D5
WESTERN AV N	LA	LA29	700	34	D5
WESTERN AV N	LA	SP	100	78	E2
WESTERN AV S	CO	GAR	13900	63	E5
WESTERN AV S	CO	LA47	10400	57	E5
WESTERN AV S	CO	WHI	6400	55	C5
WESTERN AV S	GAR	GAR	12800	57	E6
WESTERN AV S	GAR	GAR	13700	63	E5
WESTERN AV S	LA	GAR	18200	63	E5
WESTERN AV S	LA	GAR	18300	68	E2
WESTERN AV S	LA	HAC	22900	68	E6
WESTERN AV S	LA	LA04	100	34	D5
WESTERN AV S	LA	LA04	200	43	E5
WESTERN AV S	LA	LA05	600	43	E5
WESTERN AV S	LA	LA06	900	43	E5
WESTERN AV S	LA	LA18	1900	43	E5
WESTERN AV S	LA	LA20	300	43	E5
WESTERN AV S	LA	LA47	5800	51	E6
WESTERN AV S	LA	LA47	8000	57	E5
WESTERN AV S	LA	LA62	3800	51	E3
WESTERN AV S	LA	LOM	26700	73	E5
WESTERN AV S	LA	SP	100	78	E2
WESTERN AV S	LA	TOR	23600	73	E3
WESTERN AV S	LOM	LOM	26100	73	E5
WESTERN AV S	RPV	SP	26900	73	E5
WESTERN AV S	RPV	SP	28700	78	E2
WESTERN AV S	TOR	TOR	17400	63	E5
WESTERN AV S	TOR	TOR	19000	68	E2
WESTVIEW LN	LA	PP		40	C2
WESTERN HTS WK	LA	LA18	1900	43	D4
WESTFALL DR	LA	ENC	3500	21	F4
WESTFALL PL	LA	ENC	16400	21	F4
WESTFIELD PL	CLA	CLA		96	C6
WESTFIELD ST	GLEN	GL06	2300	26	A3
WESTFORD PL	CO	VAL		124	B6
WESTGATE AV	CER	ART	16600	82	C4
WESTGATE AV N	LA	LA49	100	41	B1
WESTGATE AV S	LA	LA25	1200	41	D4
WESTGATE AV S	LA	LA49	100	41	B2
WESTGATE AV S	LA	LA64	2200	41	E5
WESTGATE DR	CO	PALM		184	B3
WESTGATE ST	PAS	PAS	400	26	E2
WESTHAVEN RD	SMAR	PAS		27	D6
WESTHAVEN RD	SMAR	PAS		37	D1
WESTHAVEN ST	LA	LA16	5100	42	F5
WESTHAVEN ST	LA	LA16	4800	43	A5
WEST HILLS DR	LA	WOH		13	E2
WESTHOFF WY	WAL	WAL		93	C5
WESTHOLME AV	LA	LA24	600	41	F2
WESTHOLME AV	LA	LA25	1800	41	F2
WEST HONDO PKWY	ELM	ELM	11000	38	E3
WEST KNOLL DR	WHOL	LA48	500	33	D5
WEST KNOLL DR	WHOL	LA69	600	33	D5
WEST KNOLL DR	WHOL	LA69	8500	33	D4
WESTLAKE AV N	LA	LA26	100	44	B1
WESTLAKE AV S	LA	LA06	900	44	B2
WESTLAKE AV S	LA	LA57	100	44	B2
WESTLAKE BLVD	CO	AGO		102A	D6
WESTLAKE BLVD	CO	AGO		105	D2
WESTLAKE DR W	CO	PALM	200	183	A3
WESTLAND AV	LA	NHO	7600	16	B2
WESTLAWN AV	CO	LA66		50	A5
WESTLAWN AV	LA	LA45	7300	50	B6
WESTLAWN AV	LA	LA45	7600	56	B1
WESTLAWN AV	LA	LA66	4300	49	F4
WESTLAWN AV	LA	LA66	4700	50	A4
WESTLYN PL	CO	PAS	1200	27	D1
WESTMAN AV	CO	WHI	7600	55	B6
WESTMAN ST	SFS	WHI	8500	61	B1
WESTMINSTER AV	ALH	ALH	400	36	F5
WESTMINSTER AV	ALH	ALH	2100	45	F1
WESTMINSTER AV	CO	LB03		80	E1
WESTMINSTER AV	LA	LA20	300	43	D1
WESTMINSTER AV	LA	LA34	10700	42	A6
WESTMINSTER AV	LA	LA66	11300	49	F1
WESTMINSTER AV	LA	LA66	11200	50	A1
WESTMINSTER AV	LA	VEN	100	49	B4
WESTMINSTER CT	LA	VEN		49	B4
WESTMINSTER CT	SAD	SAD		89	D3
WESTMINSTER DR	PALM	PALM		183	E1
WESTMINSTER DR	PAS	PAS	600	26	E4
WESTMINSTER PL	LA	LA66	11900	49	F1
WESTMONT AV	POM	POM	500	94	B3
WESTMONT DR	ALH	ALH	1	36	F5
WESTMONT DR	LA	SP	700	73	E6
WESTMONT RD	WHI	WHI	5500	55	C3
WESTMORELD AV N	LA	LA04	100	34	F4
WESTMORELD AV N	LA	LA29	1100	34	F4
WESTMORELD AV S	LA	LA04	100	43	F3
WESTMORELD AV S	LA	LA05	600	43	F3
WESTMORELD AV S	LA	LA06	900	43	F3
WESTMORELD AV S	LA	LA20	300	43	F1
WESTMORELD BLVD	LA	LA06	1600	43	E4
WESTMORELAND DR	MTB	MTB	800	46	C5
WESTMORELAND PL	PAS	PAS	200	26	E3
WESTMOUNT AV	LA	LA43	3400	51	C3
WESTMOUNT CIR	WHOL	LA48		33	D5
WESTMOUNT DR	WHOL	LA48	400	33	D5
WESTMOUNT DR	WHOL	LA69	600	33	D5
WESTON PL	GLEN	GL08	2500	18	E5
WESTON PL	LA	TAR	19100	21	A3
WESTON PL	LB	LB07	3600	70	C5
WESTON RD	TOR	TOR	25200	73	B3
WESTOVER PL	PAS	PAS	500	26	E6
WEST PARK DR	LA	NHO		16	C5
WEST PARK DR	LA	NHO		23	D2
WEST PARK DR	PALM	PALM		172	B8
WESTPARK RD	LA	VN23		22	E5
WEST POINT DR	CLA	CLA	300	91	C5
WEST POINT DR	LA	LA65	3700	36	A4
WEST POINT PL	LA	LA65	3900	36	A4
WESTPORT	MB	MB		62	C3
WESTPORT ST	WCOV	WCOV		92	D5
WESTRIDGE AV	CO	COV	3600	89	A5
WESTRIDGE AV	COV	COV	100	89	A5
WESTRIDGE AV N	GLDR	GLDR	300	87	A5
WESTRIDGE AV S	GLDR	GLDR	600	87	A6
WESTRIDGE AV S	GLDR	GLDR	600	89	A2
WESTRIDGE DR	CO	VAL		126	H2
WESTRIDGE RD	LA	LA49	1900	30	E5
WESTRIDGE RD	LA	LA49	1700	40	F1
WESTRIDGE DR	LAN	LAN		159	E5
WESTRIDGE RD	WCOV	WCOV		92	E4
WESTRIDGE TER	LA	LA49	1900	30	F6
WESTSHIRE DR	LA	LA68	2700	34	D1
WESTSIDE AV	LA	LA08	3800	51	C1
WESTSIDE AV	LA	LA18	3700	51	C1
WESTSIDE DR	CO	LA22	900	54	B2
WESTSIDE DR	LAV	LAV		95A	B6
WESTSLOPE LN	LCF	LCF	5000	19	D3
WEST VAIL DR	LA	CAN		5	F3
WESTVALE CT	DUA	DUA		29	F3
WESTVALE RD	CO	PVP	26600	73	A4
WESTVALE RD	DUA	DUA		29	F3
WESTVIEW DR	PALM	PALM		172	F9
WEST VIEW ST	LA	LA16	1900	43	A5
WEST WANDA DR	LA	BH	9900	32	E2
WESTWARD AV	CAR	LB10	22000	69	E5
WESTWARD BCH RD	CO	MAL	6500	110	B5
WESTWAY LN	CLA	CLA	300	91	B4
WESTWIND CT	LA	VEN		49	D6
WESTWIND ST	LA	VEN		49	C6
WESTWINDS CIR	CER	ART	16700	66	E5
WESTWOOD BLVD	CUL	CUL	3800	50	B1
WESTWOOD BLVD	CUL	CUL	10900	50	C3
WESTWOOD BLVD	LA	LA24	900	41	E1
WESTWOOD BLVD	LA	LA25	1800	41	E2
WESTWOOD BLVD	LA	LA34	3000	42	A4
WESTWOOD BLVD	LA	LA64	2200	41	E2
WESTWOOD BLVD	LA	LA64	2600	42	A4
WESTWOOD PL	POM	POM	1700	90	E5
WESTWOOD PZ	LA	LA24		32	E6
WESTWOOD PZ	LA	LA24		41	E1
WETHERBY LN	LA	LA49		32	B2
WETHERBY RD	SMAR	PAS	2500	27	E5
WETHERHEAD DR	ALH	ALH	2400	46	B2
WETHERLY AV	LB	LB10	2700	75	A1
WETHERLY DR N	BH	BH	200	33	D6
WETHERLY DR N	BH	BH	100	42	D2
WETHERLY DR N	LA	LA48	100	33	D6
WETHERLY DR N	LA	LA69	1200	33	D4
WETHERLY DR N	WHOL	LA48	200	33	D6
WETHERLY DR N	WHOL	LA69	900	33	D4
WETHERLY DR S	BH	BH	100	42	D2
WETHERLY DR S	LA	LA35	1100	42	D2
WETHERLY DR S	LA	LA48	100	33	D6
WEXFORD AV	CO	WHI	7200	55	C6
WEXFORD DR	LA	TU	9300	11	A5
WEXFORD PL	LA	TU	6800	11	A5
WEXHAM WY	ING	IN02	1200	51	A5
WEYAND CT	LAN	LAN	42900	159	J8
WEYBRIDGE LN	LA	LA77		32	B2
WEYBRIDGE PL	ING	IN01		57	B2
WEYBURN AV	LA	LA24	10700	41	E1
WEYBURN DR	LA	LA24		41	D2
WEYBURN PL	LA	LA24		41	E2
WEYLAND CT	LAN	LAN		159	J7
WEYMOUTH AV	LA	SP	200	78	E4
WEYMOUTH PL	LA	SP		78	D3
WEYSE ST	LA	LA12	1400	44	E1
W F PALMER MTY	CO	CLA		96	C3
W F PALMR CY RD	CO	CLA		96	C2
WHALEBOAT PL	AGH	AGO		102	D3
WHALERS WALK	LA	SP		79	A5
WHALEY AV	LB	LB07	4500	70	C3
WHARF ST	LA	SP	100	79	B3
WHARFF DR	LAW	LAW		62	F2
WHARTON DR	CLA	CLA	600	91	A4
WHEATLAND AV	LA	SF	11100	10	A2
WHEATLAND AV	LA	SUN	9400	9	F3
WHEATLAND AV	LA	SUN		10	A3
WHEATLAND AV	LA	SV	8800	9	F6
WHEATLAND AV	LA	SV	7900	16	F1
WHEATLAND AV	WHI	WHI	8600	61	E1
WHEATLAND PL	LA	SV	8800	9	F6
WHEATLEY DR	WHI	WHI	17000	84	E3
WHEATON AV	CLA	CLA	1800	91	E4
WHEATSTONE AV	NWK	NWK	14300	82	B3
WHEELER AV	ARC	ARC	1	28	E4
WHEELER AV	CO	LAV		95A	C6
WHEELER AV	LA	SF	13000	2	F3
WHEELER AV	LA	SF	11300	3	D6
WHEELER AV	LAV	LAV	2100	90	C3
WHEELER AV	LAV	LAV		95A	C6
WHEELER DR	MPK	MPK	400	46	C4
WHEELER LN	PAS	PAS	600	27	A2
WHEELER PL	LA	SF	11400	3	C6
WHEELER RD	SCLR	NEW	25000	127	A4
WHEELHOUSE CT	LB	LB03		80	F1
WHEELHOUSE LN	AGH	AGO		102	D2
WHEELING WY	LA	LA42	200	36	C3
WHEELOCK CIR	CO	WHI	10700	61	A1
WHEELOCK ST	CO	WHI	11100	61	A1
WHEELOCK ST	PR	PR	9500	54	F6
WHELAN PL	CO	LA43	4500	51	A4
WHERLE CT	LB	LB04	3800	76	B4
WHERLE ST	LB	LB04		76	A4
WHETSTONE DR	CO	PALM		157	G8
WHEY DR	SCLR	SAU		124	D4
WHIETT WK	CO	CAST		123	C2
WHIFFLETREE LN	TOR	TOR		73	B2
WHIM DR	WLVL	THO		102	D2
WHIPPLE ST	LA	NHO	10300	23	E4
WHIPPOORWILL DR	CO	LPUE		98	C6
WHISPERGLEN LN	SAD	SAD		89	F1
WHISPRNG LVS DR	SCLR	SAU	26700	127	J1
WHISPRNG OAK DR	GLDR	GLDR		87	D5
WHISPRNG OAKS DR	ARC	ARC	900	28	B3
WHISPERING PINE	LPUE	LPUE		48	E6
WHISPRNG PNS CT	LA	ENC		21	C4
WHISPRNG PNS DR	ARC	ARC		28	F3
WHISPRNG PNS PL	RM	RM	8500	37	F5
WHISPRNG PNS PL	RM	RM	8500	38	A5
WHISPRNG PNS SM	ARC	ARC		28	F3
WHSPRG TREES WY	SCLR	VAL		127	A3
WHISTLER AV	ELM	ELM	4000	39	A5
WHISTLER AV	ELM	ELM	3400	47	F1
WHISTLER AV	LA	SF	13100	1	E3
WHISTLER LN	LA	SF	13200	1	E3
WHISTLING WIND	WAL	WAL		93	A6
WHITAKER AV	LA	ENC	5200	21	F1
WHITAKER AV	LA	SF	8700	7	F6
WHITAKER AV	LA	VAN	6400	14	F4
WHITBURN ST	CUL	CUL	10700	50	D3
WHITCOMB AV E	GLDR	GLDR	100	87	A4
WHITCOMB AV W	GLDR	GLDR	100	87	A4
WHITE AV	CO	COM	14400	65	C3
WHITE AV	COM	COM	900	65	C4
WHITE AV	LAV	LAV	1700	90	D3
WHITE AV	LB	LB05	6600	65	C5
WHITE AV N	POM	POM	1500	90	D5
WHITE AV N	POM	POM	100	94	E4
WHITE AV S	POM	POM	100	94	E4
WHITE CT	TOR	TOR	5000	67	E3
WHITE CT	TOR	TOR	3300	68	A3
WHITE ST	LA	SV	10800	16	E2
WHITE ST	PAS	PAS	2100	27	D3
WHITE ASH DR	PALM	PALM	39100	171	J6
WHITEBIRCH DR	WCOV	WCOV	3200	93	A2
WHITEBLUFF DR	SAD	SAD	1800	95A	B5
WHITECAP WY	CO	MAL		115	A4
WHITECLIFF DR	DBAR	POM		97A	B2
WHITECLIFF DR	RPV	PVP	5700	72	E6
WHITE CLOUD DR	CO	LPUE		85	D5
WHITE CLOUD TER	PALM	PALM		172	A9
WHITE DEER DR	LCF	LCF		19	B1
WHITE ELM WY	AGH	AGO		100A	C5
WHITE FEATHR RD	CO	ACT		182	J9
WHITEFIELD RD	PAS	PAS	100	27	D2
WHITE FIR LN	DBAR	POM		97	F3
WHITEFORD AV	CO	LPUE	100	98	E1
WHITEFOX DR	RPV	PVP	5300	72	E3
WHITE FOX LN	CO	SAU		181	C7
WHITEGATE AV	LA	SUN	10200	10	E3
WHITEGATE LN	LA	SUN	10200	10	E3
WHITEHALL CT	GLEN	GL06		26	B2
WHITEHAVEN TER	GLEN	GL07		25	D1
WHITEHEAD LN	CO	LPUE		98	A4
WHITEHILL DR	LHH	LAH	1200	98A	C2
WHITEHORN DR	RPV	PVP	26600	72	E4
WHITE HORSE CIR	WAL	WAL		93	B5
WHITE HORSE DR	WAL	WAL		93	B5
WHITEHORSE PL	SCLR	CYN		128	E1
WHITEHOUSE PL	LA	LA04	3500	34	F6
WHITEHURST DR	MPK	MPK	1700	46	C4
WHITE KNOLL DR	LA	LA12	800	44	D1
WHITELAND ST	PR	PR	9700	60	F2
WHITELAND ST	SFS	SFS	11200	60	F2
WHTLY TER STEPS	LA	LA68		34	B2
WHITEMARSH AV	COM	COM	1000	64	E4
WHITE OAK AV	LA	ENC	5600	14	D5
WHITE OAK AV	LA	ENC	4500	21	D2
WHITE OAK AV	LA	NOR	8600	7	D4
WHITE OAK AV	LA	NOR	7600	14	D4
WHITE OAK AV	LA	RES	6100	14	D3
WHITE OAK AV	LA	SF	11400	1	D6
WHITE OAK AV	LA	SF	10500	7	D4
WHITE OAK AV	LA	VAN	6100	14	D3
WHITE OAK CT	SCLR	NEW		127	B6
WHITE OAK CT	ARC	ARC	1	28	F1
WHITE OAK DR	POM	POM		90	E2
WHITE OAK PL	LA	ENC	4400	21	D3
WHITE OAK RD	WAL	WAL		93	D5
WHITE PINE PL	CO	SAU		124	C2
WHITEPOST LN	LAM	LAM	15800	83	C1
WHITE RIVER PL	WLVL	THO		102A	F5

1990 LOS ANGELES COUNTY STREET INDEX

STREET	CITY	P.O. ZONE	BLOCK	PAGE	GRID
WHITEROCK DR	LAM	LAM	13900	83	A2
WHITE ROSE WY	LA	ENC	3400	22	A5
WHITESAIL CIR	WLVL	THO		102	A4
WHITESAND PL	CO	MAL	6900	110	C5
WHITES CYN RD	SCLR	CYN	27200	124	H6
WHITESELL ST	CO	LPUE	14000	48	D1
WHITESIDE ST	CO	LA63	3200	45	C2
WHITESPEAK DR	LA	VAN	3700	22	C5
WHITES POINT DR	LA	SP		78	D5
WHITES POINT DR	RPV	PVP	29700	72	C5
WHITESPRING DR	CO	WHI	16000	84	C5
WHITE SPUR LN	CO	SAU		189	F5
WHITE STAR DR	DBAR	POM		97	D4
WHITESTONE RD	RPV	PVP	26900	72	D4
WHITEWATR CY RD	SCLR	CYN		125	D8
WHITEWING LN	WAL	WAL		93	B5
WHITEWOOD AV	DOW	DOW	12700	66	B1
WHITEWOOD AV	LB	LB08	4300	71	B3
WHITEWOOD AV	LKD	LKD	6000	66	B6
WHITEWOOD AV	LKD	LKD	4900	71	B1
WHITFIELD AV	LA	PP	14600	40	D3
WHITFIELD PL	CO	VAL		124	A7
WHITIER WDS CIR	CO	WHI		47	F6
WHITING ST	ELS	ELS	100	56	A6
WHITINGHAM DR	WCOV	WCOV	3300	97	A1
WHITING MNR LN	GLEN	GL08		18	D2
WHITING WDS RD	GLEN	GL08	100	18	C2
WHITLATCH DR	LAN	LAN		160	C7
WHITLEY AV	LA	LA68	1700	34	C2
WHITLEY AV	LA	LA68	1900	34	C2
WHITLEY ST	WHI	WHI	12300	55	C3
WHITLEY TER	LA	LA68	6600	34	B2
WHITLY CLLNS DR	RPV	PVP	29200	72	E6
WHITLOCK AV	LA	VEN	7500	55A	E2
WHITMAN AV	CLA	CLA	900	91	A3
WHITMAN AV	LA	SF	11100	8	B1
WHITMAN AV	LA	VAN	6400	15	B5
WHITMAN PL	LA	LA68	2400	34	D1
WHITMAN RD	HH	CAL		100	D2
WHITMORE AV	LA	LA39	1800	35	D4
WHITMORE ST	ELM	ELM	9200	47	B1
WHITMORE ST	MPK	MPK	1100	46	D1
WHITMORE ST	RM	RM	7400	46	E1
WHITMORE ST	RM	RM	9000	47	A1
WHITMORE TER	RM	RM	7600	46	E1
WHITNALL HWY	LA	NHO	5600	16	F6
WHITNALL HWY N	BUR	BUR	100	24	B2
WHITNALL HWY S	BUR	BUR	100	24	B2
WHITNEY AV	POM	POM		90	E3
WHITNEY CT	SAD	SAD		89	C4
WHITNEY DR	ALH	ALH	1800	46	A2
WHITNEY DR	ELM	ELM	4400	38	D4
WHITNEY LN	BUR	BUR	3200	17	C2
WHITNEY PL	MPK	MPK	400	46	B2
WHITNEY RD	CO	TOP		109	B6
WHITNEY CYN RD	CO	NEW		127	F6
WHITSETT AV	CO	LA01	7200	52	E6
WHITSETT AV	LA	NHO	5600	16	B5
WHITSETT AV	LA	NHO	4000	23	B4
WHITTIER AV	CLA	CLA	1400	91	A2
WHITTIER AV	WHI	WHI	6300	55	D5
WHITTIER BLVD	CO	LA22	4400	45	D6
WHITTIER BLVD	CO	LA22	5600	54	C1
WHITTIER BLVD	CO	LA23	3800	45	D6
WHITTIER BLVD	CO	WHI	10000	55	A3
WHITTIER BLVD	LA	LA23	2100	44	F4
WHITTIER BLVD	LA	LA23	2300	45	A5
WHITTIER BLVD	PR	PR	8200	54	C1
WHITTIER BLVD	PR	PR	9000	55	A3
WHITTIER BLVD	WHI	WHI	10200	55	E6
WHITTIER BLVD	WHI	WHI	13000	61	E1
WHITTIER BLVD	WHI	WHI	14400	84	B3
WHITTIER BLVD E	MTB	MTB	100	54	C1
WHITTIER BLVD W	MTB	MTB	100	54	C1
WHITTIER DR	BH	BH	700	33	A6
WHITTIER DR	BH	BH	600	42	A1
WHITTIER DR	CO	GL14	2400	11	E6
WHITTIER WDS DR	CO	WHI		47	F5
WHITTINGHAM CT	AGH	AGO		102	F2
WHITTLERS PL	WCOV	WCOV		98	E2
WHITTLEY AV	AVA	AVA	100	77	B5
WHITTLEY AV E	AVA	AVA		77	B5
WHITTMORE DR	CO	CAL		108	B5
WHITTWOOD DR	WHI	WHI	10000	84	B3
WHITTWOOD LN	WHI	WHI	15300	84	C3
WHITTWOOD PKWY	WHI	WHI	15400	84	B3
WHITWELL DR	LA	BH		22	F6
WHITWORTH DR	BH	BH	8800	42	D2
WHITWORTH DR	LA	LA19	5800	42	E2
WHITWORTH DR	LA	LA35	6100	42	E2
WHOLESALE ST	LA	LA21	1200	44	E4
WICK LN	CO	GLDR	700	87	D4
WICKER DR	CO	LAM	12600	83	A1
WICKER DR	CO	WHI	12300	84	A6
WICKER WY	LAV	LAV		90	C2
WICKFORD AV	LPUE	LPUE	400	98	B1
WICKHAM CT	SAD	SAD		89	D4
WICKHAM WY	GLEN	MONT		18	E3
WICKLAND RD	CO	CAL		107	F3
WICKLIFFE DR	PAS	PAS		20	B6
WICKLOW RD	LA	LA64	2900	42	B4
WICKS AV	LA	SUN		9	E4
WICKS PL	LA	SUN		9	D4
WICKS RD	PAS	PAS	1300	26	D1
WICKS ST	LA	SV	10900	9	B6
WICKS ST	LA	SV	12500	16	B1
WICKSHIRE AV	CO	LPUE	1700	85	E2
WICOPEE AV	LA	LA41	4800	26	C5
WIDELOOP RD	RH	PVP	1	78	B2
WIDENER AV	WHI	WHI	10700	84	C4
WIDMERPOOL LN	LCF	LCF		19	D5
WIDSON CT	CO	LPUE		98	A5
WIEMER AV	PAR	PAR	13400	65	F1
WIERFIELD DR	PAS	PAS	1300	26	D3
WIERSMA AV	CER	ART		71	F2
WIGAN PL	CO	LPUE		98	A5
WIGGINS	ELM	ELM		38	E6
WIGHT RD	CO	MAL		112	C6
WIGMORE DR	PAS	PAS	200	26	F6
WIGTOWN RD	LA	LA64	2700	42	B4
WIGWAM AV	ARC	ARC	900	28	E3
WILADONDA DR	LCF	LCF	800	19	B2
WILART PL	POM	POM	200	90	E6
WILBARN ST	CO	COM	4900	65	C2
WILBARN ST	PAR	PAR	8200	65	F2
WILBER PL	MTB	MTB	600	46	E6
WILBER PL	MTB	MTB	300	54	E1
WILBUR AV	COV	COV	100	89	B5
WILBUR AV	LA	NOR	11700	1	A5
WILBUR AV	LA	NOR	8700	7	B6
WILBUR AV	LA	NOR	8300	14	B2
WILBUR AV	LA	RES	6100	14	B6
WILBUR AV	LA	TAR	5600	14	B6
WILBUR AV	LA	TAR	5100	21	B2
WILBURY RD	SMAR	PAS	1300	27	E6
WILCOX AV	BELL	BELL	6200	53	D6
WILCOX AV	CDY	BELL	7300	53	D6
WILCOX AV	CDY	BELL	7500	59	D2
WILCOX AV	LA	LA04	500	34	C5
WILCOX AV	LA	LA28	1300	34	C5
WILCOX AV	LA	LA38	700	34	C5
WILCOX AV	LA	LA68	1900	34	C5
WILCOX AV	MAY	MAY	6100	53	D5
WILCOX AV	MPK	MPK	1100	46	C4
WILCOX AV	MTB	MTB	400	46	C6
WILCOX AV	MTB	MTB	100	54	C1
WILCOX PL	LA	LA38	1100	34	C4
WILD BLOSSM CIR	WAL	WAL		93	A4
WILDBRIAR DR	RPV	PVP	5700	72	E3
WILDCAT CYN RD	WAL	WAL		93	B4
WILDE AV	CO	VAL		126	G3
WILDE ST	LA	LA21	1000	44	E4
WILDER AV	LKD	LKD	20300	81	C3
WILDER AV	NWK	NWK	13500	82	C2
WILDERNESS LN	CUL	CUL		50	D2
WILDERNESS PL	POM	POM		94	E6
WILDERNESS PL	POM	POM		97A	C1
WILDFLOWER CT	PALM	PALM		172	A7
WILDFLOWER DR	CO	LPUE		48	B5
WILDFLOWER LN	ELM	ELM		48	A1
WILDFLOWER LN	WAL	WAL		97	B1
WILDFLOWER PL	POM	POM		94	E6
WILDFLOWER PL	POM	POM		97A	C1
WILDFLOWER RD	CO	ARC	11400	38	F3
WILDFLOWER RD	CO	TEC	11100	38	E3
WILDFLOWER RD	TEC	TEC	10900	38	E3
WILDHORSE LN	RHE	PVP	5000	72	F3
WILDLIFE RD	CO	MAL	6500	110	C4
WILD OAK DR	LA	LA68	2400	34	D1
WILDOMAR ST	LA	PP	600	40	C3
WILDRIDGE LN	SCLR	CYN	17700	125	B8
WILD ROSE AV	MON	MON	300	29	B3
WILD ROSE AV	POM	POM		91	A6
WILDROSE DR	CO	CAL		108	B6
WILDROSE WY	LAN	LAN		159	D9
WILDWEST	POM	POM		94	C5
WILDWIND RD	SCLR	SAU		124	H7
WILDWOOD	ELM	ELM		48	A6
WILDWOOD	WCOV	WCOV		92	D4
WILDWOOD AV	GLDR	GLDR	100	86	F5
WILDWOOD AV	LA	SV	9000	10	A6
WILDWOOD DR	CO	CAL		108	B6
WILDWOOD DR	CO	LPUE		48	B5
WILDWOOD DR	LA	LA41	1200	26	B6
WILDWOOD LN	SAD	SAD	600	90	A4
WILDWOOD RD	SCLR	NEW	24000	127	C5
WILDWOOD TR	CO	SF	12100	3	E5
WILDWOOD WY	WAL	WAL		93	D6
WILDWOOD CYN DR	GLDR	GLDR		87	F6
WILDWOOD CYN RD	BUR	BUR		17	F3
WILDWOOD CYN RD	SCLR	NEW	24000	127	C5
WILDWD FIRE RD	LA	SV		10	C6
WILDWOOD RCH RD	GLDR	GLDR	2300	87	F6
WILEY CT	CLA	CLA	100	91	B1
WILEY LN	GLEN	GL14	4200	11	C6
WILEY BURKE AV	DOW	DOW	9500	60	B2
WILEY CANYON RD	CO	NEW		127	A7
WILEY CANYON RD	SCLR	NEW	24000	127	A5
WILEY CANYON RD	SCLR	VAL	24800	127	B3
WILEY POST AV	LA	LA45	8300	56	D2
WILEY POST RD	BELL	BELL		53	E4
WILFREY AV	LAM	LAM	13400	82	E1
WILFRID CIR	LA	SF	13800	2	E1
WILHARDT ST	LA	LA12	100	44	F1
WILHELMINA AV	LA	WOH	5200	100	E1
WILKES CT	CLA	CLA		91	B1
WILKES WY	LKD	LKD	12700	81	C3
WILKIE AV	CO	GAR	14300	63	C2
WILKIE AV	GAR	GAR	12900	63	C1
WILKIE AV	HAW	HAW	12500	57	C6
WILKIE AV	HAW	IN03	11600	57	C5
WILKIE AV	ING	IN03	10800	57	C4
WILKIE AV	TOR	GAR	16200	63	C5
WILKIE AV	TOR	TOR	16800	63	C5
WILKIE DR	POM	POM	2300	90	F4
WILKINS AV	CO	LA23	1100	45	D6
WILKINS AV	LA	LA24	10400	41	E2
WILKINS AV	LA	LA24	10200	42	A1
WILKINSON AV	LA	NHO	5600	16	B6
WILKINSON AV	LA	NHO	4100	23	B4
WILLAKE ST	PR	PR	9800	60	F2
WILLAKE ST	SFS	SFS	11500	61	A3
WILLALEE AV	GLEN	GL14	4000	11	C6
WILLAMAN DR	LA	LA48	300	33	D6
WILLAMAN DR N	BH	BH	100	42	D1
WILLAMAN DR S	BH	BH	100	42	D1
WILLAMETTE LN	CLA	CLA		91	B2
WILLAPA LN	DBAR	POM		94	A5
WILLARD AV	CO	SGAB	6800	27	F6
WILLARD AV	CO	SGAB	5600	37	F3
WILLARD AV	GLEN	GL10	1000	25	A2
WILLARD AV	RM	RM	2600	37	F4
WILLARD AV	RM	RM	2600	46	F2
WILLARD AV	RM	RM	2600	47	A2
WILLARD AV	SGAB	SGAB		37	F3
WILLARD ST	LA	NHO	12000	16	A1
WILLARD ST	LA	NOR	17300	14	D1
WILLARD ST	LA	RES	17700	14	B1
WILLARD ST	LA	VAN	16900	14	F1
WILLARD ST	LA	VAN	13300	15	F1
WILLARD ST E	LB	LB06	100	75	C2
WILLARD ST W	LB	LB06	100	75	C2
WILLARD ST W	LB	LB10	1700	75	A2
WILLAT AV	CUL	CUL	3800	42	C5
WILLENS AV	LA	WOH	4400	13	A3
WILLETTA AV	CO	LAN		159	A9
WILLETTA AV	LA	LA68	2100	34	C2
WILLEY LN	WHOL	LA69	600	33	C5
WILL GEER RD	CO	TOP		109	C2
WILLIAM CT	LAN	LAN		159	G7
WILLIAM BRNT RD	HH	CAL		5	D6
WILLIAMS AV	CO	COM	12800	65	C3
WILLIAMS AV	CO	LAV	4700	95A	E6
WILLIAMS AV	LAV	LAV	3600	90	E2
WILLIAMS DR	HAW	HAW	12800	57	A6
WILLIAMS LN	BH	BH	600	33	C2
WILLIAMS PL	LA	LA32	5000	45	D1
WILLIAMS ST	LB	LB10	2000	74	F3
WILLIAMS ST	MPK	MPK	1100	46	A2
WILLIAMS ST	POM	POM	500	94	D2
WILLIAMS WK	CO	CAST		123	C2
WILLIAMS WY	WHI	WHI		55	F6
WILLIAMSBURG LN	RH	PVP	1	73	A5
WILLIAMSBURG PL	WHI	WHI		84	D4
WILLIAMSBURG WY	PALM	PALM		183	D2
WILLIAMSON AV	CO	LA22	400	46	A6
WILLIMET AV	LA	LA39	4100	25	B5
WILLINS ST	SFS	SFS	11500	61	A2
WILLIS AL	PAS	PAS	1100	26	E1
WILLIS AV	LA	SF	9600	8	D4
WILLIS AV	LA	VAN	8500	8	D6
WILLIS AV	LA	VAN	5600	15	D2
WILLIS AV	LA	VAN	4400	22	D3
WILLIS AV	LA	VAN		22	D4
WILLIS ST	SFS	SFS	10400	61	B4
WILLISTON ST	CO	PALM	1000	182	J3
WILLMONTE AV	CO	TEC	4800	38	C4
WILLMONTE AV	TEC	TEC	4800	38	C4
WILLMOTT LN	CO	MAL	26000	113	A5
WILLOUGHBY AV	LA	LA38	5800	34	A4
WILLOUGHBY AV	LA	LA46	7900	33	E4
WILLOUGHBY AV	LA	LA46	7100	34	A4
WILLOUGHBY AV	LA	LA69	8400	33	E4
WILLOUGHBY AV	WHOL	LA46	7600	33	E4
WILLOUGHBY AV	WHOL	LA46	7500	34	A4
WILLOUGHBY AV	WHOL	LA69	8300	33	E4
WILLOW	CO	LP48		98	E3
WILLOW AV	BAP	BAP	3700	39	F5
WILLOW AV	CO	BAP	1600	48	E2
WILLOW AV	CO	COV	4900	89	D3
WILLOW AV	CO	LPUE	1000	48	C4
WILLOW AV	GLDR	GLDR	700	89	D2
WILLOW AV	LPUE	LPUE	300	48	C4
WILLOW AV N	COM	COM	100	65	A3
WILLOW AV N	WCOV	WCOV	100	39	F6
WILLOW AV S	COM	COM	100	65	A3
WILLOW AV S	WCOV	WCOV	1000	48	E2
WILLOW CT	BUR	BUR	3800	24	B3
WILLOW CT	CO	LPUE		98	D5
WILLOW DR	CO	TOP	1500	109	A3
WILLOW DR	GLEN	GL08	1700	18	F5
WILLOW LN	WCOV	WCOV	2200	39	F6
WILLOW PL	LAV	LAV		90	B3
WILLOW PL	SOG	SOG	2700	58	F2
WILLOW RD	WAL	WAL		97	B1
WILLOW ST	BUR	BUR	2600	24	C2
WILLOW ST	LA	LA13	1300	44	E4
WILLOW ST	SH	LB06	600	75	E1
WILLOW ST E	LB	LB06	100	75	E1
WILLOW ST E	LB	LB15	3400	76	A1
WILLOW ST E	POM	POM	100	90	E5
WILLOW ST W	LB	LB06	100	75	A1
WILLOW ST W	LB	LB10	1200	75	A1
WILLOW ST W	POM	POM	100	90	E5
WILLOW WY	LA	PAC		3	B4
WILLOW WY	LA	PAC		9	D3
WILLOWBRAE AV	LA	CHA	10400	6	C3
WILLOW BRNCH LN	CER	ART		82	C4
WILLOWBROOK AV	CO	COM	12000	58	D4
WILLOWBROOK AV	CO	COM	12800	64	E1
WILLOWBROOK AV	CO	LA59	11500	58	D4
WILLOW BROOK AV	LA	LA29	4500	34	F4
WILLOW BROOK AV	LA	LA29	4300	35	A4
WILLOWBROOK AV	LA	LA59	10700	58	D4
WILLOWBROOK AV	PALM	PALM		171	F6
WILLOWBROOK AV	PALM	PALM		171	H6
WILLWBROOK AV N	COM	COM	100	64	F3
WILLWBROOK AV S	COM	COM	100	64	F3
WILLWBROOK AV S	COM	COM	100	64	F3
WILLOWBROOK CIR	MON	MON		29	B2
WILLOWBROOK LN	POM	POM		94	C5
WILLOW BUD DR	DBAR	WAL		97	C3
WILLOWCREEK LN	CER	ART	12400	82	B4
WILLOW CREEK RD	DBAR	POM		94	A5
WILLOWCREST AV	LA	NHO	5600	16	F6
WILLOWCREST AV	LA	NHO	3700	23	F3
WILLOWCREST LN	POM	POM		94	D6
WILLOWCREST PL	LA	NHO	10800	23	E5
WILLOWGLEN DR	DUA	DUA		29	F3
WILLOWGLEN LN	SAD	SAD		89	F1
WILLOW GLEN RD	LA	LA46	7500	33	E1
WILLOW GLEN ST	CO	CAL		100A	F5
WILLOW GLEN WK	LA	LA46	2400	33	E1
WILLOWGROVE AV	GLDR	GLDR	300	87	C5
WILLOWHAVEN DR	CO	GL14		11	E5
WILLOWOOD ST	LAM	LAM		83	C1
WILLOW RUN WY	AGH	AGO		100A	C5
WILLOW SPG LN	LA	SUN	10000	10	C3
WILLOW SPGS PL	GLDR	GLDR		87	C4
WILLOWTREE DR	AGH	AGO		102	E3
WILLOWTREE DR	RPV	PVP	6900	72	C5
WILLOWTREE LN	LA	NOR		7	B2
WILLOWVALE RD	CO	PALM		171	J7
WILLOWVALE RD	PALM	PALM		171	J7
WILLOW VIEW CIR	SCLR	VAL		124	B4
WILLOW WEED WY	SCLR	CYN		124	F8
WILLOW WEST CT	LAN	LAN	42800	159	G8
WILLOW WOOD RD	RHE	PVP	5000	72	E3
WILL ROGERS ST	LA	LA45	6000	56	C2
W RGRS ST PK RD	LA	PP	1000	40	E3
WILMA AV	CMRC	LA40	2100	53	E3
WILMA PL	LB	LB10	1800	75	A1
WILMA ST	TOR	TOR	5000	67	E2
WILMAGLEN DR	CO	WHI	15400	84	C5
WILMAR PL	RM	RM		46	E2
WILMINGTON AV	CAR	CAR	18000	64	E6
WILMINGTON AV	CAR	CAR	18400	69	E2
WILMINGTON AV	CAR	LB10	20400	69	D6
WILMINGTON AV	CAR	LB10	23500	74	C2
WILMINGTON AV	CO	COM	12300	58	E6
WILMINGTON AV	CO	LA01	5800	52	E5
WILMINGTON AV	CO	LA59	11500	58	E6
WILMINGTON AV	LA	LA02	9200	58	E6
WILMINGTON AV	LA	LA59	10700	58	E6
WILMINGTON AV	LA	WIL	24400	74	C2
WILMINGTON AV N	COM	COM	2600	58	E6
WILMINGTON AV N	COM	COM	100	64	E1
WILMINGTON AV S	COM	COM	100	64	E6
WILMINGTON BLVD	LA	WIL	200	74	B5
WILMINGTON ST	TOR	TOR	24200	72	F2
WILMOT ST	LA	LA07	1900	44	A4
WILSEY AV	LA	TU	10200	10	F3
WILSHIRE BLVD	BH	BH	9700	42	B1
WILSHIRE BLVD	LA	LA05		43	C2
WILSHIRE BLVD	LA	LA05	2800	44	B2
WILSHIRE BLVD	LA	LA10	4000	43	C2
WILSHIRE BLVD	LA	LA17	500	44	B2
WILSHIRE BLVD	LA	LA24	10200	41	E2
WILSHIRE BLVD	LA	LA24	10000	42	B1
WILSHIRE BLVD	LA	LA25	11600	41	E2
WILSHIRE BLVD	LA	LA36	5000	43	B2
WILSHIRE BLVD	LA	LA36	5700	43	A2
WILSHIRE BLVD	LA	LA48	6100	42	E1
WILSHIRE BLVD	LA	LA57	1800	44	B2
WILSHIRE BLVD	SM	SM	100	40	F6
WILSHIRE BLVD	SM	SM	700	41	A5
WILSHIRE BLVD	SM	SM	100	49	A5
WILSHIRE CT	LA	LA49		41	C3
WILSHIRE DR	WHI	WHI	12900	61	D1
WILSHIRE PL	LA	LA05	600	43	F2
WILSHIRE PL N	SM	SM		41	B4
WILSON AV	ARC	ARC	1600	28	E2
WILSON AV	BUR	BUR	1600	17	C4
WILSON AV	CO	COM	11800	65	D1
WILSON AV	CO	LA01	6900	52	E5
WILSON AV	COV	COV	100	89	B5
WILSON AV	HPK	HPK	1900	52	E5
WILSON AV	LA	VEN	2300	49	D4
WILSON AV	LYN	LYN	11800	65	D1
WILSON AV	SMAR	PAS	1400	37	B2
WILSON AV	SOG	SOG	5700	59	E6
WILSON AV E	GLEN	GL06	100	25	C4
WILSON AV N	PAS	PAS	1	27	C2
WILSON AV S	PAS	PAS	1	27	C5
WILSON AV W	GLEN	GL03	100	25	C4
WILSON CT	BUR	BUR	700	17	F5
WILSON CT	LAN	LAN		159	G6
WILSON DR	WCOV	WCOV	1000	92	C3
WILSON PL	MPK	MPK	600	46	D3
WILSON PL	SM	SM	800	49	B2
WILSON ST	CO	CAST		123	A6
WILSON ST	LA	LA21	700	44	E5
WILSON ST	POM	POM	600	94	D1
WILSON ST	SMAD	SMAD	100	28	B2
WILSON TER	GLEN	GL06	1460	25	E3
WILSON WY	IND	LPUE	400	48	F6
WILSON WY	LA	LA32		45	D1
WILSON WY	RM	RM	3100	46	E1
WILSON WY	WHI	WHI1		55	E3
WILSON WY	WHI	WHI		55	E4
WILSON CY TK TR	CO	NEW		128	A8
WILTON DR	LA	LA04	100	34	D6
WILTON PL	GAR	GAR	12800	63	D1
WILTON PL	TOR	GAR	16200	63	D5
WILTON PL	TOR	TOR	16900	63	D5
WILTON PL	TOR	TOR	18400	68	D1
WILTON PL N	LA	LA04	100	34	D5
WILTON PL N	LA	LA28	1300	34	D5
WILTON PL N	LA	LA38	700	34	D5
WILTON PL N	LA	LA68	1900	34	D5
WILTON PL S	CO	LA47	10000	57	D3
WILTON PL S	LA	LA04	100	34	D5
WILTON PL S	LA	LA05	600	43	D2
WILTON PL S	LA	LA18	3700	43	D6
WILTON PL S	LA	LA18	3700	51	D1
WILTON PL S	LA	LA19	900	43	D4
WILTON PL S	LA	LA20	300	43	D2
WILTON PL S	LA	LA47	5800	51	D5
WILTON PL S	LA	LA47	8600	57	D2
WILTON PL S	LA	LA62	3900	51	D1
WILTON ST	LB	LB04	3200	76	A3
WILTON WY	CO	VAL		124	F3
WIMBERLY AV	LA	SF	11900	2	D5
WIMBLEDON CT	WCOV	WCOV		92	D3
WIMBLEDON LN	ING	IN01		57	B2
WIMBLEDON PL	LCF	LCF	500	19	C5
WIMBLEY CT	CER	ART		66	F4
WIMMER AV	BAP	BAP	4900	39	E3
WINANS DR	LA	LA68	6000	34	C2
WINCHELL ST	CO	WHI	11400	55	B5
WINCHELL ST	PR	PR	9600	55	A5
WINCHESTER AV	ALH	ALH	200	36	F5
WINCHESTER AV	GLEN	GL01	1300	18	A6
WINCHESTER AV	GLEN	GL01	200	24	F2
WINCHESTER AV	LA	LA32	3000	36	F4
WINCHESTER CT	PALM	PALM		184	A1
WINCHESTER PL	SGAB	SGAB	200	37	F3
WINCHESTER RD	CO	CAST		123	A2
WINDCREST	PALM	PALM		171	C3
WINDCREST PL	SCLR	NEW		127	B5
WINDEMERE LN	WAL	WAL		93	D6
WINDERMERE AV	LA	LA41	5100	26	A4
WINDERMERE CT	PALM	PALM		171	H8
WINDERMERE CT	PALM	PALM		171	J6
WINDERMERE LN	GLDR	GLDR		86	E4
WINDERMERE PL	LCF	LCF		19	B5
WINDERMERE RD	SAD	SAD		89	D4
WINDFALL AV	CO	ALT	2800	20	C4
WINDHAM AV	LB	LB02		75	B6

309
1990 LOS ANGELES COUNTY STREET INDEX
WINDHAM AV — WREN AV
LOS ANGELES CO.

STREET	CITY	P.O. ZONE	BLOCK	PAGE	GRID
WINDHAM AV	LB	LB02		80A	B5
WINDHAM DR	CLA	CLA		91	C2
WINDING LN	SPAS	SPAS	1900	37	A3
WINDING WY	CO	ACT		182	G7
WINDING WY	CO	MAL	26800	112	E5
WINDING WY	PAS	PAS	1600	20A	B3
WINDNG BROOK LN	WAL	WAL		93	D4
WINDING OAK LN	MON	MON	900	29	C3
WINDING WAY LN	CO	GLDR	1500	87	D4
WINDJAMMER CT	LB	LB03		80	F1
WINDJAMMER RD	CER	ART		66	E5
WINDMILL DR	DBAR	POM		97	E6
WINDMILL RD	TOR	TOR		73	B3
WINDOM ST	LA	CAN	23400	5	E3
WINDOM ST	LA	CAN	22800	12	A3
WINDOVER RD	CO	PAS	1800	20	F6
WINDOVER WY	MPK	MPK	1200	46	A3
WINDPORT DR	RPV	PVP	29200	72	C6
WINDROSE DR	CO	LPUE		97	A5
WINDROSE DR	CO	LPUE		98	F5
WINDROSE DR	WAL	WAL		93	C6
WINDRUSH DR	CO	LPUE		85	D5
WINDRUSH RD	CO	SAU		188	B2
WINDSONG	ELM	ELM		48	A5
WINDSONG CIR	WAL	WAL		93	D6
WINDSONG CT	DBAR	POM		97A	A2
WINDSONG CT	SCLR	SAU		124	E6
WINDSONG CT	PALM	PALM		172	A7
WINDSONG LN	AGH	AGO		102	F4
WINDSOR AV	CO	ALT	2000	19	E5
WINDSOR AV	LA	LA39	3000	35	B4
WINDSOR AV	PAS	PAS	2500	19	E5
WINDSOR AV	WHI	WHI		84	D4
WINDSOR BLVD N	LA	LA04	100	34	D6
WINDSOR BLVD N	LA	LA38	700	34	D6
WINDSOR BLVD S	LA	LA04	100	34	D6
WINDSOR BLVD S	LA	LA05	600	43	C2
WINDSOR BLVD S	LA	LA19	900	43	C3
WINDSOR BLVD S	LA	LA20	300	43	C2
WINDSOR CIR	DUA	DUA		29	E4
WINDSOR CT	LAV	LAV		90	C1
WINDSOR CT	PALM	PALM		183	H8
WINDSOR DR	PALM	PALM		171	J6
WINDSOR DR	SAD	SAD		89	D4
WINDSOR LN	SMAD	SMAD	1	28	C2
WINDSOR LN	TEC	TEC		38	C4
WINDSOR PL	GLDR	GLDR	5300	89	B2
WINDSOR PL	LAN	LAN		159	G4
WINDSOR PL	LB	LB02	300	75	C6
WINDSOR PL	LCF	LCF	3400	19	C5
WINDSOR PL	POM	POM	1900	90	E5
WINDSOR PL	SPAS	SPAS	1100	36	F2
WINDSOR RD	ARC	ARC	500	28	E4
WINDSOR RD	CO	CAST		123	C3
WINDSOR RD	SMAR	PAS	1700	37	C1
WINDSOR RD E	GLEN	GL05	100	25	D5
WINDSOR RD W	GLEN	GL04	100	25	C5
WINDSOR ST	WCOV	WCOV	1200	48	E3
WINDSOR WY	CUL	CUL	5600	50	D4
WINDSOR WY	LB	LB02		80A	C5
WINDTREE CT	PALM	PALM		183	H2
WINDTREE DR	LA	LA77		22	E6
WINDWARD AV	CER	ART		66	E5
WINDWARD AV	LA	LA66	11900	49	E2
WINDWARD AV	LA	VEN	100	49	B4
WINDWARD CT	LA	VEN	10	49	B4
WINDWARD TER	BLF	BLF		66	D5
WINDWOOD DR	DBAR	WAL	800	97	D2
WINDWOOD LN	SMAD	SMAD		28	D2
WINDY CT	CO	SAU		181	F8
WINDY WY	CO	CAST		123	G2
WINEGLOW CIR	CO	WAL	1700	97	B4
WINFIELD AV	LAV	LAV	3100	90	D3
WINFIELD AV	WHI	WHI	9900	84	E3
WINFIELD RD	CO	TOP	21000	109	D3
WINFIELD ST	LA	VAN	13300	16	A1
WING LN	CO	LPUE	500	92	B5
WING ST	GLEN	GL05	300	25	E5
WINGATE PL	POM	POM	1100	94	C1
WINGATE ST	COV	COV	19500	89	A4
WINGED FOOT CIR	LA	NOR		1	A5
WINGFIELD RD	HH	CAL	24300	100	C1
WINGO ST	LA	PAC	13200	8	E5
WINGO ST	LA	PAC	12400	9	B3
WINIFRED AV	CO	PAS	1000	27	F6
WINIFRED ST	LA	TAR	19500	21	A2
WINKLER AV	LKD	LKD	20300	81	C3
WINLAN AV	LA	SF	14000	2	E1
WINLOCK DR	TOR	TOR	24400	73	B2
WINLOCK RD	TOR	TOR	2800	73	B2
WINMAR DR	LA	LA65	1600	35	F3
WINN CT	POM	POM		94	C1
WINNEBAGO AV	LA	SF	10600	8	D3
WINNERS CIR	WAL	WAL		93	D5
WINNETKA AV	LA	CAN	8400	6	E4
WINNETKA AV	LA	CAN	6200	12	F5
WINNETKA AV	LA	CHA	9100	6	E5
WINNETKA AV	LA	WOH	5600	12	F5
WINNETKA AV	LA	WOH	4500	13	F3
WINNETKA CIR	LA	WOH		13	F3
WINNETKA CT	LA	WOH	4500	13	E3
WINNETKA PL	LA	WOH		13	F3
WINNETT MTWY	WAL	WAL		92	F4
WINNETT MTWY	WAL	WAL		93	A4
WINNETT PL	SM	SM	100	40	E5
WINNIE DR	LA	LA68	3200	24	B5
WINNIE WY E	ARC	ARC	1	38	F1
WINNIE WY W	ARC	ARC	1	38	E1
WINNIPEG PL	LB	LB14		75	F5
WINODEE DR	PR	PR	6000	54	E4
WINONA AV	BUR	BUR	1600	17	A4
WINONA AV	COM	COM	100	64	F1
WINONA AV	PAS	PAS	200	26	F2
WINONA BLVD	LA	LA27	1500	34	E3
WINONA DR	WAL	WAL		93	C3
WINROCK AV	CO	ALT	2000	20	C4
WINROW CT	CO	LPUE		98	D5
WINSFORD AV	LA	LA45	7900	56	D1
WINSLOW AV	LB	LB14	300	76	C5
WINSLOW DR	LA	LA26	3400	35	A4
WINSLOW PL	CER	ART	18300	82	C6
WINSOME CIR	SCLR	SAU		127	G1
WINSTON AV	BRAD	DUA	500	29	D4
WINSTON AV	CO	PAS	500	27	E5
WINSTON AV	SMAR	PAS	540	27	E6
WINSTON AV	WCOV	WCOV	100	92	D1
WINSTON DR	ELM	ELM	3700	38	E5
WINSTON ST	LA	LA13	100	44	D3
WINSTON WY	PAS	PAS	200	28	A3
WINTER ST	CO	LA63	3200	45	C4
WINTER ST	LA	LA33	2700	45	B3
WINTER ST	LA	LA63	3000	45	B3
WINTER CYN RD	CO	MAL	3500	113	F5
WINTERDALE DR	SCLR	CYN	28700	125	C8
WINTERDALE DR	SCLR	CYN		125	C7
WINTERGREEN CT	CO	NEW		126	J4
WINTERHAVEN DR	LAV	LAV		90	C2
WINTERHAVEN LN	CO	ALT	2800	20	D4
WINTER MESA DR	CO	MAL		113	F5
WINTERSET DR	SCLR	SAU		124	E5
WINTERWOOD LN	DBAR	POM		97A	A3
WINTHROP AV	ARC	ARC	2700	38	D2
WINTHROP AV	CLA	CLA		91	B1
WINTHROP AV	LA	SF	12800	1	E3
WINTHROP DR	ALH	ALH	300	36	F5
WINTHROP DR	ALH	ALH	2000	45	F1
WINTHROP RD	SMAR	PAS	400	37	B2
WINTON AV N	CO	LPUE	100	92	C6
WINTON AV S	CO	LPUE	100	92	C6
WINTON AV S	CO	LPUE	300	98	C1
WINTON CT	CO	CAL		100	B2
WINTONWOOD AV	CO	LPUE		92	C6
WIOTA ST	LA	LA41	4800	26	C5
WISCASSET DR	LA	CAN		5	D2
WISCONSIN AV	LB	LB03	200	75	F5
WISCONSIN AV	LB	LB14	300	75	F5
WISCONSIN AV	LYN	LYN	3100	59	A3
WISCONSIN AV	SOG	SOG	2700	59	A3
WISCONSIN PL	LA	LA37	3900	51	F1
WISCONSIN PL	POM	POM	400	94	E1
WISCONSIN ST	CO	ACT	33200	189	F1
WISCONSIN ST	LA	LA07	3700	51	F1
WISCONSIN ST	LA	LA37	3800	51	F1
WISCONSIN ST	POM	POM	500	94	E2
WISE AV	LB	LB10	3400	70	B5
WISEBURN AV	HAW	HAW	5200	62	E1
WISH AV	LA	ENC	5600	14	E6
WISH AV	LA	ENC	5600	21	E1
WISH AV	LA	NOR	9100	7	E3
WISH AV	LA	SF	11400	1	E6
WISH AV	LA	SF	10300	7	E3
WISH AV	LA	VAN	6800	14	E4
WISH ST	LA	SF	17000	1	E6
WISHBONE LN	SCLR	CYN		124	E8
WISHING HILL DR	LCF	LCF	4100	19	A3
WISNER AV	LA	SF	9900	8	C3
WISNER AV	LA	SF	8300	15	C1
WISNER AV	LA	VAN	7900	15	C2
WISTARIA AV E	ARC	ARC	100	38	C1
WISTARIA AV W	ARC	ARC	1	38	E1
WISTARIA CT	LA	LA33		45	A4
WISTARIA PL	CO	ALT	400	20	B4
WISTARIA WY	SMAD	SMAD	300	28	C1
WISTERIA VLY RD	CO	CYN	14800	125	F5
WISTERLY CT	CO	SAU		124	E4
WIT PL	LA	LA29	4000	35	A4
WITHERILL PL	PALM	PALM		171	H8
WITHERILL ST	SAD	SAD	700	89	E4
WITMER CT	LA	LA26		44	C2
WITMER ST	LA	LA17	300	44	B3
WITMER ST	LA	LA26	100	44	C2
WITTICK CT	LOM	LOM	2400	73	C3
WITZEL DR	LA	VAN	3900	22	E4
WITZMAN DR	CO	LPUE	16600	92	B5
WIXOM ST	LA	NHO	11400	16	D2
WIXOM ST	LA	SV	10600	16	F2
WO-HE-LO TR	CO	CHA		1A	C6
WOKING WY	LA	LA27	4000	35	A1
WOLCOTT PL	LA	SF	10700	8	D2
WOLDORF DR	LYN	LYN	12200	65	C1
WOLDRICH ST	LA	SUN	10500	9	F1
WOLFE CIR	CO	VAL		126	H3
WOLFE ST	LKD	LKD	3000	70	F1
WOLFE ST	LKD	LKD	6399	71	C1
WOLFE WY	LA	WOH	4600	13	D3
WOLFORD LN	SPAS	SPAS		36	F3
WOLFSKILL ST	LA	SF	14300	8	D2
WOLFSKILL ST	SF	SF	100	2	E6
WOLFSKILL ST	SF	SF	700	8	E1
WOLLACOTT ST	RB	RB	1500	62	D6
WOLLAM ST	LA	LA65	1700	35	F2
WOLSEY CT	WLVL	THO		102	A4
WOLSEY LN	WCOV	WCOV		92	C5
WOLVERTON LN	CER	ART	12900	81	C2
WOLVERTON RD	GLEN	GL07		18	D6
WONDERLAND AV	LA	LA46	8500	33	D2
WONDERLND PK AV	LA	LA46	8700	33	C1
WONDERVIEW DR	CO	CAL	400	108	B5
WONDERVIEW DR	GLEN	GL02		18	C6
WONDER VIEW DR	LA	LA68	2900	24	B6
WONDER VIEW PL	LA	LA68	3400	24	B5
WONDER VIEW PZ	LA	LA68	3300	24	B6
WONG CT	SCLR	CYN		124	H6
WOOD AV	CO	LAN		146	G7
WOOD AV	SOG	SOG	5100	59	D3
WOOD AV	TOR	TOR	20500	67	E3
WOOD CT	CLA	CLA		96	C6
WOOD CT	PALM	PALM		171	E4
WOOD TER	LA	LA27	3300	35	A2
WOODACRE LN	ARC	ARC	900	28	D3
WOODACRE LN	MON	MON	200	29	C3
WOOD ACRES RD	SM	SM	800	40	E4
WOODALE AV	LA	PAC	9100	8	E4
WOODALE AV	LA	PAC	8900	9	A5
WOODALE AV	LA	SF	10600	8	D2
WOODBAY DR	LAM	LAM	14900	84	A6
WOODBEND DR	CO	CLA	1500	90	F2
WOODBEND DR	CO	CLA	3300	90	F3
WOODBINE ST	LA	LA34	10200	42	B5
WOODBINE ST	LA	LA64	3200	42	B5
WOODBINE ST	LA	LA66	11400	49	F1
WOODBLUFF AV	DUA	DUA	400	86	A4
WOODBLUFF RD	CO	CAL		108	A6
WOODBRIAR PL	AGH	AGO		102	E3
WOODBRIDGE AV	PALM	PALM		183	E1
WOODBRIDGE DR	WCOV	WCOV		92	C4
WOODBRIDGE ST	LA	NHO	10200	23	D3
WOODBRIDGE ST	LA	VAN	13300	22	F4
WOODBRIER DR	CO	WHI	16100	84	D5
WOODBROOK DR	AGH	AGO		102	E3
WOODBROOK RD	RPV	PVP	26900	72	D4
WOODBURN DR N	LA	LA49	100	41	C1
WOODBURN DR S	LA	LA49	100	41	C1
WOODBURY DR	CO	HAC	1200	73	F1
WOODBURY DR	LA	HAC	1300	68	E6
WOODBURY DR	TOR	TOR		68	B5
WOODBURY PL	CO	VAL		124	B7
WOODBURY RD	CO	ALT		19	E5
WOODBURY RD	GLEN	GL06	400	25	E3
WOODBURY RD E	CO	ALT	1	20	A5
WOODBURY RD E	CO	PAS	900	20	B6
WOODBURY RD E	PAS	PAS	400	20	A5
WOODBURY RD W	CO	ALT	1	19	E5
WOODCLIFF RD	LA	VAN	3600	22	C4
WOODCLIFFE RD	PAS	PAS	300	26	D3
WOODCOCK AV	LA	PAC	11200	9	A1
WOODCOCK AV	LA	SF	11400	2	F6
WOODCOCK AV	SF	SF40		2	E4
WOODCREEK CIR	CO	LPUE		85	D5
WOODCREEK CT	AGH	AGO		100A	A2
WOODCREST DR	CO	WHI	15400	84	B5
WOODCREST DR	LA	VAN	15500	22	B4
WOODCREST WY	WAL	WAL		93	D6
WOODCROFT AV	GLDR	GLDR	800	88	F2
WOODCROFT AV	GLDR	GLDR	300	89	B2
WOODCROFT ST E	CO	COV	18900	88	F2
WOODCROFT ST W	CO	AZU	17000	88	C2
WOODED VISTA	LA	CAN		5	C5
WOODFALL RD	SCLR	CYN	27200	125	B9
WOODFALL RD	CO	CYN		128	B1
WOODFERN DR	RPV	PVP	5800	72	D3
WOODFIELD CT	LA	LA77		22	D6
WOODFIELD DR	LA	VAN	15500	22	B4
WOODFIELD PL	LA	VAN	15500	22	B4
WOODFIELD RD	LCF	LCF	400	19	C4
WOODFORD ST	PR	PR	9400	55	B1
WOODGATE DR	WCOV	WCOV		92	D5
WOODGATE ST	LAN	LAN	700	160	A3
WOOD GLEN CT	WAL	WAL		93	C4
WOODGLEN DR	AGH	AGO		102	D2
WOODGLEN DR	SAD	SAD		89	F1
WOODGLEN LN	CO	ALT	1600	20	D4
WOODGREEN ST	LA	LA66	12400	49	E2
WOODGROVE AV	CO	COV	4000	88	B5
WOODHALL AV	LA	CAN		5	F2
WOODHAVEN DR	LA	LA68	2700	34	D1
WOODHILL CIR	DBAR	POM		97	D6
WOODHILL CYN PL	LA	NHO	3500	23	C5
WOODHILL CYN RD	LA	NHO		23	C5
WOODHOLLY CT	GLEN	GL07		25	D1
WOODHUE ST	CO	WHI	10400	55	A6
WOODHUE ST	PR	PR	9500	54	F6
WOODHURST DR	CO	COV	20900	89	C5
WOODINGTON AV	BLF	BLF		66	B3
WOODINGTON DR	LAN	LAN	500	160	C5
WOODLAKE AV	LA	CAN	6400	5	F4
WOODLAKE AV	LA	WOH	5700	5	F6
WOODLAKE AV	LA	WOH	5100	100	F2
WOODLAND AV	ARC	ARC	1	28	E3
WOODLAND AV	BUR	BUR	4100	24	A3
WOODLAND AV	GLEN	GL08	1700	18	F5
WOODLAND CT	DUA	DUA	400	86	A4
WOODLAND CT	WAL	WAL		93	C5
WOODLAND DR	BH	BH	1000	33	B4
WOODLAND DR	LA	SP	300	78	E3
WOODLAND DR	SMAD	SMAD	400	28	D1
WOODLAND LN	ARC	ARC	1	28	E3
WOODLAND LN	GLDR	GLDR	800	87	D5
WOODLAND LN	LA	LA46	8000	33	F3
WOODLAND RD	LB	LB10	1700	70	A5
WOODLAND RD	PAS	PAS		27	B6
WOODLAND WY	LA	LA68	2100	34	B2
WOODLAND WY	MPK	MPK	500	46	C5
WOODLAND CST DR	CO	WOH	21700	13	C4
WOODLAND OKS DR	SAD	SAD	100	89	F1
WOODLAND VW DR	LA	CAN	5900	5	C5
WOODLANE DR	WCOV	WCOV		92	D5
WOODLARK LN	CO	VAL		126	G1
WOODLARK ST	LAN	LAN	300	160	C6
WOODLAWN AV	BELL	BELL	6200	53	D5
WOODLAWN AV	LA	LA03	5800	52	B4
WOODLAWN AV	LA	LA11	3700	52	B2
WOODLAWN AV	LA	VEN	500	49	D4
WOODLAWN AV	LYN	LYN	3800	59	C5
WOODLAWN AV	MAY	MAY	5700	53	D5
WOODLAWN AV	SMAR	PAS	2700	37	F1
WOODLAWN CT	LA	LA11	600	52	B1
WOODLAWN CT	LA	VEN		49	D4
WOODLAWN ST	CO	SGAB	8300	37	F1
WOODLEAF DR	DBAR	POM		97	F1
WOODLEIGH LN	LCF	LCF	4100	19	C4
WOODLEY AV	LA	ENC	5600	15	A5
WOODLEY AV	LA	ENC	4400	22	A2
WOODLEY AV	LA	SF		1	F4
WOODLEY AV	LA	SF	11400	2	A5
WOODLEY AV	LA	SF	8700	8	A6
WOODLEY AV	LA	SF	8300	15	A5
WOODLEY AV	LA	VAN	6400	15	A5
WOODLEY PL	LA	SF	8300	15	A1
WOODLYN LN	BRAD	DUA	1700	29	E4
WOODLYN RD	CO	DUA	700	29	E4
WOODLYN RD	PAS	PAS	1800	27	E1
WOODMAN AV	LA	PAC	8700	8	D4
WOODMAN AV	LA	PAC	8600	15	F5
WOODMAN AV	LA	SF	10000	8	D3
WOODMAN AV	LA	VAN	5600	15	F5
WOODMAN AV	LA	VAN	4000	22	F2
WOODMAN PL	LA	VAN	7500	15	F3
WOODMAR DR	CO	WHI	4400	55	D2
WOODMERE PL	DUA	DUA	500	86	B4
WOODMONT DR	LA	NOR		1	A5
WOODMONT PL	CO	LPUE	16600	98	A3
WOODRICH LN	ELM	ELM	9800	38	C6
WOODRIDGE AV	CO	WHI	12200	61	E6
WOODRIDGE AV	LAM	LAM	12800	61	E6
WOODRIDGE AV	LAM	LAM	12900	82	E1
WOODRIDGE CIR	WCOV	WCOV		92	D5
WOODROW AV	LA	LA41	1800	26	A6
WOODROW WLSN DR	LA	LA28	6700	23	E6
WOODROW WLSN DR	LA	LA46	7400	23	E6
WOODROW WLSN DR	LA	LA46	7300	24	A6
WOODROW WLSN DR	LA	LA68	6700	24	A6
WOODRUFF AV	BLF	BLF	13400	66	D2
WOODRUFF AV	DOW	DOW	10200	60	D4
WOODRUFF AV	DOW	DOW	12700	66	D2
WOODRUFF AV	LA	LA24	1200	41	F1
WOODRUFF AV	LA	LA77	200	32	F5
WOODRUFF AV	LB	LB08	3100	71	D4
WOODRUFF AV	LB	LB15	1800	76	D1
WOODRUFF AV	LKD	LKD	5900	66	D5
WOODRUFF AV	LKD	LKD	4100	71	D4
WOODRUFF AV	TEC	TEC	9200	38	B2
WOODRUFF AV E	ARC	ARC	1	38	C2
WOODRUFF AV W	ARC	ARC	1	38	C2
WOODRUFF DR	WAL	WAL		93	C6
WOODRUFF LN	ARC	ARC	2500	38	E2
WOODRUFF PL	ARC	ARC	100	38	D2
WOODRUFF PL	BLF	BLF	14700	66	D3
WOODRUFF WY	ARC	ARC	2400	38	E2
WOODS AV	CO	LA22	100	45	F6
WOODS AV	CO	LA22	1000	53	F1
WOODS AV	MPK	MPK		45	F4
WOODS AV	NWK	NWK	12600	61	A6
WOODS DR	LA	LA69	1600	33	E3
WOODS PL	CO	LA22	1400	53	F1
WOODSHILL TR	LA	LA69	8200	33	E3
WOODSHIRE DR	LA	LA68	2700	34	C1
WOODSHIRE DR	PALM	PALM		171	C3
WOODSIDE DR	CO	SAU		124	G3
WOODSIDE DR	LA	LA65	4600	36	B3
WOODSIDE PK DR	WCOV	WCOV		98	F1
WOODSON ST	LB	LB08	8100	81	B5
WOODSPRING PL	DBAR	POM		97A	B2
WOODSTEAD AV	WHI	WHI	10000	84	B3
WOODSTOCK AV	CO	SAU		123	D5
WOODSTOCK CT	CLA	CLA		91	B1
WOODSTOCK LN	BUR	BUR		17	C3
WOODSTOCK RD	LA	LA46	2500	33	E1
WOODSTOCK RD	SMAR	PAS	1300	27	C6
WOODSTONE PL	LA	CAN		5	D3
WOODVALE CT	LA	CAN		5	F3
WOODVALE RD	LA	ENC	15600	22	B4
WOODVIEW CT	DBAR	WAL		97	C5
WOODVIEW DR	LA	LA68	3500	24	D5
WOODVILLE DR	ELM	ELM	11700	38	F5
WOODVILLE DR	ELM	ELM	12400	39	A6
WOODWARD AV	BELL	BELL	6200	53	C6
WOODWARD AV	LA	SUN	97000	10	E3
WOODWARD AV	LOM	LOM	24500	73	D3
WOODWARD AV	MAY	MAY	6000	53	C5
WOODWARD AV E	ALH	ALH	1	37	B4
WOODWARD AV W	ALH	ALH	1	37	B4
WOODWARD BLVD	CO	PAS	400	28	B5
WOODWARDIA DR	LA	LA77		22	E6
WOODWORTH AV	ING	IN03	10000	57	C4
WOODWORTH PL	SF	SF	1600	2	D6
WOODWORTH ST	LA	SF	600	2	D6
WOODWORTH ST	SF	SF	600	8	E1
WOODY TR	LA	LA68	6800	24	B6
WOODY TR	LA	LA68	6800	34	B1
WOOLFORD ST	CUL	CUL	11100	50	C3
WOOLLEY ST	TEC	TEC	9000	38	B1
WOOLSEY CYN RD	CO	CAN	23900	4	A5
WOOLSEY CYN RD	LA	CAN	23600	4	A5
WOOLWINE DR	CO	LA63	3600	45	D2
WOOSTEAD AV	WHI	WHI		84	B3
WOOSTER AV	CO	LA56	5800	50	D4
WOOSTER ST	LA	LA35	800	42	D2
WORCESTER AV	PAS	PAS	700	27	A2
WORCESTER CT	LB	LB03		76	F5
WORK ST	MTB	MTB	500	54	C2
WORKMAN AV	ARC	ARC	400	38	B2
WORKMAN AV	CO	COV	17700	88	E6
WORKMAN AV	COV	COV	100	88	E6
WORKMAN AV	TEC	TEC	9200	38	B2
WORKMAN AV E	WCOV	WCOV	1000	88	B6
WORKMAN AV W	WCOV	WCOV	1000	88	B6
WORKMAN RD	COV	COV	100	89	A6
WORKMAN ST	LA	LA31	2300	36	A6
WORKMAN ST	LA	LA31	1700	45	A2
WORKMAN ST	LA	SF	200	2	E5
WORKMAN ST	LA	SF	14600	2	D6
WORKMAN ST	LPUE	LPUE	15800	48	F6
WORKMAN ST N	SF	SF	100	2	E5
WORKMAN ST S	SF	SF	100	2	D6
WORKMAN MILL RD	CO	LPUE	700	48	A4
WORKMAN MILL RD	CO	WHI	600	48	A4
WORKMAN ML RD S	CO	WHI	1700	47	E6
WORKMAN ML RD S	CO	WHI	4000	55	C2
WORLD WY	LA	LA45	1	56	B3
WORLD WY W	LA	LA45	6800	56	A3
WORM WOOD DR	CO	LPUE		98	B4
WORNOM AV	LA	SUN	9600	10	A4
WORSHAM DR	WHI	WHI		55	F5
WORTH ST	LA	LA63	4300	45	C2
WORTHEN AV	LA	LA39	4600	35	D2
WORTHING LN	LA	LA77		32	B2
WORTHINGTON DR	CO	SGAB	8600	37	F2
WORTHINGTON DR	TEC	SGAB		38	A2
WORTHY DR N	GLDR	GLDR	600	87	C4
WORTHY DR S	GLDR	GLDR	200	87	C5
WORTSER AV	LA	NHO	7000	16	A4
WORTSER AV	LA	NHO	4400	23	A3
WORTSER AV	LA	VAN	4600	23	A3
WOTKYNS DR	PAS	PAS	1100	26	E2
WRANGLER RD	RH	PVP	1	78	A2
WRANGLER WY	WAL	WAL		93	C6
WREDE WY	WCOV	WCOV		93	A2
WREN AV	CO	LPUE	1800	92	C3

COPYRIGHT, © 1989 BY Thomas Bros Maps

INDEX

310

1990 LOS ANGELES COUNTY STREET INDEX

WREN AV — 2ND ST E

LOS ANGELES CO.

STREET	CITY	P.O. ZONE	BLOCK	PAGE	GRID
WREN AV	CO	WCOV		92	C3
WREN CT	LAV	LAV		95A	E5
WREN DR	LA	LA65	400	36	A3
WREN WY	WCOV	WCOV		92	A2
WRENCREST DR	CO	CAL		13	A4
WRENCREST DR	CO	CAL		100	F4
WRIGHT AV	PAS	PAS	700	27	B2
WRIGHT CT	POM	POM		94	B3
WRIGHT PL	ART	ART		71	F1
WRIGHT PL	SOG	SOG	4800	59	D2
WRIGHT RD	CO	COM	11700	65	C1
WRIGHT RD	LYN	LYN	11000	59	D6
WRIGHT RD	LYN	LYN	11700	65	C1
WRIGHT RD	SOG	SOG	10200	59	D4
WRIGHT ST	LA	LA15	1300	44	B4
WRIGHT ST	POM	POM	1700	94	C3
WRIGHT TER	CUL	CUL	6000	50	D1
WRIGHT WY	IND	LPUE		97	A3
WRIGHTCREST DR	CUL	CUL	5800	50	D1
WRIGHTVIEW DR	LA	NHO	3400	23	E5
WRIGHTVIEW PL	LA	NHO	3300	23	E5
WRIGHTWICK DR	CER	ART	12900	81	C2
WRIGHTWOOD CT	LA	NHO	3500	23	E5
WRIGHTWOOD DR	LA	NHO	3200	23	E5
WRIGHTWOOD LN	LA	LA28	10700	23	E5
WRIGHTWOOD LN	LA	NHO	10900	23	E5
WRIGHTWOOD PL	LA	NHO	11000	23	E5
WRIGHTWOOD WY	PALM	PALM		172	H9
WRIGHTWOOD WY	PALM	PALM		172	J9
WRIGLEY TER RD	AVA	AVA	300	77	B5
WYANDOTTE ST	LA	CAN	20200	12	A3
WYANDOTTE ST	LA	NHO	13400	15	F3
WYANDOTTE ST	LA	NHO	11500	16	D3
WYANDOTTE ST	LA	RES	17700	14	A3
WYANDOTTE ST	LA	SV	10700	16	E3
WYANDOTTE ST	LA	VAN	16700	14	E3
WYANDOTTE ST	LA	VAN	13500	15	E3
WYANT LN	WHI	WHI		55	F6
WYATT TR	CO	TOP		109	D5
WYBRO WY	CO	LA63	1400	45	E2
WYCLIFF AV N	LA	SP	200	78	D2
WYCLIFF AV S	LA	SP	900	78	D2
WYCLIFF PL	LA	SP	1600	78	D4
WYETH DR	CER	ART	11800	81	A1
WYE THE	CO	ELM	11800	39	A4
WYLAND WY E	CO	DUA	100	39	B1
WYLAND WY W	CO	MON	100	39	A1
WYLIE LN	RB	RB	900	62	D5
WYMAN AV	CO	LA22	400	45	E5
WYMORE ST	CO	COM	3700	65	B4
WYN TER	CO	WAL		97	B3
WYNCREST WY	LCF	LCF	4400	18	F2
WYNDALE PL	GLEN	GL06	2600	26	B3
WYNDHAM DR	CO	VAL		126	H2
WYNDHAM RD	LA	LA46	8300	33	E2
WYNGATE ST	LA	SUN	7900	10	D3
WYNGATE ST	LA	TU	7600	10	E3
WYNGATE ST	LA	TU	7000	11	A3
WYNGLENN LN	LA	LA23	2700	45	A6
WYNKOOP ST	LA	LA45	6400	50	B6
WYNN RD	PAS	PAS	1000	28	A1
WYNNE AV	LA	NOR	8300	14	C3
WYNNE AV	LA	RES	6300	14	C5
WYNNEWOOD DR	DBAR	POM		97A	B2
WYNOLA ST	LA	PP	400	40	C4
WYNWOOD LN	LA	LA23	2700	45	A6
WYOMING AV	BUR	BUR	2600	17	A6
WYOMING AV	LA	LA25	11500	41	D3
WYOMING ST	PAS	PAS	200	19	E6
WYSALL LN	LCF	LCF		19	D5
WYSE RD	CO	SAU		181	F6
WYSTONE AV	LA	NOR	8500	7	B6
WYSTONE AV	LA	NOR	8300	14	B1
WYSTONE AV	LA	RES	6400	14	B3
WYTON DR	LA	LA24	10300	32	E6
X					
XIMENO AV	LB	LB04	700	76	B6
XIMENO AV	LB	LB14	300	76	B6
XIMENO AV	LB	LB15	2000	76	B2
XIMENO WY	LB	LB04		76	B3
Y					
YACHT ST	LA	WIL	300	74	C6
YACHT CLUB WY	RB	RB	1	67	C2
YACHT HARBOR DR	RPV	PVP	1	77	F3
YAFFA ST	LAN	LAN		160	D7
YAGER WY	WLVL	THO		102	A5
YALE AV	CLA	CLA	100	91	B3
YALE AV	LA	VEN	2900	49	D4
YALE AV	WAL	WAL		93	B4
YALE CT	LAN	LAN		159	G7
YALE CT	LAV	LAV		90	E3
YALE CT	SM	SM		41	C4
YALE DR	GLEN	GL05	1100	25	E6
YALE ST	LA	LA12	700	44	E1
YALE ST	PAS	PAS	100	26	F2
YALE ST	SM	SM	800	41	B4
YALETON AV	CO	COV	4000	88	A4
YALETON AV	WCOV	WCOV	100	88	A6
YANCEY LN	CO	LAN		171	C2
YANKEE DR	AGH	AGO		100A	D5
YANKEY ST	DOW	DOW	7400	59	F4
YANKTON AV	CLA	CLA		96	C6
YARMOUTH AV	LA	ENC	5900	14	D6
YARMOUTH AV	LA	ENC	4700	21	D2
YARMOUTH AV	LA	RES	6100	14	D3
YARMOUTH AV	LA	SF	11500	1	D6
YARMOUTH AV	LA	SF	10300	7	D2
YARMOUTH CIR	PVE	PVP		72	A5
YARMOUTH RD	PVE	PVP	300	72	A5
YARNELL ST	LA	SF	15900	2	B2
YARNELL ST	WCOV	WCOV	1300	48	E1
YARROW DR	LAN	LAN		160	B1
YARROW ST E	CO	RM	8200	46	F3
YATES AV	CMRC	LA40	1500	54	B2
YATES ST	LA	SUN	8000	10	E3
YATES ST	LA	TU	7600	10	E3
YAVAPAI TR	CO	AGO		107	A3
YAWL ST	LA	VEN		49	C6
YBARRA DR	CO	LPUE	1500	97	A4
YBARRA RD	LA	WOH	21700	13	B3
YBARRA CYN MTWY	CO	CHA		1A	B4
YEAGER PL	LA	LA68	6800	34	B2
YEAGER WY	BELL	BELL		53	E3
YEARLING CIR	CER	ART	11400	71	F2
YEARLING PL	CER	ART	12200	81	B2
YEARLING ST	CER	ART	11200	71	F2
YEARLING ST	CER	ART	11800	81	A2
YEARLING ST	LKD	LKD	2400	70	F2
YEARLING ST	LKD	LKD	5700	71	C2
YEDOR CT	CO	PVP		73	B3
YELLOWBLUFF PL	CO	LPUE		98	E6
YELLOW BOOT LN	CAR	CAR		69	E6
YELLOWBRICK RD	DBAR	WAL		97	C2
YELLOW BRICK RD	RPV	PVP		72	E3
YELLOWBROOK LN	LAM	LAM	15300	84	B6
YLLW FEATHR CIR	WAL	WAL		93	C4
YELLOW HILL RD	CO	MAL		110	B3
YELLOWSTONE ST	LA	LA32	4300	45	C1
YELLOWWOOD DR	WLVL	THO		102A	E5
YEOMAN LN	CO	TOP	800	109	A3
YERBA ST	LA	NHO	12900	16	A2
YERBA SECA AV	AGH	AGO		100A	A2
YERMO ST	WHI	WHI	15600	84	B4
YEW ST	LAN	LAN	42800	159	F8
YNEZ AV	RB	RB	1100	67	D5
YNEZ AV N	MPK	MPK	100	46	C2
YNEZ AV S	MPK	MPK	100	46	B3
YNEZ CT	WCOV	WCOV		92	D6
YOAKUM DR	LA	BH	9600	32	F2
YOAKUM ST	LA	LA32	700	36	D4
YOCUM ST	PAS	PAS	1100	26	D1
YODER AV	CO	WHI	3600	55	C1
YOJOA PL	CO	LPUE	2700	85	E4
YOLANDA AV	LA	NOR		1	B6
YOLANDA AV	LA	NOR	8500	7	B5
YOLANDA AV	LA	NOR	8300	14	B2
YOLANDA AV	LA	RES	6100	14	B2
YOLANDA AV	LA	TAR	5700	14	B6
YOLANDA AV	LA	TAR	5100	21	B1
YOLANDA CT	WCOV	WCOV		92	D6
YOLO ST	PAS	PAS	1000	27	C3
YORBA DR	POM	POM	1600	90	E5
YORBA ST	LA	LA32	4400	36	C5
YORBITA RD	CO	LPUE	300	98	E1
YORK AV	CO	IN04	11000	57	B6
YORK AV	GLDR	GLDR	1200	89	C2
YORK AV	HAW	HAW	11400	57	B6
YORK AV	ING	IN04	11100	57	B6
YORK AV	WHI	WHI		55	F5
YORK BLVD	LA	LA41		25	E6
YORK BLVD	LA	LA41	4500	36	B1
YORK BLVD	LA	LA42	4700	36	B1
YORK BLVD	LA	LA65	3600	25	E6
YORK CIR	LAV	LAV		90	D2
YORK PL	CLA	CLA		91	B4
YORK PL	LA	LA65	4000	25	E6
YORK PL	LAN	LAN		159	J2
YORKFIELD CT	WLVL	THO		102	B4
YORK HILL PL	LA	LA41	4000	25	F6
YORKSBORO LN	LA	WOH		13	D3
YORKSHIRE AV	SM	SM	1800	41	C5
YORKSHIRE CT	SAD	SAD		89	C4
YORKSHIRE DR	ARC	ARC	1	28	E2
YORKSHIRE DR	LA	LA65	2300	35	E2
YORKSHIRE DR	PALM	PALM		183	H7
YORKSHIRE RD	CO	PAS	3300	28	A4
YORKSHIRE RD	PAS	PAS	2700	27	E4
YORKSHIRE WY	POM	POM	2300	90	F5
YORKTOWN AV	LA	LA45	7800	56	D2
YORKTOWN AV	MTB	MTB		46	D5
YORK TOWN PL	LA	LA45	7800	50	D6
YOSEMITE CT	SAD	SAD		95A	B6
YOSEMITE DR	LA	LA41	2400	25	F5
YOSEMITE DR	LA	LA41	1100	26	B5
YOSEMITE ST	CER	ART	12400	82	B5
YOSEMITE WY	LA	LA41	4600	25	F5
YOSEMITE WY	LA	LA65	3900	25	E6
YOST TR	CO	TOP	1300	109	D2
YOUNG AV	CO	RM	7700	46	E3
YOUNG CT	POM	POM		94	E5
YOUNG DR	BH	BH	9900	42	B1
YOUNG DR	CO	MONT	4400	18	F2
YOUNG ST E	LA	WIL	600	74	D3
YOUNG ST W	LA	WIL	1200	74	D3
YOUNGBERRY DR	SCLR	SAU		124	E5
YOUNGBLOOD PL	LAN	LAN	43600	159	J7
YOUNGDALE AV	LA	SF	11900	2	D5
YOUNGDALE PL	LA	SF	14900	2	D5
YOUNGDALE RD	CO	SGAB	8300	37	F1
YOUNGDALE ST	CO	SGAB	8700	38	A1
YOUNGS CYN RD	CO	ACT		189	A1
YOUNGSWORTH ST	LA	CUL	11300	50	B3
YOUNGWOOD DR	WHI	WHI	15200	84	B2
YOUNGWORTH RD	CUL	CUL	10600	50	D3
YSABEL ST	RB	RB	1000	67	E4
YSIDRO PL	LA	PP	16000	40	C4
YUBA LN	CLA	CLA		96	D6
YUCATAN AV	LA	WOH	21500	13	C3
YUCATAN PL	CER	ART	13300	82	D5
YUCATAN PL	CO	POM		97	D5
YUCCA AV	LAN	LAN	44100	160	B5
YUCCA CIR	LAV	LAV		90	D1
YUCCA LN	CO	ALT		19	E5
YUCCA PL	GLDR	GLDR	1300	89	D2
YUCCA ST	ELS	ELS	700	56	A5
YUCCA ST	LA	LA28	6000	34	C3
YUCCA TR	LA	LA46	8200	33	E3
YUCCA TR	SMAD	SMAD		20A	D3
YUCCA TR	SMAD	SMAD		28	D1
YUCCA RIDGE RD	CO	GLDR	7400	86	E4
YUCCA RIDGE RD	GLDR	GLDR	700	86	E4
YUCCA SPGS ST	CO	LAN	39900	175	B5
YUCCA TREE ST	CO	PALM	38600	171	J8
YUCCA VALLEY RD	SCLR	VAL		127	C1
YUKON AV	HAW	HAW	12500	57	B6
YUKON AV	HAW	HAW	12800	63	B2
YUKON AV	ING	IN03	10000	57	B5
YUKON AV	LAW	LAW	15200	63	B3
YUKON AV	TOR	TOR	16500	63	B6
YUKON AV	TOR	TOR	18300	68	B1
YUKON TR	CO	CAN	8400	4	A6
YUKON TR	LA	CAN	8400	5	D1
YULE LN	CO	TOP	800	109	B3
YUMA CIR	LAV	LAV		90	E1
YUMA CT	SAD	SAD	700	90	A2
YUMA PL	LA	LA46	8300	33	E2
YVETTE AV	CER	ART	17000	82	C5
YVETTE DR	CO	WHI		48	B4
YVETTE LN	SCLR	VAL		127	C2
YVETTE LN	CO	WHI	13700	48	B4
YVETTE WY	CER	ART	16600	82	C4
YVONNE AV	CO	SGAB	5200	37	F4
YVONNE ST	WCOV	WCOV		92	D6
Z					
ZACA PL	LA	LA65	4300	25	F6
ZACHRY TAYLR WY	PALM	PALM		183	D2
ZACHAU PL	LA	TU	7300	10	F2
ZADELL AV	TEC	TEC	5300	38	C3
ZAKON RD	TOR	TOR	4800	67	E6
ZALTANA ST	CO	CHA		1A	B6
ZALTANA ST	CO	CHA		6	A1
ZALVIDEA ST	LA	LA26	400	35	B6
ZAMBRANO ST	CMRC	LA40		53	F4
ZAMBRANO ST	CMRC	LA40		54	A4
ZAMORA AV	CO	COM	13900	64	D2
ZAMORA AV	CO	LA01	7400	58	D1
ZAMORA AV	CO	LA02	8600	58	D2
ZAMORA AV	LA	LA02	10300	58	D4
ZAMORA AV	LA	LA59	11100	58	D5
ZAMORA ST	LA	LA11	4100	52	C2
ZANDIA AV	LB	LB15	2100	76	B2
ZANE ST	LA	LA32	4500	36	D5
ZANE ST	LB	LB05	1	70	B2
ZANE GREY TER	CO	ALT	2800	20	C4
ZANJA ST	LA	LA66	1273	49	D3
ZANJA ST	LA	VEN	12900	49	D3
ZANJA ST	PAS	PAS	300	26	E1
ZAPATA ST	MTB	MTB		46	D6
ZARA ST	GLDR	GLDR	1500	87	D6
ZARING ST	CO	LA22	4300	45	D4
ZARING ST	CO	LA63	4100	45	D4
ZARING ST	MPK	MPK	5500	46	A5
ZASTROW AV	BLF	BLF	14700	66	C2
ZAYANTA DR	LA	VEN	7800	55A	E1
ZEIDLER RCH RD	CO	TOP		109	B4
ZEILER AV	LA	PAC	8800	8	F6
ZEILER AV	LA	VAN		15	F1
ZELDA WY	CO	CHA		4	C5
ZELLA PL	LA	LA32	4800	45	D1
ZELZAH AV	LA	ENC	5600	14	D6
ZELZAH AV	LA	ENC	4700	21	D2
ZELZAH AV	LA	NOR	8600	7	D6
ZELZAH AV	LA	NOR	8300	14	D1
ZELZAH AV	LA	RES	6100	14	D4
ZELZAH AV	LA	SF	11400	1	D6
ZELZAH AV	LA	SF	10500	7	D2
ZENITH AV	CO	LPUE	500	92	C6
ZENITH POINT RD	CO	MAL	30000	111	F5
ZENO PL	LA	VEN	2100	49	D4
ZEPHYR AV	LA	HAC	26200	73	E4
ZEPHYR CT	LA	VEN	20	49	B4
ZEPHYR CT	PALM	PALM		183	E3
ZERELDA ST	RM	RM	8600	38	A4
ZERMATT LN	CO	VAL		126	J2
ZERR CT	GLEN	GL06	200	25	E3
ZEUS	WCOV	WCOV		48	F2
ZEUS AV	NWK	NWK	11000	61	A4
ZEUS AV	NWK	NWK	11900	82	A1
ZEUS DR	LA	LA46		33	E2
ZEUS PL	LA	LA46		33	E2
ZIMMERMAN PL	CO	SAU		124	G3
ZINDELL AV	CMRC	LA40	6300	54	C6
ZINNEY RD	CO	LR	35400	184	D6
ZINNIA CT	CO	CYN		125	F4
ZINNIA LN	GLEN	GL05	500	25	E5
ZINNIA ST	PALM	PALM		183	E2
ZITOLA TER	LA	VEN	8100	55A	E1
ZITTO LN	LA	TU	9900	11	B4
ZOE AV	HPK	HPK	2000	52	E5
ZOE AV	HPK	HPK	2700	53	A5
ZOE ANNE WY	GLEN	GL14	5000	11	C4
ZOLA AV	PR	PR	5400	54	F3
ZOLA AV	PR	PR	4100	55	A1
ZOLA ST	LA	SF	17300	1	E4
ZOLTAN ST	LAN	LAN		160	E6
ZOMBAR AV	LA	VAN	7300	15	C3
ZONA CT	LB	LB02	400	75	D5
ZONAL AV	LA	LA33	1600	45	B2
ZOO DR	LA	LA27		24	E3
ZOO DR	LA	LA27		25	A3
ZOOK DR	GLEN	GL02	900	25	A2
ZORADA CT	LA	LA46	2300	33	F1
ZORADA DR	LA	LA46	2400	33	F1
ZORANA PL	LA	SP	100	78	D3
ZORILLO PL	PVE	PVP	2000	72	B5
ZORRO WY	CO	SAU		181	C7
ZUMA BAY WY	CO	MAL		110	A5
ZUMA BEACH RD	CO	MAL	30100	111	F6
ZUMA MESA DR	CO	MAL	6300	112	C6
ZUMA RIDGE MTWY	CO	MAL		105	E6
ZUMA RIDGE MTWY	CO	MAL		111	F1
ZUMA RIDGE MTWY	CO	MAL		112	A4
ZUMA RDG FRE RD	CO	MAL		105	F3
ZUMA RDG FRE RD	CO	MAL		106	A3
ZUMA VIEW PL	CO	MAL	6500	110	D4
ZUMIREZ DR	CO	MAL	6700	110	C4
ZUMIREZ DR	CO	MAL	5800	112	C6
ZUNI LN	CAR	CAR		69	E6
ZUNI ST	CO	TOP		13	C5
ZUNIGA LN	LA	LA33	1500	45	C2
ZUNIGA RD	CO	TOP	23300	108	E1
NUMERICAL STREETS					
1ST AV	CO	WHI	11300	84	D5
1ST AV	GLEN	GL14		11	C5
1ST AV	LYN	LYN	11600	59	C6
1ST AV	WHI	WHI		84	D5
1ST AV E	CO	HAC		73	F2
1ST AV N	ARC	ARC	100	28	E4
1ST AV N	COV	COV	100	88	F5
1ST AV S	ARC	ARC	100	28	E6
1ST AV S	ARC	ARC	1500	38	E1
1ST AV S	CO	COM	11700	59	C6
1ST AV S	CO	COM	11900	65	C1
1ST AV S	CO	LAM	12600	84	D5
1ST AV S	COV	COV	100	88	F5
1ST AV S	ING	IN03	10200	57	D4
1ST AV S	LYN	LYN	11600	59	C6
1ST AV S	LYN	LYN	11900	65	C1
1ST AV W	CO	HAC		73	F2
1ST CT	SM	SM		40	E6
1ST PL	HB	RB	600	67	C2
1ST PL	MB	MB	100	62	B5
1ST PL S	LB	LB02		75	D6
1ST ST	BELL	BELL		53	E3
1ST ST	DUA	DUA	1400	29	D4
1ST ST	HB	RB		67	C2
1ST ST	IRW	BAP		88	A1
1ST ST	LA	LB10		74	F2
1ST ST	LAV	LAV	1700	90	C3
1ST ST	MB	MB	100	62	B5
1ST ST	MPK	MPK	1400	45	F4
1ST ST	PAR	PAR	8000	65	F3
1ST ST	PAR	PAR		66	A3
1ST ST	SF	SF	900	2	E5
1ST ST	SFS	SFS	12400	61	C3
1ST ST E	AZU	AZU	100	88	C1
1ST ST E	CLA	CLA	100	91	B4
1ST ST E	CO	LA22	4300	45	D4
1ST ST E	CO	LA63	3600	45	C4
1ST ST E	CO	LAN	46500	148	B9
1ST ST E	LA	LA12	100	44	E3
1ST ST E	LA	LA33	1100	44	E3
1ST ST E	LA	LA33	1800	45	A3
1ST ST E	LA	LA63	3000	45	B4
1ST ST E	LA	SP	100	79	A3
1ST ST E	LB	LB02	100	75	C5
1ST ST E	LB	LB03	2100	75	D5
1ST ST E	LB	LB03	3500	76	A6
1ST ST E	LB	LB03	4700	80	B1
1ST ST E	PALM	PALM	40400	172	B4
1ST ST E	POM	POM	100	94	F2
1ST ST E	POM	POM	700	95	A2
1ST ST E	SAD	SAD	100	89	F2
1ST ST E	SAD	SAD	100	90	A2
1ST ST N	ALH	ALH	100	37	C3
1ST ST N	BUR	BUR	100	17	D5
1ST ST N	CO	ACT		189	E3
1ST ST N	LPUE	LPUE	100	48	F6
1ST ST N	MTB	MTB	100	54	E2
1ST ST S	ALH	ALH	100	37	C3
1ST ST S	BUR	BUR	100	17	D5
1ST ST S	LPUE	LPUE	100	48	F6
1ST ST S	VER	LA58		52	E4
1ST ST W	AZU	AZU	100	88	C1
1ST ST W	CLA	CLA	100	91	B4
1ST ST W	LA	LA04	3300	34	F6
1ST ST W	LA	LA12	100	44	C2
1ST ST W	LA	LA26	1200	44	C2
1ST ST W	LA	LA36	5500	34	A6
1ST ST W	LA	LA48	7900	33	E6
1ST ST W	LA	SP	500	78	E2
1ST ST W	LA	SP	100	79	A3
1ST ST W	LB	LB02	100	75	C5
1ST ST W	POM	POM	100	94	C2
1ST ST W	SAD	SAD	100	89	F2
2ND AV	GLEN	GL14		11	C5
2ND AV	LA	LA08	3800	51	D4
2ND AV	LA	LA18	1900	43	D5
2ND AV	LA	LA19	1300	43	D5
2ND AV	LA	LA43	4400	51	D4
2ND AV E	CO	HAC		73	F2
2ND AV N	ARC	ARC	100	28	E5
2ND AV N	COV	COV	100	88	E5
2ND AV S	ARC	ARC	100	28	E5
2ND AV S	ARC	ARC	1500	38	E2
2ND AV S	CO	COM	11700	59	C6
2ND AV S	CO	COM	11800	65	C1
2ND AV S	CO	LPUE	100	48	B3
2ND AV S	COV	COV	100	88	E5
2ND AV S	ING	IN03	10000	57	E4
2ND AV S	ING	IN05	8000	57	D3
2ND AV S	LYN	LYN	11700	59	C6
2ND AV S	LYN	LYN	11800	65	C1
2ND AV W	CO	HAC		73	F2
2ND PL	MB	MB	100	62	B5
2ND PL E	CO	LA63		45	D5
2ND PL S	LB	LB02		75	D6
2ND ST	BELL	BELL		53	E3
2ND ST	SCLR	NEW		127	D4
2ND ST	DUA	DUA	1500	29	D4
2ND ST	HB	RB		67	C2
2ND ST	IRW	BAP	5300	88	A2
2ND ST	LA	LB10		74	F2
2ND ST	LAV	LAV	1700	90	C3
2ND ST	MB	MB	100	62	B5
2ND ST	SF	SF	900	2	E5
2ND ST	SFS	SFS	12600	61	B3
2ND ST	SM	SM	800	40	E6
2ND ST	SM	SM	1200	49	A5
2ND ST	SM	SM	2400	49	B3
2ND ST	VER	LA58	5700	52	E4
2ND ST	WHI	WHI		61	F1
2ND ST	WHI	WHI		84	A1
2ND ST E	AZU	AZU	100	86	C6
2ND ST E	CLA	CLA	100	91	B4
2ND ST E	CO	LA22	4300	45	D5
2ND ST E	CO	LA63	3900	45	D5
2ND ST E	CO	LAN	46000	160	B1
2ND ST E	CO	PALM	38400	172	B8
2ND ST E	DOW	DOW	7500	60	B3
2ND ST E	LA	LA12	100	44	C2

INDEX

311

1990 LOS ANGELES COUNTY STREET INDEX

2ND ST E — 8TH ST W

LOS ANGELES CO.

STREET	CITY	P.O. ZONE	BLOCK	PAGE	GRID
2ND ST E	LA	LA33	1300	44	F3
2ND ST E	LA	LA33	1800	45	A3
2ND ST E	LA	LA63	3000	45	A3
2ND ST E	LA	SP	100	79	A3
2ND ST E	LAN	LAN	42400	160	B9
2ND ST E	LB	LB02	900	75	D5
2ND ST E	LB	LB03	3300	76	A6
2ND ST E	LB	LB03	5200	80	B1
2ND ST E	PAR	PAR	8000	65	F2
2ND ST E	POM	POM	500	94	F2
2ND ST E	POM	POM	1000	95	A2
2ND ST E	SAD	SAD	100	89	F2
2ND ST E	SAD	SAD	100	90	A2
2ND ST N	ALH	ALH	100	37	B3
2ND ST N	CO	ACT		189	E3
2ND ST N	LPUE	LPUE	100	48	F6
2ND ST N	MTB	MTB	600	46	E6
2ND ST N	MTB	MTB	100	54	E2
2ND ST S	ALH	ALH	100	37	B3
2ND ST S	LPUE	LPUE	100	48	F6
2ND ST S	MTB	MTB	100	54	E2
2ND ST W	AZU	AZU	100	86	C6
2ND ST W	CLA	CLA	100	91	B4
2ND ST W	LA	LA04		34	E6
2ND ST W	LA	LA04	3300	35	A6
2ND ST W	LA	LA04	3300	43	E1
2ND ST W	LA	LA04	3300	44	A1
2ND ST W	LA	LA12	100	44	C2
2ND ST W	LA	LA26	1200	44	C2
2ND ST W	LA	LA36	5500	34	B6
2ND ST W	LA	LA36	5500	43	B1
2ND ST W	LA	SP	500	78	E3
2ND ST W	LA	SP	100	79	A3
2ND ST W	POM	POM	500	94	C3
2ND ST W	SAD	SAD	100	89	F2
3RD AV	GLEN	GL14		11	C5
3RD AV	LA	LA05	800	43	D3
3RD AV	LA	LA08	3800	51	D4
3RD AV	LA	LA18	1900	43	D5
3RD AV	LA	LA19	900	43	D3
3RD AV	LA	LA43	4400	51	D4
3RD AV	LA	VEN	200	49	B3
3RD AV E	CO	HAC		73	F2
3RD AV N	ARC	ARC	100	28	F5
3RD AV N	COV	COV	100	88	E5
3RD AV S	ARC	ARC	100	28	F5
3RD AV S	ARC	ARC	1500	38	F2
3RD AV S	CO	COM	11700	59	C6
3RD AV S	CO	COM	11800	65	C1
3RD AV S	CO	LPUE	100	48	B4
3RD AV S	COV	COV	100	88	E5
3RD AV S	ING	IN03	10200	57	D4
3RD AV S	ING	IN05	7600	51	D6
3RD AV S	ING	IN05	7800	57	D3
3RD AV S	LYN	LYN	11700	59	C6
3RD AV S	LYN	LYN	11800	65	C1
3RD AV W	CO	HAC		73	F2
3RD CT	HB	RB		67	C2
3RD PL	HB	RB		67	C1
3RD PL	MB	MB	100	62	B5
3RD PL E	LA	LA63		45	C5
3RD PL S	LB	LB02		75	D6
3RD PL W	LA	LA12	400	44	D3
3RD PL W	LA	LA13	500	44	C3
3RD PL W	LA	LA17	600	44	C3
3RD ST	AVA	AVA		77	C5
3RD ST	BELL	BELL		53	E4
3RD ST	BUR	BUR	100	17	D5
3RD ST	SCLR	NEW		127	D4
3RD ST	DUA	DUA	1500	29	D4
3RD ST	HB	RB		67	C1
3RD ST	IRW	BAP		88	A2
3RD ST	LA	LB10		74	F2
3RD ST	LAV	LAV	1500	90	C3
3RD ST	MB	MB	100	62	B5
3RD ST	SF	SF	600	2	E5
3RD ST	SFS	SFS	12600	61	C3
3RD ST	SM	SM	800	40	E6
3RD ST	SM	SM	1900	49	A2
3RD ST	WHI	WHI		61	F1
3RD ST E	AZU	AZU	100	86	B6
3RD ST E	CO	LA22	4300	45	C5
3RD ST E	CO	LA63	3600	45	C5
3RD ST E	CO	LAN	42000	172	C1
3RD ST E	PALM	PALM		172	C7
3RD ST E	CO	PALM	37400	183	C1
3RD ST E	DOW	DOW	7400	60	A3
3RD ST E	LA	LA13	100	44	B2
3RD ST E	LA	LA33	1300	44	F3
3RD ST E	LA	LA33	1800	45	A3
3RD ST E	LA	LA63	3100	45	C5
3RD ST E	LA	SP	100	79	A3
3RD ST E	LAN	LAN	42000	160	B4
3RD ST E	LB	LB02	100	75	C5
3RD ST E	LB	LB14	2000	75	F5
3RD ST E	LB	LB14	3200	76	A5
3RD ST E	PALM	PALM		172	C7
3RD ST E	PALM	PALM	37600	183	C1
3RD ST E	PAR	PAR	8000	65	F2
3RD ST E	POM	POM	100	94	D3
3RD ST E	POM	POM	1000	95	A3
3RD ST E	SAD	SAD	100	89	F2
3RD ST E	SAD	SAD	100	90	A2
3RD ST N	ALH	ALH	100	37	B4
3RD ST N	CO	ACT		189	E3
3RD ST N	LPUE	LPUE	100	48	F6
3RD ST N	MTB	MTB	500	46	E6
3RD ST N	MTB	MTB	100	54	E2
3RD ST S	ALH	ALH	100	37	B4
3RD ST S	MTB	MTB	100	54	E2
3RD ST W	AZU	AZU	100	86	B6
3RD ST W	BH	BH	9100	33	C6
3RD ST W	LA	LA12	100	44	D3
3RD ST W	LA	LA13	100	44	B2
3RD ST W	LA	LA17	600	44	B2
3RD ST W	LA	LA20	3200	43	E1
3RD ST W	LA	LA20	3100	44	B2
3RD ST W	LA	LA36	6100	33	F6
3RD ST W	LA	LA36	5700	42	F1
3RD ST W	LA	LA36	5500	43	A1
3RD ST W	LA	LA48	7900	33	F6
3RD ST W	LA	LA57	1800	44	B2
3RD ST W	LA	SP	500	78	E3
3RD ST W	LA	SP	100	79	A3
3RD ST W	LAN	LAN	42000	172	B1
3RD ST W	LB	LB02	100	75	C5
3RD ST W	POM	POM	100	94	D3
3RD ST W	SAD	SAD	100	89	F2
4TH AV	CO	MDR		55A	E1
4TH AV	GLEN	GL14		11	C5
4TH AV	LA	LA08	4100	51	D4
4TH AV	LA	LA18	1900	43	D5
4TH AV	LA	LA19	900	43	D3
4TH AV	LA	LA43	4400	51	D4
4TH AV	LA	VEN	200	49	B3
4TH AV N	ARC	ARC	300	28	F4
4TH AV N	COV	COV	100	88	E5
4TH AV S	ARC	ARC	100	28	F5
4TH AV S	ARC	ARC	2600	38	F2
4TH AV S	CO	COM	11700	59	C6
4TH AV S	CO	COM	11800	65	C1
4TH AV S	CO	LPUE	100	48	B5
4TH AV S	COV	COV	100	88	E5
4TH AV S	ING	IN03	10200	57.	D4
4TH AV S	ING	IN05	8200	57	D3
4TH AV S	LYN	LYN	11700	59	C6
4TH AV S	LYN	LYN	11800	65	C1
4TH AV W	CO	HAC		73	F2
4TH CT	HB	RB		67	C2
4TH CT	SM	SM		49	B2
4TH PL	MB	MB	100	62	B5
4TH PL E	DOW	DOW	7400	60	A2
4TH PL E	LA	LA13	700	44	E3
4TH PL S	LB	LB02		75	D6
4TH ST	BELL	BELL		53	E4
4TH ST	SCLR	NEW		127	D4
4TH ST	HB	RB		67	C1
4TH ST	IRW	BAP		88	A2
4TH ST	MB	MB	100	62	B5
4TH ST	SF	SF	600	2	E5
4TH ST	SFS	SFS	12600	61	B3
4TH ST	SM	SM	200	40	F6
4TH ST	SM	SM	1200	49	A5
4TH ST	SM	SM	1400	49	A1
4TH ST E	AZU	AZU	100	86	C6
4TH ST E	CLA	CLA	100	91	B4
4TH ST E	CO	LA22	4300	45	C5
4TH ST E	CO	LA63	3600	45	C5
4TH ST E	CO	LAN	46000	160	C1
4TH ST E	CO	PALM	37400	183	C1
4TH ST E	DOW	DOW	7800	60	B3
4TH ST E	LA	LA13	100	44	E4
4TH ST E	LA	LA33	1400	44	F4
4TH ST E	LA	LA33	1800	45	A4
4TH ST E	LA	LA63	3000	45	A4
4TH ST E	LA	SP	100	79	A3
4TH ST E	LAN	LAN	43600	160	C7
4TH ST E	LAN	LAN	42000	160	C9
4TH ST E	LAN	LAN	42000	172	C1
4TH ST E	LB	LB02	100	75	D5
4TH ST E	LB	LB14	2000	75	F5
4TH ST E	LB	LB14	3200	76	A5
4TH ST E	PALM	PALM	37600	183	C1
4TH ST E	POM	POM	100	94	D3
4TH ST E	POM	POM	900	95	A3
4TH ST E	SAD	SAD	100	89	F2
4TH ST E	SAD	SAD	100	90	A2
4TH ST E	WHI	WHI		84	A1
4TH ST N	ALH	ALH	100	37	B4
4TH ST N	MTB	MTB		46	E6
4TH ST N	MTB	MTB	100	54	E2
4TH ST S	ALH	ALH	100	37	B4
4TH ST S	MTB	MTB	100	54	E2
4TH ST W	AZU	AZU	100	86	C6
4TH ST W	CLA	CLA	100	91	B4
4TH ST W	CO	PALM	36500	183	B3
4TH ST W	LA	LA13	100	44	D3
4TH ST W	LA	LA17	600	44	D3
4TH ST W	LA	LA20	3100	43	F1
4TH ST W	LA	LA20	3000	44	A1
4TH ST W	LA	LA36	5400	43	C1
4TH ST W	LA	LA48	7900	33	E6
4TH ST W	LA	LA48	7900	42	E1
4TH ST W	LA	LA57	1800	44	A1
4TH ST W	LA	SP	500	78	F3
4TH ST W	LA	SP	100	79	A3
4TH ST W	LAN	LAN	42000	172	B1
4TH ST W	LB	LB02	100	75	B5
4TH ST W	PALM	PALM		172	B9
4TH ST W	POM	POM	100	94	D3
5TH AV	GLEN	GL14		11	C5
5TH AV	LA	LA05	800	43	D3
5TH AV	LA	LA08	4100	51	C2
5TH AV	LA	LA18	1900	43	C5
5TH AV	LA	LA19	900	43	D3
5TH AV	LA	LA43	4400	51	C4
5TH AV	LA	VEN	200	49	B3
5TH AV E	CO	HAC		73	F2
5TH AV N	COV	COV	500	88	E5
5TH AV N	MON	MON	100	28	F5
5TH AV S	ARC	ARC	600	28	F6
5TH AV S	ARC	ARC	2100	38	F2
5TH AV S	CO	LPUE	100	48	C5
5TH AV S	COV	COV	100	88	E5
5TH AV S	IND	LPUE	800	48	C5
5TH AV S	ING	IN03	10200	57	C4
5TH AV S	ING	IN05	7600	51	C6
5TH AV S	ING	IN05	7800	57	C3
5TH AV S	MON	MON	100	28	F5
5TH AV W	CO	HAC		73	F2
5TH CT	HB	RB		67	C1
5TH CT	SM	SM		49	B2
5TH PL	MB	MB	100	62	B5
5TH PL E	PALM	PALM	37100	172	C9
5TH PL S	LB	LB02		75	D6
5TH PL W	PALM	PALM		172	A9
5TH ST	ARC	ARC		28	F6
5TH ST	BELL	BELL		53	E4
5TH ST	SCLR	NEW		127	C4
5TH ST	GLEN	GL01	2000	17	E5
5TH ST	GLEN	GL01	1200	25	A1
5TH ST	HB	RB		67	C1
5TH ST	LAV	LAV	1300	90	C3
5TH ST	MB	MB	100	62	C4
5TH ST	SF	SF	400	2	E4
5TH ST	SM	SM	800	40	F6
5TH ST	SM	SM	1400	49	A2
5TH ST E	AZU	AZU	100	86	C6
5TH ST E	CO	LA22	4300	45	C5
5TH ST E	CO	LA63	3600	45	C5
5TH ST E	CO	LAN	46500	148	C9
5TH ST E	CO	LAN	46000	160	C5
5TH ST E	CO	PALM	37300	183	C1
5TH ST E	DOW	DOW	7800	60	B3
5TH ST E	LA	LA13	100	44	D3
5TH ST E	LA	LA33	1200	44	F4
5TH ST E	LA	LA33	1800	45	B5
5TH ST E	LA	LA63	3000	45	B5
5TH ST E	LA	SP	100	79	A3
5TH ST E	LAN	LAN	46000	160	C9
5TH ST E	LAN	LAN	42000	172	C1
5TH ST E	LB	LB02	100	75	E5
5TH ST E	LB	LB14	2300	75	E5
5TH ST E	LB	LB14	3600	76	A5
5TH ST E	PALM	PALM	37800	172	C9
5TH ST E	PALM	PALM	37200	183	C1
5TH ST E	SAD	SAD	100	89	E2
5TH ST E	SAD	SAD	100	90	A2
5TH ST N	ALH	ALH	100	37	B4
5TH ST N	BUR	BUR	100	17	D4
5TH ST N	LPUE	LPUE	200	48	F6
5TH ST N	MTB	MTB	100	54	E2
5TH ST S	ALH	ALH	100	37	B4
5TH ST S	BUR	BUR	100	17	D4
5TH ST S	MTB	MTB	100	54	E2
5TH ST W	AZU	AZU	100	86	C6
5TH ST W	CO	PALM	37800	172	B9
5TH ST W	LA	LA13	100	44	D3
5TH ST W	LA	LA17	600	44	D3
5TH ST W	LA	LA20	3000	43	F1
5TH ST W	LA	LA20	3000	44	A1
5TH ST W	LA	LA48	6100	42	E1
5TH ST W	LA	LA57	1800	44	D3
5TH ST W	LA	SP	500	78	F3
5TH ST W	LA	SP	100	79	A3
5TH ST W	LAN	LAN	42000	160	A9
5TH ST W	LB	LB02	100	75	B5
5TH ST W	PALM	PALM	38400	172	B8
5TH ST W	SAD	SAD	100	89	E2
6TH AV	ING	IN03	10200	57	C4
6TH AV	ING	IN05	8600	57	C3
6TH AV	LA	LA08	3800	51	C1
6TH AV	LA	LA18	1900	43	C5
6TH AV	LA	LA19	1300	43	C5
6TH AV	LA	LA43	4400	51	C5
6TH AV	LA	VEN	200	49	B3
6TH AV	MON	MON	1800	28	F6
6TH AV E	CO	HAC		73	F2
6TH AV S	ARC	ARC	900	28	F6
6TH AV S	ARC	ARC	1500	38	F2
6TH AV S	CO	LPUE	100	48	C5
6TH AV S	IND	LPUE	300	48	C5
6TH CT	HB	RB		67	C1
6TH PL	MB	MB	100	62	B4
6TH PL S	LB	LB02		75	D6
6TH PL W	PALM	PALM		172	A7
6TH ST	BELL	BELL		53	E4
6TH ST	SCLR	NEW		127	D4
6TH ST	HB	RB		67	C1
6TH ST	LAV	LAV	1700	90	D3
6TH ST	MB	MB		62	B4
6TH ST	SM	SM	800	40	F6
6TH ST	SM	SM	1400	49	A2
6TH ST E	AZU	AZU	100	86	C5
6TH ST E	CLA	CLA	100	91	B3
6TH ST E	CO	LA22	4300	45	C5
6TH ST E	CO	LA22	5400	46	A6
6TH ST E	CO	LA23	3700	45	C5
6TH ST E	CO	LAN	46000	160	C1
6TH ST E	CO	PALM	38800	172	C8
6TH ST E	DOW	DOW	7800	60	B3
6TH ST E	LA	LA14	100	44	C3
6TH ST E	LA	LA21	500	44	E4
6TH ST E	LA	LA23	1600	44	E4
6TH ST E	LA	LA23	2100	45	A4
6TH ST E	LA	SP	100	79	A3
6TH ST E	LAN	LAN	42000	160	C9
6TH ST E	LAN	LAN	42000	172	C1
6TH ST E	LB	LB02	100	75	B5
6TH ST E	LB	LB14	2100	75	E5
6TH ST E	LB	LB14	3100	76	A5
6TH ST E	PALM	PALM	37600	183	C1
6TH ST E	POM	POM	100	94	E3
6TH ST E	POM	POM	1000	95	A3
6TH ST N	BUR	BUR	100	17	C4
6TH ST N	MTB	MTB	500	46	E6
6TH ST N	MTB	MTB	100	54	E2
6TH ST S	ALH	ALH	100	37	B4
6TH ST S	BUR	BUR	100	17	C4
6TH ST S	MTB	MTB	100	54	E2
6TH ST W	AZU	AZU	100	86	C5
6TH ST W	CLA	CLA	100	91	B3
6TH ST W	CO	PALM	35900	183	A4
6TH ST W	LA	LA14	100	44	C3
6TH ST W	LA	LA17	600	44	C2
6TH ST W	LA	LA20	3000	43	C1
6TH ST W	LA	LA20	2900	44	A1
6TH ST W	LA	LA36	5700	42	E1
6TH ST W	LA	LA36	5200	43	C1
6TH ST W	LA	LA48	6100	42	E1
6TH ST W	LA	LA57	1800	44	A1
6TH ST W	LA	SP	500	78	E3
6TH ST W	LA	SP	100	79	A3
6TH ST W	LAN	LAN		160	A9
6TH ST W	LB	LB02	100	75	E5
6TH ST W	PALM	PALM	40400	172	A2
6TH ST W	POM	POM	100	94	E3
6TH ST W	SAD	SAD	100	89	F2
7TH AV	ING	IN03	10200	57	C4
7TH AV	ING	IN05	7600	51	C6
7TH AV	ING	IN05	7800	57	C3
7TH AV	LA	LA08	4200	51	C4
7TH AV	LA	LA18	1900	43	C5
7TH AV	LA	LA19	1600	43	C5
7TH AV	LA	LA43	4400	51	C4
7TH AV	LA	VEN	200	49	C3
7TH AV S	ARC	ARC	1800	38	F1
7TH AV S	CO	LPUE	100	48	C5
7TH AV S	CO	LPUE	1200	85	C1
7TH AV S	IND	LPUE	300	48	C5
7TH CT	HB	RB		67	C1
7TH CT	SM	SM05		49	B2
7TH PL	ARC	ARC		38	F1
7TH PL	BUR	BUR		17	D4
7TH PL	HB	RB	1100	67	D1
7TH PL	LB	LB02		75	D6
7TH PL	MB	MB	100	62	B4
7TH PL E	LA	LA21	1600	44	E5
7TH ST	HB	RB		67	C1
7TH ST	LAV	LAV	1900	90	D3
7TH ST	MB	MB		62	B4
7TH ST	SF	SF	700	2	F4
7TH ST	SF	SF	700	3	A5
7TH ST	SM	SM	200	40	E5
7TH ST	SM	SM	1400	49	A1
7TH ST E	CLA	CLA	100	91	B3
7TH ST E	CO	LAN	46000	160	C1
7TH ST E	DOW	DOW	7800	60	B3
7TH ST E	LA	LA14	100	44	C3
7TH ST E	LA	LA21	600	44	C3
7TH ST E	LA	LA23	2100	44	E5
7TH ST E	LA	LA23	2200	45	A5
7TH ST E	LA	SP	100	79	A3
7TH ST E	LAN	LAN	42000	160	C9
7TH ST E	LAN	LAN	42000	172	C1
7TH ST E	LB	LB04	2000	75	C5
7TH ST E	LB	LB04	3100	76	A5
7TH ST E	LB	LB13	100	75	C5
7TH ST E	LB	LB15	5700	76	D4
7TH ST E	POM	POM	100	94	E3
7TH ST E	POM	POM	1000	95	A3
7TH ST E	WHI	WHI		85	A6
7TH ST N	BUR	BUR	100	17	D4
7TH ST N	LB	LB13		75	A5
7TH ST N	MTB	MTB	500	46	E6
7TH ST N	MTB	MTB	100	54	D2
7TH ST S	ALH	ALH	300	37	B6
7TH ST S	BUR	BUR	100	17	D4
7TH ST S	LB	LB13		75	A5
7TH ST S	MTB	MTB	100	54	D2
7TH ST W	CLA	CLA	100	91	B3
7TH ST W	CO	LAN	46000	160	A1
7TH ST W	CO	LAN	46000	160	A1
7TH ST W	CO	PALM		183	A1
7TH ST W	CO	SP	900	78	F3
7TH ST W	LA	LA05	2800	43	D2
7TH ST W	LA	LA05	2800	44	A2
7TH ST W	LA	LA14	100	44	C3
7TH ST W	LA	LA17	600	44	B2
7TH ST W	LA	LA57	1800	44	A2
7TH ST W	LA	SP	400	78	F3
7TH ST W	LA	SP	100	79	A3
7TH ST W	LAN	LAN	42000	160	A9
7TH ST W	LB	LB13	100	75	D5
7TH ST W	PALM	PALM	38800	172	A7
7TH ST W	POM	POM	100	94	E3
8TH AV	ING	IN03	10100	57	C4
8TH AV	ING	IN05	7600	51	C6
8TH AV	ING	IN05	7800	57	C3
8TH AV	LA	LA08	4000	51	C3
8TH AV	LA	LA18	1900	43	C5
8TH AV	LA	LA19	1800	43	C5
8TH AV	LA	LA43	4400	51	C4
8TH AV	MON	MON	1800	28	F6
8TH AV S	ARC	ARC	900	28	F6
8TH AV S	ARC	ARC	1500	38	F1
8TH AV S	CO	ARC	3000	38	F2
8TH AV S	CO	LPUE	100	48	D5
8TH CT	HB	RB		67	C1
8TH PL	HB	RB	600	67	C1
8TH PL	ING	IN03	10400	57	C4
8TH PL	MB	MB	100	62	B4
8TH PL S	LB	LB02		75	D6
8TH PL W	LA	LA17	900	44	C3
8TH ST	SCLR	NEW		127	C4
8TH ST	HB	RB	100	67	C1
8TH ST	LAV	LAV	2000	90	D3
8TH ST	LB	LB13		74	F4
8TH ST	LB	LB13		75	A4
8TH ST	MB	MB	100	62	B4
8TH ST	SF	SF	900	2	F4
8TH ST	SF	SF	400	3	A5
8TH ST E	AZU	AZU	300	86	D5
8TH ST E	CLA	CLA	100	91	B3
8TH ST E	PALM	PALM	38800	172	C7
8TH ST E	DOW	DOW	7800	60	B2
8TH ST E	LA	LA14	100	44	C3
8TH ST E	LA	LA21	600	44	C3
8TH ST E	LA	LA23	2500	44	F5
8TH ST E	LA	LA23	2600	45	A5
8TH ST E	LAN	LAN	42000	160	C9
8TH ST E	LAN	LAN	42000	172	C1
8TH ST E	LB	LB04	2000	75	D4
8TH ST E	LB	LB04	3100	76	A4
8TH ST E	LB	LB13	100	75	B4
8TH ST E	PALM	PALM	38300	172	C8
8TH ST E	POM	POM	300	94	E3
8TH ST E	POM	POM	1000	95	A3
8TH ST S	ALH	ALH	300	37	B6
8TH ST W	AZU	AZU	700	86	C5
8TH ST W	CLA	CLA	100	91	B3
8TH ST W	LA	LA05	2800	43	E2
8TH ST W	LA	LA05	2700	44	A2
8TH ST W	LA	LA14	100	44	C3
8TH ST W	LA	LA17	600	44	C3
8TH ST W	LA	LA36	5700	42	F2
8TH ST W	LA	LA36	5000	43	A2
8TH ST W	LA	LA57	1800	44	A2
8TH ST W	LA	SP	400	78	F3

INDEX

1990 LOS ANGELES COUNTY STREET INDEX

STREET	CITY	P.O. ZONE	BLOCK	PAGE	GRID
8TH ST W	LA	SP	100	79	A3
8TH ST W	LAN	LAN	42000	160	A9
8TH ST W	LB	LB13	100	75	B4
8TH ST W	POM	POM	100	94	E3
9TH AV	ARC	ARC		28	F6
9TH AV	ARC	ARC	900	29	A6
9TH AV	CO	ARC	3000	38	F2
9TH AV	LA	LA08	4000	51	C2
9TH AV	LA	LA18	2100	43	C5
9TH AV	LA	LA43	4400	51	C4
9TH AV	MON	MON		28	F6
9TH AV	MON	MON	1800	29	A6
9TH AV S	CO	LPUE	100	48	D6
9TH AV S	CO	LPUE	1100	85	C1
9TH AV S	IND	LPUE	300	48	D6
9TH CT	HB	RB		67	C1
9TH PL	MB	MB	100	62	B4
9TH PL E	LA	LA21	700	44	D4
9TH ST	CO	ACT		189	E3
9TH ST	SCLR	NEW		127	C4
9TH ST	HB	RB		67	C1
9TH ST	LAV	LAV		90	D3
9TH ST	MB	MB	100	62	B4
9TH ST	SM	SM	200	40	F5
9TH ST	SM	SM	1000	41	A6
9TH ST	SM	SM	1400	49	A1
9TH ST E	AZU	AZU	100	86	D5
9TH ST E	CLA	CLA	100	91	B3
9TH ST E	CO	PALM	38800	172	D7
9TH ST E	LA	LA15	100	44	C3
9TH ST E	LA	LA21	700	44	C3
9TH ST E	LB	LB04	3800	76	A4
9TH ST E	LB	LB13	100	75	D4
9TH ST E	LB	LB15	6700	76	E4
9TH ST E	PALM	PALM	100	172	D9
9TH ST E	POM	POM	100	94	C3
9TH ST N	BUR	BUR	100	17	E5
9TH ST S	ALH	ALH	700	37	B6
9TH ST S	BUR	BUR	100	17	E5
9TH ST W	AZU	AZU	100	86	D5
9TH ST W	CLA	CLA	100	91	B3
9TH ST W	LA	LA06	2700	43	D2
9TH ST W	LA	LA06	1800	44	C3
9TH ST W	LA	LA15	100	44	C3
9TH ST W	LA	LA19	3600	43	D2
9TH ST W	LA	LA36	5100	43	D2
9TH ST W	LA	SP	400	78	E3
9TH ST W	LA	SP	100	79	A3
9TH ST W	LB	LB13	100	75	B4
9TH ST W	POM	POM	100	94	C3
9TH ST W	POM	POM	1000	95	A3
10TH AV	ARC	ARC	900	29	A6
10TH AV	CO	ARC	800	39	A2
10TH AV	LA	LA08	4000	51	C2
10TH AV	LA	LA18	1900	43	C5
10TH AV	LA	LA43	4400	51	C5
10TH AV	MON	MON	1800	29	A6
10TH AV S	ING	IN03	10200	57	C4
10TH AV S	ING	IN05	7900	57	C2
10TH CT	HB	RB		67	C1
10TH CT	SM	SM		49	B2
10TH PL	MB	MB	100	62	B4
10TH PL E	PALM	PALM	38400	172	D8
10TH PL E	PALM	PALM	37400	183	D1
10TH PL S	LB	LB02		75	E6
10TH PL W	LA	LA15	700	44	B3
10TH ST	DOW	DOW	8500	60	C3
10TH ST	HB	RB	100	67	C1
10TH ST	LAV	LAV		90	D3
10TH ST	MB	MB	100	62	B4
10TH ST	SM	SM	200	40	F5
10TH ST	SM	SM	1000	41	A6
10TH ST	SM	SM	1500	49	A1
10TH ST E	AZU	AZU	100	86	C5
10TH ST E	CLA	CLA	100	91	B3
10TH ST E	CO	LAN	46000	160	D1
10TH ST E	CO	PALM	38800	172	D7
10TH ST E	LA	LA21	700	44	D5
10TH ST E	LB	LB04	2000	75	E4
10TH ST E	LB	LB04	3200	76	A4
10TH ST E	LB	LB13	100	75	C4
10TH ST E	LB	LB15	6800	76	E4
10TH ST E	PALM	PALM	42400	160	D9
10TH ST E	PALM	PALM	100	172	D9
10TH ST E	PALM	PALM	37200	183	D1
10TH ST E	POM	POM	100	94	D3
10TH ST N	MTB	MTB	100	54	D2
10TH ST S	MTB	MTB	100	54	D2
10TH ST W	AZU	AZU	100	86	C5
10TH ST W	CLA	CLA	100	91	B3
10TH ST W	CO	LAN		147	J8
10TH ST W	CO	LAN		148	A8
10TH ST W	CO	LAN	46000	160	A8
10TH ST W	CO	LAN	42000	172	A1
10TH ST W	CO	PALM	38800	172	A6
10TH ST W	LA	LA06	2200	44	A3
10TH ST W	LA	LA19	3400	43	C2
10TH ST W	LA	SP	400	78	F3
10TH ST W	LA	SP	100	79	A3
10TH ST W	LAN	LAN	42000	160	A8
10TH ST W	LAN	LAN	42000	172	A6
10TH ST W	LB	LB13	100	75	C4
10TH ST W	PALM	PALM	38500	172	A6
10TH ST W	POM	POM	100	94	D3
11TH AV	ING	IN05	8400	57	C2
11TH AV	LA	LA08	4100	51	C2
11TH AV	LA	LA18	2300	43	C5
11TH AV	LA	LA43	4400	51	C5
11TH CT	HB	RB		67	C1
11TH PL	HB	RB	500	67	C1
11TH PL	LA	LA15	1200	44	B3
11TH PL	MB	MB	100	62	B4
11TH PL S	LB	LB02		75	E6
11TH PL W	CO	LAN	48000	147	J7
11TH PL W	LA	LA06	1800	44	B3
11TH PL W	LA	LA19	4500	43	C3
11TH ST	SCLR	NEW		127	C4
11TH ST	DOW	DOW	8500	60	C3
11TH ST	HB	RB	100	67	C1
11TH ST	LAV	LAV		90	D2
11TH ST	MB	MB	100	62	B4
11TH ST	SM	SM	100	40	F5
11TH ST	SM	SM	900	41	A6
11TH ST	SM	SM	1700	49	B1
11TH ST E	AZU	AZU	100	86	C4
11TH ST E	CLA	CLA	100	91	B3
11TH ST E	LA	LA15	100	44	C4
11TH ST E	LA	LA21	900	44	D5
11TH ST E	LA	LA23	2700	44	F6
11TH ST E	LA	LA23	2700	45	A6
11TH ST E	LAN	LAN	44100	160	D5
11TH ST E	LB	LB04	2100	75	E4
11TH ST E	LB	LB04	3200	76	A4
11TH ST E	LB	LB13	300	75	C4
11TH ST E	LB	LB15	6800	76	E4
11TH ST E	PALM	PALM	100	172	D9
11TH ST E	POM	POM	100	94	D3
11TH ST W	AZU	AZU	100	86	C4
11TH ST W	CLA	CLA	100	91	B3
11TH ST W	CO	LAN		147	J7
11TH ST W	CO	PALM	38800	172	A7
11TH ST W	LA	LA06	2400	43	E3
11TH ST W	LA	LA06	1800	44	B3
11TH ST W	LA	LA15	100	44	C4
11TH ST W	LA	LA19	3200	43	E3
11TH ST W	LA	SP	400	78	D3
11TH ST W	LA	SP	100	79	A3
11TH ST W	LAN	LAN	46000	159	J1
11TH ST W	LB	LB13	400	75	C4
11TH ST W	PALM	PALM	40800	172	A3
11TH ST W	POM	POM	100	94	D3
12TH AV	LA	LA18	2300	43	C6
12TH AV	LA	LA19	1300	43	C3
12TH AV S	ING	IN05	8600	57	C2
12TH CT	HB	RB		67	C1
12TH CT	MB	MB	800	62	C4
12TH PL	LA	LA15	1200	44	A3
12TH PL	MB	MB	100	62	A4
12TH PL S	LB	LB02		75	E6
12TH PL W	CO	LAN	48000	147	J7
12TH PL W	LA	LA06	3000	43	E3
12TH PL W	LA	LA06	1800	44	A3
12TH ST	SCLR	NEW		127	C3
12TH ST	LAV	LAV		90	D2
12TH ST	MB	MB	100	62	B4
12TH ST	SM	SM	200	40	F5
12TH ST	SM	SM	900	41	A6
12TH ST	SM	SM	1600	49	B1
12TH ST E	CLA	CLA	100	91	B3
12TH ST E	CO	LAN	46000	148	D9
12TH ST E	CO	PALM	38800	172	D7
12TH ST E	LA	LA15	100	44	C4
12TH ST E	LA	LA21	700	44	C4
12TH ST E	LA	LA23	2700	44	F6
12TH ST E	LA	LA23	2100	45	A6
12TH ST E	LAN	LAN	45200	160	D3
12TH ST E	LB	LB13	100	75	D4
12TH ST E	PALM	PALM	100	172	D9
12TH ST E	PALM	PALM		183	D1
12TH ST E	POM	POM	100	94	E3
12TH ST N	MTB	MTB		54	D1
12TH ST W	AZU	AZU	100	86	C4
12TH ST W	CLA	CLA	100	91	B3
12TH ST W	CO	LAN	46000	159	J1
12TH ST W	CO	PALM	39400	171	J6
12TH ST W	LA	LA06	2500	43	E3
12TH ST W	LA	LA06	1800	44	A3
12TH ST W	LA	LA15	100	44	C4
12TH ST W	LA	LA19	3500	43	E3
12TH ST W	LA	SP	400	78	E4
12TH ST W	LA	SP	100	79	A4
12TH ST W	LAN	LAN	42100	159	J9
12TH ST W	LB	LB13	100	75	C4
12TH ST W	PALM	PALM	40800	171	J3
12TH ST W	POM	POM	100	94	E3
13TH AV	LA	LA18		43	C5
13TH CT	HB	RB		62	B6
13TH CT	HB	RB		67	B1
13TH PL	SCLR	NEW		127	C3
13TH PL	MB	MB		62	A4
13TH PL S	LB	LB02		75	E6
13TH PL W	LAN	LAN		159	J2
13TH ST	AZU	AZU		86	C4
13TH ST	SCLR	NEW		127	C3
13TH ST	HB	RB		67	C1
13TH ST	MB	MB		62	B4
13TH ST E	AZU	AZU	100	86	D4
13TH ST E	LA	SP	100	79	A4
13TH ST E	LAN	LAN	43500	160	D5
13TH ST E	PALM	PALM	100	172	D9
13TH ST E	PALM	PALM		183	D1
13TH ST W	CO	PALM	40000	171	J5
13TH ST W	LA	SP	400	78	E4
13TH ST W	LA	SP	100	79	A4
13TH ST W	LAN	LAN	43600	159	J6
13TH ST W	PALM	PALM	39600	171	G6
14TH CT	HB	RB		62	B6
14TH CT	HB	RB		67	B1
14TH CT	SM	SM	800	41	A5
14TH PL	MB	MB	100	62	A4
14TH PL E	LA	LA21	700	44	D5
14TH PL S	LB	LB02		75	E6
14TH PL W	LA	LA15	100	44	C4
14TH ST	SCLR	NEW		127	C3
14TH ST	HB	RB		62	C6
14TH ST	MB	MB	100	62	B4
14TH ST	MTB	MTB	1200	54	C4
14TH ST	SM	SM	100	40	F4
14TH ST	SM	SM	900	41	A5
14TH ST	SM	SM	1700	49	B1
14TH ST E	LA	LA15	100	44	C5
14TH ST E	LA	LA21	700	44	C5
14TH ST E	LA	LA23	3300	53	B1
14TH ST E	LA	SP	100	79	A4
14TH ST E	LB	LB04	2000	75	F4
14TH ST E	LB	LB04	3100	76	A4
14TH ST E	LB	LB13	100	75	B4
14TH ST W	LA	LA06	2300	43	F3
14TH ST W	LA	LA06	1800	44	A3
14TH ST W	LA	LA15	100	44	C4
14TH ST W	LA	SP	400	78	E4
14TH ST W	LA	SP	100	79	A4
14TH ST W	LB	LB13	100	75	B4
15TH CT	HB	RB		62	B6
15TH CT	HB	RB		67	B1
15TH CT	SM	SM		41	B6
15TH PL	HB	RB	900	62	C6
15TH PL	MB	MB		62	A4
15TH PL E	PALM	PALM	38000	172	E9
15TH PL S	LB	LB02		75	E6
15TH ST	SCLR	NEW		127	C3
15TH ST	HB	RB	100	62	C6
15TH ST	MB	MB	100	62	B4
15TH ST	PALM	PALM		171	J8
15TH ST	SM	SM	200	40	F4
15TH ST	SM	SM	700	41	A5
15TH ST E	CO	LAN	46000	160	D1
15TH ST E	CO	PALM	38800	172	E7
15TH ST E	LA	LA15	100	44	B4
15TH ST E	LA	LA21	700	44	B4
15TH ST E	LA	LA23	3300	53	B1
15TH ST E	LA	SP	400	78	E4
15TH ST E	LAN	LAN	43600	160	D6
15TH ST E	LB	LB04	2000	75	F3
15TH ST E	LB	LB04	3200	76	A3
15TH ST E	LB	LB13	100	75	C3
15TH ST E	PALM	PALM	38000	172	E9
15TH ST E	PALM	PALM		183	E1
15TH ST W	CO	LAN		147	J8
15TH ST W	CO	PALM	40000	171	J5
15TH ST W	LA	LA06	2200	43	F3
15TH ST W	LA	LA06	2200	44	A3
15TH ST W	LA	LA15	100	44	B4
15TH ST W	LA	LA19	3000	43	D3
15TH ST W	LA	SP	100	79	A4
15TH ST W	LAN	LAN	42000	159	J6
15TH ST W	LAN	LAN	42000	171	J1
15TH ST W	LB	LB13	100	75	B3
16TH CT	HB	RB		62	B6
16TH CT	SM	SM	1000	41	A5
16TH PL	LB	LB03		75	E6
16TH PL	MB	MB		62	A4
16TH PL W	LA	LA19	2600	43	D4
16TH PL W	LAN	LAN	42800	159	J8
16TH ST	SCLR	NEW		127	B3
16TH ST	HB	RB	100	62	C6
16TH ST	MB	MB		62	B4
16TH ST	SM	SM	100	40	F4
16TH ST	SM	SM	600	41	A5
16TH ST	SM	SM	1800	49	B1
16TH ST E	CO	LAN	46000	160	E2
16TH ST E	LA	LA15	100	44	C5
16TH ST E	LA	LA21	700	44	C5
16TH ST E	LA	LA23	3500	53	B1
16TH ST E	LAN	LAN		160	E4
16TH ST E	LB	LB04	2000	75	F3
16TH ST E	LB	LB13	100	75	C3
16TH ST E	PALM	PALM	38200	172	E9
16TH ST E	PALM	PALM		183	E1
16TH ST N	MTB	MTB	600	46	D5
16TH ST N	MTB	MTB	200	54	D1
16TH ST W	CO	LAN		147	J8
16TH ST W	CO	PALM	39800	171	J5
16TH ST W	CO	PALM	38500	172	E8
16TH ST W	CO	PALM		189	J4
16TH ST W	LA	SP	400	78	E4
16TH ST W	LA	SP	100	79	A4
16TH ST W	LAN	LAN	42100	159	J5
16TH ST W	LB	LB13	100	75	B3
16TH ST W	PALM	PALM	39600	171	J6
17TH AV	LA	VEN		49	B4
17TH CT	HB	RB		62	B6
17TH CT	SM	SM		41	A5
17TH PL	MB	MB		62	A4
17TH PL W	LA	LA06		43	F3
17TH ST	HB	RB	1	62	C6
17TH ST	MB	MB	100	62	D3
17TH ST	SM	SM	200	40	F4
17TH ST	SM	SM	600	41	A5
17TH ST	SM	SM	2100	49	B1
17TH ST E	CO	LAN	46000	160	E2
17TH ST E	CO	PALM	38600	172	E8
17TH ST E	LA	LA15	100	44	D5
17TH ST E	LA	LA21	700	44	D5
17TH ST E	LAN	LAN	42000	160	E7
17TH ST E	LB	LB04	2000	75	F3
17TH ST E	LB	LB04	3200	76	A3
17TH ST E	LB	LB13	300	75	F3
17TH ST E	PALM	PALM	38000	172	E8
17TH ST E	PALM	PALM		183	E1
17TH ST W	CO	LAN		147	H8
17TH ST W	CO	LAN	41200	171	H5
17TH ST W	CO	PALM	39800	171	J5
17TH ST W	LA	LA06	1500	43	F4
17TH ST W	LA	LA06	1300	44	A4
17TH ST W	LA	LA15	100	44	A4
17TH ST W	LA	LA19	2600	43	C4
17TH ST W	LA	SP	500	78	E4
17TH ST W	LA	SP	200	79	A4
17TH ST W	LAN	LAN	42000	159	H4
17TH ST W	LB	LB13	1900	74	F3
17TH ST W	LB	LB13	200	75	B3
17TH ST W	PALM	PALM	39600	171	J6
17TH WK	LA	SP		78	E4
18TH AV	LA	VEN		49	B4
18TH AV	LB	LB02		79	D1
18TH CT	HB	RB		62	B6
18TH CT	SM	SM	800	41	A4
18TH CT	SM	SM		49	C1
18TH PL	MB	MB	100	62	A4
18TH PL S	LB	LB03		75	E6
18TH ST	HB	RB	100	62	C6
18TH ST	MB	MB	100	62	B3
18TH ST	SM	SM	200	40	F4
18TH ST	SM	SM	600	41	A5
18TH ST	SM	SM	2100	49	B1
18TH ST E	CO	LAN	46800	148	E9
18TH ST E	CO	PALM	38600	172	E8
18TH ST E	PALM	PALM		184	A1
18TH ST E	LA	LA21	700	44	C5
18TH ST E	LAN	LAN		160	E6
18TH ST E	PALM	PALM		183	E1
18TH ST N	MTB	MTB	300	46	C6
18TH ST N	MTB	MTB	100	54	C1
18TH ST S	MTB	MTB	100	54	C1
18TH ST W	CO	LAN		147	H8
18TH ST W	CO	PALM	39800	171	H5
18TH ST W	LA	LA06	1300	44	A4
18TH ST W	LA	LA15	100	44	A4
18TH ST W	LA	LA19	5700	42	D3
18TH ST W	LA	LA19	2300	43	B4
18TH ST W	LA	LA35	5900	42	D3
18TH ST W	LA	SP	600	78	E4
18TH ST W	LA	SP	200	79	A4
18TH ST W	LAN	LAN	42100	159	H7
18TH ST W	PALM	PALM	39600	171	H6
19TH AV	LA	VEN		49	B4
19TH CT	HB	RB		62	B6
19TH CT	SM	SM	800	41	A4
19TH PL	MB	MB	100	62	A3
19TH PL S	LB	LB03		75	E6
19TH ST	HB	RB	100	62	C6
19TH ST	MB	MB	100	62	B3
19TH ST	SM	SM	200	40	F4
19TH ST	SM	SM	600	41	A5
19TH ST E	LB	LB06	100	75	C3
19TH ST E	PALM	PALM		172	E9
19TH ST E	PALM	PALM		183	C5
19TH ST E	PALM	PALM		183	E1
19TH ST E	PALM	PALM		184	A1
19TH ST E	SH	LB04	2500	75	F3
19TH ST E	SH	LB06	2000	75	E3
19TH ST N	MTB	MTB		46	C6
19TH ST N	MTB	MTB	100	54	C1
19TH ST S	MTB	MTB	100	54	C1
19TH ST W	LA	SP	600	78	E4
19TH ST W	LA	SP	300	79	A4
19TH ST W	LAN	LAN	42800	159	H8
19TH ST W	LB	LB06	200	75	C3
19TH ST W	LB	LB10	1900	74	F3
19TH ST W	LB	LB10	1200	75	A3
20TH AV	LA	VEN		49	B4
20TH CT	HB	RB		62	B6
20TH CT	SM	SM	1300	41	B5
20TH PL	HB	RB	1100	62	C6
20TH PL	MB	MB	100	62	A3
20TH PL S	LB	LB03		75	E6
20TH ST	HB	RB	100	62	C6
20TH ST	MB	MB	100	62	A3
20TH ST	SM	SM	200	40	F4
20TH ST	SM	SM	600	41	A4
20TH ST	SM	SM	2100	49	C1
20TH ST E	CO	LAN	46000	160	E6
20TH ST E	CO	PALM	38800	172	E9
20TH ST E	LA	LA11	400	44	D6
20TH ST E	LA	LA11	1500	52	D1
20TH ST E	LA	LA58	1700	44	E6
20TH ST E	LAN	LAN	42800	160	E6
20TH ST E	LB	LB06	100	75	E2
20TH ST E	PALM	PALM		172	E9
20TH ST E	PALM	PALM	37200	183	E2
20TH ST E	PALM	PALM		184	A1
20TH ST E	SH	LB04	2600	75	E2
20TH ST E	SH	LB06	1600	75	E2
20TH ST N	MTB	MTB	300	46	C6
20TH ST N	MTB	MTB	100	54	C1
20TH ST W	CO	LAN		147	H8
20TH ST W	CO	LAN	46000	159	H3
20TH ST W	CO	LAN	41200	171	H2
20TH ST W	CO	PALM	39800	171	H5
20TH ST W	LA	LA07	1200	43	F4
20TH ST W	LA	LA07	500	44	B5
20TH ST W	LA	LA16	5200	42	F4
20TH ST W	LA	LA16	4900	43	A4
20TH ST W	LA	LA18	1900	43	D4
20TH ST W	LA	SP	600	78	E4
20TH ST W	LA	SP	300	79	A4
20TH ST W	LAN	LAN	42000	159	H9
20TH ST W	LAN	LAN	42000	171	H5
20TH ST W	LB	LB06	100	75	C3
20TH ST W	LB	LB10	1900	74	F3
20TH ST W	LB	LB10	1200	75	C3
20TH ST W	PALM	PALM	39600	171	H6
21ST CT	HB	RB		62	B6
21ST CT	SM	SM	800	41	A4
21ST PL	MB	MB	100	62	A3
21ST PL	SM	SM	100	40	F4
21ST PL	SM	SM	300	41	A4
21ST ST	HB	RB	100	62	C6
21ST ST	MB	MB	100	62	C3
21ST ST	SM	SM	200	40	F4
21ST ST	SM	SM	600	41	A4
21ST ST	SM	SM	2100	49	C1
21ST ST E	CO	LAN	46000	160	E2
21ST ST E	LA	LA11	100	44	D6
21ST ST E	LA	LA11	1500	52	D1
21ST ST E	LA	LA58	1700	52	D1
21ST ST E	LAN	LAN	42800	160	E7
21ST ST E	LB	LB06	100	75	B2
21ST ST E	PALM	PALM		160	E8
21ST ST E	PALM	PALM	38400	172	E8
21ST ST E	PALM	PALM		184	A1
21ST ST E	SH	LB06	1800	75	E2
21ST ST N	MTB	MTB	300	46	C6
21ST ST N	MTB	MTB	100	54	C1
21ST ST W	LA	LA07	1200	43	E4
21ST ST W	LA	LA07	100	44	B5
21ST ST W	LA	LA16	5200	42	F4
21ST ST W	LA	LA16	4600	43	A4
21ST ST W	LA	LA18	1900	43	C4
21ST ST W	LA	SP	600	78	E4
21ST ST W	LA	SP	300	79	A4
21ST ST W	LAN	LAN	42000	159	H9
21ST ST W	LAN	LAN	42000	171	H1
21ST ST W	LB	LB06	100	75	A2
21ST ST W	LB	LB10	1200	75	A2
21ST ST W	PALM	PALM	39600	171	H6
22ND CT	HB	RB		62	B6
22ND PL W	LA	LA07	1500	43	F5

STREET	CITY	P.O. ZONE	BLOCK	PAGE	GRID
22ND PL W	LA	LA18	4000	43	C4
22ND ST	HB	RB	100	62	B6
22ND ST	MB	MB	1100	62	C3
22ND ST	SM	SM	200	40	F3
22ND ST	SM	SM	600	41	A4
22ND ST	SM	SM	2100	49	C1
22ND ST E	CO	LAN	46000	160	F2
22ND ST E	LA	LA11	400	44	D6
22ND ST E	LA	LA11	1400	52	D1
22ND ST E	LA	LA58	1700	52	D1
22ND ST E	LA	SP	200	79	A5
22ND ST E	LAN	LAN	42800	160	E7
22ND ST E	PALM	PALM	38400	172	F8
22ND ST E	PALM	PALM		184	A1
22ND ST S	MTB	MTB	100	54	C1
22ND ST W	CO	LAN	41200	171	H5
22ND ST W	CO	PALM	39800	171	H5
22ND ST W	LA	LA07	1200	43	F5
22ND ST W	LA	LA07	100	44	B5
22ND ST W	LA	LA18	1800	43	D4
22ND ST W	LA	SP	400	78	D5
22ND ST W	LA	SP	200	79	A5
22ND ST W	LAN	LAN	42000	159	H9
22ND ST W	LAN	LAN	42000	171	H5
22ND ST W	PALM	PALM	39600	171	H5
23RD AV	LA	VEN		49	B5
23RD PL	MB	MB	100	62	A3
23RD ST	HB	RB		62	B6
23RD ST	MB	MB	100	62	A3
23RD ST	SM	SM	200	40	F3
23RD ST	SM	SM	600	41	A4
23RD ST	SM	SM	2100	49	C1
23RD ST E	LA	LA11	100	44	C6
23RD ST E	LA	LA11	1300	52	D1
23RD ST E	LA	LA58	1700	52	D1
23RD ST E	LAN	LAN	43200	160	F7
23RD ST E	LB	LB06	100	75	C2
23RD ST E	LB	LB15	3700	76	A2
23RD ST E	PALM	PALM		184	A1
23RD ST E	SH	LB06	1000	75	C2
23RD ST W	LA	LA07	1200	43	F5
23RD ST W	LA	LA07	100	44	A5
23RD ST W	LA	LA16	4300	43	A4
23RD ST W	LA	LA18	1700	43	C4
23RD ST W	LA	SP	500	78	E5
23RD ST W	LA	SP	500	79	A5
23RD ST W	LAN	LAN	42100	159	G9
23RD ST W	LAN	LAN	39200	171	H7
23RD ST W	LB	LB06	100	75	A2
23RD ST W	LB	LB10	2100	74	F2
23RD ST W	LB	LB10	1200	75	A2
23RD ST W	PALM	PALM	39600	171	H6
24TH AV	LA	VEN		49	B5
24TH CT	SM	SM		41	C6
24TH PL	HB	RB	400	62	C6
24TH PL	LA	VEN		49	B5
24TH PL	MB	MB		62	A3
24TH ST	HB	RB	100	62	C6
24TH ST	MB	MB	100	62	A3
24TH ST	SM	SM	100	40	F3
24TH ST	SM	SM	300	41	A3
24TH ST	SM	SM	2400	49	C1
24TH ST E	LA	LA11	100	44	B6
24TH ST E	LA	LA11	1500	52	D1
24TH ST E	LA	LA58	1700	52	D1
24TH ST W	LA	LA07	1200	43	F5
24TH ST W	LA	LA07	100	44	B5
24TH ST W	LA	LA18	1700	43	D5
24TH ST W	LA	LA34	8900	42	D4
24TH ST W	LA	SP	500	78	E5
24TH ST W	LAN	LAN	42100	159	G9
25TH AV	LA	VEN		49	B5
25TH CT	SM	SM	800	41	B4
25TH PL	LA	VEN		49	B5
25TH PL	MB	MB	100	62	A3
25TH PL	SH	LB06		75	D2
25TH PL E	PALM	PALM	37400	183	F1
25TH PL W	LA	LA07	1100	44	A5
25TH ST	HB	RB	100	62	B5
25TH ST	MB	MB	100	62	B3
25TH ST	RPV	PVP		78	C4
25TH ST	SM	SM	200	41	A3
25TH ST	SM	SM	2500	49	D1
25TH ST E	CO	LAN	46000	160	F2
25TH ST E	CO	PALM	36400	183	F3
25TH ST E	LA	LA11	100	44	B6
25TH ST E	LA	LA11	1100	52	C1
25TH ST E	LA	LA58	2400	52	E1
25TH ST E	LAN	LAN		160	F6
25TH ST E	LB	LB06	100	75	C2
25TH ST E	LB	LB15	5100	76	B2
25TH ST E	PALM	PALM	36800	183	F2
25TH ST E	SH	LB06	900	75	D2
25TH ST E	VER	LA23	3000	53	A1
25TH ST E	VER	LA58	1900	52	E1
25TH ST W	CO	LAN	47600	147	G7

STREET	CITY	P.O. ZONE	BLOCK	PAGE	GRID
25TH ST W	CO	LAN	47300	147	G8
25TH ST W	CO	LAN	41200	171	G2
25TH ST W	CO	PALM	38400	171	G8
25TH ST W	LA	LA07	1100	43	F5
25TH ST W	LA	LA07	100	44	B6
25TH ST W	LA	LA18	1700	43	E5
25TH ST W	LA	LA34	8900	42	D4
25TH ST W	LA	SP	700	78	E5
25TH ST W	LAN	LAN	42100	159	G9
25TH ST W	LAN	LAN	42000	171	G2
25TH ST W	LB	LB06	100	75	C2
25TH ST W	LB	LB10	1900	74	F2
25TH ST W	LB	LB10	1200	75	A2
25TH ST W	PALM	PALM	39600	171	G8
25TH WY E	LB	LB06	500	75	C2
26TH AV	LA	VEN		49	C5
26TH CT	SM	SM		41	B4
26TH PL	LA	VEN		49	B5
26TH PL	MB	MB	100	62	A3
26TH PL W	LA	LA18	2100	43	D5
26TH PL W	LA	SP	1200	78	E5
26TH ST	HB	RB	100	62	B5
26TH ST	MB	MB	100	62	A3
26TH ST	SM	SM	100	41	A3
26TH ST E	BELL	BELL	4900	53	E3
26TH ST E	CMRC	LA40	5400	53	E3
26TH ST E	CMRC	LA40	5900	54	A4
26TH ST E	CO	LA22	4500	53	E3
26TH ST E	CO	LAN	46000	160	F1
26TH ST E	CO	PALM	38400	172	F8
26TH ST E	LAN	LAN		160	F6
26TH ST E	PALM	PALM		172	F9
26TH ST E	PALM	PALM	37200	183	F1
26TH ST E	VER	LA23	2700	52	E1
26TH ST E	VER	LA23	2800	53	A1
26TH ST E	VER	LA58	2400	52	E1
26TH ST W	CO	LAN	47300	147	G8
26TH ST W	LA	SP	500	78	D5
26TH ST W	LAN	LAN		159	G8
26TH ST W	PALM	PALM	39600	171	G6
26TH WY	LB	LB06		75	B1
26TH WY	LB	LB10		75	A1
27TH AV	LA	VEN		49	C5
27TH CT	HB	RB	100	62	B5
27TH DR W	LA	SP	1300	78	E5
27TH PL	LA	SP	1300	78	E5
27TH PL	LA	VEN		49	B5
27TH PL	MB	MB	100	62	A3
27TH PL E	PALM	PALM	37900	172	G9
27TH ST	HB	RB	100	62	B5
27TH ST	MB	MB	100	62	B3
27TH ST	SM	SM	2200	41	C6
27TH ST E	CO	PALM	38200	172	F8
27TH ST E	LA	LA11	100	44	B6
27TH ST E	LA	LA11	800	52	C1
27TH ST E	LAN	LAN		160	F6
27TH ST E	LB	LB06	100	75	C1
27TH ST E	LB	LB15	5100	76	B1
27TH ST E	PALM	PALM		172	F9
27TH ST E	PALM	PALM	37200	183	F1
27TH ST E	SH	LB06	600	75	E1
27TH ST E	VER	LA58	1800	52	E1
27TH ST W	CO	LAN	47300	147	G8
27TH ST W	CO	LAN	41200	171	G2
27TH ST W	CO	PALM	39800	171	G5
27TH ST W	LA	LA07	1100	43	F5
27TH ST W	LA	LA07	100	44	B6
27TH ST W	LA	LA18	1700	43	D5
27TH ST W	LA	SP	600	78	E5
27TH ST W	LAN	LAN	42000	159	G9
27TH ST W	LB	LB06	100	75	C1
27TH ST W	LB	LB10	1200	75	A1
27TH ST W	PALM	PALM	39600	171	G6
28TH AV	LA	VEN		49	C5
28TH CT	HB	RB	100	62	B5
28TH PL	LA	VEN		49	B5
28TH PL	MB	MB	100	62	A3
28TH ST	HB	RB		62	B5
28TH ST	MB	MB	100	62	A3
28TH ST	SM	SM	2200	41	C6
28TH ST	SM	SM		49	D1
28TH ST E	CO	LAN	46000	160	F3
28TH ST E	CO	PALM	38400	172	G8
28TH ST E	LA	LA11	100	44	B6
28TH ST E	LA	LA11	700	52	C1
28TH ST E	LAN	LAN	45000	160	F3
28TH ST E	LB	LB06	100	75	B1
28TH ST E	LB	LB15	5100	76	B1
28TH ST E	PALM	PALM	37400	183	G1
28TH ST E	SH	LB06	600	75	D1
28TH ST E	VER	LA58	2400	52	E1
28TH ST W	CO	ACT		182	G6
28TH ST W	LA	LA07	1100	43	F5
28TH ST W	LA	LA07	100	44	B6
28TH ST W	LA	LA16	4400	43	B5
28TH ST W	LA	LA18	2000	43	D5

STREET	CITY	P.O. ZONE	BLOCK	PAGE	GRID
28TH ST W	LA	SP	500	78	F5
28TH ST W	LAN	LAN	42100	159	G7
28TH ST W	LB	LB06	100	75	B1
28TH ST W	PALM	PALM	39600	171	G6
29TH AV	LA	VEN		49	C5
29TH CT	HB	RB	100	62	B5
29TH PL	LA	VEN		49	B5
29TH PL	MB	MB	100	62	A3
29TH PL E	PALM	PALM	37300	183	G1
29TH PL W	LA	LA18	2000	43	D5
29TH PL W	LA	SP	800	78	F5
29TH ST	HB	RB		62	B5
29TH ST	LA	SP	600	78	F5
29TH ST	LA	SP		79	A5
29TH ST	MB	MB	100	62	B3
29TH ST	SM	SM	2200	41	D6
29TH ST E	LA	LA11	100	44	B6
29TH ST E	LA	LA11	600	52	C1
29TH ST E	LB	LB06	100	75	C1
29TH ST E	LB	LB15	5100	76	B1
29TH ST E	PALM	PALM	37400	183	G2
29TH ST E	SH	LB06	600	75	E1
29TH ST W	LA	LA07	1100	43	F5
29TH ST W	LA	LA07	400	44	B6
29TH ST W	LA	LA16	4100	43	B5
29TH ST W	LA	LA18	1700	43	D5
29TH ST W	LB	LB06	100	75	C1
29TH ST W	LB	LB10	1900	74	F1
29TH ST W	LB	LB10	1300	75	A1
30TH AV	LA	VEN		49	C5
30TH PL	HB	RB	100	62	B5
30TH PL	LA	VEN		49	B5
30TH PL	LA	VEN		49	B5
30TH PL	MB	MB	100	62	A3
30TH PL W	LA	LA07	1300	43	F5
30TH ST	HB	RB		62	C5
30TH ST	LA	SP		79	A5
30TH ST	MB	MB	100	62	A3
30TH ST	SM	SM	2200	41	D6
30TH ST E	CO	LAN	46000	160	G6
30TH ST E	CO	PALM	38000	172	G8
30TH ST E	LA	LA11	100	44	A6
30TH ST E	LA	LA11	600	52	B1
30TH ST E	LAN	LAN	42800	160	G6
30TH ST E	PALM	PALM	36000	183	G4
30TH ST E	VER	LA58	2400	52	E2
30TH ST W	CO	LAN	46000	159	F6
30TH ST W	CO	LAN	41200	171	G2
30TH ST W	CO	PALM	39800	171	G5
30TH ST W	LA	LA07	1200	43	F5
30TH ST W	LA	LA07	100	44	A6
30TH ST W	LA	LA16	3800	43	B5
30TH ST W	LA	LA18	1600	43	D5
30TH ST W	LA	SP	500	78	F5
30TH ST W	LAN	LAN	42000	159	F6
30TH ST W	LAN	LAN	42000	171	G6
30TH ST W	PALM	PALM	39600	171	G6
31ST AV	LA	VEN		49	C5
31ST CT	LA	SP		79	A5
31ST PL	HB	RB	100	62	B5
31ST PL	MB	MB	100	62	A3
31ST ST	HB	RB		62	B5
31ST ST	LA	SP		79	A5
31ST ST	MB	MB	100	62	A3
31ST ST	SM	SM	2200	41	D6
31ST ST	SM	SM		49	D1
31ST ST E	CO	LAN	46500	148	G9
31ST ST E	CO	PALM	38400	172	G8
31ST ST E	LA	LA11	100	44	B6
31ST ST E	LA	LA11	400	52	B1
31ST ST E	LB	LB07	100	70	C6
31ST ST E	LB	LB07	100	70	C6
31ST ST E	PALM	PALM		183	G2
31ST ST W	CO	ACT		182	F6
31ST ST W	LA	LA07	1300	43	F5
31ST ST W	LA	LA07	100	44	B6
31ST ST W	LA	LA18	2000	43	D5
31ST ST W	LA	SP	600	78	F5
31ST ST W	LAN	LAN		159	F5
31ST ST W	LB	LB06	200	70	C6
31ST ST W	LB	LB07	100	70	C6
31ST ST W	LB	LB10	1200	70	A6
32ND PL	HB	RB		62	B5
32ND PL	MB	MB	100	62	A3
32ND ST	LA	SP		79	A6
32ND ST	MB	MB	100	62	A3
32ND ST	SM	SM	2200	41	D6
32ND ST E	CO	LAN	42800	160	G1
32ND ST E	CO	PALM	36000	183	G4
32ND ST E	LA	LA11	100	44	B6
32ND ST E	LA	LA11	300	52	B1
32ND ST E	LAN	LAN	44000	160	G5
32ND ST E	LB	LB07	300	70	C6
32ND ST E	PALM	PALM		183	G2
32ND ST E	SH	LB07	1000	70	D6
32ND ST W	CO	PALM	40800	171	F3

STREET	CITY	P.O. ZONE	BLOCK	PAGE	GRID
32ND ST W	LA	LA07	100	44	B6
32ND ST W	LA	SP	500	78	F6
32ND ST W	LAN	LAN	42400	159	F9
32ND ST W	LAN	LAN		171	F1
32ND ST W	LB	LB06	300	70	B6
32ND ST W	LB	LB10	1200	70	A6
32ND WY	LB	LB06		70	A6
33RD PL	HB	RB	100	62	B5
33RD PL	MB	MB	100	62	A3
33RD ST	HB	RB	100	62	B5
33RD ST	LA	SP		79	A6
33RD ST	MB	MB	100	62	B2
33RD ST	SM	SM	2200	41	D6
33RD ST E	CO	LAN	46000	160	G1
33RD ST E	CO	PALM	36100	183	G4
33RD ST E	LA	LA11	100	52	C1
33RD ST E	LAN	LAN	45200	160	G4
33RD ST E	LB	LB07	300	70	D6
33RD ST E	PALM	PALM		183	G2
33RD ST E	SH	LB07	600	70	D6
33RD ST W	CO	LAN		147	F2
33RD ST W	LA	LA07	100	44	A6
33RD ST W	LA	SP	600	78	F6
33RD ST W	LAN	LAN	42100	159	F3
33RD ST W	LB	LB06	300	70	B6
33RD ST W	LB	LB07	100	70	C6
33RD ST W	LB	LB10	1200	70	A6
33RD WY W	LB	LB06	700	70	B6
34TH PL	HB	RB	100	62	B5
34TH PL	MB	MB	100	62	A3
34TH ST	HB	RB	100	62	B5
34TH ST	MB	MB	100	62	A2
34TH ST	SM	SM	1800	41	D6
34TH ST E	LA	LA11	900	52	C1
34TH ST W	CO	PALM	40800	171	F3
34TH ST W	LA	SP	400	78	E5
34TH ST W	LB	LB10	1200	70	A5
35TH CT	LA	SP		79	A6
35TH CT W	LB	LB06	400	70	C5
35TH PL	HB	RB	100	62	B5
35TH PL	MB	MB	100	62	A2
35TH PL W	LA	LA07	1000	43	F6
35TH PL W	LA	LA18	1400	43	D6
35TH ST	HB	RB	100	62	B5
35TH ST	LA	SP		79	A6
35TH ST	MB	MB	100	62	B2
35TH ST E	CO	PALM		172	H9
35TH ST E	CO	PALM	37200	183	H2
35TH ST E	LA	LA11	100	52	B1
35TH ST E	LAN	LAN	43000	160	H8
35TH ST E	LB	LB07	100	70	C5
35TH ST E	PALM	PALM		183	H1
35TH ST W	LA	LA07	1100	43	F6
35TH ST W	LA	LA07	100	44	A6
35TH ST W	LA	LA18	1400	43	D6
35TH ST W	LA	SP	600	78	C5
35TH ST W	LAN	LAN	42000	159	F9
35TH ST W	LB	LB06	500	70	B5
35TH ST W	PALM	PALM	40400	171	F4
36TH CT W	LB	LB06	400	70	C5
36TH PL	MB	MB	100	62	A2
36TH PL E	LA	LA11	100	52	B1
36TH PL S	LB	LB03		80	A1
36TH PL W	LA	LA07	1000	43	D6
36TH PL W	LA	LA07	600	44	A6
36TH PL W	LA	LA18	1400	43	E6
36TH ST	LKD	LKD	2200	70	C5
36TH ST	MB	MB	100	62	A2
36TH ST E	CO	PALM	38500	172	H8
36TH ST E	LA	LA11	100	52	B1
36TH ST E	LAN	LAN	43000	160	H8
36TH ST E	LB	LB07	100	70	C5
36TH ST E	PALM	PALM		183	H1
36TH ST W	CO	LAN		171	F3
36TH ST W	LA	LA07	1100	43	E6
36TH ST W	LA	LA07	600	44	A6
36TH ST W	LA	LA07	100	52	B1
36TH ST W	LA	LA16	3600	43	B6
36TH ST W	LA	LA18	1400	43	E6
36TH ST W	LA	SP	500	78	E5
36TH ST W	LAN	LAN	42800	159	F8
36TH ST W	LB	LB06	500	70	B5
36TH ST W	LB	LB07	100	70	C5
37TH DR W	LA	LA07	1100	43	E6
37TH DR W	LA	LA18	1400	43	E6
37TH PL S	LB	LB03		80	A1
37TH PL W	LA	LA07	1100	43	F6
37TH PL W	LA	LA07	100	52	B1
37TH PL W	LA	LA18	1400	43	D6
37TH ST E	LA	LA11	100	52	B1
37TH ST E	LAN	LAN	43000	160	H8
37TH ST E	LB	LB07	100	70	C5
37TH ST E	PALM	PALM	36400	183	H4
37TH ST E	VER	LA58	2000	52	E2
37TH ST W	CO	LAN	46000	159	E2
37TH ST W	LA	LA07	1100	43	F6

STREET	CITY	P.O. ZONE	BLOCK	PAGE	GRID
37TH ST W	LA	LA07	100	52	A1
37TH ST W	LA	LA18	1400	43	D6
37TH ST W	LA	SP	400	78	F6
37TH ST W	LAN	LAN	42000	159	E8
37TH ST W	LB	LB06	400	70	C5
37TH ST W	LB	LB07	200	70	C5
38TH PL	MB	MB		62	A2
38TH PL S	LB	LB03		80	A1
38TH PL W	LA	LA08	2000	51	C1
38TH PL W	LA	LA37	1100	51	D1
38TH PL W	LA	LA62	1300	51	D1
38TH ST	CO	PALM		183	H4
38TH ST	MB	MB		62	A2
38TH ST E	LA	LA11	100	52	B1
38TH ST E	LAN	LAN	43000	160	H8
38TH ST E	VER	LA58	2000	52	E2
38TH ST W	CO	LAN	46000	159	E2
38TH ST W	CO	LAN	41200	171	E2
38TH ST W	CO	PALM	40800	171	E3
38TH ST W	LA	LA37	1000	51	E1
38TH ST W	LA	LA37	100	52	A1
38TH ST W	LA	LA62	1300	51	E1
38TH ST W	LA	SP	400	78	F6
38TH ST W	LAN	LAN	42000	159	E8
38TH ST W	LB	LB06	500	70	B5
39TH PL	LB	LB03		80	A1
39TH PL W	LA	LA37	1000	51	F1
39TH PL W	LA	LA62	1600	51	D1
39TH ST	MB	MB	100	62	A2
39TH ST W	LAN	LAN	43000	159	E8
39TH ST W	LA	LA08	2000	51	C1
39TH ST W	LA	LA37	800	51	E1
39TH ST W	LA	LA37	100	52	A1
39TH ST W	LA	LA62	1300	51	E1
39TH ST W	LA	SP	400	79	A6
39TH ST W	LAN	LAN	42000	159	E8
39TH ST W	LB	LB06	600	70	B5
40TH PL E	LA	LA11	400	52	B2
40TH PL E	LA	LA58	1700	52	D2
40TH PL W	LA	LA37	800	51	E2
40TH PL W	LA	LA37	100	52	A2
40TH ST	CO	ACT		189	E3
40TH ST	MB	MB	100	62	A2
40TH ST E	CO	LAN	4000	160	H7
40TH ST E	CO	PALM		172	H8
40TH ST E	CO	PALM	35500	183	H5
40TH ST E	LAN	LAN	42800	160	H7
40TH ST E	PALM	PALM	42000	172	H1
40TH ST W	CO	LAN	46000	159	E9
40TH ST W	CO	LAN	41200	171	E2
40TH ST W	CO	PALM	40800	171	E3
40TH ST W	LA	SP	300	78	F6
40TH ST W	LAN	LAN	42000	159	E9
40TH ST W	LAN	LAN	42000	171	E3
41ST DR W	LA	LA08	2100	51	D2
41ST DR W	LA	LA37	800	51	F2
41ST DR W	LA	LA37	500	52	A2
41ST DR W	LA	LA62	1700	51	D2
41ST PL E	LA	LA11	100	52	C2
41ST PL E	LA	LA58	1700	52	D2
41ST PL W	LA	LA37	1100	51	E2
41ST PL W	LA	LA37	100	52	A2
41ST PL W	LA	LA62	1400	51	D2
41ST ST	MB	MB	100	62	A2
41ST ST E	LA	LA11	400	52	B2
41ST ST E	LA	LA58	1700	52	B2
41ST ST E	LAN	LAN	45800	160	H2
41ST ST E	PALM	PALM		172	J8
41ST ST E	PALM	PALM	36400	183	H3
41ST ST W	LAN	LAN	42100	159	E8
41ST ST W	CO	PALM	40800	171	E3
41ST ST W	CO	SAU		189	E1
41ST ST W	LA	LA08	3200	51	C2
41ST ST W	LA	LA37	800	51	E2
41ST ST W	LA	LA37	100	52	A2
41ST ST W	LA	LA62	1700	51	D2
42ND PL E	LA	LA11	300	52	C2
42ND PL W	LA	LA37	800	51	F2
42ND PL W	LA	LA37	100	52	A2
42ND PL W	LA	LA62	1400	51	D2
42ND ST	MB	MB	100	62	A2
42ND ST E	CO	LAN		160	J2
42ND ST E	CO	PALM	35600	183	J4
42ND ST E	LA	LA11	300	52	C2
42ND ST E	LA	LA58	1700	52	D2
42ND ST E	PALM	PALM	42000	160	J9
42ND ST E	PALM	PALM		172	J9
42ND ST E	PALM	PALM		183	J1
42ND ST W	CO	LAN	41200	171	E2
42ND ST W	CO	PALM	41000	171	E3
42ND ST W	LA	LA08	2200	51	D2
42ND ST W	LA	LA37	800	51	E2
42ND ST W	LA	LA37	100	52	A2
42ND ST W	LA	LA62	1700	51	D2
43RD PL	LB	LB03		80	A1

314

1990 LOS ANGELES COUNTY STREET INDEX

43RD PL E — 71ST ST W

LOS ANGELES CO.

STREET	CITY	P.O. ZONE	BLOCK	PAGE	GRID
43RD PL E	LA	LA11	200	52	C2
43RD PL W	LA	LA08	2600	51	C2
43RD PL W	LA	LA37	800	51	F2
43RD PL W	LA	LA37	100	52	A2
43RD PL W	LA	LA62	1700	51	D2
43RD ST	MB	MB	100	62	A2
43RD ST E	CO	LAN		160	J2
43RD ST E	LA	LA11	100	52	C2
43RD ST E	LA	LA58	1700	52	D2
43RD ST E	PALM	PALM		172	J9
43RD ST W	LAN	LAN	43000	159	D8
43RD ST W	CO	PALM	40800	171	E3
43RD ST W	LA	LA08	2200	51	D2
43RD ST W	LA	LA37	800	51	F2
43RD ST W	LA	LA37	100	52	A2
43RD ST W	LA	LA62	1700	51	D2
44TH CIR	LB	LB07		70	C3
44TH ST	MB	MB	100	62	A2
44TH ST E	CO	LAN		160	J2
44TH ST E	LB	LB07	300	70	C3
44TH ST E	VER	LA58	2800	53	A2
44TH WY E	LB	LB07	300	70	C3
45TH PL	LB	LB03		80	B1
45TH ST	MB	MB	100	62	A2
45TH ST E	CO	LAN		160	J2
45TH ST E	CO	LAN		160	J5
45TH ST E	CO	PALM	36400	183	J3
45TH ST E	LAN	LAN		160	J5
45TH ST E	LA	LA11	100	52	C2
45TH ST E	LA	LA58	1700	52	D2
45TH ST E	LB	LB07	200	70	E3
45TH ST E	PALM	PALM	42000	160	J9
45TH ST E	VER	LA58		52	F2
45TH ST E	VER	LA58	3400	53	B2
45TH ST W	PALM	LAN	41200	171	D3
45TH ST W	PALM	PALM	40800	171	D3
45TH ST W	LA	LA37	900	51	D2
45TH ST W	LA	LA37	100	52	A2
45TH ST W	LA	LA62	1400	51	D2
45TH WY E	LB	LB07	1000	70	D3
46TH PL	LB	LB03		80	B1
46TH ST E	LAN	LAN		160	J5
46TH ST E	CO	LAN		160	J2
46TH ST E	LA	LA11	100	52	C2
46TH ST E	LA	LA58	1700	52	D2
46TH ST E	LB	LB07	200	70	C3
46TH ST E	VER	LA58	1900	52	E2
46TH ST E	VER	LA58	2800	53	A2
46TH ST W	CO	LAN	45200	59	D3
46TH ST W	LA	LA37	900	51	D2
46TH ST W	LA	LA37	100	52	A2
46TH ST W	LA	LA43	2800	51	C2
46TH ST W	LA	LA62	1400	51	D2
47TH PL E	LA	LA11	100	52	C3
47TH PL W	LA	LA37	100	52	A3
47TH ST	VER	LA58	3600	53	B3
47TH ST E	CO	LAN		160	J2
47TH ST E	CO	PALM		183	J6
47TH ST E	CO	PALM	34000	184	A4
47TH ST E	LAN	LAN		160	J5
47TH ST E	LA	LA11	100	52	C3
47TH ST E	LA	LA58	1700	52	C3
47TH ST E	LB	LB05		70	C3
47TH ST E	PALM	PALM	38000	173	A9
47TH ST W	CO	LAN	45200	59	D3
47TH ST W	CO	LAN	41200	171	D2
47TH ST W	PALM	PALM	40800	171	D3
47TH ST W	LA	LA37	800	51	D3
47TH ST W	LA	LA37	100	52	A3
47TH ST W	LA	LA62	1400	51	D3
47TH ST W	LB	LB05		70	C3
48TH PL	LB	LB03		80	B1
48TH PL E	LA	LA11	1300	52	D3
48TH PL E	LA	LA58	1700	52	D3
48TH ST E	LAN	LAN	44000	161	A6
48TH ST E	PALM	PALM		184	A1
48TH ST E	LA	LA11	100	52	C3
48TH ST E	VER	LA58	1900	52	E3
48TH ST E	VER	LA58		53	C3
48TH ST W	CO	LAN	45200	59	D3
48TH ST W	PALM	PALM	40800	171	D3
48TH ST W	LA	LA37	800	51	F3
48TH ST W	LA	LA37	100	52	A3
48TH ST W	LA	LA43	2100	51	C3
48TH ST W	LA	LA62	1400	51	C3
48TH ST W	LB	LB05		70	B3
49TH PL E	LA	LA11	800	52	C3
49TH PL W	LA	LA37	500	52	A3
49TH ST E	LA	LA11	100	52	C3
49TH ST E	LB	LB05		70	C3
49TH ST E	PALM	PALM		184	A5
49TH ST E	VER	LA58	2000	52	E3
49TH ST E	VER	LA58		53	C3
49TH ST W	LA	LA37	800	51	D3
49TH ST W	LA	LA37	100	52	A3
49TH ST W	LA	LA62	1400	51	D3
49TH ST W	LB	LB05		70	C3
50TH PL	LB	LB03		80	B1
50TH PL E	LA	LA11		52	D3
50TH PL E	LA	LA58		52	D3
50TH PL W	LA	LA37	800	51	F3
50TH ST E	LAN	LAN	42800	161	A8
50TH ST E	PALM	PALM	37200	184	A2
50TH ST E	LA	LA11	100	52	C3
50TH ST E	LA	LA58	1700	52	D3
50TH ST E	PALM	PALM	42000	173	A1
50TH ST E	VER	LA58	2600	52	F3
50TH ST E	VER	LA58	2800	53	A3
50TH ST W	CO	LAN	41200	171	D2
50TH ST W	LA	LA37	800	51	D3
50TH ST W	LA	LA37	100	52	A3
50TH ST W	LA	LA43	2800	51	C3
50TH ST W	LA	LA62	1400	51	D3
51ST PL W	LA	LA37	800	51	E3
51ST PL W	LA	LA62	1400	51	E3
51ST ST	CO	LA56	5200	50	E3
51ST ST E	PALM	PALM	37200	184	A2
51ST ST E	LA	LA11	100	52	C3
51ST ST E	LA	LA58	1900	52	C3
51ST ST E	LB	LB05		70	B2
51ST ST W	CO	LAN	42000	171	C1
51ST ST W	CO	LAN		171	C2
51ST ST W	LA	LA37	800	51	D3
51ST ST W	LA	LA37	100	52	A3
51ST ST W	LA	LA62	1400	51	D3
51ST ST W	LB	LB05		70	B2
52ND DR E	CO	LA22	4600	53	D3
52ND PL	LB	LB03		80	B1
52ND PL E	LA	LA11	600	52	C3
52ND PL E	MAY	MAY	4400	53	D3
52ND PL W	LA	LA37	100	52	A3
52ND ST E	CO	LA22		53	B3
52ND ST E	CO	LAN	43200	161	A7
52ND ST E	PALM	PALM	37200	184	A2
52ND ST E	CO	PALM		184	B4
52ND ST E	HPK	HPK	2600	52	F3
52ND ST E	LA	LA11	100	52	C3
52ND ST E	LA	LA58	1700	52	C3
52ND ST E	LB	LB05		70	C2
52ND ST E	MAY	MAY	3500	53	B3
52ND ST E	PALM	PALM		173	A9
52ND ST E	VER	LA58	2000	52	E3
52ND ST W	CO	LAN	42000	171	C1
52ND ST W	LA	LA37	800	51	E3
52ND ST W	LA	LA37	100	52	A3
52ND ST W	LA	LA43	2200	51	C3
52ND ST W	LA	LA62	1400	51	E3
52ND ST W	LB	LB05		70	C2
53RD PL	LB	LB03		80	B1
53RD ST E	CO	LAN	43200	161	A7
53RD ST E	PALM	PALM	37200	184	A2
53RD ST E	CO	PALM		184	B4
53RD ST E	HPK	HPK	2500	52	F3
53RD ST E	HPK	LA58		52	E3
53RD ST E	LA	LA11	100	52	C3
53RD ST E	LA	LA58	1700	52	C3
53RD ST E	LB	LB05		70	C2
53RD ST E	MAY	MAY	3500	53	B3
53RD ST E	PALM	PALM		173	A9
53RD ST E	PALM	PALM		184	A1
53RD ST E	VER	LA58	2400	52	E3
53RD ST W	CO	LAN	42100	159	C1
53RD ST W	CO	SAU		182	C9
53RD ST W	LA	LA37	800	51	E3
53RD ST W	LA	LA37	100	52	A3
53RD ST W	LA	LA62	1400	51	E3
53RD ST W	LB	LB05		70	C2
53RD ST W	PALM	PALM		171	C2
54TH PL	LB	LB03		80	B1
54TH ST	LB	LB05	2700	70	F2
54TH ST E	CO	PALM		184	B4
54TH ST E	HPK	HPK	2500	52	F3
54TH ST E	HPK	LA58		52	E3
54TH ST E	LA	LA11	100	52	B3
54TH ST E	LA	LA58	1700	52	D3
54TH ST E	MAY	MAY	3500	53	B3
54TH ST E	VER	LA58	2400	52	E3
54TH ST E	VER	LA58	2800	53	A3
54TH ST W	CO	LA56	5100	50	E3
54TH ST W	LA	LA37	800	51	E3
54TH ST W	LA	LA37	100	52	B3
54TH ST W	LA	LA43	2200	51	C3
54TH ST W	LA	LA62	1400	51	E3
55TH PL	LB	LB03		80	C2
55TH ST E	CO	PALM		184	B4
55TH ST E	HPK	HPK	2500	52	F4
55TH ST E	HPK	LA58		52	E3
55TH ST E	LA	LA11	100	52	C3
55TH ST E	LA	LA58	1700	52	C3
55TH ST E	LB	LB05		70	C1
55TH ST E	MAY	MAY	3500	53	B3
55TH ST E	PALM	PALM		184	B2
55TH ST E	VER	LA58	2000	52	E3
55TH ST W	CO	LA56	5200	50	E4
55TH ST W	LAN	LAN		159	C9
55TH ST W	CO	LAN	41600	171	C1
55TH ST W	CO	SAU		182	B9
55TH ST W	LA	LA37	800	51	E3
55TH ST W	LA	LA37	100	52	A3
55TH ST W	LA	LA62	1400	51	E3
55TH ST W	PALM	LAN	41200	171	C2
55TH WY	LB	LB05		70	F1
56TH PL	LB	LB03		80	C2
56TH ST E	LAN	LAN	46000	161	B1
56TH ST E	CO	PALM	38800	173	B7
56TH ST E	CO	PALM		184	B4
56TH ST E	HPK	LA58		52	E4
56TH ST E	LA	LA11	100	52	C4
56TH ST E	LB	LB05		70	C1
56TH ST E	MAY	MAY	3500	53	B4
56TH ST E	PALM	PALM		184	B1
56TH ST E	VER	LA58	2400	52	E4
56TH ST W	LAN	LAN	43600	159	C6
56TH ST W	LA	LA37	800	51	E4
56TH ST W	LA	LA37	100	52	A4
56TH ST W	LA	LA62	1400	51	E4
56TH WY	LB	LB05		70	F1
57TH PL	LB	LB03		80	C2
57TH ST E	LAN	LAN	46000	161	B1
57TH ST E	CO	LAN	41200	173	B2
57TH ST E	CO	PALM		184	B4
57TH ST E	HPK	HPK	2500	52	F4
57TH ST E	HPK	LA58		52	E4
57TH ST E	LA	LA11	100	52	C4
57TH ST E	LA	LA58	1700	52	C4
57TH ST E	LB	LB05	100	70	D1
57TH ST E	MAY	MAY	3500	53	B4
57TH ST E	PALM	PALM		173	B9
57TH ST E	PALM	PALM		184	B2
57TH ST E	VER	LA58	1900	52	E4
57TH ST W	CO	ACT		189	B1
57TH ST W	CO	LA43	3700	51	C4
57TH ST W	CO	LA56	4800	50	E4
57TH ST W	LAN	LAN	42100	159	B6
57TH ST W	CO	LAN		171	B1
57TH ST W	LA	LA37	800	51	E4
57TH ST W	LA	LA37	100	52	A4
57TH ST W	LA	LA43	2400	51	C4
57TH ST W	LA	LA62	1400	51	E4
58TH DR E	CO	LA01	1100	52	C4
58TH PL	LB	LB03		80	C2
58TH PL E	CO	LA01	1100	52	C4
58TH PL W	CO	LA43	4400	51	A4
58TH PL W	CO	LA56	5000	50	E4
58TH PL W	LA	LA03	100	52	B4
58TH PL W	LA	LA43	3400	51	B4
58TH PL W	LA	LA44	800	51	F4
58TH PL W	LA	LA47	1400	51	E4
58TH ST E	LAN	LAN	46000	161	B1
58TH ST E	CO	PALM	38800	173	B7
58TH ST E	HPK	HPK	2500	52	F4
58TH ST E	HPK	LA58		52	E4
58TH ST E	LA	LA11	100	52	C4
58TH ST E	MAY	MAY	3500	53	B4
58TH ST E	PALM	PALM		173	B9
58TH ST W	LAN	LAN	42100	159	B7
58TH ST W	LA	LA37	800	51	E4
58TH ST W	LA	LA37	100	52	A4
58TH ST W	LA	LA62	1400	51	E4
58TH ST W	LAN	LAN		159	B9
59TH DR W	LA	LA44	900	51	F4
59TH PL	LB	LB03		80	C2
59TH PL E	CO	LA01	1100	52	C4
59TH PL E	HPK	HPK	3500	53	B4
59TH PL E	LA	LA03	100	52	A4
59TH PL E	MAY	MAY	4400	53	D4
59TH PL W	CO	LA43	4400	51	A4
59TH PL W	LA	LA03	100	52	A4
59TH PL W	LA	LA43	3100	51	B4
59TH PL W	LA	LA44	800	51	E4
59TH PL W	LA	LA44	500	52	A4
59TH PL W	LA	LA47	1400	51	E4
59TH ST	LAN	LAN		159	B9
59TH ST E	CO	LA01	1100	52	C4
59TH ST E	LA	LA01	600	52	C4
59TH ST E	LB	LB05		70	D1
59TH ST W	CO	LA43	4400	51	A4
59TH ST W	CO	LA56	4900	50	E4
59TH ST W	LA	LA03	100	52	B4
59TH ST W	LA	LA43	2200	51	B4
59TH ST W	LA	LA44	700	51	E4
59TH ST W	LA	LA44	500	52	A4
59TH ST W	LA	LA47	1400	51	E4
60TH PL	LB	LB03		80	C2
60TH PL	MAY	MAY	4800	53	D4
60TH PL E	HPK	HPK	2900	53	B4
60TH PL W	LA	LA44	1000	51	E4
60TH PL W	LA	LA47	1400	51	E4
60TH ST E	CO	LA01	1100	52	C4
60TH ST E	CO	LA22	5200	53	C4
60TH ST E	LAN	LAN	45200	161	B3
60TH ST E	CO	PALM	36200	184	B4
60TH ST E	HPK	HPK	3500	53	C4
60TH ST E	LA	LA01	600	52	C4
60TH ST E	LA	LA03	100	52	A4
60TH ST E	LB	LB05		65	D6
60TH ST E	MAY	MAY	4300	53	C4
60TH ST E	PALM	PALM	38000	173	B8
60TH ST E	PALM	PALM	37200	184	B1
60TH ST W	CO	LA43	4400	51	A4
60TH ST W	CO	LAN	41200	171	B2
60TH ST W	LA	LA03	100	52	A4
60TH ST W	LA	LA43	2300	51	B4
60TH ST W	LA	LA44	800	51	E4
60TH ST W	LA	LA44	500	52	A4
60TH ST W	LA	LA47	1400	51	E4
60TH ST W	PALM	LAN	41200	171	B2
61ST PL	LB	LB03		80	C2
61ST PL E	HPK	HPK	3500	53	B4
61ST ST E	CMRC	LA40	5500	53	E5
61ST ST E	CO	LA01	1100	52	C4
61ST ST E	HPK	HPK	2900	53	B4
61ST ST E	LA	LA01	600	52	C4
61ST ST E	LA	LA03	100	52	A4
61ST ST E	LB	LB05	200	65	C6
61ST ST E	MAY	MAY	4300	53	B4
61ST ST E	PALM	PALM	37200	184	C1
61ST ST W	CO	LA43	4400	51	A4
61ST ST W	CO	LA56	5400	50	D4
61ST ST W	LAN	LAN	42100	159	B6
61ST ST W	LA	LA03	100	52	A4
61ST ST W	LA	LA43	3600	51	B4
61ST ST W	LA	LA44	800	51	E4
61ST ST W	LA	LA44	500	52	A4
61ST ST W	LA	LA47	1400	51	E4
62ND AV	LA	VEN		55A	D1
62ND PL	LA	LA43	4600	50	F5
62ND PL	LB	LB03		80	C2
62ND PL W	LA	LA43	4600	51	A5
62ND PL W	LA	LA44	800	51	F5
62ND ST E	CO	LA01	1100	52	C4
62ND ST E	LAN	LAN	45600	161	C2
62ND ST E	CO	PALM	36200	184	C4
62ND ST E	LA	LA01	600	52	C4
62ND ST E	LA	LA03	100	52	A4
62ND ST E	PALM	PALM	37200	184	C1
62ND ST W	CO	LA43	4400	51	A4
62ND ST W	CO	LA56	4800	50	E4
62ND ST W	CO	SAU		182	B5
62ND ST W	LA	LA03	100	52	A4
62ND ST W	LA	LA43	2400	51	C4
62ND ST W	LA	LA44	800	51	E4
62ND ST W	LA	LA44	500	52	A4
62ND ST W	LA	LA47	1400	51	E4
62ND ST W	PALM	LAN	41200	171	B3
63RD AV	LA	VEN		55A	D1
63RD PL	LB	LB03		80	C2
63RD PL N	LB	LB03		80	C3
63RD PL S	LB	LB03		80	C3
63RD PL W	LA	LA03	300	52	A5
63RD PL W	LA	LA44	500	52	A5
63RD ST E	CO	LA01	1100	52	C5
63RD ST E	LAN	LAN	45800	161	C2
63RD ST E	CO	PALM	35200	184	C6
63RD ST E	LB	LB05		65	D6
63RD ST E	PALM	PALM	37200	184	C1
63RD ST W	CO	LA56		50	D5
63RD ST W	LA	LA43	3100	51	B5
63RD ST W	LA	LA56	4800	50	F5
63RD ST W	PALM	LAN		171	A1
64TH AV	LA	VEN		55A	D1
64TH PL	LB	LB03		80	C2
64TH PL E	ING	IN02	100	50	F5
64TH PL W	ING	IN02	100	50	F5
64TH ST	HPK	HPK	1900	52	D5
64TH ST E	CO	LA01	1100	52	C5
64TH ST E	LA	LA03	100	52	B5
64TH ST E	LB	LB05		65	D5
64TH ST W	CO	LA56	5200	50	D5
64TH ST W	ING	IN02	100	50	F5
64TH ST W	ING	IN02		51	A5
64TH ST W	LA	LA03	100	52	A5
64TH ST W	LA	LA43	2700	51	C5
64TH ST W	LA	LA44	800	51	E5
64TH ST W	LA	LA47	1400	51	E5
64TH ST W	LA	LA56	5000	50	D5
65TH AV	LA	VEN		55A	D1
65TH PL	LB	LB03		80	C2
65TH PL W	LA	LA43	2200	51	D5
65TH PL W	LA	LA44	1000	51	D5
65TH PL W	LA	LA47	1400	51	D5
65TH ST	HPK	HPK	1900	52	D5
65TH ST E	CO	LA01	1100	52	C5
65TH ST E	LAN	LAN	43200	161	C7
65TH ST E	ING	IN02	700	51	B5
65TH ST E	LA	LA03	100	52	A5
65TH ST E	LB	LB05	100	65	B5
65TH ST E	PALM	PALM		173	C9
65TH ST E	PALM	PALM	37200	184	C1
65TH ST W	CO	LAN	46500	147	A4
65TH ST W	CO	LAN	42000	171	A1
65TH ST W	LA	LA03	100	52	A5
65TH ST W	LA	LA44	700	51	D5
65TH ST W	LA	LA44	500	52	A5
65TH ST W	LA	LA47	1400	51	D5
65TH ST W	LB	LB05	100	65	B5
65TH ST W	PALM	LAN		171	A2
66TH AV	LA	VEN		55A	D1
66TH PL	LB	LB03		80	C2
66TH PL W	LA	LA43	3300	51	C5
66TH ST	COM	COM		64	F6
66TH ST E	CO	LA01	1100	52	C5
66TH ST E	CO	PALM	35200	184	C6
66TH ST E	ING	IN02	900	51	B5
66TH ST E	LA	LA02	100	52	A5
66TH ST W	CO	LAN	46500	147	A4
66TH ST W	LA	LA03	100	52	A5
66TH ST W	LA	LA43	3300	51	C5
66TH ST W	LA	LA44	700	51	D5
66TH ST W	LA	LA44	500	52	A5
66TH ST W	LA	LA47	1400	51	D5
66TH WY E	LB	LB05		65	D5
67TH PL	LB	LB03		80	C2
67TH ST	HPK	HPK	1900	52	D5
67TH ST E	CO	LA01	1100	52	C5
67TH ST E	ING	IN02	500	51	B5
67TH ST E	LA	LA03	100	52	A5
67TH ST E	LB	LB05		65	B5
67TH ST E	PALM	PALM	42000	173	C1
67TH ST W	CO	LAN	46500	147	A4
67TH ST W	CO	LAN	42000	171	A1
67TH ST W	LA	LA03	100	52	A5
67TH ST W	LA	LA43	2200	51	C5
67TH ST W	LA	LA44	1000	51	D5
67TH ST W	LA	LA47	1400	51	D5
67TH ST W	PALM	LAN		171	A2
67TH WY E	LB	LB05		65	B5
67TH WY W	LB	LB05		65	B5
68TH PL	LB	LB03		80	C2
68TH ST E	CO	LA01	1100	52	C5
68TH ST E	ING	IN02	900	51	B5
68TH ST E	LA	LA03	100	52	A5
68TH ST E	LB	LB05	100	65	B5
68TH ST W	CO	LAN	46500	147	A4
68TH ST W	CO	LAN	42100	159	A6
68TH ST W	LA	LA03	200	52	A5
68TH ST W	LA	LA43	3100	51	C5
68TH ST W	LA	LA44	700	51	D5
68TH ST W	LA	LA44	500	52	A5
68TH ST W	LA	LA47	1400	51	D5
68TH ST W	LB	LB05	100	65	B5
68TH WY E	LB	LB05	100	65	B5
68TH WY W	LB	LB05	100	65	B5
69TH PL	LB	LB03		80	D2
69TH ST	LB	LB05		65	B5
69TH ST E	CO	LA01	1100	52	C5
69TH ST E	LA	LA03	100	52	A5
69TH ST W	CO	SAU		182	A6
69TH ST W	LA	LA03	100	52	A5
69TH ST W	LA	LA43	3100	51	C5
69TH ST W	LA	LA44	800	51	D5
69TH ST W	LA	LA44	500	52	A5
69TH ST W	LA	LA47	1400	51	D5
69TH WY E	LB	LB05		65	B4
70TH PL	LB	LB03		80	D2
70TH ST E	CO	LA01	1100	52	C5
70TH ST E	CO	LAN	41200	173	D2
70TH ST E	LA	LA03	100	52	A5
70TH ST E	LB	LB05	600	65	D4
70TH ST E	PALM	PALM	38000	173	D9
70TH ST E	PALM	PALM	3500	184	D5
70TH ST E	PAR	PAR	800	65	F4
70TH ST W	CO	LAN		147	A5
70TH ST W	CO	LAN	41200	171	A2
70TH ST W	LA	LA03	100	52	A5
70TH ST W	LA	LA43	2200	51	C5
70TH ST W	LA	LA44	700	51	D5
70TH ST W	LA	LA44	500	52	A5
70TH ST W	LA	LA47	1400	51	D5
70TH ST W	PALM	LAN		171	A2
70TH WY E	LB	LB05		65	D4
71ST PL	LB	LB03		80	D2
71ST PL S	LB	LB03		80	D2
71ST ST E	CO	LA01	1100	52	C5
71ST ST E	CO	PALM	40600	173	D3
71ST ST E	LA	LA03	100	52	A5
71ST ST E	LB	LB05		65	D4
71ST ST E	PALM	PALM	37200	184	D1
71ST ST W	CO	LAN	50400	146	J2

INDEX

1990 LOS ANGELES COUNTY STREET INDEX

STREET	CITY	P.O. ZONE	BLOCK	PAGE	GRID
71ST ST W	LAN	LAN	42100	158	J7
71ST ST W	LA	LA03	100	52	A5
71ST ST W	LA	LA43	3100	51	C5
71ST ST W	LA	LA44	800	51	D5
71ST ST W	LA	LA47	1400	51	D5
71ST WY E	LB	LB05		65	D4
72ND PL	LB	LB03		80	D2
72ND ST E	CO	LAN	41200	173	D4
72ND ST E	CO	LR		184	D6
72ND ST E	CO	PALM	40400	173	D2
72ND ST E	LB	LB05	600	65	D4
72ND ST E	PALM	PALM	37200	184	D1
72ND ST W	CO	LAN	50400	146	J2
72ND ST W	LAN	LAN	42100	158	J7
73RD ST E	CO	LA01	1100	52	C6
73RD ST E	CO	PALM	40800	173	D2
73RD ST E	LA	LA01	600	52	C6
73RD ST E	LA	LA03	100	52	A6
73RD ST E	PALM	PALM	37200	184	D1
73RD ST W	CO	LAN	50400	146	J2
73RD ST W	LA	LA03	100	52	A6
73RD ST W	LA	LA43	2200	51	C6
73RD ST W	LA	LA44	800	51	F6
73RD ST W	LA	LA44	500	52	A6
73RD ST W	LA	LA47	1800	51	C6
74TH PL W	ING	IN05	3500	51	B6
74TH ST E	CO	LA01	1100	52	C6
74TH ST E	LA	LA01	600	52	C6
74TH ST E	LA	LA03	100	52	A6
74TH ST W	CO	LAN	50400	146	J2
74TH ST W	LA	LA43	2200	51	C6
74TH ST W	LA	LA44	800	51	F6
74TH ST W	LA	LA44	500	52	A6
74TH ST W	LA	LA45	5600	50	D6
74TH ST W	LA	LA47	1400	51	C6
75TH PL W	ING	IN05	3500	51	B6
75TH PL W	LA	LA45	6000	50	C6
75TH ST E	CO	LA01	1100	52	C6
75TH ST E	LAN	LAN	44000	161	E5
75TH ST E	CO	LR	35000	184	E6
75TH ST E	CO	PALM		173	E2
75TH ST E	LA	LA01	600	52	C6
75TH ST E	LA	LA03	100	52	A6
75TH ST E	PALM	PALM	38000	173	E7
75TH ST W	CO	LAN	50400	146	J2
75TH ST W	LAN	LAN	45200	158	J3
75TH ST W	LA	LA03	100	52	A6
75TH ST W	LA	LA43	2200	51	C6
75TH ST W	LA	LA44	800	51	E6
75TH ST W	LA	LA44	500	52	A6
75TH ST W	LA	LA45	5700	50	D6
75TH ST W	LA	LA47	1800	51	C6
76TH PL E	CO	LA01	1100	52	C6
76TH PL E	LA	LA01	600	52	B6
76TH PL E	LA	LA03	100	52	B6
76TH PL W	LA	LA45	6000	50	D6
76TH ST E	CO	LA01	1100	52	C6
76TH ST E	CO	PALM		173	E2
76TH ST E	LA	LA01	600	52	C6
76TH ST E	LA	LA03	100	52	A6
76TH ST E	PALM	PALM	38000	173	E7
76TH ST W	CO	LAN	49400	146	J3
76TH ST W	LAN	LAN	45200	158	J3
76TH ST W	LA	LA03	100	52	A6
76TH ST W	LA	LA43	2200	51	C6
76TH ST W	LA	LA44	800	51	F6
76TH ST W	LA	LA44	500	52	A6
76TH ST W	LA	LA45	5400	50	D6
76TH ST W	LA	LA47	1400	51	C6
77TH PL E	LA	LA01	1100	52	C6
77TH PL W	LA	LA45	5800	50	D6
77TH ST E	CO	LA01	1100	52	C6
77TH ST E	CO	LR	34800	184	E6
77TH ST E	CO	PALM		173	E2
77TH ST E	LA	LA01	600	52	C6
77TH ST E	LA	LA03	100	52	A6
77TH ST E	PALM	PALM	38000	173	E7
77TH ST W	LAN	LAN	42100	158	H9
77TH ST W	ING	IN05	2200	51	C6
77TH ST W	LA	LA03	100	52	A6
77TH ST W	LA	LA43	3100	51	C6
77TH ST W	LA	LA44	800	51	E6
77TH ST W	LA	LA44	500	52	A6
77TH ST W	LA	LA45	5400	50	E6
77TH ST W	LA	LA45	5400	56	E1
77TH ST W	LA	LA47	1800	51	C6
78TH PL W	ING	IN05	2200	51	C6
78TH PL W	LA	LA43	3100	51	C6
78TH PL W	LA	LA45	5800	50	D6
78TH PL W	LA	LA47	1800	51	D6
78TH ST E	CO	LA01	1100	52	C6
78TH ST E	CO	PALM	40600	173	F4
78TH ST E	LA	LA01	600	52	C6
78TH ST E	LA	LA03	100	52	A6
78TH ST E	PALM	PALM	38000	173	E7
78TH ST W	LAN	LAN	42100	158	H9
78TH ST W	ING	IN05	2200	51	C6
78TH ST W	LA	LA03	100	52	A6
78TH ST W	LA	LA43	3100	51	C6
78TH ST W	LA	LA44	800	51	F6
78TH ST W	LA	LA44	500	52	A6
78TH ST W	LA	LA45	5500	50	D6
78TH ST W	LA	LA45	5500	56	D1
78TH ST W	LA	LA47	1400	51	C6
79TH PL	LA	LA45		50	C6
79TH ST	LA	VEN	7600	55A	E1
79TH ST E	LA	LA01	600	52	C6
79TH ST E	LA	LA03	100	52	A6
79TH ST W	ING	IN05	2200	51	D6
79TH ST W	LA	LA03	100	52	A6
79TH ST W	LA	LA43	3100	51	D6
79TH ST W	LA	LA44	800	51	F6
79TH ST W	LA	LA44	500	52	A6
79TH ST W	LA	LA45	5500	50	D6
79TH ST W	LA	LA45	5500	56	D1
79TH ST W	LA	LA47	1400	51	D6
80TH PL W	LA	LA45	6300	50	B6
80TH PL W	LA	LA45	6300	56	B1
80TH ST E	CO	LA01	1100	52	C6
80TH ST E	LAN	LAN	42800	161	E8
80TH ST E	CO	LAN	41200	173	E3
80TH ST E	CO	LR	34800	184	E6
80TH ST E	CO	PALM	40400	173	E4
80TH ST E	LA	LA01	600	52	C6
80TH ST E	LA	LA03	100	52	A6
80TH ST E	PALM	PALM	42000	173	E1
80TH ST W	CO	LAN	46600	146	H9
80TH ST W	LAN	LAN	42000	158	H8
80TH ST W	ING	IN05	2300	51	C6
80TH ST W	LA	LA03	100	52	A6
80TH ST W	LA	LA44	800	51	F6
80TH ST W	LA	LA44	500	52	A6
80TH ST W	LA	LA45	6300	50	B6
80TH ST W	LA	LA45	7400	55A	E1
80TH ST W	LA	LA47	1400	51	D6
80TH ST W	LA	VEN	7500	55A	E1
81ST PL W	LA	LA44	1000	57	F1
81ST ST	LA	VEN		55A	F1
81ST ST E	CO	LA01	1100	58	C1
81ST ST E	LAN	LAN	44200	161	E5
81ST ST E	CO	PALM		184	F1
81ST ST E	LA	LA01	600	58	B1
81ST ST E	LA	LA03	100	58	A1
81ST ST E	PALM	PALM	38800	173	E7
81ST ST E	PALM	PALM		184	F1
81ST ST W	CO	LAN	46600	146	H9
81ST ST W	ING	IN05	2200	57	C1
81ST ST W	LA	LA03	100	58	A1
81ST ST W	LA	LA44	800	57	F1
81ST ST W	LA	LA44	500	58	A1
81ST ST W	LA	LA45	7400	55A	F1
81ST ST W	LA	LA45	6300	56	B1
81ST ST W	LA	LA47	1400	57	D1
82ND PL E	CO	LA01	1500	58	D1
82ND PL E	LA	LA03	100	58	B1
82ND PL W	ING	IN05	2600	57	C1
82ND ST E	CO	LA01	1100	58	C1
82ND ST E	LAN	LAN	44200	161	F5
82ND ST E	CO	LR	34800	184	F6
82ND ST E	CO	PALM	36400	184	F5
82ND ST E	LA	LA01	600	58	B1
82ND ST E	LA	LA03	100	58	B1
82ND ST E	PALM	PALM	38800	173	F8
82ND ST E	PALM	PALM		184	F1
82ND ST W	CO	LAN	46600	146	H9
82ND ST W	LAN	LAN	42100	158	H5
82ND ST W	ING	IN05	2500	57	C1
82ND ST W	LA	LA03	100	58	B1
82ND ST W	LA	LA44	800	57	F1
82ND ST W	LA	LA44	500	58	A1
82ND ST W	LA	LA45	7400	55A	F1
82ND ST W	LA	LA45	5300	56	E1
82ND ST W	LA	LA47	1400	57	D1
83RD PL W	LA	LA44	1300	57	E1
83RD PL W	LA	LA45	6000	56	C1
83RD ST E	CO	LA01	1100	58	C1
83RD ST E	LAN	LAN	44200	161	F5
83RD ST E	CO	PALM	36600	184	F3
83RD ST E	LA	LA01	600	58	B1
83RD ST E	LA	LA03	100	58	B1
83RD ST W	LAN	LAN	42100	158	G2
83RD ST W	ING	IN05	2200	57	C1
83RD ST W	LA	LA03	100	58	A1
83RD ST W	LA	LA44	800	57	D1
83RD ST W	LA	LA44	500	58	A1
83RD ST W	LA	LA45	7400	55A	F1
83RD ST W	LA	LA45	5400	56	D1
83RD ST W	LA	LA47	1400	57	D1
83RD ST W	LA	VEN	7500	55A	F1
84TH PL E	CO	LA01	1100	58	C1
84TH PL E	LA	LA01	600	58	B1
84TH PL E	LA	LA03	100	58	B1
84TH PL W	ING	IN05	2200	57	C1
84TH PL W	LA	LA03	100	58	B1
84TH PL W	LA	LA44	1000	57	D1
84TH PL W	LA	LA45	6300	56	B1
84TH PL W	LA	LA47	1400	57	D1
84TH ST E	CO	LA01	1100	58	C1
84TH ST E	LA	LA01	600	58	B1
84TH ST E	LA	LA03	100	58	B1
84TH ST W	ING	IN05	2600	57	C1
84TH ST W	LA	LA03	100	58	A1
84TH ST W	LA	LA44	800	57	F1
84TH ST W	LA	LA44	500	58	A1
84TH ST W	LA	LA45	5900	56	D1
84TH ST W	LA	LA47	1400	57	D1
85TH PL W	LA	LA03	100	58	B1
85TH PL W	LA	LA45	5700	56	C1
85TH ST	CO	LAN		161	F5
85TH ST	LAN	LAN		161	F5
85TH ST E	CO	LA01	1100	58	C1
85TH ST E	CO	LR	35200	184	F6
85TH ST E	CO	PALM	36400	184	F6
85TH ST E	LA	LA01	600	58	B1
85TH ST E	LA	LA03	100	58	B1
85TH ST W	LAN	LAN	42800	158	G8
85TH ST W	ING	IN05	2400	57	C1
85TH ST W	LA	LA03	100	58	B1
85TH ST W	LA	LA44	800	57	F1
85TH ST W	LA	LA44	500	58	A1
85TH ST W	LA	LA45	7400	55A	F1
85TH ST W	LA	LA45	6300	56	C1
85TH ST W	LA	LA47	1400	57	D1
85TH ST W	LA	VEN	7500	55A	F1
86TH PL W	LA	LA03	100	58	B1
86TH PL W	LA	LA45	5900	56	D2
86TH ST E	LAN	LAN	44400	161	F5
86TH ST E	CO	PALM	36400	184	F3
86TH ST W	LAN	LAN	42100	158	G3
87TH PL E	CO	LA02	1100	58	C2
87TH PL E	LA	LA02	600	58	C2
87TH PL E	LA	LA03	100	58	B2
87TH PL W	LA	LA03	100	58	B2
87TH PL W	LA	LA45	7400	55A	F2
87TH PL W	LA	LA45	6400	56	C2
87TH ST E	CO	LA02	1100	58	C2
87TH ST E	LAN	LAN	44400	161	F5
87TH ST E	CO	LR	34600	184	F7
87TH ST E	CO	PALM	36800	184	F2
87TH ST E	LA	LA02	600	58	C2
87TH ST E	LA	LA03	100	58	A2
87TH ST W	CO	LA44	1000	57	E2
87TH ST W	LAN	LAN	42100	158	G8
87TH ST W	CO	PALM	39600	171I	G5
87TH ST W	LA	LA03	100	58	A2
87TH ST W	LA	LA44	500	58	A2
87TH ST W	LA	LA45	7400	55A	F2
87TH ST W	LA	LA47	1400	57	E2
88TH PL E	CO	LA02	1100	58	C2
88TH PL E	LA	LA02	600	58	C2
88TH PL E	LA	LA03	100	58	B2
88TH PL W	LA	LA03	100	58	B2
88TH PL W	LA	LA44	500	58	B2
88TH PL W	LA	LA45	7400	55A	F2
88TH PL W	LA	LA45	6400	56	C2
88TH PL W	LA	LA47	1400	57	E2
88TH ST E	CO	LA02	1100	58	C2
88TH ST E	CO	LAN		161	G5
88TH ST E	CO	PALM	38400	173	G8
88TH ST E	LA	LA02	800	58	C2
88TH ST E	LA	LA03	100	58	A2
88TH ST W	CO	LA44	1000	57	E2
88TH ST W	LAN	LAN	42100	158	G8
88TH ST W	ING	IN05	2200	57	C2
88TH ST W	LA	LA03	100	58	A2
88TH ST W	LA	LA44	800	57	E2
88TH ST W	LA	LA44	500	58	A2
88TH ST W	LA	LA45	7400	55A	F2
88TH ST W	LA	LA45	5800	56	D2
88TH ST W	LA	LA47	1400	57	E2
89TH ST E	CO	LA02	1100	58	C2
89TH ST E	CO	LR	35200	184	G5
89TH ST E	LA	LA02	600	58	C2
89TH ST E	LA	LA03	100	58	B2
89TH ST W	CO	LA44	1000	57	E2
89TH ST W	LA	LA03	100	58	B2
89TH ST W	LA	LA44	500	58	B2
89TH ST W	LA	LA45	7300	55A	F2
89TH ST W	LA	LA45	6200	56	C2
89TH ST W	LA	LA47	1400	57	E2
90TH PL W	CO	LA44	1000	57	E2
90TH PL W	LA	LA47	1400	57	E2
90TH ST E	CO	LA02	1100	58	C2
90TH ST E	CO	LAN	42800	161	G6
90TH ST E	CO	PALM	36400	184	F3
90TH ST E	LA	LA02	600	58	C2
90TH ST E	LA	LA03	100	58	B2
90TH ST E	PALM	PALM	42000	173	G1
90TH ST W	CO	LA44	1000	57	E2
90TH ST W	LAN	LAN	42500	158	F8
90TH ST W	CO	PALM	40000	171I	G5
90TH ST W	ING	IN05	2200	57	C2
90TH ST W	LA	LA03	100	58	B2
90TH ST W	LA	LA44	800	57	E2
90TH ST W	LA	LA44	500	58	B2
90TH ST W	LA	LA45	7300	55A	F2
90TH ST W	LA	LA45	6400	56	C2
90TH ST W	LA	LA47	1400	57	E2
91ST PL W	LA	LA03	300	58	A2
91ST PL W	LA	LA45		55A	F2
91ST PL W	LA	LA45	6400	56	C2
91ST PL W	LA	LA47	1400	57	E2
91ST ST E	CO	LA02	1100	58	C2
91ST ST E	CO	PALM	38400	173	G8
91ST ST E	LA	LA02	600	58	C2
91ST ST E	LA	LA03	100	58	B2
91ST ST E	PALM	PALM	42400	161	G9
91ST ST W	CO	LA44	1000	57	E2
91ST ST W	CO	LAN	47200	146	F8
91ST ST W	LAN	LAN		158	F6
91ST ST W	LA	LA03	100	58	B2
91ST ST W	LA	LA44	700	57	F2
91ST ST W	LA	LA44	750	58	A2
91ST ST W	LA	LA45	7300	55A	F2
91ST ST W	LA	LA45	7100	56	A2
91ST ST W	LA	LA47	1400	57	E2
92ND ST	LA	PDR		55A	F2
92ND ST E	CO	LA02	1100	58	D2
92ND ST E	CO	LAN	42100	161	G4
92ND ST E	CO	LR	35600	184	G5
92ND ST E	CO	PALM	36400	184	G5
92ND ST E	LA	LA02	600	58	C2
92ND ST E	LA	LA03	100	58	B2
92ND ST E	PALM	PALM	42400	161	G9
92ND ST W	CO	LA44	1000	57	E2
92ND ST W	CO	LAN	47200	146	F8
92ND ST W	CO	PALM	40000	171I	F5
92ND ST W	LA	LA03	100	58	B2
92ND ST W	LA	LA44	700	57	F2
92ND ST W	LA	LA44	500	58	B2
92ND ST W	LA	LA45	7300	55A	F2
92ND ST W	LA	LA45	6300	56	C2
92ND ST W	LA	LA47	1400	57	E2
93RD PL W	LA	LA45	7400	55A	F2
93RD PL W	LA	LA45	7100	56	A2
93RD ST E	CO	LA02	2200	58	E2
93RD ST E	CO	PALM	38400	173	G8
93RD ST E	LA	LA02	600	58	C2
93RD ST E	LA	LA03	100	58	B2
93RD ST E	PALM	PALM	42400	161	G9
93RD ST W	CO	LA44	1000	57	E2
93RD ST W	CO	LAN	47200	146	F8
93RD ST W	ING	IN01	400	56	F2
93RD ST W	LAN	LAN		158	F6
93RD ST W	LA	LA03	100	58	B2
93RD ST W	LA	LA44	900	57	E2
93RD ST W	LA	LA44	500	58	B2
93RD ST W	LA	LA45	5200	56	E2
93RD ST W	LA	LA47	1400	57	D2
94TH PL W	LA	LA45	7100	56	A2
94TH PL W	LA	LA47	1400	57	E2
94TH ST E	CO	LA02	1200	58	D2
94TH ST E	CO	LR	35600	184	H5
94TH ST E	CO	PALM	36400	184	H5
94TH ST E	ING	IN01	100	57	A2
94TH ST E	LA	LA02	600	58	C2
94TH ST E	LA	LA03	100	58	B2
94TH ST W	CO	LA44	1000	57	E2
94TH ST W	ING	IN01	200	56	F2
94TH ST W	ING	IN05	2800	57	C2
94TH ST W	LA	LA03	100	58	B2
94TH ST W	LA	LA44	700	57	E2
94TH ST W	LA	LA44	500	58	B2
94TH ST W	LA	LA45	5200	56	E2
94TH ST W	LA	LA47	1400	57	E2
95TH PL E	LA	LA02	1600	58	D2
95TH PL W	LA	LA45	5200	56	E3
95TH ST E	CO	LA02	2100	58	E2
95TH ST E	CO	LAN	44400	161	H7
95TH ST E	CO	LR		173	H9
95TH ST E	CO	PALM		173	H9
95TH ST E	CO	PALM	37100	184	H2
95TH ST E	LA	LA02	600	58	C3
95TH ST E	LA	LA03	100	58	B3
95TH ST E	PALM	PALM	42000	161	H9
95TH ST E	PALM	PALM	42000	173	H1
95TH ST W	CO	LA44	1000	57	E3
95TH ST W	CO	LA47	1400	57	E3
95TH ST W	CO	LAN	42100	158	F4
95TH ST W	CO	PALM	40000	171I	F5
95TH ST W	ING	IN01	400	56	F3
95TH ST W	ING	IN05	2800	57	C3
95TH ST W	LAN	LAN		158	E7
95TH ST W	LA	LA03	100	58	B3
95TH ST W	LA	LA44	700	57	F3
95TH ST W	LA	LA44	500	58	A3
95TH ST W	LA	LA45	5200	56	E3
95TH ST W	LA	LA47	1500	57	D3
96TH PL	LA	LA45		56	D3
96TH PL E	CO	LA02	2300	58	E3
96TH PL W	CO	LAN	44400	158	E5
96TH PL W	LA	LA47	2000	57	D3
96TH ST E	CO	LA02	1200	58	D3
96TH ST E	CO	LAN	44400	161	H7
96TH ST E	CO	LR	33600	184	H9
96TH ST E	CO	PALM	36400	184	H5
96TH ST E	LA	LA02	1400	58	D3
96TH ST E	PALM	PALM	42000	173	H1
96TH ST W	CO	LA44	1000	57	E3
96TH ST W	CO	LA47	1400	57	E3
96TH ST W	LAN	LAN	44400	158	E5
96TH ST W	ING	IN01	400	56	F3
96TH ST W	LA	LA45	5200	56	E3
96TH ST W	LA	LA47	1500	57	E3
97TH PL W	LA	LA45	5200	56	E3
97TH ST E	CO	LA02	2300	58	D3
97TH ST E	CO	LAN	44400	161	H7
97TH ST E	CO	LR		173	H9
97TH ST E	CO	PALM		173	H9
97TH ST E	CO	LR	37200	184	H2
97TH ST E	ING	IN01	300	57	A3
97TH ST E	LA	LA02	600	58	C3
97TH ST E	LA	LA03	100	58	B3
97TH ST E	PALM	PALM	42000	173	H1
97TH ST W	CO	LA44	1000	57	E3
97TH ST W	CO	LA47	1400	57	E3
97TH ST W	CO	LAN	50500	146	E1
97TH ST W	LAN	LAN	44400	158	E5
97TH ST W	CO	PALM	40000	171I	F5
97TH ST W	ING	IN01	400	56	F3
97TH ST W	LA	LA03	100	58	B3
97TH ST W	LA	LA44	700	57	E3
97TH ST W	LA	LA44	500	58	B3
97TH ST W	LA	LA45	5200	56	E3
97TH ST W	LA	LA47	1500	57	E3
98TH PL W	CO	LAN	44400	158	E5
98TH ST E	CO	LA02	1200	58	D3
98TH ST E	CO	PALM	36400	184	H3
98TH ST E	ING	IN01	100	57	A3
98TH ST E	LA	LA02	600	58	C3
98TH ST E	LA	LA03	100	58	B3
98TH ST E	PALM	PALM	42000	173	H1
98TH ST W	CO	LA44	1000	57	E3
98TH ST W	CO	LA47	1400	57	E3
98TH ST W	CO	LAN	50500	146	E1
98TH ST W	LAN	LAN	44400	158	E5
98TH ST W	CO	PALM	40000	171I	F5
98TH ST W	ING	IN01	100	56	F3
98TH ST W	LA	LA03	100	58	B3
98TH ST W	LA	LA44	700	57	E3
98TH ST W	LA	LA44	500	58	B3
98TH ST W	LA	LA45	5200	56	E3
98TH ST W	LA	LA47	1500	57	E3
99TH PL E	LA	LA02		58	E3
99TH PL W	LA	LA45	5300	56	E3
99TH ST E	CO	LA02	1200	58	D3
99TH ST E	ING	IN01	300	57	A3
99TH ST E	LA	LA02	600	58	C3
99TH ST E	LA	LA03	100	58	A3
99TH ST E	PALM	PALM	42000	173	H1
99TH ST W	CO	LA44	1000	57	E3
99TH ST W	CO	LA47	1400	57	E3
99TH ST W	CO	LAN	50500	146	E1
99TH ST W	CO	LAN	44400	158	E5
99TH ST W	ING	IN01	400	56	F3
99TH ST W	ING	IN05	3100	57	C3
99TH ST W	LA	LA03	100	58	A3
99TH ST W	LA	LA44	700	57	E3
99TH ST W	LA	LA44	500	58	A3
99TH ST W	LA	LA45	5300	56	E3
99TH ST W	LA	LA47	1500	57	E3
100TH ST E	CO	LA02	1200	58	D3
100TH ST E	CO	LAN	42800	161	H6
100TH ST E	CO	LR		171	H9
100TH ST E	CO	PALM		171	H9
100TH ST E	CO	LR	37200	184	H1
100TH ST E	LA	LA02	1400	58	D3
100TH ST E	PALM	LR		173	H1
100TH ST E	PALM	PALM	42000	173	H1
100TH ST W	LAN	LAN	44400	158	E5
100TH ST W	CO	PALM	40000	171I	E5
101ST ST E	CO	LR	33600	184	J9
101ST ST E	CO	PALM	36400	184	J3
101ST ST E	LA	LA02	700	58	C3
101ST ST E	LA	LA03	100	58	A3
101ST ST E	PALM	PALM		173	J1
101ST ST W	CO	IN04	5000	56	E3
101ST ST W	CO	LA44	1000	57	E3
101ST ST W	CO	LA47	1400	57	E3

1990 LOS ANGELES COUNTY STREET INDEX

STREET	CITY	P.O. ZONE	BLOCK	PAGE	GRID
101ST ST W	CO	LAN	47600	146	E7
101ST ST W	ING	IN03	2300	57	C3
101ST ST W	ING	IN04	4000	57	A3
101ST ST W	LA	LA03	100	58	A3
101ST ST W	LA	LA44	700	57	E3
101ST ST W	LA	LA44	500	58	A3
102ND ST E	CO	LR		171	J9
102ND ST E	CO	PALM		171	J9
102ND ST E	CO	PALM	37200	184	J1
102ND ST E	LA	LA02	700	58	C3
102ND ST E	LA	LA03	100	58	A3
102ND ST E	PALM	PALM		173	J1
102ND ST W	CO	LA44	1000	57	E3
102ND ST W	CO	LA47	1400	57	E3
102ND ST W	CO	LAN	47600	146	E7
102ND ST W	LAN	LAN	42800	158	E8
102ND ST W	ING	IN03	2200	57	C3
102ND ST W	ING	IN04	4000	57	A3
102ND ST W	LA	LA03	100	58	A3
102ND ST W	LA	LA44	700	57	E3
102ND ST W	LA	LA44	500	58	A3
102ND ST W	LA	LA45	5200	56	E3
103RD PL E	LA	LA02	700	58	C3
103RD PL W	CO	LA47	2000	57	D3
103RD ST E	CO	LA02	1200	58	C3
103RD ST E	CO	PALM	36400	184	J3
103RD ST E	LA	LA02	600	58	C3
103RD ST E	LA	LA03	100	58	A3
103RD ST E	PALM	PALM		173	J1
103RD ST W	CO	LA44	1000	57	D3
103RD ST W	CO	LA47	1400	57	D3
103RD ST W	CO	LAN	47600	146	D7
103RD ST W	LAN	LAN	42800	158	E8
103RD ST W	ING	IN04	4000	57	A3
103RD ST W	LA	LA03	100	58	A3
103RD ST W	LA	LA44	700	57	D3
103RD ST W	LA	LA44	500	58	A3
103RD ST W	LA	LA47	1500	57	D3
104TH PL	LA	LA44	500	58	A3
104TH PL E	LA	LA02	1500	58	D4
104TH PL W	LA	LA44	500	57	F3
104TH ST E	LA	LA02	600	58	C3
104TH ST E	LA	LA03	100	58	A3
104TH ST E	PALM	PALM		173	J1
104TH ST W	CO	LA44	1000	57	E3
104TH ST W	CO	LA47	1400	57	E3
104TH ST W	CO	LAN	47600	146	D7
104TH ST W	LAN	LAN	42800	158	D8
104TH ST W	ING	IN02	4500	56	F3
104TH ST W	ING	IN02	4000	57	A3
104TH ST W	ING	IN03	3100	57	C3
104TH ST W	ING	IN04	4000	57	A3
104TH ST W	LA	LA03	100	58	A3
104TH ST W	LA	LA44	700	57	E3
104TH ST W	LA	LA44	500	58	A3
104TH ST W	LA	LA45	5200	56	E3
104TH ST W	LA	LA47	1600	57	E3
105TH ST E	CO	LR		171	J9
105TH ST E	CO	PALM		171	J9
105TH ST E	CO	PALM	37200	184	J1
105TH ST E	LA	LA02	600	58	B4
105TH ST E	LA	LA03	100	58	B4
105TH ST E	PALM	PALM		173	J1
105TH ST W	CO	IN04	4000	57	A4
105TH ST W	CO	LA44	1000	57	E4
105TH ST W	CO	LA47	1400	57	E4
105TH ST W	CO	LAN	47600	146	D7
105TH ST W	LAN	LAN	42800	158	D8
105TH ST W	ING	IN03	3600	57	A4
105TH ST W	LA	LA03	100	58	A4
105TH ST W	LA	LA44	700	57	E4
105TH ST W	LA	LA44	500	58	A4
105TH ST W	LA	LA45	5400	56	E4
106TH ST E	CO	LR	30500	192	A6
106TH ST E	CO	PALM	36400	184	J4
106TH ST E	LA	LA02	600	58	B4
106TH ST E	LA	LA03	100	58	B4
106TH ST E	PALM	PALM		173	J1
106TH ST W	CO	IN04	4900	56	E4
106TH ST W	CO	IN04	4000	57	A4
106TH ST W	CO	LA44	1000	57	E4
106TH ST W	CO	LA47	1400	57	E4
106TH ST W	CO	LAN	50500	146	D1
106TH ST	LAN	LAN		158	D6
106TH ST W	ING	IN03	3600	57	A4
106TH ST W	LA	LA03	100	58	A4
106TH ST W	LA	LA44	700	57	E4
106TH ST W	LA	LA44	500	58	A4
106TH ST W	LA	LA47	1800	57	E4
107TH PL	LYN	LYN		58	F4
107TH PL E	CO	LA59	2400	58	F4
107TH ST E	CO	LR		185	A3
107TH ST E	LA	LA02	600	58	B4
107TH ST E	LA	LA03	100	58	A4
107TH ST E	PALM	PALM	41500	174	A1
107TH ST W	CO	IN04	4000	57	A4

STREET	CITY	P.O. ZONE	BLOCK	PAGE	GRID
107TH ST W	CO	LA44	1000	57	E4
107TH ST W	CO	LA47	1400	57	E4
107TH ST W	CO	LAN	50500	146	D1
107TH ST W	ING	IN03	3100	57	C4
107TH ST W	LAN	LAN		158	D6
107TH ST W	LA	LA03	100	58	A4
107TH ST W	LA	LA44	700	57	E4
107TH ST W	LA	LA44	500	58	A4
108TH ST E	CO	LA59	2400	58	E4
108TH ST E	CO	LR		185	A3
108TH ST E	CO	PEAR	33700	185	A9
108TH ST E	LA	LA59	600	58	B4
108TH ST E	LA	LA61	100	58	B4
108TH ST E	LYN	LYN	2600	58	F4
108TH ST E	PALM	PALM	41500	174	A1
108TH ST W	CO	LA44	1000	57	E4
108TH ST W	CO	LA47	1400	57	E4
108TH ST W	CO	LAN	50500	146	D1
108TH ST W	CO	LAN	44400	158	D5
108TH ST W	ING	IN03	2300	57	B4
108TH ST W	LA	LA44	700	57	E4
108TH ST W	LA	LA44	500	58	B4
108TH ST W	LA	LA47	1800	57	E4
108TH ST W	LA	LA61	100	58	B4
109TH PL E	LA	LA59	600	58	B4
109TH PL E	LA	LA61	100	58	B4
109TH PL W	CO	LA44	1000	57	E4
109TH PL W	CO	LA47	1400	57	E4
109TH PL W	LA	LA44	700	57	E4
109TH PL W	LA	LA44	500	58	A4
109TH PL W	LA	LA61	100	58	A4
109TH ST E	CO	LA59	2400	58	F4
109TH ST E	CO	LR		185	A3
109TH ST E	LA	LA59	600	58	C4
109TH ST E	LA	LA61	100	58	A4
109TH ST E	LYN	LYN	2600	58	F4
109TH ST W	CO	IN04	4900	56	E4
109TH ST W	CO	LA44	1000	57	E4
109TH ST W	CO	LA47	1600	57	E4
109TH ST W	CO	LAN	48000	146	D6
109TH ST W	ING	IN03	2300	57	B4
109TH ST W	LA	LA44	700	57	E4
109TH ST W	LA	LA44	500	58	A4
109TH ST W	LA	LA61	100	58	A4
110TH PL W	CO	LA47	1400	57	E4
110TH ST E	CO	LA59	2400	58	F4
110TH ST E	CO	LR		185	A3
110TH ST E	CO	PEAR	34400	185	A7
110TH ST E	LA	LA59	600	58	B4
110TH ST E	LA	LA61	100	58	B4
110TH ST E	LYN	LYN	2600	58	F4
110TH ST E	PALM	PALM	38800	174	A8
110TH ST W	CO	IN04	4800	56	F4
110TH ST W	CO	LA44	1000	57	E4
110TH ST W	CO	LA47	1400	57	E4
110TH ST W	CO	LAN	43000	158	C8
110TH ST W	ING	IN03	3100	57	B4
110TH ST W	LA	LA44	700	57	E4
110TH ST W	LA	LA44	500	58	A4
110TH ST W	LA	LA61	100	58	A4
111TH DR E	LA	LA59	800	58	C4
111TH PL E	LA	LA59	600	58	B4
111TH PL E	LA	LA61	100	58	B4
111TH PL W	CO	IN04	4800	56	F4
111TH PL W	CO	IN04	4300	57	A4
111TH PL W	CO	LA47	1400	57	E4
111TH PL W	ING	IN03	3100	57	B4
111TH PL W	LA	LA44	500	58	A4
111TH PL W	LA	LA61	100	58	A4
111TH ST	LA	LA45	5200	56	E4
111TH ST E	CO	LA59	2400	58	F4
111TH ST E	CO	LR		185	A3
111TH ST E	CO	PALM	38500	174	A8
111TH ST E	LA	LA59	600	58	B4
111TH ST E	LA	LA61	100	58	B4
111TH ST E	LYN	LYN	2600	58	F4
111TH ST E	PALM	PALM	41800	174	A1
111TH ST W	CO	IN04	4500	56	F4
111TH ST W	CO	IN04	4000	57	A4
111TH ST W	CO	LA44	1000	57	E4
111TH ST W	CO	LA47	1400	57	E4
111TH ST W	CO	LAN	50000	146	C2
111TH ST W	ING	IN03	2200	57	D4
111TH ST W	LA	LA44	700	57	F4
111TH ST W	LA	LA44	500	58	A4
111TH ST W	LA	LA61	100	58	A4
112TH PL E	CO	LA59	2400	58	E4
112TH ST	HAW	IN03	4100	57	A4
112TH ST E	CO	LR		185	A3
112TH ST E	CO	LR		192	A6
112TH ST E	CO	PEAR	34400	185	A7
112TH ST E	LA	LA59	600	58	C4
112TH ST E	LA	LA61	100	58	A4
112TH ST E	LYN	LYN	2600	58	F4
112TH ST E	PALM	PALM	38800	174	A7
112TH ST W	CO	IN04	4800	56	F4

STREET	CITY	P.O. ZONE	BLOCK	PAGE	GRID
112TH ST W	CO	IN04	4100	57	A4
112TH ST W	CO	LA44	1000	57	E4
112TH ST W	CO	LA47	1400	57	E4
112TH ST W	CO	LAN	50000	146	C2
112TH ST W	ING	IN03	2300	57	B4
112TH ST W	LA	LA44	700	57	F4
112TH ST W	LA	LA44	500	58	A4
112TH ST W	LA	LA61	100	58	A4
113TH ST E	CO	LA59	2400	58	E4
113TH ST E	CO	LR	34100	185	B8
113TH ST E	CO	LR	31000	192	B6
113TH ST E	CO	PALM	36900	185	B2
113TH ST E	LA	LA59	600	58	C5
113TH ST E	LA	LA61	100	58	A5
113TH ST E	PALM	PALM	38800	174	A7
113TH ST W	CO	IN04	4800	56	F4
113TH ST W	CO	LA47	1400	57	E5
113TH ST W	CO	LAN	50000	146	C2
113TH ST W	ING	IN03	3100	57	B5
113TH ST W	LA	LA44	700	57	F5
113TH ST W	LA	LA44	500	58	A5
113TH ST W	LA	LA61	100	58	A5
114TH ST E	CO	LA59	2400	58	E5
114TH ST E	CO	LR	34100	185	B8
114TH ST E	LA	LA59	900	58	C5
114TH ST W	CO	LAN	50000	146	C2
115TH PL	HAW	IN03	2300	57	D5
115TH PL E	CO	LA59	2400	58	F5
115TH PL W	LA	LA44	800	57	F5
115TH PL W	LA	LA61	300	58	A5
115TH ST	HAW	HAW	4500	56	F5
115TH ST	HAW	HAW	3600	57	A5
115TH ST	HAW	IN03	2200	57	D5
115TH ST	HAW	LA47	2000	57	D5
115TH ST E	CO	LA59	2400	58	E5
115TH ST E	CO	LR	34100	185	B8
115TH ST E	LA	LA59	600	58	B5
115TH ST E	LA	LA61	300	58	B5
115TH ST E	PALM	LR		174	A9
115TH ST E	PALM	PALM	38800	174	A7
115TH ST W	CO	LA47	1800	57	D5
115TH ST W	CO	LAN	50000	146	C2
115TH ST W	CO	LAN	44800	158	C4
115TH ST W	ING	IN03	3200	57	B5
115TH ST W	LA	HAW	4800	56	E5
115TH ST W	LA	LA44	700	57	F5
115TH ST W	LA	LA44	500	58	A5
115TH ST W	LA	LA45	5000	56	E5
115TH ST W	LA	LA61	100	58	A5
116TH PL E	CO	LA59	1500	58	D5
116TH PL E	LA	LA59	600	58	B5
116TH PL W	LA	LA61	100	58	A5
116TH ST	HAW	HAW	4500	56	F5
116TH ST	HAW	HAW	3700	57	A5
116TH ST	HAW	IN03	2200	57	D5
116TH ST	HAW	LA47	2000	57	D5
116TH ST E	CO	LR	34100	185	B8
116TH ST E	CO	LR		192	B6
116TH ST E	CO	PALM	36400	185	B3
116TH ST E	LA	LA59	600	58	B5
116TH ST E	LA	LA61	100	58	B5
116TH ST E	PALM	PALM	38800	174	A7
116TH ST W	CO	IN04	5200	56	E5
116TH ST W	CO	LAN	50200	146	B2
116TH ST W	ING	IN03	3000	57	B5
116TH ST W	LA	HAW	4800	56	E5
116TH ST W	LA	LA44	700	57	F5
116TH ST W	LA	LA44	500	58	A5
116TH ST W	LA	LA45	5000	56	E5
116TH ST W	LA	LA61	100	58	A5
117TH PL E	CO	LA59	1500	58	D5
117TH PL W	ING	IN03	3200	57	C5
117TH ST	HAW	HAW	4500	56	F5
117TH ST	HAW	HAW	3700	57	A5
117TH ST	HAW	IN03	2300	57	D5
117TH ST E	CO	LA59	1500	58	D5
117TH ST E	CO	PALM	36400	185	B3
117TH ST E	CO	PEAR	34300	185	B8
117TH ST E	LA	LA59	600	58	A5
117TH ST E	LA	LA61	100	58	A5
117TH ST W	CO	HAW	5000	56	E5
117TH ST W	CO	IN04	5200	56	E5
117TH ST W	CO	LA44	1000	57	F5
117TH ST W	CO	LA47	1900	57	D5
117TH ST W	CO	LAN	50200	146	B2
117TH ST W	ING	IN03	3000	57	B5
117TH ST W	LA	LA44	700	57	F5
117TH ST W	LA	LA44	500	58	A5
117TH ST W	LA	LA61	100	58	A5
118TH DR E	LA	LA59	800	58	C5
118TH PL	HAW	HAW	4800	56	F5
118TH PL	HAW	HAW	3700	57	B5
118TH PL	HAW	IN03	2500	57	D5
118TH PL E	CO	LA59	1500	58	D5
118TH PL E	LA	LA59	600	58	C5
118TH PL E	LA	LA61	100	58	A5

STREET	CITY	P.O. ZONE	BLOCK	PAGE	GRID
118TH PL W	CO	HAW	5000	56	F5
118TH PL W	CO	IN04	5200	56	E5
118TH PL W	ING	IN03	3000	57	B5
118TH PL W	LA	LA61	100	58	A5
118TH ST	HAW	HAW	4500	56	E5
118TH ST	HAW	HAW	3700	57	A5
118TH ST	HAW	IN03	2400	57	D5
118TH ST E	CO	LA59	1200	58	D5
118TH ST E	CO	LR		192	B6
118TH ST E	CO	PALM	37600	185	B1
118TH ST E	LA	LA59	600	58	B5
118TH ST E	LA	LA61	100	58	B5
118TH ST E	PALM	PALM	38800	174	B7
118TH ST W	CO	HAW	5000	56	E5
118TH ST W	CO	IN04	5200	56	E5
118TH ST W	CO	LA44	1200	57	F5
118TH ST W	CO	LA47	1800	57	D5
118TH ST W	CO	LAN	50700	146	B1
118TH ST W	ING	IN03	3200	57	B5
118TH ST W	LA	LA44	700	57	F5
118TH ST W	LA	LA44	500	58	A5
118TH ST W	LA	LA61	100	58	B5
119TH PL	HAW	HAW	4800	56	F5
119TH PL	HAW	HAW	3700	57	B5
119TH PL W	CO	HAW	5000	56	F5
119TH PL W	CO	IN04	5200	56	E5
119TH PL W	CO	LA44	1000	57	F5
119TH PL W	ING	IN03	3100	57	C5
119TH ST	HAW	HAW	4800	56	F5
119TH ST	HAW	HAW	3700	57	A5
119TH ST	HAW	IN03	2200	57	C5
119TH ST E	CO	LA59	1500	58	D5
119TH ST E	LA	LA59	600	58	B5
119TH ST E	LA	LA61	100	58	B5
119TH ST W	CO	HAW	5000	56	F5
119TH ST W	CO	IN04	5200	56	E5
119TH ST W	CO	LA44	1000	57	F5
119TH ST W	CO	LAN	50000	146	B2
119TH ST W	ING	IN03	3200	57	C5
119TH ST W	LA	LA44	500	58	A5
119TH ST W	LA	LA61	100	58	B5
120TH ST	HAW	HAW	4500	56	F5
120TH ST	HAW	HAW	2200	57	A5
120TH ST	HAW	LA47	2000	57	D5
120TH ST E	CO	LA59	1200	58	C5
120TH ST E	CO	LAN	38800	174	C5
120TH ST E	CO	PALM	37600	185	C1
120TH ST E	LA	LA59	600	58	A5
120TH ST E	LA	LA61	100	58	A5
120TH ST W	CO	HAW	5000	56	F5
120TH ST W	CO	IN04	5200	56	E5
120TH ST W	CO	LA44	1000	57	E5
120TH ST W	CO	LA47	1400	57	E5
120TH ST W	CO	LAN	43600	158	B6
120TH ST W	ING	IN03	3100	57	C5
120TH ST W	LA	LA44	700	57	E5
120TH ST W	LA	LA44	500	58	A5
120TH ST W	LA	LA61	100	58	A5
121ST PL E	CO	LA59	600	58	C6
121ST PL W	CO	LA61	100	58	B6
121ST ST	HAW	HAW	4800	56	F6
121ST ST E	CO	COM	2200	58	E6
121ST ST E	CO	LA59	600	58	A6
121ST ST E	CO	LA61	100	58	A6
121ST ST E	CO	LAN	39200	174	C6
121ST ST E	CO	LR	30500	192	C6
121ST ST E	CO	PALM	38000	174	C9
121ST ST E	CO	PEAR		185	C9
121ST ST E	CO	PEAR	32500	192	C2
121ST ST W	CO	HAW	5000	56	E5
121ST ST W	CO	LA44	1000	57	E5
121ST ST W	CO	LA47	1400	57	E5
121ST ST W	CO	LA61	100	58	A6
121ST ST W	CO	LAN	43600	158	B6
121ST ST W	LA	LA44	500	58	A6
122ND PL E	CO	LA59	1400	58	D6
122ND ST	HAW	HAW	4800	56	E6
122ND ST	HAW	HAW	4000	57	A6
122ND ST E	CO	COM	1900	58	E6
122ND ST E	CO	LA59	600	58	A6
122ND ST E	CO	LA61	100	58	A6
122ND ST E	CO	LAN	39200	174	C6
122ND ST E	CO	PALM	38000	174	C9
122ND ST E	CO	PEAR		185	C1
122ND ST E	CO	PEAR	32500	192	C2
122ND ST W	CO	HAW	5000	56	E6
122ND ST W	CO	LA44	1000	57	E6
122ND ST W	CO	LA47	1400	57	E6
122ND ST W	CO	LA61	100	58	A6
122ND ST W	CO	LAN	43600	158	B6
123RD PL	HAW	HAW	4800	56	E6
123RD PL W	CO	HAW	5000	56	E6
123RD ST	HAW	HAW	4800	56	E6
123RD ST E	CO	COM	2100	58	E6
123RD ST E	CO	LA59	1100	58	C6
123RD ST E	CO	LAN	39400	174	C6

STREET	CITY	P.O. ZONE	BLOCK	PAGE	GRID
123RD ST E	CO	LR	30500	192	C6
123RD ST E	CO	PALM	38000	174	C9
123RD ST E	CO	PEAR	32500	192	C2
123RD ST W	CO	HAW	5000	56	E6
123RD ST W	CO	LA44	1000	57	E6
123RD ST W	CO	LA47	1400	57	E6
123RD ST W	CO	LA61	100	58	B6
123RD ST W	CO	LAN	49300	146	A4
123RD ST W	LA	LA44	700	57	E6
124TH PL W	CO	HAW	5200	56	E6
124TH ST	HAW	HAW	4800	56	E6
124TH ST E	CO	COM	1600	58	D6
124TH ST E	CO	LA59	1100	58	C6
124TH ST E	CO	LA61	100	58	B6
124TH ST E	CO	PALM	38000	174	C9
124TH ST E	CO	PEAR		185	C7
124TH ST W	CO	HAW	5000	56	E6
124TH ST W	CO	LA44	1000	57	E6
124TH ST W	CO	LA47	1400	57	E6
124TH ST W	CO	LA61	100	58	B6
124TH ST W	CO	LAN	49300	146	A4
124TH ST W	LA	LA44	700	57	F6
124TH ST W	LA	LA44	500	58	A6
125TH ST	HAW	HAW	4600	56	F6
125TH ST E	CO	COM	1400	58	D6
125TH ST E	CO	LA59	1100	58	D6
125TH ST E	CO	LAN	38800	174	C5
125TH ST E	CO	LR	30500	192	C6
125TH ST E	CO	PALM	38000	174	C9
125TH ST W	CO	HAW	5000	56	E6
125TH ST W	CO	LA44	1000	57	E6
125TH ST W	CO	LA47	1400	57	E6
125TH ST W	CO	LAN	49300	146	A4
125TH ST W	LA	LA44	800	57	F6
126TH ST	HAW	HAW	3600	57	A6
126TH ST E	CO	COM	1400	58	D6
126TH ST E	CO	LA59	800	58	C6
126TH ST E	CO	LA61	100	58	B6
126TH ST E	CO	LAN	45200	174	D7
126TH ST E	CO	LR	30500	192	D6
126TH ST E	CO	PALM	35400	185	C3
126TH ST E	CO	PEAR		185	D8
126TH ST E	CO	PEAR	33200	192	C1
126TH ST W	CO	HAW	5000	56	E6
126TH ST W	CO	LA44	1000	57	E6
126TH ST W	CO	LA47	1400	57	E6
126TH ST W	CO	LA61	100	58	B6
126TH ST W	CO	LAN	49300	146	A4
126TH ST W	LA	LA44	700	57	F6
127TH PL E	COM	COM	1600	58	D6
127TH PL W	CO	HAW	5200	56	E6
127TH ST E	CO	COM	1400	58	D6
127TH ST E	CO	LA59	1100	58	D6
127TH ST E	CO	LA61	100	58	B6
127TH ST E	CO	LAN	39000	174	D7
127TH ST E	CO	PALM	37900	174	D9
127TH ST E	CO	PEAR		185	D8
127TH ST E	CO	PEAR		192	D6
127TH ST W	CO	HAW	5200	56	E6
127TH ST W	CO	LA44	1000	57	E6
127TH ST W	CO	LA47	1400	57	E6
127TH ST W	CO	LA61	100	58	B6
127TH ST W	CO	LAN	49300	146	A4
127TH ST W	COM	COM	900	58	D6
127TH ST W	LA	LA44	500	58	A6
128TH ST E	CO	LAN	39000	174	D7
128TH ST E	CO	PALM	37900	174	D9
128TH ST E	CO	PEAR		185	D8
128TH ST W	CO	LAN	49300	146	A4
128TH ST W	CO	LAN	43600	158	A6
129TH PL	GAR	GAR	3000	63	C1
129TH PL E	COM	COM	1600	64	D1
129TH ST	HAW	HAW	4600	62	F1
129TH ST	HAW	HAW	4000	63	A1
129TH ST E	CO	COM	2500	58	F6
129TH ST E	CO	LA61	300	64	B1
129TH ST E	CO	PEAR		185	D8
129TH ST W	CO	GAR	1100	63	F1
129TH ST W	CO	HAW	4700	62	F1
129TH ST W	CO	LA61	300	64	A1
129TH ST W	CO	LAN	49300	146	A4
129TH ST W	COM	COM	900	58	D6
129TH ST W	GAR	GAR	1000	63	D1
130TH ST	HAW	HAW	4600	62	F1
130TH ST	HAW	HAW	3700	63	A1
130TH ST E	CO	COM	2000	64	E1
130TH ST E	CO	LA59	900	64	C1
130TH ST E	CO	LA61	100	64	B1
130TH ST E	CO	LAN	40400	174	D4
130TH ST E	CO	PALM	37200	185	D2
130TH ST E	CO	PEAR		185	D8
130TH ST W	CO	HAW	4800	62	F1
130TH ST W	CO	LA61	300	64	B1
130TH ST W	CO	LAN	45200	158	A3
130TH ST W	COM	COM	800	64	D1

COPYRIGHT, © 1989 BY Thomas Bros Maps

STREET	CITY	P.O. ZONE	BLOCK	PAGE	GRID
130TH ST W	LA	GAR	700	63	F1
131ST ST	HAW	HAW	4600	62	F1
131ST ST	HAW	HAW	3100	63	A1
131ST ST E	CO	COM	2000	64	E1
131ST ST E	CO	LA59	700	64	C1
131ST ST E	CO	LA61	300	64	B1
131ST ST E	CO	PALM	38400	174	D8
131ST ST E	CO	PEAR	32400	192	D2
131ST ST E	CO	VAL	30500	192	D6
131ST ST W	CO	GAR	1000	63	F1
131ST ST W	CO	HAW	4800	62	F1
131ST ST W	CO	LA61	100	64	A1
131ST ST W	CO	LAN	44400	157	J2
131ST ST W	COM	COM	800	64	D1
131ST ST W	LA	GAR	700	63	F1
132ND PL	GAR	GAR		63	C1
132ND PL	HAW	HAW	3600	63	B1
132ND ST	HAW	HAW	4600	62	F1
132ND ST	HAW	HAW	3600	63	A1
132ND ST E	CO	LA61	100	64	B1
132ND ST E	CO	LA61	100	64	B1
132ND ST E	CO	LAN	40500	174	D4
132ND ST E	CO	PALM	37200	185	D1
132ND ST E	CO	PEAR	33500	185	D9
132ND ST E	COM	LA59	800	64	C1
132ND ST W	CO	HAW	4700	62	E1
132ND ST W	CO	HAW	3100	63	B1
132ND ST W	CO	LA61	300	64	A1
132ND ST W	CO	LA61	300	64	A1
132ND ST W	CO	LAN	44400	157	J3
132ND ST W	COM	COM	800	64	D1
132ND ST W	GAR	GAR	1000	63	D1
132ND ST W	LA	GAR	700	63	F1
133RD ST	HAW	HAW	4600	62	F1
133RD ST	HAW	HAW	3600	63	A1
133RD ST E	CO	COM	2500	64	F1
133RD ST E	CO	LAN	40400	174	D4
133RD ST E	CO	PEAR		185	E9
133RD ST E	CO	PEAR		192	E6
133RD ST E	COM	COM	1500	64	D1
133RD ST W	CO	HAW	4700	62	E1
133RD ST W	CO	HAW	3100	63	C1
133RD ST W	CO	LA61	300	64	A1
133RD ST W	CO	LAN	44400	157	J2
133RD ST W	GAR	GAR	1000	63	F1
133RD ST W	LA	GAR	700	63	F1
134TH PL	HAW	HAW	5400	62	E1
134TH PL	HAW	HAW	3800	63	B1
134TH PL E	COM	COM	1600	64	D1
134TH PL W	CO	HAW	4700	62	E1
134TH PL W	CO	HAW	3100	63	C1
134TH PL W	GAR	GAR	1000	63	F1
134TH ST	GAR	GAR	1200	63	E1
134TH ST	HAW	HAW	4600	62	F1
134TH ST	HAW	HAW	3500	63	B1
134TH ST E	CO	COM	2500	64	F1
134TH ST E	CO	LAN	40400	174	E4
134TH ST E	CO	PEAR		185	E9
134TH ST W	CO	HAW	4700	62	E1
134TH ST W	CO	HAW	3100	63	B1
134TH ST W	CO	LA61	100	64	A1
134TH ST W	CO	LAN	44400	157	J2
134TH ST W	COM	COM	800	64	D1
134TH ST W	COM	LA59	2100	64	C1
134TH ST W	LA	GAR	700	63	F1
135TH PL	GAR	GAR		63	C1
135TH ST	HAW	HAW	4600	62	F1
135TH ST	HAW	HAW	3500	63	B1
135TH ST E	CO	COM	2500	64	F1
135TH ST E	CO	LA59	600	64	B1
135TH ST E	CO	LA61	100	64	B1
135TH ST E	CO	PEAR		185	E9
135TH ST E	COM	LA59	2100	64	B1
135TH ST W	CO	HAW	4700	62	E1
135TH ST W	CO	LA61	300	64	B1
135TH ST W	CO	LAN	44400	157	J2
135TH ST W	GAR	GAR	1000	63	E1
135TH ST W	HAW	HAW	3100	63	B1
135TH ST W	LA	GAR	700	63	F1
135TH ST W	LA	GAR	500	64	B1
136TH ST	GAR	GAR		63	C1
136TH ST	HAW	HAW	4600	62	F1
136TH ST	HAW	HAW	4000	63	A1
136TH ST E	CO	LA59	600	64	C1
136TH ST E	CO	LA61	100	64	B1
136TH ST E	CO	LAN	38800	174	E7
136TH ST E	CO	PALM	35200	185	E4
136TH ST E	CO	PEAR		185	E9
136TH ST W	CO	HAW	4700	62	E1
136TH ST W	COM	COM	800	64	D1
136TH ST W	LA	GAR	700	63	F1
137TH PL	HAW	HAW	4600	62	F2
137TH PL	HAW	HAW	4400	63	A2
137TH PL W	CO	GAR	1100	63	F2
137TH PL W	CO	HAW	4700	62	F2
137TH PL W	LA	GAR	700	63	F2

STREET	CITY	P.O. ZONE	BLOCK	PAGE	GRID
137TH ST	GAR	GAR		63	C1
137TH ST	HAW	HAW	4600	62	F1
137TH ST	HAW	HAW	4000	63	A2
137TH ST E	CO	LA59	600	64	C1
137TH ST E	CO	LA61	100	64	B1
137TH ST E	CO	LAN	38800	174	E7
137TH ST E	CO	PALM	37200	185	E2
137TH ST E	CO	PEAR	34600	185	E7
137TH ST W	CO	HAW	4700	62	E1
137TH ST W	COM	COM	1000	64	D1
137TH ST W	GAR	GAR	1200	63	F2
137TH ST W	LA	GAR	700	63	F2
138TH PL	HAW	HAW	5300	62	E2
138TH ST	GAR	GAR	1100	63	F2
138TH ST	HAW	HAW	4600	62	F2
138TH ST	HAW	HAW	4000	63	A2
138TH ST	LA	GAR		64	A2
138TH ST E	CO	LA59	600	64	C2
138TH ST E	CO	LA61	200	64	B2
138TH ST E	CO	LAN	38800	174	E6
138TH ST W	CO	HAW	4700	62	E2
138TH ST W	COM	COM	1000	64	D2
138TH ST W	LA	GAR	700	63	F2
139TH PL	GAR	GAR		63	C2
139TH ST	HAW	HAW	5300	62	E2
139TH ST	HAW	HAW	3100	63	B2
139TH ST E	CO	LA59	600	64	C2
139TH ST E	CO	LA61	100	64	B2
139TH ST W	CO	HAW	4700	62	E2
139TH ST W	GAR	GAR	1200	63	E2
139TH ST W	LA	GAR	700	63	F2
140TH ST	HAW	HAW	4600	62	F2
140TH ST	HAW	HAW	4400	63	A2
140TH ST E	CO	COM	1200	64	C2
140TH ST E	CO	LA61	400	64	B2
140TH ST E	CO	LAN	38800	174	F7
140TH ST E	CO	PALM	37200	185	F2
140TH ST W	CO	HAW	4700	62	E2
140TH ST W	CO	LA61	200	64	B2
140TH ST W	GAR	GAR		63	C2
140TH ST W	LA	GAR	700	63	F2
140TH ST W	LA	GAR	500	64	A2
141ST PL	GAR	GAR	1300	63	C2
141ST ST	GAR	GAR		63	C2
141ST ST	HAW	HAW	4600	62	F2
141ST ST	HAW	HAW	4000	63	A2
141ST ST E	CO	COM	1200	64	C2
141ST ST E	CO	LAN	38800	174	F7
141ST ST E	CO	PALM	35200	185	F7
141ST ST E	CO	PEAR	34800	185	F7
141ST ST W	CO	HAW	4700	62	E2
141ST ST W	LA	GAR	700	63	F2
142ND PL	HAW	HAW	5300	62	E2
142ND ST	HAW	HAW	4600	62	F2
142ND ST	HAW	HAW	4000	63	A2
142ND ST E	CO	COM	1200	64	C2
142ND ST E	CO	LAN	38800	174	F7
142ND ST E	CO	PALM	37200	185	F2
142ND ST W	CO	HAW	4700	62	E2
142ND ST W	LA	GAR	700	63	F2
142ND WY	HAW	HAW	5300	62	E2
143RD PL W	CO	GAR	2900	63	C2
143RD ST E	CO	LAN	38800	174	F7
144TH PL	GAR	GAR	1200	63	F2
144TH PL	HAW	HAW	3600	63	B2
144TH ST	GAR	GAR		63	F2
144TH ST	HAW	HAW	3600	63	B2
144TH ST E	CO	COM	1100	64	C2
144TH ST E	PAR	PAR	8100	65	F2
144TH ST W	CO	GAR	1700	63	D2
144TH ST W	CO	LAW	5300	62	E2
144TH ST W	LA	GAR	700	63	F2
145TH PL	GAR	GAR	1300	63	E2
145TH ST	GAR	GAR	1100	63	F2
145TH ST	HAW	HAW	3600	63	B2
145TH ST	HAW	LAW	4800	62	F2
145TH ST E	CO	COM	700	64	C2
145TH ST E	CO	LAN	39300	174	F7
145TH ST E	CO	PALM	37200	185	F1
145TH ST W	CO	GAR	2000	63	D2
145TH ST W	CO	LAW	5300	62	E2
145TH ST W	COM	COM	1500	64	D2
145TH ST W	LA	GAR	700	63	F2
145TH ST W	LAW	LAW	4500	62	F2
145TH ST W	LAW	LAW	4000	63	A2
146TH PL W	CO	GAR	2000	63	D2
146TH ST	CO	COM	800	64	C2
146TH ST	GAR	GAR		63	F2
146TH ST	HAW	HAW	3600	63	B2
146TH ST E	CO	PALM	38000	174	G8
146TH ST E	CO	PEAR	33200	185	G6
146TH ST W	CO	GAR	2000	63	D2
146TH ST W	CO	GAR	100	64	B2
146TH ST W	CO	LAW	5300	62	E2
146TH ST W	LA	GAR	700	63	F2
146TH ST W	LA	GAR	500	64	A2

STREET	CITY	P.O. ZONE	BLOCK	PAGE	GRID
147TH PL	HAW	HAW	3800	63	B3
147TH ST	GAR	GAR		63	E2
147TH ST	HAW	LAW	4800	62	F2
147TH ST E	CO	LAN	38800	174	G5
147TH ST E	CO	PALM	38000	174	G8
147TH ST W	CO	GAR	3100	63	C2
147TH ST W	CO	HAW	3300	63	C2
147TH ST W	CO	LAN	46000	157	G1
147TH ST W	LA	GAR	700	63	F2
147TH ST W	LA	GAR	500	64	A2
147TH ST W	LAW	LAW	4500	62	F2
147TH ST W	LAW	LAW	4000	63	A2
148TH DR W	LA	GAR	700	63	F3
148TH PL	GAR	GAR		63	E3
148TH PL	HAW	HAW	3600	63	B3
148TH PL W	LA	GAR	700	63	F3
148TH ST	GAR	GAR		63	D3
148TH ST	HAW	HAW	3800	63	B3
148TH ST E	CO	COM	900	64	C2
148TH ST E	CO	LAN	38800	174	G4
148TH ST E	CO	PALM	38000	174	G8
148TH ST W	LA	GAR	700	63	F2
148TH ST W	LA	GAR	500	64	A2
148TH ST W	LAW	LAW	4600	62	F3
149TH DR W	LA	GAR	700	63	F3
149TH ST	GAR	GAR		63	D3
149TH ST	HAW	HAW	3900	63	B3
149TH ST E	CO	COM	1000	64	C3
149TH ST E	CO	GAR	400	64	B3
149TH ST E	CO	PALM	38000	174	G8
149TH ST W	LA	GAR	700	63	F3
149TH ST W	LA	GAR	500	64	A3
149TH ST W	LAW	LAW	4500	62	F3
149TH ST W	LAW	LAW	4000	63	A3
150TH ST	GAR	GAR	1100	63	D3
150TH ST E	CO	COM	1000	64	C3
150TH ST E	CO	LAN	40400	174	G4
150TH ST E	CO	PALM	38000	174	G8
151ST ST E	CO	LAN	40600	174	G2
151ST ST E	CO	PALM	38000	174	G8
151ST ST W	COM	COM	900	64	D3
152ND PL W	CO	GAR	3100	63	C3
152ND ST	GAR	GAR		63	D3
152ND ST E	CO	GAR	100	64	B3
152ND ST E	CO	LAN	40400	174	G4
152ND ST E	CO	PALM	38400	174	H8
152ND ST W	CO	GAR	2200	63	C3
152ND ST W	CO	LAN	46000	157	F1
152ND ST W	CO	LAW	3600	63	B3
152ND ST W	COM	COM	900	64	D3
152ND ST W	LA	GAR	500	64	A3
152ND ST W	LAW	LAW	4500	62	F3
153RD PL W	LAW	LAW	4500	62	F3
153RD ST	CO	GAR	3200	63	C3
153RD ST	GAR	GAR		63	D3
153RD ST E	CO	LAN	38800	174	H5
153RD ST E	CO	PALM	37800	174	H9
153RD ST E	CO	PALM	38400	174	H8
153RD ST W	COM	COM	1200	64	D3
153RD ST W	LAW	LAW	4500	62	F3
153RD ST W	LAW	LAW	4100	63	A3
154TH PL	GAR	GAR		63	D3
154TH PL W	CO	GAR	3200	63	C3
154TH ST	GAR	GAR		63	D3
154TH ST E	CO	COM	600	64	B3
154TH ST E	CO	GAR	500	64	B3
154TH ST E	CO	LAN	40500	174	H4
154TH ST E	CO	PALM	38400	174	H8
154TH ST W	CO	GAR	2200	63	C3
154TH ST W	CO	GAR	100	64	B3
154TH ST W	CO	LAW	3600	63	A3
154TH ST W	COM	COM	1200	64	D3
154TH ST W	LA	GAR	700	63	F3
154TH ST W	LAW	LAW	4500	62	F3
154TH ST W	LAW	LAW	4000	63	A3
155TH CT	GAR	GAR	1800	63	D3
155TH ST	GAR	GAR		63	E3
155TH ST E	CO	LAN	40400	174	H4
155TH ST E	CO	PALM	38400	174	H8
155TH ST W	CO	GAR	2200	63	C3
155TH ST W	CO	GAR	100	64	A3
155TH ST W	COM	COM	1200	64	D3
155TH ST W	LA	GAR	700	63	F3
155TH ST W	LA	GAR	500	64	A3
156TH CT	GAR	GAR	1800	63	D3
156TH PL	GAR	GAR	1100	63	F3
156TH ST	GAR	GAR		63	F3
156TH ST E	CO	LAN	38400	174	H5
156TH ST E	CO	PALM	38400	174	H8
156TH ST W	CO	GAR	2200	63	C3
156TH ST W	CO	LAW	3600	63	B3
156TH ST W	COM	COM	800	64	C3
156TH ST W	LA	GAR	700	63	F3
156TH ST W	LA	GAR	500	64	A3
156TH ST W	LAW	LAW	4500	62	F3
156TH ST W	LAW	LAW	4100	63	A3

STREET	CITY	P.O. ZONE	BLOCK	PAGE	GRID
157TH ST E	CO	COM	600	64	C3
157TH ST E	CO	GAR	100	64	A3
157TH ST E	CO	LLAN	32200	192	H3
157TH ST E	CO	PALM	38400	174	H8
157TH ST E	CO	VAL	30900	192	H6
157TH ST W	CO	GAR	100	64	A3
157TH ST W	CO	LAW	3600	63	B4
157TH ST W	COM	COM	2000	64	D3
157TH ST W	GAR	GAR	2000	63	D4
157TH ST W	LA	GAR	700	63	F3
157TH ST W	LA	GAR	500	64	A3
158TH ST	COM	COM	2000	64	D3
158TH ST E	CO	GAR		64	B4
158TH ST E	CO	LAN	40400	174	H4
158TH ST E	CO	PALM	38400	174	H8
158TH ST W	GAR	GAR	1100	63	F4
158TH ST W	LA	GAR	600	63	F4
158TH ST W	LA	GAR	500	64	A4
159TH PL W	LA	GAR	500	64	A4
159TH ST	COM	COM	2000	64	D3
159TH ST	RB	RB		62	F4
159TH ST E	CO	GAR		64	B4
159TH ST E	CO	LAN	40500	174	H3
159TH ST E	CO	PALM	38400	174	H8
159TH ST W	GAR	GAR	1000	63	F4
159TH ST W	LA	GAR	700	63	F4
159TH ST W	LA	GAR	500	64	A4
159TH ST W	LAW	LAW	4500	62	F4
159TH ST W	LAW	LAW	4000	63	A4
160TH ST	RB	RB		62	F4
160TH ST E	CO	LAN	38800	174	J7
160TH ST E	CO	LLAN		192	J3
160TH ST E	CO	PALM		174	J7
160TH ST E	NWK	NWK	11400	82	A4
160TH ST W	CO	LAN	46000	157	E1
160TH ST W	GAR	GAR	1000	63	F4
160TH ST W	LA	GAR	500	64	A4
160TH ST W	LAW	LAW	4500	62	F4
160TH ST W	LAW	LAW	4000	63	A4
161ST ST E	CO	LAN	38800	174	J7
161ST ST E	CO	PALM		174	J7
161ST ST E	NWK	NWK	11400	82	A4
161ST ST W	GAR	GAR	1000	63	F4
161ST ST W	LAW	LAW	4500	62	F4
161ST ST W	LAW	LAW	4000	63	A4
162ND ST	GAR	GAR	1000	63	F4
162ND ST	NWK	NWK	11800	82	A4
162ND ST E	CAR	GAR	100	64	B4
162ND ST E	CO	LAN	38800	174	J7
162ND ST E	CO	PALM		174	J7
162ND ST W	CO	LAN	46000	157	D1
162ND ST W	LAW	LAW	4500	62	F4
162ND ST W	LAW	LAW	4000	63	A4
163RD ST	CAR	CAR	900	64	C4
163RD ST	COM	COM	1200	64	D4
163RD ST E	CAR	GAR	100	64	B4
163RD ST E	CO	LAN	38800	174	J7
163RD ST E	CO	LLAN		192	J2
163RD ST E	CO	PALM		174	J7
163RD ST E	NWK	NWK	11800	82	A4
163RD ST W	GAR	GAR	1000	63	F4
163RD ST W	LA	GAR	800	63	F4
163RD ST W	LAW	LAW	4500	62	F4
163RD ST W	LAW	LAW	4000	63	A4
163RD ST W	TOR	GAR		63	C4
164TH ST E	CO	LAN	38800	174	J7
164TH ST E	CO	PALM		174	J7
164TH ST W	CAR	GAR	400	64	A4
164TH ST W	LA	GAR	700	63	F4
164TH ST W	LA	GAR	600	64	A4
164TH ST W	LAW	LAW	4500	62	F4
164TH ST W	LAW	LAW	4000	63	A4
164TH ST W	NWK	NWK	11800	82	A4
164TH ST W	TOR	GAR	2000	63	D4
165TH PL W	GAR	GAR	1000	63	F4
165TH PL W	LA	GAR	700	63	F4
165TH ST	NWK	NWK	11800	82	A4
165TH ST E	CO	LAN	39500	175	A5
165TH ST E	CO	LLAN	34400	192	J4
165TH ST E	CO	PALM		174	J7
165TH ST E	CO	PALM		185	J3
165TH ST W	COM	COM	1400	64	D4
165TH ST W	LAW	LAW	4500	62	F4
165TH ST W	LAW	LAW	4000	63	A4
165TH ST W	TOR	GAR	2200	63	D4
166TH PL	TOR	TOR	2500	63	D5
166TH ST	CER	ART		82	C4
166TH ST	COM	COM	1200	64	D4
166TH ST E	ART	ART	11300	66	E4
166TH ST E	ART	ART	11500	82	C4
166TH ST E	CO	LAN	39000	175	A7
166TH ST E	CO	PALM	39000	175	A7
166TH ST E	NWK	NWK	10600	66	E4
166TH ST E	NWK	NWK	11500	82	C4
166TH ST W	GAR	GAR	1100	63	E4
166TH ST W	LAW	LAW	4500	62	F4

STREET	CITY	P.O. ZONE	BLOCK	PAGE	GRID
166TH ST W	LAW	LAW	4000	63	A4
166TH ST W	TOR	GAR	2000	63	C4
166TH ST W	TOR	TOR	3100	63	C4
167TH ST	TOR	TOR		63	C5
167TH ST E	ART	ART	11800	82	A5
167TH ST E	CO	LAN	38800	175	A7
167TH ST E	CO	PALM	39000	175	A7
167TH ST E	NWK	NWK	11200	66	F5
167TH ST W	CO	LAN	46000	157	D1
167TH ST W	GAR	GAR	1000	63	F4
167TH ST W	LA	GAR	700	63	F4
167TH ST W	LAW	LAW	4500	62	F5
167TH ST W	LAW	LAW	4000	63	A5
168TH PL	LA	GAR	600	64	A5
168TH ST	ART	ART	11500	66	F5
168TH ST	ART	ART	11800	82	A5
168TH ST	CER	ART	12100	82	A5
168TH ST E	CAR	CAR	700	64	B4
168TH ST E	CO	LAN	38800	175	A7
168TH ST E	CO	PALM	39000	175	A7
168TH ST W	CAR	GAR	100	64	A4
168TH ST W	GAR	GAR	1000	63	F5
168TH ST W	LA	GAR	700	63	F4
168TH ST W	LA	GAR	500	64	A4
168TH ST W	LAW	LAW	4500	62	F5
168TH ST W	LAW	LAW	4000	63	A5
168TH ST W	TOR	TOR	2500	63	B5
169TH PL W	GAR	GAR	1300	63	E5
169TH PL W	LA	GAR	800	63	F5
169TH PL W	TOR	TOR	2100	63	D5
169TH ST	ART	ART	11500	66	F5
169TH ST	ART	ART	11500	82	A5
169TH ST E	CAR	CAR	300	64	B5
169TH ST E	CO	PALM	39000	175	A7
169TH ST W	GAR	GAR	1400	63	E5
169TH ST W	LA	GAR	700	63	F5
169TH ST W	LA	GAR	500	64	A5
169TH ST W	LAW	LAW	4000	63	A5
169TH ST W	TOR	TOR	3600	63	B5
170TH ST	LAM	LAM		83	A5
170TH ST E	ART	ART	11800	82	A5
170TH ST E	CO	LAN	38400	175	A8
170TH ST E	CO	PALM	37800	175	A8
170TH ST W	CO	LAN	46000	157	C2
170TH ST W	GAR	GAR	1000	63	F5
170TH ST W	LA	GAR	500	64	A5
170TH ST W	LAW	LAW	4500	62	F5
170TH ST W	LAW	LAW	4100	63	A5
170TH ST W	TOR	TOR	2500	63	B5
171ST ST	GAR	GAR	1400	63	E5
171ST ST	LA	GAR	600	64	A5
171ST ST E	CO	LAN	38400	175	A9
171ST ST E	CO	PALM	38000	175	A9
171ST ST W	LAW	LAW	4500	62	F5
171ST ST W	LAW	LAW	4200	63	A5
171ST ST W	TOR	TOR	2500	63	B5
172ND PL	GAR	GAR		63	E5
172ND ST E	CO	LAN	38400	175	B9
172ND ST E	CO	LAN		175	B4
172ND ST E	CO	PALM	38000	175	B9
172ND ST W	GAR	GAR	1400	63	E5
172ND ST W	LA	GAR	500	64	A5
172ND ST W	LAW	LAW	4500	62	F5
172ND ST W	LAW	LAW	4400	63	A5
172ND ST W	TOR	TOR	1000	63	B5
173RD PL W	LA	GAR	700	63	F5
173RD PL W	LA	GAR	700	64	A5
173RD PL W	TOR	TOR	4000	63	A5
173RD ST	ART	ART		66	F5
173RD ST E	CO	LAN		175	B4
173RD ST E	CO	LAN	38400	175	B9
173RD ST E	CO	PALM	38100	175	B9
173RD ST W	GAR	GAR		63	E5
173RD ST W	GAR	GAR	1400	63	E5
173RD ST W	LA	GAR	700	63	F5
173RD ST W	LAW	LAW	4500	62	F5
173RD ST W	LAW	LAW	4400	63	A5
173RD ST W	TOR	TOR	2200	63	B5
174TH ST E	CO	LAN		175	B4
174TH ST E	CO	LAN	39500	175	B6
175TH PL W	TOR	TOR	4000	63	A5
175TH ST E	ART	ART	11600	82	A5
175TH ST E	CO	LAN		175	B4
175TH ST E	CO	LAN	38400	175	B7
175TH ST W	TOR	TOR	2600	63	C5
176TH CT	TOR	TOR		63	B5
176TH ST	ART	ART		66	F5
176TH ST	CER	ART	12300	82	B5
176TH ST E	ART	ART	11600	82	A5
176TH ST E	CO	LAN		175	B4
176TH ST E	CO	LAN	39900	175	B5
176TH ST W	TOR	TOR		63	C5
177TH ST	ART	ART		66	F5
177TH ST	CER	ART	11300	66	F5
177TH ST E	CO	LAN		175	B4

1990 LOS ANGELES COUNTY STREET INDEX

STREET	CITY	P.O. ZONE	BLOCK	PAGE	GRID
177TH ST E	CO	LAN	40000	175	B4
177TH ST W	LA	GAR	1100	63	F5
177TH ST W	TOR	TOR	2000	63	D6
178TH ST E	ART	ART	11400	66	F6
178TH ST E	ART	ART	11600	82	A6
178TH ST E	CO	LAN		175	B4
178TH ST E	CO	LAN	39600	175	B6
178TH ST W	GAR	GAR	1400	63	E6
178TH ST W	TOR	TOR	2000	63	D6
179TH PL	GAR	GAR		63	E6
179TH ST E	ART	ART	12100	82	B6
179TH ST E	CO	LAN	39600	175	C5
179TH ST W	GAR	GAR	1400	63	E6
179TH ST W	TOR	TOR	1700	63	D6
180TH PL	TOR	TOR	1700	63	D6
180TH ST E	ART	ART	11500	82	B6
180TH ST E	CO	LAN	38400	175	C7
180TH ST W	GAR	GAR	1400	63	E6
180TH ST W	TOR	TOR	1700	63	D6
181ST ST	ART	ART	11500	66	F6
181ST ST E	CAR	GAR	300	64	B6
181ST ST E	CO	LAN	40400	175	C4
181ST ST E	CO	LLAN		175	C4
181ST ST W	TOR	TOR	1700	63	D6
182ND PL	RB	RB		62	F6
182ND ST	RB	RB	2600	62	F6
182ND ST E	CAR	GAR	300	64	B6
182ND ST E	CO	LAN	38800	175	C7
182ND ST W	GAR	GAR	1000	63	E6
182ND ST W	LA	GAR	600	63	F6
182ND ST W	LA	GAR	600	64	A6
182ND ST W	TOR	TOR	2200	63	B6
183RD ST	CER	ART	10900	66	E6
183RD ST	CER	ART	12300	82	C6
183RD ST	RB	RB		62	F6
183RD ST E	ART	ART	11400	66	E6
183RD ST E	ART	ART	11500	82	C6
183RD ST W	LA	GAR	1400	63	E6
183RD ST W	TOR	TOR	1900	63	D6
184TH ST	RB	RB	2500	62	F6
184TH ST E	ART	ART	11700	82	A6
184TH ST E	CAR	CAR	200	64	B6
184TH ST E	CO	LAN	40400	175	C3
184TH ST W	LA	GAR	1000	63	E6
184TH ST W	LA	GAR	500	64	A6
184TH ST W	LA	GAR	1000	68	F1
184TH ST W	TOR	TOR	1900	63	D6
184TH ST W	TOR	TOR	1900	68	D1
185TH PL	TOR	TOR		68	E1
185TH PL E	ART	ART	12200	82	B6
185TH ST	RB	RB	2500	62	F6
185TH ST E	ART	ART	11600	66	F6
185TH ST E	ART	ART	11600	82	A6
185TH ST E	CAR	CAR	200	69	B1
185TH ST E	CO	LAN	38800	175	C7
185TH ST W	LA	GAR	900	63	F6
185TH ST W	LA	GAR	900	68	F1
185TH ST W	TOR	TOR	1700	63	B6
185TH ST W	TOR	TOR	1700	68	D1
186TH ST	RB	RB	4400	67	F1
186TH ST E	ART	ART	11500	66	F6
186TH ST E	ART	ART	11500	82	A6
186TH ST E	CAR	CAR	200	69	B1
186TH ST E	CO	LAN	41600	175	D1
186TH ST W	LA	GAR	1400	68	E1
186TH ST W	TOR	TOR	2200	68	C1
187TH PL	LA	GAR	900	68	E1
187TH ST	ART	ART	11500	81	A1
187TH ST	ART	ART	11500	82	A6
187TH ST	CAR	GAR	600	69	C1
187TH ST E	ART	ART	11400	71	F1
187TH ST E	CO	LAN	41600	175	D1
187TH ST W	LA	GAR	900	68	E1
187TH ST W	TOR	TOR	1700	68	B1
188TH ST E	ART	ART	11600	81	A1
188TH ST E	CO	LAN	41600	175	D1
188TH ST W	CO	LH	44000	157	A6
188TH ST W	TOR	TOR	3100	68	B1
189TH ST E	CAR	CAR	100	69	B1
189TH ST E	CO	LAN	41600	175	D1
189TH ST W	TOR	TOR	3100	68	C1
190TH ST E	CO	LAN	41600	175	D1
190TH ST E	CO	PALM	38800	175	D7
190TH ST W	LA	GAR	600	68	E1
190TH ST W	LA	GAR	500	69	A1
190TH ST W	TOR	TOR	1700	68	B1
191ST ST	TOR	TOR	4500	67	F1
191ST ST E	ART	ART	12100	81	B1
191ST ST E	CO	LAN	40000	175	D5
192ND ST E	ART	ART	12100	81	B1
192ND ST E	CAR	CAR	100	69	B1
192ND ST E	CO	LAN	40000	175	E5
193RD ST E	ART	ART	12200	81	B1
193RD ST E	CER	ART	12600	81	C1
194TH ST E	ART	ART	12200	81	B2
194TH ST E	CO	LAN	40000	175	E5
195TH ST	CER	ART	11000	71	E2
195TH ST	TOR	TOR		68	D2
195TH ST E	CER	ART	11500	81	C2
195TH ST E	CO	LAN	38800	175	E7
195TH ST E	GAR	GAR	800	68	F1
196TH ST	CO	TOR		68	F2
196TH ST	LA	TOR		68	F2
196TH ST E	CO	LAN	38800	175	E7
197TH ST	CO	TOR	1100	68	F2
197TH ST E	CO	LAN	38800	175	E7
200TH ST E	CO	LAN		175	F1
201ST ST E	CO	LAN		175	F1
202ND ST E	CO	LAN		175	F1
203RD ST E	CO	LAN	40500	175	F3
204TH ST	CO	TOR	20300	68	F3
204TH ST W	LA	TOR	1400	68	E3
205TH ST	LKD	LKD	11400	71	F3
205TH ST	TOR	TOR		68	D3
205TH ST E	CO	LAN	39200	175	G6
205TH ST E	LKD	LKD	11600	81	A3
205TH ST W	LA	TOR	1500	68	E3
206TH ST	LKD	LKD	11400	71	F3
206TH ST E	LKD	LKD	11600	81	A3
206TH ST W	LA	TOR	1500	68	E3
207TH ST	LKD	LKD	11400	81	A3
207TH ST E	LKD	LKD	11500	71	F3
207TH ST W	LA	TOR	1500	68	E3
208TH ST	LKD	LKD	11600	81	A3
208TH ST	TOR	TOR		68	C3
208TH ST E	CAR	LB10	2900	70	A3
208TH ST E	LKD	LKD	11500	71	F3
208TH ST W	LA	TOR	1300	68	E3
209TH ST	CAR	LB10	2400	69	F3
209TH ST	LKD	LKD		71	F3
209TH ST E	LKD	LKD	11600	81	A3
209TH ST W	CO	TOR	600	68	F3
209TH ST W	LA	TOR	1300	68	E3
210TH ST	CO	TOR		68	F3
210TH ST	LA	TOR		68	E3
210TH ST E	CO	LAN	39200	175	G6
211TH ST E	CAR	CAR	200	69	B3
211TH ST E	HG	LKD	12200	81	B3
211TH ST E	LKD	LKD	11300	71	F4
211TH ST E	LKD	LKD	12400	81	B3
211TH ST E	LKD	LKD	12500	81	C3
211TH ST W	CO	TOR	1000	68	F3
211TH ST W	LA	TOR	1300	68	E3
212TH ST E	CO	COM	200	69	B4
212TH ST E	HG	LKD		81	A4
212TH ST E	LKD	LKD	11300	71	F4
212TH ST E	LKD	LKD	12400	81	B4
212TH ST E	LKD	LKD	11900	81	A4
212TH ST W	CAR	CAR	300	69	A4
212TH ST W	CO	TOR	600	68	F4
212TH ST W	LA	TOR	1300	68	E4
212TH ST W	TOR	TOR	1800	68	D4
213TH PL W	CAR	CAR	100	69	A4
213TH ST	LKD	LKD	11300	71	F4
213TH ST E	CAR	CAR	100	69	B4
213TH ST E	HG	LKD	12200	81	B4
213TH ST E	LKD	LKD	12600	81	C4
213TH ST W	CAR	CAR	400	69	B4
213TH ST W	CO	TOR	1000	68	F4
213TH ST W	LA	TOR	1300	68	E4
213TH ST W	TOR	TOR	1700	68	E4
214TH ST E	CAR	CAR	100	69	B4
214TH ST E	HG	LKD		81	B4
214TH ST E	LKD	LKD	11300	71	F4
214TH ST E	LKD	LKD	11600	81	A4
214TH ST W	CAR	CAR	100	69	B4
214TH ST W	CO	TOR	700	68	F4
214TH ST W	LA	TOR	1300	68	E4
215TH PL E	CAR	CAR	1100	69	D4
215TH ST	LKD	LKD	11600	81	A4
215TH ST E	CAR	CAR	100	69	B4
215TH ST E	CO	LAN		175	H3
215TH ST E	HG	LKD	12100	81	B4
215TH ST E	LKD	LKD	11300	71	F4
215TH ST E	LKD	LKD	12300	81	B4
215TH ST W	CAR	CAR	400	69	B4
215TH ST W	LA	TOR	1300	68	E4
216TH ST	HG	LKD	12100	81	B4
216TH ST	LKD	LKD	11600	81	A4
216TH ST	LKD	LKD	11600	81	A4
216TH ST E	CAR	CAR	100	69	B4
216TH ST E	LKD	LKD	11300	71	F4
216TH ST W	CAR	CAR	600	69	A4
216TH ST W	CO	TOR	1000	68	E4
216TH ST W	LA	TOR	1300	68	E4
217TH ST E	CO	LAN		175	H1
218TH PL	CAR	LB10	2600	69	F4
218TH PL E	CAR	CAR	100	69	B4
218TH PL W	CAR	CAR	400	69	A4
218TH ST	CAR	LB10	2600	69	F4
218TH ST E	CO	TOR	100	69	B4
218TH ST W	CAR	CAR	300	69	A4
218TH ST W	LA	TOR	1300	68	E4
218TH ST W	TOR	TOR	1800	68	D4
219TH PL	CAR	LB10	2600	69	F4
219TH PL W	CAR	CAR	100	69	A4
219TH ST	CAR	LB10	2600	69	F4
219TH ST E	CAR	CAR	200	69	B4
219TH ST E	HG	LKD	11800	81	A4
219TH ST W	CAR	CAR	200	69	A4
219TH ST W	CO	TOR	700	68	F4
219TH ST W	LA	TOR	1300	68	E4
220TH PL	CAR	LB10	2700	69	F5
220TH ST E	CAR	LB10	1900	69	F4
220TH ST E	CAR	LB10	2600	70	A4
220TH ST E	CO	LAN	39600	175	J5
220TH ST E	CO	TOR	100	69	A5
220TH ST W	CO	TOR	700	68	F4
220TH ST W	CO	TOR	100	69	A5
220TH ST W	LA	TOR	1300	68	F4
220TH ST W	TOR	TOR	1700	68	D4
221ST PL	CAR	LB10	2600	69	F5
221ST ST E	CAR	CAR	100	69	B5
221ST ST E	CAR	LB10	2600	69	F5
221ST ST E	HG	LKD	12200	81	B5
221ST ST E	LKD	LKD	11800	81	B5
221ST ST W	LA	TOR	1000	68	E5
222ND ST E	CAR	CAR	300	69	B5
222ND ST E	HG	LKD	12200	81	B5
222ND ST W	CAR	CAR	100	69	B5
222ND ST W	CO	TOR	1000	68	F5
222ND ST W	LA	TOR	1300	68	E5
222ND ST W	TOR	TOR	1800	68	D5
223RD ST E	CAR	CAR	100	69	B5
223RD ST E	CAR	LB10	1900	69	B5
223RD ST E	HG	LKD	11800	81	A5
223RD ST E	LA	LB10	2200	69	B5
223RD ST W	CAR	CAR	100	69	B5
223RD ST W	CO	TOR	700	68	E5
223RD ST W	LA	TOR	1300	68	E5
223RD ST W	TOR	TOR	1700	68	E5
224TH PL E	CAR	CAR	600	69	C5
224TH PL W	CAR	CAR	100	69	A5
224TH ST E	CAR	CAR	300	69	B5
224TH ST E	HG	LKD	12200	81	B5
224TH ST W	CAR	CAR	300	69	A5
224TH ST W	LA	TOR	1300	68	E5
224TH ST W	TOR	TOR	3200	68	A5
225TH PL	TOR	TOR	2500	68	C5
225TH ST E	CAR	CAR	600	69	C5
225TH ST E	CO	LAN	39600	175	J5
225TH ST W	CAR	CAR	100	69	A5
225TH ST W	CO	TOR	1000	68	E5
225TH ST W	LA	TOR	1300	68	E5
225TH ST W	TOR	TOR	2600	68	C5
226TH PL E	CAR	CAR	600	69	C5
226TH PL W	CAR	CAR	100	69	B5
226TH ST	HG	LKD	12200	81	B5
226TH ST E	CAR	CAR	600	69	C5
226TH ST W	CAR	CAR	100	69	A5
226TH ST W	CO	TOR	700	68	F5
226TH ST W	LA	TOR	1500	68	E5
226TH ST W	TOR	TOR	4100	67	F5
226TH ST W	TOR	TOR	2600	68	C5
227TH PL	TOR	TOR	3200	68	B5
227TH PL W	CO	TOR	800	68	F5
227TH ST E	CAR	CAR	100	69	B5
227TH ST W	CO	TOR	800	68	F5
227TH ST W	TOR	TOR	2200	68	C5
228TH PL	TOR	TOR		67	F5
228TH PL	TOR	TOR	3200	68	B5
228TH ST E	CAR	CAR	100	69	A5
228TH ST W	CO	TOR	700	68	E6
228TH ST W	CO	TOR	100	69	A5
228TH ST W	LA	TOR	1300	68	E6
228TH ST W	TOR	TOR	2200	68	C6
229TH PL	CAR	CAR	100	69	A6
229TH PL	TOR	TOR	2200	68	C6
229TH PL E	CAR	CAR	100	69	B6
229TH ST	TOR	TOR		67	F5
229TH ST E	CAR	CAR	100	69	B6
229TH ST W	CAR	CAR	300	69	A6
229TH ST W	CO	TOR	700	68	F6
229TH ST W	TOR	TOR	2100	68	C6
230TH PL	TOR	TOR	4000	67	F6
230TH PL	TOR	TOR	1900	68	D6
230TH ST	TOR	TOR	4100	67	F6
230TH ST	TOR	TOR	1900	68	D6
230TH ST E	CAR	CAR	100	69	B6
230TH ST W	CAR	CAR	100	69	A6
230TH ST W	TOR	TOR	1900	68	D6
231ST PL	TOR	TOR		68	A6
231ST ST E	CAR	CAR	100	69	B6
231ST ST W	CAR	CAR	100	69	A6
231ST ST W	CO	TOR	1000	68	E6
231ST ST W	CO	TOR	600	69	A6
231ST ST W	LA	TOR	1300	68	E6
231ST ST W	TOR	TOR	4000	67	F6
231ST ST W	TOR	TOR	2000	68	C6
232ND PL E	CAR	CAR	100	69	B6
232ND PL W	CAR	CAR	100	69	A6
232ND ST	CO	TOR	600	69	A6
232ND ST	TOR	TOR	1900	68	D6
232ND ST E	CAR	CAR	100	69	B6
232ND ST W	CAR	CAR	100	69	A6
232ND ST W	CO	TOR	900	68	F6
232ND ST W	TOR	TOR	3800	67	F6
233RD ST E	CAR	CAR	100	69	B6
233RD ST W	CAR	CAR	200	69	A6
233RD ST W	TOR	TOR	4300	67	F6
233RD ST W	TOR	TOR	1800	68	C6
234TH PL	TOR	TOR	4200	67	F6
234TH PL	TOR	TOR	3800	68	A6
234TH PL E	CAR	CAR	100	69	B6
234TH PL W	CAR	CAR	100	69	A6
234TH ST E	CAR	CAR	100	69	B6
234TH ST E	CAR	CAR	500	69	B6
234TH ST W	CAR	CAR	100	69	A6
234TH ST W	TOR	TOR	3800	67	F6
234TH ST W	TOR	TOR	1700	68	D6
235TH PL	CAR	CAR		74	B1
235TH PL	TOR	TOR		73	C1
235TH ST E	CAR	CAR	100	69	B6
235TH ST W	CAR	CAR	100	69	A6
235TH ST W	TOR	TOR	1700	68	C6
236TH CT	CAR	CAR	100	69	A6
236TH CT	CAR	CAR	100	74	A1
236TH PL	TOR	TOR		73	C1
236TH ST	TOR	TOR		67	F6
236TH ST	TOR	TOR	1700	72	F1
236TH ST E	CAR	CAR	100	74	B1
236TH ST W	TOR	TOR	1800	68	C6
237TH PL	TOR	TOR		73	C1
237TH ST	LA	HAC		73	E1
237TH ST E	CAR	CAR	200	69	B6
237TH ST W	TOR	TOR	1900	73	C1
238TH PL E	CAR	CAR	200	74	B1
238TH ST	LA	HAC		73	E1
238TH ST	TOR	TOR		67	F6
238TH ST	TOR	TOR	1900	72	F1
238TH ST E	CAR	CAR	200	74	B1
238TH ST W	TOR	TOR	1600	73	D1
239TH ST W	LA	TOR		73	C1
239TH ST W	TOR	TOR	1600	73	C1
240TH ST	TOR	TOR	3600	72	F1
240TH ST W	CO	TOR	1700	73	D1
240TH ST W	LA	HAC		73	E1
240TH ST W	LA	LOM		73	E1
240TH ST W	LOM	LOM		73	D1
240TH ST W	TOR	TOR	3600	73	A1
241ST ST W	LA	LOM		73	D1
241ST ST W	LOM	LOM		73	C1
241ST ST W	TOR	TOR	1700	73	D1
242ND PL	LA	LOM		73	D1
242ND PL	LOM	LOM		73	E1
242ND PL	TOR	TOR		73	D1
242ND PL W	LA	HAC		73	E1
242ND ST W	LA	LOM	1700	73	D1
242ND ST W	LOM	LOM		73	D1
242ND ST W	TOR	TOR	1700	73	D1
242ND ST W	TOR	TOR	3600	73	A1
243RD PL	LOM	LOM		73	D1
243RD PL	TOR	TOR		73	D1
243RD ST	CO	HAC		73	F1
243RD ST W	LA	HAC	1700	73	E1
243RD ST W	LA	LOM	1700	73	C1
243RD ST W	LOM	LOM		73	C1
243RD ST W	TOR	TOR	1700	73	C1
244TH ST	CO	HAC		73	F2
244TH ST W	CAR	CAR	300	74	B1
244TH ST W	LA	HAC	1700	73	E1
244TH ST W	LA	LOM	1700	73	E1
244TH ST W	TOR	TOR	1700	73	E1
244TH ST W	TOR	TOR	3600	73	A2
245TH PL W	TOR	TOR	1800	73	E2
245TH ST	CO	HAC		73	F2
245TH ST W	CAR	CAR	400	74	B1
245TH ST W	LA	LOM	1400	73	D2
245TH ST W	LA	LOM	1600	73	E2
245TH ST W	LOM	LOM	2100	73	D2
245TH ST W	TOR	TOR	1700	73	E2
246TH PL	CAR	CAR	400	74	B2
246TH PL W	LOM	LOM	2300	73	C2
246TH ST E	LA	WIL	100	74	B2
246TH ST W	CAR	CAR	400	74	B2
246TH ST W	LA	HAC		73	E2
246TH ST W	LA	LOM	1700	73	C2
246TH ST W	LA	WIL	100	74	B2
246TH ST W	LOM	LOM	1800	73	C2
247TH PL W	LA	HAC		73	D2
247TH PL W	LOM	LOM	1800	73	E2
247TH ST	TOR	TOR		73	C2
247TH ST E	CAR	CAR	300	74	B2
247TH ST E	LA	WIL	600	74	C2
247TH ST W	LA	HAC	1500	73	D2
247TH ST W	LA	LOM	1700	73	D2
247TH ST W	LOM	LOM	1700	73	D2
248TH ST	LA	WIL		74	C2
248TH ST E	LA	WIL	500	73	C2
248TH ST W	LA	HAC	1500	73	D2
248TH ST W	LA	LOM	1700	73	E2
248TH ST W	LOM	LOM	1800	73	E2
249TH ST E	CAR	CAR	300	74	B2
249TH ST E	LA	WIL	600	74	C2
249TH ST W	LA	HAC	1600	73	E2
249TH ST W	LOM	LOM	2300	73	E2
250TH ST W	LOM	LOM	2000	73	C2
251ST ST W	LA	HAC	900	73	E2
251ST ST W	LA	LOM	1700	73	C2
251ST ST W	LOM	LOM	1800	73	C2
252ND ST W	LA	HAC	900	73	E2
252ND ST W	LA	LOM	1700	73	D2
252ND ST W	LOM	LOM	1800	73	D2
253RD PL W	LOM	LOM	1900	73	D3
253RD ST W	LA	HAC	700	73	E2
253RD ST W	LA	LOM	1700	73	C2
253RD ST W	LOM	LOM	1800	73	C2
254TH ST W	LA	HAC	1000	73	E3
254TH ST W	LA	LOM	1700	73	C3
254TH ST W	LOM	LOM	1800	73	C3
255TH ST	LA	HAC		74	A3
255TH ST W	LA	HAC	700	73	E3
255TH ST W	LA	LOM	1700	73	C3
255TH ST W	LOM	LOM	1800	73	C3
255TH ST W	TOR	TOR	2500	73	C3
256TH ST W	LA	HAC	900	73	F3
256TH ST W	LA	LOM	1700	73	C3
256TH ST W	LOM	LOM	1800	73	C3
257TH ST W	LA	HAC	1000	73	D3
257TH ST W	LA	LOM	1700	73	D3
257TH ST W	LOM	LOM	1800	73	D3
258TH PL W	LA	HAC	900	73	E3
258TH PL W	LOM	LOM		73	D3
259TH PL W	LA	HAC	1600	73	D3
259TH PL W	LOM	LOM		73	D3
259TH ST W	LA	HAC	900	73	E3
259TH ST W	LA	LOM	1700	73	E3
259TH ST W	LOM	LOM		73	E3
260TH ST W	LA	HAC	1400	73	D3
260TH ST W	LA	LOM	1700	73	D3
260TH ST W	LOM	LOM		73	D3
261ST ST W	LA	HAC	1400	73	D3
261ST ST W	LOM	LOM		73	D3
262ND ST W	LA	HAC	1500	73	D4
262ND ST W	LOM	LOM	1700	73	D4
263RD ST W	LOM	LOM	1700	73	D4
264TH ST	LA	HAC		73	E4
264TH ST W	LOM	LOM		73	D4
265TH ST W	LA	LA	1600	73	E4
266TH ST W	LA	LA	1600	73	E4

AIRPORTS (SEE TRANSPORTATION)

BEACHES & HARBORS

PAGE	GRID	NAME	ADDRESS	CITY	PHONE
		BEACH & SURF CONDITION			213457 9701
77	D3	ABALONE COVE CO BEACH	6000 PALOS VERDES DR	RO PALOS VERD	
80	C1	ALAMITOS BAY	2ND ST	LONG BEACH	
113	E5	AMARILLO BEACH	24300 MALIBU RD	L A COUNTY	
77	B4	AVALON BAY	AVALON	CATALINA IS	213510 0535
115	A5	BIG ROCK BEACH	20600 PACIFIC COAST HY	L A COUNTY	
72	B3	BLUFF COVE	1000 PALOS VERDES DR W	PALOS VERDES	
79	A6	CABRILLO BEACH	36TH ST	SAN PEDRO	213832 1130
79	A5	CABRILLO MARINA	225 E 22ND ST	SAN PEDRO	213519 3566
114	D4	CARBON BEACH	22200 PACIFIC COAST HY	L A COUNTY	
115	F4	CASTLE ROCK BEACH	PACIFIC COAST HWY	CASTELLAMARE	
67	D5	CLIFTON BEACH PARK	ESPLANADE & AVE A	REDONDO BEACH	
113	C5	CORRAL BEACH	CORRAL CYN RD	L A COUNTY	
113	B5	DAN BLOCKER STATE BCH	PACIFIC COAST HWY	LA COUNTY	
55A	E4	DOCKWEILER STATE BEACH	WEST END OF IMP HWY	LOS ANGELES	
110	C6	DUME COVE	POINT DUME	L A COUNTY	
74	C6	EAST BASIN	CANAL ST	WILMINGTON	
112	F6	ESCONDIDO BEACH	ESCONDIDO BEACH RD	L A COUNTY	
62	B5	HERMOSA BEACH	33RD PL	HERMOSA BEACH	213372 2166
67	B3	KING HARBOR	BERYL ST	REDONDO BEACH	
114	E5	LA COSTA BEACH	21400 PACIFIC COAST HY	L A COUNTY	
114	F5	LAS FLORES BEACH	20900 PACIFIC COAST HY	L A COUNTY	
115	C5	LAS TUNAS STATE BEACH	19500 PACIFIC COAST HY	L A COUNTY	
110	B3	LEO CARRILLO STATE BCH	35000 PACIFIC COAST HY	L A COUNTY	
79	E2	LONG BEACH HARBOR	SEASIDE BLVD	LONG BEACH	213437 0041
80	D2	LONG BEACH MARINA	2ND ST	LONG BEACH	213594 0951
79	B6	LOS ANGELES HARBOR	SEASIDE AV	E SAN PEDRO	213519 3400
72	A5	LUNADA BAY	PASEO LUNADO	PALOS VERDES	
72	C2	MALAGA COVE	PASEO DEL MAR	PALOS VERDES	
114	A5	MALIBU BEACH	MALIBU COLONY DR	MALIBU BEACH	213457 9891
114	B5	MALIBU LAGOON ST BEACH	23200 PACIFIC COAST HY	L A COUNTY	
62	A4	MANHATTAN STATE BEACH	MANHATTAN BEACH BLVD	MANHATTAN BCH	213545 4502
49	D5	MARINA DEL REY	VIA MARINA	L A COUNTY	213823 4571
110	E4	NICHOLAS CYN CO BEACH	34000 PACIFIC COAST HY	L A COUNTY	
110	D4	PARADISE COVE	PACIFIC COAST HWY	L A COUNTY	
110	A5	POINT DUME STATE BEACH	WESTWARD BEACH RD	LA COUNTY	
77	F3	PORTUGUESE BEND	5000 PALOS VERDES DR	RO PALOS VERD	
113	D5	PUERCO BEACH	PUERCO CYN RD	L A COUNTY	
67	C4	REDONDO STATE BEACH	AINSWORTH CT	REDONDO BEACH	
111	A5	RH MEYER MEM ST BEACH	PACIFIC COAST HWY	LA COUNTY	
78	C5	ROYAL PALMS ST BEACH	PASEO DEL MAR	LOS ANGELES	
40	D6	SANTA MONICA STATE BCH	PALISADES BEACH RD	SANTA MONICA	213394 3264
115	E5	TOPANGA STATE BEACH	TOPANGA CYN BLVD	L A COUNTY	
67	C6	TORRANCE BEACH PARK	VIA RIVERA	TORRANCE	
111	E5	TRANCAS BEACH	GUERNSEY AV	L A COUNTY	
74	F5	TURNING BASIN	WATER ST	LONG BEACH	
49	B4	VENICE CITY BEACH	OCEAN FRONT WALK	VENICE	
74	B6	WEST BASIN	WEST BASIN AV	WILMINGTON	
110	D5	WESTWARD BEACH	WESTWARD BEACH RD	W OF PT DUME	
40	A5	WILL ROGERS STATE BCH	PACIFIC COAST HWY	LOS ANGELES	
111	F6	ZUMA BEACH	30000 PACIFIC COAST HY	L A COUNTY	

BUILDINGS

PAGE	GRID	NAME	ADDRESS	CITY	PHONE
42	A2	ABI TOWER	10100 SANTA MONICA	CENTURY CITY	
44	B2	ADAMS PLAZA	1545 WILSHIRE BLVD	LOS ANGELES	213483 2742
56	C5	AIRPORT IMPERIAL TWRS	2230 E IMPERIAL HWY	EL SEGUNDO	213772 1193
44	C5	ALLIED CRAFTS	407 E PICO BLVD	LOS ANGELES	213749 2789
44	B2	ALLIED PROPERTIES	1930 WILSHIRE BLVD	LOS ANGELES	
28	A2	ALLSTATE INS COMP BLDG	600 SIERRA MADRE VILLA	PASADENA	818351 3511
33	B6	AMERICAN MEDICAL INT	414 N CAMDEN DR	BEVERLY HILLS	213278 6200
75	C5	ANDRUS BLDG	215 LONG BEACH BL	LONG BEACH	213432 7221
44	C4	APPAREL MART BLDG	112 W 9TH ST	LOS ANGELES	
27	B4	ARCADE LANE BLDG	696 E COLORADO	PASADENA	818792 9910
28	C6	ARCADIA PROFESSNL CNTR	650 W DUARTE RD	ARCADIA	818447 3559
27	A4	ARROYO SECO BLDG	117 E COLORADO BLVD	PASADENA	
81	A1	ARTESIA CITY HALL	18747 CLARKSDALE AV	ARTESIA	213865 6262
44	C3	A T & T BUILDING	611 W 6TH ST	LOS ANGELES	
44	C3	ATLANTIC RICHFIELD PZ	515 S FLOWER	LOS ANGELES	213625 2132
41	F4	AVCO CENTER BLDG	10850 WILSHIRE	W LOS ANGELES	
44	D3	BANCO POPULAR BLDG	354 S SPRING STREET	LOS ANGELES	
44	D3	BANK OF AMERICA	525 S FLOWER ST	LOS ANGELES	213228 4567
27	B4	BANK OF AMERICA	530 E COLORADO BLVD	PASADENA	818578 5025
44	D2	B OF A DATA CENTER	1000 W TEMPLE ST	LOS ANGELES	
44	C3	BANK OF CALIFORNIA	550 S FLOWER ST	LOS ANGELES	213972 2000
22	C3	BANK OF CALIFORNIA	15250 VENTURA BLVD	SHERMAN OAKS	
42	F1	BANKERS LIFE	6404 WILSHIRE BLVD	LOS ANGELES	213651 3601
44	D3	BANKS HUNTLEY	634 S SPRING	LOS ANGELES	
42	E1	BARCLAY BLDG	111 NO LA CIENEGA BLVD	BEVERLY HILLS	
21	C1	BARCLAYS BANK	18321 VENTURA BLVD	TARZANA	818345 8980
41	C3	BARRINGTON PLAZA	11740 WILSHIRE BLVD	W LOS ANGELES	213272 9647
44	D4	BARTLETT, A G	215 W 7TH	LOS ANGELES	213680 9006
42	B1	BEDFORD, WILSHIRE BLDG	360 NO BEDFORD DR	BEVERLY HILLS	213276 0414
54	A6	BELL GARDENS CITY HALL	5960 1/2 E FLORENCE AV	BELL GARDENS	213562 2830
76	B6	BELMONT MEDICAL BLDG	4817 EAST 2 ND	LONG BEACH	

PAGE	GRID	NAME	ADDRESS	CITY	PHONE
44	C5	BENDIX BLDG	1206 MAPLE AVE	LOS ANGELES	
43	E2	BENEFICIAL INSUR GROUP	3700 WILSHIRE BLVD	LOS ANGELES	213381 8011
44	D2	BEST BANKERS BLDG	629 S HILL ST	LOS ANGELES	
26	F2	BEVERLY ENTERPRISES	873 S FAIR OAKS AV	PASADENA	818684 1100
33	C6	BEVERLY HILLS CTY HALL	450 CRESCENT DR	BEVERLY HILLS	213550 4700
42	C2	BEVERLY HILLS LAW BLDG	424 S BEVERLY DR	BEVERLY HILLS	213553 8533
42	B1	BEVERLY HILLS MED BLDG	133 S LASKY DR	BEVERLY HILLS	213879 3700
33	C4	BEVERLY SUNSET	9201 W SUNSET BLVD	BEVERLY HILLS	213272 2911
70	D4	BIXBY KNOLLS MED CTR	4130 ATLANTIC AV	LONG BEACH	
44	C3	BIXEL BUILDING	1055 WILSHIRE BLVD	LOS ANGELES	
44	D3	BRADBURY	304 S BROADWAY	LOS ANGELES	213489 1411
41	C3	BRENTWOOD SQUARE BLDG	11661 SAN VICENTE BLVD	BRENTWOOD	213820 7646
44	D3	BROADWAY ARCADE	542 S BROADWAY	LOS ANGELES	
44	D2	BROADWAY HILL	233 S BROADWAY	LOS ANGELES	
44	C3	BROADWAY PLAZA	700 FLOWER ST	LOS ANGELES	213624 2891
44	D2	BROADWAY TEMPLE	229 N BROADWAY	LOS ANGELES	
44	C3	BROCKMAN	520 W 7TH	LOS ANGELES	
44	E3	BRUNSWIG SQUARE	360 W 2ND ST	LOS ANGELES	
42	B1	BUCKEYE REALTY	8500 WILSHIRE BLVD	BEVERLY HILLS	213652 1411
44	D4	BUILDERS EXCHANGE	656 S LOS ANGELES	LOS ANGELES	
44	B3	BLDG INDUSTRY CENTER	1625 W OLYMPIC BLVD	LOS ANGELES	
44	C3	BULLOCK'S CORP HQ	800 S HOPE ST	LOS ANGELES	
44	D3	BUNKER HILL E OFFICE	311 S SPRING ST	LOS ANGELES	213624 3426
44	D2	BUNKER HILL TOWERS	800 W 1ST ST	LOS ANGELES	
17	E5	BURBANK CITY HALL	275 E OLIVE	BURBANK	818847 8600
44	C4	BURNS, L L	910 S BROADWAY	LOS ANGELES	
44	D4	CAIRNS	108 W 6TH	LOS ANGELES	
34	F3	CALIFORNIA FED S & L	4705 SUNSET BLVD	LOS ANGELES	213663 8221
43	A2	CALIFORNIA FED S & L	5670 WILSHIRE BLVD	LOS ANGELES	213932 4321
44	C3	CALIFORNIA JEWLRY MART	607 S HILL ST	LOS ANGELES	213627 2831
44	C4	CALIFORNIA MART	110 E 9TH ST	LOS ANGELES	213620 0260
44	B5	CALIFORNIA MEDICAL	1401 S HOPE	LOS ANGELES	213749 2458
44	D3	CALIFORNIA STATE	107 S BROADWAY	LOS ANGELES	
44	D3	CALTRANS	120 S SPRING ST	LOS ANGELES	213620 3550
44	D3	CANADIAN	432 S MAIN	LOS ANGELES	213624 9524
34	C3	CAPITOL RECORDS, INC	1750 N VINE ST	LOS ANGELES	213462 6252
43	C1	CARNATION	5045 WILSHIRE BLVD	LOS ANGELES	213932 6000
27	B4	CARRINGTON BLDG	960 E GREEN ST	PASADENA	
70	D4	CARSON PROFESSIONAL	1230 E CARSON	LONG BEACH	
42	F2	CARTHAY CENTER PROF	6318 SAN VICENTE BLVD	LOS ANGELES	
42	A2	CENTURY CITY	1801 CENTURY PARK	CENTURY CITY	213277 8907
42	A2	CENTURY PARK PLAZA	1801 CENTURY PARK	CENTURY CITY	213552 1801
59	C5	CENTURYWOOD MED CTR	3737 E CENTURY BLVD	LYNWOOD	213774 4754
22	D3	CERTIFIED LIFE TOWER	14724 VENTURA BLVD	SHERMAN OAKS	818981 9000
44	C4	CHAPMAN	756 S BROADWAY	LOS ANGELES	
13	D1	CHAZAN	21031 VENTURA BLVD	WOODLAND HILS	
44	D3	CHESTER WILLIAMS	525 S SPRING	LOS ANGELES	213628 3125
44	D3	CITIZENS BUILDING	453 S SPRING ST	LOS ANGELES	
27	A4	CITIZENS COM T&S BANK	225 E COLORADO BLVD	PASADENA	818795 3000
44	D3	CITIZENS NATIONAL BANK	453 S SPRING	LOS ANGELES	
56	C3	CITIZENS SAVINGS&LOAN	9800 SEPULVEDA BLVD	LOS ANGELES	213642 0200
42	B1	CITY NATIONAL BANK	400 N ROXBURY DR	BEVERLY HILLS	213550 5400
33	C4	CITY NATIONAL BANK	9229 W SUNSET BLVD	BEVERLY HILLS	213550 5785
44	C3	CITY NATIONAL BANK	606 S OLIVE ST	LOS ANGELES	213629 1134
41	A6	CITY NATIONAL BANK	600 WILSHIRE BLVD	SANTA MONICA	213393 6701
44	C4	COAST FEDERAL BLDG	315 W 9TH ST	LOS ANGELES	213623 1351
44	C3	COLDWELL BANKER BLDG	533 S FREMONT AV	LOS ANGELES	213613 3644
53	F3	COMMERCE CITY HALL	2535 COMMERCE WY	COMMERCE	213722 4805
53	F3	COMMERCE SQUARE	6055 E WASHINGTON BLVD	COMMERCE	213722 7427
44	C4	COMMERCIAL CLUB	1106 S BROADWAY	LOS ANGELES	
44	C4	COMMERCIAL EXCHANGE	416 W 8TH	LOS ANGELES	213623 3702
44	D3	COMMERCIAL LOFT	239 S LOS ANGELES	LOS ANGELES	
56	C5	COMPUTER SCIENCES	650 N SEPULVEDA BLVD	EL SEGUNDO	213615 0311
44	C3	CONSOLIDATED	607 S HILL	LOS ANGELES	
44	D2	CONSUMER AFFAIRS	107 S BROADWAY	LOS ANGELES	213952 5225
44	B2	CONTINENTAL INSURANCE	1520 WILSHIRE BLVD	LOS ANGELES	
44	C4	COOPER	860 S LOS ANGELES	LOS ANGELES	213622 1139
42	C1	CORINNE GRIFFITH COR	195 S BEVERLY DR	BEVERLY HILLS	
44	C4	CORPORATION	724 S SPRING	LOS ANGELES	
44	D3	COTTON EXCHANGE	106 W 3RD	LOS ANGELES	213623 1780
75	C5	COUNTY COURT	415 W OCEAN BLVD	LONG BEACH	
59	F5	COUNTY COURTHOUSE	IMPERIAL HWY	DOWNEY	
44	D2	COUNTY COURT HOUSE	111 N HILL ST	LOS ANGELES	213974 1234
43	F1	COUNTY ENGINEERING	550 S VERMONT AV	LOS ANGELES	213738 2365
51	B1	CRENSHAW MEDICAL CENTR	3741 STOCKER	LOS ANGELES	213292 0405
51	B2	CRENSHW PLZA MED CENTR	3751 STOCKER ST	LOS ANGELES	
44	C3	CROCKER NATIONAL BANK	611 W 6TH ST	LOS ANGELES	213612 8211
34	B3	CROSS ROADS OF THE WLD	1575 CRSS RDS OF T WLD	HOLLYWOOD	213463 5611
44	C3	CUTTS	706 S HILL ST	LOS ANGELES	
42	E1	DANIELS HELD BLDG	6380 WILSHIRE BLVD	LOS ANGELES	
75	D5	DAVIES, J R	730 E 3RD	LONG BEACH	
68	A4	DEL AMO FINANCIAL CTR	21515 HAWTHORNE BLVD	TORRANCE	213540 9300
44	D2	DEPT OF WATER & POWER	111 N HOPE ST	LOS ANGELES	213481 4211
44	D3	DESIGN CENTER OF LA	433 S SPRING ST	LOS ANGELES	213625 1100
43	A2	DOMINGUEZ WILSHIRE	5410 WILSHIRE BLVD	LOS ANGELES	
44	D3	DOUGLAS	257 S SPRING	LOS ANGELES	
44	D4	DOUGLAS OIL BLDG	530 W 6TH ST	LOS ANGELES	
44	C4	EASTERN-COLUMBIA BLDG	849 S BROADWAY	LOS ANGELES	213623 7242
44	C3	EDISON	601 W 5TH	LOS ANGELES	
44	C3	EDWARDS AND WILDEY	609 S GRAND AVE	LOS ANGELES	
44	C3	EIGHTH AND FIGUEROA	751 S FIGUEROA	LOS ANGELES	213623 1275

1990 LOS ANGELES COUNTY POINTS OF INTEREST

PAGE	GRID	NAME	ADDRESS	CITY	PHONE
44	D4	EMPIRE LIFE BLDG	611 WILSHIRE BLVD	LOS ANGELES	213626 4374
44	B5	EMPLOYMENT DEVELOPMENT	1525 S BROADWAY	LOS ANGELES	213744 2121
22	A3	ENCINO MEDICAL TOWER	16260 VENTURA BLVD	ENCINO	818986 0692
34	C3	EQUITABLE	6253 HOLLYWOOD BLVD	LOS ANGELES	213463 9389
43	E2	EQUITABLE LIFE	3435 WILSHIRE BLVD	LOS ANGELES	213381 5432
42	B1	EXECUTIVE LIFE	9777 WILSHIRE BLVD	BEVERLY HILLS	213273 4202
75	C5	F & M	320 PINE AV	LONG BEACH	213432 8475
44	B3	FAB ENTERPRISES	1605 W OLYMPIC BLVD	LOS ANGELES	213380 4660
44	D3	FARMERS & MERCHANTS BK	401 S MAIN	LOS ANGELES	
44	D3	FASHION LEAGUE	333 W 3RD	LOS ANGELES	
44	D3	FAY, F P	326 W 3RD	LOS ANGELES	
75	C5	FEDERAL	300 LONG BEACH BLVD	LONG BEACH	213688 3800
44	D3	FEDERAL BLDG	300 N LOS ANGELES ST	LOS ANGELES	213688 3800
41	D2	FEDERAL OFFICE BLDG	11000 WILSHIRE BLVD	WESTWOOD	213688 3800
44	C4	FEDERAL RESERVE	409 W OLYMPIC BLVD	LOS ANGELES	213683 8449
44	C3	FEDERAL SAVINGS	645 S HILL	LOS ANGELES	
44	D3	FERGUSEN	307 S HILL	LOS ANGELES	
44	D3	FIDELITY	548 S SPRING	LOS ANGELES	
75	D6	FIDELITY FEDERAL PLAZA	555 E OCEAN BLVD	LONG BEACH	213436 9696
28	B4	FIELD BLDG	3820 E COLORADO BLVD	PASADENA	
43	B2	FIFTY FOUR TEN WILSHRE	5410 WILSHIRE BLVD	LOS ANGELES	213936 8686
43	F4	FILM EXCHANGE	1584 W WASHINGTON BLVD	LOS ANGELES	213732 0574
44	C4	FINANCIAL CENTER	704 S SPRING	LOS ANGELES	
44	C4	FINE CRAFTS	309 E 8TH	LOS ANGELES	
75	D5	FIVE POINTS	555 ALAMITOS AV	LONG BEACH	
34	B3	FOLB BUILDING	1800 N HIGHLAND	HOLLYWOOD	
44	C3	FOREMAN	707 S HILL	LOS ANGELES	
44	C3	FORRESTER	640 S BROADWAY	LOS ANGELES	
44	C3	FOX, WILLIAM	608 S HILL	LOS ANGELES	213627 8907
33	C6	FREDERICK BLDG	222 N CANON DR	BEVERLY HILLS	
44	B2	FREMONT BLDG	1709 W 8TH ST	LOS ANGELES	
44	C3	FUR FASHION MART	635 S HILL ST	LOS ANGELES	
44	C5	FURNITURE EXCHANGE	1206 SANTEE	LOS ANGELES	
44	C4	GARFIELD	403 W 8TH	LOS ANGELES	213627 5152
44	C4	GARLAND	740 S BROADWAY	LOS ANGELES	
44	C4	GARLAND, WM H	117 W 9TH	LOS ANGELES	
41	C4	GARMENT CAPITOL	217 E 8TH	LOS ANGELES	
42	A2	GATEWAY WEST OFF BLDG	1800 AV OF THE STARS	CENTURY CITY	
75	C5	GENERAL TELEPHONE	200 W OCEAN BLVD	LONG BEACH	
44	C4	GERRY	746 S LOS ANGELES ST	LOS ANGELES	213623 4219
42	E1	GERSHON	6399 WILSHIRE BLVD	LOS ANGELES	
44	C3	GIANNINI, A P	649 S OLIVE	LOS ANGELES	
42	C1	GIBRALTAR SAVINGS&LOAN	9111 WILSHIRE BLVD	BEVERLY HILLS	213278 8720
42	C1	GLENDALE FEDERAL	9450 WILSHIRE BLVD	BEVERLY HILLS	213274 9826
25	C3	GLENDALE FEDERAL S & L	401 N BRAND BLVD	GLENDALE	818956 3800
44	C3	GLOBAL MARINE INC	811 W 7TH ST	LOS ANGELES	213680 9550
24	F2	GRAND CENTRAL BLDG	1310 AIR WY	GLENDALE	818245 7581
44	C3	GRAND FINANCIAL PLAZA	EIGHTH ST & GRAND AV	LOS ANGELES	
44	D4	GRAYCO	754 LOS ANGELES S	LOS ANGELES	
42	E1	GREAT WESTERN	8484 WILSHIRE BLVD	BEVERLY HILLS	213852 3411
34	C3	GUARANTY	6331 HOLLYWOOD BLVD	LOS ANGELES	
44	D4	HAAS BLDG	219 W 7TH ST	LOS ANGELES	
44	D2	HALL ADMINISTRATION	500 TEMPLE	LOS ANGELES	
44	D2	HALL OF JUSTICE	211 TEMPLE	LOS ANGELES	
44	D2	HALL OF RECORDS	320 TEMPLE ST	LOS ANGELES	
79	E4	HARBOR ADMINISTRATIVE	925 HARBOR PLAZA S	LONG BEACH	213437 0041
44	C4	HARRIS	110 W 11TH	LOS ANGELES	
44	C3	HARRIS & FRANK	635 S HILL	LOS ANGELES	
44	C4	HARRIS NEWMARK	127 E 9TH	LOS ANGELES	213623 6047
81	A4	HAWAIIAN GDNS CITY HLL	21815 PIONEER BLVD	HAWAIIAN GDNS	213420 2641
44	C2	HEALTH ADMIN COUNTY	313 N FIGUEROA ST	LOS ANGELES	213974 7711
21	D2	HEES PROPERTIES INC	16033 VENTURA BLVD	ENCINO	
33	E6	HEES PROPERTIES INC	435 S LA CIENEGA BLVD	LOS ANGELES	213271 6620
44	D3	HIGGINS	108 W 2ND	LOS ANGELES	
44	C3	HILTON CENTER	900 WILSHIRE	LOS ANGELES	213628 6231
44	C3	HOLLINGSWORTH CORP THE	1052 W 6TH ST	LOS ANGELES	
34	B3	HOLLYWOOD CENTER	1655 N CHEROKEE AV	LOS ANGELES	
34	B3	HOLLYWOOD PROFESSIONAL	7046 HOLLYWOOD BLVD	LOS ANGELES	
34	C3	HOLLYWOOD SECURITY	6381 HOLLYWOOD BLVD	LOS ANGELES	
34	B4	HOLLYWOOD STORAGE	1025 N HIGHLAND AV	LOS ANGELES	
34	C3	HOLLYWOOD STUDIO	6560 HOLLYWOOD BLD	LOS ANGELES	
34	D3	HOLLYWOOD WESTERN	5504 HOLLYWOOD BLVD	LOS ANGELES	
34	C3	HOLLYWOOD WHITLEY	6605 HOLLYWOOD BLVD	LOS ANGELES	
44	C3	HOME SAVINGS	654 S FIGUEROA ST	LOS ANGELES	213627 7991
56	C5	HUGHES ADMINISTRATION	1950 E IMPERIAL HWY	EL SEGUNDO	213648 2345
43	E2	I B M	3424 WILSHIRE BLVD	LOS ANGELES	213736 4000
44	C3	IMPERIAL	810 W 6TH	LOS ANGELES	
43	B2	IMPERIAL S & L ASSN	4929 WILSHIRE BLVD	LOS ANGELES	213938 3741
44	C4	INSURANCE EXCHANGE	318 W 9TH	LOS ANGELES	
75	C5	INSURANCE EXCHANGE	205 E BROADWAY	LONG BEACH	
44	C3	INTERNATIONAL TOWER	888 FIGUEROA	LOS ANGELES	
44	C4	ISAACS	739 S BROADWAY	LOS ANGELES	
44	C3	JEWELERS EXCHANGE	747 S HILL	LOS ANGELES	
44	D3	JEWELRY TRADES	220 W 5TH	LOS ANGELES	213680 0313
44	D3	JOHNSON, O T	356 S BROADWAY	LOS ANGELES	
75	C4	JONES BROS	302 E ANAHEIM	LONG BEACH	
44	D3	KAJIMA BUILDING	250 E 1ST ST	LOS ANGELES	213624 7353
75	C5	KAVANAUGH	603 W 5TH	LONG BEACH	
34	C3	K-B SUNSET & VINE BLDG	6255 SUNSET BLVD	HOLLYWOOD	
43	F2	K-B WILSHIRE NEW HAMP	3255 WILSHIRE	LOS ANGELES	
42	C1	KENTON CENTER	9595 WILSHIRE BL	BEVERLY HILLS	

PAGE	GRID	NAME	ADDRESS	CITY	PHONE
41	E2	KIRKEBY CENTER	10889 WILSHIRE BLVD	W LOS ANGELES	213208 4416
44	C3	KNICKERBOCKER	643 S OLIVE	LOS ANGELES	
70	D5	KNOLLS PROFESSIONAL	3848 A ATLANTIC AV	LONG BEACH	
75	C4	LABOR TEMPLE	1231 LOCUST AV	LONG BEACH	
44	D4	LABOR TEMPLE AF OF L	532 MAPLE	LOS ANGELES	
43	B1	LABREA ARCADE	624 S LA BREA	LOS ANGELES	
42	C1	LADD ENTERPRISES INC	9250 WILSHIRE BLVD	BEVERLY HILLS	213272 6613
27	B4	LAKE & COLORADO BLDG	880 E COLORADO BLVD	PASADENA	
76	B6	LAMBERT	200 NIETO AV	LONG BEACH	
44	D4	LANE MORTGAGE	208 W 8TH	LOS ANGELES	213623 4418
34	C6	LARCHMONT MEDICAL CTR	321 N LARCHMONT BLVD	LOS ANGELES	213463 3954
48	F6	LA PUENTE CITY HALL	15900 E MAIN ST	LA PUENTE	818330 4511
44	D3	LAUGHLIN HOMER	315 S BROADWAY	LOS ANGELES	
44	D3	LAW	139 N BROADWAY	LOS ANGELES	
42	F4	LAWRENCE	5746 VENICE BLVD	LOS ANGELES	213939 7603
43	A2	LEE TOWER	5455 WILSHIRE BLVD	LOS ANGELES	213938 5271
44	C4	LINCOLN	742 S HILL	LOS ANGELES	
22	F3	LINCOLN S & L	13701 RIVERSIDE DR	SHERMAN OAKS	818783 3130
42	B1	LINDEN WILSHIRE	1880 CENTURY PARK E	BEVERLY HILLS	213553 6304
44	D3	LISSNER	524 S SPRING	LOS ANGELES	
75	C5	LONG BEACH CITY HALL	333 W OCEAN BLVD	LONG BEACH	213590 6555
44	D2	L A CITY BD OF EDUCATN	450 N GRAND AV	LOS ANGELES	213625 6000
44	D3	L A CITY HALL	200 N SPRING	LOS ANGELES	213485 2121
44	D3	L A CITY HALL ANNEX SQ	111 E 1ST ST	LOS ANGELES	213485 2121
44	D3	L A CITY POLICE ADMIN	150 N LOS ANGELES	LOS ANGELES	213485 2121
44	D2	LOS ANGELES CIVIC CTR	200 N SPRING	LOS ANGELES	213485 2121
44	D2	L A COUNTY ADMIN	500 W TEMPLE ST	LOS ANGELES	213974 1811
44	B5	L A HOME FURNISHINGS	1933 S BROADWAY	LOS ANGELES	213749 7911
59	B5	LYNWOOD CITY HALL	11330 BULLIS RD	LYNWOOD	213537 0800
23	F4	M C A BLDG	100 UNIVERSITY CITY	UNIVERSAL CTY	818985 4321
75	C4	MACHINISTS	728 ELM AV	LONG BEACH	
44	B5	MALOUF	155 W WASHINGTON BLVD	LOS ANGELES	
75	D4	MALOUF	919 ATLANTIC AV	LONG BEACH	
49	E5	MARINA AIRPORT BLDG	4676 ADMIRALTY	MARINA DL REY	
70	C5	MASONIC TEMPLE	3610 LOCUST	LONG BEACH	213427 0821
34	B3	MAX FACTOR	1655 MCCADDEN PL	HOLLYWOOD	213462 6131
44	D4	MAXFIELD	819 SANTEE	LOS ANGELES	
44	C4	MCCOMAS	120 E 8TH	LOS ANGELES	
71	A4	MCDONNELL-DOUGLAS CORP	3855 N LAKEWOOD BLVD	LONG BEACH	213593 5511
43	D1	MEDBROOK MEDICAL GROUP	4732 E 3RD ST	LOS ANGELES	213269 1154
70	D5	MEDICAL	3810 ATLANTIC AV	LONG BEACH	
23	E4	MEDICAL ARTS BLDG	4418 VINELAND AV	NO HOLLYWOOD	818761 0073
75	C3	MEDICAL DENTAL	1933 PACIFIC AV	LONG BEACH	
44	C3	MEDICAL OFFICE	1136 W 6TH	LOS ANGELES	213482 9731
44	C3	MEDICO DENTAL	947 W 8TH	LOS ANGELES	
75	C2	MEDICO DENTAL	2333 PACIFIC AV	LONG BEACH	
27	B3	MELVIN BLDG	739 E WALNUT ST	PASADENA	818796 2689
44	D4	MERCANTILE CENTER	122 E 7TH	LOS ANGELES	213623 1066
44	C3	MERCHANDISE MART	712 S OLIVE	LOS ANGELES	213629 1201
44	D4	MERCHANTS EXCHANGE	719 S LOS ANGELES	LOS ANGELES	
44	D3	METROPOLITAN	315 W 5TH	LOS ANGELES	213624 1500
44	D1	METRO WATER DISTRICT	1111 SUNSET BLVD	LOS ANGELES	213485 9038
42	E1	MID WILSHIRE MEDICAL	6317 WILSHIRE BLVD	LOS ANGELES	213653 8377
44	C4	MILLINERY CENTER	739 S BROADWAY	LOS ANGELES	
44	C3	MOBIL	612 S FLOWER	LOS ANGELES	213683 5711
34	B3	MUIR MEDICAL CENTER	7080 HOLLYWOOD BLVD	HOLLYWOOD	213464 0111
34	C5	MUSICIANS LOCAL	817 VINE ST	LOS ANGELES	213462 2161
43	A2	MUTUAL BENEFIT LIFE	5900 WILSHIRE BLVD	LOS ANGELES	213937 8400
43	B2	MUTUAL OF OMAHA	5225 WILSHIRE BLVD	LOS ANGELES	213933 9381
27	A4	MUTUAL SAVINGS & LOAN	315 E COLORADO BLVD	PASADENA	818684 1500
44	D3	NATIONAL AUTO&CASUALTY	639 S SPRING	LOS ANGELES	
44	C4	NATIONAL CITY BANK	810 S SPRING	LOS ANGELES	
44	C3	NATIONAL OIL	609 S GRAND AVE	LOS ANGELES	
43	C2	NATIONAL TITLE	3540 WILSHIRE BLVD	LOS ANGELES	
75	B6	NAVY LANDING	350 S MAGNOLIA AV	LONG BEACH	
44	D3	NELSON	355 S BROADWAY	LOS ANGELES	
44	C4	NEW ORPHEUM	846 S BROADWAY	LOS ANGELES	
44	C4	NINTH & HILL	315 W 9TH	LOS ANGELES	
44	C4	NINTH& BROADWAY BLDG	850 S BROADWAY	LOS ANGELES	
64	A6	NISSAN MOTOR CORP	18501 S FIGUEROA ST	CARSON	213532 3111
44	C4	OCCIDENTAL CENTER	1150 S OLIVE ST	LOS ANGELES	213742 2111
75	C5	OCEAN CENTER	110 W OCEAN BLVD	LONG BEACH	213436 2470
44	D3	OHIO OIL	437 S HILL	LOS ANGELES	
44	C4	OLYMPIC	1013 S LOS ANGELES	LOS ANGELES	213748 6081
75	C5	ONE FIFTEEN PINE AV	115 PINE AV	LONG BEACH	
44	C3	ONE WILSHIRE BLDG	624 S GRAND AV	LOS ANGELES	213629 4831
43	F2	ONE L A PLAZA	3250 WILSHIRE	LOS ANGELES	213487 4444
34	B3	OUTPOST	6715 HOLLYWOOD BLVD	LOS ANGELES	
44	A3	OVERLAND TERMINAL	1807 E OLYMPIC BLVD	LOS ANGELES	213623 5221
44	C3	OVIATT JAMES	617 S OLIVE	LOS ANGELES	213623 5050
44	C3	PACIFIC BELL	1010 WILSHIRE BLVD	LOS ANGELES	213488 6500
33	D5	PACIFIC DESIGN CENTER	8687 MELROSE AV	W HOLLYWOOD	213657 0800
44	D3	PACIFIC ELECTRIC	610 S MAIN	LOS ANGELES	
43	D3	PACIFIC EMPLOYERS INS	4050 WILSHIRE BLVD	LOS ANGELES	213480 4600
34	B3	PACIFIC FEDERAL BLDG	6801 HOLLYWOOD BLVD	HOLLYWOOD	213463 4141
43	E3	PACIFIC INDEMNITY	3200 WILSHIRE BLVD	LOS ANGELES	213385 2700
44	C3	PACIFIC MUTUAL	523 W 6TH	LOS ANGELES	213625 1211
44	D3	PACIFIC SOUTHWEST	215 W 6TH	LOS ANGELES	213613 6211
44	C2	PACIFIC STOCK EXCHANGE	233 S BEAUDRY ST	LOS ANGELES	213977 4500
79	A3	PACIFIC TRADE CENTER	255 W 5TH ST	SAN PEDRO	213832 3040
44	C3	PADEN PELTON	728 S HILL	LOS ANGELES	

1990 LOS ANGELES COUNTY POINTS OF INTEREST

PAGE	GRID	NAME	ADDRESS	CITY	PHONE
34	C3	PALMER	6362 HOLLYWOOD BLVD	LOS ANGELES	
15	D1	PANORAMA TOWERS	8155 VAN NUYS BLVD	LOS ANGELES	213873 5957
44	C3	PARK CENTRAL	412 W 6TH	LOS ANGELES	213627 3996
44	A2	PARK WILSHIRE PROF	2412 W 7TH	LOS ANGELES	
27	A4	PASADENA CITY HALL	100 N GARFIELD AV	PASADENA	818577 4000
44	B5	PATRIOTIC HALL	1816 S FIGUEROA	LOS ANGELES	213747 5361
44	C3	PECK NORMAN BLDG	700 WILSHIRE BLVD	LOS ANGELES	213624 7001
43	E2	PELLISSIER	3780 WILSHIRE BLVD	LOS ANGELES	
42	B1	PERPETUAL SAVINGS&LOAN	9720 WILSHIRE BLVD	BEVERLY HILLS	213274 6066
44	D3	PERSHING SQUARE	448 S HILL	LOS ANGELES	213627 5117
44	C4	PETROL	950 S BROADWAY	LOS ANGELES	
44	C4	PETROLEUM	714 W OLYMPIC BLVD	LOS ANGELES	213749 7887
75	C4	PETROLEUM	929 LONG BEACH BLVD	LONG BEACH	
44	D3	PHILLIPS	224 S SPRING	LOS ANGELES	
43	E2	PIERCE NATIONAL LIFE	3807 WILSHIRE BLVD	LOS ANGELES	213381 7393
44	D3	PIONEER	317 S HILL	LOS ANGELES	
44	C4	PLATT	834 S BROADWAY	LOS ANGELES	
34	C3	POSTAL UNION LIFE INS	6305 YUCCA	LOS ANGELES	
44	D3	PREMIERE TOWERS	621 S SPRING ST	LOS ANGELES	
75	C5	PRESS TELEGRAM	604 PINE AV	LONG BEACH	
44	B3	PRODUCE	1315 E 7TH	LOS ANGELES	
44	C3	PROFESSIONAL	1052 W 6TH	LOS ANGELES	
75	C4	PROFESSIONAL	117 E 8TH	LONG BEACH	213436 2972
75	C4	PROFESSIONAL ANNEX	812 PINE AV	LONG BEACH	
27	B4	PROFESSIONAL BLDG	65 N MADISON AV	PASADENA	818792 5701
70	D3	PROFESSIONAL CENTER	125 E 8TH	LONG BEACH	
44	C2	PROMENADE TOWERS	123 S FIGUEROA ST	LOS ANGELES	213481 1769
70	D3	PRUDENTIAL	4320 ATLANTIC AV	LONG BEACH	213427 8931
43	A2	PRUDENTIAL SQUARE	5757 WILSHIRE BLVD	LOS ANGELES	
75	C5	PUBLIC SAFETY	400 W BROADWAY	LONG BEACH	
44	C3	QUINBY	650 S GRAND AV	LOS ANGELES	213623 2669
34	C3	R C A	6363 W SUNSET BLVD	LOS ANGELES	213468 4000
27	A4	REALTY BLDG	385 E GREEN ST	PASADENA	
76	B4	RECREATION PARK CLUB	5000 E ANAHEIM	LONG BEACH	
44	D3	RELNA	430 S BROADWAY	LOS ANGELES	
44	A2	RIVERSIDE CEMENT	2404 WILSHIRE BLVD	LOS ANGELES	213383 6348
44	D3	RIVES, JUDSON C	424 S BROADWAY	LOS ANGELES	
44	C3	ROOSEVELT	727 W 7TH	LOS ANGELES	213627 3096
44	D3	ROWAN	458 S SPRING	LOS ANGELES	213628 7737
44	C3	ST VINCENTS SQUARE	7TH & BROADWAY	LOS ANGELES	
44	D3	SAN FERNANDO	406 S MAIN	LOS ANGELES	213620 0498
44	E4	SANTA FE	121 E 6TH	LOS ANGELES	
41	A6	SANTA MONICA MED PLAZA	1260 15TH ST	SANTA MONICA	213394 0743
44	C3	SAWYER BLDG	812 W 8TH	LOS ANGELES	
75	C4	SCOTTISH RITE CATH	356 E 9TH	LONG BEACH	
37	A5	SEARS ADMINISTRATION	900 S FREMONT AV	ALHAMBRA	818576 4831
44	D3	SECURITY	510 S SPRING	LOS ANGELES	
75	C5	SECURITY	110 PINE AV	LONG BEACH	213436 4466
27	A4	SECURITY BLDG	234 E COLORADO	PASADENA	818796 2681
44	C3	SECURITY PACIFIC BANK	600 S GRAND AV	LOS ANGELES	
44	C3	SECURITY PAC BANK HQ	333 S HOPE ST	LOS ANGELES	213613 6211
25	C3	SECURITY PACIFIC BANK	601 N BRAND	GLENDALE	
44	C3	SECURITY PACIFIC BANK	800 6TH STREET	LOS ANGELES	
44	C3	SECURITY TITLE INS	530 W 6TH	LOS ANGELES	
44	D3	SEVERANCE	105 W 6TH	LOS ANGELES	
75	C5	SHARON	205 CHESTNUT AV	LONG BEACH	
44	C3	SIGNAL OIL & GAS	1010 WILSHIRE BLVD	LOS ANGELES	
44	C4	SINGER	806 S BROADWAY	LOS ANGELES	213627 3701
27	B4	SINGER BLDG	16 S OAKLAND AV	PASADENA	
44	D4	SIXTH AND SAN PEDRO	421 E 6TH ST	LOS ANGELES	213628 6723
42	E1	SIXTY-FIVE-O-FIVE	6505 WILSHIRE BLVD	BEVERLY HILLS	
75	C5	SOUTHERN CALIF EDISON	100 LONG BEACH BLVD	LONG BEACH	213432 9411
44	C3	SOUTHERN CALIF GAS CO	810 S FLOWER ST	LOS ANGELES	213689 2345
44	C3	SPRECKELS	714 S HILL	LOS ANGELES	213624 4088
44	D3	SPRING ARCADE	541 S SPRING	LOS ANGELES	
44	E4	STACK, H D	228 W 4TH	LOS ANGELES	
44	C4	STANDARD OIL	605 W OLYMPIC BLVD	LOS ANGELES	
44	C3	STATE MUTUAL S & L	626 WILSHIRE BLVD	LOS ANGELES	213625 7463
44	D3	STATE OFFICE BLDG #2	107 S BROADWAY	LOS ANGELES	
27	A4	STEVENSON BLDG	30 N RAYMOND AV	PASADENA	818793 4868
44	D4	STEWART DAWES	805 SANTEE	LOS ANGELES	
44	D3	STIMSON	129 W 3RD	LOS ANGELES	
44	D3	STORY, WALTER P	610 S BROADWAY	LOS ANGELES	
44	D5	STRONG, F R	703 S CENTRAL	LOS ANGELES	
44	D3	SUBWAY TERMINAL	417 S HILL	LOS ANGELES	213625 5825
34	B3	SUNSET CENTER	6725 SUNSET BLVD	HOLLYWOOD	
33	C4	SUNSET-DOHENY WEST	9255 SUNSET BLVD	BEVERLY HILLS	
34	C3	SUNSET MEDICAL	6642 W SUNSET BLVD	LOS ANGELES	
34	C3	SUNSET-VINE TOWER	6290 W SUNSET BLVD	LOS ANGELES	213464 0244
62	E3	T R W ADMINISTRATION	1 SPACE PARK DR	REDONDO BEACH	213535 4321
44	B2	T W A TOWER	1545 WILSHIRE BLVD	LOS ANGELES	213483 1100
34	C3	TAFT	1680 VINE	LOS ANGELES	
75	C4	TEAMSTERS	1314 ELM AV	LONG BEACH	
53	B4	TERMINAL	4814 LOMA VISTA AV	LOS ANGELES	
44	E5	TERMINAL SALES	747 WAREHOUSE	LOS ANGELES	
43	F2	TEXACO	3350 WILSHIRE BLVD	LOS ANGELES	213385 0515
44	C4	TEXTILE CENTER	746 S LOS ANGELES ST	LOS ANGELES	213623 4219
33	E6	THE CENTER	LA CIENEGA & BEVERLY	LOS ANGELES	
71	B2	THE CENTRE SYCAMORE PZ	5000 N CLARK AV	LAKEWOOD	213804 4434
44	D3	THIRD AND BROADWAY	306 W 3RD	LOS ANGELES	
42	E2	TICOR BLDG	6300 WILSHIRE BLVD	LOS ANGELES	213852 6300

PAGE	GRID	NAME	ADDRESS	CITY	PHONE
44	D3	TIMES MIRROR	TIMES MIRROR-SQUARE	LOS ANGELES	213972 5000
43	F2	TISHMAN	3440-50-60 WILSHIRE BL	LOS ANGELES	
56	D3	TISHMAN AIRPORT CENTER	6151 W CENTURY BLVD	LOS ANGELES	213776 3000
44	C3	TISHMAN DOWNTOWN	615 S FLOWER	LOS ANGELES	213628 2440
41	F4	TISHMAN WESTWOOD	10960 WILSHIRE BLVD	WESTWOOD	213477 0033
43	E2	TRAVELERS INSURANCE	3600 WILSHIRE BLVD	LOS ANGELES	213381 0011
44	C3	TRINITY AUDITORIUM	847 GRAND AV	LOS ANGELES	
44	B2	TWENTY TEN WILSHIRE BL	1930 WILSHIRE BLVD	LOS ANGELES	
27	B4	UNION BANK PLAZA	201 S LAKE AV	PASADENA	818578 7501
22	C3	UNION BANK PLAZA	15233 VENTURA BLVD	SHERMAN OAKS	818995 2061
44	C3	UNION BANK SQUARE	445 S FIGUEROA ST	LOS ANGELES	213687 6877
44	D3	UNION FEDERAL	426 S SPRING	LOS ANGELES	213688 8555
44	C2	UNION OIL CENTER	461 S BOYLSTON	LOS ANGELES	213489 1100
44	D4	UNION PACIFIC	422 W 6TH	LOS ANGELES	
44	C3	UNITED CALIF BANK HQ	707 WILSHIRE	LOS ANGELES	213614 4111
42	B1	UNITED CALIFORNIA BANK	9601 WILSHIRE BLVD	BEVERLY HILLS	213858 5478
21	F2	UNITED CALIFORNIA BANK	16633 VENTURA BLVD	ENCINO	818788 0500
44	D3	UNITED CALIFORNIA BANK	600 S SPRING	LOS ANGELES	
43	D2	UNITED OF AMERICA	4055 WILSHIRE BLVD	LOS ANGELES	
43	F2	U S BORAX	3075 WILSHIRE BLVD	LOS ANGELES	213381 5311
44	D2	U S COURTHOUSE	TEMPLE & SPRING	LOS ANGELES	
16	C5	VALLEY PLAZA TOWER	12160 VICTORY BLVD	N HOLLYWOOD	
44	D4	VAN NUYS 1 N	210 W 7TH	LOS ANGELES	213627 6126
75	C5	VETERANS MEMORIAL	245 W BROADWAY	LONG BEACH	213436 4019
34	C3	VINE TOWER BLDG	6305 YUCCA ST	HOLLYWOOD	213461 4253
44	D3	WASHINGTON	311 S SPRING	LOS ANGELES	
44	C3	WELLS FARGO BANK	770 WILSHIRE BLVD	LOS ANGELES	213683 7123
44	C4	WESTERN PACIFIC	1031 S BROADWAY	LOS ANGELES	
44	D4	WESTINGHOUSE ELECTRIC	420 S SAN PEDRO	LOS ANGELES	
44	B2	WESTLAKE MEDICAL	1913 WILSHIRE BLVD	LOS ANGELES	
44	B2	WESTLAKE PARK	2024 W 6TH	LOS ANGELES	
44	B2	WESTLAKE PROFESSIONAL	2007 WILSHIRE BLVD	LOS ANGELES	
41	E2	WESTWOOD CENTER	1100 GLENDON AV	W LOS ANGELES	213477 5585
44	D5	WHOLESALE TERMINAL	746 S CENTRAL AV	LOS ANGELES	
44	D3	WILCOX	206 S SPRING	LOS ANGELES	213972 5000
44	C3	WILFLOWER	615 S FLOWER	LOS ANGELES	
43	B2	WILSHIRE CENTER	5371 WILSHIRE BLVD	LOS ANGELES	
42	C1	WILSHIRE DOHENY PLAZA	9100 WILSHIRE BL	BEVERLY HILLS	
44	B2	WILSHIRE MEDICAL	1930 WILSHIRE BLVD	LOS ANGELES	213483 4186
43	F2	WILSHIRE PLAZA	3303 WILSHIRE BLVD	LOS ANGELES	213385 1381
43	D2	WILSHIRE PROFESSIONAL	3875 WILSHIRE BLVD	LOS ANGELES	213386 8745
42	E1	WILSHIRE SN VICENTE PZ	8383 WILSHIRE BLVD	BEVERLY HILLS	213653 1985
43	F2	WILSHIRE SQUARE	3345 WILSHIRE BLVD	LOS ANGELES	213383 4124
41	F4	WILSHIRE WEST PLAZA	10880 WILSHIRE BLVD	WESTWOOD	
44	D3	WILSON	132 W 1ST	LOS ANGELES	213628 6452
76	B5	WOODLAND CLUB HOUSE	5000 E 7TH	LONG BEACH	
44	C2	WORLD TRADE CENTER	333 S FLOWER ST	LOS ANGELES	213489 3330
44	D3	WRIGHT AND CALLENDER	405 S HILL	LOS ANGELES	
27	A4	Y M C A	235 E HOLLY	PASADENA	818793 3131
68	B5	Y M C A	2900 W SEPULVEDA	TORRANCE	213325 5885
44	C3	617 W SEVENTH	617 W SEVENTH	LOS ANGELES	213626 1899
44	C3	800 WILSHIRE BLDG	800 WILSHIRE BLVD	LOS ANGELES	213627 5626
44	C4	929 S BROADWAY	929 S BROADWAY	LOS ANGELES	
44	B3	1830 W 8TH ST BLDG	1830 W 8TH	LOS ANGELES	
44	B3	1836 W 8TH ST BLDG	1836 W 8TH	LOS ANGELES	
42	A2	1900 AVE OF THE STARS	1900 AVE OF THE STARS	CENTURY CITY	213557 0890
42	E1	6363 WILSHIRE	6363 WILSHIRE BLVD	LOS ANGELES	

CEMETERIES

PAGE	GRID	NAME	ADDRESS	CITY	PHONE
45	D6	AGUDATH ACHIM	1022 S DOWNEY RD	L A COUNTY	213653 8886
70	E3	ALL SOULS CEMETERY	4400 CHERRY AV	LONG BEACH	213424 8601
65	B3	ANGELES ABBEY MEM PK	1515 E COMPTON BLVD	COMPTON	213631 1141
45	D6	BETH ISRAEL CEMETERY	1068 S DOWNEY RD	LOS ANGELES	213653 8886
34	C4	BETH OLAM CEMETERY	900 N GOWER ST	LOS ANGELES	213469 2322
45	D5	CALVARY CEMETERY	4201 WHITTIER BLVD	E LOS ANGELES	213261 3106
183	F2	DESERT LAWN MEM PARK	2200 E AV S	PALMDALE	805947 7177
8	C1	EDEN MEMORIAL PARK	11500 SEPULVEDA BLVD	MISSION HILLS	818361 7161
38	B5	EL MONTE CEMETERY	9263 VALLEY BLVD	ROSEMEAD	818287 4838
127	E6	ETERNAL VALLEY MEM PK	23287 N SIERRA HWY	NEWHALL	805259 0800
45	B4	EVERGREEN CEMETERY	204 N EVERGREEN	LOS ANGELES	213268 6714
93	C2	FOREST LAWN MEM PARK	21300 E VIA VERDE	COVINA	818966 3671
25	D6	FOREST LAWN MEM PARK	1712 S GLENDALE AV	GLENDALE	818254 3131
24	C4	FOREST LAWN MEM PARK	6300 FOREST LAWN DR	LOS ANGELES	213254 7251
3	E3	GLENHAVEN MEMORIAL PK	13017 N LOPEZ CYN RD	SAN FERNANDO	818899 5211
73	D5	GREEN HILLS MEM PARK	27501 S WESTERN AV	RO PALOS VERD	213831 0311
50	C5	HILLSIDE MEMORIAL PK	6001 W CENTINELA AV	CULVER CITY	213836 7860
34	D4	HOLLYWOOD MEM PARK	6000 SANTA MONICA BLVD	HOLLYWOOD	213469 1181
50	D3	HOLY CROSS CEMETERY	5835 W SLAUSON AV	CULVER CITY	213670 7697
94	F5	HOLY CROSS CEMETERY	444 E LEXINGTON AV	POMONA	714627 3602
45	D6	HOME OF PEACE MEM PK	4334 WHITTIER BLVD	E LOS ANGELES	213261 6135
51	B6	INGLEWOOD PARK CEM	720 E FLORENCE AV	INGLEWOOD	213412 6500
160	D4	JOSHUA MEMORIAL PARK	808 E LANCASTER BLVD	LANCASTER	805942 8125
90	D2	LA VERNE CEMETERY	3201 B ST	LA VERNE	714593 1415
64	D4	LINCOLN MEMORIAL PARK	16701 S CENTRAL AV	CARSON	213636 7141
29	B6	LIVE OAK MEMORIAL PARK	200 E DUARTE RD	MONROVIA	818359 5311
75	D1	LONG BEACH CEMETERY	1095 E WILLOW ST	LONG BEACH	213424 2639
19	F5	MOUNTAIN VIEW CEMETERY	2400 N FAIR OAKS	ALTADENA	818794 7133
54	A5	MT CARMEL	6501 E GAGE AV	COMMERCE	213653 8886
54	B5	MT OLIVE MEMORIAL PARK	7231 E SLAUSON AV	COMMERCE	213721 4729
24	D4	MT SINAI MEMORIAL PARK	5950 FOREST LAWN DR	LOS ANGELES	213469 6000

—Z— COPYRIGHT, © 1989 BY Thomas Bros Maps

1990 LOS ANGELES COUNTY POINTS OF INTEREST

PAGE	GRID	NAME	ADDRESS	CITY	PHONE
89	A2	OAKDALE MEMORIAL PARK	1401 S GRAND AV	GLENDORA	818335 0281
6	A3	OAKWOOD MEMORIAL PARK	22600 LASSEN ST	CHATSWORTH	818341 0344
45	C6	ODD FELLOWS CEMETERY	3640 WHITTIER BLVD	LOS ANGELES	213261 6156
83	A2	OLIVE LAWN MEMORIAL PK	13926 S LA MIRADA BLVD	LA MIRADA	213943 1718
62	F6	PACIFIC CREST CEMETERY	1400 INGLEWOOD AV	REDONDO BEACH	213370 5891
60	F4	PARADISE MEMORIAL PARK	11541 E FLORENCE	SANTA FE SPGS	213864 7316
54	B5	PARK LAWN MEM PARK	6555 GAGE AV	COMMERCE	213773 3220
16	F5	PIERCE BROS VALHALLA	10621 VICTORY BLVD	N HOLLYWOOD	818763 9121
94	F4	POMONA CEMETERY	502 E FRANKLIN AV	POMONA	714622 2029
98	D4	QUEEN OF HEAVEN CEM	2161 S FULLERTON RD	ROWLAND HTS	818964 1291
46	E4	RESURRECTION CEMETERY	966 N POTRERO GRNDE DR	MONTEBELLO	213728 1231
63	F6	ROOSEVELT MEMORIAL PK	18255 S VERMONT AV	GARDENA	213329 1113
43	E4	ROSEDALE CEMETERY	1831 W WASHINGTON BLVD	LOS ANGELES	213734 3155
55	D2	ROSE HILLS MEM PARK	3900 S WORKMAN MILL RD	WHITTIER	213699 0921
8	C1	SAN FERNANDO MISSION	11160 STANWOOD AV	LOS ANGELES	213361 7387
37	D2	SAN GABRIEL CEMETERY	601 ROSES RD	SAN GABRIEL	818282 2764
3	E3	SHOLOM MEMORIAL PARK	13017 N LOPEZ CYN RD	SAN FERNANDO	818899 5211
75	D1	SUNNYSIDE CEMETERY	1095 E WILLOW	LONG BEACH	213424 2639
70	E3	SUNNYSIDE MEM GARDENS	4725 CHERRY	LONG BEACH	213424 1631
102	C3	VALLEY OAKS MEM PK	5600 N LINDERO CYN RD	WESTLAKE VLGE	213889 0902
11	A2	VERDUGO HILLS CEMETERY	7000 PARSONS TR	TUJUNGA	818352 6123
41	D2	VETERANS ADMINISTRATN	950 SEPULVEDA BLVD	WESTWOOD	213824 4311
41	E2	WESTWOOD MEMORIAL PARK	1218 GLENDON AV	WESTWOOD	213474 1579
74	C3	WILMINGTON CEMETERY	605 EAST O ST	WILMINGTON	213834 4442
41	B6	WOODLAWN CEMETERY	1847 14TH ST	SANTA MONICA	213450 0781
64	D4	WOODLAWN MEMORIAL PARK	1715 W GREENLEAF DR	COMPTON	213636 1696
66	D1	YOUNG ISRAEL	13622 CURTIS & KING RD	NORWALK	213653 8886

CHAMBERS OF COMMERCE

PAGE	GRID	NAME	ADDRESS	CITY	PHONE
100A	D4	AGOURA HILLS	28128 AGOURA RD	AGOURA HILLS	818889 1327
102	F4	AGOURA LAS VIRGINES	29252 CANWOOD ST	AGOURA	818889 3150
37	C4	ALHAMBRA	104 S FIRST ST	ALHAMBRA	818282 8481
20	B5	ALTADENA	2526 N EL MOLINO AV	ALTADENA	818794 3988
28	D5	ARCADIA	388 W HUNTINGTON DR	ARCADIA	818447 2159
82	A6	ARTESIA	18634 S PIONEER	ARTESIA	213924 6397
77	B5	AVALON CATALINA ISLAND	#1 PLEASURE PIER	AVALON	213510 1520
58	B6	AVALON-EL SEGUNDO	12811 S AVALON BLVD	LOS ANGELES	213292 7000
86	D5	AZUSA	568 E FOOTHILL BLVD	AZUSA	818334 1507
39	E5	BALDWIN PARK	14327 E RAMONA BLVD	BALDWIN PARK	818960 4848
53	C5	BELL	6415 S ATLANTIC AV	BELL	213560 8755
66	C4	BELLFLOWER	9729 E FLOWER AV	BELLFLOWER	213867 1744
53	E6	BELL GARDENS	7113 EASTERN AV	BELL GARDENS	213773 3708
42	C1	BEVERLY HILLS	239 S BEVERLY DR	BEVERLY HILLS	213271 8126
17	D6	BURBANK	200 W MAGNOLIA BLVD	BURBANK	818846 3111
12	C3	CANOGA PARK	7248 OWENSMOUTH AV	CANOGA PARK	818884 4222
125	A8	CANYON COUNTRY	17956 SIERRA HWY	CYN COUNTRY	805252 4131
69	A4	CARSON	426 W CARSON ST	CARSON	213320 0551
42	A2	CENTURY CITY	2020 AVE OF THE STARS	CENTURY CITY	213553 4062
82	C5	CERRITOS	13017 ARTESIA BLVD	CERRITOS	213926 8506
6	C3	CHATSWORTH	21740 DEVONSHIRE ST	CHATSWORTH	213341 2428
53	F4	CITY OF COMMERCE	5800 EASTERN AV	COMMERCE	213724 1067
91	B4	CLAREMONT	215 W SECOND	CLAREMONT	714624 1681
65	A3	COMPTON	499 E COMPTON BLVD	COMPTON	213631 8611
88	E5	COVINA	101 N CITRUS AV	COVINA	818967 4191
51	C3	CRENSHAW	4716 CRENSHAW BLVD	LOS ANGELES	
50	C4	CULVER CITY	5901 GREEN VALLEY CIR	CULVER CITY	213417 3919
60	C4	DOWNEY	11131 BROOKSHIRE AV	DOWNEY	213923 2191
29	E5	DUARTE	2229 E HUNTINGTON DR	DUARTE	818357 3333
38	D6	EL MONTE	10820 VALLEY MALL	EL MONTE	818444 4561
56	A6	EL SEGUNDO	427 MAIN	EL SEGUNDO	213322 1220
21	F2	ENCINO	4933 BALBOA BLVD	ENCINO	213789 4711
63	D4	GARDENA	1919 W REDONDO BCH BL	GARDENA	213532 9905
25	C4	GLENDALE	200 S LOUISE ST	GLENDALE	818240 7870
87	A5	GLENDORA	224 N GLENDORA AV	GLENDORA	213963 4128
7	D2	GRANADA HILLS	10727 WHITE OAK AV#100	SAN FERNANDO	818368 3235
73	E2	HARBOR CITY	1437 W LOMITA BLVD	LOS ANGELES	213325 3310
81	A4	HAWAIIAN GARDENS	21815 PIONEER BLVD	HAWAIIAN GDNS	213421 1632
57	A6	HAWTHORNE	12427 S HAWTHORNE BLVD	HAWTHORNE	213676 1163
67	C1	HERMOSA BEACH	323 PIER AV	HERMOSA BEACH	213376 0951
36	C2	HIGHLAND PARK	131 S AVENUE 57	LOS ANGELES	213256 0920
34	C3	HOLLYWOOD	6290 SUNSET BLVD	HOLLYWOOD	213469 8311
52	F5	HUNTINGTON PARK	2650 ZOE AV	HUNTINGTON PK	213585 1155
48	E6	INDUSTRY	255 N HACIENDA BLVD	INDUSTRY	818968 3737
57	A1	INGLEWOOD	330 E QUEEN ST	INGLEWOOD	213677 1121
88	B2	IRWINDALE	16116 E ARROW HWY	IRWINDALE	818960 6606
19	B3	LA CANADA	1327 FOOTHILL BLVD	LA CANADA	818790 4289
11	D6	LA CRESCENTA	3131 FOOTHILL BLVD	LA CRESCENTA	818248 4957
71	C2	LAKEWOOD	5445 DEL AMO BLVD	LAKEWOOD	213920 7737
84	C6	LA MIRADA	15707 E IMPERIAL HWY	LA MIRADA	213943 3748
48	F6	LA PUENTE	15917 E MAIN ST	LA PUENTE	818330 3216
160	A4	LANCASTER	44943 N 10TH ST W	LANCASTER	805948 4518
90	D3	LA VERNE	2078 BONITA AV	LA VERNE	714593 5265
63	A3	LAWNDALE	14704 S HAWTHORNE BLVD	LAWNDALE	213679 3306
73	D2	LOMITA	24300 NARBONNE AV	LOMITA	213326 6378
75	B6	LONG BEACH	330 GOLDEN SHORE	LONG BEACH	213436 1251
44	C2	LOS ANGELES	404 S BIXEL ST	LOS ANGELES	213629 0711
43	B3	LOS ANGELES MID-CITY	4729 W VENICE BLVD	LOS ANGELES	213937 3532
59	B5	LYNWOOD	3651 E IMPERIAL HWY	LYNWOOD	213537 6484
114	D4	MALIBU	22235 PACIFIC COAST HY	MALIBU	213456 9025
62	B4	MANHATTAN BEACH	425 15TH ST	MANHATTAN BCH	213545 5313
49	D4	MARINA DEL REY	14014 TAHITI WY	MARINA DL REY	213821 0555
8	C2	MISSION HILLS	10646 1/2 SEPULVEDA BL	MISSION HILLS	818361 8888
29	B4	MONROVIA	111 W COLORADO BLVD	MONROVIA	818358 1159
54	D1	MONTEBELLO	1304 W BEVERLY BLVD	MONTEBELLO	213721 1153
46	C2	MONTEREY PARK	163 W GARVEY AV	MONTEREY PARK	818280 3864
18	F3	MONTROSE	3808 OCEAN VIEW BLVD	MONTROSE	818249 7171
127	C4	NEWHLL-SAUGUS-VALENCIA	24275 WALNUT AV	NEWHALL	805259 4787
23	E2	NORTH HOLLYWOOD	5019 LANKERSHIM BLVD	N HOLLYWOOD	818508 5155
7	C6	NORTHRIDGE	8801 RESEDA BLVD	NORTHRIDGE	818349 5676
82	B2	NORWALK	12040 E FOSTER RD	NORWALK	213864 7785
40	D4	PACIFIC PALISADES	15330 ANTIOCH ST	PACIFIC PALSD	213495 7963
9	B1	PACOIMA	11243 GLEN OAKS BLVD	PACOIMA	818899 7401
172	D8	PALMDALE	712 E PALMDALE BLVD	PALMDALE	805273 3232
72	F5	PALOS VERDES PENINSULA	927 DEEP VALLEY DR	ROLLG HLS EST	213377 8111
15	D1	PANORAMA CITY	14600 ROSCOE BLVD	PANORAMA CITY	818891 3996
65	F3	PARAMOUNT	15357 PARAMOUNT BLVD	PARAMOUNT	213634 3980
27	A4	PASADENA	199 S LOS ROBLES AV	PASADENA	818795 3355
54	E5	PICO RIVERA	9122 E WASHINGTON BLVD	PICO RIVERA	213949 2473
94	E3	POMONA	260 S GAREY AV	POMONA	714622 1256
67	C2	REDONDO BEACH	1215 N CATALINA AV	REDONDO BEACH	213376 6911
14	C3	RESEDA	18546 SHERMAN WY	RESEDA	818345 1920
38	A5	ROSEMEAD	8780 E VALLEY BLVD	ROSEMEAD	818288 0811
89	F3	SAN DIMAS	111 S MONTE VISTA AV	SAN DIMAS	714592 3818
2	E6	SAN FERNANDO	747 SAN FERNANDO RD	SAN FERNANDO	818361 1184
14	E1	SAN FERNANDO VALLEY	8238 LOUISE AV	NORTHRIDGE	818708 2391
37	D3	SAN GABRIEL	534 W MISSION DR	SAN GABRIEL	818576 2525
37	D1	SAN MARINO	2304 HUNTINGTON DR	SAN MARINO	818286 1022
79	A3	SAN PEDRO	390 W 7TH ST	SAN PEDRO	213832 7272
61	A3	SANTA FE SPRINGS	11736 E TELEGRAPH RD	SANTA FE SPGS	213868 6736
49	A1	SANTA MONICA	1460 4TH ST	SANTA MONICA	213393 9825
22	C3	SHERMAN OAKS	15301 VENTURA BLVD	SHERMAN OAKS	818783 3100
28	C2	SIERRA MADRE	245 W SIERRA MADRE BL	SIERRA MADRE	818355 7141
75	E2	SIGNAL HILL	1919 E HILL ST	SIGNAL HILL	213424 6489
59	A3	SOUTH GATE	3350 TWEEDY BLVD	SOUTH GATE	213567 1203
36	F1	SOUTH PASADENA	1005 FAIR OAKS AV	S PASADENA	818799 7161
23	E4	STUDIO CITY	11201 VENTURA BLVD	STUDIO CITY	818769 3213
16	E1	SUN VALLEY	8113 SUNLAND BL	SUN VALLEY	213768 2014
2	F3	SYLMAR	13251 GLADSTONE AV	SYLMAR	818367 1177
21	B1	TARZANA	18705 VENTURA BLVD	TARZANA	818343 3687
38	B2	TEMPLE CITY	5827 N TEMPLE CITY BL	TEMPLE CITY	818286 3101
24	A3	TOLUCA LAKE	10000 RIVERSIDE DR	TOLUCA LAKE	818761 6594
108	F3	TOPANGA	23370 RED ROCK RD	TOPANGA	213455 1442
68	A4	TORRANCE	3400 TORRANCE BL	TORRANCE	213540 5858
15	D5	VAN NUYS	14545 VICTORY BLVD	VAN NUYS	818989 0300
49	D4	VENICE	681 VENICE BLVD	VENICE	213827 2366
52	E2	VERNON	3801 SANTA FE AV	VERNON	213583 3313
97	B1	WALNUT VALLEY	374 S LEMON AV	WALNUT	714595 6138
56	C2	WESTCHESTER	8833 SEPULVEDA BLVD	WESTCHESTER	213645 5151
92	A1	WEST COVINA	811 S SUNSET AV	WEST COVINA	818338 8496
33	E4	WEST HOLLYWOOD	8350 SANTA MONICA BLVD	LOS ANGELES	213654 9213
41	E2	WESTERN L A REGIONAL	10880 WILSHIRE BLVD	WESTWOOD	213475 4574
61	E1	WHITTIER AREA	8158 S PAINTER AV	WHITTIER	213698 9554
74	C4	WILMINGTON	544 N AVALON BLVD	WILMINGTON	213834 8586
43	D2	WILSHIRE CENTER	3875 WILSHIRE BLVD	LOS ANGELES	213386 8224
12	C6	WOODLAND HILLS	21600 OXNARD ST	WOODLAND HLLS	818347 4737

CITY HALLS

PAGE	GRID	NAME	ADDRESS	CITY	PHONE
102	D4	AGOURA HILLS	30101 W AGOURA RD	AGOURA HILLS	818889 9114
37	C4	ALHAMBRA	111 S 1ST ST	ALHAMBRA	818570 5007
28	D5	ARCADIA	240 W HUNTINGTON	ARCADIA	818574 5400
81	A1	ARTESIA	18747 CLARKSDALE AV	ARTESIA	213865 6262
77	B5	AVALON	209 METROPOLE AV	AVALON	213510 0220
86	D5	AZUSA	213 E FOOTHILL BLVD	AZUSA	818334 5125
39	E5	BALDWIN PARK	14403 PACIFIC AV	BALDWIN PARK	818960 4011
53	C5	BELL	6330 PINE AV	BELL	213588 6211
66	C4	BELLFLOWER	16600 CIVIC CENTER DR	BELLFLOWER	213804 1424
54	A6	BELL GARDENS	5960 1/2 E FLORENCE AV	BELL GARDENS	714562 2830
33	C6	BEVERLY HILLS	450 CRESCENT DR	BEVERLY HILLS	213550 4700
17	E5	BRADBURY	600 WINSTON AV	BRADBURY	818847 8600
69	C4	CARSON	701 E CARSON ST	CARSON	213830 7600
81	D5	CERRITOS	18125 S BLOOMFIELD AV	CERRITOS	213860 0311
91	B4	CLAREMONT	207 HARVARD AV	CLAREMONT	714624 4531
53	F3	COMMERCE	2535 COMMERCE WY	COMMERCE	213722 4805
64	F3	COMPTON	205 S WILLOWBROOK AV	COMPTON	213605 5500
88	E5	COVINA	125 E COLLEGE ST	COVINA	818331 0111
59	D1	CUDAHY	5220 SANTA ANA ST	CUDAHY	213773 5143
42	C6	CULVER CITY	9770 CULVER BLVD	CULVER CITY	213837 5211
60	C4	DOWNEY	11111 S BROOKSHIRE AV	DOWNEY	213869 7331
29	D4	DUARTE	1600 HUNTINGTON DR	DUARTE	818357 7931
47	E1	EL MONTE	11333 VALLEY BLVD	EL MONTE	818580 2019
56	A6	EL SEGUNDO	350 MAIN ST	EL SEGUNDO	213322 4670
63	E4	GARDENA	1700 W 162ND ST	GARDENA	213217 9500
25	D4	GLENDALE	613 E BROADWAY	GLENDALE	818956 4000
87	B5	GLENDORA	116 E FOOTHILL BLVD	GLENDORA	818914 8200
81	A4	HAWAIIAN GARDENS	21815 PIONEER BLVD	HAWAIIAN GDNS	213420 2641
57	A6	HAWTHORNE	4455 W 126TH ST	HAWTHORNE	213970 7902
62	C6	HERMOSA BEACH	1315 VALLEY DR	HERMOSA BCH	213376 6984
100	D1	HIDDEN HILLS	2454 LONG VALLEY RD	HIDDEN HILLS	213888 9281
53	A5	HUNTINGTON PARK	6550 MILES AV	HUNTINGTON PK	213582 6161
48	F6	INDUSTRY	15651 E STAFFORD ST	INDUSTRY	818333 2211

PAGE	GRID	NAME	ADDRESS	CITY	PHONE
57	A1	INGLEWOOD	1 MANCHESTER BLVD	INGLEWOOD	213412 5300
88	B3	IRWINDALE	5050 N IRWINDALE AV	IRWINDALE	818962 3381
19	B3	LA CANADA-FLINTRIDGE	1327 FOOTHILL BLVD	LA CANADA	818790 8880
84	E3	LA HABRA HEIGHTS	1245 N HACIENDA BLVD	LA HABRA HTS	213694 6302
71	B2	LAKEWOOD	5050 N CLARK AV	LAKEWOOD	213866 9771
83	A1	LA MIRADA	13700 S LA MIRADA BLVD	LA MIRADA	213943 0131
160	A4	LANCASTER	44933 N FERN AV	LANCASTER	805945 7811
48	F6	LA PUENTE	15900 E MAIN ST	LA PUENTE	818330 4511
90	D2	LA VERNE	3660 D ST	LA VERNE	714596 1913
63	A3	LAWNDALE	14717 BURIN AV	LAWNDALE	213973 4321
73	D1	LOMITA	24300 NARBONNE AV	LOMITA	213325 7110
75	C5	LONG BEACH	333 W OCEAN BLVD	LONG BEACH	213590 6555
44	D3	LOS ANGELES	200 N SPRING ST	LOS ANGELES	213485 2121
59	B5	LYNWOOD	11330 BULLIS RD	LYNWOOD	213537 0800
62	B4	MANHATTAN BEACH	1400 HIGHLAND AV	MANHATTAN BCH	213545 5621
53	C4	MAYWOOD	4319 E SLAUSON AV	MAYWOOD	213562 5000
29	B4	MONROVIA	415 S IVY AV	MONROVIA	818359 3231
46	D6	MONTEBELLO	1600 W BEVERLY BLVD	MONTEBELLO	213725 1200
46	C2	MONTEREY PARK	320 W NEWMARK AV	MONTEREY PK	818307 1458
61	B6	NORWALK	12700 S NORWALK BLVD	NORWALK	213829 2677
172	C8	PALMDALE	708 E PALMDALE BLVD	PALMDALE	805273 3162
77	B2	PALOS VERDES ESTATES	340 PALOS VERDES DR W	PALO VERD EST	213378 0383
65	F4	PARAMOUNT	16400 COLORADO AV	PARAMOUNT	213531 3503
27	A4	PASADENA	100 N GARFIELD AV	PASADENA	818577 4000
55	F5	PICO RIVERA	6615 S PASSONS	PICO RIVERA	213942 2000
94	E3	POMONA	505 S GAREY AV	POMONA	714620 2311
55	F5	RANCHO PALOS VERDES	30940 HAWTHORNE BLVD	RO PALO VRDS	213377 0360
67	D3	REDONDO BEACH	415 DIAMOND	REDONDO BEACH	213372 1171
73	B4	ROLLING HILLS	2 PORTUGUESE BEND RD	ROLLING HILLS	213377 1521
73	A4	ROLLING HILLS ESTATES	4045 PALOS VERDES DR N	ROLLNG HL EST	213377 1577
38	A5	ROSEMEAD	8838 VALLEY BLVD	ROSEMEAD	818288 6671
90	A3	SAN DIMAS	245 E BONITA AV	SAN DIMAS	714599 6713
2	E6	SAN FERNANDO	117 N MACNEIL	SAN FERNANDO	818898 1200
37	D3	SAN GABRIEL	532 W MISSION DR	SAN GABRIEL	818308 2800
37	D1	SAN MARINO	2000 HUNTINGTON DR	SAN MARINO	818300 0700
124	F8	SANTA CLARITA	21021 SOLEDAD CYN RD	SANTA CLARITA	805259 2489
61	A1	SANTA FE SPRINGS	11710 E TELEGRAPH RD	SANTA FE SPGS	213868 0511
49	A1	SANTA MONICA	1685 MAIN ST	SANTA MONICA	213393 9975
28	C2	SIERRA MADRE	232 W SIERRA MADRE BL	SIERRA MADRE	818355 7135
75	E2	SIGNAL HILL	2175 CHERRY AV	SIGNAL HILL	213426 7333
47	D3	SOUTH EL MONTE	1415 SANTA ANITA AV	S EL MONTE	818579 6540
59	B2	SOUTH GATE	8650 CALIFORNIA AV	SOUTH GATE	213563 9500
36	F1	SOUTH PASADENA	1424 MISSION	S PASADENA	818799 9101
38	C2	TEMPLE CITY	9701 LAS TUNAS DR	TEMPLE CITY	818285 2171
68	B4	TORRANCE	3031 TORRANCE BLVD	TORRANCE	213328 5310
52	E2	VERNON	4305 S SANTA FE AV	VERNON	213583 8811
93	D5	WALNUT	21201 LA PUENTE RD	WALNUT	213595 7543
92	A1	WEST COVINA	1444 W GARVEY AV	WEST COVINA	818814 8400
33	D5	WEST HOLLYWOOD	8611 SANTA MONICA BLVD	W HOLLYWOOD	213854 7400
102	B4	WESTLAKE VILLAGE	31824 VILLAGE CTR DR	WESTLAKE VLG	818706 1613
55	E5	WHITTIER	13230 E PENN	WHITTIER	213945 8200

COLLEGES & UNIVERSITIES

PAGE	GRID	NAME	ADDRESS	CITY	PHONE
26	F4	AMBASSADOR COLLEGE	300 W GREEN	PASADENA	818304 6000
26	C1	ART CENTER COLLEGE	1700 LIDA ST	PASADENA	818577 1700
86	E6	AZUSA PACIFIC UNIV	18527 ALOSTA	AZUSA	213969 3434
83	A1	BIOLA UNIVERSITY	13800 BIOLA AV	LA MIRADA	714944 0351
27	C5	CAL INST OF TECHNOLOGY	1201 E CALIFORNIA BLVD	PASADENA	818356 6811
126	J2	CALIF INST OF THE ARTS	24700 MCBEAN PKWY	VALENCIA	805255 1050
93	E3	CALIF STATE POLYT UNIV	3801 W TEMPLE AV	POMONA	714598 4592
64	C6	CAL STATE DOMNGUZ HLLS	1000 E VICTORIA ST	CARSON	213516 3300
76	D4	CAL STATE U LONG BEACH	1250 BELLFLOWER BLVD	LONG BEACH	213498 4111
45	E1	CAL STATE U LS ANGELES	5151 STATE UNIV DR	LOS ANGELES	213224 0111
7	C4	CAL STATE U NORTHRIDGE	18111 NORDHOFF ST	NORTHRIDGE	818885 1200
66	E4	CERRITOS COLLEGE	11110 E ALONDRA BLVD	NORWALK	213860 2451
86	E5	CITRUS COLLEGE	1000 W FOOTHILL BLVD	GLENDORA	213335 0521
91	C3	CLAREMONT-MCKENNA COL	747 N DARTMOUTH AV	CLAREMONT	714621 8000
34	F5	CLEVELAND CHIROPRACTIC	590 N VERMONT AV	LOS ANGELES	213660 6166
126	J1	COLLEGE OF THE CANYONS	26455 N ROCKWLL CYN RD	VALENCIA	805259 7800
65	A5	COMPTON COLLEGE	1111 E ARTESIA BLVD	COMPTON	213637 2660
45	F4	EAST LOS ANGELES	1301 E BROOKLYN	MONTEREY PARK	213265 8650
63	C4	EL CAMINO COLLEGE	16007 CRENSHAW BLVD	GARDENA	213532 3670
44	C3	FASHION INSTITUTE	818 W 7TH ST	LOS ANGELES	213624 1200
22	E2	FASHION INSTITUTE	13701 RIVERSIDE DR	SHERMAN OAKS	818990 2133
27	B4	FULLER THEOLOGICAL SEM	135 N OAKLAND AV	PASADENA	818449 1745
25	F1	GLENDALE COLLEGE	1500 N VERDUGO RD	GLENDALE	818240 1000
25	D3	GLEN UNIV COLL OF LAW	220 N GLENDALE AV	GLENDALE	818247 0770
91	C3	HARVEY MUDD COLLEGE	12TH & DARTMOUTH	CLAREMONT	714621 8000
41	E1	JULES STEIN EYE INST	800 WESTWOOD PLAZA	W LOS ANGELES	213825 8556
71	B4	LONG BEACH CITY	4901 E CARSON	LONG BEACH	213420 4111
84	D5	LA COL OF CHIROPRACTIC	16200 E AMBER VLY DR	L A COUNTY	213947 8755
34	F4	LOS ANGELES CITY COL	855 N VERMONT AV	LOS ANGELES	213669 4000
74	A4	LOS ANGELES HARBOR COL	1111 FIGUEROA PL	WILMINGTON	213518 1000
2	E6	L A MISSION COLLEGE	1245 SAN FERNANDO RD	SAN FERNANDO	818365 8271
57	E5	L A SOUTHWEST COLLEGE	1600 W IMPERIAL HWY	LOS ANGELES	213777 2225
44	B5	L A TRADE TECH COLLEGE	400 W WASHINGTON BLVD	LOS ANGELES	213746 0800
16	A6	LOS ANGELES VALLEY COL	5800 FULTON AV	VAN NUYS	818781 1200
44	B3	LOYOLA LAW SCHOOL	1441 W OLYMPIC BLVD	LOS ANGELES	213736 1000
50	A6	LOYOLA MARYMOUNT UNIV	7101 W 80TH	WESTCHESTER	213642 2700
78	C3	MARYMOUNT PAL VER COL	30800 PALOS VER DR E	RO PALOS VRDS	213377 5501
127	D4	MASTERS COLLEGE	21726 PLACERITA CYN	NEWHALL	805259 3540
32	B5	MOUNT SAINT MARYS	12001 CHALON RD	W LOS ANGELES	213476 2237
93	C4	MT SAN ANTONIO	1100 N GRAND AV	WALNUT	714594 5611
56	E2	NORTHROP UNIVERSITY	5800 ARBOR VITA E ST	INGLEWOOD	213776 3410
26	A6	OCCIDENTAL	1600 CAMPUS RD	EAGLE ROCK	213259 2974
44	A2	OTIS ART-PARSONS	2401 WILSHIRE	LOS ANGELES	213387 5288
43	E3	PACIFIC STATES UNIV	1516 S WESTERN AV	LOS ANGELES	213731 2383
27	C4	PASADENA CITY	1570 E COLORADO BLVD	PASADENA	818578 7123
113	E4	PEPPERDINE UNIVERSITY	24255 W PAC COAST HWY	MALIBU	213456 4000
12	D5	PIERCE	6201 WINNETKA AV	WOODLAND HILL	818347 0551
91	C3	PITZER COLLEGE	747 N DARTMOUTH	CLAREMONT	714621 8000
91	C4	POMONA COLLEGE	10TH & COLLEGE	CLAREMONT	714621 8000
47	E6	RIO HONDO COLLEGE	3600 S WORKMAN MILL RD	WHITTIER	213692 0921
49	C1	SANTA MONICA COLLEGE	1900 PICO BLVD	SANTA MONICA	213450 5150
91	C3	SCRIPPS COLLEGE	747 N DARTMOUTH AV	CLAREMONT	714621 8000
43	F2	SOUTHWESTERN UNIV	675 S WESTMORELAND AV	LOS ANGELES	213738 6700
32	E6	UNIV CALIF AT LA	405 HILGARD AV	WESTWOOD	213825 4321
22	B6	UNIVERSITY OF JUDAISM	15600 MULHOLLAND DR	LOS ANGELES	213879 4114
90	C3	UNIVERSITY OF LA VERNE	1950 3RD AV	LA VERNE	714593 3511
44	A6	UNIV OF SO CALIF	3551 UNIVERSITY AV	LOS ANGELES	213743 6741
45	B2	USC SCHOOL OF MEDICINE	2025 ZONAL AV	LOS ANGELES	213224 7622
50	B2	UNIVERSITY OF W LA	10811 WASHINGTON BLVD	CULVER CITY	213204 0000
43	F1	WEST COAST UNIVERSITY	440 SHATTO PL	LOS ANGELES	213487 4433
50	D2	W LOS ANGELES COLLEGE	4800 FRESHMAN DR	CULVER CITY	213836 7110
55	F5	WHITTIER	13406 PHILADELPHIA ST	WHITTIER	213693 0771
34	B6	WHITTIER SCHL OF LAW	5353 W THIRD ST	LOS ANGELES	
44	C3	WOODBURY	1027 WILSHIRE BLVD	LOS ANGELES	213482 8491

GOLF COURSES

PAGE	GRID	NAME	ADDRESS	CITY	PHONE
37	D4	ALHAMBRA MUN GOLF CRSE	630 S ALMANSOR ST	ALHAMBRA	818570 5059
63	B4	ALONDRA PARK GOLF CRSE	16400 S PRAIRIE AV	LAWNDALE	213327 5699
20	C5	ALTADENA GOLF COURSE	1456 E MENDOCINO ST	ALTADENA	818797 3821
26	D4	ANNANDALE GOLF COURSE	1 N SAN RAFAEL AV	PASADENA	818795 8253
172	A5	ANTELOPE VALLEY C C	39800 N CNTRY CLUB DR	PALMDALE	805947 3400
38	F3	ARCADIA PAR 3 GOLF CSE	620 E LIVE OAK AV	ARCADIA	818443 9367
36	E1	ARROYO SECO GOLF CRSE	1055 LOHMAN LN	S PASADENA	213255 2822
86	C4	AZUSA GREENS C C	919 W SIERRA MADRE AV	AZUSA	818969 1727
21	F1	BALBOA GOLF COURSE	16821 BURBANK BLVD	ENCINO	818995 1170
32	D5	BEL AIR COUNTRY CLUB	10768 BELLAGIO RD	BEL AIR EST	213472 0414
66	B3	BELLFLOWER GOLF CENTER	9030 COMPTON BLVD	BELLFLOWER	213867 6333
76	D5	BIXBY VILLAGE GOLF CRS	6180 BIXBY VILLAGE DR	LONG BEACH	213498 7003
21	B4	BRAEMAR COUNTRY CLUB	4001 RESEDA BLVD	TARZANA	818345 6520
41	B3	BRENTWOOD COUNTRY CLUB	590 BURLINGAME AV	LOS ANGELES	213451 8011
26	E1	BROOKSIDE GOLF COURSE	1133 ROSEMONT AV	PASADENA	818796 0177
47	F4	CALIFORNIA COUNTRY CLB	1509 S WORKMAN MILL RD	WHITTIER	213692 0421
100	D4	CALABASAS PARK G CRSE	4515 N PARK ENTRADA	CALABASAS	818888 8811
61	E4	CANDLEWOOD CNTRY CLUB	14000 E TELEGRAPH RD	WHITTIER	213941 5310
77	B6	CATALINA ISLAND G CLUB	100 COUNTRY CLUB DR	AVALON	213510 0530
57	D6	CHESTER L WASHNGTN GC	1930 W 120TH ST	LOS ANGELES	213756 2516
26	B1	CHEVY CHASE CNTRY CLUB	3067 E CHEVY CHASE DR	GLENDALE	818244 8461
91	B2	CLAREMONT GOLF COURSE	1550 N INDIAN HILL	CLAREMONT	714624 2748
65	D3	COMPTON PAR 3 G COURSE	6400 E COMPTON BLVD	COMPTON	213633 6721
192	H2	CRYSTALAIRE C C	15701 BOCA RATON AV	LLANO	805944 2111
17	E3	DE BELL MUN GOLF CRSE	1200 HARVARD DR	BURBANK	818845 0022
172	H6	DESERT AIRE GOLF CRSE	3620 E AVE P	PALMDALE	805947 6728
97	F1	DIAMOND BAR G COURSE	22751 GOLDEN SPGS DR	DIAMOND BAR	818964 0300
69	A2	DOMINGUEZ GOLF COURSE	19800 S MAIN ST	CARSON	213323 9115
28	A2	EATON CYN GOLF COURSE	1150 SRA MADRE VILLA	PASADENA	818791 1142
21	C3	EL CABALLERO C C	18300 TARZANA DR	TARZANA	818345 2770
3	A2	EL CARISO GOLF COURSE	13100 ELDRIDGE AV	SYLMAR	818367 6157
76	F1	EL DORADO GOLF COURSE	2400 STUDEBAKER RD	LONG BEACH	213594 6908
62	C1	EL SEGUNDO GOLF COURSE	366 S SEPULVEDA BLVD	EL SEGUNDO	213651 0116
22	A1	ENCINO GOLF COURSE	16821 BURBANK BLVD	ENCINO	818995 1170
59	F2	FORD PARK GOLF COURSE	8000 S PARK LN	BELL GARDENS	213927 8811
84	C1	FRIENDLY HILLS C CLUB	8500 VILLAVERDE DR	WHITTIER	213693 3623
127	H1	FRIENDLY VALLEY G CRSE	19345 W AV OF THE OAKS	NEWHALL	805252 9859
87	E6	GLENDORA COUNTRY CLUB	310 S AMELIA AV	GLENDORA	818335 3713
89	A1	GLENOAKS GOLF COURSE	200 W DAWSON	GLENDORA	818335 7565
98A	A1	HACIENDA GOLF CLUB	718 EAST RD	LA HABRA HTS	213694 1081
9	C3	HANSEN DAM GOLF COURSE	10400 GLENOAKS BLVD	PACOIMA	818896 0050
74	A3	HARBOR PARK GOLF CRSE	1221 FIGUEROA PL	WILMINGTON	213830 2145
24	F4	HARDING MUN GOLF CRSE	4730 CRYSTAL SPRINGS	LOS ANGELES	818663 2555
71	E4	HEARTWELL PK GOLF CRSE	6700 E CARSON ST	LONG BEACH	213421 8855
42	B3	HILLCREST COUNTRY CLUB	10000 W PICO BLVD	LOS ANGELES	213553 8911
92	C6	INDUSTRY HILLS GOLF	111 S AZUSA AV	INDUSTRY	818965 0861
57	D3	JACK THOMPSON GLF CRSE	9637 S WESTERN AV	LOS ANGELES	213757 1650
1	F5	KNOLLWOOD COUNTRY CLUB	12040 BALBOA BLVD	GRANADA HILLS	818368 5709
19	C2	LA CANADA FLINTRIDGE	5500 GODBEY DR	LA CANADA	818790 0155
157	H3	LAKE ELIZABETH G CLUB	14700 ELIZABETH LK RD	ELIZABETH LK	805724 1441
102	D3	LAKE LINDERO CNTRY CLB	5719 LAKE LINDERO DR	AGOURA	818889 1158
24	A4	LAKESIDE COUNTRY CLUB	4201 CLYBOURN AV	N HOLLYWOOD	818877 1301
71	A4	LAKEWOOD GOLF COURSE	3101 CARSON BLVD	LAKEWOOD	213429 3606
83	B1	LA MIRADA GOLF COURSE	15501 E ALICANTE RD	LA MIRADA	714943 1090
59	E4	LOS AMIGOS CO GLF CRSE	7295 E QUILL DR	DOWNEY	213869 0302
42	A1	LOS ANGELES CNTRY CLB	10101 WILSHIRE BLVD	LOS ANGELES	213276 6104
97	B3	LOS ANGELES NATL GOLF	20055 E COLIMA RD	WALNUT	714965 1634
25	B6	LOS FELIZ GOLF COURSE	LOS FELIZ BLVD	LOS ANGELES	213663 7758
77	C2	LOS VERDES GOLF COURSE	7000 W LOS VERDES DR	RO PALOS VRDS	213377 0338
95A	E4	MARSHALL CYN GOLF CRSE	6100 N STEPHNS RNCH RD	LA VERNE	714593 8211
46	B5	MONTEBELLO MUN G CRSE	901 VIA SAN CLEMENTE	MONTEBELLO	213723 2971

PAGE	GRID	NAME	ADDRESS	CITY	PHONE
45	E2	MONTEREY PARK G COURSE	3600 RAMONA RD	MONTEREY PARK	213266 4632
32	A2	MOUNTAINGATE G CRSE N	12445 MOUNTAINGATE DR	LOS ANGELES	213476 6215
32	A3	MOUNTAINGATE G CRSE S	12445 MOUNTAINGATE DR	LOS ANGELES	213476 0557
90	C5	MTN MEADOWS GOLF CRSE	1875 GANESHA BLVD	POMONA	714629 1166
82	C1	NORWALK GOLF COURSE	13717 S SHOEMAKER AV	NORWALK	213921 6500
18	E4	OAKMONT COUNTRY CLUB	3100 COUNTRY CLUB DR	GLENDALE	818242 2050
94	D4	PALM LAKE GOLF CLUB	1300 W PHILLIPS BLVD	POMONA	714629 2852
72	D2	PALOS VERDES GOLF CLUB	3301 VIA CAMPESINA	PALO VERD EST	213375 2759
49	C2	PENMAR GOLF COURSE	1233 ROSE AV	VENICE	213396 6228
47	C6	PICO RIVERA GOLF CRSE	3260 FAIRWAY DR	PICO RIVIERA	818692 9933
1	A6	PORTER VALLEY CNTRY CL	19216 SINGING HILLS DR	LOS ANGELES	818360 1071
62	D2	RADISSON PZ GOLF CRSE	1400 PARK VIEW AV	MANHATTAN BCH	213546 4551
42	A4	RANCHO PK & GOLF COURS	10460 W PICO BLVD	LOS ANGELES	213838 7373
76	B5	RECREATION PARK GOLF	5000 E ANAHEIM ST	LONG BEACH	213494 5000
76	B4	RECREATION PARK GOLF	5000 E 7TH ST	LONG BEACH	213438 4012
60	A2	RIO HONDO GOLF COURSE	10626 S OLD RIV SCH RD	DOWNEY	213927 2329
40	F3	RIVIERA COUNTRY CLUB	1250 CAPRI DR	PAC PALISADES	213454 6591
73	C4	ROLLING HILLS CNTRY CL	27000 PALOS VERDS DR E	ROLLNG HL EST	213326 4343
34	F1	ROOSEVELT MUN G COURSE	GRIFFITH PARK	LOS ANGELES	818665 2011
95A	C5	SAN DIMAS CYN GOLF CSE	2100 TERREBONE AV	SAN DIMAS	714599 2313
37	E2	SAN GABRIEL CNTRY CLB	411 E LAS TUNAS DR	SAN GABRIEL	818287 9671
28	D5	SANTA ANITA GOLF CRSE	405 S SANTA ANITA AV	ARCADIA	818447 7156
67	E5	SEA-AIRE GOLF COURSE	22730 LUPINE DR	TORRANCE	213316 9779
26	C2	SCHOLL CANYON GLF CRSE	3800 E GLENOAKS BLVD	GLENDALE	818240 9551
95A	D5	SIERRA LA VERNE GLF CL	6300 COUNTRY CLUB DR	LA VERNE	
71	B5	SKYLINKS GOLF COURSE	4800 E WARDLOW RD	LONG BEACH	213429 0030
59	D3	SOUTH GATE GOLF COURSE	9615 PINEHURST AV	SOUTH GATE	213564 1434
92	E2	SOUTH HILLS CNTRY CLUB	2655 E CITRUS ST	WEST COVINA	818339 1231
23	B4	STUDIO CITY G C	4141 WHITSETT AV	N HOLLYWOOD	818877 3777
123	H8	VALENCIA GOLF COURSE	27330 TOURNEY RD	VALENCIA	818365 9341
15	A4	VAN NUYS GOLF COURSE	6550 ODESSA AV	VAN NUYS	818785 3685
11	A5	VERDUGO HLLS GOLF CRSE	6433 LA TUNA CANYON RD	TUJUNGA	818352 1100
89	D5	VIA VERDE COUNTRY CLUB	1400 AVD ENTRADA	SAN DIMAS	714599 7977
69	B2	VICTORIA GOLF COURSE	348 E 192ND STREET	CARSON	213323 6981
70	C4	VIRGINIA COUNTRY CLUB	4602 VIRGINIA RD	LONG BEACH	213424 5211
126	J3	VISTA VALENCIA G CRSE	24700 W TREVINO DR	VALENCIA	805365 3322
56	B2	WESTCHESTER GOLF COURS	6900 W MANCHESTER AV	LOS ANGELES	213670 5110
102	B3	WESTLAKE VILLAGE G CRS	4812 LAKEVIEW CYN RD	WESTLAKE VLLG	818889 0770
47	A3	WHITTIER NARROWS G CRS	8640 RUSH ST	ROSEMEAD	213288 1044
34	C5	WILSHIRE COUNTRY CLUB	301 N ROSSMORE	LOS ANGELES	213934 1121
24	F5	WILSON MUN GOLF COURSE	GRIFFITH PARK DR	LOS ANGELES	818663 2555
13	D3	WOODLAND HILLS C C	21150 DUMETZ RD	WOODLAND HLLS	818347 1476
15	A5	WOODLEY GOLF COURSE	6331 WOODLEY AV	VAN NUYS	818780 6886

HOSPITALS

PAGE	GRID	NAME	ADDRESS	CITY	PHONE
		*EMERGENCY SERVICES	AVAILABLE		
37	A4	*ALHAMBRA COMMUNITY	100 S RAYMOND AV	ALHAMBRA	818570 1606
159	J5	ANTELOPE VALLEY	1600 W AVENUE J	LANCASTER	805949 5000
77	B5	AVALON MUNICIPAL HOSP	100 FALLS CANYON RD	AVALON	213510 0700
35	D6	BARLOW HOSPITAL	2000 STADIUM WY	LOS ANGELES	213250 4200
73	E2	*BAY HARBOR HOSPITAL	1437 W LOMITA BLVD	HARBOR CITY	213325 1221
66	C5	BELLFLOWER DOCTORS	9542 E ARTESIA BLVD	BELLFLOWER	213925 8355
66	D5	BELLWOOD GENERAL	10250 E ARTESIA AV	BELLFLOWER	213866 9028
54	E1	BEVERLY HOSPITAL	309 W BEVERLY BLVD	MONTEBELLO	213726 1222
42	A3	BEVERLY GLEN HOSPITAL	10361 W PICO BLVD	LOS ANGELES	213277 5111
42	A2	BEVERLY HILLS HOSP	10390 STA MONICA BLVD	LOS ANGELES	213277 5000
42	C2	BEVERLY HILLS MED CTR	1177 S BEVERLY DR	LOS ANGELES	213553 5155
58	A3	BROADWAY COMMUNITY	9500 S BROADWAY	LOS ANGELES	213777 2222
42	C6	*BROTMAN MEDICAL CENTR	3828 DELMAS TER	CULVER CITY	213836 7000
17	E5	*BURBANK COMMUNITY HOS	466 E OLIVE AV	BURBANK	818953 6500
44	B4	*CALIFORNIA MED CENTER	1414 S HOPE ST	LOS ANGELES	213748 2411
12	D3	*CANOGA PARK HOSPITAL	20800 SHERMAN WY	CANOGA PARK	818348 0200
33	D6	*CEDARS-SINAI MED CTR	8700 BEVERLY BLVD	LOS ANGELES	213855 5000
57	A3	*CENTINELA HOSPITAL	555 E HARDY ST	INGLEWOOD	213673 4660
56	C3	CENTINELA HOSP-AIRPRT	9601 S SEPULVEDA BLVD	LOS ANGELES	213215 6020
42	B2	CENTURY CITY HOSPITAL	2070 CENTURY PARK E	LOS ANGELES	213553 6211
81	A4	*CHARTER COMMUNITY HOS	21530 S PIONEER BLVD	HAWAIIAN GDNS	213860 0401
67	F5	*CHARTER PACIFIC HOSP	4025 W 226TH ST	TORRANCE	213373 7733
65	E4	*CHARTER SUBURBAN	16453 S COLORADO AV	PARAMOUNT	213531 3110
34	F3	*CHILDRENS HOSPITAL	4650 W SUNSET	LOS ANGELES	213660 2450
44	C1	CIGNA HOSPITAL OF L A	1711 W TEMPLE ST	LOS ANGELES	213413 1313
29	D6	CITY OF HOPE	1500 E DUARTE RD	DUARTE	818359 8111
66	E1	*COAST PLAZA MED CTR	13100 STUDEBAKER RD	NORWALK	213868 3751
16	A5	COLDWATER CANYON HOSP	6421 COLDWATER CYN AV	N HOLLYWOOD	818984 2000
63	F3	COMMUNITY OF GARDENA	1246 W 155TH ST	GARDENA	213323 5330
52	F4	COM HOSP HUNTINGTN PK	2623 E SLAUSON AV	HUNTINGTON PK	213583 1931
37	D3	*COM HOSP SAN GABRIEL	218 S STA ANITA ST	SAN GABRIEL	818289 5454
88	C5	COVINA VLY COM HOSP	845 N LARK ELLEN AV	WEST COVINA	818339 5451
51	B2	CRENSHAW CENTER HOSP	3831 STOCKER ST	LOS ANGELES	213292 0221
57	B1	*DANIEL FREEMAN MEM	333 N PRAIRIE AV	INGLEWOOD	213674 7050
71	A1	*DOCTORS HOS OF LAKEWD	3700 E SOUTH ST	LAKEWOOD	213531 2550
65	B5	DOMINGUEZ VALLEY HOSP	3100 SUSANA RD	COMPTON	213639 5151
60	B4	*DOWNEY COMMUNITY HOSP	11500 S BROOKSHIRE	DOWNEY	213806 5000
45	C6	*EAST L A DOCTORS HOSP	4060 WHITTIER BLVD	LOS ANGELES	213268 5514
22	A3	*ENCINO HOSPITAL	16237 VENTURA	ENCINO	818995 5000
87	A5	*FOOTHILL PRESBYTERIAN	250 S GRAND AV	GLENDORA	818963 8411
49	E5	*FREEMAN MARINA HOSP	4650 LINCOLN BLVD	MARINA DL REY	213823 8911
44	E1	FRENCH HOSPITAL	531 W COLLEGE ST	LOS ANGELES	213624 8411
63	F3	*GARDENA MEMORIAL HOSP	1145 W REDONDO BCH BL	GARDENA	213532 4200
46	C1	*GARFIELD MEDICAL CTR	525 N GARFIELD	MONTEREY PARK	818573 2222
25	E3	*GLENDALE ADVENTIST	1509 WILSON TER	GLENDALE	818240 8000
25	C6	*GLENDALE MEMORIAL	1420 S CENTRAL AV	GLENDALE	818502 1900
87	A6	*GLENDORA COMMUNITY	150 W ALOSTA AV	GLENDORA	818335 0231
44	B3	GOOD SAMARITAN HOSP	616 S WITMER ST	LOS ANGELES	213977 2121
7	E3	*GRANADA HILLS COM HOS	10445 BALBOA BLVD	GRANADA HILLS	818360 1021
47	D3	GREATER EL MONTE COMM	1701 SANTA ANITA AV	S EL MONTE	818579 7777
68	F4	*HARBOR UCLA MED CTR	1000 W CARSON ST	TORRANCE	213533 2345
63	A1	HAWTHORNE MEM HOSP	13300 S HAWTHORNE BLVD	HAWTHORNE	213679 3321
127	A2	*HENRY MAYO NEWHALL	23845 W MCBEAN PKWY	VALENCIA	805253 8000
34	C3	HOLLYWOOD COMMUNITY	6245 DE LONGPRE AV	LOS ANGELES	213462 2271
34	F3	*HOLLYWOOD PRESBYTRIAN	1300 N VERMONT AV	LOS ANGELES	213660 3530
2	C6	*HOLY CROSS HOSPITAL	15031 RINALDI ST	MISSION HILLS	818365 8051
12	A3	HUMANA WEST HILLS	7300 MEDICAL CENTER DR	CANOGA PARK	818884 7060
26	F5	*HUNTINGTON MEM HOSP	100 CONGRESS ST	PASADENA	818440 5000
88	E5	INTER-COMMUNITY MED C	303 N THIRD AV	COVINA	213331 7331
66	B2	KAISER FOUNDATION HOS	9400 E ROSECRANS AV	BELLFLOWER	213920 4321
73	F3	KAISER FOUNDATION HOS	25825 S VERMONT AV	HARBOR CITY	213325 5111
34	F3	KAISER FOUNDATION HOS	4867 SUNSET BLVD	HOLLYWOOD	213667 4011
57	C1	KAISER FOUNDATION HOS	3425 W MANCHESTER BLVD	INGLEWOOD	213667 6445
42	E4	KAISER FOUNDATION HOS	6041 CADILLAC AV	LOS ANGELES	213857 2201
60	E6	KAISER FOUNDATION HOS	12500 S HOXIE AV	NORWALK	213920 4321
15	F1	KAISER FOUNDATION HOS	13652 CANTARA	PANORAMA CITY	818908 2000
13	D1	KAISER FOUNDATION HOS	5601 DE SOTO AV	WOODLAND HLLS	818719 2000
50	D4	LADERA HGTS COMM HOSP	5525 SLAUSON AV	LOS ANGELES	213410 0999
3	D6	LAKE VIEW MEDICAL CTR	11600 ELDRIDGE AV	LAKE VIEW TER	818896 1121
84	A6	LA MIRADA MEDICAL CTR	14900 E IMPERIAL HWY	LA MIRADA	714941 2251
160	A6	LANCASTER COMMUNITY	43830 N 10TH ST W	LANCASTER	805948 4781
27	F4	LAS ENCINAS HOSPITAL	2900 E DEL MAR BLVD	PASADENA	818795 9901
19	F2	LA VINA HOSPITAL	3900 N LINCOLN AV	ALTADENA	818791 1241
45	A4	LINCOLN HOSPITAL	443 S SOTO	LOS ANGELES	213261 1181
45	A4	LINDA VISTA COMMUNITY	610 S ST LOUIS ST	LOS ANGELES	213265 0789
67	F4	*LITTLE COMPNY OF MARY	4101 TORRANCE BLVD	TORRANCE	213540 7676
76	A3	*LONG BEACH COMMUNITY	1720 TERMINO AV	LONG BEACH	213498 1000
76	D4	*LONG BEACH VET ADMIN	5901 E 7TH ST	LONG BEACH	213494 2611
45	C6	LOS ANGELES COMMUNITY	4081 E OLYMPIC BLVD	E LOS ANGELES	213267 0477
45	B2	*LA CO USC MED CENTER	1200 N STATE ST	LOS ANGELES	213226 2345
43	E5	LOS ANGELES DOCTORS	2231 S WESTERN AV	LOS ANGELES	213737 7372
58	D6	*MARTIN L KING JR GEN	12021 S WILMINGTON AV	LOS ANGELES	213603 4321
21	C1	*MEDICAL CTR TARZANA	18321 CLARK ST	TARZANA	818881 0800
75	D1	*MEMORIAL HOSP MED CTR	2801 ATLANTIC AV	LONG BEACH	213595 2311
28	D5	*METHODIST HOSP S CAL	300 W HUNTINGTON DR	ARCADIA	818445 4441
42	F2	MIDWAY HOSPITAL	5925 W SAN VICENTE BL	LOS ANGELES	213938 3161
159	B4	MIRA LOMA HOSPITAL	44900 N 60TH ST W	LANCASTER	805945 8300
53	A6	MISSION HOSPITAL	3111 E FLORENCE AV	HUNTINGTON PK	213582 8261
29	B4	MONROVIA COMM HOSP	323 S HELIOTROPE AV	MONROVIA	818359 8341
46	B3	MONTEREY PARK HOSP	900 S ATLANTIC BLVD	MONTEREY PARK	818570 9000
100	F3	MOTION PICTURE HOSP	23450 CALABASAS RD	WOODLAND HLLS	818347 1591
127	D4	NEWHALL COMM HOSPITAL	24237 SAN FERNANDO RD	NEWHALL	805259 6300
23	B2	*N HOLLYWOOD MED CTR	12629 RIVERSIDE DR	N HOLLYWOOD	213980 9200
14	C1	*NORTHRIDGE HOSPITAL	18300 ROSCOE BLVD	NORTHRIDGE	818885 8500
82	C1	NORWALK COMMUNITY	13222 BLOOMFIELD AV	NORWALK	213863 4763
2	D1	OLIVE VIEW MED CENTER	14445 OLIVE VIEW DR	SYLMAR	818367 2231
15	D3	OLIVE VIEW MED CENTER	7533 VAN NUYS BLVD	VAN NUYS	818901 3201
94	E1	ORANGE GROVE COMM	1225 NORTH PARK AV	POMONA	714629 4033
44	B5	ORTHOPAEDIC HOSPITAL	2400 S FLOWER ST	LOS ANGELES	213742 1000
75	C1	*PACIFIC HOSPITAL L B	2776 PACIFIC AV	LONG BEACH	213595 1911
183	D2	*PALMDALE MEDICAL CTR	1212 E AV S	PALMDALE	805273 2211
15	D1	*PANORAMA COMMUNITY	14850 ROSCOE BLVD	PANORAMA CITY	818787 2222
35	A4	PARK VIEW HOSPITAL	1021 N HOOVER ST	LOS ANGELES	213666 1551
19	F6	PASADENA COMMUNITY	1845 N FAIR OAKS	PASADENA	818798 7811
55	A3	*PICO RIVERA COM HOSP	5216 S ROSEMEAD BLVD	PICO RIVERA	213948 1121
82	A6	*PIONEER HOSPITAL	17831 S PIONEER BLVD	ARTESIA	213865 6291
90	E6	*POMONA VLY COM HOSP	1798 N GAREY AV	POMONA	714623 8715
55	D6	*PRESBYTERIAN INTER-CO	12401 E WASHINGTON BL	WHITTIER	213698 0811
35	B6	*QUEEN OF ANGELS MED C	2301 BELLEVUE AV	LOS ANGELES	213413 3000
48	F2	*QUEEN OF THE VLY HOSP	1115 S SUNSET AV	WEST COVINA	818962 4011
21	F2	*RANCHO ENCINO	5333 BALBOA BLVD	ENCINO	818788 4400
59	F5	RANCHO LOS AMIGOS	7601 E IMPERIAL HWY	DOWNEY	213922 7111
60	D1	RIO HONDO MEMORIAL	8300 E TELEGRAPH RD	DOWNEY	213806 1821
56	F5	R F KENNEDY MED CTR	4500 W 116TH ST	HAWTHORNE	213973 1711
59	B5	*ST FRANCIS MED CENTER	3630 E IMPERIAL HWY	LYNWOOD	213603 6000
41	B5	*ST JOHNS HOSPITAL	1328 22ND	SANTA MONICA	213829 5511
24	C3	ST JOSEPH MEDICAL CTR	501 S BUENA VISTA ST	BURBANK	818843 5111
27	E1	*ST LUKES HOSPITAL	2632 E WASHINGTON BLVD	PASADENA	818797 1141
75	D4	*ST MARYS MEDICAL CTR	1050 LINDEN AV	LONG BEACH	213491 9000
44	B1	ST VINCENT MED CTR	2131 W 3RD ST	LOS ANGELES	213484 7111
89	D4	*SAN DIMAS COMMUNITY	1350 W COVINA BLVD	SAN DIMAS	714599 6811
2	E6	*SAN FERNANDO COM HOSP	732 MOTT ST	SAN FERNANDO	818361 7331
78	E3	*SAN PEDRO PENINSULA	1300 W 7TH ST	SAN PEDRO	213832 3311
45	E4	*SANTA MARTA HOSPITAL	319 N HUMPHREYS AV	LOS ANGELES	213266 6500
41	A5	*SANTA MONICA MED CTR	1225 15TH ST	SANTA MONICA	213319 4000
29	D4	*SANTA TERESITA	1210 ROYAL OAKS DR	DUARTE	818359 3243
8	B4	*SEPULVEDA V A HOSP	16111 PLUMMER	SEPULVEDA	818891 7711
9	C5	*SERRA MEM HEALTH CTR	9449 SN FERNANDO RD	SUN VALLEY	818767 3310
22	D2	*SHERMAN OAKS COMM	4929 VAN NUYS BLVD	SHERMAN OAKS	818981 7111
44	A1	SHRINER CRIPPLD CHILD	3160 GENEVA ST	LOS ANGELES	213388 3151
28	C2	SIERRA MADRE COM HOSP	225 W SIERRA MADRE BL	SIERRA MADRE	213355 7181
67	D2	*SOUTH BAY HOSPITAL	514 N PROSPECT AV	REDONDO BEACH	213376 9474
35	A6	TEMPLE COMMUNITY HOSP	235 N HOOVER ST	LOS ANGELES	213382 7252
48	D2	*TERRACE PLAZA MED CTR	14148 E FRNCISQUITO AV	BALDWIN PARK	818338 1101
68	B6	*TORRANCE MEM HOSP	3330 W LOMITA BLVD	TORRANCE	213325 9110

1990 LOS ANGELES COUNTY POINTS OF INTEREST

PAGE	GRID	NAME	ADDRESS	CITY	PHONE
71	F4	U S NAVAL HOSPITAL	7500 E CARSON	LONG BEACH	213651 3158
41	E1	UCLA MEDICAL CENTER	10833 LE CONTE AV	W LOS ANGELES	213825 9111
15	D3	*VALLEY MEDICAL CENTER	14500 SHERMAN CIR	VAN NUYS	818997 0101
12	B4	*VALLEY PARK MED CTR	7011 SHOUP AV	CANOGA PARK	818348 0500
15	C4	*VALLEY PRESBYTERIAN	15107 VANOWEN ST	VAN NUYS	818782 6600
37	E3	VALLEY VISTA	115 E BROADWAY	SAN GABRIEL	818287 6191
15	D6	VAN NUYS COMM HOSP	14433 EMELITA ST	VAN NUYS	818787 1511
19	A3	*VERDUGO HILLS HOSP	1812 VERDUGO BLVD	GLENDALE	818790 7100
41	D3	*WADSWORTH HOS VET ADM	11000 WILSHIRE BLVD	W LOS ANGELES	213478 3711
49	F3	WASHINGTON MED CTR	12101 WASHINGTON BLVD	CULVER CITY	213391 0601
48	F1	WEST COVINA HOSPITAL	725 S ORANGE AV	WEST COVINA	818338 8481
34	B4	WEST HOLLYWOOD	1233 N LA BREA AV	W HOLLYWOOD	213874 6111
102	A4	*WESTLAKE COMM HOSP	4415 LAKEVIEW CYN RD	WESTLAKE VLLG	805497 7806
12	B1	*WEST PARK HOSPITAL	22141 ROSCOE BLVD	CANOGA PARK	818340 0580
42	F2	*WESTSIDE HOSPITAL	910 S FAIRFAX	LOS ANGELES	213938 3431
45	A3	*WHITE MEMORIAL MED	1720 BROOKLYN AV	LOS ANGELES	213268 5000
84	B2	*WHITTIER HOSPITAL	15151 E JANINE DR	WHITTIER	213945 3561
71	D5	WOODRUFF COMMUNITY	3800 WOODRUFF AV	LONG BEACH	213421 8241
		HOTELS			
56	E3	AIRPORT CENTURY INN	5547 W CENTURY BLVD	LOS ANGELES	213649 4000
56	E3	L A AIRPORT HILTON	5711 W CENTURY BLVD	LOS ANGELES	213410 4000
57	B2	AIRPORT PARK HOTEL	600 S PRAIRIE AV	INGLEWOOD	213673 5151
56	A2	AMFAC HOTEL	8601 LINCOLN BLVD	LOS ANGELES	213670 8111
62	C2	BARNABEYS HOTEL	3501 N SEPULVEDA BLVD	MANHATTAN BCH	213545 8466
32	E4	BEL AIR HOTEL	701 STONE CANYON	BEL AIR ESTS	213472 1211
32	C6	BEL AIR SUMMIT HOTEL	11461 SUNSET BLVD	LOS ANGELES	213476 6571
23	E4	BEVERLY GARLAND	4222 VINELAND	N HOLLYWOOD	818980 8000
42	C2	BEVERLY HILLCREST	1224 S BEVERWIL DR	LOS ANGELES	213277 2800
33	B5	BEVERLY HILLS	9641 SUNSET BLVD	BEVERLY HILLS	213276 2251
42	B1	BEVERLY HILTON	9876 WILSHIRE BLVD	BEVERLY HILLS	213274 7777
33	C6	BEVERLY PLAZA HOTEL	8384 W 3RD ST	BEVERLY HILLS	213658 6600
42	C1	BEVERLY WILSHIRE	9500 WILSHIRE BLVD	BEVERLY HILLS	213275 4282
44	C3	BILTMORE	515 S OLIVE	LOS ANGELES	213624 1011
44	C3	BONAVENTURE	401 S FLOWER ST	LOS ANGELES	213624 1000
17	A4	BURBANK AIRPORT HILTON	2500 HOLLYWOOD WY	BURBANK	818843 6000
42	A2	CENTURY PLAZA	2025 AV OF THE STARS	LOS ANGELES	213277 2000
41	E2	CENTURY WILSHIRE HOTEL	10776 WILSHIRE BLVD	W LOS ANGELES	213474 4506
57	A5	COCKATOO INN	IMPERIAL & HAWTHORNE	HAWTHORNE	213679 2291
33	E2	CONTINENTAL HYATT	8401 SUNSET BLVD	LOS ANGELES	213656 4101
56	E3	DAYS INN	5101 CENTURY BLVD	INGLEWOOD	213419 1234
28	F4	EMBASSY SUITES	211 E HUNTINGTON DR	ARCADIA	818445 8525
93	B1	EMBASSY SUITES HOTEL	1211 E GARVEY ST	COVINA	818915 3441
56	B5	EMBASSY SUITES	1440 IMPERIAL HWY	EL SEGUNDO	213414 0080
160	A4	ESSEX HOUSE HOTEL	44916 N 10TH ST W	LANCASTER	805948 0961
56	C6	HACIENDA HOTEL	525 SEPULVEDA BLVD	EL SEGUNDO	213615 0015
22	B3	HILTON VALLEY INN	15433 VENTURA BLVD	SHERMAN OAKS	818981 5400
32	C6	HOLIDAY INN	170 N CHURCH ST	BRENTWOOD	818476 6411
44	C4	HOLIDAY INN	1020 S FIGUEROA	CONVENTN CNTR	213748 1291
44	B3	HOLIDAY INN	750 GARLAND	DOWNTOWN LA	213628 5242
25	B4	HOLIDAY INN	600 N PACIFIC AV	GLENDALE	818956 0202
34	B3	HOLIDAY INN	1755 N HIGHLAND	HOLLYWOOD	213462 7181
76	B1	HOLIDAY INN	2640 LAKEWOOD BLVD	LONG BEACH	213597 4401
45	A2	HOLIDAY INN	1640 MARENGO ST	LOS ANGELES	213223 3841
56	D3	HOLIDAY INN	9901 LA CIENGA BLVD	LOS ANGELES	213649 5151
54	C5	HOLIDAY INN	7709 TELEGRAPH RD	MONTEBELLO	213724 1400
27	B4	HOLIDAY INN	303 E CORDOVA ST	PASADENA	818449 4000
49	A1	HOLIDAY INN	120 COLORADO AV	SANTA MONICA	213451 0676
68	A4	HOLIDAY INN	21333 HAWTHORNE BLVD	TORRANCE	213540 0500
68	F2	HOLIDAY INN	19800 S VERMONT AV	TORRANCE	213781 9100
15	B1	HOLIDAY INN	8244 ORION AV	VAN NUYS	818989 5010
41	F4	HOLIDAY INN	10740 WILSHIRE BLVD	W LOS ANGELES	213475 8711
13	D1	HOLIDAY INN	21101 VENTURA BLVD	WOODLAND HLLS	818883 6110
49	A2	HOLIDAY INN-BAYVIEW PZ	530 PICO BLVD	SANTA MONICA	213399 9344
56	D3	HOLIDAY INN-CROWNE PZ	5985 CENTURY BLVD	LOS ANGELES	213642 7500
76	B1	HOLIDAY INN-LB AIRPORT	2640 LAKEWOOD BLVD	LONG BEACH	213597 4401
34	B3	HOLLYWOOD ROOSEVELT	7000 HOLLYWOOD BLVD	HOLLYWOOD	213466 7000
34	D3	HOTEL HOLLYWOOD	5825 SUNSET BLVD	HOLLYWOOD	213463 4000
44	E3	HOTEL TOKYO	318 E 1ST ST	LOS ANGELES	213680 1766
23	E4	HOWARD JOHNSON LODGE	4222 VINELAND AV	N HOLLYWOOD	818980 8000
50	C5	HOWARD JOHNSONS	5990 GREEN VLY CIR	CULVER CITY	213641 7740
40	F6	HUNTLEY HOTEL	1111 2ND ST	SANTA MONICA	213394 5454
80	D1	HYATT EDGEWATER	6400 E PACIFIC CST HWY	LONG BEACH	213434 8451
54	B3	HYATT HOUSE	6300 TELEGRAPH RD	COMMERCE	213722 7200
56	C3	HYATT HOUSE L A INTL	6225 W CENTURY BLVD	LOS ANGELES	213670 9000
33	F3	HYATT ON SUNSET	8401 SUNSET BLVD	HOLLYWOOD	213656 4101
75	C6	HYATT REGENCY	200 PINE AV	LONG BEACH	213491 1234
44	C3	HYATT REGENCY	711 S HOPE AV	LOS ANGELES	213683 1234
43	E2	HYATT WILSHIRE	3515 WILSHIRE BLVD	LOS ANGELES	213381 7411
49	D5	JAMAICA BAY INN	4175 ADMIRALTY WY	MARINA DL REY	213823 5333
33	D5	LE BEL AGE	1020 N SAN VICENTE	W HOLLYWOOD	213854 1111
33	F3	LE MONDRIAN	8440 SUNSET BLVD	LOS ANGELES	213650 8999
33	D4	LE PARC	733 WEST KNOLL	W HOLLYWOOD	213855 8888
33	C6	L'ERMITAGE	9291 BURTON WY	BEVERLY HILLS	213278 3344
49	A2	LOEWS BEACH HOTEL	1700 OCEAN AV	SANTA MONICA	213458 6700
44	C3	LOS ANGELES HILTON	930 WILSHIRE BLVD	LOS ANGELES	213629 4321
49	E5	MARINA DEL REY HOTEL	13534 BALI WY	MARINA DL REY	213822 1010
49	D4	MARINA INTERNATIONAL	4200 ADMIRALTY WY	MARINA DL REY	213822 1010
71	B6	MARRIOTT HOTEL	4700 AIRPORT PLAZA DR	LONG BEACH	213425 5210
56	D3	MARRIOTT HOTEL	AIRPORT BL & CENTURY	LOS ANGELES	213641 5700

PAGE	GRID	NAME	ADDRESS	CITY	PHONE
68	A4	MARRIOTT HOTEL	3635 FASHION WY	TORRANCE	213316 3636
12	C6	MARRIOTT HOTEL	21850 OXNARD ST	WOODLAND HLLS	818887 4800
49	E4	MARRIOTT INN	13480 MAXELLA AV	MARINA DL REY	213822 8555
42	B2	MARRIOTT-CENTURY CITY	2151 AV OF THE STARS	LOS ANGELES	213201 0440
49	E4	MARRIOTT-MARINA DL REY	13480 MAXELLA AV	MARINA DL REY	213822 8555
44	B3	MAYFAIR HOTEL	1256 W 7TH ST	LOS ANGELES	213484 9614
34	F5	MID TOWN HILTON	400 N VERMONT AV	LOS ANGELES	213662 4888
40	F4	MIRAMAR SHERATON	101 WILSHIRE BLVD	SANTA MONICA	213394 3731
44	D3	NEW OTANI HOTEL	120 S LOS ANGELES ST	LOS ANGELES	213629 1200
40	E6	OCEANA	849 OCEAN AVE	SANTA MONICA	213393 0486
50	C5	PACIFICA HOTEL	6161 CENTINELA AV	CULVER CITY	213649 1776
27	B4	PASADENA HILTON HOTEL	150 S LOS ROBLES	PASADENA	818577 1000
56	E3	QUALITY INN	5249 W CENTURY BLVD	LOS ANGELES	213645 2200
62	D2	RADISSON PLAZA	1400 PARKVIEW AV	MANHATTAN BCH	213546 7511
50	C5	RAMADA INN	6333 BRISTOL PKWY	CULVER CITY	213670 3200
42	C2	RAMADA INN	1150 S BEVERLY DR	LOS ANGELES	213553 6561
56	D3	RAMADA INN	9620 AIRPORT	WESTCHESTER	213670 1600
33	D4	RAMADA INN	8732 W SUNSET	W HOLLYWOOD	213659 1910
23	F5	REGISTRY HOTEL	555 UNIVERSAL TER PKWY	UNIVERSAL CTY	818506 2500
76	A1	RESIDENCE INN	4111 E WILLOW ST	LONG BEACH	213595 0909
62	C3	RESIDENCE INN	1700 SEPULVEDA BLVD	MANHATTAN BCH	213546 7627
68	A3	RESIDENCE INN	3701 TORRANCE BLVD	TORRANCE	213543 4566
44	C2	SHERATON GRANDE	333 S FIGUEROA ST	LOS ANGELES	213617 1133
92	C6	SHERATON PK RESORT	1 INDUSTRY HILLS PKWY	INDUSTRY	818965 0861
56	C3	SHERATON PZ-LA REINA	6101 W CENTURY BLVD	LOS ANGELES	213642 1111
67	C3	SHEARTON-REDONDO BEACH	300 N HARBOR DR	REDONDO BEACH	213318 8888
44	A2	SHERATON TOWN HOUSE	2961 WILSHIRE BLVD	LOS ANGELES	213382 7171
23	F5	SHERATON UNIVERSAL	333 UNIVERSAL TER PKWY	UNIVERSAL CTY	818980 1212
23	B4	SPORTSMENS LODGE	12825 VENTURA BLVD	LOS ANGELES	213769 4700
56	D3	STOUFFER CONCOURSE	5400 W CENTURY BLVD	LOS ANGELES	213216 5858
44	A6	UNIVERSITY HILTON	3540 S FIGUEROA ST	LOS ANGELES	213748 4141
22	B3	VALLEY HILTON	15433 VENTURA BLVD	SHERMAN OAKS	818981 5400
80A	C4	VISCOUNT HOTEL	700 QUEENSWAY DR	LONG BEACH	213435 7676
56	D3	VISCOUNT HOTEL	9750 AIRPORT BLVD	LOS ANGELES	213645 4600
12	E3	WARNER PALMS SUITE HTL	20200 SHERMAN WY	CANOGA PARK	818883 8250
41	E1	WESTWOOD MARQUIS	930 HILGARD AV	WESTWOOD	213208 8765
55	E5	WHITTIER HILTON	7320 GREENLEAF AV	WHITTIER	213945 8511
44	A2	WILSHIRE ROYALE HOTEL	2619 WILSHIRE BLVD	LOS ANGELES	213387 5311
		LIBRARIES			
58	B6	A C BILBREW	150 E EL SEGUNDO BLVD	LOS ANGELES	213538 3350
75	E5	ALAMITOS	1836 E 3RD ST	LONG BEACH	213436 6448
46	A1	ALHAMBRA BRANCH LIB	2037 S FREMONT AV	ALHAMBRA	818570 5098
37	C3	ALHAMBRA MAIN LIBRARY	410 W MAIN ST	ALHAMBRA	818570 5008
27	A6	ALLENDALE	1130 S MARENGO	PASADENA	818799 2519
82	B4	ALONDRA	11949 E ALONDRA BLVD	NORWALK	213868 7771
20	B5	ALTADENA LIBRARY	600 E MARIPOSA	ALTADENA	818798 0833
51	C3	ANGELES MESA	2700 W 52ND ST	LOS ANGELES	213292 4328
71	B2	ANGELO M IACABONI	4990 CLARK AV	LAKEWOOD	213866 1777
45	D4	ANTHONY QUINN	3965 BROOKLYN AV	LOS ANGELES	213264 7715
28	E6	ARCADIA	20 W DUARTE RD	ARCADIA	818446 7111
36	C2	ARROYO SECO REGIONAL	6145 N FIGUEROA ST	LOS ANGELES	213237 1181
81	A1	ARTESIA	18722 S CLARKDALE AV	ARTESIA	213865 6614
52	A5	ASCOT	256 W 70TH ST	LOS ANGELES	213759 4817
53	E2	ATLANTIC LIBRARY	2262 S ATLANTIC BLVD	COMMERCE	213268 9351
35	C1	ATWATER	3229 GLENDALE BLVD	LOS ANGELES	213664 1353
77	B5	AVALON	215 SUMNER AV	AVALON	213510 1050
86	D5	AZUSA PUBLIC LIBRARY	729 N DALTON AV	AZUSA	213334 0338
71	C4	BACH	4055 BELLFLOWER BLVD	LONG BEACH	213421 5411
43	A5	BALDWIN HILLS	2906 S LA BREA	BALDWIN HILLS	213733 1196
39	E4	BALDWIN PARK	4181 BALDWIN PARK BL	BALDWIN PARK	818962 6947
80	C1	BAY SHORE	195 BAY SHORE AV	LONG BEACH	213438 3501
53	C5	BELL	4411 E GAGE AV	BELL	213560 2149
59	F1	BELL GARDENS	7110 S GARFIELD AV	BELL GARDENS	213927 1309
45	D4	BELVEDERE	3965 E BROOKLYN AV	LOS ANGELES	213264 7715
45	A4	BENJAMIN FRANKLIN	2200 EAST 1ST ST	LOS ANGELES	213263 6901
33	C6	BEVERLY HILLS	444 N REXFORD DR	BEVERLY HILLS	213550 4721
18	B5	BRAND LIBRARY	1601 W MOUNTAIN STREET	GLENDALE	818956 2051
41	C3	BRENTWOOD	11820 SAN VICENTE BLVD	W LOS ANGELES	213826 6579
76	A4	BREWITT	4036 E ANAHEIM ST	LONG BEACH	213498 0770
24	C2	BUENA VISTA	401 N BUENA VISTA	BURBANK	818953 9747
17	E5	BURBANK CENTRAL	110 N GLEN OAKS BLVD	BURBANK	818953 9737
75	D2	BURNETT	560 E HILL ST	LONG BEACH	213591 8614
34	F4	CAHUENGA	4591 SANTA MONICA BLVD	LOS ANGELES	213664 6418
12	C3	CANOGA PARK	7260 OWENSMOUTH	CANOGA PARK	818887 0320
125	A9	CANYON COUNTRY LIBRARY	18536 SOLEDAD CANYON	CYN COUNTRY	805251 2720
69	B4	CARSON	151 E CARSON ST	CARSON	213830 0901
25	C2	CASA VERDUGO	1151 N BRAND BLVD	GLENDALE	818956 2047
44	C3	CENTRAL LIBRARY	630 W 5TH ST	LOS ANGELES	213612 3200
82	C6	CERRITOS	18025 BLOOMFIELD AV	CERRITOS	213924 5775
89	B3	CHARTER OAK	20562 ARROW HIGHWAY	CHARTER OAK	818339 2151
6	D3	CHATSWORTH	21052 DEVONSHIRE ST	CHATSWORTH	818341 4276
54	C3	CHET HOLIFIELD	1060 S GREENWOOD AV	MONTEBELLO	213728 0421
26	B1	CHEVY CHASE	3301 E CHEVY CHASE DR	GLENDALE	818956 2046
44	E1	CHINATOWN	536 W COLLEGE ST	LOS ANGELES	213620 0925
45	D2	CITY TERRACE	4025 E CITY TERRACE DR	CITY TERRACE	213261 0295
68	B4	CIVIC CENTER LIBRARY	3301 TORRANCE BLVD	TORRANCE	213618 5959
91	B4	CLAREMONT	208 N HARVARD AV	CLAREMONT	714621 4902
66	C4	CLIFTON A BRAKENSIEK	9945 E FLOWER ST	BELLFLOWER	213925 5543
53	F3	COMMERCE CENTRAL LIB	5655 JILLSON ST	COMMERCE	213722 6600

1990 LOS ANGELES COUNTY POINTS OF INTEREST

PAGE	GRID	NAME	ADDRESS	CITY	PHONE
64	F3	COMPTON	240 W COMPTON BLVD	COMPTON	213637 0202
88	E5	COVINA LIBRARY	234 N 2ND	COVINA	818967 3935
57	C4	CRENSHAW-IMPERIAL	11141 CRENSHAW BLVD	INGLEWOOD	213412 5403
18	E3	CRESCENTA VALLEY	2465 HONOLULU AV	MONTROSE	818956 2048
59	D1	CUDAHY	5218 SANTA ANA ST	CUDAHY	213771 1345
50	C2	CULVER CITY LIBRARY	4975 OVERLAND AV	CULVER CITY	213559 1676
35	F4	CYPRESS PARK	3320 PEPPER AV	LOS ANGELES	213225 0989
70	D5	DANA	3680 ATLANTIC AV	LONG BEACH	213424 4828
46	E1	DEL MAR	3132 N DEL MAR AV	ROSEMEAD	818280 4422
97	F2	DIAMOND BAR	1061 S GRAND AV	DIAMOND BAR	714861 4978
70	A4	DOMINGUEZ	2719 E CARSON ST	LONG BEACH	213518 7800
60	C4	DOWNEY CITY LIBRARY	11121 S BROOKSHIRE	DOWNEY	213923 3256
29	D5	DUARTE	1301 BUENA VISTA AV	DUARTE	818358 1865
26	A5	EAGLE ROCK	5027 CASPAR AV	LOS ANGELES	213258 8078
65	C3	EAST COMPTON	4205 E COMPTON BLVD	COMPTON	213632 6193
45	E5	EAST LOS ANGELES	4801 E 3RD ST	LOS ANGELES	213264 0155
44	C1	ECHO PARK	515 N LAVETA TER	LOS ANGELES	213250 7808
88	A5	EDGEWOOD LIBRARY	1435 W PUENTE AV	WEST COVINA	818962 4069
45	D6	EL CAMINO REAL	4264 E WHITTIER BLVD	LOS ANGELES	213269 8102
76	E1	EL DORADO	2900 STUDEBAKER	LONG BEACH	213429 1814
47	D1	EL MONTE	3224 N TYLER AV	EL MONTE	818444 9506
67	E6	EL RETIRO	126 VISTA DEL PARQUE	TORRANCE	213375 0922
56	A5	EL SEGUNDO	111 W MARIPOSA	EL SEGUNDO	213322 4121
36	D4	EL SERENO	4990 HUNTINGTON DR SO	LOS ANGELES	213225 9201
21	C2	ENCINO-TARZANA	18231 VENTURA BLVD	TARZANA	818343 1983
43	F6	EXPOSITION PARK REG	3665 S VERMONT AV	LOS ANGELES	213732 0169
34	A6	FAIRFAX	161 S GARDNER	LOS ANGELES	213936 6191
49	C1	FAIRVIEW	2101 OCEAN PARK BLVD	SANTA MONICA	213450 0443
44	A2	FELIPE DE NEVE	2820 W 6TH ST	LOS ANGELES	213384 7676
52	D5	FLORENCE	1610 E FLORENCE AV	LOS ANGELES	213581 8028
63	E4	GARDENA LIBRARY	1731 W GARDENA BLVD	GARDENA	213323 6363
71	E3	GEORGE NYE, JR	6600 DEL AMO BLVD	LAKEWOOD	213421 8497
25	D4	GLENDALE LIBRARY	222 E HARVARD ST	GLENDALE	818956 2020
87	B5	GLENDORA CITY LIBRARY	140 S GLENDORA AV	GLENDORA	213963 4168
34	C3	GOLDWYN HOLLYWOOD REGL	1623 IVAR AV	LOS ANGELES	213467 1821
58	E2	GRAHAM	1900 E FIRESTONE BLVD	LOS ANGELES	213582 2903
7	F2	GRANADA HILLS	10640 PETIT AV	GRANADA HILLS	818368 5687
25	A1	GRANDVIEW	1535 5TH ST	GLENDALE	818956 2049
54	B6	GREENWOOD	6134 S GREENWOOD AV	COMMERCE	213927 1516
85	E3	HACIENDA HEIGHTS	16010 LA MONDE ST	HACIENDA HTS	818968 9356
75	A1	HARTE LIBRARY	1595 W WILLOW	LONG BEACH	213424 2345
27	F2	HASTINGS	3325 E ORANGE GROVE BL	PASADENA	818792 0945
81	B4	HAWAIIAN GARDENS LIB	12100 CARSON #E	HAWAIIAN GDNS	213496 1212
57	A6	HAWTHORNE LIBRARY	12700 S GREVILLEA AV	HAWTHORNE	213679 8193
62	C6	HERMOSA BEACH	550 PIER AV	HERMOSA BEACH	213379 8475
27	C4	HILL AVENUE	55 S HILL AV	PASADENA	818796 1276
59	E6	HOLLYDALE	12000 GARFIELD AV	SOUTH GATE	213634 0156
57	D5	HOLLY PARK	2150 W 120TH ST	HAWTHORNE	213757 1735
53	A5	HUNTINGTON PARK	6518 MILES AV	HUNTINGTON PK	213583 1461
51	C5	HYDE PARK	6527 CRENSHAW BLVD	LOS ANGELES	213750 7241
57	A1	INGLEWOOD LIBRARY	101 W MANCHESTER BLVD	INGLEWOOD	213412 5380
88	B3	IRWINDALE	5050 N IRWINDALE AV	IRWINDALE	818962 5255
67	F3	ISABEL HENDERSON	4805 EMERALD ST	TORRANCE	213371 2075
43	D6	JEFFERSON	2211 W JEFFERSON BLVD	LOS ANGELES	213734 8573
34	C5	JOHN C FREMONT	6121 MELROSE AV	LOS ANGELES	213465 9593
51	F5	JOHN MUIR	1005 W 64TH ST	LOS ANGELES	213759 4184
52	A2	JUNIPERO SERRA	4255 S OLIVE ST	LOS ANGELES	213234 1685
19	C3	LA CANADA-FLINTRIDGE	4545 N OAKWOOD AV	LA CANADA	818790 3330
18	E1	LA CRESCENTA	4521 LA CRESCENTA AV	LA CRESCENTA	818248 5313
27	E4	LAMANDA PARK	140 S ALTADENA DR	PASADENA	818793 5672
83	A1	LA MIRADA LIBRARY	13800 LA MIRADA BLVD	LA MIRADA	714943 0277
159	J5	LANCASTER	1150 W AVENUE J	LANCASTER	805948 5029
27	A1	LA PINTORESCA	1355 N RAYMOND AV	PASADENA	818797 1873
48	F6	LA PUENTE	15920 E CENTRAL AV	LA PUENTE	818968 4613
102	F4	LAS VIRGENES LIBRARY	29130 W ROADSIDE DR	AGOURA HILLS	818889 2278
90	D2	LA VERNE	3640 D STREET	LA VERNE	714596 1934
63	A2	LAWNDALE	14615 BURIN AV	LAWNDALE	213676 0177
59	B3	LELAND R WEAVER	4035 TWEEDY BLVD	SOUTH GATE	213567 8853
57	A4	LENNOX	4359 LENNOX BLVD	LENNOX	213674 0385
36	A6	LINCOLN HEIGHTS	2530 WORKMAN ST	LOS ANGELES	213225 3977
26	D1	LINDA VISTA	1281 BRYANT ST	PASADENA	818793 1808
184	E6	LITTLEROCK	8135 PEARBLOSSOM HWY	LITTLEROCK	805944 4138
39	A2	LIVE OAK LIBRARY	4153-55 LIVE OAK AV	ARCADIA	818446 8803
73	D1	LOMITA	24200 NARBONNE AV	LOMITA	213539 4515
75	C5	LONG BEACH	101 PACIFIC AV	LONG BEACH	213437 2949
76	C2	LOS ALTOS	5614 BRITTON DR	LONG BEACH	213596 7370
52	A1	LOS ANGELES	3516 S HOPE ST	LOS ANGELES	213744 2004
44	D3	L A COUNTY LAW LIBRARY	301 W 1ST ST	LOS ANGELES	213629 3531
35	A2	LOS FELIZ	1939 1/2 HILLHURST AV	LOS ANGELES	213664 2903
61	B1	LOS NIETOS	11644 E SLAUSON AV	LOS NIETOS	213695 0708
56	A2	LOYOLA VILLAGE	7114 W MANCHESTER AV	LOS ANGELES	213670 5436
59	B5	LYNWOOD	11320 BULLIS RD	LYNWOOD	213635 7121
45	B3	MALABAR	2801 WABASH AV	LOS ANGELES	213268 0874
72	C2	MALAGA COVE PLAZA	2400 VIA CAMPESINA	PALO VERD EST	213377 9584
114	A5	MALIBU	23519 W CIVIC CTR WY	MALIBU	213456 6438
62	B4	MANHATTAN BEACH	1320 HIGHLAND AV	MANHATTAN BCH	213545 8595
62	D4	MANHATTAN HEIGHTS	1560 MANHATTAN BCH BL	MANHATTAN BCH	213379 8401
49	E5	MARINA DEL REY	4533 ADMIRALTY WY	MARINA DL REY	213821 3415
75	D4	MARK TWAIN	1325 E ANAHEIM ST	LONG BEACH	213591 7412
58	A3	MARK TWAIN	9621 S FIGUEROA ST	LOS ANGELES	213755 4088
49	F2	MAR VISTA	12006 VENICE BLVD	LOS ANGELES	213390 3454
63	C2	MASAO W SATOW	14433 S CRENSHAW BLVD	GARDENA	213679 0638
53	C4	MAYWOOD	4323 E SLAUSON AV	MAYWOOD	213771 8600
43	C2	MEMORIAL	4625 W OLYMPIC BLVD	LOS ANGELES	213934 0855
78	C1	MIRALESTE	29089 PALOS VERDS DR E	RO PALOS VERD	213377 9584
29	B4	MONROVIA	321 S MYRTLE AV	MONROVIA	818358 0174
41	A5	MONTANA	1704 MONTANA AV	SANTA MONICA	213829 7081
46	D6	MONTEBELLO	1550 BEVERLY BLVD	MONTEBELLO	213722 6551
45	F1	MONTEREY PARK	318 RAMONA RD	MONTEREY PARK	818307 1333
57	C1	MORNINGSIDE PARK	3202 W 85TH ST	INGLEWOOD	213412 5400
127	C4	NEWHALL LIBRARY	22704 W 9TH ST	NEWHALL	805259-0750
23	D2	NORTH HOLLYWOOD REG	5211 TUJUNGA AV	N HOLLYWOOD	818766 7185
70	D1	NORTH LONG BEACH	5571 ORANGE AV	LONG BEACH	213422 1927
62	E5	NORTH REDONDO	2000 ARTESIA BLVD	REDONDO BEACH	213374 0218
7	C5	NORTHRIDGE	9051 DARBY AV	NORTHRIDGE	818886 3640
63	B5	NORTH TORRANCE LIBRARY	3604 W ARTESIA BLVD	TORRANCE	213323 7200
53	E2	NORTHWEST	1466 S MCDONNELL AV	COMMERCE	213265 1787
17	A5	NORTHWEST PARK	3323 VICTORY BLVD	BURBANK	818953 9750
61	B6	NORWALK	12350 IMPERIAL HWY	NORWALK	213868 0775
38	F5	NORWOOD	4550 N PECK RD	EL MONTE	818443 3147
49	A2	OCEAN PARK	2601 MAIN ST	SANTA MONICA	213396 2741
8	F2	PACOIMA	13605 VAN NUYS BLVD	PACOIMA	818899 5203
40	D4	PALISADES	861 ALMA REAL DR	PACIFIC PALIS	213459 2754
172	C8	PALMDALE	700 E PALMDALE BLVD	PALMDALE	805273 2820
42	A5	PALMS-RANCHO PARK	2920 OVERLAND AV	LOS ANGELES	213838 2157
15	E1	PANORAMA CITY	14345 ROSCOE BLVD	PANORAMA CITY	818894 4071
65	F4	PARAMOUNT	16254 COLORADO AV	PARAMOUNT	213630 3171
27	A3	PASADENA MAIN LIBRARY	285 E WALNUT ST	PASADENA	818405 4052
72	E5	PENINSULA CENTER	650 DEEP VALLEY DR	ROLLNG HL EST	213377 9584
54	F4	PICO RIVERA	9001 MINES AV	PICO RIVERA	213942 7394
43	F3	PIO PICO	2631 OLYMPIC BL	LOS ANGELES	213381 1453
110	C5	POINT DUME LIBRARY	6955 FERNHILL DR	MALIBU	213457 6913
94	E3	POMONA	625 S GAREY AV	POMONA	714620 2043
68	D4	POST AVENUE LIBRARY	1345 POST AV	TORRANCE	213328 5392
171	D1	QUARTZ HILL	42018 N 50TH ST W	QUARTZ HILL	805943 2454
67	D4	REDONDO BEACH	309 ESPLANADE	REDONDO BEACH	213376 8723
54	E6	RIVERA	7828 S SERAPIS AV	PICO RIVERA	213949 5485
42	D3	ROBERTSON	1719 S ROBERTSON BLVD	LOS ANGELES	213837 1239
45	B5	ROBERT LOUIS STEVENSON	803 S SPENCE ST	LOS ANGELES	213268 4710
38	A5	ROSEMEAD	8800 VALLEY BLVD	ROSEMEAD	818573 5220
98	F4	ROWLAND HEIGHTS	1850 NOGALES ST	ROWLAND HTS	818912 5348
90	A3	SAN DIMAS LIBRARY	145 N WALNUT	SAN DIMAS	714599 6738
2	E5	SAN FERNANDO LIBRARY	1050 LIBRARY ST	SAN FERNANDO	818365 6928
37	E3	SAN GABRIEL	500 S DEL MAR AV	SAN GABRIEL	818287 0761
37	D1	SAN MARINO	1890 HUNTINGTON DR	SAN MARINO	818282 8484
78	F3	SAN PEDRO REGIONAL	931 S GAFFEY	SAN PEDRO	213548 7779
26	D5	SAN RAFAEL	1240 NITHSDALE RD	PASADENA	818795 7974
27	B1	SANTA CATALINA	999 E WASHINGTON BLVD	PASADENA	818794 1219
61	A3	SANTA FE SPRINGS	11700 E TELEGRAPH RD	SANTA FE SPGS	213868 7738
49	A1	SANTA MONICA MAIN LIB	1343 6TH ST	SANTA MONICA	213451 5751
22	E3	SHERMAN OAKS	14245 MOORPARK ST	SHERMAN OAKS	818981 7850
28	B2	SIERRA MADRE	440 W SIERRA MADRE BLD	SIERRA MADRE	818355 7186
55	C5	SORENSEN	11405 E ROSEHEDGE DR	WHITTIER	213692 7742
47	D3	SOUTH EL MONTE	1430 N CENTRAL AV	S EL MONTE	818443 4158
36	F1	SOUTH PASADENA	1100 OXLEY	S PASADENA	818799 9108
61	F5	SOUTH WHITTIER	14433 S LEFFINGWELL RD	WHITTIER	213946 4415
68	D6	SOUTHEAST TORRANCE	23115 ARLINGTON AV	TORRANCE	213530 5044
23	B3	STUDIO CITY	4400 BABCOCK AV	STUDIO CITY	818769 5212
48	D2	SUNKIST	840 N PUENTE AV	LA PUENTE	818960 2707
10	E3	SUNLAND-TUJUNGA	7771 FOOTHILL BLVD	TUJUNGA	818352 4481
28	A4	SUNNYSLOPE	346 S ROSEMEAD BLVD	PASADENA	818792 5733
16	E2	SUN VALLEY	7935 VINELAND AV	SUN VALLEY	818764 7907
2	D3	SYLMAR	13059 GLENOAKS BLD	SYLMAR	818367 6102
38	C2	TEMPLE CITY	5939 GOLDEN WEST AV	TEMPLE CITY	818285 2136
124	B9	VALENCIA LIBRARY	23743 W VALENCIA BLVD	VALENCIA	805259 8942
16	B4	VALLEY PLAZA	12311 VANOWEN ST	N HOLLYWOOD	818765 0805
15	E5	VAN NUYS	6250 SYLMAR AV	VAN NUYS	818989 8453
49	C4	VENICE	610 CALIFORNIA AV	VENICE	213821 1769
51	F3	VERMONT SQUARE	1201 W 48TH ST	LOS ANGELES	213293 7138
52	C2	VERNON BRANCH	4504 S CENTRAL AV	LOS ANGELES	213234 9106
64	B6	VICTORIA PARK	17906 S AVALON BLVD	CARSON	213327 4830
51	B3	VIEW PARK	3854 W 54TH ST	LOS ANGELES	213293 5371
69	B6	VILLA CARSON	23317 S AVALON BLVD	CARSON	213830 5561
93	D5	WALNUT	21155 LA PUENTE RD	WALNUT	714595 0757
73	A1	WALTERIA	3815 W 242ND ST	TORRANCE	213375 8418
43	D4	WASHINGTON IRVING	1803 S ARLINGTON AV	LOS ANGELES	213734 6303
58	D3	WATTS LIBRARY	1501 E 103RD	WATTS	213567 2297
81	B3	WEINGART LIBRARY	12301 E 207TH ST	LAKEWOOD	213860 3431
56	C2	WESTCHESTER	8946 SEPULVEDA EAST WY	WESTCHESTER	213645 6082
92	A1	WEST COVINA LIBRARY	1601 W COVINA PKWY	WEST COVINA	818962 3541
33	D5	WEST HOLLYWOOD	715 N SAN VICENTE BLVD	W HOLLYWOOD	213652 5340
41	D3	WEST LOS ANGELES REG	11360 SANTA MONICA BL	W LOS ANGELES	213312 8323
14	B4	WEST VALLEY REGIONAL	19036 VANOWEN ST	RESEDA	818345 4393
55	E5	WHITTIER CENTRAL	7344 S WASHINGTON AV	WHITTIER	213698 8181
84	C4	WHITTWOOD	10537 S STA GERTRUDES	WHITTIER	213947 5417
34	A3	WILL & ARIEL DRANT	1403 N GARDNER	HOLLYWOOD	213876 2741
58	E5	WILLOWBROOK	11838 WILMINGTON AV	LOS ANGELES	213564 5698
74	C4	WILMINGTON LIBRARY	309 W OPP	WILMINGTON	213834 1082
34	D6	WILSHIRE	149 N ST ANDREWS PL	LOS ANGELES	213467 7343
62	E1	WISEBURN	5335 W 135TH ST	HAWTHORNE	213643 8880
57	E4	WOODCREST	1340 W 106TH ST	LOS ANGELES	213757 9373
13	B1	WOODLAND HILLS	22200 VENTURA BLVD	WOODLAND HLLS	818887 0160

1990 LOS ANGELES COUNTY POINTS OF INTEREST

PARK & RIDE

PAGE	GRID	NAME	ADDRESS	CITY	PHONE
100A	A4	AGOURA HILLS PK &RIDE	KANAN RD & 101 FRWY	AGOURA HILLS	
102	F4	AGOURA PARK AND RIDE	CANWOOD WEST OF KANAN	LA COUNTY	
39	F4	BALDWIN PARK	BADILLO ST & RAMONA BL	BALDWIN PARK	
65	C5	BUTLER AV	BUTLER AV & ARTESIA BL	LONG BEACH	
69	C3	CARSON PARK& RIDE	DOMINGNEZ ST&LEAPWD AV	CARSON	
86	E6	CITRUS COLLEGE	FOOTHLL BL & CITRUS AV	AZUSA	
56	A2	CONG CHURCH OF MESSIAH	7300 W MANCHESTER AV	WESTCHESTER	
72	E5	COURTYARD, THE	550 DEEP VALLEY DR	ROLLNG HL EST	
93	D1	COVINA PARK & RIDE	VIA VERDE & 10 FRWY	COVINA	
93	F6	DIAMOND BAR BLVD	DIAMOND BAR BL AT 60	DIAMOND BAR	
60	D2	DOWNEY PARK & RIDE	LAKEWOOD BL & I-5 FWY	DOWNEY	
38	D6	EL MONTE BUS STATION	3501 SANTA ANITA AV	EL MONTE	
38	D6	EL MONTE FIRE STATION	3613 SANTA ANITA AV	EL MONTE	
38	D6	EL MONTE PARK & RIDE	SANTA ANITA AV	EL MONTE	
21	F2	ENCINO PARK & RIDE	HAYVENHURST & MAGNOLIA	LOS ANGELES	
12	A4	FALLBROOK SQUARE	FALBROK AV & CRSWEL ST	CANOGA PARK	
12	E3	FIRST BAPTIST CHURCH	SHERMAN WY & MASON AV	LOS ANGELES	
28	A2	FIRST CHURCH NAZARENE	3700 E SIERRA MADRE BL	PASADENA	
63	E4	GARDENA VLY BAPTIST CH	15804 DENKER AV	GARDENA	
11	B6	GLENDALE	RT 210 AT LOWELL AV	GLENDALE	
77	B2	GOLDEN COVE SHOPNG CTR	PALOS VRDS DR/HAWTHRNE	RO PALOS VERD	
7	A4	HANDYMAN, THE	SHIRLEY AV AND PLUMMER	NORTHRIDGE	
76	A1	JEWISH COMMUNITY CTR	3801 E WILLOW ST	LONG BEACH	
19	A2	LA CANADA	RT 2 AT FOOTHILL BLVD	LA CANADA	
83	B3	LA MIRADA PARK & RIDE	ASH GRV DR&ADELFA DR	LA MIRADA	
159	J6	LANCASTER PARK & RIDE	AVENUE K & 14 FRWY	LANCASTER	
94	A5	LANTERMAN STATE HOSP	RT 57 AT HOSP OVERCROS	POMONA	
172	C5	LOCKHEED CORPORATION	TRISTAR WY & 6TH ST E	PALMDALE	
89	D1	LONEHILL AV	RT 210 AT LONEHILL AV	GLENDORA	
23	E4	LOS ANGELES PK & RIDE	BLUFFSIDE DR&RIVERTON	LOS ANGELES	
90	D6	LA COUNTY FAIRGROUNDS	MCKINLEY AV	POMONA	
3	B5	PACOIMA	RTE 210 AT PAXTON ST	LOS ANGELES	
26	F4	PARSONS COMPANY	PASADENA AV & UNION ST	PASADENA	
98	C3	PUENTE HILLS MALL	ALBATROSS AT CASTLETON	INDUSTRY	
62	F6	REDONDO BEACH	1601 KINGSDALE AV	REDONDO BEACH	
22	B6	RIMERTON RD	RTE 405 AT RIMERTON RD	LOS ANGELES	
90	E6	ROUTE 10	GAREY AV & MCKINLEY	POMONA	
78	F1	ROUTE 110	BATTERY ST & GAFFEY ST	SAN PEDRO	
16	C6	ROUTE 170	RTE 170 AT OXNARD	N HOLLYWOOD	
42	A5	ST JOHN'S PRSBYTRAN CH	11000 NATIONAL BLVD	PALMS	
127	F6	SAN FERNANDO RD	EAST OF RTE 14	NEWHALL	
127	F5	SAN FERNANDO RD	WEST OF RTE 14	NEWHALL	
37	E6	SAN GABRIEL PARK &RIDE	DEL MAR AV&MARSHALL ST	SAN GABRIEL	
127	E6	SANTA CLARITA PK &RIDE	SN FRNADO RD&SIERRA HY	SANTA CLARITA	
12	C5	TOPANGA PLAZA	TOPGA CYN BL & VCTY BL	CANOGA PARK	
92	D2	UNITED METHODIST CHRCH	718 AZUSA AV	WEST COVINA	
15	D2	VAN NUYS BLVD	7724 VAN NUYS BLVD	PANORAMA CITY	
127	J1	VIA PRINCESSA	S OF SIERRA HWY	NEWHALL	
88	F6	WEST COVINA PARK &RIDE	ESTLND TER&BRRANCA AV	WEST COVINA	
92	D2	WEST COVINA PARK &RIDE	CAMERON AV & AZUSA AV	WEST COVINA	
56	C2	1ST BAPTIST CHURCH	8540 LA TIJERA BLVD	WESTCHESTER	
39	D4	1ST PRESBYTERIAN CHRCH	4428 STEWART AV	BALDWIN PARK	

PARKS

PAGE	GRID	NAME	ADDRESS	CITY	PHONE
100A	B4	AGOURA	5217 N CHESBRO RD	AGOURA	818889 5131
27	A6	ALLENDALE PARK	ALLENDALE RD&EUCLID AV	PASADENA	
37	D4	ALMANSOR PARK	ALMANSOR AV	ALHAMBRA	
63	B4	ALONDRA	3850 MANHATTAN BCH BL	LAWNDALE	213323 8125
19	F5	ALTADENA PARK	65 MOUNTAIN VIEW ST	ALTADENA	
61	D5	AMELIA MAYBERRY PARK	13201 E MEYER RD	SANTA FE SPGS	213944 7241
8	C2	ANDREAS PICO ADOBE	10940 SEPULVEDA BLVD	MISSION HILLS	818365 7810
78	F6	ANGELS GATE PARK	930 PASEO DEL MAR	LOS ANGELES	
174	H1	ANTLPE VLY INDIAN MUS	15701 E AVENUE M	LANCASTER	805946 2554
59	F5	APOLLO PARK	12458 RIVES AV	DOWNEY	213862 2269
147	E8	APOLLO PARK	4445 W AVE G	LANCASTER	805948 2257
28	E5	ARCADIA COUNTY PARK	405 S SANTA ANITA AV	ARCADIA	818445 9133
43	E3	ARDMORE PLAYGROUND	3250 SAN MARINO ST	LOS ANGELES	213383 7549
36	E1	ARROYO SECO PARK	ARROYO DR AT PASDNA AV	S PASADENA	
56	E2	ASHWOOD PARK	201 S ASH	INGLEWOOD	
58	A6	ATHENS PARK	12603 SO BROADWAY	LOS ANGELES	
45	F6	ATLANTIC AVENUE PARK	570 ATLANTIC AVENUE	E LOS ANGELES	
1	E6	BABBITT PARK	BABBITT & SIMONDS	MISSION HILLS	
42	F6	BALDWIN HILLS PLGD	5401 HIGHLIGHT PL	LOS ANGELES	213934 8422
46	C2	BARNES MEMORIAL PARK	400 S MCPHERRIN AV	MONTEREY PARK	818573 1216
34	F3	BARNSDALL PARK	4800 HOLLYWOOD BLVD	LOS ANGELES	213660 4254
48	C3	BASSETT PARK	510 N VINELAND AV	LA PUENTE	818968 4289
54	A6	BELL GARDENS PARK	6662 LOVELAND ST	BELL GARDENS	213927 1451
35	A5	BELLEVUE PARK	EDGECLIFFE & MARCIA DR	LOS ANGELES	213664 2468
45	F4	BELVEDERE PARK	4914 E BROOKLYN AV	E LOS ANGELES	213268 7264
47	D1	BICENTENNIAL PARK	3400 SAN GABRIEL PKWY	PICO RIVERA	213695 4536
81	B4	BILLY MILFORD PARK	NORWALK BLVD	HAWAIIAN GDNS	
70	F2	BISCAILUZ PARK	2601 DOLLAR ST	LAKEWOOD	213634 3348
70	D3	BIXBY KNOLLS PARK	1000 SAN ANTONIO DR	LONG BEACH	213438 9071
50	D1	BLAIR HILLS PARK	ROBSTONE DR	CULVER CITY	
50	C3	BLANCO PARK	OVERLAND AV&STEVER ST	CULVER CITY	
63	C3	BODGER PARK	14900 SO YUKON AV	HAWTHORNE	213676 2085
90	A6	BONELLI REGIONAL CO PK	120 PARK RD	SAN DIMAS	714599 8411

PAGE	GRID	NAME	ADDRESS	CITY	PHONE
45	A5	BOYLE HTS SPORTS CTR	933 S MOTT ST	LOS ANGELES	213264 5136
17	C2	BRACE CANYON PARK	SCOTT RD & LAMER ST	BURBANK	
18	B4	BRAND PARK	1601 W MOUNTAIN ST	GLENDALE	818243 8177
8	C1	BRAND PARK	15174 SN FRNDO MSN BL	MISSION HILLS	818361 1377
9	A6	BRANFORD PARK	13310 BRANFORD ST	LOS ANGELES	818767 0347
26	F2	BRENNER PARK	LINCOLN AV&MOUNTAIN ST	PASADENA	
53	E1	BRISTOW PARK	1466 S MCDONNELL AV	COMMERCE	213269 5603
55	E4	BROADWAY PARK	BROADWAY&NEWLIN AV	WHITTIER	
26	E3	BROOKSIDE PARK	ARROYO BL & PK RDWY A	PASADENA	
92	C2	CAMERON PARK	700 LARKELLEN AV	WEST COVINA	
64	C2	CAMPANELLA	14812 STANFORD AV	COMPTON	213631 6757
36	A3	CARLIN SMITH PLAYGRND	511 W AVENUE 46	LOS ANGELES	818225 4960
69	B4	CARSON PARK	21411 SO ORRICK AV	CARSON	213830 4925
42	E2	CARTHAY CIRCLE PARK	RAMONA WY&FOSTER DR	LOS ANGELES	
58	D5	CARVER PARK	1400 E 118TH ST	LOS ANGELES	213566 2039
H		CASTAIC LAKE STATE REC	32100 RIDGE ROUTE	CASTAIC	805257 4050
5	D3	CASTLE PEAK PARK	VALLEY CIRCLE BLVD	LOS ANGELES	
51	B6	CENTINELA PARK	700 WARREN LN	INGLEWOOD	213649 7407
55	E4	CENTRAL PARK	13200 BAILEY ST	WHITTIER	
44	D6	CENTRAL PLAYGROUND	1357 E 22ND ST	LOS ANGELES	213749 9711
82	D4	CERRITOS PARK EAST	13200 166TH ST	CERRITOS	
81	C2	CERRITOS REGIONAL PARK	19700 S BLOOMFIELD AV	CERRITOS	213924 5144
111	A3	CHARMLEE COUNTY PARK	ENCINAL CANYON RD	MALIBU	
89	B3	CHARTER OAK	20261 E COVINA BLVD	COVINA	818339 0411
6	A2	CHATSWORTH PARK	22300 CHATSWORTH ST	CHATSWORTH	818341 6595
42	B3	CHEVIOT HILLS PK & REC	2551 MOTOR AV	LOS ANGELES	213837 5186
45	D3	CITY TERRACE	1126 NO HAZARD AV	E LOS ANGELES	213261 0291
65	C5	COOLIDGE PARK	352 E NEECE ST	LONG BEACH	213423 0123
50	C2	COOMBS PARK	FARRAGUT DR	CULVER CITY	
32	A6	CRESCENT HILLS PARK	1000 HANLEY AV	LOS ANGELES	213472 5223
18	C1	CRESCENTA VALLEY	3901 NEW YORK AV	LA CRESCENTA	818249 5940
59	E1	CUDAHY NEIGHBORHOOD PK	5200 SANTA ANA ST	CUDAHY	
35	B2	CULTURAL ART CENTER	3224 RIVERSIDE DR	LOS ANGELES	213666 0221
35	F4	CYPRESS PARK	2630 PEPPER	CYPRESS PARK	213221 7821
88	E1	DALTON PARK	18867 E ARMSTEAD ST	AZUSA	818963 9512
57	C2	DARBY PARK	3400 ARBOR VITAE ST	INGLEWOOD	213649 7391
56	E6	DEL AIRE	12601 SO IRIS AV	HAWTHORNE	213676 4661
34	B3	DELONGPRE PARK	DELNGPRE AV&CHERKEE AV	HOLLYWOOD	
55A	D1	DEL REY LAGOON	6660 ESPLANADE WY	PLAYA DEL REY	213823 9677
43	E6	DENKER RECREATION CTR	1550 W 35TH PL	LOS ANGELES	213732 4905
63	D5	DESCANSO PARK	2500 DESCANSO WY	TORRANCE	
J		DEVILS PUNCHBOWL	28000 DEVILS PNCHBL RD	PEARBLOSSOM	805944 2743
3	E4	DEXTER	11053 N TRAIL LKVW TER	SAN FERNANDO	818896 3210
50	C1	DR PAUL CARLSON MEM PK	BRADDOCK DR & MOTOR AV	CULVER CITY	
70	A4	DOMINGUEZ	21330 S SANTA FE AV	CARSON	213549 3962
67	E1	DOMINGUEZ PARK	BERYL ST&190TH ST	REDONDO BEACH	
41	B4	DOUGLAS PARK	1155 CHELSEA AV	SANTA MONICA	213828 9912
29	D5	DUARTE PARK	1200 BUENA VISTA ST	DUARTE	
159	F7	DUNTLEY RAWLEY PARK	AV K AT 35 TH ST W	LANCASTER	
26	C4	EAGLEROCK REC CENTER	1100 EAGLE VISTA DR	EAGLE ROCK	818257 6948
27	F4	EATON BLANCHE PARK	DEL MAR BL&LAPRESDA DR	PASADENA	
20	E6	EATON CANYON PARK	1750 ALTADENA DR	PASADENA	818794 1866
35	C6	ECHO PARK	1632 BELLEVUE AV	LOS ANGELES	213626 2585
88	E4	EDNA PARK	EDNA PL & VALENCIA	COVINA	
28	E4	EISENHOWER PARK	500 2ND ST	ARCADIA	
3	A2	EL CARISO REGIONAL PK	13100 HUBBARD ST	SYLMAR	818367 7050
160	C5	EL DORADO	PONDERA ST & 5TH ST	LANCASTER	805425 4712
76	E1	EL DORADO	2760 STUDEBAKER RD	LONG BEACH	213421 9431
76	F1	EL DORADO NATURE CTR	7550 E SPRING ST	LONG BEACH	213425 8569
63	A6	EL NIDO PARK	18301 KINGSDALE AV	TORRANCE	213542 2550
24	A5	EL PASEO DE CAHUENGA	CAHUENGA & HOLLYWD FRY	LOS ANGELES	
44	E2	EL PUEBLO D LS ANGELES	SUNSET BLVD & BROADWAY	LOS ANGELES	213620 3342
58	D6	EL SEGUNDO PARK	130TH ST & COMPTON AV	COMPTON	
36	D5	EL SERENO REC CTR	4721 KLAMATH ST	EL SERENO	818225 3517
35	D5	ELYSIAN PARK	929 ACADEMY RD	LOS ANGELES	213225 2044
64	C1	ENTERPRISE PARK	13055 CLOVIS ST	LOS ANGELES	213635 0688
36	C3	ERNEST E DEBS REG	4235 MONTEREY RD	LOS ANGELES	818223 2721
16	A5	ERWIN PARK	ERWIN ST & ETHEL AV	LOS ANGELES	
44	D1	EVERETT PARK	EVERETT ST	LOS ANGELES	
45	B4	EVERGREEN REC CENTER	2844 E 2ND ST	LOS ANGELES	213262 0397
52	A1	EXPOSITION PARK	EXPOSITION BLVD	LOS ANGELES	
20	B3	FARNSWORTH	568 E MT CURVE AV	ALTADENA	818798 6335
9	B6	FERNANGELES REC CTR	8851 LAUREL CYN BLVD	SUN VALLEY	818767 9123
59	F2	FORD REGIONAL CO PARK	8000 S SCOUT AV	BELL GARDENS	213927 4435
63	D3	FREEMAN PARK	2100 W 154TH PL	GARDENA	213327 0220
25	B3	FREMONT PARK	PATTERSON AV	GLENDALE	
45	B5	FRESNO RECREATION CTR	1016 S FRESNO ST	LOS ANGELES	213265 4755
55	E5	FRIENDS PARK	13300 MAR VISTA ST	WHITTIER	
78	C4	FRIENDSHIP	PALOS VERDES DR-WESTRN	RO PALOS VERD	
60	B2	FURMAN PARK	10419 RIVES AV	DOWNEY	213862 0918
92	D4	GALSTER WILDERNESS PK	AROMA DR	WEST COVINA	
37	A1	GARFIELD PARK	815 S MISSION AV	S PASADENA	
46	E1	GARVEY MEM REC CENTER	7933 E EMERSON PL	S SAN GABRIEL	
46	D3	GARVEY RANCH PARK	ORANGE AV & GRAVES AV	MONTEREY PARK	
69	B6	GENERAL SCOTT PARK	23410 CATSKILL AV	CARSON	213830 8310
46	C4	GEORGE E ELDER	1950 WILCOX AV	MONTEREY PARK	213573 1218
159	C9	GEORGE LANE	5520 W AVENUE L-8	LANCASTER	805945 8491
52	B2	GILBRT LINDSAY COM CTR	4211 AVALON BLVD	LOS ANGELES	213233 0552
25	C4	GLENDALE CENTRAL PARK	COLORADO ST & BRAND AV	GLENDALE	
2	F4	GLENOAKS PARK	HARDING AV - LUCAS ST	SAN FERNANDO	
64	D2	GONZALES PARK COM CTR	1101 W CRESSY ST	COMPTON	213638 1007

1990 LOS ANGELES COUNTY POINTS OF INTEREST

PAGE	GRID	NAME	ADDRESS	CITY	PHONE
7	F2	GRANADA HILLS REC CTR	16730 CHATSWORTH ST	GRANADA HILLS	818363 3556
46	A1	GRANADA PARK	HELLMAN AV & PALM AV	ALHAMBRA	
29	C2	GRAND AV	GRAND AV	MONROVIA	
27	C4	GRANT PARK	CORDOVA ST&CHESTER AV	PASADENA	
54	F1	GRANT REA MEMORIAL PK	BEVERLY BLVD & REA DR	MONTEBELLO	
36	A4	GREAVER OAK PARK	FIGUEROA ST & 37TH	LOS ANGELES	
33	C4	GREYSTONE PARK	501 N DOHENY RD	BEVERLY HILLS	213550 4769
71	F2	GRIDLEY	GRIDLEY AT BERTHA	CERRITOS	
34	E1	GRIFFITH PARK	N END VERMONT AV	LOS ANGELES	213665 5188
63	D6	GUENSER PARK	17800 S GRAMERCY PL	TORRANCE	213515 9114
61	E3	GUNN AVENUE PARK	10130 SO GUNN AV	WHITTIER	213698 7645
59	D6	HAM MEMORIAL PARK	5300 COURTLAND AV	LYNWOOD	
42	F1	HANCOCK PARK	5801 WILSHIRE BLVD	LOS ANGELES	
9	D2	HANSEN DAM PARK	11850 FOOTHILL BLVD	SN FERNDO VLY	818899 5752
74	A4	HARBOR PARK	1221 FIGUEROA PL	WILMINGTON	213830 9126
57	B6	HAWTHORNE MEM PARK	3901 EL SEGUNDO BLVD	HAWTHORNE	213676 1181
71	C4	HEARTWELL PARK	5801 PARKCREST ST	LONG BEACH	213423 7924
57	F6	HELEN KELLER	1045 W 126TH ST	LOS ANGELES	213756 3506
44	F4	HOLLENBECK PARK	415 S ST LOUIS ST	LOS ANGELES	213261 0113
57	D6	HOLLY PARK	2000 W 120TH	HAWTHORNE	
32	F6	HOLMBY PARK	400 BEVERLY GLEN DRIVE	LOS ANGELES	
44	A5	HOOVER RECREATION CTR	1010 W 25TH ST	LOS ANGELES	213749 8896
65	D6	HOUGHTON PARK	6301 MYRTLE AV	N LONG BEACH	213422 3584
H		HUNGRY VY VEH REC AREA	HWY 5 AND HWY 138	LA COUNTY	
57	B5	IMPERIAL PARK	120TH ST & YUKON AV	INGLEWOOD	213566 4247
60	C6	INDEPENDENCE PARK	12334 BELLFLOWER BLVD	DOWNEY	
123	B8	INDIAN DUNES PARK	28700 HENRY MAYO DR	VALENCIA	805259 8000
42	C4	IRVING SCHACHTER	BEVERWIL DR	LOS ANGELES	
88	B3	IRWINDALE PARK	5050 IRWINDALE AV	IRWINDALE	
57	D3	JESSE OWENS CO PARK	9637 S WESTERN AV	LOS ANGELES	213757 2488
49	B2	JOSLYN PARK CENTER	KENSNGTN RD & BEVLY AV	SANTA MONICA	213396 1763
65	C4	KELLY PARK	2319 E CALDWELL ST	COMPTON	213635 2417
190	C2	KENTUCKY SPRINGS PARK	ANGELES FOREST HWY	L A COUNTY	
5	D5	KNAPP PARK	25000 KITTRIDGE ST	CANOGA PARK	818887 9800
42	E2	LA CIENEGA PARK	8400 GREGORY WY	BEVERLY HILLS	213550 4775
37	C1	LACY PARK	3300 MONTEREY RD	SAN MARINO	
50	F4	LADERA PARK	6027 LADERA PARK AV	LOS ANGELES	213294 0626
46	D4	LA LOMA PARK	FULTON AV & IRIS WY	MONTEREY PARK	
38	F5	LAMBERT PARK	11431 MCGIRK AV	EL MONTE	818575 2322
83	B2	LA MIRADA PARK	13701 S ADELFA DR	LA MIRADA	213943 6978
12	C2	LANARK REC CENTER	21816 LANARK ST	CANOGA PARK	818883 1503
48	F5	LA PUENTE PARK	500 GLENDORA AV	LA PUENTE	
27	A1	LA PINTORESCA PARK	1400 FAIR OAKS AV	PASADENA	
2	D5	LAS PALMAS PARK	505 HUNTINGTON ST	SAN FERNANDO	818365 3011
2	E5	LAYNE PARK	1ST ST - FERMOORE ST	SAN FERNANDO	
81	C5	LEE WARE PARK	WARDHAM AV	HAWAIIAN GDNS	
78	F2	LELAND	863 S HERBERT AV	SAN PEDRO	213548 9295
34	E4	LEMON GROVE REC CTR	4949 LEMON GROVE AV	LOS ANGELES	213666 4144
56	F4	LENNOX	10828 CONDON AV	LENNOX	213677 0827
40	F6	LINCOLN PARK	WILSHIRE & LINCOLN	SANTA MONICA	213394 4282
45	B1	LINCOLN PARK	3501 VALLEY BLVD	LOS ANGELES	213223 3595
50	C2	LINDBERG PARK	RHODA WY & STUDIO DR	CULVER CITY	
61	A4	LITTLE LAKE PARK	10900 PIONEER BLVD	SANTA FE SPGS	213944 6011
62	B3	LIVE OAK PARK	ARDMORE AV	MANHATTAN BCH	
19	F3	LOMA ALTA	3330 NO LINCOLN ST	ALTADENA	818794 8811
78	F6	LOOKOUT POINT	GAFFEY ST & 35TH ST	SAN PEDRO	
70	B5	LOS CERRITOS PARK	500 W SAN ANTONIO DR	LONG BEACH	
21	F2	LOS ENCINOS ST HIST PK	VENTURA BL	LOS ANGELES	818784 4849
61	A2	LOS NIETOS PARK	11143 CHARLESWORTH RD	SANTA FE SPGS	213692 8621
85	C1	LOS ROBLES CO PARK	14906 E LOS ROBLES	HACIENDA HTS	818330 3052
65	B2	LUEDERS PARK COMM CTR	1500 ROSECRANS AV	COMPTON	213638 4821
59	B5	LYNWOOD PARK	3798 CENTURY BLVD	LYNWOOD	213537 0800
44	A2	MACARTHUR PARK	WILSHIRE BLVD	LOS ANGELES	
68	B5	MADRONA MRSH NTR PRES	22300 MADRONA AV	TORRANCE	
5	E4	MAE BOYAR REC CTR	23936 HIGHLANDER RD	CANOGA PARK	818347 9263
110	C5	MALIBU COMMUNITY CTR	6955 FERNHILL DR	MALIBU	213457 1558
107	B4	MALIBU CREEK STATE PK	LAS VIRGENES RD	LA COUNTY	
62	D4	MANHATTAN HEIGHTS PARK	MANHATTAN BEACH BLVD	MANHATTAN BCH	
85	D2	MANZANITA	1747 SO KWIS AV	LA PUENTE	818336 6246
49	C2	MARINE PARK CENTER	1406 MARINE ST	SANTA MONICA	213396 2764
160	A2	MARIPOSA PARK	45755 N FIG AV	LANCASTER	805942 4435
95A	F3	MARSHALL CYN COUNTY PK	6550 STEPHENS RANCH RD	LA VERNE	
49	A2	MARY HITCHCOCK PARK	4TH ST & STRAND ST	SANTA MONICA	
52	C4	MARY MCCLEOD BETHUNE	1244 E 61ST ST	LOS ANGELES	213234 8349
6	E3	MASON RECREATION CTR	10400 MASON ST	CHATSWORTH	818998 6377
172	G9	MCADAM MEMORIAL PARK	38115 30TH ST E	PALMDALE	805947 1454
17	D4	MCCAMBRIDGE PARK	1515 N GLENOAKS BLVD	BURBANK	818847 9506
10	F4	MCGROARTY CULTURAL CTR	7570 MCGROARTY TER	TUJUNGA	818352 5285
42	E5	MCMANUS PARK	3459 MCMANUS AV	CULVER CITY	213558 9497
41	B6	MEMORIAL PARK	14TH & OLYMPIC	SANTA MONICA	213450 0555
28	B5	MICHILLINDA PARK	3800 MICHILLINDA DR	PASADENA	
58	E6	MONA	2291 E 121ST ST	COMPTON	213639 2413
54	D1	MONTEBELLO PARK	WHITTIER BL & PARK AV	MONTEBELLO	
23	C3	MOORPARK PARK	12000 MOORPARK ST	STUDIO CITY	
39	E5	MORGAN PARK	14100 RAMONA BLVD	BALDWIN PARK	
47	F2	MOUNTAIN VIEW PARK	12127 ELLIOTT AV	EL MONTE	818575 2292
37	D5	MUNICIPAL PARK	WELLS & RAMONA	SAN GABRIEL	
127	B3	NEWHALL MEMORIAL PARK	24923 N NEWHALL AVE	NEWHALL	805259 4990
23	D2	NORTH HOLLYWOOD PARK	5301 TUJUNGA AV	N HOLLYWOOD	818763 7651
124	H8	NORTH OAKS PARK	27824 N CAMP PLENTY RD	SAUGUS	805251 2050
7	C3	NORTHRIDGE REC CTR	10058 RESEDA BLVD	NORTHRIDGE	818349 7341

PAGE	GRID	NAME	ADDRESS	CITY	PHONE
19	D4	OAK GROVE PARK	4550 OAK GROVE DR	PASADENA	
45	D4	OBREGON	4021 E 1ST ST	LOS ANGELES	213264 2646
127	B4	OLD ORCHARD PARK	25051 N AVE ROTELLA	VALENCIA	805259 8424
24	D1	OLIVE AVENUE PARK	OLIVE AVE	LOS ANGELES	
1	D2	OMELVENY PARK	VAN GOGH & SESNON	LOS ANGELES	
48	F2	ORANGEWOOD PARK	1600 MERCED AV	WEST COVINA	
5	E1	ORCUTT RCH HORTICULT	23555 JUSTICE ST	LAKESIDE PARK	818883 6641
98	B4	OTTERBEIN ST REC CTR	17250 E COLIMA RD	ROWLAND HTS	
17	A5	PACIFIC PARK	501 S PACIFIC AV	BURBANK	818956 2009
9	A2	PACOIMA PLAYGROUND	10943 HERRICK AV	PACOIMA	818899 1950
40	D5	PALISADES PARK	851 ALMA REAL DR	LOS ANGELES	213454 1412
55	C3	PALM PARK	PALM AV & FLORAL DR	WHITTIER	
42	A5	PALMS PARK	2950 OVERLAND AV	LOS ANGELES	213838 3838
173	B9	PALMS PARK	5600 AVE R	PALMDALE	
88	C5	PALM VIEW PARK	1300 PUENTE AV	WEST COVINA	
8	E6	PANORAMA REC CENTER	8600 HAZELTINE AV	PANORAMA	818892 9300
67	F4	PARADISE PARK	5006 LEE ST	TORRANCE	213391 9331
65	F2	PARAMOUNT	14410 PARAMOUNT BLVD	PARAMOUNT	213531 3503
27	A4	PASADENA CENTRAL PARK	FAIR OAKS AV & DEL MAR	PASADENA	
27	A3	PASADENA MEMORIAL PARK	WALNUT ST & RAYMOND AV	PASADENA	
10	E4	PASKO PARK	MCGROARTY ST	LOS ANGELES	
81	B1	PAT NIXON PARK	PATRICIA DR	CERRITOS	
8	E2	PAXTON PARK & REC CTR	10731 LAUREL CYN BLVD	PACOIMA	818896 2811
185	C8	PEARBLOSSOM	33922 121ST ST E	PEARBLOSSOM	805944 2988
78	E2	PECK PARK & REC CTR	560 N WESTERN AV	SAN PEDRO	213548 7580
38	F3	PECK ROAD PARK	5401 N PECK RD	ARCADIA	818444 1340
25	A2	PELANCONI PARK	1000 GRANDVIEW AV	GLENDALE	
62	E6	PERRY PARK	GRANT AV & SLAUSON LN	REDONDO BEACH	
44	C3	PERSHING SQUARE	532 S OLIVE ST	LOS ANGELES	213628 6010
55	B2	PICO PARK	9520 BEVERLY BLVD	PICO RIVERA	213692 3222
55	B3	PIO PICO STATE HIS PK	6003 S PIONEER BLVD	WHITTIER	213695 1217
127	J4	PLACERITA CYN STATE PK	19150 PLACERITA CYN RD	NEWHALL	805259 7721
34	A4	PLUMMER	1200 N VISTA ST	LOS ANGELES	213876 1725
7	A2	PORTER RANCH PARK	TAMPA AV & TUNNEY AV	NORTHRIDGE	
43	C3	QUEEN ANNE REC CENTER	1240 WEST BLVD	LOS ANGELES	213934 0130
62	F1	RAMONA PARK	137TH ST	HAWTHORNE	
65	F5	RAMONA PARK	3301 E 65TH ST	LONG BEACH	213422 1960
42	A3	RANCHO PARK	2459 MOTOR AV	LOS ANGELES	
43	A6	RO CIENEGA SPORTS CTR	5001 RODEO RD	LOS ANGELES	213294 6788
77	C2	RANCHO PALOS VERDES	30359 S HAWTHORNE BLVD	RO PALOS VERD	213377 2290
2	F6	RECREATION PARK	PARK AV - 1ST ST	SAN FERNANDO	
76	B4	RECREATION PARK	GRANADA AV	LONG BEACH	
14	C5	RESEDA PARK & REC CTR	18411 VICTORY BLVD	RESEDA	818881 3882
160	A5	REYNOLDS PARK	716 W OLDFIELD ST	LANCASTER	805942 4417
92	C5	RIMGROVE DR	747 N RIMGROVE DRIVE	LA PUENTE	818336 0416
54	F1	RIO HONDO PARK	4628 S ORANGE ST	PICO RIVERA	213695 9604
60	D5	RIO SAN GABRIEL PARK	9612 ARDINE	DOWNEY	213861 5914
34	D6	ROBERT BURNS PARK	BEVERLY BL&VAN NESS AV	LOS ANGELES	
9	C3	ROGER JESSUP REC CTR	12467 W OSBORNE ST	PACOIMA	818896 6215
63	B3	ROGERS-ANDERSON PK	PRAIRIE AV	LAWNDALE	
52	D6	ROOSEVELT	7600 GRAHAM AV	LOS ANGELES	213581 3766
26	B5	ROSEMARY PLAYGROUND	YOSEMITE DR	EAGLE ROCK	
38	B4	ROSEMEAD PARK	MISSION - ENCINITA	ROSEMEAD	
53	F2	ROSEWOOD PARK	5600 HARBOR	COMMERCE	213721 5281
63	D1	ROWLEY PARK	13220 VAN NESS AV	GARDENA	213515 9456
42	B2	ROXBURY REC CENTER	471 S ROXBURY DR	BEVERLY HILLS	213550 4761
12	E3	RUNNYMEADE REC CTR	RUNNYMDE ST&WINNTKA AV	LOS ANGELES	
34	A2	RUNYON CANYON PK	2000 FULLER AV	LOS ANGELES	
30	E6	RUSTIC CANYON PARK	SANTA MONICA MTNS	LOS ANGELES	
J		SADDLEBACK BUTTE ST PK	4555 W AVE G	LANCASTER	805942 0662
45	C6	SALAZAR PARK	3864 WHITTIER BLVD	E LOS ANGELES	213264 4607
95A	A6	SAN DIMAS CANYON	1512 N SYCAMORE CYN RD	SAN DIMAS	714599 7512
124	C5	SANTA CLARITA	27285 N SECO CANYON RD	SAUGUS	805259 3566
88	A1	SANTA FE DAM REC AREA	200 S PECKAM RD	AZUSA	818334 0713
40	A1	SANTA YNEZ	CYN PK & PACIFIC PALIS	LOS ANGELES	
127	E3	SAXONIA PARK	QUIGLEY & CLEARDALE	NEWHALL	
70	D3	SCHERER PARK	4600 LONG BEACH BLVD	LONG BEACH	213422 7070
14	E5	SEPULVEDA DAM REC AREA	17015 BURBANK BLVD	ENCINO	818343 4143
8	C6	SEPULVEDA REC CENTER	8801 KESTER AV	SEPULVEDA	818893 3700
46	A2	SEQUOIA PARK	RIDGECREST-CREST VISTA	MONTEREY PARK	
12	A4	SHADOW RANCH PARK	22633 VANOWEN ST	CANOGA PARK	818347 9126
70	A6	SILVERADO PARK	1545 W 31ST ST	LONG BEACH	213424 7108
56	F3	SIMINSKI PARK	9717 INGLEWOOD AV	INGLEWOOD	213649 7455
66	B4	SIMMS PARK	16614 S CLARK AV	BELLFLOWER	213866 7510
70	F3	SIMON BOLIVAR PARK	3300 DEL AMO BLVD	LAKEWOOD	
26	F5	SINGER PARK	CALIFORNIA BL&JOHN AV	PASADENA	
37	E3	SMITH PARK	200 W BROADWAY	SAN GABRIEL	818287 9421
44	D4	SIXTH & GLADYS	6TH & GLADYS ST	LOS ANGELES	
55	C5	SORENSEN	11419 ROSEHEDGE DR	WHITTIER	213692 9717
65	A4	SOUTH PARK	SANTA FE AV&JOHNSON ST	COMPTON	
52	B3	SOUTH PARK	345 E 51ST ST	LOS ANGELES	213232 2696
63	F5	SOUTH GARDENA PARK	SOUTH PARK LN	GARDENA	
59	D3	SOUTH GATE PARK	4900 SOUTHERN AV	SOUTH GATE	213567 1331
89	B1	SOUTH HILLS PARK	FOOTHILL FRWY	GLENDORA	
76	B2	STEARNS PARK	4520 E 23RD ST	LONG BEACH	213597 4713
85	E2	STIMSON AV PARK	1545 S STIMSON AV	LA PUENTE	818330 9477
9	E4	STONEHURST REC CENTER	9901 DRONEFIELD AV	SUN VALLEY	818767 0314
17	E3	STOUGH PARK	WALNUT AV	BURBANK	
16	B2	STRATHERN PLGD	STRATHRN ST&WHTSETT AV	LOS ANGELES	
23	B3	STUDIO CITY REC CTR	12621 RYE ST	STUDIO CITY	818769 4415
10	D3	SUNLAND PK & REC CTR	8651 FOOTHILL BLVD	SUNLAND	818352 5282

COPYRIGHT, © 1989 BY Thomas Bros Maps

PAGE	GRID	NAME	ADDRESS	CITY	PHONE
114	B5	SURFRIDER BCH ST PK	PACIFIC COAST HWY	MALIBU BEACH	
36	B3	SYCAMORE GROVE PARK	4702 N FIGUEROA ST	LOS ANGELES	213256 7721
2	E3	SYLMAR PARK	13109 BORDEN AV	SYLMAR	818367 5656
107	E5	TAPIA CO PARK	884 LAS VIRGENES RD	CALABASAS	
14	B6	TARZANA PARK	5665 VANALDEN AV	TARZANA	818343 5946
44	E2	THE PLAZA	SUNSET BLVD & MAIN ST	LOS ANGELES	
66	C2	THOMPSON PARK	14001 S BELLFLOWER BL	BELLFLOWER	213925 6601
63	D3	THORNBURG PARK	2320 W 149TH ST	GARDENA	213515 9456
160	F4	TIERRA BONITA	30TH ST	LANCASTER	
44	A4	TOBERMAN PLGD	1725 TOBERMAN ST	LOS ANGELES	213485 6896
40	D1	TOPANGA STATE PARK	SANTA MONICA MOUNTAINS	LOS ANGELES	
27	C5	TOURNAMENT PARK	1100 CALIFORNIA BLVD	PASADENA	
54	B6	TREASURE ISLAND PARK	9300 BLUFF RD	DOWNEY	213927 3212
44	C6	TRINITY REC CENTER	2415 TRINITY ST	LOS ANGELES	213485 4195
11	E6	TWO STRIKE PARK	5107 ROSEMONT AV	LA CRESCENTA	818248 4145
127	B2	VALENCIA GLEN	23750 VIA GAVOLA	VALENCIA	805259 4577
127	A2	VALENCIA MEADOWS	25671 N FEDALA RD	VALENCIA	805259 9007
16	B4	VALLEY PLAZA PARK	12240 ARCHWOOD ST	N HOLLYWOOD	818765 5885
123	A5	VAL VERDE PARK	30300 W ARLINGTON ST	VAL VERDE	805259 2421
63	D1	VAN NESS PARK	VAN NESS AV & 135TH ST	GARDENA	
15	E4	VAN NUYS REC CTR	14301 VANOWEN ST	VAN NUYS	818781 3331
22	E2	VAN NUYS-SHERMAN OAKS	14201 HUSTON ST	SHERMAN OAKS	818783 5121
188	D2	VASQUEZ ROCKS PARK	10700 W ESCNDDO CYN RD	SAUGUS	805268 0991
17	B1	VERDUGO MOUNTAIN PARK	SO OF LA TUNA CYN RD	LOS ANGELES	
24	B2	VERDUGO PARK	3201 W VERDUGO AV	BURBANK	818847 9510
25	E1	VERDUGO PARK	1401 N VERDUGO RD	GLENDALE	818956 2010
54	C6	VETERANS MEMORIAL PARK	6364 ZINDELL AV	COMMERCE	213927 1515
3	A1	VETERANS MEMORIAL PARK	13000 SAYER ST	SYLMAR	818367 1957
50	B1	VETERANS MEMORIAL PARK	4117 OVERLAND AV	CULVER CITY	213558 9497
17	B5	VICKROY PARK	MONTERY AV&BRIGHTON ST	BURBANK	
67	F3	VICTOR PARK	4727 EMERALD ST	TORRANCE	213371 9261
69	B1	VICTORIA PARK	419 E 192ND ST	CARSON	213532 9050
27	E2	VICTORY PARK	2575 PALOMA ST	PASADENA	818798 0865
67	D3	VINCENT PARK	600 VINCENT ST	REDONDO BEACH	
45	B3	WABASH REC CENTER	2765 WABASH AV	LOS ANGELES	213262 6534
12	C6	WARNER RANCH PARK	5800 TOPANGA CYN BLVD	LOS ANGELES	
34	A2	WATTLES GARDEN PARK	1850 N CURSON AV	HOLLYWOOD	213876 9911
58	D4	WATTS TOWERS ST HIS PK	1765 E 107TH ST	WATTS	
27	B1	WASHINGTON PARK	600 WASHINGTON BLVD	PASADENA	
23	F4	WEDDINGTON PARK	VLYHEART & HOLLYWD FRY	LOS ANGELES	
64	C4	WEST PARK	ALONDRA BL & WADSWORTH	COMPTON	
56	A2	WESTCHESTER REC CTR	7000 MANCHESTER AV	LOS ANGELES	213670 7473
49	F3	WEST END PARK	MOORE & WADE STS	CULVER CITY	
33	D5	WEST HOLLYWOOD PARK	647 N SAN VICENTE BLVD	W HOLLYWOOD	213652 3063
52	E5	WESTSIDE PARK	GAGE AV & COTTAGE ST	HUNTINGTON PK	
34	A6	WEST WILSHIRE REC CTR	141 S GARDNER ST	LOS ANGELES	213939 8874
78	D5	WHITE POINT PARK	2000 PASEO DEL MAR	LOS ANGELES	
47	A3	WHITTIER NARROWS	1000 N DURFEE AV	S EL MONTE	818444 1872
67	E4	WILDERNESS PARK	1102 CAMINO REAL	REDONDO BEACH	
20A	F6	WILDERNESS PARK	HIGHLAND VISTA DR	ARCADIA	
33	E4	WILLIAM S HART PARK	SUNSET BL & FLORES ST	LOS ANGELES	
127	D5	WILLIAM S HART PARK	24151 NEWHALL AV	NEWHALL	805259 0855
55	F5	WILLIAM PENN PARK	13900 PENN ST	WHITTIER	
58	C6	WILLOWBROOK PARK	EL SEGUNDO BLVD	L A COUNTY	
58	D3	WILL ROGERS MEM PK	1333 E 103RD ST	WATTS	213566 8284
40	E2	WILL ROGERS ST HIS PK	14253 SUNSET BLVD	PAC PALISADES	213454 8212
12	E1	WINNETKA REC CENTER	8401 WINNETKA AV	CANOGA PARK	818341 1430
23	E3	WOODBRIDGE PARK	ELMER AV&WOODBRIDGE ST	LOS ANGELES	
12	B6	WOODLAND HILLS REC CTR	5858 SHOUP AV	WOODLAND HLLS	818883 9370
15	B5	WOODLEY AV PARK	6350 WOODLEY AV	VAN NUYS	818994 2420
88	C1	ZACATECAS PARK	1ST ST & BARBARA AV	AZUSA	
1	D6	ZELZAH PARK	ZELZAH AV & LERDO AV	LOS ANGELES	

POINTS OF INTEREST

PAGE	GRID	NAME	ADDRESS	CITY	PHONE
35	A3	ABC TV CENTER	4151 PROSPECT AV	LOS ANGELES	213557 7777
90	F4	ADOBE DE PALOMARES	490 E ARROW HWY	POMONA	
75	F2	ALAMITOS DISCOVRY WELL	HILL ST & TEMPLE AV	SIGNAL HILL	
174	B4	ALPNE BUTTE WLDLF SANC	145TH ST E AVENUE P	PALMDALE	
8	C2	ANDREAS PICO ADOBE	10940 SEPULVEDA BLVD	MISSION HILLS	818365 7810
19	C1	ANGELES NATL FOREST			
H		ANTLPE VLY POPPY PRSRV	LANCASTER RD	L A COUNTY	
28	C4	ARBORETUM, STATE-LA CO	301 N BALDWIN AV	ARCADIA	818446 8251
68	F1	ASCOT PARK RACEWAY	18320 S VERMONT AV	LOS ANGELES	213321 1100
74	C3	BANNING MUSEUM	401 EAST M ST	WILMINGTON	213548 7777
80	A1	BELMONT PIER	39TH PL	LONG BEACH	
6	D4	BOYS TOWN OF THE WEST	21000 PLUMMER	CHATSWORTH	818341 3476
24	B4	BURBANK STUDIOS	4000 WARNER BLVD	BURBANK	818954 6000
79	A6	CABRILLO MARINE MUSEUM	3720 STEPHN M WHITE RD	SAN PEDRO	213831 3207
126	J2	CALIF INST OF THE ARTS	24700 W MCBEAN PKWY	VALENCIA	805255 1050
79	B2	CATALINA AIR-SEA TERML	BERTH 96	SAN PEDRO	213547 1161
77	A4	CATALINA ISLAND	26 MI S W LA HARBOR	L A COUNTY	
33	F6	CBS TELEVISION CITY	7800 BEVERLY BLVD	LOS ANGELES	213852 2345
34	C3	CBS TV CITY	6121 SUNSET BLVD	HOLLYWOOD	818460 3000
42	A2	CENTURY CITY	10200 SANTA MONICA BL	LOS ANGELES	
44	E1	CHINATOWN	NORTH BROADWAY	LOS ANGELES	
44	D2	CIVIC CENTER PLAZA	TEMPLE & HILL	LOS ANGELES	
34	B3	CROSSROADS OF THE WLD	SUNSET BL & CHEROKEE	LOS ANGELES	
19	A3	DESCANSO GARDENS	1418 DESCANSO DR	LA CANADA	818790 5571
7	D3	DEVONSHIRE DOWNS	18000 DEVONSHIRE	NORTHRIDGE	818363 8181
24	C3	DISNEY STUDIOS	500 S BUENA VISTA	BURBANK	
35	D6	DODGER STADIUM	1000 ELYSIAN PK	LOS ANGELES	213224 1400
74	C4	DRUM BARRACKS MUSEUM	1052 BANNING BLVD	WILMINGTON	213548 7509
33	F6	FARMERS MARKET	3RD ST & FAIRFAX AV	LOS ANGELES	213933 9211
44	C4	FEDERAL RESERVE	409 W OLYMPIC BLVD	LOS ANGELES	213683 8449
49	E6	FISHERMAN'S VILLAGE	13723 FIJI WY	MARINA DL REY	213823 5411
78	D5	FORT MCARTHUR MIL RES	WESTERN AV	SAN PEDRO	
44	D2	FT MOORE PIONEER MEM	HILL ST & SUNSET BLVD	LOS ANGELES	
57	B2	FORUM, THE	MANCHESTER & PRAIRIE	INGLEWOOD	213419 3100
54	B6	GOVERNOR GAGE MANSION	7000 GAGE AV	BELL GARDENS	
26	E3	GAMBLE HOUSE	4 WESTMORELAND PL	PASADENA	818793 3334
25	A4	GENE AUTRY WESTERN MUS	4700 ZOO DR	LOS ANGELES	213667 2000
115	F4	GETTY, J PAUL MUSEUM	17985 W PAC COAST HWY	MALIBU	213459 8402
44	D3	GRAND CENTRAL MARKET	315 S BROADWAY	LOS ANGELES	213624 2378
34	F1	GREEK THEATRE	2700 N VERMONT AV	LOS ANGELES	213660 8400
33	C4	GREYSTONE MANSION	501 N DOHENY RD	BEVERLY HILLS	213550 4864
34	E1	GRIFFITH PARK	N END VERMONT AV	LOS ANGELES	213665 5188
91	B3	GRISWOLD OLD SCH HOUSE	555 W FOOTHILL BLVD	CLAREMONT	714626 2411
36	B4	HERITAGE SQUARE	3800 HOMER ST	LOS ANGELES	213222 3150
67	B1	HERMOSA BEACH PIER	PIER AV	HERMOSA BEACH	
34	F3	HOLLYHOCK HOUSE	4800 HOLLYWOOD BLVD	LOS ANGELES	213662 7272
34	B2	HOLLYWOOD BOWL	2301 N HIGHLAND AV	HOLLYWOOD	213876 8742
34	B2	HOLLYWOOD BOWL MUSEUM	2301 N HIGHLAND AV	HOLLYWOOD	213850 2058
34	C3	HOLLYWOOD PALLADIUM	6215 SUNSET BLVD	HOLLYWOOD	213466 4311
57	B2	HOLLYWOOD PARK	1050 PRAIRIE AV	INGLEWOOD	213419 1500
34	C4	HOLLYWOOD RANCH MARKET	1248 VINE ST	LOS ANGELES	213469 1424
34	B3	HOLLYWOOD WAX MUSEUM	6767 HOLLYWOOD BLVD	LOS ANGELES	213462 8860
27	D6	HUNTINGTON LIB&ART GAL	1151 OXFORD RD	SAN MARINO	818405 2100
92	B6	INDUSTRY HILLS REC CTR	TEMPLE AND AZUSA AV	INDUSTRY	
63	D4	JAPANESE CULTURAL INS	16215 S GRAMERCY PL	GARDENA	213324 6611
19	E3	JET PROPULSION LAB	4800 OAK GROVE DR	PASADENA	818354 4321
93	E2	KELLOGG ARABIAN HSE FM	CAL POLY COLLEGE	POMONA	714598 4153
78	F6	KOREAN FRIENDSHIP BELL	930 PASEO DEL MAR	LOS ANGELES	
43	E2	KOREATOWN	WESTERN&OLYMPIC	LOS ANGELES	
42	F1	LA BREA FOSSIL PITS	5801 WILSHIRE BLVD	LOS ANGELES	213936 2230
35	F6	LAWRYS CALIFORNIA CTR	568 SAN FERNANDO RD	LOS ANGELES	213225 2491
44	E3	LITTLE TOKYO	1ST & SAN PEDRO STS	LOS ANGELES	
100	E3	LEONIS ADOBE	23537 CALABASAS RD	CALABASAS	818346 3683
73	D2	LOMITA RAILROAD MUSEUM	250TH & WOODWARD AV	LOMITA	213326 6255
80A	C5	LONDONTOWNE	QUEENS HWY	LONG BEACH	
75	C6	L B CONVENTION CENTER	300 E OCEAN BLVD	LONG BEACH	213436 3636
75	E6	L B MUSEUM OF ART	2300 E OCEAN BLVD	LONG BEACH	213439 2119
44	D3	L A CHILDREN'S MUSEUM	310 N MAIN ST	LOS ANGELES	213687 8800
52	A1	LOS ANGELES COLISEUM	EXPOSITION PARK	LOS ANGELES	213748 6131
44	B4	L A CONVENTION CENTER	1201 S FIGUEROA	LOS ANGELES	213748 8531
90	D5	L A COUNTY FAIR	WHITE AV	POMONA	714623 3111
44	D2	LOS ANGELES MALL	MAIN ST & TEMPLE ST	LOS ANGELES	
42	F1	L A CO MUSEUM OF ART	5905 WILSHIRE BLVD	LOS ANGELES	213937 2590
79	B3	L A MARITIME MUSEUM	BERTH 84	SAN PEDRO	213548 7618
52	A1	L A SPORTS ARENA	3939 FIGUEROA ST	LOS ANGELES	213748 6131
44	C3	L A WORLD TRADE CENTER	350 S FIGUEROA ST	LOS ANGELES	213489 3330
24	F4	LOS ANGELES ZOO	5333 ZOO DR	GRIFFITH PARK	213666 4090
44	A2	MACARTHUR PARK	WILSHIRE BL & ALVARADO	LOS ANGELES	
123	G7	MAGIC MOUNTAIN	26101 MAGIC MTN PKWY	VALENCIA	805255 4111
75	C6	MAGNOLIA PIER	LONG BEACH BLVD	LONG BEACH	
114	B5	MALIBU PIER	23000 PACIFIC COAST HY	MALIBU	
62	D2	MANHATTAN BCH C CLUB	1330 PARKVIEW AV	MANHATTAN BCH	213546 5656
62	B4	MANHATTAN BEACH PIER	MANHATTAN BEACH BLVD	MANHATTAN BCH	
76	C6	MARINE STADIUM	COLORADO ST	LONG BEACH	
50	B1	MGM STUDIOS	10202 WASHINGTON BLVD	CULVER CITY	
67	C3	MONSTAD PIER	CORAL WY	REDONDO BEACH	
41	F3	MORMON TEMPLE	10777 SANTA MONICA BL	W LOS ANGELES	213474 1549
20A	C1	MT WILSON OBSERVATORY	MT WILSON RD	LA COUNTY	805440 1136
33	C1	MULHOLLAND DR	STA MONICA HILLS	LOS ANGELES	
34	F3	MUNICIPAL ART GALLERY	4804 HOLLYWOOD BLVD	LOS ANGELES	213660 4254
44	E3	MUS OF CONTMPORARY ART	250 S GRAND AV	LOS ANGELES	
52	A1	MUS OF NATURAL HISTORY	EXPOSITION PARK	LOS ANGELES	213744 3411
52	A1	MUS OF SCI & INDUSTRY	EXPOSITION PARK	LOS ANGELES	213744 7400
44	C2	MUSIC CENTER	135 N GRAND AV	LOS ANGELES	213972 7211
24	B3	NBC STUDIO	3000 W ALAMEDA AV	BURBANK	818840 4444
26	F4	NORTON SIMON MUSEUM	411 W COLORADO BLVD	PASADENA	818449 3730
44	E2	OLVERA ST	PLAZA	LOS ANGELES	
44	B5	OLYMPIC AUDITORIUM	1801 S GRAND AV	LOS ANGELES	213749 5171
27	A4	PACIFIC ASIAN MUSEUM	46 N LOS ROBLES AV	PASADENA	818449 2742
42	F1	PAGE MUSEUM	5801 WILSHIRE BLVD	LOS ANGELES	213936 2230
110	D4	PARADISE COVE PIER	28128 PACIFIC COAST HY	MALIBU	
34	D5	PARAMOUNT STUDIOS	5451 MARATHON ST	LOS ANGELES	213468 5000
27	A4	PASADENA CENTER	300 E GREEN ST	PASADENA	818577 4343
34	E1	PLANETARIUM	GRIFFITH PARK	LOS ANGELES	213664 1191
100	E3	PLUMMER HOUSE	23537 CALABASAS RD	CALABASAS PK	818346 3683
77	B3	PNT VCNTE FISHING ACSS	PALOS VERDE DR AT P VE	PLS VRDS PEN	
79	B4	PORTS O'CALL VILLAGE	BERTH 77 L A HARBOR	SAN PEDRO	213831 0287
44	E2	PUEBLO DE LOS ANGELES	PLAZA	LOS ANGELES	
80A	C4	QUEEN MARY	QUEENS HIGHWAY	LONG BEACH	213435 3511
75	C6	QUEENS PARK	SEASIDE WY	LONG BEACH	
89	F4	RAGING WATERS	111 RAGING WATERS DR	SAN DIMAS	714599 1251
70	C3	RO LOS CERRITOS MUSEUM	4600 VIRGINIA RD	LONG BEACH	213424 9423
91	B2	RO STA ANA BOTANC GRDN	1500 N COLLEGE AV	CLAREMONT	714626 3922
67	C3	REDONDO BEACH MUN PIER	HARBOR DR	REDONDO BEACH	
42	E1	RESTAURANT ROW	LA CIENEGA BLVD	BEVERLY HILLS	
26	E2	ROSE BOWL	ARROYO SECO PARK	PASADENA	818577 7208
34	A4	SAMUEL GOLDWYN STUDIOS	1041 N FORMOSA AV	HOLLYWOOD	213650 2500

330 1990 LOS ANGELES COUNTY POINTS OF INTEREST

LOS ANGELES CO.

INDEX

PAGE	GRID	NAME	ADDRESS	CITY	PHONE
44	F1	SAN ANTONIO WINERY	737 LAMAR	LOS ANGELES	213223 1401
8	C1	SAN FERNANDO MISSION	15101 MISSION BLVD	SAN FERNANDO	818361 0186
37	D3	SAN GABRIEL MISSION	MISSION DR	SAN GABRIEL	818282 5191
28	D5	SANTA ANITA PARK	285 W HUNTINGTON DR	ARCADIA	818574 7223
49	A2	SANTA MONICA CIVIC AUD	1855 MAIN	SANTA MONICA	213393 9961
49	A6	SANTA MONICA MUNI PIER	COLORADO AV	SANTA MONICA	
124	C9	SAUGUS SPEEDWAY	22234 SOLEDAD CYN RD	SAUGUS	805259 3886
73	B4	S COAST BOTANIC GARDEN	26300 CRENSHAW BLVD	PAL VER PENIN	213377 0468
36	B3	SOUTHWEST MUSEUM	234 MUSEUM DR	LOS ANGELES	213221 2163
47	D5	SPORTS ARENA	605 FWY & ROSE HILLS	PICO RIVERA	213692 0829
80A	C5	SPRUCE GOOSE, THE	QUEENS HIGHWAY	LONG BEACH	213435 3511
46	E6	TAYLOR RANCH HOUSE	737 N MONTEBELLO BLVD	MONTEBELLO	213722 3410
58	D4	TOWERS OF SIMON RODIA	1765 E 107TH ST	WATTS	
24	E3	TRAVELTOWN MUSEUM	5200 FOREST LAWN DR	GRIFFITH PARK	213662 5874
23	F4	UNIVERSAL STUDIOS	100 UNIVERSITY CITY PZ	UNIVERSL CITY	818508 9600
41	D1	UCLA	405 HILGARD AV	WESTWOOD	213825 4321
41	E1	UCLA BOTANICAL GARDENS	405 HILGARD AV	WESTWOOD	
44	A6	USC	3551 UNIVERSITY AV	LOS ANGELES	213741 2311
49	C5	VENICE PIER	WASHINGTON&PACIFIC AV	LOS ANGELES	
77	E2	WAYFARERS CHAPEL	5755 RO PALOS VRDS DR	RO PALOS VERD	213377 1650
48	E6	WORKMN TMPLE HMSTD MUS	15415 E DON JULIAN RD	INDUSTRY	818968 8492
47	A3	WHITTIER NARROWS REC	1000 N DURFEE AV	S EL MONTE	818444 1872

RAILROADS (SEE TRANSPORTATION)

SHOPPING CENTERS

PAGE	GRID	NAME	ADDRESS	CITY	PHONE
73	C3	AIRPORT PLAZA	PAC CST HWY & CRENSHAW	TORRANCE	
37	C4	ALHAMBRA PLACE	GARFIELD AND MAIN	ALHAMBRA	
82	A4	ALONDRA SQUARE	ALONDRA BL & PIONEER	NORWALK	
159	J6	ANTELOPE VALLEY CENTER	AV K & ANTELOPE VLY FY	LANCASTER	
7	F1	BALBOA MISSION HILLS	SF MISSION BL & BALBOA	GRANADA HILLS	
48	E1	BALDWIN PK TOWNE CTR	MERCED AV & GARVEY AV	BALDWIN PARK	818303 1610
33	D6	BEVERLY CENTER	BEVERLY BL&LA CIENEGA	LOS ANGELES	213854 0070
42	C1	BEVERLY HILLS	WILSHIRE BL & CANON DR	BEVERLY HILLS	
44	C3	BROADWAY PLAZA	7TH ST & FLOWER ST	LOS ANGELES	213624 2891
17	D5	BURBANK CENTER	MAGNOLIA & GLENOAKS	BURBANK	
69	C3	CARSON MALL	20700 S AVALON BLVD	CARSON	213327 4822
42	A2	CENTURY SQUARE	10250 SANTA MONICA BL	LOS ANGELES	213552 8155
51	B1	CRENSHAW SHOPPING CTR	CRENSHAW & STA BARBARA	LOS ANGELES	
68	A4	DEL AMO	21880 HAWTHORNE BLVD	TORRANCE	213370 7548
68	A4	DEL AMO FASION CENTER	3 DEL AMO FASHION SQ	TORRANCE	213542 8525
25	F4	EAGLE ROCK PLAZA	2700 COLORADO BLVD	EAGLE ROCK	213256 2147
88	F6	EASTLAND CENTER	2648 E WORKMAN AV	COVINA	818331 1408
43	A2	EAST MIRACLE MILE	WILSHIRE & CLOVERDALE	LOS ANGELES	
38	F6	EL MONTE CENTER	PECK RD & ALLOWAY ST	EL MONTE	
28	B5	EL RANCHO-SANTA ANITA	HUNTINGTON & SUNSET	ARCADIA	
12	A5	FALLBROOK SQUARE	FALLBROOK AV	CANOGA PARK	818340 5872
50	C4	FOX HILLS MALL	200 FOX HILLS MALL	CULVER CITY	213390 7833
63	A6	GALLERIA AT SOUTH BAY	2031 HAWTHORNE BLVD	REDONDO BEACH	213722 1481
63	F3	GARDENA VLY SHOPPG CTR	NORMANDIE&REDONDO BCH	GARDENA	
25	D4	GLENDALE FASHION CTR	200 N GLENDALE AV	GLENDALE	818245 5403
25	C4	GLENDALE GALLERIA	135 GLENDALE GALLERIA	GLENDALE	818246 2401
25	C4	GLENDALE GALLERIA II	CENTRAL AV & HAWTHORNE	GLENDALE	
7	D2	GRANADA HILLS	CHATSWORTH & ZELZAH	LOS ANGELES	
28	B3	HASTINGS RANCH	3743 E FOOTHILL BLVD	PASADENA	818477 9055
57	A6	HAWTHORNE PLAZA	12124 HAWTHORNE BLVD	HAWTHORNE	213675 4427
34	C3	HOLLYWOOD & VINE	HOLLYWOOD BL & VINE ST	HOLLYWOOD	
34	E3	HOLLYWOOD & WESTERN	WESTERN & HOLLYWOOD BL	LOS ANGELES	
95	B2	INDIAN HILL VILLAGE	1531 INDIAN HILL VLG	POMONA	714629 2539
71	B2	LAKEWOOD CENTER MALL	LAKEWOOD & DEL AMO	LAKEWOOD	213633 0437
71	A2	LAKEWOOD SQUARE	LAKEWD BL & DEL AMO BL	LAKEWOOD	
159	J6	LANCASTER	LIGHTWOOD AV & K AV	LANCASTER	
159	G8	LANCASTER PLAZA	AVENUE L & 30TH ST W	LANCASTER	
16	C5	LAUREL PLAZA	6100 LAUREL CYN BLVD	N HOLLYWOOD	818769 3200
75	C5	LONG BEACH PLAZA	LONG BEACH BL & 6TH ST	LONG BEACH	
76	C2	LOS ALTOS SHOPPING CTR	2100 BELLFLOWER BLVD	LONG BEACH	
71	F1	LOS CERRITOS CENTER	239 LOS CERRITOS CENTR	CERRITOS	213860 0341
62	C2	MANHATTAN VILLAGE	3300 N SEPULVEDA BL	MANHATTAN BCH	213546 5555
76	D6	MARINA PACIFICA MALL	6300 E PAC COAST HWY	LONG BEACH	213598 9625
43	F2	MID-WILSHIRE	WILSHIRE BL & VIRGIL	LOS ANGELES	
46	F5	MONTEBELLO CENTER	MONTEBELLO BLVD	MONTEBELLO	
70	C2	NORTH LONG BEACH	LONG BEACH BL & 53RD	LONG BEACH	
7	A5	NORTHRIDGE FASHION CTR	9301 TAMPA AV	NORTHRIDGE	818885 9700
82	A2	NORWALK SQUARE	ROSECRANS & PIONEER BL	NORWALK	
68	A2	OLD TOWNE MALL	19800 HAWTHORNE BLVD	TORRANCE	213542 1506
52	F4	PACIFIC CENTER	SLAUSON & PACIFIC BLVD	HUNTINGTON PK	
61	B6	PADDISON SQUARE	IMPERIAL & NORWALK	NORWALK	
15	D1	PANORAMA CITY	ROSCOE & VAN NUYS	PANORAMA CITY	818892 2102
27	A4	PASADENA	COLORADO & LOS ROBLES	PASADENA	
72	E5	PENINSULA CENTER	HAWTHORNE & INDIAN PK	ROL HILLS EST	
94	C5	PHILLIPS RANCH CENTER	VILLAGE LOOP RD	POMONA	
54	F2	PICO RIVERA PLAZA	WHITTIER & PARAMOUNT	PICO RIVERA	
98	B3	PUENTE HILLS MALL	449 PUENTE HILLS MALL	INDUSTRY	818965 5875
38	B6	ROSEMEAD SQUARE	ROSEMEAD-SN BERNDO FWY	ROSEMEAD	
28	C5	SANTA ANITA FASHION PK	400 S BALDWIN AV	ARCADIA	818445 3116
61	D3	SANTA FE SPRINGS MALL	13350 E TELEGRAPH RD	SANTA FE SPGS	
49	A1	SANTA MONICA PLACE	COLORADO AV & 2ND ST	SANTA MONICA	
34	D4	SANTA MONICA-WESTERN	SANTA MONICA & WESTERN	LOS ANGELES	
44	C3	SEVENTH MARKET PL	725 S FIGUEROA	LOS ANGELES	213955 7150
22	E3	SHERMAN OAKS FASHN SQ	RIVERSIDE & WOODMAN	SHERMAN OAKS	818783 0550
22	C3	SHERMAN OAKS GALLERIA	VENTURA BL & SEPULVEDA	SHERMAN OAKS	818783 3550
75	C6	SHORELINE VILLAGE	419 SHORELINE VLG DR	LONG BEACH	213435 5911
60	C4	STONEWOOD	9066 E STONEWOOD ST	DOWNEY	213861 9233
72	E5	THE COURTYARD	550 DEEP VALLEY	ROL HILLS EST	213541 0688
76	E4	THE MARKET PLACE	911 STUDEBAKER RD	LONG BEACH	213493 1475
27	A4	THE PLAZA PASADENA	COLORADO BL&LOS ROBLES	PASADENA	
12	C5	THE PROMENADE	TOPANGA CYN & VICTORY	WOODLAND HILS	818884 7090
78	E1	THE TERRACES AT S BAY	WESTERN AV&CADDINGTON	RO PALOS VERD	
12	C5	TOPANGA PLAZA	6600 TOPANGA CYN BLVD	CANOGA PARK	818883 9670
63	E3	TOZAI PLAZA	15504 S WESTERN AV	GARDENA	213538 9063
16	C5	VALLEY PLAZA	VICTORY & LAUREL CYN	N HOLLYWOOD	
42	D4	WARD PLAZA	LA CIENEGA BLVD	W LOS ANGELES	
28	C5	WEST ARCADIA CENTER	BALDWIN & GOLDEN WEST	ARCADIA	
56	C2	WESTCHESTER CENTER	SEPULVEDA & LA TIJERA	WESTCHESTER	
92	B1	WEST COVINA FASHION PZ	1200 W COVINA PKWY	WEST COVINA	818960 1881
42	F1	WEST MIRACLE MILE	WILSHIRE BL & FAIRFAX	LOS ANGELES	
41	F4	WESTSIDE PAVILION	OVERLAND AV & AYRES AV	W LOS ANGELES	
41	E2	WESTWOOD VILLAGE	WESTWOOD & GAYLEY	WESTWOOD	
61	E1	WHITTIER QUAD	8434 B QUADWAY	WHITTIER	213693 4113
84	C3	WHITTWOOD MALL	15601 E WHITTWOOD LN	WHITTIER	213947 2871
66	E4	WOOLCO CENTER	ALONDRA & STUDEBAKER	CERRITOS	

THEATERS

PAGE	GRID	NAME	ADDRESS	CITY	PHONE
42	A2	ABC ENTERTAINMENT CTR	2040 AV OF THE STARS	LOS ANGELES	213557 7777
44	D2	AHMANSON THEATER	135 N GRAND AV	LOS ANGELES	213972 7211
26	F4	AMBASSADOR AUDITORIUM	ST JOHN AV	PASADENA	818304 6161
34	C3	AQUARIUS THEATER	6230 SUNSET BLVD	HOLLYWOOD	213460 6700
44	C2	BAKER MARIONETTE THTR	1345 W 1ST ST	LOS ANGELES	213250 9995
42	C1	BEVERLY THEATRE	9404 WILSHIRE BLVD	BEVERLY HILLS	213274 5865
34	B3	CHINESE THEATER	6925 HOLLYWOOD BLVD	HOLLYWOOD	213464 8111
34	D3	CINERAMA DOME	6360 SUNSET BLVD	HOLLYWOOD	213466 3401
44	D2	DOROTHY CHANDLER PAV	135 N GRAND AV	LOS ANGELES	213972 7211
34	B3	EGYPTIAN THEATER	6712 HOLLYWOOD BLVD	HOLLYWOOD	213467 6167
34	C1	JOHN ANSON FORD THEATR	2580 CAHUENGA BLVD	LOS ANGELES	213972 7211
34	F1	GREEK THEATER	2700 N VERMONT	LOS ANGELES	213660 8400
34	B2	HOLLYWOOD BOWL	2301 N HIGHLAND	HOLLYWOOD	213856 5400
34	E3	HOLLYWOOD PACIFIC	6433 HOLLYWOOD BLVD	HOLLYWOOD	213464 4111
34	C3	HUNTINGTON HARTFORD	1615 N VINE ST	HOLLYWOOD	213462 6666
43	F3	INNER CITY CULTURAL	1308 S NEW HAMPSHIRE	LOS ANGELES	213387 1161
34	C3	IVAR THEATER	1605 IVAR AV	HOLLYWOOD	213464 7121
42	C1	LA STAGE CO WEST	205 N CANON DR	BEVERLY HILLS	213859 2646
44	D3	LA THEATER CENTER	51 S SPRING	LOS ANGELES	
44	D2	MARK TAPER FORUM	135 N GRAND AV	LOS ANGELES	213972 7211
44	D2	MUSIC CENTER	135 N GRAND AV	LOS ANGELES	213972 7211
34	C3	PANTAGES	6233 HOLLYWOOD BLVD	HOLLYWOOD	213462 3104
34	B3	PARAMOUNT THEATER	6838 HOLLYWOOD BLVD	LOS ANGELES	213463 3263
27	A4	PASADENA CIVIC AUD	300 E GREEN ST	PASADENA	818449 7360
28	A3	PASADENA HASTINGS	355 N ROSEMEAD BLVD	PASADENA	818351 8888
41	F4	PICWOOD THEATRE	10872 W PICO	W LOS ANGELES	213272 8239
41	D3	ROYAL THEATER	11523 SANTA MONICA AV	W LOS ANGELES	213477 5581
37	E3	SN GBRL V CIV LT OPERA	320 W MISSION DR	SAN GABRIEL	818308 2865
49	A2	SANTA MONICA CIVIC AUD	1855 MAIN ST	SANTA MONICA	213393 9961
44	A6	SHRINE AUDITORIUM	649 W JEFFERSON BLVD	LOS ANGELES	213749 5123
42	A2	SHUBERT THEATER	2020 AV OF THE STARS	CENTURY CITY	213553 9000
75	C6	TERRACE THEATER	300 E OCEAN BLVD	LONG BEACH	213436 3660
23	F4	UNIVERSAL AMPHITHEATER	100 UNIVERSAL CITY PZ	UNIVERSAL CTY	818980 9421
43	C2	WILSHIRE EBELL	4401 W 8TH ST	LOS ANGELES	213939 1128
42	E1	WILSHIRE THEATER	8440 WILSHIRE BLVD	BEVERLY HILLS	213852 1900

TRANSPORTATION

PAGE	GRID	NAME	ADDRESS	CITY	PHONE
25	C6	AMTRAK GLENDALE	W CERRITOS & RAILROAD	GLENDALE	818246 4455
27	A4	AMTRAK PASADENA	222 S RAYMOND AV	PASADENA	818796 0211
90	E4	AMTRAK POMONA	2701 N GAREY AV	POMONA	714593 1311
44	E2	AMTRAK UNION STATION	800 N ALAMEDA ST	LOS ANGELES	213624 0171
90	B4	BRACKETT FIELD	1615 MCKINLEY AV	LA VERNE	714331 4003
17	A4	BURBK-GLNDLE-PAS AIRPT	2627 N HOLLYWOOD WY	BURBANK	818840 8847
64	D3	COMPTON AIRPORT	901 W ALONDRA BLVD	COMPTON	213603 7090
38	E5	EL MONTE AIRPORT	4233 SANTA ANITA AV	EL MONTE	818448 6129
44	D4	GREYHOUND BUS STATION	600 S MAIN ST	LOS ANGELES	213623 6177
57	B6	HAWTHORNE MUN AIRPORT	12101 CRENSHAW BLVD	HAWTHORNE	213970 7215
71	A5	LONG BEACH MUN AIRPORT	4100 DONALD DOUGLAS DR	LONG BEACH	213421 8293
56	C3	L A INTERNATL AIRPORT	WORLD WAY	LOS ANGELES	213646 5252
172	D3	PALMDALE AIR TERMINAL	STATE HWY 14	PALMDALE	805947 3181
49	D1	STA MONICA MUN AIRPORT	3200 AIRPORT DR	SANTA MONICA	
73	B2	TORRANCE MUN AIRPORT	3115 AIRPORT DR	TORRANCE	213325 0191
44	E2	UNION STATION	800 N ALAMEDA ST	LOS ANGELES	213624 0171
15	A2	VAN NUYS AIRPORT	6950 HAYVENHURST ST	VAN NUYS	818785 8838
9	B2	WHITEMAN AIRPARK	12653 OSBORN PL	PACOIMA	818896 5271

Thomas Bros. Maps ®

THE BUSINESS TOOLS OF CONFIDENCE

For over seventy years, businesses and travellers have relied on Thomas Bros. Maps to supply them with the tools to get to their destinations with confidence. Our popular Thomas Guides, Wall Maps and California Road Atlas have become the standard for accurate, reliable, up-to-date street map information. This level of excellence has been extended into a broad line of specialized map products to further service the needs of businesses and professionals for geographic information.

ZIP GUIDES

The Thomas Guide® overprinted with the U.S. Postal Service zip code boundaries and numbers. These Zip Guides are the perfect tools for direct mail marketing, general mailing, sales management and delivery services.

CENSUS TRACT GUIDES

These Thomas Guides are overprinted with the U.S. Census Bureau census tract boundary lines and numbers. The Census Tract Guides are extremely useful to those involved in real estate, market research, political canvassing and financial analysis.

COMMERCIAL GUIDE EDITIONS

These larger printed page formats of The Thomas Guide® are heavy duty bound and are available for selected counties.* They are made for those who are involved in daily real estate and property activity. Special editions contain overlays of county assessor boundaries or aerial photos matching each map page.

CUSTOM MAP PRODUCTS

The map publishing and technical capabilities of Thomas Bros. Maps are available for the design, production, and printing of custom products, such as folded pocket maps, sheet maps, map enlargements and promotional inserts from available map data.

PC SOFTWARE PRODUCTS

PC STREET INDEX™ AND PC GEOFINDER™ are new software products for selected counties* that display the features of The Thomas Guide® and the Page/Grid System™ on the IBM/PC.

THOMAS BROS. MAPS—Committed to getting you there with confidence in CALIFORNIA, WASHINGTON, OREGON AND ARIZONA. For your nearest authorized dealer, call:

(800) 432-8430
in California

(714) 863-1984
Outside California

* For Los Angeles/Orange Counties.

ORANGE COUNTY
1990 *Thomas Guide* ®

TABLE OF CONTENTS

ORANGE-LOS ANGELES COMBINATION **$22.95**
TBM 4055
SAN DIEGO-ORANGE COMBINATION **$21.95**
TBM 4057
ORANGE **$13.95**
TBM 3055

HOW TO USE THE THOMAS GUIDE PAGE AND GRID SYSTEM

Finding Your Destination

- Use the Street Index to find the page number and grid location of a street name.

- Use the Cities and Communities or Points of Interest Index to find the page number and grid of a specific destination.

Planning Your Route

- Use the Key Maps or the Foldout Map to go from city to city, or to find what page your destination is on.

- Follow a street page to page by using the "See Map" page number in the border of each page.

COMO USAR EL SISTEMA DE PAGINA Y CUADRADO DEL THOMAS GUIDE

Encontrando Su Destinación

- Se puede usar el Indice de Calle para encontrar el número de página y locación del cuadrado del nombre de la calle.

- Se puede usar los Indices de las Ciudades y las Comunidades, o de Puntos de Interés para encontrar el número de página y el cuadrado de la destinación específica.

Planeando Su Ruta

- Se puede usar el Mapa Clave o el Mapa Doblado para viajar de ciudad a ciudad, o para encontrar la página de su destinación.

- Se puede usar el número de página con las palabras "See Map" se encuentran al borde de cada página para seguir una calle de página a página.

LIST OF ABBREVIATIONS

AL.....................ALLEY	CR.....................CRESCENT	KPN.....KEY PENINSULA NORTH	RDG.....................RIDGE
AR.....................ARROYO	CRES.....................CRESCENT	KPS.....KEY PENINSULA SOUTH	RES.....................RESERVOIR
ARR.....................ARROYO	CSWY.....................CAUSEWAY	L.....................LA	RIV.....................RIVER
AV.....................AVENUE	CT.....................COURT	LN.....................LANE	RV.....................RIVER
AVD.....................AVENIDA	CTE.....................CORTE	LP.....................LOOP	RO.....................RANCHO
AVD D LS.....AVENIDA DE LOS	CTO.....................CUT OFF	LS.....................LAS, LOS	S.....................SOUTH
BCH.....................BEACH	CTR.....................CENTER	MDW.....................MEADOW	SN.....................SAN
BL.....................BOULEVARD	CV.....................COVE	MHP.....MOBILE HOME PARK	SPG.....................SPRING
BLVD.....................BOULEVARD	CY.....................CANYON	MNR.....................MANOR	SPGS.....................SPRINGS
CEM.....................CEMETERY	CYN.....................CANYON	MT.....................MOUNT	SQ.....................SQUARE
CIR.....................CIRCLE	D.....................DE	MTN.....................MOUNTAIN	SRA.....................SIERRA
CK.....................CREEK	DL.....................DEL	MTWY.....................MOTORWAY	ST.....................SAINT
CL.....................CALLE	DR.....................DRIVE	MTY.....................MOTORWAY	ST.....................STREET
CL DL.....................CALLE DEL	DS.....................DOS	N.....................NORTH	STA.....................SANTA
CL D LS.............CALLE DE LAS	E.....................EAST	PAS.....................PASEO	STA.....................STATION
CALLE DE LOS	EST.....................ESTATE	PAS DE.....................PASEO DE	TER.....................TERRACE
CL EL.....................CALLE EL	EXPWY.....EXPRESSWAY	PAS DL.....................PASEO DEL	THTR.....................THEATER
CLJ.....................CALLEJON	EXT.....................EXTENSION	PAS D LS.........PASEO DE LAS	TK TR.....................TRUCK TRAIL
CL LA.....................CALLE LA	FRWY.....................FREEWAY	PASEO DE LOS	TR.....................TRAIL
CL LS.....................CALLE LAS	FRW.....................FREEWAY	PGD.....................PLAYGROUND	VIA D.....................VIA DE
CALLE LOS	FY.....................FREEWAY	PK.....................PARK	VIA D LS.....VIA DE LAS
CM.....................CAMINO	GN.....................GLEN	PK.....................PEAK	VIA DE LOS
CM D.....................CAMINO DE	GRDS.....................GROUNDS	PKWY.....................PARKWAY	VIA DL.....................VIA DEL
CM D LA.........CAMINO DE LA	GRN.....................GREEN	PL.....................PLACE	VIS.....................VISTA
CM D LS.......CAMINO DE LAS	GRV.....................GROVE	PT.....................POINT	VLG.....................VILLAGE
CAMINO DE LOS	HTS.....................HEIGHTS	PY.....................PARKWAY	VLY.....................VALLEY
CMTO.....................CAMINITO	HWY.....................HIGHWAY	PZ.....................PLAZA	VW.....................VIEW
CN.....................CANAL	HY.....................HIGHWAY	RCH.....................RANCH	W.....................WEST
COM.....................COMMON	JCT.....................JUNCTION	RCHO.....................RANCHO	WK.....................WALK

LEGEND

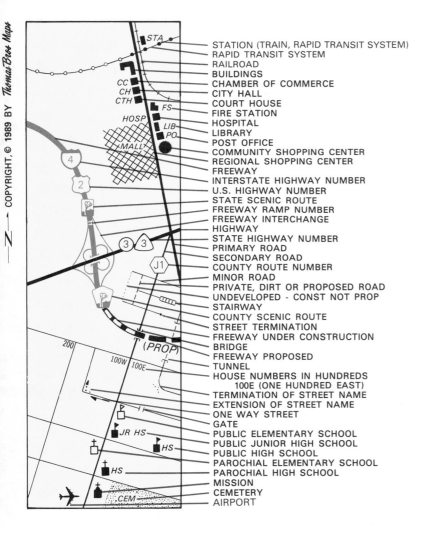

STATION (TRAIN, RAPID TRANSIT SYSTEM)
RAPID TRANSIT SYSTEM
RAILROAD
BUILDINGS
CHAMBER OF COMMERCE
CITY HALL
COURT HOUSE
FIRE STATION
HOSPITAL
LIBRARY
POST OFFICE
COMMUNITY SHOPPING CENTER
REGIONAL SHOPPING CENTER
FREEWAY
INTERSTATE HIGHWAY NUMBER
U.S. HIGHWAY NUMBER
STATE SCENIC ROUTE
FREEWAY RAMP NUMBER
FREEWAY INTERCHANGE
HIGHWAY
STATE HIGHWAY NUMBER
PRIMARY ROAD
SECONDARY ROAD
COUNTY ROUTE NUMBER
MINOR ROAD
PRIVATE, DIRT OR PROPOSED ROAD
UNDEVELOPED - CONST NOT PROP
STAIRWAY
COUNTY SCENIC ROUTE
STREET TERMINATION
FREEWAY UNDER CONSTRUCTION
BRIDGE
FREEWAY PROPOSED
TUNNEL
HOUSE NUMBERS IN HUNDREDS
    100E (ONE HUNDRED EAST)
TERMINATION OF STREET NAME
EXTENSION OF STREET NAME
ONE WAY STREET
GATE
PUBLIC ELEMENTARY SCHOOL
PUBLIC JUNIOR HIGH SCHOOL
PUBLIC HIGH SCHOOL
PAROCHIAL ELEMENTARY SCHOOL
PAROCHIAL HIGH SCHOOL
MISSION
CEMETERY
AIRPORT

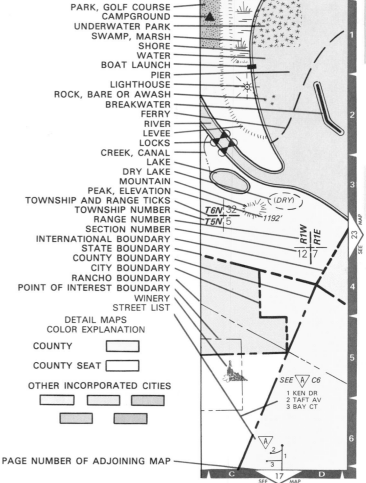

PARK, GOLF COURSE
CAMPGROUND
UNDERWATER PARK
SWAMP, MARSH
SHORE
WATER
BOAT LAUNCH
PIER
LIGHTHOUSE
ROCK, BARE OR AWASH
BREAKWATER
FERRY
RIVER
LEVEE
LOCKS
CREEK, CANAL
LAKE
DRY LAKE
MOUNTAIN
PEAK, ELEVATION
TOWNSHIP AND RANGE TICKS
TOWNSHIP NUMBER
RANGE NUMBER
SECTION NUMBER
INTERNATIONAL BOUNDARY
STATE BOUNDARY
COUNTY BOUNDARY
CITY BOUNDARY
RANCHO BOUNDARY
POINT OF INTEREST BOUNDARY
WINERY
STREET LIST

DETAIL MAPS
COLOR EXPLANATION

COUNTY

COUNTY SEAT

OTHER INCORPORATED CITIES

PAGE NUMBER OF ADJOINING MAP

1 KEN DR
2 TAFT AV
3 BAY CT

SCALE OF MAP PAGES
(UNLESS OTHERWISE SHOWN)

MAJOR DEPARTMENT STORES
B	BROADWAY
BF	BUFFUMS
BK	BULLOCKS
IM	I MAGNIN
M	MAY CO
MW	MONTGOMERY WARD
NM	NEIMAN-MARCUS
N	NORDSTROM
O	OHRBACHS
P	J C PENNEY
R	ROBINSONS
S	SEARS
SF	SAKS FIFTH AV

1990 ORANGE COUNTY
CITIES AND COMMUNITIES INDEX

ESTIMATED POPULATION INCORPORATED CITIES   2,025,909
ESTIMATED POPULATION UNINCORPORATED AREAS   254,491
ESTIMATED TOTAL POPULATION   2,280,400

COMMUNITY NAME	ABBR.	POST OFFICE NAME	P.O. ABBR.	ZIP CODE	MILES TO S.A.	EST. POP.	AREA SQ. MI.	MAP PAGE
ALISO VIEJO		LAGUNA BEACH	LB	92656	27.0			29C
* ANAHEIM	ANA	ANAHEIM	AN	92801	6.2	244,300	43.5	11
ANAHEIM HILLS		ANAHEIM	AN	92807	7.0			13
ATWOOD		ATWOOD	ATW	92601	10.6			7
BALBOA		NEWPORT BEACH	NB	92661	11.5			33
BALBOA ISLAND		NEWPORT BEACH	NB	92662	10.1			31
* BREA	BREA	BREA	BREA	92621	12.1	33,550	10.3	2
* BUENA PARK	BPK	BUENA PARK	BP	90620	11.0	66,200	10.8	5
CAPISTRANO BEACH		SAN CLEMENTE	SCL	92624	25.3			38
CORONA DEL MAR		CORONA DEL MAR	CDLM	92625	10.2			33
* COSTA MESA	CM	COSTA MESA	CM	92626	8.2	92,900	15.8	31
COTO DE CAZA		SN JUAN CAPISTRNO	SJ	92679	39.0			59
COWAN HEIGHTS		SANTA ANA	SA	92705	6.1			18
* CYPRESS	CYP	CYPRESS	CYP	90630	12.3	45,350	6.3	9
* DANA POINT	DPT	DANA POINT	DPT	92629	26.0	29,180	6.2	37
EAST IRVINE		EAST IRVINE	EIRV	92650	6.0			29
EAST LAKE		YORBA LINDA	YL	92686	13.5			8
EAST TUSTIN		TUSTIN	TUS	92680	3.1			24
EL MODENA		ORANGE	OR	92669	6.3			18
EL TORO		EL TORO	ET	92630	16.2			29A
EL TORO USMC AIR STN	ETMC	SANTA ANA	SA	92709	16.0			51
EMERALD BAY	EBAY	LAGUNA BEACH	LB	92651	21.2			34
* FOUNTAIN VALLEY	FTNV	SANTA ANA	SA	92708	8.1	56,100	9.7	26
* FULLERTON	FUL	FULLERTON	FL	92631	9.0	111,700	22.1	6
* GARDEN GROVE	GGR	GARDEN GROVE	GG	92640	5.7	134,800	17.0	16
* HUNTINGTON BEACH	HTB	HUNTINGTON BEACH	HB	92646	12.6	188,700	28.0	26
* IRVINE	IRV	SANTA ANA	SA	92715	8.1	100,500	42.8	29
* LAGUNA BEACH	LAG	LAGUNA BEACH	LB	92651	23.8	24,550	5.6	34
LAGUNA HILLS		LAGUNA BEACH	LB	92653	13.5			29A
LAGUNA NIGUEL		LAGUNA BEACH	LB	92677	26.0			35
* LA HABRA	LAH	LA HABRA	LAH	90631	15.9	49,000	7.05	2
LAKE FOREST		EL TORO	ET	92630	14.5			29A
* LA PALMA	LAP	BUENA PARK	BP	90623	12.7	16,100	1.7	9
LEISURE WORLD		LAGUNA BEACH	LB	92653	13.5			29A
LEISURE WORLD		SEAL BEACH	SB	90740	13.7			14
LEMON HEIGHTS		SANTA ANA	SA	92705	5.8			18
LIDO ISLE		NEWPORT BEACH	NB	92660	10.5			31
* LOS ALAMITOS	LALM	LOS ALAMITOS	LALM	90720	14.1	12,150	2.25	14
MIDWAY CITY		MIDWAY CITY	MDWY	92655	7.8			21
* MISSION VIEJO	MVJO	SN JUAN CAPISTRNO	SJ	92690	19.1	71,329	16.0	29D
MODJESKA		ORANGE	OR	92669	31.1			49
* NEWPORT BEACH	NB	NEWPORT BEACH	NB	92660	10.2	69,900	15.7	31
NEWPORT CENTER		NEWPORT BEACH	NB	92660	9.3			32
NORTHWOOD		SANTA ANA	SA	92714	4.0			24
OLINDA		BREA	BREA	92621	13.8			3
OLIVE		ORANGE	OR	92665	6.4			12
* ORANGE	OR	ORANGE	OR	92666	3.4	106,400	22.6	17
- -ORANGE COUNTY	CO					2,280,400	798.5	
ORANGE PARK ACRES		ORANGE	OR	92669	7.6			13
* PLACENTIA	PLA	PLACENTIA	PLA	92670	8.7	41,650	6.7	7
RANCHO SANTA MARGARITA		SN JUAN CAPISTRNO	SJ	92688	38.5			56
RED HILL		SANTA ANA	SA	92705	5.2			24
ROSSMOOR		LOS ALAMITOS	LALM	90720	13.7			14
* SAN CLEMENTE	SCL	SAN CLEMENTE	SC	92672	29.0	39,100	19.5	39
* SAN JUAN CAPISTRANO	SJC	SN JUAN CAPISTRNO	SJ	92675	23.0	24,500	13.49	38
SAN JUAN HOT SPRINGS		SN JUAN CAPISTRNO	SJ	92675	36.0			62
* SANTA ANA	SA	SANTA ANA	SA	92701		237,300	27.3	23
SANTA ANA GARDENS		SANTA ANA	SA	92704	3.5			22
* SEAL BEACH	SB	SEAL BEACH	SB	90740	14.2	27,350	10.7	19
SILVERADO CANYON		SILVERADO	SIL	92676	29.4			53
SOUTH LAGUNA		LAGUNA	LB	92677	27.7			35
* STANTON	STN	STANTON	STN	90680	9.2	28,350	3.1	15
SUNSET BEACH		SUNSET BEACH	SUNB	90742	13.4			20
SURFSIDE		SURFSIDE	SURF	90743	13.4			20
THREE ARCH BAY		LAGUNA BEACH	LB	92677	33.1			37
TRABUCO CANYON		SN JUAN CAPISTRNO	SJ	92679	39.0			56
TURTLE ROCK		SANTA ANA	SA	92715	9.1			32A
* TUSTIN	TUS	TUSTIN	TUS	92680	2.8	46,800	10.2	23
* VILLA PARK	VPK	ORANGE	OR	92667	7.9	6,950	2.1	13
* WESTMINSTER	WSTM	WESTMINSTER	WSTM	92683	8.2	73,300	10.9	15
WOODBRIDGE		SANTA ANA	SA	92714	8.5			29
* YORBA LINDA	YL	YORBA LINDA	YL	92686	13.3	47,900	18.0	7

* INDICATES INCORPORATED CITY   MILES ARE ESTIMATED FROM DOWNTOWN SANTA ANA

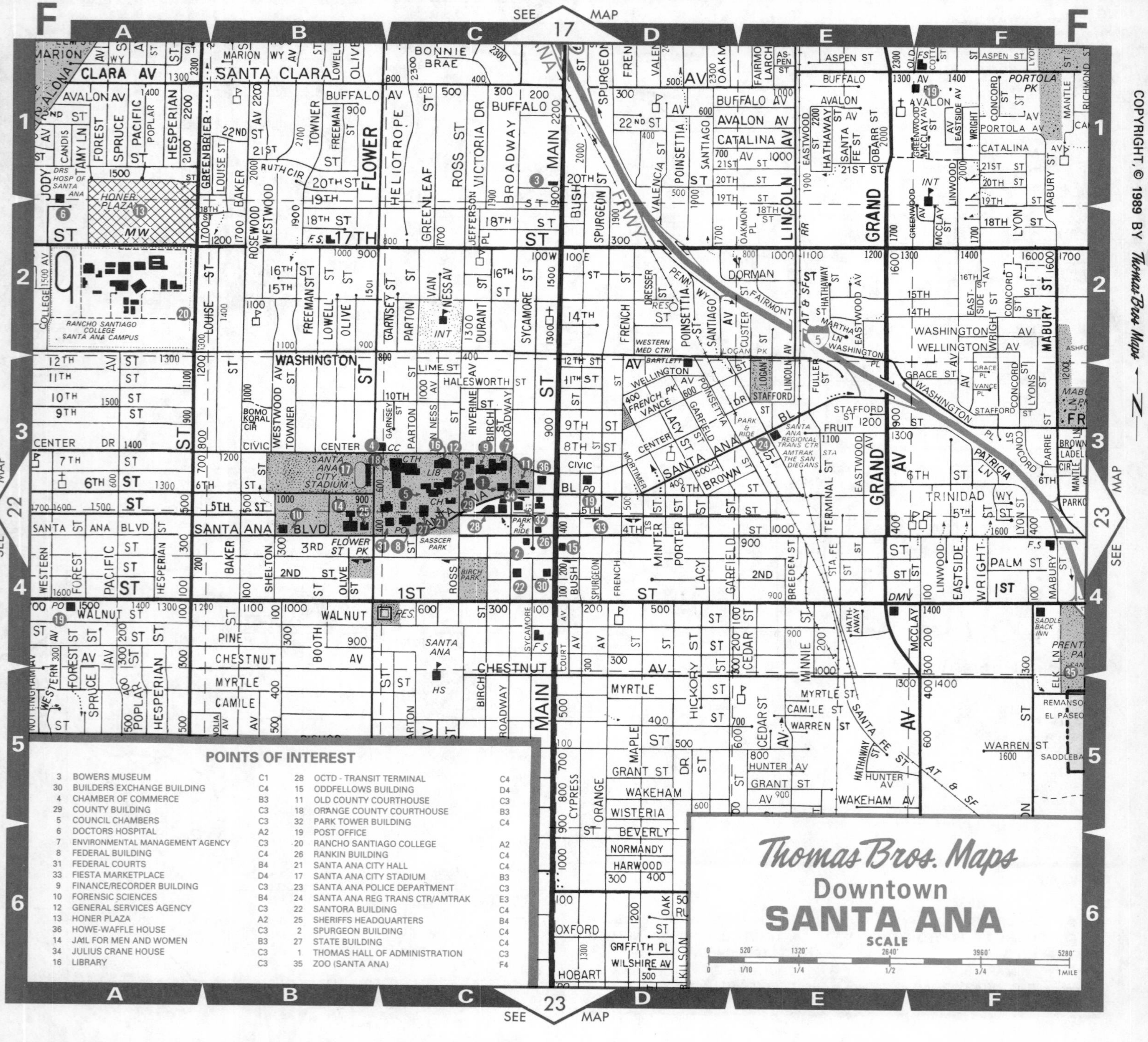

POINTS OF INTEREST

#	Name	Grid	#	Name	Grid
3	BOWERS MUSEUM	C1	28	OCTD - TRANSIT TERMINAL	C4
30	BUILDERS EXCHANGE BUILDING	C4	15	ODDFELLOWS BUILDING	D4
4	CHAMBER OF COMMERCE	B3	11	OLD COUNTY COURTHOUSE	C3
29	COUNTY BUILDING	C3	18	ORANGE COUNTY COURTHOUSE	B3
6	COUNCIL CHAMBERS	C3	32	PARK TOWER BUILDING	C4
6	DOCTORS HOSPITAL	A2	19	POST OFFICE	
8	ENVIRONMENTAL MANAGEMENT AGENCY	C4	20	RANCHO SANTIAGO COLLEGE	A2
8	FEDERAL BUILDING	C3	26	RANKIN BUILDING	C4
33	FEDERAL COURTS	B4	21	SANTA ANA CITY HALL	C4
33	FIESTA MARKETPLACE	D4	17	SANTA ANA CITY STADIUM	B3
10	FINANCE/RECORDER BUILDING	C3	23	SANTA ANA POLICE DEPARTMENT	C3
10	FORENSIC SCIENCES	B4	24	SANTA ANA REG TRANS CTR/AMTRAK	E3
12	GENERAL SERVICES AGENCY	C3	22	SANTORA BUILDING	C4
13	HONER PLAZA	A2	25	SHERIFFS HEADQUARTERS	B4
36	HOWE-WAFFLE HOUSE	C3	2	SPURGEON BUILDING	C4
34	JAIL FOR MEN AND WOMEN	B3	27	STATE BUILDING	C4
34	JULIUS CRANE HOUSE	C3	1	THOMAS HALL OF ADMINISTRATION	C3
16	LIBRARY	C3	35	ZOO (SANTA ANA)	F4

Thomas Bros. Maps

Downtown SANTA ANA

SCALE

ORANGE CO.

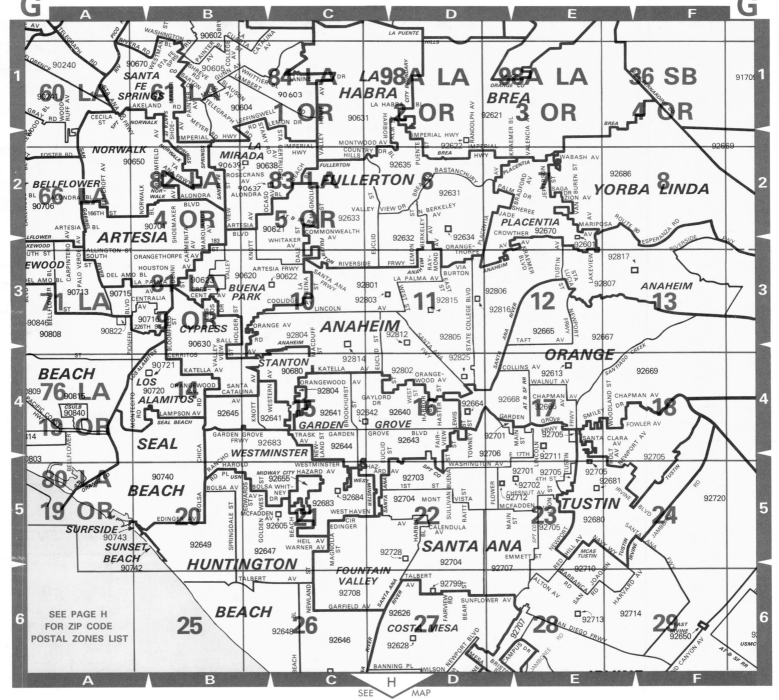

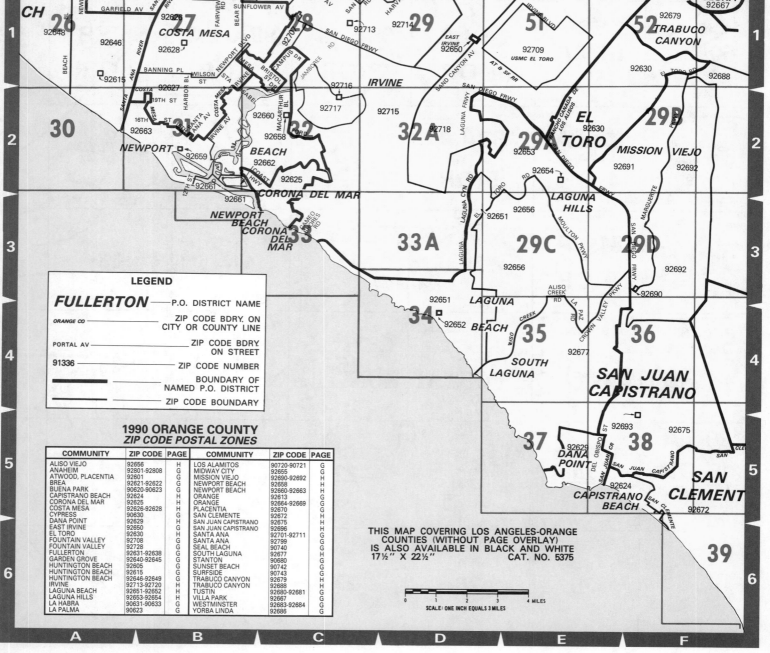

This map covering Los Angeles-Orange Counties (without page overlay) is also available in black and white 17½" x 22½". Cat. No. 5375

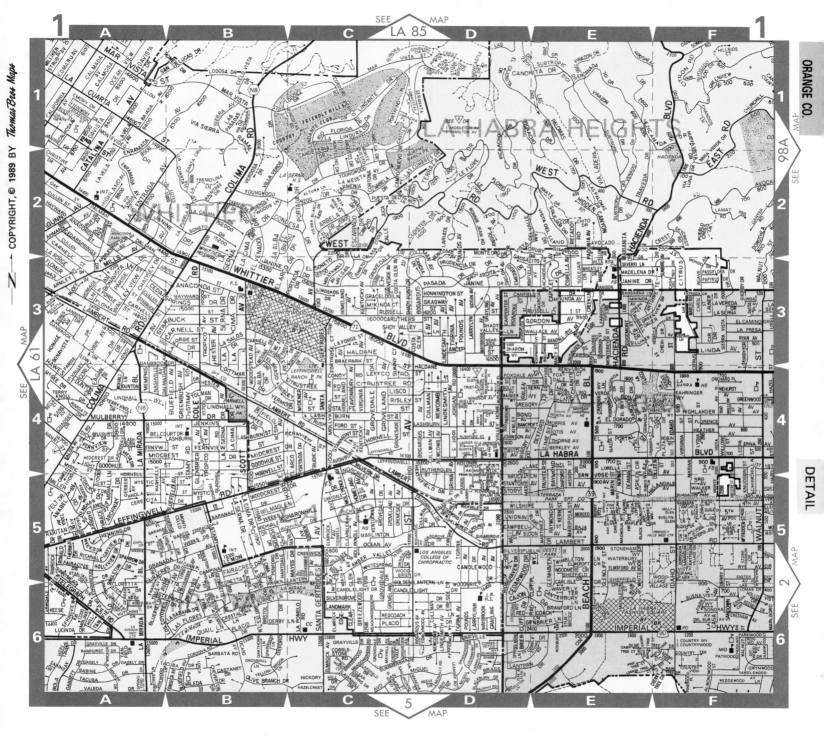

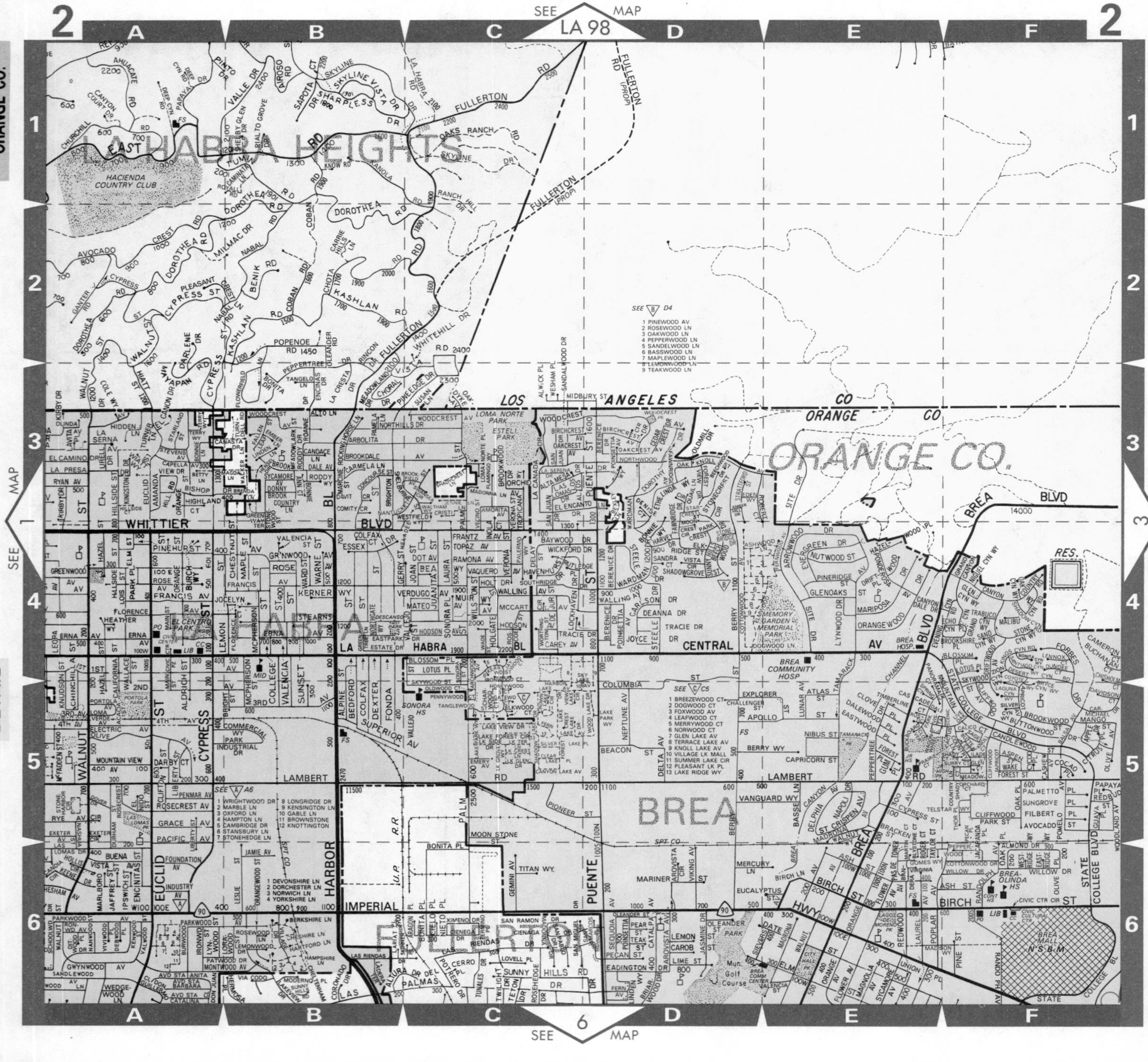

ORANGE CO.

DETAIL

SEE MAP LA 98

COPYRIGHT, © 1989 BY *Thomas Bros Maps*

EAST LA HABRA HEIGHTS

HACIENDA COUNTRY CLUB

LOS ANGELES CO. / ORANGE CO.

ORANGE CO.

WHITTIER BLVD

LA HABRA

BREA

FULLERTON

SEE MAP 6

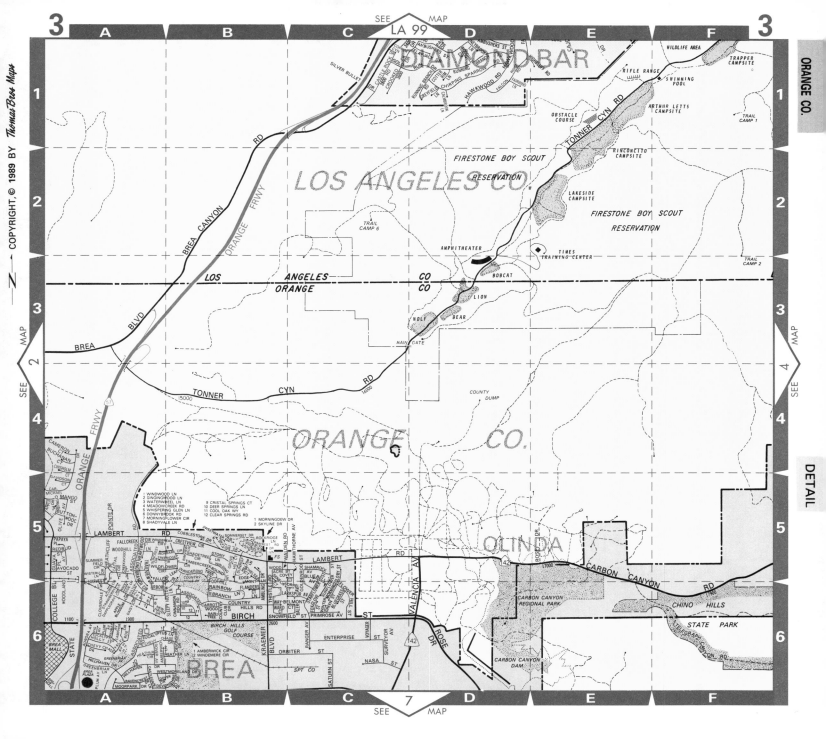

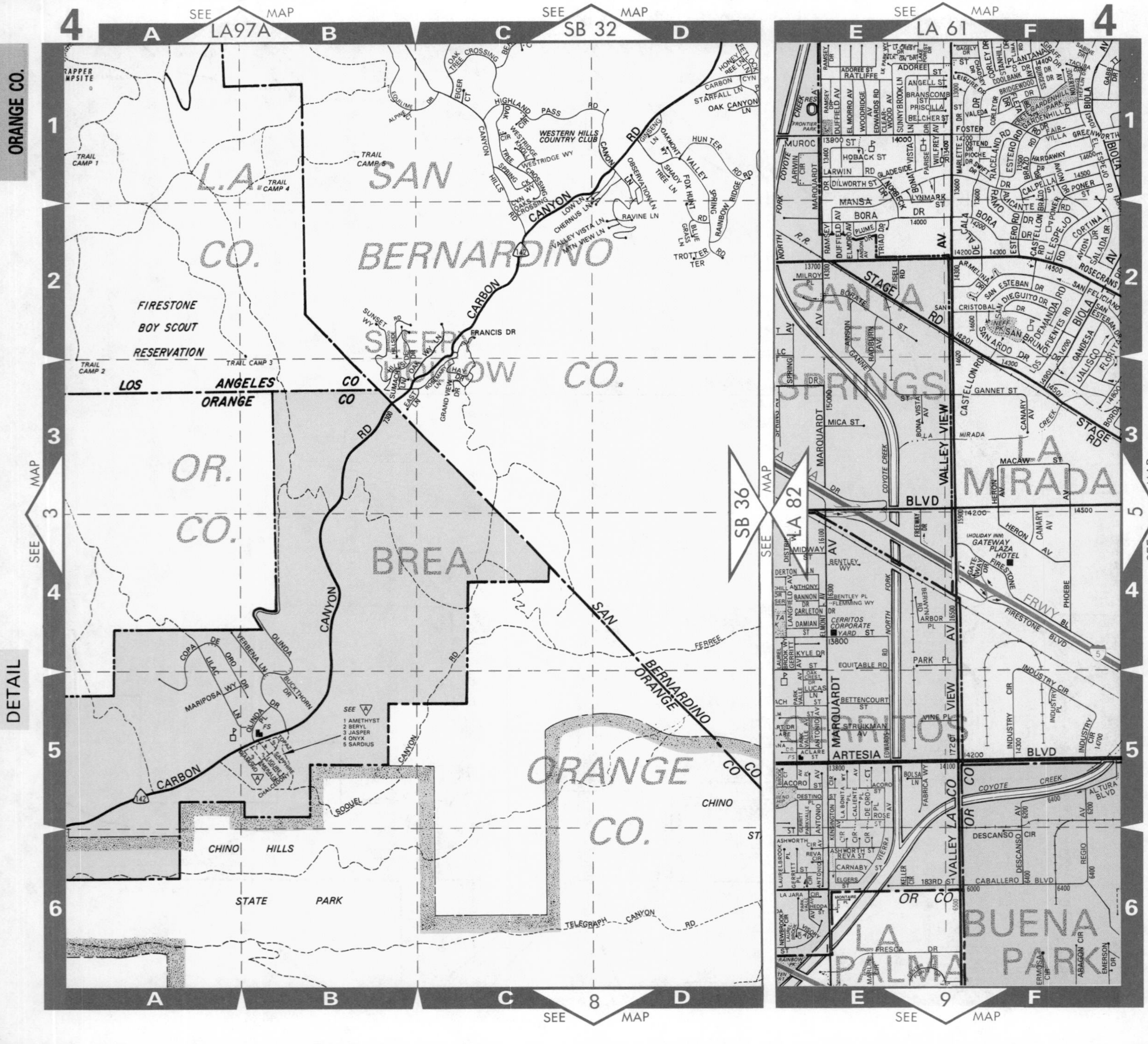

SEE MAP LA97A

SEE MAP SB 32

SEE MAP LA 61

COPYRIGHT, © 1989 BY *Thomas Bros. Maps* —N—

DETAIL

L.A. CO.

SAN BERNARDINO CO.

FIRESTONE BOY SCOUT RESERVATION

TRAIL CAMP 1
TRAIL CAMP 2
TRAIL CAMP 3
TRAIL CAMP 4

WESTERN HILLS COUNTRY CLUB

LOS ANGELES CO.
ORANGE CO.

OR. CO.

BREA

CARBON CANYON RD

CHINO HILLS STATE PARK

ORANGE CO.

CHINO

TELEGRAPH CANYON RD.

SAN BERNARDINO CO.
ORANGE CO.

SANTA FE SPRINGS

LA MIRADA

CERRITOS

LA PALMA

BUENA PARK

FIRESTONE FRWY

SEE MAP SB 36 / LA 82

SEE MAP 8

SEE MAP 9

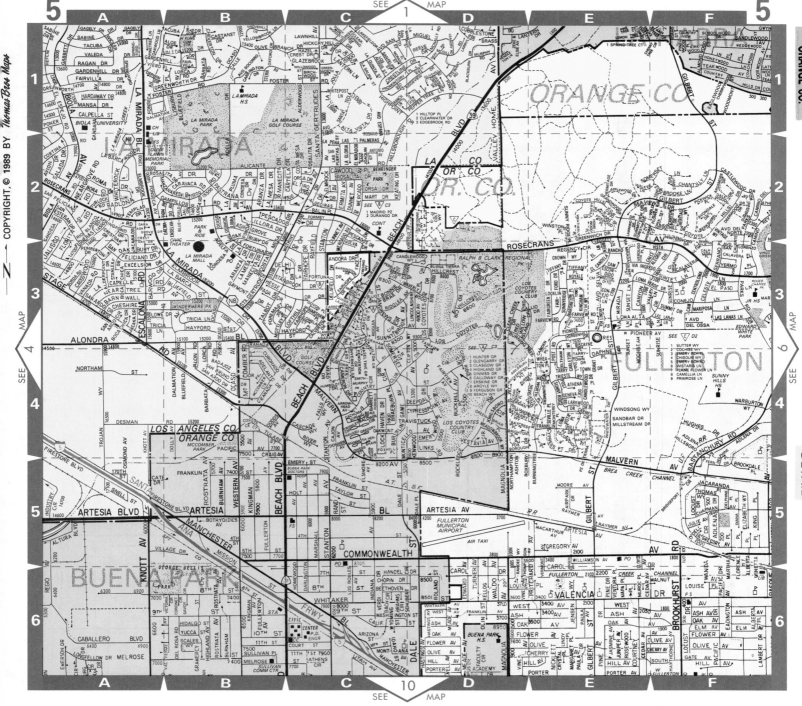

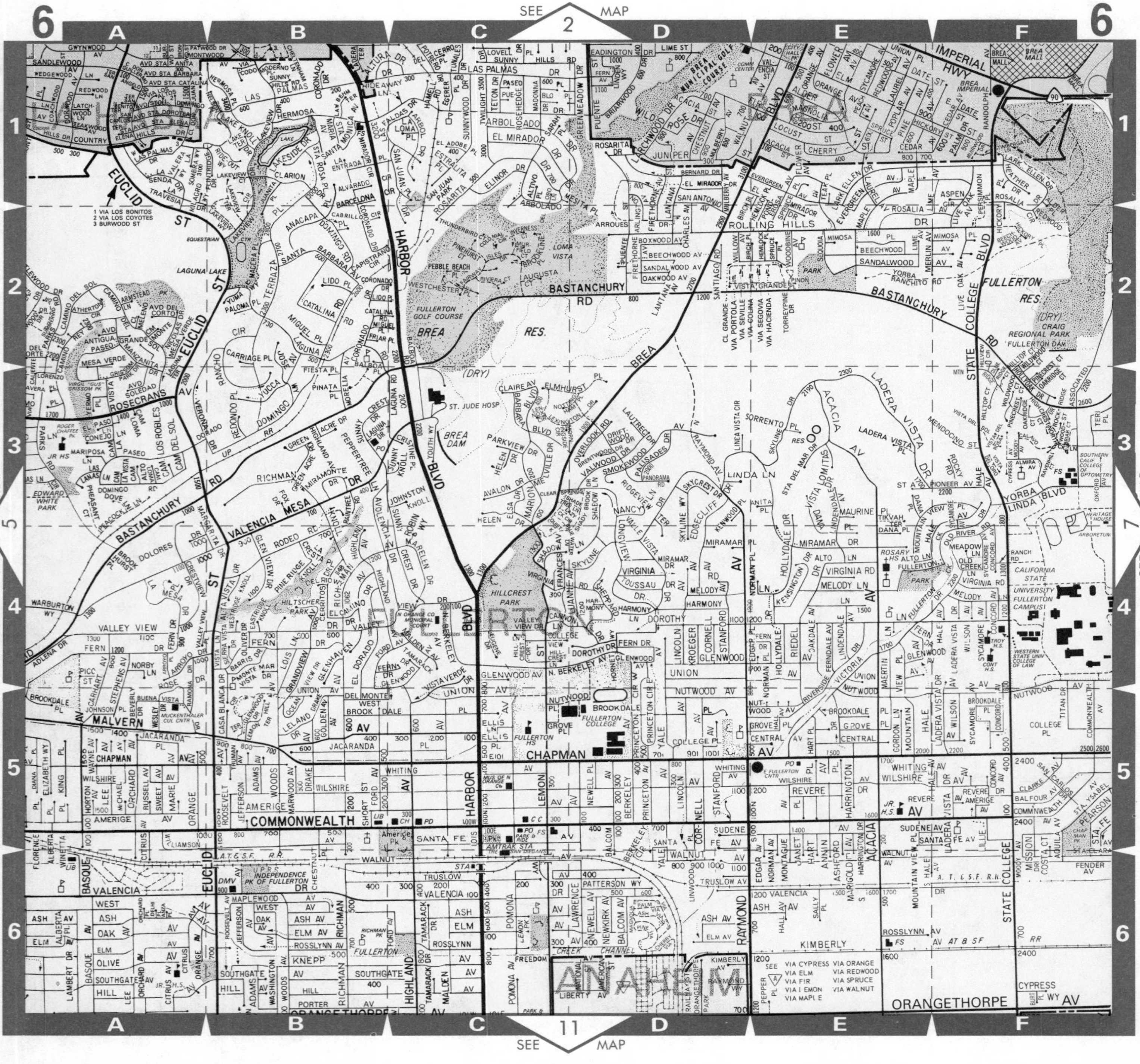
SEE MAP 2
SEE MAP 5
SEE MAP 7
SEE MAP 11
A
B
C
D
E
F
1
2
3
4
5
6
FULLERTON
BREA
ANAHEIM
BREA RES. (DRY)
BREA DAM
FULLERTON GOLF COURSE
BREA MUNICIPAL GOLF COURSE
CRAIG REGIONAL PARK
FULLERTON DAM
FULLERTON RES. (DRY)
HILLCREST PARK
CALIFORNIA STATE UNIVERSITY FULLERTON CAMPUS
FULLERTON COLLEGE
FULLERTON HS
ST. JUDE HOSP
AMTRAK STA
INDEPENDENCE PK OF FULLERTON
WESTERN STATE UNIV COLLEGE OF LAW
SOUTHERN CALIF COLLEGE OF OPTOMETRY
LAGUNA LAKE
EDWARD WHITE PARK
HARBOR BLVD
EUCLID ST
BASTANCHURY RD
STATE COLLEGE BLVD
IMPERIAL HWY
COMMONWEALTH
CHAPMAN AV
ORANGETHORPE AV
VALENCIA MESA DR
ROSECRANS AV
MALVERN AV
YORBA LINDA BLVD
1 VIA LOS BONITOS
2 VIA LOS COYOTES
3 BURWOOD ST
SEE VIA CYPRESS VIA ORANGE
VIA ELM VIA REDWOOD
VIA FIR VIA SPRUCE
VIA LEMON VIA WALNUT
VIA MAPLE

SEE 3 MAP

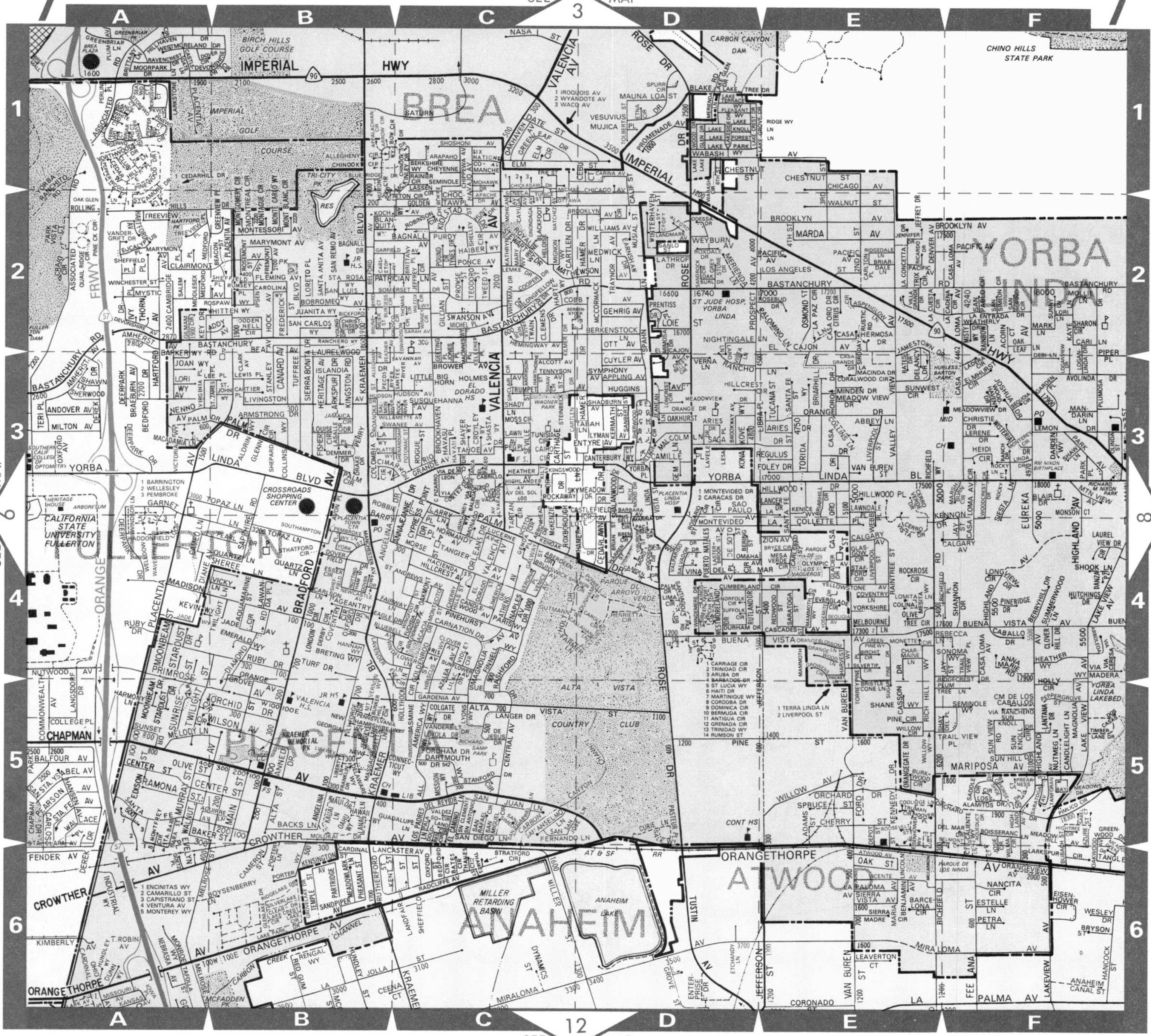

SEE 6 MAP

SEE 8 MAP

SEE 12 MAP

ORANGE CO.

DETAIL

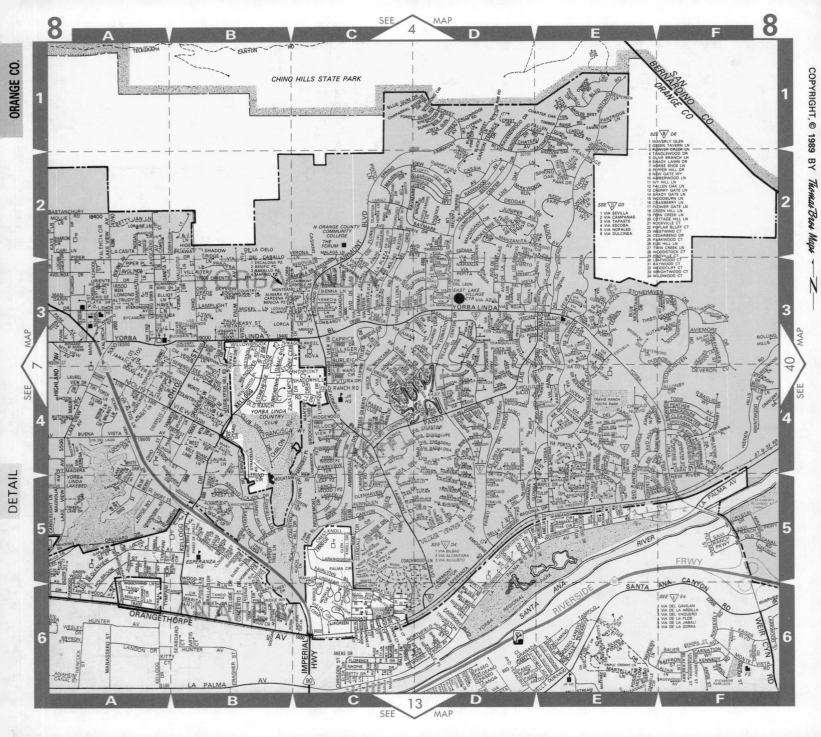

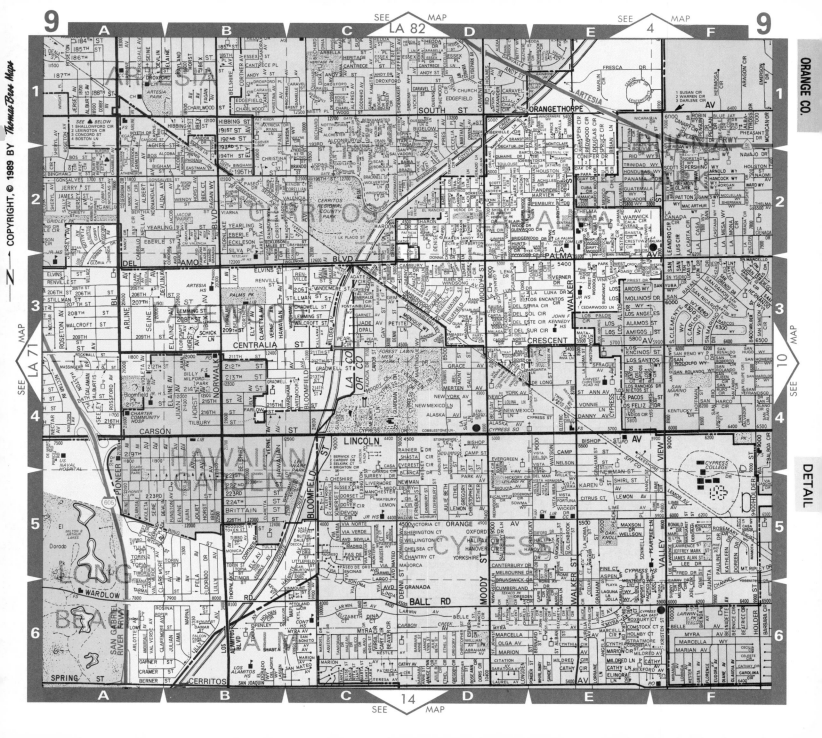

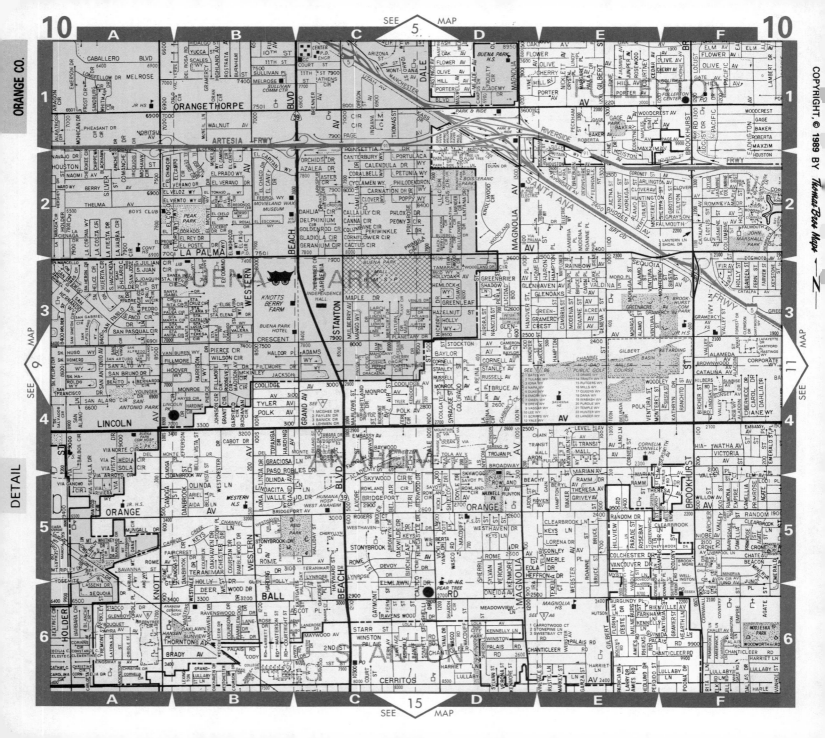

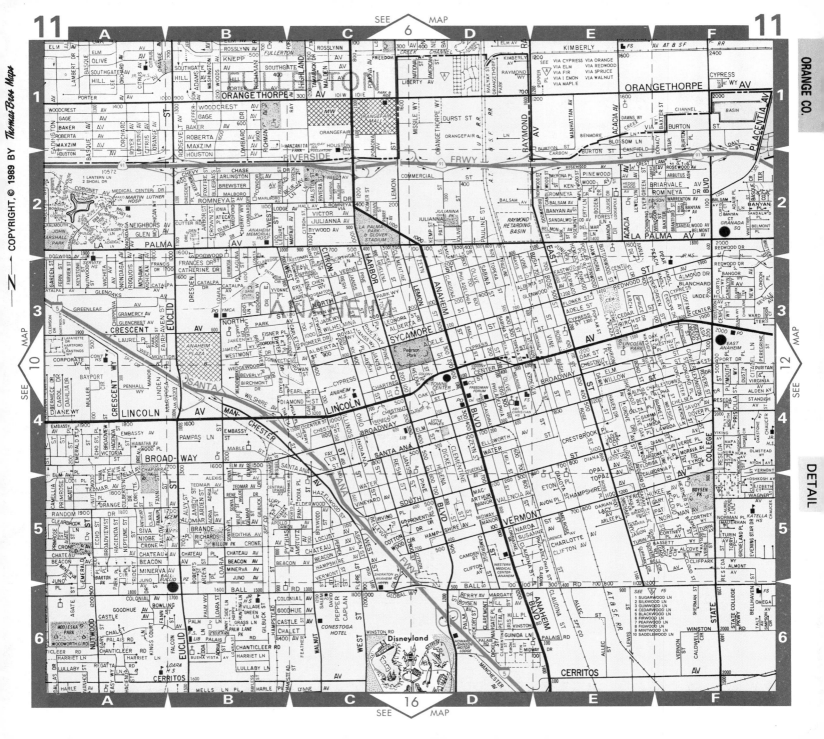

ORANGE CO.

DETAIL

ANAHEIM

SEE MAP 7

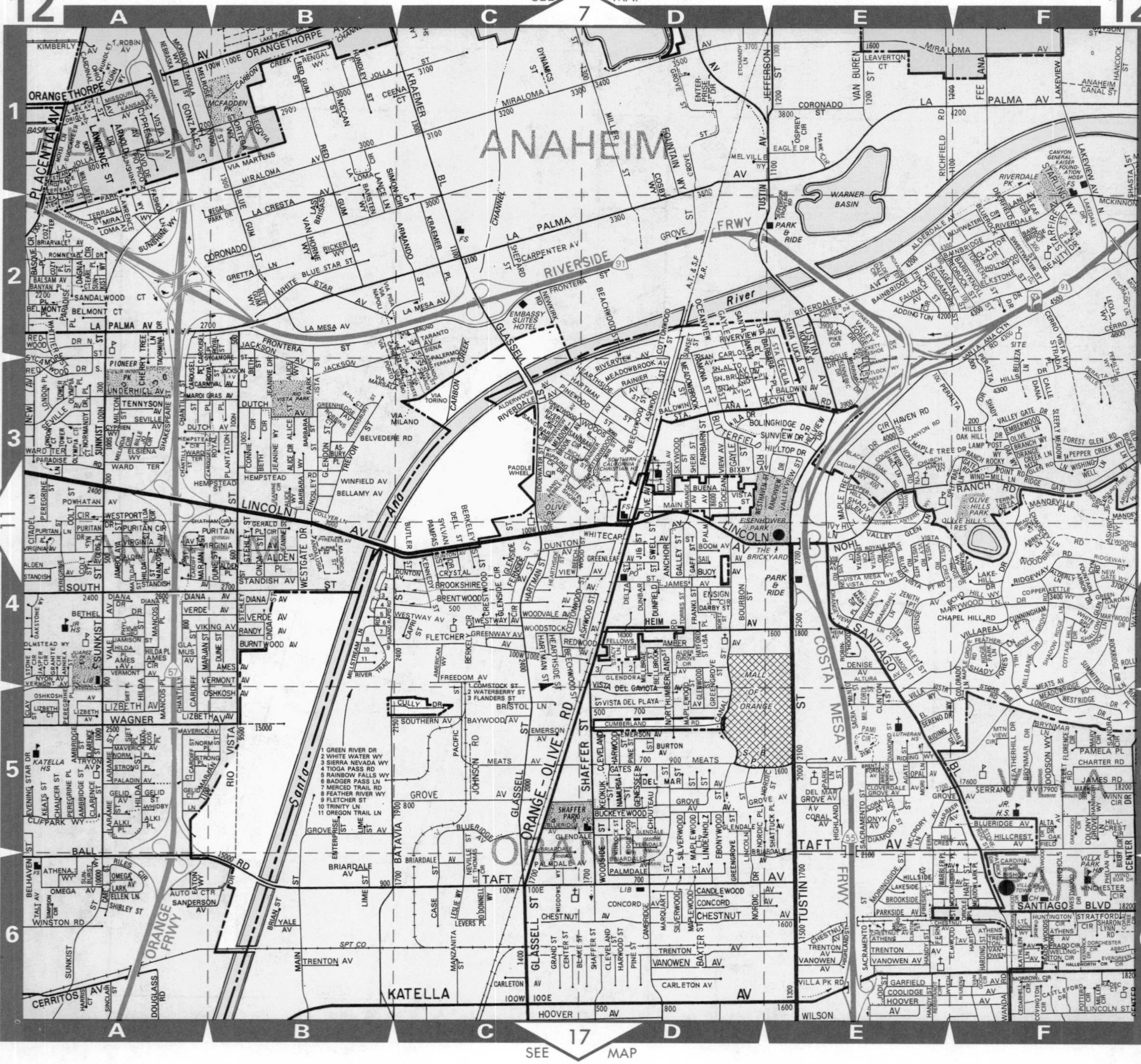

SEE MAP 11

SEE MAP 13

SEE MAP 17

KATELLA

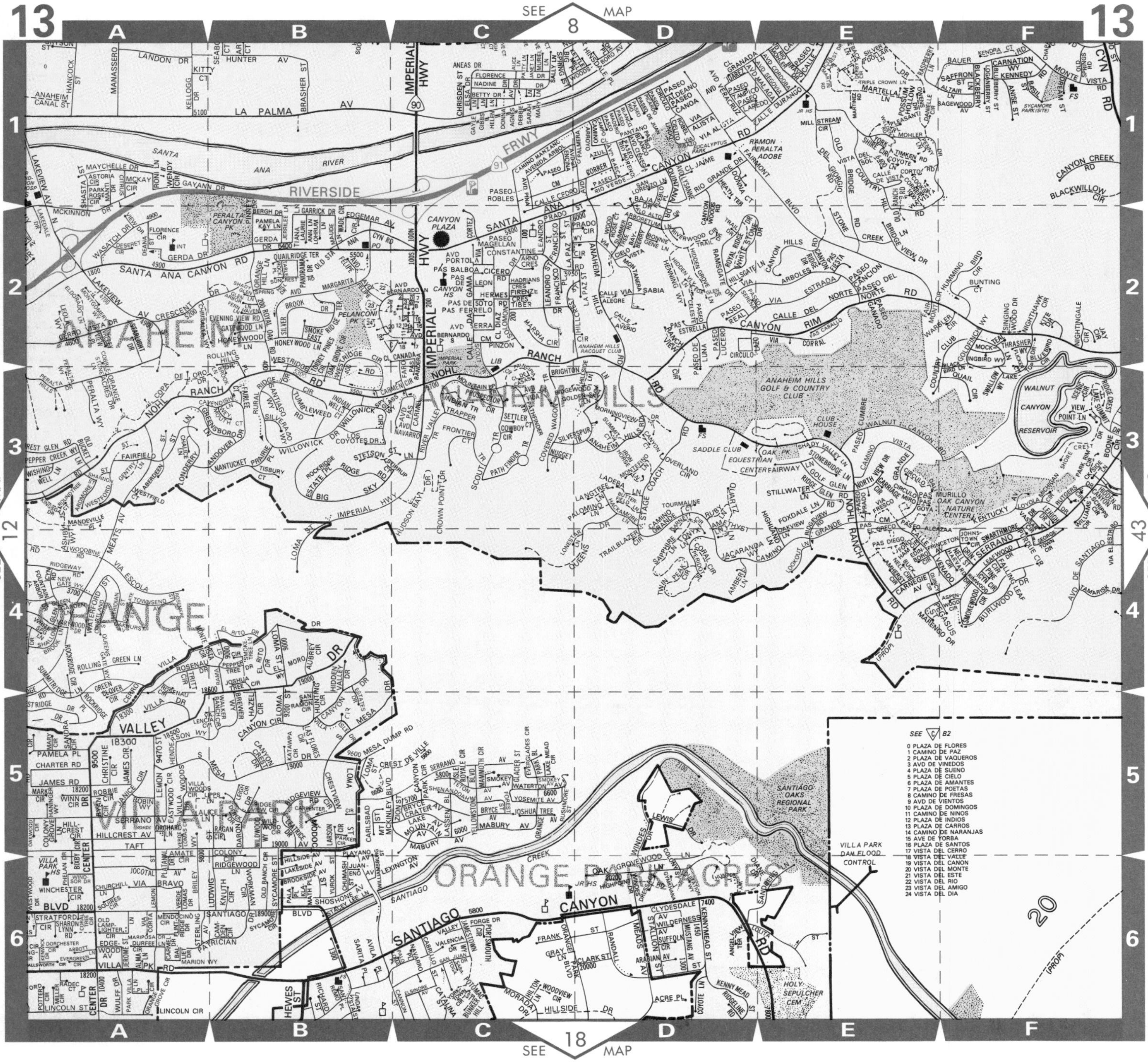
SEE MAP 8
SEE MAP 12
SEE MAP 43
SEE MAP 18
A B C D E F
1 2 3 4 5 6
ANAHEIM
ANAHEIM HILLS
ORANGE
VILLA PARK
ORANGE PARK ACRES
LA PALMA AV
SANTA ANA RIVER
RIVERSIDE FRWY
91
IMPERIAL HWY
90
SANTA ANA CANYON RD
NOHL RANCH RD
CANYON RIM RD
SERRANO AV
SANTIAGO CANYON RD
VILLA PARK RD
CANYON PLAZA
PERALTA CANYON PK
PELANCONI PK
EUCALYPTUS PARK
RAMON PERALTA ADOBE
ANAHEIM HILLS GOLF & COUNTRY CLUB
CLUB HOUSE
SADDLE CLUB
EQUESTRIAN CENTER
OAK CANYON NATURE CENTER
WALNUT CANYON RESERVOIR
ANAHEIM HILLS RACQUET CLUB
SANTIAGO OAKS REGIONAL PARK
VILLA PARK DAM FLOOD CONTROL
HOLY SEPULCHER CEM
CANYON HS
VILLA PARK HS
SYCAMORE PARK(SITE)
20
SEE C B2
0 PLAZA DE FLORES
1 CAMINO DE PAZ
2 PLAZA DE VAQUEROS
3 AVD DE VINEDOS
4 PLAZA DE SUENO
5 PLAZA DE CIELO
6 PLAZA DE AMANTES
7 PLAZA DE POETAS
8 CAMINO DE FRESAS
9 AVD DE VIENTOS
10 PLAZA DE DOMINGOS
11 CAMINO DE NINOS
12 PLAZA DE INDIOS
13 PLAZA DE CARROS
14 CAMINO DE NARANJAS
15 AVE DE YORBA
16 PLAZA DE SANTOS
17 VISTA DEL CERRO
18 VISTA DEL VALLE
19 VISTA DEL CANON
20 VISTA DEL MONTE
21 VISTA DEL ESTE
22 VISTA DEL RIO
23 VISTA DEL AMIGO
24 VISTA DEL DIA

ORANGE CO.

DETAIL

13

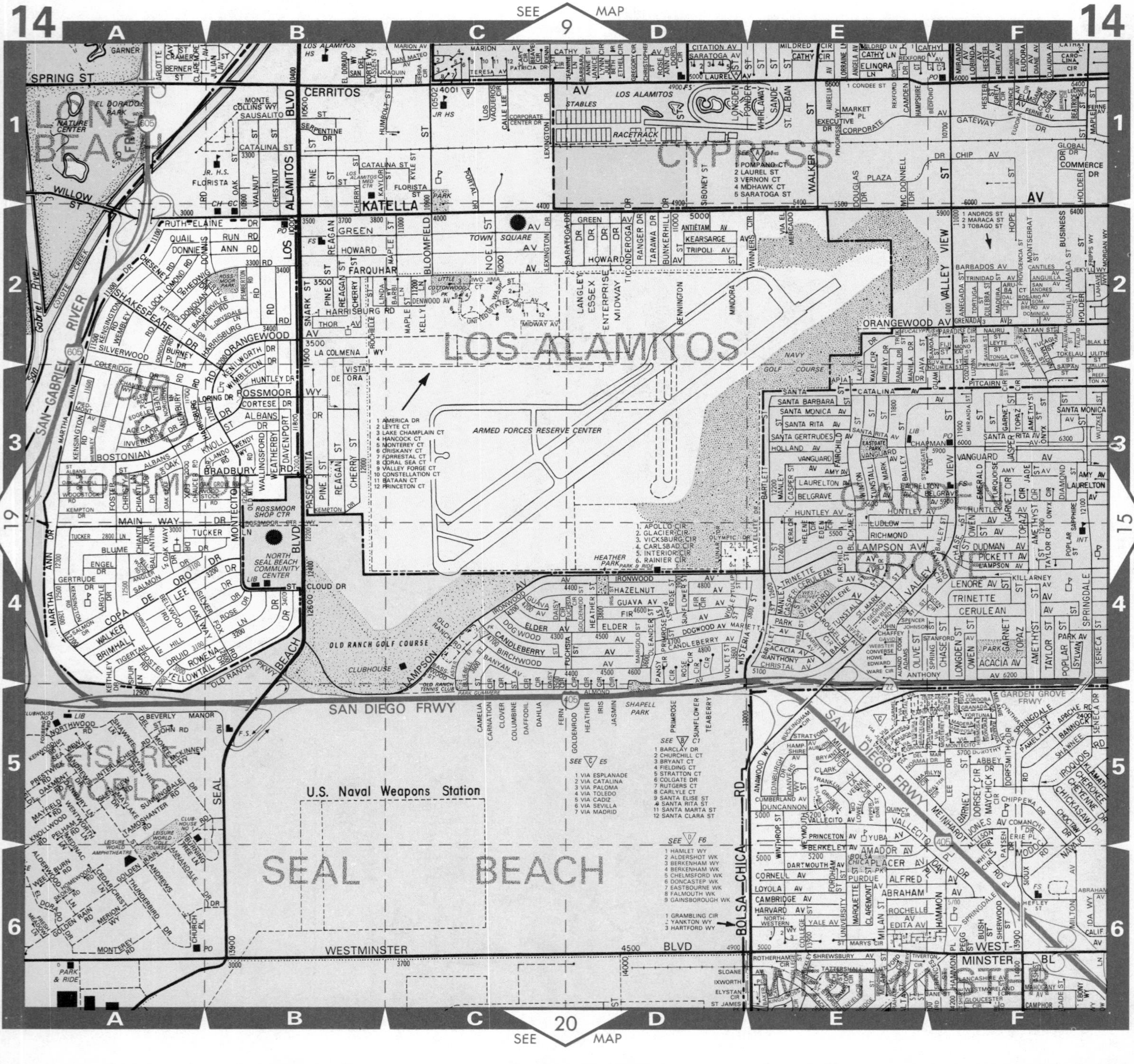

ORANGE CO.

DETAIL

LONG BEACH

CYPRESS

LOS ALAMITOS

Armed Forces Reserve Center

SEAL BEACH

U.S. Naval Weapons Station

WESTMINSTER

GARDEN GROVE

LEISURE WORLD

ROSSMOOR

Old Ranch Golf Course

North Seal Beach Community Center

Racetrack

Los Alamitos

SPRING ST

CERRITOS

KATELLA

WILLOW ST

SAN DIEGO FRWY

WESTMINSTER BLVD

WEST MINSTER BL

MAIN WAY

San Gabriel River

Coyote Creek

1. AMERICA DR
2. LEYTE CT
3. LAKE CHAMPLAIN CT
4. HANCOCK CT
5. MONTEREY CT
6. ORISKANY CT
7. FORRESTAL CT
8. CORAL SEA CT
9. VALLEY FORGE CT
10. CONSTELLATION CT
11. BATAAN CT
12. PRINCETON CT

1. APOLLO CIR
2. GLACIER CIR
3. VICKSBURG CIR
4. CARLSBAD CIR
5. INTERIOR CIR
6. RAINIER CIR

SEE E5
1 VIA ESPLANADE
2 VIA CATALINA
3 VIA PALOMA
4 VIA TOLEDO
5 VIA CADIZ
6 VIA SEVILLA
7 VIA MADRID

SEE F5
1 BARCLAY DR
2 CHURCHILL CT
3 BRYANT CT
4 FIELDING CT
5 STRATTON CT
6 COLGATE DR
7 RUTGERS CT
8 CARLYLE CT
9 SANTA ELISE ST
10 SANTA RITA ST
11 SANTA MARTA ST
12 SANTA CLARA ST

SEE F6
1 HAMLET WY
2 ALDERSHOT WK
3 BERKENHAM WK
4 BERKENHAM WK
5 CHELMSFORD WK
6 DONCASTEP WK
7 EASTBOURNE WK
8 FALMOUTH WK
9 GAINSBOROUGH WK

1 GRAMBLING CIR
2 YANKTON WY
3 HARTFORD WY

SEE MAP 19

SEE MAP 15

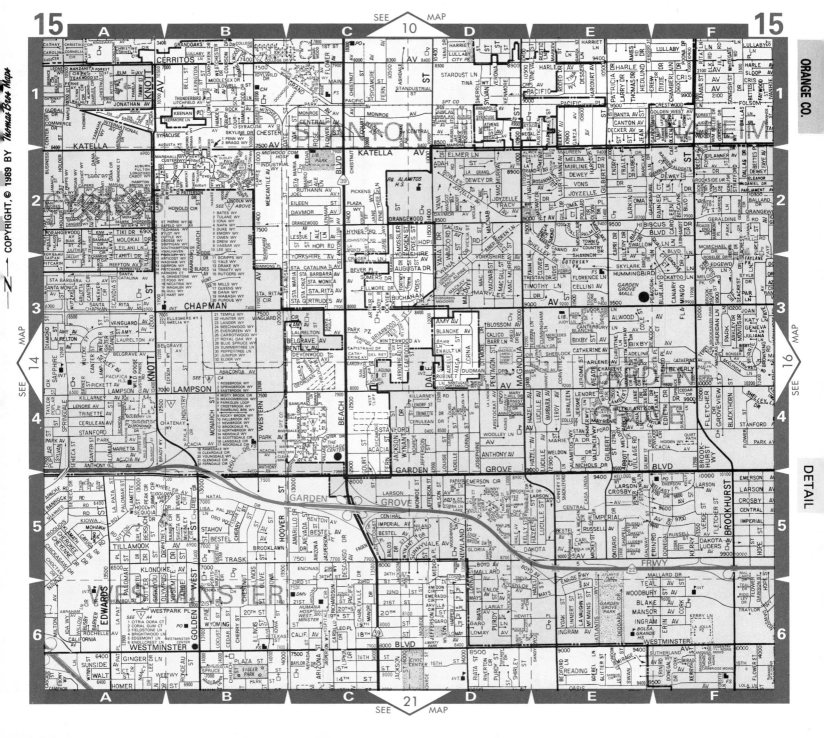

ORANGE CO.

DETAIL

SEE MAP 11

SEE MAP 15

SEE MAP 17

SEE MAP 22

ANAHEIM

Disneyland

ORANGE

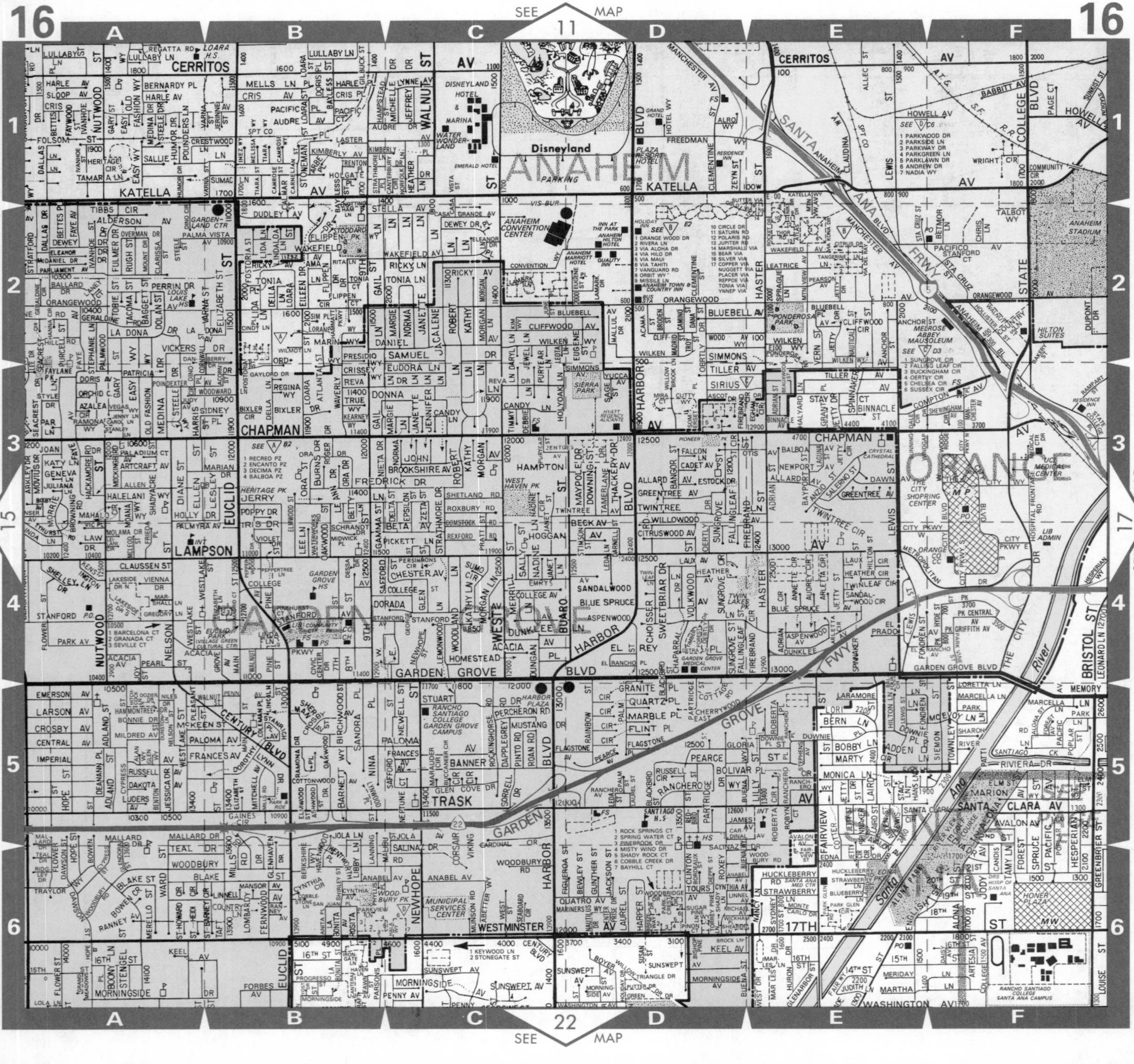

GARDEN GROVE

WESTMINSTER

SANTA ANA

CERRITOS AV

KATELLA AV

CHAPMAN AV

LAMPSON

GARDEN GROVE BLVD

TRASK

17TH ST

WASHINGTON AV

HARBOR BLVD

EUCLID ST

BROOKHURST ST

NUTWOOD

BRISTOL ST

STATE COLLEGE BLVD

Anaheim Stadium

Santa Ana Fwy

The City Shopping Center

UCI Medical Center

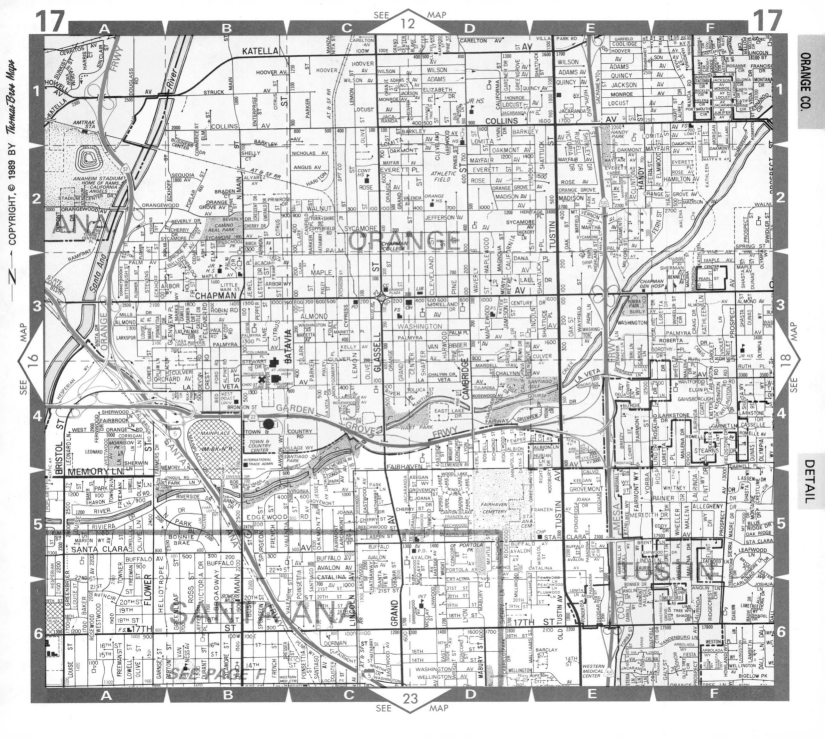

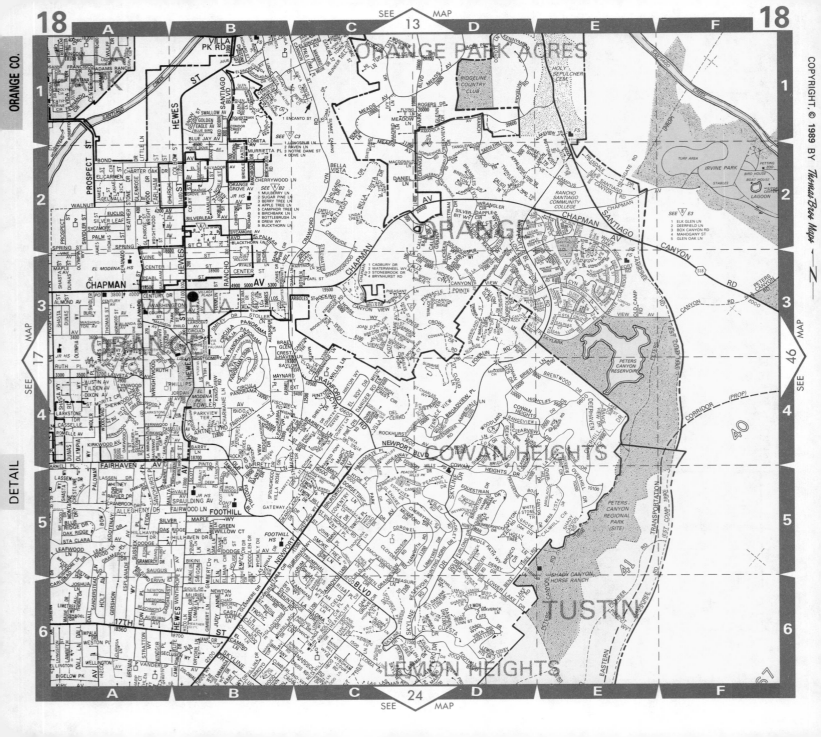

SEE MAP
LA 71

SEE MAP
19 LT

ORANGE CO.

DETAIL

ORANGE CO.

Spring St

El Dorado Park

Golf Course

Nature Center

LONG BEACH

STEARNS ST

California State University Long Beach

Long Beach Veterans Administration Hospital

WALTER B HILL JR HS

Bixby Village Golf Course

Belmont Shores Mobile Estates

Marina Pacifica Mall

WESTMINSTER AV

SEE MAP 19 RT
SEE MAP

SAN GABRIEL RIVER

SEE MAP LA 80

SEE MAP LA 76

Westminster

Hyatt Hotel

The Market Place

Long Beach Marina Seaport Village

Long Beach Yacht Club

Gum Grove Park

SEAL BEACH

BOLSA AV

U.S. Naval Weapons Station

Municipal Pier

Eisenhower Park

ANAHEIM BAY

ROCKWELL INT FACILITY

PARK & RIDE

Regency Dr

1 ISLAND VILLAGE DR
2 SEAWIND DR
3 SPINNAKER WY
4 MARINER WY
5 ANCHOR WY
6 TRIDENT WY
7 COMPASS CT
8 WINDJAMMER CT
9 TOP SIDE CT
10 WHEELHOUSE
11 KEEL CT
12 OUTRIGGER CT
13 SEACREST CT
14 SANDCASTLE CT

SEE MAP 20

PARK & RIDE

1 WORCESTER CT
2 HOLBROOK CT
3 BROCTON CT
4 WARE CT
5 MILTON CT
6 PITTSFIELD CT
7 LEXINGTON CT
8 STONEHAM CT
9 CHELSEA CT
10 CRANSTON CT
11 MARBORA CT
12 PROVIDENCE CT
13 PASEO DORADO

BEACH COMBER AV
CRYSTAL COVE DR
CORAL DR
DOLPHIN DR
DRIFTWOOD DR
EMERALD COVE DR
GOLDEN SANDS DR
JADE COVE DR
MARINA VIEW DR
SAND PIPER DR
SEA BREEZE DR
SILVER SHOALS DR

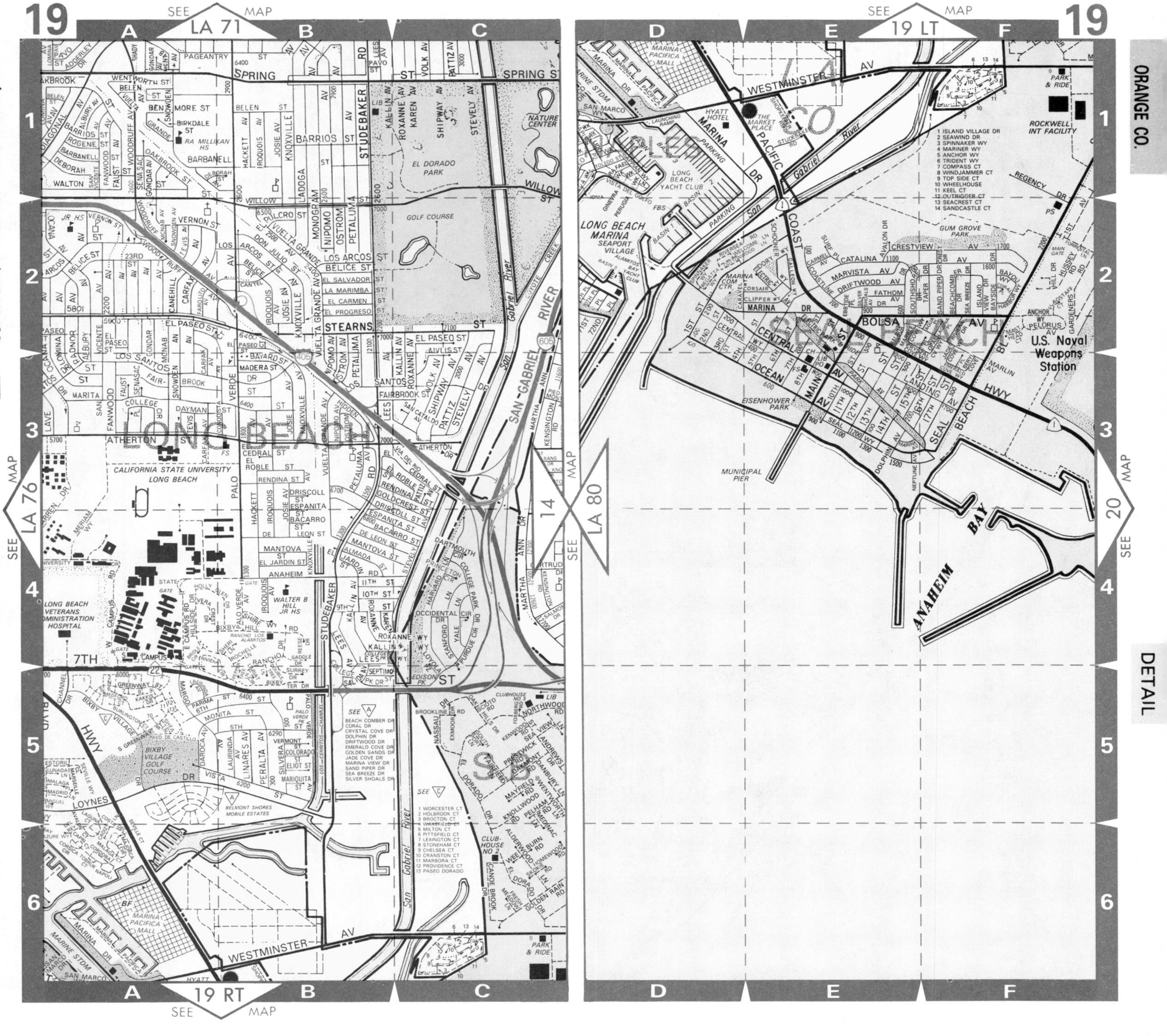

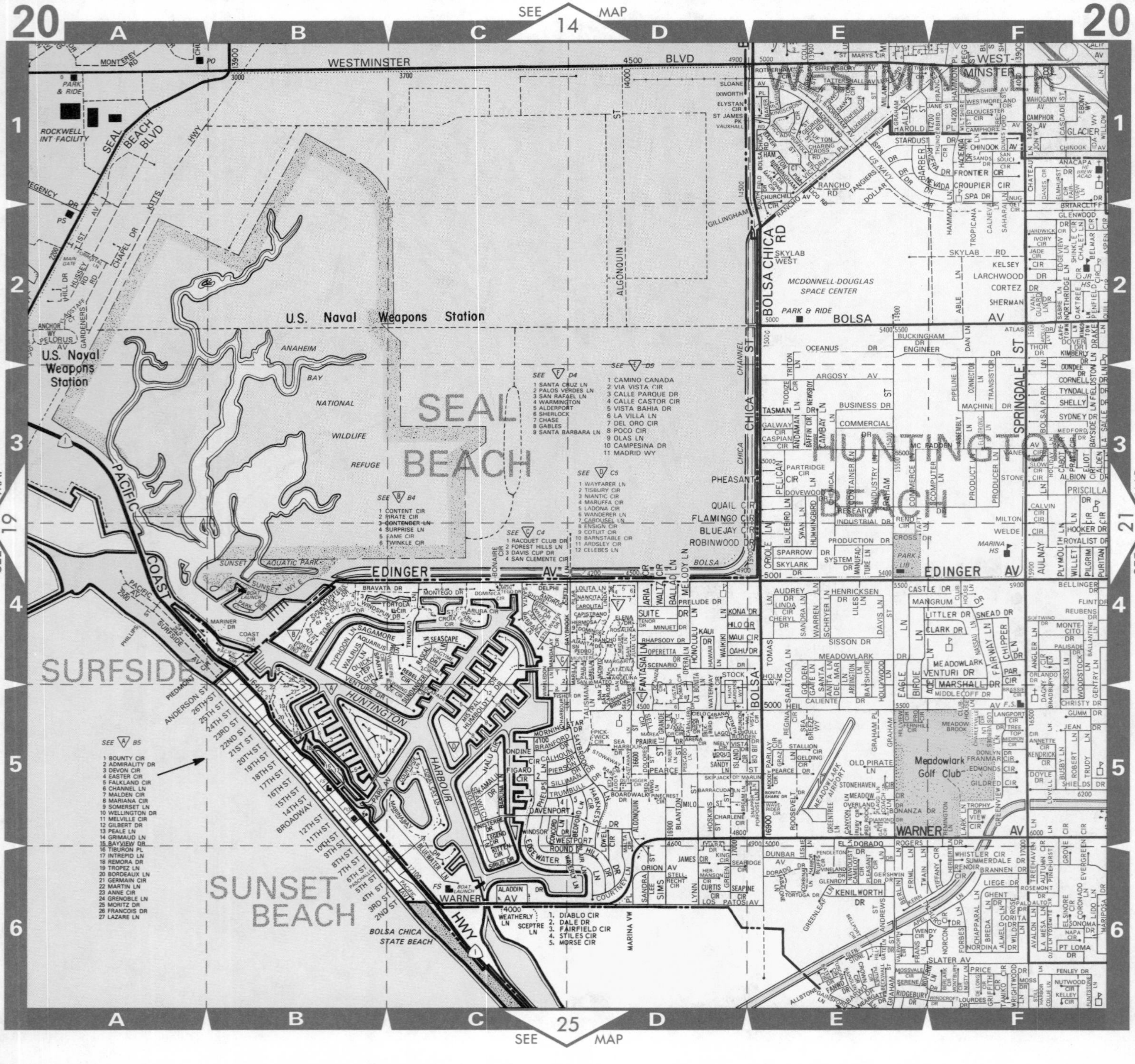

WESTMINSTER BLVD

WESTMINSTER

ROCKWELL INT FACILITY

SEAL BEACH BLVD

PARK & RIDE
PO

U.S. Naval Weapons Station

U.S. Naval Weapons Station

ANAHEIM BAY

NATIONAL WILDLIFE REFUGE

SEAL BEACH

McDONNELL-DOUGLAS SPACE CENTER

SKYLAB WEST

BOLSA CHICA RD

PARK & RIDE

BOLSA AV

HUNTINGTON BEACH

PACIFIC COAST HWY

SURFSIDE

SUNSET AQUATIC PARK

EDINGER AV

SEASCAPE

HUNTINGTON HARBOUR

SUNSET BEACH

MEADOWLARK GOLF CLUB

WARNER AV

BOLSA CHICA STATE BEACH

WARNER AV

SLATER AV

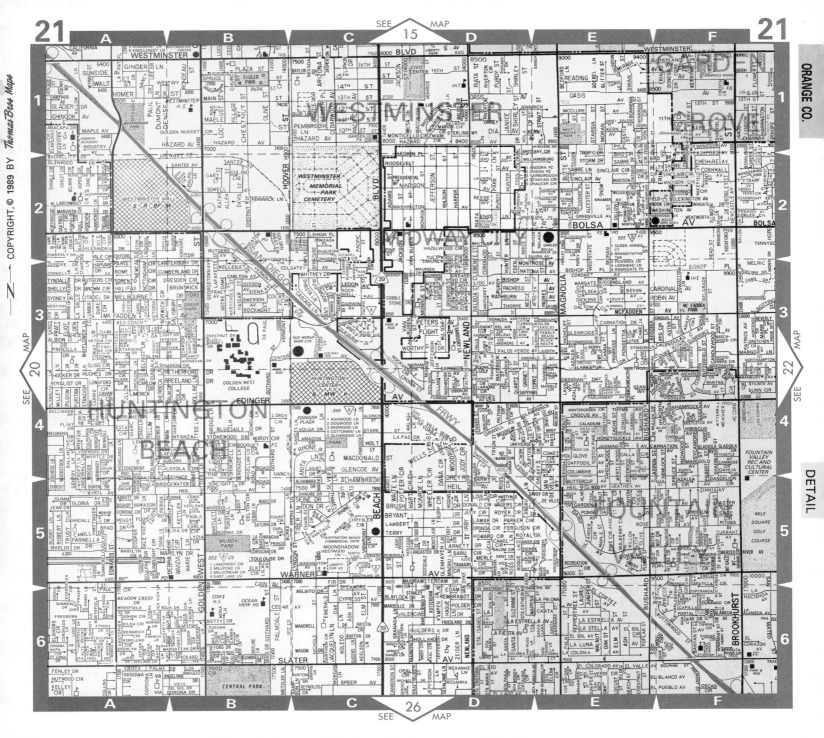

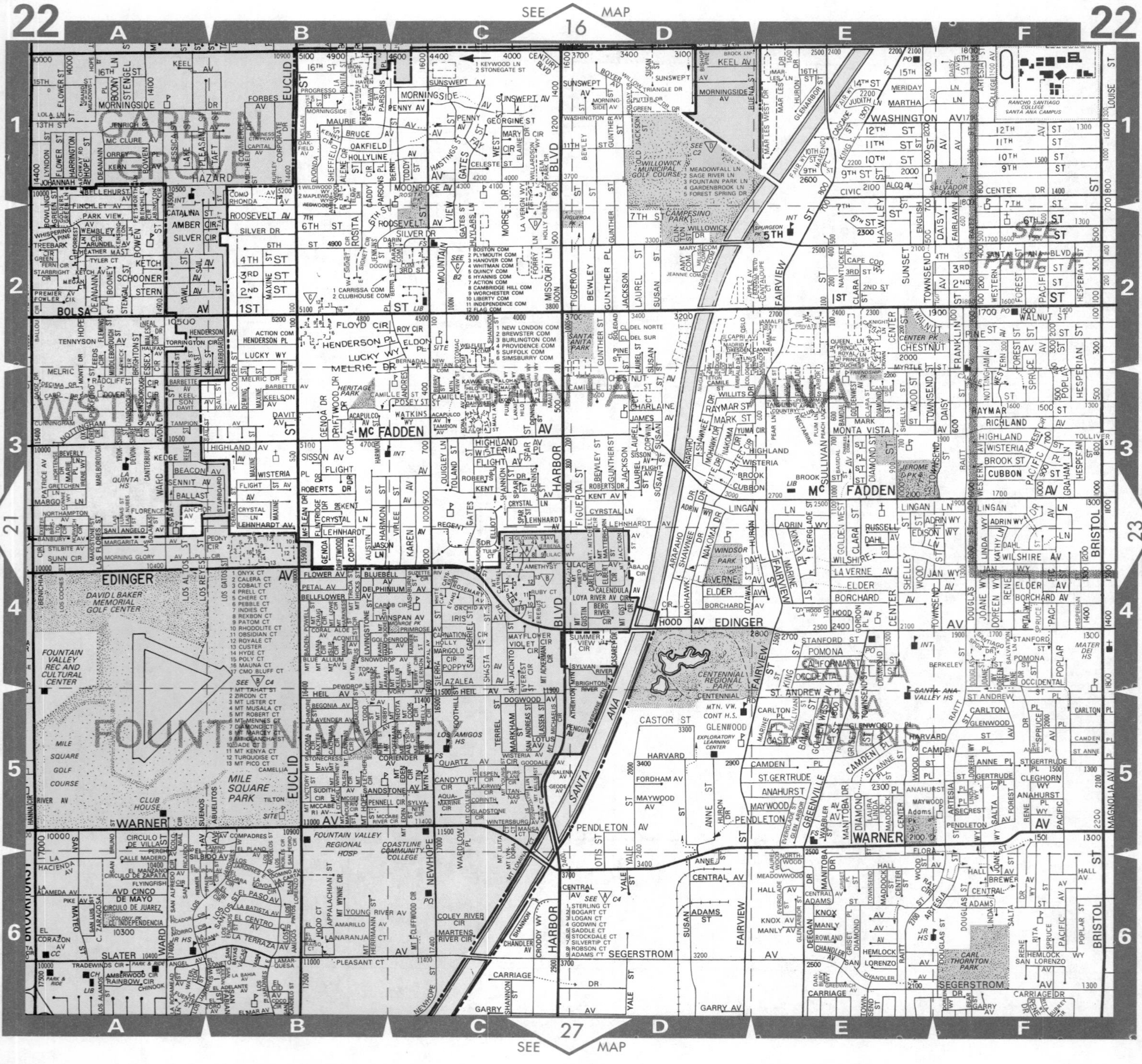

ORANGE CO.

DETAIL

GARDEN GROVE

SANTA ANA

W STA

FOUNTAIN VALLEY

EDINGER

SANTA ANA GARDENS

BOLSA

WARNER

SLATER

SEE MAP 21

SEE MAP 23

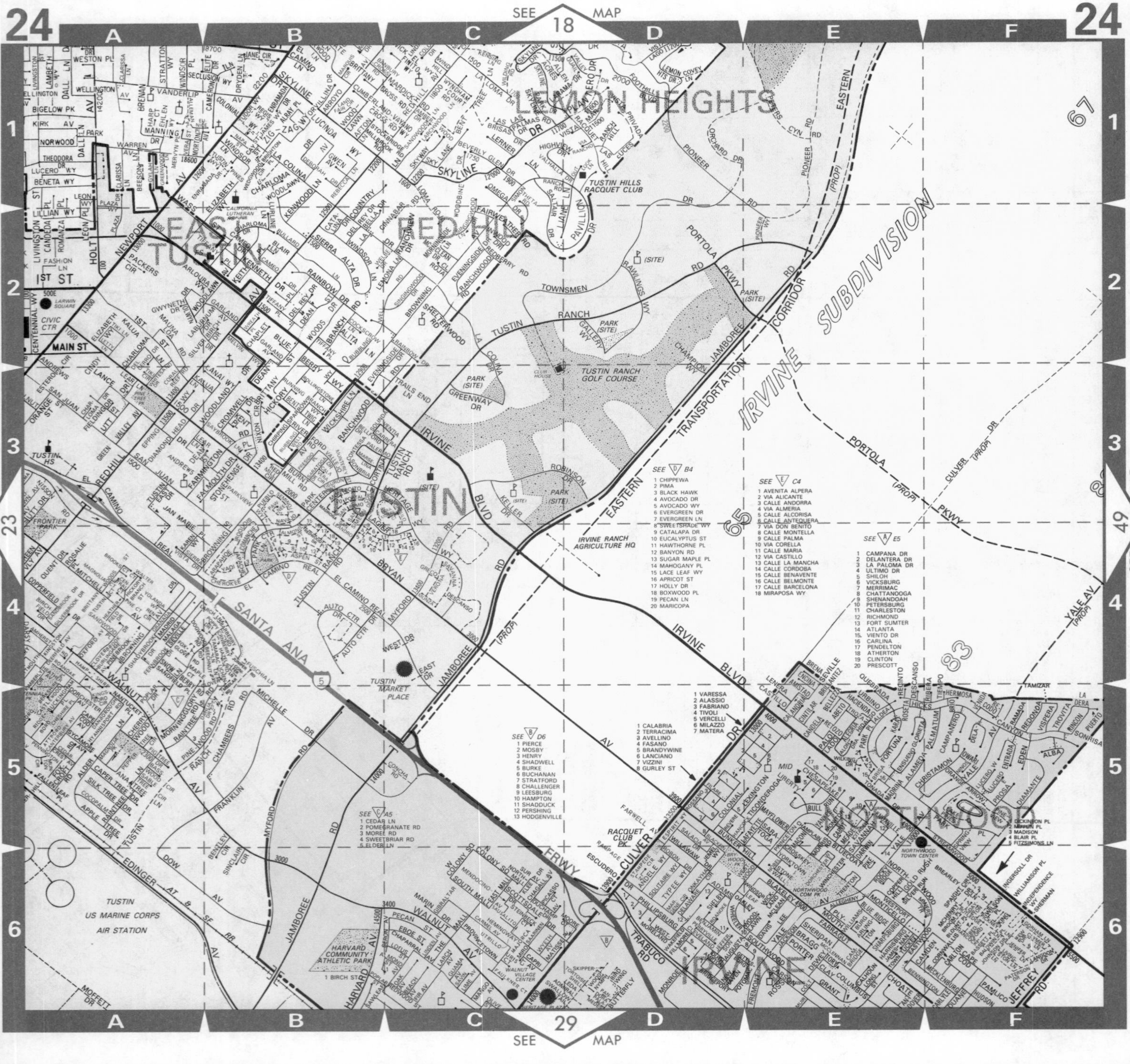

ORANGE CO.

DETAIL

LEMON HEIGHTS

EAST TUSTIN

RED HILL

Tustin Hills Racquet Club

TUSTIN

Tustin Ranch Golf Course

IRVINE SUBDIVISION

IRVINE RANCH AGRICULTURE HQ

Tustin Market Place

NORTHWOOD

Northwood Town Center

TUSTIN HS

FRONTIER PARK

Racquet Club Pk

TUSTIN US MARINE CORPS AIR STATION

HARVARD COMMUNITY ATHLETIC PARK

IRVINE

SEE 23 MAP

SEE 49 MAP

SEE B4
1 CHIPPEWA
2 PIMA
3 BLACK HAWK
4 AVOCADO DR
5 AVOCADO WY
6 EVERGREEN DR
7 EVERGREEN LN
8 SWEETSHADE WY
9 CATALAPA DR
10 EUCALYPTUS ST
11 HAWTHORNE PL
12 BANYON RD
13 SUGAR MAPLE PL
14 MAHOGANY PL
15 LACE LEAF WY
16 APRICOT ST
17 HOLLY DR
18 BOXWOOD PL
19 PECAN LN
20 MARICOPA

SEE C4
1 AVENITA ALPERA
2 VIA ALICANTE
3 VIA ALMERIA
4 CALLE ALCORISA
5 CALLE ANTEQUERA
6 VIA DON BENITO
7 CALLE MONTELLA
8 CALLE PALMA
9 CALLE CORELLA
10 CALLE MARIA
11 VIA CASTILLO
12 CALLE LA MANCHA
13 CALLE CORDOBA
14 CALLE BENAVENTE
15 CALLE BELMONTE
16 CALLE BARCELONA
17 MIRAPOSA WY

SEE E5
1 CAMPANA DR
2 DELANTERA DR
3 LA PALOMA DR
4 ULTIMO DR
5 SHILOH
6 VICKSBURG
7 MERRIMAC
8 CHATTANOOGA
9 SHENANDOAH
10 PETERSBURG
11 CHARLESTON
12 RICHMOND
13 FORT SUMTER
14 ATLANTA
15 VIENTO DR
16 CARLINA
17 PENDELTON
18 ATHERTON
19 CLINTON
20 PRESCOTT

SEE D6
1 PIERCE
2 MOSBY
3 HENRY
4 SHADWELL
5 BURKE
6 BUCHANAN
7 STRATFORD
8 CHALLENGER
9 LEESBURG
10 HAMPTON
11 SHADDUCK
12 PERSHING
13 HODGENVILLE

SEE A5
1 CEDAR LN
2 POMEGRANATE RD
3 MOREE RD
4 SWEETBRIAR RD
5 ELDER LN

1 VARESSA
2 ALASSIO
3 FABRIANO
4 TIVOLI
5 VERCELLI
6 MILAZZO
7 MATERA

1 CALABRIA
2 TERRACIMA
3 AVELLINO
4 FASANO
5 BRANDYWINE
6 LANCIANO
7 VIZZINI
8 GURLEY ST

1 BIRCH LN

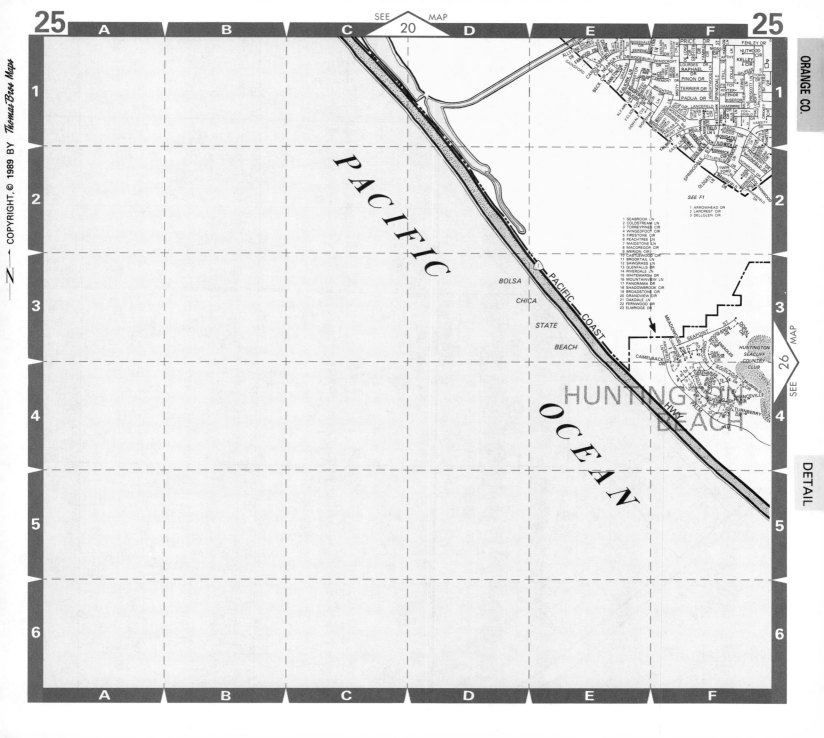

ORANGE CO.

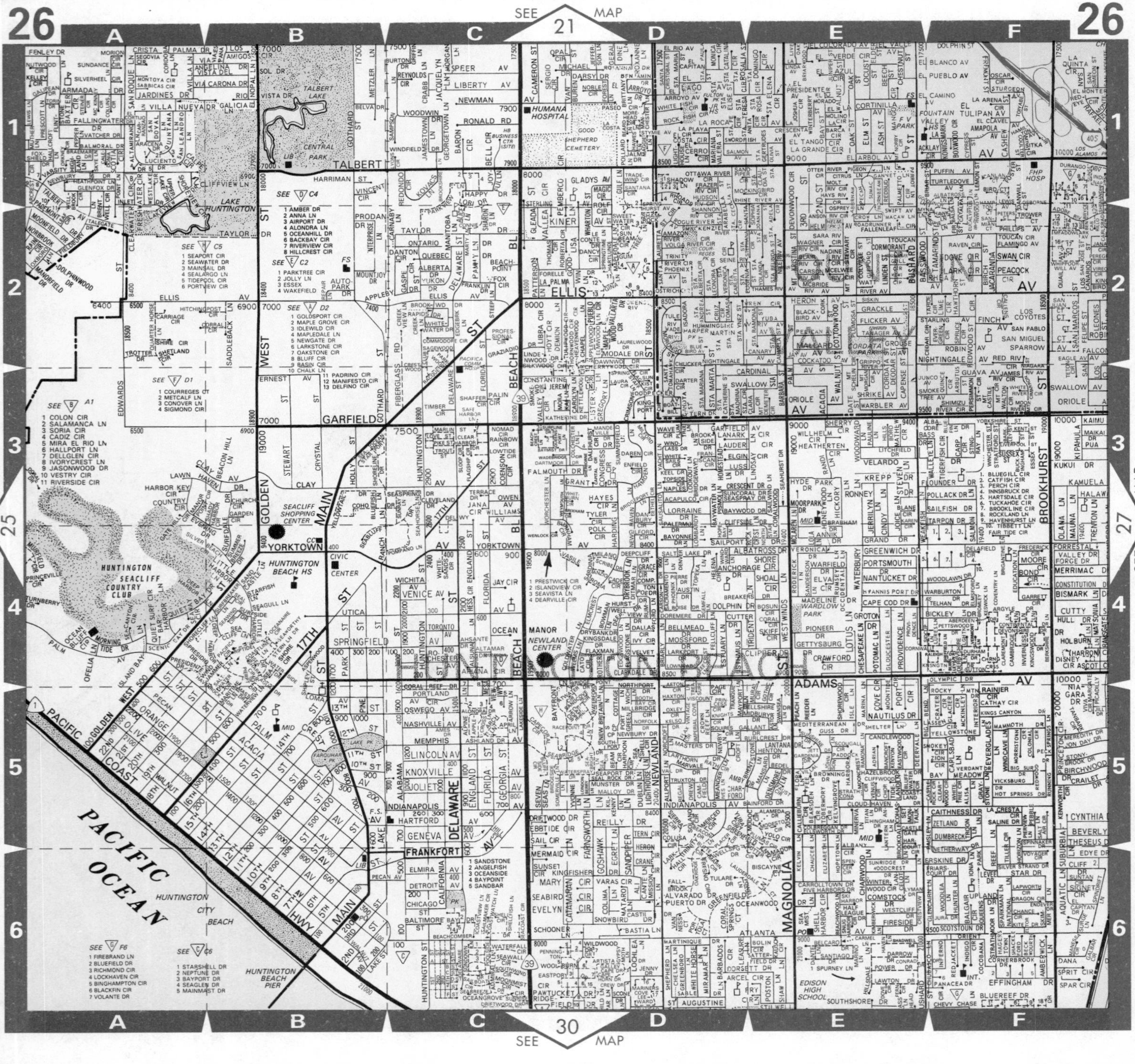

DETAIL

PACIFIC OCEAN

HUNTINGTON BEACH

SEE MAP 22

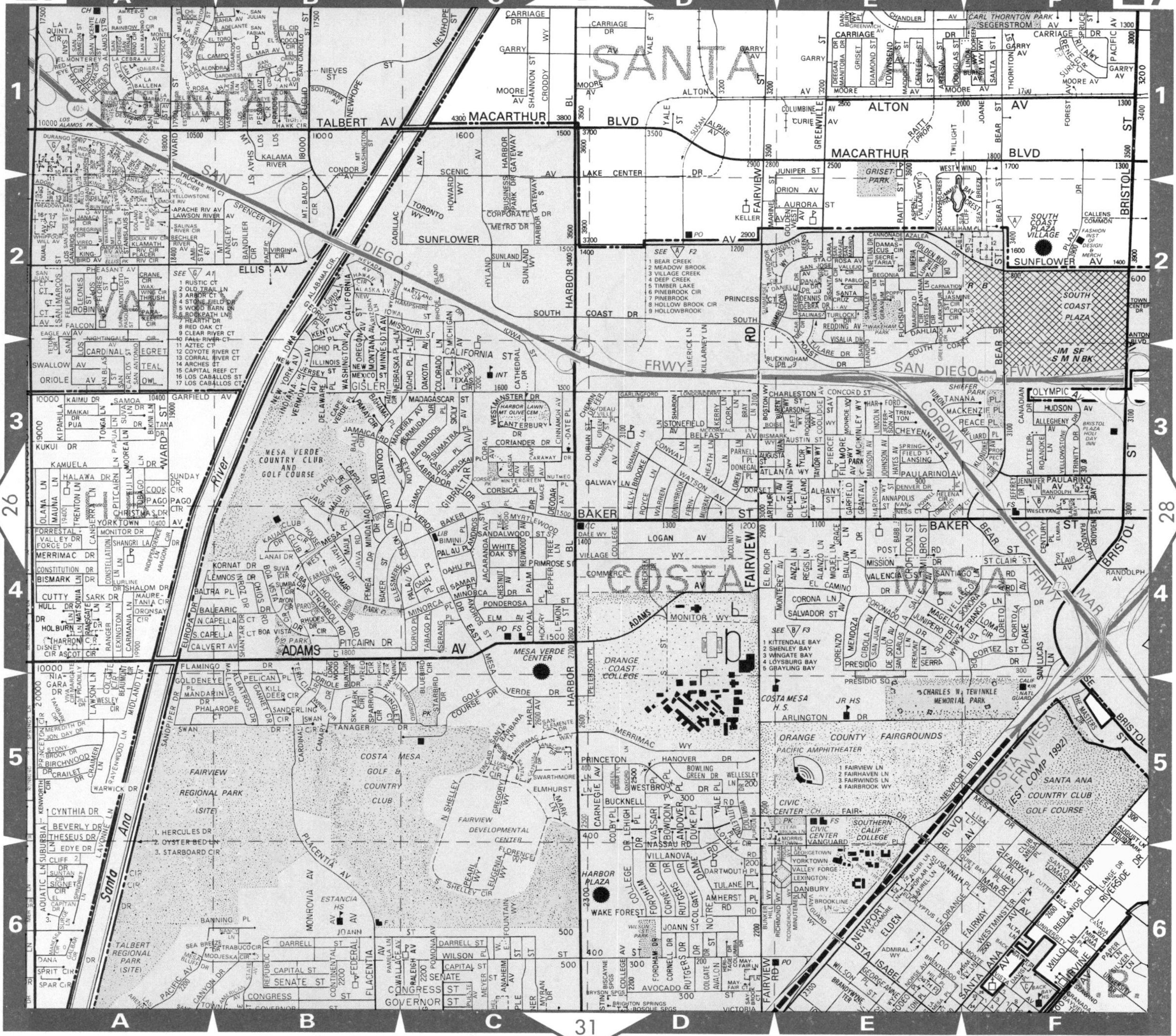
A B C D E F
1 2 3 4 5 6
SANTA ANA
FOUNTAIN VALLEY
COSTA MESA
SEE MAP 26
SEE MAP 28
SEE MAP 31
TALBERT AV
MACARTHUR BLVD
ALTON AV
SAN DIEGO FRWY
SOUTH COAST DR
SOUTH COAST PLAZA
SOUTH COAST PLAZA VILLAGE
CORONA DEL MAR FRWY
COSTA MESA FRWY (EST COMP 1992)
HARBOR BL
FAIRVIEW RD
BRISTOL ST
BAKER ST
ADAMS AV
NEWPORT BLVD
Santa Ana River
MESA VERDE COUNTRY CLUB AND GOLF COURSE
MESA VERDE CENTER
ORANGE COAST COLLEGE
ORANGE COUNTY FAIRGROUNDS
PACIFIC AMPHITHEATER
CHARLES W. TEWINKLE MEMORIAL PARK
COSTA MESA H.S.
COSTA MESA GOLF & COUNTRY CLUB
FAIRVIEW REGIONAL PARK (SITE)
FAIRVIEW DEVELOPMENTAL CENTER
TALBERT REGIONAL PARK (SITE)
SANTA ANA COUNTRY CLUB GOLF COURSE
SOUTHERN CALIF COLLEGE
HARBOR PLAZA
ESTANCIA HS
GRISET PARK
CARL THORNTON PARK
SEGERSTROM
SEE G A1
1 RUSTIC CT
2 OLD TRAIL LN
3 ARBOR CT
4 STONE FIELD DR
5 WOOD BARN LN
6 ROCKPATH LN
7 HEARTH DR
8 RED OAK CT
9 CLEAR RIVER CT
10 FALL RIVER CT
11 AZTEC CT
12 COYOTE RIVER CT
13 CORRAL RIVER CT
14 ARCHES CT
15 CAPITAL REEF CT
16 LOS CABALLOS CT
17 LOS CABALLOS CT
SEE A F2
1 BEAR CREEK
2 MEADOW BROOK
3 VILLAGE CREEK
4 DEEP CREEK
5 TIMBER LAKE
6 PINEBROOK CIR
7 PINEBROOK
8 HOLLOW BROOK CIR
9 HOLLOWBROOK
SEE B F3
1 KITTENDALE BAY
2 SHENLEY BAY
3 WINGATE BAY
4 LOYSBURG BAY
5 GRAYLING BAY
1 FAIRVIEW LN
2 FAIRHAVEN LN
3 FAIRWINDS LN
4 FAIRBROOK WY
1. HERCULES DR
2. OYSTER BED LN
3. STARBOARD CIR

SEE MAP 31

ORANGE CO.

DETAIL

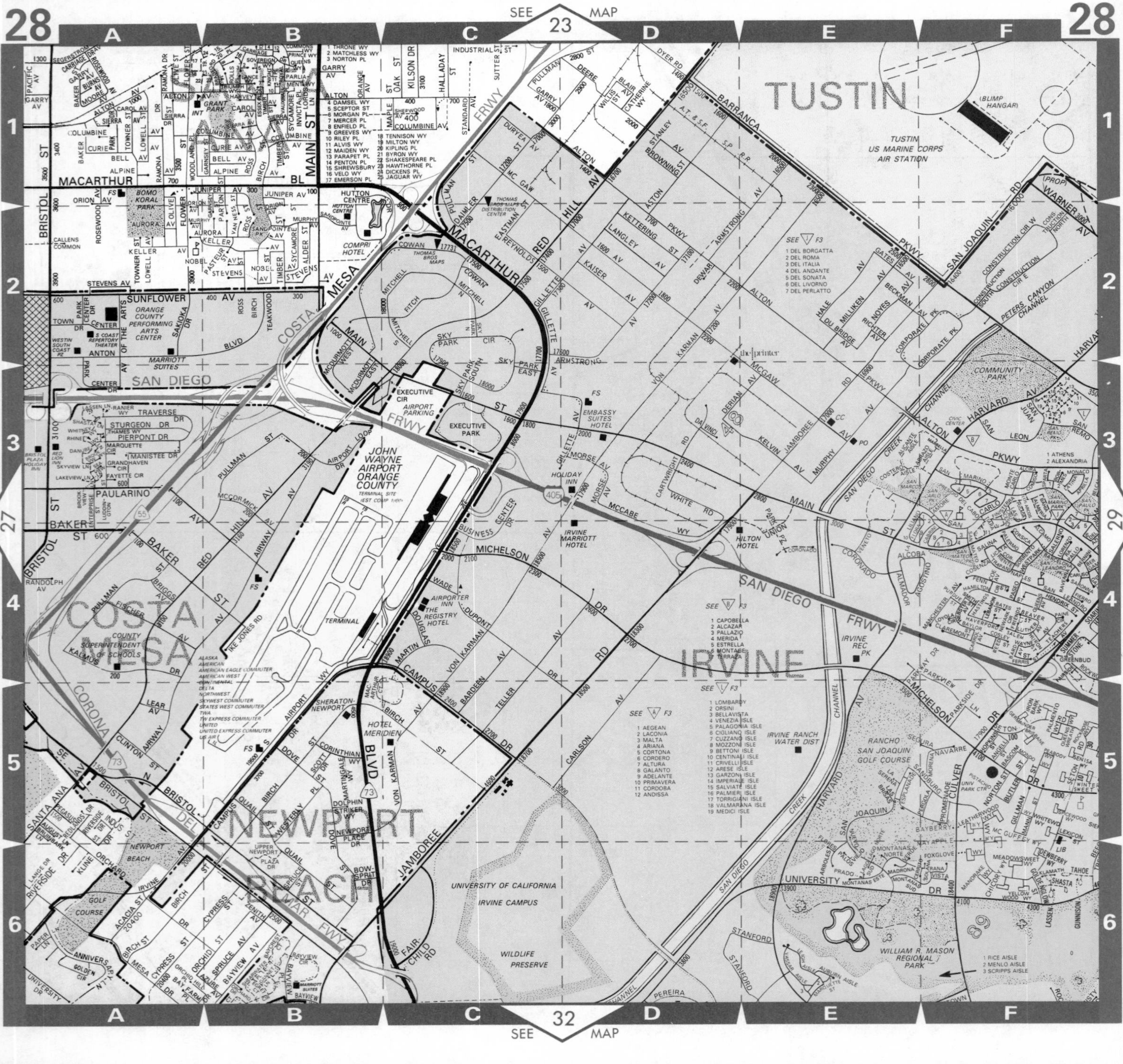

TUSTIN

TUSTIN US MARINE CORPS AIR STATION

(BUMP HANGAR)

COSTA MESA

MACARTHUR

SUNFLOWER

SAN DIEGO FRWY

JOHN WAYNE AIRPORT ORANGE COUNTY TERMINAL SITE

IRVINE

COSTA MESA

NEWPORT BEACH

UNIVERSITY OF CALIFORNIA IRVINE CAMPUS

WILDLIFE PRESERVE

WILLIAM R. MASON REGIONAL PARK

RANCHO SAN JOAQUIN GOLF COURSE

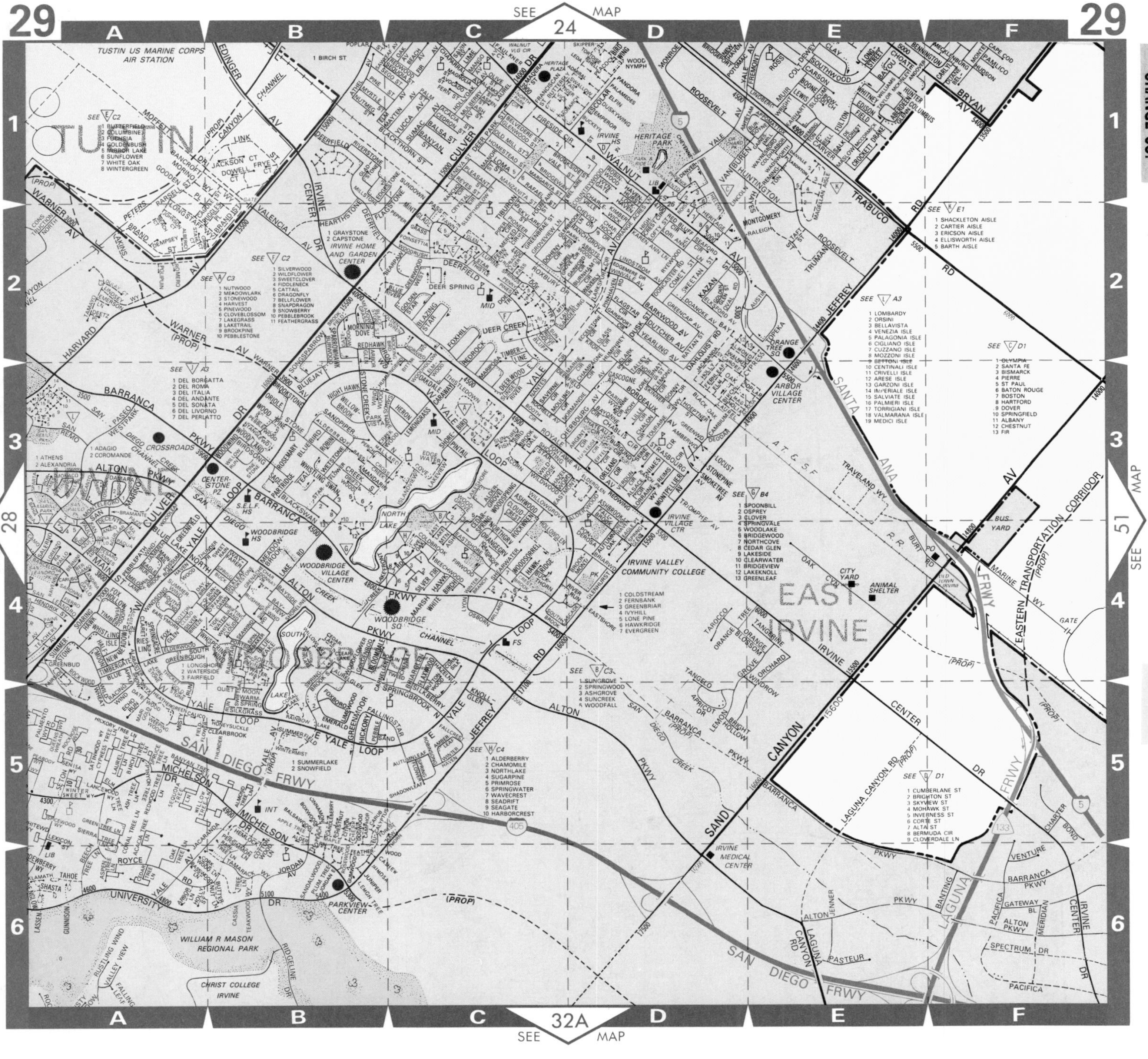

ORANGE CO.

DETAIL

COPYRIGHT © 1989 BY Thomas Bros. Maps

—N→

TUSTIN

TUSTIN US MARINE CORPS AIR STATION

SEE C2
1 BUTTERFLY LN
2 COLUMBINE
3 FUCHSIA
4 GOLDENBUSH
5 ARBOR LANE
6 SUNFLOWER
7 WHITE OAK
8 WINTERGREEN

SEE C2
1 GRAYSTONE DR
2 CAPSTONE

IRVINE HOME AND GARDEN CENTER

SEE C3
1 NUTWOOD
2 MEADOWLARK
3 STONEWOOD
4 HARVEST
5 PINEWOOD
6 CLOVEBLOSSOM
7 LAKEGRASS
8 LAKETRAIL
9 BROOKPINE
10 PEBBLESTONE

1 SILVERWOOD
2 WILDFLOWER
3 SWEETCLOVER
4 FIDDLENECK
5 CATTAIL
6 DRAGONFLY
7 BELLFLOWER
8 SNAPDRAGON
9 SNOWBERRY
10 FEATHERGRASS

SEE A3
1 DEL BORGATTA
2 DEL ROMA
3 DEL ITALIA
4 DEL ANDANTE
5 DEL SONATA
6 DEL LIVORNO
7 DEL PERLATTO

1 ATHENS
2 ALEXANDRIA
1 ADAGIO
2 COROMANDE

WOODBRIDGE

WOODBRIDGE VILLAGE CENTER

IRVINE VALLEY COMMUNITY COLLEGE

1 COLDSTREAM
2 FERNBANK
3 GREENBRIAR
4 IVYHILL
5 LONE PINE
6 HAWKRIDGE
7 EVERGREEN

SEE C3
1 SUNGROVE
2 SPRINGWOOD
3 ASHGROVE
4 SUNCREEK
5 WOODFALL

EAST IRVINE

SEE B4
1 SPOONBILL
2 OSPREY
3 CLOVER
4 SPRINGVALE
5 WOODLAKE
6 BRIDGEWOOD
7 NORTHCOVE
8 CEDAR GLEN
9 LAKESIDE
10 CLEARWATER
11 BRIDGEVIEW
12 LAKEKNOLL
13 GREENLEAF

SEE A3
1 LOMBARDY
2 ORSINI
3 BELLAVISTA
4 VENEZIA ISLE
5 PALAGONIA ISLE
6 CIGLIANO ISLE
7 CUZZANO ISLE
8 MOZZONI ISLE
9 CENTINAIA ISLE
10 CRIVELLI ISLE
11 ARESE ISLE
12 GARZONI ISLE
13 IMPERIALE ISLE
14 SALVIATE ISLE
15 PALMIERI ISLE
16 TORRIGIANI ISLE
17 VALMARANA ISLE
18 MEDICI ISLE

SEE D1
1 OLYMPIA
2 SANTA FE
3 BISMARCK
4 PIERRE
5 ST PAUL
6 BATON ROUGE
7 BOSTON
8 HARTFORD
9 DOVER
10 SPRINGFIELD
11 ALBANY
12 CHESTNUT
13 FIR

SEE E1
1 SHACKLETON AISLE
2 CARTIER AISLE
3 ERICSON AISLE
4 ELLISWORTH AISLE
5 BARTH AISLE

SEE D1
1 CUMBERLANE ST
2 BRIGHTON ST
3 SKYVIEW ST
4 MOHAWK ST
5 INVERNESS ST
6 CORTE ST
7 ALTA ST
8 BERMUDA CIR
9 CLOVERDALE LN

SEE C4
1 ALDERBERRY
2 CHAMOMILE
3 NORTHLAKE
4 SUGARPINE
5 PRIMROSE
6 SPRINGWATER
7 WAVECREST
8 SEADRIFT
9 SEAGATE
10 HARBORCREST

SEE C4
1 SUMMERLAKE
2 SNOWFIELD

WILLIAM R MASON REGIONAL PARK

CHRIST COLLEGE IRVINE

IRVINE MEDICAL CENTER

PARKVIEW CENTER

ARBOR VILLAGE CENTER

ORANGE TREE SQ

IRVINE VILLAGE CTR

CENTERSTONE PZ

CROSSROADS

ALTON PKWY

BARRANCA PKWY

SAN DIEGO FRWY

MICHELSON DR

UNIVERSITY DR

MARINE WAY

EASTERN TRANSPORTATION CORRIDOR (PROP)

ANIMAL SHELTER

CITY YARD

BUS YARD

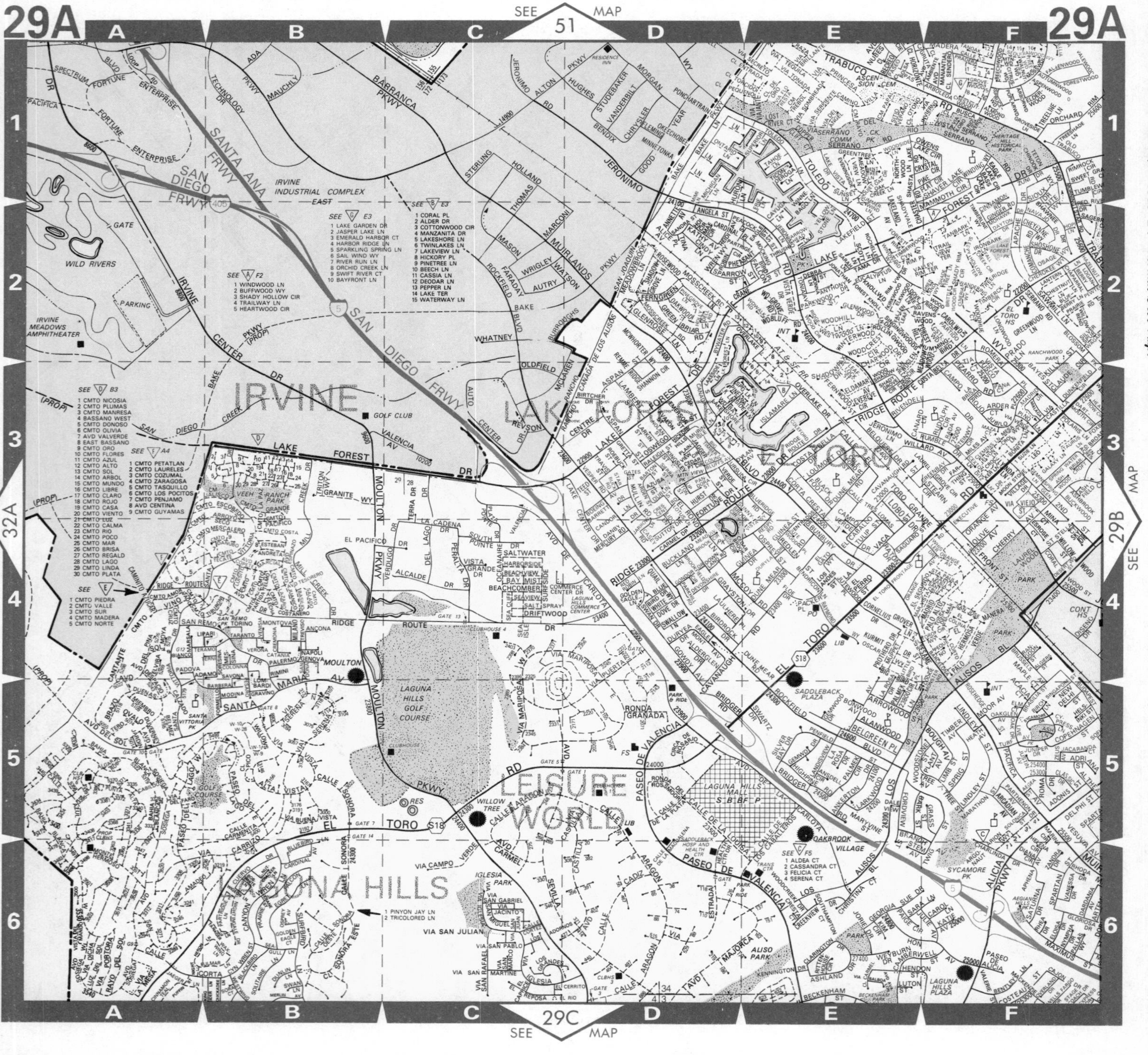

ORANGE CO.

DETAIL

IRVINE

LAKE FOREST / EL TORO

LAGUNA HILLS GOLF COURSE

LEISURE WORLD

LAGUNA HILLS

SANTA ANA FRWY

SAN DIEGO FRWY

IRVINE INDUSTRIAL COMPLEX EAST

IRVINE MEADOWS AMPHITHEATER

WILD RIVERS

BARRANCA PKWY

GOLF CLUB

LAGUNA HILLS MALL

OAKBROOK VILLAGE

SADDLEBACK PLAZA

LAGUNA HILLS PLAZA

ALISO PARK

SYCAMORE PK

WILLOW TREE

CLUBHOUSE

RANCH PARK

SEE F2
1 WINDWOOD LN
2 BUFFWOOD WY
3 SHADY HOLLOW CIR
4 TRAILWAY LN
5 HEARTWOOD CIR

SEE E3
1 LAKE GARDEN DR
2 JASPER LAKE LN
3 EMERALD HARBOR CT
4 HARBOR RIDGE LN
5 SPARKLING SPRING LN
6 SAIL WIND WY
7 RIVER RUN LN
8 ORCHID CREEK LN
9 SWIFT RIVER CT
10 BAYFRONT LN

SEE E3
1 CORAL PL
2 ALDER DR
3 COTTONWOOD CIR
4 MANZANITA DR
5 LAKESHORE LN
6 TWINLAKES LN
7 LAKEVIEW LN
8 HICKORY PL
9 PINETREE LN
10 BEECH LN
11 CASSIA LN
12 DEODAR LN
13 PEPPER LN
14 LAKE TER
15 WATERWAY LN

SEE B3
1 CMTO NICOSIA
2 CMTO PLUMAS
3 CMTO MANRESA
4 BASSANO WEST
5 CMTO DONOSO
6 CMTO OLIVIA
7 AVD VALVERDE
8 EAST BASSANO
9 CMTO ORO
10 CMTO FLORES
11 CMTO AZUL
12 CMTO ALTO
13 CMTO SOL
14 CMTO ARBOL
15 CMTO MUNDO
16 CMTO LIBRE
17 CMTO CLARO
18 CMTO ROJO
19 CMTO CASA
20 CMTO VIENTO
21 CMTO ESTE
22 CMTO CALMA
23 CMTO RIO
24 CMTO POCO
25 CMTO MAR
26 CMTO BRISA
27 CMTO REGALD
28 CMTO LAGO
29 CMTO LINDA
30 CMTO PLATA

SEE A4
1 CMTO PETATLAN
2 CMTO LAURELES
3 CMTO COZUMEL
4 CMTO ZARAGOSA
5 CMTO TASQUILLO
6 CMTO LOS POCITOS
7 CMTO PENJAMO
8 AVD CENTINA
9 CMTO GUYAMAS

SEE
1 CMTO PIEDRA
2 CMTO VALLE
3 CMTO SUR
4 CMTO MADERA
5 CMTO NORTE

FS
1 ALDBA CT
2 CASSANDRA CT
3 FELICIA CT
4 SERENA CT

1 PINYON JAY LN
2 TRICOLORED LN

1 ALDBA CT
2 CASSANDRA CT
3 FELICIA CT
4 SERENA CT

VIA SAN JULIAN

IGLESIA PARK

LAGUNA HILLS HOSP AND HEALTH

PASEO DE VALENCIA

MOULTON PKWY

LAKE FOREST DR

EL TORO RD

SEE MAP 32A
SEE MAP 29B

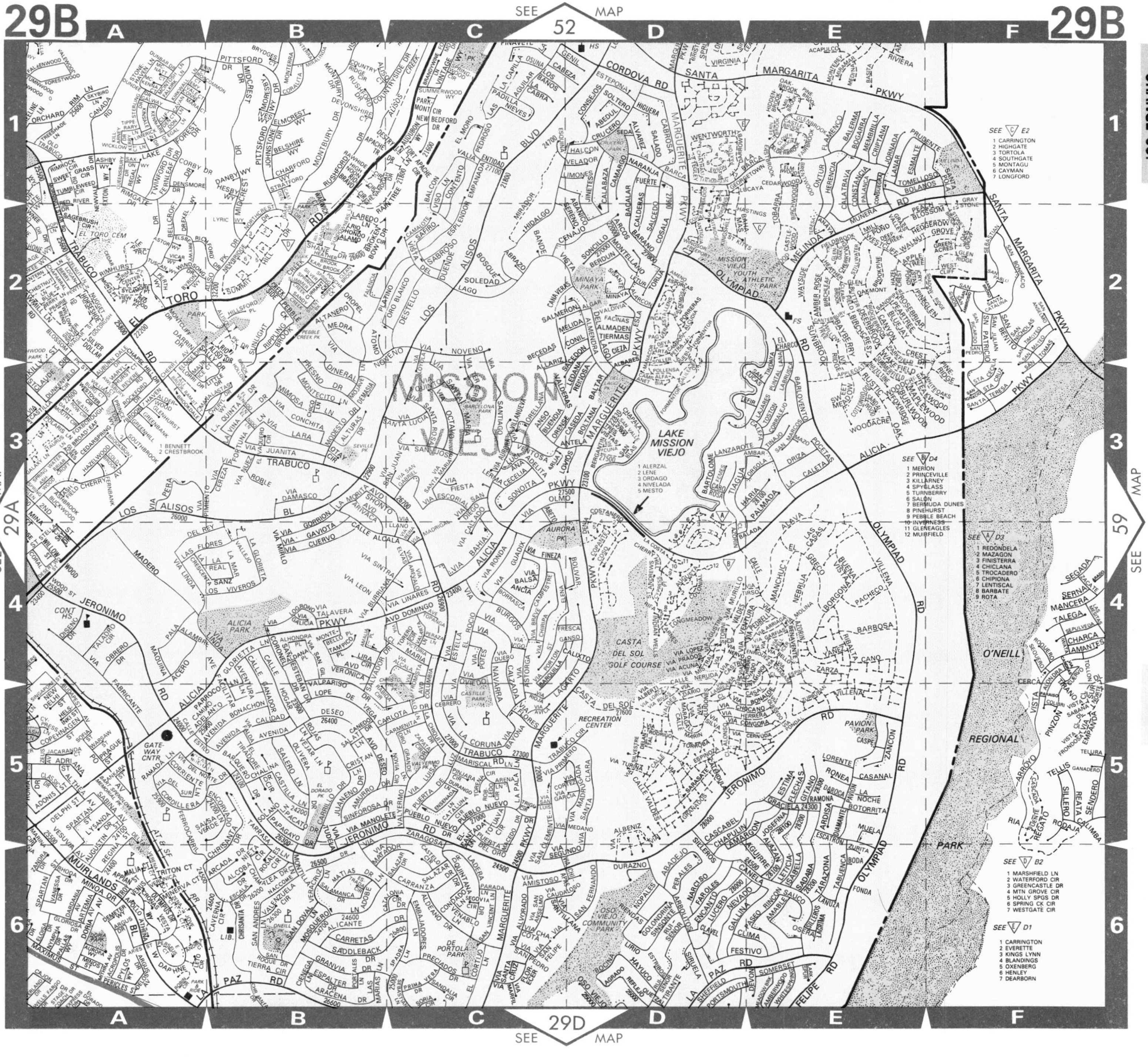
SEE 52 MAP
A
B
C
D
E
F
1
2
3
4
5
6
MISSION VIEJO
LAKE MISSION VIEJO
1 ALERZAL
2 LENE
3 ORDAGO
4 NIVELADA
5 MESTO
SEE C E2
1 CARRINGTON
2 HIGHGATE
3 TORTOLA
4 SOUTHGATE
5 MONTAGU
6 CAYMAN
7 LONGFORD
SEE B D4
1 MERION
2 PRINCEVILLE
3 KILLARNEY
4 SPYGLASS
5 TURNBERRY
6 SALON
7 BERMUDA DUNES
8 PINEHURST
9 PEBBLE BEACH
10 INVERNESS
11 GLENEAGLES
12 MUIRFIELD
SEE A D3
1 REDONDELA
2 MAZAGON
3 FINISTERRA
4 CHICLANA
5 TROCADERO
6 CHIPIONA
7 LENTISCAL
8 BARBATE
9 ROTA
SEE D B2
1 MARSHFIELD LN
2 WATERFORD CIR
3 GREENCASTLE DR
4 MTN GROVE CIR
5 HOLLY SPGS DR
6 SPRING CK CIR
7 WESTGATE CIR
SEE E D1
1 CARRINGTON
2 EVERETTE
3 KINGS LYNN
4 BLANDINGS
5 OXENBERG
6 HENLEY
7 DEARBORN
SANTA MARGARITA PKWY
OLYMPIAD RD
ALICIA PKWY
TRABUCO RD
LOS ALISOS BL
JERONIMO RD
MARGUERITE PKWY
LA PAZ RD
EL TORO RD
CASTA DEL SOL GOLF COURSE
O'NEILL REGIONAL PARK
ALICIA PARK
AURORA PK
MINAYA PARK
MISSION VIEJO YOUTH ATHLETIC PARK
RECREATION CENTER
PAVION PARK
OSO VIEJO COMMUNITY PARK
DE PORTOLA PARK
CASTILLE PARK
EL TORO CEM
GATE-WAY CNTR
SEE 29A MAP
SEE 59 MAP
SEE 29D MAP

DETAIL

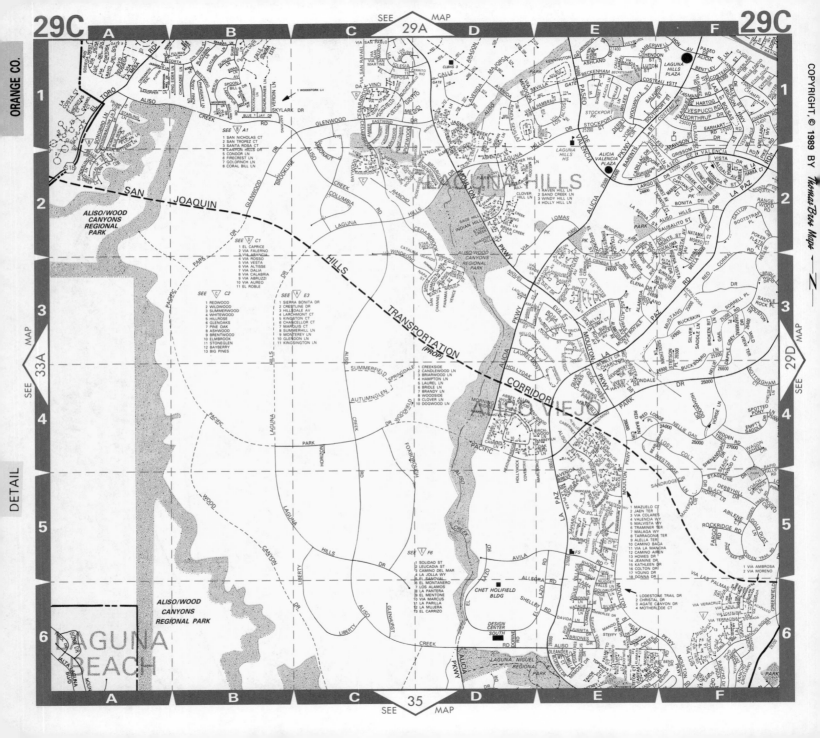

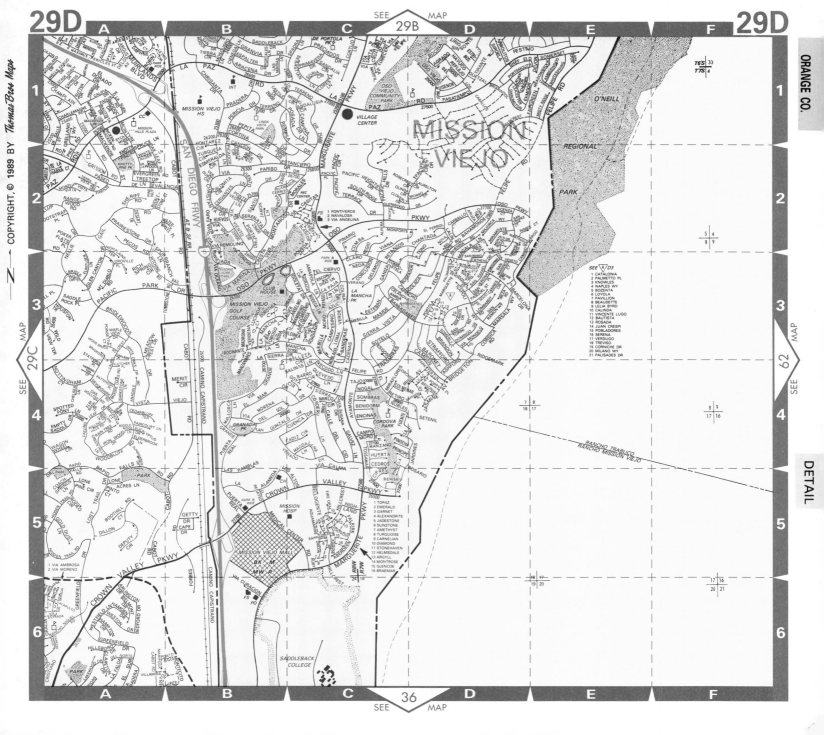

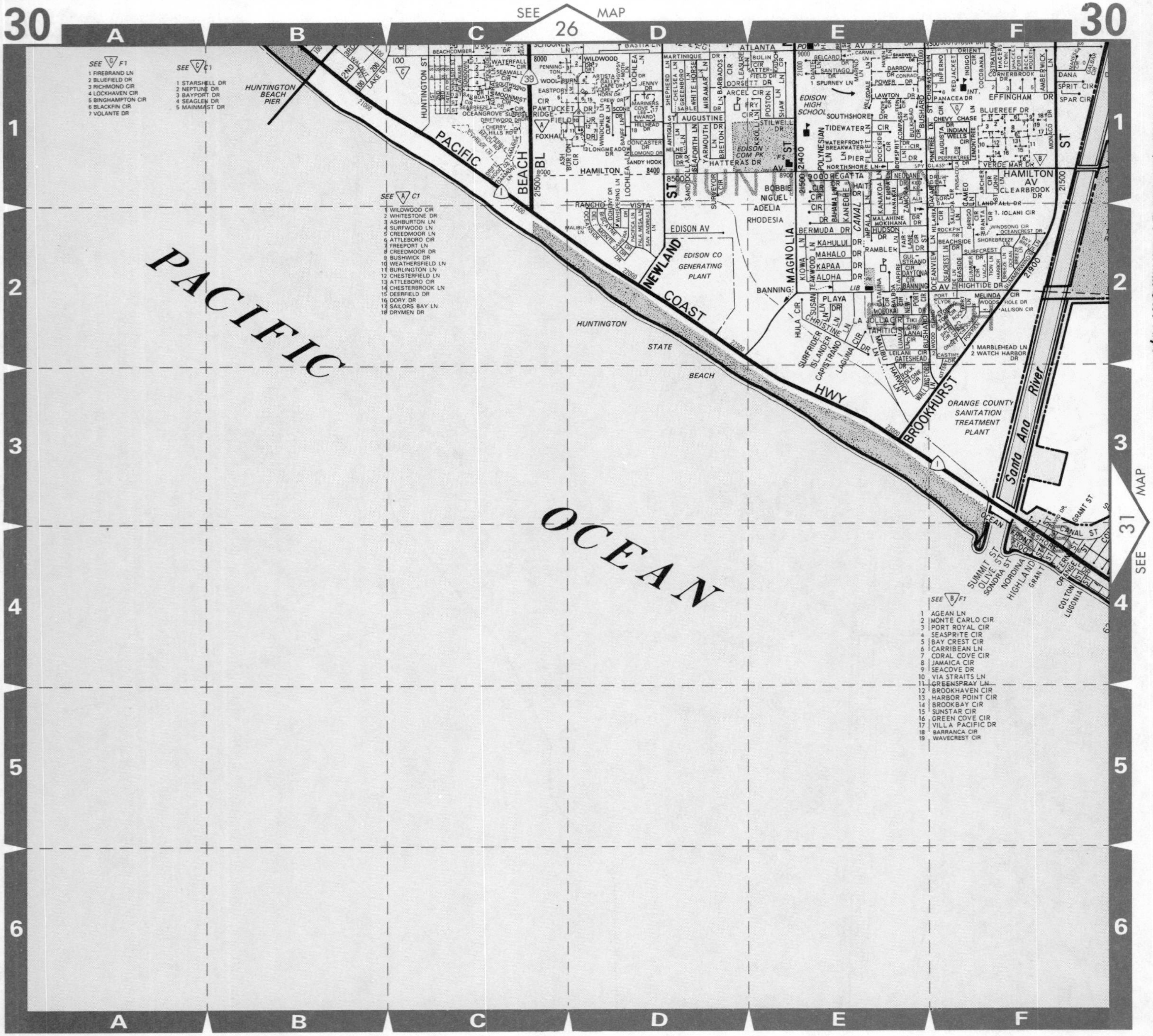
SEE MAP 26
SEE MAP 31
A B C D E F
1 2 3 4 5 6
ORANGE CO.
DETAIL
PACIFIC OCEAN
HUNTINGTON BEACH PIER
HUNTINGTON STATE BEACH
PACIFIC COAST HWY
BEACH BL
NEWLAND ST
MAGNOLIA ST
BROOKHURST ST
HAMILTON AV
EDISON AV
ATLANTA AV
EDISON HIGH SCHOOL
EDISON COM PK
EDISON CO GENERATING PLANT
ORANGE COUNTY SANITATION TREATMENT PLANT
Santa Ana River
BANNING
SEE G F1
1 FIREBRAND LN
2 BLUEFIELD DR
3 RICHMOND CIR
4 LOCKHAVEN CIR
5 BINGHAMPTON CIR
6 BLACKFIN CIR
7 VOLANTE DR
SEE C C1
1 STARSHELL DR
2 NEPTUNE DR
3 BAYPORT DR
4 SEAGLEN DR
5 MAINMAST DR
SEE A C1
1 WILDWOOD CIR
2 WHITESTONE DR
3 ASHBURTON LN
4 SURFWOOD LN
5 CREEDMOOR LN
6 ATTLEBORO CIR
7 FREEPORT LN
8 CREEDMOOR DR
9 BUSHWICK DR
10 WEATHERSFIELD LN
11 BURLINGTON LN
12 CHESTERFIELD LN
13 ATTLEBORO CIR
14 CHESTERBROOK LN
15 DEERFIELD DR
16 DORY DR
17 SAILORS BAY LN
18 DRYMEN DR
SEE B F1
1 AGEAN LN
2 MONTE CARLO CIR
3 PORT ROYAL CIR
4 SEASPRITE CIR
5 BAY CREST CIR
6 CARRIBEAN LN
7 CORAL COVE CIR
8 JAMAICA CIR
9 SEACOVE DR
10 VIA STRAITS LN
11 GREENSPRAY LN
12 BROOKHAVEN CIR
13 HARBOR POINT CIR
14 BROOKBAY CIR
15 SUNSTAR CIR
16 GREEN COVE CIR
17 VILLA PACIFIC DR
18 BARRANCA CIR
19 WAVECREST CIR
1 MARBLEHEAD LN
2 WATCH HARBOR DR

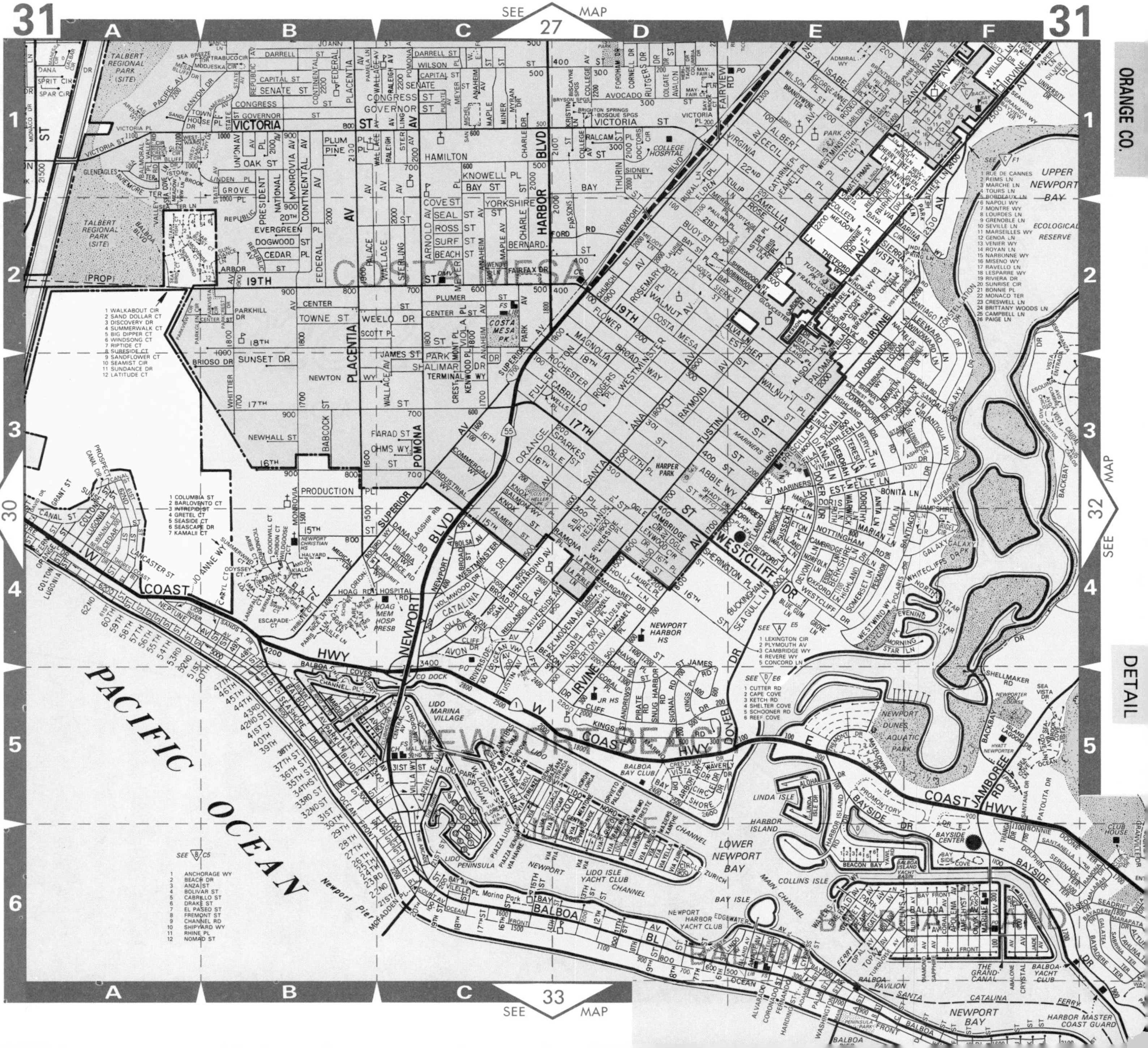

ORANGE CO.

DETAIL

— N → COPYRIGHT, © 1989 BY Thomas Bros Maps

COSTA MESA

PACIFIC OCEAN

NEWPORT BEACH

BALBOA ISLAND

UPPER NEWPORT BAY

ECOLOGICAL RESERVE

LOWER NEWPORT BAY

NEWPORT DUNES AQUATIC PARK

Legend (A2):
1 WALKABOUT CIR
2 SAND DOLLAR CT
3 DISCOVERY DR
4 SUMMERWALK CT
5 BIG DIPPER CT
6 RIPTIDE CT
7 SUBSIDE CT
8 SANDFLOWER CT
9 SEAMIST CT
10 SEAMIST CIR
11 SUNDANCE CT
12 LATITUDE CT

Legend (B3):
1 COLUMBIA ST
2 BARLOVENTO CT
3 GRETEL CT
4 GRETEL CT
5 SEASIDE CT
6 SEASCAPE DR
7 KAMALI CT

Legend (B6) SEE B/C5:
1 ANCHORAGE WY
2 BEACH DR
3 ANZA ST
4 BOLIVAR ST
5 CABRILLO ST
6 DRAKE ST
7 EL PASEO ST
8 FREMONT ST
9 CHANNEL RD
10 SHIPYARD WY
11 RHINE PL
12 NOMAD ST

Legend (E5) E6:
1 CUTTER RD
2 CAPE COVE
3 KETCH RD
4 SHELTER COVE
5 SCHOONER RD
6 REEF COVE

Legend (E6):
1 LEXINGTON CIR
2 PLYMOUTH AV
3 CAMBRIDGE WY
4 REVERE WY
5 CONCORD LN

Legend (F1):
1 RUE DE CANNES
2 REIMS LN
3 MARCHE LN
4 TOURS LN
5 BORDEAUX LN
6 NAPOLI WY
7 MONTRE WY
8 LOURDES LN
9 GRENOBLE LN
10 SEVILLE LN
11 MARSEILLES WY
12 GENOA LN
13 VENIER WY
14 ROYAN LN
15 NARBONNE WY
16 MISENO WY
17 RAVELLO LN
18 LESPARRE WY
19 RIVIERA DR
20 SUNRISE CIR
21 BONNIE PL
22 MONACO TER
23 CRESWELL LN
24 BRITTANY WOODS LN
25 CAMPBELL LN
26 PAIGE LN

TALBERT REGIONAL PARK (SITE)

HOAG MEM HOSP PRESB

COSTA MESA PK

HARPER PARK

NEWPORT HARBOR HS

LIDO MARINA VILLAGE

LIDO ISLE YACHT CLUB

NEWPORT HARBOR YACHT CLUB

BALBOA BAY CLUB

BAY ISLE

COLLINS ISLE

LINDA ISLE

HARBOR ISLAND

BAYSIDE CENTER

CLUB HOUSE

NEWPORT BAY

BALBOA YACHT CLUB

THE GRAND CANAL

BALBOA PAVILION

HARBOR MASTER COAST GUARD

SEE MAP 30

SEE MAP 32

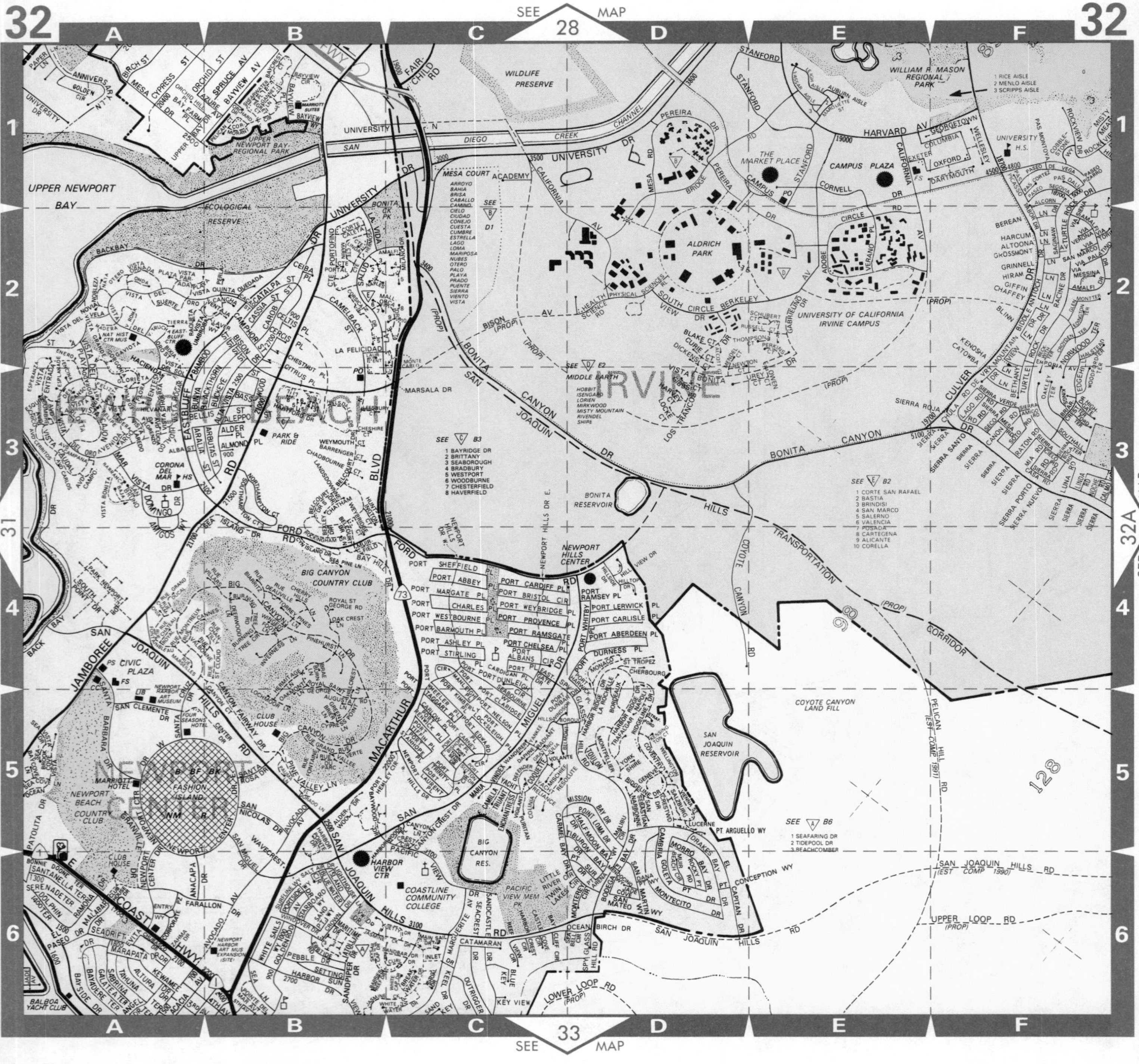

UPPER NEWPORT BAY

WILDLIFE PRESERVE

WILLIAM R. MASON REGIONAL PARK
1 RICE AISLE
2 MENLO AISLE
3 SCRIPPS AISLE

ECOLOGICAL RESERVE

NEWPORT BEACH

IRVINE

THE MARKET PLACE

CAMPUS PLAZA

ALDRICH PARK

UNIVERSITY OF CALIFORNIA IRVINE CAMPUS

MIDDLE EARTH
HOBBIT
ISENGARD
LOREN
MIRKWOOD
MISTY MOUNTAIN
RIVENDEL
SHIRE

SEE B3
1 BAYRIDGE DR
2 BRITTANY
3 SEABROUGH
4 BRADBURY
5 WESTPORT
6 WOODBURNE
7 CHESTERFIELD
8 HAVERFIELD

SEE B2
1 CORTE SAN RAFAEL
2 BASTIA
3 BRINDISI
4 SAN MARCO
5 SALERNO
6 VALENCIA
7 POSADA
8 CARTEGENA
9 ALICANTE
10 CORELLA

BONITA RESERVOIR

NEWPORT HILLS CENTER

BIG CANYON COUNTRY CLUB

ROYAL ST GEORGE RD

COYOTE CANYON LAND FILL

SAN JOAQUIN RESERVOIR

SEE B6
1 SEAFARING DR
2 TIDEPOOL DR
3 BEACHCOMBER

NEWPORT BEACH COUNTRY CLUB

FASHION ISLAND

CIVIC PLAZA

CLUB HOUSE

MARRIOTT HOTEL

BIG CANYON RES.

HARBOR VIEW CTR

COASTLINE COMMUNITY COLLEGE

PACIFIC VIEW MEM

SAN JOAQUIN HILLS RD

UPPER LOOP RD (PROP)

LOWER LOOP RD (PROP)

BALBOA YACHT CLUB

ORANGE CO.

COPYRIGHT, © 1989 BY Thomas Bros. Maps

—N—

SEE MAP 32

SEE MAP 29A

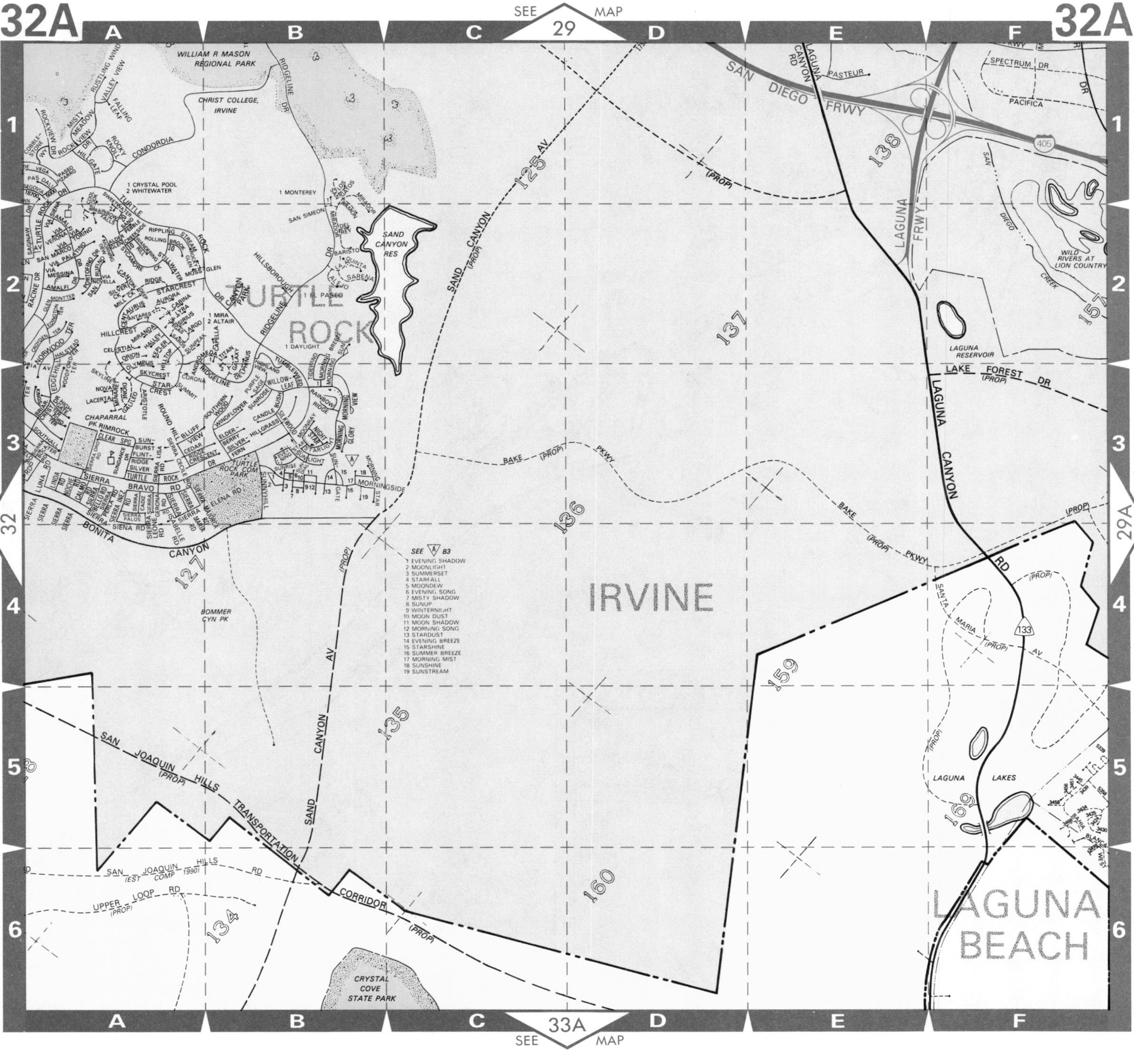

DETAIL

WILLIAM R MASON REGIONAL PARK

CHRIST COLLEGE, IRVINE

SAN DIEGO FRWY

PASTEUR

PACIFICA

SPECTRUM DR

405

LAGUNA CANYON RD

138

LAGUNA FRWY

405

WILD RIVERS AT LION COUNTRY

LAGUNA RESERVOIR

LAKE FOREST DR (PROP)

TURTLE ROCK

SAND CANYON RES

1 Monterey
1 Crystal Pool
2 Whitewater

1 Daylight

HILLCREST

CHAPARRAL

TURTLE ROCK COM PARK

BONITA

CANYON

BOMMER CYN PK

137

136

135

125 AV

SAND CANYON (PROP)

BAKE (PROP) PKWY

BAKE (PROP) PKWY

IRVINE

133

SANTA MARIA (PROP)

LAGUNA CANYON RD

159

SEE B3
1 EVENING SHADOW
2 MOONLIGHT
3 SUMMERSET
4 STARFALL
5 MOONDEW
6 EVENING SONG
7 MISTY SHADOW
8 SUNUP
9 WINTERNIGHT
10 MOON DUST
11 MOON SHADOW
12 MORNING SONG
13 STARDUST
14 EVENING BREEZE
15 STARSHINE
16 SUMMER BREEZE
17 MORNING MIST
18 SUNSHINE
19 SUNSTREAM

SAN JOAQUIN HILLS (PROP)

SAN JOAQUIN HILLS (EST COMP 1990)

UPPER LOOP RD (PROP)

134

TRANSPORTATION CORRIDOR (PROP)

SAND CANYON AV

160

LAGUNA LAKES

161

LAGUNA BEACH

CRYSTAL COVE STATE PARK

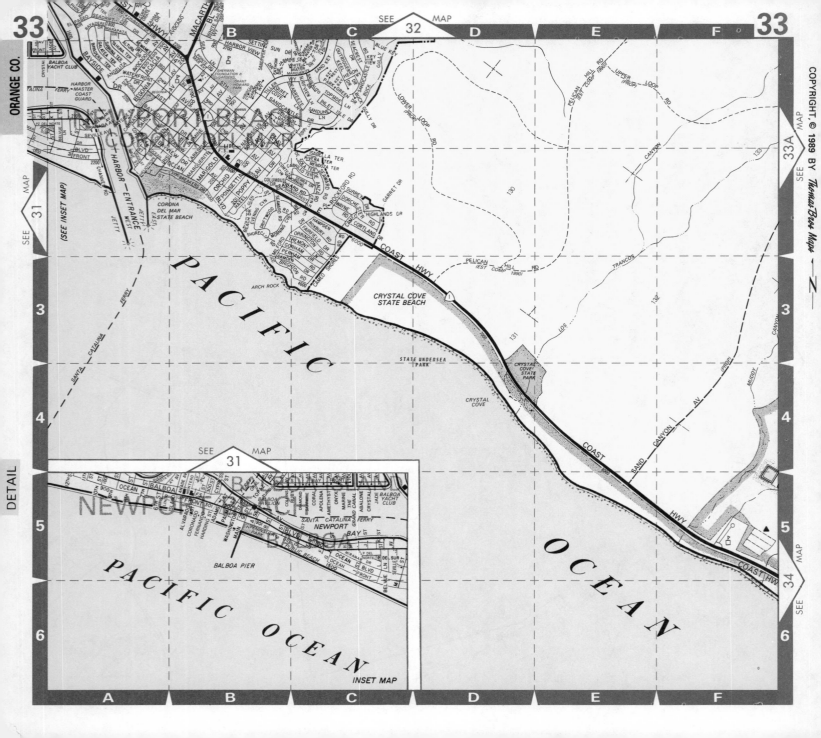

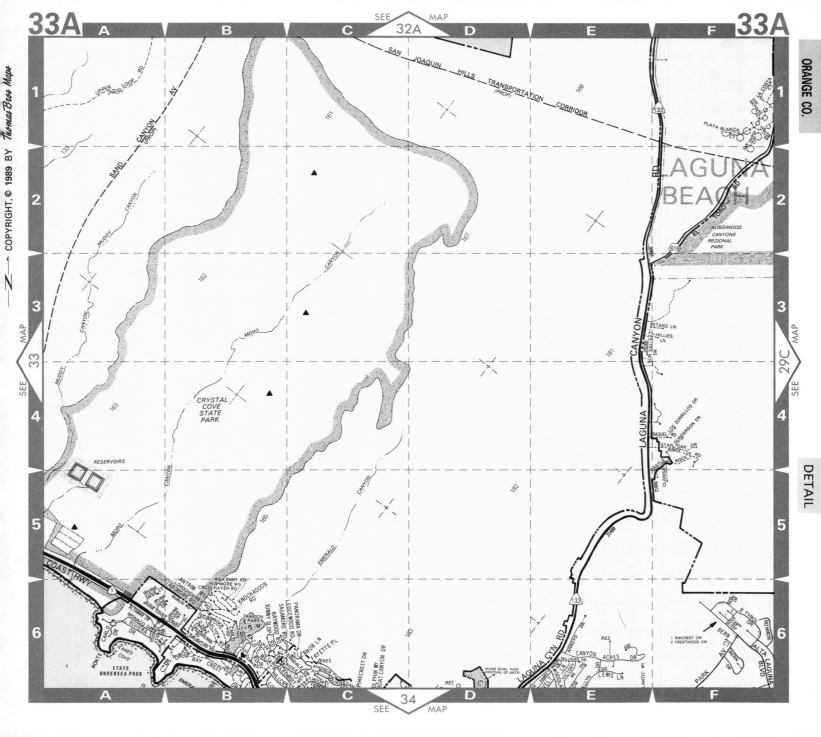

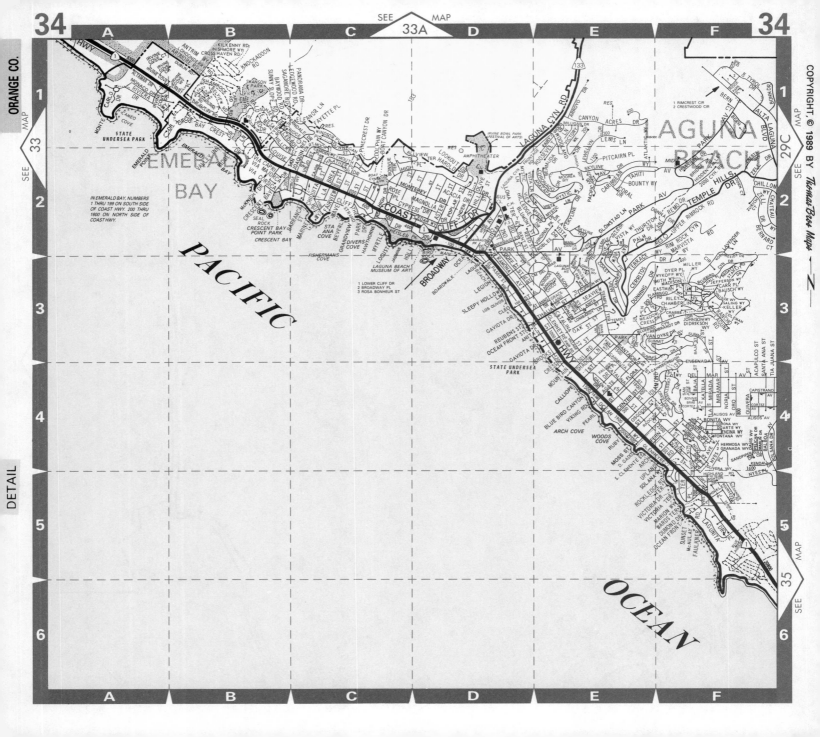

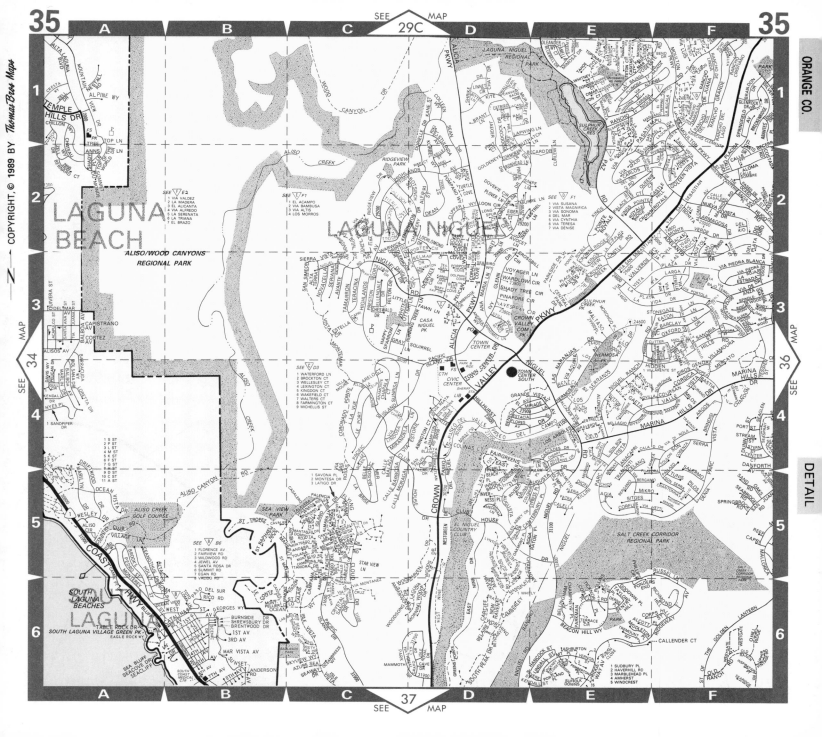

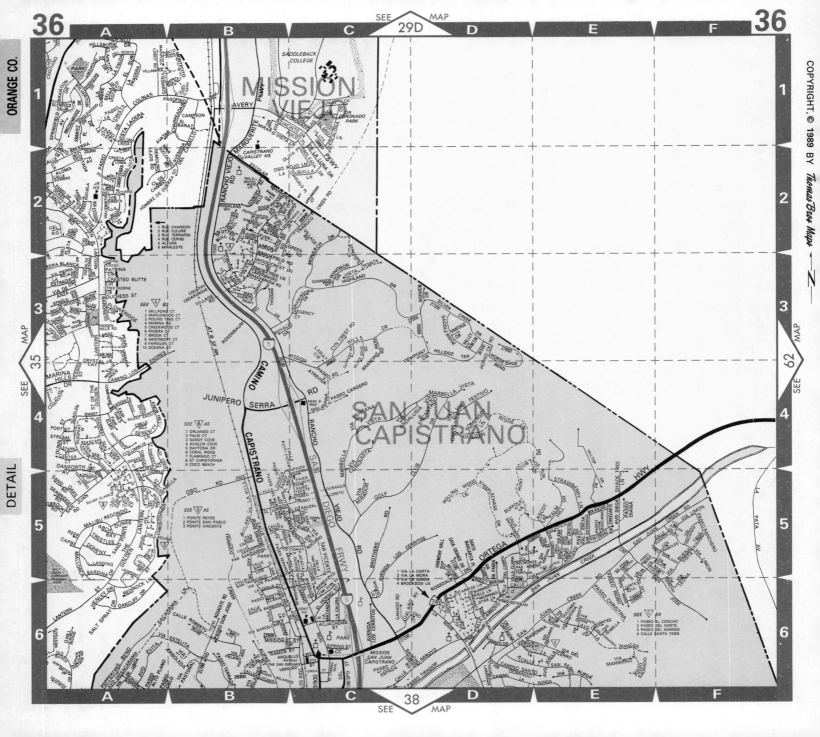

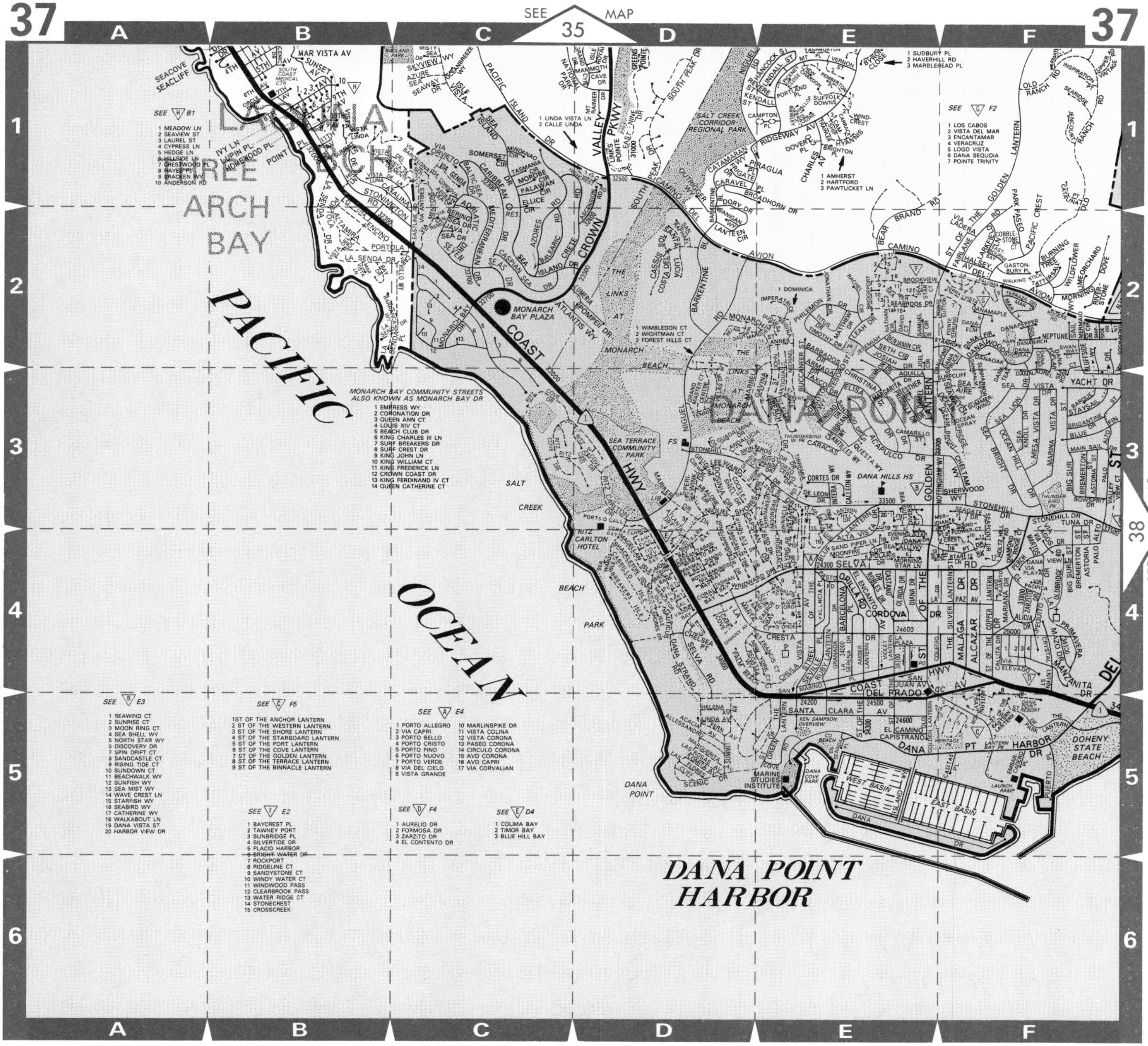

ORANGE CO.

DETAIL

N — COPYRIGHT, © 1989 BY Thomas Bros Maps

PACIFIC

OCEAN

LAGUNA BEACH

TREE ARCH BAY

DANA POINT

SEE H B1
1 MEADOW LN
2 SEAVIEW ST
3 LAUREL ST
4 CYPRESS LN
5 HEDGE LN
6 HILLSIDE LN
7 CRESTWOOD PL
8 HAYES PL
9 BRACKEN LN
10 ANDERSON RD

SEE G F2
1 LOS CABOS
2 VISTA DEL MAR
3 ENCANTAMAR
4 VERACRUZ
5 LOGO VISTA
6 DANA SEQUOIA
7 POINTE TRINITY

1 SUDBURY PL
2 HAVERHILL RD
3 MARBLEHEAD PL

1 AMHERST
2 HARTFORD
3 PAWTUCKET LN

1 LINDA VISTA LN
2 CALLE LINDA

MONARCH BAY PLAZA

1 WIMBLEDON CT
2 WIGHTMAN CT
3 FOREST HILLS CT

1 DOMINICA

MONARCH BAY COMMUNITY STREETS
ALSO KNOWN AS MONARCH BAY DR
1 EMPRESS WY
2 CORONATION DR
3 QUEEN ANN CT
4 LOUIS XIV CT
5 BEACH CLUB DR
6 KING CHARLES DR LN
7 SURF BREAKERS DR
8 SURF CREST DR
9 KING JOHN LN
10 KING WILLIAM CT
11 KING FREDERICK LN
12 CROWN COAST DR
13 KING FERDINAND IV CT
14 QUEEN CATHERINE CT

SEA TERRACE COMMUNITY PARK

SALT CREEK

BEACH PARK

RITZ CARLTON HOTEL

PORTS O CALL

DANA POINT

MARINE STUDIES INSTITUTE

DOHENY STATE BEACH

DANA POINT HARBOR

WEST BASIN

EAST BASIN

SEE B E3
1 SEAWIND CT
2 SUNRISE CT
3 MOON RING CT
4 SEA SHELL WY
5 NORTH STAR WY
6 DISCOVERY DR
7 SPIN DRIFT CT
8 SANDCASTLE CT
9 RISING TIDE CT
10 SUNDOWN CT
11 BEACHWALK WY
12 SUNFISH WY
13 SEA MIST WY
14 WAVE CREST LN
15 STARFISH WY
16 SEABIRD WY
17 CATHERINE WY
18 WALKABOUT LN
19 DANA VISTA ST
20 HARBOR VIEW DR

1ST OF THE ANCHOR LANTERN
2 ST OF THE WESTERN LANTERN
3 ST OF THE SHORE LANTERN
4 ST OF THE STARBOARD LANTERN
5 ST OF THE PORT LANTERN
6 ST OF THE COVE LANTERN
7 ST OF THE GOLDEN LANTERN
8 ST OF THE TERRACE LANTERN
9 ST OF THE BINNACLE LANTERN
SEE C F5

SEE A E4
1 PORTO ALLEGRO
2 VIA DELLA
3 PORTO BELLO
4 PORTO CRISTO
5 PORTO FINO
6 PORTO NUOVO
7 PORTO VERDE
8 VIA DEL CIELO
9 VISTA GRANDE
10 MARLINSPIKE DR
11 VISTA COLINA
12 VISTA CORONA
13 PASEO CORONA
14 CIRCULO CORONA
15 AVD CORONA
16 AVD CAPRI
17 VIA CORVALIAN

SEE D E2
1 BAYCREST PL
2 TAWNEY PORT
3 SUNBRIDGE PL
4 SILVERTIDE DR
5 BRIGHT WATER DR
6 ROCKPORT
7 RIDGELINE CT
8 SANDYSTONE CT
9 WINDY WATER CT
10 WINDWOOD PASS
11 CLEARBROOK PASS
12 WATER RIDGE CT
13 STONECREST
14 CROSSCREEK

SEE D F4
1 AURELIO DR
2 FORMOSA DR
3 ZARZITO DR
4 EL CONTENTO DR

SEE E D4
1 COLIMA BAY
2 TIMOR BAY
3 BLUE HILL BAY

A   B   C   D   E   F

ORANGE CO.

DETAIL

DPT

PACIFIC OCEAN

SAN CLEMENTE

SHORECLIFF GOLF COURSE

PRIMA DESHECHA CANADA BEACH

1 BAY DR
2 SHELL DR
3 PACIFIC DR
4 OCEAN DR
5 SURF DR
6 PALM DR
7 SEA BREEZE DR
8 EBB TIDE DR
9 BEACH DR
10 BREAKER DR
11 DOLPHIN DR
12 SANDY DR

SEE B/D4
1 CAPISTRANO LN
2 SANTA ANA LN
3 S ALAMEDA LN
4 N ALAMEDA LN
5 CORONADO LN
6 MONTEREY LN
7 POCO PASEO
8 LA RAMBLA
9 VISTA MARINA
10 CORONA LN
11 ELENA LN
12 AVD DEL MAR

AMTRAK STA
THE SAN DIEGANS

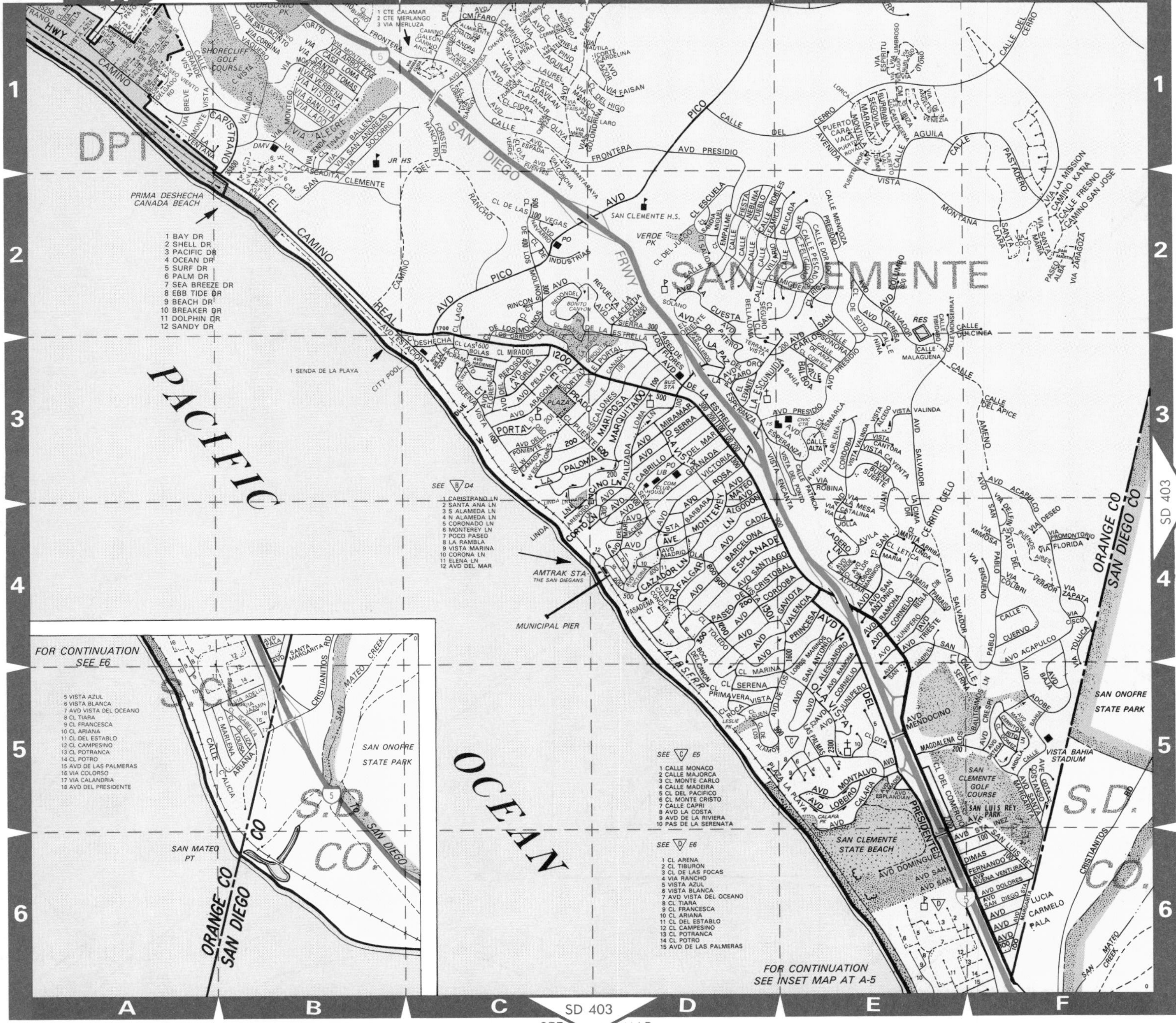

MUNICIPAL PIER

SAN DIEGO FRWY

FOR CONTINUATION SEE E6

5 VISTA AZUL
6 VISTA BLANCA
7 AVD VISTA DEL OCEANO
8 CL TIARA
9 CL FRANCESCA
10 CL ARIANA
11 CL DEL ESTABLO
12 CL CAMPESINO
13 CL POTRANCA
14 CL POTRO
15 AVD DE LAS PALMERAS
16 VIA COLORSO
17 VIA CALANDRIA
18 AVD DEL PRESIDENTE

SAN MATEO PT

SAN ONOFRE STATE PARK

ORANGE CO / SAN DIEGO CO

S.D. CO

SEE C/E5
1 CALLE MONACO
2 CALLE MAJORCA
3 CL MONTE CARLO
4 CALLE MADEIRA
5 CL DEL PACIFICO
6 CL MONTE CRISTO
7 CALLE CAPRI
8 AVD LA COSTA
9 AVD DE LA RIVIERA
10 PAS DE LA SERENATA

SEE D/E6
1 CL ARENA
2 CL TIBURON
3 CL DE LAS FOCAS
4 VIA RANCHO
5 VISTA AZUL
6 VISTA BLANCA
7 AVD VISTA DEL OCEANO
8 CL TIARA
9 CL FRANCESCA
10 CL ARIANA
11 CL DEL ESTABLO
12 CL CAMPESINO
13 CL POTRANCA
14 CL POTRO
15 AVD DE LAS PALMERAS

SAN ONOFRE STATE PARK

VISTA BAHIA STADIUM

SAN CLEMENTE GOLF COURSE

SAN LUIS REY PARK

SAN CLEMENTE STATE BEACH

PRESIDENTE

FOR CONTINUATION SEE INSET MAP AT A-5

A   B   C   D   E   F

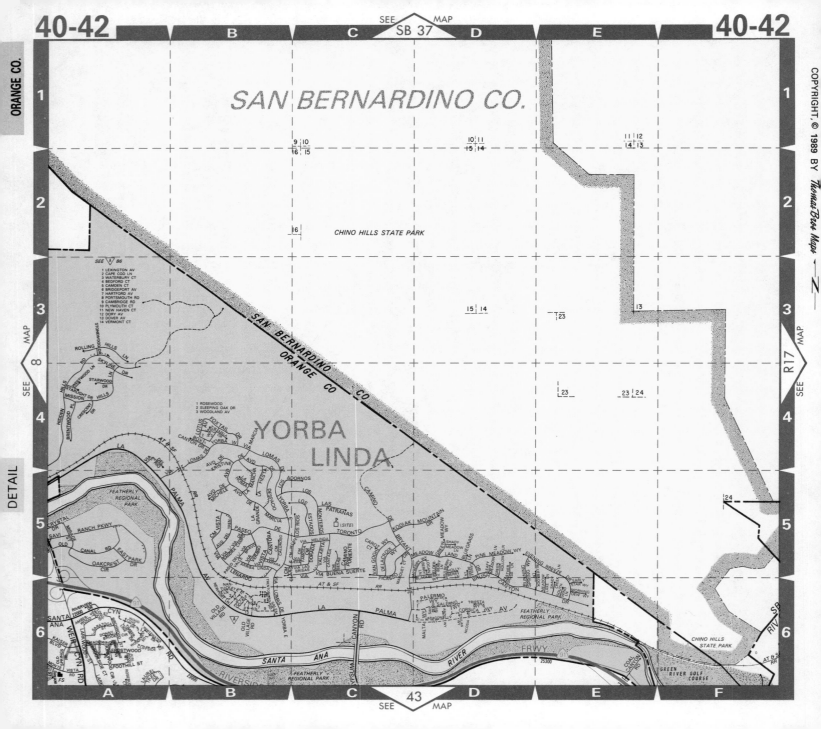

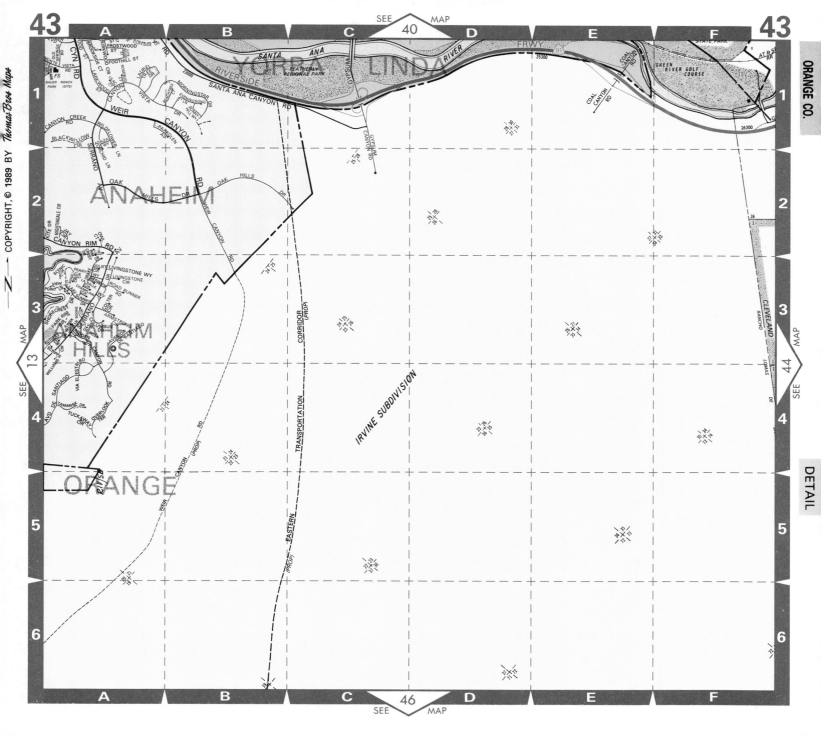

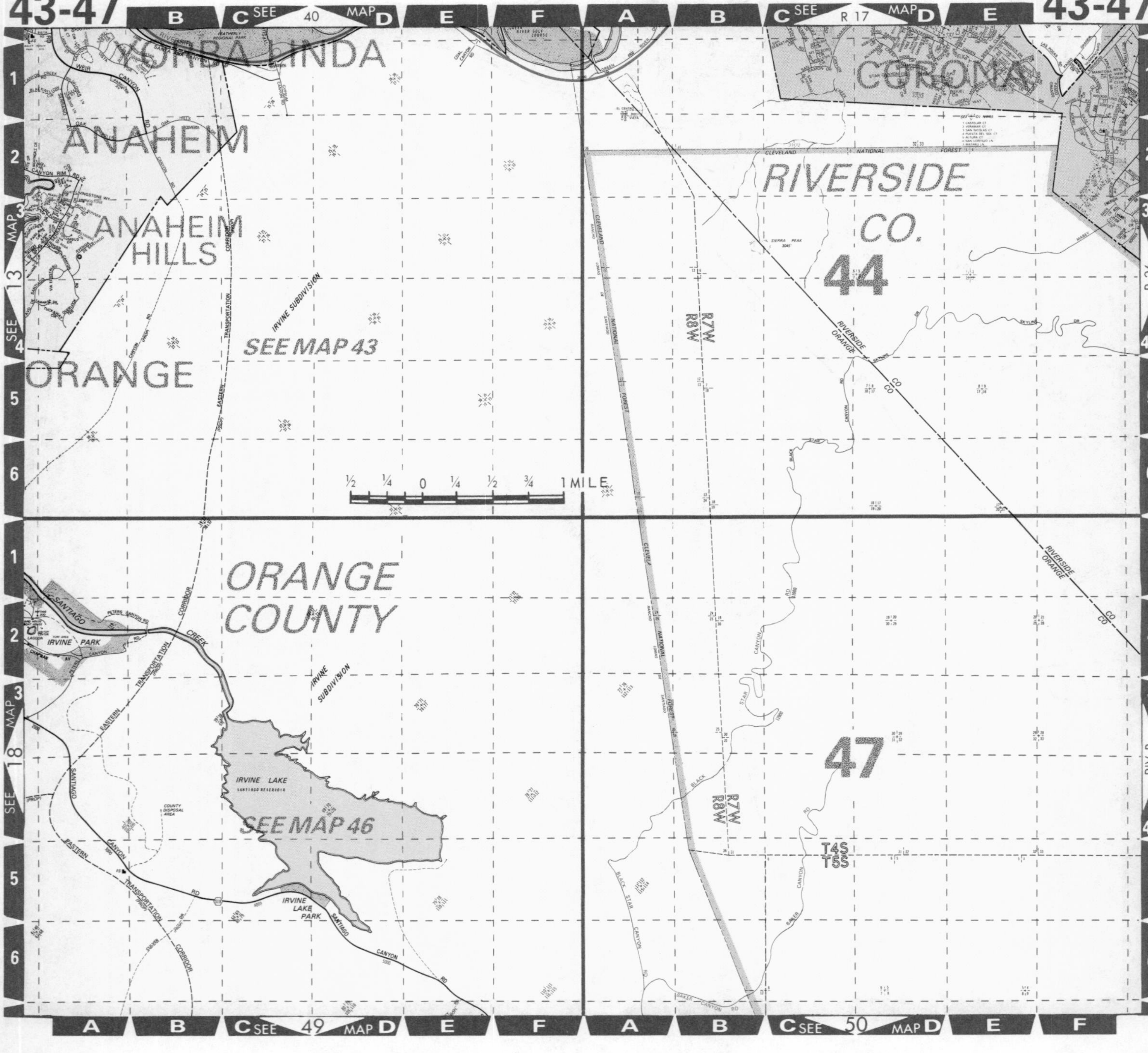

ORANGE CO.

DETAIL

SEE MAP 40

SEE R 17 MAP

YORBA LINDA

ANAHEIM

ANAHEIM HILLS

ORANGE

SEE MAP 43

IRVINE SUBDIVISION

SANTA ANA RIVER GOLF COURSE

CORONA

RIVERSIDE CO.

44

CLEVELAND NATIONAL FOREST

SIERRA PEAK 3045

R7W
R8W

RIVERSIDE
ORANGE
CO
CO

SEE R 26 MAP

½ ¼ 0 ¼ ½ ¾ 1 MILE

ORANGE COUNTY

SANTIAGO

IRVINE PARK

CREEK

IRVINE SUBDIVISION

IRVINE LAKE
SANTIAGO RESERVOIR

COUNTY DISPOSAL AREA

SEE MAP 46

IRVINE LAKE PARK

SANTIAGO CANYON RD

TRANSPORTATION

EASTERN

CORRIDOR

CLEVELAND NATIONAL FOREST

BLACK STAR CANYON

47

R7W
R8W

T4S
T5S

RIVERSIDE
ORANGE
CO
CO

BLACK STAR CANYON RD

SILVERADO CANYON

SEE 18 MAP

SEE RIV B MAP

SEE 49 MAP

SEE 50 MAP

A B C D E F A B C D E F

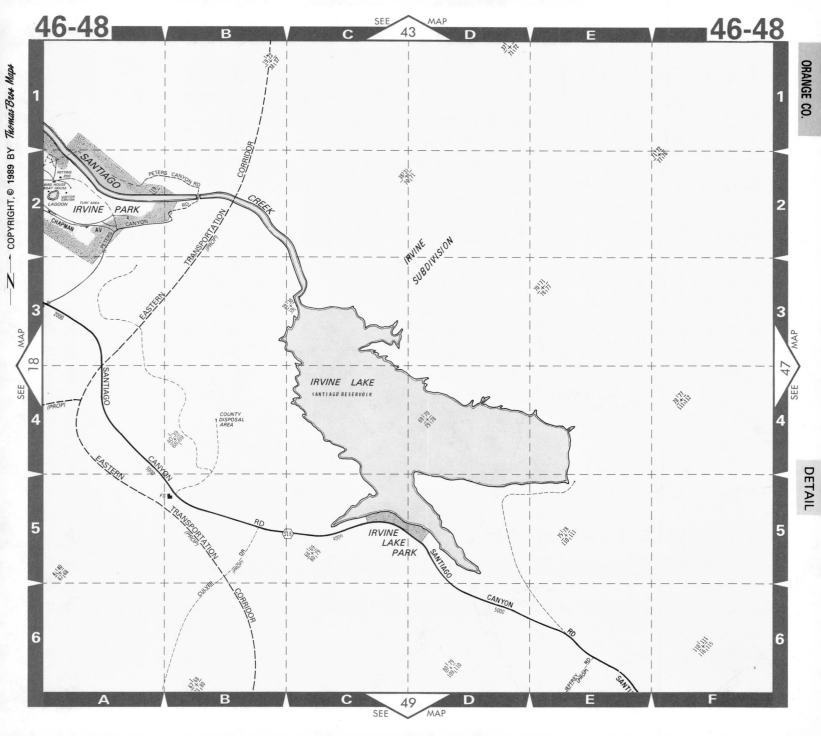

ORANGE CO.

DETAIL

SEE MAP 43

SANTIAGO

PETERS CANYON RD

IRVINE PARK

PETTING ZOO

BIRD HOUSE
BOAT HOUSE

VISITOR CENTER

TURF AREA

LAGOON

CHAPMAN

AV

CANYON

PETERS

RD

TRANSPORTATION

EASTERN

(PROP)

CORRIDOR

CREEK

IRVINE
SUBDIVISION

IRVINE LAKE
SANTIAGO RESERVOIR

SANTIAGO

2000

(PROP)

CANYON

3000

FS

COUNTY
DISPOSAL
AREA

EASTERN

TRANSPORTATION

(PROP)

CULVER (PROP) DR

RD

S18

4000

IRVINE
LAKE
PARK

SANTIAGO

CANYON

5000

RD

CORRIDOR

JEFFREY RD (PROP)

SANTI

SEE MAP 18

SEE MAP 47

SEE MAP 49

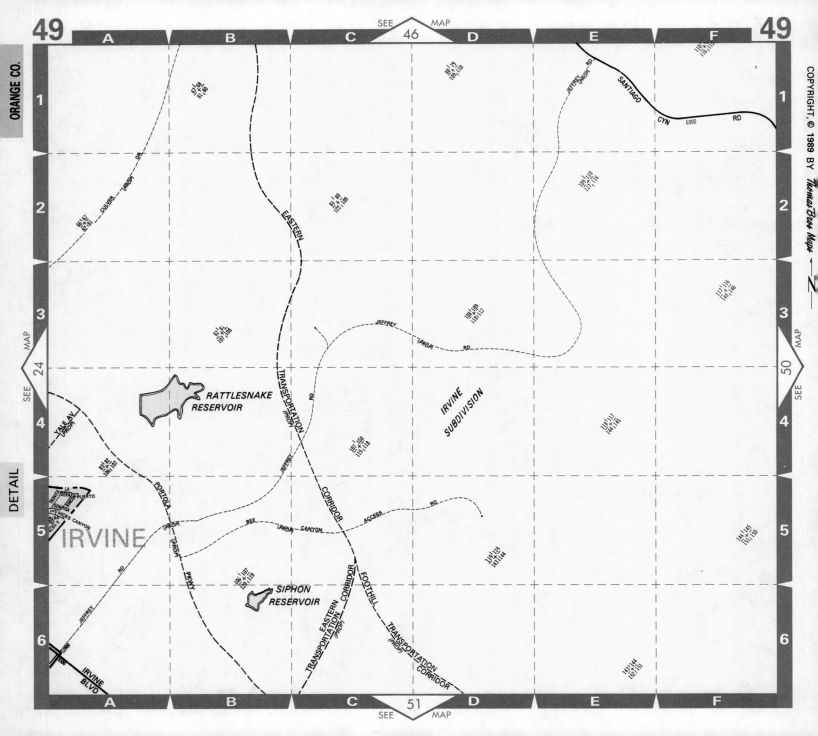

ORANGE CO.

DETAIL

SEE MAP 46

A   B   C   D   E   F

1

2

3

4

5

6

SEE MAP 24

SEE MAP 50

SEE MAP 51

CULVER DR (PROP)

EASTERN

TRANSPORTATION (PROP)

RATTLESNAKE RESERVOIR

JEFFREY (PROP) RD

IRVINE SUBDIVISION

SANTIAGO CYN 6000 RD

JEFFREY (PROP) RD

CORRIDOR

IRVINE

YALE AV (PROP)

PORTOLA (PROP) PKWY

JEFFREY (PROP)

LA DERNIE PUERTO
SONRISA
HICKS CANYON

BEE (PROP) CANYON ACCESS RD

SIPHON RESERVOIR

EASTERN TRANSPORTATION (PROP) CORRIDOR

FOOTHILL TRANSPORTATION (PROP) CORRIDOR

JEFFREY RD

IRVINE BLVD

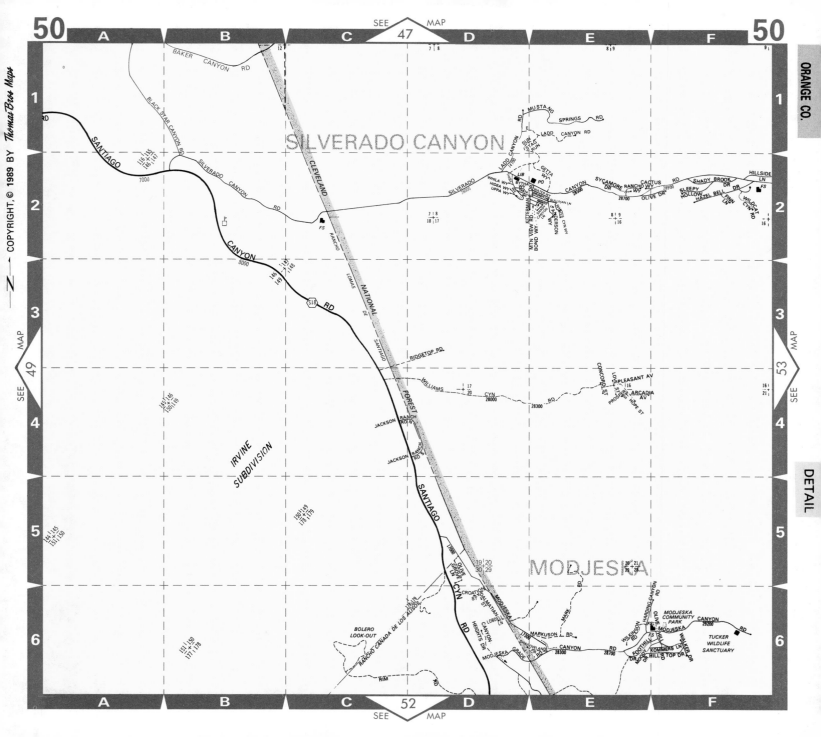

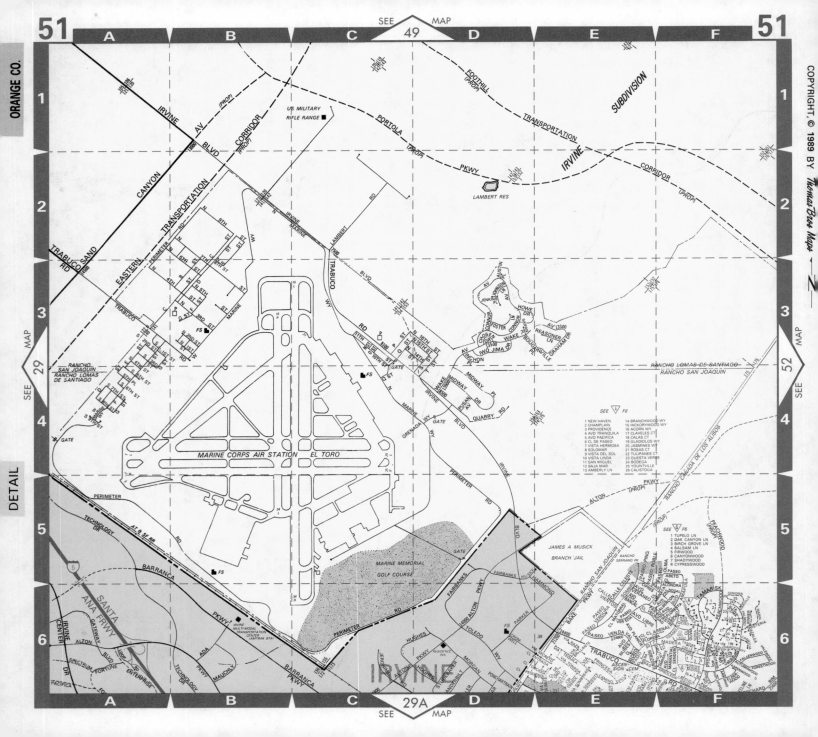

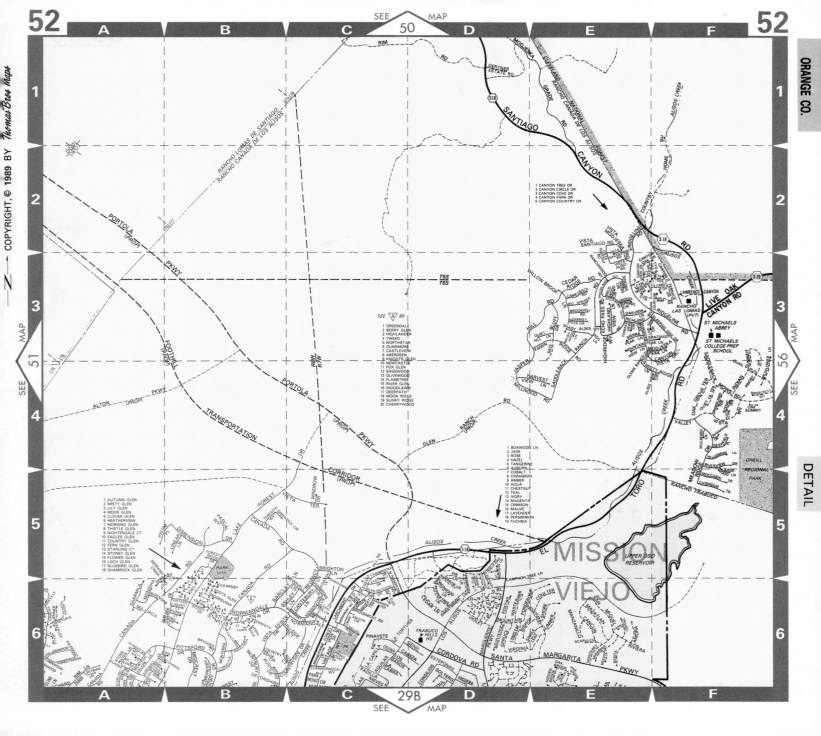

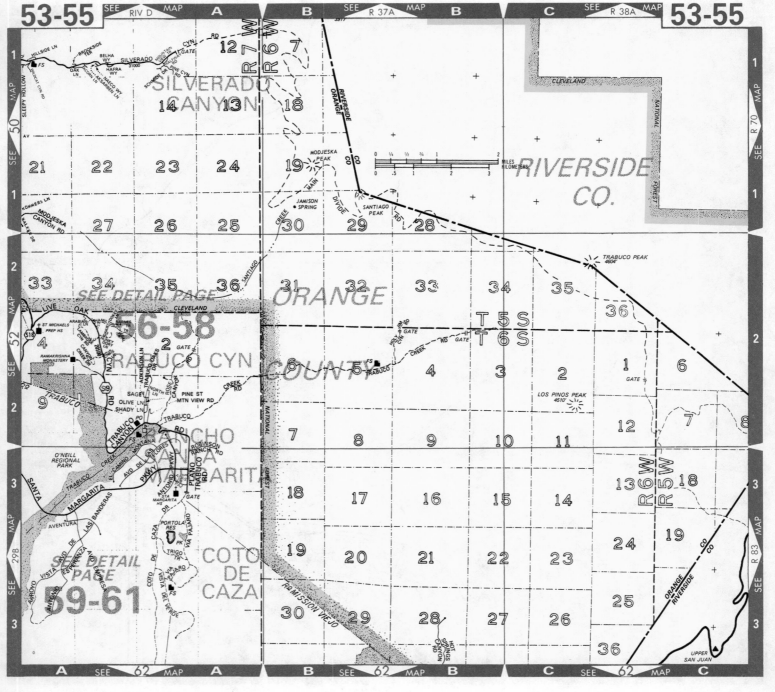

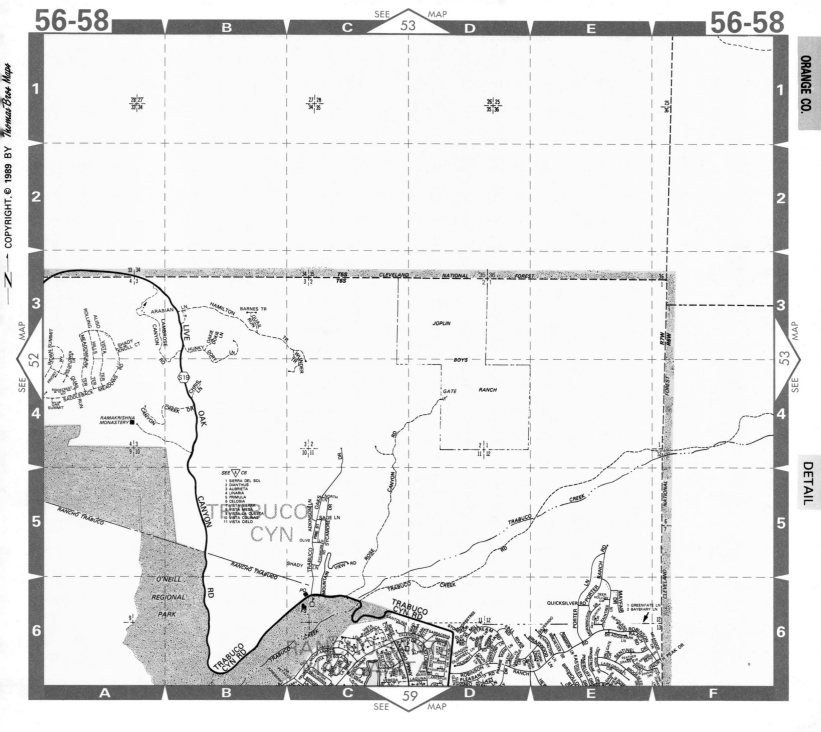

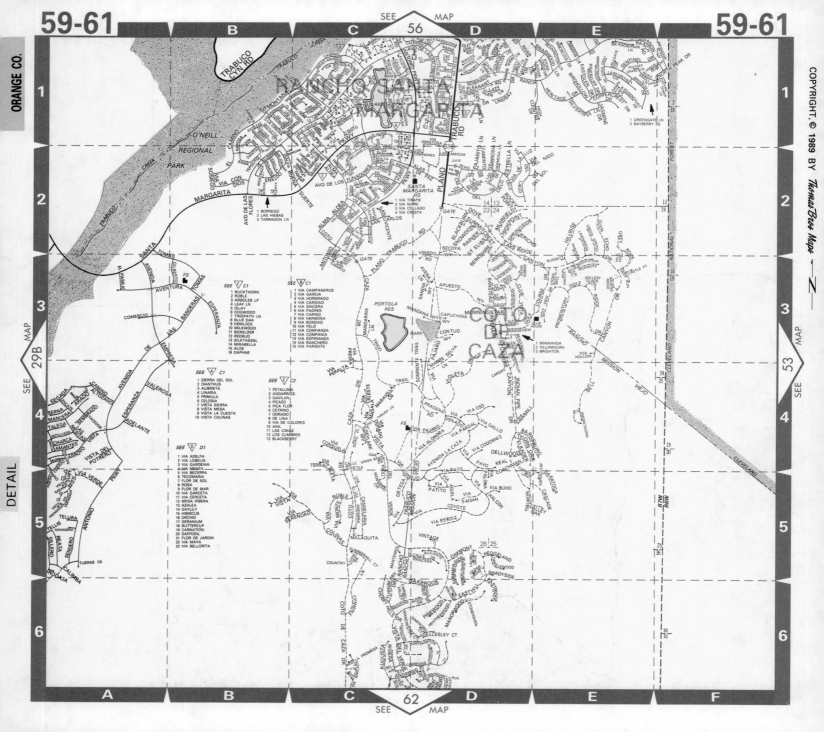

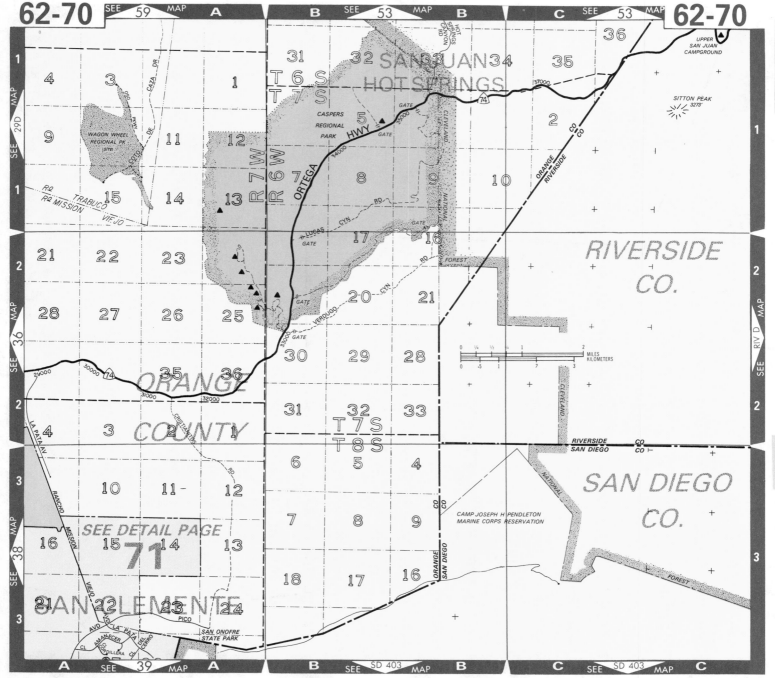

ORANGE CO.

DETAIL

SEE 59 MAP A
SEE 53 MAP B
SEE 53 MAP C

UPPER SAN JUAN CAMPGROUND

4   3   1
31   32   SAN 33 JUAN 34   35   36

T 6 S
T 7 S   HOT SPRINGS

SITTON PEAK 3273'

9   WAGON WHEEL REGIONAL PK (SITE)   11   12   CASPERS REGIONAL PARK   5   2   1

R 7 W   R 6 W   ORTEGA   HWY   GATE

15   14   13   7   8   9   10

TRABUCO   MISSION VIEJO

LUCAS GATE   CYN   RD   GATE

21   22   23   17   17   16

ORANGE   RIVERSIDE   CO   CO   CLEVELAND   NATIONAL

RIVERSIDE CO.

28   27   26   25   20   CYN   21

VERDUGO   GATE

30   29   28

0 ¼ ½ ¾ 1   2   MILES
0 .5 1   2   3   KILOMETERS

35   36   31   32   33

ORANGE

74

COUNTY

T 7 S
T 8 S

RIVERSIDE   CO
SAN DIEGO   CO

SAN DIEGO CO.

4   3   1   6   5   4

LA PATA AV   CRISTIANITOS   RD

10   11   12   7   8   9

CAMP JOSEPH H PENDLETON MARINE CORPS RESERVATION

SEE DETAIL PAGE 71

16   15   14   13   18   17   16

ORANGE   SAN DIEGO   CO   CO

CLEVELAND   NATIONAL   FOREST

SAN CLEMENTE
21   22   23   24

AVD LA PATA   PICO

SAN ONOFRE STATE PARK

SEE 39 MAP A
SEE SD 403 MAP B
SEE SD 403 MAP C

1

SAN JUAN CAPISTRANO

CRISTIANITOS RD

$\frac{2|1}{11|12}$

$\frac{1}{12}$

R7W | R6W

2

$\frac{6}{7}$

$\frac{11|12}{14|13}$

$\frac{12}{13}$

SEE MAP 38

3

SEE MAP 62

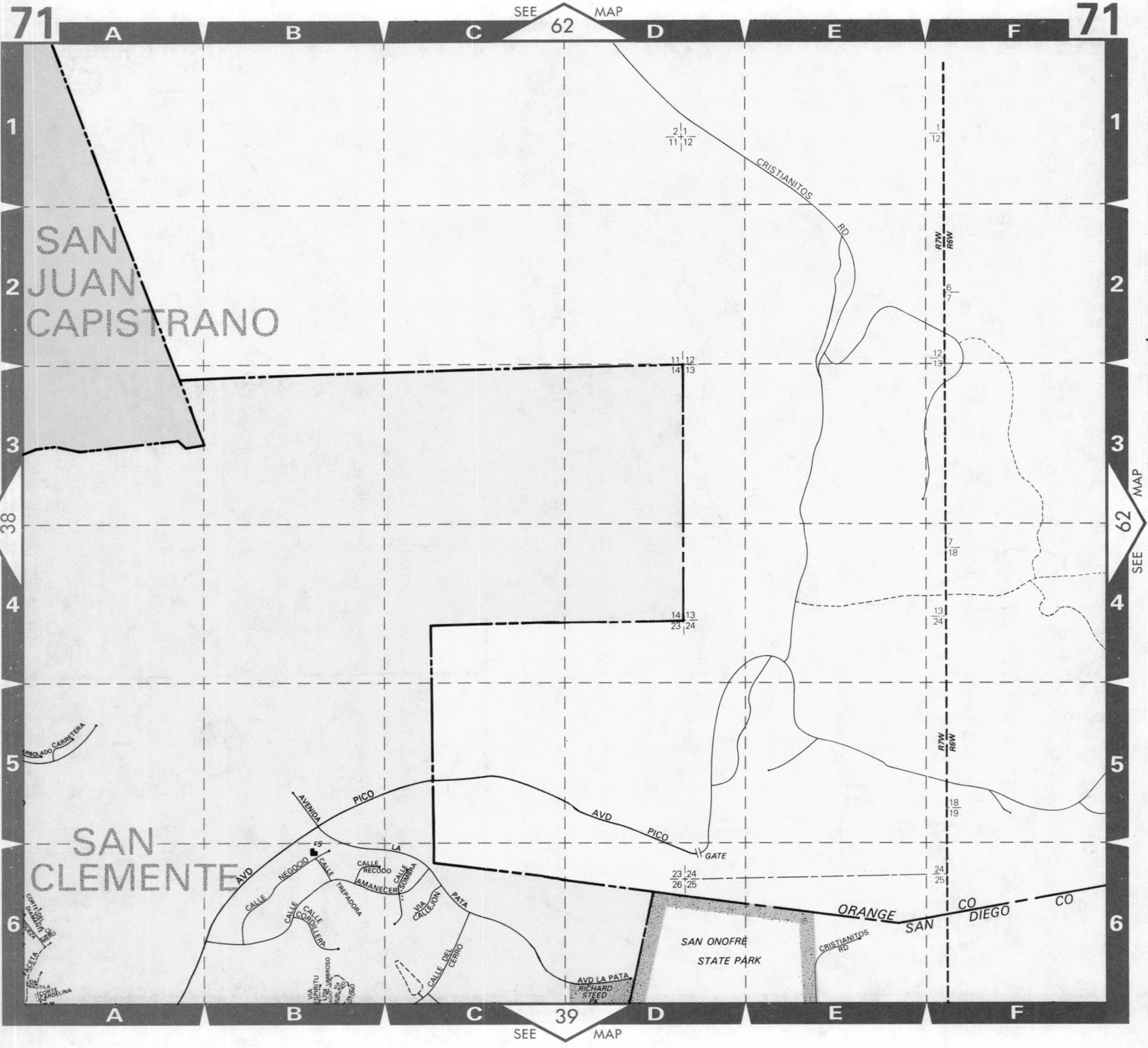

$\frac{7}{18}$

4

$\frac{14|13}{23|24}$

$\frac{13}{24}$

ARBOLADO CARRETERA

5

PICO
AVENIDA

AVD PICO

R7W | R6W

$\frac{18}{19}$

SAN CLEMENTE

AVD
CALLE NEGOCIO
CALLE
CALLE TREPADORA
CALLE RECODO
AMANECER
CALLE SOMBRA
VIA CALLEJON
PATA

GATE

$\frac{23|24}{26|25}$

$\frac{24}{25}$

ORANGE SAN CO DIEGO CO

6

COMPLEJO DEL PLANTA PRIMO
ACETA
VIA ESPIRITU
VIA LUMINOSO
CALLE CORDILLERA
CALLE DEL CERRO

AVD LA PATA
RICHARD STEED

SAN ONOFRE STATE PARK

CRISTIANITOS RD

ORANGE CO.

FRWY ACCESS

ORANGE COUNTY FREEWAY ACCESS MAP

□ ON RAMP   ■ OFF RAMP   ▣ BOTH ON & OFF RAMP

THINK OF THE SYMBOLS AS A LIGHTBULB, WHITE IS ON AND BLACK IS OFF.
USE THE SYMBOLS ON THE RIGHT-HAND SIDE OF THE FREEWAY IN THE DIRECTION YOU ARE TRAVELING

FREEWAY INTERCHANGE

THE RECTANGULAR EXTENSIONS AT THE END OF THE FREEWAY SHOW THE DIRECTIONS IN WHICH YOU MAY TRAVEL.

4.5 ITALICIZED NUMBERS ALONG THE FREEWAY INDICATE THE DISTANCE (IN MILES) BETWEEN FREEWAY INTERCHANGES.

(12) THE NUMBER IN PARENTHESES FOLLOWING EACH STREET NAME REFERS TO THE ATLAS PAGE ON WHICH IT APPEARS.

PACIFIC

5	SANTA ANA FRWY / SAN DIEGO FRWY
22	GARDEN GROVE FRWY
55	COSTA MESA FRWY
57	ORANGE FRWY
73	CORONA DEL MAR FRWY
90	IMPERIAL HWY
91	RIVERSIDE FRWY / ARTESIA FRWY
605	SAN GABRIEL RIVER FRWY
405	SAN DIEGO FRWY
133	LAGUNA FRWY

73
A ST
1990 ORANGE COUNTY STREET INDEX
ALLTHORN DR
ORANGE CO.

A

STREET	CITY	P.O. ZONE	BLOCK	PAGE	GRID
A ST	HTB	HB47	16800	21	C5
A ST	HTB	HB		26	C6
A ST	LAG	LB77		35	A4
A ST	NB	NB	100	33	B5
A ST N	TUS	TUS	100	23	E2
A ST S	TUS	TUS	100	23	E2
ABADEJO	MVJO	SJ92		29B	D6
ABAJO CIR	FTNV	SA08	16000	22	D4
ABALONE AV	NB	NB	100	31	F6
ABALONE AV	NB	NB	100	33	C5
ABALONE DR	DPT	LB77		37	D3
ABALONE DR	NB	NB	300	31	F6
ABALONE LN	HTB	HB		20	E6
ABALONE PL	NB	NB	1100	31	F6
ABANICO	MVJO	SJ91	27400	29B	D2
ABANITA WY	CO	LB77		35	C6
ABANTES PL	CO	LB77	38600	36	A1
ABARAN WY	BPK	BP		5	C3
ABBEY DR	WSTM	WSTM	5700	14	F5
ABBEY LN	CO	LB		29C	E4
ABBEY LN	OR	OR		12	F4
ABBEY LN	YL	YL		7	E3
ABBEYWOOD LN	CO	LB		29C	D4
ABBIE WY	CM	CM27	400	31	D3
ABBOT DR	HTB	HB47	6500	21	A5
ABBOTSWOOD CIR	IRV	SA	4500	29	D2
ABBOTT CT	GGR	GG	12900	15	E4
ABBOTT LN	VPK	OR67	18200	13	A6
ABBOTT ST	GGR	GG	12700	15	E4
ABEDUL	MVJO	SJ91	21600	29B	D1
ABERDEEN	CO	ET		52	C4
ABERDEEN	IRV	SA		29	E1
ABERDEEN	MVJO	SJ91		29D	C5
ABERDEEN DR	HTB	HB	9800	26	F4
ABERDEEN DR	PLA	PLA	600	7	C4
ABERDEEN LN	GGR	GG	11400	15	D2
ABERDEEN LN	VPK	OR67	17900	17	F1
ABERDEEN ST	ANA	AN		13	A3
ABERDENE MTN	FTNV	SA08		22	D5
ABETO	IRV	SA		24	E5
ABETO	MVJO	SJ91		29B	C3
A BETTER WY	GGR	GG	13700	16	C6
ABILENE CT	CO	LB53		29C	F5
ABINGTON CIR	WSTM	WSTM	14500	22	A2
ABINGTON CT	CO	LB	30000	35	D4
ABLE LN	HTB	HB	14500	20	F2
ABOTSINCH ST	CO	LB		35	D2
ABRAHAM AV	CYP	CYP	4800	9	D6
ABRAHAM AV	WSTM	WSTM	5500	14	E6
ABRAHAM AV	WSTM	WSTM	6200	15	A6
ABRAZO	MVJO	SJ91		29B	C2
ABRAZO AISLE	IRV	SA14		28	F3
ACACIA	IRV	SA		29	D3
ACACIA AV	ANA	AN	800	11	E2
ACACIA AV	DPT	DPT		37	D5
ACACIA AV	FUL	FL	800	11	E1
ACACIA AV	GGR	GG45	5300	14	E4
ACACIA AV	GGR	GG	6300	15	C4
ACACIA AV	GGR	GG	10500	16	A4
ACACIA AV	NB	NB	700	32	A6
ACACIA AV	NB	NB	400	33	A1
ACACIA AV	OR	OR	1000	17	B3
ACACIA AV	STN	GG41	8000	15	C4
ACACIA AV E	HTB	HB	100	26	B5
ACACIA AV N	FUL	FL	100	6	E6
ACACIA AV S	FUL	FL	100	6	E6
ACACIA AV W	HTB	HB	100	26	B5
ACACIA CT	CO	SJ91		29A	F5
ACACIA DR	CYP	CYP	8500	9	C4
ACACIA DR	LAG	LB51	100	34	D2
ACACIA DR	PLA	PLA	700	7	C4
ACACIA DR	TUS	TUS	14200	23	F1
ACACIA LN	CO	LB		29C	E1
ACACIA LN	YL	YL		8	C5
ACACIA PKWY	GGR	GG40	10700	16	A4
ACACIA PL	SA	SA	2600	17	A5
ACACIA ST	BREA	BREA	100	6	E1
ACACIA ST	CO	SA07	20000	28	A6
ACACIA ST	CYP	CYP	8000	9	C3
ACACIA ST	FTNV	SA08	18900	26	E3
ACACIA ST	IRV	SA	3800	29	C1
ACACIA ST	LAH	LAH	300	2	A5
ACACIA HILL DR	YL	YL		8	C5
ACACIA TREE LN	IRV	SA		29	A6
ACADEMY	IRV	SA17		32	C1
ACADEMY AV	ANA	AN	2800	10	C4
ACADEMY DR	BPK	BP	8700	10	D1
ACAMA ST	ANA	AN	2100	16	D2

STREET	CITY	P.O. ZONE	BLOCK	PAGE	GRID
ACANTILADO	SCL	SC72		38	F5
ACAPULCO	MVJO	SJ92		52	E6
ACAPULCO AV	SA	SA	4400	22	B3
ACAPULCO CIR	HTB	HB	8500	26	D3
ACAPULCO DR	DPT	DPT	33300	37	E3
ACAPULCO ST	LAG	LB51	800	34	F4
ACAPULCO ST	LAG	LB51	800	35	A3
ACASO	CO	LB56		29C	E3
ACE LN	HTB	HB	16400	20	E5
ACEBO LN	SCL	SC72	300	39	D4
ACECA DR	CO	LALM	2800	14	A3
ACERO	MVJO	SJ91		29B	A4
ACHILLES CIR	LAP	BP23	5300	9	E2
ACJACHEMA ST	SJC	SJ75	26700	36	C6
ACKLAY CIR	FTNV	SA08		26	F1
ACME PL	ANA	AN	3100	10	C6
ACONITE AV	FTNV	SA08	11200	22	B4
ACORN	CO	LB56		29C	C2
ACORN	IRV	SA		29	C3
ACORN CIR	BREA	BREA		3	A6
ACORN CT	YL	YL		7	F2
ACORN LN	CO	SIL		53	A1
ACORN ST	GGR	GG	11600	16	B3
ACORN WY	CO	ET		51	F4
ACRE PL	CO	OR	20200	13	D6
ACROPOLIS DR	CO	SJ91		29B	A6
ACROPOLIS DR	CO	SJ91		29D	A1
ADA	IRV	SA18		29A	B1
ADA	IRV	SA18		51	B6
ADAGIO	IRV	SA14		29	A3
ADAH ST	GGR	GG	8500	15	D2
ADAIR PL	ANA	AN	1100	11	F2
ADAMO	CO	LB		29A	A4
ADAMS	IRV	SA		24	D6
ADAMS AV	CM	CM	1400	27	D4
ADAMS AV	HTB	HB	9000	26	E4
ADAMS AV	HTB	HB46	10000	27	B4
ADAMS AV E	HTB	HB	10000	26	E4
ADAMS AV E	OR	OR	100	17	E1
ADAMS AV N	FUL	FL	300	6	B5
ADAMS AV S	FUL	FL	500	6	B6
ADAMS AV S	FUL	FL	1100	11	B1
ADAMS AV W	HTB	HB	100	26	E4
ADAMS CIR	VPK	OR67	10600	18	A1
ADAMS CT	FTNV	SA08	15900	22	D6
ADAMS ST	ANA	AN	300	11	B4
ADAMS ST	CO	MDWY	14600	21	C2
ADAMS ST	GGR	GG45	12500	14	E4
ADAMS ST	NB	NB	100	33	B5
ADAMS ST	PLA	PLA		7	E5
ADAMS ST E	SA	SA	100	23	C6
ADAMS ST W	SA	SA	1400	22	F6
ADAMS WY	BPK	BP	7800	10	C3
ADAMS RANCH RD	VPK	OR67	18300	18	A1
ADDEN CIR	GGR	GG	13200	16	E2
ADDINGTON CIR	ANA	AN	100	12	E2
ADDINGTON DR	ANA	AN	3900	12	E2
ADDISON RD	CO	SA	11200	18	C5
ADDY AV	PLA	PLA	600	7	B2
ADELANTE	CO	SJ88		59	A4
ADELANTE	IRV	SA14		28	D5
ADELANTO DR	BPK	BP	7500	5	B4
ADELANTO DR	CO	LB	25000	35	F2
ADELE ST	OR	OR	700	17	F2
ADELE ST E&W	ANA	AN	100	11	D3
ADELIA CIR	HTB	HB	9000	30	E1
ADELINE AV	GGR	GG	9500	15	E3
ADELITA	MVJO	SJ91		29B	C3
ADELLE ST	GGR	GG	12200	15	D4
ADKINSON LN	CO	SJ	20300	56	C5
ADLAND ST	GGR	GG	13000	16	A5
ADLENA DR N	FUL	FL33	200	5	F5
ADLENA DR N	FUL	FL	900	6	A4
ADLENA PL	FUL	FL33	1800	5	F4
ADMIRAL	IRV	SA		29	D1
ADMIRAL LN	ANA	AN	1800	11	A2
ADMIRAL LN	HTB	HB		30	C1
ADMIRAL WY	CM	CM		27	E6
ADMIRAL WY	DPT	DPT	25700	38	A3
ADMIRALTY CT	SJC	SJ75		38	A2
ADMIRALTY DR	HTB	HB	3100	20	A5
ADOBE LN	MVJO	SJ91	24500	29B	B6
ADOBE CIRCLE RD	IRV	SA		32	E2
ADOBE RIVER AV	FTNV	SA08	10000	27	A2
ADONIS ST	CO	SJ91	25400	29A	F5
ADORE CIR	CYP	CYP	10000	9	E6
ADRIA PL	ANA	AN	400	11	B5
ADRIA ST	ANA	AN	600	11	B5
ADRIAN CIR	GGR	GG43		16	E4
ADRIAN CIR	HTB	HB	20300	26	E5
ADRIAN ST	GGR	GG	11800	16	E3

STREET	CITY	P.O. ZONE	BLOCK	PAGE	GRID
ADRIANA ST	CO	SJ91	24100	29A	F5
ADRIANA ST	CO	SJ91	25400	29B	A5
ADRIATIC DR	DPT	LB77	32400	37	C2
ADRIN WY	SA	SA	1700	22	E3
AEGEA ST	CO	SJ91	25300	29A	F5
AEGEAN	IRV	SA14		28	D5
AEGEAN SEA DR	DPT	LB77	22900	37	C1
AERO DR	GGR	GG	12100	15	D3
AETNA ST	ANA	AN	1200	10	E2
AFLORAMIENTO	SCL	SC72		38	E4
AFTON CIR	HTB	HB	8500	26	D5
AFTON LN	CO	SA	12200	24	B1
AGATE	IRV	SA		29	A4
AGATE AV	NB	NB	100	31	E6
AGATE CIR	CYP	CYP	4200	9	C3
AGATE CIR	HTB	HB	16900	20	E5
AGATE PL	ANA	AN	100	10	F5
AGATE PL	ANA	AN	100	11	A5
AGATE ST	ANA	AN	200	10	F6
AGATE ST	ANA	AN	200	11	A6
AGATE ST	LAG	LB51	100	34	E4
AGATE ST	OR	OR	1900	12	E5
AGATE CANYON DR	CO	LB56		29C	E6
AGEAN LN	HTB	HB	21300	30	F4
AGIA	CO	LB77		35	E5
AGNES AV	ANA	AN		13	C1
AGNES STNLEY ST	GGR	GG	12600	15	D4
AGOSTINO	IRV	SA14		28	F4
AGRADO	MVJO	SJ92	27500	29B	D6
AGRADO	MVJO	SJ92	27500	29D	D1
AGUA DR	HTB	HB		26	B4
AGUA PL	SB	SB	600	19	F2
AGUACATE RD	SJC	SJ75	31500	36	B6
AGUACATE RD	SJC	SJ75	31400	38	B1
AGUILAR	MVJO	SJ91	21300	29B	C1
AGUILAR	MVJO	SJ91	21300	52	C6
AGUILLAR	IRV	SA14		29	A4
AGUIRRE	MVJO	SJ92	24500	29B	E6
AGUIRRE LN	PLA	PLA		7	A5
AHSANTE DR	HTB	HB	500	26	C4
AIDA LN	ANA	AN	3300	10	B5
AINSWORTH LN	LAP	BP23	8000	9	C3
AIRPARK DR	FUL	FL33	300	5	E5
AIRPORT DR	HTB	HB		26	B2
AIRPORT WY N	CO	SA07		28	C4
AIRPORT WY S	CO	SA07		28	B5
AIRPORTER WY	CO	LB56		29C	E5
AIRPORT LOOP DR	CM	CM26	3100	28	B3
AIRWAY AV	CM	SA07	2900	28	A5
AKINS	IRV	SA14		29	A2
AKSARBEN LN	CO	SIL	30300	53	A1
ALABAMA CIR	CM	CM		27	B2
ALABAMA ST	HTB	HB	19200	26	C5
ALABAMA ST N	HTB	HB	100	26	C5
ALABASTER	IRV	SA		29	A4
ALADDIN DR	ANA	AN	100	10	F4
ALADDIN DR	HTB	HB	4000	20	C6
ALADDIN ST	ANA	AN	300	10	F4
ALAMANDA	MVJO	SJ91		29D	B2
ALAMBRE	MVJO	SJ91		29B	A4
ALAMEDA	IRV	SA		24	E5
ALAMEDA AV	ANA	AN	2000	10	F3
ALAMEDA AV	CO	LB		29C	E3
ALAMEDA DR	HTB	HB		26	D5
ALAMEDA LN N	SCL	SC72	100	39	C4
ALAMEDA LN S	SCL	SC72	100	39	C4
ALAMEDA WY	BPK	BP		5	C3
ALAMITOS WY	GGR	GG	12700	15	E4
ALAMO CIR	CO	ET	26600	29B	B2
ALAMO LN	YL	YL		8	B5
ALAMO ST	ANA	AN	600	10	E2
ALAMO ST	IRV	SA	3900	29	C1
ALAN WY	GGR	GG	13200	16	A5
ALANDA AV	OR	OR	3700	18	A3
ALANWOOD ST	CO	ET	24600	29A	E5
ALANZO LN	CM	CM	2800	27	E4
ALARCON	MVJO	SJ91	27600	29B	E6
ALAS DE PAZ	CO	SJ		59	D2
ALASKA AV	CM	CM		27	B2
ALASKA AV	CO	CYP	4700	9	D4
ALASSIO	IRV	SA		24	D5
ALAVA	MVJO	SJ92	28100	29B	E3
ALAZAN	MVJO	SJ92	28100	29B	F5
ALBA E&W	IRV	SA		24	F5
ALBA ST	NB	NB	700	32	A3
ALBACORE DR	HTB	HB	9500	26	E3
ALBANY	IRV	SA14		29	F3
ALBANY CIR	HTB	HB	9100	26	E6
ALBANY CIR	VPK	OR67	10500	17	F1
ALBANY ST	CM	CM	1000	27	E3

STREET	CITY	P.O. ZONE	BLOCK	PAGE	GRID
ALBARES	MVJO	SJ91	22500	29B	D2
ALBATROSS DR	BPK	BP	7000	9	F1
ALBATROSS DR	CM	CM	2600	27	B5
ALBATROSS DR	HTB	HB	8800	26	E4
ALBATROSS LN	FTNV	SA08	9500	26	F1
ALBERICI	TUS	SA10		29	A2
ALBERT PL	CM	CM27	100	31	E1
ALBERTA DR	HTB	HB	7600	26	C2
ALBERTA PL N	FUL	FL33	200	5	F6
ALBERTA PL S	FUL	FL33	600	5	F6
ALBERTA ST E&W	ANA	AN	100	11	C3
ALBILLO CT	CO	LB56		29C	E5
ALBION AV	SA	SA	1700	17	E4
ALBION DR	HTB	HB47	6100	21	A3
ALBION LN	OR	OR	1500	17	D4
ALCIRA	IRV	SA		28	F3
ALCALDE DR	CO	LB	23000	29A	C4
ALCAMO	IRV	SA14		28	F4
ALCAZAR	IRV	SA14		28	D4
ALCAZAR DR	DPT	DPT	33700	37	F4
ALCESTER ST	WSTM	WSTM	14600	21	E2
ALCIMA DR	OR	OR69		18	C1
ALCO AV	SA	SA	2000	22	E1
ALCOBA	IRV	SA14		28	E4
ALCOBA DR	MVJO	SJ91	24600	29B	B6
ALCORN LN	IRV	SA		32	F1
ALCOTT AV	PLA	PLA	600	7	C3
ALCOTT CT	IRV	SA		32	D2
ALCOTT PL	CO	LB		35	E6
ALCOVE WY	ANA	AN	1400	11	F5
ALCUDIA	MVJO	SJ92		29B	D2
ALDANA PL	MVJO	SJ91		29B	B4
ALDEA	IRV	SA		24	E5
ALDEA CT	CO	SJ91		29A	E6
ALDEAN PL	NB	NB	600	31	D4
ALDEANO	SCL	SC72		38	E4
ALDEANO DR	MVJO	SJ91		29B	C6
ALDEBARAN CIR	NB	NB	900	31	F3
ALDEN AV	ANA	AN	2100	11	F4
ALDEN AV	ANA	AN	2300	12	A4
ALDEN LN	HTB	HB	15500	20	F3
ALDEN PL	ANA	AN	2500	12	A4
ALDER	IRV	SA		29	B5
ALDER AV	YL	YL		8	E2
ALDER DR	CO	ET	24400	29A	C2
ALDER LN	CM	CM		27	E6
ALDER LN	LAP	BP23	5000	9	D2
ALDER LN	TUS	TUS	14500	24	A5
ALDER PL	FUL	FL	2900	6	F2
ALDER PL	NB	NB	900	32	B3
ALDER ST	BREA	BREA	100	6	E1
ALDER ST	SA	SA	3800	28	B2
ALDER WY	CO	SJ		52	E3
ALDERBERRY	IRV	SA		29	C5
ALDERBROOK	IRV	SA		29	B3
ALDERBROOK	MVJO	SJ92		29B	E1
ALDERBURY ST	CYP	CYP	9200	9	D5
ALDERDALE AV	ANA	AN	3900	12	E2
ALDERDALE CIR	ANA	AN	900	12	E2
ALDER GLEN	IRV	SA		32A	A2
ALDERGLEN DR	CO	ET	24000	29A	D4
ALDERGROVE	IRV	SA		29	C3
ALDER GROVE CIR	OR	OR		12	D4
ALDERLY LN	OR	OR	3500	12	F4
ALDERPORT	HTB	HB		20	C3
ALDERSHOT WK	WSTM	WSTM		14	D6
ALDERSON AV	GGR	GG	10500	16	A2
ALDERWOOD	CO	ET	25900	29B	A3
ALDERWOOD	CO	LB77		35	F3
ALDERWOOD	CO	LB77		36	A3
ALDERWOOD	IRV	SA		29	D3
ALDERWOOD AV	OR	OR	100	12	C3
ALDERWOOD DR	NB	NB		32	B5
ALDERWOOD LN	SB	SB	13600	14	A6
ALDGATE AV	GGR	GG	9800	15	F2
ALDRICH ST	HTB	HB47	7900	21	C4
ALDRICH ST N&S	LAH	LAH	100	2	A5
ALDRIN WY	PLA	PLA	1500	7	B3
ALDWOOD AV	GGR	GG	9500	15	E3
ALE LN	STN	STN	11200	15	C2
ALEGRIA	IRV	SA		24	E5
ALEJO	IRV	SA		32A	B2
ALELLA TER	CO	LB56		29C	E5
ALENE CIR	SA	SA	900	22	B1
ALEPPO ST	NB	NB	700	32	B3
ALERIA	CO	LB77		35	E5
ALERT LN	HTB	HB		20	B4
ALERZAL	MVJO	SJ92		29B	D3
ALEXANDER LN	CO	SA	12100	18	B3
ALEXANDER RD	LAG	LB51	2800	34	F5
ALEXANDRIA	IRV	SA14		28	F3

STREET	CITY	P.O. ZONE	BLOCK	PAGE	GRID
ALEXANDRIA DR	HTB	HB47	6300	21	A2
ALEXANDRITE	MVJO	SJ91		29D	C5
ALEXIS AV	ANA	AN	1500	11	B5
ALFABIA	MVJO	SJ92	27700	29B	D3
ALFAWN CIR	HTB	HB		25	E1
ALFIERI ST	CO	LB77		35	D2
ALFORD CIR	YL	YL	3900	7	D2
ALFORJA	SCL	SC72		38	E3
ALFRED AV	WSTM	WSTM	5500	14	E6
ALGAR	MVJO	SJ91	22400	29B	D2
ALGARROBO	CO	LB	5300	29A	A5
ALGIRS	IRV	SA14		28	F3
ALGIERS ST	CO	SJ91		29A	F4
ALGONQUIN ST	HTB	HB	16200	20	D5
ALGONQUIN ST	SB	SB	14000	20	D2
ALHAMBRA DR	HTB	HB47	7500	21	C5
ALHONDRA PL	MVJO	SJ91		29B	B4
ALIANO	YL	YL		8	B3
ALICANTE	CO	SJ79		59	D5
ALICANTE	NB	NB60		32	E4
ALICANTE DR	MVJO	SJ91	26500	29B	B6
ALICANTE LN	HTB	HB	20800	26	D6
ALICANTE AISLE	IRV	SA14		28	E3
ALICE AV	CO	ET	24000	29A	D2
ALICE CIR	ANA	AN	200	12	B3
ALICE CIR	CYP	CYP	10000	9	E6
ALICE LN	ANA	AN		8	C6
ALICE LN	HTB	HB		26	C2
ALICE LN	VPK	OR67	18600	13	A5
ALICE ST N	ANA	AN	100	12	B3
ALICE WY	ANA	AN	400	12	B3
ALICIA DR	DPT	DPT	25000	37	F4
ALICIA DR	DPT	DPT	25100	38	A4
ALICIA PKWY	CO	SJ91	25400	29A	F6
ALICIA PKWY	CO	LB		29C	E2
ALICIA PKWY	CO	LB	23500	35	D3
ALICIA PKWY	MVJO	SJ91	27500	29B	A5
ALICIA PKWY	MVJO	SJ92		29B	C4
ALIENTO	CO	SJ		59	C1
ALII CIR	HTB	HB	9400	30	E1
ALIPAZ ST	DPT	DPT		38	A4
ALIPAZ ST	SJC	SJ75	31500	36	B6
ALIPAZ ST	SJC	SJ75	32000	38	B2
ALISA LN	HTB	HB	20400	26	F5
ALISAL AV	CO	LB	25400	29C	F2
ALISMA	CO	SJ		59	C1
ALISO AV	CM	CM27	1600	31	E3
ALISO AV	NB	NB	300	31	D4
ALISO CIR	LAG	LB	31000	35	A5
ALISO CT	CO	ET		52	B6
ALISO PL	ANA	AN	3100	10	C6
ALISO WY	LAG	LB		35	A5
ALISO CANYON RD	LAG	LB		35	B5
ALISO CREEK RD	CO	LB		29C	D6
ALISO HILLS DR	CO	LB		29C	F2
ALISO NIGUEL	CO	LB		29C	E4
ALISO PARK DR	CO	ET		29B	B2
ALISOS AV	LAG	LB51	900	34	F4
ALISOS AV	LAG	LB51	1700	35	A3
ALISO VIEW CIR	CO	SJ79		52	E4
ALISO VISTA TER	CO	SJ79		56	A3
ALITA LN	CO	SA	1800	24	B2
ALKI PL	ANA	AN	2600	12	A5
ALL AMERICA WY	PLA	PLA	100	7	C5
ALLARD AV	GGR	GG	12700	16	D3
ALLARIZ	MVJO	SJ91	27300	29B	C2
ALLEC ST	ANA	AN	1200	11	E6
ALLEGHENY	IRV	SA		24	E6
ALLEGHENY AV	CM	CM	700	27	F3
ALLEGHENY AV	PLA	PLA		7	B3
ALLEGHENY CIR	PLA	PLA	200	7	B1
ALLEGHENY DR	CO	SA	17500	17	F5
ALLEGHENY DR	CO	SA	18200	18	A5
ALLEGHENY WY	PLA	PLA	2400	7	B1
ALLEGRA RD	CO	LB		29C	E6
ALLEMAN PL	CO	SA	12200	24	A1
ALLEN DR	GGR	GG	10400	16	A3
ALLEN ST	WSTM	WSTM	14600	21	B2
ALLEN ACRES	CO	SA		18	C6
ALLENWOOD LN	CO	LB		29C	D4
ALLESSANDRO	DPT	DPT		37	D5
ALLEY PZ	OR	OR		17	C3
ALLIANCE AV	TUS	TUS	16600	23	E3
ALLISON CIR	HTB	HB	9600	30	F2
ALLISON CIR	OR	OR		18	C3
ALLISON CIR	WSTM	WSTM	5700	14	F5
ALLONBY CIR	YL	YL		8	F4
ALLPORT LN	HTB	HB	20300	26	D5
ALLSTONE DR	HTB	HB		20	E6
ALLSTONE DR	HTB	HB		25	E1
ALLTHORN DR	CO	SA	13800	18	A6

INDEX

—Z— COPYRIGHT, © 1989 BY Thomas Bros Maps

STREET	CITY	P.O. ZONE	BLOCK	PAGE	GRID
ALLVIEW PL	LAG	LB51	600	34	D2
ALLVIEW TER	LAG	LB51	22500	34	C2
ALLWOOD CIR	ANA	AN		8	E5
ALLYSSUM	CO	SJ		56	D6
ALLYSSUM	CO	SJ		59	D1
ALMA LN	VPK	OR67	10300	13	A6
ALMA ALDEA	CO	TRA		59	C2
ALMADEN	MVJO	SJ91	22400	29B	D2
ALMADOR	IRV	SA14		28	E4
ALMARA LN	CO	LB	22900	35	C5
ALMARA PZ	YL	YL		8	C3
ALMELO LN	HTB	HB	17300	20	F6
ALMENDRA	MVJO	SJ91	27400	29B	D2
ALMERIA	IRV	SA14		28	F3
ALMIRA	CO	LB		35	E4
ALMIRA AV	FUL	FL	1600	6	F3
ALMOND AV	SB	SB	4000	14	D5
ALMOND AV E	OR	OR	3500	18	A3
ALMOND AV E&W	OR	OR	100	17	C3
ALMOND DR	ANA	AN	1800	11	F3
ALMOND DR	BREA	BREA	800	2	F6
ALMOND PL	NB	NB	900	32	B3
ALMOND ST	CYP	CYP	10500	15	A1
ALMOND ST	FTNV	SA08	16400	21	E4
ALMOND ST	IRV	SA		24	C6
ALMOND ST	IRV	SA	3800	29	D2
ALMOND ST	TUS	TUS		24	B4
ALMONDINE DR	GGR	GG	6800	15	A4
ALMOND TREE LN	ANA	AN		10	D2
ALMOND TREE LN	IRV	SA		29	B5
ALMONDWOOD	CO	ET		29A	F1
ALMONDWOOD ST	LAH	LAH	1400	5	F1
ALMONT AV	ANA	AN	1700	11	F5
ALMSIDE DR	TUS	TUS	1200	23	F3
ALOE	CO	SJ		59	B3
ALOHA DR	HTB	HB	9000	30	E2
ALOHA DR	NB	NB		31	E5
ALOHA LN	SA	SA		22	C3
ALOHA ST	SA	SA		22	C3
ALOMA AV	CO	LB	29000	35	F2
ALOMAR AV	ANA	AN	1600	11	B5
ALONA PL	ANA	AN	900	10	E3
ALONA ST	SA	SA	1700	16	F6
ALONDRA	CO	SJ88		29B	F4
ALONDRA	CO	LB		35	E4
ALONDRA	IRV	SA		24	E5
ALONDRA DR	HTB	HB	500	26	C5
ALONDRA LN	HTB	HB		26	B2
ALONZO COOK ST	GGR	GG45		14	E4
ALOYSIA	CO	SJ		59	C1
ALPERA	MVJO	SJ92		29D	C2
ALPHA LN	ANA	AN	1500	11	F4
ALPHA PL	ANA	AN	1400	11	E4
ALPINE AV	ANA	AN06		12	B3
ALPINE AV	SA	SA04		27	D1
ALPINE AV	SA	SA	300	28	B1
ALPINE LN	HTB	HB	1300	26	C5
ALPINE RD	OR	OR	400	17	B4
ALPINE ST	LAH	LAH	100	2	B5
ALPINE ST	OR	OR	500	17	B2
ALPINE WY	LAG	LB51	2900	35	A1
ALRAY PL	CO	TUS	12300	24	B1
ALRO AV	ANA	AN	100	16	D1
ALSACE CIR	IRV	SA	15400	29	D3
ALSUNA LN	HTB	HB	1700	26	C4
ALTA DR	VPK	OR67	17900	12	F5
ALTA LN	CM	CM		27	F6
ALTA ST	IRV	SA14	14500	29	E5
ALTA ST	PLA	PLA	100	7	B5
ALTA ST	WSTM	WSTM	14200	20	E1
ALTADENA DR	TUS	TUS	17000	23	E4
ALTAIR	IRV	SA		32A	B2
ALTAIR LN	ANA	AN		8	F6
ALTAIR LN	ANA	AN		13	A6
ALTA LAGUNA BL	LAG	LB51	3200	29C	A6
ALTA LAGUNA BL	LAG	LB51	2800	34	F1
ALTA LAGUNA BL	LAG	LB51	2800	35	A1
ALTA LAGUNA BL	LAG	LB	28700	35	A3
ALTA LOMA	CO	ET		51	F6
ALTA LOMA CT	CO	LB		29C	E3
ALTA LOMA DR	LAG	LB	31400	35	B6
ALTAMAR DR	HTB	HB	600	26	C4
ALTAMAR DR	LAG	LB51	2500	34	A1
ALTA MESA DR	BREA	BREA	1200	2	C3
ALTA MESA WY	BREA	BREA	1400	2	D3
ALTAMIRA DR	CO	LB	24800	29C	F3
ALTAMIRA RD	LAG	LB77		37	B2
ALTAMIRANO LN	HTB	HB	17800	26	A1
ALTANERO	MVJO	SJ91		29B	B2
ALTA PANORAMA	CO	SA	19000	18	B4
ALTA PINE LN	SJC	SJ75	32600	38	A2

STREET	CITY	P.O. ZONE	BLOCK	PAGE	GRID
ALTA TERRA	CO	LB77		35	C3
ALTA VISTA	CO	LB		29A	B5
ALTA VISTA	DPT	SC24	27200	38	C5
ALTA VISTA CIR	HTB	HB47	17400	21	A6
ALTA VISTA DR	DPT	DPT	24300	37	E4
ALTA VISTA DR	FUL	FL	1100	6	B4
ALTA VISTA DR	NB	NB	2100	32	B3
ALTA VISTA ST	PLA	PLA	300	7	C5
ALTA VISTA WY	LAG	LB51	200	34	F5
ALTHEA AV	CO	SJ91	25500	29B	A5
ALTIVO PL	FUL	FL	2700	6	C1
ALTO LN	FUL	FL	1400	6	E4
ALTO LN	LAH	LAH	1100	2	B3
ALTON AV E	SA	SA	100	28	B1
ALTON AV W	SA	SA04	1500	27	D1
ALTON AV W	SA	SA	200	28	B1
ALTON PKWY	CO	SA18		29A	B1
ALTON PKWY	IRV	SA		28	F3
ALTON PKWY	IRV	SA	4000	29	B4
ALTON PKWY	IRV	SA18		29A	A1
ALTON PKWY	IRV	SA18		51	A6
ALTOONA LN	IRV	SA		32	F2
ALTRUDY LN	YL	YL	18500	8	A3
ALTURA	CO	LB77		36	A2
ALTURA	IRV	SA14		28	D5
ALTURA	SCL	SC72		38	E4
ALTURA AV	OR	OR	2000	12	E4
ALTURA BLVD	BPK	BP	6200	5	A5
ALTURA DR	FUL	FL35	200	2	B6
ALTURA DR	NB	NB	1900	32	A6
ALTURA DR	NB	NB		33	A1
ALTURAS DR	MVJO	SJ91		29B	B3
ALUMBRE	CO	SJ88		59	B2
ALVA LN	CM	CM27	300	31	E2
ALVARADO CIR	FUL	FL	100	6	B1
ALVARADO DR	HTB	HB	8300	26	D6
ALVARADO PL	NB	NB	300	31	E6
ALVARADO ST	NB	NB	300	31	E6
ALVARADO ST	NB	NB	100	33	B5
ALVAREZ	MVJO	SJ91	21600	29B	D1
ALVAREZ AV	OR	OR	1300	17	B2
ALVEAR	MVJO	SJ92		52	E6
ALVIS WY	SA	SA	200	28	B1
ALVY ST	ANA	AN	600	11	B5
ALWICK CIR	GGR	GG	9100	15	E2
ALWOOD AV	GGR	GG	9500	15	E3
AMABLE	MVJO	SJ92	28100	29B	E6
AMA DAISY	CO	SJ		59	C1
AMADO	TUS	TUS		23	D3
AMADOR AV	WSTM	WSTM	5500	14	E6
AMADOR CIR	HTB	HB		26	E6
AMAGANSET WY	TUS	TUS	17200	23	F1
AMALFI	NB	NB60		32	C2
AMALFI DR	IRV	SA	3100	32	F2
AMALFI DR	SA	SA		22	E2
AMALIA PL	MVJO	SJ91		29B	B4
AMALIA ST	CO	LB56		29C	D3
AMANDA CIR	ANA	AN		8	E5
AMANDA LN	LAH	LAH	900	2	A3
AMANTES	CO	SJ88		59	A4
AMAPOLA AV	CO	OR	20000	18	D1
AMAPOLA AV	OR	OR	7000	18	D1
AMAPOLA LN	MVJO	SJ91		29D	C3
AMARANTE	CO	LAG		35	F4
AMARGON	MVJO	SJ92	28000	29B	D5
AMARILLO DR	WSTM	WSTM	13200	15	C5
AMARITA LN	ANA	AN	1500	16	B2
AMATE CIR	VPK	OR67	18600	13	A5
AMAZON DR	HTB	HB47	7500	21	C4
AMAZON RIV CIR	FTNV	SA08	8500	26	D2
AMBAR	MVJO	SJ92	28000	29B	E3
AMBASSADOR DR	FTNV	SA08		21	E4
AMBASSADOR DR	WSTM	WSTM	9200	21	E4
AMBASSADOR WY	CO	LB56		29C	E5
AMBER	CO	LB56		29C	C1
AMBER	MVJO	SJ91		52	D5
AMBER AV	OR	OR	16200	12	D4
AMBER CIR	GGR	GG43	10600	22	A2
AMBER DR	HTB	HB		26	B2
AMBER LN	ANA	AN07		13	D4
AMBERDALE DR	YL	YL	5900	8	C5
AMBER HILL DR	BREA	BREA		2	D3
AMBERLEAF	IRV	SA		29	C5
AMBER LANTRN ST	DPT	DPT	33900	37	E5
AMBERLY LN	CO	ET		51	E4
AMBER ROSE	MVJO	SJ92		29B	E2
AMBERTON LN	HTB	HB	17700	25	E1
AMBERVALE LN	CO	SA05		18	D4
AMBERWICK CIR	BREA	BREA		3	B6
AMBERWICK CIR	CYP	CYP	9600	9	D5
AMBERWICK LN	ANA	AN	1300	10	F6

STREET	CITY	P.O. ZONE	BLOCK	PAGE	GRID
AMBERWICK LN	BREA	BREA		3	A6
AMBERWICK LN	CO	TUS	14500	23	F1
AMBERWICK LN	HTB	HB	21000	26	F6
AMBERWICKE	CO	SJ79		59	D3
AMBERWOOD	IRV	SA		29	D3
AMBERWOOD	MVJO	SJ92		29B	E6
AMBERWOOD	MVJO	SJ92		29D	E1
AMBERWOOD AV	LAP	BP23	4500	9	D3
AMBERWOOD CIR	FTNV	SA08		22	A6
AMBERWOOD DR	CO	SA	1500	24	C1
AMBERWOOD DR	CO	LB		35	C6
AMBERWOOD DR	SA	SA		22	B1
AMBERWOOD LN	YL	YL	6400	8	F2
AMBERWOOD ST	ANA	AN08		40	E6
AMBERWOOD ST	OR	OR69		18	E3
AMBIA	MVJO	SJ92		29D	C3
AMBLING DR	BREA	BREA		3	B6
AMBOY ST	ANA	AN	600	11	B5
AMBRIDGE ST	ANA	AN	900	12	A5
AMBROSIA LN	CO	SJ79		59	D2
AMBY DR	HTB	HB	8800	26	D5
AMELIA ST	ANA	AN		8	E5
AMELIA WY	CYP	CYP	11300	15	B3
AMENO	MVJO	SJ92	29800	29B	D2
AMERICA DR	LALM	LALM		14	C3
AMERICAN AV	CM	CM27	2100	31	B1
AMERICAN PL	CM	CM27	1000	31	A1
AMERICAN ST	ANA	AN	1700	11	D1
AMERICAN WY	OR	OR		12	C4
AMERIGE AV E&W	FUL	FL	100	6	B5
AMES AV	ANA	AN	2500	12	A4
AMES CIR	ANA	AN	2600	12	A4
AMES DR	HTB	HB		26	C5
AMETHYST	BREA	BREA	18700	4	B5
AMETHYST	MVJO	SJ91		29D	C5
AMETHYST AV	NB	NB	100	31	F6
AMETHYST CIR	GGR	GG45	12200	14	F4
AMETHYST CT	FTNV	SA08	11800	22	C4
AMETHYST LN	ANA	AN		13	D3
AMETHYST ST	GGR	GG45	11800	14	F4
AMHERST	CO	LB77		35	E6
AMHERST	CO	LB77		37	E1
AMHERST	CYP	CYP	6500	15	A2
AMHERST AV	FUL	FL	2600	7	A2
AMHERST CIR	ANA	AN		13	E4
AMHERST CIR	WSTM	WSTM	15100	21	C3
AMHERST PL	CM	CM	200	27	D6
AMHERST RD	CM	CM	200	27	D6
AMHERST RD	TUS	TUS	1600	23	F4
AMIDON CIR	WSTM	WSTM	8300	15	D6
AMIDON PL	WSTM	WSTM	8400	15	D6
AMIES RD	CO	AN04	10300	10	E6
AMIES RD	CO	AN04	10400	15	E1
AMIGOS WY	NB	NB		32	A3
AMISTAD	IRV	SA		24	E4
AMISTAD ST	FTNV	SA08	18400	27	A2
AMORA	MVJO	SJ92		52	E6
AMORE	IRV	SA14		28	F3
AMORITA AV	LAH	LAH	2200	2	C3
AMOS ST	OR	OR	2300	12	E4
AMSTERDAM DR	HTB	HB47	8200	21	D5
AMSTUTZ AV	ANA	AN	700	11	C5
AMUNDSEN BAY	DPT	LB77		37	D4
AMURRO DR	MVJO	SJ91		29B	B5
AMY AV	CO	GG41	8500	15	D3
AMY AV	GGR	GG45	5300	14	F3
AMY AV	GGR	GG	6300	15	A3
AMY AV	STN	GG41	7700	15	C3
AMY COM	SA	SA03		22	D2
ANABEL AV	GGR	GG	11200	16	C6
ANABELLA	SCL	SCL		38	E4
ANACAPA DR	CM	CM26		27	C5
ANACAPA DR	HTB	HB	6000	20	F1
ANACAPA DR	NB	NB		32	A6
ANACAPA PL	FUL	FL	2700	6	B2
ANACAPA ST	CO	LB		29C	E2
ANACAPA WY	LAG	LB51	600	34	E2
ANACAPRI	CO	LB77		35	E4
ANACONDA AV	GGR	GG	7000	15	B4
ANADALE DR	CO	LB53		29D	A4
ANADE AV	NB	NB	300	31	E6
ANAHEIM AV	CM	CM	2200	27	C6
ANAHEIM AV	CM	CM27	1700	31	C1
ANAHEIM BLVD	OR	OR68	300	16	F2
ANAHEIM BLVD S	ANA	AN05	100	11	D3
ANAHEIM BLVD S	ANA	AN	100	11	E6
ANAHEIM BLVD S	ANA	AN	1500	16	E1
ANAHEIM CN ST	ANA	AN	4500	12	F1
ANAHEIM CN ST	ANA	AN	4700	13	A1
ANAHEIM HLLS RD	ANA	AN		13	D2

STREET	CITY	P.O. ZONE	BLOCK	PAGE	GRID
ANAHURST PL E&W	SA	SA	100	23	A5
ANAHURST PL W	SA	SA	1500	22	F5
ANA MARIA LN	CO	LB	29700	35	D3
ANAMONTE	CO	LB77		35	C4
ANA TREE LN	TUS	TUS	2200	24	A5
ANAWOOD WY	WSTM	WSTM	13200	14	E5
ANAYA	MVJO	SJ92		29B	E2
ANCHOR AV	GGR	GG43	10600	22	A3
ANCHOR AV	OR	OR	2600	12	D4
ANCHOR CIR	HTB	HB	20400	26	E5
ANCHOR CIR	SJC	SJ75		38	A2
ANCHOR ST	ANA	AN	2100	16	E2
ANCHOR WY	NB	NB	2000	31	E3
ANCHOR WY	SB	SB		19	F2
ANCHOR WY	SB	SB		20	A2
ANCHORAGE CIR	PLA	PLA	900	12	A1
ANCHORAGE DR	HTB	HB	8800	26	D4
ANCHORAGE WY	NB	NB		31	A6
ANCHOR LNTRN ST	DPT	DPT		37	B5
ANCIA LN	MVJO	SJ91		29B	C4
ANCONA	CO	LB		29A	B4
ANDALUCIA	IRV	SA14		29	A4
ANDALUCIA DR	DPT	LB77		37	D3
ANDALUSIA CIR	MVJO	SJ91	26900	29D	C1
ANDALUSIA ST	ANA	AN06		12	B4
ANDAMAN LN	HTB	HB	15300	20	E3
ANDARA RD	CO	LB		35	C5
ANDARRIOS	CO	SJ88		59	B5
ANDELE WY	IRV	SA		24	D6
ANDERSON RD	LAG	LB77	31800	37	A1
ANDERSON ST	CO	SUNB	16300	20	A5
ANDERSON ST	PLA	PLA	1700	7	C3
ANDERSON WY	CO	SIL	14900	50	E2
ANDISSA	IRV	SA14		28	D5
ANDORA	WSTM	WSTM		21	E2
ANDORA DR	CO	LAM	8000	5	C3
ANDOVER	IRV	SA		24	E6
ANDOVER	IRV	SA		29	E1
ANDOVER AV	FUL	FL	2600	7	A3
ANDOVER CIR	FTNV	SA08	15800	21	F4
ANDOVER DR	ANA	AN		13	B3
ANDOVER PL	CM	CM	2400	27	D5
ANDRE LN	LAP	BP23	8000	9	D3
ANDREA CT	CO	SJ91	25800	29B	A6
ANDREA LN	ANA	AN		8	E5
ANDREA ST	CO	LB56		29C	D3
ANDREA WY	CO	LB	23700	35	D3
ANDRES PL	SA	SA	100	22	C3
ANDRES PICO RD	SJC	SJ75	31200	36	C6
ANDREW CIR	LAP	BP23	5000	9	D2
ANDREW DR	GGR	GG43		16	E1
ANDREW DR	LAP	BP23	5000	9	E2
ANDREW WY	CYP	CYP	6900	15	A2
ANDREWS ST	TUS	TUS	1300	24	B2
ANDRIA	IRV	SA14		29	A4
ANDRIA PL	CO	LB	23000	35	C5
ANDROMEDA	IRV	SA		32A	A2
ANDROS DR	HTB	HB49		20	C4
ANDROS ST	CM	CM	2800	27	C4
ANDROS ST	CYP	CYP	11400	14	F2
ANEAS DR	ANA	AN		8	C6
ANEAS DR	ANA	AN		13	C1
ANEGADA ST	CYP	CYP	11100	14	F2
ANGEL AV	FTNV	SA08	10500	22	A6
ANGELA AV	CYP	CYP	10100	9	E6
ANGELA ST	CO	ET	24000	29A	D2
ANGELFISH	HTB	HB		26	C6
ANGELINA DR	HTB	HB		20	D4
ANGELINA DR N&S	PLA	PLA	100	7	B5
ANGELITA DR	NB	NB	500	32	A6
ANGELITA DR	NB	NB	400	33	A1
ANGELL ST	IRV	SA	17900	28	F5
ANGEL VIEW TER	OR	OR		13	D6
ANGLER LN	CO	LALM	2800	14	A4
ANGLER LN	HTB	HB	16200	20	F4
ANGLIN CIR	TUS	TUS		17	E6
ANGLIN LN	TUS	TUS		17	F6
ANGUILLA AV	CYP	CYP	6200	14	F2
ANGUS AV	OR	OR	800	17	C2
ANGUS CT	GGR	GG	8800	15	D2
ANIL	CO	SJ88		59	B4
ANISE ST	ANA	AN		8	F6
ANISE ST	ANA	AN		13	F1
ANITA CIR	WSTM	WSTM	15000	21	C2
ANITA DR	OR	OR	100	17	A3
ANITA LN	HTB	HB47	7600	21	C4
ANITA LN	NB	NB	1500	31	E3
ANITA PL	FUL	FL	1200	6	E3
ANITA PL	GGR	GG	13900	16	B6
ANITA ST	LAG	LB51	100	34	D3
ANKARA ST	CO	SJ91	2400	29B	A5

STREET	CITY	P.O. ZONE	BLOCK	PAGE	GRID
ANKERTON DR	CO	ET	24100	29A	E5
ANNA DR N&S	ANA	AN	600	11	E2
ANNA DR W	ANA	AN	1600	11	E2
ANNA LN	HTB	HB		26	B2
ANNAGLEN LN	LAH	LAH	800	1	F5
ANNAJEANNE DR	PLA	PLA	1400	7	C4
ANNA MARIA RD	CO	LB	29700	35	D3
ANNA MARIE RD E	YL	YL	17800	7	F4
ANNANDALE DR	SB	SB	13600	14	A6
ANNAPOLIS AV	CO	AN04	8700	15	D1
ANNAPOLIS ST	CM	CM	1000	27	E3
ANNAPOLIS ST	SA	SA	2800	17	D5
ANN CROSS DR	GGR	GG		15	D4
ANNE CIR	HTB	HB		20	B6
ANNE ST	SA	SA	2000	22	D5
ANNED DR	PLA	PLA	100	7	B5
ANNETTE AV	CO	ET	21900	29A	D2
ANNETTE CIR	GGR	GG	12600	16	E4
ANNETTE CIR	HTB	HB	6000	20	F5
ANNIK DR	HTB	HB	9000	26	E4
ANNIKA ST	ANA	AN	900	12	A4
ANNIN AV N&S	FUL	FL	100	6	E6
ANNIVERSARY LN	NB	NB	2100	32	A1
ANNS LN	LAG	LB51	21500	35	A2
ANSDELL CIR	CO	ET	24500	29A	E5
ANSELMO	MVJO	SJ91		29D	C3
ANSO	MVJO	SJ91		29B	C3
ANSON RIVER CIR	FTNV	SA08		26	E2
ANTARES	IRV	SA		32A	A2
ANTELA	MVJO	SJ91		29B	D3
ANTELOPE RIV AV	FTNV	SA08	10300	27	A2
ANTHONY AV	GGR	GG41		15	B4
ANTHONY AV	GGR	GG41	6300	15	D4
ANTHONY AV	GGR	GG45	5300	14	E4
ANTHONY CIR	LAP	BP23	7500	9	D2
ANTHONY DR	CO	ET	22000	29A	E2
ANTHONY DR	HTB	HB47	8700	21	D5
ANTHONY ST	ANA	AN	500	11	A5
ANTIBES	CO	LB		35	C5
ANTICOST WY	CYP	CYP	11400	15	B3
ANTIETAM	IRV	SA		29	D1
ANTIETAM AV	LALM	LALM	5000	14	D2
ANTIGUA	DPT	DPT		37	E3
ANTIGUA	MVJO	SJ92		29B	D2
ANTIGUA CIR	NB	NB	1800	31	F3
ANTIGUA CIR	PLA	PLA	1200	7	E5
ANTIGUA LN	HTB	HB	21400	30	D1
ANTIGUA ST	CO	AN04	10000	10	F6
ANTIGUA WY	NB	NB	1400	31	F3
ANTILLES WY	DPT	DPT		37	E3
ANTIOCH DR	IRV	SA		32	F2
ANTOINETTE DR	LAH	LAH	1300	1	E3
ANTON BLVD	CM	CM26	600	28	A2
ANTONIO PKWY	CO	SJ		56	D6
ANTONIO PKWY	CO	SJ88		59	A5
ANTONIO PKWY	CO	SJ		59	D1
ANTRIM CIR	HTB	HB47	6400	21	A3
ANTRIM WY	EBAY	LB51	700	34	B1
ANZA LN	CM	CM	2800	27	E4
ANZA PL	FUL	FL	600	6	A6
ANZA ST	NB	NB		31	A6
ANZIO	HTB	HB		26	D4
ANZIO	IRV	SA14		29	A4
ANZIO ST	GGR	GG	13000	16	E3
ANZIO WY	YL	YL		40	D6
APACHE	TUS	TUS		24	B4
APACHE DR	BPK	BP	7300	10	A2
APACHE DR	CO	ET		29A	F2
APACHE DR	PLA	PLA	500	7	C2
APACHE RD	WSTM	WSTM	6000	14	F5
APACHE RD	WSTM	WSTM	6200	15	A5
APACHE RIVER AV	FTNV	SA08	10300	27	A2
APACHE TRAIL DR	CO	ET	26800	29B	B1
APEL LN	HTB	HB	5600	20	E6
APHENA AV	CO	SJ91	24000	29A	F6
APIA DR	CYP	CYP	5500	14	E3
APOLENA AV	NB	NB	100	31	F6
APOLLO	CO	SJ91	24500	29B	A6
APOLLO AV	ANA	AN	1200	11	B5
APOLLO CIR	LALM	LALM	5100	14	D4
APOLLO LN	HTB	HB	15000	20	F2
APOLLO ST	BREA	BREA		2	D5
APPALACHIAN CIR	PLA	PLA	200	7	B1
APPALACHIAN ST	FTNV	SA08	17400	22	B6
APPALOOSA PL	CO	LB		29C	F3
APPALOOSA TR	OR	OR	7700	18	D2
APPIAN WY	CO	SA	1100	18	C6
APPIAN WY	CO	SJ91	25700	29B	A6
APPLE AV	SA	SA		22	D2
APPLE DR	BREA	BREA	500	2	F5
APPLE LN	SA	SA		22	E3

75
APPLE ST

1990 ORANGE COUNTY STREET INDEX

AUTUMNGLEN

ORANGE CO.

STREET	CITY	P.O. ZONE	BLOCK	PAGE	GRID
APPLE ST	FTNV	SA08	16500	21	F5
APPLE BLSSM CIR	BREA	BREA		3	A6
APPLEBY DR	HTB	HB	7500	26	B2
APPLE CREEK LN	YL	YL		8	C5
APPLECROSS LN	HTB	HB	1300	26	C5
APPLEGATE	MVJO	SJ92		29B	E3
APPLE TREE	IRV	SA15		29	B5
APPLETREE	MVJO	SJ92		29B	E2
APPLE TREE DR	TUS	TUS	2100	24	A5
APPLE TREE LN	CO	OR	18900	18	B2
APPLETREE LN	OR	OR69		18	D2
APPLEWOOD CIR	FUL	FL33		5	E2
APPLEWOOD CIR	HTB	HB	18600	26	D2
APPLEWOOD CT	SJC	SJ75		36	C2
APPLING AV	PLA	PLA	900	7	D3
APPOMATTOX	IRV	SA		29	E1
APRICOT AV	BREA	BREA	400	2	F5
APRICOT CIR	FTNV	SA08	17000	21	F6
APRICOT DR	IRV	SA		29	D5
APRICOT ST	TUS	TUS		24	D4
APRIL LN	HTB	HB	500	26	C5
APRILLA	IRV	SA14		28	F3
APSLEY RD	CO	SA	10000	18	D5
APUESTO WY	CO	SJ		59	D3
AQUA	MVJO	SJ91		52	D5
AQUA WY	OR	OR69		18	B3
AQUAMARINE	MVJO	SJ91		29D	C5
AQUAMARINE CIR	FTNV	SA08	11500	22	C5
AQUAMARINE ST	PLA	PLA	900	7	B4
AQUARIUS DR	HTB	HB		20	C4
AQUATIC LN	HTB	HB46	20800	27	A6
AQUEDUCT CT	PLA	PLA		7	F5
AQUEDUCT DR	CYP	CYP	10100	9	C6
AQUEDUCT DR	PLA	PLA		7	F5
AQUILA AV	FUL	FL	2500	6	F6
AQUILLA DR	DPT	DPT	24600	37	E3
ARABIAN AV	OR	OR		13	D6
ARABIAN LN	CO	SJ		56	A3
ARACENA DR	HTB	HB47	6600	26	A1
ARACENA DR	MVJO	SJ91	26600	29B	B6
ARACENA DR	MVJO	SJ91	26500	29D	B1
ARADO	CO	SJ88		59	A4
ARAGON CIR	BPK	BP	6600	9	F1
ARAGON CIR	HTB	HB46	19500	27	A4
ARAGON PL	FUL	FL35	3900	2	C6
ARAGON WY	YL	YL		40	D6
ARALIA ST	NB	NB	2100	32	A3
ARAPAHO DR	SA	SA	400	22	D4
ARAPAHO PL	PLA	PLA	400	7	C1
ARAPAHOE	TUS	TUS		24	B4
ARBE PL	ANA	AN	1600	16	B1
ARBELLA RD	CO	LB		35	C5
ARBOL DR	FUL	FL	3000	6	C1
ARBOLADA WY	CO	TUS	17600	17	F6
ARBOLADO	SCL	SC72		38	F5
ARBOLADO DR	FUL	FL	500	6	C2
ARBOLES	IRV	SA		28	E6
ARBOLES LP	CO	SJ		59	B3
ARBOLITA DR	LAH	LAH	1000	2	B3
ARBOLITOS	MVJO	SJ92		29B	D6
ARBOLITOS	MVJO	SJ92		29D	D1
ARBOR CIR	BREA	BREA		3	A6
ARBOR CIR	HTB	HB47	7800	21	C5
ARBOR CT	FTNV	SA08		27	A2
ARBOR DR	NB	NB	2500	31	D5
ARBOR LN	IRV	SA		29	A6
ARBOR RD	SJC	SJ75		36	B2
ARBOR ST	ANA	AN	1100	11	B2
ARBOR ST	CM	CM27	800	31	B2
ARBOR WY	CO	LB77		35	F3
ARBOR WY	OR	OR	1000	17	B3
ARBORETUM RD	ANA	AN		13	D1
ARBORGLEN	IRV	SA		29	B2
ARBORWOOD	CO	ET		29A	F1
ARBORWOOD	CO	ET		51	F6
ARBUTAS ST	NB	NB	2100	32	B3
ARBUTUS AV	ANA	AN	1600	11	F2
ARBUTUS ST	FTNV	SA08	18800	26	F3
ARC WY	ANA	AN	800	10	A6
ARC WY	YL	YL	5800	8	A5
ARCADA DR	MVJO	SJ91	26000	29B	B6
ARCADIA AV	CO	SA	18800	50	E4
ARCADIAN AV	CO	SJ91	25400	29A	F5
ARCEL CIR	HTB	HB	8700	30	D1
ARCH LN	HTB	HB	500	26	C5
ARCH ST	LAG	LB51	200	34	E5
ARCH BAY	CO	LB77		36	A5
ARCHER CIR	HTB	HB	21500	30	F1
ARCHER ST	ANA	AN	300	10	F5
ARCHES CT	FTNV	SA08		27	A3
ARCHFIELD LN	HTB	HB		25	F3
ARCHWAY RD	WSTM	WSTM	14500	22	A1
ARCHWOOD AV	BREA	BREA		2	C4
ARCOS	MVJO	SJ91		29B	D2
ARDEMORE DR	FUL	FL33		5	F2
ARDEN PL	ANA	AN	900	11	B5
ARDEN ST	ANA	AN	600	11	B5
ARDEN ST	CO	ET		29A	D3
ARDEN ST	SA	SA	2200	16	E5
ARDER CT	CO	ET	22700	29A	F3
ARDILLA LN	SCL	SC72	500	39	F5
ARDIS DR	GGR	GG	11700	15	E3
ARDISA	MVJO	SJ92	24300	29B	E5
ARDMORE RD	EBAY	LB51	700	34	B1
ARDMORE ST	ANA	AN		13	A3
ARDSLEY CIR	HTB	HB	16300	20	D4
ARELO CT	CO	LB77		35	C4
ARENA CIR	HTB	HB	4700	20	D5
ARENA LN	MVJO	SJ91		29B	C5
ARENILLAS	SCL	SC72		38	E4
ARENOSO LN	SCL	SC72	300	39	C4
ARESE ISLE	IRV	SA14		28	D5
ARGENT CIR	IRV	SA	15400	29	D3
ARGENTINA CIR	BPK	BP23	7100	9	E1
ARGO	IRV	SA		32A	A2
ARGO CIR	HTB	HB47	17200	21	B6
ARGONAUT	CO	LB56		29C	C2
ARGONAUT DR	CO	SJ91		29A	F6
ARGOS	CO	LB77		35	F4
ARGOSY AV	HTB	HB	5000	20	E3
ARGUELLO WY	SJC	SJ75	26700	36	B6
ARGUS DR	CO	SJ91		29B	A6
ARGUS DR	CO	SJ91		29D	A1
ARGYLE DR	BPK	BP	4700	5	C3
ARGYLE DR	CO	LALM	11600	14	A4
ARGYLE DR	HTB	HB	9700	26	F4
ARGYLE WY	BPK	BP	4900	5	D4
ARGYLL	MVJO	SJ91		29D	C6
ARIA CIR	HTB	HB	16000	20	D4
ARIANA	IRV	SA14		28	D5
ARIANA CIR	HTB	HB	500	26	C4
ARIANA LN	CO	LB	30900	35	C5
ARIEL PL	ANA	AN	3400	10	B5
ARIES CT	NB	NB		31	B4
ARIES DR	YL	YL	16800	7	D3
ARIES ST	CO	SJ91	25500	29B	A6
ARIES ST	CO	SJ91		29D	A1
ARIJA	MVJO	SJ91	22900	29B	C3
ARION WY	CO	SJ91		29A	F5
ARISTOCRAT AV	GGR	GG	12500	15	D4
ARISTOTLE	IRV	SA		32A	A3
ARIZONA LN	CM	CM	3200	27	B2
ARIZONA PL	ANA	AN	1200	11	E4
ARIZONA ST	BPK	BP	6600	5	C6
ARIZONA ST	BPK	BP	6700	10	C1
ARIZONA ST	WSTM	WSTM	13200	15	C5
ARIZONA ST	WSTM	WSTM	13900	21	C1
ARJAY WY	CO	LB77		35	D2
ARKLEY DR	GGR	GG	12100	15	F3
ARLEE PL	ANA	AN	900	11	E5
ARLENE AV	GGR	GG	9500	15	E4
ARLETTA CIR	GGR	GG	12600	16	E4
ARLINGTON	IRV	SA		24	E6
ARLINGTON AV	ANA	AN	2200	10	E2
ARLINGTON AV	ANA	AN	1000	11	B2
ARLINGTON AV	FUL	FL	2900	6	D2
ARLINGTON DR	CM	CM	900	27	E5
ARLINGTON DR	CO	LB		29D	A6
ARLINGTON LN	HTB	HB	16300	20	E5
ARLINGTON RD	OR	OR	500	17	F4
ARLOURA WY	TUS	TUS	1300	24	A2
ARMADA DR	DPT	DPT		37	E2
ARMADA DR	HTB	HB	6200	26	A1
ARMAGOSA DR	CO	LB	25000	35	F2
ARMANDO ST	ANA	AN	400	12	C2
ARMSTEAD LN	FUL	FL		6	A2
ARMSTRONG AV	IRV	SA	17100	28	D2
ARMSTRONG CIR	ANA	AN		43	A3
ARMSTRONG DR	PLA	PLA	300	7	B3
ARNES	MVJO	SJ92		29B	D4
ARNETT DR	HTB	HB47	8400	21	D5
ARNETT DR	SA	SA	2400	17	B5
ARNO CRESCENT	ANA	AN	5900	13	C2
ARNOLD AV	CM	CM27	1900	31	C2
ARNOLD DR	PLA	PLA	1000	12	A1
ARNOLD WY	BPK	BP	6200	9	F2
ARON PL	ANA	AN	200	10	D4
ARON ST	ANA	AN	500	10	D5
AROVISTA AV	BREA	BREA	300	2	D6
AROVISTA CIR	BREA	BREA	200	2	D6
ARREOS	SCL	SC72		38	E4
ARRIBA LINDA	CO	LB77		36	A2
ARRIBA LINDA	SCL	SC72		39	E4
ARROUES DR	FUL	FL	900	6	D2
ARROW CIR	PLA	PLA	2400	7	B1
ARROW LN	HTB	HB	1300	26	C5
ARROWHEAD AV	BPK	BP	5300	5	C4
ARROWHEAD DR	CO	SJ79		56	E6
ARROWHEAD DR	HTB	HB	6000	25	F2
ARROWHEAD DR	PLA	PLA	1300	7	C4
ARROWHEAD LN	CO	ET	22000	29A	E2
ARROWHEAD ST	STN	STN	12200	15	C4
ARROWOOD ST	CO	ET	24600	29A	E5
ARROWWOOD DR	BREA	BREA	1000	2	E4
ARROYO	SCL	SC72		38	E4
ARROYO AV	CO	SA	10000	18	C6
ARROYO AV	CO	SA	12000	24	B1
ARROYO CIR	LAP	BP23	7600	9	D2
ARROYO DR	FUL	FL	1000	6	A4
ARROYO DR	LAG	LB51	1400	34	E1
ARROYO PL	FUL	FL	300	6	A4
ARROYO ST	YL	YL	4800	8	A3
ARROYO CAJON DR	YL	YL		8	B5
ARROYO CHICO DR	LAG	LB51	400	34	E3
ARROYO LINDO DR	CO	SA	1200	18	C6
ARROYO VISTA	CO	SJ88		29B	F5
ARROYO VISTA	CO	SJ88		59	A4
ARTA	MVJO	SJ92	27700	29B	D2
ARTCRAFT AV	GGR	GG	10500	16	A3
ARTEMIA AV	CO	SJ91		29B	A6
ARTESIA AV	FUL	FL33	2300	5	D5
ARTESIA BLVD	BPK	BP	7000	5	B5
ARTESIA FRWY	BPK	BP		10	B1
ARTESIA ST N	SA	SA	1600	16	F6
ARTESIA ST S	SA	SA	1900	22	F5
ARTESIA ST S	SA	SA04	3000	27	F1
ARTHUR AV	CM	CM	3000	27	E3
ARTHUR DR	CO	AN04	11900	15	C3
ARTIS CT	ANA	AN		8	B6
ARTISTA DR	HTB	HB	8200	30	D1
ARTNELL RD	CO	SA	12800	18	B4
ARUBA	CO	LB77		36	A3
ARUBA CIR	HTB	HB	3800	20	C4
ARUBA CT	CYP	CYP	6200	14	F2
ARUBA DR	PLA	PLA	1200	7	D4
ARUNDEL AV	WSTM	WSTM	10000	22	A2
ARUZA	MVJO	SJ92		29D	D2
ARVILLA CIR	WSTM	WSTM	8300	15	D6
ARVILLA PL	WSTM	WSTM	8400	15	D6
ASARI LN	HTB	HB47	16900	21	D5
ASBURY AV	STN	STN	10500	15	B1
ASBURY CIR	WSTM	WSTM	9200	21	E3
ASBURY PL	ANA	AN	2900	12	B3
ASCENSION DR	DPT	LB77	32400	37	D2
ASCOT CIR	HTB	HB46	10000	27	A4
ASCOT DR	GGR	GG	12800	16	D3
ASCOT LN	SJC	SJ75		36	E5
ASCOT PL	ANA	AN	3100	10	C6
ASCOT WY	STN	STN		15	B2
ASH AV E&W	FUL	FL	100	6	C6
ASH AV W	FUL	FL33	1600	5	D6
ASH CIR	YL	YL		8	D2
ASH DR	LAP	BP23	7800	9	D2
ASH LN	CO	SJ91		29A	F5
ASH PL	ANA	AN	1300	11	F2
ASH ST	ANA	AN	100	11	F3
ASH ST	FTNV	SA08	17300	21	E6
ASH ST	FTNV	SA08	17700	26	E1
ASH ST	HTB	HB47	17000	21	C6
ASH ST	IRV	SA	3900	29	C1
ASH ST	OR	OR	300	17	B3
ASH ST	WSTM	WSTM	14000	20	F1
ASH ST E&W	BREA	BREA	100	2	E6
ASH WY	LAH	LAH	400	1	E5
ASHBORNE RD	EBAY	LB51	700	34	B1
ASHBROOK	CO	ET		29A	F3
ASHBROOK	CO	ET	25500	29B	A3
ASHBROOK	IRV	SA		29	D3
ASHBURTON AV	TUS	TUS	1500	23	F4
ASHBURTON CIR	HTB	HB	8100	30	D1
ASHBURTON LN	HTB	HB	21000	30	C2
ASHBURTON PL	CO	LB		35	E6
ASHBURTON PL	CO	LB77		37	E1
ASHBURY AV	CYP	CYP	4600	9	D5
ASHBY WY	CO	ET		29B	A1
ASHBY WY	OR	OR		12	F4
ASHBY WY	OR	OR		13	A4
ASH CREEK LN	CO	LB		29C	D2
ASHDALE ST	STN	STN	10200	10	C6
ASHDALE ST	STN	STN	10400	15	C1
ASHFIELD	CO	ET		29A	F3
ASHFIELD	CO	ET	23000	29B	A3
ASHFORD	MVJO	SJ92		29D	D4
ASHFORD AV	WSTM	WSTM	9700	21	F1
ASHFORD CT	SA	SA		23	D1
ASHFORD LN	NB	NB	1200	31	F3
ASHFORD PL N	FUL	FL	100	6	E6
ASHFORD PL S	FUL	FL	200	6	E6
ASHGROVE	IRV	SA		29	D5
ASHINGTON LN	ANA	AN	1400	10	F6
ASHLAND DR	CO	LB	24700	29A	E6
ASHLAND DR	CO	LB		29C	E1
ASHLAND DR	HTB	HB	500	26	C5
ASHLEY CIR	LAH	LAH	300	1	E5
ASHLEY CIR	WSTM	WSTM	15500	21	F3
ASHLEY LN	CO	ET		52	B6
ASHMORE CIR	WSTM	WSTM	6800	21	A2
ASHTON CIR	CO	ET	27100	52	C6
ASHTON DR	LAG	LB51	300	34	F5
ASHTON PL	FUL	FL33	700	5	D5
ASH TREE LN	IRV	SA		29	A5
ASH VIA	FUL	FL		6	D6
ASHWOOD	CO	ET	22900	29A	F3
ASHWOOD	CO	LB56		29C	B3
ASHWOOD	IRV	SA		29	C3
ASHWOOD LN	BREA	BREA		2	D4
ASHWOOD LN	WSTM	WSTM		21	C4
ASHWOOD ST	GGR	GG	13400	16	B5
ASHWOOD ST	OR	OR	2400	12	D4
ASPAN ST	CO	ET	23000	29A	D3
ASPEN CIR	FUL	FL	1900	6	F1
ASPEN CIR	HTB	HB47	14600	21	A2
ASPEN CIR	LAP	BP23	7300	9	E1
ASPEN LN	CM	CM		27	E6
ASPEN ST	ANA	AN	800	11	C5
ASPEN ST	BREA	BREA	500	2	F5
ASPEN ST	CYP	CYP	5500	9	E5
ASPEN ST	FTNV	SA08	16300	21	F4
ASPEN ST	IRV	SA	3900	29	C1
ASPEN ST	OR	OR69		18	E3
ASPEN ST	SA	SA	1000	17	C5
ASPEN ST	TUS	TUS		24	B4
ASPEN WY	SJC	SJ75		36	B2
ASPEN WY	STN	STN	7800	15	C1
ASPEN WY	YL	YL		8	E2
ASPEN CREEK LN	CO	LB		29C	D2
ASPENGLOW CIR	YL	YL		7	E2
ASPENGLOW LN	YL	YL		7	E2
ASPEN LEAF	CO	SJ79		59	E5
ASPEN TREE LN	IRV	SA15		29	A6
ASPEN VILLGE WY	SA	SA04		27	E2
ASPENWOOD	CO	ET		29A	F1
ASPENWOOD	CO	ET		51	F6
ASPENWOOD	HTB	HB		26	B4
ASPENWOOD AV	GGR	GG	13000	16	E4
ASPENWOOD AV	WSTM	WSTM	8300	21	D3
ASPENWOOD CIR	ANA	AN		13	F4
ASPENWOOD LN	GGR	GG	12500	16	D4
ASSEMBLY LN	HTB	HB		20	F3
ASSOCIATED RD	FUL	FL	1600	6	F3
ASSOCIATED RD	FUL	FL	2400	7	A1
ASSOCIATED RD N	BREA	BREA	100	3	A5
ASSOCIATED RD S	BREA	BREA	100	3	A6
ASSOCIATED RD S	BREA	BREA	300	7	A1
ASTER CIR	BPK	BP	7800	10	C2
ASTER CIR	FTNV	SA08	9900	21	F5
ASTER LN	YL	YL		8	C3
ASTER PL	CM	CM27	2100	31	E2
ASTER ST	LAG	LB51	300	34	D2
ASTER ST	SB	SB	12800	14	C4
ASTER ST	WSTM	WSTM	15500	21	F3
ASTI WY	CO	LB77		35	C2
ASTON ST	IRV	SA	15000	28	D1
ASTOR LN	HTB	HB	20100	26	E5
ASTOR WY	CO	ET		29B	A2
ASTORIA	CO	SJ79		59	E3
ASTORIA CIR	ANA	AN		13	A1
ASTORIA ST	DPT	LB77		37	F3
ASTORIA ST	DPT	DPT	33200	38	A3
ATCHISON ST	OR	OR	100	17	C3
ATCHISON ST N&S	ANA	AN	100	11	D3
ATECA PL	ANA	AN	1400	11	B2
ATHEL AV	IRV	SA	14800	29	B1
ATHENA	CO	SJ91	24600	29B	A6
ATHENA DR	HTB	HB47	6300	21	A6
ATHENA PL	FUL	FL33		5	E4
ATHENA WY	ANA	AN		12	A6
ATHENIA CIR	CYP	CYP	10000	9	E6
ATHENS	IRV	SA14		28	F3
ATHENS AV	OR	OR	2100	12	E6
ATHENS AV	PLA	PLA	1100	7	C4
ATHENS AV	VPK	OR67	18000	12	F6
ATHENS CIR	BPK	BP	7900	5	C6
ATHENS CIR	BPK	BP	7800	10	C1
ATHENS CIR	LAP	BP23	5300	9	E2
ATHENS CT	CO	AN04	8700	15	D1
ATHENS CT	CO	SJ92		29D	E3
ATHERSTON	MVJO	SJ92		29D	D1
ATHERTON	IRV	SA		24	E4
ATHERTON AV	CO	LB		29C	E2
ATHERTON CIR	FUL	FL		6	A2
ATHERTON LN	TUS	TUS	14400	23	F4
ATHERTON MTN	FTNV	SA08		22	D4
ATLANTA	IRV	SA		24	E4
ATLANTA AV	HTB	HB	8000	26	E6
ATLANTA AV	HTB	HB46		30	D1
ATLANTA AV E	HTB	HB	100	26	C6
ATLANTA ST	ANA	AN	2100	16	B2
ATLANTA WY	CM	CM	1100	27	E3
ATLANTIC DR	DPT	LB77	33500	37	D3
ATLANTIC WY	LAG	LB51		34	E1
ATLANTIS WY	DPT	LB77		37	C2
ATLANTIS WY	GGR	GG		15	E6
ATLAS DR	ANA	AN		16	E2
ATLAS DR	HTB	HB	6000	20	F2
ATLAS ST	BREA	BREA		2	E5
ATOLL DR	DPT	DPT	33300	38	B4
ATOLL DR	NB	CDLM		32	B6
ATOMO	MVJO	SJ91		29B	B2
ATTBORO PL	TUS	TUS	14800	24	A5
ATTLEBORO CIR	HTB	HB	21100	30	D1
ATTLEBORO LN	HTB	HB	21200	30	D1
ATWATER CIR	HTB	HB		26	C5
ATWOOD AV	PLA	PLA	1600	7	E6
AUBREY CIR	VPK	OR67	9000	13	B4
AUBREY PL	FUL	FL33		5	D4
AUBRIETA	CO	TRA		56	B5
AUBRIETA	CO	TRA		59	B4
AUBURN	MVJO	SJ91		52	D4
AUBURN AV	CO	SA	18400	18	A6
AUBURN CIR	WSTM	WSTM	5300	14	E5
AUBURN DR	HTB	HB47	6700	21	B4
AUBURN WY	STN	STN	7000	15	A2
AUBURN AISLE	IRV	SA15		32	E1
AUBURN DALE DR	CO	ET	22500	29B	A3
AUDRE AV	ANA	AN	1600	16	B1
AUDRE DR	ANA	AN	1200	16	B1
AUDREY CIR	GGR	GG	12600	16	E4
AUDREY DR	HTB	HB	5000	20	E4
AUDUBON WY	CO	ET	21500	29B	C1
AUGUST LN	CO	SA07		27	F5
AUGUST LN	CO	SA07		28	A5
AUGUSTA	CO	SJ79		59	C6
AUGUSTA	IRV	SA		24	D6
AUGUSTA	MVJO	SJ92		29B	D4
AUGUSTA CIR	HTB	HB	21400	30	F1
AUGUSTA CT	CYP	CYP		9	C5
AUGUSTA CT	FUL	FL		6	C2
AUGUSTA DR	CO	AN04	8200	15	D3
AUGUSTA DR	CO	LB		35	D5
AUGUSTA LN	NB	NB		32	B5
AUGUSTA ST	CM	CM	1100	27	E3
AUGUSTA WY	STN	STN	11000	15	B2
AUGUSTIN ST	CO	SJ91	24100	29B	A6
AUKLET LN	CO	LB	29400	35	D2
AULNAY LN	HTB	HB	15500	20	F4
AURELIA AV	CYP	CYP	10100	9	E6
AURELIO DR	DPT	DPT	34000	37	C5
AURORA	IRV	SA		32A	A2
AURORA AV	BREA	BREA	200	3	A5
AURORA AV	SA	SA	200	28	B2
AURORA ST	ANA	AN	600	10	D3
AURORA ST	SA	SA04	2600	27	E2
AURORA ST	SA	SA	700	28	A2
AURORA WY	CO	SJ91		29B	A6
AURORA WY	CO	SJ91		29D	A1
AUSTIN	IRV	SA		29	E2
AUSTIN AV	OR	OR	3400	18	A4
AUSTIN DR	HTB	HB	8500	26	D4
AUSTIN PL	ETMC	SA09		51	D3
AUSTIN ST	CM	CM	1100	27	E3
AUSTIN ST	SA	SA	800	22	B4
AUSTIN WY	STN	STN	11100	15	A2
AUTO CENTER DR	ANA	AN		12	B6
AUTO CENTER DR	IRV	SA18		29A	C3
AUTO CENTER DR	TUS	TUS		24	B4
AUTO MALL DR	SA	SA		23	D4
AUTOPARK DR	HTB	HB48		26	B2
AUTRY	IRV	SA18		29A	C2
AUTRY DR	ANA	AN		8	E6
AUTUMN CIR	HTB	HB	17100	20	F6
AUTUMN DR	ANA	AN	900	11	C3
AUTUMN LN	STN	STN	8200	15	C3
AUTUMNGLEN	CO	LB56		29C	C4

INDEX

AUTUMN GLEN

1990 ORANGE COUNTY STREET INDEX

76

BAKE LN

COPYRIGHT, © 1989 BY Thomas Bros Maps

ORANGE CO.

INDEX

STREET	CITY	P.O. ZONE	BLOCK	PAGE	GRID
AUTUMN GLEN	CO	ET		52	A5
AUTUMN HILL LN	CO	LB		29C	D2
AUTUMN HILL WY	OR	SA05		18	D3
AUTUMNLEAF	IRV	SA		29	C5
AUTUMN OAK	IRV	SA		29	D4
AUTUMNWOOD	CO	ET		29A	F1
AUTUMNWOOD	CO	ET		51	F6
AVALON AV	CO	SA06	13000	16	E5
AVALON AV	LAG	LB51	900	34	E3
AVALON AV E	SA	SA	800	17	C5
AVALON AV W	SA	SA	1600	16	F5
AVALON DR	FUL	FL	100	6	C3
AVALON DR	SB	SB	100	19	E2
AVALON LN	HTB	HB	17300	20	F6
AVALON ST	CM	CM	2200	27	D6
AVALON ST	CM	CM27	2200	31	D1
AVALON ST	CO	ET	24000	29A	D3
AVALON COVE	CO	LB77		36	B4
AVANTE	CO	LB77		35	C3
AVATAR	CO	LB77		36	A1
AVELLINO	IRV	SA		24	D5
AVENA LN	CO	SJ		59	D3
AVD ACAPULCO	SCL	SC72		39	F3
AVENIDA ADOBE	SCL	SC72		39	F5
AVENIDA ADOBE	YL	YL		8	E4
AVD AEROPUERTO	SJC	SJ75		38	B3
AVD ALBERCON	CO	ET		51	F6
AVD ALESSANDRO	SCL	SC72	100	39	E5
AVENIDA ALGODON	SCL	SC72	100	39	D3
AVENITA ALPERA	TUS	TUS		24	E3
AVENIDA AMADIS	SCL	SC72	100	39	E5
AVENIDA AMAPOLA	CO	ET	20800	51	F6
AVD AMBIENTE	CO	ET		29A	F1
AVD AMBIENTE	CO	ET	21300	51	F6
AVENIDA AMOR	YL	YL		8	D4
AVENIDA ANITA	SCL	SC72		39	C3
AVENIDA ANTIGUA	FUL	FL		6	A2
AVENIDA ANTIGUA	YL	YL		8	E5
AVENIDA ARAGON	SCL	SC72	100	39	C3
AVENIDA ARBOL	ANA	AN	5900	13	C1
AVENIDA ARIVACA	MVJO	SJ91		29B	B3
AVENIDA ARLENA	SCL	SC72		39	E3
AVENIDA ARMIJO	CO	LB53		29C	E6
AVENIDA AVALON	CO	LB53		29A	E6
AVENIDA AVALON	CO	LB53		29C	E1
AVENIDA AVILLA	SJC	SJ75	31600	36	E6
AVENIDA AVILLA	SJC	SJ75		38	E1
AVENIDA AZOR	SCL	SC72		38	F6
AVENIDA AZOR	SCL	SC72		39	D1
AVENIDA BAJA	SCL	SC72		39	F5
AVENIDA BANCAL	CO	ET		51	E6
AVENIDA BARCA	ANA	AN		13	D1
AVD BARCELONA	SCL	SC72	100	39	D4
AVD BARCELONA	YL	YL		8	F5
AVD BERNARDO N	ANA	AN	5600	13	C2
AVD BERNARDO S	ANA	AN	5600	13	C2
AVD BONACHON	MVJO	SJ91	26100	29B	B5
AVENIDA BREVE	CO	LB		29C	E5
AVD BUENA SUERT	SCL	SC72		39	E3
AVD BUENA VNTRA	SCL	SC72	100	39	F6
AVD BUENOS AIRS	SCL	SC72		39	F4
AVD CABALLEROS	SCL	SC72	100	39	D3
AVD CABRILLO	SJC	SJ75	25800	38	A2
AVD CABRLLO N&S	SCL	SC72	100	39	D3
AVD CADIZ E&W	SCL	SC72	100	39	D4
AVENIDA CALAFIA	SCL	SC72	100	39	E5
AVENIDA CALIDAD	MVJO	SJ91	26100	29B	B5
AVENIDA CALITA	SJC	SJ75	33500	38	C3
AVENIDA CAMPANA	NB	NB		32	A3
AVENIDA CAMPO	NB	NB		32	A3
AVENIDA CAPRI	DPT	DPT		37	C5
AVENIDA CARLOS	NB	NB		32	A3
AVENIDA CARMEL	CO	LB	275	29A	C5
AVENIDA CARMEL	CYP	CYP	4300	9	C5
AVENIDA CARMELO	SCL	SC72	100	39	F6
AVD CASTILLA	CO	LB	300	29A	D6
AVENIDA CENTINA	CO	LB		29A	A3
AVD CERRITOS	NB	NB		32	A3
AVENIDA CHICA	SCL	SC72		39	C3
AVENIDA CHICO	NB	NB		32	A3
AVENIDA CIENEGA	ANA	AN		13	D1
AVD CINCO D MYO	FTNV	SA08	10300	22	A6
AVD COLUMBIA	MVJO	SJ91		29B	C4
AVENIDA COLUMBO	SCL	SC72		39	E2
AVENIDA COPETE	CO	LB		29A	B4
AVENIDA CORDOBA	ANA	AN		8	E6
AVD CORDOBA E&W	SCL	SC72	100	39	D4
AVD CORNELIO E	SCL	SC72	100	39	E4
AVD CORNELIO W	SCL	SC72	100	39	E5
AVENIDA CORONA	DPT	DPT	24000	37	C5
AVD COSTANERO	CO	LB		29A	B4

STREET	CITY	P.O. ZONE	BLOCK	PAGE	GRID
AVD COSTANSO	SCL	SC72	300	39	F5
AVENIDA COTA	SCL	SC72	100	39	F5
AVENIDA CRESPI	SCL	SC72	200	39	F5
AVENIDA CUMBRE	NB	NB		31	F3
AVENIDA CUMBRE	NB	NB		32	A3
AVENIDA DAROCA	CO	TRA		59	C6
AVENIDA DAROCA	CO	TRA		62	A1
AVD DE DESPACIO	YL	YL		40	B5
AVD DE KRISTINE	YL	YL		40	B4
AVD D L CARLOTA	CO	LB	22900	29A	C4
AVD D L ESTRL N	SCL	SC72	100	39	D3
AVD D L ESTRL S	SCL	SC72	100	39	D3
AVD D LA GRULLA	SCL	SC72	100	39	C3
AVD DE LA LUZ	YL	YL		8	D3
AVD DE LA PAZ	SCL	SC72	100	39	D2
AVD DE LA PLATA	CO	LB		29C	E5
AVD D L RIVIERA	SCL	SC72	200	39	D5
AVD D LS BANDRS	CO	SJ88		59	A3
AVD D LAS ESTRL	YL	YL		8	D3
AVD D LS FLORES	CO	LB		29C	E5
AVD D LS FLORES	CO	SJ		56	D6
AVD D LS FLORES	CO	SJ		59	C1
AVD D LS FLORES	YL	YL	4200	8	C3
AVD D LS PALMRS	SCL	SC72		39	A5
AVD D LS PALMRS	SCL	SC72		39	D6
AVD DE LA VISTA	SJC	SJ75		36	B5
AVD DEL CABALLO	CO	LB77	25900	36	B2
AVD DEL CORRO	CO	TRA		62	A1
AVD DEL CORTO	FUL	FL		6	A2
AVD DEL ESTE	YL	YL	4400	8	D2
AVENIDA DEL MAR	SCL	SC72	100	39	D3
AVD DEL NORTE	FUL	FL33	1100	5	F2
AVD DEL NORTE	YL	YL	20000	8	C2
AVD DL PRESDNTE	SCL	SCL		39	A5
AVD D LS ARBOLS	YL	YL		8	D3
AVD D LS CERITO	SJC	SJ75	3100	36	C6
AVD D LS FUNDAD	CO	SJ		59	C2
AVD D L LOBOS M	SCL	SC72	100	39	E5
AVD D LOS NINOS	CO	LB		29C	E5
AVD D LOS REYES	YL	YL		8	D3
AVD DEL OSSA	FUL	FL33		5	F3
AVD D LS SUENOS	YL	YL		8	D3
AVD DL PONIENTE	SCL	SC72	100	39	C3
AVD DEL REPOSO	SCL	SC72	100	39	C3
AVENIDA DEL REY	YL	YL	4400	8	C3
AVD DEL ROSAL	SJC	SJ75	33000	38	A2
AVENIDA DEL SOL	CO	LB	23000	29A	A5
AVENIDA DL TREN	YL	YL		40	B5
AVD DEL VALLE	YL	YL	4800	8	D3
AVD DEL VERDOR	SCL	SC72		39	F4
AVD DE MARCIA	YL	YL		40	B4
AVD DE MICHELE	YL	YL		40	B5
AVD DE PIO PICO	PLA	PLA	1000	12	A1
AVD DL PRESDNTE	SCL	SC72		39	E4
AVD DE SACARAMA	SJC	SJ75	31900	36	A6
AVD DE SACARAMA	SJC	SJ75	31900	38	A1
AVD DE SANTIAGO	ANA	AN		13	F4
AVD DE SANTIAGO	ANA	AN		43	A4
AVD DESCANSO	SJC	SJ75	32700	38	A2
AVENIDA DESEO	MVJO	SJ91	26000	29B	B5
AVD DESPACIO	CO	LB	23000	29A	A4
AVD DE VIENTOS	ANA	AN		13	E5
AVD DE VINEDOS	ANA	AN		13	E5
AVENIDA D YORBA	ANA	AN		13	E5
AVENIDA DOLORES	SCL	SC72	100	39	F6
AVENIDA DOMINGO	MVJO	SJ91		29B	C4
AVD DOMINGUEZ	SCL	SC72	100	39	E6
AVENIDA EL CID	YL	YL		8	D4
AVENIDA EMPRESA	CO	SJ88		59	A3
AVENIDA ENCINA	ANA	AN	100	13	C1
AVENIDA ESPADA	SCL	SC72		39	C1
AVD ESPINAZO	CO	LB		29A	B4
AVD ESPLANDIAN	SCL	SC72	2500	39	E5
AVD ESTACION	SCL	SC72		39	C3
AVENIDA EVITA	SJC	SJ75	32000	36	A6
AVENIDA EVITA	SJC	SJ75	32000	38	A1
AVENIDA FACETA	SCL	SC72		39	C1
AVD FACILITAR	MVJO	SJ91	23800	29B	B4
AVENIDA FARO	ANA	AN		13	C3
AVENIDA FELIPE	ANA	AN		13	B2
AVD FLORENCIA	SCL	SC72	100	39	C3
AVD FLORENCIA	YL	YL		8	E4
AVD FLORESTA	CO	ET		51	F6
AVENIDA FUENTES	SCL	SC72		39	C1
AVENIDA GAVIOTA	SCL	SC72	100	39	D4
AVD GOLONDRINA	SJC	SJ75	26800	38	C1
AVENIDA GRANADA	CYP	CYP	4300	9	C6
AVENIDA GRANADA	SCL	SC72	100	39	D3
AVENIDA GRANADA	YL	YL		8	E5
AVD HACIENDA	SCL	SC72	1500	39	C3
AVENIDA JUAREZ	ANA	AN		13	D1

STREET	CITY	P.O. ZONE	BLOCK	PAGE	GRID
AVD JUNIPERO E	SCL	SC72	100	39	E4
AVD JUNIPERO W	SCL	SC72	100	39	E5
AVENIDA LA CAZA	CO	SJ		59	D4
AVD LA COSTA	SCL	SC72	200	39	D5
AVD LA CUESTA	SCL	SC72	100	39	D2
AVENIDA LADERA	NB	NB	500	32	A3
AVD LA MANCHA	SJC	SJ75		36	E6
AVD LA MANCHA	SJC	SJ75		38	E1
AVD LA PALOMA	SJC	SJ75	26800	38	C1
AVENIDA LA PATA	SCL	SC72		39	F1
AVENIDA LA PATA	SCL	SC72		71	B5
AVD LA PROMESA	CO	TRA		59	C6
AVD LA PROMESA	CO	TRA		62	A1
AVENIDA LARGA	SJC	SJ75	27300	38	D1
AVENIDA LARGO	NB	NB	500	32	A3
AVD LAS PALMAS	DPT	SC24	26400	38	C5
AVENIDA LA VIDA	ANA	AN		13	C3
AVENIDA LEANDRO	SJC	SJ75		38	B1
AVENIDA LIBRE	CO	ET		51	E6
AVENIDA LOBEIRO	SCL	SC72	200	39	E5
AVENIDA LORENZO	NB	NB	500	32	A3
AVD LOS AMIGOS	SJC	SJ75	32100	38	C1
AVENIDA LUCIA	NB	NB		32	A3
AVENIDA LUCIA	SCL	SC72	100	39	F6
AVENIDA LYSANNE	ANA	AN		13	D1
AVENIDA MADRID	CYP	CYP	4200	9	C5
AVENIDA MADRID	SCL	SC72	200	39	D4
AVD MAGDALENA E	SCL	SC72	100	39	E5
AVD MAGDALENA W	SCL	SC72	100	39	E5
AVD MAGNIFICA	CO	ET		51	F6
AVENIDA MAJORCA	CO	LB	174	29A	D6
AVENIDA MAJORCA	CO	LB	500	29C	D1
AVENIDA MALAGA	ANA	AN		13	D1
AVD MANANTIAL	CO	ET		29A	F1
AVD MANANTIAL	CO	ET	21300	51	F6
AVD MAREJADA	SCL	SC72		38	E6
AVD MAREJADA	SCL	SC72		39	C1
AVD MARGARITA	ANA	AN		13	B2
AVD MARIPOSA	SJC	SJ75	25900	38	A2
AVENIDA MATEO	CYP	CYP	9700	9	C5
AVENIDA MATEO	SCL	SC72	100	39	D3
AVD MENDOCINO	SCL	SC72		39	E5
AVENIDA MESITA	SCL	SC72		38	E5
AVENIDA MIRAMAR	SCL	SC72	100	39	D3
AVD MONTALVO	SCL	SC72	100	39	E5
AVD MONTEREY	CYP	CYP	9500	9	C5
AVD MONTEREY	SCL	SC72	100	39	D4
AVENIDA NARCISO	CO	ET	25100	51	F6
AVENIDA NAVARRO	ANA	AN		13	C3
AVENIDA NAVARRO	SCL	SC72		39	C2
AVENIDA NUBES	CO	ET	21200	51	E6
AVENIDA OLIVA	SCL	SC72		39	C1
AVENIDA OLIVERA	SJC	SJ75	32800	38	B2
AVENIDA ORTEGA	SCL	SC72	300	39	F5
AVD PACIFICA	CO	ET		51	E4
AVENIDA PADRE	SJC	SJ75	26800	38	C1
AVD PAJARITO	DPT	OR	19000	37	F4
AVENIDA PALA	SCL	SC72	100	39	F6
AVD PALIZDA E&W	SCL	SC72	100	39	D3
AVENIDA PALMAR	CO	OR	22900	18	B2
AVENIDA PALMAR	OR	OR		18	B2
AVENIDA PALMERA	ANA	AN	100	13	D1
AVD PTRO DL ORO	SCL	SC72		39	D2
AVD PEDREGAL	SJC	SJ75		38	A2
AVENIDA PELAYO	SCL	SC72	100	39	C3
AVD PESCADOR	SJC	SJ75		38	C4
AVENIDA PICO	CO	SC72		71	B6
AVENIDA PICO	SCL	SC72	400	39	D1
AVENIDA PICO	SCL	SC72		71	D5
AVENIDA PINA	ANA	AN	100	13	C1
AVENIDA PINO	SCL	SC72		38	F6
AVENIDA PINO	SCL	SC72		39	C1
AVENIDA PIZZARO	SCL	SC72	100	39	D3
AVD PLANICIE	CO	ET	21200	51	E6
AVD PLATANAR	SCL	SC72		39	C1
AVENIDA PORTOLA	ANA	AN		13	C2
AVD PRESIDIO	SCL	SC72	100	39	E3
AVD PRINCESA	SCL	SC72	100	39	E4
AVD PSTA DL SOL	YL	YL	19900	8	C3
AVD RAMONA E	SCL	SC72	100	39	E4
AVD RAMONA W	SCL	SC72	100	39	E5
AVD RIO BRAVO	ANA	AN		8	E6
AVD RIO DEL ORO	YL	YL	4300	8	C3
AVENIDA RIVIERA	CO	LB56		35	E2
AVENIDA ROMERO	SJC	SJ75	25900	38	B2
AVENIDA ROSA	SCL	SC72	100	39	D3
AVD SALVADOR	SCL	SC72	100	39	E2
AVD SN ANTNIO E	SCL	SC72	100	39	E4
AVD SN ANTNIO W	SCL	SC72	100	39	E5
AVD SAN CARLOS	SCL	SC72	200	39	E2

STREET	CITY	P.O. ZONE	BLOCK	PAGE	GRID
AVD SAN DIEGO	SCL	SC72	100	39	F6
AVD SAN DIMAS	SCL	SC72	100	39	E6
AVD SN FERNANDO	SCL	SC72	100	39	E6
AVD SN GBRIEL E	SCL	SC72	100	39	E5
AVENIDA SN JUAN	SCL	SC72		39	E4
AVD SAN LORENZO	FUL	FL33	1800	5	F3
AVD SN LUIS REY	SCL	SC72	100	39	F6
AVD SAN PABLO	SCL	SC72	100	39	F4
AVD SANTA ANITA	LAH	LAH		2	A6
AVD SANTA ANITA	LAH	LAH		6	A1
AVD STA BARBARA	LAH	LAH		2	A6
AVD STA BARBARA	LAH	LAH		6	A1
AVD STA BARBARA	SCL	SC72	200	39	D4
AVD STA CATALNA	LAH	LAH		2	A6
AVD STA CATALNA	LAH	LAH		6	A1
AVD STA DOROTEA	LAH	LAH	200	6	A1
AVD SANTA ELENA	LAH	LAH	200	6	A1
AVD SANTA INEZ	SCL	SC72	100	39	F5
AVD STA MARGRTA	SCL	SC72	100	39	F6
AVD SANTIAGO	SCL	SC72	100	39	D4
AVD STO DOMINGO	LAH	LAH	200	6	A1
AVENIDA SEGOVIA	ANA	AN		8	E6
AVENIDA SELVA	FUL	FL33	1500	5	E3
AVENIDA SERRA	ANA	AN		13	C2
AVENIDA SERRA	SCL	SC72	100	39	D3
AVENIDA SEVILLA	CO	LB	266	29A	C6
AVENIDA SEVILLA	CO	LB	400	29C	D1
AVENIDA SEVILLA	CYP	CYP	4100	9	C5
AVENIDA SHONTO	MVJO	SJ91		29B	B3
AVENIDA SIEGA	SJC	SJ75		36	E5
AVENIDA SIERRA	SCL	SC72	100	39	D2
AVENIDA SOLEDAD	FUL	FL	1000	6	A3
AVENIDA SOSIEGA	CO	LB	24000	29A	A5
AVENIDA SOSIEGA	CO	LB		29C	A1
AVD SOSIEGA W	CO	LB		29A	A6
AVD SOSIEGA W	CO	LB		29C	A1
AVENIDA TERESA	SCL	SC72		39	E2
AVD TESORERO	CO	LB		29A	B4
AVENIDA TOPANGA	MVJO	SJ91		29B	C4
AVD TRANQUILA	CO	ET		51	E4
AVENIDA TRIESTE	SCL	SC72		39	E4
AVD VALENCIA	SCL	SC72	100	39	D4
AVD VALVERDE	CO	LB		29A	A3
AVENIDA VAQUERO	SCL	SC72		38	D6
AVENIDA VAQUERO	SCL	SC72	300	39	B1
AVD VERACRUZ	ANA	AN		13	D1
AVENIDA VERANEO	CO	ET		51	E6
AVENIDA VERDE	SCL	SC72	100	39	E4
AVD VERONICA	MVJO	SJ91		29B	B4
AVD VICTORIA	SCL	SC72	100	39	D3
AVD VIS DL OCNO	SCL	SC72		39	D6
AVD VIS HERMOSA	SCL	SC72		38	F6
AVD VIS HERMOSA	SCL	SC72		39	C1
AVD VIS MONTANA	SCL	SC72		39	E1
AVENTURA	CO	SJ88		59	B3
AVENTURA LN	MVJO	SJ91		29B	B4
AV ABUELITOS	FTNV	SA08		22	B5
AV ALVARADO	PLA	PLA		7	C3
AV COMPADRES	FTNV	SA08		22	B5
AV DEL SOL	PLA	PLA	3500	7	C3
AV DE VACA	PLA	PLA	14000	7	C3
AV MENDOCINO	IRV	SA	14100	24	C6
AV OF THE ARTS	CM	CM26		28	A2
AV SAUSALITO	IRV	SA	3700	24	C6
AV SUENOS	FTNV	SA08		22	A5
AVENUE SUR	IRV	SA	3700	24	C6
AVENUE W	LAG	LB51	400	34	F4
AVERY PKWY	MVJO	SJ92	29000	36	B1
AVIEMORE DR	YL	YL		8	F3
AVIEMORE TER	CM	CM27	1100	31	A1
AVILA PL	OR	OR	1200	13	B6
AVILA PL	OR	OR		18	C1
AVILA RD	CO	LB		29C	D5
AVILA WY	BPK	BP		5	C3
AVILLA LN	HTB	HB	17500	26	A1
AVOCADO AV	NB	NB	600	32	B6
AVOCADO AV	NB	NB	100	33	A1
AVOCADO AV	YL	YL	4200	8	A2
AVOCADO DR	TUS	TUS		24	D3
AVOCADO LN	SJC	SJ75		36	B2
AVOCADO ST	ANA	AN	800	11	E4
AVOCADO ST	BREA	BREA	1000	2	F5
AVOCADO ST	BREA	BREA	1100	3	A5
AVOCADO ST	CM	CM27	200	31	D1
AVOCADO ST	FTNV	SA08	16500	21	E5
AVOCADO ST	IRV	SA	3800	29	C1
AVOCADO WY	ANA	AN	1000	11	F5
AVOCADO WY	TUS	TUS		24	B4
AVOCET LN	CO	LB		35	D2
AVOLENCIA DR	FUL	FL	1300	6	B3
AVOLINDA DR	YL	YL	18000	7	F3

STREET	CITY	P.O. ZONE	BLOCK	PAGE	GRID
AVOLINDA DR	YL	YL	18100	8	A3
AVON CIR	ANA	AN	2100	10	F5
AVON CIR	LAP	BP23	5100	9	D4
AVON CIR	WSTM	WSTM	15400	22	A3
AVON PL	ANA	AN	500	11	E5
AVON PL	PLA	PLA	1200	7	B4
AVON ST	NB	NB	2600	31	C4
AVONDALE AV	ANA	AN	2500	10	E2
AVONDALE DR	CO	LB	24700	29C	E4
AVONDALE DR	FUL	FL33		5	F2
AVONDALE PL	ANA	AN	2500	10	E2
AWLSBURY CIR	FUL	FL33		5	D4
AWLSBURY CT	CO	ET	25700	29B	A3
AYAMONTE	MVJO	SJ92		29D	C4
AYON CIR	CM	CM	1900	27	B4
AZAL CT	CO	LB56		29C	E4
AZALEA	CO	ET		51	F6
AZALEA	CO	ET		52	A6
AZALEA	CO	SJ88		59	B5
AZALEA AV	FTNV	SA08	9500	21	F4
AZALEA AV	FTNV	SA08	11500	22	C4
AZALEA AV	PLA	PLA	800	7	C5
AZALEA CIR	FTNV	SA08	9600	21	F4
AZALEA CIR	GGR	GG	10300	16	A3
AZALEA DR	BPK	BP	7800	10	C2
AZALEA DR	CM	CM	900	27	E2
AZALEA WY	ANA	AN08		43	A1
AZALEA WY	WSTM	WSTM	15600	21	E3
AZELA CIR	YL	YL		40	B4
AZITA CT	GGR	GG		15	D5
AZORES RD	DPT	LB77	32400	37	C2
AZTEC CIR	SA	SA	2800	22	D3
AZTEC CT	FTNV	SA08		27	A3
AZUER	MVJO	SJ91		29D	C3
AZUL DR	DPT	SC24		38	C6
AZURE AV	CO	SA	2300	32	B1
AZURE ST	ANA	AN	1700	7	F5
AZURE SEA	CO	LB77		35	C6
AZURE SEA	DPT	LB77		37	C1
AZUSA CIR	CO	SA		18	B4
AZUSA ST	CO	ET	23400	29A	D3
B					
B ST	ETMC	SA09		51	B3
B ST	HTB	HB47	16800	21	C5
B ST	HTB	HB		26	C6
B ST	NB	NB	100	33	B5
B ST	TUS	TUS	15500	23	F3
B ST N&S	TUS	TUS	100	23	F3
BABB ST	CM	CM	2900	27	E3
BABBITT AV	ANA	AN	1500	16	F1
BABCOCK ST	CM	CM27	1600	31	B3
BACALAR	MVJO	SJ91	21800	29B	D1
BACH CIR	BPK	BP	6400	5	C6
BACHMAN DR	SA	SA	100	17	B5
BACKBAY CIR	HTB	HB		26	B2
BACK BAY DR	NB	NB	22500	31	F3
BACK BAY DR	NB	NB	20600	32	A4
BACK BAY LP	CM	CM		27	F6
BACKS LN	PLA	PLA		7	B5
BADAJOZ DR	BPK	BP	7500	5	B4
BADGER PASS	IRV	SA		29	C2
BADGER PASS LN	OR	OR		12	B5
BAFFIN CIR	HTB	HB	15300	20	E3
BAGGETT ST	GGR	GG	11400	16	A2
BAGNALL AV	PLA	PLA	200	7	C2
BAGNALL DR	PLA	PLA	200	7	B2
BAHAMA LN	HTB	HB	21500	30	E1
BAHAMA PL	CM	CM	1700	27	B3
BAHAMAS	MVJO	SJ92		29B	E2
BAHAMONDE	MVJO	SJ92		29D	D2
BAHIA	IRV	SA14		28	F3
BAHIA BLANCA	CO	LB	21000	29A	A5
BAHIA BLANCA E	CO	LB		29A	A5
BAHIA BLANCA W	CO	LB	21500	29A	A5
BAHIA BLANCA W	CO	LB53	21500	32A	F5
BAHIA MESA CT	IRV	SA		32	C1
BAILEY DR	OR	OR	2100	12	F5
BAILEY ST	GGR	GG45	11800	14	E3
BAILEY ST	OR	OR	2300	12	E4
BAINBRIDGE AV	ANA	AN	3900	12	E2
BAINBRIDGE CIR	ANA	AN	300	12	F2
BAINFORD DR	HTB	HB	8800	26	E5
BAJA	NB	NB		32	A3
BAJA AV	LAH	LAH	2000	1	E5
BAJA DR	ANA	AN		13	D1
BAJA ST	LAG	LB51	800	34	F4
BAJA MAR	CO	ET		51	E4
BAJA PANORAMA	CO	SA	18900	18	B3
BAKE LN	CO	ET		29A	D1

1990 ORANGE COUNTY STREET INDEX

STREET	CITY	P.O. ZONE	BLOCK	PAGE	GRID
BAKE PKWY	CO	ET		29A	D1
BAKE PKWY	IRV	SA18		29A	C2
BAKER AV	FUL	FL33	1500	10	E1
BAKER AV	FUL	FL	400	11	B1
BAKER DR	ANA	AN	200	10	C4
BAKER DR	HTB	HB47	6800	21	A6
BAKER ST	ANA	AN	500	10	E5
BAKER ST	CM	CM	700	27	D4
BAKER ST	CM	CM26	600	28	A4
BAKER ST	PLA	PLA	300	7	A5
BAKER ST	WSTM	WSTM	14100	20	E1
BAKER ST N	SA	SA	1700	17	A6
BAKER ST N&S	SA	SA	100	23	A2
BAKER ST S	SA	SA	3400	28	A1
BAKER CANYON RD	CO			47	B6
BAKER CANYON RD	CO			50	B1
BAKERY ST	OR	OR68	3600	16	F3
BALADA	MVJO	SJ92	28000	29B	D4
BALADRE RD	SJC	SJ75		38	B3
BALANTREE CIR	YL	YL		8	F3
BALBOA AV	GGR	GG	13100	16	E3
BALBOA AV	LAG	LB51	900	34	F4
BALBOA AV	LAG	LB51	300	35	A4
BALBOA AV	NB	NB	600	31	F6
BALBOA BLVD	NB	NB		31	A2
BALBOA BLVD E&W	NB	NB	100	31	B5
BALBOA BLVD W	NB	NB	200	33	A5
BALBOA CIR	HTB	HB	22000	30	E2
BALBOA DR	SB	SB	400	19	E3
BALBOA LN	TUS	TUS		23	E3
BALBOA PL	FUL	FL	200	6	B3
BALBOA PZ	ANA	AN		16	B3
BALBOA RD	FUL	FL	2200	6	C2
BALBOA ST	WSTM	WSTM	15300	21	D3
BALBOA WY	CYP	CYP	9800	9	F6
BALBOA COVES	NB	NB	3800	31	B4
BALCOM AV N&S	FUL	FL	100	6	D6
BALCON	MVJO	SJ91		29B	C1
BALDWIN AV	OR	OR	1200	12	E3
BALDWIN CIR	BPK	BP	8200	5	C4
BALDWIN PL	IRV	SA		24	F6
BALDWIN ST	CO	LAH	1200	1	E3
BALEARIC DR	CM	CM	1900	27	A4
BALEARIC RD	DPT	LB77	32500	37	C2
BALER AV	BREA	BREA		3	C6
BALERMA	MVJO	SJ92	21500	29B	E1
BALFOUR AV	FUL	FL	2400	6	F5
BALFOUR AV	FUL	FL	2600	7	A5
BALFOUR CIR	GGR	GG		16	E4
BALGAIR CIR	HTB	HB	20800	26	F6
BALI CIR	CM	CM	3000	27	B3
BALI ST	SA	SA		22	C3
BALL RD	BPK	BP	6000	9	D6
BALL RD	BPK	BP	6500	10	B6
BALL RD	CO	AN04	9500	10	B6
BALL RD	CO	AN06	15000	12	A5
BALL RD	CYP	CYP	4000	9	D6
BALL RD	LALM	LALM	3800	9	D6
BALL RD E	ANA	AN	2400	12	A5
BALL RD E&W	ANA	AN	100	11	B6
BALL RD W	ANA	AN	2100	10	B6
BALLAD DR	ANA	AN	1700	8	B6
BALLAD LN	HTB	HB	16000	20	D4
BALLANTINE DR	CO	LALM	12000	14	A4
BALLANTINE LN	HTB	HB47	16000	21	A4
BALLARD DR	GGR	GG	10300	16	A2
BALLAST AV	GGR	GG43	10500	22	A3
BALLAST AV	SA	SA	5200	22	A3
BALLAST LN	ANA	AN	1800	11	A2
BALLIET DR	VPK	OR67	10300	13	A6
BALLOCH ST	CO	LB		35	C2
BALLOU CIR	WSTM	WSTM	19400	21	F2
BALLOW LN	CM	CM	2800	27	E4
BALMORAL DR	HTB	HB	6300	26	A1
BALMORAL PL	CM	CM27	2000	31	A1
BALOS DR	GGR	GG	13300	15	C5
BALSA AV	BREA	BREA	400	2	F5
BALSA LN	FTNV	SA08	18100	26	F2
BALSA ST	IRV	SA	3800	29	C1
BALSAM AV	ANA	AN	800	11	D2
BALSAM AV	ANA	AN	2200	12	A2
BALSAM LN	CO	ET		51	F5
BALSAWOOD	IRV	SA		29	B5
BALTA	CO	LB77		35	D6
BALTAR	MVJO	SJ91	22600	29B	D3
BALTIC SEA DR	DPT	LB77	32300	37	C1
BALTIMORE AV	HTB	HB	200	26	C6
BALTRA PL	CM	CM	2000	27	A4
BAMBOO ST	NB	NB	2500	32	A2
BAMDAL ST	SA	SA	600	22	E5
BANANA BLVD	SA	SA		22	E2
BANANA ST	FTNV	SA08	16000	21	F4
BANBURY AV	WSTM	WSTM	10000	22	A4
BANBURY CIR	ANA	AN	2100	10	F5
BANBURY CIR	LAP	BP23	5100	9	D3
BANBURY CRSS RD	CO	SA05	1100	18	B6
BANBURY CRSS RD	CO	SA05	1200	24	B1
BANCROFT AV	LAH	LAH	2400	1	D4
BANCROFT CIR	HTB	HB	20300	26	E5
BANCROFT WY	TUS	SA10	3000	29	A1
BANDE	MVJO	SJ91	22100	29B	C2
BANDERA WY	BREA	BREA		2	E6
BANDERAS	MVJO	SJ91		29D	C3
BANDILIER CIR	FTNV	SA08	18400	27	B2
BANDIT CIR	HTB	HB		20	B4
BANFF LN	HTB	HB	21300	30	D1
BANFF ST	STN	STN	10200	10	C6
BANGOR ST	GGR	GG	12100	16	D3
BANGOR WY	ANA	AN	2100	11	F3
BANICK DR	ANA	AN	100	10	C4
BANKTON DR	HTB	HB		25	E1
BANNER AV	GGR	GG	11500	16	C5
BANNER DR	GGR	GG	11500	16	C5
BANNING AV	HTB	HB	8500	30	E2
BANNING PL	CM	CM	900	27	C6
BANNING PL	CO	CM27	900	27	B6
BANNOCK RD	WSTM	WSTM	6000	14	F5
BANNOCK RD	WSTM	WSTM	6200	15	A5
BANSTEAD	CO	SJ79		59	D3
BANTA AV	CO	AN04	9500	15	E1
BANTING	IRV	SA18		29	F6
BANYAN AV	ANA	AN	1200	11	E2
BANYAN AV	SB	SB	4100	14	C4
BANYAN CT	ANA	AN	2500	12	A2
BANYAN LN	ANA	AN	2100	11	F2
BANYAN LN	ANA	AN	2100	12	A2
BANYAN PL	ANA	AN	2100	11	F2
BANYAN PL	ANA	AN	2200	12	A2
BANYAN ST	FTNV	SA08	17200	21	F6
BANYAN ST	IRV	SA	3800	29	C1
BANYAN TREE LN	IRV	SA		29	A5
BANYON RD	TUS	TUS		24	D4
BANYON RIM RD	YL	YL		8	D1
BARANO	MVJO	SJ91		29B	D2
BARBADANES	MVJO	SJ92		29D	C3
BARBADOS	MVJO	SJ92		29B	D1
BARBADOS AV	CYP	CYP	6000	14	F2
BARBADOS CIR	HTB	HB	21000	30	D1
BARBADOS DR	DPT	DPT		37	E2
BARBADOS DR	PLA	PLA	800	7	D4
BARBADOS PL	CM	CM	3100	27	C3
BARBARA AV	GGR	GG	12500	15	E4
BARBARA AV E	PLA	PLA	900	7	D3
BARBARA BLVD	FUL	FL	100	6	C3
BARBARA CIR	BPK	BP	10000	10	A6
BARBARA ST N	ANA	AN	100	12	B3
BARBARA WY	ANA	AN	400	12	B3
BARBARA ANNE ST	CYP	CYP	10100	9	D6
BARBARAGLEN LN	LAH	LAH	900	1	F5
BARBATE	MVJO	SJ92	27800	29B	F4
BARBER ST	WSTM	WSTM	14100	20	E1
BARBERA	CO	LB		29A	B5
BARBERRY RD	TUS	TUS		24	B4
BARBETTE AV	GGR	GG43	10500	22	A3
BARBETTE AV	SA	SA	5200	22	A3
BARBI LN	LALM	LALM	11200	14	C2
BARBI LN	LAP	BP23	7400	9	D2
BARBOSA	MVJO	SJ92	28400	29B	E4
BARCELONA	CO	ET		29A	F4
BARCELONA	IRV	SA14		28	F4
BARCELONA	WSTM	WSTM		21	E2
BARCELONA CIR	FUL	FL	100	6	B1
BARCELONA CIR	LAP	BP23	5200	9	D2
BARCELONA CIR	PLA	PLA		7	E6
BARCELONA CT	GGR	GG		16	A4
BARCELONA DR	MVJO	SJ92		29D	E3
BARCELONA LN	CYP	CYP	9800	9	E6
BARCELONA LN	HTB	HB47	17100	21	D6
BARCELONA PL	DPT	DPT	33800	37	E4
BARCLAY CT	SA	SA		23	E1
BARCLAY DR	CYP	CYP	4000	14	D5
BARCLAY DR	GGR	GG	11000	15	E2
BARCLAY LN	CO	LAG		35	F3
BARCLAY LN	CO	ET		52	B6
BARD AV	IRV	SA	17500	28	F4
BARDEEN AV	IRV	SA	18800	28	C5
BARDON LN	HTB	HB47	16800	21	B5
BAREFOOT CIR	HTB	HB	16700	20	D5
BARENTS ST	CO	LB		29C	E2
BAR HARBOR LN	HTB	HB		26	A4
BARISTO	IRV	SA		32A	B2
BARK ST	CO	ET	24200	29A	E5
BARKENTINE BLVD	CO	LB77		37	D2
BARKENTINE BLVD	DPT	DPT		37	D2
BARKER CIR	WSTM	WSTM	13800	15	A6
BARKER ST	GGR	GG	12400	15	A4
BARKER WY	PLA	PLA	800	7	A3
BARKLEY AV E	OR	OR	300	17	D1
BARKLEY AV W	OR	OR	700	17	D1
BARKLEY ST	HTB	HB46		26	F3
BARKSTONE LN	CO	LB53		29D	A4
BARKWOOD AV	IRV	SA	4900	29	D2
BARLOVENTO	MVJO	SJ92	22600	29B	E3
BARLOVENTO CT	NB	NB		31	A3
BARNEBURG	CO	SJ79		59	D4
BARNES TR	CO	SJ		56	B3
BARNETT ST	ANA	AN	500	11	F4
BARNETT WY	GGR	GG	13200	16	B5
BARNEY CIR	GGR	GG	13800	16	A6
BARNEY ST	GGR	GG	13900	16	A6
BARNEY ST	WSTM	WSTM	13200	14	F5
BARNSDALE ST	ANA	AN	600	10	F5
BARNSTABLE CIR	HTB	HB	16300	20	D4
BARON CIR	HTB	HB	17900	26	C1
BARONESS	CO	LB77		36	A3
BARONET	MVJO	SJ92		29D	D4
BARONET PL	FUL	FL33		5	E3
BARQUE WY	DPT	DPT	25200	37	F3
BARQUE WY	DPT	DPT		38	A3
BARQUERO DR	MVJO	SJ91	24000	29B	B5
BARQUILLA	MVJO	SJ91		29B	C4
BARR LN	CO	GG41	8500	15	D3
BARR LN	GGR	GG	8800	15	D3
BARRACUDA LN	HTB	HB		20	D5
BARRACUDA WY	LAG	LB51	600	35	A4
BARRANCA	NB	NB		32	A3
BARRANCA CIR	HTB	HB		30	F5
BARRANCA PKWY	IRV	SA	1500	28	D1
BARRANCA PKWY	IRV	SA		29	B3
BARRANCA PKWY	IRV	SA18		29A	B1
BARRANCA PKWY	IRV	SA18		51	A5
BARRANCA RD	IRV	SA	3900	29	C5
BARRANCA ST	LAG	LB51	100	34	B2
BARRANCA WY	LAG	LB77		37	B2
BARRENGER CT	NB	NB		32	B3
BARRETT CIR	BPK	BP	5200	5	C4
BARRETT DR	CO	ET	23700	29A	D3
BARRETT LN	CO	SA	12600	18	B5
BARRETT ST	CO	SA	10600	18	B5
BARRETT HLL CIR	CO	SA	13000	18	B5
BARRIER REEF DR	NB	CDLM		32	B6
BARRINGTON CT	FUL	FL	2800	7	A3
BARRINGTON DR	CO	LAM	8000	5	C3
BARRIS DR	FUL	FL	700	6	B4
BARRO CIR	MVJO	SJ91		29D	C4
BARRY DR	CYP	CYP	6000	9	F6
BARRY LN	CO	SA	18600	18	B4
BARRY PL	PLA	PLA	400	7	B4
BARRY PL	WSTM	WSTM	8500	21	D5
BARRYKNOLL ST	ANA	AN	100	12	F2
BARSTEN WY	ANA	AN		12	B1
BART DR	GGR	GG	11500	15	E2
BARTH AISLE	IRV			29	F2
BARTLETT LN	HTB	HB47	16500	21	B5
BARTLETT ST	GGR	GG45	11800	14	E3
BARTOLOME	MVJO	SJ92	22900	29B	D3
BARTON DR	HTB	HB47	7700	21	C6
BARTON ST	CO	ET	23500	29A	D3
BARUNA CT	NB	NB		31	B4
BARUNA LN	HTB	HB	16600	20	C5
BARWOOD DR	HTB	HB		25	E1
BASCOM ST	IRV	SA	17900	28	F5
BASIL ST	ANA	AN		8	F6
BASIL ST	ANA	AN		13	F1
BASIL ST	FTNV	SA08	16000	21	F4
BASIN CIR	HTB	HB		26	B3
BASITA	MVJO	SJ92		52	E6
BASKERVILLE RD	CO	LALM	11300	14	A2
BASQUE AV S	FUL	FL	1000	11	A1
BASQUE CIR	ANA	AN	1300	11	F2
BASQUE CIR	ANA	AN	1300	12	A2
BASQUE PL	ANA	AN	1100	11	F2
BASQUE PL	ANA	AN	1100	12	A2
BASQUE AV N&S	FUL	FL	100	6	A6
BASS	IRV	SA		29	B3
BASS DR	HTB	HB	9500	26	E3
BASSANO E	CO	LB		29A	A3
BASSANO W	CO	LB		29A	A3
BASSE LN	BREA	BREA	200	2	E5
BASSETT PL	IRV	SA		24	F6
BASSETT WY	ANA	AN	1400	11	F5
BASS LAKE CIR	CO	ET		29A	F1
BASSWOOD AV	SB	SB	4000	14	C4
BASSWOOD CIR	TUS	TUS	2300	24	A5
BASSWOOD LN	BREA	BREA		2	D2
BASSWOOD LN	IRV	SA		29	A6
BASSWOOD ST	FTNV	SA08	18200	26	F2
BASSWOOD ST	NB	NB	900	32	B3
BASTANCHURY RD	CO	YL	16500	7	E2
BASTANCHURY RD	YL	YL	16500	7	E2
BASTANCHURY RD	YL	YL	18100	8	A2
BASTANCHRY RD E	FUL	FL	100	6	C2
BASTANCHRY RD E	FUL	FL	2600	7	A2
BASTANCHRY RD E	PLA	PLA	100	7	B2
BASTANCHRY RD W	FUL	FL33	900	5	F4
BASTANCHRY RD W	PLA	PLA	100	7	B2
BASTIA	CO	LAG		35	F4
BASTIA	NB	NB60		32	E3
BASTIA LN	HTB	HB	20900	26	D6
BATAAN CT	LALM	LALM		14	C3
BATAAN ST	CYP	CYP	6300	14	F2
BATAVIA ST	CO	OR65	9100	12	C5
BATAVIA ST	CO	OR69	10300	17	C3
BATAVIA ST N	OR	OR	1400	12	C5
BATAVIA ST N&S	OR	OR	100	17	C3
BATES CIR	ANA	AN	1700	7	C6
BATES CIR	HTB	HB		20	E6
BATES CIR	HTB	HB		25	E1
BATES DR	YL	YL	4400	7	E3
BATES ST	IRV	SA	3600	28	F4
BATES WY	STN	STN		10	E4
BATES WY	STN	STN		15	B2
BATON ROUGE	IRV	SA14		29	F3
BATTERY ST	SJC	SJ75	27000	38	C1
BAUER RD	ANA	AN		8	F6
BAUSCH WY	LAG	LB51	1000	34	F3
BAUTISTA	MVJO	SJ92		29D	F3
BAUTISTA DR	CO	LB	25200	29D	A1
BAWLEY	CO	LB77		37	E1
BAXTER CIR	HTB	HB	17700	26	A1
BAXTER ST	ANA	AN	1000	11	F2
BAXTER ST	FUL	FL	1600	11	F1
BAXTER ST	OR	OR	1400	12	D6
BAY	IRV	SA		29	D2
BAY AV E&W	NB	NB	100	31	C6
BAY AV W	NB	NB	400	31	D6
BAY CIR	FTNV	SA08	17700	26	E1
BAY DR	LAG	LB77	1	37	B2
BAY DR	HTB	HB		26	C6
BAY DR	SCL	SC72		39	A2
BAY ST	FTNV	SA08	17700	26	E1
BAY ST E&W	CM	CM27	100	31	C1
BAYADERE DR	NB	CDLM	1900	32	A6
BAYADERE TER	NB	CDLM	1500	33	A1
BAYBERRY	CO	LB56		29C	C2
BAYBERRY	MVJO	SJ92		29B	E2
BAYBERRY CT	ANA	AN		13	D2
BAYBERRY LN	CO	SJ79		56	E6
BAYBERRY ST	OR	OR69		18	E3
BAYBERRY WY	FUL	FL33	2100	5	D4
BAYBERRY WY	IRV	SA	18100	28	F5
BAYBERRY WY	YL	YL		40	D5
BAY BREEZE DR	HTB	HB	9500	30	F2
BAY CLIFF CIR	NB	CDLM		32	C6
BAY COVE LN	NB	NB		31	F5
BAY COVE LN	NB	NB		32	A5
BAY CREST	SA	SA04		27	F2
BAY CREST CIR	HTB	HB	12300	30	F4
BAYCREST CT	NB	SA07		28	B6
BAYCREST DR	EBAY	LB51	100	34	B2
BAYCREST PL	DPT	DPT		37	B5
BAYCREST PL	FUL	FL33	2100	5	D4
BAYCREST RD	NB	NB	2100	31	E3
BAYES ST	CO	ET		29A	F3
BAY FARM PL	CO	SA	2300	32	A1
BAY FRONT N	NB	NB	100	31	E6
BAY FRONT S	NB	NB	100	31	F6
BAY FRONT S	NB	NB		33	C5
BAYFRONT LN	CO	ET		29A	D3
BAYFRONT LN	HTB	HB		26	C5
BAYHILL CT	GGR	GG		16	D6
BAY HILL DR	NB	NB		32	B4
BAY LEAF ST	CO	SJ88		59	B1
BAYLESS ST	ANA	AN	1400	11	B6
BAYLESS ST	ANA	AN	1500	16	B1
BAYLOR AV	ANA	AN	2600	10	D3
BAYLOR CIR	ANA	AN	2600	10	D3
BAYLOR CIR	HTB	HB47	13000	21	A2
BAYLOR DR	WSTM	WSTM	7600	21	C1
BAYLOR ST	IRV	SA	3600	28	F4
BAYMARE DR	YL	YL		8	D2
BAY MEADOW DR	HTB	HB	9500	26	F5
BAY MEADOWS DR	PLA	PLA	200	7	F5
BAYMIST	CO	LB	5100	29A	C4
BAYMIST DR	HTB	HB46		26	C3
BAYONNE CIR	IRV	SA	5100	29	D3
BAYONNE DR	HTB	HB	8500	26	D4
BAYOU	IRV	SA		29	E1
BAYOU WY	SB	SB	1700	19	F2
BAYPOINT	HTB	HB		26	C6
BAYPORT CIR	ANA	AN	1800	11	A4
BAYPORT DR	HTB	HB		26	A6
BAYPORT DR	HTB	HB		30	C1
BAYPORT ST	GGR	GG	12000	16	E3
BAYPORT WY	DPT	DPT		38	D3
BAYPORT WY	NB	NB	2000	31	E2
BAYRIDGE DR	NB	NB		32	C3
BAYSHORE DR	ANA	AN	1100	11	A2
BAY SHORE DR	NB	NB	2400	31	D5
BAYSHORE LN	CO	ET		29A	D3
BAY SHORE LN	HTB	HB	16300	20	E5
BAYSIDE	IRV	SA		29	B4
BAYSIDE DR	NB	NB	300	31	F6
BAYSIDE DR	NB	CDLM	1400	32	A6
BAYSIDE DR	NB	CDLM	1900	33	A1
BAYSIDE DR	SB	SB	600	19	F2
BAYSIDE LN	DPT	DPT		38	D3
BAYSIDE LN	HTB	HB47	15400	21	A3
BAYSIDE PL	NB	CDLM	200	33	A1
BAYSIDE COVE E	NB	NB		31	F6
BAYSIDE COVE W	NB	NB		31	F6
BAYTREE RD	SJC	SJ75		36	B2
BAYVIEW	IRV	SA		29	B4
BAYVIEW AV	CO	SA	20000	32	B1
BAYVIEW CIR	NB	NB60		28	B6
BAYVIEW CIR	NB	NB60		32	B1
BAYVIEW DR	CO	SUNB	16600	20	B5
BAYVIEW DR	HTB	HB	16600	20	B5
BAYVIEW DR	NB	CDLM	2500	33	A1
BAY VIEW PL	LAG	LB51	600	34	E2
BAYVIEW PL	NB	SA07		28	B6
BAYVIEW PL	NB	SA07		32	B1
BAYVIEW TER	CM	CM27		31	F1
BAYVIEW WY	NB	SA07		32	B1
BAYWATER LN	HTB	HB		26	D4
BAYWOOD	CO	LB56		29C	C2
BAYWOOD AV	ANA	AN	2900	10	C4
BAYWOOD AV	OR	OR65		12	C5
BAYWOOD CT	CO	YL		8	F3
BAYWOOD DR	BREA	BREA	1200	2	C4
BAYWOOD DR	FUL	FL33		5	E2
BAYWOOD DR	HTB	HB		26	D3
BAYWOOD DR	NB	NB		32	B5
BAYWOOD RD	EBAY	LB51	200	34	B1
BEA WY	LAH	LAH	1700	2	C4
BEACH AV	IRV	SA	14600	24	C6
BEACH AV	IRV	SA	14700	29	C1
BEACH BLVD	BPK	BP	4600	5	B5
BEACH BLVD	BPK	BP	6700	10	B2
BEACH BLVD	CO	LAH	3200	1	E6
BEACH BLVD	CO	BP21	4500	5	C2
BEACH BLVD	CO	LAH	3300	5	C2
BEACH BLVD	CO	GG41	12400	15	C4
BEACH BLVD	CO	WSTM	15200	21	C5
BEACH BLVD	GGR	GG	13000	15	C5
BEACH BLVD	HTB	HB47	15700	21	C1
BEACH BLVD	HTB	HB	17500	26	C3
BEACH BLVD	HTB	HB	21000	30	C1
BEACH BLVD	STN	STN	10100	10	C6
BEACH BLVD	STN	GG41	12500	15	C4
BEACH BLVD	STN	STN	10500	15	C4
BEACH BLVD	WSTM	WSTM	13400	15	C5
BEACH BLVD	WSTM	WSTM	14000	21	C5
BEACH BLVD N&S	ANA	AN	100	10	C6
BEACH BLVD N&S	LAH	LAH	100	1	E6
BEACH CT	TUS	SA10		29	A2
BEACH DR	NB	NB		31	A6
BEACH DR	NB	CDLM	100	33	B2
BEACH DR	SCL	SC72		39	A2
BEACH RD	DPT	SC24	34800	38	B6
BEACH ST	CM	CM27	600	31	C2
BEACH ST	LAH	LAH	800	1	E3
BEACH ST N&S	LAG	LB51	100	34	D3
BEACH WY	BPK	BP	4700	5	D4
BEACH CLUB DR	DPT	LB77	32900	37	B3
BEACHCOMBER	CO	LB		29A	C4
BEACHCOMBER DR	HTB	HB		26	C6
BEACHCOMBER DR	NB	CDLM		32	E5
BEACHCOMBER DR	SB	SB	600	19	F2
BEACHCREST LN	HTB	HB46		26	C3
BEACHMONT AV	CO	SA	18400	18	A6
BEACHSIDE DR	HTB	HB	9500	30	F2
BEACH TER DR	GGR	GG		15	C5
BEACHTREE CT	ANA	AN08		43	B1

STREET	CITY	P.O. ZONE	BLOCK	PAGE	GRID
BEACHVIEW	CO	LB		29A	C4
BEACHWALK WY	DPT	DPT		37	A5
BEACHWOOD LN	HTB	HB	20800	26	E6
BEACHWOOD ST	OR	OR	4100	12	D2
BEACHY PL	ANA	AN	2500	10	D5
BEACON AV	ANA	AN	2000	10	F5
BEACON AV	ANA	AN	1100	11	B5
BEACON AV	GGR	GG43	10500	22	A3
BEACON DR	HTB	HB		26	D5
BEACON ST	BREA	BREA		2	D5
BEACON ST	FUL	FL	2500	7	B2
BEACON ST	NB	NB	2200	31	C4
BEACON BAY	NB	NB	300	31	E6
BEACON HILL LN	HTB	HB		26	B3
BEACON HILL WY	CO	LB77		35	E6
BEACONSFIELD	CO	SJ79		59	D3
BEAL AV	PLA	PLA	100	7	B2
BEAM CIR	HTB	HB		26	D5
BEAR ST	CM	CM	3000	27	F4
BEAR ST	SA	SA04	3000	27	F1
BEAR BRAND RD	CO	LB77		37	E2
BEAR CREEK	CM	CM		27	D2
BEARD LN	HTB	HB	17800	26	D1
BEARDSLEY CIR	VPK	OR67	10400	17	F1
BEARGRASS CIR	CO	LB	24000	29C	E4
BEARPAW	IRV	SA		29	C2
BEARSDEN CIR	HTB	HB	20500	26	E5
BEARTREE LN	OR	OR69		18	E2
BEAR VIA	ANA	AN		16	D2
BEATON WY	OR	OR	2400	17	A2
BEATRICE CIR	BPK	BP	10000	9	F6
BEATRICE ST	CYP	CYP	10500	14	F1
BEAUDETTE	MVJO	SJ92		29D	F3
BEAUMONT CIR	HTB	HB46	20000	27	A5
BEAUMONT CT	NB	NB		32	B3
BEAUTY DR	ANA	AN	4500	12	F2
BEAUXWOOD ST	GGR	GG	11700	16	E3
BEAVER CIR	CYP	CYP	10100	9	C6
BEAVER ST	IRV	SA	3800	28	F4
BECARD DR	CO	LB	24100	35	D2
BECCA DR	GGR	GG	11000	15	F2
BECEDAS	MVJO	SJ91		29B	C2
BECHLER RIV AV	FTNV	SA08	10500	27	A2
BECK AV	GGR	GG	12300	16	D4
BECK CIR	HTB	HB		25	E1
BECKENHAM ST	CO	LB		29C	E1
BECKLEY CIR	VPK	OR67	17800	17	F1
BECKMAN AV	IRV	SA	2500	28	E2
BECKNOLL LN	CO	SA	11000	18	D5
BECKWALL LN	HTB	HB		25	E1
BECKWITH TER	IRV	SA	10400	32	F2
BECKWOURTH CIR	HTB	HB	21000	26	F6
BEDEL DR	HTB	HB	8900	26	E5
BEDFORD CIR	ANA	AN	1700	7	C6
BEDFORD CT	CYP	CYP	10400	14	F1
BEDFORD CT	YL	YL		40	A3
BEDFORD DR	CO	LB		29D	A6
BEDFORD DR	FUL	FL	2200	7	A3
BEDFORD DR	IRV	SA		24	F6
BEDFORD LN	HTB	HB	16900	20	D5
BEDFORD LN	NB	NB	1600	31	E4
BEDFORD LN	WSTM	WSTM	14100	15	E6
BEDFORD LN	WSTM	WSTM	14100	21	E1
BEDFORD RD	OR	OR	300	17	B4
BEDFORD ST N	LAH	LAH	300	2	B5
BEDFORD ST S	LAH	LAH	100	2	B5
BEECH AV	YL	YL		8	D2
BEECH LN	CO	ET	22400	29A	C2
BEECH ST	FTNV	SA08	17700	26	E1
BEECHNUT RD	TUS	TUS	2100	24	B4
BEECH TREE LN	IRV	SA		29	A6
BEECHWOOD	CO	LB56		29C	E6
BEECHWOOD	IRV	SA		29	C4
BEECHWOOD AV	FUL	FL	800	6	D2
BEECHWOOD AV	FUL	FL35		6	F2
BEECHWOOD CIR	WSTM	WSTM	9900	21	F3
BEECHWOOD DR	BREA	BREA		2	D4
BEECHWOOD ST	ANA	AN		11	F3
BEECHWOOD ST	OR	OR	2400	12	C4
BEECHWOOD ST	SA	SA	1000	17	C5
BEECHWOOD WY	CO	ET		51	F6
BEECHWOOD WY	STN	STN	7700	15	B3
BEESON LN	CO	TUS	14500	24	A1
BEESON LN	SA	SA	2500	23	C6
BEETHOVEN DR	BPK	BP	8200	5	C6
BEGONIA AV	CM	CM	900	27	E2
BEGONIA AV	FTNV	SA08	11000	22	B5
BEGONIA AV	NB	CDLM	400	33	A1
BEGONIA CIR	BPK	BP	7900	10	D2
BEGONIA DR	YL	YL		8	D5
BEGONIA PL	MVJO	SJ92		29D	D4

STREET	CITY	P.O. ZONE	BLOCK	PAGE	GRID
BEGONIA ST	WSTM	WSTM	15500	21	F3
BEL-AIR	CO	SJ79		59	C6
BEL AIR CIR	WSTM	WSTM	8600	21	D3
BEL AIR ST	BPK	BP	8600	10	C4
BEL AIR ST N	ANA	AN	100	10	C4
BEL AIR ST S	ANA	AN	300	10	C5
BELAIRE	CO	LB77		35	D6
BEL AIRE ST	IRV	SA	14600	29	D1
BELCANTO	IRV	SA14		29	A3
BELCARO DR	HTB	HB46		26	E6
BELCOURT DR N	NB	NB		32	B3
BELCOURT DR S	NB	NB		32	B3
BELCREST	CO	LB77		35	D5
BELDAY ST	CO	CYP	8700	9	D4
BELFAST AV	CM	CM	1200	27	D3
BELFAST DR	GGR	GG	9700	15	F5
BELFAST LN	HTB	HB47	15800	21	A3
BELFAST WY	EBAY	LB51	700	34	B1
BELFORD AV	PLA	PLA	2000	7	B2
BELFORD DR	SJC	SJ75	31200	36	D5
BELGRADE ST	WSTM	WSTM		21	F3
BELGRAVE AV	GGR	GG45	5300	14	F3
BELGRAVE AV	GGR	GG	6300	15	A3
BELGRAVE AV	STN	GG41	7700	15	C3
BELGREEN PL	CO	ET	24500	29A	E5
BELHA WY	CO	SIL		53	A1
BELHAVEN ST	ANA	AN	1100	11	F6
BELINDA CIR	ANA	AN	100	10	E4
BELL	IRV	SA		29	E1
BELL AV	ANA	AN	1200	11	F5
BELL AV	SA	SA	400	28	B1
BELL AV	TUS	TUS	1000	23	E5
BELL CIR	HTB	HB	17900	26	C1
BELL ST	STN	STN	10500	15	B1
BELLA DR	CO	ET		29A	E3
BELLAGIO	CO	LB77		35	E4
BELLAGIO RD	OR	OR69		18	C2
BELLAMY AV	ANA	AN	2900	12	B3
BELLA VISTA	CO	LB77		36	A1
BELLAVISTA	IRV	SA14		28	D5
BELLA VISTA DR	OR	OR69		18	C2
BELLA VISTA ST	ANA	AN	100	10	B5
BELLBROOK ST	OR	OR	2300	12	D4
BELL CANYON DR	CO	SJ79		59	E4
BELLCROFT DR	CO	ET		29B	A2
BELLE AV	BPK	BP	6000	9	F6
BELLE AV	CYP	CYP	5000	9	D6
BELLEFORD DR	TUS	SA	2000	24	B3
BELLEHURST AV	WSTM	WSTM	10200	22	A1
BELLE ISLE DR	CO	LAG		36	A5
BELLE LOMA	CO	LB77		36	A2
BELLE MAISON	CO	LB77		35	C5
BELLERIVE CIR	CO	LB	24100	35	E4
BELLEVUE DR	ANA	AN	600	11	C5
BELLEVUE PL	ANA	AN	800	11	C5
BELLEZA CIR	MVJO	SJ91		29D	C3
BELLEZA LN	ANA	AN		12	F3
BELLEZZA	IRV	SA		24	E5
BELLFIELD LN	HTB	HB		25	F1
BELLFLOWER	IRV	SA		29	B2
BELLFLOWER AV	FTNV	SA08	11000	22	B4
BELLFLOWER DR	BPK	BP	7700	10	D2
BELLHAVEN ST	ANA	AN	1100	11	F6
BELLHAVEN ST	LAP	BP23	8200	9	D3
BELLINGER DR	HTB	HB47	6200	21	A4
BELLINGHAM PL	CO	LB77		35	E6
BELLIS ST	NB	NB	700	32	A3
BELLMEAD DR	HTB	HB	8500	26	D4
BELLO PL	CO	LB	30000	35	E3
BELLOGENTE	MVJO	SJ91		29D	C5
BELLO PANORAMA	SCL	SC72		38	F5
BELLOTA	MVJO	SJ92	25000	29D	D1
BELLPORT CIR	HTB	HB	17400	20	E6
BELLSHIRE DR	HTB	HB	8800	26	E5
BELLS VIREO LN	CO	LB56		29C	A2
BELLWOOD RD	CO	LALM	12300	14	A4
BELMAR CIR	HTB	HB	14600	20	F2
BELMAR DR	CO	LB		35	D3
BELMEZ	CO	LB	23000	29A	A5
BELMONT	NB	NB		32	C5
BELMONT AV	ANA	AN	1200	11	E2
BELMONT CT	ANA	AN	2400	12	A2
BELMONT CT	BREA	BREA		3	C6
BELMONT CT	PLA	PLA		7	F5
BELMONT DR	CO	LB		29D	A6
BELMONT LN	PLA	PLA		7	F5
BELMONT PL	ANA	AN	2200	11	F2
BELMONT PL	ANA	AN	2200	12	A2
BELMONT ST	CO	CYP	8500	9	D4
BELMONT WY	PLA	PLA		7	F5
BELMONTE	IRV	SA20		29	F1

STREET	CITY	P.O. ZONE	BLOCK	PAGE	GRID
BELMONTE	MVJO	SJ92		29D	D2
BELMONTE RD	CO	LB	22900	35	C5
BELQUEST DR	CO	ET	24700	29A	E3
BELSHIRE WY	CO	ET		29B	B1
BELSITO DR	HTB	HB47	7600	21	C6
BELTY CIR	WSTM	WSTM	9500	21	F2
BELVA DR	HTB	HB		26	B1
BELVEDERE RD	ANA	AN	2900	12	B3
BELVEDERE ST	IRV	SA	4000	29	C1
BELVIEW RD	LAG	LB	700	34	B1
BELVUE LN	NB	CDLM		33	A1
BELVUE LN	NB	NB		33	C6
BEN AV	STN	STN		15	D1
BENCHLEY CIR	WSTM	WSTM	14500	22	A2
BENDIX	IRV	SA18		29A	D1
BENDRICON LN	CO	ET	24500	29A	E4
BENECIA AV	CO	LB	30300	35	E4
BENETA WY	CO	TUS	18000	23	F1
BENETA WY	CO	TUS	18100	24	A1
BENETA WY	TUS	TUS	200	23	F1
BENICHIA CIR	FTNV	SA08	15900	22	A4
BENICIA PZ	YL	YL		8	C3
BENIDORM	MVJO	SJ92		29D	C4
BENISA	MVJO	SJ92		29D	C5
BENJAMIN	IRV	SA		24	D6
BENJAMIN AV	PLA	PLA		7	E6
BENJAMIN CIR	DPT	DPT	24500	37	E2
BENJAMIN DR	HTB	HB	8400	26	D1
BEN LOMOND LN	YL	YL	18700	8	A3
BENMORE LN	ANA	AN	1500	11	E1
BENNETT	CO	ET		29B	A3
BENNETT AV	OR	OR	2700	17	F3
BENNINGTON	IRV	SA		24	E6
BENNINGTON	IRV	SA		29	E1
BENNINGTON DR	CO	SA		18	C5
BENNINGTON ST	LALM	LALM	17000	14	D2
BENT ST	LAG	LB51	400	34	D3
BENTLEY CIR	TUS	TUS		24	B5
BENTLEY LN	CO	LB		29A	F6
BENTLEY LN	CO	LB		29C	F1
BENTLY AV	STN	GG41	7700	15	C3
BENTON AV	WSTM	WSTM	7500	15	C5
BENTON ST	GGR	GG	13000	16	A5
BENTON WY	SA	SA	2200	17	B5
BENT TREE LN	CO	SA	11000	18	D6
BENT TREE LN	CO	SA	11800	24	C1
BENT TREE LN	CO	ET		29A	E1
BENT TREE RD	CO	SA05		18	D6
BENT TWIG LN	CO	TUS	1700	24	B3
BENTWOOD	CO	LB77		35	F3
BENTWOOD CT	CO	YL		8	C6
BENTWOOD LN	CO	LB		29C	D4
BENWOOD DR	ANA	AN	300	10	D5
BERDUN	MVJO	SJ91	27500	29B	D2
BEREAN LN	IRV	SA		32	F2
BERENICE DR	BREA	BREA	800	2	D4
BERGAMO	CO	LB77		35	F5
BERGAMO	IRV	SA14		29	A4
BERGANTIN	MVJO	SJ92	22700	29B	D3
BERGEN CIR	TUS	TUS	17200	23	E1
BERGENIA	CO	SJ		59	C1
BERGH DR	ANA	AN	5300	13	B1
BERG RIVER CIR	FTNV	SA08		22	D4
BERING ST	PLA	PLA	1200	7	D4
BERING SEA DR	DPT	LB77	23000	37	C2
BERKELEY AV	FUL	FL	100	6	D5
BERKELEY AV	IRV	SA17		32	E2
BERKELEY AV	WSTM	WSTM	5000	14	E6
BERKELEY AV N	FUL	FL	100	6	C4
BERKELEY CIR	FUL	FL	100	6	D6
BERKELEY CIR	OR	OR	2500	12	C4
BERKELEY ST	OR	OR	2700	12	C3
BERKELEY ST	SA	SA		22	F4
BERKELEY ST E	SA	SA	100	23	A4
BERKELEY ST W	SA	SA	900	23	A4
BERKENHAM WY	WSTM	WSTM	13900	14	D6
BERKENHAM WK	WSTM	WSTM		14	D6
BERKENSTOCK CIR	PLA	PLA	800	7	C2
BERKENSTOCK LN	PLA	PLA	600	7	D2
BERKLEY AV	LAH	LAH	2300	1	E4
BERKLEY ST	ANA	AN	1200	10	A6
BERKSHIRE	CO	SJ79		59	D3
BERKSHIRE DR	FUL	FL33		5	F2
BERKSHIRE LN	HTB	HB	19800	26	F4
BERKSHIRE LN	LAH	LAH		2	B6
BERKSHIRE LN	NB	NB	1100	31	E4
BERKSHIRE LN	SJC	SJ75		36	C2
BERKSHIRE PL	TUS	TUS	14600	23	F5
BERKSHIRE WY	GGR	GG	13600	16	B6
BERKSHIRE WY	PLA	PLA	300	7	C1

STREET	CITY	P.O. ZONE	BLOCK	PAGE	GRID
BERLARK CIR	HTB	HB	17500	25	F1
BERLIN LN	HTB	HB	17000	20	E6
BERMUDA AV	WSTM	WSTM	8500	21	D3
BERMUDA CIR	IRV	SA	4300	29	E5
BERMUDA CIR	PLA	PLA	1200	7	D5
BERMUDA DR	CM	CM	3100	27	C3
BERMUDA DR	HTB	HB	9000	30	E2
BERMUDA DR	LAG	LB51	1300	34	E2
BERMUDA DUNES	MVJO	SJ92		29B	E3
BERN CT	LAG	LB51	3000	34	F1
BERN DR	LAG	LB51	3000	34	F1
BERN LN	SA	SA	2300	16	E5
BERNADAL PL	SA	SA	4500	22	C2
BERNADETTE AV	BPK	BP	10000	9	F6
BERNARD CT	LAG	LB51	2800	35	A2
BERNARD DR	FUL	FL	900	6	D1
BERNARD ST	CM	CM27	400	31	C2
BERNARD ST	CYP	CYP		9	D6
BERNARDY PL	ANA	AN	1800	16	A1
BERNAY	CO	LB77		35	E5
BERNI ST	SA	SA	300	22	B1
BERNICE CIR	BPK	BP	10000	9	F6
BERNICE CIR	CYP	CYP	10500	14	F1
BERNIECE DR	ANA	AN	100	10	F4
BERNIECE DR	ANA	AN	200	11	A4
BERNINI	IRV	SA14		29	A4
BERRENDO	CO	LB56		29C	E3
BERRY AV	ANA	AN	300	11	D6
BERRY AV	BPK	BP	6500	10	A2
BERRY AV	CO	AN04	10700	15	E1
BERRY RD	TUS	SA10		23	F5
BERRY ST	BREA	BREA	200	2	D4
BERRY ST	SA	SA	400	22	C3
BERRY WY	BREA	BREA	500	2	D5
BERRY WY	LAH	LAH	400	1	E5
BERRY GLEN	CO	ET		52	C3
BERRYHILL DR	YL	YL		7	F4
BERRY TREE LN	CO	OR	18900	18	B2
BERSHIRE DR	HTB	HB		25	F1
BERSUCH ST	WSTM	WSTM	13300	15	A5
BERTON CIR	LAP	BP23	4800	9	D2
BERWICK	MVJO	SJ91		29D	C5
BERWICK CT	CYP	CYP	4000	9	C4
BERYL	BREA	BREA	18700	4	B5
BERYL AV	ANA	AN	2500	10	E5
BERYL LN	NB	NB	1800	31	E3
BERYL COVE WY	SB	SB	400	19	F3
BESTEL AV	GGR	GG	8000	15	E5
BESTEL AV	WSTM	WSTM	6500	15	B5
BETA AV	GGR	GG	11500	16	C4
BETA PL	ANA	AN	1400	11	E4
BETANZOS	MVJO	SJ92		29D	C3
BETH CIR	ANA	AN	200	12	B3
BETH ST	ANA	AN	400	12	B3
BETHANY	CO	LB77		35	D6
BETHANY DR	IRV	SA		32	F3
BETHEL CIR	HTB	HB	19300	26	D3
BETHEL DR	ANA	AN	2400	12	A4
BETMOR LN	ANA	AN		16	F2
BETTES PL	ANA	AN04	1500	15	F1
BETTES PL	ANA	AN	1500	16	A1
BETTES PL	GGR	GG	11000	16	A2
BETTONI ISLE	IRV	SA14		28	D5
BETTY DR	ANA	AN		13	C1
BETTY DR	HTB	HB47	7000	21	B6
BETTY LN	GGR	GG	12200	16	B3
BETTY LN	LAH	LAH	100	2	A3
BEVAN AV	WSTM	WSTM	9200	21	E3
BEVER PL	STN	STN	8000	15	C3
BEVERLY DR	ANA	AN	1400	11	B4
BEVERLY DR	FUL	FL	700	6	A5
BEVERLY DR	HTB	HB46	10000	27	A5
BEVERLY DR	OR	OR	1200	17	B2
BEVERLY LN	GGR	GG	9800	15	F4
BEVERLY LN	WSTM	WSTM	10100	22	A3
BEVERLY PL	SA	SA	300	23	C3
BEVERLY ST	LAG	LB51	100	34	C2
BEVERLY GLEN DR	CO	SA	1700	24	C1
BEVERLY MANR RD	SB	SB	3400	14	A5
BEWLEY ST	GGR	GG	13700	16	D6
BEWLEY ST N	SA	SA	100	22	D2
BEWLEY ST S	SA	SA	900	22	D2
BEXLEY DR	NB	NB		32	B3
BEXLEY LN	CO	BREA	1400	2	D3
BEXLEY ST	WSTM	WSTM	14000	20	E1
BIAK ST	CYP	CYP	6500	15	A2
BIANCO	CO	LB	20000	29A	A4
BICKFORD ST	PLA	PLA	100	7	B2
BICKLEY CIR	GGR	GG	9100	15	E2
BICKLEY DR	HTB	HB	9500	26	F4
BIDDLE DR	IRV	SA	20000	32	F2

STREET	CITY	P.O. ZONE	BLOCK	PAGE	GRID
BIENVILLE AV	CO	AN04	9600	10	F6
BIG BEAR CIR	BPK	BP	8200	5	C4
BIG BEN CT	FTNV	SA08		26	F2
BIG BEND DR	CO	LB		29C	F6
BIG BEND DR	CO	LB		35	E1
BIGBEND LN	HTB	HB	20000	26	F5
BIG BIRD LN	CO	ET		29A	E4
BIG CANYON DR	NB	NB		32	B4
BIG DIPPER CT	NB	NB63		31	A2
BIGELOW PARK	CO	TUS	17700	23	F1
BIGELOW PARK	CO	TUS	18100	24	A1
BIG PINES	CO	LB56		29C	B3
BIG SKY LN	ANA	AN		13	B3
BIG SPRING DR	YL	YL	2000	8	C5
BIG SPRING ST	ANA	AN	800	13	C1
BIG SPRINGS RD	CO	SJ79		52	E3
BIG SUR DR	HTB	HB	9800	26	F5
BIG SUR ST	CO	LB56		29C	D3
BIG SUR ST	DPT	DPT	33000	37	F3
BIG SUR ST	DPT	DPT	33000	38	A3
BIG TIMBER ST	CO	ET	24100	29A	D3
BIKINI LN	HTB	HB46	19000	27	A3
BIKINI PL	CO	SA	18700	18	B5
BIKINI ST	CYP	CYP	1600	14	F3
BILLIE JO CIR	ANA	AN	100	12	A3
BILTMORE LN	CO	LB56		29C	E5
BIMINI DR	CO	SA	11000	18	C5
BIMINI LN	HTB	HB	16000	20	C4
BIMINI PL	CM	CM	1600	27	C4
BINGHAMPTON CIR	HTB	HB48	21100	26	A6
BINNACLE AV	GGR	GG	13000	16	E3
BINNACLE AV	OR	OR68	4400	16	E3
BINNACLE RD	DPT	LB77		37	E4
BINNACLE WY	ANA	AN	1300	10	F2
BINNACLE WY	ANA	AN	1200	11	A2
BINNACLE LTN ST	DPT	DPT		37	B5
BIOLA LN	GGR	GG		15	E5
BIRCH	IRV	SA		29	D3
BIRCH AV	OR	OR	1200	17	B2
BIRCH CIR	YL	YL		8	D2
BIRCH LN	BREA	BREA	300	2	E6
BIRCH LN	CO	SJ91		29A	F5
BIRCH PL	FUL	FL	2800	6	D2
BIRCH ST	ANA	AN	1500	11	E3
BIRCH ST	CO	SA07	20000	28	A6
BIRCH ST	CYP	CYP	8300	9	C3
BIRCH ST	FTNV	SA08	18200	26	F2
BIRCH ST	IRV	SA	3500	24	B6
BIRCH ST	NB	NB60		28	B5
BIRCH ST E	BREA	BREA	1000	3	B6
BIRCH ST E&W	BREA	BREA	100	2	E6
BIRCH ST N&S	SA	SA	100	23	B4
BIRCH ST S	SA	SA	3400	28	B1
BIRCHBARK LN	CO	OR	11700	18	B2
BIRCHCREST	MVJO	SJ92		29B	E2
BIRCHCREST AV	BREA	BREA	1000	2	D3
BIRCHCREST CIR	BREA	BREA	1600	2	D3
BIRCHER ST	ANA	AN	200	10	F4
BIRCHFIELD DR	TUS	TUS	1500	24	A4
BIRCH GROVE LN	CO	ET		51	F5
BIRCHIT CIR	YL	YL		7	E4
BIRCHLEAF	MVJO	SJ92		29B	E2
BIRCHLEAF DR	ANA	AN	600	10	C5
BIRCHMONT	CO	LB56		29C	C1
BIRCHMONT DR	ANA	AN	1400	11	B4
BIRCH TREE CT	LAH	LAH		1	E6
BIRCH TREE LN	IRV	SA		29	A5
BIRCHWOOD	MVJO	SJ92		29B	E2
BIRCHWOOD AV	SB	SB	4200	14	C4
BIRCHWOOD CIR	LAP	BP23		9	E2
BIRCHWOOD DR	HTB	HB	10000	26	F5
BIRCHWOOD LN	CO	LB		29C	E4
BIRCHWOOD PL	TUS	TUS	14700	23	F5
BIRCHWOOD RD	OR	OR		18	B2
BIRCHWOOD ST	ANA	AN08		40	A6
BIRCHWOOD ST	GGR	GG	13000	16	B5
BIRD AV	CO	MDWY	8500	21	D2
BIRD AV	WSTM	WSTM	9500	21	E2
BIRD CIR	GGR	GG	9600	21	F2
BIRD CIR	WSTM	WSTM	9300	21	E1
BIRD CT	FTNV	SA08		26	F1
BIRDHOLLOW DR	CO	SJ79		59	E1
BIRDIE LN	HTB	HB	16100	20	E4
BIRDROCK DR	CO	ET	24100	29A	D4
BIRDSONG	IRV	SA		29	B3
BIRD WING	IRV	SA		29	D1
BIRENDRA	CO	ET		52	A6
BIRMINGHAM DR	WSTM	WSTM		20	E1
BIRMINGHAM PL	TUS	TUS	14400	23	F4
BIRTCHER DR	CO	ET		29A	D3
BIRTCHER DR	SA	SA		23	C6

STREET	CITY	P.O. ZONE	BLOCK	PAGE	GRID
BISCAYNE BLVD	GGR	GG	11300	15	F2
BISCAYNE CT	ANA	AN04	1700	15	F1
BISCAYNE CT	GGR	GG	11100	15	F2
BISCAYNE CT	HTB	HB	8800	26	E6
BISCAYNE DR	HTB	HB		30	D2
BISCAYNE PL	FUL	FL33		5	E3
BISCAYNE SPGS	CM	CM27		31	D1
BISHOP	MVJO	SJ92		52	D6
BISHOP AV	CO	MDWY	8000	21	D3
BISHOP AV	WSTM	WSTM	8600	21	D3
BISHOP CIR	VPK	OR67	17600	12	F6
BISHOP DR	HTB	HB47	6500	21	A5
BISHOP DR	LAH	LAH	100	2	A3
BISHOP PL	WSTM	WSTM	9000	21	E3
BISHOP ST	CO	CYP	4900	9	D4
BISHOP ST	CYP	CYP	5500	9	E4
BISHOP ST E&W	SA	SA	100	23	A3
BISHOP PINE LN	GGR	SA03		16	D6
BISMARCK	IRV	SA14		29	F3
BISMARK DR	HTB	HB	10000	26	F4
BISMARK WY	CM	CM	1100	27	E3
BISON AV	NB	NB	700	32	B2
BISQUINE	CO	LB77		37	E1
BITTERBUSH ST	OR	OR	100	17	A3
BITTERN LN	CO	LB		35	D1
BITTEROOT CIR	FTNV	SA08	9000	21	E4
BITTERWOOD	IRV	SA		29	C3
BIXBY AV	GGR	GG	9200	15	E3
BIXBY AV	OR	OR	1000	12	D3
BIXBY CIR	VPK	OR67		13	A6
BIXIA ST	NB	NB	700	32	A2
BIXLER CIR	GGR	GG	11000	16	B3
BIXLER DR	GGR	GG	11200	16	B3
BLACKBEARD	HTB	HB		20	D5
BLACKBERRY	CO	SJ88		59	B5
BLACKBERRY CIR	BPK	BP	7900	10	D2
BLACKBERRY LN	ANA	AN		8	F6
BLACKBERRY LN	ANA	AN		13	F1
BLACKBERRY WY	YL	YL		40	D5
BLACKBERRY COVE	OR	SA05		18	D3
BLACKBIRD	TUS	SA10		23	E6
BLACKBIRD AV	FTNV	SA08	9000	26	E2
BLACKBIRD LN	ANA	AN		13	F2
BLACKBIRD LN	CO	LB53		29A	B6
BLACKBIRD ST	GGR	GG	13000	16	D5
BLACKBURN	CO	SJ79		59	D2
BLACKFIN AV	IRV	SA	4000	24	D5
BLACKFIN CIR	HTB	HB48	9500	26	A6
BLACKFOOT AV	PLA	PLA	2400	7	C2
BLACKFOOT DR	CO	ET	24400	29A	E3
BLACK FOREST LN	YL	YL		8	D1
BLACK HAWK	TUS	TUS		24	B4
BLACK HAWK	TUS	TUS		24	D3
BLACKHAWK CIR	BPK	BP	7300	10	A2
BLACKHEATH CIR	WSTM	WSTM	8900	21	E3
BLACK HORSE LN	CO	LB53		29C	F5
BLACKMER ST	CYP	CYP		14	E3
BLACKMER ST	GGR	GG45	11800	14	E4
BLACK OAK	IRV	SA		29	D3
BLACK OAK RD	ANA	AN	300	12	E3
BLACK PINE CIR	YL	YL		8	D1
BLACKPOOL RD	WSTM	WSTM	14100	20	E1
BLACK RIVER CT	FTNV	SA08	10300	27	A1
BLACK STAR LN	LAP	BP23	7400	9	D2
BLCK STAR CY RD	CO	OR69		44	C6
BLCK STAR CY RD	CO	SA		47	A5
BLCK STAR CY RD	CO			50	A1
BLACKSTONE ST	IRV	SA		29	B2
BLACKSWAN	IRV	SA		29	B3
BLACKTHORN LN	OR	OR		18	B2
BLACKTHORN ST	GGR	GG	12500	15	F4
BLACKTHORN ST	IRV	SA	3600	29	C1
BLACKTHORN ST	NB	NB	2500	32	B3
BLACK WALNUT WY	LAH	LAH	400	1	E5
BLACKWILLOW CIR	ANA	AN08		43	A1
BLACKWOOD LN	ANA	AN		11	E6
BLADES AV	GGR	GG		15	B3
BLAIR AV	SA	SA		28	D1
BLAIR DR	YL	YL	18000	7	F3
BLAIR LN	CO	TUS	1400	24	B2
BLAIR LN	HTB	HB	17000	20	D6
BLAIR PL	IRV	SA		24	F5
BLAIR RIVER CIR	FTNV	SA08		26	E2
BLAIRWOOD DR	LAP	BP23	5200	9	D2
BLAKE AV	GGR	GG	9500	15	F6
BLAKE CT	IRV	SA		32	D2
BLAKE CT	SA	SA		23	E1
BLAKE RD	BREA	BREA	3800	7	D1
BLAKE ST	GGR	GG	10400	16	A6
BLAKE ST	OR	OR	1400	12	D6
BLAKE ST S	LAH	LAH	500	1	E5
BLAKE ST W	LAH	LAH	2300	1	E5
BLAKELEY	IRV	SA		24	E6
BLANCA DR	CYP	CYP	4500	9	C5
BLANCHARD AV	ANA	AN	2100	11	F3
BLANCHE AV	CO	GG41	8500	15	D3
BLANCHE AV	GGR	GG	9200	15	E3
BLANCHE CIR	BPK	BP	10000	10	A6
BLANDINGS	MVJO	SJ92		29B	F6
BLANE CIR	HTB	HB	9400	26	E3
BLANQUITA WY	PLA	PLA	200	7	B2
BLANTON ST	HTB	HB	16600	20	D5
BLASCOS	MVJO	SJ91		29D	C2
BLAYLOCK PL	HTB	HB47	8000	21	C6
BLAZING STAR	IRV	SA	15300	29	C2
BLESSINGTON LN	SJC	SJ75		38	D4
BLINN LN	IRV	SA		32	F2
BLISS LN	TUS	TUS	15900	23	E4
BLOOMDALE	IRV	SA		29	B4
BLOOMFIELD ST	CYP	CYP	9000	9	C5
BLOOMFIELD ST	LALM	LALM	9700	9	C5
BLOOMFIELD ST	LALM	LALM	10400	14	C2
BLOSSOM AV	GGR	GG	8800	15	D3
BLOSSOM LN	ANA	AN	1500	11	E1
BLOSSOM PL E	BREA	BREA	300	2	F4
BLOSSOM PL W	BREA	BREA	2900	2	C4
BLOSSOM PARK ST	CO	ET		29B	A2
BLOUNT PL	IRV	SA		24	F6
BLUE ALLIUM AV	FTNV	SA08	11000	22	B4
BLUEBELL AV	ANA	AN	100	16	D2
BLUEBELL AV	BREA	BREA		3	C5
BLUEBELL AV	FTNV	SA08	11300	22	B4
BLUEBELL AV	GGR	GG	12000	16	C2
BLUEBELL AV	PLA	PLA	300	7	B4
BLUEBELL DR	BPK	BP	8500	10	D2
BLUEBELL DR	CO	LB	28200	29C	E6
BLUEBELL PL	ANA	AN	400	16	E2
BLUEBELL ST	SB	SB	12900	14	C4
BLUEBERRY LN	CO	ET		29A	F2
BLUEBERRY LN	CO	ET		29B	A2
BLUEBERRY LN	SA	SA		16	E6
BLUEBERRY ST	ANA	AN		8	F6
BLUEBERRY ST	ANA	AN		13	F1
BLUEBERRY ST	YL	YL		8	A5
BLUEBERRY WY	CO	TUS	1600	24	B2
BLUEBIRD	IRV	SA		29	B3
BLUEBIRD AV	FTNV	SA08	8600	26	D2
BLUE BIRD AV	OR	OR	4500	18	B1
BLUEBIRD CIR	ANA	AN		13	F2
BLUEBIRD CIR	CM	CM	2700	27	C5
BLUE BIRD DR	CO	ET	23400	29A	D4
BLUEBIRD LN	CO	LB53		29A	B6
BLUEBIRD LN	HTB	HB	15600	20	E4
BLUEBIRD LN	LAP	BP23	8000	9	C3
BLUEBIRD CYN DR	LAG	LB51	100	34	E4
BLUEBIRD CYN LN	LAG	LB51		34	E4
BLUEBIRD GLEN	CO	ET		52	A5
BLUEBONNET DR	HTB	HB47	15500	21	B3
BLUEBROOK LN	YL	YL		40	E6
BLUECOAT	IRV	SA		24	E5
BLUEFIELD DR	HTB	HB48	9700	26	A6
BLUEFIELD PZ	YL	YL	19800	8	C4
BLUE FIN DR	DPT	DPT	25200	38	A3
BLUE FIN DR	SJC	SJ75		38	A3
BLUEFIN LN	HTB	HB	19000	26	F3
BLUE FIN COVE	CO	LB		35	D3
BLUEFISH LN	HTB	HB		26	B3
BLUE FOX CIR	HTB	HB47	7200	21	A6
BLUEGATE LN	HTB	HB		25	F1
BLUEGILL CIR	HTB	HB	19400	26	F3
BLUEGRASS LN	YL	YL		40	D5
BLUEGRASS ST	ANA	AN	1200	11	B2
BLUEGRASS ST	BREA	BREA		3	C6
BLUE GUM DR	YL	YL		8	C1
BLUE GUM LN	NB	NB		31	E4
BLUE GUM ST	ANA	AN	1000	12	B2
BLUE GUM WY	ANA	AN	1000	12	B2
BLUE HERON LN	CO	LB56		29C	A1
BLUEHILL BAY	DPT	LB77	23500	37	C5
BLUEJAY	IRV	SA		29	B3
BLUEJAY	MVJO	SJ92		29B	E2
BLUE JAY AV	OR	OR	4500	18	B1
BLUEJAY CIR	HTB	HB	5000	20	D3
BLUE JAY DR	BPK	BP	6200	9	F1
BLUE JAY DR	CO	LB56		29C	B1
BLUEJAY LN	ANA	AN	1200	11	C2
BLUEJAY LN	GGR	GG	11500	15	F3
BLUE KEY	NB	CDLM		32	C6
BLUE KEY	NB	NB		33	C1
BLUE LAGOON	LAG	LB51		34	F5
BLUE LAKE	IRV	SA		29	B4
BLUE LAKE N	IRV	SA		29	A4
BLUE LAKE S	IRV	SA		29	A4
BLUE LANTERN ST	DPT	DPT	33500	37	E4
BLUE MTN DR	YL	YL		8	E3
BLUE OAK	CO	SJ		59	B3
BLUEREEF DR	HTB	HB	9700	30	F1
BLUE RIDGE	IRV	SA		24	E6
BLUERIDGE AV	OR	OR	100	12	C5
BLUERIDGE CT	CO	YL		8	C6
BLUERIDGE CT	FUL	FL		6	F3
BLUE RIDGE DR	CO	SA	18100	18	A5
BLUE RIDGE DR	PLA	PLA	2300	7	B1
BLUERIDGE RD	CO	ET	25100	29A	E3
BLUE RIVER	IRV	SA		29	B2
BLUEROCK ST	ANA	AN	100	12	F2
BLUE SAIL DR	DPT	DPT	38	38	B4
BLUESAILS DR	HTB	HB47	7000	21	B4
BLUE SPRUCE AV	GGR	GG	12500	16	E4
BLUE SPRUCE WY	STN	STN	7800	15	B3
BLUE STAR ST	ANA	AN	2800	12	B2
BLUEWATER CIR	ANA	AN	4300	12	F2
BLUE WATER DR	NB	CDLM	2600	32	B6
BLUEWATER LN	DPT	DPT		38	D3
BLUE WATER LN	FUL	FL		6	D4
BLUEWATER LN	HTB	HB		20	C6
BLUFF CIR	HTB	HB		26	B2
BLUFF DR	LAG	LB	31400	35	A6
BLUFF DR E	NB	NB	2000	32	A2
BLUFFSIDE CIR	HTB	HB		26	C5
BLUFFSIDE DR	DPT	LB77		37	F2
BLUFFSIDE DR	DPT	DPT	32900	38	A2
BLUFF VIEW	IRV	SA		32A	A3
BLUFFWATER CIR	HTB	HB	20400	26	E5
BLUME DR	CO	LALM	2700	14	A4
BLUMONT ST	LAG	LB51	400	34	D2
BLYSTONE CT	BREA	BREA		2	E6
BOARDWALK	LAG	LB51	300	34	D3
BOARDWALK DR	HTB	HB	4400	20	D5
BOATBILL CIR	FTNV	SA08	8500	26	D3
BOAT CANYON DR	LAG	LB51	200	34	C2
BOATMAN AV	STN	STN	10900	15	C1
BOATSWAIN CIR	ANA	AN	1100	11	A2
BOA VISTA CIR	CM	CM	1800	27	B4
BOA VISTA DR	CM	CM	1900	27	B4
BOBBIE CIR	HTB	HB	9000	30	E1
BOBBY LN	SA	SA	2200	16	E5
BOBOLINK DR	CO	LB	29100	35	D2
BOBWHITE LN	CO	LB53		29A	B6
BOBWHITE WY	OR	OR	100	18	B3
BOCA CANYON DR	CO	SA	10500	18	D5
BOCA D L PLAYA	SCL	SC72	100	39	C3
BOCA DEL CANON	SCL	SC72	1200	39	D4
BOCA RATON PL	CO	LB	31000	35	E5
BOCINA	MVJO	SJ92	27500	29B	D6
BOCINA	MVJO	SJ92	27500	29D	D1
BOCK AV	STN	STN	7200	15	B1
BODA	MVJO	SJ92	28400	29B	E6
BODEGA	CO	ET		51	E4
BODEGA LN	MVJO	SJ91		29D	C3
BODEGA BAY DR	NB	CDLM		32	D6
BODEN DR	ANA	AN	1100	11	E2
BOEING AV	CO	ET	23600	29A	D3
BOEING AV	YL	YL	18500	8	A3
BOGARRA ST	MVJO	SJ92	21500	29B	E1
BOGART CT	FTNV	SA08	15900	22	D6
BOISE	IRV	SA		29	D2
BOISE DR	HTB	HB	8500	26	D4
BOISE WY	CM	CM	1100	27	D3
BOISSERANC DR	ANA	AN	4800	8	A5
BOISSERANC LN	PLA	PLA	1900	7	F5
BOISSERANC ST	CO	AN07	6400	8	A6
BOISSERANC WY	ANA	AN		8	A5
BOLANOS	MVJO	SJ92	28600	29B	E1
BOLEADA DR	MVJO	SJ92		36	C2
BOLERO LN	HTB	HB	16600	20	C6
BOLERO WY	NB	NB	400	31	B4
BOLEYN CIR	CO	TUS	15500	23	E3
BOLIN CIR	HTB	HB	8800	30	E1
BOLINGRIDGE DR	OR	OR	1600	12	D3
BOLIVAR	MVJO	SJ91		29B	D4
BOLIVAR CIR	GGR	GG	12800	16	D5
BOLIVAR PL	GGR	GG	12600	16	D5
BOLIVAR ST	NB	NB		31	C5
BOLIVIA DR	BPK	BP	5700	9	E1
BOLSA AV	CO	MDWY	8000	21	E2
BOLSA AV	GGR	GG43	10500	22	B2
BOLSA AV	HTB	HB	5000	20	E2
BOLSA AV	HTB	HB47	6200	21	E2
BOLSA AV	NB	NB	400	31	C4
BOLSA AV	SB	SB	900	19	E2
BOLSA AV	WSTM	WSTM	6500	21	E2
BOLSA AV	WSTM	WSTM	10000	22	B2
BOLSA WY	LAG	LB51	800	34	E3
BOLSA CHICA RD	SB	SB	14600	20	E1
BOLSA CHICA RD	WSTM	WSTM	13000	14	D6
BOLSA CHICA RD	WSTM	WSTM	14000	20	E2
BOLSA CHICA ST	HTB	HB	14600	20	E5
BOLSANA DR	LAG	LB51	400	34	F4
BOLSANA DR	LAG	LB51	400	35	A4
BOLSA PARK LN	HTB	HB	15200	20	F2
BOLTANA	MVJO	SJ91	22700	29B	D3
BOLTON CIR	HTB	HB		25	F1
BOMO KORAL CIR	SA	SA		23	A1
BONAIRE CIR	HTB	HB	16000	20	C4
BONAIRE WY	NB	NB	2000	31	E2
BONANZA	SCL	SCL		38	E3
BONANZA DR	HTB	HB	5300	20	E5
BONAVENTURE DR	CO	LB56		29C	E5
BOND	IRV	SA18		29	F5
BOND AV	CO	OR	18600	18	A2
BOND AV	LAH	LAH	2400	1	D4
BOND AV	OR	OR	3600	18	A2
BOND CIR	HTB	HB	9800	26	F4
BOND ST	ANA	AN	300	11	E4
BOND WY	CO	SIL	28200	50	E2
BONDURANT CIR	HTB	HB47	16000	21	A4
BONITA DR	HTB	HB		20	E5
BONITA LN	CO	ET		29A	F3
BONITA LN	NB	NB		31	E3
BONITA PL	FUL	FL35	3900	2	C6
BONITA ST	TUS	TUS	1000	23	F3
BONITA WY	LAG	LB51	1000	34	F4
BONITA CYN DR	IRV	SA		32	C2
BONITA CYN DR	IRV	SA		32A	A3
BONITA CYN WY	BREA	BREA		2	F4
BONITA HTS DR	CO	SA	12700	18	B4
BONN DR	LAG	LB51	3100	29C	A6
BONN DR	LAG	LB51	3100	34	F1
BONNEMA ST	WSTM	WSTM	14300	21	E1
BONNER DR	CO	TUS	17500	17	E6
BONNER DR	TUS	TUS	17400	17	E6
BONNIE DR	GGR	GG	10300	16	A5
BONNIE DR	HTB	HB47	6800	21	A5
BONNIE LN	CO	LB53		29C	E6
BONNIE LN E	LAH	LAH	300	2	A3
BONNIE LN N	LAH	LAH	1300	2	A3
BONNIE PL	CM	CM27	2400	31	F1
BONNIE WY	BREA	BREA	900	2	D4
BONNIE ANN CT	LAH	LAH		2	B3
BONNIE BRAE	SA	SA	2400	17	B5
BONNIE BRAE AV	LAG	LB51	900	34	F4
BONNIE BRAE DR	BPK	BP	8300	5	C3
BONNIE DOON TER	NB	NB	1000	31	F6
BONNIE DOON TER	NB	CDLM	1300	32	A6
BONNIE GENE LN	ANA	AN		13	D2
BONSER AV	GGR	GG	10000	15	F3
BON VILLA CIR	LAP	BP23	7200	9	E1
BONVUE TER	LAG	LB51	700	34	C2
BONWOOD AV	CO	ET	24700	29A	E5
BOOM AV	OR	OR	1100	12	D4
BOONE	IRV	SA		29	E1
BOONE CIR	ANA	AN		13	F3
BOONE CIR	WSTM	WSTM		21	D4
BOONE PL	CO	LB		29C	E2
BOONEY ST	WSTM	WSTM	14800	22	A2
BOONY LN	GGR	GG43	14100	22	A1
BOOTH CIR	IRV	SA		29	C3
BOOTH ST	SA	SA	100	23	A2
BOOTHBAY CIR	HTB	HB	8400	26	D5
BOOTHILL CT	CO	LB	27400	29D	A5
BOOTSTRAP PL	CO	LB		29C	F2
BORBA CIR	HTB	HB	9500	30	F1
BORCHARD AV E	SA	SA	700	23	C4
BORCHARD AV W	SA	SA	1300	22	E4
BORCHARD AV W	SA	SA	100	23	A4
BORCHARD CIR	SA	SA	3100	22	D4
BORDEAUX	NB	CDLM		32	D5
BORDEAUX AV	IRV	SA	5100	29	D3
BORDEAUX LN	CM	CM27	300	31	F2
BORDEAUX LN	HTB	HB	16300	20	A6
BORDEAUX ST	GGR	GG	13700	16	D6
BORGONA	MVJO	SJ92	28300	29B	E4
BORMER	IRV	SA14		28	F3
BORRASCA	MVJO	SJ91		29B	C4
BORREGO	CO	SJ		59	B2
BORREGO CT	CO	LB		35	E1
BORREGO DR	LAP	BP23	4900	9	D2
BORROMEO AV	PLA	PLA	100	7	B2
BORTZ ST	OR	OR	2500	12	D4
BOSQUE	MVJO	SJ91		29B	C2
BOSQUE SPRINGS	CM	CM27		31	D1
BOSTON	IRV	SA		29	E2
BOSTON COM	SA	SA		22	C2
BOSTON WY	CM	CM	3100	27	D3
BOSTONIAN DR	CO	LALM	2600	14	A3
BOSUN CIR	HTB	HB	8900	26	E4
BOTHNIA BAY	DPT	LB77		37	D4
BOTORRITA	MVJO	SJ92	28300	29B	E5
BOTRYOIDES AV	BPK	BP	6000	5	B5
BOTTLEBRUSH LN	CO	OR	11700	18	B2
BOUGAINVLLEA RD	SJC	SJ75		38	A3
BOUGAINVILLE PL	ETMC	SA09		51	D3
BOUGH AV	CO	SJ91		29A	F5
BOUMA CIR	LAP	BP23	7700	9	E2
BOUNTY CIR	HTB	HB	3200	20	A5
BOUNTY WY	LAG	LB51	1300	34	E2
BOUQUET AV	ANA	AN	3600	10	A6
BOUQUET DR	HTB	HB47	7200	21	B4
BOURBON LN	LAP	BP23	7400	9	D1
BOURBON ST	CO	OR65	2500	12	D4
BOUVAIS RD	CO	AN04	10200	10	E6
BOW CIR	PLA	PLA	2400	7	B1
BOW PL	CO	SA	13100	18	A5
BOWDITCH	IRV	SA		29	E1
BOWDOIN PL	CM	CM	2400	27	D5
BOWEN CIR	GGR	GG	10500	16	A6
BOWEN ST	GGR	GG	13000	16	A6
BOWEN ST	GGR	GG43	14100	22	A1
BOWEN ST	WSTM	WSTM	14800	22	A2
BOWIE CIR	YL	YL		8	C2
BOWIE ST	WSTM	WSTM		21	D4
BOWLES AV	GGR	GG	11100	15	D2
BOWLING ST	ANA	AN	1700	11	A6
BOWLING GRN DR	CM	CM	200	27	D5
BOWLING GRN ST	WSTM	WSTM	14500	22	A2
BOWMAN LN	HTB	HB		26	D4
BOWSPRIT DR	DPT	DPT		37	F3
BOWSPRIT DR	DPT	DPT	25200	38	A3
BOWSPRIT DR	NB	NB60	19400	28	B6
BOWSPRIT LN	ANA	AN	2000	10	F2
BOWSPRIT LN	ANA	AN	2000	11	A2
BOWSPRIT LN	HTB	HB	21300	30	E1
BOX CANYON DR	YL	YL		40	B4
BOX CANYON RD	OR	OR69		18	F2
BOXELDER	CO	SJ		59	B3
BOXTHORN	CO	SJ		59	C1
BOXWOOD	IRV	SA		29	B5
BOXWOOD AV	FUL	FL	800	6	D2
BOXWOOD CIR	FTNV	SA08	17900	26	F1
BOXWOOD LN	MVJO	SJ91		52	D4
BOXWOOD PL	TUS	TUS		24	D4
BOXWOOD ST	ANA	AN	600	11	C5
BOYD AV	GGR	GG	8500	15	D5
BOYD ST	SA	SA	1600	23	E4
BOYER AV	SA	SA	3500	22	D1
BOYSEN AV	ANA	AN	400	11	D6
BOYSENBERRY LN	PLA	PLA		7	A6
BOZENTA	MVJO	SJ92		29D	F3
BRABHAM DR	HTB	HB	9000	26	E4
BRACKEN ST	BREA	BREA	100	2	E5
BRACKEN WY	LAG	LB77	31900	37	A1
BRAD DR	HTB	HB47	6500	21	A5
BRADBURY	NB	NB		32	C3
BRADBURY CT	OR	OR		12	F3
BRADBURY LN	HTB	HB	16300	20	F4
BRADBURY RD	CO	LALM	3100	14	B3
BRADBURY RD	LALM	LALM	3500	14	B3
BRADCLIFF	CO	SA		18	C4
BRADCLIFF DR	CO	SA	10900	18	C5
BRADEN CT	OR	OR		17	B2
BRADFORD AV	FUL	FL	1500	7	B4
BRADFORD AV N&S	PLA	PLA	100	7	B4
BRADFORD LN	CO	LB53		29D	A4
BRADFORD PL	SA	SA		23	B6
BRADFORD PL	SA	SA		28	B1
BRADFORD PL	STN	STN	11000	15	B2
BRADFORD ST	STN	STN	11000	15	B2
BRADFORD MDWS	GGR	GG		15	F6
BRADFORD MDWS	GGR	GG		21	F1
BRADLEY DR	BPK	BP	7300	9	F2
BRADY AV	ANA	AN	3300	10	B6
BRADY WY	GGR	GG	12700	15	A4
BRAEBURN AV	FUL	FL	2200	7	A3
BRAEBURN CIR	BPK	BP	5100	5	C4
BRAEBURN LN	NB	NB		32	B4
BRAEBURN PL	BPK	BP	5200	5	C4
BRAEBURN RD	TUS	TUS	14700	23	F4
BRAEBURN ST	ANA	AN	1300	10	E2
BRAE GLEN	CO	SA	19200	18	B3
BRAEMAR	MVJO	SJ91		29D	C6
BRAEMAR DR	HTB	HB	6300	26	A1
BRAEMAR WY	NB	NB	2100	31	E2
BRAESWOOD WY	STN	STN	10600	15	C1

STREET	CITY	P.O. ZONE	BLOCK	PAGE	GRID
BRAGG	IRV	SA		24	E6
BRAGG WY	STN	STN	11000	15	B2
BRAHMS CIR	BPK	BP	6400	5	C6
BRAMANTE	IRV	SA14		29	A3
BRAMBLE LN	CO	LB		29C	D4
BRAMBLE WY	FUL	FL33		5	E4
BRAMBLES WY	OR	OR	500	18	D2
BRANBURY PL	TUS	TUS	14700	23	F5
BRANCH AV	CO	ET	24800	29A	F6
BRANCH LN	BREA	BREA		3	B6
BRANCHWOOD WY	CO	ET		51	E4
BRAND ST	TUS	SA10	15500	29	B2
BRANDE AV	ANA	AN	1500	11	B5
BRANDNG IRON RD	SJC	SJ75	27000	36	C4
BRANDON	MVJO	SJ92		29D	D3
BRANDON CIR	ANA	AN07		8	B5
BRANDON DR	CO	LB	28400	35	F1
BRANDON DR	CO	LB77		36	A1
BRANDON LN	SJC	SJ75		38	D4
BRANDON LN	WSTM	WSTM		21	F2
BRANDY LN	CO	LB		29C	D4
BRANDYWINE	IRV	SA		24	D5
BRANDYWINE LN	CO	ET	21300	29B	C1
BRANDYWINE LN	CO	ET		52	C6
BRANDYWYNE TER	CM	CM27		31	E1
BRANDYWYNE TER	GGR	GG		21	E2
BRANFORD DR	HTB	HB	4100	20	C5
BRANFORD LN	LAH	LAH	2200	1	E6
BRANGWYN WY	LAG	LB51	1200	34	E3
BRANNEN DR	HTB	HB	5800	20	F6
BRANSFORD DR	LAP	BP23	5300	9	D1
BRANT LN	CO	LB		35	D1
BRANTA CIR	HTB	HB	21600	30	F2
BRANTFORD ST	ANA	AN		11	F2
BRASHER ST	ANA	AN		8	B6
BRASHER ST	ANA	AN		13	B1
BRASILIA ST	CO	SJ91		29A	F5
BRASSIE CIR	HTB	HB	5900	20	F5
BRASS LTRN DR S	LAH	LAH	1200	1	D6
BRASS LTRN DR W	LAH	LAH	2300	1	D6
BRAVATA DR	HTB	HB		20	B4
BRAVO LN	LAP	BP23		9	E3
BRAXTON DR	CO	LB		35	C3
BRAY LN	CM	CM	3100	27	D3
BRAZIL DR	BPK	BP	5700	9	E1
BRAZO	CO	LB	23000	29A	A5
BREA BLVD	CO	BREA	14000	2	F3
BREA BLVD	CO	BREA	14500	3	A3
BREA BLVD	FUL	FL	100	6	D3
BREA BLVD N&S	BREA	BREA	100	2	E5
BREA BLVD S	BREA	BREA	600	6	D3
BREA GLEN	CO	SA	10300	18	B3
BREAKER DR	SCL	SC72		39	A2
BREAKERS DR	HTB	HB	8900	26	D4
BREAKERS DR	NB	CDLM	3100	33	B2
BREAKERS ISLE	DPT	LB77	33300	37	D4
BREAKWATER CIR	HTB	HB	9400	30	F1
BREAKWATER DR	DPT	DPT		38	D3
BREAKWATER DR	NB	CDLM		32	C6
BREAKWATER DR	NB	CDLM		33	C1
BREAM LN	HTB	HB		20	D5
BREARLEY LN	IRV	SA		24	F6
BRECKENRIDGE DR	CO	LB77	28400	36	A1
BRECKENRIDGE ST	OR	OR	2000	12	E5
BREDA LN	HTB	HB	17300	20	F6
BREEDEN ST	SA	SA	300	23	C2
BREELAND DR	HTB	HB47	6700	21	B4
BREEZEWOOD CT	BREA	BREA		2	D5
BREEZEWOOD ST	DPT	DPT		38	D3
BREEZWAY CT	GGR	GG		16	D6
BREEZY PL	DPT	DPT	33300	38	A3
BREEZY WY	CO	OR69	12500	17	E4
BREEZY WY	OR	OR	600	17	E4
BREIGHTON CIR	OR	OR	7100	18	D2
BREMERTON ST	DPT	DPT	33200	38	A3
BREMERTON ST	DPT	LB77		37	F3
BRENA	IRV	SA		24	E5
BRENAN WY	CO	SA	13800	18	A6
BRENAN WY	CO	TUS	14300	24	A1
BRENDA AV	BPK	BP	10000	9	F6
BRENDA LN	CO	LAH		2	B3
BRENNER AV	BPK	BP	6700	10	C1
BRENT CIR	HTB	HB47	16200	21	A4
BRENT CIR	PLA	PLA	900	7	D4
BRENT LN	TUS	TUS	17500	17	F5
BRENTFORD AV	OR	OR	2100	12	E5
BRENTHAVEN PL	ANA	AN	500	11	B3
BRENTSTONE LN	HTB	HB	20200	26	E5
BRENTWELL CIR	HTB	HB	18000	26	A2
BRENTWOOD	CO	LB56		29C	B3
BRENTWOOD	MVJO	SJ92		29B	E1

STREET	CITY	P.O. ZONE	BLOCK	PAGE	GRID
BRENTWOOD AV E	OR	OR	100	12	C4
BRENTWOOD AV W	OR	OR	100	12	C4
BRENTWOOD DR	CO	SA	9800	18	E4
BRENTWOOD DR	FUL	FL	700	6	D3
BRENTWOOD DR	LAG	LB77	31500	35	B6
BRENTWOOD LN	WSTM	WSTM		15	B6
BRENTWOOD PL	ANA	AN	200	11	A4
BRENTWOOD PL	CM	CM	2400	27	E6
BRENTWOOD PL	YL	YL		8	F4
BRENTWOOD PL	YL	YL		40	A4
BRENTWOOD ST	CM	CM27	200	31	E1
BRESSEL LN	HTB	HB47	16900	21	D5
BRETING WY	PLA	PLA	200	7	B4
BRETON CIR	OR	OR		18	C3
BRETON LN	HTB	HB	21100	30	D1
BRETON WY	CYP	CYP	6900	15	A2
BREWER AV	SA	SA	1900	22	F6
BREWER WY	VPK	OR67	9200	13	B5
BREWSTER AV	ANA	AN	1000	11	B2
BREWSTER COM	SA	SA		22	C2
BREWSTER CT	CYP	CYP	6600	15	A2
BRIAN LN	ANA	AN		11	E5
BRIAN LN	LAP	BP23	7300	9	E1
BRIAN ST	OR	OR		12	B6
BRIAN ST N	PLA	PLA	1200	7	D4
BRIAR ST	FTNV	SA08	18000	26	F1
BRIARCLIFF DR	HTB	HB	6000	20	F1
BRIARCLIFF PL	TUS	TUS	14800	23	F5
BRIARCLIFF ST	WSTM	WSTM	15500	21	E3
BRIAR CREEK LN	CO	LB		29C	D2
BRIAR CREEK PL	OR	OR69		18	E3
BRIARCREST DR	IRV	SA		32A	A3
BRIARCREST LN	OR	OR69		18	D2
BRIARCROFT	CO	ET	22900	29A	F3
BRIARDALE AV E	OR	OR	100	12	C5
BRIARDALE AV W	OR	OR	1000	12	B6
BRIARDALE LN	YL	YL		7	E2
BRIARGLEN	CO	LB56		29C	D2
BRIARGLEN	IRV	SA		29	C4
BRIARGLEN LP	STN	STN		15	C4
BRIARHILL DR	YL	YL	4500	7	E3
BRIARLY LN	HTB	HB	19700	26	D4
BRIARVALE AV	ANA	AN	1600	11	F2
BRIARVALE AV	ANA	AN	2200	12	A2
BRIARWOOD	IRV	SA		29	D4
BRIARWOOD	MVJO	SJ92		29D	D1
BRIARWOOD E	STN	STN		10	C6
BRIARWOOD E	STN	STN		15	C1
BRIARWOOD W	STN	STN		10	C6
BRIARWOOD W	STN	STN		15	C1
BRIARWOOD CT	FUL	FL		7	A1
BRIARWOOD DR	BREA	BREA	500	2	D6
BRIARWOOD DR	BREA	BREA	600	6	D1
BRIARWOOD DR	HTB	HB47	6800	21	B3
BRIARWOOD LN	CO	LB		29C	D4
BRIARWOOD LN	CO	SJ79		56	E6
BRIARWOOD LN	CO	SJ79		59	E1
BRIARWOOD LN	SJC	SJ75		36	B2
BRIARWOOD RD	OR	OR69		18	E3
BRIARWOOD ST	ANA	AN	1100	11	E2
BRIARWOOD ST	FTNV	SA08	17500	26	E1
BRIARWOOD ST	STN	STN	12000	15	C3
BRIDGE LN	HTB	HB47	16100	21	B4
BRIDGE RD	IRV	SA		32	D1
BRIDGE RD	LAG	LB51		34	F2
BRIDGEMONT RD	CO	ET	27100	52	C6
BRIDGE POINT DR	HTB	HB		26	D5
BRIDGEPORT	DPT	DPT		37	E2
BRIDGEPORT	IRV	SA		24	D6
BRIDGEPORT	IRV	SA		29	D1
BRIDGEPORT AV	ANA	AN	2700	10	C5
BRIDGEPORT AV	YL	YL		40	A3
BRIDGEPORT CIR	FUL	FL33		5	F5
BRIDGEPORT LN	HTB	HB	8400	26	D3
BRIDGEPORT RD	TUS	TUS	14700	23	F5
BRIDGEPORT ST	FTNV	SA08	16700	21	F5
BRIDGEPORT WY	ANA	AN	500	10	B5
BRIDGER RD	CO	ET	23900	29A	D5
BRIDGESIDE LN	HTB	HB46		26	C5
BRIDGETON	MVJO	SJ92		29D	D4
BRIDGEVIEW	IRV	SA		29	E4
BRIDGE VIEW DR	ANA	AN		13	E2
BRIDGEWATER DR	HTB	HB47	6700	21	A5
BRIDGEWATER LN	DPT	DPT		38	D3
BRIDGEWAY LN	HTB	HB	19000	26	D3
BRIDGEWAY ST	IRV	SA	4200	29	C1
BRIDGEWOOD	IRV	SA		29	E4
BRIDGEWOOD DR	LAP	BP23	5200	9	D2
BRIDINGTON	CO	LB77		35	D5
BRIDLE CIR	CO	YL	6300	8	C6
BRIDLE LN	CO	LB		29C	D4

STREET	CITY	P.O. ZONE	BLOCK	PAGE	GRID
BRIDLE LN	YL	YL		8	B5
BRIDLE PATH	OR	OR		18	B2
BRIDLE PATH WY	CO	SA		18	D5
BRIDLEWOOD DR	CO	LB		29C	F3
BRIDLEWOOD DR	CO	LB53		29D	A3
BRIER LN	CO	SA	9700	18	D4
BRIERCLIFF	CO	SJ79		59	D3
BRIERCLIFF DR	LAH	LAH	900	1	D6
BRIGANTINE DR	DPT	DPT		37	F3
BRIGANTINE DR	DPT	LB77	25200	37	D4
BRIGANTINE DR	DPT	DPT		38	A3
BRIGANTINE LN	HTB	HB	19400	26	F4
BRIGGS AV	CM	CM26	200	28	A4
BRIGHT ST	LAH	LAH	200	2	A5
BRIGHT HOLLOW	IRV	SA		29	D5
BRIGHTON	CO	SJ79		59	E3
BRIGHTON CIR	CYP	CYP	4000	9	C4
BRIGHTON DR	CO	SA		18	D5
BRIGHTON DR	HTB	HB	5600	25	F1
BRIGHTON LN	ANA	AN		13	C3
BRIGHTON LN	CO	ET		52	C5
BRIGHTON PL	CO	TUS		24	B1
BRIGHTON PL	CO	LB77		37	E1
BRIGHTON PL	FUL	FL33	2100	5	D4
BRIGHTON RD	NB	CDLM	4500	33	B3
BRIGHTON ST	IRV	SA14	14500	29	E5
BRIGHTON ST	LAH	LAH	800	2	B3
BRIGHTON ST	WSTM	WSTM	15200	22	A4
BRIGHTON RIVER	FTNV	SA08		22	D4
BRIGHTON SPGS	CM	CM27		31	D1
BRIGHT WATER DR	DPT	DPT		37	B5
BRIGHTWOOD CT	CO	YL		8	C6
BRIGHTWOOD DR	CO	SA	10000	18	D4
BRIGHTWOOD LN	GGR	GG		15	A6
BRILEY WY	VPK	OR67	9700	13	A6
BRILLANTEZ	IRV	SA		24	E5
BRIMHALL DR	CO	LALM	2600	14	A4
BRIMHALL LN	HTB	HB47	16100	21	A4
BRINDISI	CO	LB77		35	F4
BRINDISI	NB	NB60		32	E3
BRIO	IRV	SA		24	F5
BRIONES DR	CO	LB53		29C	E6
BRIOSO DR	CM	CM27		31	A3
BRISA	IRV	SA		24	E5
BRISA DEL LAGO	CO	SJ		59	C1
BRISA RIBERA	CO	SJ88		59	B5
BRISBANE WY	IRV	SA	4000	28	F5
BRISBANE WY	YL	YL		8	E3
BRISBANE BAY	DPT	LB77		37	D4
BRISTLECONE	MVJO	SJ92		52	D6
BRISTLE CONE LN	YL	YL		7	E4
BRISTOL CIR	WSTM	WSTM	15800	22	A4
BRISTOL DR	ANA	AN		10	C4
BRISTOL LN	OR	OR		12	C5
BRISTOL ST	CM	CM	2700	27	F3
BRISTOL ST	CM	CM26	200	28	A5
BRISTOL ST	CO	CM27	3100	27	F3
BRISTOL ST	CO	SA07	1500	28	A5
BRISTOL ST	NB	NB60	2700	28	B6
BRISTOL ST	NB	NB		32	B1
BRISTOL ST N	NB	NB60		28	B6
BRISTOL ST N	SA	SA	1700	17	A4
BRISTOL ST N&S	SA	SA	100	23	A6
BRISTOL ST S	SA	SA04	2800	27	F3
BRISTOL ST SE	CM	CM26		27	F5
BRISTOL ST SE	CM	CM26		28	A5
BRITAIN WY	ANA	AN	2500	10	E1
BRITTANY	NB	NB		32	C3
BRITTANY CIR	WSTM	WSTM	8700	21	D1
BRITTANY LN	BREA	BREA	300	7	A1
BRITTANY LN	HTB	HB	17600	26	D1
BRITTANY LN	STN	STN	8300	15	C3
BRITTANY PL	PLA	PLA	2000	7	C2
BRITTANY WY	CYP	CYP		9	E4
BRITTNY CRSS RD	CO	SA05	1200	18	B6
BRITTANY WDS DR	CO	SA	12800	24	B3
BRITTANY WDS DR	CO	TUS	13000	24	B3
BRITTANY WDS LN	NB	NB		31	F2
BRITTANY WDS ST	TUS	TUS		24	A4
BRITTLEWOOD CIR	CO	ET		29A	F2
BRIXHAM CIR	HTB	HB	8200	26	D3
BROAD ST	NB	NB	2800	31	C4
BROADHORN DR	CO	LB77		37	D1
BROADLEAF	CO	ET	22800	29B	A3
BROADMOOR ST	FUL	FL33		5	E4
BROADMOOR TR	OR	OR	500	18	D2
BROADSTONE CIR	HTB	HB48		25	E3
BROADVIEW PL	ANA	AN	800	11	A5
BROADVIEW PL	CO	SA	10100	18	D4
BROADVIEW ST	ANA	AN	100	11	A5

STREET	CITY	P.O. ZONE	BLOCK	PAGE	GRID
BROADWAY	CM	CM27	100	31	D2
BROADWAY	CO	AN04	9900	10	D4
BROADWAY	CO	SUNB	16700	20	B5
BROADWAY	LAG	LB51	100	34	D3
BROADWAY E	ANA	AN	100	11	E3
BROADWAY N	SA	SA	1600	17	B6
BROADWAY N&S	SA	SA01	100	23	B1
BROADWAY W	ANA	AN	2100	10	D4
BROADWAY W	ANA	AN	100	11	C3
BROADWAY PL	LAG	LB51	100	34	C3
BROADWAY PL	SA	SA	2200	23	B5
BROCK LN	GGR	GG		16	D6
BROCKTON CT	CO	LB		35	C4
BRODEN ST	ANA	AN	2100	16	D2
BRODER ST	ANA	AN	300	10	C5
BROKEN BIT LN	CO	LB	26400	29C	F3
BROKEN BOW DR	CO	ET	21900	29B	B2
BROKENHILL CT	CO	YL	5300	8	B4
BROMLEY LN	HTB	HB46		26	F4
BROMLEY ST	WSTM	WSTM	14600	21	F2
BRONCO CIR	CO	SA		18	D5
BRONCO CIR	YL	YL		8	D2
BRONSON ST	OR	OR	1600	17	B4
BRONWYN DR	ANA	AN	600	10	C5
BROOK CT	SJC	SJ75		36	A3
BROOK LN	ANA	AN		13	B3
BROOK ST	SA	SA	1600	22	F3
BROOK ST	SA	SA	900	23	A3
BROOKBAY CIR	HTB	HB	9700	30	F5
BROOKDALE	CO	ET		29B	A3
BROOKDALE	IRV	SA		29	C3
BROOKDALE AV	LAH	LAH	800	2	B3
BROOKDALE DR	GGR	GG	8900	15	D5
BROOKDALE LN	HTB	HB	20500	26	E6
BROOKDALE PL	STN	STN		15	B4
BROOKDALE PL E	FUL	FL	100	6	B5
BROOKDALE PL W	FUL	FL33	1600	5	F5
BROOKDALE PL W	FUL	FL	100	6	B5
BROOKE AV	WSTM	WSTM		21	D4
BROOKE LN	FUL	FL33		5	F2
BROOKFIELD	IRV	SA		29	B2
BROOKFIELD AV	LAH	LAH	1500	2	C3
BROOKFIELD CIR	CO	ET	23400	29A	D4
BROOKFIELD RD	SJC	SJ75		36	B2
BROOK GLEN LN	OR	OR69		18	E2
BROOKHAVEN	CO	ET	22600	29B	A3
BROOKHAVEN AV	PLA	PLA	1500	7	C2
BROOKHAVEN CIR	HTB	HB	9700	30	F5
BROOKHAVEN ST	GGR	GG	11900	15	F3
BROOKHAVEN PARK	GGR	GG40		15	F3
BROOKHILL DR	CO	YL	5400	8	C4
BROOKHILL RD	CO	SJ79		52	E3
BROOK HOLLOW	CO	ET	26200	29B	B3
BROOKHOLLOW DR	SA	SA		23	D5
BROOKHURST PL W	FUL	FL	1600	6	A4
BROOKHURST RD N	FUL	FL33	100	5	F6
BROOKHURST RD S	FUL	FL33	100	5	F6
BROOKHURST RD S	FUL	FL33	1000	10	F5
BROOKHURST ST	FTNV	SA08	15800	21	F6
BROOKHURST ST	FTNV	SA08	17600	26	F3
BROOKHURST ST	GGR	GG	11000	15	F5
BROOKHURST ST	GGR	GG	14000	21	F6
BROOKHURST ST	HTB	HB	19000	26	F3
BROOKHURST ST	HTB	HB		30	E3
BROOKHURST ST	WSTM	WSTM	14600	21	F6
BROOKHURST ST N	ANA	AN	100	10	F5
BROOKHURST ST S	ANA	AN	100	10	F5
BROOKHURST ST S	ANA	AN04	1500	15	F1
BROOKHURST WY	GGR	GG	12700	15	F4
BROOKLAWN DR	WSTM	WSTM	7300	15	B5
BROOKLINE	CO	LB51		29C	B2
BROOKLINE CIR	HTB	HB	19500	26	F3
BROOKLINE LN	CM	CM	100	27	E6
BROOKLINE PL	FUL	FL		6	C2
BROOKLINE RD	SB	SB	1000	19	C5
BROOKLINE WY	TUS	TUS	14600	23	F1
BROOKLYN AV	YL	YL	17500	7	E2
BROOKLYN AV E	PLA	PLA	800	7	D2
BROOKLYN CIR	PLA	PLA	2300	7	D2
BROOKMONT	CO	ET	25700	29B	A3
BROOKMONT	IRV	SA		29	D4
BROOKMONT DR	YL	YL	5900	8	C5
BROOKMORE AV	ANA	AN	2100	10	F5
BROOKPINE	IRV	SA		29	B2
BROOKPINE	MVJO	SJ92		29B	E2
BROOKS CT	TUS	TUS		24	A4
BROOKS ST	LAG	LB	31000	35	A5
BROOKS ST	LAG	LB51	100	34	E4
BROOKSEED DR	CO	SJ79		56	E6
BROOKSHIRE AV	GGR	GG	11600	16	C3
BROOKSHIRE AV	TUS	TUS	1800	23	F5

STREET	CITY	P.O. ZONE	BLOCK	PAGE	GRID
BROOKSHIRE AV E	OR	OR	200	12	C4
BROOKSHIRE AV W	OR	OR	100	12	C4
BROOKSHIRE LN	HTB	HB		26	C1
BROOKSHIRE PL	BREA	BREA		2	F4
BROOKSIDE AV	OR	OR	2200	12	E6
BROOKSIDE AV	OR	OR	19000	13	B6
BROOKSIDE CT	ANA	AN08		40	A6
BROOKSIDE CT	ANA	AN		43	A1
BROOKSIDE DR	GGR	GG	10000	15	F2
BROOKSIDE DR	HTB	HB	8500	26	D3
BROOKSIDE LN	BREA	BREA		3	A6
BROOKSIDE LN	SJC	SJ75		36	C6
BROOKSIDE ST	IRV	SA	4200	29	C1
BROOKSIDE TER	CO	SIL		53	A1
BROOKSTONE	CO	SJ79		59	E3
BROOKSTONE	IRV	SA		29	B3
BROOKTRAIL LN	HTB	HB48		25	E3
BROOKVIEW	DPT	DPT		37	E2
BROOKVIEW LN	CM	CM26		28	A3
BROOKVIEW WY	CM	CM26		28	A3
BROOKWAY AV	YL	YL	4700	7	D3
BROOKWOOD DR	HTB	HB		26	C2
BROOKWOOD DR	LAH	LAH	1400	2	C3
BROOKWOOD ST	BREA	BREA	900	2	F5
BROOM PL	IRV	SA		24	F6
BROTHERS RD	SJC	SJ75	31000	36	C5
BROWER AV	PLA	PLA	400	7	C3
BROWN CIR	HTB	HB47	6300	21	A3
BROWN ST	SA	SA	800	23	C1
BROWNCROFT RD	LAG	LB51	600	34	E3
BROWNING	IRV	SA		28	D1
BROWNING AV	TUS	SA05	12200	24	C2
BROWNING AV	CO	TUS	12000	24	C2
BROWNING AV	TUS	TUS	13400	24	B4
BROWNING DR	HTB	HB	9000	26	E5
BROWNING RD	GGR	GG	12200	16	A3
BROWNLEE RD	GGR	GG	11600	15	F3
BROWNSTONE	LAH	LAH		2	B5
BROWNSTONE CIR	CYP	CYP	9100	9	D4
BROWNSTONE LN	WSTM	WSTM		21	E2
BROWNWOOD AV	ANA	AN	2100	10	F3
BRUCE AV	ANA	AN	2600	10	D4
BRUCE AV	SA	SA	4800	22	B1
BRUCE LN	LAH	LAH	2500	1	D5
BRUCE PL	ANA	AN	900	10	E3
BRUCE ST	ANA	AN	500	10	E5
BRUINBARK LN	CO	SA07		27	F5
BRUINBARK LN	CO	SA07		28	A5
BRUNEMEIER ST	PLA	PLA	1900	7	B2
BRUNSWICK AV	PLA	PLA	600	7	C4
BRUNSWICK DR	CYP	CYP	5000	9	D5
BRUNSWICK DR	HTB	HB47	6900	21	B3
BRUNSWICK WY	CO	SA	11000	18	C5
BRUSH DR	HTB	HB47	8000	21	C5
BRUSH CANYON DR	YL	YL		40	D6
BRUSHWOOD LN	CO	SJ79		52	E3
BRUSSELS AV	CO	SJ91		29A	F4
BRYAN AV	CO	SA20	3000	24	B4
BRYAN AV	IRV	SA	6000	29	F1
BRYAN AV	TUS	TUS	1000	24	B4
BRYANT CIR	WSTM	WSTM	5300	14	E5
BRYANT CT	CYP	CYP	10400	14	D5
BRYANT DR	HTB	HB47	8200	21	C5
BRYCE AV	OR	OR		13	C5
BRYCE CIR	PLA	PLA	1500	7	E4
BRYCE CT	FTNV	SA08		26	F2
BRYCE PL	CO	SA	13500	17	F5
BRYCE CANYON WY	BREA	BREA		2	F4
BRYDGES CT	CO	ET		52	B6
BRYNHURST RD	OR	OR		18	C3
BRYNMAR DR	VPK	OR67	9500	12	F5
BRYNMAR LN	VPK	OR67		12	F5
BRYNWOOD ST	SA	SA	2500	17	C5
BRYSON ST	ANA	AN		8	A6
BRYSON SPRINGS	CM	CM27		31	D1
BUARO ST	GGR	GG	12000	16	C4
BUBACH ST	ANA	AN	1700	7	F6
BUBBLNG WELL RD	CO	SA	12500	24	B2
BUBBLNG WELL RD	CO	TUS	13200	24	B2
BUCCANEER CIR	GGR	GG	13300	16	C5
BUCCANEER CT	SJC	SJ75		38	A3
BUCCANEER DR	PLA	PLA	1000	12	A1
BUCCANEER ST	DPT	DPT		37	E3
BUCHANAN	IRV	SA		24	C5
BUCHANAN CIR	BPK	BP	8700	10	B4
BUCHANAN CT	BREA	BREA		2	F4
BUCHANAN DR	CO	AN04	8300	15	D3
BUCHANAN WY	CM	CM	3000	27	E3
BUCKBOARD CT	BREA	BREA		2	E5
BUCKBOARD LN	CO	LB	24700	29C	F4
BUCKEYE	IRV	SA		29	D1

— Z — COPYRIGHT, © 1989 BY Thomas Bros Maps

STREET	CITY	P.O. ZONE	BLOCK	PAGE	GRID
BUCKEYE CIR	FTNV	SA08	16700	21	F5
BUCKEYE ST	NB	NB	2500	32	B3
BUCKEYEWOOD AV	OR	OR	500	12	D5
BUCK GULLY DR	NB	CDLM		33	C1
BUCKHAVEN ST	CO	LB		35	C2
BUCKHILL AV	BPK	BP	5200	5	D4
BUCKHILL PL	BPK	BP	5300	5	D4
BUCKINGHAM CIR	GGR	GG	11900	16	F3
BUCKINGHAM CIR	WSTM	WSTM	13200	14	E5
BUCKINGHAM DR	CM	CM		27	E3
BUCKINGHAM DR	HTB	HB		20	E2
BUCKINGHAM DR	SJC	SJ75		36	C3
BUCKINGHAM LN	NB	NB	1000	31	E4
BUCKINGHAM PL	TUS	TUS	14500	23	F5
BUCKINGHAM RD	FUL	FL33	3600	10	E1
BUCKINGHAM ST	FUL	FL33	1400	10	E1
BUCKINGHAM ST	HTB	HB46		26	F3
BUCKLAND LN	CO	ET	23600	29A	D4
BUCKLESTONE CT	CO	LB	25700	29D	A2
BUCKNELL CIR	ANA	AN		13	E4
BUCKNELL CIR	WSTM	WSTM	15100	21	C3
BUCKNELL RD	CM	CM	200	27	D5
BUCKSKIN CIR	YL	YL		8	B3
BUCKSKIN DR	CO	LB	24800	29C	F3
BUCKSKIN WY	OR	OR	100	18	D3
BUCKTHORN	CO	SJ		59	B3
BUCKTHORN	IRV	SA		29	C4
BUCKTHORN DR	BREA	BREA	100	4	B5
BUCKTHORN LN	CO	OR	11600	18	B2
BUCKWOOD	CO	ET		29A	F3
BUCKWOOD	CO	ET	25400	29B	A3
BUDAPEST AV	CO	SJ91		29B	A5
BUDLONG CIR	ANA	AN		8	B5
BUDLONG ST	ANA	AN		8	A5
BUENA ST	GGR	GG43	14000	22	D1
BUENA WY	GGR	GG	13200	16	D6
BUENA SUERTE	CO	SJ88		59	B2
BUENA TIERR CIR	BPK	BP		5	D3
BUENA TIERRA PL	BPK	BP	8500	5	D3
BUENA VISTA	MVJO	SJ92		29B	E4
BUENA VISTA	SCL	SC72	800	39	C3
BUENA VISTA	TUS	TUS		23	D3
BUENA VISTA AV	ANA	AN	1600	11	B6
BUENA VISTA AV	LAH	LAH	600	1	F6
BUENA VISTA AV	LAH	LAH	100	2	A6
BUENA VISTA AV	PLA	PLA	1200	7	D4
BUENA VISTA AV	YL	YL	17000	7	D4
BUENA VISTA AV	YL	YL	17300	7	F4
BUENA VISTA AV	YL	YL	18200	8	A4
BUENA VISTA BL	NB	NB	500	31	D6
BUENA VISTA DR	CO	LB	25900	29C	F3
BUENA VISTA DR	FUL	FL	1200	6	A5
BUENA VISTA ST	CO	OR65	16400	12	D3
BUENA VISTA WY	LAG	LB51	500	34	E2
BUENDIA	MVJO	SJ91		29B	C3
BUFFALO AV E	SA	SA	300	17	B5
BUFFALO AV W	SA	SA	100	17	B5
BUFFWOOD WY	CO	ET	25000	29A	B2
BULKHEAD CIR	HTB	HB	21300	30	E1
BULL RUN	IRV	SA		24	E5
BULLARD LN	CO	SA	1500	24	B2
BULLARD LN	CO	TUS	1300	24	B2
BUMBLEBEE RD	TUS	SA10		23	E6
BUNBURY DR	CO	ET	24500	29A	E4
BUNKER HILL	IRV	SA		24	D5
BUNKER HILL	OR	OR	5900	13	C6
BUNKER HILL CIR	PLA	PLA	600	7	B5
BUNKERHILL DR	LALM	LALM	11000	14	D2
BUNKER HILL PL	ANA	AN	4000	12	E3
BUNKER HILL WY	CM	CM	2300	27	D6
BUNTING AV	FTNV	SA08	10100	27	A2
BUNTING CIR	CM	CM	2700	27	B5
BUNTING CIR	FTNV	SA08		27	A2
BUNTING CT	ANA	AN		13	F2
BUNYA ST	NB	NB	2500	32	A3
BUOY AV	OR	OR	1000	12	D4
BUOY ST	CM	CM27	200	31	D2
BURCH WY	LAH	LAH	700	2	A4
BURDIE LN	CO	OR69	17300	17	E4
BURDIE LN	OR	OR	1900	17	E4
BURGESS CIR	PLA	PLA		7	B2
BURGESS CIR	WSTM	WSTM		21	D4
BURGOYNE	IRV	SA		29	E1
BURGUNDY CIR	IRV	SA	5200	29	D3
BURGUNDY PL	CO	AN04	10000	10	E6
BURGUNDY WY	PLA	PLA	1400	7	C4
BURKE	IRV	SA		24	C5
BURKE LN	HTB	HB47		21	B5
BURKWOOD CIR	YL	YL		7	E5
BURLCREST DR	HTB	HB	8700	26	E5
BURLEIGH DR	YL	YL	19900	8	C3

STREET	CITY	P.O. ZONE	BLOCK	PAGE	GRID
BURLINGAME AV	BPK	BP	5200	5	C4
BURLINGAME AV	TUS	TUS	14500	24	A4
BURLINGTON COM	SA	SA		22	C2
BURLINGTON LN	HTB	HB	21300	30	C2
BURLWOOD	MVJO	SJ92		29B	E3
BURLWOOD DR	ANA	AN		13	F4
BURLY AV	OR	OR	2500	17	F3
BURLY AV	OR	OR	3500	18	A3
BURNEY PL	CO	LALM	3100	14	A2
BURNHAM AV	BPK	BP	5700	5	B6
BURNHAM AV	BPK	BP	6700	10	B1
BURNHAM CIR	HTB	HB	8100	26	C4
BURNHAM CIR	IRV	SA	14900	29	D2
BURNING TREE	CO	LB77		37	F2
BURNING TRE CIR	NB	NB		32	B4
BURNING TREE LN	SB	SB	13600	14	A6
BURNING TREE RD	FUL	FL33	700	5	E5
BURNING TREE RD	NB	NB		32	B4
BURNING TREE ST	WSTM	WSTM	15500	21	E3
BURNLEY LN	HTB	HB	19900	26	F4
BURNS AV	SA	SA04	1300	27	F1
BURNS AV	SA	SA	1300	28	A1
BURNS DR	GGR	GG	12000	16	B3
BURNSIDE DR	LAG	LB	31500	35	B6
BURNSIDE PL	LAG	LB	31500	35	B6
BURNT MILL RD	CO	TUS	1800	24	B3
BURNT MILL RD	TUS	TUS		24	B3
BURNTWOOD	CO	LB77		36	A3
BURNTWOOD AV	ANA	AN	2800	12	B4
BURRIANA	SCL	SC72		39	E1
BURROUGHS	IRV	SA18		29A	C2
BURT PL	FUL	FL	1200	11	F1
BURT RD	IRV	EIRV	6000	29	E4
BURTON AV	OR	OR	800	12	D5
BURTON DR	HTB	HB47		21	C6
BURTON DR	HTB	HB		26	C1
BURTON PL	ANA	AN	1400	11	F1
BURTON ST	ANA	AN	1400	11	E1
BURTON WY	STN	STN	7100	15	B2
BURWOOD	IRV	SA		29	B2
BURWOOD ST	FUL	FL	3600	6	A2
BURWOOD ST	LAH	LAH	1200	2	A6
BUSBY CIR	WSTM	WSTM	13800	15	A6
BUSBY LN	HTB	HB	16500	20	F5
BUSCADOR	MVJO	SJ92		29D	D3
BUSH ST	OR	OR	100	17	B4
BUSH ST	WSTM	WSTM	13900	14	F6
BUSH ST N	ANA	AN	300	11	E3
BUSH ST N	SA	SA	1600	17	B6
BUSH ST N	SA	SA	100	23	B2
BUSH ST S	ANA	AN	100	11	E3
BUSHARD ST	FTNV	SA08	15900	21	E6
BUSHARD ST	FTNV	SA08	17600	26	E1
BUSHARD ST	HTB	HB	19000	26	E6
BUSHARD ST	HTB	HB	21300	30	E2
BUSHARD ST	WSTM	WSTM	14000	21	E2
BUSHWICK DR	HTB	HB	8100	30	C2
BUSINESS DR	HTB	HB	5300	20	E3
BUSINESS CTR DR	CYP	CYP		14	F2
BUSINESS CTR DR	IRV	SA		28	C4
BUSINESS CTR DR	OR	OR		17	B1
BUSINESS CTR PY	GGR	GG43		22	B1
BUSINESS PK DR	CM	CM		27	C2
BUTLER ST	IRV	SA	17900	28	F5
BUTLER ST	OR	OR	2600	12	C4
BUTTE CIR	HTB	HB		26	D6
BUTTE CT	BREA	BREA	500	2	F5
BUTTE ST	WSTM	WSTM	14300	21	E2
BUTTERCUP	CO	SJ88		59	B5
BUTTERCUP AV	FTNV	SA08	9000	21	E4
BUTTERFIELD	IRV	SA		29	A1
BUTTERFIELD	MVJO	SJ92		29B	E2
BUTTERFIELD LN	ANA	AN		13	D3
BUTTERFIELD RD	OR	OR	3800	12	D3
BUTTERFIELD ST	FTNV	SA08	15800	21	F4
BUTTERFIELD ST	WSTM	WSTM	15600	21	F4
BUTTERFLY	IRV	SA		29	C1
BUTTERNUT CIR	FTNV	SA08	16700	21	F5
BUTTERNUT LN	IRV	SA		29	B6
BUTTONBRUSH TR	OR	OR	600	18	E2
BUTTONSHELL LN	NB	NB	1800	31	F3
BUTTONWOOD	IRV	SA		29	C5
BUTTONWOOD DR	BREA	BREA	100	2	F5
BUTTONWOOD DR	BREA	BREA	1000	3	A5
BUTTONWOOD ST	ANA	AN	500	11	E2
BUTTONWOOD ST	FTNV	SA08	17000	21	F6
BYCROFT CIR	YL	YL	3900	7	D2
BYLOT WY	CYP	CYP	11400	15	B2
BYRD CT	PLA	PLA		7	B2
BYRNE DR	LAP	BP23	5500	9	E2
BYRON WY	CO	ET		29B	A2

STREET	CITY	P.O. ZONE	BLOCK	PAGE	GRID
BYRON WY	SA	SA		28	C1
BYRON CLOSE	CO	LB		35	E6
BYRON CLOSE	CO	LB77		37	E1
BYTHA WY	CO	SIL	28200	50	D2
BYWATER RD	CO	ET		29A	D2
BYWOOD AV	ANA	AN	800	11	C2
C					
C ST	ETMC	SA09		51	A3
C ST	HTB	HB		26	C6
C ST	LAG	LB51		35	A4
C ST	NB	NB	100	33	B5
C ST	TUS	TUS	14000	23	F3
C ST N&S	TUS	TUS	100	23	F3
CABALLERO BLVD	BPK	BP	6000	5	A6
CABALLERO BLVD	BPK	BP	6500	10	A1
CABALLERO DR	HTB	HB	16500	20	D5
CABALLO DR	YL	YL		7	F4
CABANA	HTB	HB		20	D5
CABARET CT	CO	SA	13000	18	A5
CABERNET CT	CO	LB56		29C	E4
CABEZA	MVJO	SJ91		29B	C1
CABEZA	MVJO	SJ91	27400	52	C6
CABILDO	CO	LB	3300	29A	A5
CABLLSTA DL NRT	SCL	SC72		38	E3
CABLLSTA DL SUR	SCL	SC72		38	E3
CABO DR	WSTM	WSTM		21	F3
CABO ROSA	MVJO	SJ92	27900	29B	D3
CABOT	IRV	SA		24	E5
CABOT CIR	HTB	HB	15500	20	F3
CABOT DR	ANA	AN	3200	10	B4
CABOT RD	CO	LB	27900	29D	A5
CABOT RD	CO	LB77		36	A1
CABOT WY	STN	STN	7000	15	A2
CABRILLO CIR	FUL	FL	100	6	B2
CABRILLO CT	FTNV	SA08	18200	27	A2
CABRILLO ST	CM	CM27	100	31	D3
CABRILLO ST	NB	NB		31	A6
CABRILLO ST	OR	OR	1200	13	C6
CABRILLO TER	NB	CDLM	400	33	C2
CABRILLO WY	LAG	LB77		37	C2
CABRILLO WY	CYP	CYP	9800	9	E6
CABRILLO ISLE	DPT	LB77		37	D4
CABRILLO PK DR	SA	SA	900	23	D1
CABRINI	IRV	SA14		28	F4
CABROSA	MVJO	SJ91	21500	29B	D1
CACAO ST	NB	NB	700	32	B2
CACERES CIR	MVJO	SJ91	26800	29D	C1
CACHE ST	FTNV	SA08	16000	21	E4
CACHUMA CIR	BPK	BP	8100	5	C4
CACHUMA CIR	FTNV	SA08		22	B5
CACTUS	BREA	BREA		2	F5
CACTUS CIR	BPK	BP	8000	10	C2
CACTUS WY	CO	SIL	28800	50	E2
CADBURY DR	OR	OR		18	C3
CADDY CIR	SA	SA	900	22	B1
CADE CIR	HTB	HB		26	D4
CADENA	SCL	SC72		38	E3
CADENAS	MVJO	SJ91		29D	C3
CADET AV	GGR	GG	12700	16	D3
CADILLAC AV	CM	CM		27	B2
CADILLAC DR	CO	LB		29C	E2
CADIZ CIR	HTB	HB	6500	26	A3
CADIZ CIR	LAP	BP23	5000	9	D3
CADIZ CIR	MVJO	SJ91		29D	C4
CADIZ DR	WSTM	WSTM		21	F3
CAESARS PL	CO	LB56		29C	E5
CAGNEY LN	NB	NB		31	B4
CAIN AV	HTB	HB47	7400	21	B5
CAIRO CIR	CO	PLA	16200	7	C3
CAITHNESS DR	HTB	HB	9500	26	F5
CAJON AV	BPK	BP		5	C4
CAJON DR	CO	LB		29A	F6
CAJON DR	CO	LB	25000	29C	F1
CAJON DR	CO	SJ91		29B	A6
CAJON DR S	LAH	LAH	1000	1	D6
CAJON DR W	LAH	LAH	2300	1	D6
CAJON ST	LAG	LB51	200	34	C2
CAJON TER	LAG	LB51		34	C2
CALABAZA	MVJO	SJ91	21700	29B	D1
CALABRIA	IRV	SA		24	D5
CALADIUM AV	FTNV	SA08	9000	21	E4
CALA D OR	CO	LB77		35	F4
CALAIS	CO	LB		35	C6
CALA MOREYA ST	CO	LB77		35	E4
CALANDRIA	IRV	SA		24	E5
CALAS CT	CO	ET		51	E4
CALATRAVA	MVJO	SJ92	21700	29B	E1
CALAVERA CIR	TUS	TUS		24	B3

STREET	CITY	P.O. ZONE	BLOCK	PAGE	GRID
CALAVERA PL	FUL	FL33	1800	5	F3
CALAVERAS CIR	LAP	BP23	5800	9	E2
CALAVO AV	FUL	FL	2400	6	F3
CALDERAS	MVJO	SJ91	21800	29B	D2
CALDWELL CIR	ANA	AN	1400	11	F6
CALEDONIA CIR	HTB	HB	17900	26	A1
CALEFA	MVJO	SJ92		29B	E3
CALELLA	CO	LB77		35	E5
CALENDULA	CO	SJ		56	D6
CALENDULA	MVJO	SJ92	24000	29B	D5
CALENDULA AV	FTNV	SA08	12100	22	D4
CALENDULA AV	WSTM	WSTM	9500	21	F3
CALENDULA DR	BPK	BP	8000	10	C2
CALERA CT	FTNV	SA08	15800	22	B4
CALERO AV	CO	LB	25000	29C	F2
CALGARY AV	YL	YL	17300	7	E4
CALHOUN	IRV	SA		24	E6
CALHOUN	IRV	SA		29	E1
CALHOUN DR	HTB	HB	4100	20	C5
CALICO	IRV	SA		29	A5
CALICO AV	GGR	GG	8800	15	D3
CALICO CIR	ANA	AN	900	10	D6
CALICO CT	BREA	BREA	400	2	F5
CALICO TR	OR	OR		18	D2
CALIENTE CT	PLA	PLA		7	F5
CALIENTE DR	HTB	HB	5100	20	E5
CALIENTE WY	PLA	PLA		7	F5
CALIFIA DR	CO	LB	25400	29D	A1
CALIFORNIA AV	IRV	SA17		32	C1
CALIFORNIA AV	IRV	SA		32	E1
CALIFORNIA AV	WSTM	WSTM	6200	15	A6
CALIFORNIA PL	ANA	AN	1200	11	E4
CALIFORNIA ST	BPK	BP	8200	5	C6
CALIFORNIA ST	CM	CM	3600	27	C3
CALIFORNIA ST	HTB	HB	200	26	C6
CALIFORNIA ST	LAH	LAH	100	2	A5
CALIFORNIA ST	PLA	PLA	2300	7	D1
CALIFORNIA ST	SA	SA	2400	22	E4
CALIFORNIA ST	TUS	TUS	300	23	E3
CALIFORNIA ST	TUS	TUS	15700	23	E3
CALIFORNIA ST N	OR	OR	100	17	D3
CALIFORNIA ST S	OR	OR	300	17	D3
CALIMBA	CO	SJ88		29B	F5
CALINDA	MVJO	SJ92		29D	F3
CALISTOGA	CO	ET		51	E4
CALIXTO	MVJO	SJ91		29B	D4
CALLA CIR	FTNV	SA08	9400	21	E4
CALLAHAN LN	PLA	PLA		7	D4
CALLA LILY CIR	BPK	BP	8000	10	C2
CALLE ABRIL	SCL	SC72	3900	38	C4
CL ACCORDARSE	SJC	SJ75	33800	38	C4
CALLE ADOBE	CO	SJ		59	C2
CALLE AGUA	SCL	SC72		38	D4
CALLE AGUILA	SCL	SC72		39	E1
CALLE ALBARDA	CO	TRA		59	C2
CALLE ALCALA	MVJO	SJ91		29B	B4
CALLE ALCAZAR	SCL	SC72		39	E4
CALLE ALCAZAR	YL	YL		8	F4
CALLE ALCORISA	TUS	TUS		24	E3
CALLE ALEGRE	ANA	AN		13	D2
CALLE ALEGRIA	FUL	FL33	1800	5	F3
CALLE ALICIA	SCL	SC72		39	B5
CALLE ALIMAR	CO	TRA		59	C2
CALLE ALMANZA	DPT	SC24	26700	38	C5
CALLE ALMIRANTE	SCL	SC72		38	F6
CALLE ALMIRANTE	SCL	SC72		39	C1
CALLE ALONDRA	CO	ET	25100	51	F6
CALLE ALONSO	MVJO	SJ92	23900	29B	D5
CALLE ALPINIA	CO	SJ		56	D6
CALLE ALPINIA	CO	SJ		59	D1
CALLE ALTA	OR	OR	6900	18	D3
CALLE ALTA	SCL	SC72		39	E3
CALLE AMABLE	SCL	SC72		38	E5
CALLE AMANECER	SCL	SC72		71	B6
CALLE AMENO	SCL	SC72		39	F3
CALLE AMIGO	SCL	SC72		38	E6
CALLE ANDALUCIA	SCL	SC72	3900	38	C4
CALLE ANDORRA	TUS	TUS		24	E3
CALLE ANEJO	DPT	SC24		38	C6
CL ANTEQUERA	TUS	TUS		24	E3
CALLE ARAGON	CO	LB		29A	C5
CALLE ARAGON	CO	LB		29C	D1
CALLE ARCO	SCL	SC72	27000	38	D6
CALLE ARENA	SCL	SC72		39	D6
CALLE ARENAL	CO	ET	24900	51	F6
CALLE ARIANA	SCL	SC72		39	D6
CALLE ARROYO	SJC	SJ75		36	D6
CALLE ARROYO	SJC	SJ75		38	C1
CALLE ASPERO	SJC	SJ75		36	A6
CALLE ASPERO	SJC	SJ75		38	A1
CALLE AVERIO	ANA	AN		13	D2

STREET	CITY	P.O. ZONE	BLOCK	PAGE	GRID
CALLE AVIADOR	SJC	SJ75	33100	38	B3
CALLE AZORIN	MVJO	SJ92	23000	29B	E4
CALLE AZUL	CO	LB	24000	29A	A5
CALLE BAHIA	SCL	SC72	400	39	F5
CALLE BAJA	OR	OR		18	D2
CALLE BALANDRA	SCL	SC72		38	E6
CALLE BALANDRA	SCL	SC72		39	C1
CALLE BALBOA	SCL	SC72		39	E3
CALLE BARANDA	SCL	SC72		38	E6
CALLE BARBOSA	CO	LB77		35	C5
CALLE BARCELONA	TUS	TUS		24	E4
CALLE BECERRA	CO	LB77		36	A2
CALLE BELLA	YL	YL		8	D5
CL BELLA LOMA	SCL	SC72		39	D2
CALLE BELMONTE	SJC	SJ75		36	D5
CALLE BELMONTE	TUS	TUS		24	E4
CALLE BENAVENTE	TUS	TUS		24	E4
CALLE BIELDO	CO	TRA		59	C2
CL BIENVENIDO	SCL	SC72	4000	38	C4
CALLE BOLSA	CO	ET		29A	E1
CALLE BOLSA	CO	ET	21200	51	E6
CALLE BONITA	SJC	SJ75	26700	36	B5
CALLE BONITA	YL	YL		8	D3
CALLE BONITO	SCL	SC72	1300	39	C2
CALLE BORREGO	SCL	SC72		38	D6
CALLE BORREGO	SJC	SJ75		38	C4
CALLE BRISA	SCL	SC72		38	E5
CALLE BURRO	SCL	SC72		38	E6
CALLE BURRO	SCL	SC72		39	B1
CALLE BUSCA	CO	ET	25100	29A	F1
CALLE CABALLERO	SJC	SJ75	27000	38	C2
CALLE CADIZ	CO	LB	46	29A	D6
CALLE CAMBIO	DPT	SC24		38	C5
CALLE CAMENORO	SCL	SC72		38	F6
CALLE CAMINATA	CO	ET		51	F6
CALLE CAMISA	SCL	SC72		38	C5
CALLE CAMPANA	SCL	SC72	34600	38	D5
CALLE CAMPESINO	SCL	SC72		39	D6
CALLE CAMPO	SCL	SC72	100	39	D2
CALLE CANADA	ANA	AN		13	C2
CALLE CANASTA	SCL	SC72	34600	38	D5
CALLE CANDELA	FUL	FL33	1900	5	E3
CALLE CANELA	SCL	SC72		38	F6
CALLE CANTO	SJC	SJ75	26800	38	C3
CALLE CAPRI	SCL	SC72	2300	39	D5
CALLE CARMEL	CO	LB53		29A	E6
CALLE CARMEL	CO	LB53		29C	E1
CALLE CARMELITA	DPT	SC24	34300	38	C5
CALLE CARMENITA	CO	LB	5400	29A	B5
CALLE CARTAGENA	SJC	SJ75	27800	36	D6
CALLE CASAL	MVJO	SJ92	27600	29B	D5
CALLE CASALERO	CO	LB		35	F2
CALLE CASINO	SCL	SC72		38	D5
CALLE CASITA	SCL	SC72		38	D5
CALLE CASTILE	CO	SJ79		59	C4
CL CASTOR CIR	HTB	HB		20	D3
CALLE CEDRO	ANA	AN	5900	13	C1
CALLE CELESTE	CO	ET		51	E6
CALLE CERRITOS	SJC	SJ75		38	B2
CALLE CETRO	SCL	SC72		38	C5
CALLE CHAYOTE	SCL	SC72		38	F6
CALLE CHAYOTE	SCL	SC72		39	C1
CALLE CHUECA	SCL	SC72		38	E6
CALLE CHUECA	SJC	SJ75	30600	36	B5
CALLE CIDRA	SCL	SC72		39	C1
CALLE CITA	LAG	LB77	32200	37	B1
CALLE CITA	SCL	SC72	2400	39	E5
CALLE COLINA	SCL	SC72	200	39	C3
CALLE CONCHITA	SCL	SC72	1000	39	D4
CALLE CONEJO	SJC	SJ75		38	C4
CALLE CONTENTA	SCL	SC72		38	E5
CL CORDILLERA	SCL	SC72		71	B6
CALLE CORDOBA	TUS	TUS		24	E4
CALLE CORRAL	SCL	SC72		38	E6
CALLE CORTA	CO	LB	21000	29A	A6
CALLE CORTA	CO	LB		29C	A1
CALLE CORTEZ	CO	LB		29A	C6
CALLE CORTEZ	SCL	SC72	100	39	E3
CALLE CORTEZ	YL	YL		8	A5
CALLE COTURNO	CO	TRA		59	C2
CALLE CRISTINA	CO	SJ		59	C1
CALLE CUADRA	SCL	SC72		38	E6
CALLE CUERVO	SCL	SC72		39	F4
CALLE CUERVO	YL	YL		8	F5
CALLE CUMBRE	SCL	SC72		38	E5
CALLE DA GAMA	ANA	AN		13	C2
CALLE DANA	ANA	AN		12	F3
CALLE DE ANZA	PLA	PLA		7	C3
CALLE DE ANZA	SCL	SC72	200	39	E3
CL DE BONANZA	SJC	SJ75	33800	38	C4
CALLE DE BRYAN	YL	YL	19200	8	B2

1990 ORANGE COUNTY STREET INDEX

STREET	CITY	P.O. ZONE	BLOCK	PAGE	GRID
CALLE DE CAMBIO	CO	LB77	28900	36	A2
CALLE DE CASAS	ANA	AN		13	C3
CL D INDUSTRIAS	SCL	SC72	100	39	C2
CL DE LA LADERA	YL	YL		8	D4
CL DE LA LOUISA	CO	LB	23500	29A	D5
CL D L MAGDALNA	CO	LB	23900	29A	D6
CALLE DEL APICE	SCL	SC72		39	F3
CL DE LA PLATA	CO	LB	23900	29A	D5
CL DE LAS FOCAS	SCL	SC72		39	D6
CL DE LAS VEGAS	SCL	SC72	100	39	C2
CALLE DEL CAMPO	SJC	SJ75	31500	36	D6
CL DEL CERRITO	SCL	SC72	600	39	F5
CALLE DEL CERRO	SCL	SC72		39	D1
CALLE DEL CERRO	SCL	SC72		71	C6
CALLE DEL CID	MVJO	SJ91		29D	C4
CL DEL COMERCIO	SCL	SC72	2500	39	E5
CL DEL CORONADO	PLA	PLA		7	C3
CL DEL ESTABLO	SCL	SC72		39	D6
CALLE DELGADO	SJC	SJ75		38	C3
CALLE DELGADO	YL	YL		8	E4
CALLE DEL HIGO	SCL	SC72		39	D1
CALLE DELICADA	SCL	SC72		39	E2
CALLE DEL JUEGO	SCL	SC72		39	D2
CALLE DEL LAGO	CO	ET		51	F6
CALLE DEL MAR	CO	LB56		29C	F6
CALLE DEL NORTE	ANA	AN		13	E2
CALLE DEL NORTE	CO	SJ88		59	A5
CALLE DEL NORTE	SA	SA		22	D2
CL D LOS ALAMOS	SCL	SC72	1500	39	D5
CL D LS CABLROS	CO	LB	24000	29A	E6
CL D LS MOLINOS	SCL	SC72	100	39	C2
CL DEL PACIFICO	SCL	SC72	2300	39	D5
CALLE DELPHINA	SJC	SJ75	26400	38	B1
CALLE DEL RITO	SCL	SC72	500	39	F5
CALLE DEL SOL	DPT	SC24	34700	38	C5
CALLE DEL SUR	CO	SJ88		59	A5
CALLE DEL SUR	SA	SA		22	D2
CALLE DL TESORO	SJC	SJ75	33200	38	A2
CALLE DE ORO	CO	ET		29A	E1
CALLE DE ORO	CO	ET		51	E6
CALLE DE PASEO	CO	ET		51	E4
CL DE PRINCESA	CO	SJ79		59	D5
CALLE DESCANSO	SCL	SC72		38	E6
CALLE DESHECHA	SCL	SC72	1700	39	C3
CALLE DE SOTO	SCL	SC72		39	E2
CALLE DE VISTA	ANA	AN		13	E1
CALLE DIAZ	ANA	AN		13	C2
CALLE DIVINO	SCL	SC72	27300	38	C5
CALLE DOLORES	DPT	SC24	26900	38	C5
CALLE DON CARLO	SJC	SJ75	26900	38	C3
CALLE DONCELLO	SCL	SC72		38	F5
CL DON GUILLRMO	LAH	LAH		2	A6
CL DON GUILLRMO	LAH	LAH		6	A1
CALLE DON JUAN	LAH	LAH		2	A6
CALLE DON JUAN	LAH	LAH		6	A1
CALLE DORADO	SCL	SC72	200	39	E2
CALLE DORADO	SJC	SJ75		38	C4
CALLE DULCE	SCL	SC72		38	E5
CALLE DULCINEA	SCL	SC72		39	F2
CALLE DURANGO	ANA	AN		8	E6
CALLE DURANGO	ANA	AN		13	E1
CALLE EL SAUZAL	SJC	SJ75		36	C5
CL EL TORO GRND	CO	ET	24600	29A	E3
CL EMBOCADURA	SCL	SC72		38	E5
CALLE EMILIA	SCL	SCL		38	E4
CALLE EMPALME	SCL	SC72		39	D2
CALLE ENTRADA	CO	ET		29A	E1
CALLE ENTRADA	CO	ET		51	E6
CALLE ENTRADA	YL	YL		8	E5
CALLE ENTRADERO	SJC	SJ75		36	D5
CALLE ESCAMILA	SJC	SJ75		38	B1
CALLE ESCUELA	SCL	SC72		39	D2
CALLE ESMARCA	SCL	SC72		39	E3
CALLE ESPERANZA	SJC	SJ75		38	C3
CALLE ESPINA	MVJO	SJ92	28000	29B	E4
CALLE ESPOLON	CO	TRA		59	C2
CALLE ESTEBAN	SCL	SC72		38	E5
CALLE ESTILO	MVJO	SJ91	23800	29B	A5
CALLE ESTRIBO	CO	SJ		59	C2
CALLE FAMILIA	SCL	SC72		39	D2
CALLE FELICIDAD	SCL	SC72		39	E2
CALLE FELIZ	YL	YL		8	D3
CALLE FIERROS	SCL	SC72		38	E5
CALLE FIESTA	SCL	SC72		39	D2
CALLE FLORERA	CO	ET	24900	51	E6
CALLE FORTUNA	DPT	SC24	34300	38	C5
CALLE FRANCESCA	CO	SJ		59	C1
CALLE FRANCESCA	SCL	SC72		39	A5
CALLE FRANCESCA	SCL	SC72		39	D6
CALLE FRESNO	SCL	SCL		39	F2
CALLE FRONTERA	SCL	SC72		38	E6

STREET	CITY	P.O. ZONE	BLOCK	PAGE	GRID
CALLE FRONTERA	SCL	SC72		39	B1
CALLE GANADERO	SCL	SC72		38	E5
CALLE GANADOR	MVJO	SJ91	23800	29B	B4
CALLE GAUCHO	SCL	SC72		38	E6
CALLE GOMERO	SCL	SC72		38	D4
CALLE GOMEZ	SCL	SC72	400	39	F5
CALLE GRANADA	ANA	AN08		8	D6
CALLE GRANADA	DPT	SC24		38	C5
CALLE GRANADA	DPT	SC24		38	C5
CALLE GRANDE	FUL	FL		6	D2
CALLE GRANDE	OR	OR		18	D2
CL GRANDE VISTA	SCL	SC72		38	D6
CL GRANDE VISTA	SCL	SC72		39	A1
CALLE GRUTA	CO	ET	21200	51	F6
CL GUADALAJARA	SCL	SC72		38	E6
CALLE GUAYMAS	SCL	SC72		38	C6
CALLE HERALDO	SCL	SC72		38	F5
CALLE HERMOSA	DPT	SC24	26800	38	C6
CALLE HIDALGO	SCL	SC72		38	E6
CALLE HOGAR	MVJO	SJ91	23800	29B	B4
CALLE HORCA	CO	TRA		59	C2
CALLE HORIZONTE	CO	ET	21200	51	E6
CL INDEPENDNCIA	FTNV	SA08	10300	22	A6
CALLE ISABELLA	SCL	SC72		39	B5
CALLE JAIME	ANA	AN		13	D1
CALLE JARDIN	SJC	SJ75		38	A3
CALLE JUANITA	DPT	SC24	26700	38	C5
CALLE JUAREZ	SCL	SC72		38	D6
CALLE JUCA	CO	LB		35	F2
CALLE JUNO	SCL	SC72	3900	38	C4
CALLE KATRINA	CO	SJ		59	C1
CALLE LA BOMBA	SJC	SJ75		36	C5
CALLE LA FUENTE	SJC	SJ75		38	A2
CALLE LAGO	DPT	SC24		38	B5
CALLE LAGO	SCL	SC72		39	C2
CALLE LA MANCHA	TUS	TUS		24	E4
CL LA PRIMAVERA	DPT	DPT	33700	37	F4
CL LA PURISIMA	SJC	SJ75		36	B6
CALLE LA QUINTA	SCL	SC72		38	D5
CALLE LARKSPUR	CO	SJ88		59	D1
CALLE LAS BOLAS	SCL	SC72		39	C3
CALLE LA SERNA	SCL	SC72	2300	39	E4
CL LAS FLORES	DPT	SC24	34600	38	B5
CALLE LAS NUBES	SCL	SC72		39	E6
CL LAS PALMAS	SCL	SC72	2300	39	E5
CALLE LASUEN	SCL	SC72	200	39	D5
CALLE LA VETA	SCL	SC72		38	C6
CALLE LEE	LALM	LALM		14	C1
CALLE LETICIA	SCL	SC72		39	E4
CALLE LIMA	SCL	SC72		38	C5
CALLE LINDA	DPT	LB77		37	C1
CALLE LISA	SCL	SC72		39	B5
CALLE LOBINA	SCL	SC72		39	C1
CALLE LOMA	DPT	SC24	34600	38	C5
CALLE LORENZO	SJC	SJ75	30800	36	B5
CL LOS ALAMOS	DPT	SC24	26700	38	C5
CL LOS OLIVOS	SCL	SC72		38	D5
CL LOS ROBLES	DPT	SC24	34600	38	C5
CALLE LOUISA	SCL	SC72		39	B5
CALLE LUCANA	SJC	SJ75	26300	36	B6
CALLE LUCANA	SJC	SJ75	26300	38	B1
CALLE LUEGO	SCL	SC72		38	E6
CALLE MACHO	SCL	SC72		38	E6
CALLE MADEIRA	SCL	SC72	2400	39	D5
CALLE MADERA	CO	ET	25000	51	F6
CALLE MADERO	FTNV	SA08	10400	22	A6
CALLE MADRIGAL	SJC	SJ75		38	B2
CALLE MAJORCA	SCL	SC72	2400	39	D5
CALLE MALAGA	CO	LB77		35	C5
CALLE MALAGUENA	SCL	SC72		39	E3
CALLE MANZANA	YL	YL		8	D3
CALLE MARBELLA	CO	SJ		59	C1
CALLE MARIA	CO	SJ		59	C1
CALLE MARIA	DPT	SC24	26700	38	C5
CALLE MARIA	MVJO	SJ91	26700	29B	C4
CALLE MARIA	SCL	SC72	100	39	E4
CALLE MARIA	TUS	TUS		24	E4
CALLE MARIN	MVJO	SJ92		29B	D5
CALLE MARINA	SCL	SC72	200	39	D5
CALLE MARISMA	SJC	SJ75		38	B1
CALLE MARLENA	SCL	SC72		39	B5
CALLE MATORRAL	CO	ET		51	E6
CALLE MAYITA	SCL	SC72		39	E4
CALLE MAYO	SCL	SC72	3900	38	C4
CALLE MELENO	FUL	FL		6	A2
CALLE MELINDA	CO	SJ		59	C1
CALLE MENDOZA	SCL	SC72		39	E2
CALLE MERO	SCL	SC72		38	F6
CALLE MERO	SCL	SC72		71	A6
CALLE MIGUEL	SCL	SC72		39	D2
CALLE MIGUEL	SJC	SJ75	32800	38	A2

STREET	CITY	P.O. ZONE	BLOCK	PAGE	GRID
CALLE MIRADOR	SCL	SC72	1400	39	C3
CALLE MIRADOR	YL	YL		8	A5
CALLE MIRAMAR	SJC	SJ75	33700	38	C3
CALLE MIRANDA	FUL	FL33	1800	5	F3
CALLE MONACO	SCL	SC72	2300	39	D5
CALLE MONSERATE	SJC	SJ75		38	B2
CALLE MONSERRAT	SCL	SC72		39	E2
CALLE MONTE	DPT	SC24		38	B5
CL MONTE CARLO	SCL	SC72	2400	39	D5
CL MONTE CRISTO	SCL	SC72	2300	39	D5
CALLE MONTELLA	TUS	TUS		24	E4
CALLE MONTEREY	DPT	SC24	26800	38	C4
CALLE MONTEREY	SCL	SC72	26800	38	C4
CALLE MORAGA	CO	LB77		35	C5
CALLE NARANJA	DPT	SC24	34200	38	C5
CALLENDER CT	CO	LB		35	F6
CALLE NEBLINA	SCL	SC72		39	D2
CALLE NEGOCIO	SCL	SC72		71	B6
CALLE NERUDA	MVJO	SJ92		29B	D4
CALLE NINA	SCL	SC72		39	E3
CALLE NISPERO	SCL	SC72		38	F6
CALLE NISPERO	SCL	SC72		39	C1
CALLENS CIR	FTNV	SA08		26	F2
CALLENS COMMON	SA	SA04		27	F2
CALLE NUEVO	SCL	SC72		38	E4
CALLE OCASO	CO	ET		51	F6
CALLE OLA VERDE	SCL	SC72		39	C1
CALLE OLIVIA	CO	ET		51	F6
CALLE OSO	SCL	SC72		39	C3
CALLE OTONO	CO	ET		29A	E1
CALLE PAISANO	SCL	SC72		38	E6
CALLE PALMA	TUS	TUS		24	E4
CALLE PALOMA	DPT	SC24	34500	38	C5
CALLE PANTANO	ANA	AN		13	D1
CALLE PARQUE DR	HTB	HB		20	D3
CL PASSIFLORA	CO	SJ		56	D6
CL PASSIFLORA	CO	SJ		59	D1
CALLE PASTADERO	SCL	SC72		39	F1
CALLE PATRICIA	SCL	SC72		39	E3
CALLE PEQUENO	CO	ET		29A	D1
CALLE PEQUENO	CO	ET		51	D6
CALLE PERA	YL	YL		8	D3
CALLE PERFECTO	SJC	SJ75	33100	38	B3
CALLE PERLINO	SCL	SC72	27300	38	C5
CALLE PESCADOR	SCL	SC72		39	E2
CALLE PICO	CO	LB	5400	29A	B5
CALLE PIEDRAS	SCL	SC72		38	E5
CALLE PIZARRO	PLA	PLA		7	C3
CALLE PLAYA	CO	LB56		29C	F6
CALLE PLUMA	SCL	SC72		38	D5
CALLE PORTOLA	DPT	SC24	34200	38	C5
CALLE POSADA	SJC	SJ75		36	F5
CALLE POTRANCA	SCL	SC72		39	D6
CALLE POTRO	SCL	SC72		39	D6
CALLE PRADERA	CO	ET		29A	F1
CALLE PRADERA	CO	ET	25100	51	F6
CALLE PRIMA	DPT	SC24		38	D6
CALLE PRIMA	DPT	SC24		39	A1
CALLE PRIMAVERA	SCL	SC72	200	39	D5
CALLE PRINCIPIA	ANA	AN		13	C2
CALLE PUEBLO	SCL	SC72		39	D2
CALLE PUENTE	SCL	SC72	600	39	C3
CALLE QUIETO	SCL	SC72		38	D6
CALLE RAMADA	SCL	SC72		39	A5
CALLE RAMONA	DPT	SC24	34700	38	B5
CALLE RANCHERA	CO	SJ		59	C1
CALLE RAQUEL	SJC	SJ75		36	E5
CALLE REAL	DPT	SC24	26700	38	C6
CALLE REAL	SCL	SC72	3900	38	C5
CALLE REATA	SCL	SC72		38	E6
CALLE RECODO	SCL	SC72		71	B6
CALLE RECREO	CO	ET	21200	51	E6
CALLE REDONDEL	SCL	SC72	100	39	C2
CL RESPLENDOR	SJC	SJ75	30700	36	B4
CALLE REYNALDA	SJC	SJ75	31900	38	B1
CALLE RICA	SCL	SC72	200	39	E2
CALLE RICARDO	SJC	SJ75	25000	38	A1
CALLE RIENDA	CO	SJ		59	C2
CALLE RIO VISTA	SJC	SJ75		36	B6
CALLE RIO VISTA	SJC	SJ75		38	B1
CALLE ROBERTO	SJC	SJ75	22500	36	B6
CALLE ROBLES	SCL	SC72		39	D2
CALLE ROCA VIS	SCL	SC72	200	39	D5
CALLE ROJA	CO	SA	1900	24	D5
CALLE ROLANDO	SJC	SJ75		38	B2
CALLE ROSITA	DPT	SC24	34500	38	C5
CL SACRAMENTO	SCL	SC72	1500	39	C3
CALLE SALIDA	DPT	SC24		38	B5
CALLE SALIDA	SCL	SC72		39	D2
CL SAN ANTONIO	SJC	SJ75		36	B5

STREET	CITY	P.O. ZONE	BLOCK	PAGE	GRID
CALLE SANDIA	SCL	SC72		39	D2
CALLE SAN DIEGO	SJC	SJ75		36	B5
CL SAN FELIPE	SJC	SJ75		36	C5
CL SN FRANCISCO	SJC	SJ75		36	B6
CALLE SAN JUAN	DPT	SC24	34300	38	C5
CALLE SAN JUAN	SJC	SJ75		36	B5
CALLE SAN LUIS	SJC	SJ75		36	B5
CL SAN MARCOS	SJC	SJ75	32800	38	A2
CALLE SAN PEDRO	SJC	SJ75		36	C5
CALLE SAN REMO	SJC	SJ75	27800	36	D6
CALLE SAN REMO	SJC	SJ75		38	D1
CL STA BARBARA	SJC	SJ75		36	B6
CL STA ROSALIA	SJC	SJ75		36	B5
CALLE STA YNES	SJC	SJ75	27800	36	E6
CALLE STA YNES	SJC	SJ75	27800	38	F1
CALLE SEGURO	SCL	SC72		39	D2
CALLE SENDERO	CO	ET		29A	F1
CALLE SENDERO	CO	ET	21200	51	F6
CALLE SERENA	FUL	FL33	1900	5	F3
CALLE SERENA	SCL	SC72	200	39	D5
CALLE SEVILLE	SCL	SC72	100	39	D3
CALLE SIERRA	CO	AN07		44	A2
CALLE SOLEDAD	SA	SA		22	D2
CALLE SOMBRA	SCL	SC72		71	C6
CALLE SOMBRE	CO	LB77		36	A2
CALLE SONORA	CO	LB		29A	B5
CALLE SONORA	CO	LB		29C	B1
CALLE SONORA	SCL	SC72	200	39	E3
CALLE SONORA	YL	YL		8	F4
CL SONORA ESTE	CO	LB		29A	B6
CL SONORA ESTE	CO	LB		29C	B1
CL SONORA OESTE	CO	LB		29A	B6
CL SONORA OESTE	CO	LB		29C	B1
CALLE SORPRESO	SCL	SC72		38	E6
CALLE SUSANNA	SJC	SJ75		36	F5
CALLE TIARA	SCL	SC72		39	D6
CALLE TIBIDABO	SCL	SC72		39	E2
CALLE TIBURON	SCL	SC72		39	D6
CALLE TIMONERO	SCL	SC72		38	E5
CALLE TIMONERO	SCL	SC72		39	A4
CALLE TINAJA	SCL	SC72	200	39	B1
CALLE TOGA	DPT	SC24		38	C5
CALLE TOLEDO	SCL	SC72	1000	39	D4
CALLE TORCIDO	CO	ET		29A	D1
CALLE TORCIDO	CO	ET		51	D6
CL TRANQUILLO	YL	YL		8	D3
CALLE TREPADORA	SCL	SC72		71	B6
CL TRES LOMAS	CO	ET	24700	29A	E3
CALLE ULTIMA	DPT	SC24		38	C5
CALLE ULTIMO	FUL	FL33	1900	5	F3
CALLE VALDES	MVJO	SJ92	27600	29B	D4
CALLE VALLARTA	SCL	SC72		38	F5
CALLE VALLE	SCL	SC72	1300	39	C2
CALLE VAQUETA	CO	SJ		59	C1
CALLE VECINIDAD	CO	ET		51	E6
CALLE VELEZ	DPT	SC24	34300	38	C5
CALLE VENADO	ANA	AN		13	E4
CALLE VENEZIA	SCL	SC72		39	E1
CALLE VERANO	DPT	SC24	26700	38	C6
CALLE VERANO	SCL	SC72		38	D5
CALLE VICENTE	SCL	SC72	34900	38	D5
CALLE VIEJA	CO	LB	24900	35	F3
CALLE VIENTOS	CO	ET		51	E6
CL VILLA CLARA	SJC	SJ75		36	D5
CALLE VILLARIO	SCL	SC72		39	D2
CALLE VISTA	CO	LB		35	F1
CL VISTA ALEGRE	YL	YL		8	D4
CALLE VIS LINDA	YL	YL		8	D4
CL VISTA TORITO	SCL	SC72	300	39	B1
CALLE WINONA	SJC	SJ75	31800	38	B1
CALLE ZARAGOSA	FTNV	SA08	17200	22	A6
CALLE ZORRA	SCL	SC72		38	D5
CALLIEBURN CIR	HTB	HB	20500	26	E5
CALLIOPE ST	LAG	LB51	100	34	E4
CALLITA DR	DPT	DPT	34000	37	F4
CALMAR ST	ANA	AN	1800	16	B1
CALMHILL CIR	CO	SA	10500	18	E5
CALNAN ST	TUS	SA10		23	F6
CALNEVA LN	HTB	HB	14300	20	F1
CALPE CIR	HTB	HB	6800	26	A1
CALTECH CIR	WSTM	WSTM	15800	21	D4
CALVERT AV	CM	CM	2000	27	A4
CALVERTON CIR	CO	LB		35	D3
CALVIN CIR	HTB	HB	6000	20	F3
CALVO DR	CO	SA	17100	17	E5
CALZADO	CO	LB	23000	29A	A5
CAMALOTE	MVJO	SJ91		29B	C2
CAMARGO	MVJO	SJ91	21800	29B	D1
CAMARILLO ST	DPT	DPT		37	E3
CAMARILLO ST	PLA	PLA	300	7	A6
CAMAROSA DR	YL	YL	4500	8	C3

STREET	CITY	P.O. ZONE	BLOCK	PAGE	GRID
CAMBAY LN	HTB	HB	15300	20	E3
CAMBERA LN	CO	SA	1000	18	C5
CAMBERLEY	CO	LB77		35	D6
CAMBERWELL ST	CO	LB		29A	E6
CAMBERWELL ST	CO	LB		29C	E1
CAMBIUM	IRV	SA		29	D3
CAMBRIA CIR	OR	OR	7100	18	D2
CAMBRIA DR	HTB	HB		30	D2
CAMBRIA DR	NB	CDLM		32	D5
CAMBRIA LN	CO	LB		29C	D4
CAMBRIA PL	ANA	AN	1000	10	E2
CAMBRIA ST	ANA	AN	600	10	E3
CAMBRIDGE	IRV	SA		24	E6
CAMBRIDGE AV	FUL	FL	2200	7	A2
CAMBRIDGE AV	PLA	PLA	1700	7	A2
CAMBRIDGE AV	WSTM	WSTM	5000	14	E6
CAMBRIDGE CIR	CM	CM27	400	31	D4
CAMBRIDGE CIR	CO	LB		35	D3
CAMBRIDGE CT	CO	SJ79		59	D6
CAMBRIDGE DR	LAH	LAH		2	B5
CAMBRIDGE LN	HTB	HB	19500	26	F4
CAMBRIDGE LN	NB	NB	1000	31	E4
CAMBRIDGE RD	YL	YL		40	A3
CAMBRIDGE ST	ANA	AN	1000	11	D5
CAMBRIDGE ST	CYP	CYP	9200	9	C5
CAMBRIDGE ST	SA	SA	2700	17	D4
CAMBRIDGE ST N	OR	OR	1400	12	D6
CAMBRIDGE ST N	OR	OR	100	17	D4
CAMBRIDGE ST S	OR	OR	100	17	D4
CAMBRIDGE WY	NB	NB		31	E4
CAMBRIDG HL COM	SA	SA		22	C2
CAMBRIDGE MDWS	GGR	GG		15	F6
CAMBRIDGE MDWS	GGR	GG		21	F1
CAMBURY DR	LAP	BP23	4500	9	D3
CAMDEN	CO	ET		29B	B1
CAMDEN	IRV	SA		24	E6
CAMDEN	MVJO	SJ92		29D	D3
CAMDEN CIR	LAP	BP23	7900	9	E2
CAMDEN CIR	VPK	OR67	10200	13	B6
CAMDEN CT	CO	LB77		35	E4
CAMDEN CT	YL	YL		40	A3
CAMDEN DR	CO	SA		18	C5
CAMDEN DR	CYP	CYP	10400	14	E1
CAMDEN DR	NB	CDLM	4500	33	B2
CAMDEN DR	PLA	PLA	1000	7	D4
CAMDEN PL	FUL	FL33		5	E4
CAMDEN PL	LAG	LB51	300	34	C2
CAMDEN PL	SA	SA	1300	22	E5
CAMDEN PL	SA	SA	1000	23	A5
CAMDEN ST	ANA	AN	200	11	D5
CAMDEN WY	PLA	PLA	1200	7	D4
CAMDEN WY	STN	STN		15	B2
CAMDEN MEADOWS	GGR	GG		15	F6
CAMDEN MEADOWS	GGR	GG		21	F1
CAMEL CIR	HTB	HB47	8600	21	D5
CAMELA ST	YL	YL	4300	8	A2
CAMELBACK DR	HTB	HB		25	E3
CAMELBACK RD	CO	SJ79		52	E3
CAMELBACK ST	NB	NB	1000	32	B2
CAMELIA LN	WSTM	WSTM	15500	21	E3
CAMELIA ST	SB	SB	12900	14	C5
CAMELLA CT	CO	LB	28000	29C	E6
CAMELLIA	CO	ET		51	F6
CAMELLIA	CO	ET		52	A6
CAMELLIA	CO	SJ		56	D6
CAMELLIA AV	FTNV	SA08	11000	22	B5
CAMELLIA DR	BPK	BP	7400	10	C2
CAMELLIA LN	CM	CM27	200	31	E2
CAMELLIA LN	FUL	FL33		5	F4
CAMELLIA ST	ANA	AN	200	10	F5
CAMELOT CIR	HTB	HB	17100	20	E6
CAMEL POINT DR	LAG	LB	31200	35	A5
CAMEO DR	CO	SA	1500	24	B2
CAMEO DR	CO	TUS	1300	24	B2
CAMEO LN	FUL	FL	1400	7	A4
CAMEO LN	HTB	HB	21500	30	F1
CAMEO HGHLDS DR	NB	CDLM	400	33	C2
CAMEO SHORES RD	NB	CDLM	100	33	C3
CAMERON CT	ANA	AN		10	D3
CAMERON DR	BPK	BP	5000	5	C4
CAMERON LN	CO	SA	14100	18	A6
CAMERON LN	CO	TUS	14200	24	A1
CAMERON ST	HTB	HB47	17500	21	C6
CAMERON ST	HTB	HB	17600	26	C1
CAMERON ST	PLA	PLA		7	B6
CAMERONA RD	CO	LB		35	C5
CAMFIELD LN	HTB	HB	20300	26	D5
CAMILE PL	SA	SA	1600	22	F3
CAMILE ST E&W	SA	SA	100	23	A3
CAMILE ST W	SA	SA	2200	22	C3
CAMILLE CIR	OR	OR	200	17	B3

1990 ORANGE COUNTY STREET INDEX

STREET	CITY	P.O. ZONE	BLOCK	PAGE	GRID
CAMILLE DR	HTB	HB47	6400	21	A5
CAMILLE PL	YL	YL	16600	7	D3
CAMILLE ST W	SA	SA	3300	22	C3
CAMINANTE	SCL	SC72		38	E4
CAMINITO ALTO	CO	LB		29A	A3
CAMINITO AMOR	CO	LB	22000	29A	A4
CMTO ANDRETA	CO	LB		29A	B4
CAMINITO ARBOL	CO	LB		29A	A3
CMTO ARR SECO	CO	LB		29A	B3
CAMINITO AZUCAR	CO	LB		29A	A4
CAMINITO AZUL	CO	LB		29A	A3
CMTO BASILIO	CO	LB		29A	B4
CAMINITO BRISA	CO	LB		29A	A4
CAMINITO CALMA	CO	LB		29A	A4
CAMINITO CASA	CO	LB		29A	A3
CAMINITO CLARO	CO	LB		29A	A3
CAMINITO COSTA	CO	LB	22400	29A	B4
CMTO COZUMAL	CO	LB		29A	A3
CAMINITO CRUZ	CO	LB		29A	A4
CAMINITO DANUBO	CO	LB		29A	B4
CAMINITO DONOSO	CO	LB	22900	29A	A3
CMTO ESCOBEDO	CO	LB		29A	B3
CMTO ESTEBAN	CO	LB		29A	B4
CAMINITO FLECHA	CO	LB		29A	B4
CAMINITO FLORES	CO	LB		29A	A3
CAMINITO GRANDE	CO	LB	22400	29A	B3
CMTO GUYAMAS	CO	LB		29A	A3
CMTO JUANICO	CO	LB		29A	B4
CAMINITO LAGO	CO	LB		29A	A4
CAMINITO LA PAZ	CO	LB		29A	B3
CMTO LAURELES	CO	LB		29A	A3
CAMINITO LAZARO	CO	LB		29A	B4
CAMINITO LIBRE	CO	LB		29A	A3
CAMINITO LINDA	CO	LB		29A	A4
CMTO LS POCITOS	CO	LB		29A	A3
CMTO LUISITO	CO	LB		29A	B4
CAMINITO LUZ	CO	LB		29A	A3
CAMINITO MADERA	CO	LB	22300	29A	A4
CMTO MANRESA	CO	LB		29A	A3
CAMINITO MAR	CO	LB		29A	A4
CMTO MARCIAL	CO	LB		29A	B4
CMTO MESCALERO	CO	LB		29A	B4
CAMINITO MUNDO	CO	LB		29A	A3
CMTO NICOSIA	CO	LB	22900	29A	A3
CAMINITO NORTE	CO	LB	23400	29A	A4
CAMINITO OLIVIA	CO	LB	22900	29A	A3
CAMINITO ORO	CO	LB		29A	A3
CMTO PACIFICO	CO	LB	22400	29A	B3
CMTO PARTIDA	CO	LB		29A	B4
CMTO PENJAMO	CO	LB		29A	A3
CMTO PETATLAN	CO	LB		29A	A3
CAMINITO PIEDRA	CO	LB		29A	A4
CAMINITO PLATA	CO	LB		29A	A4
CAMINITO PLUMAS	CO	LB	22900	29A	A3
CAMINITO POCO	CO	LB		29A	A4
CAMINITO REGALD	CO	LB		29A	A4
CAMINITO RIO	CO	LB		29A	A4
CAMINITO ROJO	CO	LB		29A	A3
CAMINITO SALADO	CO	LB		29A	B4
CAMINITO SOL	CO	LB		29A	A3
CAMINITO SUR	CO	LB		29A	A4
CMTO TASQUILLO	CO	LB		29A	A3
CAMINITO TECATE	CO	LB		29A	B4
CAMINITO TELMO	CO	LB		29A	B4
CMTO TIBURON	CO	LB	22100	29A	B4
CAMINITO VADO	CO	LB		29A	A4
CAMINITO VALLE	CO	LB	23400	29A	A4
CAMINITO VIENTO	CO	LB		29A	A3
CAMINITO VINO	CO	LB	22000	29A	A4
CMTO ZARAGOZA	CO	LB		29A	A3
CAMINO AV	SA	SA	1700	17	D5
CAMINO ST	ANA	AN	2100	16	D2
CAMINO ADELANTO	MVJO	SJ91	23200	29B	A5
CAMINO AIREN	CO	LB56		29C	E5
CAMINO ALONDRA	SCL	SC72		38	D6
CAMINO ALTO	FUL	FL	1500	6	A3
CAMINO ALTOZANO	CO	SJ88		59	A4
CAMINO ANCLA	SCL	SC72		38	E6
CAMINO ANCLA	SCL	SC72		39	C1
CAMINO ARROYO	ANA	AN	100	13	D1
CAMINO BAGA	CO	LB56		29C	E5
CAMINO BARCELOS	CO	LB56		29C	E4
CAMINO BESAR	YL	YL		40	C5
CAMINO BUCANERO	SCL	SC72		38	E6
CAMINO CALUROSO	YL	YL		40	B5
CM CANADA LN	HTB	HB		20	D3
CM CAPISTRANO	CO	LB77		29D	A6
CM CAPISTRANO	CO	LB53	26900	29D	B4
CM CAPISTRANO	DPT	SC24	34500	38	B5
CM CAPISTRANO	DPT	SC24	36600	39	A1
CM CAPISTRANO	MVJO	LB53		29D	B4

STREET	CITY	P.O. ZONE	BLOCK	PAGE	GRID
CM CAPISTRANO	SCL	SC72		39	B1
CM CAPISTRANO	SJC	SJ75	29400	36	B4
CM CAPISTRANO	SJC	SJ75	31900	38	B3
CM CENTRO LOMA	FUL	FL33	1700	5	F3
CAMINO CHICO	SCL	SC72		39	E1
CAMINO CHICO	SJC	SJ75		36	F5
CAMINO CLARO	YL	YL		40	B5
CAMINO CORRER	ANA	AN	5900	13	C1
CM CORSA RIO	SCL	SC72		38	F6
CM DE BRYANT	YL	YL		40	D6
CM DE ESTRELLA	DPT	SC24	26800	38	C6
CM DE ESTRELLA	SCL	SC72	27000	38	C6
CM DE FRESAS	ANA	AN		13	E5
CM D LA MANZANA	SCL	SC72		38	D4
CAMINO DL AVION	CO	LB77		37	D1
CAMINO DL AVION	DPT	DPT	25400	38	A2
CAMINO DL AVION	SJC	SJ75	25600	38	A2
CAMINO DL CIELO	CO	SJ79		59	D2
CAMINO DEL MAR	CO	LB56		29C	F6
CM D LS CABLLOS	YL	YL	17900	7	F5
CM D LOS CANTOS	YL	YL		8	D3
CM DE LOS MARES	SCL	SC72	34400	38	D5
CM DEL RANCHO	SCL	SC72		39	C2
CAMINO DEL SOL	FUL	FL	2000	6	A2
CM DE NARANJAS	ANA	AN		13	E5
CAMINO DE NINOS	ANA	AN		13	E5
CAMINO DE PAZ	ANA	AN		13	E5
CAMINO DE VISTA	SJC	SJ75		38	B4
CAMINO DORADA	YL	YL		40	C5
CM EL MOLINO	DPT	SC24	34100	38	B4
CM ESCONDIDO	FUL	FL33	2300	5	E3
CAMINO FAMOSA	YL	YL		40	C5
CAMINO FARO	SCL	SC72		38	F6
CAMINO GALEON	SCL	SC72		38	E6
CAMINO GRANDE	ANA	AN		13	E3
CAMINO IBIZA	SCL	SC72		39	E1
CAMINO JALISCO	CO	LB		29A	B3
CAMINO KATIA	SCL	SCL		39	F2
CAMINO LARGO	MVJO	SJ92		29D	E3
CAMINO LA RONDA	SJC	SJ75		36	D6
CAMINO LA RONDA	SJC	SJ75		38	D1
CM LAS RAMBLAS	SJC	SJ75	26600	38	B4
CAMINO LAUREL	SCL	SC72		38	F6
CAMINO LAUREL	SCL	SC72		39	C1
CAMINO LA VISTA	FUL	FL	1500	6	A3
CAMINO LOMA	FUL	FL	1500	6	A3
CM LOS PADRES	CO	LB77		36	A4
CM LOS ROBLES	FUL	FL	1500	6	A3
CAMINO MANZANO	ANA	AN	5900	13	C1
CAMINO MESA CT	IRV	SA		32	C2
CM MIRA COSTA	SCL	SC72		38	C6
CAMINO MONTE	FUL	FL		6	A2
CAMINO PAPAL	CO	ET		29A	E1
CAMINO PINZON	ANA	AN		13	C2
CAMINO PONIENTE	YL	YL		40	C5
CAMINO RAYO	CO	ET		29A	E1
CAMINO REAL	FTNV	SA08		22	A5
CM RECONDITO	FUL	FL33	2300	5	E3
CAMINO REY	FUL	FL33	2100	5	F3
CAMINO RIOJA	CO	LB56		29C	E4
CAMINO SANCHO	SJC	SJ75		36	F6
CM SAN CLEMENTE	SCL	SC72	100	39	B2
CAMINO SAN JOSE	SCL	SCL		39	F2
CAMINO SAN JOSE	SJC	SJ75		36	E5
CM SNTO DOMINGO	SJC	SJ75	27600	36	D6
CM SNTO DOMINGO	SJC	SJ75	27600	38	D1
CAMINO TAMPICO	ANA	AN		8	E6
CAMINO TECATE	YL	YL		40	B5
CAMINO TREBOL	CO	ET		29A	E1
CAMINO VALVERDE	SJC	SJ75		38	B2
CM VERA CRUZ	SCL	SC72		38	E4
CAMINO VERDE	YL	YL	19000	8	B3
CAMINO VILLA	CO	ET		29A	E1
CAMINO VILLA	CO	ET		51	E6
CAMINO VISTA	ANA	AN		13	E3
CAMINO VISTA	YL	YL		40	B5
CAMINTO DR	CO	SJ79		59	D2
CAMO BLUFF CT	FTNV	SA08	15800	22	B4
CAMP ST	CO	CYP	4900	9	D4
CAMP ST	CYP	CYP	5500	9	E4
CAMPANA DR	IRV	SA		24	E4
CAMPANA WY	CO	LB		35	C6
CAMPANERO	IRV	SA		24	F5
CAMPANET	MVJO	SJ92	27700	29B	D3
CAMPANILLA	SCL	SC72		38	D5
CAMPBELL AV	LAH	LAH	2400	1	D5
CAMPBELL DR	ANA	AN	600	10	F5
CAMPBELL LN	CM	CM27		31	F2
CAMPEON	CO	LB77		36	B1
CAMPESINA DR	HTB	HB	16500	20	D5
CAMPESINO	MVJO	SJ91		29D	C3

STREET	CITY	P.O. ZONE	BLOCK	PAGE	GRID
CAMPESTRE	MVJO	SJ91		29B	C4
CAMPHOR	IRV	SA		29	B5
CAMPHOR AV	WSTM	WSTM	5700	20	F1
CAMPHOR AV	YL	YL		8	D2
CAMPHOR CIR	BREA	BREA	200	3	A6
CAMPHOR ST	NB	NB	700	32	B2
CAMPHOR TREE LN	CO	OR	11700	18	B2
CAMPHOR TREE LN	MVJO	SJ91		52	D6
CAMPINA DR	MVJO	SJ91	25100	29D	C1
CAMPO MORO	MVJO	SJ92		29D	C4
CAMPO RASO	SCL	SC72		38	F4
CAMPO ROJO	CO	ET	25100	29A	F3
CAMPOS	MVJO	SJ92	22500	29B	D2
CAMPO VERDE	CO	ET	24600	29A	E3
CAMPTON PL	CO	LB77		37	E1
CAMPUS DR	BPK	BP	6900	10	D1
CAMPUS DR	CO	AN04	9700	10	F5
CAMPUS DR	IRV	SA	2000	28	C4
CAMPUS DR	IRV	SA		32	E1
CAMPUS DR	NB	NB60	19000	28	B5
CAMPUS DR	OR			18	E2
CAMROSE CIR	FTNV	SA08	9800	21	F4
CAMROSE ST	ANA	AN	1700	16	B1
CAMROSE WY	ANA	AN	1600	16	B1
CAMSHIP	CO	LB77		37	E1
CAMUS LN	STN	GG41	12500	15	C4
CANADA E	SCL	SC72	100	39	D3
CANADA W	SCL	SC72	100	39	C3
CANADA CT S	CO	ET	23200	29A	D3
CANADA RD	CO	ET		52	A6
CANADIAN DR	CM	CM	3100	27	F3
CANAL CIR	NB	NB	500	31	A3
CANAL ST	CO	OR65	8700	12	D4
CANAL ST	NB	NB63	100	30	F4
CANAL ST	NB	NB	300	31	A4
CANAL ST	OR	OR	2100	12	D4
CANARD AV	PLA	PLA	1700	7	B3
CANARD LN	CO	ET	22800	29A	E3
CANARY AV	FTNV	SA08	8900	26	E2
CANARY CIR	BPK	BP	6100	9	F1
CANARY CT	CO	ET		52	B6
CANARY CT	CO	LB77		35	D2
CANARY DR	CM	CM	2600	27	B5
CANARY LN	GGR	GG	11700	15	F3
CANASTA DR	CO	LAH	11000	2	A3
CANAVERAS	MVJO	SJ91	22200	29B	C2
CANBERRA LN	HTB	HB46	19500	27	A4
CANCHA	NB	NB		32	B2
CANCION DR	MVJO	SJ91	26400	29D	B2
CANCUN	MVJO	SJ92		52	E6
CANDACE LN	LAH	LAH	1000	2	B3
CANDEDA PL	CO	TUS	14600	23	F2
CANDELA	IRV	SA		24	E5
CANDIA CIR	LAH	LAH	600	1	F6
CANDIS AV	SA	SA	2100	16	F6
CANDLE CIR	HTB	HB		25	E1
CANDLEBERRY	IRV	SA		29	B5
CANDLEBERRY AV	SB	SB	4000	14	D4
CANDLEBERRY CIR	OR	OR69		18	E3
CANDLEBERRY LN	YL	YL		40	D5
CANDLEBUSH	IRV	SA		32A	B3
CANDLELIGHT CIR	HTB	HB47	7000	21	B4
CANDLELIGHT LN	YL	YL	6000	7	F5
CANDLESTICK LN	CYP	CYP	9100	9	D4
CANDLESTICK LN	NB	NB	1600	31	F3
CANDLEWOOD AV	OR	OR	800	12	D6
CANDLEWOOD AV	PLA	PLA	500	7	C4
CANDLEWOOD CIR	ANA	AN		8	B6
CANDLEWOOD DR	FUL	FL33		5	E4
CANDLEWOOD DR	HTB	HB	9300	26	E5
CANDLEWOOD DR	LAH	LAH	700	1	D5
CANDLEWOOD LN	CO	LB		29C	D4
CANDLEWOOD ST	ANA	AN	1200	11	E2
CANDLEWOOD ST	BREA	BREA	500	2	F5
CANDLEWOOD ST	WSTM	WSTM	15500	21	F3
CANDLEWOOD WY	BPK	BP	4500	5	D3
CANDLEWOOD WY	LAH	LAH	2600	1	D5
CANDOR LN	CO	ET	23700	29A	D4
CANDY LN	GGR	GG	11500	16	C3
CANDYTUFT CIR	FTNV	SA08	11500	22	C5
CANEDO DR	MVJO	SJ91		29B	B5
CANELA	MVJO	SJ92	24500	29B	D6
CANFIELD DR	CO	LAH	9300	1	D3
CANFIELD DR	LAH	LAH	2400	1	D3
CANFIELD LN	ANA	AN	1600	11	E1
CANFIELD PL	OR	OR		17	C2
CANGAS	MVJO	SJ92		29D	D2
CANIS CIR	HTB	HB47	6900	21	B6
CANNA CIR	BPK	BP	8000	10	C2
CANNA CIR	HTB	HB47	17300	21	B6

STREET	CITY	P.O. ZONE	BLOCK	PAGE	GRID
CANNA WY	WSTM	WSTM	15500	21	E3
CANNERY ST	GGR	GG	13000	15	E5
CANNES	LAG	LB		35	B6
CANNES	IRV	SA14		29	A4
CANNES CIR	MVJO	SJ92		29D	E3
CANNES DR	SA	SA		22	E2
CANNON LN	FUL	FL	300	6	C4
CANNON ST	OR	OR	1100	13	C6
CANNONADE CIR	CM	CM	900	27	E2
CANO	MVJO	SJ92	28400	29B	E4
CANOE BROOK DR	SB	SB	13700	19	C6
CANOGA PL	ANA	AN	200	10	A4
CANOGA ST	ANA	AN	400	10	A5
CANTALOUPE CT	SA	SA		22	E2
CANTANTE	CO	LB	23000	29A	A4
CANTARA LN	CO	LB	22900	35	C5
CANTER CIR	GGR	GG	11800	15	A3
CANTER LN	YL	YL		8	D2
CANTER ST	GGR	GG	12100	15	A3
CANTERA	SA	SA03		16	B6
CANTERBURY	MVJO	SJ92		29B	E2
CANTERBURY AV	TUS	TUS	14600	24	A5
CANTERBURY CIR	ANA	AN	1700	16	B1
CANTERBURY CIR	WSTM	WSTM	15400	22	A3
CANTERBURY CT	PLA	PLA	1500	7	D3
CANTERBURY DR	CM	CM	1560	27	C3
CANTERBURY DR	CYP	CYP	5000	9	D5
CANTERBURY DR	HTB	HB47	6700	21	A2
CANTEBURY LN	CO	ET		52	C6
CANTERBURY LN	GGR	GG	9300	15	E3
CANTERBURY LN	LAH	LAH	2200	1	E6
CANTERBURY PL	CO	LB	30800	35	D5
CANTERBURY WY	BPK	BP	8000	10	C2
CANTERBURY WY	PLA	PLA		7	D3
CANTERRA	CO	ET		52	B6
CANTILENA	SCL	SC72		38	D5
CANTILES AV	CYP	CYP	6200	14	F2
CANTON AV	CO	AN04	9500	15	E1
CANVASBACK CIR	CO	LB	24000	35	D1
CANYON CIR	ANA	AN		8	B5
CANYON CIR	VPK	OR67	18800	13	B5
CANYON CT	ANA	AN		13	D3
CANYON CT	FTNV	SA08	18200	27	A2
CANYON CT	NB	NB		32	B5
CANYON DR	CM	CM27	2100	31	A1
CANYON DR	CO	CM27	2200	27	A6
CANYON DR	CO	CM27	2100	31	A1
CANYON DR	FUL	FL33	1600	5	F3
CANYON DR	VPK	OR67	19000	13	B5
CANYON DR	YL	YL	19600	8	C5
CANYON LN	HTB	HB	16900	20	E6
CANYON LN	NB	NB		32	C5
CANYON TER	CO	SA		18	C3
CANYON ACRES DR	LAG	LB51	100	34	E1
CYN CIRCLE DR	CO	SJ		52	E2
CYN COUNTRY DR	CO	SJ79		52	E2
CYN COUNTRY RD	BREA	BREA		2	F4
CANYON COURT DR	CO	SJ		52	F3
CANYON COVE DR	CO	SJ		52	E2
CANYON CREEK DR	CO	SJ		56	A4
CANYON CREEK RD	ANA	ANA		43	A1
CANYON CREST DR	ANA	AN		8	E6
CANYON CREST DR	CO	SJ		52	F3
CANYON CREST DR	MVJO	SJ92		29B	E2
CANYON CREST DR	NB	NB		32	C5
CANYON CREST DR	VPK	OR67		13	B5
CANYON CREST RD	SJC	SJ75	27000	36	C3
CANYONDALE DR	BREA	BREA	100	2	E4
CYN FAIRWAY DR	NB	NB		32	B4
CYN HEIGHTS DR	CO	OR67		50	D6
CANYON HILL DR	CO	SJ		52	F3
CANYON HILLS DR	LAG	LB51		29C	B1
CANYON HILLS RD	ANA	AN		13	E2
CYN ISLAND DR	NB	NB		32	B4
CANYON LAKE	SA	SA		17	D5
CANYON LAKE AV	BREA	BREA		2	C5
CANYON LAKE DR	CO	SJ		52	E3
CYN MEADOWS DR	CO	SJ		52	E3
CANYON OAK DR	CO	SJ		52	E3
CANYON PARK	IRV	SA15		32A	B2
CANYON PARK CIR	OR	OR	1900	13	C5
CANYON PARK DR	CO	SJ		52	E2
CANYON RIDGE	IRV	SA		32A	A2
CANYON RIDGE	OR	OR69		18	D3
CANYON RIDGE DR	ANA	AN		13	E2
CANYON RIDGE DR	CO	SJ		52	F3
CANYON RIM DR	CO	SJ		52	E3
CANYON RIM PL	CO	ET30		29A	E2
CANYON RIM RD	ANA	AN		13	E2
CANYON RIM RD	ANA	AN		43	A2
CYN TERRACE DR	CO	SJ		52	F3

STREET	CITY	P.O. ZONE	BLOCK	PAGE	GRID
CYN TERRACE DR	YL	YL		8	D1
CANYON TREE DR	CO	SJ		52	E2
CANYON VIEW AV	CO	SA		18	D3
CANYON VIEW AV	OR	OR		18	D3
CANYON VIEW DR	ANA	AN		13	E4
CANYON VIEW DR	CO	SJ		52	E3
CANYON VIEW DR	LAG	LB51	600	34	E3
CANYON VISTA DR	ANA	AN08		43	A1
CANYON VISTA DR	CO	SJ79		52	F3
CANYON WREN LN	CO	LB53		29A	B6
CANYON WREN ST	CO	LB56		29C	B1
CANYONWOOD	CO	ET		29A	F1
CANYONWOOD	CO	ET		51	F5
CANYON WOODS RD	ANA	AN		13	D2
CAOBA RD	SJC	SJ75		38	B3
CAPE CIR	HTB	HB		26	D4
CAPE DR	CO	LB	26000	29D	B5
CAPE WY	CYP	CYP	11200	15	A2
CAPE BAY PL	DPT	DPT	33400	38	A3
CAPE COD	IRV	SA		24	F6
CAPE COD	IRV	SA		29	F1
CAPE COD AV	TUS	TUS	1900	24	A5
CAPE COD DR	HTB	HB	9300	26	E4
CAPE COD LN	YL	YL		40	A3
CAPE COD WY	SA	SA		22	E2
CAPECORAL CIR	HTB	HB		26	C5
CAPE COTTAGE LN	HTB	HB	20000	26	D5
CAPE COVE	DPT	LB77		37	D4
CAPE COVE	NB	NB60		31	E6
CAPEHOPE CIR	HTB	HB		26	D5
CAPE HORN DR	HTB	HB	8200	30	D1
CAPELLA	IRV	SA		32A	B2
CAPELLA AV	LAH	LAH	100	2	A3
CAPELLA CT N	CM	CM	2000	27	B4
CAPELLA CT S	CM	CM	2000	27	B4
CAPELLO WY	OR	OR69		18	C2
CAPE MAY LN	HTB	HB	22000	30	F2
CAPE NEWBURY DR	HTB	HB	8400	26	D5
CAPENSE ST	FTNV	SA08	18700	26	E3
CAPERS WY	CYP	CYP	6600	15	A2
CAPER TREE DR	TUS	TUS	2100	24	A5
CAPE SPLIT CIR	HTB	HB	9500	30	F2
CAPETOWN LN	HTB	HB	15000	20	F2
CAPE VERDE PL	CM	CM	3100	27	B3
CAPISTRANO AV	LAG	LB51	900	34	F4
CAPISTRANO AV	LAG	LB51	1700	35	A3
CAPISTRANO CIR	FUL	FL	100	6	B2
CAPISTRANO DR	HTB	HB		20	D4
CAPISTRANO DR	STN	STN	8100	15	C3
CAPISTRANO LN	HTB	HB	22000	30	E2
CAPISTRANO LN	SCL	SC72	100	39	C3
CAPISTRANO PL	OR	OR		18	B1
CAPISTRANO ST	PLA	PLA	300	7	A6
CAPSTRN BLFS RD	DPT	SC24	27300	38	D6
CAPSTRN BLFS RD	DPT	SC24		39	A1
CAPITAL AV	GGR	GG43		22	B1
CAPITAL CIR	HTB	HB	19300	26	D3
CAPITAL REEF CT	FTNV	SA08		27	A3
CAPITOL ST	CM	CM27	600	31	B1
CAPLAN ST	ANA	AN	900	11	C6
CAPOBELLA	IRV	SA14		28	D4
CAPOTE DE PASEO	SJC	SJ75	27000	38	C2
CAPRI	CO	LB77		35	F5
CAPRI	CO	LB77		36	A5
CAPRI	MVJO	SJ92		52	E6
CAPRI AV	IRV	SA	3900	24	C6
CAPRI AV	SA	SA		22	D2
CAPRI CIR	CM	CM	1800	27	B3
CAPRI CIR	CYP	CYP	9800	9	E6
CAPRI CIR	HTB	HB47	15400	21	A3
CAPRI CT	CO	LB77		35	C3
CAPRI DR	GGR	GG	11500	15	E2
CAPRI LN	CM	CM	3000	27	B3
CAPRI ST	OR	OR	9000	12	C4
CAPRICE CIR	LAP	BP23	7200	9	E1
CAPRICE DR	YL	YL	19900	8	C3
CAPRICHO	MVJO	SJ92		29D	C3
CAPRICORN ST	BREA	BREA		2	E5
CAPSTAN DR	DPT	LB77		37	D3
CAPSTONE	IRV	SA		29	B2
CAPSTONE DR	HTB	HB47	6800	21	B6
CAPTAINS LN	DPT	DPT		38	D3
CAPUCHINA WY	CO	SJ		59	D3
CARACAS DR	PLA	PLA	1200	7	D3
CARACAS ST	DPT	DPT		37	E3
CARAVACA	SCL	SC72		39	E1
CARAVEL PL	CO	LB77		37	D1
CARAVEL WY	SB	SB	600	19	E2
CARAWAY	IRV	SA		29	C3
CARAWAY DR	CM	CM	1500	27	C3
CARBALLO	MVJO	SJ92		29D	D2

84

CARBECK DR

CELANOVA

1990 ORANGE COUNTY STREET INDEX

STREET	CITY	P.O. ZONE	BLOCK	PAGE	GRID
CARBECK DR	HTB	HB		25	F1
CARBON CIR	LAP	BP23	7600	9	D2
CARBON CYN RD	BREA	BREA	7000	3	E5
CARBON CYN RD	BREA	BREA		4	A5
CARBON CYN RD	CO	BREA	18000	3	E5
CARDENA	YL	YL		8	B3
CARDENIO	MVJO	SJ91		29D	C3
CARDIFF	CO	LB77		35	D6
CARDIFF	CO	SJ79		59	D4
CARDIFF CIR	HTB	HB	17800	25	E1
CARDIFF DR	CYP	CYP	4000	9	C4
CARDIFF DR	STN	STN	8100	15	C4
CARDIFF DR	YL	YL		8	F3
CARDIFF ST	ANA	AN	800	12	A5
CARDILLO DR	WSTM	WSTM	13900	15	C6
CARDINAL	CO	SJ88		59	C2
CARDINAL AV	CO	LB53		29A	B6
CARDINAL AV	FTNV	SA08	8700	26	E3
CARDINAL AV	FTNV	SA08	10200	27	A3
CARDINAL AV	GGR	GG	12500	16	D5
CARDINAL AV	WSTM	WSTM	9500	21	F3
CARDINAL CIR	GGR	GG	11900	16	C6
CARDINAL CIR	VPK	OR67	17600	12	F6
CARDINAL DR	CM	CM	2600	27	B5
CARDINAL PL	CO	ET		29A	D2
CARDINAL ST	ANA	AN		7	B6
CARDINAL ST	PLA	PLA	800	12	A1
CARERON CT	BREA	BREA		2	F4
CAREY AV	BREA	BREA	1400	2	C4
CARFAX AV	TUS	TUS	14000	23	F3
CARHART AV	FUL	FL	700	6	A5
CARI LN	YL	YL	18200	7	F2
CARIBBEAN CT	CO	LB77		36	A5
CARIBBEAN DR	DPT	LB77	32300	37	C1
CARIBBEAN WY	DPT	DPT		37	E3
CARIBBEAN WY	LAG	LB51	1500	34	E2
CARIBOU ST	FTNV	SA08	16000	21	E4
CARIE LN	STN	STN	7400	15	B2
CARINA	IRV	SA		32A	A2
CARINA AV E	PLA	PLA	800	7	D1
CARL LN	GGR	GG	9300	15	E5
CARL ST	ANA	AN		12	A6
CARLA CIR	HTB	HB47	6900	21	B5
CARLA ST	STN	GG41	7700	15	C4
CARLANN CIR	CO	TUS	17000	23	E3
CARLETON AV	ANA	AN	100	11	C4
CARLETON AV	OR	OR	800	12	D6
CARLETON CIR	PLA	PLA	2000	7	B2
CARLETON ST	FTNV	SA08	16000	22	D4
CARLETON WY	FUL	FL33		5	E4
CARLINA	IRV	SA		24	E4
CARLISLE AV	CO	SA	11700	18	B6
CARLISLE CIR	LAH	LAH	2200	1	E5
CARLO RD	EBAY	LB51	700	34	B1
CARLOS RD	YL	YL		8	E4
CARLOTA DR	MVJO	SJ91		29B	B5
CARLOTTA	NB	NB		32	A3
CARLOTTA AV	BPK	BP	10200	10	A6
CARLOTTA ST	GGR	GG	11800	15	A3
CARLOW DR	HTB	HB47	6700	21	A4
CARLSBAD CIR	LALM	LALM	5200	14	D4
CARLSBAD CT	FTNV	SA08	18200	27	A2
CARLSBAD DR	CO	SA	17800	17	F6
CARLSBAD DR	CO	SA	18100	18	A6
CARLSBAD LN	HTB	HB	20200	26	F5
CARLSBAD ST	OR	OR		13	B5
CARLSBAD ST	PLA	PLA	1200	7	E4
CARLSON AV	IRV	SA	18500	28	D5
CARLSON CT	CO	LB53		29D	A3
CARLSON DR	BREA	BREA	800	2	D4
CARLSON LN	PLA	PLA	100	7	B4
CARLTON	IRV	SA		24	F6
CARLTON AV	WSTM	WSTM	7100	21	B3
CARLTON CT	CO	LB56		29C	E5
CARLTON PL	CM	CM27	2300	31	E1
CARLTON PL	SA	SA	1300	22	E5
CARLTON PL	SA	SA	1000	23	A5
CARLTON PL	YL	YL		7	E2
CARLTON WY	STN	STN	11000	15	B2
CARLYLE	IRV	SA		24	F6
CARLYLE	IRV	SA		29	F1
CARLYLE CT	CYP	CYP	4000	14	D5
CARMA CT	CO	LB77		35	F3
CARMANIA LN	HTB	HB46	19700	27	A4
CARMEL AV	IRV	SA	3400	24	C6
CARMEL AV	SB	SB	700	19	E2
CARMEL CIR	FUL	FL33		5	E4
CARMEL CIR	WSTM	WSTM	8700	21	D3
CARMEL CT	LAG	LB51		29C	A1
CARMEL DR	CM	CM	3200	27	E2
CARMEL DR	CO	ET		29A	D4
CARMEL DR	STN	STN	8100	15	C4
CARMEL DR	VPK	OR67	10300	13	A6
CARMEL LN	HTB	HB46		26	E6
CARMEL ST	CO	LB56		29C	D3
CARMEL WY	CO	SA	12500	18	B4
CARMELA LN	LAH	LAH	1200	2	B3
CARMEL BAY DR	NB	CDLM		32	C5
CARMELITA ST	LAG	LB51	1300	34	E4
CARMEL VALLEY	CO	SJ79		59	C6
CARMEN CIR	ANA	AN		13	B3
CARMEN CIR	OR	OR	200	17	B3
CARMENITA LN	MVJO	SJ91		29B	C5
CARMESI	CO	SJ88		59	C2
CARMICHAEL DR	BREA	BREA		2	F5
CARMONITA LN	YL	YL		8	B3
CARNABY LN	HTB	HB	18300	26	C2
CARNATION	CO	SJ88		59	B5
CARNATION AV	CM	CM	900	27	E2
CARNATION AV	FTNV	SA08	9500	21	F4
CARNATION AV	NB	CDLM	200	33	A1
CARNATION CIR	FTNV	SA08	11500	22	C4
CARNATION CIR	SB	SB	12900	14	C5
CARNATION DR	BPK	BP	8000	10	C2
CARNATION DR	PLA	PLA	400	7	C4
CARNATION DR	WSTM	WSTM	9000	21	E3
CARNATION WY	ANA	AN		8	F6
CARNATION WY	ANA	AN		13	A6
CARNEGIE AV	ANA	AN		13	E4
CARNEGIE AV	CM	CM	2500	27	D5
CARNEGIE AV	SA	SA	1700	23	D6
CARNEGIE AV	WSTM	WSTM	8200	21	D3
CARNELIAN	IRV	SA		29	B4
CARNELIAN	MVJO	SJ91		29D	C5
CARNELIAN ST	ANA	AN	1600	16	B1
CARNIVAL AV	ANA	AN	2700	12	A3
CAROB	IRV	SA		29	B5
CAROB CIR	FTNV	SA08	11200	22	B4
CAROB LN	MVJO	SJ91		52	D6
CAROB ST	BREA	BREA	800	2	D6
CAROB ST	CYP	CYP	8100	9	C4
CAROB ST	NB	NB	2700	32	B2
CAROL AV	SA	SA	300	28	B1
CAROL DR	ANA	AN	100	10	F4
CAROL DR	ANA	AN	200	11	A4
CAROL DR	FUL	FL33	1800	5	E6
CAROL LN	CO	LB	24900	29A	F6
CAROL LN	GGR	GG	10500	16	A3
CAROL ST	LAH	LAH	1000	1	F3
CAROL WY	CO	SA	11200	18	D6
CAROLE CIR	PLA	PLA		7	D4
CAROLE LN	OR	OR	100	17	E3
CAROLEEN LN	ANA	AN04	1700	15	F1
CAROLEEN LN	GGR	GG	11200	15	F2
CAROLET LN	OR	OR	400	17	F4
CAROLINA CIR	BPK	BP	6400	9	F6
CAROLINA WY	PLA	PLA	300	7	B2
CAROLITA LN	HTB	HB		20	D4
CAROLWOOD	CO	ET	25100	29A	F2
CAROLYN CIR	LAP	BP23	7900	9	D3
CAROLYN CIR	VPK	OR67	18000	17	F1
CAROLYN LN	HTB	HB	18800	26	D3
CAROLYN WY	ANA	AN	200	11	F3
CAROT CT	YL	YL		40	C5
CAROUSEL CIR	GGR	GG45	5600	14	E4
CAROUSEL LN	HTB	HB	16600	20	D4
CAROUSEL PL	ANA	AN	500	12	A3
CAROUSEL ST S	ANA	AN	100	12	A3
CARP CIR	HTB	HB	19000	26	F3
CARPENTER AV	ANA	AN	3200	12	C2
CARPENTER CIR	VPK	OR67	19200	13	B5
CARPENTER ST	LAH	LAH	1300	1	D3
CARPINTERIA CT	CO	LB	28000	29C	E6
CARRACK	CO	LB77		37	E1
CARR PL	LAG	LB51	1000	34	F3
CARRANZA DR	MVJO	SJ91	26300	29B	C6
CARRANZA LN	HTB	HB	17800	26	A1
CARRARA RD	CO	LB	30900	35	C5
CARRAVACA	SCL	SC72		39	E1
CARRERA	TUS	TUS		24	B3
CARRETAS DR	MVJO	SJ91	26300	29B	B6
CARRETERA	SCL	SC72		38	F5
CARRETERA	SCL	SC72		71	A5
CARRETERRA DR	SJC	SJ75	32600	38	A2
CARREY AV	CO	LAM	8000	5	C3
CARRIAGE CIR	ANA	AN		13	E3
CARRIAGE CIR	HTB	HB48		26	A2
CARRIAGE CIR	YL	YL		7	D4
CARRIAGE DR	SA	SA	300	23	B6
CARRIAGE DR	SA	SA04	1500	27	F1
CARRIAGE DR	SA	SA		28	A1
CARRIAGE PL	FUL	FL	800	6	B2
CARRIAGE HLL LN	CO	LB		29C	D2
CARRIBEAN LN	HTB	HB	21300	30	F4
CARRIE AV	OR	OR		17	E2
CARRIE LN	HTB	HB47	15800	21	A4
CARRILLO DR	MVJO	SJ91		29B	B5
CARRINGTON	MVJO	SJ92		29B	F1
CARRINGTON	MVJO	SJ92		29B	F6
CARRISSA COM	SA	SA		22	C2
CARROL AV	IRV	SA14		28	F4
CARROLL WY	TUS	TUS	13500	17	E5
CARROLLTOWN DR	HTB	HB	9000	26	E6
CARROTWOOD CT	ANA	AN		10	E6
CARROTWOOD DR	BREA	BREA		3	B6
CARROTWOOD WY	STN	STN	10500	15	B3
CARSON	IRV	SA		24	E6
CARSON	IRV	SA		29	E1
CARSON DR	HTB	HB	8500	26	D4
CARSON ST	CM	CM	1100	27	D3
CARSON RIV CIR	FTNV	SA08		26	E2
CARTAGENA	LAP	BP23		9	D3
CARTAGENA	SCL	SC72		39	E1
CARTEGENA	NB	NB60		32	E4
CARTHAGE ST	CO	PLA	4900	7	C3
CARTHAY CIR	GGR	GG	12200	15	E3
CARTIER PL	PLA	PLA	500	7	B3
CARTIER AISLE	IRV			29	F2
CARTLEN DR	CO	PLA	4700	7	C3
CARTLEN DR N	PLA	PLA	1700	7	C2
CARTWRIGHT RD	IRV	SA		28	D3
CARUSO	IRV	SA14		29	A4
CARVER	IRV	SA		29	E1
CARY CIR	CYP	CYP	10100	9	C6
CARYL CT	NB	NB	200	31	B4
CASA BLANCA DR	FUL	FL	600	6	B5
CASA GRANDE AV	ANA	AN	1100	16	C2
CASA GRANDE CIR	CYP	CYP	4400	9	C4
CASA GRANDE DR	SJC	SJ75	31100	36	D5
CASA GRANDE DR	YL	YL	17300	7	E3
CASA HERMOSA DR	YL	YL	17300	7	E2
CASALERO DR	CO	LB		35	C5
CASA LINDA CIR	OR	OR	1800	17	B3
CASALINDA LN	GGR	GG	12900	15	E5
CASA LOMA AV	YL	YL	4000	7	F4
CASA LOMA CIR	YL	YL		7	F4
CASANAL	MVJO	SJ92	28400	29B	E5
CASA NUEVO LN	MVJO	SJ91	23400	29B	A5
CASA ORO DR	YL	YL	4400	7	E4
CASAREY DR	CO	SA04		22	D4
CASA VERDE	CYP	CYP	6400	9	F5
CASA VISTA ST	ANA	AN	1800	16	C2
CASCABEL	MVJO	SJ92	27900	29B	D5
CASCADA	CO	SJ88		29B	F5
CASCADE	CO	SJ79		59	E5
CASCADE	IRV	SA		29	C4
CASCADE CT	BREA	BREA		2	E5
CASCADE LN	HTB	HB47	15200	21	C3
CASCADE ST	HTB	HB	14300	20	F1
CASCADE ST	SA	SA	1200	22	E1
CASCADE ST	WSTM	WSTM	14100	20	F1
CASCADE WY	BPK	BP		5	C4
CASCADES AV	PLA	PLA	17000	7	E4
CASCADES AV	YL	YL	17000	7	E4
CASCADES DR	CO	LB	24100	35	E4
CASE ST	OR	OR	1600	12	C6
CASEDA	MVJO	SJ91	22700	29B	D3
CASEY RD	CO	ET	23600	29A	D4
CASHEW	IRV	SA		29	B6
CASHEW AV	BREA	BREA	400	2	F5
CASHEW ST	FTNV	SA08	17700	26	F1
CASIANO DR	YL	YL	4300	8	C2
CASINO RIDGE RD	YL	YL		8	E1
CASITAS CT	CO	LB		29C	E6
CASITAS CT	CO	LB	28000	35	E1
CASITAS PL	DPT	DPT		37	F5
CASPE	MVJO	SJ92		29B	E5
CASPER ST	GGR	GG45	12200	14	E4
CASPERS CIR	HTB	HB47	17400	21	A6
CASPIAN CIR	HTB	HB	5000	20	E3
CASPIAN SEA DR	DPT	LB77	32700	37	C2
CASSANDRA CT	CO	SJ91		29A	E6
CASSANDRA BAY	DPT	LB77		37	D4
CASSANO DR	CO	LB	23000	35	C5
CASSELLE AV	CO	SA	18000	17	F4
CASSELLE AV	OR	OR	3400	17	F4
CASSELLE AV	OR	OR	3700	18	A4
CASSIA AV	CM	CM	3000	27	C3
CASSIA LN	CO	ET	22400	29A	C2
CASSIA LN	YL	YL		8	D2
CASSIA ST	NB	NB	2700	32	B2
CASSIA TREE LN	IRV	SA		29	B6
CASSIS	DPT	DPT		37	D2
CASSON DR	YL	YL	5700	7	E5
CASTA DEL SOL	MVJO	SJ92	27600	29B	D5
CASTANO	CO	SJ88		59	C2
CASTANO DR	DPT	DPT	33700	37	E4
CASTAWAY LN	HTB	HB	16700	20	D5
CASTELLANA PZ	YL	YL		8	C3
CASTELO CIR	MVJO	SJ91		29B	C6
CASTILE LN	MVJO	SJ91	26600	29D	B1
CASTILIAN DR	HTB	HB	8300	26	D6
CASTILLA LN	MVJO	SJ91	24000	29B	B5
CASTILLO	IRV	SA		24	E5
CASTINE DR	HTB	HB	9500	30	F2
CASTLE AV	ANA	AN	1300	11	A6
CASTLE CIR	OR	OR	200	17	B3
CASTLE DR	HTB	HB	5500	20	E4
CASTLE LN	SA	SA		22	E2
CASTLE RD	CO	LB		35	E2
CASTLE ST	WSTM	WSTM	14400	21	E1
CASTLE WY	SA	SA		23	B6
CASTLEBROOK	MVJO	SJ92		29B	E1
CASTLE COVE CIR	NB	CDLM		32	C6
CASTLEFIELD DR	CO	PLA	16200	7	D3
CASTLEFORD DR	VPK	OR67	17800	17	F1
CASTLE GATE AV	TUS	TUS	14900	23	F5
CASTLEGATE DR	HTB	HB	9300	26	E5
CASTLE GATE LN	BREA	BREA	300	7	A1
CASTLEGATE LN	CO	SA	1000	18	B6
CASTLE HILL	CO	LB		35	F2
CASTLE POINT	CO	SJ79		59	E3
CASTLE ROCK CIR	HTB	HB	20400	26	F5
CASTLEROCK LN	CO	SA		18	D3
CASTLEROCK LN	OR	SA05		18	D3
CASTLE ROCK RD	CO	LB51	21100	33A	F5
CASTLE ROCK RD	YL	YL		8	E1
CASTLEVIEW	CO	ET		52	C4
CASTLEWOOD	CO	ET	25000	29A	F2
CASTLEWOOD	MVJO	SJ92		29B	E2
CASTLEWOOD AV	TUS	TUS	14500	24	A5
CASTLEWOOD CIR	HTB	HB48		25	E3
CASTLEWOOD DR	FUL	FL33		5	F2
CASTOR ST	SA	SA	3400	22	D5
CASWELL CT	CO	LB		35	E1
CATALINA AV	ANA	AN	2100	10	F3
CATALINA AV	LAG	LB	31500	35	A6
CATALINA AV	SA	SA	700	17	C6
CATALINA AV	SB	SB	700	19	E2
CATALINA CIR	HTB	HB	22000	30	E2
CATALINA DR	CO	SA	12500	24	B2
CATALINA DR	HTB	HB		20	D4
CATALINA DR	NB	NB	300	31	C4
CATALINA RD	FUL	FL	100	6	B2
CATALINA ST	GGR	GG43	10600	22	B2
CATALINA ST	LAG	LB51	400	34	E3
CATALINA ST	LALM	LALM	3200	14	B1
CATALINA ST	OR	OR	1100	13	C6
CTLNA ISLNDS ST	CO	LB56		29C	D3
CATALONIA CIR	MVJO	SJ91	24600	29B	B6
CATALONIA CT	MVJO	SJ92		29D	F3
CATALPA AV	BREA	BREA	300	2	D6
CATALPA AV N	ANA	AN	1200	10	F2
CATALPA AV W	ANA	AN	1500	11	A3
CATALPA DR	ANA	AN	1400	11	A3
CATALAPA DR	TUS	TUS		24	D3
CATALPA LN	FTNV	SA08	18100	26	F2
CATALPA ST	NB	NB	2700	32	B2
CATALUNA CIR	MVJO	SJ91	24000	29B	C5
CATAMARAN DR	NB	CDLM		32	C6
CATAMARAN LN	HTB	HB	20800	26	D6
CATAMARAN WY	CO	LB77		37	D1
CATANIA	CO	LB		29A	B4
CATBIRD CT	CO	LB		35	D1
CATE DR	BPK	BP	7000	5	A5
CATFISH CIR	HTB	HB	19400	26	F3
CATHAY CIR	BPK	BP	6400	9	F6
CATHAY CIR	HTB	HB	9700	26	F5
CATHEDRAL DR	CM	CM	3100	27	C3
CATHERINE AV	GGR	GG	9200	15	E3
CATHERINE AV	STN	STN	8000	15	C3
CATHERINE CIR	VPK	OR67	18000	17	F1
CATHERINE DR	ANA	AN	1400	11	B3
CATHERINE WY	DPT	DPT		37	A5
CATHERINE WY	SA	SA		28	D1
CATHRINE PL	CM	CM27	2200	31	E1
CATHY AV	CYP	CYP	4500	9	E6
CATHY AV	CYP	CYP		14	E1
CATHY CIR	CYP	CYP	5500	9	E6
CATHY LN	CYP	CYP	5600	9	E6
CATO CIR	HTB	HB		26	D4
CATOWBA LN	IRV	SA		32	F2
CATSKILL ST	FTNV	SA08	16000	22	C4
CATTAIL	IRV	SA		29	B2
CATTAIL CIR	BREA	BREA		3	A5
CAUDLE ST	TUS	SA10	15500	29	A2
CAVALIER	LAG	LB		35	B5
CAVALLO LN	CO	LB		35	C6
CAVAN CIR	HTB	HB47	6400	21	A4
CAVAN LN	CO	ET		29B	A1
CAVANAUGH RD	CO	ET	24800	29A	D4
CAVENDISH LN	ANA	AN		13	A3
CAVENDISH ST	WSTM	WSTM	14000	20	E1
CAVERNA CIR	MVJO	SJ91	24600	29B	B6
CAVON PL	ANA	AN	900	10	E3
CAY ST	CO	TUS	12500	24	B1
CAYMAN	MVJO	SJ92		29B	F1
CAYMUS CT	CO	TRA		59	C2
CAYUGA AV	PLA	PLA	2400	7	C2
CAYUGA DR	WSTM	WSTM	6300	15	A5
CAYUGA LN	CO	ET	22000	29A	E2
CAZADOR LN	SCL	SC72	300	39	D4
CEANOTHUS DR	LAG	LB	31500	35	A5
CEBOLLA	CO	SJ88		59	B2
CEBU CT N	PLA	PLA	2400	7	D1
CECELIA	MVJO	SJ91		29B	C3
CECIL PL	CM	CM27	100	31	E1
CECILIA CIR	BPK	BP	6400	9	F6
CEDAR AV	BREA	BREA	400	6	E1
CEDAR AV	FUL	FL33	200	5	E6
CEDAR AV	FUL	FL33	1000	10	E1
CEDAR AV	HTB	HB47	6400	21	B6
CEDAR AV	YL	YL	4600	8	A3
CEDAR CIR	FTNV	SA08	16600	21	F5
CEDAR CIR	FTNV	SA08	18600	26	F2
CEDAR CIR	GGR	GG		15	F4
CEDAR CT	CYP	CYP	9800	9	E6
CEDAR DR	BPK	BP	8600	10	C3
CEDAR LN	MVJO	SJ91		52	D6
CEDAR LN	TUS	TUS	2100	24	B5
CEDAR PL	CM	CM27	900	31	B2
CEDAR ST	ANA	AN	1500	11	E3
CEDAR ST	NB	NB	100	31	A4
CEDAR ST	OR	OR	300	17	B3
CEDAR ST	SA	SA	100	23	C2
CEDAR ST	STN	STN	10700	15	C1
CEDAR ST	WSTM	WSTM	13100	15	B6
CEDAR WY	LAG	LB51	100	34	D2
CEDARBEND DR	CO	YL	4300	8	F2
CEDARBLUFF TER	CO	LB53		29D	A4
CEDARBROOK	CO	LB56		29C	C1
CEDARBROOK	CO	LB56		29C	C1
CEDARBROOK	CO	LB56		29C	D3
CEDAR BROOK CIR	CO	ET	24300	29A	D4
CEDAR CREEK CIR	ANA	AN		8	B5
CEDAR CREEK WY	OR	OR69		18	D2
CEDARCREST AV	TUS	TUS	1900	24	A5
CEDAR CREST DR	BREA	BREA		2	D3
CEDAR CREST LN	SB	SB	13500	14	A6
CEDAR GLEN	IRV	SA		29	E4
CEDAR GLENN DR	ANA	AN		8	B6
CEDARGROVE	CO	TRA		59	D5
CEDARGROVE CT	CO	YL		8	C6
CEDAR GROVE CT	SJC	SJ75		36	B3
CEDAR HAVEN WY	ANA	AN	400	12	E3
CEDARHILL E	FUL	FL		7	A1
CEDARHILL W	FUL	FL		7	A1
CEDARHILL CIR	VPK	OR67	10600	17	F1
CEDARHILL DR	FUL	FL		7	A1
CEDARHILL LN	FUL	FL		7	A1
CEDARHILL PL	FUL	FL		7	A1
CEDARLAKE	IRV	SA		29	B4
CEDARLAWN DR	CO	PLA	5000	7	D4
CEDAR POINT	CO	ET		29B	A2
CEDAR POINT CIR	CO	ET	22900	29A	D3
CEDAR RIDGE	IRV	SA		32A	A3
CEDAR RIDGE RD	CO	SJ79		52	E3
CEDARSPRING	CO	ET	22800	29B	A3
CEDARSPRING	IRV	SA		29	C4
CEDAR TREE LN	IRV	SA15		29	A6
CEDARVIEW	CO	CYP		9	D3
CEDARWOOD	MVJO	SJ92		29B	E1
CEDARWOOD AV	CO	MDWY	15200	21	C3
CEDARWOOD AV	WSTM	WSTM	14000	21	C1
CEDARWOOD DR	LAH	LAH	700	1	D5
CEDARWOOD LN	ANA	AN		11	E6
CEDARWOOD LN	LAP	BP23		9	E3
CEDARWOOD ST	OR	OR	800	18	A5
CEDRON ST	IRV	SA	3800	29	C1
CEDROS	MVJO	SJ92		29D	C4
CEENA CT	ANA	AN	3000	12	B1
CEIBA PL	NB	NB	900	32	B2
CELANO	CO	LB77		35	E4
CELANOVA	MVJO	SJ92		29D	C3

ORANGE CO.

INDEX

85
CELESTE CIR

1990 ORANGE COUNTY STREET INDEX

CHRISTIANA WY

ORANGE CO.

STREET	CITY	P.O. ZONE	BLOCK	PAGE	GRID
CELESTE CIR	BPK	BP	6400	9	F6
CELESTE LN	FUL	FL33	1800	5	F3
CELESTE ST	SA	SA	4000	22	C1
CELESTIAL	IRV	SA		32A	A2
CELLINI	CO	LB56		29C	C1
CELLINI AV	GGR	GG	9200	15	E3
CELOSIA	CO	TRA		56	B5
CELOSIA	CO	TRA		59	B4
CELTIS PL	NB	NB	900	32	B2
CEMETERY RD	ANA	AN	100	11	E3
CENAJO	MVJO	SJ91	27400	29B	D2
CENPLA WY	ANA	AN	100	11	F3
CENTAURUS	IRV	SA		32A	A2
CENTELLA PL	NB	NB	2000	31	E2
CENTENNIAL RD	SA	SA	2800	22	D4
CENTENNIAL WY	TUS	TUS	100	23	F2
CENTER AV	HTB	HB47		21	B3
CENTER CT	CO	LB77		35	F4
CENTER CT	CO	LB77		36	A4
CENTER DR	NB	NB		32	B5
CENTER DR	VPK	OR67	9500	13	A6
CENTER DR	VPK	OR67	10400	18	A1
CENTER ST	ANA	AN	1100	11	C4
CENTER ST	ANA	AN05		11	D4
CENTER ST	ANA	AN		11	F3
CENTER ST	CM	CM27	500	31	C2
CENTER ST	CO	OR69		17	F3
CENTER ST	CO	OR	18500	18	A3
CENTER ST	LAG	LB51	200	34	E4
CENTER ST	OR	OR	1400	12	C6
CENTER ST	SA	SA	100	22	E2
CENTER ST	SA	SA04	3000	27	E1
CENTER ST E&W	PLA	PLA	100	7	B5
CENTER ST N&S	OR	OR	100	17	D4
CENTER POINT	CO	ET		29B	A2
CENTERPOINTE DR	LAP	BP23		9	E1
CENTINALI ISLE	IRV	SA14		28	D5
CENTRAL AV	BREA	BREA	100	2	D4
CENTRAL AV	FUL	FL	1200	6	E5
CENTRAL AV	GGR	GG	8000	15	C5
CENTRAL AV	GGR	GG	10200	16	A5
CENTRAL AV	NB	NB	3600	31	C5
CENTRAL AV	PLA	PLA	100	7	C5
CENTRAL AV	SB	SB	100	19	E2
CENTRAL AV	STN	STN	7600	15	C1
CENTRAL AV E&W	SA	SA	100	23	B6
CENTRAL AV W	SA	SA	1300	22	D6
CENTRAL CT	TUS	TUS		24	A4
CENTRAL WY	SB	SB	100	19	E2
CENTRAL PARK AV	ANA	AN	500	11	B5
CENTRAL PARK DR	CO	LB		35	E3
CENTRE CT	DPT	LB77		37	D3
CENTRE DR	CO	ET		29A	D3
CENTURY AV	OR	OR	3700	18	A3
CENTURY BLVD	GGR	GG	13000	16	B5
CENTURY BLVD	SA	SA	3800	16	C6
CENTURY CIR	CO	LB56		29C	E5
CENTURY BLVD	SA	SA	1600	22	C1
CENTURY DR	ANA	AN	500	11	E3
CENTURY DR	OR	OR	1500	17	D3
CENTURY DR	OR	OR	4100	18	A3
CENTURY PL	CM	CM	2900	27	F4
CERCA	CO	SJ88		29B	F4
CERCA	SCL	SC72		38	F4
CERCADO	SCL	SC72		38	E4
CERCIS PL	NB	NB	900	32	B2
CERRITO	IRV	SA		28	F6
CERRITO	MVJO	SJ91		29D	B2
CERRITO CIELO	SCL	SC72	200	39	E4
CERRITOS AV	ANA	AN		16	A1
CERRITOS AV	CO	AN06	14400	12	A6
CERRITOS AV	CO	AN04	9500	15	E1
CERRITOS AV	CYP	CYP	4000	9	B6
CERRITOS AV	CYP	CYP	4000	14	B1
CERRITOS AV	CYP	CYP	6400	15	A1
CERRITOS AV	LALM	LALM	3200	14	B1
CERRITOS AV	STN	STN	7000	15	A1
CERRITOS AV	STN	AN04	8800	15	A1
CERRITOS AV E	ANA	AN	100	11	E6
CERRITOS AV W	ANA	AN	2000	10	A6
CERRITOS AV W	ANA	AN	1200	11	A6
CERRITOS DR	FUL	FL	1000	6	B4
CERRITOS DR	LAG	LB51	1200	34	E3
CERRITOS DR	OR	OR		18	B1
CERRO VERDE DR	YL	YL	17500	7	E3
CERRO VILLA DR	VPK	OR67	18300	13	A4
CERRO VISTA DR	ANA	AN	4700	13	A2
CERRO VISTA DR	YL	YL	17500	7	E4
CERRO VISTA WY	ANA	AN		12	F2
CERULEAN AV	GGR	GG45	5300	14	F4
CERULEAN AV	GGR	GG	6300	15	A4

STREET	CITY	P.O. ZONE	BLOCK	PAGE	GRID
CERULEAN DR	GGR	GG	8400	15	D4
CERVANTES LN	MVJO	SJ91	25600	29D	B2
CETRINO	CO	SJ88		59	B4
CEXTON LN	CO	ET		29A	F3
CEYLON DR	CM	CM	2900	27	B4
CEYLON RD	CM	CM	3000	27	C3
CHABLIS CIR	IRV	SA	5200	29	D3
CHADBOURNE CT	NB	NB		32	B3
CHADBOURNE LN	CO	SA	18900	18	B6
CHADWICK LN	CO	SA	1200	18	B6
CHAFFEY LN	IRV	SA		32	F2
CHAGALL AV	IRV	SA		24	C6
CHAIN AV	ANA	AN	2400	10	E4
CHALCEDONY	BREA	BREA	18700	4	B5
CHALET AV	ANA	AN	2100	10	F6
CHALET AV	ANA	AN	1300	11	A6
CHALET LN	HTB	HB	14600	20	F2
CHALICE LN	ANA	AN		13	A3
CHALINA DR	MVJO	SJ91	26000	29B	B5
CHALK LN	HTB	HB		26	B3
CHALLENGER	IRV	SA		24	C5
CHALLENGER ST	BREA	BREA		2	D5
CHALLIS ST	FTNV	SA08	16000	21	E4
CHALON CIR	IRV	SA	15100	29	D3
CHALON RD	CO	YL	5600	8	B4
CHALYNN AV	OR	OR	1300	17	D4
CHALYNN CIR	OR	OR	500	17	D4
CHAMALEA DR	MVJO	SJ91	24200	29B	B6
CHAMBERLAIN DR	CO	AN04	10500	15	F1
CHAMBERLIN WY	LAG	LB51	1100	34	F3
CHAMBERS RD	TUS	TUS	14500	24	B5
CHAMOIS CIR	CYP	CYP	6600	15	A3
CHAMOMILE	IRV	SA		29	C5
CHAMONIX	CO	LB77		35	E4
CHAMPAGNE CIR	CO	YL	19700	8	C6
CHAMPAGNE CIR	IRV	SA	15100	29	D3
CHAMPION AV	WSTM	WSTM	8800	21	E2
CHAMPION LN	HTB	HB		25	F3
CHAMPION WY	TUS	TUS		24	D2
CHAMPLAIN	CO	ET		51	E4
CHAMPLAIN	IRV	SA		24	E5
CHAMPLAIN CIR	ANA	AN		43	A3
CHAMPLAIN RD	CO	LB	25400	29C	F1
CHAMPLAIN RD	CO	LB		29D	A1
CHAMPNEY PL	CO	LB77		35	E6
CHANCE CIR	HTB	HB	9800	26	F6
CHANCELLOR CT	CO	LB56		29C	C3
CHANDLER AV	SA	SA	1300	22	E6
CHANDLER RCH RD	OR	OR	300	18	D2
CHANDON	CO	LB77		35	F4
CHANNEL LN	HTB	HB	16500	20	A5
CHANNEL PL	NB	NB	3800	31	B5
CHANNEL RD	NB	NB		31	A6
CHANNEL RD	NB	CDLM	2200	33	A2
CHNNL ISLNDS ST	CO	LB56		29C	D3
CHANNEL VIEW	CO	LB		35	C6
CHANNING AV	WSTM	WSTM	8800	21	E2
CHANNING WY	CO	LALM	2600	14	A3
CHANTADA	MVJO	SJ92		29D	D2
CHANTICLEER RD	ANA	AN	2000	10	F6
CHANTICLEER RD	ANA	AN	1500	11	A6
CHANTICLEER RD	CO	AN04	9500	10	F6
CHANTICLEER RD	STN	STN	8300	10	D6
CHANTILLY CIR	CO	SA		18	D3
CHANTILLY LN	FUL	FL33		5	F2
CHANTILLY ST N	ANA	AN	500	12	A3
CHANTILLY ST S	ANA	AN	100	12	A3
CHANTONNAY	CO	LB77		35	F5
CHANTRY CT	CYP	CYP	4500	9	D5
CHANTRY DR	LAH	LAH	600	1	E4
CHAPALA	MVJO	SJ92	27600	29B	D3
CHAPALA CT	CO	LB77		35	C4
CHAPARRAL AV	IRV	SA	3500	24	C6
CHAPARRAL AV	IRV	SA	3600	29	C1
CHAPARRAL CT	ANA	AN		8	F6
CHAPARRAL DR	GGR	GG	12500	16	D4
CHAPARRAL LN	CO	ET		29A	F2
CHAPARRAL PL	CO	LB	26400	29C	F3
CHAPARRL RDG DR	YL	YL		8	C1
CHAPARRO RD	SJC	SJ75		38	B3
CHAPEL DR	SB	SB		20	A2
CHAPEL LN	HTB	HB	18500	26	D2
CHAPEL HILL DR	CO	ET	25800	29B	A2
CHAPEL HILL RD	OR	OR	2900	12	F4
CHAPLET PL	CO	SA	12800	24	B2
CHAPLET PL	CO	TUS	13000	24	B2
CHAPMAN AV	CO	GG41	8500	15	B3
CHAPMAN AV	CO	OR	18500	18	C3
CHAPMAN AV	CO	OR69		46	A2
CHAPMAN AV	CO	SA	21100	18	D2
CHAPMAN AV	GGR	GG45	5500	14	E3

STREET	CITY	P.O. ZONE	BLOCK	PAGE	GRID
CHAPMAN AV	GGR	GG	6500	15	B3
CHAPMAN AV	GGR	GG	10200	16	B3
CHAPMAN AV	STN	AN04	8000	15	B3
CHAPMAN AV	STN	STN	7900	15	B3
CHAPMAN AV E	FUL	FL	2500	7	A5
CHAPMAN AV E	OR	OR	3400	18	A3
CHAPMAN AV E&W	FUL	FL	100	6	C5
CHAPMAN AV E&W	OR	OR	100	17	B3
CHAPMAN AV E&W	PLA	PLA	100	7	A5
CHAPMAN AV W	FUL	FL33	1600	5	F5
CHAPMAN AV W	OR	OR68	3600	16	E3
CHAPPARAL LN	HTB	HB	17200	20	F6
CHAPULIN	MVJO	SJ92	27900	29B	D5
CHARCA	CO	SJ88		59	A4
CHARCO	SCL	SC72		38	F5
CHARDONNAY	IRV	SA		29	B4
CHARFORD DR	HTB	HB	8600	26	D5
CHARFORD WY	CO	ET		29B	B1
CHARING CRSS DR	HTB	HB	9700	26	F4
CHARING CRSS RD	WSTM	WSTM		20	E1
CHARLAINE AV	SA	SA	3300	22	D3
CHARLE DR	CM	CM27	2100	31	C1
CHARLE ST	CM	CM27	1900	31	C2
CHARLEMAGNE RD	CO	LB		29C	F1
CHARLEMAGNE RD	CO	LB	25400	29D	A1
CHARLENE CIR	GGR	GG	9500	15	E4
CHARLENE CIR	HTB	HB	4800	20	D5
CHARLENE TER	ANA	AN	200	11	F3
CHARLES AV	CO	LB77		37	E1
CHARLES AV	FUL	FL	2900	6	D2
CHARLES CIR	CYP	CYP	10600	15	A1
CHARLES LN	HTB	HB47	16500	21	C5
CHARLES COMMON	SA	SA03		22	E3
CHARLESTON	IRV	SA		24	E4
CHARLESTON ST	CM	CM	1100	27	D3
CHARLESTOWN DR	ANA	AN	1600	11	F4
CHARLEVILLE CIR	IRV	SA	4400	29	D2
CHARLEVILLE DR	WSTM	WSTM	13500	15	C6
CHARLEYVLLE CIR	HTB	HB	16500	20	F5
CHARLINDA DR	CO	SJ91	25000	29A	F6
CHARLOMA DR	TUS	TUS	14600	23	F4
CHARLOMA DR	TUS	TUS	14000	23	F3
CHARLOMA DR	TUS	TUS	13100	24	A2
CHARLOTTE AV	ANA	AN	200	11	E5
CHARLOTTE ST	SA	SA	300	17	B5
CHARLTON DR	CO	LB	24500	29C	E4
CHARMAINE LN	CO	SA	12600	18	B4
CHARMAINE LN	YL	YL	17500	7	E4
CHARMONY	CO	LB77		35	D5
CHARNOCK DR	IRV	SA	4500	29	D2
CHARREADAS	CO	LB77		36	B1
CHARRO DR	SJC	SJC	25400	38	A2
CHARTER	IRV	SA18		29	F5
CHARTER RD	VPK	OR67	18100	13	A5
CHARTER OAK DR	OR	OR	4000	18	A2
CHARTER OAK TER	YL	YL		8	E1
CHARTRES LN	LAP	BP23	7400	9	D2
CHARTRES ST	ANA	AN	100	11	C4
CHARWOOD CIR	CO	ET	22800	29A	E2
CHARWOOD CT	BREA	BREA		2	C5
CHARWOOD LN	CO	SA	1000	18	B6
CHARWOOD LN	HTB	HB	20700	26	E6
CHASE	HTB	HB		20	C3
CHASE ST	GGR	GG45	12300	14	F4
CHASTER RD	CO	ET		29A	E2
CHAT DR	CO	LB	28300	35	D1
CHATEAU AV	ANA	AN	2000	10	F5
CHATEAU AV	ANA	AN	1100	11	A5
CHATEAU AV	YL	YL		8	D1
CHATEAU CIR	IRV	SA	5100	29	D3
CHATEAU LN	HTB	HB	14300	20	F1
CHATEAU PL	ANA	AN	1600	11	B5
CHATEAU WY	LAG	LB51	2100	34	F2
CHATENAY WY	GGR	GG	12500	15	A4
CHATHAM	MVJO	SJ92		29B	D1
CHATHAM CIR	ANA	AN	400	12	A3
CHATHAM CT	NB	NB		32	B3
CHATHAM DR	CO	TUS	17500	23	F1
CHATTANOOGA	IRV	SA		24	E4
CHAUCER CIR	WSTM	WSTM	14800	21	E2
CHAUCER LN	HTB	HB	20600	26	E6
CHAUCER RD	CO	LALM	12000	14	A3
CHAUCER ST	ANA	AN	700	11	F4
CHAUCER ST	ANA	AN	600	12	A5
CHAUNCEY LN	OR	OR		12	F3
CHELE CIR	HTB	HB47	6600	21	A5
CHELMSFORD WK	WSTM	WSTM		14	D6
CHELSEA CIR	GGR	GG	12800	16	F3
CHELSEA CIR	WSTM	WSTM	9100	21	E3
CHELSEA CT	BREA	BREA		3	B5

STREET	CITY	P.O. ZONE	BLOCK	PAGE	GRID
CHELSEA CT	CYP	CYP	4500	9	D5
CHELSEA DR	ANA	AN	1600	11	F4
CHELSEA LN	CO	LB53		29C	F4
CHELSEA LN	HTB	HB	21200	30	D1
CHELSEA POINT	DPT	DPT		37	D4
CHELTAM WY	DPT	DPT	33300	37	F3
CHELTENHAM LN	LAH	LAH		6	B1
CHEMICAL LN	HTB	HB	15000	20	E3
CHEMIN DE FER	CM	CM26	3100	27	D3
CHENILE	IRV	SA		29	C4
CHENILLE AV	FTNV	SA08	9600	21	F4
CHERBOURG	NB	CDLM		32	D4
CHERBOURG AV	IRV	SA	15200	29	D3
CHERE CT	FTNV	SA08	10700	22	B4
CHERI DR	LAH	LAH	1000	1	F3
CHEROKEE	TUS	TUS		24	B4
CHEROKEE AV	PLA	PLA	2400	7	C2
CHEROKEE CIR	BPK	BP	7300	10	A2
CHEROKEE DR	WSTM	WSTM	6100	14	F5
CHEROKEE DR	WSTM	WSTM	6100	15	A5
CHEROKEE WY	CO	ET		29A	F2
CHERRY	IRV	SA		29	B5
CHERRY AV	CO	ET	23000	29A	F4
CHERRY AV	CO	ET	22400	29B	A3
CHERRY AV	FUL	FL33	3600	5	E6
CHERRY AV	FUL	FL33	1800	10	F1
CHERRY CIR	BPK	BP	8300	10	C3
CHERRY DR	OR	OR	1100	17	B2
CHERRY ST	ANA	AN	100	11	C4
CHERRY ST	BREA	BREA	300	6	E1
CHERRY ST	CO	SA		17	D5
CHERRY ST	LALM	LALM	10700	14	B2
CHERRY ST	PLA	PLA		7	E5
CHERRY ST	SA	SA	1000	17	C5
CHERRY ST	WSTM	WSTM	13100	15	B6
CHERRY WY	ANA	AN	1100	11	B2
CHERRY GATE LN	YL	YL	20400	8	F2
CHERRY HILL	MVJO	SJ92		29B	D4
CHERRYHILL DR	CO	SA	11000	18	C5
CHERRYHILL LN	HTB	HB		25	F3
CHERRY HILL PL	OR	OR69		18	C2
CHERRY HILLS DR	CO	SJ79		59	C6
CHERRY HILLS LN	NB	NB		32	B4
CHERRY HILLS PL	CO	LB	24100	35	E4
CHERRY HILLS RD	HTB	HB		30	C1
CHERRY HILLS ST	PLA	PLA	1100	7	C4
CHERRYLEE LN	YL	YL	5500	8	A4
CHERRY TREE CIR	LAH	LAH		1	F6
CHERRY TREE LN	ANA	AN	500	12	A3
CHERRY TREE LN	CO	NB	300	31	E1
CHERRY VIA	FUL	FL		6	D6
CHERRYWOOD	CO	ET		52	C4
CHERRYWOOD	MVJO	SJ92		29B	E2
CHERRYWOOD	CO	LB56		29C	D2
CHERRYWOOD E	GGR	GG		16	D5
CHERRYWOOD E	OR	OR69		18	B2
CHERRYWOOD CIR	HTB	HB	8300	26	D3
CHERRYWOOD LN	SJC	SJ75	29300	36	C2
CHERRYWOOD LN	TUS	TUS	14500	24	A5
CHERRYWOOD ST	LAH	LAH	1900	5	F1
CHERTA	MVJO	SJ92		29B	D4
CHERYL DR	HTB	HB	5000	20	E4
CHERYL WY	CO	ET	22600	29B	B3
CHERYLLYN LN	ANA	AN	3000	10	C5
CHESAPEAKE	IRV	SA		24	E5
CHESAPEAKE LN	HTB	HB	19800	26	E4
CHESENEY DR	CO	LALM	2800	14	A2
CHESHAM AV	LAH	LAH	500	1	F6
CHESHIRE	MVJO	SJ92		29D	D1
CHESHIRE AV	WSTM	WSTM	9700	21	F2
CHESHIRE CIR	LAP	BP23	8000	9	D3
CHESHIRE CT	NB	NB		32	B3
CHESHIRE DR	CYP	CYP	4000	9	C5
CHESHIRE LN	LAH	LAH		2	B6
CHESHIRE PL	TUS	TUS	14600	24	A5
CHESTER AV	GGR	GG	11500	16	C4
CHESTER AV	STN	STN	7700	15	B1
CHESTER DR	CO	LB	26600	29C	E4
CHESTERBROOK LN	HTB	HB	21000	30	C2
CHESTERFIELD	NB	NB		32	C3
CHESTRFIELD CIR	CO	SA		18	D3
CHESTERFIELD LN	HTB	HB	21200	30	C2
CHESTNUT	IRV	SA		29	B5
CHESTNUT	IRV	SA14		29	F3
CHESTNUT	MVJO	SJ91		52	D5
CHESTNUT AV	BREA	BREA	700	6	D1
CHESTNUT AV	CM	CM	2900	27	C4
CHESTNUT AV	OR	OR	100	12	D6
CHESTNUT AV	STN	STN	10500	15	C1
CHESTNUT AV E&W	SA	SA	100	23	B2
CHESTNUT AV W	SA	SA	1700	22	E2

STREET	CITY	P.O. ZONE	BLOCK	PAGE	GRID
CHESTNUT CIR	BPK	BP	8300	10	C3
CHESTNUT DR	HTB	HB47	6900	21	B3
CHESTNUT LN	CO	ET		29A	F2
CHESTNUT PL	ANA	AN	1500	11	F3
CHESTNUT PL	FUL	FL	100	6	B6
CHESTNUT PL	NB	NB	900	32	B2
CHESTNUT ST	CO	LAH	1300	2	B4
CHESTNUT ST	CO	PLA		7	D1
CHESTNUT ST	CO	YL	16800	7	D1
CHESTNUT ST	CYP	CYP	10500	15	A1
CHESTNUT ST	FTNV	SA08	17500	21	E6
CHESTNUT ST	FTNV	SA08	17600	26	E1
CHESTNUT ST	LAH	LAH	500	2	B4
CHESTNUT ST	LALM	LALM	10500	14	B1
CHESTNUT ST	WSTM	WSTM	13100	15	B6
CHESTNUT ST	WSTM	WSTM	14000	21	B1
CHESTNUT ST	YL	YL		7	E1
CHESTNUT ST E	ANA	AN	1200	11	E3
CHESTNUT ST W	ANA	AN	100	11	C4
CHESTNUTWOOD	CO	ET		29A	F1
CHESTNUTWOOD	CO	ET		51	F6
CHESWALD DR	CO	LB		35	C3
CHEVIOT DR	IRV	SA	4400	29	D2
CHEVY CHASE DR	ANA	AN	900	11	B2
CHEVY CHASE DR	BREA	BREA	1200	3	A6
CHEVY CHASE DR	HTB	HB	9500	30	F1
CHEYENNE	IRV	SA		29	D1
CHEYENNE DR	WSTM	WSTM	6100	14	F5
CHEYENNE DR	WSTM	WSTM	6100	15	A5
CHEYENNE PL	PLA	PLA	400	7	C1
CHEYENNE ST	CM	CM	900	27	E3
CHEYENNE WY	CO	ET		29A	F2
CHEYENNE WY	FUL	FL33		5	D2
CHIANTI DR	CO	LALM	12000	14	A4
CHICAGO AV	YL	YL	17200	7	E1
CHICAGO AV E	PLA	PLA	800	7	D1
CHICAGO AV E&W	HTB	HB	100	26	C6
CHICKADEE LN	CO	LB56		29C	B1
CHICKASAW DR	PLA	PLA	600	7	C1
CHICKASAW DR	WSTM	WSTM	6100	14	F5
CHICLANA	MVJO	SJ92	27900	29B	F4
CHICO LN	MVJO	SJ91		29B	B3
CHICORY WY	IRV	SA	18100	28	F6
CHILE CIR	BPK	BP	7500	9	E2
CHILLON WY	LAG	LB51	2800	34	F2
CHILLON WY	LAG	LB51	2100	35	A1
CHIMNEY RCK CIR	CO	SJ79		52	E3
CHINCHILLA ST	LAH	LAH	200	1	F5
CHINOOK AV	FTNV	SA08	10500	22	A6
CHINOOK AV	WSTM	WSTM	6000	20	F1
CHINOOK CIR	PLA	PLA	200	7	B1
CHINOOK DR	CO	ET		29A	F1
CHINOOK DR	HTB	HB	5800	20	F1
CHINOOK DR	PLA	PLA	200	7	C1
CHIOS	CO	LB77		35	E5
CHIOS RD	CM	CM	2900	27	B4
CHIP AV	CYP	CYP		14	F1
CHIPIONA	MVJO	SJ92	27800	29B	F4
CHIPPER LN	HTB	HB	16200	20	F4
CHIPPEWA	TUS	TUS		24	D3
CHIPPEWA AV	ANA	AN	600	11	A3
CHIPPEWA AV	PLA	PLA	2500	7	C1
CHIPPEWA CIR	BPK	BP	7300	10	A2
CHIPPEWA DR	WSTM	WSTM	6000	14	F5
CHIPWOOD ST	OR	OR	500	18	A4
CHIQUITA	SCL	SC72		39	D3
CHIQUITA ST	LAG	LB51	100	34	C2
CHIRPNG SPRW WY	CO	TUS	13000	24	B3
CHISHOLM CT	BREA	BREA		2	F4
CHISHOLM TR	CO	SJ79		52	F5
CHISOLM WY	FUL	FL33		5	F4
CHOATE	IRV	SA		24	E6
CHOATE	IRV	SA		29	E1
CHOCTAW DR	WSTM	WSTM	6000	14	F5
CHOCTAW DR	WSTM	WSTM	6100	15	A5
CHOCTAW PL	PLA	PLA	400	7	C2
CHOISSER RD	GGR	GG	12400	16	D4
CHOPIN DR	BPK	BP	8200	5	C6
CHOSEN DR	ETMC	SA09		51	D3
CHOUTEAU ST	OR	OR	1800	12	D5
CHRIS LN	ANA	AN		16	F2
CHRIS LN	CO	SJ		56	B4
CHRISALTA WY	ANA	AN		13	A2
CHRISANTA DR	MVJO	SJ91	24100	29B	B6
CHRISANTA DR	MVJO	SJ91	25000	29D	B1
CHRISDEN ST	ANA	AN		13	C1
CHRISTAL AV	GGR	GG45	5100	14	E4
CHRISTAL DR	CO	LB53		29C	E6
CHRISTAMON	IRV	SA		24	F5
CHRISTENSEN DR	PLA	PLA	100	7	B2
CHRISTIANA WY	CO	LB77		35	C2

INDEX

STREET	CITY	P.O. ZONE	BLOCK	PAGE	GRID
CHRISTIE DR	YL	YL	17700	7	F3
CHRISTINA CT	CO	LB	24500	29A	E6
CHRISTINA DR	DPT	DPT		37	E3
CHRISTINE AV	OR	OR	1200	18	B1
CHRISTINE CIR	ANA	AN	3600	10	A6
CHRISTINE CIR	BPK	BP	6500	10	A6
CHRISTINE CIR	VPK	OR67	9500	13	A5
CHRISTINE DR	HTB	HB	9000	30	E2
CHRISTINE LN	GGR	GG	12200	15	E3
CHRISTINE ST	OR	OR	300	18	B2
CHRISTMAS DR	HTB	HB46	10300	27	A4
CHRISTOPHER ST	CYP	CYP	9100	9	D6
CHRISTY DR	HTB	HB47	6100	21	A5
CHRISTY LN	CO	LALM	12000	14	A3
CHRISTY ST	STN	STN		15	D1
CHRYSLER	IRV	SA18		29A	D1
CHRYSLER CIR	HTB	HB47	7800	21	C4
CHUBASCO DR	NB	CDLM	2000	32	A6
CHUBASCO LN	HTB	HB	21000	26	F6
CHUCKER CIR	FTNV	SA08	8500	26	D3
CHULA VISTA AV	DPT	DPT	33600	37	E4
CHUMASH ST	OR	OR		13	B6
CHURCH CIR	HTB	HB		26	B3
CHURCH PL	SB	SB	13900	14	A6
CHURCH ST	CM	CM27	1900	31	D2
CHURCH ST	CO	OR	11200	18	A2
CHURCH ST	WSTM	WSTM	14100	21	B1
CHURCH HAVEN WY	ANA	AN	4000	12	E3
CHURCHILL	CO	SJ79		59	E3
CHURCHILL AV	WSTM	WSTM		20	E1
CHURCHILL CIR	ANA	AN	2100	10	F5
CHURCHILL CT	CYP	CYP	10400	14	D5
CHURCHILL LN	VPK	OR67	18300	13	A6
CIBOLA AV	CM	CM	2700	27	E4
CICERO RD	ANA	AN	5900	13	C2
CIELITO LINDO	ANA	AN		13	D1
CIELO	CO	LB		35	E4
CIELO DR	HTB	HB	4700	20	D5
CIELO PL	CO	SA	11400	18	C6
CIELO PL	FUL	FL35	3900	2	C6
CIELO VISTA	ANA	AN		13	D2
CIENAGA DR	FUL	FL35	300	2	C6
CIENEGA LN	MVJO	SJ91		29B	B6
CIENEGA LN	MVJO	SJ91	24800	29D	B1
CIEZA	MVJO	SJ91	22500	29B	D2
CIGLIANO ISLE	IRV	SA14		28	D5
CIMARRON AV	PLA	PLA	200	7	B3
CIMARRON CT	CO	LB	24000	35	E1
CIMARRON PL	YL	YL		8	F4
CIMMARON LN	CO	SJ79		56	E6
CIMMARON LN	CO	SJ79		59	E1
CINDA ST	ANA	AN	500	12	B4
CINDY LN	ANA	AN	11000	16	B2
CINDY LN	CO	ET	24000	29A	D2
CINDY LN	HTB	HB	19300	26	E3
CINDY LN	TUS	TUS	13400	24	A2
CINDY PL	ANA	AN	11500	16	B2
CINERIA WY	CO	ET	25100	29A	F2
CINNABAR RD	CO	SA	12200	24	C1
CINNAMON	IRV	SA		29	B5
CINNAMON	MVJO	SJ91		52	D5
CINNAMON AV	CM	CM	3000	27	C3
CINNAMON RD	CO	ET	25000	29A	F1
CINNAMON RDG RD	BREA	BREA		3	B6
CINNAMON TEAL	CO	LB56		29A	A6
CINTILAR	IRV	SA		24	E5
CIPRES	MVJO	SJ92		29D	C5
CIRCA DL ROSRIO	CO	LB		29A	D5
CIRCLE DR	ANA	AN		16	D2
CIRCLE DR	LAG	LB	100	34	B2
CIRCLE DR	LAG	LB77	31800	37	B1
CIRCLE DR	NB	NB	2500	31	D5
CIRCLE DR N	LAH	LAH	1000	1	F3
CIRCLE DR W	LAH	LAH	900	1	F3
CIRCLE WY	LAG	LB51	1300	34	B2
CIRCLE C	BPK	BP	8200	10	C1
CIRCLE HAVEN RD	ANA	AN	4000	12	E3
CIRCLE HILL	CO	LB77		36	A4
CIRCLE M	BPK	BP	8200	10	C1
CIRCLE VW DR N	IRV	SA		32	D1
CIRCLE VW DR S	IRV	SA		32	E2
CIRCLE ZURICH	NB	NB	900	31	D6
CIRCULA PANORMA	CO	SA	12200	18	B3
CIRCULO WY	OR	OR	4500	18	B3
CIRCULO BAJO	YL	YL		8	D4
CIRCULO CORONA	DPT	DPT	33500	37	C5
CIRCULO DALI	ANA	AN		13	E3
CIRCLO D JUAREZ	FTNV	SA08	10200	22	A6
CIRCLO DEL SOL	YL	YL		8	D4
CIRCULO D VILLA	FTNV	SA08		22	A6
CIRCLO D ZAPATA	FTNV	SA08		22	A6

STREET	CITY	P.O. ZONE	BLOCK	PAGE	GRID
CIRCULO DURANGO	YL	YL		8	E4
CIRCULO LAZO	ANA	AN		13	D2
CIRCULO LOMA	YL	YL		8	D5
CIRCULO MIRO	ANA	AN		13	E3
CIRCULO NUEVO	YL	YL		8	E4
CIRCULO ROBEL	ANA	AN		13	D1
CIRCULO VISTA	YL	YL		8	D5
CITADEL	IRV	SA		24	E5
CITADEL CIR	WSTM	WSTM	15100	21	C2
CITADEL DR	HTB	HB47	6200	21	A3
CITADEL LN	ANA	AN	500	11	F4
CITADEL LN	ANA	AN	400	12	A4
CITATION AV	CYP	CYP	5000	9	D6
CITRIA DORA CT	GGR	GG45	6900	15	A6
CITRIO DORA AV	YL	YL	4600	8	A3
CITRON	IRV	SA		29	B5
CITRON LN	ANA	AN	1200	11	C2
CITRON ST N&S	ANA	AN	100	11	C2
CITRUS AV S	FUL	FL	100	6	A6
CITRUS AV S	FUL	FL	600	11	A1
CITRUS CIR	YL	YL		7	E2
CITRUS CT	CYP	CYP	5500	9	E5
CITRUS DR	ANA	AN		16	E2
CITRUS DR	CO	LAH	1000	1	F3
CITRUS DR	LAH	LAH	800	1	F3
CITRUS LN	FTNV	SA08	18000	26	E1
CITRUS PL	BREA	BREA	400	2	F5
CITRUS PL	BREA	BREA	500	3	A5
CITRUS PL	NB	NB	900	32	B2
CITRUS ST N&S	OR	OR	100	17	B2
CITRUS EDGE CIR	ANA	AN		8	B5
CITRUS VIEW DR	ANA	AN	200	13	A1
CITRUSWOOD AV	GGR	GG	12500	16	D4
CITRUSWOOD WY	CO	ET		29A	F1
CITRUSWOOD WY	CO	ET		51	F6
CITY BLVD E	OR	OR68	200	16	F4
CITY DR	OR	OR68	100	16	F4
CITY PKWY E	OR	OR68	3600	16	F4
CITY PKWY N	OR	OR68		16	F4
CITY PKWY S	OR	OR68	500	16	F4
CITY PKWY W	OR	OR68	3900	16	E4
CIUDAD MESA CT	IRV	SA		32	C2
CIVIC CTR CIR	BREA	BREA		2	F6
CIVIC CENTER DR	GGR	GG	12900	16	B4
CIVIC CENTER DR	SA	SA	1300	22	E1
CIVIC CENTER DR	SA	SA	300	23	A1
CIVIC CENTER PZ	LAH	LAH		2	A4
CLAIRE AV	FUL	FL	300	6	C3
CLAIREMONT PL	CO	ET	27100	52	C6
CLAIRMONT AV	FUL	FL	2900	7	A2
CLAIRMONT AV	PLA	PLA	500	7	A2
CLARA ST	ANA	AN	600	11	A5
CLARA ST N	SA	SA	100	22	E2
CLARA ST S	SA	SA	500	22	E2
CLARE CIR	WSTM	WSTM	15700	21	E3
CLARE DR	HTB	HB47	6500	21	A4
CLAREDGE DR	ANA	AN	1200	11	B3
CLAREMONT LN	HTB	HB	19800	26	F4
CLAREMONT ST	ANA	AN	1200	11	D6
CLAREMONT ST	IRV	SA	3600	28	F4
CLAREMONT ST	WSTM	WSTM	13600	14	E6
CLARENCE ST	ANA	AN	900	12	A5
CLARENDON ST	FTNV	SA08	15800	21	F4
CLARENDON ST	WSTM	WSTM	15600	21	F4
CLARET	IRV	SA		29	A4
CLARETON DR	CO	LB		29D	A6
CLARETON DR	CO	LB77		36	A1
CLARINGTON DR	CO	LB	24700	29A	E6
CLARINGTON DR	CO	LB		29C	E1
CLARION DR	FUL	FL	800	6	B1
CLARISA	CO	LB51		33A	F5
CLARISSA LN	CO	SA	14100	18	A6
CLARISSA LN	CO	TUS	14200	24	A1
CLARISSA ST	GGR	GG	11100	16	A2
CLARK AV	PLA	PLA	1700	7	B3
CLARK CIR	IRV	SA	15000	29	D2
CLARK CIR	WSTM	WSTM	5300	14	E5
CLARK DR	HTB	HB	5600	20	F4
CLARK ST	CO	OR	20000	13	D6
CLARK ST N	OR	OR	200	17	C4
CLARK ST S	OR	OR	100	17	C4
CLARK TER	ANA	AN	200	11	F3
CLARK WY	BPK	BP	6100	9	F2
CLARKDALE DR	HTB	HB		26	D4
CLARKE AV	FUL	FL	2400	6	F5
CLARO	MVJO	SJ92		29D	C3
CLASSIC DR	CO	SJ91	25400	29A	F5
CLAUDE CIR	CO	ET		29A	F3
CLAUDE CIR	CO	ET		29B	A3
CLAUDIA AV	BPK	BP	10200	9	F6
CLAUDIA CIR	CYP	CYP	10500	14	F1

STREET	CITY	P.O. ZONE	BLOCK	PAGE	GRID
CLAUDINA PL	ANA	AN		11	E5
CLAUDINA ST N	ANA	AN	100	11	D3
CLAUDINA ST S	ANA	AN	100	11	D4
CLAUDINA WY	ANA	AN		16	E1
CLAUSSEN ST	GGR	GG	10500	16	A4
CLAVEL	MVJO	SJ92	24800	29B	D6
CLAVELES CT	CO	ET		51	E4
CLAY	IRV	SA		29	E1
CLAY AV	HTB	HB	6800	26	A3
CLAY ST	ANA	AN	900	11	F5
CLAY ST	ANA	AN	900	12	A5
CLAY ST	NB	NB	900	31	C4
CLAYTOR CIR	ANA	AN	4300	12	F2
CLEAN BROOK	CO	ET	22100	29B	B2
CLEARBROOK	IRV	SA		29	A5
CLEARBROOK	MVJO	SJ92		29B	E2
CLEARBROOK DR	HTB	HB	9600	30	F1
CLEARBROOK LN	ANA	AN	2000	10	E5
CLEARBROOK LN	ANA	AN	1900	11	A5
CLEARBROOK LN	CM	CM	100	27	E5
CLEARBROOK LN	CO	AN04	9700	10	F5
CLEARBROOK WY	STN	STN		15	C4
CLEARBROOK PASS	DPT	DPT		37	B5
CLEAR CREEK DR	FUL	FL33		5	D3
CLEAR CREEK LN	CO	LB		29C	D1
CLEARDALE CIR	STN	STN		15	B4
CLEAR HARBOR DR	HTB	HB		26	C3
CLEAR HAVEN DR	YL	YL		8	E2
CLEARLAKE	IRV	SA		29	B4
CLEARLAKE CIR	PLA	PLA		7	B6
CLEAR LAKE PL	BREA	BREA		2	C5
CLEAR RIVER CT	FTNV	SA08	10200	27	A2
CLEAR RIVER LN	YL	YL		8	C5
CLEAR SPRING	IRV	SA		32A	A3
CLEAR SPGS DR	FUL	FL		6	C3
CLEAR SPGS RD	BREA	BREA		3	B5
CLEARVIEW DR	YL	YL		8	D2
CLEARVIEW LN	CO	SA	10000	18	D4
CLEARWATER	IRV	SA		29	E4
CLEARWATER CIR	HTB	HB	18000	26	A2
CLEARWATER CT	CO	LB77		36	A5
CLEARWATER DR	YL	YL		8	F4
CLEARWOOD CIR	HTB	HB	20400	26	F5
CLEGHORN WY	SA	SA	1500	22	F5
CLEMENS DR	PLA	PLA	1800	7	C2
CLEMENS LN	CO	ET	23100	29A	F3
CLEMENSEN AV	SA	SA	1600	17	C5
CLEMENTE ST	WSTM	WSTM	15000	21	D3
CLEMENTINE CIR	BPK	BP	6500	10	A6
CLEMENTINE ST N	ANA	AN	100	11	C3
CLEMENTINE ST S	ANA	AN	100	11	D4
CLEMENTINE ST S	ANA	AN	1500	16	D1
CLEMONS CIR	IRV	SA	15000	29	D3
CLEMSON DR	ANA	AN		10	F3
CLEMSON DR	ANA	AN		11	A3
CLEMSON ST	WSTM	WSTM	15100	21	C3
CLEO ST	LAG	LB51	100	34	D3
CLERMONT	LAG	LB		35	B6
CLEVELAND	IRV	SA		24	D6
CLEVELAND AV	CM	CM	3000	27	E3
CLEVELAND DR	HTB	HB	7600	26	C3
CLEVELAND ST N	OR	OR	1400	12	D5
CLEVELAND ST N	OR	OR	100	17	D2
CLIFDEN CT	CO	ET		29B	A1
CLIFF	DPT	DPT		37	D5
CLIFF DR	HTB	HB46	10000	27	A6
CLIFF DR	LAG	LB51	100	34	C2
CLIFF DR	NB	NB	200	31	C4
CLIFFROSE ST	ANA	AN	100	11	F3
CLIFFSIDE DR	ANA	AN08		40	A6
CLIFFSIDE DR	HTB	HB		26	D4
CLIFFSITE PL	YL	YL	6100	8	C5
CLIFF VIEW LN	HTB	HB	18000	26	B1
CLIFFWOOD AV	BREA	BREA	200	2	F5
CLIFFWOOD AV	GGR	GG	12000	16	C2
CLIFFWOOD AV E	ANA	AN	400	16	D2
CLIFFWOOD AV W	ANA	AN	100	16	D2
CLIFFWOOD CIR	ANA	AN	500	16	D2
CLIFFWOOD DR	HTB	HB	9300	26	E5
CLIFFWOOD PK ST	BREA	BREA	100	2	F5
CLIFPARK CIR	ANA	AN	1000	11	F5
CLIFPARK WY	ANA	AN	1200	11	F5
CLIFPARK WY	ANA	AN	2200	12	A5
CLIFTON AV E	ANA	AN	100	11	D5
CLIFTON AV W	ANA	AN	200	11	E5
CLIFTON ST	LAH	LAH	500	2	A5
CLIFTON WY	BPK	BP	5100	5	D4
CLIMA	MVJO	SJ92	28000	29B	D6
CLINTON	IRV	SA		24	E4
CLINTON ST	CM	CM26	1500	28	A5

STREET	CITY	P.O. ZONE	BLOCK	PAGE	GRID
CLINTON ST	GGR	GG	13200	16	D6
CLINTON ST	OR	OR	1500	12	E5
CLINTON ST	OR	OR	500	17	E2
CLINTON ST	SA	SA	500	22	D2
CLIPPER DR	HTB	HB	8800	26	D4
CLIPPER LN	ANA	AN	1900	10	F2
CLIPPER LN	ANA	AN	1900	11	A2
CLIPPER WY	CO	LB		35	D2
CLIPPER WY	SB	SB	200	19	E2
CLOUDCREST	IRV	SA		29	C3
CLOUD CREST CIR	ANA	AN		8	B5
CLOUDHAVEN DR	HTB	HB	9200	26	E5
CLOVE PL	BREA	BREA	200	2	E5
CLOVEBLOSSOM	IRV	SA		29	B2
CLOVER	IRV	SA		29	E4
CLOVER AV	ANA	AN	2000	10	F2
CLOVER AV	FTNV	SA08	9300	21	E5
CLOVER AV	PLA	PLA	400	7	C4
CLOVER CIR	SB	SB	12900	14	C5
CLOVER CT	BREA	BREA		2	E5
CLOVER CT	CO	SA	19400	18	B3
CLOVER DR	TUS	TUS		24	B4
CLOVER LN	CO	LB		29C	D4
CLOVER LN	GGR	GG	11700	15	E3
CLOVER WY	BPK	BP	8000	10	C2
CLOVERBROOK	MVJO	SJ92		29B	E1
CLOVERBROOK DR	TUS	TUS	14300	24	A4
CLOVERDALE AV	OR	OR	2100	12	E5
CLOVERDALE AV	WSTM	WSTM	9700	21	F3
CLOVERDALE DR	BREA	BREA		3	A5
CLOVERDALE LN	IRV	SA14	14700	29	E5
CLOVER GLEN	CO	ET		52	A5
CLOVER HILL DR	YL	YL		7	F4
CLOVER HILL LN	CO	LB		29C	D2
CLOVERLY DR	MVJO	SJ92		29D	C2
CLOYDEN RD	CO	SA	1400	18	C5
CLUB	HTB	HB		26	C2
CLUB DR	FUL	FL		7	A1
CLUBHOUSE AV	NB	NB	500	31	C5
CLUB HOUSE CIR	CM	CM	1800	27	B4
CLUBHOUSE COM	SA	SA		22	C2
CLUB HOUSE DR	CO	LB		35	D5
CLUBHOUSE DR	NB	CDLM	800	32	A6
CLUBHOUSE LN	HTB	HB	16000	20	F5
CLUB HOUSE RD	CM	CM	2800	27	B4
CLUB MESA PL	CM	CM	2600	27	F6
CLUB TERRACE DR	YL	YL	5000	8	B3
CLUB VIEW DR	CO	YL	5400	8	B4
CLUB VISTA	CO	SJ79		59	D3
CLUSTER PINES	GGR	GG	12500	15	A4
CLYDESDALE AV	OR	OR		13	D6
CLYMER LN	IRV	SA		24	F6
COACH LN	HTB	HB	16900	20	E5
COACHMAN	CO	SJ79		59	D4
COACHMAN WY	CO	ET	27100	52	C6
COACHSPRINGS LN	CO	LB53		29C	F5
COACHSPRINGS LN	CO	LB53		29D	A5
COACHWOOD LN	YL	YL		8	C5
COACHWOOD ST	LAH	LAH	1500	6	A1
COAL CANYON RD	CO	AN07		43	E1
COAL CANYON RD	YL	YL		43	E1
COAST BLVD	NB	NB		31	A4
COAST CIR	HTB	HB		20	B4
COAST HWY	CO	LB51	6000	33	E5
COAST HWY	CO	LB51	9000	33A	A5
COAST HWY	CO	LB	100	34	C2
COAST HWY	DPT	DPT	34000	37	E4
COAST HWY	DPT	LB77	32000	37	C2
COAST HWY	HTB	HB	21700	30	C1
COAST HWY	LAG	LB77	30800	35	A5
COAST HWY	SCL	SC72	34400	38	B6
COAST HWY E	NB	CDLM	1600	32	A6
COAST HWY E	NB	CDLM	2600	33	C2
COAST HWY E&W	NB	NB	100	31	E5
COAST HWY N	LAG	LB51	100	34	C2
COAST HWY S	LAG	LB51	100	34	C2
COAST ST	GGR	GG	13000	15	C5
COAST ST	STN	GG41	12900	15	C5
COASTLAND DR	HTB	HB	9400	26	F5
COASTLINE DR	SB	SB	100	19	E2
COASTLINE LN	HTB	HB		26	B4
COAST VIEW DR	LAG	LB51	700	34	E3
COASTVIEW LN	HTB	HB		26	C6
COASTWATCH LN	HTB	HB		26	C6
COATE RD	OR	OR	400	17	F4
COBALT	MVJO	SJ91		52	D5
COBALT CT	FTNV	SA08	10700	22	B4
COBB AV	PLA	PLA	700	7	C2
COBBLE CREEK DR	GGR	GG		16	D6
COBBLER RD	WSTM	WSTM		21	E2
COBBLESTONE CT	CO	LAG		37	F2

STREET	CITY	P.O. ZONE	BLOCK	PAGE	GRID
COBBLESTONE DR	CO	MDWY		21	C3
COBBLESTONE DR	BREA	BREA		3	B5
COBBLESTONE DR	OR	OR		18	D3
COBBLESTONE LN	ANA	AN		13	A2
COBBLESTONE LN	CYP	CYP		9	D4
COBBLESTONE LN	GGR	GG		16	B6
COBBLESTONE RD	LAH	LAH	2300	1	E6
COBBLESTONE WY	BREA	BREA		3	A5
COBBLESTONE WY	IRV	SA		32A	A1
COBRA LN	HTB	HB47	17200	21	A6
COCAO PL	BREA	BREA	1000	2	F5
COCHISE WY	FUL	FL33		5	F3
COCKATOO AV	FTNV	SA08	9000	26	E2
COCKATOO LN	GGR	GG	9800	15	F3
COCKLESHELL DR	DPT	LB77		37	D3
COCKSCROW LN	CO	SA	1800	24	B2
COCOBANA LN	HTB	HB	2100	26	F6
COCO BEACH	CO	LB77		36	B4
COCOPALM DR	TUS	TUS	2100	24	A5
COD CIR	HTB	HB47	16900	21	A5
CODY AV	WSTM	WSTM		21	D4
CODY DR	STN	STN	7500	10	B6
COE AV	IRV	SA	17400	28	F4
COENSON CIR	HTB	HB	2900	26	C3
COFFMAN AV	ANA	AN	100	11	F3
COHASSET LN	HTB	HB	20500	26	E5
COHO DR	HTB	HB		26	B3
COLBOW ST	CO	OR	11200	18	B2
COLBREGGAN DR	HTB	HB	9000	26	E5
COLBY CIR	WSTM	WSTM	7400	21	B3
COLBY PL	CM	CM	2500	27	D5
COLBY ST	OR	OR	500	18	B2
COLCHESTER AV	WSTM	WSTM	8800	21	E2
COLCHESTER DR	ANA	AN	2200	10	E5
COLCHESTER DR	CO	AN04	9500	10	E5
COLCHESTER LN	HTB	HB	19000	26	D3
COLDBROOK	CO	ET	25700	29B	A3
COLDBROOK	IRV	SA		29	C4
COLDHARBOR	IRV	SA		29	E1
COLDSTREAM	IRV	SA		29	D4
COLDSTREAM LN	HTB	HB48		25	E2
COLDWATER LN	HTB	HB		26	D4
COLE ST	GGR	GG	12000	15	E3
COLE WY	LAH	LAH	1300	2	A3
COLEBROOK DR	CO	LB77		35	C3
COLEFORD ST	CO	ET	24600	29A	E3
COLEGIO DR	DPT	DPT	33700	37	F4
COLEMAN PL	GGR	GG	13100	16	B5
COLEMAN WY	LAG	LB51	1200	34	F3
COLERIDGE CT	SA	SA		23	E1
COLERIDGE DR	CO	LALM	2600	14	A3
COLEY RIVER CIR	FTNV	SA08	11500	22	C6
COLFAX CT	LAH	LAH	1300	2	B4
COLFAX ST N	LAH	LAH	300	2	B5
COLFAX ST S	LAH	LAH	100	2	B5
COLGATE AV	WSTM	WSTM	7500	21	B3
COLGATE CIR	HTB	HB46	20000	27	A5
COLGATE DR	CM	CM	2300	27	D6
COLGATE DR	CM	CM27	2200	31	D1
COLGATE DR	CYP	CYP	10400	14	D5
COLGATE DR	PLA	PLA	500	7	C5
COLGATE ST	ANA	AN	200	10	D4
COLGATE WY	PLA	PLA	500	7	C5
COLIBRI	CO	SJ88		29B	F5
COLIMA LN	HTB	HB	20800	26	C6
COLIMA BAY	DPT	LB77	23500	37	C5
COLINA DR	MVJO	SJ91		29D	C3
COLINA DR	YL	YL	17400	7	E4
COLLEEN PL	CO	NB60	300	31	E2
COLLEEN ST	LAH	LAH	100	1	F4
COLLEEN WY	CO	LB77		35	D1
COLLEGE AV	CM	CM	2200	27	D6
COLLEGE AV	CM	CM27	2100	31	D1
COLLEGE AV	GGR	GG	11000	16	B4
COLLEGE AV	SA	SA	1300	22	F1
COLLEGE DR	CM	CM	2300	27	D6
COLLEGE DR	STN	STN		15	B1
COLLEGE PL	FUL	FL	300	6	D5
COLLEGE PL	FUL	FL	2500	7	A5
COLLEGE ST	CM	CM	2900	27	D3
COLLEGE ST	GGR	GG	9200	15	E4
COLLEGE ST	SA	SA	1700	16	F6
COLLEGE ST	WSTM	WSTM	13800	14	E6
COLLEGE ST	WSTM	WSTM	14000	20	E1
COLLEGE ST N&S	LAH	LAH	100	2	B5
COLLEGE PARK DR	SB	SB	12500	19	C4
COLLEGE VIEW	FUL	FL	300	6	C4
COLLETA PL	WSTM	WSTM	14700	21	E2
COLLIE LN	HTB	HB		20	F6
COLLIE LN	HTB	HB	17500	25	F1
COLLIER LN	WSTM	WSTM		21	E2

Thomas Bros Maps — COPYRIGHT, © 1989 BY

ORANGE CO.

INDEX

STREET	CITY	P.O. ZONE	BLOCK	PAGE	GRID
COLLINS AV	NB	NB	100	31	E6
COLLINS AV E&W	OR	OR	100	17	B1
COLLINS CIR	HTB	HB	17700	26	A1
COLLINS LN	HTB	HB	17500	26	A1
COLLINS LN	YL	YL	4700	7	E3
COLLINS WY	PLA	PLA	1500	7	B3
COLLYER LN	ANA	AN	2900	12	B3
COLMENAR	MVJO	SJ92		29D	C4
COLOGNE DR	SA	SA		22	D2
COLOMA WY	CO	TRA		59	C2
COLOMBIA CIR	PLA	PLA	1400	7	B3
COLOMBIA DR	BPK	BP	7100	9	E2
COLOMBO LN	TUS	TUS		23	E3
COLON CIR	HTB	HB	6500	26	A3
COLONIAL	IRV	SA		24	D5
COLONIAL	MVJO	SJ92		29B	E4
COLONIAL AV	ANA	AN	1300	11	A6
COLONIAL CIR	FTNV	SA08	17000	22	A5
COLONIAL CIR	FUL	FL		6	C2
COLONIAL CIR	HTB	HB	20200	26	F5
COLONIAL DR	WSTM	WSTM	14500	21	D1
COLONIAL PL	CO	LB	30800	35	D5
COLONIAL WY	CO	TUS		24	B1
COLONNA	CO	LB		29A	B4
COLONY CIR	VPK	OR67	18700	13	B5
COLONY DR	CO	SA	11800	18	C6
COLONY SQ N	IRV	SA	3500	24	C6
COLONY SQ W	IRV	SA	14100	24	C6
COLONY ST	ANA	AN	800	10	F5
COLONY ST	CO	AN04	9700	10	F5
COLONY ST	OR	OR		13	D5
COLONY GROVE LN	VPK	OR67	9700	13	A5
COLORADO LN	CM	CM	3200	27	C3
COLORADO LN	OR	OR	2300	12	F5
COLORADO PL	CM	CM	3200	27	C3
COLORADO ST	ANA	AN	200	10	D4
COLT	IRV	SA		24	E6
COLT	IRV	SA		29	E1
COLT ST	ANA	AN	400	12	A4
COLT WY	FUL	FL33		5	D2
COLTER CIR	ANA	AN		43	A3
COLTON DR	CO	LB56		29C	E5
COLTON ST	NB	NB	100	31	A4
COLUMBIA	CO	LB56		29C	C1
COLUMBIA	IRV	SA		32	F1
COLUMBIA CIR	PLA	PLA		7	B3
COLUMBIA DR	BPK	BP23		9	E2
COLUMBIA DR	CM	CM	2200	27	D5
COLUMBIA DR	CM	CM27	2200	31	D1
COLUMBIA LN	HTB	HB47	15000	21	A3
COLUMBIA PL	OR	OR	1300	17	B3
COLUMBIA PL	YL	YL		8	F4
COLUMBIA ST	BREA	BREA		2	D5
COLUMBIA ST	NB	NB		31	A3
COLUMBIA RIV CT	FTNV	SA08	10300	27	A1
COLUMBINE	CO	SJ79		59	D3
COLUMBINE	IRV	SA		29	A1
COLUMBINE AV	FTNV	SA08	9000	21	E4
COLUMBINE AV	SA	SA04		27	E1
COLUMBINE AV	SA	SA	100	28	B1
COLUMBINE AV	SA	SA	100	28	C1
COLUMBINE CIR	BPK	BP	8000	10	A5
COLUMBINE PL	ANA	AN	1200	10	F2
COLUMBINE ST	ANA	AN	1100	10	F2
COLUMBINE ST	SA	SA	700	28	A1
COLUMBINE ST	SB	SB	12900	14	C5
COLUMBUS	CO	LB77		36	A4
COLUMBUS	IRV	SA		29	E1
COLUMBUS AV	GGR	GG44		15	D5
COLUMBUS CIR	NB	CDLM	400	33	B2
COLUMBUS DR	ANA	AN		43	A3
COLUMBUS WY	ANA	AN		43	A3
COLUSA CIR	HTB	HB		26	D5
COLVILLE ST	FTNV	SA08	18300	26	E2
COMANCHE	TUS	TUS		24	B4
COMANCHE DR	BPK	BP	7300	10	A2
COMANCHE DR	PLA	PLA	500	7	C1
COMANCHE DR	WSTM	WSTM	6000	14	F5
COMANCHE RD	CO	ET		29A	F2
COMBA	MVJO	SJ92		29D	C2
COMERCIO	CO	SJ88		59	A3
COMET CIR	WSTM	WSTM	8900	21	E4
COMET ST	IRV	SA	14500	29	D2
COMISO	IRV	SA14		28	F3
COMITY CIR	LAH	LAH	1300	2	B3
COMMERCE DR	CYP	CYP		14	F1
COMMERCE DR	CYP	CYP	6400	15	A1
COMMERCE DR	GGR	GG43		22	B1
COMMERCE LN	HTB	HB	15500	20	E3
COMMERCE ST	OR	OR		17	B2
COMMERCE WY	CM	CM	1200	27	D4

STREET	CITY	P.O. ZONE	BLOCK	PAGE	GRID
COMMERCE CTR DR	CO	LB		29A	D4
COMMERCIAL DR	HTB	HB	5300	20	E3
COMMERCIAL ST	SA	SA	100	23	B4
COMMERCIAL ST E	ANA	AN	100	11	D2
COMMERCIAL ST W	ANA	AN	100	11	D2
COMMERCIAL WY	CM	CM27	100	31	C3
COMMERCIAL WY	LAH	LAH		2	B5
COMMODORE CIR	HTB	HB	7600	26	C2
COMMODORE CT	SJC	SJ75		38	A3
COMMODORE RD	NB	NB	1800	31	E3
COMMONS WY	SA	SA		23	B6
COMMONWEALTH AV	BPK	BP	7500	5	C5
COMMONWLTH AV E	FUL	FL	100	6	B5
COMMONWLTH AV N	FUL	FL	500	7	A5
COMMONWLTH AV W	FUL	FL33	1600	5	C5
COMMONWLTH AV W	FUL	FL	100	6	B5
COMMONWEALTH PL	WSTM	WSTM	15700	21	E4
COMMUNITY CIR	ANA	AN		16	F1
COMO AV	SA	SA	5200	22	B1
COMPADRE	CO	LB77		36	A4
COMPASS LN	ANA	AN	2000	10	F2
COMPASS LN	ANA	AN		11	A2
COMPASS LN	HTB	HB	21300	30	E1
COMPASS WY	SJC	SJ75		38	A2
COMPOSTELA	MVJO	SJ92		29D	C3
COMPTON AV	OR	OR68	3700	16	F3
COMPTON DR	HTB	HB		26	D4
COMPUTER LN	HTB	HB	15500	20	F3
COMSTOCK CIR	LAP	BP23	7900	9	E2
COMSTOCK CT	CYP	CYP	5700	9	E6
COMSTOCK DR	HTB	HB	9300	26	E6
COMSTOCK RD	GGR	GG	11700	16	C4
COMSTOCK ST	OR	OR	2300	12	C4
CONCERTO DR	ANA	AN	1700	8	B6
CONCHA RD	IRV	SA		24	C5
CONCORD AV	FUL	FL	200	6	F4
CONCORD AV	GGR	GG	8600	15	D5
CONCORD AV	OR	OR	800	12	D6
CONCORD LN	CO	LB		35	D5
CONCORD LN	HTB	HB	16900	20	C5
CONCORD LN	NB	NB		31	E5
CONCORD PL	ANA	AN	500	11	F4
CONCORD ST	CM	CM	1000	27	E3
CONCORD ST	CO	SA		50	E4
CONCORD ST	SA	SA	2200	17	D6
CONCORD ST	SA	SA	700	23	D1
CONCORD WY	LAH	LAH	1000	1	D6
CONCORDIA	IRV	SA		32A	A1
CONCORDIA PL	WSTM	WSTM	7600	21	C2
CONCOURSE ST	LAH	LAH	800	2	B3
CONCOURSE ST E	LAH	LAH	1400	2	B3
CONDADO LN	MVJO	SJ91		29B	C6
CONDEE ST	CYP	CYP	10300	9	E6
CONDON CIR	WSTM	WSTM	15700	21	F3
CONDOR AV	FTNV	SA08	11000	27	B2
CONDOR LN	CO	LB51		29C	B2
CONDOR ST	ANA	AN	1300	11	B2
CONDOR CREST AV	OR	OR		18	B1
CONDOR RIDGE RD	YL	YL		8	E1
CONEJO	CO	LB56		29C	E3
CONEJO LN	FUL	FL33	1800	5	F3
CONEJO LN	FUL	FL	1300	6	A3
CONESTOGA WY	ANA	AN	3900	12	E2
CONGRESS CIR	HTB	HB	19300	26	D3
CONGRESS ST	CM	CM27	600	31	C1
CONIFER DR	LAP	BP23	5500	9	E2
CONIFER LN	TUS	TUS		24	B4
CONIFER ST	ANA	AN	400	11	F3
CONIL	MVJO	SJ91	22500	29B	D2
CONLEY AV	ANA	AN	2500	10	E5
CONNECTICUT AV	ANA	AN	1100	11	B3
CONNECTICUT WY	PLA	PLA		7	B5
CONNECTOR LN	HTB	HB		20	F3
CONNEMARA CT	CO	ET		29B	A1
CONNEMARA CT	CO	ET		52	A6
CONNEMARA DR	SJC	SJ75		38	C4
CONNER CIR	WSTM	WSTM	9400	15	D6
CONNER DR	HTB	HB47	8700	21	D5
CONNIE CIR	ANA	AN	200	12	B3
CONNIE DR	HTB	HB		26	C2
CONNIE WY	WSTM	WSTM	15700	22	A3
CONNOR AV	ETMC	SA09		51	D3
CONOVER LN	FTNV	SA08		26	A3
CONSEJOS	MVJO	SJ91	21500	29B	D1
CONSEJOS	MVJO	SJ91		52	D6
CONSTANCE CIR	BPK	BP	6500	10	A6
CONSTANCIA	MVJO	SJ92	21700	29B	E1
CONSTANTINE DR	HTB	HB	8000	26	C3
CONSTANTINE RD	ANA	AN	5900	13	C2
CONSTELLATON CT	LALM	LALM		14	C3
CONSTELLTION DR	NB	NB60	2000	31	F2

STREET	CITY	P.O. ZONE	BLOCK	PAGE	GRID
CONSTELLATON LN	HTB	HB46	19500	27	A4
CONSTITUTION AV	OR	OR	4300	18	B3
CONSTITUTION DR	HTB	HB	9800	26	F4
CONSTITUTION DR	HTB	HB46	10000	27	A4
CONSTRUCTION N	IRV	SA		28	F2
CONSTRUCTION S	IRV	SA		28	F2
CONSTRCTN CIR E	IRV	SA		28	F2
CONSTRCTN CIR W	IRV	SA		28	F2
CONSUEGRA	MVJO	SJ92	21700	29B	E1
CONSUELO	TUS	TUS		23	D3
CONSUELO PL	MVJO	SJ92		36	C2
CONTAINER LN	HTB	HB	15000	20	E3
CONTENDER LN	HTB	HB		20	B3
CONTENT CIR	HTB	HB		20	B3
CONTENTO	MVJO	SJ91		29B	C1
CONTESSA	TUS	TUS		24	B3
CONTIJO WY	CO	SJ		59	D3
CONTINENTAL AV	CM	CM	2200	27	B6
CONTINENTAL AV	CM	CM27	1900	31	B1
CONTINENTAL DR	HTB	HB	9800	26	F4
CONVENTION WY	ANA	AN	600	16	C2
CONVERSE HOWE	GGR	GG45		14	E4
CONWAY AV	CM	CM	1200	27	D3
COOK CIR	HTB	HB46	10400	27	A3
COOK LN	SJC	SJ75	32000	38	A1
COOKIE MNSTR RD	CO	ET		29A	F4
COOKS CORNER	ANA	AN	1000	13	E1
COOL BROOK	IRV	SA		32A	A1
COOLIDGE AV	ANA	AN01	200	10	C4
COOLIDGE AV	ANA	AN	2800	10	B4
COOLIDGE AV	CM	CM	3000	27	E3
COOLIDGE AV	OR	OR		12	E6
COOLIDGE AV	OR	OR	2200	17	F1
COOLIDGE LN	PLA	PLA		7	E5
COOL OAK WY	BREA	BREA		3	B5
COOPER DR	PLA	PLA	600	7	C2
COOPER DR	SA	SA	100	22	B2
COOPER LN	HTB	HB47	16500	21	A5
COOPER ST	SA	SA	100	22	B3
COPA DE ORO DR	ANA	AN07		13	A3
COPA DE ORO DR	BREA	BREA	200	4	A4
COPA DE ORO DR	CO	LALM	2600	14	A4
COPANTE	MVJO	SJ92	23200	29B	D4
COPELAND	TUS	SA10		23	F6
COPENHAGEN ST	CO	SJ91		29A	F5
COPENHAGEN ST	CO	SJ91		29B	A5
COPLEY PL	CO	LB		35	E6
COPPER CLIFF CT	CO	ET		29A	E1
COPPERCREST DR	CO	SJ79		59	E1
COPPERFIELD DR	TUS	TUS	1500	24	A4
COPPERFIELD RD	OR	OR		17	C2
COPPER HILL	IRV	SA		24	E6
COPPR KETTLE WY	OR	OR	3400	12	F4
COPPER LNTRN ST	DPT	DPT	33700	37	F4
COPPER VIA	ANA	AN		16	D2
COPPS HILL ST	CO	LB		35	F6
CORAL AV	CM	CM	3000	27	C3
CORAL AV	NB	NB	100	31	F6
CORAL AV	OR	OR	1600	12	E5
CORAL CIR	ANA	OR67		13	D4
CORAL CIR	HTB	HB	8900	26	E4
CORAL DR	LAG	LB51	1300	34	E2
CORAL PL	CO	ET	22600	29A	C2
CORAL PL	NB	NB	1300	31	D5
CORAL PL	SB	SB	1700	19	F2
CORAL WY	LAG	LB51		34	E2
CORAL ALOE AV	FTNV	SA08	11000	22	B4
CORAL BAY	DPT	LB77		37	D4
CORALBELL WY	BPK	BP	8000	10	C2
CORAL BILL LN	CO	LB51		29C	B2
CORAL CAY LN	HTB	HB		20	C5
CORAL COVE	CO	LB		35	D3
CORAL COVE CIR	HTB	HB	9800	30	F4
CORAL RIDGE	CO	LB77		36	B4
CORAL GARDENS	MVJO	SJ92		29B	D2
CORAL GUM CT	GGR	GG	6900	15	A6
CORALINO	CO	SJ88		59	C2
CORALITA	CO	ET		29B	E1
CORALITA	CO	ET		52	B6
CORAL LAKE	IRV	SA		29	B5
CORAL REACH ST	DPT	DPT	33300	38	A3
CORAL REEF DR	HTB	HB		26	C5
CORAL REEF RD	TUS	TUS	13300	24	A2
CORAL RIDGE CIR	BPK	BP	5200	5	D4
CORAL SEA	CO	LB77		36	A4
CORAL SEA CT	LALM	LALM		14	C3
CORAL SPGS CT	HTB	HB	20800	26	D6
CORAL TREE CIR	VPK	OR67		13	A6
CORAL TREE LN	IRV	SA		29	A6
CORALWIND	CO	LB56		29C	C1

STREET	CITY	P.O. ZONE	BLOCK	PAGE	GRID
CORALWOOD CIR	YL	YL	17200	7	E3
CORALWOOD DR	CO	SA		18	C4
CORALWOOD LN	HTB	HB		26	E4
CORAL WOOD ST	CO	ET	25400	29A	F4
CORBINA LN	HTB	HB		20	E6
CORBY DR	CO	ET		29B	A1
CORCUBION	MVJO	SJ92		29D	C3
CORDATA ST	FTNV	SA08	18800	26	E3
CORDAWAY AV	WSTM	WSTM	8600	21	D4
CORDERO	IRV	SA14		28	D5
CORDERO	TUS	TUS		24	B3
CORDERO LN	MVJO	SJ91		29D	C4
CORDOBA	IRV	SA14		28	D5
CORDILLERA DR	MVJO	SJ91	25900	29B	A5
CORDOBA CIR	LAP	BP23	5000	9	D3
CORDOBA DR	PLA	PLA		7	D5
CORDOBA LN	HTB	HB47	17500	21	A6
CORDOVA DR	DPT	DPT	24600	37	E4
CORDOVA LN	YL	YL	4600	8	C3
CORDOVA PZ	WSTM	WSTM		21	E2
CORDOVA RD	MVJO	SJ91		29B	D1
CORDOVA RD	MVJO	SJ91		52	D6
CORELLA	NB	NB60		32	E4
CORFU	CO	LB77		35	F5
CORIANDER DR	CM	CM	1500	27	C3
CORIENDER AV	FTNV	SA08	16600	22	B5
CORINNE CIR	BPK	BP	6500	10	A6
CORINTH CIR	FTNV	SA08	17000	22	C5
CORINTHIAN WY	NB	NB60		28	B5
CORK CIR	YL	YL		8	E2
CORK DR	HTB	HB47	6600	21	A3
CORK LN	CM	CM	3100	27	D3
CORK ST	FTNV	SA08	18500	26	E2
CORK ST	GGR	GG	13300	15	F6
CORK ST	GGR	GG	14000	21	F2
CORKWOOD LN	IRV	SA		29	A6
CORLA AV	TUS	TUS	17200	23	E3
CORMORANT CIR	FTNV	SA08	9400	26	E2
CORMORANT CIR	NB	SA07		32	B1
CORMORANT LN	CO	LB	23900	35	D2
CORNELIA CIR	ANA	AN	3600	10	A6
CORNELIA CIR	BPK	BP	6500	10	A6
CORNELIUS DR	CO	ET	24700	29A	E4
CORNELL	IRV	SA		32	E1
CORNELL AV	ANA	AN	2600	10	D3
CORNELL AV	WSTM	WSTM	5000	14	E6
CORNELL AV N&S	FUL	FL	100	6	D4
CORNELL DR	CM	CM	2300	27	D6
CORNELL DR	CM	CM27	2200	31	D1
CORNELL DR	HTB	HB47	6000	21	A3
CORNELL PL	ANA	AN	2700	10	D3
CORNER ST	ANA	AN	200	10	E4
CORNERBROOK DR	HTB	HB	9700	26	F6
CORNET CIR	ANA	AN		8	A5
CORNET CIR	CO	AN07	6400	8	A6
CORNET PL	ANA	AN	6200	8	A5
CORNFLOWER CIR	BPK	BP	8000	10	C2
CORNICHE DR	MVJO	SJ92		29D	F3
CORNSILK	IRV	SA		29	C4
CORNWALL AV	WSTM	WSTM	9700	21	F2
CORNWALL CIR	LAP	BP23	8500	9	D4
CORNWALL DR	ANA	AN	800	10	F6
CORNWALL DR	HTB	HB	9500	26	F4
CORNWALL DR	LAP	BP23	5100	9	D4
CORNWALL LN	NB	NB	1500	31	E4
CORNWALL SQ	SA	SA		23	D2
CORNWALL ST	GGR	GG	11600	16	A2
CORNWALLIS	IRV	SA		24	F6
COROMANDE	IRV	SA14		29	A3
CORONA	IRV	SA		32A	A3
CORONA LN	CM	CM	1000	27	E4
CORONA LN	SCL	SC72	100	39	C4
CORONA LN	TUS	TUS		23	E3
CORONA WY	LAG	LB51	1000	34	F4
CORONA DL MR FY	CM			27	E3
CORONA DL MR FY	CO			28	A5
CORONA DL MR FY	NB			32	B2
CORONADO	IRV	SA		28	E4
CORONADO DR	BPK	BP	7500	5	B4
CORONADO DR	CM	CM	900	27	E4
CORONADO DR	FUL	FL	2300	6	B2
CORONADO DR	LAG	LB51	600	34	E2
CORONADO LN	HTB	HB47	17300	21	A6
CORONADO LN	SCL	SC72	100	39	C4
CORONADO LN	TUS	TUS		23	E3
CORONADO ST	ANA	AN	2600	12	B2
CORONADO ST	NB	NB	100	33	B5
CORONADO ST	WSTM	WSTM	15000	21	D3
CORONADO POINTE	CO	LB77		35	C4
CORONATION DR	DPT	LB77	32700	37	B3
CORONEL DR	MVJO	SJ91		29B	B4

STREET	CITY	P.O. ZONE	BLOCK	PAGE	GRID
CORONEL RD	CO	SA	1300	18	C5
CORONET AV	ANA	AN	2000	10	E2
CORONET AV	ANA	AN		11	A2
CORONET AV	WSTM	WSTM	9100	21	E3
CORONET CIR	BPK	BP	6400	5	B6
COROT DR	LAG	LB51	700	34	E3
CORPORATE AV	CYP	CYP		14	E1
CORPORATE DR	CM	CM		27	C2
CORPORATE DR	GGR	GG43		22	B1
CORPORATE PZ	NB	NB		32	A6
CORPORATE WY	ANA	AN		10	F3
CORPORATE WY	ANA	AN		11	A3
CORPORTE CTR DR	LALM	LALM		14	C1
CORPORATE PARK	IRV	SA		28	E2
CORRAL CIR	HTB	HB48		26	B2
CORRALEJO	MVJO	SJ92		29B	E3
CORRAL RIVER CT	FTNV	SA08		27	A3
CORRIDA PL	OR	OR	1000	18	B1
CORRIENTE	IRV	SA14		28	F4
CORRIENTE LN	MVJO	SJ91	25900	29B	A5
CORRIGAN AV	SA	SA	900	17	A4
CORRINE CIR	HTB	HB47	6500	21	A5
CORSAIR	CO	LAG		35	F3
CORSAIR CIR	GGR	GG	13300	16	C5
CORSAIR WY	SB	SB	200	19	E2
CORSICA	CO	LAG		35	F4
CORSICA	IRV	SA14		28	F4
CORSICA DR N	NB	NB60		32	B2
CORSICA DR S	NB	NB60		32	B2
CORSICA PL	CM	CM	1500	27	C3
CORSICA RD	MVJO	SJ92		29D	E3
CORSICA WY	YL	YL		40	D6
CORSICAN DR	HTB	HB47	7200	21	B5
CORTA DR	SA	SA	600	22	B3
CORTA CRESTA DR	CO	ET	24300	29A	E3
CORTE ST	IRV	SA14		29	E5
CORTE AURORA	SJC	SJ75		36	F5
CORTE AZUL	SJC	SJ75		36	E6
CORTE CALAMAR	SCL	SCL		38	C6
CORTE CALAMAR	SCL	SCL		39	C1
CORTE CALETA	NB	NB60		32	B2
CORTE CARDELINA	SCL	SC72		38	F6
CORTE CARDELINA	SCL	SC72		39	D1
CORTE CARDELINA	SCL	SC72		71	A6
CTE DL DIAMANTE	SCL	SC72		38	F6
CTE DL DIAMANTE	SCL	SC72		71	A6
CORTE HERMOSA	NB	NB60		32	B2
CORTE LINDA	NB	NB60		32	B2
CORTE MARIN	NB	NB60		32	B2
CORTE MERLANGO	SCL	SCL		38	C6
CORTE MERLANGO	SCL	SCL		39	C1
CORTE PORTAL	NB	NB60		32	B2
CORTE PORTOFINO	NB	NB60		32	B2
CTE SAN RAFAEL	NB	NB60		32	E3
CORTES DR	DPT	DPT		37	E3
CORTESE DR	CO	LALM	3300	14	B3
CORTEZ AV	GGR	GG44		15	D5
CORTEZ AV	LAG	LB51	900	34	F4
CORTEZ AV	LAG	LB51	1700	35	A3
CORTEZ CIR	NB	CDLM	400	33	B2
CORTEZ DR	HTB	HB	6000	20	F2
CORTEZ LN	TUS	TUS		23	E3
CORTEZ ST	CM	CM	800	27	F4
CORTINA	TUS	TUS		24	B3
CORTINA DR	MVJO	SJ91	26300	29D	B1
CORTLAND DR	NB	CDLM	4500	33	C2
CORTNEY PL	ANA	AN	1300	11	F5
CORTNEY WY	ANA	AN	1700	11	F5
CORTO	CO	ET		29A	F4
CORTO LN	SCL	SC72	400	39	C4
CORTO RD	ANA	AN	6500	13	E1
CORTO WY	LAH	LAH	800	1	E4
CORTONA	IRV	SA14		28	D5
CORVETTE ST	GGR	GG	12100	15	E4
CORVO PL	CM	CM	2800	27	C4
CORWIN CT	SA	SA	600	22	D3
CORY CIR	LAP	BP23	7300	9	D2
CORY DR	HTB	HB47	6600	21	A6
COSALA	MVJO	SJ91	21800	29B	D2
COSBY WY	ANA	AN	1100	12	D1
COSENZA	CO	LB77		35	F4
COSENZA	IRV	SA14		28	F4
COSLEY ST	IRV	SA	3700	28	F4
COSO	MVJO	SJ92	23200	29B	D4
COSTA	SCL	SC72		38	F5
COSTA CT	FUL	FL	200	6	F6
COSTA BELLA DR	CO	ET	22700	29A	F3
COSTADA RD	CO	LB77		36	A2
COSTA DEL SOL	DPT	DPT		37	D2
COSTA MESA FWY	CM			28	B2
COSTA MESA FWY	CO			27	F5

COPYRIGHT, © 1989 BY Thomas Bros Maps

INDEX

STREET	CITY	P.O. ZONE	BLOCK	PAGE	GRID
COSTA MESA FWY	OR			12	E6
COSTA MESA FWY	SA			23	D6
COSTA MESA FWY	TUS			17	E6
COSTA MESA ST	CM	CM27	100	31	D2
COSTANERO	MVJO	SJ92	27500	29B	D3
COSTEAU ST	CO	LB		29A	F6
COSTEAU ST	CO	LB	25100	29C	F1
COSTERO AISLE	IRV	SA14		28	E3
COTO DE CAZA DR	CO	SJ79		59	C5
COTO DE CAZA DR	CO	SJ79		62	A1
COTTAGE PL	CM	CM27	200	31	E2
COTTAGE RD	GGR	GG		16	D5
COTTAGE HILL DR	OR	OR		12	F4
COTTAGE HILL LN	YL	YL	20200	8	F2
COTTER ST	SA	SA	2100	16	E5
COTTLE WY	CYP	CYP	6600	15	B2
COTTONCLOUD	IRV	SA		29	A4
COTTONTAIL RD	CO	SA		18	D5
COTTONWOOD	MVJO	SJ92		29B	E3
COTTONWOOD AV	BREA	BREA		2	D4
COTTONWOOD AV	GGR	GG	11000	16	B5
COTTONWOOD CIR	ANA	AN	800	11	C5
COTTONWOOD CIR	CO	ET	22500	29A	C2
COTTONWOOD CIR	HTB	HB47	15400	21	C3
COTTONWOOD DR	BREA	BREA	600	2	F6
COTTONWOOD DR	CO	SA		18	B5
COTTONWOOD LN	IRV	SA		29	B6
COTTONWOOD LN	LAP	BP23	5000	9	D2
COTTONWOOD LN	SB	SB		19	D3
COTTONWOOD LN	WSTM	WSTM		21	C4
COTTONWOOD RD	YL	YL	20780	8	D5
COTTONWOOD ST	FTNV	SA08	18500	26	E2
COTTONWOOD ST	OR	OR	2500	12	C4
COTTONWOOD ST	SA	SA	2300	17	D5
COTUIT CIR	HTB	HB	16400	20	D4
COULTER	MVJO	SJ92		52	E6
COUNCIL BLFS AV	CO	ET	22900	29A	D3
COUNT CIR	HTB	HB47	7400	21	B5
COUNTESS DR	HTB	HB		20	B4
COUNTRY CIR	HTB	HB		26	A3
COUNTRY CT	SJC	SJ75		36	B3
COUNTRY LN	BREA	BREA	400	2	F5
COUNTRY LN	CO	SA	12100	24	B1
COUNTRY LN	GGR	GG	10700	16	B6
COUNTRY LN	LAH	LAH	900	2	B3
COUNTRY LN	OR	OR68	3600	16	F2
COUNTRY TER	LAH	LAH		1	F6
COUNTRY WY	LAH	LAH		1	F6
COUNTRY CYN RD	ANA	AN	4000	12	E3
COUNTRY CLUB DR	BPK	BP	8000	5	C4
COUNTRY CLUB DR	BREA	BREA		3	B6
COUNTRY CLUB DR	CM	CM	2900	27	B3
COUNTRY CLUB DR	MVJO	SJ91		29D	C3
COUNTRY CLUB LN	ANA	AN		13	F2
COUNTRY CLUB LN	SA	SA		22	E3
COUNTRY CLUB LN	YL	YL	19000	8	B4
COUNTRY CLUB RD	LAG	LB		35	A5
COUNTRY FARM LN	CO	SJ		56	D6
COUNTRY FARM LN	CO	SJ		59	D1
COUNTRY GLEN	CO	ET		52	A5
COUNTRY HAVEN	CO	SA	10900	18	C4
COUNTRY HILL RD	ANA	AN	1000	13	E1
COUNTRY HLLS DR	CO	SA		18	D5
COUNTRY HLLS DR	LAH	LAH	500	5	F1
COUNTRY HLLS DR	LAH	LAH	200	6	A1
COUNTRY HLLS RD	BREA	BREA		3	B6
COUNTRY HLLS RD	SJC	SJ75		36	B2
COUNTRY HOLLOW	CO	OR		18	B2
COUNTRY HLLW LN	CO	SJ		56	D6
COUNTRY HLLW LN	CO	SJ		59	D1
COUNTRY HOME RD	CO	OR67		52	E2
COUNTRY RDG CIR	CO	ET		52	B6
COUNTRYSIDE DR	CO	ET		29B	B1
COUNTRYSIDE DR	CO	ET		52	B6
COUNTRY VIEW	LAH	LAH		1	F6
COUNTRY VIEW	LAH	LAH		5	F1
COUNTRY VIEW DR	CO	SJ79		59	C5
COUNTRY VIEW DR	YL	YL		8	B5
COUNTRYWOOD	LAH	LAH		1	F6
COUNTRYWOOD DR	YL	YL		8	B3
COUNTRYWOOD LN	IRV	SA	14500	29	D1
COUNTY LN	CO	SA	10900	18	C4
COURREGES CT	NB	NB63		26	A3
COURSAN	CO	LAG		35	F4
COURSON DR	ANA	AN	700	10	B5
COURSON DR	STN	STN	10300	10	B6
COURSON DR	STN	STN	10500	15	B1
COURT AV	NB	NB63	1900	31	C6
COURT AV	SA	SA	100	23	B2
COURT LN	CO	AN04	11700	15	C3
COURT LN	STN	STN	11500	15	C3

STREET	CITY	P.O. ZONE	BLOCK	PAGE	GRID
COURT ST	BPK	BP	7700	5	C6
COURT ST	BPK	BP	7800	10	C1
COURT ST	OR	OR	4100	18	A3
COURT ST	STN	STN	10300	10	C6
COURT ST	STN	STN	10500	15	C2
COURT ST	STN	GG41	12700	15	C2
COURTLAND ST	OR	OR67		13	A4
COURTNEY AV	FUL	FL33	300	5	E6
COURTNEY AV	FUL	FL33	1000	10	E1
COURTNEY LN	HTB	HB	16900	20	D6
COURTNEY PL	FUL	FL33	200	5	E6
COURTRIGHT RD	STN	STN	10300	10	B6
COURTRIGHT ST	ANA	AN	1200	10	B6
COURTSIDE LN	HTB	HB		20	C5
COVE	IRV	SA		29	C3
COVE CIR	HTB	HB	20000	26	E5
COVE RD	DPT	DPT	24100	37	E5
COVE ST	CM	CM27	600	31	C2
COVE ST	NB	CDLM	2600	33	A1
COVE ISLAND PL	DPT	DPT	33300	38	A3
COVE LANTERN ST	DPT	DPT	34300	37	B5
COVENTRY	NB	NB		32	D5
COVENTRY	SA	SA		23	D1
COVENTRY CIR	FUL	FL33		5	E2
COVENTRY CIR	LAP	BP23	7000	9	E1
COVENTRY CIR	PLA	PLA	1000	7	B4
COVENTRY DR	ANA	AN	700	10	F6
COVENTRY LN	CO	ET		52	C6
COVENTRY LN	CO	LB		29C	D5
COVENTRY LN	HTB	HB	19900	26	F4
COVENTRY LN	YL	YL	17300	7	E4
COVENTRY PL	CO	SA	10900	18	C5
COVENTRY MDWS	GGR	GG		15	F6
COVERD WAGON TR	ANA	AN		13	C3
COVEY CT	BREA	BREA		3	C5
COVEY LN	CO	SA		18	D6
COVEY LN	CO	SA		24	D1
COVEY LN	TUS	SA05		18	D6
COVEY LN	TUS	SA05		24	D1
COVINGTON CIR	VPK	OR67	10600	17	F1
COWAN	IRV	SA		28	C2
COWAN CYN CIR	OR	OR69		18	D3
COWAN HTS DR	CO	SA	9800	18	D4
COWAN HTS DR SE	CO	SA	10100	18	D4
COWAN HTS DR SW	CO	SA	1300	18	D4
COWBOY CIR	ANA	AN		13	C3
COYAN WY	CO	LB56		29C	E6
COYOTE LN	ANA	AN	1100	13	E1
COYOTE LN	OR	OR		13	D6
COYOTE LN	OR	OR		18	D1
COYOTE CYN RD	IRV	SA	5000	32	D4
COYOTE CYN WY	BREA	BREA		2	F4
COYOTE CREEK CT	BPK	BP		5	B4
COYOTE HILLS DR	FUL	FL33		5	E2
COYOTE RIVER CT	FTNV	SA08		27	A3
COZUMEL ST	CYP	CYP	11500	14	F3
COZY PL	ANA	AN	1100	11	F2
COZY PL	ANA	AN	1100	12	A2
COZY TER	ANA	AN	1300	11	F2
COZY TER	ANA	AN	1300	12	A2
COZY GLEN LN	CO	SJ		59	D1
CRABB LN	HTB	HB	17600	26	C1
CRABBE WY	LAG	LB51	1100	34	F3
CRAGER LN	CO	AN04	8000	15	C3
CRAGER LN	STN	STN	8000	15	C3
CRAIG AV	BPK	BP	7700	5	B4
CRAIG CIR	FUL	FL	2400	7	A2
CRAIG DR E	OR	OR	3100	17	F3
CRAIG DR S	OR	OR	100	17	F3
CRAIG LN	HTB	HB47	16000	21	A4
CRAILET DR	HTB	HB46	10000	27	A5
CRAIMER LN	HTB	HB46	20300	27	A5
CRANBERRY LN	YL	YL	20300	8	F2
CRANBERRY RD	TUS	TUS		24	B4
CRANBRIDGE DR	CO	ET	21000	52	C6
CRANBROOK DR	CO	SA	18300	18	A5
CRANBROOK PL	FUL	FL33		5	D4
CRANBROOKE DR	CO	ET		52	C5
CRANDALL DR	HTB	HB47	6400	21	A5
CRANE CIR	FTNV	SA08	10400	27	A2
CRANE CIR	HTB	HB	8400	26	D6
CRANE ST	CO	LB53		29A	B6
CRANE ST	CO	ET	22200	29A	E2
CRATER CIR	HTB	HB	20000	26	F5
CRATER LAKE AV	OR	OR	5500	13	C5
CRATER LAKE CT	FTNV	SA08	10300	27	A2
CRAWFORD CIR	HTB	HB	9100	26	E4
CRAWFORD CYN RD	CO	SA		18	C4
CRAWFORD CYN RD	OR	OR69	100	18	C2
CREEDMOOR DR	HTB	HB	8100	30	B2
CREEK DR	CO	LB	25000	29C	F2

STREET	CITY	P.O. ZONE	BLOCK	PAGE	GRID
CREEK LN	CO	LAH	1000	1	E3
CREEK LN	HTB	HB		26	C2
CREEK RD	IRV	SA		29	B4
CREEKSIDE	CO	ET		29B	B2
CREEKSIDE	CO	LB		29C	D4
CREEKSIDE	OR	OR		18	C2
CREEKSIDE DR	FUL	FL33		5	E4
CREEKSIDE DR	IRV	SA	26300	32A	A2
CREEK SIDE LN	ANA	AN		13	F3
CREEK SIDE LN	ANA	AN		43	A3
CREEKVIEW DR	CO	LB	24400	29A	E6
CREEK VIEW DR	GGR	GG		15	D5
CREEKVIEW DR	OR	OR		18	D2
CREEKVIEW LN	HTB	HB		26	C2
CREEKWOOD	IRV	SA		29	B3
CREEKWOOD CT	BREA	BREA		3	A5
CREEKWOOD CT	SJC	SJ75		36	A3
CREMONA	CO	LB		29A	B4
CRESCENT AV	ANA	AN	2100	10	B3
CRESCENT AV	ANA	AN	1600	11	A3
CRESCENT AV	BPK	BP	5300	9	E3
CRESCENT AV	BPK	BP	6500	10	B3
CRESCENT AV	CO	CYP	4400	9	E3
CRESCENT AV	LAP	BP23	4700	9	B3
CRESCENT CIR	GGR	GG45	5900	14	E4
CRESCENT DR	ANA	AN	5200	13	A2
CRESCENT DR	HTB	HB		26	D3
CRESCENT DR	OR	OR	400	17	B2
CRESCENT DR	YL	YL		8	F4
CRESCENT DR	YL	YL		40	A4
CRESCENT LN	OR	OR		18	A4
CRESCENT RD	CO	ET	23500	29A	D3
CRESCENT WY	ANA	AN	100	11	A4
CRESCENT BAY DR	LAG	LB51	100	34	B2
CRESS PL	LAG	LB51	1200	34	E3
CRESS ST	LAG	LB51	100	34	E4
CREST AV	HTB	HB	200	26	B5
CREST CIR	LAP	BP23	8000	9	E3
CREST CIR	NB	NB		32	C5
CREST DR	SB	SB	200	19	F2
CREST DR	YL	YL		8	D1
CREST RD	OR	OR	300	17	B4
CRESTA CT	CO	LB	24600	29A	E6
CRESTA WY	LAG	LB51	3000	34	F2
CRESTA WY	LAG	LB51	3000	35	A1
CRESTA BLLA CIR	YL	YL		7	D3
CRESTA LOMA	CO	LB77		36	A2
CRESTA VERDE	MVJO	SJ91	26000	29D	B3
CRESTA DEL SOL	SCL	SC72		38	D5
CRESTBROOK	CO	ET		29B	A3
CRESTBROOK	IRV	SA		29	C4
CRESTBROOK PL	ANA	AN	1200	11	E4
CRESTBROOK WY	STN	STN		15	B4
CREST DE VILLE	OR	OR	5400	13	C5
CRESTD BUTE CIR	CO	LB77		36	A3
CRESTHAVEN	IRV	SA		29	D4
CRESTHAVEN LN	CO	SA	10500	18	B3
CRESTHILL DR	ANA	AN	18900	8	B5
CRESTI LN	LAH	LAH	11800	2	C3
CRESTKNOLL DR	YL	YL	19900	8	C5
CRESTLAKE CIR	PLA	PLA		7	B6
CREST LAKE DR	BREA	BREA		2	C5
CRESTLANE AV	ANA	AN	1500	11	E2
CRESTLANE PL	ANA	AN	1300	11	E2
CRESTLINE DR	CO	SA	13100	18	A5
CRESTLINE DR	CO	LB56		29C	C3
CRESTMONT PL	CM	CM27	1900	31	C3
CRESTMOOR LN	HTB	HB	17600	25	E1
CRESTRIDGE PL	ANA	AN	1300	11	E2
CRESTVIEW AV	SB	SB	1000	19	F2
CRESTVIEW CIR	BREA	BREA		3	B5
CRESTVIEW CIR	LAP	BP23	5700	9	E2
CRESTVIEW CIR	VPK	OR67	9600	13	B5
CRESTVIEW DR	FUL	FL	1000	6	A4
CRESTVIEW DR	LAG	LB51	2000	34	F4
CRESTVIEW DR	NB	NB	2400	31	D5
CRESTVIEW LN	HTB	HB	20500	26	E6
CRESTVIEW PL	LAG	LB51	2100	34	F4
CRESTWOOD	HTB	HB		26	C3
CRESTWOOD CIR	GGR	GG	12700	15	F5
CRESTWOOD CIR	LB	LB51		33A	F6
CRESTWOOD DR	NB	CDLM		32	D5
CRESTWOOD LN	ANA	AN04	1700	15	F1
CRESTWOOD LN	ANA	AN	2000	16	A1
CRESTWOOD LN	CO	AN04	9500	15	F1
CRESTWOOD PL	LAG	LB77	31900	37	A1
CRESTWOOD ST	OR	OR	2500	12	C4
CRESWELL LN	NB	NB		31	F2
CRETE LN	HTB	HB49		20	C4
CRETE RD	DPT	LB77	32400	37	C2

STREET	CITY	P.O. ZONE	BLOCK	PAGE	GRID
CREW DR	CO	AN04	10600	15	F1
CREW DR	HTB	HB		30	D1
CRIMSON	HTB	HB		26	D3
CRIMSON	MVJO	SJ91		52	D5
CRIOLLO CIR	OR	OR	7200	18	D2
CRIPPLE CREEK	CO	ET	22200	29B	B2
CRIPTANA	MVJO	SJ92	21600	29B	E1
CRIS AV	ANA	AN04	2000	15	F1
CRIS AV	ANA	AN	1900	16	A1
CRIS AV	CO	AN04	9800	15	F1
CRIS AV	STN	AN04	9000	15	E1
CRIS PL	ANA	AN	1500	16	B1
CRISSEY WY	GGR	GG	11400	16	B3
CRISTAL SPGS CT	BREA	BREA		3	B5
CRISTAN LN	MVJO	SJ91		29B	B5
CRISTA PALMA DR	HTB	HB	6500	26	A1
CRISTIANITOS RD	CO			62	A2
CRISTINE PL	FUL	FL	100	6	C3
CRIVELLI ISLE	IRV	SA14		28	D5
CROATIAN ST	CO	OR67		50	D6
CROCKER LN	CO	ET	25000	29A	F3
CROCKETT	IRV	SA		29	E1
CROCKETT CIR	WSTM	WSTM		21	D4
CROCKETT DR	ANA	AN	4000	12	E2
CROCUS AV	FTNV	SA08	9000	21	E4
CROCUS CIR	BPK	BP	7900	10	C2
CROCUS CIR	CM	CM	900	27	E2
CROCUS CIR	LAP	BP23	5800	9	E3
CRODDY WY	SA	SA	2400	22	C6
CRODDY WY	SA	SA04	3000	27	C1
CROFT LN	HTB	HB	20200	26	D5
CROFTDON ST	CM	CM	2900	27	E4
CROL LN	CO	ET		29A	F3
CROMWELL	IRV	SA18		51	D6
CROMWELL	SA	SA		23	D1
CROMWELL CIR	WSTM	WSTM	15700	21	F3
CROMWELL DR	TUS	TUS		24	B3
CRONAS	CO	SJ91	24500	29B	A6
CRONE AV	ANA	AN	2000	10	F5
CRONE AV	ANA	AN	1300	11	A5
CROSBY AV	GGR	GG	9500	15	E5
CROSBY AV	GGR	GG	10200	16	B5
CROSS DR	HTB	HB	5500	20	E4
CROSS ST	TUS	SA10		23	F6
CROSSBILL CIR	CO	LB	23900	35	D3
CROSSBOW LN	ANA	AN	900	10	E6
CROSSCREEK	DPT	DPT		37	B5
CROSS CREEK	IRV	SA		29	B3
CROSSGATE ST	OR	OR67		13	A4
CROSSHAVEN RD	EBAY	LB51	700	34	B1
CROSSJACK DR	DPT	LB77		37	E4
CROSSKEY	IRV	SA		24	E6
CROUPIER CIR	HTB	HB	5800	20	F1
CROW LN	FTNV	SA08	9200	26	E2
CROWLEY CIR	BPK	BP	8100	5	C4
CROWLEY WY	PLA	PLA	1500	7	C3
CROWN CIR	HTB	HB		25	E1
CROWN CT	WSTM	WSTM		21	D4
CROWN DR	NB	CDLM	2500	32	B6
CROWN DR N	NB	CDLM	1200	32	B6
CROWN LN	SA	SA		22	E2
CROWN ST	ANA	AN	1100	11	B2
CROWN WY	FUL	FL33		5	E3
CROWN WY	SA	SA		23	B6
CROWN COAST DR	DPT	LB77	32700	37	B3
CROWN CREEK	CO	LB		35	E3
CROWN HILL	CO	LB		35	E2
CROWN LAKE CIR	BREA	BREA		2	C5
CROWN POINT DR	ANA	AN07		13	C3
CROWN REEF LN	HTB	HB	20000	26	D5
CROWN RIDGE	CO	LB		35	E2
CROWN ROYALE	CO	LB		35	F2
CROWN VLY PKWY	CO	LB	27900	29D	A6
CROWN VLY PKWY	CO	LB	29000	35	D5
CROWN VLY PKWY	DPT	LB77	31900	37	D2
CROWN VLY PKWY	MVJO	SJ91		29D	B5
CROWN VLY PKWY	MVJO	SJ92		29D	B5
CROWTHER AV	ANA	AN	3100	7	B5
CROWTHER AV E&W	PLA	PLA	100	7	A6
CROYDEN TER	IRV	SA		32	F2
CROYDEN BAY	CM	CM		27	F3
CRUCERO	MVJO	SJ91	27600	29B	D1
CRUCILLO	CO	SJ		59	C1
CRYSTAL AV	NB	NB	100	31	F6
CRYSTAL CIR	CO	ET		29A	F1
CRYSTAL CIR	CYP	CYP	4200	9	C3
CRYSTAL CIR	IRV	SA	15000	29	C2
CRYSTAL DR	ANA	AN07		8	F5
CRYSTAL DR	YL	YL		40	A5
CRYSTAL LN	SA	SA	3500	22	B3
CRYSTAL PL	FUL	FL33	900	10	E1

STREET	CITY	P.O. ZONE	BLOCK	PAGE	GRID
CRYSTAL PL	SB	SB	400	19	F2
CRYSTAL ST	HTB	HB	18800	26	B3
CRYSTAL CAY	CO	LB77		36	A3
CRYSTAL COVE	CO	LB51		33	E4
CRYSTAL COVE WY	SB	SB	1200	19	F2
CRYSTAL LNTN ST	DPT	DPT	33900	37	F4
CRYSTAL POND	MVJO	SJ92		29B	E2
CRYSTAL POOL	IRV	SA		32A	A1
CRYSTL SANDS DR	CO	LB	31500	35	C6
CRYSTAL VW AV E	OR	OR	200	12	C4
CRYSTAL VW AV W	OR	OR	100	12	C4
CUBA CIR	BPK	BP	5500	9	E2
CUBBON ST E&W	SA	SA	100	23	A3
CUBBON ST W	SA	SA	1400	22	D3
CUENCA DR	MVJO	SJ91		29D	C4
CUERVO	CO	SJ88		29B	F4
CUERVO DR	CO	LB53		29A	B6
CULBERTSON DR	ANA	AN	500	11	A5
CUL DE SAC AV	ANA	AN	4600	12	F2
CULEBRA ST	CYP	CYP	11200	14	F2
CULLY DR	CO	OR65	15500	12	C5
CULPEPPER CIR	HTB	HB47	16200	21	A4
CULVER AV E&W	OR	OR	100	17	B4
CULVER DR	IRV	SA	12900	24	D6
CULVER DR	IRV	SA	17500	28	F5
CULVER DR	IRV	SA	14300	29	A4
CULVER DR	IRV	SA	4000	32	F3
CUMBERLAND	CO	SJ79		59	E5
CUMBERLAND AV	WSTM	WSTM	5000	14	E5
CUMBERLAND CIR	YL	YL	16800	7	D4
CUMBERLAND DR	CYP	CYP	5000	9	D6
CUMBERLAND DR	HTB	HB47	6700	21	B3
CUMBERLAND LN	NB	NB	1500	31	E4
CUMBERLAND RD	CO	OR65	16200	12	D5
CUMBRLD CRSS RD	CO	SA05	1200	18	B6
CUMBRLD CRSS RD	CO	SA05	1300	24	B1
CUMBERLANE ST	IRV	SA	14500	29	E5
CUMMINGS PL	LAG	LB51	900	34	E3
CUMMINS DR	CO	LB56		29C	E6
CUNNINGHAM AV	WSTM	WSTM	10000	22	A3
CUNNINGHAM CT	OR	OR		12	F4
CUNNINGHAM LN	GGR	GG	12200	15	E3
CUPAR LN	HTB	HB	21300	30	D1
CUPRIEN WY	LAG	LB51	600	34	E3
CURACAO	CO	LB77		36	A4
CURIE AV	SA	SA04		27	E1
CURIE AV	SA	SA	500	28	A1
CURIE CT	IRV	SA		32	D2
CURIE LN	PLA	PLA	1100	7	D5
CURL DR	NB	CDLM		32	C6
CURLEW LN	CO	LB	28800	35	E2
CURRANT AV	FTNV	SA08	9900	21	F5
CURRANT CREEK	CO	ET	22100	29B	B2
CURRIE CIR	CO	SA	13700	18	B6
CURTIS CIR	HTB	HB		20	D6
CURTIS CT	ANA	AN	1100	11	F2
CURTIS WY N	ANA	AN	200	11	F3
CUSTER CT	FTNV	SA08	15900	22	B4
CUSTER ST	SA	SA	1300	17	C6
CUSTER ST	SA	SA	1000	23	C1
CUSTER WY	STN	STN	7100	15	A2
CUTTER	CO	LAG		35	F3
CUTTER DR	HTB	HB	8800	26	D4
CUTTER RD	ANA	AN	1600	11	B2
CUTTER RD	NB	NB60		31	E6
CUTTER WY	CO	CM27		27	F6
CUTTY WY	ANA	AN		16	D3
CUTTYHUNK CT	CYP	CYP	11300	15	A2
CUTTY SARK DR	HTB	HB46	10000	27	A4
CUYLER AV	PLA	PLA	900	7	D3
CUZZANO ISLE	IRV	SA14		28	D5
CYCLAMEN WY	BPK	BP	7800	10	C2
CYCOD PL	BREA	BREA	400	2	F5
CYMBAL PL	ANA	AN	6200	8	A5
CYMBAL ST	CO	AN07	6400	8	A6
CYMBAL WY	ANA	AN	4800	8	A5
CYNTHIA AV	GGR	GG	11200	16	B6
CYNTHIA CIR	CYP	CYP	5500	9	E6
CYNTHIA CIR	GGR	GG	11000	16	B6
CYNTHIA CT	CM	CM27	2300	31	E1
CYNTHIA DR	HTB	HB46	10000	27	A5
CYNTHIA DR	WSTM	WSTM	13100	14	F5
CYNTHIA LN	CYP	CYP	5600	9	E6
CYPRESS	IRV	SA		29	E3
CYPRESS AV	CYP	CYP	8600	9	E4
CYPRESS AV	FUL	FL	1700	6	F3
CYPRESS AV	HTB	HB47	7600	21	C6
CYPRESS AV	PLA	PLA	1000	12	A1
CYPRESS AV	SA	SA	100	23	B3
CYPRESS DR	LAG	LB51	100	34	C2
CYPRESS LN	CO	SJ91		29A	F5

STREET	CITY	P.O. ZONE	BLOCK	PAGE	GRID
CYPRESS LN	LAG	LB77	31800	37	A1
CYPRESS LN	HTB	HB		30	C1
CYPRESS LN	YL	YL		8	D1
CYPRESS PL	CO	LB		35	D5
CYPRESS ST	BREA	BREA	100	2	E5
CYPRESS ST	CO	LAH	1000	2	A5
CYPRESS ST	CO	SA07	20000	28	A6
CYPRESS ST	CO	SA	20300	32	A1
CYPRESS ST	CYP	CYP	5200	9	E4
CYPRESS ST	FTNV	SA08	17900	26	F1
CYPRESS ST	GGR	GG	13000	16	A5
CYPRESS ST	NB	NB	200	33	B5
CYPRESS ST E&W	ANA	AN	100	11	D3
CYPRESS ST N&S	LAH	LAH	100	2	A5
CYPRESS ST N&S	OR	OR	100	17	C3
CYPRESS WY	FUL	FL	2400	6	F6
CYPRESS WY	FUL	FL	2400	11	F1
CYPRESS POINT	CO	SJ79		59	D6
CYPRESS POINT	MVJO	SJ92		29B	D4
CYPRESS PT AV	BPK	BP	8500	5	D4
CYPRESS PT DR	FUL	FL33		5	E4
CYPRESS PT DR	PLA	PLA	1100	7	C4
CYPRESS PT LN	NB	NB		32	B5
CYPRESS TREE LN	IRV	SA		29	A5
CYPRESSWOOD	CO	ET		51	F5
CYPRIEN WY	ANA	AN	2500	12	A3
D					
D ST	LAG	LB		35	A4
D ST	ETMC	SA09		51	A4
D ST	HTB	HB		26	C6
D ST	NB	NB	100	33	C5
D ST N&S	TUS	TUS	200	23	F2
DA VINCI	CO	LB56		29C	C1
D'BAGLIO WY	YL	YL		8	F4
DABNY LN	LAP	BP23	8000	9	D3
DADE LN	GGR	GG	10000	15	F2
DAFFODIL	CO	SJ88		59	B6
DAFFODIL	NB	CDLM		33	B1
DAFFODIL AV	FTNV	SA08	9000	21	E4
DAFFODIL CIR	SB	SB	12900	14	C5
DAFFODIL PL	MVJO	SJ92		29D	D4
DAGNA PL	ANA	AN	1100	12	A2
DAGNY CIR	HTB	HB	6000	20	F4
DAGNY CIR	HTB	HB	16300	20	F4
DAHL LN	SA	SA	1400	22	D4
DAHLIA	CO	LB56		29C	D2
DAHLIA AV	CM	CM	900	27	E2
DAHLIA AV	NB	CDLM	100	33	A1
DAHLIA CIR	BPK	BP	7800	10	C2
DAHLIA CIR	FTNV	SA08	9800	21	F4
DAHLIA CIR	SB	SB	12900	14	C5
DAHLIA DR	ANA	AN	100	10	F4
DAHLIA DR	ANA	AN	100	11	A4
DAHLIA DR	TUS	TUS		24	A5
DAHLIA PL	NB	NB	2500	33	A1
DAHLQUIST RD	IRV	SA	14700	29	D2
DAIMLER ST	IRV	SA	17100	28	C2
DAIMLER ST	SA	SA		23	D6
DAIMLER ST	SA	SA	3000	28	C2
DAIRYVIEW CIR	HTB	HB47	17400	21	C6
DAISY AV	FTNV	SA08	9200	21	E5
DAISY AV N	SA	SA	1600	16	F6
DAISY AV N&S	SA	SA	100	22	F1
DAISY CIR	LAP	BP23	5800	9	E3
DAISY CIR	BREA	BREA		3	A6
DAISY CIR	SB	SB	12600	14	C4
DAISY ST	SB	SB	12800	14	C4
DAKAR LN	HTB	HB	21500	30	F1
DAKOTA AV	CM	CM	3200	27	C3
DAKOTA AV	GGR	GG	8700	15	D5
DAKOTA AV	GGR	GG	10200	16	A5
DAKOTA ST	ANA	AN	800	11	E5
DAKOTA ST	FTNV	SA08	18900	26	D3
DALCA CT	CYP	CYP	6200	14	F2
DALE	STN	STN		15	D1
DALE CT	BREA	BREA		2	E5
DALE DR	CO	LB		29C	E3
DALE DR	HTB	HB	4100	20	C6
DALE PL	BPK	BP		5	D5
DALE ST	BPK	BP	6000	5	D6
DALE ST	BPK	BP	6700	10	D1
DALE ST	CO	AN04	11500	15	D4
DALE ST	CO	GG41		15	D4
DALE ST	GGR	GG	11000	15	D4
DALE ST	STN	STN	10100	10	D4
DALE ST	STN	GG41	12000	15	D4
DALE ST N&S	ANA	AN	100	10	D4
DALE WY	CM	CM	1400	27	D4
DALEHURST CIR	HTB	HB	19000	26	D3

STREET	CITY	P.O. ZONE	BLOCK	PAGE	GRID
DALEVIEW DR	CO	ET	24800	29A	E5
DALE VISTA LN	HTB	HB47	16500	21	A5
DALEWOOD DR	FUL	FL33		5	F2
DALEWOOD LN	WSTM	WSTM	15500	21	F3
DALEWOOD PL	BREA	BREA	200	2	E5
DALL LN	CO	SA	13500	18	A6
DALL LN	CO	TUS	14000	18	A6
DALL LN	CO	TUS	14100	24	A1
DALLAS CIR	HTB	HB		26	D4
DALLAS DR	ANA	AN	1400	10	F6
DALLAS DR	ANA	AN04	1600	15	F1
DALLAS DR	GGR	GG	11000	15	F2
DALLAS DR	LAP	BP23	7000	9	E2
DALMATIAN ST	CO	OR67		50	D6
DALTON CIR	WSTM	WSTM	9100	21	E3
DALY ST	ANA	AN		11	F1
DAMARA	IRV	SA14		29	A3
DAMASCUS CIR	CM	CM	900	27	E2
DAMASK DR	HTB	HB47	7900	21	C5
DAMON AV	ANA	AN	1200	11	B5
DAMSEL WY	SA	SA		28	B1
DAN LN	HTB	HB		20	F2
DANA AV	OR	OR	2100	17	E3
DANA CIR	CYP	CYP		15	A2
DANA CIR	WSTM	WSTM	16400	21	D4
DANA DR	CM	CM26	1000	27	E2
DANA DR	DPT	DPT	24500	37	E5
DANA DR	HTB	HB46	10000	31	A1
DANA DR	LAP	BP23	4600	9	D2
DANA PL	FUL	FL	1300	6	E4
DANA PL	OR	OR		17	E3
DANA RD	NB	NB	4300	31	C4
DANA ST	ANA	AN	2100	16	D2
DANA WY	STN	STN		10	E4
DANA WY	CYP	CYP		15	A2
DANA WY	STN	STN		15	B3
DANABIRCH	DPT	DPT		37	F2
DANA BLUFFS	DPT	SC24		38	B5
DANACEDAR	DPT	DPT		37	F2
DANACORAL	DPT	DPT		37	F2
DANAELM	DPT	DPT		37	F2
DANAFIR	DPT	DPT		37	F2
DANALAUREL	DPT	DPT		37	F3
DANAMAPLE	DPT	DPT		37	F2
DANA MESA DR	SJC	SJ75	25500	38	A2
DANAOAK	DPT	DPT		37	F2
DANAPALM	DPT	DPT		37	F3
DANAPEPPER	DPT	DPT		37	F2
DANAPINE	DPT	DPT		37	F2
DANA POINT DR	DPT	DPT		37	E4
DANA POINT WY	NB	CDLM		32	D6
DANA PT HRBR DR	DPT	DPT	33600	37	E5
DANAPOPLAR	DPT	DPT		37	F2
DANA SEQUOIA	DPT	DPT		37	F1
DANASPRUCE	DPT	DPT		37	F2
DANA STRAND RD	DPT	DPT	33900	37	D4
DANATEAK	DPT	DPT		37	F3
DANA VIEW LN	DPT	DPT		37	F4
DANA VISTA ST	DPT	DPT		37	A5
DANA WOODS	DPT	DPT		37	F2
DANBERRY CIR	TUS	TUS	14600	23	F4
DANBERRY DR	GGR	GG	10800	16	A2
DANBOROUGH RD	TUS	TUS	14600	24	A5
DANBOROUGH ST	WSTM	WSTM	15200	22	A2
DANBROOK AV	ANA	AN	3400	10	B4
DANBROOK DR	ANA	AN	800	10	B5
DANBROOK ST	ANA	AN	300	10	B5
DANBURY CIR	HTB	HB	8400	26	D4
DANBURY LN	CM	CM	100	27	E6
DANBURY LN	SB	SB	13300	14	A5
DANBURY ST	CYP	CYP	9200	9	D5
DANBURY WY	SA	SA04		22	E6
DANBY DR	CO	ET	23700	29A	D4
DANBY WY	CO	ET		29B	B1
DANCY CIR	HTB	HB	8200	26	D2
DANDELION AV	FTNV	SA08	9700	21	F5
DANDELION CIR	FTNV	SA08	9800	21	F5
DANE CT	CO	LB77		35	D2
DANES CIR	HTB	HB	14300	20	F1
DANFORTH AV	CO	LB77		35	F4
DANFORTH AV	CO	LB77		36	A4
DAN GURNEY DR	SA	SA		23	D4
DANIEL AV	GGR	GG	11500	16	C2
DANIEL DR	DPT	DPT	32900	37	E3
DANIEL LN	CO	OR		18	C2
DANIELLE CIR	ANA	AN		13	E1
DANIELLE DR	CM	CM	1000	27	D2
DANIGER RD	CO	SA	12300	18	C4
DANITA LN	YL	YL	4400	8	A3
DANNEN DR	CO	SA	11300	18	D6
DANNY AV	CYP	CYP	5500	9	E4

STREET	CITY	P.O. ZONE	BLOCK	PAGE	GRID
DANTA	CO	SJ		59	B2
DANTE LN	HTB	HB46		26	E6
DANTON CIR	HTB	HB	7500	26	C2
DANUBE DR	HTB	HB47	7500	21	B5
DANUBE WY	CM	CM26		28	A3
DANVERS DR	GGR	GG	6800	15	A4
DANVERS WY	WSTM	WSTM	13300	14	E5
DANVILLE	IRV	SA		29	E1
DANWILL ST	FTNV	SA08		26	F2
DANZA PZ	YL	YL	5400	8	A4
DANZIG BAY	DPT	LB77		37	D4
DAPHNE	CO	SJ		59	B3
DAPHNE E	CO	SJ91	24500	29B	A6
DAPHNE W	CO	SJ91	24500	29B	A6
DAPHNE W	CO	SJ91		29D	A1
DAPHNE PL	FUL	FL33	2500	5	E4
DAPPLE CIR	OR	OR	7200	18	D2
DAPPLEGRAY CIR	BREA	BREA		3	A6
DAPPLE GREY DR	CO	LB	26300	29C	F3
DAPPLEGREY RD	GGR	GG	13100	16	C5
DARBY CT	LAH	LAH	100	2	A5
DARBY ST	OR	OR	1000	12	D4
DARDANIA AV	CO	SJ91		29A	F6
DARDANIA AV	CO	SJ91	24500	29B	A6
DARDEN WY	YL	YL	4800	7	F3
DAREN CIR	HTB	HB	8300	26	D3
DARIAN RD	ANA	AN		11	E5
DARIN ST	SA	SA	500	22	B2
DARIN WY	CYP	CYP		15	A2
DARLENE CIR	LAP	BP23	7400	9	F1
DARLENE DR	CO	SA	11200	18	D6
DARLINGTON	MVJO	SJ92		29D	D1
DARLINGTON AV	BPK	BP	5700	5	C6
DARMEL PL	CO	SA	1800	17	F5
DARNELL ST	GGR	GG	12300	16	D4
DAROCA	MVJO	SJ92	28300	29B	E5
DAROCA WY	BPK	BP		5	C3
DARON DR	VPK	OR67	9700	13	B5
DARRELL ST	CM	CM	600	27	B6
DARRIN DR	CO	ET	26000	29B	A2
DARROW DR	HTB	HB46		26	E6
DARROWBY	MVJO	SJ92		29B	D1
DARSY CIR	TUS	TUS	1600	23	F4
DARSY DR	HTB	HB	8300	26	D1
DARTER CIR	FTNV	SA08	8500	26	D3
DARTMOOR DR	HTB	HB	8100	26	C3
DARTMOOR ST	LAG	LB51	300	34	C2
DARTMOUTH	HTB	HB		20	D5
DARTMOUTH	IRV	SA		32	F1
DARTMOUTH AV	WSTM	WSTM	5500	14	E6
DARTMOUTH CIR	CO	ET		29A	F3
DARTMOUTH CIR	CO	ET		29B	A3
DARTMOUTH CIR	SB	SB	1000	19	C4
DARTMOUTH CIR	TUS	TUS	14600	23	F4
DARTMOUTH DR	PLA	PLA	500	7	C5
DARTMOUTH PL	CM	CM	200	27	D6
DARTMOUTH WY	ANA	AN		10	F3
DARTMOUTH WY	ANA	AN		11	A3
DARTMOUTH WY	PLA	PLA	200	7	C5
DARWIN	IRV	SA		24	E6
DARWIN AV	CO	MDWY	7700	21	C3
DARYL LN	GGR	GG	11600	16	C2
DASYA CIR	DPT	LB77		37	D3
DATE PL	CM	CM	1500	27	C3
DATE ST	BREA	BREA	800	6	F1
DATE ST	BREA	BREA	3300	7	C1
DATE ST	FTNV	SA08	18900	26	E3
DATE ST	STN	STN	10500	15	C2
DATE ST E&W	ANA	AN	200	11	F3
DATE ST E&W	BREA	BREA	100	2	E6
DATEWOOD	IRV	SA		29	A5
DAUPHIN	DPT	DPT		37	D2
DAVENPORT DR	HTB	HB	4000	20	C5
DAVENPORT RD	CO	LALM	11200	14	B3
DAVID AV	LAH	LAH	2500	1	D4
DAVID CIR	DPT	DPT		37	E2
DAVID DR	NB	NB63		30	F3
DAVID ST	ANA	AN	900	11	C6
DAVIDA LN	CO	LB53		29C	E6
DAVIDSON CT	BREA	BREA		2	F5
DAVID WEBSTER	GGR	GG45		14	E2
DA VINCI	IRV	SA		28	D3
DAVIS	IRV	SA		24	E6
DAVIS LN	HTB	HB	16000	20	E4
DAVIS PL	CM	CM	2500	27	F6
DAVIS ST	WSTM	WSTM	14600	21	B2
DAVIS WY	LAG	LB51	600	34	F4
DAVIS CUP DR	HTB	HB		20	C4
DAVIT AV	GGR	GG43	10500	22	A3
DAVIT AV	SA	SA	5100	22	B3

STREET	CITY	P.O. ZONE	BLOCK	PAGE	GRID
DAVIT CIR	LAH	LAH	1300	2	B3
DAVMOR AV	GGR	GG	8500	15	D2
DAVMOR AV	STN	STN	7600	15	C2
DAWN AV	GGR	GG	13200	16	E3
DAWN CIR	LAP	BP23	5100	9	D3
DAWN ST	ANA	AN	300	11	E4
DAWNS WY	FUL	FL		11	E1
DAWNVIEW LN	CO	NB60	300	31	E1
DAWNVIEW LN	CO	SJ79		56	E6
DAWNWOOD DR	HTB	HB	8300	26	D2
DAWSON LN	HTB	HB47	15700	21	B3
DAWSON ST	GGR	GG	13500	16	A6
DAY PL	WSTM	WSTM	13300	15	A5
DAYBREAK	IRV	SA		29	A4
DAYLIGHT	IRV	SA		32A	B2
DAYLILY	CO	SJ88		59	B5
DAYNA ST	SA	SA	2700	17	D5
DAYNA ST	SA	SA	900	23	E1
DAYTON	IRV	SA		24	F6
DAYTON DR	CO	ET	25000	29A	F2
DAYTONA CIR	HTB	HB	9400	30	E2
DAYTONA DR	CO	LB77		36	B4
DEADWOOD DR	SJC	SJ75	32600	38	A2
DEAN ST	CO	LB77		35	D2
DEAN ST	CO	SA	12700	24	B2
DEAN ST	CO	TUS	13000	24	B2
DEAN ST	TUS	TUS	13500	24	A3
DEANA ST	ANA	AN		13	A2
DEANANN PL	GGR	GG	13200	16	A5
DEANANN PL	GGR	GG43	14100	22	A1
DEANANN PL	WSTM	WSTM	14800	22	A2
DEANNA DR	BREA	BREA	900	2	D4
DEANNA ST	LAH	LAH	100	1	E5
DE ANZA CIR	HTB	HB		20	D5
DE ANZA RD	NB	CDLM	400	33	C2
DE ANZA LN	TUS	TUS		23	E3
DEARBORN	MVJO	SJ92		29B	F6
DEAUVILLE DR	HTB	HB	8200	26	C3
DEAUVILLE PL	CM	CM	1400	27	D3
DEBBIE DR	ANA	AN		13	C1
DEBBIE LN	GGR	GG	11700	16	C3
DEBI LN	YL	YL	18000	7	F3
DEBJOIS AV	FTNV	SA08	9800	21	F4
DEBORAH DR	CO	SA05	1400	24	B1
DEBORAH DR	CO	TUS	1200	24	B1
DEBORAH LN	NB	NB	1800	31	E3
DEBORAH LN	OR	OR	2000	17	E4
DEBORAH ST	CYP	CYP	9500	9	F5
DEBRA CIR	HTB	HB47	16800	21	B5
DEBRA DR	CM	CM26	1000	27	E2
DEBRA ST	CO	ET	22100	29A	E2
DEBUSK LN	TUS	TUS	14000	23	F3
DEBWOOD PL	LAH	LAH	1200	2	A6
DECATUR DR	LAP	BP23	5000	9	D1
DECENTE	IRV	SA14		29	A4
DECIMA DR	WSTM	WSTM		21	F3
DECIMA PZ	ANA	AN		16	B3
DECKER AV	CO	AN04	9500	15	E1
DEE LN	YL	YL	19000	8	B4
DEEDEE DR	CM	CM	3300	27	E2
DEEGAN DR	SA	SA	2400	22	E6
DEEGAN DR	SA	SA04	3000	27	E1
DEEPCLIFF DR	HTB	HB		26	D4
DEEP CREEK	CM	CM		27	D2
DEEPCREEK	IRV	SA		32A	A2
DEEPCREEK	MVJO	SJ92		29B	E2
DEEPDALE AV	BPK	BP	8400	5	D4
DEEP HARBOR DR	HTB	HB		26	B4
DEEP HARBOR LN	HTB	HB		26	B4
DEEP SPRING RD	OR	OR69		18	E2
DEEPVIEW DR	HTB	HB		26	D4
DEEP WELL RD	CO	SA		18	B5
DEERBROOK	MVJO	SJ92		29B	E2
DEER CREEK	IRV	SA		29	C2
DEER CREEK CIR	ANA	AN	8400	8	B5
DEER CREEK LN	CO	LB		29C	D1
DEERCREEK LN	YL	YL		8	E1
DEERE AV	IRV	SA	1500	28	D1
DEERE AV	SA	SA	1800	28	D1
DEERFIELD	IRV	SA		29	C2
DEERFIELD AV	IRV	SA	4900	29	C3
DEERFIELD AV	TUS	TUS	14600	23	F4
DEERFIELD DR	HTB	HB	8100	30	C2
DEERFIELD LN	OR	OR69		18	F2
DEERFIELD PL	CO	SJ79		52	F4
DEERFIELD ST	ANA	AN		12	F2
DEERFOOT LN	YL	YL		8	B5
DEERHAVEN DR	CO	SA	9700	18	E4
DEERHAVEN LN	ANA	AN		10	D2
DEERHILL DR	CO	SA	10000	18	D4
DEERHOLLOW CIR	CO	SJ79		56	E6

STREET	CITY	P.O. ZONE	BLOCK	PAGE	GRID
DEERHURST	CO	LB56		29C	C5
DEERPARK DR	FUL	FL	1400	7	A3
DEER PARK ST	IRV	SA	14500	29	C1
DEERPATH	CO	ET		52	C4
DEER RUN	CO	SJ79		59	E3
DEER SPRING	IRV	SA		29	C2
DEER SPRINGS LN	BREA	BREA		3	B5
DEERVALE CIR	CO	LB		35	D3
DEERVALE LN	HTB	HB	20300	26	E5
DEERWOOD E	IRV	SA		29	C3
DEERWOOD W	IRV	SA		29	C2
DEERWOOD DR	ANA	AN	3300	10	B6
DEERWOOD DR	FUL	FL33		5	F2
DEERWOOD DR	OR	OR69		18	E2
DEERWOOD LN	NB	NB		32	B4
DEERWOOD ST	OR	OR69		18	E3
DEETZ PL	IRV	SA14		29	A2
D ESTE DR	CO	AN04	10200	10	E6
DEFIANCE DR	HTB	HB47	6700	21	B4
DE FOREST	IRV	SA		29	E1
DE JESUS DR	PLA	PLA	700	7	C5
DE JUR ST	BREA	BREA	800	2	C4
DEL WY	HTB	HB		26	C4
DELACROIX WY	YL	YL		40	C5
DELAFIELD CIR	HTB	HB	9600	26	F4
DELAFIELD DR	CO	LAM	4500	5	C3
DE LA LUNA DR	MVJO	SJ92		36	C2
DELAMESA	IRV	SA		24	F5
DEL AMO AV	CO	TUS	14500	23	E4
DEL AMO AV	TUS	TUS	14000	23	F3
DELANCY DR	YL	YL	4400	7	E3
DEL ANDANTE	IRV	SA14		29	A3
DELANO DR	CYP	CYP	10100	9	C6
DELANO LN	CYP	CYP	10000	9	C6
DELANO ST S	ANA	AN	100	10	C4
DELANTAL	MVJO	SJ92	23900	29B	D5
DELANTERA DR	IRV	SA		24	E4
DE LAS BANDERAS	CO	SJ88		59	B3
DELAWARE	IRV	SA		24	D6
DELAWARE PL	CM	CM	3200	27	B3
DELAWARE ST	HTB	HB	18200	26	C5
DELAWARE ST N	HTB	HB	400	26	C5
DELAWARE WY	PLA	PLA	300	7	B5
DELAY ST	BREA	BREA	1000	2	C4
DEL AZUL	IRV	SA14		29	A4
DEL BORGATTA	IRV	SA14		29	A3
DEL CARBO	IRV	SA14		28	F3
DEL CERRO	CO	LB77		36	A2
DEL CERRO DR	TUS	TUS	13400	24	A2
DEL CERRO PL	FUL	FL	300	6	C1
DEL CIELO	CO	LB56		35	F1
DEL COBRE	CO	LB77		36	A2
DEL CORONADO DR	CO	LB56		29C	E5
DELEMOS	MVJO	SJ92		29D	C3
DE LEON DR	DPT	DPT		37	E3
DEL ESTE CIR	LAP	BP23	5100	9	D3
DELFINO CIR	HTB	HB		26	B2
DELFT AV	SA	SA		22	E2
DEL GADO	LAG	LB51	2200	34	E4
DEL GADO RD	SCL	SC72		39	A1
DEL GIORGIO RD	ANA	AN	20900	13	E1
DELHI PL	FUL	FL	600	6	A6
DELICIA DR	CO	SJ79		59	D2
DE LINA	CO	SJ88		59	B4
DE LINO	CO	SJ88		59	C2
DEL ITALIA	IRV	SA14		29	A3
DEL LIVORNO	IRV	SA14		29	A3
DELL ST	OR	OR	2700	12	C3
DELLA LN	ANA	AN	2000	16	B3
DELLA LN	GGR	GG	11700	16	B3
DEL LAGO DR	CO	LB	23000	29A	C4
DELLGLEN CIR	HTB	HB		25	F2
DELLGLEN CIR	HTB	HB		26	A3
DELLWOOD	CO	SJ79		59	D4
DEL MAR	CO	LB56		35	E2
DEL MAR AV	CM	CM	100	27	E6
DEL MAR AV	CO	CM27	300	27	E6
DEL MAR AV	LAG	LB51	900	34	F4
DEL MAR AV	LAG	LB51	1700	35	A3
DEL MAR AV	OR	OR	600	12	D5
DEL MAR DR	PLA	PLA		7	F5
DEL MAR LN	ANA	AN	1400	11	E2
DEL MAR LN	HTB	HB	16300	20	E5
DEL MAR LN	LAP	BP23	7300	9	E2
DEL MONTE W	FUL	FL	400	6	B5
DEL MONTE DR	ANA	AN	3100	10	B4
DEL MONTE DR	HTB	HB		30	D2
DEL MONTE DR	SB	SB	13000	14	B2
DEL MONTE ST	CO	LB	24800	29C	F2
DEL NORTE	CO	LB		29D	A6
DEL NORTE	CO	LB77		36	A1
DEL NORTE CIR	LAP	BP23	5100	9	D3

STREET	CITY	P.O. ZONE	BLOCK	PAGE	GRID
DEL NORTE WY	LALM	LALM		9	B6
DEL NORTE WY	LALM	LALM		14	B1
DEL OBISPO ST	DPT	DPT	33100	38	A4
DEL OBISPO ST	SJC	SJ75	31800	38	B1
DEL OBISPO ST	SJC	SJ75		36	C6
DEL OBISPO ST	SJC	SJ75	26700	38	B1
DE LONG CIR	HTB	HB	17500	20	F6
DE LONG ST	CYP	CYP	5200	9	E4
DEL ORO	CO	LB77		36	A2
DEL ORO CIR	HTB	HB		20	D3
DEL ORO LN	FUL	FL	2700	6	C2
DEL ORO LN	LAP	BP23	8200	9	D3
DELOS AV	CO	SJ91		29B	A6
DELOS AV	CO	SJ91		29D	A1
DEL PERLATTO	IRV	SA14		29	A3
DELPHI DR	HTB	HB49		20	C4
DELPHI ST	CO	SJ91		29A	F5
DELPHI ST	CO	SJ91	24100	29B	A5
DELPHIA AV	BREA	BREA	200	2	E5
DELPHINE PL	FUL	FL33	400	5	F5
DELPHINIUM AV	FTNV	SA08	11300	22	B4
DELPHINIUM CIR	BPK	BP	7800	10	C2
DELPHINUS	IRV	SA		32A	B3
DEL PLATA	CO	LB77		36	A2
DEL PONIENTE	CO	LB77		36	A2
DEL PRADO AV	DPT	DPT	24200	37	E5
DELRAY CIR	WSTM	WSTM	8600	21	D3
DELIA LN	CO	OR69	17300	17	E4
DEL REY	DPT	SC24		38	D6
DEL REY	DPT	SC24		39	A1
DEL REY	IRV	SA		32A	B2
DEL REY	MVJO	SJ91		29B	A4
DEL REY DR	CO	SA	12500	24	B2
DEL REY DR	PLA	PLA	500	7	C5
DEL REY DR	STN	STN	8100	15	C3
DEL RIO	CO	LB		35	F2
DEL RIO	CO	LB77		36	A1
DEL RIO WY	CYP	CYP	9800	9	E6
DEL RIO WY	FUL	FL	500	6	B4
DEL ROMA	IRV	SA14		29	A3
DEL ROSA RD	BPK	BP	6500	5	B6
DEL ROSA RD	BPK	BP	6600	10	B1
DEL SERRA CIR	LAP	BP23	5100	9	D3
DEL SOL CIR	LAP	BP23	5100	9	D3
DEL SONATA	IRV	SA14		29	A3
DEL SUR AV	LAH	LAH	900	1	F6
DEL SUR CIR	LAP	BP23	5100	9	D3
DELTA AV	BREA	BREA		2	D5
DELTA AV	CO	SJ91	25600	29B	A5
DELTA PL	ANA	AN	1400	11	E4
DELTA ST	GGR	GG	12200	16	C3
DELTA ST	OR	OR	2500	12	D4
DELTA RIVER CT	FTNV	SA08	10300	27	A2
DELTON CIR	HTB	HB47	16500	21	B5
DEL VALLE AV	OR	OR	3600	18	A2
DEMASIA	MVJO	SJ91		29B	B3
DEMETER WY	CO	SJ91		29B	A6
DEMING ST	SA	SA	400	22	B3
DEMION LN	HTB	HB	18500	26	C2
DEMMER DR	PLA	PLA	100	7	B3
DEMMER PL	PLA	PLA	200	7	B3
DEMPSEY	TUS	SA10		29	A2
DENBIGH LN	TUS	TUS	14400	23	F4
DENIA	CO	LB77		35	F5
DENIA	MVJO	SJ92	23100	29B	D3
DENISE AV	OR	OR	2200	12	E4
DENISE CIR	LAP	BP23	7800	9	D2
DENISE CT	BREA	BREA	1300	2	D3
DENISE DR	WSTM	WSTM	14200	21	A1
DENNI ST	CO	CYP	8100	9	C3
DENNI ST	CYP	CYP	9000	9	C6
DENNI ST	CYP	CYP	10400	14	C1
DENNI ST	LAP	BP23	7800	9	C2
DENNIS DR	CM	CM	1000	27	D2
DENNIS ST	SA	SA	800	22	C3
DENSMORE DR	CO	ET		29B	A1
DENSMORE LN	HTB	HB	20300	26	E5
DENVALE CIR	HTB	HB		25	E1
DENVER	IRV	SA		29	D1
DENVER AV	YL	YL	4000	7	E2
DENVER DR	CM	CM		27	E3
DENVER LN	HTB	HB	19500	26	D4
DENWOOD AV	LALM	LALM	3800	14	C2
DEODAR	IRV	SA		29	D3
DEODAR AV	CM	CM	3000	27	C4
DEODAR DR	YL	YL		8	D2
DEODAR LN	CO	ET	22400	29A	C2
DEODAR ST	CO	SA	13000	17	E6
DEODAR ST	FTNV	SA08	18800	26	E3
DEODAR ST	SA	SA	2000	17	E5
DEODARA DR	GGR	GG	13700	15	E6

STREET	CITY	P.O. ZONE	BLOCK	PAGE	GRID
DE PAUL ST	WSTM	WSTM	15400	21	B3
DEPOT ST	PLA	PLA		7	E5
DEPUTY CIR	CO	LB	27500	29D	A5
DERBY CIR	ANA	AN		8	E6
DERBY CIR	ANA	AN		13	E1
DERBY CIR	CO	LB		29C	E1
DERBY CIR	PLA	PLA	1000	7	B4
DERBY DR	CO	SA		18	D5
DERBYHILL DR	CO	LB56		29C	F5
DERBYSHIRE LN	HTB	HB	19900	26	F4
DEREK CIR	HTB	HB47	8700	21	D5
DEREK DR	FUL	FL31	200	7	A3
DEREK DR	VPK	OR67	18800	13	B5
DERIAN AV	IRV	SA	17200	28	D3
DERNE PL	CO	LB77		35	E6
DERRY ST	LAH	LAH	800	1	F5
DESAI PL	DPT	SC24		38	D6
DESAI PL	DPT	SC24		39	A1
DE SALLE ST	CO	LB	24900	29C	F1
DESCANSO	IRV	SA		24	E5
DESCANSO	NB	NB	2100	32	A3
DESCANSO	TUS	TUS		24	C4
DESCANSO AV	BPK	BP20	6200	4	F6
DESCANSO CIR	BPK	BP20	6200	4	F6
DESCANSO DR	WSTM	WSTM	13500	15	C5
DESERET CIR	ANA	AN	4700	13	A2
DESERT TR	CO	LB	25800	29D	A2
DESERT CYN RD	BREA	BREA		2	F4
DESERT THORN	CO	SJ		59	C1
DESERT WOOD ST	CO	ET	23300	29A	F4
DESMOND ST	GGR	GG	11300	15	E2
DE SOLA TER	NB	CDLM	400	33	C2
DE SOTO AV	CM	CM	2700	27	E4
DESOTO LN	TUS	TUS		23	E3
DESOTO ST	PLA	PLA	1200	7	D4
DESOTO WY	DPT	DPT		37	E3
DESSA DR	GGR	GG		16	B4
DESSER LN	CO	AN04	10500	15	E1
DESTELLO	MVJO	SJ91		29B	C2
DESTRY CIR	HTB	HB47	17300	21	A6
DESTRY LN	CO	ET	26800	29B	B1
DETRA LN	GGR	GG		16	D4
DETROIT AV	HTB	HB	200	26	C6
DEVERON COVE	YL	YL		8	F4
DE VILLE CIR	HTB	HB47	8700	21	E5
DE VILLE DR	YL	YL	18700	8	A3
DEVILWOOD CIR	WSTM	WSTM	8200	21	D3
DEVON	MVJO	SJ92		29B	E6
DEVON	MVJO	SJ92		29D	E1
DEVON	SA	SA		23	D1
DEVON CIR	CYP	CYP	4200	9	C5
DEVON CIR	HTB	HB	3200	20	A5
DEVON CIR	LAP	BP23	8600	9	D4
DEVON LN	GGR	GG		15	D5
DEVON LN	NB	NB	1100	31	E4
DEVON RD	OR	OR	300	17	B4
DEVONPORT CIR	CO	LB	24600	29C	E4
DEVONPORT CIR	YL	YL		8	F3
DEVONSHIRE	MVJO	SJ92		29D	E3
DEVONSHIRE AV	FUL	FL	2800	7	A2
DEVONSHIRE AV	TUS	TUS	14500	23	F4
DEVONSHIRE CIR	BREA	BREA	300	7	A1
DEVONSHIRE CIR	WSTM	WSTM	15400	22	A3
DEVONSHIRE CT	CO	ET		29B	B1
DEVONSHIRE CT	CO	ET		52	B6
DEVONSHIRE DR	BREA	BREA	2000	3	B6
DEVONSHIRE DR	BREA	BREA	2000	7	A1
DEVONSHIRE DR	CO	ET	23600	29A	D4
DEVONSHIRE DR	HTB	HB	9700	26	F4
DEVONSHIRE LN	LAH	LAH		2	B6
DEVONSHIRE RD	ANA	AN	1300	10	E2
DEVONSHIRE RD	CO	LB53		29D	A4
DEVONWOOD AV	STN	GG41	7700	15	C3
DEVONWOOD CIR	FTNV	SA08	18200	26	E2
DEVOY DR	ANA	AN	2800	10	C5
DE VRIES LN	LAP	BP23	8000	9	E3
DE VRY DR	IRV	SA		32	F3
DEWAR	IRV	SA		28	D2
DEWBERRY	CO	SJ		59	C1
DEWBERRY WY	IRV	SA	4300	28	F6
DEWDROP AV	FTNV	SA08	11200	22	B4
DEWEY	IRV	SA		24	E6
DEWEY	IRV	SA		29	E1
DEWEY DR	ANA	AN	1100	16	C2
DEWEY DR	GGR	GG	8600	15	D2
DEWEY DR	GGR	GG	10200	16	A2
DEWEY PL	ANA	AN	1100	16	C2
DEXFORD DR N&S	LAH	LAH	100	1	E4
DEXTER ST N	LAH	LAH	300	2	B5
DEXTER ST S	LAH	LAH	100	2	B5
DEYA	MVJO	SJ92	27700	29B	D2

STREET	CITY	P.O. ZONE	BLOCK	PAGE	GRID
DIA AV	WSTM	WSTM	8600	21	D1
DIABLO CIR	HTB	HB	4000	20	C6
DIAMANTE	IRV	SA		24	F5
DIAMANTE	MVJO	SJ92	24300	29B	E5
DIAMOND	MVJO	SJ91		29D	C6
DIAMOND S	BREA	BREA	100	4	B5
DIAMOND AV	NB	NB	100	31	F6
DIAMOND CIR	LAP	BP23	7400	9	E2
DIAMOND CT	FTNV	SA08	11800	22	B5
DIAMOND DR	HTB	HB	5400	20	E5
DIAMOND RD	PLA	PLA	700	7	B4
DIAMOND ST	ANA	AN	1100	11	C4
DIAMOND ST	GGR	GG45	11800	14	F3
DIAMOND ST	LAG	LB51	100	34	E4
DIAMOND ST	OR	OR	1800	12	E5
DIAMOND ST	SA	SA	500	22	E3
DIAMOND ST	SA	SA04		22	E6
DIAMOND ST	SA	SA04	3000	27	E1
DIAMOND ST	WSTM	WSTM	15700	21	E4
DIAMOND HEAD DR	CO	TUS	13400	24	A3
DIAMOND HEAD DR	TUS	TUS	13400	24	A3
DIAMOND RDGE CT	DPT	DPT		37	F4
DIANA AV	ANA	AN	1200	11	F4
DIANA AV	ANA	AN	2700	12	B4
DIANA CIR	CO	SJ91	25000	29A	F6
DIANA DR	ANA	AN	2500	12	A4
DIANA DR	DPT	DPT	33700	37	E4
DIANA LN	NB	NB	1900	31	E3
DIANA PL	ANA	AN	800	11	F4
DIANA PL	ANA	AN	2600	12	A4
DIANA PL	FUL	FL33	300	5	F5
DIANE AV	BPK	BP	10200	9	F6
DIANE AV	PLA	PLA	1000	7	A4
DIANE CIR	CYP	CYP	10500	14	F1
DIANE DR	OR	OR	7600	13	D6
DIANE LN	HTB	HB47	16700	21	A5
DIANE ST	GGR	GG	12000	16	A3
DIANE WY	ANA	AN	2000	10	F4
DIANE WY	ANA	AN	2000	11	A4
DIANNE ST	SA	SA	400	23	E2
DIANTHUS	CO	TRA		56	B5
DIANTHUS	CO	TRA		59	B4
DICKEL ST N	ANA	AN	800	11	C2
DICKEL ST S	ANA	AN	500	11	D4
DICKENS CIR	WSTM	WSTM	9100	21	E3
DICKENS CT	IRV	SA		32	D2
DICKENS PL	SA	SA		23	B6
DICKENS PL	SA	SA		28	C1
DICKINSON PL	IRV	SA		24	F5
DIDRIKSON WY	LAG	LB51	1000	34	F3
DIEPPE ST	GGR	GG	13700	16	D6
DIJE CT	SCL	SC72	200	39	C3
DILLON RD	CO	LB	25500	29D	A5
DILLOW ST	WSTM	WSTM	14700	21	E2
DIMENSION DR	CO	ET		52	B5
DINA CT	CYP	CYP	4300	9	C6
DINERAL	MVJO	SJ91		29B	B3
DION	CO	LB77		35	E5
DINO CIR	GGR	GG	11000	16	A2
DINO PL	GGR	GG	11700	16	A3
DIONE	IRV	SA		32A	A3
DIRIGO CIR	HTB	HB	21600	30	F2
DIRK CIR	LAP	BP23		9	E2
DISCOVERY DR	DPT	DPT		37	A5
DISCOVERY DR	CO	TRA		56	E6
DISCOVERY DR	NB	NB		31	A2
DISENO DR	MVJO	SJ91		29A	F4
DISENO DR	MVJO	SJ91		29B	A4
DISNEY CIR	HTB	HB46	10000	27	A4
DITMAR LN	HTB	HB		26	D4
DITMORE DR	GGR	GG	12100	15	D3
DITWOOD PL	LAH	LAH	1200	2	A6
DITZ LN	CO	ET		29A	F3
DIVERS CT	DPT	DPT		37	E3
DIXIE	FTNV	SA08	17400	21	F6
DIXIE DR	CO	AN04	10600	15	F1
DIXON AV	OR	OR	3400	18	A4
DOANOKE AV	IRV	SA	5100	29	D2
DOCKSIDE CIR	HTB	HB	21400	30	E1
DOCTORS CIR	CM	CM27	2100	31	D1
DODDS AV	BPK	BP	5400	5	B4
DODGE AV	CO	SA	18400	18	A5
DODSON WY	VPK	OR67	9700	12	F5
DOE RUN	CO	SA	19200	18	B5
DOE TR E	IRV	SA		29	C2
DOE TR W	IRV	SA		29	C2
DOGWOOD	CO	SJ		59	B3
DOGWOOD	IRV	SA		29	B5
DOGWOOD AV	ANA	AN	2100	10	F2
DOGWOOD AV	ANA	AN	1900	11	A2

STREET	CITY	P.O. ZONE	BLOCK	PAGE	GRID
DOGWOOD AV	FTNV	SA08	11800	22	C5
DOGWOOD AV	SB	SB	4000	14	D4
DOGWOOD CIR	YL	YL		8	E2
DOGWOOD COM	SA	SA		22	B2
DOGWOOD CT	BREA	BREA		2	D5
DOGWOOD LN	BREA	BREA		2	D4
DOGWOOD LN	CO	LB		29C	D4
DOGWOOD LN	WSTM	WSTM		21	C4
DOGWOOD RD	TUS	TUS	2100	24	B4
DOGWOOD ST	ANA	AN	1600	11	B2
DOGWOOD ST	CM	CM27	900	31	B2
DOGWOOD ST	OR	OR69		18	E3
DOGWOOD ST	WSTM	WSTM	15200	21	D3
DOGWOOD WY	STN	STN	10600	15	C1
DOHENY	CO	LB77		36	A5
DOHENY CIR	IRV	SA	14900	29	C2
DOHENY DR	HTB	HB		30	D2
DOHENY PL	DPT	SC24	34700	38	B5
DOHENY PARK RD	DPT	SC24	34000	38	A5
DOHRN CIR	HTB	HB47	6500	21	A6
DOIG DR	GGR	GG		15	B2
DOLAN ST	GGR	GG	11400	16	A2
DOLLAR DR	HTB	HB	5400	20	E1
DOLLY AV	BPK	BP	5500	5	B4
DOLORES CIR	PLA	PLA	300	7	C5
DOLORES DR	FUL	FL	1000	6	A4
DOLORES ST	ANA	AN		8	D5
DOLORES ST	HTB	HB	16600	20	D5
DOLORES ST	LAH	LAH	900	1	E3
DOLOROSA	MVJO	SJ91		29D	C3
DOLPHIN AV E&W	SB	SB	100	19	E3
DOLPHIN CT	SJC	SJ75		38	A3
DOLPHIN DR	HTB	HB	8800	26	D4
DOLPHIN DR	SCL	SC72		39	A2
DOLPHIN ST	FTNV	SA08	9600	21	F6
DOLPHIN TER	NB	NB	1000	31	F6
DOLPHIN TER	NB	CDLM	1300	32	A6
DOLPHIN WY	LAG	LB51	200	34	C2
DOLPHIN COVE	CO	LB	23000	35	D3
DOLPHIN STKR WY	NB	NB60	19400	28	B5
DOLPHINWOOD DR	HTB	HB		25	F2
DOLPHINWOOD DR	HTB	HB		26	A2
DOMADOR	SCL	SC72		38	E4
DOMINICA	DPT	DPT		37	E3
DOMINGEZ DR	HTB	HB		20	D4
DOMINGO AV	DPT	SC24	25800	38	A4
DOMINGO DR	MVJO	SJ92		29D	E3
DOMINGO DR	NB	NB		32	A3
DOMINGO PL	FUL	FL	200	6	B2
DOMINGO RD	FUL	FL	1100	6	B3
DOMINGUEZ ST	CO	LB56		29C	D3
DOMNGUEZ RCH RD	YL	YL		8	E4
DOMINICA AV	CYP	CYP	6200	14	F2
DOMINICA CIR	HTB	HB	3900	20	C4
DOMINICA CIR	PLA	PLA	1200	7	D5
DOMINION WY	SJC	SJ75		36	C3
DOMINITA RD	CO	LB		35	C5
DON DR	HTB	HB47	7600	21	C5
DONACY WY	ANA	AN	1500	11	F1
DONALD CIR	HTB	HB47	8500	21	D5
DONALD PL	NB	NB		31	D4
DONATELLO	CO	LB56		29C	C1
DONATELLO	IRV	SA14		29	A4
DONCASTER	HTB	HB	8400	30	D1
DONCASTER RD	IRV	SA	14600	29	D2
DONCASTER WK	WSTM	WSTM		14	D6
DONEGAL DR	GGR	GG	13100	15	F5
DONEGAL DR	GGR	GG	14100	21	F1
DONEGAL DR	WSTM	WSTM	14600	21	F2
DONEGAL LN	CO	ET		29B	A1
DONEGAL LN	SJC	SJ75		38	C4
DONEGAL PL	CM	CM	1200	27	D3
DON JUAN AV	SJC	SJ75	31200	36	C6
DONLYN DR	HTB	HB	5900	20	F5
DONNA AV	OR	OR	3800	18	A3
DONNA CT	ANA	AN		13	D1
DONNA DR	ANA	AN		13	C1
DONNA DR	CO	LB56		29C	E5
DONNA DR	LAG	LB51	2000	34	E2
DONNA DR	LAP	BP23	4800	9	D3
DONNA LN	CO	ET	24500	29A	E2
DONNA LN	GGR	GG	11500	16	B3
DONNAGLEN LN	LAH	LAH	800	1	F5
DONNER AV	BPK	BP		5	C4
DONNER CT	CO	LB	24000	35	E1
DONNEYBROOKE ST	OR	OR	200	17	A3
DONNIE RD	CO	NB60	2200	31	E2
DONNIE ANN RD	CO	LALM	3100	14	A2
DONNIS RD	CO	LALM	11000	14	A2
DONNYBROOK AV	LAH	LAH	800	2	B3
DONNYBROOK CIR	ANA	AN08		40	A6

STREET	CITY	P.O. ZONE	BLOCK	PAGE	GRID
DONNYBROOK LN	CM	CM	3000	27	D3
DONNYBROOK RD	BREA	BREA		3	A5
DONOVAN RD	CO	LALM	11200	14	A2
DONWEST	CO	TUS		23	E2
DORADA AV	GGR	GG	11600	16	B4
DORADO	CO	SJ88		59	B4
DORADO DR	HTB	HB		20	E6
DORAL CT	CO	YL	19400	8	B3
DORAL DR	HTB	HB		25	F3
DORAL PL	CO	LB		35	D5
DORCHESTER E&W	IRV	SA		24	E6
DORCHESTER AV	TUS	TUS	1800	24	A5
DORCHESTER CIR	VPK	OR67	18100	13	A6
DORCHESTER LN	LAH	LAH		2	B6
DORCHESTER RD	NB	NB	4500	33	C2
DORCHESTER ST	ANA	AN	500	11	F4
DOREEN DR	CYP	CYP	9700	9	F5
DOREEN WY	SA	SA	1300	22	F4
DOREEN WY	SA	SA04	3000	27	F1
DOREMERE DR	HTB	HB	8500	26	D4
DORFSMITH DR	WSTM	WSTM	13300	14	F5
DORIA AV	CO	SJ91		29B	A6
DORIA AV	CO	SJ91		29D	A1
DORIANE CIR	HTB	HB47	6500	21	A4
DORIELLE DR	CO	LB77		35	D1
DORINDA RD	YL	YL		8	E3
DORINE RD	CO	LB		29C	D6
DORIS AV	GGR	GG	10300	16	A3
DORIS CIR	CYP	CYP	10300	9	D6
DORIS LN	NB	NB	1700	31	E3
DORIS PL	ANA	AN	1500	16	B1
DORIS WY	CO	SA		18	C4
DORISGLEN LN	LAH	LAH	600	1	F5
DORITA DR	HTB	HB	5900	20	F6
DORMAN ST	SA	SA	800	23	C1
DORN CT	LAG	LB51	2900	34	F2
DOROTHEA	MVJO	SJ91		29D	B3
DOROTHY AV	GGR	GG	10600	16	B5
DOROTHY AV	OR	OR	4100	18	A3
DOROTHY CIR	VPK	OR67	10700	17	F1
DOROTHY DR	BREA	BREA	900	2	D3
DOROTHY DR	FUL	FL	400	6	D4
DOROTHY DR	OR	OR	2500	17	F3
DOROTHY DR	OR	OR	3700	18	A3
DOROTHY DR	WSTM	WSTM	5700	14	F5
DOROTHY LN	FUL	FL	700	6	D4
DOROTHY LN	NB	NB	1500	31	E3
DOROTHY PL	OR	OR	2700	17	F3
DORSET DR	CYP	CYP	4200	9	C5
DORSET LN	CM	CM	1100	27	D3
DORSETSHIRE LN	CO	SA	1000	18	C5
DORSETT DR	HTB	HB	8600	30	D1
DORSEY CIR	WSTM	WSTM	13300	14	F5
DORTHEA ST	YL	YL	4200	8	B2
DORWOOD AV	LAH	LAH	1400	6	A1
DORY AV	YL	YL		40	A3
DORY DR	CO	LB77		37	D1
DORY DR	HTB	HB	8400	30	D1
DORY WY	SB	SB	300	19	E2
DOS CASAS LN	YL	YL	18200	7	F5
DOSINIA DR	DPT	LB77		37	D3
DOT AV	LAH	LAH	1800	2	C4
DOTTIE CIR	GGR	GG		15	E4
DOUGLAS	IRV	SA		28	C4
DOUGLAS CIR	LAP	BP23	7300	9	E1
DOUGLAS DR	CM	CM		27	C5
DOUGLAS DR	CYP	CYP		14	E1
DOUGLAS LN	YL	YL	5300	8	A4
DOUGLAS ST	SA	SA	1100	22	F4
DOUGLAS ST	SA	SA04	3000	27	F1
DOUGLASS RD	ANA	AN	1600	12	A6
DOUGLASS RD	ANA	AN06		17	A1
DOVE	CO	SJ		59	C1
DOVE CIR	FTNV	SA08	9700	26	F2
DOVE CIR	HTB	HB46		30	E6
DOVE CIR	LAP	BP23	4700	9	D3
DOVE LN	FUL	FL		6	A3
DOVE LN	OR	OR69		18	C2
DOVE LN	YL	YL		8	E1
DOVE PL	ANA	AN	1000	11	F5
DOVE ST	NB	NB60	2000	28	B5
DOVE ST	OR	OR69		18	C3
DOVE CANYON DR	CO	SJ79		59	D2
DOVECOTE LN	ANA	AN	2300	10	E5
DOVEKIE CIR	CO	LB	23900	35	D2
DOVER	CO	SJ79		59	D3
DOVER	IRV	SA14		29	F3
DOVER AV	BREA	BREA		3	A6
DOVER CIR	ANA	AN	1000	11	E5
DOVER CIR	BREA	BREA	2000	3	A6
DOVER CIR	CYP	CYP	4200	9	C5

ORANGE CO.

INDEX

STREET	CITY	P.O. ZONE	BLOCK	PAGE	GRID
DOVER CIR	WSTM	WSTM	10400	22	A3
DOVER DR	HTB	HB	6100	20	F2
DOVER DR	LAH	LAH	100	2	A5
DOVER DR	LAP	BP23	5100	9	D3
DOVER DR	NB	NB	500	31	E3
DOVER LN	YL	YL		40	A3
DOVER PL	ANA	AN	1900	11	F4
DOVER PL	CO	LB77		37	E1
DOVER ST	ANA	AN	700	11	F4
DOVER WY	PLA	PLA	1100	7	B4
DOVER WY	STN	STN		15	B2
DOVERFIELD DR	PLA	PLA	200	7	B4
DOVE TREE LN	CO	ET	24900	29A	E2
DOVEWOOD DR	HTB	HB	5000	20	E3
DOW AV	TUS	TUS		24	A6
DOWELL CT	TUS	SA10		29	B1
DOWN DR	HTB	HB47	6400	21	A3
DOWNEY PL	ANA	AN	900	10	F6
DOWNIE PL	GGR	GG	12700	16	E5
DOWNIE PL	SA	SA	2200	16	E5
DOWNING CIR	WSTM	WSTM	9200	21	E3
DOWNING ST	ANA	AN		11	E2
DOWNING ST	GGR	GG	11900	16	D3
DOWNLAND RD	CO	ET	23400	29A	D4
DOYLE DR	ANA	AN	300	10	D5
DOYLE DR	HTB	HB	6000	20	F5
DOZIER DR	GGR	GG		16	A5
DRACAENA ST	BPK	BP	8200	10	C4
DRAGON CIR	HTB	HB	9800	26	F6
DRAGONFLY	IRV	SA		29	B2
DRAKE	CO	LB77		36	A4
DRAKE	IRV	SA		29	E1
DRAKE AV	CM	CM	2700	27	F4
DRAKE AV	FUL	FL	100	6	B5
DRAKE DR	ANA	AN		13	F3
DRAKE DR	ANA	AN		43	A3
DRAKE DR	PLA	PLA	1400	7	B3
DRAKE LN	HTB	HB47	15000	21	A2
DRAKE ST	GGR	GG44		15	D5
DRAKE ST	NB	NB		31	A6
DRAKE WY	STN	STN		10	E4
DRAKE WY	STN	STN		15	B3
DRAKES BAY DR	NB	CDLM		32	D5
DRAYTON AV	TUS	TUS	1100	23	E4
DREAM ST	ANA	AN		8	F6
DREAM ST	ANA	AN		13	F1
DREAM ST	ANA	AN08		40	A6
DREAM ST	ANA	AN		43	A1
DRESDEN AV	SA	SA		22	D2
DRESDEN CIR	CYP	CYP	5200	9	D6
DRESDEN CIR	HTB	HB47	6900	21	B3
DRESDEN PL	ANA	AN	1200	11	B2
DRESDEN ST	ANA	AN	900	11	B3
DRESSAGE	OR	OR		13	D6
DRESSER ST	SA	SA	1600	17	B6
DRESSER ST	SA	SA	1500	23	B1
DREW CIR	HTB	HB	20400	26	D5
DREW WY	STN	STN		10	E4
DREW WY	CO	OR		18	B2
DREW WY	STN	STN		15	B2
DREXEL WY	CO	ET		29B	A2
DREY LN	HTB	HB47	17300	21	B6
DREY RD	WSTM	WSTM	8400	21	D5
DRIFTING SAND	IRV	SA		29	B5
DRIFTWOOD	CO	LB		29A	C4
DRIFTWOOD	IRV	SA		29	B3
DRIFTWOOD AV	BREA	BREA	700	2	F4
DRIFTWOOD AV	LAP	BP23		9	E2
DRIFTWOOD AV	SB	SB	700	19	E2
DRIFTWOOD CIR	PLA	PLA	1000	12	A2
DRIFTWOOD CT	SJC	SJ75	33000	38	A3
DRIFTWOOD DR	LAG	LB	30600	35	A6
DRIFTWOOD DR	FUL	FL	800	6	D3
DRIFTWOOD DR	HTB	HB	8000	26	C5
DRIFTWOOD DR	HTB	HB		30	C1
DRIFTWOOD DR	SA	SA	600	22	B3
DRIFTWOOD LN	WSTM	WSTM		21	C3
DRIFTWOOD PL	BREA	BREA		2	E4
DRIFTWOOD RD	NB	CDLM	200	33	B2
DRIFTWOOD ST	OR	OR		12	C3
DRIZA	MVJO	SJ92	28200	29B	E3
DRUID LN	CO	LALM	2900	14	A4
DRUMBEAT DR	HTB	HB	9500	30	F1
DRUMCLIFF RD	EBAY	LB51	700	34	B1
DRYBANK DR	HTB	HB		26	D4
DRYBROOK LN	HTB	HB		26	D4
DRY CREEK LN	CO	LB		29C	D1
DRYDEN LN	CO	SA	14000	18	B6
DRY DOCK COVE	CO	LB		35	D2
DRYMEN DR	HTB	HB	8300	30	D1
DRYSDALE LN	CO	LALM	11300	14	B2

STREET	CITY	P.O. ZONE	BLOCK	PAGE	GRID
DUANE	IRV	SA		24	F6
DUANE	IRV	SA		29	F1
DUARTE	NB	NB		32	A3
DUARTE WY	LAG	LB51	1000	34	F4
DUBLIN LN	HTB	HB	20400	26	D5
DUBLIN RD	EBAY	LB51	700	34	B1
DUBLIN ST	CM	CM	3100	27	C3
DUBLIN ST	CO	ET	23000	29A	D3
DU BRIDGE AV	IRV	SA		28	E2
DUCHAMP DR	IRV	SA		24	C6
DUCHESS LN	HTB	HB		20	F4
DUCHESS LN	HTB	HB47	16200	21	A4
DUCHESS LN	SA	SA		22	E2
DUCHESS ST	CO	LB77		36	A3
DUDLEY AV	ANA	AN	1500	16	B2
DUDLEY WY	STN	STN	7200	15	B2
DUDMAN AV	GGR	GG45	6000	14	F4
DUDMAN DR	CO	GG41	8600	15	D4
DUDMAN DR	GGR	GG	8700	15	D4
DUELLO LN	HTB	HB47	17400	21	B6
DUENAS	CO	LB	21000	29A	A5
DUENDE	MVJO	SJ91		29B	C2
DUKE WY	STN	STN		10	E4
DUKE CIR	HTB	HB47	15400	21	A3
DUKE DR	WSTM	WSTM	9500	21	F3
DUKE LN	SA	SA		22	E2
DUKE PL	ANA	AN	900	10	E3
DUKE PL	CM	CM	2400	27	D5
DUKE ST	GGR	GG	13400	16	C5
DUKE WY	STN	STN		15	B2
DULAY CT	IRV	SA14		29	A2
DULCINEA	MVJO	SJ91		29D	C3
DUMAINE DR	LAP	BP23	5000	9	D2
DUMBRECK DR	HTB	HB	9500	26	F5
DUMOND DR	LAG	LB51	2800	34	F5
DUMONT LN	WSTM	WSTM	14200	21	A1
DUMONT ST	GGR	GG	12700	15	A4
DUNAS DR	CO	SA	12600	18	A4
DUNAS RD	OR	OR	400	17	F4
DUNAS ST N	OR	OR	200	17	F3
DUNAS ST S	OR	OR	100	17	F3
DUNBAR DR	CO	ET		52	A6
DUNBAR ST	HTB	HB	5000	20	E6
DUNBAR ST	OR	OR	2500	12	D4
DUNCANNON AV	WSTM	WSTM	5000	14	E5
DUNDALK LN	HTB	HB47	15800	21	A3
DUNDEE CT	BREA	BREA		2	F4
DUNDEE DR	CO	ET		29B	A1
DUNDEE DR	CO	ET		52	A6
DUNDEE DR	HTB	HB	6000	20	F2
DUNE LN	HTB	HB		26	C6
DUNE ST	ANA	AN	600	12	B4
DUNE MEAR RD	CO	ET	22900	29A	E4
DUNES	CO	LB77		36	A5
DUNES LN	HTB	HB	14300	20	F1
DUNFIELD ST	OR	OR	2600	12	D4
DUNGAN LN	GGR	GG	12600	16	C4
DUNGARVIN LN	SJC	SJ75		38	D4
DUNHAM LN	PLA	PLA		7	D4
DUNKENFIELD CIR	CO	ET		29A	F3
DUNKENFIELD CIR	CO	ET		29B	A3
DUNKLEE AV	GGR	GG	13000	16	E4
DUNKLEE LN	GGR	GG	12000	16	C4
DUNLIN LN	CO	LB53		29A	B6
DUNN DR	ANA	AN	2600	10	D2
DUNN DR	HTB	HB47	6400	21	A3
DUNN ST	CO	LB		35	F4
DUNN ST	CO	LB77		36	A4
DUNN WY	PLA	PLA	700	12	A1
DUNNEGAN DR	LAG	LB51	500	34	C2
DUNNEGAN PL	LAG	LB51	500	34	C2
DUNNING DR	LAG	LB51	1200	34	E3
DUNROBIN WY	YL	YL		8	E3
DUNSMORE	CO	ET		52	C3
DUNSMUIR PZ	YL	YL	19800	8	C4
DUNSTON LN	GGR	GG		16	A5
DUNTON AV E&W	OR	OR	100	12	C4
DUPONT DR	ANA	AN06		17	A2
DUPONT DR	IRV	SA	2000	28	C4
DUQUESA	DPT	DPT		37	E2
DUQUESNE PL	WSTM	WSTM	7600	21	C2
DURANGO DR	BPK	BP	7600	5	C3
DURANGO LN	MVJO	SJ91		29B	C5
DURANGO RIVR CT	FTNV	SA08	10200	27	A1
DURANT ST	SA	SA	1600	17	B6
DURANT ST	SA	SA	1300	23	B1
DURAZNO	MVJO	SJ92		29B	D6
DURFEE CIR	VPK	OR67	18300	13	A6
DURFEE LN	VPK	OR67	18400	13	A6
DURHAM DR	HTB	HB	9600	26	F4
DURHAM DR	YL	YL	16800	7	D4

STREET	CITY	P.O. ZONE	BLOCK	PAGE	GRID
DURHAM ST	LAH	LAH	700	2	A5
DURST ST	ANA	AN	300	11	D1
DURYEA AV	IRV	SA	1000	28	C1
DURYEA DR	CO	ET	23400	29A	D4
DUSK ST	IRV	SA	14800	29	D2
DUSKYWING	IRV	SA		29	D1
DUSTIN PL	ANA	AN	500	11	F4
DUSTY RD	WSTM	WSTM		21	E2
DUTCH AV	ANA	AN	2700	12	B3
DUTCHER AV	IRV	SA	5000	29	D2
DUVERNEY	CO	LB	23000	29A	A5
DWYER DR	ANA	AN	400	11	B3
DWYER PL	ANA	AN	300	11	B4
DYER PL	LAG	LB51	1000	34	F3
DYER RD	CO	SA05	15600	23	B6
DYER RD	SA	SA	100	23	B6
DYLAN AV	CO	ET	24100	29A	D3
DYNAMICS ST	ANA	AN	1300	12	C1
E					
E ST	ETMC	SA09		51	A3
E ST	HTB	HB		26	C6
E ST	NB	NB	100	33	C5
EADINGTON AV	FUL	FL33	300	5	F6
EADINGTON AV	FUL	FL33	1000	10	F1
EADINGTON DR	BREA	BREA	900	2	D6
EAGLE AV	FTNV	SA08	10100	27	A2
EAGLE CIR	OR	OR	500	17	D4
EAGLE DR	ANA	AN	3700	12	E1
EAGLE DR	BPK	BP	7000	9	F1
EAGLE DR	GGR	GG	12900	15	B4
EAGLE DR	PLA	PLA	300	7	B4
EAGLE LN	HTB	HB	16000	20	E4
EAGLE PT	IRV	SA		29	D4
EAGLE RUN	IRV	SA		29	A4
EAGLE ST	CO	ET		29A	E2
EAGLE CREST DR	CO	SJ79		59	D6
EAGLECREST DR	HTB	HB48		25	F4
EAGLE LAKE CIR	CO	ET		29A	F1
EAGLEMONT AV	CO	ET	24000	29A	D4
EAGLEROCK WY	LAG	LB	31600	35	A6
EAGLES GLEN	CO	ET		52	A5
EAGLES NEST DR	YL	YL		8	E1
EAGLES POINT	OR	SA05		18	C4
EAGLEWOOD PL	LAH	LAH	1500	5	F1
EARHART	IRV	SA		29	E1
EARHART RD	CO	LB		29C	F1
EARL CIR	ANA	AN	1200	12	A2
EARL CIR	HTB	HB47	7400	21	B5
EARL CIR	WSTM	WSTM	15700	21	F3
EARL LN	SA	SA		22	E3
EARL PL	ANA	AN	1100	12	A2
EARLE DR	GGR	GG	13200	15	E5
EARLHAM ST	CO	OR	11700	18	A3
EARLHAM ST	CO	SA	13000	18	A5
EARLHAM ST N	OR	OR	300	18	A2
EARLHAM ST S	OR	OR	100	18	A3
EARLYMORN	IRV	SA		29	A4
EARLY STAR WY	YL	YL		40	E6
EARNSHAW DR	PLA	PLA	2000	7	D2
EAST DR	TUS	TUS		24	C4
EAST ST N&S	ANA	AN	100	11	E3
EAST BAY FRONT	NB	NB62		31	F6
EASTBLUFF DR	NB	NB	2000	32	A2
EASTBOURNE BAY	CO	LAG		37	F2
EASTBOURNE WK	WSTM	WSTM		14	D6
EASTBROOK	MVJO	SJ92		29B	E1
EASTBROOK WY	STN	STN		15	B4
EASTER CIR	HTB	HB	3200	20	A5
EASTER HILL DR	CO	SA	10490	18	C4
EASTRN LNTRN ST	DPT	DPT		37	F5
EASTGATE DR	NB	NB	3100	32	C4
EASTGATES ST	ANA	AN	1200	10	C6
EASTGLEN DR	CO	SJ79		59	E1
EASTLAKE	IRV	SA		29	C4
EAST LAKE DR	OR	OR		17	D4
EASTLAKE LN	HTB	HB47		21	C5
EASTLINE RD	DPT	LB77	32200	37	C2
EAST MALL	IRV	SA		24	C6
EASTMAN ST	IRV	SA	17200	28	C2
EASTMAN WY	LAG	LB51	1000	34	F3
EASTMONT	IRV	SA		29	C3
EAST NINE DR	CO	LB	31700	35	D6
EAST NINE DR	CO	LB77	31700	37	D1
EASTON ST	PLA	PLA	900	12	A1
EASTPARK DR	LAH	LAH	1300	2	B4
EASTPARK DR	YL	YL		40	A5
EASTPORT DR	HTB	HB	8100	30	C1
EASTRIDGE	CO	TRA		59	D6

STREET	CITY	P.O. ZONE	BLOCK	PAGE	GRID
EASTHILL	CO	TRA		59	D6
EASTRIDGE DR	CO	ET		52	C6
EASTRIDGE WY	BREA	BREA	200	2	F6
EASTRIDGE KNOLL	FUL	FL	1000	6	B4
EASTSHORE	IRV	SA		29	C4
EASTSIDE AV	SA	SA	1600	17	D5
EASTSIDE AV	SA	SA	100	23	D2
EASTSIDE ST	SA	SA	2700	17	D5
EASTVIEW	CO	LB		29C	E3
EASTVIEW CT	SJC	SJ75		36	B3
EASTWIND	CO	LB56		29C	C1
EASTWIND DR	DPT	DPT		38	A4
EASTWIND DR	PLA	PLA	900	12	A1
EASTWING	CO	LB56		29C	B1
EASTWOOD AV N	SA	SA	400	23	C1
EASTWOOD AV S	SA	SA	2300	17	C6
EASTWOOD CIR	HTB	HB	20300	26	E5
EASTWOOD CIR	VPK	OR67	9600	13	A5
EASTWOOD DR	ANA	AN	1200	11	E3
EASTWOOD PL	BREA	BREA	200	2	E5
EASTWOOD RD	IRV	SA		24	F6
EASTWOOD ST	SA	SA	2100	17	C6
EASTWOOD ST	SA	SA	2000	23	D5
EASY LN	HTB	HB		25	F2
EASY ST	YL	YL	19300	8	B3
EASY WY	ANA	AN	1300	11	A6
EASY WY	ANA	AN	1600	16	A1
EASY WY	GGR	GG	11600	16	A3
EATON LN	CO	LAG		35	F3
EATON WY	CO	AN06	10000	12	A6
EATON WY	STN	STN		15	B2
EBBTIDE CIR	HTB	HB	8000	26	C5
EBB TIDE DR	SCL	SC72		39	A2
EBBTIDE PL	SB	SB	800	19	E2
EBBTIDE RD	NB	CDLM	1100	32	B6
EBBTIDE WY	ANA	AN		11	A2
EBEL RD	TUS	TUS	15600	23	E3
EBOE ST	IRV	SA	3500	24	C6
EBONY WY	WSTM	WSTM	14100	21	A1
EBONYWOOD ST	OR	OR	1700	12	D5
EBSON	MVJO	SJ92		29B	D1
ECCELSTONE CIR	IRV	SA	15000	29	D2
ECHO PL	ANA	AN	100	11	A4
ECHO RUN	IRV	SA		29	A5
ECHO ST	ANA	AN	200	11	A4
ECHO CANYON PL	BREA	BREA		2	F4
ECHO HILL LN	YL	YL		8	C5
ECHO HILL WY	OR	OR	2900	12	F4
ECHO PASS RD	CO	SJ		52	E3
ECHO RIVER CT	FTNV	SA08		27	A2
ECKENRODE WY	PLA	PLA		7	D4
ECKHOFF ST	CO	OR69	11000	17	B2
ECKHOFF ST	OR	OR	100	17	B2
EDAM CIR	HTB	HB47	8300	21	D6
ED BANE CIR	WSTM	WSTM		21	D4
EDDA LN	ANA	AN	1300	11	B6
EDDY DR	CO	SA	17500	17	F5
EDELWEISS CT	CO	LB		29C	E6
EDEN	IRV	SA		24	F5
EDEN CIR	GGR	GG45	12200	14	E4
EDEN ST	CO	MDWY	14700	21	D2
EDEN ST	WSTM	WSTM	15000	21	D3
EDEN WY	BREA	BREA		2	D3
EDENDALE CT	SA	SA	400	23	B4
EDGAR AV	FUL	FL	200	6	E6
EDGAR PL	FUL	FL	1000	6	E4
EDGEBROOK DR	GGR	GG	8600	15	D5
EDGEBROOK LN	HTB	HB		26	C2
EDGECLIFF DR	FUL	FL	1100	6	D4
EDGECLIFF DR	YL	YL	5500	8	B4
EDGEHILL DR	IRV	SA		32	F3
EDGELEY PL	CO	LALM	2900	14	A3
EDGEMAR AV	ANA	AN	5500	13	B2
EDGEMAR CIR	ANA	AN	100	13	B2
EDGEMERE DR	IRV	SA	4800	29	D2
EDGEMONT CIR	CYP	CYP	5300	9	D5
EDGEMONT CIR	WSTM	WSTM	8500	21	D3
EDGEMONT DR	HTB	HB47	6500	21	A4
EDGEMONT LN	BREA	BREA		3	B5
EDGEMONT LN	GGR	GG		15	A6
EDGEMONT ST	LAH	LAH	1000	1	E3
EDGESTONE	IRV	SA		29	B1
EDGEVIEW DR	CO	SA	1100	18	C5
EDGEVIEW LN	HTB	HB	14600	20	F2
EDGE WATER	IRV	SA		29	C3
EDGEWATER AV E	NB	NB	100	31	E6
EDGEWATER AV W	NB	NB	500	31	E6
EDGEWATER DR	DPT	DPT		38	D3
EDGEWATER LN	HTB	HB	16600	20	C6
EDGEWATER ST	OR	OR		12	C3
EDGEWOOD AV	VPK	OR67	18300	13	A6

STREET	CITY	P.O. ZONE	BLOCK	PAGE	GRID
EDGEWOOD CIR	GGR	GG	11900	15	F3
EDGEWOOD LN	GGR	GG	10000	15	F3
EDGEWOOD LN	HTB	HB		26	D4
EDGEWOOD RD	SA	SA	100	17	B5
EDGEWOOD RD	SJC	SJ75		36	B2
EDIETH DR	GGR	GG	12500	15	F4
EDINBORO CIR	ANA	AN		13	E4
EDINBURGH DR	WSTM	WSTM	13300	14	E5
EDINGER AV	CO	SA04	12000	22	D4
EDINGER AV	FTNV	SA08	9500	21	B4
EDINGER AV	FTNV	SA08	10000	22	A4
EDINGER AV	HTB	HB	3300	20	F4
EDINGER AV	HTB	HB47	6200	21	B4
EDINGER AV	SB	SB	3500	20	C4
EDINGER AV	TUS	TUS		23	E4
EDINGER AV	TUS	SA05		24	A6
EDINGER AV	TUS	SA10		29	B1
EDINGER AV	WSTM	WSTM	8000	21	B4
EDINGER AV E&W	SA	SA	100	23	A4
EDINGER AV W	SA	SA	1500	22	D4
EDINGTON TER	IRV	SA		32	F2
EDISON	IRV	SA		29	E1
EDISON AV	HTB	HB	8500	30	D2
EDISON ST	PLA	PLA	200	7	A5
EDISON WY	GGR	GG	12200	15	B3
EDISON WY	SA	SA	1900	22	E4
EDITA AV	WSTM	WSTM	5500	14	E6
EDITHIA AV	ANA	AN	1500	11	B5
EDMONDS CIR	HTB	HB	5900	20	F5
EDNA DR	SA	SA	1600	16	E6
EDUCATION LN	HTB	HB	19600	26	F4
EDWARD AV	FUL	FL33	100	5	D6
EDWARDS ST	HTB	HB47	14500	21	A5
EDWARDS ST	HTB	HB	17500	26	A3
EDWARDS ST	WSTM	WSTM	13000	15	A6
EDWARDS ST	WSTM	WSTM	14000	21	A5
EDWARDSON CIR	PLA	PLA	1900	7	C2
EDWARD WARE CIR	GGR	GG45		14	E4
EDWINA LN	GGR	GG	9300	15	E4
EDYE DR	HTB	HB46	10000	27	A6
EFFINGHAM DR	HTB	HB	9800	26	F6
EGAN AV	DPT	SC24	34200	38	B5
EGAN RD	LAG	LB	31500	35	B5
EGERER PL	FUL	FL	3300	6	C1
EGHAM CIR	GGR	GG	11800	16	E3
EGRET AV	FTNV	SA08	10400	27	A3
EGRET CT	NB	SA07		28	B6
EGRET CT	NB	SA07		32	B1
EGRET LN	CO	LB53		29A	B6
EGRET LN	HTB	HB	20500	26	D6
EHLEN WY	CO	TUS	14300	24	A1
EIDER CT	CO	LB	23900	35	D2
EIFFEL CIR	IRV	SA	15400	29	D3
EILEEN DR	ANA	AN	1800	16	B2
EILEEN ST	STN	STN	7600	15	C2
EIRE CIR	HTB	HB47	6500	21	A3
EISENHOWER CIR	ANA	AN		7	F6
EISENHOWER WY	PLA	PLA		7	E5
EISNER PL	ANA	AN	1100	11	B3
EIVON LN	CO	ET	300	29A	F3
EL ACAMPO	CO	LB56		29C	F6
EL ADELANTE AV	FTNV	SA08	10600	27	A1
EL ADOBE PL	FUL	FL	300	6	C1
EL ADOLFO	CO	LB56		35	E2
ELAINE DR	CO	LB56		29C	E5
ELAINE DR	SA	SA	900	22	C1
EL ALICANTA	CO	LB56		35	E1
EL AMARILLO AV	FTNV	SA08	11000	22	B6
EL APAJO	CO	LB56		35	E2
EL ARBOL AV	FTNV	SA08	9300	26	E1
EL ARREO	CO	SJ		59	B1
EL ARROYO AV	FTNV	SA08	8500	26	D1
EL ARROYO DR	HTB	HB	8400	26	D1
EL AZUL CIR	FTNV	SA08	9300	26	E1
ELBA CIR	CM	CM	1800	27	B4
ELBA DR	CO	LB77		35	C2
EL BARAT	CO	LB77		36	B1
ELBE CIR	HTB	HB47	16500	21	C5
ELBEN DR	LAP	BP23	4600	9	D3
ELBERT CIR	FTNV	SA08	16000	22	D4
EL BLANCO AV	FTNV	SA08	9300	21	E6
EL BOSQUE	LAG	LB51	400	34	D3
EL BRAZO	CO	LB56		35	E1
EL CABALLO ST	CO	ET	24900	29A	E4
EL CABRILLO	PLA	PLA		7	C3
EL CAJON AV	CO	YL	16700	7	E2
EL CAJON AV	YL	YL	16600	7	E2
EL CAMINO AV	FTNV	SA08	9300	26	F1
EL CAMINO CIR	BPK	BP	7400	10	B2
EL CAMINO DR	CM	CM	900	27	E4
EL CAMINO DR	FUL	FL	500	6	B4

STREET	CITY	P.O. ZONE	BLOCK	PAGE	GRID
EL CAMINO DR	LAH	LAH	500	1	F3
EL CAMINO LN	CO	SA	1000	18	B6
EL CAMINO LN	CO	SA	1000	24	B1
EL CAMINO LN	PLA	PLA	100	7	C5
EL CAMINO WY	TUS	TUS		23	F3
EL CM CAPISTRNO	DPT	DPT	24600	37	E5
EL CM DEL MAR	LAG	LB51	400	34	D3
EL CM MONTANA	CO	SJ		56	C6
EL CM MONTANA	CO	SJ		59	C1
EL CAMINO REAL	SJC	SJ75	31300	36	C6
EL CAMINO REAL	SJC	SJ75	31800	38	C1
EL CAMINO REAL	TUS	TUS	100	23	F3
EL CAMINO REAL	TUS	TUS		24	A3
EL CAM REAL N&S	SCL	SC72	100	39	B2
EL CAMPO AV	FTNV	SA08	10600	27	A1
EL CAMPO CIR	BPK	BP	7400	10	B2
EL CANEY DR	BPK	BP	7500	10	B2
EL CANON DR	CO	LAH	1000	2	A3
EL CANON DR	LAH	LAH	100	2	A3
ELCANTADA LN	MVJO	SJ91		29B	C5
EL CANTO DR	CO	LB		35	F2
EL CANTO DR	CO	LB77		36	A1
EL CAPITAN AV	FTNV	SA08	8600	26	D1
EL CAPITAN DR	HTB	HB46	10000	27	A6
EL CAPITAN DR	NB	CDLM		32	D5
EL CAPITAN LN	CO	LB	25000	29C	F2
EL CAPITAN WY	BPK	BP	7500	10	B2
EL CAPRICE	CO	LB		29A	C6
EL CAPRICE	CO	LB56		29C	B1
EL CARMEN AV	CO	OR	18600	18	A2
EL CARMEN AV	OR	OR	3600	18	A2
EL CARRIZO	CO	LB56		29C	F6
EL CEDRO CIR	BPK	BP	7400	10	B2
EL CENTRO	CO	AN07		44	A1
EL CENTRO AV	FTNV	SA08	10800	22	B6
EL CENTRO WY	BPK	BP	7400	10	B2
EL CERRITO	CO	LB		29A	C6
EL CERRITO	CO	LB		29C	C1
EL CERRO CIR	FTNV	SA08	8600	26	D1
EL CERRO DR	BPK	BP	7000	10	B1
EL CHACO DR	BPK	BP	7500	10	B2
EL CHARCO	MVJO	SJ92		29B	E2
EL CHINO AV	FTNV	SA08	10900	27	B1
EL CHINO CIR	BPK	BP	7400	10	A2
EL CID AV	FTNV	SA08	10900	27	B1
EL CIELO CIR	BPK	BP	7200	10	B2
EL CIERVO LN	MVJO	SJ91		29D	C3
EL CLAVEL AV	FTNV	SA08	9800	26	F1
EL COCO CIR	FTNV	SA08	10900	27	B1
EL COCO WY	BPK	BP	7700	10	B2
EL COLINA	CO	ET		29A	F4
EL COLORADO AV	FTNV	SA08	9100	21	E6
EL CONEJO LN	CO	LB	25000	29C	F2
EL CONTENTO DR	DPT	DPT	34000	37	C5
EL CORAZON AV	FTNV	SA08	10000	22	A6
EL CORTEZ AV	FTNV	SA08	9100	21	E6
EL CORTEZ CIR	BPK	BP	7400	10	B2
EL CORTIJO DR	HTB	HB	6500	26	A1
EL CORTIJO LN	MVJO	SJ91		29B	C6
EL CORTIJO LN	MVJO	SJ91	24900	29D	C1
EL COSTA CIR	FTNV	SA08	8600	26	D1
ELDAMAR AV	CO	ET		29A	E3
ELDEN AV	CM	CM	2400	27	E6
ELDEN AV	CM	CM27	2100	31	E1
ELDER AV	SA	SA	1300	22	D4
ELDER AV	SA	SA	600	23	C4
ELDER AV	SB	SB	4200	14	D4
ELDER LN	TUS	TUS	2300	24	B5
ELDER ST	ANA	AN	300	11	F3
ELDER ST	FTNV	SA08	17500	21	E6
ELDER WY	GGR	GG		15	B2
ELDER WY	STN	STN	7800	15	B3
ELDERBERRY	IRV	SA		32A	B3
ELDERBERRY LN	YL	YL		40	D5
ELDERBERRY ST	CO	SJ88		59	B1
ELDERBROOK LN	CO	LB53		29D	A4
ELDERGLEN	IRV	SA		29	D3
ELDER GLEN CIR	ANA	AN		8	B5
ELDERWOOD	CO	ET		29A	F1
ELDERWOOD	CO	ET		51	F6
ELDERWOOD	IRV	SA		29	A4
ELDERWOOD AV	ANA	AN	1100	11	C5
ELDERWOOD AV	OR	OR69		18	E3
EL DIABLO CIR	BPK	BP	7600	10	B2
EL DOMINO AV	FTNV	SA08	10800	22	B6
EL DOMINO WY	BPK	BP	7800	10	B3
EL DON DR	LAH	LAH	1500	1	E4
ELDON PL	SA	SA	4500	22	C2
EL DORADO AV	LAH	LAH	1500	1	E4
EL DORADO DR	BPK	BP	7000	10	B2
EL DORADO DR	CO	LB	25100	29D	A1

STREET	CITY	P.O. ZONE	BLOCK	PAGE	GRID
EL DORADO DR	FUL	FL	800	6	B4
EL DORADO DR	HTB	HB	5400	20	E6
EL DORADO DR	SB	SB	13100	14	A6
ELDORADO LN	ANA	AN		13	A2
EL DORADO LN	NB	NB		32	B5
EL DORADO ST	PLA	PLA	1100	7	C4
EL DORADO WY	LALM	LALM		9	B6
EL DORADO WY	LALM	LALM		14	B1
EL DURANGO CIR	FTNV	SA08	9700	21	F6
ELEANOR DR	ANA	AN	1100	16	C2
ELEANOR DR	GGR	GG	10300	15	F2
ELEANOR DR	GGR	GG	10300	16	A2
ELEANOR LN	LAG	LB51	1600	34	C1
ELECTRIC AV	LAH	LAH	100	2	A5
ELECTRIC AV	SB	SB	500	19	E2
ELECTRIC AV	STN	STN	7800	15	C1
ELECTRIC ST	CYP	CYP	8900	9	E4
ELECTRIC WY	ANA	AN	2500	10	D2
ELECTRONIC LN	HTB	HB		20	F3
ELENA DR	CO	LB	24800	29C	E3
ELENA DR	HTB	HB		20	D4
ELENA LN	SCL	SC72	600	39	C4
EL ENCANTO AV	DPT	DPT	33700	37	E4
EL ENCANTO DR	BREA	BREA	1200	2	C3
EL ESCORIAL WY	BPK	BP	7500	10	B2
EL ESTE AV	FTNV	SA08	10500	27	A1
EL FERROL	MVJO	SJ92		29D	D2
EL FERROL WY	BPK	BP	7500	10	B2
ELFIN	IRV	SA		29	D1
EL FINITO WY	CO	SA	1200	18	C6
EL FINITO WY	CO	SA	1300	24	C1
EL GATO WY	CO	ET	23300	29A	E4
ELGIN CIR	HTB	HB	8700	26	D3
ELGIN PL	OR	OR	3000	17	F4
EL GORRA CIR	FTNV	SA08	10700	22	B6
EL GRECO	MVJO	SJ92	23200	29B	E4
EL GRECO CIR	FTNV	SA08	9700	21	F5
EL HORNO ST	SJC	SJ75	31200	36	C6
ELINOR DR	FUL	FL	500	6	C1
ELINORA LN	CYP	CYP	5600	9	E6
ELIOT CIR	HTB	HB	15500	20	F3
ELISA DR	DPT	DPT		37	E3
ELITE DR	CO	SA	14100	18	A6
ELITE DR E	CO	SA	18700	18	A6
ELIZABETH CT	CYP	CYP	4200	9	C6
ELIZABETH DR	OR	OR	500	17	D1
ELIZABETH LN	GGR	GG	12700	16	B4
ELIZABETH LN	HTB	HB	20600	26	E6
ELIZABETH PL	GGR	GG	13400	16	B5
ELIZABETH PL	OR	OR	1000	17	D1
ELIZABETH ST	GGR	GG	11500	16	B2
ELIZABETH WY	CO	TUS	12500	24	A1
ELIZABETH WY	FUL	FL33	300	5	F5
ELIZABETH WY	TUS	SA05	13400	24	A2
ELK CIR	HTB	HB47	7200	21	B5
ELK LN	SA	SA	100	23	D2
ELK RD	ANA	AN	1500	10	F6
ELK RD	ANA	AN04	1500	15	F1
ELKADER	CO	SJ79		59	D4
ELK GLEN LN	OR	OR69		18	F2
ELKRIDGE ST	BREA	BREA		2	D4
ELK RIVER CT	FTNV	SA08		27	A2
ELKSFORD AV	IRV	SA	5000	29	D2
ELKSTONE AV	ANA	AN	4200	12	F2
ELKWOOD	CO	ET	22200	29A	E2
ELKWOOD CT	BREA	BREA		2	C5
EL LAGO AV	FTNV	SA08	8500	26	D1
EL LAZO	CO	SJ		59	B1
EL LAZO RD	CO	LB		29C	D6
ELLEN ST	GGR	GG	12000	16	A3
ELLENDALE DR	CO	LB	29600	35	C3
ELLERY DR	GGR	GG	11500	15	E2
ELLESMERE AV	CM	CM	2800	27	B4
ELLESMERE WY	CYP	CYP	6900	15	B3
EL LEVANTE	SCL	SC72	100	39	D3
EL LIBRO AV	FTNV	SA08	8500	21	D6
ELLICE CIR	DPT	LB77		37	C1
ELLINGTON LN	WSTM	WSTM		21	F2
ELLIOT	BPK	BP	8100	5	C3
ELLIOT LN	YL	YL	18700	8	A3
ELLIOTT PL	GGR	GG	13800	15	D6
ELLIOTT PL	SA	SA	800	22	C3
ELLIS AV	FTNV	SA08	8500	26	D2
ELLIS AV	FTNV	SA08	10000	27	B2
ELLIS AV	HTB	HB	6500	26	B2
ELLIS LN	FUL	FL	100	6	C5
ELLIS PL	FUL	FL	100	6	C5
ELLIS ST	FTNV	SA08	10000	27	A2
ELLISWRTH AISLE	IRV			29	F2
ELLMAR CIR	CO	SA	13700	18	B5
ELLSWORTH AV	ANA	AN	100	11	D4

STREET	CITY	P.O. ZONE	BLOCK	PAGE	GRID
ELLSWORTH DR	HTB	HB	9000	26	E5
EL LUCERO CIR	BPK	BP	7200	10	B2
ELM	IRV	SA		29	D3
ELM AV	ANA	AN	2100	10	F4
ELM AV	ANA	AN	1700	11	A4
ELM AV	CM	CM	1500	27	C4
ELM AV	CYP	CYP	6200	14	F1
ELM AV	CYP	CYP	6700	15	A1
ELM AV	FUL	FL33	1600	10	F1
ELM AV	IRV	SA	14800	29	B1
ELM AV E&W	FUL	FL	100	6	C6
ELM AV W	FUL	FL33	1600	5	F6
ELM CIR	BPK	BP	8500	10	C3
ELM CIR	BREA	BREA	500	7	C1
ELM CIR	FTNV	SA08	16500	21	E5
ELM CT	CO	SJ91		29A	F5
ELM PL W	ANA	AN	1900	10	F4
ELM PL W	ANA	AN	1900	11	A4
ELM ST	FTNV	SA08	17200	21	E6
ELM ST	FTNV	SA08	17700	26	E1
ELM ST	HTB	HB47	17000	21	C6
ELM ST	LAH	LAH	700	2	A4
ELM ST	OR	OR	300	17	B3
ELM ST	SA	SA	1300	16	F5
ELM ST E	ANA	AN	1200	11	E4
ELM ST E&W	BREA	BREA	100	2	E6
ELM ST W	ANA	AN	100	11	D4
ELM ST W	BREA	BREA	300	6	E1
ELM ST W	BREA	BREA	3300	7	C1
EL MANERA	CO	ET		29A	F4
EL MANZANO	CO	LB56		35	F1
EL MANZANO AV	FTNV	SA08	10500	22	A6
EL MAR AV	FTNV	SA08	10700	27	B1
EL MAR DR	MVJO	SJ91		29D	B4
ELM BANK DR	CO	LB53		29D	A4
ELMBROOK	CO	LB56		29C	B3
ELM CREEK LN	CO	LB		29C	D2
ELMCREST LN	HTB	HB		26	D4
ELMCREST WY	CO	ET		29B	B1
ELMCROFT CIR	LAH	LAH	2000	1	E5
ELMDALE WY	STN	STN		15	C4
ELMER LN	GGR	GG	8500	15	D2
ELM HILL LN	YL	YL	20400	8	F2
EL MENTONE	CO	LB56		29C	F6
ELMHURST CIR	HTB	HB	14300	20	F1
ELMHURST CIR	YL	YL	17700	7	F3
ELMHURST CT	CO	YL		8	C6
ELMHURST LN	CM	CM	400	27	C5
ELMHURST PL	FUL	FL35		6	C3
EL MIO LN	MVJO	SJ92		36	C1
ELMIRA AV	HTB	HB	200	26	C5
ELMIRA ST	ANA	AN	1300	10	E2
ELMIRA BAY	CM	CM		27	F4
EL MIRADOR DR	FUL	FL	500	6	C1
EL MIRAGE AV	CO	LB	23900	35	E4
ELMLAWN DR	ANA	AN	2800	10	C5
EL MODENA AV	NB	NB	300	31	D4
EL MOLINO CIR	FTNV	SA08	9200	26	E1
EL MONTANERO	CO	LB56		29C	F6
EL MONTE AV	FTNV	SA08	10400	27	A1
EL MONTE DR	BPK	BP	7500	10	B2
EL MONTEREY AV	FTNV	SA08	10100	27	A1
EL MORADO	FTNV	SA08	9200	26	E1
EL MORO	MVJO	SJ91		29B	C1
EL MORO WY	VPK	OR67	18900	13	B4
EL MOROCCO WY	BPK	BP	7800	10	B2
EL MORRO CIR	FTNV	SA08	10600	22	A6
EL MORRO WY	BPK	BP	7400	10	B2
ELM PARK DR	SA	SA		22	C1
ELMRIDGE DR	HTB	HB48		25	E3
ELMSFORD AV	LAH	LAH	1500	1	E5
ELMSFORD LN	HTB	HB	19700	26	F4
ELM TREE LN	IRV	SA		29	A5
ELMWOOD	MVJO	SJ92		29B	E1
ELMWOOD	IRV	SA		29	C3
ELMWOOD AV	BREA	BREA		2	D4
ELMWOOD DR	SA	SA		22	B1
ELMWOOD LN	HTB	HB	18700	26	D2
ELMWOOD ST	ANA	AN	600	11	E3
ELMWOOD ST	GGR	GG	12200	16	B3
ELMWOOD ST	OR	OR	600	12	F6
ELMWOOD ST	OR	OR		17	F2
EL NIDO LN	MVJO	SJ91	26200	29B	B3
EL NIDO ST	LAH	LAH	700	2	A5
EL NOPAL LN	HTB	HB	17500	26	B1
EL OESTE	CO	LB77		36	A1
ELOISA DR	CO	SJ91	24500	29A	F6
ELOISE DR	CO	ET	22400	29B	A3
EL ORIENTE E	SCL	SC72	100	39	D2
EL PACIFICO DR	CO	LB		29A	B4

STREET	CITY	P.O. ZONE	BLOCK	PAGE	GRID
EL PARAISO CT	FTNV	SA08	11000	22	B6
EL PASEO	IRV	SA		32A	B2
EL PASEO ST	LAG	LB51	300	34	D3
EL PASEO	PLA	PLA		7	C3
EL PASEO	TUS	TUS		23	D3
EL PASEO DR	NB	CDLM	500	32	A6
EL PASEO ST	NB	NB		31	A6
EL PASILLO	CO	SJ88		59	A3
EL PASO AV	FTNV	SA08	10800	22	B6
EL PASO CIR	BPK	BP	7800	10	B2
EL PASO LN	FUL	FL33	1800	5	F3
EL PASO LN	FUL	FL	1300	6	A3
EL PEPPINO	CO	LB56		35	F1
EL PERRO ST	CO	ET	23300	29A	E4
EL PESCADOR LN	LAP	BP23	8200	9	D3
EL PICADOR CIR	FTNV	SA08	10600	22	A6
EL PICADOR LN	MVJO	SJ91	25400	29D	B2
EL PILAR	CO	LB		29C	E4
EL PLANO	MVJO	SJ92		29B	E2
EL PLANO AV	FTNV	SA08	10900	22	B6
EL PORTAL	SCL	SC72	100	39	C3
EL PORTAL AV	FTNV	SA08	9600	21	F6
EL PORTAL CIR	FTNV	SA08		21	F6
EL PORTAL CT	LAH	LAH	1600	1	E4
EL PORTAL DR N	LAH	LAH	100	1	E4
EL PORTAL DR W	LAH	LAH	1500	1	E4
EL PORTICO	CO	LB56		35	F1
EL POSTE DR	BPK	BP	7100	10	B2
EL PRADO	SCL	SC72	900	39	C3
EL PRADO AV	GGR	GG	13400	16	E4
EL PRADO AV	OR	OR68	4000	16	F4
EL PRADO ST	CO	LB		29C	E3
EL PRADO WY	BPK	BP	7200	10	B2
EL PRESIDNTE AV	FTNV	SA08	8800	26	E1
EL PROVO CIR	BPK	BP	7000	10	A2
EL PUEBLO AV	FTNV	SA08	9400	26	F1
EL RANCHO AV	FTNV	SA08	8500	21	D6
EL RANCHO AV	OR	OR68	4000	16	F4
EL RANCHO DR	LAH	LAH	200	1	E4
EL RANCHO PL	GGR	GG	12400	16	D4
EL RO VERDE DR	LAP	BP23	4700	9	D2
EL RANCHO VISTA	FUL	FL33	2000	5	E3
EL REDONDO CIR	BPK	BP	7200	10	B2
EL REGATEO	MVJO	SJ91		29D	B5
EL REPOSA	CO	LB		29A	C6
EL REPOSA	CO	LB		29C	C1
EL RETIRO	MVJO	SJ92		29D	C4
EL REY	FTNV	SA08	9500	21	F6
EL REY AV	FTNV	SA08		21	F6
EL REY CIR	FTNV	SA08		21	F6
EL REY DR	BPK	BP	7100	10	B2
EL REY DR	LAH	LAH	700	1	E4
EL REY PL	GGR	GG	12400	16	D4
EL RIO	CO	LB		29A	D6
EL RIO	CO	LB		29C	D1
EL RIO AV	FTNV	SA08	8500	26	D1
EL RIO CIR	CM	CM	2800	27	D4
EL RITO DR	VPK	OR67	9600	13	B4
EL ROBLE	CO	LB56		29C	B2
ELROND LN	CO	ET	24600	29A	D3
EL ROSAL CIR	BPK	BP	7300	10	B2
EL ROVIA CIR	BPK	BP	7600	10	B2
EL ROY DR	CO	SA	12300	18	C4
EL RUBI CIR	FTNV	SA08	10600	22	B6
ELSA DR	ANA	AN		13	C1
ELSA DR	FUL	FL	200	6	C3
EL SALVADOR AV	CO	OR	18700	18	B2
EL SALVADOR AV	OR	OR	4600	18	B2
EL SANDOVAL	CO	LB56		29C	F6
EL SARRENTO	CO	LB56		35	E1
ELSBERRY WY	CO	ET		29B	A2
EL SEGUNDO	CO	ET		29A	E4
EL SEGUNDO ST	CO	LB	25800	29C	E2
EL SERENO DR	OR	OR	2400	12	E5
ELSIENA WY	ANA	AN	2500	12	A3
EL SILBIDO AV	FTNV	SA08	10600	22	A6
ELSINORE AV	BPK	BP	5500	5	C5
ELSINORE AV	OR	OR		13	C6
ELSINORE AV	OR	OR	4900	18	B1
ELSINORE CIR	HTB	HB	17300	20	F6
EL SOL AV	FTNV	SA08	9000	21	E6
EL SOL CIR	FTNV	SA08	9400	21	E6
EL SONETO AV	FTNV	SA08	10600	22	B6
EL SUR	CO	LB		29D	A6
EL SUR	CO	LB77		36	A1
EL TAMBOR AV	FTNV	SA08	9500	21	F6
EL TANGO CIR	FTNV	SA08	9200	26	E1
ELTHAM PL	FUL	FL33		5	E4
EL TIBURON AV	FTNV	SA08	10600	22	A5
EL TIEMPO LN	MVJO	SJ91	25400	29D	B2
EL TIRADORE CIR	MVJO	SJ91	24000	29B	B5

STREET	CITY	P.O. ZONE	BLOCK	PAGE	GRID
EL TOBOSO	MVJO	SJ91		29D	B3
EL TOMASO WY	BPK	BP	7200	10	B2
EL TORO AV	FTNV	SA08	10600	27	A1
EL TORO CIR	CO	ET		29A	F4
EL TORO LN	FTNV	SA08	20900	26	F6
EL TORO RD	CO	ET	22700	29A	E4
EL TORO RD	CO	ET	20800	29B	A2
EL TORO RD	CO	LB53	23000	29A	B5
EL TORO RD	CO	ET		52	E5
EL TORO RD	CO	LB53	22000	29C	A1
EL TORO RD	LAG	LB51	21000	29C	A1
EL TORO RD	LAG	LB51	20000	33A	F2
EL TORO WY	BPK	BP	7800	10	B2
EL TORO WY	CO	ET		29A	F4
EL TORO FRTG RD	CO	ET		29A	E4
EL TULIPAN AV	FTNV	SA08	9800	26	F1
ELVA CIR	HTB	HB	9100	26	E4
EL VALLE AV	FTNV	SA08	9300	21	F6
EL VAQUERO	CO	SJ		59	C1
EL VAQUERO CIR	MVJO	SJ91	22700	29B	B3
EL VELOZ WY	BPK	BP	7000	10	B2
EL VENADO LN	MVJO	SJ91	26200	29B	B3
EL VERANO DR	BPK	BP	7000	10	B2
EL VERDE CIR	FTNV	SA08	9200	21	E6
EL VIENTO WY	BPK	BP	7000	10	B2
EL VINO WY	BPK	BP	7600	10	B2
ELVIRA	CO	LB	22000	29A	A4
ELVIRA AV	WSTM	WSTM	8600	21	E2
ELYSTAN CIR	WSTM	WSTM		14	D6
ELYSTAN CIR	WSTM	WSTM	14100	20	D1
EMBAJADORES LN	MVJO	SJ91	26900	29B	C6
EMBARCADERO PL	DPT	DPT		37	F5
EMBASSY AV	ANA	AN	2100	10	F4
EMBASSY AV	ANA	AN	1800	11	A4
EMBASSY CIR	LAP	BP23		9	D3
EMBASSY ST	ANA	AN	1500	11	B4
EMBASSY WY	CO	LB56		29C	E5
EMBASSY WY	CYP	CYP		9	D4
EMBER LN	LAH	LAH	600	2	B3
EMBERWOOD LN	ANA	AN		12	F3
EMBURY DR	CO	SA	18400	18	A5
EMERADO CIR	WSTM	WSTM	8300	15	D6
EMERADO PL	WSTM	WSTM	8400	15	D6
EMERALD	IRV	SA		29	B5
EMERALD	MVJO	SJ91		29D	C5
EMERALD S	BREA	BREA	100	4	B5
EMERALD AV	CO	MDWY	8900	21	D3
EMERALD AV	NB	NB	100	31	E6
EMERALD AV	WSTM	WSTM	8500	21	D3
EMERALD CIR	CYP	CYP	4200	9	C3
EMERALD DR	EBAY	LB51		34	A2
EMERALD DR	EBAY	LB51	200	34	B1
EMERALD DR	OR	OR	400	17	B2
EMERALD DR	SA	SA		22	D2
EMERALD LN	HTB	HB47	17000	21	C6
EMERALD LN	SA	SA		22	D2
EMERALD PL	ANA	AN	100	10	F4
EMERALD PL	ANA	AN	100	11	A4
EMERALD PL	SB	SB	400	19	F3
EMERALD ST	ANA	AN	200	10	F4
EMERALD ST	ANA	AN	200	11	A4
EMERALD ST	GGR	GG45	11800	14	F3
EMERALD WY	PLA	PLA	200	7	B4
EMERALD COVE WY	SB	SB	1400	19	F3
EMERALD HRBR CT	CO	ET		29A	D3
EMERALD PT DR	LAG	LB		34	A2
EMERSON AV	GGR	GG	10100	15	F5
EMERSON AV	GGR	GG	10300	16	A5
EMERSON AV	OR	OR	100	12	D5
EMERSON AV	WSTM	WSTM	7100	21	B3
EMERSON CIR	GGR	GG	8500	15	D5
EMERSON DR	BPK	BP	6700	10	A1
EMERSON LN	IRV	SA14		29	A2
EMERSON PL	GGR	GG	9600	15	F5
EMERSON PL	SA	SA		23	B6
EMERSON PL	SA	SA		28	B1
EMERSON ST	CM	CM27	400	31	E2
EMERSON ST	CO	ET		29A	D3
EMERSON WY	STN	STN	11100	15	B2
EMERY AV	LAH	LAH	2000	2	C5
EMERY CT	FTNV	SA08	9300	21	E5
EMERY ST	BPK	BP	7700	5	C5
EMERY RANCH PL	FUL	FL33		5	F4
EMERY RANCH RD	FUL	FL33		5	F4
EMERYWOOD DR	BPK	BP	5300	5	D4
EMERYWOOD RD	TUS	TUS	14500	23	F4
EMILY ST N	ANA	AN	100	11	D2
EMILY ST S	ANA	AN	600	11	D4
EMINENCIA DL NR	SCL	SC72		38	E3
EMINENCIA DL SR	SCL	SC72		38	E3
EMMETT ST	SA	SA	600	23	C6

1990 ORANGE COUNTY STREET INDEX

STREET	CITY	P.O. ZONE	BLOCK	PAGE	GRID
EMMONS CIR	FTNV	SA08		21	F5
EMOGENE ST	ANA	AN		8	D5
EMORY WY	STN	STN		10	E4
EMORY WY	STN	STN		15	B2
EMPANADA	MVJO	SJ91		29B	C1
EMPEROR	IRV	SA		29	D1
EMPEROR DR	CO	SA	18900	18	B5
EMPIRE LN	WSTM	WSTM	15700	21	F3
EMPIRE ST	ANA	AN	100	10	F5
EMPORIA AV	IRV	SA		32	F2
EMPRESA	MVJO	SJ91		29D	F2
EMPRESS WY	DPT	LB77	32600	37	B3
EMPTY SADDLE DR	CO	LB	25000	29C	F4
EMRYS AV	GGR	GG	12000	16	C4
EMYVALE CT	CO	ET		29B	A1
EMYVALE CT	CO	ET		52	A6
ENAULT LN	CO	GG41	8500	15	D3
ENCANTAMAR	DPT	DPT		37	F1
ENCANTO	MVJO	SJ92	27900	29B	D6
ENCANTO	TUS	TUS		23	D3
ENCANTO CT	CO	LB	25700	29C	F2
ENCANTO PZ	ANA	AN		16	B3
ENCANTO ST	OR	OR	1000	18	B1
ENCINA	IRV	SA		24	E4
ENCINA	NB	NB		32	A2
ENCINA WY	LAG	LB51	1000	34	F4
ENCINAS	MVJO	SJ92		29D	C4
ENCINAS CIR	WSTM	WSTM	7700	15	C5
ENCINITAS CT	LAG	LB51		29C	A1
ENCINITAS ST	LAH	LAH	900	2	A6
ENCINITAS WY	PLA	PLA	500	7	A6
ENCINO N&S	LAG	LB77	1	37	B2
ENCINO CIR	HTB	HB47	17400	21	A6
ENCINO LN	SCL	SC72	300	39	D3
ENCORE CT	NB	NB		31	B4
ENCORVADO LN	MVJO	SJ91	24100	29B	B5
ENDERLE WY	TUS	TUS	13900	17	E6
ENDEVER DR	HTB	HB	9900	26	F6
ENDRY ST	CO	AN04	10800	15	E2
ENDRY ST	GGR	GG	11100	15	E2
ENEBRO RD	SJC	SJ75		38	B3
ENELDO	CO	SJ88		59	B2
ENEO PL	GGR	GG	12300	15	F4
ENERO	NB	NB		32	A3
ENFIELD CIR	HTB	HB	8300	26	D3
ENFIELD CIR	WSTM	WSTM	14100	20	E1
ENFIELD PL	SA	SA		28	B1
ENGEL DR	CO	LALM	2700	14	A4
ENGINEER DR	HTB	HB		20	F2
ENGLAND AV	WSTM	WSTM	9200	21	E3
ENGLAND ST	HTB	HB	19400	26	C4
ENGLAND ST N	HTB	HB	900	26	C5
ENGLEWOOD CIR	HTB	HB47	17000	21	A6
ENGLEWOOD DR	CO	LB77	25400	36	A1
ENGLISH ST	SA	SA	1700	16	E6
ENGLISH ST	SA	SA	500	22	E2
ENID LN	CO	MDWY	8500	21	D2
ENLOE AV	GGR	GG	8600	15	D6
ENLOE WY	GGR	GG	9000	15	E6
ENRAMADA DR	CO	TUS	12200	24	A1
ENRIQUE	SCL	SCL		38	E4
ENSARRIA	MVJO	SJ92		29B	E2
ENSENADA	SCL	SC72		38	E3
ENSENADA AV	LAG	LB51	900	34	F3
ENSENADA LN	MVJO	SJ91		29B	C5
ENSENADA PL	DPT	DPT		37	E5
ENSIGN CIR	HTB	HB	16600	20	D4
ENSIGN CIR	OR	OR	1100	12	D4
ENSUENO	IRV	SA		24	E5
ENTERPRISE	IRV	SA18		51	A6
ENTERPRISE DR	ANA	AN06		12	D1
ENTERPRISE DR	GGR	GG		16	D6
ENTERPRISE DR	LALM	LALM	11000	14	D2
ENTERPRISE LN	HTB	HB	18300	26	B2
ENTERPRISE ST	BREA	BREA		3	C6
ENTERPRISE ST	CM	CM26	3000	28	A4
ENTERPRISE ST	OR	OR		12	B5
ENTERPRISE ST	OR	OR	900	17	B1
ENTIDAD	MVJO	SJ91		29B	C1
ENTRADA	IRV	SA		24	F5
ENTRADA DR	LAH	LAH	900	1	F3
ENTRADA PARAISO	SCL	SC72	1900	39	E4
ENTRADOS DR	CO	ET	23300	29A	E4
ENTRY WY	NB	NB		32	A6
ENTYRE AV	CO	PLA	16300	7	D3
EOLA DR	ANA	AN	2500	10	D5
EPPING WY	TUS	SA05	13400	24	A3
EPSILON ST	GGR	GG	12200	16	C3
EQUADOR WY	BPK	BP	5700	9	E2
EQUESTRIAN DR	CO	SA	10700	18	D5
EQUESTRIAN DR	OR	OR		18	D2

STREET	CITY	P.O. ZONE	BLOCK	PAGE	GRID
EQUESTRIAN LN	CO	OR		18	B1
EQUITATION WY	OR	OR		13	D6
ERIC CT	ANA	AN		11	E5
ERICSON WY	CO	LB	25000	29C	F1
ERICSON AISLE	IRV			29	F2
ERIE LN	CO	ET	22000	29A	E1
ERIE PL	WSTM	WSTM	6000	14	E6
ERIE ST	PLA	PLA	700	7	C1
ERIN CT	CO	ET		29B	A1
ERIN CT	CO	ET		52	B6
ERIN RD	GGR	GG	13300	15	F6
ERIN RD	GGR	GG	14100	21	F1
ERIN RD	WSTM	WSTM	14500	21	F1
ERIN ST	GGR	GG	13600	15	F6
ERIN WY	EBAY	LB51	700	34	B1
ERNA AV E&W	LAH	LAH	100	2	B4
ERNA AV W	LAH	LAH	500	1	F4
ERNEST AV	HTB	HB	7000	26	B3
ERNEST FULSM DR	GGR	GG		15	D4
ERNESTINE CT	CO	LB	25800	29C	E2
ERSKINE DR	HTB	HB	9500	26	F6
ERSKINE GREEN	BPK	BP	8100	5	D4
ERVIN LN	CO	SA	18400	18	A6
ERWIN LN	HTB	HB47	17200	21	A6
ESCALA DR	MVJO	SJ91		29B	B6
ESCALONA DR	MVJO	SJ92		36	C1
ESCALONA PZ	YL	YL		8	C3
ESCALONES E	SCL	SC72	100	39	D3
ESCALONES W	SCL	SC72	100	39	C3
ESCAPADE CIR	HTB	HB		20	C5
ESCAPADE CT	NB	NB		31	B4
ESCARLATA	CO	SJ88		59	C2
ESCATRON	MVJO	SJ92		29B	E5
ESCOLAR	IRV	SA		29	D1
ESCONDIDO LN	MVJO	SJ91		29D	C3
ESCUDERO DR	IRV	SA	4000	24	D6
ESCUNA	MVJO	SJ92	27500	29B	D3
ESGOS	MVJO	SJ92		29D	C3
ESLA	MVJO	SJ91	27600	29B	D2
ESMALTE	MVJO	SJ92	21600	29B	E1
ESMERALDA CIR	MVJO	SJ91	26200	29D	B2
ESPALTER DR	MVJO	SJ91	26600	29B	B6
ESPALTER DR	MVJO	SJ91	26300	29D	B1
ESPANITA AV S	OR	OR	100	18	B3
ESPANITA ST	CO	OR	11200	18	B2
ESPANITA ST N	OR	OR	500	18	B2
ESPANITA ST S	OR	OR	200	18	B3
ESPEN CIR	FTNV	SA08	11600	22	C5
ESPERANZA	CO	SJ88		59	A4
ESPERANZA	CO	SJ88		59	B3
ESPERANZA	NB	NB		31	F2
ESPERANZA	NB	NB		32	A3
ESPERANZA AV	FTNV	SA08	9600	21	F6
ESPERANZA RD	CO	YL	19400	8	D5
ESPINOZA	MVJO	SJ92	27700	29B	D5
ESPIRIT WY	IRV	SA		24	D5
ESPLANADE	IRV	SA		28	E5
ESPLANADE	NB	NB		32	A3
ESPLANADE E&W	SCL	SC72	100	39	D4
ESPLANADE AV	CO	OR	11700	18	A3
ESPLANADE AV	CO	SA	11800	18	A6
ESPLANADE ST N	OR	OR	100	18	A3
ESPLANADE ST S	OR	OR	100	18	A3
ESPLENDOR	MVJO	SJ91		29B	C2
ESPORLAS	MVJO	SJ92		29B	D2
ESQUINA	MVJO	SJ91	27400	29B	C1
ESQUINA	NB	NB		31	F3
ESQUINA	NB	NB		32	A3
ESROSE CT	CO	ET	25300	29A	F4
ESSEX	HTB	HB		26	B2
ESSEX CIR	ANA	AN	2100	10	F6
ESSEX CIR	PLA	PLA	100	7	B4
ESSEX CIR	WSTM	WSTM	15200	22	A2
ESSEX DR	LAH	LAH	1300	2	B4
ESSEX DR	LALM	LALM	11000	14	D2
ESSEX LN	NB	NB	1100	31	E4
ESSEX PL	SA	SA	3000	28	B1
ESSEX ST	HTB	HB46		26	F3
ESSEX WY	CO	LAG		35	F3
ESTA CIR	HTB	HB47	6500	21	A4
ESTACIA AV	CO	LB	23800	35	D4
ESTALLENS	MVJO	SJ92	22400	29B	D2
ESTAMPIDA	SCL	SC72		38	E3
ESTANCIA	SCL	SC72		38	E4
ESTANCIERO DR	MVJO	SJ91	26300	29D	C2
ESTATE DR	LAH	LAH	1300	2	B4
ESTATE RIDGE RD	ANA	AN	5400	13	B3
ESTATES DR	VPK	OR67		13	B5
ESTEBAN	MVJO	SJ92		29D	C3
ESTELLA CIR	CO	LB77		35	C4
ESTELLE LN	NB	NB	1300	31	E3

STREET	CITY	P.O. ZONE	BLOCK	PAGE	GRID
ESTELLE LN	PLA	PLA		7	F6
ESTEPONA	MVJO	SJ91		29B	D1
ESTEPONA	MVJO	SJ91	27600	52	D6
ESTEPONA WY	BPK	BP		5	C3
ESTERO CIR	TUS	TUS	13600	24	A3
ESTES CIR	WSTM	WSTM	13000	15	B5
ESTES WY	CO	SA	18100	18	A5
ESTHER CIR	CYP	CYP	10100	9	D6
ESTHER CT	DPT	DPT	23000	37	E3
ESTHER ST	CM	CM27	200	31	E2
ESTHER ST	CYP	CYP	9100	9	D5
ESTIMA	MVJO	SJ92		29B	E5
ESTOCK DR	GGR	GG	12800	16	D3
ESTRADA CIR	MVJO	SJ91	26300	29B	B6
ESTRADA DR	CO	LB77		36	A3
ESTRALITA PL	FUL	FL	400	6	C1
ESTRELLA	CO	LB		35	E4
ESTRELLA	IRV	SA14		28	D4
ESTRELLA	TUS	TUS		23	D3
ESTRELLA LN	CO	SJ79		59	D2
ESTRIBO	SCL	SC72		38	F3
ESTRIBOS	MVJO	SJ92	24900	29B	D6
ESTRIBOS	MVJO	SJ92	24900	29D	D1
ESTUARY LN	HTB	HB	19700	26	D4
ETCHANDY LN	ANA	AN		7	D6
ETCHANDY LN	ANA	AN	1300	12	D1
ETHEL CIR	CYP	CYP	10400	9	D6
ETHELBEE WY	CO	SA	13000	17	E5
ETHELINDA WY	BREA	BREA	900	2	D3
ETHYL PL	ANA	AN	300	11	A4
ETNA CIR	BREA	BREA	300	7	D1
ETNA CIR	HTB	HB47	7700	21	C3
ETON CIR	HTB	HB47	15000	21	A2
ETON PL	ANA	AN	500	11	E5
ETON PL	NB	NB	1500	31	E4
ETON PL E	CO	SA	18400	18	A5
ETON PL N	CO	SA	13000	18	A5
EUCALYPTUS	IRV	SA		29	B5
EUCALYPTUS CIR	CYP	CYP	5000	9	D5
EUCALYPTUS DR	ANA	AN	21200	8	E6
EUCALYPTUS DR	CO	LB53		29	A4
EUCALYPTUS LN	BREA	BREA	1400	3	A6
EUCALYPTUS LN	CM	CM		27	E6
EUCALYPTUS LN	CO	ET	22200	29A	E6
EUCALYPTUS LN	FTNV	SA08	18100	26	F2
EUCALYPTUS PL	FUL	FL		7	A2
EUCALYPTUS ST	BREA	BREA	400	2	D6
EUCALYPTUS ST	BREA	BREA	1600	3	A6
EUCALYPTUS ST	TUS	TUS		24	D4
EUCALYPTUS TR	OR	OR		18	E2
EUCALYPTUS WY	ANA	AN		8	E6
EUCALYPTUS WY	LAH	LAH	400	1	E5
EUCALYPTS HL RD	YL	YL	5300	8	B4
EUCLID AV	OR	OR	3600	18	A2
EUCLID ST	CO	LAH	1300	2	A3
EUCLID ST	FTNV	SA08	15900	22	B5
EUCLID ST	FTNV	SA08	17600	27	B2
EUCLID ST	GGR	GG	11000	16	B6
EUCLID ST	GGR	GG43	14100	22	B1
EUCLID ST N&S	ANA	AN	100	11	B6
EUCLID ST N&S	FUL	FL	100	6	A6
EUCLID ST N&S	LAH	LAH	100	2	A6
EUCLID ST N&S	SA	SA	100	22	B5
EUCLID ST S	ANA	AN02	1400	16	B3
EUCLID ST S	FUL	FL	1000	11	B3
EUCLID ST S	LAH	LAH	1400	6	A1
EUCLID WY	ANA	AN	200	11	B4
EUDORA AV	BPK	BP	10200	9	F6
EUDORA CIR	CYP	CYP	10500	14	F1
EUDORA LN	GGR	GG	11500	16	C3
EUGENE DR	FUL	FL	1000	6	C4
EUGENE PL	ANA	AN	700	16	D2
EUGENE ST	ANA	AN	2000	16	D2
EUGENE ST	GGR	GG	11500	16	D2
EUGENIA WY	CM	CM		27	C6
EUNICE CIR	LAH	LAH	300	1	E5
EUNICE PL	CO	TUS	18600	24	A1
EUREKA AV	YL	YL	4200	7	F3
EUROPA DR	CM	CM	2800	27	E4
EVA ST	CO	LB56		29C	E3
EVANS CIR	FTNV	SA08	16100	22	C4
EVANS CIR	WSTM	WSTM	13100	15	B5
EVANSTON CIR	TUS	TUS	14600	23	F1
EVE CIR	PLA	PLA	400	7	B4
EVELYN CIR	HTB	HB	8200	26	C6
EVELYN DR	ANA	AN	100	11	F3
EVELYN PL	PLA	PLA	400	7	A6
EVELYNGLEN LN	LAH	LAH	900	1	F5
EVENING BREEZE	IRV	SA		32A	C4
EVNG BREEZE DR	YL	YL		40	E5

STREET	CITY	P.O. ZONE	BLOCK	PAGE	GRID
EVENING CYN RD	BREA	BREA	900	2	E4
EVENING CYN RD	NB	CDLM	200	33	B2
EVENING HILL DR	HTB	HB		26	A4
EVENING SHADOW	IRV	SA		32A	C4
EVENINGSIDE DR	CO	SA	12800	24	B3
EVENINGSIDE LN	CO	ET		29A	E1
EVENING SONG	IRV	SA		32A	C4
EVENINGSONG LN	ANA	AN08		43	B1
EVENING STAR	IRV	SA		32A	B3
EVENING STAR DR	ANA	AN	1100	11	F5
EVENING STAR DR	DPT	DPT		37	E4
EVENING STAR LN	NB	NB	700	31	E4
EVENING VIEW RD	ANA	AN	5300	13	B2
EVEREST CIR	CYP	CYP	4500	9	C4
EVEREST CIR	FTNV	SA08	16400	22	C4
EVEREST CIR	HTB	HB47	7700	21	C3
EVEREST ST	FTNV	SA08	16400	22	C4
EVERETT AV	OR	OR	2200	17	E2
EVERETT PL	OR	OR	100	17	C2
EVERETTE	MVJO	SJ92		29B	F6
EVEREVE CIR	CO	ET		29A	E3
EVERGLADE CIR	PLA	PLA	1500	7	E4
EVERGLADE ST	SA	SA	400	22	E4
EVERGLADES CIR	OR	OR		13	C5
EVERGLADES LN	HTB	HB	20100	26	F5
EVERGREEN	IRV	SA		29	D4
EVERGREEN AV	CYP	CYP	5000	9	D4
EVERGREEN AV	FUL	FL	1300	6	E2
EVERGREEN AV	YL	YL	18500	8	A3
EVERGREEN CIR	FTNV	SA08	16600	21	F5
EVERGREEN CIR	FTNV	SA08	18600	26	F2
EVERGREEN CIR	HTB	HB	17000	20	F6
EVERGREEN CIR	VPK	OR67		13	A6
EVERGREEN DR	BREA	BREA	1100	2	E4
EVERGREEN DR	CYP	CYP	9100	9	D5
EVERGREEN DR	TUS	TUS		24	D3
EVERGREEN LN	TUS	TUS		24	B4
EVERGREEN PL	CM	CM27	900	31	B2
EVERGREEN RD	CO	LB		29D	A2
EVERGREEN RD	SJC	SJ75		36	B2
EVERGREEN ST	ANA	AN	100	11	E2
EVERGREEN ST	SA	SA	1200	23	C5
EVERGREEN WY	STN	STN	7800	15	B3
EVERGREEN MDWS	GGR	GG		15	D3
EVITA DR	NB	NB	700	32	A6
EVON LN	SA	SA	1900	16	E5
EVONDA ST	SA	SA	900	22	B1
EVORA	WSTM	WSTM		21	E2
EWELL WY	STN	STN	7300	15	B2
EXBURY CT	SA	SA01		23	E1
EXECUTIVE CIR	IRV	SA		28	C3
EXECUTIVE DR	CO	ET		29A	F3
EXECUTIVE DR	CYP	CYP		14	E1
EXECUTIVE PARK	IRV	SA		28	C3
EXETER	IRV	SA		32	E1
EXETER AV	LAH	LAH	500	1	F5
EXETER AV	LAH	LAH		2	A5
EXETER CIR	LAH	LAH	400	2	A5
EXETER PL	OR	OR	600	17	F4
EXETER ST	WSTM	WSTM	15700	22	A4
EXMOOR	MVJO	SJ92		29D	D1
EXMOOR DR	SB	SB	13000	19	C5
EXPLORER ST	BREA	BREA	500	2	D5
EXPRESS DR	CO	LB		29C	F1
EXPRESS DR	CO	LB	25400	29D	A1
EXTON WY	CO	ET		29B	A1

F

STREET	CITY	P.O. ZONE	BLOCK	PAGE	GRID
F ST	LAG	LB		35	A4
F ST	ETMC	SA09		51	A4
F ST	HTB	HB		26	C6
F ST	NB	NB	100	33	C5
F ST	TUS	CDLM	300	23	F2
FABRIANO	IRV	SA		24	D5
FACINAS	MVJO	SJ91	22500	29B	D2
FACULTY CIR	BPK	BP	6900	10	D1
FAEROE BAY	DPT	LB77		37	E4
FAGAN PL	GGR	GG	8000	15	C5
FAHRINGER WY	LAH	LAH	1200	1	F4
FAHRION PL	ANA	AN	100	11	E3
FAIR DR	CM	CM	100	27	E5
FAIR WY	SA	SA	900	22	E1
FAIRBAIRN ST	OR	OR	3800	12	D3
FAIRBANKS	CO	SA		51	D5
FAIRBANKS	IRV	SA18		51	D6
FAIRBROOK	MVJO	SJ92		29B	E1
FAIRBROOK LN	SA	SA	900	17	A4
FAIRBROOK WY	CM	CM		27	E5
FAIRCHILD RD	IRV	SA		28	C6
FAIRCHILD ST	GGR	GG45	11800	14	E3

STREET	CITY	P.O. ZONE	BLOCK	PAGE	GRID
FAIRCOURT LN	CO	LB53		29D	A4
FAIRCREST DR	ANA	AN	3200	10	A5
FAIRDAWN	IRV	SA		29	B4
FAIR ELMS	CO	LB77		36	A4
FAIRFAX DR	CM	CM27	500	31	C2
FAIRFIELD	IRV	SA		29	A4
FAIRFIELD CIR	HTB	HB	16900	20	C6
FAIRFIELD DR	NB	CDLM	4500	33	C2
FAIRFIELD LN	SB	SB	13100	19	C5
FAIRFIELD ST	ANA	AN		13	A3
FAIRFIELD WY	CYP	CYP		9	C5
FAIRFORD DR	FUL	FL33		5	E3
FAIRGLEN CT	SJC	SJ75		36	A3
FAIRGREEN	MVJO	SJ92		29D	E1
FAIRGREEN AV	CO	YL	19700	8	C6
FAIRGREEN DR	FUL	FL33		5	E3
FAIRGREENS E	CO	LB		35	D4
FAIRGREENS W	CO	LB		35	D4
FAIRHAVEN AV	CO	SA	16800	17	C4
FAIRHAVEN AV	CO	SA	18100	18	A4
FAIRHAVEN AV	OR	OR	1700	17	C4
FAIRHAVEN AV	SA	SA	1100	17	C4
FAIRHAVEN LN	CM	CM		27	E5
FAIRHAVEN ST	ANA	AN	400	11	A3
FAIRHAVEN EXT	CO	SA	12900	18	B4
FAIRHILL DR	CO	NB60	2300	31	E2
FAIRHOPE DR	CO	LAM	4500	5	C3
FAIRLAKE	IRV	SA		29	B4
FAIRLANE CIR	HTB	HB	21800	30	E2
FAIRLANE RD	CO	LAG		37	F2
FAIRLAWN ST	SA	SA	500	22	F2
FAIRLEE CT	ANA	AN		13	B3
FAIRLYNN BLVD	CO	YL	6200	8	C5
FAIRLYNN BLVD	YL	YL	6000	8	C5
FAIRMONT	CO	LB77		35	D5
FAIRMONT AV	SA	SA	2300	17	C5
FAIRMONT BLVD	ANA	AN	800	8	D6
FAIRMONT BLVD	ANA	AN08	100	13	D1
FAIRMONT BLVD	YL	YL	4200	8	C3
FAIRMONT BLVD	YL	YL		8	D1
FAIRMONT CIR	ANA	AN		13	E2
FAIRMONT CIR	WSTM	WSTM	8500	21	D3
FAIRMONT ST	OR	OR	300	17	E4
FAIRMONT ST	SA	SA	1600	17	C6
FAIRMONT WY	CO	OR69	12500	17	E5
FAIRMONT WY	CO	SA	13000	17	E5
FAIRMONT WY	OR	OR	600	17	E4
FAIRMONT WY	TUS	TUS	13500	17	E5
FAIR OAKS	CO	LB77		36	A4
FAIRSIDE	IRV	SA		29	A4
FAIR TIDE CIR	HTB	HB	9700	26	F4
FAIRVIEW AV	BPK	BP	5200	5	D4
FAIRVIEW CIR	BPK	BP	5100	5	D3
FAIRVIEW LN	CM	CM		27	E5
FAIRVIEW LN	HTB	HB	14300	20	F1
FAIRVIEW RD	CM	CM	2200	27	D4
FAIRVIEW RD	CM	CM27	2200	31	D1
FAIRVIEW RD	LAG	LB	31600	35	B5
FAIRVIEW ST	ANA	AN	900	10	F3
FAIRVIEW ST	ANA	AN	900	11	A3
FAIRVIEW ST	CO	SA06	13600	16	E6
FAIRVIEW ST	GGR	GG	13000	16	E6
FAIRVIEW ST	LAG	LB51	100	34	C2
FAIRVIEW ST N	SA	SA	1600	16	E6
FAIRVIEW ST N&S	SA	SA	100	22	E2
FAIRVIEW ST S	SA	SA04	2800	27	D2
FAIRWAY DR	CM	CM	2400	27	F6
FAIRWAY DR E	OR	OR	700	17	D4
FAIRWAY DR W	OR	OR	300	17	C4
FAIRWAY LN	ANA	AN		13	E3
FAIRWAY LN	HTB	HB	16200	20	F4
FAIRWAY LN	PLA	PLA	300	7	B4
FAIRWAY PL	CM	CM	200	27	F6
FAIRWY ISLES DR	FUL	FL		6	C2
FAIRWAY LN	CO	SJ79		59	C6
FAIRWAY VIEW DR	CO	YL	5000	8	B3
FAIRWAY VIEW DR	YL	YL	5000	8	B3
FAIRWEATHER RD	CO	SA	1900	24	C2
FAIRWINDS LN	CM	CM		27	E5
FAIRWOOD LN	CO	SA	18600	18	B5
FAIRYWOOD LN	LAG	LB51	1200	34	E2
FALCON AV	FTNV	SA08	10300	27	A2
FALCON DR	BPK	BP	7000	9	F1
FALCON LN	GGR	GG	12700	16	D3
FALCON ST	ANA	AN	300	11	A5
FALCON ST	CO	ET		29A	E2
FALCON CREST LN	CO	LB56		29C	A2
FALCONRIDGE RD	YL	YL		8	D1
FALENCIA	MVJO	SJ91		29B	B2
FALKIRK	MVJO	SJ91		29D	C5
FALKIRK LN	CO	ET		29B	A1

COPYRIGHT, © 1989 BY Thomas Bros Maps

1990 ORANGE COUNTY STREET INDEX

STREET	CITY	P.O. ZONE	BLOCK	PAGE	GRID
FALKIRK LN	CO	ET		52	A6
FALKIRK LN	HTB	HB	17600	25	E1
FALKLAND CIR	HTB	HB	3200	20	A5
FALL PL	ANA	AN	900	11	C3
FALLBROOK	CO	ET		29B	A3
FALLBROOK	HTB	HB		26	D6
FALLBROOK	IRV	SA		29	D3
FALLBROOK DR	SA	SA	2900	17	A4
FALLBROOK WY	STN	STN		15	B4
FALLCREEK CIR	BREA	BREA		3	A5
FALL CREEK CIR	CO	ET		29A	F2
FALLCREST	IRV	SA		29	C5
FALLENLEAF CIR	FTNV	SA08		26	E2
FALLEN LEAF PL	TUS	TUS	1900	24	A5
FALLEN LEAF RD	CO	ET	22300	29A	E2
FALLEN LEAF RD	YL	YL		8	E1
FALLEN LEAF ST	LAH	LAH	1300	2	B3
FALLEN OAK	CO	LB77		36	A3
FALLEN OAK LN	YL	YL	20300	8	F2
FALLENWOOD	CO	ET		29A	F1
FALLENWOOD	CO	ET		29B	A1
FALLENWOOD	CO	ET		51	F6
FALLENWOOD	CO	ET		52	A6
FALLING LEAF	IRV	SA		32A	A1
FALLING LEAF CIR	ANA	AN		13	F4
FALLING LEAF CIR	BREA	BREA		3	A5
FALLINGLEAF CIR	GGR	GG	11800	16	F2
FALLING LEAF DR	CO	LB53		29D	A4
FALLINGLEAF ST	GGR	GG	12000	16	D4
FALLING STAR	IRV	SA		29	C5
FALLINGWATER DR	HTB	HB	6200	26	A1
FALL RIVER CT	FTNV	SA08		27	A2
FALL RIVER RD	CO	SJ		56	D6
FALLS WY	BPK	BP		5	C4
FALMOUTH AV	ANA	AN	2000	10	F2
FALMOUTH AV	ANA	AN		11	A2
FALMOUTH DR	HTB	HB	8100	26	C3
FALMOUTH DR	TUS	TUS	13500	24	A3
FALMOUTH PL	TUS	TUS	13400	24	B3
FALMOUTH WK	WSTM	WSTM		14	D6
FAME CIR	HTB	HB	16000	20	C4
FANN PL	ANA	AN	600	11	A5
FANN ST	ANA	AN	300	11	A5
FANTASIA LN	HTB	HB	16000	20	D4
FANWOOD DR	HTB	HB		25	E1
FARAD ST	CM	CM27	700	31	C3
FARADAY	IRV	SA18		29A	C2
FARALLON DR	CM	CM	1800	27	B4
FARALLON DR	NB	NB		32	A6
FAREN DR	CO	SA	1200	18	C6
FARGO RD	CO	LB53		29C	F5
FARINELLA DR	HTB	HB47	6200	21	A5
FARMER LN	PLA	PLA		7	C4
FARMERS DR	SA	SA	2700	17	A5
FARMINGHAM CT	CO	LB		35	C4
FARMINGTON RD	TUS	TUS	13300	24	B3
FARNHAM AV	LALM	LALM	3400	9	C6
FARNHAM LN	CO	AN04	9600	10	E6
FARNHAM ST	FTNV	SA08	16300	22	B4
FARNSWORTH LN	HTB	HB	20500	26	D6
FAROLES	MVJO	SJ92	27800	29B	D6
FARQUHAR AV	LALM	LALM	3500	14	B2
FARRAGUT	IRV	SA		24	E6
FARRINGTON DR	LAH	LAH	1100	1	E3
FARTHING ST	CO	ET	25000	29A	F3
FARVIEW RD	FUL	FL33		5	E3
FARWELL AV	IRV	SA		24	D5
FASANO	IRV	SA		24	D5
FASHION LN	ANA	AN	1300	12	A2
FASHION LN	TUS	TUS	100	24	A2
FASHION ISLAND	NB	NB		32	A5
FASHION PARK ST	OR	OR	500	17	C4
FASHION SQ LN	LAH	LAH	1900	1	E6
FATHOM AV	SB	SB	900	19	E2
FATHOM CT	SJC	SJ75		38	A2
FATHOM DR	NB	CDLM		33	B1
FATHOM LN	ANA	AN	2000	10	F2
FATHOM LN	ANA	AN	2000	11	A2
FAULKNER CT	IRV	SA	3700	24	C6
FAULKNER DR	PLA	PLA	1800	7	C2
FAULKNER RD	IRV	LAG	30500	34	F5
FAUN LN	GGR	GG	11600	15	D3
FAUNA AV	ANA	AN	3900	12	E2
FAUST CIR	HTB	HB	8900	26	E5
FAWN	CO	ET		52	B6
FAWN CIR	YL	YL		8	E1
FAWN ST	SA	SA	1300	22	B1
FAWN GLEN	IRV	SA		29	C2
FAWNRIDGE AV	BREA	BREA		2	D3
FAWNRIDGE DR	BREA	BREA		2	D4
FAWN RIDGE RD	CO	SJ79		52	E3

STREET	CITY	P.O. ZONE	BLOCK	PAGE	GRID
FAWNWOOD LN	OR	OR69		18	E2
FAY CIR	SA	SA	4000	22	C1
FAY LN	ANA	AN	1100	11	C4
FAYE AV	GGR	GG	11000	16	A2
FAYETTE CIR	CM	CM26	600	28	A3
FAYETTE PL	LAG	LB51	1500	34	C2
FAYLEN DR	ANA	AN	200	10	C4
FAYWOOD AV	ANA	AN04	1600	15	F1
FAYWOOD AV	ANA	AN	1600	16	A1
FEATHER AV	PLA	PLA		7	B3
FEATHER AV	YL	YL		8	C4
FEATHER ST	ANA	AN	1200	11	C6
FEATHERGRASS	IRV	SA		29	B2
FTHR GRASS CIR	CO	SJ79		56	E6
FTHR GRASS LN	YL	YL		40	D6
FEATHERHILL DR	OR	OR		12	F4
FEATHERHILL DR	VPK	OR67	9500	12	F5
FEATHERHILL RD	TUS	TUS	14800	23	F5
FEATHER RIV WY	OR	OR		12	B5
FEATHERWOOD	IRV	SA		29	B6
FEDERAL AV	CM	CM	2200	27	B6
FEDERAL AV	CM	CM27	1900	31	B2
FEE LN	HTB	HB	20400	26	E5
FEE ANA ST	ANA	AN	900	12	F1
FEE ANA ST	PLA	PLA	600	7	F6
FELDNER RD N&S	OR	OR	100	17	B3
FELICIA CT	CO	SJ91		29A	E6
FELICIA DR	YL	YL		8	C3
FELICIDAD CIR	ANA	AN	2600	10	D3
FELICIDAD ST	ANA	AN	800	10	D3
FELIPA RD	YL	YL		8	E3
FELIPE	NB	NB	2100	32	A3
FELIPE	SCL	SCL		38	E4
FELIPE RD	MVJO	SJ92		29B	E6
FELIPE RD	MVJO	SJ92		29D	C4
FELIZ	NB	NB	400	32	A3
FELLCLIFF LN	HTB	HB	19700	26	D4
FELLOWS DR	CO	OR65	16300	12	D4
FELSON CIR	HTB	HB		25	E1
FELTHAM CIR	WSTM	WSTM		21	D4
FELTON DR	CO	LB	29600	35	C3
FEMES	MVJO	SJ92		29B	D3
FEN WY	LAG	LB51	800	34	E3
FENDER AV	FUL	FL	2400	6	F6
FENLEY DR	HTB	HB	6000	25	F1
FENLEY DR	LALM	LALM	3600	9	B6
FENN ST	IRV	SA	3500	28	F4
FENWAY DR	WSTM	WSTM	7000	15	B6
FENWICK DR	HTB	HB47	6700	21	A6
FENWICK LN	WSTM	WSTM	7100	21	B2
FENWICK PL	CO	SA	11100	18	C5
FEOLA CIR	HTB	HB47	15900	21	B4
FERGUSON CIR	HTB	HB47	8600	21	D5
FERGUSON GREEN	BPK	BP	8100	5	D4
FERN AV	BREA	BREA	1100	6	D1
FERN AV	DPT	DPT		37	D5
FERN AV	OR	OR	1800	12	E5
FERN AV	STN	STN	10100	10	C6
FERN AV	STN	STN	10500	15	C1
FERN CIR	HTB	HB46		30	E6
FERN CIR	SB	SB	12900	14	C5
FERN CIR	YL	YL		8	D2
FERN DR E	FUL	FL	500	6	D4
FERN DR W	FUL	FL33	1600	5	F5
FERN DR W	FUL	FL	300	6	B4
FERN ST	ANA	AN	1200	10	C6
FERN ST	ANA	AN	900	10	F3
FERN ST	ANA	AN	900	11	A3
FERN ST	GGR	GG	12700	15	C4
FERN ST	IRV	SA	3800	29	C1
FERN ST	LAG	LB51	200	34	E4
FERN ST	NB	NB63	100	30	F4
FERN ST	NB	NB	100	31	A4
FERN ST	STN	GG41	12700	15	C4
FERN ST N	OR	OR	1400	12	E6
FERN ST N	OR	OR	300	17	F2
FERN WY	LAH	LAH	2300	1	E4
FERNANDO AV	LAG	LB51	900	34	F3
FERNANDO CIR	VPK	OR67	18100	18	A1
FERNANDO ST	NB	NB	300	33	B5
FERNBANK	CO	ET	25600	29B	A3
FERNBANK	IRV	SA		29	D4
FERNBROOK	MVJO	SJ92		29B	E1
FERNBROOK DR	TUS	TUS	14100	24	A4
FERNBURY ST	CYP	CYP	9200	9	D5
FERN CANYON	IRV	SA		29	C2
FERN CREEK LN	YL	YL	20200	8	F2
FERNDALE AV	FUL	FL	900	6	E4
FERNDALE AV	OR	OR	700	12	D5
FERNDALE CIR	STN	STN		15	B4
FERNDALE DR	GGR	GG	13000	15	D5

STREET	CITY	P.O. ZONE	BLOCK	PAGE	GRID
FERNDALE PL	EBAY	LB51	200	34	B2
FERNDALE ST	ANA	AN	1300	10	E2
FERNE AV	CYP	CYP	6200	14	F1
FERNE AV	CYP	CYP	6500	15	A1
FERN GLEN	CO	ET		52	A5
FERNGLEN DR	YL	YL	19900	8	C5
FERNGREEN LN	CO	ET	22800	29A	D2
FERN HAVEN LN	ANA	AN	5300	13	B2
FERNHEATH LN	CM	CM	3000	27	D3
FERNHILL CIR	HTB	HB	5500	20	E5
FERN HILL LN	ANA	AN	400	12	E3
FERN LAKE AV	BREA	BREA		2	C5
FERNLEAF	IRV	SA		29	D3
FERNLEAF AV	NB	CDLM	100	33	A1
FERNLEAF DR	CO	ET		29B	A1
FERNPOINT CIR	HTB	HB		25	F1
FERNSIDE CIR	OR	OR	2500	12	C4
FERNSIDE ST	OR	OR	2600	12	C4
FERNWOOD AV	BREA	BREA		2	E4
FERNWOOD AV	OR	OR	3700	18	A4
FERNWOOD CT	FUL	FL		7	A1
FERNWOOD DR	GGR	GG	13600	16	B6
FERNWOOD DR	HTB	HB48		25	E3
FERNWOOD DR	SA	SA	2900	17	A4
FERNWOOD PZ	YL	YL	19800	8	C4
FERNWOOD ST	ANA	AN	500	11	E3
FERNWOOD ST	CO	ET		29A	E3
FERRARI LN	GGR	GG	12100	15	E3
FERRIS LN	GGR	GG	9200	15	E3
FERRIS ST	IRV	SA	3900	28	F4
FERROCARRIL	MVJO	SJ91	24300	29B	A5
FESTIVAL CIR	LAP	BP23	5300	9	E2
FESTIVO	MVJO	SJ92	27800	29B	D6
FESTIVO	MVJO	SJ92		29D	D1
FIBERGLASS RD	HTB	HB	18500	26	C3
FICHOT WY	CYP	CYP	11500	15	A2
FIDDLENECK	IRV	SA		29	B2
FIELD	IRV	SA		29	E1
FIELDBROOK	MVJO	SJ92		29B	E2
FIELDBROOK LN	CYP	CYP	4600	9	D4
FIELDBROOK LN	WSTM	WSTM	9400	21	F2
FIELDBURY LN	ANA	AN		13	E4
FIELDBURY LN	HTB	HB	18000	26	A2
FIELDCREST	MVJO	SJ92		29D	D1
FIELDCREST LN	OR	OR69		18	E3
FIELDFLOWER	IRV	SA		29	A5
FIELDGATE ST	GGR	GG	12200	15	C4
FIELDGATE ST	STN	GG41	12200	15	C4
FIELDING CT	CYP	CYP	10400	14	D5
FIELDING DR	TUS	TUS	13700	24	A3
FIELDPOINT	CO	SJ79		59	E3
FIELDSTON LN	HTB	HB47	15300	21	A3
FIELDSTONE DR	CO	SA	12800	17	F4
FIELDSTONE LN	GGR	GG		15	A6
FIERRO	IRV	SA14		29	A4
FIESTA	NB	NB	2200	32	A3
FIESTA PL	FUL	FL	400	6	B3
FIESTA WY	CO	TUS	17600	17	F6
FIESTA WY	CO	TUS	17500	23	F1
FIG AV	BREA	BREA	200	3	A6
FIG ST	FTNV	SA08	16200	21	E4
FIGARO CIR	HTB	HB	4000	20	C5
FIG TREE DR	TUS	TUS	2100	24	A5
FIGUEROA ST	GGR	GG	13700	16	C6
FIGUEROA ST N&S	SA	SA	100	22	C2
FIGWOOD LN	ANA	AN		11	E6
FIJI LN	HTB	HB46	19300	27	A3
FIJI ST	CYP	CYP	5900	14	F2
FILARE	IRV	SA		24	D5
FILBERT PL	BREA	BREA	1000	2	F5
FILBERT ST	FTNV	SA08	16300	21	F4
FILLMORE	IRV	SA		24	D6
FILLMORE CIR	BPK	BP	8600	10	B4
FILLMORE DR	BPK	BP	7000	10	B3
FILLMORE DR	CO	AN04	8100	15	C3
FILLMORE DR	STN	STN	8000	15	C3
FILLMORE WY	CM	CM	3000	27	E3
FINCH AV	FTNV	SA08	9800	26	F2
FINCH ST	ANA	AN	100	12	E2
FINCHLEY AV	WSTM	WSTM	10100	22	A2
FINISTERRA	MVJO	SJ92	27800	29B	F4
FINISTERRA	IRV	SA14		28	F3
FINISTERRE DR	HTB	HB	3800	20	C5
FINLEY AV	NB	NB	3200	31	B5
FINN LN	CO	SIL	29300	50	F2
FINNELL WY	PLA	PLA	900	7	C4
FIR	IRV	SA14		29	F3
FIR AV	ANA	AN	2100	10	F3
FIR AV	IRV	SA	14500	24	C6
FIR AV	IRV	SA	14700	29	C1

STREET	CITY	P.O. ZONE	BLOCK	PAGE	GRID
FIR AV	SB	SB	4200	14	D4
FIR CIR	LAP	BP23	5500	9	E1
FIR CIR	SB	SB	12700	14	D4
FIR CIR	YL	YL		8	D2
FIR DR	HTB	HB47	7600	21	C5
FIR LN	CO	LB		29D	A2
FIR ST	FTNV	SA08	18200	26	F1
FIR ST	OR	OR	100	17	B3
FIR ST E&W	BREA	BREA	100	6	E1
FIR WY	LAH	LAH	400	1	E5
FIRCREST DR	YL	YL	5400	8	B4
FIREBIRD	IRV	SA		29	C3
FIREBRAND CIR	GGR	GG	11800	16	D4
FIREBRAND LN	HTB	HB48	21000	26	A6
FIREBRAND ST	GGR	GG	12000	16	D4
FIRECREST LN	CO	LB51		29C	B2
FIRENZE ST	CO	LAG		35	F3
FIRENZE CRES	ANA	AN	5900	13	C2
FIRE OPAL	MVJO	SJ91		29D	C5
FIRESIDE AV	OR	OR	1600	12	E6
FIRESIDE CIR	IRV	SA	4100	29	C1
FIRESIDE DR	HTB	HB	9300	26	E6
FIRESTONE	IRV	SA		29	A4
FIRESTONE BLVD	BPK	BP	5800	5	A5
FIRESTONE CIR	HTB	HB48		25	E2
FIRESTONE CT	FTNV	SA08		27	A1
FIRETHORN	CO	SJ		59	C1
FIRETHORNE AV	FUL	FL	2600	6	D2
FIRETHORNE ST	BREA	BREA	800	6	D2
FIRTH GREEN	BPK	BP	8100	5	C3
FIRWOOD	CO	LB56		29C	C2
FIRWOOD	CO	ET		51	F5
FIRWOOD	IRV	SA		29	C4
FIRWOOD LN	ANA	AN		11	E6
FISCHBECK RD	CO	SA		18	B4
FISCHER AV	CM	CM26	200	28	A4
FISHER CIR	PLA	PLA	1500	7	B3
FISHER DR	HTB	HB	4100	20	C5
FISHER LN	CO	SA		18	B4
FISHERMANS DR	DPT	DPT		38	D3
FITCH	IRV	SA		28	C2
FITZSIMONS LN	IRV	SA		24	F5
FIVE HARBORS DR	HTB	HB	9000	26	E6
FLAG COM	SA	SA		22	C2
FLAGG LN	HTB	HB	16900	20	E5
FLAGSHIP CIR	HTB	HB	19000	26	C3
FLAGSHIP RD	NB	NB	400	31	C4
FLAGSTAFF CT	SB	SB		19	F2
FLAGSTAFF CT	SB	SB		20	A2
FLAGSTAFF LN	HTB	HB		26	D3
FLAGSTAR CIR	IRV	SA	4900	29	D2
FLAGSTONE	IRV	SA		29	B2
FLAGSTONE AV	GGR	GG	12000	16	C5
FLAGSTONE LN	HTB	HB		26	D4
FLAGSTONE PL	GGR	GG	12400	16	D5
FLAME FLOWER LN	FUL	FL33		5	F4
FLAMENCO	MVJO	SJ92	21500	29B	E1
FLAMETREE	CO	ET		52	C4
FLAME TREE CIR	FTNV	SA08		21	F6
FLAME TREE ST	FTNV	SA08	17200	21	F6
FLAMINGO AV	FTNV	SA08	9800	26	F2
FLAMINGO CIR	HTB	HB	5000	20	D3
FLAMINGO CT	CO	LB77		36	B4
FLAMINGO DR	BPK	BP	6000	9	F1
FLAMINGO DR	CM	CM	1900	27	B5
FLAMINGO DR	GGR	GG	11600	15	F3
FLAMINGO RD	LAG	LB51	900	34	E3
FLAMINGO WY	LAH	LAH	900	2	C3
FLAMINIAN WY	CO	SA	1100	18	B6
FLANDERS CT	BREA	BREA		3	B6
FLANDERS ST	OR	OR	2300	12	C5
FLANNER AV	GGR	GG	10000	15	F2
FLAX CIR	HTB	HB	20200	26	D5
FLAXMAN DR	HTB	HB		26	D4
FLAXWOOD	IRV	SA		29	C4
FLECHAS	MVJO	SJ92	28200	29B	E5
FLEET LN	HTB	HB	21300	30	E1
FLEET RD	VPK	OR67	9700	12	F5
FLEETWOOD AV	CYP	CYP	4000	9	C5
FLEETWOOD ST	CYP	CYP	9200	9	C5
FLEMING	IRV	SA18		29A	D1
FLEMING AV	PLA	PLA	300	7	B2
FLEMING ST	WSTM	WSTM		22	A2
FLETCHER AV	CO	OR65	15700	12	C4
FLETCHER AV E&W	OR	OR	100	12	C4
FLETCHER DR	GGR	GG	12500	15	F4
FLETCHER PL	CO	LB53		29D	A4
FLETCHER ST	GGR	GG	13200	15	F5
FLETCHER ST	OR	OR		12	B5
FLETCHER GREEN	BPK	BP	8100	5	C4
FLICKER AV	FTNV	SA08	9200	26	E2

STREET	CITY	P.O. ZONE	BLOCK	PAGE	GRID
FLICKER CT	ANA	AN		13	F2
FLIGHT AV	CO	MDWY	8300	21	D3
FLIGHT AV	SA	SA	3300	22	B3
FLINT CIR	GGR	GG	12300	16	D5
FLINT DR	CO	SA	12800	17	F5
FLINT DR	HTB	HB47	6200	21	A4
FLINT DR	TUS	TUS	13500	17	F5
FLINT PL	GGR	GG	12400	16	D5
FLINTLOCK LN	CO	LB		29D	A3
FLINTLOCK WY	ANA	AN	4000	12	E3
FLINTRIDGE	IRV	SA		32A	A3
FLINTRIDGE DR	FUL	FL	3100	6	A1
FLINTRIDGE DR	SA	SA	4900	22	B3
FLINTRIDGE DR	VPK	OR67	10200	13	A6
FLINTSTONE LN	HTB	HB		20	F6
FLINTSTONE LN	HTB	HB	17500	26	A1
FLINTWOOD	IRV	SA		29	B1
FLIPPEN CIR	ANA	AN	1500	16	B2
FLIPPEN CT	ANA	AN	1500	16	B2
FLIPPEN DR	ANA	AN	1800	16	B2
FLIPPEN WY	ANA	AN	1500	16	B2
FLOE DR	CO	ET	24200	29A	E4
FLORA DR	YL	YL	18300	8	A4
FLORA LN	HTB	HB	20300	26	E5
FLORA ST	LAG	LB51	300	34	E4
FLORA ST E	SA	SA	100	23	B5
FLORA ST W	SA	SA	1500	22	E6
FLORAMAR	CO	SJ		56	C1
FLORAMAR	CO	SJ		59	C1
FLOR DE JARDIN	CO	SJ88		59	B5
FLOR DE MAR	CO	SJ88		59	B5
FLOR DE SOL	CO	SJ88		59	B5
FLORE ST	ANA	AN	900	11	C5
FLORECITA	CO	SJ		59	D1
FLORENCE AV	ANA	AN	200	11	E5
FLORENCE AV	BPK	BP	10100	9	F6
FLORENCE AV	LAG	LB	31600	35	B5
FLORENCE AV	CYP	CYP	10500	14	F1
FLORENCE AV	WSTM	WSTM	10400	22	A3
FLORENCE AV E&W	LAH	LAH	100	2	A4
FLORENCE AV W	LAH	LAH	500	1	F4
FLORENCE CIR	ANA	AN		13	A2
FLORENCE CIR	HTB	HB47	15400	21	A3
FLORENCE CIR	VPK	OR67	9000	12	F5
FLORENCE CT	LAH	LAH	300	2	B4
FLORENCE DR	ANA	AN		8	C6
FLORENCE DR	ANA	AN		13	C1
FLORENCE LN	GGR	GG	9200	15	E3
FLORENCE PL	FUL	FL33	200	5	F6
FLORENCE WY	CM	CM26		27	C6
FLORES	IRV	SA		28	E6
FLORES AV	CO	LB	23800	35	E4
FLORESTA LN	MVJO	SJ91	25000	29D	C1
FLORETTE ST	ANA	AN	200	11	A5
FLORIDA CIR	CM	CM		27	B2
FLORIDA PL	ANA	AN	1200	11	E4
FLORIDA ST	HTB	HB	19200	26	C4
FLORIDA ST N	HTB	HB	800	26	C5
FLORIN LN	CO	AN04	10200	10	E6
FLORISTA ST	LALM	LALM	3300	14	A1
FLOSSMOOR	CO	SJ79		59	D3
FLOUNDER DR	HTB	HB	9500	26	E3
FLOWER AV	BREA	BREA	100	2	E6
FLOWER AV	BREA	BREA	600	6	E1
FLOWER AV	FTNV	SA08	11000	22	B4
FLOWER AV	FUL	FL33	1400	5	E6
FLOWER AV	FUL	FL33	1600	10	D1
FLOWER AV	STN	STN	10500	15	C2
FLOWER CIR	OR	OR		17	B4
FLOWER LN	HTB	HB47		21	B6
FLOWER ST	ANA	AN	1200	11	E3
FLOWER ST	CM	CM27	100	31	D2
FLOWER ST	GGR	GG	12500	15	F4
FLOWER ST	GGR	GG		16	A4
FLOWER ST	GGR	GG	14100	21	F1
FLOWER ST	GGR	WSTM		15	F6
FLOWER ST	GGR	WSTM		16	A6
FLOWER ST	GGR	WSTM		21	F1
FLOWER ST N	SA	SA	1700	17	A6
FLOWER ST N&S	OR	OR	100	17	A3
FLOWER ST N&S	SA	SA	100	23	A4
FLOWER ST S	SA	SA	2800	28	A2
FLOWER CREEK LN	YL	YL	6200	8	F2
FLOWER GATE LN	YL	YL	20300	8	F2
FLOWER GLEN	CO	ET		52	A5
FLOWER HILL ST	BREA	BREA		3	C6
FLOWERIDGE CIR	CO	LB77		36	A3
FLOWERWOOD AV	OR	OR69		18	E3
FLOYD AV	ANA	AN	2900	10	C4
FLOYD CIR	SA	SA	4600	22	B2
FLYING CLOUD DR	CO	LB	31500	35	C6

1990 ORANGE COUNTY STREET INDEX

STREET	CITY	P.O. ZONE	BLOCK	PAGE	GRID
FLYING E LN	CO	OR		18	C1
FLYINGFISH CIR	FTNV	SA08	10500	22	A6
FLYING JIB DR	DPT	LB77		37	E4
FLYNN LN	GGR	GG	11000	15	F2
FOGO WY	CYP	CYP	6900	15	B3
FOLEY DR	YL	YL	17000	7	E3
FOLEY PL	OR	OR	200	17	C3
FOLKSTONE CIR	HTB	HB		30	E3
FOLSOM ST	ANA	AN04	2000	15	F1
FOLSOM ST	ANA	AN	1900	16	A1
FONDA	MVJO	SJ92		29B	E6
FONDA ST N	LAH	LAH	100	2	B5
FONDA ST S	LAH	LAH	100	2	B5
FONDREN ST	GGR	GG	13000	16	E5
FONDREN ST	OR	OR68	800	16	E4
FONTAINBLEAU AV	CYP	CYP	4200	9	C3
FONTAINBLEAU WY	CO	CO	4500	9	D3
FONTAINE AV	IRV	SA	15400	29	C3
FONTANA WY	LAG	LB51	600	34	F4
FONTIVEROS	MVJO	SJ91		29D	C2
FOOTHILL BLVD	CO	SA	12900	18	B5
FOOTHILL BLVD	CO	SA	1900	24	D1
FOOTHILL BLVD	TUS	TUS		24	D1
FOOTHILL BLVD E	CO	SA	18700	18	B5
FOOTHILL DR	CO	OR67	28700	50	E6
FOOTHILL DR	FUL	FL33		5	F2
FOOTHILL LN	BREA	BREA		3	B6
FOOTHILL LN	CO	SA		18	C6
FOOTHILL ST	ANA	AN08		40	A6
FOOTHILL ST	ANA	AN		43	A1
FOOTHILL ST	FTNV	SA08	16400	22	C5
FORBES AV	GGR	GG43		22	B1
FORBES DR	BREA	BREA		2	F4
FORBES LN	HTB	HB	17300	20	F6
FORBES RD	CO	LB	27900	29D	B6
FORD AV N	FUL	FL	300	6	B4
FORD AV S	FUL	FL	500	6	B5
FORD DR	HTB	HB47	7000	21	B6
FORD DR	PLA	PLA		7	E5
FORD RD	CM	CM27	400	31	D2
FORD RD	NB	NB		32	B4
FORDHAM AV	SA	SA		22	D5
FORDHAM CIR	ANA	AN		13	E4
FORDHAM DR	CM	CM	2200	27	D6
FORDHAM DR	PLA	PLA	500	7	C5
FORDHAM ST	WSTM	WSTM	13600	14	E6
FORDVIEW ST	CO	ET	24100	29A	E5
FORELLE DR	HTB	HB	8000	26	C2
FOREST	IRV	SA		29	B5
FOREST AV	LAG	LB51	200	34	D2
FOREST AV	SA	SA04	3200	27	F1
FOREST AV	YL	YL		8	D1
FOREST AV N	SA	SA	1700	16	F6
FOREST AV S	SA	SA	400	22	F5
FOREST CIR	SA	SA	700	22	F3
FOREST DR	GGR	GG		16	D4
FOREST LN	ANA	AN	1400	11	E2
FOREST LN	ANA	AN04	2000	15	F1
FOREST LN	HTB	HB	17600	26	D1
FOREST PL	BREA	BREA	200	2	E5
FOREST ST	CYP	CYP	6600	15	A1
FOREST ST	OR	OR		13	C5
FOREST ST	SA	SA	300	22	F2
FORESTERRA LN	TUS	TUS	1300	23	F4
FOREST GLEN RD	ANA	AN		12	F3
FOREST GLEN RD	YL	YL		8	D1
FOREST HILL	CO	ET	22400	29A	F2
FOREST HILLS CT	DPT	LB77		37	D2
FOREST HILLS LN	HTB	HB		20	C4
FOREST KNOLL LN	CO	ET	24700	29A	E2
FOREST LAKE	SA	SA		17	D5
FOREST LAKE DR	BREA	BREA		2	C5
FOREST MEADOW	CO	ET	21200	52	C6
FOREST RIDGE DR	CO	ET		52	B5
FOREST RIM CIR	CO	ET		29A	E2
FOREST SPG DR	SA	SA		22	D1
FORESTVIEW DR	BREA	BREA		2	D3
FORESTWOOD	CO	ET		29A	F1
FORESTWOOD	CO	ET		51	F6
FORESTWOOD	CO	ET		52	A6
FORESTWOOD DR	FUL	FL33		5	E2
FORMELLO	CO	LB		29A	B5
FORMENTOR	MVJO	SJ92	22400	29B	D3
FORMOSA DR	DPT	DPT	34000	37	C5
FORREST LN	WSTM	WSTM	14600	22	A2
FORRESTAL CT	LALM	LALM		14	C3
FORRESTAL DR	HTB	HB	10000	26	F4
FORRESTAL LN	SB	SB		20	A2
FORRY LN	SA	SA	300	22	C2
FORSTER ST	SJC	SJ75	26800	38	C1
FORSTER CYN RD	SJC	SJ75	32700	38	C2

STREET	CITY	P.O. ZONE	BLOCK	PAGE	GRID
FORSTER RCH RD	SCL	SC72		39	C1
FORSTER RCH RD	SJC	SJ75		38	B3
FORSYTH LN	GGR	GG	14100	21	F1
FORT RD	OR	OR69		18	E3
FORT APACHE CIR	CO	ET	26900	29B	C1
FORTNEY DR	CO	AN04	11700	15	C3
FORTROSE	MVJO	SJ91		29D	C5
FORT SUMTER	IRV	SA		24	E4
FORTUNA	IRV	SA		24	E5
FORTUNA	NB	NB	2200	32	A3
FORTUNA LN	MVJO	SJ91	22800	29B	B3
FORTUNE	IRV	SA18		51	A6
FORTUNE DR	CO	ET		29A	D3
FORUM WY	CO	SA	11500	18	C5
FOSS LN	HTB	HB		25	F2
FOSTER LN	ETMC	SA09		51	D3
FOSTER RD	CO	LALM	11200	14	A3
FOSTER ST	FTNV	SA08		26	F1
FOSTORIA ST	ANA	AN	1900	16	B2
FOSTORIA ST	GGR	GG	11100	16	B2
FOUNDATION AV	LAH	LAH	100	2	A6
FOUNTAIN LN	HTB	HB47	16500	21	A5
FOUNTAIN ST	IRV	SA		29	C2
FOUNTAIN WY	ANA	AN	1100	12	D1
FOUNTAIN WY E	CM	CM	2200	27	C6
FOUNTAIN WY W	CM	CM	2200	27	C6
FOUNTN ARBOR DR	OR	OR	2500	12	F4
FOUNTN ARBOR DR	OR	OR		13	A4
FOUNTAIN PK LN	SA	SA		22	D1
FOWLER AV	CO	SA	18600	18	B4
FOWLER CIR	WSTM	WSTM	10000	21	F2
FOX CIR	HTB	HB	7800	26	C2
FOX DR	FUL	FL	1400	6	B3
FOXBERG RD	SB	SB	1000	19	C5
FOXBORO	IRV	SA		29	B5
FOXBOROUGH	CO	LB56		29C	C4
FOXBOROUGH CT	CO	YL		8	C6
FOXBOROUGH PL	FUL	FL33	2100	5	D4
FOXBOROUGH WY	CO	ET		29B	A3
FOXCROFT RD	TUS	TUS	14800	24	A5
FOXDALE AV	LAH	LAH	2400	1	D4
FOXDALE DR	LAH	LAH	2100	1	E4
FOXDALE LN	ANA	AN		13	E3
FOXFIELD LN	YL	YL		8	B5
FOXFIRE ST	ANA	AN	1200	11	B2
FOX GLEN	CO	ET		52	C4
FOXGLEN	IRV	SA		29	A4
FOX GLEN DR	ANA	AN		13	D2
FOXGLOVE AV	FTNV	SA08	9000	21	E4
FOXGLOVE RD	TUS	TUS	14000	24	A4
FOXGLOVE ST	BREA	BREA		3	C6
FOXGLOVE WY	IRV	SA	18100	28	F6
FOXHALL DR	HTB	HB	8100	30	C1
FOXHILL	IRV	SA	15300	29	C2
FOX HILLS AV	BPK	BP	5100	5	C4
FOX HILLS PL	BPK	BP	8200	5	C4
FOX HILLS ST	WSTM	WSTM	15500	21	D3
FOX HOLLOW	CO	SJ79		59	E3
FOX HOLLOW	IRV	SA		29	A4
FOXHOLLOW DR	YL	YL		8	E1
FOXRIDGE	MVJO	SJ92		29B	E3
FOX RUN LN	OR	OR69		18	E2
FOX RUN LN	SJC	SJ75		36	E4
FOXRUN RD	CO	SA		18	D4
FOXSHIELD DR	HTB	HB		25	F1
FOX SPRINGS RD	CO	SA	10000	18	E4
FOXTAIL	MVJO	SJ92		52	D6
FOXTAIL DR	YL	YL		40	B4
FOXTON CIR	ANA	AN		8	E5
FOXWOOD	MVJO	SJ92		29B	E2
FOXWOOD AV	BREA	BREA		2	D5
FOXWOOD DR	FUL	FL33		5	E2
FOXWOOD PL	FUL	FL33		5	E2
FRALEY ST	CO	AN04	10900	15	E2
FRALEY ST	GGR	GG	11000	15	E2
FRAMPTON AV	OR	OR	200	17	B3
FRANCES AV	FUL	FL	1200	6	C4
FRANCES AV	GGR	GG	10600	16	A5
FRANCES DR	ANA	AN	1400	11	B3
FRANCES ST	WSTM	WSTM	14000	20	E1
FRANCIS AV E&W	LAH	LAH	100	2	A4
FRANCIS DR	ANA	AN	1700	11	A3
FRANCIS LN	CM	CM	2800	27	F4
FRANCISCA WY	CO	YL	19300	8	B4
FRANCISCAN CIR	HTB	HB	8500	26	D3
FRANCISCAN ST	IRV	SA	14500	29	C1
FRANCISCO DR	NB	NB	400	31	E2
FRANCISCO DR	NB	NB	2100	31	E2
FRANCISCO DR	VPK	OR67	18100	18	A1
FRANCISCO PL	ANA	AN	200	13	C2
FRANCISCO ST	ANA	AN	100	13	C2

STREET	CITY	P.O. ZONE	BLOCK	PAGE	GRID
FRANCOIS DR	HTB	HB		20	B6
FRANK ST	CO	OR	20000	13	C6
FRANKFORT AV E	HTB	HB	100	26	C6
FRANKFORT AV W	HTB	HB	100	26	C6
FRANKI ST	OR	OR	2500	12	D4
FRANKLIN AV	FUL	FL33	3700	5	D6
FRANKLIN AV	TUS	TUS	14500	24	B5
FRANKLIN CIR	WSTM	WSTM	13400	14	E5
FRANKLIN DR	HTB	HB	7700	26	C2
FRANKLIN DR	PLA	PLA	300	7	B5
FRANKLIN ST	BPK	BP	7300	5	B5
FRANKLIN ST	SA	SA	400	22	F2
FRANKLIN HLS DR	FUL	FL33		5	E4
FRANMAR CIR	HTB	HB	5900	20	F5
FRANS LN	HTB	HB	17300	20	E6
FRANTZ AV	LAH	LAH	2000	2	C4
FRANZEN AV	SA	SA	1500	17	D5
FRASER LN	HTB	HB47	17200	21	A6
FRAZER RIV CIR	FTNV	SA08	8600	26	D1
FRED DR	CYP	CYP	6000	9	F5
FREDERICK CIR	HTB	HB	9800	26	F4
FREDERICK ST	PLA	PLA	1900	7	B2
FREDRICK DR	GGR	GG	11200	16	B3
FREDRICK DR	VPK	OR67	10400	17	F1
FREEBORN DR	HTB	HB47	6300	21	A6
FREEDMAN WY	ANA	AN	500	16	D1
FREEDOM AV	ANA	AN	300	11	C1
FREEDOM AV	OR	OR65	600	12	C4
FREEMAN LN	SA	SA	2600	17	A5
FREEMAN ST	SA	SA	2000	17	A6
FREEMAN ST	SA	SA	800	23	A1
FREEPORT	MVJO	SJ92		29B	D2
FREEPORT LN	HTB	HB	21000	30	C2
FREMONT	IRV	SA		29	E1
FREMONT AV	PLA	PLA	2100	7	B2
FREMONT LN	CM	CM	2700	27	E4
FREMONT ST	ANA	AN	1300	10	A6
FREMONT ST	FTNV	SA08	17500	26	F1
FREMONT ST	NB	NB		31	A6
FREMONT WY	BPK	BP	6100	9	F2
FRENCH ST	SA	SA	1600	17	B5
FRENCH ST	SA	SA	100	23	B2
FRESCA	MVJO	SJ91		29B	C4
FRESCA DR	LAP	BP23	5900	9	E1
FRESE LN	LAP	BP23		9	E3
FRESH MEADOW LN	SB	SB	13800	19	C6
FRESHWATER CIR	HTB	HB	18000	26	A2
FRESNO CIR	HTB	HB		26	D6
FRESNO DR	MVJO	SJ91		29B	B3
FRIAR PL	FUL	FL	100	6	B2
FRIARSCOURT DR	HTB	HB	9500	26	F6
FRIEDA PL	GGR	GG	12400	16	A4
FRIENDS CT	IRV	SA	17500	28	F4
FRIESLAND DR	HTB	HB47	8200	21	C6
FRIGATE DR	CO	LB77		37	D1
FRIML LN	HTB	HB	17000	20	E6
FRIPPS WY	CYP	CYP	11600	15	A2
FRITCH DR	HTB	HB	6000	25	F1
FRONT ST	CO	ET	25000	29A	F4
FRONTERA ST	ANA	AN	3000	12	C2
FRONTIER CIR	HTB	HB	5800	20	F1
FRONTIER CT	ANA	AN		13	C3
FROST CIR	BPK	BP	6800	10	A1
FROSTWOOD ST	ANA	AN08		40	A6
FROSTWOOD ST	ANA	AN		43	A1
FRUIT ST	SA	SA	1000	23	C1
FRY CIR	HTB	HB	8800	30	E1
FRYE CT	TUS	SA10		29	B1
FUCHSIA	IRV	SA		29	A1
FUCHSIA	MVJO	SJ91		52	D5
FUCHSIA CIR	PLA	PLA	1000	7	C4
FUCHSIA CIR	SB	SB	12600	14	C4
FUCHSIA ST	CM	CM	3300	27	E2
FUCHSIA ST	SB	SB	12700	14	C4
FUENTE	CO	SJ88		29B	F5
FUENTES	NB	NB	2100	32	A3
FUERTE	MVJO	SJ91		29B	D1
FUJI WY	SA	SA		22	C3
FULCRUM PL	ANA	AN	2500	10	E4
FULLER ST	SA	SA	1000	23	C1
FULLERTON AV	BPK	BP	5500	5	B5
FULLERTON AV	CM	CM27	1700	31	C3
FULLERTON AV	NB	NB	300	31	D4
FULLERTON CK DR	FUL	FL	2000	6	E4
FULMER DR	GGR	GG	11100	16	A2
FULMAR LN	CO	LB56		29A	A6
FULTON	IRV	SA		29	E1
FULTON ST	ANA	AN	1200	10	F2
FULTON WY	STN	STN	7000	15	A2
FURLONG DR	CO	SA		18	D5

STREET	CITY	P.O. ZONE	BLOCK	PAGE	GRID
FURMAN AV	WSTM	WSTM	8200	21	D4
FURMAN RD	LAP	BP23	7700	9	E2
FURNACE CK RD	YL	YL	5700	8	C5
FUSCHIA LN	TUS	TUS		24	B4
FUTURA DR	YL	YL	19900	8	C4
G					
G ST	LAG	LB		35	A4
G ST	ETMC	SA09		51	A4
G ST	NB	NB	100	33	C5
GABLE LN	LAH	LAH		2	B5
GABLE ST	DPT	SC24		38	D6
GABLE ST	DPT	SC24	27500	39	A1
GABLES	HTB	HB		20	C3
GABLES LN	WSTM	WSTM		21	E2
GABRIELINO DR	IRV	SA17		32	E2
GAETA	CO	LB77		35	E4
GAFF ST	OR	OR	2600	12	D4
GAGE AV	FUL	FL33	1500	10	E1
GAGE AV	FUL	FL	500	11	A1
GAGE PL	FUL	FL33	2300	10	E1
GAIL LN	ANA	AN	1800	16	B2
GAIL LN	GGR	GG	11500	16	B3
GAIN ST	ANA	AN	100	10	E5
GAINES CIR	GGR	GG	13600	16	B5
GAINES WY	BPK	BP	6200	9	F2
GAINESMILL	IRV	SA		29	E1
GAINFORD CIR	IRV	SA	14900	29	D2
GAINSBOROUGH DR	LAG	LB51	500	34	E4
GAINSBOROUGH PL	LAG	LB51	600	34	E4
GAINSBOROUGH RD	OR	OR	3000	17	F4
GAINSBOROUGH WY	LAG	LB51	600	34	E4
GAINSBOROUGH WK	WSTM	WSTM		14	D6
GAINSFORD LN	HTB	HB		25	E1
GAINSPORT CIR	IRV	SA	4900	29	D2
GALANO WY	SJC	SJ75	31400	36	C6
GALANTO	IRV	SA14		28	D5
GALAPAGOS LN	DPT	DPT		38	A2
GALATEA TER	NB	CDLM	1900	32	A6
GALAXY	IRV	SA		32A	B2
GALAXY CIR	BPK	BP	8300	10	C3
GALAXY DR	NB	NB	1400	31	F3
GALAXY DR	WSTM	WSTM	16300	21	E4
GALAXY LN	CO	ET	23000	29A	F3
GALBAR CIR	HTB	HB46	10000	31	A1
GALEN DR	LAG	LB51	1500	34	E4
GALEN DR N	LAH	LAH	700	1	D4
GALEN DR W	LAH	LAH	2400	1	D4
GALENA AV	FTNV	SA08	11800	22	C5
GALICIA LN	HTB	HB	17700	26	B1
GALILEA	MVJO	SJ92	22500	29B	D3
GALILEO	IRV	SA		32A	A3
GALINA WY	CO	LB77		35	C2
GALIPEAN DR	HTB	HB		25	F1
GALIPEAN DR	HTB	HB	6100	25	F2
GALLANT DR	HTB	HB	8800	26	E5
GALLARDOS	MVJO	SJ92		29B	E2
GALLATIN ST	FTNV	SA08	16000	21	E4
GALLEON WY	DPT	DPT		37	E3
GALLEON WY	SB	SB	200	19	E2
GALLEON WY	SJC	SJ75		38	A2
GALLERY WY	TUS	TUS		24	D2
GALLEY AV	OR	OR	2600	12	D4
GALLEY DR	HTB	HB	8300	30	D1
GALLINA	MVJO	SJ92	27900	29B	D6
GALLIO DR	FUL	FL33		5	D3
GALLOWAY GREEN	BPK	BP21	8100	5	D4
GALLUP CIR	CO	LB	25400	29C	F2
GALVEZ LN	MVJO	SJ91		29D	C4
GALWAY CIR	HTB	HB	5000	20	E3
GALWAY DR	CO	ET		29B	A1
GALWAY DR	CO	ET		52	A6
GALWAY LN	CM	CM	1300	27	D3
GALWAY ST	GGR	GG	12900	15	E5
GALWAY ST	PLA	PLA	1400	7	C4
GALWAY ST	WSTM	WSTM	14500	21	F1
GALY ST	CO	TUS	14200	23	F1
GAMBLE AV	GGR	GG	9800	15	F2
GAMMA PL	ANA	AN	400	11	E4
GAMMA ST	GGR	GG	12200	16	B4
GANADERO	CO	SJ88		59	A5
GANADO	SCL	SC72		38	E4
GANADO DR	SJC	SJ75		36	D6
GANADO RD	SJC	SJ75	31400	36	C6
GANGES LN	HTB	HB47	16100	21	C4
GANIZA	MVJO	SJ92		29D	C3
GANNET DR	CM	CM	2600	27	B5
GANNET LN	FTNV	SA08	9200	26	E1
GANNET LN	NB	SA07		28	B6
GANNET LN	NB	SA07		32	B1

STREET	CITY	P.O. ZONE	BLOCK	PAGE	GRID
GANSO	MVJO	SJ91		29B	C4
GARD CT	TUS	SA10		29	A2
GARDEN CIR	HTB	HB		26	B3
GARDEN DR	ANA	AN04	1600	15	F1
GARDEN DR	GGR	GG	11000	15	F1
GARDEN LN	CM	CM27	2000	31	E2
GARDEN LN	CO	CM27	2000	31	E2
GARDEN PL	YL	YL	17900	7	F3
GARDEN ST	ANA	AN	900	10	F3
GARDEN ST	ANA	AN	900	11	A3
GARDENAIRE LN	ANA	AN04	1700	15	E2
GARDENAIRE LN	GGR	GG	11100	15	E2
GARDENBROOK LN	SA	SA		22	D1
GARDENERS RD	SB	SB		20	A2
GARDEN GROVE BL	CO	GG41	8500	15	B5
GARDEN GROVE BL	GGR	GG	5700	15	B5
GARDEN GROVE BL	GGR	GG	10300	16	C4
GARDEN GROVE BL	OR	OR68	3700	16	E4
GARDEN GROVE BL	STN	GG41	8000	15	B5
GARDEN GROVE BL	WSTM	WSTM	6000	15	B5
GARDEN GROVE FY	GGR			15	B5
GARDEN GROVE FY	GGR			16	C6
GARDEN GROVE FY	OR			17	C4
GARDEN GROVE FY	WSTM			14	F5
GARDENIA AV	FTNV	SA08	9000	21	F5
GARDENIA AV	PLA	PLA	500	7	C5
GARDENIA DR	BPK	BP	7700	10	C3
GARDENIA DR	HTB	HB	9000	26	E5
GARDENIA WY	NB	CDLM		33	B1
GARDINERS CT	CYP	CYP	11300	15	A2
GARDNER DR N	OR	OR	1100	17	D1
GARDNER DR S	OR	OR	200	17	D3
GARDNER ST	OR	OR	400	17	D4
GARFIELD AV	CM	CM	3000	27	E3
GARFIELD AV	FTNV	SA08	8500	26	B3
GARFIELD AV	FTNV	SA08	10000	27	A3
GARFIELD AV	HTB	HB	6000	26	B3
GARFIELD AV	HTB	HB46	10000	27	A3
GARFIELD AV	OR	OR		12	E6
GARFIELD AV	OR	OR	2200	17	E1
GARFIELD AV	PLA	PLA	200	7	B2
GARFIELD CIR	BPK	BP	8700	10	B4
GARFIELD ST	SA	SA	100	23	C1
GARIBALDI AV	DPT	LB77		37	E4
GARLAND AV	TUS	TUS	1200	24	A2
GARLAND CIR	ANA	AN		8	A5
GARLAND CIR	WSTM	WSTM	15500	21	F3
GARLAND LN	ANA	AN	6200	8	A5
GARLAND ST	ANA	AN	4800	8	A5
GARLINGFORD ST	CM	CM	1300	27	D3
GARNET	MVJO	SJ91		29D	C5
GARNET AV	CYP	CYP	4200	9	C3
GARNET AV	NB	NB	100	31	E6
GARNET CIR	ANA	AN07	6100	13	D3
GARNET CIR	GGR	GG45	11800	14	F3
GARNET LN	FUL	FL	2800	7	A3
GARNET LN	OR	OR	3000	17	F4
GARNET ST	GGR	GG45	12500	14	F4
GARNET ST	WSTM	WSTM	15700	21	D4
GARNSEY ST N	SA	SA	1400	17	A6
GARNSEY ST N	SA	SA	300	23	A1
GARNSEY ST S	SA	SA	300	23	A4
GARNSEY ST S	SA	SA	3400	28	B1
GARO LN	GGR	GG	8500	15	D6
GARO PL	WSTM	WSTM	8400	15	D6
GARRET DR	NB	CDLM	400	33	C2
GARRETT CIR	HTB	HB	9800	26	F4
GARRETT RD	STN	STN	10300	10	B6
GARRETT ST	ANA	AN	1300	10	B6
GARRETT ST	STN	STN	10700	15	B1
GARRICK DR	ANA	AN	5400	13	B1
GARRY AV	SA	SA		23	A6
GARRY AV	SA	SA		23	B6
GARRY AV	SA	SA04	1400	27	F1
GARRY AV	SA	SA		28	A1
GARRY AV	SA	SA	1800	28	C1
GARY PL	ANA	AN	1300	11	F5
GARY PL	NB	NB	600	31	D4
GARY ST	ANA	AN	1300	11	A6
GARY ST	ANA	AN	1600	16	A1
GARY ST	GGR	GG	11600	16	A3
GARY ST	WSTM	WSTM	7000	21	B2
GARZA AV	CO	AN04	10700	15	E1
GARZA ST	ANA	AN	1400	10	E6
GARZA ST	ANA	AN04	1400	15	E1
GARZONI ISLE	IRV	SA14		28	D5
GASCOGNE AV	IRV	SA	4800	29	D3
GAS LIGHT DR	HTB	HB47	6800	21	A3
GASPE CIR	HTB	HB	18300	26	C2
GASTONBURY PL	CO	LB		37	F2
GATA	MVJO	SJ92		29B	E3

GATE HILL CIR

1990 ORANGE COUNTY STREET INDEX

96

GRANADA DR

ORANGE CO.

INDEX

STREET	CITY	P.O. ZONE	BLOCK	PAGE	GRID
GATE HILL CIR	HTB	HB		26	A4
GATES AV	IRV	SA		28	E2
GATES AV	OR	OR	600	12	D5
GATES ST	CO	ET	23400	29A	D3
GATES ST N	SA	SA	600	22	C1
GATES ST S	SA	SA	700	22	C1
GATESHEAD DR	HTB	HB		30	E2
GATEWAY BLVD	IRV	SA		29	F6
GATEWAY BLVD	IRV	SA18		51	A6
GATEWAY DR	CO	SA	19500	18	B5
GATEWAY DR	CYP	CYP		14	F1
GATEWAY DR	CYP	CYP		15	A1
GATEWOOD	IRV	SA		29	B2
GATEWOOD CT	BREA	BREA		2	C5
GATEWOOD LN	ANA	AN	5300	13	B2
GAVILAN	CO	SJ88		59	B5
GAVINA	DPT	LB77		37	E3
GAVIOTA	CO	SJ		59	C1
GAVIOTA	NB	NB		32	A2
GAVIOTA DR	LAG	LB51	1000	34	D3
GAY ST	CO	CYP	8000	9	C3
GAYANN DR	ANA	AN		13	A1
GAYLE LN	ANA	AN		13	C1
GAYLE ST	OR	OR	3800	12	D3
GAYLORD DR	GGR	GG	11100	16	B3
GAYMONT ST	ANA	AN	600	10	C6
GEETING PL	PLA	PLA	1800	7	C2
GEHRIG AV	PLA	PLA	900	7	D2
GELDING CIR	HTB	HB	5000	20	E5
GELID AV	ANA	AN	2500	12	A5
GELID CT	ANA	AN	2600	12	A5
GELID ST	ANA	AN	2500	12	A5
GELIDUM CIR	DPT	LB77		37	D3
GEM AV	CYP	CYP		9	C3
GEM LN	YL	YL	4900	7	D3
GEMFALL LN	HTB	HB	19700	26	D4
GEMINI AV	BREA	BREA	100	2	C6
GEMINI LN	CO	ET	25000	29A	F3
GEMINI LN	HTB	HB47		21	B5
GEMWOOD DR	CO	ET	24000	29A	E5
GENE ST	CYP	CYP	9800	9	F6
GENESEE ST	OR	OR	1900	12	D5
GENEVA AV	HTB	HB	100	26	C5
GENEVA LN	GGR	GG	10300	15	F3
GENEVA PL	FUL	FL33		5	E4
GENEVA ST	ANA	AN	600	10	E3
GENEVA ST	IRV	SA	14900	29	C1
GENEVE	NB	CDLM		32	D5
GENIL	MVJO	SJ91		29B	C1
GENIL	MVJO	SJ91	27400	52	D6
GENOA	CO	LAG		35	F4
GENOA CIR	HTB	HB47	15000	21	A2
GENOA DR	SA	SA	700	22	B3
GENOA LN	CM	CM27	300	31	F2
GENOA PL	PLA	PLA	1400	7	C4
GENOVA	CO	LB		29A	B4
GENTRY LN	ANA	AN		13	A3
GENTRY LN	HTB	HB47	16200	21	A5
GENTRY WY	STN	STN	11000	15	B2
GEODE AV	FTNV	SA08	11800	22	C5
GEORGE ST	GGR	GG	12400	16	C4
GEORGEANNE PL	CM	CM27	100	31	E1
GEO REYBURN RD	GGR	GG45		14	E4
GEORGES WY	LAG	LB	22300	35	B6
GEORGETOWN	IRV	SA		32	F1
GEORGETOWN	MVJO	SJ92		29B	D1
GEORGETOWN AV	WSTM	WSTM	7000	21	B3
GEORGETOWN CIR	ANA	AN		13	F4
GEORGETOWN LN	CM	CM	100	27	E6
GEORGETOWN LN	HTB	HB		26	C1
GEORGIA CIR	PLA	PLA	300	7	B5
GEORGIA PL	CM	CM	3200	27	B2
GEORGIA ST	HTB	HB	900	26	C5
GEORGIAN ST	STN	GG41	12200	15	C4
GEORGIA SUE DR	CO	LB	24700	29A	E6
GEORGINE ST	SA	SA	4000	22	C1
GERALD CIR	ANA	AN	2800	12	B4
GERALDINE CIR	GGR	GG	11300	15	F2
GERALDINE LN	HTB	HB47	17500	21	D6
GERALDINE RD	GGR	GG	10000	15	F2
GERALDINE RD	GGR	GG	10300	16	A2
GERALDO	SCL	SCL		38	E4
GERANIUM	CO	SJ		59	E1
GERANIUM	NB	CDLM		33	B1
GERANIUM AV	FTNV	SA08	9400	21	E4
GERANIUM CIR	BPK	BP	7800	10	C2
GERANIUM CIR	FTNV	SA08	9400	21	E4
GERANIUM ST	CM	CM		27	E2
GERDA DR	ANA	AN	4900	13	B2
GERMAIN CIR	HTB	HB		20	A6
GERMAINDER WY	IRV	SA	4000	28	F5

STREET	CITY	P.O. ZONE	BLOCK	PAGE	GRID
GERRY ST	LAH	LAH	500	2	B4
GERSHON PL	CO	SA	13500	18	A6
GERSHWIN DR	HTB	HB	5500	20	E6
GERTNER EST RD	CO	OR67		52	D1
GERTRUDE DR	CO	LALM	2600	14	A4
GETTA WY	CO	SIL		50	E2
GETTY DR	CO	LB	26000	29D	B5
GETTYSBURG	IRV	SA		24	D6
GETTYSBURG DR	HTB	HB	9000	26	E4
GHENT DR	HTB	HB	5900	20	F6
GIARC LN	HTB	HB47	16000	21	A4
GIBBS CT	IRV	SA		32	D3
GIBBS LN	ANA	AN		13	C1
GIBRALTAR AV	CM	CM	3000	27	C3
GIBRALTAR AV	IRV	SA	14300	24	C6
GIBSON CIR	HTB	HB47	17300	21	B6
GIFFIN LN	IRV	SA		32	F2
GIFFORD ST	FTNV	SA08	18300	26	E2
GIGI DR	CO	SA	11400	18	C5
GILA WY	PLA	PLA	200	7	B3
GILBERT DR	HTB	HB	3300	20	A5
GILBERT ST	CO	AN04	9300	10	E6
GILBERT ST	CO	AN04	10600	15	E4
GILBERT ST	GGR	GG	12740	15	E4
GILBERT ST N&S	ANA	AN	100	10	E6
GILBERT ST N&S	FUL	FL33	100	5	E5
GILBERT ST S	FUL	FL33	1000	10	E1
GILBERT ST W	FUL	FL33		5	E3
GILBERTO	CO	SJ88		59	B3
GILBUCK DR	ANA	AN	600	11	B5
GILBUCK ST	ANA	AN	1300	11	B6
GILDRED CIR	HTB	HB	5900	20	F5
GILFORD CIR	HTB	HB	8400	26	D4
GILL DR	GGR	GG	11400	15	E2
GILLETTE AV	IRV	SA	17200	28	C2
GILLILAN ST	PLA	PLA	1900	7	C2
GILLINGHAM CIR	WSTM	WSTM		20	D2
GILLMAN ST	IRV	SA	17900	28	F5
GILMAN CIR	PLA	PLA	1900	7	A2
GILMAR ST	ANA	AN	600	11	B4
GIMBERT LN	CO	SA	13300	18	B6
GIMKHANA	OR	OR		13	D6
GINA LN	HTB	HB		26	D2
GINGER AV	CM	CM	3000	27	C3
GINGER LN	WSTM	WSTM	6500	21	A1
GINGER RD	CO	ET	25000	29A	F2
GINGERWOOD CIR	FUL	FL		7	A1
GINNISS GREEN	BPK	BP21	8100	5	D4
GIOTTO	CO	LB56		29C	C1
GISLER AV	CM	CM	700	27	B3
GITANO	MVJO	SJ92	28300	29B	E5
GIVENS PL	WSTM	WSTM	14700	21	E2
GLACIER CIR	HTB	HB	20000	26	F5
GLACIER CIR	LALM	LALM	12400	14	D4
GLACIER CT	FTNV	SA08		27	A2
GLACIER DR	PLA	PLA	1200	7	E4
GLACIER DR	WSTM	WSTM	6000	20	F1
GLACIER DR	WSTM	WSTM	6100	21	A1
GLACIER ST	OR	OR		13	C5
GLADE CT	BREA	BREA	400	2	F5
GLADIOLA AV	FTNV	SA08	9700	21	F4
GLADIOLA CIR	BPK	BP	7800	10	C2
GLADIOLA CIR	FTNV	SA08	9800	21	F4
GLADIOLUS WY	CO	ET		51	E4
GLADSTONE	IRV	SA		29	B1
GLADSTONE CIR	FTNV	SA08	17000	22	C5
GLADSTONE DR	CO	SA	11800	18	B6
GLADYS AV	HTB	HB	8300	26	D1
GLAMUS AV	ANA	AN	2700	12	A4
GLASGOW CIR	HTB	HB47	8500	21	D5
GLASGOW CIR	YL	YL	17300	7	E4
GLASGOW GREEN	BPK	BP21	8100	5	D4
GLASS CIR	IRV	SA	15000	29	D2
GLASSELL	CO	OR65	8700	12	C3
GLASSELL ST	OR	OR	1300	12	C5
GLASSELL ST N&S	OR	OR	100	17	C5
GLASS MTN ST	FTNV	SA08		22	B5
GLEADA ST	HTB	HB	18100	26	C2
GLEN AV	ANA	AN	2100	10	F2
GLEN AV	ANA	AN	1700	11	A2
GLEN CIR	CM	CM27		31	A1
GLEN CT	BREA	BREA	300	2	F5
GLEN DR	ANA	AN	1300	11	B2
GLEN DR	HTB	HB47	6500	21	A3
GLEN DR	NB	CDLM	300	33	B2
GLEN PL	YL	YL	6000	8	C5
GLEN ST	GGR	GG	12400	16	C4
GLEN WY	GGR	GG	13200	16	A5
GLEN ABBEY	CO	SJ79		59	D3
GLEN ABBEY DR	CO	LB		35	D5
GLEN ACRES	CO	ET		29A	F3

STREET	CITY	P.O. ZONE	BLOCK	PAGE	GRID
GLEN ACRES	CO	ET	25500	29B	A3
GLENAIRE DR	CO	SA	1100	18	C5
GLEN ALBYN LN	CO	OR	19000	18	B1
GLEN ALBYN LN	OR	OR	4900	18	B1
GLEN ARBOR	SA	SA04		22	E3
GLEN ARBOR LN	ANA	AN	5600	13	B2
GLEN ARBOR ST	SA	SA	400	22	E5
GLENARIFF LN	SJC	SJ75		38	C4
GLEN ARRAN LN	CO	OR	19000	18	B1
GLENBROOK	MVJO	SJ92		29B	E1
GLENBROOK LN	IRV	SA	14700	29	C2
GLENBROOK ST	CYP	CYP	9600	9	E5
GLENCAIRN LN	HTB	HB	20600	26	F6
GLEN CANYON CT	CO	LB		29C	F3
GLEN CANYON DR	CO	LB	25000	29D	A3
GLEN CANYON RD	OR	OR	2500	12	F4
GLEN CANYON RD	OR	OR	2500	13	A4
GLEN CANYON WY	BREA	BREA		2	F4
GLENCLIFF ST	LAH	LAH	800	1	E5
GLENCOE	MVJO	SJ91		29D	C6
GLENCOE AV	HTB	HB47	7700	21	C4
GLEN COVE	CO	LB77		36	A5
GLEN COVE DR	GGR	GG	11500	16	B5
GLENCREST AV	ANA	AN	2400	10	D3
GLENCREST AV	ANA	AN	1800	11	A3
GLENDALE AV	OR	OR	500	12	D5
GLENDALE CIR	STN	STN		15	B4
GLENDALE CT	SA	SA	400	23	B3
GLENDALE DR	OR	OR		12	C5
GLENDALE DR	YL	YL	6300	8	C5
GLENDON LN	CO	LB56		29C	C3
GLENDON ST N&S	ANA	AN	100	12	B3
GLENDORA AV	OR	OR	500	12	D4
GLENDORA ST	GGR	GG	13600	16	A6
GLEN EAGLES	CO	SJ79		59	D6
GLENEAGLES	MVJO	SJ92		29B	E4
GLENEAGLES CIR	HTB	HB		25	F3
GLENEAGLES CIR	WSTM	WSTM	8900	21	E3
GLENEAGLES TER	CM	CM27	1100	31	A1
GLEN ECHO	CO	SJ79		59	E2
GLENFALLS DR	HTB	HB48		25	E3
GLENFOX DR	HTB	HB	6200	26	A1
GLENGARRY GREEN	BPK	BP21	8100	5	D4
GLENHAVEN AV	ANA	AN	2500	10	E3
GLENHAVEN AV	FUL	FL	800	6	B4
GLENHAVEN DR	GGR	GG	13600	16	B6
GLENHAVEN DR	LAH	LAH	800	1	E5
GLENHAVEN DR	YL	YL	19900	8	C5
GLENHAVEN LN	HTB	HB47	16700	21	D5
GLEN HOLLY DR	ANA	AN	3000	10	B5
GLENHURST	CO	ET	25800	29B	A3
GLENHURST	CO	LB56		29C	C6
GLENHURST	IRV	SA		29	D4
GLEN IRIS	CO	SJ79		59	D3
GLENKNOLL DR	CO	YL	6000	8	C5
GLEN LAKE AV	BREA	BREA		2	D5
GLENLAKE DR	PLA	PLA		7	B6
GLENMEADOW DR	CO	ET		52	C6
GLENMERE DR	CO	SA	13900	18	B6
GLENMONT TER	IRV	SA		32	F2
GLENN	IRV	SA		29	E1
GLENN CIR	PLA	PLA	1500	7	B3
GLENN DR	CO	OR	10800	18	D1
GLENNEYRE ST	LAG	LB51	300	34	E4
GLENN RANCH WY	CO	SJ79		52	E4
GLEN OAK LN	OR	OR69		18	F2
GLENOAKS	CO	LB56		29C	B3
GLENOAKS	MVJO	SJ92		29B	E2
GLENOAKS AV	ANA	AN	2400	10	E3
GLENOAKS AV	ANA	AN	1700	11	A3
GLENOAKS ST	BREA	BREA	400	2	E4
GLEN RIDGE	MVJO	SJ92		29B	F2
GLENRIDGE AV	WSTM	WSTM	9000	21	E3
GLEN ROBIN LN	CO	OR	10900	18	B1
GLENROCK DR	CO	LB		35	F1
GLENROCK DR	CO	LB77		36	A1
GLENROSE DR	OR	OR	500	18	A2
GLENROSE LN	CO	ET		29A	D2
GLENROSE ST	OR	OR	300	18	A2
GLENROY AV	ANA	AN	3600	10	A6
GLENROY DR	HTB	HB	5300	20	E6
GLENROY PL	CO	LALM	2900	14	A3
GLENSIDE CIR	OR	OR	2500	12	C4
GLENSIDE ST	OR	OR	2700	12	C4
GLENSTONE DR	HTB	HB	5300	20	E6
GLENVIEW AV	ANA	AN	1700	8	A5
GLENVIEW CIR	ANA	AN	6200	8	A5
GLENVIEW DR	FUL	FL	900	6	B4
GLENVIEW PL	OR	OR	200	17	B3
GLENVIEW RD	SB	SB	1500	14	A5

STREET	CITY	P.O. ZONE	BLOCK	PAGE	GRID
GLENWOOD AV	ANA	AN	1200	11	E3
GLENWOOD AV E	FUL	FL	100	6	C4
GLENWOOD AV W	FUL	FL	200	6	C4
GLENWOOD CIR	FUL	FL		6	B5
GLENWOOD CIR	LAP	BP23	5200	9	D2
GLENWOOD DR	CO	ET	24700	29A	E2
GLENWOOD DR	CO	LB56		29C	C1
GLENWOOD DR	FUL	FL		6	B5
GLENWOOD DR	HTB	HB	6000	20	F2
GLENWOOD DR	MVJO	SJ92		29D	C2
GLENWOOD LN	NB	NB	1700	31	F3
GLENWOOD PL	ANA	AN	600	11	E3
GLENWOOD PL E	SA	SA	900	23	A5
GLENWOOD PL	SA	SA07		23	C5
GLENWOOD PL W	SA	SA	1300	22	D5
GLENWOOD ST	IRV	SA	4000	29	C1
GLENWOOD ST	OR	OR	2200	12	D5
GLENWOOD TER	FUL	FL		6	B5
GLITTER ST	WSTM	WSTM	14100	15	E6
GLITTER ST	WSTM	WSTM	14100	21	E1
GLOBAL DR	CYP	CYP		14	F1
GLOBAL DR	CYP	CYP	6400	15	A1
GLOBAL WY	ANA	AN	700	11	C6
GLOCAMORA LN	SJC	SJ75		38	C4
GLOMSTAD LN	LAG	LB51	600	34	E2
GLORIA AV	GGR	GG	8500	15	D5
GLORIA CIR	VPK	OR67	18000	17	F1
GLORIA DR	HTB	HB47	6200	21	A5
GLORIA ST	GGR	GG	12500	16	D5
GLORIETA	IRV	SA		24	E5
GLORIETA	NB	NB		32	A3
GLORIETTA LN	MVJO	SJ91		29B	B4
GLORIOSA DR	CO	SJ91	25500	29A	F6
GLOUCESTER CIR	WSTM	WSTM	5700	20	F1
GLOUCESTER DR	CM	CM27	400	31	E2
GLOUCESTER LN	HTB	HB	19700	26	E4
GLOXINIA AV	FTNV	SA08	11700	22	C4
GLOXINIA DR	YL	YL		8	D5
GODWIN CT	FTNV	SA08	15900	22	D6
GOEBEL LN	WSTM	WSTM	14100	15	E6
GOEBEL LN	WSTM	WSTM	14100	21	E1
GOETZ AV	SA	SA	100	23	B6
GOETZ PL	PLA	PLA	400	7	A6
GOFF ST	LAG	LB51	400	34	D3
GOLADA	MVJO	SJ92		29D	D3
GOLD CIR	HTB	HB47	16000	21	A4
GOLD BLUFF	IRV	SA		29	C2
GOLD DUST LN	CO	LB53		29C	F5
GOLDEN AV	FUL	FL	600	6	B5
GOLDEN AV E	PLA	PLA	200	7	C2
GOLDEN CIR	NB	NB	2200	32	A1
GOLDEN WY	PLA	PLA		7	C2
GOLDENBUSH	IRV	SA		29	A1
GOLDEN CIR DR	SA	SA	400	23	E2
GOLDEN EAGLE AV	OR	OR	4600	18	B1
GOLDEN EAGLE CT	CO	LB53		29A	B6
GOLDEN EAGLE LN	CO	ET	23900	29A	D4
GOLDENEYE AV	FTNV	SA08	10800	27	B1
GOLDENEYE CIR	CO	LB		35	D2
GOLDENEYE DR	CO	LB	23900	35	D2
GOLDENEYE PL	CM	CM	2000	27	A5
GOLDEN GATE LN	HTB	HB	16300	20	E4
GOLDEN GLEN ST	IRV	SA	5100	29	D2
GOLDENGLOW ST	IRV	SA	4300	28	F6
GOLDEN LNTRN ST	CO	LB77		35	F6
GOLDEN LNTRN ST	CO	LB77		36	A4
GOLDEN LNTRN ST	CO	LB77		37	F2
GOLDEN LNTRN ST	DPT	DPT	33700	37	E4
GOLDEN NUGT CIR	WSTM	WSTM	7000	21	B1
GOLDEN RAIN RD	SB	SB	1200	14	A6
GOLDEN RIDGE LN	SJC	SJ75		36	D4
GOLDENROD	IRV	SA		29	B4
GOLDENROD AV	FTNV	SA08	11300	22	B4
GOLDENROD AV	NB	CDLM	900	32	B6
GOLDENROD AV	NB	CDLM	100	33	A1
GOLDENROD CIR	BPK	BP	7800	10	C2
GOLDENROD CIR	SB	SB	12900	14	D5
GOLDENROD DR	CM	CM	900	27	E2
GOLDEN ROD CIR	CO	LB53		29D	A4
GOLDENROD ST	BREA	BREA		3	C6
GOLDENROD ST	PLA	PLA	700	7	C4
GOLDENROD ST	SB	SB	12500	14	D4
GOLDEN SKY LN	ANA	AN		13	C3
GOLDENSPRING DR	DPT	DPT	25500	38	A3
GOLDENSPUR WY	OR	OR	100	18	D3
GOLDEN STAR	IRV	SA		29	C2
GOLDEN VIEW LN	HTB	HB47	17200	21	A6
GOLDEN VISTA	CO	LB		35	F2
GOLDEN WEST AV	ANA	AN04	1700	15	F1
GOLDEN WEST AV	SA	SA	600	22	E4
GOLDEN WEST AV	SA	SA04	3800	27	E2

STREET	CITY	P.O. ZONE	BLOCK	PAGE	GRID
GOLDEN WEST CIR	WSTM	WSTM	15000	21	B2
GOLDEN WEST ST	HTB	HB47	15000	21	B6
GOLDEN WEST ST	HTB	HB48	17500	26	B3
GOLDEN WEST ST	WSTM	WSTM	13000	15	B6
GOLDEN WEST ST	WSTM	WSTM	14000	21	B1
GOLDEN WST ST N	HTB	HB	100	26	A5
GOLDENWREN	IRV	SA		29	C2
GOLDERS GRN LN	WSTM	WSTM	14500	22	A2
GOLDFINCH LN	CO	LB51		29C	B2
GOLD FINCH LN	FTNV	SA08	9500	26	F2
GOLDFINCH WY	ANA	AN		13	F2
GOLD RUSH	CO	ET	22500	29B	A2
GOLD RUSH	IRV	SA		24	E6
GOLDRUSH RDG LN	CO	LB56		29C	E6
GOLDSPORT CIR	HTB	HB	18100	26	B2
GOLD STAR LN	CO	SA	11000	18	D5
GOLDSTONE	IRV	SA		29	A5
GOLD VIA	ANA	AN		16	D2
GOLETA DR	MVJO	SJ91		29D	C3
GOLETA POINT	NB	CDLM		32	D6
GOLF CLUB DR	SJC	SJ75		36	C5
GOLF COURSE DR	CM	CM	2600	27	C5
GOLF COURSE DR	CO	SJ79		59	D3
GOLF GLEN RD	ANA	AN		13	E3
GOLF RIDGE DR	CO	SJ79		59	E3
GOLF VIEW DR	CO	SJ79		59	E3
GOLONDRINA	MVJO	SJ92		29B	D6
GOMES WY	BREA	BREA		2	E6
GONDOR DR	CO	ET	23400	29A	D4
GONZAGA PL	WSTM	WSTM	7600	21	C2
GONZALES ST	PLA	PLA	900	12	A1
GOODALE AV	FTNV	SA08	11800	22	C5
GOODEN PL	TUS	SA10	3000	29	A1
GOODHUE AV	ANA	AN	1300	11	A6
GOODWILL CT	NB	NB		31	B4
GOODWIN LN	HTB	HB	18400	26	D2
GOODWIN PL	CO	LB77		35	E6
GOODYEAR	IRV	SA18		29A	D1
GORDON AV	CO	LAH	9100	1	E3
GORDON AV	LAH	LAH	2500	1	E3
GORDON LN	FUL	FL	500	6	E5
GORDON LN	YL	YL	19000	8	B4
GORDON PL	ANA	AN	1100	11	B3
GORDON PL	SA	SA	1400	22	E4
GORDON RD	CO	LB		29C	E3
GORDON GRN	BPK	BP	8100	5	C3
GORGONIA	NB	NB		32	A2
GORHAM DR	NB	CDLM	4500	33	C2
GORHAM LN	IRV	SA		24	F6
GOSHAWK LN	HTB	HB	20500	26	D6
GOTHARD ST	HTB	HB47	16000	21	B4
GOTHARD ST	HTB	HB	17500	26	B3
GOTHIC CIR	HTB	HB	20000	26	E5
GOURAMI BAY	DPT	LB77		37	E4
GOVERNOR ST	CM	CM27	600	31	B1
GOVIN CIR	HTB	HB47	6400	21	A4
GOWDY AV	CO	ET	23800	29A	D4
GOYA CIR	MVJO	SJ91		29D	C4
GRACE AV	CO	CYP	4700	9	D4
GRACE AV	LAH	LAH	300	2	A5
GRACE CIR	HTB	HB		26	D4
GRACE LN	CM	CM	2900	27	E4
GRACE PL	SA	SA	1500	23	D1
GRACE ST	SA	SA	1300	23	D1
GRACE HAVEN WY	YL	YL	19800	8	C5
GRACELAND DR	LAG	LB51	400	34	E3
GRACIELA	MVJO	SJ92	24300	29B	E5
GRACIOSA LN	ANA	AN	3100	10	B4
GRACKLE AV	FTNV	SA08	9200	26	E2
GRAFTON PL	ANA	AN	700	11	C3
GRAHAM CIR	CYP	CYP	9200	9	E4
GRAHAM DR	ETMC	SA09		51	E3
GRAHAM LN	SA	SA	800	22	F3
GRAHAM PL	HTB	HB	16500	20	E5
GRAHAM ST	CYP	CYP	9200	9	E4
GRAHAM ST	HTB	HB	14900	20	E5
GRAHAM ST	HTB	HB	17500	25	E1
GRAHAM ST	WSTM	WSTM		20	E1
GRAHAM GREEN	BPK	BP21	8100	5	C3
GRAMBLING CIR	WSTM	WSTM	13800	14	D6
GRAMERCY AV	ANA	AN	2300	10	E3
GRAMERCY AV	ANA	AN	1800	11	A3
GRAMERCY DR	CO	SA	18200	18	A5
GRAMERCY CIR	BPK	BP	6400	5	B6
GRAMERCY ST	BPK	BP	6700	10	B1
GRANADA	TUS	TUS		24	A4
GRANADA AV	NB	CDLM	2100	33	A1
GRANADA CT	GGR	GG		16	A4
GRANADA CT	LAH	LAH	1500	1	E4
GRANADA DR	BPK	BP	7500	5	B4
GRANADA DR	DPT	DPT	33800	37	E4

1990 ORANGE COUNTY STREET INDEX

STREET	CITY	P.O. ZONE	BLOCK	PAGE	GRID
GRANADA DR	LAH	LAH	300	1	E4
GRANADA DR	OR	OR	1000	18	B1
GRANADA DR	YL	YL	4500	8	C3
GRANADA LN	HTB	HB47	17100	21	C6
GRANADA WY	CM	CM27	300	31	F1
GRANADA WY	LAG	LB51	2400	34	F4
GRANBY DR	YL	YL		8	F4
GRAND AV	BPK	BP	8500	10	C4
GRAND AV	CO	SA	13100	17	D5
GRAND AV	STN	STN	8000	15	C1
GRAND AV N	SA	SA	1600	17	C6
GRAND AV N&S	ANA	AN	100	10	C4
GRAND AV N&S	SA	SA	100	23	C1
GRAND DR	HTB	HB	9300	26	E4
GRAND ST N	OR	OR	1400	12	C6
GRAND ST N&S	OR	OR	100	17	C4
GRAND CANYON	BREA	BREA		2	F4
GRAND CANYON DR	CO	LB77	31700	37	D1
GRANDE VISTA AV	CO	LB	30200	35	E4
GRAND HAVEN CIR	CM	CM26	600	28	A3
GRAND MANAN DR	CYP	CYP	6500	15	A2
GRAND MASTER CT	DPT	DPT		37	D3
GRAND MEADOWS	GGR	GG43		22	A1
GRAND OAKS CIR	TUS	TUS	1600	23	F5
GRANDOAKS DR	STN	STN	7100	10	B6
GRAND RAPID RD	OR	OR		12	B4
GRANDVIEW AV	FUL	FL	800	6	B4
GRANDVIEW AV	YL	YL	5000	8	A5
GRANDVIEW CIR	HTB	HB48		25	E3
GRANDVIEW ST	LAG	LB51	200	34	C2
GRANDVW AV EXT	YL	YL		8	B5
GRANDWOOD DR	FUL	FL33		5	E2
GRANITE CIR	ANA	AN	900	12	A4
GRANITE CIR	GGR	GG	12300	16	D5
GRANITE PL	GGR	GG	12400	16	D5
GRANITE WY	CO	LB		29A	B3
GRANT	IRV	SA		24	E6
GRANT	IRV	SA		29	E1
GRANT AV	CM	CM	3000	27	E3
GRANT CIR	BPK	BP	8700	10	B4
GRANT DR	HTB	HB	8200	26	D3
GRANT PL	OR	OR68	100	16	E3
GRANT ST	FUL	FL33	700	5	E4
GRANT ST	NB	NB63	100	30	F4
GRANT ST	NB	NB	100	31	A3
GRANT ST	SA	SA	300	23	B3
GRANT WY	STN	STN	11000	15	B2
GRANVIA DR	MVJO	SJ91	26300	29B	B6
GRANVIA DR	MVJO	SJ91		29D	B1
GRANVILLE DR	NB	CDLM		32	A5
GRASS CIR	HTB	HB47		21	B6
GRASS LN	ANA	AN	1500	11	B6
GRASS ST	CO	ET	24200	29A	F5
GRASSLAND TER	CO	SJ79		52	F4
GRASSMERE LN	TUS	TUS	14300	23	F4
GRASS VALLEY	MVJO	SJ92		29B	E2
GRAVIER ST	CO	AN04	10000	10	F6
GRAVINO	CO	LB		29A	B5
GRAY LN	CO	OR		13	C6
GRAYLING BAY	CM	CM		27	E4
GRAYSON AV	ANA	AN	2000	10	F2
GRAY SQUIRRL LN	CO	LB	23000	35	C3
GRAYSTON DR	CO	ET	24100	29A	D4
GRAYSTONE	IRV	SA		29	B2
GRAYSTONE	MVJO	SJ92		29B	F1
GRAYSTONE LN	HTB	HB	20400	26	F5
GRAYVILLE DR	LAH	LAH	2300	1	D6
GRAZ CIR	HTB	HB		20	E5
GRAZIADIO DR	HTB	HB	8000	26	C2
GREASEWOOD CIR	WSTM	WSTM	8400	21	D3
GRECO	TUS	TUS		24	C4
GREEN AV	LALM	LALM	3500	14	B2
GREEN DR	SA	SA		16	D6
GREEN DR	SA	SA		22	D1
GREEN ST	CM	CM	3100	27	D3
GREEN ST	HTB	HB	16600	20	D6
GREENACRE AV	ANA	AN	2200	10	E3
GREEN ACRE DR	FUL	FL	500	6	B3
GREEN ACRE RD	FUL	FL	2100	6	B3
GREENACRES	MVJO	SJ92		29B	F2
GREENBANK	CO	ET		29B	A3
GREENBAY DR	CO	ET	25000	29A	F3
GREENBORO LN	HTB	HB	21000	30	D1
GREENBOUGH	IRV	SA		29	A4
GREENBRAE ST	IRV	SA		29	C2
GREENBRIAR	IRV	SA		29	D4
GREENBRIAR DR	YL	YL		8	F4
GREENBRIAR LN	BREA	BREA	1200	3	A6
GREENBRIAR LN	BREA	BREA	300	7	A1
GREENBRIAR LN	CM	CM	2500	27	D5
GREENBRIAR PL	BPK	BP	8900	5	D4

STREET	CITY	P.O. ZONE	BLOCK	PAGE	GRID
GREENBRIAR RD	CO	ET	24100	29A	D2
GREENBRIER	CO	SJ79		59	D3
GREENBRIER AV	ANA	AN	2400	10	D3
GREEN BRIER CIR	CO	SJ79		59	C4
GREENBRIER DR	HTB	HB48		25	F4
GREENBRIER LN	LAH	LAH	2200	1	E6
GREEN BRIER LN	NB	NB		32	B5
GREENBRIER RD	CO	SA	10300	18	D4
GREENBRIER ST	SA	SA	1900	17	A6
GREENBROOK DR	CM	CM26		27	E3
GREENBUD	IRV	SA		29	A4
GREENCAP AV	IRV	SA	5100	29	D2
GREENCASTLE DR	MVJO	SJ92		29B	E6
GRN CLOVER CIR	OR	OR		13	A4
GREEN COVE CIR	HTB	HB	21400	30	F5
GREENDALE	CO	ET		52	C3
GREENFERN CIR	WSTM	WSTM	10000	22	A2
GREENFIELD	IRV	SA		29	A4
GREENFIELD DR	CO	LB77		29C	F6
GREENFIELD DR	CO	LB		29D	A6
GREENFIELD LN	HTB	HB	20800	26	D6
GREEN GARDEN LN	OR	OR	3600	13	A4
GREENGATE LN	CO	SJ79		56	E6
GREENGROVE DR	OR	OR	200	17	E4
GREENGROVE ST	OR	OR	1700	12	D6
GREENGROVE ST	OR	OR	1100	17	E4
GREENGROVE ST	SA	SA	2800	17	E5
GREENHAVEN LN	ANA	AN		10	D1
GREENHAVEN ST	YL	YL		8	F3
GREENHEDGE AV	ANA	AN	2900	12	B3
GREENHILL	CO	ET	25800	29B	A3
GREENHILL DR	FUL	FL33		5	E3
GREEN HILL LN	YL	YL	20200	8	F2
GREEN HILLS LN	CO	LB53		29D	A4
GREEN HOLLOW LN	YL	YL		40	D5
GRN LANTERN ST	DPT	DPT	34000	37	E5
GREENLEAF	IRV	SA		29	E4
GREENLEAF AV	ANA	AN	2400	10	D3
GREENLEAF AV	ANA	AN	1800	11	A3
GREENLEAF AV	BPK	BP	8500	10	D3
GREENLEAF AV	OR	OR	700	12	C4
GREENLEAF DR	BREA	BREA	500	7	C1
GREENLEAF LN	HTB	HB	17100	20	E6
GREENLEAF PZ	YL	YL	19600	8	C5
GREENLEAF ST	FTNV	SA08	17000	21	F6
GREENLEAF ST	SA	SA	1700	17	B6
GREENMEADOW AV	TUS	TUS	1600	23	F5
GREENMEADOW DR	FUL	FL	3300	6	D1
GREEN MEADOW WY	YL	YL		40	D5
GREENMOOR	IRV	SA		29	B5
GREEN PINE WY	YL	YL		7	E4
GREEN RIVER DR	OR	OR		12	B5
GREENSBORO LN	ANA	AN		13	A3
GREENS EAST DR	CO	LB		35	D5
GREENS POINTE	CO	LB	31800	35	D6
GREENS POINTE	CO	LB77	31800	37	D1
GREENSPRAY LN	HTB	HB	21300	30	F4
GREEN SPRING	CO	SJ79		59	E2
GREEN TAVERN LN	YL	YL	6200	8	F1
GREENTREE AV	GGR	GG	12600	16	D3
GREENTREE CIR	ANA	AN		10	A6
GREENTREE LN	CO	ET		29A	E1
GREENTREE LN	HTB	HB	17000	20	E5
GREEN TREE LN	IRV	SA		29	A5
GREENTREE LN	LAH	LAH	100	2	B4
GREEN VALLEY AV	TUS	TUS	14100	23	F4
GREEN VALLEY AV	TUS	TUS	13600	24	A3
GREEN VALLEY LN	GGR	GG		15	D4
GREENVIEW DR	LAH	LAH	1200	1	F3
GREENVIEW DR	OR	OR	1300	17	E4
GREENVIEW LN	HTB	HB	16600	20	F5
GREENVIEW PL	FUL	FL		7	B2
GREENVILLE AV	WSTM	WSTM	9000	21	E2
GREENVILLE ST	SA	SA	1500	22	E5
GREENVILLE ST	SA	SA04	2800	27	E1
GREENWALD LN	CO	SA	12300	18	C4
GREENWAY AV	OR	OR	100	12	C4
GREENWAY DR	TUS	TUS		24	C3
GREENWAY TER	LAH	LAH		2	B3
GREENWICH AV	SA	SA04		22	E6
GREENWICH CIR	YL	YL		7	D4
GREENWICH DR	FUL	FL33		5	E2
GREENWICH DR	HTB	HB	9300	26	E4
GREENWICH LN	CO	AN04	9600	10	E5
GREENWICH ST	ANA	AN	500	10	E5
GREENWICH ST	CO	AN04	9300	10	E5
GREEN WILLOW CT	CO	SA	18800	18	B5
GREEN WILLOW DR	GGR	GG	12500	15	A4
GREENWOOD	IRV	SA		29	D3
GREENWOOD AV	OR	OR	3900	18	A4
GREENWOOD AV	SA	SA	1800	17	D5

STREET	CITY	P.O. ZONE	BLOCK	PAGE	GRID
GREENWOOD AV E	LAH	LAH	100	2	B4
GREENWOOD AV W	LAH	LAH	500	1	F4
GREENWOOD AV W	LAH	LAH	100	2	B4
GREENWOOD CT	FUL	FL33		5	E2
GREENWOOD DR	ANA	AN	4600	8	A5
GREENWOOD LN	CO	TUS	14500	24	A1
GREENWOOD LN	CO	ET		29A	F2
GREENWOOD LN	SA	SA	2300	23	D6
GREEVES	SA	SA		23	B6
GREEVES WY	SA	SA		28	B1
GREGORY AV	FUL	FL33	1600	5	E5
GREGORY CIR	BPK	BP	8200	5	C4
GREGORY CIR	CYP	CYP	10400	9	D6
GREGORY LN	GGR	GG	10600	16	A4
GREGORY LN	HTB	HB	18800	26	D3
GREGORY LN	LAH	LAH	1800	1	D4
GREGORY ST	CYP	CYP	9100	9	D6
GREGORY WY	CM	CM		27	C5
GRENACHE	IRV	SA		29	B4
GRENADA	CO	LB77		36	A3
GRENADA AV	CYP	CYP	6000	14	F2
GRENADA CIR	PLA	PLA	800	7	D5
GRENADA WY	CO	SA09		51	C4
GRENOBLE LN	CM	CM27	300	31	F2
GRENOBLE LN	HTB	HB		20	B6
GRETA AV	BPK	BP	10200	9	F6
GRETA CIR	CYP	CYP	10500	14	F1
GRETCHEN LN	WSTM	WSTM	10100	22	A3
GRETCHEN WY	ANA	AN	800	11	C3
GRETEL CT	NB	NB		31	A4
GRETTA LN	ANA	AN	2700	12	B2
GRETTA ST	CO	ET	23000	29A	D3
GREY OAKS ST	WSTM	WSTM	15600	21	F3
GREY ROCK	CO	SJ79		59	E2
GREY STONE DR	YL	YL		7	D2
GRIFFIN LN	HTB	HB47		21	C6
GRIFFIN LN	HTB	HB		26	C1
GRIFFITH CIR	HTB	HB	17500	20	F6
GRIFFITH PL	LAG	LB51	800	34	E3
GRIFFITH PL	SA	SA	400	23	C4
GRIFFITH WY	LAG	LB51	600	34	E3
GRIMAUD LN	HTB	HB	16300	20	A6
GRIMSBY DR	HTB	HB		25	F1
GRINDLAY ST	CYP	CYP	9100	9	E5
GRINDSTONE WY	CYP	CYP	11400	15	B3
GRINNELL CIR	WSTM	WSTM	13500	14	E5
GRINNELL LN	IRV	SA		32	F2
GRINNELL ST	ANA	AN		13	F4
GRIPPO RIVER AV	FTNV	SA08		26	E3
GRISET PL	SA	SA	2400	22	E6
GRISET PL	SA	SA04	3000	27	E1
GRISET ST	SA	SA	1900	22	E5
GRISSOM CIR	CO	LB		29C	E2
GRISSOM RD	CO	LB	25000	29C	E2
GRISSOM RD	CO	LB	25800	29D	A2
GRISSOM PARK DR	FUL	FL	1000	6	A3
GRIVEY AV	ANA	AN	2400	10	E5
GROSBEAK CIR	CO	LB		35	D1
GROSSE WY	CYP	CYP	6600	15	B2
GROSSMONT AV	IRV	SA		32	F2
GROTON DR	HTB	HB	9200	26	E4
GROTON ST	ANA	AN	1200	10	F2
GROUSE AV	FTNV	SA08	9400	26	E2
GROUSE CT	GGR	GG	11700	15	F3
GROVE AV	ANA	AN	500	11	E4
GROVE AV	GGR	GG	12900	16	A4
GROVE AV E	OR	OR	100	12	C5
GROVE AV W	OR	OR	100	12	C5
GROVE CIR	HTB	HB	17000	20	F6
GROVE LN	NB	NB		31	E4
GROVE PL	CM	CM27	900	31	B1
GROVE PL	FUL	FL	300	6	C5
GROVE ST	ANA	AN	1000	12	D2
GROVE HILL CT	BREA	BREA		3	B5
GROVELAKE DR	PLA	PLA		7	B6
GROVELAND PL	ANA	AN	1100	11	F5
GROVEMONT ST	CO	SA	17000	17	E5
GROVEMONT ST	SA	SA	700	17	C5
GROVE OAK DR	CO	SA	10800	18	D5
GROVER LN	CO	ET		29A	E4
GROVESIDE LN	CO	ET	25300	29A	F1
GROVESITE DR	CO	TUS	13600	17	F6
GROVESITE DR	TUS	TUS		17	F6
GROVEVIEW LN	IRV	SA	14700	29	C2
GROVEVIEW ST	GGR	GG	12400	15	F4
GROVEWOOD	CO	ET		29A	F1
GROVEWOOD	CO	ET		51	F6
GROVEWOOD LN	OR	OR	7400	13	D5
GROWERS CIR	YL	YL		7	E4
GRUNDY LN	CO	SIL	28200	50	E2

STREET	CITY	P.O. ZONE	BLOCK	PAGE	GRID
GRUNION	HTB	HB		20	D5
GUADALAJARA WY	BPK	BP		5	C3
GUADALMINA DR	DPT	LB77		37	D3
GUADALUPE LN	PLA	PLA	500	7	C5
GUADALUPE ST	SJC	SJ75	31300	36	C6
GUADIANA	MVJO	SJ91		29D	C3
GUAM	CYP	CYP	11400	14	F3
GUAMA AV	IRV	SA	14500	24	C6
GUATEMALA WY	BPK	BP	5700	9	E2
GUAVA AV	BPK	BP	8200	10	D3
GUAVA AV	SB	SB	4200	14	D4
GUAVA PL	BREA	BREA	200	3	A5
GUAVA ST	FTNV	SA08		26	F3
GUIANA CIR	BPK	BP	7100	9	E1
GUILDERS DR	HTB	HB47	8200	21	D6
GUILLEMOT LN	CO	LB56		29C	B1
GUINEA DR	CO	ET	23400	29A	E4
GUINEA ST	CO	ET	23400	29A	E4
GUINIDA LN	ANA	AN	100	11	D6
GUINIDA LN	CO	AN04	9500	10	F6
GULF LN	HTB	HB	18000	26	D1
GULINO CIR	WSTM	WSTM	7000	21	B2
GULL	HTB	HB		20	D5
GULL CIR	FTNV	SA08	9400	26	E2
GULL CIR	LAG	LB51	1600	34	F4
GULL CIR	LAG	LB51	1600	35	A3
GULL WY	CYP	CYP	11400	15	B3
GULLWING AV	CO	LAG		36	A5
GULSTRAND CIR	HTB	HB	9400	30	E2
GUM CIR	FTNV	SA08	17300	21	F6
GUM CIR	YL	YL		8	D2
GUM PL	BREA	BREA	400	2	E5
GUMM DR	HTB	HB	6100	20	F5
GUMM DR	HTB	HB47	6200	21	A5
GUM TREE LN	HTB	HB	18100	26	D2
GUMWOOD	IRV	SA		29	B6
GUMWOOD CIR	WSTM	WSTM	8200	21	D3
GUMWOOD LN	ANA	AN		11	E6
GUNDERSON DR	CO	SA15	21000	33A	F4
GUNNISON	IRV	SA		29	A6
GUNNISON CT	CO	LB	28000	29C	E6
GUNTHER PL	SA	SA	100	22	D2
GUNTHER ST	GGR	GG	13700	16	D6
GUNTHER ST N	SA	SA	500	22	D2
GUNTHER ST S	SA	SA	100	22	D2
GURLEY ST	IRV	SA	13500	24	D5
GURNEY LN	HTB	HB47	17300	21	A6
GURNEY, DAN DR	SA	SA		23	D4
GUSS DR	HTB	HB	9000	26	F5
GUTMANN LN	PLA	PLA		7	C4
GWEN AV	CO	TUS	1400	24	B1
GWYNETH DR	TUS	TUS	13100	24	A2
GWYNWOOD AV	LAH	LAH	100	2	A6
GYLAH LN	TUS	TUS	14500	24	A1
GYMKHANA	OR	OR		13	D6
GYPSUM CYN RD	CO	AN07		43	C1
GYPSUM CYN RD	YL	YL		43	C1
GYPSY MOTH LN	HTB	HB	21100	30	D1
H					
H ST	LAG	LB		35	A4
H ST	NB	NB	500	33	C5
HACIENDA	IRV	SA		24	E5
HACIENDA	NB	NB	600	32	A3
HACIENDA DR	HTB	HB	5700	20	F1
HACIENDA DR	LAH	LAH	400	1	E4
HACIENDA LN	YL	YL	18900	8	A3
HACIENDA PL	ANA	AN04	900	11	A4
HACIENDA RD	CO	LAH	1000	1	E3
HACIENDA RD	LAH	LAH	800	1	E3
HACIENDA ST	ANA	AN	200	11	A4
HACIENDA ST	PLA	PLA	1100	7	C4
HACKAMORE LN	ANA	AN07		13	D3
HACKAMORE LN	YL	YL		8	D2
HACKAMORE RD	GGR	GG	12000	16	A3
HADDONFIELD LP	FUL	FL	2800	7	A4
HADRIANS CRES	ANA	AN	5900	13	C2
HAFRA WY	CO	SIL	30600	53	A1
HAGA ST	CO	GG41	12000	15	D4
HAGERSTOWN CIR	HTB	HB	21000	26	F6
HAGUE LN	HTB	HB47	17000	21	D6
HAIBER CIR	PLA	PLA	2100	7	C2
HAIBER WY	PLA	PLA	500	7	C2
HAITI CIR	CM	CM	3100	27	B3
HAITI DR	HTB	HB	9100	30	E1
HAITI DR	PLA	PLA	800	7	D5
HALA WY	GGR	GG43		16	C6
HALAWA DR	HTB	HB46	10000	27	A3
HALAWA LN	CYP	CYP	11500	15	A2
HALCON	MVJO	SJ91	27500	29B	D1

STREET	CITY	P.O. ZONE	BLOCK	PAGE	GRID
HALDOR PL	BPK	BP	7700	10	B3
HALE AV	FUL	FL		6	E4
HALE AV	GGR	GG	13300	15	D5
HALE AV	IRV	SA		28	E2
HALE AV N	FUL	FL	300	6	F4
HALE AV S	FUL	FL	300	6	E6
HALE CIR	GGR	GG	13700	15	D6
HALEKULANI DR	GGR	GG	9600	15	E4
HALELANI WY	GGR	GG	10500	16	A3
HALERO RD	WSTM	WSTM	13500	15	D5
HALESWORTH ST	SA	SA	300	23	B1
HALF LEAGUE DR	HTB	HB	9100	26	E6
HALFMOON	IRV	SA		29	A4
HALFMOON CT	SJC	SJ75	33000	38	B2
HALF MN BAY DR	NB	CDLM		32	D5
HALFWAY RD	CO	SIL	31300	53	A1
HALIFAX AV	WSTM	WSTM	10400	22	A2
HALIFAX CIR	CYP	CYP	5000	9	D5
HALIFAX DR	CYP	CYP	5200	9	E5
HALIFAX DR	HTB	HB47	6500	21	A3
HALL AV	ANA	AN	700	11	C2
HALL AV	SA	SA	1400	22	E6
HALL AV N	FUL	FL	700	6	E5
HALL AV S	FUL	FL	500	6	E5
HALL CIR	TUS	TUS	100	23	F2
HALL PL	LAG	LB51	1000	34	F3
HALLADAY ST	SA	SA	100	23	C4
HALLADAY ST	SA	SA	2900	28	C1
HALLCROFT LN	HTB	HB		25	F1
HALLEY	IRV	SA		32A	A2
HALLIDAY ST	ANA	AN	800	10	C6
HALLPORT LN	HTB	HB	18000	26	A2
HALLSWORTH CIR	VPK	OR67	18100	13	A6
HALSEY AV	CO	LAG		37	F2
HALSTEAD TER	IRV	SA		32A	A2
HALYARD	NB	NB		31	B4
HALYARD DR	DPT	LB77		37	E3
HALYARD LN	GGR	GG	11800	16	E3
HAMBLETONIAN PL	CO	SA	10700	18	D5
HAMDEN AV	STN	STN	10600	15	B1
HAMDEN DR	CO	LB		29D	A6
HAMDEN LN	HTB	HB	19000	26	D3
HAMELL RD	FUL	FL	3300	6	C1
HAMER DR	CO	PLA	4700	7	D3
HAMER DR N	PLA	PLA	1700	7	D2
HAMER LN	CO	PLA	5000	7	D4
HAMILTON AV	FTNV	SA08		26	F1
HAMILTON AV	HTB	HB	8000	30	D1
HAMILTON AV	OR	OR	2200	17	E2
HAMILTON ST	CM	CM27	700	31	C1
HAMILTON ST	IRV	SA	3600	28	F4
HAMILTON TR	CO	SJ		56	B3
HAMILTON GRN	BPK	BP	5000	5	C4
HAMLET LN	TUS	TUS	14200	23	F3
HAMLET WY	WSTM	WSTM	5500	14	D6
HAMLIN ST N	OR	OR	400	18	B2
HAMLIN ST S	OR	OR	100	18	B2
HAMMATT PKWY	ANA	AN		16	B2
HAMMON LN	HTB	HB	14300	20	F2
HAMMON PL	WSTM	WSTM	13600	14	F6
HAMMON PL	WSTM	WSTM	14000	20	F1
HAMMOND	CO	SA		51	E6
HAMMONTREE DR	GGR	GG		16	A5
HAMPDEN AV	TUS	SA10	1600	23	F4
HAMPDEN RD	NB	CDLM	4500	33	C2
HAMPDEN TER	CO	ET	27200	52	C6
HAMPSHIRE AV	WSTM	WSTM	5200	14	E5
HAMPSHIRE AV E	ANA	AN	1200	11	C5
HAMPSHIRE CIR	LAP	BP23		9	D3
HAMPSHIRE CIR	NB	NB	900	31	F4
HAMPSHIRE CT	CYP	CYP	10400	14	E1
HAMPSHIRE CT	NB	NB	800	31	F4
HAMPSHIRE LN	LAH	LAH		2	B6
HAMPSHIRE LN	NB	NB	1000	31	F3
HAMPSHIRE RD	TUS	TUS	1800	24	A4
HAMPSTEAD ST	ANA	AN	700	11	B6
HAMPSTEAD ST	WSTM	WSTM	1500	16	B1
HAMPTON	IRV	SA		24	C5
HAMPTON	SA	SA		23	D1
HAMPTON AV	GGR	GG	12200	16	C3
HAMPTON CT	FTNV	SA08		26	F2
HAMPTON CT	WSTM	WSTM	5000	20	E1
HAMPTON DR	CO	LB		29D	A6
HAMPTON LN	CO	LB		29C	D4
HAMPTON LN	LAH	LAH		2	B5
HAMPTON PL	ANA	AN	900	10	E3
HAMPTON RD N	CO	LB	30000	35	D4
HAMPTON ST S	ANA	AN	100	10	E5
HAMPTON WY	STN	STN	7000	15	A2
HAMPTON WY N	CO	ET		52	C6
HAMSHIRE DR	HTB	HB		25	F1

COPYRIGHT, © 1989 BY Thomas Bros Maps

STREET	CITY	P.O. ZONE	BLOCK	PAGE	GRID
HANAKAI LN	HTB	HB	21500	30	E1
HANCOCK	IRV	SA		24	D5
HANCOCK CT	LALM	LALM		14	C3
HANCOCK LN	IRV	SA		24	F6
HANCOCK ST	ANA	AN		8	A6
HANCOCK ST	CO	LB		35	E6
HANCOCK ST	CO	LB77		37	E1
HANCOCK WY	BPK	BP	6200	9	F2
HANDEL DR	BPK	BP	8200	5	C6
HANDY ST	OR	OR	1300	12	E6
HANDY ST	OR	OR	300	17	E2
HANDY CREEK RD	OR	OR69		18	E3
HANINGER WY	VPK	OR67	9600	13	A5
HANLINE WY	LAH	LAH	1300	1	F4
HANNA CIR	GGR	GG	11500	15	F2
HANNAH WY	PLA	PLA	200	7	B4
HANOVER CIR	CYP	CYP	5000	9	D5
HANOVER COM	SA	SA		22	C2
HANOVER DR	CM	CM	200	27	D5
HANOVER DR	CYP	CYP	5200	9	D5
HANOVER LN	CO	LB		29C	E3
HANOVER LN	HTB	HB47	15000	21	A3
HANOVER PL	ANA	AN	900	10	D3
HANOVER ST	ANA	AN	400	10	D3
HANS LN	SA	SA	2300	16	E5
HANSEN AV	FUL	FL	2500	7	A5
HAPPY DR	HTB	HB		26	C1
HAPPY HUNTNG LN	ANA	AN	1200	11	B6
HAPPY SPARRW LN	CO	LB	29000	35	C3
HARBOR BLVD	CM	CM	2600	27	C5
HARBOR BLVD	CM	CM27	1800	31	C2
HARBOR BLVD	CO	SA04	16000	22	C6
HARBOR BLVD	FTNV	SA08	15800	22	C6
HARBOR BLVD	GGR	GG	12000	16	C6
HARBOR BLVD N&S	ANA	AN	100	11	C3
HARBOR BLVD N&S	FUL	FL	100	6	C5
HARBOR BLVD N&S	LAH	LAH	100	2	B6
HARBOR BLVD N&S	SA	SA	100	22	C3
HARBOR BLVD S	ANA	AN	1500	16	D3
HARBOR BLVD S	FUL	FL	1000	11	C3
HARBOR BLVD S	SA	SA04	3500	27	C5
HARBOR PL	ANA	AN05	400	11	D4
HARBOR WY	SB	SB	1700	19	F2
HARBOR BLFS CIR	HTB	HB		20	E6
HARBR BREEZE LN	HTB	HB	21500	30	F2
HARBORCREST	IRV	SA		29	C5
HARBOR CRST CIR	NB	CDLM		32	C6
HARBR GATEWAY N	CM	CM		27	C1
HARBR GATEWAY S	CM	CM		27	C2
HARBOR ISLND DR	NB	NB		31	E6
HARBOR ISLND RD	NB	NB	500	31	E5
HARBOR ISLE LN	HTB	HB	20000	26	E5
HARBOR KEY CIR	HTB	HB		26	A3
HARBOR LAKE AV	BREA	BREA		2	C5
HARBOR PT CIR	HTB	HB		30	F5
HARBOR POINT DR	DPT	DPT		38	D3
HARBOR POINT DR	NB	CDLM		32	B5
HARBOR RIDGE DR	NB	CDLM		32	D5
HARROR RIDGE LN	CO	ET		29A	D3
HARBORSIDE	CO	LB		29A	C4
HARBOR VIEW	DPT	SC24		38	B5
HARBOR VIEW DR	DPT	DPT		37	A5
HARBOR VIEW DR	NB	CDLM	2500	32	B6
HARBOR VIEW DR	NB	CDLM	3000	33	B1
HARBOR WOODS PL	NB	NB		32	C5
HARBOUR LN	HTB	HB	16400	20	C5
HARCOURT AV	CO	AN04	10500	15	E2
HARCOURT AV	GGR	GG	11000	15	E2
HARCOURT CIR	HTB	HB	9400	26	E5
HARCOURT ST	ANA	AN	400	10	E3
HARCUM LN	IRV	SA		32	F2
HARDEE WY	STN	STN	11100	15	B2
HARDING AV	ANA	AN	100	10	B4
HARDING CYN RD	CO	OR67		50	E6
HARDING CIR	BPK	BP	7100	10	B4
HARDING LN	HTB	HB	19300	26	D4
HARDING ST	NB	NB	400	33	B5
HARDING ST	OR	OR	1300	12	F6
HARDING ST	OR	OR	1100	17	F1
HARDING WY	CM	CM	3000	27	E3
HARDWICK CIR	HTB	HB	6000	20	F2
HARHAY AV	CO	MDWY	7700	21	C3
HARIA	MVJO	SJ92	28000	29B	E3
HARITON ST	OR	OR	600	17	C2
HARKERS CT	CYP	CYP	11400	15	B3
HARKNESS CIR	HTB	HB	16700	20	D5
HARLA AV	CM	CM	2600	27	C5
HARLE AV	ANA	AN04	2000	15	E1
HARLE AV	ANA	AN	1900	16	A1
HARLE AV	CO	AN04	9300	15	E1
HARLE PL	ANA	AN	1500	16	B1

STREET	CITY	P.O. ZONE	BLOCK	PAGE	GRID
HARMON ST	SA	SA	800	22	B3
HARMONY CIR	HTB	HB47	6400	21	A2
HARMONY LN	FUL	FL	700	6	D4
HARMONY LN	PLA	PLA	600	7	A5
HARMONY PL	FUL	FL31	500	6	D4
HARMONY PL	GGR	GG	11500	15	F2
HARMONY HALL CT	SJC	SJ75	31100	36	D5
HAROLD DR	LAG	LB51	200	34	D2
HAROLD PL	HTB	HB	5400	20	E1
HAROLD PL	WSTM	WSTM	5400	20	E1
HARON ST	ANA	AN	900	10	E3
HARP CT	CO	TUS	14300	24	A1
HARPER ST	CO	MDWY	14500	21	D2
HARPER ST	GGR	GG	13700	16	D6
HARPER ST	WSTM	WSTM	13600	15	D6
HARPER ST	WSTM	WSTM	15000	21	D2
HARPOON CIR	HTB	HB		26	D5
HARRIET LN	ANA	AN	1800	10	F6
HARRIET LN	ANA	AN	1500	11	A6
HARRIET LN	CO	AN04	9500	10	E6
HARRIET LN	STN	STN	8500	10	D6
HARRIMAN AV	HTB	HB	7400	26	B1
HARRINGTON CT	CO	LB53		29D	A4
HARRINGTON DR N	FUL	FL	100	6	E5
HARRINGTON DR S	FUL	FL	100	6	E5
HARRINGTON ST	GGR	GG43	14200	22	A1
HARRIS CT	ANA	AN		12	A6
HARRIS CT	ANA	AN06		17	A1
HARRIS ST	GGR	GG	11900	16	A3
HARRISBURG	IRV	SA		24	E6
HARRISBURG RD	CO	LALM	11400	14	A3
HARRISBURG RD	LALM	LALM	11300	14	B2
HARRISON WY	BPK	BP	8600	10	B4
HARROGATE PL	CO	SA	10900	18	C4
HARRON CIR	HTB	HB46	10100	27	A4
HARROW PL	NB	NB	1500	31	E3
HART CIR	HTB	HB47	16500	21	C5
HART PL N	FUL	FL	100	6	E5
HART PL S	FUL	FL	200	6	E5
HART ST	OR	OR	1400	12	F6
HART ST	OR	OR	600	17	F2
HART WY	CYP	CYP	11400	15	B3
HARTE WY	PLA	PLA	2000	7	C2
HARTFIELD CIR	HTB	HB		25	F1
HARTFORD	CO	LB77		37	E1
HARTFORD	IRV	SA		29	F3
HARTFORD AV	FUL	FL	2200	7	A3
HARTFORD AV E&W	HTB	HB	100	26	C5
HARTFORD CT	CO	SJ79		59	D6
HARTFORD DR	NB	NB		32	B3
HARTFORD LN	LAH	LAH		2	B6
HARTFORD PL	ANA	AN		10	F3
HARTFORD PL	ANA	AN		11	A3
HARTFORD RD	OR	OR	3000	17	F4
HARTFORD RD	YL	YL		40	A3
HARTFORD WY	CM	CM	900	27	E3
HARTFORD WY	WSTM	WSTM	5000	14	D6
HARTLUND ST	HTB	HB	18000	26	D2
HARTMAN ST	OR	OR	2400	12	C4
HARTOG ST	CO	LB	25100	29C	F1
HARTSDALE CIR	HTB	HB	19500	26	F3
HARVARD AV	IRV	SA	14000	24	B6
HARVARD AV	IRV	SA	17800	28	E5
HARVARD AV	IRV	SA	15000	29	A2
HARVARD AV	IRV	SA		32	E1
HARVARD AV	TUS	SA10		29	A2
HARVARD AV	WSTM	WSTM	5000	14	E6
HARVARD CIR	ANA	AN		13	F4
HARVARD CIR	HTB	HB47	6300	21	A2
HARVARD LN	SB	SB	12200	19	C4
HARVARD ST	SA	SA	1700	22	D5
HARVEST	IRV	SA		29	B2
HARVEST LN	BREA	BREA		3	A5
HARVEST LN	CO	AN04	9500	10	E6
HARVEST WY	YL	YL		7	E4
HARVEST VIEW LN	CO	SJ79		52	E4
HARVEY AV	SA	SA	200	28	B1
HARVEY CT	IRV	SA		32	D3
HARVEY DR	BREA	BREA	900	2	D4
HARVEY LN	GGR	GG	12300	15	E4
HARWICH LN	HTB	HB		30	E3
HARWOOD PL	SA	SA	300	23	B3
HARWOOD ST N	OR	OR	1400	12	D5
HARWOOD ST N&S	OR	OR	100	17	D3
HASELTINE GREEN	BPK	BP21	5000	5	C4
HASTER ST	ANA	AN	1600	16	E4
HASTER ST	CO	GG	12400	16	E4
HASTER ST	GGR	GG	11700	16	E4
HASTINGS	CO	LB77		35	D5
HASTINGS	MVJO	SJ92		29B	E2
HASTINGS AV	FUL	FL33	300	5	D6

STREET	CITY	P.O. ZONE	BLOCK	PAGE	GRID
HASTINGS AV	FUL	FL33	1000	10	D1
HASTINGS AV	IRV	SA	17500	28	F4
HASTINGS CIR	HTB	HB47	8600	21	D5
HASTINGS DR	VPK	OR67	10700	17	F1
HASTINGS ST	SA	SA	1200	22	C1
HASTINGS WY	ANA	AN		10	F3
HASTINGS WY	ANA	AN		11	A3
HATHAWAY DR	OR	OR		17	C2
HATHAWAY ST N	SA	SA	2100	17	C6
HATHAWAY ST N&S	SA	SA	100	23	C2
HATTERAS DR	HTB	HB	8600	30	D1
HAVASU CIR	BPK	BP	8100	5	C4
HAVASU DR	PLA	PLA	1400	7	C3
HAVASU PL	PLA	PLA	1400	7	C3
HAVEN DR	ANA	AN	1200	11	E4
HAVEN LN	HTB	HB46		26	E6
HAVEN LN	SA	SA		16	B6
HAVEN LN	SA	SA		22	B1
HAVEN LN	YL	YL	18700	8	A3
HAVEN PL	NB	NB	1400	31	D4
HAVENHURST CIR	IRV	SA	4500	29	D1
HAVENHURST DR	BREA	BREA	1100	2	C4
HAVENHURST LN	HTB	HB	19600	26	F4
HAVEN ROCK DR	HTB	HB		26	B5
HAVEN WOOD	IRV	SA		29	A4
HAVENWOOD CIR	OR	OR	800	18	A4
HAVENWOOD DR	GGR	GG	13300	16	B6
HAVERFIELD	NB	NB		32	C3
HAVERFORD ST	IRV	SA	3600	28	F4
HAVERHILL RD	CO	LB		35	E6
HAWAII CIR	CM	CM		27	B2
HAWAII LN	HTB	HB	16200	20	D4
HAWAII WY	PLA	PLA	300	7	B5
HAWES LN	HTB	HB	17800	26	D1
HAWK CIR	ANA	AN	1100	12	E1
HAWK LN	FTNV	SA08	9500	26	F1
HAWKRIDGE	IRV	SA		29	C4
HAWLEY ST	SA	SA	500	22	E2
HAWTHORN	IRV	SA		29	C5
HAWTHORN ST	ANA	AN	500	11	E2
HAWTHORN ST	FTNV	SA08	18500	26	F2
HAWTHORNE AV	BREA	BREA		3	C5
HAWTHORNE AV	FUL	FL33	600	5	F6
HAWTHORNE AV	FUL	FL33	900	10	F1
HAWTHORNE PL	SA	SA		28	C1
HAWTHORNE PL	TUS	TUS		24	D4
HAWTHORNE RD	LAG	LB51	300	34	C2
HAWTHORNE ST	PLA	PLA	1700	7	C3
HAXTON CIR	HTB	HB	8500	26	D5
HAYES AV	CM	CM	3000	27	E3
HAYES CIR	BPK	BP	7100	10	B4
HAYES CIR	HTB	HB	8300	26	D3
HAYES PL	LAG	LB77	31900	37	A1
HAYES ST	IRV	SA		29	E2
HAYFORD ST	OR	OR	2400	12	D4
HAYS RIVER CIR	FTNV	SA08		26	E1
HAYUCO	MVJO	SJ92	24900	29B	D6
HAYUCO	MVJO	SJ92	24900	29D	D1
HAYWARD ST	ANA	AN	800	10	C6
HAZARD AV	CO	WSTM	9500	21	D2
HAZARD AV	GGR	GG	9700	21	D2
HAZARD AV	GGR	GG43	10200	22	A1
HAZARD AV	SA	SA	3500	22	A1
HAZARD AV	WSTM	WSTM	6700	21	B1
HAZARD AV	WSTM	WSTM	10000	22	A1
HAZEL	MVJO	SJ91		52	D4
HAZEL AV	GGR	GG	12500	15	D4
HAZEL CIR	VPK	OR67	9200	13	B5
HAZEL DR	NB	CDLM	200	33	B2
HAZEL RD	TUS	TUS		24	B4
HAZEL ST	GGR	GG	13100	15	E6
HAZEL ST N&S	LAH	LAH	100	2	A5
HAZEL BELL DR	CO	SIL	29100	50	F2
HAZELBROOK DR	HTB	HB	9300	26	E5
HAZEL CREST	MVJO	SJ92		29B	E2
HAZELNUT	IRV	SA		29	C4
HAZELNUT AV	SB	SB	4200	14	D4
HAZELNUT LN	CO	ET		29B	A2
HAZELNUT ST	BPK	BP	8600	10	D3
HAZELTINE	MVJO	SJ92		29B	E3
HAZELWOOD	CO	ET	22800	29B	A3
HAZELWOOD	FTNV	SA08	17300	21	F6
HAZELWOOD	IRV	SA		29	C3
HAZELWOOD CIR	WSTM	WSTM	8300	21	D2
HAZELWOOD PL	BREA	BREA	1100	2	E4
HAZELWOOD ST	ANA	AN	500	11	C5
HEAD ST	WSTM	WSTM		21	F2
HEADLAND DR	CO	SJ79		56	E6
HEALEY AV	GGR	GG	6700	15	A4
HEALTH CTR DR	CO	LB		29A	D6

STREET	CITY	P.O. ZONE	BLOCK	PAGE	GRID
HEALTH SCI RD	IRV	SA		32	D2
HEALY DR	GGR	GG	9000	15	E3
HEARTH DR	FTNV	SA08		27	A2
HEARTH LN	CO	AN04	10000	10	F6
HEARTHSIDE ST	OR	OR	2400	12	C4
HEARTHSTONE	IRV	SA		29	B2
HEARTWOOD CIR	BREA	BREA		3	A5
HEARTWOOD CIR	CO	ET		29A	B2
HEATH AV	CO	SJ91	24900	29A	F5
HEATH TER	ANA	AN		13	D1
HEATHCLIFF DR	CO	SA	11600	18	C6
HEATHCLIFF PL	BREA	BREA		3	A5
HEATHER AV	FTNV	SA08	9300	21	E5
HEATHER AV	GGR	GG	12800	16	D4
HEATHER AV	LAH	LAH	500	1	F4
HEATHER AV	PLA	PLA	600	7	C3
HEATHER AV	TUS	TUS	1600	23	F4
HEATHER AV	TUS	TUS	1700	24	A4
HEATHER CIR	BPK	BP	7600	10	C2
HEATHER CIR	BREA	BREA	1400	3	A6
HEATHER CIR	GGR	GG	13200	16	E4
HEATHER CIR	SB	SB	3500	14	D5
HEATHER CT	WSTM	WSTM	10000	22	A2
HEATHER DR	FUL	FL	3000	6	F1
HEATHER LN	ANA	AN	1600	16	C1
HEATHER LN	BREA	BREA	1200	3	B6
HEATHER LN	NB	NB	2200	31	F1
HEATHER PL	LAG	LB51	300	34	C2
HEATHER ST	ANA	AN	800	11	F5
HEATHER ST	SB	SB	3800	14	D4
HEATHER WY	LAH	LAH	300	2	A4
HEATHER WY	YL	YL	18000	7	F4
HEATHER BROOK	CO	ET	26500	29B	B2
HEATHERFIELD DR	TUS	TUS	14200	24	A4
HEATHER GLEN	CO	SA		18	B6
HEATHER GLEN	MVJO	SJ92		29B	E2
HEATHERGREEN	IRV	SA		29	A5
HEATHER HILL LN	CO	LB		29C	D2
HEATHER RIDGE	CO	LB		29C	D4
HEATHERIDGE DR	YL	YL		8	F3
HEATHERSTONE DR	OR	OR	500	18	A2
HEATHERSTONE ST	OR	OR	800	18	A4
HEATHERTEN CIR	HTB	HB	9100	26	E3
HEATHERVIEW	CO	ET		52	A5
HEATHERWOOD	CO	TRA		59	D6
HEATHER WOOD LN	YL	YL		8	F3
HEATHPOINT LN	HTB	HB	18000	26	A1
HEATHROW CIR	CO	ET		29B	A3
HEAVENWOOD CIR	HTB	HB	18700	26	D2
HEDGE LN	LAG	LB77	31800	37	A1
HEDGELAND	CO	TRA		59	D5
HEDGEMONT WY	CO	ET	21200	52	C6
HEDGEROW	MVJO	SJ92		29B	E2
HEDGEWOOD AV	ANA	AN	1500	11	E2
HEDIN CIR	ANA	AN		43	A3
HEDLUND DR	CO	AN04	10400	15	E1
HEDLUND RD	CO	AN04	10500	10	E6
HEDWIG RD	CO	LALM	3200	14	A2
HEFFRON DR	ANA	AN	2500	10	E5
HEFLEY ST	WSTM	WSTM	6000	14	F6
HEIDI AV	CO	ET	21900	29A	D2
HEIDI CIR	GGR	GG	13800	16	A6
HEIDI CIR	YL	YL	17500	7	F3
HEIDI ST	GGR	GG	13900	16	A6
HEIGHTS DR	TUS	TUS	14500	23	E1
HEIL AV	FTNV	SA08	9000	21	C5
HEIL AV	FTNV	SA08	10000	22	B5
HEIL AV	HTB	HB	4100	20	E5
HEIL AV	HTB	HB47	6200	21	B5
HEIL AV	WSTM	WSTM	8000	21	C5
HEIM AV	CO	OR65	16300	12	D4
HEIM AV	OR	OR	1400	12	D4
HELEN DR	FUL	FL	200	6	C3
HELEN LN	ANA	AN		13	C1
HELENA	IRV	SA		29	D1
HELENA AV	DPT	DPT		37	D5
HELENA CIR	CM	CM		27	E3
HELENA CIR	CO	SJ91	25000	29A	F5
HELENA CIR	FTNV	SA08	16900	21	F5
HELENA CIR	HTB	HB	19500	26	D4
HELENA CIR	VPK	OR67	17800	17	F1
HELENA PL	CM	CM		27	E3
HELENA ST N&S	ANA	AN	100	11	D4
HELENBROOK LN	HTB	HB49		25	F1
HELENE CIR	GGR	GG45	12200	14	E4
HELENE ST	GGR	GG45	12600	14	E4
HELIANTHUS	CO	SJ		59	C1
HELIOPSIS	CO	SJ		59	C1
HELIOTROPE AV	NB	CDLM	100	33	A2
HELIOTROPE DR	SA	SA	1700	17	A6
HELM AV	FTNV	SA08	9000	26	E2

STREET	CITY	P.O. ZONE	BLOCK	PAGE	GRID
HELMSDALE	MVJO	SJ91		29D	C6
HELMSIDE DR	HTB	HB	5600	25	E1
HELOISE WY	PLA	PLA	2100	7	C2
HELSINKI ST	CO	SJ91		29A	F5
HELSINKI ST	CO	SJ91		29B	A5
HEMINGWAY AV	IRV	SA		24	C6
HEMINGWAY AV	PLA	PLA	600	7	C2
HEMINGWAY CT	IRV	SA	3800	24	C6
HEMLOCK	CO	SJ		59	B3
HEMLOCK	IRV	SA		29	B5
HEMLOCK CIR	FTNV	SA08	16500	21	F5
HEMLOCK PL	ANA	AN	700	11	E2
HEMLOCK PL	FUL	FL	2800	6	E2
HEMLOCK ST	FTNV	SA08	16300	21	F4
HEMLOCK ST	OR	OR	200	17	B3
HEMLOCK WY	BPK	BP	8600	10	D3
HEMLOCK WY	SA	SA	1400	22	E6
HEMLOCK WY	SA	SA	800	23	A6
HEMP CIR	FTNV	SA08	16100	21	F4
HEMPSTEAD CIR	ANA	AN	2700	12	A3
HEMPSTEAD RD	ANA	AN	2800	12	B3
HEMPSTEAD ST	ANA	AN	2700	12	A3
HENDERSON AV	GGR	GG43	10600	22	A2
HENDERSON PL	SA	SA	4600	22	B2
HENDERSON WY	LAH	LAH	1200	1	F4
HENDERSON WY	VPK	OR67	9400	13	A5
HENDERSON GRN	BPK	BP	5000	5	C4
HENDON ST	CO	LB		29A	E6
HENDON ST	CO	LB		29C	E1
HENDRIX ST	IRV	SA	3700	28	F4
HENDRIX ST	IRV	SA		29	A4
HENLEY	MVJO	SJ92		29B	F6
HENLEY DR	CO	LB77		36	A6
HENLEY DR	WSTM	WSTM		21	E2
HENNING WY	ANA	AN		13	D2
HENRICKSEN DR	HTB	HB	5300	20	E4
HENRIETTA CIR	PLA	PLA		7	D4
HENRY	IRV	SA		24	C5
HENSEL DR	CO	LAH		2	B3
HENSHAW CIR	BPK	BP	8200	5	C4
HENSTRIDGE CIR	TUS	TUS	13800	17	F6
HENTON DR	HTB	HB	8800	26	E5
HERBERT LN	HTB	HB	17000	20	F6
HERCULES DR	HTB	HB46	10000	27	A6
HEREFORD ST	WSTM	WSTM	14200	20	F1
HERENCIA	MVJO	SJ92	21700	29B	E1
HERITAGE	IRV	SA		29	D2
HERITAGE AV	PLA	PLA	1700	7	B3
HERITAGE CIR	ANA	AN	1800	16	A1
HERITAGE DR	CM	CM		27	D6
HERITAGE DR	CO	SJ79		59	E1
HERITAGE LN	HTB	HB47	16700	21	C5
HERITAGE PL	OR	OR		17	E2
HERITAGE WY	FUL	FL33		5	F2
HERITAGE WY	TUS	TUS		24	C3
HERMANSON CIR	HTB	HB		20	D6
HERMES RD	ANA	AN	5900	13	C2
HERMIT CIR	HTB	HB47	16700	21	C5
HERMITAGE DR	FUL	FL33		5	E2
HERMITAGE LN	NB	NB		32	B5
HERMOSA	CO	ET		29A	F4
HERMOSA	IRV	SA		24	F5
HERMOSA CIR	BPK	BP	6600	9	F1
HERMOSA DR	ANA	AN	1000	11	B3
HERMOSA DR	HTB	HB		20	D4
HERMOSA DR E&W	FUL	FL	100	6	B1
HERMOSA LN	CO	SJ79		59	D2
HERMOSA PL	FUL	FL	3700	6	B1
HERMOSA WY	LAG	LB51	700	34	F4
HERON	IRV	SA		29	C3
HERON AV	FTNV	SA08	9000	26	E2
HERON CIR	HTB	HB	8400	26	D6
HERON WY	NB	CDLM		33	C1
HERSHEY DR	BPK	BP	7400	9	F2
HESBY WY	CO	ET		29B	B1
HESPERIAN ST N	SA	SA	2000	16	F6
HESPERIAN ST N	SA	SA	100	22	F2
HESPERIAN ST S	SA	SA	300	23	A3
HESPERIAN WY	SA	SA		17	A4
HESS CIR	HTB	HB	2100	26	C4
HESSELL ST	ANA	AN	300	11	B4
HESTER AV	BPK	BP	10200	9	F6
HESTER PL	GGR	GG	12200	15	F3
HESTER ST	CYP	CYP	10500	14	F1
HEWES AV	CO	OR	11200	18	A6
HEWES AV	CO	SA	12600	18	A6
HEWES ST	CO	OR	200	18	B3
HEWES ST N&S	OR	OR	100	18	B4
HEWITT LN	GGR	GG	8700	15	D6
HEWITT PL	GGR	GG	8700	15	D6
HIALEAH DR	CYP	CYP	10100	9	C6

1990 ORANGE COUNTY STREET INDEX

STREET	CITY	P.O. ZONE	BLOCK	PAGE	GRID
HIAWATHA AV	ANA	AN	2100	10	F4
HIAWATHA AV	ANA	AN	1800	11	A4
HIBISCUS	CO	SJ88		59	B5
HIBISCUS AV	FTNV	SA08	9700	21	F4
HIBISCUS CIR	YL	YL		8	C3
HIBISCUS CT	NB	CDLM		33	B1
HIBISCUS DR	CO	LB	28000	29C	E6
HIBISCUS DR	GGR	GG	9700	15	F2
HIBISCUS WY	PLA	PLA	700	7	C5
HICKOCK RD	STN	STN	10200	10	C6
HICKORY	IRV	SA		29	B5
HICKORY CIR	CYP	CYP	5100	9	D5
HICKORY DR	BPK	BP	8000	10	D3
HICKORY DR	YL	YL		8	D5
HICKORY LN	HTB	HB	19300	26	E3
HICKORY LN	OR	OR	1300	17	E2
HICKORY PL	CM	CM	2800	27	C4
HICKORY PL	CO	ET	22500	29A	C2
HICKORY PL	FUL	FL	2900	6	F2
HICKORY ST	ANA	AN	1300	11	D6
HICKORY ST	BREA	BREA	900	6	E1
HICKORY ST	FTNV	SA08	16300	21	E4
HICKORY ST	SA	SA	100	23	C2
HICKORY BRCH LN	OR	OR69		18	E2
HICKORY BRCH RD	CO	SA	12800	24	B3
HICKORY BRCH RD	CO	TUS	13000	24	B3
HICKORY BRCH ST	TUS	TUS		24	A4
HICKORY HLLS AV	CO	ET	22800	29A	D3
HICKORY TREE LN	IRV	SA		29	A5
HICKORY TREE LN	YL	YL		8	E2
HICKORYWOOD WY	CO	ET		51	E4
HICKS CANYON	IRV	SA		24	E5
HICKS CANYON	IRV	SA20		49	A5
HIDALGO	IRV	SA	27700	24	E5
HIDALGO	MVJO	SJ91	22000	29B	C2
HIDALGO	NB	NB	2400	32	A3
HIDALGO ST	BPK	BP	7100	5	B6
HIDDEN LN	CO	LAH	1000	2	A3
HIDDEN TR	OR	OR		18	B2
HIDDEN WY	GGR	GG		15	F4
HIDDENBROOK	MVJO	SJ92		29B	E1
HIDDENBROOK	MVJO	SJ92		52	E6
HIDDEN CANYON	OR	OR69		18	D3
HIDDEN CYN RD	ANA	AN		13	F3
HIDDEN CYN RD	ANA	AN		43	A3
HIDDEN CREEK LN	CO	LB		29C	D2
HIDDEN CREST	CO	LB77		36	A3
HIDDEN GROVE LN	ANA	AN		13	D2
HIDDEN HILL AV	TUS	TUS	14900	23	F5
HIDDEN HILLS RD	CO	LB		35	F3
HIDDEN HILLS RD	CO	LB77		36	A3
HIDDEN HILLS RD	YL	YL		8	F4
HIDDEN HILLS RD	YL	YL		40	A4
HIDDEN SPG LN	CO	SJ		56	D6
HIDDEN SPG LN	CO	SJ		59	D1
HIDDEN TRAIL RD	CO	LB	27000	29C	F4
HIDDEN VLY DR	VPK	OR67	9200	13	B4
HIDDEN VLY LN	ANA	AN		13	D2
HIDDN VLY CY RD	LAG	LB51	2000	34	F2
HIDDEN VLG RD	GGR	GG		15	F4
HIDDENWOOD	CO	LB77		35	F3
HIDDENWOOD	CO	LB77		36	A3
HIDEA WY	CO	SIL	28100	50	D2
HIDEAWAY DR	CO	SA		18	C4
HIDEAWAY DR	YL	YL	18800	8	B2
HIDEAWAY LN	FUL	FL	3300	6	B1
HIDEOUT	HTB	HB		20	D5
HIERRO	SCL	SC72		38	E4
HIGGINS CIR	HTB	HB47	16500	21	D5
HIGH DR	LAG	LB51	100	34	C2
HIGH ST	ANA	AN		11	C3
HIGHBROOK RD	OR			18	E2
HIGHBROOK WY	STN	STN		15	C4
HIGHCLIFF DR	CO	SA	9900	18	D4
HIGHCLIFF ST	WSTM	WSTM	15500	21	E3
HIGH COUNTRY DR	CO	SJ		59	E1
HIGH CREST CIR	CO	SA		18	C4
HIGHCREST CIR	IRV	SA	14500	29	D2
HIGHCREST CT	FUL	FL		6	F3
HIGHCREST LN	FUL	FL		6	F3
HIGHCREST RD	CO	LB77		37	D1
HIGHGATE	MVJO	SJ92		29B	F1
HIGHGATE TER	IRV	SA		32A	A3
HIGHLAND	MVJO	SJ91		29D	C5
HIGHLAND AV	BPK	BP	6400	5	B6
HIGHLAND AV	BPK	BP	6700	10	B1
HIGHLAND AV	PLA	PLA	6400	7	F5
HIGHLAND AV	SA	SA	4100	22	C3
HIGHLAND AV	YL	YL	5000	7	F4
HIGHLAND AV N&S	FUL	FL	100	6	C6
HIGHLAND AV S	FUL	FL	1000	11	C1

STREET	CITY	P.O. ZONE	BLOCK	PAGE	GRID
HIGHLAND CT	LAH	LAH	200	2	A3
HIGHLAND DR	NB	NB	1100	31	E3
HIGHLAND DR	SJC	SJ75	27000	36	C3
HIGHLAND LN	ANA	AN		13	E3
HIGHLAND LN	CO	SA05		18	C6
HIGHLAND LN	HTB	HB47		26	A1
HIGHLAND RD	LAG	LB51	100	34	F5
HIGHLAND ST	NB	NB63	100	30	F4
HIGHLAND ST	OR	OR	1800	12	E5
HIGHLAND ST	OR	OR	200	17	E3
HIGHLAND ST	SA	SA	1300	22	E3
HIGHLAND ST	SA	SA	100	23	E3
HIGHLAND WY	LAG	LB51	2700	34	F5
HIGHLAND WY	SJC	SJ92		36	B2
HIGHLANDER	CO	ET		52	C3
HIGHLANDER AV	LAH	LAH	500	1	F4
HIGHLANDER AV	PLA	PLA	600	7	C3
HIGHLAND GREEN	BPK	BP21		5	D4
HIGHLANDS AV	CO	LB	22700	35	C3
HIGHLAND VIEW	IRV	SA		32A	B2
HIGHLAND VW LN	CO	SJ		52	E3
HIGH NOON CIR	CO	ET	26700	29B	B1
HIGHPINE RD	CO	ET	24300	29A	E5
HIGHPLAINS TER	CO	LB		29D	A2
HIGHPOINT	CO	SJ79		59	D2
HIGHPOINT RD	OR	OR		13	D6
HIGHRIDGE WY	CO	SJ		52	E3
HIGHTIDE DR	HTB	HB	9500	30	F2
HIGHTREE CIR	ANA	AN	4600	7	F5
HIGHVIEW CIR	SJC	SJ75	29800	36	D3
HIGHVIEW DR	CO	SA	2000	24	C1
HIGHWOOD CIR	CO	LB	26000	29C	F4
HIGUERA	MVJO	SJ91		29B	D1
HIGUERA	MVJO	SJ91		52	D6
HILARIA CIR	HTB	HB	21600	30	F2
HILARIA WY	NB	NB	4100	31	C4
HILBERS RD	ANA	AN	2100	10	F4
HILDA CIR	ANA	AN	400	12	A3
HILDA CT	ANA	AN	500	12	A4
HILDA ST	ANA	AN	500	12	A5
HILGARD DR	OR	OR69		18	C2
HILL AV	ANA	AN	100	11	D6
HILL AV	FUL	FL33		10	D1
HILL AV	FUL	FL	100	11	A1
HILL DR	SB	SB		20	A2
HILL LN	LAG	LB77		37	B1
HILL PL	ANA	AN	100	11	D6
HILL PL	CM	CM27	200	31	E1
HILL RD	GGR	GG	10000	15	F2
HILL RD	LAH	LAH	900	2	A3
HILL ST	HTB	HB	600	26	C5
HILL ST	LAG	LB51	400	34	D2
HILL ST	OR	OR	400	18	B4
HILLANDALE AV	LAH	LAH	1400	1	F5
HILLARY LN	CO	LB		29C	F2
HILLCREST	IRV	SA		32A	A2
HILLCREST	MVJO	SJ91		29D	C5
HILLCREST AV	OR	OR	2500	12	E5
HILLCREST AV	PLA	PLA	400	7	C4
HILLCREST AV	VPK	OR67	18300	13	A5
HILLCREST CIR	ANA	AN		13	D2
HILLCREST CIR	BPK	BP	4800	5	D3
HILLCREST CIR	HTB	HB		26	B2
HILLCREST CIR	VPK	OR67	18200	13	A5
HILLCREST CIR	YL	YL	16900	7	D3
HILLCREST DR	LAG	LB	2000	34	B1
HILLCREST DR	FUL	FL	100	6	C4
HILLCREST DR	LAG	LB51	700	34	B1
HILLCREST DR S	CO	LB		35	E2
HILLCREST LN	FUL	FL	300	6	C4
HILLCREST LN	NB	NB		32	B4
HILLCREST RD	BPK	BP	8600	5	D3
HILLCREST ST	ANA	AN		13	D2
HILLCREST ST	CO	LAH	2200	1	F5
HILLEDGE DR	LAG	LB51	400	34	D2
HILLGATE	IRV	SA		32A	A1
HILLGATE CIR	CO	SJ79		56	E6
HILLGATE LN	HTB	HB	17400	20	E6
HILLGRASS	IRV	SA		32A	B3
HILLHAVEN CIR	BREA	BREA	200	3	A6
HILLHAVEN DR	BREA	BREA	1200	3	A6
HILLHAVEN DR	BREA	BREA		7	A1
HILLHAVEN DR	CO	SA	18400	18	A5
HILLHEAD DR	HTB	HB	8400	30	D1
HILLHURST DR	CO	LB	23600	35	D4
HILLIES LN	CO	LB51		33A	F4
HILLMAN CIR	OR	OR		12	E4
HILLOCK VIEW PZ	YL	YL	19600	8	C4
HILLRISE	CO	SJ79		59	E2
HILLROSE	CO	LB56		29C	B3
HILL ROSE DR	CO	LALM	2800	14	A4

STREET	CITY	P.O. ZONE	BLOCK	PAGE	GRID
HILLSBORO CIR	HTB	HB	19000	26	E3
HILLSBORO DR	CO	LB		29D	A6
HILLSBORO PL	FUL	FL33	800	5	F5
HILLSBORO PL	TUS	TUS	14800	23	F5
HILLSBORO RD	CO	SA	10500	18	D4
HILLSBOROUGH	IRV	SA15		32A	B2
HILLSBOROUGH	NB	NB		32	C5
HILLSDALE AV	CO	LB56		29C	C3
HILLSDALE DR	NB	NB		32	B3
HILLSDALE DR	OR			18	E2
HILLSDALE LN	HTB	HB46		30	E6
HILLSFORD PL	CO	ET	26000	29B	B2
HILLSGATE LN	ANA	AN		13	D2
HILLSGATE RD	OR			18	E2
HILLSIDE AV	OR	OR	2400	12	E6
HILLSIDE AV	OR	OR	19000	13	B5
HILLSIDE CT	CO	ET		52	C6
HILLSIDE CT	LAH	LAH	200	2	A3
HILLSIDE DR	CO	OR	19800	13	C6
HILLSIDE DR	CO	OR	19800	18	C1
HILLSIDE DR	NB	NB		32	D4
HILLSIDE DR	YL	YL	6200	8	C5
HILLSIDE LN	ANA	AN		13	D3
HILLSIDE LN	LAG	LB77	31800	37	A1
HILLSIDE LN	CO	SIL	29300	50	F2
HILLSIDE LN	CO	SIL	29300	53	A1
HILLSIDE ST	LAH	LAH	600	2	A3
HILLSIDE TER	SJC	SJ75	29800	36	D3
HILLSIDE WY	LAG	LB51	1100	34	F3
HILLTOP	IRV	SA		32A	A2
HILLTOP CT	FUL	FL		6	F2
HILL TOP DR	CO	OR67	28800	50	F6
HILLTOP DR	NB	NB		32	D4
HILLTOP DR	OR	OR	1600	12	E3
HILLTOP DR	SJC	SJ75		36	E4
HILLTOP LN	BREA	BREA		3	B5
HILLTOP PL	YL	YL		8	C5
HILLVIEW CIR	FUL	FL		6	E3
HILLVIEW CIR	HTB	HB	16500	20	E5
HILLVIEW DR	CO	LB		35	E3
HILLVIEW DR	LAG	LB51		34	F2
HILLVIEW DR	NB	NB		32	D4
HILLVIEW DR	OR	OR	3900	12	E3
HILLVIEW RD	ANA	AN	300	10	E5
HILLVIEW RD	CO	AN04	9300	10	E5
HILLWOOD DR	YL	YL	17000	7	E3
HILLWOOD PL	YL	YL	17300	7	E3
HILO CIR	HTB	HB	4900	20	D4
HILO LN	CO	SA	13900	18	B6
HILO ST	SA	SA		22	C3
HILO WY	SA	SA		22	C3
HILTON LN	CO	OR		18	C1
HILTON LN	GGR	GG	13000	16	E5
HILTON LN	HTB	HB47	16000	21	A4
HILTON LN	OR	OR		13	C6
HILTON ST	GGR	GG	12500	16	E4
HILTON WY	CO	LB56		29C	E5
HILVANAR	NB	NB	600	32	A3
HINGHAM DR	HTB	HB	9300	26	E5
HINKLE PL	LAG	LB51	300	34	F5
HINSDALE PL	ANA	AN	800	13	D1
HINTON WY	CO	SA	12300	18	C4
HIRAM LN	IRV	SA		32	F2
HIRAM ST	FTNV	SA08	15900	21	F4
HITCHCOCK LN	GGR	GG		16	A5
HITCHNGPOST CIR	HTB	HB48		26	A2
HITCHNG RAIL RD	CO	LB	25800	29D	A3
HI TOP LN	CO	OR		18	C1
HOAG RD	NB	NB		31	B4
HOBART LN	HTB	HB47	16400	21	B5
HOBART ST	SA	SA	100	23	B4
HOBART BAY	DPT	LB77		37	D4
HOCK AV	PLA	PLA	1900	7	B2
HODGENVILLE	IRV	SA		24	C5
HODSON AV	BREA	BREA	1400	2	C4
HODSON AV	LAH	LAH	1600	2	C4
HOEPTNER ST	IRV	SA	5200	29	D3
HOFFMAN ST	BPK	BP	8900	9	F4
HOGGAN AV	GGR	GG	12200	16	C4
HOI CIR	CO	ET	21900	29A	D2
HOLBROOK ST	ANA	AN	1700	8	A5
HOLBURN DR	HTB	HB46	10000	27	A4
HOLDEN CIR	LALM	LALM	10000	9	B6
HOLDER ST	BPK	BP	7000	9	F2
HOLDER ST	CYP	CYP	9100	9	F6
HOLDER ST	CYP	CYP	10500	14	F1
HOLDER ST	CYP	CYP		15	A2
HOLGATE DR	ANA	AN	1200	16	B1
HOLGATE PL	ANA	AN	1500	16	B1
HOLGATE ST	LAH	LAH	100	2	C4

STREET	CITY	P.O. ZONE	BLOCK	PAGE	GRID
HOLIDAY DR	SA	SA		16	D6
HOLIDAY DR	SA	SA		22	D1
HOLIDAY LN	CO	SA		18	C4
HOLIDAY LN	HTB	HB	15400	20	F3
HOLIDAY RD	NB	NB	1700	31	F3
HOLLAND	IRV	SA18		29A	C1
HOLLAND AV	GGR	GG45	5300	14	E3
HOLLAND DR	HTB	HB47	8000	21	C6
HOLLIS CIR	LAH	LAH	400	2	A6
HOLLISTER ST	OR	OR68		16	F2
HOLLOW BROOK	CM	CM		27	D2
HOLLW BROOK CIR	CM	CM		27	D2
HOLLOWGLEN	IRV	SA		29	C4
HOLLY	IRV	SA		29	D3
HOLLY AV	FTNV	SA08	11500	22	C4
HOLLY AV	LAH	LAH	2500	1	D4
HOLLY CIR	YL	YL	18000	7	F4
HOLLY DR	GGR	GG	10800	16	A3
HOLLY DR	LAG	LB77	31000	35	A5
HOLLY DR	LAP	BP23	7900	9	D2
HOLLY DR	TUS	TUS		24	D4
HOLLY LN	NB	NB	2200	31	D4
HOLLY ST	ANA	AN	900	10	F2
HOLLY ST	BREA	BREA	1200	3	A6
HOLLY ST	HTB	HB	19000	26	B3
HOLLY ST	IRV	SA		29	A6
HOLLY ST	LAG	LB51	300	34	C3
HOLLY ST	OR	OR	100	17	B3
HOLLY WY	BPK	BP	8600	10	D3
HOLLYBERRY LN	YL	YL		40	D5
HOLLYCREEK DR	SA	SA		22	C2
HOLLYDALE DR	FUL	FL	1000	6	E4
HOLLY DELL RD	CO	ET	22800	29A	D2
HOLLY HILL LN	CO	LB		29C	E2
HOLLYHOCK AV	FTNV	SA08	9400	21	E4
HOLLYHOCK AV	TUS	TUS	14900	23	F5
HOLLYHOCK LN	CO	LB		29C	D5
HOLLYHOCK LN	PLA	PLA	900	7	C5
HOLLYLINE AV	SA	SA	4500	22	B1
HOLLYOAK	CO	LB		29C	D4
HOLLYOAK AV	BPK	BP	8600	10	D3
HOLLY OAK AV	IRV	SA	14700	29	C1
HOLLYOAK DR	FUL	FL		6	F3
HOLLY OAK LN	MVJO	SJ91		52	D5
HOLLY SPGS DR	MVJO	SJ92		29B	F6
HOLLY TREE LN	CO	SA	1700	18	D5
HOLLYWOOD LN	HTB	HB	16300	20	E5
HOLMBY CT	CYP	CYP	5700	9	E6
HOLMES AV	PLA	PLA	600	7	C3
HOLMWOOD DR	NB	NB	300	31	C4
HOLT AV	CO	SA	13500	18	A6
HOLT AV	CO	TUS	14200	24	A2
HOLT AV	HTB	HB47	7900	21	C4
HOLT AV	TUS	TUS	100	24	A2
HOLT DR	LAH	LAH	2100	2	C4
HOLT DR	PLA	PLA		7	C4
HOLT ST	BPK	BP	7700	5	C5
HOLTWOOD AV	ANA	AN	4300	12	F2
HOLTZ HILL RD	DPT	DPT		37	F4
HOLY JIM CYN RD	CO			53	B2
HOLYOAK LN	GGR	GG	11700	16	C3
HMBR D GUERR RD	CO	LB77	28900	36	A2
HOME PL	ANA	AN	900	10	E3
HOMER ST	ANA	AN	1000	11	C2
HOMER ST	WSTM	WSTM	6500	21	A1
HOMESTEAD E	OR	OR		17	F1
HOMESTEAD W	OR	OR		17	F1
HOMESTEAD LN	HTB	HB	19000	26	D3
HOMESTEAD RD	GGR	GG	11700	16	C4
HOMESTEAD ST	IRV	SA	4000	29	C1
HOMEWAY DR	GGR	GG	11100	15	E2
HOMEWOOD AV	BPK	BP	5700	5	C6
HOMEWOOD LN	ANA	AN		8	B5
HOMEWOOD PL	LAG	LB77	31900	37	B1
HOMEWOOD PL	FUL	FL33		5	E2
HOMEWOOD RD	SB	SB	1400	14	A6
HON AV	CO	LB		29A	E6
HON AV	CO	LB	24800	29C	F1
HONDO ST	ANA	AN	700	8	D6
HONDURAS WY	BPK	BP	5700	9	E2
HONEYSUCKLE	IRV	SA		29	B5
HONEYSUCKLE AV	FTNV	SA08	9200	21	E4
HONEYWOOD CT	BREA	BREA		2	C5
HONEYWOOD LN	ANA	AN		13	B2
HONEYWOOD LN	HTB	HB	19500	26	E4
HONEYWOOD LN	LAH	LAH	400	5	F1
HONEYWOOD LN E	ANA	AN		13	B2
HONOLD CIR	GGR	GG		15	B2
HONOLULU LN	HTB	HB	16200	20	D4
HOOD AV E	SA	SA	500	23	C4
HOOD AV W	SA	SA	2400	22	E4

STREET	CITY	P.O. ZONE	BLOCK	PAGE	GRID
HOOD CT	FTNV	SA08	17400	22	B6
HOOD DR	WSTM	WSTM	6700	15	A5
HOOD LN	STN	STN	11100	15	B2
HOOKER DR	HTB	HB47	6200	21	A4
HOOVER AV E	OR	OR		12	E6
HOOVER AV E&W	OR	OR	100	17	B1
HOOVER PL	PLA	PLA		7	E5
HOOVER ST	WSTM	WSTM	13000	15	B5
HOOVER ST	WSTM	WSTM	14000	21	B2
HOOVER WY	BPK	BP	7000	10	B4
HOPE ST	CO	SA	15900	50	E4
HOPE ST	CYP	CYP		14	F2
HOPE ST	GGR	GG	13000	16	A5
HOPE ST	GGR	GG43	14100	22	A1
HOPE ST	WSTM	WSTM	14700	22	A2
HOPEBAY LN	HTB	HB		26	D4
HOPETOWN LN	HTB	HB	20600	26	E6
HOPI LN	CO	ET		29A	F2
HOPI RD	CO	AN04	8400	15	D2
HOPI RD	GGR	GG	8500	15	D2
HOPI RD	STN	STN	7600	15	C2
HOPKINS ST	IRV	SA	17900	28	F5
HORIZON	CO	LB56		29C	C4
HORIZON LN	HTB	HB	20600	26	F6
HORNBEAM LN	FTNV	SA08	18000	26	E2
HORNET WY	FUL	FL	1000	6	D4
HORNO CREEK RD	SJC	SJ75	27700	36	D3
HORSESHOE	CO	ET	25000	29B	A2
HORSESHOE CIR	PLA	PLA	1900	7	F5
HORSESHOE DR	PLA	PLA	100	7	F5
HORSESHOE LN	ANA	AN	4000	12	E2
HORSE SHOE LN	YL	YL	6400	8	F2
HORSESHOE RD	OR	OR		18	D2
HORSESHOE TR	OR	OR	7900	18	D2
HORSESHOE BEND	SJC	SJ75	27600	36	D3
HORSETREE CIR	CO	SJ		56	D6
HORSHAM AV	WSTM	WSTM	5200	20	E1
HORSHAM PL	SA	SA		23	B6
HORTENSE DR	WSTM	WSTM	15500	22	A3
HORTON AV	FUL	FL	200	6	A5
HOSKINS ST	HTB	HB	16700	20	D5
HOSPITAL CIR	WSTM	WSTM	200	15	C6
HOSPITAL RD	NB	NB	4100	31	C4
HOSPITL FRNT RD	OR	OR68		16	F3
HOTEL WY	ANA	AN	1500	16	D1
HOTEL TER DR	SA	SA		23	C6
HOT SPRINGS DR	HTB	HB	9700	26	F5
HOT SPGS CYN RD	CO	SA		62	B1
HOUSTON AV	FUL	FL33	1500	10	E2
HOUSTON AV	FUL	FL	100	11	B2
HOUSTON AV	LAP	BP23	5000	9	E2
HOUSTON ST	BPK	BP	6500	9	F2
HOUSTON ST	CO	FL33	9900	10	F2
HOUSTON ST	FUL	FL33	1900	10	F2
HOUSTON TR	CO	LB		29C	F3
HOUSTON TR	CO	LB		29D	A3
HOWARD AV	LALM	LALM	3500	14	B2
HOWARD CIR	GGR	GG	13800	16	A6
HOWARD CIR	HTB	HB47	8500	21	D5
HOWARD ST	GGR	GG	13900	16	A6
HOWARD WY	CM	CM		27	C2
HOWE DR	ETMC	SA09		51	D3
HOWELL AV	ANA	AN	2000	16	E1
HOWELL AV	ANA	AN06	2000	17	A1
HOWELL AV	CO	AN06	14200	17	A1
HOWES DR	CO	LB56		29C	E5
HOWLAND LN	HTB	HB47	16100	21	A4
HOWLAND WY	CO	TUS	14000	17	F6
HOWLAND WY	CO	TUS	14100	23	F1
HOYT CIR	HTB	HB	18700	26	C2
HUBBELL WY	ANA	AN	1200	10	E2
HUBER CT	CO	AN04	10900	15	E2
HUBER ST	GGR	GG	11100	15	E2
HUCKLEBERRY RD	SA	SA	2500	16	E6
HUDSON	IRV	SA		24	F6
HUDSON	IRV	SA		29	F1
HUDSON AV	CM	CM	700	27	F3
HUDSON AV	PLA	PLA	200	7	C3
HUDSON DR	HTB	HB	9300	30	E2
HUDSON DR	PLA	PLA	200	7	C3
HUDSON DR	PLA	PLA		7	B3
HUDSON BAY DR	ANA	AN		13	C3
HUDSON RIV CIR	FTNV	SA08	8600	26	D1
HUERTA	MVJO	SJ92		29D	C4
HUEVOS CIR	MVJO	SJ91	26500	29D	B2
HUGGINS AV	YL	YL	16700	7	D3
HUGGINS AV E	PLA	PLA	900	7	D3
HUGHES	IRV	SA18		29A	D1
HUGHES	IRV	SA18		51	D6
HUGHES DR	ANA	AN	3000	10	C4
HUGHES DR	FUL	FL33		5	F4

1990 ORANGE COUNTY STREET INDEX

STREET	CITY	P.O. ZONE	BLOCK	PAGE	GRID
HUGHES DR	HTB	HB47	6400	21	A4
HUGO RD	CO	LB		35	F2
HUGO RD	CO	LB77		36	A1
HUKEE AV	ANA	AN	1300	11	F5
HULA CIR	HTB	HB	22000	30	E2
HULL DR	HTB	HB46	10000	27	A4
HUMBOLDT AV	WSTM	WSTM	6500	15	A6
HUMBOLDT DR	BPK	BP		5	C4
HUMBOLDT DR	HTB	HB	3800	20	C5
HUMBOLT ST	LALM	LALM	10100	9	B6
HUMBOLT ST	LALM	LALM		14	B1
HUMMINGBIRD	IRV	SA		29	B3
HUMMINGBIRD AV	FTNV	SA08	8700	26	D2
HUMMING BRD CIR	ANA	AN		13	F2
HUMMINGBIRD CIR	LAP	BP23	8000	9	C3
HUMMINGBIRD DR	CM	CM	1700	27	B5
HUMMINGBIRD LN	CO	ET	22400	29A	F2
HUMMINGBIRD LN	CO	LB56		29C	A1
HUMMINGBIRD LN	GGR	GG	9800	15	E3
HUMMINGBIRD LN	HTB	HB	15600	20	E4
HUMMINGBIRD LN	YL	YL	18700	8	A3
HUMOR DR	ANA	AN	1600	16	A1
HUMPHREY CIR	IRV	SA	15000	29	D2
HUNDLEY ST	ANA	AN	1300	12	B1
HUNDLEY WY	PLA	PLA	700	7	A6
HUNDLEY WY	PLA	PLA	700	12	A1
HUNKY DORY LN	CO	SJ		56	B3
HUNT AV	GGR	GG		15	B3
HUNT DR	PLA	PLA	2200	7	C2
HUNT CLUB DR	SJC	SJ75		36	D5
HUNTER	IRV	SA		29	E1
HUNTER AV	ANA	AN		8	B6
HUNTER AV	ANA	AN		13	B1
HUNTER AV	SA	SA	900	23	C3
HUNTER LN	CO	MDWY	14500	21	D2
HUNTER LN	HTB	HB	20800	26	F6
HUNTER LN	WSTM	WSTM	15000	21	D1
HUNTER WY	STN	STN		10	E4
HUNTER WY	OR	OR		13	D6
HUNTER WY	STN	STN		15	B3
HUNTER GREEN	BPK	BP21	4900	5	D4
HUNTING CIR	VPK	OR67		13	B5
HUNTING HORN DR	CO	SA	10900	18	D5
HUNTINGTON	IRV	SA		29	D1
HUNTINGTON AV	ANA	AN	2100	10	E2
HUNTINGTON CIR	VPK	OR67	17900	12	F6
HUNTINGTON CT	NB	NB		32	B3
HUNTINGTON PL	HTB	HB47	7000	21	B5
HUNTINGTON ST	HTB	HB	18200	26	C4
HUNTINGTON ST N	HTB	HB	100	26	C6
HUNTGTN GDNS WY	HTB	HB	16300	20	D5
HUNTNGTN VLG LN	HTB	HB47		21	C3
HUNTKNOLL LN	CO	SJ79		56	E6
HUNTLEY AV	GGR	GG45	5300	14	E3
HUNTLEY DR	CO	LALM	3300	14	B3
HUNTRIDGE RD	CO	SA	1000	18	B6
HUNTSMAN RD	CO	SA	1600	18	D5
HUNTSWOOD CIR	LAP	BP23	5200	9	D2
HURLEY ST N	SA	SA	800	22	B1
HURLEY ST S	SA	SA	300	22	B2
HURON CIR	PLA	PLA	2300	7	B1
HURON DR	SA	SA	400	22	D4
HURON LN	CO	ET		29A	D1
HURON ST	IRV	SA	3900	28	F4
HURST DR	CO	ET		29A	D3
HURSTWELL DR	HTB	HB		26	D4
HUSSEY RD	SB	SB		20	A2
HUTCHINGS DR	YL	YL	18200	7	F4
HUTSON LN	CO	AN04	9500	10	E6
HUTTON CTR DR	SA	SA		28	B1
HUXFORD LN	ANA	AN		8	D6
HUXLEY CIR	WSTM	WSTM		21	D4
HUYLARS LN	SA	SA	500	22	C2
HYACINTH CIR	FTNV	SA08	16000	21	F4
HYANNIS	CO	LB77		37	E1
HYANNIS COM	SA	SA		22	C2
HYANNIS PORT DR	HTB	HB	9300	26	E4
HYANNISPORT RD	TUS	TUS	14600	24	A5
HYATT CT	CO	LB56		29C	E5
HYDE CT	CM	CM		27	E3
HYDE CT	FTNV	SA08	10700	22	B4
HYDE PARK DR	CO	SA	1000	18	C5
HYDE PARK DR	HTB	HB	9000	26	E3
HYLAND AV	CM	CM	3300	27	C2
HYNES RD	STN	STN	8000	15	C2
I					
I ST	NB	NB	100	33	C5
IBERVILLE CIR	LAP	BP23	5100	9	D1
IBEZA RD	MVJO	SJ92		29D	E3

STREET	CITY	P.O. ZONE	BLOCK	PAGE	GRID
IBIS CT	CO	LB		35	D1
IDA WY	WSTM	WSTM		14	F6
IDA WY	WSTM	WSTM	13800	15	A6
IDA WY	WSTM	WSTM	14200	21	A1
IDAHO LN	CM	CM	3200	27	C3
IDAHO PL	CM	CM	3200	27	C3
IDAHO ST	BPK	BP	6700	10	C1
IDAHO ST	CO	LAH	1000	1	F6
IDAHO ST N&S	LAH	LAH	100	1	F6
IDLEWILD CIR	HTB	HB	8400	26	B2
IDYLWILD DR	STN	STN	7300	15	B1
IKE JONES RD	CO	SA07		28	B4
ILA DR	OR	OR	1500	12	D3
ILLINOIS ST	CM	CM	1800	27	B3
ILLINOIS ST	WSTM	WSTM	13100	15	B6
ILLINOIS ST S	ANA	AN	100	11	C4
IMA LOA CT	NB	NB		31	B4
IMPALA DR	CO	TUS	10200	18	A6
IMPALA LN	HTB	HB	21700	30	E2
IMPERATRICE	DPT	DPT		37	E2
IMPERIAL AV	GGR	GG	8000	15	C5
IMPERIAL AV	GGR	GG	10200	16	A5
IMPERIAL DR	CO	LB		29C	E3
IMPERIAL DR	SJC	SJ75		36	B3
IMPERIAL HWY	ANA	AN	1600	8	C6
IMPERIAL HWY	ANA	AN	100	13	C2
IMPERIAL HWY	CO	YL	16600	7	D1
IMPERIAL HWY	LAH	LAH	500	1	E6
IMPERIAL HWY	PLA	PLA	16500	7	D1
IMPERIAL HWY	YL	YL	16800	7	D1
IMPERIAL HWY	YL	YL	18100	8	C6
IMPERIAL HWY E	FUL	FL35	100	2	B6
IMPERIAL HY E&W	BREA	BREA	100	2	B6
IMPERIAL HY E&W	LAH	LAH	100	2	B6
IMPERIAL HWY W	BREA	BREA	1000	6	F1
IMPERIAL HWY W	BREA	BREA	1100	7	A1
IMPERIAL CV LN	HTB	HB46	20000	26	D5
IMPERIALE ISLE	IRV	SA14		28	D5
IMPERIAL TER LN	ANA	AN07	1700	8	C6
INCA	MVJO	SJ92	27700	29B	D2
INCHON PL	ETMC	SA09		51	D3
INCLINADO	SCL	SC72		38	E4
INDEPENDNCE COM	SA	SA		22	C2
INDEPENDENCE LN	HTB	HB46	19500	27	A4
INDEPENDENCE WY	IRV	SA		24	F6
INDIAN TR	ANA	AN		13	C3
INDIANA AV	BPK	BP	5400	5	C6
INDIANA AV	BPK	BP	6700	10	C1
INDIANA AV	CM	CM	3200	27	B3
INDIANA ST	ANA	AN	300	11	C4
INDIANAPOLIS AV	HTB	HB	8000	26	D5
INDIANAPOLIS AV	HTB	HB46	10000	27	A5
INDIANAPLS AV W	HTB	HB	100	26	C5
INDIAN CREEK LN	CO	LB		29C	D1
INDIAN HILL LN	CO	LB		29C	D2
INDIAN PIPE	CO	SJ79		59	D4
INDIAN RIVER CT	FTNV	SA08	10300	27	A1
INDIAN SPG LN	NB	NB		31	F2
INDIAN SUMMIT	CO	SJ79		52	F4
INDIAN WELLS	MVJO	SJ92		29B	D4
INDIAN WLLS CIR	HTB	HB	9500	30	F1
INDIAN WELLS CT	ANA	AN		13	B3
INDIES CT	FTNV	SA08	15800	22	B4
INDIGO CIR	HTB	HB	21000	26	F6
INDIGO LN	LAP	BP23	7500	9	D2
INDUS ST	CO	SA07	1600	28	A5
INDUSTRIAL DR	HTB	HB		20	E3
INDUSTRIAL DR	TUS	TUS	1300	23	E5
INDUSTRIAL ST	SA	SA	1200	23	C6
INDUSTRIAL WY	CM	CM27	100	31	C3
INDUSTRIAL WY	PLA	PLA	400	7	A6
INDUSTRIAL WY	STN	STN	7500	15	B2
INDUSTRY AV	LAH	LAH	100	2	A6
INDUSTRY LN	HTB	HB	15000	20	E3
INDUSTRY ST	GGR	GG	12000	15	B4
INDUSTRY WY	WSTM	WSTM	6300	21	A1
INEZ WY	ANA	AN	1600	16	B1
INFERNO LN	HTB	HB	21000	26	F6
INGERSOLL DR	IRV	SA		24	F6
INGRAM AV	GGR	GG	9000	15	E6
INGRAM CIR	WSTM	WSTM	8000	21	D3
INISHMORE WY	EBAY	LB51	700	34	B1
INLET DR	HTB	HB	6400	26	A1
INLET DR	NB	CDLM		32	C6
INLET ISLE DR	NB	CDLM		33	C1
INNISBROOK LN	CO	LB		35	D5
INNSBRUCK DR	HTB	HB	9500	26	F3
INOLA CT	LAH	LAH	800	2	C4
INROZ DR	CM	CM	2900	27	B4
INSPIRATION PT	CO	LB77		35	F6
INSPIRATION PT	CO	LB77		36	A6

STREET	CITY	P.O. ZONE	BLOCK	PAGE	GRID
INSPIRATION PT	CO	LB77		37	F1
INSPIRATION PT	CO	LB77		38	A1
INTERA WY	DPT	DPT		37	E3
INTERIOR CIR	LALM	LALM	12500	14	D4
INTERIOR LN	HTB	HB	20000	26	F5
INTERLACHEN RD	SB	SB	1500	14	A5
INTERNATIONL AV	CYP	CYP		15	A1
INTREPID LN	HTB	HB		20	A6
INTREPID ST	NB	NB		31	A4
INVERARY	CO	SJ79		59	D3
INVERNESS	MVJO	SJ92		29B	E3
INVERNESS CT	FUL	FL35		6	C2
INVERNESS DR	CO	LALM	2800	14	A3
INVERNESS LN	HTB	HB	19800	26	F4
INVERNESS LN	NB	NB		32	B4
INVERNESS PL	CO	LB		35	D5
INVERNESS ST	IRV	SA14	14700	29	E5
INVERNESS GRN	BPK	BP	5000	5	C4
INVICTA PL	SA	SA		28	B1
INWOOD DR	CO	SA	2000	24	C2
INWOOD LN	LAP	BP23	7700	9	D2
IOLANI CIR	HTB	HB	9400	30	F1
IONA LN	HTB	HB	20600	26	F6
IONA WY	STN	STN		10	E4
IONA WY	STN	STN		15	B2
IONIA PL	ANA	AN	1400	11	B2
IONIAN BAY	DPT	LB77		37	D4
IOWA PL	PLA	PLA	800	12	A1
IOWA ST	CM	CM	3200	27	B3
IOWA ST	WSTM	WSTM	13100	15	B6
IPSEN WY	PLA	PLA	2000	7	B2
IPSWICH ST	LAH	LAH	900	2	A6
IPSWICH ST	WSTM	WSTM	14100	20	E1
IRA CT	ANA	AN	800	10	D6
IRBY LN	HTB	HB47	16500	21	D5
IRELAND LN	HTB	HB47	17400	21	A6
IRENE PL	ANA	AN	1000	10	E3
IRENE WY	PLA	PLA	2100	7	C2
IRENE WY	WSTM	WSTM	15500	22	A3
IRIS AV	FTNV	SA08	11500	22	C4
IRIS AV	MVJO	SJ92		29D	D4
IRIS AV	NB	CDLM	100	33	A2
IRIS AV	PLA	PLA	400	7	C4
IRIS CIR	LAP	BP23		9	E2
IRIS CIR	SB	SB	3500	14	D5
IRIS CIR	WSTM	WSTM	15500	21	F3
IRIS DR	GGR	GG	11000	16	B4
IRIS PL	CM	CM27	2100	31	E2
IRIS ST	ANA	AN	1100	11	D6
IRIS ST	SB	SB	3900	14	D4
IRIS WY	LAG	LB51	2300	34	F4
IRONBARK CIR	BREA	BREA		3	A5
IRONBARK LN	CO	ET		29A	F2
IRONBARK WY	IRV	SA	17800	28	F5
IRON GATE CIR	HTB	HB		25	F1
IRONGATE LN	SA	SA		16	B6
IRONGATE LN	SA	SA		22	B1
IRONHEAD LN	CO	LB	23900	35	D2
IRON HORSE LN	ANA	AN		13	D3
IRON PIKE CIR	ANA	AN	3900	12	E2
IRONSIDES DR	SJC	SJ75		38	B4
IRONWOOD	IRV	SA		29	B2
IRONWOOD AV	OR	OR69		18	E3
IRONWOOD AV	SB	SB	4000	14	D4
IRONWOOD CIR	CO	SJ79		59	C5
IRONWOOD CT	BREA	BREA		2	C4
IRON WOOD DR	CO	LB53		29D	A4
IRONWOOD LN	CO	SA		18	B5
IRONWOOD LN	FTNV	SA08	18100	26	F2
IRONWOOD LN	HTB	HB48		25	F4
IRONWOOD ST	LAH	LAH	1200	2	A6
IRONWOOD ST	LAH	LAH		6	A1
IROQUOIS	TUS	TUS		24	B6
IROQUOIS AV	ANA	AN	900	11	A3
IROQUOIS AV	PLA	PLA	2400	7	C1
IROQUOIS DR	BPK	BP	7300	10	A2
IROQUOIS RD	WSTM	WSTM	5700	14	F5
IROQUOIS RD	WSTM	WSTM	6200	15	A5
IRVINE AV	CM	CM27	800	31	D5
IRVINE AV	CO	CM27	2600	27	F6
IRVINE AV	CO	SA07	20100	28	A6
IRVINE AV	NB	NB	2000	31	E2
IRVINE AV	NB	NB	300	31	E2
IRVINE BLVD	CO	SA	1500	24	C3
IRVINE BLVD	CO	SA		49	A6
IRVINE BLVD	CO	SA		51	A1
IRVINE BLVD	IRV	SA20	4000	24	D4
IRVINE BLVD	TUS	TUS	17200	23	F2
IRVINE BLVD	TUS	TUS	1000	24	C3
IRVINE CTR DR	CO	SA		29	E4

STREET	CITY	P.O. ZONE	BLOCK	PAGE	GRID
IRVINE CTR DR	CO	SA		51	A6
IRVINE CTR DR	IRV	SA		24	B6
IRVINE CTR DR	IRV	SA		29	B2
IRVINE CTR DR	IRV	LB53		29A	A2
IRVINE COVE CIR	LAG	LB51		34	A1
IRVINE COVE CT	LAG	LB51		34	A1
IRVINE COVE DR	LAG	LB51	100	34	A1
IRVINE COVE PL	LAG	LB51		34	B1
IRVINE COVE WY	LAG	LB51	100	34	A1
IRVINE CV CREST	LAG	LB51		34	A1
IRVING PL	ANA	AN	800	11	C5
IRWIN DR	STN	STN	7200	15	B2
ISABELLA	MVJO	SJ92	28200	29B	E6
ISABELLA DR	HTB	HB		20	D4
ISABELLA TER	NB	CDLM	400	33	C2
ISELA CT	CO	LB56		29C	E6
ISLAMARE LN	CO	ET	23100	29A	E3
ISLAND AV	NB	NB	100	31	E6
ISLAND CIR	HTB	HB		20	D5
ISLAND DR	FUL	FL33		5	D3
ISLAND WY	DPT	DPT		37	E5
ISLAND BAY LN	HTB	HB		26	A4
ISLANDER LN	HTB	HB	22000	30	E2
ISLANDIA DR	PLA	PLA	100	7	B3
ISLND LAGOON DR	NB	NB		31	F5
ISLANDVIEW	IRV	SA		29	C3
ISLANDVIEW CIR	HTB	HB46		26	C4
ISLAND VIEW DR	NB	CDLM	2600	32	B6
ISLAND VIEW DR	SB	SB	600	19	F2
ISLAY	CO	SJ		59	B3
ISLE ROYAL DR	CO	LB		35	D6
ISLE ROYAL DR	CO	LB77	31700	37	D1
ISLE ROYALE CIR	OR	OR	1900	13	C5
ISLE VISTA	CO	LB		35	C6
ISLE VISTA	CO	LB77		37	C1
ISTHMUS LN	HTB	HB46	19700	26	D4
IVANHOE ST	ANA	AN	1400	11	A6
IVANHOE ST	ANA	AN	1500	16	A1
IVANHOE ST	GGR	GG	11100	16	A2
IVERNESS WY	TUS	TUS	14600	23	F1
IVES LN	HTB	HB	20400	26	D5
IVES WY	CO	ET		29B	B1
IVORY	MVJO	SJ91		52	D5
IVORY AV	FTNV	SA08	11000	22	C5
IVORY CIR	HTB	HB	6000	20	F2
IVORY CREST LN	HTB	HB		25	F2
IVORY CREST LN	HTB	HB		26	A3
IVY CIR	HTB	HB		26	D4
IVY CIR	YL	YL		8	E4
IVY LN	ANA	AN	900	10	F3
IVY LN	CO	OR		18	C1
IVY LN	LAG	LB77	31800	37	B1
IVY PL	FUL	FL	2400	7	A2
IVY PL	LAH	LAH	2300	1	E4
IVY GLEN LN	GGR	GG		15	D4
IVY GLENN DR	CO	LB	29700	35	D3
IVYHILL	IRV	SA		29	D4
IVY HILL LN	OR	OR	2000	12	E4
IVY HILL LN	YL	YL	20300	8	F2
IVY RIDGE	MVJO	SJ92		29B	E2
IVYWOOD DR	LAP	BP23	5200	9	D2
IWATA	CO	SJ88		59	A4
IWO JIMA CT	LALM	LALM		14	C2
IWO JIMA DR	ETMC	SA09		51	D3
IXWORTH PL	WSTM	WSTM		14	D6
IXWORTH PL	WSTM	WSTM	5000	20	D1
J					
J ST	NB	NB	400	33	C5
J & J LN	YL	YL	18900	8	B2
JACALENE LN	ANA	AN	1800	16	C2
JACALENE LN	GGR	GG	11200	16	C2
JACANA CIR	CO	LB	24000	35	D1
JACARANDA	IRV	SA		29	A5
JACARANDA	IRV	SA		29	D3
JACARANDA AV	CM	CM	2900	27	C4
JACARANDA AV	OR	OR	100	17	D1
JACARANDA AV	TUS	TUS	17300	23	E1
JACARANDA CT	CO	SJ91		29A	F5
JACARANDA LN	YL	YL		8	D5
JACARANDA PL	BREA	BREA	200	2	F6
JACARANDA PL W	FUL	FL33	1600	5	F5
JACARANDA PL W	FUL	FL	200	6	A5
JACARANDA ST	FTNV	SA08	18200	26	F2
JACARANDA ST	SA	SA	2500	17	C5
JACARANDA WY	ANA	AN07		13	D4
JACINTO DR	MVJO	SJ92		36	C1
JACK RD	GGR	GG	9200	15	E3
JACKSON	IRV	SA		24	E6
JACKSON AV	ANA	AN	2700	12	B3

STREET	CITY	P.O. ZONE	BLOCK	PAGE	GRID
JACKSON AV	OR	OR	300	17	D1
JACKSON CT	TUS	SA10		29	B1
JACKSON RD N	CO			50	C4
JACKSON ST	CO	MDWY	14600	21	C2
JACKSON ST	GGR	GG	12600	15	C6
JACKSON ST	GGR	GG	13700	16	D6
JACKSON ST	WSTM	WSTM	13500	15	C6
JACKSON ST	WSTM	WSTM	14000	21	C1
JACKSON ST N	SA	SA	100	22	D2
JACKSON ST S	SA	SA	400	22	D2
JACKSON WY	BPK	BP	7500	10	B4
JACKSN RCH RD N	CO			50	C4
JACKSN RCH RD S	CO			50	C4
JACQUELYN LN	HTB	HB47		21	C6
JACQUELYN LN	HTB	HB	17300	26	C1
JADE	MVJO	SJ91		52	D4
JADE AV	CYP	CYP	4200	9	C3
JADE AV	NB	NB	100	33	C5
JADE AV	PLA	PLA	200	7	B4
JADE CIR	HTB	HB	6000	20	F2
JADE CIR	PLA	PLA	900	7	B4
JADE CIR	WSTM	WSTM	8900	21	E3
JADE CT	FTNV	SA08	11800	22	B5
JADE ST	GGR	GG45	12100	14	F3
JADE WY	ANA	AN	800	11	C3
JADE WY	FUL	FL	3000	7	A4
JADE COVE	NB	CDLM		32	D6
JADE COVE WY	SB	SB	400	19	F3
JADESTONE	MVJO	SJ91		29D	C5
JAEGER DR	CO	LB	28800	35	D1
JAEGER LN	CO	LB56		29A	A6
JAEN TER	CO	LB56		29C	E5
JAFFREY ST	LAH	LAH	900	2	A6
JAGGER ST	CO	ET	24000	29A	D3
JAGUAR WY	SA	SA	300	28	C1
JALM DR	HTB	HB	8400	26	D1
JALUIT ST	CYP	CYP	6500	15	A3
JAMAICA CIR	BPK	BP	7600	9	E2
JAMAICA CIR	HTB	HB	9800	30	F4
JAMAICA CIR	PLA	PLA	100	7	B3
JAMAICA RD	CM	CM	1700	27	B3
JAMAICA ST	CYP	CYP	11100	14	F2
JAMAICA ST	CYP	CYP		15	A2
JAMAICA TER	YL	YL	5200	8	A3
JAMBOLAYA ST	ANA	AN	400	12	A4
JAMBOREE BLVD	TUS	TUS	14900	24	C4
JAMBOREE RD	IRV	SA14	19000	24	B6
JAMBOREE RD	IRV	SA15	19000	28	C6
JAMBOREE RD	NB	NB	22500	31	F5
JAMBOREE RD	NB	NB	20000	32	A4
JAMBOREE RD	TUS	TUS	13000	24	D3
JAMES AV	GGR	GG	12600	16	D5
JAMES AV	SA	SA	3300	22	D3
JAMES CIR	HTB	HB		20	D6
JAMES CIR	VPK	OR67	9400	13	A5
JAMES PL	ANA	AN	600	11	B3
JAMES RD	VPK	OR67	18000	12	F5
JAMES RD	VPK	OR67	18100	13	A5
JAMES ST	CM	CM27	700	31	C3
JAMES ST N	OR	OR	300	18	A3
JAMES ST S	OR	OR	100	18	A3
JAMES WY	ANA	AN	1200	11	B3
JAMES WY	FUL	FL33		5	F2
JAMES ALAN ST	CYP	CYP	6000	9	F5
JAMESON ST	OR	OR	200	17	D3
JAMES RIVER CIR	FTNV	SA08		26	F3
JAMESTOWN	IRV	SA		24	E6
JAMESTOWN DR	YL	YL	4400	7	E2
JAMESTOWN LN	HTB	HB		26	C1
JAMESTOWN WY	OR	OR	1200	13	C6
JAMESTOWN WY	OR	OR		18	C1
JAMIE AV	LAH	LAH		2	B6
JAMISON ST	ANA	AN	2500	12	A4
JAMON LN	MVJO	SJ91	25900	29D	B2
JAN WY	SA	SA	1600	22	F4
JANA CIR	HTB	HB	7800	26	C3
JANACA CIR	FTNV	SA08	10100	27	A2
JANE AV	STN	STN		15	D1
JANE CIR	CO	SA	18800	18	B6
JANE DR	GGR	GG	12500	15	E4
JANE ST	WSTM	WSTM	5600	20	F1
JANE WY	CO	AN04	11700	15	C3
JANE WY	STN	STN	11300	15	C3
JANEEN CIR	LAP	BP23	8000	9	E3
JANEEN WY	ANA	AN	1200	11	B3
JANET CIR	GGR	GG	12400	15	E4
JANET LN	ANA	AN		8	C6
JANET LN	GGR	GG	12500	16	C4
JANET PL N	FUL	FL	100	6	E6
JANET PL S	FUL	FL	200	6	E6
JANET ST	GGR	GG	12300	16	C4

101

1990 ORANGE COUNTY STREET INDEX

JANETTE LN — KEMPER AV

ORANGE CO.

STREET	CITY	P.O. ZONE	BLOCK	PAGE	GRID
JANETTE LN	ANA	AN	1800	16	C2
JANETTE LN	GGR	GG	11500	16	C3
JANICE CIR	VPK	OR67	9600	13	A5
JANICE ST	WSTM	WSTM	14200	21	D1
JANICE LYNN CIR	CYP	CYP	10400	9	D6
JANICE LYNN ST	CYP	CYP	10100	9	D6
JANISON DR	CO	LAH	9500	1	E3
JAN MARIE PL	TUS	TUS	1800	24	A3
JANSS ST N	ANA	AN	100	11	C3
JANSS ST S	ANA	AN	500	11	C4
JANSS WY	ANA	AN	500	11	C3
JARDIN	CO	LB	23000	29A	A5
JARDINES	MVJO	SJ92		29D	D4
JARDINES DR	HTB	HB	6500	26	A1
JAROD WY	CO	LB77		35	D2
JARRETT CIR	CO	LB		35	D3
JARRETT CIR	HTB	HB47	8700	21	D5
JARROW LN	CO	ET	23600	29A	D4
JASMIN CIR	SB	SB	3500	14	D5
JASMINE AV	FTNV	SA08	9300	21	E4
JASMINE AV	FUL	FL33	600	5	E6
JASMINE AV	FUL	FL33	600	10	E1
JASMINE AV	MVJO	SJ92		29D	D4
JASMINE AV	NB	CDLM	100	33	B1
JASMINE CIR	CM	CM	900	27	E2
JASMINE CIR	FTNV	SA08	9400	21	E4
JASMINE CIR	PLA	PLA	700	7	C5
JASMINE DR	BREA	BREA	300	2	D6
JASMINE DR	CO	SJ79		59	E1
JASMINE PL	ANA	AN	1200	10	F2
JASMINE ST	ANA	AN	1100	10	F2
JASMINE ST	LAG	LB51	100	34	C3
JASMINE CK DR	NB	CDLM		32	B6
JASMINE CK LN	CO	LB		29C	D1
JASMINE CK RD	NB	CDLM		33	B1
JASMINES WY	CO	ET		51	E4
JASON CT	GGR	GG		15	D5
JASON DR	ANA	AN		11	E5
JASON LN	SA	SA	4700	22	B4
JASONWOOD DR	HTB	HB		25	F1
JASONWOOD DR	HTB	HB		26	A2
JASPER	BREA	BREA	100	4	B5
JASPER	MVJO	SJ91		29D	C5
JASPER CIR	ANA	AN	900	12	A4
JASPER ST	GGR	GG45	11800	14	F3
JASPER HILL RD	CO	SJ79		52	E4
JASPER LAKE LN	CO	ET		29A	D3
JASPERSON WY	WSTM	WSTM	13200	15	C6
JASPERSON WY	WSTM	WSTM	13900	21	C1
JAVA RD	CM	CM	2900	27	B4
JAVA ST	CYP	CYP	11500	14	E3
JAVA SEA DR	DPT	LB77	23000	37	C2
JAY AV	FTNV	SA08	9000	26	E2
JAY CIR	ANA	AN		13	F2
JAY CIR	ANA	AN		43	A2
JAY CIR	HTB	HB	900	26	C4
JAY ST	STN	STN		15	D1
JAY ST	YL	YL	5100	7	F4
JAYWOOD CT	BREA	BREA		2	C4
JEAN DR	HTB	HB	6100	20	F5
JEAN ST	CO	AN04	10800	15	E1
JEANEAN LN	YL	YL	4700	7	D3
JEANETTE PL	CM	CM27	2200	31	E1
JEANINE CIR	ANA	AN		12	B3
JEANINE DR	ANA	AN	400	12	B3
JEANINE DR	CO	LB56		29C	E5
JEANINE LN	CYP	CYP	10300	14	D1
JEANINE ST	ANA	AN	400	12	B4
JEANINE WY	ANA	AN	200	12	B3
JEANNIE COM	SA	SA03		22	D2
JEFFERSON	IRV	SA		24	D6
JEFFERSON AV	CM	CM	3100	27	E3
JEFFERSON AV	OR	OR	500	17	D2
JEFFERSON AV N	FUL	FL	100	6	B5
JEFFERSON AV S	FUL	FL	500	6	B6
JEFFERSON AV S	FUL	FL	1300	11	B1
JEFFERSON DR	BPK	BP	8700	10	B4
JEFFERSON LN	HTB	HB	17500	26	D1
JEFFERSON PL	SA	SA	1700	17	B6
JEFFERSON ST	ANA	AN	1300	7	E6
JEFFERSON ST	ANA	AN	1200	12	E1
JEFFERSON ST	CO	MDWY	14500	21	D2
JEFFERSON ST	GGR	GG	12800	15	D4
JEFFERSON ST	PLA	PLA	5400	7	E5
JEFFERSON ST	WSTM	WSTM	13500	15	D6
JEFFERSON ST	YL	YL	5000	7	D5
JEFFERSON WY	LAG	LB51	1100	34	F3
JEFFRSN FRTG RD	ANA	AN		12	E2
JEFFREY CIR	HTB	HB47	16700	21	D5
JEFFREY CIR	PLA	PLA	2000	7	C2
JEFFREY DR	ANA	AN	1500	16	C1

STREET	CITY	P.O. ZONE	BLOCK	PAGE	GRID
JEFFREY DR	CM	CM		27	F3
JEFFREY DR	YL	YL	4000	7	E2
JEFFREY RD	CO	SA		49	A6
JEFFREY RD	IRV	SA	13000	24	F6
JEFFREY RD	IRV	SA	13000	29	C5
JEFFREY MARK ST	CYP	CYP	6000	9	F5
JEKYLL WY	CYP	CYP	6500	15	A2
JEMEL WY	IRV	SA	13500	24	D6
JENCOURT	CO	LB77		37	F1
JENCOURT	CO	LB77		38	A1
JENET CIR	CO	SA	13700	18	B6
JENIFER DR	ANA	AN		8	F5
JENIFER LN	IRV	SA		24	F6
JENKINS PL	ETMC	SA09		51	D3
JENKINS ST	SA	SA	500	22	B2
JENNER	CO	ET		51	F6
JENNER	CO	ET		52	A6
JENNER	IRV	SA18		29	E6
JENNER ST	WSTM	WSTM		21	D4
JENNIE LN	LAH	LAH	11800	2	C3
JENNIFER CIR	LAP	BP23	7800	9	D2
JENNIFER DR	YL	YL	17500	7	E2
JENNIFER LN	CM	CM		27	F3
JENNIFER LN	GGR	GG	11800	16	C3
JENNIFER LN	OR	OR	100	17	E3
JENNRICH AV	GGR	GG43	10100	22	A1
JENNRICH AV	WSTM	WSTM	8500	21	E1
JENNY DR	HTB	HB	8400	30	D1
JENNY LN	GGR	GG	10500	16	A3
JENSEN WY	FUL	FL33	100	5	E6
JENTGES AV	GGR	GG	12200	16	C3
JEPSEN CIR	HTB	HB47	17400	21	A6
JEREMIAH DR	DPT	DPT	24500	37	E2
JEREMY LN	HTB	HB		26	C3
JEREVA CIR	HTB	HB47	16000	21	A4
JERICHO	CO	SJ79		59	D2
JERINNE ST	ANA	AN	1600	16	A1
JEROME LN	GGR	GG	12500	15	E4
JEROME ST	GGR	GG	12200	15	E4
JEROME ST	VPK	OR67	10300	13	A6
JERONIMO LN	CO	ET		29A	E2
JERONIMO RD	CO	ET	22800	29A	D1
JERONIMO RD	IRV	SA18		29A	C1
JERONIMO RD	IRV	SA18		51	C6
JERONIMO RD	MVJO	SJ91	25500	29A	D1
JERONIMO RD	MVJO	SJ91	24000	29B	A4
JERONIMO RD	MVJO	SJ92	26000	29B	D5
JERRILEE LN	ANA	AN	100	13	B2
JERRILYN LN	HTB	HB	19300	26	E3
JERRY LN	GGR	GG	11000	16	B3
JERSEY CIR	HTB	HB47	6400	21	A4
JESSEE DR	SA	SA	2600	17	C5
JESSICA DR	GGR	GG	13300	16	A5
JESSICA ST	GGR	GG43	14300	22	A1
JETT DR	HTB	HB	9000	26	F5
JETTY CIR	GGR	GG	12000	16	E3
JETTY CIR	SA	SA	2100	16	E6
JETTY DR	ANA	AN	2100	16	E2
JETTY DR	NB	CDLM		32	C6
JETTY DR	OR	OR68	100	16	E3
JETTY DR	SA	SA	2300	16	E5
JETTY ST	GGR	GG	12500	16	E4
JETTY ST	SA	SA	2200	16	E5
JEWEL AV	LAG	LB	31500	35	B5
JEWEL LN	GGR	GG	11600	16	C2
JEWEL PL	OR	OR	100	17	B3
JIB CIR	HTB	HB		20	E5
JIB ST	OR	OR	2700	12	D4
JILL DR	HTB	HB46		27	A5
JILL RD	ANA	AN	1500	10	F6
JILL RD	ANA	AN04	1500	15	F1
JILL ST	CYP	CYP	10600	15	A1
JIM ST	WSTM	WSTM	16200	21	D4
JINETE	SCL	SC72		38	E3
JINETES	MVJO	SJ91	21700	29B	D1
JOAN CIR	LAP	BP23	8000	9	E3
JOAN DR	GGR	GG	10200	15	F3
JOAN DR	GGR	GG	10300	16	A3
JOAN ST	LAH	LAH	500	2	C4
JOAN WY	PLA	PLA	800	7	A3
JOANA DR	SA	SA	1000	17	C5
JOAN D'ARC CIR	OR	OR		18	C3
JOANE WY	SA	SA	1300	22	F4
JOANE WY	SA	SA04	3000	27	F1
JOANN WY	NB	NB63	200	31	A4
JOANN ST	CM	CM26	200	27	D6
JOANNE WY	YL	YL		8	E4
JOCELYN DR	LAH	LAH	500	2	A4
JOCOTAL AV	VPK	OR67	18300	13	A6
JODI ST	OR	OR		12	E6
JODI ST	OR	OR		17	E1

STREET	CITY	P.O. ZONE	BLOCK	PAGE	GRID
JODY AV	SA	SA	2100	16	F6
JODY CIR	WSTM	WSTM	16400	21	D4
JOEL AV	STN	STN	7600	15	C2
JOEL CIR	CYP	CYP	9800	9	F6
JOEL CIR	DPT	DPT	32900	37	E2
JOHANNAH AV	GGR	GG	9700	21	F1
JOHANNAH AV	GGR	GG43	10100	22	A1
JOHN AV	GGR	GG	11600	16	C3
JOHN CHFFEY CIR	GGR	GG45		14	E4
JOHNSON AV	CM	CM	3000	27	E3
JOHNSON AV	LAH	LAH	2500	1	D4
JOHNSON CIR	BPK	BP	8700	10	B4
JOHNSON CT	TUS	SA10		29	A2
JOHNSON DR	IRV	SA		24	F6
JOHNSON LN	ETMC	SA09		51	D3
JOHNSON LN	HTB	HB	20200	26	E5
JOHNSON PL	FUL	FL	1500	6	A5
JOHNSON RD	OR	OR	2000	12	C5
JOHNSON WY	LAG	LB51	1000	34	F3
JOHNSTON RD	STN	STN	8000	15	C2
JOHNSTONE DR	CO	ET		29B	B1
JOHNSTON KNOLL	FUL	FL	200	6	C3
JOHNSTOWN CIR	ANA	AN		13	F4
JOICE LN	HTB	HB	19300	26	E3
JOJOBA AV	FTNV	SA08	9300	21	E4
JOLA AV	GGR	GG	11300	16	C5
JOLA LN	GGR	GG	11200	16	B5
JOLIET AV	HTB	HB	200	26	C5
JOLIET CIR	ANA	AN		43	A3
JOLLY LN	HTB	HB		26	B2
JON WY	WSTM	WSTM	14200	20	F1
JONATHAN AV	CO	ET	24600	29A	E2
JONATHAN AV	CYP	CYP	6800	15	A1
JONATHAN CIR	DPT	DPT		37	E2
JON DAY DR	HTB	HB46	10000	27	A5
JONES AV	WSTM	WSTM	5700	14	F5
JONES DR	OR	OR	100	18	B3
JONES PL	PLA	PLA	1800	7	C2
JONESBORO CIR	BPK	BP	8900	5	D4
JONESBORO WY	BPK	BP	5300	5	D4
JONESPORT LN	HTB	HB	22000	30	F2
JONQUIL AV	WSTM	WSTM	9500	21	F3
JONQUIL RD E	SA	SA	800	17	B5
JONQUIL RD W	SA	SA	400	17	B5
JORDAN E	IRV	SA		29	B6
JORDAN AV	IRV	SA		29	B6
JORDAN AV	OR	OR	4100	18	A4
JORIE DR	CO	LB	24600	29A	E6
JORNADA	MVJO	SJ92	21600	29B	E1
JOSE WY	FUL	FL	500	6	B2
JOSEFINA	MVJO	SJ92	28100	29B	E5
JOSEPH CT	LAH	LAH	1500	1	E3
JOSEPHINE ST	GGR	GG	12900	15	D4
JOSHUA CIR	BPK	BP	8100	10	C3
JOSHUA CIR	FTNV	SA08	17500	26	E1
JOSHUA DR	CO	SJ		59	D1
JOSHUA DR	YL	YL	17700	7	F3
JOSHUA LN	CO	SA	18100	18	A6
JOSHUA TREE AV	OR	OR		13	C5
JOSHUA TREE CIR	VPK	OR67		13	B4
JOSIAH DR	DPT	DPT		37	E2
JOSIE CIR	PLA	PLA	300	7	F6
JOVE CT	CO	SJ91	24500	29B	A6
JOY ST	GGR	GG	12900	16	A4
JOYCE AV	WSTM	WSTM	14200	21	C1
JOYCE DR	BREA	BREA	900	2	D4
JOYFUL LN	HTB	HB		26	C1
JOYZELLE DR	GGR	GG	8500	15	D2
JUAN CRESPI	MVJO	SJ92		29D	F3
JUANENO AV	OR	OR		13	B6
JUANENO DR	MVJO	SJ91		29B	B5
JUANITA DR	CO	LB53		29C	E6
JUANITA DR	HTB	HB		20	D4
JUANITA PL	FUL	FL	2800	6	B1
JUANITA ST	CYP	CYP	9500	9	F6
JUANITA ST	LAH	LAH	300	2	C4
JUANITA WY	LAG	LB51	2300	34	F4
JUANITA WY	PLA	PLA	200	7	B2
JUBILO PL	CO	ET	22700	29A	F3
JUDITH CIR	WSTM	WSTM	9000	21	E3
JUDITH LN	ANA	AN04	1700	15	F1
JUDITH LN	SA	SA	2200	22	E1
JUDSON AV	WSTM	WSTM	7100	21	B3
JUDWICK CIR	HTB	HB		25	F2
JUDY AV	GGR	GG	10700	16	A3
JUDY CIR	HTB	HB47	8500	21	D5
JUDY LN	GGR	GG	9200	15	E3
JUDY ANNE LN	CO	SA	13700	18	B6
JULIANA LN	GGR	GG	10300	15	F3
JULIANNA ST E	ANA	AN	200	11	D2

STREET	CITY	P.O. ZONE	BLOCK	PAGE	GRID
JULIANNA ST W	ANA	AN	500	11	C2
JULIE AV	CO	LB	24600	29A	F6
JULIE AV	FUL	FL33	1900	5	F5
JULIE AV	OR	OR	4800	18	B1
JULIE BETH CIR	CYP	CYP	10400	9	D6
JULIE BETH ST	CYP	CYP	9100	9	D6
JULIEN CIR	HTB	HB47	6600	21	A4
JULIET LOW DR	HTB	HB47	7600	21	C4
JULIP LN	HTB	HB47	7200	21	B6
JUNCO AV	FTNV	SA08	9400	26	F3
JUNE	HTB	HB	8200	26	D2
JUNE AV	STN	STN		15	D1
JUNE DR	HTB	HB47	6300	21	A6
JUNE PL	ANA	AN		16	C2
JUNE ST	GGR	GG	11500	16	C2
JUNEBERRY	CO	SJ		59	B1
JUNIPER	IRV	SA		29	B6
JUNIPER AV	FUL	FL33	600	5	E6
JUNIPER AV	FUL	FL33	600	10	E1
JUNIPER AV	OR	OR	3100	17	F1
JUNIPER AV	SA	SA	200	28	B2
JUNIPER AV	YL	YL		8	D2
JUNIPER CIR	LAP	BP23	5000	9	D2
JUNIPER DR	CO	SJ91		29A	F5
JUNIPER LN	CO	SJ		59	B1
JUNIPER PL	ANA	AN	700	11	E2
JUNIPER RD	TUS	TUS		24	B4
JUNIPER ST	BREA	BREA	100	6	D1
JUNIPER ST	FTNV	SA08	17000	21	E6
JUNIPER ST	SA	SA04	2600	27	E1
JUNIPER WY	LAH	LAH	400	1	E5
JUNIPER WY	STN	STN	10500	15	B3
JUNIPERO DR	CM	CM	900	27	E4
JUNIPRO SRRA RD	SJC	SJ75	26700	36	B4
JUNO AV	ANA	AN	2100	10	F5
JUNO AV	ANA	AN	1500	11	A5
JUNO PL	ANA	AN	2000	10	F5
JUNO PL	ANA	AN	2000	11	A5
JUPITER CIR	WSTM	WSTM	16400	21	D4
JUPITER DR	BPK	BP	8400	10	D3
JUPITER RD	ANA	AN		16	D2
JURA DR	HTB	HB	9600	26	F6
JUSTICE CIR	OR	OR		18	B3
JUSTIN AV	CO	SJ91	25300	29A	F5
JUTEWOOD PL	CO	ET	24500	29A	E4
JUTEWOOD ST	ANA	AN08		40	A6
JUTEWOOD ST	ANA	AN		43	A1
K					
K ST	LAG	LB		35	A4
K ST	NB	NB	500	33	C5
KAHULUI DR	HTB	HB	9000	30	E2
KAIMU DR	HTB	HB46	10000	27	A3
KAISER AV	IRV	SA	1600	28	D2
KAISER BLVD	ANA	AN		8	F6
KALAMA RIVER	FTNV	SA08	10800	27	B1
KALMUS DR	CM	CM26	200	28	A4
KALUA LN	TUS	TUS	1200	24	A2
KAMALII CT	NB	NB		31	A4
KAMALII DR	HTB	HB	3900	20	C5
KAMEHA CIR	CO	YL	6000	8	C5
KAMPEN LN	HTB	HB47	17000	21	D6
KAMUELA DR	HTB	HB46	10000	27	A3
KANAKOA LN	HTB	HB	21500	30	E2
KANE ST	CO	LB77		35	D1
KANEOHE LN	HTB	HB	21500	30	E1
KANSAS AV	PLA	PLA	200	12	A1
KAPAA DR	HTB	HB	9000	30	E2
KARA	IRV	SA		24	E5
KARA BAY	DPT	LB77		37	D4
KARAN LN	OR	OR	2000	17	E4
KAREN AV	CYP	CYP	5500	9	E5
KAREN AV	SA	SA	800	22	C4
KAREN CIR	HTB	HB	9400	26	E3
KAREN CIR	LAP	BP23	4800	9	D2
KAREN PL	ANA	AN	1000	11	C3
KAREN WY	TUS	TUS	13800	24	A4
KAREN ANN CIR	CO	LB77		35	D3
KAREN ANN LN	IRV	SA	5000	29	D2
KARI BROOK	CO	ET	26400	29B	E3
KASS DR	BPK	BP	8300	10	C1
KASSY DR	CO	SA		18	B4
KATAWPA CIR	VPK	OR67	9500	13	B5
KATELLA AV	CO	AN04	8800	15	C2
KATELLA AV	CO	STN	7200	15	B1
KATELLA AV	CO	AN06	15000	17	A1
KATELLA AV	CYP	CYP	4500	14	B2
KATELLA AV	CYP	CYP	6500	15	A2
KATELLA AV	GGR	GG	8500	15	A1
KATELLA AV	LALM	LALM	2800	14	B2

STREET	CITY	P.O. ZONE	BLOCK	PAGE	GRID
KATELLA AV	STN	STN	7000	15	A2
KATELLA AV	STN	AN04	8700	15	A2
KATELLA AV E	ANA	AN06	2100	17	A1
KATELLA AV E&W	ANA	AN	100	16	A1
KATELLA AV E&W	OR	OR	100	12	C6
KATELLA AV E&W	OR	OR	100	17	B1
KATELLA AV W	ANA	AN	1900	16	A1
KATELLA ST	LAG	LB51	800	34	F4
KATELLA WY	ANA	AN		16	E1
KATHERINE DR	HTB	HB	8200	26	D3
KATHLEEN DR	CO	LB56		29C	E5
KATHLEEN DR	CYP	CYP	9700	9	F5
KATHLEEN LN	CO	OR69	11800	17	F3
KATHLEEN LN	NB	NB	1500	31	E3
KATHLEEN LN N	OR	OR	1300	12	F6
KATHLEEN LN S	OR	OR	100	17	F3
KATHLEEN ST	OR	OR	700	17	F2
KATHRYN DR	ANA	AN	100	10	F4
KATHRYN WY	PLA	PLA	2100	7	C2
KATHY AV	CO	ET	24100	29A	D2
KATHY DR	LAP	BP23		9	C2
KATHY LN	ANA	AN	1900	16	C2
KATHY LN	GGR	GG	11400	16	C2
KATHY LN	SA	SA	1100	22	F4
KATHY ST	WSTM	WSTM	14600	21	B2
KATIE AV	CO	LB	24900	29A	F6
KATY LN	GGR	GG	10300	15	F3
KATYGLEN LN	LAH	LAH	600	1	F5
KAUAI DR	SA	SA		22	C3
KAUAI LN	PLA	PLA	200	7	B5
KAUAI PL	CM	CM	2900	27	B4
KAUI DR	HTB	HB	4700	20	D4
KAUSCH CIR	HTB	HB	21000	30	E1
KAWAI CT	FTNV	SA08		22	C5
KAWAII ST	SA	SA		22	C3
KAYE LN	YL	YL	4200	7	F2
KAYLOR AV	LALM	LALM	3400	9	B6
KAYLOR ST	LALM	LALM	10800	14	B1
KAZAN ST	IRV	SA	14500	29	D2
KEARNEY WY	GGR	GG	11400	16	B3
KEARSARGE AV	LALM	LALM	5000	14	D2
KEATS CIR	WSTM	WSTM		21	E4
KEATS CT	SA	SA01		23	D1
KEATS ST	ANA	AN	1100	12	A5
KEDGE AV	GGR	GG43	10500	22	A3
KEDGE AV	SA	SA	5500	22	A3
KEEGAN WY	CO	SA	17000	17	E5
KEEGAN WY	SA	SA	1400	17	D5
KEEL AV	GGR	GG	10500	16	A6
KEEL DR	HTB	HB	8500	26	D3
KEEL DR	NB	CDLM		32	C6
KEEL DR	NB	NB		33	C1
KEELSON AV	GGR	GG43	10500	22	A3
KEELSON AV	SA	SA	5200	22	A3
KEELSON LN	HTB	HB47	17300	21	C6
KEENAN PL	STN	STN		15	B1
KEENE DR S	LAH	LAH	900	2	A6
KEENE DR W	LAH	LAH	100	1	F6
KEITH CIR	LAP	BP23	7500	9	D2
KEITH PL	CO	TUS	12800	24	B2
KEITH GRN	BPK	BP	5000	5	C4
KEITHLEY DR	CO	LALM	2600	14	A4
KELLE ST	CO	LB77		35	D2
KELLEHER PL	PLA	PLA	1800	7	C2
KELLER AV	SA	SA04	2800	27	D2
KELLER AV	SA	SA	200	28	B2
KELLER DR	TUS	TUS		24	C3
KELLER RD	TUS	SA10		23	E5
KELLER WY	LAG	LB51	1100	34	F3
KELLEY CIR	HTB	HB	6100	25	F1
KELLEY CIR	HTB	HB	6100	26	A1
KELLOG CIR	HTB	HB47	16500	21	B5
KELLOGG AV	FUL	FL33	100	5	D6
KELLOGG DR	ANA	AN	1800	8	B5
KELLOGG DR	ANA	AN	1600	13	A1
KELLOGG DR	CO	YL	5600	8	B4
KELLOGG DR	YL	YL	5500	8	B4
KELLOGG WY	GGR	GG		15	E5
KELLY AV	OR	OR	300	17	C3
KELLY CIR	LAP	BP23	7800	9	D2
KELLY LN	LALM	LALM	11200	14	C2
KELLY PL	GGR	GG41	13000	15	F5
KELLY ST	GGR	GG	13200	15	D5
KELSEY CIR	HTB	HB	6000	20	F2
KELSO DR	HTB	HB	8500	26	D5
KELTON WY	STN	STN	11100	15	B2
KELVIN AV	IRV	SA	2700	28	E3
KELVIN LN	HTB	HB	20600	26	E6
KELVINGROVE LN	HTB	HB	20400	26	E5
KEMP ST	ANA	AN	1100	11	D2
KEMPER AV	SA	SA	1800	17	D4

INDEX

STREET	CITY	P.O. ZONE	BLOCK	PAGE	GRID
KEMPTON DR	CO	LALM	2600	14	A3
KEMPTON DR	LALM	LALM	3500	14	B3
KEN WY	ANA	AN	800	11	C3
KENBROOK DR	HTB	HB		25	F1
KENDALL CIR	FTNV	SA08	9900	21	F4
KENDALL DR	LAG	LB51	1600	34	F4
KENDALL DR	LAG	LB51	1600	35	A4
KENDALL ST	CO	LB		35	E6
KENDALL ST	CO	LB77		37	E1
KENDOR CIR	BPK	BP	8400	10	C4
KENDOR DR	ANA	AN	300	10	C4
KENDOR DR	BPK	BP	8500	10	C4
KENDRA CT	ANA	AN08		8	F6
KENDRICK CIR	HTB	HB	6000	20	F5
KENILWORTH DR	CO	LALM	3200	14	B3
KENILWORTH DR	HTB	HB	5300	20	E6
KENMARE DR	CO	ET		29B	A1
KENMORE LN	CO	STN	7000	15	B1
KENMORE ST	ANA	AN	300	10	D5
KENMORE ST	ANA	AN04	1400	15	D1
KENMORE ST	STN	AN04	10200	15	D1
KENNEBEC DR	ANA	AN	200	12	E3
KENNEDY DR	PLA	PLA		7	E5
KENNEDY RD	ANA	AN		8	F6
KENNEDY RD	ANA	AN		13	F1
KENNEDY ST	OR	OR	2600	12	C4
KENNELLY LN	CO	AN04	9700	10	E6
KENNELLY LN	STN	AN04	8700	10	D6
KENNETH DR	CO	TUS	1300	24	B2
KENNETH DR	CO	SA	1500	24	B2
KENNINGTON DR	CO	LB		29A	E6
KENNINGTON DR	CO	LB		29C	E1
KENNON DR	YL	YL	17600	7	F3
KENNY CIR	SA	SA	5000	22	B1
KENNYMEAD ST	OR	OR	10200	13	D6
KENNYMEAD ST	OR	OR		18	D1
KENOAK DR	CO	PLA	16200	7	D4
KENOAK DR E	PLA	PLA	600	7	C4
KENOSHA LN	IRV	SA		32	F2
KENRICH CT	LAH	LAH	2100	1	E4
KENSING LN	CO	SA	1500	24	C1
KENSINGTON AV	ANA	AN	3000	7	B6
KENSINGTON CT	NB	NB		32	D5
KENSINGTON DR	CO	LB		35	D2
KENSINGTON DR	FUL	FL	1300	6	E4
KENSINGTON DR	HTB	HB	9500	26	F4
KENSINGTON LN	CO	ET		52	C6
KENSINGTON LN	GGR	GG	10400	16	A4
KENSINGTON LN	LAH	LAH		2	B5
KENSINGTON LN	WSTM	WSTM		22	A2
KENSINGTON RD	CO	LALM	11200	14	A3
KENSINGTON RD	OR	OR	500	17	F4
KENT AV	SA	SA	3500	22	B3
KENT CIR	HTB	HB47	8600	21	D5
KENT CIR	LAP	BP23		9	D3
KENT LN	NB	NB	1500	31	E3
KENT PL	TUS	TUS	1700	24	B3
KENT ST	ANA	AN	1700	7	B6
KENT ST	HTB	HB46		26	F3
KENT ST	WSTM	WSTM	14600	21	F2
KENT WY	CYP	CYP	6900	15	A2
KENT WY	STN	STN		15	B2
KENTUCKY AV	ANA	AN		13	F3
KENTUCKY DR	BPK	BP	6100	9	F4
KENTUCKY PL	CM	CM	1800	27	B2
KENTWATER PL	CO	YL	5300	8	B4
KENWICK CIR	HTB	HB		25	F2
KENWICK DR	VPK	OR67	10300	13	A6
KENWOOD AV	ANA	AN	1200	11	E2
KENWOOD AV	BPK	BP	5200	5	D4
KENWOOD LN	CO	TUS	12500	24	B1
KENWOOD PL	ANA	AN	1200	11	E2
KENWOOD PL	CM	CM27	1900	31	C2
KENWOOD PL	FUL	FL	1100	6	D3
KENWOOD RD	SB	SB	1200	14	A5
KENWOOD ST	LAH	LAH	1200	2	A6
KENWORTH CIR	HTB	HB	20400	26	F5
KENYON DR	TUS	TUS	17000	23	E4
KENYON LN	HTB	HB	20400	26	F5
KENYON PL	OR	OR	4800	18	B2
KEOKI DR	HTB	HB	9400	30	E1
KEOKUK ST	OR	OR	1900	12	D5
KEPLER	IRV	SA		32A	E2
KERMATH ST	CO	PLA	4700	7	D3
KERMORE LN	CO	STN	7000	15	B1
KERMORE LN	STN	STN	7200	15	B1
KERN AV	GGR	GG	9700	21	F1
KERN AV	GGR	GG43	10200	22	A1
KERN AV	WSTM	WSTM	8800	21	E1
KERN DR	HTB	HB	5500	20	E6
KERN ST	LAH	LAH	500	1	E5

STREET	CITY	P.O. ZONE	BLOCK	PAGE	GRID
KERN ST	YL	YL		8	F4
KERNER WY	LAH	LAH	1100	2	B4
KERR GREEN	BPK	BP21	5000	5	C4
KERRWOOD	CO	LB56		29C	C2
KERRWOOD ST	BREA	BREA		2	C4
KERRY CT	CO	ET		29B	A1
KERRY LN	CM	CM	3100	27	D3
KERRY LN	GGR	GG		15	F6
KERRY ST	GGR	GG	13000	15	F6
KERRY ST	GGR	GG	14000	21	F1
KERTH DR	CO	LALM	3100	14	A2
KESTREL LN	CO	LB	29200	35	D2
KESWICK LN	HTB	HB	19800	26	F4
KETCH AV	GGR	GG43	10500	22	A2
KETCH AV	WSTM	WSTM	10100	21	F2
KETCH AV	WSTM	WSTM	10200	22	A2
KETCH RD	NB	NB60		31	E6
KETTERING ST	IRV	SA	1600	28	D2
KETTLE MILL PL	ANA	AN	800	13	D1
KETTLER LN	HTB	HB47	16500	21	B5
KEVIN LN	LAP	BP23		9	E2
KEVIN WY	PLA	PLA	500	7	B4
KEWAMEE DR	NB	NB	2000	32	A6
KEY DR	PLA	PLA	1900	7	A2
KEY BAY	NB	NB		33	C1
KEYS LN	ANA	AN	2500	10	B5
KEYSTONE ST	ANA	AN	900	11	A3
KEY VIEW	NB	NB		33	C1
KEY WEST	CO	LB77		36	A5
KEY WEST	NB	NB		33	C1
KEYWOOD LN	SA	SA		16	C6
KEYWOOD LN	SA	SA		22	C1
KIALOA CT	NB	NB		31	B4
KIAMA PL	ANA	AN	1400	11	B5
KIAMA ST	ANA	AN	600	11	B5
KIBBINS CIR	STN	STN	7200	15	B2
KIERSY PL	CO	SA		18	C5
KILDA CIR	HTB	HB47	6500	21	A6
KILDARE LN	SJC	SJ75		38	D4
KILKARNEY	CO	ET		52	B6
KILKENNY LN	HTB	HB	20400	26	D5
KILKENNY RD	EBAY	LB51	700	34	B1
KILLARNEY	MVJO	SJ92		29B	E3
KILLARNEY AV	GGR	GG45	6000	14	F4
KILLARNEY AV	GGR	GG	6500	15	A4
KILLARNEY DR	CO	ET		29B	A1
KILLARNEY LN	CM	CM	3100	27	D3
KILLARNEY LN	SJC	SJ75		38	C4
KILLARNEY RD	GGR	GG	8400	15	C4
KILLDEER CIR	CM	CM	1900	27	B5
KILLINGSWRTH AV	OR	OR	2700	17	F3
KILLY ST	CO	ET		29A	F3
KILLY ST	CO	ET		29B	A2
KILLYBROOKE LN	CM	CM	3000	27	D4
KILMER DR	PLA	PLA	1800	7	C2
KILO WY	LAG	LB51	2400	34	F4
KILSON DR	SA	SA	700	23	C4
KILSON DR	SA	SA	2900	28	C1
KILT AV	PLA	PLA	1400	7	C3
KIM CIR	CO	LB	24600	29A	E6
KIM LN	HTB	HB47	16200	21	C4
KIM WY	GGR	GG	11500	16	C2
KIMBERLEE DR	CO	LB53		29C	E6
KIMBERLY AV	FUL	FL	1200	6	E6
KIMBERLY AV	FUL	FL	2300	7	A6
KIMBERLY AV	PLA	PLA		7	A6
KIMBERLY AV E	ANA	AN	700	11	E1
KIMBERLY AV W	ANA	AN	1500	16	B1
KIMBERLY CIR	TUS	TUS	14600	23	F5
KIMBERLY DR	HTB	HB	6000	20	F2
KIMBERLY LN	ANA	AN	1300	16	C1
KIMBERLY LN	SJC	SJ75		36	B2
KIMBERLY PL	ANA	AN	1200	16	C1
KIMBERWICK CIR	IRV	SA	4500	29	D2
KIMBERWICK LN	HTB	HB	20900	26	E6
KIMBERWICKE DR	CO	SA	1600	18	D5
KINCAID DR	CM	CM		27	C5
KINER AV	HTB	HB	8000	26	D2
KING	IRV	SA		24	F6
KING CIR	ANA	AN	1000	11	F5
KING CIR	HTB	HB		20	D6
KING CIR	WSTM	WSTM	15800	21	E4
KING PL	FUL	FL	300	6	A5
KING ST	SA	SA	1300	22	E1
KING ST	SA	SA	1200	22	E4
KING ST	YL	YL		8	F4
KINGBIRD AV	FTNV	SA08	10100	27	A2
KNG CHAS III LN	DPT	LB77	32800	37	B3
KINGDON CT	CO	LB		35	C4
KING EIDER LN	CO	LB56		29C	B1
KING FRND IV CT	DPT	LB77	32800	37	B3

STREET	CITY	P.O. ZONE	BLOCK	PAGE	GRID
KINGFISHER DR	HTB	HB	8200	26	D6
KING FREDRCK LN	DPT	LB77	32800	37	B3
KINGHAM WY	FUL	FL33		5	E3
KING JOHN LN	DPT	LB77	22800	37	B3
KINGLET CT	CM	CM	1700	27	B5
KINGLET CT	CO	LB	29300	35	D2
KINGMAN AV	BPK	BP	5500	5	B5
KINGPORT	HTB	HB		26	D3
KINGS CT	CM	CM		27	E2
KINGS PL	NB	NB	100	31	D5
KINGS RD	CO	LB		35	E2
KINGS RD	NB	NB	300	31	D5
KINGS ST	LALM	LALM	10100	9	C6
KINGSBORO CIR	TUS	TUS	1900	24	A5
KINGSBRIAR DR	YL	YL	5500	8	C5
KINGS BRIDGE RD	CO	SA		18	D3
KINGS CANYON DR	HTB	HB	9700	26	F5
KINGS CANYON RD	BREA	BREA		2	F4
KINGS CANYON ST	FTNV	SA08	18000	27	A3
KINGS COURT DR	ANA	AN	1200	11	A6
KINGS COURT LN	ANA	AN	1300	11	A6
KINGSCROSS RD	WSTM	WSTM	5000	20	E1
KINGS CROWN RD	CO	SA		18	D4
KINGS CROWN RD	OR	OR		18	C3
KINGSDALE DR	HTB	HB		26	D4
KINGSFORD TER	IRV	SA		32A	A3
KINGSGATE DR	OR	OR		12	F3
KINGSGATE DR	OR	OR	2800	13	A3
KINGSHILL	MVJO	SJ92		29B	D2
KINGSINGTON LN	CO	LB56		29C	C3
KINGSLEY ST	CO	ET	24000	29A	D3
KINGSLEY ST N&S	ANA	AN	100	12	B3
KINGS LYNN	MVJO	SJ92		29B	F6
KINGS POINTE	CO	LB		35	E2
KINGSPORT DR	YL	YL		7	D4
KINGS RIVER CT	FTNV	SA08	10300	27	A2
KINGSTON AV	TUS	TUS	14500	24	A4
KINGSTON CT	CO	LB56		29C	C3
KINGSTON DR	LAH	LAH	1100	2	A3
KINGSTON LN	HTB	HB	15200	20	F2
KINGSTON RD	PLA	PLA	1600	7	B3
KINGSTON ST	CM	CM		27	E2
KINGS VIEW	CO	LB		35	E3
KINGSVIEW RD	CO	SA		18	B4
KINGSWAY AV	ANA	AN	3600	10	A6
KINGSWOOD CT	FUL	FL		7	A1
KINGSWOOD DR	CO	PLA	16200	7	C3
KINGSWOOD DR E	PLA	PLA	900	7	C3
KINGSWOOD LN	HTB	HB	19800	26	F4
KINGTON WY	LAP	CYP	8400	9	E3
KING WILLIAM CT	DPT	LB77	32900	37	C3
KINKERRY LN	SJC	SJ75		38	D4
KINLEY ST	LAH	LAH	300	1	D4
KINMOUNT ST	LALM	LALM	8300	9	C6
KINSALE DR	CO	ET		29B	A1
KIOLSTAD DR	PLA	PLA	400	7	C2
KIOWA LN	HTB	HB	21800	30	E2
KIOWA RD	WSTM	WSTM	6100	15	A5
KIPAHULU LN	HTB	HB46	19000	27	A3
KIPLING CIR	WSTM	WSTM		21	E4
KIPLING LN	TUS	TUS	14200	23	F4
KIPLING PL	SA	SA		28	C1
KIRBY DR	LAH	LAH	800	1	F3
KIRBY WY	STN	STN	7300	15	B2
KIRK AV	CO	TUS	18000	23	F1
KIRK AV	CO	TUS	18100	24	A1
KIRKLUND CIR	HTB	HB47	6500	21	A6
KIRKWALL LN	CO	ET		29B	A1
KIRKWALL LN	CO	ET		52	A6
KIRKWOOD	CO	ET	22300	29A	E2
KIRKWOOD AV	CO	SA	18200	18	A4
KIRKWOOD AV	OR	OR	1800	17	E4
KIRKWOOD AV	OR	OR	3400	18	A4
KIRKWOOD CIR	ANA	AN08		40	A6
KIRKWOOD CIR	ANA	AN		43	A1
KIRKWOOD LN	LAH	LAH	400	5	F1
KIRWIN CIR	FTNV	SA08	17000	22	C5
KISER DR	HTB	HB	6000	25	F1
KITE DR	ANA	AN		13	F2
KITE DR	ANA	AN		43	A2
KITE DR	HTB	HB	9800	26	F6
KITE HILL DR	CO	LB	29200	35	D2
KITRIDGE	MVJO	SJ92		29B	D2
KITTEN CIR	HTB	HB	3900	20	C5
KITTENDALE BAY	CM	CM		27	E4
KITTERMAN DR	CO	SIL	14900	50	D2
KITTERY CIR	HTB	HB	22200	30	F3
KITTRICK DR	CO	LALM	2900	14	A2
KITTS HWY	SB	SB		20	A1
KITTY CT	ANA	AN		8	A6

STREET	CITY	P.O. ZONE	BLOCK	PAGE	GRID
KITTY CT	ANA	AN		13	A1
KIWI CIR	CYP	CYP	6600	15	A2
KIWI CIR	FTNV	SA08	9400	26	E2
KIWI LN	GGR	GG		15	D5
KLAMATH	IRV	SA		28	F6
KLAMATH CT	CO	LB	28000	29C	E6
KLAMATH DR	WSTM	WSTM	13300	14	F5
KLAMATH DR	WSTM	WSTM	13400	15	A5
KLAMATH PL	OR	OR		13	B6
KLAMATH RIV CIR	FTNV	SA08	10300	27	A2
KLEE DR	IRV	SA	14000	24	C6
KLINE DR	CO	SA07	20000	28	A6
KLONDIKE AV	CM	CM		27	E3
KLONDIKE AV	WSTM	WSTM	6500	15	A5
KNAVE PL	SA	SA	2800	23	B6
KNEPP AV	FUL	FL	100	11	B1
KNEPP AV W	FUL	FL	100	6	B6
KNIGHT LN	SA	SA		22	E2
KNIGHT PL	SA	SA	2900	23	B6
KNIGHT PL	SA	SA	3000	28	B1
KNIGHTS CIR	HTB	HB	8600	26	D5
KNIGHTS GLEN	CO	ET		52	C4
KNIGHTS BRDG RD	OR	OR		18	C3
KNOB HILL	CO	LB77		36	A4
KNOCKADOON RD	EBAY	LB51	700	34	B1
KNOLL CT	BREA	BREA	400	2	F5
KNOLLCREST LN	GGR	GG		15	A6
KNOLLGLEN	IRV	SA		29	C5
KNOLL LAKE	SA	SA		17	D5
KNOLL LAKE AV	BREA	BREA		2	D5
KNOLLWOOD	CO	ET	24800	29A	E2
KNOLLWOOD CIR	ANA	AN	1100	10	D2
KNOLLWOOD CT	BPK	BP		5	C3
KNOLLWOOD DR	OR	OR69		18	D3
KNOLLWOOD RD	SB	SB	1200	19	C5
KNOLLWOOD WY	BPK	BP	8200	5	C3
KNOTT AV	BPK	BP	6000	5	A6
KNOTT AV	BPK	BP	6600	10	A6
KNOTT AV	CO	STN	10800	15	A2
KNOTT AV	CYP	CYP	10500	15	A2
KNOTT AV	STN	STN	10400	15	A2
KNOTT AV S	ANA	AN	100	10	A6
KNOTT ST	GGR	GG	11200	15	A4
KNOTTINGTON	LAH	LAH		2	B5
KNOTTY PINE RD	CO	LB		29D	A2
KNOWELL PL	CM	CM27	500	31	C1
KNOWLES	MVJO	SJ92		29D	F3
KNOX AV	SA	SA	1300	22	E6
KNOX PL	CM	CM27	200	31	C3
KNOX ST	CM	CM27	200	31	C3
KNOXVILLE	IRV	SA		24	E5
KNOXVILLE AV E	HTB	HB	100	26	C5
KNOXVILLE AV W	HTB	HB	100	26	C5
KNUDSON ST	LAH	LAH	200	1	F5
KNUTH CIR	VPK	OR67	10100	13	B6
KOCH AV	PLA	PLA		7	B2
KODIAK ST	ANA	AN	100	12	E2
KODIAK MTN DR	YL	YL		40	C5
KOLEDO LN	HTB	HB47	17300	21	C6
KOMMERS LN	CO	OR67		50	F6
KONA AV	SA	SA		22	C3
KONA DR	HTB	HB	4900	20	D4
KONA LN	GGR	GG	12600	15	E4
KONA LN	SA	SA		22	C3
KONA KOVE WY	YL	YL	4800	7	D3
KONIGSMARK ST	FTNV	SA08		26	F1
KOOPMANS WY	CO	LAH	1300	1	E3
KOOTENAY DR	CO	SA	13100	18	A5
KORBEL WY	CO	LB77		35	D2
KORNAT DR	CM	CM	1900	27	B4
KOSO PL	CO	TRA		59	C2
KOURI LN	ANA	AN	800	10	B5
KOVACS	HTB	HB		26	C1
KRAEMER BLVD	ANA	AN	1700	7	B5
KRAEMER BLVD	ANA	AN	1500	12	C1
KRAEMER BLVD	BREA	BREA	3000	3	B6
KRAEMER BL N&S	PLA	PLA	100	7	B3
KRAEMER PL	ANA	AN	1100	12	C2
KRAFT ST	SA	SA	1200	22	B1
KRAMER AV	WSTM	WSTM	9300	21	E2
KRATON	CO	LB77		35	D6
KREPP DR	HTB	HB	9300	26	E3
KRISTEN ST	CYP	CYP	10300	9	F6
KRISTI LN	SA	SA	2200	23	E1
KRISTIN CIR	HTB	HB47	7800	21	C6
KRISTIN LN	CM	CM27		31	D1
KRISTOPHER LN	HTB	HB47	17000	21	A6
KROEGER AV	FUL	FL	1000	6	D4
KROEGER ST S	ANA	AN	100	11	D4
KROLL LN	HTB	HB	21200	30	D1
KRON ST	IRV	SA	4800	29	D2

STREET	CITY	P.O. ZONE	BLOCK	PAGE	GRID
K THANGA DR	NB	CDLM	700	31	F5
KUDRON WY	ANA	AN05	200	11	E3
KUKUI DR	HTB	HB46	10000	27	A3
KURMIT DR	CO	ET		29A	E4
KURT LN	HTB	HB47	17400	21	A6
KYLE ST	LALM	LALM	10700	14	C1
KYLE ST N	LALM	LALM	10700	9	C6
L					
L ST	LAG	LB		35	A4
L ST	NB	NB	100	33	A1
LA ALAMEDA	MVJO	SJ91		29D	B5
LA ALAMEDA AV	FTNV	SA08	9800	21	F6
LA ALAMEDA AV	FTNV	SA08	10000	22	A6
LA ALCALA	CO	LB56		35	F1
LA ALONDRA AV	FTNV	SA08	10600	27	A1
LA AMAPOLA AV	FTNV	SA08	9800	26	F1
LA ARENA CIR	FTNV	SA08	9800	26	F1
LA AZTECA	CO	LB56		35	E1
LA BAJADA	CO	LB56		35	E1
LA BAHIA AV	FTNV	SA08	10600	27	A1
LA BALLENA CIR	FTNV	SA08	10300	27	A1
LA BARCA	MVJO	SJ91	28300	29B	D1
LA BARCA	MVJO	SJ92		29B	E1
LA BARCA CIR	FTNV	SA08	9200	26	E1
LA BATISTA AV	FTNV	SA08	10800	22	B6
LA BAYA AV	FTNV	SA08	8500	21	D6
LA BELLA DR	CO	SA	12400	24	B2
LA BONITA AV	GGR	GG	13900	16	B6
LA BONITA LN	HTB	HB		20	D5
LA BONITA ST	SA	SA	1300	22	B1
LABRADOR DR	CM	CM	1600	27	C3
LA BREA ST	LAG	LB51	100	34	C2
LA BRISA RD	CO	ET	22700	29A	F3
LA BRISAS CIR	CO	LB77		35	C6
LA BRISE	CO	LB77		35	C5
LABRUSCA	MVJO	SJ92		29B	E3
LABURNAM LN	FTNV	SA08	18000	26	E2
LABURNUM DR	TUS	TUS	13200	24	A2
LA CABRA	MVJO	SJ91	27300	29B	C1
LA CABRA	MVJO	SJ91		52	C6
LA CADENA CIR	YL	YL	4200	7	F2
LA CADENA DR	CO	LB	23000	29A	C3
LA CADENA WY	LAH	LAH	500	1	E4
LA CALERA ST	SJC	SJ75	31300	36	C6
LA CALETA	MVJO	SJ92	28200	29B	E3
LA CALMA DR	SJC	SJ75	32500	38	A2
LA CANADA CIR	BPK	BP	6000	9	F2
LA CANADA DR	BREA	BREA	1500	2	C3
LA CANADA WY	CO	CM27	300	27	F6
LA CANTO	CO	SJ88		59	C1
LA CAPILLA	MVJO	SJ91		29B	C1
LA CAPILLA	MVJO	SJ91		52	C6
LA CAPILLA AV	FTNV	SA08	9500	21	F6
LA CARRETERRA	CO	LB77		36	A2
LA CARTA AV	FTNV	SA08	10900	22	B6
LA CARTA CIR	BPK	BP	7700	9	F2
LA CASA AV	LAH	LAH	900	1	F6
LA CASA WY	BPK	BP	7700	9	F2
LA CASADA	CO	SJ88		59	C1
LA CASITA AV	FTNV	SA08	8500	21	D6
LA CASITA AV	YL	YL	18600	8	A2
LA CASTANA WY	BPK	BP	7700	9	F2
LACEBARK LN	MVJO	SJ91		52	D6
LA CEBRA AV	FTNV	SA08	10300	27	A1
LACE LEAF WY	TUS	TUS		24	D4
LACERTA	IRV	SA		32A	A3
LA CHIQUITA DR	MVJO	SJ91		29B	C5
LA CIENAGA DR	BPK	BP	6100	9	F2
LA CIENAGA DR	BPK	BP	6500	10	A2
LA CIENEGA ST	CO	LB		29C	E3
LA CIMA	CO	LB77		36	A2
LA CIMA DR	SCL	SC72		39	E4
LA CINCHA	CO	SJ		59	B1
LA COLINA DR	CO	TUS	1000	24	B1
LA COLINA DR	CO	SA	1400	24	B1
LA COLLETTE PL	YL	YL	17000	7	E4
LA COLLINA ST	CO	LB77		35	F3
LA COLMENA WY	LALM	LALM	3600	14	B2
LA COLONIA AV	FTNV	SA08	8600	21	D6
LA CONCETTA DR	YL	YL	4200	7	E2
LACONIA	IRV	SA14		28	D5
LACONIA DR	VPK	OR67	10700	17	F1
LA CORONA WY	BPK	BP	7700	10	A2
L CORTINILLA AV	FTNV	SA08	9300	26	E1
LA COSTA	MVJO	SJ91		29B	D4
LA COSTA CIR	BPK	BP	7700	10	A2
LA COSTA CT	CM	CM27		31	D2
LA COSTA CT	LAG	LB51		29C	A1
LA COSTA LN	HTB	HB		26	D1

1990 ORANGE COUNTY STREET INDEX

STREET	CITY	P.O. ZONE	BLOCK	PAGE	GRID
LA CRESCENTA	FTNV	SA08	9000	26	E1
LA CRESCENTA	MVJO	SJ91		29B	A4
LA CRESTA AV	ANA	AN	2800	12	B2
LA CRESTA CIR	HTB	HB	9700	26	F5
LA CRESTA DR	DPT	DPT	24200	37	E4
LA CRESTA DR	DPT	LB77		37	E4
LA CRESTA PL	FUL	FL	1000	6	B4
LA CUESTA AV	CO	LB	25900	29C	F2
LA CUESTA CIR	YL	YL	4200	7	E2
LA CUESTA DR	CO	SA	1800	18	D6
LA CUEVA	CO	SJ88		59	C1
LA CUMBRE	CO	LB77		36	A1
LA CUMBRE DR	OR	OR	6600	18	D3
LACY AV	ANA	AN	900	11	E5
LACY ST	SA	SA	100	23	C2
LADD CANYON RD	CO	SIL	14500	50	D2
LADD CYN RD E	CO	SIL		50	E1
LADELL CIR	SA	SA	1700	23	D1
LA DERA	IRV	SA		24	F5
LA DERA	IRV	SA20		49	A5
LADERA CIR	YL	YL	17700	7	F3
LADERA DR	MVJO	SJ91		29B	C6
LADERA LN	ANA	AN		13	D3
LADERA TER	LAH	LAH	1400	2	B6
LADERA SENDA	CO	SA	10200	18	D5
LADERA VISTA DR	FUL	FL	100	6	F5
LADERA VISTA PL	FUL	FL	1700	6	E3
LADERO LN	SCL	SC72	100	39	E4
LA DESPENSA AV	FTNV	SA08	10300	27	A1
LA DONA AV	GGR	GG	10900	16	A2
LADONA CIR	HTB	HB	16600	20	D3
LA DONA CT	FTNV	SA08	8900	21	E6
LA DONA DR	GGR	GG	10500	16	A2
LAEL DR	OR	OR	1400	17	E3
LA ENTRADA CIR	ANA	AN	1100	11	B3
LA ENTRADA DR	YL	YL	17500	7	F2
LA ENTRADA PL E	FUL	FL	100	6	B1
LA ENTRADA PL W	FUL	FL	100	6	B1
LA ESCONDIDA	SCL	SC72		39	D3
LA ESPERANZA	FTNV	SA08		21	F6
LA ESPERANZA N	SCL	SC72	100	39	D3
LA ESPERANZA S	SCL	SC72	100	39	D3
LA ESTRADA DR	CO	LB		35	F3
LA ESTRELLA AV	FTNV	SA08	8600	21	E6
LA FALDA	CO	LB		29D	A6
LA FALDA	CO	LB77		36	A1
LAFAYETTE	IRV	SA		24	D5
LAFAYETTE AV	NB	NB	2600	31	C5
LAFAYETTE DR	ANA	AN		10	F3
LAFAYETTE DR	ANA	AN		11	A3
LAFAYETTE DR	HTB	HB47	6700	21	B4
LAFAYETTE ST	WSTM	WSTM	15100	21	B3
LA FELICIDAD	NB	NB		32	B2
LA FIESTA	YL	YL		40	B5
LA FIESTA AV	FTNV	SA08	8500	21	D6
LA FIESTA DR	BPK	BP	7700	10	A2
LA FLEUR	CO	LB77		35	C4
LA FLOR AV	FTNV	SA08	10900	27	B1
LA FLORA	IRV	SA14		28	E4
LA FONDA CIR	FTNV	SA08	10900	22	B6
LA FUENTE	MVJO	SJ92		29D	C4
LA FUENTE ST	FTNV	SA08	10500	27	B1
LA GALLINA	CO	LB56		29C	F6
LAGARTO	MVJO	SJ91		29B	C5
LAGIER WY	TUS	TUS		24	B3
LA GLORIETA	MVJO	SJ91		29B	B4
LAGO	HTB	HB		20	D5
LAGO NORTE	IRV	SA		28	E6
LAGO SUD	IRV	SA		28	E6
LA GRACIA	CO	LB56		29C	E6
LA GRANADA AV	FTNV	SA08	9600	21	F6
LA GRANADA CIR	LAP	BP23	8200	9	D3
LA GRAND AV	GGR	GG	8600	15	D2
LA GRANDE	YL	YL		40	B5
LA GRANDE CIR	FTNV	SA08	9200	26	E1
LAGRIMA	MVJO	SJ92	24700	29B	E6
LAGUNA AV	LAG	LB51	100	34	D3
LAGUNA CIR	HTB	HB	22100	30	E2
LAGUNA CT	CO	LB56		29C	D3
LAGUNA CT	STN	STN	8100	15	C4
LAGUNA DR	FUL	FL	200	6	B3
LAGUNA DR	LAH	LAH	1700	1	E3
LAGUNA FRWY	CO			29	F6
LAGUNA FRWY	CO			32A	E2
LAGUNA FRWY	IRV			29	F6
LAGUNA PL	ANA	AN	900	11	B3
LAGUNA PL	SB	SB	600	19	F2
LAGUNA RD	FUL	FL	200	6	B2
LAGUNA ST	ANA	AN	1000	11	B3
LAGUNA ST	GGR	GG	12000	16	E3
LAGUNA TER	FUL	FL		6	A3
LAGUNA WY	CYP	CYP	5700	9	E6
LAGUNA CYN RD	IRV	SA	16100	29	E6
LAGUNA CYN RD	IRV	SA		32A	F3
LAGUNA CYN RD	LAG	LB51		32A	F3
LAGUNA CYN RD	LAG	LB51	22500	33A	E4
LAGUNA CYN RD	LAG	LB51	600	34	D1
LAGUNA CYN WY	BREA	BREA		2	F5
LAGUNA HILLS DR	CO	LB56		29C	B3
LAGUNA VISTA	CO	LB		35	F2
LAGUNA WOODS DR	CO	LB		35	D6
LAGUNITA	LAG	LB	30600	34	F5
LAGUNITA DR	LAG	LB	30500	34	F5
LAGUNITA PL	LAG	LB	30500	34	F5
LA HABRA BL E&W	LAH	LAH	100	2	B4
LA HABRA BLVD W	LAH	LAH	500	1	E4
LA HABRA CIR	BPK	BP	7700	10	A2
LA HABRA CT	CO	LB	25400	29C	F2
LA HABRA PL	LAH	LAH	300	2	A4
LA HACIENDA AV	FTNV	SA08	10000	22	A6
LAHAVE WY	CYP	CYP	11400	15	A2
LA HERMOSA AV	CO	LB	23800	35	E4
LA HERRADURA	CO	TRA		59	C1
LA HOMA	YL	YL		40	B5
LA HOMA ST	CYP	CYP	8500	9	E3
LAIRD CIR	SA	SA	2100	16	E6
LAIRD ST	GGR	GG	13000	16	E5
LAIRD ST	SA	SA	2200	16	E5
LAJARES	MVJO	SJ92		29B	E3
LA JOLLA CIR	HTB	HB	9300	30	E2
LA JOLLA DR	NB	NB	200	31	C4
LA JOLLA PZ	GGR	GG		15	F6
LA JOLLA ST	ANA	AN	2900	7	B6
LA JOLLA ST	ANA	AN	2800	12	B1
LA JOLLA ST E&W	PLA	PLA	100	12	A1
LA JOLLA WY	CO	LB56		29C	F6
LA JOLLA WY	CYP	CYP	5700	9	E6
LAKE AV	NB	NB	3200	31	B5
LAKE DR	OR	OR		17	D4
LAKE RD	IRV	SA		29	B4
LAKE ST	GGR	GG43	14000	22	A1
LAKE ST	HTB	HB48		26	B6
LAKE TER	CO	ET		29A	C2
LAKE TER	FUL	FL	500	6	B1
LAKE CENTER DR	CO	ET		29A	D3
LAKE CENTER DR	SA	SA04	3700	27	D1
LK CHAMPLAIN CT	LALM	LALM		14	C3
LAKE COURT RD	CO	SA		18	D6
LAKECREST CIR	CO	SA	9800	18	E4
LAKE CREST DR	YL	YL	3700	7	D1
LAKE CREST LN	LAH	LAH	2200	2	C5
LAKEDALE DR	ANA	AN		12	F2
LAKEDALE DR	ANA	AN		13	A2
LAKEFIELD ST	CO	ET		29A	E2
LAKE FOREST CIR	LAH	LAH	2200	2	C5
LAKE FOREST DR	CO	ET	23100	29A	D3
LAKE FOREST DR	CO	ET		52	B5
LAKE FOREST DR	CO	LB	22800	29A	B3
LAKE FOREST LN	CO	ET		29A	D2
LAKE FOREST LN	YL	YL	16700	7	D1
LAKEFRONT	IRV	SA		29	B4
LAKEFRONT CIR	HTB	HB47		21	B5
LAKE GARDEN DR	CO	ET		29A	D3
LAKE GLEN DR	LAH	LAH	2200	2	C5
LAKE GLEN DR	YL	YL	3700	7	D1
LAKEGRASS	IRV	SA		29	B2
LAKE GROVE DR	YL	YL	3600	7	E1
LAKE GROVE WY	LAH	LAH	500	2	C5
LAKE HAVEN WY	YL	YL	5800	8	A5
LAKEHILL DR	OR	OR	2900	12	F4
LAKEKNOLL	IRV	SA		29	E4
LAKE KNOLL AV	GGR	GG		15	D5
LAKE KNOLL DR	FUL	FL	500	6	B1
LAKE KNOLL LN	YL	YL	16700	7	D1
LAKELAND AV	CO	ET		29A	E1
LAKE MEAD CIR	OR	OR		13	C5
LAKEMONT LN	HTB	HB47	16300	21	A4
LA KENICE WY	YL	YL	17000	7	E3
LAKE PARK DR	PLA	PLA		7	B6
LAKE PARK LN	NB	NB	2200	31	F2
LAKE PARK WY	BREA	BREA		2	D5
LAKE PARK WY	LAH	LAH	400	2	C5
LAKE PARK WY	YL	YL	16700	7	D1
LAKE PINES	IRV	SA		24	F5
LAKE PLEASANT	YL	YL	16700	7	D1
LAKEPOINT LN	HTB	HB	18000	26	A2
LAKE RIDGE	CO	SJ79		59	D2
LAKE RIDGE WY	LAH	LAH	400	2	D5
LAKE RIDGE WY	YL	YL	16700	7	D1
LAKESHORE	IRV	SA		29	C3
LAKESHORE DR	CYP	CYP	6000	9	E4
LAKESHORE LN	CO	ET		29A	C2
LAKE SHORE LN	YL	YL	5800	8	A5
LAKESIDE	IRV	SA18		29	E4
LAKESIDE AV	OR	OR	2300	12	E6
LAKESIDE AV	OR	OR	19000	13	B6
LAKESIDE DR	FUL	FL	500	6	B1
LAKE SIDE DR	LAH	LAH	2000	2	C5
LAKESIDE DR	YL	YL	3700	7	D1
LAKESIDE DR N	GGR	GG		16	A4
LAKESIDE DR S	GGR	GG		16	A4
LAKESIDE LN	CO	ET		29A	D3
LAKESIDE LN	HTB	HB		26	C5
LAKE SUMMIT DR	ANA	AN		13	F3
LAKE SUMMIT DR	ANA	AN		43	A3
LAKE TERRACE LN	LAH	LAH	2200	2	C5
LAKE TERRACE WY	YL	YL	16700	7	D1
LAKETOP DR	ANA	AN		13	F3
LAKETRAIL	IRV	SA		29	B2
LAKETREE DR	YL	YL	16700	7	D1
LAKEVIEW	IRV	SA		29	C3
LAKEVIEW AV	ANA	AN	1200	7	F6
LAKEVIEW AV	CO	PLA	6100	7	F6
LAKEVIEW AV	PLA	PLA	6400	7	F6
LAKEVIEW AV	YL	YL	4200	8	A4
LAKEVIEW AV N	ANA	AN	100	12	F1
LAKEVIEW AV N	ANA	AN		13	A1
LAKEVIEW AV S	ANA	AN	100	13	A2
LAKEVIEW CIR	FUL	FL	3000	6	B1
LAKEVIEW CT	FUL	FL	600	6	B1
LAKEVIEW DR	FUL	FL35	3200	2	B6
LAKEVIEW DR	FUL	FL	2700	6	B1
LAKEVIEW DR	HTB	HB	6600	26	A2
LAKEVIEW DR	LAH	LAH	1200	2	B6
LAKEVIEW LN	CM	CM26		28	A3
LAKEVIEW LN	CO	ET		29A	C2
LAKEVIEW RD	SJC	SJ75		36	B3
LAKEVIEW TER	FUL	FL	3000	6	B1
LAKEVIEW TR	OR	OR		18	E1
LAKEVIEW WY	FUL	FL	2900	6	B2
LAKE VISTA DR	CO	ET	21000	29A	E1
LAKEWOOD DR	CO	LB		29D	A6
LAKEWOOD DR	CO	LB77		36	A1
LAKE WOOD DR	YL	YL	3700	7	D1
LAKIA DR	CYP	CYP		14	E3
LA LILA LN	FTNV	SA08	10500	27	A1
LA LIMA LN	FTNV	SA08	17800	27	B1
LA LIMONAR RD	CO	SA	1000	18	C5
LALIN	MVJO	SJ92		29D	D2
LA LINDA AV	FTNV	SA08	9000	26	E1
LA LINDA CIR	GGR	GG		15	D4
LA LINDA CT	CO	CM27	2200	31	E2
LA LINDA DR	OR	OR	200	17	B3
LA LINDA PL	CM	CM27	2300	31	E1
LA LITA LN	MVJO	SJ92	28800	36	C1
LA LOMA CIR	ANA	AN		12	B1
LA LOMA DR	CO	SA	1000	18	C6
LA LOMA DR	CO	SA	1600	24	C1
LA LOMA PL	FUL	FL35	3200	6	C1
LA LUNA AV	FTNV	SA08	9000	21	E6
LA LUNA DR	LAP	BP23	5000	9	D3
LA MACINDA DR	YL	YL		7	E3
LA MADERA	CO	LB56		35	E1
LA MANCHA	MVJO	SJ91		29D	B3
LA MANCHA	YL	YL		40	B5
LA MANCHA CIR	HTB	HB47	7300	21	B5
LA MANGUSTA	CO	LB56		29C	F6
LA MAR	MVJO	SJ91		29B	B4
LAMAR CIR	HTB	HB47	8500	21	D5
LAMAR ST	ANA	AN04	1600	15	F1
LAMARK DR	ANA	AN	700	16	D2
LAMARK LN	ANA	AN	1000	16	C2
LAMARK WY	LAH	LAH	500	1	E4
LA MARMOTA AV	FTNV	SA08	10400	27	A1
LA MARQUESA AV	FTNV	SA08	10700	22	B6
LA MATANZA	SJC	SJ75	31300	36	C6
LAMBDA LN	ANA	AN	1500	11	F4
LAMBDA PL	ANA	AN	1400	11	E4
LAMBERT CIR	GGR	GG	12200	15	E4
LAMBERT DR	FUL	FL33	500	5	F6
LAMBERT DR	FUL	FL33	500	10	F1
LAMBERT DR	FUL	FL	1000	11	A1
LAMBERT DR	HTB	HB47	8200	21	C5
LAMBERT RD	CO	LAH	9800	1	E5
LAMBERT RD	CO	SA	12900	51	C2
LAMBERT RD E&W	BREA	BREA	100	2	E5
LAMBERT RD E&W	LAH	LAH	100	2	B5
LAMBERT RD W	BREA	BREA	1100	3	A5
LAMBERT RD W	LAH	LAH	500	1	E5
LAMBERT ST	CO	ET		29A	D3
LAMBERT WY	STN	STN	11100	15	A2
LAMBETH WY	CO	TUS	14000	17	F6
LAMBETH WY	CO	TUS	14100	23	F1
LAMBROSE CYN RD	CO	SJ		56	B3
LA MESA AV	ANA	AN	3100	12	C2
LA MESA AV	CO	AN06		12	B2
LA MESA CT	CM	CM27		31	E1
LA MESA DR	FUL	FL	1000	6	A4
LA MESA LN	HTB	HB	17200	20	F6
LA MESA PL	FUL	FL	1100	6	A4
LA MESA WY	BPK	BP	7700	9	F2
LA MIRADA BLVD	BPK	BP	7500	5	B3
LA MIRADA CIR	BPK	BP	7700	9	F2
LA MIRADA LN	OR	OR		18	A4
LA MIRADA ST	CO	LB	25000	29C	F2
LA MIRADA ST	LAG	LB51	800	34	F4
LA MIRADA ST	LAH	LAH	900	1	E3
LA MONA CIR	BPK	BP	7700	9	F2
LA MONTE RD	STN	STN	8000	15	C2
LA MONTROSA	CO	LB56		35	E1
LAMORA CIR	FTNV	SA08	9600	21	F6
LA MORADA CIR	MVJO	SJ91	26000	29D	C3
LA MORITA DR	MVJO	SJ91		29B	B3
LAMPLIGHT LN	YL	YL	19000	8	B3
LAMPLIGHTER ST	GGR	GG	11800	15	A4
LAMP POST LN	YL	YL		8	C5
LAMP POST WY	ANA	AN		12	F3
LAMPSON AV	CO	GG41	7700	15	B4
LAMPSON AV	CO	GG	13000	16	A4
LAMPSON AV	GGR	GG45	5300	14	E4
LAMPSON AV	GGR	GG	6300	15	B4
LAMPSON AV	GGR	GG	10200	16	A4
LAMPSON AV	SB	SB	3500	14	C5
LAMPSON AV	STN	GG41	7700	15	B4
LA MUJERA	CO	LB56		29C	F6
LA NAE CIR	OR	OR	500	18	A2
LANAI CIR	HTB	HB	9400	30	E2
LANAI DR	CM	CM	1900	27	B4
LANAI LN	PLA	PLA	200	7	B5
LANAI ST	SA	SA		22	C3
LANAI WY	SA	SA		22	C3
LANAI WY	TUS	TUS	1500	24	A2
LANAKILA LN	GGR	GG	9700	15	F4
LANAR	MVJO	SJ92	21600	29B	E1
LA NARANJA CT	FTNV	SA08	11000	22	B6
LANARK CIR	HTB	HB	8700	26	D3
LANCASHIRE AV	WSTM	WSTM	5700	20	F1
LANCASHIRE CIR	LAP	BP23		9	D3
LANCASTER AV	ANA	AN	3100	7	B6
LANCASTER DR	HTB	HB47	8200	21	C5
LANCASTER ST	NB	NB	6100	31	A4
LANCE DR	TUS	TUS	1300	24	A3
LANCE LN	ANA	AN	1200	12	B1
LANCE WY	SA	SA	200	23	B6
LANCE WY	SA	SA	200	28	B1
LANCEFIELD DR	HTB	HB		25	F1
LANCELOT LN	HTB	HB	20700	26	E6
LANCER DR	ANA	AN	700	11	B3
LANCER DR	YL	YL	17000	7	D3
LANCEWOOD CT	FUL	FL		7	A1
LANCEWOOD PZ	YL	YL	19600	8	C5
LANCEWOOD WY	IRV	SA	4300	29	A5
LANCIANO	IRV	SA		24	D5
LAND LN	ANA	AN	200	10	E4
LANDAU LN	HTB	HB47	16500	21	D5
LANDER WY	STN	STN		10	E4
LANDER WY	STN	STN		15	B3
LANDERS DR	CO	MDWY	8500	21	D2
LANDFAIR CIR	CO	SA	1200	24	B1
LANDFAIR ST	ANA	AN	1700	7	C6
LANDFALL CT	NB	NB		31	B4
LANDFALL DR	HTB	HB	9500	30	F1
LANDING	CO	LB77		36	A5
LANDING AV	SB	SB	1200	19	F3
LANDISVIEW AV	CO	ET	23700	29A	E5
LANDMARK AV	YL	YL	16600	7	D2
LANDON DR	ANA	AN07		8	A6
LANDOVER RD	CO	LB		29C	E3
LANDSDOWNE RD	TUS	SA10		23	E5
LANDSDOWNNE DR	NB	NB		32	B3
LANEROSE DR	ANA	AN	3100	10	B6
LANETT ST	CO	CYP	8700	9	D4
LANEY CT	GGR	GG	11300	16	A2
LANGDALE LN	TUS	TUS	1200	23	F4
LANGDON DR	IRV	SA		24	F6
LANGE DR	CO	SA07	20400	27	F6
LANGER DR	PLA	PLA	500	7	C5
LANGLEY AV	IRV	SA	1600	28	D2
LANGLEY DR	LALM	LALM	11000	14	D2
LANGPORT CIR	HTB	HB	5900	20	E5
LANGREO	MVJO	SJ92		29B	D6
LANGREO	MVJO	SJ92		29D	D1
LANGS BAY	CM	CM		27	F3
LANGSDORF DR	FUL	FL	500	7	A5
LANGTREE LN	ANA	AN07		13	D3
LANI AV	ANA	AN		12	F2
LANNING ST	GGR	GG	13500	16	B6
LA NOCHE	MVJO	SJ92	28400	29B	E5
LA NOVIA AV	SJC	SJ75	31500	36	D6
LA NOVIA AV	SJC	SJ75		38	D2
LANSDALE CIR	STN	STN		15	B4
LANSDOWNE LN	CO	SA	1400	18	C6
LANSING LN	CM	CM	900	27	E3
LANTANA AV	BREA	BREA	700	6	D2
LANTANA AV	FUL	FL	2600	6	D2
LANTANA DR	BPK	BP	7600	10	D2
LANTANA DR	HTB	HB	9000	26	E5
LANTANA DR	YL	YL		7	F5
LANTANA LN	CM	CM	3300	27	E2
LANTEEN CIR	CO	LB77		37	D2
LANTERN LN	ANA	AN	2000	11	A2
LANTERN LN	CO	ET		29A	F2
LANTERN BAY DR	DPT	DPT		37	F5
LANTERN HILL DR	DPT	DPT		37	E3
LANUZA	MVJO	SJ92	28300	29B	E6
LANZAROTE	MVJO	SJ92		29B	D3
LA PAJA LN	MVJO	SJ91		29D	C3
LA PALA LN	MVJO	SJ91		29B	C5
LA PALMA AV	ANA	AN	2100	11	A2
LA PALMA AV	ANA	AN	2200	12	A2
LA PALMA AV	BPK	BP	6000	9	E3
LA PALMA AV	BPK	BP	6500	10	B2
LA PALMA AV	LAP	BP23	4500	9	E3
LA PALMA AV	YL	YL		40	A4
LA PALMA AV E	ANA	AN	4700	13	A1
LA PALMA AV W	ANA	AN01	2000	11	A2
LA PALMA DR	HTB	HB	8000	26	C2
LA PALOMA	DPT	DPT		37	F2
LA PALOMA	SCL	SC72	200	39	C3
LA PALOMA AV	FTNV	SA08	8900	21	E6
LA PALOMA AV	PLA	PLA		7	E6
LA PALOMA DR	IRV	SA		24	E4
LA PANTERA	CO	LB56		29C	F6
LA PARILLA	CO	LB56		29C	F6
LA PAT CT	WSTM	WSTM	6500	21	A1
LA PAT PL	WSTM	WSTM	13400	15	A6
LA PAT PL	WSTM	WSTM	14000	21	A1
LA PATA AV	CO	SA		36	F5
LA PATA AV	CO	SA		62	A2
LA PATA ST	WSTM	WSTM	13000	15	A5
LA PAZ AV	DPT	DPT	24700	37	F4
LA PAZ CIR	ANA	AN	200	13	C2
LA PAZ CIR	YL	YL	4400	7	E2
LA PAZ DR	HTB	HB47	8100	21	C4
LA PAZ LN	LAP	BP23	7100	9	E1
LA PAZ LN	YL	YL	4400	7	E2
LA PAZ RD	CO	LB		29C	E5
LA PAZ RD	CO	LB	25100	35	E1
LA PAZ RD	MVJO	SJ91	26000	29B	B6
LA PAZ RD	MVJO	SJ91	26100	29D	B1
LA PAZ RD	MVJO	SJ92		29B	D6
LA PAZ RD	MVJO	SJ92		29D	C1
LA PAZ RD	PLA	PLA	900	7	D4
LA PAZ ST	ANA	AN	100	13	C2
LA PAZ WY	ANA	AN	6000	13	C2
LA PERLA AV	FTNV	SA08	10500	27	A1
LA PERLA ST	ANA	AN	800	10	D3
LA PERLE LN	CM	CM27	300	31	D4
LA PERLE PL	CM	CM27	300	31	D4
LA PLACENTIA	SCL	SC72	100	39	D2
LA PLATA DR	CO	LB	24600	35	F3
LA PLAYA AV	DPT	SC24	25900	38	B5
LA PLAYA CIR	FTNV	SA08	8700	26	D1
LA PLAZA	ANA	AN	100	11	E3
LA PLAZA	DPT	DPT	24600	37	E4
LA PLAZA CT	LAH	LAH	300	1	F4
LA PLAZA DR	LAH	LAH	100	1	F4
LA PLUMOSA	CO	LB56		35	E1
LA PORTERO ST	CO	LAG		35	F3
LA PRADERA	CO	LB77		36	A1
LA PRADERA	YL	YL	19000	8	B3
LA PRESA DR E	LAH	LAH	200	2	A3
LA PRESA DR W	LAH	LAH	400	1	F3
LA PUEBLA	MVJO	SJ92		29B	D2
LA PUERTA	CO	SJ88		59	B2
LAPWING LN	CO	LB	24000	35	D1
LAPWORTH CIR	HTB	HB	9800	26	F6
LA QUILLA LN	MVJO	SJ92		36	C2
LA QUINTA	IRV	SA		32A	B2
LA QUINTA CIR	FTNV	SA08	10000	27	A1
LA QUINTA DR	MVJO	SJ91	22800	29B	B3
LARAMA DR	CO	SA	11500	18	C6
LA RAMBLA	SCL	SC72	200	39	C4
LARAMIE CIR	WSTM	WSTM		21	D4

STREET	CITY	P.O. ZONE	BLOCK	PAGE	GRID
LARAMIE ST	ANA	AN	900	12	A5
LARAMORE LN	GGR	GG	13500	16	E5
LARAMORE LN	SA	SA	1700	16	E5
LARCH AV	IRV	SA	14500	24	C6
LARCH CIR	BPK	BP	8100	10	C3
LARCH LN	TUS	TUS		24	B4
LARCH ST	ANA	AN	100	11	E3
LARCHMONT AV	SA	SA	2300	17	C5
LARCHMONT CT	CO	LB56		29C	C3
LARCHMONT DR	CO	ET	21000	52	C6
LARCHWOOD DR	BREA	BREA	500	6	D1
LARCHWOOD DR	HTB	HB47	6000	21	A2
LARCHWOOD LN	CO	SA	12000	24	C1
LARCREST CIR	HTB	HB		25	F1
LA REAL	MVJO	SJ91		29B	B4
LAREDO LN	CO	ET	26600	29B	B2
LA REINA CIR	ANA	AN	100	10	D4
LA REINA ST	ANA	AN	300	10	D4
LARGO	CO	LB77		36	A3
LARGO DR	CO	LB	24000	29C	E2
LARIAT AV	GGR	GG	8600	15	D6
LARIAT CIR	SJC	SJ75	27000	36	C3
LARIAT DR	YL	YL		8	C2
LARIAT LN	CO	SA05		18	B5
LARIAT PL	FUL	FL35		2	B6
LARK AV	PLA	PLA	900	12	A1
LARK CIR	FTNV	SA08	9700	26	F2
LARK LN	HTB	HB	16900	20	F6
LARK ST	ANA	AN	1000	11	E2
LARK ELLEN DR	FUL	FL	1600	6	E1
LARK ELLEN LN	ANA	AN		12	A6
LARKFIELD DR	YL	YL	19600	8	C5
LARKFIELD LN	CO	LAG		37	F2
LARKFIELD PZ	YL	YL	19600	8	C5
LARKGROVE CIR	CO	SJ79		56	E6
LARKHALL CIR	HTB	HB		26	D6
LARKIN DR	GGR	GG	11400	15	E2
LARKIN ST	CO	ET	24000	29A	D3
LARKMONT DR	HTB	HB49		25	F1
LARKPORT DR	HTB	HB	8500	26	D4
LARKRIDGE DR	CO	YL	19700	8	C5
LARKSPUR	MVJO	SJ92		29B	E6
LARKSPUR	MVJO	SJ92		29D	E1
LARKSPUR AV	BREA	BREA		3	C6
LARKSPUR AV	NB	NB	200	33	B2
LARKSPUR CIR	ANA	AN	4600	7	F6
LARKSPUR CIR	HTB	HB47	6400	21	A2
LARKSPUR CIR	IRV	SA	14900	29	D2
LARKSPUR DR	BPK	BP	7500	10	C2
LARKSPUR DR	CO	LB56		29C	B1
LARKSPUR DR	OR	OR	2100	17	A3
LARKSPUR DR	PLA	PLA	1700	7	B3
LARKSPUR DR	WSTM	WSTM	9000	21	D3
LARKSPUR ST	CM	CM	3300	27	E2
LARKSTONE AV	OR	OR	4100	18	A4
LARKSTONE CIR	HTB	HB		26	B2
LARKSTONE CIR	OR	OR	4200	18	A4
LARKSTONE DR	CO	SA	18000	18	A4
LARKSTONE DR	OR	OR	1900	17	F4
LARKSTONE DR	OR	OR	3700	18	A4
LARKSTONE LN	BREA	BREA	300	7	A1
LARKWOOD DR	FUL	FL33		5	E4
LARKWOOD LN	CO	ET	23800	29A	E5
LARKWOOD ST	ANA	AN		8	F6
LARKWOOD ST	ANA	AN08		40	A6
LARKWOOD ST	ANA	AN08		43	A1
LARO LN	YL	YL	4400	7	D3
LA ROCA AV	FTNV	SA08	8800	26	D1
LA ROCHELLE	NB	CDLM		32	D5
LA RODA	MVJO	SJ91		29D	B3
LA RONDA	SCL	SC72		39	D3
LA RONDA	TUS	TUS		23	D3
LA ROSA CIR	FTNV	SA08	10500	27	A1
LA ROSA DR	CO	ET	23700	29A	E5
LA ROSA LN	FTNV	SA08	17600	27	A1
LARRY DR	CO	AN04	10300	10	E6
LARRY DR	CO	AN04	10600	15	E1
LARRY LN	PLA	PLA	400	7	C3
LARSON AV	GGR	GG	8100	15	C5
LARSON AV	GGR	GG	10200	16	A5
LARSON CIR	VPK	OR67	9800	13	B5
LARTHORN DR	HTB	HB	8700	26	D5
LARWIN AV	CYP	CYP	4000	9	C6
LARWIN LN	CYP	CYP	4800	9	D6
LAS ALFORJAS	CO	SJ88		59	B1
LA SALLE AV	CM	CM	2800	27	E4
LA SALLE CIR	ANA	AN		43	A3
LASALLE CIR	PLA	PLA	1500	7	B3
LA SALLE LN	CO	CYP	8800	9	D4
LA SALLE LN	HTB	HB47	15300	21	A3
LA SALLE ST	CO	CYP	8500	9	D4

STREET	CITY	P.O. ZONE	BLOCK	PAGE	GRID
LAS ALTURAS AV	CO	LB		29C	E3
LAS ALTURAS CT	CO	LB		29C	E3
LA SALUD	NB	NB		32	B2
LAS AMIGAS	CO	SJ88		59	D2
LA SARAGOSA	CO	LB56		35	F1
LAS ARENAS WY	CM	CM27		31	A1
LAS ARUBAS	CO	LB56		35	F1
LAS BOLSAS ST	CO	LB	25000	29C	F1
LAS BRISAS	ANA	AN		12	B2
LAS BRISAS	IRV	SA		28	E5
LAS BRISAS DR	CO	SA	1800	24	C1
LAS CABOS	CO	LB56		35	F1
LAS CASAS	MVJO	SJ92	28200	29B	E4
LAS CIMAS	CO	SJ88		59	B4
LAS COLINAS CT	CO	LB	23500	35	D4
LAS CRUCES	CO	LB	29300	35	F2
LAS CRUCES	IRV	SA14		28	F3
LA SENDA DR	FUL	FL	1000	6	A1
LA SENDA DR N&S	LAG	LB77		37	B2
LA SENDA PL	LAG	LB77		37	C2
LA SERENA	IRV	SA		28	E5
LA SERENA DR	BREA	BREA	1400	2	C3
LA SERENA DR	DPT	DPT	33900	37	E4
LA SERENATA	CO	LB56		35	E1
LA SERNA AV	LAH	LAH	400	1	F3
LA SERNA AV	LAH	LAH	300	2	A3
LA SERRA ST	CO	LB	25800	29C	E2
LAS ESPECIAS	CO	SJ88		59	C2
LAS FALDAS DR	FUL	FL	200	6	B1
LAS FLORES	DPT	DPT		37	D5
LAS FLORES	MVJO	SJ91		29B	A4
LAS FLORES AV	DPT	SC24	26000	38	A4
LAS FLORES CIR	VPK	OR67		13	B5
LAS FLORES ST	FTNV	SA08	15800	22	A4
LAS FLORES ST	WSTM	WSTM	15800	22	A4
LAS HIEBAS	CO	SJ88		59	B2
LA SIENA	CO	LB56		35	E2
LA SIERRA DR	MVJO	SJ91		29D	B3
LA SIERRA PL	CO	SA	1700	18	E4
LAS LANAS CIR	FUL	FL33		5	F3
LAS LANAS LN	FUL	FL33	1800	5	F3
LAS LANAS LN	FUL	FL		6	A3
LAS LOMAS DR	BREA	BREA	1200	2	C3
LAS LOMAS DR	LAH	LAH	500	1	F6
LAS LOMAS DR	LAH	LAH	100	2	A6
LAS LUCES	CO	SA		24	D1
LAS LUNAS ST	WSTM	WSTM	15800	22	A3
LAS MARIAS LN	MVJO	SJ91		29B	B6
LAS MARIAS LN	MVJO	SJ91	24900	29D	B1
LAS MESITAS	CO	SJ88		59	A4
LAS NARANJAS DR	CO	LB	24100	35	E4
LAS NIEVES	MVJO	SJ91		29B	C1
LAS NINAS DR	CO	SA	13600	18	B6
LAS NUBES DR	CO	SJ79		59	D2
LAS NUBES ST	WSTM	WSTM	15800	22	A3
LA SOMBRA AV	FTNV	SA08	10300	27	A1
LA SOMBRA WY	FUL	FL	3100	6	A1
LAS ONDAS DR	MVJO	SJ92		36	C1
LAS PALMAS	CO	LB56		29C	E3
LAS PALMAS CIR	OR	OR	1800	17	B3
LAS PALMAS DR	CO	SA	11700	24	C1
LAS PALMAS DR E	FUL	FL	100	6	B1
LAS PALMAS DR W	FUL	FL	100	6	C1
LAS PATRANAS	YL	YL		40	C5
LAS PIEDRAS	CO	SJ88		59	C1
LAS RAMBLAS	MVJO	SJ91		29D	B5
LAS RIENDAS DR	FUL	FL35	300	2	C6
LAS RIENDAS DR	LAH	LAH	1200	2	B6
LAS ROSAS AV	DPT	DPT		37	D5
LASSEN	IRV	SA		29	A6
LASSEN BLVD	OR	OR	1700	13	C5
LASSEN CIR	BPK	BP	9900	10	A6
LASSEN CIR	HTB	HB	9500	26	F5
LASSEN CIR	PLA	PLA	300	7	C1
LASSEN DR	BPK	BP	6600	10	A6
LASSEN DR	CO	SA	18000	17	F5
LASSEN DR	CO	SA	18100	18	A5
LASSEN LN	CM	CM26		28	A3
LASSEN ST	FTNV	SA08	16500	22	C5
LASSEN ST	LALM	LALM	10400	9	B6
LASSEN WY	CO	SA	13100	17	F5
LAS SOLANOS ST	WSTM	WSTM	15800	22	A3
LA STELLA AV	FTNV	SA08	8900	21	E6
LASTER AV	ANA	AN	1200	16	B1
LASTERBROOK ST	PLA	PLA	1200	7	D4
LAS TUNAS DR	MVJO	SJ92		36	C1
LA SUBIDA DR	CO	SJ79		59	D2
LA SUEN RD	CO	LB	25200	29D	A1
LAS VEGAS AV	DPT	SC24	25800	38	A4
LATCHWOOD LN	LAH	LAH	300	6	A1
LATEEN DR	DPT	LB77		37	D4

STREET	CITY	P.O. ZONE	BLOCK	PAGE	GRID
LA TEHAMA CIR	FTNV	SA08	10600	22	A6
LA TERRAZA AV	FTNV	SA08	10800	22	B6
LATHROP DR	CO	YL	16500	7	D2
LATHROP DR	YL	YL	16500	7	D2
LATHROP DR E	PLA	PLA	1000	7	D2
LA TIERRA AV	FTNV	SA08	9800	21	F6
LA TIERRA CIR	FTNV	SA08		21	F6
LA TIERRA LN	YL	YL	19700	8	C3
LATIGO DR	CO	LB		35	C5
LATINA	IRV	SA14		28	F3
LATITUDE CT	NB	NB		31	A3
LATONA ST	ANA	AN	1300	10	A6
LA TORTOLA AV	FTNV	SA08	10300	27	A1
LA TORTOLA CIR	FTNV	SA08	10300	27	A1
LA TORTUGA	MVJO	SJ91	21300	52	C6
LA TRAVESIA DR	FUL	FL	800	6	A1
LA TRIANA	CO	LB56		35	E2
LATUS PL	ANA	AN04	1700	15	F1
LAUDER CIR	HTB	HB	8700	26	D3
LAUDERDALE CT	HTB	HB	8800	26	D6
LAULHERE PL	CO	ET	24100	29A	D4
LAUNER DR	LAH	LAH	1300	1	F3
LAURA CIR	HTB	HB	8300	26	D3
LAURA LN	YL	YL		8	B4
LAURA ST	LAH	LAH	500	2	C4
LAURA WY	WSTM	WSTM	16400	21	D4
LAURA LINDA LN	SA	SA	2200	22	E5
LAUREL	IRV	SA		29	D3
LAUREL AV	CYP	CYP	5000	14	D1
LAUREL AV	FUL	FL	2900	6	E1
LAUREL AV	IRV	SA	14600	29	C1
LAUREL AV N&S	BREA	BREA	100	2	E6
LAUREL AV S	BREA	BREA	500	6	E1
LAUREL CT	SA	SA	600	22	D3
LAUREL DR	OR	OR	900	17	F1
LAUREL LN	CM	CM		27	E6
LAUREL LN	CO	LB		29C	D4
LAUREL PL	ANA	AN	1700	11	A3
LAUREL PL	NB	NB	2200	31	D4
LAUREL RD	CO	SJ		59	C1
LAUREL ST	LAG	LB77	31800	37	A1
LAUREL ST	CYP	CYP	10400	14	E1
LAUREL ST	FTNV	SA08	17000	21	E6
LAUREL ST	GGR	GG	13400	16	D6
LAUREL ST N	SA	SA	100	22	D2
LAUREL ST S	SA	SA	400	22	D2
LAUREL WY	LAH	LAH	400	1	E5
LAUREL CREEK LN	CO	LB		29C	D2
LAUREL CREST DR	CO	LB53		29D	A4
LAURELGATE	CO	TRA		59	D5
LAURELGLEN	IRV	SA		29	B4
LAURELGROVE CIR	CO	ET	22900	29A	F3
LAURELGROVE CIR	IRV	SA	14900	29	C2
LAURELHURST DR	HTB	HB47	6700	21	B4
LAURELMONT	CO	LB		29C	D3
LAURELTON AV	GGR	GG45	5300	14	E3
LAURELTON AV	GGR	GG	6300	15	A3
LAURELTON AV	STN	GG41	7700	15	C3
LAURELTON CIR	MVJO	SJ92		29D	C2
LAUREL TREE DR	ANA	ANA		43	A1
LAUREL TREE LN	IRV	SA		29	A5
LAUREL VIEW CIR	YL	YL		8	A4
LAUREL VIEW DR	YL	YL		8	A4
LAURELWOOD	SA	SA		22	E6
LAURELWOOD AV E	PLA	PLA	100	7	B2
LAURELWOOD AV W	PLA	PLA	100	7	B2
LAURELWOOD DR	HTB	HB	8300	26	D2
LAURELWOOD LN	ANA	AN		11	F5
LAURELWOOD LN	LAP	BP23	7600	9	D2
LAURELWOOD LN	SJC	SJ75		36	B2
LAURELWOOD ST	CO	ET	23200	29A	F4
LAURENT	BN	NB60		32	B2
LAURIANNE AV	GGR	GG	11000	15	E2
LAURIE LN	CM	CM27	2000	31	D2
LAURIE LN	CO	TUS	17600	17	F6
LAURIE LN	TUS	TUS	17300	17	F5
LAURIE ANN LN	ANA	AN	100	13	B2
LAURINDA LN	OR	OR	400	17	F4
LAURINDA WY	CO	SA	13000	17	F4
LAURINDA WY	CO	TUS	13500	17	F6
LAURINDA WY	CO	TUS	14300	23	F1
LAURINDA WY	TUS	TUS	13500	17	F6
LAUTREC DR	FUL	FL	200	6	D3
LAUX AV	GGR	GG	12500	16	D4
LAUX CIR	GGR	GG	13200	16	E4
LAVA WY	CO	MDWY	15900	21	E4
LAVA WY	WSTM	WSTM	15900	21	E4
LA VACA ST	CO	ET	23100	29A	E4
LA VAUGHN DR	GGR	GG	13000	15	E5
LA VAUGHN ST	GGR	GG	13700	15	E6

STREET	CITY	P.O. ZONE	BLOCK	PAGE	GRID
LAVELE DR	YL	YL	4800	7	D3
LAVENDER	MVJO	SJ91		52	D5
LAVENDER AV	FTNV	SA08	11000	22	B5
LAVENDER CIR	ANA	AN		10	D2
LAVENDER CIR	BPK	BP	7600	10	D2
LAVENDER LN	CM	CM		27	E2
LAVENDER LN	LAG	LB51	2400	34	F2
LAVENDER LN	PLA	PLA	900	7	B4
LA VENTANA	SCL	SC72	3000	39	A1
LAVER WY	NB	NB		32	B2
LA VEREDA DR	CO	SA	11200	18	C6
LA VEREDA DR	LAH	LAH	600	1	F3
LA VERGN WY	SA	SA	800	22	C2
LA VERNE AV	SA	SA	2200	22	D4
LA VERNE CIR	WSTM	WSTM	5400	14	E5
LA VERNE ST W	ANA	AN	100	11	C3
LA VETA AV	CO	OR69	17200	17	E4
LA VETA AV E	OR	OR	3500	18	A4
LA VETA AV E&W	OR	OR	100	17	B4
LA VETA DR	OR	OR		18	A4
LA VETA PK CIR	OR	OR	500	17	C4
LA VIDA	NB	NB		32	B2
LA VIDA DR	CO	LB	24600	35	F3
LA VILLA LN	HTB	HB		20	D3
LA VINA DR	MVJO	SJ91	22800	29B	B3
LAVINA LN	GGR	GG	12300	15	E4
LA VISTA DR	LAG	LB51	900	34	E2
LA VITA PL	LAH	LAH	1300	1	F3
LAVONNE LN	HTB	HB46	20500	27	A6
LA VUE	CO	LB77		35	C4
LAW DR	GGR	GG	10300	16	A4
LAWANDA PL	PLA	PLA	1000	7	B4
LAW BEHM TER	FUL	FL	3700	6	B1
LAWN AV	PLA	PLA	600	7	C3
LAWNDALE PL	YL	YL	17300	7	E3
LAWN HAVEN DR	HTB	HB	6800	26	A3
LAWNRIDGE	CO	SJ79		59	E2
LAWNWOOD DR	FUL	FL33		5	E2
LAWRENCE AV	ANA	AN	1300	12	A2
LAWRENCE AV	WSTM	WSTM		21	E4
LAWRENCE AV N&S	FUL	FL	100	6	D6
LAWRENCE DR	CYP	CYP	8600	9	F5
LAWRENCE ST	CYP	CYP	6000	9	F5
LAWRENCE ST	PLA	PLA	900	12	A1
LAWRENCE CANYON	CO	OR67		52	F3
LAWSON LN	HTB	HB46	20000	27	A5
LAWSON WY	OR	OR	700	17	B4
LAWSON WY	SA	SA	2700	17	B4
LAWSON RIVER AV	FTNV	SA08	10500	27	A2
LAWTON DR	HTB	HB46		30	E6
LAXORE ST	ANA	AN	100	10	C5
LA ZANA CT	FTNV	SA08	8700	21	E6
LA ZANJA ST	SJC	SJ75	26700	36	B6
L ZAPATILLA CIR	FTNV	SA08	9700	21	F5
LAZARE LN	HTB	HB		20	B6
LAZY CREEK CIR	FUL	FL		6	D3
LAZY GLEN LN	CO	SJ		59	D1
LAZY MEADOW RD	OR	OR69		18	E2
LEAF	IRV	SA		24	D6
LEAF CIR	ANA	AN		12	F2
LEAF CIR	HTB	HB		25	F2
LEAF CIR	HTB	HB		26	A2
LEAF LN	CO	SJ		59	B3
LEAFLOCK ST	CO	ET		29A	E2
LEAFWOOD CIR	HTB	HB47	16700	21	C5
LEAFWOOD CT	BREA	BREA		2	D5
LEAFWOOD CT	CO	YL		8	F3
LEAFWOOD DR	ANA	AN		13	F4
LEAFWOOD DR	TUS	TUS	17500	17	E5
LEAFWOOD LN	CO	TUS	17700	17	F5
LEAFWOOD LN	CO	SA	18100	18	A5
LEAFWOOD ST	STN	STN	12100	15	C4
LEAFY MEADOW LN	YL	YL		40	D5
LEAH DR	DPT	DPT		37	E2
LEANDRO ST S	ANA	AN	100	13	C2
LE ANN DR	GGR	GG	12000	16	B3
LEAR AV	CM	CM26	1500	28	A5
LEAR LN	TUS	TUS	1300	24	A3
LEASURE LN	HTB	HB	21000	30	D1
LEATHERWOOD WY	IRV	SA	18100	28	F5
LEATRICE DR	VPK	OR67	9700	13	B5
LEATRICE LN E	ANA	AN	100	16	E2
LEAVERTON CT	ANA	AN		7	E6
LEAVERTON CT	ANA	AN	4000	12	E1
LEBANON CIR	IRV	SA	17500	28	F4
LE CONTE	LAG	LB		35	B6
LE CONTE DR	HTB	HB	8200	26	D2
LEDA	IRV	SA		24	D6
LEDA LN	GGR	GG	12500	16	D4
LEDA ST	GGR	GG		16	D5
LEDANA	MVJO	SJ91	22500	29B	D3

STREET	CITY	P.O. ZONE	BLOCK	PAGE	GRID
LEDGEWOOD RD	EBAY	LB51	200	34	B1
LEDON AV	CO	MDWY	7700	21	C3
LEDROIT LN	LAG	LB51	400	34	B2
LEDROIT ST	LAG	LB51	200	34	B2
LEE	IRV	SA		24	E6
LEE AV N	FUL	FL	200	6	A5
LEE AV S	FUL	FL	600	6	A5
LEE AV S	FUL	FL	1000	11	A1
LEE CIR	HTB	HB47	17300	21	B6
LEE DR	BPK	BP	7400	9	F2
LEE DR	CYP	CYP	6000	9	F5
LEE DR	WSTM	WSTM	13200	14	F5
LEE LN	GGR	GG	12400	16	B4
LEE PL	PLA	PLA	600	7	B3
LEE ST	CYP	CYP	9700	9	F5
LEE WY	STN	STN		10	E4
LEE WY	STN	STN		15	B3
LEECREST LN	HTB	HB	19900	26	D4
LEEDS CIR	WSTM	WSTM	15200	22	A2
LEESBURG	IRV	SA		24	C5
LEESBURY CT	NB	NB		32	B3
LEEWARD DR	DPT	LB77		37	D3
LEEWARD DR	DPT	DPT		38	B4
LEEWARD DR	HTB	HB	8400	30	D1
LEEWARD LN	NB	NB	2000	31	F2
LEEWARD WY	ANA	AN		11	A2
LEGEND CIR	HTB	HB	3900	20	C5
LEGGETT LN	FUL	FL33		5	E3
LEGION PL	CO	MDWY	8000	21	C1
LEGION ST	LAG	LB51	100	34	D3
LE GRANDE LN	HTB	HB	16500	20	D5
LEHIGH DR	ANA	AN		13	F3
LEHIGH PL	CM	CM	2500	27	D5
LEHIGH PL	WSTM	WSTM	7600	21	C2
LEHMEN DR	ANA	AN	3000	10	C4
LEHNHARDT AV	FTNV	SA08	10700	22	B3
LEHNHARDT AV	SA	SA	3500	22	D3
LEHUA LN	HTB	HB	21500	30	E1
LEICESTER	MVJO	SJ92		29D	D1
LEIGH AISLE	IRV	SA15		28	E6
LEIGH AISLE	IRV	SA15		32	E1
LEIGH CIR	VPK	OR67	9600	13	B5
LEIGHTON LN	HTB	HB	19800	26	F4
LEILA LN	NB	NB	1400	31	E3
LEILANI CIR	GGR	GG	10500	16	A4
LEILANI DR	HTB	HB	9300	30	E2
LEILANI LN	CYP	CYP	6700	15	A2
LEISURE CT	ANA	AN	1100	11	B2
LELAND DR	FUL	FL	600	6	B5
LELIA BYRD	MVJO	SJ92		29D	F3
LE MANS CIR	YL	YL	19900	8	C4
LE MAY CT	OR	OR	300	17	E3
LE MER	CO	LB77		35	C4
LEMKE DR	PLA	PLA	600	7	C2
LEMNOS DR	CM	CM	1900	27	B4
LEMON AV	CYP	CYP	4500	9	E5
LEMON CIR	BPK	BP	8100	10	C3
LEMON CIR	CO	SA		18	C5
LEMON DR	YL	YL	18000	7	F3
LEMON DR	YL	YL	18100	8	A3
LEMON ST	BREA	BREA	800	2	D6
LEMON ST	CM	CM	2800	27	C5
LEMON ST	FTNV	SA08	18000	26	F1
LEMON ST	LAH	LAH	100	2	A4
LEMON ST	VPK	OR67	9500	13	A6
LEMON ST N&S	ANA	AN	100	11	C2
LEMON ST N&S	FUL	FL	100	6	C5
LEMON ST N&S	OR	OR	100	17	C1
LEMON ST S	FUL	FL	1000	11	C2
LEMON TER	CO	SA		18	D6
LEMONA LN	CO	SA	12500	24	B2
LEMON CREEK CIR	OR	SA05		18	D3
LEMONGRASS	IRV	SA		29	C3
LEMON GROVE	IRV	SA		29	D5
LEMON HTS DR	CO	SA	1600	18	D5
LEMON HTS DR	CO	SA	2000	24	D1
LEMON HILL DR	CO	SA		18	C5
LEMON HILL TER	FUL	FL	600	6	B5
LEMON HILL TR	OR	OR		18	E2
LEMON LEAF LN	CO	SA		18	C5
LEMON TREE	IRV	SA		29	B6
LEMON TREE CT	LAH	LAH		1	E6
LEMON TREE DR	LAH	LAH		1	E6
LEMONTREE LN	HTB	HB	21400	30	F1
LEMONWOOD CIR	LAP	BP23		9	E2
LEMONWOOD DR	LAH	LAH		2	B6
LEMONWOOD LN	BREA	BREA		2	D2
LEMONWOOD LN	GGR	GG	12700	16	C4
LENA DR	LAP	BP23	5100	9	D3
LENE	MVJO	SJ92	27500	29B	D3
LENERA	IRV	SA		24	E4

1990 ORANGE COUNTY STREET INDEX

STREET	CITY	P.O. ZONE	BLOCK	PAGE	GRID
LENIS CIR	HTB	HB47	6900	21	B5
LENITA LN	SA	SA	2200	17	E6
LENMAR ST	STN	STN	11400	15	C2
LENNOX CIR	FUL	FL35		6	C3
LENNOX CT	BREA	BREA		2	F4
LENNOX DR	HTB	HB47	6500	21	A4
LENORE AV	GGR	GG45	6000	14	F4
LENORE AV	GGR	GG	6500	15	A4
LENORE DR	GGR	GG	9300	15	E4
LENORE ST	GGR	GG	8400	15	D4
LENTISCAL	MVJO	SJ92	27800	29B	F4
LENWOOD CIR	CM	CM27	400	31	D4
LENWOOD DR	CM	CM27	400	31	D4
LENZ DR	ANA	AN	800	11	C3
LEO LN	CO	ET	23000	29A	F3
LEO PL	WSTM	WSTM	7700	15	C6
LEOLA WY	ANA	AN		12	F2
LEOLA WY	ANA	AN		13	A2
LEON PL	CO	TUS	14600	24	A2
LEON WY	CO	TUS	18200	24	A2
LEONADO	CO	SJ88		59	C2
LEONARD LN	SA	SA		17	A4
LEONE WY	CYP	CYP		14	F1
LEONE WY	CYP	CYP		15	A1
LEONHARDT CIR	GGR	GG	11500	15	F2
LEONORA ST	ANA	AN	400	11	C3
LEORA AV	LAH	LAH	100	1	F4
LEOTA LN	GGR	GG	11600	16	C3
LE PARC	CO	ET		29B	A2
LE PORT	CO	LB77		35	C4
LERENE DR	YL	YL	17700	7	F3
LERMA	MVJO	SJ91		29B	C3
LERNER LN	CO	SA	1800	24	C1
LEROY AV	GGR	GG	12500	15	E4
LEROY ST	GGR	GG	12700	15	E4
LESA PL	YL	YL	4800	7	D3
LESLEY ST	GGR	GG	12200	16	A3
LESLIE LN	HTB	HB	17000	20	E6
LESLIE ST	LAH	LAH	900	2	B6
LESLIE WY	OR	OR	1600	12	C6
LE SOLEIL	CO	LB77		35	C4
LES PARRE WY	CM	CM27	2400	31	F2
LESSUE AV	STN	STN	7600	15	C2
LESTER DR	OR	OR	100	17	B3
LETICIA	MVJO	SJ92	28200	29B	E6
LETO CIR	CO	SJ91	24900	29B	A6
LETO CIR	CO	SJ91		29D	A1
LETTY LN	TUS	TUS	1100	24	A2
LETUR	MVJO	SJ91	22200	29B	D2
LEUCADIA ST	CO	LB56		29C	F6
LEVEE DR	HTB	HB	9700	26	F6
LEVEL AV	ANA	AN	2400	10	E4
LEVEL PL	ANA	AN	2400	10	E4
LEVERS PL	OR	OR	300	12	C6
LEWELLYN AV	ANA	AN	1200	11	E2
LEWELLYN DR	LAG	LB51	1100	34	E2
LEWIS	IRV	SA		29	E1
LEWIS AV	FTNV	SA08		26	F2
LEWIS DR	CO	OR	7400	13	D5
LEWIS DR	OR	OR	9900	13	D5
LEWIS LN	HTB	HB	17800	25	F1
LEWIS LN	LAG	LB51	300	34	E2
LEWIS PL	PLA	PLA	500	7	B3
LEWIS ST	ANA	AN	1200	11	E6
LEWIS ST	ANA	AN	1500	16	E4
LEWIS ST	GGR	GG	13000	16	E5
LEWIS ST	SA	SA	2100	16	E5
LEWIS ST N&S	OR	OR68	100	16	E4
LEXICON ST	IRV	SA		28	F6
LEXICON ST	IRV	SA		29	A5
LEXINGTON	IRV	SA		24	E5
LEXINGTON AV	GGR	GG	9600	21	F2
LEXINGTON AV	OR	OR		13	B6
LEXINGTON AV	YL	YL		40	A3
LEXINGTON CIR	CO	ET		52	C6
LEXINGTON DR	FUL	FL35		6	C3
LEXINGTON CIR	NB	NB		31	E4
LEXINGTON CT	CO	LB		35	C4
LEXINGTON DR	LALM	LALM	11000	14	C2
LEXINGTON LN	CM	CM	100	27	E6
LEXINGTON LN	HTB	HB46	19600	27	A4
LEXINGTON PL	ANA	AN	500	11	F4
LEXINGTON ST	CYP	CYP	9200	9	C5
LEXINGTON ST	STN	STN	10400	10	B6
LEXINGTON ST	STN	STN	10500	15	B1
LEXINGTON WY	CO	SJ79		59	C6
LEYTE CT	LALM	LALM		14	C3
LEYTE ST	CYP	CYP	6100	14	F2
LIANE LN	CO	SA	2000	24	C2
LIARD PL	CM	CM	900	27	F3
LIATRIS CIR	FTNV	SA08	9000	21	E4

STREET	CITY	P.O. ZONE	BLOCK	PAGE	GRID
LIBBY LN	GGR	GG	13500	16	B6
LIBERTY	CO	LB56		29C	C6
LIBERTY	IRV	SA		24	E5
LIBERTY AV	ANA	AN	300	11	C1
LIBERTY AV	HTB	HB	7600	26	C1
LIBERTY COM	SA	SA		22	C2
LIBERTY LN	ANA	AN	1000	11	E2
LIBERTY LN	PLA	PLA	300	7	B5
LIBERTY ST	LAH	LAH	500	2	A5
LIBERTY WY	OR	OR		18	A3
LIBERTY WY	PLA	PLA		7	B5
LIBRA CIR	HTB	HB	18500	26	C2
LIBRA PL	YL	YL	4700	7	E3
LICATA	IRV	SA14		28	F4
LICHEN LN	TUS	TUS		24	B4
LIDA LN	ANA	AN	1900	16	B2
LIDA LN	GGR	GG	11100	16	B2
LIDO AV	WSTM	WSTM	8500	21	D3
LIDO DR	SA	SA	400	22	D2
LIDO LN	ANA	AN	800	11	B3
LIDO LN	CO	ET		29A	D3
LIDO LN	HTB	HB47	17300	21	A6
LIDO PL	ANA	AN	1200	11	B3
LIDO PL	FUL	FL	100	6	B2
LIDO ST	ANA	AN	1000	11	B3
LIDO WY	CYP	CYP	9800	9	F6
LIDO PARK DR	NB	NB	600	31	C5
LIDO SANDS DR	NB	NB		31	A4
LIEGE DR	HTB	HB	5800	20	F6
LIGHTHOUSE AV	ANA	AN		11	A2
LIGHTHOUSE CT	SJC	SJ75	33000	38	B2
LIGHTHOUSE DR	DPT	DPT		38	D3
LIGHTHOUSE LN	ANA	AN	1200	10	F2
LIGHTHOUSE LN	FTNV	SA08	17900	26	D1
LIGHTHOUSE LN	HTB	HB46		26	D5
LIGHTHOUSE LN	NB	CDLM	2600	32	B6
LIGHTHOUSE LN N	NB	CDLM	1400	32	B6
LIGURE	BREA	BREA	200	4	B5
LILAC	NB	CDLM		33	B1
LILAC AV	FTNV	SA08	11700	22	D4
LILAC AV	HTB	HB47	16900	21	B5
LILAC AV	MVJO	SJ92		29D	D4
LILAC CIR	BPK	BP	7600	10	D2
LILAC CIR	WSTM	WSTM	9400	21	E3
LILAC CT	ANA	AN08		43	A1
LILAC DR	PLA	PLA	700	7	C5
LILAC LN	BREA	BREA	100	4	A4
LILAC LN	CM	CM27	200	31	E2
LILAC LN	OR	OR	400	17	A4
LILAC WY	FTNV	SA08	11700	22	C4
LILES LN	HTB	HB	16000	20	E4
LILIANO	IRV	SA14		28	E4
LILLE CIR	IRV	SA	15100	29	D3
LILLE LN	NB	NB		31	B4
LILLIAN PL	CM	CM	200	27	F6
LILLIAN WY	CO	TUS	18000	23	F2
LILLIAN WY	CO	TUS	18100	24	A2
LILLIE AV N&S	FUL	FL	100	6	F6
LILLY ST	GGR	GG	13100	16	E5
LILY GLEN	CO	ET		52	A5
LIMA CIR	PLA	PLA	1200	7	D4
LIMB ST	CO	SJ91		29A	F5
LIMBER	MVJO	SJ92		52	E6
LIME	IRV	SA	14500	24	C6
LIME	IRV	SA		29	C1
LIME AV	CYP	CYP	5500	9	E5
LIME AV	FUL	FL	2700	6	E2
LIME CIR	BPK	BP	8000	10	C3
LIME CIR	CYP	CYP	9200	9	F5
LIME CIR	FTNV	SA08	18500	26	F2
LIME ST	ANA	AN	800	11	F4
LIME ST	BREA	BREA	700	2	D6
LIME ST	LAH	LAH	200	1	E4
LIME ST	SA	SA	500	23	B1
LIME ST N	OR	OR	1700	12	B6
LIME ST N	OR	OR	200	17	B3
LIME ST S	OR	OR	100	17	B3
LIMELIGHT CIR	HTB	HB47	16900	21	A5
LIME ORCHARD	CO	LB77		37	F2
LIME ORCHARD	CO	LB77		38	A2
LIMERICK DR	HTB	HB47	6500	21	A4
LIMERICK DR	PLA	PLA	1100	7	C4
LIMERICK LN	CM	CM	3100	27	D3
LIMERICK LN	CO	ET		29B	A1
LIMERICK LN	SJC	SJ75		38	D4
LIMETREE DR	CO	SA	11000	18	D5
LIMETREE WY	CO	SA	18100	17	F6
LIMETREE WY	TUS	TUS	17700	17	F6
LIMEWOOD	IRV	SA		29	B5
LIMONES	MVJO	SJ91	27400	29B	D1
LINARIA	CO	TRA		56	B5

STREET	CITY	P.O. ZONE	BLOCK	PAGE	GRID
LINARIA	CO	TRA		59	B4
LINCOLN	IRV	SA		29	D1
LINCOLN AV	BPK	BP	5700	9	C4
LINCOLN AV	BPK	BP	6500	10	A4
LINCOLN AV	CO	CYP	5000	9	C4
LINCOLN AV	CO	OR65	15400	12	B3
LINCOLN AV	CO	SA	13000	17	C6
LINCOLN AV	CYP	CYP	4000	9	C4
LINCOLN AV	HTB	HB	200	26	C5
LINCOLN AV	SA	SA	1600	17	C6
LINCOLN AV	SA	SA	900	23	C1
LINCOLN AV E	ANA	AN	2200	12	B3
LINCOLN AV E	ANA	AN	4600	13	B3
LINCOLN AV E&W	ANA	AN	100	11	A4
LINCOLN AV E&W	OR	OR	100	12	D4
LINCOLN AV N&S	FUL	FL	100	6	D4
LINCOLN AV W	ANA	AN	2100	10	A4
LINCOLN CIR	VPK	OR67	18300	18	A1
LINCOLN CT	BPK	BP	8900	9	F4
LINCOLN LN	NB	NB	1400	31	E4
LINCOLN ST	GGR	GG	13000	16	B5
LINCOLN ST	PLA	PLA		7	E6
LINCOLN ST	VPK	OR67	17800	17	F1
LINCOLN ST	VPK	OR67	18100	18	A1
LINCOLN ST N	OR	OR	1700	12	D5
LINCOLN ST N	OR	OR	300	17	E2
LINCOLN ST S	OR	OR	100	17	E2
LINCOLN WY	CM	CM	3100	27	E3
LINCOLN WY	GGR	GG		15	B2
LINCOLN PZ WY	CYP	CYP	9000	9	C4
LINCOLNSHIRE AV	BPK	BP	4700	5	D3
LINDA AV	DPT	DPT		37	D5
LINDA AV	LAH	LAH	600	1	F3
LINDA CIR	HTB	HB	5000	20	D4
LINDA DR	YL	YL		7	F3
LINDA LN	CO	TUS	17600	17	F5
LINDA LN	CYP	CYP	9500	9	F5
LINDA LN	FUL	FL	1200	6	D3
LINDA LN	GGR	GG40		16	B4
LINDA LN	HTB	HB		20	D4
LINDA LN	LAP	BP23	7800	9	D2
LINDA LN	NB	NB	2100	31	E3
LINDA LN	SCL	SC72	300	39	C4
LINDA LN	TUS	TUS	17500	17	F5
LINDA WY	LALM	LALM	11200	14	B2
LINDA WY	SA	SA	1100	22	F4
LINDA WY	SA	SA04	3000	27	E1
LINDACITA LN	ANA	AN	3100	10	B5
LINDA CREST CIR	OR	OR69		18	C2
LINDAFAIR LN	CO	YL	19600	8	C5
LINDA FLORA ST	CO	LB	24500	29C	E2
LINDA ISLE DR	NB	NB	200	31	E5
LINDALE LN	CO	SA	13600	18	B6
LINDALL ST	CO	LB		35	E6
LINDALL ST	CO	LB77		37	E1
LINDALOA ST	GGR	GG	11100	16	B2
LINDAUER DR	LAH	LAH	1400	1	E3
LINDA VERDE ST	YL	YL		8	A4
LINDA VISTA CIR	FUL	FL	2100	6	D3
LINDA VISTA DR	CO	LB	25000	29C	F2
LINDA VISTA LN	DPT	LB77		37	C1
LINDA VISTA ST	OR	OR	1000	18	B1
LINDA VISTA ST	PLA	PLA	1300	7	D3
LINDBERG	IRV	SA		29	E1
LINDEN AV	IRV	SA	14500	24	C6
LINDEN CIR	BPK	BP	8100	10	C3
LINDEN LN	LAH	LAH	800	2	B3
LINDEN PL	ANA	AN	300	11	A4
LINDEN PL	CM	CM27	900	31	B1
LINDEN ST	FTNV	SA08	18200	26	E2
LINDEN ST	LAG	LB51	400	34	D2
LINDEN WY	BREA	BREA	500	6	D1
LINDENDALE AV	FUL	FL	1000	6	E4
LINDENHOLZ ST	OR	OR	1600	12	D5
LINDENWOOD DR	HTB	HB	8200	26	C2
LINDFORD LN	YL	YL	5400	8	A4
LINDLEY ST	CO	SJ91		29A	F5
LINDO AV	NB	NB	300	31	E6
LINDSAY DR	CO	SJ		59	D1
LINDSAY LN	HTB	HB	19000	26	E3
LINDSAY RD	ANA	AN	2100	10	F4
LINDSAY ST	ANA	AN	200	10	F4
LINDSEY WY	IRV	SA14		29	A2
LINDSTROM AV	IRV	SA	5000	29	D2
LINDY PL	FUL	FL33	700	5	E6
LINDY PL	FUL	FL33	700	10	E1
LINDY WY	GGR	GG		15	D6
LINEAR LN	CO	ET		52	B5
LINGAN LN	SA	SA	1400	22	E3
LINK ST	TUS	SA10		29	B1

STREET	CITY	P.O. ZONE	BLOCK	PAGE	GRID
LINKS RD	BPK	BP	8500	5	D4
LINKS POINTE	CO	LB77	32100	37	D1
LINMAR MEADOWS	GGR	GG		15	D3
LINNELL AV	GGR	GG	10500	16	B6
LINNERT ST	GGR	GG	13600	15	E6
LINNET CIR	CO	LB	23800	35	D1
LINWOOD AV N	SA	SA	1500	17	D6
LINWOOD AV N	SA	SA	300	23	D2
LINWOOD AV S	SA	SA	1000	23	D3
LINWOOD PL	FUL	FL	100	6	D6
LINWOOD ST	SA	SA	2600	17	D5
LIONHEAD LN	GGR	GG		21	E2
LIPARI	CO	LB		29A	A4
LIPKIN DR	WSTM	WSTM	13900	15	C6
LIPKIN DR	WSTM	WSTM	13900	21	C1
LIPPS LN	VPK	OR67	18600	13	A5
LIPTON ST	CO	ET		29A	D3
LIRA CIR	MVJO	SJ91		29B	B4
LIRIO	MVJO	SJ92		29B	D6
LIRIO	MVJO	SJ92		29D	D1
LISA LN	CM	CM	100	27	F5
LISA LN	HTB	HB	18100	26	D2
LISA LN	WSTM	WSTM	7000	15	B5
LISA PL	OR	OR	2500	12	D4
LISABETH COM	SA	SA03		22	D2
LISTER LN	HTB	HB	18800	26	D3
LITCHFIELD AV	STN	STN	10700	15	B1
LITCHFIELD DR	HTB	HB	9300	26	E3
LITTLE DR	CO	ET	22500	29B	B3
LITTLE LN	OR	OR		18	A2
LTL BIG HORN AV	PLA	PLA	1700	7	C3
LITTLE BIRD PL	CO	ET		29A	E4
LITTLE CYN LN	YL	YL		8	E1
LITTLE FAWN LN	CO	LB	23000	35	C3
LITTLEFIELD DR	HTB	HB		25	F2
LITTLE HARBOR	HTB	HB		26	B4
LITTL HARBOR LN	HTB	HB		26	B4
LITTLE JOHN WY	VPK	OR67	17000	12	F6
LITTLE MAIN ST	OR	OR	100	17	B3
LITTLER DR	HTB	HB	5600	20	F4
LITTLER DR	HTB	HB	16200	20	F4
LITTLE RIV CIR	NB	CDLM		32	C6
LITTLETON CIR	CM	CM		27	D5
LITTLETON PL	CM	CM	2400	27	D5
LIVEOAK	IRV	SA		29	C4
LIVE OAK AV	FUL	FL	2800	6	F2
LIVE OAK CIR	CO	SJ		52	F3
LIVEOAK CIR	FTNV	SA08	17500	26	E1
LIVE OAK CT	ANA	AN	1200	11	E4
LIVE OAK DR	ANA	AN	600	11	E4
LIVE OAK DR	CO	SJ91		29A	F5
LIVE OAK DR	OR	OR69		18	D2
LIVE OAK LN	YL	YL		8	D2
LIVE OAK ST	BREA	BREA	400	2	E5
LIVE OAK CYN RD	CO	SJ		52	F3
LIVE OAK CYN RD	CO	SJ	20300	56	B3
LIVERMORE PL	CYP	CYP	4200	9	C5
LIVERPOOL LN	ANA	AN	2100	10	F5
LIVERPOOL ST	HTB	HB46		26	F3
LIVERPOOL ST	YL	YL	5200	7	E4
LIVINGSTON AV E	PLA	PLA	100	7	B3
LIVINGSTON AV W	PLA	PLA	100	7	B3
LIVINGSTON CIR	ANA	AN		43	A3
LIVINGSTON LN	IRV	SA		24	F6
LIVINGSTON ST	CO	TUS	14000	17	F6
LIVINGSTON ST	CO	TUS	14100	23	F2
LIVINGSTON WY	ANA	AN		43	A3
LIVINGSTONE ST	FTNV	SA08	16000	22	B4
LIVINGSTON MDWS	GGR	GG		15	F6
LIVINGSTON MDWS	GGR	GG		21	F1
LIZBETH AV	ANA	AN	2400	12	A5
LIZBETH CT	ANA	AN	2300	12	A5
LLANO DEL NORTE	SCL	SC72		38	E4
LLANO DEL SUR	SCL	SC72		38	F4
LLOYD AV	FUL	FL33	100	5	E6
LOARA ST	GGR	GG	11100	16	B2
LOARA ST N&S	ANA	AN	100	11	B5
LOARA ST S	ANA	AN	1500	16	B1
LOBDELL LN	CO	OR67		50	D6
LOBELIA	CO	TRA		56	C6
LOBELIA	CO	TRA		59	C1
LOBO DR	CO	ET	24700	29A	E3
LOBO ST	SJC	SJ75		36	B6
LOCH GLEN	CO	ET		52	A5
LOCHLEA LN	HTB	HB	21000	30	D1
LOCHLOMOND DR	CO	LB		35	D2
LOCH LOMOND RD	CO	LALM	11300	14	A2
LOCHMOOR LN	NB	NB		32	B5
LOCKE CT	IRV	SA		32	D3
LOCKHAVEN CIR	HTB	HB48	21100	26	A6
LOCKHAVEN CIR	IRV	SA	4500	29	D2

STREET	CITY	P.O. ZONE	BLOCK	PAGE	GRID
LOCKHAVEN DR	BPK	BP	5300	5	C4
LOCKHAVEN DR	BREA	BREA	1000	2	C4
LOCKHAVEN WY	GGR	GG	11100	15	F2
LOCKLIN WY	FUL	FL33		5	E3
LOCKWOOD PK PL	TUS	TUS	100	23	F2
LOCUST	IRV	SA		29	D3
LOCUST AV	ANA	AN	1100	11	C5
LOCUST AV	OR	OR	100	17	D1
LOCUST CIR	WSTM	WSTM		15	B6
LOCUST DR	BPK	BP	8200	10	C3
LOCUST DR N	FUL	FL33	400	5	F5
LOCUST DR S	FUL	FL33	500	5	F6
LOCUST DR S	FUL	FL33	900	10	F1
LOCUST ST	BREA	BREA	100	6	E1
LOCUST ST	FTNV	SA08	17500	26	E1
LOCUST ST	LAG	LB51	300	34	C3
LOCUST ST	WSTM	WSTM	13700	15	B6
LOCUST ST	WSTM	WSTM	14000	21	B1
LODESTONE TR DR	CO	LB56		29C	E6
LODGE AV	ANA	AN	1000	11	B2
LODGEPOLE ST	ANA	AN		11	E2
LODI PL	ANA	AN	1900	10	F5
LODI PL	ANA	AN	1900	11	A5
LOFTY ST	IRV	SA	14500	29	D2
LOFTY VIEW DR	YL	YL		8	D2
LOGAN AV	CM	CM	1200	27	D4
LOGAN CT	FTNV	SA08	15900	22	D6
LOGAN ST	SA	SA	600	23	C1
LOGANA	YL	YL		8	B3
LOGANBERRY LN	CO	ET		29A	F2
LOGANBERRY LN	CO	ET		29B	A2
LOGANBERRY LN	YL	YL		40	D5
LOGANBERRY ST	ANA	AN		8	F6
LOGANBERRY ST	ANA	AN		13	F1
LOGANLINDA DR	YL	YL	4500	7	F3
LOGANVIEW DR	YL	YL	4500	7	F3
LOGO VISTA	DPT	DPT		37	F1
LOHRUM LN	ANA	AN	100	13	B2
LOIE ST	CO	YL	16700	7	D2
LOIE ST	YL	YL	16700	7	D2
LOIRE CIR	HTB	HB47	16500	21	C5
LOIS CIR	HTB	HB47	8500	21	D5
LOIS LN	FUL	FL	800	6	B4
LOIS ST	LAH	LAH	100	2	A4
LOLA AV	STN	STN	8300	10	C6
LOLA LN	GGR	GG		21	F1
LOLA LN	HTB	HB	19400	26	E4
LOLINA LN	CO	CYP	5000	9	D4
LOLA LN	GGR	WSTM		21	F1
LOLITA LN	HTB	HB		20	D4
LOLITA ST	CO	OR	10200	13	E6
LOLITA ST	OR	OR	10200	13	E6
LOLO CIR	FTNV	SA08	9500	21	F5
LOMA AV	HTB	HB	200	26	B5
LOMA CIR	CM	CM	800	27	F4
LOMA LN	SCL	SC72	100	39	D3
LOMA ST	IRV	SA	4000	29	C1
LOMA ST	OR	OR67		13	B4
LOMA ST	VPK	OR67	9000	13	B5
LOMA TER	LAG	LB51	300	34	D2
LOMA ALTA DR	FUL	FL33	1700	5	E3
LOMA LINDA	CO	LB77		36	A1
LOMA LINDA DR	ANA	AN	200	10	B5
LOMA LINDA WY	CO	SA	11800	18	C6
LOMA NORTE PL	LAH	LAH		2	C3
LOMAR LN	CO	SA	13900	18	B6
LOMA ROJA	CO	SA	1600	24	C1
LOMA VERDE	MVJO	SJ91		29D	C3
LOMA VERDE AV W	LAH	LAH	300	2	A5
LOMA VERDE DR	FUL	FL33	1900	5	E3
LOMA VERDE LN	CO	SA	1200	18	C6
LOMA VISTA PL	FUL	FL33		5	E4
LOMAY AV	GGR	GG	8500	15	D6
LOMAY AV	WSTM	WSTM	8400	15	D6
LOMBARD CT	CM	CM		27	E3
LOMBARD DR	ANA	AN	1100	11	B2
LOMBARD DR	FUL	FL	1400	11	B1
LOMBARD PL	ANA	AN	1200	11	B2
LOMBARDI	CO	LB		29A	B4
LOMBARDY	IRV	SA14		28	D5
LOMBARDY LN	HTB	HB	19000	26	D4
LOMBARDY LN	LAG	LB51	500	34	E3
LOMBARDY LN	YL	YL	19700	8	C3
LOMBARDY RD	GGR	GG	13600	16	B6
LOMBARDY RD	MVJO	SJ92		29D	E3
LOMITA AV	CO	OR	19000	18	B1
LOMITA AV	DPT	DPT		37	D5
LOMITA AV	OR	OR	100	17	D1
LOMITA DR	CO	SJ79		59	D2
LOMITA LN	YL	YL	17400	7	E4
LOMITA PL	ANA	AN	1200	11	B3

1990 ORANGE COUNTY STREET INDEX

ORANGE CO. · INDEX

1990 ORANGE COUNTY STREET INDEX

STREET	CITY	P.O. ZONE	BLOCK	PAGE	GRID
MADISON AV	OR	OR	1100	17	E2
MADISON AV	SA	SA	1200	23	C4
MADISON AV	WSTM	WSTM	8000	21	E2
MADISON AV E&W	PLA	PLA	100	7	A4
MADISON CIR	BPK	BP	7400	10	B4
MADISON CIR	GGR	GG	9600	21	F2
MADISON CIR	WSTM	WSTM	9500	21	E2
MADISON PL	LAG	LB51	900	34	F3
MADISON WY	BREA	BREA		2	E6
MADONNA CT	CO	LB56		29C	E5
MADONNA DR	FUL	FL35		2	C6
MADONNA DR	FUL	FL	2700	6	C1
MADONNA LN	LAH	LAH	2000	2	C3
MADRAS PL	GGR	GG	12200	15	F3
MADRE SELVA LN	CO	SJ		59	D3
MADRID	CO	ET		29A	F4
MADRID	TUS	TUS		24	A4
MADRID AV	SA	SA		22	D2
MADRID CIR	CYP	CYP	9800	9	E6
MADRID CT	GGR	GG		16	B4
MADRID DR	CO	ET		29A	F3
MADRID LN	CO	OR		18	C1
MADRID PZ	BPK	BP		5	C3
MADRID RD	CO	LB		35	F2
MADRID ST	ANA	AN	2100	16	D2
MADRID WY	HTB	HB	4600	20	D5
MADRIGAL	SCL	SC72		38	D5
MADRINA	IRV	SA		24	E5
MADRONA	CO	SJ		56	D6
MADRONA	IRV	SA		28	E6
MADRONA	MVJO	SJ91		29D	B3
MADRONA	TUS	TUS		24	B3
MADRONA AV N&S	BREA	BREA	100	2	E6
MADRONA AV S	BREA	BREA	400	6	D1
MADRONE CIR	FTNV	SA08	16700	21	F5
MAE CIR	CO	ET	22000	29A	D2
MAERTIN LN	FUL	FL	600	6	E4
MAGALA LN	CO	SJ92		29D	E2
MAGALEN WY	CYP	CYP	11400	15	B3
MAGDA LN	CO	LAH	11000	2	A3
MAGDA LN	LAH	LAH		2	A3
MAGDALENA LN	MVJO	SJ91		29D	C4
MAGELLAN LN	HTB	HB47	16200	21	B4
MAGELLAN ST	CM	CM	800	27	E4
MAGELLAN AISLE	IRV			29	E2
MAGELLAN ISLE	DPT	LB77		37	D4
MAGENTA	MVJO	SJ91		52	D5
MAGGIE LN	HTB	HB		26	D1
MAGIC CIR	HTB	HB	8300	26	D1
MAGIC LANTRN LN	HTB	HB47	17300	21	C6
MAGNOLIA	IRV	SA		29	D3
MAGNOLIA AV	BREA	BREA	300	2	E6
MAGNOLIA AV	BREA	BREA	500	6	E1
MAGNOLIA AV	CO	OR65	8500	12	D3
MAGNOLIA AV	OR	OR	3300	12	D3
MAGNOLIA AV	PLA	PLA	700	7	C4
MAGNOLIA AV	SA	SA	400	23	A4
MAGNOLIA AV	YL	YL		7	F5
MAGNOLIA AV N	ANA	AN01	100	10	D2
MAGNOLIA AV N&S	FUL	FL33	100	5	D6
MAGNOLIA AV S	ANA	AN04		10	D6
MAGNOLIA AV S	FUL	FL33	1000	10	D1
MAGNOLIA CT	CO	LB53		29D	A4
MAGNOLIA CT	TUS	TUS		24	A4
MAGNOLIA DR	LAG	LB51	300	34	D2
MAGNOLIA ST	BPK	BP	4400	5	D5
MAGNOLIA ST	CM	CM27	100	31	D2
MAGNOLIA ST	CO	AN04	10800	15	D4
MAGNOLIA ST	FTNV	SA08	16000	21	E3
MAGNOLIA ST	FTNV	SA08	17600	26	E6
MAGNOLIA ST	GGR	GG	11000	15	D4
MAGNOLIA ST	HTB	HB	19000	26	E6
MAGNOLIA ST	HTB	HB	21200	30	E2
MAGNOLIA ST	IRV	SA	3800	29	C1
MAGNOLIA ST	OR	OR	200	17	D3
MAGNOLIA ST	STN	AN04	10500	15	D4
MAGNOLIA ST	WSTM	WSTM	14000	21	E3
MAGNOLIA WY	LAH	LAH	400	1	E5
MAGNOLIA WY	YL	YL		7	F5
MAGNOLIA VIA	FUL	FL		6	D6
MAGPIE LN	FTNV	SA08	9500	26	F2
MAHALO CIR	GGR	GG	12300	16	A3
MAHALO DR	HTB	HB	9000	30	E2
MAHALO WY	GGR	GG	10300	16	A3
MAHOGANY AV	FTNV	SA08	16300	21	E4
MAHOGANY AV	WSTM	WSTM	6000	20	F1
MAHOGANY CIR	BPK	BP	8100	10	C3
MAHOGANY CIR	YL	YL		8	D2
MAHOGANY PL	TUS	TUS		24	D4
MAHOGANY ST	OR	OR69		18	F2
MAHOGANY RUN	CO	SJ79		59	D6

STREET	CITY	P.O. ZONE	BLOCK	PAGE	GRID
MAIDEN WY	SA	SA		28	B1
MAIDSTONE LN	HTB	HB48		25	E2
MAIDSTONE ST	FTNV	SA08	15900	22	A4
MAIDSTONE ST	WSTM	WSTM	15700	22	A4
MAIKAI DR	HTB	HB46	10000	27	A3
MAIN ST	CO	OR65	16400	12	D3
MAIN ST	CO	OR69	10600	17	B2
MAIN ST	GGR	GG	12500	16	B4
MAIN ST	HTB	HB	18500	26	B4
MAIN ST	IRV	SA	1000	28	B2
MAIN ST	IRV	SA	4000	29	A4
MAIN ST	NB	NB	100	33	B5
MAIN ST	SB	SB	100	19	E3
MAIN ST	STN	STN	7800	15	C1
MAIN ST	WSTM	WSTM	7000	21	B1
MAIN ST	YL	YL	4700	8	A3
MAIN ST E&W	TUS	TUS	100	23	D2
MAIN ST N	HTB	HB	100	26	B6
MAIN ST N	OR	OR	1300	12	B6
MAIN ST N	SA	SA	1600	17	B6
MAIN ST N&S	LAH	LAH	100	2	A5
MAIN ST N&S	OR	OR	100	17	B3
MAIN ST N&S	PLA	PLA	100	7	B5
MAIN ST N&S	SA	SA	100	23	B5
MAIN ST S	SA	SA	2800	28	B1
MAIN ST W	TUS	TUS	1100	24	A2
MAIN DIVIDE RD	CO			53	B1
MAIN GATE	SB	SB		20	A2
MAINMAST DR	HTB	HB		26	A6
MAINMAST DR	HTB	HB		30	A1
MAINPLACE DR	SA	SA01		17	B4
MAINSAIL	IRV	SA		29	A4
MAIN SAIL DR	DPT	LB77		37	F3
MAIN SAIL DR	DPT	DPT	25200	38	A3
MAINSAIL DR	HTB	HB46		26	A2
MAIN SAIL DR	NB	CDLM		32	C6
MAINSAIL WY	DPT	DPT		38	D3
MAIN WAY DR	CO	LALM	2600	14	A4
MAJOR CIR	HTB	HB47		21	C5
MAJORCA	CO	ET		52	A6
MAJORCA AV	IRV	SA	14300	24	C6
MAJORCA LN	YL	YL	19700	8	C3
MAJORCA ST	ANA	AN06		12	B3
MAJORCA WY	CO	SJ92		29D	E2
MAKO LN	ANA	AN		11	A2
MAL CT	ANA	AN	100	12	B3
MALABAR DR	NB	CDLM	600	32	A6
MALAGA	IRV	SA14		29	A4
MALAGA	TUS	TUS		24	A4
MALAGA	WSTM	WSTM		21	E2
MALAGA DR	DPT	DPT	33700	37	F4
MALAGA DR	LAP	BP23	5000	9	D3
MALAGA LN	HTB	HB47	16000	21	C4
MALAGA LN	YL	YL	19800	8	C2
MALAGA WY	CO	ET		29A	F3
MALAGA WY	CO	LB56		29C	E5
MALAHINE DR	HTB	HB	9300	30	E2
MALAQUITA	CO	SJ79		59	C5
MALASPINA RD	SJC	SJ75		36	C4
MALBORO AV	ANA	AN	1000	11	B2
MALCOLM LN	YL	YL	16600	7	D3
MALDEN AV N&S	FUL	FL	100	6	C6
MALDEN CIR	HTB	HB	16400	20	A5
MALDEN ST	CYP	CYP	11500	14	F2
MALEA	CO	LB77		35	F4
MALENA DR	CO	SA	12800	17	F4
MALENA DR	TUS	TUS	13500	17	F5
MALENA DR N	OR	OR	100	17	F3
MALENA DR S	OR	OR	200	17	F3
MALENA ST	OR	OR	100	17	F2
MALIA CT	CO	SJ91	25800	29B	A6
MALIBU	CO	LB77		36	A5
MALIBU CIR	NB	CDLM		32	D5
MALIBU CIR	WSTM	WSTM	14300	21	D1
MALIBU DR	STN	STN	12200	15	C3
MALIBU LN	HTB	HB	22000	30	E2
MALIBU ST	GGR	GG	13600	16	B6
MALIBU CYN RD	BREA	BREA		2	F4
MALIBU CYN WY	BREA	BREA		2	F4
MALINDA LN	GGR	GG	10100	15	F4
MALL AV	ANA	AN	2300	10	E4
MALL PL	ANA	AN	200	10	E4
MALL PL W	ANA	AN	2500	10	E4
MALL WY	ANA	AN	200	10	E4
MALLARD	IRV	SA		29	B3
MALLARD AV	FTNV	SA08	9000	26	E2
MALLARD AV	GGR	GG	8500	15	D5
MALLARD DR	CM	CM	2700	27	B5
MALLARD DR	CO	LB56		29C	B1
MALLARD DR	GGR	GG	10000	15	F5
MALLARD DR	GGR	GG	10300	16	A5

STREET	CITY	P.O. ZONE	BLOCK	PAGE	GRID
MALLARD ST	OR	OR	700	17	F1
MALLORCA	CO	LB77		35	F5
MALLORCA	CO	LB77		36	A5
MALLORCA DR	NB	NB60		32	C2
MALLORCA LN	MVJO	SJ91		29D	B4
MALLOY DR	HTB	HB	8100	26	D5
MALL THE	IRV	SA		24	C6
MALLUL DR	ANA	AN	2200	16	D2
MALM CIR	HTB	HB47	15900	21	B4
MALTA	IRV	SA14		28	D5
MALTA CIR	HTB	HB	6900	20	D6
MALTA ST	CO	SA	13200	18	A5
MALTA WY	YL	YL		40	D6
MALTASO PL	CO	LB	29900	35	E3
MALVERN AV	BPK	BP	8000	5	C4
MALVERN AV W	FUL	FL33	1600	5	E5
MALVERN AV W	FUL	FL	100	6	A5
MALVISTA WY	CO	LB56		29C	E5
MAMBRINO	MVJO	SJ91		29D	C3
MAMMOTH CIR	BPK	BP	8100	5	C4
MAMMOTH CIR	CO	ET		29A	F1
MAMMOTH CIR	OR	OR		13	C5
MAMMOTH CIR	PLA	PLA	17100	7	E4
MAMMOTH CT	FTNV	SA08	18000	27	A1
MAMMOTH DR	HTB	HB	9700	26	F5
MAMMOTH ST	YL	YL	5500	7	E4
MAMMOTH WY	PLA	PLA	5500	7	E4
MAMMOTH CAVE DR	CO	LB77	23400	37	D1
MAMOTA WY	CYP	CYP	9600	9	F5
MANACOR	MVJO	SJ92	22400	29B	D2
MANALASTAS DR	CO	ET	22600	29B	B3
MANASSERO ST	ANA	AN		13	A1
MANCERA	CO	SJ88		59	A4
MANCHESTER AV	BPK	BP	6000	5	B5
MANCHESTER AV	IRV	SA	17400	28	F4
MANCHESTER AV	PLA	PLA	1200	7	B4
MANCHESTER AV N	ANA	AN	100	11	B4
MANCHESTER AV S	ANA	AN	100	11	B4
MANCHESTER AV S	ANA	AN	1500	16	E2
MANCHESTER BLVD	BPK	BP	6700	10	C1
MANCHESTER CT	CO	SJ79		59	D6
MANCHESTER LN	HTB	HB	17800	26	D1
MANCHESTER PL	CYP	CYP	4200	9	C5
MANCHESTER PL	OR	OR68		16	F3
MANCHUCA	MVJO	SJ92	28100	29B	E4
MANCOS AV	ANA	AN	400	12	A4
MANCOS PL	ANA	AN	500	12	A5
MANDALAY	CO	LB77		35	D6
MANDALAY CIR	HTB	HB		20	C4
MANDARIN	IRV	SA		29	B3
MANDARIN DR	CM	CM	2000	27	A5
MANDARIN LN	YL	YL	18100	7	F3
MANDARINA LN	CO	SJ		59	C3
MANDEVILLA	CO	SJ		56	D6
MANDEVILLA	CO	SJ		59	D1
MANDEVILLE DR	CO	LB		29C	E3
MANDEVILLE DR	HTB	HB	8300	26	D3
MANDEVILLE PL	OR	OR	3300	12	F3
MANDEVILLE PL	OR	OR	3800	13	A3
MANDO DR	CO	LB56		29C	E6
MANDRAKE WY	IRV	SA	18100	28	F6
MANDRELL DR	HTB	HB47	7700	21	C6
MANESSA CIR	HTB	HB46	21000	31	A1
MANGO AV	IRV	SA	14600	24	C6
MANGO AV	IRV	SA	14600	29	C1
MANGO CIR	FTNV	SA08	17700	26	E1
MANGO ST	BREA	BREA	1000	2	F5
MANGO ST	BREA	BREA	1200	3	A5
MANGO WY	BPK	BP	8300	10	C3
MANGRUM DR	HTB	HB	5500	20	E4
MANHATTAN AV	FUL	FL	1300	11	E1
MANHATTAN DR	HTB	HB47	6700	21	A6
MANIFESTO CIR	HTB	HB		26	B2
MANILA DR	CYP	CYP	11500	14	E3
MANISTEE DR	CM	CM26		28	A3
MANITOBA DR	SA	SA	2200	22	E5
MANITOBA DR	SA	SA04	3000	27	E1
MANITOBA LN	HTB	HB	18300	26	C2
MANLEY ST	GGR	GG45	11900	14	E4
MANLY AV	SA	SA	1300	22	E6
MANN ST	IRV	SA	17900	28	F5
MANNING DR	CO	TUS	18400	24	A1
MANOR DR	WSTM	WSTM	13700	15	C6
MANOR ST	ANA	AN	400	11	A4
MANOR ST	IRV	SA	14900	29	C1
MANORFIELD DR	HTB	HB		25	F2
MANORFIELD DR	HTB	HB		26	A2
MANOR POINT CIR	HTB	HB		26	A3
MANOR VIEW DR	YL	YL	5300	8	C4
MANORWOOD	CO	TRA		59	D6

STREET	CITY	P.O. ZONE	BLOCK	PAGE	GRID
MANSA CT	FTNV	SA08		22	C5
MANSARD LN	HTB	HB	20300	26	E5
MANSILLA ST	CO	LAG		35	F3
MANSOR AV	GGR	GG	9500	15	E6
MANSOR AV	GGR	GG	10800	16	B6
MANTA CT	DPT	LB77		37	D4
MANTANZA DR	CO	LB		35	C5
MANTENIDA	CO	SJ79		59	C5
MANTI DR	ANA	AN	400	13	A1
MANTLE LN N	SA	SA	600	23	D1
MANTLE LN S	SA	SA	1100	23	D3
MANTLE ST	SA	SA	2200	17	D5
MANUFACTURE LN	HTB	HB		20	E4
MANZANA WY	CO	SJ		59	D3
MANZANARES	MVJO	SJ91		29D	B4
MANZANILLO	MVJO	SJ92		52	E6
MANZANITA AV	YL	YL		8	D2
MANZANITA CIR	CYP	CYP	6500	15	A1
MANZANITA DR	CO	ET	24300	29A	C2
MANZANITA DR	DPT	DPT	25100	37	F4
MANZANITA DR	FUL	FL	2000	6	A2
MANZANITA DR	LAG	LB51	700	34	E3
MANZANITA RD	SJC	SJ75		38	B3
MANZANITA ST	IRV	SA	4000	29	C1
MANZANITA ST	OR	OR	1300	12	C6
MANZANO	MVJO	SJ92		29D	C4
MAPACHE	CO	SJ		59	B1
MAPLE	IRV	SA		29	B5
MAPLE AV	BREA	BREA	400	6	E1
MAPLE AV	CM	CM	1200	27	D4
MAPLE AV	CM	CM27	1900	31	C2
MAPLE AV	CO	OR69	17800	17	F3
MAPLE AV	FUL	FL	2800	6	E2
MAPLE AV	WSTM	WSTM	6300	21	A1
MAPLE AV E&W	OR	OR	100	17	C3
MAPLE CIR	YL	YL		8	E5
MAPLE CT	CO	SJ91		29A	F4
MAPLE CT	TUS	TUS		24	A4
MAPLE DR	BPK	BP	8000	10	C3
MAPLE ST	ANA	AN	900	10	F3
MAPLE ST	CM	CM	2200	27	C6
MAPLE ST	CM	CM27	2100	31	C1
MAPLE ST	CYP	CYP		14	F1
MAPLE ST	CYP	CYP	10500	15	A1
MAPLE ST	FTNV	SA08	16700	21	E5
MAPLE ST	LAH	LAH	500	2	B4
MAPLE ST	LALM	LALM	3400	9	C6
MAPLE ST	LALM	LALM	11000	14	B2
MAPLE ST	SA	SA	100	23	B3
MAPLE ST	SA	SA	3000	28	C1
MAPLE ST	WSTM	WSTM	7000	21	B1
MAPLE CREST DR	ANA	AN		8	B6
MAPLEDALE LN	HTB	HB	18200	26	D2
MAPLEGROVE CIR	HTB	HB	18100	26	B2
MAPLEGROVE CT	CO	YL		8	C6
MAPLE GROVE RD	OR	OR		12	F4
MAPLE TREE CT	LAH	LAH		1	F6
MAPLE TREE DR	ANA	AN	4000	12	E3
MAPLE TREE DR	OR	OR	2700	12	E3
MAPLE VIEW DR	CO	LB53		29D	A3
MAPLEWOOD	MVJO	SJ92		29B	E3
MAPLEWOOD AV	FUL	FL	500	6	B6
MAPLEWOOD AV	LAP	BP23		9	E2
MAPLEWOOD CIR	HTB	HB	18600	26	D2
MAPLEWOOD CT	SJC	SJ75		36	A3
MAPLEWOOD LN	BREA	BREA		2	D2
MAPLEWOOD LN	WSTM	WSTM		21	C3
MAPLEWOOD PL	OR	OR	1000	17	D3
MAPLEWOOD ST	ANA	AN	1200	11	E2
MAPLEWOOD ST N	OR	OR	1600	12	D6
MAPLEWOOD ST N	OR	OR	100	17	D3
MAPLEWOOD ST S	OR	OR	200	17	D3
MAPLEWOOD WY	SA	SA		22	B1
MAQUINA	MVJO	SJ91		29B	A4
MAR DR	GGR	GG		15	D5
MARA PL	ANA	AN05		11	E5
MARACA ST	CYP	CYP	11400	14	F2
MARACAY	SCL	SC72		39	E1
MARALESTE DR	CO	LB	23000	35	C5
MARANA	SCL	SC72		38	D5
MARAPATA DR	NB	CDLM	1800	32	A6
MARATHON ST	CO	SJ91	25300	29A	F5
MARAUDER CIR	GGR	GG	13300	16	C5
MARAVILLA LN	CO	SJ		59	C4
MARBELLA	DPT	LB77		37	D3
MARBELLA	IRV	SA14		28	F3
MARBELLA	MVJO	SJ91		29D	C3
MARBELLA	SCL	SC72		38	D4
MARBELLA VISTA	SJC	SJ75		36	D4
MARBER LN	HTB	HB		25	F1
MAR BIZCOCHO RD	CO	LB77	28900	36	A1

STREET	CITY	P.O. ZONE	BLOCK	PAGE	GRID
MARBLE CIR	GGR	GG	12300	16	D5
MARBLE CIR	WSTM	WSTM	8900	21	E4
MARBLE LN	LAH	LAH		2	B5
MARBLE PL	GGR	GG	12400	16	D5
MARBLE ARCH DR	CO	SA	11500	18	C6
MARBLE COVE WY	SB	SB	400	19	E2
MARBLEHEAD LN	HTB	HB46	22000	30	F2
MARBLEHEAD PL	CO	LB		35	E6
MARBLEHEAD PL	CO	LB77		37	E1
MAREBLU	CO	LB56		29C	E4
MARBROOK WY	STN	STN		15	C4
MARCELLA AV	CYP	CYP	5000	9	D6
MARCELLA CIR	CYP	CYP	5600	9	E6
MARCELLA LN	SA	SA	1400	16	F5
MARCELLA WY	BPK	BP	6000	9	F6
MARCELLENA DR	HTB	HB47	6300	21	A6
MARCHAND AV	GGR	GG	9000	15	E2
MARCHE LN	CM	CM27	300	31	F2
MARCIA DR	LAH	LAH	1300	1	E3
MARCINE ST	LAH	LAH	1000	2	B3
MARCONI	IRV	SA18		29A	C2
MARCUS AV	NB	NB	3200	31	B5
MARCY DR	CO	SA	19300	18	C5
MARCY RANCH RD	CO	SA		18	C4
MARDA AV	YL	YL	17200	7	E2
MARDEL DR	CYP	CYP	10100	9	C6
MARDELL AV	OR	OR	900	17	D4
MAR DE REY	SCL	SC72		38	D5
MARDICK RD	CO	SA	1400	24	C1
MARDI GRAS AV	ANA	AN	2700	12	A3
MARDINA WY	LAH	LAH	2100	1	E4
MAREA DR	HTB	HB	4600	20	D5
MARELEN DR	FUL	FL	1400	6	C4
MARELL CIR	CO	SA	13900	18	B6
MARENGO DR	ANA	AN		13	E4
MARENGO PL	SA	SA	900	22	E1
MARGARET DR	NB	NB	2200	31	D4
MARGARET PL	FUL	FL33	900	10	E1
MARGARET ST	CYP	CYP	9500	9	F5
MARGARITA AV	FTNV	SA08	10300	22	A4
MARGARITA DR	FUL	FL	1300	6	A3
MARGARITA DR	HTB	HB		20	D4
MARGARITA LN	HTB	HB47	17300	21	A6
MARGARITA ST	DPT	DPT		37	E3
MARGARITA ST	IRV	SA		29	C1
MARGATE CIR	WSTM	WSTM	9100	21	E3
MARGATE DR	ANA	AN	100	11	D6
MARGATE LN	HTB	HB46	19800	27	A4
MARGATE PL	ANA	AN	1300	11	D6
MARGENE CIR	IRV	SA	13700	24	D6
MARGIE LN	ANA	AN	1800	16	B2
MARGIE LN	GGR	GG	11500	16	B3
MARGO LN	WSTM	WSTM	9900	21	F3
MARGO LN	WSTM	WSTM		22	A3
MARGUERITA AV	DPT	DPT		37	D5
MARGUERITE AV	NB	CDLM	1200	32	C6
MARGUERITE AV	NB	NB	100	33	B1
MARGUERITE PKWY	MVJO	SJ91	22200	29B	C5
MARGUERITE PKWY	MVJO	SJ91	25000	29D	C5
MARGUERITE PKWY	MVJO	SJ91		52	D6
MARGUERITE PKWY	MVJO	SJ92		29B	C5
MARGUERITE PKWY	MVJO	SJ92		29D	C2
MARGUERITE PKWY	MVJO	SJ92		36	B1
MARGUERITE PKWY	MVJO	SJ92		52	D6
MARGUERITE PKWY	SJC	SJ75		36	B3
MARIA AV	PLA	PLA	6500	7	E6
MARIAN AV	ANA	AN	2400	10	E4
MARIAN AV	BPK	BP	6000	9	F6
MARIAN AV	CO	AN04	9800	10	E4
MARIAN DR	GGR	GG	10800	16	A3
MARIAN LN	NB	NB	1000	31	E4
MARIAN ST N&S	LAH	LAH	100	1	F4
MARIAN WY	ANA	AN	800	10	A6
MARIANA CIR	HTB	HB	16500	20	A5
MARIANA DR	DPT	DPT	33700	37	F4
MARIANO DR	CO	LB		35	C5
MARICOPA	TUS	TUS		24	D4
MARICOPA	TUS	TUS		24	D4
MARIE AV	FUL	FL	200	6	A5
MARIE LN	GGR	GG	9000	15	E3
MARIE LN	HTB	HB47	16500	21	B5
MARIE PL	OR	OR	200	17	A3
MARIE PL	WSTM	WSTM	15300	22	A3
MARIE ST	LAH	LAH	300	1	D5
MARIETTA AV	GGR	GG45	5200	14	E4
MARIETTA AV	GGR	GG	6600	15	A4
MARIETTA AV	OR	OR	700	17	C3
MARIETTA DR	GGR	GG	9200	15	E4
MARIETTA PL	OR	OR	400	17	C3
MARIGOLD	CO	LB51		29C	C2
MARIGOLD	IRV	SA		29	A5

1990 ORANGE COUNTY STREET INDEX

108

MARIGOLD AV — MEADOW LN

ORANGE CO.

COPYRIGHT, © 1989 BY Thomas Bros Maps

STREET	CITY	P.O. ZONE	BLOCK	PAGE	GRID
MARIGOLD AV	FTNV	SA08	9600	21	F4
MARIGOLD AV	FTNV	SA08	11700	22	C4
MARIGOLD AV	FUL	FL	200	6	E6
MARIGOLD AV	NB	CDLM	200	33	B2
MARIGOLD CIR	CM	CM	3300	27	E2
MARIGOLD CIR	FTNV	SA08	11500	22	C4
MARIGOLD ST	SB	SB	3600	14	D4
MARILLA DR	HTB	HB		20	D4
MARILYN CIR	GGR	GG	12300	15	E4
MARILYN CIR	WSTM	WSTM	5500	14	E5
MARILYN DR	LAG	LB	30600	35	A5
MARILYN DR	CYP	CYP	6000	9	F5
MARILYN DR	HTB	HB47	6500	21	B5
MARIN	CO	ET		51	F6
MARIN	CO	ET		52	A6
MARIN CIR	HTB	HB		26	D6
MARIN CT	ANA	AN		10	C6
MARIN CT	CO	LB	25000	29C	F2
MARIN DR	IRV	SA	3400	24	C6
MARIN ST	LAH	LAH	200	1	E5
MARIN WY	GGR	GG	11400	16	B2
MARINA CIR	CO	SJ91	25000	29A	F5
MARINA CIR	CO	SJ91		29B	A5
MARINA DR	PLA	PLA		7	D4
MARINA DR	SB	SB	100	19	E2
MARINA LN	HTB	HB	20000	26	E5
MARINA RD	SJC	SJ75		36	A3
MARINA WY	GGR	GG		15	D5
MARINABAY DR	HTB	HB		20	C5
MARINA HILLS DR	CO	LB77		35	E4
MARINA HILLS DR	CO	LB77		36	A4
MARINA VIEW PL	HTB	HB	17200	20	D6
MARINA VISTA DR	DPT	DPT	33100	37	F3
MARINE AV	NB	NB	100	31	F6
MARINE AV	SB	SB	1500	19	F3
MARINE DR	LAG	LB51	1000	34	C2
MARINE DR	PLA	PLA		7	D4
MARINE ST	SA	SA	400	22	E4
MARINE ST	SA	SA04	3800	27	D2
MARINE WY	CO	SA	6500	29	F4
MARINE WY	LAG	LB51	1000	34	C2
MARINE WY N	ETMC	SA09		51	C2
MARINE WY W	ETMC	SA09		51	B3
MARINER DR	DPT	LB77		37	D3
MARINER DR	HTB	HB	16000	20	B4
MARINER DR	SJC	SJ75		38	A3
MARINER LN	WSTM	WSTM	14300	21	D1
MARINER ST	BREA	BREA	700	2	D6
MARINER WY	ANA	AN	1300	10	F2
MARINER WY	ANA	AN	1300	11	A2
MARINERS DR	NB	NB	1000	31	E3
MARINERS WY	GGR	GG		16	D6
MARINERS COVE	HTB	HB	8400	30	D1
MARINO	CO	SJ88		59	C2
MARINO	YL	YL		8	B3
MARINO DR	NB	NB	2400	31	D5
MARINO LN	HTB	HB46		26	E6
MARINO PZ	YL	YL		8	C3
MARIO LN	STN	STN	11200	15	C2
MARION AV	CYP	CYP	4000	9	D6
MARION AV	LALM	LALM	3900	9	C6
MARION BLVD	FUL	FL	100	6	C3
MARION CIR	CYP	CYP	5600	9	E6
MARION CIR	WSTM	WSTM	8300	21	D1
MARION ST	CO	BP23	7800	9	C2
MARION WY	CM	CM27	2000	31	D2
MARION WY	LAG	LB51	2800	34	F5
MARION WY	SA	SA	1300	16	F5
MARION WY	SA	SA	1200	17	A5
MARION WY	VPK	OR67	18500	13	A6
MARIPOSA	CO	LB		29D	A6
MARIPOSA	CO	LB77		36	A1
MARIPOSA	CO	SJ79		59	E2
MARIPOSA	IRV	SA		29	C3
MARIPOSA E	SCL	SC72	100	39	D3
MARIPOSA W	SCL	SC72	100	39	D3
MARIPOSA AV	FTNV	SA08	9500	21	F5
MARIPOSA AV	PLA	PLA		7	F5
MARIPOSA AV	YL	YL	17600	7	F5
MARIPOSA DR	BREA	BREA	1000	2	E4
MARIPOSA DR	HTB	HB	6200	20	F6
MARIPOSA DR	VPK	OR67	18500	13	A6
MARIPOSA LN	FUL	FL33	1800	5	F3
MARIPOSA LN	FUL	FL	1300	6	A3
MARIPOSA PL	ANA	AN	300	11	A4
MARIPOSA ST	LAH	LAH	500	1	E5
MARIPOSA WY	BREA	BREA	100	4	A5
MARISA ST	STN	GG41	7700	15	C4
MARISCAL LN	MVJO	SJ91	27000	29B	C5
MARITA LN	ANA	AN		8	B6
MARITIME DR	NB	CDLM		32	B6

STREET	CITY	P.O. ZONE	BLOCK	PAGE	GRID
MARITIME LN	HTB	HB		26	B5
MARJAN LN	HTB	HB47	16000	21	B4
MARJAN ST	ANA	AN	600	12	A5
MARK CIR	LAP	BP23	7500	9	D2
MARK CIR	OR	OR76		13	A5
MARK CIR	VPK	OR67	17900	12	F5
MARK LN	ANA	AN		8	E5
MARK LN	CM	CM		27	C5
MARK LN	HTB	HB47	16400	21	C5
MARK LN	YL	YL	18000	7	F2
MARK RD	CO	OR67		50	E6
MARK ST	SA	SA	1900	22	E3
MARKEN LN	HTB	HB47	17300	21	C6
MARKET PL	CYP	CYP		14	E1
MARKEV ST	ANA	AN	1400	10	E6
MARKEV ST	ANA	AN04		15	E1
MARKEV ST	CO	SA	10900	15	D1
MARKEV ST	GGR	GG	10800	15	E1
MARKEV ST	STN	AN04	10800	15	D1
MARKHAM ST	FTNV	SA08	16500	22	C5
MARKON DR	GGR	GG		15	B3
MARKS WY	OR	OR	100	17	B3
MARKUSON RD	CO	OR67		50	E6
MARKWOOD ST	OR	OR	700	17	E2
MARLBORO AV	ANA	AN		11	B2
MARLBORO LN	CO	LB		29C	E5
MARLBORO ST	LAH	LAH	900	2	A6
MARLBOROUGH CIR	WSTM	WSTM	15400	22	A3
MARLEI RD	LAH	LAH	1300	1	F3
MARLENE AV	GGR	GG	9000	15	E4
MAR LES DR	SA	SA	1600	16	E6
MAR LES DR	SA	SA	1600	22	E1
MAR LES DR W	SA	SA	1000	22	E1
MAR LES LN	SA	SA	2700	16	E6
MAR LES LN	SA	SA	2700	22	E1
MARLIN AV	SB	SB	1200	19	F3
MARLIN CIR	LAP	BP23	8700	9	E1
MARLIN DR	HTB	HB		20	E5
MARLIN DR	LAG	LB51	400	34	F4
MARLIN ST	HTB	HB		26	C3
MARLIN WY	NB	NB	1700	31	E3
MARLIN COVE	CO	LB		35	D2
MARLINSPIKE DR	DPT	LB77		37	C5
MARLOWE CIR	WSTM	WSTM		20	E1
MARLOWE DR	GGR	GG	12000	15	E3
MARLOWE ST	ANA	AN		10	C4
MARMARA BAY	DPT	LB77		37	D4
MARMON AV	OR	OR	4000	18	A3
MARNE CIR	IRV	SA	15100	29	D3
MAROON DR	LAP	BP23	4500	9	C2
MARQUART ST	OR	OR	1600	12	D6
MARQUESA	DPT	DPT		37	E2
MARQUET CT	YL	YL		40	C6
MARQUETTE	IRV	SA15		32	E1
MARQUETTE	MVJO	SJ92		29D	E3
MARQUETTE CIR	CM	CM26	600	28	A3
MARQUETTE ST	IRV	SA15		28	E6
MARQUETTE ST	IRV	SA15		32	E1
MARQUETTE ST	WSTM	WSTM	13600	14	E6
MARQUIS CIR	CO	SA	12000	18	B6
MARQUIS CT	CO	LB56		29C	C3
MARQUITA E	SCL	SC72	100	39	D3
MARQUITA W	SCL	SC72	100	39	D3
MARRIOTT CT	CO	LB56		29C	E5
MARRYAT WY	STN	STN	11100	15	B2
MARS DR	BPK	BP	8200	10	C3
MARS DR	HTB	HB47		21	B5
MARS ST	WSTM	WSTM	16200	21	D4
MARSALA	CO	LB		29A	A4
MARSALA DR	NB	NB60		32	C3
MARSALA DR	YL	YL	19600	8	C3
MARSALA WY	MVJO	SJ92		29D	E3
MARSEILLE	LAG	LB		35	B5
MARSEILLE DR	HTB	HB47	8100	21	C6
MARSEILLES WY	CM	CM27	2400	31	F2
MARSELINA	TUS	TUS		24	B3
MARSHA AV	STN	STN		15	D1
MARSHA CIR	ANA	AN		13	C2
MARSHALL AV	BPK	BP	5700	5	C5
MARSHALL DR	HTB	HB	5600	20	F4
MARSHALL LN	GGR	GG	10600	16	A4
MARSHALL LN	TUS	TUS	13500	17	E5
MARSHALL WY	STN	STN	7100	15	A2
MARSHALL VIA	ANA	AN		16	D2
MARSHBURN CIR	YL	YL		7	F3
MARSHFIELD LN	MVJO	SJ92		29B	F6
MARSH HAWK	IRV	SA		29	C4
MARTELLA LN	ANA	AN		8	E6
MARTELLA LN	ANA	AN		13	E1
MARTENS RIV CIR	FTNV	SA08	11500	22	C6
MARTHA AV	OR	OR	1900	17	E2

STREET	CITY	P.O. ZONE	BLOCK	PAGE	GRID
MARTHA LN	SA	SA	1300	22	E1
MARTHA LN	SA	SA	1100	23	C1
MARTHA PL	FUL	FL33	200	5	F6
MARTHA ANN DR	CO	LALM	11100	14	A3
MARTHA ANNE DR	CO	TUS	18000	23	F1
MARTIN	IRV	SA		28	C4
MARTIN AV	FTNV	SA08	8900	26	D2
MARTIN CT	BREA	BREA		2	E6
MARTIN LN	HTB	HB		20	B6
MARTIN LN	OR	SA05	19400	18	C4
MARTINEZ DR	LAH	LAH	500	1	E5
MARTINEZ RD	ANA	AN		8	E6
MARTINEZ RD	ANA	AN		13	E1
MARTINGALE PL	CO	SA		18	D5
MARTINGALE WY	NB	NB60	19400	28	B5
MARTINIQUE	CO	LB77		36	A4
MARTINIQUE DR	CO	SJ92		29D	E2
MARTINIQUE DR	HTB	HB	8600	30	D1
MARTINIQUE WY	CO	CYP	8300	9	D4
MARTINIQUE WY	PLA	PLA	800	7	D5
MARTY LN	GGR	GG	13200	16	E5
MARTY LN	HTB	HB		26	C2
MARTY LN	SA	SA	1800	16	E5
MARUFFA CIR	HTB	HB	16400	20	D3
MARVALE DR	HTB	HB	8500	26	D5
MARVIEW DR	LAP	BP23	5200	9	E2
MAR VISTA	CO	ET		29A	F4
MAR VISTA AV	LAG	LB	22200	35	B6
MAR VISTA AV	LAG	LB77	31700	37	B1
MAR VISTA AV	SB	SB	700	19	E2
MARVISTA DR	HTB	HB47	6100	21	A2
MAR VISTA DR	NB	NB	600	32	A3
MAR VISTA LN	LAG	LB77		37	B2
MARVISTA WY	LAG	LB51	1900	34	F3
MARWOOD AV	FUL	FL	300	6	B5
MARY CIR	HTB	HB	8200	26	C6
MARY CIR	SA	SA	4000	22	C1
MARY CIR	VPK	OR67	9000	12	F5
MARY CIR	VPK	OR67	9000	13	A5
MARY COM	SA	SA03		22	D2
MARY LN	ANA	AN		13	C1
MARY WY	PLA	PLA	2100	7	C2
MARY ELLEN LN	YL	YL		8	B4
MARYGLEN LN	LAH	LAH	900	1	F5
MARY HILL DR	GGR	GG		15	D4
MARY JANE LN	YL	YL	18600	8	A2
MARY KAY CIR	CO	LB77		35	D3
MARYKNOLL ST	WSTM	WSTM	15200	21	B3
MARYLAND CIR	CM	CM		27	C2
MARYLEE DR	GGR	GG	8500	15	D3
MARYLHURST CT	CO	ET	22500	29B	A3
MARYMONT AV	FUL	FL		7	A2
MARYMONT AV	PLA	PLA	500	7	B2
MARYNELL DR	CO	YL	5300	8	C4
MARYPORT DR	HTB	HB	5500	25	E1
MAR Y SOL	DPT	DPT		37	F2
MARYVINE ST	CO	ET	24500	29A	E5
MARYWOOD DR	OR	OR	2900	12	F4
MARYWOOD DR	OR	OR		13	A4
MASHIE CIR	HTB	HB47	17400	21	B6
MASIDE	MVJO	SJ92		29D	C3
MASLOW	IRV	SA		29	E1
MASON	IRV	SA18		29A	C2
MASON DR	HTB	HB47	6700	21	A5
MASSACHUSTTS LN	PLA	PLA	200	7	B5
MAST AV	GGR	GG43	10500	22	A2
MAST AV	WSTM	WSTM	10200	22	A2
MAST DR	HTB	HB		26	B5
MASTERS DR	HTB	HB	8600	26	D5
MASTERS LN	ANA	AN	1200	10	B6
MASTERSON RD	STN	STN	10300	10	B6
MASTERSON ST	ANA	AN	1300	10	B6
MASTHEAD CT	SB	SB		19	F2
MATALON LN	LAP	CYP	5500	9	E3
MATARO LN	HTB	HB	20800	26	D6
MATCHLESS WY	SA	SA		28	B1
MATEO AV	LAH	LAH	1600	2	C4
MATERA	IRV	SA		24	D5
MATHEW CIR	HTB	HB	19000	26	E3
MATHEWSON AV	PLA	PLA	700	7	C2
MATIAS DR	MVJO	SJ91	24500	29B	B6
MATILDA ST	ANA	AN	600	12	A4
MATINICUS CT	CYP	CYP	11300	15	A2
MATISSE AV	IRV	SA	14100	24	C6
MATRYCE WY	CO	TUS	14000	17	F6
MATSONIA LN	HTB	HB	19700	26	F4
MATTHEW DR	DPT	DPT		37	E2
MAUCHLY	IRV	SA18		29A	B1
MAUCHLY	IRV	SA18		51	B6
MAUDE LN	ANA	AN	100	13	B2

STREET	CITY	P.O. ZONE	BLOCK	PAGE	GRID
MAUERHAN PL	ANA	AN	2000	11	F5
MAUI AV	SA	SA		22	C3
MAUI CIR	CM	CM	2900	27	B4
MAUI CIR	HTB	HB	4900	20	D4
MAUI DR	PLA	PLA	300	7	B5
MAUI PL	CM	CM	1900	27	B4
MAUI WY	SA	SA		22	C3
MAUNA CT	FTNV	SA08	15800	22	B4
MAUNA LN	HTB	HB46	19300	27	A4
MAUNA LN	SA	SA		22	C3
MAUNA KEA PL	CO	LB	30800	35	D5
MAUNA LOA RD	TUS	TUS	1200	24	A2
MAUNA LOA ST	BREA	BREA	3600	7	D1
MAUREEN DR	CO	MDWY		21	D3
MAUREEN DR	GGR	GG	9200	15	E2
MAURETANIA CIR	HTB	HB46	10400	27	A4
MAURICE CT	CO	ET	22500	29B	A3
MAURIE AV	SA	SA	4300	22	B1
MAURINE PL	FUL	FL	1500	6	E3
MAUVE	MVJO	SJ91		52	D5
MAUVE DR	CO	SA	13800	18	A6
MAVERICK AV	ANA	AN	2500	12	A5
MAVERICK CIR	CO	LB53		29C	F5
MAVERICK DR	YL	YL		8	C2
MAVERICK LN	CO	SA		18	D6
MAVIS ST	ANA	AN	700	11	D3
MAWSON DR	CO	LB	25000	29C	F1
MAXIMUS ST	CO	SJ91		29A	F6
MAXIMUS ST	CO	SJ91		29B	A6
MAXIMUS ST	CO	SJ91		29D	A1
MAXINE ST N	SA	SA	100	22	B3
MAXINE ST S	SA	SA	300	22	B3
MAXSON DR	CYP	CYP	5700	9	E5
MAXWELL AV	FUL	FL33	1100	10	D1
MAXZIM AV	FUL	FL33	1600	10	E1
MAXZIM AV	FUL	FL	400	11	B1
MAYAPPLE WY	IRV	SA	18100	28	F6
MAYBERRY CIR	WSTM	WSTM	15100	21	B2
MAYBROOK ST	WSTM	WSTM	15800	21	D4
MAYBURY CIR	CYP	CYP	4500	9	C5
MAYCHELLE DR	ANA	AN	4700	13	A1
MAYCHICK CIR	WSTM	WSTM	13300	14	F5
MAYFAIR AV	ANA	AN	1100	11	C2
MAYFAIR AV E&W	OR	OR	100	17	D2
MAYFAIR CT	CM	CM		27	D6
MAYFAIR CT	CM	CM27		31	D1
MAYFAIR DR	CO	SJ79		56	E6
MAYFAIR LN	CM	CM		27	D6
MAYFAIR LN	CM	CM27		31	D1
MAYFIELD RD	SB	SB	1200	14	A5
MAYFLOWER	IRV	SA		24	E5
MAYFLOWER CIR	FTNV	SA08	11700	22	C4
MAYFLOWER DR	NB	NB		31	E5
MAYFLOWER LN	HTB	HB47	15500	21	A3
MAYFLOWER ST	ANA	AN	1000	10	E3
MAYLAKE DR	SB	SB	13400	14	A5
MAYNARD WY	CO	SA	10300	18	B4
MAYOR LN	HTB	HB47	17400	21	A6
MAYPOLE DR	GGR	GG	12400	16	D3
MAYPORT LN	HTB	HB	20000	26	D5
MAYRENE AV	GGR	GG	9300	15	E4
MAYS AV	GGR	GG	8500	15	E6
MAYTEN AV	IRV	SA14	14800	29	C1
MAYWOOD AV	ANA	AN	3100	10	B6
MAYWOOD AV E	SA	SA	1300	23	C5
MAYWOOD AV W	SA	SA	2500	22	E5
MAYWOOD PL	SA	SA	1900	22	F5
MAYWOOD ST	ANA	AN	800	11	E4
MAZA CIR	FTNV	SA08	9000	21	E5
MAZA CT	CO	ET	25200	29A	F3
MAZAGON	MVJO	SJ92	27800	29B	F4
MAZATLAN	MVJO	SJ92		52	E6
MAZATLAN DR	CO	LB		35	D4
MAZO	MVJO	SJ92	22800	29B	E3
MAZO DR	DPT	DPT	34000	37	F4
MAZUELO CT	CO	LB56		29C	E5
MCAULAY PL	LAG	LB51	100	34	F5
MCBRIDE RIV CIR	FTNV	SA08		26	E2
MCCABE WY	IRV	SA	2100	28	D3
MCCABE RIVER AV	FTNV	SA08		22	B5
MCCABE RIV CIR	FTNV	SA08		22	B5
MCCAIN SMITH	TUS	SA10		23	E5
MCCAN ST	ANA	AN	1000	12	B1
MCCARRON WY	PLA	PLA		7	E6
MCCART AV	BREA	BREA	1400	2	C4
MCCART AV	LAH	LAH	2300	2	C4
MCCART CIR	BREA	BREA	1000	2	C4
MCCARTHY DR	HTB	HB	6000	25	F1
MCCARTHY LN	YL	YL	19000	8	B4
MCCLAY ST N	SA	SA	1700	17	D6
MCCLAY ST N&S	SA	SA	100	23	D2

STREET	CITY	P.O. ZONE	BLOCK	PAGE	GRID
MC CLEAN DR	CO	SA	1900	24	C2
MCCLELLAN WY	BPK	BP	6300	9	F2
MC CLENNAN	IRV	SA		24	E6
MCCLINTOCK WY	CM	CM	2900	27	D4
MCCLOUD CT	CO	LB		29C	E6
MCCLOUD CT	CO	LB		35	E1
MCCLOUD ST	ANA	AN	900	11	F5
MCCLURE AV	GGR	GG43	10200	22	A1
MCCLURE AV	WSTM	WSTM	8900	21	E1
MCCOMBER RD	BPK	BP	5000	5	B4
MCCORD CIR	FTNV	SA08	15900	21	F4
MC CORMACK LN	CM	CM	1200	27	D3
MCCORMACK LN	CO	PLA	4700	7	D2
MCCORMACK LN N	PLA	PLA	1700	7	D2
MCCORMICK	IRV	SA		29	E1
MCCORMICK AV	CM	CM26	200	28	B3
MCCOY RD	CO	ET	24200	29A	E4
MCCOY RD	OR	OR	200	17	B3
MCCRORY LN	OR	OR	1800	12	E5
MCDANIEL DR	GGR	GG	10300	16	A2
MCDERMITT ST	FTNV	SA08		21	F4
MCDONNELL DR	CYP	CYP		14	E1
MCDURMOTT E	IRV	SA		28	B3
MCDURMOTT W	IRV	SA		28	B3
MCELWEE RIV CIR	FTNV	SA08		26	E2
MCEVOY LN	GGR	GG	13500	16	F5
MCEVOY LN	SA	SA	1700	16	F5
MCFADDEN AV	CO	MDWY	8100	21	A3
MCFADDEN AV	CO	WSTM	7700	21	A3
MCFADDEN AV	GGR	GG43	10500	22	A3
MCFADDEN AV	HTB	HB	5000	20	E3
MCFADDEN AV	HTB	HB47	6200	21	A3
MCFADDEN AV	TUS	TUS	16500	23	E3
MCFADDEN AV	WSTM	WSTM	7000	21	E3
MCFADDEN AV	WSTM	WSTM	10000	22	B3
MCFADDEN AV E&W	SA	SA	100	23	C3
MCFADDEN AV W	SA	SA	1300	22	E3
MCFADDEN PL	NB	NB	100	31	C6
MCFADDEN ST	LAH	LAH	400	1	F5
MCGAW AV	IRV	SA	1000	28	C1
MCGEE RIVER CIR	FTNV	SA08		22	B5
MCGHEE DR	ANA	AN	200	10	C4
MCGUFFEY WY	IRV	SA	4200	28	F5
MCHENRY DR	IRV	SA		24	F6
MCINTOSH LN	CO	ET		29B	A1
MCINTOSH LN	CO	ET		52	A6
MCINTYRE ST	CO	LB	25200	29D	A1
MCKAY CIR	ANA	AN	4700	13	A1
MCKEEN ST	GGR	GG	10600	16	A5
MCKENNA CT	CO	ET		29B	A1
MCKENNA CT	CO	ET		52	A6
MCKENZIE DR	CO	PLA	5000	7	C4
MCKENZIE DR N	PLA	PLA	1300	7	C4
MCKINLEY	IRV	SA		29	E1
MCKINLEY CIR	BPK	BP	7400	10	B4
MCKINLEY CIR	WSTM	WSTM	13300	15	B5
MC KINLEY DR	PLA	PLA	2300	7	C1
MCKINLEY LN	HTB	HB	20000	26	F5
MCKINLEY WY	CM	CM	3100	27	E3
MCKINNEY CIR	HTB	HB	17700	26	A1
MCKINNEY WY	SB	SB	1800	14	A5
MCKINNON DR	ANA	AN	4700	13	A2
MCKNIGHT DR	LAG	LB51	100	34	B2
MCLAREN	IRV	SA18		29A	C3
MCLAREN LN	HTB	HB	19300	26	E4
MCLEAN	IRV	SA		24	E6
MCLEAN DR N	SA	SA	1100	22	B1
MCLEAN DR S	SA	SA	1000	22	B3
MCLEOD ST	GGR	GG	12400	16	A4
MCMAINS ST	GGR	GG	13600	15	E6
MCMICHAEL DR	GGR	GG	10000	15	F2
MCNATT CT	CO	ET		29B	A1
MCNATT CT	CO	ET		52	A6
MCNEIL LN	BPK	BP	7000	10	B1
MCNEIL LN	NB	NB		31	B4
MCNEIL WY	BPK	BP	7400	10	B2
MCNUTT WY	CYP	CYP	6500	15	A2
MCPHERSON RD	CO	OR69	11900	17	F3
MCPHERSON RD	OR	OR	100	17	F3
MCPHERSON ST	LAH	LAH	100	2	B4
MCWHORTER WY	CO	ET		29A	D2
MEAD DR	BPK	BP		5	C4
MEAD ST	FTNV	SA08	17500	22	A6
MEADE	IRV	SA		24	E5
MEADE AV	FUL	FL33	300	5	D6
MEADE AV	FUL	FL33	1000	10	D1
MEADE ST	GGR	GG	12200	15	E4
MEADOW CIR	HTB	HB		20	E5
MEADOW CT	BREA	BREA	300	2	F5
MEADOW LN	CO	OR	19900	18	C1
MEADOW LN	CO	CM27	300	31	E2

INDEX

STREET	CITY	P.O. ZONE	BLOCK	PAGE	GRID
MEADOW LN	LAG	LB77	31800	37	A1
MEADOW LN	FUL	FL	2200	6	F4
MEADOW BROOK	CM	CM		27	D2
MEADOWBROOK	IRV	SA		29	B4
MEADOWBROOK	MVJO	SJ92		29B	E6
MEADOWBROOK	MVJO	SJ92		29D	E1
MEADOW BROOK AV	GGR	GG		15	D5
MEADOWBROOK AV	OR	OR	4000	12	D3
MEADOWBROOK CIR	CO	ET	23400	29A	D4
MEADOWBROOK DR	HTB	HB	5800	20	F5
MEADOWBROOK LN	CO	ET	22800	29A	D2
MEADOWBROOK PL	ANA	AN	400	11	B4
MEADWBROOK ST E	OR	OR	400	12	D3
MEADOWBROOK WY	BPK	BP	8800	5	D4
MEADOWBROOK WY	STN	STN		15	B4
MEADOWCREEK RD	BREA	BREA		3	A5
MEADOW CREST DR	CO	LB53		29D	A3
MEADOW CREST DR	HTB	HB47	6400	21	A6
MEADOWFALL LN	SA	SA		22	D1
MEADOWGLEN DR	ANA	AN	4600	8	A6
MEADOW GRASS	IRV	SA		29	B2
MEADOW GROVE RD	OR	OR	2600	12	F4
MEADOWHILL AV	ANA	AN	4600	7	F5
MEADOW LAKE LN	YL	YL		40	E6
MEADOW LAND DR	YL	YL		40	D5
MEADOWLARK	IRV	SA		29	B2
MEADOWLARK AV	FTNV	SA08	10000	27	A2
MEADOWLARK DR	HTB	HB	5100	20	E4
MEADOWLARK DR	LAG	LB51	1000	34	E3
MEADOWLARK LN	ANA	AN		7	B6
MEADOWLARK LN	CO	CM27	300	31	E1
MEADOWLARK LN	LAG	LB51	1000	34	E3
MEADOWLARK LN	LAP	BP23	8000	9	D3
MEADOWLARK PL	OR	OR	1600	12	F6
MEADOWLARK ST	LAH	LAH	900	2	B3
MEADOWLARK TER	CO	SJ79		56	A3
MEADOWOOD	CO	LB56		29C	D2
MEADOWOOD CIR	HTB	HB		25	F3
MEADOWPARK LN	CO	TRA		56	E6
MEADOW RIDGE DR	CO	SJ79		52	F5
MEADOWRIDGE RD	OR	OR		12	F5
MEADOWRIDGE ST	ANA	AN08		40	A6
MEADOWSWEET WY	IRV	SA	18100	28	F6
MEADOWVIEW DR	YL	YL	16700	7	F3
MEADOWVIEW LN	ANA	AN	2600	10	D6
MEADOW VIEW LN	CM	CM27		31	A1
MEADOW VIEW LN	CO	ET		29A	E1
MEADOWWOOD	CO	ET	22500	29A	F2
MEADOWWOOD	SA	SA		22	E6
MEADOW WOOD DR	CO	SJ79		59	C6
MEADS AV	CO	OR	10200	13	D6
MEADS AV	CO	OR	10500	18	C1
MEADS AV	OR	OR	19000	13	D6
MEAGHER ST	FTNV	SA08	15900	21	F4
MEANDER LN	HTB	HB	20200	26	D5
MEANDOR LN	CO	SJ79		56	F6
MEAR LN	TUS	TUS	1200	23	E4
MEASOR ST	SA	SA	2500	23	B6
MEATH CIR	HTB	HB47	6500	21	A3
MEATS AV	ANA	AN		13	A4
MEATS AV	OR	OR		13	A4
MEATS AV	VPK	OR67		12	F4
MEATS AV E	OR	OR	400	12	D5
MECKLENBURG	IRV	SA		24	F6
MECKLENBURG	IRV	SA		29	F1
MEDALLION AV	TUS	TUS	17000	23	E3
MEDFORD AV	CO	TUS	17100	17	F6
MEDFORD AV	CO	SA	18500	18	A6
MEDFORD AV	TUS	TUS	17400	17	E6
MEDFORD DR	HTB	HB	6000	20	F3
MEDFORD PL	FUL	FL	2500	7	A2
MEDFORD ST	ANA	AN	1100	11	B2
MEDIA PANORAMA	CO	SA	18900	18	B4
MEDICAL LN	NB	NB	800	31	B4
MEDICAL CTR DR	ANA	AN	1700	11	A2
MEDICAL CTR DR	OR	OR68		16	F3
MEDICAL CTR RD	MVJO	SJ91		29D	B5
MEDICI	CO	LB56		29C	C1
MEDICI ISLE	IRV	SA14		28	D5
MEDINA	MVJO	SJ92		52	E6
MEDINA DR	ANA	AN	1600	16	A1
MEDINA DR	GGR	GG	11600	16	A3
MEDINAC LN	SB	SB	13500	14	A6
MEDINAH LN	CO	LB		35	D5
MEDITERRANEN DR	DPT	LB77	32400	37	C2
MEDITERRANEN DR	HTB	HB	9000	26	E5
MEDLAR RD	TUS	TUS		24	B5
MEDORA PL	WSTM	WSTM	13500	15	D5
MEDRA	MVJO	SJ91		29B	B2
MEDWICK LN	PLA	PLA	900	7	D2
MEER CIR	HTB	HB47	17400	21	D6
MEGAN CT	WSTM	WSTM	10000	22	A2
MEINHARDT RD	WSTM	WSTM	5500	14	F5
MEJORANA	CO	SJ88		59	B2
MELADEE	LAH	LAH	800	2	B4
MELANIE DR	ANA	AN		8	E5
MELANIE LN	WSTM	WSTM	13000	14	F5
MELBA DR	GGR	GG	9200	15	E2
MELBOURNE DR	CYP	CYP	5000	9	D5
MELBOURNE DR	HTB	HB47	6500	21	A3
MELBOURNE LN	YL	YL	17300	7	E4
MELIDA	MVJO	SJ91	22400	29B	D2
MELINDA CIR	ANA	AN	100	12	A3
MELINDA CIR	HTB	HB	9600	30	F2
MELINDA RD	MVJO	SJ92	28900	29B	E2
MELISSA COM	SA	SA03		22	D2
MELISSA LN	YL	YL	4200	7	D3
MELISSA WY	ANA	AN	1600	16	B1
MELLS LN	ANA	AN	1600	16	B1
MELLS PL	ANA	AN	1500	16	B1
MELODY CIR	GGR	GG	11700	15	F3
MELODY DR	GGR	GG	12700	15	E4
MELODY LN	CM	CM27	100	31	D2
MELODY LN	FUL	FL	900	6	E4
MELODY LN	HTB	HB	16000	20	D4
MELODY LN	PLA	PLA	500	7	A5
MELODY HILL LN	CO	LB		29C	D2
MELODYLANE	IRV	SA		29	A4
MELODY PARK DR	GGR	GG	10000	15	F3
MELRIC AV	GGR	GG43	10500	22	A3
MELRIC AV	WSTM	WSTM	10300	22	A2
MORNINGSIDE CIR	FUL	FL35		6	C3
MELRIC DR	SA	SA	4600	22	B2
MELROSE CIR	WSTM	WSTM	8400	21	D1
MELROSE ST	BPK	BP	7000	5	A6
MELROSE ST	BPK	BP	7000	10	A1
MELROSE ST N	PLA	PLA	100	7	A6
MELROSE ST S	ANA	AN	100	11	D4
MELROSE ST S	PLA	PLA	300	7	A6
MELROSE ST S	PLA	PLA	900	12	A1
MELVILLE CIR	HTB	HB	16600	20	A5
MELVILLE DR	FUL	FL	200	6	C3
MELVILLE WY	ANA	AN	3500	12	D1
MELVIN WY	CO	TUS	1500	24	B2
MEMBRILLA	MVJO	SJ92	21500	29B	E1
MEMORY LN	OR	OR		17	C4
MEMORY LN	SA	SA	1200	16	F5
MEMORY LN	SA	SA	600	17	A5
MEMPHIS AV E&W	HTB	HB	100	26	C5
MENDEL CT	IRV	SA17		32	D2
MENDOCINO	IRV	SA		24	C6
MENDOCINO AV	CO	LB		29C	E2
MENDOCINO CIR	VPK	OR67	18500	13	A6
MENDOCINO CT	CO	LB	24600	29C	E2
MENDOCINO ST	FUL	FL31		6	F3
MENDOZA DR	CM	CM	2700	27	E4
MENDOZA TER	NB	CDLM	400	33	C2
MENLO AISLE	IRV	SA15		32	F1
MENUDA PANORAMA	CO	SA	19000	18	B3
MERANO	CO	LB77		35	E5
MERASHEEN WY	CYP	CYP	6800	15	A2
MERCADO AV	CO	LAM	4500	5	C2
MERCANTILE AV	STN	STN	11000	15	B2
MERCATO	CO	LAG		35	F4
MERCATOR ISLE	DPT	LB77		37	D4
MERCED AV	LAH	LAH	1100	1	E5
MERCED CIR	HTB	HB		26	D5
MERCED CIR	IRV	SA		29	C2
MERCEDES CIR	GGR	GG	9100	15	E3
MERCED RIVER AV	FTNV	SA08		21	F5
MERCED TRAIL RD	OR	OR		12	B5
MERCER PL	SA	SA	3000	28	B1
MERCIER LN	HTB	HB47	16300	21	A5
MERCURY DR	BPK	BP	8300	10	C3
MERCURY DR	WSTM	WSTM	16300	21	D4
MERCURY LN	BREA	BREA	500	2	D6
MERCURY RD	CO	ET		29A	D4
MEREDITH DR	CO	SA	17500	17	E5
MEREDITH DR	HTB	HB46	10000	27	A5
MERELET LN	OR	OR	300	17	F4
MERELLO ST	GGR	GG	13800	16	A6
MERIDA	IRV	SA14		28	D4
MERIDA PZ	YL	YL		8	C3
MERIDAY LN	SA	SA	1800	22	E1
MERIDIAN	CO	SJ79		59	D3
MERIDIAN	IRV	SA		29	F6
MERIDIAN DR	DPT	DPT		37	F3
MERIDIAN DR	CYP	CYP		15	A1
MERIDIAN ST	OR	OR67		13	A4
MERIDIAN WY	CO	LB56		29C	E5
MERIENDA	CO	LB56		29C	E3
MERIENDA LN	CO	YL	3500	7	D1
MERIENDA LN	YL	YL	3900	7	D2
MERINO CIR	MVJO	SJ91	26800	29D	C1
MERION	MVJO	SJ92		29B	E3
MERION CIR	HTB	HB48		25	E2
MERION WY	SB	SB	1400	14	A6
MERIT CIR	MVJO	LB53		29D	B4
MERLE CIR	HTB	HB47	8500	21	D5
MERLE PL	ANA	AN	2500	10	E5
MERLIN AV	CO	LB56		29C	B1
MERLIN AV	FUL	FL	2800	6	E2
MERMAID CIR	DPT	DPT		37	F2
MERMAID CIR	DPT	DPT		38	A2
MERMAID CIR	HTB	HB	8000	26	C6
MERMAID ST	LAG	LB51	300	34	D3
MERONA PL	ANA	AN	1300	11	E2
MERONA ST	ANA	AN	1200	11	E2
MERRILL PL	CM	CM27	100	31	D1
MERRILL ST	GGR	GG	12300	16	C4
MERRIMAC	IRV	SA		24	E4
MERRIMAC DR	ANA	AN	100	12	E3
MERRIMAC DR	HTB	HB	10000	26	F4
MERRIMAC WY	CM	CM	1200	27	D5
MERRYWOOD CT	BREA	BREA		2	D5
MERTEN AV	CO	CYP	4700	9	D4
MERVYN PL	CO	TUS	14300	24	A1
MESA CIR	WSTM	WSTM	14400	21	C1
MESA DR	CM	CM	100	27	F5
MESA DR	CO	SA07	1000	27	F5
MESA DR	CO	SA07	2100	28	A6
MESA DR	CO	SA	2200	32	A1
MESA DR S	VPK	OR67	18600	13	B5
MESA RD	IRV	SA	20000	32	D1
MESA RD E	LAG	LB	100	34	B2
MESA WY	CO	ET		29A	F3
MESA BLUFF DR	CM	CM		27	A6
MESA BLUFF DR	CM	CM27		31	A1
MESA DUMP RD	OR	OR		13	B5
MESA VERDE	FUL	FL	1100	6	A2
MESA VERDE CIR	PLA	PLA	1400	7	E4
MESA VERDE CT	FTNV	SA08	18200	27	A2
MESA VERDE DR E	CM	CM	1500	27	B4
MESA VERDE DR W	CM	CM	2800	27	B4
MESA VISTA DR	DPT	DPT	33100	37	F3
MESILLA	MVJO	SJ91		29D	C3
MESITA PL	FUL	FL	800	6	D1
MESITA WY	YL	YL	5300	7	E4
MESQUITE CIR	FTNV	SA08	16100	21	F4
MESQUITE ST	FTNV	SA08	16100	21	F4
MESSERSMITH AV	CO	AN04	9800	10	F4
MESSINA	CO	LB		29A	B4
MESTO	MVJO	SJ92	23100	29B	D3
METCALF LN	FTNV	SA08		26	A3
METRO DR	CM	CM		27	C2
METROPOLITAN DR	OR	OR68	3600	16	E4
METZLER LN	HTB	HB47	17500	21	B6
MEXICO WY	BPK	BP	7600	9	E2
MEYER PL	CM	CM	2200	27	C6
MEYER PL	CM	CM27	1900	31	C2
MIAMI CIR	WSTM	WSTM	8300	21	D1
MIA VIA	DPT	SC24		38	C6
MICHAEL AV	FUL	FL	200	6	A5
MICHAEL AV	GGR	GG	12600	16	D6
MICHAEL DR	HTB	HB47	8100	21	D6
MICHAEL PL	NB	NB	600	31	D4
MICHAEL ST	SA	SA	800	22	B1
MICHAEL WY	ANA	AN		11	E5
MICHEL PL	PLA	PLA	400	7	C2
MICHEL WY	PLA	PLA	1900	7	C2
MICHELANGELO	CO	LB56		29C	C1
MICHELLE DR	ANA	AN	1500	16	B1
MICHELLE DR	IRV	SA		24	B5
MICHELLE DR	TUS	TUS	2300	24	B5
MICHELLIS ST	CO	LB77		35	D3
MICHELSON DR	IRV	SA	2000	28	C4
MICHELSON DR	IRV	SA	4300	29	A5
MICHIGAN AV	CM	CM	3200	27	C3
MICHIGAN CIR	ANA	AN		13	F3
MICHIGAN LN	CO	ET		29A	D1
MICKEL LN	YL	YL	19200	8	B3
MICKEY ST	GGR	GG	13400	15	E5
MICMAC DR	PLA	PLA	800	7	C1
MIDBURY DR	HTB	HB	8700	26	E5
MIDCREST DR	CO	ET		29B	B1
MIDCREST DR	CO	ET		52	B6
MIDDLEBOROUGH	WSTM	WSTM	15100	22	A2
MIDDLEBURY CIR	CYP	CYP	4500	9	C5
MIDDLECOFF DR	HTB	HB	5500	20	F5
MIDDLERIDGE LN	CO	LB53		29D	A4
MIDDLESEX DR	STN	STN	7200	15	B1
MIDDLESEX PL	FUL	FL	2500	7	A2
MIDDLETON PL	CO	LB		35	E6
MIDDLETON ST	LAH	LAH	900	1	E6
MIDDLETOWN LN	WSTM	WSTM	8200	21	D1
MIDIRON CIR	HTB	HB	5900	20	F5
MIDLAND LN	HTB	HB46	20000	27	A5
MIDLOTHIAN	CO	SJ79		59	D3
MIDWAY AV	LALM	LALM		14	C2
MIDWAY DR	ANA	AN	100	11	D6
MIDWAY DR	CYP	CYP	11500	14	E3
MIDWAY DR	ETMC	SA09		51	D4
MIDWAY DR	HTB	HB		25	F1
MIDWAY DR	LALM	LALM	11000	14	D2
MIDWAY PL	CO	MDWY	15000	21	C2
MIDWAY PL	ETMC	SA09		51	D4
MIDWAY MANOR	ANA	AN	100	11	D5
MIDWICK PL	GGR	GG	11300	16	B4
MIDWOOD LN	ANA	AN04	2000	15	F1
MIEMBRO	CO	LB	23000	29A	A5
MIFFLIN PL	IRV	SA		24	F5
MIGNON WY	PLA	PLA	2100	7	C2
MIGUEL LN	CM	CM	2800	27	E4
MIGUEL PL	FUL	FL	100	6	B2
MIGUELITA RD	SJC	SJ75	32100	38	C1
MIKANOS DR	MVJO	SJ92		29D	E3
MIKINDA AV	CO	LAH	9300	1	E3
MIKINDA AV	LAH	LAH	1400	1	E3
MIKRO	CO	LB77		35	F5
MILAGRO WY	FUL	FL	3100	6	A1
MILAN AV	SA	SA		22	D3
MILAN PL	ANA	AN	300	10	D4
MILAN ST	WSTM	WSTM	13100	14	E5
MILAN ST	WSTM	WSTM		20	E1
MILANO	CO	LB		29A	B4
MILANO	HTB	HB		26	D4
MILANO DR	NB	NB60		32	C2
MILANO WY	MVJO	SJ92		29D	F3
MILAZZO	IRV	SA		24	D5
MILBRO ST	CM	CM	2900	27	E4
MILDRED AV	CYP	CYP	5900	9	E6
MILDRED AV	GGR	GG	10400	16	A5
MILDRED CIR	CYP	CYP	5500	9	E6
MILDRED LN	CYP	CYP	5600	9	E6
MILES AV	CO	ET	25100	29A	F3
MILFORD CIR	CO	SA	13400	18	A5
MILFORD CIR	HTB	HB	8400	26	D3
MILFORD DR	NB	CDLM	100	33	B2
MILFORD ST	OR	OR	1500	12	E5
MILFORD ST	OR	OR	200	17	E3
MILKWOOD	CO	SJ		59	B3
MILKY WY	WSTM	WSTM	8900	21	E4
MILL CIR	HTB	HB47	17300	21	B6
MILLBANK DR	OR	OR		12	F4
MILLBRAE ST	OR	OR	2300	12	D4
MILLBRIDGE CIR	HTB	HB	8400	26	D5
MILLBROOK	MVJO	SJ92		29B	E1
MILLBROOK	MVJO	SJ92		52	E6
MILLBROOK RD	CO	SA	1400	24	B1
MILL CREEK	IRV	SA		32A	A2
MILL CREEK DR	CO	LB		29A	B4
MILLER CIR	VPK	OR67	10400	18	A1
MILLER DR	TUS	TUS	17600	23	F2
MILLER ST	ANA	AN	1400	7	C6
MILLER ST	ANA	AN	1300	12	D1
MILLER ST	BPK	BP	7200	9	F2
MILLER WY	LAG	LB51	1000	34	F3
MILLIGAN DR	LAG	LB51	100	34	E1
MILLIKEN AV	IRV	SA		28	E2
MILL POND	MVJO	SJ92		29B	E2
MILLPOND CT	SJC	SJ75		36	A3
MILL POND LN	HTB	HB47		21	C5
MILL POND RD E	DPT	SC24	27000	38	C6
MILL POND RD W	DPT	SC24	26900	38	C6
MILLS CIR	WSTM	WSTM	15800	21	D4
MILLS DR	ANA	AN	300	11	D2
MILLS DR	CO	OR	19600	18	C3
MILLS DR	OR	OR	2500	17	A3
MILLS RD	GGR	GG	13500	16	B6
MILLS WY	STN	STN		10	E4
MILLS WY	STN	STN		15	B3
MILLS END	CO	AN04	9500	10	F5
MILLSTONE	IRV	SA		29	B1
MILLSTONE PL	YL	YL		8	F4
MILL STREAM CIR	ANA	AN		13	E1
MILLSTREAM DR	FUL	FL33		5	E4
MILLSTREAM LN	HTB	HB47		21	C5
MILLSTREAM LN	OR	OR		12	B4
MILL STREAM RD	CO	SJ		56	D6
MILLWOOD LN	ANA	AN		8	D6
MILLWOOD RD	CO	SJ79		52	E4
MILLWOOD ST	SA	SA	1900	17	D6
MILNE DR	HTB	HB	8500	30	D1
MILNEBURG ST	CO	AN04	10000	10	E6
MILO ST	HTB	HB	4700	20	D5
MILOS	CO	LAG		35	F4
MILTON AV	FUL	FL	2600	7	A3
MILTON AV	WSTM	WSTM		14	F6
MILTON AV	WSTM	WSTM	13500	15	A6
MILTON CIR	CYP	CYP	9800	9	F6
MILTON CIR	HTB	HB	6000	20	F3
MILTON ST	ANA	AN	200	12	A3
MILTON WY	SA	SA		28	C1
MIMBRERA RD	SJC	SJ75		38	B3
MIMI LN	CO	ET	21900	29A	D1
MIMOSA	IRV	SA		29	B6
MIMOSA DR	CO	YL	4556	7	D2
MIMOSA DR	CO	LB	24100	29C	E6
MIMOSA DR	YL	YL	4540	7	D2
MIMOSA LN	MVJO	SJ91		29B	B3
MIMOSA LN	TUS	TUS	14200	23	E1
MIMOSA PL	FUL	FL	1400	6	F2
MINA	CO	ET		29B	A3
MINA CT	CO	ET	25400	29A	F3
MINARET	IRV	SA		32A	A3
MINAYA	MVJO	SJ91		29B	D2
MINDANAO CIR	DPT	LB77		37	C1
MINDANAO DR	CM	CM	2900	27	B4
MINDANAO ST	CYP	CYP	11600	14	F2
MINDEN DR	YL	YL	17200	7	E3
MINDORA ST	LALM	LALM	11000	14	D2
MINER ST	CM	CM	2200	27	C6
MINER ST	CM	CM27	2100	31	C1
MINERS TR	IRV	SA		24	E6
MINERVA AV	ANA	AN	2000	10	F5
MINERVA AV	ANA	AN	1500	11	A5
MINERVA CT	CO	SJ91		29B	A6
MINERVA LN	HTB	HB	20400	26	E5
MINERVA PL	ANA	AN	2000	10	F5
MINERVA PL	ANA	AN	1900	11	A5
MINIKAHDA	CO	SJ79		59	D3
MINIKAHDA	CO	SJ79		59	E3
MINNESOTA AV	CM	CM	3200	27	B3
MINNETONKA LN	CO	ET		29A	D1
MINNIE ST	SA	SA	100	23	C2
MINOA DR	CO	SJ91	25600	29B	A6
MINORCA DR	CM	CM	1500	27	C4
MINORCA PL	CM	CM	1600	27	B4
MINORCA WY	BPK	BP		5	C3
MINORCA WY	SJC	SJ75		38	B2
MINORI	CO	LB77		35	F5
MINORU LN	HTB	HB47	16800	21	D5
MINOS ST	CO	SJ91		29B	A6
MINOS ST	CO	SJ91		29D	A1
MINOT ST	ANA	AN	1200	10	E2
MINT AV	FTNV	SA08	9000	21	E4
MINT AV	WSTM	WSTM		21	E4
MINTEER ST	ANA	AN	1200	11	B2
MINTER ST N	SA	SA	400	23	C2
MINTER ST S	SA	SA	1400	23	C4
MINT GLADE	IRV	SA		29	C2
MINTWOOD LN	ANA	AN		11	E6
MINUET DR	HTB	HB	4500	20	D4
MINUET LN	ANA	AN	5300	8	B6
MINUET LN	CO	AN07	18400	8	A6
MINUTEMEN WY	CM	CM	2300	27	E6
MIRA	IRV	SA		32A	B2
MIRA CT	ANA	AN		16	D3
MIRA ADELANTE	SCL	SC72		38	E5
MIRA ALLENDE	SCL	SC72		38	E5
MIRABEL DR	CO	LB	22900	35	C5
MIRABELLA	CO	SJ		59	B3
MIRA COLLADO	SCL	SC72		38	E5
MIRA DEL NORTE	SCL	SC72		38	E5
MIRA DEL OESTE	SCL	SC72		38	E5
MIRA DEL SUR	SCL	SC72		38	E5
MIRADOR	IRV	SA		32A	B2
MIRADOR	MVJO	SJ91		29B	C2
MIRADOR CIR	FUL	FL	3000	6	B1
MIRADOR CT	CO	LB	30400	35	D4
MIRA EL RIO LN	HTB	HB	17900	26	A3
MIRAFLORES	MVJO	SJ92		29D	C4
MIRAGE AV	GGR	GG	9500	15	E6
MIRAGE AV	WSTM	WSTM	9200	21	E1
MIRAGE CIR	GGR	GG	9700	21	F1
MIRAGE ST	YL	YL		40	A5
MIRALAGO PL	CO	SA	10400	18	E5
MIRA LAS OLAS	SCL	SC72		38	E5
MIRALESTE	CO	LB77		36	A2
MIRALINDA	CO	ET		52	B6
MIRALOMA AV	ANA	AN	3300	7	C6
MIRALOMA AV	ANA	AN	2600	12	B1
MIRALOMA AV	PLA	PLA		7	E6
MIRALOMA AV	PLA	PLA	1650	12	E1

INDEX

1990 ORANGE COUNTY STREET INDEX

STREET	CITY	P.O. ZONE	BLOCK	PAGE	GRID
MIRA LOMA CIR	HTB	HB47	17400	21	A6
MIRA LOMA PL	CO	CM27	300	27	F6
MIRALOMA WY	ANA	AN	2500	12	A2
MIRAMAR	MVJO	SJ92		52	E6
MIRAMAR CIR	CO	SA05		18	D4
MIRAMAR DR	FUL	FL	700	6	D4
MIRAMAR DR	NB	CDLM	2000	33	A1
MIRAMAR DR	NB	NB	1500	33	C5
MIRAMAR LN	HTB	HB	21000	30	D1
MIRAMAR PL	FUL	FL	1000	6	D4
MIRAMAR ST	LAG	LB51	800	34	F4
MIRA MONTE	TUS	TUS		24	C3
MIRAMONTE DR	CO	SJ92		29D	E2
MIRAMONTE DR	FUL	FL	1200	6	B3
MIRANDA	IRV	SA		32A	A2
MIRANDA AV	BPK	BP	10200	9	F6
MIRANDA ST	GGR	GG45	11800	14	F3
MIRANDELA LN	CO	LB77		35	C4
MIRAPOSA WY	TUS	TUS		24	E4
MIRA PUERTA	SCL	SC72		38	E5
MIRAR VISTA DR	MVJO	SJ92		36	B1
MIRAR VISTA LN	MVJO	SJ92		36	B1
MIRASOL ST	SA	SA	2000	17	E5
MIRASOL ST	SA	SA	900	23	E1
MIRA VELERO	SCL	SC72		38	E5
MIRAVERDE	CO	LB		35	E4
MIRA VISTA	CO	LB77		36	A2
MIRA VISTA DR	CO	SA	10400	18	E5
MIRIAM PL	CO	SA	13000	18	B4
MIRKWOOD RUN	YL	YL		8	D2
MIRLO	CO	SJ		59	C1
MIRLO CIR	MVJO	SJ91		29D	C4
MIRO CT	IRV	SA	3900	24	C6
MIRROR CIR	WSTM	WSTM	9300	15	E6
MIRROR LAKE	IRV	SA		29	A1
MISCOU WY	CYP	CYP	11400	15	A2
MISENO WY	CM	CM27	2400	31	F2
MISSILE LN	ANA	AN		16	D2
MISSILE WY	ANA	AN	1600	11	D1
MISSION DR	CM	CM	900	27	E4
MISSION DR N&S	FUL	FL	100	6	F6
MISSION LN	HTB	HB	20800	26	D6
MISSION ST	BPK	BP	7300	5	B5
MISSION ST	LAH	LAH	100	1	E5
MISSION ST	SJC	SJ75	22600	36	B6
MISSION WY	PLA	PLA	100	7	C5
MISSION BAY DR	NB	CDLM		32	D5
MISSION HLLS DR	SJC	SJ75	27000	36	C3
MISSION HLLS LN	YL	YL		8	F4
MISSION HLLS LN	YL	YL		40	A4
MISSOURI AV	PLA	PLA	200	7	A6
MISSOURI AV	PLA	PLA	200	12	A1
MISSOURI LN	SA	SA	300	22	C2
MISSOURI ST	CM	CM	1700	27	B2
MISTLETOE AV	FTNV	SA08	9700	21	F4
MISTLETOE ST	CO	SJ88		59	B1
MISTRAL DR	HTB	HB	3800	20	C5
MISTY LN	HTB	HB	17500	20	F6
MISTY RUN	IRV	SA		29	A5
MISTY WY	YL	YL		7	F2
MISTY BROOK CIR	STN	STN		15	B4
MISTY CREEK LN	CO	LB		29C	D1
MISTY GLEN	CO	ET		52	A5
MISTY MEADOW	IRV	SA		32A	A1
MISTY RIDGE LN	CO	SJ79		52	D4
MISTY RIDGE	MVJO	SJ92		29D	E1
MISTY SEA DR	CO	LB		35	C6
MISTY SEA DR	CO	LB77		37	C1
MISTY SHADOW	IRV	SA		32A	C4
MISTY WIND DR	GGR	GG		16	D6
MITCHELL	IRV	SA		28	C2
MITCHELL N	IRV	SA		28	C2
MITCHELL S	IRV	SA		28	C2
MITCHELL AV	GGR	GG	13300	16	B5
MITCHELL AV	TUS	TUS	1200	23	F3
MITCHELL AV	TUS	TUS	1500	24	A4
MITCHELL DR	STN	STN	10700	15	B1
MITHRA AV	CO	SJ91		29B	A6
MITHRA AV	CO	SJ91		29D	A1
MITTERBILL ST	FTNV	SA08	15900	21	F4
MITTMAN LN	SA	SA		18	B4
MOANA WY	GGR	GG	12200	16	A4
MOAT PL	SA	SA		23	B6
MOBERLY CT	CO	LB77		35	F3
MOCCASIN TR	CO	SJ79		52	F5
MOCKING BIRD	IRV	SA		29	C2
MOCKINGBIRD CIR	FTNV	SA08	8800	26	E1
MOCKINGBIRD CT	GGR	GG	12100	16	A3
MOCKINGBIRD LN	CO	LB56		29C	B1
MOCKINGBIRD PL	CO	ET		29A	E2
MOCKINGBIRD PL	OR	OR	1600	12	F6
MOCKINGBIRD WY	ANA	AN		13	F2
MODAC	FTNV	SA08	17300	21	F6
MODALE DR	HTB	HB	8200	26	D2
MODENA PL	ANA	AN	1000	10	E2
MODENA ST	ANA	AN	600	10	E3
MODERNO PL	FUL	FL35		2	B6
MODESTO CIR	HTB	HB		26	E5
MODESTO DR	MVJO	SJ91		29B	B3
MODINA	CO	LB		29A	B5
MODJESKA CIR	CM	CM		27	A6
MODJESKA CYN RD	CO	OR67		50	D6
MODJESKA CYN RD	CO	OR67		53	A1
MODJESKA GRD RD	CO	OR67		50	D6
MODJESKA GRD RD	CO	OR67		52	D1
MODJSKA PEAK LN	CO	SJ		52	F3
MODOC CIR	HTB	HB		26	E5
MODOC DR	CO	LB	25200	29D	A1
MODOC DR	WSTM	WSTM	6000	14	F6
MODOC ST	OR	OR		13	B5
MOEN ST	CO	AN04	11500	15	D2
MOFFETT DR	TUS	SA10		23	E5
MOFFETT DR	TUS	SA10		29	A1
MOHAWK AV	ANA	AN	900	11	A3
MOHAWK CIR	BPK	BP	7300	10	A2
MOHAWK CT	CYP	CYP	10400	14	E1
MOHAWK DR	CO	ET		29A	F2
MOHAWK DR	PLA	PLA	500	7	C1
MOHAWK DR	SA	SA	500	22	D4
MOHAWK RD	WSTM	WSTM	6300	15	A5
MOHAWK ST	IRV	SA14	14600	29	F3
MOHICAN AV	ANA	AN	900	11	A3
MOHICAN AV	PLA	PLA	2400	7	C2
MOHICAN DR	BPK	BP	6500	10	A1
MOHICAN WY	ANA	AN	1100	11	A2
MOHLER DR	ANA	AN	1000	13	E1
MOIR CT	CO	TUS		23	E2
MOISI LN	PLA	PLA	1000	12	A1
MOJAVE LN	MVJO	SJ91		29B	B3
MOJO CT	NB	NB		31	B4
MOKIHANNA DR	HTB	HB	9300	30	E2
MOLAMA CIR	GGR	GG	10500	16	A4
MOLLIE LN	YL	YL		7	F2
MOLOKAI DR	CYP	CYP	6700	15	A2
MOLOKAI DR	HTB	HB	9300	30	E2
MOLOKAI DR	PLA	PLA	300	7	B5
MOLOKAI PL	CM	CM	3100	27	C3
MOLT RIVER CIR	FTNV	SA08		26	E1
MONA LN	HTB	HB47	17300	21	B6
MONACO	IRV	SA14		28	F3
MONACO	NB	CDLM		32	D4
MONACO CIR	PLA	PLA	1400	7	C4
MONACO DR	HTB	HB		30	F1
MONACO DR	LAG	LB51	2400	34	A1
MONACO DR	SA	SA		22	E2
MONACO TER	CM	CM27	2400	31	F1
MONARCH	IRV	SA		29	C1
MONARCH DR	SJC	SJ75		36	C3
MONARCH ST	GGR	GG	12500	15	B4
MONARCH BAY DR	DPT	LB77	32900	37	C2
MONARCH BCH DR	DPT	LB77		37	E3
MONDO WY	IRV	SA	4000	28	F5
MONETTE CIR	YL	YL		7	E4
MONFORTE	MVJO	SJ92		29D	C2
MONICA LN	SA	SA	1900	16	E5
MONIQUE WY	CO	CYP	4500	9	D3
MONISHA	CO	ET		52	A6
MONITA CIR	CO	LB56		29C	E6
MONITOR	IRV	SA		24	E5
MONITOR DR	HTB	HB46	10200	27	A4
MONITOR WY	CM	CM		27	D4
MONO PL	WSTM	WSTM	13200	15	A5
MONO KAI ST	CYP	CYP	6000	14	F2
MONROE	IRV	SA		24	D6
MONROE AV	ANA	AN	2700	10	D4
MONROE AV	BPK	BP	7000	10	B4
MONROE AV	OR	OR	300	17	D1
MONROE AV	STN	STN	7700	15	C1
MONROE CIR	BPK	BP	8700	10	B4
MONROE LN	HTB	HB47	16500	21	D5
MONROE LN	WSTM	WSTM	14400	21	D1
MONROE PL	ANA	AN	2700	10	D4
MONROE ST	CO	MDWY	14500	21	D3
MONROE ST	GGR	GG	12500	15	D5
MONROE ST	WSTM	WSTM	13600	15	D6
MONROE ST	WSTM	MDWY	15400	21	D3
MONROE WY	CM	CM	3100	27	E3
MONROE WY	PLA	PLA	700	7	A6
MONROE WY	PLA	PLA	700	12	A1
MONROVIA AV	CM	CM	2200	27	B6
MONROVIA AV	CM	CM27	1600	31	B1
MONROVIA AV	NB	NB	1500	31	B4
MONSON CT	YL	YL		7	F3
MONTAGE	IRV	SA14		28	D4
MONTAGNE DR	CO	SA	13200	17	F5
MONTAGU	MVJO	SJ92		29B	F1
MONTAGUE AV N&S	FUL	FL	100	6	E6
MONTAGUE CIR	PLA	PLA	2200	7	B2
MONTAIRE PL	LAP	BP23		4	E6
MONTALVO RD	CO	LB		35	C5
MONTANA	SCL	SC72		38	E4
MONTANA AV	BPK	BP	8300	10	C1
MONTANA AV	CM	CM	3200	27	B3
MONTANA CIR	VPK	OR67	18100	17	F1
MONTANA CIR	VPK	OR67	18100	18	A1
MONTANAS ESTE	IRV	SA		28	E6
MONTANAS NORTE	IRV	SA		28	E6
MONTANAS SUD	IRV	SA		28	E6
MONTANOSO DR	MVJO	SJ91	25400	29D	B2
MONTAREZ CIR	MVJO	SJ91	26200	29D	B1
MONTAUK CIR	HTB	HB	20500	26	E5
MONTA VISTA AV	SA	SA	1800	22	E3
MONT BLANC CIR	PLA	PLA	2200	7	B2
MONTBURY CIR	HTB	HB	17500	25	F1
MONTBURY DR	CO	ET		29B	B1
MONTBURY DR	CO	ET		52	B6
MONTCLAIR CIR	LAP	BP23	5300	9	E1
MONTCLAIR CT	GGR	GG	11400	15	E2
MONTCLAIR LN	HTB	HB47	16700	21	D5
MONTCLIFF DR	CO	ET		29B	A2
MONTE DR	WSTM	WSTM		22	A3
MONTEAGO RD	CO	LB		35	C5
MONTEANO LN	YL	YL		8	B3
MONTEBELLO PL	MVJO	SJ91		29B	B4
MONTE CARLO	IRV	SA14		28	F3
MONTE CARLO	NB	NB60		32	C2
MONTE CARLO CIR	HTB	HB	9700	30	F4
MONTE CARLO DR	LAG	LB51	100	34	A1
MONTE CARLO DR	SA	SA	2500	16	E6
MONTE CARLO WY	MVJO	SJ92		29D	E2
MONTE CARLO WY	PLA	PLA	2200	7	B2
MONTECITO	CO	LB		29D	B6
MONTECITO	CO	LB77		36	B1
MONTECITO	GGR	GG	10000	15	F2
MONTECITO	TUS	TUS		24	B3
MONTECITO DR	HTB	HB	6000	20	F4
MONTECITO DR	NB	CDLM		32	D6
MONTECITO DR	YL	YL	19000	8	B4
MONTECITO LN	MVJO	SJ91		29B	B3
MONTECITO PL	OR	OR		18	C1
MONTECITO RD	CO	LALM	11500	14	B4
MONTECITO ST	PLA	PLA	1100	7	C4
MONTECITO WY	CYP	CYP	5700	9	E6
MONTE COLLNS WY	LALM	LALM		14	B1
MONTEFINO LN	ANA	AN		13	D3
MONTEGO DR	HTB	HB	3700	20	C4
MONTEGO WY	TUS	TUS	16600	23	E3
MONTEGO BAY	DPT	LB77		37	D4
MONTE HERMOSO	CO	LB	21000	29A	A6
MONTELEGRO	IRV	SA14		29	A3
MONTELLANO	MVJO	SJ91	22100	29B	D2
MONTEMAR	CO	LB77		36	B1
MONTE MR VIS DR	FUL	FL	700	6	B4
MONTERAS ST	CO	LAG		35	F3
MONTEREY	IRV	SA		32A	B1
MONTEREY	MVJO	SJ92		52	E6
MONTEREY AV	CM	CM	2700	27	E4
MONTEREY CIR	NB	CDLM		32	D6
MONTEREY CIR	PLA	PLA	300	7	A5
MONTEREY CIR	WSTM	WSTM	8700	21	D3
MONTEREY CIR	YL	YL		7	F3
MONTEREY CT	LALM	LALM		14	C3
MONTEREY DR	LAG	LB51	100	34	C2
MONTEREY LN	CO	LB56		29C	C3
MONTEREY LN	HTB	HB49	16000	20	D4
MONTEREY LN	LAP	BP23	7200	9	E1
MONTEREY LN	SCL	SC72	400	39	C4
MONTEREY PL	FUL	FL33		5	E4
MONTEREY RD	OR	OR	100	17	D3
MONTEREY RD	SB	SB	1300	14	A6
MONTEREY ST	ANA	AN	100	10	F3
MONTEREY ST	LAG	LB	31000	35	A5
MONTEREY ST	LAH	LAH	900	1	E3
MONTEREY ST	TUS	TUS		24	B3
MONTEREY WY	PLA	PLA	300	7	B6
MONTERO AV	NB	NB		31	E6
MONTE ROYALE DR	MVJO	SJ92		29D	E2
MONTE ROYALE ST	CO	LB		29C	E3
MONTERRA	CO	ET		29B	B1
MONTERRA	CO	ET		52	B6
MONTESA DR	CO	LB	30900	35	C5
MONTESSORI AV	PLA	PLA	300	7	B2
MONTE VERDE DR	CO	LB	24800	35	F2
MONTEVIDEO AV E	PLA	PLA	1200	7	D4
MONTEVIDEO DR	PLA	PLA	1100	7	D4
MONTE VISTA	CO	LB53		29D	A2
MONTE VISTA	SCL	SC72	200	39	A1
MONTE VISTA AV	CM	CM	100	27	F6
MONTE VISTA AV	CM	CM27	200	31	F1
MONTE VISTA AV	CO	LAH	2000	1	F5
MONTE VISTA AV	CO	CM27	300	31	F1
MONTE VIS AV N	LAH	LAH	100	1	F5
MONTE VIS AV S	LAH	LAH	100	1	F5
MONTE VISTA CIR	VPK	OR67	18700	13	A4
MONTE VISTA RD	ANA	AN		8	F6
MONTE VISTA RD	ANA	AN08		40	A6
MONTE VISTA RD	ANA	AN		43	A1
MONTEZUMA CIR	FTNV	SA08	10000	27	A1
MONTGOMERY	IRV	SA		29	D2
MONTGOMERY CIR	PLA	PLA	2200	7	B2
MONTGOMERY DR	WSTM	WSTM		14	E6
MONTGOMERY DR	WSTM	WSTM		20	E1
MONTGOMERY PL E	OR	OR	4700	18	B4
MONTGOMERY PL S	OR	OR	400	17	C4
MONTGOMERY WY	ANA	AN07		13	A2
MONTICELLO	IRV	SA		24	E6
MONTICELLO AV	BPK	BP	5500	5	D4
MONTICELLO CIR	WSTM	WSTM	8100	21	C1
MONTICELLO ST	CO	LAG		35	F3
MONTIEL	MVJO	SJ91	26000	29D	C3
MONTILLA	SCL	SC72		39	E1
MONTILLA LN	MVJO	SJ91	24300	29B	B6
MONTLAKE DR	GGR	GG	11500	15	E2
MONTOVA	CO	LB		29A	B4
MONTOYA CIR	HTB	HB	6500	26	A1
MONTPELLIER	LAG	LB		35	B6
MONTPELLIER	NB	NB60		32	D5
MONTPELLIER AV	IRV	SA	15200	29	D3
MONT POINT	CO	ET		29B	A2
MONTRE WY	CM	CM27	2400	31	F2
MONTREAL CIR	PLA	PLA	2200	7	B2
MONTROSE	MVJO	SJ91		29D	C6
MONTROSE AV	WSTM	WSTM	8700	21	D2
MONTSERRAT ST	CYP	CYP	11200	14	F2
MONTWOOD AV E&W	LAH	LAH	100	2	A6
MONTY LN	CO	SIL	28200	50	D2
MONUMENT ST	ANA	AN	200	10	E4
MONZA	TUS	TUS		24	C4
MOODY AV N	FUL	FL	2600	6	F3
MOODY AV S	FUL	FL	200	6	F6
MOODY CIR	HTB	HB		20	E5
MOODY DR	CO	OR67	28800	50	E6
MOODY ST	CO	CYP	8200	9	D6
MOODY ST	CYP	CYP	9100	9	D6
MOODY ST	LAP	BP23	7000	9	D3
MOONBEAM DR	HTB	HB47	6900	21	B3
MOONBEAM DR	PLA	PLA	300	7	A5
MOONBEAM PL	FUL	FL33	1600	5	E4
MOONBEAM ST	PLA	PLA	500	7	A4
MOONCREST CIR	BREA	BREA		2	D4
MOONCREST CIR	HTB	HB	20400	26	E5
MOONCREST ST	WSTM	WSTM	14000	21	E1
MOONDEW	IRV	SA		32A	C4
MOON DUST	IRV	SA		32A	C4
MOONFIELD DR	HTB	HB		25	F2
MOONFIELD DR	HTB	HB		26	A2
MOONFIRE DR	DPT	DPT		37	E4
MOONGLOW LN	HTB	HB47	16100	21	B4
MOONGLOW LN	SJC	SJ75		36	D6
MOONLIGHT	IRV	SA		32A	C4
MOONLIGHT CIR	HTB	HB47	7000	21	B4
MOONMIST CIR	HTB	HB		30	C1
MOONRAY	IRV	SA		32A	B3
MOON RIDGE	CO	ET		52	C4
MOONRIDGE AV	SA	SA	4300	22	C1
MOON RING CT	DPT	DPT		37	A5
MOONRISE CT	NB	NB63		31	A2
MOON RIVER CIR	FTNV	SA08		26	F3
MOONSAIL DR	DPT	LB77		37	E3
MOON SHADOW	IRV	SA		32A	C4
MOONSHADOW CIR	HTB	HB47		21	C5
MOONSTONE LN	CO	ET	23000	29A	F3
MOONSTONE ST	ANA	AN	1300	10	A6
MOONSTONE ST	ANA	AN04		15	A1
MOON STONE ST	BREA	BREA		2	C5
MOONTIDE CIR	HTB	HB	20000	26	E5
MOOR AV	CO	SJ91		29A	F5
MOORDALE CIR	STN	STN		15	B4
MOORE AV	FUL	FL33	1800	5	E5
MOORE AV	SA	SA04	1500	27	F1
MOORE AV	SA	SA		28	A1
MOORE CIR	HTB	HB	9800	26	F4
MOORE CT	IRV	SA	3900	24	C6
MOOREA LN	HTB	HB46	19100	27	A3
MOOREA WY	LAG	LB51		34	E2
MOORE OAKS RD	CO	LB53		29D	A4
MOORGATE DR	LAP	BP23	4500	9	C3
MOOR GLEN	CO	ET		52	A5
MOORHEN LN	CO	LB56		29C	B1
MOORPARK DR	BREA	BREA	1700	7	A1
MOORPARK DR	HTB	HB	9000	26	E3
MOORSVIEW	CO	ET		52	B6
MOPAN RIVER AV	FTNV	SA08		27	A2
MORADA DR	CO	OR	10500	13	C6
MORADA DR	CO	OR	10600	18	C1
MORAGA ST	ANA	AN	600	10	E3
MORA KAI LN	HTB	HB	18900	26	C3
MORAL RD	SJC	SJ75		38	B3
MORALES	MVJO	SJ91	25000	29D	C2
MORAN ST	WSTM	WSTM	14300	21	E1
MORAVA AV	ANA	AN	1800	11	F4
MORAVA PL	ANA	AN	1600	11	F4
MOREHEAD DR	HTB	HB	8400	26	D1
MOREL RD	TUS	TUS	2400	24	B5
MORELAND DR	OR	OR	600	17	D3
MORELIA AV	FUL	FL	2200	6	B3
MORENA	IRV	SA		28	F5
MORENA DR	MVJO	SJ91		29D	B4
MORESBY WY	CO	ET		29B	B1
MORESBY WY	CO	ET		52	B6
MORGAN	IRV	SA18		29A	D1
MORGAN	IRV	SA18		51	D6
MORGAN CIR	TUS	TUS	1300	23	E5
MORGAN LN	ANA	AN	1900	16	C2
MORGAN LN	GGR	GG	11400	16	C3
MORGAN LN	HTB	HB47	17500	21	C6
MORGAN LN	HTB	HB	17500	26	C1
MORGAN PL	SA	SA	3000	28	B1
MORGAN ST	OR	OR	700	17	F1
MORGAN WY	BPK	BP	6200	9	F2
MORGAN WY	CYP	CYP	11600	15	A2
MORI LN	OR	OR	2000	12	E5
MORINO WY	TUS	SA10	3000	29	A1
MORION CIR	HTB	HB	6400	26	A1
MORITZ DR	HTB	HB		20	A6
MORNING BREEZE	IRV	SA		32A	B3
MORNING CYN RD	NB	CDLM	200	33	B2
MORNING DEW	IRV	SA		32A	A2
MORNING DEW DR	BREA	BREA		3	B5
MORNING DEW WY	YL	YL		40	E6
MORNING DOVE	CO	LB77		37	F2
MORNING DOVE	CO	LB77		38	A2
MORNING DOVE	IRV	SA		29	B2
MORNINGFLWR CIR	BREA	BREA		3	A5
MORNING GLEN	CO	ET		52	A5
MORNING GLORY	IRV	SA		32A	B3
MORNING GLRY AV	FTNV	SA08	10300	22	A4
MORNING GLY CIR	FTNV	SA08	10500	22	A4
MORNING GLRY PL	FTNV	SA08	10400	22	A4
MORNING GLRY RD	TUS	TUS	14100	24	A5
MORNING GLRY ST	BREA	BREA		3	C6
MORNINGLORY WY	OR	OR		18	D3
MORNING MIST	IRV	SA		32A	C4
MORNING RIDGE	CO	LB		29C	D4
MORNINGSIDE	IRV	SA		32A	B3
MORNINGSIDE AV	GGR	GG	12500	16	D6
MORNINGSIDE AV	SA	SA		16	C6
MORNINGSIDE AV	SA	SA	3500	22	C1
MORNINGSIDE CIR	LAG	LB51	1500	34	F3
MORNINGSIDE DR	GGR	GG43	10200	22	A1
MORNINGSIDE DR	LAG	LB51	1000	34	F3
MORNINGSIDE DR	LAG	LB51	2500	35	A2
MORNINGSIDE LN	CO	SA	12300	24	C2
MORNINGSIDE ST	OR	OR	1600	12	E6
MORNING SONG	IRV	SA		32A	C4
MORNINGSTAR	CO	SJ79		59	D3
MORNING STAR	IRV	SA		32A	B3
MORNINGSTAR DR	ANA	AN08		43	B1
MORNING STAR DR	HTB	HB	4000	20	C5
MORNING STAR LN	DPT	DPT		37	E4
MORNING STAR LN	NB	NB	700	31	E4
MORNINGSTAR LN	SJC	SJ75		36	D6
MORNING STAR RD	CO	ET		29A	F1
MORNINGSTAR RD	CO	ET	25400	29B	A1
MORNING SUN	IRV	SA		32A	B3
MORNING TIDE DR	HTB	HB		26	A4
MORNING VIEW	IRV	SA		32A	B3
MORNINGVIEW DR	ANA	AN		13	D3
MORNING WOOD DR	CO	LB		35	D6
MORO CIR	PLA	PLA	1200	7	D4
MORO LN	ANA	AN	900	10	E3
MORO PL	ANA	AN	2300	10	E3
MORO AZUL	MVJO	SJ91		29D	C3
MOROBE CIR	DPT	LB77		37	C1

111
ORANGE CO.

1990 ORANGE COUNTY STREET INDEX

MORONGO PL
NEWCASTLE AV

STREET	CITY	P.O. ZONE	BLOCK	PAGE	GRID
MORONGO PL	CO	LB	29900	35	E3
MORONGO ST	FTNV	SA08	8500	26	D2
MORRIE LN	GGR	GG	11700	15	F4
MORRIS AV	LAH	LAH	2200	1	E4
MORRIS RD	IRV	SA		24	E6
MORRISTOWN CIR	HTB	HB	20200	26	F5
MORRISTOWN LN	CM	CM	100	27	E6
MORRO CT	CO	LB	25000	29C	F2
MORRO CT	CO	LB	28000	29C	E6
MORRO DR	MVJO	SJ92		29D	C2
MORRO BAY DR	NB	CDLM		32	D5
MORRO BAY LN	HTB	HB47	17400	21	A6
MORROW CIR	VPK	OR67		12	F6
MORSE AV	IRV	SA		28	D3
MORSE AV	PLA	PLA	300	7	C4
MORSE CIR	HTB	HB	16700	20	C6
MORSE DR	SA	SA	800	22	C2
MORTIMER ST	SA	SA	400	23	B1
MORTON ST	CO	TUS	14300	24	A1
MOSBY	IRV	SA		24	C5
MOSELLE CIR	CO	YL	6400	8	C6
MOSHER DR	TUS	TUS	15400	23	E5
MOSQUERO LN	MVJO	SJ91	24600	29B	B6
MOSQUERO LN	MVJO	SJ91		29D	B1
MOSS CIR	PLA	PLA	600	7	C3
MOSS DR	HTB	HB	5900	20	E6
MOSS ST	LAG	LB51	100	34	E4
MOSSCREEK RD	CO	ET	24100	29A	D2
MOSSFORD DR	HTB	HB	8500	26	D4
MOSS GLEN	IRV	SA		32A	A2
MOSS GLEN AV	FTNV	SA08	9500	21	F4
MOSS HILL LN	CO	LB		29C	D2
MOSSLER ST	CO	AN04	11500	15	C2
MOSSVALE CIR	HTB	HB	5500	25	E1
MOSSWOOD DR	ANA	AN		8	E5
MOSSWOOD WY	CO	ET		29A	F1
MOSSWOOD WY	CO	ET		51	F6
MOSTRAZA	CO	SJ88		59	B2
MOTHERLODE CT	CO	LB56		29C	E6
MOTZ ST	GGR	GG	11200	15	E2
MOULINS CIR	IRV	SA	15300	29	C3
MOULTON PKWY	CO	LB	23500	29A	B5
MOULTON PKWY	CO	LB	22000	29A	B3
MOULTON PKWY	CO	LB	24900	29C	D2
MOULTON PKWY	CO	LB56		29C	F6
MOULTON PKWY	CO	LB		35	F1
MOUNT DR	GGR	GG	11100	16	A2
MT ACKERMAN CIR	FTNV	SA08		22	C4
MT ACOMA CIR	FTNV	SA08	16600	22	B5
MOUNTAIN	MVJO	SJ92		52	D6
MOUNTAIN AV	OR	OR		13	C5
MOUNTAIN CT	BREA	BREA	600	2	F5
MOUNTAIN RD	LAG	LB51	100	34	E4
MOUNTAIN ASH	IRV	SA		29	C4
MOUNTAIN GN CIR	CO	ET		52	C6
MOUNTAIN GN RD	ANA	AN07		12	F3
MTN GROVE CIR	MVJO	SJ92		29B	F6
MOUNTAIN LAUREL	IRV	SA		29	C2
MOUNTAIN LP TR	ANA	AN		13	C3
MOUNTAIN RDG RD	FUL	FL		6	F3
MOUNTAIN VIA	ANA	AN	2700	10	D4
MOUNTAIN VIEW	IRV	SA		32	F2
MOUNTAIN VW AV	ANA	AN	1700	16	E2
MOUNTAIN VW AV	CO	YL	5592	8	A4
MOUNTAIN VW AV	YL	YL	5000	8	A3
MTN VIEW AV S	LAH	LAH	600	2	A5
MTN VIEW AV W	LAH	LAH	100	2	A5
MOUNTAIN VW CIR	VPK	OR67		12	F5
MOUNTAIN VW CT	OR	SA05		18	C3
MOUNTAIN VW DR	LAG	LB51	3100	29C	A6
MOUNTAIN VW DR	LAG	LB51	2900	35	A1
MOUNTAIN VW DR	TUS	TUS	100	23	E2
MOUNTAIN VW LN	CO	SJ		52	E3
MOUNTAINVIEW LN	HTB	HB48		25	E3
MOUNTAIN VW PL	YL	YL	5500	8	B4
MTN VIEW PL N	FUL	FL	300	6	E5
MTN VIEW PL S	FUL	FL	100	6	E6
MOUNTAIN VW RD	CO	SIL		50	E2
MOUNTAIN VW RD	CO	SJ	31100	56	C6
MTN VIEW ST N	SA	SA	100	22	C2
MTN VIEW ST S	SA	SA	400	22	C2
MTN VIEW ST S	SA	SA03		22	C3
MOUNTAIN VW TR	CO	SIL		53	A1
MOUNTAINWOOD WY	CO	ET		29A	F1
MOUNTAINWOOD WY	CO	ET		51	F6
MT ALLYSON CIR	FTNV	SA08	16800	22	C5
MT ARARAT CIR	FTNV	SA08	16400	22	B4
MT BDN-POWLL ST	FTNV	SA08	16100	22	B4
MOUNT BALDY CIR	BPK	BP	9600	10	A5
MT BALDY CIR	FTNV	SA08	18200	27	B2
MT BARNARD DR	BPK	BP	9600	10	A5

STREET	CITY	P.O. ZONE	BLOCK	PAGE	GRID
MT BAXTER CIR	FTNV	SA08	16600	22	B5
MT BODIE ST	FTNV	SA08	16200	22	C4
MT CACHUMA CIR	FTNV	SA08	16600	22	B5
MT CARMEL CT	FTNV	SA08	16000	22	C4
MT CASTILE CIR	FTNV	SA08		26	F3
MT CHERIE CIR	FTNV	SA08		27	A2
MT CIMARRON ST	FTNV	SA08		26	F3
MT CITADEL ST	FTNV	SA08		22	B5
MT CLIFFWD CIR	FTNV	SA08		22	C6
MT COLLIEN ST	FTNV	SA08	16800	22	C5
MT COOK CIR	FTNV	SA08	16500	22	C5
MT COULTER ST	FTNV	SA08		26	F1
MT CRAIG CIR	FTNV	SA08	16200	22	B4
MT DANA CIR	BPK	BP	9600	10	A5
MT DANA CIR	FTNV	SA08	16200	22	B4
MT DARWIN CIR	FTNV	SA08	16600	22	B5
MT DEMETER CIR	FTNV	SA08		26	E3
MT DIABLO RD	CO	LB		29D	A3
MT DUNHAVEN ST	FTNV	SA08	16400	22	B4
MT EDEN CIR	FTNV	SA08	16800	22	C5
MT EDEN ST	FTNV	SA08	16900	22	C5
MT EMMA ST	FTNV	SA08	16300	22	B4
MT EREBUS CT	FTNV	SA08	16100	22	C4
MT ERIN CIR	FTNV	SA08	16800	22	C5
MT FLETCHER CIR	FTNV	SA08		22	B5
MT GALE CIR	FTNV	SA08		21	F5
MT GIST CIR	FTNV	SA08		22	D4
MT GUSTIN ST	FTNV	SA08		22	D4
MT HANNA CIR	FTNV	SA08		21	F5
MT HARKNESS ST	FTNV	SA08	16100	22	B4
MT HENRY ST	FTNV	SA08		21	F6
MT HERRMANN ST	FTNV	SA08		22	B6
MT HICKS ST	FTNV	SA08	16000	22	B4
MT HOFFMAN CIR	FTNV	SA08	16600	22	B5
MT HOOD DR	CO	SA	13200	17	F5
MT HOPE ST	FTNV	SA08	16900	22	B5
MT HUTCHINGS ST	FTNV	SA08	16800	22	C6
MT ISLIP CIR	FTNV	SA08	16200	22	B4
MT JACKSON ST	FTNV	SA08	15900	22	D4
MOUNTJOY DR	HTB	HB	7400	26	B2
MT KELLER	FTNV	SA08	16400	22	C4
MT KENYA CT	FTNV	SA08	16100	22	B5
MT KIBBY ST	FTNV	SA08	16500	22	B5
MT KRISTINA ST	FTNV	SA08		26	E2
MT LANGLEY ST	FTNV	SA08	18200	27	B2
MT LILITA CT	FTNV	SA08		22	C5
MT LISTER CT	FTNV	SA08	16000	22	B5
MT LOMINA CT	FTNV	SA08		22	C6
MT LOWE CIR	FTNV	SA08	16100	22	B4
MT LOWE DR	BPK	BP	6600	10	A5
MT LYNDORA CT	FTNV	SA08		22	C6
MT MARCEY CT	FTNV	SA08	16100	22	B5
MT MARCUS ST	FTNV	SA08		22	B5
MT MATTERHRN ST	FTNV	SA08	15900	22	D4
MT MCKINLEY BL	OR	OR		13	B5
MT MENNES CT	FTNV	SA08	16100	22	B5
MT MICHAELS CIR	FTNV	SA08		22	C5
MT MILLS ST	FTNV	SA08	16800	22	C5
MT MITCHELL CIR	FTNV	SA08	15900	22	D4
MT MORGAN CIR	FTNV	SA08		26	E3
MT MUSALA CT	FTNV	SA08	16100	22	B5
MT NEOTA ST	FTNV	SA08	16500	22	C5
MT NEWBERRY CIR	FTNV	SA08	16400	22	C4
MT NIMBUS CIR	FTNV	SA08	16100	22	B4
MT NIMBUS ST	FTNV	SA08	16300	22	B4
MT NORBY CIR	FTNV	SA08		26	E1
MT OLANCHA ST	FTNV	SA08	16100	22	B5
MT OLSEN CIR	FTNV	SA08		22	B5
MT PALOMAR DR	BPK	BP	6500	10	A5
MT PICO CT	FTNV	SA08	16000	22	B5
MT PRIETO CIR	FTNV	SA08		22	D4
MT RAINIER DR	CO	LB77	31900	37	D1
MT RIPLEY DR	BPK	BP	6500	10	A5
MT RIPLEY DR	CYP	CYP	6200	9	F5
MT ROBERT CT	FTNV	SA08	11700	22	B5
MT SCHELIN CIR	FTNV	SA08		26	E3
MT SHASTA CIR	BPK	BP	9600	10	A5
MT SHAY ST	FTNV	SA08	18000	27	B1
MT SHELLY CIR	FTNV	SA08	16500	22	C5
MT SHERROD CIR	FTNV	SA08	16500	21	F5
MT STEWART CIR	FTNV	SA08		26	E2
MT TAHAT ST	FTNV	SA08	15900	22	B5
MT TODD ST	FTNV	SA08	16500	22	B5
MT TRICIA ST	FTNV	SA08	10600	22	B4
MT VERNON AV	OR	OR	1900	17	E2
MT VERNON ST	CO	LB		35	E6
MT VERNON ST	CO	LB77		37	E1
MT VERNON WY	PLA	PLA	600	7	B5
MT VICTORY ST	FTNV	SA08	16800	22	B5
MT WALTON CIR	FTNV	SA08		26	F3
MT WASHINGTN ST	FTNV	SA08	18000	27	B1

STREET	CITY	P.O. ZONE	BLOCK	PAGE	GRID
MT WATERMAN DR	BPK	BP	9600	10	A5
MT WATERMAN ST	FTNV	SA08		27	A2
MT WHITNEY DR	BPK	BP	6500	10	A5
MT WHITNEY ST	FTNV	SA08	16800	22	B5
MT WYNNE CIR	FTNV	SA08		22	B6
MT YOUNIS ST	FTNV	SA08	16700	22	C5
MOVIUS DR	GGR	GG	12000	15	F3
MOYA	CO	LB	23000	29A	A4
MOZER DR	CO	LB56		29C	E4
MOZZONI ISLE	IRV	SA14		28	D5
MUELA	MVJO	SJ92	24400	29B	E5
MUIR	IRV	SA20		24	E6
MUIR	IRV	SA		29	E1
MUIR DR	BPK	BP		5	C4
MUIR DR	OR	OR		18	B1
MUIR WY	LAH	LAH	2100	2	C4
MUIR BEACH CIR	NB	CDLM		32	D6
MUIRFIELD	CO	SJ79		59	D2
MUIRFIELD	MVJO	SJ92		29B	E4
MUIRFIELD	NB	NB		32	B4
MUIRFIELD CIR	HTB	HB		25	F4
MUIRLANDS BLVD	CO	ET	23800	29A	D2
MUIRLANDS BLVD	CO	SJ91	25500	29B	A6
MUIRLANDS BLVD	CO	SJ91	25900	29D	A1
MUIRLANDS BLVD	IRV	SA18		29A	C2
MUIRWOOD DR	BREA	BREA		6	F1
MUIR WOODS CT	FTNV	SA08	18000	27	A2
MUJICA PL	BREA	BREA		7	D1
MULBERRY AV	BPK	BP	8200	10	C3
MULBERRY AV	BREA	BREA	700	6	D1
MULBERRY AV	FUL	FL	3000	6	D1
MULBERRY AV	IRV	SA	14700	29	C1
MULBERRY CIR	FTNV	SA08	16700	21	E5
MULBERRY LN	CO	OR	18900	18	B2
MULBERRY LN	CO	SJ79		52	F4
MULBERRY LN	GGR	GG	6900	15	A4
MULBERRY ST	CYP	CYP		9	C3
MULBERRY ST	OR	OR69		18	E3
MULBERRY WY	YL	YL		40	D5
MULLEIN CIR	FTNV	SA08	16000	21	F4
MULLER ST	ANA	AN	100	11	A4
MULLIN RD	CO	ET	23400	29A	D3
MUMFORD DR	CO	SA	1300	18	C5
MUNERA	MVJO	SJ92	28400	29B	E2
MUNGALL DR	ANA	AN	3500	10	A5
MUNSON RD	GGR	GG	13900	16	C6
MUNSTER DR	HTB	HB	8100	26	D5
MUNTON CIR	TUS	TUS	1900	24	A5
MUPPET WY	CO	ET		29A	E4
MURAL CIR	HTB	HB	20000	26	E5
MURDY CIR	HTB	HB47	7300	21	B4
MURFIELD CT	FUL	FL		6	C2
MURIEL LN	ANA	AN		8	C6
MURIEL PL	CO	SA	18700	18	B6
MURIN ISLE LN	CO	ET	23500	29A	D3
MURLINE DR	GGR	GG	9200	15	E2
MURO	MVJO	SJ92		29B	D2
MUROC PL	FUL	FL33	200	5	E6
MURPHY AV	IRV	SA	17300	28	E3
MURPHY AV	SA	SA	100	28	B2
MURRAY LN	CM	CM	3000	27	D3
MURRAY LN	CO	SA	11300	18	D6
MURRAY ST	PLA	PLA	100	7	A5
MURRE LN	CO	LB	29100	35	D2
MURRELET DR	CO	LB	28500	35	D1
MURRIETTA PL	OR	OR		18	B2
MUSIAL ST	PLA	PLA	2200	7	D2
MUSICK	CO	SA		51	D5
MUSTANG AV	OR	OR	1300	13	D6
MUSTANG DR	CO	LB	24900	29C	F3
MUSTANG DR	GGR	GG	11900	16	C5
MUSTANG DR	YL	YL		8	C2
MUSTANG SPGS RD	CO	SIL		50	E1
MUTHER LN	HTB	HB	17900	25	F1
MYKONOS	CO	LB77		35	E4
MYCROFT LN	HTB	HB47	16400	21	A5
MYFORD RD	TUS	TUS		24	C4
MYNA LN	FTNV	SA08	9500	26	F1
MYRA AV	ANA	AN	3600	10	A6
MYRA AV	BPK	BP	6000	9	F6
MYRA AV	BPK	BP	6500	10	A6
MYRA AV	CYP	CYP	4000	9	C6
MYRA AV	LALM	LALM	3800	9	C6
MYRAN DR	CM	CM27	2100	31	C1
MYRTLE AV	TUS	TUS	100	23	E2
MYRTLE AV	TUS	TUS	15700	23	E3
MYRTLE DR	HTB	HB47	6200	21	A4
MYRTLE ST	IRV	SA	3500	29	B1
MYRTLE ST	LAG	LB51	100	34	C2
MYRTLE ST E	SA	SA	100	23	A2

STREET	CITY	P.O. ZONE	BLOCK	PAGE	GRID
MYRTLE ST W	SA	SA	1300	22	E2
MYRTLE ST W	SA	SA	700	23	A2
MYRTLEWOOD CIR	WSTM	WSTM	8200	21	D3
MYRTLEWOOD ST	CM	CM	1500	27	C4
MYRTLEWOOD ST	FTNV	SA08	16300	21	E4
MYSTIC AV	FUL	FL	2800	7	A2
MYSTIC LN	ANA	AN	2300	10	E5
MYSTIC LN	CO	AN04	9700	10	E5
MYSTIC LN	CO	SA	10600	18	C4
MYSTIC LN	LAG	LB51	700	34	E2
MYSTIC WY	LAG	LB51	500	34	E2
MYSTIC VIEW	LAG	LB51	600	34	D2
MYTINGER LN	HTB	HB47	16500	21	A5
N					
N ST	ETMC	SA09		51	C3
N ST	NB	CDLM	2100	33	A1
NACCOME DR	MVJO	SJ91	26100	29B	B6
NADA LN	HTB	HB47		21	D4
NADA ST	LAH	LAH	200	1	E4
NADIA WY	GGR	GG43		16	E1
NADINE CIR	GGR	GG	12200	16	C3
NADINE DR	ANA	AN		13	C1
NADINE LN	GGR	GG	12500	16	C4
NADINE RIV CIR	FTNV	SA08		26	E2
NAECO WY	CO	SIL	30400	53	A1
NAKOMA DR	SA	SA	500	22	D4
NALU CIR	HTB	HB	16600	20	C5
NAMURIA ST	OR	OR	1900	12	D5
NANCE CIR	OR	OR69		18	C3
NANCITA CIR	PLA	PLA		7	F6
NANCITA LN	HTB	HB		20	D4
NANCITA ST	ANA	AN	600	10	D3
NANCY CIR	LAP	BP23	7800	9	D2
NANCY DR	HTB	HB47	7500	21	B4
NANCY LN	CM	CM	1000	27	B6
NANCY LN	FUL	FL	700	6	D3
NANCY LN	SA	SA	1700	16	E6
NANCY ST	CYP	CYP	9200	9	E5
NANCY JANE CT	DPT	DPT	33500	38	A3
NANCY LEE DR	WSTM	WSTM	14000	21	A1
NANTES CIR	IRV	SA	15100	29	C3
NANTUCKET	ANA	AN		13	B3
NANTUCKET	IRV	SA		24	E6
NANTUCKET CT	CYP	CYP	11300	15	A2
NANTUCKET DR	HTB	HB	9300	26	E4
NANTUCKET LN	YL	YL		40	B6
NANTUCKET PL	SA	SA		22	E2
NANTUCKET PL	TUS	TUS	1900	24	A5
NANTUCKET ST	LAH	LAH	1000	2	B3
NANTUCKET ST	WSTM	WSTM	15300	21	D3
NANTUCKET WY	GGR	GG		15	D4
NANWOOD ST	LAH	LAH	1200	2	A6
NAOMI AV	BPK	BP	6500	10	A2
NAPA CIR	HTB	HB	6100	20	F6
NAPA PL	ANA	AN	2000	11	F4
NAPA PL	FUL	FL33	200	5	E6
NAPA ST	CO	TUS	1000	24	B1
NAPA ST	CO	LB56		29C	D3
NAPA WY	STN	STN		10	E4
NAPA WY	STN	STN		15	B2
NAPA RIVER CT	FTNV	SA08	10200	27	A1
NAPLES	NB	NB60		32	B2
NAPLES AV	PLA	PLA	1100	7	C4
NAPLES DR	HTB	HB	8500	26	D3
NAPLES PL	FUL	FL33	1300	10	E1
NAPLES WY	MVJO	SJ92		29D	F3
NAPOLI	CO	LB		29A	B4
NAPOLI	NB	CDLM		32	D5
NAPOLI DR	BREA	BREA	200	2	E5
NAPOLI WY	CM	CM27	2400	31	F1
NAPOLI WY	MVJO	SJ92		29D	E3
NARANJA	MVJO	SJ91	27700	29B	D1
NARANJA RD	SJC	SJ75	2400	38	B3
NARBONNE	CO	LB77		35	E4
NARBONNE	NB	CDLM		32	D5
NARBONNE WY	CM	CM27	2400	31	F1
NARCISO	MVJO	SJ92	27800	29B	D6
NARCISSUS AV	NB	CDLM	200	33	B2
NARCISSUS ST	WSTM	WSTM	15500	21	F3
NARDA ST	ANA	AN	200	11	D5
NASA ST	BREA	BREA		3	C6
NASHAWENA CT	CYP	CYP	11300	15	A2
NASHUA ST	LAH	LAH	800	1	F5
NASHUA ST	LAH	LAH		2	A5
NASHVILLE AV	HTB	HB	200	26	C5
NASSAU DR	CM	CM	200	27	D6
NASSAU DR	SB	SB	13000	19	C5
NASSAU LN	HTB	HB	16100	20	F4
NASSAU RD	CM	CM	300	27	D6

STREET	CITY	P.O. ZONE	BLOCK	PAGE	GRID
NATA	NB	NB		32	A2
NATAL DR	WSTM	WSTM	7000	15	B5
NATALIE RAE LN	CO	LB53		29C	E6
NATAMA CT	CO	LB	25000	29C	F2
NATCHEZ AV	PLA	PLA	2400	7	C2
NATHAN CIR	DPT	DPT		37	E2
NATIONAL AV	CM	CM27	2000	31	B1
NATIONAL LN	HTB	HB	20800	26	F6
NATIONAL ST	ANA	AN	1700	11	D1
NATIONAL PK DR	CO	LB	31900	35	D6
NATIONAL PK DR	CO	LB77	31700	37	C1
NATOMA AV	WSTM	WSTM	8500	21	D3
NAURU ST	CYP	CYP	6100	14	F2
NAUTICAL ST	ANA	AN	2000	16	E2
NAUTICUS ISLE	DPT	LB77		37	D4
NAUTILUS DR	GGR	GG		16	D6
NAUTILUS DR	HTB	HB	9300	26	E5
NAUTILUS LN	NB	NB	2000	31	E2
NAUTILUS WY	SJC	SJ75		38	A2
NAVAJO	TUS	TUS		24	B3
NAVAJO AV	PLA	PLA	2400	7	C2
NAVAJO DR	BPK	BP	6500	10	A2
NAVAJO DR	CO	ET		29A	F2
NAVAJO RD	WSTM	WSTM	6000	14	F6
NAVAJO RD	WSTM	WSTM	6200	15	A6
NAVALOSA	MVJO	SJ91		29D	C2
NAVARRE	IRV	SA		28	F5
NAVARRO PL	OR	OR	1200	13	C6
NAVARRO PL	OR	OR		18	C1
NAYSHON CT	CYP	CYP	11300	15	A2
NEAL DR	WSTM	WSTM		22	A2
NEARFIELD LN	LAP	BP23	7600	9	D2
NEARGATE DR	HTB	HB		20	E6
NEARGATE DR	HTB	HB		25	E1
NEARING DR	CO	AN04	11500	15	C3
NEBRASKA AV	PLA	PLA	800	12	A1
NEBRASKA LN	CM	CM	3200	27	B3
NEBRASKA PL	CM	CM	3200	27	B3
NEBRIJA	MVJO	SJ92	28200	29B	E4
NECATINA WY	CYP	CYP	6900	15	B3
NECTARINE LN	SA	SA		22	E3
NECTARINE ST	FTNV	SA08	17000	21	F5
NEDA	MVJO	SJ92		29D	C3
NEDRA PL	ANA	AN04	1700	15	F1
NEECE ST	WSTM	WSTM	15000	21	D2
NEELEY CIR	HTB	HB	4800	20	D5
NEIGHBORS AV	ANA	AN	1800	11	A2
NELL CIR	PLA	PLA	500	7	B2
NELLIE GAIL RD	CO	LB	24000	29C	F4
NELLIE GAIL RD	CO	LB	25600	29D	A2
NELSON PL	FUL	FL	3400	6	B1
NELSON ST	CYP	CYP	5500	9	E4
NELSON ST	GGR	GG	12000	16	A4
NELSON ST	WSTM	WSTM		21	E4
NENNO AV	PLA	PLA	700	7	A3
NEOLANI DR	HTB	HB	9300	30	E1
NEPTUNE AV	BREA	BREA		2	D5
NEPTUNE AV	NB	NB	4600	31	A4
NEPTUNE AV	SB	SB	100	19	F3
NEPTUNE CIR	WSTM	WSTM	8900	21	E4
NEPTUNE CT	GGR	GG	13400	16	C5
NEPTUNE DR	BPK	BP	8400	10	C3
NEPTUNE DR	DPT	DPT		37	F2
NEPTUNE DR	HTB	HB		30	C1
NEPTUNE PL	ANA	AN	900	11	A5
NEPTUNE ST	ANA	AN	600	11	A5
NESTALL RD	LAG	LB51	3000	35	A1
NESTLE AV	CYP	CYP	4300	9	C6
NETHERWAY DR	HTB	HB	9500	26	F6
NETTLEWOOD CIR	HTB	HB	18700	26	D3
NEVADA AV	CM	CM		27	B2
NEVADA DR	HTB	HB	5500	20	F1
NEVADA ST	WSTM	WSTM	13200	15	C5
NEVADA ST	WSTM	WSTM	13900	21	C1
NEVADO	MVJO	SJ92	27900	29B	D6
NEVILLE ST	OR	OR	1700	12	C6
NEVIS CIR	CM	CM	2800	27	B4
NEW AV	ANA	AN	300	11	F3
NEWARK CIR	IRV	SA	17500	28	F4
NEW BEDFORD DR	CO	ET	26900	29B	C1
NEW BEDFORD WY	GGR	GG		15	D4
NEWBRIDGE DR	CO	ET		29B	B2
NEW BRITAIN COM	SA	SA		22	C2
NEW BRTAIN LN N	HTB	HB	20000	26	D5
NEW BRTAIN LN S	HTB	HB	20100	26	D5
NEWBROOK WY	STN	STN		15	B4
NEWBURY DR	HTB	HB	6200	26	A1
NEWBURY RD	CO	LALM	11700	14	A3
NEWBY LN	HTB	HB	20200	26	D5
NEWCASTLE	CO	ET		52	C4
NEWCASTLE AV	PLA	PLA	200	7	B4

INDEX

STREET	CITY	P.O. ZONE	BLOCK	PAGE	GRID
NEWCASTLE AV	WSTM	WSTM	9800	21	F2
NEWCASTLE DR	ANA	AN	600	10	D5
NEWCASTLE DR	PLA	PLA	200	7	B4
NEWCASTLE LN	CYP	CYP	9800	9	C5
NEWCASTLE LN	FUL	FL33	800	5	E4
NEWCASTLE LN	HTB	HB47	15100	21	A3
NEW CHARDON	CO	LB		35	E6
NEW CHARDON	CO	LB77		37	E1
NEWDALE WY	STN	STN		15	B4
NEW DELHI ST	CO	SJ91		29A	F5
NEW DELHI ST	CO	SJ91		29B	A5
NEWELL AV	FUL	FL	500	6	B4
NEWELL PL	FUL	FL	500	6	C5
NEWELL ST	GGR	GG	13100	16	C5
NEWFAME CIR	FTNV	SA08	9500	21	F4
NEWGATE DR	HTB	HB		26	B2
NEW GATE WY	OR	OR		12	C2
NEW GATE WY	OR	OR	3600	13	A4
NEW GATE WY	YL	YL	6400	8	F2
NEWHALL LN	CM	CM		52	C6
NEWHALL ST	CM	CM27	900	31	B3
NEW HAMPSHIRE CIR	CM	CM		27	B2
NEW HAMPSHIRE WY	PLA	PLA	300	7	B5
NEW HAVEN	CO	ET		51	E4
NEW HAVEN	IRV	SA		24	D6
NEW HAVEN	IRV	SA		29	D1
NEW HAVEN	CO	LB77		35	D6
NEW HAVEN	YL	YL		40	B4
NEWHAVEN DR	BREA	BREA		3	A4
NEWHAVEN DR	CO	SA	13000	18	A5
NEWHAVEN DR	OR	OR	800	18	A4
NEW HAVEN LN	HTB	HB	19300	26	D4
NEWHOPE ST	CM	CM	3000	27	C1
NEWHOPE ST	FTNV	SA08	16000	22	C6
NEWHOPE ST	FTNV	SA08	17500	27	C1
NEWHOPE ST	GGR	GG	12800	16	C6
NEWHOPE ST N&S	SA	SA	100	22	C6
NEWHOPE ST S	SA	SA04	3200	27	C1
NEW JERSEY LN	PLA	PLA	200	7	B5
NEW JERSEY ST	CM	CM	1800	27	B3
NEWKIRK AV	FUL	FL	500	6	D6
NEWKIRK RD	ANA	AN	400	12	C2
NEWLAND ST	CO	MDWY	14500	21	D6
NEWLAND ST	GGR	GG	13000	15	D5
NEWLAND ST	HTB	HB	16500	21	D6
NEWLAND ST	HTB	HB	17600	26	D2
NEWLAND ST	HTB	HB	21200	30	D2
NEWLAND ST	WSTM	WSTM	13500	15	D5
NEWLAND ST	WSTM	WSTM	14000	21	D6
NEW LONDON COM	SA	SA		22	C2
NEWMAN AV	CYP	CYP	4500	9	C5
NEWMAN AV	HTB	HB	7700	26	C1
NEWMAN ST	CYP	CYP	5500	9	E4
NEWMEADOW	IRV	SA		29	A4
NEW MEXICO	CO	CYP	4700	9	D4
NEW MEXICO ST	CM	CM	1800	27	B3
NEW MOON LN	HTB	HB		25	F2
NEWPORT AV	CO	SA	11000	18	B5
NEWPORT AV	CO	TUS	12200	24	A2
NEWPORT AV	CO	TUS	14200	24	A2
NEWPORT AV	GGR	GG	13200	16	C4
NEWPORT AV	NB	NB	100	31	C4
NEWPORT AV	TUS	TUS	13200	24	A3
NEWPORT AV	TUS	TUS	12900	24	A2
NEWPORT BLVD	CM	CM	2300	27	C4
NEWPORT BLVD	CM	CM27	1500	31	D2
NEWPORT BLVD	CO	OR		18	D3
NEWPORT BLVD	CO	SA		18	C4
NEWPORT BLVD	NB	NB	2100	31	C4
NEWPORT BLVD	OR	OR		18	D3
NEWPORT CIR	HTB	HB	22000	30	F4
NEWPORT CIR	SA	SA	1800	23	D5
NEWPORT LN	YL	YL		40	B6
NEWPORT WY	CO	LB56		29C	E6
NEWPORT WY	CYP	CYP	9800	9	B4
NEWPORT CTR DR E	NB	CDLM	500	32	A6
NEWPRT CTR DR W	NB	CDLM	500	32	A6
NEWPORTER WY	CO	LB56		29C	E6
NEWPORT GLEN CT	SA	NB		31	F1
NEWPRT HLS DR E	NB	NB	21500	32	C4
NEWPRT HLS DR W	NB	NB	21500	32	C4
NEWPORT PL DR	NB	NB60	19400	28	C6
NEWPRT SHORS DR	NB	NB	6200	31	A4
NEWQUIST ST	HTB	HB	17000	26	F2
NEW RIVER	YL	YL		8	F5
NEWSBOY	HTB	HB		20	D5
NEWTON AV	CO	SA	18400	18	A6
NEWTON CT	IRV	SA17		32	D2
NEWTON WY	CM	CM27	700	31	B3
NEWTON WY	STN	STN	7200	15	B2

STREET	CITY	P.O. ZONE	BLOCK	PAGE	GRID
NEWVALE DR	CO	ET		29B	A1
NEW YORK AV	CM	CM	3200	27	B3
NEW YORK AV	CO	CYP	4700	9	D4
NEW YORK CT	DPT	LB77		37	E4
NEW ZEALAND ST	CYP	CYP	11500	15	A2
NIAGARA DR	HTB	HB46	10200	27	A5
NIAGARA WY	CM	CM	2400	27	D6
NIAGARA WY	SA	SA		22	D2
NIAGARA RIV AV	FTNV	SA08		26	D2
NIANTIC CIR	HTB	HB	16400	20	D3
NIANTIC PL	YL	YL	4300	8	A2
NIBUS ST	BREA	BREA		2	E5
NICARAGUA CIR	BPK	BP	7100	9	F1
NICE DR	SA	SA		22	D2
NICE LN	NB	NB		31	B4
NICHOLAS AV	CO	ET	800	17	C2
NICHOLAS AV	VPK	OR67	9700	12	F6
NICHOLS DR	GGR	GG	9200	15	E4
NICHOLS ST	HTB	HB47	17000	21	C6
NICKLETT AV	FUL	FL33	1000	10	E1
NICOLAS DR	FUL	FL		6	A2
NICOLE DR	CO	LB56		29C	E5
NICOSIA	CO	LB77		35	F5
NICOSIA WY	YL	YL		40	D6
NIDO WY	LAG	LB51	2500	34	F4
NIETA CIR	MVJO	SJ91	26100	29B	B6
NIETA DR	GGR	GG	12000	16	B3
NIETO PL	FUL	FL35	3900	2	C6
NIEVES ST	FTNV	SA08	17700	27	B1
NIGHTENGALE CT	CO	ET		52	A5
NIGHTHAWK	IRV	SA		29	B3
NIGHTHAWK CIR	ANA	AN		13	F2
NIGHTHAWK CIR	FTNV	SA08	11000	27	B1
NIGHT HERON LN	CO	LB56		29A	A6
NIGHTINGALE AV	FTNV	SA08	8700	26	D2
NIGHTINGALE CIR	ANA	AN		13	F2
NIGHTINGALE CIR	FTNV	SA08	10300	27	A2
NIGHTINGALE DR	CO	ET		43	A2
NIGHTINGALE DR	CO	ET	27000	52	C6
NIGHTINGALE LN	YL	YL	16800	7	F3
NIGHT STAR	IRV	SA		32A	B3
NIGUEL CIR	HTB	HB	9000	30	E1
NIGUEL DR	LAP	BP23	5200	9	F3
NIGUEL RD	CO	LB	23700	35	D1
NIGUEL RD	CO	LB77		37	D1
NIGUEL RD	DPT	LB77	33800	37	D1
NIGUEL CYN WY	BREA	BREA		2	F4
NIGUEL HTS BL	CO	LB56		29C	E6
NIGUEL POINTE	CO	LB77		36	F5
NIGUEL RANCH RD	CO	LB		35	E4
NIGUEL SHORS DR	DPT	LB77		37	D3
NIGUEL VILLG DR	CO	LB53		29C	C6
NIGUEL VISTA	CO	LB		35	F2
NIKE DR	ANA	AN		16	F3
NILAND WY	GGR	GG	8200	15	D5
NILE CIR	HTB	HB47	16600	21	C5
NILE RIVER AV	FTNV	SA08	8900	26	D2
NILES DR	GGR	GG		16	A3
NIMBLE CIR	HTB	HB		20	C4
NIMES CIR	IRV	SA	15300	29	B3
NIMES CT	CO	SJ92		29D	E2
NIMROD DR	HTB	HB47	7000	26	B6
NINA PL	ANA	AN	300	11	A4
NINA PL	GGR	GG	13000	16	B5
NINOS	IRV	SA		24	F5
NIOBE AV	ANA	AN	2000	10	F5
NIOBE AV	ANA	AN	1700	11	A5
NIOBE PL	ANA	AN	1800	10	F5
NIRA AV	STN	STN		15	D1
NISSON RD	TUS	TUS		24	E3
NISSON RD	TUS	SA05	1600	24	A3
NIVELADA	MVJO	SJ92	27500	29B	D2
NIXON CIR	TUS	TUS	13300	24	B3
NOBEL	IRV	SA		24	C6
NOBEL AV	SA	SA	100	28	B4
NOBLE CIR	HTB	HB	8300	26	D1
NOBLE ST	OR	OR	400	18	B1
NOEL PL	CYP	CYP	10100	9	C6
NOEL ST	LALM	LALM	11000	14	F1
NOGAL	MVJO	SJ92		29D	C4
NOGAL AV	YL	YL	4300	8	D6
NOHL CANYON RD	ANA	AN	17500	12	E3
NOHL CANYON RD	OR	OR	2000	12	D5
NOHL RANCH RD	ANA	AN	2300	12	E4
NOHL RANCH RD	ANA	AN	4600	13	A3
NOHL RANCH RD	ANA	AN	2100	12	F4
NOLA ST	WSTM	WSTM	14300	21	D1
NOLAN ST	CO	ET	24000	29A	C1
NOMAD CIR	HTB	HB	7500	26	C3

STREET	CITY	P.O. ZONE	BLOCK	PAGE	GRID
NOMAD ST	NB	NB		31	A6
NOPALES	MVJO	SJ92		29B	D6
NORANN CIR	LAP	BP23	7800	9	D2
NORBROOK DR	HTB	HB		25	F2
NORBROOK DR	HTB	HB		26	A2
NORBY LN	FUL	FL	1200	6	A4
NORCON CIR	HTB	HB	17300	20	F6
NORCRIS LN	YL	YL	5400	8	A4
NORCROFT LN	HTB	HB	20200	26	D1
NORD DR	HTB	HB47		21	D4
NORDIC DR	OR	OR	1700	12	D5
NORDIC PL	OR	OR	1700	12	D5
NORDIC ST	OR	OR	2000	12	E5
NORDICA LN	ANA	AN	800	11	F4
NORDICA ST	ANA	AN	800	11	F4
NORDINA DR	HTB	HB	5800	20	F6
NORDINA ST	NB	NB63	100	31	B4
NORE DR	CO	LB	1600	34	F1
NORFOLK CIR	YL	YL	16900	7	D4
NORFOLK DR	CO	SA		18	D3
NORFOLK DR	HTB	HB	8400	26	D5
NORFOLK DR	OR	SA05		18	D3
NORFOLK LN	ANA	AN	1600	16	C1
NORFOLK LN	NB	NB	1400	31	C1
NORGROVE CIR	HTB	HB47	16200	21	A4
NORGROVE LN	CO	LALM	11700	14	A3
NORIA ST	LAG	LB51	804	34	F4
NORINO DR	HTB	HB47	6700	21	A6
NORITSU AV	BPK	BP		10	A1
NORMA DR	ANA	AN	2500	11	F4
NORMA DR	HTB	HB47	7000	21	B5
NORMA DR	WSTM	WSTM	5500	14	B5
NORMA LN	ANA	AN	1800	16	C2
NORMA LN	GGR	GG	11500	16	C3
NORMA ST	LAH	LAH	200	1	F5
NORMAN AV	FUL	FL	200	6	E6
NORMAN AV	ANA	AN	1300	11	F5
NORMAN PL	ANA	AN	2000	11	F5
NORMAN PL	FUL	FL	1000	6	E5
NORMANDALE DR	CO	ET	27000	52	C6
NORMANDIE AV	IRV	SA	15000	29	D3
NORMANDIE CIR	OR	OR69		18	C3
NORMANDY AV	PLA	PLA	400	7	C4
NORMANDY CT	ANA	AN	100	12	A3
NORMANDY DR	ANA	AN	100	12	A3
NORMANDY LN	HTB	HB47	16300	21	A5
NORMANDY PL	ANA	AN	300	12	A3
NORMANDY PL E	SA	SA	300	23	B3
NORMANDY WY	CYP	CYP	4500	9	D5
NORRIS ST	IRV	SA	5000	29	D3
NORSE AV	CM	CM	2400	27	E1
NORSE AV	ANA	AN	700	11	F4
NORSE CIR	ANA	AN	700	11	F4
NORSE WY	CM	CM27	2300	31	E1
NORSTADT WY	BPK	BP	6100	9	F2
NORTH LN	CO	SJ	31000	56	C5
NORTH ST E&W	ANA	AN	100	11	C5
NORTHAMPTON AV	WSTM	WSTM	10000	22	A3
NORTHAMPTON ST	NB	NB		32	B3
NORTHAMPTON PL	CO	SJ79		59	D6
NORTHAMPTON WY	FUL	FL33	800	5	E4
NORTHBROOK WY	STN	STN		15	B4
NORTHCOVE	IRV	SA		29	E4
NORTH CREEK LN	FUL	FL		6	F3
NORTHCREST DR	CO	ET		29B	B2
NORTHFIELD AV	ANA	AN	6100	8	D6
NORTHFIELD LN	HTB	HB47	17000	21	C4
NORTHGATE LN	ANA	AN	700	11	C2
NORTHGATE WY	LAH	LAH	200	2	B4
NORTHGROVE	IRV	SA		29	E4
NORTHILLS DR	LAH	LAH	1200	2	B3
NORTHLAKE	IRV	SA		29	D1
NORTHLAKE	HTB	HB		20	B3
NORTH MALL	SA	SA		24	C6
NORTH PARK BLVD	CO	SA	2300	17	D5
NORTH PARK CIR	SA	SA	4000	29	C1
NORTH PEAK DR	CO	SJ79		56	F6
NORTHPORT DR	HTB	HB	8300	26	D5
NORTHRIDGE LN	HTB	HB	14800	20	F2
NORTHRIDGE RD	WSTM	WSTM		21	F2
NORTHRUP DR	CO	LB	25000	29C	E1
NORTHSHORE LN	HTB	HB	21300	30	E1
NORTHSTAR	CO	ET		12	D5
NORTHSTAR LN	ANA	AN		26	E4
NORTH STAR WY	DPT	DPT		37	A5
NORTHUMBLRND AV	WSTM	WSTM		21	F2
NORTHUMBLRND RD	CO	OR65	9300	12	D5
NORTHUMBLRND RD	CO	OR	2200	12	D5
NORTH VIEW DR	ANA	AN		13	E3
NORTHWESTERN WY	WSTM	WSTM	5000	14	E6

STREET	CITY	P.O. ZONE	BLOCK	PAGE	GRID
NORTHWIND CT	NB	NB63		31	A2
NORTHWOOD	IRV	SA		24	E6
NORTHWOOD	SA	SA		22	E6
NORTHWOOD AV	BREA	BREA	900	2	D3
NORTHWOOD CT	FUL	FL		7	A1
NORTHWOOD DR	FUL	FL		7	A1
NORTHWOOD LN	CO	ET		29A	E1
NORTHWOOD RD	SB	SB	1400	14	A5
NORTHWOOD RD	SB	SB	1100	19	C5
NORTON PL	SA	SA		28	B1
NORTON ST	IRV	SA	17900	28	F5
NORWICH CIR	HTB	HB47	15400	21	A3
NORWICH CIR	WSTM	WSTM	15800	22	A4
NORWICH LN	LAH	LAH		2	B6
NORWOOD CT	BREA	BREA		2	D5
NORWOOD ST	OR	OR	200	18	A3
NORWOOD TER	ANA	AN	1200	11	E2
NORWOOD PARK	CO	TUS	17500	23	F1
NORWOOD PARK	CO	TUS	18100	24	A1
NORWOOD PARK PL	TUS	TUS	17200	23	E1
NOTRE DAME RD	CM	CM	2300	27	D6
NOTRE DAME ST	CO	OR69		18	C3
NOTRE DAME ST	CO	OR69		18	C2
NOTTINGHAM AV	WSTM	WSTM	15200	21	B3
NOTTINGHAM AV	SA	SA	500	22	F3
NOTTINGHAM CT	CO	LB53		29C	F4
NOTTINGHAM LN	ANA	AN		16	B1
NOTTINGHAM LN	HTB	HB	15100	21	A3
NOTTINGHAM PL	FUL	FL35		6	C3
NOTTINGHAM RD	NB	NB	1000	31	B4
NOTTINGHAM WY	DPT	DPT		37	F3
NOUMEA ST	CYP	CYP	5900	14	F3
NOVA	IRV	SA		32A	A3
NOVA DR	YL	YL	19900	8	C3
NOVACELLA	CO	LB77		35	C3
NOVIA	NB	NB		32	A2
NOVIA CIR	MVJO	SJ91		29B	C5
NOVILLA	CO	LB77		35	F3
NOVILLA	SCL	SC72		38	E3
NOVILUNIO	SCL	SC72		38	E5
NOYA	MVJO	SJ92		29D	D2
NOYES AV	IRV	SA		28	D2
NUBE LN	HTB	HB	16500	20	D5
NUBIAN LN	OR	OR	1500	17	A4
NUBLADO	MVJO	SJ91		29D	C3
NUBLES	MVJO	SJ92		29D	C4
NUEVA VISTA	CO	LB		35	F2
NUEVA VISTA DR	CO	LB	25000	35	F2
NUEVO	IRV	SA		28	E6
NUGGET	CO	ET	25000	29B	E2
NUGGET CIR	HTB	HB	5900	20	F1
NUGGET CT	ANA	AN		13	C3
NUGGET FALLS LN	CO	LB56		29C	E6
NUGGETT VIA	ANA	AN		16	D2
NURA AV	ANA	AN	2100	11	F4
NURA PL	ANA	AN	2100	11	F4
NUTCRACKER LN	CO	LB53		29A	B6
NUTHATCH LN	CO	LB	24000	35	F1
NUTMEG LN	YL	YL		7	F5
NUTMEG PL	CM	CM	1500	27	C3
NUTMEG ST	IRV	SA	3500	29	B1
NUTWOOD AV	FUL	FL	800	6	D5
NUTWOOD AV	FUL	FL	2500	7	A4
NUTWOOD CIR	HTB	HB	6100	26	F1
NUTWOOD PL	ANA	AN	1800	11	A5
NUTWOOD PL	FUL	FL	300	6	C5
NUTWOOD ST	BREA	BREA	400	2	E4
NUTWOOD ST	GGR	GG	12000	16	A4
NUTWOOD ST	OR	OR	300	18	A4
NUTWOOD ST N	ANA	AN	800	11	A3
NUTWOOD ST S	ANA	AN	800	11	A6
NUTWOOD ST S	ANA	AN	1500	16	A1
NYANZA DR	HTB	HB47	6800	21	B4
NYES PL	LAG	LB51	1700	35	A4
NYES PL	LAG	LB51	100	35	A4
NYMPHA DR	CO	SJ91		29A	F6
NYMPHA DR	CO	SJ91		29B	A6
NYMPHA DR	CO	SJ91		29D	A1
NYON AV	ANA	AN	2100	11	F4
NYON AV	ANA	AN	2300	12	A4
NYON PL	ANA	AN	2100	11	F4

O

STREET	CITY	P.O. ZONE	BLOCK	PAGE	GRID
O ST	ETMC	SA09		51	C3
O ST	CO	TRA		59	D5

STREET	CITY	P.O. ZONE	BLOCK	PAGE	GRID
OAHU PL	CM	CM	1600	27	C4
OAHU ST	SA	SA		22	C3
OAHU WY	PLA	PLA	100	7	B5
OAHU WY	SA	SA		22	C3
OAK AV	IRV	SA		29	D3
OAK AV	FUL	FL33	1500	5	E6
OAK AV	FUL	FL	700	6	A6
OAK AV	FUL	FL33	4000	10	D1
OAK AV	IRV	SA	14600	24	C6
OAK AV	IRV	SA	14700	29	C1
OAK AV	FTNV	SA08	16500	21	E5
OAK CIR	LAP	BP23	5500	9	F2
OAK DR	CO	SA	13400	18	B5
OAK LN	CO	SIL	30000	53	A1
OAK LN	HTB	HB47	17000	21	C6
OAK LN	OR	OR	20100	13	D6
OAK PL	ANA	AN	200	18	A3
OAK PL	BREA	BREA	200	2	F6
OAK PL	WSTM	WSTM	13600	14	F6
OAK ST	CM	CM27	800	31	B1
OAK ST	FTNV	SA08	17300	21	E6
OAK ST	FTNV	SA08	17600	26	E1
OAK ST	HTB	HB47	17000	21	C6
OAK ST	LAG	LB51	100	34	E3
OAK ST	LALM	LALM	10500	14	B1
OAK ST	PLA	PLA		7	E6
OAK ST	SA	SA	100	23	C3
OAK ST	SA	SA	2900	28	C1
OAK ST	STN	STN	10700	15	C1
OAK ST E	ANA	AN	1200	11	E3
OAK ST N	OR	OR	200	17	E2
OAK ST S W	ANA	AN	200	11	E3
OAK WY	LAH	LAH	400	1	E5
OAKBROOK	CO	SJ79		59	C6
OAKBROOK	MVJO	SJ92		29B	E1
OAKBROOK	MVJO	SJ92		52	E6
OAKBROOK CIR	HTB	HB		25	F3
OAK BURL DR	YL	YL		7	D2
OAK CANYON	IRV	SA		29	E4
OAK CANYON LN	CO	ET		51	F5
OAK CANYON WY	BREA	BREA		2	F4
OAKCLIFF DR	CO	LB77		36	A6
OAKCREST AV	WSTM	WSTM	15200	21	E1
OAKCREST CIR	YL	YL		40	A5
OAK CREST LN	NB	NB		32	B4
OAKCREST PL	ANA	AN	900	10	C6
OAKDALE	IRV	SA		29	C3
OAKDALE AV	FUL	FL	900	6	A4
OAKDALE DR	GGR	GG	8900	15	D5
OAKDALE LN	HTB	HB48		25	E3
OAKFIELD AV	SA	SA	4300	22	B1
OAKFIELD DR	VPK	OR67	17900	12	F5
OAKGLEN AV	CO	SJ91		29A	F5
OAKGLEN LN	FUL	FL		7	A2
OAK GROVE	MVJO	SJ92		29B	F2
OAK GROVE	IRV	SA		29	C4
OAK GROVE CIR	CO	SA	400	13	B2
OAK GROVE CIR	HTB	HB47	6500	21	A4
OAKGROVE CIR	CO	LALM	3100	14	B3
OAK GROVE RD	CO	SJ79		52	F4
OAK GROVE TER	CO	LB		29	

STREET	CITY	P.O. ZONE	BLOCK	PAGE	GRID
OAKHAVEN AV	BREA	BREA	300	7	C1
OAKHAVEN DR	ANA	AN	1300	10	B5
OAKHAVEN DR	STN	STN	10400	15	B1
OAK HILL DR	ANA	AN		12	F3
OAK HILLS DR	OR	OR		43	A2
OAK HILLS DR	SB	SB	13000	19	C5
OAK HOLLOW RD	CO	LB53		29D	A4
OAKHURST CIR	OR	OR67		13	A4
OAKHURST DR	YL	YL		7	D3
OAKIE DOKEY LN	CO	SJ		31	B3
OAK KNOLL	CO	SJ79		59	C4
OAK KNOLL DR	ANA	AN		8	B6
OAK KNOLL DR	CO	LALM	2600	14	A3
OAKKNOLL ST	BREA	BREA		2	D3
OAKLAND DR	LAH	LAH	300	1	D4
OAKLAND DR W	LAH	LAH	2100	1	D4
OAK LEAF DR	CO	LALM	12200	14	A3
OAK LEAF DR	YL	YL	17900	7	D2
OAK LEAF RD	CO	LB		29D	A1
OAKLEY AV	IRV	SA		24	D6
OAKLEY TER	IRV	SA		32	F3
OAK MEADOW DR	MVJO	SJ92	5600	8	C5
OAKMONT	CO	OR		59	D5
OAKMONT AV	CO	TRA	300	17	D2

STREET	CITY	P.O. ZONE	BLOCK	PAGE	GRID
OAKMONT AV	SA	SA	2300	17	C5
OAKMONT DR	SB	SB	1100	19	C5
OAKMONT LN	HTB	HB47	16300	21	A4
OAKMONT LN	HTB	HB		30	C1
OAKMONT LN	NB	NB		32	B5
OAKMONT PL	BPK	BP	8200	5	C4
OAKMONT PL	CO	LB		35	D5
OAKMONT PL	SA	SA	1600	17	C6
OAKMONT RD	SB	SB	1400	14	A5
OAKMONT ST	PLA	PLA	1100	7	C4
OAKMOUNT ST	CYP	CYP	9600	9	E5
OAKPARK DR	CO	ET		29B	B2
OAKRIDGE CT	FUL	FL		6	F3
OAK RIDGE DR	CO	SA	18100	17	F5
OAK RIDGE DR	CO	SA	18200	18	A5
OAKRIDGE LN	CO	SJ		56	D6
OAKRIDGE LN	CO	SJ		59	D1
OAKRIDGE LN	HTB	HB	8600	26	D6
OAKSHIRE LN	HTB	HB47	15500	21	A3
OAK SPRING LN	CO	LB		29C	E4
OAKSTONE CIR	HTB	HB		26	B2
OAKSTONE WY	ANA	AN	800	11	F4
OAKSTONE WY	ANA	AN	700	12	A4
OAK SUMMIT	CO	SJ79		52	F4
OAKTREE CIR	HTB	HB	14900	20	F2
OAK TREE CT	LAH	LAH		1	E6
OAK TREE CT	YL	YL	18500	8	A3
OAK TREE LN	IRV	SA		29	A6
OAK TREE LN	OR	SA05		18	D3
OAKVALE DR	CO	YL	19700	8	C6
OAKVIEW LN	ANA	AN		13	E3
OAKVIEW LN	CO	SJ		52	E3
OAKVILLE	CO	ET		51	F6
OAKVILLE	CO	ET		52	A6
OAK WAY DR	CO	LALM	12400	14	A4
OAKWILDE DR	ANA	AN	600	10	C5
OAKWOOD AV	ANA	AN	1700	8	A6
OAKWOOD AV	FUL	FL	800	6	D2
OAKWOOD CIR	VPK	OR67	9700	12	F5
OAKWOOD CT	SJC	SJ75		36	B2
OAKWOOD LN	BREA	BREA		2	D2
OAKWOOD LN	CO	ET	22800	29A	D2
OAKWOOD ST	GGR	GG	12200	16	B4
OAKWOOD ST	OR	OR	700	18	A4
OASIS AV	GGR	GG	9500	21	E1
OASIS AV	WSTM	WSTM	8500	21	D1
OBARR ST	SA	SA	2000	17	C6
OBERLIN AV	WSTM	WSTM	8300	21	D4
OBERLIN CT	CO	LAG		35	F3
OBRAJERO	SCL	SC72		38	E3
OBRERO DR	MVJO	SJ91		29B	A4
OBSIDIAN CT	FTNV	SA08	10900	22	B4
OBSIDIAN DR	WSTM	WSTM	9000	21	E4
OCASO AV	BPK	BP	5000	5	B4
OCCIDENTAL DR	SB	SB	1000	19	C4
OCCIDENTAL LN	HTB	HB	19500	26	E4
OCCIDENTAL ST E	SA	SA	100	23	A4
OCCIDENTAL ST W	SA	SA	1500	22	E4
OCCIDENTAL ST W	SA	SA	900	23	A4
OCEAN AV	LAG	LB51	100	34	D3
OCEAN AV E&W	SB	SB	100	19	E3
OCEAN BLVD	NB	CDLM	2500	33	B2
OCEAN BLVD	NB	NB	2000	33	A2
OCEAN BLVD	NB	NB	1500	33	C5
OCEAN DR	NB	CDLM	2800	33	A2
OCEAN DR	SCL	SC72		39	A2
OCEAN PL	HTB	HB47	7000	21	B5
OCEAN WY	LAG	LB		35	B6
OCEAN WY	LAG	LB51	1700	34	E4
OCEANA CT	SJC	SJ75		36	A3
OCEANAIRE	CO	LB		29A	C4
OCEANAIRE CIR	HTB	HB		26	B4
OCEAN BIRCH DR	NB	CDLM		32	D6
OCEAN BLUFF CIR	HTB	HB		26	A4
OCEAN BREEZE DR	GGR	GG	12500	15	E4
OCEAN BREEZE LN	HTB	HB	21500	30	F2
OCEANBREEZE WY	CO	LB		35	C6
OCEANBREEZE WY	CO	LB77		37	C1
OCEAN BRIGHT	DPT	DPT		37	F3
OCEAN CREST	SA	SA04		27	E2
OCEAN CREST DR	HTB	HB	9500	30	F2
OCEAN FRONT ST	LAG	LB51	900	34	D3
OCEAN FRONT	NB	NB63	6900	30	F3
OCEAN FRONT	NB	NB	3200	31	B5
OCEAN FRONT	NB	NB	2000	33	A2
OCEAN FRONT	NB	NB	900	33	A5
OCEANGROVE CIR	HTB	HB		30	C1
OCEAN HILL DR	DPT	DPT	33100	37	F3
OCEANHILL DR	HTB	HB48		26	B2
OCEAN MANOR	HTB	HB	900	26	C4
OCEANO CIR	HTB	HB	4600	20	D5
OCEANPORT	HTB	HB		26	B3
OCEAN RIDGE	DPT	DPT		37	F3
OCEANSIDE	HTB	HB		26	C6
OCEANSIDE DR	HTB	HB		30	D2
OCEAN SPRAY	DPT	DPT		37	F3
OCEANUS	CO	LAG		35	F3
OCEANUS DR	HTB	HB		20	E2
OCEAN VIA	ANA	AN	2700	10	D4
OCEAN VIEW AV	CO	OR65	8500	12	D3
OCEAN VIEW AV	NB	NB	200	31	C4
OCEAN VIEW AV	OR	OR		12	D3
OCEAN VIEW DR	FUL	FL	600	6	B5
OCEANVIEW LN	HTB	HB	21700	30	F2
OCEAN VIEW ST	LAG	LB	31400	35	B6
OCEANVIEW ST	OR	OR	3800	12	D2
OCEAN VISTA	NB	NB		31	F5
OCEAN VISTA	NB	NB		32	A5
OCEAN VISTA DR	LAG	LB	21400	35	A5
OCEANWOOD DR	DPT	DPT		38	D3
OCEANWOOD DR	HTB	HB	9000	26	E6
O DELL PL	FUL	FL33	1900	5	F5
ODESSA DR	YL	YL	4000	7	D2
ODONNELL WY	OR	OR	1600	12	C6
ODYSSEY CT	NB	NB		31	B4
OERTLY CIR	GGR	GG	11800	16	F3
OERTLY DR	ANA	AN	2100	16	D3
OERTLY DR	GGR	GG	12300	16	D4
OFELIA LN	HTB	HB		26	A4
OGDEN PL	STN	STN	7500	15	B3
OGLE CIR	CM	CM27	400	31	D3
OGLE ST	CM	CM27	200	31	C3
O HILL RIDGE	CO	LB77		35	F6
OHIO AV	PLA	PLA	800	12	A1
OHIO PL	CM	CM	1800	27	B3
OHIO ST	YL	YL	4200	8	B4
OHIO ST N&S	ANA	AN	100	11	C4
OHMER WY	GGR	GG	12500	15	E4
OHMS WY	CM	CM27	1600	31	C3
OJAI CT	CO	TRA		59	C1
OJAI LN	HTB	HB	17400	20	F6
OKEECHOBEE LN	CO	ET		29A	D1
OLANA LN	HTB	HB	19300	26	F4
OLANA PZ	YL	YL		8	C3
OLANA WY	ANA	AN	100	11	F3
OLAS LN	HTB	HB	4600	20	D5
OLA VISTA N	SCL	SC72	100	39	D4
OLA VISTA S	SCL	SC72	100	39	E5
OLD BRIDGE RD	ANA	AN		13	E1
OLDBRIDGE RD	DPT	DPT		37	F4
OLD BUCKET LN	ANA	AN		13	A3
OLD CAMP RD	OR	OR69		18	E3
OLD CANAL RD	YL	AN07		8	F5
OLD CANAL RD	YL	YL		40	A5
OLD CHAPMAN AV	CO	OR		18	C3
OLD CREEK LN	FUL	FL	2200	6	F4
OLD FASHION WY	ANA	AN	1500	16	A1
OLD FASHION WY	GGR	GG	11600	16	A3
OLDFIELD	IRV	SA18		29A	C2
OLD FOOTHILL BL	CO	SA	12800	18	B5
OLDGATE LN	HTB	HB		25	F2
OLDGLEN LN	HTB	HB		25	F1
OLD GOLDN LNTRN	DPT	DPT		37	E5
OLD GRAND ST	SA	SA		17	D5
OLD HICKORY RD	CO	SJ		56	D6
OLD HICKORY RD	CO	SJ		59	D1
OLD JACKSON ST	SA	SA	1100	22	D1
OLD LAMPLTR CIR	VPK	OR67		13	A6
OLD LAMPLITR LN	VPK	OR67	10200	13	A6
OLDMILL DR	BREA	BREA		2	D3
OLD MILL RD	CO	LALM	12000	14	B3
OLD MILL ST	IRV	SA	4000	29	C1
OLD OAK RD	CO	SJ		56	D6
OLD OAK RD	CO	SJ		59	D1
OLD ORCHARD LN	OR	OR67		17	D1
OLD PIRATE LN	HTB	HB	5400	20	E5
OLD RANCH CIR	VPK	OR67	10100	13	B6
OLD RANCH PKWY	SB	SB		14	B4
OLD RANCH RD	ANA	AN	900	13	E2
OLD RANCH RD	CO	YL	19300	8	B4
OLD RANCH RD	CO	LB77		35	F6
OLD RANCH RD	CO	LB77		36	A6
OLD RANCH RD	CO	LB77		37	F1
OLD RANCH RD	CO	LB77		38	A1
OLD RANCH RD	SB	SB		14	C4
OLD RIVER RD	FUL	FL	2000	6	F4
OLD STA ANA CYN	ANA	AN		13	B2
OLD SPRINGS RD	ANA	AN		8	F6
OLD TRABUCO RD	CO	ET		29A	F1
OLD TRABUCO RD	CO	ET		29B	A1
OLD TRAIL LN	FTNV	SA08		27	A2
OLD TUSTIN AV	SA	SA	1700	17	E6
OLD VILLAGE RD	YL	YL		40	B6
OLDWOOD CT	BREA	BREA		2	C5
OLEANDER CIR	BPK	BP	7800	10	C3
OLEANDER CIR	FTNV	SA08	16700	21	E5
OLEANDER ST	BREA	BREA	600	2	D6
OLEANDER ST	SB	SB	3600	14	D4
OLEANDER WY	CO	LB	24100	29C	E6
OLGA AV	CYP	CYP	5000	9	D6
OLIN ST	FUL	FL33	300	5	D6
OLINDA AV	LAH	LAH	200	2	A3
OLINDA CIR	MVJO	SJ92		29D	C2
OLINDA DR	BREA	BREA	100	4	B4
OLINDA DR	DPT	DPT	33700	37	E4
OLINDA LN	ANA	AN	3100	10	B5
OLINDA PL	BREA	BREA	100	4	B5
OLINDA ST	YL	YL	4700	8	A3
OLIVA PL	MVJO	SJ92		36	B2
OLIVE AV	BREA	BREA	400	3	A5
OLIVE AV	CO	OR65	8600	12	D3
OLIVE AV	CO	ET	23100	29A	F4
OLIVE AV	FUL	FL33	1500	5	E6
OLIVE AV	FUL	FL	1000	6	A6
OLIVE AV	FUL	FL33	1600	10	E1
OLIVE AV	FUL	FL	1000	11	A1
OLIVE AV	HTB	HB	100	26	A5
OLIVE AV	OR	OR	2800	12	D3
OLIVE AV E&W	LAH	LAH	100	2	A5
OLIVE CIR	FTNV	SA08	16600	21	E5
OLIVE DR	CO	SIL	28800	50	F2
OLIVE LN	CO	SJ	31000	56	C5
OLIVE LN	SA	SA	2300	17	A5
OLIVE PL	BREA	BREA	200	2	F6
OLIVE ST	FTNV	SA08	16700	21	E5
OLIVE ST	GGR	GG45	12700	14	E4
OLIVE ST	IRV	SA	3900	24	C6
OLIVE ST	IRV	SA	3900	29	C1
OLIVE ST	LAG	LB51	500	34	D2
OLIVE ST	NB	NB63	100	30	F4
OLIVE ST	PLA	PLA	400	7	A5
OLIVE ST	WSTM	WSTM	13400	15	B6
OLIVE ST	WSTM	WSTM	14000	21	B1
OLIVE ST N	SA	SA	1700	17	A6
OLIVE ST N	SA	SA	100	23	A4
OLIVE ST N&S	ANA	AN	100	11	D3
OLIVE ST N&S	OR	OR	100	17	C4
OLIVE ST S	SA	SA	900	23	A4
OLIVE ST S	SA	SA	2800	28	A2
OLIVE BRANCH LN	YL	YL	6400	8	F2
OLIVE BRANCH WY	ANA	AN		12	F3
OLIVEBROOK CT	WSTM	WSTM		15	D5
OLIVE GROVE LN	CO	OR67		50	D5
OLIVE HILL RD	CO	OR67	17300	50	F6
OLIVER DR	ANA	AN	3000	10	C4
OLIVER DR	FUL	FL	900	6	B4
OLIVERA DR	MVJO	SJ91	24000	29B	B5
OLIVERA WY	LAG	LB51	2600	34	F4
OLIVE TREE CIR	CO	TUS	14200	23	F1
OLIVE TREE CIR	YL	YL		7	E4
OLIVE TREE DR	LAH	LAH	1200	1	E6
OLIVEWOOD	CO	ET		52	C4
OLIVEWOOD LN	WSTM	WSTM		21	C4
OLIVO RD	SJC	SJ75		38	B3
OLMSTEAD WY	ANA	AN	2200	11	F4
OLSON DR	GGR	GG	11400	15	E2
OLWYN DR	TUS	TUS	1200	24	A2
OLYMPIA	IRV	SA14		29	F2
OLYMPIA CT	ANA	AN	100	12	A3
OLYMPIA PL	ANA	AN	300	12	A3
OLYMPIA WY	CO	SA	12600	18	A4
OLYMPIA WY N	OR	OR	200	18	A3
OLYMPIA WY S	OR	OR	100	18	A3
OLYMPIAD RD	MVJO	SJ92		29B	D2
OLYMPIC AV	CO	CM27	700	27	F3
OLYMPIC AV	PLA	PLA	1500	7	E4
OLYMPIC CT	FTNV	SA08	10300	27	A2
OLYMPIC DR	HTB	HB	9500	26	F5
OLYMPIC DR	LALM	LALM	5100	14	D4
OLYMPIC PL	CO	LB	30800	35	E5
OLYMPUS	IRV	SA		32A	A2
OLYMPUS DR	CO	SJ91	25500	29B	A6
OLYMPUS DR	WSTM	WSTM	13400	15	A6
OMA PL	GGR	GG	9200	15	E2
OMAHA AV	PLA	PLA	1300	7	D4
OMEGA AV	ANA	AN	2300	11	F6
OMEGA AV	ANA	AN	2200	12	A6
OMEGA DR	CO	SA	1900	24	C1
ONDA	NB	NB		32	A2
ONDINE CIR	HTB	HB	4000	20	C5
ONEIDA AV	ANA	AN	2600	10	D6
ONKAYHA CIR	IRV	SA	13500	24	D6
ONONDAGA AV	ANA	AN	900	11	A3
ONONDAGA AV	PLA	PLA	2400	7	C2
ONSET CIR	HTB	HB	9500	30	F2
ONTARIO CIR	WSTM	WSTM	14400	21	E2
ONTARIO DR	GGR	GG	13200	15	E5
ONTARIO DR	HTB	HB	7500	26	C2
ONTARIO DR	WSTM	WSTM	14500	21	E2
ONTARIO LN	CO	ET		29A	D1
ONTUR	MVJO	SJ92	21700	29B	E1
ONYX	BREA	BREA	100	4	B5
ONYX	IRV	SA		29	A5
ONYX AV	NB	NB	100	31	F6
ONYX AV	OR	OR	2100	12	E5
ONYX AV	WSTM	WSTM	8600	21	D3
ONYX CIR	GGR	GG45	12200	14	F3
ONYX CT	FTNV	SA08	10800	22	B4
ONYX LN	ANA	AN07		13	D3
ONYX ST	CYP	CYP	11500	14	F2
ONYX ST	GGR	GG45	11800	14	F3
OPAL AV	ANA	AN	1200	11	E4
OPAL AV	CYP	CYP	4200	9	C3
OPAL AV	FTNV	SA08	11400	22	C4
OPAL AV	NB	NB	100	31	E6
OPAL AV	OR	OR	2400	12	E5
OPAL CIR	HTB	HB47	8100	21	C6
OPAL CIR	WSTM	WSTM	8900	21	E4
OPAL COVE WY	SB	SB	400	19	F2
OPAL HILL CT	CO	LB56		29C	E5
OPEN SKY DR	FUL	FL33		5	F2
OPERA LN	HTB	HB	16200	20	D4
OPERETTA DR	HTB	HB	4500	20	D4
OPORTO	WSTM	WSTM		21	E2
ORA DR	GGR	GG	11200	16	B3
ORA ST	GGR	GG	12000	16	B3
ORAN CIR	BPK	BP	6900	10	B1
ORANGE AV	ANA	AN	1900	10	D5
ORANGE AV	ANA	AN	1800	11	A5
ORANGE AV	BPK	BP	6500	10	A5
ORANGE AV	CM	CM	2400	27	E6
ORANGE AV	CM	CM27	1500	31	C3
ORANGE AV	CO	AN04	9500	10	D5
ORANGE AV	CO	OR65	8500	12	D3
ORANGE AV	CO	ET	23100	29A	E4
ORANGE AV	CYP	CYP	4000	9	D5
ORANGE AV	HTB	HB	200	26	A5
ORANGE AV	NB	NB	400	31	C3
ORANGE AV	OR	OR	3000	12	D3
ORANGE AV	SA	SA	100	23	B5
ORANGE AV	SA	SA	2700	28	B1
ORANGE AV N&S	BREA	BREA	100	2	E6
ORANGE AV N&S	FUL	FL	100	6	A5
ORANGE AV S	BREA	BREA	500	6	E1
ORANGE AV S	FUL	FL	1300	11	A1
ORANGE DR	YL	YL	16700	7	D3
ORANGE FRWY	CO			12	A6
ORANGE FRWY	FUL			7	A4
ORANGE FRWY	OR			17	A3
ORANGE ST	FTNV	SA08	17100	21	F6
ORANGE ST	LAH	LAH	100	2	A4
ORANGE ST	NB	NB	100	31	A4
ORANGE ST	TUS	TUS	13900	23	F3
ORANGE ST	TUS	TUS		24	A3
ORANGE ST N&S	OR	OR	100	17	C4
ORANGE ACRES DR	ANA	AN	17600	13	A3
ORANGE ACRES LN	IRV	SA	14500	29	D2
ORANGE ARROW	IRV	SA		24	F5
ORANGE BLOSSOM	IRV	SA		29	E4
ORANGEBLOSOM LN	YL	YL		7	E4
ORG CO TECH CTR	SA	SA		23	C6
ORANGE CREEK LN	ANA	AN		12	F3
ORANGEFAIR AV E	FUL	FL	100	11	C1
ORANGEFAIR AV W	FUL	FL	100	11	C1
ORANGEFAIR LN	ANA	AN	1100	11	D1
ORANGEGATE DR	YL	YL		7	E5
ORANGEGROVE	IRV	SA		29	C4
ORANGE GROVE AV	PLA	PLA	100	7	B4
ORANGE GRV AV E	OR	OR	1100	17	E2
ORANGE GRV AV E	OR	OR	1100	17	E2
ORANGE GRV AV W	OR	OR	1500	17	B2
ORANGEGROVE CIR	VPK	OR67	10400	18	A1
ORANGEHILL LN	OR	OR		12	E4
ORANGE HLL LN S	ANA	AN	100	13	B2
ORANGE KNOLL DR	CO	SA	11300	18	B5
ORANGE OAK	CO	LB		35	F3
ORANGE OAK	CO	LB77		36	A3
ORANGE OLIVE RD	OR	OR	2800	12	C5
ORANGE PARK BL	CO	OR	10200	13	C6
ORANGE PARK BL	CO	OR	10500	18	D2
ORANGE PARK BL	OR	OR		13	C5
ORANGETHORPE AV	ANA	AN	3100	7	B6
ORANGETHORPE AV	ANA	AN	16500	7	D6
ORANGETHORPE AV	ANA	AN	4700	8	A6
ORANGETHORPE AV	ANA	AN	300	11	B1
ORANGETHORPE AV	BPK	BP	6000	9	E1
ORANGETHORPE AV	BPK	BP	6500	10	B1
ORANGETHORPE AV	CO	AN07	18400	8	A6
ORANGETHORPE AV	FUL	FL	16500	7	A6
ORANGETHORPE AV	LAP	BP23	5000	9	E1
ORANGETHORPE AV	PLA	PLA	1400	7	D6
ORANGETHORPE AV	PLA	PLA	100	12	A1
ORANGTHRPE AV E	FUL	FL	100	11	E1
ORANGETHRP AV E	PLA	PLA	100	7	A6
ORANGTHRPE AV W	FUL	FL33	1500	10	B1
ORANGTHRPE AV W	FUL	FL	100	11	B1
ORANGETHRP AV W	PLA	PLA	100	7	A6
ORANGETHORPE WY	ANA	AN	1500	11	D1
ORANGETHORPE PK	ANA	AN01		6	D6
ORANGETHORPE PK	ANA	AN	1700	11	D1
ORANGE TREE	IRV	SA		29	D4
ORANGE TREE LN	CO	TUS	17500	23	F1
ORANGETREE LN	OR	OR		17	D1
ORANGEVIEW AV	PLA	PLA	2000	7	F6
ORANGEVIEW LN	OR	OR		12	E4
ORANGEVIEW RD	CO	SA	11200	18	C6
ORANGEWOOD	SA	SA		23	D4
ORANGEWOOD AV	CO	LALM	3200	14	B2
ORANGEWOOD AV	CO	OR69	14800	17	A2
ORANGEWOOD AV	CYP	CYP	5600	14	E2
ORANGEWOOD AV	CYP	CYP	6400	15	B2
ORANGEWOOD AV	GGR	GG	7500	15	B2
ORANGEWOOD AV	GGR	GG	10200	16	A2
ORANGEWOOD AV	LALM	LALM		14	E2
ORANGEWOOD AV	LALM	LALM	3500	14	B2
ORANGEWOOD AV	OR	OR	1200	17	A2
ORANGEWOOD AV	STN	STN	7500	15	B2
ORANGEWOOD AV E	ANA	AN	100	16	D2
ORANGEWOOD AV W	ANA	AN	100	16	D2
ORANGE WOOD DR	ANA	AN		16	D2
ORANGEWOOD DR	BREA	BREA	1000	2	E4
ORANGEWOOD LN	TUS	TUS	100	23	F2
ORANGEWOOD LN	YL	YL		7	E4
ORANGEWOOD RD	SJC	SJ75	26500	36	B2
ORANGEWOOD ST	LAH	LAH		2	B6
ORBIT WY	ANA	AN		16	D2
ORBITA	MVJO	SJ91		29D	C2
ORBITER ST	BREA	BREA		3	B6
ORCAS DR	CM	CM	1700	27	C3
ORCHARD	IRV	SA		29	E4
ORCHARD AV	OR	OR	2100	17	A4
ORCHARD AV N&S	FUL	FL	100	6	A5
ORCHARD AV S	FUL	FL	1100	11	A1
ORCHARD CT	BREA	BREA	400	2	F5
ORCHARD DR	CO	YL	18000	8	B4
ORCHARD DR	CO	SA07	1500	28	A6
ORCHARD DR	CO	SA	2500	32	B1
ORCHARD DR	PLA	PLA		7	F5
ORCHARD DR	TUS	TUS		24	D1
ORCHARD DR	YL	YL	18300	8	A5
ORCHARD LN	VPK	OR67		13	A5
ORCHARD PL	FUL	FL	600	6	A6
ORCHARD PL	LAH	LAH	600	1	F4
ORCHARD RIM LN	CO	ET	25400	29A	F1
ORCHID	CO	SJ		59	B5
ORCHID AV	FTNV	SA08	11500	22	C4
ORCHID AV	LAH	LAH	2200	2	C3
ORCHID AV	MVJO	SJ92		29D	D4
ORCHID AV	NB	CDLM	200	33	B2
ORCHID CIR	GGR	GG	10300	16	A3
ORCHID CIR	PLA	PLA	500	7	B5
ORCHID DR	BPK	BP	7800	10	C2
ORCHID DR	PLA	PLA	100	7	B5
ORCHID DR	WSTM	WSTM	9100	21	E3
ORCHID LN	ANA	AN08		13	A2
ORCHID ST	CO	SA07	20000	28	B6
ORCHID CREEK LN	CO	ET		29A	D3
ORCHID HILL PL	CO	SA	2300	32	A1
ORCHILA ST	CYP	CYP	11400	14	F2
ORD WY	ANA	AN	1500	16	B2
ORD WY	GGR	GG	11300	16	B2
ORD WY	WSTM	WSTM		21	D4
ORDAGO	MVJO	SJ92		29B	D3
OREGON AV	CM	CM	3200	27	B3
OREGON ST	BPK	BP	6700	10	C1
OREGON TRAIL LN	OR	OR		12	B5
ORELLANA	MVJO	SJ91		29B	C3
ORELLANO WY	CO	LB		29C	F1
ORELLANO WY	CO	LB	25200	29D	A1
ORENSE	MVJO	SJ91	22700	29B	C3
ORIENT DR	HTB	HB	9500	26	F6
ORIENTE DR	YL	YL	18500	8	A3
ORILLA RD	DPT	DPT	33700	37	E4
ORINDA CIR	HTB	HB47	8500	21	D5

1990 ORANGE COUNTY STREET INDEX

STREET	CITY	P.O. ZONE	BLOCK	PAGE	GRID
ORINDA RD	SJC	SJ75		36	B3
ORIOLE	IRV	SA		29	B3
ORIOLE AV	FTNV	SA08	9100	26	E3
ORIOLE AV	FTNV	SA08	10300	27	A3
ORIOLE AV	PLA	PLA	800	12	A1
ORIOLE DR	BPK	BP	7000	9	F1
ORIOLE DR	CM	CM	1700	27	B5
ORIOLE DR	LAG	LB51	900	34	E3
ORIOLE LN	HTB	HB	15800	20	E4
ORIOLE PL	ANA	AN	1200	10	A6
ORIOLE PL	OR	OR	1600	12	F6
ORIOLE ST	ANA	AN	1300	10	A6
ORION	IRV	SA		32A	A2
ORION AV	SA	SA04	2600	27	E2
ORION AV	SA	SA	1000	28	A2
ORION ST	HTB	HB	4500	20	D6
ORION WY	NB	NB	400	31	B4
ORISKANY CT	LALM	LALM		14	C3
ORKNEY CIR	HTB	HB	17900	26	A1
ORLANDO CT	CO	LB77		36	B4
ORLANDO DR	HTB	HB	6000	20	F4
ORLANDO DR	YL	YL	4600	8	C3
ORLANDO RD	CO	LALM	3200	14	B3
ORLEANS CIR	IRV	SA	15400	29	D3
ORLEANS DR	PLA	PLA	1300	7	C4
ORLEANS LN	LAP	BP23	7400	9	D2
ORME ST	ANA	AN04	1700	15	F1
ORO PL	SJC	SJ75	31400	36	D6
ORO ST	LAG	LB51	800	34	F4
ORO BLANCO	MVJO	SJ91		29B	C2
ORO GRANDE LN	MVJO	SJ91		29B	C5
ORONSAY CIR	HTB	HB46	10400	27	A4
OROPEL	MVJO	SJ91		29B	E2
OROSCO CIR	PLA	PLA	1900	7	B2
ORO VERDE LN	YL	YL	19000	8	B3
OROVILLE PL	CO	LB		29D	A3
ORREY PL	GGR	GG43	10200	22	A1
ORREY PL	WSTM	WSTM	8800	21	D1
ORRINGTON RD	NB	NB	4500	33	C2
ORRS CT	CYP	CYP	11300	15	A2
ORRWAY DR	STN	GG41	12500	15	C4
ORSINI	IRV	SA14		28	D5
ORSOLA	MVJO	SJ92	28000	29B	E3
ORTEGA HWY	CO	SA	29000	62	B1
ORTEGA HWY	SJC	SJ75	26800	36	E5
ORTEGA WY	PLA	PLA	1000	12	B1
ORVILLINA DR	CO	SA	12100	24	B1
ORWELL AV	WSTM	WSTM		21	D4
OSAGE WY	CO	ET		29A	F2
OSBORN	IRV			29	C4
OSBORNE CT	FTNV	SA08		26	F2
OSBORNE ST	WSTM	WSTM		21	E4
OSCAR CIR	FTNV	SA08	9500	26	F1
OSCAR WY	CO	ET		29A	E4
OSERA	MVJO	SJ92	28200	29B	E6
OSGOOD CT	LAG	LB51	300	34	E4
OSHKOSH AV	ANA	AN	2300	12	A5
OSHKOSH CIR	ANA	AN	2100	11	F5
OSLO CIR	BPK	BP	6900	10	B1
OSMOND ST	YL	YL	4300	7	E2
OSO PKWY	CO	LB		29D	A3
OSO PKWY	MVJO	SJ91	26700	29D	B3
OSO RD	CO	SJ75		36	B5
OSO RD	SJC	SJ75	26600	36	B5
OSO WY	WSTM	WSTM	7100	15	B5
OSOBERRY ST	CO	SJ88		59	B1
OSO ROJO LN	MVJO	SJ92		36	B2
OSO VIEJO	MVJO	SJ92	25000	29B	D6
OSO VIEJO	MVJO	SJ92	25000	29D	D1
OSPREY	IRV	SA		29	E3
OSPREY AV	CO	LB53		29A	B6
OSPREY CIR	ANA	AN		12	E1
OSPREY LN	FTNV	SA08	9200	26	E2
OSPREY ST	CO	ET	24100	29A	E4
OSSABAW CT	CYP	CYP	6800	15	A2
OSTRICH CIR	FTNV	SA08	8500	26	D2
OSUNA	MVJO	SJ91		29B	C1
OSUNA	MVJO	SJ91	27300	52	C6
OSWEGO AV E&W	HTB	HB	100	26	C5
OSWEGO ST	CO	ET	23300	29A	D3
OTAY CIR	MVJO	SJ91		29B	B3
OTERO	NB	NB		32	A2
OTERO	SCL	SC72		38	E5
OTIS AV	GGR	GG	12800	16	D3
OTIS AV	LAH	LAH	2000	1	E4
OTIS ST	SA	SA	2300	22	D5
OTT AV	PLA	PLA	900	7	D2
OTTAWA DR	PLA	PLA	800	7	C2
OTTAWA ST	SA	SA	1400	22	D4
OTTAWA RIV CIR	FTNV	SA08	8600	26	D1
OTTER RIVER CIR	FTNV	SA08		26	E1

STREET	CITY	P.O. ZONE	BLOCK	PAGE	GRID
OUTER WY	CYP	CYP	11500	15	A2
OUTLOOK LN	CO	SA	11900	24	D1
OUTPOST RD	SJC	SJ75		36	C4
OUTRIDER ST	OR	OR		18	D3
OUTRIGGER CIR	HTB	HB	4400	20	D5
OUTRIGGER CT	SJC	SJ75		38	A3
OUTRIGGER DR	NB	CDLM		33	C1
OUTRIGGER WY	ANA	AN	1800	11	A2
OUTRIGGER WY	CO	LB77		37	D1
OVAL RD	IRV	SA	5100	29	D2
OVALO	CO	LB	21000	29A	A5
OVERBROOK DR	CO	SA		18	C4
OVERHILL DR	CO	SA	9700	18	E4
OVERLAKE DR	CO	ET	24500	29A	E2
OVERLAND	IRV	SA		29	A4
OVERLAND CIR	ANA	AN		13	D3
OVERLAND DR	CO	LB		29A	F6
OVERLAND DR	CO	LB	25400	29C	F1
OVERLAND DR	HTB	HB	5300	20	E5
OVERLOOK RD	FUL	FL	700	6	D3
OVERLOOK TER	ANA	AN		43	A4
OVERMAN DR	GGR	GG	10500	16	A2
OVERTON ST	FTNV	SA08	15900	21	F4
OVERVIEW CIR	CO	SA	1800	18	E4
OVIEDA PZ	WSTM	WSTM		21	E2
OWARI	IRV	SA		24	F5
OWEN AV	HTB	HB	7900	26	C3
OWEN CT	IRV	SA17		32	E3
OWEN ST	GGR	GG45	12300	14	F4
OWEN WY	STN	STN		10	E4
OWEN WY	STN	STN		15	B2
OWENS DR	ANA	AN		13	E1
OWENS DR	SA	SA	100	17	B5
OWENS ST	BPK	BP		5	C4
OWENS LAKE CIR	CO	ET		29A	F1
OWENS RIVER CIR	FTNV	SA08	18500	26	D2
OWL CIR	FTNV	SA08	10400	27	A3
OWL CT	ANA	AN		43	A2
OWL CT	CO	ET		52	B6
OWL HILL LN	CO	LB		29C	D2
OX RD	ANA	AN	900	11	C6
OXBORO LN	HTB	HB		25	F2
OXBORO LN	HTB	HB		26	A2
OXBOW CREEK LN	CO	LB		29C	D1
OXBRIDGE CIR	CO	SA		18	D3
OXENBERG	MVJO	SJ92		29B	F6
OXFORD	IRV	SA		32	F1
OXFORD AV	FUL	FL	1700	7	A3
OXFORD AV	TUS	TUS	14400	24	A4
OXFORD CIR	WSTM	WSTM	15400	22	A3
OXFORD DR	CO	LAG		35	F3
OXFORD DR	CYP	CYP	5000	9	D5
OXFORD DR	HTB	HB47	6500	21	A2
OXFORD DR	PLA	PLA	1000	7	B4
OXFORD LN	CM	CM	2500	27	D5
OXFORD LN	LAH	LAH		2	B5
OXFORD LN	NB	NB	1000	31	E4
OXFORD ST	ANA	AN	1700	7	C6
OXFORD ST	SA	SA	100	23	B4
OXLEY CIR	HTB	HB	8500	26	D5
OYSTER BED LN	HTB	HB46	20700	27	A6

P

STREET	CITY	P.O. ZONE	BLOCK	PAGE	GRID
P ST	LAG	LB		35	A4
P ST	ETMC	SA09		51	C3
PABLO RD	YL	YL		8	E4
PACATO DR	MVJO	SJ91		29B	B5
PACEMONT DR	HTB	HB		25	F2
PACEMONT DR	HTB	HB		26	A2
PACHECO	MVJO	SJ92	28400	29B	E4
PACHECO AV	WSTM	WSTM	8600	21	D3
PACIFIC AV	ANA	AN04	2100	15	E1
PACIFIC AV	BPK	BP	7400	5	B4
PACIFIC AV	CO	LAH	10800	2	A5
PACIFIC AV	CO	AN04	9000	15	E1
PACIFIC AV	CO	SUNB	2600	20	C6
PACIFIC AV	CO	CM27	2200	27	A6
PACIFIC AV	CO	CM27	2100	31	A1
PACIFIC AV	LAG	LB51	1400	34	E2
PACIFIC AV	LAH	LAH	300	2	A5
PACIFIC AV	SB	SB	2500	20	A4
PACIFIC AV	STN	AN04	7800	15	E1
PACIFIC AV	WSTM	WSTM	13600	15	C6
PACIFIC AV	WSTM	WSTM	14000	21	C1
PACIFIC AV	YL	YL	17500	7	E2
PACIFIC AV N	SA	SA	2000	16	F6
PACIFIC AV N&S	SA	SA	100	22	F3
PACIFIC AV S	SA	SA04	2800	27	F1
PACIFIC CIR	HTB	HB47		20	B4
PACIFIC CIR	MVJO	SJ92		29D	C2

STREET	CITY	P.O. ZONE	BLOCK	PAGE	GRID
PACIFIC CT	ANA	AN	1500	16	B1
PACIFIC DR	FUL	FL33	200	5	F6
PACIFIC DR	FUL	FL33	1000	10	F1
PACIFIC DR	NB	CDLM	2200	33	A1
PACIFIC DR	SCL	SC72		39	A2
PACIFIC PL	ANA	AN	1500	16	B1
PACIFIC PL	CO	AN04	9200	15	E1
PACIFIC PL	MVJO	SJ92		29D	C2
PACIFIC ST	CO	MDWY	15200	21	C3
PACIFIC ST	CO	WSTM	15000	21	C2
PACIFIC ST	FTNV	SA08	18300	27	B2
PACIFIC ST	OR	OR	2100	12	C5
PACIFIC ST	STN	STN	7900	15	C1
PACIFIC ST	TUS	TUS	100	23	E2
PACIFICA	IRV	SA		29	F6
PACIFICA	IRV	SA18		51	A6
PACIFICA AV	CO	SJ91	25200	29A	F5
PACIFICA CIR	HTB	HB		26	B4
PACIFICA DR	PLA	PLA	1000	7	D4
PACIFICA LN	HTB	HB		30	D2
PACIFIC CST HWY	CO	SUNB	2500	20	A3
PACIFIC CST HWY	HTB	HB	15900	20	A3
PACIFIC CST HWY	HTB	HB	17500	25	E3
PACIFIC CST HWY	HTB	HB48		26	A5
PACIFIC CST HWY	HTB	HB	21700	30	C1
PACIFIC CST HWY	SB	SB	100	19	E1
PACIFIC CST HWY	SB	SB	2300	20	A3
PACIFIC CREST	CO	LAG		37	F2
PACIFIC CRST DR	MVJO	SJ92		29D	C2
PACIFIC HTS DR	MVJO	SJ92		29D	C2
PACIFIC HLS DR	MVJO	SJ92		29D	C2
PACIFIC ISLD DR	CO	LB	31600	35	C6
PACIFIC ISLD DR	CO	LB77	31900	37	C1
PACIFICO AV	ANA	AN	800	16	E2
PACIFICO WY	CYP	CYP	9800	9	E6
PACIFIC PARK DR	CO	LB56		29C	B4
PACIFIC PARK DR	CO	LB53		29D	A3
PACIFIC PT	MVJO	SJ92		29D	C2
PACIFIC TER DR	MVJO	SJ92		29D	C2
PACIFIC VIEW DR	NB	CDLM	3000	32	C5
PACIFIC VIEW ST	DPT	SC24		38	B5
PACKER PL	CO	ET	23400	29A	E4
PACKERS CIR	TUS	TUS	1000	24	A2
PADDLE WHEL CIR	OR	OR		12	C3
PADDOCK CIR	HTB	HB	9100	26	E5
PADDOCK LN	CO	SA		18	D5
PADDOCK LN	YL	YL		8	D2
PADILLA	MVJO	SJ91		29B	C1
PADILLA	MVJO	SJ91		52	C6
PADINA CIR	DPT	LB77		37	E3
PADOVA	CO	LB		29A	A4
PADRES ST	WSTM	WSTM	15200	21	E3
PADRINO CIR	HTB	HB		26	B2
PADUA	IRV	SA14		29	A4
PADUA DR	CO	LB	25400	29D	A1
PADUA DR	HTB	HB	5800	25	F1
PAGE AV	BPK	BP	7800	10	C1
PAGE AV	CO	FL33	9800	10	F1
PAGE AV	FUL	FL33	1900	10	F1
PAGE CIR	HTB	HB	8600	26	D5
PAGE CT	ANA	AN	1600	16	F1
PAGEANT ST	ANA	AN	100	12	E2
PAGEANTRY DR	PLA	PLA	100	7	B4
PAGO PAGO CIR	HTB	HB46	10400	27	A3
PAGUERA	MVJO	SJ92	27700	29B	D2
PAIGE CIR	CO	LB	24600	29A	E6
PAIGE LN	CM	CM27		31	F1
PAINE CIR	IRV	SA		28	F4
PAINE CIR	IRV	SA		29	A4
PAINTED PONY LN	CO	SA		18	C4
PAINTER ST	LAH	LAH	200	1	E5
PAISLEY LN	HTB	HB	20500	26	F5
PAJARITO LN	CO	SJ79		59	D2
PAL WY	WSTM	WSTM	7100	15	B5
PALA	MVJO	SJ91		29B	A4
PALA CIR	PLA	PLA	200	7	C5
PALA DR	GGR	GG	12600	15	B4
PALA PL	OR	OR		13	B6
PALA WY	LAG	LB51	2600	34	F4
PALACE AV	CM	CM27	1900	31	B2
PALACE CT	CO	LB		35	E2
PALACE LN	SA	SA		22	E2
PALACE WY	TUS	TUS	13800	17	E6
PALADIN AV	ANA	AN	2500	12	A5
PALADIN CT	ANA	AN	2700	12	A5
PALADIUM AV	GGR	GG	10500	16	A3
PALADIUM CT	GGR	GG	10600	16	A3
PALAGONIA ISLE	IRV	SA14		28	D5
PALAIS RD	CO	AN04	9700	10	F6
PALAIS RD	STN	STN	7300	10	B6

STREET	CITY	P.O. ZONE	BLOCK	PAGE	GRID
PALAIS RD E	ANA	AN	100	11	E6
PALAIS RD W	ANA	AN	2100	10	D6
PALAIS RD W	ANA	AN	200	11	B6
PALAMEDES	IRV	SA		29	D1
PALA MESA LN	HTB	HB		30	D2
PALAMOS PL	MVJO	SJ92		29D	E2
PALAMINO CIR	CO	YL	6400	8	C6
PALANCA	MVJO	SJ92	21800	29B	E1
PALAU PL	CM	CM	1600	27	C4
PALAU ST	CYP	CYP	6100	14	F3
PALAWAN CIR	DPT	LB77		37	C1
PALAWAN ST	CYP	CYP	11500	14	F2
PALENCIA LN	CO	LB		35	C5
PALERMO	CO	LB		29A	B4
PALERMO	IRV	SA14		28	F4
PALERMO	TUS	TUS		24	B3
PALERMO DR	HTB	HB	8500	26	D4
PALERMO ST	CO	LAG		35	F3
PALERMO WY	LAH	LAH	500	2	C4
PALERMO WY	YL	YL		40	D6
PALI ST	SA	SA		22	C3
PALIN CIR	HTB	HB		26	C3
PALISADE DR	HTB	HB	6000	20	F4
PALISADES DR	DPT	SC24	26400	38	B5
PALISADES DR	FUL	FL	2000	6	D3
PALISADES DR	MVJO	SJ92		29D	F3
PALLAS WY	CO	SJ91		29A	F6
PALLAS WY	CO	SJ91		29B	A6
PALLAS WY	CO	SJ91		29D	A1
PALLAZIO	IRV	SA14		28	D4
PALLAZO	CO	LB77		35	F5
PALM AV	CO	OR65	8500	12	D4
PALM AV	HTB	HB		25	F4
PALM AV	HTB	HB	200	26	B5
PALM AV	OR	OR		12	D4
PALM AV	YL	YL	4200	8	B3
PALM AV E	OR	OR	3600	18	A2
PALM AV E&W	OR	OR	100	17	A3
PALM CIR	PLA	PLA	100	7	B3
PALM CT	CO	LB77		36	B4
PALM DR	BREA	BREA	500	6	F1
PALM DR	FUL	FL		7	B3
PALM DR	LAG	LB51	1700	34	E3
PALM DR	OR	OR	200	17	B3
PALM DR	SCL	SC72		39	A2
PALM DR E&W	PLA	PLA	100	7	B3
PALM LN	ANA	AN	1600	11	B6
PALM PL	OR	OR	700	17	D3
PALM ST	BREA	BREA	500	2	C5
PALM ST	CO	LAH	1200	2	C3
PALM ST	FTNV	SA08	17100	21	E6
PALM ST	FTNV	SA08	18500	26	E3
PALM ST	FUL	FL35	2600	2	C5
PALM ST	GGR	GG	12700	16	D5
PALM ST	IRV	SA	3700	29	C1
PALM ST	NB	NB	100	33	B5
PALM ST	SA	SA	1500	23	D2
PALM ST N	LAH	LAH	100	2	C5
PALM ST S	ANA	AN	1100	11	D6
PALM ST S	LAH	LAH	400	2	C5
PALM WY	ANA	AN	1200	11	B6
PALMA CIR	CO	YL	6400	8	C6
PALMA DR	CO	LB	22900	35	C5
PALMADA	MVJO	SJ92	28000	29B	E3
PALMATUM	IRV	SA		24	F5
PALMA VALLEY	CO	SJ79		59	D6
PALMA VISTA AV	GGR	GG	10800	16	A2
PALMA VISTA ST	GGR	GG	11000	16	A2
PALM BEACH CT	DPT	LB77		37	D4
PALMDALE AV	OR	OR	100	12	C6
PALMDALE ST	HTB	HB47	17000	21	B6
PALMEK CIR	CO	ET	23800	29A	E5
PALMENTO WY	IRV	SA	17800	29	A5
PALMER PL	LAG	LB51	400	34	E4
PALMER ST	CM	CM27	200	31	C3
PALMERA	CO	SJ		59	C1
PALMERA RD	SJC	SJ75		38	B3
PALMETTO CIR	FTNV	SA08	18000	26	E1
PALMETTO CT	CO	LB	28000	29C	E6
PALMETTO PL	BREA	BREA	1000	2	F5
PALMETTO PL	CO	LB	30800	35	E5
PALMETTO PL	MVJO	SJ92		29D	F3
PALM HILL DR	SJC	SJ75		36	E5
PALMIERI ISLE	IRV	SA14		28	D5
PALM VIA	FUL	FL		6	D6
PALM VISTA	YL	YL		8	B3
PALMWOOD	CO	ET		51	F6
PALMWOOD DR	GGR	GG	11000	16	A3
PALMYRA AV	GGR	GG	10900	16	A4
PALMYRA AV E	OR	OR	3500	18	A3
PALMYRA AV E&W	OR	OR	100	17	C3

STREET	CITY	P.O. ZONE	BLOCK	PAGE	GRID
PALMYRA PL	OR	OR	1300	17	B3
PALO DR	CO	LB		35	F3
PALO DR	CO	LB77		36	A3
PALO LN	MVJO	SJ91	23900	29B	C5
PALO ALTO	CO	ET		29A	F4
PALO ALTO DR	ANA	AN		13	D2
PALO ALTO DR	HTB	HB	6000	20	F6
PALO ALTO PL	OR	OR		18	B1
PALO ALTO ST	DPT	LB77		37	F3
PALO ALTO ST	DPT	DPT	33000	38	A4
PALO LADO	IRV	SA		24	E5
PALO LOMA PL	OR	OR	1200	13	C6
PALO LOMA PL	OR	OR		18	C1
PALOMA AV	GGR	GG	10500	16	A5
PALOMA DR	CM	CM27	2000	31	E3
PALOMA DR	NB	NB	2000	31	E3
PALOMA LN	YL	YL	4400	8	B3
PALOMA PL	FUL	FL	900	6	B2
PALOMAR CT	CO	LB		29C	E5
PALOMAR CT	CO	LB	28000	35	E1
PALOMAR ST	GGR	GG	12500	15	A4
PALOMAR ST	WSTM	WSTM	13000	15	A6
PALOMAR WY	CO	SA	12900	18	A5
PALOMARES	MVJO	SJ92		29D	E3
PALOMINO LN	ANA	AN07		13	D3
PALOMINO LN	YL	YL	4300	7	E2
PALOMITA CIR	MVJO	SJ91	26300	29D	B2
PALOS	IRV	SA		28	E6
PALOS VERDES AV	WSTM	WSTM	8500	21	D3
PALOS VERDES LN	HTB	HB		20	C3
PALO VERDE	CO	ET		29A	F4
PAMELA LN	CM	CM27	2200	31	B1
PAMELA LN	LAH	LAH	1400	2	B3
PAMELA LN	WSTM	WSTM	6000	14	F5
PAMELA PL	VPK	OR67	17900	12	F5
PAMELA PL	VPK	OR67	17900	13	A5
PAMELA ST	CYP	CYP	10600	15	A1
PAMELA KAY LN	ANA	AN	5300	13	B2
PAMI CIR	OR	OR	2100	12	E5
PAMLICO	IRV	SA		24	F6
PAMLICO	IRV	SA		29	F1
PAMMY LN	HTB	HB	18200	26	C2
PAMPAS LN	ANA	AN	1600	11	B4
PAMPAS ST	OR	OR	2600	12	C4
PAMPERO CIR	MVJO	SJ91	25400	29D	B2
PANA CT	CO	ET	25200	29A	F3
PANACEA DR	HTB	HB	9500	26	F6
PANADERO	SCL	SC72		38	E4
PANAMA DR	BPK	BP	5500	9	E2
PANAMA ST	CO	LB56		29C	D3
PANAY CIR	CM	CM	1800	27	B3
PANAY ST	CYP	CYP	11500	15	A2
PANDORA	IRV	SA		29	D1
PANDORA LN	CO	AN04	9700	10	E5
PANDORA PL	ANA	AN	600	11	C5
PANDORA ST	CO	ET		29A	D3
PANORAMA CT	BREA	BREA		2	E4
PANORAMA DR	ANA	AN		13	B2
PANORAMA DR	HTB	HB48		25	E3
PANORAMA DR	LAG	LB51	400	34	C1
PANORAMA PL	CO	SA	12700	18	B4
PANORAMA RD	FUL	FL	600	6	C3
PANORAMA CREST	CO	SA	12700	18	B4
PANORAMA VW DR	CO	SA	12600	18	B4
PANSY CIR	SB	SB	3500	14	D4
PANSY LN	CM	CM	3300	27	E3
PANSY ST	SB	SB	3800	14	D4
PANTANO	CO	SJ		59	C1
PANTANO	SCL	SC72		38	F4
PAPAGAYO DR	MVJO	SJ91	26300	29B	B5
PAPAYA LN	GGR	GG		15	D5
PAPAYA PL	BREA	BREA	1200	2	F5
PAPAYA PL	BREA	BREA	1200	3	A5
PAPER LN	NB	NB60	2900	27	F6
PAPER LN	NB	NB	2900	31	F1
PAPUA LN	HTB	HB46	19000	27	A3
PAR CIR	HTB	HB	5900	20	F4
PAR LN	GGR	GG	10300	15	F3
PARADA LN	MVJO	SJ91		29B	C6
PARADE ST	CO	AN04	9500	10	E5
PARADISE CIR	CYP	CYP	5900	14	F2
PARADISE CT	ANA	AN	1300	12	A2
PARADISE LN S	ANA	AN	100	12	A3
PARADISE PL	ANA	AN	1000	12	A2
PARADISE RD	ANA	AN	2300	12	A3
PARADISE ST	ANA	AN	1100	12	A2
PARAGUAY DR	BPK	BP	5500	9	E2
PARAISO	CO	SJ88		29B	F5
PARAKEET CIR	FTNV	SA08	10400	27	A2
PARAPET PL	SA	SA		28	B1
PARC VISTA	CO	LAG		35	F4

COPYRIGHT, © 1989 BY Thomas Bros Maps

115
1990 ORANGE COUNTY STREET INDEX
PARC VISTA — PAT PL
ORANGE CO.

STREET	CITY	P.O. ZONE	BLOCK	PAGE	GRID
PARC VISTA	CO	LB77		35	F4
PARDELLA LN	CO	LB		35	C6
PARIS CIR	HTB	HB47	6500	21	A2
PARIS LN	NB	NB		31	B4
PARIS WY	IRV	SA	5100	29	D3
PARIS WY	PLA	PLA	600	7	C4
PARISO DR	MVJO	SJ91	26500	29D	B2
PARK AV	ANA	AN	1100	11	B3
PARK AV	CM	CM27	1800	31	C2
PARK AV	CO	SUNB	16900	20	B5
PARK AV	CYP	CYP	4700	9	D5
PARK AV	GGR	GG45	5300	14	E4
PARK AV	GGR	GG	6300	15	A4
PARK AV	GGR	GG	10200	16	A4
PARK AV	LAG	LB51	200	34	F1
PARK AV	LAH	LAH	1000	1	F6
PARK AV	NB	NB	100	31	E6
PARK AV	STN	STN	8000	15	C1
PARK AV	YL	YL	4800	7	F3
PARK AV	YL	YL	4900	8	A3
PARK BLVD	SA	SA	2300	17	B5
PARK CIR	ANA	AN	900	11	A6
PARK CIR	SJC	SJ75		36	B2
PARK DR	CM	CM27	500	31	C3
PARK DR	LAG	LB51	100	34	C2
PARK DR	SA	SA	1500	23	A4
PARK DR	SA	SA	3400	28	A1
PARK LN	ANA	AN	2500	12	A1
PARK LN	BREA	BREA		2	E5
PARK LN	CO	MDWY		21	D2
PARK LN	GGR	GG	11300	15	F3
PARK LN	NB	NB	3600	31	B5
PARK LN E	SA	SA	700	17	C5
PARK LN N	OR	OR	2000	12	E5
PARK LN N	OR	OR	200	17	E2
PARK LN S	OR	OR	200	17	E2
PARK LN W	SA	SA	1300	16	F5
PARK LN W	SA	SA	400	17	A5
PARK PL	CM	CM27	500	31	C3
PARK PL	IRV	SA		24	E5
PARK PL	LAG	LB51		34	F1
PARK PL	LAH	LAH	500	2	A4
PARK PL	NB	NB63		31	C5
PARK PL	OR	OR		18	A4
PARK PL	YL	YL	4900	7	F3
PARK PZ	IRV	SA		28	E4
PARK PZ	STN	STN		15	C3
PARK ST	HTB	HB	1000	26	B4
PARK ST	OR	OR	100	18	A4
PARK ST	WSTM	WSTM	7100	21	B1
PARK WY	ANA	AN	400	11	C3
PARK WY	LAH	LAH	900	1	F6
PARK BALBOA AV	OR	OR68		16	F4
PARK CENTER DR	CM	CM26		28	A3
PARKCENTER DR	SA	SA		23	E2
PARKCENTER LN	TUS	SA05		24	B4
PARK CENTRAL AV	OR	OR68		16	F4
PARK CIRCLE DR	SB	SB		20	B4
PARKCOURT PL	SA	SA	1700	23	D2
PARK CREST	BREA	BREA		2	D4
PARKCREST DR	CM	CM27	1800	31	B2
PARKCREST DR	GGR	GG		16	D6
PARKDALE DR	ANA	AN		10	D2
PARKER	IRV	SA18		51	D6
PARKER CIR	HTB	HB47	8600	21	D5
PARKER CIR	VPK	OR67	19200	13	B5
PARKER DR	TUS	TUS	17300	23	E1
PARKER ST N&S	OR	OR	100	17	C1
PARKFIELD	MVJO	SJ92		29B	E2
PARKGLEN CIR	CM	CM27	1800	31	A2
PARKGLEN CIR	IRV	SA	4400	29	D2
PARK GLEN CIR	SA	SA		16	E6
PARK GLEN RD	SA	SA		16	E6
PARKGLEN LOOP	STN	STN		15	B4
PARK GREEN DR	NB	CDLM		33	C1
PARKGREEN LN	GGR	GG43	11000	16	E1
PK GRIFFITH AV	OR	OR68		16	F4
PARKHAVEN DR	ANA	AN		10	D2
PARKHILL DR	CM	CM27	1000	31	B2
PARKHILL RD	CO	ET	24300	29A	D4
PARKHURST PL	YL	YL		8	C4
PARK HYDE ST	OR	OR68		16	F4
PK INDSTRIAL DR	LAH	LAH		2	B5
PARK LAKE	SA	SA		17	D5
PARKLAND ST	YL	YL		8	B5
PARK LANTERN ST	DPT	DPT		37	F5
PARK LAWN DR	GGR	GG43		16	E1
PARKMAN RD	CO	LB77		35	E6
PK MCCOMBER CIR	BPK	BP	5200	5	B4
PARKMONT CIR	CO	ET	26900	29B	C1
PARKMONT CIR	CO	ET		52	C6

STREET	CITY	P.O. ZONE	BLOCK	PAGE	GRID
PARK NEWPORT DR	NB	NB		32	A4
PARK PASEO	CO	LAG		37	F2
PARK PLACE DR	CO	LB		35	E3
PARK RIDGE AV	CO	YL	19400	8	B3
PARK RIM CIR	ANA	AN		13	F3
PARK RIM CIR	ANA	AN		43	A3
PARK ROSE CIR	ANA	AN		13	A1
PARKS RD	FUL	FL		6	A3
PARKSIDE AV	OR	OR	2100	12	E6
PARKSIDE DR	IRV	SA	17900	28	F5
PARKSIDE DR	YL	YL		8	B5
PARKSIDE DR E	CO	LB		35	E3
PARKSIDE DR W	CO	LB		35	E3
PARKSIDE LN	ANA	AN		10	D2
PARKSIDE LN	GGR	GG43	11000	16	E1
PARKSIDE LN	HTB	HB47	16100	21	C4
PARK SKYLINE RD	CO	SA	1700	18	C6
PARK SKYLINE RD	CO	SA	1800	24	C1
PARK TERRACE LN	MVJO	SJ92		29D	D4
PARKTREE CIR	HTB	HB		26	B2
PARKVIEW AV	WSTM	WSTM	10000	22	A2
PARKVIEW CIR	ANA	AN	3100	10	B5
PARKVIEW CIR	CM	CM27	1800	31	A2
PARK VIEW DR	FUL	FL	100	6	C3
PARKVIEW LN	GGR	GG	11000	16	B6
PARKVIEW LN	HTB	HB		26	C2
PARKVIEW LN	IRV	SA	3600	28	F5
PARKVIEW ST	ANA	AN	600	10	B5
PARKVIEW TER	CO	SA	18900	18	B4
PARKVIEW TER	YL	YL	19800	8	C4
PARKVIEW WY	TUS	TUS		24	B3
PARK VILLA CIR	VPK	OR67	10400	13	A6
PARK VILLA LN	VPK	OR67	10400	13	A6
PARK VILLA PL	VPK	OR67	18200	13	A6
PARK VINE ST	OR	OR68		16	F4
PARK VISTA	IRV	SA		29	B3
PARKVISTA CIR	CM	CM27	1800	31	B2
PARK VISTA CT	FUL	FL	2400	7	A2
PARK VISTA ST	ANA	AN	400	12	B3
PARKWAY DR	GGR	GG	13900	16	B6
PARKWAY DR	IRV	SA	17900	28	E5
PARKWAY LOOP	TUS	SA10		23	F5
PARKWEST CIR	LAP	BP23		9	E3
PARKWOOD	CO	LB56		29C	C1
PARKWOOD	HTB	HB		26	C2
PARKWOOD AV E	LAH	LAH	300	2	A6
PARKWOOD AV W	LAH	LAH	500	1	F6
PARKWOOD AV W	LAH	LAH	100	2	A6
PARKWOOD CT	CO	YL		8	F2
PARKWOOD CT	FUL	FL		7	A1
PARKWOOD DR	GGR	GG43	13900	16	E1
PARKWOOD ST	ANA	AN	400	11	A3
PARKWOOD ST	CO	ET		29A	E2
PARLAY CIR	HTB	HB		20	E5
PARLIAMENT AV	GGR	GG	10000	15	F2
PARLIAMENT AV	GGR	GG	10300	16	A2
PARLIAMENT AV	WSTM	WSTM	9100	21	E4
PARLIAMENT WY	SA	SA		23	B6
PARLIAMENT WY	SA	SA	200	28	B1
PARMLEY LN	CM	CM		27	F6
PARNELL PL	CM	CM	1200	27	D3
PAROS CIR	CM	CM	1800	27	B4
PARRIE ST	SA	SA	600	23	D1
PARROCO LN	MVJO	SJ91		29B	A5
PARROT CT	CO	ET		52	B6
PARROT LN	FTNV	SA08	9200	26	E1
PARRY AV	ANA	AN	1000	11	C2
PARSELL ST	TUS	SA10	15500	29	A1
PARSONS PL	GGR	GG43	14000	22	B1
PARSONS PL	SA	SA	900	22	B1
PARSONS ST	CM	CM27	1900	31	D2
PARSONS ST	LAH	LAH	300	1	D4
PARTHENON AV	CO	SJ91	25400	29A	F5
PARTIDO LN	CO	ET	25100	29A	F2
PARTON ST N	SA	SA	1700	17	B6
PARTON ST N	SA	SA	300	23	B1
PARTON ST S	SA	SA	300	23	B4
PARTON ST S	SA	SA	3500	28	B2
PARTRIDGE	IRV	SA		29	B3
PARTRIDGE CIR	CO	ET		29A	D2
PARTRIDGE CIR	HTB	HB	5000	20	E3
PARTRIDGE CIR	LAP	BP23	4700	9	D3
PARTRIDGE LN	CO	LB53		29A	B6
PARTRIDGE LN	OR	OR	5400	18	C3
PARTRIDGE LN	YL	YL		8	E1
PARTRIDGE ST	ANA	AN		7	B6
PARTRIDGE ST	GGR	GG	13000	16	D5
PASADA VALIENTE	CO	SJ		59	C2
PASADENA AV	CO	SA	13700	17	E6
PASADENA AV	CO	TUS	15500	23	E3
PASADENA AV	SA	SA	2200	17	E6

STREET	CITY	P.O. ZONE	BLOCK	PAGE	GRID
PASADENA AV	TUS	TUS	100	23	E2
PASADENA CT	SCL	SC72	400	39	D4
PASATIEMPO	MVJO	SJ92	27000	29D	D1
PASATIEMPO DR	CO	YL	27500	8	B4
PASCAL WY	CO	ET		52	B5
PASCHALLS LN	CO	SUNB		20	B6
PASEO CIR	HTB	HB	8400	26	D1
PASEO PL	FUL	FL	600	6	C1
PASEO ABETO	CO	ET	25100	51	F5
PASEO ACACIA	SJC	SJ75	31200	36	C5
PASEO ACTIVO	SJC	SJ75		38	C4
PASEO ADELANTO	SJC	SJ75		38	C1
PASEO AGUILA	SCL	SC72		38	D6
PASEO ALBA	SCL	SCL		39	F2
PASEO ALBA	SJC	SJ75		36	E5
PASEO ALCAZAA	ANA	AN		13	E3
PASEO ALDEANO	ANA	AN		13	D1
PASEO ALDONZA	SJC	SJ75		36	E6
PASEO ALEGRIA	SJC	SJ75	33900	38	C4
PASEO ALONDRA	SJC	SJ75		38	D1
PASEO ALTO	YL	YL		8	D3
PAS ALTO PLANO	SJC	SJ75		36	A6
PAS ALTO PLANO	SJC	SJ75		38	A1
PASEO AMADOR	SJC	SJ75		38	D2
PASEO AMANTE	SJC	SJ75		38	D1
PASEO AMAPOLA	SJC	SJ75	31200	36	B5
PASEO ANDANTE	SJC	SJ75		36	E6
PASEO ANDORRA	SJC	SJ75		38	B2
PASEO ARBOLEDA	CO	ET	24900	29A	F1
PASEO ARBOLEDA	CO	ET		51	F6
PASEO ARNALDO	YL	YL		8	C4
PASEO ATREVIDA	SJC	SJ75		36	C4
PASEO AZAELA	SJC	SJ75		38	D1
PASEO AZTECA	SJC	SJ75		36	E5
PASEO BAHAIA	SJC	SJ75		36	E5
PASEO BALBOA	ANA	AN		13	C2
PASEO BANDERA	ANA	AN		13	C2
PASEO BARONA	SJC	SJ75	27600	36	D6
PASEO BARRANCA	SJC	SJ75		36	E5
PASEO BELARDES	SJC	SJ75		36	B6
PASEO BELARDES	SJC	SJ75		38	B1
PASEO BLANCO	SJC	SJ75		38	A3
PASEO BONITA	LALM	LALM	11600	14	B3
PASEO BOSCANA	SJC	SJ75		36	E5
PASEO BRILLO	SJC	SJ75	26600	38	B4
PASEO BURLADERO	SJC	SJ75	27000	38	C2
PASEO CABALLO	ANA	AN		13	E2
PASEO CADIZ	SJC	SJ75		36	F5
PASEO CALIENTE	YL	YL		8	E4
PASEO CAMALU	SJC	SJ75		36	C5
PASEO CAMPO	ANA	AN		13	D1
PASEO CANCION	ANA	AN		13	E2
PASEO CANOA	ANA	AN		13	D1
PASEO CARDERO	SJC	SJ75		36	C4
PASEO CARMEL	ANA	AN		13	C3
PASEO CARMEL	SJC	SJ75		36	B5
PASEO CAROLINA	SJC	SJ75	32000	38	B1
PASEO CASTILE	SJC	SJ75		38	D2
PASEO CELESTE	ANA	AN	24900	13	D2
PASEO CERVEZA	SJC	SJ75	33100	38	B3
PASEO CHRISTINA	SJC	SJ75		36	E6
PASEO CIELO	SJC	SJ75		36	A6
PASEO CIELO	SJC	SJ75		38	A1
PASEO CIPRES	CO	ET		51	E6
PASEO CIRCULO	TUS	TUS		24	C3
PASEO CLAVEL	SJC	SJ75		38	D1
PASEO COLONIAL	SJC	SJ75		38	A2
PASEO CORONA	DPT	DPT		37	C5
PASEO CORRALES	SJC	SJ75		38	E1
PASEO CORTEZ	IRV	SA		32	F1
PASEO CORTO	TUS	TUS	1300	23	E1
PASEO CUMBRE	ANA	AN		13	E3
PASEO DALI	IRV	SA		32A	A1
PAS D ALESSNDRO	SJC	SJ75	32000	38	A1
PASEO DE ALICIA	CO	LB		29A	B6
PASEO DE ALICIA	CO	LB		29C	F1
PASEO D COLINAS	CO	LB77		36	A2
PAS D CRISTOBAL	SCL	SC72	100	39	D4
PASEO DE DECORA	SJC	SJ75	33800	38	C4
PASEO DE ELENA	SJC	SJ75	32000	38	A1
PASEO DE GRACE	ANA	AN		8	B5
PASEO D HERMOSA	SJC	SJ75	32000	38	A1
PASEO DE JUAN	ANA	AN		13	D1
PASEO D JUANITA	SJC	SJ75	25000	38	A1
PAS D LA CUMBRE	YL	YL		8	D5
PASEO DEL AMOR	SJC	SJ75	25600	38	A2
PASEO DE LA PAZ	SJC	SJ75		38	A1
PAS DE LA PLAYA	CO	LB		35	C6
PAS D LA RAMBLA	YL	YL		8	D4
PAS D L SERENTA	SCL	SC72	100	39	D5

STREET	CITY	P.O. ZONE	BLOCK	PAGE	GRID
PAS D LS PALOMS	YL	YL		8	C4
PASEO DEL CAMPO	CO	LB	23700	35	D4
PASEO DE LEON	ANA	AN		13	C2
PASEO DEL ESTE	SJC	SJ75		38	C3
PASEO DL LAGO E	CO	LB	23900	29A	B5
PASEO DL LAGO W	CO	LB	23900	29A	A5
PASEO DL LUCERO	SJC	SJ75		38	A3
PASEO DEL MAR	CO	LB		35	C5
PASEO DEL MAR	SJC	SJ75		38	B4
PASEO DL MARINO	SJC	SJ75	27900	36	E6
PASEO DL MARINO	SJC	SJ75		38	F1
PASEO DL NIGUEL	CO	LB	30700	35	D5
PASEO DEL NORTE	ANA	AN		13	E2
PASEO DEL NORTE	SJC	SJ75		36	E6
PASEO DEL NORTE	SJC	SJ75	27900	38	F1
PAS D LS FLORES	SCL	SC72		39	D3
PASEO DEL PRADO	YL	YL		8	D5
PASEO DL RETIRO	YL	YL		8	D5
PASEO DEL SOL	CO	LB		35	C6
PASEO DE LUNA	ANA	AN		13	D2
PASEO DEL VALLE	CO	LB	30300	35	D4
PASEO DEL VALLE	YL	YL		40	B5
PASEO DE MANUEL	SJC	SJ75	32000	38	A1
PASEO DE OCASO	CO	LB77		36	A2
PASEO DE ORO	CYP	CYP	4000	9	C5
PASEO DE PLATA	CYP	CYP	4200	9	C5
PASEO DE SOTO	ANA	AN		13	C2
PASEO DE TANIA	SJC	SJ75	32000	38	A1
PASEO DE TONER	BREA	BREA	100	2	E6
PAS DE TORONTO	YL	YL		40	B5
PAS DE VALENCIA	CO	LB	25000	29A	D6
PAS DE VALENCIA	CO	LB	25800	29C	F2
PAS DE VALENCIA	CO	LB		29D	A2
PASEO DE VEGA	IRV	SA		32	F1
PASEO DIANA	SJC	SJ75		36	E5
PASEO DIEGO	ANA	AN		13	E4
PASEO DON JOSE	SJC	SJ75	31500	36	B6
PASEO DORADO	FUL	FL	1100	6	A3
PASEO DURAN	SJC	SJ75	31400	36	D6
PASEO DURANGO	SJC	SJ75		36	C5
PASEO EL ARCO	SJC	SJ75		36	B5
PASEO EL CONCHO	SJC	SJ75		36	E6
PASEO EL CONCHO	SJC	SJ75	27900	38	F1
PASEO EL GRECO	ANA	AN		13	E3
PASEO EL MARMOL	SJC	SJ75		36	B5
PASEO EL SIENA	CO	LB77		36	B1
PASEO ENSENADA	SJC	SJ75		36	C4
PASEO EQUESTRE	CO	ET		51	F6
PASEO ESCUELA	CO	LB77		36	A2
PASEO ESPADA	SJC	SJ75		36	C6
PASEO ESPADA	SJC	SJ75		38	C1
PASEO ESTABLO	SJC	SJ75		38	E1
PASEO ESTEBAN	SJC	SJ75	27700	36	D6
PASEO ESTRELLA	ANA	AN		13	D2
PASEO FERRELO	ANA	AN		13	C2
PASEO FIESTA	ANA	AN		13	E2
PASEO FIESTA	SJC	SJ75		38	D2
PASEO FLAMENCO	SCL	SC72		38	D6
PASEO GALLITA	SCL	SC72		38	D6
PASEO GALLITA	SCL	SC72		39	A1
PASEO GANADO	ANA	AN		13	E2
PASEO GANSO	SCL	SC72		38	D6
PASEO GILBERTO	YL	YL		8	C4
PASEO GOYA	ANA	AN		13	E3
PASEO GRANDE	FUL	FL	1100	6	A2
PASEO HALCON	SCL	SC72		38	D6
PASEO ISABELLA	SJC	SJ75		36	E6
PASEO JOAQUIN	YL	YL		8	C4
PASEO LABRANZA	SJC	SJ75		36	D6
PASEO LABRANZA	SJC	SJ75		38	D1
PASEO LA CRESTA	CO	LB77		36	A1
PASEO LAGUNA	SJC	SJ75		38	C2
PASEO LAREDO	ANA	AN		8	E6
PASEO LAREDO	ANA	AN		13	D1
PASEO LARO	SCL	SC72		39	C1
PASEO LA RONDA	SJC	SJ75		38	D1
PASEO LA SERNA	SJC	SJ75		38	C2
PASEO LA VISTA	CO	LB77		36	A1
PASEO LINDERO	SJC	SJ75		38	D2
PASEO LOMITA	CO	LB		35	F2
PASEO LOMITA	CO	LB77		36	A2
PASEO LOMITA	SJC	SJ75		38	C2
PASEO LORENZO	YL	YL		8	C4
PASEO LORETO	SJC	SJ75		36	C5
PASEO LUCERO	ANA	AN		13	D2
PASEO LUIS	YL	YL		8	C4
PASEO MADERO	ANA	AN		13	D1
PASEO MAGELLAN	ANA	AN		13	C2
PASEO MANANA	SJC	SJ75	25900	38	B1
PASEO MAR AZUL	SJC	SJ75		36	B5
PASEO MARBELLA	SJC	SJ75	26200	38	B2

STREET	CITY	P.O. ZONE	BLOCK	PAGE	GRID
PASEO MIMOSA	SJC	SJ75		38	D2
PASEO MINERO	SJC	SJ75		38	B1
PAS MIRAFLORES	SJC	SJ75	33200	38	A3
PASEO MIRALOMA	SJC	SJ75		36	E5
PASEO MOLINOS	SJC	SJ75		38	A3
PASEO MONO	SJC	SJ75		38	A3
PAS MONTE VISTA	SJC	SJ75		38	B1
PASEO MONTOYA	IRV	SA		32	F1
PASEO MURILLO	ANA	AN		13	E3
PASEO NARANJA	SJC	SJ75	31200	36	C6
PASEO NICOLE	SJC	SJ75		36	D5
PASEO NOGAL	CO	ET	20900	51	F6
PASEO NOGAL	SJC	SJ75	31200	36	C5
PASEO OLIVOS	SJC	SJ75	31200	36	C5
PASEO OLMA	CO	ET	20800	51	F5
PASEO PAMELA	SJC	SJ75	26400	38	B1
PASEO PANORAMA	YL	YL		8	D4
PASEO PERDIDO	SJC	SJ75		38	B2
PASEO PEREGRINO	SJC	SJ75		38	C4
PASEO PICARDO	ANA	AN		13	D1
PASEO PICASSO	IRV	SA		32	F1
PASEO PINO	CO	ET	20800	51	E5
PASEO PINTO	SJC	SJ75		38	B2
PASEO PINZON	DPT	SC24		38	C6
PASEO PIZARRO	IRV	SA		32	F1
PASEO PLACENTIA	SJC	SJ75		38	D2
PASEO PRADO	ANA	AN		13	E3
PASEO PUEBLO	CO	SJ		59	C2
PASEO RANCHERO	SJC	SJ75		36	F5
PASEO RAVENNA	SJC	SJ75		38	D2
PASEO REAL	ANA	AN		13	D2
PASEO REPOSO	SJC	SJ75		36	D5
PASEO RICO	YL	YL		8	E3
PASEO RINCON	MVJO	SJ92	28000	29B	E6
PASEO RIO AZUL	ANA	AN		13	C1
PAS RIO BLANCO	ANA	AN		13	D1
PASEO RIOBO	SJC	SJ75		36	E6
PAS RIO MORENO	ANA	AN		13	D1
PASEO RIO VERDE	ANA	AN		13	D1
PASEO RITA	SJC	SJ75	31500	36	B6
PASEO ROBLE	CO	ET	20800	51	E5
PASEO ROBLES	ANA	AN	200	13	C1
PASEO ROSARITO	SJC	SJ75		36	C5
PASEO SAGRADO	SJC	SJ75		36	E6
PASEO SAGRADO	SJC	SJ75		38	E1
PASEO SANCHEZ	SJC	SJ75	32000	38	B1
PAS SAN GABRIEL	SJC	SJ75		36	B5
PAS SANTA CLARA	SJC	SJ75	26500	36	B6
PASEO SANTIAGO	SJC	SJ75		36	B5
PASEO SEGOVIA	IRV	SA		32	F1
PASEO SEGOVIA	SJC	SJ75		38	D2
PASEO SERENA	ANA	AN		13	D2
PASEO SERENO	SJC	SJ75	31200	36	B5
PASEO SERRA	YL	YL		8	D4
PASEO SIENNA	SJC	SJ75		38	D2
PASEO SOMBRA	CO	ET		51	E6
PASEO SONATA	SJC	SJ75		38	D2
PASEO TAMARA	SJC	SJ75		38	D1
PASEO TAMPICO	ANA	AN		13	D1
PASEO TECATE	SJC	SJ75		36	C5
PASEO TELAVERA	SJC	SJ75		38	D2
PASEO TERRAZA	SJC	SJ75		36	B6
PASEO TERRAZA	SJC	SJ75		38	B1
PASEO TIARA	SJC	SJ75		38	D2
PASEO TIRADOR	SJC	SJ75		36	D6
PASEO TOLUCA	SJC	SJ75		38	D2
PASEO TORTUGA	SJC	SJ75		36	D5
PASEO TORTUGA	YL	YL		8	E4
PASEO TRANQUILO	CO	ET	21000	51	F6
PASEO TRIADOR	SJC	SJ75		38	C1
PASEO VALENCIA	SJC	SJ75		36	E5
PASEO VERANO	SJC	SJ75		38	D2
PASEO VENDAVAL	CO	ET	24600	51	E6
PASEO VENTURA	SJC	SJ75		36	E5
PASEO VERDE	SJC	SJ75		36	E5
PASEO VERDE	TUS	TUS	1400	23	E1
PASEO VERDURA	CO	ET		51	E6
PASEO VEREDA	CO	ET		51	E6
PASEO VIENTO	DPT	SC24		39	A1
PASEO VIOLETA	SJC	SJ75		38	D1
PASEO WESTPARK	IRV	SA		28	F4
PASEO WESTPARK	IRV	SA		29	A3
PASEO ZORRO	YL	YL		8	E6
PASO DEL SUR	LAG	LB	22100	35	B6
PASOFINO	CO	LB77		36	B1
PASO ROBLES DR	ANA	AN	3100	10	B4
PASTEUR	IRV	SA18		29	E6
PASTEUR PL	PLA	PLA	200	7	D5
PASTEUR ST	SA	SA	3700	28	B2
PASTO RD	DPT	DPT	24300	37	E4
PAT PL	ANA	AN	1300	11	F5

INDEX

STREET	CITY	P.O. ZONE	BLOCK	PAGE	GRID
PATERSON DR	IRV	SA		24	F6
PATHFINDER TR	ANA	AN		13	C3
PATOLITA DR	NB	NB	600	31	F5
PATOM CT	FTNV	SA08	15800	22	B4
PATRA	CO	LB77		35	E5
PATRIA CT	OR	OR		18	C1
PATRICE AV	WSTM	WSTM	15700	22	A3
PATRICE RD	NB	NB	4200	31	C4
PATRICIA CIR	CYP	CYP	4500	9	C6
PATRICIA CIR	LAP	BP23		9	D2
PATRICIA DR	CO	AN04	10300	10	E6
PATRICIA DR	CO	AN04	10500	15	E1
PATRICIA DR	CYP	CYP	4400	9	C6
PATRICIA DR	GGR	GG	10300	16	A3
PATRICIA LN	HTB	HB47	16500	21	A5
PATRICIA LN	SA	SA	1600	23	D1
PATRICIA ST	CO	LB56		29C	E3
PATRICIAGLEN LN	LAH	LAH	400	1	F5
PATRICIAN DR	VPK	OR67	18700	13	A6
PATRICIAN LN	PLA	PLA	200	7	B2
PATRICK DR	VPK	OR67	9800	12	F6
PATRINA CIR	CO	LB77		36	A3
PATRIOT WY	TUS	TUS		18	E6
PATT ST	ANA	AN	1100	11	D2
PATTERSON DR	GGR	GG	7000	15	B2
PATTERSON LN	HTB	HB	18300	26	C2
PATTERSON PL	CO	LB53		29D	A4
PATTERSON WY	FUL	FL	400	6	D6
PATTI LN	SA	SA	2600	16	F5
PATTON WY	BPK	BP	6000	9	F2
PATTY LN	ANA	AN		8	C6
PATWOOD DR E	LAH	LAH	200	2	A6
PATWOOD DR W	LAH	LAH	200	2	A6
PAUL DR	WSTM	WSTM	14200	21	A1
PAUL RD	OR	OR	1600	17	B3
PAULA AV	FUL	FL33	400	5	E6
PAULA CIR	HTB	HB47	6900	21	B5
PAULA DR	FUL	FL33	900	5	E6
PAULA DR	FUL	FL33	900	10	E1
PAULA DR	HTB	HB		20	D4
PAULA LN	ANA	AN		11	E5
PAULARINO AV	CO	CM27	13500	27	E3
PAULARINO AV E	CM	CM26	1000	28	A3
PAULARINO AV W	CM	CM	600	27	E3
PAULARINO AV W	CM	CM26	400	28	A3
PAULINE DR	CYP	CYP	9600	9	F5
PAULINE LN	FTNV	SA08	18900	26	E3
PAULINE LN	HTB	HB	19000	26	E3
PAULINE PL	CM	CM27	200	31	D2
PAULINE ST	ANA	AN	300	11	D3
PAULOWNIA	CO	SJ		59	C1
PAUMA LN	NB	NB		32	B5
PAVILLION	MVJO	SJ92		29D	F3
PAVILLION DR	CO	SA	2000	24	D2
PAVION	MVJO	SJ92	24000	29B	E5
PAVONIA CIR	BPK	BP	7700	10	D2
PAVOREAL	SCL	SCL		38	E4
PAWLET CIR	FTNV	SA08	9800	21	F4
PAWNEE	TUS	TUS		24	B3
PAWTUCKET CIR	HTB	HB	8100	30	C1
PAWTUCKET DR	HTB	HB	8200	30	C1
PAWTUCKET LN	CO	LB77		37	E1
PAXTON	MVJO	SJ92		29B	D1
PAYASO LN	MVJO	SJ91		29D	C3
PAYSEN DR	WSTM	WSTM	13500	14	F6
PAZZI	IRV	SA14		29	A4
PEABODY WY	IRV	SA	4100	28	F5
PEACE PL	CM	CM	900	27	F3
PEACH	IRV	SA		29	B5
PEACH AV	BREA	BREA	600	6	E1
PEACH LN	HTB	HB	20200	26	E5
PEACH LN	SA	SA		22	E3
PEACH ST	CYP	CYP	9200	9	E5
PEACH BLOSSOM	MVJO	SJ92		29B	E2
PEACH KNOLL	ANA	AN	200	11	F2
PEACHTREE LN	CO	NB60	300	31	E1
PEACHTREE LN	HTB	HB48		25	E2
PEACHWOOD	CO	ET		51	F6
PEACHWOOD CIR	WSTM	WSTM	8400	21	D3
PEACHWOOD LN	SA	SA	2100	17	E6
PEACOCK	IRV	SA		29	D1
PEACOCK CIR	FTNV	SA08	9800	26	F2
PEACOCK CT	CO	LB56		29C	B1
PEACOCK CT	GGR	GG	11700	15	F3
PEACOCK LN	FUL	FL		6	A3
PEACOCK LN	OR	OR69		18	E3
PEACOCK ST	CO	ET		29A	E2
PEACOCK HILL DR	CO	SA		18	D5
PEAK CIR	WSTM	WSTM	13200	15	A5
PEALE LN	HTB	HB	16400	20	A6
PEAR LN	SA	SA		22	E3

STREET	CITY	P.O. ZONE	BLOCK	PAGE	GRID
PEAR ST	BREA	BREA	900	2	D6
PEARCE AV	GGR	GG	12300	16	D5
PEARCE DR	HTB	HB		20	E5
PEARCE ST	GGR	GG	12400	16	D5
PEARCE ST	HTB	HB	4500	20	D5
PEAR KNOLL	ANA	AN	200	11	F3
PEARL	CO	LB77		36	A3
PEARL AV	FTNV	SA08	16900	21	F5
PEARL AV	NB	NB	100	31	E6
PEARL CIR	CYP	CYP	4200	9	C3
PEARL CT	CYP	CYP	4300	9	C3
PEARL DR	FUL	FL	3000	7	B4
PEARL ST	ANA	AN	1100	11	C4
PEARL ST	CO	OR69	17700	17	F3
PEARL ST	CO	OR	18500	18	A3
PEARL ST	GGR	GG	10600	16	A4
PEARL ST	LAG	LB51	100	34	E4
PEARL ST	OR	OR	5300	18	C3
PEARL WY	CM	CM		27	C6
PEARSON AV	FUL	FL	2500	6	F5
PEARSON AV	FUL	FL	2600	7	A5
PEARSON AV E	ANA	AN	100	16	E2
PEARTREE	MVJO	SJ92		29B	E2
PEARTREE LN	CYP	CYP	9600	9	E5
PEARWOOD LN	ANA	AN		11	E6
PEARWOOD LN	SA	SA	2100	17	E6
PEARY WY	ANA	AN		43	A3
PEBBLE	IRV	SA		29	B5
PEBBLE CT	FTNV	SA08	10800	22	B4
PEBBLE DR	NB	CDLM	2700	32	B6
PEBBLE LN	HTB	HB	20500	26	F5
PEBBLE BEACH	MVJO	SJ92		29B	E3
PEBBLE BCH CIR	WSTM	WSTM	8900	21	E3
PEBBLE BEACH CT	BPK	BP		5	C3
PEBBLE BEACH DR	BPK	BP	8200	5	C3
PEBBLE BEACH LN	YL	YL	5500	8	A4
PEBBLE BEACH PL	CO	LB		35	D5
PEBBLE BEACH PL	FUL	FL		6	C2
PEBBLE BEACH RD	HTB	HB		30	C1
PEBBLEBROOK	IRV	SA		29	B2
PEBBLE CREEK	CO	ET	26300	29B	B2
PEBBLEPATH	IRV	SA		29	A4
PEBBLESTONE	IRV	SA		29	B2
PEBBLEWOOD	IRV	SA		29	B3
PECAN AV E&W	HTB	HB	100	26	A5
PECAN LN	FTNV	SA08	18000	26	E1
PECAN LN	TUS	TUS		24	D4
PECAN PL	BREA	BREA	200	2	F5
PECAN ST	BREA	BREA	600	2	D6
PECAN ST	CYP	CYP	9200	9	D5
PECAN ST	IRV	SA	3500	24	C6
PECAN WY	LAH	LAH	400	1	E5
PECK DR	HTB	HB	9700	26	F5
PECKHAM ST	FUL	FL33	1300	10	E1
PECOS RD	CO	LB	25700	29D	A2
PECOS RIVER	PLA	PLA	1700	7	B3
PEDRO ST	LAG	LB	31100	35	A5
PEDROSO	MVJO	SJ91		29B	C1
PEG PL	PLA	PLA	600	7	C3
PEGASUS	IRV	SA		32A	A2
PEGASUS ST	ANA	AN07		13	F4
PEGASUS ST	CO	SA07	1500	28	A5
PEGG ST	WSTM	WSTM	13900	14	F6
PEGGY CIR	HTB	HB47	6500	21	A5
PELHAM RD	SB	SB	1400	14	A5
PELICAN AV	FTNV	SA08	9000	26	E2
PELICAN CT	NB	SA07		28	B6
PELICAN CT	NB	SA07		32	B1
PELICAN DR	BPK	BP	7000	9	F1
PELICAN DR	LAG	LB51	600	34	F4
PELICAN LN	HTB	HB	15500	20	E3
PELICAN PL	CM	CM	1900	27	B5
PELICAN WY	CO	LB		35	D3
PELODO	SCL	SC72		38	E4
PELORUS AV	SB	SB		19	F2
PELORUS AV	SB	SB		20	A2
PEMBA DR	CM	CM	2800	27	B4
PEMBERO CIR	HTB	HB	18100	26	D2
PEMBERTON PL	CO	LB		35	E6
PEMBERTON PL	CO	LB77		37	E1
PEMBERTON RD	CO	LALM	11200	14	B2
PEMBROKE CT	FUL	FL	2800	7	A3
PEMBROKE DR	CO	SA	10900	18	C5
PEMBROKE LN	CO	ET		52	C6
PEMBROKE LN	NB	NB	1100	31	E4
PEMBROKE LN	PLA	PLA	200	7	B4
PEMBROKE PL	PLA	PLA	1200	7	B4
PEMBROOK LN	WSTM	WSTM	7700	21	C1
PEMBROOKE LN	ANA	AN	1300	10	F6
PEMBURY DR	LAP	BP23	5300	9	E2
PENASCO	SCL	SC72		38	F5

STREET	CITY	P.O. ZONE	BLOCK	PAGE	GRID
PENDELTON	IRV	SA		24	E4
PENDLETON AV	SA	SA	1700	22	D5
PENDLETON DR	HTB	HB	5400	20	E6
PENDLETON LN	LAH	LAH		1	D6
PENDLETON LN	LAH	LAH		5	D1
PENFIELD CIR	HTB	HB47	14900	21	A2
PENFIELD ST	CO	ET	24400	29A	E5
PENGUIN AV	FTNV	SA08		22	C5
PENGUIN DR	BPK	BP	7000	9	F1
PENHALL WY	ANA	AN	1800	11	A4
PENMAR AV	LAH	LAH	100	2	A5
PENN AV	GGR	GG	10900	16	B5
PENN DR	OR	OR	300	17	D3
PENN WY	SA	SA	1600	17	C6
PENN WY	SA	SA	1500	23	C1
PENN WY	STN	STN	7200	15	B2
PENNELL CIR	FTNV	SA08	11300	22	B5
PENNINGTON AV	TUS	TUS	1800	24	A5
PENNINGTON DR	HTB	HB	8100	26	C6
PENNINGTON LN	CO	SJ79		56	E6
PENNINGTON LN	CO	SJ79		59	E1
PENNSYLVANIA WY	PLA	PLA	300	7	B5
PENNY AV	SA	SA	4200	22	B1
PENNY LN	ANA	AN		13	E1
PENNY PINES	IRV	SA		29	C2
PENNYWOOD CT	BREA	BREA		2	C5
PENRITH LN	TUS	TUS	1300	23	F4
PENSACOLA CIR	HTB	HB	21400	30	F1
PENSACOLA ST	WSTM	WSTM	15500	21	D4
PENTAGON ST	GGR	GG	12300	15	D4
PENTON PL	SA	SA		28	B1
PEONY CIR	BPK	BP	8400	10	C2
PEONY CIR	FTNV	SA08	10700	22	B4
PEPITA DR	MVJO	SJ91	26400	29D	B1
PEPPER AV	YL	YL		8	D2
PEPPER CIR	BPK	BP	8100	10	C3
PEPPER LN	CO	ET	22300	29A	C2
PEPPER LN	HTB	HB	17800	26	A1
PEPPER PL	FUL	FL	1200	11	E1
PEPPER ST	ANA	AN	900	11	C6
PEPPER ST	OR	OR	100	17	B3
PEPPER CREEK WY	ANA	AN		12	F3
PEPPERDINE CIR	WSTM	WSTM	13500	14	E5
PEPPERDINE LN	GGR	GG		15	E5
PEPPER GRASS	IRV	SA		29	C2
PEPPERGROVE ST	YL	YL		7	F5
PEPPER HILL DR	OR	OR	2000	12	E3
PEPPER HILL DR	YL	YL	6400	8	F2
PEPPERTREE CIR	TUS	TUS	14500	24	A5
PEPPER TREE DR	ANA	AN		10	D2
PEPPERTREE DR	BREA	BREA	400	2	E5
PEPPERTREE DR	HTB	HB	9500	30	F1
PEPPERTREE DR	OR	OR		13	B4
PEPPER TREE LN	CM	CM	2900	27	C4
PEPPERTREE LN	FUL	FL	1200	6	B3
PEPPERTREE LN	GGR	GG		16	B4
PEPPERTREE LN	MVJO	SJ91	21100	52	D6
PEPPERTREE LN	STN	STN	10500	15	B3
PEPPER TREE LN	YL	YL		8	B5
PEPPERTREE ST	FTNV	SA08	17100	21	E6
PEPPERTREE BEND	SJC	SJ75		36	A6
PEPPERTREE BEND	SJC	SJ75		38	A1
PEPPERWOOD	CO	LB		29C	E3
PEPPERWOOD E	FUL	FL	1600	7	A1
PEPPERWOOD W	FUL	FL	1600	7	A1
PEPPERWOOD CIR	WSTM	WSTM	8400	21	D3
PEPPERWOOD CT	FUL	FL		7	A1
PEPPERWOOD DR	BREA	BREA	600	2	F6
PEPPERWOOD DR	GGR	GG		16	B4
PEPPERWOOD LN	BREA	BREA		2	D2
PEPPERWOOD LN	SJC	SJ75		36	B2
PEPPERWOOD PL	FUL	FL		7	A1
PEQUENO	CO	ET		29A	F4
PEQUITO DR	DPT	DPT	33800	37	F4
PERALES	MVJO	SJ92		29B	D6
PERALTA DR	CO	LB	23100	29A	C4
PERALTA WY	ANA	AN		13	A3
PERALTA HLLS DR	ANA	AN	100	12	F3
PERALTA HLLS DR	ANA	AN	4700	13	A3
PERALTA RIV CIR	FTNV	SA08		21	F6
PERAZA LN	MVJO	SJ91		29B	C4
PERCH	IRV	SA		29	B3
PERCH AV	FTNV	SA08	10500	22	A5
PERCH CIR	HTB	HB	19400	26	F3
PERCH DR	DPT	DPT	25300	37	F4
PERCHERON RD	GGR	GG	11800	16	C5
PERCY DR	WSTM	WSTM		21	E2
PERDIDO ST	CO	AN04	10000	10	F6
PEREGRINE CIR	FTNV	SA08	10100	27	A2
PEREGRINE PL	ANA	AN	900	12	A5

STREET	CITY	P.O. ZONE	BLOCK	PAGE	GRID
PEREGRINE ST	ANA	AN	200	11	F3
PEREGRINE ST	ANA	AN	400	12	A3
PEREIRA DR	IRV	SA17		32	D1
PERGOLA	IRV	SA		28	F5
PERHAM RD	NB	CDLM	4500	33	C2
PERICIA DR	MVJO	SJ91	25100	29D	B1
PERICLES ST	CO	SJ91		29B	A6
PERICLES ST	CO	SJ91		29D	A1
PERIDOT PL	ANA	AN07		13	D4
PERIMETER RD	ETMC	SA09		51	C6
PERIMETER RD	CO	SA09		51	A2
PERIWINKLE DR	BPK	BP	8100	10	C2
PERIWINKLE DR	CO	SA	12500	18	C4
PERIWINKLE DR	DPT	LB77		37	D3
PERKINS CT	IRV	SA17		32	E2
PERLA	NB	NB		32	B2
PERLIN PL	FUL	FL		7	A1
PERRIN DR	GGR	GG	10500	16	A2
PERRY DR	PLA	PLA	1500	7	B3
PERRY DR	TUS	SA10		23	E6
PERRYVILLE	IRV	SA		24	D6
PERSEUS CT	CO	SJ91	24500	29B	A6
PERSEUS CT	CO	SJ91		29D	A1
PERSHING	IRV	SA		24	C5
PERSHING WY	BPK	BP	6100	9	F2
PERSIMMON	MVJO	SJ91		52	D5
PERSIMMON CIR	FTNV	SA08	18800	26	F3
PERSIMMON LN	IRV	SA		29	B5
PERSIMMON LN	SA	SA		22	E3
PERSIMMON PL	FUL	FL		6	F2
PERSIMMON ST	FTNV	SA08	18900	26	F3
PERSIMMONS CIR	GGR	GG	12500	16	C4
PERTH WY	CO	ET		29B	A2
PERTH BAY	DPT	LB77		37	D4
PERU CIR	BPK	BP	7500	9	E2
PESARO	IRV	SA14		29	A4
PESCADO LN	HTB	HB	16600	20	D5
PESCADOR DR	NB	NB	1100	31	E4
PETAL AV	FTNV	SA08	11000	22	B4
PETAL PL	ANA	AN	1300	11	D6
PETALUMA CT	CO	TRA		59	B5
PETERS AV	CO	MDWY	8300	21	D3
PETERSBURG	IRV	SA		24	E4
PETERS CT	FTNV	SA08		26	F2
PETERS CYN RD	CO	OR	8800	18	E4
PETERS CYN RD	CO	OR69		46	A2
PETERS CYN RD	TUS	TUS		18	E5
PETERSON PL	CM	CM	2700	27	C5
PETITE LN	CO	CYP	4500	9	C3
PETRA	MVJO	SJ92	22400	29B	D2
PETRA LN	PLA	PLA		7	F6
PETREL CT	CO	LB		35	D2
PETSWORTH LN	WSTM	WSTM	14500	22	A2
PETTSWOOD DR	HTB	HB	9500	26	F4
PETUNIA AV	FTNV	SA08	9800	21	F5
PETUNIA WY	BPK	BP	8200	10	C2
PEWTER LN	CO	ET		29B	A2
PHAEDRA	CO	LB77		35	F5
PHALAROPE CT	CM	CM	2000	27	A5
PHEASANT AV	FTNV	SA08	10200	27	A2
PHEASANT CIR	BPK	BP	7100	9	F1
PHEASANT CIR	HTB	HB	5000	20	E3
PHEASANT CT	FUL	FL		6	A3
PHEASANT DR	BPK	BP	6200	9	F1
PHEASANT DR	BPK	BP	6400	10	A1
PHEASANT LN	CO	LB56		29C	B1
PHEASANT LN	OR	OR69		18	C3
PHEASANT ST	ANA	AN		7	B6
PHEASANT ST	CO	ET	22000	29A	D2
PHELAN DR	VPK	OR67	10000	12	F6
PHELAN DR	VPK	OR67	10000	13	A6
PHELPS LN	HTB	HB	16600	20	C5
PHILDLPHIA ST N	ANA	AN	100	11	D3
PHILDLPHIA ST S	ANA	AN	100	11	D4
PHILEMON DR	DPT	DPT		37	E2
PHILIPS PL	OR	OR	4700	18	B4
PHILLIPS AV	FTNV	SA08		26	F2
PHILLIPS CIR	CO	LB		35	E5
PHILLIPS ST	SB	SURF	15600	20	A4
PHILLIPSBURG	IRV	SA		24	D6
PHILO AV	CYP	CYP	5900	9	E4
PHILO AV	OR	OR	4400	18	B3
PHILODENDRON WY	BPK	BP	8200	10	C2
PHLOX DR	BPK	BP	8400	10	C2
PHOEBE CT	CO	LB56		29C	A2
PHOENIX	IRV	SA		29	D1
PHOENIX AV	FTNV	SA08	8500	26	D2
PHOENIX LN	HTB	HB	19600	26	D4
PHYLLIS CIR	ANA	AN	800	12	A4
PHYLLIS PL	GGR	GG	13800	16	B6
PHY SCIENCES RD	IRV	SA		32	D2

STREET	CITY	P.O. ZONE	BLOCK	PAGE	GRID
PIAZZA GENOA	NB	NB	400	31	C6
PIAZZA LIDO	NB	NB	300	31	C6
PICADILLY LN	HTB	HB46	19900	27	A4
PICADILLY WY	ANA	AN	2500	10	E1
PICADILLY WY	CO	FL33	9200	10	E1
PICA FLOR	CO	SJ		59	B5
PICASSO CT	IRV	SA		24	C6
PICASSO DR	YL	YL		40	C6
PICAZO	CO	SJ		59	B5
PICCADILLY CIR	WSTM	WSTM	14200	20	E1
PICKENS LN	STN	STN	8100	15	C2
PICKETT AV	GGR	GG45	6000	14	F4
PICKETT AV	GGR	GG	6500	15	A4
PICKETT LN	GGR	GG	11700	16	C4
PICKFORD ST	WSTM	WSTM	15300	22	A3
PICKNEY LN	IRV	SA		24	F6
PICKNEY CLOSE	CO	LB		35	E6
PICKNEY CLOSE	CO	LB77		37	E1
PICKWICK CIR	HTB	HB	4300	20	D5
PICKWICK LN	GGR	GG		21	E2
PICKWICK PL	FUL	FL33		5	F2
PICO ST	FUL	FL	1300	6	A4
PIEDMONT AV	CO	LALM	2600	14	A3
PIEDMONT CIR	HTB	HB		20	A5
PIEDMONT DR	ANA	AN		8	D5
PIER DR	HTB	HB	9300	30	E1
PIERCE	IRV	SA		24	C5
PIERCE AV	CM	CM	3100	27	E3
PIERCE CIR	BPK	BP	7200	10	B3
PIERCE DR	BPK	BP	8300	10	B4
PIERPOINT DR	HTB	HB		26	B4
PIERPONT DR	CM	CM26	500	28	A3
PIERRE	IRV	SA		29	E2
PIERRE DR	HTB	HB	8500	26	D4
PIERRE WY	CYP	CYP	14500	15	A2
PIERSON DR	HTB	HB	4100	20	C5
PIERVIEW LN	HTB	HB	20500	26	F5
PIGEON LN	FTNV	SA08	7200	26	E1
PIKE	IRV	SA		24	E6
PIKE AV	FTNV	SA08	10100	22	A6
PIKE RD	CO	LB		29C	F2
PIKE RD	CO	LB	25200	29D	A2
PIKE ST	HTB	HB		26	C3
PILAR LN	HTB	HB		20	D4
PILGRIM CIR	HTB	HB47	15800	21	A4
PILOS	CO	LB77		35	F5
PIMA	TUS	TUS		24	D3
PIMA CT	CO	TRA		59	C2
PIMILCO DR	CYP	CYP	10100	9	C6
PIMLICO CIR	PLA	PLA		7	F5
PIMLICO RD	WSTM	WSTM	5200	20	E1
PINA	CO	LB	23000	29A	A4
PINAFORE CIR	CO	LB	23800	35	D3
PINARIO	MVJO	SJ92		29D	C2
PINATA CIR	MVJO	SJ91	25400	29D	B2
PINATA PL	FUL	FL	400	6	B3
PINAVETE	MVJO	SJ91	27300	52	C6
PINCIAN WY	CO	SA	11600	18	C6
PINCKNEY WY	CYP	CYP	11400	15	B3
PINE AV	BREA	BREA	400	2	F6
PINE AV	BREA	BREA	500	6	E1
PINE CIR	FTNV	SA08	16700	21	E5
PINE CIR	LAP	BP23	5000	9	D2
PINE CIR	YL	YL	17500	7	E5
PINE CT	TUS	TUS		24	A4
PINE CT	CYP	CYP	5600	9	E5
PINE DR	FUL	FL33	200	5	E6
PINE DR	FUL	FL33	1000	10	E1
PINE DR	LAH	LAH	1100	1	E5
PINE PL	ANA	AN	600	11	C3
PINE PL	CM	CM27	800	31	B1
PINE ST	BREA	BREA	200	2	F6
PINE ST	CO	MDWY	8000	21	C2
PINE ST	CO	SJ		56	C5
PINE ST	GGR	GG	12200	16	B4
PINE ST	HTB	HB	1500	26	B5
PINE ST	IRV	SA	3500	29	B1
PINE ST	LALM	LALM	10700	14	B2
PINE ST	PLA	PLA	1200	7	D5
PINE ST	WSTM	WSTM	13300	15	B6
PINE ST	WSTM	WSTM	14000	21	B1
PINE ST E&W	SA	SA	100	23	A2
PINE ST N	ANA	AN	300	11	C3
PINE ST N	OR	OR	1400	12	D5
PINE ST N&S	OR	OR	100	17	D3
PINE ST S	ANA	AN	600	11	D5
PINE ST W	SA	SA	1300	22	F2
PINE WY	ANA	AN	500	11	C3
PINEBLUFF DR	CO	SJ79		59	E1
PINEBROOK	CM	CM		27	D2
PINEBROOK	MVJO	SJ92		29B	E1

STREET	CITY	P.O. ZONE	BLOCK	PAGE	GRID
PINEBROOK	MVJO	SJ92		52	E6
PINEBROOK CIR	CM	CM		27	D2
PINEBROOK DR	GGR	GG		16	D6
PINEBROOK DR	TUS	TUS	14400	24	A4
PINE CANYON CIR	ANA	AN		13	F4
PINE CANYON RD	CO	SA	19600	18	C4
PINE CANYON RD	CO	SIL		53	A1
PINE COVE CIR	ANA	AN		8	B5
PINE CREEK CIR	FUL	FL		7	A2
PINECREEK DR	CM	CM		27	D4
PINECREST	MVJO	SJ92		52	E6
PINECREST CIR	HTB	HB		20	D5
PINECREST CIR	YL	YL		8	E1
PINECREST CT	FUL	FL		6	F3
PINECREST DR	LAG	LB51	300	34	C2
PINE FLAT CIR	CO	ET		29A	F1
PINEGLEN	MVJO	SJ92		29B	F2
PINEGROVE LN	CO	ET	24100	29A	D2
PINEHAVEN RD	IRV	SA	14800	29	D2
PINEHURST	MVJO	SJ92		29B	E3
PINEHURST AV	PLA	PLA	400	7	C4
PINEHURST AV E	LAH	LAH	100	2	A4
PINEHURST AV W	LAH	LAH	600	1	F4
PINEHURST AV W	LAH	LAH	100	2	A4
PINEHURST CIR	WSTM	WSTM	8900	21	E3
PINEHURST CT	FUL	FL		6	C2
PINEHURST CT	GGR	GG		16	B4
PINEHURST LN	CO	LB	24000	35	E4
PINEHURST LN	HTB	HB	17000	20	F6
PINEHURST LN	NB	NB		32	B4
PINE LAKE LN	CO	ET		29A	D3
PINE MEADOW WY	YL	YL		40	D5
PINE NUT RD	CO	LB		29D	A2
PINE OAK	CO	LB56		29C	B3
PINERIDGE	MVJO	SJ92		29B	F3
PINERIDGE DR	LAP	BP23	5500	9	E3
PINERIDGE DR	YL	YL	17600	7	F4
PINERIDGE ST	BREA	BREA	400	2	E4
PINE RIDGE WY	ANA	AN		8	B6
PINE RDGE KNOLL	FUL	FL	700	6	B4
PINESTONE	IRV	SA		29	B3
PINESTRAP CIR	CO	LB53		29C	F5
PINE TREE CT	LAH	LAH		1	E6
PINETREE LN	CO	ET	22400	29A	C2
PINETREE LN	HTB	HB	21300	30	F1
PINETREE LN	MVJO	SJ91		52	D6
PINE TREE LN	STN	STN	11300	15	C2
PINE VALLEY	CO	SJ79		59	D6
PINE VALLEY LN	NB	NB		32	B5
PINE VIA	FUL	FL		6	D6
PINEVIEW	IRV	SA		24	F5
PINEVILLE CT	CO	YL		8	F3
PINEWOOD	CO	TRA		59	D6
PINEWOOD	IRV	SA		29	B2
PINEWOOD AV	ANA	AN	1400	11	E2
PINEWOOD AV	BREA	BREA		2	D2
PINEWOOD CT	FUL	FL		7	A1
PINEWOOD DR	FUL	FL		7	A1
PINEWOOD LN	CO	LB		29D	A2
PINEWOOD LN	SJC	SJ75	29300	36	B2
PINEWOOD PL	LAH	LAH	1400	1	F6
PINEWOOD PL	LAH	LAH		5	F1
PINEWOOD RD	TUS	TUS	14100	24	A5
PINEWOOD ST	OR	OR	3000	12	C3
PINJARA CIR	MVJO	SJ91		29B	C5
PINNACLE DR	CO	SJ79		56	E6
PINNACLE POINTE	OR	OR69		18	D3
PINNACLES CT	CO	LB	28000	29C	E6
PINNEY DR	ANA	AN	100	13	B2
PINO LN	CO	ET	25200	29A	F3
PINO RD	SJC	SJ75		38	B3
PINOCHA	MVJO	SJ92		29D	C4
PINON CT	GGR	SA03		16	D6
PINON DR	HTB	HB	5800	25	F1
PINON PL	FUL	FL		6	E2
PINON TREE LN	CM	CM		27	E6
PINTAIL	IRV	SA		29	C3
PINTAIL CIR	CO	LB	29000	35	D2
PINTO CT	CO	LB	25600	29D	A5
PINTO LN	CO	SA05		18	B4
PINTO LN	YL	YL		8	C2
PINTO RD	GGR	GG	13200	16	C5
PINTO WY	OR	OR	7300	18	D3
PINTO RIVER CT	FTNV	SA08	10300	27	A1
PINUELA	MVJO	SJ92		29D	C5
PINYON CIR	FTNV	SA08	16500	21	E5
PINYON ST	BPK	BP	8600	10	C4
PINYON JAY LN	CO	LB53		29A	C6
PINYON TREE LN	IRV	SA		29	A5
PINZON	CO	SJ88		29B	F5
PIONEER AV	FUL	FL	2000	6	F3

STREET	CITY	P.O. ZONE	BLOCK	PAGE	GRID
PIONEER AV W	FUL	FL33	2000	5	E3
PIONEER DR	ANA	AN	900	11	C3
PIONEER DR	HTB	HB	9000	26	E4
PIONEER RD	TUS	TUS		24	D1
PIONEER ST	BREA	BREA		2	C5
PIONEER ST	IRV	SA		29	C2
PIONEER WY	TUS	TUS		24	E2
PIPELINE LN	HTB	HB		20	F3
PIPER CIR	IRV	SA		29	C2
PIPER PL	YL	YL	18300	8	A3
PIPESTONE ST	FTNV	SA08	10000	27	A1
PIPIT CT	CO	LB		35	D1
PIRAGUA PL	CO	LB77		37	D1
PIRATE CIR	HTB	HB		20	C4
PIRATE RD	NB	NB	300	31	D5
PISMO LN	HTB	HB		26	D3
PISTACHIO WY	IRV	SA	4100	28	F5
PITCAIRN DR	CM	CM	1700	27	B4
PITCAIRN LN	HTB	HB46	19300	27	A3
PITCAIRN PL	LAG	LB51	1300	34	E2
PITCAIRN ST	CYP	CYP	6000	14	F3
PITMAN LN	HTB	HB47	16000	21	A4
PITTSFORD DR	CO	ET		29B	B1
PITTSFORD DR	CO	ET		52	B6
PIUTE DR	SA	SA	800	22	D3
PIXLEY ST N&S	OR	OR	100	17	C4
PIZZARRO AV	GGR	GG44		15	D5
PIZARRO RD	CO	ET	25100	29A	F3
PLACENTIA AV	ANA	AN	1200	12	A1
PLACENTIA AV	CM	CM	2200	27	B6
PLACENTIA AV	CM	CM27	1600	31	B3
PLACENTIA AV	FUL	FL	1200	7	A4
PLACENTIA AV	NB	NB	4300	31	B3
PLACENTIA AV N	PLA	PLA	100	7	A4
PLACENTIA AV S	PLA	PLA	100	7	A4
PLACENTIA AV S	PLA	PLA	900	11	F1
PLACENTIA AV S	PLA	PLA	900	12	A1
PLACER AV	WSTM	WSTM	5500	14	E6
PLACER CIR	HTB	HB		26	D6
PLACER RIV CIR	FTNV	SA08	10300	27	A2
PLACER VIA	ANA	AN		16	D2
PLACERVILLE PL	YL	YL	5700	8	C4
PLACID CIR	HTB	HB47	15500	21	A3
PLACIDA AV	CO	LB	28600	35	F2
PLACID HARBOR	DPT	DPT		37	B5
PLAINVIEW CIR	CO	ET	22800	29A	D3
PLANETARY DR	BPK	BP	8200	10	C3
PLANO TRABUC RD	CO	SJ	31900	59	D2
PLANT AV	CO	SJ91		29A	F5
PLANTATION PL N	ANA	AN	100	12	B3
PLANTATION PL S	ANA	AN	100	12	B3
PLANTERO DR	CO	SA	11500	18	D6
PLANTERO DR	CO	SA	11500	24	D1
PLATA	NB	NB		32	A2
PLATA PL	MVJO	SJ92		36	B1
PLATANAL DR	VPK	OR67	9900	13	A5
PLATINO	MVJO	SJ91		29B	B2
PLATTE DR	CM	CM	3000	27	F3
PLATTE ST	YL	YL		8	F4
PLATTE WY	PLA	PLA	200	7	B3
PLAYA	NB	NB		32	A2
PLAYA DR	HTB	HB	9100	30	E2
PLAYA WY	CYP	CYP	5700	9	E6
PLAYA BLANCA CT	LAG	LB51		33A	F1
PLAYA BLANCA DR	CO	LB		35	D4
PLAYANO AV	OR	OR		13	B5
PLAZA DR	CYP	CYP		14	E1
PLAZA DR	SA	SA04	3600	27	F2
PLAZA DR	TUS	TUS	14600	24	A2
PLAZA SQ	OR	OR		17	C3
PLAZA ST	WSTM	WSTM	7100	15	B6
PLAZA ST	WSTM	WSTM	7100	21	B1
PLAZA WY	STN	STN	8000	15	C2
PLAZA WY	TUS	TUS	18200	24	A1
PLAZA D AMANTES	ANA	AN		13	E5
PLAZA DE CARROS	ANA	AN		13	E5
PLAZA DE CIELO	ANA	AN		13	E5
PZ DE DOMINGOS	ANA	AN		13	E5
PLAZA DE FLORES	ANA	AN		13	E5
PLAZA DE INDIOS	ANA	AN		13	E5
PLAZA DEL NORTE	NB	NB	1800	33	A1
PLAZA DEL NORTE	NB	NB	1700	33	C5
PLAZA DEL SUR	NB	NB	1800	33	A1
PLAZA DEL SUR	NB	NB	1700	33	C5
PLAZA DE POETAS	ANA	AN		13	E5
PLAZA DE SANTOS	ANA	AN		13	E5
PLAZA DE SUENO	ANA	AN		13	E5
PLAZA DE TIERRA	FUL	FL33		5	E5
PZ DE VAQUEROS	ANA	AN		13	E5
PLAZA DE VISTA	FUL	FL33		5	E4
PLAZA ESCONDIDO	FUL	FL33		5	E4

STREET	CITY	P.O. ZONE	BLOCK	PAGE	GRID
PLAZA ESTIVAL	SCL	SC72	27000	38	C6
PLAZA LA PLAYA	SCL	SC72		39	E5
PLAZA POINTE DR	CO	LB		29A	C3
PLEASANT AV	CO	SA		50	E4
PLEASANT CIR	HTB	HB	17100	20	E6
PLEASANT CT	FTNV	SA08	17400	22	B6
PLEASANT PL	ANA	AN	6400	13	E1
PLEASANT PL	GGR	GG	12400	15	F4
PLEASANT ST	GGR	GG	13000	16	A5
PLEASANT ST	GGR	GG43	14100	22	A1
PLEASANT ST	IRV	SA	4000	29	C1
PLEASANT GN RD	CO	SJ		59	D1
PLEASANT HLL RD	CO	ET	21000	52	C6
PLEASANT LK PL	BREA	BREA		2	D5
PLEASONTON	IRV	SA		29	E1
PLOVER LN	CO	LB	23900	35	D2
PLUM AV	BREA	BREA	200	3	A6
PLUM LN	OR	OR	400	17	A4
PLUM LN	SA	SA		22	E3
PLUM PL	CM	CM27	800	31	B1
PLUMAS CIR	HTB	HB		26	D5
PLUMAS CT	FTNV	SA08	16900	21	E5
PLUMER ST	CM	CM27	500	31	C2
PLUMERIA PL	CM	CM	3400	27	E2
PLUMOSA DR	YL	YL	4200	8	A3
PLUMOSA ST	FTNV	SA08	18600	26	E2
PLUM TREE	IRV	SA		29	B6
PLUM TREE LN	ANA	AN		10	D2
PLUM TREE LN	HTB	HB	19000	26	D3
PLUM TREE LN	YL	YL	17600	7	F5
PLUMWOOD AV	WSTM	WSTM	15700	21	D4
PLUMWOOD LN	SA	SA	2100	17	E6
PLYMOUTH	IRV	SA		24	E6
PLYMOUTH AV	NB	NB		31	E4
PLYMOUTH COM	SA	SA		22	C2
PLYMOUTH CT	YL	YL		40	A3
PLYMOUTH LN	HTB	HB	15600	20	F4
PLYMOUTH PL	ANA	AN	500	11	F4
PO AV	CO	SJ91	25600	29B	A5
POBLADORES	MVJO	SJ92		29D	F3
POCETAS	MVJO	SJ92	22800	29B	E3
POCO CIR	HTB	HB		20	D3
POCO PL	MVJO	SJ92		36	C1
POCO PASEO	SCL	SC72	300	39	C4
POE DR	HTB	HB		26	D4
POES ST	CO	AN04	11500	15	D2
POINDEXTER AV	GGR	GG	10700	16	A3
POINSETTIA	IRV	SA		29	C2
POINSETTIA AV	FTNV	SA08	9200	21	E5
POINSETTIA AV	NB	CDLM	200	33	B2
POINSETTIA AV N	BREA	BREA	800	2	D4
POINSETTIA AV S	BREA	BREA	300	2	D6
POINSETTIA CT	CO	LB53		29D	A3
POINSETTIA DR	BPK	BP	7800	10	C1
POINSETTIA DR	OR	OR	200	17	A3
POINSETTIA LN	BPK	BP	7400	10	C1
POINSETTIA ST	SA	SA	1700	17	C6
POINSETTIA ST	SA	SA	400	23	C1
POINSETTIA WY	WSTM	WSTM	15200	21	E3
POINT PL	LAG	LB77	32000	37	B1
PT ARENA WY	NB	CDLM		32	D6
PT ARGUELLO WY	NB	CDLM		32	D5
PT ARGUELLO WY	NB	NB		32	D5
PT CATALINA	CO	LB77		37	F1
PT CATALINA	CO	LB77		38	A1
PT CONCPTION WY	NB	CDLM		32	D6
POINTE DR	BREA	BREA		3	A5
PTE DEL MAR AV	NB	CDLM		32	B6
PTE DEL MAR AV	NB	CDLM		33	B1
POINTE REYES	CO	LB77		36	B5
POINTE ROYALE	CO	LB		35	E2
POINTE SN PABLO	CO	LB77		36	B5
POINTE STIRLING	DPT	DPT		37	F2
POINTE SUTTON	DPT	DPT		37	F2
POINTE TRINITY	DPT	DPT		37	F1
POINTE VINCENTE	CO	LB77		36	B5
POINT LOMA DR	HTB	HB	6000	20	F6
POINT LOMA DR	HTB	HB47		21	A6
POINT LOMA DR	NB	CDLM		32	D5
PT MENDOCINO WY	NB	CDLM		32	D6
POINT SUR DR	NB	CDLM		32	D6
POKER FLATS PL	CO	LB		29C	F2
POKER FLATS PL	CO	LB		29D	A2
POLARIS DR	BPK	BP	8400	10	D3
POLARIS DR	DPT	DPT		37	E4
POLARIS DR	NB	NB	900	31	E4
POLARIS LN	CO	ET	25000	29A	F3
POLARIS RD	ANA	AN		16	D2
POLDER CIR	HTB	HB47	8400	21	D6
POLK AV	ANA	AN	2200	10	B4

STREET	CITY	P.O. ZONE	BLOCK	PAGE	GRID
POLK CIR	HTB	HB	8300	26	D4
POLIPUIN	IRV	SA14		29	A2
POLLACK DR	HTB	HB	9500	26	F3
POLLARD DR	GGR	GG	11400	15	E2
POLLARD LN	HTB	HB	17800	26	D1
POLLENSA	MVJO	SJ92	27700	29B	D3
POLY CT	FTNV	SA08	10700	22	B4
POLYNESIAN LN	HTB	HB	21500	30	E1
POMEGRANATE RD	TUS	TUS	2100	24	A4
POMELO AV	BREA	BREA	200	2	F5
POMONA AV	CM	CM	2200	27	C6
POMONA AV	CM	CM27	1600	31	C3
POMONA AV N&S	FUL	FL	100	6	C6
POMONA AV S	FUL	FL	800	11	C1
POMONA LN	HTB	HB47	16300	21	B4
POMONA ST	SA	SA07		23	C4
POMONA ST E&W	SA	SA	100	23	B4
POMONA ST W	SA	SA	1500	22	E4
POMPANO CT	CYP	CYP	10400	14	E1
POMPANO LN	HTB	HB		26	C4
POMPANO WY	CO	LB	29000	35	D2
POMPEII DR	DPT	LB77		37	D2
PONCE AV	PLA	PLA	300	7	C2
PONCE CT	CO	LB	25400	29C	F2
PONCHARTRAIN LN	CO	ET		29A	D1
PONCHA SPRING	CO	ET	22200	29B	B2
PONDER ST	CYP	CYP	10200	9	E6
PONDEROSA	MVJO	SJ92		52	D6
PONDEROSA	IRV	SA		29	D4
PONDEROSA AV	BREA	BREA	200	2	E4
PONDEROSA AV	FTNV	SA08	16300	21	E4
PONDEROSA AV	FUL	FL	1300	6	E2
PONDEROSA LN	ANA	AN		16	E2
PONDEROSA ST	CM	CM	1500	27	C4
PONDEROSA ST	CO	SA	13000	17	E6
PONDEROSA ST	OR	OR	1300	17	E5
PONDEROSA ST	SA	SA	2000	17	E5
PONDERS END	CO	LB77		35	E6
PONTEVEDRA LN	MVJO	SJ91	26600	29D	B2
PONY CT	OR	OR	7200	18	D2
POOLSIDE LN	HTB	HB		26	C6
POONA DR	CO	AN04	10300	10	F6
POONA DR	CO	AN04	10400	15	F1
POPE CT	SA	SA		23	E1
POPLAR	IRV	SA		29	E3
POPLAR AV N&S	BREA	BREA	100	2	E6
POPLAR AV S	BREA	BREA	500	6	E1
POPLAR DR	TUS	TUS	14400	24	A5
POPLAR LN	CM	CM		27	E6
POPLAR PL	ANA	AN	700	11	E2
POPLAR ST	ANA	AN	300	11	E3
POPLAR ST	FTNV	SA08	17300	21	E6
POPLAR ST	GGR	GG45	12400	14	F4
POPLAR ST	IRV	SA14	3500	24	B6
POPLAR ST	IRV	SA	3500	29	B1
POPLAR ST	LAG	LB51	300	34	D2
POPLAR ST	OR	OR	200	17	A3
POPLAR ST N	SA	SA	2000	16	F6
POPLAR ST S	SA	SA	300	22	F3
POPLAR BLUFF CT	CO	YL		8	F2
POPLARWOOD	CO	ET		29A	F1
POPLIN	IRV	SA		29	B4
POPPY	NB	CDLM		33	C1
POPPY AV	FTNV	SA08	11500	22	C4
POPPY AV	NB	CDLM	200	33	B2
POPPY CIR	CM	CM		27	E2
POPPY CIR	FTNV	SA08	9600	21	F4
POPPY CIR	WSTM	WSTM	9200	21	E3
POPPY DR	GGR	GG	11000	16	B3
POPPY DR	TUS	TUS		24	B4
POPPY LN	NB	CDLM		33	C1
POPPY PL	MVJO	SJ92		29D	D4
POPPY WY	BPK	BP	8200	10	C2
POPPY WY	WSTM	WSTM	15600	21	E3
PORPOISE LN	HTB	HB		20	D5
PORPOISE COVE	CO	LB		35	D3
PORRERAS	MVJO	SJ92	22400	29B	D2
PORT CIR	HTB	HB	20000	26	E5
PORT ST	CO	LB		35	F4
PORT ST	CO	LB77		36	A4
PORT ABBEY PL	NB	NB	2500	32	C4
PORT ABRDEEN PL	NB	NB		32	D4
PORTAFINO DR	MVJO	SJ91	26000	29D	B2
PORTAGE ST	YL	YL		8	F4
PORTAL E	SCL	SC72	100	39	D3
PORTAL W	SCL	SC72	100	39	C3
PORTAL DR	LALM	LALM	10900	14	C1
PORT ALBANS CIR	NB	NB	3100	32	C4
PORT ALBANS PL	NB	NB	3100	32	C4
PORTALES LN	MVJO	SJ91		29B	B6
PORTALES LN	MVJO	SJ91	26600	29D	B1

STREET	CITY	P.O. ZONE	BLOCK	PAGE	GRID
PORT ANTONIO	CO	LB77		35	C2
PORT ASHLEY PL	NB	NB	2500	32	C4
PRT BARMOUTH PL	NB	NB	2500	32	C4
PORT BISHOP PL	NB	NB		32	C5
PRT BRISTOL CIR	NB	NB	3100	32	C4
PORT CARDIFF PL	NB	NB	3100	32	C4
PRT CARDIGAN PL	NB	NB	3100	32	C4
PRT CARLISLE PL	NB	NB		32	D4
PORT CARLOW PL	NB	NB		32	C5
PORT CARNEY PL	NB	NB	2600	32	C5
PORT CHARLES PL	NB	NB	2500	32	C4
PORT CHELSEA PL	NB	NB	3100	32	C4
PRT CLARIDGE PL	NB	NB	2500	32	C5
PORT CLYDE DR	HTB	HB	9500	30	F2
PORT DUNBAR DR	NB	NB		32	D4
PORT DUNLGH CIR	NB	NB	2000	32	C4
PORT DURNESS PL	NB	NB		32	D4
PORT EDWARD CIR	NB	NB		32	C5
PORT EDWARD PL	NB	NB		32	C5
PORTER	IRV	SA		24	E6
PORTER AV	FUL	FL33	2000	10	E1
PORTER AV	FUL	FL	300	11	B1
PORTER CIR	CO	LB		35	D2
PORTER LN	CO	SJ79		56	E6
PORTER LN	PLA	PLA	400	7	B6
PORTER ST	SA	SA	400	23	C2
PORTER WY	PLA	PLA	500	7	B6
PORTER RANCH RD	CO	SJ79		56	E6
PRT GREENWCH LN	HTB	HB	20100	26	D5
PORT HARWICK PL	NB	NB		32	D4
PORT HEMLEY CIR	NB	NB		32	B5
PORTAL	TUS	TUS		24	B3
PORTIA CIR	GGR	GG	11500	15	E2
PORTCO DL NORTE	SCL	SC72		38	E3
PORTICO DEL SUR	SCL	SC72		38	E4
PRT KIMBERLY PL	NB	NB		32	C5
PORTLAND AV	HTB	HB	200	26	C5
PORTLAND CIR	HTB	HB	300	26	C5
PORTLAND PL	CO	LB		35	E6
PORTLAND PL	CO	LB77		37	E1
PORT LANTERN ST	DPT	DPT	34300	37	B5
PORT LAURENT PL	NB	NB		32	C5
PORT LERWICK PL	NB	NB		32	D4
PRT LOCKSLGH PL	NB	NB	400	32	C5
PORT MANLGH CIR	NB	NB		32	C4
PRT MANLEIGH PL	NB	NB		32	C4
PORT MARGATE PL	NB	NB	2500	32	C4
PORT MARINE DR	DPT	DPT		38	D3
PORT NELSON PL	NB	NB60	1900	32	C5
PORTO PL	ANA	AN	600	11	C5
PORTO ALLEGRO	DPT	LB77	24200	37	C5
PORTO BELLO	DPT	LB77	24200	37	C5
PORTO CERVO DR	DPT	DPT		37	E3
PORTO CRISTO	DPT	LB77	24200	37	C5
PORTOFINO	CO	LB		29D	A6
PORTOFINO	CO	LB77		36	B1
PORTO FINO	DPT	LB77	24200	37	C5
PORTOFINO CIR	HTB	HB49		20	B4
PORTOFINO DR	IRV	SA		32A	A2
PORTOFINO PL	MVJO	SJ92		29D	E3
PORTOLA	MVJO	SJ92		29D	E3
PORTOLA N&S	LAG	LB77		37	B2
PORTOLA AV	SA	SA	1600	17	D5
PORTOLA AV W	LAH	LAH	300	2	A5
PORTOLA CT	HTB	HB	20900	26	D6
PORTOLA DR	CM	CM	2700	27	F4
PORTOLA LN	TUS	TUS		23	E3
PORTOLA PKWY	TUS	TUS		24	D2
PORTO NUOVO	DPT	LB77	24200	37	C5
PORTO VERDE	DPT	LB77	24200	37	C5
PRT PROVENCE PL	NB	NB	3100	32	C4
PORT RAMSEY PL	NB	NB		32	D4
PRT RAMSGATE PL	NB	NB	3100	32	C4
PORT RENWICK PL	NB	NB		32	C5
PORT ROYAL CIR	HTB	HB	9700	30	F4
PORT ROYAL WY	CO	LB77		35	C3
PRT SEABOURN WY	NB	NB		32	C4
PORT SHEFFLD PL	NB	NB	2500	32	C4
PORTSIDE	IRV	SA		29	B5
PORTSIDE CIR	HTB	HB		25	F1
PORTSIDE WY	NB	CDLM	1200	32	B6
PORTSMOUTH	MVJO	SJ92		29B	D6
PORTSMOUTH	MVJO	SJ92		29D	D1
PORTSMOUTH CIR	OR	OR		13	C6
PORTSMOUTH CIR	VPK	OR67	17800	17	F1
PORTSMOUTH CIR	WSTM	WSTM	13500	15	B6
PORTSMOUTH DR	HTB	HB	9300	26	E4
PORTSMOUTH PL	CO	SJ79		59	D6
PORTSMOUTH RD	YL	YL		40	A3
PORTSMOUTH WY	GGR	GG		15	D4
PORTS O CALL	DPT	LB77		37	D3

COPYRIGHT, © 1989 BY Thomas Bros Maps

PRT STANHOPE PL

1990 ORANGE COUNTY STREET INDEX

118

RAMADA LN

STREET	CITY	P.O. ZONE	BLOCK	PAGE	GRID
PRT STANHOPE PL	NB	NB		32	C5
PRT STIRLING PL	NB	NB	2500	32	C4
PORT SUTTON DR	NB	NB		32	C5
PORT TAGGART PL	NB	NB		32	C5
PORT TIFFIN PL	NB	NB		32	C5
PRT TWNSEND CIR	NB	NB60		32	C5
PRT TRINITY CIR	NB	NB	1200	32	C5
PORT TRINITY PL	NB	NB		32	C5
PORTULACA WY	BPK	BP	8200	10	C2
PORTVIEW CIR	HTB	HB46		26	A2
PORT WESTBRN PL	NB	NB	2500	32	C4
PORT WEYBRDG PL	NB	NB	3100	32	C4
PORT WHEELER PL	NB	NB	2500	32	C4
PORT WHITBY PL	NB	NB		32	D4
POSADA	IRV	SA14		28	F3
POSADA	NB	NB60		32	E3
POSADA LN	MVJO	SJ91	25200	29D	C1
POSEIDON	CO	LB77		35	E3
POSEY ST	SA	SA	4500	22	B3
POSSUM RUN	IRV	SA		29	A4
POSSUM HOLLOW	ANA	AN		13	E1
POST LN	ANA	AN	6400	8	B6
POST RD	CM	CM	900	27	E4
POST RD	FUL	FL33		5	E4
POSTON LN	HTB	HB	21100	30	E1
POTOMAC	IRV	SA		24	E6
POTOMAC	IRV	SA		29	D1
POTOMAC AV	YL	YL		8	F4
POTOMAC CIR	ANA	AN		8	D5
POTOMAC COM	SA	SA		22	C2
POTOMAC LN	HTB	HB	19700	26	E4
POTOMAC ST	OR	OR		13	C6
POTOMAC ST	PLA	PLA	1500	7	C3
POTRERO DR	FUL	FL35	3600	2	C6
POTTER CIR	HTB	HB47	16500	21	C5
POTTER CIR	VPK	OR67	10600	18	A1
POUND DR	PLA	PLA	2100	7	C2
POUNDERS LN	ANA	AN	1600	16	A1
POVEDA	MVJO	SJ91		29D	C2
POWDER HORN DR	ANA	AN	3900	12	E2
POWDRHRN RIV CT	FTNV	SA08	10300	27	A2
POWELL CT	CM	CM		27	E3
POWELL DR	PLA	PLA		7	D4
POWELL LN	HTB	HB		26	D6
POWELL PL	NB	NB	600	31	D4
POWER DR	HTB	HB46		26	E6
POWHATAN AV	ANA	AN	2400	12	A3
PRADERA DR	MVJO	SJ91	25100	29D	B1
PRADERA RD	CO	SJ		59	D4
PRADO	IRV	SA		28	E6
PRADO CIR	ANA	AN	6000	13	D2
PRADO CIR	VPK	OR67	17900	12	F6
PRADO LN	CO	ET	22700	29A	F2
PRADO ST	ANA	AN	5900	13	C2
PRADO WOODS DR	VPK	OR67	10200	12	F6
PRAGUE ST	CO	SJ91		29B	A5
PRAIRIE CT	BREA	BREA	400	2	E5
PRAIRIE DR	HTB	HB	4500	20	D5
PRAIRIE PL	ANA	AN		13	B3
PRAIRIE RD	CO	ET	22000	29B	A2
PRAIRIE FALCON	CO	LB53		29A	B6
PRAIRIESTONE DR	CO	LB	25700	29D	A2
PRAIRIE VIEW LN	CO	SJ		56	D6
PRAIRIE VIEW LN	CO	SJ		59	D1
PRATT CIR	HTB	HB	15500	20	F3
PRATT ST	GGR	GG	12300	16	C4
PREAKNESS CT	PLA	PLA		7	F5
PREAKNESS DR	PLA	PLA	100	7	F5
PREBLE DR	TUS	TUS	200	23	F2
PRECIADOS DR	MVJO	SJ91		29B	C6
PRECIADOS DR	MVJO	SJ91	26700	29D	C1
PRECIPICE	CO	LB77		36	A4
PRELL CT	FTNV	SA08	15800	22	B4
PRELUDE DR	ANA	AN	1700	8	B6
PRELUDE DR	HTB	HB	4500	20	D4
PREMIER AV	WSTM	WSTM	10000	22	A2
PRENTISS DR	YL	YL	4100	7	D2
PRENTISS PL	YL	YL		7	D2
PRESCOTT	IRV	SA		24	E4
PRESCOTT LN	HTB	HB	17500	25	F1
PRESIDENT PL	CM	CM27	2000	31	B2
PRESIDENTE DR	HTB	HB		26	A4
PRESIDENTIAL WY	CO	MDWY		21	C2
PRESIDIO	IRV	SA14		28	F3
PRESIDIO DR	CM	CM	700	27	E4
PRESIDIO DR	CO	LB	25400	29D	A1
PRESIDIO DR	HTB	HB		26	A4
PRESIDIO PL	TUS	TUS		24	B3
PRESIDIO SQ	CM	CM	2600	27	E5
PRESIDIO WY	GGR	GG	11400	16	B2
PRESIDIO WY	OR			18	E3

STREET	CITY	P.O. ZONE	BLOCK	PAGE	GRID
PRESTON DR	CO	LB	22900	35	C3
PRESTWICK CIR	HTB	HB	8200	26	C3
PRESTWICK RD	SB	SB	1300	19	C5
PRICE DR	HTB	HB	5800	20	F6
PRIEST DR	BPK	BP		9	E3
PRIMAVERA	IRV	SA15		28	D5
PRIMAVERA DR	MVJO	SJ91		29B	C6
PRIMAVERA DR	MVJO	SJ91		29D	C1
PRIMROSE	CO	LB56		29C	E4
PRIMROSE	IRV	SA		29	C5
PRIMROSE AV	BREA	BREA		3	C6
PRIMROSE AV	FTNV	SA08	11300	22	B4
PRIMROSE AV	PLA	PLA	100	7	A4
PRIMROSE CIR	SB	SB	3500	14	D5
PRIMROSE DR	BPK	BP	7400	10	C2
PRIMROSE DR	OR	OR	1100	17	B2
PRIMROSE LN	FUL	FL33		5	F4
PRIMROSE LN	MVJO	SJ91		52	D6
PRIMROSE LN	WSTM	WSTM	15500	21	E3
PRIMROSE ST	ANA	AN	200	10	F5
PRIMROSE ST	ANA	AN	200	11	A5
PRIMROSE ST	CM	CM	1500	27	C4
PRIMROSE ST	SB	SB	3700	14	D4
PRIMULA	CO	TRA		56	B5
PRIMULA	CO	TRA		59	B4
PRIMULA CIR	BPK	BP	8400	10	C2
PRINCE CIR	WSTM	WSTM	15800	21	E4
PRINCE DR	HTB	HB47	7400	21	B5
PRINCE LN	SA	SA		22	E2
PRINCE WY	SA	SA		23	B6
PRINCESS CIR	HTB	HB	8600	26	D5
PRINCESS CT	CM	CM		27	D2
PRINCESS LN	SA	SA		22	E2
PRINCETON	IRV	SA		24	E5
PRINCETON AV	ANA	AN		13	E4
PRINCETON AV	WSTM	WSTM	5000	14	E5
PRINCETON AV N	FUL	FL	100	6	D5
PRINCETON AV S	FUL	FL	100	6	D5
PRINCETON CIR	HTB	HB46	20200	27	A5
PRINCETON CIR	SB	SB	1000	19	C4
PRINCETON CIR E	FUL	FL	500	6	D5
PRINCETON CIR W	FUL	FL	500	6	D5
PRINCETON CT	LALM	LALM		14	C3
PRINCETON DR	CM	CM	200	27	C5
PRINCETON WY	CO	ET	25700	29B	A3
PRINCEVILLE	MVJO	SJ92		29B	E3
PRINCEVILLE CIR	HTB	HB		25	F4
PRINCIPE	MVJO	SJ92		29D	C4
PRIORY WY	CO	SJ79		52	F4
PRISCILLA DR	DPT	DPT	24500	37	E3
PRISCILLA DR	HTB	HB	6000	20	F3
PRISCILLA LN	NB	NB	1400	31	E3
PRISCILLA ST	ANA	AN	600	11	F4
PRISCILLA WY	ANA	AN	500	11	F4
PRISM PL	CO	ET		52	A5
PRITCHARD AV N	FUL	FL33	100	5	E6
PRITCHARD AV S	FUL	FL33	100	5	E6
PRITCHARD WY	CYP	CYP	11400	15	B3
PRIVATE DR E	SA	SA		22	E2
PRIVATE DR S	SA	SA		22	E2
PRIVATE DR W	SA	SA		22	E2
PRIVATE RD	NB	NB60	2300	31	E2
PRO CIR	HTB	HB	16500	20	E5
PRODAN DR	HTB	HB	7400	26	B2
PRODUCER LN	HTB	HB	15500	20	F3
PRODUCT LN	HTB	HB	15500	20	F3
PRODUCTION DR	HTB	HB		20	E4
PRODUCTION PL	NB	NB	800	31	B3
PROFESSIONL CIR	HTB	HB48		26	C2
PROGRESS WY	CYP	CYP		14	E1
PROGRESSO ST	SA	SA	5000	22	B1
PROMENADE	IRV	SA		28	F5
PROMENADE AV	PLA	PLA	1000	7	D1
PROMONTORY	CO	SJ79		59	E3
PROMONTORY DR E	NB	NB		31	E5
PROMONTORY DR W	NB	NB		31	E5
PROSA	IRV	SA		24	F5
PROSPECT AV	CO	SA	13000	17	F5
PROSPECT AV	CO	TUS	14000	17	F5
PROSPECT AV	CO	TUS	14200	23	F1
PROSPECT AV	YL	YL	3700	7	D2
PROSPECT AV N&S	OR	OR	100	17	F4
PROSPECT AV N&S	TUS	TUS	100	23	F2
PROSPECT PL	CM	CM		27	F3
PROSPECT ST	CO	OR	11000	18	A2
PROSPECT ST	NB	NB	100	31	A3
PROSPECT ST	OR	OR	500	18	A2
PROSPECT ST	VPK	OR67	10600	17	F1
PROSPECTOR CIR	ANA	AN		13	C3
PROSPECT PARK N	TUS	TUS	200	23	F2
PROSPECT PARK S	TUS	TUS	200	23	F2

STREET	CITY	P.O. ZONE	BLOCK	PAGE	GRID
PROSPER ST	CO	SA		50	E4
PROTHERO DR	CO	ET	23600	29A	E4
PROVENTIAL DR	ANA	AN	600	11	D5
PROVIDENCE	CO	ET		51	E4
PROVIDENCE COM	SA	SA		22	C2
PROVIDENCE DR	VPK	OR67	10500	17	F1
PROVIDENCE LN	HTB	HB	19700	26	E4
PROVIDENCIA ST	CYP	CYP	11300	14	F2
PROVINCETOWN AV	IRV	SA	3600	24	C6
PROWSE ST	PLA	PLA	2000	7	C2
PRUDENTE	MVJO	SJ92	28700	29B	E1
PRUNUS ST	FTNV	SA08	18500	26	E2
PRYOR AV	DPT	SC24	26000	38	B4
PUA DR	HTB	HB46	10000	27	A3
PUEBLO	TUS	TUS		24	B3
PUEBLO CIR	HTB	HB		26	D2
PUEBLO PL	ANA	AN		13	D1
PUEBLO PL	FUL	FL	600	6	C1
PUEBLO NUEVO DR	MVJO	SJ91	26900	29B	C5
PUENTE AV	CM	CM27	2100	31	C1
PUENTE LN	BREA	BREA		2	D3
PUENTE ST	BREA	BREA	100	2	D6
PUENTE ST	CO	BREA	1000	2	D3
PUENTE ST	FUL	FL35	3700	2	D6
PUENTE ST	FUL	FL	2600	6	D1
PUERTA DEL ORO	MVJO	SJ91		29B	C5
PUERTA DE LUZ	MVJO	SJ91	24000	29B	C5
PUERTA REAL	MVJO	SJ91		29D	B5
PUERTO	IRV	SA		24	F5
PUERTO	IRV	SA20		49	A5
PUERTO DR	HTB	HB	8400	26	D6
PUERTO PL	DPT	DPT	34400	37	F5
PUERTO CARAVACA	SCL	SCL		39	E1
PUERTO MORANT	SCL	SC72		39	E1
PUERTO NATALES	PLA	PLA	1200	7	D4
PUERTO RICO DR	BPK	BP	7500	9	E2
PUERTO RICO DR	LAP	BP23	7400	9	E2
PUERTO ROYAL	SCL	SC72		39	E1
PUERTO VALDEMO	SCL	SC72		39	E1
PUERTO VALLARTA	CO	LB	30000	35	E4
PUFFIN AV	FTNV	SA08	9500	26	F1
PUFFIN ST	CO	LB56		29C	A1
PULLMAN ST	ANA	AN07		8	F5
PULLMAN ST	CM	CM26	3000	28	A4
PULLMAN ST	CO	SA07	17100	28	C1
PULLMAN ST	SA	SA	2300	23	D6
PULLMAN ST	SA	SA	2900	28	C1
PUNTA ALTA	CO	LB	21000	29A	A5
PUNTA DE VISTA	YL	YL		8	D3
PUNTAL LANA	MVJO	SJ92		29B	E3
PURCELL ST	GGR	GG	11500	16	A2
PURDUE AV	WSTM	WSTM	5400	14	E6
PURDUE CIR	ANA	AN		13	F4
PURDUE CIR	SB	SB	400	19	C4
PURDUE DR	CM	CM		27	D5
PURDUE ST	IRV	SA	3500	28	F4
PURDUE WY	STN	STN		10	E4
PURDUE WY	STN	STN		15	B3
PURDY AV	PLA	PLA	300	7	C2
PURDY ST	CO	MDWY	14500	21	D2
PURDY ST	GGR	GG	13500	15	D6
PURDY ST	WSTM	WSTM	14200	15	D6
PURDY ST	WSTM	WSTM	14300	21	D3
PURITAN CIR	ANA	AN	2500	12	A4
PURITAN CIR	HTB	HB47	15800	21	A4
PURITAN DR	ANA	AN	2300	12	A4
PURITAN LN	ANA	AN	2300	12	A4
PURITAN PL	ANA	AN	2700	12	B4
PURPLE SAGE	IRV	SA		32A	B3
PURPLE SAGE LN	SJC	SJ75	25500	38	A2
PURSLANE CIR	FTNV	SA08	11700	22	C5
PURYEAR LN	GGR	GG	11700	16	C3
PURYEAR ST	GGR	GG	12000	16	C3
PUSAN AV	ETMC	SA09		51	D4
PUTNEY CIR	HTB	HB		25	E1
PUTTER DR	SA	SA		16	D6
PUTTER DR	SA	SA		22	D1
PYLE CIR	GGR	GG	9600	21	F1
PYLE CIR	WSTM	WSTM	9300	21	F1
PYLE WY	CO	MDWY	8500	21	D1
PYLOS WY	CO	SJ91		29B	A6
PYRACANTHA CIR	BPK	BP	7700	10	D2
PYRENEES AV	ANA	AN06		12	B4
PYTHIAS AV	ANA	AN	500	11	B5

Q

STREET	CITY	P.O. ZONE	BLOCK	PAGE	GRID
Q ST	ETMC	SA09		51	C3
QUADRILLE PL	CO	SA	10900	18	D5
QUAIL AV	FTNV	SA08	10000	26	F2

STREET	CITY	P.O. ZONE	BLOCK	PAGE	GRID
QUAIL CIR	ANA	AN		13	F3
QUAIL CIR	BREA	BREA		2	D3
QUAIL CIR	HTB	HB	5000	20	D3
QUAIL CIR	YL	YL		8	E1
QUAIL CT	FTNV	SA08	10000	26	F2
QUAIL CT	GGR	GG	11700	15	F2
QUAIL DR	LAP	BP23	4700	9	D3
QUAIL LN	BREA	BREA		2	D3
QUAIL LN	OR	OR	100	18	B3
QUAIL PL	CO	SJ79		59	C4
QUAIL ST	NB	NB60	2000	28	B5
QUAIL WY	CO	ET	23500	29A	D4
QUAIL CREEK	CO	LB		29C	E4
QUAIL LAKES	CO	LB		29C	E4
QUAIL RIDGE CIR	FUL	FL		7	A2
QUAIL RIDGE TER	ANA	AN		13	B2
QUAIL RUN	CO	SA		18	D4
QUAIL RUN	CO	SJ79		52	F4
QUAIL RUN	CO	SJ79		56	A4
QUAIL RUN	CO	SJ79		56	B3
QUAIL RUN	DPT	DPT		38	A4
QUAIL RUN RD	CO	LALM	3100	14	A2
QUARRY RD	CO	ET		51	D4
QUARRY VIEW DR	YL	YL		8	D2
QUARTERHORSE LN	HTB	HB		26	A2
QUARTERHORSE LN	YL	YL		8	C2
QUARTZ AV	FTNV	SA08	11500	22	C5
QUARTZ CIR	FTNV	SA08	11700	22	C5
QUARTZ CIR	GGR	GG	12300	16	D5
QUARTZ LN	ANA	AN		13	D3
QUARTZ LN	FUL	FL	3000	7	B4
QUARTZ PL	GGR	GG	12400	16	D5
QUARTZ ST	WSTM	WSTM	15700	21	D4
QUATRO AV	GGR	GG	12000	16	D6
QUEBEC DR	HTB	HB	7600	26	C2
QUEBRADA	IRV	SA		24	E5
QUEDA WY	LAG	LB51	2600	34	F4
QUEDADA	NB	NB		32	B2
QUEEN CIR	WSTM	WSTM	15900	21	E4
QUEEN LN	SA	SA		22	E2
QUEEN ANN CT	DPT	LB77	32700	37	B3
QUEEN ANNES CT	GGR	GG		21	E2
QN CATHERINE CT	DPT	LB77	32600	37	B3
QUEENS AV	IRV	SA		28	F4
QUEENS CT	CM	CM		27	E2
QUEENS CT	CO	LB		35	E2
QUEENS DR	ANA	AN07	6000	13	D4
QUEENS LN	HTB	HB47	17300	21	C6
QUEENS WY	SA	SA		23	B6
QUEENS WY	STN	STN		10	E4
QUEENS WY	STN	STN		15	B3
QUEENSBOROUGH ST	WSTM	WSTM	15200	22	A3
QUEENSBURY DR	CO	ET		29B	A1
QUEENSBURY ST N	ANA	AN	100	12	B3
QUEENS GATE WY	OR	OR		13	A4
QUEENS PARK LN	HTB	HB	20600	26	F6
QUEENSPORT LN	HTB	HB46		26	C3
QUEENS WRETH WY	IRV	SA	17800	28	F5
QUEENS WRETH WY	IRV	SA	17800	29	A5
QUENT DR	TUS	TUS	14000	24	A4
QUESTA WY	DPT	DPT		37	E3
QUESTA VERDE	CO	ET		51	E4
QUETZAL	MVJO	SJ92	25000	29D	D1
QUEVEDO LN	MVJO	SJ91		29D	C4
QUICKSILVER RD	CO	TRA		56	E6
QUICKSTEP CIR	HTB	HB		20	B4
QUIET BAY DR	HTB	HB		26	A4
QUIET BAY LN	CM	CM27		27	F5
QUIET BROOK CIR	FUL	FL		6	C3
QUIET COVE	NB	CDLM	3400	33	B1
QUIET CK TER	CO	SJ79		52	F4
QUIET HILL LN	CO	SJ79		52	E3
QUIET MOON	IRV	SA		29	B5
QUIET OAK DR	CO	ET		29A	E1
QUIET PATH	GGR	GG		15	F4
QUIET SURF CIR	HTB	HB		26	A4
QUIGLEY DR	CO	LB		35	C2
QUIGLEY LN	SA	SA	700	22	C3
QUILL CIR	HTB	HB47	14900	21	A2
QUINCE CIR	FTNV	SA08	18800	26	F3
QUINCY AV	OR	OR	100	17	C1
QUINCY CIR	ANA	AN		13	E4
QUINCY CIR	WSTM	WSTM	5500	14	E5
QUINCY COM	SA	SA		22	C2
QUINTANA DR	ANA	AN		13	D1
QUINTANA DR	MVJO	SJ91		29B	C6
QUINTANA LN	HTB	HB	17800	26	A1
QUIRPON WY	CYP	CYP	11400	15	B3
QUIVERA ST	LAG	LB51	800	34	F4

R

STREET	CITY	P.O. ZONE	BLOCK	PAGE	GRID
RABASADA	MVJO	SJ92		29B	F3
RABAUL RD	CYP	CYP	11500	14	E3
RABIDA CIR	MVJO	SJ91	23900	29B	B4
RACEPOINT DR	HTB	HB		26	C5
RACHAEL VISTA	CO	LB		35	E1
RACHEL CIR	DPT	DPT		37	E2
RACINE DR	IRV	SA		32	F2
RACING WIND	IRV	SA		29	A5
RACQUET	HTB	HB		26	C3
RACQUET CLUB DR	HTB	HB		20	C4
RACQUET HILL	CO	SA		24	D1
RADA AV	CO	ET	25000	29A	F3
RADCLIFF CIR	WSTM	WSTM	10400	22	A3
RADCLIFF CT	LAG	LB51	300	34	E4
RADCLIFF PL	LAH	LAH	1000	1	E6
RADCLIFF WY	STN	STN		15	B2
RADCLIFFE AV	ANA	AN	3100	7	C6
RADEC CT	VPK	OR67		12	F6
RADEC CT	VPK	OR67	18100	13	A6
RADEC CT	VPK	OR67		17	F1
RADEC CT	VPK	OR67		18	A1
RAELYN PL	GGR	GG	10000	15	F4
RAFAEL ST	IRV	SA		29	C1
RAGAN CIR	VPK	OR67	18500	13	B5
RAGTIME CIR	HTB	HB		20	C4
RAIL CIR	CO	LB	24000	35	D1
RAILWAY ST	ANA	AN	1700	11	D1
RAIN CIR	HTB	HB		26	A2
RAINBOW	FTNV	SA08	10200	22	A6
RAINBOW AV	ANA	AN	2400	10	E3
RAINBOW CIR	FTNV	SA08		22	A6
RAINBOW CIR	FTNV	SA08	10200	27	A1
RAINBOW CIR	HTB	HB	7500	26	C3
RAINBOW DR	CO	SA	1500	24	B2
RAINBOW LN	BREA	BREA		3	B6
RAINBOW LN	YL	YL		7	F2
RAINBOW ST	GGR	GG	13000	16	D5
RAINBOW FALLS	IRV	SA		32A	A2
RAINBOW FLLS WY	OR	OR		12	B5
RAINBOW LAKE	IRV	SA		29	B5
RAINBOW RIDGE	IRV	SA		32A	B3
RAINGLEN LN	HTB	HB		25	E1
RAINIER	CO	SJ79		59	D2
RAINIER AV	OR	OR	300	12	D3
RAINIER CIR	HTB	HB	9700	26	F5
RAINIER CIR	LALM	LALM	12500	14	D4
RAINIER CIR	PLA	PLA	300	7	C1
RAINIER CIR	WSTM	WSTM	13300	15	B5
RAINIER CT	ANA	AN04	1700	15	F2
RAINIER CT	GGR	GG	11100	15	F2
RAINIER DR	CO	SA	17300	17	F5
RAINIER DR	CO	SA	18100	18	A5
RAINIER DR	CYP	CYP	4500	9	C4
RAINIER ST	FTNV	SA08	16300	22	C4
RAINIER WY	LAH	LAH	2500	1	D4
RAINSTAR	IRV	SA		29	B4
RAINTREE DR	BREA	BREA		3	B6
RAIN TREE DR	LAH	LAH		1	F6
RAINTREE LN	CO	ET	21800	29B	B1
RAINTREE LN	CO	TRA		56	E6
RAIN TREE LN	IRV	SA		29	B6
RAINTREE LN	TUS	TUS		24	A5
RAIN TREE RD	CO	LB53		29D	A4
RAINTREE RD	FUL	FL	1200	6	B3
RAIN TREE RD	OR	OR69		18	E3
RAINTREE RD	TUS	TUS	14100	24	A5
RAINTREE ST	YL	YL	5200	7	E4
RAINWOOD	CO	LB77		35	F3
RAINWOOD	CO	LB56		29C	C2
RAINWOOD	CO	LB77		36	A3
RAINWOOD AV	YL	YL		8	D2
RAIN WOOD CIR	ANA	AN		8	B6
RAITT ST N&S	SA	SA	100	22	F3
RALCAM PL	CM	CM27	300	31	D1
RALEIGH	IRV	SA		29	E2
RALEIGH AV	CM	CM	2200	27	C6
RALEIGH AV	CM	CM27	2100	31	C1
RALEIGH CT	GGR	GG44		15	D5
RALEIGH DR	HTB	HB	9500	26	E4
RALEIGH PL	TUS	TUS	14000	23	F3
RALEIGH ST	ANA	AN	1200	11	C2
RALEIGH ST	CO	ET	23500	29A	D3
RALPH LN	WSTM	WSTM	14600	21	B2
RALSTON ST	ANA	AN	1200	11	C2
RAMA ST	VPK	OR67	9500	13	B4
RAMADA	IRV	SA		24	F5
RAMADA CT	CO	LB56		29C	E5
RAMADA LN	MVJO	SJ91	23400	29B	A5

COPYRIGHT, © 1989 BY Thomas Bros Maps

ORANGE CO.

INDEX

STREET	CITY	P.O. ZONE	BLOCK	PAGE	GRID
RAMADA PZ	FUL	FL33		5	E4
RAMBLER DR	HTB	HB	9400	30	E2
RAMBLEWOOD DR	ANA	AN	800	10	B5
RAMBLEWOOD DR	STN	STN	10300	10	B6
RAMBLEWOOD DR	STN	STN	10500	15	B1
RAMBLING LN	CO	LB		29C	D4
RAMBLING BRK WY	STN	STN		15	B4
RAMJIT CT	CO	ET	26000	29B	A3
RAMM DR	ANA	AN	2300	10	E5
RAMM DR	CO	AN04	9800	10	E5
RAMONA	MVJO	SJ92		29B	E5
RAMONA AV	LAG	LB51	400	34	D3
RAMONA AV	LAH	LAH	2000	2	C4
RAMONA CT	ANA	AN	300	10	F5
RAMONA DR	FUL	FL	700	6	A5
RAMONA DR	GGR	GG	13300	16	B5
RAMONA DR	NB	CDLM	600	32	A6
RAMONA DR	SA	SA	2300	23	A6
RAMONA DR	SA	SA	2800	28	A1
RAMONA LN	HTB	HB	20300	26	E5
RAMONA PL	CM	CM27	300	31	C4
RAMONA PL	GGR	GG	13300	16	B5
RAMONA RD	YL	YL		8	E5
RAMONA ST	ANA	AN	400	10	F5
RAMONA ST	CO	LB56		29C	D3
RAMONA ST	OR	OR	4000	12	D3
RAMONA ST	PLA	PLA	400	7	A5
RAMONA WY	CM	CM27	300	31	C4
RAMONA WY	GGR	GG	10300	16	A3
RAMOS ST	SJC	SJ75	26500	36	B6
RAMOS ST	SJC	SJ75	26500	38	B1
RAMPAGE LN	IRV	SA	4000	24	D6
RAMPART LN	LAP	BP23	7300	9	D1
RAMPART PL	SA	SA		23	B6
RAMPART ST	ANA	AN06		17	A3
RAMPART ST	OR	OR		17	A3
RAMSDALE WY	STN	STN		15	B4
RAMSGATE DR	ANA	AN		13	D2
RAMSGATE LN	HTB	HB46	19800	27	A4
RAMSGATE PZ	GGR	GG		21	E3
RANA	CO	SJ		59	B2
RANA	IRV	SA		28	F6
RANCH DR	YL	YL		7	F3
RANCH LN	HTB	HB		26	B4
RANCH RD	FUL	FL	2300	6	F4
RANCHERO AV	GGR	GG	12300	16	D5
RANCHERO PL	GGR	GG	13200	16	E5
RANCHERO WY	GGR	GG	12400	16	D5
RANCHERO WY	PLA	PLA	1800	7	B2
RANCHERO WY	SA	SA	2400	16	E5
RANCH GATE RD	ANA	AN		12	F3
RANCHGROVE DR	IRV	SA	4400	29	D2
RANCH HILL	CO	SA	11500	24	D1
RANCHITO ST	ANA	AN	200	10	F4
RANCHO	TUS	TUS		23	D3
RANCHO CIR	FUL	FL	800	6	B3
RANCHO CIR	IRV	SA	15000	29	C1
RANCHO LN	YL	YL	16800	7	D3
RANCHO RD	HTB	HB47		20	E1
RANCHO RD	WSTM	WSTM	5000	14	F6
RANCHO RD	WSTM	WSTM	5700	20	E1
RANCHO WY	CO	SIL	28700	50	E2
RANCHO AZUL	CO	LB56		29C	F6
RANCHO AZUL	CO	LB56		29D	A6
RANCHO CIELO	CO	SJ79		59	D2
RCHO CIRCLE LN	YL	YL		8	A2
RANCHO CLEMENTE	CO	LB		35	F1
RCHO CRISTIANO	CO	LB		29C	F6
RCHO CRISTIANO	CO	LB		35	F1
RANCHO DE JUANA	CO	LB		35	F1
RANCHO DE LINDA	CO	LB56		29C	F6
RANCHO DE LINDA	CO	LB		35	F1
RANCHO DEL LAGO	CO	LB56		35	F1
RANCHO DEL REY	HTB	HB		20	D4
RANCHO DEL SOL	CO	LB		35	F1
RANCHO GRANDE	CO	LB56		29C	F6
RANCHO GRANDE	CO	LB		35	F1
RANCHO LAGUNA	CO	LB		35	F2
RCHO LAGUNA RD	LAG	LB51	1200	34	F3
RANCHO MARALENA	CO	LB		35	F1
RCHO NIGUEL RD	CO	LB56		29C	F6
RCHO NIGUEL RD	CO	LB56		35	E1
RANCHO PAMELITA	CO	LB		29C	F6
RANCHO PAMELITA	CO	LB		35	F1
RO SANTIAGO BL	CO	OR	10300	18	B3
RO SANTIAGO BL	OR	OR	100	18	B3
RANCHO VIEJO RD	CO	SJ75		36	B2
RANCHO VIEJO RD	SJC	SJ92		36	B2
RANCHO VIEJO RD	SJC	SJ75	30000	36	C4
RANCHO VIEJO RD	SJC	SJ75		38	D1
RANCHO VISTA	HTB	HB		30	D2

STREET	CITY	P.O. ZONE	BLOCK	PAGE	GRID
RANCHROAD DR	OR	OR		18	B2
RANCH VIEW CIR	ANA	AN		13	D2
RANCHVIEW DR	CO	SA	12400	24	C2
RANCHVIEW DR	OR	OR	3900	12	E3
RANCHWOOD RD	TUS	SA05	12900	24	B3
RANCH WOOD TR	OR	OR	600	18	D2
RANCHWOOD WY	CO	SJ79		52	E3
RAND ST	BPK	BP	5800	5	C5
RANDALL AV	CO	LAH	9000	1	E3
RANDALL AV N	CO	LAH	1000	1	E3
RANDALL ST	CO	LAH		1	E3
RANDALL ST	CO	OR	10300	13	D6
RANDALL ST	OR	OR		13	D6
RANDALL WY	LAG	LB51	500	34	E3
RANDEE WY	FUL	FL33		5	D6
RANDI LN	HTB	HB	19000	26	E3
RANDOLPH AV	BREA	BREA	500	6	F1
RANDOLPH AV	CM	CM	2800	27	F4
RANDOLPH AV N&S	BREA	BREA	100	2	F6
RANDOM DR	ANA	AN	2000	10	F5
RANDOM DR	ANA	AN	1700	11	A5
RANDOM DR	CO	AN04	9500	10	E5
RANDY AV	ANA	AN	2800	12	B4
RANGER AV	BREA	BREA	3000	3	C6
RANGER DR	LALM	LALM	11000	14	D2
RANGER LN	HTB	HB46	19800	27	A4
RANGEVIEW	CO	SJ79		59	D3
RANGEVIEW DR	CO	SA	9800	18	D4
RANGEWOOD RD	CO	LB	25400	29D	A2
RANGOON ST	CO	SJ91		29A	F4
RANIER WY	CM	CM26		28	A3
RANNEY AV	GGR	GG	10400	16	A6
RAPALLO	IRV	SA14		29	A4
RAPALLO PZ	YL	YL		8	C3
RAPHAEL DR	HTB	HB	5800	25	F1
RAPID FALLS RD	CO	LB	25400	29C	F4
RAPID FALLS RD	CO	LB		29D	A5
RAPIDS DR	HTB	HB		26	C2
RAPOSA	CO	SJ		59	B1
RAQUEL RD	CO	SA15	21000	33A	F4
RAQUETA	NB	NB		32	A2
RARITAN AV	FTNV	SA08	9800	21	F4
RASCAL LN	HTB	HB		20	C4
RASHFORD DR	PLA	PLA	1000	7	C4
RASPBERRY LN	ANA	AN		8	E6
RASPBERRY LN	ANA	AN		13	E1
RATH CIR	HTB	HB	8700	26	D5
RATHBURN AV	WSTM	WSTM	8600	21	D3
RATON DR	CO	ET	24700	29A	E4
RATTAN ST	IRV	SA	14800	29	D2
RAVELLO	CO	LB77		35	F5
RAVELLO LN	CM	CM27	300	31	F2
RAVEN CIR	FTNV	SA08	9700	26	F2
RAVEN CT	OR	OR69		18	C3
RAVEN LN	OR	OR69		18	C2
RAVENCREST DR	BREA	BREA	1700	7	A1
RAVENCREST RD	CO	SA	1000	18	B6
RAVENHILL CT	FUL	FL		6	F3
RAVEN HILL LN	CO	LB		29C	E2
RAVENNA	IRV	SA14		29	A4
RAVENNA DR	YL	YL	19800	8	C3
RAVENNA RD	CO	SJ92		29D	E2
RAVENNA ST	ANA	AN	1200	11	C2
RAVENSRIDGE	CO	SJ79		59	E3
RAVENSCROFT RD	CO	OR		18	D3
RAVENSWOOD	CO	ET	24900	29A	F2
RAVENSWOOD DR	ANA	AN	2800	10	B6
RAVENSWOOD DR	YL	YL		8	D1
RAVENWOOD CT	FUL	FL		7	A1
RAVENWOOD LN	HTB	HB46	20300	27	A5
RAVENWOOD ST	IRV	SA	14500	29	D1
RAWHIDE CIR	CO	ET	26700	29B	B1
RAWLINGS WY	TUS	TUS		24	D2
RAY AV	FUL	FL	1100	11	C1
RAY CIR	SA	SA	2100	22	E6
RAYMAR ST	SA	SA	1300	22	F3
RAYMAR ST	SA	SA	1200	23	A3
RAYMER AV	FUL	FL33	1800	5	E5
RAYMOND AV	ANA	AN	1000	11	D1
RAYMOND AV	CM	CM27	1700	31	D3
RAYMOND AV N&S	FUL	FL	100	6	D6
RAYMOND AV S	FUL	FL	1000	11	D1
RAYMOND CIR	GGR	GG45	12500	14	F4
RAYMOND ST	LAH	LAH	200	1	E5
RAYMOND WY	ANA	AN01	700	6	D6
RAYMOND WY	ANA	AN	700	11	D1
RAYMOND WY	CO	ET	24500	29A	E4
RAYO DEL SOL	CO	LB		29A	A6
RAYO DEL SOL	CO	LB		29C	A1
REA CIR	GGR	GG	12200	15	E4
READING AV	GGR	GG	9500	21	E1

STREET	CITY	P.O. ZONE	BLOCK	PAGE	GRID
READING AV	WSTM	WSTM	9000	21	E1
REAGAN ST	LALM	LALM	10600	14	B2
REASONER LN	ETMC	SA09		51	E3
REATA	CO	SJ88		29B	F5
REBANO	SCL	SC72		38	E3
REBECCA DR	LAH	LAH	1000	1	F3
REBECCA LN	CO	SA	1500	24	B1
REBECCA LN	YL	YL		7	F4
REBEL CIR	HTB	HB		20	C4
RECINTO	IRV	SA		24	E5
RECODO	IRV	SA		24	F5
RECODO LN	MVJO	SJ91		29D	C4
RECREATION CIR	FTNV	SA08	9000	21	E5
RECREO PZ	ANA	AN		16	B3
RED BARN CIR	CO	LB	27000	29C	E4
REDBAY AV	BREA	BREA	200	3	A6
REDBERRY RD	CO	SA	2000	24	C2
REDBIRD ST	GGR	GG	13300	16	D5
RED BLUFF CIR	IRV	SA	4800	29	D2
RED BLUFF DR	CO	SJ79		52	E3
REDBUD	CO	SJ		59	B3
REDBUD CIR	FTNV	SA08	18000	26	E1
REDBUD ST	BREA	BREA	1200	3	A5
RED COACH DR	HTB	HB47	6500	21	A3
REDCOACH LN	LAH	LAH	2300	1	D6
RED CORRAL RD	CO	LB		29C	F3
REDDING AV	CM	CM	1000	27	E2
RED EYE CIR	FTNV	SA08	10000	27	A1
REDFORD LN	LAP	BP23	8000	9	D3
REDGROVE CIR	HTB	HB47	6500	21	A4
RED GUM ST	ANA	AN	1300	7	B6
RED GUM ST	ANA	AN	1000	12	B1
REDHAWK	IRV	SA		29	B2
RED HILL AV	CM	CM26	3000	28	A4
RED HILL AV	CO	SA	11500	18	C6
RED HILL AV	CO	SA05	14400	23	D6
RED HILL AV	CO	TUS	14000	23	D6
RED HILL AV	CO	SA	11800	24	A3
RED HILL AV	CO	SA	16500	24	A3
RED HILL AV	CO	TUS	12500	28	C2
RED HILL AV	IRV	SA	16500	28	C2
RED HILL AV	TUS	TUS	14500	23	D6
RED HILL AV	TUS	TUS	13300	24	A3
RED JACKET CIR	HTB	HB	21000	26	F6
REDLANDS AV	NB	NB	400	31	C4
REDLANDS DR	CO	CM27	2600	27	F6
REDLANDS DR	CO	SA07	20200	28	A5
REDLANDS DR	CO	NB60	2300	31	E2
REDLANDS LN	HTB	HB47	16300	21	A4
REDLANDS PL	CM	CM27	1500	31	D4
REDLANDS ST	WSTM	WSTM	15800	21	D4
REDLEN ST	CO	ET	24500	29A	E4
RED LODGE PL	CO	LB	24000	29C	E4
RED MILL CIR	TUS	TUS	1900	24	B3
RED OAK CT	FTNV	SA08		27	A2
REDONDA	IRV	SA		24	F5
REDONDELA	MVJO	SJ92	27800	29B	F4
REDONDO	CO	LB77		36	A5
REDONDO CIR	HTB	HB	18000	26	C1
REDONDO DR E	ANA	AN	800	11	B3
REDONDO DR W	ANA	AN	800	11	B3
REDONDO PL	FUL	FL	1500	6	B3
RED RIVER CIR	FTNV	SA08		26	F2
RED RIVER DR	CO	ET	21800	29B	A1
RED ROBIN LN	CO	ET	23300	29A	D4
RED ROBIN ST	OR	OR	800	18	B1
REDROCK	IRV	SA	15300	29	C2
RED ROCK CIR	HTB	HB	16900	20	E5
RED ROCK LN	CO	LB77		36	A6
REDROCK ST	ANA	AN	100	12	F2
RED WILLOW RD	FUL	FL33		5	D3
REDWING	IRV	SA		29	D3
REDWING CIR	CM	CM	2700	27	B4
REDWING LN	HTB	HB		20	D5
REDWOOD	CO	LB56		29C	B3
REDWOOD AV	ANA	AN	1500	11	E3
REDWOOD AV	BREA	BREA	100	2	E6
REDWOOD AV	BREA	BREA	500	6	E1
REDWOOD AV	CM	CM	2900	27	C4
REDWOOD AV	OR	OR	300	12	C4
REDWOOD CIR	FTNV	SA08	16500	21	F5
REDWOOD CIR	FTNV	SA08	18500	26	F2
REDWOOD CIR	FUL	FL	2900	6	F2
REDWOOD CIR	LAP	BP23	7300	9	E1
REDWOOD DR	SA	SA		22	B1
REDWOOD DR	TUS	TUS		24	B4
REDWOOD DR N	ANA	AN	2000	11	F2
REDWOOD DR N	ANA	AN	2300	12	A2
REDWOOD DR S	ANA	AN	2000	11	F3
REDWOOD DR S	ANA	AN	2300	12	A3

STREET	CITY	P.O. ZONE	BLOCK	PAGE	GRID
REDWOOD LN	HTB	HB	20300	26	F5
REDWOOD LN	LAH	LAH	200	6	A1
REDWOOD LN	MVJO	SJ91		52	D6
REDWOOD LN	WSTM	WSTM		21	C4
REDWOOD PL N	ANA	AN	400	11	F2
REDWOOD PL S	ANA	AN	300	11	F3
REDWOOD ST	CYP	CYP	9300	9	D5
REDWOOD ST	FTNV	SA08	16300	21	F4
REDWOOD ST	FTNV	SA08	18600	26	F2
REDWOOD ST	IRV	SA	3500	24	C6
REDWOOD ST	IRV	SA	3500	29	C1
REDWOOD ST	YL	YL	5400	7	E4
RED WOOD POINT	CO	ET		29B	A2
REDWOOD TREE LN	IRV	SA		29	A5
REED AV	ANA	AN	600	11	C2
REED AV	IRV	SA	17500	28	F4
REED ST	LAG	LB51	500	34	D3
REEDER LN	HTB	HB	20200	26	E5
REEF	CO	LB77		35	F5
REEF	CO	LB77		36	A5
REEF CIR	PLA	PLA	900	12	A1
REEF LN	HTB	HB	20500	26	F6
REEF BAY PL	DPT	DPT	33300	38	A3
REEF COVE	NB	NB60		31	E6
REEFTON AV	CYP	CYP	6500	14	F3
REEFTON AV	CYP	CYP	6600	15	A3
REEF VIEW CIR	NB	CDLM		32	C6
REESE WY	CO	MDWY	8500	21	D2
REEVE ST	GGR	GG43	15100	22	A2
REEVES PL	CO	OR69		18	C1
REFLEJO	MVJO	SJ92	24900	29B	D6
REFLEJO	MVJO	SJ92	24900	29D	D1
REGAL AV	CO	AN04	8700	15	D1
REGAL CIR	HTB	HB	20400	26	D5
REGAL WY	CO	ET		29B	A1
REGAL OAKS DR	YL	YL		8	D2
REGAL PARK DR	ANA	AN	2600	12	B2
REGATO	CO	SJ88		29B	F5
REGATTA CT	SJC	SJ75	33000	38	B2
REGATTA DR	HTB	HB	9000	30	E1
REGATTA RD	ANA	AN	1800	11	A6
REGATTA RD	LAG	LB51	1400	34	F3
REGATTA WY	DPT	LB77		37	D4
REGATTA WY	SB	SB		19	D2
REGENCY CIR	FUL	FL33		5	E3
REGENCY CT	SJC	SJ75		36	C3
REGENCY DR	SB	SB		19	F1
REGENCY LN	CO	ET		52	C6
REGENCY ST	LAP	BP23	8200	9	D3
REGENT DR	SA	SA	4200	22	C3
REGGAE CT	CO	LB77		36	A5
REGINA	DPT	DPT		37	E2
REGINA CIR	HTB	HB	16500	20	E5
REGINA ST	CO	SJ91	24400	29B	A6
REGINA WY	GGR	GG	11100	16	B3
REGIO	MVJO	SJ92		29D	C2
REGIO AV	BPK	BP	6400	5	A6
REGIS LN	CM	CM	2800	27	E4
REGIS WY	CO	TUS		24	B1
REGISTRY CT	CO	LB56		29C	E5
REGLA CIR	SCL	SC72		39	E4
REGULUS DR	YL	YL	17000	7	E3
REILLY DR	HTB	HB	8200	26	D5
REIMER ST	FTNV	SA08	10800	22	A6
REIMS CIR	IRV	SA	15300	29	D3
REIMS LN	CM	CM27	300	31	C3
REIMS LN	NB	NB		31	B4
REINA	DPT	DPT		37	D2
REINOSA	MVJO	SJ91	22600	29B	D3
REMANSO	TUS	TUS		23	D3
REMBRANDT CIR	OR	OR		12	F6
REMBRANDT CIR	OR	OR	1200	17	F1
REMBRANDT DR	FTNV	SA08	8500	21	D6
REMBRANDT DR	HTB	HB47	8400	21	D6
REMBRANDT DR	LAG	LB51	700	34	E3
REMESA DR	MVJO	SJ91	25200	29D	B1
REMINGTON	IRV	SA		29	E1
REMINGTON LN	HTB	HB	17000	20	E5
REMME RIDGE	CO	ET		29A	D2
REMOLINO LJS RD	CO	LB77	28900	36	A2
REMORA DR	HTB	HB		20	A6
REN CIR	TUS	TUS	1900	24	A4
RENE DR	ANA	AN		11	B5
RENE DR	SA	SA	1100	22	F6
RENE DR	SA	SA04	2800	27	F1
RENEE ST	OR	OR	100	18	B3
RENGAL WY	ANA	AN	2900	12	B1
RENNRICK CIR	HTB	HB47	6500	21	A6
RENO CIR	HTB	HB	5500	20	E3
RENOAK ST	ANA	AN	200	10	D4
RENOIR CIR	HTB	HB	5700	20	F6

STREET	CITY	P.O. ZONE	BLOCK	PAGE	GRID
RENZ CIR	FUL	FL33		5	E4
REPAIR LN	HTB	HB48		26	B2
REPPOE VIA	ANA	AN		16	D2
REPUBLIC AV	CM	CM	2200	27	B6
REPUBLIC AV	CM	CM27	1900	31	B2
RESEARCH DR	HTB	HB	5500	20	E3
RESEDA PL	ANA	AN	2000	11	F4
RESEDA ST	ANA	AN	500	11	F4
RESERVOIR RD	CO	SA	11300	18	C6
RESH PL	ANA	AN	500	11	C3
RESH ST N	ANA	AN	100	11	C4
RESH ST S	ANA	AN	500	11	C4
RESPIT RD	CO	ET	23400	29A	E4
RETHERFORD DR	HTB	HB47	6700	21	B4
RETOZO	IRV	SA		24	E5
REUBENS CIR	OR	OR		12	F6
REUBENS DR	HTB	HB47	6200	21	A4
REUBENS ST	LAG	LB51	100	34	D3
REVA DR	GGR	GG	11400	16	B3
REVERE	IRV	SA		24	D5
REVERE AV	FUL	FL	2200	6	E5
REVERE DR	FUL	FL	1400	6	E5
REVERE DR	WSTM	WSTM	14500	21	E2
REVERE RD	CO	ET	22500	29B	A3
REVERE ST	ANA	AN	500	11	F4
REVERE ST	CO	LB		35	E6
REVERE ST	CO	LB77		37	E1
REVERE WY	NB	NB		31	E4
REVSON	IRV	SA18		29A	C3
REVUELTA CT	SCL	SC72		39	D2
REXBON CT	FTNV	SA08	10700	22	B4
REXFORD AV	CYP	CYP	5900	14	E1
REXFORD CT	CYP	CYP	10400	14	E1
REXFORD DR	CYP	CYP	10400	14	E1
REXFORD RD	GGR	GG	11700	16	C4
REY DR	HTB	HB	4700	20	D5
REYES ST	IRV	SA	4000	29	C1
REYNOLDS AV	IRV	SA	1300	28	C2
REYNOLDS CIR	HTB	HB47		21	C6
REYNOLDS CIR	HTB	HB		26	C1
REYNOLDS PL	ANA	AN	500	12	A4
RHAPSODY DR	HTB	HB	4500	20	D4
RHEA AV	FTNV	SA08	9500	26	F2
RHEA DR	CO	SJ91		29A	F6
RHIEMS RD	CO	AN04	10300	10	E6
RHINE CIR	HTB	HB47	16500	21	C5
RHINE DR	HTB	HB47	7500	21	C5
RHINE LN	CM	CM26		28	A3
RHINE PL	NB	NB		31	A6
RHINE RIVER AV	FTNV	SA08	8900	26	E2
RHOADS CIR	FTNV	SA08		26	D1
RHODA DR	CO	SJ91	25500	29A	F6
RHODE ISLND CIR	CM	CM		27	C2
RHODES AV	ANA	AN	2200	10	E2
RHODES DR	CM	CM	1800	27	B4
RHODESIA DR	HTB	HB	9000	30	E2
RHODOLITE CT	FTNV	SA08	15900	22	B4
RHONA DR	CO	LB56		29C	E5
RHONDA AV	GGR	GG43	10600	22	B1
RHONDA AV	SA	SA	5400	22	B1
RHONE LN	HTB	HB47	16200	21	B5
RHONE LN	HTB	HB47	7600	21	B5
RIA	CO	SJ88		29B	F5
RIACHUELO	SCL	SC72		38	F4
RIATA DR	WSTM	WSTM	14000	15	D6
RIATA ST	CO	MDWY	14500	21	D2
RIATA ST	GGR	GG	13600	15	D6
RIATA ST	WSTM	WSTM	14200	21	D2
RIBALTA	MVJO	SJ92	23400	29B	E4
RIBERA	IRV	SA		24	F5
RICARDO DR	YL	YL	4100	7	E2
RICE AISLE	IRV	SA15		32	F1
RICE CIR	HTB	HB47	15000	21	A2
RICHARD ST	OR	OR	1200	13	B6
RICHARD ST	OR	OR	300	18	B2
RICHARDS PL	ANA	AN	1600	11	B5
RICHARDSON ST	SA	SA	1200	22	C4
RICHARDSON WY	WSTM	WSTM	13500	15	C6
RICHFIELD RD	ANA	AN	1100	12	E1
RICHFIELD RD	PLA	PLA	6200	7	E6
RICHFIELD RD	YL	YL	5000	7	E6
RICHFIELD WY	YL	YL	4900	7	E3
RICHFORD DR	CO	ET		29B	A2
RICH HILL WY	YL	YL	5600	7	E5
RICHLAND AV	SA	SA	1300	22	F3
RICHLAND AV	SA	SA	900	23	A3
RICHLAND ST	OR	OR		12	C3
RICHLAND ST	SA	SA	100	23	A3
RICHLAND WY	CO	SJ		52	E3
RICHMAN AV N&S	FUL	FL	100	6	B6
RICHMAN AV S	FUL	FL	1000	11	B1

INDEX

1990 ORANGE COUNTY STREET INDEX

STREET	CITY	P.O. ZONE	BLOCK	PAGE	GRID
RICHMAN KNOLL	FUL	FL	1000	6	B3
RICHMOND	IRV	SA		24	E4
RICHMOND AV	GGR	GG45	5300	14	E4
RICHMOND CIR	HTB	HB48	21100	26	A6
RICHMOND DR N	PLA	PLA	1400	7	D3
RICHMOND ST	SA	SA	2200	17	D5
RICHMOND WY	CM	CM	2300	27	E6
RICHMOND HILL	CO	LAG		35	F6
RICHMONT DR	ANA	AN	100	10	C4
RICH SPRING CIR	CO	LB	25900	29D	A3
RICHTER AV	IRV	SA	2500	28	E2
RICK ST	OR	OR	500	18	A2
RICKENBACKER RD	CO	LB	25200	29D	A1
RICKER WY	ANA	AN07		12	B2
RICKY AV	ANA	AN	1500	16	B2
RICKY AV	GGR	GG	11800	16	C2
RICKY LN	ANA	AN	1300	16	C2
RICO RD	LAG	LB	22100	35	B6
RICOH PLAZA	SA	SA05		23	E6
RIDE OUT WY	FUL	FL	800	6	B1
RIDGE DR	LB	LB51		33A	F6
RIDGE LN	CO	ET	23100	29A	E3
RIDGE LN	LAG	LB	100	34	B2
RIDGE RD	SJC	SJ75	29400	36	B2
RIDGE WY	YL	YL	5900	8	A5
RIDGEBORO PL	TUS	TUS	14800	23	F5
RIDGEBORO PL	TUS	TUS	14800	24	A5
RIDGEBROOK	MVJO	SJ92		29B	E2
RIDGEBURY DR	HTB	HB	5500	25	E1
RIDGECREST CIR	ANA	AN		43	A3
RIDGECREST CIR	CM	CM27		31	A1
RIDGECREST CIR	TUS	TUS		17	F6
RIDGECREST DR	YL	YL	17600	7	E4
RIDGECREST LN	OR	OR		12	E4
RIDGECREST WY	CO	SJ79		52	F4
RIDGEDALE LN	YL	YL		7	E2
RIDGEFIELD DR	HTB	HB	8100	30	C1
RIDGE GATE RD	ANA	AN		12	F3
RIDGEGLEN RD	ANA	AN		13	E3
RIDGEHAVEN DR	LAH	LAH	700	1	D5
RIDGELAKE DR	PLA	PLA		7	B6
RIDGELINE	IRV	SA		32A	A3
RIDGELINE CT	DPT	DPT		37	B5
RIDGELINE DR	IRV	SA		29	B6
RIDGELINE DR	IRV	SA		32A	B1
RIDGELINE DR	NB	CDLM		32	D5
RIDGELINE RD	CO	SJ		52	F3
RIDGELINE RD	OR	OR		18	D1
RIDGE MANOR WY	YL	YL	19800	8	C5
RIDGEMARK	MVJO	SJ92		29D	D3
RIDGE PARK DR	YL	YL		8	E2
RIDGE PARK LN	OR	OR		12	F4
RIDGEROCK	CO	LB77		36	A4
RIDGE ROUTE DR	CO	ET	22700	29A	D4
RIDGE ROUTE DR	CO	LB	22900	29A	B4
RIDGETOP RD	CO	SA		50	D3
RIDGEVIEW CIR	HTB	HB47	14900	21	A2
RIDGEVIEW CIR	VPK	OR67		13	B5
RIDGEVIEW DR	CO	LB	29000	35	C2
RIDGEVIEW DR	OR	OR		18	C3
RIDGEVIEW RD	ANA	AN		13	E3
RIDGEVIEW RD	VPK	OR67	19000	13	B5
RIDGEVIEW TER	FUL	FL	1300	6	D3
RIDGEWAY AV	CO	LB		35	E6
RIDGEWAY AV	CO	LB77		37	E1
RIDGEWAY DR	BPK	BP	7400	9	F2
RIDGEWAY DR	CO	SA	10500	18	C4
RIDGEWAY RD	OR	OR	3100	12	F4
RIDGEWAY RD	OR	OR	3600	13	A4
RIDGEWAY ST	ANA	AN	200	10	C4
RIDGEWOOD CIR	CO	ET	24500	29A	E2
RIDGEWOOD CT	ANA	AN		13	C3
RIDGEWOOD LN	VPK	OR67	18700	13	B6
RIDGEWOOD PL	YL	YL	19800	8	C4
RIDGEWOOD ST	OR	OR	1700	12	D5
RIDGEWOOD ST	SA	SA	2200	17	D5
RIDGLEA AV	BPK	BP	4700	5	C3
RIDGLEY DR	GGR	GG	10000	15	F6
RIDGWAY LN	LAH	LAH	500	1	E2
RIDING WY	OR	OR	2400	12	E5
RIEDEL DR	FUL	FL	900	6	E4
RIENDAS	MVJO	SJ92		29B	D6
RIESLING	IRV	SA		29	A4
RIFA	MVJO	SJ92		29B	D4
RIGEL CIR	NB	NB	800	31	F3
RIGGER	CO	LAG		35	F3
RIGHTER CIR	SA	SA	2800	17	E5
RIGSBY ST	LAH	LAH	100	1	D4
RIKI CT	CO	LB77		35	D1
RILES CIR	ANA	AN		12	A6
RILEY PL	LAG	LB51	1000	34	F3

STREET	CITY	P.O. ZONE	BLOCK	PAGE	GRID
RILEY PL	SA	SA	3000	28	B1
RIM PT	CO	ET		29B	A2
RIM RD	CO	SA		50	D6
RIM RD	YL	YL		8	E1
RIMCREST CIR	LB	LB51		33A	F6
RIM CREST DR	ANA	AN		43	A2
RIM CREST DR	YL	YL		8	D1
RIMCREST RD	BREA	BREA		3	B5
RIMGATE DR	CO	ET		29B	A1
RIMHURST DR	CO	ET		29B	A2
RIMI CT	CO	LB77		35	D2
RIMINI	CO	LB		29A	B4
RIMROCK	IRV	SA		32A	A3
RIMROCK CIR	CO	ET	21700	29B	A1
RIM ROCK CYN RD	LAG	LB51	1500	34	E3
RIM VIEW DR	CO	ET		29A	E2
RIMVIEW LN	BREA	BREA		3	B5
RIMWOOD DR	ANA	AN		13	F4
RINCON	IRV	SA		24	F5
RINCON	IRV	SA20		49	A5
RINCON	TUS	TUS		23	D2
RINCON CT	SCL	SC72	100	39	C2
RINDGE CIR	FTNV	SA08	15800	21	F4
RING BIT DR	YL	YL		8	C2
RINGO CIR	HTB	HB47	6400	21	A4
RIO WY	BPK	BP	5700	9	E2
RIO ALISO DR	CO	ET		29B	B2
RIO BRAVO CIR	CO	ET	26700	29B	B1
RIO DE ORO DR	YL	YL	18400	8	A3
RIO DE PLATA DR	YL	YL	18400	8	A3
RIO GRANDE AV	CO	LB		29C	E3
RIO GRANDE AV	PLA	PLA	300	7	C3
RIO GRANDE CIR	CO	ET	22000	29B	B2
RIO GRANDE CT	FTNV	SA08		27	A2
RIO GRANDE DR	ANA	AN		13	D1
RIO HONDO CIR	CO	ET	26600	29B	B2
RIO VERDE	CO	ET	21500	29A	F1
RIO VERDE DR	LAH	LAH	2000	1	E4
RIO VISTA	CO	AN07		44	A1
RIO VISTA DR	HTB	HB	6900	26	B1
RIO VISTA ST	CO	AN06	9000	12	B5
RIO VSTA ST N&S	ANA	AN	100	12	B5
RIPPLING BROOK	CO	ET	22300	29B	B2
RIPPLING CK DR	OR	OR		12	C3
RIPPLING STREAM	IRV	SA		32A	A2
RIPTIDE CIR	HTB	HB		26	B4
RIPTIDE CT	NB	NB63		31	A2
RISA PL	CO	SA	1100	18	C5
RISING TIDE CT	DPT	DPT		37	A5
RITA LN	ANA	AN	1500	10	F6
RITA LN	ANA	AN04	1500	15	F1
RITA WY	SA	SA	1100	22	F4
RITA WY	SA	SA04	2800	27	F1
RITCHEY ST	SA	SA	1200	23	D5
RITTENHOUSE CIR	CO	LB		29A	E6
RITTENHOUSE CIR	CO	LB		29C	E1
RITTER ST	CYP	CYP	10500	15	A1
RITZ-CARLTON DR	DPT	LB77		37	D3
RITZ COVE DR	DPT	LAG		37	C3
RIVA LN	CYP	CYP		9	E3
RIVENDELL DR	CO	ET	22700	29A	E3
RIVER AV	NB	NB	3900	31	A4
RIVER AV	OR	OR	100	17	C4
RIVER LN	SA	SA	1200	16	F5
RIVER LN	SA	SA	900	17	A5
RIVER WY	BPK	BP		5	C4
RIVERA LN	ANA	AN		16	D2
RIVERA PL	CO	LB	30800	35	D5
RIVERA TER	NB	CDLM	400	33	C2
RIVERBEND	HTB	HB47		21	E5
RIVERBOAT WY	OR	OR		12	D3
RIVERDALE AV	ANA	AN	3800	12	E2
RIVERDALE AV	OR	OR	100	12	C3
RIVERDALE LN	HTB	HB48		25	E3
RIVERDALE WY	STN	STN		15	C4
RIVER FORD RD	CO	TUS	1800	24	B3
RIVER GLEN	CO	ET		52	C4
RIVERINE AV	SA	SA	1000	23	B1
RIVER MIST CIR	OR	OR		12	C3
RIVERRUN	IRV	SA		29	D4
RIVER RUN LN	CO	ET		29A	D3
RIVERSEA RD	SB	SB		19	D3
RIVERSIDE AV	NB	NB	100	31	C4
RIVERSIDE CIR	HTB	HB		25	F2
RIVERSIDE CIR	HTB	HB		26	A3
RIVERSIDE DR	CO	CM27	2600	27	F6
RIVERSIDE DR	CO	SA07	20200	28	A6
RIVERSIDE DR	FUL	FL	1200	6	E5
RIVERSIDE DR	SA	SA	2300	17	B5
RIVERSIDE FRWY	ANA			8	E6
RIVERSIDE FRWY	ANA			11	C2

STREET	CITY	P.O. ZONE	BLOCK	PAGE	GRID
RIVERSIDE FRWY	ANA			12	C2
RIVERSIDE FRWY	ANA			13	B1
RIVERSIDE FRWY	CO			40	B6
RIVERSIDE FRWY	CO			43	B1
RIVERSIDE FRWY	FUL	FL33		10	E1
RIVERSIDE FRWY	FUL			11	C2
RIVERSIDE PL	CM	CM27	1500	31	D4
RIVERSTONE	CO	LB77		37	F2
RIVERSTONE	CO	LB77		38	A2
RIVERSTONE	IRV	SA		29	B1
RIVERTON CIR	WSTM	WSTM	14200	21	D1
RIVER TRAIL RD	OR	OR		12	B4
RIVER VALLEY TR	ANA	AN		13	C3
RIVERVIEW AV	OR	OR	400	12	D2
RIVERVIEW CIR	HTB	HB		26	B2
RIVERVIEW DR	ANA	AN		8	F6
RIVERVIEW DR	ANA	AN08		40	A6
RIVERVIEW DR	CO	SJ79		52	F4
RIVERVIEW DR	YL	YL	19900	8	C5
RIVERWOOD CIR	ANA	AN		13	D2
RIVIERA	CO	SJ79		59	C6
RIVIERA	MVJO	SJ92		52	E6
RIVIERA CT	FUL	FL		6	C2
RIVIERA CT	SJC	SJ75	300	36	A3
RIVIERA DR	CM	CM27	300	31	F1
RIVIERA DR	HTB	HB	14300	20	F1
RIVIERA DR	LAG	LB51	2400	34	A1
RIVIERA DR	SA	SA	1400	16	F5
RIVIERA DR	SA	SA	900	17	A5
RIVIERA DR	SB	SB	500	19	F2
RIVIERA ST	ANA	AN	1200	11	C2
RIVIERA WY	LAG	LB51	100	34	A1
ROAD A	HTB	HB47		21	B4
ROAD B	HTB	HB47		21	B4
ROAD C	HTB	HB47		21	B5
ROADRUNNER LN	CO	LB56		29C	B1
ROADRUNNER LN	FTNV	SA08	9200	26	E2
ROAD RUNNER RD	ANA	AN		43	B3
ROADS END DR	GGR	GG	10000	15	F2
ROAN RD	GGR	GG	13100	16	C5
ROANE CIR	CO	SA05		18	B5
ROANNE CIR	IRV	SA	15100	29	D3
ROANNE DR	LAH	LAH	1300	2	B3
ROANNE PL N	ANA	AN	1000	10	E2
ROANNE ST N	ANA	AN	800	10	E3
ROANNE ST S	ANA	AN	600	10	E5
ROANOKE	CO	SJ79		59	E3
ROANOKE	IRV	SA		24	D6
ROANOKE AV	LAH	LAH	1200	1	D3
ROANOKE AV	TUS	SA10	1600	23	F4
ROANOKE AV	TUS	SA05	1900	24	A4
ROANOKE AV	YL	YL		8	F4
ROANOKE CT	CYP	CYP	11300	15	A2
ROANOKE LN	CM	CM	3000	27	F3
ROANOKE ST	LAH	LAH	1300	1	D3
ROANOKE ST	PLA	PLA	1600	7	B3
ROB WY	ANA	AN	100	10	F4
ROBBIE CIR	VPK	OR67	18300	13	A5
ROBBIE PL	PLA	PLA	400	7	B3
ROBBINS CT	ANA	AN	100	12	B3
ROBERT CT	BREA	BREA		2	E3
ROBERT DR	ANA	AN	3000	10	C4
ROBERT LN	ANA	AN	1900	16	C2
ROBERT LN	GGR	GG	11400	16	C3
ROBERT LN	HTB	HB	16500	20	F5
ROBERTA AV	FUL	FL33	1500	10	E1
ROBERTA AV	FUL	FL	400	11	B1
ROBERTA CIR	GGR	GG	13400	16	E6
ROBERTA CIR	HTB	HB	18200	26	D2
ROBERTA DR	OR	OR	2500	17	F3
ROBERTA DR	OR	OR	3700	18	A3
ROBERTA PL	GGR	GG	13000	16	E5
ROBERTO	SCL	SCL		38	E4
ROBERTO ST	VPK	OR67	10700	17	F1
ROBERTO ST	VPK	OR67	10900	18	A1
ROBERTS DR	SA	SA	3300	22	C3
ROBERTS ST	ANA	AN	900	11	B5
ROBIDOUX DR	HTB	HB47	8000	21	C5
ROBIN	IRV	SA		29	B3
ROBIN AV	FTNV	SA08	9500	26	F2
ROBIN AV	FTNV	SA08	10200	27	A2
ROBIN AV	PLA	PLA	800	12	A1
ROBIN AV	WSTM	WSTM	9500	21	F3
ROBIN CIR	CO	SJ91		29B	A6
ROBIN CIR	CO	SJ91		29D	A1
ROBIN CIR	YL	YL		8	A4
ROBIN DR	LAP	BP23	4300	9	C3
ROBIN LN	YL	YL	5400	8	A4
ROBIN PL	ANA	AN	900	11	B2
ROBIN RD	OR	OR	1500	17	B3

STREET	CITY	P.O. ZONE	BLOCK	PAGE	GRID
ROBIN ST	ANA	AN	1200	11	B2
ROBIN ST	CO	ET		29A	D2
ROBIN WY	BPK	BP	6100	9	F1
ROBIN WY	FUL	FL	1500	6	C4
ROBIN WY	LAH	LAH	1200	1	F4
ROBIN WY	VPK	OR67	18500	13	A5
ROBINET LN	CO	GG41	8500	15	D4
ROBIN HILL LN	CO	LB		29C	D4
ROBIN HOOD CIR	VPK	OR67	10200	12	F6
ROBINHOOD LN	CM	CM27	200	31	E2
ROBINHOOD PL	CM	CM27	200	31	D2
ROBINHOOD PL	OR	OR	2400	12	E4
ROBINSON CIR	PLA	PLA		7	C2
ROBINSON DR	STN	STN		15	B2
ROBINSON DR	TUS	TUS		24	C3
ROBINSONG	IRV	SA		29	C5
ROBINSON RCH RD	CO	SJ		56	D6
ROBINSON RCH RD	CO	SJ		59	D1
ROBINWOOD CIR	IRV	SA	4400	29	D1
ROBINWOOD DR	HTB	HB	5000	20	D4
ROBLE	CO	SJ		59	B3
ROBLEDO CIR	MVJO	SJ91	24000	29B	C5
ROBLES DR	DPT	DPT	33700	37	E4
ROBON CT	NB	NB		31	B4
ROBON DR	IRV	SA		24	D6
ROBROY CIR	HTB	HB47	17300	21	B6
ROBSON CT	FTNV	SA08	15900	22	D6
ROBWOOD CIR	ANA	AN		8	E5
ROBYN CT	GGR	GG		16	E5
ROCHELLE AV	IRV	SA	4900	29	C3
ROCHELLE AV	WSTM	WSTM	5500	14	E6
ROCHELLE AV	WSTM	WSTM	6200	15	A6
ROCHELLE LN	CO	ET	24700	29A	E2
ROCHELLE ST	CO	LB56		29C	E5
ROCHELLE ST	LALM	LALM	11200	14	B2
ROCHELLE ST	STN	STN		15	D1
ROCHESTER AV	HTB	HB	200	26	C4
ROCHESTER ST	CM	CM27	100	31	D3
ROCHESTER ST	WSTM	WSTM	15800	21	D4
ROCINANTE	MVJO	SJ91		29D	B3
ROCK ST	NB	CDLM	2700	33	A2
ROCKAWAY DR	CO	PLA	16100	7	C3
ROCKAWAY DR E	PLA	PLA	600	7	C3
ROCKCREEK CIR	HTB	HB47		21	E5
ROCKCREST LN	HTB	HB		26	E4
ROCKET DR	ANA	AN		16	E2
ROCKFIELD BLVD	CO	ET	23100	29A	E5
ROCKFIELD BLVD	IRV	SA18		29A	C2
ROCK FISH CIR	FTNV	SA08	8500	26	D1
ROCKFORD DR	CO	ET	22600	29B	A3
ROCKFORD LN	WSTM	WSTM		21	F2
ROCKFORD PL	NB	CDLM	4500	33	C2
ROCKFORD RD	NB	CDLM	400	33	C2
ROCKHAMPTON CT	YL	YL		8	F3
ROCKHURST AV	CO	SA	10600	18	C4
ROCKINGHAM DR	NB	NB		32	B4
ROCKING HRSE LN	CO	LB	26000	29C	F4
ROCKING HRSE LN	LAH	LAH	1100	2	B3
ROCKINGHORSE RD	CO	SA		18	C5
ROCKINGHORSE RD	GGR	GG	13000	16	C5
ROCKING HRSE WY	OR	OR		18	C3
ROCKLAND LN	HTB	HB	19500	26	F3
ROCKLEDGE DR	BPK	BP	5300	5	D5
ROCKLEDGE RD	LAG	LB51	100	34	E5
ROCKLEDGE TER	LAG	LB51	100	34	E5
ROCKMONT AV	WSTM	WSTM	7100	21	B3
ROCKPATH LN	FTNV	SA08		27	A2
ROCKPOINT DR	HTB	HB	9500	30	F2
ROCKPORT	DPT	DPT		37	B5
ROCKPORT LN	HTB	HB	22000	30	F2
ROCKRIDGE CIR	OR	OR		12	F4
ROCKRIDGE CIR	OR	OR		13	A5
ROCKRIDGE LN	BREA	BREA		3	B5
ROCKRIDGE PL	ANA	AN		13	B3
ROCKRIDGE PL	OR	OR		13	A5
ROCKRIDGE RD	CO	LB53		29C	F5
ROCKRIDGE ST	FUL	FL		6	F3
ROCK RIVER	PLA	PLA	1600	7	C3
ROCKROSE CIR	YL	YL		7	E4
ROCKROSE WY	IRV	SA	17800	29	A5
ROCK SPRINGS	IRV	SA		29	C2
ROCK SPRINGS CT	GGR	GG		16	D5
ROCKVIEW CIR	WSTM	WSTM		21	C3
ROCKVIEW DR	CO	AN04	11900	15	C3
ROCKVIEW DR	IRV	SA		32A	A1
ROCKVILLE CT	CO	YL		8	F2
ROCKWELL AV	CO	MDWY	7700	21	C3
ROCKWOOD	IRV	SA		29	A4
ROCKWOOD DR	YL	YL		8	B5
ROCKWREN	IRV	SA		29	C4
ROCKY	IRV	SA		32A	A2

STREET	CITY	P.O. ZONE	BLOCK	PAGE	GRID
ROCKY CT	FTNV	SA08	15900	22	C4
ROCKY CT	GGR	GG	8700	15	D6
ROCKY LN	YL	YL		7	F3
ROCKY RD	CO	SA	19100	18	B4
ROCKY RD	FUL	FL	1700	6	F3
ROCKY BEACH LN	DPT	DPT	25500	38	B4
ROCKY BROOK WY	STN	STN		15	B4
ROCKY CREEK LN	CO	LB		29C	D1
ROCKY GLEN	IRV	SA		32A	A2
ROCKY GROVE CT	CO	YL		8	C6
ROCKY KNOLL	IRV	SA		32A	A1
ROCKY MTN DR	HTB	HB	9500	26	F5
ROCKY POINT	CO	SJ79		59	D2
ROCKY POINT	YL	YL	4700	7	F3
ROCKY POINT RD	ANA	AN		12	F3
ROCKY POINT RD	NB	CDLM		32	D6
ROCKY RIDGE	IRV	SA		24	E6
RODAJA	CO	SJ88		29B	F5
RODDY DR	LAH	LAH	1000	2	B3
RODDY WY	LAH	LAH	1000	2	B3
RODEO CIR	CO	LB53		29D	A5
RODEO CIR	OR	OR		18	D2
RODEO CT	CYP	CYP	10000	9	E6
RODEO DR	CO	AN04	10500	15	E1
RODEO PL	CM	CM27	2400	31	E1
RODEO RD	FUL	FL	600	6	B4
RODERICK LN	HTB	HB	19500	26	E4
ROE DR	SA	SA	100	17	B5
ROEBUCK ST	CO	ET	23100	29A	D3
ROGER CT	BREA	BREA		2	E6
ROGER DR	GGR	GG	12000	16	B3
ROGERS CT	ANA	AN	2900	10	C5
ROGERS DR	CO	OR	20000	18	D1
ROGERS DR	HTB	HB	5500	20	E6
ROGERS PL	CM	CM27	1800	31	D3
ROGERS RD	DPT	DPT		37	F2
ROGUE DR	ANA	AN	3800	12	E2
ROGUE ST	PLA	PLA	1500	7	C3
ROGUE RIVER AV	FTNV	SA08	8500	26	D2
ROJAS LN	MVJO	SJ91		29B	B5
ROLAND ST	BPK	BP	8500	5	D6
ROLF CIR	HTB	HB	8300	26	D2
ROLLING BROOK	IRV	SA		32A	A2
ROLLING GRN LN	OR	OR		13	A4
ROLLING HLLS DR	ANA	AN		13	B2
ROLLING HLLS DR	FUL	FL	800	6	D2
ROLLING HLLS DR	FUL	FL	2600	7	A2
ROLLING HLLS LN	YL	YL		8	F3
ROLLING HLLS LN	YL	YL		40	A3
ROLLING HLLS PL	ANA	AN07		13	B2
ROLLING HLLS RD	CO	LB53		29D	A4
ROLLING HLS TER	CO	SJ79		56	A3
ROLLINGSTONE LN	CO	TUS	1800	24	B3
ROLLING WOOD LN	SJC	SJ75		36	D5
ROLLINGWOOD RD	CO	ET	24600	29A	E2
ROLLINS LN	HTB	HB47	15800	21	B4
ROLLINS PL	CO	LB77		35	E6
ROLLO CIR	CO	SA	11700	18	C6
ROLLS PL	SA	SA	3000	28	B1
ROMA	HTB	HB		26	D4
ROMA DR	CO	SJ91	24000	29A	F5
ROMAINE WY	GGR	GG	12500	15	A4
ROMANZA PL	CO	TUS	14600	23	F2
ROME AV	ANA	AN	2500	10	B5
ROME AV	CYP	CYP	5200	9	E5
ROME CIR	HTB	HB47	6500	21	A3
ROME PL	ANA	AN	800	10	A5
ROME ST	CYP	CYP	9800	9	E5
ROMELLE AV	CO	SA	17800	17	F4
ROMELLE AV	CO	SA	18100	18	A4
ROMELLE AV	OR	OR	2000	17	F4
ROMERA PL	CO	ET	25100	29A	F2
ROMERO	CO	SJ88		59	B2
ROMERO	IRV	SA14		29	A2
ROMNEYA DR E	ANA	AN	1200	11	E2
ROMNEYA DR E	ANA	AN	2200	12	A2
ROMNEYA DR W	ANA	AN	2000	10	F2
ROMNEYA DR W	ANA	AN	200	11	B2
ROMNEYA VIA	ANA	AN	500	11	C2
RONALD CIR	CYP	CYP	6000	9	F5
RONALD DR	CYP	CYP	6100	9	F5
RONALD RD	HTB	HB	7700	26	C1
RNDA DL ROSSMOR	CO	LB	23000	29A	D5
RONDA GRANADA	CO	LB	2071	29A	D5
RONDA MENDOZA	CO	LB	801	29C	E1
RONDA SEVILLA	CO	LB	835	29C	D1
RONDEAU ST	WSTM	WSTM	14000	21	B1
RONDEL PL	CO	TUS	14200	23	F1
RONEA	MVJO	SJ92	28300	29B	E5
RONI LN	ANA	AN		13	A1
RONNEY DR	HTB	HB	9400	26	E3

STREET	CITY	P.O. ZONE	BLOCK	PAGE	GRID
RONWOOD AV	LAH	LAH	400	2	A6
ROOK DR	HTB	HB47	6700	21	A6
ROOSEVELT	IRV	SA		29	D1
ROOSEVELT AV	CO	MDWY	8000	21	C2
ROOSEVELT AV	SA	SA	4300	22	B2
ROOSEVELT AV N	FUL	FL	100	6	B5
ROOSEVELT AV S	FUL	FL	500	6	B6
ROOSEVELT AV S	FUL	FL	1400	11	B1
ROOSEVELT CIR	BPK	BP	8600	10	B4
ROOSEVELT LN	HTB	HB	16500	20	E5
ROOSEVELT LN	LAG	LB51	1200	34	E2
ROOSEVELT RD	ANA	AN		8	F6
ROOSEVELT ST	PLA	PLA		7	E5
ROOSEVELT WY	CM	CM	3100	27	E3
ROQUE LN	HTB	HB47	16800	21	D5
ROQUERO	CO	SJ88		29B	F4
ROSA	CO	SJ		59	B5
ROSA ST	CO	LB56		29C	E3
ROSA BONHEUR ST	LAG	LB51	100	34	C3
ROSADA	MVJO	SJ92		29D	F3
ROSALES CIR	MVJO	SJ91	26100	29B	B6
ROSALIA AV	FUL	FL	1700	6	E2
ROSALIA DR	FUL	FL	2400	6	F1
ROSALIE PL	TUS	SA	14000	24	A4
ROSALINA DR	HTB	HB		20	D4
ROSALIND DR	CO	OR69	12400	17	F5
ROSALIND DR	CO	SA	12800	17	F5
ROSALIND DR	OR	OR	200	17	F3
ROSALIND DR	TUS	TUS	13700	17	F6
ROSALINDA	SCL	SCL		38	E4
ROSANNA AV	GGR	GG	9000	15	E2
ROSANNA DR	HTB	HB	8300	26	D1
ROSANNE CIR	VPK	OR67	18000	17	F1
ROSARIO	MVJO	SJ92		29D	D5
ROSARIO AV	CYP	CYP	6200	14	F2
ROSARIO CIR	PLA	PLA	1300	7	D3
ROSARIO ST	PLA	PLA	1300	7	D3
ROSARITA DR	FUL	FL	500	6	C2
ROSAS CT	CO	ET		51	E4
ROSCOE ST	LAH	LAH	100	2	C4
ROSCOMMON CT	CO	ET		29B	A1
ROSCOMMON CT	CO	ET		52	B6
ROSE	MVJO	SJ91		52	D4
ROSE AV	FTNV	SA08	9400	21	F5
ROSE AV	STN	STN	10500	15	C1
ROSE AV E&W	OR	OR	100	17	D2
ROSE AV W	LAH	LAH	500	2	A4
ROSE CIR	SB	SB	3500	14	D4
ROSE DR	BREA	BREA	100	3	D6
ROSE DR	BREA	BREA	500	7	D1
ROSE DR	CO	BREA	3100	3	E5
ROSE DR	FUL	FL	1100	6	A4
ROSE DR	PLA	PLA	400	7	D5
ROSE DR	YL	YL	3700	7	D2
ROSE LN	CM	CM27	200	31	E2
ROSE LN	WSTM	WSTM	15600	21	E3
ROSE PL	ANA	AN	800	11	E5
ROSE PL	LAG	LB51	500	34	C2
ROSE ST	LAP	BP23	8000	9	E3
ROSE ST	SB	SB	3800	14	D4
ROSE ST	STN	STN	10500	15	C1
ROSE ST N&S	ANA	AN	100	11	E3
ROSE ANN CIR	CYP	CYP	10400	9	D6
ROSEBAY ST	ANA	AN	300	10	E5
ROSEBAY ST	CO	AN04	9500	10	E5
ROSEBRIAR	MVJO	SJ92		29B	E2
ROSEBROOK WY	STN	STN		15	B4
ROSEBUD CT	ANA	AN08		43	A1
ROSEBUD DR	YL	YL	17000	7	E2
ROSE CANYON RD	CO	SJ	20100	56	C5
ROSECRANS AV	BPK	BP	8000	5	D2
ROSECRANS AV	FUL	FL33	1600	5	D2
ROSECRANS AV	FUL	FL	1000	6	A3
ROSECREST AV E	LAH	LAH	100	2	A5
ROSECREST AV S	LAH	LAH	700	2	A5
ROSECREST AV W	LAH	LAH	100	2	A5
ROSECREST CIR	MVJO	SJ92		29D	C2
ROSEDALE DR	SJC	SJ75	27500	36	D6
ROSEHEDGE DR	FUL	FL35	3700	2	C6
ROSEHEDGE DR	FUL	FL	3300	6	C1
ROSEHEDGE ST	CO	SJ91		29A	F5
ROSELEAF AV	TUS	TUS	17200	23	E2
ROSELEE DR	GGR	GG	10000	15	F3
ROSEMARY	IRV	SA		29	B3
ROSEMARY AV	FTNV	SA08	11500	22	C4
ROSEMARY DR	CYP	CYP	6100	9	F5
ROSEMARY PL	CM	CM27	1900	31	D2
ROSEMERE ST	OR	OR67		13	A4
ROSEMONT DR	HTB	HB	6000	20	F6
ROSEMONT ST	ANA	AN	1000	11	E2
ROSEMONT ST	PLA	PLA	2100	7	B2

STREET	CITY	P.O. ZONE	BLOCK	PAGE	GRID
ROSEMOUNT DR	CO	SJ79		56	E6
ROSENAU CIR	VPK	OR67		13	A4
ROSENAU DR	VPK	OR67	18600	13	A4
ROSENBAUM RD	SJC	SJ75		36	B3
ROSEPATH	CO	ET		52	B6
ROSETA	IRV	SA		24	E5
ROSE TREE RD	SJC	SJ75	29800	36	B3
ROSEWOOD	CO	LB56		29C	D2
ROSEWOOD	IRV	SA		29	B6
ROSEWOOD	YL	YL		40	B4
ROSEWOOD AV	ANA	AN	1400	11	E2
ROSEWOOD AV	FUL	FL33	600	5	E6
ROSEWOOD AV	FUL	FL33	600	10	E1
ROSEWOOD AV	SA	SA	3600	28	A2
ROSEWOOD AV E	OR	OR	900	17	D4
ROSEWOOD AV N	SA	SA	1700	17	A6
ROSEWOOD AV S	SA	SA07	2200	23	A5
ROSEWOOD AV W	OR	OR	300	17	C4
ROSEWOOD CT	SA	SA	2400	23	A6
ROSEWOOD LN	BREA	BREA		2	D2
ROSEWOOD LN	CO	ET	24100	29A	D2
ROSEWOOD LN	LAH	LAH		2	B6
ROSEWOOD LN	WSTM	WSTM		21	F2
ROSEWOOD ST	FTNV	SA08	16300	21	E4
ROSITA PL	GGR	GG	13900	16	B6
ROSITA ST	SA	SA	500	22	B2
ROSPAW WY	PLA	PLA	500	7	B2
ROSS	IRV	SA		24	E6
ROSS	IRV	SA		29	E1
ROSS CIR	WSTM	WSTM	16400	21	D5
ROSS LN	HTB	HB47	16500	21	D5
ROSS ST	CM	CM27	600	31	C2
ROSS ST	FTNV	SA08	17000	21	D5
ROSS ST N	SA	SA	1600	17	B6
ROSS ST N&S	SA	SA	100	23	B4
ROSS ST S	SA	SA	3400	28	B1
ROSSANO	IRV	SA		24	D5
ROSSCOMMON LN	SJC	SJ75		38	C4
ROSSLYNN AV E&W	FUL	FL	100	6	B6
ROSSMOOR WY	CO	LALM	3300	14	B3
ROSSMOOR WY	LALM	LALM	3500	14	B3
ROSSMOOR CTR WY	SB	SB	3200	14	B4
ROSTRATA AV	BPK	BP	5600	5	B5
ROSWELL ST	SA	SA	2800	17	D4
ROSY FINCH LN	CO	LB56		29C	B1
ROTA	MVJO	SJ92	27700	29B	F4
ROTH LN	OR	OR	100	18	C3
ROTHERHAM CIR	WSTM	WSTM	5000	20	E1
ROTHERT LN	HTB	HB		26	D4
ROTTERDAM LN	HTB	HB47	17000	21	D6
ROUND HILL	IRV	SA		32A	A3
ROUNDHILL DR	HTB	HB	16900	20	C6
ROUNDTREE CT	BREA	BREA		3	B5
ROUNDTREE CT	OR	OR	3600	12	F3
ROUNDTREE CT	OR	OR	3600	13	A3
ROUND TREE CT	SJC	SJ75		36	A3
ROUNDTREE LN	ANA	AN		10	D2
ROUNDUP WY	OR	OR	6900	18	D2
ROUNSEVEL TER	LAG	LB51	2800	34	F5
ROUSSELLE ST	SA	SA	1600	23	C5
ROUTT ST	FTNV	SA08	16100	21	E4
ROVEN AV	ANA	AN	2500	10	E5
ROWAN ST	ANA	AN	500	11	C4
ROWE LN	LAP	BP23		9	E2
ROWENA DR	CO	LALM	3000	14	A4
ROWLAND AV	ANA	AN	2500	10	D5
ROWLAND AV	SA	SA	1300	22	E6
ROWLAND AV	SA	SA	700	23	B6
ROWLAND CIR	ANA	AN	2700	10	C5
ROXANNE DR	WSTM	WSTM	14000	21	A1
ROXANNE LN	HTB	HB47	17500	21	D6
ROXANNE ST	ANA	AN	400	12	E2
ROXBORO ST	ANA	AN		11	F2
ROXBOROUGH DR	CO	PLA	5000	7	C4
ROXBOROUGH DR N	PLA	PLA	1300	7	C4
ROXBURY CT	CYP	CYP	5700	9	E6
ROXBURY DR	FUL	FL33	700	5	E5
ROXBURY DR	IRV	SA	4400	29	C2
ROXBURY RD	GGR	GG	11700	16	C3
ROXBURY RD	NB	CDLM	4500	33	C2
ROXBURY TER	LAH	LAH	1100	1	E6
ROXBURY WY	STN	STN		15	B2
ROXDALE DR	YL	YL	16700	7	D2
ROXEY DR	GGR	GG	13200	16	D6
ROY CIR	SA	SA	4500	22	C2
ROYAL DR	HTB	HB47	8700	21	D5
ROYAL LN	SA	SA		22	E2
ROYAL PL	SA	SA		23	B6
ROYAL PL	WSTM	WSTM	15900	21	E4
ROYAL PL N	ANA	AN	100	12	B3
ROYAL PL S	ANA	AN	100	12	B3

STREET	CITY	P.O. ZONE	BLOCK	PAGE	GRID
ROYAL ST	ANA	AN	400	12	A3
ROYAL WY	ANA	AN	800	11	C3
ROYALE AV	IRV	SA	5100	29	C3
ROYALE CT	FTNV	SA08	15900	22	B4
ROYALE DR	SJC	SJ75		36	B3
ROYALE PL	FUL	FL33		5	E3
ROYALE RIDGE	CO	LB		35	E2
ROYAL HILL	CO	LB		35	E2
ROYALIST DR	HTB	HB47	6000	21	A4
ROYAL OAK CT	CO	YL		8	C6
ROYAL OAK DR	HTB	HB47	6200	21	A2
ROYAL OAK DR	OR	OR69		18	E2
ROYAL OAK RD	ANA	AN	100	13	B2
ROYAL OAK RD	TUS	TUS	1800	23	F5
ROYAL OAK WY	STN	STN	10500	15	B3
ROYAL PALM BLVD	GGR	GG	9200	15	E2
ROYAL PALM DR	CM	CM	2800	27	C4
ROYAL RIDGE DR	ANA	AN		13	D2
ROYAL ST GEO RD	NB	NB		32	B4
ROYAL STEWRT DR	PLA	PLA	600	7	C2
ROYAL TERN LN	CO	LB56		29C	A2
ROYAN LN	CM	CM27	300	31	F2
ROYCE LN	CM	CM	3000	27	D3
ROYCE PL	ANA	AN	200	10	D4
ROYCE RD	IRV	SA		29	A6
ROYCROFT LN	LAP	BP23	7600	9	E2
ROYER AV	FUL	FL	1600	11	A1
ROYER CIR	HTB	HB47	8600	21	D5
RUBICON CT	CO	LB	28000	35	E1
RUBIDOUX	MVJO	SJ92		29D	F3
RUBY	MVJO	SJ91		29D	C5
RUBY AV	NB	NB	100	31	F6
RUBY CIR	HTB	HB	16900	20	E5
RUBY CT	FTNV	SA08	11900	22	C4
RUBY DR	FUL	FL	2900	7	A4
RUBY DR	PLA	PLA	100	7	B4
RUBY LN	ANA	AN		13	D3
RUBY PL	LAG	LB51	2100	34	F4
RUBY ST	LAG	LB51	100	34	E4
RUBY LANTERN ST	DPT	DPT	34000	37	E4
RUDDER DR	HTB	HB		20	D5
RUDOLPH CIR	CO	ET	25000	29A	F3
RUE CIR	FTNV	SA08	16100	21	F4
RUEBENS CIR	OR	OR	1200	17	F1
RUE BIARRITZ	NB	NB		32	B4
RUE CANNES	NB	NB		32	A4
RUE CERISE	CO	LB77		36	A2
RUE CHAMONIX	NB	NB		32	A4
RUE CHANSON	CO	LB77		36	A2
RUE CHANTILLY	NB	NB		32	B4
RUE CHATU ROYAL	NB	NB		32	A4
RUE DEAUVILLE	NB	NB		32	B4
RUE DE CANNES	CM	CM27	2400	31	E1
RUE DU PARC	NB	NB		32	B5
RUE FLEURIE	CO	LB77		36	A2
RUE FNTAINBLEAU	NB	NB		32	A4
RUE FONTAINE	NB	NB		32	B5
RUE GRAND DUCAL	NB	NB	11100	32	A4
RUE GRND VALLEE	NB	NB		32	B5
RUE MARSEILLES	NB	NB		32	A4
RUE MONTREUX	NB	NB		32	A4
RUE ST CLOUD	NB	NB		32	B4
RUE TERRARSE	CO	LB77		36	A2
RUE VALBONNE	NB	NB		32	A4
RUE VERTE	NB	NB		32	B5
RUE VILLARS	NB	NB		32	B4
RUGGLES PL	TUS	SA10	15500	29	B2
RUGH ST	GGR	GG	11100	16	A2
RUISENOR	MVJO	SJ92		29B	D6
RUISENOR	MVJO	SJ92	27000	29D	D1
RUMBLE DR	CO	ET	22800	29A	F3
RUMFORD LN	HTB	HB		26	D4
RUMSEY LN	HTB	HB	19600	26	E4
RUMSEY PL	PLA	PLA	500	7	B2
RUMSON ST	YL	YL		7	D5
RUNNING BRCH WY	CO	TUS	1800	24	B3
RUNNING DEER LN	CO	LB	29000	35	D3
RUNNING SPG WY	YL	YL		40	D6
RUNNING SPGS LN	HTB	HB	20100	26	F5
RUNNING TDE CIR	HTB	HB		20	C5
RUNYON PL	ANA	AN	2500	10	D5
RURAL LN	CM	CM27	2100	31	D1
RURAL PL	CM	CM27	2100	31	D1
RURAL RIDGE CIR	ANA	AN	5200	13	B3
RURAL RIDGE DR	ANA	AN	400	13	B3
RUSH	SA	SA		23	D1
RUSH ST	GGR	GG	11100	15	E2
RUSHFORD DR	CO	ET		29B	B1
RUSHFORD DR	CO	ET		52	B6
RUSHING WIND	IRV	SA		29	B4

STREET	CITY	P.O. ZONE	BLOCK	PAGE	GRID
RUSHMOOR LN	HTB	HB47	15200	21	C3
RUSHMORE LN	CO	SA	17800	17	F5
RUSHMORE ST	FTNV	SA08	16500	22	B5
RUSHMORE ST	OR	OR		13	C5
RUSSEL LN	CO	LB		35	F5
RUSSELL AV	ANA	AN	2600	10	D4
RUSSELL AV	FUL	FL	200	6	A5
RUSSELL AV	GGR	GG	9300	15	F5
RUSSELL AV	GGR	GG	10200	16	A5
RUSSELL AV E	SA	SA	400	23	A3
RUSSELL AV W	SA	SA	2200	22	E4
RUSSELL AV W	SA	SA	100	23	A3
RUSSELL CIR	GGR	GG	12600	16	D5
RUSSELL CIR	PLA	PLA	900	7	D4
RUSSELL CT	IRV	SA17		32	E2
RUSSELL DR	OR	OR	700	17	E1
RUSSELL PL	ANA	AN	2700	10	D4
RUSSELL ST	CO	LAH	9300	1	E3
RUSSELL ST	STN	STN		15	D1
RUSSELL ST N	LAH	LAH	900	1	E3
RUSSELL ST W	LAH	LAH	1200	1	E3
RUSSETT	CO	SJ79		59	E3
RUSTIC CT	BREA	BREA		2	E5
RUSTIC CT	FTNV	SA08		27	A2
RUSTIC LN	ANA	AN	1400	10	E6
RUSTIC LN	ANA	AN04	1400	15	E1
RUSTIC LN	CO	AN04	10800	15	E1
RUSTIC RD	YL	YL		7	E2
RUSTIC GATE WY	OR	OR	2800	12	E3
RUSTIC OAK	CO	LB		35	F3
RUSTIC OAK	CO	LB77		36	A3
RUSTIC OAK	MVJO	SJ92		29B	E3
RUSTLING WIND	IRV	SA		29	A6
RUSTY ANCHOR ST	DPT	DPT	25500	38	B4
RUTGERS AV	WSTM	WSTM	7000	21	B2
RUTGERS CIR	ANA	AN		13	F3
RUTGERS CIR	ANA	AN		43	A3
RUTGERS CIR	HTB	HB47	6300	21	A3
RUTGERS CT	CYP	CYP	10400	14	D5
RUTGERS DR	ANA	AN		13	F3
RUTGERS DR	CM	CM	2300	27	D6
RUTGERS DR	CM	CM27	2200	31	D1
RUTGERS WY	ANA	AN07		43	A3
RUTGERS WY	STN	STN		10	E4
RUTGERS WY	STN	STN		15	B3
RUTH CIR	SA	SA	1100	17	A6
RUTH DR	HTB	HB47	6800	21	A5
RUTH LN	NB	NB	1400	31	E4
RUTH PL	OR	OR	2700	17	F4
RUTH PL	OR	OR	3700	18	A4
RUTHANN AV	STN	STN	7600	15	C2
RUTH ELAINE DR	CO	LALM	3100	14	A2
RUTHERFORD ST	ANA	AN	1700	7	B6
RUTLAND DR	YL	YL	5400	7	D4
RUTLAND RD	NB	NB	1000	31	E4
RUTLEDGE AV	STN	STN	11100	15	B2
RUTLEDGE LN	IRV	SA		24	F6
RUTLEDGE PL	BREA	BREA	1300	2	C4
RYALS LN	CO	OR	19000	18	B3
RYAN AV	LAH	LAH	500	1	F3
RYAN CIR	VPK	OR67		13	A5
RYAN DR	CO	LB56		29C	E5
RYCROFT RD	CO	SA	11700	18	B6
RYE AV	LAH	LAH	500	1	F5
RYE CIR	LAH	LAH	400	2	A5
RYEWOOD ST	IRV	SA	14500	29	D2

S

STREET	CITY	P.O. ZONE	BLOCK	PAGE	GRID
S ST	CM	CM		27	D4
S ST	LAG	LB		35	A4
S ST	ETMC	SA09		51	D4
SAARINEN AV	IRV	SA		24	C6
SAARINEN CT	IRV	SA	3800	24	C6
SABBICAS CIR	HTB	HB	6500	26	A1
SABEL CT	ANA	AN07		7	F5
SABINA AV	CO	SJ91		29B	A5
SABINA ST	ANA	AN	300	11	D3
SABLE DR	HTB	HB	8600	30	D1
SABLE TREE CIR	TUS	TUS	2300	24	A5
SABOT LN	HTB	HB47	16400	21	B4
SABRE AV	GGR	GG	9600	21	F2
SABRE LN	HTB	HB	14800	20	F2
SABRE LN	WSTM	WSTM	9000	21	E2
SABRINA TER	NB	CDLM	1900	33	A1
SABROSO	MVJO	SJ91		29B	C2
SACARAMA LN	SJC	SJ75	31500	36	A6
SACEDON	MVJO	SJ91		29B	D2
SACRAMENTO	IRV	SA		29	D1
SACRAMENTO LN	HTB	HB	19500	26	D4
SACRAMENTO ST	OR	OR	1300	12	E5

STREET	CITY	P.O. ZONE	BLOCK	PAGE	GRID
SACRAMENTO ST	OR	OR	100	17	E2
SACUILLO ST	FTNV	SA08	17700	27	B1
SACUL PL	CO	LB		35	F2
SADABA	MVJO	SJ92	24300	29B	E6
SADDLE CT	FTNV	SA08	15900	22	D6
SADDLE DR	PLA	PLA	100	7	F5
SADDLEBACK DR	MVJO	SJ91	26300	29B	B6
SADDLEBACK DR	MVJO	SJ91		29D	B1
SADDLEBACK DR	OR	OR		18	D2
SADDLEBACK LN	ANA	AN		8	E6
SADDLEBACK LN	HTB	HB48		26	B2
SADDLEBACK RD	TUS	TUS		23	D3
SDDLBCK MDWS RD	CO	SJ79		52	F4
SDDLBCK MDWS RD	CO	SJ79		56	A4
SADDLBCK RCH RD	CO	SJ		52	E4
SADDLEHILL TR	OR	OR	7300	18	D2
SADDLEHORN LN	CO	LB	26500	29C	F3
SADDLEHORN WY	OR	OR	7300	18	D2
SADDLERIDGE DR	SJC	SJ75	29900	36	D3
SADDLE ROCK PL	CO	LB		29C	F3
SADDLE ROCK PL	CO	LB		29D	A3
SADDLERY RD	CO	SA		18	D5
SADDLETREE LN	YL	YL		8	B5
SADDLEWOOD LN	ANA	AN		11	E6
SAFE HARBOR LN	HTB	HB	19000	26	C3
SAFFORD ST	GGR	GG	12500	16	B4
SAFFORD ST E	GGR	GG	12800	16	B4
SAFFORD ST W	GGR	GG	12800	16	B4
SAFFRON ST	ANA	AN		8	F6
SAFFRON ST	ANA	AN		13	F1
SAFIRO	MVJO	SJ91		29B	C2
SAGA DR	YL	YL	16800	7	D3
SAGAMORE DR	HTB	HB		20	B4
SAGAMORE RD	LAG	LB	200	34	B1
SAGAMORE ST	ANA	AN	100	12	E2
SAGE	IRV	SA		29	B3
SAGE CIR	FTNV	SA08	9900	21	F5
SAGE CT	BREA	BREA	600	2	F5
SAGE CT	CO	LB		29C	E3
SAGE LN	CO	SJ	30100	56	C5
SAGE ST	GGR	GG	11700	16	D3
SAGEBRUSH CIR	CO	ET	21900	29B	A2
SAGE HILL LN	CO	LB		29C	D2
SAGE HILLS RD	OR	OR69		18	E3
SAGE RIVER LN	SA	SA		22	D1
SAGEWOOD	CO	ET		52	C4
SAGEWOOD	HTB	HB		26	C2
SAGEWOOD AV	ANA	AN		8	F6
SAGEWOOD CIR	ANA	AN		13	F1
SAGEWOOD LN	CO	SJ79		52	F5
SAGEWOOD ST	OR	OR69		18	E3
SAGINAW DR	IRV	SA		32	F2
SAGUARO ST	CO	ET	23000	29A	E4
SAHARA LN	HTB	HB	14400	20	F2
SAHARA PL	CO	LB56		29C	E5
SAIGON LN	CO	SA	13600	18	B6
SAIL AV	OR	OR	1100	12	D4
SAIL CIR	HTB	HB	8000	26	C6
SAIL ST	GGR	GG43	14500	22	A2
SAIL ST	SA	SA	400	22	A3
SAIL WY	DPT	DPT		37	F2
SAILBOAT CIR	HTB	HB		30	C1
SAILFISH DR	HTB	HB	9500	26	F3
SAILMAKER CIR	HTB	HB		26	C6
SAILORS BAY LN	HTB	HB	21100	30	D1
SAILPORT DR	HTB	HB		26	D4
SAILWIND LN	HTB	HB		26	E3
SAIL WIND WY	CO	ET		29A	D3
ST AGNES CIR	CYP	CYP	10000	9	E6
ST ALBAN ST	CYP	CYP	10100	9	E6
ST ALBANS DR	CO	LALM	2600	14	A3
ST ANDREW PL E	SA	SA07	100	23	A5
ST ANDREW PL E	SA	SA05	1800	23	D5
ST ANDREW PL W	SA	SA	1300	22	E5
ST ANDREW PL W	SA	SA	100	23	A5
ST ANDREWS	CO	SJ79		59	C6
ST ANDREWS	MVJO	SJ92		29B	D4
ST ANDREWS AV	BPK	BP	4600	5	C3
ST ANDREWS AV	PLA	PLA	400	7	C4
ST ANDREWS AV	WSTM	WSTM	8600	21	D3
ST ANDREWS CIR	BPK	BP	8300	5	C3
ST ANDREWS DR	SB	SB	13100	14	A6
ST ANDREWS LN	HTB	HB	17000	20	E6
ST ANDREWS RD	NB	NB	200	31	D5
ST ANN AV	CYP	CYP	5500	9	E4
ST ANNE PL	SA	SA	1300	22	E5
ST ANNE PL	SA	SA	1200	23	A5
ST ANNES	CO	SJ79		59	D3
ST ANNES	DPT	DPT		37	E2
ST ANNS DR	LAG	LB51	100	34	E3
ST AUGUSTINE DR	HTB	HB	8600	30	D1

STREET	CITY	P.O. ZONE	BLOCK	PAGE	GRID
ST BERNARD ST	CYP	CYP	10100	9	E6
ST CHARLES AV	CYP	CYP	10000	9	D6
ST CHARLES WY	CO	SA	10320	18	D4
ST CHRISTOPHER	CO	LB77		36	A5
ST CLAIR ST	CM	CM	700	27	F4
ST CLOUD CIR	HTB	HB47	16700	21	D5
ST CLOUD DR	CO	LALM	3200	14	B4
ST CLOUD LN	CO	SA		18	D4
ST CRISPEN AV	BREA	BREA	200	2	E5
ST CROIX	CO	LB77		36	A4
ST CROIX CIR	HTB	HB	3800	20	C4
ST ELENA	MVJO	SJ91		29B	C4
ST ELIAS	CO	SJ79		59	D2
ST ELIZABETH	CO	LB77		36	A4
ST ELIZABTH CIR	CYP	CYP	10000	9	E6
ST FRANCIS CIR	CYP	CYP	10000	9	D6
ST FRANCIS CT	DPT	LB77		37	E4
ST GEORGE CIR	CYP	CYP	9800	9	D5
ST GEORGE LN	HTB	HB47	17000	21	A5
ST GEORGE RD	WSTM	WSTM		20	E1
ST GERMAIN	CO	LB77		35	F4
ST GERMAIN CIR	OR	OR69		18	C3
ST GERTRDE PL E	SA	SA	100	23	A5
ST GERTRDE PL W	SA	SA	1300	22	E5
ST GERTRDE PL W	SA	SA	100	23	A5
ST ISABELLA	CO	LB77		36	A5
ST JAMES AV	OR	OR	700	12	D4
ST JAMES PL	PLA	PLA	1700	7	B3
ST JAMES RD	NB	NB	600	31	D4
ST JAMES WY	CO	TUS		24	B1
ST JAMES PARK	WSTM	WSTM	5000	20	D1
ST JOAN ST	CYP	CYP	10100	9	D6
ST JOHN	DPT	DPT		37	E3
ST JOHN CIR	CYP	CYP	9800	9	E6
ST JOHN DR	GGR	GG		15	D6
ST JOHN LN	HTB	HB	21500	30	F1
ST JOHN PL	CO	SA	1000	18	C5
ST JOHN RD	SB	SB	1700	14	A5
ST JOHN WY	PLA	PLA	600	7	B3
ST JUDE DR	CO	SA	19400	18	C4
ST KITTS	DPT	DPT		37	E3
ST KITTS	MVJO	SJ92		29B	D2
ST LO	CO	LB		35	C6
ST LUCIA WY	PLA	PLA	800	7	D5
ST MARK ST	GGR	GG45	11800	14	E3
ST MARKS DR	CO	SA	13000	18	B5
ST MARTIN	CO	LB77		36	A5
ST MARYS CIR	CO	SAO5		18	D3
ST MARYS CIR	WSTM	WSTM	5000	14	E6
ST MARYS DR	CO	SA	13000	18	B5
ST MAXIME	LAG	LB		35	B5
ST MICHAEL	DPT	DPT		37	E3
ST MICHAEL CIR	CYP	CYP	10000	9	E6
ST MORITZ CIR	CO	SA	18100	18	A4
ST PAUL	IRV	SA		29	E2
ST PAUL CIR	HTB	HB47	6400	21	A5
ST PIERRE	CO	SJ79		59	D3
ST PIERRE WY	CYP	CYP	11400	15	B2
ST RAPHAEL	LAG	LB		35	B5
ST REGIS PL	CO	SA	1000	18	B6
ST ROBERT	DPT	DPT		37	E3
ST SOPHIA CIR	CYP	CYP	10000	9	D6
ST STEPHEN CIR	CYP	CYP	10000	9	D6
ST THOMAS	CO	LB77		36	A4
ST THOMAS CIR	OR	OR65		12	C6
ST THOMAS DR	CO	SA	13000	18	C5
ST TROPEZ	LAG	LB		35	B5
ST TROPEZ	NB	CDLM		32	D4
ST VINCENT	CO	LB77		36	A4
ST VINCENT CIR	CYP	CYP	10000	9	D6
ST VINCENT PL	CO	SA	1000	18	C5
SAIPAN PL	ETMC	SA09		51	D3
SAIPAN ST	CYP	CYP	6300	14	F3
SAKIOKA DR	CM	CM26		28	A2
SALACIA DR	IRV	SA	4000	24	D5
SALADO	MVJO	SJ91	21700	29B	D1
SALAMANCA DR	MVJO	SJ91	26300	29B	B6
SALAMANCA LN	HTB	HB	17900	26	A2
SALAT LN	MVJO	SJ91		29B	B5
SALAZAR DR	MVJO	SJ91		29B	C6
SALCEDO	MVJO	SJ91	21900	29B	D2
SALEM AV	WSTM	WSTM	9300	21	E1
SALEM CIR	HTB	HB47	8600	21	D5
SALEM PL	FUL	FL	2500	7	A2
SALEM RD	YL	YL		40	B6
SALEM ST	ANA	AN	900	11	C6
SALEM ST	IRV	SA	3800	28	F4
SALERMO	CO	LB77		35	F5
SALERNO	IRV	SA14		28	F4
SALERNO	NB	NB60		32	E3
SALERNO ST	GGR	GG	13100	16	E3

STREET	CITY	P.O. ZONE	BLOCK	PAGE	GRID
SALERNO WY	YL	YL		40	D6
SALERO LN	MVJO	SJ91	23900	29B	B5
SALFORD ST	CO	LB		29C	E1
SALINA	IRV	SA14		28	F4
SALINAS AV	CM	CM	1100	27	E2
SALINAS LN	MVJO	SJ91		29D	C4
SALINAS RIV CIR	FTNV	SA08	10300	27	A2
SALINAZ DR	GGR	GG	11300	16	C6
SALINE DR	HTB	HB	9700	26	F5
SALING WY	LAG	LB51	1100	34	F3
SALISBURY CIR	LAP	BP23	5200	9	D4
SALISBURY LN	CYP	CYP	9500	9	D5
SALISBURY LN	HTB	HB47	15400	21	B3
SALISBURY LN	LAP	BP23	8500	9	D4
SALISH AV	GGR	GG	8600	15	D2
SALK	IRV	SA		29	E1
SALK WY	PLA	PLA	200	7	D5
SALLIE LN	ANA	AN	1600	16	A1
SALLY DR	CO	ET	26100	29B	A2
SALLY LN	ANA	AN		8	C6
SALLY LN	ANA	AN		13	C1
SALLY PL	FUL	FL31	500	6	E6
SALLY ST	GGR	GG	12500	16	C4
SALMERON	MVJO	SJ91	22300	29B	C2
SALMON AV	FTNV	SA08	8700	26	D1
SALMON DR	CO	LALM	2600	14	A4
SALMON LN	HTB	HB	19300	26	F4
SALMON WY	CM	CM27	200	31	C3
SALMON RIVER	PLA	PLA	1600	7	B3
SALON	MVJO	SJ92		29B	E3
SALSA VERDE	MVJO	SJ91	26000	29B	A5
SALTA ST	SA	SA	2100	22	F6
SALTA ST	SA	SA04	3000	27	F1
SALT AIR CIR	HTB	HB	20500	26	F5
SALT AIR CIR	NB	NB	2500	32	B6
SALTAIR DR	CO	SA	2000	24	C1
SALTAIR DR	CYP	CYP	10100	9	E6
SALT AIR DR	NB	CDLM		32	B6
SALTAIRE DR	CO	LAG		36	A5
SALT LAKE DR	HTB	HB	8500	26	D4
SALTSPRAY	CO	LB		29A	C4
SALT SPRAY DR	CO	LB77		36	A6
SALTWATER	CO	LB		29A	C4
SALTWATER CIR	HTB	HB		26	B5
SALTWATER DR	DPT	DPT	25500	38	B4
SALUDA CIR	HTB	HB	21600	30	F2
SALVADOR DR	MVJO	SJ91		29B	B4
SALVADOR DR	PLA	PLA	1200	7	D4
SALVADOR DR E	PLA	PLA	1200	7	D4
SALVADOR ST	CM	CM	1000	27	E4
SALVADOR BAY	DPT	DPT		37	D4
SALVATION LN	SA	SA	1500	22	F4
SALVIA	CO	SJ88		59	B2
SALVIATE ISLE	IRV	SA14		28	D5
SALZBURG	NB	CDLM		32	D5
SAMANTHA CIR	ANA	AN		8	E5
SAMAR DR	CM	CM	1600	27	B4
SAMAR PL	CM	CM	1600	27	C4
SAMBAR CIR	CYP	CYP	6600	15	A2
SAMOA DR	HTB	HB46	10300	27	A3
SAMOA PL	CM	CM	3000	27	C3
SAMOA ST	CYP	CYP	11500	14	F2
SAMOA WY	LAG	LB51	1400	34	E2
SAMPSON LN	HTB	HB47		21	C6
SAMPSON LN	HTB	HB		26	C1
SAMUEL CIR	DPT	DPT		37	E2
SAMUEL DR	GGR	GG	11500	16	C2
SAMURA PL	STN	GG41	7700	15	C4
SAN ADRIANO WY	BPK	BP	6900	10	A3
SAN ALANO AV	OR	OR	1500	12	D3
SAN ALANO CIR	BPK	BP	6500	10	A4
SAN ALANO LN	BPK	BP	8700	10	A4
SAN ALANO PL	OR	OR	1600	12	D3
SAN ALFREDO CIR	BPK	BP	6900	10	A3
SAN ALFREDO CIR	FTNV	SA08	17100	22	A6
SAN ALTO AV	OR	OR	1500	12	D3
SAN ALTO PL	OR	OR	1600	12	D3
SAN ALTO WY	BPK	BP	6700	10	A3
SAN AMADEO	CO	LB	22000	29A	A6
SAN AMBROSIO	CO	SJ88		29B	F2
SAN ANDREAS	CO	SJ88		59	C2
SAN ANDREAS LN	HTB	HB		30	D2
SAN ANDRES AV	CYP	CYP	6200	14	F2
SAN ANDRES AV	CYP	CYP		15	A2
SAN ANDRES LN	MVJO	SJ91	24800	29B	B6
SAN ANDRES ST	FTNV	SA08	16500	22	C5
SAN ANGELO AV	WSTM	WSTM	10300	22	A3
SAN ANGELO DR	HTB	HB47	8100	21	C4
SAN ANSELMO	CO	SJ88		29B	F2
SAN ANSELMO LN	PLA	PLA	100	7	C5
SAN ANTONIO AV	BPK	BP	8500	10	A4

STREET	CITY	P.O. ZONE	BLOCK	PAGE	GRID
SAN ANTONIO AV	FUL	FL	1000	6	D1
SAN ANTONIO CIR	PLA	PLA	100	7	C5
SAN ANTONIO RD	YL	YL		8	E1
SAN ANTONIO RD	YL	YL		8	E3
SAN ANTONIO ST	FTNV	SA08	18500	27	A3
SAN ARDO DR	BPK	BP	7500	5	B4
SAN ARTURO CIR	BPK	BP	6700	10	A3
SAN BAYAS ST	FTNV	SA08	17400	22	B6
SAN BENITO	CO	SJ88		29B	F2
SAN BENITO WY	BPK	BP	6700	10	A4
SN BERNARDNO AV	NB	NB63	300	31	C4
SN BERNRDNO CIR	FTNV	SA08	17600	27	A1
SN BERNARDO CIR	BPK	BP	6800	10	A4
SN BERNARDNO PL	CM	CM27	1500	31	D4
SANBERT ST	CO	PLA	4700	7	D3
SAN BITTERN LN	CO	LB56		29C	A1
SAN BLAS	MVJO	SJ92	27500	29B	D3
SAN BLAS ST	FTNV	SA08	18900	27	A3
SAN BONIFACIO	CO	SJ88		29B	F2
SAN BONITO AV	LALM	LALM	3900	9	C6
SAN BRISO PL	CO	LB77	29300	35	F2
SAN BRUNO	CO	SJ88		29B	F2
SAN BRUNO	NB	NB		32	A3
SAN BRUNO AV	OR	OR	1500	12	D3
SAN BRUNO DR	BPK	BP	6700	10	A4
SAN BRUNO ST	FTNV	SA08	17000	22	A6
SAN CALVINO CIR	BPK	BP	8500	10	A3
SAN CANDELO ST	FTNV	SA08	17600	27	B1
SN CAPISTRNO WY	BPK	BP	8300	10	A3
SAN CARLO	IRV	SA		28	F4
SAN CARLOS	CO	SJ88		59	C2
SAN CARLOS AV	OR	OR	1500	12	D2
SAN CARLOS DR	FUL	FL	2500	6	F5
SAN CARLOS LN	CM	CM	2700	27	E4
SAN CARLOS LN	HTB	HB		20	D5
SAN CARLOS PL	OR	OR	1600	12	D2
SAN CARLOS ST	FTNV	SA08	18800	27	A3
SAN CARLOS WY	BPK	BP	8300	9	F3
SAN CARLOS WY	PLA	PLA	200	7	B2
SN CLEMENTE CIR	HTB	HB		20	C4
SAN CLEMENTE DR	CM	CM26		27	C5
SAN CLEMENTE DR	NB	NB		32	A5
SAN CLEMENTE LN	PLA	PLA	100	7	C5
SAN CLEMENTE ST	FTNV	SA08	17700	27	A1
SAN CLEMENTE ST	LAG	LB51	2200	34	E4
SAN CLEMENTE WY	BPK	BP	8300	9	F3
SAN CORZO ST	FTNV	SA08	17700	27	B1
SAND	IRV	SA		29	B5
SAND ST	CO	LB77		36	A5
SANDALIA CIR	MVJO	SJ91		29B	C6
SANDALIA CIR	MVJO	SJ91		29D	C1
SANDALWOOD	CO	LB56		29C	C2
SANDALWOOD	IRV	SA		29	B6
SANDALWOOD	MVJO	SJ92		29B	E3
SANDALWOOD AV	ANA	AN	1200	11	E2
SANDALWOOD AV	FUL	FL	800	6	D2
SANDALWOOD CIR	GGR	GG	13200	16	E4
SANDALWOOD CIR	WSTM	WSTM	8300	21	D3
SANDALWOOD CT	ANA	AN	2500	12	A2
SANDALWOOD CT	SJC	SJ75		36	B2
SANDALWOOD DR	BREA	BREA	1500	2	C3
SANDALWOOD LN	CO	SA	12000	24	C1
SANDALWOOD LN	GGR	GG	12500	16	D4
SANDALWOOD LN	NB	NB	1700	31	F3
SANDALWOOD PL	ANA	AN	2200	11	F2
SANDALWOOD PL	ANA	AN	2200	12	A2
SANDALWOOD ST	CM	CM	1500	27	C4
SANDALWOOD ST	FTNV	SA08	16300	21	E4
SANDALWOOD WY	STN	STN	7700	15	B1
SANDBAR	HTB	HB		26	C6
SAND BAR CIR	OR	OR		12	C3
SANDBAR DR	FUL	FL33		5	E4
SANDBAR DR	NB	CDLM		32	C6
SANDBERG LN	CO	OR		13	E6
SANDBERG LN	OR	OR	7800	13	E6
SANDBROOK DR	TUS	TUS	14300	23	F4
SANDBURG CIR	BPK	BP	6400	10	A1
SANDBURG DR	BPK	BP	6800	10	A1
SANDBURG WY	IRV	SA	4100	28	F5
SAND CANYON AV	CO	SA	14100	29	D5
SAND CANYON AV	CO	SA	13000	51	A2
SAND CANYON AV	IRV	SA	14000	29	D5
SAND CANYON RD	IRV	SA		32A	C3
SAND CANYON WY	BREA	BREA		2	F4
SANDCASTLE CT	DPT	DPT		37	A5
SANDCASTLE DR	NB	CDLM		32	C6
SANDCASTLE DR	NB	CDLM	800	33	B1
SANDCASTLE LN	HTB	HB		26	B4
SANDCOVE CIR	HTB	HB		26	D5
SAND CREEK LN	CO	LB		29C	E2

STREET	CITY	P.O. ZONE	BLOCK	PAGE	GRID
SAND DOLLAR CT	NB	NB		31	A2
SAND DOLLAR LN	HTB	HB	21300	30	D1
SAND DUNES CT	FTNV	SA08		27	A1
SANDE ST	CYP	CYP	10200	9	E6
SANDELWOOD LN	BREA	BREA		2	D2
SANDERLING	IRV	SA		29	C2
SANDERLING CIR	CM	CM	1900	27	B5
SANDERLING LN	CO	LB56		29C	A2
SANDERSON AV	ANA	AN		12	A6
SANDERSON LN	HTB	HB	19600	26	E4
SANDERSTEAD RD	CO	SA	13600	18	A6
SANDFIELD PL	TUS	TUS	2000	24	A4
SANDFLOWER CT	DPT	DPT		37	F3
SANDFLOWER CT	NB	NB		31	A3
SANDHURST PL	CO	SA	13000	18	A6
SANDI LN	CM	CM27		31	A1
SANDIA CT	CO	LB	25100	29C	F2
SANDIA WY	CO	SJ		59	D3
SAN DIEGO CIR	FTNV	SA08	17600	27	A1
SAN DIEGO DR	BPK	BP	6500	10	A3
SAN DIEGO FRWY	CM	CM26		28	A3
SAN DIEGO FRWY	CO			29D	B4
SAN DIEGO FRWY	FTNV	SA08		27	B2
SAN DIEGO FRWY	IRV			29	A5
SAN DIEGO FRWY	IRV			29A	B2
SAN DIEGO FRWY	IRV			32A	E1
SAN DIEGO FRWY	SCL	SC72		39	C1
SAN DIEGO FRWY	SB	SB		14	B5
SAN DIEGO FRWY	SJC			36	C4
SAN DIEGO FRWY	SJC			38	B4
SAN DIEGO FRWY	WSTM			14	E5
SAN DIEGO FRWY	WSTM			21	B2
SAN DIEGO LN	PLA	PLA	500	7	C5
SAN DIMAS CIR	BPK	BP	8000	10	A3
SAND KEY	NB	CDLM		33	C1
SANDLEWOOD AV	LAH	LAH	500	5	F1
SANDLEWOOD AV	LAH	LAH	100	6	A1
SANDLING CT	CO	LB77		35	F3
SAND OAKS RD	CO	LB77		35	F5
SAN DONA	CO	LB		29A	B4
SAN DOVAL LN	HTB	HB	17800	26	A1
SAN DOVAL LN	MVJO	SJ91	24600	29B	B6
SANDOWN ST	LAH	LAH	1000	1	F6
SANDPEBBLE	IRV	SA		32A	A2
SANDPEBBLE LN	BREA	BREA		3	B5
SAND PEBBLE WY	OR	OR		12	C3
SANDPIPER	IRV	SA		29	B3
SANDPIPER	MVJO	SJ92		29B	E2
SANDPIPER AV	ANA	AN		7	B6
SANDPIPER CIR	FTNV	SA08	8800	26	E1
SANDPIPER CIR	OR	OR	200	18	B3
SANDPIPER CT	SJC	SJ75		38	B2
SANDPIPER DR	CM	CM	2600	27	A5
SANDPIPER DR	LAG	LB51		34	F4
SANDPIPER DR	LAG	LB51		35	A4
SANDPIPER DR	LAP	BP23	4900	9	D3
SANDPIPER DR	NB	CDLM	1000	32	B6
SANDPIPER DR	SB	SB	600	19	F2
SANDPIPER LN	CO	LB56		29C	A1
SAND PIPER LN	DPT	DPT		37	E4
SANDPIPER LN	HTB	HB	20500	26	D6
SAND POINT WY	NB	CDLM	1200	32	B6
SAND POINTE	CO	LB77		36	A5
SANDPOINTE AV	SA	SA		28	B2
SANDRA CIR	VPK	OR67	9000	12	F5
SANDRA CIR	VPK	OR67	9000	13	A5
SANDRA CT	BREA	BREA	900	2	D4
SANDRA DR	YL	YL	5900	8	A5
SANDRA LN	HTB	HB	16000	20	E4
SANDRA PL	GGR	GG	13000	16	B5
SANDRA ST	CO	ET	21900	29A	D2
SANDRAGLEN LN	LAH	LAH	400	1	F5
SANDRA LEE ST	HTB	HB	17000	20	D6
SANDRIDGE CIR	CO	LB56		29C	E5
SAND ROCK CIR	YL	YL		7	D2
SANDS DR	HTB	HB	5700	20	F1
SANDSPOINT CT	CO	YL	19400	8	C4
SANDSTONE	HTB	HB		26	C6
SANDSTONE	IRV	SA		29	B3
SANDSTONE AV	FTNV	SA08	11300	22	B5
SANDUNE LN	NB	CDLM		33	C1
SANDUSKY LN	WSTM	WSTM	15500	21	D3
SANDWOOD LN	CO	SA	12000	24	C1
SANDWOOD PL	TUS	TUS	1800	24	A4
SANDY CIR	LAP	BP23	4900	9	D2
SANDY DR	CO	AN04	11900	15	C3
SANDY DR	SCL	SC72		39	A2
SANDY LN	HTB	HB		20	D5
SANDY WY	GGR	GG		15	E6
SANDY BEACH PL	DPT	DPT	33200	38	B4
SANDY COVE	CO	LB77		36	B4

STREET	CITY	P.O. ZONE	BLOCK	PAGE	GRID
SANDY CREEK	CO	ET	26400	29B	B2
SANDY HILL LN	YL	YL		8	B5
SANDY HOOK DR	HTB	HB	8500	30	D1
SANDYSTONE CT	DPT	DPT		37	B5
SAN ESTEBAN DR	MVJO	SJ91		29B	B4
SAN FABIAN ST	FTNV	SA08	17600	22	B6
SAN FABIAN ST	FTNV	SA08	17600	27	B1
SAN FABIO CIR	BPK	BP	8800	9	F4
SAN FELIPE CIR	BPK	BP	8800	9	F4
SAN FELIPE CIR	BPK	BP		10	A4
SAN FELIPE DR	CO	LB		35	D4
SAN FELIPE ST	FTNV	SA08	18500	27	A3
SAN FERNANDO LN	PLA	PLA	500	7	C5
SAN FIDEL ST	FTNV	SA08	17900	27	A1
SN FRANCISCO DR	BPK	BP	6200	9	F4
SN FRANCISCO DR	BPK	BP	6500	10	A4
SN FRANCISCO ST	FTNV	SA08	17600	27	A1
SAN GABRIEL CIR	BPK	BP	6500	10	A3
SAN GABRIEL LN	PLA	PLA	100	7	C5
SAN GABRIEL ST	FTNV	SA08	16200	22	C4
SANGALLO	IRV	SA14		29	A4
SAN GONZALO DR	MVJO	SJ91		29D	B4
SN HACIENDA CIR	BPK	BP	8000	10	A3
SAN HARCO CIR	BPK	BP	6100	9	F4
SAN HAROLDO WY	BPK	BP	6500	10	A4
SAN HELICE CIR	BPK	BP	8000	10	A3
SN HERNANDO WY	BPK	BP	6600	10	A3
SAN HERON CIR	BPK	BP	8000	10	A3
SAN HILARIO CIR	BPK	BP	8000	10	A3
SAN HOMERO WY	BPK	BP	6500	10	A3
SAN HUERTA CIR	BPK	BP	8000	10	A3
SAN HUGO LN	FTNV	SA08	17400	21	D6
SAN HUGO WY	BPK	BP	6500	10	A3
SAN IGNACIO	CO	SJ88		29B	F3
SAN JACINTO CIR	FTNV	SA08	16100	22	C4
SAN JACINTO LN	HTB	HB		20	D4
SAN JACINTO ST	FTNV	SA08	16200	22	C4
SAN JOAQUIN	IRV	SA15		28	E5
SAN JOAQUIN AV	LALM	LALM	3800	9	B6
SAN JOAQUIN AV	LALM	LALM	3700	14	B1
SAN JOAQUIN CIR	BPK	BP	6900	10	A3
SAN JOAQUIN ST	LAG	LB51	200	34	B2
SN JQUIN HLS RD	NB	CDLM	2500	32	B6
SN JQUIN HLS RD	NB	NB	1500	32	A4
SAN JOSE	CO	ET		29A	F4
SAN JOSE AV	CM	CM	1100	27	E2
SAN JOSE AV	LAH	LAH	1800	1	E4
SAN JOSE CIR	BPK	BP	8000	10	A3
SAN JOSE LN	PLA	PLA	100	7	C5
SAN JOSE ST	FTNV	SA08	18300	26	F2
SAN JOSE ST	LAG	LB51	800	34	F4
SAN JUAN	IRV	SA		28	F3
SAN JUAN AV	DPT	DPT	24600	37	E4
SAN JUAN CIR	BPK	BP	6900	10	A3
SAN JUAN CIR	LAP	BP23	4900	9	D2
SAN JUAN CT	FTNV	SA08	10000	26	F2
SAN JUAN CT	FTNV	SA08		27	A2
SAN JUAN DR	BREA	BREA	1400	2	C3
SAN JUAN DR	FUL	FL	2900	6	C1
SAN JUAN DR	OR	OR	5600	13	C6
SAN JUAN LN	CM	CM	2700	27	E4
SAN JUAN LN	HTB	HB		20	D4
SAN JUAN LN	PLA	PLA	500	7	C5
SAN JUAN PL	FUL	FL	2900	6	C1
SAN JUAN PL	GGR	GG	11100	16	B6
SAN JUAN RD	CO	LB77		36	A5
SAN JUAN ST	CO	TUS	1000	23	F3
SAN JUAN ST	CO	TUS	1400	24	A3
SAN JUAN CK RD	SJC	SJ75	27300	36	D6
SAN JUAN CK RD	SJC	SJ75	27000	38	C2
SAN JULIAN	CO	SJ88		29B	F2
SAN JULIAN CIR	BPK	BP	6900	10	A3
SAN JULIAN ST	FTNV	SA08	17500	27	B1
SAN LAZARO CIR	BPK	BP	8000	9	F3
SAN LEANDRO	IRV	SA		28	F4
SAN LEANDRO	IRV	SA		29	A4
SAN LEANDRO	TUS	TUS		24	B3
SAN LEANDRO CIR	BPK	BP	8000	9	F3
SAN LEANDRO LN	CM	CM	3200	27	E3
SAN LEANDRO LN	HTB	HB	17800	26	A1
SAN LEON	IRV	SA		28	F3
SAN LEON AV	FTNV	SA08	10800	27	B1
SAN LEON CIR	BPK	BP	8000	9	F3
SANLO ST	CO	YL	16500	7	D2
SAN LORENZO AV	SA	SA	1500	22	F6
SAN LORENZO AV	SA	SA	1100	23	A6
SAN LORENZO CIR	FTNV	SA08	17200	22	B6
SAN LORENZO DR	BPK	BP	6000	9	F3
SAN LORENZO LN	ANA	AN		13	D1
SAN LUCAS	MVJO	SJ92	28100	29B	E3
SAN LUCAS CIR	BPK	BP	8000	9	F3

123

1990 ORANGE COUNTY STREET INDEX

SAN LUCAS LN — SATURN ST

ORANGE CO.

STREET	CITY	P.O. ZONE	BLOCK	PAGE	GRID
SAN LUCAS LN	CM	CM	2700	27	F4
SAN LUIS CIR	BPK	BP	8000	9	F3
SAN LUIS DR	OR			18	E3
SAN LUIS ST	FTNV	SA08	17200	22	A6
SAN LUIS WY	PLA	PLA	100	7	B2
SAN MAIZ ST	FTNV	SA08	17800	27	B1
SN MARCELLO CIR	BPK	BP	6500	10	A3
SAN MARCO	CO	SJ88		59	C3
SAN MARCO	NB	NB60		32	E3
SAN MARCOS	MVJO	SJ92	28200	29B	E3
SAN MARCOS DR	STN	STN	12300	15	C4
SAN MARCOS PL	FUL	FL35		2	D6
SAN MARCOS ST	FTNV	SA08	18500	26	F2
SAN MARCOS WY	BPK	BP	6300	9	F3
SAN MARINO	IRV	SA		28	F3
SAN MARINO	IRV	SA		29	A3
SAN MARINO CIR	BPK	BP	6400	9	F3
SAN MARINO CIR	CM	CM	3300	27	E2
SAN MARINO CIR	FTNV	SA08	17600	27	A1
SAN MARINO CT	MVJO	SJ92		29D	E3
SAN MARINO DR	BPK	BP	7800	9	F3
SAN MARINO PL	DPT	DPT	24200	37	E4
SAN MARTIN	MVJO	SJ92		29B	E2
SAN MARTIN	SCL	SCL		39	F2
SAN MARTIN WY	BPK	BP	6300	9	F3
SAN MARTIN WY	NB	CDLM		32	D6
SAN MATEO	CO	SJ88		29B	F2
SAN MATEO	IRV	SA		28	F4
SAN MATEO AV	LALM	LALM	3900	9	C6
SAN MATEO CIR	BPK	BP	6500	9	F3
SAN MATEO LN	BPK	BP	6300	9	F3
SAN MATEO LN	HTB	HB		20	D4
SAN MATEO ST	FTNV	SA08	17000	22	A6
SAN MATEO WY	NB	CDLM		32	D6
SANMIAN CT	FTNV	SA08		26	F2
SAN MICHEL	CM	CM27		31	C1
SAN MIGUEL	CO	ET		51	E4
SAN MIGUEL	CO	TRA		62	A1
SAN MIGUEL	MVJO	SJ92		52	E6
SAN MIGUEL CIR	BPK	BP	6500	9	F3
SAN MIGUEL CIR	PLA	PLA	100	7	C5
SAN MIGUEL CT	FTNV	SA08	10000	26	F2
SAN MIGUEL DR	FUL	FL35		2	C6
SAN MIGUEL DR	NB	NB	2100	32	B5
SAN MIGUEL LN	HTB	HB		20	D4
SAN MINISO CIR	FTNV	SA08	17800	27	B1
SAN NICHOLAS	CO	SJ88		29B	F2
SAN NICHOLAS CT	LAG	LB51		33A	F1
SAN NICOLAS DR	NB	NB	2100	32	B5
SANORIA ST	CO	LAG		35	F3
SAN PABLO	CO	SJ88		29B	F2
SAN PABLO CIR	CM	CM	1100	27	E2
SAN PABLO CIR	YL	YL	4200	7	F2
SAN PABLO CT	FTNV	SA08	10000	26	F2
SAN PABLO DR	BPK	BP	8000	10	A3
SAN PABLO DR	FUL	FL35		2	C6
SN PACIFICO CIR	BPK	BP	8200	10	A3
SAN PACO AV	FTNV	SA08	10800	27	B1
SAN PACO CIR	BPK	BP	6800	10	A3
SAN PACO LN	BPK	BP	8300	10	A3
SAN PADRE CIR	BPK	BP	6900	10	A3
SAN PALO CIR	BPK	BP	8200	10	A3
SAN PASQUAL CIR	BPK	BP	6800	10	A3
SAN PASQUAL LN	BPK	BP	8400	10	A3
SAN PASQUAL ST	FTNV	SA08	18700	27	A2
SAN PASQUEL ST	MVJO	SJ92		29D	E3
SAN PATRICIO	CO	SJ88		29B	F2
SAN PAULO	IRV	SA		29	A4
SAN PEDRO	CO	SJ88		29B	F2
SAN PEDRO AV	CO	LB		29C	E2
SAN PEDRO CIR	BPK	BP	6900	10	A3
SAN PEDRO CIR	FTNV	SA08	17100	22	B6
SAN PEDRO DR	HTB	HB		20	D4
SAN RAFAEL CIR	CM	CM	3300	27	E2
SAN RAFAEL CIR	PLA	PLA	100	7	C5
SAN RAFAEL DR	BPK	BP	7200	9	F3
SAN RAFAEL DR	MVJO	SJ92		29D	E3
SAN RAFAEL LN	HTB	HB		20	C3
SAN RAFAEL PL	CO	LB56		35	F1
SAN RAFAEL ST	FTNV	SA08	17600	27	A1
SAN RAMON	IRV	SA		32A	B1
SAN RAMON CIR	VPK	OR67		13	B5
SAN RAMON DR	FUL	FL35		2	C6
SAN RAMON WY	BPK	BP	6100	9	F3
SAN RAMON WY	MVJO	SJ92		29D	E3
SAN RAPHAEL	DPT	DPT		37	D2
SAN REMO	CO	SJ92		29D	E3
SAN REMO	IRV	SA		28	F3
SAN REMO	IRV	SA		29	A3
SAN REMO	SCL	SC72		38	D5
SAN REMO	TUS	TUS		24	B3

STREET	CITY	P.O. ZONE	BLOCK	PAGE	GRID
SAN REMO AV	PLA	PLA	2000	7	B2
SAN REMO DR	CO	LB		29A	A4
SAN REMO DR	LAG	LB51	1900	34	F2
SAN REMO PL	OR	OR		13	B6
SAN REMO PL	OR	OR	1200	18	B1
SAN REMO WY	BPK	BP	6000	9	F3
SAN REMO WY	YL	YL		40	D6
SAN RENALDO CIR	BPK	BP	6200	9	F3
SAN RICARDO	CO	SJ88		29B	F2
SAN RICARDO CIR	FTNV	SA08	17100	22	A6
SAN RICARDO ST	FTNV	SA08	17000	22	A6
SAN RICARDO WY	BPK	BP	6200	9	F3
SAN RIO DR	BPK	BP	8500	9	F4
SAN ROBERTO CIR	BPK	BP	6200	9	F3
SAN RODOLFO WY	BPK	BP	6000	9	F3
SAN ROLANDO CIR	BPK	BP	6200	9	F4
SAN ROLANDO WY	BPK	BP	6000	9	F4
SAN ROMOLO WY	BPK	BP	8500	9	F3
SAN ROQUE DR	MVJO	SJ91	26100	29B	B6
SAN ROQUE DR	MVJO	SJ91		29D	B1
SAN ROQUE LN	HTB	HB	17500	26	A1
SAN RUBEN CIR	BPK	BP	6200	9	F4
SAN RUFINO CIR	YL	YL	4200	7	F2
SAN RUFINO DR	IRV	SA		32A	A2
SAN RUFO CIR	BPK	BP	6200	9	F4
SN SALVADOR CIR	BPK	BP	8800	9	F4
SAN SEBASTIAN	CO	SJ88		29B	F2
SAN SEBASTIAN	NB	CDLM		32	D5
SAN SIMEON	CO	LB77		35	C4
SAN SIMEON	IRV	SA		32A	B2
SAN SIMEON	TUS	TUS		24	B3
SAN SIMEON CIR	BPK	BP	8600	10	A3
SAN SIMEON CIR	PLA	PLA	500	7	C5
SAN SIMEON CIR	YL	YL	4200	7	F2
SAN SIMEON DR	LAP	BP23	5700	9	E2
SAN SIMEON ST	CO	LB56		29C	D3
SAN SIMEON ST	FTNV	SA08	17600	27	A1
SAN SIMON	CO	SJ88		29B	F2
SANSINENA LN	LAH	LAH	1400	1	E3
SAN SOUCI CIR	HTB	HB	5900	20	F1
SAN SOUCI PL	MVJO	SJ92		29D	E3
SANTA ADELA CIR	FTNV	SA08	18100	26	E2
STA ALBERTA CIR	FTNV	SA08	18400	26	D2
SANTA ANA AV	CM	CM	2500	27	F6
SANTA ANA AV	CM	CM27	1500	31	D3
SANTA ANA AV	CO	SA07	20200	27	F6
SANTA ANA AV	CO	SA07	20000	28	A5
SANTA ANA AV	NB	NB	200	31	D3
SANTA ANA BL E	SA	SA	100	23	B2
SANTA ANA BL W	SA	SA	1300	22	F2
SANTA ANA BL W	SA	SA	100	23	B2
SANTA ANA CIR	BPK	BP	7000	10	A3
SANTA ANA FRWY	ANA			10	E2
SANTA ANA FRWY	ANA			11	B4
SANTA ANA FRWY	ANA			16	E1
SANTA ANA FRWY	BPK			5	A5
SANTA ANA FRWY	CO			29A	B1
SANTA ANA FRWY	CO			51	A5
SANTA ANA FRWY	IRV			29	E3
SANTA ANA FRWY	SA			17	B4
SANTA ANA FRWY	SA			23	D2
SANTA ANA FRWY	TUS			24	B4
SANTA ANA LN	SCL	SC72	100	39	C4
SANTA ANA ST	LAG	LB51	800	34	F4
STA ANA ST E&W	ANA	AN	100	11	C4
STA ANA CYN RD	ANA	AN	21900	8	E6
STA ANA CYN RD	ANA	AN	3800	12	F2
STA ANA CYN RD	ANA	AN	4800	13	A2
STA ANA CYN RD	ANA	AN08		40	A6
STA ANA CYN RD	CO	AN07		43	B1
SANTA ANDREA ST	FTNV	SA08	18500	26	D2
SANTA ANITA AV	PLA	PLA	2000	7	B2
SANTA ANITA CIR	BPK	BP	7000	10	A3
SANTA ANITA CIR	FTNV	SA08	17800	26	E1
SANTA ANITA LN	HTB	HB	16300	20	E5
SANTA ANITA ST	OR	OR	4000	12	D2
STA ARABELLA ST	FTNV	SA08	18000	26	D2
SANTA BARBARA	CO	SJ88		59	C2
STA BARBARA AV	FUL	FL	500	6	B2
STA BARBARA AV	GGR	GG45	5300	14	E3
STA BARBARA AV	GGR	GG	6300	15	A3
STA BARBARA AV	STN	STN	7700	15	C3
STA BARBARA DR	NB	NB		32	A4
STA BARBARA LN	CM	CM26		27	C5
STA BARBARA LN	HTB	HB		20	C3
STA BARBARA LN	HTB	HB		20	C4
STA BARBARA PL	CO	LB56		35	F2
STA BARBARA PL	OR	OR	4000	12	D2
STA BARBARA ST	FTNV	SA08	17100	21	E6
STA BARBARA ST	FTNV	SA08	18800	26	E3
STA BARBARA ST	PLA	PLA	300	7	A5

STREET	CITY	P.O. ZONE	BLOCK	PAGE	GRID
STA BELINDA ST	FTNV	SA08	18200	26	E2
SANTA BERTA WY	BPK	BP	8300	10	B3
STA CARLOTTA ST	FTNV	SA08	18200	26	D2
STA CARMELA ST	FTNV	SA08	18500	26	E2
SANTA CATALINA	CO	SJ88		29B	F2
STA CATALINA AV	GGR	GG45	5300	14	E3
STA CATALINA AV	GGR	GG	6300	15	A3
STA CATALINA AV	STN	STN	7600	15	C3
STA CATALNA CIR	BPK	BP	7200	10	B3
STA CATALNA CIR	FTNV	SA08	17500	26	D1
STA CATALINA DR	CM	CM26		27	C5
STA CATHERIN ST	FTNV	SA08	17000	21	D6
STA CATHERIN ST	FTNV	SA08	18900	26	D3
SANTA CATRINA	CO	SJ88		59	C2
SANTA CECILIA	CO	SJ88		29B	F3
STA CECILIA CIR	FTNV	SA08	18100	26	D2
STA CECILIA ST	FTNV	SA08	18000	26	D2
STA CECILIA ST	OR	OR	4000	12	E2
SANTA CLARA	SCL	SCL		39	F2
SANTA CLARA AV	CO	SA	16100	17	E5
SANTA CLARA AV	CO	SA	18100	18	A5
SANTA CLARA AV	DPT	DPT	24100	37	E5
SANTA CLARA AV	FUL	FL	2400	6	F6
SANTA CLARA AV	FUL	FL	2600	7	A6
SANTA CLARA AV	TUS	TUS	17400	17	D5
STA CLARA AV W	SA	SA	1300	16	F5
SANTA CLARA CIR	CM	CM	3300	27	E2
SANTA CLARA CIR	FTNV	SA08	18900	26	E3
SANTA CLARA CIR	SA	SA	1900	16	E5
SANTA CLARA PL	FUL	FL	200	7	A6
SANTA CLARA ST	CO	LB56		29C	D3
SANTA CLARA ST	BPK	BP	7200	10	B3
SANTA CLARA ST	CYP	CYP	10400	14	D5
SANTA CLARA ST	FTNV	SA08	17100	21	E6
STA CLAUDIA ST	FTNV	SA08	18000	26	E1
STA CRISTOBL ST	FTNV	SA08	17500	21	D6
STA CRISTOBL ST	FTNV	SA08	17600	26	D1
SANTA CRUZ	CO	ET		29A	F4
SANTA CRUZ	CO	SJ88		29B	F3
SANTA CRUZ AV	OR			18	E3
SANTA CRUZ CIR	BPK	BP	7200	10	B3
SANTA CRUZ CIR	CM	CM	1100	27	E2
SANTA CRUZ CIR	FTNV	SA08	18500	26	D2
SANTA CRUZ DR	NB	NB	22200	32	A5
SANTA CRUZ LN	HTB	HB		20	C3
SANTA CRUZ ST	ANA	AN		16	F2
SANTA CRUZ ST	LAG	LB51	1400	34	E4
SANTA CRUZ ST	STN	STN	11500	15	C3
STA DOMINGO CIR	FTNV	SA08	18500	21	E6
STA DOMINGO WY	BPK	BP		10	B3
SANTA ELENA	CO	SJ88		59	C2
SANTA ELENA CIR	FTNV	SA08	17500	21	E6
SANTA ELENA DR	BPK	BP	7200	10	B3
SANTA ELENA ST	FTNV	SA08	17600	21	E6
SANTA ELENA ST	FTNV	SA08	17600	26	E1
SANTA ELISE CIR	BPK	BP	8300	10	B3
SANTA ELISE ST	CYP	CYP	10400	14	D5
SANTA ELISE ST	FTNV	SA08	17600	26	D1
SANTA ELVIRA WY	BPK	BP	8300	10	B3
STA EUGENIA ST	FTNV	SA08	18400	26	E2
SANTA FE	IRV	SA14		29	F3
SANTA FE AV	DPT	SC24	34200	38	A5
SANTA FE AV	PLA	PLA	100	7	A5
SANTA FE AV E&W	FUL	FL	100	6	C5
SANTA FE AV W	FUL	FL	2500	7	A5
SANTA FE CIR	FTNV	SA08	17800	26	D1
SANTA FE DR	BPK	BP	8300	10	B3
SANTA FE DR	TUS	TUS	1300	23	E5
SANTA FE ST	SA	SA	2000	17	C6
SANTA FE ST	YL	YL	4600	7	E4
SANTA FE ST N	ANA	AN	100	11	D3
SANTA FE ST N&S	SA	SA	100	23	C3
STA GERTRUDS AV	GGR	GG45	5300	14	E3
STA GERTRUDS AV	STN	STN	7600	15	C3
STA GERTRDS CIR	FTNV	SA08	17800	26	E1
SANTA INEZ CIR	BPK	BP	7100	10	B3
SANTA INEZ DR	BPK	BP	8000	10	B3
SANTA INEZ PL	BPK	BP	8100	10	B3
SANTA INEZ WY	BPK	BP	8000	10	B3
SANTA IRENE CIR	BPK	BP	7000	10	B3
SANTA ISABEL	CO	SJ88		59	C2
SANTA ISABEL AV	CM	CM27	100	31	E1
SANTA ISABEL AV	NB	NB	2200	31	E1
STA ISABEL CIR	BPK	BP	7000	10	A3
SANTA ISABEL DR	BPK	BP	7100	10	B3
SANTA ISABEL ST	FTNV	SA08	17000	21	D6
STA ISADORA ST	FTNV	SA08	18500	26	D2
STA JOANANA CIR	FTNV	SA08	18200	26	E2
STA JOANANA ST	FTNV	SA08	18100	26	E2
STA LAURETTA CR	FTNV	SA08	18200	26	D2

STREET	CITY	P.O. ZONE	BLOCK	PAGE	GRID
STA LAURETTA ST	FTNV	SA08	18200	26	D2
STA LEONORA CIR	FTNV	SA08	18400	26	D2
SANTA LORETTA	CO	SJ88		59	C3
SANTA LUCIA	DPT	DPT		37	D2
SANTA LUCIA CIR	BPK	BP	7100	10	B3
SANTA LUCIA ST	FTNV	SA08	17000	21	D6
SANTA LUCIA ST	OR	OR	4000	12	E2
STA MADRINA CIR	FTNV	SA08	18900	26	D3
STA MADRINA ST	FTNV	SA08	17000	21	D6
STA MARGRITA LN	LAP	BP23	8200	9	D3
STA MARGRITA PY	CO	SJ88		59	A3
STA MARGRITA PY	MVJO	SJ92		29B	F1
STA MARGRITA PY	MVJO	SJ91		29B	D1
STA MARGRITA PY	MVJO	SJ92		29B	D1
STA MARGRITA PY	MVJO	SJ91		52	D6
STA MARGRITA PY	MVJO	SJ92		52	D6
STA MARGRITA PL	SJC	SJ75	31100	36	D5
SANTA MARIA	CO	ET		29A	F4
SANTA MARIA AV	CO	LB	21000	29A	B5
SANTA MARIA AV	FUL	FL	3600	6	B1
SANTA MARIA ST	FTNV	SA08	17300	21	D6
SANTA MARIA ST	FTNV	SA08	17600	26	D1
SANTA MARIA ST	OR			18	E3
SANTA MARIA ST	STN	STN	11200	15	C3
STA MARIANA ST	FTNV	SA08	17900	26	D1
SANTA MARTA CIR	BPK	BP	7000	10	A3
SANTA MARTA ST	CYP	CYP	10400	14	D5
SANTA MARTA ST	FTNV	SA08	18800	26	D3
SANTA MONICA AV	FUL	FL	3600	6	B1
SANTA MONICA AV	GGR	GG45	5300	14	E3
SANTA MONICA AV	GGR	GG	6300	15	A3
SANTA MONICA AV	STN	STN	7700	15	C3
STA MONICA CIR	FTNV	SA08	17500	21	D6
SANTA MONICA ST	CO	LB56		29C	D3
SANTANA CIR	HTB	HB	8300	26	D1
SANTANA DR	NB	NB	700	31	F5
SANTANELLA TER	NB	NB	1300	31	F6
SANTANELLA TER	NB	NB	1300	32	A6
SANTA OLIVIA ST	FTNV	SA08	17900	26	E1
SANTA PAULA	CO	ET		29A	F4
SANTA PAULA CIR	BPK	BP	7000	10	A3
SANTA PAULA CIR	FTNV	SA08	17500	21	D6
SANTA PAULA ST	FTNV	SA08	17600	26	D1
SANTA PAULA ST	STN	STN	11700	15	C3
SANTA POLA	MVJO	SJ92	21700	29B	F1
SANTA RAMONA ST	FTNV	SA08	18500	26	E2
SANTA RITA AV	GGR	GG45	5300	14	E3
SANTA RITA AV	GGR	GG	6300	15	A3
SANTA RITA AV	STN	STN	7700	15	C3
SANTA RITA CIR	BPK	BP	7000	10	A3
SANTA RITA CIR	GGR	GG	7500	15	B3
SANTA RITA ST	CYP	CYP	10400	14	D5
SANTA RITA ST	FTNV	SA08	17000	21	D6
SANTA ROSA	CO	SJ88		59	C3
SANTA ROSA AV	CM	CM	1000	27	E2
SANTA ROSA AV	CO	LB		29C	E3
SANTA ROSA CIR	FTNV	SA08	17600	26	E1
SANTA ROSA CT	LAG	LB51		29C	B1
SANTA ROSA DR	LAG	LB	31500	35	B5
SANTA ROSA DR	NB	NB		32	B5
SANTA ROSA PL	FUL	FL	3000	6	B1
SANTA ROSA WY	PLA	PLA	100	7	B2
STA ROSALIA ST	FTNV	SA08	17500	21	D6
STA ROSALIA ST	GGR	GG	12000	15	B3
STA ROSALIA ST	STN	STN	11200	15	B3
STA ROSALIA ST	STN	GG41	12000	15	B3
STA SOPHIA CIR	FTNV	SA08	18100	26	E2
STA STEPHNA CIR	FTNV	SA08	18200	26	E2
STA SUSANA CIR	MVJO	SJ91		29D	C4
STA SUZANNE ST	FTNV	SA08	17000	21	D6
SANTA TERESA	CO	SJ88		29B	F3
STA TERESA CIR	BPK	BP	7100	10	B3
STA TERESA CIR	FTNV	SA08	17600	26	D1
STA TOMASA CIR	FTNV	SA08	18500	26	D2
SANTA VALERA ST	BPK	BP	7300	10	B3
SANTA VALERA ST	FTNV	SA08	17900	26	D1
STA VERONICA ST	FTNV	SA08	18400	26	D2
STA VITTORIA DR	CO	LB	23000	29A	A5
SANTA YNEZ DR	HTB	HB47	6300	21	A6
SANTA YNEZ ST	FTNV	SA08	18500	26	D2
STA YOLANDA CIR	FTNV	SA08	18400	26	E2
SANTA YSABEL AV	FUL	FL	2400	6	F5
SANTA YSABEL AV	FUL	FL	2600	7	A5
SANTEE AV	WSTM	WSTM	6700	21	B2
SANTEE RIVER	PLA	PLA	1700	7	C3
SANTIAGO AV	SA	SA	1600	17	C6
SANTIAGO AV	SA	SA	600	23	C1
SANTIAGO BLVD	CO	OR	10200	13	B6
SANTIAGO BLVD	OR	OR	1600	12	E4
SANTIAGO BLVD	VPK	OR67	17800	12	E4
SANTIAGO BLVD	VPK	OR67	18100	13	B6

STREET	CITY	P.O. ZONE	BLOCK	PAGE	GRID
SANTIAGO DR	DPT	DPT		37	E3
SANTIAGO DR	HTB	HB46		26	E6
SANTIAGO DR	LAP	BP23	4700	9	D2
SANTIAGO DR	NB	NB	1000	31	F2
SANTIAGO DR	PLA	PLA	1100	7	D4
SANTIAGO RD	CM	CM	800	27	E4
SANTIAGO RD	FUL	FL	2700	6	D2
SANTIAGO WY	ANA	AN	500	13	B3
SANTIAGO CYN RD	CO	OR	20600	13	C6
SANTIAGO CYN RD	CO	OR	2100	18	E2
SANTIAGO CYN RD	CO	SA	1500	18	E2
SANTIAGO CYN RD	CO		2000	46	A4
SANTIAGO CYN RD	CO			49	E1
SANTIAGO CYN RD	CO	SA	6000	50	B2
SANTIAGO CYN RD	CO	OR67		52	D1
SANTIAGO CYN RD	OR	OR	5500	13	C6
SANTIAGO CYN WY	BREA	BREA		2	F4
SANTIAGO SPG DR	SA	SA		22	F4
SAN TIMOTEO	CO	SJ88		29B	F2
SANTO DR	MVJO	SJ91	25600	29D	B2
SANTOLINA	CO	SJ		56	C6
SAN TOMAS	CO	SJ88		29B	F2
SANTO TOMAS ST	CM	CM	200	27	F6
SAN TORINI RD	MVJO	SJ92		29D	E3
SAN TROPEZ CT	CO	SJ92		29D	E2
SAN TROPEZ CT	LAG	LB51		33A	F1
SAN VALLE	MVJO	SJ92	27600	29B	D3
SAN VINCENTE	CO	SJ88		59	C2
SAN VICENTE ST	FTNV	SA08	17600	27	A1
SAN VINCENT LN	MVJO	SJ91		29B	C6
SAN YSIDRO CIR	BPK	BP	6000	9	F3
SAN YSIDRO LN	FTNV	SA08	17400	21	E6
SAN YUBA WY	BPK	BP	6000	9	F3
SANZ	MVJO	SJ91		29B	B4
SAO PAULO AV E	PLA	PLA	1200	7	D3
SAO PAULO CIR	PLA	PLA	1300	7	D3
SAPELO WY	CYP	CYP	11500	15	B2
SAPPHIRE	BREA	BREA	200	4	B5
SAPPHIRE	MVJO	SJ91		29D	C5
SAPPHIRE AV	NB	NB	100	31	F6
SAPPHIRE AV	WSTM	WSTM	8700	21	D4
SAPPHIRE LN	ANA	AN07		13	D4
SAPPHIRE RD	FUL	FL	1500	7	B4
SAPPHIRE ST	GGR	GG45	12100	14	F4
SARA LN	CO	LB	24800	29A	E6
SARABETH LN	CO	LB56		29C	E6
SARAH AV	PLA	PLA	200	7	C2
SARAH LN	ANA	AN		13	C1
SARAH LN	CO	ET	24700	29A	E2
SARAH PL	FUL	FL	3200	6	C1
SARAH WY	ANA	AN		11	E5
SARAH WY	PLA	PLA	1900	7	C2
SARAHGLEN LN	LAH	LAH	600	1	F5
SARA RIVER CIR	FTNV	SA08		26	E2
SARATOGA	CO	SJ79		59	E5
SARATOGA	IRV	SA		24	E5
SARATOGA AV	CO	LB		29C	E3
SARATOGA AV	CYP	CYP	5000	14	D1
SARATOGA AV	PLA	PLA	100	7	F5
SARATOGA DR	LALM	LALM	11000	14	C2
SARATOGA DR	TUS	TUS		24	B3
SARATOGA LN	HTB	HB	16300	20	E4
SARATOGA ST	ANA	AN08		40	A6
SARATOGA ST	CYP	CYP	10400	14	E1
SARATOGA ST	OR	OR	1800	13	C6
SARATOGA ST	YL	YL	5400	7	E4
SARATOGA WY	CM	CM		27	E6
SARATOGA WY	PLA	PLA		7	F5
SARCO ST	CYP	CYP	11700	15	A3
SARCO ST	GGR	GG	11800	15	A3
SARDINA	CO	LB77		36	A5
SARDINIA	HTB	HB		26	D4
SARDIUS	BREA	BREA	100	4	B5
SARENA	IRV	SA		32A	B2
SARITA DR	CO	LB	25400	29C	F2
SARITA PL	OR	OR	1200	13	B6
SARITA PL	OR	OR		18	B1
SARMENTOSO	SCL	SC72		38	F4
SARONNA	IRV	SA14		29	A4
SAROS	IRV	SA		32A	A2
SARRACENIA	CO	SJ		56	D6
SARU CIR	HTB	HB47	8400	21	D5
SATELLITE DR	LALM	LALM	12400	14	E4
SATINWOOD CIR	WSTM	WSTM	8300	21	D2
SATINWOOD WY	IRV	SA	4300	29	A5
SATTERFIELD DR	HTB	HB	8800	30	E1
SATURN DR	BPK	BP	8300	10	C3
SATURN DR	HTB	HB47		21	B5
SATURN RD	ANA	AN		16	D2
SATURN ST	BREA	BREA		3	C6
SATURN ST	BREA	BREA		7	C1

INDEX

1990 ORANGE COUNTY STREET INDEX

STREET	CITY	P.O. ZONE	BLOCK	PAGE	GRID
SATURNA DR	CO	SJ91		29A	F6
SAUCO	MVJO	SJ92	24700	29B	E6
SAUGUS AV	CO	SA	18500	18	A6
SAUSALITO	IRV	SA		24	C6
SAUSALITO CIR	LAP	BP23	5000	9	D3
SAUSALITO DR	NB	CDLM	3600	33	C1
SAUSALITO LN	HTB	HB	19000	26	D4
SAUSALITO ST	CO	LB	24800	29C	F2
SAUSALITO ST	LALM	LALM	3200	14	B1
SAVAII ST	CYP	CYP	11500	14	F2
SAVANNA ST	ANA	AN	3500	10	A5
SAVANNAH	IRV	SA		24	E5
SAVANNA	TUS	TUS		24	C4
SAVANNAH AV	PLA	PLA		7	C3
SAVERNE CIR	IRV	SA	15300	29	C3
SAVIN AV	IRV	SA	14600	24	C6
SAVIN AV	IRV	SA	14600	29	C1
SAVI RANCH PKY	ANA	AN07		8	F5
SAVI RANCH PKWY	YL	YL		40	A5
SAVONA	CO	LB		29A	B4
SAVONA PL	CO	LB	23000	35	C5
SAVOY AV	ANA	AN	1800	11	F4
SAVOY CIR	BPK	BP	6400	5	B6
SAVOY CIR	HTB	HB47	8700	21	E5
SAVOY PL	ANA	AN	2700	10	D5
SAWGRASS LN	HTB	HB48		25	E3
SAWLEAF AV	IRV	SA	14500	24	B6
SAWMILL	CO	SJ79		59	D4
SAWMILL LN	CO	ET		29A	F2
SAWSTON CIR	WSTM	WSTM	14100	20	E1
SAXON WY	CO	ET		29B	A1
SAYBROOK CT	CM	CM		27	D6
SAYBROOK CT	CM	CM27		31	D1
SAYBROOK LN	CM	CM		27	D6
SAYBROOK LN	CM	CM27		31	D1
SAYBROOK LN	HTB	HB	16200	20	C5
SAYBROOK LN	TUS	TUS	1700	24	B3
SAYLOR TER	CO	SA	10300	18	B4
SCALES WY	BPK	BP	7100	5	B6
SCANDIA ST	CYP	CYP	11700	15	A3
SCANDIA ST	GGR	GG	11800	15	A4
SCANLAN CT	FTNV	SA08		26	F1
SCARBOROUGH LN	ANA	AN	1400	10	F6
SCENARIO DR	HTB	HB	4500	20	D4
SCENIC AV	CM	CM		27	C1
SCENIC CIR	ANA	AN		13	F3
SCENIC CIR	ANA	AN		43	A3
SCENIC DR	DPT	DPT		37	D5
SCENIC DR	LAG	LB	31500	35	B6
SCENIC WY	BREA	BREA		2	E5
SCENIC BAY DR	HTB	HB		26	A4
SCENIC CYN TER	CO	SJ79		52	F4
SCENIC VIEW DR	YL	YL	5500	8	A4
SCEPTOR ST	SA	SA		28	B1
SCEPTRE LN	HTB	HB	17200	20	C6
SCHENLEY BAY	CM	CM		27	E4
SCHERER PL	TUS	TUS	1200	23	F4
SCHMIDT DR	CO	SIL	31200	53	A1
SCHOLZ PZ	NB	NB		31	B4
SCHOOL LN	TUS	TUS	14700	23	E4
SCHOOL ST	YL	YL	4600	8	A3
SCHOOLWOOD DR	LAH	LAH		1	F6
SCHOOLWOOD DR	LAH	LAH		5	F1
SCHOONER AV	GGR	GG43	10500	22	A2
SCHOONER AV	WSTM	WSTM	10400	22	A2
SCHOONER LN	ANA	AN		11	A2
SCHOONER LN	HTB	HB	20900	26	C6
SCHOONER RD	NB	NB60		31	E6
SCHOONER WY	SB	SB	100	19	E2
SCHOONER COVE	CO	LB		35	D2
SCHRANDT DR	GGR	GG	11400	16	B3
SCHRYER LN	HTB	HB	16000	20	E4
SCHUBERT CIR	BPK	BP	6300	5	D6
SCHUBERT CT	IRV	SA17		32	E2
SCHUG ST	OR	OR	400	18	A4
SCIOTO RD	SB	SB	1200	19	C5
SCONE DR	HTB	HB	8300	30	D1
SCOTCH CIR	PLA	PLA	1300	7	C4
SCOTCH PINE ST	FTNV	SA08	16300	21	E4
SCOTIA CIR	HTB	HB	17900	26	A1
SCOTSDALE CIR	HTB	HB47	16700	21	D5
SCOTS GLEN	CO	ET		52	B6
SCOTSTOUN DR	HTB	HB	9500	26	F6
SCOTT	CO	SA05		18	B5
SCOTT CIR	CYP	CYP	6800	15	A1
SCOTT CIR	LAP	BP23	5000	9	D2
SCOTT DR	NB	NB60	19400	28	B5
SCOTT LN	ANA	AN	600	10	D5
SCOTT LN	CO	ET	24700	29A	E2
SCOTT PL	CM	CM27	900	31	B2
SCOTT WY	BPK	BP	6000	9	F2

STREET	CITY	P.O. ZONE	BLOCK	PAGE	GRID
SCOTTSDALE CIR	STN	STN		15	B4
SCOTTSDALE DR	IRV	SA	3600	24	C6
SCOTTYS COVE DR	DPT	DPT		38	D3
SCOUGALL CIR	HTB	HB	9100	26	E5
SCOUT TR	ANA	AN		13	C3
SCRIBE DR	HTB	HB		26	D4
SCRIPPS CIR	ANA	AN		13	F3
SCRIPPS CIR	ANA	AN		43	A3
SCRIPPS WY	STN	STN		10	E4
SCRIPPS WY	STN	STN		15	B3
SCRIPPS AISLE	IRV	SA15		32	F1
SCULPIN DR	HTB	HB47	16900	21	A5
SEA CIR	HTB	HB		26	D5
SEA LN	NB	CDLM	900	32	B6
SEA ST	CO	LB77		36	A4
SEA TER	DPT	DPT		37	E2
SEA WY	SB	SUNB	15600	20	A4
SEA AIRE	DPT	DPT		37	F3
SEA BELL CIR	NB	CDLM		32	D6
SEABIRD CIR	HTB	HB	8200	26	D6
SEABIRD CT	NB	NB27		31	A2
SEA BIRD WY	CO	LB		35	D3
SEABIRD WY	DPT	DPT		37	A5
SEA BLUFF DR	CM	CM27	300	31	A1
SEABLUFF DR	HTB	HB		26	B4
SEA BLUFF LN	LAG	LB	31600	35	B6
SEABOARD CIR	GGR	GG		16	C6
SEABOARD CIR	STN	STN		15	B2
SEABOARD CT	ANA	AN		8	B6
SEABOROUGH	NB	NB		32	C3
SEA BREEZE	SA	SA04		27	F2
SEA BREEZE CT	SJC	SJ75		38	A3
SEA BREEZE DR	CM	CM	1000	27	A6
SEABREEZE DR	HTB	HB		30	C1
SEABREEZE LN	NB	CDLM	3500	33	C1
SEA BREEZE LN	SCL	SC72		39	A2
SEA BREEZE LN	SB	SB	600	19	F2
SEA BREEZE WY	HTB	HB	16500	20	E5
SEABRIDGE LN	HTB	HB		26	C5
SEABRIDGE RD	CO	LB77		35	F5
SEA BRIGHT DR	DPT	DPT	33100	37	F3
SEABRIGHT LN	HTB	HB46		26	D5
SEABROOK DR	DPT	DPT		37	E2
SEABROOK LN	HTB	HB48		25	E2
SEABROOK WY	CYP	CYP	6700	15	A2
SEABROOK COVE	NB	NB		31	F5
SEABROOK COVE	NB	NB		32	A5
SEACALL WY	DPT	DPT		37	E4
SEA CANYON CIR	HTB	HB		26	A4
SEA CLIFF	CO	LB		29A	C4
SEACLIFF	CO	SJ79		59	C6
SEA CLIFF	SA	SA04		27	E2
SEACLIFF DR	LAG	LB	31600	35	B6
SEACLIFF DR	LAG	LB77		37	A1
SEA CLIFF LN	HTB	HB		26	B4
SEACOAST CIR	HTB	HB		26	C6
SEACOVE DR	LAG	LB	31600	35	A6
SEA COVE DR	DPT	DPT	24900	37	F3
SEACOVE DR	HTB	HB	9900	30	F4
SEACOVE DR	LAG	LB77		37	A1
SEA COVE LN	CM	CM27		31	A1
SEA COVE LN	NB	NB		31	F5
SEA COVE LN	NB	NB		32	A5
SEACREST CIR	GGR	GG	11500	15	F2
SEA CREST DR	DPT	DPT		37	F4
SEACREST DR	GGR	GG	11600	15	F3
SEACREST DR	NB	CDLM		32	C6
SEACREST DR	NB	CDLM		33	C1
SEACREST LN	HTB	HB	21800	30	F2
SEADRIFT	IRV	SA		29	C5
SEADRIFT DR	NB	CDLM	1800	32	A6
SEAFARE	CO	LB77		36	A4
SEAFARING DR	NB	CDLM		32	E5
SEAFORD CIR	IRV	SA	6000	29	D2
SEAFORTH LN	HTB	HB	21300	30	D1
SEAGATE	IRV	SA		29	C5
SEAGATE DR	DPT	DPT		37	F3
SEAGLEN	CO	LB77		36	A4
SEAGLEN DR	HTB	HB		26	A6
SEAGLEN DR	HTB	HB		30	C1
SEA GULL CT	DPT	DPT		37	E3
SEAGULL LN	CO	LB53		29A	B6
SEAGULL LN	HTB	HB		26	B4
SEA GULL LN	NB	NB	800	31	E4
SEA HARBOUR DR	HTB	HB	4400	20	D5
SEAHORSE LN	HTB	HB		26	C4
SEA HORSE COVE	CO	LB		35	D3
SEAHURST DR	HTB	HB		26	E3
SEA ISLAND DR	DPT	LB77	32400	37	C1
SEA ISLAND DR	NB	NB		32	B3
SEA ISLE	CO	LB		29A	C4

STREET	CITY	P.O. ZONE	BLOCK	PAGE	GRID
SEA KNOLL DR	DPT	DPT	33100	37	F3
SEALARGO LN	HTB	HB46		26	A2
SEAL CIR	HTB	HB		26	B4
SEAL ST	CM	CM27	600	31	C2
SEAL WY	SB	SB	200	19	E3
SEAL BEACH BLVD	SB	SB	12000	14	B5
SEAL BEACH BLVD	SB	SB		19	F3
SEAL BEACH BLVD	SB	SB		20	A1
SEA LION DR	DPT	DPT	33100	37	F3
SEAL ROCK DR	HTB	HB		26	D5
SEAMIST CIR	NB	NB		31	A3
SEA MIST LN	HTB	HB	20800	26	E6
SEA MIST WY	DPT	DPT		37	A5
SEAN DR	CO	LB77		35	D1
SEAN WY	WSTM	WSTM	9400	21	F4
SEAPINE CIR	HTB	HB		20	D6
SEA PINE LN	NB	NB		32	B4
SEA POINT DR	DPT	DPT		37	F3
SEAPOINT ST	HTB	HB		25	F3
SEAPORT	CO	LB77		36	A4
SEAPORT CIR	HTB	HB46		26	A2
SEAPORT DR	HTB	HB		26	D5
SEARIDGE	CO	LB77		35	F6
SEARIDGE	CO	LB77		36	A6
SEARIDGE	CO	LB77		37	F1
SEARIDGE	CO	LB77		38	A1
SEARIDGE CIR	HTB	HB	4800	20	D6
SEAROSE CT	DPT	DPT	25200	37	F3
SEASAND	CO	LB77		36	A4
SEASCAPE	CO	LB77		36	A4
SEASCAPE CIR	DPT	SC24		39	A1
SEASCAPE DR	HTB	HB		20	C4
SEASCAPE DR	NB	NB		31	B4
SEA SHADOWS WY	CO	LB77		35	C6
SEA SHARK CIR	HTB	HB		26	B4
SEASHELL CIR	HTB	HB		26	D5
SEA SHELL WY	DPT	DPT		37	A5
SEASHORE CIR	HTB	HB		26	B4
SEASHORE DR	NB	NB63	7000	30	F4
SEASHORE DR	NB	NB	700	31	B5
SEASIDE CT	NB	NB		31	A4
SEASIDE DR	DPT	DPT		38	D3
SEASIDE LN	HTB	HB	21600	30	F2
SEASPRAY E	CO	LB77		36	A4
SEASPRAY N	CO	LB77		36	A4
SEASPRAY S	CO	LB77		36	A4
SEASPRAY DR	HTB	HB		26	D3
SEASPRAY LN	CO	LB77		36	A4
SEASPRING DR	HTB	HB		26	C3
SEASPRITE CIR	HTB	HB	21300	30	F4
SEASTAR	HTB	HB		26	B3
SEASTAR CT	DPT	DPT		37	E2
SEA TERRACE LN	CM	CM27		31	A2
SEAVIEW	CO	LB		29A	C4
SEAVIEW	HTB	HB		20	D5
SEAVIEW AV	NB	CDLM	2500	33	B2
SEAVIEW CIR	PLA	PLA	900	12	A1
SEAVIEW DR	DPT	SC24		38	D6
SEAVIEW DR	DPT	SC24		39	A1
SEAVIEW DR	FUL	FL33		5	E2
SEAVIEW LN	CM	CM26		28	A3
SEA VIEW LN	SB	SB	13100	14	A5
SEAVIEW ST	LAG	LB77	31800	37	A1
SEAVIEW ST	LAG	LB51	400	34	E3
SEA VISTA DR	DPT	DPT	25000	37	F3
SEA VISTA DR	NB	NB		31	F5
SEA VISTA DR	NB	NB		32	A5
SEAVISTA LN	HTB	HB46		26	C4
SEAWALL CIR	HTB	HB		30	C1
SEAWARD RD	NB	CDLM	300	33	B2
SEAWARD ISLE	DPT	LB77	33900	37	D4
SEAWATCH	DPT	DPT		37	F3
SEAWATER DR	HTB	HB46		26	A2
SEAWAY CIR	HTB	HB		26	A4
SEAWAY DR	CO	LB		35	C6
SEAWAY DR	CO	LB77		37	C1
SEAWIND	IRV	SA14		29	B4
SEAWIND CIR	HTB	HB		26	B4
SEAWIND CT	DPT	DPT		37	A5
SEAWIND DR	CO	CM27		27	F6
SEAWIND DR	CO	CM27		31	F1
SEAWITCH LN	HTB	HB	16600	20	C5
SEAWOOD CT	FUL	FL		7	A1
SEAWORTHY DR	HTB	HB		26	B4
SEBA AV	OR	OR	1700	17	E4
SEBASTIAN LN	MVJO	SJ91		29B	C6
SEBASTIAN LN	MVJO	SJ91		29D	C1
SECLUSION WY	CO	SA	18700	18	A6
SECOYA WY	CO	SJ		59	D2
SECREST WY	SA	SA	1500	22	F5

STREET	CITY	P.O. ZONE	BLOCK	PAGE	GRID
SECRETARIAT CIR	CM	CM	900	27	E2
SEDA	MVJO	SJ91	27700	29B	D1
SEDGEWICK CIR	CO	LB		35	D2
SEGADA	CO	SJ88		59	A4
SEGERSTROM AV	SA	SA	1300	22	F6
SEGERSTROM AV	SA	SA	700	23	A6
SEGERSTROM AV	SA	SA		28	A1
SEGO ST	IRV	SA	3500	29	B1
SEGOVIA	IRV	SA	18700	32	F1
SEGOVIA	SCL	SC72		39	E1
SEGOVIA CIR	HTB	HB	6500	26	A1
SEGOVIA CIR	MVJO	SJ91		29B	C6
SEGOVIA CIR	PLA	PL70		12	B1
SEGOVIA LN	YL	YL	19600	8	C3
SEGURA	IRV	SA		28	F5
SEINE CIR	IRV	SA	15300	29	D3
SEINE CIR	MVJO	SJ92		29D	E3
SEINE DR	HTB	HB47	7500	21	C5
SEINE RIVER AV	FTNV	SA08	8800	26	D2
SELKIRK CT	CYP	CYP	4000	9	C4
SELKIRK DR	HTB	HB		25	E1
SELL CIR	HTB	HB	16500	20	D5
SELVA RD	DPT	LB77		37	D4
SELVA RD	DPT	DPT	24300	37	E4
SEMBRADO	CO	SJ88		59	A4
SEMINOLE	TUS	TUS		24	B3
SEMINOLE AV	PLA	PLA	400	7	C1
SEMINOLE PL	CO	LB		35	D5
SEMINOLE WY	YL	YL	17600	7	F5
SENATE ST	CM	CM27	600	31	B1
SENDA D L PLAYA	SCL	SC72		39	B3
SENDERO	CO	SJ88		59	A5
SENECA CIR	ANA	AN		11	C4
SENECA CT	BREA	BREA		3	B5
SENECA DR	WSTM	WSTM	13000	15	A5
SENECA ST	PLA	PLA	600	7	C2
SENISA WY	IRV	SA	4300	29	A5
SENNIT AV	GGR	GG43	10500	22	A3
SENTINEL DR	CO	SJ79		56	E6
SENTRY DR	STN	STN	10300	10	C6
SENTRY HILL	CO	LB77		35	E6
SEPULVEDA	CO	SJ88		59	A4
SEPULVEDA AV	DPT	SC24	34000	38	B4
SEQUERO	CO	SJ88		29B	F4
SEQUOIA AV	ANA	AN	2200	10	E3
SEQUOIA AV	BREA	BREA	300	2	D6
SEQUOIA AV	CYP	CYP	5000	9	D5
SEQUOIA AV	FUL	FL	2800	6	E2
SEQUOIA AV	OR	OR	1800	17	B2
SEQUOIA AV	PLA	PLA	1500	7	E4
SEQUOIA CIR	YL	YL	4500	7	F3
SEQUOIA DR	BPK	BP	6500	10	A6
SEQUOIA DR	WSTM	WSTM	6700	15	A5
SEQUOIA LN	MVJO	SJ91		52	D5
SEQUOIA ST	FTNV	SA08	16500	21	F5
SEQUOIA ST	IRV	SA	3500	29	C1
SEQUOIA WY	SA	SA		22	D2
SEQUOIA TREE LN	IRV	SA		29	A5
SEQUOIAWOOD WY	CO	ET		29A	F1
SEQUOIAWOOD WY	CO	ET		51	F6
SERANADO ST	OR	OR	100	18	A3
SERANG PL	CM	CM	2800	27	C4
SERENA	MVJO	SJ92		29D	F3
SERENA CT	CO	SJ91		29A	E6
SERENA CT	NB	NB		31	B4
SERENADE LN	HTB	HB47	16200	21	B4
SERENADE TER	NB	CDLM	1400	32	A6
SERENATA DR	MVJO	SJ91	25800	29D	B2
SERENE DR	HTB	HB	5700	20	E6
SERENE DR	HTB	HB	5500	25	E1
SERENITY LN	CO	LB77		36	A4
SERENO	MVJO	SJ91	27400	29B	D2
SERENO	TUS	TUS		23	D3
SERENO PL	ANA	AN	2600	10	D4
SERGIO CIR	HTB	HB47		21	C6
SERGIO CIR	HTB	HB47		26	C1
SERIANA	CO	LB77		35	C3
SERNA	CO	SJ88		59	A4
SERON AV	IRV	SA	14400	24	B6
SERPENTINE DR	LALM	LALM	3500	14	B1
SERRA DR	NB	CDLM	400	33	C2
SERRA LN	TUS	TUS		23	E3
SERRA WY	CM	CM	900	27	E4
SERRANO AV	ANA	AN		13	F4
SERRANO AV	ANA	ANA		43	A1
SERRANO AV	ANA	AN		43	A2
SERRANO AV	NB	CDLM	2100	33	A1
SERRANO AV	OR	OR	19400	13	C5
SERRANO AV E	VPK	OR67	17600	12	F5
SERRANO AV E	VPK	OR67	18200	13	A5
SERRANO CT	CO	ET		52	A6

STREET	CITY	P.O. ZONE	BLOCK	PAGE	GRID
SERRANO PL	FUL	FL33	2100	5	F3
SERRANO RD	CO	ET		29A	E1
SERRANO RD	CO	ET		29B	A2
SERRANO CK RD	CO	ET		52	A5
SERRA VISTA	CO	ET		51	F6
SERRENTE PZ	YL	YL		8	C3
SERVICE RD	TUS	TUS		23	E4
SESAME ST	CO	ET		29A	F4
SETENIL	MVJO	SJ92		29D	D4
SETH CIR	DPT	DPT	24500	37	E2
SETON RD	IRV	SA	10	28	F5
SETON RD	IRV	SA	10	29	A5
SETTING SUN DR	NB	CDLM	3000	32	B6
SETTLER CT	ANA	AN		13	C3
SEVEN SEAS DR	DPT	LB77	32400	37	C2
SEVEN SEAS LN	HTB	HB	20400	26	C5
SEVERYNS	TUS	SA10		23	F6
SEVILLA CIR	HTB	HB47	15000	21	A2
SEVILLE	IRV	SA		24	E4
SEVILLE	TUS	TUS		24	A4
SEVILLE	WSTM	WSTM		21	E2
SEVILLE AV	ANA	AN	2300	12	A3
SEVILLE AV	NB	CDLM	400	33	A1
SEVILLE AV	NB	NB	2100	33	C5
SEVILLE CIR	LAP	BP23	5300	9	E1
SEVILLE CT	GGR	GG		16	A4
SEVILLE LN	CM	CM27	300	31	F2
SEVILLE LN	DPT	DPT	33800	37	E4
SEVILLE PL	FUL	FL33	800	5	E4
SEVILLE ST	PLA	PLA	1500	7	C3
SEXTANT DR	DPT	LB77		37	E3
SHACKLEFORD CIR	HTB	HB	21000	26	F6
SHACKLEFORD LN	GGR	GG	12900	15	E5
SHACKLETN AISLE	IRV			29	F2
SHACKLETON ISLE	DPT	LB77	33300	37	D4
SHADBURN AV	CO	PLA	16300	7	D3
SHADBUSH ST	FTNV	SA08	16400	21	F4
SHADDUCK	IRV	SA		24	C5
SHADEL DR	CO	SA	18100	17	F6
SHADEL DR	TUS	TUS	17700	17	F6
SHADETREE CIR	BREA	BREA		3	B5
SHADETREE LN	ANA	AN		10	D2
SHADE TREE LN	CO	ET		29A	F2
SHADE TREE LN	FUL	FL		6	D3
SHADE TREE LN	SJC	SJ75		36	E5
SHADOW LN	ANA	AN	2600	10	D3
SHADOW LN	FTNV	SA08		26	D1
SHADOW LN	FUL	FL	1300	6	C4
SHADOW LN	LAG	LB51	400	34	E4
SHADOW LN	STN	STN	8100	15	C3
SHADOWBROOK CIR	HTB	HB48		25	E3
SHADOW CYN RD	BREA	BREA		2	F4
SHADOWFAX DR	CO	ET		29A	E3
SHADOWGROVE LN	CO	ET		29A	D2
SHADOWGROVE ST	BREA	BREA		2	D4
SHADOW HILL DR	CO	YL	19300	8	C4
SHADOW HILL LN	CO	LB		29C	D2
SHADOW LAKE	SA	SA		17	D5
SHADOW LAKE DR	BREA	BREA		2	C5
SHADOWLAND CIR	CO	OR67		50	D6
SHADOWLEAF	IRV	SA		29	C5
SHADOW OAK DR	CO	SJ		52	E3
SHADOW OAK DR	YL	YL		8	E2
SHADOW PINES RD	OR	OR69		18	E3
SHADOW RIDGE	MVJO	SJ92		29B	F2
SHADOW RIDGE LN	OR	OR		12	F4
SHADOW RIDGE LN	YL	YL		8	B2
SHADOW ROCK LN	CO	TRA		56	E6
SHADWELL	IRV	SA		24	C5
SHADWELL DR	HTB	HB46		26	E6
SHADY CT	BREA	BREA	300	2	F5
SHADY DR	CM	CM27	400	31	D3
SHADY LN	CO	SJ	31000	56	C5
SHADY LN	GGR	GG	13900	16	D6
SHADY LN	LAG	LB56	28700	35	A2
SHADY LN	PLA	PLA	600	7	C3
SHADY PL	LAG	LB51	28700	35	A2
SHADYACRE ST	GGR	GG	12000	16	A3
SHADY BROOK DR	CO	SIL	29100	50	F2
SHADY BROOK DR	FUL	FL		6	D4
SHADYBROOK DR	TUS	TUS	14100	24	A4
SHADYBROOK RD	SJC	SJ75		36	B3
SHADY CANYON LN	CO	SIL		50	E2
SHADY CANYON RD	CO	SA		18	E5
SHADY CREEK LN	YL	YL		40	E6
SHADYCREST LN	CO	LAH	11800	2	C3
SHADY FOREST LN	OR	OR	2500	12	F4
SHADY GATE LN	YL	YL	6500	8	F2
SHADY GLEN LN	ANA	AN	18700	13	B2
SHADY GLEN LN	OR	OR	2000	12	E3
SHADY GLEN PL	YL	YL		8	C4

Z — COPYRIGHT, © 1989 BY Thomas Bros Maps

125

1990 ORANGE COUNTY STREET INDEX

SHADY GROVE CIR — SIMPSON CIR

ORANGE CO.

STREET	CITY	P.O. ZONE	BLOCK	PAGE	GRID
SHADY GROVE CIR	CO	ET	22600	29A	E3
SHADY HARBR CIR	HTB	HB48		26	B3
SHADY HOLLW CIR	CO	ET	25000	29A	B2
SHADY KNOLL	YL	YL		8	A4
SHADY KNOLL CT	CO	SJ79		56	A3
SHADY LAWN DR	YL	YL	6400	8	F2
SHADY MEADOW LN	YL	YL		40	D5
SHADY OAK WY	ANA	AN		12	F3
SHADYRIDGE DR	CO	SA	10600	18	D4
SHADY RIDGE LN	CO	SJ79		52	E3
SHADY RIM CIR	CO	ET		29A	F2
SHADY ROCK CT	GGR	GG43		16	D6
SHADYSIDE	CO	TRA		59	D5
SHADY TREE CIR	CO	LB	23800	35	E3
SHADYVALE LN	BREA	BREA		3	A5
SHADYVALE LN	CO	ET		29A	E2
SHADY VALLEY LN	ANA	AN		13	E3
SHADY VALLEY LN	LAH	LAH	2500	1	D3
SHADYWOOD	CO	LB		35	F3
SHADYWOOD	CO	LB77		36	A3
SHADYWOOD	CO	ET		51	F5
SHAFFER CIR	HTB	HB	7500	26	C3
SHAFFER ST	OR	OR	1400	12	D5
SHAFFER ST N&S	OR	OR	100	17	D4
SHAKESPEARE DR	CO	LALM	2700	14	A2
SHAKESPEARE PL	SA	SA		28	C1
SHAKESPEARE ST	ANA	AN	100	12	A3
SHALANWOOD LN N	PLA	PLA	1400	7	D3
SHALIMAR DR	CM	CM27	600	31	C3
SHALLOP	CO	LB77		37	E1
SHALLW BROOK LN	OR	OR		12	F4
SHALLW BROOK LN	OR	OR		13	A4
SHALOM DR	HTB	HB46	10400	27	A4
SHAMLEY CIR	HTB	HB		25	F1
SHAMROCK AV	BREA	BREA		3	C5
SHAMROCK AV	FTNV	SA08	9500	21	F4
SHAMROCK CIR	HTB	HB	8400	26	D2
SHAMROCK LN	CM	CM28	1400	27	D3
SHAMROCK LN	SJC	SJ75		38	C4
SHAMROCK LN	YL	YL		8	B4
SHAMROCK RD	LAG	LB	700	34	B1
SHAMROCK ST	PLA	PLA	1000	12	A1
SHAMROCK GLEN	CO	ET		52	A5
SHANE DR	CO	ET	26500	29B	B2
SHANE WY	YL	YL	17500	7	E5
SHANGRI LA DR	HTB	HB46	10300	27	A4
SHANNON AV	GGR	GG	9200	15	E3
SHANNON CIR	CO	ET		29A	D3
SHANNON DR	HTB	HB47	6700	21	B4
SHANNON DR	YL	YL		7	F4
SHANNON LN	CM	CM	1300	27	D3
SHANNON LN	SJC	SJ75		38	D4
SHANNON ST	ANA	AN		13	A3
SHANNON ST	SA	SA	100	22	C3
SHANNON ST	SA	SA04		27	C1
SHANNON RIV CIR	FTNV	SA08	8600	26	D2
SHANNY AV	DPT	LB77		37	D4
SHANTAR DR	CM	CM	2800	27	B4
SHAPELL ST	GGR	GG	13200	15	E5
SHARK DR	HTB	HB		20	E5
SHARMILA	CO	ET		52	A6
SHARON CIR	ANA	AN	1200	10	D6
SHARON CIR	PLA	PLA		7	D4
SHARON CIR	YL	YL	18200	7	F2
SHARON DR	LAP	BP23	4500	9	D2
SHARON LN	CM	CM	3100	27	D3
SHARON LN	CO	SA		18	D6
SHARON LN	HTB	HB		26	C2
SHARON RD	SA	SA	1300	16	F5
SHARON RD	SA	SA	900	17	A5
SHARON WY	CO	LAH	9000	1	D3
SHARON LYNN RD	VPK	OR67	18300	13	A6
SHARPLESS ST	CO	LAH	1100	1	D3
SHARPLESS ST	LAH	LAH	1300	1	D3
SHARPSBURG	IRV	SA		24	E6
SHASTA	IRV	SA		29	A6
SHASTA AV	LALM	LALM	3900	9	B6
SHASTA CIR	CYP	CYP	4500	9	C4
SHASTA CIR	LAP	BP23	5700	9	E2
SHASTA CIR	WSTM	WSTM	13300	15	B5
SHASTA LN	CM	CM26		28	A3
SHASTA LN	HTB	HB47	15200	21	C3
SHASTA ST	ANA	AN	200	13	A1
SHASTA ST	FTNV	SA08	16000	22	C4
SHASTA ST N	OR	OR	200	17	F3
SHASTA ST S	OR	OR	100	17	F3
SHASTA WY	CO	SA	12600	17	F5
SHASTA WY	CO	SA	12600	18	A4
SHASTA WY	CO	TUS	14200	23	F1
SHASTA WY	PLA	PLA	1500	7	C3
SHASTA WY	TUS	TUS	800	23	F1

STREET	CITY	P.O. ZONE	BLOCK	PAGE	GRID
SHASTA WY S	OR	OR	500	17	F4
SHASTA LAKE RD	CO	ET		29A	E1
SHATTUCK PL N	OR	OR	1800	12	E5
SHATTUCK PL N	OR	OR	100	17	E3
SHATTUCK PL S	OR	OR	200	17	E3
SHATTUCK ST	OR	OR	1800	17	E1
SHAVER WY	PLA	PLA	1400	7	C3
SHAVER LAKE CIR	CO	ET		29A	F1
SHAW CIR	PLA	PLA	1700	7	C3
SHAW LN	HTB	HB	21000	30	E1
SHAW LN	YL	YL	4800	7	F3
SHAWN LN	FUL	FL	2700	7	A3
SHAWNEE DR	CO	ET		29A	F2
SHAWNEE DR	SA	SA	500	22	D4
SHAWNEE LN	SB	SB	13100	14	A5
SHAWNEE RD	WSTM	WSTM	6000	14	F5
SHAWNEE RD	WSTM	WSTM	6200	15	A5
SHAY DEL PL	YL	YL	6100	7	F5
SHAYNE DR	HTB	HB47	6200	21	A5
SHEARER LN	GGR	GG		16	D6
SHEARWATER	IRV	SA		29	C4
SHEARWATER PL	NB	SA07		28	B6
SHEARWATER PL	NB	SA07		32	B1
SHEFFIELD	MVJO	SJ92		29B	D6
SHEFFIELD	MVJO	SJ92		29D	D1
SHEFFIELD DR	LAH	LAH	1500	1	E5
SHEFFIELD LN	HTB	HB	19900	26	F4
SHEFFIELD PL	FUL	FL	2800	7	B2
SHEFFIELD ST	ANA	AN	1700	7	C6
SHEFFIELD ST	PLA	PLA	1100	7	B4
SHEFFIELD ST	SA	SA	900	22	B1
SHEFFIELD ST	WSTM	WSTM	14500	21	F1
SHELBURNE ST	LAH	LAH	900	2	B3
SHELBY	IRV	SA		24	D6
SHELL CIR	HTB	HB		26	C6
SHELL CIR	WSTM	WSTM	9400	21	E2
SHELL DR	DPT	DPT		38	D3
SHELL DR	SCL	SC72		39	A2
SHELL ST	NB	CDLM	2600	33	A1
SHELL COVE	CO	LB		35	D2
SHELLEY CIR S	CM	CM		27	C6
SHELLEY DR	GGR	GG	10200	16	A4
SHELLEY RD	CO	LB		29C	D6
SHELLEY ST	PLA	PLA	2100	7	C2
SHELLEY ST	SA	SA	500	22	E4
SHELLFISH LN	HTB	HB		26	C6
SHELL HARBR CIR	HTB	HB	20800	26	E6
SHELLI DR	ANA	AN	1200	10	D6
SHELLMAKER RD	NB	NB		31	F5
SHELLY CT	OR	OR68		17	B2
SHELLY DR	GGR	GG	9000	15	E2
SHELLY DR	HTB	HB47	6000	21	A3
SHELLY LN	CO	SA		18	C4
SHELTER LN	HTB	HB	20200	26	E5
SHELTER COVE	NB	NB60		31	E6
SHELTERWOOD RD	CO	SA	2200	24	C2
SHELTON ST N&S	SA	SA	100	23	A4
SHENANDOAH	IRV	SA		24	E4
SHENANDOAH AV	OR	OR	5800	13	C5
SHENANDOAH DR	CO	ET	21800	29B	B1
SHENANDOAH DR	CO	LB	27000	29C	F4
SHENANDOAH ST	FTNV	SA08	18000	27	A2
SHENANDOAH ST	PLA	PLA	1400	7	C3
SHENLYN DR	HTB	HB47	6500	21	A6
SHEPARD CIR	PLA	PLA	1500	7	B3
SHEPARD ST	ANA	AN	900	12	C2
SHEPARD WY	CO	SA	11300	18	C5
SHEPHERD LN	HTB	HB	21000	30	D1
SHEPPARD CIR	GGR	GG		15	D5
SHEPPARD DR	FUL	FL	1100	6	D4
SHER LN	HTB	HB47	16000	21	C4
SHERBECK LN	HTB	HB47	15800	21	B4
SHERBORNE LN	HTB	HB	19200	26	C4
SHERBROOK DR	CO	TUS	17500	23	F1
SHEREE LN	PLA	PLA	500	7	B4
SHERI ST	OR	OR	3800	12	D3
SHERIDAN	IRV	SA		24	E6
SHERIDAN DR	CO	LB77		36	A1
SHERIDAN LN	GGR	GG	12000	15	F3
SHERIDAN RD	FUL	FL33	2100	5	D4
SHERIDAN WY	BPK	BP	600	9	F1
SHERIFF RD	CO	LB	25800	29D	A2
SHERINGHAM AV	OR	OR68	3700	16	F3
SHERINGTON CT	CYP	CYP	4500	9	D5
SHERINGTON PL	NB	NB	1600	31	D4
SHERLOCK	HTB	HB		20	C3
SHERLOCK CIR	GGR	GG	9000	15	D3
SHERLOCK LN	GGR	GG	9100	15	E3
SHERMAN	IRV	SA		24	F6
SHERMAN AV	GGR	GG	10600	16	B5
SHERMAN AV	OR	OR	2700	17	F3

STREET	CITY	P.O. ZONE	BLOCK	PAGE	GRID
SHERMAN DR	HTB	HB	6000	20	F2
SHERMAN ST	ANA	AN	1200	11	F6
SHERMAN WY	BPK	BP	6300	9	F2
SHERMAN WY	STN	STN	11000	15	B2
SHERRILL ST	ANA	AN	600	10	D5
SHERRILL ST	STN	AN04	10100	10	D6
SHERRILL ST	STN	AN04	10500	15	D1
SHERRY CIR	HTB	HB	9100	26	E3
SHERRY LN	SA	SA	1700	17	D6
SHERRY LN	SA	SA	600	23	D1
SHERRYGLEN LN	LAH	LAH	800	1	F5
SHERRY LYNN DR	CO	SA		18	C4
SHERWIN LN	SA	SA	900	17	A4
SHERWOOD AV	ANA	AN	500	11	E4
SHERWOOD AV	FUL	FL	2600	7	A3
SHERWOOD AV	OR	OR	3900	18	A4
SHERWOOD AV	PLA	PLA	700	7	A3
SHERWOOD AV	SA	SA	100	28	B1
SHERWOOD CIR	VPK	OR67	10200	12	F6
SHERWOOD DR	YL	YL		8	D1
SHERWOOD LN	SA	SA	900	17	A4
SHERWOOD PL	CM	CM27	200	31	D2
SHERWOOD ST	CM	CM27	200	31	D2
SHERWOOD ST	WSTM	WSTM	13800	14	F6
SHERWOOD WY	DPT	DPT		37	F3
SHERWD VLLG CIR	PLA	PLA	1500	7	D3
SHETLAND CIR	HTB	HB		26	A2
SHETLAND DR	ANA	AN		10	C4
SHETLAND LN	CO	OR		18	C2
SHETLAND RD	GGR	GG	11700	16	C3
SHIELDS DR	ANA	AN	300	10	D5
SHIELDS DR	HTB	HB	6000	20	F5
SHIELDS DR	HTB	HB47	6200	21	A5
SHILOH	IRV	SA		24	E4
SHILOH PL	ANA	AN	700	8	D6
SHIMIZU RIV CIR	FTNV	SA08	9600	26	F3
SHINKLE CIR	HTB	HB	14500	20	F2
SHIPLEY ST	HTB	HB	1600	26	B5
SHIPPIGAN WY	CYP	CYP	11400	15	B2
SHIPSIDE DR	DPT	DPT		37	F2
SHIPSIDE DR	DPT	DPT		38	A2
SHIPWAY LN	NB	NB	1900	31	E3
SHIPYARD WY	NB	NB	200	31	A6
SHIRE CIR	HTB	HB		26	A2
SHIRL ST	CYP	CYP	5700	9	E5
SHIRLEEN CT	CO	LB77		35	D3
SHIRLEY DR	LAP	BP23	5000	9	D2
SHIRLEY DR	OR	OR	700	17	E1
SHIRLEY ST	ANA	AN		12	A6
SHIRLEY ST	GGR	GG	13800	16	B6
SHIRLEY ST	WSTM	WSTM	14000	21	D1
SHOAL CIR	HTB	HB	8900	26	D4
SHOAL DR	ANA	AN		11	A2
SHOAL DR	NB	CDLM		32	C6
SHOAL DR	NB	CDLM		33	C1
SHOOK LN	YL	YL	18200	8	A4
SHOOTING STAR	IRV	SA		29	C3
SHOOTNG STR CIR	WSTM	WSTM		15	B5
SHORE	MVJO	SJ92		52	E6
SHORE AV	NB	CDLM	2900	33	A2
SHORE CIR	HTB	HB	8900	26	E4
SHOREBIRD	HTB	HB		20	D5
SHOREBIRD	IRV	SA		29	C3
SHOREBREAK DR	HTB	HB		20	C4
SHOREBREEZE DR	HTB	HB		30	F2
SHORECLIFF LN	HTB	HB		26	A4
SHORECLIFF RD	NB	NB	4100	33	B2
SHORECREST DR	ANA	AN		13	F3
SHORECREST DR	ANA	AN		43	A3
SHORECREST LN	NB	CDLM	3800	33	B2
SHOREHAM LN	HTB	HB	17800	25	E1
SHORE LANTRN ST	DPT	DPT	34300	37	B5
SHORELINE	IRV	SA		29	B4
SHORELINE DR	DPT	LB77		37	D3
SHORELINE DR	HTB	HB		26	B3
SHOREVIEW CIR	HTB	HB	18000	26	A1
SHOREWOOD CIR	HTB	HB	20000	26	E5
SHORT ST	FUL	FL	100	6	B5
SHORT ST	LAG	LB51	600	34	E3
SHORT ST	NB	NB	3200	31	B5
SHORT ST	YL	YL	5700	8	A5
SHOSHONE AV	OR	OR		13	B6
SHOSHONE DR	CO	ET		29A	F2
SHOSHONE WY	BPK	BP	6700	10	A1
SHOSHONI AV	PLA	PLA	400	7	C1
SHREWSBURY AV	WSTM	WSTM	5300	20	E1
SHREWSBURY DR	LAG	LB	31500	35	B6
SHREWSBURY PL	SA	SA		23	B6
SHREWSBURY PL	SA	SA		28	B1
SHRIKE AV	FTNV	SA08	9200	26	E3

STREET	CITY	P.O. ZONE	BLOCK	PAGE	GRID
SHRIKE DR	CO	LB	28400	35	D1
SHRINER CIR	FTNV	SA08	9800	21	F6
SIBONEY ST	LALM	LALM	11000	14	D1
SICILY AV	CM	CM	3100	27	C3
SICOMORO RD	SJC	SJ75		38	B3
SIDCUP LN	HTB	HB	19900	26	F4
SIDNEY LN	CM	CM27		31	D1
SIDNEY PL	GGR	GG	10800	16	A3
SIDNEY BAY	DPT	DPT		37	D4
SIDON AV	LAH	LAH	2000	1	D5
SIEGA	CO	SJ88		59	A4
SIEMON ST	GGR	GG	13000	16	F5
SIEMON ST	SA	SA	2300	16	F5
SIENA AV	WSTM	WSTM	7100	21	B3
SIENNA LN	YL	YL	19700	8	C3
SIERKS ST	CM	CM27	200	31	D2
SIERRA AV	SA	SA	200	28	B1
SIERRA CIR	HTB	HB		26	D5
SIERRA CIR	LAP	BP23	7600	9	D2
SIERRA CIR	LALM	LALM		14	C1
SIERRA AV	SA	SA07	300	28	B1
SIERRA PL	ANA	AN	2000	10	F2
SIERRA ST	CO	ET	24000	29A	D3
SIERRA ST	FTNV	SA08	16100	22	C4
SIERRA ALTA DR	CO	SA	1500	24	B2
SIERRA ALTA DR	CO	TUS	1200	24	B2
SIERRA AMIGO RD	IRV	SA		32	F3
SIERRA BELLO RD	IRV	SA15	19000	32A	A3
SIERRA BOCA RD	IRV	SA		32	F3
SRA BONITA DR	CO	LB56		29C	C3
SRA BONITA DR	PLA	PLA	1600	7	B3
SIERRA BRAVO RD	IRV	SA		32A	A3
SIERRA CADIZ RD	IRV	SA		32A	A3
SIERRA CALMO RD	IRV	SA	13200	32A	A3
SIERRA CANON RD	IRV	SA		32	F3
SIERRA CASA RD	IRV	SA		32	F3
SIERRA CECILE	IRV	SA		32A	A3
SIERRA CHULA RD	IRV	SA		32	F3
SIERRA CIELO RD	IRV	SA		32	F3
SIERRA DEL SOL	CO	SJ		56	B5
SIERRA DEL SOL	CO	SJ		59	B4
SIERRA ELENA RD	IRV	SA		32A	A3
SRA GERONA RD	IRV	SA		32A	A3
SIERRA INEZ RD	IRV	SA		32A	A3
SIERRA ISABELLE	IRV	SA		32A	A3
SIERRA LAGO	IRV	SA		32	F3
SIERRA LAGO RD	IRV	SA		32	F3
SIERRA LEONE RD	IRV	SA		32A	A3
SIERRA LINDA RD	IRV	SA		32	F3
SIERRA LISA RD	IRV	SA		32A	A3
SIERRA LUNA RD	IRV	SA		32	F3
SRA MADRE CIR	PLA	PLA	1600	7	E6
SIERRA MADRE DR	CO	SA	13200	17	F5
SIERRA MAJORCA	IRV	SA		32A	A3
SIERRA MARIA RD	IRV	SA		32A	A3
SIERRA MESA RD	IRV	SA		32	F3
SIERRA MIA RD	IRV	SA		32	F3
SRA NEVADA WY	OR	OR		12	B5
SIERRA NOCHE RD	IRV	SA		32	F3
SIERRA NUEVO RD	IRV	SA		32	F3
SIERRA ORO RD	IRV	SA		32A	A3
SIERRA PALOS RD	IRV	SA		32A	A3
SIERRA PEAK LN	CO	SJ		52	E3
SIERRA PERLA RD	IRV	SA		32A	A3
SIERRA PORTO RD	IRV	SA		32	F3
SIERRA RATON RD	IRV	SA		32	F3
SIERRA RIDGE	CO	ET		52	B6
SIERRA ROJA RD	IRV	SA		32	F3
SIERRA SANTO RD	IRV	SA		32	F3
SIERRA SECO RD	IRV	SA		32	F3
SIERRA SIENA RD	IRV	SA		32A	A3
SIERRA SOTO RD	IRV	SA		32	F3
SIERRA TREE LN	IRV	SA		29	A5
SIERRA VERDE RD	IRV	SA		32	F3
SIERRA VISTA	CO	LB77		35	C4
SIERRA VISTA	MVJO	SJ92		29D	C3
SIERRA VISTA	NB	NB	2500	31	E2
SIERRA VISTA AV	PLA	PLA	1600	7	E6
SIERRA VISTA DR	FUL	FL	800	6	B4
SIERRA VISTA DR	LAH	LAH	900	1	F3
SIERRA VISTA DR	TUS	TUS	1800	24	A4
SIESTA LN	YL	YL	5000	7	F4
SIESTA ST	ANA	AN	1000	10	F3
SIET PL	ANA	AN	900	12	A5
SIEVERS AV	BREA	BREA	200	2	D6
SIGMOND CIR	FTNV	SA08		26	A3
SIGNAL RD	NB	NB	200	31	D5
SIGNET CIR	HTB	HB46	10000	27	A6
SIGNET CIR E	SA	SA		22	B2
SIGNET CIR W	SA	SA		22	B2
SILENT BROOK	CO	ET	22200	29B	B2

STREET	CITY	P.O. ZONE	BLOCK	PAGE	GRID
SILENT KNOLL	CO	LAG		36	A4
SILENT SPG LN	CO	SJ		56	D6
SILENT SPG LN	CO	SJ		59	D1
SILKBERRY	IRV	SA		29	C5
SILKGRASS	IRV	SA		29	B5
SILKLEAF	IRV	SA		29	B4
SILKTASSEL	CO	SJ		59	B3
SILKTREE CIR	OR	OR	500	17	B4
SILK TREE DR	TUS	TUS	2100	24	A5
SILKTREE ST	FTNV	SA08	16500	21	F5
SILKWOOD	IRV	SA		32A	B3
SILKWOOD CIR	HTB	HB	8100	26	C2
SILKWOOD LN	ANA	AN		11	E6
SILLERO	CO	SJ88		29B	F5
SILLEROS	MVJO	SJ92		29B	D5
SILLIKER AV	LAH	LAH	1200	1	E3
SILLIMAN DR	HTB	HB	4100	20	C5
SILVER CIR	GGR	GG43	10600	22	A2
SILVER DR	SA	SA	4300	22	C2
SILVER LN	HTB	HB47	16400	21	C5
SILVER LN	NB	NB60		27	F6
SILVER LN	NB	NB	2900	31	F1
SILVER RUN	IRV	SA		24	E6
SILVER ST	BPK	BP	7500	10	A2
SILVERADO DR	CO	TRA		56	E6
SILVERADO DR	HTB	HB		25	F4
SILVERADO LN	LAP	BP23	7400	9	D2
SILVERADO WY	ANA	AN		13	B3
SILVERADO CY RD	CO	SIL		50	B2
SILVERADO CY RD	CO	SIL		53	A1
SILVER BAY DR	CO	ET	23800	29A	E5
SILVER BCH CIR	HTB	HB		26	A4
SILVER BIRCH DR	TUS	TUS	13200	24	A2
SILVERBIT WY	OR	OR		18	D2
SILVERBREEZE	IRV	SA		29	A4
SILVERBROOK DR	ANA	AN		13	B2
SILVERBROOK DR	TUS	TUS	14300	24	A4
SILVER CYN WY	BREA	BREA		2	F5
SILVER CREEK	IRV	SA		32A	A2
SILVER CREEK DR	SJC	SJ75	27300	36	D3
SILVER CRESCENT	IRV	SA		32A	A3
SILVERDOLLAR	CO	ET	25000	29B	A2
SILVR DOLLAR LN	ANA	AN		8	E6
SILVERFERN	IRV	SA		32A	B3
SILVER FIR	IRV	SA		29	C4
SILVER FOX RD	CO	LALM	11600	14	A3
SILVER GLADE DR	CO	LB77		36	A5
SILVER HEEL CIR	HTB	HB	6400	26	A1
SILVERLAKE DR	PLA	PLA		7	B6
SILVER LAKE PL	BREA	BREA		2	C5
SILVER LNTRN ST	DPT	DPT	33700	37	F4
SILVER LEAF AV	OR	OR	3700	18	A2
SILVERLEAF LN	CO	LB		29C	E1
SILVER MAPLE DR	LAH	LAH	1100	1	E5
SILVER MAPLE WY	CO	SA	18600	18	B5
SILVEROAK	CO	LB56		29C	C2
SILVER SADDLE	CO	LB	26400	29C	F3
SILVR SHOALS AV	SB	SB	800	19	E2
SILVER SPRING	CO	ET	26400	29B	B2
SILVER SPUR	CO	ET	25000	29B	A2
SILVER SPUR LN	CO	LB56		29C	E6
SILVERSPUR LN	LAH	LAH	2400	1	D5
SILVER SPUR RD	SJC	SJ75	27000	36	C4
SILVERSPUR TR	ANA	AN		13	C3
SILVERSPUR WY	LAH	LAH	700	1	D5
SILVER SPURS LN	YL	YL		8	B3
SILVER STRND DR	HTB	HB	9700	26	F6
SILVERTIDE DR	DPT	DPT		37	B5
SILVER TIP CIR	YL	YL		7	E4
SILVERTIP CT	FTNV	SA08	15900	22	D6
SILVERTON DR	CO	LB77	28400	36	A1
SILVERTREE LN	CO	SJ79		59	E1
SILVER VIA	ANA	AN		16	D2
SILVERWOOD	IRV	SA		29	B2
SILVERWOOD DR	CO	LALM	2700	14	A2
SILVERWOOD DR	HTB	HB47	6200	21	A4
SILVERWOOD ST	OR	OR	1600	12	D6
SIM PL	ANA	AN	1500	16	B2
SIMEON DR	DPT	DPT		37	E3
SIMI PL	FUL	FL33	1300	10	E1
SIMMONE LN	HTB	HB47	16500	21	B5
SIMMONS AV	GGR	GG	12200	16	D3
SIMMONS AV E	ANA	AN	100	16	D3
SIMMONS AV W	ANA	AN	200	16	D3
SIMMONS PL	STN	STN	7500	15	B3
SIMON CIR	ANA	AN		12	B1
SIMONE WY	CO	CYP	4600	9	D3
SIMON RANCH RD	CO	SA	2000	24	C1
SIMPATICA CIR	CO	ET		52	C5
SIMPSON CIR	ANA	AN		11	F6
SIMPSON CIR	ANA	AN		12	A6

INDEX

STREET	CITY	P.O. ZONE	BLOCK	PAGE	GRID
SIMS ST	HTB	HB	16600	20	D6
SIMSBURRY COM	SA	SA		22	C2
SINCLAIR AV	WSTM	WSTM	9000	21	E2
SINCLAIR CIR	GGR	GG	9600	21	F2
SINCLAIR CIR	PLA	PLA	1700	7	C3
SINCLAIR CIR	TUS	TUS		24	B6
SINCLAIR CIR	WSTM	WSTM	9300	21	E2
SINCLAIR ST	ANA	AN		12	A6
SINCLAIR ST	ANA	AN06		17	A1
SINFOROSA DR	MVJO	SJ91		29B	B5
SINGAPORE ST	CO	SJ91		29A	F5
SINGING WOOD	IRV	SA		29	B4
SINGNG WOOD CIR	CO	SJ79		52	E3
SINGING WOOD DR	ANA	AN		13	F2
SINGINGWOOD DR	CO	SA	12100	24	C2
SINGINGWOOD DR	YL	YL		8	D1
SINGINGWOOD LN	BREA	BREA		3	A5
SINGINGWOOD LN	CO	SA	12200	24	C2
SINGINGWOOD ST	OR	OR		18	C3
SINGINGWOODS DR	CO	ET	24900	29A	E2
SINGLELEAF	MVJO	SJ92		52	E6
SINSONTE	MVJO	SJ92		29B	D6
SINSONTE	MVJO	SJ92		29D	D1
SIOUX DR	CO	SA	18700	18	B6
SIOUX DR	CO	ET	21800	29A	F1
SIOUX RD	WSTM	WSTM	13300	14	F6
SIOUX RIVER CIR	FTNV	SA08	10300	27	A2
SIRIUS	IRV	SA		32A	A2
SIRIUS AV	GGR	GG	13000	16	D3
SIRIUS AV	OR	OR68	4100	16	D3
SIRIUS AV E&W	ANA	AN	100	16	D3
SIRIUS DR	HTB	HB	3800	20	C6
SIRODAY	YL	YL	4500	7	E3
SIROS	CO	LAG		35	F4
SIRRINE DR	CO	SA	1600	18	E4
SIRUELA	MVJO	SJ92		29B	D6
SIRUELA	MVJO	SJ92		29D	D2
SISANTE	MVJO	SJ91		29B	D2
SISKIN AV	FTNV	SA08	9200	26	E2
SISKIYOU ST	WSTM	WSTM	13100	15	A6
SISSON AV	SA	SA	5100	22	B3
SISSON DR	HTB	HB	5000	20	E4
SITE DR	BREA	BREA	1000	2	E4
SITE DR	CO	BREA	1100	2	E3
SITGES	CO	LB77		35	F5
SITIO VERANO	CO	ET		29A	E1
SITKA CIR	FTNV	SA08		26	F1
SIVA AV	ANA	AN	1700	11	A5
SIX NATIONS AV	PLA	PLA	500	7	C1
SKIFF CIR	HTB	HB	8900	26	E4
SKI HARBOR CIR	HTB	HB	9100	26	E6
SKIMMER LN	HTB	HB	20800	26	F6
SKINNER PL	FUL	FL35		2	B6
SKINNER ST	IRV	SA	5100	29	D3
SKIPJACK DR	HTB	HB		20	D5
SKIPPER	IRV	SA		29	D1
SKOKIE RD	SB	SB	1300	14	A6
SKY DR	CO	ET	23200	29A	F4
SKY LN	CO	SA	12000	24	C1
SKYBIRD LN	CO	ET	25600	29B	A1
SKYBIRD LN	CO	ET		52	A6
SKY COUNTRY CIR	CO	TRA		56	E6
SKYCREST	IRV	SA		32A	A3
SKYCREST DR	FUL	FL	1800	6	D3
SKYE LN	HTB	HB	17900	26	A1
SKYHILL WY	CO	SA		18	D6
SKYLAB RD	HTB	HB47		20	F2
SKYLAB WEST	HTB	HB47		20	E2
SKY LAKE AV	BREA	BREA		2	C4
SKYLARK BLVD	GGR	GG	9300	15	E3
SKYLARK CIR	CM	CM	2700	27	B5
SKYLARK DR	CO	ET		52	B6
SKYLARK DR	CO	LB56		29C	B1
SKYLARK DR	HTB	HB	5000	20	E4
SKYLARK LN	GGR	GG	9900	15	E3
SKYLARK LN	NB	NB	1600	31	E3
SKYLARK PL	OR	SA05		18	E3
SKYLARK ST	IRV	SA		29	C2
SKYLARK WY	CO	SJ79		59	C4
SKYLINE	IRV	SA		32A	A3
SKYLINE DR	BREA	BREA		3	B5
SKYLINE DR	CO	SA	1800	24	C1
SKYLINE DR	FUL	FL	1300	6	D4
SKYLINE DR	LAG	LB51	900	34	E2
SKYLINE DR	STN	STN		15	B1
SKYLINE DR	YL	YL		40	A4
SKYLINE DR SE	CO	SA	1000	18	C6
SKYLINE DR SW	CO	SA	1300	18	C6
SKYLINE LN	HTB	HB47		21	B6
SKYLINE TER	LAG	LB51	900	34	E2
SKYLINE WY	FUL	FL	1300	6	D4

STREET	CITY	P.O. ZONE	BLOCK	PAGE	GRID
SKYLINE VIEW DR	CO	SA		18	D6
SKYLINKS CIR	WSTM	WSTM	15600	21	D3
SKYMEADOW DR	CO	PLA	16300	7	D3
SKYMEADOW DR E	PLA	PLA	900	7	D3
SKY PARK BLVD	IRV	SA14		28	C2
SKY PARK EAST	IRV	SA		28	C3
SKY PARK NORTH	IRV	SA		28	C2
SKY PARK SOUTH	IRV	SA		28	C3
SKYSAIL DR	NB	CDLM		32	B6
SKYVIEW DR	HTB	HB47	6700	21	A3
SKYVIEW DR	OR	OR69		18	E2
SKYVIEW LN	CM	CM26		28	A3
SKYVIEW ST	IRV	SA14	14600	29	E5
SKYVIEW WY	CO	LB		35	C6
SKYVIEW WY	CO	LB77		37	C1
SKYVIEW KNOLL	YL	YL	19200	8	B3
SKYWAY DR	CO	SA	12000	24	C1
SKYWOOD CIR	ANA	AN	2800	10	C5
SKYWOOD PL	ANA	AN	2600	10	D4
SKYWOOD ST	OR	OR	3800	12	D3
SKYWOOD ST E	BREA	BREA	300	2	F4
SKYWOOD ST N	OR	OR	1200	12	D3
SKYWOOD ST W	BREA	BREA	1800	2	C4
SLATER AV	FTNV	SA08	8500	21	B6
SLATER AV	FTNV	SA08	10000	22	A6
SLATER AV	HTB	HB	6200	20	F6
SLATER AV	HTB	HB47	5700	21	B6
SLEEPING OAK DR	CO	SJ		52	F3
SLEEPING OAK DR	YL	YL		40	B4
SLEEPY GLEN LN	CO	SJ		59	D1
SLEEPY HOLLOW	CO	SIL	29100	50	F2
SLEEPY HOLLW LN	BREA	BREA		3	B6
SLEEPY HOLLW LN	LAG	LB51	500	34	D3
SLEEPYHOLLOW ST	IRV	SA	14900	29	C2
SLEEPYHOLLW TER	CO	ET		29A	F2
SLEEPY MDW LN	ANA	AN		12	F3
SLIGO CIR	HTB	HB47	6400	21	A3
SLOANE AV	WSTM	WSTM		14	D6
SLOANE AV	WSTM	WSTM	5000	20	D1
SLOCUM	IRV	SA		29	E1
SLOOP AV	ANA	AN04	2000	15	F1
SLOOP AV	ANA	AN	1900	16	A1
SLOOP CIR	HTB	HB	19000	26	C3
SMALLEY RD	CM	CM	3300	27	E2
SMILEY DR	CO	SA	18900	18	B3
SMITH ST	IRV	SA	3600	28	F4
SMITH WY	LAG	LB51	1000	34	F3
SMOKERIDGE TER	ANA	AN		13	B2
SMOKE RIVER CT	FTNV	SA08		27	A2
SMOKESTONE	IRV	SA		29	B4
SMOKETHORN	CO	SJ79		59	E5
SMOKE TREE AV	FTNV	SA08	9500	26	F3
SMOKETREE AV	IRV	SA	5300	29	D3
SMOKETREE AV	YL	YL		8	D2
SMOKETREE CIR	VPK	OR67		13	B4
SMOKE TREE CT	LAH	LAH		1	E6
SMOKE TREE DR	LAH	LAH		1	E6
SMOKE TREE LN	CO	SA	1000	18	C5
SMOKETREE LN	SJC	SJ75		36	B3
SMOKETREE LN	VPK	OR67		13	B4
SMOKEWOOD AV	FUL	FL	600	6	D3
SMOKEWOOD CIR	ANA	AN		13	F4
SMOKEWOOD CIR	HTB	HB	18800	26	C3
SMOKEWOOD DR	CO	SA	1400	18	C5
SMOKEWOOD DR	VPK	OR67	9700	12	F6
SMOKEY AV	OR	OR		13	C5
SMOKEY CIR	HTB	HB	9500	26	F5
SNAPDRAGON	IRV	SA		29	B2
SNAPPER LN	HTB	HB		20	D6
SNARK ST	LALM	LALM	11400	14	B2
SNEAD DR	HTB	HB	5800	20	F4
SNIPE LN	CO	LB	24000	35	D2
SNOW ST	WSTM	WSTM	14500	21	E2
SNOWAPPLE	IRV	SA		29	A4
SNOWBERRY	CO	SJ		59	C1
SNOWBERRY	IRV	SA		29	B2
SNOWBERRY RD	TUS	TUS		24	A4
SNOWBIRD DR	HTB	HB	8200	26	D6
SNOWDON	CO	SJ79		59	D2
SNOWDROP AV	FTNV	SA08	11200	22	B4
SNOWFIELD	IRV	SA		29	B5
SNOWFIELD ST	BREA	BREA		3	B6
SNOW GOOSE ST	OR	OR	800	18	B1
SNOW WOOD CIR	ANA	AN		8	B6
SNUG HARBOR CIR	HTB	HB	20000	26	E6
SNUG HARBOR RD	NB	NB	300	31	D5
SOARING HAWK	IRV	SA		29	A4
SOFIA ST	CO	SJ91		29B	A5
SOFTWIND DR	HTB	HB	6000	20	F4
SOLANA	IRV	SA		28	F6
SOLANA DR	CO	SA	12000	18	B3

STREET	CITY	P.O. ZONE	BLOCK	PAGE	GRID
SOLANA WY	LAG	LB51	2600	34	E5
SOLANO	SCL	SC72		39	D2
SOLANO CIR	HTB	HB		26	D5
SOLANO CIR	PLA	PLA	600	7	C5
SOLANO CT	CO	LB	24700	29C	E3
SOLANO LN	MVJO	SJ91		29B	B5
SOLANO RIVER CT	FTNV	SA08		27	A2
SOLEDAD	MVJO	SJ91		29B	C2
SOLERA DR	CO	LB	22900	35	C5
SOLIDAD ST	CO	LB56		29C	F6
SOLINDA	TUS	TUS		24	B3
SOLITAIRE LN	CO	LB53		29A	B6
SOLITAIRE WY	IRV	SA		24	D6
SOLLER	MVJO	SJ92	27700	29B	D2
SOLOMAR	CO	ET		51	E4
SOLOMON DR N	ANA	AN	100	13	C2
SOLOMON DR S	ANA	AN	100	13	C2
SOLONICA ST	CO	SJ91	25300	29A	F5
SOLRID ST	MVJO	SJ92		29D	E3
SOLTERO	MVJO	SJ91	27600	29B	D1
SOLTERO	MVJO	SJ91		52	D6
SOMBRAS	MVJO	SJ92		29D	C4
SOMBREADO	SCL	SC72		38	E4
SOMBRERO AV	CYP	CYP	6200	14	F2
SOMERDALE LN	LAP	BP23	8200	9	D3
SOMERLY	MVJO	SJ92		29D	D3
SOMERS DR	CO	AN04	8100	15	C3
SOMERSET	CO	SJ79		59	D3
SOMERSET	MVJO	SJ92		29B	E6
SOMERSET	MVJO	SJ92		29D	E1
SOMERSET CIR	BPK	BP	8300	5	C4
SOMERSET CIR	DPT	LB77		37	C1
SOMERSET DR	PLA	PLA	200	7	B2
SOMERSET LN	CYP	CYP	9200	9	C5
SOMERSET LN	FUL	FL33		5	F2
SOMERSET LN	HTB	HB	16400	20	A5
SOMERSET LN	NB	NB	1100	31	E4
SOMERSET LN	SJC	SJ75		36	D4
SOMERSET PL	GGR	GG	11800	16	D3
SOMERSET ST	BPK	BP	4900	5	C4
SOMERSET ST	WSTM	WSTM	5100	20	E1
SOMERSET WY	SA	SA		23	B6
SOMERVILLE LN	HTB	HB	20400	26	D5
SOMMERSET CIR	LAP	BP23	7000	9	E1
SOMMERSET DR	BREA	BREA		3	B5
SOMMERSET LN	CO	ET		52	C6
SOMMERVILLE CIR	YL	YL	20000	8	C5
SOMMET DU MONDE	LAG	LB51		35	A2
SONATA LN	ANA	AN	5400	8	B6
SON BON	CO	LB77		35	E4
SONBRIA	TUS	TUS		24	B3
SONCILLO	MVJO	SJ91		29B	D2
SONGBIRD LN	CO	LB56		29C	A1
SONGISH ST	ANA	AN04	1600	15	F1
SONGISH ST	GGR	GG	11000	15	F2
SONGSPARROW	IRV	SA		29	B3
SON MORELL	CO	LB77		35	E4
SONNETT ST	STN	STN	10100	10	D6
SONNY CIR	IRV	SA	15000	29	D3
SONOITA	MVJO	SJ91		29B	C3
SONOMA	CO	ET30		51	F6
SONOMA DR	HTB	HB	6100	20	F6
SONOMA ST	CO	LB56		29C	D3
SONOMA WY	SJC	SJ75		36	B2
SONOMA WY	YL	YL	17600	7	F4
SONORA AV	LAH	LAH	900	1	F6
SONORA LN	TUS	TUS		23	E3
SONORA PL	LAH	LAH	300	2	C4
SONORA RD	CM	CM	700	27	F4
SONORA ST	BREA	BREA	600	2	C4
SONORA ST	NB	NB63	100	30	F4
SONORA WY	CYP	CYP	6400	9	F5
SONRIENTE TR	CO	SJ		59	D4
SONRISA	IRV	SA		24	F5
SONRISA	IRV	SA20		49	A5
SONRISA E	IRV	SA		24	F5
SONRISA W	IRV	SA		24	F5
SONRISA LN	CO	LB77		35	C4
SON SERRA	CO	LB77		35	F4
SONWELL PL	CYP	CYP	9500	9	E5
SONYA PL	ANA	AN	600	11	B5
SONYA ST	ANA	AN	300	11	B5
SOQUEL CYN RD	BREA	BREA		4	B5
SOQUEL CYN RD	CO	YL		4	B5
SORA CT	CO	LB56		29A	B6
SORBONNE	CO	LAG		35	F4
SORCE LN	CO	LB51		33A	F4
SORENTO CIR	HTB	HB47	6500	21	A3
SORESINA	CO	LB		29A	B4
SORIA CIR	HTB	HB	6700	26	A3

STREET	CITY	P.O. ZONE	BLOCK	PAGE	GRID
SORIA CIR	MVJO	SJ91	25000	29D	C1
SORREL ST	BREA	BREA		3	C6
SORREL ST	FTNV	SA08	9600	21	F4
SORRELL DR	GGR	GG	13300	16	C5
SORRELL PL	CO	LB	26300	29C	F3
SORRENTO	CO	LB77		36	A1
SORRENTO	IRV	SA14		28	F4
SORRENTO CIR	LAP	BP23	5200	9	D2
SORRENTO PL	FUL	FL	1300	6	E3
SOTELO	MVJO	SJ92		29D	E3
SOTO GRANDE DR	DPT	LB77		37	E3
SOUD DR	HTB	HB47		21	D4
SOUTH ST E	ANA	AN	2000	12	A4
SOUTH ST E&W	ANA	AN	100	11	C5
SOUTHALL TER	IRV	SA		32	F3
SOUTHAMPTON	IRV	SA		24	D6
SOUTHAMPTON CT	CO	LB	24500	29A	E6
SOUTHAMPTON CT	NB	NB		32	B3
SOUTHAMPTON DR	CYP	CYP	6800	15	B2
SOUTHAMPTON WY	PLA	PLA	200	7	B4
SOUTHBROOK	CO	ET	25800	29B	A3
SOUTHBROOK	IRV	SA		29	C4
SOUTH COAST DR	CM	CM	900	27	E3
SOUTHERN AV	OR	OR	800	12	C5
SOUTHERN WOOD	IRV	SA		32A	B3
SOUTHFIELD DR	WSTM	WSTM		20	E1
SOUTHGATE	MVJO	SJ92		29B	F1
SOUTHGATE AV	FUL	FL	100	6	B6
SOUTHGATE AV	FUL	FL33	1800	10	E1
SOUTHGATE AV	FUL	FL	100	11	B1
SOUTHGATE AV W	FUL	FL33	1600	5	F6
SOUTHLAKE DR	HTB	HB47		21	C5
SOUTH MALL	IRV	SA		24	C6
SOUTHPARK AV	FTNV	SA08		27	B1
SOUTH PEAK	CO	LB		35	D6
SOUTH PEAK	CO	LB77		37	D1
SOUTH POINT DR	NB	NB		32	A4
SOUTH POINTE DR	CO	LB		29A	C4
SOUTHPORT DR	HTB	HB	8200	26	D5
SOUTH PORT LN	SB	SB	13100	19	C5
SOUTHPORT ST	CO	LB		29C	E1
SOUTHRIDGE DR	BREA	BREA	1200	2	C4
SOUTH RIDGE DR	MVJO	SJ92		29D	C2
SOUTHSAND	IRV	SA		29	A4
SOUTHSHORE DR	HTB	HB	9300	30	E1
SOUTHSHORE DR	SB	SB	600	19	F2
SOUTHWIND	IRV	SA		29	B4
SOUTHWIND CIR	HTB	HB		30	C1
SOUTHWIND CT	SJC	SJ75	33000	38	B2
SOUTHWIND LN	YL	YL		40	E6
SOUTHWOOD	IRV	SA		24	E6
SOUTHWOOD	IRV	SA		29	E1
SOUZA AV	GGR	GG	9500	15	E5
SOVEREIGN WY	SA	SA		23	B6
SOWELL AV	WSTM	WSTM	6800	21	E2
SOWMA WY	CYP	CYP	5200	9	D5
SPA DR	HTB	HB	5400	20	F1
SPADRA LN	MVJO	SJ91	24700	29B	C6
SPADRA LN	MVJO	SJ91	24900	29D	C1
SPAHN LN	PLA	PLA	1700	7	D2
SPAIGHT CIR	IRV	SA		24	F6
SPAR CIR	HTB	HB	10000	26	F6
SPAR ST	GGR	GG43	15100	22	A3
SPAR ST	SA	SA	700	22	C3
SPARKES ST	CM	CM27	200	31	D3
SPARKLEBERRY ST	FTNV	SA08	17000	21	F6
SPARKLER DR	HTB	HB		20	B4
SPARKLNG SPG LN	CO	ET		29A	D3
SPARKMAN LN	HTB	HB	20800	26	F6
SPARROW AV	FTNV	SA08	10000	26	F2
SPARROW CIR	CM	CM	2700	27	B5
SPARROW DR	HTB	HB	5000	20	E4
SPARROW LN	LAP	BP23	8000	9	D3
SPARROW ST	CO	ET	24200	29A	D2
SPARROWHAWK	IRV	SA		29	B2
SPARROW HILL LN	CO	LB		29C	D2
SPARTA	IRV	SA14		28	F3
SPARTAN CIR	HTB	HB		20	B4
SPARTAN ST	CO	SJ91		29A	F6
SPARTAN ST	CO	SJ91	24100	29B	A5
SPAULDING AV	CO	SA	18600	18	B5
SPECTRUM	IRV	SA18		51	A6
SPECTRUM DR	IRV	SA		29	F6
SPEER AV	HTB	HB	7500	26	C1
SPENCER AV	FTNV	SA08	10800	27	B2
SPENCER CIR	HTB	HB	9100	26	E6
SPENCER DR	GGR	GG	12000	15	E3
SPENCER JOHNSON	GGR	GG45		14	E4
SPICEWOOD	CO	LB56		29C	C1
SPICEWOOD WY	IRV	SA	4300	28	F5
SPICEWOOD WY	IRV	SA		29	A5

STREET	CITY	P.O. ZONE	BLOCK	PAGE	GRID
SPICKARD DR	HTB	HB47	6800	21	B6
SPINDLE CIR	DPT	LB77		37	D3
SPINDLEWOOD	CO	LB		35	F3
SPINDLEWOOD	CO	LB77		36	A3
SPIN DRIFT CT	DPT	DPT		37	A5
SPINDRIFT LN	HTB	HB46	20800	27	A6
SPINDRIFT WY	NB	NB	4200	31	C4
SPINNAKER	IRV	SA		29	B5
SPINNAKER DR	HTB	HB	9800	26	F6
SPINNAKER DR	SJC	SJ75		38	A2
SPINNAKER DR N	DPT	LB77		37	E3
SPINNAKER DR S	DPT	LB77		37	E3
SPINNAKER ST	ANA	AN	1900	16	E3
SPINNAKER ST	GGR	GG	12500	16	E4
SPINNAKER ST	OR	OR68	100	16	E3
SPINNAKER ST	SA	SA	2200	16	E5
SPINNAKER WY	SB	SB		19	D2
SPLIT RAIL LN	ANA	AN		12	F3
SPOONBILL	IRV	SA		29	E3
SPOONBILL DR	CO	LB56		29C	B1
SPOTTED BULL LN	SJC	SJ75	29500	36	B2
SPOTTED BULL WY	SJC	SJ75	29300	36	B2
SPOTTED PONY LN	CO	LB		29C	F4
SPOTTED PONY LN	CO	LB	25000	29D	A4
SPRAGUE AV	CYP	CYP	5500	9	E4
SPRAGUE LN	ANA	AN	1900	16	E2
SPRIG ST	CO	SJ91		29A	F5
SPRING CIR	HTB	HB		26	D3
SPRING ST	ANA	AN05	900	11	C3
SPRING CT	BREA	BREA		2	E5
SPRING ST	CO	OR	18500	18	A2
SPRING ST	GGR	GG45	12700	14	F4
SPRING ST	OR	OR	3300	17	F2
SPRING ST	OR	OR	3500	18	A2
SPRING ST	SJC	SJ75	26800	36	C6
SPRINGACRE	IRV	SA		29	A4
SPRINGBROOK N	IRV	SA		29	C5
SPRINGBROOK S	IRV	SA		29	B4
SPRINGBROOK RD	CO	LB77		35	F5
SPRINGBROOK WY	STN	STN		15	B4
SPRING BUCK	IRV	SA		29	B4
SPRING CK CIR	MVJO	SJ92		29B	F6
SPRINGDALE	CO	LB56		29C	C4
SPRINGDALE DR	WSTM	WSTM	13000	14	F5
SPRINGDALE PL	WSTM	WSTM	13600	14	F6
SPRINGDALE ST	GGR	GG45	11800	14	F4
SPRINGDALE ST	HTB	HB	14300	20	F3
SPRINGDALE ST	HTB	HB	17500	25	F1
SPRINGDALE ST	WSTM	WSTM	13000	14	F5
SPRINGFIELD	IRV	SA14		29	F3
SPRINGFLD AV E	HTB	HB	100	26	B4
SPRINGFLD AV W	HTB	HB	100	26	B4
SPRINGFIELD DR	CO	LB	28400	35	F1
SPRINGFIELD DR	CO	LB77		36	A1
SPRINGFIELD ST	CM	CM	900	27	E3
SPRINGFLOWER	IRV	SA		29	C5
SPRING GLEN	CO	ET	25400	29A	F3
SPRING GLEN	IRV	SA		29	D4
SPRING HILL DR	ANA	AN	5300	13	B2
SPRING HILL LN	CO	LB		29C	D2
SPRINGHURST AV	HTB	HB	8400	26	D2
SPRING LAKE LN	CO	ET		29A	E3
SPRING OAK	YL	YL		8	E2
SPRING PINES	CO	LB		29C	E4
SPRINGSIDE	CO	SJ79		59	D2
SPRINGTIME LN	HTB	HB	18300	26	D2
SPRING TREE CT	LAH	LAH		1	F6
SPRINGVALE	IRV	SA		29	E4
SPRINGVIEW	IRV	SA		24	F5
SPRING VIEW DR	YL	YL		8	C2
SPRINGWATER	CO	ET	22800	29A	F3
SPRINGWATER	IRV	SA		29	C5
SPRING WATER CT	GGR	GG		16	D6
SPRINGWOOD	CO	LB77		35	F3
SPRINGWOOD	CO	LB77		36	A3
SPRINGWOOD	IRV	SA		29	D5
SPRINGWOOD CIR	CO	ET	27000	29B	C1
SPRINGWOOD CIR	CO	ET		52	C6
SPRINGWOOD DR	CO	SA	12800	18	B4
SPRIT CIR	HTB	HB	10000	26	F6
SPRUCE	MVJO	SJ92		52	D6
SPRUCE AV	CO	SA07	20000	28	B6
SPRUCE AV	CO	SA	20200	32	B1
SPRUCE AV	OR	OR	200	17	B3
SPRUCE CIR	FTNV	SA08	16600	21	F5
SPRUCE CIR	FTNV	SA08	18600	26	F2
SPRUCE CIR	LAP	BP23	7300	9	E1
SPRUCE CT	CYP	CYP	9800	9	E6
SPRUCE DR	ANA	AN	200	11	E3
SPRUCE LN	CO	LB		29D	A2
SPRUCE PL	FUL	FL	2800	6	E2

1990 ORANGE COUNTY STREET INDEX

STREET	CITY	P.O. ZONE	BLOCK	PAGE	GRID
SPRUCE ST	BREA	BREA	600	6	E1
SPRUCE ST	FTNV	SA08	16400	21	F5
SPRUCE ST	GGR	GG		15	F4
SPRUCE ST	NB	NB60	19800	28	B6
SPRUCE ST	PLA	PLA	17100	7	E5
SPRUCE ST	WSTM	WSTM	7000	21	B1
SPRUCE ST N	SA	SA	2000	16	F6
SPRUCE ST S	SA	SA	200	22	F4
SPRUCE WY	LAH	LAH	400	1	E5
SPRUCE TREE LN	IRV	SA		29	A5
SPRUCEWOOD	CO	ET		29A	F1
SPRUCEWOOD	CO	ET		51	F6
SPRUCEWOOD AV	OR	OR69		18	E3
SPUR LN	CO	LALM	2700	14	A4
SPUR BRANCH LN	CO	LB	26000	29D	A3
SPURGEON ST N	SA	SA	1600	17	B6
SPURGEON ST N	SA	SA	100	23	B2
SPURNEY LN	HTB	HB46		30	E6
SPURR CIR	BREA	BREA	3600	7	D1
SPYGLASS	MVJO	SJ92		29B	E3
SPYGLASS CT	SJC	SJ75		38	A2
SPYGLASS LN	HTB	HB	21400	30	F1
SPYGLASS WY	ANA	AN		13	B3
SPYGLASS HIL RD	NB	NB		32	D5
SPYGLASS HIL RD	NB	CDLM		32	D6
SQUIRES CIR	HTB	HB	8600	26	D5
SQUIRES CIR	VPK	OR67	10100	13	A6
SQUIRES DR	CO	SA	11400	18	C6
STACY LN	CO	OR65		12	D4
STACEY LEE LN	OR	OR		13	B6
STACIE LN	STN	STN		15	E1
STACY LN	SA	SA	2300	16	E5
STADCO DR	ANA	AN	3600	10	A6
STADIUM WY	ANA	AN06		17	A2
STADIUM CTR DR	ANA	AN06		17	A2
STADIUM VIEW	ANA	AN06		17	A1
STAEDLER CIR	FTNV	SA08	10800	22	A6
STAEDLER ST	FTNV	SA08	10800	22	A6
STAFFORD CIR	YL	YL	17300	7	E4
STAFFORD ST	SA	SA	200	23	C1
STAGE RD	BPK	BP	7500	5	A3
STAGE COACH DR	CO	SJ91		29B	A6
STAGE COACH DR	CO	LB		29C	F1
STAGE COACH DR	CO	LB	25400	29D	A1
STAGE COACH RD	ANA	AN		13	D3
STAGELINE DR	CO	LB	25000	29C	F5
STAGEWOOD CT	CO	LB	27200	29C	F4
STAHL CT	TUS	SA10		29	A2
STAHOV AV	WSTM	WSTM	7000	15	B5
STALLION CIR	HTB	HB	5000	20	E5
STALLION ST	OR	OR		13	D6
STAMPEDE CIR	IRV	SA	13700	24	D6
STANDARD AV N&S	SA	SA	100	23	C5
STANDARD AV S	SA	SA	3200	28	C1
STANDISH AV	ANA	AN	2200	11	F4
STANDISH AV	ANA	AN	2300	12	A4
STANDISH LN	HTB	HB47	15800	21	A4
STANDUSTRIAL ST	STN	STN	8300	15	C1
STANFIELD CIR	HTB	HB49		25	F1
STANFORD	IRV	SA		28	E6
STANFORD	IRV	SA		32	E1
STANFORD AV	FUL	FL	200	6	D4
STANFORD AV	GGR	GG45	5300	14	E4
STANFORD AV	GGR	GG	6300	15	C4
STANFORD AV	GGR	GG	10300	16	A4
STANFORD AV	SA	SA	600	23	C4
STANFORD AV	STN	GG41	8000	15	C4
STANFORD CIR	PLA	PLA	700	7	C5
STANFORD CT	ANA	AN		16	F2
STANFORD DR	PLA	PLA	600	7	C5
STANFORD LN	HTB	HB47	15300	21	A3
STANFORD LN	SB	SB	12500	19	C4
STANFORD ST	LAH	LAH	200	1	E5
STANFORD ST E	SA	SA	100	23	A4
STANFORD ST W	SA	SA	1500	22	E4
STANFORD ST W	SA	SA	100	23	A4
STANFORD WY	STN	STN	11100	15	B2
STANHOPE	DPT	DPT		37	F2
STANISLAUS ST	FTNV	SA08	18400	27	A2
STANLEY	IRV	SA		28	D1
STANLEY AV	ANA	AN	2600	10	D4
STANLEY AV	PLA	PLA	1700	7	B3
STANLEY LN	GGR	GG	10500	16	A3
STANLEY PL	ANA	AN	2700	10	D4
STANLEY WK	HTB	HB47	17000	21	B5
STAN OAK DR	CO	SA15	21000	33A	F4
STANRICH PL	GGR	GG	10900	16	B5
STANS LN	CO	SA15	21300	33A	F3
STANSBURY LN	LAH	LAH		2	B5
STANTON	CO	SA05		18	B5
STANTON AV	BPK	BP	5100	5	C5

STREET	CITY	P.O. ZONE	BLOCK	PAGE	GRID
STANTON AV	LAH	LAH	2400	1	D5
STANTON AV	STN	STN	11200	15	C2
STANYAN CIR	WSTM	WSTM	14800	21	E2
STAR DR	HTB	HB	9700	26	F6
STARBIRD DR	CM	CM	2600	27	C5
STARBOARD CIR	HTB	HB46	10000	27	A6
STARBOARD DR	DPT	DPT	25500	38	B4
STARBOARD DR	GGR	GG43	14700	22	A2
STARBOARD ST	SA	SA	400	22	B3
STARBOARD WY	NB	CDLM	1200	32	B6
STARBRD LNTN ST	DPT	DPT	24700	37	B5
STARBRIGHT CIR	WSTM	WSTM	10000	22	A2
STARBUCK RD	CO	ET	23400	29A	D3
STARBURST CT	NB	NB63		31	A2
STARCREST	CO	LB56		29C	D2
STARCREST	IRV	SA		32A	A2
STARCREST ST	BREA	BREA		2	D3
STARDUST	IRV	SA		32A	C4
STARDUST CT	CO	LB56		29C	E5
STARDUST DR	HTB	HB	5400	20	F1
STARDUST DR	PLA	PLA	300	7	A4
STARDUST LN	STN	AN04	8700	15	D1
STARE LN	NB	NB		31	B4
STARFALL	IRV	SA		32A	C4
STARFIRE LN	HTB	HB	21800	30	E2
STARFIRE ST	ANA	AN	100	12	F2
STARFISH AV	FTNV	SA08	9700	21	F6
STARFISH CT	NB	NB		31	A2
STARFISH LN	HTB	HB		26	B4
STARFISH WY	DPT	DPT		37	A5
STARFLOWER	IRV	SA		29	B3
STARFLOWER ST	BREA	BREA		3	C6
STARK ST	HTB	HB47	7900	21	C4
STARLAND ST	LAH	LAH	1300	2	A3
STARLIGHT	IRV	SA		32A	B3
STARLIGHT CIR	HTB	HB47	7000	21	B4
STARLIGHT CIR	NB	NB	1600	31	E3
STARLIGHT DR	ANA	AN		13	A2
STARLIGHT DR	YL	YL		8	F4
STARLIGHT DR	YL	YL		40	A4
STARLING AV	FTNV	SA08	9500	26	E2
STARLING CIR	LAP	BP23		9	D3
STARLING CT	CO	ET		52	A5
STARLING LN	CO	LB56		29C	A1
STARLING WY	ANA	AN	200	12	F1
STARLIT DR	LAG	LB51	1400	34	F3
STARMONT LN	HTB	HB		25	F1
STAR PINE RD	OR	OR69		18	E2
STARR ST	STN	STN	8000	10	C6
STARRISE LN	SJC	SJ75		36	D6
STARSHELL DR	HTB	HB		26	A6
STARSHELL DR	HTB	HB		30	C1
STARSHINE	IRV	SA		32A	C4
STARSHINE DR	HTB	HB47	6500	21	A3
STARSIA ST	WSTM	WSTM	14300	21	E1
STAR THISTLE	IRV	SA		29	C2
STARVIEW LN	CO	LB	31500	35	C5
STARWOOD DR	YL	YL		40	A4
STATE AV	CM	CM	2200	27	B6
STATE AV	CM	CM27	2000	31	B1
STATE COLLGE BL	OR	OR	100	17	A3
STATE COLG BL N	ANA	AN	100	11	F6
STATE COLG BL N	BREA	BREA	100	2	F6
STATE COLG BL N	BREA	BREA		3	A6
STATE COLG BL N	FUL	FL	100	6	F6
STATE COLG BL S	ANA	AN	100	11	F6
STATE COLG BL S	ANA	AN	1600	16	F2
STATE COLG BL S	BREA	BREA	100	2	F6
STATE COLG BL S	BREA	BREA		3	A6
STATE COLG BL S	FUL	FL	100	6	F6
STATE COLG BL S	FUL	FL	1600	11	F6
STATE COLLG PKY	ANA	AN		11	F6
STAY CT	OR	OR68	4400	16	E3
STAYSAIL DR	DPT	DPT	25200	37	F3
STAYSAIL DR	DPT	DPT	32900	38	A3
STEARN CIR	CO	ET		29A	F3
STEARNS AV	LAH	LAH	600	2	B4
STEARNS AV	OR	OR	1800	17	E4
STEARNS DR	CO	SA	17900	17	F4
STEARNS DR	OR	OR	3000	17	F4
STEARNS DR	OR	OR	4000	18	A4
STEELE DR	ANA	AN	1600	16	A1
STEELE DR	BREA	BREA	800	2	D4
STEELE DR	GGR	GG	11600	16	A3
STEELE ST	GGR	GG	11100	16	A2
STEELE WY	GGR	GG	11900	16	A3
STEEP LN	HTB	HB	18400	26	C2
STEEPLECHASE DR	SJC	SJ75		36	D5
STEFFY DR	CO	LB56		29C	E6
STEHLEY ST	ANA	AN	500	12	B4
STEINBECK CT	IRV	SA	3800	24	C6

STREET	CITY	P.O. ZONE	BLOCK	PAGE	GRID
STEINBECK ST	PLA	PLA	1700	7	C3
STEINER CIR	HTB	HB	17700	26	A1
STEINWAY CIR	CO	ET	25100	29A	F3
STELLA AV	ANA	AN	1200	16	B2
STELLA CT	CO	ET	23100	29A	F4
STELLRECHT CIR	HTB	HB49		20	D6
STEM AV	CO	ET	24800	29A	E6
STENGAL ST	WSTM	WSTM	14800	22	A2
STENGEL ST	GGR	GG43	14100	22	A1
STEPHANIE LN	GGR	GG	11500	16	A3
STEPHENS AV	FUL	FL	700	6	A5
STEPHENS AV	GGR	GG	13200	16	E5
STERLING	IRV	SA18		29A	C1
STERLING AV	CM	CM27	1900	31	C2
STERLING AV	HTB	HB	8000	26	C2
STERLING AV	VPK	OR67	10200	13	A6
STERLING CT	FTNV	SA08	15900	22	D6
STERLING DR	CO	ET		29B	A1
STERLING WY	WSTM	WSTM	8400	21	D1
STERN AV	GGR	GG43	10500	22	A2
STERN AV	WSTM	WSTM	10200	22	A2
STERN LN	HTB	HB		26	B4
STERN ST	CO	LB		35	F4
STERN ST	CO	LB77		36	A4
STERN WAVE PL	DPT	DPT	33300	38	B4
STETSON CT	ANA	AN		13	B3
STETSON PL	CO	LB	26500	29C	F4
STEVEN LN	HTB	HB	19200	26	E3
STEVENS AV	LAH	LAH	100	2	A3
STEVENS AV	SA	SA	100	28	B2
STEVENS LN	GGR	GG	13000	15	E5
STEVENS ST	OR	OR	100	17	A3
STEWART DR	OR	OR	1300	17	B4
STEWART ST	HTB	HB	18800	26	B3
STILBITE AV	FTNV	SA08	10000	22	A4
STILES CIR	HTB	HB	16700	20	C6
STILL HARBOR LN	HTB	HB		20	F6
STILL HARBOR LN	HTB	HB	17500	25	F1
STILLWATER	IRV	SA		32A	A2
STILLWATER	MVJO	SJ92		29B	E2
STILLWATER AV	OR	OR		18	C3
STILLWATER DR	HTB	HB		20	C4
STILLWATER LN	ANA	AN		13	E3
STILLWATER LN	CO	LB	23800	35	D3
STILWELL DR	HTB	HB	8800	30	E1
STIMSON ST	GGR	GG	12400	16	D4
STINGRAY LN	HTB	HB	19000	26	F3
STINSON LN	WSTM	WSTM	9400	21	E3
STINSON ST	ANA	AN	100	10	D4
STIRLNGBRDG CIR	YL	YL		8	F3
STIRRUP CT	ANA	AN		13	B3
STIRRUP LN	CO	SA		18	D5
STOCKBRIDGE RD	CO	SA	1400	24	B1
STOCKDALE ST	FTNV	SA08	15900	22	D6
STOCKHOLM WY	HTB	HB	5000	20	D4
STOCKPORT ST	CO	LB		29C	E1
STOCKTON AV	ANA	AN	2600	10	D3
STOLLER LN	CO	SA	19300	18	B3
STONE CIR	ANA	AN	900	12	A4
STONE CIR	HTB	HB	6000	20	F3
STONEBRIDGE DR	BREA	BREA		2	D4
STONEBRIDGE LN	ANA	AN		13	E3
STONEBROOK DR	OR	OR		18	C3
STONEBROOK LN	CM	CM27		31	A1
STONE CANYON AV	CO	YL	5000	8	B4
STONE CANYON WY	BREA	BREA		2	F4
STONE CREEK N	IRV	SA		29	B3
STONE CREEK S	IRV	SA		29	B3
STONECREEK DR	CO	SJ79		56	E6
STONECREEK DR	CO	SJ79		59	E1
STONE CREEK LN	ANA	AN		13	E2
STONE CREEK LN	CO	LB		29C	D2
STONECRESS AV	FTNV	SA08	11000	22	B5
STONECREST	DPT	DPT		37	B5
STONECREST CIR	BREA	BREA		2	D3
STONECREST LN	YL	YL		8	B5
STONEFIELD AV	CM	CM	1300	27	D3
STONE FIELD DR	FTNV	SA08		27	A2
STONEGATE LN	CO	LB77		35	F3
STONEGATE LN	GGR	GG45	11900	14	E3
STONEGATE ST	SA	SA		16	C6
STONEGATE ST	SA	SA		22	C1
STONEGLASS	CO	TUS		23	E2
STONEGLEN	CO	LB56		29C	B3
STONEHAM WY	LAH	LAH	1500	1	E5
STONE HARBR CIR	LAH	LAH		1	F5
STONE HARBR CIR	LAH	LAH		2	A5
STONEHAVEN	CO	TRA		59	D6
STONEHAVEN	MVJO	SJ91		29D	C6
STONEHAVEN CIR	GGR	GG	9400	15	E4

STREET	CITY	P.O. ZONE	BLOCK	PAGE	GRID
STONEHAVEN CIR	HTB	HB		20	E5
STONEHAVEN DR	YL	YL		8	F4
STONEHAVEN LN	CO	ET		29B	A1
STONEHAVEN LN	CO	ET		52	A6
STONEHEDGE CT	CO	YL	5300	8	B4
STONEHEDGE LN	LAH	LAH		2	B5
STONEHEDGE LN	WSTM	WSTM		21	E2
STONEHENGE DR	TUS	TUS	1700	24	B3
STONEHENGE LN	CYP	CYP	9000	9	D4
STONEHILL DR	DPT	LB77		37	F3
STONEHILL DR	DPT	LB77	24000	37	D3
STONEHILL DR	DPT	DPT	33400	38	A4
STONEHURST PZ	YL	YL	6000	8	C5
STONEMAN PL	ANA	AN	1500	16	B1
STONEMAN ST	ANA	AN	1600	16	B1
STONEMILL	CO	SJ79		59	E3
STONEPINE	IRV	SA		29	D3
STONEPINE CT	CO	YL		8	C6
STONEPINE LN	ANA	AN		10	E6
STONE PINE RD	OR	OR		12	F5
STONERIDGE AV	WSTM	WSTM	9000	21	E3
STONERIDGE ST	OR	OR	1800	12	F5
STONE RIVER CT	FTNV	SA08		27	A2
STONETOWER LN	CO	SJ79		56	E6
STONEWALL	IRV	SA		24	E6
STONEWOOD	IRV	SA		29	B2
STONEWOOD CT	FUL	FL		7	A1
STONEWOOD DR	HTB	HB47	7000	21	B4
STONEWOOD DR	YL	YL		40	A3
STONEWOOD ST	LAH	LAH	800	2	B4
STONEYBROOK	MVJO	SJ92		29B	F2
STONEY CREEK RD	CO	SJ		56	D6
STONEY GLEN	CO	ET		52	A5
STONINGTON CIR	HTB	HB	9500	30	F2
STONINGTON RD	LAG	LB77	32100	37	B1
STONY LN	BREA	BREA		3	B5
STONY PL	ANA	AN	700	10	B5
STONYBROOK DR	ANA	AN	2400	10	C5
STONYBROOK DR	CO	AN04	9500	10	C5
STONYBROOK DR	HTB	HB46	10000	27	A5
STONYHAVEN LN	ANA	AN		10	D1
STORDAHL CIR	CO	LB	29800	35	D3
STORM DR	WSTM	WSTM	9100	21	E2
STORY AV	LAH	LAH	2000	1	D5
STOWAWAY CIR	HTB	HB	4400	20	D5
STRADA PL	ANA	AN		12	F2
STRADA CENTRO	NB	NB	300	31	C5
STRADA HAVRE	NB	NB	200	31	D5
STRADELLA AV	CO	YL	5600	8	B4
STRAFFORD	MVJO	SJ92		29D	D3
STRAFFORD	NB	NB60		32	D5
STRAFORD PL	CO	LB53		29D	A4
STRAIT PL	WSTM	WSTM	14400	21	E2
STRAIT ST	WSTM	WSTM	14300	21	E1
STRAND TER	CO	SA	10390	18	D4
STRASBOURG AV	IRV	SA	5300	29	D3
STRATFORD	CO	ET		29B	B1
STRATFORD	IRV	SA		24	C5
STRATFORD AV	WSTM	WSTM	5200	14	E5
STRATFORD CIR	ANA	AN	1700	7	C6
STRATFORD CIR	LAP	BP23	5100	9	D3
STRATFORD CIR	PLA	PLA	100	7	B4
STRATFORD CIR	VPK	OR67	18100	12	F6
STRATFORD CIR	VPK	OR67	17900	13	A6
STRATFORD CT	SA	SA		23	E2
STRATFORD ST	HTB	HB46		26	F3
STRATFORD WY	GGR	GG	11000	15	F2
STRATHCONA DR	HTB	HB	9100	26	E5
STRATHMOOR LN	HTB	HB	21000	26	F6
STRATHMORE DR	GGR	GG	12200	16	C4
STRATHMORE PL	ANA	AN	1700	16	B1
STRATMORE AV	CYP	CYP	5700	9	E6
STRATTFORD ST	BREA	BREA		2	D3
STRATTON CT	CYP	CYP	4000	14	D5
STRATTON LN	CO	LB77		35	E4
STRATTON WY	CO	SA	13900	18	A6
STRATTON WY	CO	SA	14100	24	A1
STRAWBERRY LN	BREA	BREA		3	A6
STRAWBERRY LN	SJC	SJ75		36	E5
STRAWBERRY LN	SA	SA	2500	16	E6
STRAWBERRY RDG	OR	SA05		18	D3
STREAM ST	CO	LB		35	F4
STREAM ST	CO	LB77		36	A4
STREAMWOOD	IRV	SA		24	F5
STREET A	FUL	FL		6	E3
STREET A	NB	NB60		32	A2
ST AMBER LANTRN	DPT	DPT	33900	37	E5
ST ANCHOR LNTRN	DPT	DPT		37	B5
ST BINNACLE LAN	DPT	DPT		37	B5
ST BLUE LANTERN	DPT	DPT	33500	37	E4
ST COPPER LNTRN	DPT	DPT	33700	37	F4

STREET	CITY	P.O. ZONE	BLOCK	PAGE	GRID
ST COVE LANTERN	DPT	DPT	34300	37	B5
ST CRYSTAL LTRN	DPT	DPT	33900	37	F4
ST EASTERN LTRN	DPT	DPT		37	F5
ST GOLDEN LNTRN	CO	LB77		35	F6
ST GOLDEN LNTRN	CO	LB77		37	F2
ST GOLDEN LNTRN	DPT	DPT	33700	37	E4
ST GOLDEN LNTRN	CO	LB77		36	A2
ST GREEN LANTRN	DPT	DPT	33300	37	E5
ST PARK LANTERN	DPT	DPT		37	F5
ST PORT LANTERN	DPT	DPT	34300	37	B5
ST RUBY LANTERN	DPT	DPT	34000	37	E4
ST SHORE LANTRN	DPT	DPT	34300	37	B5
ST SILVER LNTRN	DPT	DPT	33700	37	F4
ST STARBRD LTRN	DPT	DPT	24700	37	B5
ST TERRACE LTRN	DPT	DPT		37	B5
ST VIOLET LNTRN	DPT	DPT	33900	37	E4
ST WESTERN LTRN	DPT	DPT	34300	37	B5
STROMBOLI RD	CM	CM	2800	27	B4
STRONG PL	ANA	AN	2500	12	A5
STRUCK AV	CO	OR69	15000	17	B1
STRUCK AV	OR	OR	1000	17	B1
STUART DR	GGR	GG	11500	16	C5
STUDEBAKER	IRV	SA18		29A	D1
STUECKLE AV	ANA	AN	100	11	D4
STULINDA AV	CO	LB77		35	D1
STURBRIDGE DR	LAH	LAH	700	1	E6
STURGEON AV	FTNV	SA08	9500	26	F1
STURGEON DR	CM	CM26	500	28	A3
STYLE DR	GGR	GG	10200	15	F3
STYMIE AV	HTB	HB	8400	26	D1
SUBURBIA LN	HTB	HB46	20500	27	A6
SUBURNAS WY	CO	SA	11500	18	C5
SUDBURY PL	CO	LB		35	E6
SUDBURY PL	CO	LB77		37	E1
SUDENE AV	FUL	FL	1100	6	D5
SUDITH AV	FTNV	SA08	11000	22	B5
SUE DR	PLA	PLA	700	7	C5
SUFFIELD ST	LAP	BP23	8200	9	D3
SUFFOLK CIR	OR	OR		13	D6
SUFFOLK CIR	YL	YL	16900	7	D4
SUFFOLK COM	SA	SA		22	C2
SUFFOLK LN	SJC	SJ75		36	D5
SUFFOLK ST	WSTM	WSTM		20	E1
SUFFOLK DOWNS	CO	LB		35	E6
SUFFOLK DOWNS	CO	LB77		37	E1
SUGAR AV	CO	MDWY	8100	21	C3
SUGARBUSH CIR	CO	SJ79		56	E6
SUGARBUSH CIR	CO	SJ79		59	E1
SUGARLOAF ST	FTNV	SA08	16500	22	B5
SUGAR MAPLE PL	TUS	TUS		24	D4
SUGARPINE	IRV	SA		29	C5
SUGARPINE DR	CO	SJ79		52	F4
SUGAR PINE DR	YL	YL		7	E4
SUGAR PINE LN	CO	OR		18	B2
SUGAR PINE WY	GGR	SA03		16	D6
SUGARWOOD LN	ANA	AN		11	E6
SUITE DR	HTB	HB	4500	20	D4
SULLIVAN PL	BPK	BP21		10	B1
SULLIVAN ST N&S	SA	SA	100	22	E3
SUMAC AV	IRV	SA	14800	29	C1
SUMAC LN	ANA	AN	1500	16	B1
SUMAC LN	FTNV	SA08	18000	26	E1
SUMAC RIDGE DR	CO	YL	5000	8	B4
SUMATRA PL	CM	CM	3100	27	C3
SUMBA CIR	CM	CM	1900	27	B4
SUMMER CIR	HTB	HB	21900	30	F2
SUMMER ST	ANA	AN	900	11	C3
SUMMER BREEZE	IRV	SA		32A	C4
SUMMR BREEZE DR	HTB	HB		26	B4
SUMMER CLOUD LN	HTB	HB47	16600	21	A5
SUMMER CREEK	CO	ET	26400	29B	B2
SUMMERDALE DR	HTB	HB	6000	20	F6
SUMMERFIELD	CO	LB56		29C	C4
SUMMERFIELD	IRV	SA		29	B5
SUMMERFIELD	MVJO	SJ92		29B	E2
SUMMERFIELD CIR	BREA	BREA		3	A5
SUMMERFIELD LN	HTB	HB	19000	26	D3
SUMMERFIELD LN	SJC	SJ75		36	D6
SUMMERHILL CT	CO	SJ79		59	C5
SUMMERHILL LN	CO	LB56		29C	C3
SUMMERLAKE	IRV	SA		29	B5
SUMMER LAKE CIR	BREA	BREA		2	D5
SUMMERSET	IRV	SA		32A	C4
SUMMERSET CIR	CM	CM		27	D2
SUMMERSHADE DR	LAH	LAH	2400	1	D6
SUMMERSIDE	CO	TRA		59	D5
SUMMERSTONE	IRV	SA		29	A4
SUMMERSWORTH PL	FUL	FL33		5	E4
SUMMERTREE LN	STN	STN	10500	15	B3
SUMMERTREE RD	ANA	AN		13	D2
SUMMER VIEW CIR	CO	SA04		22	D4

COPYRIGHT, © 1989 BY Thomas Bros Maps

STREET	CITY	P.O. ZONE	BLOCK	PAGE	GRID
SUMMERVILLE AV	TUS	TUS	1700	23	F5
SUMMERWALK CT	NB	NB		31	A2
SUMMERWIND	DPT	DPT		37	F3
SUMMERWIND	IRV	SA		29	A4
SUMMER WIND	SA	SA04		27	E2
SUMMERWIND CT	NB	NB		31	B4
SUMMERWIND LN	CO	ET		29A	E1
SUMMERWIND LN	HTB	HB	21500	30	F2
SUMMERWOOD	CO	LB56		29C	B3
SUMMERWOOD DR	FUL	FL33		5	F2
SUMMERWOOD LN	YL	YL		7	F4
SUMMERWOOD WY	CO	ET	26900	29B	C1
SUMMERWOOD WY	CO	ET		52	C6
SUMMIT	IRV	SA		32A	A3
SUMMIT AV	DPT	DPT		37	D5
SUMMIT CIR	FUL	FL33	1900	5	F3
SUMMIT CIR	WSTM	WSTM	13200	15	A5
SUMMIT CT	ANA	AN		13	D3
SUMMIT DR	LAG	LB51	700	34	E4
SUMMIT DR	YL	YL		8	A3
SUMMIT LN	LAG	LB77		37	B1
SUMMIT PL	LAG	LB51	1100	34	F3
SUMMIT RD	LAG	LB	31500	35	B5
SUMMIT ST	NB	NB63	100	30	F4
SUMMIT WY	LAG	LB51	900	34	F3
SUMMIT CAMINO	OR	OR69		18	C1
SUMMITCREST	CO	SJ79		59	D2
SUMMIT HILL DR	CO	ET		29B	B2
SUMMIT LAKE DR	ANA	AN		13	F3
SUMMITRIDGE LN	OR	OR		12	F4
SUMMITRIDGE LN	OR	OR		13	A4
SUMMITVIEW DR	FUL	FL33		5	E2
SUMNER PL	CO	CYP	8500	9	D4
SUMO CIR	GGR	GG	11800	16	C4
SUN DR	HTB	HB47	6600	21	A5
SUNBEAM CIR	HTB	HB	8300	26	D2
SUNBREEZE DR	HTB	HB47		21	B6
SUNBRIDGE PL	DPT	DPT		37	B5
SUNBROOK	MVJO	SJ92		29B	E2
SUNBURST	IRV	SA		32A	A3
SUNBURST AV	CO	LB		29C	F2
SUNBURST LN	HTB	HB47	6900	21	B3
SUNBURST WY	ANA	AN		12	A6
SUNCORAL DR	HTB	HB		26	D3
SUNCREEK	IRV	SA		29	D5
SUNCREST CIR	BREA	BREA		3	A5
SUNCREST RD	ANA	AN		13	E2
SUNDANCE AV	CO	LB		29C	E3
SUNDANCE CIR	HTB	HB	6400	26	A1
SUNDANCE CIR	OR	OR		18	D2
SUNDANCE DR	IRV	SA		32A	A3
SUNDANCE DR	NB	NB		31	A3
SUNDANCE DR	SJC	SJ75		36	D6
SUNDANCE LN	CM	CM27		31	B2
SUNDANCE LN	LAP	BP23		9	E3
SUNDANCER LN	HTB	HB		20	C5
SUNDAY DR	HTB	HB46	10400	27	A3
SUNDERLAND ST	CO	SA		18	D3
SUNDIAL	IRV	SA		32A	B3
SUNDOWN CT	DPT	DPT		37	A5
SUNDOWN LN	ANA	AN		8	B5
SUNDOWN LN	HTB	HB		26	C6
SUNDOWN LN	YL	YL	19000	8	B3
SUNDOWNER DR	CO	LB	27100	29D	A4
SUNDOWNERS LN	CO	ET	21900	29B	B2
SUNDOWN PASS	IRV	SA		29	C1
SUNFISH	IRV	SA		29	C3
SUNFISH WY	DPT	DPT		37	A5
SUNFLOWER	IRV	SA		29	A1
SUNFLOWER AV	CM	CM	1500	27	C2
SUNFLOWER AV	CM	CM26	13900	28	A2
SUNFLOWER AV	CO	SA07	12000	27	C2
SUNFLOWER AV	PLA	PLA	500	7	C4
SUNFLOWER AV	SA	SA04	12000	27	D2
SUNFLOWER CIR	SB	SB	3500	14	D5
SUNFLOWER LN	HTB	HB47	15600	21	B3
SUNFLOWER LN	LAP	BP23		9	E2
SUNFLOWER ST	BREA	BREA		3	C6
SUNFLOWER ST	SB	SB	3800	14	D4
SUNGATE	IRV	SA		32A	B3
SUNGROVE	IRV	SA		29	D5
SUNGROVE CIR	GGR	GG	11800	16	F2
SUNGROVE PL	BREA	BREA	1000	2	F5
SUNGROVE ST	GGR	GG	12100	16	D4
SUNHARBOR	DPT	DPT		37	F3
SUN HILL DR	YL	YL	17700	7	F5
SUNKIST CIR	HTB	HB		26	D3
SUNKIST ST	ANA	AN06		17	A1
SUNKIST ST N&S	ANA	AN	100	12	A4
SUNKIST WY	ANA	AN	1100	12	A2
SUN KNOLL CIR	YL	YL	5800	7	F5
SUN KNOLL DR	YL	YL	17900	7	F5
SUNLAND LN	CM	CM		27	C2
SUNLAND WY	CM	CM		27	C2
SUNLIGHT	IRV	SA		32A	B3
SUNLIGHT DR	HTB	HB47	7000	21	B4
SUNLIGHT CREEK	CO	ET	22200	29B	B2
SUNMIST DR	YL	YL	5700	8	B5
SUNMIST LN	YL	YL		8	B4
SUNN CIR	FTNV	SA08	10000	22	A4
SUNNINGDALE CIR	OR	OR68	100	16	E3
SUNNINGDALE RD	SB	SB	1600	14	A5
SUNNY CIR	CYP	CYP	9800	9	F6
SUNNY LN	YL	YL	4100	7	F2
SUNNYBROOK AV	BPK	BP	8300	5	C3
SUNNYBROOK CIR	BPK	BP	4900	5	C3
SUNNYBROOK CIR	CO	ET	25100	29A	E3
SUNNYBROOK CIR	GGR	GG		15	D5
SUNNYBROOK DR	LAH	LAH	800	1	E4
SUNNY CREST DR	FUL	FL	1300	6	B3
SUNNYCREST LN	HTB	HB47	14600	21	A2
SUNNYGLEN AV	CO	LB		29C	E3
SUNNYHILL	IRV	SA		32A	B3
SUNNYHILL WY	ANA	AN08		43	B1
SUNNYHILLS AV	BREA	BREA		2	D4
SUNNY HILLS RD	FUL	FL	400	6	C1
SUNNY HLLS RD E	FUL	FL35	500	2	C6
SUNNY KNOLL	FUL	FL	200	6	C3
SUNNY RIDGE	CO	ET		52	C4
SUNNY RIDGE DR	FUL	FL33		5	E4
SUNNY RIDGE PL	FUL	FL33		5	E2
SUNNYSIDE DR	YL	YL		8	D1
SUNNY SIDE LN	ANA	AN	13100	11	E6
SUNNY SLOPE RD	LAG	LB	200	34	B1
SUNNYVALE AV	GGR	GG	13400	15	D5
SUNNYVALE AV	WSTM	WSTM	13500	15	D5
SUNNYVIEW CIR	YL	YL	5400	8	B5
SUNNYWOOD DR	FUL	FL	2800	6	C1
SUNPEAK	IRV	SA		32A	A2
SUNRAY LN	HTB	HB		26	C3
SUNRIDGE	IRV	SA		29	C2
SUNRIDGE DR	DPT	DPT		38	B4
SUNRIDGE DR	HTB	HB	9300	26	E6
SUNRISE	IRV	SA		32A	B3
SUNRISE AV	ANA	AN	2100	10	F4
SUNRISE CIR	CM	CM27		31	F1
SUNRISE CT	DPT	DPT		37	A5
SUNRISE DR	HTB	HB		30	C1
SUNRISE LN	CO	SA	9800	18	D4
SUNRISE LN	FUL	FL33	1600	5	F3
SUNRISE PL	YL	YL	19000	8	B3
SUNRISE RD	BREA	BREA		3	B5
SUNRISE ST	PLA	PLA	100	7	A5
SUNRISE WY	PLA	PLA	500	7	A5
SUNRISE VIA	ANA	AN	100	10	D4
SUNRIVER	IRV	SA		29	A4
SUNROSE	IRV	SA		32A	B3
SUNSET AV	ANA	AN	2100	10	F4
SUNSET AV	LAG	LB	31700	35	B6
SUNSET AV	LAG	LB77	31800	37	B1
SUNSET CIR	HTB	HB	8000	26	C6
SUNSET CT	FTNV	SA08	18000	27	A1
SUNSET DR	CM	CM27	900	31	B3
SUNSET DR	NB	NB	6600	31	A3
SUNSET DR	PLA	PLA	600	7	A5
SUNSET LN	CO	ET		29A	E1
SUNSET LN	FUL	FL33	1500	5	F3
SUNSET LN	YL	YL	5500	8	A4
SUNSET PL	CO	LB	24000	29C	E1
SUNSET PL E	CO	LB	24000	29C	E1
SUNSET PL W	CO	LB	24000	29C	E1
SUNSET ST	OR	OR	4000	12	D2
SUNSET ST	SA	SA	500	22	E2
SUNSET ST N	LAH	LAH	100	2	B5
SUNSET ST S	LAH	LAH	300	2	B5
SUNSET TER	LAG	LB51	100	34	F5
SUNSET WY E	SB	SB		20	B4
SUNSET RIDGE DR	LAG	LB51	1600	34	B2
SUNSET RIDGE RD	LAG	LB	200	34	B2
SUNSET RIVER	IRV	SA		29	C3
SUNSET VIA	ANA	AN	100	10	D4
SUNSHINE	IRV	SA		32A	C4
SUNSHINE DR	HTB	HB	9000	26	E5
SUNSHINE WY	ANA	AN	1300	12	A2
SUNSIDE AV	WSTM	WSTM	6400	21	A1
SUN STAG RUN	CO	SIL		50	D1
SUNSTAR CIR	HTB	HB	9800	30	F5
SUNSTAR LN	DPT	DPT		37	F4
SUNSTONE	MVJO	SJ91		29D	C5
SUNSTREAM	IRV	SA		32A	C4
SUNSWEPT AV	GGR	GG	12500	16	D6
SUNSWEPT AV	SA	SA	3500	22	C1
SUNTAN CIR	HTB	HB46	10000	27	A6
SUNUP	IRV	SA		32A	C4
SUN VALLEY DR	CO	SA15	20300	33A	E4
SUNVIEW DR	ANA	AN	3200	10	B6
SUNVIEW DR	HTB	HB47	6700	21	A3
SUNVIEW DR	OR	OR	1500	12	E3
SUN VIEW RD	YL	YL	5800	7	F5
SUNWEST CIR	YL	YL		7	E3
SUNWOOD LN	ANA	AN		8	B5
SUPERIOR AV	CM	CM27	1500	31	C4
SUPERIOR AV	LAH	LAH	1200	2	B5
SUPERIOR AV	NB	NB	400	31	B4
SUPERIOR LN	CO	ET		29A	E1
SUR AV	IRV	SA		24	C6
SURF DR	ANA	AN	1200	11	A2
SURF DR	SCL	SC72		39	A2
SURF PL	SB	SB	100	19	E2
SURF ST	CM	CM27	600	31	C2
SURFBIRD LN	CO	LB53		29A	B6
SURFBREAKER LN	HTB	HB		26	B4
SURF BREAKRS DR	DPT	LB77		37	B3
SURFCLIFF	DPT	DPT		37	F3
SURF COVE	CO	LB		35	D2
SURF CREST DR	DPT	LB77	23100	37	C3
SURFCREST DR	HTB	HB46	9600	30	F2
SURFDALE DR	HTB	HB		26	B4
SURFLINE DR	HTB	HB46		26	C3
SURFLINE WY	NB	CDLM	1200	32	B6
SURFRIDER CT	SJC	SJ75		38	B2
SURFRIDER LN	HTB	HB	22000	30	E2
SURF SHOAL PL	DPT	DPT	33400	38	B4
SURFSIDE	CO	LB		29A	C4
SURFSIDE AV	HTB	HB	2500	20	A4
SURFSIDE AV	SB	SURF	2600	20	A4
SURFSIDE CT	NB	NB63		31	A2
SURFSIDE DR	DPT	DPT		38	D3
SURFSIDE DR	HTB	HB		26	B4
SURFVIEW LN	NB	CDLM	3500	33	C1
SURFWOOD LN	HTB	HB	21000	30	C2
SURGE LN	HTB	HB46	20900	27	A6
SURPRISE LN	HTB	HB		20	B3
SURREY CIR	SA	SA	1500	22	F6
SURREY CIR	SA	SA04	1500	27	F1
SURREY DR	CYP	CYP	4200	9	C5
SURREY DR	NB	CDLM	4500	33	C2
SURRY CT	BREA	BREA	300	2	F5
SURVEYOR AV	BREA	BREA		3	C6
SURVEYOR CIR	HTB	HB		30	D1
SUSAN CIR	GGR	GG	9800	15	F4
SUSAN CIR	LAP	BP20	7400	9	F1
SUSAN LN	GGR	GG	12600	15	F4
SUSAN LN	HTB	HB	22000	30	E2
SUSAN LN	LAH	LAH	1400	2	C3
SUSAN ST	SA	SA		16	D6
SUSAN ST	SA	SA	2000	22	D6
SUSAN ST	SA	SA04	2800	27	D1
SUSANGLEN CIR	LAH	LAH	600	1	F5
SUSANNAH PL	CM	CM	200	27	E6
SUSANNE AV	ANA	AN	200	11	D5
SUSQUEHANNA AV	PLA	PLA	1700	7	C3
SUSSEX CIR	CYP	CYP	4200	9	C5
SUSSEX CIR	GGR	GG	12800	16	F3
SUSSEX CIR	HTB	HB47	15000	21	B2
SUSSEX LN	NB	NB	1200	31	E4
SUSSEX PL	CO	SA	13100	18	A5
SUSSEX PL E	CO	SA	18500	18	A5
SUSSEX ST	HTB	HB46		26	F3
SUTHERLAND DR	YL	YL		8	E3
SUTHERLAND WY	GGR	GG	9500	21	F1
SUTHERLAND WY	WSTM	WSTM	9400	21	F1
SUTTER CIR	HTB	HB		26	E6
SUTTER DR	CO	LB	25400	29D	A1
SUTTER DR	WSTM	WSTM	13400	15	A6
SUTTER ST	GGR	GG	12700	15	A4
SUTTER ST	SA	SA	2800	23	C6
SUTTER ST	SA	SA	2900	28	C1
SUTTER WY	CM	CM	2800	27	E4
SUTTER WY	FUL	FL33		5	F3
SUTTER CREEK RD	ANA	AN	900	10	F6
SUTTER VIA	ANA	AN		16	D1
SUTTON DR	CO	ET	23600	29A	D4
SUTTON LN	CO	LB77		35	E4
SUTTON LN	HTB	HB	19900	26	F4
SUTTON ST	WSTM	WSTM	13300	15	A5
SUVA CIR	CM	CM	1900	27	B4
SUVA LN	HTB	HB46	19000	27	A3
SUVA ST	CYP	CYP	5900	14	F2
SUZETTE RIV CIR	FTNV	SA08		22	C4
SUZI LN	WSTM	WSTM		21	C1
SUZIE LN	CO	ET		29A	F3
SWALLOW AV	FTNV	SA08	8800	26	E3
SWALLOW AV	FTNV	SA08	10200	27	A3
SWALLOW AV	OR	OR	4600	18	B1
SWALLOW LN	CO	ET	23500	29A	D4
SWALLOW LN	GGR	GG	9500	15	E2
SWALLOW LN	WSTM	WSTM	15200	21	F3
SWALLOW WY	ANA	AN		13	F3
SWALLOWTAIL	IRV	SA		29	D1
SWALLOWTAIL DR	CO	LB	23900	35	D1
SWAN CIR	CM	CM	1900	27	B5
SWAN CIR	FTNV	SA08	9800	26	F2
SWAN CIR	LAP	BP23	8000	9	C3
SWAN DR	CM	CM	1900	27	A5
SWAN DR	CO	ET	23900	29A	D4
SWAN LN	CO	LB53		29A	B6
SWAN LN	HTB	HB	15600	20	E4
SWAN ST	ANA	AN	1000	11	C2
SWAN ST	OR	OR	700	18	B2
SWAN ST	WSTM	WSTM	14000	15	E6
SWAN ST	WSTM	WSTM	14100	21	E2
SWANEE AV	PLA	PLA	200	7	B3
SWANSEA CIR	LAH	LAH	1700	2	B3
SWANSEA LN	HTB	HB	20100	26	E5
SWANSON AV	PLA	PLA	300	7	C2
SWANWAY CT	DPT	DPT	25200	37	F2
SWARTHMORE DR	ANA	AN		13	F4
SWARTHMORE LN	CM	CM	400	27	C5
SWARTZ DR	CO	ET	23600	29A	E5
SWEET AV	FUL	FL	200	6	A5
SWEETAN ST	IRV	SA	14500	29	D2
SWEETBAY CT	ANA	AN		10	E6
SWEETBRIAR DR	GGR	GG	12500	16	D4
SWEETBRIAR LN	HTB	HB47	15600	21	A3
SWEETBRIAR RD	TUS	TUS	2100	24	A5
SWEETBRIER LN	MVJO	SJ91		52	D6
SWEETCLOVER	IRV	SA		29	B2
SWEET GRASS CIR	CO	ET	21700	29B	A1
SWEETLEAF ST	FTNV	SA08	16000	21	E4
SWEET MEADOW	CO	LB77		36	A4
SWEET MEADOW	MVJO	SJ92		29B	E3
SWEET RAIN	IRV	SA		29	B4
SWEETSHADE WY	TUS	TUS		24	D3
SWEETWATER	IRV	SA		32A	A1
SWEETWATER CIR	HTB	HB	8300	26	D2
SWEETWATER DR	BREA	BREA		3	B5
SWEETWATER LN	OR	OR69		18	E3
SWEETWATER PL	YL	YL	5700	8	C4
SWEETWATER ST N	ANA	AN	100	12	F2
SWELL ST	OR	OR	2700	12	D4
SWIDLER PL	CO	SA	12600	18	A4
SWIDLER PL	OR	OR	100	18	A3
SWIDLER ST	OR	OR	300	18	A2
SWIFT AV	FTNV	SA08	9400	26	E2
SWIFT CT	NB	NB		31	B4
SWIFT RIVER CT	CO	ET		29A	D3
SWIFTSAIL	IRV	SA		29	B5
SWORDFISH AV	FTNV	SA08	8700	26	D1
SYCAMORE	IRV	SA		29	D2
SYCAMORE AV	BREA	BREA	300	2	E6
SYCAMORE AV	BREA	BREA	500	6	E1
SYCAMORE AV	FUL	FL	700	6	F5
SYCAMORE AV	HTB	HB47	7700	21	C5
SYCAMORE AV	LAH	LAH	800	2	B3
SYCAMORE AV	STN	STN	10500	15	C1
SYCAMORE AV	TUS	TUS	1200	23	E4
SYCAMORE AV	TUS	TUS	1900	24	A5
SYCAMORE AV E	OR	OR	3600	18	A2
SYCAMORE AV E&W	OR	OR	100	17	C2
SYCAMORE CIR	VPK	OR67	10200	13	B6
SYCAMORE CIR	YL	YL	18500	8	A3
SYCAMORE CT	FUL	FL		7	A2
SYCAMORE DR	CO	SJ91		29A	F5
SYCAMORE DR	CO	SIL	28600	50	E2
SYCAMORE DR	CO	SJ		56	C5
SYCAMORE DR	FUL	FL		7	A2
SYCAMORE LN	CM	CM		27	E6
SYCAMORE LN	CO	LB		29D	A1
SYCAMORE PL	FUL	FL		7	A2
SYCAMORE PT	CO	ET		29B	A2
SYCAMORE RD	CO	SJ		56	C5
SYCAMORE ST	FTNV	SA08	16300	21	F4
SYCAMORE ST	STN	GG41	12700	15	C4
SYCAMORE ST	VPK	OR67	9900	13	B6
SYCAMORE ST E	ANA	AN	2000	12	A3
SYCAMORE ST E&W	ANA	AN	100	11	C3
SYCAMORE ST N	SA	SA	1500	17	B6
SYCAMORE ST N	SA	SA	100	23	B4
SYCAMORE ST S	SA	SA	100	23	B4
SYCAMORE ST S	SA	SA	3200	28	B1
SYCAMORE CYN DR	CO	SJ79		59	D3
SYCAMORE CREEK	IRV	SA		32A	A2
SYCAMORE GN DR	CO	SJ		52	E3
SYDNEY DR	HTB	HB	6000	20	F3
SYDNEY ST	SA	SA	1700	16	E6
SYLVAN DR	OR	OR	2700	12	C4
SYLVAN ST	ANA	AN	600	10	D5
SYLVAN ST	ANA	AN04	1400	15	D1
SYLVAN ST	GGR	GG45	12600	14	F4
SYLVAN ST	STN	AN04	10500	10	D6
SYLVAN ST	STN	AN04	10500	15	D1
SYLVANITE CIR	FTNV	SA08	11400	22	C5
SYLVAN RIVER	FTNV	SA08		22	D4
SYLVIA DR	HTB	HB47	6800	21	A5
SYLVIA LN	NB	NB	1500	31	E3
SYMPHONY AV	PLA	PLA	800	7	D3
SYMPHONY ST	ANA	AN		8	A5
SYRACUSE AV	CO	AN04	8700	15	D1
SYRACUSE AV	STN	STN	7000	15	A1
SYRACUSE ST	ANA	AN	100	10	D4
SYRACUSE ST	WSTM	WSTM	15000	21	C3
SYSTEM DR	HTB	HB		20	E4
T					
T ST	ETMC	SA09		51	D4
T ST	NB	CDLM	2900	33	A2
TABAGO PL	CM	CM	2800	27	C4
TABAH LN	CO	PLA	16200	7	D3
TABLE ROCK DR	LAG	LB	31500	35	A6
TABLEROCK PL	ANA	AN		13	B2
TABOR DR	IRV	SA		32	F2
TABUENCA	MVJO	SJ92	24500	29B	E6
TACOMA CIR	VPK	OR67	17800	17	F1
TACOMA ST	GGR	GG	11400	16	A2
TAFOLLA ST	PLA	PLA	800	12	A1
TAFT AV	OR	OR		12	C6
TAFT AV	VPK	OR67	17900	12	E5
TAFT AV	VPK	OR67	18300	13	B5
TAFT AV E&W	OR	OR	100	12	E6
TAFT LN	HTB	HB	15800	20	E4
TAFT ST	GGR	GG	13000	16	B6
TAFT ST	GGR	GG43	14100	22	A1
TAFT ST	IRV	SA		29	E2
TAFT WY	CM	CM	3100	27	E3
TAHITI AV	LAG	LB51	1500	34	E2
TAHITI CIR	HTB	HB	9300	30	E2
TAHITI DR	CM	CM	1800	27	B4
TAHITI DR	CYP	CYP	6700	15	A3
TAHITIAN CIR	CO	YL	6400	8	C6
TAHOE	IRV	SA		29	A6
TAHOE AV	PLA	PLA	400	7	C3
TAHOE CIR	BPK	BP	5600	5	C4
TAHOE CIR	FTNV	SA08	18500	26	F2
TAHOE CIR	LAP	BP23	5600	9	E2
TAHOE CT	CO	LB		29C	E6
TAHOE CT	CO	LB	24000	35	E1
TAHOE DR	PLA	PLA	500	7	C3
TAHOE LN	CO	ET		29A	E1
TAHOE ST	WSTM	WSTM	13400	15	B6
TAHOMA ST	FTNV	SA08		21	F5
TAHUNA TER	NB	CDLM	1900	32	A6
TAHUNA TER	NB	NB	2100	33	A1
TAJO	MVJO	SJ92		29D	C4
TALADRO CIR	MVJO	SJ91		29B	A4
TALAUD ST	CYP	CYP	11500	14	F2
TALAVERA DR	CO	LB		35	C5
TALBERT AV	CM	CM	900	27	B1
TALBERT AV	FTNV	SA08	8600	26	C1
TALBERT AV	FTNV	SA08	10000	27	B1
TALBERT AV	HTB	HB		25	F1
TALBERT AV	HTB	HB	6200	26	C1
TALBOT WY	ANA	AN		16	F2
TALEGA	CO	SJ88		59	A4
TALEGA AV	CO	LB		29C	E3
TALEGATE DR	HTB	HB		26	A2
TALISMAN LN	HTB	HB	16500	20	D5
TALLEY ST	IRV	SA	15000	29	D3
TALT AV	ANA	AN	1300	11	F6
TALT AV	ANA	AN	1200	12	A6
TAMA DR	CO	ET	22100	29A	E6
TAMA LN	CO	LB53		29C	E6
TAMARA DR	ANA	AN	3000	10	C4
TAMARA LN	ANA	AN	1800	16	C1
TAMARAC LN	TUS	TUS	2100	24	B4
TAMARACK AV	BREA	BREA	800	2	E4
TAMARACK DR N	FUL	FL	900	6	C4
TAMARACK DR S	FUL	FL	500	6	C6
TAMARACK DR S	FUL	FL	1000	11	C1
TAMARACK WY	BPK	BP	8500	10	D3
TAMARACK WY	IRV	SA		29	B6
TAMARACK WY	STN	STN	10600	15	C1
TAMARIND	MVJO	SJ92		29D	E1

ORANGE CO. — INDEX

COPYRIGHT © 1989 BY Thomas Bros. Maps — Z

1990 ORANGE COUNTY STREET INDEX

STREET	CITY	P.O. ZONE	BLOCK	PAGE	GRID
TOLLON	CO	SJ88		59	A4
TOLUCA CT	CO	LB	25900	29C	E2
TOLUCA ST	OR	OR	300	17	D4
TOMAHAWK ST	FTNV	SA08	18700	26	D3
TOMAS	CO	SJ88		59	A2
TOMAS LN	HTB	HB	16000	20	E4
TOMBSTONE RD	CO	LB		29D	A3
TOMELLOSO	MVJO	SJ92	28600	29B	E1
TONADA DR	IRV	SA		24	E5
TONGA CIR	CYP	CYP	6100	14	F2
TONGA LN	HTB	HB46	19000	27	A3
TONIA AV	CO	ET	24500	29A	E2
TONIA CT	ANA	AN	1500	16	B2
TONIA LN	ANA	AN	1300	16	C2
TONIA PL	ANA	AN	1600	16	B2
TONIA VIA	ANA	AN		16	D2
TONNER CYN RD	CO	BREA	15000	3	B4
TONO	MVJO	SJ92		29D	D2
TOPANGA DR	ANA	AN	100	10	B4
TOPAZ	BREA	BREA	100	4	B5
TOPAZ	MVJO	SJ91		29D	C5
TOPAZ AV	ANA	AN	1200	11	E5
TOPAZ AV	FTNV	SA08	11200	22	B4
TOPAZ AV	LAH	LAH	2000	2	C4
TOPAZ AV	NB	NB	100	31	E6
TOPAZ CIR	GGR	GG45	11900	14	F3
TOPAZ LN	FUL	FL	3000	7	A3
TOPAZ ST	GGR	GG45	12300	14	F4
TOPAZ ST	OR	OR	1900	12	E5
TOPAZ ST	WSTM	WSTM	15700	21	E4
TOPEKA	IRV	SA		29	E2
TOPEKA LN	HTB	HB	19500	26	D4
TOPEKA ST	ANA	AN	100	11	D3
TOPO ST	ANA	AN	200	10	E4
TOP O T WRLD DR	LAG	LB51	28700	35	A2
TOPONAS CT	CO	LB		29C	E6
TOPONAS CT	CO	LB	24000	35	E1
TOPSAIL	CO	LAG		35	F3
TOPSIDE CIR	HTB	HB	8500	26	D3
TOPSIDE LN	NB	CDLM		33	C1
TORCHWOOD CIR	WSTM	WSTM	8300	21	D3
TORENA CIR	MVJO	SJ91	24000	29B	C5
TORERO CIR	MVJO	SJ91		29B	C4
TORIDA WY	YL	YL	4600	7	E3
TORIJA	MVJO	SJ91	27600	29B	D2
TORIN DR	HTB	HB	6200	25	F1
TORINA LN	CO	LB	23000	35	C5
TORINO	CO	LB		29A	B4
TORJIAN LN	HTB	HB47	16500	21	A5
TORONTO AV	HTB	HB	200	26	C4
TORONTO WY	CM	CM		27	C2
TORRENS ST	ANA	AN	200	12	F2
TORRENTERRA	SCL	SC72		38	F4
TORRES ST	OR	OR	2400	12	D4
TORREY CIR	CO	LB77		35	E6
TORREYPINE DR	FUL	FL		6	E2
TORREY PINE LN	GGR	SA03		16	D6
TORREY PINE LN	MVJO	SJ91		52	D6
TORREY PINE PL	YL	YL		7	E5
TORREY PNES CIR	ANA	AN07	400	13	B2
TORREYPINES CIR	HTB	HB48		25	E2
TORREY PINES LN	NB	NB		32	B4
TORRIGIANI ISLE	IRV	SA14		28	D5
TORRINGTON CIR	WSTM	WSTM		22	A2
TORROBA	MVJO	SJ92	27700	29B	D5
TORRY PL	ANA	AN	1100	11	F5
TORTOISE SHELL	IRV	SA		29	D1
TORTOLA	MVJO	SJ92		29B	F1
TORTOLA CIR	HTB	HB	3700	20	C4
TORTUGA DR	HTB	HB		20	E6
TORTUGA ST	CYP	CYP	11200	14	F2
TORY	IRV	SA		24	E6
TOSCANY	IRV	SA14		29	A3
TOSSA DEL MAR	CO	ET		29A	F4
TOSSAMAR	MVJO	SJ92		29D	C4
TOSTON	MVJO	SJ92		29B	E3
TOTO LOMA LN	LAG	LB	31500	35	B6
TOTUAVA CIR	MVJO	SJ91		29B	C5
TOUCAN AV	FTNV	SA08	9200	26	F2
TOUCAN CIR	FTNV	SA08	9800	26	F2
TOUCHSTONE DR	GGR	GG	12000	15	E3
TOULAN WY	YL	YL		40	D6
TOULON	CO	LB77		35	F4
TOULON	LAG	LB		35	B6
TOULON	NB	CDLM		32	D5
TOULOUSE CIR	IRV	SA	15400	29	D3
TOULOUSE DR	HTB	HB47	7200	21	B5
TOULOUSE DR	LAP	BP23	5000	9	D2
TOURAINE WY	IRV	SA	15100	29	D3
TOURMALINE CT	ANA	AN		13	D3
TOURS AV	GGR	GG	12500	16	D6
TOURS LN	CM	CM27	300	31	F2
TOUSSAU DR	FUL	FL	700	6	D4
TOWAY LN	HTB	HB47	15500	21	A3
TOWER CT	ANA	AN	100	12	A3
TOWER PL	ANA	AN	300	12	A3
TOWN&COUNTRY DR	GGR	GG	9300	15	E2
TOWN&COUNTRY RD	OR	OR	1000	17	B4
TOWN CENTER DR	CM	CM26		28	A2
TOWN CENTER DR	CO	LB		35	D4
TOWNE ST	CM	CM27	900	31	B2
TOWNE CENTRE PL	ANA	AN06		17	A2
TOWNER LN N	SA	SA	2600	17	A5
TOWNER ST N	SA	SA	1700	17	A6
TOWNER ST N	SA	SA	800	23	A4
TOWNER ST S	SA	SA	1100	23	A4
TOWNER ST S	SA	SA	3400	28	A1
TOWN HOUSE DR	CM	CM27		31	A1
TOWNHOUSE DR	TUS	TUS	1000	23	E3
TOWNLEY ST	SA	SA	2400	16	F5
TOWNSEND AV	OR	OR67		13	A4
TOWNSEND ST N	SA	SA	100	22	E3
TOWNSEND ST S	SA	SA	500	22	E3
TOWNSEND ST S	SA	SA04	3000	27	E1
TOWNSMEN DR	TUS	TUS		24	D2
TOYON DR	SJC	SJ75		36	E5
TOYON LN	NB	NB	1800	31	E2
TOYON TER	YL	YL		8	C5
TRABUCO CIR	CM	CM		27	A6
TRABUCO CIR	MVJO	SJ92	27000	29B	C5
TRABUCO LN	LAP	BP23	7400	9	D2
TRABUCO RD	CO	SA	5500	29	E1
TRABUCO RD	CO	ET		29A	E1
TRABUCO RD	CO	ET	25000	29B	A2
TRABUCO RD	CO	ET		51	E6
TRABUCO RD	CO	SA		51	A3
TRABUCO RD	IRV	SA	4200	24	D6
TRABUCO RD	IRV	SA	4400	29	E1
TRABUCO RD	MVJO	SJ91	24600	29B	B3
TRABUCO CYN RD	CO	SJ	20300	56	B6
TRABUCO CYN RD	CO	SJ		59	B1
TRABUCO CYN WY	BREA	BREA		2	F4
TRABUCO CK RD	CO	SJ		53	B2
TRABUCO CK RD	CO	SJ		56	C6
TRABUCO CK RD	SJC	SJ75		36	C2
TRABUCO OAKS DR	CO	SJ	20300	56	C5
TRACIE DR	BREA	BREA	900	2	C4
TRACY AV	GGR	GG	8800	15	D2
TRACY AV	WSTM	WSTM	7100	21	B3
TRACY LN	LAP	BP23	7300	9	D2
TRACY LN	OR	OR	100	17	E3
TRADEWIND CIR	HTB	HB	8300	26	D1
TRADEWIND CT	SJC	SJ75	33000	38	B2
TRADEWINDS CIR	FTNV	SA08		22	A6
TRADEWINDS LN	NB	NB	1600	31	E2
TRAFALGAR	NB	CDLM		32	D5
TRAFALGAR DR	LAP	BP23	4600	9	D3
TRAFALGAR LN	SCL	SC72	100	39	D4
TRAIL DR	ANA	AN		13	D2
TRAILBLAZER CIR	ANA	AN07		13	D4
TRAIL CREST LN	YL	YL		8	B5
TRAIL RIDGE	YL	YL		8	E2
TRAILS DR	FUL	FL33		5	F2
TRAILS END LN	CO	SA	2000	24	C3
TRAILS END LN	OR	OR69		18	E2
TRAIL SIDE RD	YL	YL		8	E4
TRAILVIEW CIR	BREA	BREA		3	A5
TRAIL VIEW PL	YL	YL	17600	7	F4
TRAILVIEW TER	CO	ET	25000	29A	F2
TRAILWAY LN	CO	ET	21900	29A	B2
TRAMINER TER	CO	LB56		29C	E5
TRAMONTI	CO	LB77		35	E5
TRANQUIL LN	HTB	HB	20000	26	D5
TRANSISTOR LN	HTB	HB		20	F3
TRANSIT AV	ANA	AN	2300	10	E4
TRANSIT PL	ANA	AN	2500	10	E4
TRAPANI	CO	LB77		35	F4
TRAPANI	IRV	SA14		28	F4
TRAPPER TR	ANA	AN		13	C3
TRASK AV	GGR	GG	8000	15	B5
TRASK AV	GGR	GG	10200	16	C5
TRASK AV	SA	SA	1800	16	C5
TRASK AV	WSTM	WSTM	6500	15	B5
TRASMIRAS	MVJO	SJ92		29D	C4
TRAVELAND WY	IRV	SA20		29	E3
TRAVERSE DR	CM	CM26	500	28	A3
TRAVERTINE PL	CO	SA	10200	18	D5
TRAVIS RD	YL	YL		8	D5
TRAVIS ST	CO	ET	23000	29A	D3
TRAVISTUCK PL	BPK	BP	8500	5	D4
TRAWLER	CO	LB77		37	E1
TRAYLOR WY	GGR	GG	10000	15	F6
TRAYLOR WY	GGR	GG	10200	16	A6
TRAYNOR AV	PLA	PLA	2000	7	D2
TREASURE CIR	HTB	HB	20000	26	D5
TREASURE LN	CO	SA	1200	18	C6
TREE AV	CO	SJ91		29A	F5
TREE ST	CO	SJ91		29A	F5
TREEBARK CIR	WSTM	WSTM	10000	22	A2
TREEHAVEN LN	HTB	HB	17100	20	F6
TREELINE LN	CO	ET	21600	29A	F1
TREEPATH LN	CO	SJ		59	B3
TREERIDGE CIR	BREA	BREA		3	A5
TREERIDGE LN	CO	ET	22100	29A	F2
TREESHADE LN	CO	ET	21500	29A	F1
TREETHORNE CIR	CO	LB77		36	A3
TREETOP CIR	HTB	HB	5900	20	F5
TREETOP LN	CO	LB		29D	A2
TREE TOP LN	LAG	LB51	21500	35	A1
TREEVIEW PL	FUL	FL		7	A2
TREEWOOD WY	CO	ET		29A	F1
TREEWOOD WY	CO	ET		51	F6
TREMONT DR	NB	NB		31	E5
TREMONT LN	NB	CDLM	4500	33	C2
TREMOUNT WY	CO	LB		35	E6
TRENTON	IRV	SA		24	E6
TRENTON AV E	OR	OR	100	12	D6
TRENTON AV W	OR	OR	1100	12	B6
TRENTON DR	ANA	AN	1300	16	C1
TRENTON LN	HTB	HB46	19500	27	A4
TRENTON PL	ANA	AN	1500	16	B1
TRENTON RD	YL	YL		40	B6
TRENTON WY	CM	CM	900	27	E3
TRESTLES	CO	LB77		36	A5
TRES VISTAS	MVJO	SJ92	27500	29B	D3
TREVA CIR	GGR	GG		15	D5
TREVINO WY	BPK	BP		5	C3
TREVISO	CO	LB		29A	B4
TREVISO	MVJO	SJ92		29D	F3
TREVOR ST N&S	ANA	AN	100	12	B3
TRIANGLE DR	SA	SA		16	D6
TRIANGLE DR	SA	SA		22	D1
TRIBUTE CT	NB	NB		31	B4
TRICOLORED LN	CO	LB53		29A	C6
TRIDENT LN	HTB	HB	19500	26	E4
TRIDENT ST	ANA	AN	600	11	A5
TRIESTA WY	YL	YL		40	D6
TRIESTE WY	FUL	FL33		5	E4
TRIGO CIR	MVJO	SJ91		29B	C5
TRIGO TR	CO	SJ		59	C3
TRILLIUM AV	FTNV	SA08	9700	21	F5
TRINETTE AV	GGR	GG45	5300	14	F4
TRINETTE AV	GGR	GG	6300	15	A4
TRINETTE DR	GGR	GG	8400	15	D4
TRINI CIR	WSTM	WSTM		21	E3
TRINIDAD AV	CYP	CYP	6000	14	F2
TRINIDAD CIR	PLA	PLA	1200	7	D5
TRINIDAD DR	DPT	DPT		37	E3
TRINIDAD LN	HTB	HB	16000	20	C4
TRINIDAD WY	BPK	BP	5700	9	E2
TRINIDAD WY	PLA	PLA		7	D4
TRINIDAD WY	SA	SA	1600	23	D2
TRINITY	HTB	HB		26	D5
TRINITY DR	CM	CM	3000	27	F3
TRINITY LN	LAP	BP23	7800	9	D2
TRINITY LN	OR	OR		12	B5
TRINITY WY	STN	STN		10	E4
TRINITY WY	STN	STN		15	B3
TRINITY RIV CIR	FTNV	SA08	8500	26	D2
TRINO CIR	CO	YL	19300	8	B5
TRIOMPHE AV	IRV	SA	5400	29	D3
TRIPLE CROWN LN	ANA	AN		8	E6
TRIPOLI AV	LALM	LALM	5000	14	D2
TRIPP CIR	HTB	HB47	16500	21	D5
TRISTAN DR	GGR	GG	9000	15	E3
TRITON CT	CO	SJ91	25800	29B	A6
TRITON LN	HTB	HB		20	E2
TRITON WY	CO	LB		29A	B3
TRITT CIR	VPK	OR67	9100	13	A4
TRIUMPH WY	SA	SA	300	28	B1
TRIUMPHAL WY	CO	SA	1000	18	C5
TRIVOLI	MVJO	SJ92		52	E6
TRIX CIR	YL	YL	4200	7	E2
TROCADERO	MVJO	SJ92	27800	29B	F4
TROJAN CIR	HTB	HB47	14900	21	A2
TROJAN PL	ANA	AN	2600	10	D4
TROJAN ST	ANA	AN	200	10	D4
TROJAN WY	STN	STN		15	B2
TROON LN	HTB	HB	20500	26	F5
TROON ST	CO	LB		35	C2
TROPEA	CO	LB77		35	F4
TROPEZ LN	HTB	HB	16300	20	A6
TROPHY DR	HTB	HB	5800	20	F5
TROPIC DR	WSTM	WSTM	9100	21	E1
TROPIC LN	CO	SA	1000	18	B6
TROPICANA LN	CO	SA	11200	18	C5
TROPICANA LN	HTB	HB	14300	20	F2
TROPICANA PL	CO	LB56		29C	E5
TROPICANA WY	LAH	LAH	800	2	C3
TROTTER AV	SA	SA	1400	23	E4
TROTTER DR	HTB	HB		26	A2
TROUT ST	HTB	HB		26	C3
TROVITA	IRV	SA		24	F5
TROWER CT	FTNV	SA08		26	F2
TROY ST	ANA	AN		16	D2
TROY ST	CO	SJ91	24300	29B	A6
TROZA	IRV	SA		24	E5
TRUCKEE ST	YL	YL		8	F4
TRUCKEE RIVR CT	FTNV	SA08		27	A1
TRUDY LN	HTB	HB	16500	20	F5
TRUE WY	GGR	GG	11400	16	B3
TRUK ST	CYP	CYP	11500	14	E2
TRUMAN	IRV	SA		29	E2
TRUMAN AV	FUL	FL	300	6	B5
TRUMAN CIR	PLA	PLA		7	E5
TRUMBULL DR	HTB	HB	4100	20	C5
TRUMPET AV	PLA	PLA	600	7	C3
TRUMPETER LN	CO	LB56		29C	A1
TRUSLOW AV E&W	FUL	FL	100	6	C6
TRUXTON DR	HTB	HB	8500	26	D5
TRYON AV	ANA	AN	2400	12	A5
TRYON ST	WSTM	WSTM	16400	21	D4
TUCANA DR	HTB	HB47	6900	21	B6
TUCANA ST	YL	YL	4700	7	E3
TUCKAHOE CIR	HTB	HB	19500	26	F3
TUCKAWAY CIR	ANA	AN		43	A4
TUCKER LN	CO	LALM	2600	14	A4
TUDOR LN	GGR	GG	9300	15	E3
TUDOR PL	ANA	AN	600	11	C3
TUDOR WY	CO	TUS		24	B1
TUFFREE BLVD	PLA	PLA	1600	7	B3
TUFTON ST	WSTM	WSTM		20	E1
TUFTS LN	HTB	HB47	16300	21	A4
TULAGI ST	CYP	CYP	6300	14	F2
TULANE PL	CM	CM26	200	27	D6
TULANE RD	CM	CM	200	27	D5
TULANE ST	WSTM	WSTM	13500	14	E5
TULANE WY	STN	STN		10	E4
TULANE WY	STN	STN		15	B2
TULARE DR	CM	CM	1100	27	E3
TULARE DR	HTB	HB		26	D6
TULARE ST	BPK	BP	7500	5	B4
TULAROSA AV E	OR	OR	700	17	D4
TULAROSA AV W	OR	OR	300	17	C4
TULE RIVER CIR	FTNV	SA08	8500	26	D2
TULIP CIR	YL	YL		8	E5
TULIP CT	FTNV	SA08	11700	22	C4
TULIP LN	CM	CM27	100	31	D1
TULIP ST	CO	ET	23100	29A	E4
TULIP ST	SB	SB	3900	14	D4
TULIPANES CT	CO	ET		51	E4
TULIPWOOD CIR	HTB	HB	18700	26	D2
TULIPWOOD CIR	WSTM	WSTM	8300	21	D2
TULLOW LN	HTB	HB47	15800	21	A4
TUMBLE WEED	IRV	SA		32A	B2
TUMBLEWEED CIR	CO	ET	21800	29B	A1
TUMBLEWEED RD	ANA	AN	500	13	B3
TUNA DR	DPT	LB77		37	F3
TUNA DR	DPT	DPT	25200	38	A3
TUNALES DR	FUL	FL35	3600	2	C6
TUNGWOOD ST	WSTM	WSTM	15000	21	D3
TUNICE ST	PLA	PLA	700	7	C2
TUNIS	CO	LB77		35	F5
TUNISIA CIR	CO	PLA	16200	7	C3
TUNSTALL CIR	GGR	GG45	12400	14	E3
TUNSTALL LN	HTB	HB47	16500	21	B5
TUNSTALL ST	GGR	GG45	11800	14	E3
TUPELO LN	CO	ET		51	F5
TUPELO LN	TUS	TUS	14200	23	F3
TURANO	CO	LAG		35	F4
TURF AV	CO	SJ91		29A	F5
TURF DR	PLA	PLA	200	7	B4
TURIN AV	ANA	AN	1200	11	F5
TURLOCK CT	CO	LB	28000	29C	E6
TURLOCK DR	CM	CM	3200	27	E2
TURNABOUT RD	OR	OR		18	D2
TURNBERRY	MVJO	SJ92		29B	E3
TURNBERRY DR	CO	SJ79		59	C6
TURNBERRY DR	HTB	HB		25	F4
TURNDELL RD	CO	LAH	1000	2	B3
TURNER AV	FUL	FL33	100	5	D6
TURNER LN	CO	LAH	1000	2	A3
TURQUESA CIR	MVJO	SJ91	26200	29D	B2
TURQUOISE	MVJO	SJ91		29D	C5
TURQUOISE AV	NB	NB	100	31	E6
TURQUOISE CT	FTNV	SA08	11800	22	B5
TURQUOISE ST	ANA	AN	800	11	E4
TURQUOISE ST	GGR	GG45	11800	14	F3
TURTLE COVE	CO	LB	23700	35	D2
TURTLEDOVE AV	FTNV	SA08	9500	26	F1
TURTLE ROCK DR	IRV	SA	18500	32	F2
TURTLE ROCK DR	IRV	SA		32A	A3
TUSCAN CIR	HTB	HB		20	E6
TUSCAN CIR	HTB	HB		25	E1
TUSCAN WY	CO	ET		29B	A2
TUSTIN AV	ANA	AN		7	D6
TUSTIN AV	ANA	AN	1300	12	D1
TUSTIN AV	CM	CM27	1500	31	D3
TUSTIN AV	CO	SA05	14900	23	E3
TUSTIN AV	CO	CM27	2000	31	F1
TUSTIN AV	NB	NB	100	31	D3
TUSTIN AV	TUS	TUS	100	23	E2
TUSTIN AV N	SA	SA	1700	17	E5
TUSTIN AV N&S	SA	SA	100	23	E2
TUSTIN CT	TUS	TUS		24	A4
TUSTIN ST N	OR	OR67	1400	12	E6
TUSTIN ST N	OR	OR	100	17	E2
TUSTIN EAST DR	TUS	TUS		24	A3
TUSTIN PINES WY	CO	TUS	1000	24	B1
TUSTIN RANCH RD	TUS	TUS		24	B4
TUSTIN VLLGE WY	TUS	TUS	15500	23	E3
TWAIN LN	HTB	HB	17000	20	E6
TWAIN PL	PLA	PLA	1800	7	C2
TWANA DR	GGR	GG	8500	15	D3
TWEED	CO	ET		52	C3
TWEED	IRV	SA		29	C4
TWEED ST	PLA	PLA	2000	7	C2
TWIG ST	CO	ET	24200	29A	F6
TWILIGHT	SA	SA04		27	E2
TWILIGHT DR	FUL	FL35	3800	2	C6
TWILIGHT DR	FUL	FL	3000	6	C1
TWILIGHT LN	PLA	PLA	900	7	B4
TWILIGHT ST	PLA	PLA	100	7	A5
TWINBERRY	CO	LB56		29C	D2
TWIN CREEK LN	YL	YL		8	F2
TWINFORD DR	CO	ET		29B	A1
TWINFORD LN	HTB	HB		25	F2
TWIN HILLS DR	SB	SB	13200	14	A5
TWINKLE CIR	HTB	HB		20	B3
TWIN LAKES CIR	NB	CDLM		32	C6
TWIN LAKES DR	CYP	CYP		9	E4
TWINLAKES LN	CO	ET		29A	C2
TWINLEAF CIR	GGR	GG	13200	16	E4
TWINLEAF LN	GGR	GG	12500	16	D4
TWINLEAF TR	OR	OR	7600	18	D2
TWIN OAK	YL	YL		8	E2
TWIN PEAK CIR	ANA	AN07		13	D4
TWINSPAN AV	FTNV	SA08	11200	22	B4
TWINTREE AV	GGR	GG	12200	16	D3
TWINTREE CIR	GGR	GG	13200	16	E4
TWINTREE LN	GGR	GG	12500	16	D3
TYBURN RD	CO	LB	200	34	C1
TYEE LN	HTB	HB47	16200	21	B4
TYHURST RD	GGR	GG	10200	15	F4
TYLER AV	ANA	AN	2800	10	B4
TYLER CIR	HTB	HB	8300	26	D3
TYLER CT	WSTM	WSTM	10000	22	A2
TYLER WY	CM	CM	3000	27	E3
TYMPANI CIR	ANA	AN		8	A6
TYMPANI ST	ANA	AN	4800	8	A5
TYNDALL DR	HTB	HB47	6000	21	A3
TYNES DR	PLA	PLA	2100	7	C2
TYPEE WY	IRV	SA		24	D6
TYPHOON LN	HTB	HB		20	B4
TYROL AV	ANA	AN	1600	11	F4
TYROL DR	LAG	LB51	3100	29C	A6
TYROL DR	LAG	LB51	3100	34	F1
TYROL PL	ANA	AN	1800	11	F4
TYRONE CIR	HTB	HB47	6400	21	A3
U					
ULITHI ST	CYP	CYP	6500	15	A2
ULTIMO DR	IRV	SA		24	E4
UNDERHILL AV	ANA	AN	2100	11	F3
UNDERHILL AV	ANA	AN	2200	12	A3
UNDERHILL LN	HTB	HB47	16200	21	A5
UNION	IRV	SA		28	E4
UNION AV	CM	CM27	2100	31	B1
UNION AV	LAH	LAH	2500	1	D5
UNION AV E&W	FUL	FL	100	6	C5
UNION PL	BREA	BREA	400	2	E6
UNITD STATES DR	LALM	LALM		14	C2
UNIVERSE AV	WSTM	WSTM	8700	21	D4

ORANGE CO.

STREET	CITY	P.O. ZONE	BLOCK	PAGE	GRID
UNIVERSITY DR	CO	CM27	300	27	F6
UNIVERSITY DR	IRV	SA	18000	28	E6
UNIVERSITY DR	IRV	SA	17400	29	A6
UNIVERSITY DR	IRV	SA		32	C1
UNIVERSITY DR	NB	NB	2500	31	F1
UNIVERSITY DR	NB	NB		32	B2
UNIVERSITY DR N	IRV	SA	1200	32	B1
UNIVERSITY DR N	NB	NB		32	B1
UNIVERSITY ST	WSTM	WSTM	13400	14	E6
UPLAND DR	HTB	HB	9700	26	F6
UPLAND RD	LAG	LB51	100	34	E5
UPPA WY	CO	SIL	28100	50	D2
UPPER BAY DR	CO		20400	32	A1
UPPERLAKE CIR	HTB	HB	18000	26	A1
UPPER LOOP RD	CO			32	F6
UPPER LOOP RD	CO			32A	A6
UPPER LOOP RD	CO			33	E1
UPPER LOOP RD	CO			33A	A1
UPR NWPRT PZ DR	NB	NB60		28	B6
UPPER INN ROCK	LAG	LB51	1900	34	E2
UPPR VINTAGE RD	CO	LB77		37	F1
UPPR VINTAGE RD	CO	LB77		38	A1
UPTON DR	LAH	LAH	1900	1	E6
URBINO	IRV	SA		24	E5
URELL DR	LAH	LAH	1100	2	A3
UREY CT	IRV	SA17		32	E3
URIS CT	IRV	SA	3700	24	C6
URSULA CIR	CO	ET		29A	D3
UTAH AV	BPK	BP	8100	10	C1
UTAH CIR	CM	CM	1600	27	C3
UTE WY	CO	ET	21800	29A	F1
UTICA AV E&W	HTB	HB	100	26	B4
UTRILLO DR	IRV	SA	14100	24	C6
UTT DR	CO	TUS	13700	24	A3
UTT DR	TUS	TUS	14000	23	F3
UTT DR	TUS	TUS	13500	24	A3
UXBRIDGE PL	SA	SA		23	B6
UXBRIDGE ST	WSTM	WSTM	14000	20	E1
V					
VACAS CIR	FTNV	SA08	17400	22	B6
VACATION LN	HTB	HB	21900	30	F2
VACUNO	SCL	SC72		38	E4
VAIL DR	HTB	HB	8500	26	D5
VALARTA LN	MVJO	SJ91		29B	C4
VALDEMOSA	MVJO	SJ92	22300	29B	D2
VALDERAS	MVJO	SJ92		29B	C3
VALDEZ CIR	PLA	PLA	600	7	C5
VALDINA AV	ANA	AN	2200	10	E3
VALDIVIA	MVJO	SJ91	22300	29B	D2
VALE AV	ANA	AN	700	12	A4
VALE AV	CO	SA	18700	18	B5
VALE ST	IRV	SA	4200	29	C1
VALENCIA	CO	LB		29A	C3
VALENCIA	NB	NB60		32	E3
VALENCIA AV	BREA	BREA	300	3	C1
VALENCIA AV	CO	BREA		3	D6
VALENCIA AV	IRV	SA		29	B2
VALENCIA AV	IRV	LB53	10200	29A	C2
VALENCIA AV	OR	OR	300	17	C2
VALENCIA AV	PLA	PLA	1200	7	C4
VALENCIA AV	TUS	TUS	1000	23	E5
VALENCIA AV E&W	ANA	AN	100	11	D5
VALENCIA CIR	VPK	OR67		13	A5
VALENCIA CIR	YL	YL	4500	8	A2
VALENCIA DR	HTB	HB47	8100	21	C6
VALENCIA DR	OR			13	C6
VALENCIA DR E&W	FUL	FL	100	6	A6
VALENCIA DR R&W	FUL	FL33	1400	5	F6
VALENCIA PL	DPT	DPT	33800	37	E4
VALENCIA PL	LAH	LAH	700	2	B4
VALENCIA PZ	WSTM	WSTM		21	E2
VALENCIA ST	BREA	BREA	200	6	E1
VALENCIA ST	CM	CM	900	27	C6
VALENCIA ST	SA	SA06	1800	17	C6
VALENCIA ST N	LAH	LAH	100	2	B4
VALENCIA ST S	LAH	LAH	100	2	B5
VALENCIA WY	CO	LB56		29C	E5
VALENCIA M DR E	GGR	GG	12700	15	E4
VALENCIA M DR W	FUL	FL	100	6	A4
VALENTINE DR	HTB	HB47	7400	21	B4
VALENZUELA CIR	MVJO	SJ91	26100	29B	B6
VALERA WY	FUL	FL	3100	6	A1
VALERIE ST	CO	LB		29A	F6
VALERIE ST	CO	LB		29C	F1
VALERIO CT	CO	LB	29300	35	F1
VALEWOOD	CO	ET		29A	F1
VALEWOOD	CO	ET		51	F6
VALEWOOD	CO	ET		52	A6
VALEWORTH CIR	HTB	HB	17400	26	A1
VALHALLA DR	CO	SA	2000	24	C1
VALIA	MVJO	SJ91		29B	C1
VALIDO RD	LAG	LB	31500	35	B5
VALLARTA DR	CO	LB		35	D5
VALLARTA DR	HTB	HB		26	D2
VALLE CIR	HTB	HB46	18100	26	C2
VALLECITO AV	WSTM	WSTM	5000	14	E1
VALLECITO DR	WSTM	WSTM		14	E1
VALLECITO DR	YL	YL		8	B3
VALLECITO LN	YL	YL	4600	8	B3
VALLE CIR	HTB	HB	18900	26	C3
VALLEJO	MVJO	SJ91		29B	B4
VALLEJO CIR	CM	CM	1000	27	E2
VALLEJO DR	ANA	AN	3100	10	B5
VALLEJO DR	TUS	TUS		24	B3
VALLEJO ST	BREA	BREA	600	2	C5
VALLEJO ST	LAH	LAH	200	2	C4
VALLE VISTA	CO	LB77		35	F4
VALLE VISTA DR	FUL	FL	1100	6	B2
VALLEY CIR	CM	CM27	1100	27	A2
VALLEY CIR	HTB	HB46		26	C3
VALLEY CIR	VPK	OR67	18300	13	A5
VALLEY LN	FUL	FL33	1700	5	F6
VALLEY PL	ANA	AN	2100	10	F4
VALLEY RD	CM	CM27	2000	31	A2
VALLEY ST S	ANA	AN	700	10	F5
VALLEY FORGE CT	LALM	LALM		14	C3
VALLEY FORGE DR	ANA	AN		12	A2
VALLEY FORGE DR	HTB	HB46	3900	27	A4
VALLEY FORGE DR	OR	OR	5800	13	C6
VALLEY FORGE DR	PLA	PLA	500	7	B5
VALLEY FORGE LN	CM	CM	100	27	E6
VALLEY GATE DR	ANA	AN		12	F3
VALLEY GLEN LN	OR	OR	2100	12	A4
VALLEYMONT RD	LAG	LB		34	B2
VALLEY OAK	CO	SJ79	27000	52	C6
VALLEY QUAIL DR	CO	SA		18	D6
VALLEY RIM CIR	SJC	SJ75	27500	36	D3
VALLEY RIM TER	CO	ET		29A	F2
VALLEY VIEW	IRV	SA		32A	A1
VALLEY VIEW AV	YL	YL	4000	7	E3
VALLEY VIEW DR	DPT	DPT		38	A3
VALLEY VW DR E	FUL	FL	100	6	C4
VALLEY VW DR W	FUL	FL	300	6	A4
VALLEY VIEW PL	ANA	AN		13	A2
VALLEY VIEW PL	FUL	FL	900	6	A3
VALLEY VIEW ST	BPK	BP	6500	9	F2
VALLEY VIEW ST	BPK	BP	7600	9	F1
VALLEY VIEW ST	CYP	CYP	9100	9	F5
VALLEY VIEW ST	CYP	CYP	10500	9	F4
VALLEY VIEW ST	GGR	GG45	11800	14	E4
VALLEVIEW ST	OR		3900	12	E3
VALLEY VISTA WY	WSTM	WSTM	13000	14	E4
VALLEY VISTA WY	CO			25	D5
VALMARANA ISLE	IRV	SA14		28	D5
VALPARAISO DR E	PLA	PLA	1200	7	B4
VALPARAISO DR N	PLA	PLA	1200	7	C4
VALPARAISO WY	PLA	PLA	1200	7	C4
VALPARISO DR	MVJO	SJ91	26600	29B	B4
VALEROSA	CO	SJ88		59	A4
VAL VERDE AV	BPK	BP	6500	3	B6
VALVERDE AV	BREA	BREA		6	E3
VAL VERDE CT	CO	LB		29C	E3
VALWOOD DR	FUL	FL	600	6	A6
VALWOOD ST	LAH	LAH	1200	2	A6
VALYERMO DR	MVJO	SJ91		29B	D5
VAN BIBBER AV	OR	OR	500	17	D1
VAN BUREN	IRV	SA		29	D1
VAN BUREN ST	ANA	AN	1300	10	F1
VAN BUREN ST	ANA	AN	1300	11	E1
VAN BUREN ST	HTB	HB47	17500	21	D6
VAN BUREN ST	HTB	HB	17500	26	D1
VAN BUREN ST	PLA	PLA		7	E5
VAN BUREN ST	WSTM	WSTM	15500	21	C3
VAN BUREN WY	YL	YL	4800	7	D3
VAN BUREN WY	BPK	BP	7000	10	A3
VANCE PL	SA	SA	1500	23	D1
VANCE ST	SA	SA	200	23	D1
VANCOUVER DR	ANA	AN	2100	16	A1
VANCOUVER DR	CO	AN04	9500	10	E5
VANDENBERG LN	TUS	TUS	17300	17	F6
VANDERBILT DR	IRV	SA18		28	F6
VANDERBILT DR	PLA	PLA	500	7	C5
VANDERGRIFT DR	FUL	FL		7	A2
VANDERLIP AV	CO	TUS	18200	18	A6
VANDERLIP AV	CO	TUS	18200	24	A1
VAN DEVELDE WY	WSTM	WSTM	16300	21	F1
VAN DYKE CIR	LAP	BP23		9	E2
VAN DYKE CIR	LAG	LB51	1000	34	E3
VAN DYKE LN	HTB	HB47	17000	21	D6
VANE CIR	HTB	HB	6000	20	F3
VANESSA DR	CO	SJ91	24500	29A	F6
VAN GOGH CIR	OR	OR		12	F1
VAN GOGH CIR	OR	OR	1200	17	F1
VAN GOGH WY	YL	YL		40	C5
VANGUARD AV	GGR	GG45	5300	14	F3
VANGUARD CIR	GGR	GG	6500	15	A3
VANGUARD CIR	GGR	GG	7700	15	C3
VANGUARD LN	HTB	HB	14900	20	F2
VANGUARD PL	CM	CM26		27	E5
VANGUARD RD	ANA	AN		16	D2
VANGUARD WY	BREA	BREA	100	2	D5
VAN HORNE WY	CM	CM	2300	27	E6
VAN NESS AV N	SA	SA	1600	17	B6
VAN NESS AV N	SA	SA	300	23	B1
VAN NESS AV S	SA	SA	500	23	B4
VAN NESS CT	CM	CM		27	E3
VAN NESS ST	HTB	HB	20900	26	D6
VAN NESS ST	SA	SA	3600	28	B2
VANOWEN AV	OR	OR	800	12	D6
VANTAGE CIR	SJC	SJ75	27400	36	D3
VANTAGE DR	HTB	HB47	7500	21	C5
VANTAGE PL	HTB	HB	7500	26	C1
VAQUERO AV	LAH	LAH	2000	2	C4
VARAS CIR	HTB	HB	8300	26	D6
VARESSA	IRV	SA		29	D1
VARNA ST	ANA	AN	1600	16	A1
VARNA ST	GGR	GG	11500	16	A1
VARSITY DR	HTB	HB		25	F1
VARSITY DR	HTB	HB	6200	26	A1
VASILE	ANA	AN		16	D4
VASSAR CIR	ANA	AN		34	B2
VASSAR PL	CM	CM	2400	27	D5
VASSAR ST	WSTM	WSTM	15300	21	A3
VASSAR WY	STN	STN		10	E4
VASSAR WY	STN	STN		15	B2
VASSAR AISLE	IRV	SA15		28	E6
VASSAR AISLE	IRV	SA15		32	E1
VATCHER DR	HTB	HB	6200	20	A1
VAUXHALL PL	SA	SA	3000	28	B1
VAUXHALL RD	WSTM	WSTM	5000	20	D1
VAYANO WY	CO	SA	1300	24	C1
VECINO LN	CO	LAH	10000	1	F3
VECINO ST	LAH	LAH	800	2	C3
VEEH DR	TUS	TUS	1200	23	F3
VEGAS WY	GGR	GG	10500	16	A1
VEJAR LN	MVJO	SJ91	27400	29B	B5
VELADOR	MVJO	SJ91		29B	D1
VELARDO DR	HTB	HB	9300	25	D1
VELARE ST	ANA	AN	600	10	F5
VELASCO LN	CM	CM	2800	27	E4
VELASQUEZ RD	CO	LB	25000	29C	F1
VELO WY	SA	SA		28	C1
VELVA PL	ANA	AN	300	11	A5
VELVET CIR	HTB	HB		26	A4
VENABLO LN	MVJO	SJ91		29B	C5
VENADO DR	CO	SJ91		29D	B4
VENDRELL	MVJO	SJ91		29B	B2
VENECIA LN	YL	YL	19600	8	C3
VENER DR	GGR	GG	13100	15	E5
VENETIAN DR	CM	CM	3300	27	E2
VENETO	IRV	SA		28	E4
VENEZIA ISLE	IRV	SA14		28	D5
VENICE AV	HTB	HB	200	26	A4
VENICE AV	PLA	PLA	1200	7	C4
VENICE ST	CO	LB56		29C	D3
VENIDA	SA	SA		24	F5
VENIER WY	CM	CM27	2400	31	A1
VENISIA	NB	NB		32	B2
VENTA	TUS	TUS		24	B3
VENTOSA	MVJO	SJ91	27300	29B	A6
VENTURA AV	PLA	PLA	500	7	A6
VENTURA PL	FUL	FL33	200	5	E5
VENTURA ST	ANA	AN	1100	10	E3
VENTURE	IRV	SA18		29	F6
VENTURE DR	HTB	HB		20	B5
VENTURI DR	HTB	HB	5500	20	A5
VENUS	CO	SJ91	24500	29B	A6
VENUS CIR	HTB	HB	20400	26	C6
VENUS CIR	BPK	BP	8400	10	C3
VENUS DR	WSTM	WSTM	16300	21	D4
VERA CIR	GGR	GG45	12300	14	E4
VERA ST	CO	TUS	14400	24	A1
VERA ST	GGR	GG45	12700	14	E4
VERACRUZ	DPT	DPT		37	F1
VERACRUZ LN	MVJO	SJ91	26500	29B	B6
VERANADA RD	CO	LB		35	C5
VERANO	MVJO	SJ91		29D	C3
VERANO PL	IRV	SA		32	E1
VERBENA	MVJO	SJ91		29D	B3
VERBENA CT	FTNV	SA08	11800	22	F6
VERBENA LN	BREA	BREA	200	4	A4
VERCELLI	IRV	SA		24	D5
VERDANT DR	HTB	HB	9700	26	F5
VERDE	IRV	SA		28	E6
VERDE AV	ANA	AN	2700	12	B4
VERDE CIR	ANA	AN	1600	11	F4
VERDE LN	HTB	HB47		21	D4
VERDE LN	ANA	AN	1800	11	F4
VERDE ST	ANA	AN	800	11	F4
VERDE ST	CO	ET		29A	D3
VERDE ST	GGR	GG	13200	15	F5
VERDE ST	GGR	GG	14400	21	F1
VERDE LOMAS CIR	VPK	OR67	9700	13	A5
VERDE LOMAS DR	VPK	OR67	10100	13	A6
VERDE MAR DR	HTB	HB	9700	30	F1
VERDI DR	BPK	BP	6300	5	C6
VERDIN LN	CO	LB56		29C	B1
VERDUGO	MVJO	SJ92		29D	F3
VERDUGO AV	LAH	LAH	1600	2	B4
VERDUGO PL	FUL	FL33	1900	5	E3
VERDUGO ST	SJC	SJ75	26700	36	B6
VERDUGO ST	SJC	SJ75	26700	38	C1
VERDUGO CYN RD	SJC	SJ75		62	B2
VERDUN CIR	IRV	SA	15400	29	D3
VERDURA CIR	MVJO	SJ91	26200	29D	B2
VEREDA LAGUNA	CO	SJ		59	F1
VERENA CT	CO	SJ91	24300	29B	A5
VERLENE CIR	HTB	HB47	6900	21	B4
VERMONT AV	CM	CM	3200	27	B3
VERMONT AV E	ANA	AN	2300	12	A4
VERMONT AV E&W	ANA	AN	100	11	D5
VERMONT AV N&S	FUL	FL33	100	5	E5
VERMONT CT	YL	YL	40	8	F6
VERMONT LN	HTB	HB	19800	26	F4
VERMONT ST	WSTM	WSTM	15100	21	B3
VERN ST	ANA	AN	2100	16	D2
VERNA LN	YL	YL	16700	7	D3
VERNER DR	LAP	BP23	5300	9	E1
VERNON CT	CYP	CYP	10400	14	F1
VERNON DR	ANA	AN	1400	11	F6
VERNON ST	FTNV	SA08	16300	22	E1
VERNON ST	LAH	LAH	900	2	E3
VERONA	TUS	TUS		24	C4
VERONA DR	FUL	FL	1500	6	A3
VERONA LN	YL	YL	19600	8	C1
VERONA PL	MVJO	SJ92		29D	C4
VERONA PL	PLA	PLA	1200	7	C4
VERONA ST	ANA	AN	600	10	D5
VERONA ST	LAH	LAH	500	2	C4
VERONICA CT	CO	SJ91	24500	29B	A5
VERONICA DR	HTB	HB	9000	26	E4
VERRAZANNO BAY	DPT	LB77		37	D4
VESPER CIR	HTB	HB47	6500	21	A3
VESPER RD	CO	ET		29A	D3
VESPUCCI RD	CO	LB	25100	29C	F1
VESTA	CO	SJ91	24600	29B	A6
VESTAVIA AV	BPK	BP	8700	5	D4
VESTAVIA CIR	BPK	BP	5500	5	D4
VESTRY CIR	HTB	HB	200	26	A4
VESTRY CIR	HTB	HB		26	A3
VESUVIA AV	CO	SJ91		29B	D2
VESUVIO CIR	YL	YL		8	F6
VESUVIUS DR	BREA	BREA	360	7	D1
VIA ABEDUL	SCL	SC72		38	F6
VIA ABRUZZI	CO	LB56		29C	B2
VIA ACAPULCO	CO	LB53		29C	B4
VIA ACASO	CO	SJ		59	B4
VIA ACUATICA	CO	SJ		59	C1
VIA ACUNA	MVJO	SJ92	23500	29D	D4
VIA ADELA	YL	YL		8	C4
VIA ADELFA	CO	SJ		59	B4
VIA ADELIA	CO	SJ		59	B4
VIA AGUILA	CO	SC72		59	F6
VIA AGUILA	SCL	SC72		59	F6
VIA AGUSTINI	CO	SJ91	27500	29B	D4
VIA ALAMEDA	YL	YL	19900	8	C3
VIA ALANO	SJC	SJ75	22500	36	B6
VIA ALBENIZ	MVJO	SJ92		29B	D5
VIA ALBERTI	MVJO	SJ92		29B	D5
VIA ALCALA	MVJO	SJ92		29B	B4
VIA ALCANTARA	YL	YL		8	D5
VIA ALCAZAR AV	CO	LB	30300	35	F1
VIA ALEGRE	SCL	SC72	300	39	B1
VIA ALEGRE	YL	YL	5300	8	C2
VIA ALFONSE	CO	LB56		35	F1
VIA ALFREDO	CO	LB56		35	E1
VIA ALHAMBRA	CO		675	29C	E7
VIA ALICANTE	TUS	TUS		24	E3
VIA ALICIA	SJC	SJ75	32000	38	A1
VIA ALISA	YL	YL		8	C3
VIA ALISTA	ANA	AN		13	D1
VIA ALISTA	CO	SJ79		59	D2
VIA ALLEGRE	CO	SJ79		59	D2
VIA ALMERIA	TUS	TUS		24	E3
VIA ALMERIA	YL	YL		8	C4
VIA ALONDRA	CO	SJ		59	D4
VIA ALTIS	CO	LB56		35	F1
VIA ALTISSE	CO	LB56		29C	B2
VIA ALTO CERRO	CO	LB56		35	F3
VIA ALTO CERRO	CO	LB77		36	A3
VIA ALVARADO	YL	YL		8	D3
VIA ALVORADO	MVJO	SJ92	24000	29B	C6
VIA AMANTE	YL	YL		8	D4
VIA AMAPOLA	YL	YL		38	E5
VIA AMARILLA	YL	YL		8	D3
VIA AMATE	SCL	SC72		38	F6
VIA AMATE	SCL	SC72		39	E1
VIA AMBROSA	CO	LB53		29C	F6
VIA AMISTOSA	CO	SJ		59	F6
VIA ANA	SJC	SJ75	31500	36	B6
VIA ANDALUSIA	YL	YL		8	A4
VIA ANDALUSIA	YL	YL		8	A4
VIA ANDORRA	SJC	SJ79	27800	59	C5
VIA ANGELINA	YL	YL		8	A4
VIA ANGELINA	MVJO	SJ91	26800	29D	C2
VIA ANGELINA DR	HTB	HB47	6800	26	A1
VIA ANTIBES	DPT	LB77		37	F1
VIA ANTIBES	NB	NB	100	31	F5
VIA APOLINA	YL	YL		8	C4
VIA AQUARA AV	SJC	SJ75		36	E5
VIA ARAGON	CO	LB56	24200	35	E4
VIA ARBOLEDA	ANA	AN		13	D2
VIA ARBOLEDA	SCL	LB56		29C	E2
VIA ARBOLEDA	SCL	SC72	2700	39	B1
VIA ARBOLEDA	SJC	SJ75		38	B1
VIA ARBOLEDA	YL	YL		8	A4
VIA AREVALO	MVJO	SJ91		29B	D4
VIA ARNAZ	YL	YL		8	C4
VIA ARRIAGA	MVJO	SJ92		29B	A4
VIA ARRIBA LNDA	YL	YL		8	A4
VIA ARROYO DR	BPK	BP	6500	10	A4
VIA ASTORGA	MVJO	SJ91	23000	29B	B4
VIA ASTURIAS	CO	SJ91	24500	29B	D4
VIA ATHENA	CO	LB56		29C	C4
VIA AUGUSTO	CO	LB56		29C	B2
VIA AUREO	CO	LB56		29C	B2
VIA AVENTURA PL	MVJO	SJ91	23000	29B	A6
VIA AVILA	SA	SA	12900	18	B4
VIA AVILA	MVJO	SJ91	25000	29B	C5
VIA AZAFRAN	SCL	SC72		39	E4
VIA AZUL	CO	LB56		29C	F6
VIA BADALONA	YL	YL		8	A4
VIA BAHIA	MVJO	SJ91	27000	29B	A6
VIA BAJO CERRO	CO	LB		35	F3
VIA BALBOA	CO	LB53		29C	A4
VIA BALBOA	CO	LB53		29C	A4
VIA BALBOA	PLA	PLA		7	C3
VIA BALBOA	WSTM	WSTM		14	E5
VIA BALBOA CIR	BPK	BP	9100	10	A4
VIA BALSA	SCL	SC72	200	39	B1
VIA BAMBUSA	SCL	SC72		39	E4
VIA BANDITA	SCL	SC72		29C	F6
VIA BARCAZA	CO	TRA		59	C6
VIA BARCAZA	CO	TRA		62	A1
VIA BARCELONA	DPT	LB77		37	C1
VIA BARCELONA	GGR	GG45		14	E5

STREET	CITY	P.O. ZONE	BLOCK	PAGE	GRID
VIA BARCELONA	NB	NB	100	31	C5
VIA BARCELONA	SJC	SJ75		36	B6
VIA BARCELONA	YL	YL		8	D5
VIA BARRACUDA	SCL	SC72		38	C6
VIA BARRACUDA	SCL	SC72		39	C1
VIA BARRIDA	SJC	SJ75	32200	38	D1
VIA BAYONA	MVJO	SJ91	24000	29B	C5
VIA BECERRA	CO	SJ		59	B5
VIA BELARDES	SJC	SJ75		36	B6
VIA BELARDES	SJC	SJ75	31800	38	B1
VIA BELARMINO	YL	YL		8	D4
VIA BELLA	DPT	SC24		38	C6
VIA BELLA	DPT	SC24		39	A1
VIA BELLA VISTA	YL	YL	4400	8	C3
VIA BELLAZA	CO	LB56		29C	F6
VIA BELLEZA	YL	YL		8	D4
VIA BELLO	MVJO	SJ92	23500	29B	E4
VIA BELLORITA	CO	SJ88		59	B5
VIA BELLOTA	SCL	SC72		38	E5
VIA BENAVENTE	MVJO	SJ92		29B	E4
VIA BERNARDO	YL	YL		8	E4
VIA BERNRDO CIR	YL	YL		8	E4
VIA BILBAO	YL	YL		8	D5
VIA BLANCO	SCL	SC72		38	F5
VIA BONALDE	MVJO	SJ92		29B	D5
VIA BONDAD	CO	SJ		59	C3
VIA BONITA	CO	LB	25000	35	F2
VIA BRAVO	VPK	OR67	18300	13	A6
VIA BRAVO	YL	YL		40	B5
VIA BRENDA	BPK	BP	5000	9	D4
VIA BREVE	ANA	AN		8	C6
VIA BREVE	MVJO	SJ91		29B	C4
VIA BREVE	SCL	SC72		39	A1
VIA BREVE	YL	YL		8	D4
VIA BRIER	CO	SA		18	D4
VIA BRILLANTE	CO	ET		29A	E1
VIA BRILLANTE	CO	ET		51	E6
VIA BRONCA	SJC	SJ75		38	C2
VIA BRUMOSA	YL	YL		8	D3
VIA BRUNO	ANA	AN		12	C2
VIA BUENA	SJC	SJ75	32000	38	D1
V BUENA SUERTE	YL	YL		40	C6
VIA BUENA VISTA	CO	LB		29A	B5
VIA BUENA VISTA	SJC	SJ75		36	F5
VIA BUHO	CO	SJ		59	D5
VIA BURGOS	MVJO	SJ91	23000	29B	C4
VIA BURGOS	YL	YL		8	D5
VIA BURRIANA	MVJO	SJ91		29B	B4
VIA BURTON ST	ANA	AN	1700	11	F1
VIA CABALLO	CO	SJ		59	C2
VIA CABEZA	YL	YL		8	D3
VIA CADIZ	YL	YL		8	D4
VIA CADIZ	WSTM	WSTM		14	D5
VIA CALABRIA	CO	LB56		29C	B2
VIA CALANDRIA	SCL	SCL		39	A5
VIA CALDERON	YL	YL		8	D4
VIA CALIENTE	FUL	FL33	2100	5	F3
VIA CALIFORNIA	DPT	SC24	26100	38	B5
VIA CALIFORNIA	SJC	SJ75	26600	38	B4
VIA CALLADO	MVJO	SJ91	23000	29B	C3
VIA CALLEJON	SCL	SC72		71	C6
VIA CALLEJON	SJC	SJ75	27200	38	C1
VIA CALMA	MVJO	SJ91		29D	C4
VIA CALMA	TUS	TUS	300	23	E1
VIA CALZADA	MVJO	SJ91	23000	29B	C4
VIA CAMPANAS	YL	YL		8	E2
VIA CAMPANEROS	CO	SJ		59	C3
VIA CAMPO VERDE	CO	LB		29A	C6
VIA CANARIAS	YL	YL		8	D5
VIA CANCHA	SCL	SC72		38	D5
VIA CANDELARIA	CO	SJ79		59	C5
VIA CANDRAS	CO	SJ88		29B	F4
VIA CANELA	SJC	SJ75		38	D1
VIA CANON	DPT	SC24	26200	38	B5
VIA CANON	YL	YL		8	E4
VIA CANTABRIA	SJC	SJ75		36	D4
VIA CANTADA	YL	YL		40	C5
VIA CAPISTRANO	WSTM	WSTM		14	F5
VIA CAPOTE	SJC	SJ75	27100	38	C2
VIA CAPRI	ANA	AN		12	C2
VIA CAPRI	DPT	LB77	33700	37	C5
VIA CAPRI	LAG	LB51	1500	34	B2
VIA CAPRI	SJC	SJ75		38	C2
VIA CARIDAD	CO	SJ		59	C3
VIA CARINO	CO	SJ		59	C3
VIA CARLOS	CO	LB56		35	E2
VIA CARLOS	SJC	SJ75	32000	38	B1
VIA CARMEL	WSTM	WSTM		14	E5
VIA CARONA DR	HTB	HB	6800	26	B1
VIA CARRETAS	YL	YL		8	D3
VIA CARRISSA	CO	SJ88		59	D1

STREET	CITY	P.O. ZONE	BLOCK	PAGE	GRID
VIA CARRIZO	CO	LB		29A	B6
VIA CARTAGENA	YL	YL		8	D4
VIA CASA LOMA	SCL	SC72	2700	39	B1
VIA CASCADA	SJC	SJ75	33600	38	C4
VIA CASCADITA	SCL	SC72	2700	39	B1
VIA CASCO	YL	YL		8	E3
VIA CASITAS	MVJO	SJ92		29D	C2
VIA CASTELLON	YL	YL		8	D4
VIA CASTILE	YL	YL		8	D4
VIA CASTILLA	CO	ET		29A	F3
VIA CASTILLA	CO	LB	1	29A	D5
VIA CASTILLO	TUS	TUS		24	E4
VIA CASTRO	MVJO	SJ92	28000	29B	D4
VIA CATALINA	CO	LB56		29C	F6
VIA CATALINA	DPT	SC24	34400	38	B5
VIA CATALINA	SCL	SC72		39	E4
VIA CATALINA	WSTM	WSTM		14	D5
VIA CATALONIA	SJC	SJ75		38	B1
VIA CAUDALOSO	MVJO	SJ92	25000	29B	C6
VIA CEBOLLA	CO	LB		35	F3
VIA CEBRERO	MVJO	SJ91	27000	29B	C5
VIA CELESTE	CO	SJ		59	C4
VIA CELESTINA	YL	YL		8	D4
VIA CERCETA	CO	SJ		59	B5
VIA CERESA	YL	YL		8	A4
VIA CEREZA	MVJO	SJ91		29B	B3
VIA CEREZA	SCL	SC72		39	C1
VIA CERMENA	SCL	SC72		38	F6
VIA CERMENA	SCL	SC72		39	C1
VIA CERNUDA	MVJO	SJ92		29B	D5
VIA CERRITO	CO	LB77		36	A2
VIA CERRO REBEL	SJC	SJ75		38	D2
VIA CERVANTES	SJC	SJ75		36	E6
VIA CERVANTES	YL	YL		8	D4
VIA CHABAS	MVJO	SJ92	23500	29B	E4
VIA CHACOTA	MVJO	SJ92	25000	29B	C6
VIA CHALUPA	SCL	SC72		38	F6
VIA CHAPALA	SCL	SC72		38	D5
VIA CHIAPAS	MVJO	SJ92	24000	29B	C6
VIA CHICO PL	CO	LB	30300	35	E4
VIA CHICUELINA	SJC	SJ75	27000	38	C2
VIA CHIQUERO	SJC	SJ75	27000	38	C2
VIA CHIRIPA	MVJO	SJ91		29B	C4
VIA CHOCANO	MVJO	SJ92		29B	D5
VIA CHUEÇA	SCL	SC72		38	E6
VIA CISCO	SCL	SC72		39	F4
VIA COCIDA	SJC	SJ75	27000	38	C2
VIA COCO	SCL	SCL		39	F2
VIA CODO	FUL	FL		6	B1
VIA CODORNIZ	CO	SJ		59	D4
VIA COLARES	CO	LB56		29C	E5
VIA COLIBRI	SCL	SC72		39	F4
VIA COLINA	FUL	FL		6	D2
VIA COLINAS	CO	SJ79		59	C5
VIA COLLADO	CO	SJ88		59	C2
VIA COLORSO	SCL	SCL		39	A5
VIA COMPANIA	CO	SJ		59	C3
VIA CONCHA	MVJO	SJ91		29D	B3
VIA CONCHA	SCL	SC72		39	C1
VIA CONCHITA	MVJO	SJ91		29B	B3
VIA CON DIOS	CO	SJ88		59	B2
VIA CONEJO	CO	SJ		59	C4
VIA CONFIANZA	CO	SJ		59	C3
VIA CONGORA	MVJO	SJ92		29B	D5
VIA CONIFERO	SCL	SC72		38	F6
VIA CONIFERO	SCL	SC72		39	C1
VIA CONQUISTA	SJC	SJ75		36	C4
VIA CONSUELA	CO	SJ79		59	C4
VIA CONTENTO	YL	YL		8	E3
VIA CORBINA	SCL	SC72		38	D6
VIA CORBINA	SCL	SC72	3000	39	B1
VIA CORDOBA	GGR	GG45		14	F5
VIA CORDOVA	DPT	LB77		37	C1
VIA CORDOVA	NB	NB	100	31	C5
VIA CORDOVA	SJC	SJ75		36	E5
VIA CORELLA	TUS	TUS		24	E4
VIA CORONA	CO	LB		35	D4
VIA CORONA	DPT	SC24	26100	38	B5
VIA CORONA	YL	YL		8	E3
VIA CORONADO	GGR	GG45		14	E5
VIA CORONADO	MVJO	SJ92		36	C1
VIA CORONADO	YL	YL		8	E3
VIA CORRAL	ANA	AN		13	E2
VIA CORRILLO	YL	YL		8	E4
VIA CORSICA	LAG	LB51	1500	34	B2
VIA CORTA	SJC	SJ75		38	C4
VIA CORTA	VPK	OR67	10200	13	A6
VIA CORTEZ	ANA	AN		13	C2
VIA CORTEZ	MVJO	SJ92	27000	29B	C5
VIA CORTEZ	PLA	PLA		7	C3
VIA CORVALIAN	DPT	DPT	33500	37	C5

STREET	CITY	P.O. ZONE	BLOCK	PAGE	GRID
VIA CORZO	YL	YL		8	E3
VIA COTA	YL	YL		8	E4
VIA COYOTE	CO	SJ		59	D5
VIA CRESPI	CO	LB56		29C	F6
VIA CRESTA	CO	LB77		36	A2
VIA CRESTA	CO	SJ88		59	C2
VIA CRISTAL	SJC	SJ75		36	E5
VIA CRISTAL	YL	YL		8	D4
VIA CRUZ	CO	LB		35	C5
VIA CRUZADA	SJC	SJ75		36	E6
VIA CUARTEL	SJC	SJ75	31200	36	D5
VIA CUERVO	MVJO	SJ91	27000	29B	B4
VIA CURACION	MVJO	SJ91		29D	B6
VIA CYNTHIA	CO	LB56		35	E2
VIA CYPRESS	ANA	AN	1700	11	E1
VIA DALIA	CO	LB56		29C	B2
VIA DAMASCO	MVJO	SJ91	26000	29B	B3
VIA DANIEL	YL	YL		8	D3
VIA DARIO	MVJO	SJ92		29B	D5
VIA DE AGUA	SJC	SJ75	33500	38	C4
VIA DE AGUILA	SJC	SJ75	30000	38	B1
VIA DE ANGELES	SCL	SC72		39	E1
VIA DE ANZA	CO	LB		35	F3
VIA DE ANZA	CO	LB77		36	A3
VIA DE ANZA	SJC	SJ75		38	B3
VIA DE CAMPO	YL	YL		40	B5
VIA DE COLORES	CO	SJ88		59	B4
VIA DE DAUM	DPT	SC24	35400	38	D6
VIA DE GAVILAN	SJC	SJ75	26000	38	B1
VIA D L ARDILLA	YL	YL		8	F6
VIA DEL ACERO	YL	YL		8	E4
VIA D L ESCUELA	YL	YL		8	E4
VIA D L ESPUELA	YL	YL		8	E3
VIA DE LA FLOR	YL	YL		8	F6
VIA DEL AGUA	CO	LB56		29C	F6
VIA DEL AGUA	YL	YL		8	E3
VIA DEL AGUILA	YL	YL		8	E4
VIA D LA JABALI	YL	YL		8	F6
VIA DE LA LUNA	YL	YL	4600	8	C3
VIA DE LA LUZ	CO	SJ79		59	D2
VIA DE LA LUX	DPT	DPT		37	E3
VIA DE LA MESA	CO	SJ		59	C1
VIA DEL AMO	SJC	SJ75	32700	38	B2
VIA DE LA MULA	YL	YL		8	D3
VIA DEL ANGEL	CO	ET		29A	E1
VIA DE LA PLAZA	YL	YL	4400	8	C3
VIA DE LA REATA	YL	YL		8	E3
VIA DE LA ROCA	YL	YL		8	E3
VIA D LS MONTAN	YL	YL	19900	8	C3
VIA DE LA ZORRA	YL	YL		8	F4
VIA DEL BISONTE	YL	YL		8	E4
VIA DEL BUEY	YL	YL		8	D3
VIA DEL CABALLO	YL	YL	19300	8	B3
VIA DEL CAMPO	SCL	SC72	3900	38	C4
VIA DEL CAZADOR	YL	YL		8	E5
VIA DEL CERRO	SJC	SJ75	27800	36	D6
VIA DEL CERRO	SJC	SJ75		38	E1
VIA DEL CERRO	YL	YL		8	E3
VIA DEL CIELO	DPT	LB77	33800	37	C5
VIA DEL CONEJO	YL	YL		8	E4
VIA DEL CORRAL	YL	YL		8	E3
VIA DEL COYOTE	YL	YL		8	E4
VIA DEL CUERVO	YL	YL		8	E4
VIA DEL FARO	CO	LB	22000	29A	A5
VIA DEL FIERRO	YL	YL		8	E3
VIA DELFIN	SCL	SC72		39	F4
VIA DL GANADERO	YL	YL	4300	8	C2
VIA DEL GAVILAN	YL	YL		8	F6
VIA DEL HALCON	YL	YL		8	E4
VIA DE LINDA	SJC	SJ75	32000	36	A6
VIA DE LINDA	SJC	SJ75	32000	38	A1
VIA DEL JINETE	YL	YL		8	E5
VIA DEL LAGO	CO	SJ79		59	D2
VIA DEL LEON	YL	YL		7	C3
VIA DEL LEON	YL	YL		8	D3
VIA DEL LOBO	YL	YL		8	E5
VIA DEL MAR	GGR	GG45		14	E5
VIA DEL NIDO	CO	SJ79		59	D2
VIA DEL NORTE	MVJO	SJ91	25900	29B	A5
VIA DEL NORTE	TUS	TUS		23	F3
VIA DEL OBISPO	YL	YL		8	D2
VIA DEL ORO	CO	LB56		35	E2
VIA D LS ROBLES	YL	YL	4300	8	C2
VIA DEL PALMAR	YL	YL		8	D3
VIA DEL PARQUE	YL	YL		8	E4
VIA DEL POTRERO	YL	YL		8	E4
VIA DEL PRADO	YL	YL	4400	8	C3
VIA DEL PUENTE	YL	YL		8	E3
VIA DEL PUMA	YL	YL		8	E4
VIA DEL RANCHO	YL	YL	4600	8	C3

STREET	CITY	P.O. ZONE	BLOCK	PAGE	GRID
VIA DEL RAY	ANA	AN		16	E2
VIA DEL REY	SJC	SJ75	25700	38	A3
VIA DEL RIO	CO	ET	25000	29A	E1
VIA DEL RIO	YL	YL		40	A4
VIA DEL SOL	CO	SJ79		59	D2
VIA DEL SOL	MVJO	SJ91		29D	B4
VIA DEL SUD	TUS	TUS		23	F3
VIA DEL SUR	MVJO	SJ91	25900	29B	A5
VIA DL TECOLOTE	YL	YL		8	E5
VIA DEL TESORO	SCL	SC72		38	D5
VIA DE LUNA	CO	LB56		35	F2
VIA DEL VALLE	YL	YL	4400	8	C3
VIA DEL VAQUERO	YL	YL		8	F6
VIA DEL VENADO	YL	YL		8	E5
VIA DEL VIENTO	CO	SJ79		59	D2
VIA DENISE	CO	LB56		35	E2
VIA DE OLIVA	SJC	SJ75	32000	38	B1
VIA DE ORO	YL	YL	5500	8	A4
VIA DE ROSA	ANA	AN		43	A3
VIA DESCANSO	GGR	GG45		14	E5
VIA DESEO	SCL	SC72		39	F4
VIA DE TOLEDO	SJC	SJ75	25900	38	B1
VIA DIANZA	YL	YL		8	E4
VIA DICHA	CO	LB		29A	A6
VIA DICHA	CO	LB		29C	A1
VIA DIEGO	YL	YL		8	E3
VIA DIEGO CIR	YL	YL		8	E3
VIA DIJON	NB	NB	100	31	C5
VIA DI NOLA	CO	LB77		35	F4
VIA DONALDO	YL	YL		8	D3
VIA DON BENITO	TUS	TUS		24	E4
VIA DON JUAN	YL	YL		8	D3
VIA DON QUIJOTE	YL	YL		8	D3
VIA DORADO	CO	SJ		59	C4
VIA DUERO	MVJO	SJ91	27000	29B	C4
VIA DULCINEA	SJC	SJ75		36	E6
VIA DULCINEA	YL	YL		8	E2
VIA EBOLI	NB	NB	100	31	C5
VIA EL ESTRIBO	ANA	AN		13	F4
VIA EL ESTRIBO	ANA	AN		43	A4
VIA ELEVADO	DPT	DPT	25100	37	F4
VIA ELM	ANA	AN	1700	11	E1
VIA EL MERCADO	LALM	LALM	11000	14	E2
VIA EL MODENA	OR	OR		18	B3
VIA EL MOLINO	YL	YL	4400	8	C3
VIA EL ROCIO	MVJO	SJ91	23500	29B	C4
VIA EL ROSARIO	SJC	SJ75		36	B5
VIA CARISSA	CO	LB56		35	E1
VIA EL SOCORRO	SJC	SJ75		36	C5
VIA EL TAJO	YL	YL		8	D5
VIA ELVAS	MVJO	SJ91		29B	C4
VIA EMPANADA	CO	SJ88		59	A5
VIA ENCANTADO	SJC	SJ75		36	D4
VIA ENCANTO	SJC	SJ75		36	E5
VIA ENCANTO	YL	YL	19000	8	A4
VIA ENCINAS	CYP	CYP	4000	9	C5
VIA ENCINO	GGR	GG45		14	F5
VIA ENRIQUEZ	MVJO	SJ92	23500	29B	E4
VIA ENSUENO	SCL	SC72		39	F4
VIA ENTRADA	CO	LB56		29C	F6
VIA ENTRADA	CYP	CYP	9500	9	C5
VIA ENTRADA	TUS	TUS		23	F3
VIA ERRECARTE	SJC	SJ75		36	E5
VIA ESCOBA	YL	YL		8	E2
VIA ESCOLA	OR	OR67		13	A4
VIA ESCOLAR	SJC	SJ92		36	B2
VIA ESCORIAL	MVJO	SJ91	27000	29B	C3
VIA ESPANA	HTB	HB47	17400	21	B6
VIA ESPANA	YL	YL		8	D2
VIA ESPANA LN	HTB	HB	17500	26	B1
VIA ESPERANZA	CO	SJ		59	C3
VIA ESPINOZA	DPT	SC24	34500	38	B5
VIA ESPIRITU	SCL	SC72		39	E1
VIA ESPIRITU	SCL	SC72		71	B6
VIA ESPLANADE	WSTM	WSTM		14	D5
VIA ESTANCIA	SJC	SJ75		38	D1
VIA ESTANCIA	YL	YL		8	E3
VIA ESTE	YL	YL		8	E4
VIA ESTELITA	SJC	SJ75		36	A6
VIA ESTELITA	SJC	SJ75		38	B1
VIA ESTELLA	MVJO	SJ91	23000	29B	C4
VIA ESTENAGA	SJC	SJ75		36	E5
VIA ESTER	YL	YL		8	C4
VIA ESTORIL	CO	LB77		35	C4
VIA ESTRADA	ANA	AN		13	E2
VIA ESTRADA	CO	LB	98	29A	D6
VIA ESTRADA	SJC	SJ75		38	B2
VIA ESTUDIO	CO	LB77		36	A2
VIA FABRICANTE	MVJO	SJ91		29B	A4
VIA FAISAN	CO	SJ		59	D5
VIA FAISAN	SCL	SC72		39	D1

STREET	CITY	P.O. ZONE	BLOCK	PAGE	GRID
VIA FAJITA	SJC	SJ75		36	F5
VIA FALDA	MVJO	SJ91	23900	29B	B5
VIA FALERNO	CO	LB56		29C	B1
VIA FARO	MVJO	SJ91		29D	B2
VIA FELICIA	CO	SJ		56	D6
VIA FELICIA	CO	SJ		59	D1
VIA FELIZ	CO	SJ		59	C3
VIA FERMO	NB	NB	100	31	C5
VIA FERNANDO	SJC	SJ75		36	E6
VIA FERRARI	ANA	AN	2900	12	C3
VIA FESTIVO	SJC	SJ75		36	D4
VIA FIERO	CO	LB56		29C	F6
VIA FIERRO	SJC	SJ75		38	D1
VIA FIESTA	MVJO	SJ91	26000	29B	C3
VIA FINEZA	MVJO	SJ91		29B	C4
VIA FIR	ANA	AN	1800	11	E1
VIA FIRENZE	NB	NB	200	31	C5
VIA FLORECER	MVJO	SJ92	25000	29B	C6
VIA FLORECER	MVJO	SJ92		29D	C1
VIA FLORENCE	NB	NB	100	31	C5
VIA FLORES	MVJO	SJ91	23000	29B	C5
VIA FLORES	SJC	SJ75		38	D1
VIA FLORESTA	CO	ET		29A	E1
VIA FLORESTA	CO	ET		51	E6
VIA FLORIDA	SCL	SC72		39	F4
VIA FLORITAS	SCL	SC72		38	D4
VIA FLOTA	SCL	SC72		38	F6
VIA FONTE	YL	YL		8	D4
VIA FORTUNA	DPT	SC24	34300	38	B5
VIA FORTUNA	GGR	GG45		14	F5
VIA FORTUNA	SJC	SJ75		38	D2
VIA FRANCISCO	YL	YL		8	E3
VIA FRESCO	ANA	AN		13	E3
VIA FROMISTA	MVJO	SJ91		29B	C4
VIA FRONDOSA	YL	YL	4600	8	C3
VIA GALICIA	MVJO	SJ91	23000	29B	B4
VIA GALLO	CO	SJ		59	D4
VIA GANCHO CIR	BPK	BP	6500	10	A5
VIA GARCETA	CO	SJ		59	B5
VIA GARCIA	CO	SJ		59	C3
VIA GARCIA	MVJO	SJ92	27000	29B	C5
VIA GARDENIA	CO	SJ		59	B4
VIA GARFIAS	MVJO	SJ92	28000	29B	E4
VIA GAVILAN	SCL	SC72		39	C1
VIA GAVIOTA	MVJO	SJ91		29B	B4
VIA GENOA	DPT	LB77		37	C1
VIA GENOA	NB	NB	100	31	C5
VIA GERALDINA	YL	YL		8	C4
VIA GLORIA	SCL	SC72		38	D5
VIA GLORIA	YL	YL		8	C3
VIA GOLETA	SCL	SC72		38	D5
VIA GOLONDRINA	SCL	SC72		39	D1
VIA GOMEZ	DPT	SC24	34400	38	B5
VIA GORRION	MVJO	SJ91		29B	B4
VIA GRANADA	GGR	GG45		14	F5
VIA GRANADOS	MVJO	SJ92	27800	29B	D5
VIA GRANDE	MVJO	SJ91		29D	B4
VIA GRAZIANA	NB	NB	200	31	C5
VIA GUADALUPE	YL	YL		8	D4
VIA GUADIX	MVJO	SJ91	23000	29B	C4
VIA HABANA	YL	YL		8	D4
VIA HACIENDA	FUL	FL		6	E2
VIA HACIENDA	SJC	SJ75		36	F5
VIA HALCON	CO	SJ		59	D5
VIA HAVRE	NB	NB	100	31	C5
VIA HELENA	LAP	BP23	5000	9	D3
VIA HERMOSA	CO	SJ		59	C3
VIA HERMOSA	GGR	GG45		14	F5
VIA HERRERA	MVJO	SJ92		29B	D5
VIA HIDALGO	SCL	SC72		38	E6
VIA HIERRO	MVJO	SJ92	23000	29B	D4
VIA HILO DR	ANA	AN		16	D2
VIA HONESTO	CO	TRA		59	C2
VIA HORNRADO	CO	SJ		59	C3
VIA IGLESIA	CO	LB		29A	C6
VIA IGLESIA	CO	LB		29C	C1
VIA INEZ	YL	YL		8	E4
VIA INEZ RD	SJC	SJ75	25500	38	A2
VIA INFANTA	YL	YL		8	D5
VIA INGRESO	CYP	CYP	4000	9	C5
VIA INGRESO	FUL	FL33	2200	5	E3
VIA INGRESO	YL	YL		8	D3
VIA INVIERNO	CO	ET		29A	F1
VIA IRANA	STN	STN		15	A1
VIA ISABELLA	YL	YL		8	D3
VIA ITHACA	NB	NB63	100	31	C5
VIA JACARA	STN	STN		15	A1
VIA JACINTO	CO	LB		29A	C6
VIA JANEIRO	CO	LB56		29C	F6
VIA JAQUIMA	CO	SJ		59	B1
VIA JARDIN	STN	STN		15	A1

STREET	CITY	P.O. ZONE	BLOCK	PAGE	GRID
VIA JARDIN	YL	YL		8	D4
VIA JAZMIN	SCL	SCL		39	B5
VIA JOAQUIN	CO	SJ		59	C2
VIA JUANA	YL	YL		8	C3
VIA JUANITA	MVJO	SJ91	26200	29B	B3
VIA JUAREZ	SCL	SC72		38	D6
VIA JUCAR	NB	NB	100	31	C5
VIA JUNIPERO	WSTM	WSTM		14	E5
VIA KANNELA	STN	STN		15	A1
VIA KONA DR	ANA	AN		16	E2
VIA KORON	NB	NB	100	31	C5
VIA KRISTINA	CO	LB56		35	F1
VIA LA CANADA	OR	OR		18	B3
VIA LA CARTA	SJC	SJ75		36	C5
VIA LA CORUNA	MVJO	SJ91	23000	29B	C5
VIA LADERA	CO	LAG		37	F2
VIA LADO	SCL	SC72	2700	39	B1
VIA LAGOS	DPT	DPT	33600	37	F4
VIA LA GRANJA	YL	YL		8	D3
VIA LAGUNA	CO	LB77		36	A5
VIA LAGUNARIA	CO	LB56		35	F1
VIA LA JOLLA	SCL	SC72	200	39	E4
VIA LA MANCHA	CO	LB56		29C	E5
VIA LA MANCHA	YL	YL		8	D3
VIA LA MESA	CO	LB		29A	A6
VIA LA MESA	CO	LB		29C	A1
VIA LA MESA	SCL	SC72		39	E3
VIA LA MIRADA	SJC	SJ75		38	C3
VIA LA MISSION	SCL	SCL		39	F2
VIA LA MORA	SJC	SJ75		36	C5
VIA LA NARANJA	YL	YL		8	D3
VIA LANTANA	CO	SJ		56	D6
VIA LANTANA	CO	SJ		59	D1
VIA LA PALOMA	OR	OR		18	B3
VIA LA PLATA	SJC	SJ75	31900	38	D1
VIA LA PLUMA	SJC	SJ75		38	A3
VIA L PRIMAVERA	YL	YL	4600	8	C3
VIA LA QUINTA	YL	YL	4600	8	C3
VIA LARA	MVJO	SJ91	26200	29B	B3
VIA LARDO	OR	OR	4500	18	B3
VIA LARGA	CO	LB		35	F3
VIA LARGO	CYP	CYP	4300	9	C6
VIA LARREA	MVJO	SJ92		29B	D5
VIA LAS BRISAS	YL	YL		40	C5
VIA LA SENDA	SJC	SJ75		36	C5
VIA LAS PALMAS	CO	LB56		29C	F6
VIA LAS PALMAS	SJC	SJ75		36	E6
VIA LAS ROSAS	CO	LB77		35	C4
VIA LAS VILLAS	YL	YL		8	D4
VIA LATIGO	CO	SJ		59	C2
VIA LAVENDERA	CO	SJ		59	C1
VIA LA VIEJA	YL	YL		8	D5
VIA LEMON	ANA	AN	1700	11	E1
VIA LENARDO	YL	YL		40	B5
VIA LENITA	DPT	DPT	33200	38	A3
VIA LENITA	SJC	SJ75		38	A3
VIA LEON	MVJO	SJ91		29B	B4
VIA LEONA	SJC	SJ75		36	F5
VIA LERIDA	YL	YL		8	D4
VIA LIDO	NB	NB	3300	31	C5
VIA LIDO NORD	NB	NB	100	31	D5
VIA LIDO SOUD	NB	NB	100	31	C5
VIA LINARES	MVJO	SJ91		29B	C4
VIA LINARES	YL	YL		8	D5
VIA LINDA	MVJO	SJ91		29B	A4
VIA LINDA	CYP	CYP	9900	9	C6
VIA LINDA	FUL	FL33		5	E3
VIA LINDO	TUS	TUS	300	23	E1
VIA LLANO	MVJO	SJ91		29B	C3
VIA LOBELIA	CO	SJ		59	B4
VIA LOBO	CO	ET	21500	29A	F1
VIA LOGRONO	MVJO	SJ91	26000	29B	B4
VIA LIMON	SJC	SJ75		36	F5
VIA LINDOSA	CO	LB77		35	C4
VIA LOMA	CO	LB77		36	A5
VIA LOMA LINDA	YL	YL	4500	8	D3
VIA LOMAS	CO	LB		29C	D2
V LOMAS D YORBA	YL	YL		40	B5
V LOMAS D YRB E	YL	YL		40	B6
V LOMAS D YRB W	YL	YL		40	A5
VIA LOPEZ	DPT	SC24	34200	38	B5
VIA LOPEZ	MVJO	SJ92	23500	29B	D4
VIA LORADO	SJC	SJ75	32800	38	B2
VIA LORCA	MVJO	SJ92		29B	D5
VIA LORCA	NB	NB	100	31	D5
VIA LORO	SCL	SC72		38	D6
VIA LOS ALISOS	GGR	GG45		14	F5
VIA LOS ALTOS	CO	LB	662	29C	E1
VIA LOS ALTOS	LAH	LAH		6	A1
VIA LOS ARBOLES	SJC	SJ75		36	F5
VIA LOS BONITOS	LAH	LAH	1700	6	A2
VIA LOS COYOTES	LAH	LAH	1700	6	A2
VIA LOS PAJAROS	SJC	SJ75	26700	36	B6
VIA LOURDES	YL	YL		8	D3
VIA LOYOLA	MVJO	SJ91		29B	C2
VIA LUCERA	ANA	AN		12	C2
VIA LUCIA	YL	YL		8	D3
VIA LUCIO	TUS	TUS	1400	23	E1
VIA LUGO	YL	YL		8	E3
VIA LUGONES	MVJO	SJ92		29B	D5
VIA LUIS	CO	LB56		29C	F6
VIA LUISA	MVJO	SJ91		29B	C5
VIA MACHADO	MVJO	SJ92		29B	D4
VIA MADERA	GGR	GG45		14	F5
VIA MADERA	SJC	SJ75		36	E5
VIA MADERA	YL	YL		8	A4
VIA MADONNA	SJC	SJ75	31600	36	E6
VIA MADONNA	SJC	SJ75	31600	38	D1
VIA MADRID	WSTM	WSTM		14	D5
VIA MADRID	YL	YL		8	D3
VIA MADRIGAL	MVJO	SJ91		29B	C4
VIA MADRIGAL	SJC	SJ75		38	B2
VIA MADRINA	SJC	SJ75		38	D1
VIA MADRUGADA	MVJO	SJ92	24000	29B	D5
VIA MAGDALENA	CO	LB56		29C	F6
VIA MAGNOLIA	CO	SJ		59	D1
VIA MAJORCA	CYP	CYP	4300	9	C5
VIA MAJORCA	LAG	LB51	1500	34	B2
VIA MALAGA	NB	NB	500	31	C5
VIA MALAGA	SJC	SJ75		38	B2
VIA MALAGA	YL	YL		8	D5
VIA MAMBRINO	SJC	SJ75		36	E6
VIA MAMBRINO	SJC	SJ75		38	E1
VIA MANGO	SCL	SC72		39	C1
VIA MANOLETE	MVJO	SJ91		29B	B5
VIA MANRESA	YL	YL		8	D5
VIA MANTARAYA	SCL	SC72		39	C1
VIA MANZANA	SCL	SC72	3900	38	C4
VIA MANZANILLO	YL	YL		8	C5
VIA MAPLE	ANA	AN	1700	11	E1
VIA MARAGALL	MVJO	SJ92		29B	D5
VIA MARAVILLA	CO	LB56		35	E1
VIA MARCO	ANA	AN	300	12	C3
VIA MARCOS	YL	YL		8	E3
VIA MARCUS	CO	LB56		29C	F6
VIA MAREJADA	MVJO	SJ91		29D	B2
VIA MARFIL	MVJO	SJ92	24000	29B	C6
VIA MARFIL	MVJO	SJ92		29D	C1
VIA MARGARITA	YL	YL		8	C4
VIA MARIA	LAP	BP23	5000	9	D4
VIA MARIA	YL	YL		8	C4
VIA MARIANO	YL	YL		8	E3
VIA MARINA	MVJO	SJ91		29D	B3
VIA MARINA WY	NB	NB	2500	31	F2
VIA MARINI	CO	LB77		35	F5
VIA MARIPOSA	CO	SJ		59	D1
VIA MARIPOSA	GGR	GG45		14	F5
VIA MARIPOSA	YL	YL		8	E4
VIA MARIPOSA E	CO	LB	2000	29A	D4
VIA MARIPOSA W	CO	LB		29A	C5
VIA MARISA	YL	YL		8	E2
VIA MARSALA	ANA	AN		12	B3
VIA MARTENS	ANA	AN		12	B1
VIA MARTOS	DPT	DPT	33600	37	F4
VIA MARWAH	YL	YL		8	D3
VIA MASALA	CO	SJ		59	C4
VIA MATADOR	MVJO	SJ91		29B	B6
VIA MAUI	ANA	AN		16	D2
VIA MAYA	CO	SJ		59	B5
VIA MAYOR	SJC	SJ75		38	A3
VIA MECHA	SCL	SC72		39	C3
VIA MEDANO	MVJO	SJ92	27000	29B	C5
VIA MEDIA	CYP	CYP	9700	9	C5
VIA MEDIA	TUS	TUS		23	F3
VIA MEDIA CIR	BPK	BP	6700	10	A4
VIA MELINDA	YL	YL		40	C5
VIA MENDOZA	CO	LB	667	29C	D1
VIA MENTA	CO	SJ		59	B4
VIA MENTONE	DPT	LB77		37	C2
VIA MENTONE	NB	NB	100	31	D5
VIA MERCED	SCL	SC72		38	D5
VIA MERLA	SCL	SC72		39	C1
VIA MERLUZA	SCL	SCL		38	C6
VIA MERLUZA	SCL	SCL		39	C1
VIA MESSINA	IRV	SA		32A	A2
VIA MIGUEL	YL	YL		8	D2
VIA MESETA	CO	SJ88		59	C2
VIA MILANO	ANA	AN	300	12	C3
VIA MILANO	CO	LB77		35	C2
VIA MIMOSA	SCL	SC72		39	F4
VIA MINORCA	SJC	SJ75		38	B2
VIA MIRADA	FUL	FL33	160	5	E3
VIA MIRADOR	SJC	SJ75		36	C5
VIA MIRAMAR	CO	LB		35	C6
VIA MIRAMAR	YL	YL		8	C4
VIA MIRADA	CO	LB56		29C	F6
VIA MIRLO	MVJO	SJ91		29B	B4
VIA MISTRAL	MVJO	SJ92	23500	29B	D4
VIA MISTRAL	SJC	SJ75		38	B2
VIA MOLINA	MVJO	SJ92		29B	E4
VIA MONDELO	MVJO	SJ92		29D	E3
VIA MONITA	YL	YL		8	C4
VIA MONTANERA	ANA	AN		13	D2
VIA MONTANERO	CO	SJ		56	C6
VIA MONTANERO	CO	SJ		59	C1
VIA MONTANEZ	CO	LB		35	C5
VIA MONTE	CO	SJ79		59	C5
VIA MONTECITO	GGR	GG45		14	F5
VIA MONTECITO	SCL	SC72	2700	39	B1
VIA MONTEGO	SCL	SC72	300	39	B1
VIA MONTEREY	GGR	GG45		14	F5
VIA MONTEREY	SJC	SJ75		38	B2
VIA MONTEZUMA	SCL	SC72		38	E6
VIA MONTEZUMA	SCL	SC72	2700	39	B1
VIA MONTOYA	SJC	SJ75		38	D2
VIA MONTURA	SJC	SJ75		38	E1
VIA MORADA	SCL	SC72		38	E4
VIA MORENA	YL	YL		8	C4
VIA MORENO	CO	LB53		29C	F6
VIA MURCIA	YL	YL		8	D4
VIA MURILLO	MVJO	SJ92		29B	D4
VIANA	MVJO	SJ92		29D	C2
VIA NADA	SCL	SC72	300	39	B1
VIA NANDINA	CO	LB56		35	E1
VIA NANDIA	CO	SJ		56	D6
VIA NANDIA	CO	SJ		59	D1
VIA NAPOLI	ANA	AN		12	B2
VIA NAPOLI	CO	LB77		35	C2
VIA NATALIE	YL	YL		8	C4
VIA NAUTILA	SCL	SC72		38	F6
VIA NAUTILA	SCL	SC72		39	C1
VIA NAVARRA	MVJO	SJ91	23000	29B	C4
VIA NAVARRA	YL	YL		8	D2
VIA NERVO	MVJO	SJ92	28000	29B	D4
VIA NIARA	CO	TRA		59	C2
VIA NICE	NB	NB	100	31	D5
VIA NIETOS	YL	YL		8	E5
VIA NOPALES	YL	YL		8	E2
VIA NORIEGA	YL	YL		8	E3
VIA NORTE	CYP	CYP	4200	9	C5
VIA NORTE CIR	BPK	BP	6700	10	A4
VIA NOVA	CO	LB53		29D	A2
VIA NOVELLA	IRV	SA		32A	A2
VIA NOVENO	MVJO	SJ91		29B	C2
VIA NUBLADO	SCL	SC72		39	E1
VIA NUBLADO	SCL	SC72		71	B6
VIA NUEVA	YL	YL		40	C5
VIA NUEZ	MVJO	SJ91	26000	29B	B3
VIA OCEANO	MVJO	SJ91		29D	B3
VIA OCTAVO	MVJO	SJ91		29B	C3
VIA OESTE	YL	YL		8	E4
VIA OLAS	SCL	SC72		38	D5
VIA OLMO	MVJO	SJ91		29B	C3
VIA OLOROSA	CO	SJ		59	D1
VIA ONTIVEROS	YL	YL		8	E4
VIA OPORTO	NB	NB	3200	31	C5
VIA OPORTO	YL	YL		8	C4
VIA ORANGE	ANA	AN	1700	11	E1
VIA ORDAZ	SJC	SJ75		36	E5
VIA ORONTES	SJC	SJ75		38	B2
VIA ORTEGA	CO	SJ		59	C5
VIA ORVIETO	DPT	LB77		37	C1
VIA ORVIETO	NB	NB	100	31	D5
VIA OSO	CO	SJ		59	D4
VIA OTONO	SCL	SC72		39	E1
VIA OTONO	SCL	SC72		71	B6
VIA OVIEDO	MVJO	SJ91	27000	29B	C4
VIA PACIFICA	DPT	DPT	25100	37	F4
VIA PADRES	CO	SJ		59	C3
VIA PAJARO	CO	SJ		59	D4
VIA PAJARO	SCL	SC72		38	D6
VIA PALATINO	IRV	SA	5100	32A	A2
VIA PALERMO	ANA	AN	3400	12	C2
VIA PALERMO	NB	NB	100	31	D5
VIA PALMA	ANA	AN	2500	10	D2
VIA PALMA	CO	LB77		36	A5
VIA PALMITO	SCL	SC72		38	F6
VIA PALMITO	SCL	SC72		39	C1
VIA PALOMA	CO	SJ		59	D4
VIA PALOMA	WSTM	WSTM		14	D5
VIA PALOMINO	CO	LB56		29C	E4
VIA PAMPLONA	YL	YL		8	D3
VIA PAN	CO	LB		35	F3
VIA PANSA	CO	LB56		29C	E4
VIA PARDAL	CO	SJ		59	D4
VIA PARIENTE	CO	SJ88		59	C3
VIA PARRA	SJC	SJ75	31200	36	D5
VIA PASA	SCL	SC72		38	D5
VIA PASADA	CO	LB		35	F2
VIA PASADA	CO	LB77		36	A2
VIA PASADA	TUS	TUS	1400	23	F1
VIA PASATIEMPO	CO	LB56		35	E2
VIA PASTORAL	SJC	SJ75		36	B6
VIA PASTORAL	SJC	SJ75		38	B1
VIA PATITO	CO	SJ		59	D5
VIA PATO	CO	SJ		59	D4
VIA PATO	SCL	SC72		38	D6
VIA PAVON	SCL	SC72		38	D6
VIA PAVO REAL	CO	SJ		59	D4
VIA PEDRELL	MVJO	SJ92		29B	E4
VIA PELLICER	MVJO	SJ92	28000	29B	E4
VIA PEPITA	YL	YL		8	D3
VIA PEQUENO	CO	LB56		35	E2
VIA PERA	MVJO	SJ91		29B	A3
VIA PERA	SCL	SC72		38	F6
VIA PERA	SCL	SC72		39	C1
VIA PERALTA	CO	SJ79		59	C4
VIA PERDIZ	CO	SJ		59	D5
VIA PERLA	SJC	SJ75		36	E5
VIA PERLA	YL	YL		8	D4
VIA PETALOS	CO	SJ		59	C1
VIA PETRA	SJC	SJ75		38	D2
VIA PICHON	SCL	SC72		38	D6
VIA PIEDRA	YL	YL		8	E3
V PIEDRA BLANCA	CO	LB		35	F3
VIA PIEDRA ROJA	CO	LB		35	F3
VIA PIEDRA ROJA	CO	LB77		36	A3
VIA PIMIENTO	MVJO	SJ91		29B	A3
VIA PISA	ANA	AN		12	B2
VIA PIZARRO	YL	YL		8	D3
VIA PLAYA	DPT	DPT	25100	37	F4
VIA PONDAL	MVJO	SJ92		29B	E5
VIA PORTAL	WSTM	WSTM		14	E5
VIA PORTO	ANA	AN		12	B2
VIA PORTOLA	CO	LB	29300	35	F3
VIA PORTOLA	FUL	FL		6	D2
VIA PORTOLA	YL	YL		8	E4
VIA PORTON	MVJO	SJ91		29B	C4
VIA PORTORA	CO	LB		29A	A6
VIA PORTORA	CO	LB		29C	A1
VIA POTES	MVJO	SJ91	23600	29B	C4
VIA PRADO	CO	SJ88		59	C2
VIA PRADOS	MVJO	SJ92	27500	29B	D4
VIA PRESEA	CO	SJ79		59	C3
VIA PRESIDIO	YL	YL		8	E5
VIA PRIMARIA	YL	YL		8	D3
VIA PRIMAVERA	SJC	SJ75		36	E5
VIA PRIMERO	MVJO	SJ92		29B	C5
VIA PRINCESA	CO	ET		29A	E1
VIA PRINCESA	CO	ET		51	E6
VIA PROMONTORIO	SCL	SC72		39	F4
VIA PUERTA	CO	LB		29A	D4
VIA PUNTERO	SJC	SJ75		38	D1
VIA QUEBRADA	SJC	SJ75		38	B1
VIA QUEVEDO	MVJO	SJ92		29B	E5
VIA QUINTO	MVJO	SJ91		29B	C3
VIA QUITO	NB	NB	100	31	D6
VIA QUIXOTE	SJC	SJ75		36	E6
VIA RAMON	YL	YL		8	E4
VIA RAMONA	GGR	GG45		14	F5
VIA RANCHERO	CO	SJ		59	C3
VIA RANCHERO	YL	YL		7	F5
VIA RANCHO	CO	SA		24	D1
VIA RANCHO	SCL	SC72		39	D6
VIA RAVENNA	NB	NB	100	31	D6
VIA RAZA	CO	ET		51	E6
VIA REATA	CO	LB		35	D4
VIA REDONDO	SJC	SJ75		38	D2
VIA REDWOOD	ANA	AN	1700	11	E1
VIA REINA	MVJO	SJ91		29B	C4
VIA REMO	ANA	AN	300	12	C3
VIA REMOLINO	MVJO	SJ91		29D	B2
VIA RENE	YL	YL		8	D4
VIA RIBAZO	ANA	AN		13	D1
VIA RICARDO	CO	SJ		59	C1
VIA RICARDO	YL	YL		8	D3
VIA RINCON	YL	YL		8	E5
VIA RIOJA	MVJO	SJ91	27000	29B	C5
VIA RIVAS	MVJO	SJ92		29B	D5
VIA RIVERA	YL	YL		8	D3
VIA RIVIERA WY	BPK	BP	9200	10	A5
VIA ROBINA	SCL	SC72		39	E3
VIA ROBLE	CO	SJ79		59	C5
VIA ROBLE	MVJO	SJ91	23000	29B	B3
VIA ROBLE	YL	YL		8	E5
VIA RODRIGO	MVJO	SJ92	27600	29B	D5
VIA ROJA	YL	YL		8	D3
VIA ROMA	ANA	AN	500	12	C3
VIA ROMA	CO	SJ92		29D	E2
VIA ROMERO	YL	YL		8	E5
VIA ROMONA	SJC	SJ75		38	D2
VIA RONDA	MVJO	SJ91	23500	29B	C4
VIA ROSA	YL	YL		8	E3
VIA ROSSO	CO	LB56		29C	B2
VIA RUBI	SJC	SJ75		36	E5
VIA RUEDA	SJC	SJ75		36	E6
VIA RUEDA	SJC	SJ75		38	E1
VIA SABIA	ANA	AN		13	D2
VIA SACRAMENTO	DPT	SC24	26300	38	B5
VIA SACRAMENTO	SCL	SC72	26600	38	C4
VIA SAMUEL	YL	YL		8	D3
VIA SAN ANDREAS	SCL	SC72	200	39	B1
VIA SAN ANSELMO	MVJO	SJ92	24000	29B	C6
VIA SN CLEMENTE	MVJO	SJ92	24000	29B	C6
VIA SAN DIEGO	MVJO	SJ91	23000	29B	C3
VIA SANDRA	YL	YL		40	B5
VIA SAN FELIPE	MVJO	SJ92	24000	29B	C6
VIA SAN FELIPE	MVJO	SJ92		29D	C1
VIA SN FERNANDO	MVJO	SJ92	25000	29B	C6
VIA SAN GABRIEL	CO	LB		29A	C6
VIA SAN GABRIEL	MVJO	SJ91	27000	29B	C3
VIA SAN GIL	MVJO	SJ91		29B	B4
VIA SN GORGONIO	SCL	SC72		38	D6
VIA SN GORGONIO	SCL	SC72	3000	39	B1
VIA SAN JACINTO	SCL	SC72		38	D6
VIA SAN JACINTO	SCL	SC72	3000	39	B1
VIA SAN JOSE	MVJO	SJ91		29B	C3
VIA SAN JUAN	CO	LB		29A	C6
VIA SAN JUAN	DPT	SC24	34300	38	B5
VIA SAN JUAN	MVJO	SJ91	23000	29B	C3
VIA SAN JULIAN	CO	LB		29A	C6
VIA SANLUCAR	YL	YL		8	C5
VIA SAN LUIS	MVJO	SJ92	27000	29B	C5
VIA SAN MARCO	CO	LB		29A	C6
VIA SAN MARCO	CO	LB		29C	C1
VIA SAN MARCO	IRV	SA	5100	32	F2
VIA SAN MARTINE	CO	LB		29A	C6
VIA SAN MARTINE	CO	LB		29C	C1
VIA SAN MIGUEL	CO	LB		29A	C6
VIA SAN PABLO	CO	LB		29A	C6
VIA SAN PABLO	CO	LB		29C	C1
VIA SAN PEDRO	MVJO	SJ92	25000	29B	C6
VIA SAN PEDRO	MVJO	SJ92		29D	C1
VIA SAN RAFAEL	CO	LB		29A	C6
VIA SAN RAFAEL	CO	LB		29C	C1
VIA SAN REMO	DPT	LB77		37	C2
VIA SAN REMO	NB	NB	100	31	D5
VIA SN SEBSTIAN	CO	LB	29500	35	E3
VIA SANTA CLARA	MVJO	SJ92	24000	29B	D5
VIA SANTA CRUZ	MVJO	SJ92	25000	29B	C6
VIA SANTA CRUZ	MVJO	SJ92		29D	C1
VIA SANTA LUCIA	MVJO	SJ91		29B	C3
VIA SANTA MARIA	MVJO	SJ91	23000	29B	C3
VIA SANTA MARIA	SCL	SCL		39	F2
VIA SANTA MARIA	SJC	SJ75		36	E6
VIA SANTA MARIA	YL	YL		8	D5
VIA SANTANA	YL	YL		8	E5
VIA SANTANDER	YL	YL		8	D4
VIA SANTA ROSA	DPT	SC24	34100	38	B4
VIA SANTA ROSA	MVJO	SJ91		29B	C3
VIA SANTIAGO	GGR	GG45		14	E5
VIA SANTIAGO	MVJO	SJ91		29B	C3
VIA SANTIAGO	YL	YL		8	E5
VIA SANTILLANA	MVJO	SJ92	25000	29B	C6
VIA SANTO TOMAS	SCL	SC72	2700	39	B1
VIA SANTO TOMAS	SJC	SJ75		36	B5
VIA SAN VICENTE	SJC	SJ75		36	C5
VIA SARA	YL	YL		8	C4
VIA SARASATE	MVJO	SJ92	27800	29B	D5
VIA SARGO	SCL	SC72		39	C1
VIA SECRETO	CO	ET		29A	E1
VIA SECRETO	CO	ET		51	E6
VIA SEGOVIA	FUL	FL		6	E2
VIA SEGUNDO	MVJO	SJ92	27000	29B	C6
VIA SENDA	SCL	SC72	200	39	B1
VIA SEPULVEDA	YL	YL		8	E4
VIA SEQUOIA	SJC	SJ75		38	D2
VIA SERENA	CO	SJ88		59	B2
VIA SERENA N	CO	LB		29A	B5
VIA SERENA S	CO	LB		29A	B5
VIA SERENIDAD	CO	SJ79		59	C5
VIA SERENO	YL	YL	19000	8	B4
VIA SERPIENTE	CO	ET		29A	E1
VIA SERRA	DPT	SC24	26000	38	B4

VIA SEVILLA

1990 ORANGE COUNTY STREET INDEX

134

VISTA MADERA

STREET	CITY	P.O. ZONE	BLOCK	PAGE	GRID
VIA SEVILLA	WSTM	WSTM		14	D5
VIA SEVILLA	YL	YL		8	E2
VIA SEVILLA DR	BPK	BP	9200	10	A5
VIA SEVILLE	FUL	FL		6	D2
VIA SIENA	ANA	AN	3400	12	C2
VIA SIENA	IRV	SA	5100	32	F2
VIA SILVA	MVJO	SJ92		29B	D5
VIA SILVESTRE	MVJO	SJ92	24000	29B	D5
VIA SINCERA	CO	SJ		59	C3
VIA SINTRA	MVJO	SJ91		29B	B4
VIA SOCORRO	SCL	SC72	200	39	B1
VIA SOLA CIR	BPK	BP	6700	10	A4
VIA SOLANA	SJC	SJ75		36	E5
VIA SOLANO	CO	SJ		56	C6
VIA SOLANO	CO	SJ		59	C1
VIA SOLIS	SJC	SJ75		38	A3
VIA SOMBREADA	CO	ET		29A	E1
VIA SONADOR	YL	YL		8	D4
VIA SONOMA	CO	LB56		35	E2
VIA SONOMA	CYP	CYP	9800	9	C6
VIA SONORA	GGR	GG45		14	F5
VIA SONORA	SJC	SJ75		36	D5
VIA SONORA	YL	YL		8	E5
VIA SONRISA	YL	YL		8	D3
VIA SOSIEGO	CO	SJ88		59	B2
VIA SPRUCE	ANA	AN	1700	11	E1
VIA STORNI	MVJO	SJ92	23500	29B	D4
VIA STRAITS LN	HTB	HB	21300	30	F4
VIA SUENO	SCL	SC72		38	D5
VIA SUSANA	CO	LB56		35	E2
VIA TAHITI	ANA	AN		16	D2
VIA TALAVERA	MVJO	SJ91	26000	29B	B4
VIA TALAVERA	YL	YL		8	D4
VIA TAPASTE	YL	YL		8	E2
VIA TARANTO	ANA	AN	3400	12	C2
VIA TARARA	YL	YL		8	D5
VIA TARRAGONA	YL	YL		8	D5
VIA TECA	SCL	SC72		39	C1
VIA TENORIO	YL	YL		8	D5
VIA TEODOCIO	YL	YL		8	E3
VIA TEQUILA	CO	ET		29A	E1
VIA TEQUILA	CO	ET		51	E6
VIA TERCERO	MVJO	SJ91		29B	C3
VIA TERESA	CO	LB56		35	E2
VIA TERRACALETA	CO	TRA		59	C4
VIA TERRACINA	CO	LB56		29C	F6
VIA TERRANO	CO	SJ88		59	C2
VIA TINA	LAP	BP23	8500	9	D3
VIA TIRAPIE	CO	TRA		59	C2
VIA TIRSO	MVJO	SJ92		29B	E4
VIA TOLEDO	WSTM	WSTM		14	D5
VIA TOLEDO	YL	YL		8	E3
VIA TOLUCA	SCL	SC72		39	F4
VIA TOMAS	YL	YL		8	E3
VIA TONADA	CO	ET		29A	E1
VIA TONADA	CO	ET		51	E6
VIA TONADA	SJC	SJ75	32000	38	B1
VIA TORINO	ANA	AN	300	12	C3
VIA TORINO	IRV	SA	5100	32A	A2
VIA TORRALBA	YL	YL		8	D5
VIA TORTUGA	CO	SJ		59	C1
VIA TRIESTE	ANA	AN	300	12	C3
VIA TRIESTE	NB	NB	100	31	D5
VIA TRINIDAD	YL	YL		8	D2
VIA TROVADOR	YL	YL		8	D5
VIA TUDELA	MVJO	SJ91		29B	B5
VIA TUNAS	SCL	SC72		38	D5
VIA TURINA	MVJO	SJ92	27600	29B	D5
VIA TURQUEZA	SCL	SC72		38	F6
VIA TUSCANY	CO	LB77		35	C2
VIA ULMARIA	CO	SJ		59	D1
VIA UMBROSO	SCL	SC72		39	E1
VIA UMBROSO	SCL	SC72		71	B6
VIA UNAMUNO	MVJO	SJ92	28000	29B	D4
VIA UNDINE	NB	NB	100	31	D6
VIA URIBE	CO	LB56		29C	F6
VIA VALDEZ	CO	LB56		35	E1
VIA VALENCIA	WSTM	WSTM		14	E5
VIA VALLARTA	YL	YL		40	C6
VIA VALLE	CO	LB		35	D4
VIA VALOR	DPT	SC24		38	D6
VIA VALOR	DPT	SC24	27400	39	A1
VIA VALVERDE	CO	LB	29400	35	E3
VIA VARADERO	YL	YL		8	D4
VIA VELEZ	DPT	SC24	34100	38	C4
VIA VENADO	CO	SJ		59	D4
VIA VENETA	CO	LB56		29C	C1
VIA VENETO	MVJO	SJ92		29D	E3
VIA VENEZIA	NB	NB	100	31	D6
VIA VENIDA	CO	LB		35	D4
VIA VENTANA	SJC	SJ75		36	C4

STREET	CITY	P.O. ZONE	BLOCK	PAGE	GRID
VIA VENTANA	YL	YL		8	D3
VIA VENTOSA	YL	YL		8	D3
VIA VENTURA	GGR	GG45		14	E5
VIA VENTURA	MVJO	SJ92		29B	D4
VIA VERACRUZ	CO	LB56		29C	F6
VIA VERANO	YL	YL		40	B5
VIA VERBENA	SCL	SC72	2700	39	B1
VIA VERDE	CO	ET		29A	F3
VIA VERDE	CO	SJ88		59	A4
VIA VERDE	CYP	CYP	4200	9	C5
VIA VERDE	DPT	SC24	25800	38	B5
VIA VERONA	IRV	SA	18700	32	F2
VIA VESTA	CO	LB56		29C	B2
VIA VETTI	CO	LB77		35	F5
VIA VIAJANTE	CO	ET		29A	E1
VIA VICENTE	YL	YL		8	E4
VIA VICO CIR	BPK	BP	9300	10	A5
VIA VICTORIA	MVJO	SJ91	26700	29B	C4
VIA VIEJO	CO	ET		29A	F3
VIA VIEJO	SJC	SJ75		38	B2
VIA VIENTE	SJC	SJ75		38	B1
VIA VIENTO	MVJO	SJ91	25600	29D	B2
VIA VIENTO	YL	YL		8	D3
VIA VIGO	MVJO	SJ91	27000	29B	C4
VIA VIGO	YL	YL		8	D4
VIA VILLAGIO	SCL	SC72		39	E1
VIA VIOLETA	CO	SJ		59	D1
VIA VIRGINIA	YL	YL		8	C4
VIA VISTA	ANA	AN	1000	13	E1
VIA VISTA	CO	ET	22000	29A	B5
VIA VISTA	CO	LB		29A	B5
VIA VISTA	CO	SJ79		59	B5
VIA VISTA CIR	HTB	HB	16400	20	D3
VIA VISTA DR	BPK	BP	8900	10	A5
VIA VISTOSA	SCL	SC72	2700	39	B1
VIA VIVA	MVJO	SJ91	26500	29D	B2
VIA WALNUT	ANA	AN	1700	11	E1
VIA WAZIERS	NB	NB	100	31	D6
VIA XANTHE	NB	NB	100	31	D6
VIA YELLA	NB	NB	100	31	D6
VIA ZAPADOR	CO	SJ		59	C2
VIA ZAPATA	SCL	SC72		39	F4
VIA ZARAGOSA	MVJO	SJ91		29B	B5
VIA ZARAGOZA	SCL	SCL		39	F2
VIA ZARAGOZA	YL	YL		8	D5
VIA ZUMAQUE	SCL	SC72		39	C1
VIA ZURICH	NB	NB	100	31	D6
VIC PL	GGR	GG	10400	16	A4
VICAR WY	CO	ET		29B	A2
VICENTE LUGO	MVJO	SJ92		29D	F3
VICENZA CT	CO	SJ92		29D	E2
VICEROY	IRV	SA		29	C1
VICEROY CIR	HTB	HB47	8600	21	D5
VICHY CIR	IRV	SA	15200	29	D3
VICILIA ST	GGR	GG	11200	15	D2
VICKERS AV	GGR	GG	10700	16	A2
VICKI LN	ANA	AN	300	10	D5
VICKIE LN	CO	OR		18	C1
VICKSBURG	IRV	SA		24	E4
VICKSBURG CIR	LALM	LALM	12400	14	D4
VICKSBURG DR	HTB	HB	9700	26	F5
VICKY LN	PLA	PLA	500	7	B4
VICTOR AV	ANA	AN	500	11	C2
VICTORIA AV	ANA	AN	2100	10	F4
VICTORIA BLVD	DPT	SC24	25800	38	A4
VICTORIA CIR	BPK	BP	6400	5	B6
VICTORIA CT	CYP	CYP	4500	9	D5
VICTORIA DR	FUL	FL	1300	6	E4
VICTORIA DR	LAG	LB51	100	34	E5
VICTORIA DR	OR	OR	700	17	E1
VICTORIA DR	SA	SA	1900	17	B6
VICTORIA LN	HTB	HB47	15000	21	A3
VICTORIA PL	CM	CM27	1100	31	A1
VICTORIA PL	CO	CM27	1100	31	A1
VICTORIA PL	LAG	LB51	200	34	E5
VICTORIA PL	WSTM	WSTM	14500	20	E1
VICTORIA ST	ANA	AN	1800	11	A4
VICTORIA ST	CM	CM27	200	31	B1
VICTORIA ST	DPT	DPT		38	A4
VICTORIA WY	PLA	PLA	1500	7	A3
VICTORY WK	LAG	LB51	1100	34	E2
VIDA DR	VPK	OR67	10700	17	F1
VIDA DR	VPK	OR67	10700	18	A1
VIEJO	IRV	SA		28	E6
VIEJO ST	LAG	LB51	200	34	C2
VIEJO WY	SJC	SJ75		38	B2
VIELLE PL	NB	NB	1800	31	C6
VIENNA DR	GGR	GG	10600	16	A4
VIENNA DR	SA	SA		22	D2
VIENNA ST	NB	NB		32	D5
VIENTO DR	IRV	SA		24	E4

STREET	CITY	P.O. ZONE	BLOCK	PAGE	GRID
VIEW CIR	HTB	HB	5800	20	F5
VIEW DR	LAH	LAH	100	2	A3
VIEW LAKE	SA	SA		17	D5
VIEW LAKE CIR	BREA	BREA		2	C5
VIEW PARK DR	YL	YL		8	E2
VIEW POINT	CO	ET		29B	A2
VIEWPOINT CIR	SJC	SJ75	27200	36	C3
VIEW POINT DR	DPT	SC24		38	B5
VIEW POINT LN	ANA	AN		13	F3
VIEW POINT LN	ANA	AN		43	A3
VIEWPOINT LN	HTB	HB47	16700	21	C5
VIEWPOINT PL	CO	LAG		36	A5
VIEW RIDGE DR	CO	SA	12800	18	B4
VIKING AV	ANA	AN	200	11	F4
VIKING AV	ANA	AN	2100	12	A4
VIKING AV	BREA	BREA	100	2	D6
VIKING CIR	GGR	GG	13300	16	C5
VIKING CIR	HTB	HB47	6400	21	A2
VIKING RD	LAG	LB51	1600	34	E4
VILA MOURA	CO	LB77		35	C4
VILELLE PL	NB	NB	1800	31	C6
VILLA DR	VPK	OR67	9500	13	A5
VILLA LN	VPK	OR67	18500	13	A6
VILLA PL	ANA	AN	100	11	C4
VILLA TER	YL	YL	18900	8	B3
VILLA WY	CYP	CYP	5300	9	E5
VILLA WY	NB	NB	2800	31	C5
VILLAMOURA	CO	LAG		35	F4
VILLAMOURA	CO	SJ79		59	D3
VILLAMOURA	CO	SJ79		59	E3
VILLA DEL CERRO	CO	SA		18	C4
VILLAGE DR	BPK	BP		5	A5
VILLAGE DR	CO	ET	22900	29A	F3
VILLAGE DR	HTB	HB	9000	26	E5
VILLAGE DR	LAH	LAH	1200	2	B6
VILLAGE DR	TUS	TUS	17300	23	E1
VILLAGE LN	LAG	LB		35	A5
VILLAGE RD	GGR	GG	12700	15	E4
VILLAGE RD	SJC	SJ75		36	B3
VILLAGE WY	CM	CM		27	D4
VILLAGE WY	OR	OR	900	17	C4
VILLAGE WY	SA	SA	1200	23	E4
VILLAGE WY	WSTM	WSTM	14200	21	B1
VILLAGE CTR DR	STN	GG41		15	C4
VILLAGE CTR DR	YL	YL		8	D3
VILLAGE CREEK	CM	CM		27	D2
VILLAGEGLEN DR	LAH	LAH	600	1	F5
VILLAGEGLEN LN	LAH	LAH	800	1	F5
VILLAGE GRN LN	ANA	AN	1400	11	B6
VILLAGE LK MALL	BREA	BREA		2	D5
VILLAGER CIR	YL	YL	19900	8	C3
VILLAGE WOOD LN	CO	ET	24800	29A	E3
VILLA GRANDE DR	YL	YL	4200	7	E2
VILLA ISLE CIR	VPK	OR67		13	B5
VILLA ISLE DR	VPK	OR67		13	B5
VILLAMIRA	CO	LB		29D	A6
VILLAMIRA	CO	LB77		36	A1
VILLANOVA CIR	WSTM	WSTM	15800	21	D4
VILLANOVA RD	CM	CM	200	27	D6
VILLANUEVA	MVJO	SJ91		29B	C3
VILLA NUEVA DR	HTB	HB	6500	26	A1
VILLA PACIFC DR	HTB	HB	9700	30	F5
VILLA PARK RD	CO	OR		18	B1
VILLA PARK RD	OR	OR	1700	12	E6
VILLA PARK RD	VPK	OR67	18100	13	A6
VILLA REAL	CO	ET		51	F6
VILLAREAL DR	OR	OR	2400	12	F4
VILLARENTE ST	CO	LAG		35	F4
VILLA ROSE DR	CO	SA	12900	18	B5
VILLA VISTA TER	CO	OR		18	B1
VILLA VISTA WY	OR	OR	2000	12	E5
VILLA VISTA WY	VPK	OR67		12	F5
VILLA WOODS CIR	VPK	OR67	18500	13	A5
VILLA WOODS DR	VPK	OR67	9600	13	A5
VILLA YORBA	HTB	HB47	16000	21	D4
VILLENA	MVJO	SJ92	23300	29B	E5
VIOLADO	CO	SJ88		59	C2
VINA DL MR AV E	PLA	PLA	1300	7	D4
VINA DL MAR CIR	PLA	PLA	1100	7	D4
VINA DEL MAR PL	PLA	PLA	1100	7	D4
VINALHAVEN CT	CYP	CYP	6700	15	B2
VINCENT CIR	HTB	HB48		26	B1
VINCENTE AV	PLA	PLA		7	E6
VINE AV	CO	OR69	17800	17	F3
VINE AV	FUL	FL33	200	5	E6
VINE AV	FUL	FL33	1000	10	D1
VINE AV	OR	OR	3300	17	F2
VINE ST	CO	OR	18500	18	A3
VINE ST N&S	ANA	AN	100	11	D3
VINEDO RD	CO	SJ		59	D2

STREET	CITY	P.O. ZONE	BLOCK	PAGE	GRID
VINELAND DR	HTB	HB	5300	20	E6
VINEVALE CIR	LAP	BP23	5600	9	E3
VINEVALE ST	ANA	AN	1400	10	E6
VINEVALE ST	ANA	AN04	1300	15	E1
VINEVALE ST	GGR	GG	11200	15	D2
VINEVALE ST	STN	AN04	10600	15	E1
VINEWOOD AV	TUS	TUS	17300	23	E2
VINEYARD AV	ANA	AN	1000	11	C5
VINTAGE	CO	LB77		35	D6
VINTAGE	CO	TRA		59	D5
VINTAGE LN	ANA	AN		11	E3
VINTAGE LN	HTB	HB	20000	26	D5
VINTAGE WY	CO	ET	21200	29B	C1
VINTAGE WY	CO	ET		52	C6
VINTAGE WY	FUL	FL33		5	F2
VINTAGE WDS RD	CO	ET		52	B6
VIOLA PL	CM	CM27	1800	31	C2
VIOLA ST	ANA	AN	4800	8	A5
VIOLET CIR	FTNV	SA08	11700	22	C4
VIOLET	MVJO	SJ91		52	D6
VIOLET CIR	PLA	PLA	900	7	C4
VIOLET DR	GGR	GG	11600	16	B4
VIOLET LN	OR	OR	100	17	F3
VIOLET ST	SB	SB	3600	14	D4
VIOLETA LN	CO	SJ		59	D4
VIOLET LNTRN ST	DPT	DPT	33900	37	E4
VIREO CIR	CM	CM	2700	27	B5
VIREO CIR	FTNV	SA08	10100	27	A2
VIRGIL CIR	CYP	CYP	10100	9	C6
VIRGINIA	MVJO	SJ92		52	D6
VIRGINIA AV	ANA	AN	2100	11	F4
VIRGINIA AV	ANA	AN	2200	12	A4
VIRGINIA AV	SA	SA	300	17	B5
VIRGINIA CIR	FTNV	SA08	10800	27	B2
VIRGINIA PL	ANA	AN	500	12	A4
VIRGINIA PL	CM	CM27	100	31	E1
VIRGINIA PL	PLA	PLA	1700	7	A3
VIRGINIA RD	FUL	FL	300	6	D4
VIRGINIA ST	LAH	LAH	100	1	F4
VIRGINIA WY	BREA	BREA		2	E6
VIRGINIA WY	LAG	LB	31500	35	B6
VIRGINIA WY	LAG	LB77	31900	37	B1
VIRGINIA PK DR	LAG	LB51	400	34	E2
VIRLEE ST	SA	SA	800	22	B4
VISALIA DR	CM	CM	1000	27	E2
VISCOUNT DR	HTB	HB	8600	26	D5
VISO LN	MVJO	SJ91		29B	C1
VISPERA	IRV	SA		24	F5
VISTA	IRV	SA		28	F6
VISTA AV	PLA	PLA	1000	12	A1
VISTA CIR	BREA	BREA		2	D4
VISTA CIR	OR	OR		12	E4
VISTA CT	BREA	BREA		2	F5
VISTA CT	OR	OR		12	E4
VISTA DR	DPT	SC24		38	B5
VISTA DR	HTB	HB	4800	20	D5
VISTA DR	NB	NB	2500	31	D5
VISTA LN	FUL	FL	900	6	B4
VISTA LN	LAG	LB51	600	34	D2
VISTA LN	YL	YL	4400	7	D3
VISTA PL	ANA	AN	1300	11	F1
VISTA TER	CO	ET		52	C5
VISTA WY	CO	ET		29A	C1
VISTA WY	YL	YL		8	D2
VISTA ALCEDO	SCL	SC72		39	E3
VISTA ALISO RD	CO	TRA		52	E3
VISTA AZUL	DPT	SC24		38	C6
VISTA AZUL	DPT	SC24		39	A1
VISTA AZUL	SCL	SC72		39	D6
VISTA BAHIA DR	HTB	HB		20	D3
VISTA BARRANCA	CO	SJ88		56	C6
VISTA BAYA CIR	CO	CM27	300	31	E2
VISTA BAYA CIR	NB	NB	2500	31	E2
VISTA BLANCA	SCL	SC72		39	E6
VISTA BLUFF RD	OR	OR		12	E4
VISTA BONITA	CYP	CYP	9300	9	E5
VISTA BONITA	NB	NB	2000	32	A3
VISTA BONITA DR	IRV	SA17		32	D3
VISTA CAJON	NB	NB	2000	32	A3
VISTA CANTORA	SCL	SC72		39	E3
VISTA CANTORA	YL	YL		40	B5
VISTA CANYON RD	OR	OR		12	E4
VISTA CARILLO	CO	LB77		35	C4
VISTA CAUDAL	NB	NB	2000	32	A3
VISTA CAYENTA	SCL	SC72		39	E3
VISTA CIELO	CO	SJ88		56	B5
VISTA COLINA	DPT	DPT		37	C5
VISTA COLINAS	CO	SJ88		56	B5
VISTA COLINAS	CO	SJ88		59	B4
VISTA CORONA	DPT	DPT		37	C5
VISTA CREST RD	OR	OR		12	E4

STREET	CITY	P.O. ZONE	BLOCK	PAGE	GRID
VIS DE CATALINA	LAG	LB77	32000	37	B1
VISTA DE DONS	DPT	SC24	27500	38	D6
VIS DE LA LUNA	LAG	LB77	32100	37	B1
VISTA DEL AMIGO	ANA	AN		13	E6
VISTA DEL AMIGO	YL	YL		8	D3
VISTA DEL CANON	ANA	AN		13	E6
VISTA DEL CERRO	ANA	AN		13	E5
VISTA DEL DIA	ANA	AN		13	E6
VISTA DEL DONS	DPT	SC24		39	A1
VISTA DEL ESTE	ANA	AN		13	E6
VIS DEL GAVIOTA	OR	OR	500	12	D4
VISTA DEL LAGO	CO	SA	11200	18	D6
VISTA DEL LAGO	MVJO	SJ91	27400	29B	D2
VISTA DEL LAGO	MVJO	SJ92		29B	D2
VISTA DEL LAGO	YL	YL	5500	8	A4
VISTA DEL MANDO	CO	LB		29A	A6
VISTA DEL MAR	CYP	CYP	5300	9	E5
VISTA DEL MAR	DPT	DPT		37	F1
VISTA DEL MAR	DPT	SC24	26700	38	C6
VISTA DEL MAR	YL	YL		8	C4
VISTA DL MAR DR	FUL	FL	1300	6	E3
VISTA DEL MONTE	ANA	AN		13	E6
VISTA DEL NORTE	YL	YL		8	D2
VISTA DEL ORO	FUL	FL	2100	6	F3
VISTA DEL ORO	NB	NB	2000	31	F2
VISTA DEL ORO	NB	NB	2000	32	A3
VISTA DL PARADA	NB	NB		32	A2
VISTA DEL PLAYA	NB	NB	2200	32	A2
VISTA DEL PLAYA	OR	OR	500	12	D5
VISTA DEL PONTO	SCL	SC72		39	E3
VIS DEL POTRERO	CO	SJ88		59	A4
VISTA DEL RIO	ANA	AN		13	E6
VISTA DEL ROSA	FUL	FL	1900	6	F3
VIS DL SN CLMNT	DPT	LB77	32200	37	C1
VISTA DEL SOL	ANA	AN	6400	13	E1
VISTA DEL SOL	CO	ET		51	E4
VISTA DEL SOL	CYP	CYP	5300	9	E4
VISTA DEL SOL	FUL	FL	2100	6	F3
VISTA DEL SOL	LAG	LB77	22500	37	B1
VISTA DEL SOL	NB	NB	3100	32	A2
VISTA DEL SOL	YL	YL		8	D3
VISTA DEL SOL W	DPT	LB77	32200	37	C1
VISTA DL SOL DR	HTB	HB	6800	26	B1
VISTA DEL VALLE	ANA	AN		13	E5
VISTA DEL VALLE	CO	SA05		18	C4
VISTA DEL VELA	NB	NB		32	A2
VISTA DEL VERDE	CO	TRA		59	C4
VISTA DEL VERDE	CO	TRA		62	A1
VISTA DE ORA	LALM	LALM	3700	14	B3
VISTA DE TODO	DPT	SC24	35200	38	D6
VISTA DE TODO	DPT	SC24		39	A1
VISTA D'ONDE	DPT	LB77	24100	37	E4
VISTA DORADO	NB	NB	2100	32	A2
VISTA D'ORO	DPT	LB77	24100	37	E4
VISTA ENCANTA	SCL	SC72		39	E3
VISTA ENSILLADO	CO	SJ		56	C6
VISTA ENSILLADO	CO	SJ		59	C1
VISTA ENTRADA	NB	NB		31	F3
VISTA ENTRADA	NB	NB	2000	32	A3
VISTA ESTATE DR	CO	ET		29B	B1
VISTA ESTATE DR	CO	ET		52	B6
VISTA FIRENZE	CO	LB53		29D	A2
VISTA FLORA	NB	NB	2100	32	A3
VISTA FORTUNA	CYP	CYP	5400	9	E5
VISTA FRONDOSA	CO	SJ88		59	A5
VISTA FUSCO	CO	ET	25100	29A	F2
VISTA GLEN CIR	YL	YL		8	D1
VISTA GLEN RD	OR	OR		12	E4
VISTA GRANDE	DPT	LB77	33800	37	C5
VISTA GRANDE	FUL	FL		6	D2
VISTA GRANDE	NB	NB		32	A2
VISTA GRANDE DR	CO	LB		29A	C4
VISTA HTS RD	OR	OR		12	E4
VISTA HERMOSA	CO	ET		51	E4
VISTA HERMOSA	CO	ET		51	F6
VISTA HERMOSA	CYP	CYP	5300	9	E5
VISTA HOGAR	NB	NB	2000	32	A3
VISTA HUERTA	NB	NB	2000	32	A3
VISTA KNOLL RD	OR	OR		12	E4
VISTA LA CUESTA	CO	SJ88		56	B5
VISTA LA CUESTA	CO	SJ88		59	B4
VISTA LADERA	CO	LB77		36	A1
VISTA LAGO	CO	SJ		59	C1
VISTA LAGUNA	YL	YL		8	C4
VISTA LAMPARA	YL	YL		40	B5
VISTA LAREDO	NB	NB	2000	32	A3
VISTA LINDA	CO	ET		51	E4
VISTA LINDA	LAG	LB77		37	B1
VISTA LOMA	CO	YL		8	C6
VIS LOMITAS DR	FUL	FL	2000	6	E3
VISTA MADERA	NB	NB		32	A2

ORANGE CO.

INDEX

STREET	CITY	P.O. ZONE	BLOCK	PAGE	GRID
VISTA MAGNIFICA	CO	LB56		35	E2
VISTA MAR	CO	SA	11500	24	D1
VISTAMAR DR	CO	LAG		36	A5
VISTA MARINA	NB	NB	2000	31	E2
VISTA MARINA	SCL	SC72	1000	39	C4
VISTA MESA	CO	SJ88		56	B5
VISTA MESA	CO	SJ88		59	B4
VISTA MESA	CYP	CYP	9300	9	E5
VISTA MESA WY	OR	OR		12	E4
VIS MODJESKA RD	CO	TRA		52	E2
VISTA MONTANA	YL	YL		8	C4
VISTA MONTEMAR	CO	LB77		35	C3
VISTA NIGUEL	CO	LB77		36	A5
VISTA NOBLEZA	NB	NB		32	A2
VISTA ORNADA	NB	NB		32	A2
VISTA PANORAMA	CO	SA	19000	18	B4
VISTA PARADA	NB	NB60		32	A2
VISTA PARK AV	OR	OR		12	E4
VISTA PLAZA DR	CO	LB	29500	35	F3
VISTA POINT RD	OR	OR		12	E4
VISTA POINTE	SJC	SJ75		36	C3
VIS PORTOLA RD	CO	TRA		52	E2
VISTA PRIVADA	CO	SA	2100	24	D1
VISTA QUINTA	NB	NB		32	B2
VISTA RANCHO	CO	LB		35	F2
VISTA REAL	CYP	CYP	5300	9	E4
VISTA REAL	YL	YL	19000	8	B4
VISTA RIDGE DR	OR	OR		12	E4
VISTA ROMA	NB	NB		32	A2
VISTA ROMA CIR	HTB	HB		20	D5
VISTA ROYALE DR	OR	OR		12	E4
VISTA SABANA	CO	SJ88		59	A5
VIS SADLBACK RD	CO	TRA		52	E2
VIS SANTIAGO RD	CO	TRA		52	E2
VISTA SERENA	CYP	CYP	9300	9	E5
VISTA SERRANO	CO	ET	25100	29A	F1
VISTA SIERRA	CO	TRA		56	B5
VISTA SIERRA	CO	TRA		59	B4
VISTA SIERRA	CYP	CYP	9400	9	E5
VISTA SUERTE	NB	NB		32	A2
VISTA SUMMIT WY	OR	OR		12	F4
VISTA TORITO	SCL	SC72		38	D6
VISTA TRUCHA	NB	NB		32	A2
VISTA UMBROSA	NB	NB		32	B2
VISTA VALINDA	SCL	SC72		39	E3
VISTA VALLEY RD	OR	OR		12	E4
VISTA VERDE DR	CO	ET	22200	29A	E2
VISTA VERDE DR	FUL	FL	200	6	C4
VISTA VIEJO	MVJO	LB53		29D	B4
VITTORIA ST	CO	LB77		35	F3
VIVA CIR	HTB	HB46		27	A5
VIVA LN	HTB	HB47		21	D4
VIVIAN LN	NB	NB	1400	31	E3
VIVIWOOD PL	LAH	LAH	1200	2	A6
VIZZINI	IRV	SA		24	D5
VOGEL AV	WSTM	WSTM		21	D4
VOLANTE DR	HTB	HB48	9500	26	A6
VOLGA DR	HTB	HB47	7500	21	C4
VOLGA RIVER CIR	FTNV	SA08	8500	26	D2
VOLKWOOD ST	GGR	GG	12300	16	D4
VON CIR	WSTM	WSTM	14500	21	E2
VON KARMAN AV	IRV	SA	18300	28	C4
VON KARMAN AV	NB	NB60	19000	28	C5
VONNIE LN	CYP	CYP	5500	9	E4
VONS DR	GGR	GG	9000	15	E2
VOYAGER AV	BREA	BREA	3000	3	C6
VOYAGER CIR	HTB	HB	9900	26	F6
VOYAGER LN	ANA	AN	1900	11	A2
VOYAGER LN	CO	LB	23800	35	E3
VUELTA LOMA	DPT	SC24		38	B5
VUELTA RICA	DPT	SC24		38	B5
W					
WAAL CIR	HTB	HB47	17400	21	D6
WABASH AV	CO	YL	17000	7	D1
WABASH AV	YL	YL	16900	7	D1
WABASH AV E	PLA	PLA	10000	7	D1
WABASH CIR	PLA	PLA	2300	7	D1
WABASH WY	STN	STN		10	E4
WABASH WY	STN	STN		15	B3
WACO AV	PLA	PLA	2400	7	C1
WADE	IRV	SA15		28	C4
WADE CIR	ANA	AN	200	13	B2
WADE ST	LAH	LAH	100	2	C4
WADEBRIDGE CIR	HTB	HB	8100	26	C3
WADE RIVER CIR	FTNV	SA08	8500	26	D2
WADHAM WY	CYP	CYP	11400	15	B3
WADSWORTH	IRV	SA		29	E1
WAGAR ST	CO	ET		29B	A2
WAGERS CIR	HTB	HB47	8600	21	D5

STREET	CITY	P.O. ZONE	BLOCK	PAGE	GRID
WAGNER AV	ANA	AN	2100	11	F5
WAGNER AV	ANA	AN	2300	12	A5
WAGNER AV	CO	AN06	15000	12	A5
WAGNER RIV CIR	FTNV	SA08		26	E2
WAGON DR	HTB	HB47	7600	21	C6
WAGON WHEEL CIR	CO	LB53		29C	F4
WAGON WHEEL CIR	CO	LB53	25000	29D	A4
WAGON WHEEL CT	BREA	BREA		2	E5
WAGON WHEEL DR	CO	YL	5000	8	B3
WAGON WHEEL LN	CO	SJ		56	D6
WAGON WHEEL LN	CO	SJ		59	D1
WAIKIKI LN	HTB	HB	16000	20	D4
WAIKIKI WY	SA	SA		22	C3
WAINWRIGHT DR	BPK	BP	7400	9	F2
WAITE LN	HTB	HB47	16500	21	C5
WAKE AV	ETMC	SA09	13300	51	D4
WAKE CIR	CYP	CYP	11500	14	E3
WAKEFIELD	HTB	HB		26	B2
WAKEFIELD	IRV	SA		24	D6
WAKEFIELD	MVJO	SJ92		29B	E2
WAKEFIELD AV	GGR	GG	11000	16	B2
WAKEFIELD AV E	ANA	AN	100	16	E2
WAKEFIELD AV W	ANA	AN	1100	16	B2
WAKEFIELD CT	CO	LB		35	C4
WAKEFIELD PL	ANA	AN	1100	16	B2
WAKEFIELD ST	WSTM	WSTM	14500	21	F2
WAKE FOREST DR	ANA	AN		10	F3
WAKE FOREST RD	CM	CM	200	27	D6
WAKE FOREST ST	BREA	BREA	500	2	F5
WAKEHAM AV	SA	SA	300	23	C3
WAKEHAM PL	CM	CM	900	27	E2
WAKEHAM PL	SA	SA04	2000	27	E2
WAKONDA	CO	SJ79		59	D3
WALDEN LN	ANA	AN		8	D6
WALDEN LN	TUS	TUS	1200	23	F3
WALDEN RD	BREA	BREA		3	B5
WALDO AV	FUL	FL33	100	5	D6
WALES CIR	WSTM	WSTM	15000	22	A2
WALKABOUT CIR	NB	NB		31	A2
WALKABOUT LN	DPT	DPT		37	A5
WALKER AV	LAH	LAH	900	1	F5
WALKER CIR	WSTM	WSTM		21	D4
WALKER CT	CYP	CYP		9	E5
WALKER DR	CO	OR67		50	F6
WALKER LN	CO	LAH	1200	2	B3
WALKER LN	FUL	FL33		5	E2
WALKER ST	BPK	BP	7500	9	E3
WALKER ST	CYP	CYP	8800	9	E3
WALKER ST	CYP	CYP	10500	14	E1
WALKER ST	LAP	BP23	6500	9	E6
WALKER LEE DR	CO	LALM	2600	14	A4
WALKER RCH CIR	VPK	OR67		13	A5
WALKING STICK	CO	LB77		37	F2
WALL ST	LAH	LAH	500	1	D5
WALLACE AV	CM	CM27	1700	31	B1
WALLACE AV	CO	LAH	9100	1	E3
WALLACE AV	FUL	FL	2500	7	A5
WALLACE ST	LAH	LAH	100	2	A5
WALLEYE LN	HTB	HB	19000	26	F3
WALLGREEN ST	PLA	PLA	100	12	A1
WALLING AV	BREA	BREA	1000	2	D4
WALLING AV	LAH	LAH	2200	2	C4
WALLINGFORD LN	HTB	HB		30	E3
WALLINGSFORD LN	WSTM	WSTM		21	E2
WALLINGSFORD RD	CO	LALM	11200	14	B3
WALNUT	IRV	SA		29	D2
WALNUT AV	BPK	BP	7200	10	B1
WALNUT AV	CO	OR69	17800	17	F2
WALNUT AV	CO	OR	18100	18	A2
WALNUT AV	GGR	GG	12200	16	B4
WALNUT AV	HTB	HB	100	26	A5
WALNUT AV	IRV	SA	3000	24	B6
WALNUT AV	IRV	SA	4000	29	D1
WALNUT AV	TUS	TUS	1500	23	F3
WALNUT AV	TUS	TUS	1900	24	A4
WALNUT AV E	OR	OR	3600	18	A2
WALNUT AV E&W	FUL	FL	100	6	B6
WALNUT AV E&W	OR	OR	100	17	C2
WALNUT AV N&S	BREA	BREA	100	2	E6
WALNUT AV N&S	PLA	PLA	100	7	A5
WALNUT AV S	BREA	BREA	400	6	D1
WALNUT AV W	FUL	FL33	1600	5	F6
WALNUT LN	YL	YL		8	A4
WALNUT PL	CM	CM27	400	31	E3
WALNUT ST	ANA	AN	100	11	C6
WALNUT ST	ANA	AN	1500	16	C1
WALNUT ST	CM	CM27	100	31	D2
WALNUT ST	CO	LAH	1000	2	A5
WALNUT ST	CYP	CYP	6500	15	A1
WALNUT ST	FTNV	SA08	16500	21	E6
WALNUT ST	FTNV	SA08	17600	26	E3

STREET	CITY	P.O. ZONE	BLOCK	PAGE	GRID
WALNUT ST	GGR	GG	10600	16	A5
WALNUT ST	LALM	LALM	10300	14	B1
WALNUT ST	NB	NB	100	31	A4
WALNUT ST	OR	OR68	300	16	F2
WALNUT ST	TUS	TUS	1000	23	F3
WALNUT ST	YL	YL	17400	7	E2
WALNUT ST E&W	SA	SA	100	23	A2
WALNUT ST N&S	LAH	LAH	100	1	F5
WALNUT ST W	SA	SA	1300	22	F2
WALNUT WY	BREA	BREA	200	2	E5
WALNUT WY	FUL	FL		6	C6
WALNUT CYN RD	ANA	AN		13	E3
WALNUT CREEK RD	YL	YL	5800	8	C5
WALNUT GROVE	MVJO	SJ92		29B	E2
WALNUT RIDGE RD	OR	OR69		18	E3
WALNUTWOOD WY	CO	ET		29A	F1
WALNUTWOOD WY	CO	ET		51	F6
WALRUS LN	HTB	HB		20	B4
WALT ST	WSTM	WSTM	6400	21	A1
WALTER AV	TUS	TUS	1100	23	F3
WALTER CIR	WSTM	WSTM	5500	14	F5
WALTER CT	TUS	TUS		24	A4
WALTERS CT	CO	LB		35	C4
WALTHAM WY	LAH	LAH	1700	2	C3
WALTON DR	HTB	HB47	6500	21	A4
WALTZ AV	ANA	AN	1700	8	B6
WALTZ CIR	HTB	HB	16000	20	D4
WANDA CIR	HTB	HB47	16800	21	B5
WANDA DR	ANA	AN	1000	11	E2
WANDA DR N	FUL	FL33	200	5	F6
WANDA DR S	FUL	FL33	200	5	F6
WANDA RD	OR	OR	1300	12	F6
WANDA RD	OR	OR	900	17	F1
WANDA RD	VPK	OR67	10200	12	F6
WANDERER LN	HTB	HB	16600	20	D3
WANDERING LN	BREA	BREA		3	B5
WANDERING LN	CO	ET	25100	29A	F2
WANDERING RILL	IRV	SA		32A	A2
WANIGAN WY	CO	LB77		37	D2
WARBLER AV	HTB	HB	9200	26	E3
WARBLER AV	OR	OR	1600	12	E5
WARBLER CIR	ANA	AN		13	E2
WARBLER PL	OR	OR	1600	12	E6
WARBLER ST	SA	SA	2300	22	E5
WARBURTON DR	HTB	HB	9500	26	F4
WARBURTON WY	FUL	FL33	1400	5	F4
WARD CIR	CYP	CYP	6800	15	A1
WARD ST	FTNV	SA08	15800	22	A6
WARD ST	FTNV	SA08	17600	27	A2
WARD ST	GGR	GG	13600	16	A6
WARD ST	GGR	GG43	14200	22	A3
WARD ST	HTB	HB46	19000	27	A3
WARD ST	LAH	LAH	500	2	B4
WARD ST	WSTM	WSTM	14500	22	A3
WARD TER	ANA	AN	2100	11	F3
WARD TER	ANA	AN	2300	12	A3
WARD WY	BPK	BP	6400	9	F2
WARDLOW CIR	CO	LB	23800	35	E3
WARDLOW PL	FTNV	SA08	17000	22	C6
WARDMAN DR	BREA	BREA	900	2	D4
WARDS TER	LAG	LB51	2800	34	F5
WARFIELD DR	HTB	HB	9000	26	E4
WARMINGTON	HTB	HB		20	C3
WARMSPRING	IRV	SA		29	B5
WARNE ST	LAH	LAH	500	2	B4
WARNER AV	TUS	SA05	15800	23	D5
WARNER AV	FTNV	SA08	8500	21	C5
WARNER AV	FTNV	SA08	10000	22	A5
WARNER AV	HTB	HB	3700	20	E5
WARNER AV	HTB	HB47	6200	21	C5
WARNER AV	IRV	SA	3000	28	F1
WARNER AV	IRV	SA	3100	29	A1
WARNER AV	TUS	SA10	1000	23	D5
WARNER AV E&W	SA	SA	100	23	A5
WARNER AV W	SA	SA	1300	22	E5
WARREN AV	CO	TUS	18200	24	A1
WARREN CIR	LAP	BP23	7400	9	F1
WARREN LN	CM	CM	3000	27	D3
WARREN LN	HTB	HB	16000	20	E4
WARREN ST	PLA	PLA	1200	7	D4
WARREN ST	SA	SA	900	23	C3
WARREN ST	WSTM	WSTM	14300	21	E1
WARRENTON AV	ANA	AN		11	F2
WARSAW ST	CO	SJ91		29B	A5
WARWICK CIR	LAP	BP23	5800	9	E2
WARWICK CIR	WSTM	WSTM	15200	22	A2
WARWICK CT	CO	ET		29B	B1
WARWICK DR	CO	LB		35	D2
WARWICK DR	HTB	HB46	10300	27	A5
WARWICK LN	NB	NB	1400	31	E3

STREET	CITY	P.O. ZONE	BLOCK	PAGE	GRID
WASATCH DR N	ANA	AN	4900	13	A2
WASCO RD	ANA	AN	600	10	D5
WASCO RD	GGR	GG	11000	15	D2
WASCO RD	STN	STN	10100	10	D6
WASCO ST	GGR	GG	11300	15	D2
WASHBURN ST	FTNV	SA08	16000	22	C4
WASHINGTON AV	CM	CM	3200	27	B3
WASHINGTON AV	CO	MDWY	8000	21	C2
WASHINGTON AV	FUL	FL	600	6	B6
WASHINGTON AV	FUL	FL	1000	11	B1
WASHINGTON AV	GGR	GG	9500	21	F2
WASHINGTON AV	HTB	HB47	7500	21	C5
WASHINGTON AV	WSTM	WSTM	8000	21	E2
WASHINGTON AV E	OR	OR	100	17	C3
WASHINGTON AV E	OR	OR	3500	18	A3
WASHINGTON AV W	OR	OR	700	17	C3
WASHINGTON AV W	SA	SA	1300	22	E1
WASHINGTON PL	SA	SA	1300	23	C1
WASHINGTON ST	BPK	BP	6600	5	C6
WASHINGTON ST	NB	NB	100	33	B5
WASHINGTON AV E	SA	SA	100	23	A1
WASHINGTON AV W	SA	SA	100	23	A1
WASP ST	LALM	LALM		14	C2
WASS ST	CO	TUS	1000	24	A1
WASS ST	TUS	TUS	12300	24	A1
WATCH HARBOR DR	HTB	HB46	9500	30	F2
WATER ST	OR	OR	100	17	D3
WATER ST E&W	ANA	AN	100	11	C5
WATER WY	CO	SIL	28200	50	E2
WATERBERRY ST	OR	OR	2300	12	C5
WATERBURY CT	YL	YL		40	A3
WATERBURY LN	HTB	HB	19300	26	E3
WATERBURY WY	LAH	LAH	1500	1	E5
WATERFALL CIR	HTB	HB		30	C1
WATERFALL LN	BREA	BREA		3	A6
WATERFORD CIR	MVJO	SJ92		29B	F6
WATERFORD DR	YL	YL		8	E3
WATERFORD LN	CO	LB		35	C4
WATERFORD LN	HTB	HB		26	D5
WATERFORD ST	OR	OR67		13	A4
WATERFRONT DR	HTB	HB	9400	30	F1
WATERFRONT DR	NB	CDLM	2200	33	A1
WATERMAN WY	CM	CM27	2200	31	E1
WATER RIDGE CT	DPT	DPT		37	B5
WATERS WY	NB	NB		31	E6
WATERSIDE	IRV	SA		29	B4
WATERSIDE DR	HTB	HB		26	B4
WATERSIDE LN	CO	ET		29A	E3
WATERSPRAY DR	HTB	HB46		26	C5
WATERTON AV	OR	OR		13	C5
WATERTON ST	FTNV	SA08	17500	22	A6
WATERVIEW LN	HTB	HB		26	B5
WATERWAY	IRV	SA		29	B4
WATERWAY CIR	HTB	HB		20	D5
WATERWAY LN	CO	ET		29A	C2
WATERWHEEL LN	BREA	BREA		3	A5
WATERWHEEL PL	CO	LB	20600	29D	A2
WATERWHEEL WY	OR	OR		18	C3
WATERWORKS RD	GGR	GG	12900	16	B4
WATKINS WY	SA	SA	4500	22	C3
WATSON	IRV	SA18		29A	D2
WATSON AV	CM	CM	1200	27	D3
WATSON CIR	WSTM	WSTM		21	D4
WATSON ST	CYP	CYP	8800	9	E4
WATT RIVER AV	FTNV	SA08	9200	26	E2
WAVE CIR	HTB	HB	8500	26	D3
WAVE ST	LAG	LB51	100	34	C2
WAVE ST	NB	CDLM	2700	33	A2
WAVECREST	IRV	SA		29	C5
WAVECREST CIR	HTB	HB	21300	30	F1
WAVECREST DR	NB	CDLM	2500	32	B6
WAVE CREST LN	DPT	DPT		37	A5
WAVERIDER CIR	HTB	HB49		20	E5
WAVERLY CIR	BPK	BP	8300	5	C3
WAVERLY DR	ANA	AN	2000	16	B3
WAVERLY DR	BPK	BP	8400	5	D3
WAVERLY DR	GGR	GG	11600	16	B3
WAVERLY DR	NB	NB	2600	31	D5
WAVERLY LN	HTB	HB	17000	20	C6
WAVERLY LN	IRV	SA	14800	29	D2
WAVERLY PL	BPK	BP	4700	5	D3
WAVERLY ST	SA	SA	2800	17	D5
WAVERLY ST N&S	OR	OR	100	17	D5
WAVERLY TER	LAH	LAH	2200	1	E6
WAVERLY GLEN	YL	YL	20000	8	F1
WAVERTREE LN	FUL	FL	1400	7	A4
WAVESPRAY CIR	CO	LB	23800	35	D3
WAXWING CIR	CM	CM	2700	27	B5
WAXWING CIR	FTNV	SA08	10400	27	A2
WAXWING LN	CO	LB56		29A	B6
WAY LN	NB	CDLM	2600	33	A1

STREET	CITY	P.O. ZONE	BLOCK	PAGE	GRID
WAYFARER	IRV	SA		29	B4
WAYFARER LN	HTB	HB	16300	20	D3
WAYFIELD CIR	OR	OR	200	17	E3
WAYFIELD ST N	OR	OR	200	17	E2
WAYFIELD ST S	OR	OR	100	17	E2
WAYNE AV	FUL	FL	300	6	A5
WAYNE AV	IRV	SA	17200	28	F4
WAYNE RD	NB	CDLM	4500	33	C2
WAYNESBORO	IRV	SA		29	E1
WAYSIDE	MVJO	SJ92		29B	E2
WAYSIDE PL	ANA	AN	200	11	E3
WAYSIDE ST	ANA	AN	500	11	F4
WAYWARD CT	BREA	BREA		3	B6
WEAKFISH AV	HTB	HB	19300	26	E4
WEARE AV	FTNV	SA08	9600	21	F4
WEATHERBY RD	CO	LALM	11200	14	B3
WEATHERLY DR	YL	YL		7	F2
WEATHERLY LN	HTB	HB	17200	20	C6
WEATHERLY PL	FUL	FL33		5	E2
WEATHRSFIELD LN	HTB	HB	21300	30	C2
WEATHERWOOD	CO	LB		35	F3
WEAVER CIR	GGR	GG	11800	15	A3
WEAVER ST	GGR	GG	12200	15	A4
WEBB PL	YL	YL		7	E4
WEBBER PL	WSTM	WSTM	14000	21	C1
WEBER CIR	HTB	HB47	6400	21	A5
WEBER CIR	SA	SA	2200	17	E5
WEBSTER AV	ANA	AN	600	10	E6
WEBSTER AV	IRV	SA	17500	28	F4
WEBSTER ST	WSTM	WSTM	15300	21	E3
WEDGEWOOD CIR	CO	TUS		24	B1
WEDGEWOOD DR	ANA	AN	1500	11	B4
WEDGEWOOD LN	LAH	LAH	500	5	F1
WEDGEWOOD LN	LAH	LAH	200	6	A1
WEDGEWOOD LN	WSTM	WSTM		21	E2
WEE WY	WSTM	WSTM	6700	21	A1
WEE BURN RD	SB	SB	1200	14	A6
WEELO DR	CM	CM27	700	31	B2
WEEMS LN	HTB	HB		26	D4
WEEPING WLLW LN	ANA	AN		10	D1
WEEPINGWOOD	IRV	SA		29	A5
WEIR CANYON RD	ANA	AN		8	F5
WEIR CANYON RD	ANA	AN08		40	A6
WELBE DR	CO	SA		24	B2
WELCOME LN	SB	SB		19	D3
WELDE CIR	HTB	HB	6000	20	F4
WELDON DR	GGR	GG	9200	15	E4
WELFLEET COM	SA	SA		22	C2
WELLBANK LN	HTB	HB		25	F1
WELLBROOK CIR	HTB	HB	18000	26	A2
WELLDOW LN	FUL	FL	1400	7	A4
WELLESLEY	IRV	SA		32	F1
WELLESLEY AV	WSTM	WSTM	7000	21	B3
WELLESLEY CT	CO	LB		35	C4
WELLESLEY CT	CO	SJ79		59	D6
WELLESLEY CT	FUL	FL	2800	7	A3
WELLESLEY LN	CM	CM	200	27	D5
WELLINGTON AV	CO	TUS	17500	17	F6
WELLINGTON AV	CO	TUS	18100	18	A6
WELLINGTON AV	SA	SA		17	D6
WELLINGTON AV	SA	SA		23	D1
WELLINGTON CIR	ANA	AN	2100	10	F5
WELLINGTON CIR	VPK	OR67	17900	12	F6
WELLINGTON CT	CYP	CYP	4500	9	D5
WELLINGTON CT	NB	NB		32	D5
WELLINGTON DR	HTB	HB	16600	20	A5
WELLINGTON RD	OR	OR	400	17	F4
WELLS PL	CM	CM27	100	31	C3
WELLS RD	WSTM	WSTM	8200	21	D4
WELLS FARGO DR	CO	SJ91		29B	A6
WELLS FARGO DR	CO	LB53		29B	A6
WELLS FARGO DR	CO	LB		29C	F1
WELLS FARGO DR	CO	LB	25400	29D	A1
WELLSON DR	CYP	CYP	5700	9	E5
WELLSPRING DR	HTB	HB		26	D6
WEMBLEY CIR	CO	LB	24500	29C	E3
WEMBLEY CIR	WSTM	WSTM		22	A2
WEMBLEY RD	CO	LALM	11300	14	A3
WENDOVER RD	CO	YL	5500	8	B4
WENDT TER	LAG	LB51	600	34	E3
WENDY CIR	ANA	AN		13	A1
WENDY CIR	FTNV	SA08	9000	21	E5
WENDY CIR	HTB	HB	5500	20	E6
WENDY LN	CM	CM27		31	C2
WENDY WY	CO	LALM	3200	14	B3
WENLOCK CIR	HTB	HB	8100	26	C4
WENTWORTH	MVJO	SJ92		29B	D1
WENTWORTH DR	WSTM	WSTM		21	F2
WENTWORTH LN	SB	SB	13400	14	A5
WENTWORTH PL	GGR	GG	11000	16	B6
WESENBERG CIR	LAP	BP23		9	F3

1990 ORANGE COUNTY STREET INDEX
136
WESLEY CIR
WINDCROFT DR

COPYRIGHT, © 1989 BY Thomas Bros Maps

STREET	CITY	P.O. ZONE	BLOCK	PAGE	GRID
WESLEY CIR	HTB	HB46	10200	27	A5
WESLEY CIR	OR	OR		18	A4
WESLEY DR	ANA	AN07		8	A6
WESLEY DR	LAG	LB	21500	35	A5
WESLEY DR	FUL	FL	700	6	A5
WESLEYAN BAY	CM	CM		27	F3
WEST AV	FUL	FL33	1500	5	E6
WEST AV	FUL	FL	300	6	A6
WEST DR	TUS	TUS		24	C4
WEST ST	GGR	GG40	11200	16	C4
WEST ST	LAG	LB	31400	35	B6
WEST ST	SA	SA	900	22	C1
WEST ST N&S	ANA	AN	100	11	C3
WEST ST S	ANA	AN	1500	16	C4
WESTBORNE DR	DPT	DPT	25300	38	A2
WESTBOURNE CT	CYP	CYP		9	C5
WESTBROOK PL	CM	CM	300	27	D5
WESTBROOK WY	STN	STN		15	C4
WESTBURY LN	TUS	TUS	17600	23	F1
WESTCHESTER DR	ANA	AN	100	10	B6
WESTCHESTER DR	STN	STN	10300	10	B6
WESTCHESTER LN	CO	LB		29C	E3
WESTCHESTER PL	FUL	FL		6	C2
WESTCLIFF	CO	LB77		35	D5
WESTCLIFF	MVJO	SJ92		29B	E2
WESTCLIFF DR	HTB	HB	9300	26	E6
WESTCLIFF DR	NB	NB	900	31	E4
WESTCLIFF DR	STN	STN	12300	15	C4
WESTERLY PL	NB	NB60	3900	28	B5
WESTERN AV	BPK	BP	5500	5	B5
WESTERN AV	BPK	BP	6700	10	B3
WESTERN AV	GGR	GG	11700	15	B4
WESTERN AV	STN	STN	10300	10	B5
WESTERN AV	STN	STN	10500	15	B4
WESTERN AV	WSTM	WSTM	13000	15	B4
WESTERN AV N	SA	SA	100	22	F3
WESTERN AV N&S	ANA	AN	100	10	B5
WESTERN AV S	SA	SA	300	22	F3
WESTERN WY	CO	LB56		29C	E5
WESTRN LNTRN ST	DPT	DPT	34300	37	B5
WESTFALL RD	TUS	TUS	14500	23	F4
WESTFIELD CT	ANA	AN		13	A3
WESTFIELD DR	CO	LB		29D	A6
WESTFIELD ST	YL	YL		8	F4
WESTFIELD WY	LAH	LAH	1700	2	B3
WESTFORD ST	ANA	AN		13	A3
WESTGATE	CO	LB77		35	F6
WESTGATE	CO	LB77		36	A6
WESTGATE	CO	LB77		37	F1
WESTGATE DR	ANA	AN	500	12	B4
WESTGREEN DR	CO	LB		35	D5
WESTGROVE CIR	MVJO	SJ92		29B	F6
WESTHAVEN CIR	ANA	AN	600	10	B5
WESTHAVEN CIR	WSTM	WSTM	9800	21	F3
WESTHAVEN CT	ANA	AN		10	C5
WESTHAVEN DR	ANA	AN	2600	10	C5
WEST HAVEN DR	CO	LB	26600	29C	E4
WESTHAVEN ST	OR	OR	3800	12	D3
WESTKNOLL DR	CO	YL	5000	8	B3
WESTLAKE CIR	HTB	HB	18000	26	A1
WESTLAKE ST	GGR	GG	12500	16	A5
WESTMINSTER AV	CM	CM	2500	27	F6
WESTMINSTER AV	CM	CM27	1500	31	D3
WESTMINSTER AV	CO	GG41	10000	15	A6
WESTMINSTER AV	CO	GG	10000	16	C6
WESTMINSTER AV	GGR	GG	8500	15	F6
WESTMINSTER AV	GGR	GG	10200	16	C6
WESTMINSTER AV	NB	NB	400	31	C4
WESTMINSTER AV	SA	SA	2300	16	C6
WESTMINSTER BL	SB	SB		14	B6
WESTMINSTER BL	SB	SB	3000	14	B6
WESTMINSTER BL	WSTM	WSTM	5000	14	F6
WESTMINSTER BL	WSTM	WSTM	6100	15	A6
WESTMINSTER DR	CM	CM	1600	27	C3
WESTMINSTER PL	CM	CM	2600	27	F6
WESTMONT CT	SJC	SJ75		36	A3
WESTMONT DR	ANA	AN	1100	11	A3
WESTMORELAND	IRV	SA		24	D6
WESTMORELND CIR	WSTM	WSTM	5700	20	F1
WESTMORELAND DR	BREA	BREA	1900	7	A1
WESTMORELAND DR	YL	YL	5400	7	D4
WEST NINE DR	CO	LB		35	D6
WESTON DR	CO	LB		29D	A6
WESTON PL	CO	TUS	18000	17	F6
WESTON PL	CO	TUS	18100	18	A6
WESTON SQ	SA	SA		23	D1
WEST ORANGE RD	SA	SA	900	17	A4
WESTOVER CIR	CO	ET		29B	A3
WESTPARK PL	WSTM	WSTM	6700	15	A6
WESTPORT	IRV	SA		24	E6
WESTPORT	NB	NB		32	C3

STREET	CITY	P.O. ZONE	BLOCK	PAGE	GRID
WESTPORT CIR	ANA	AN	2400	12	A3
WESTPORT DR	ANA	AN	2100	11	F3
WESTPORT DR	ANA	AN	2300	12	A3
WESTPORT DR	HTB	HB	16900	20	C6
WESTRA LN	LAP	BP23	7800	9	E2
WESTRIDGE CIR	ANA	AN	400	13	B2
WESTRIDGE DR	OR	OR		12	F5
WESTRIDGE LN	CO	LB53	27000	29C	F4
WESTRIDGE RD	ANA	AN	5300	13	B2
WESTRIDGE WY	BREA	BREA	200	2	F6
WESTRIDGE KNOLL	FUL	FL	1000	6	B4
WESTSTATE ST	WSTM	WSTM	15000	21	E2
WESTVALE DR	ANA	AN	700	10	B6
WEST VALE LN	YL	YL		8	B4
WEST VIEW DR	OR	OR		18	C3
WESTWARD LN	CM	CM27		31	A1
WESTWARD WY	CM	CM27		31	A1
WESTWAY AV	OR	OR	100	12	C4
WEST WIND	SA	SA04		27	E1
WESTWIND CIR	PLA	PLA	900	12	A1
WESTWIND CT	CO	YL		8	F2
WESTWIND WY	NB	NB	1000	31	E4
WESTWINDS LN	HTB	HB	19500	26	E4
WESTWING	CO	LB56		29C	B1
WESTWOOD	IRV	SA		24	D6
WESTWOOD AV N	SA	SA	1700	17	A6
WESTWOOD AV N	SA	SA	800	23	A1
WESTWOOD DR	VPK	OR67	10200	12	F6
WESTWOOD DR	WSTM	WSTM	9500	21	E3
WESTWOOD LN	CO	ET	22700	29A	E2
WESTWOOD LN	HTB	HB47		21	C5
WESTWOOD LN	YL	YL		8	F4
WESTWOOD LN	YL	YL		40	A4
WESTWOOD PL	ANA	AN	700	11	C3
WESTWOOD ST N	SA	SA	2600	17	A5
WETSTONE	IRV	SA		29	B3
WEYBRIDGE CT	CYP	CYP		9	C5
WEYBRIDGE CT	NB	NB		32	B3
WEYBURN AV	YL	YL	16700	7	D2
WEYBURN DR	CO	LB	24700	29A	E6
WEYBURN DR	CO	LB		29C	E1
WEYMOUNT PL	CO	SA		18	D5
WEYMOUTH CT	ANA	AN		13	B3
WEYMOUTH CT	NB	NB		32	B3
WEYMOUTH LN	HTB	HB	19200	26	C3
WEYMOUTH PL	LAG	LB51	300	34	C2
WEYMOUTH ST	WSTM	WSTM	13200	14	E5
WHALE COVE	CO	LB		35	D2
WHARTON ST	HTB	HB	18100	26	D2
WHATNEY	IRV	SA18		29A	C2
WHEATON CIR	WSTM	WSTM	7100	21	B2
WHEATON PL	FUL	FL33		5	E4
WHEATON TER	CO	ET	21000	52	C6
WHEELER	IRV	SA		24	D6
WHEELER AV	WSTM	WSTM	6800	15	A5
WHEELER CIR	HTB	HB47	16500	21	D5
WHEELER CIR	OR	OR	200	17	F3
WHEELER PL	CO	SA	12800	17	F5
WHEELER PL	OR	OR	200	17	F4
WHEELER PL	TUS	TUS	13500	17	F5
WHEELER ST	OR	OR	100	17	F3
WHEMBLY DR	CO	SA	13500	18	B5
WHETMORE LN	HTB	HB47	17300	21	B6
WHIDBY LN	ANA	AN	2500	12	A5
WHILA WY	CO	SIL	28100	50	D2
WHIPPOORWILL AV	FTNV	SA08	10000	26	F2
WHIPPOORWILL LN	CO	LB56		29C	A1
WHIPSTONE TR	CO	SA	1800	18	D5
WHIRLAWAY ST	CYP	CYP	10200	9	E6
WHISLER DR	CO	ET	24900	29A	F4
WHISPERING LN	HTB	HB		30	D2
WHISPERNG GN LN	BREA	BREA		3	A5
WHSPRNG PIN CIR	WSTM	WSTM	10000	22	A2
WHISPERING WIND	IRV	SA		29	A4
WHISTLER CIR	HTB	HB	5700	20	F6
WHISTLING ISLE	IRV	SA		29	A4
WHISTLING SWAN	IRV	SA		29	B3
WHITAKER AV	FUL	FL33		5	D6
WHITAKER ST	BPK	BP	7700	5	C6
WHITBURN CIR	HTB	HB	8200	26	D3
WHITBY CIR	TUS	TUS	17000	23	E3
WHITE CIR	WSTM	WSTM	5700	14	F6
WHITE RD	IRV	SA	2200	28	D3
WHITE ALDER LN	CO	LB		29D	A2
WHITEBARK	MVJO	SJ92		52	D6
WHITE BIRCH	IRV	SA		29	C4
WHITEBOOK DR	LAH	LAH	700	1	E5
WHITECAP AV	OR	OR	700	12	D4
WHITECAP CIR	FTNV	SA08	16100	22	C4
WHITECAP	CO	LAG		35	F3
WHITECAP DR	NB	CDLM		32	C6

STREET	CITY	P.O. ZONE	BLOCK	PAGE	GRID
WHITECAP DR	NB	CDLM		33	C1
WHITECAP LN	HTB	HB		20	C4
WHITECLIFFS DR	NB	NB	1200	31	F4
WHITECLOUD	IRV	SA		29	B4
WHITE DOVE AV	OR	OR	4500	18	B2
WHITE DOVE DR	CO	ET	23400	29A	D4
WHITE FIR LN	MVJO	SJ91		52	D6
WHITE FISH CIR	FTNV	SA08	8500	26	D1
WHITEGATE RD	ANA	AN	1400	10	F6
WHITEGATE RD	ANA	AN04	1500	15	F1
WHITEHOLLOW	CO	TRA		59	D6
WHITE HORSE LN	HTB	HB	21000	26	D6
WHITE LANTRN WY	OR	OR	2100	12	E3
WHITEMARSH DR	HTB	HB48		25	E3
WHITEMARSH DR	HTB	HB		25	F4
WHITE OAK	IRV	SA		29	A1
WHITE OAK DR	YL	YL		8	A4
WHITEOAK LN	HTB	HB47	15500	21	A3
WHITE OAK ST	CM	CM	1500	27	C4
WHITE OAK RIDGE	OR	OR		18	D3
WHITEOAKS	MVJO	SJ92		29B	F3
WHITE OAKS DR	CO	LB53		29D	A4
WHITE OTTER LN	CO	LB	29000	35	C3
WHITE PELICN LN	CO	LB56		29C	A2
WHITE RIVER CIR	FTNV	SA08		26	F3
WHITESAILS CIR	HTB	HB	8500	26	D3
WHITE SAILS LN	NB	CDLM	1000	32	B6
WHITE SAND DR	TUS	TUS	13300	24	A2
WHITESANDS DR	HTB	HB		26	C4
WHITE SANDS ST	DPT	DPT	25600	38	A3
WHITES CYN WY	CO	SIL	14900	50	E2
WHITE SHORES DR	OR	OR		12	C3
WHITESPRING	MVJO	SJ92		29B	E6
WHITESPRING	MVJO	SJ92		29D	E1
WHITE SPRING LN	OR	OR		12	F4
WHITE SPRING LN	YL	YL	19800	8	C6
WHITE STAR AV	ANA	AN	2800	12	B2
WHITE STAR AV	CO	AN06	15000	12	B2
WHITE STONE DR	ANA	AN		13	D2
WHITESTONE DR	HTB	HB	8100	30	C2
WHITESTONE TR	CO	SA	1700	18	D5
WHITETREE CIR	HTB	HB	20400	26	F5
WHITEWATER	IRV	SA		32A	A1
WHITEWATER DR	ANA	AN08		40	A6
WHITEWATER DR	FUL	FL33		5	E4
WHITE WATER DR	HTB	HB		26	C2
WHITEWATER DR	NB	CDLM		32	C6
WHITEWATER DR	NB	CDLM		33	B1
WHITEWATER ST	YL	YL		8	F4
WHITEWATER WY	NB	CDLM		32	C6
WHITEWATER WY	NB	CDLM		33	B1
WHITE WATER WY	OR	OR		12	B5
WHITEWOOD	CO	LB56		29C	B3
WHITEWOOD CT	FUL	FL		7	A1
WHITEWOOD WY	IRV	SA15	4300	28	F5
WHITFORD LN	HTB	HB	17800	25	F1
WHITING AV E&W	FUL	FL	100	6	D5
WHITLEY AV	WSTM	WSTM	8500	21	D2
WHITLY	CO	LB77		35	D6
WHITMAN CIR	BPK	BP	6700	10	A1
WHITMAN COM	SA	SA		22	C2
WHITMAN DR	BPK	BP	6800	10	A1
WHITMAN DR	PLA	PLA	1900	7	C2
WHITNEY	IRV	SA		29	E1
WHITNEY CIR	WSTM	WSTM	13300	15	B5
WHITNEY CT	CO	LB	24000	35	E1
WHITNEY DR	CO	SA	17600	17	F5
WHITNEY DR	CO	SA	18300	18	A5
WHITNEY DR	HTB	HB47	7500	21	C3
WHITNEY WY	CM	CM26		28	A3
WHITNEY WY	CYP	CYP	9100	9	D5
WHITTEN WY	PLA	PLA	600	7	B2
WHITTIER AV	CM	CM27	1600	31	B3
WHITTIER BLVD	BREA	BREA	1200	2	A3
WHITTIER BL E&W	LAH	LAH	100	2	A3
WHITTIER BLVD W	LAH	LAH	500	1	B3
WHITTIER LN	GGR	GG		15	E5
WHITTIER LN	HTB	HB47	16300	21	B5
WHITTIER ST	ANA	AN	500	11	F2
WHITTIER ST	ANA	AN	500	12	A2
WIATT WY	CO	LAH	10700	2	A3
WICHITA AV	ANA	AN	900	11	A3
WICHITA AV	HTB	HB	100	26	C4
WICKER DR	CYP	CYP	5400	9	E5
WICKFORD DR	BREA	BREA	1200	2	C4
WICKFORD DR	CO	SA	11000	18	C5
WICKHAM LN	LAP	BP23	8200	9	D3
WICKHAM PL	GGR	GG		16	D6
WICKLAND	IRV	SA		24	E6
WICKLOW LN	CO	ET		29B	A1

STREET	CITY	P.O. ZONE	BLOCK	PAGE	GRID
WICKLOW LN	HTB	HB47	15800	21	A3
WICKSHIRE LN	TUS	SA05	13000	24	B3
WIDDOWS WY	OR	OR	1700	12	C6
WIGEON LN	CO	LB53		29A	B6
WIGHTMAN CT	DPT	LB77		37	D2
WILBERTA LN	ANA	AN	2700	10	D5
WILCOX CIR	PLA	PLA	1950	7	C2
WILCOX WY	LAG	LB51	600	34	E2
WILCOX WY	PLA	PLA		7	C2
WILDBROOK	IRV	SA		29	A4
WILDCAT CYN RD	CO	SIL	14800	50	F2
WILDCAT CYN RD	CO	SIL	14800	53	A1
WILD CHERRY CIR	HTB	HB47	15500	21	A3
WILDFLOWER LN	ANA	AN08		43	A1
WILDFLOWER LN	CO	SJ79		52	F4
WILDE PL	ANA	AN	600	11	B5
WILDE ST	ANA	AN	300	11	B5
WILDERNESS AV	OR	OR		13	D6
WILDEVE LN	TUS	TUS	14300	23	F4
WILDFIRE CIR	HTB	HB		20	B4
WILDFLOWER	CO	LB77		37	F2
WILDFLOWER	IRV	SA		29	B2
WILDFLOWER AV	OR	SA05		18	D3
WILDFLOWER CIR	BREA	BREA		3	A5
WILDFLOWER DR	FUL	FL33		5	F2
WILDGOOSE CT	NB	NB		31	B4
WILDGOOSE ST	GGR	GG	11900	15	A4
WILDHORSE CIR	OR	OR		18	D2
WILD HORSE LP	CO	SJ		59	C1
WILDING RD	CO	SA	11500	18	C6
WILD PLUM CIR	HTB	HB47	15500	21	A3
WILDROSE	IRV	SA		29	C3
WILD ROSE DR	BREA	BREA	500	6	D1
WILDROSE LN	HTB	HB	17200	20	F6
WILD VIEW TER	CO	LB		29C	F3
WILD VIEW TER	CO	LB		29D	A3
WILDWHEAT	IRV	SA		29	A5
WILDWOOD	CO	LB56		29C	B3
WILDWOOD	IRV	SA		29	C3
WILDWOOD CIR	CO	SJ79		52	E3
WILDWOOD CIR	HTB	HB	8100	30	B2
WILDWOOD CIR	VPK	OR67	18900	13	B5
WILDWOOD CT	CO	YL		8	F3
WILDWOOD CT	FUL	FL		6	F3
WILDWOOD DR	HTB	HB	8200	30	D1
WILDWOOD LN	ANA	AN		10	D1
WILDWOOD LN	SJC	SJ92		36	B2
WILDWOOD RD	LAG	LB	31500	35	B5
WILDWOOD WY	SA	SA		22	B1
WILDWOOD WY	VPK	OR67	9700	13	B5
WILGAR DR	LAH	LAH	100	1	E4
WILHELMINA ST E	ANA	AN	100	11	C3
WILHELMINA ST W	ANA	AN	100	11	C3
WILKEN WY	GGR	GG	12000	16	C2
WILKEN WY E&W	ANA	AN	100	16	E2
WILKES PL	CO	LB	25200	29C	F1
WILKING DR	IRV	SA		24	E5
WILKINSON RD	CO	OR67		50	E6
WILLAMETTE AV	PLA	PLA	200	7	B3
WILLAMETTE DR	ANA	AN		8	D5
WILLAMETTE DR	WSTM	WSTM	13400	15	A6
WILLAMETTE ST	WSTM	WSTM	13000	15	A6
WILLARD	IRV			29	C4
WILLARD AV	CO	ET	22800	29A	E3
WILLARDSON WY	SA	SA	900	22	C1
WILLAWAW DR	IRV	SA		24	D5
WILLDAN RD	ANA	AN08		13	E1
WILLET CIR	ANA	AN		8	E5
WILLET LN	CO	LB56		29C	A2
WILLET LN	HTB	HB47	15800	21	A4
WILLHELM CIR	HTB	HB	9100	26	E3
WILLIAM AV	CYP	CYP	4800	9	D6
WILLIAM MILL DR	ANA	AN04	1600	15	F1
WILLIAMS	IRV	SA		29	E1
WILLIAMS AV	HTB	HB	7900	26	C4
WILLIAMS AV	PLA	PLA	900	7	D2
WILLIAMS CIR	ANA	AN		13	F3
WILLIAMS CIR	ANA	AN		43	A4
WILLIAMS ST	SA	SA	1500	17	D6
WILLIAMS ST	TUS	TUS	15200	23	D3
WILLIAMSBURG	IRV	SA		24	E6
WILLIAMSBURG AV	WSTM	WSTM	8700	21	E1
WILLIAMSBURG CT	CO	ET		29B	A3
WILLIAMSBURG RD	FUL	FL33	2100	5	D4
WILLIAMSBURG ST	OR	OR		13	B6
WILLIAMS CYN RD	CO	SA		50	D4
WILLIAMSON AV	FUL	FL33	2300	5	E5
WILLIAMSON AV	FUL	FL	500	6	A5
WILLIAMSON PL	IRV	SA		24	F6
WILLIS LN	CO	SA	12300	18	C4
WILLIS ST	SA	SA		28	D1

STREET	CITY	P.O. ZONE	BLOCK	PAGE	GRID
WILLITS ST W	SA	SA	1300	22	E3
WILLIWAW DR	IRV	SA		24	D5
WILLO LN	CO	CM27	2500	27	F6
WILLOW AV	ANA	AN	1900	10	F5
WILLOW AV	FUL	FL	2800	6	D2
WILLOW AV	OR	OR	200	17	B3
WILLOW AV	PLA	PLA		7	E5
WILLOW CIR	FTNV	SA08	16700	21	E5
WILLOW CIR	YL	YL	17500	7	E5
WILLOW DR	BREA	BREA	600	2	F6
WILLOW DR	SA	SA		16	D6
WILLOW DR	SA	SA		22	D1
WILLOW LN	LAP	BP23	7700	9	D2
WILLOW LN	TUS	TUS	14200	23	E1
WILLOW LN	WSTM	WSTM	13700	15	A6
WILLOW LN	WSTM	WSTM	13900	21	A1
WILLOW RUN	IRV	SA		29	B3
WILLOW ST	ANA	AN	1200	11	E4
WILLOW ST	LAH	LAH	100	1	F4
WILLOW WY	YL	YL	17500	7	E5
WILLOW BEND	CO	ET		29A	F2
WILLOWBROOK	IRV	SA		29	B3
WILLOWBROOK AV	CO	YL	19300	8	B3
WILLOWBROOK LN	ANA	AN		16	D3
WILLOW BROOK LN	CO	SJ79		52	E3
WILLOWBROOK RD	WSTM	WSTM		21	E2
WILLOWGLADE	CO	SJ79		59	E3
WILLOW GLEN CIR	CO	SA		18	D3
WILLOWGROVE	IRV	SA		29	C3
WILLOWICK CIR	ANA	AN		13	B3
WILLOWICK CT	CO	YL		8	C6
WILLOWICK DR	ANA	AN		13	B3
WILLOWICK DR	SA	SA	3000	22	D2
WILLOWLAKE	IRV	SA		29	B4
WILLOWLEAF	IRV	SA		32A	B3
WILLOWOOD	CO	LB		29C	D3
WILLOWOOD AV	GGR	GG	12500	16	D4
WILLOWS	CO	LB	22000	29A	B5
WILLOWS DR	GGR	GG	8600	15	D5
WILLOW SPGS RD	OR	OR		18	D2
WILLOWTREE	MVJO	SJ92		29B	E2
WILLOW TREE LN	CO	LB53		29D	A4
WILLOW TREE LN	IRV	SA		29	A5
WILLOW TREE LN	YL	YL		8	E2
WILLOW WOOD ST	CO	ET	25400	29A	F4
WILLOW WOODS DR	ANA	AN		8	B6
WILLOW WOODS LN	ANA	AN		8	B6
WILMA CIR	PLA	PLA	300	7	F6
WILMOT LN	ANA	AN02		16	B2
WILSHIRE AV	ANA	AN	1400	11	B4
WILSHIRE AV	LAH	LAH	2000	1	D5
WILSHIRE AV E	SA	SA	500	23	B4
WILSHIRE AV E&W	FUL	FL	100	6	B5
WILSHIRE AV W	SA	SA	1300	22	F4
WILSHIRE AV W	SA	SA	100	23	A4
WILSHIRE PL	SA	SA	2600	22	E4
WILSON AV	FUL	FL	500	6	F5
WILSON AV	PLA	PLA	100	7	B5
WILSON AV E&W	OR	OR	100	17	C1
WILSON CIR	BPK	BP	7200	10	B3
WILSON CIR	PLA	PLA	400	7	B5
WILSON PL	IRV	SA		24	F6
WILSON ST	CO	MDWY	14500	21	D2
WILSON ST	CO	CM27	900	31	B1
WILSON ST	GGR	GG	13000	15	D5
WILSON ST	LAG	LB51	600	34	E3
WILSON ST	LAH	LAH	300	2	C4
WILSON ST	WSTM	WSTM	13600	15	D6
WILSON ST	WSTM	WSTM	14400	21	D1
WILSON ST E	CM	CM27	200	31	C1
WILSON ST E&W	CM	CM	100	27	C6
WILTON WY	LAH	LAH	1500	1	E6
WILTSHIRE ST	WSTM	WSTM	14100	20	F1
WIMBLEDON CT	DPT	LB77		37	D2
WIMBLEDON LN	HTB	HB		20	C4
WIMBLEDON WY	CM	CM		27	E2
WIMBLETON DR	CO	LALM	3200	14	B3
WIMBLETON LN	LAH	LAH	2200	1	E5
WINCHESTER	IRV	SA		24	E6
WINCHESTER CIR	VPK	OR67	18200	13	A6
WINCHESTER DR	CO	SJ79		56	E6
WINCHESTER DR	CO	SJ79		59	E1
WINCHESTER LN	YL	YL		8	B5
WINCHESTER ST	FUL	FL	2800	7	A2
WINCHESTER ST	HTB	HB46		26	F3
WINDBREAK CIR	BREA	BREA		3	A5
WIND CAVE LN	HTB	HB	20200	26	F5
WINDCHILD LN	HTB	HB	21100	30	D1
WINDCREST	CO	LB77		35	E6
WINDCREST	CO	LB77		37	E1
WINDCROFT DR	HTB	HB49		20	F6

ORANGE CO.
INDEX

STREET	CITY	P.O. ZONE	BLOCK	PAGE	GRID
WINDCROFT DR	HTB	HB49		25	F1
WINDEMEIR LN	HTB	HB47	16000	21	A4
WINDEMERE CIR	CO	ET		52	C6
WINDEMERE DR	YL	YL		7	D4
WINDEMERE LN	TUS	TUS	1300	23	F4
WINDEMERE WY	STN	STN		15	B2
WINDERMERE CIR	BREA	BREA		3	B6
WINDERMERE WY	LAP	BP23	5000	9	E1
WINDES DR	CO	OR	9500	13	D5
WINDES DR	OR	OR	10000	13	D6
WINDFIELD DR	HTB	HB		26	C1
WINDFLOWER	CO	LB56		29C	C1
WINDFLOWER	CO	TRA		59	D5
WINDFLOWER	IRV	SA		32A	B3
WINDFLOWER CIR	PLA	PLA	900	7	B4
WINDFLOWER LN	PLA	PLA	900	7	B4
WINDGAP DR	OR	OR68	100	16	E3
WINDHILL RD	CO	SA	11800	18	C6
WINDHILL WY	CO	SA	1400	24	C1
WINDING LN	BREA	BREA		3	B5
WINDING WY	CO	ET		29A	F1
WINDJAMMER	IRV	SA		29	A4
WINDJAMMER DR	DPT	LB77		37	D4
WINDJAMMER DR	SJC	SJ75		38	A2
WINDJAMMER LN	HTB	HB		26	B4
WINDJAMMER LN	WSTM	WSTM		21	B1
WINDLASS DR	DPT	LB77		37	D3
WINDLASS DR	HTB	HB	8500	26	D3
WINDMILL LN	ANA	AN		12	F3
WINDMILL LN	CO	LB	23800	35	D3
WINDOVER DR	NB	CDLM	2500	32	B6
WINDROW	IRV	SA		29	E4
WINDROW DR	CO	ET		52	C5
WINDSONG	IRV	SA		29	A4
WINDSONG AV	LAP	BP23	4600	9	D3
WINDSONG CIR	HTB	HB	21700	30	F2
WINDSONG CIR	YL	YL		8	D1
WINDSONG CT	NB	NB63		31	A2
WINDSONG DR	CO	ET		29B	A2
WINDSONG DR	SJC	SJ75		36	D6
WINDSONG WY	FUL	FL33		5	E4
WINDSOR	IRV	SA		24	E6
WINDSOR	MVJO	SJ92		29B	D2
WINDSOR	NB	NB		32	C5
WINDSOR AV	WSTM	WSTM	9700	21	F1
WINDSOR CIR	CYP	CYP	9100	9	D5
WINDSOR CIR	LAP	BP23	5100	9	D4
WINDSOR CT	CM	CM		27	D2
WINDSOR DR	HTB	HB	4200	20	C5
WINDSOR DR	SJC	SJ75		36	C3
WINDSOR DR	VPK	OR67	18200	13	A6
WINDSOR LN	CO	SA	1500	24	B2
WINDSOR LN	CO	TUS	1000	24	B2
WINDSOR LN	FUL	FL	1400	7	A4
WINDSOR PL	CO	SA	14000	18	A6
WINDSOR PL	CO	SA	14100	24	B1
WINDSOR PL	LAG	LB51	400	34	C2
WINDSOR ST	ANA	AN		11	F2
WINDSPUN DR	HTB	HB		20	B4
WINDSTREAM CIR	CO	SJ79		59	E1
WINDWARD DR	ANA	AN	1900	11	A2
WINDWARD DR	DPT	LB77		37	D4
WINDWARD LN	HTB	HB	19500	26	D4
WINDWARD LN	NB	NB	2000	31	F3
WINDWARD WY	CO	ET		29A	E2
WINDWOOD	IRV	SA		29	B3
WINDWOOD LN	BREA	BREA		3	A5
WINDWOOD LN	CO	ET	25100	29A	B2
WINDWOOD PASS	DPT	DPT		37	B5
WINDY CIR	YL	YL		40	B4
WINDY HILL LN	CO	LB		29C	E2
WINDY KNOLL	YL	YL	19000	8	B4
WINDY POINTE	OR	OR69		18	D3
WINDY SANDS CIR	HTB	HB47	8000	21	C6
WINDY SEA CIR	HTB	HB47	8000	21	C6
WINDY WATER CT	DPT	DPT		37	B5
WINEMAST ST	FTNV	SA08	17300	21	F6
WINETTA PL	FUL	FL	200	6	A6
WINFIELD AV	ANA	AN	2900	12	B3
WINFIELD CT	CO	YL		8	C6
WINGATE DR	WSTM	WSTM		21	F2
WINGATE BAY	CM	CM		27	E4
WINGEDFOOT CIR	HTB	HB48		25	E2
WINGED FOOT LN	NB	NB		32	B4
WINGFOOT ST	PLA	PLA	1000	7	C4
WINLOCK ST	OR	OR	1700	12	D5
WINN CIR	VPK	OR67	18200	13	A5
WINNEBAGO LN	CO	ET		29A	E1
WINNERS CIR	LALM	LALM		14	E2
WINNEY CIR	PLA	PLA	1900	7	C2
WINNWOOD LN	CO	SA	18700	18	B4

STREET	CITY	P.O. ZONE	BLOCK	PAGE	GRID
WINSLOW DR	HTB	HB	6000	20	F3
WINSTON PL	FUL	FL33		5	E2
WINSTON RD	STN	STN	8300	10	C6
WINSTON RD E	ANA	AN	1600	11	F6
WINSTON RD E	ANA	AN	2000	12	A6
WINSTON RD W	ANA	AN	2400	10	D6
WINSTON RD W	ANA	AN	100	11	D6
WINTER ST	ANA	AN	900	11	C2
WINTERBERRY ST	FTNV	SA08	17500	26	E1
WINTERBRANCH	IRV	SA		29	C4
WINTERGREEN	IRV	SA		29	A1
WINTERGREEN CIR	FTNV	SA08	9100	21	E4
WINTERGREEN DR	HTB	HB	6000	25	F1
WINTERGREEN PL	CM	CM		27	C3
WINTERGREEN ST	BREA	BREA		3	C6
WINTERHAVEN	IRV	SA		29	C5
WINTERHAVEN ST	YL	YL	4000	7	D2
WINTERMIST	IRV	SA		29	B5
WINTERNIGHT	IRV	SA		32A	C4
WINTERS PL	HTB	HB47	7000	21	B5
WINTERSBURG AV	FTNV	SA08	11800	22	C5
WINTERSWEET WY	IRV	SA	4300	29	A5
WINTERWOOD AV	STN	STN	8200	15	C3
WINTERWOOD CIR	HTB	HB	9300	26	E6
WINTERWOOD DR	CO	ET	22200	29A	E2
WINTERWOOD DR	FUL	FL33		5	F2
WINTHROP CIR	FTNV	SA08		21	F5
WINTHROP ST	WSTM	WSTM	13500	14	E6
WINTHROPE ST	CO	SA	13300	18	A6
WINTHROPE ST	OR	OR	800	18	B4
WINTON ST	GGR	GG45	11800	14	E3
WINVALE AV	IRV	SA	4800	29	D2
WISHING WELL LN	ANA	AN		12	F3
WISHINGWELL LN	HTB	HB47	16200	21	B4
WISTARIA LN	FUL	FL33		5	F4
WISTERIA	CO	ET		51	F6
WISTERIA	CO	ET		52	A6
WISTERIA AV	FTNV	SA08	11800	22	C5
WISTERIA CIR	CM	CM	3300	27	E2
WISTERIA DR	YL	YL		7	F3
WISTERIA LN	BREA	BREA		3	A5
WISTERIA LN	TUS	TUS	14200	23	E1
WISTERIA PL E	SA	SA	300	23	B3
WISTERIA PL W	SA	SA	4100	22	C3
WISTERIA ST	SB	SB	3600	14	D4
WONDER VIEW DR	CO	OR		18	B1
WOOD ST	SA	SA	500	22	E3
WOODACRE	MVJO	SJ92		29B	E3
WOODACRE ST	BREA	BREA		3	B5
WOOD BARN LN	FTNV	SA08		27	A2
WOODBINE AV	FUL	FL	2800	6	E2
WOODBINE DR	CO	SA	12100	24	C1
WOODBINE RD	OR	OR		12	F4
WOODBINE RD	OR	OR		13	A4
WOODBLUFF RD	CO	ET	22300	29A	E2
WOODBLUFF RD	CO	LB53		29D	A4
WOODBORO DR	HTB	HB	5700	25	F1
WOODBRIAR CT	FUL	FL		6	F3
WOODBRIDGE DR	GGR	GG		16	D6
WOODBRIER DR	LAH	LAH	2600	1	D5
WOODBROOK DR	GGR	GG	13000	15	D5
WOOD BROOK RD	CO	LB53		29D	A3
WOODBURN LN	YL	YL	6500	8	F2
WOODBURNE	NB	NB		32	C3
WOODBURY AV	GGR	GG	9400	15	E6
WOODBURY DR	OR	OR	12900	17	E5
WOODBURY RD	GGR	GG	10200	16	A6
WOOD CANYON DR	CO	LB56		29C	B5
WOOD CANYON DR	CO	LB56		35	C1
WOODCLIFF CT	CO	YL		8	F3
WOODCOCK DR	CO	LB	28800	35	D1
WOOD COVE DR	ANA	AN08		40	A6
WOODCREEK	MVJO	SJ92		29B	E3
WOODCREEK DR	CO	LB	24500	29A	E6
WOODCREEK RD	ANA	AN08		40	A6
WOODCREST AV	BREA	BREA	1200	2	C3
WOODCREST AV	FUL	FL33	1600	10	E1
WOODCREST AV	FUL	FL	500	11	B1
WOODCREST AV	LAH	LAH	600	2	B3
WOODCREST CIR	CO	ET	22800	29A	E2
WOODCREST CIR	YL	YL		7	F3
WOODCREST DR	HTB	HB	9300	26	E6
WOODCREST DR	YL	YL	5000	7	F3
WOODCREST LN	SJC	SJ75		36	B3
WOODEN DR	PLA	PLA	500	7	B2
WOODFALL	IRV	SA		29	D5
WOODFERN	IRV	SA		29	A4
WOODFERN LN	HTB	HB	17500	25	E1
WOODFIELD	CO	LB56		29C	D4
WOODFIELD DR	BREA	BREA		3	B5
WOODFLOWER	IRV	SA		29	B4

STREET	CITY	P.O. ZONE	BLOCK	PAGE	GRID
WOODFORD TER	IRV	SA	600	32	F3
WOODFORD TER	IRV	SA		32	F3
WOODGATE DR	CO	YL	19700	8	C6
WOODGLEN CIR	CO	ET	22700	29A	E2
WOODGLEN CIR	LAP	BP23		9	E3
WOODGLEN DR	ANA	AN		8	E5
WOODGLEN DR	CO	SA	13500	18	B5
WOODGROVE	IRV	SA		29	C3
WOODGROVE RD	CO	ET	22300	29A	E2
WOODHAVEN DR	CO	LB		35	D6
WOODHAVEN DR	YL	YL	4600	7	F3
WOODHILL LN	BREA	BREA		3	A5
WOODHILL LN	CO	ET	24600	29A	E2
WOODHOLLOW	IRV	SA		29	C3
WOOD HOLLOW LN	CO	SJ		56	D6
WOOD HOLLOW LN	CO	SJ		59	D1
WOODHUE CT	CO	ET	22300	29A	F2
WOOD ISLAND LN	HTB	HB	22100	30	F2
WOODLAKE	IRV	SA		29	E4
WOOD LAKE	SA	SA		17	D5
WOODLAKE CT	SJC	SJ75		36	B3
WOOD LAKE DR	BREA	BREA		2	D5
WOODLAKE DR	HTB	HB47		21	C5
WOOD LAKE LN	CO	ET		29A	D3
WOODLAND	IRV	SA		29	B3
WOODLAND AV	BREA	BREA	200	3	A6
WOODLAND AV	YL	YL		40	B4
WOODLAND DR	ANA	AN	1100	10	D2
WOODLAND DR	BPK	AN01		10	D3
WOODLAND DR	LAG	LB51	100	34	E2
WOODLAND DR	TUS	TUS	13500	24	A3
WOODLAND LN	CO	SA	10200	18	D4
WOODLAND LN	GGR	GG	12500	16	C4
WOODLAND PL	CM	CM27	400	31	E2
WOODLAND PL	CO	CM27	300	31	E2
WOODLAND PL	SA	SA	1500	23	A5
WOODLAND PL	SA	SA	3400	28	A1
WOODLAND ST	OR	OR	500	18	A4
WOODLAND WY	CO	SJ79		52	E3
WOODLANDS DR	HTB	HB		25	F3
WOODLAWN	CO	ET		52	C4
WOODLAWN	IRV	SA		24	E6
WOODLAWN AV	CO	SA	11800	24	B1
WOODLAWN AV	TUS	TUS	14000	23	F3
WOODLAWN AV	TUS	TUS	13000	24	A2
WOODLAWN DR	CO	TUS	12300	24	A2
WOODLAWN DR	HTB	HB	9500	26	F4
WOODLAWN DR	OR	OR	100	18	B3
WOODLEA LN	HTB	HB	20800	26	F6
WOODLEAF	IRV	SA		29	A3
WOODLEY AV	ANA	AN	2200	10	E4
WOODMERE CIR	LAH	LAH	2200	1	E5
WOODMERE CIR	WSTM	WSTM	9900	21	F3
WOODMONT PL	LAH	LAH	1700	5	F1
WOOD NYMPH	IRV	SA		29	D1
WOODPECKER AV	FTNV	SA08	8500	26	D3
WOODPINE	IRV	SA		29	B3
WOODRIDGE	CO	ET	25000	29A	F2
WOODRIDGE CIR	FTNV	SA08	16700	21	F5
WOODRIDGE CIR	OR	OR68	100	16	F3
WOODROSE CT	ANA	AN		13	D2
WOODRUFF ST	WSTM	WSTM	16300	21	D4
WOODRUSH	IRV	SA		29	C2
WOODS AV N	FUL	FL	100	6	B5
WOODS AV S	FUL	FL	1000	11	B1
WOODS LN	SJC	SJ75		36	C6
WOODS ST	OR	OR	3000	12	D3
WOODSBORO AV	ANA	AN		8	D6
WOODSBORO AV	ANA	AN	6000	13	D1
WOOD SHADOW LN	CO	ET	22500	29A	E3
WOODS HOLE DR	HTB	HB	9600	30	F2
WOODSIDE	CO	LB		29C	D4
WOODSIDE CIR	HTB	HB47	6500	21	A3
WOODSIDE DR	PLA	PLA	1200	7	D4
WOODSIDE LN	CO	ET		29A	E1
WOODSIDE ST	OR	OR	1700	12	D6
WOODSONG DR	CO	LB		35	C6
WOODSORREL	IRV	SA		29	C4
WOODSPRING	IRV	SA		29	C3
WOODSPRING CIR	CO	SJ		52	E3
WOODSTOCK AV	OR	OR	100	12	C4
WOODSTOCK CT	CO	YL		8	F2
WOODSTOCK LN	HTB	HB	16200	20	F4
WOODSTOCK RD	CO	LALM	2600	14	A3
WOODSTONE ST	CO	SJ91		29A	F5
WOODSTORK LN	CO	LB56		29C	C1
WOODSTREAM CIR	HTB	HB47		21	E5
WOODSWALLOW LN	CO	LB56		29C	A1
WOOD THRUSH LN	CO	SJ79		59	C4
WOODVALE AV	OR	OR	100	12	C4

STREET	CITY	P.O. ZONE	BLOCK	PAGE	GRID
WOODVIEW CIR	CO	OR		13	C6
WOODVIEW CIR	CO	OR		18	C1
WOODWALK RD	CO	ET	24300	29A	E2
WOODWARD CIR	GGR	GG	11800	16	A3
WOODWARD LN	GGR	GG	10800	16	A3
WOODWARD LN	HTB	HB	19000	26	E3
WOODWIND	IRV	SA		29	B3
WOODWIND AV	OR	OR69		18	E3
WOODWIND DR	HTB	HB		26	C1
WOODWIND LN	ANA	AN	4800	8	B5
WOODWIND LN	CO	AN07	6300	8	A6
WOODWIND WY	ANA	AN		8	A6
WOODWORTH RD	ANA	AN	1900	10	F6
WOOLBURN DR	HTB	HB	8100	26	C6
WOOLLEY LN	GGR	GG	8700	15	D4
WOOLSEY	SA	SA		23	E1
WOOLWICH ST	CO	LB		29C	E1
WORCHESTER COM	SA	SA		22	C2
WORCHESTER LN	HTB	HB	19200	26	C4
WORKMAN CIR	VPK	OR67	10100	13	B6
WORTH AV	LAH	LAH	2200	1	E4
WORTHING	CO	LB77		35	D6
WORTHINGTON ST	BREA	BREA	800	2	C4
WORTHY DR	CO	MDWY	8100	21	C3
WRANGLER CIR	OR	OR	7200	18	D2
WREATH PL	CO	TUS	13000	24	B2
WREN AV	FTNV	SA08	8900	26	E2
WREN CIR	CM	CM	1800	27	B5
WREN CIR	FTNV	SA08	8900	26	E2
WREN ST	ANA	AN	1300	11	C2
WREN WY	CO	ET		29A	D2
WREN WY	FUL	FL33		5	E3
WRENFIELD DR	HTB	HB47	6500	21	A6
WRIGHT	IRV	SA		29	E1
WRIGHT CIR	ANA	AN	900	16	F1
WRIGHT ST N	SA	SA	1300	17	D6
WRIGHT ST N	SA	SA	100	23	D2
WRIGHT ST S	SA	SA	2200	23	D5
WRIGHT ST S	SA	SA	1200	23	D4
WRIGHTWOOD CT	CO	YL		8	F3
WRIGHTWOOD DR	LAH	LAH		2	B5
WRIGHTWOOD DR	OR	OR	500	18	A2
WRIGHTWOOD LN	HTB	HB	17500	20	F6
WRIGHTWOOD LN	HTB	HB	17600	25	F1
WRIGHTWOOD ST N	OR	OR	300	18	A2
WRIGHTWOOD ST S	OR	OR	300	18	A4
WRIGLEY	IRV	SA18		29A	C2
WULFF DR	VPK	OR67	10400	13	A6
WULFF DR	VPK	OR67	10400	18	A1
WUNDER TR	CO	SJ79		59	C3
WUTZKE ST	GGR	GG	11800	15	A3
WYANDOTE AV	PLA	PLA	2300	7	C1
WYATT RD	STN	STN	10300	10	B6
WYCKERSHAM PL	FUL	FL33		5	D4
WYETH AV	IRV	SA		24	C6
WYETH CIR	OR	OR		12	F6
WYETH CIR	OR	OR	1200	17	F1
WYKOFF WY	LAG	LB51	1000	34	F3
WYNANT DR	GGR	GG	12600	15	C4
WYNANT DR	WSTM	WSTM	13500	15	C5
WYNDHAM CT RD	CO	SA	1500	18	B6
WYNGATE CIR	IRV	SA	4400	29	D1
WYNGATE RD	OR	OR	2800	12	E3
WYNN ST	WSTM	WSTM	14100	21	A1
WYOMING CIR	CM	CM		27	B2
WYOMING ST	BPK	BP	6600	5	C6
WYOMING ST	WSTM	WSTM	7000	15	B6
X					
XAVIER CIR	WSTM	WSTM	15100	21	C3
XIMENO DR	FUL	FL35	400	2	C6
Y					
Y PL	LAG	LB51	300	34	D2
YACEDOR	CO	SJ88		59	A4
YACHT DR	DPT	LB77		37	F3
YACHT DR	DPT	DPT	25200	38	A3
YACHT LN	HTB	HB	19000	26	D3
YACHT CAMILLA	NB	NB		32	C5
YACHT COLINIA	NB	NB		32	C5
YACHT COQUETTE	NB	NB		32	C5
YACHT DAPHNE	NB	NB		32	C5
YACHT DEFENDER	NB	NB		32	C5
YACHT ENCHANTRS	NB	NB		32	C5
YACHT GRAYLING	NB	NB		32	C5
YACHT JULIA	NB	NB		32	C5
YACHT MARIA	NB	NB		32	C5
YACHT MISCHIEF	NB	NB		32	C5
YACHT PURITAN	NB	NB		32	C5

STREET	CITY	P.O. ZONE	BLOCK	PAGE	GRID
YACHT RADIANT	NB	NB		32	C5
YACHT RELIANCE	NB	NB		32	C5
YACHT RESOLUTE	NB	NB		32	C5
YACHT TRUANT	NB	NB		32	C5
YACHT VIGILANT	NB	NB		32	C5
YACHT VINDEX	NB	NB		32	C5
YACHT VOLANTE	NB	NB		32	C5
YACHT WANDERER	NB	NB		32	C5
YACHT YANKEE	NB	NB		32	C5
YALE AV	ANA	AN	2600	10	D4
YALE AV	IRV	SA	12900	24	E6
YALE AV	IRV	SA		29	A6
YALE AV	IRV	SA	13900	29	D1
YALE AV	OR	OR		12	B6
YALE AV	WSTM	WSTM	5200	14	E6
YALE AV N&S	FUL	FL	100	6	D6
YALE CIR	HTB	HB47	6300	21	A2
YALE CIR	SB	SB	1000	19	C4
YALE LN	SB	SB	100	19	C4
YALE PL	CM	CM	2500	27	D5
YALE ST	SA	SA	2000	22	D5
YALE ST	SA	SA04	3400	27	D1
YALE WY	STN	STN		10	E4
YALE WY	STN	STN		15	B3
YALE LOOP E	IRV	SA		29	C4
YALE LOOP W	IRV	SA		29	A4
YAMAHA WY	CYP	CYP		15	A1
YANA DR	ANA	AN	700	10	D5
YANA DR	GGR	GG	11000	15	D3
YANA DR	STN	STN	10100	10	D6
YANA DR	STN	STN	10400	15	D1
YANEZ	MVJO	SJ92	28200	29B	E4
YANKEE	IRV	SA		24	E5
YANKTON ST	PLA	PLA	700	7	C1
YANKTON WY	WSTM	WSTM	13800	14	D6
YAP ST	CYP	CYP	11500	14	F2
YAQUI	TUS	TUS		24	B4
YARBOROUGH ST	WSTM	WSTM	14200	21	E2
YARDLEY ST	CO	AN04	9700	10	E6
YARMOUTH LN	HTB	HB	21200	30	D1
YARMOUTH RD	CO	SA	11000	18	C5
YAWL RD	NB	NB60		31	E6
YAWL ST	GGR	GG43	14700	22	A2
YEARLING AV	IRV	SA	5000	29	D2
YELLOWPINE LN	CO	SJ79		52	F4
YELLOWSTONE AV	PLA	PLA	1500	7	E4
YELLOWSTONE AV	YL	YL	17300	7	E4
YELLOWSTONE BL	OR	OR		13	C5
YELLOWSTONE CT	FTNV	SA08		27	A2
YELLOWSTONE DR	CM	CM	3000	27	F3
YELLOWSTONE DR	CO	SA	13500	17	F6
YELLOWSTONE DR	HTB	HB	9500	26	F5
YELLOWSTONE LN	CO	ET		29A	E2
YELLOWTAIL DR	CO	LALM	2900	14	A4
YELLOWTAIL DR	HTB	HB		26	B3
YELLOWWOOD WY	IRV	SA	4300	28	F6
YERMO CIR	GGR	GG	9600	21	F2
YERMO PL	FUL	FL33	1800	5	F3
YERMO PL	FUL	FL	2000	6	A3
YERMO WY	WSTM	WSTM	9000	21	E2
YNNEP VIA	ANA	AN		16	D2
YOAK ST	GGR	GG	13600	15	E6
YOCKEY ST	GGR	GG	13000	15	D6
YOLANDA ST	CO	LB56		29C	D3
YOLANDA WY	TUS	TUS	1900	24	A4
YOLO CIR	HTB	HB		26	E5
YORBA LN	GGR	GG		15	D5
YORBA LN	YL	YL	4600	8	B3
YORBA PL	PLA	PLA	900	7	D3
YORBA ST	CO	OR69	12100	17	E5
YORBA ST	CO	SA	12800	17	E5
YORBA ST	OR	OR	100	17	E5
YORBA ST	SJC	SJ75	26800	36	C6
YORBA ST	SJC	SJ75	26800	38	C1
YORBA ST	TUS	TUS	13500	17	E6
YORBA ST	TUS	TUS	100	23	E2
YORBA LINDA BL	CO	PLA	16200	7	D3
YORBA LINDA BL	FUL	FL	2400	6	F3
YORBA LINDA BL	FUL	FL	2600	7	A3
YORBA LINDA BL	YL	YL	16600	7	D3
YORBA LINDA BL	YL	YL	18000	8	A3
YORBA LNDA BL E	PLA	PLA	100	7	D3
YORBA RANCH RD	YL	YL		8	E4
YORBA RCHITO RD	FUL	FL	1200	6	E2
YORBA RCHITO RD	FUL	FL	2700	7	A1
YORK	SA	SA		23	D1
YORK CIR	ANA	AN	2100	10	F6
YORK CIR	CO	LB		29C	E1
YORK CIR	LAP	BP23	5100	9	D4
YORK DR	PLA	PLA	100	7	B4
YORKSHIRE	NB	CDLM		32	D5

STREET	CITY	P.O. ZONE	BLOCK	PAGE	GRID
YORKSHIRE AV	CO	AN04	8300	15	C3
YORKSHIRE AV	GGR	GG	8700	15	D3
YORKSHIRE AV	STN	STN	7600	15	C3
YORKSHIRE AV	YL	YL	17300	7	E4
YORKSHIRE CIR	ANA	AN		13	E1
YORKSHIRE CIR	LAP	BP23		9	D3
YORKSHIRE DR	CYP	CYP	5000	9	D5
YORKSHIRE LN	HTB	HB47	15100	21	B2
YORKSHIRE LN	LAH	LAH		2	B6
YORKSHIRE PL	OR	OR		17	C2
YORKSHIRE ST	CM	CM27	500	31	C2
YORKSHIRE ST	HTB	TB46		26	F3
YORKSHIRE ST	WSTM	WSTM	15400	22	A3
YORKTOWN	IRV	SA		24	E6
YORKTOWN AV	HTB	HB	8000	26	C4
YORKTOWN AV	HTB	HB46	10000	27	A4
YORKTOWN AV E	HTB	HB	200	26	C4
YORKTOWN CIR	OR	OR	5900	13	C6
YORKTOWN LN	CM	CM	100	27	E6
YOSEMITE AV	OR	OR		13	C5
YOSEMITE CIR	HTB	HB	17300	20	F6
YOSEMITE CT	FTNV	SA08	18000	27	A1
YOSEMITE DR	BPK	BP	6500	10	A5
YOSEMITE DR	PLA	PLA	1100	7E	E4
YOSEMITE DR	WSTM	WSTM	13400	15	B6
YOSEMITE RD	CO	LB		29C	E6
YOSEMITE RD	CO	LB		35	E1
YOST DR	SA	SA	1300	22	B1
YOUNG CIR	OR	OR	600	17	E4
YOUNG DR	CO	LB56		29C	E5
YOUNG DR	PLA	PLA	1900	7	B2
YOUNG LN	CO	SA05		18	B5
YOUNG ST	SA	SA	600	23	C6
YOUNGDALE WY	STN	STN		15	B4
YOUNGER DR	BPK	BP	6800	10	A4
YOUNG RIVER AV	FTNV	SA08		22	B6
YOUNTVILLE	CO	ET		51	E4
YOUTH WY	FUL	FL	2000	6	C3
YSIDORA ST	SJC	SJ75	31200	36	C5
YUBA AV	WSTM	WSTM	5500	14	E5
YUBA CIR	HTB	HB		26	D5
YUBA RIVER AV	FTNV	SA08	8900	26	E2
YUCCA AV	FUL	FL	2200	6	B3
YUCCA AV	GGR	GG	12400	16	D3
YUCCA AV	IRV	SA	14800	29	C1
YUCCA CIR	FTNV	SA08	16500	21	E5
YUCCA CIR	HTB	HB47	14600	21	A2
YUCCA RD	SJC	SJ75		38	A3
YUCCA ST	BPK	BP	7100	5	B6
YUKON AV	CM	CM	3000	27	E3
YUKON CIR	CM	CM		27	E3
YUKON DR	HTB	HB	7600	26	C2
YUMA CIR	SA	SA	2800	22	D3
YUMA PL	WSTM	WSTM	13000	15	A5
YUMA WY	FUL	FL	2200	6	B2
YUROK ST	OR	OR		13	B6
YVONNE LN	HTB	HB	20400	26	D5
YVONNE PL	ANA	AN	1100	11	B3

Z

STREET	CITY	P.O. ZONE	BLOCK	PAGE	GRID
ZACATE	CO	SJ88		59	A4
ZAHMA DR	NB	CDLM	700	32	A6
ZAMORA LN	HTB	HB	21500	30	E1
ZANCON	MVJO	SJ92	24000	29B	E5
ZANDRA DR	CO	SJ91	24400	29A	F6
ZANDRA DR	CO	SJ91		29B	A6
ZANE CIR	HTB	HB47	14600	21	A2
ZAPATA CIR	MVJO	SJ91		29B	C5
ZARZA	MVJO	SJ92	28200	29B	E4
ZARZITO DR	DPT	DPT		37	C5
ZARZITO DR	DPT	DPT	33700	37	F4
ZEIDER LN	HTB	HB47	17300	21	D6
ZEKE & ELSIE AV	LAH	LAH	1400	5	D1
ZELL DR	LAG	LB51	2800	34	F2
ZELLA LN	YL	YL	4500	8	A3
ZENA CT	CO	SJ91		29B	A6
ZENITH AV	CO	SA07	2300	28	B6
ZENITH POINT RD	OR	OR		12	E4
ZETA ST	GGR	GG	12200	16	C3
ZETLAND DR	HTB	HB	9500	26	F5
ZEUS AV	CO	SJ91		29A	F5
ZEUS AV	CO	SJ91	25300	29B	A5
ZEYN ST	ANA	AN	500	11	D3
ZEYN ST S	ANA	AN	500	11	D4
ZEYN ST S	ANA	AN	1700	16	D1
ZIGZAG WY	CO	TUS	12400	24	B1
ZINNIA AV	FTNV	SA08	9900	21	F5
ZION AV E	PLA	PLA	1400	7	E4
ZION CIR	HTB	HB	9500	26	F5
ZION CT	FTNV	SA08	16300	27	A1
ZION ST	OR	OR	1800	13	C5
ZION WY	SA	SA		22	D2
ZION CANYON WY	BREA	BREA		2	F4
ZIRCON	MVJO	SJ91		29D	C5
ZIRCON CT	FTNV	SA08	11700	22	B5
ZOCALA	SCL	SC72		38	D5
ZORAIDA	MVJO	SJ91		29D	C3
ZUMAYA CT	CO	LB	24800	29C	F3
ZUNI DR	CO	ET	21800	29A	F1
ZUNI PL	WSTM	WSTM	13000	15	A5
ZURBURAN	MVJO	SJ92	28100	29B	E5
ZURICH CIR	NB	NB	900	31	D6
ZURICH CT	LAG	LB51	2900	34	F2
ZURITA	MVJO	SJ92	28400	29B	E6

NUMERICAL STREETS

STREET	CITY	P.O. ZONE	BLOCK	PAGE	GRID
1ST AV	CO	LAH	10300	1	F4
1ST AV	LAG	LB77	22200	35	B6
1ST AV	NB	CDLM	2300	33	A1
1ST AV	SB	SB		20	A2
1ST AV E&W	LAH	LAH	100	2	A4
1ST AV W	LAH	LAH	500	1	F4
1ST ST	CO	OR69	11700	17	F3
1ST ST	CO	SA05	17000	23	F2
1ST ST	FTNV	SA08	18200	26	E2
1ST ST	SB	SB	100	19	D2
1ST ST	STN	STN	7800	10	C6
1ST ST E	SA	SA01	100	23	A2
1ST ST E	TUS	TUS	100	23	F2
1ST ST N	ETMC	SA09		51	B3
1ST ST S	ETMC	SA09		51	A3
1ST ST W	SA	SA03	1300	22	E2
1ST ST W	SA	SA03	900	23	A2
1ST ST W	TUS	TUS	100	23	F2
1ST ST W	TUS	TUS	1100	24	A2
2ND AV	LAG	LB77	31500	35	B6
2ND AV	NB	CDLM	2200	33	A1
2ND AV E&W	LAH	LAH	100	2	A5
2ND ST	CO	SUNB	17100	20	B6
2ND ST	CO	ET	25300	29A	F3
2ND ST	FTNV	SA08	18000	26	E2
2ND ST	HTB	HB48	100	26	B6
2ND ST	LAG	LB51	300	34	D3
2ND ST	SB	SB	100	19	D2
2ND ST	STN	STN	7700	10	C6
2ND ST	YL	YL	4000	7	E2
2ND ST E	SA	SA01	100	23	C2
2ND ST E&W	TUS	TUS	100	23	E2
2ND ST N	ETMC	SA09		51	B3
2ND ST S	ETMC	SA09		51	A3
2ND ST W	SA	SA03	1300	22	F2
2ND ST W	SA	SA03	900	23	A2
3RD AV	LAG	LB77	22400	35	B6
3RD AV	NB	CDLM	2200	33	A1
3RD AV E	LAH	LAH	500	2	B5
3RD AV W	LAH	LAH	600	1	F5
3RD ST	CO	SUNB	17100	20	B6
3RD ST	FTNV	SA08	18000	26	E2
3RD ST	HTB	HB48	100	26	B6
3RD ST	LAG	LB51	300	34	D2
3RD ST	SB	SB	100	19	D2
3RD ST	YL	YL	3700	7	E2
3RD ST E	SA	SA01	100	23	A2
3RD ST E&W	TUS	TUS	100	23	E2
3RD ST N	ETMC	SA09		51	B3
3RD ST S	ETMC	SA09		51	A3
3RD ST W	SA	SA03	1300	22	F2
3RD ST W	SA	SA03	900	23	A2
4TH AV	LAG	LB77	31700	35	B6
4TH AV	LAG	LB77		37	B1
4TH AV	NB	CDLM	2200	33	B1
4TH AV W	LAH	LAH	500	1	F5
4TH ST	BPK	BP21	7300	5	C5
4TH ST	CO	SUNB	17000	20	B6
4TH ST	HTB	HB48		26	C6
4TH ST	SB	SB	100	19	D3
4TH ST	YL	YL	4000	7	E2
4TH ST E	SA	SA01	100	23	B2
4TH ST N	ETMC	SA09		51	A3
4TH ST S	ETMC	SA09		51	A3
4TH ST W	SA	SA03	1800	22	F2
5TH AV	LAG	LB77	31700	37	B1
5TH AV	NB	CDLM	2400	33	B1
5TH AV W	LAH	LAH	700	1	F5
5TH PL	ETMC	SA09		51	A4
5TH ST	BPK	BP21	7500	5	B5
5TH ST	CO	SUNB	17000	20	B6
5TH ST	HTB	HB48	100	26	B6
5TH ST	SB	SB	100	19	E3
5TH ST E	SA	SA01	100	23	B2
5TH ST N	ETMC	SA09		51	B3
5TH ST S	ETMC	SA09		51	A4
5TH ST W	SA	SA03	1300	22	E2
5TH ST W	SA	SA03	950	23	A2
6TH AV	LAG	LB77		35	B6
6TH AV	LAG	LB77		37	B1
6TH ST	CO	SUNB	17000	20	B6
6TH ST	HTB	HB48	100	26	B6
6TH ST	NB	NB61	100	31	D6
6TH ST	PLA	PLA		7	D1
6TH ST	SB	SB	100	19	E3
6TH ST E	SA	SA01	500	23	C2
6TH ST E&W	TUS	TUS	100	23	E3
6TH ST N	ETMC	SA09		51	B3
6TH ST S	ETMC	SA09		51	A4
6TH ST W	SA	SA03	1300	22	F2
6TH ST W	SA	SA03	900	23	A2
7TH AV	LAG	LB77	31800	37	B1
7TH ST	BPK	BP21	7500	5	C6
7TH ST	CO	SUNB	16900	20	B6
7TH ST	GGR	GG40	12500	16	B4
7TH ST	HTB	HB48	100	26	B6
7TH ST	NB	NB61	100	31	D6
7TH ST	SB	SB	100	19	E3
7TH ST N	ETMC	SA09		51	B3
7TH ST S	ETMC	SA09		51	A4
7TH ST W	SA	SA03	1300	22	F2
8TH AV	LAG	LB77	31800	37	B1
8TH ST	BPK	BP21	6600	5	C6
8TH ST	CO	SUNB	16900	20	B6
8TH ST	GGR	GG40	12600	16	B4
8TH ST	HTB	HB48	100	26	B6
8TH ST	NB	NB61	100	31	D6
8TH ST	SB	SB	100	19	E3
8TH ST E	SA	SA01	100	23	B1
8TH ST N	ETMC	SA09		51	B3
8TH ST S	ETMC	SA09		51	A4
9TH AV	LAG	LB77	31800	37	B1
9TH ST	ANA	AN02	1500	16	B2
9TH ST	BPK	BP21	7000	5	A6
9TH ST	CO	SUNB	16900	20	B6
9TH ST	GGR	GG40	11600	16	B4
9TH ST	HTB	HB48	100	26	B6
9TH ST	NB	NB61	100	31	D6
9TH ST E	SA	SA01	100	23	B1
9TH ST N	ETMC	SA09		51	B2
9TH ST S	ETMC	SA09		51	A4
9TH ST W	SA	SA03	1300	22	F1
10TH AV	LAG	LB77	31800	37	B1
10TH ST	BPK	BP21	7500	5	B6
10TH ST	CO	SUNB	16900	20	B5
10TH ST	ETMC	SA09		51	C3
10TH ST	HTB	HB48	100	26	B5
10TH ST	NB	NB61	100	31	D6
10TH ST	SB	SB	100	19	E3
10TH ST	WSTM	WSTM	7700	21	C1
10TH ST E	SA	SA01	100	23	A1
10TH ST W	SA	SA03	1300	22	E1
10TH ST W	SA	SA03	900	23	A1
11TH AV	LAG	LB77	32000	37	B1
11TH ST	BPK	BP21	7500	5	B6
11TH ST	CO	SUNB	16800	20	B5
11TH ST	GGR	GG44	9600	21	F1
11TH ST	GGR	WSTM		21	F1
11TH ST	HTB	HB48	100	26	B5
11TH ST	NB	NB61	100	31	D6
11TH ST	SB	SB	100	19	E3
11TH ST	WSTM	WSTM	7700	21	C1
11TH ST E	SA	SA01	100	23	B1
11TH ST N	ETMC	SA09		51	C3
11TH ST W	SA	SA03	1300	22	F1
12TH ST	CO	SUNB	16800	20	B5
12TH ST	HTB	HB48	100	26	B5
12TH ST	NB	NB61	100	31	D6
12TH ST	SB	SB		19	E3
12TH ST	WSTM	WSTM	7700	21	C1
12TH ST E	SA	SA01	100	23	B1
12TH ST W	SA	SA03	1300	22	E1
13TH ST	CO	SUNB		20	B5
13TH ST	CO	WSTM	9700	21	F1
13TH ST	HTB	HB48	100	26	B5
13TH ST	NB	NB63	100	31	D6
13TH ST	SB	SB		19	E3
13TH ST	WSTM	WSTM	7700	21	C1
14TH ST	CO	SUNB	16700	20	B5
14TH ST	HTB	HB48	100	26	B5
14TH ST	NB	NB63	100	31	C6
14TH ST	SB	SB	100	19	E3
14TH ST	WSTM	WSTM	7700	21	C1
14TH ST E	SA	SA01	100	23	B1
14TH ST N	ETMC	SA09		51	D3
14TH ST W	SA	SA06	2200	22	E1
15TH ST	CO	SUNB	16700	20	B5
15TH ST	GGR	GG43	10000	15	F6
15TH ST	GGR	GG43	10100	16	A6
15TH ST	GGR	WSTM	11000	16	A6
15TH ST	HTB	HB48	100	26	A5
15TH ST	NB	NB63	800	31	B4
15TH ST	SB	SB	200	19	E3
15TH ST	WSTM	WSTM	7700	21	C1
15TH ST E	SA	SA01	100	23	D1
15TH ST E&W	SA	SA06	100	23	A1
15TH ST N	ETMC	SA09		51	D3
15TH ST N	NB	NB63	100	31	C6
15TH ST W	NB	NB63	400	31	B4
15TH ST W	SA	SA06	1700	22	E1
16TH PL	CM	CM27	200	31	C3
16TH ST	CO	SUNB	16600	20	B5
16TH ST	GGR	GG43	10200	16	A6
16TH ST	HTB	HB48	100	26	A5
16TH ST	NB	NB63	100	31	C6
16TH ST	NB	NB63	800	31	D4
16TH ST	SA	SA06	1800	16	F6
16TH ST	SA	SA01	100	17	B6
16TH ST	SB	SB	200	19	F3
16TH ST	WSTM	WSTM	7700	21	C1
16TH ST N	ETMC	SA09		51	D3
16TH ST W	CM	CM27	700	31	B3
16TH ST W	NB	NB63	800	31	D4
16TH ST W	SA	SA06	400	17	B6
17TH PL	CM	CM27	300	31	D3
17TH ST	CO	SA01	17000	17	D6
17TH ST	CO	SA	18100	18	A6
17TH ST	CO	SUNB	16600	20	B5
17TH ST	HTB	HB48	19000	26	B5
17TH ST	NB	NB63	100	31	C6
17TH ST	SB	SB	200	19	F5
17TH ST	TUS	SA05	17200	17	E6
17TH ST E	CM	CM27	100	31	D3
17TH ST E&W	SA	SA01	100	17	A6
17TH ST N	HTB	HB48	100	26	B5
17TH ST W	CM	CM27	600	31	D3
17TH ST W	SA	SA06	1300	16	E6
17TH ST W	SA	SA06	300	17	A6
18TH ST	CO	SUNB	16600	20	B5
18TH ST	HTB	HB48	100	26	A5
18TH ST	NB	NB63	100	31	C6
18TH ST	WSTM	WSTM	7800	15	C6
18TH ST E	CM	CM27	100	31	B2
18TH ST E	SA	SA01	1500	17	D6
18TH ST E&W	SA	SA06	100	17	B6
18TH ST W	CM	CM27	500	31	B2
18TH ST W	SA	SA06	1700	16	F6
19TH ST	CO	SUNB	16600	20	B5
19TH ST	HTB	HB48	100	26	A5
19TH ST	NB	NB63	100	31	C6
19TH ST	WSTM	WSTM	7700	15	C6
19TH ST E	SA	SA06	700	17	C6
19TH ST E	SA	SA01	1400	17	C6
19TH ST E&W	CM	CM27	100	31	B2
19TH ST W	SA	SA06	1600	16	F6
19TH ST W	SA	SA06	100	17	A6
20TH PL	WSTM	WSTM	8400	15	C6
20TH ST	CO	SUNB	16500	20	B5
20TH ST	HTB	HB48	100	26	A5
20TH ST	NB	NB63	100	31	C6
20TH ST	WSTM	WSTM	7200	15	B6
20TH ST E	CM	CM27	100	31	D2
20TH ST E	SA	SA01	1400	17	D6
20TH ST E&W	SA	SA06	100	17	B6
20TH ST W	CM	CM27	700	31	D2
20TH ST W	SA	SA06	1800	16	F6
21ST ST	CM	CM27	100	31	D2
21ST ST	CO	SUNB	16500	20	B5
21ST ST	HTB	HB48	100	26	A5
21ST ST	NB	NB63	200	31	C6
21ST ST	WSTM	WSTM	7000	15	C6
21ST ST E	SA	SA01	1100	17	C6
21ST ST E	SA	SA06	700	17	C6
21ST ST W	SA	SA06	1300	16	F6
21ST ST W	SA	SA06	900	17	A6
22ND ST	CM	CM27	100	31	E1
22ND ST	CO	SUNB	16500	20	B5
22ND ST	CO	CM27	300	31	E1
22ND ST	HTB	HB48	100	26	A5
22ND ST	NB	NB63	100	31	B6
22ND ST	NB	NB60	400	31	E1
22ND ST	WSTM	WSTM	7700	15	C6
22ND ST E	SA	SA06	300	17	B5
22ND ST W	SA	SA06	1200	16	F6
22ND ST W	SA	SA06	1200	17	A6
23RD ST	CM	CM27	100	31	E1
23RD ST	CO	SUNB	16400	20	B5
23RD ST	CO	CM27	300	31	E1
23RD ST	NB	NB63	100	31	B6
23RD ST	NB	NB60	100	31	E1
23RD ST	WSTM	WSTM	7500	15	C6
24TH PL	CM	CM27	200	31	E1
24TH ST	CO	SUNB	16400	20	A5
24TH ST	NB	NB63	100	31	B6
24TH ST	SA	SA06	100	17	B5
24TH ST	WSTM	WSTM	7700	15	C6
25TH ST	CO	SUNB	16300	20	A5
25TH ST	NB	NB63	100	31	B6
26TH ST	CO	SUNB	16300	20	A5
26TH ST	NB	NB63	100	31	B6
27TH ST	NB	NB63	100	31	B6
28TH ST	NB	NB63	100	31	B6
29TH ST	NB	NB63	100	31	B6
30TH ST	NB	NB63	100	31	B5
31ST ST	NB	NB63	100	31	B5
32ND ST	NB	NB63	100	31	B5
33RD ST	NB	NB63	100	31	B5
34TH ST	NB	NB63	100	31	B5
35TH ST	NB	NB63	100	31	B5
36TH ST	NB	NB63	100	31	B5
37TH ST	NB	NB63	100	31	B5
38TH ST	NB	NB63	100	31	B5
39TH ST	NB	NB63	100	31	B5
40TH ST	NB	NB63	100	31	B5
41ST ST	NB	NB63	100	31	B5
42ND ST	ANA	AN05		11	D4
42ND ST	NB	NB63	100	31	B5
43RD ST	NB	NB63	100	31	B5
44TH ST	NB	NB63	100	31	B5
45TH ST	NB	NB63	100	31	B5
46TH ST	NB	NB63	100	31	B5
47TH ST	NB	NB63	100	31	B5
48TH ST	NB	NB63	100	31	B4
49TH ST	NB	NB63	100	31	B4
50TH ST	NB	NB63	100	31	A5
51ST ST	NB	NB63	100	31	A5
52ND ST	NB	NB63	100	31	A4
53RD ST	NB	NB63	100	31	A4
54TH ST	NB	NB63	100	31	A4
55TH ST	NB	NB63	100	31	A4
56TH ST	NB	NB63	100	31	A4
57TH ST	NB	NB63	100	31	A4
58TH ST	NB	NB63	100	31	A4
59TH ST	NB	NB63	100	31	A4
60TH ST	NB	NB63	100	31	A4
61ST ST	NB	NB63	100	31	A4
62ND ST	NB	NB63	100	31	A4

1990 ORANGE COUNTY POINTS OF INTEREST

PAGE	GRID	NAME	ADDRESS	CITY	PHONE
		AIRPORTS (SEE TRANSPORTATION)			
		BEACHES AND HARBORS			
35	A5	ALISO BEACH	PACIFIC COAST HWY	LAGUNA BEACH	
19	F4	ANAHEIM BAY		SEAL BEACH	
31	E5	BALBOA MARINA	2751 W COAST HWY	NEWPORT BEACH	
25	D3	BOLSA CHICA STATE BCH	COAST HWY & WARNER AV	HUNTNGTON BCH	846 3460
38	B6	CAPISTRANO BEACH	COAST HWY	DANA POINT	
33	A2	CORONA DL MAR STAT BCH	OCEAN BLVD & LARKSPUR	CORONA DL MAR	
33	D4	CRYSTAL COVE STATE BCH	COAST HWY	ORANGE CO	
37	E5	DANA POINT BEACH	DANA POINT COVE RD	DANA POINT	
37	D6	DANA POINT HARBOR	25002 DANA DR	DANA POINT	496 6411
38	A5	DOHENY STATE BEACH	34320 DEL OBISPO ST	DANA POINT	496 6171
26	B6	HUNTINGTON CITY BEACH	COAST HWY & MAIN ST	HUNTNGTON BCH	
30	D2	HUNTINGTON STATE BEACH	COAST HWY AT BEACH BL	HUNTNGTON BCH	536 3053
34	D3	LAGUNA BEACH MUN BEACH	PACIFIC CST HY & BRDWY	LAGUNA BEACH	
31	C5	LIDO CHANNEL	FOOT OF LIDO PARK DR	NEWPORT BEACH	
31	D6	NEWPORT BAY		NEWPORT BEACH	
33	B5	NEWPORT BEACH MUN BCH	BALBOA BLVD	NEWPORT BEACH	
31	E5	NEWPORT DUNES AQUAT PK	COAST HWY & JAMBOREE	NEWPORT BEACH	
33	A1	NEWPORT HARBOR	1901 BAYSIDE DR	NEWPORT BEACH	834 6106
37	C3	SALT CREEK BEACH PARK	OFF COAST HWY	DANA POINT	
39	E6	SAN CLEMENTE STATE BCH	225 AVENIDA CALAFIA	SAN CLEMENTE	492 3156
19	E3	SEAL BEACH MUNI BEACH	OCEAN AV & NEPTUNE AV	SEAL BEACH	
34	D4	STATE UNDERWATER PARK	PACIFIC COAST HWY	LAGUNA BEACH	
20	B4	SUNSET AQUATIC PARK	2901 EDINGER AV	SUNSET BEACH	
31	F1	UPPER NEWPORT BAY		NEWPORT BEACH	
		BUILDINGS			
23	C2	ADVERTISING ARTS	1058 E 1ST ST	SANTA ANA	
11	D5	ANAHEIM ECON DEV OFFCE	600 S HARBOR BLVD	ANAHEIM	635 5800
32	A5	AVCO BUILDING	620 NEWPORT CENTER DR	NEWPORT BEACH	644 5800
17	B6	BOWERS MUSEUM	2002 N MAIN ST	SANTA ANA	547 8304
F	F5	BUILDERS EXCHANGE	208 N MAIN ST	SANTA ANA	
29C	D6	CHET HOLIFIELD FED BLD	24000 AVILA RD	LAGUNA NIGUEL	831 4220
23	A1	COMMUNITY CENTER	20 CIVIC CENTER PLAZA	SANTA ANA	834 4144
23	B1	CONTRACTORS EXCHANGE	801 BUSH ST	SANTA ANA	
23	B3	COUNTY ADMINISTRATION	10 CIVIC CENTER PLAZA	SANTA ANA	834 2345
23	B2	COUNTY COURT HOUSE	700 CIVIC CENTER DR W	SANTA ANA	834 3575
28	A4	CO SUPERINTNDT SCHOOLS	200 KALMUS DR	COSTA MESA	
23	B1	DR HOWE-WAFFLE HOUSE	120 E CIVIC CENTER DR	SANTA ANA	
23	B2	HALL OF RECORDS	630 N BROADWAY	SANTA ANA	834 2500
24	D3	JULIUS CRANE HOUSE	518 N BROADWAY	SANTA ANA	
23	B2	LLOYDS BANK CALIFORNIA	102 W 4TH ST	SANTA ANA	541 5151
17	C2	MEDICAL ARTS BUILDING	1125 E 17TH ST	SANTA ANA	
23	B2	MUCKENTHALER	325 N BROADWAY	SANTA ANA	
6	C4	N ORANGE CO MUNI COURT	1275 N BERKELEY AV	FULLERTON	773 4555
F	F5	ODDFELLOWS BUILDING	309 N MAIN ST	SANTA ANA	
6	C5	ONE TEN BUILDING	222 N HARBOR BLVD	FULLERTON	525 1784
23	B1	OTIS BUILDING	408 N MAIN ST	SANTA ANA	
15	F3	PLAZA PROFESSIONL BLDG	9872 CHAPMAN AV	GARDEN GROVE	
23	B2	POLICE BUILDING	24 CIVIC CENTER PLAZA	SANTA ANA	647 5021
F	F6	RANKIN BUILDING	117 W 4TH ST	SANTA ANA	
F	F6	SANTORA BUILDING	201 N BROADWAY	SANTA ANA	
23	B2	SOCIAL SERVICES BLDG	601 N ROSS ST	SANTA ANA	834 2270
F	F6	SPURGEON BUILDING	206 4TH ST	SANTA ANA	
16	E3	THE CITY	4000 W CHAPMAN AV	ORANGE	
32	A5	THE TOWERS	550 NEWPORT CENTER DR	NEWPORT BEACH	
32	A5	UNION BANK BUILDING	600 NEWPORT CENTER DR	NEWPORT BEACH	558 5310
23	B3	UNION BANK SQUARE	500 S MAIN ST	ORANGE	547 0807
23	B1	UNITED CALIF BANK BLDG	1018 N MAIN ST	SANTA ANA	558 5112
15	F5	WRIGHT PROF BUILDING	13169 BROOKHURST ST	GARDEN GROVE	
		CEMETERIES			
11	E3	ANAHEIM CEMETERY	1400 E SYCAMORE ST	ANAHEIM	535 4928
29A	E1	ASCENSION CEMETERY	24754 TRABUCO RD	EL TORO	837 1331
29B	A2	EL TORO MEMORIAL PARK	25751 TRABUCO RD	EL TORO	951 8244
17	D5	FAIRHAVEN MEMORIAL PK	1702 E FAIRHAVEN AV	SANTA ANA	633 1442
9	C3	FOREST LAWN CYPRESS	4471 LINCOLN AV	CYPRESS	828 3131
26	D1	GOOD SHEPHERD CEMETERY	17952 BEACH BLVD	HUNTNGTON BCH	847 8546
27	C3	HARBOR LAWN-MT OLIVE	1625 GISLER AV	COSTA MESA	540 5554
13	E6	HOLY SEPULCHER CEM	7845 SANTIAGO CYN RD	ORANGE	532 6551
6	C2	LOMA VISTA MEMORIAL PK	701 E BASTANCHURY RD	FULLERTON	525 1575
15	D3	MAGNOLIA MEMORIAL PARK	12241 MAGNOLIA ST	GARDEN GROVE	539 1771
16	F2	MELROSE ABBEY MEM PARK	2303 S MANCHESTER AV	ANAHEIM	634 1981
2	E4	MEMORY GARDEN MEM PARK	455 W CENTRAL AV	BREA	529 3961
32	C6	PACIFIC VIEW MEM PARK	3500 PACIFIC VIEW DR	NEWPORT BEACH	644 2700
17	D5	SANTA ANA CEMETERY	1919 E SANTA CLARA AV	SANTA ANA	953 2959
21	C2	WESTMINSTER MEM PARK	14801 BEACH BLVD	WESTMINSTER	893 2421
		CHAMBERS OF COMMERCE			
11	D4	ANAHEIM	100 S ANAHEIM BLVD	ANAHEIM	758 0222
31	F6	BALBOA ISLAND	333 MARINE AV	BALBOA ISLAND	675 6871
2	F6	BREA	1 CIVIC CENTER CIR	BREA	529 4938
5	C6	BUENA PARK	6696 BEACH BLVD	BUENA PARK	521 0261
33	B2	CORONA DEL MAR	2855 E COAST HWY	CORONA DL MAR	673 4050
31	D2	COSTA MESA	1901 NEWPORT BLVD	COSTA MESA	650 1490
9	E5	CYPRESS	9471 WALKER ST	CYPRESS	827 2430
37	E4	DANA POINT	34221 GOLDEN LANTERN	DANA POINT	496 1555
22	B6	FOUNTAIN VALLEY	10101 SLATER AV	FOUNTAIN VLY	962 4441
6	C5	FULLERTON	219 E COMMONWEALTH AV	FULLERTON	871 3100
16	B4	GARDEN GROVE	11400 STANFORD AV	GARDEN GROVE	638 7950

PAGE	GRID	NAME	ADDRESS	CITY	PHONE
26	B6	HUNTINGTON BEACH	2213 MAIN ST	HUNTNGTON BCH	536 8888
28	E3	IRVINE	2815 MCGAW	IRVINE	660 9112
34	D2	LAGUNA BEACH	357 GLENNEYRE ST	LAGUNA BEACH	494 1018
2	A4	LA HABRA	321 E LA HABRA BLVD	LA HABRA	992 4702
9	E2	LA PALMA	7822 WALKER ST	LA PALMA	739 1450
32	A4	NEWPORT BEACH	1470 JAMBOREE RD	NEWPORT BEACH	644 8211
17	D3	ORANGE	80 PLAZA SQUARE	ORANGE	538 3581
16	F4	ORANGE COUNTY	1 CITY BLVD W	ORANGE	634 2900
7	B5	PLACENTIA	119 N BRADFORD AV	PLACENTIA	528 1873
29D	A1	SADDLEBACK VALLEY	25301 CABOT RD	LAGUNA HILLS	837 3000
39	D3	SAN CLEMENTE	1100 N EL CAMINO REAL	SAN CLEMENTE	492 1131
36	C6	SAN JUAN CAPISTRANO	31682 EL CAMINO REAL	SN J CAPSTRNO	493 4700
23	A1	SANTA ANA	801 W CIVIC CTR DR	SANTA ANA	541 5353
23	F2	TUSTIN	399 EL CAMINO REAL	TUSTIN	544 5341
21	C2	WESTMINSTER	14491 BEACH BLVD	WESTMINSTER	898 9648
8	A3	YORBA LINDA	4854 MAIN ST	YORBA LINDA	777 3507
		CITY HALLS			
11	D4	ANAHEIM	200 S ANAHEIM BLVD	ANAHEIM	999 5100
2	F6	BREA	CIVIC CENTER CIR	BREA	990 7600
5	C6	BUENA PARK	6650 BEACH BLVD	BUENA PARK	521 9900
27	E5	COSTA MESA	77 FAIR DR	COSTA MESA	754 5223
9	D5	CYPRESS	5275 ORANGE AV	CYRPESS	828 2200
22	A6	FOUNTAIN VALLEY	10200 SLATER AV	FOUNTAIN VLY	963 8321
6	C5	FULLERTON	303 W COMMONWEALTH AV	FULLERTON	738 6300
16	B4	GARDEN GROVE	11391 ACACIA PKWY	GARDEN GROVE	638 6639
26	B4	HUNTINGTON BEACH	2000 MAIN ST CIVIC CTR	HUNTNGTON BCH	
28	E3	IRVINE	2815 MCGAW AV	IRVINE	660 9112
34	D2	LAGUNA BEACH	505 FOREST AV	LAGUNA BEACH	497 3311
2	A4	LA HABRA	201 E LA HABRA BLVD	LA HABRA	694 1011
9	E2	LA PALMA	7822 WALKER ST	LA PALMA	523 7700
14	B2	LOS ALAMITOS	3191 KATELLA AV	LOS ALAMITOS	827 8670
29D	B5	MISSION VIEJO	26522 VIA ALAMEDA	MISSION VIEJO	582 2489
31	C5	NEWPORT BEACH	3300 NEWPORT BLVD	NEWPORT BEACH	644 3017
17	D3	ORANGE	300 E CHAPMAN AV	ORANGE	532 0341
7	B5	PLACENTIA	401 E CHAPMAN AV	PLACENTIA	993 8231
39	D3	SAN CLEMENTE	100 AVENIDA PRESIDIO	SAN CLEMENTE	361 8200
38	C1	SAN JUAN CAPISTRANO	32400 PASEO ADELANTO	SN J CAPSTRNO	493 1171
23	B2	SANTA ANA	20 CIVIC CENTER PLAZA	SANTA ANA	647 5200
19	E3	SEAL BEACH	211 8TH ST	SEAL BEACH	431 2527
15	B1	STANTON	10660 WESTERN AV	STANTON	220 2220
23	F2	TUSTIN	300 CENTENNIAL WY	TUSTIN	544 8890
12	F6	VILLA PARK	17855 SANTIAGO BLVD	VILLA PARK	998 1500
15	D6	WESTMINSTER	8200 WESTMINSTER BLVD	WESTMINSTER	898 3311
7	F3	YORBA LINDA	4845 CASA LOMA AV	YORBA LINDA	961 7100
		COLLEGES & UNIVERSITIES			
6	F4	CAL STATE UNIV,FULLRTN	800 N STATE COLLEGE BL	FULLERTON	773 2011
17	C2	CHAPMAN COLLEGE	333 N GLASSELL ST	ORANGE	997 6710
22	A6	COASTLINE COLLEGE	11460 WARNER AV	FOUNTAIN VLY	546 7600
9	F4	CYPRESS COLLEGE	9200 VALLEY VIEW ST	CYPRESS	826 2220
27	F2	FASHION INSTITUTE	3850 PLAZA DR	SANTA ANA	546 0930
6	D5	FULLERTON COLLEGE	321 E CHAPMAN AV	FULLERTON	871 8000
21	B6	GOLDEN WEST COLLEGE	15744 GOLDEN WEST AV	HUNTNGTON BCH	892 7711
29	D4	IRVINE VALLEY COLLEGE	5500 IRVINE CENTER DR	IRVINE	559 9300
27	D4	ORANGE COAST COLLEGE	2701 FAIRVIEW RD	COSTA MESA	566 5651
16	C5	RCHO SANTIAGO-GGR	13162 NEWHOPE ST	GARDEN GROVE	537 9260
18	E2	RCHO SANTIAGO-OR	8045 E CHAPMAN AV	ORANGE	667 3167
16	F6	RCHO SANTIAGO-SA	W 17TH ST AT BRISTOL	SANTA ANA	667 3000
29D	C6	SADDLEBACK COLLEGE	28000 MARGUERITE PKWY	MISSION VIEJO	831 4500
27	E6	SOUTHERN CALIF COLLEGE	55 FAIR DR	COSTA MESA	556 3610
6	F3	S CALIF COL OPTOMETRY	2001 ASSOCIATED RD	FULLERTON	870 7226
32	D2	UNIV OF CALIF, IRVINE	UNIVERSITY DR	IRVINE	833 5011
17	B4	WEST COAST UNIVERSITY	550 S MAIN ST	ORANGE	953 2700
		GOLF COURSES			
35	A5	ALISO CREEK	31106 S PACIFIC CST HY	LAGUNA BEACH	499 1919
7	C5	ALTA VISTA	777 ALTA VISTA DR	PLACENTIA	528 1103
13	E3	ANAHEIM HILLS	6501 E NOHL RANCH RD	ANAHEIM	637 7311
32	B4	BIG CANYON	BIG CANYON RD	NEWPORT BEACH	644 5404
5	C4	BIG TEE	5151 BEACH BLVD	BUENA PARK	521 6300
3	B6	BIRCH HILLS	2250 E BIRCH ST	BREA	990 0201
6	D1	BREA	501 W FIR ST	BREA	529 3003
29B	D4	CASTA DEL SOL	27601 CASTA DEL SOL	MISSION VIEJO	581 0940
27	B5	COSTA MESA	1701 GOLF COURSE DR	COSTA MESA	754 5267
22	A4	DAVID L BAKER GOLF CTR	10410 EDINGER AV	FOUNTAIN VLY	531 5885
30	C1	DRIFTWOOD BEACH CLUB	21462 PACIFIC CST HY	HUNTNGTON BCH	536 8871
35	D5	EL NIGUEL	23700 CLUB HOUSE DR	LAGUNA NIGUEL	496 5767
51	C5	EL TORO MARINE MEM	MARINE CORPS AIR STATN	EL TORO	559 2577
6	C2	FULLERTON MUNICIPAL	2700 N HARBOR BLVD	FULLERTON	871 5141
40	F6	GREEN RIVER GOLF CLUB	GREEN RIV DR AT 91 FWY	SANTA ANA CYN	970 8411
10	E3	H G DAD MILLER PUBLIC	430 N GILBERT ST	ANAHEIM	991 5530
26	A4	HUNTINGTON SEACLIFF	3000 PALM AV	HUNTNGTON BCH	536 7575
7	B1	IMPERIAL	2200 E IMPERIAL HWY	BREA	529 3923
29A	C5	LAGUNA HILLS	EL TORO RD & MOULTN PY	LAGUNA HILLS	837 7630
14	A5	LEISURE WORLD	1661 GOLDEN RAIN RD	SEAL BEACH	431 6586
14	D1	LOS ALAMITOS	4561 E KATELLA AV	LOS ALAMITOS	828 0402
5	D3	LOS COYOTES	8888 LOS COYOTES DR	BUENA PARK	523 7780
20	E5	MEADOWLARK	16782 GRAHAM ST	HUNTNGTON BCH	846 1364
27	B3	MESA VERDE	3000 CLUB HOUSE RD	COSTA MESA	549 0377
22	A5	MILE SQUARE	10401 WARNER AV	FOUNTAIN VLY	968 4556
29D	B3	MISSION VIEJO	26742 OSO PKWY	MISSION VIEJO	831 1020
14	E2	NAVAL BASE	5660 ORANGEWOOD AV	LOS ALAMITOS	527 4401
28	A6	NEWPORT BEACH	3100 IRVINE AV	NEWPORT BEACH	852 8681
32	A5	NEWPORT BCH CNTRY CLUB	1600 E COAST HWY	NEWPORT BEACH	644 9550
31	F5	NEWPORTER	1107 JAMBOREE RD	NEWPORT BEACH	644 1700

PAGE	GRID	NAME	ADDRESS	CITY	PHONE
14	B4	OLD RANCH	3901 LAMPSON AV	SEAL BEACH	847 8524
28	E5	RANCHO SAN JOAQUIN	5 SANDBURG WY	IRVINE	786 5522
18	D1	RIDGELINE COUNTRY CLUB	10604 MEADS AV	ORANGE	538 5030
16	F5	RIVER VIEW	1800 W 22ND ST	SANTA ANA	543 1115
39	F5	SAN CLEMENTE MUNICIPAL	150 E AVD MAGDALENA	SAN CLEMENTE	492 3943
38	C2	SAN JUAN HILLS	32120 SAN JUAN CK RD	SN J CAPSTRNO	837 0361
27	F5	SANTA ANA COUNTRY CLUB	20382 NEWPORT BLVD	SANTA ANA	545 7260
17	E4	SANTIAGO	580 S TUSTIN AV	ORANGE	532 3762
38	D5	SHORECLIFF GOLF CLUB	501 AVENIDA VAQUERO	SAN CLEMENTE	492 1177
37	D2	THE LINKS-MONARCH BCH	23841 STONEHILL DR	DANA POINT	
24	D3	TUSTIN RCH GOLF COURSE	12442 TUSTIN RANCH RD	TUSTIN	730 1611
22	D1	WILLOWICK MUNICIPAL	3017 W 5TH ST	SANTA ANA	531 0678
8	B5	YORBA LINDA	19400 E MOUNTAIN VW AV	YORBA LINDA	779 2467
		HOSPITALS			
		*EMERGENCY SERVICES	AVAILABLE		
10	B6	*ANAHEIM GENERAL HOSP	3350 W BALL RD	ANAHEIM	827 6700
11	B2	*ANAHEIM MEMORIAL HOSP	1111 W LA PALMA AV	ANAHEIM	774 1450
2	E4	BREA COMMUNITY HOSP	380 W CENTRAL AV	BREA	529 0211
10	A4	*BUENA PARK COMMUNITY	6850 LINCOLN AV	BUENA PARK	827 1161
5	C5	*BUENA PK DOCTORS HOSP	5742 BEACH BLVD	BUENA PARK	521 4770
12	F1	*CANYON GENERAL-KAISER	441 N LAKEVIEW AV	ANAHEIM	978 4000
17	E3	*CHAPMAN GENERAL HOSP	2601 E CHAPMAN AV	ORANGE	633 0011
17	B4	*CHILDRENS HOSP OF O C	455 S MAIN ST	ORANGE	997 3000
23	A6	*COASTAL COMMUNITIES	2701 S BRISTOL ST	SANTA ANA	754 5454
31	D1	COLLEGE HOSPITAL	301 VICTORIA ST	COSTA MESA	642 2734
16	F6	*DOCTORS HOSP STA ANA	1901 COLLEGE AV	SANTA ANA	547 2565
26	F1	*F H P HOSPITAL	9920 TALBERT AV	FOUNTAIN VLY	962 4677
22	B5	*FOUNTAIN VLY REGIONAL	17100 EUCLID ST	FOUNTAIN VLY	979 1211
1	F5	FRNDLY HLS REG MED CTR	1251 W LAMBERT RD	LA HABRA	870 5090
16	D4	*GARDEN GROVE MED CTR	12601 GARDEN GROVE BL	GARDEN GROVE	537 5160
23	E4	*HLTH CARE M CTR-TUSTN	14662 NEWPORT AV	TUSTIN	838 9600
31	C4	*HOAG MEM HOSP PRESB	301 NEWPORT BLVD	NEWPORT BEACH	645 8600
26	C1	*HUMANA-HUNTINGTON BCH	17772 BEACH BLVD	HUNTNGTON BCH	842 1473
10	C5	*HUMANA HOSPITAL-WEST	3033 W ORANGE AV	ANAHEIM	827 3000
15	C6	*HUMANA-WESTMINSTER	200 HOSPITAL CIR	WESTMINSTER	893 4541
29	D6	IRVINE MEDICAL CENTER	16200 SAND CANYON AV	IRVINE	857 6500
9	E2	*LA PALMA INTERCOMMNTY	7901 WALKER AV	LA PALMA	670 7400
14	B1	*LOS ALAMITOS MED CTR	3751 KATELLA AV	LOS ALAMITOS	598 1311
11	A2	*MARTIN LUTHER HOSP	1830 W ROMNEYA DR	ANAHEIM	491 5200
15	C2	*MIDWOOD COMMUNITY	7770 KATELLA AV	STANTON	898 0300
29D	C5	*MISSION HOSPITAL	27700 MEDICAL CTR RD	MISSION VIEJO	582 2300
26	C2	*PACIFICA COMMUNITY	18792 DELAWARE ST	HUNTNGTON BCH	842 0611
7	D3	*PLACENTIA LINDA COMM	1301 N ROSE DR	PLACENTIA	993 2000
29A	D6	*SADDLEBACK HOSPITAL	24451 HEALTH CTR DR	LAGUNA HILLS	837 4500
16	E6	SANTA ANA MEDICAL CTR	1901 N FAIRVIEW ST	SANTA ANA	554 1653
17	B4	*ST JOSEPH HOSPITAL	1100 W STEWART DR	ORANGE	633 9111
6	C3	*ST JUDE HOSPITAL	101 E VALENCIA MESA DR	FULLERTON	871 3280
7	D2	*ST JUDE-YORBA LINDA	16850 E BASTANCHURY RD	YORBA LINDA	993 3000
38	D5	*SAN CLEMENTE GENERAL	654 CAMINO D LOS MARES	SAN CLEMENTE	496 1122
35	B6	*SOUTH COAST MED CTR	31872 COAST HWY	LAGUNA BEACH	499 1311
16	F3	*U C IRVINE MED CTR	101 THE CITY DR	ORANGE	634 6011
11	D5	*WESTERN MEDICAL CTR	1025 S ANAHEIM BLVD	ANAHEIM	533 6220
23	E1	*WESTERN MEDICAL CTR	1001 N TUSTIN AV	SANTA ANA	835 3555
		HOTELS			
28	C4	AIRPORTER INN	18700 MACARTHUR BLVD	IRVINE	833 2770
16	D2	ANAHEIM MARRIOTT HOTEL	700 CONVENTION WY	ANAHEIM	750 8000
33	B5	BALBOA INN	105 MAIN ST	BALBOA	675 8740
28	A2	BEVERLY HERITAGE	3350 AV OF THE ARTS	COSTA MESA	751 5100
27	F3	BRISTOL PZ HOLIDAY INN	3131 BRISTOL ST	COSTA MESA	557 3000
10	B3	BUENA PARK HOTEL	7675 CRESCENT AV	BUENA PARK	995 1111
28	B2	COMPRI HOTEL	7 HUTTON CENTER DR	SANTA ANA	751 2400
11	C6	CONESTOGA HOTEL	1240 S WALNUT ST	ANAHEIM	535 0300
59	D4	COTO DE CAZA	PLANO TRABUCO	COTO DE CAZA	586 0761
37	F5	DANA POINT RESORT	25135 PARK LANTERN ST	DANA POINT	661 5000
23	D2	DAYS INN	1600 E 1ST ST	SANTA ANA	835 3051
16	C1	DISNEYLAND HOTEL	1150 W CERRITOS AV	ANAHEIM	635 8600
16	F4	DOUBLETREE HOTEL	100 THE CITY DR	ORANGE	634 4500
12	C2	EMBASSY SUITES HOTEL	3100 E FRONTERA	ANAHEIM	632 1221
10	C2	EMBASSY SUITES HOTEL	7762 BEACH BLVD	BUENA PARK	739 5600
28	D3	EMBASSY SUITES HOTEL	2120 MAIN ST	IRVINE	553 8332
23	C6	EMBASSY SUITES HOTEL	1325 E DYER RD	SANTA ANA	241 3800
16	C1	EMERALD HOTEL	1717 S WEST ST	ANAHEIM	670 1991
32	A5	FOUR SEASONS HOTEL	690 NEWPORT CENTER DR	NEWPORT BEACH	759 0808
16	D1	GRAND HOTEL	1 HOTEL WY	ANAHEIM	772 7777
11	E1	GRISWOLD'S HOTEL	1500 S RAYMOND AV	FULLERTON	636 9000
28	E4	HILTON HOTEL	17900 JAMBOREE BLVD	IRVINE	660 0931
16	F2	HILTON SUITES HOTEL	400 N STATE COLLEGE BL	ANAHEIM	938 1111
16	C2	HILTON TOWERS	777 W CONVENTION WY	ANAHEIM	750 4321
16	D2	HOLIDAY INN	1850 S HARBOR BLVD	ANAHEIM	750 2801
10	C1	HOLIDAY INN	7000 BEACH BLVD	BUENA PARK	522 7000
11	C2	HOLIDAY INN	222 W HOUSTON AV	FULLERTON	992 1700
21	C3	HOLIDAY INN	7667 CENTER AV	HUNTNGTON BCH	891 0123
28	D3	HOLIDAY INN	17941 VON KARMAN AV	IRVINE	863 1999
29D	B1	HOLIDAY INN	25205 LA PAZ RD	LAGUNA HILLS	586 5000
16	D1	HOTEL IBIS	100 W FREEMAN WY	ANAHEIM	520 9696
28	C5	HOTEL MERIDIEN	4500 MACARTHUR BLVD	NEWPORT BEACH	476 2001
34	D3	HOTEL SAN MAARTEN	696 S COAST HWY	LAGUNA BEACH	494 9436
11	D6	HOWARD JOHNSONS	1380 S HARBOR BLVD	ANAHEIM	776 6120
31	E5	HYATT NEWPORTER	1107 JAMBOREE RD	NEWPORT BEACH	644 1700
16	D3	HYATT REGENCY ALICANTE	100 PLAZA ALICANTE	GARDEN GROVE	971 3000
16	D2	INN AT THE PARK	1855 S HARBOR BLVD	ANAHEIM	750 1811
28	C4	IRVINE MARRIOTT	18000 VON KARMAN AV	IRVINE	553 0100
32	A5	MARRIOTT HOTEL	900 NEWPORT CTR DR W	NEWPORT BEACH	640 4000
28	A2	MARRIOTT SUITES	500 ANTON BLVD	COSTA MESA	
32	B1	MARRIOTT SUITES	500 BAYVIEW CIR	NEWPORT BEACH	854 4500

PAGE	GRID	NAME	ADDRESS	CITY	PHONE
31	B6	OCEAN FRONT HOTEL	2306 W OCEAN FRONT	NEWPORT BEACH	673 1241
16	D1	PLAZA RESORT HOTEL	1700 S HARBOR BLVD	ANAHEIM	772 5900
16	C2	QUALITY INN	616 W CONVENTION WY	ANAHEIM	750 3131
10	B2	QUALITY INN	7555 BEACH BLVD	BUENA PARK	522 7360
23	D6	RAMADA HOTEL	2726 S GRAND AV	SANTA ANA	966 1955
16	E1	RAMADA INN	1331 E KATELLA AV	ANAHEIM	978 8088
28	A3	RED LION INN	3050 BRISTOL ST	COSTA MESA	540 7000
28	C4	REGISTRY	18800 MACARTHUR BLVD	IRVINE	752 8777
51	D6	RESIDENCE INN	10 MORGAN ST	IRVINE	380 3000
37	D4	RITZ CARLTON	33533 SHORELINE DR	DANA POINT	240 2000
23	D2	SADDLEBACK INN	1660 E FIRST ST	SANTA ANA	835 3311
34	E4	SURF & SAND	1555 S COAST HWY	LAGUNA BEACH	497 4477
16	D1	THE RESIDENCE INN	1700 S CLEMENTINE ST	ANAHEIM	533 3555
16	F3	THE RESIDENCE INN	201 N STATE COLLEGE BL	ORANGE	978 7700
11	C6	SHERATON-ANAHEIM	1015 W BALL RD	ANAHEIM	778 1700
28	B5	SHERATON-NEWPORT BEACH	4545 MACARTHUR BLVD	NEWPORT BEACH	833 0570
34	D3	VACATION VILLAGE	647 S COAST HWY	LAGUNA BEACH	494 8566
28	A2	WESTIN-SOUTH COAST PZ	666 ANTON BLVD	COSTA MESA	540 2500
		LIBRARIES			
11	C4	ANAHEIM PUBLIC	500 W BROADWAY	ANAHEIM	999 1880
31	E6	BALBOA	100 E BALBOA BLVD	NEWPORT BEACH	640 2241
30	E2	BANNING ANNEX	9281 BANNING AV	HUNTNGTON BCH	962 6664
2	F6	BREA	CIVIC CENTER CIR	BREA	671 1722
10	B3	BUENA PARK	7150 LA PALMA AV	BUENA PARK	826 4100
13	C2	CANYON HILLS	400 SCOUT TR	ANAHEIM	974 7630
15	E3	CHAPMAN BRANCH	9182 CHAPMAN AV	GARDEN GROVE	539 2115
33	B2	CORONA DEL MAR	420 MARIGOLD AV	NEWPORT BEACH	640 2191
31	C2	COSTA MESA	1855 PARK AV	COSTA MESA	646 8845
35	D4	CROWN VALLEY	30341 CROWN VALLEY PWY	LAGUNA NIGUEL	249 5252
9	E5	CYPRESS	5331 ORANGE AV	CYPRESS	826 0350
37	D3	DANA NIGUEL	33840 NIGUEL RD	DANA POINT	496 5517
10	D4	E L HASKETT READNG CTR	2650 W BROADWAY	ANAHEIM	821 0553
18	B3	EL MODENA BRANCH	380 S HEWES ST	ORANGE	639 7181
29A	E4	EL TORO	24672 RAYMOND WY	EL TORO	855 8173
11	B6	EUCLID BRANCH	1340 S EUCLID ST	ANAHEIM	533 0160
22	A6	FOUNTAIN VALLEY	17565 LOS ALAMOS ST	FOUNTAIN VLY	962 1324
6	B5	FULLERTON MAIN	353 COMMONWEALTH AV	FULLERTON	738 6333
16	B4	GARDEN GROVE	11200 STANFORD AV	GARDEN GROVE	530 0711
14	F3	GARDEN GROVE WEST	11962 BAILEY ST	GARDEN GROVE	897 2594
20	E4	GRAHAM ANNEX	15882 GRAHAM ST	HUNTNGTON BCH	894 1307
29	D1	HERITAGE PARK	14361 YALE AV	IRVINE	551 7151
6	A6	HUNT BRANCH	201 S BASQUE AV	FULLERTON	871 9450
26	B1	HUNTINGTON BEACH	7111 TALBERT AV	HUNTNGTON BCH	842 4481
34	D2	LAGUNA BEACH	363 GLENNEYRE ST	LAGUNA BEACH	497 1733
2	A4	LA HABRA	221 LA HABRA BLVD	LA HABRA	526 7728
9	E2	LA PALMA	7842 WALKER ST	LA PALMA	523 8585
14	A5	LEISURE WORLD	2300 BEVERLY MANOR RD	SEAL BEACH	598 2431
16	F4	LIBRARY ADMIN OFFICES	431 S THE CITY DR	ORANGE	834 6841
14	B4	LOS ALAMITOS-ROSSMOOR	12700 MONTECITO RD	SEAL BEACH	846 3240
26	B6	MAIN ANNEX	525 MAIN ST	HUNTNGTON BCH	960 3344
31	E3	MARINERS BRANCH	2005 DOVER DR	NEWPORT BEACH	640 2141
19	E3	MARY WILSON BRANCH	707 ELECTRIC AV	SEAL BEACH	840 6759
22	E3	MCFADDEN BRANCH	2627 W MCFADDEN AV	SANTA ANA	834 4085
27	C4	MESA VERDE	2969 MESA VERDE DR	COSTA MESA	546 5274
29B	B6	MISSION VIEJO	24851 CHRISANTA DR	MISSION VIEJO	830 7100
22	C2	NEWHOPE BRANCH	122 N NEWHOPE ST	SANTA ANA	554 3411
32	A5	NEWPORT CENTER	856 SAN CLEMENTE DR	NEWPORT BEACH	640 2246
17	D3	ORANGE MAIN	101 N CENTER ST	ORANGE	532 0391
7	C5	PLACENTIA	411 E CHAPMAN AV	PLACENTIA	528 1906
39	D3	SAN CLEMENTE	242 AVENIDA DEL MAR	SAN CLEMENTE	492 3493
36	C6	SAN JUAN CAPISTRANO	31495 EL CAMINO REAL	SN J CAPSTRNO	493 3984
23	B1	SANTA ANA	26 CIVIC CENTER PZ	SANTA ANA	834 4013
50	D2	SILVERADO	28192 SILVERADO CYN RD	SILVERADO	649 2216
15	C2	STANTON	7850 KATELLA AV	STANTON	898 3302
12	A4	SUNKIST BRANCH	901 S SUNKIST ST	ANAHEIM	956 3501
12	D6	TAFT	740 E TAFT AV	ORANGE	532 0421
23	F2	TUSTIN	345 E MAIN ST	TUSTIN	544 7725
28	F6	UNIVERSITY PARK	4512 SANDBURG WY	IRVINE	786 4001
12	F6	VILLA PARK	17865 SANTIAGO BLVD	VILLA PARK	998 0861
21	D1	WESTMINSTER	8180 13TH ST	WESTMINSTER	893 5057
8	A3	YORBA LINDA	18262 LEMON DR	YORBA LINDA	528 7039
		MOTELS			
27	E5	ALI BABA	2250 NEWPORT BLVD	COSTA MESA	645 7700
29A	D3	BEST WESTERN LAGUNA	23702 ROCKFIELD BLVD	EL TORO	458 1900
17	B5	BEST WESTERN INN	2600 N MAIN ST	SANTA ANA	836 5141
16	D1	CANDY CANE	1747 S HARBOR BLVD	ANAHEIM	774 5284
36	D5	CAPISTRANO INN	27174 ORTEGA HWY	SN J CAPSTRNO	493 5661
10	C6	COMFORT INN	11632 BEACH BLVD	ANAHEIM	891 7688
29A	C4	COMFORT INN	23061 AVD D LA CARLOTA	LAGUNA HILLS	859 0166
16	E1	COSMIC AGE	1717 S HARBOR BLVD	ANAHEIM	635 6550
38	B6	COUNTRY BAY INN	34862 COAST HWY	CAPISTRNO BCH	496 6656
31	D1	COZY INN	325 W BAY ST	COSTA MESA	650 2055
10	B3	FARM DE VILLE	7800 CRESCENT AV	BUENA PARK	527 2201
10	C1	HAMPTON INN	7828 ORANGETHORPE AV	BUENA PARK	670 7200
16	C1	HEIDE	815 W KATELLA AV	ANAHEIM	533 1979
23	D6	IRVINE HOST HOTEL	1717 E DYER RD	SANTA ANA	261 1515
16	D1	JOLLY ROGER INN	640 W KATELLA AV	ANAHEIM	772 7621
29A	D5	LAGUNA HLS HYATT LODGE	23932 PASEO D VALENCIA	LAGUNA HILLS	830 2550
29A	D3	LAGUNA HLLS TRAVELODGE	23150 LAKE CENTER DR	EL TORO	855 1000
29	E4	LA QUINTA INN	14972 SAND CANYON AV	IRVINE	551 0909
27	C2	LA QUINTA MOTOR INN	1515 SOUTH COAST DR	COSTA MESA	957 5841
37	E5	MARINA INN	34902 DEL OBISPO ST	DANA POINT	496 2353
36	C6	MISSION INN	26891 ORTEGA HWY	SN J CAPSTRNO	493 1151
23	C6	QUALITY SUITES	2701 HOTEL TERRACE DR	SANTA ANA	957 9200
39	C2	RAMADA INN	35 CALLE DE INDUSTRIAS	SAN CLEMENTE	498 8800

PAGE	GRID	NAME	ADDRESS	CITY	PHONE
16	C4	RODEWAY INN	12052 GARDEN GROVE BL	GARDEN GROVE	636 1555
23	C6	SUPER 8 LODGE	2700 HOTEL TER	SANTA ANA	432 8888

PARKS

PAGE	GRID	NAME	ADDRESS	CITY	PHONE
29C	D3	ALISO/WOOD CYNS REGL	ALICIA PKWY	ORANGE CO	
2	D6	AROVISTA	W IMPERIAL HWY	BREA	
5	B6	BELLIS	7171 8TH ST	BUENA PARK	521 3466
9	E1	BETTENCOURT	ORANGETHORPE & WALKER	LA PALMA	
32	B1	BONITA CREEK PARK	UNIVERSITY & LA VIDA	NEWPORT BEACH	
24	D6	BRYWOOD PARK	BRYAN AV	IRVINE	
3	E6	CARBON CANYON REGIONAL	17002 CARBON CANYON RD	BREA	996 5252
63	B1	CASPERS, RONALD W REGL	33401 ORTEGA HWY	SN JN HOT SPG	496 4212
22	D4	CENTENNIAL REGIONAL	3000 CENTENNIAL	SANTA ANA	
26	B1	CENTRAL	GOLDEN WEST & TALBERT	HUNTNGTON BCH	960 8847
6	F6	CHAPMAN	SN CARLOS & STA YSABEL	FULLERTON	
8	B1	CHINO HILLS STATE	TELEGRAPH CANYON RD	ORANGE CO	
2	E6	CIVIC CENTER	BREA BLVD & DATE ST	BREA	
31	C2	COSTA MESA	570 W 18TH ST	COSTA MESA	
6	F2	CRAIG REGIONAL	3300 STATE COLLEGE BL	FULLERTON	990 0271
35	D3	CROWN VALLEY COMMUNITY	CROWN VLY PKY & NIGUEL	LAGUNA NIGUEL	495 5130
33A	A4	CRYSTAL COVE STATE	COAST HWY	ORANGE CO	
9	E3	CYPRESS	WATSON & CRESCENT	CYPRESS	
23	C5	DELHI	2314 HALLADAY ST	SANTA ANA	
26	A5	DWYER	17TH ST & ORANGE AV	HUNTNGTON BCH	
14	E3	EASTGATE	121001 ST MARK ST	GARDEN GROVE	
11	F2	EDISON	ROMNEYA DR & BAXTER ST	ANAHEIM	
12	D3	EISENHOWER	LINCOLN AV	ORANGE	
18	B4	EL MODENA	555 S HEWES AV	ORANGE	
22	F1	EL SALVADOR	1825 CIVIC CENTER DR W	SANTA ANA	543 2168
27	A5	FAIRVIEW REGIONAL	PLACENTIA AV	COSTA MESA	
26	B5	FARQUHAR	12TH ST & CREST AV	HUNTNGTON BCH	
15	F3	FAYLANE	11700 SEACREST DR	GARDEN GROVE	
43	C1	FEATHERLY REGIONAL	24001 SANTA ANA CYN RD	YORBA LINDA	637 0210
15	E6	GARDEN GROVE	9301 WESTMINSTER AV	GARDEN GROVE	
21	B3	GOLDENWEST PARK	SUGAR & GOLDEN WEST ST	WESTMINSTER	
6	A2	GRISSOM, VIRGIL	ROSECRANS AV	FULLERTON	
15	E3	GUTOWSKY	9201 FERRIS LN	GARDEN GROVE	
17	D4	HART, W O	701 S GLASSELL ST	ORANGE	
24	B6	HARVARD COMM ATHLETIC	HARVARD AV	IRVINE	
29	D1	HERITAGE	WALNUT AV & YALE AV	IRVINE	
6	C4	HILLCREST	HARBOR & VALLEY VW DR	FULLERTON	
6	B4	HILTSCHER	EUCLID & VALLEY VW DR	FULLERTON	
29A	C6	IGLESIA COMM PARK	24671 VIA IGLESIA	LAGUNA HILLS	830 8318
13	C2	IMPERIAL PARK	NOHL RCH RD IMPERIAL	ANAHEIM	
18	F2	IRVINE REGIONAL	21401 CHAPMAN AV	ORANGE	633 8072
22	E3	JEROME	2115 W MCFADDEN AV	SANTA ANA	541 9665
12	A4	JUAREZ	SUNKIST ST&VERMONT AV	ANAHEIM	
1	F4	LA BONITA	IDAHO ST	LA HABRA	
6	B2	LAGUNA LAKE	LAKEVIEW DR	FULLERTON	
35	D1	LAGUNA NIGUEL REGIONAL	28241 LA PAZ RD	LAGUNA NIGUEL	831 2790
26	B5	LAKE	12TH & MAIN ST	HUNTNGTON BCH	
11	C2	LA PALMA	HARBOR BL & LEMON ST	ANAHEIM	
18	A4	LA VETA	3705 E LA VETA AV	ORANGE	
6	C6	LEMON	LEMON ST & ASH AV	FULLERTON	
11	E4	LINCOLN	BROADWAY & EAST ST	ANAHEIM	
23	C4	MADISON	1528 S STANDARD AV	SANTA ANA	
31	C6	MARINA	1601 BALBOA BLVD	BALBOA	
10	F2	MARSHALL, JOHN	LA PALMA & COLUMBINE	ANAHEIM	
28	E6	MASON, WILLIAM R REGL	18712 UNIVERSITY DR	IRVINE	833 1933
22	A4	MILE SQUARE	16801 EUCLID ST	FOUNTAIN VLY	962 5549
32	A5	NEWPORT BEACH COUNTRY	1600 E COAST HWY	NEWPORT BEACH	
31	E5	NEWPORT DUNES AQUATIC	COAST HWY&JAMBOREE RD	NEWPORT BEACH	644 0510
29	D1	ORCHARD PARK	ROOSEVELT & YALE AV	IRVINE	
56	B6	O'NEILL REGIONAL	30892 TRABUCO CYN RD	TRABUCO OAKS	586 7962
32	C5	PACIFIC VIEW	PACIFIC VIEW DR	NEWPORT BEACH	
11	B6	PALM LANE	PALM LN & EUCLID AV	ANAHEIM	
10	B2	PEAK PARK	7225 EL DORADO DR	BUENA PARK	522 5482
11	C3	PEARSON	HARBOR BL & CYPRESS AV	ANAHEIM	
18	E5	PETERS CANYON REGIONAL	10500 PETERS CANYON RD	TUSTIN	
23	D2	PRENTICE	1700 E FIRST ST	SANTA ANA	836 4000
5	D3	RALPH B CLARK	8800 ROSECRANS AV	BUENA PARK	670 8045
9	D2	RANCHO VERDE	MOODY ST & SHARON DR	LA PALMA	
46	A3	SADDLEBACK	N SANTIAGO RD	ORANGE CO	
35	E6	SALT CREEK CORRIDOR	NIGUEL RD	ORANGE CO	
39	E6	SAN CLEMENTE STATE		SAN CLEMENTE	
6	C1	SAN JUAN	SAN JUAN PL	FULLERTON	
28	F4	SAN MATEO PARK	SAN MATEO & MAIN ST	IRVINE	
17	B5	SANTIAGO	2535 N MAIN ST	SANTA ANA	
18	E2	SANTIAGO HILLS PARK	WHITE OAK RIDGE	ORANGE	
18	B1	SANTIAGO OAKS REGIONAL	HEWES ST	ORANGE	
12	C5	SHAFFER	1930 N SHAFFER ST	ORANGE	
14	D5	SHAPELL	ALMOND AV&OLEANDER ST	SEAL BEACH	
21	B1	SIGLER	PARK ST & OLIVE ST	WESTMINSTER	
20	B4	SUNSET AQUATIC	2901 EDINGER AV	SUNSET BEACH	846 2873
20	D4	SWANSON		LAGUNA BEACH	
17	B2	SYCAMORE	1550 W SYCAMORE AV	ORANGE	
27	E5	TEWINKLE, CHARLES MEM	ARLINGTON & JUNIPERO	COSTA MESA	
18	F1	VILLA PARK DAM	CHAPMAN AV	OR PARK ACRES	
6	A3	WHITE, EDWARD	BROOKHURST RD	FULLERTON	
5	B3	WINDERMERE	15200 BARNWALL ST	LA MIRADA	
8	D6	YORBA REGIONAL	7600 E LA PALMA AV	ANAHEIM	970 1460

POINTS OF INTEREST

PAGE	GRID	NAME	ADDRESS	CITY	PHONE
11	D4	ANAHEIM CIVIC CENTER	200 S ANAHEIM BLVD	ANAHEIM	999 5100
16	C2	ANAHEIM CONVENTION CTR	800 W KATELLA AV	ANAHEIM	999 8999
12	D6	ANAHEIM LAKE	ORANGTHRPE & TUSTIN AV	ANAHEIM	524 7100
17	A2	ANAHEIM STADIUM	2000 STATE COLLEGE BL	ANAHEIM	634 2000
31	D5	BALBOA BAY CLUB	1221 W COAST HWY	NEWPORT BEACH	645 5000
33	A1	BALBOA YACHT CLUB	1801 BAYSIDE DR	NEWPORT BEACH	673 3515
17	B6	BOWERS MUSEUM	2002 N MAIN ST	SANTA ANA	547 8304
16	E3	CRYSTAL CATHEDRAL	4201 CHAPMAN AV	GARDEN GROVE	971 4000
27	D4	DIEGO SEPULVEDA ADOBE	1900 ADAMS AV	COSTA MESA	
11	C6	DISNEYLAND	1313 S HARBOR BLVD	ANAHEIM	999 4565
29A	F1	HERITAGE HILL HIST PK	25151 SERRANO RD	EL TORO	855 2028
34	D2	IRVINE BOWL	650 LAGUNA CANYON RD	LAGUNA BEACH	494 1145
29A	A2	IRVINE MDWS AMPHITHEATR	8800 IRVINE CENTER DR	IRVINE	855 6111
10	B3	KNOTTS BERRY FARM	8039 BEACH BLVD	BUENA PARK	827 1776
34	D2	LAGUNA MUSEUM OF ART	307 CLIFF DR	LAGUNA BEACH	494 6531
4	B4	LA VIDA HOT SPRINGS	6155 CARBON CANYON RD	BREA	528 7861
14	D1	LOS ALAMITOS RACETRACK	4961 KATELLA AV	LOS ALAMITOS	995 1234
36	C6	MSSN SN JUAN CAPISTRNO	ORTEGA HWY&CM CAPSTRNO	SN J CAPSTRNO	493 1111
10	B2	MOVIELAND WAX MUSEUM	7711 BEACH BLVD	BUENA PARK	522 1154
6	A5	MUCKENTHALR CULTRL CTR	1201 W MALVERN AV	FULLERTON	738 6595
6	C5	MUSEUM OF N ORANGE CO	301 N POMONA AV	FULLERTON	738 6545
32	A2	NATURAL HISTORY CENTER	2627 VISTA DEL ORO	NEWPORT BEACH	640 7120
31	F5	NEWPORT DUNES AQUAT PK	E COAST HWY & JAMBOREE	NEWPORT BEACH	644 0510
32	A4	NEWPORT HARBOR ART MUS	850 SAN CLEMENTE DR	NEWPORT BEACH	759 1122
7	F3	NIXON, R M BIRTHPLACE	18061 YORBA LINDA BLVD	YORBA LINDA	
29	F4	OLD TOWN IRVINE	SAND CYN AV & I-5	IRVINE	551 0909
21	C3	OLD WORLD SHOPPING CTR	7561 CENTER AV	HUNTINGTON BCH	897 4086
28	E5	ORANGE CO FAIRGROUNDS	88 FAIR DR	COSTA MESA	751 3247
27	E5	PACIFIC AMPHITHEATER	100 FAIR DR	COSTA MESA	546 6141
13	E1	RAMON PERALTA ADOBE	FAIRMONT BLVD	ANAHEIM	
23	A1	SANTA ANA MUNI STADIUM	6TH ST & FLOWER ST	SANTA ANA	
23	D2	SANTA ANA ZOO	1801 E CHESTNUT AV	SANTA ANA	835 7484
33	B5	SANTA CATALINA FERRY	BALBOA PIER-400 MAIN	NEWPORT BEACH	673 5245
33	B1	SHERMAN FOUNDTN&GARDNS	2619 E COAST HWY	CORONA DL MAR	673 2261
50	H6	TUCKER WILDLIFE SANCT	29322 MADJESKA CYN RD	MODJESKA CYN	649 2760
32	C1	WILDLIFE PRESERVE	JAMBOREE BLVD	IRVINE	
29A	A2	WILD RIVERS	8800 IRVINE CENTER DR	IRVINE	768 9453

SHOPPING CENTERS

PAGE	GRID	NAME	ADDRESS	CITY	PHONE
11	B3	ANAHEIM PLAZA	500 N EUCLID ST	ANAHEIM	635 3431
2	F6	BREA MALL	IMPERIAL&STATE COLLEGE	BREA	990 2732
10	C3	BUENA PARK MALL	STANTON & LA PALMA	BUENA PARK	
32	A5	FASHION ISLAND	62 FASHION ISLAND	NEWPORT BEACH	644 2020
13	C1	HONER PLAZA	1509 W 17TH ST	SANTA ANA	
21	C4	HUNTINGTON CENTER	7777 EDINGER AV	HUNTINGTON BCH	897 2533
29A	D5	LAGUNA HILLS MALL	24155 LAGUNA HLLS MALL	LAGUNA HILLS	586 8282
1	E6	LA HABRA FASHION SQ	BEACH & IMPERIAL	LA HABRA	525 1105
17	B4	MAINPLACE	STA AND & GARDEN GV FY	SANTA ANA	542 2368
12	B5	MALL OF ORANGE	2298 ORANGE MALL	ORANGE	998 0440
29D	B5	MISSION VIEJO MALL	SN DIEGO FWY&CROWN VLY	MISSION VIEJO	
11	C1	ORANGEFAIR MALL	240 ORANGEFAIR MALL	FULLERTON	871 3422
27	F2	SOUTH COAST PLAZA	3333 BRISTOL ST	COSTA MESA	546 6682
16	F3	THE CITY	GARDEN GROVE FWY	ORANGE	634 8500
24	C4	TUSTIN MARKET PLACE	JAMBOREE & EL CM REAL	TUSTIN	
21	A2	WESTMINSTER MALL	195 WESTMINSTER MALL	WESTMINSTER	894 5107

THEATERS

PAGE	GRID	NAME	ADDRESS	CITY	PHONE
2	F6	CABARET REP THEATRE	800 E BIRCH ST	BREA	879 6865
27	D4	CHILDRENS THEATR GUILD	1240 LOGAN AV	COSTA MESA	540 7450
9	D5	CYPRESS CIVIC THEATRE	5172 ORANGE AV	CYPRESS	527 1949
11	D4	FREEDMAN FORUM	224 E BROADWAY	ANAHEIM	535 2000
6	B5	FUL-CIVIC LIGHT OPERA	218 W COMMONWEALTH AV	FULLERTON	526 3832
16	B4	GEM THEATRE	12852 MAIN ST	GARDEN GROVE	636 7213
34	C2	LAGUNA MOULTON PLAYHSE	606 LAGUNA CANYON RD	LAGUNA BEACH	494 8021
11	D4	MEDIEVAL TIMES	7662 BEACH BLVD	BUENA PARK	521 4740
27	D4	OR CO COLLG THEATRE	2701 FAIRVIEW RD	COSTA MESA	556 5651
28	A2	OR CO PRFRMNG ARTS CTR	611 ANTON BLVD	COSTA MESA	556 2121
39	D3	SN CLEMNTE COM THEATRE	202 AVENIDA CABRILLO	SAN CLEMENTE	492 0465
28	A2	S COAST REP THEATER	655 TOWN CENTER DR	COSTA MESA	957 4033
32	D1	U C EXT THEATRE GROUP	U C IRVINE CAMPUS	IRVINE	833 6617
21	B1	U C IRVINE COM THEATR	7272 MAPLE ST	WESTMINSTER	893 8626

TRANSPORTATION

PAGE	GRID	NAME	ADDRESS	CITY	PHONE
32	B3	AERONAUTC FOR PK&RIDE	JAMBOREE & FORD RD	NEWPORT BEACH	
16	F1	AMTRAK STN - ANAHEIM	2150 E KATELLA AV	ANAHEIM	385 1448
16		AMTRAK STN - FULLERTON	SANTA FE & HARBOR BLVD	FULLERTON	992 0530
39	D4	AMTRAK STN-SN CLEMENTE	MUNICIPAL PIER	SAN CLEMENTE	
36	C6	AMTRAK STN-SN JN CPSTR	26762 VERDUGO ST	SN J CAPSTRNO	661 8835
23	C1	AMTRAK STN - SANTA ANA	1000 E SANTA ANA BLVD	SANTA ANA	547 8389
29D	B5	CROWN VLY SHOP PK&RIDE	CROWN VALLEY PKWY	MISSION VIEJO	
14	D4	FEDERAL SW REG LAB P&R	4665 LAMPSON AV	LOS ALAMITOS	
5	D5	FULLERTON MUNI AIRPORT	4011 W COMMONWEALTH AV	FULLERTON	738 6323
10	D1	FULLERTON PARK & RIDE	ORANGETHRPE & MAGNOLIA	FULLERTON	
6	C5	FUL TRAN CTR PK&RIDE	HARBOR & COMMONWEALTH	FULLERTON	
51	B6	IRV MULTI MODAL TRANS	ADA & BARRANCA PKWY	IRVINE	
24	B5	IRVINE PARK & RIDE	MYFORD RD & MICHELLE	IRVINE	
28	B5	JOHN WAYNE-OR CO AIRPT	18741 AIRPORT WY	SANTA ANA	834 2400
38	C6	K-MART PLAZA PARK&RIDE	CM D ESTRLL&MIRA CSTA	SAN CLEMENTE	
29A	E6	LAGUNA HILLS MALL P&R	PASEO DE VALENCIA	LAGUNA HILLS	
12	E2	LEVITZ FURNITURE P&R	1000 N TUSTIN AV	ANAHEIM	
20	E2	MCDONNELL DOUGLAS P&R	BOLSA & BOLSA CHICA RD	HUNTINGTON BCH	
20	E5	MEADOWLARK AIRPORT	5141 WARNER AV	HUNTINGTON BCH	840 1122
12	E4	ORANGE PARK & RIDE	55 FWY AT LINCOLN	ORANGE	
23	D1	REGIONAL TRANS CTR P&R	1000 E SANTA ANA BLVD	SANTA ANA	
10	D1	ROUTE 91 PARK & RIDE	RTE 91 AT MAGNOLIA	FULLERTON	
29A	D2	ST GEORGE'S PARK&RIDE	23802 AVD D LA CARLOTA	LAGUNA HILLS	
23	B2	SANTA ANA PARK & RIDE	BROADWAY AND 6TH ST	SANTA ANA	
36	C4	SN JUAN CAPISTRANO P&R	RTE 5 & JUNIPERO SERRA	SN J CAPSTRNO	
10	D2	WICKES FURNITURE P & R	1256 MAGNOLIA AV	ANAHEIM	
11	C1	ZODYS PARK & RIDE	120 E ORANGETHORPE AV	ANAHEIM	